Collins

OFFICIAL
SCRABBLE™
WORDS

Published by Collins
An imprint of HarperCollins Publishers
Westerhill Road
Bishopbriggs
Glasgow G64 2QT

HarperCollins Publishers
Macken House, 39/40 Mayor Street Upper
Dublin 1, D01 C9W8, Ireland

Seventh Edition 2024

10 9 8 7 6 5 4 3 2 1

© HarperCollins Publishers 2004, 2005,
2006, 2007, 2011, 2015, 2019, 2022, 2024

ISBN 978-0-00-866072-7

Collins® is a registered trademark of
HarperCollins Publishers Limited

© 2024 Mattel. SCRABBLE™ and
SCRABBLE tiles, including S1 tiles,
are trademarks of Mattel.

www.collins.co.uk/scrabble

Typeset by Davidson Publishing Solutions,
Glasgow

Printed in India

Entered words that we have reason to
believe constitute trademarks have been
designated as such. However, neither the
presence nor absence of such designation
should be regarded as affecting the legal
status of any trademark.

The contents of this publication are
believed correct at the time of printing.
Nevertheless the Publisher can accept no
responsibility for errors or omissions,
changes in the detail given or for any
expense or loss thereby caused.

HarperCollins does not warrant that any
website mentioned in this title will be
provided uninterrupted, that any website
will be error free, that defects will be
corrected, or that the website or the server
that makes it available are free of viruses or
bugs. For full terms and conditions please
refer to the site terms provided on the
website.

A catalogue record for this book is available
from the British Library.

If you would like to comment on any aspect
of this book, please contact us at the given
address or online.
E-mail: dictionaries@harpercollins.co.uk

MIX
Paper | Supporting
responsible forestry
FSC™ C007454
FSC
www.fsc.org

This book is produced from independently certified FSC™ paper
to ensure responsible forest management.

For more information visit: www.harpercollins.co.uk/green

Contents

Rules for the word list

- Only includes words of between 2 and 15 letters in length

- Does not include proper nouns, place names, and words with an initial capital letter, unless such words can also be spelt with a lower-case initial letter

- Does not include abbreviations, prefixes, suffixes, or words requiring apostrophes or hyphens

- Includes foreign words that are considered to have been absorbed into the English language

- Includes inflected forms, such as plurals and verb forms, eg plumb, plumbs, plumbed, plumbing

- Includes words that are old, obsolete, dialectal, historical and/or literary

- Includes World English, including spelling and variants from the US, South Africa, Australia, New Zealand, etc

- Includes words that are denoted contractions, short forms and slang

- Includes words that may be deemed rude or derogatory

Disclaimer
While every effort has been made to exclude words in the category of hate speech, no other word is excluded on the grounds of religion, gender, race, or for any reason other than that it is an invalid word form for Scrabble™ game play. The presence or exclusion of any word does not in any way represent the views of the Publisher, HarperCollins.

Other resources

Associations

World English-Language Scrabble Players Association (WESPA) –
www.wespa.org

The WESPA website also provides access to resources for national associations, tournament organizers, players and youth players.

Association of British Scrabble Players (ABSP) – www.absp.org.uk

The ABSP website includes details of UK clubs and tournaments.

North American Scrabble Players Association (NASPA) –
www.scrabbleplayers.org

The NASPA website contains numerous word lists and lists of further resources.

Collins Scrabble game tools online

https://scrabble.collinsdictionary.com

Check valid words at: https://scrabble.collinsdictionary.com/check

Get some suggestions for your letters with Collins hints tool:
https://scrabble.collinsdictionary.com/hints

Improve your skills with Collins training tool:
https://scrabble.collinsdictionary.com/train

Helpful lists of valid words are collected here:
https://scrabble.collinsdictionary.com/word-lists

Other tools are available from here: https://scrabble.collinsdictionary.com/tools

Alphabetical list of two letter words

AA	EA	IN	OD	TA
AB	ED	IO	OE	TE
AD	EE	IS	OF	TI
AE	EF	IT	OH	TO
AG	EH	JA	OI	UG
AH	EL	JO	OK	UH
AI	EM	KA	OM	UM
AL	EN	KI	ON	UN
AM	ER	KO	OO	UP
AN	ES	KY	OP	UR
AR	ET	LA	OR	US
AS	EW	LI	OS	UT
AT	EX	LO	OU	WE
AW	FA	MA	OW	WO
AX	FE	ME	OX	XI
AY	FY	MI	OY	XU
BA	GI	MM	PA	YA
BE	GO	MO	PE	YE
BI	GU	MU	PI	YO
BO	HA	MY	PO	YU
BY	HE	NA	QI	ZA
CH	HI	NE	RE	ZE
DA	HM	NO	SH	ZO
DE	HO	NU	SI	
DI	ID	NY	SO	
DO	IF	OB	ST	

Alphabetical list of three letter words

AAH	ALE	ASS	BAY	BRU
AAL	ALL	ATE	BED	BUB
AAS	ALP	ATS	BEE	BUD
ABA	ALS	ATT	BEG	BUG
ABB	ALT	AUA	BEL	BUM
ABS	ALU	AUE	BEN	BUN
ABY	AMA	AUF	BES	BUR
ACE	AME	AUK	BET	BUS
ACH	AMI	AVA	BEY	BUT
ACK	AMP	AVE	BEZ	BUY
ACT	AMU	AVI	BIB	BYE
ADD	ANA	AVO	BID	BYS
ADO	AND	AWA	BIG	CAA
ADS	ANE	AWE	BIN	CAB
ADZ	ANI	AWK	BIO	CAD
AFF	ANN	AWL	BIS	CAF
AFT	ANS	AWN	BIT	CAG
AGA	ANT	AXE	BIZ	CAL
AGE	ANY	AYE	BOA	CAM
AGO	APE	AYS	BOB	CAN
AGS	APO	AYU	BOD	CAP
AHA	APP	AZO	BOG	CAR
AHI	APT	BAA	BOH	CAT
AHS	ARB	BAC	BOI	CAW
AIA	ARC	BAD	BOK	CAY
AID	ARD	BAE	BON	CAZ
AIL	ARE	BAG	BOO	CEE
AIM	ARF	BAH	BOP	CEL
AIN	ARK	BAL	BOR	CEP
AIR	ARM	BAM	BOS	CHA
AIS	ARO	BAN	BOT	CHE
AIT	ARS	BAO	BOW	CHI
AJI	ART	BAP	BOX	CID
AKA	ARY	BAR	BOY	CIG
AKE	ASH	BAS	BRA	CIS
ALA	ASK	BAT	BRO	CIT
ALB	ASP	BAW	BRR	CLY

COB	DEF	DSO	ELK	FAG
COD	DEG	DUB	ELL	FAH
COG	DEI	DUD	ELM	FAM
COL	DEL	DUE	ELS	FAN
CON	DEN	DUG	ELT	FAP
COO	DEP	DUH	EME	FAR
COP	DEV	DUI	EMO	FAS
COR	DEW	DUM	EMS	FAT
COS	DEX	DUN	EMU	FAV
COT	DEY	DUO	END	FAW
COW	DIB	DUP	ENE	FAX
COX	DID	DUR	ENG	FAY
COY	DIE	DUX	ENS	FED
COZ	DIF	DYE	EON	FEE
CRU	DIG	DZO	ERA	FEG
CRY	DIM	EAN	ERE	FEH
CUB	DIN	EAR	ERF	FEM
CUD	DIP	EAS	ERG	FEN
CUE	DIS	EAT	ERK	FER
CUM	DIT	EAU	ERM	FES
CUP	DIV	EBB	ERN	FET
CUR	DOB	ECH	ERR	FEU
CUT	DOC	ECO	ERS	FEW
CUZ	DOD	ECU	ESS	FEY
CWM	DOE	EDH	EST	FEZ
DAB	DOF	EDS	ETA	FIB
DAD	DOG	EEK	ETH	FID
DAE	DOH	EEL	EUK	FIE
DAG	DOL	EEN	EVE	FIG
DAH	DOM	EEW	EVO	FIL
DAK	DON	EFF	EWE	FIN
DAL	DOO	EFS	EWK	FIR
DAM	DOP	EFT	EWT	FIT
DAN	DOR	EGG	EWW	FIX
DAP	DOS	EGO	EXO	FIZ
DAS	DOT	EHS	EYE	FLU
DAW	DOW	EIK	FAA	FLY
DAY	DOX	EKE	FAB	FOB
DEB	DOY	ELD	FAD	FOE
DEE	DRY	ELF	FAE	FOG

FOH	GEY	HAE	HON	ISH
FON	GHI	HAG	HOO	ISM
FOO	GIB	HAH	HOP	ISO
FOP	GID	HAJ	HOS	ITA
FOR	GIE	HAM	HOT	ITS
FOU	GIF	HAN	HOW	IVY
FOX	GIG	HAO	HOX	IWI
FOY	GIN	HAP	HOY	JAB
FRA	GIO	HAS	HUB	JAG
FRO	GIP	HAT	HUE	JAI
FRY	GIS	HAW	HUG	JAK
FUB	GIT	HAY	HUH	JAM
FUD	GJU	HEH	HUI	JAP
FUG	GNU	HEM	HUM	JAR
FUM	GOA	HEN	HUN	JAW
FUN	GOB	HEP	HUP	JAY
FUR	GOD	HER	HUT	JEE
GAB	GOE	HES	HYE	JET
GAD	GON	HET	HYP	JEU
GAE	GOO	HEW	ICE	JIB
GAG	GOR	HEX	ICH	JIG
GAK	GOS	HEY	ICK	JIN
GAL	GOT	HIC	ICY	JIZ
GAM	GOV	HID	IDE	JOB
GAN	GOX	HIE	IDS	JOE
GAP	GRR	HIM	IFF	JOG
GAR	GUB	HIN	IFS	JOL
GAS	GUE	HIP	IGG	JOR
GAT	GUL	HIS	ILK	JOT
GAU	GUM	HIT	ILL	JOW
GAW	GUN	HMM	IMP	JOY
GAY	GUP	HOA	ING	JUD
GED	GUR	HOB	INK	JUG
GEE	GUS	HOC	INN	JUN
GEL	GUT	HOD	INS	JUS
GEM	GUV	HOE	INT	JUT
GEN	GUY	HOG	ION	KAB
GEO	GYM	HOH	IOS	KAE
GER	GYP	HOI	IRE	KAF
GET	HAD	HOM	IRK	KAI

KAK	LAM	LOW	MHO	NAB
KAM	LAP	LOX	MIB	NAE
KAS	LAR	LOY	MIC	NAG
KAT	LAS	LUD	MID	NAH
KAW	LAT	LUG	MIG	NAM
KAY	LAV	LUM	MIL	NAN
KEA	LAW	LUN	MIM	NAP
KEB	LAX	LUR	MIR	NAS
KED	LAY	LUV	MIS	NAT
KEF	LEA	LUX	MIX	NAV
KEG	LED	LUZ	MIZ	NAW
KEN	LEE	LYE	MMM	NAY
KEP	LEG	LYM	MNA	NEB
KET	LEI	MAA	MOA	NED
KEX	LEK	MAC	MOB	NEE
KEY	LEP	MAD	MOC	NEF
KHI	LET	MAE	MOD	NEG
KID	LEU	MAG	MOE	NEK
KIF	LEV	MAK	MOG	NEP
KIN	LEW	MAL	MOI	NET
KIP	LEX	MAM	MOL	NEW
KIR	LEY	MAN	MOM	NIB
KIS	LIB	MAP	MON	NID
KIT	LID	MAR	MOO	NIE
KOA	LIE	MAS	MOP	NIL
KOB	LIG	MAT	MOR	NIM
KOI	LIN	MAW	MOS	NIP
KON	LIP	MAX	MOT	NIS
KOP	LIS	MAY	MOU	NIT
KOR	LIT	MED	MOW	NIX
KOS	LOB	MEE	MOY	NOB
KOW	LOC	MEG	MOZ	NOD
KUE	LOD	MEH	MUD	NOG
KYE	LOG	MEL	MUG	NOH
KYU	LOO	MEM	MUM	NOM
LAB	LOP	MEN	MUN	NON
LAC	LOR	MES	MUS	NOO
LAD	LOS	MET	MUT	NOR
LAG	LOT	MEU	MUX	NOS
LAH	LOU	MEW	MYC	NOT

NOW	OLD	OWL	PIA	PUS
NOX	OLE	OWN	PIC	PUT
NOY	OLM	OWO	PIE	PUY
NTH	OMA	OWT	PIG	PWN
NUB	OMS	OXO	PIN	PYA
NUG	ONE	OXY	PIP	PYE
NUN	ONO	OYE	PIR	PYX
NUR	ONS	OYS	PIS	QAT
NUS	ONY	PAC	PIT	QIN
NUT	OOF	PAD	PIU	QIS
NYE	OOH	PAH	PIX	QUA
NYM	OOM	PAK	PLU	RAD
NYS	OON	PAL	PLY	RAG
OAF	OOP	PAM	POA	RAH
OAK	OOR	PAN	POD	RAI
OAR	OOS	PAP	POH	RAJ
OAT	OOT	PAR	POI	RAM
OBA	OPA	PAS	POL	RAN
OBE	OPE	PAT	POM	RAP
OBI	OPS	PAV	POO	RAS
OBO	OPT	PAW	POP	RAT
OBS	ORA	PAX	POS	RAV
OCA	ORB	PAY	POT	RAW
OCH	ORC	PEA	POW	RAX
ODA	ORD	PEC	POX	RAY
ODD	ORE	PED	POZ	REB
ODE	ORF	PEE	PRE	REC
ODS	ORG	PEG	PRO	RED
OES	ORS	PEH	PRY	REE
OFF	ORT	PEL	PSI	REF
OFT	OSE	PEN	PST	REG
OHM	OUD	PEP	PUB	REH
OHO	OUK	PER	PUD	REI
OHS	OUP	PES	PUG	REM
OIK	OUR	PET	PUH	REN
OIL	OUS	PEW	PUL	REO
OIS	OUT	PHI	PUN	REP
OKA	OVA	PHO	PUP	RES
OKE	OWE	PHT	PUR	RET

REV	SAE	SIK	SUI	TET
REW	SAG	SIM	SUK	TEW
REX	SAI	SIN	SUM	TEX
REZ	SAL	SIP	SUN	THE
RHO	SAM	SIR	SUP	THO
RHY	SAN	SIS	SUQ	THY
RIA	SAP	SIT	SUR	TIC
RIB	SAR	SIX	SUS	TID
RID	SAT	SKA	SWY	TIE
RIF	SAU	SKI	SYE	TIG
RIG	SAV	SKY	SYN	TIK
RIM	SAW	SLY	TAB	TIL
RIN	SAX	SMA	TAD	TIN
RIP	SAY	SNY	TAE	TIP
RIT	SAZ	SOB	TAG	TIS
RIZ	SEA	SOC	TAI	TIT
ROB	SEC	SOD	TAJ	TIX
ROC	SED	SOG	TAK	TIZ
ROD	SEE	SOH	TAM	TOC
ROE	SEG	SOL	TAN	TOD
ROK	SEI	SOM	TAO	TOE
ROM	SEL	SON	TAP	TOG
ROO	SEN	SOP	TAR	TOM
ROT	SER	SOS	TAS	TON
ROW	SET	SOT	TAT	TOO
RUB	SEV	SOU	TAU	TOP
RUC	SEW	SOV	TAV	TOR
RUD	SEX	SOW	TAW	TOT
RUE	SEY	SOX	TAX	TOW
RUG	SEZ	SOY	TAY	TOY
RUM	SHA	SOZ	TEA	TRY
RUN	SHE	SPA	TEC	TSK
RUT	SHH	SPY	TED	TUB
RYA	SHO	SRI	TEE	TUG
RYE	SHY	STY	TEF	TUI
RYU	SIB	SUB	TEG	TUM
SAB	SIC	SUD	TEL	TUN
SAC	SIF	SUE	TEN	TUP
SAD	SIG	SUG	TES	TUT

TUX	VAC	WAI	WRY	YON
TWA	VAE	WAN	WUD	YOU
TWO	VAG	WAP	WUS	YOW
TWP	VAN	WAR	WUZ	YUG
TYE	VAR	WAS	WYE	YUK
TYG	VAS	WAT	WYN	YUM
UDO	VAT	WAW	XED	YUP
UDS	VAU	WAX	XIS	YUS
UEY	VAV	WAY	YAD	ZAG
UFO	VAW	WAZ	YAE	ZAP
UGH	VAX	WEB	YAG	ZAS
UGS	VEE	WED	YAH	ZAX
UKE	VEG	WEE	YAK	ZEA
ULE	VET	WEM	YAM	ZED
ULU	VEX	WEN	YAP	ZEE
UME	VIA	WET	YAR	ZEK
UMM	VID	WEX	YAS	ZEL
UMP	VIE	WEY	YAW	ZEN
UMS	VIG	WHA	YAY	ZEP
UMU	VIM	WHO	YEA	ZEX
UNI	VIN	WHY	YEH	ZHO
UNS	VIS	WIG	YEN	ZIG
UPO	VLY	WIN	YEP	ZIN
UPS	VOE	WIS	YER	ZIP
URB	VOG	WIT	YES	ZIT
URD	VOL	WIZ	YET	ZIZ
URE	VOM	WOE	YEW	ZOA
URN	VOR	WOF	YEX	ZOL
URP	VOW	WOK	YEZ	ZOO
USE	VOX	WON	YGO	ZOS
UTA	VUG	WOO	YIN	ZUZ
UTE	VUM	WOP	YIP	ZZZ
UTS	WAB	WOS	YOB	
UTU	WAD	WOT	YOD	
UVA	WAE	WOW	YOK	
UWU	WAG	WOX	YOM	

Two and three letter words with J, Q, X, and Z

Two letter words with J
JA   JO

Three letter words with J
AJI	JAM	JEU	JOG	JUG
GJU	JAP	JIB	JOL	JUN
HAJ	JAR	JIG	JOR	JUS
JAB	JAW	JIN	JOT	JUT
JAG	JAY	JIZ	JOW	RAJ
JAI	JEE	JOB	JOY	TAJ
JAK	JET	JOE	JUD	

Two letter words with Q
QI

Three letter words with Q
QAT	QIN	QIS	QUA	SUQ

Two letter words with X
AX	EX	OX	XI	XU

Three letter words with X
AXE	GOX	MUX	REX	VEX
BOX	HEX	NIX	SAX	VOX
COX	HOX	NOX	SEX	WAX
DEX	KEX	OXO	SIX	WEX
DOX	LAX	OXY	SOX	WOX
DUX	LEX	PAX	TAX	XED
EXO	LOX	PIX	TEX	XIS
FAX	LUX	POX	TIX	YEX
FIX	MAX	PYX	TUX	ZAX
FOX	MIX	RAX	VAX	ZEX

Two letter words with Z

ZA	ZE	ZO

Three letter words with Z

ADZ	JIZ	TIZ	ZED	ZIP
AZO	LUZ	WAZ	ZEE	ZIT
BEZ	MIZ	WIZ	ZEK	ZIZ
BIZ	MOZ	WUZ	ZEL	ZOA
CAZ	POZ	YEZ	ZEN	ZOL
COZ	REZ	ZAG	ZEP	ZOO
CUZ	RIZ	ZAP	ZEX	ZOS
DZO	SAZ	ZAS	ZHO	ZUZ
FEZ	SEZ	ZAX	ZIG	ZZZ
FIZ	SOZ	ZEA	ZIN	

TWO TO NINE
LETTER WORDS

AA	ABAMPS	ABATTISES	ABDOMINAL	ABETMENT
AAH	ABAND	ABATTOIR	ABDUCE	ABETMENTS
AAHED	ABANDED	ABATTOIRS	ABDUCED	ABETS
AAHING	ABANDING	ABATTU	ABDUCENS	ABETTAL
AAHS	ABANDON	ABATURE	ABDUCENT	ABETTALS
AAL	ABANDONED	ABATURES	ABDUCES	ABETTED
AALII	ABANDONEE	ABAXIAL	ABDUCING	ABETTER
AALIIS	ABANDONER	ABAXILE	ABDUCT	ABETTERS
AALS	ABANDONS	ABAYA	ABDUCTED	ABETTING
AARDVARK	ABANDS	ABAYAS	ABDUCTEE	ABETTOR
AARDVARKS	ABAPICAL	ABB	ABDUCTEES	ABETTORS
AARDWOLF	ABAS	ABBA	ABDUCTING	ABEYANCE
AARGH	ABASE	ABBACIES	ABDUCTION	ABEYANCES
AARRGH	ABASED	ABBACY	ABDUCTOR	ABEYANCY
AARRGHH	ABASEDLY	ABBAS	ABDUCTORS	ABEYANT
AARTI	ABASEMENT	ABBATIAL	ABDUCTS	ABFARAD
AARTIS	ABASER	ABBE	ABEAM	ABFARADS
AAS	ABASERS	ABBED	ABEAR	ABHENRIES
AASVOGEL	ABASES	ABBES	ABEARING	ABHENRY
AASVOGELS	ABASH	ABBESS	ABEARS	ABHENRYS
AATMAN	ABASHED	ABBESSES	ABED	ABHOR
AATMANS	ABASHEDLY	ABBEY	ABEGGING	ABHORRED
AB	ABASHES	ABBEYS	ABEIGH	ABHORRENT
ABA	ABASHING	ABBOT	ABELE	ABHORRER
ABAC	ABASHLESS	ABBOTCIES	ABELES	ABHORRERS
ABACA	ABASHMENT	ABBOTCY	ABELIA	ABHORRING
ABACAS	ABASIA	ABBOTS	ABELIAN	ABHORS
ABACI	ABASIAS	ABBOTSHIP	ABELIAS	ABID
ABACK	ABASING	ABBS	ABELMOSK	ABIDANCE
ABACS	ABASK	ABCEE	ABELMOSKS	ABIDANCES
ABACTINAL	ABATABLE	ABCEES	ABER	ABIDDEN
ABACTOR	ABATE	ABCOULOMB	ABERNETHY	ABIDE
ABACTORS	ABATED	ABDABS	ABERRANCE	ABIDED
ABACUS	ABATEMENT	ABDICABLE	ABERRANCY	ABIDER
ABACUSES	ABATER	ABDICANT	ABERRANT	ABIDERS
ABAFT	ABATERS	ABDICANTS	ABERRANTS	ABIDES
ABAKA	ABATES	ABDICATE	ABERRATE	ABIDING
ABAKAS	ABATING	ABDICATED	ABERRATED	ABIDINGLY
ABALONE	ABATIS	ABDICATES	ABERRATES	ABIDINGS
ABALONES	ABATISES	ABDICATOR	ABERS	ABIES
ABAMP	ABATOR	ABDOMEN	ABESSIVE	ABIETES
ABAMPERE	ABATORS	ABDOMENS	ABESSIVES	ABIETIC
ABAMPERES	ABATTIS	ABDOMINA	ABET	ABIGAIL

ABIGAILS	ABLET	ABOMASA	ABRACHIAS	ABROAD
ABILITIES	ABLETS	ABOMASAL	ABRADABLE	ABROADS
ABILITY	ABLING	ABOMASI	ABRADANT	ABROGABLE
ABIOGENIC	ABLINGS	ABOMASUM	ABRADANTS	ABROGATE
ABIOSES	ABLINS	ABOMASUS	ABRADE	ABROGATED
ABIOSIS	ABLOOM	ABOMINATE	ABRADED	ABROGATES
ABIOTIC	ABLOW	ABONDANCE	ABRADER	ABROGATOR
ABITUR	ABLUENT	ABOON	ABRADERS	ABROOKE
ABITURS	ABLUENTS	ABORAL	ABRADES	ABROOKED
ABJECT	ABLUSH	ABORALLY	ABRADING	ABROOKES
ABJECTED	ABLUTED	ABORD	ABRAID	ABROOKING
ABJECTING	ABLUTION	ABORDED	ABRAIDED	ABROSIA
ABJECTION	ABLUTIONS	ABORDING	ABRAIDING	ABROSIAS
ABJECTLY	ABLY	ABORDS	ABRAIDS	ABRUPT
ABJECTS	ABMHO	ABORE	ABRAM	ABRUPTER
ABJOINT	ABMHOS	ABORIGEN	ABRASAX	ABRUPTEST
ABJOINTED	ABNEGATE	ABORIGENS	ABRASAXES	ABRUPTION
ABJOINTS	ABNEGATED	ABORIGIN	ABRASION	ABRUPTLY
ABJURE	ABNEGATES	ABORIGINE	ABRASIONS	ABRUPTS
ABJURED	ABNEGATOR	ABORIGINS	ABRASIVE	ABS
ABJURER	ABNORMAL	ABORNE	ABRASIVES	ABSCESS
ABJURERS	ABNORMALS	ABORNING	ABRAXAS	ABSCESSED
ABJURES	ABNORMITY	ABORT	ABRAXASES	ABSCESSES
ABJURING	ABNORMOUS	ABORTED	ABRAY	ABSCIND
ABLATE	ABOARD	ABORTEE	ABRAYED	ABSCINDED
ABLATED	ABODE	ABORTEES	ABRAYING	ABSCINDS
ABLATES	ABODED	ABORTER	ABRAYS	ABSCISE
ABLATING	ABODEMENT	ABORTERS	ABRAZO	ABSCISED
ABLATION	ABODES	ABORTING	ABRAZOS	ABSCISES
ABLATIONS	ABODING	ABORTION	ABREACT	ABSCISIC
ABLATIVAL	ABOHM	ABORTIONS	ABREACTED	ABSCISIN
ABLATIVE	ABOHMS	ABORTIVE	ABREACTS	ABSCISING
ABLATIVES	ABOIDEAU	ABORTS	ABREAST	ABSCISINS
ABLATOR	ABOIDEAUS	ABORTUARY	ABREGE	ABSCISS
ABLATORS	ABOIDEAUX	ABORTUS	ABREGES	ABSCISSA
ABLAUT	ABOIL	ABORTUSES	ABRI	ABSCISSAE
ABLAUTS	ABOITEAU	ABOUGHT	ABRICOCK	ABSCISSAS
ABLAZE	ABOITEAUS	ABOULIA	ABRICOCKS	ABSCISSE
ABLE	ABOITEAUX	ABOULIAS	ABRIDGE	ABSCISSES
ABLED	ABOLISH	ABOULIC	ABRIDGED	ABSCISSIN
ABLEGATE	ABOLISHED	ABOUND	ABRIDGER	ABSCOND
ABLEGATES	ABOLISHER	ABOUNDED	ABRIDGERS	ABSCONDED
ABLEISM	ABOLISHES	ABOUNDING	ABRIDGES	ABSCONDER
ABLEISMS	ABOLITION	ABOUNDS	ABRIDGING	ABSCONDS
ABLEIST	ABOLLA	ABOUT	ABRIM	ABSEIL
ABLEISTS	ABOLLAE	ABOUTS	ABRIN	ABSEILED
ABLER	ABOLLAS	ABOVE	ABRINS	ABSEILER
ABLES	ABOMA	ABOVES	ABRIS	ABSEILERS
ABLEST	ABOMAS	ABRACHIA	ABROACH	ABSEILING

ABSEILS	ABSTRACTS	ABUTTER	ACANTHI	ACCEDING
ABSENCE	ABSTRICT	ABUTTERS	ACANTHIN	ACCEND
ABSENCES	ABSTRICTS	ABUTTING	ACANTHINE	ACCENDED
ABSENT	ABSTRUSE	ABUZZ	ACANTHINS	ACCENDING
ABSENTED	ABSTRUSER	ABVOLT	ACANTHOID	ACCENDS
ABSENTEE	ABSURD	ABVOLTS	ACANTHOUS	ACCENSION
ABSENTEES	ABSURDER	ABWATT	ACANTHS	ACCENT
ABSENTER	ABSURDEST	ABWATTS	ACANTHUS	ACCENTED
ABSENTERS	ABSURDISM	ABY	ACAPNIA	ACCENTING
ABSENTING	ABSURDIST	ABYE	ACAPNIAS	ACCENTOR
ABSENTLY	ABSURDITY	ABYED	ACARBOSE	ACCENTORS
ABSENTS	ABSURDLY	ABYEING	ACARBOSES	ACCENTS
ABSEY	ABSURDS	ABYES	ACARI	ACCENTUAL
ABSEYS	ABTHANE	ABYING	ACARIAN	ACCEPT
ABSINTH	ABTHANES	ABYS	ACARIASES	ACCEPTANT
ABSINTHE	ABUBBLE	ABYSM	ACARIASIS	ACCEPTED
ABSINTHES	ABUILDING	ABYSMAL	ACARICIDE	ACCEPTEE
ABSINTHS	ABULIA	ABYSMALLY	ACARID	ACCEPTEES
ABSIT	ABULIAS	ABYSMS	ACARIDAN	ACCEPTER
ABSITS	ABULIC	ABYSS	ACARIDANS	ACCEPTERS
ABSOLUTE	ABUNA	ABYSSAL	ACARIDEAN	ACCEPTING
ABSOLUTER	ABUNAS	ABYSSES	ACARIDIAN	ACCEPTIVE
ABSOLUTES	ABUNDANCE	ACACIA	ACARIDS	ACCEPTOR
ABSOLVE	ABUNDANCY	ACACIAS	ACARINE	ACCEPTORS
ABSOLVED	ABUNDANT	ACADEME	ACARINES	ACCEPTS
ABSOLVENT	ABUNE	ACADEMES	ACAROID	ACCESS
ABSOLVER	ABURST	ACADEMIA	ACAROLOGY	ACCESSARY
ABSOLVERS	ABUSABLE	ACADEMIAS	ACARPOUS	ACCESSED
ABSOLVES	ABUSAGE	ACADEMIC	ACARUS	ACCESSES
ABSOLVING	ABUSAGES	ACADEMICS	ACATER	ACCESSING
ABSONANT	ABUSE	ACADEMIES	ACATERS	ACCESSION
ABSORB	ABUSED	ACADEMISM	ACATES	ACCESSORY
ABSORBANT	ABUSER	ACADEMIST	ACATHISIA	ACCIDENCE
ABSORBATE	ABUSERS	ACADEMY	ACATOUR	ACCIDENT
ABSORBED	ABUSES	ACAI	ACATOURS	ACCIDENTS
ABSORBENT	ABUSING	ACAIS	ACAUDAL	ACCIDIA
ABSORBER	ABUSION	ACAJOU	ACAUDATE	ACCIDIAS
ABSORBERS	ABUSIONS	ACAJOUS	ACAULINE	ACCIDIE
ABSORBING	ABUSIVE	ACALCULIA	ACAULOSE	ACCIDIES
ABSORBS	ABUSIVELY	ACALEPH	ACAULOUS	ACCINGE
ABSTAIN	ABUT	ACALEPHAE	ACCA	ACCINGED
ABSTAINED	ABUTILON	ACALEPHAN	ACCABLE	ACCINGES
ABSTAINER	ABUTILONS	ACALEPHE	ACCAS	ACCINGING
ABSTAINS	ABUTMENT	ACALEPHES	ACCEDE	ACCIPITER
ABSTERGE	ABUTMENTS	ACALEPHS	ACCEDED	ACCITE
ABSTERGED	ABUTS	ACANTH	ACCEDENCE	ACCITED
ABSTERGES	ABUTTAL	ACANTHA	ACCEDER	ACCITES
ABSTINENT	ABUTTALS	ACANTHAE	ACCEDERS	ACCITING
ABSTRACT	ABUTTED	ACANTHAS	ACCEDES	ACCLAIM

ACCLAIMED	ACCOUTRES	ACED	ACETIFY	ACHINESS
ACCLAIMER	ACCOY	ACEDIA	ACETIN	ACHING
ACCLAIMS	ACCOYED	ACEDIAS	ACETINS	ACHINGLY
ACCLIMATE	ACCOYING	ACELDAMA	ACETONE	ACHINGS
ACCLIVITY	ACCOYLD	ACELDAMAS	ACETONES	ACHIOTE
ACCLIVOUS	ACCOYS	ACELLULAR	ACETONIC	ACHIOTES
ACCLOY	ACCREDIT	ACENTRIC	ACETOSE	ACHIRAL
ACCLOYED	ACCREDITS	ACENTRICS	ACETOUS	ACHKAN
ACCLOYING	ACCRETE	ACEPHALIC	ACETOXYL	ACHKANS
ACCLOYS	ACCRETED	ACEQUIA	ACETOXYLS	ACHOLIA
ACCOAST	ACCRETES	ACEQUIAS	ACETUM	ACHOLIAS
ACCOASTED	ACCRETING	ACER	ACETYL	ACHOO
ACCOASTS	ACCRETION	ACERATE	ACETYLATE	ACHOOS
ACCOIED	ACCRETIVE	ACERATED	ACETYLENE	ACHROMAT
ACCOIL	ACCREW	ACERB	ACETYLIC	ACHROMATS
ACCOILS	ACCREWED	ACERBATE	ACETYLIDE	ACHROMIC
ACCOLADE	ACCREWING	ACERBATED	ACETYLS	ACHROMOUS
ACCOLADED	ACCREWS	ACERBATES	ACH	ACHY
ACCOLADES	ACCROIDES	ACERBER	ACHAENIA	ACICLOVIR
ACCOMPANY	ACCRUABLE	ACERBEST	ACHAENIUM	ACICULA
ACCOMPT	ACCRUAL	ACERBIC	ACHAGE	ACICULAE
ACCOMPTED	ACCRUALS	ACERBITY	ACHAGES	ACICULAR
ACCOMPTS	ACCRUE	ACEROLA	ACHALASIA	ACICULAS
ACCORAGE	ACCRUED	ACEROLAS	ACHAR	ACICULATE
ACCORAGED	ACCRUES	ACEROSE	ACHARNE	ACICULUM
ACCORAGES	ACCRUING	ACEROUS	ACHARS	ACICULUMS
ACCORD	ACCUMBENT	ACERS	ACHARYA	ACID
ACCORDANT	ACCURACY	ACERVATE	ACHARYAS	ACIDAEMIA
ACCORDED	ACCURATE	ACERVULI	ACHATES	ACIDEMIA
ACCORDER	ACCURSE	ACERVULUS	ACHE	ACIDEMIAS
ACCORDERS	ACCURSED	ACES	ACHED	ACIDER
ACCORDING	ACCURSES	ACESCENCE	ACHENE	ACIDEST
ACCORDION	ACCURSING	ACESCENCY	ACHENES	ACIDHEAD
ACCORDS	ACCURST	ACESCENT	ACHENIA	ACIDHEADS
ACCOST	ACCUSABLE	ACESCENTS	ACHENIAL	ACIDIC
ACCOSTED	ACCUSABLY	ACETA	ACHENIUM	ACIDIER
ACCOSTING	ACCUSAL	ACETABULA	ACHENIUMS	ACIDIEST
ACCOSTS	ACCUSALS	ACETAL	ACHES	ACIDIFIED
ACCOUNT	ACCUSANT	ACETALS	ACHIER	ACIDIFIER
ACCOUNTED	ACCUSANTS	ACETAMID	ACHIEST	ACIDIFIES
ACCOUNTS	ACCUSE	ACETAMIDE	ACHIEVE	ACIDIFY
ACCOURAGE	ACCUSED	ACETAMIDS	ACHIEVED	ACIDITIES
ACCOURT	ACCUSER	ACETATE	ACHIEVER	ACIDITY
ACCOURTED	ACCUSERS	ACETATED	ACHIEVERS	ACIDLY
ACCOURTS	ACCUSES	ACETATES	ACHIEVES	ACIDNESS
ACCOUTER	ACCUSING	ACETIC	ACHIEVING	ACIDOPHIL
ACCOUTERS	ACCUSTOM	ACETIFIED	ACHILLEA	ACIDOSES
ACCOUTRE	ACCUSTOMS	ACETIFIER	ACHILLEAS	ACIDOSIS
ACCOUTRED	ACE	ACETIFIES	ACHIMENES	ACIDOTIC

ACIDS	ACOLUTHIC	ACQUITTAL	ACRONYM	ACTINIUMS
ACIDULATE	ACOLYTE	ACQUITTED	ACRONYMIC	ACTINOID
ACIDULENT	ACOLYTES	ACQUITTER	ACRONYMS	ACTINOIDS
ACIDULOUS	ACOLYTH	ACRASIA	ACROPETAL	ACTINON
ACIDURIA	ACOLYTHS	ACRASIAS	ACROPHOBE	ACTINONS
ACIDURIAS	ACONITE	ACRASIN	ACROPHONY	ACTINOPOD
ACIDY	ACONITES	ACRASINS	ACROPOLIS	ACTINS
ACIERAGE	ACONITIC	ACRATIC	ACROS	ACTION
ACIERAGES	ACONITINE	ACRAWL	ACROSOMAL	ACTIONED
ACIERATE	ACONITUM	ACRE	ACROSOME	ACTIONER
ACIERATED	ACONITUMS	ACREAGE	ACROSOMES	ACTIONERS
ACIERATES	ACORN	ACREAGES	ACROSPIRE	ACTIONING
ACIFORM	ACORNED	ACRED	ACROSS	ACTIONIST
ACINAR	ACORNS	ACRES	ACROSTIC	ACTIONS
ACING	ACOSMISM	ACRID	ACROSTICS	ACTIVATE
ACINI	ACOSMISMS	ACRIDER	ACROTER	ACTIVATED
ACINIC	ACOSMIST	ACRIDEST	ACROTERIA	ACTIVATES
ACINIFORM	ACOSMISTS	ACRIDIN	ACROTERS	ACTIVATOR
ACINOSE	ACOUCHI	ACRIDINE	ACROTIC	ACTIVE
ACINOUS	ACOUCHIES	ACRIDINES	ACROTISM	ACTIVELY
ACINUS	ACOUCHIS	ACRIDINS	ACROTISMS	ACTIVES
ACK	ACOUCHY	ACRIDITY	ACRYLATE	ACTIVISE
ACKEE	ACOUSTIC	ACRIDLY	ACRYLATES	ACTIVISED
ACKEES	ACOUSTICS	ACRIDNESS	ACRYLIC	ACTIVISES
ACKER	ACQUAINT	ACRIMONY	ACRYLICS	ACTIVISM
ACKERS	ACQUAINTS	ACRITARCH	ACRYLYL	ACTIVISMS
ACKNEW	ACQUEST	ACRITICAL	ACRYLYLS	ACTIVIST
ACKNOW	ACQUESTS	ACRO	ACT	ACTIVISTS
ACKNOWING	ACQUIESCE	ACROBAT	ACTA	ACTIVITY
ACKNOWN	ACQUIGHT	ACROBATIC	ACTABLE	ACTIVIZE
ACKNOWNE	ACQUIGHTS	ACROBATS	ACTANT	ACTIVIZED
ACKNOWS	ACQUIRAL	ACRODONT	ACTANTS	ACTIVIZES
ACLINIC	ACQUIRALS	ACRODONTS	ACTED	ACTON
ACMATIC	ACQUIRE	ACRODROME	ACTIN	ACTONS
ACME	ACQUIRED	ACROGEN	ACTINAL	ACTOR
ACMES	ACQUIREE	ACROGENIC	ACTINALLY	ACTORISH
ACMIC	ACQUIREES	ACROGENS	ACTING	ACTORLIER
ACMITE	ACQUIRER	ACROLECT	ACTINGS	ACTORLY
ACMITES	ACQUIRERS	ACROLECTS	ACTINIA	ACTORS
ACNE	ACQUIRES	ACROLEIN	ACTINIAE	ACTRESS
ACNED	ACQUIRING	ACROLEINS	ACTINIAN	ACTRESSES
ACNES	ACQUIS	ACROLITH	ACTINIANS	ACTRESSY
ACNODAL	ACQUIST	ACROLITHS	ACTINIAS	ACTS
ACNODE	ACQUISTS	ACROMIA	ACTINIC	ACTUAL
ACNODES	ACQUIT	ACROMIAL	ACTINIDE	ACTUALISE
ACOCK	ACQUITE	ACROMION	ACTINIDES	ACTUALIST
ACOELOUS	ACQUITES	ACRONIC	ACTINISM	ACTUALITE
ACOEMETI	ACQUITING	ACRONICAL	ACTINISMS	ACTUALITY
ACOLD	ACQUITS	ACRONYCAL	ACTINIUM	ACTUALIZE

ACTUALLY	ACYLOIN	ADDEEMS	ADDUCERS	ADHAN
ACTUALS	ACYLOINS	ADDEND	ADDUCES	ADHANS
ACTUARIAL	ACYLS	ADDENDA	ADDUCIBLE	ADHARMA
ACTUARIES	AD	ADDENDS	ADDUCING	ADHARMAS
ACTUARY	ADAGE	ADDENDUM	ADDUCT	ADHERABLE
ACTUATE	ADAGES	ADDENDUMS	ADDUCTED	ADHERE
ACTUATED	ADAGIAL	ADDER	ADDUCTING	ADHERED
ACTUATES	ADAGIO	ADDERBEAD	ADDUCTION	ADHERENCE
ACTUATING	ADAGIOS	ADDERS	ADDUCTIVE	ADHEREND
ACTUATION	ADAMANCE	ADDERWORT	ADDUCTOR	ADHERENDS
ACTUATOR	ADAMANCES	ADDIBLE	ADDUCTORS	ADHERENT
ACTUATORS	ADAMANCY	ADDICT	ADDUCTS	ADHERENTS
ACTURE	ADAMANT	ADDICTED	ADDY	ADHERER
ACTURES	ADAMANTLY	ADDICTING	ADEEM	ADHERERS
ACUATE	ADAMANTS	ADDICTION	ADEEMED	ADHERES
ACUATED	ADAMSITE	ADDICTIVE	ADEEMING	ADHERING
ACUATES	ADAMSITES	ADDICTS	ADEEMS	ADHESION
ACUATING	ADAPT	ADDIES	ADELGID	ADHESIONS
ACUITIES	ADAPTABLE	ADDING	ADELGIDS	ADHESIVE
ACUITY	ADAPTED	ADDINGS	ADEMPTION	ADHESIVES
ACULEATE	ADAPTER	ADDIO	ADENINE	ADHIBIT
ACULEATED	ADAPTERS	ADDIOS	ADENINES	ADHIBITED
ACULEATES	ADAPTING	ADDITION	ADENITIS	ADHIBITS
ACULEI	ADAPTION	ADDITIONS	ADENOID	ADHOCRACY
ACULEUS	ADAPTIONS	ADDITIVE	ADENOIDAL	ADIABATIC
ACUMEN	ADAPTIVE	ADDITIVES	ADENOIDS	ADIAPHORA
ACUMENS	ADAPTOGEN	ADDITORY	ADENOMA	ADIEU
ACUMINATE	ADAPTOR	ADDLE	ADENOMAS	ADIEUS
ACUMINOUS	ADAPTORS	ADDLED	ADENOMATA	ADIEUX
ACUPOINT	ADAPTS	ADDLEMENT	ADENOSES	ADIOS
ACUPOINTS	ADAW	ADDLES	ADENOSINE	ADIOSES
ACUSHLA	ADAWED	ADDLING	ADENOSIS	ADIPIC
ACUSHLAS	ADAWING	ADDOOM	ADENYL	ADIPOCERE
ACUTANCE	ADAWS	ADDOOMED	ADENYLATE	ADIPOCYTE
ACUTANCES	ADAXIAL	ADDOOMING	ADENYLIC	ADIPOSE
ACUTE	ADAYS	ADDOOMS	ADENYLS	ADIPOSES
ACUTELY	ADBLOCKER	ADDORSED	ADEPT	ADIPOSIS
ACUTENESS	ADBOT	ADDRESS	ADEPTER	ADIPOSITY
ACUTER	ADBOTS	ADDRESSED	ADEPTEST	ADIPOUS
ACUTES	ADD	ADDRESSEE	ADEPTLY	ADIPSIA
ACUTEST	ADDABLE	ADDRESSER	ADEPTNESS	ADIPSIAS
ACYCLIC	ADDAX	ADDRESSES	ADEPTS	ADIT
ACYCLOVIR	ADDAXES	ADDRESSOR	ADEQUACY	ADITS
ACYL	ADDEBTED	ADDREST	ADEQUATE	ADJACENCE
ACYLATE	ADDED	ADDS	ADERMIN	ADJACENCY
ACYLATED	ADDEDLY	ADDUCE	ADERMINS	ADJACENT
ACYLATES	ADDEEM	ADDUCED	ADESPOTA	ADJACENTS
ACYLATING	ADDEEMED	ADDUCENT	ADESSIVE	ADJECTIVE
ACYLATION	ADDEEMING	ADDUCER	ADESSIVES	ADJIGO

ADJIGOS	ADMIN	ADONISE	ADRATES	ADULTING
ADJOIN	ADMINICLE	ADONISED	ADREAD	ADULTINGS
ADJOINED	ADMINS	ADONISES	ADREADED	ADULTLIKE
ADJOINING	ADMIRABLE	ADONISING	ADREADING	ADULTLY
ADJOINS	ADMIRABLY	ADONIZE	ADREADS	ADULTNESS
ADJOINT	ADMIRAL	ADONIZED	ADRED	ADULTRESS
ADJOINTS	ADMIRALS	ADONIZES	ADRENAL	ADULTS
ADJOURN	ADMIRALTY	ADONIZING	ADRENALIN	ADUMBRAL
ADJOURNED	ADMIRANCE	ADOORS	ADRENALLY	ADUMBRATE
ADJOURNS	ADMIRE	ADOPT	ADRENALS	ADUNC
ADJUDGE	ADMIRED	ADOPTABLE	ADRIFT	ADUNCATE
ADJUDGED	ADMIRER	ADOPTED	ADROIT	ADUNCATED
ADJUDGES	ADMIRERS	ADOPTEE	ADROITER	ADUNCITY
ADJUDGING	ADMIRES	ADOPTEES	ADROITEST	ADUNCOUS
ADJUNCT	ADMIRING	ADOPTER	ADROITLY	ADUST
ADJUNCTLY	ADMISSION	ADOPTERS	ADRY	ADUSTED
ADJUNCTS	ADMISSIVE	ADOPTING	ADS	ADUSTING
ADJURE	ADMIT	ADOPTION	ADSCRIPT	ADUSTS
ADJURED	ADMITS	ADOPTIONS	ADSCRIPTS	ADVANCE
ADJURER	ADMITTED	ADOPTIOUS	ADSORB	ADVANCED
ADJURERS	ADMITTEE	ADOPTIVE	ADSORBATE	ADVANCER
ADJURES	ADMITTEES	ADOPTS	ADSORBED	ADVANCERS
ADJURING	ADMITTER	ADORABLE	ADSORBENT	ADVANCES
ADJUROR	ADMITTERS	ADORABLY	ADSORBER	ADVANCING
ADJURORS	ADMITTING	ADORATION	ADSORBERS	ADVANTAGE
ADJUST	ADMIX	ADORBS	ADSORBING	ADVECT
ADJUSTED	ADMIXED	ADORE	ADSORBS	ADVECTED
ADJUSTER	ADMIXES	ADORED	ADSPEAK	ADVECTING
ADJUSTERS	ADMIXING	ADORER	ADSPEAKS	ADVECTION
ADJUSTING	ADMIXT	ADORERS	ADSUKI	ADVECTIVE
ADJUSTIVE	ADMIXTURE	ADORES	ADSUKIS	ADVECTS
ADJUSTOR	ADMONISH	ADORING	ADSUM	ADVENE
ADJUSTORS	ADMONITOR	ADORINGLY	ADUKI	ADVENED
ADJUSTS	ADNASCENT	ADORKABLE	ADUKIS	ADVENES
ADJUTAGE	ADNATE	ADORN	ADULARIA	ADVENING
ADJUTAGES	ADNATION	ADORNED	ADULARIAS	ADVENT
ADJUTANCY	ADNATIONS	ADORNER	ADULATE	ADVENTIVE
ADJUTANT	ADNEXA	ADORNERS	ADULATED	ADVENTS
ADJUTANTS	ADNEXAL	ADORNING	ADULATES	ADVENTURE
ADJUVANCY	ADNOMINAL	ADORNMENT	ADULATING	ADVERB
ADJUVANT	ADNOUN	ADORNS	ADULATION	ADVERBIAL
ADJUVANTS	ADNOUNS	ADOS	ADULATOR	ADVERBS
ADLAND	ADO	ADOWN	ADULATORS	ADVERSARY
ADLANDS	ADOBE	ADOZE	ADULATORY	ADVERSE
ADMAN	ADOBELIKE	ADPRESS	ADULT	ADVERSELY
ADMASS	ADOBES	ADPRESSED	ADULTED	ADVERSER
ADMASSES	ADOBO	ADPRESSES	ADULTERER	ADVERSEST
ADMEASURE	ADOBOS	ADRAD	ADULTERY	ADVERSITY
ADMEN	ADONIS	ADRATE	ADULTHOOD	ADVERT

ADVERTED	ADYNAMIC	AEON	AEROBUS	AEROSTAT
ADVERTENT	ADYTA	AEONIAN	AEROBUSES	AEROSTATS
ADVERTING	ADYTUM	AEONIC	AERODART	AEROTAXES
ADVERTISE	ADZ	AEONS	AERODARTS	AEROTAXIS
ADVERTIZE	ADZE	AEPYORNIS	AERODROME	AEROTONE
ADVERTS	ADZED	AEQUORIN	AERODUCT	AEROTONES
ADVEW	ADZELIKE	AEQUORINS	AERODUCTS	AEROTRAIN
ADVEWED	ADZES	AERADIO	AERODYNE	AERUGO
ADVEWING	ADZING	AERADIOS	AERODYNES	AERUGOS
ADVEWS	ADZUKI	AERATE	AEROFOIL	AERY
ADVICE	ADZUKIS	AERATED	AEROFOILS	AESC
ADVICEFUL	AE	AERATES	AEROGEL	AESCES
ADVICES	AECIA	AERATING	AEROGELS	AESCULIN
ADVISABLE	AECIAL	AERATION	AEROGRAM	AESCULINS
ADVISABLY	AECIDIA	AERATIONS	AEROGRAMS	AESIR
ADVISE	AECIDIAL	AERATOR	AEROGRAPH	AESTHESES
ADVISED	AECIDIUM	AERATORS	AEROLITE	AESTHESIA
ADVISEDLY	AECIUM	AERIAL	AEROLITES	AESTHESIS
ADVISEE	AEDES	AERIALIST	AEROLITH	AESTHETE
ADVISEES	AEDICULE	AERIALITY	AEROLITHS	AESTHETES
ADVISER	AEDICULES	AERIALLY	AEROLITIC	AESTHETIC
ADVISERS	AEDILE	AERIALS	AEROLOGIC	AESTIVAL
ADVISES	AEDILES	AERIE	AEROLOGY	AESTIVATE
ADVISING	AEDINE	AERIED	AEROMANCY	AETATIS
ADVISINGS	AEFALD	AERIER	AEROMETER	AETHER
ADVISOR	AEFAULD	AERIES	AEROMETRY	AETHEREAL
ADVISORS	AEGIRINE	AERIEST	AEROMOTOR	AETHERIC
ADVISORY	AEGIRINES	AERIFIED	AERONAUT	AETHERS
ADVOCAAT	AEGIRITE	AERIFIES	AERONAUTS	AETIOLOGY
ADVOCAATS	AEGIRITES	AERIFORM	AERONOMER	AFALD
ADVOCACY	AEGIS	AERIFY	AERONOMIC	AFAR
ADVOCATE	AEGISES	AERIFYING	AERONOMY	AFARA
ADVOCATED	AEGLOGUE	AERILY	AEROPAUSE	AFARAS
ADVOCATES	AEGLOGUES	AERO	AEROPHAGY	AFARS
ADVOCATOR	AEGROTAT	AEROBAT	AEROPHOBE	AFAWLD
ADVOUTRER	AEGROTATS	AEROBATIC	AEROPHONE	AFEAR
ADVOUTRY	AEGYO	AEROBATS	AEROPHORE	AFEARD
ADVOWSON	AEGYOS	AEROBE	AEROPHYTE	AFEARED
ADVOWSONS	AEMULE	AEROBES	AEROPLANE	AFEARING
ADWARD	AEMULED	AEROBIA	AEROPULSE	AFEARS
ADWARDED	AEMULES	AEROBIC	AEROS	AFEBRILE
ADWARDING	AEMULING	AEROBICS	AEROSAT	AFF
ADWARDS	AENEI	AEROBIONT	AEROSATS	AFFABLE
ADWARE	AENEOUS	AEROBIUM	AEROSCOPE	AFFABLY
ADWARES	AENEUS	AEROBOMB	AEROSHELL	AFFAIR
ADWOMAN	AENEUSES	AEROBOMBS	AEROSOL	AFFAIRE
ADWOMEN	AEOLIAN	AEROBOT	AEROSOLS	AFFAIRES
ADYNAMIA	AEOLIPILE	AEROBOTS	AEROSPACE	AFFAIRS
ADYNAMIAS	AEOLIPYLE	AEROBRAKE	AEROSPIKE	AFFEAR

AFFEARD	AFFIXERS	AFFRIGHT	AFTEREYES	AGAMONTS
AFFEARE	AFFIXES	AFFRIGHTS	AFTERGAME	AGAMOUS
AFFEARED	AFFIXIAL	AFFRONT	AFTERGLOW	AGAPAE
AFFEARES	AFFIXING	AFFRONTE	AFTERHEAT	AGAPAI
AFFEARING	AFFIXMENT	AFFRONTED	AFTERINGS	AGAPE
AFFEARS	AFFIXTURE	AFFRONTEE	AFTERLIFE	AGAPEIC
AFFECT	AFFLATED	AFFRONTS	AFTERMAST	AGAPES
AFFECTED	AFFLATION	AFFUSION	AFTERMATH	AGAR
AFFECTER	AFFLATUS	AFFUSIONS	AFTERMOST	AGARIC
AFFECTERS	AFFLICT	AFFY	AFTERNOON	AGARICS
AFFECTING	AFFLICTED	AFFYDE	AFTERPAIN	AGAROSE
AFFECTION	AFFLICTER	AFFYING	AFTERPEAK	AGAROSES
AFFECTIVE	AFFLICTS	AFGHAN	AFTERS	AGARS
AFFECTS	AFFLUENCE	AFGHANI	AFTERSHOW	AGARWOOD
AFFEER	AFFLUENCY	AFGHANIS	AFTERSUN	AGARWOODS
AFFEERED	AFFLUENT	AFGHANS	AFTERSUNS	AGAS
AFFEERING	AFFLUENTS	AFIELD	AFTERTAX	AGAST
AFFEERS	AFFLUENZA	AFIRE	AFTERTIME	AGASTED
AFFERENT	AFFLUX	AFLAJ	AFTERWARD	AGASTING
AFFERENTS	AFFLUXES	AFLAME	AFTERWORD	AGASTS
AFFIANCE	AFFLUXION	AFLATOXIN	AFTMOST	AGATE
AFFIANCED	AFFOGATO	AFLOAT	AFTOSA	AGATES
AFFIANCES	AFFOGATOS	AFLUTTER	AFTOSAS	AGATEWARE
AFFIANT	AFFOORD	AFOCAL	AG	AGATISE
AFFIANTS	AFFOORDED	AFOOT	AGA	AGATISED
AFFICHE	AFFOORDS	AFORE	AGACANT	AGATISES
AFFICHES	AFFORCE	AFOREHAND	AGACANTE	AGATISING
AFFIDAVIT	AFFORCED	AFORESAID	AGACERIE	AGATIZE
AFFIED	AFFORCES	AFORETIME	AGACERIES	AGATIZED
AFFIES	AFFORCING	AFOUL	AGAIN	AGATIZES
AFFILIATE	AFFORD	AFRAID	AGAINST	AGATIZING
AFFINAL	AFFORDED	AFREET	AGALACTIA	AGATOID
AFFINE	AFFORDING	AFREETS	AGALLOCH	AGAVE
AFFINED	AFFORDS	AFRESH	AGALLOCHS	AGAVES
AFFINELY	AFFOREST	AFRIT	AGALWOOD	AGAZE
AFFINES	AFFORESTS	AFRITS	AGALWOODS	AGAZED
AFFINITY	AFFRAP	AFRO	AGAMA	AGE
AFFIRM	AFFRAPPED	AFRONT	AGAMAS	AGED
AFFIRMANT	AFFRAPS	AFROS	AGAMETE	AGEDLY
AFFIRMED	AFFRAY	AFT	AGAMETES	AGEDNESS
AFFIRMER	AFFRAYED	AFTER	AGAMI	AGEE
AFFIRMERS	AFFRAYER	AFTERBODY	AGAMIC	AGEING
AFFIRMING	AFFRAYERS	AFTERBURN	AGAMID	AGEINGS
AFFIRMS	AFFRAYING	AFTERCARE	AGAMIDS	AGEISM
AFFIX	AFFRAYS	AFTERCLAP	AGAMIS	AGEISMS
AFFIXABLE	AFFRENDED	AFTERDAMP	AGAMOGONY	AGEIST
AFFIXAL	AFFRET	AFTERDECK	AGAMOID	AGEISTS
AFFIXED	AFFRETS	AFTEREYE	AGAMOIDS	AGELAST
AFFIXER	AFFRICATE	AFTEREYED	AGAMONT	AGELASTIC

AGELASTS
AGELESS
AGELESSLY
AGELONG
AGEMATE
AGEMATES
AGEN
AGENCIES
AGENCY
AGENDA
AGENDAS
AGENDER
AGENDUM
AGENDUMS
AGENE
AGENES
AGENESES
AGENESIA
AGENESIAS
AGENESIS
AGENETIC
AGENISE
AGENISED
AGENISES
AGENISING
AGENIZE
AGENIZED
AGENIZES
AGENIZING
AGENT
AGENTED
AGENTIAL
AGENTING
AGENTINGS
AGENTIVAL
AGENTIVE
AGENTIVES
AGENTRIES
AGENTRY
AGENTS
AGER
AGERATUM
AGERATUMS
AGERS
AGES
AGEUSIA
AGEUSIAS
AGFLATION
AGGADA

AGGADAH
AGGADAHS
AGGADAS
AGGADIC
AGGADOT
AGGADOTH
AGGER
AGGERS
AGGIE
AGGIER
AGGIES
AGGIEST
AGGRACE
AGGRACED
AGGRACES
AGGRACING
AGGRADE
AGGRADED
AGGRADES
AGGRADING
AGGRATE
AGGRATED
AGGRATES
AGGRATING
AGGRAVATE
AGGREGATE
AGGRESS
AGGRESSED
AGGRESSES
AGGRESSOR
AGGRI
AGGRIEVE
AGGRIEVED
AGGRIEVES
AGGRO
AGGROS
AGGRY
AGGY
AGHA
AGHAS
AGHAST
AGILA
AGILAS
AGILE
AGILELY
AGILENESS
AGILER
AGILEST
AGILITIES

AGILITY
AGIN
AGING
AGINGS
AGINNER
AGINNERS
AGIO
AGIOS
AGIOTAGE
AGIOTAGES
AGISM
AGISMS
AGIST
AGISTED
AGISTER
AGISTERS
AGISTING
AGISTMENT
AGISTOR
AGISTORS
AGISTS
AGITA
AGITABLE
AGITANS
AGITAS
AGITATE
AGITATED
AGITATES
AGITATING
AGITATION
AGITATIVE
AGITATO
AGITATOR
AGITATORS
AGITPOP
AGITPOPS
AGITPROP
AGITPROPS
AGLARE
AGLEAM
AGLEE
AGLET
AGLETS
AGLEY
AGLIMMER
AGLITTER
AGLOO
AGLOOS
AGLOSSAL

AGLOSSATE
AGLOSSIA
AGLOSSIAS
AGLOW
AGLU
AGLUS
AGLY
AGLYCON
AGLYCONE
AGLYCONES
AGLYCONS
AGMA
AGMAS
AGMINATE
AGNAIL
AGNAILS
AGNAME
AGNAMED
AGNAMES
AGNATE
AGNATES
AGNATHAN
AGNATHANS
AGNATHOUS
AGNATIC
AGNATICAL
AGNATION
AGNATIONS
AGNISE
AGNISED
AGNISES
AGNISING
AGNIZE
AGNIZED
AGNIZES
AGNIZING
AGNOLOTTI
AGNOMEN
AGNOMENS
AGNOMINA
AGNOMINAL
AGNOSIA
AGNOSIAS
AGNOSIC
AGNOSTIC
AGNOSTICS
AGO
AGOG
AGOGE

AGOGES
AGOGIC
AGOGICS
AGOING
AGON
AGONAL
AGONE
AGONES
AGONIC
AGONIES
AGONISE
AGONISED
AGONISES
AGONISING
AGONISM
AGONISMS
AGONIST
AGONISTES
AGONISTIC
AGONISTS
AGONIZE
AGONIZED
AGONIZES
AGONIZING
AGONS
AGONY
AGOOD
AGORA
AGORAE
AGORAS
AGOROT
AGOROTH
AGOUTA
AGOUTAS
AGOUTI
AGOUTIES
AGOUTIS
AGOUTY
AGRAFE
AGRAFES
AGRAFFE
AGRAFFES
AGRAPHA
AGRAPHIA
AGRAPHIAS
AGRAPHIC
AGRAPHON
AGRARIAN
AGRARIANS

AGRASTE	AGUACATE	AHOY	AILANTHIC	AIRBRUSH
AGRAVIC	AGUACATES	AHS	AILANTHUS	AIRBURST
AGREE	AGUE	AHULL	AILANTO	AIRBURSTS
AGREEABLE	AGUED	AHUNGERED	AILANTOS	AIRBUS
AGREEABLY	AGUELIKE	AHUNGRY	AILED	AIRBUSES
AGREED	AGUES	AHURU	AILERON	AIRBUSSES
AGREEING	AGUEWEED	AHURUHURU	AILERONS	AIRCHECK
AGREEMENT	AGUEWEEDS	AHURUS	AILETTE	AIRCHECKS
AGREES	AGUISE	AI	AILETTES	AIRCOACH
AGREGE	AGUISED	AIA	AILING	AIRCON
AGREGES	AGUISES	AIAS	AILMENT	AIRCONS
AGREMENS	AGUISH	AIBLINS	AILMENTS	AIRCRAFT
AGREMENT	AGUISHLY	AID	AILS	AIRCREW
AGREMENTS	AGUISING	AIDA	AIM	AIRCREWS
AGRESTAL	AGUIZE	AIDANCE	AIMED	AIRDASH
AGRESTIAL	AGUIZED	AIDANCES	AIMER	AIRDASHED
AGRESTIC	AGUIZES	AIDANT	AIMERS	AIRDASHES
AGRIA	AGUIZING	AIDANTS	AIMFUL	AIRDATE
AGRIAS	AGUNA	AIDAS	AIMFULLY	AIRDATES
AGRIFOOD	AGUNAH	AIDE	AIMING	AIRDRAWN
AGRIFOODS	AGUNOT	AIDED	AIMLESS	AIRDROME
AGRIMONY	AGUNOTH	AIDER	AIMLESSLY	AIRDROMES
AGRIN	AGUTI	AIDERS	AIMS	AIRDROP
AGRINS	AGUTIS	AIDES	AIN	AIRDROPS
AGRIOLOGY	AGYRIA	AIDFUL	AINE	AIRED
AGRISE	AGYRIAS	AIDING	AINEE	AIRER
AGRISED	AH	AIDLESS	AINGA	AIRERS
AGRISES	AHA	AIDMAN	AINGAS	AIREST
AGRISING	AHADITH	AIDMEN	AINS	AIRFARE
AGRIZE	AHCHOO	AIDOI	AINSELL	AIRFARES
AGRIZED	AHEAD	AIDOS	AINSELLS	AIRFIELD
AGRIZES	AHEAP	AIDS	AIOLI	AIRFIELDS
AGRIZING	AHED	AIERIES	AIOLIS	AIRFLOW
AGRO	AHEIGHT	AIERY	AIR	AIRFLOWS
AGRODOLCE	AHEM	AIGA	AIRBAG	AIRFOIL
AGROLOGIC	AHEMERAL	AIGAS	AIRBAGS	AIRFOILS
AGROLOGY	AHENT	AIGHT	AIRBALL	AIRFRAME
AGRONOMIC	AHI	AIGLET	AIRBALLED	AIRFRAMES
AGRONOMY	AHIGH	AIGLETS	AIRBALLS	AIRGAP
AGROS	AHIMSA	AIGRET	AIRBASE	AIRGAPS
AGROUND	AHIMSAS	AIGRETS	AIRBASES	AIRGLOW
AGRYPNIA	AHIND	AIGRETTE	AIRBOARD	AIRGLOWS
AGRYPNIAS	AHING	AIGRETTES	AIRBOARDS	AIRGRAPH
AGRYZE	AHINT	AIGUILLE	AIRBOAT	AIRGRAPHS
AGRYZED	AHIS	AIGUILLES	AIRBOATS	AIRGUN
AGRYZES	AHISTORIC	AIKIDO	AIRBORNE	AIRGUNS
AGRYZING	AHOLD	AIKIDOS	AIRBOUND	AIRHEAD
AGS	AHOLDS	AIKONA	AIRBRICK	AIRHEADED
AGTERSKOT	AHORSE	AIL	AIRBRICKS	AIRHEADS

AIRHOLE	AIRSCREWS	AIRWOMAN	AKEAKE	ALAIMENT
AIRHOLES	AIRSHAFT	AIRWOMEN	AKEAKES	ALAIMENTS
AIRIER	AIRSHAFTS	AIRWORTHY	AKEBIA	ALALAGMOI
AIRIEST	AIRSHED	AIRY	AKEBIAS	ALALAGMOS
AIRILY	AIRSHEDS	AIS	AKED	ALALIA
AIRINESS	AIRSHIP	AISLE	AKEDAH	ALALIAS
AIRING	AIRSHIPS	AISLED	AKEDAHS	ALAMEDA
AIRINGS	AIRSHOT	AISLELESS	AKEE	ALAMEDAS
AIRLESS	AIRSHOTS	AISLES	AKEES	ALAMO
AIRLIFT	AIRSHOW	AISLEWAY	AKELA	ALAMODE
AIRLIFTED	AIRSHOWS	AISLEWAYS	AKELAS	ALAMODES
AIRLIFTS	AIRSICK	AISLING	AKENE	ALAMORT
AIRLIKE	AIRSIDE	AISLINGS	AKENES	ALAMOS
AIRLINE	AIRSIDES	AIT	AKENIAL	ALAN
AIRLINER	AIRSOFT	AITCH	AKES	ALAND
AIRLINERS	AIRSOFTS	AITCHBONE	AKHARA	ALANDS
AIRLINES	AIRSOME	AITCHES	AKHARAS	ALANE
AIRLOCK	AIRSPACE	AITS	AKIMBO	ALANG
AIRLOCKS	AIRSPACES	AITU	AKIN	ALANGS
AIRMAIL	AIRSPEED	AITUS	AKINESES	ALANIN
AIRMAILED	AIRSPEEDS	AIVER	AKINESIA	ALANINE
AIRMAILS	AIRSTOP	AIVERS	AKINESIAS	ALANINES
AIRMAN	AIRSTOPS	AIYEE	AKINESIS	ALANINS
AIRMEN	AIRSTREAM	AIZLE	AKINETIC	ALANNAH
AIRMOBILE	AIRSTRIKE	AIZLES	AKING	ALANNAHS
AIRN	AIRSTRIP	AJAR	AKIRAHO	ALANS
AIRNED	AIRSTRIPS	AJEE	AKIRAHOS	ALANT
AIRNING	AIRT	AJI	AKITA	ALANTS
AIRNS	AIRTED	AJIES	AKITAS	ALANYL
AIRPARK	AIRTH	AJIS	AKKAS	ALANYLS
AIRPARKS	AIRTHED	AJIVA	AKOLUTHOI	ALAP
AIRPLANE	AIRTHING	AJIVAS	AKOLUTHOS	ALAPA
AIRPLANES	AIRTHS	AJOWAN	AKRASIA	ALAPAS
AIRPLAY	AIRTIGHT	AJOWANS	AKRASIAS	ALAPS
AIRPLAYS	AIRTIME	AJUGA	AKRATIC	ALAR
AIRPORT	AIRTIMES	AJUGAS	AKVAVIT	ALARM
AIRPORTS	AIRTING	AJUTAGE	AKVAVITS	ALARMABLE
AIRPOST	AIRTRAM	AJUTAGES	AL	ALARMED
AIRPOSTS	AIRTRAMS	AJWAN	ALA	ALARMEDLY
AIRPOWER	AIRTS	AJWANS	ALAAP	ALARMING
AIRPOWERS	AIRVAC	AKA	ALAAPS	ALARMISM
AIRPROOF	AIRVACS	AKARYOTE	ALABAMINE	ALARMISMS
AIRPROOFS	AIRWARD	AKARYOTES	ALABASTER	ALARMIST
AIRPROX	AIRWARDS	AKARYOTIC	ALACHLOR	ALARMISTS
AIRPROXES	AIRWAVE	AKAS	ALACHLORS	ALARMS
AIRS	AIRWAVES	AKATEA	ALACK	ALARUM
AIRSCAPE	AIRWAY	AKATEAS	ALACKADAY	ALARUMED
AIRSCAPES	AIRWAYS	AKATHISIA	ALACRITY	ALARUMING
AIRSCREW	AIRWISE	AKE	ALAE	ALARUMS

ALARY	ALBINOISM	ALCHEMIC	ALDOXIMES	ALES
ALAS	ALBINOS	ALCHEMIES	ALDRIN	ALETHIC
ALASKA	ALBINOTIC	ALCHEMISE	ALDRINS	ALEURON
ALASKAS	ALBITE	ALCHEMIST	ALE	ALEURONE
ALASTOR	ALBITES	ALCHEMIZE	ALEATORIC	ALEURONES
ALASTORS	ALBITIC	ALCHEMY	ALEATORY	ALEURONIC
ALASTRIM	ALBITICAL	ALCHERA	ALEBENCH	ALEURONS
ALASTRIMS	ALBITISE	ALCHERAS	ALEC	ALEVIN
ALATE	ALBITISED	ALCHYMIES	ALECITHAL	ALEVINS
ALATED	ALBITISES	ALCHYMY	ALECK	ALEW
ALATES	ALBITIZE	ALCID	ALECKS	ALEWASHED
ALATION	ALBITIZED	ALCIDINE	ALECOST	ALEWIFE
ALATIONS	ALBITIZES	ALCIDS	ALECOSTS	ALEWIVES
ALAY	ALBIZIA	ALCO	ALECS	ALEWS
ALAYED	ALBIZIAS	ALCOHOL	ALECTRYON	ALEXANDER
ALAYING	ALBIZZIA	ALCOHOLIC	ALEE	ALEXIA
ALAYS	ALBIZZIAS	ALCOHOLS	ALEF	ALEXIAS
ALB	ALBRICIAS	ALCOLOCK	ALEFS	ALEXIC
ALBA	ALBS	ALCOLOCKS	ALEFT	ALEXIN
ALBACORE	ALBUGO	ALCOOL	ALEGAR	ALEXINE
ALBACORES	ALBUGOS	ALCOOLS	ALEGARS	ALEXINES
ALBARELLI	ALBUM	ALCOPOP	ALEGGE	ALEXINIC
ALBARELLO	ALBUMEN	ALCOPOPS	ALEGGED	ALEXINS
ALBAS	ALBUMENS	ALCORZA	ALEGGES	ALEYE
ALBATA	ALBUMIN	ALCORZAS	ALEGGING	ALEYED
ALBATAS	ALBUMINS	ALCOS	ALEHOUSE	ALEYES
ALBATROSS	ALBUMOSE	ALCOVE	ALEHOUSES	ALEYING
ALBE	ALBUMOSES	ALCOVED	ALEMBIC	ALFA
ALBEDO	ALBUMS	ALCOVES	ALEMBICS	ALFAKI
ALBEDOES	ALBURNOUS	ALDEA	ALEMBROTH	ALFAKIS
ALBEDOS	ALBURNUM	ALDEAS	ALENCON	ALFALFA
ALBEE	ALBURNUMS	ALDEHYDE	ALENCONS	ALFALFAS
ALBEIT	ALBUTEROL	ALDEHYDES	ALENGTH	ALFAQUI
ALBERGHI	ALCADE	ALDEHYDIC	ALEPH	ALFAQUIN
ALBERGO	ALCADES	ALDER	ALEPHS	ALFAQUINS
ALBERT	ALCAHEST	ALDERFLY	ALEPINE	ALFAQUIS
ALBERTITE	ALCAHESTS	ALDERMAN	ALEPINES	ALFAS
ALBERTS	ALCAIC	ALDERMEN	ALERCE	ALFERECES
ALBESCENT	ALCAICS	ALDERN	ALERCES	ALFEREZ
ALBESPINE	ALCAIDE	ALDERS	ALERION	ALFILARIA
ALBESPYNE	ALCAIDES	ALDICARB	ALERIONS	ALFILERIA
ALBICORE	ALCALDE	ALDICARBS	ALERT	ALFORJA
ALBICORES	ALCALDES	ALDOL	ALERTED	ALFORJAS
ALBINAL	ALCARRAZA	ALDOLASE	ALERTER	ALFREDO
ALBINESS	ALCATRAS	ALDOLASES	ALERTEST	ALFRESCO
ALBINIC	ALCAYDE	ALDOLS	ALERTING	ALGA
ALBINISM	ALCAYDES	ALDOSE	ALERTLY	ALGAE
ALBINISMS	ALCAZAR	ALDOSES	ALERTNESS	ALGAECIDE
ALBINO	ALCAZARS	ALDOXIME	ALERTS	ALGAL

ALGAROBA	ALIASING	ALIGNER	ALIZARIS	ALKYNE
ALGAROBAS	ALIASINGS	ALIGNERS	ALKAHEST	ALKYNES
ALGARROBA	ALIBI	ALIGNING	ALKAHESTS	ALL
ALGARROBO	ALIBIED	ALIGNMENT	ALKALI	ALLANITE
ALGAS	ALIBIES	ALIGNS	ALKALIC	ALLANITES
ALGATE	ALIBIING	ALIKE	ALKALIES	ALLANTOIC
ALGATES	ALIBIS	ALIKENESS	ALKALIFY	ALLANTOID
ALGEBRA	ALIBLE	ALIMENT	ALKALIN	ALLANTOIN
ALGEBRAIC	ALICANT	ALIMENTAL	ALKALINE	ALLANTOIS
ALGEBRAS	ALICANTS	ALIMENTED	ALKALIS	ALLATIVE
ALGERINE	ALICYCLIC	ALIMENTS	ALKALISE	ALLATIVES
ALGERINES	ALIDAD	ALIMONIED	ALKALISED	ALLAY
ALGESES	ALIDADE	ALIMONIES	ALKALISER	ALLAYED
ALGESIA	ALIDADES	ALIMONY	ALKALISES	ALLAYER
ALGESIAS	ALIDADS	ALINE	ALKALIZE	ALLAYERS
ALGESIC	ALIEN	ALINED	ALKALIZED	ALLAYING
ALGESIS	ALIENABLE	ALINEMENT	ALKALIZER	ALLAYINGS
ALGETIC	ALIENAGE	ALINER	ALKALIZES	ALLAYMENT
ALGICIDAL	ALIENAGES	ALINERS	ALKALOID	ALLAYS
ALGICIDE	ALIENATE	ALINES	ALKALOIDS	ALLCOMERS
ALGICIDES	ALIENATED	ALINING	ALKALOSES	ALLEDGE
ALGID	ALIENATES	ALIPED	ALKALOSIS	ALLEDGED
ALGIDITY	ALIENATOR	ALIPEDS	ALKALOTIC	ALLEDGES
ALGIDNESS	ALIENED	ALIPHATIC	ALKANE	ALLEDGING
ALGIN	ALIENEE	ALIQUANT	ALKANES	ALLEE
ALGINATE	ALIENEES	ALIQUOT	ALKANET	ALLEES
ALGINATES	ALIENER	ALIQUOTS	ALKANETS	ALLEGE
ALGINIC	ALIENERS	ALISMA	ALKANNIN	ALLEGED
ALGINS	ALIENING	ALISMAS	ALKANNINS	ALLEGEDLY
ALGO	ALIENISM	ALISON	ALKENE	ALLEGER
ALGOID	ALIENISMS	ALISONS	ALKENES	ALLEGERS
ALGOLOGY	ALIENIST	ALIST	ALKIE	ALLEGES
ALGOMETER	ALIENISTS	ALIT	ALKIES	ALLEGGE
ALGOMETRY	ALIENLY	ALITERACY	ALKINE	ALLEGGED
ALGOR	ALIENNESS	ALITERATE	ALKINES	ALLEGGES
ALGORISM	ALIENOR	ALIUNDE	ALKO	ALLEGGING
ALGORISMS	ALIENORS	ALIVE	ALKOS	ALLEGIANT
ALGORITHM	ALIENS	ALIVENESS	ALKOXIDE	ALLEGING
ALGORS	ALIF	ALIYA	ALKOXIDES	ALLEGORIC
ALGOS	ALIFORM	ALIYAH	ALKOXY	ALLEGORY
ALGUACIL	ALIFS	ALIYAHS	ALKY	ALLEGRO
ALGUACILS	ALIGARTA	ALIYAS	ALKYD	ALLEGROS
ALGUAZIL	ALIGARTAS	ALIYOS	ALKYDS	ALLEL
ALGUAZILS	ALIGHT	ALIYOT	ALKYL	ALLELE
ALGUM	ALIGHTED	ALIYOTH	ALKYLATE	ALLELES
ALGUMS	ALIGHTING	ALIZARI	ALKYLATED	ALLELIC
ALIAS	ALIGHTS	ALIZARIN	ALKYLATES	ALLELISM
ALIASED	ALIGN	ALIZARINE	ALKYLIC	ALLELISMS
ALIASES	ALIGNED	ALIZARINS	ALKYLS	ALLELS

ALLELUIA	ALLNESS	ALLOTTED	ALLUVIAL	ALMONRY
ALLELUIAH	ALLNESSES	ALLOTTEE	ALLUVIALS	ALMOST
ALLELUIAS	ALLNIGHT	ALLOTTEES	ALLUVION	ALMOUS
ALLEMANDE	ALLOBAR	ALLOTTER	ALLUVIONS	ALMS
ALLENARLY	ALLOBARS	ALLOTTERS	ALLUVIUM	ALMSGIVER
ALLERGEN	ALLOCABLE	ALLOTTERY	ALLUVIUMS	ALMSHOUSE
ALLERGENS	ALLOCARPY	ALLOTTING	ALLY	ALMSMAN
ALLERGIC	ALLOCATE	ALLOTYPE	ALLYING	ALMSMEN
ALLERGICS	ALLOCATED	ALLOTYPES	ALLYL	ALMSWOMAN
ALLERGIES	ALLOCATES	ALLOTYPIC	ALLYLIC	ALMSWOMEN
ALLERGIN	ALLOCATOR	ALLOTYPY	ALLYLS	ALMUCE
ALLERGINS	ALLOD	ALLOVER	ALLYOU	ALMUCES
ALLERGIST	ALLODIA	ALLOVERS	ALLYSHIP	ALMUD
ALLERGY	ALLODIAL	ALLOW	ALLYSHIPS	ALMUDE
ALLERION	ALLODIUM	ALLOWABLE	ALMA	ALMUDES
ALLERIONS	ALLODIUMS	ALLOWABLY	ALMAGEST	ALMUDS
ALLETHRIN	ALLODS	ALLOWANCE	ALMAGESTS	ALMUG
ALLEVIANT	ALLODYNIA	ALLOWED	ALMAH	ALMUGS
ALLEVIATE	ALLOGAMY	ALLOWEDLY	ALMAHS	ALNAGE
ALLEY	ALLOGENIC	ALLOWING	ALMAIN	ALNAGER
ALLEYCAT	ALLOGRAFT	ALLOWS	ALMAINS	ALNAGERS
ALLEYCATS	ALLOGRAPH	ALLOXAN	ALMANAC	ALNAGES
ALLEYED	ALLOMERIC	ALLOXANS	ALMANACK	ALNICO
ALLEYS	ALLOMETRY	ALLOY	ALMANACKS	ALNICOS
ALLEYWAY	ALLOMONE	ALLOYED	ALMANACS	ALOCASIA
ALLEYWAYS	ALLOMONES	ALLOYING	ALMANDINE	ALOCASIAS
ALLHEAL	ALLOMORPH	ALLOYS	ALMANDITE	ALOD
ALLHEALS	ALLONGE	ALLOZYME	ALMAS	ALODIA
ALLIABLE	ALLONGED	ALLOZYMES	ALME	ALODIAL
ALLIAK	ALLONGES	ALLS	ALMEH	ALODIUM
ALLIAKS	ALLONGING	ALLSEED	ALMEHS	ALODIUMS
ALLIANCE	ALLONS	ALLSEEDS	ALMEMAR	ALODS
ALLIANCES	ALLONYM	ALLSORTS	ALMEMARS	ALOE
ALLICE	ALLONYMS	ALLSPICE	ALMERIES	ALOED
ALLICES	ALLOPATH	ALLSPICES	ALMERY	ALOES
ALLICHOLY	ALLOPATHS	ALLUDE	ALMES	ALOESWOOD
ALLICIN	ALLOPATHY	ALLUDED	ALMIGHTY	ALOETIC
ALLICINS	ALLOPATRY	ALLUDES	ALMIRAH	ALOETICS
ALLIED	ALLOPHANE	ALLUDING	ALMIRAHS	ALOFT
ALLIES	ALLOPHONE	ALLURE	ALMNER	ALOGIA
ALLIGARTA	ALLOPLASM	ALLURED	ALMNERS	ALOGIAS
ALLIGATE	ALLOSAUR	ALLURER	ALMOND	ALOGICAL
ALLIGATED	ALLOSAURS	ALLURERS	ALMONDIER	ALOHA
ALLIGATES	ALLOSTERY	ALLURES	ALMONDITE	ALOHAS
ALLIGATOR	ALLOT	ALLURING	ALMONDS	ALOIN
ALLIS	ALLOTMENT	ALLUSION	ALMONDY	ALOINS
ALLISES	ALLOTROPE	ALLUSIONS	ALMONER	ALONE
ALLIUM	ALLOTROPY	ALLUSIVE	ALMONERS	ALONELY
ALLIUMS	ALLOTS	ALLUVIA	ALMONRIES	ALONENESS

ALONG	ALSO	ALTITUDE	ALURE	AMARELLE
ALONGSIDE	ALSOON	ALTITUDES	ALURES	AMARELLES
ALONGST	ALSOONE	ALTO	ALUS	AMARETTI
ALOO	ALT	ALTOIST	ALVAR	AMARETTO
ALOOF	ALTAR	ALTOISTS	ALVARS	AMARETTOS
ALOOFLY	ALTARAGE	ALTOS	ALVEARIES	AMARNA
ALOOFNESS	ALTARAGES	ALTRICES	ALVEARY	AMARONE
ALOOS	ALTARS	ALTRICIAL	ALVEATED	AMARONES
ALOPECIA	ALTARWISE	ALTRUISM	ALVEOLAR	AMARYLLID
ALOPECIAS	ALTCOIN	ALTRUISMS	ALVEOLARS	AMARYLLIS
ALOPECIC	ALTCOINS	ALTRUIST	ALVEOLATE	AMAS
ALOPECOID	ALTER	ALTRUISTS	ALVEOLE	AMASS
ALOUD	ALTERABLE	ALTS	ALVEOLES	AMASSABLE
ALOW	ALTERABLY	ALU	ALVEOLI	AMASSED
ALOWE	ALTERANT	ALUDEL	ALVEOLUS	AMASSER
ALP	ALTERANTS	ALUDELS	ALVINE	AMASSERS
ALPACA	ALTERCATE	ALULA	ALWAY	AMASSES
ALPACAS	ALTERED	ALULAE	ALWAYS	AMASSING
ALPACCA	ALTERER	ALULAR	ALYSSUM	AMASSMENT
ALPACCAS	ALTERERS	ALULAS	ALYSSUMS	AMATE
ALPARGATA	ALTERING	ALUM	AM	AMATED
ALPEEN	ALTERITY	ALUMIN	AMA	AMATES
ALPEENS	ALTERN	ALUMINA	AMABILE	AMATEUR
ALPENGLOW	ALTERNANT	ALUMINAS	AMADAVAT	AMATEURS
ALPENHORN	ALTERNAT	ALUMINATE	AMADAVATS	AMATING
ALPHA	ALTERNATE	ALUMINE	AMADODA	AMATION
ALPHABET	ALTERNATS	ALUMINES	AMADOU	AMATIONS
ALPHABETS	ALTERNE	ALUMINIC	AMADOUS	AMATIVE
ALPHAS	ALTERNES	ALUMINIDE	AMAH	AMATIVELY
ALPHASORT	ALTERS	ALUMINISE	AMAHS	AMATOL
ALPHATEST	ALTESSE	ALUMINIUM	AMAIN	AMATOLS
ALPHORN	ALTESSES	ALUMINIZE	AMAKHOSI	AMATORIAL
ALPHORNS	ALTEZA	ALUMINOUS	AMAKOSI	AMATORIAN
ALPHOSIS	ALTEZAS	ALUMINS	AMALGAM	AMATORY
ALPHYL	ALTEZZA	ALUMINUM	AMALGAMS	AMAUROSES
ALPHYLS	ALTEZZAS	ALUMINUMS	AMANDINE	AMAUROSIS
ALPINE	ALTHAEA	ALUMISH	AMANDINES	AMAUROTIC
ALPINELY	ALTHAEAS	ALUMIUM	AMANDLA	AMAUT
ALPINES	ALTHEA	ALUMIUMS	AMANDLAS	AMAUTI
ALPINISM	ALTHEAS	ALUMNA	AMANITA	AMAUTIK
ALPINISMS	ALTHO	ALUMNAE	AMANITAS	AMAUTIKS
ALPINIST	ALTHORN	ALUMNI	AMANITIN	AMAUTIS
ALPINISTS	ALTHORNS	ALUMNUS	AMANITINS	AMAUTS
ALPS	ALTHOUGH	ALUMROOT	AMARACUS	AMAZE
ALREADY	ALTIGRAPH	ALUMROOTS	AMARANT	AMAZED
ALRIGHT	ALTIMETER	ALUMS	AMARANTH	AMAZEDLY
ALS	ALTIMETRY	ALUMSTONE	AMARANTHS	AMAZEMENT
ALSIKE	ALTIPLANO	ALUNITE	AMARANTIN	AMAZES
ALSIKES	ALTISSIMO	ALUNITES	AMARANTS	AMAZING

AMAZINGLY	AMBIPOLAR	AMBUSHER	AMENS	AMIDOL
AMAZON	AMBIT	AMBUSHERS	AMENT	AMIDOLS
AMAZONIAN	AMBITION	AMBUSHES	AMENTA	AMIDONE
AMAZONITE	AMBITIONS	AMBUSHING	AMENTAL	AMIDONES
AMAZONS	AMBITIOUS	AME	AMENTIA	AMIDS
AMBACH	AMBITS	AMEARST	AMENTIAS	AMIDSHIP
AMBACHES	AMBITTY	AMEBA	AMENTS	AMIDSHIPS
AMBAGE	AMBIVERT	AMEBAE	AMENTUM	AMIDST
AMBAGES	AMBIVERTS	AMEBAN	AMERCE	AMIE
AMBAGIOUS	AMBLE	AMEBAS	AMERCED	AMIES
AMBAN	AMBLED	AMEBEAN	AMERCER	AMIGA
AMBANS	AMBLER	AMEBIASES	AMERCERS	AMIGAS
AMBARI	AMBLERS	AMEBIASIS	AMERCES	AMIGO
AMBARIES	AMBLES	AMEBIC	AMERCING	AMIGOS
AMBARIS	AMBLING	AMEBOCYTE	AMERICIUM	AMILDAR
AMBARY	AMBLINGS	AMEBOID	AMES	AMILDARS
AMBASSAGE	AMBLYOPIA	AMEER	AMESACE	AMIN
AMBASSIES	AMBLYOPIC	AMEERATE	AMESACES	AMINE
AMBASSY	AMBO	AMEERATES	AMETHYST	AMINES
AMBATCH	AMBOINA	AMEERS	AMETHYSTS	AMINIC
AMBATCHES	AMBOINAS	AMEIOSES	AMETROPIA	AMINITIES
AMBEER	AMBOINES	AMEIOSIS	AMETROPIC	AMINITY
AMBEERS	AMBOS	AMELCORN	AMI	AMINO
AMBER	AMBOYNA	AMELCORNS	AMIA	AMINOS
AMBERED	AMBOYNAS	AMELIA	AMIABLE	AMINS
AMBERGRIS	AMBRIES	AMELIAS	AMIABLY	AMIR
AMBERIER	AMBROID	AMEN	AMIANTHUS	AMIRATE
AMBERIES	AMBROIDS	AMENABLE	AMIANTUS	AMIRATES
AMBERIEST	AMBROSIA	AMENABLY	AMIAS	AMIRIGHT
AMBERINA	AMBROSIAL	AMENAGE	AMICABLE	AMIRITE
AMBERINAS	AMBROSIAN	AMENAGED	AMICABLY	AMIRS
AMBERITE	AMBROSIAS	AMENAGES	AMICE	AMIS
AMBERITES	AMBROTYPE	AMENAGING	AMICES	AMISES
AMBERJACK	AMBRY	AMENAUNCE	AMICI	AMISS
AMBEROID	AMBSACE	AMEND	AMICUS	AMISSES
AMBEROIDS	AMBSACES	AMENDABLE	AMID	AMISSIBLE
AMBEROUS	AMBULACRA	AMENDE	AMIDASE	AMISSING
AMBERS	AMBULANCE	AMENDED	AMIDASES	AMITIES
AMBERY	AMBULANT	AMENDER	AMIDE	AMITOSES
AMBIANCE	AMBULANTS	AMENDERS	AMIDES	AMITOSIS
AMBIANCES	AMBULATE	AMENDES	AMIDIC	AMITOTIC
AMBIENCE	AMBULATED	AMENDING	AMIDIN	AMITROLE
AMBIENCES	AMBULATES	AMENDMENT	AMIDINE	AMITROLES
AMBIENT	AMBULATOR	AMENDS	AMIDINES	AMITY
AMBIENTS	AMBULETTE	AMENE	AMIDINS	AMLA
AMBIGRAM	AMBUSCADE	AMENED	AMIDMOST	AMLAS
AMBIGRAMS	AMBUSCADO	AMENING	AMIDO	AMMAN
AMBIGUITY	AMBUSH	AMENITIES	AMIDOGEN	AMMANS
AMBIGUOUS	AMBUSHED	AMENITY	AMIDOGENS	AMMETER

AMMETERS	AMNIONIC	AMORISTIC	AMPHIBOLE	AMRITAS
AMMINE	AMNIONS	AMORISTS	AMPHIBOLY	AMRITATVA
AMMINES	AMNIOS	AMORNINGS	AMPHIGORY	AMRITS
AMMINO	AMNIOTE	AMOROSA	AMPHIOXI	AMSINCKIA
AMMIRAL	AMNIOTES	AMOROSAS	AMPHIOXUS	AMTMAN
AMMIRALS	AMNIOTIC	AMOROSITY	AMPHIPATH	AMTMANS
AMMO	AMNIOTOMY	AMOROSO	AMPHIPOD	AMTRAC
AMMOCETE	AMOEBA	AMOROSOS	AMPHIPODS	AMTRACK
AMMOCETES	AMOEBAE	AMOROUS	AMPHOLYTE	AMTRACKS
AMMOCOETE	AMOEBAEAN	AMOROUSLY	AMPHORA	AMTRACS
AMMOLITE	AMOEBAN	AMORPHISM	AMPHORAE	AMTRAK
AMMOLITES	AMOEBAS	AMORPHOUS	AMPHORAL	AMTRAKS
AMMON	AMOEBEAN	AMORT	AMPHORAS	AMU
AMMONAL	AMOEBIC	AMORTISE	AMPHORIC	AMUCK
AMMONALS	AMOEBOID	AMORTISED	AMPING	AMUCKS
AMMONATE	AMOK	AMORTISES	AMPLE	AMULET
AMMONATES	AMOKS	AMORTIZE	AMPLENESS	AMULETIC
AMMONIA	AMOKURA	AMORTIZED	AMPLER	AMULETS
AMMONIAC	AMOKURAS	AMORTIZES	AMPLEST	AMUS
AMMONIACS	AMOLE	AMOSITE	AMPLEXUS	AMUSABLE
AMMONIAS	AMOLES	AMOSITES	AMPLIDYNE	AMUSE
AMMONIATE	AMOMUM	AMOTION	AMPLIFIED	AMUSEABLE
AMMONIC	AMOMUMS	AMOTIONS	AMPLIFIER	AMUSED
AMMONICAL	AMONG	AMOUNT	AMPLIFIES	AMUSEDLY
AMMONIFY	AMONGST	AMOUNTED	AMPLIFY	AMUSEMENT
AMMONITE	AMOOVE	AMOUNTING	AMPLITUDE	AMUSER
AMMONITES	AMOOVED	AMOUNTS	AMPLOSOME	AMUSERS
AMMONITIC	AMOOVES	AMOUR	AMPLY	AMUSES
AMMONIUM	AMOOVING	AMOURETTE	AMPOULE	AMUSETTE
AMMONIUMS	AMORAL	AMOURS	AMPOULES	AMUSETTES
AMMONO	AMORALISM	AMOVE	AMPS	AMUSIA
AMMONOID	AMORALIST	AMOVED	AMPUL	AMUSIAS
AMMONOIDS	AMORALITY	AMOVES	AMPULE	AMUSIC
AMMONS	AMORALLY	AMOVING	AMPULES	AMUSING
AMMOS	AMORANCE	AMOWT	AMPULLA	AMUSINGLY
AMNESIA	AMORANCES	AMOWTS	AMPULLAE	AMUSIVE
AMNESIAC	AMORANT	AMP	AMPULLAR	AMYGDAL
AMNESIACS	AMORCE	AMPACITY	AMPULLARY	AMYGDALA
AMNESIAS	AMORCES	AMPASSIES	AMPULS	AMYGDALAE
AMNESIC	AMORET	AMPASSY	AMPUTATE	AMYGDALE
AMNESICS	AMORETS	AMPED	AMPUTATED	AMYGDALES
AMNESTIC	AMORETTI	AMPERAGE	AMPUTATES	AMYGDALIN
AMNESTIED	AMORETTO	AMPERAGES	AMPUTATOR	AMYGDALS
AMNESTIES	AMORETTOS	AMPERE	AMPUTEE	AMYGDULE
AMNESTY	AMORINI	AMPERES	AMPUTEES	AMYGDULES
AMNIA	AMORINO	AMPERSAND	AMREETA	AMYL
AMNIC	AMORISM	AMPERZAND	AMREETAS	AMYLASE
AMNIO	AMORISMS	AMPHIBIA	AMRIT	AMYLASES
AMNION	AMORIST	AMPHIBIAN	AMRITA	AMYLENE

AMYLENES	ANAEROBIA	ANALYSAND	ANAPLASTY	ANCESTOR
AMYLIC	ANAEROBIC	ANALYSE	ANAPTYXES	ANCESTORS
AMYLOGEN	ANAGEN	ANALYSED	ANAPTYXIS	ANCESTRAL
AMYLOGENS	ANAGENS	ANALYSER	ANARCH	ANCESTRY
AMYLOID	ANAGLYPH	ANALYSERS	ANARCHAL	ANCHO
AMYLOIDAL	ANAGLYPHS	ANALYSES	ANARCHIAL	ANCHOR
AMYLOIDS	ANAGLYPHY	ANALYSING	ANARCHIC	ANCHORAGE
AMYLOPSIN	ANAGOGE	ANALYSIS	ANARCHIES	ANCHORED
AMYLOSE	ANAGOGES	ANALYST	ANARCHISE	ANCHORESS
AMYLOSES	ANAGOGIC	ANALYSTS	ANARCHISM	ANCHORET
AMYLS	ANAGOGIES	ANALYTE	ANARCHIST	ANCHORETS
AMYLUM	ANAGOGY	ANALYTES	ANARCHIZE	ANCHORING
AMYLUMS	ANAGRAM	ANALYTIC	ANARCHS	ANCHORITE
AMYOTONIA	ANAGRAMS	ANALYTICS	ANARCHY	ANCHORMAN
AMYTAL	ANAL	ANALYZE	ANARTHRIA	ANCHORMEN
AMYTALS	ANALCIME	ANALYZED	ANARTHRIC	ANCHORS
AN	ANALCIMES	ANALYZER	ANAS	ANCHOS
ANA	ANALCIMIC	ANALYZERS	ANASARCA	ANCHOVETA
ANABAENA	ANALCITE	ANALYZES	ANASARCAS	ANCHOVIES
ANABAENAS	ANALCITES	ANALYZING	ANASTASES	ANCHOVY
ANABANTID	ANALECTA	ANAMNESES	ANASTASIS	ANCHUSA
ANABAS	ANALECTIC	ANAMNESIS	ANASTATIC	ANCHUSAS
ANABASES	ANALECTS	ANAMNIOTE	ANATA	ANCHUSIN
ANABASIS	ANALEMMA	ANAN	ANATAS	ANCHUSINS
ANABATIC	ANALEMMAS	ANANA	ANATASE	ANCHYLOSE
ANABIOSES	ANALEPTIC	ANANAS	ANATASES	ANCIENT
ANABIOSIS	ANALGESIA	ANANASES	ANATEXES	ANCIENTER
ANABIOTIC	ANALGESIC	ANANDA	ANATEXIS	ANCIENTLY
ANABLEPS	ANALGETIC	ANANDAS	ANATHEMA	ANCIENTRY
ANABOLIC	ANALGIA	ANANDROUS	ANATHEMAS	ANCIENTS
ANABOLISM	ANALGIAS	ANANKE	ANATMAN	ANCILE
ANABOLITE	ANALITIES	ANANKES	ANATMANS	ANCILIA
ANABRANCH	ANALITY	ANANTHOUS	ANATOMIC	ANCILLA
ANACHARIS	ANALLY	ANAPAEST	ANATOMIES	ANCILLAE
ANACLINAL	ANALOG	ANAPAESTS	ANATOMISE	ANCILLARY
ANACLISES	ANALOGA	ANAPEST	ANATOMIST	ANCILLAS
ANACLISIS	ANALOGIC	ANAPESTIC	ANATOMIZE	ANCIPITAL
ANACLITIC	ANALOGIES	ANAPESTS	ANATOMY	ANCLE
ANACONDA	ANALOGISE	ANAPHASE	ANATOXIN	ANCLES
ANACONDAS	ANALOGISM	ANAPHASES	ANATOXINS	ANCOME
ANACRUSES	ANALOGIST	ANAPHASIC	ANATROPY	ANCOMES
ANACRUSIS	ANALOGIZE	ANAPHOR	ANATTA	ANCON
ANADEM	ANALOGON	ANAPHORA	ANATTAS	ANCONAL
ANADEMS	ANALOGONS	ANAPHORAL	ANATTO	ANCONE
ANAEMIA	ANALOGOUS	ANAPHORAS	ANATTOS	ANCONEAL
ANAEMIAS	ANALOGS	ANAPHORIC	ANAXIAL	ANCONES
ANAEMIC	ANALOGUE	ANAPHORS	ANBURIES	ANCONOID
ANAEROBE	ANALOGUES	ANAPLASIA	ANBURY	ANCORA
ANAEROBES	ANALOGY	ANAPLASMA	ANCE	ANCRESS

ANCRESSES
AND
ANDANTE
ANDANTES
ANDANTINI
ANDANTINO
ANDESINE
ANDESINES
ANDESITE
ANDESITES
ANDESITIC
ANDESYTE
ANDESYTES
ANDIRON
ANDIRONS
ANDOUILLE
ANDRADITE
ANDRO
ANDROECIA
ANDROGEN
ANDROGENS
ANDROGYNE
ANDROGYNY
ANDROID
ANDROIDS
ANDROLOGY
ANDROMEDA
ANDROS
ANDS
ANDVILE
ANDVILES
ANE
ANEAR
ANEARED
ANEARING
ANEARS
ANEATH
ANECDOTA
ANECDOTAL
ANECDOTE
ANECDOTES
ANECDOTIC
ANECDYSES
ANECDYSIS
ANECHOIC
ANELACE
ANELACES
ANELASTIC
ANELE

ANELED
ANELES
ANELING
ANELLI
ANEMIA
ANEMIAS
ANEMIC
ANEMOGRAM
ANEMOLOGY
ANEMONE
ANEMONES
ANEMOSES
ANEMOSIS
ANENST
ANENT
ANERGIA
ANERGIAS
ANERGIC
ANERGIES
ANERGY
ANERLY
ANEROID
ANEROIDS
ANES
ANESTRA
ANESTRI
ANESTROUS
ANESTRUM
ANESTRUS
ANETHOL
ANETHOLE
ANETHOLES
ANETHOLS
ANETIC
ANEUPLOID
ANEURIN
ANEURINS
ANEURISM
ANEURISMS
ANEURYSM
ANEURYSMS
ANEW
ANGA
ANGAKOK
ANGAKOKS
ANGANWADI
ANGARIA
ANGARIAS
ANGARIES

ANGARY
ANGAS
ANGASHORE
ANGEKKOK
ANGEKKOKS
ANGEKOK
ANGEKOKS
ANGEL
ANGELED
ANGELFISH
ANGELHOOD
ANGELIC
ANGELICA
ANGELICAL
ANGELICAS
ANGELING
ANGELS
ANGELUS
ANGELUSES
ANGER
ANGERED
ANGERING
ANGERLESS
ANGERLY
ANGERS
ANGICO
ANGICOS
ANGINA
ANGINAL
ANGINAS
ANGINOSE
ANGINOUS
ANGIOGRAM
ANGIOLOGY
ANGIOMA
ANGIOMAS
ANGIOMATA
ANGISHORE
ANGKLUNG
ANGKLUNGS
ANGLE
ANGLED
ANGLEDUG
ANGLEDUGS
ANGLEPOD
ANGLEPODS
ANGLER
ANGLERS
ANGLES

ANGLESITE
ANGLEWISE
ANGLEWORM
ANGLICE
ANGLICISE
ANGLICISM
ANGLICIST
ANGLICIZE
ANGLIFIED
ANGLIFIES
ANGLIFY
ANGLING
ANGLINGS
ANGLIST
ANGLISTS
ANGLO
ANGLOPHIL
ANGLOS
ANGOLA
ANGOPHORA
ANGORA
ANGORAS
ANGOSTURA
ANGRIER
ANGRIES
ANGRIEST
ANGRILY
ANGRINESS
ANGRY
ANGST
ANGSTED
ANGSTIER
ANGSTIEST
ANGSTING
ANGSTROM
ANGSTROMS
ANGSTS
ANGSTY
ANGUIFORM
ANGUINE
ANGUIPED
ANGUIPEDE
ANGUIPEDS
ANGUISH
ANGUISHED
ANGUISHES
ANGULAR
ANGULARLY
ANGULATE

ANGULATED
ANGULATES
ANGULOSE
ANGULOUS
ANHEDONIA
ANHEDONIC
ANHEDRAL
ANHEDRALS
ANHINGA
ANHINGAS
ANHUNGRED
ANHYDRASE
ANHYDRIDE
ANHYDRITE
ANHYDROUS
ANI
ANICCA
ANICCAS
ANICONIC
ANICONISM
ANICONIST
ANICUT
ANICUTS
ANIDROSES
ANIDROSIS
ANIGH
ANIGHT
ANIL
ANILE
ANILIN
ANILINE
ANILINES
ANILINGUS
ANILINS
ANILITIES
ANILITY
ANILS
ANIMA
ANIMACIES
ANIMACY
ANIMAL
ANIMALIAN
ANIMALIC
ANIMALIER
ANIMALISE
ANIMALISM
ANIMALIST
ANIMALITY
ANIMALIZE

ANIMALLY	ANISOLES	ANNATS	ANNUALIZE	ANODYNIC
ANIMALS	ANKER	ANNATTA	ANNUALLY	ANOESES
ANIMAS	ANKERITE	ANNATTAS	ANNUALS	ANOESIS
ANIMATE	ANKERITES	ANNATTO	ANNUITANT	ANOESTRA
ANIMATED	ANKERS	ANNATTOS	ANNUITIES	ANOESTRI
ANIMATELY	ANKH	ANNEAL	ANNUITISE	ANOESTRUM
ANIMATER	ANKHS	ANNEALED	ANNUITIZE	ANOESTRUS
ANIMATERS	ANKLE	ANNEALER	ANNUITY	ANOETIC
ANIMATES	ANKLEBONE	ANNEALERS	ANNUL	ANOINT
ANIMATEUR	ANKLED	ANNEALING	ANNULAR	ANOINTED
ANIMATI	ANKLES	ANNEALS	ANNULARLY	ANOINTER
ANIMATIC	ANKLET	ANNECTENT	ANNULARS	ANOINTERS
ANIMATICS	ANKLETS	ANNELID	ANNULATE	ANOINTING
ANIMATING	ANKLING	ANNELIDAN	ANNULATED	ANOINTS
ANIMATION	ANKLONG	ANNELIDS	ANNULATES	ANOLE
ANIMATISM	ANKLONGS	ANNEX	ANNULET	ANOLES
ANIMATIST	ANKLUNG	ANNEXABLE	ANNULETS	ANOLYTE
ANIMATO	ANKLUNGS	ANNEXE	ANNULI	ANOLYTES
ANIMATOR	ANKUS	ANNEXED	ANNULLED	ANOMALIES
ANIMATORS	ANKUSES	ANNEXES	ANNULLING	ANOMALOUS
ANIMATOS	ANKUSH	ANNEXING	ANNULMENT	ANOMALY
ANIME	ANKUSHES	ANNEXION	ANNULOSE	ANOMIC
ANIMES	ANKYLOSE	ANNEXIONS	ANNULS	ANOMIE
ANIMI	ANKYLOSED	ANNEXMENT	ANNULUS	ANOMIES
ANIMIS	ANKYLOSES	ANNEXURE	ANNULUSES	ANOMY
ANIMISM	ANKYLOSIS	ANNEXURES	ANOA	ANON
ANIMISMS	ANKYLOTIC	ANNICUT	ANOAS	ANONYM
ANIMIST	ANLACE	ANNICUTS	ANOBIID	ANONYMA
ANIMISTIC	ANLACES	ANNO	ANOBIIDS	ANONYMAS
ANIMISTS	ANLAGE	ANNONA	ANODAL	ANONYMISE
ANIMOSITY	ANLAGEN	ANNONAS	ANODALLY	ANONYMITY
ANIMUS	ANLAGES	ANNOTATE	ANODE	ANONYMIZE
ANIMUSES	ANLAS	ANNOTATED	ANODES	ANONYMOUS
ANION	ANLASES	ANNOTATES	ANODIC	ANONYMS
ANIONIC	ANN	ANNOTATOR	ANODISE	ANOOPSIA
ANIONS	ANNA	ANNOUNCE	ANODISED	ANOOPSIAS
ANIRIDIA	ANNAL	ANNOUNCED	ANODISER	ANOPHELES
ANIRIDIAS	ANNALISE	ANNOUNCER	ANODISERS	ANOPIA
ANIRIDIC	ANNALISED	ANNOUNCES	ANODISES	ANOPIAS
ANIS	ANNALISES	ANNOY	ANODISING	ANOPSIA
ANISE	ANNALIST	ANNOYANCE	ANODIZE	ANOPSIAS
ANISEED	ANNALISTS	ANNOYED	ANODIZED	ANORAK
ANISEEDS	ANNALIZE	ANNOYER	ANODIZER	ANORAKS
ANISES	ANNALIZED	ANNOYERS	ANODIZERS	ANORECTAL
ANISETTE	ANNALIZES	ANNOYING	ANODIZES	ANORECTIC
ANISETTES	ANNALS	ANNOYS	ANODIZING	ANORETIC
ANISIC	ANNAS	ANNS	ANODONTIA	ANORETICS
ANISOGAMY	ANNAT	ANNUAL	ANODYNE	ANOREXIA
ANISOLE	ANNATES	ANNUALISE	ANODYNES	ANOREXIAS

ANOREXIC	ANTAR	ANTHELIA	ANTIATOMS	ANTIELITE
ANOREXICS	ANTARA	ANTHELION	ANTIAUXIN	ANTIENT
ANOREXIES	ANTARAS	ANTHELIX	ANTIBAC	ANTIENTS
ANOREXY	ANTARCTIC	ANTHEM	ANTIBIAS	ANTIFA
ANORTHIC	ANTARS	ANTHEMED	ANTIBLACK	ANTIFAS
ANORTHITE	ANTAS	ANTHEMIA	ANTIBODY	ANTIFAT
ANOSMATIC	ANTBEAR	ANTHEMIC	ANTIBOSS	ANTIFLU
ANOSMIA	ANTBEARS	ANTHEMING	ANTIBUG	ANTIFOAM
ANOSMIAS	ANTBIRD	ANTHEMION	ANTIBUSER	ANTIFOG
ANOSMIC	ANTBIRDS	ANTHEMIS	ANTIC	ANTIFRAUD
ANOTHER	ANTE	ANTHEMS	ANTICAL	ANTIFUR
ANOUGH	ANTEATER	ANTHER	ANTICALLY	ANTIGANG
ANOUROUS	ANTEATERS	ANTHERAL	ANTICAR	ANTIGAY
ANOVULANT	ANTECEDE	ANTHERID	ANTICHLOR	ANTIGEN
ANOVULAR	ANTECEDED	ANTHERIDS	ANTICISE	ANTIGENE
ANOW	ANTECEDES	ANTHERS	ANTICISED	ANTIGENES
ANOXAEMIA	ANTECHOIR	ANTHESES	ANTICISES	ANTIGENIC
ANOXAEMIC	ANTED	ANTHESIS	ANTICITY	ANTIGENS
ANOXEMIA	ANTEDATE	ANTHILL	ANTICIVIC	ANTIGLARE
ANOXEMIAS	ANTEDATED	ANTHILLS	ANTICIZE	ANTIGRAFT
ANOXEMIC	ANTEDATES	ANTHOCARP	ANTICIZED	ANTIGUN
ANOXIA	ANTEED	ANTHOCYAN	ANTICIZES	ANTIHELIX
ANOXIAS	ANTEFIX	ANTHODIA	ANTICK	ANTIHERO
ANOXIC	ANTEFIXA	ANTHODIUM	ANTICKE	ANTIHUMAN
ANS	ANTEFIXAE	ANTHOID	ANTICKED	ANTIJAM
ANSA	ANTEFIXAL	ANTHOLOGY	ANTICKES	ANTIKING
ANSAE	ANTEFIXES	ANTHOTAXY	ANTICKING	ANTIKINGS
ANSAPHONE	ANTEING	ANTHOZOAN	ANTICKS	ANTIKNOCK
ANSATE	ANTELOPE	ANTHOZOIC	ANTICLINE	ANTILABOR
ANSATED	ANTELOPES	ANTHRACES	ANTICLING	ANTILEAK
ANSATZ	ANTELUCAN	ANTHRACIC	ANTICLY	ANTILEFT
ANSATZES	ANTENATAL	ANTHRAX	ANTICODON	ANTILIFE
ANSERINE	ANTENATI	ANTHRAXES	ANTICOLD	ANTILIFER
ANSERINES	ANTENNA	ANTHRO	ANTICOUS	ANTILOCK
ANSEROUS	ANTENNAE	ANTHROPIC	ANTICRACK	ANTILOG
ANSWER	ANTENNAL	ANTHROS	ANTICRIME	ANTILOGS
ANSWERED	ANTENNARY	ANTHURIUM	ANTICS	ANTILOGY
ANSWERER	ANTENNAS	ANTI	ANTICULT	ANTIMACHO
ANSWERERS	ANTENNULE	ANTIABUSE	ANTICULTS	ANTIMALE
ANSWERING	ANTEPAST	ANTIACNE	ANTIDORA	ANTIMAN
ANSWERS	ANTEPASTS	ANTIAGING	ANTIDORON	ANTIMASK
ANT	ANTERIOR	ANTIAIR	ANTIDOTAL	ANTIMASKS
ANTA	ANTEROOM	ANTIALIEN	ANTIDOTE	ANTIMEN
ANTACID	ANTEROOMS	ANTIAR	ANTIDOTED	ANTIMERE
ANTACIDS	ANTES	ANTIARIN	ANTIDOTES	ANTIMERES
ANTAE	ANTETYPE	ANTIARINS	ANTIDRAFT	ANTIMERIC
ANTALGIC	ANTETYPES	ANTIARMOR	ANTIDRUG	ANTIMINE
ANTALGICS	ANTEVERT	ANTIARS	ANTIDUNE	ANTIMONIC
ANTALKALI	ANTEVERTS	ANTIATOM	ANTIDUNES	ANTIMONY

ANTIMONYL	ANTIQUES	ANTITRADE	ANTSY	ANZIANI
ANTIMUON	ANTIQUEY	ANTITRAGI	ANTWACKIE	AORIST
ANTIMUONS	ANTIQUIER	ANTITRUST	ANUCLEATE	AORISTIC
ANTIMUSIC	ANTIQUING	ANTITUMOR	ANURA	AORISTS
ANTIMYCIN	ANTIQUITY	ANTITYPAL	ANURAL	AORTA
ANTING	ANTIRADAR	ANTITYPE	ANURAN	AORTAE
ANTINGS	ANTIRAPE	ANTITYPES	ANURANS	AORTAL
ANTINODAL	ANTIRED	ANTITYPIC	ANURESES	AORTAS
ANTINODE	ANTIRIOT	ANTIULCER	ANURESIS	AORTIC
ANTINODES	ANTIROCK	ANTIUNION	ANURETIC	AORTITIS
ANTINOISE	ANTIROLL	ANTIURBAN	ANURIA	AOUDAD
ANTINOME	ANTIROYAL	ANTIVAX	ANURIAS	AOUDADS
ANTINOMES	ANTIRUST	ANTIVAXER	ANURIC	APACE
ANTINOMIC	ANTIRUSTS	ANTIVENIN	ANUROUS	APACHE
ANTINOMY	ANTIS	ANTIVENOM	ANUS	APACHES
ANTINOVEL	ANTISAG	ANTIVIRAL	ANUSES	APADANA
ANTINUKE	ANTISCIAN	ANTIVIRUS	ANVIL	APADANAS
ANTINUKER	ANTISENSE	ANTIWAR	ANVILED	APAGE
ANTINUKES	ANTISERA	ANTIWEAR	ANVILING	APAGOGE
ANTIPAPAL	ANTISERUM	ANTIWEED	ANVILLED	APAGOGES
ANTIPARTY	ANTISEX	ANTIWHITE	ANVILLING	APAGOGIC
ANTIPASTI	ANTISHAKE	ANTIWOMAN	ANVILS	APAID
ANTIPASTO	ANTISHARK	ANTIWORLD	ANVILTOP	APANAGE
ANTIPATHY	ANTISHIP	ANTLER	ANVILTOPS	APANAGED
ANTIPHON	ANTISHOCK	ANTLERED	ANXIETIES	APANAGES
ANTIPHONS	ANTISKID	ANTLERS	ANXIETY	APAREJO
ANTIPHONY	ANTISLEEP	ANTLIA	ANXIOUS	APAREJOS
ANTIPILL	ANTISLIP	ANTLIAE	ANXIOUSLY	APART
ANTIPODAL	ANTISMOG	ANTLIATE	ANY	APARTHEID
ANTIPODE	ANTISMOKE	ANTLIKE	ANYBODIES	APARTMENT
ANTIPODES	ANTISMUT	ANTLION	ANYBODY	APARTNESS
ANTIPOLAR	ANTISNOB	ANTLIONS	ANYHOO	APATETIC
ANTIPOLE	ANTISNOBS	ANTONYM	ANYHOW	APATHATON
ANTIPOLES	ANTISOLAR	ANTONYMIC	ANYMORE	APATHETIC
ANTIPOPE	ANTISPAM	ANTONYMS	ANYON	APATHIES
ANTIPOPES	ANTISPAST	ANTONYMY	ANYONE	APATHY
ANTIPORN	ANTISTAT	ANTPITTA	ANYONES	APATITE
ANTIPOT	ANTISTATE	ANTPITTAS	ANYONS	APATITES
ANTIPRESS	ANTISTATS	ANTRA	ANYPLACE	APATOSAUR
ANTIPYIC	ANTISTICK	ANTRAL	ANYROAD	APAY
ANTIPYICS	ANTISTORY	ANTRE	ANYTHING	APAYD
ANTIQUARK	ANTISTYLE	ANTRES	ANYTHINGS	APAYING
ANTIQUARY	ANTITANK	ANTRORSE	ANYTIME	APAYS
ANTIQUATE	ANTITAX	ANTRUM	ANYWAY	APE
ANTIQUE	ANTITHEFT	ANTRUMS	ANYWAYS	APEAK
ANTIQUED	ANTITHET	ANTS	ANYWHEN	APED
ANTIQUELY	ANTITHETS	ANTSIER	ANYWHERE	APEDOM
ANTIQUER	ANTITOXIC	ANTSIEST	ANYWHERES	APEDOMS
ANTIQUERS	ANTITOXIN	ANTSINESS	ANYWISE	APEEK

APEHOOD	APHELIAN	APHTHOUS	APLOMB	APOLLO
APEHOODS	APHELION	APHYLLIES	APLOMBS	APOLLOS
APELIKE	APHELIONS	APHYLLOUS	APLUSTRE	APOLOG
APEMAN	APHERESES	APHYLLY	APLUSTRES	APOLOGAL
APEMEN	APHERESIS	APIACEOUS	APNEA	APOLOGIA
APEPSIA	APHERETIC	APIAN	APNEAL	APOLOGIAE
APEPSIAS	APHESES	APIARIAN	APNEAS	APOLOGIAS
APEPSIES	APHESIS	APIARIANS	APNEIC	APOLOGIES
APEPSY	APHETIC	APIARIES	APNEUSES	APOLOGISE
APER	APHETISE	APIARIST	APNEUSIS	APOLOGIST
APERCU	APHETISED	APIARISTS	APNEUSTIC	APOLOGIZE
APERCUS	APHETISES	APIARY	APNOEA	APOLOGS
APERIENT	APHETIZE	APICAL	APNOEAL	APOLOGUE
APERIENTS	APHETIZED	APICALLY	APNOEAS	APOLOGUES
APERIES	APHETIZES	APICALS	APNOEIC	APOLOGY
APERIODIC	APHICIDE	APICES	APO	APOLUNE
APERITIF	APHICIDES	APICIAN	APOAPSES	APOLUNES
APERITIFS	APHID	APICULATE	APOAPSIS	APOMICT
APERITIVE	APHIDES	APICULI	APOCARP	APOMICTIC
APERS	APHIDIAN	APICULUS	APOCARPS	APOMICTS
APERT	APHIDIANS	APIECE	APOCARPY	APOMIXES
APERTNESS	APHIDIOUS	APIEZON	APOCOPATE	APOMIXIS
APERTURAL	APHIDS	APIMANIA	APOCOPE	APOOP
APERTURE	APHIS	APIMANIAS	APOCOPES	APOPHASES
APERTURED	APHOLATE	APING	APOCOPIC	APOPHASIS
APERTURES	APHOLATES	APIOL	APOCRINE	APOPHATIC
APERY	APHONIA	APIOLOGY	APOCRYPHA	APOPHENIA
APES	APHONIAS	APIOLS	APOD	APOPHONY
APESHIT	APHONIC	APIPHOBE	APODAL	APOPHYGE
APETALIES	APHONICS	APIPHOBES	APODE	APOPHYGES
APETALOUS	APHONIES	APIPHOBIA	APODES	APOPHYSES
APETALY	APHONOUS	APIPHOBIC	APODICTIC	APOPHYSIS
APEX	APHONY	APISH	APODOSES	APOPLAST
APEXES	APHORISE	APISHLY	APODOSIS	APOPLASTS
APGAR	APHORISED	APISHNESS	APODOUS	APOPLEX
APHAGIA	APHORISER	APISM	APODS	APOPLEXED
APHAGIAS	APHORISES	APISMS	APOENZYME	APOPLEXES
APHAKIA	APHORISM	APIVOROUS	APOGAEIC	APOPLEXY
APHAKIAS	APHORISMS	APLANAT	APOGAMIC	APOPTOSES
APHANITE	APHORIST	APLANATIC	APOGAMIES	APOPTOSIS
APHANITES	APHORISTS	APLANATS	APOGAMOUS	APOPTOTIC
APHANITIC	APHORIZE	APLANETIC	APOGAMY	APORETIC
APHASIA	APHORIZED	APLASIA	APOGEAL	APORIA
APHASIAC	APHORIZER	APLASIAS	APOGEAN	APORIAS
APHASIACS	APHORIZES	APLASTIC	APOGEE	APORT
APHASIAS	APHOTIC	APLENTY	APOGEES	APOS
APHASIC	APHRODITE	APLITE	APOGEIC	APOSITIA
APHASICS	APHTHA	APLITES	APOGRAPH	APOSITIAS
APHELIA	APHTHAE	APLITIC	APOGRAPHS	APOSITIC

A

APOSPORIC	APPARITOR	APPETENCE	APPORTION	APPUIS
APOSPORY	APPAY	APPETENCY	APPORTS	APPULSE
APOSTACY	APPAYD	APPETENT	APPOSABLE	APPULSES
APOSTASY	APPAYING	APPETIBLE	APPOSE	APPULSIVE
APOSTATE	APPAYS	APPETISE	APPOSED	APPUY
APOSTATES	APPEACH	APPETISED	APPOSER	APPUYED
APOSTATIC	APPEACHED	APPETISER	APPOSERS	APPUYING
APOSTIL	APPEACHES	APPETISES	APPOSES	APPUYS
APOSTILLE	APPEAL	APPETITE	APPOSING	APRACTIC
APOSTILS	APPEALED	APPETITES	APPOSITE	APRAXIA
APOSTLE	APPEALER	APPETIZE	APPRAISAL	APRAXIAS
APOSTLES	APPEALERS	APPETIZED	APPRAISE	APRAXIC
APOSTOLIC	APPEALING	APPETIZER	APPRAISED	APRES
APOTHECE	APPEALS	APPETIZES	APPRAISEE	APRICATE
APOTHECES	APPEAR	APPLAUD	APPRAISER	APRICATED
APOTHECIA	APPEARED	APPLAUDED	APPRAISES	APRICATES
APOTHEGM	APPEARER	APPLAUDER	APPREHEND	APRICOCK
APOTHEGMS	APPEARERS	APPLAUDS	APPRESS	APRICOCKS
APOTHEM	APPEARING	APPLAUSE	APPRESSED	APRICOT
APOTHEMS	APPEARS	APPLAUSES	APPRESSES	APRICOTS
APOZEM	APPEASE	APPLE	APPRISE	APRIORISM
APOZEMS	APPEASED	APPLECART	APPRISED	APRIORIST
APP	APPEASER	APPLEJACK	APPRISER	APRIORITY
APPAID	APPEASERS	APPLES	APPRISERS	APRON
APPAIR	APPEASES	APPLET	APPRISES	APRONED
APPAIRED	APPEASING	APPLETINI	APPRISING	APRONFUL
APPAIRING	APPEL	APPLETS	APPRIZE	APRONFULS
APPAIRS	APPELLANT	APPLEY	APPRIZED	APRONING
APPAL	APPELLATE	APPLIABLE	APPRIZER	APRONLIKE
APPALL	APPELLEE	APPLIANCE	APPRIZERS	APRONS
APPALLED	APPELLEES	APPLICANT	APPRIZES	APROPOS
APPALLING	APPELLOR	APPLICATE	APPRIZING	APROTIC
APPALLS	APPELLORS	APPLIED	APPRO	APSARAS
APPALOOSA	APPELS	APPLIER	APPROACH	APSARASES
APPALS	APPEND	APPLIERS	APPROBATE	APSE
APPALTI	APPENDAGE	APPLIES	APPROOF	APSES
APPALTO	APPENDANT	APPLIEST	APPROOFS	APSIDAL
APPANAGE	APPENDED	APPLIQUE	APPROS	APSIDES
APPANAGED	APPENDENT	APPLIQUED	APPROVAL	APSIDIOLE
APPANAGES	APPENDING	APPLIQUES	APPROVALS	APSIS
APPARAT	APPENDIX	APPLY	APPROVE	APSO
APPARATS	APPENDS	APPLYING	APPROVED	APSOS
APPARATUS	APPERIL	APPOINT	APPROVER	APT
APPAREL	APPERILL	APPOINTED	APPROVERS	APTAMER
APPARELED	APPERILLS	APPOINTEE	APPROVES	APTAMERS
APPARELS	APPERILS	APPOINTER	APPROVING	APTED
APPARENCY	APPERTAIN	APPOINTOR	APPS	APTER
APPARENT	APPESTAT	APPOINTS	APPUI	APTERAL
APPARENTS	APPESTATS	APPORT	APPUIED	APTERIA

APTERISM	AQUARIANS	ARABISE	ARAYSE	ARBOVIRUS
APTERISMS	AQUARIIST	ARABISED	ARAYSED	ARBS
APTERIUM	AQUARIST	ARABISES	ARAYSES	ARBUSCLE
APTEROUS	AQUARISTS	ARABISING	ARAYSING	ARBUSCLES
APTERYX	AQUARIUM	ARABIZE	ARB	ARBUTE
APTERYXES	AQUARIUMS	ARABIZED	ARBA	ARBUTEAN
APTEST	AQUAROBIC	ARABIZES	ARBALEST	ARBUTES
APTING	AQUAS	ARABIZING	ARBALESTS	ARBUTUS
APTITUDE	AQUASCAPE	ARABLE	ARBALIST	ARBUTUSES
APTITUDES	AQUASHOW	ARABLES	ARBALISTS	ARC
APTLY	AQUASHOWS	ARACEOUS	ARBAS	ARCADE
APTNESS	AQUATIC	ARACHIS	ARBELEST	ARCADED
APTNESSES	AQUATICS	ARACHISES	ARBELESTS	ARCADES
APTOTE	AQUATINT	ARACHNID	ARBITER	ARCADIA
APTOTES	AQUATINTA	ARACHNIDS	ARBITERS	ARCADIAN
APTOTIC	AQUATINTS	ARACHNOID	ARBITRAGE	ARCADIANS
APTS	AQUATONE	ARAGONITE	ARBITRAL	ARCADIAS
APYRASE	AQUATONES	ARAHUANA	ARBITRARY	ARCADING
APYRASES	AQUAVIT	ARAHUANAS	ARBITRATE	ARCADINGS
APYRETIC	AQUAVITS	ARAISE	ARBITRESS	ARCANA
APYREXIA	AQUEDUCT	ARAISED	ARBITRIUM	ARCANAS
APYREXIAS	AQUEDUCTS	ARAISES	ARBLAST	ARCANE
AQUA	AQUEOUS	ARAISING	ARBLASTER	ARCANELY
AQUABATIC	AQUEOUSLY	ARAK	ARBLASTS	ARCANIST
AQUABOARD	AQUIFER	ARAKS	ARBOR	ARCANISTS
AQUACADE	AQUIFERS	ARALIA	ARBOREAL	ARCANUM
AQUACADES	AQUILEGIA	ARALIAS	ARBORED	ARCANUMS
AQUADROME	AQUILINE	ARAME	ARBOREOUS	ARCATURE
AQUAE	AQUILON	ARAMES	ARBORES	ARCATURES
AQUAFABA	AQUILONS	ARAMID	ARBORET	ARCCOSINE
AQUAFABAS	AQUIVER	ARAMIDS	ARBORETA	ARCED
AQUAFARM	AR	ARANCINI	ARBORETS	ARCH
AQUAFARMS	ARAARA	ARANEID	ARBORETUM	ARCHAEA
AQUAFER	ARAARAS	ARANEIDAN	ARBORIO	ARCHAEAL
AQUAFERS	ARABA	ARANEIDS	ARBORIOS	ARCHAEAN
AQUAFIT	ARABAS	ARANEOUS	ARBORISE	ARCHAEANS
AQUAFITS	ARABESK	ARAPAIMA	ARBORISED	ARCHAEI
AQUALUNG	ARABESKS	ARAPAIMAS	ARBORISES	ARCHAEON
AQUALUNGS	ARABESQUE	ARAPONGA	ARBORIST	ARCHAEUS
AQUANAUT	ARABIC	ARAPONGAS	ARBORISTS	ARCHAIC
AQUANAUTS	ARABICA	ARAPUNGA	ARBORIZE	ARCHAICAL
AQUAPHOBE	ARABICAS	ARAPUNGAS	ARBORIZED	ARCHAISE
AQUAPLANE	ARABICISE	ARAR	ARBORIZES	ARCHAISED
AQUAPONIC	ARABICIZE	ARAROBA	ARBOROUS	ARCHAISER
AQUAPORIN	ARABILITY	ARAROBAS	ARBORS	ARCHAISES
AQUARELLE	ARABIN	ARARS	ARBOUR	ARCHAISM
AQUARIA	ARABINOSE	ARAUCARIA	ARBOURED	ARCHAISMS
AQUARIAL	ARABINS	ARAWANA	ARBOURS	ARCHAIST
AQUARIAN	ARABIS	ARAWANAS	ARBOVIRAL	ARCHAISTS

ARCHAIZE	ARCHLIKE	ARDENCIES	ARENE	ARGENTAL
ARCHAIZED	ARCHLUTE	ARDENCY	ARENES	ARGENTIC
ARCHAIZER	ARCHLUTES	ARDENT	ARENITE	ARGENTINE
ARCHAIZES	ARCHLY	ARDENTLY	ARENITES	ARGENTITE
ARCHANGEL	ARCHNESS	ARDOR	ARENITIC	ARGENTOUS
ARCHDRUID	ARCHOLOGY	ARDORS	ARENOSE	ARGENTS
ARCHDUCAL	ARCHON	ARDOUR	ARENOUS	ARGENTUM
ARCHDUCHY	ARCHONS	ARDOURS	AREOLA	ARGENTUMS
ARCHDUKE	ARCHONTIC	ARDRI	AREOLAE	ARGH
ARCHDUKES	ARCHOSAUR	ARDRIGH	AREOLAR	ARGHAN
ARCHEAN	ARCHRIVAL	ARDRIGHS	AREOLAS	ARGHANS
ARCHED	ARCHSTONE	ARDRIS	AREOLATE	ARGIL
ARCHEI	ARCHWAY	ARDS	AREOLATED	ARGILLITE
ARCHENEMY	ARCHWAYS	ARDUOUS	AREOLE	ARGILS
ARCHER	ARCHWISE	ARDUOUSLY	AREOLES	ARGINASE
ARCHERESS	ARCIFORM	ARE	AREOLOGY	ARGINASES
ARCHERIES	ARCING	AREA	AREOMETER	ARGININE
ARCHERS	ARCINGS	AREACH	AREOMETRY	ARGININES
ARCHERY	ARCKED	AREACHED	AREOSTYLE	ARGLE
ARCHES	ARCKING	AREACHES	AREPA	ARGLED
ARCHEST	ARCKINGS	AREACHING	AREPAS	ARGLES
ARCHETYPE	ARCMIN	AREAD	ARERE	ARGLING
ARCHEUS	ARCMINS	AREADING	ARES	ARGOL
ARCHFIEND	ARCMINUTE	AREADS	ARET	ARGOLS
ARCHFOE	ARCO	AREAE	ARETE	ARGON
ARCHFOES	ARCOGRAPH	AREAL	ARETES	ARGONAUT
ARCHFOOL	ARCOLOGY	AREALLY	ARETHUSA	ARGONAUTS
ARCHFOOLS	ARCOS	AREAR	ARETHUSAS	ARGONON
ARCHI	ARCS	AREARS	ARETS	ARGONONS
ARCHICARP	ARCSEC	AREAS	ARETT	ARGONS
ARCHIL	ARCSECOND	AREAWAY	ARETTED	ARGOSIES
ARCHILOWE	ARCSECS	AREAWAYS	ARETTING	ARGOSY
ARCHILS	ARCSINE	ARECA	ARETTS	ARGOT
ARCHIMAGE	ARCSINES	ARECAS	AREW	ARGOTIC
ARCHINE	ARCTIC	ARECOLINE	ARF	ARGOTS
ARCHINES	ARCTICS	ARED	ARFS	ARGUABLE
ARCHING	ARCTIID	AREDD	ARGAL	ARGUABLY
ARCHINGS	ARCTIIDS	AREDE	ARGALA	ARGUE
ARCHITECT	ARCTOID	AREDES	ARGALAS	ARGUED
ARCHITYPE	ARCTOPHIL	AREDING	ARGALI	ARGUER
ARCHIVAL	ARCUATE	AREFIED	ARGALIS	ARGUERS
ARCHIVE	ARCUATED	AREFIES	ARGALS	ARGUES
ARCHIVED	ARCUATELY	AREFY	ARGAN	ARGUFIED
ARCHIVES	ARCUATION	AREFYING	ARGAND	ARGUFIER
ARCHIVING	ARCUS	AREG	ARGANDS	ARGUFIERS
ARCHIVIST	ARCUSES	AREIC	ARGANS	ARGUFIES
ARCHIVOLT	ARD	ARENA	ARGEMONE	ARGUFY
ARCHLET	ARDEB	ARENAS	ARGEMONES	ARGUFYING
ARCHLETS	ARDEBS	ARENATION	ARGENT	ARGUING

ARGULI	ARILLODE	ARMBAND	ARMORERS	AROIDS
ARGULUS	ARILLODES	ARMBANDS	ARMORIAL	AROINT
ARGUMENT	ARILLOID	ARMCHAIR	ARMORIALS	AROINTED
ARGUMENTA	ARILLUS	ARMCHAIRS	ARMORIES	AROINTING
ARGUMENTS	ARILS	ARMED	ARMORING	AROINTS
ARGUS	ARIOSE	ARMER	ARMORIST	AROLLA
ARGUSES	ARIOSI	ARMERIA	ARMORISTS	AROLLAS
ARGUTE	ARIOSO	ARMERIAS	ARMORLESS	AROMA
ARGUTELY	ARIOSOS	ARMERS	ARMORS	AROMANTIC
ARGYLE	ARIOT	ARMET	ARMORY	AROMAS
ARGYLES	ARIPPLE	ARMETS	ARMOUR	AROMATASE
ARGYLL	ARIS	ARMFUL	ARMOURED	AROMATIC
ARGYLLS	ARISE	ARMFULS	ARMOURER	AROMATICS
ARGYRIA	ARISEN	ARMGAUNT	ARMOURERS	AROMATISE
ARGYRIAS	ARISES	ARMGUARD	ARMOURIES	AROMATIZE
ARGYRITE	ARISH	ARMGUARDS	ARMOURING	AROS
ARGYRITES	ARISHES	ARMHOLE	ARMOURS	AROSE
ARHAT	ARISING	ARMHOLES	ARMOURY	AROUND
ARHATS	ARISTA	ARMIES	ARMOZEEN	AROUSABLE
ARHATSHIP	ARISTAE	ARMIGER	ARMOZEENS	AROUSAL
ARHYTHMIA	ARISTAS	ARMIGERAL	ARMOZINE	AROUSALS
ARHYTHMIC	ARISTATE	ARMIGERO	ARMOZINES	AROUSE
ARIA	ARISTO	ARMIGEROS	ARMPIT	AROUSED
ARIARIES	ARISTOS	ARMIGERS	ARMPITS	AROUSER
ARIARY	ARISTOTLE	ARMIL	ARMREST	AROUSERS
ARIAS	ARK	ARMILLA	ARMRESTS	AROUSES
ARID	ARKED	ARMILLAE	ARMS	AROUSING
ARIDER	ARKING	ARMILLARY	ARMSFUL	AROW
ARIDEST	ARKITE	ARMILLAS	ARMURE	AROWANA
ARIDITIES	ARKITES	ARMILS	ARMURES	AROWANAS
ARIDITY	ARKOSE	ARMING	ARMY	AROYNT
ARIDLY	ARKOSES	ARMINGS	ARMYWORM	AROYNTED
ARIDNESS	ARKOSIC	ARMISTICE	ARMYWORMS	AROYNTING
ARIE	ARKS	ARMLESS	ARNA	AROYNTS
ARIEL	ARLE	ARMLET	ARNAS	ARPA
ARIELS	ARLED	ARMLETS	ARNATTO	ARPAS
ARIETTA	ARLES	ARMLIKE	ARNATTOS	ARPEGGIO
ARIETTAS	ARLING	ARMLOAD	ARNICA	ARPEGGIOS
ARIETTE	ARM	ARMLOADS	ARNICAS	ARPEN
ARIETTES	ARMADA	ARMLOCK	ARNOTTO	ARPENS
ARIGHT	ARMADAS	ARMLOCKED	ARNOTTOS	ARPENT
ARIKI	ARMADILLO	ARMLOCKS	ARNUT	ARPENTS
ARIKIS	ARMAGNAC	ARMOIRE	ARNUTS	ARPILLERA
ARIL	ARMAGNACS	ARMOIRES	ARO	ARQUEBUS
ARILED	ARMAMENT	ARMONICA	AROBA	ARRABIATA
ARILLARY	ARMAMENTS	ARMONICAS	AROBAS	ARRACACHA
ARILLATE	ARMATURE	ARMOR	AROHA	ARRACK
ARILLATED	ARMATURED	ARMORED	AROHAS	ARRACKS
ARILLI	ARMATURES	ARMORER	AROID	ARRAH

ARRAIGN	ARRIAGE	ARROYO	ARTAL	ARTIST
ARRAIGNED	ARRIAGES	ARROYOS	ARTEFACT	ARTISTE
ARRAIGNER	ARRIBA	ARROZ	ARTEFACTS	ARTISTES
ARRAIGNS	ARRIDE	ARROZES	ARTEL	ARTISTIC
ARRANGE	ARRIDED	ARS	ARTELS	ARTISTRY
ARRANGED	ARRIDES	ARSE	ARTEMISIA	ARTISTS
ARRANGER	ARRIDING	ARSED	ARTERIAL	ARTLESS
ARRANGERS	ARRIERE	ARSEHOLE	ARTERIALS	ARTLESSLY
ARRANGES	ARRIERO	ARSEHOLED	ARTERIES	ARTMAKER
ARRANGING	ARRIEROS	ARSEHOLES	ARTERIOLE	ARTMAKERS
ARRANT	ARRIS	ARSENAL	ARTERITIS	ARTMAKING
ARRANTLY	ARRISES	ARSENALS	ARTERY	ARTOCARPI
ARRAS	ARRISH	ARSENATE	ARTESIAN	ARTS
ARRASED	ARRISHES	ARSENATES	ARTFUL	ARTSIE
ARRASENE	ARRIVAL	ARSENIATE	ARTFULLY	ARTSIER
ARRASENES	ARRIVALS	ARSENIC	ARTHOUSE	ARTSIES
ARRASES	ARRIVANCE	ARSENICAL	ARTHOUSES	ARTSIEST
ARRAUGHT	ARRIVANCY	ARSENICS	ARTHRITIC	ARTSINESS
ARRAY	ARRIVE	ARSENIDE	ARTHRITIS	ARTSMAN
ARRAYAL	ARRIVED	ARSENIDES	ARTHRODIA	ARTSMEN
ARRAYALS	ARRIVER	ARSENIOUS	ARTHROPOD	ARTSY
ARRAYED	ARRIVERS	ARSENITE	ARTHROSES	ARTWORK
ARRAYER	ARRIVES	ARSENITES	ARTHROSIS	ARTWORKS
ARRAYERS	ARRIVING	ARSENO	ARTI	ARTY
ARRAYING	ARRIVISME	ARSENOUS	ARTIC	ARUANA
ARRAYMENT	ARRIVISTE	ARSES	ARTICHOKE	ARUANAS
ARRAYS	ARROBA	ARSEY	ARTICLE	ARUGOLA
ARREAR	ARROBAS	ARSHEEN	ARTICLED	ARUGOLAS
ARREARAGE	ARROCES	ARSHEENS	ARTICLES	ARUGULA
ARREARS	ARROGANCE	ARSHIN	ARTICLING	ARUGULAS
ARRECT	ARROGANCY	ARSHINE	ARTICS	ARUHE
ARREEDE	ARROGANT	ARSHINES	ARTICULAR	ARUHES
ARREEDES	ARROGATE	ARSHINS	ARTIER	ARUM
ARREEDING	ARROGATED	ARSIER	ARTIES	ARUMS
ARREST	ARROGATES	ARSIEST	ARTIEST	ARUSPEX
ARRESTANT	ARROGATOR	ARSINE	ARTIFACT	ARUSPICES
ARRESTED	ARROW	ARSINES	ARTIFACTS	ARVAL
ARRESTEE	ARROWED	ARSING	ARTIFICE	ARVEE
ARRESTEES	ARROWHEAD	ARSINO	ARTIFICER	ARVEES
ARRESTER	ARROWIER	ARSIS	ARTIFICES	ARVICOLE
ARRESTERS	ARROWIEST	ARSON	ARTIGI	ARVICOLES
ARRESTING	ARROWING	ARSONIST	ARTIGIS	ARVO
ARRESTIVE	ARROWLESS	ARSONISTS	ARTILLERY	ARVOS
ARRESTOR	ARROWLIKE	ARSONITE	ARTILY	ARY
ARRESTORS	ARROWROOT	ARSONITES	ARTINESS	ARYBALLOI
ARRESTS	ARROWS	ARSONOUS	ARTIS	ARYBALLOS
ARRET	ARROWWOOD	ARSONS	ARTISAN	ARYL
ARRETS	ARROWWORM	ARSY	ARTISANAL	ARYLS
ARRHIZAL	ARROWY	ART	ARTISANS	ARYTENOID

ARYTHMIA	ASCITES	ASHED	ASINICOS	ASPECTS
ARYTHMIAS	ASCITIC	ASHEN	ASININE	ASPECTUAL
ARYTHMIC	ASCITICAL	ASHERIES	ASININELY	ASPEN
AS	ASCLEPIAD	ASHERY	ASININITY	ASPENS
ASAFETIDA	ASCLEPIAS	ASHES	ASK	ASPER
ASANA	ASCOCARP	ASHET	ASKANCE	ASPERATE
ASANAS	ASCOCARPS	ASHETS	ASKANCED	ASPERATED
ASAR	ASCOGONIA	ASHFALL	ASKANCES	ASPERATES
ASARUM	ASCON	ASHFALLS	ASKANCING	ASPERGE
ASARUMS	ASCONCE	ASHIER	ASKANT	ASPERGED
ASBESTIC	ASCONOID	ASHIEST	ASKANTED	ASPERGER
ASBESTINE	ASCONS	ASHINE	ASKANTING	ASPERGERS
ASBESTOS	ASCORBATE	ASHINESS	ASKANTS	ASPERGES
ASBESTOUS	ASCORBIC	ASHING	ASKARI	ASPERGILL
ASBESTUS	ASCOSPORE	ASHIVER	ASKARIS	ASPERGING
ASCARED	ASCOT	ASHKEY	ASKED	ASPERITY
ASCARID	ASCOTS	ASHKEYS	ASKER	ASPERMIA
ASCARIDES	ASCRIBE	ASHLAR	ASKERS	ASPERMIAS
ASCARIDS	ASCRIBED	ASHLARED	ASKESES	ASPEROUS
ASCARIS	ASCRIBES	ASHLARING	ASKESIS	ASPERS
ASCARISES	ASCRIBING	ASHLARS	ASKEW	ASPERSE
ASCAUNT	ASCUS	ASHLER	ASKEWNESS	ASPERSED
ASCEND	ASDIC	ASHLERED	ASKING	ASPERSER
ASCENDANT	ASDICS	ASHLERING	ASKINGS	ASPERSERS
ASCENDED	ASEA	ASHLERS	ASKLENT	ASPERSES
ASCENDENT	ASEISMIC	ASHLESS	ASKOI	ASPERSING
ASCENDER	ASEITIES	ASHMAN	ASKOS	ASPERSION
ASCENDERS	ASEITY	ASHMEN	ASKS	ASPERSIVE
ASCENDEUR	ASEMANTIC	ASHORE	ASLAKE	ASPERSOIR
ASCENDING	ASEPALOUS	ASHPAN	ASLAKED	ASPERSOR
ASCENDS	ASEPSES	ASHPANS	ASLAKES	ASPERSORS
ASCENSION	ASEPSIS	ASHPLANT	ASLAKING	ASPERSORY
ASCENSIVE	ASEPTATE	ASHPLANTS	ASLANT	ASPHALT
ASCENT	ASEPTIC	ASHRAF	ASLEEP	ASPHALTED
ASCENTS	ASEPTICS	ASHRAM	ASLOPE	ASPHALTER
ASCERTAIN	ASEXUAL	ASHRAMA	ASLOSH	ASPHALTIC
ASCESES	ASEXUALLY	ASHRAMAS	ASMEAR	ASPHALTS
ASCESIS	ASEXUALS	ASHRAMITE	ASMOULDER	ASPHALTUM
ASCETIC	ASH	ASHRAMS	ASOCIAL	ASPHERIC
ASCETICAL	ASHAKE	ASHTANGA	ASOCIALS	ASPHERICS
ASCETICS	ASHAME	ASHTANGAS	ASP	ASPHODEL
ASCI	ASHAMED	ASHTRAY	ASPARAGUS	ASPHODELS
ASCIAN	ASHAMEDLY	ASHTRAYS	ASPARKLE	ASPHYXIA
ASCIANS	ASHAMES	ASHY	ASPARTAME	ASPHYXIAL
ASCIDIA	ASHAMING	ASIAGO	ASPARTATE	ASPHYXIAS
ASCIDIAN	ASHCAKE	ASIAGOS	ASPARTIC	ASPHYXIED
ASCIDIANS	ASHCAKES	ASIDE	ASPECT	ASPHYXIES
ASCIDIATE	ASHCAN	ASIDES	ASPECTED	ASPHYXY
ASCIDIUM	ASHCANS	ASINICO	ASPECTING	ASPIC

ASPICK	ASSAILANT	ASSERTERS	ASSISTER	ASSUME
ASPICKS	ASSAILED	ASSERTING	ASSISTERS	ASSUMED
ASPICS	ASSAILER	ASSERTION	ASSISTING	ASSUMEDLY
ASPIDIA	ASSAILERS	ASSERTIVE	ASSISTIVE	ASSUMER
ASPIDIOID	ASSAILING	ASSERTOR	ASSISTOR	ASSUMERS
ASPIDIUM	ASSAILS	ASSERTORS	ASSISTORS	ASSUMES
ASPINE	ASSAIS	ASSERTORY	ASSISTS	ASSUMING
ASPINES	ASSAM	ASSERTS	ASSIZE	ASSUMINGS
ASPIRANT	ASSAMS	ASSES	ASSIZED	ASSUMPSIT
ASPIRANTS	ASSART	ASSESS	ASSIZER	ASSURABLE
ASPIRATA	ASSARTED	ASSESSED	ASSIZERS	ASSURANCE
ASPIRATAE	ASSARTING	ASSESSES	ASSIZES	ASSURE
ASPIRATE	ASSARTS	ASSESSING	ASSIZING	ASSURED
ASPIRATED	ASSASSIN	ASSESSOR	ASSLESS	ASSUREDLY
ASPIRATES	ASSASSINS	ASSESSORS	ASSLIKE	ASSUREDS
ASPIRATOR	ASSAULT	ASSET	ASSOCIATE	ASSURER
ASPIRE	ASSAULTED	ASSETLESS	ASSOIL	ASSURERS
ASPIRED	ASSAULTER	ASSETS	ASSOILED	ASSURES
ASPIRER	ASSAULTS	ASSEVER	ASSOILING	ASSURGENT
ASPIRERS	ASSAY	ASSEVERED	ASSOILS	ASSURING
ASPIRES	ASSAYABLE	ASSEVERS	ASSOILZIE	ASSUROR
ASPIRIN	ASSAYED	ASSEZ	ASSONANCE	ASSURORS
ASPIRING	ASSAYER	ASSHAT	ASSONANT	ASSWAGE
ASPIRINS	ASSAYERS	ASSHATS	ASSONANTS	ASSWAGED
ASPIS	ASSAYING	ASSHOLE	ASSONATE	ASSWAGES
ASPISES	ASSAYINGS	ASSHOLES	ASSONATED	ASSWAGING
ASPISH	ASSAYS	ASSIDUITY	ASSONATES	ASSWIPE
ASPLENIUM	ASSEGAAI	ASSIDUOUS	ASSORT	ASSWIPES
ASPORT	ASSEGAAIS	ASSIEGE	ASSORTED	ASTABLE
ASPORTED	ASSEGAI	ASSIEGED	ASSORTER	ASTANGA
ASPORTING	ASSEGAIED	ASSIEGES	ASSORTERS	ASTANGAS
ASPORTS	ASSEGAIS	ASSIEGING	ASSORTING	ASTARE
ASPOUT	ASSEMBLE	ASSIENTO	ASSORTIVE	ASTART
ASPRAWL	ASSEMBLED	ASSIENTOS	ASSORTS	ASTARTED
ASPREAD	ASSEMBLER	ASSIGN	ASSOT	ASTARTING
ASPRO	ASSEMBLES	ASSIGNAT	ASSOTS	ASTARTS
ASPROS	ASSEMBLY	ASSIGNATS	ASSOTT	ASTASIA
ASPROUT	ASSENT	ASSIGNED	ASSOTTED	ASTASIAS
ASPS	ASSENTED	ASSIGNEE	ASSOTTING	ASTATIC
ASQUAT	ASSENTER	ASSIGNEES	ASSUAGE	ASTATIDE
ASQUINT	ASSENTERS	ASSIGNER	ASSUAGED	ASTATIDES
ASRAMA	ASSENTING	ASSIGNERS	ASSUAGER	ASTATINE
ASRAMAS	ASSENTIVE	ASSIGNING	ASSUAGERS	ASTATINES
ASS	ASSENTOR	ASSIGNOR	ASSUAGES	ASTATKI
ASSAGAI	ASSENTORS	ASSIGNORS	ASSUAGING	ASTATKIS
ASSAGAIED	ASSENTS	ASSIGNS	ASSUASIVE	ASTEISM
ASSAGAIS	ASSERT	ASSIST	ASSUETUDE	ASTEISMS
ASSAI	ASSERTED	ASSISTANT	ASSUMABLE	ASTELIC
ASSAIL	ASSERTER	ASSISTED	ASSUMABLY	ASTELIES

A

ASTELY	ASTOOP	ASURA	ATAP	ATHEIST
ASTER	ASTOUND	ASURAS	ATAPS	ATHEISTIC
ASTERIA	ASTOUNDED	ASWARM	ATARACTIC	ATHEISTS
ASTERIAS	ASTOUNDS	ASWAY	ATARAXIA	ATHEIZE
ASTERID	ASTRACHAN	ASWIM	ATARAXIAS	ATHEIZED
ASTERIDS	ASTRADDLE	ASWING	ATARAXIC	ATHEIZES
ASTERISK	ASTRAGAL	ASWIRL	ATARAXICS	ATHEIZING
ASTERISKS	ASTRAGALI	ASWOON	ATARAXIES	ATHELING
ASTERISM	ASTRAGALS	ASYLA	ATARAXY	ATHELINGS
ASTERISMS	ASTRAKHAN	ASYLEE	ATAVIC	ATHEMATIC
ASTERN	ASTRAL	ASYLEES	ATAVISM	ATHENAEUM
ASTERNAL	ASTRALLY	ASYLLABIC	ATAVISMS	ATHENEUM
ASTEROID	ASTRALS	ASYLUM	ATAVIST	ATHENEUMS
ASTEROIDS	ASTRAND	ASYLUMS	ATAVISTIC	ATHEOLOGY
ASTERS	ASTRANTIA	ASYMMETRY	ATAVISTS	ATHEOUS
ASTERT	ASTRAY	ASYMPTOTE	ATAXIA	ATHERINE
ASTERTED	ASTRICT	ASYNAPSES	ATAXIAS	ATHERINES
ASTERTING	ASTRICTED	ASYNAPSIS	ATAXIC	ATHEROMA
ASTERTS	ASTRICTS	ASYNDETA	ATAXICS	ATHEROMAS
ASTHANGA	ASTRIDE	ASYNDETIC	ATAXIES	ATHETESES
ASTHANGAS	ASTRINGE	ASYNDETON	ATAXY	ATHETESIS
ASTHENIA	ASTRINGED	ASYNERGIA	ATCHIEVE	ATHETISE
ASTHENIAS	ASTRINGER	ASYNERGY	ATCHIEVED	ATHETISED
ASTHENIC	ASTRINGES	ASYSTOLE	ATCHIEVES	ATHETISES
ASTHENICS	ASTROCYTE	ASYSTOLES	ATE	ATHETIZE
ASTHENIES	ASTRODOME	ASYSTOLIC	ATEBRIN	ATHETIZED
ASTHENY	ASTROFELL	AT	ATEBRINS	ATHETIZES
ASTHMA	ASTROID	ATAATA	ATECHNIC	ATHETOID
ASTHMAS	ASTROIDS	ATAATAS	ATECHNICS	ATHETOSES
ASTHMATIC	ASTROLABE	ATABAL	ATELIC	ATHETOSIC
ASTHORE	ASTROLOGY	ATABALS	ATELIER	ATHETOSIS
ASTHORES	ASTRONAUT	ATABEG	ATELIERS	ATHETOTIC
ASTICHOUS	ASTRONOMY	ATABEGS	ATEMOYA	ATHIRST
ASTIGMIA	ASTROPHEL	ATABEK	ATEMOYAS	ATHLETA
ASTIGMIAS	ASTROTURF	ATABEKS	ATEMPORAL	ATHLETAS
ASTILBE	ASTRUT	ATABRIN	ATENOLOL	ATHLETE
ASTILBES	ASTUCIOUS	ATABRINE	ATENOLOLS	ATHLETES
ASTIR	ASTUCITY	ATABRINES	ATES	ATHLETIC
ASTOMATAL	ASTUN	ATABRINS	ATHAME	ATHLETICS
ASTOMOUS	ASTUNNED	ATACAMITE	ATHAMES	ATHODYD
ASTONE	ASTUNNING	ATACTIC	ATHANASY	ATHODYDS
ASTONED	ASTUNS	ATAGHAN	ATHANOR	ATHRILL
ASTONES	ASTUTE	ATAGHANS	ATHANORS	ATHROB
ASTONIED	ASTUTELY	ATALAYA	ATHEISE	ATHROCYTE
ASTONIES	ASTUTER	ATALAYAS	ATHEISED	ATHWART
ASTONING	ASTUTEST	ATAMAN	ATHEISES	ATIGI
ASTONISH	ASTYLAR	ATAMANS	ATHEISING	ATIGIS
ASTONY	ASUDDEN	ATAMASCO	ATHEISM	ATILT
ASTONYING	ASUNDER	ATAMASCOS	ATHEISMS	ATIMIES

ATIMY	ATOMISM	ATRIAL	ATTAINT	ATTICISED
ATINGLE	ATOMISMS	ATRIP	ATTAINTED	ATTICISES
ATISHOO	ATOMIST	ATRIUM	ATTAINTS	ATTICISM
ATISHOOS	ATOMISTIC	ATRIUMS	ATTAP	ATTICISMS
ATLANTES	ATOMISTS	ATROCIOUS	ATTAPS	ATTICIST
ATLAS	ATOMIZE	ATROCITY	ATTAR	ATTICISTS
ATLASES	ATOMIZED	ATROPHIA	ATTARS	ATTICIZE
ATLATL	ATOMIZER	ATROPHIAS	ATTASK	ATTICIZED
ATLATLS	ATOMIZERS	ATROPHIC	ATTASKED	ATTICIZES
ATMA	ATOMIZES	ATROPHIED	ATTASKING	ATTICS
ATMAN	ATOMIZING	ATROPHIES	ATTASKS	ATTING
ATMANS	ATOMS	ATROPHY	ATTASKT	ATTIRE
ATMAS	ATOMY	ATROPIA	ATTED	ATTIRED
ATMOLOGY	ATONABLE	ATROPIAS	ATTEMPER	ATTIRES
ATMOLYSE	ATONAL	ATROPIN	ATTEMPERS	ATTIRING
ATMOLYSED	ATONALISM	ATROPINE	ATTEMPT	ATTIRINGS
ATMOLYSES	ATONALIST	ATROPINES	ATTEMPTED	ATTITUDE
ATMOLYSIS	ATONALITY	ATROPINS	ATTEMPTER	ATTITUDES
ATMOLYZE	ATONALLY	ATROPISM	ATTEMPTS	ATTOLASER
ATMOLYZED	ATONE	ATROPISMS	ATTEND	ATTOLLENS
ATMOLYZES	ATONEABLE	ATROPOUS	ATTENDANT	ATTOLLENT
ATMOMETER	ATONED	ATS	ATTENDED	ATTOMETER
ATMOMETRY	ATONEMENT	ATT	ATTENDEE	ATTOMETRE
ATMOS	ATONER	ATTABOY	ATTENDEES	ATTONCE
ATMOSES	ATONERS	ATTABOYS	ATTENDER	ATTONE
ATOC	ATONES	ATTACH	ATTENDERS	ATTONED
ATOCIA	ATONIA	ATTACHE	ATTENDING	ATTONES
ATOCIAS	ATONIAS	ATTACHED	ATTENDS	ATTONING
ATOCS	ATONIC	ATTACHER	ATTENT	ATTORN
ATOK	ATONICITY	ATTACHERS	ATTENTAT	ATTORNED
ATOKAL	ATONICS	ATTACHES	ATTENTATS	ATTORNEY
ATOKE	ATONIES	ATTACHING	ATTENTION	ATTORNEYS
ATOKES	ATONING	ATTACK	ATTENTIVE	ATTORNING
ATOKOUS	ATONINGLY	ATTACKED	ATTENTS	ATTORNS
ATOKS	ATONY	ATTACKER	ATTENUANT	ATTOTESLA
ATOLL	ATOP	ATTACKERS	ATTENUATE	ATTRACT
ATOLLS	ATOPIC	ATTACKING	ATTERCOP	ATTRACTED
ATOM	ATOPIES	ATTACKMAN	ATTERCOPS	ATTRACTER
ATOMIC	ATOPY	ATTACKMEN	ATTEST	ATTRACTOR
ATOMICAL	ATRAMENT	ATTACKS	ATTESTANT	ATTRACTS
ATOMICITY	ATRAMENTS	ATTAGIRL	ATTESTED	ATTRAHENS
ATOMICS	ATRAZINE	ATTAGIRLS	ATTESTER	ATTRAHENT
ATOMIES	ATRAZINES	ATTAIN	ATTESTERS	ATTRAP
ATOMISE	ATREMBLE	ATTAINDER	ATTESTING	ATTRAPPED
ATOMISED	ATRESIA	ATTAINED	ATTESTOR	ATTRAPS
ATOMISER	ATRESIAS	ATTAINER	ATTESTORS	ATTRIBUTE
ATOMISERS	ATRESIC	ATTAINERS	ATTESTS	ATTRIST
ATOMISES	ATRETIC	ATTAINING	ATTIC	ATTRISTED
ATOMISING	ATRIA	ATTAINS	ATTICISE	ATTRISTS

ATTRIT	AUCUBA	AUDITS	AULIC	AURELIANS
ATTRITE	AUCUBAS	AUE	AULNAGE	AURELIAS
ATTRITED	AUDACIOUS	AUF	AULNAGER	AUREOLA
ATTRITES	AUDACITY	AUFGABE	AULNAGERS	AUREOLAE
ATTRITING	AUDAD	AUFGABES	AULNAGES	AUREOLAS
ATTRITION	AUDADS	AUFS	AULOI	AUREOLE
ATTRITIVE	AUDIAL	AUGEND	AULOS	AUREOLED
ATTRITS	AUDIBLE	AUGENDS	AUMAIL	AUREOLES
ATTRITTED	AUDIBLED	AUGER	AUMAILED	AUREOLING
ATTUENT	AUDIBLES	AUGERS	AUMAILING	AURES
ATTUITE	AUDIBLING	AUGH	AUMAILS	AUREUS
ATTUITED	AUDIBLY	AUGHT	AUMBRIES	AURIC
ATTUITES	AUDIENCE	AUGHTS	AUMBRY	AURICLE
ATTUITING	AUDIENCES	AUGITE	AUMIL	AURICLED
ATTUITION	AUDIENCIA	AUGITES	AUMILDAR	AURICLES
ATTUITIVE	AUDIENT	AUGITIC	AUMILDARS	AURICULA
ATTUNE	AUDIENTS	AUGMENT	AUMILS	AURICULAE
ATTUNED	AUDILE	AUGMENTED	AUNE	AURICULAR
ATTUNES	AUDILES	AUGMENTER	AUNES	AURICULAS
ATTUNING	AUDING	AUGMENTOR	AUNT	AURIFIED
ATUA	AUDINGS	AUGMENTS	AUNTER	AURIFIES
ATUAS	AUDIO	AUGUR	AUNTERS	AURIFORM
ATWAIN	AUDIOBOOK	AUGURAL	AUNTHOOD	AURIFY
ATWEEL	AUDIOGRAM	AUGURED	AUNTHOODS	AURIFYING
ATWEEN	AUDIOLOGY	AUGURER	AUNTIE	AURIS
ATWITTER	AUDIOPHIL	AUGURERS	AUNTIES	AURISCOPE
ATWIXT	AUDIOS	AUGURIES	AUNTLIER	AURIST
ATYPIC	AUDIOTAPE	AUGURING	AUNTLIEST	AURISTS
ATYPICAL	AUDIPHONE	AUGURS	AUNTLIKE	AUROCHS
AUA	AUDISM	AUGURSHIP	AUNTLY	AUROCHSES
AUAS	AUDISMS	AUGURY	AUNTS	AURORA
AUBADE	AUDIST	AUGUST	AUNTY	AURORAE
AUBADES	AUDISTS	AUGUSTE	AURA	AURORAL
AUBERGE	AUDIT	AUGUSTER	AURAE	AURORALLY
AUBERGES	AUDITABLE	AUGUSTES	AURAL	AURORAS
AUBERGINE	AUDITED	AUGUSTEST	AURALITY	AUROREAN
AUBRETIA	AUDITEE	AUGUSTLY	AURALLY	AUROUS
AUBRETIAS	AUDITEES	AUGUSTS	AURAR	AURUM
AUBRIETA	AUDITING	AUK	AURAS	AURUMS
AUBRIETAS	AUDITINGS	AUKLET	AURATE	AUSFORM
AUBRIETIA	AUDITION	AUKLETS	AURATED	AUSFORMED
AUBURN	AUDITIONS	AUKS	AURATES	AUSFORMS
AUBURNS	AUDITIVE	AULA	AUREATE	AUSLANDER
AUCEPS	AUDITIVES	AULARIAN	AUREATELY	AUSPEX
AUCEPSES	AUDITOR	AULARIANS	AUREI	AUSPICATE
AUCTION	AUDITORIA	AULAS	AUREITIES	AUSPICE
AUCTIONED	AUDITORS	AULD	AUREITY	AUSPICES
AUCTIONS	AUDITORY	AULDER	AURELIA	AUSTENITE
AUCTORIAL	AUDITRESS	AULDEST	AURELIAN	AUSTERE

AUSTERELY	AUTOBANKS	AUTOICOUS	AUTOPSY	AUXINIC
AUSTERER	AUTOBODY	AUTOING	AUTOPTIC	AUXINS
AUSTEREST	AUTOBUS	AUTOLATRY	AUTOPUT	AUXOCYTE
AUSTERITY	AUTOBUSES	AUTOLOAD	AUTOPUTS	AUXOCYTES
AUSTRAL	AUTOCADE	AUTOLOADS	AUTOREPLY	AUXOMETER
AUSTRALES	AUTOCADES	AUTOLOGY	AUTOROUTE	AUXOSPORE
AUSTRALIS	AUTOCAR	AUTOLYSE	AUTOS	AUXOTONIC
AUSTRALS	AUTOCARP	AUTOLYSED	AUTOSAVE	AUXOTROPH
AUSUBO	AUTOCARPS	AUTOLYSES	AUTOSAVED	AVA
AUSUBOS	AUTOCARS	AUTOLYSIN	AUTOSAVES	AVADAVAT
AUTACOID	AUTOCIDAL	AUTOLYSIS	AUTOSCOPY	AVADAVATS
AUTACOIDS	AUTOCLAVE	AUTOLYTIC	AUTOSOMAL	AVAIL
AUTARCH	AUTOCOID	AUTOLYZE	AUTOSOME	AVAILABLE
AUTARCHIC	AUTOCOIDS	AUTOLYZED	AUTOSOMES	AVAILABLY
AUTARCHS	AUTOCRACY	AUTOLYZES	AUTOSPORE	AVAILE
AUTARCHY	AUTOCRAT	AUTOMAGIC	AUTOSPORT	AVAILED
AUTARKIC	AUTOCRATS	AUTOMAKER	AUTOTELIC	AVAILES
AUTARKIES	AUTOCRIME	AUTOMAN	AUTOTEST	AVAILFUL
AUTARKIST	AUTOCRINE	AUTOMAT	AUTOTESTS	AVAILING
AUTARKY	AUTOCROSS	AUTOMATA	AUTOTIMER	AVAILS
AUTECIOUS	AUTOCUE	AUTOMATE	AUTOTOMIC	AVAL
AUTECISM	AUTOCUES	AUTOMATED	AUTOTOMY	AVALANCHE
AUTECISMS	AUTOCUTIE	AUTOMATES	AUTOTOXIC	AVALE
AUTEUR	AUTOCYCLE	AUTOMATIC	AUTOTOXIN	AVALED
AUTEURISM	AUTODIAL	AUTOMATON	AUTOTROPH	AVALEMENT
AUTEURIST	AUTODIALS	AUTOMATS	AUTOTUNE	AVALES
AUTEURS	AUTODROME	AUTOMEN	AUTOTUNES	AVALING
AUTHENTIC	AUTODYNE	AUTOMETER	AUTOTYPE	AVANT
AUTHOR	AUTODYNES	AUTONOMIC	AUTOTYPED	AVANTI
AUTHORED	AUTOECISM	AUTONOMY	AUTOTYPES	AVANTIST
AUTHORESS	AUTOED	AUTONYM	AUTOTYPIC	AVANTISTS
AUTHORIAL	AUTOFILL	AUTONYMS	AUTOTYPY	AVARICE
AUTHORING	AUTOFILLS	AUTOPEN	AUTOVAC	AVARICES
AUTHORISE	AUTOFLARE	AUTOPENS	AUTOVACS	AVAS
AUTHORISH	AUTOFOCI	AUTOPHAGY	AUTUMN	AVASCULAR
AUTHORISM	AUTOFOCUS	AUTOPHOBY	AUTUMNAL	AVAST
AUTHORITY	AUTOGAMIC	AUTOPHONY	AUTUMNIER	AVATAR
AUTHORIZE	AUTOGAMY	AUTOPHYTE	AUTUMNS	AVATARS
AUTHORS	AUTOGENIC	AUTOPILOT	AUTUMNY	AVAUNT
AUTISM	AUTOGENY	AUTOPISTA	AUTUNITE	AVAUNTED
AUTISMS	AUTOGIRO	AUTOPLAY	AUTUNITES	AVAUNTING
AUTIST	AUTOGIROS	AUTOPLAYS	AUXESES	AVAUNTS
AUTISTIC	AUTOGRAFT	AUTOPOINT	AUXESIS	AVE
AUTISTICS	AUTOGRAPH	AUTOPSIA	AUXETIC	AVEL
AUTISTS	AUTOGUIDE	AUTOPSIAS	AUXETICS	AVELLAN
AUTO	AUTOGYRO	AUTOPSIC	AUXILIAR	AVELLANE
AUTOBAHN	AUTOGYROS	AUTOPSIED	AUXILIARS	AVELS
AUTOBAHNS	AUTOHARP	AUTOPSIES	AUXILIARY	AVENGE
AUTOBANK	AUTOHARPS	AUTOPSIST	AUXIN	AVENGED

A

AVENGEFUL	AVERTS	AVIGATORS	AVOUCH	AWAKE
AVENGER	AVES	AVINE	AVOUCHED	AWAKED
AVENGERS	AVGAS	AVION	AVOUCHER	AWAKEN
AVENGES	AVGASES	AVIONIC	AVOUCHERS	AWAKENED
AVENGING	AVGASSES	AVIONICS	AVOUCHES	AWAKENER
AVENIR	AVI	AVIONS	AVOUCHING	AWAKENERS
AVENIRS	AVIAN	AVIOPHOBE	AVOURE	AWAKENING
AVENS	AVIANISE	AVIRULENT	AVOURES	AWAKENS
AVENSES	AVIANISED	AVIS	AVOUTERER	AWAKES
AVENTAIL	AVIANISES	AVISANDUM	AVOUTRER	AWAKING
AVENTAILE	AVIANIZE	AVISE	AVOUTRERS	AWAKINGS
AVENTAILS	AVIANIZED	AVISED	AVOUTRIES	AWANTING
AVENTRE	AVIANIZES	AVISEMENT	AVOUTRY	AWARD
AVENTRED	AVIANS	AVISES	AVOW	AWARDABLE
AVENTRES	AVIAPHOBE	AVISING	AVOWABLE	AWARDED
AVENTRING	AVIARIES	AVISO	AVOWABLY	AWARDEE
AVENTURE	AVIARIST	AVISOS	AVOWAL	AWARDEES
AVENTURES	AVIARISTS	AVITAL	AVOWALS	AWARDER
AVENTURIN	AVIARY	AVIZANDUM	AVOWED	AWARDERS
AVENUE	AVIATE	AVIZE	AVOWEDLY	AWARDING
AVENUES	AVIATED	AVIZED	AVOWER	AWARDS
AVER	AVIATES	AVIZEFULL	AVOWERS	AWARE
AVERAGE	AVIATIC	AVIZES	AVOWING	AWARENESS
AVERAGED	AVIATING	AVIZING	AVOWRIES	AWARER
AVERAGELY	AVIATION	AVO	AVOWRY	AWAREST
AVERAGER	AVIATIONS	AVOCADO	AVOWS	AWARN
AVERAGERS	AVIATOR	AVOCADOES	AVOYER	AWARNED
AVERAGES	AVIATORS	AVOCADOS	AVOYERS	AWARNING
AVERAGING	AVIATRESS	AVOCATION	AVRUGA	AWARNS
AVERMENT	AVIATRICE	AVOCET	AVRUGAS	AWASH
AVERMENTS	AVIATRIX	AVOCETS	AVULSE	AWATCH
AVERRABLE	AVICULAR	AVODIRE	AVULSED	AWATO
AVERRED	AVID	AVODIRES	AVULSES	AWATOS
AVERRING	AVIDER	AVOID	AVULSING	AWAVE
AVERS	AVIDEST	AVOIDABLE	AVULSION	AWAY
AVERSE	AVIDIN	AVOIDABLY	AVULSIONS	AWAYDAY
AVERSELY	AVIDINS	AVOIDANCE	AVUNCULAR	AWAYDAYS
AVERSION	AVIDITIES	AVOIDANT	AVYZE	AWAYES
AVERSIONS	AVIDITY	AVOIDED	AVYZED	AWAYNESS
AVERSIVE	AVIDLY	AVOIDER	AVYZES	AWAYS
AVERSIVES	AVIDNESS	AVOIDERS	AVYZING	AWDL
AVERT	AVIETTE	AVOIDING	AW	AWDLS
AVERTABLE	AVIETTES	AVOIDS	AWA	AWE
AVERTED	AVIFAUNA	AVOISION	AWAIT	AWEARIED
AVERTEDLY	AVIFAUNAE	AVOISIONS	AWAITED	AWEARY
AVERTER	AVIFAUNAL	AVOPARCIN	AWAITER	AWEATHER
AVERTERS	AVIFAUNAS	AVOS	AWAITERS	AWED
AVERTIBLE	AVIFORM	AVOSET	AWAITING	AWEE
AVERTING	AVIGATOR	AVOSETS	AWAITS	AWEEL

AWEIGH	AWNIER	AXIOMATIC	AYGRE	AZOTED
AWEING	AWNIEST	AXIOMS	AYIN	AZOTEMIA
AWELESS	AWNING	AXION	AYINS	AZOTEMIAS
AWES	AWNINGED	AXIONS	AYONT	AZOTEMIC
AWESOME	AWNINGS	AXIS	AYRE	AZOTES
AWESOMELY	AWNLESS	AXISED	AYRES	AZOTH
AWESTRIKE	AWNS	AXISES	AYRIE	AZOTHS
AWESTRUCK	AWNY	AXITE	AYRIES	AZOTIC
AWETO	AWOKE	AXITES	AYS	AZOTISE
AWETOS	AWOKEN	AXLE	AYU	AZOTISED
AWFUL	AWOL	AXLED	AYURVEDA	AZOTISES
AWFULLER	AWOLS	AXLES	AYURVEDAS	AZOTISING
AWFULLEST	AWORK	AXLETREE	AYURVEDIC	AZOTIZE
AWFULLY	AWRACK	AXLETREES	AYUS	AZOTIZED
AWFULNESS	AWRONG	AXLIKE	AYWORD	AZOTIZES
AWFY	AWRY	AXMAN	AYWORDS	AZOTIZING
AWHAPE	AWSOME	AXMEN	AZALEA	AZOTOUS
AWHAPED	AX	AXOID	AZALEAS	AZOTURIA
AWHAPES	AXAL	AXOIDS	AZAN	AZOTURIAS
AWHAPING	AXE	AXOLEMMA	AZANS	AZUKI
AWHATO	AXEBIRD	AXOLEMMAS	AZEDARACH	AZUKIS
AWHATOS	AXEBIRDS	AXOLOTL	AZEOTROPE	AZULEJO
AWHEEL	AXED	AXOLOTLS	AZEOTROPY	AZULEJOS
AWHEELS	AXEL	AXON	AZERTY	AZURE
AWHETO	AXELIKE	AXONAL	AZIDE	AZUREAN
AWHETOS	AXELS	AXONE	AZIDES	AZURES
AWHILE	AXEMAN	AXONEMAL	AZIDO	AZURIES
AWHIRL	AXEMEN	AXONEME	AZIMUTH	AZURINE
AWING	AXENIC	AXONEMES	AZIMUTHAL	AZURINES
AWK	AXES	AXONES	AZIMUTHS	AZURITE
AWKS	AXIAL	AXONIC	AZINE	AZURITES
AWKWARD	AXIALITY	AXONS	AZINES	AZURN
AWKWARDER	AXIALLY	AXOPLASM	AZIONE	AZURY
AWKWARDLY	AXIL	AXOPLASMS	AZIONES	AZYGIES
AWL	AXILE	AXSEED	AZLON	AZYGOS
AWLBIRD	AXILEMMA	AXSEEDS	AZLONS	AZYGOSES
AWLBIRDS	AXILEMMAS	AY	AZO	AZYGOUS
AWLESS	AXILLA	AYAH	AZOIC	AZYGOUSLY
AWLS	AXILLAE	AYAHS	AZOLE	AZYGY
AWLWORT	AXILLAR	AYAHUASCA	AZOLES	AZYM
AWLWORTS	AXILLARS	AYAHUASCO	AZOLLA	AZYME
AWMOUS	AXILLARY	AYATOLLAH	AZOLLAS	AZYMES
AWMRIE	AXILLAS	AYAYA	AZON	AZYMITE
AWMRIES	AXILS	AYAYAS	AZONAL	AZYMITES
AWMRY	AXING	AYE	AZONIC	AZYMOUS
AWN	AXINITE	AYELP	AZONS	AZYMS
AWNED	AXINITES	AYENBITE	AZOTAEMIA	
AWNER	AXIOLOGY	AYENBITES	AZOTAEMIC	
AWNERS	AXIOM	AYES	AZOTE	

B

BA	BABBLY	BABUISM	BACCATE	BACKBARS
BAA	BABE	BABUISMS	BACCATED	BACKBEAT
BAAED	BABEL	BABUL	BACCHANAL	BACKBEATS
BAAING	BABELDOM	BABULS	BACCHANT	BACKBENCH
BAAINGS	BABELDOMS	BABUS	BACCHANTE	BACKBEND
BAAL	BABELISH	BABUSHKA	BACCHANTS	BACKBENDS
BAALEBOS	BABELISM	BABUSHKAS	BACCHIAC	BACKBIT
BAALIM	BABELISMS	BABY	BACCHIAN	BACKBITE
BAALISM	BABELS	BABYCCINO	BACCHIC	BACKBITER
BAALISMS	BABES	BABYCINO	BACCHII	BACKBITES
BAALS	BABESIA	BABYCINOS	BACCHIUS	BACKBLOCK
BAAS	BABESIAE	BABYDADDY	BACCIES	BACKBOARD
BAASKAAP	BABESIAS	BABYDOLL	BACCIFORM	BACKBOND
BAASKAAPS	BABICHE	BABYDOLLS	BACCO	BACKBONDS
BAASKAP	BABICHES	BABYFOOD	BACCOES	BACKBONE
BAASKAPS	BABIED	BABYFOODS	BACCOS	BACKBONED
BAASSKAP	BABIER	BABYHOOD	BACCY	BACKBONES
BAASSKAPS	BABIES	BABYHOODS	BACH	BACKBURN
BABA	BABIEST	BABYING	BACHA	BACKBURNS
BABACO	BABIRUSA	BABYISH	BACHARACH	BACKCAST
BABACOOTE	BABIRUSAS	BABYISHLY	BACHAS	BACKCASTS
BABACOS	BABIRUSSA	BABYLIKE	BACHATA	BACKCHAT
BABACU	BABKA	BABYMOON	BACHATAS	BACKCHATS
BABACUS	BABKAS	BABYMOONS	BACHCHA	BACKCHECK
BABALAS	BABLAH	BABYPROOF	BACHCHAS	BACKCLOTH
BABAS	BABLAHS	BABYSAT	BACHED	BACKCOMB
BABASSU	BABOO	BABYSIT	BACHELOR	BACKCOMBS
BABASSUS	BABOOL	BABYSITS	BACHELORS	BACKCOURT
BABBELAS	BABOOLS	BAC	BACHES	BACKCROSS
BABBITRY	BABOON	BACALAO	BACHING	BACKDATE
BABBITT	BABOONERY	BACALAOS	BACHS	BACKDATED
BABBITTED	BABOONISH	BACALHAU	BACILLAR	BACKDATES
BABBITTRY	BABOONS	BACALHAUS	BACILLARY	BACKDOOR
BABBITTS	BABOOS	BACCA	BACILLI	BACKDOWN
BABBLE	BABOOSH	BACCAE	BACILLUS	BACKDOWNS
BABBLED	BABOOSHES	BACCALA	BACK	BACKDRAFT
BABBLER	BABOUCHE	BACCALAS	BACKACHE	BACKDROP
BABBLERS	BABOUCHES	BACCARA	BACKACHES	BACKDROPS
BABBLES	BABU	BACCARAS	BACKACTER	BACKDROPT
BABBLIER	BABUCHE	BACCARAT	BACKARE	BACKED
BABBLIEST	BABUCHES	BACCARATS	BACKBAND	BACKEND
BABBLING	BABUDOM	BACCARE	BACKBANDS	BACKENDS
BABBLINGS	BABUDOMS	BACCAS	BACKBAR	BACKER

BACKERS	BACKLOG	BACKSTAMP	BACTERIAL	BADMEN
BACKET	BACKLOGS	BACKSTAY	BACTERIAN	BADMINTON
BACKETS	BACKLOT	BACKSTAYS	BACTERIAS	BADMOUTH
BACKFALL	BACKLOTS	BACKSTOP	BACTERIC	BADMOUTHS
BACKFALLS	BACKMOST	BACKSTOPS	BACTERIN	BADNESS
BACKFAT	BACKOUT	BACKSTORY	BACTERINS	BADNESSES
BACKFATS	BACKOUTS	BACKSTRAP	BACTERISE	BADS
BACKFIELD	BACKPACK	BACKSWEPT	BACTERIUM	BADWARE
BACKFILE	BACKPACKS	BACKSWING	BACTERIZE	BADWARES
BACKFILES	BACKPEDAL	BACKSWORD	BACTEROID	BAE
BACKFILL	BACKPIECE	BACKTALK	BACULA	BAEL
BACKFILLS	BACKPLANE	BACKTALKS	BACULINE	BAELS
BACKFIRE	BACKPLATE	BACKTRACK	BACULITE	BAES
BACKFIRED	BACKREST	BACKUP	BACULITES	BAETYL
BACKFIRES	BACKRESTS	BACKUPS	BACULUM	BAETYLS
BACKFISCH	BACKRONYM	BACKVELD	BACULUMS	BAFF
BACKFIT	BACKROOM	BACKVELDS	BAD	BAFFED
BACKFITS	BACKROOMS	BACKWALL	BADAMASH	BAFFIES
BACKFLIP	BACKRUSH	BACKWALLS	BADASS	BAFFING
BACKFLIPS	BACKS	BACKWARD	BADASSED	BAFFLE
BACKFLOW	BACKSAW	BACKWARDS	BADASSES	BAFFLED
BACKFLOWS	BACKSAWS	BACKWASH	BADDER	BAFFLEGAB
BACKHAND	BACKSEAT	BACKWATER	BADDEST	BAFFLER
BACKHANDS	BACKSEATS	BACKWIND	BADDIE	BAFFLERS
BACKHAUL	BACKSET	BACKWINDS	BADDIES	BAFFLES
BACKHAULS	BACKSETS	BACKWOOD	BADDISH	BAFFLING
BACKHOE	BACKSEY	BACKWOODS	BADDY	BAFFS
BACKHOED	BACKSEYS	BACKWORD	BADE	BAFFY
BACKHOES	BACKSHISH	BACKWORDS	BADGE	BAFT
BACKHOUSE	BACKSHORE	BACKWORK	BADGED	BAFTA
BACKIE	BACKSIDE	BACKWORKS	BADGELESS	BAFTAS
BACKIES	BACKSIDES	BACKWRAP	BADGER	BAFTS
BACKING	BACKSIGHT	BACKWRAPS	BADGERED	BAG
BACKINGS	BACKSLAP	BACKYARD	BADGERING	BAGARRE
BACKLAND	BACKSLAPS	BACKYARDS	BADGERLY	BAGARRES
BACKLANDS	BACKSLASH	BACLAVA	BADGERS	BAGASS
BACKLASH	BACKSLID	BACLAVAS	BADGES	BAGASSE
BACKLESS	BACKSLIDE	BACLOFEN	BADGING	BAGASSES
BACKLIFT	BACKSPACE	BACLOFENS	BADINAGE	BAGATELLE
BACKLIFTS	BACKSPEER	BACNE	BADINAGED	BAGEL
BACKLIGHT	BACKSPEIR	BACNES	BADINAGES	BAGELED
BACKLINE	BACKSPIN	BACON	BADINERIE	BAGELING
BACKLINER	BACKSPINS	BACONER	BADIOUS	BAGELLED
BACKLINES	BACKSPLIT	BACONERS	BADLAND	BAGELLING
BACKLIST	BACKSTAB	BACONS	BADLANDS	BAGELS
BACKLISTS	BACKSTABS	BACRONYM	BADLY	BAGFUL
BACKLIT	BACKSTAGE	BACRONYMS	BADMAN	BAGFULS
BACKLOAD	BACKSTAIR	BACS	BADMASH	BAGGAGE
BACKLOADS	BACKSTALL	BACTERIA	BADMASHES	BAGGAGES

BAGGED	BAGWIGS	BAILORS	BAKEBOARD	BALASES
BAGGER	BAGWORM	BAILOUT	BAKED	BALATA
BAGGERS	BAGWORMS	BAILOUTS	BAKEHOUSE	BALATAS
BAGGIE	BAH	BAILS	BAKELITE	BALAYAGE
BAGGIER	BAHADA	BAILSMAN	BAKELITES	BALAYAGED
BAGGIES	BAHADAS	BAILSMEN	BAKEMEAT	BALAYAGES
BAGGIEST	BAHADUR	BAININ	BAKEMEATS	BALBOA
BAGGILY	BAHADURS	BAININS	BAKEN	BALBOAS
BAGGINESS	BAHOOKIE	BAINITE	BAKEOFF	BALCONET
BAGGING	BAHOOKIES	BAINITES	BAKEOFFS	BALCONETS
BAGGINGS	BAHT	BAIRN	BAKER	BALCONIED
BAGGIT	BAHTS	BAIRNISH	BAKERIES	BALCONIES
BAGGITS	BAHU	BAIRNLIER	BAKERS	BALCONING
BAGGY	BAHUS	BAIRNLIKE	BAKERY	BALCONY
BAGH	BAHUT	BAIRNLY	BAKES	BALD
BAGHOUSE	BAHUTS	BAIRNS	BAKESHOP	BALDACHIN
BAGHOUSES	BAHUVRIHI	BAISA	BAKESHOPS	BALDAQUIN
BAGHS	BAIDAR	BAISAS	BAKESTONE	BALDED
BAGIE	BAIDARKA	BAISEMAIN	BAKEWARE	BALDER
BAGIES	BAIDARKAS	BAIT	BAKEWARES	BALDEST
BAGLESS	BAIDARS	BAITED	BAKGAT	BALDFACED
BAGLIKE	BAIGNOIRE	BAITER	BAKHSHISH	BALDHEAD
BAGMAN	BAIJIU	BAITERS	BAKING	BALDHEADS
BAGMEN	BAIJIUS	BAITFISH	BAKINGS	BALDICOOT
BAGNETTE	BAIL	BAITH	BAKKIE	BALDIE
BAGNETTES	BAILABLE	BAITING	BAKKIES	BALDIER
BAGNIO	BAILBOND	BAITINGS	BAKLAVA	BALDIES
BAGNIOS	BAILBONDS	BAITS	BAKLAVAS	BALDIEST
BAGPIPE	BAILED	BAIZA	BAKLAWA	BALDING
BAGPIPED	BAILEE	BAIZAS	BAKLAWAS	BALDISH
BAGPIPER	BAILEES	BAIZE	BAKSHEESH	BALDLY
BAGPIPERS	BAILER	BAIZED	BAKSHISH	BALDMONEY
BAGPIPES	BAILERS	BAIZES	BAL	BALDNESS
BAGPIPING	BAILEY	BAIZING	BALACLAVA	BALDPATE
BAGS	BAILEYS	BAJADA	BALADIN	BALDPATED
BAGSFUL	BAILIE	BAJADAS	BALADINE	BALDPATES
BAGSIED	BAILIES	BAJAN	BALADINES	BALDRIC
BAGSIES	BAILIFF	BAJANS	BALADINS	BALDRICK
BAGSY	BAILIFFS	BAJILLION	BALAFON	BALDRICKS
BAGSYING	BAILING	BAJRA	BALAFONS	BALDRICS
BAGUET	BAILIWICK	BAJRAS	BALALAIKA	BALDS
BAGUETS	BAILLI	BAJREE	BALANCE	BALDY
BAGUETTE	BAILLIAGE	BAJREES	BALANCED	BALE
BAGUETTES	BAILLIE	BAJRI	BALANCER	BALECTION
BAGUIO	BAILLIES	BAJRIS	BALANCERS	BALED
BAGUIOS	BAILLIS	BAJU	BALANCES	BALEEN
BAGWASH	BAILMENT	BAJUS	BALANCING	BALEENS
BAGWASHES	BAILMENTS	BAKE	BALANITIS	BALEFIRE
BAGWIG	BAILOR	BAKEAPPLE	BALAS	BALEFIRES

BALEFUL	BALLANT	BALLONET	BALMINESS	BAMPOT
BALEFULLY	BALLANTED	BALLONETS	BALMING	BAMPOTS
BALER	BALLANTS	BALLONNE	BALMLIKE	BAMS
BALERS	BALLAST	BALLONNES	BALMORAL	BAN
BALES	BALLASTED	BALLONS	BALMORALS	BANAK
BALING	BALLASTER	BALLOON	BALMS	BANAKS
BALINGS	BALLASTS	BALLOONED	BALMY	BANAL
BALISAUR	BALLAT	BALLOONS	BALNEAL	BANALER
BALISAURS	BALLATED	BALLOT	BALNEARY	BANALEST
BALISE	BALLATING	BALLOTED	BALONEY	BANALISE
BALISES	BALLATS	BALLOTEE	BALONEYS	BANALISED
BALISTA	BALLBOY	BALLOTEES	BALOO	BANALISES
BALISTAE	BALLBOYS	BALLOTER	BALOOS	BANALITY
BALISTAS	BALLCLAY	BALLOTERS	BALS	BANALIZE
BALK	BALLCLAYS	BALLOTING	BALSA	BANALIZED
BALKANISE	BALLCOCK	BALLOTINI	BALSAM	BANALIZES
BALKANIZE	BALLCOCKS	BALLOTS	BALSAMED	BANALLY
BALKED	BALLED	BALLOW	BALSAMIC	BANANA
BALKER	BALLER	BALLOWS	BALSAMIER	BANANAS
BALKERS	BALLERINA	BALLPARK	BALSAMING	BANAUSIAN
BALKIER	BALLERINE	BALLPARKS	BALSAMS	BANAUSIC
BALKIEST	BALLERS	BALLPEEN	BALSAMY	BANC
BALKILY	BALLET	BALLPOINT	BALSAS	BANCHAN
BALKINESS	BALLETED	BALLROOM	BALSAWOOD	BANCO
BALKING	BALLETIC	BALLROOMS	BALTHASAR	BANCOS
BALKINGLY	BALLETING	BALLS	BALTHAZAR	BANCS
BALKINGS	BALLETS	BALLSED	BALTI	BAND
BALKLINE	BALLFIELD	BALLSES	BALTIC	BANDA
BALKLINES	BALLGAME	BALLSIER	BALTIS	BANDAGE
BALKS	BALLGAMES	BALLSIEST	BALU	BANDAGED
BALKY	BALLGIRL	BALLSING	BALUN	BANDAGER
BALL	BALLGIRLS	BALLSY	BALUNS	BANDAGERS
BALLABILE	BALLGOWN	BALLUP	BALUS	BANDAGES
BALLABILI	BALLGOWNS	BALLUPS	BALUSTER	BANDAGING
BALLAD	BALLHAWK	BALLUTE	BALUSTERS	BANDAID
BALLADE	BALLHAWKS	BALLUTES	BALZARINE	BANDALORE
BALLADED	BALLIER	BALLY	BAM	BANDANA
BALLADEER	BALLIES	BALLYARD	BAMBI	BANDANAS
BALLADES	BALLIEST	BALLYARDS	BAMBINI	BANDANNA
BALLADIC	BALLING	BALLYHOO	BAMBINO	BANDANNAS
BALLADIN	BALLINGS	BALLYHOOS	BAMBINOS	BANDAR
BALLADINE	BALLISTA	BALLYRAG	BAMBIS	BANDARI
BALLADING	BALLISTAE	BALLYRAGS	BAMBOO	BANDARIS
BALLADINS	BALLISTAS	BALM	BAMBOOS	BANDARIYA
BALLADIST	BALLISTIC	BALMACAAN	BAMBOOZLE	BANDARS
BALLADRY	BALLIUM	BALMED	BAMMED	BANDAS
BALLADS	BALLIUMS	BALMIER	BAMMER	BANDBOX
BALLAN	BALLOCKS	BALMIEST	BAMMERS	BANDBOXES
BALLANS	BALLON	BALMILY	BAMMING	BANDBRAKE

B

BANDEAU	BANDORAS	BANGS	BANKROLL	BANSHIES
BANDEAUS	BANDORE	BANGSRING	BANKROLLS	BANT
BANDEAUX	BANDORES	BANGSTER	BANKRUPT	BANTAM
BANDED	BANDPASS	BANGSTERS	BANKRUPTS	BANTAMS
BANDEIRA	BANDROL	BANGTAIL	BANKS	BANTED
BANDEIRAS	BANDROLS	BANGTAILS	BANKSIA	BANTENG
BANDELET	BANDS	BANI	BANKSIAS	BANTENGS
BANDELETS	BANDSAW	BANIA	BANKSIDE	BANTER
BANDELIER	BANDSAWED	BANIAN	BANKSIDES	BANTERED
BANDER	BANDSAWN	BANIANS	BANKSMAN	BANTERER
BANDEROL	BANDSAWS	BANIAS	BANKSMEN	BANTERERS
BANDEROLE	BANDSHELL	BANING	BANKSTER	BANTERING
BANDEROLS	BANDSMAN	BANISH	BANKSTERS	BANTERS
BANDERS	BANDSMEN	BANISHED	BANLIEUE	BANTIES
BANDFISH	BANDSTAND	BANISHER	BANLIEUES	BANTING
BANDH	BANDSTER	BANISHERS	BANNABLE	BANTINGS
BANDHS	BANDSTERS	BANISHES	BANNED	BANTLING
BANDICOOT	BANDURA	BANISHING	BANNER	BANTLINGS
BANDIED	BANDURAS	BANISTER	BANNERALL	BANTS
BANDIER	BANDURIST	BANISTERS	BANNERED	BANTY
BANDIES	BANDWAGON	BANJAX	BANNERET	BANTZ
BANDIEST	BANDWIDTH	BANJAXED	BANNERETS	BANXRING
BANDINESS	BANDY	BANJAXES	BANNERING	BANXRINGS
BANDING	BANDYING	BANJAXING	BANNEROL	BANYA
BANDINGS	BANDYINGS	BANJO	BANNEROLS	BANYAN
BANDIT	BANDYMAN	BANJOES	BANNERS	BANYANS
BANDITO	BANDYMEN	BANJOIST	BANNET	BANYAS
BANDITOS	BANE	BANJOISTS	BANNETS	BANZAI
BANDITRY	BANEBERRY	BANJOLELE	BANNING	BANZAIS
BANDITS	BANED	BANJOS	BANNINGS	BAO
BANDITTI	BANEFUL	BANJULELE	BANNISTER	BAOBAB
BANDITTIS	BANEFULLY	BANK	BANNOCK	BAOBABS
BANDLIKE	BANES	BANKABLE	BANNOCKS	BAOS
BANDMATE	BANG	BANKBOOK	BANNS	BAP
BANDMATES	BANGALAY	BANKBOOKS	BANOFFEE	BAPS
BANDOBAST	BANGALAYS	BANKCARD	BANOFFEES	BAPTISE
BANDOBUST	BANGALORE	BANKCARDS	BANOFFI	BAPTISED
BANDOG	BANGALOW	BANKED	BANOFFIS	BAPTISER
BANDOGS	BANGALOWS	BANKER	BANQUET	BAPTISERS
BANDOLEER	BANGBELLY	BANKERLY	BANQUETED	BAPTISES
BANDOLEON	BANGED	BANKERS	BANQUETER	BAPTISIA
BANDOLERO	BANGER	BANKET	BANQUETS	BAPTISIAS
BANDOLIER	BANGERS	BANKETS	BANQUETTE	BAPTISING
BANDOLINE	BANGING	BANKING	BANS	BAPTISM
BANDONEON	BANGKOK	BANKINGS	BANSELA	BAPTISMAL
BANDONION	BANGKOKS	BANKIT	BANSELAS	BAPTISMS
BANDOOK	BANGLE	BANKITS	BANSHEE	BAPTIST
BANDOOKS	BANGLED	BANKNOTE	BANSHEES	BAPTISTRY
BANDORA	BANGLES	BANKNOTES	BANSHIE	BAPTISTS

BAPTIZE	BARBERRY	BARDIC	BARFLY	BARKAN
BAPTIZED	BARBERS	BARDIE	BARFS	BARKANS
BAPTIZER	BARBES	BARDIER	BARFUL	BARKED
BAPTIZERS	BARBET	BARDIES	BARGAIN	BARKEEP
BAPTIZES	BARBETS	BARDIEST	BARGAINED	BARKEEPER
BAPTIZING	BARBETTE	BARDING	BARGAINER	BARKEEPS
BAPU	BARBETTES	BARDISM	BARGAINS	BARKEN
BAPUS	BARBICAN	BARDISMS	BARGANDER	BARKENED
BAR	BARBICANS	BARDLING	BARGE	BARKENING
BARACAN	BARBICEL	BARDLINGS	BARGED	BARKENS
BARACANS	BARBICELS	BARDO	BARGEE	BARKER
BARACHOIS	BARBIE	BARDOS	BARGEES	BARKERS
BARAGOUIN	BARBIES	BARDS	BARGEESE	BARKHAN
BARASINGA	BARBING	BARDSHIP	BARGELIKE	BARKHANS
BARATHEA	BARBITAL	BARDSHIPS	BARGELLO	BARKIER
BARATHEAS	BARBITALS	BARDY	BARGELLOS	BARKIEST
BARATHRUM	BARBITONE	BARE	BARGEMAN	BARKING
BARAZA	BARBLESS	BAREBACK	BARGEMEN	BARKLESS
BARAZAS	BARBOLA	BAREBACKS	BARGEPOLE	BARKLIKE
BARB	BARBOLAS	BAREBOAT	BARGES	BARKS
BARBAL	BARBOT	BAREBOATS	BARGEST	BARKY
BARBARIAN	BARBOTINE	BAREBONE	BARGESTS	BARLEDUC
BARBARIC	BARBOTS	BAREBONED	BARGHEST	BARLEDUCS
BARBARISE	BARBOTTE	BAREBONES	BARGHESTS	BARLESS
BARBARISM	BARBOTTES	BARED	BARGING	BARLEY
BARBARITY	BARBS	BAREFACED	BARGOON	BARLEYS
BARBARIZE	BARBULE	BAREFIT	BARGOONS	BARLOW
BARBAROUS	BARBULES	BAREFOOT	BARGOOSE	BARLOWS
BARBASCO	BARBUT	BAREGE	BARGUEST	BARM
BARBASCOS	BARBUTS	BAREGES	BARGUESTS	BARMAID
BARBASTEL	BARBWIRE	BAREGINE	BARHOP	BARMAIDS
BARBATE	BARBWIRES	BAREGINES	BARHOPPED	BARMAN
BARBATED	BARBY	BAREHAND	BARHOPS	BARMBRACK
BARBE	BARCA	BAREHANDS	BARIATRIC	BARMEN
BARBECUE	BARCAROLE	BAREHEAD	BARIC	BARMIE
BARBECUED	BARCAS	BARELAND	BARILLA	BARMIER
BARBECUER	BARCHAN	BARELY	BARILLAS	BARMIEST
BARBECUES	BARCHANE	BARENESS	BARING	BARMILY
BARBED	BARCHANES	BARER	BARISH	BARMINESS
BARBEL	BARCHANS	BARES	BARISTA	BARMKIN
BARBELL	BARCODE	BARESARK	BARISTAS	BARMKINS
BARBELLS	BARCODED	BARESARKS	BARITE	BARMPOT
BARBELS	BARCODES	BAREST	BARITES	BARMPOTS
BARBEQUE	BARD	BARF	BARITONAL	BARMS
BARBEQUED	BARDASH	BARFED	BARITONE	BARMY
BARBEQUES	BARDASHES	BARFI	BARITONES	BARN
BARBER	BARDE	BARFING	BARIUM	BARNACLE
BARBERED	BARDED	BARFIS	BARIUMS	BARNACLED
BARBERING	BARDES	BARFLIES	BARK	BARNACLES

BARNBOARD	BAROQUELY	BARREED	BARRULETS	BASALTS
BARNBRACK	BAROQUES	BARREFULL	BARRY	BASAN
BARNED	BAROSAUR	BARREING	BARS	BASANITE
BARNET	BAROSAURS	BARREL	BARSTOOL	BASANITES
BARNETS	BAROSCOPE	BARRELAGE	BARSTOOLS	BASANS
BARNEY	BAROSTAT	BARRELED	BARTEND	BASANT
BARNEYED	BAROSTATS	BARRELFUL	BARTENDED	BASANTS
BARNEYING	BAROTITIS	BARRELING	BARTENDER	BASAS
BARNEYS	BAROUCHE	BARRELLED	BARTENDS	BASCINET
BARNIER	BAROUCHES	BARRELS	BARTER	BASCINETS
BARNIEST	BARP	BARREN	BARTERED	BASCULE
BARNING	BARPERSON	BARRENER	BARTERER	BASCULES
BARNLIKE	BARPS	BARRENEST	BARTERERS	BASE
BARNS	BARQUE	BARRENLY	BARTERING	BASEBALL
BARNSTORM	BARQUES	BARRENS	BARTERS	BASEBALLS
BARNWOOD	BARQUETTE	BARRES	BARTISAN	BASEBAND
BARNWOODS	BARRA	BARRET	BARTISANS	BASEBANDS
BARNY	BARRABLE	BARRETOR	BARTIZAN	BASEBOARD
BARNYARD	BARRACAN	BARRETORS	BARTIZANS	BASEBORN
BARNYARDS	BARRACANS	BARRETRY	BARTON	BASED
BAROCCO	BARRACE	BARRETS	BARTONS	BASEEJ
BAROCCOS	BARRACES	BARRETTE	BARTSIA	BASEHEAD
BAROCK	BARRACK	BARRETTER	BARTSIAS	BASEHEADS
BAROCKS	BARRACKED	BARRETTES	BARWARE	BASELARD
BAROGRAM	BARRACKER	BARRICADE	BARWARES	BASELARDS
BAROGRAMS	BARRACKS	BARRICADO	BARWOOD	BASELESS
BAROGRAPH	BARRACOON	BARRICO	BARWOODS	BASELINE
BAROLO	BARRACUDA	BARRICOES	BARYE	BASELINER
BAROLOS	BARRAGE	BARRICOS	BARYES	BASELINES
BAROMETER	BARRAGED	BARRIE	BARYON	BASELOAD
BAROMETRY	BARRAGES	BARRIER	BARYONIC	BASELOADS
BAROMETZ	BARRAGING	BARRIERED	BARYONS	BASELY
BARON	BARRANCA	BARRIERS	BARYTA	BASEMAN
BARONAGE	BARRANCAS	BARRIES	BARYTAS	BASEMEN
BARONAGES	BARRANCO	BARRIEST	BARYTE	BASEMENT
BARONESS	BARRANCOS	BARRING	BARYTES	BASEMENTS
BARONET	BARRAS	BARRINGS	BARYTIC	BASEN
BARONETCY	BARRASWAY	BARRIO	BARYTON	BASENESS
BARONETS	BARRAT	BARRIOS	BARYTONE	BASENJI
BARONG	BARRATED	BARRIQUE	BARYTONES	BASENJIS
BARONGS	BARRATER	BARRIQUES	BARYTONS	BASEPATH
BARONIAL	BARRATERS	BARRISTER	BAS	BASEPATHS
BARONIES	BARRATING	BARRO	BASA	BASEPLATE
BARONNE	BARRATOR	BARROOM	BASAL	BASER
BARONNES	BARRATORS	BARROOMS	BASALLY	BASES
BARONS	BARRATRY	BARROW	BASALT	BASEST
BARONY	BARRATS	BARROWFUL	BASALTES	BASH
BAROPHILE	BARRE	BARROWS	BASALTIC	BASHAW
BAROQUE	BARRED	BARRULET	BASALTINE	BASHAWISM

BASHAWS	BASILS	BASSETS	BASTIS	BATHERS
BASHED	BASIN	BASSETT	BASTLE	BATHES
BASHER	BASINAL	BASSETTED	BASTLES	BATHETIC
BASHERS	BASINED	BASSETTS	BASTO	BATHHOUSE
BASHES	BASINET	BASSI	BASTOS	BATHING
BASHFUL	BASINETS	BASSIER	BASTS	BATHINGS
BASHFULLY	BASINFUL	BASSIEST	BASUCO	BATHLESS
BASHING	BASINFULS	BASSINET	BASUCOS	BATHMAT
BASHINGS	BASING	BASSINETS	BAT	BATHMATS
BASHLESS	BASINLIKE	BASSING	BATABLE	BATHMIC
BASHLIK	BASINS	BASSIST	BATARD	BATHMISM
BASHLIKS	BASION	BASSISTS	BATARDS	BATHMISMS
BASHLYK	BASIONS	BASSLINE	BATATA	BATHOLITE
BASHLYKS	BASIPETAL	BASSLINES	BATATAS	BATHOLITH
BASHMENT	BASIS	BASSLY	BATAVIA	BATHORSE
BASHMENTS	BASK	BASSNESS	BATAVIAS	BATHORSES
BASHO	BASKED	BASSO	BATBOY	BATHOS
BASHTAG	BASKET	BASSOON	BATBOYS	BATHOSES
BASHTAGS	BASKETFUL	BASSOONS	BATCH	BATHROBE
BASIC	BASKETRY	BASSOS	BATCHED	BATHROBES
BASICALLY	BASKETS	BASSWOOD	BATCHER	BATHROOM
BASICITY	BASKING	BASSWOODS	BATCHERS	BATHROOMS
BASICS	BASKS	BASSY	BATCHES	BATHS
BASIDIA	BASMATI	BAST	BATCHING	BATHTUB
BASIDIAL	BASMATIS	BASTA	BATCHINGS	BATHTUBS
BASIDIUM	BASNET	BASTARD	BATE	BATHWATER
BASIFIED	BASNETS	BASTARDLY	BATEAU	BATHYAL
BASIFIER	BASOCHE	BASTARDRY	BATEAUX	BATHYBIUS
BASIFIERS	BASOCHES	BASTARDS	BATED	BATHYLITE
BASIFIES	BASON	BASTARDY	BATELESS	BATHYLITH
BASIFIXED	BASONS	BASTE	BATELEUR	BATIK
BASIFUGAL	BASOPHIL	BASTED	BATELEURS	BATIKED
BASIFY	BASOPHILE	BASTER	BATEMENT	BATIKING
BASIFYING	BASOPHILS	BASTERS	BATEMENTS	BATIKS
BASIJ	BASQUE	BASTES	BATES	BATING
BASIL	BASQUED	BASTI	BATFISH	BATISTE
BASILAR	BASQUES	BASTIDE	BATFISHES	BATISTES
BASILARY	BASQUINE	BASTIDES	BATFOWL	BATLER
BASILECT	BASQUINES	BASTILE	BATFOWLED	BATLERS
BASILECTS	BASS	BASTILES	BATFOWLER	BATLET
BASILIC	BASSE	BASTILLE	BATFOWLS	BATLETS
BASILICA	BASSED	BASTILLES	BATGIRL	BATLIKE
BASILICAE	BASSER	BASTINADE	BATGIRLS	BATMAN
BASILICAL	BASSERS	BASTINADO	BATH	BATMEN
BASILICAN	BASSES	BASTING	BATHCUBE	BATOLOGY
BASILICAS	BASSEST	BASTINGS	BATHCUBES	BATON
BASILICON	BASSET	BASTION	BATHE	BATONED
BASILISK	BASSETED	BASTIONED	BATHED	BATONING
BASILISKS	BASSETING	BASTIONS	BATHER	BATONNIER

B

BATONS	BATTIEST	BAUDRONS	BAWDKINS	BAYLE
BATOON	BATTIK	BAUDS	BAWDRIC	BAYLES
BATOONED	BATTIKS	BAUERA	BAWDRICS	BAYMAN
BATOONING	BATTILL	BAUERAS	BAWDRIES	BAYMEN
BATOONS	BATTILLED	BAUHINIA	BAWDRY	BAYNODDY
BATRACHIA	BATTILLS	BAUHINIAS	BAWDS	BAYONET
BATS	BATTILY	BAUK	BAWDY	BAYONETED
BATSHIT	BATTINESS	BAUKED	BAWK	BAYONETS
BATSMAN	BATTING	BAUKING	BAWKS	BAYOU
BATSMEN	BATTINGS	BAUKS	BAWL	BAYOUS
BATSWING	BATTLE	BAULK	BAWLED	BAYS
BATSWOMAN	BATTLEAX	BAULKED	BAWLER	BAYSIDE
BATSWOMEN	BATTLEAXE	BAULKER	BAWLERS	BAYSIDES
BATT	BATTLEBUS	BAULKERS	BAWLEY	BAYT
BATTA	BATTLED	BAULKIER	BAWLEYS	BAYTED
BATTALIA	BATTLER	BAULKIEST	BAWLING	BAYTING
BATTALIAS	BATTLERS	BAULKILY	BAWLINGS	BAYTS
BATTALION	BATTLES	BAULKING	BAWLS	BAYWOOD
BATTAS	BATTLING	BAULKLINE	BAWN	BAYWOODS
BATTEAU	BATTOLOGY	BAULKS	BAWNEEN	BAYWOP
BATTEAUX	BATTS	BAULKY	BAWNEENS	BAYWOPS
BATTED	BATTU	BAUR	BAWNS	BAYYAN
BATTEL	BATTUE	BAURS	BAWR	BAYYANS
BATTELED	BATTUES	BAUSOND	BAWRS	BAZAAR
BATTELER	BATTUTA	BAUXITE	BAWS	BAZAARS
BATTELERS	BATTUTAS	BAUXITES	BAWSUNT	BAZAR
BATTELING	BATTUTO	BAUXITIC	BAWTIE	BAZARS
BATTELLED	BATTUTOS	BAVARDAGE	BAWTIES	BAZAZZ
BATTELS	BATTY	BAVAROIS	BAWTY	BAZAZZES
BATTEMENT	BATWING	BAVIN	BAXTER	BAZILLION
BATTEN	BATWOMAN	BAVINED	BAXTERS	BAZOO
BATTENED	BATWOMEN	BAVINING	BAY	BAZOOKA
BATTENER	BAUBEE	BAVINS	BAYADEER	BAZOOKAS
BATTENERS	BAUBEES	BAW	BAYADEERS	BAZOOM
BATTENING	BAUBLE	BAWBAG	BAYADERE	BAZOOMS
BATTENS	BAUBLES	BAWBAGS	BAYADERES	BAZOOS
BATTER	BAUBLING	BAWBEE	BAYAMO	BAZOUKI
BATTERED	BAUCHLE	BAWBEES	BAYAMOS	BAZOUKIS
BATTERER	BAUCHLED	BAWBLE	BAYARD	BAZZ
BATTERERS	BAUCHLES	BAWBLES	BAYARDS	BAZZAZZ
BATTERIE	BAUCHLING	BAWCOCK	BAYBERRY	BAZZAZZES
BATTERIES	BAUD	BAWCOCKS	BAYE	BAZZED
BATTERING	BAUDEKIN	BAWD	BAYED	BAZZES
BATTERO	BAUDEKINS	BAWDIER	BAYER	BAZZING
BATTEROS	BAUDRIC	BAWDIES	BAYES	BDELLIUM
BATTERS	BAUDRICK	BAWDIEST	BAYEST	BDELLIUMS
BATTERY	BAUDRICKE	BAWDILY	BAYFRONT	BE
BATTIER	BAUDRICKS	BAWDINESS	BAYFRONTS	BEACH
BATTIES	BAUDRICS	BAWDKIN	BAYING	BEACHBALL

B

BEACHBOY	BEAGLINGS	BEANING	BEARWOOD	BEAUFFETS
BEACHBOYS	BEAK	BEANLIKE	BEARWOODS	BEAUFIN
BEACHCOMB	BEAKED	BEANO	BEAST	BEAUFINS
BEACHED	BEAKER	BEANOS	BEASTED	BEAUISH
BEACHES	BEAKERFUL	BEANPOLE	BEASTHOOD	BEAUS
BEACHGOER	BEAKERS	BEANPOLES	BEASTIE	BEAUT
BEACHHEAD	BEAKIER	BEANS	BEASTIES	BEAUTEOUS
BEACHIER	BEAKIEST	BEANSTALK	BEASTILY	BEAUTER
BEACHIEST	BEAKLESS	BEANY	BEASTING	BEAUTEST
BEACHING	BEAKLIKE	BEAR	BEASTINGS	BEAUTIED
BEACHSIDE	BEAKS	BEARABLE	BEASTLIER	BEAUTIES
BEACHWEAR	BEAKY	BEARABLY	BEASTLIKE	BEAUTIFUL
BEACHY	BEAL	BEARBERRY	BEASTLY	BEAUTIFY
BEACON	BEALING	BEARBINE	BEASTS	BEAUTS
BEACONED	BEALINGS	BEARBINES	BEAT	BEAUTY
BEACONING	BEALS	BEARCAT	BEATABLE	BEAUTYING
BEACONS	BEAM	BEARCATS	BEATBOX	BEAUX
BEAD	BEAMED	BEARD	BEATBOXED	BEAUXITE
BEADBLAST	BEAMER	BEARDED	BEATBOXER	BEAUXITES
BEADED	BEAMERS	BEARDIE	BEATBOXES	BEAVER
BEADER	BEAMIER	BEARDIER	BEATDOWN	BEAVERED
BEADERS	BEAMIEST	BEARDIES	BEATDOWNS	BEAVERIES
BEADHOUSE	BEAMILY	BEARDIEST	BEATEN	BEAVERING
BEADIER	BEAMINESS	BEARDING	BEATER	BEAVERS
BEADIEST	BEAMING	BEARDLESS	BEATERS	BEAVERY
BEADILY	BEAMINGLY	BEARDLIKE	BEATH	BEBEERINE
BEADINESS	BEAMINGS	BEARDS	BEATHED	BEBEERU
BEADING	BEAMISH	BEARDY	BEATHING	BEBEERUS
BEADINGS	BEAMISHLY	BEARE	BEATHS	BEBLOOD
BEADLE	BEAMLESS	BEARED	BEATIER	BEBLOODED
BEADLEDOM	BEAMLET	BEARER	BEATIEST	BEBLOODS
BEADLES	BEAMLETS	BEARERS	BEATIFIC	BEBOP
BEADLIKE	BEAMLIKE	BEARES	BEATIFIED	BEBOPPED
BEADMAN	BEAMS	BEARGRASS	BEATIFIES	BEBOPPER
BEADMEN	BEAMY	BEARHUG	BEATIFY	BEBOPPERS
BEADROLL	BEAN	BEARHUGS	BEATING	BEBOPPING
BEADROLLS	BEANBAG	BEARING	BEATINGS	BEBOPS
BEADS	BEANBAGS	BEARINGS	BEATITUDE	BEBUNG
BEADSMAN	BEANBALL	BEARISH	BEATLESS	BEBUNGS
BEADSMEN	BEANBALLS	BEARISHLY	BEATNIK	BECALL
BEADWORK	BEANED	BEARLIKE	BEATNIKS	BECALLED
BEADWORKS	BEANERIES	BEARNAISE	BEATS	BECALLING
BEADY	BEANERY	BEARPAW	BEATY	BECALLS
BEAGLE	BEANFEAST	BEARPAWS	BEAU	BECALM
BEAGLED	BEANIE	BEARS	BEAUCOUP	BECALMED
BEAGLER	BEANIER	BEARSKIN	BEAUCOUPS	BECALMING
BEAGLERS	BEANIES	BEARSKINS	BEAUFET	BECALMS
BEAGLES	BEANIEST	BEARWARD	BEAUFETS	BECAME
BEAGLING	BEANINESS	BEARWARDS	BEAUFFET	BECAP

BECAPPED	BECLOTHES	BEDAMNS	BEDELS	BEDLAMPS
BECAPPING	BECLOUD	BEDARKEN	BEDELSHIP	BEDLAMS
BECAPS	BECLOUDED	BEDARKENS	BEDEMAN	BEDLESS
BECARPET	BECLOUDS	BEDASH	BEDEMEN	BEDLIKE
BECARPETS	BECLOWN	BEDASHED	BEDERAL	BEDLINER
BECASSE	BECLOWNED	BEDASHES	BEDERALS	BEDLINERS
BECASSES	BECLOWNS	BEDASHING	BEDES	BEDMAKER
BECAUSE	BECOME	BEDAUB	BEDESMAN	BEDMAKERS
BECCACCIA	BECOMES	BEDAUBED	BEDESMEN	BEDMATE
BECCAFICO	BECOMING	BEDAUBING	BEDEVIL	BEDMATES
BECHALK	BECOMINGS	BEDAUBS	BEDEVILED	BEDOTTED
BECHALKED	BECOWARD	BEDAWIN	BEDEVILS	BEDOUIN
BECHALKS	BECOWARDS	BEDAWINS	BEDEW	BEDOUINS
BECHAMEL	BECQUEREL	BEDAZE	BEDEWED	BEDPAN
BECHAMELS	BECRAWL	BEDAZED	BEDEWING	BEDPANS
BECHANCE	BECRAWLED	BEDAZES	BEDEWS	BEDPLATE
BECHANCED	BECRAWLS	BEDAZING	BEDFAST	BEDPLATES
BECHANCES	BECRIME	BEDAZZLE	BEDFELLOW	BEDPOST
BECHARM	BECRIMED	BEDAZZLED	BEDFRAME	BEDPOSTS
BECHARMED	BECRIMES	BEDAZZLES	BEDFRAMES	BEDQUILT
BECHARMS	BECRIMING	BEDBATH	BEDGOWN	BEDQUILTS
BECK	BECROWD	BEDBATHS	BEDGOWNS	BEDRAGGLE
BECKE	BECROWDED	BEDBOARD	BEDHEAD	BEDRAIL
BECKED	BECROWDS	BEDBOARDS	BEDHEADS	BEDRAILS
BECKES	BECRUST	BEDBUG	BEDIAPER	BEDRAL
BECKET	BECRUSTED	BEDBUGS	BEDIAPERS	BEDRALS
BECKETS	BECRUSTS	BEDCHAIR	BEDIDE	BEDRAPE
BECKING	BECUDGEL	BEDCHAIRS	BEDIGHT	BEDRAPED
BECKON	BECUDGELS	BEDCOVER	BEDIGHTED	BEDRAPES
BECKONED	BECURL	BEDCOVERS	BEDIGHTS	BEDRAPING
BECKONER	BECURLED	BEDDABLE	BEDIM	BEDRENCH
BECKONERS	BECURLING	BEDDED	BEDIMMED	BEDREST
BECKONING	BECURLS	BEDDER	BEDIMMING	BEDRESTS
BECKONS	BECURSE	BEDDERS	BEDIMPLE	BEDRID
BECKS	BECURSED	BEDDING	BEDIMPLED	BEDRIDDEN
BECLAMOR	BECURSES	BEDDINGS	BEDIMPLES	BEDRIGHT
BECLAMORS	BECURSING	BEDE	BEDIMS	BEDRIGHTS
BECLAMOUR	BECURST	BEDEAFEN	BEDIRTIED	BEDRITE
BECLASP	BED	BEDEAFENS	BEDIRTIES	BEDRITES
BECLASPED	BEDABBLE	BEDECK	BEDIRTY	BEDRIVEL
BECLASPS	BEDABBLED	BEDECKED	BEDIZEN	BEDRIVELS
BECLOAK	BEDABBLES	BEDECKING	BEDIZENED	BEDROCK
BECLOAKED	BEDAD	BEDECKS	BEDIZENS	BEDROCKS
BECLOAKS	BEDAGGLE	BEDEGUAR	BEDLAM	BEDROLL
BECLOG	BEDAGGLED	BEDEGUARS	BEDLAMER	BEDROLLS
BECLOGGED	BEDAGGLES	BEDEHOUSE	BEDLAMERS	BEDROOM
BECLOGS	BEDAMN	BEDEL	BEDLAMISM	BEDROOMED
BECLOTHE	BEDAMNED	BEDELL	BEDLAMITE	BEDROOMS
BECLOTHED	BEDAMNING	BEDELLS	BEDLAMP	BEDROP

B

BEDROPPED	BEDUNG	BEEFINESS	BEESOME	BEFLEAED
BEDROPS	BEDUNGED	BEEFING	BEESTING	BEFLEAING
BEDROPT	BEDUNGING	BEEFLESS	BEESTINGS	BEFLEAS
BEDRUG	BEDUNGS	BEEFS	BEESTUNG	BEFLECK
BEDRUGGED	BEDUST	BEEFSTEAK	BEESWAX	BEFLECKED
BEDRUGS	BEDUSTED	BEEFWOOD	BEESWAXED	BEFLECKS
BEDS	BEDUSTING	BEEFWOODS	BEESWAXES	BEFLOWER
BEDSHEET	BEDUSTS	BEEFY	BEESWING	BEFLOWERS
BEDSHEETS	BEDWARD	BEEGAH	BEESWINGS	BEFLUM
BEDSIDE	BEDWARDS	BEEGAHS	BEET	BEFLUMMED
BEDSIDES	BEDWARF	BEEHIVE	BEETED	BEFLUMS
BEDSIT	BEDWARFED	BEEHIVED	BEETFLIES	BEFOAM
BEDSITS	BEDWARFS	BEEHIVES	BEETFLY	BEFOAMED
BEDSITTER	BEDWARMER	BEEKEEPER	BEETING	BEFOAMING
BEDSKIRT	BEDWETTER	BEELIKE	BEETLE	BEFOAMS
BEDSKIRTS	BEDYDE	BEELINE	BEETLED	BEFOG
BEDSOCK	BEDYE	BEELINED	BEETLER	BEFOGGED
BEDSOCKS	BEDYED	BEELINES	BEETLERS	BEFOGGING
BEDSONIA	BEDYEING	BEELINING	BEETLES	BEFOGS
BEDSONIAS	BEDYES	BEEN	BEETLING	BEFOOL
BEDSORE	BEE	BEENAH	BEETROOT	BEFOOLED
BEDSORES	BEEBEE	BEENAHS	BEETROOTS	BEFOOLING
BEDSPREAD	BEEBEES	BEENTO	BEETS	BEFOOLS
BEDSPRING	BEEBREAD	BEENTOS	BEEVES	BEFORE
BEDSTAND	BEEBREADS	BEEP	BEEYARD	BEFORTUNE
BEDSTANDS	BEECH	BEEPED	BEEYARDS	BEFOUL
BEDSTEAD	BEECHEN	BEEPER	BEEZER	BEFOULED
BEDSTEADS	BEECHES	BEEPERS	BEEZERS	BEFOULER
BEDSTRAW	BEECHIER	BEEPING	BEFALL	BEFOULERS
BEDSTRAWS	BEECHIEST	BEEPS	BEFALLEN	BEFOULING
BEDTICK	BEECHMAST	BEER	BEFALLING	BEFOULS
BEDTICKS	BEECHNUT	BEERAGE	BEFALLS	BEFRET
BEDTIME	BEECHNUTS	BEERAGES	BEFANA	BEFRETS
BEDTIMES	BEECHWOOD	BEERFEST	BEFANAS	BEFRETTED
BEDU	BEECHY	BEERFESTS	BEFELD	BEFRIEND
BEDUCK	BEEDI	BEERHALL	BEFELL	BEFRIENDS
BEDUCKED	BEEDIE	BEERHALLS	BEFFANA	BEFRINGE
BEDUCKING	BEEDIES	BEERIER	BEFFANAS	BEFRINGED
BEDUCKS	BEEF	BEERIEST	BEFINGER	BEFRINGES
BEDUIN	BEEFALO	BEERILY	BEFINGERS	BEFUDDLE
BEDUINS	BEEFALOES	BEERINESS	BEFINNED	BEFUDDLED
BEDUMB	BEEFALOS	BEERMAT	BEFIT	BEFUDDLES
BEDUMBED	BEEFCAKE	BEERMATS	BEFITS	BEG
BEDUMBING	BEEFCAKES	BEERNUT	BEFITTED	BEGAD
BEDUMBS	BEEFEATER	BEERNUTS	BEFITTING	BEGALL
BEDUNCE	BEEFED	BEERS	BEFLAG	BEGALLED
BEDUNCED	BEEFIER	BEERSIES	BEFLAGGED	BEGALLING
BEDUNCES	BEEFIEST	BEERY	BEFLAGS	BEGALLS
BEDUNCING	BEEFILY	BEES	BEFLEA	BEGAN

BEGAR	BEGIRDLE	BEGUILER	BEHIGHTS	BEINGS
BEGARS	BEGIRDLED	BEGUILERS	BEHIND	BEINING
BEGAT	BEGIRDLES	BEGUILES	BEHINDS	BEINKED
BEGAZE	BEGIRDS	BEGUILING	BEHOLD	BEINNESS
BEGAZED	BEGIRT	BEGUIN	BEHOLDEN	BEINS
BEGAZES	BEGLAD	BEGUINAGE	BEHOLDER	BEJABBERS
BEGAZING	BEGLADDED	BEGUINE	BEHOLDERS	BEJABERS
BEGEM	BEGLADS	BEGUINES	BEHOLDING	BEJADE
BEGEMMED	BEGLAMOR	BEGUINS	BEHOLDS	BEJADED
BEGEMMING	BEGLAMORS	BEGULF	BEHOOF	BEJADES
BEGEMS	BEGLAMOUR	BEGULFED	BEHOOFS	BEJADING
BEGET	BEGLERBEG	BEGULFING	BEHOOVE	BEJANT
BEGETS	BEGLOOM	BEGULFS	BEHOOVED	BEJANTS
BEGETTER	BEGLOOMED	BEGUM	BEHOOVES	BEJASUS
BEGETTERS	BEGLOOMS	BEGUMS	BEHOOVING	BEJASUSES
BEGETTING	BEGNAW	BEGUN	BEHOTE	BEJEEBERS
BEGGAR	BEGNAWED	BEGUNK	BEHOTES	BEJEEZUS
BEGGARDOM	BEGNAWING	BEGUNKED	BEHOTING	BEJESUIT
BEGGARED	BEGNAWS	BEGUNKING	BEHOVE	BEJESUITS
BEGGARIES	BEGO	BEGUNKS	BEHOVED	BEJESUS
BEGGARING	BEGOES	BEHALF	BEHOVEFUL	BEJESUSES
BEGGARLY	BEGOGGLED	BEHALVES	BEHOVELY	BEJEWEL
BEGGARS	BEGOING	BEHAPPEN	BEHOVES	BEJEWELED
BEGGARY	BEGONE	BEHAPPENS	BEHOVING	BEJEWELS
BEGGED	BEGONIA	BEHATTED	BEHOWL	BEJUMBLE
BEGGING	BEGONIAS	BEHAVE	BEHOWLED	BEJUMBLED
BEGGINGLY	BEGORAH	BEHAVED	BEHOWLING	BEJUMBLES
BEGGINGS	BEGORED	BEHAVER	BEHOWLS	BEKAH
BEGHARD	BEGORRA	BEHAVERS	BEIGE	BEKAHS
BEGHARDS	BEGORRAH	BEHAVES	BEIGEL	BEKISS
BEGIFT	BEGOT	BEHAVING	BEIGELED	BEKISSED
BEGIFTED	BEGOTTEN	BEHAVIOR	BEIGELING	BEKISSES
BEGIFTING	BEGRIM	BEHAVIORS	BEIGELLED	BEKISSING
BEGIFTS	BEGRIME	BEHAVIOUR	BEIGELS	BEKNAVE
BEGILD	BEGRIMED	BEHEAD	BEIGER	BEKNAVED
BEGILDED	BEGRIMES	BEHEADAL	BEIGES	BEKNAVES
BEGILDING	BEGRIMING	BEHEADALS	BEIGEST	BEKNAVING
BEGILDS	BEGRIMMED	BEHEADED	BEIGIER	BEKNIGHT
BEGILT	BEGRIMS	BEHEADER	BEIGIEST	BEKNIGHTS
BEGIN	BEGROAN	BEHEADERS	BEIGNE	BEKNOT
BEGINNE	BEGROANED	BEHEADING	BEIGNES	BEKNOTS
BEGINNER	BEGROANS	BEHEADS	BEIGNET	BEKNOTTED
BEGINNERS	BEGRUDGE	BEHELD	BEIGNETS	BEKNOWN
BEGINNES	BEGRUDGED	BEHEMOTH	BEIGY	BEL
BEGINNING	BEGRUDGER	BEHEMOTHS	BEIN	BELABOR
BEGINS	BEGRUDGES	BEHEST	BEINED	BELABORED
BEGIRD	BEGS	BEHESTS	BEING	BELABORS
BEGIRDED	BEGUILE	BEHIGHT	BEINGLESS	BELABOUR
BEGIRDING	BEGUILED	BEHIGHTED	BEINGNESS	BELABOURS

B

BELACE	BELEED	BELLEEKS	BELONGS	BEMBIXES
BELACED	BELEEING	BELLEND	BELONS	BEMEAN
BELACES	BELEES	BELLENDS	BELOVE	BEMEANED
BELACING	BELEMNITE	BELLES	BELOVED	BEMEANING
BELADIED	BELEMNOID	BELLETER	BELOVEDS	BEMEANS
BELADIES	BELFRIED	BELLETERS	BELOVES	BEMEANT
BELADY	BELFRIES	BELLHOP	BELOVING	BEMEDAL
BELADYING	BELFRY	BELLHOPS	BELOW	BEMEDALED
BELAH	BELGA	BELLIBONE	BELOWS	BEMEDALS
BELAHS	BELGARD	BELLICOSE	BELS	BEMETE
BELAMIES	BELGARDS	BELLIED	BELT	BEMETED
BELAMOUR	BELGAS	BELLIES	BELTED	BEMETES
BELAMOURE	BELGICISM	BELLING	BELTER	BEMETING
BELAMOURS	BELIE	BELLINGS	BELTERS	BEMINGLE
BELAMY	BELIED	BELLINI	BELTING	BEMINGLED
BELAR	BELIEF	BELLINIS	BELTINGS	BEMINGLES
BELARS	BELIEFS	BELLMAN	BELTLESS	BEMIRE
BELATE	BELIER	BELLMEN	BELTLIKE	BEMIRED
BELATED	BELIERS	BELLOCK	BELTLINE	BEMIRES
BELATEDLY	BELIES	BELLOCKED	BELTLINES	BEMIRING
BELATES	BELIEVE	BELLOCKS	BELTMAN	BEMIST
BELATING	BELIEVED	BELLOW	BELTMEN	BEMISTED
BELAUD	BELIEVER	BELLOWED	BELTS	BEMISTING
BELAUDED	BELIEVERS	BELLOWER	BELTWAY	BEMISTS
BELAUDING	BELIEVES	BELLOWERS	BELTWAYS	BEMIX
BELAUDS	BELIEVING	BELLOWING	BELUGA	BEMIXED
BELAY	BELIKE	BELLOWS	BELUGAS	BEMIXES
BELAYED	BELIQUOR	BELLPULL	BELVEDERE	BEMIXING
BELAYER	BELIQUORS	BELLPULLS	BELYING	BEMIXT
BELAYERS	BELITTLE	BELLS	BEMA	BEMOAN
BELAYING	BELITTLED	BELLWORT	BEMAD	BEMOANED
BELAYS	BELITTLER	BELLWORTS	BEMADAM	BEMOANER
BELCH	BELITTLES	BELLY	BEMADAMED	BEMOANERS
BELCHED	BELIVE	BELLYACHE	BEMADAMS	BEMOANING
BELCHER	BELL	BELLYBAND	BEMADDED	BEMOANS
BELCHERS	BELLBIND	BELLYBOAT	BEMADDEN	BEMOCK
BELCHES	BELLBINDS	BELLYFLOP	BEMADDENS	BEMOCKED
BELCHING	BELLBIRD	BELLYFUL	BEMADDING	BEMOCKING
BELDAM	BELLBIRDS	BELLYFULS	BEMADS	BEMOCKS
BELDAME	BELLBOY	BELLYING	BEMAS	BEMOIL
BELDAMES	BELLBOYS	BELLYINGS	BEMATA	BEMOILED
BELDAMS	BELLBUOY	BELLYLIKE	BEMAUL	BEMOILING
BELEAGUER	BELLBUOYS	BELOMANCY	BEMAULED	BEMOILS
BELEAP	BELLCAST	BELON	BEMAULING	BEMONSTER
BELEAPED	BELLCOTE	BELONG	BEMAULS	BEMOUTH
BELEAPING	BELLCOTES	BELONGED	BEMAZED	BEMOUTHED
BELEAPS	BELLE	BELONGER	BEMBEX	BEMOUTHS
BELEAPT	BELLED	BELONGERS	BEMBEXES	BEMUD
BELEE	BELLEEK	BELONGING	BEMBIX	BEMUDDED

BEMUDDING	BENDERS	BENIGNER	BENZAL	BEPIMPLED
BEMUDDLE	BENDIER	BENIGNEST	BENZALS	BEPIMPLES
BEMUDDLED	BENDIEST	BENIGNITY	BENZENE	BEPITIED
BEMUDDLES	BENDINESS	BENIGNLY	BENZENES	BEPITIES
BEMUDS	BENDING	BENIS	BENZENOID	BEPITY
BEMUFFLE	BENDINGLY	BENISEED	BENZIDIN	BEPITYING
BEMUFFLED	BENDINGS	BENISEEDS	BENZIDINE	BEPLASTER
BEMUFFLES	BENDLET	BENISON	BENZIDINS	BEPLUMED
BEMURMUR	BENDLETS	BENISONS	BENZIL	BEPOMMEL
BEMURMURS	BENDS	BENITIER	BENZILS	BEPOMMELS
BEMUSE	BENDWAYS	BENITIERS	BENZIN	BEPOWDER
BEMUSED	BENDWISE	BENJ	BENZINE	BEPOWDERS
BEMUSEDLY	BENDY	BENJAMIN	BENZINES	BEPRAISE
BEMUSES	BENDYS	BENJAMINS	BENZINS	BEPRAISED
BEMUSING	BENE	BENJES	BENZOATE	BEPRAISES
BEMUZZLE	BENEATH	BENNE	BENZOATES	BEPROSE
BEMUZZLED	BENEDICK	BENNES	BENZOIC	BEPROSED
BEMUZZLES	BENEDICKS	BENNET	BENZOIN	BEPROSES
BEN	BENEDICT	BENNETS	BENZOINS	BEPROSING
BENADRYL	BENEDICTS	BENNI	BENZOL	BEPUFF
BENADRYLS	BENEDIGHT	BENNIES	BENZOLE	BEPUFFED
BENAME	BENEFACT	BENNIS	BENZOLES	BEPUFFING
BENAMED	BENEFACTS	BENNY	BENZOLINE	BEPUFFS
BENAMES	BENEFIC	BENOMYL	BENZOLS	BEQUEATH
BENAMING	BENEFICE	BENOMYLS	BENZOYL	BEQUEATHS
BENCH	BENEFICED	BENS	BENZOYLS	BEQUEST
BENCHED	BENEFICES	BENT	BENZYL	BEQUESTS
BENCHER	BENEFIT	BENTGRASS	BENZYLIC	BERAKE
BENCHERS	BENEFITED	BENTHAL	BENZYLS	BERAKED
BENCHES	BENEFITER	BENTHIC	BEPAINT	BERAKES
BENCHIER	BENEFITS	BENTHOAL	BEPAINTED	BERAKING
BENCHIEST	BENEMPT	BENTHON	BEPAINTS	BERASCAL
BENCHING	BENEMPTED	BENTHONIC	BEPAT	BERASCALS
BENCHLAND	BENES	BENTHONS	BEPATCHED	BERATE
BENCHLESS	BENET	BENTHOS	BEPATS	BERATED
BENCHMARK	BENETS	BENTHOSES	BEPATTED	BERATES
BENCHTOP	BENETTED	BENTIER	BEPATTING	BERATING
BENCHTOPS	BENETTING	BENTIEST	BEPEARL	BERAY
BENCHY	BENGA	BENTO	BEPEARLED	BERAYED
BEND	BENGALINE	BENTONITE	BEPEARLS	BERAYING
BENDABLE	BENGAS	BENTOS	BEPELT	BERAYS
BENDAY	BENI	BENTS	BEPELTED	BERBER
BENDAYED	BENIGHT	BENTWOOD	BEPELTING	BERBERE
BENDAYING	BENIGHTED	BENTWOODS	BEPELTS	BERBERES
BENDAYS	BENIGHTEN	BENTY	BEPEPPER	BERBERIN
BENDED	BENIGHTER	BENUMB	BEPEPPERS	BERBERINE
BENDEE	BENIGHTS	BENUMBED	BEPESTER	BERBERINS
BENDEES	BENIGN	BENUMBING	BEPESTERS	BERBERIS
BENDER	BENIGNANT	BENUMBS	BEPIMPLE	BERBERS

BERBICE	BERHYMED	BERRYINGS	BESEEKES	BESINGING
BERCEAU	BERHYMES	BERRYLESS	BESEEKING	BESINGS
BERCEAUX	BERHYMING	BERRYLIKE	BESEEM	BESIT
BERCEUSE	BERIBERI	BERSEEM	BESEEMED	BESITS
BERCEUSES	BERIBERIS	BERSEEMS	BESEEMING	BESITTING
BERDACHE	BERIMBAU	BERSERK	BESEEMLY	BESLAVE
BERDACHES	BERIMBAUS	BERSERKER	BESEEMS	BESLAVED
BERDASH	BERIME	BERSERKLY	BESEEN	BESLAVER
BERDASHES	BERIMED	BERSERKS	BESEES	BESLAVERS
BERE	BERIMES	BERTH	BESES	BESLAVES
BEREAVE	BERIMING	BERTHA	BESET	BESLAVING
BEREAVED	BERINGED	BERTHAGE	BESETMENT	BESLIME
BEREAVEN	BERK	BERTHAGES	BESETS	BESLIMED
BEREAVER	BERKELIUM	BERTHAS	BESETTER	BESLIMES
BEREAVERS	BERKO	BERTHE	BESETTERS	BESLIMING
BEREAVES	BERKS	BERTHED	BESETTING	BESLOBBER
BEREAVING	BERLEY	BERTHES	BESHADOW	BESLUBBER
BEREFT	BERLEYED	BERTHING	BESHADOWS	BESMEAR
BERES	BERLEYING	BERTHINGS	BESHAME	BESMEARED
BERET	BERLEYS	BERTHS	BESHAMED	BESMEARER
BERETS	BERLIN	BERYL	BESHAMES	BESMEARS
BERETTA	BERLINE	BERYLINE	BESHAMING	BESMILE
BERETTAS	BERLINES	BERYLLIA	BESHINE	BESMILED
BERG	BERLINS	BERYLLIAS	BESHINES	BESMILES
BERGALL	BERM	BERYLLIUM	BESHINING	BESMILING
BERGALLS	BERME	BERYLS	BESHIVER	BESMIRCH
BERGAMA	BERMED	BES	BESHIVERS	BESMOKE
BERGAMAS	BERMES	BESAINT	BESHONE	BESMOKED
BERGAMASK	BERMING	BESAINTED	BESHOUT	BESMOKES
BERGAMOT	BERMS	BESAINTS	BESHOUTED	BESMOKING
BERGAMOTS	BERMUDAS	BESANG	BESHOUTS	BESMOOTH
BERGANDER	BERNICLE	BESAT	BESHREW	BESMOOTHS
BERGEN	BERNICLES	BESAW	BESHREWED	BESMUDGE
BERGENIA	BEROB	BESCATTER	BESHREWS	BESMUDGED
BERGENIAS	BEROBBED	BESCORCH	BESHROUD	BESMUDGES
BERGENS	BEROBBING	BESCOUR	BESHROUDS	BESMUT
BERGERE	BEROBED	BESCOURED	BESIDE	BESMUTCH
BERGERES	BEROBS	BESCOURS	BESIDES	BESMUTS
BERGFALL	BEROUGED	BESCRAWL	BESIEGE	BESMUTTED
BERGFALLS	BERRET	BESCRAWLS	BESIEGED	BESNOW
BERGHAAN	BERRETS	BESCREEN	BESIEGER	BESNOWED
BERGHAANS	BERRETTA	BESCREENS	BESIEGERS	BESNOWING
BERGMEHL	BERRETTAS	BESEE	BESIEGES	BESNOWS
BERGMEHLS	BERRIED	BESEECH	BESIEGING	BESOGNIO
BERGOMASK	BERRIES	BESEECHED	BESIGH	BESOGNIOS
BERGS	BERRIGAN	BESEECHER	BESIGHED	BESOIN
BERGYLT	BERRIGANS	BESEECHES	BESIGHING	BESOINS
BERGYLTS	BERRY	BESEEING	BESIGHS	BESOM
BERHYME	BERRYING	BESEEKE	BESING	BESOMED

BESOMING	BESPREADS	BESTREWS	BETES	BETOKENED
BESOMS	BESPRENT	BESTRID	BETH	BETOKENS
BESONIAN	BEST	BESTRIDE	BETHANK	BETON
BESONIANS	BESTAD	BESTRIDES	BETHANKED	BETONIES
BESOOTHE	BESTADDE	BESTRODE	BETHANKIT	BETONS
BESOOTHED	BESTAIN	BESTROW	BETHANKS	BETONY
BESOOTHES	BESTAINED	BESTROWED	BETHEL	BETOOK
BESORT	BESTAINS	BESTROWN	BETHELS	BETOSS
BESORTED	BESTAR	BESTROWS	BETHESDA	BETOSSED
BESORTING	BESTARRED	BESTS	BETHESDAS	BETOSSES
BESORTS	BESTARS	BESTUCK	BETHINK	BETOSSING
BESOT	BESTEAD	BESTUD	BETHINKS	BETRAY
BESOTS	BESTEADED	BESTUDDED	BETHORN	BETRAYAL
BESOTTED	BESTEADS	BESTUDS	BETHORNED	BETRAYALS
BESOTTING	BESTED	BESUITED	BETHORNS	BETRAYED
BESOUGHT	BESTEST	BESUNG	BETHOUGHT	BETRAYER
BESOULED	BESTI	BESWARM	BETHRALL	BETRAYERS
BESPAKE	BESTIAL	BESWARMED	BETHRALLS	BETRAYING
BESPANGLE	BESTIALLY	BESWARMS	BETHS	BETRAYS
BESPAT	BESTIALS	BET	BETHUMB	BETREAD
BESPATE	BESTIARY	BETA	BETHUMBED	BETREADS
BESPATTER	BESTICK	BETACISM	BETHUMBS	BETRIM
BESPEAK	BESTICKS	BETACISMS	BETHUMP	BETRIMMED
BESPEAKS	BESTIE	BETAINE	BETHUMPED	BETRIMS
BESPECKLE	BESTIES	BETAINES	BETHUMPS	BETROD
BESPED	BESTILL	BETAKE	BETHWACK	BETRODDEN
BESPEED	BESTILLED	BETAKEN	BETHWACKS	BETROTH
BESPEEDS	BESTILLS	BETAKES	BETID	BETROTHAL
BESPICE	BESTING	BETAKING	BETIDE	BETROTHED
BESPICED	BESTIR	BETAS	BETIDED	BETROTHS
BESPICES	BESTIRRED	BETATOPIC	BETIDES	BETS
BESPICING	BESTIRS	BETATRON	BETIDING	BETTA
BESPIT	BESTIS	BETATRONS	BETIGHT	BETTAS
BESPITS	BESTORM	BETATTER	BETIME	BETTED
BESPOKE	BESTORMED	BETATTERS	BETIMED	BETTER
BESPOKEN	BESTORMS	BETAXED	BETIMES	BETTERED
BESPORT	BESTOW	BETCHA	BETIMING	BETTERING
BESPORTED	BESTOWAL	BETE	BETING	BETTERS
BESPORTS	BESTOWALS	BETED	BETISE	BETTIES
BESPOT	BESTOWED	BETEEM	BETISES	BETTING
BESPOTS	BESTOWER	BETEEME	BETITLE	BETTINGS
BESPOTTED	BESTOWERS	BETEEMED	BETITLED	BETTONG
BESPOUSE	BESTOWING	BETEEMES	BETITLES	BETTONGS
BESPOUSED	BESTOWS	BETEEMING	BETITLING	BETTOR
BESPOUSES	BESTREAK	BETEEMS	BETOIL	BETTORS
BESPOUT	BESTREAKS	BETEL	BETOILED	BETTY
BESPOUTED	BESTREW	BETELNUT	BETOILING	BETUMBLED
BESPOUTS	BESTREWED	BETELNUTS	BETOILS	BETWEEN
BESPREAD	BESTREWN	BETELS	BETOKEN	BETWEENS

B

BETWIXT	BEWEEP	BEZ	BHARALS	BIASEDLY
BEUNCLED	BEWEEPING	BEZANT	BHAT	BIASES
BEURRE	BEWEEPS	BEZANTS	BHATS	BIASING
BEURRES	BEWENT	BEZAZZ	BHAVAN	BIASINGS
BEVATRON	BEWEPT	BEZAZZES	BHAVANS	BIASNESS
BEVATRONS	BEWET	BEZEL	BHAWAN	BIASSED
BEVEL	BEWETS	BEZELLESS	BHAWANS	BIASSEDLY
BEVELED	BEWETTED	BEZELS	BHEESTIE	BIASSES
BEVELER	BEWETTING	BEZES	BHEESTIES	BIASSING
BEVELERS	BEWHORE	BEZIL	BHEESTY	BIATCH
BEVELING	BEWHORED	BEZILS	BHEL	BIATCHES
BEVELLED	BEWHORES	BEZIQUE	BHELPURI	BIATHLETE
BEVELLER	BEWHORING	BEZIQUES	BHELPURIS	BIATHLON
BEVELLERS	BEWIG	BEZOAR	BHELS	BIATHLONS
BEVELLING	BEWIGGED	BEZOARDIC	BHIKHU	BIAXAL
BEVELMENT	BEWIGGING	BEZOARS	BHIKHUS	BIAXIAL
BEVELS	BEWIGS	BEZONIAN	BHIKKHUNI	BIAXIALLY
BEVER	BEWILDER	BEZONIANS	BHINDI	BIB
BEVERAGE	BEWILDERS	BEZZANT	BHINDIS	BIBACIOUS
BEVERAGES	BEWINGED	BEZZANTS	BHISHTI	BIBASIC
BEVERED	BEWITCH	BEZZAZZ	BHISHTIS	BIBATION
BEVERING	BEWITCHED	BEZZAZZES	BHISTEE	BIBATIONS
BEVERS	BEWITCHER	BEZZIE	BHISTEES	BIBB
BEVIES	BEWITCHES	BEZZIES	BHISTI	BIBBED
BEVOMIT	BEWORM	BEZZLE	BHISTIE	BIBBER
BEVOMITED	BEWORMED	BEZZLED	BHISTIES	BIBBERIES
BEVOMITS	BEWORMING	BEZZLES	BHISTIS	BIBBERS
BEVOR	BEWORMS	BEZZLING	BHOONA	BIBBERY
BEVORS	BEWORRIED	BEZZY	BHOONAS	BIBBING
BEVUE	BEWORRIES	BHAGEE	BHOOT	BIBBINGS
BEVUES	BEWORRY	BHAGEES	BHOOTS	BIBBLE
BEVVIED	BEWRAP	BHAI	BHUNA	BIBBLES
BEVVIES	BEWRAPPED	BHAIS	BHUNAS	BIBBS
BEVVY	BEWRAPS	BHAJAN	BHUT	BIBCOCK
BEVVYING	BEWRAPT	BHAJANS	BHUTS	BIBCOCKS
BEVY	BEWRAY	BHAJEE	BI	BIBE
BEWAIL	BEWRAYED	BHAJEES	BIACETYL	BIBELOT
BEWAILED	BEWRAYER	BHAJI	BIACETYLS	BIBELOTS
BEWAILER	BEWRAYERS	BHAJIA	BIACH	BIBES
BEWAILERS	BEWRAYING	BHAJIS	BIACHES	BIBFUL
BEWAILING	BEWRAYS	BHAKTA	BIALI	BIBFULS
BEWAILS	BEY	BHAKTAS	BIALIES	BIBIMBAP
BEWARE	BEYLIC	BHAKTI	BIALIS	BIBIMBAPS
BEWARED	BEYLICS	BHAKTIS	BIALY	BIBLE
BEWARES	BEYLIK	BHANG	BIALYS	BIBLES
BEWARING	BEYLIKS	BHANGRA	BIANNUAL	BIBLESS
BEWEARIED	BEYOND	BHANGRAS	BIANNUALS	BIBLICAL
BEWEARIES	BEYONDS	BHANGS	BIAS	BIBLICISM
BEWEARY	BEYS	BHARAL	BIASED	BIBLICIST

B

BIBLIKE	BICYCLE	BIENNALE	BIFTAHS	BIGHAS
BIBLIOTIC	BICYCLED	BIENNALES	BIFTER	BIGHEAD
BIBLIST	BICYCLER	BIENNIA	BIFTERS	BIGHEADED
BIBLISTS	BICYCLERS	BIENNIAL	BIFURCATE	BIGHEADS
BIBS	BICYCLES	BIENNIALS	BIG	BIGHORN
BIBULOUS	BICYCLIC	BIENNIUM	BIGA	BIGHORNS
BICAMERAL	BICYCLING	BIENNIUMS	BIGAE	BIGHT
BICARB	BICYCLIST	BIER	BIGAMIES	BIGHTED
BICARBS	BID	BIERS	BIGAMIST	BIGHTING
BICAUDAL	BIDARKA	BIERWURST	BIGAMISTS	BIGHTS
BICCIES	BIDARKAS	BIESTINGS	BIGAMOUS	BIGLY
BICCY	BIDARKEE	BIFACE	BIGAMY	BIGMOUTH
BICE	BIDARKEES	BIFACES	BIGARADE	BIGMOUTHS
BICENTRIC	BIDDABLE	BIFACIAL	BIGARADES	BIGNESS
BICEP	BIDDABLY	BIFARIOUS	BIGAROON	BIGNESSES
BICEPS	BIDDEN	BIFF	BIGAROONS	BIGNONIA
BICEPSES	BIDDER	BIFFED	BIGARREAU	BIGNONIAS
BICES	BIDDERS	BIFFER	BIGEMINAL	BIGOS
BICHIR	BIDDIES	BIFFERS	BIGEMINY	BIGOSES
BICHIRS	BIDDING	BIFFIES	BIGENDER	BIGOT
BICHORD	BIDDINGS	BIFFIN	BIGENER	BIGOTED
BICHROME	BIDDY	BIFFING	BIGENERIC	BIGOTEDLY
BICIPITAL	BIDE	BIFFINS	BIGENERS	BIGOTRIES
BICKER	BIDED	BIFFO	BIGEYE	BIGOTRY
BICKERED	BIDENT	BIFFOS	BIGEYES	BIGOTS
BICKERER	BIDENTAL	BIFFS	BIGFEET	BIGRAM
BICKERERS	BIDENTALS	BIFFY	BIGFOOT	BIGRAMS
BICKERING	BIDENTATE	BIFID	BIGFOOTED	BIGS
BICKERS	BIDENTS	BIFIDA	BIGFOOTS	BIGSTICK
BICKIE	BIDER	BIFIDITY	BIGG	BIGTIME
BICKIES	BIDERS	BIFIDLY	BIGGED	BIGUANIDE
BICOASTAL	BIDES	BIFIDUM	BIGGER	BIGUINE
BICOLOR	BIDET	BIFIDUMS	BIGGEST	BIGUINES
BICOLORED	BIDETS	BIFIDUS	BIGGETIER	BIGWIG
BICOLORS	BIDI	BIFIDUSES	BIGGETY	BIGWIGS
BICOLOUR	BIDING	BIFILAR	BIGGIE	BIHOURLY
BICOLOURS	BIDINGS	BIFILARLY	BIGGIES	BIJECTION
BICONCAVE	BIDIS	BIFLEX	BIGGIN	BIJECTIVE
BICONVEX	BIDON	BIFOCAL	BIGGING	BIJOU
BICORN	BIDONS	BIFOCALED	BIGGINGS	BIJOUS
BICORNATE	BIDS	BIFOCALS	BIGGINS	BIJOUX
BICORNE	BIELD	BIFOLD	BIGGISH	BIJUGATE
BICORNES	BIELDED	BIFOLDS	BIGGITIER	BIJUGOUS
BICORNS	BIELDIER	BIFOLIATE	BIGGITY	BIJURAL
BICRON	BIELDIEST	BIFORATE	BIGGON	BIJWONER
BICRONS	BIELDING	BIFORKED	BIGGONS	BIJWONERS
BICURIOUS	BIELDS	BIFORM	BIGGS	BIKE
BICUSPID	BIELDY	BIFORMED	BIGGY	BIKED
BICUSPIDS	BIEN	BIFTAH	BIGHA	BIKER

B

BIKERS	BILIMBING	BILLIONTH	BIMESTERS	BINGEABLE
BIKES	BILIMBIS	BILLMAN	BIMETAL	BINGED
BIKEWAY	BILINEAR	BILLMEN	BIMETALS	BINGEING
BIKEWAYS	BILING	BILLON	BIMETHYL	BINGEINGS
BIKIE	BILINGUAL	BILLONS	BIMETHYLS	BINGER
BIKIES	BILIOUS	BILLOW	BIMINI	BINGERS
BIKING	BILIOUSLY	BILLOWED	BIMINIS	BINGES
BIKINGS	BILIRUBIN	BILLOWIER	BIMODAL	BINGIES
BIKINI	BILITERAL	BILLOWING	BIMONTHLY	BINGING
BIKINIED	BILK	BILLOWS	BIMORPH	BINGINGS
BIKINIS	BILKED	BILLOWY	BIMORPHS	BINGLE
BIKKIE	BILKER	BILLS	BIN	BINGLED
BIKKIES	BILKERS	BILLY	BINAL	BINGLES
BILABIAL	BILKING	BILLYBOY	BINARIES	BINGLING
BILABIALS	BILKS	BILLYBOYS	BINARISM	BINGO
BILABIATE	BILL	BILLYCAN	BINARISMS	BINGOED
BILANDER	BILLABLE	BILLYCANS	BINARY	BINGOES
BILANDERS	BILLABONG	BILLYCOCK	BINATE	BINGOING
BILATERAL	BILLBOARD	BILLYO	BINATELY	BINGOS
BILAYER	BILLBOOK	BILLYOH	BINAURAL	BINGS
BILAYERS	BILLBOOKS	BILLYOHS	BIND	BINGY
BILBERRY	BILLBUG	BILLYOS	BINDAAS	BINIOU
BILBIES	BILLBUGS	BILOBAR	BINDAASES	BINIOUS
BILBO	BILLED	BILOBATE	BINDABLE	BINIT
BILBOA	BILLER	BILOBATED	BINDASS	BINITS
BILBOAS	BILLERS	BILOBED	BINDASSES	BINK
BILBOES	BILLET	BILOBULAR	BINDER	BINKS
BILBOS	BILLETED	BILOCULAR	BINDERIES	BINMAN
BILBY	BILLETEE	BILSTED	BINDERS	BINMEN
BILE	BILLETEES	BILSTEDS	BINDERY	BINNACLE
BILECTION	BILLETER	BILTONG	BINDHI	BINNACLES
BILED	BILLETERS	BILTONGS	BINDHIS	BINNED
BILES	BILLETING	BIMA	BINDI	BINNING
BILESTONE	BILLETS	BIMAH	BINDING	BINOCLE
BILEVEL	BILLFISH	BIMAHS	BINDINGLY	BINOCLES
BILEVELS	BILLFOLD	BIMANAL	BINDINGS	BINOCS
BILGE	BILLFOLDS	BIMANOUS	BINDIS	BINOCULAR
BILGED	BILLHEAD	BIMANUAL	BINDLE	BINOMIAL
BILGES	BILLHEADS	BIMAS	BINDLES	BINOMIALS
BILGIER	BILLHOOK	BIMBASHI	BINDS	BINOMINAL
BILGIEST	BILLHOOKS	BIMBASHIS	BINDWEED	BINOVULAR
BILGING	BILLIARD	BIMBETTE	BINDWEEDS	BINS
BILGY	BILLIARDS	BIMBETTES	BINE	BINTURONG
BILHARZIA	BILLIE	BIMBLE	BINER	BINUCLEAR
BILIAN	BILLIES	BIMBO	BINERS	BIO
BILIANS	BILLING	BIMBOES	BINERVATE	BIOACTIVE
BILIARIES	BILLINGS	BIMBOS	BINES	BIOASSAY
BILIARY	BILLION	BIMENSAL	BING	BIOASSAYS
BILIMBI	BILLIONS	BIMESTER	BINGE	BIOBANDED

BIOBANK	BIOLOGIC	BIOPSIED	BIOWEAPON	BIRDCALLS
BIOBANKS	BIOLOGICS	BIOPSIES	BIPACK	BIRDDOG
BIOBLAST	BIOLOGIES	BIOPSY	BIPACKS	BIRDDOGS
BIOBLASTS	BIOLOGISM	BIOPSYING	BIPAROUS	BIRDED
BIOCENOSE	BIOLOGIST	BIOPTIC	BIPARTED	BIRDER
BIOCHEMIC	BIOLOGY	BIOREGION	BIPARTITE	BIRDERS
BIOCHIP	BIOLYSES	BIORHYTHM	BIPARTY	BIRDFARM
BIOCHIPS	BIOLYSIS	BIOS	BIPED	BIRDFARMS
BIOCIDAL	BIOLYTIC	BIOSAFETY	BIPEDAL	BIRDFEED
BIOCIDE	BIOMARKER	BIOSCOPE	BIPEDALLY	BIRDFEEDS
BIOCIDES	BIOMASS	BIOSCOPES	BIPEDS	BIRDHOUSE
BIOCLEAN	BIOMASSES	BIOSCOPY	BIPHASIC	BIRDIE
BIOCYCLE	BIOME	BIOSECURE	BIPHENYL	BIRDIED
BIOCYCLES	BIOMES	BIOSENSOR	BIPHENYLS	BIRDIEING
BIODATA	BIOMETER	BIOSOCIAL	BIPHOBIA	BIRDIES
BIODIESEL	BIOMETERS	BIOSOLID	BIPHOBIAS	BIRDING
BIODOT	BIOMETRIC	BIOSOLIDS	BIPHOBIC	BIRDINGS
BIODOTS	BIOMETRY	BIOSPHERE	BIPINNATE	BIRDLIFE
BIOENERGY	BIOMINING	BIOSTABLE	BIPKWELE	BIRDLIFES
BIOETHIC	BIOMORPH	BIOSTATIC	BIPLANE	BIRDLIKE
BIOETHICS	BIOMORPHS	BIOSTROME	BIPLANES	BIRDLIME
BIOFACT	BIONIC	BIOTA	BIPOD	BIRDLIMED
BIOFACTS	BIONICS	BIOTAS	BIPODS	BIRDLIMES
BIOFIBERS	BIONOMIC	BIOTECH	BIPOLAR	BIRDMAN
BIOFIBRES	BIONOMICS	BIOTECHS	BIPRISM	BIRDMEN
BIOFILM	BIONOMIES	BIOTERROR	BIPRISMS	BIRDS
BIOFILMS	BIONOMIST	BIOTIC	BIPYRAMID	BIRDSEED
BIOFOULER	BIONOMY	BIOTICAL	BIRACIAL	BIRDSEEDS
BIOFUEL	BIONT	BIOTICS	BIRADIAL	BIRDSEYE
BIOFUELED	BIONTIC	BIOTIN	BIRADICAL	BIRDSEYES
BIOFUELS	BIONTS	BIOTINS	BIRAMOSE	BIRDSFOOT
BIOG	BIOPARENT	BIOTITE	BIRAMOUS	BIRDSHOT
BIOGAS	BIOPHILIA	BIOTITES	BIRCH	BIRDSHOTS
BIOGASES	BIOPHILIC	BIOTITIC	BIRCHBARK	BIRDSONG
BIOGASSES	BIOPHOR	BIOTOPE	BIRCHED	BIRDSONGS
BIOGEN	BIOPHORE	BIOTOPES	BIRCHEN	BIRDWATCH
BIOGENIC	BIOPHORES	BIOTOXIN	BIRCHES	BIRDWING
BIOGENIES	BIOPHORS	BIOTOXINS	BIRCHING	BIRDWINGS
BIOGENOUS	BIOPIC	BIOTRON	BIRCHINGS	BIREME
BIOGENS	BIOPICS	BIOTRONS	BIRCHIR	BIREMES
BIOGENY	BIOPIRACY	BIOTROPH	BIRCHIRS	BIRETTA
BIOGRAPH	BIOPIRATE	BIOTROPHS	BIRCHWOOD	BIRETTAS
BIOGRAPHS	BIOPLASM	BIOTURBED	BIRD	BIRIANI
BIOGRAPHY	BIOPLASMS	BIOTYPE	BIRDBATH	BIRIANIS
BIOGS	BIOPLAST	BIOTYPES	BIRDBATHS	BIRIYANI
BIOHACKER	BIOPLASTS	BIOTYPIC	BIRDBRAIN	BIRIYANIS
BIOHAZARD	BIOPLAY	BIOVULAR	BIRDCAGE	BIRK
BIOHERM	BIOPLAYS	BIOWASTE	BIRDCAGES	BIRKEN
BIOHERMS	BIOPSIC	BIOWASTES	BIRDCALL	BIRKIE

BIRKIER	BIRTHINGS	BISMUTHAL	BITCHY	BITTERNUT
BIRKIES	BIRTHMARK	BISMUTHIC	BITCOIN	BITTERS
BIRKIEST	BIRTHNAME	BISMUTHS	BITCOINS	BITTIE
BIRKS	BIRTHRATE	BISNAGA	BITE	BITTIER
BIRL	BIRTHROOT	BISNAGAS	BITEABLE	BITTIES
BIRLE	BIRTHS	BISOM	BITEPLATE	BITTIEST
BIRLED	BIRTHWORT	BISOMS	BITER	BITTILY
BIRLER	BIRYANI	BISON	BITERS	BITTINESS
BIRLERS	BIRYANIS	BISONS	BITES	BITTING
BIRLES	BIS	BISONTINE	BITESIZE	BITTINGS
BIRLIEMAN	BISCACHA	BISPHENOL	BITEWING	BITTOCK
BIRLIEMEN	BISCACHAS	BISQUE	BITEWINGS	BITTOCKS
BIRLING	BISCOTTI	BISQUES	BITING	BITTOR
BIRLINGS	BISCOTTO	BISSON	BITINGLY	BITTORS
BIRLINN	BISCUIT	BISSONED	BITINGS	BITTOUR
BIRLINNS	BISCUITS	BISSONING	BITLESS	BITTOURS
BIRLS	BISCUITY	BISSONS	BITMAP	BITTS
BIRO	BISE	BIST	BITMAPPED	BITTUR
BIROS	BISECT	BISTABLE	BITMAPS	BITTURS
BIRR	BISECTED	BISTABLES	BITO	BITTY
BIRRED	BISECTING	BISTATE	BITONAL	BITUMED
BIRRETTA	BISECTION	BISTER	BITOS	BITUMEN
BIRRETTAS	BISECTOR	BISTERED	BITOU	BITUMENS
BIRRIA	BISECTORS	BISTERS	BITRATE	BITURBO
BIRRIAS	BISECTRIX	BISTORT	BITRATES	BITURBOS
BIRRING	BISECTS	BISTORTS	BITS	BITWISE
BIRROTCH	BISERIAL	BISTOURY	BITSER	BIUNIQUE
BIRRS	BISERIATE	BISTRE	BITSERS	BIVALENCE
BIRSE	BISERRATE	BISTRED	BITSIER	BIVALENCY
BIRSED	BISES	BISTRES	BITSIEST	BIVALENT
BIRSES	BISEXUAL	BISTRO	BITSTOCK	BIVALENTS
BIRSIER	BISEXUALS	BISTROIC	BITSTOCKS	BIVALVATE
BIRSIEST	BISH	BISTROS	BITSTREAM	BIVALVE
BIRSING	BISHES	BISULCATE	BITSY	BIVALVED
BIRSLE	BISHOP	BISULFATE	BITT	BIVALVES
BIRSLED	BISHOPDOM	BISULFIDE	BITTACLE	BIVARIANT
BIRSLES	BISHOPED	BISULFITE	BITTACLES	BIVARIATE
BIRSLING	BISHOPESS	BIT	BITTE	BIVIA
BIRSY	BISHOPING	BITABLE	BITTED	BIVINYL
BIRTH	BISHOPRIC	BITCH	BITTEN	BIVINYLS
BIRTHDATE	BISHOPS	BITCHED	BITTER	BIVIOUS
BIRTHDAY	BISK	BITCHEN	BITTERED	BIVIUM
BIRTHDAYS	BISKS	BITCHERY	BITTERER	BIVOUAC
BIRTHDOM	BISMAR	BITCHES	BITTEREST	BIVOUACKS
BIRTHDOMS	BISMARCK	BITCHFEST	BITTERING	BIVOUACS
BIRTHED	BISMARCKS	BITCHIER	BITTERISH	BIVVIED
BIRTHER	BISMARS	BITCHIEST	BITTERLY	BIVVIES
BIRTHERS	BISMILLAH	BITCHILY	BITTERN	BIVVY
BIRTHING	BISMUTH	BITCHING	BITTERNS	BIVVYING

BIWEEKLY	BLACKCAPS	BLADDING	BLAMABLY	BLANQUET
BIYEARLY	BLACKCOCK	BLADE	BLAME	BLANQUETS
BIZ	BLACKDAMP	BLADED	BLAMEABLE	BLARE
BIZARRE	BLACKED	BLADELESS	BLAMEABLY	BLARED
BIZARRELY	BLACKEN	BLADELIKE	BLAMED	BLARES
BIZARRES	BLACKENED	BLADER	BLAMEFUL	BLARING
BIZARRO	BLACKENER	BLADERS	BLAMELESS	BLARNEY
BIZARROS	BLACKENS	BLADES	BLAMER	BLARNEYED
BIZAZZ	BLACKER	BLADEWORK	BLAMERS	BLARNEYS
BIZAZZES	BLACKEST	BLADIER	BLAMES	BLART
BIZCACHA	BLACKFACE	BLADIEST	BLAMING	BLARTED
BIZCACHAS	BLACKFIN	BLADING	BLAMMED	BLARTING
BIZE	BLACKFINS	BLADINGS	BLAMMING	BLARTS
BIZES	BLACKFISH	BLADS	BLAMS	BLASE
BIZJET	BLACKFLY	BLADY	BLANCH	BLASH
BIZJETS	BLACKGAME	BLAE	BLANCHED	BLASHED
BIZNAGA	BLACKGUM	BLAEBERRY	BLANCHER	BLASHES
BIZNAGAS	BLACKGUMS	BLAER	BLANCHERS	BLASHIER
BIZONAL	BLACKHEAD	BLAES	BLANCHES	BLASHIEST
BIZONE	BLACKING	BLAEST	BLANCHING	BLASHING
BIZONES	BLACKINGS	BLAFF	BLANCO	BLASHY
BIZZAZZ	BLACKISH	BLAFFED	BLANCOED	BLASPHEME
BIZZAZZES	BLACKJACK	BLAFFING	BLANCOING	BLASPHEMY
BIZZES	BLACKLAND	BLAFFS	BLANCOS	BLAST
BIZZIES	BLACKLEAD	BLAG	BLAND	BLASTED
BIZZO	BLACKLEG	BLAGGED	BLANDED	BLASTEMA
BIZZOS	BLACKLEGS	BLAGGER	BLANDER	BLASTEMAL
BIZZY	BLACKLIST	BLAGGERS	BLANDEST	BLASTEMAS
BLAB	BLACKLY	BLAGGING	BLANDING	BLASTEMIC
BLABBED	BLACKMAIL	BLAGGINGS	BLANDISH	BLASTER
BLABBER	BLACKNESS	BLAGS	BLANDLY	BLASTERS
BLABBERED	BLACKOUT	BLAGUE	BLANDNESS	BLASTHOLE
BLABBERS	BLACKOUTS	BLAGUER	BLANDS	BLASTIE
BLABBIER	BLACKPOLL	BLAGUERS	BLANK	BLASTIER
BLABBIEST	BLACKS	BLAGUES	BLANKED	BLASTIES
BLABBING	BLACKSPOT	BLAGUEUR	BLANKER	BLASTIEST
BLABBINGS	BLACKTAIL	BLAGUEURS	BLANKEST	BLASTING
BLABBY	BLACKTIP	BLAH	BLANKET	BLASTINGS
BLABS	BLACKTIPS	BLAHED	BLANKETED	BLASTMENT
BLACK	BLACKTOP	BLAHER	BLANKETS	BLASTOFF
BLACKBALL	BLACKTOPS	BLAHEST	BLANKETY	BLASTOFFS
BLACKBAND	BLACKWASH	BLAHING	BLANKIE	BLASTOID
BLACKBIRD	BLACKWOOD	BLAHS	BLANKIES	BLASTOIDS
BLACKBODY	BLAD	BLAIN	BLANKING	BLASTOMA
BLACKBOY	BLADDED	BLAINS	BLANKINGS	BLASTOMAS
BLACKBOYS	BLADDER	BLAISE	BLANKLY	BLASTOPOR
BLACKBUCK	BLADDERED	BLAIZE	BLANKNESS	BLASTS
BLACKBUTT	BLADDERS	BLAM	BLANKS	BLASTULA
BLACKCAP	BLADDERY	BLAMABLE	BLANKY	BLASTULAE

B

BLASTULAR	BLAZING	BLECH	BLESS	BLINDAGES
BLASTULAS	BLAZINGLY	BLED	BLESSED	BLINDED
BLASTY	BLAZON	BLEE	BLESSEDER	BLINDER
BLAT	BLAZONED	BLEED	BLESSEDLY	BLINDERS
BLATANCY	BLAZONER	BLEEDER	BLESSER	BLINDEST
BLATANT	BLAZONERS	BLEEDERS	BLESSERS	BLINDFISH
BLATANTLY	BLAZONING	BLEEDING	BLESSES	BLINDFOLD
BLATE	BLAZONRY	BLEEDINGS	BLESSING	BLINDGUT
BLATED	BLAZONS	BLEEDS	BLESSINGS	BLINDGUTS
BLATER	BLEACH	BLEEP	BLEST	BLINDING
BLATES	BLEACHED	BLEEPED	BLET	BLINDINGS
BLATEST	BLEACHER	BLEEPER	BLETHER	BLINDLESS
BLATHER	BLEACHERS	BLEEPERS	BLETHERED	BLINDLY
BLATHERED	BLEACHERY	BLEEPING	BLETHERER	BLINDNESS
BLATHERER	BLEACHES	BLEEPS	BLETHERS	BLINDS
BLATHERS	BLEACHING	BLEES	BLETS	BLINDSIDE
BLATING	BLEAK	BLELLUM	BLETTED	BLINDWORM
BLATS	BLEAKER	BLELLUMS	BLETTING	BLING
BLATT	BLEAKEST	BLEMISH	BLEUATRE	BLINGED
BLATTANT	BLEAKISH	BLEMISHED	BLEW	BLINGER
BLATTED	BLEAKLY	BLEMISHER	BLEWART	BLINGEST
BLATTER	BLEAKNESS	BLEMISHES	BLEWARTS	BLINGIER
BLATTERED	BLEAKS	BLENCH	BLEWIT	BLINGIEST
BLATTERS	BLEAKY	BLENCHED	BLEWITS	BLINGING
BLATTING	BLEAR	BLENCHER	BLEWITSES	BLINGLISH
BLATTS	BLEARED	BLENCHERS	BLEY	BLINGS
BLAUBOK	BLEARER	BLENCHES	BLEYS	BLINGY
BLAUBOKS	BLEAREST	BLENCHING	BLIGHT	BLINI
BLAUD	BLEAREYED	BLEND	BLIGHTED	BLINIS
BLAUDED	BLEARIER	BLENDABLE	BLIGHTER	BLINK
BLAUDING	BLEARIEST	BLENDE	BLIGHTERS	BLINKARD
BLAUDS	BLEARILY	BLENDED	BLIGHTIES	BLINKARDS
BLAW	BLEARING	BLENDER	BLIGHTING	BLINKED
BLAWED	BLEARS	BLENDERS	BLIGHTS	BLINKER
BLAWING	BLEARY	BLENDES	BLIGHTY	BLINKERED
BLAWN	BLEAT	BLENDING	BLIKSEM	BLINKERS
BLAWORT	BLEATED	BLENDINGS	BLIMBING	BLINKING
BLAWORTS	BLEATER	BLENDS	BLIMBINGS	BLINKS
BLAWS	BLEATERS	BLENNIES	BLIMEY	BLINNED
BLAY	BLEATING	BLENNIOID	BLIMP	BLINNING
BLAYS	BLEATINGS	BLENNY	BLIMPED	BLINS
BLAZAR	BLEATS	BLENT	BLIMPERY	BLINTZ
BLAZARS	BLEB	BLEOMYCIN	BLIMPING	BLINTZE
BLAZE	BLEBBIER	BLERT	BLIMPISH	BLINTZES
BLAZED	BLEBBIEST	BLERTS	BLIMPS	BLINY
BLAZER	BLEBBING	BLESBOK	BLIMY	BLIP
BLAZERED	BLEBBINGS	BLESBOKS	BLIN	BLIPPED
BLAZERS	BLEBBY	BLESBUCK	BLIND	BLIPPING
BLAZES	BLEBS	BLESBUCKS	BLINDAGE	BLIPS

BLIPVERT	BLOBBIEST	BLOKART	BLOODWORK	BLOTCHY
BLIPVERTS	BLOBBING	BLOKARTS	BLOODWORM	BLOTLESS
BLISS	BLOBBY	BLOKE	BLOODWORT	BLOTS
BLISSED	BLOBS	BLOKEDOM	BLOODY	BLOTTED
BLISSES	BLOC	BLOKEDOMS	BLOODYING	BLOTTER
BLISSFUL	BLOCK	BLOKEISH	BLOOEY	BLOTTERS
BLISSING	BLOCKABLE	BLOKES	BLOOIE	BLOTTIER
BLISSLESS	BLOCKADE	BLOKEY	BLOOK	BLOTTIEST
BLIST	BLOCKADED	BLOKIER	BLOOKS	BLOTTING
BLISTER	BLOCKADER	BLOKIEST	BLOOM	BLOTTINGS
BLISTERED	BLOCKADES	BLOKISH	BLOOMED	BLOTTO
BLISTERS	BLOCKAGE	BLONCKET	BLOOMER	BLOTTY
BLISTERY	BLOCKAGES	BLOND	BLOOMERS	BLOUBOK
BLIT	BLOCKBUST	BLONDE	BLOOMERY	BLOUBOKS
BLITE	BLOCKED	BLONDER	BLOOMIER	BLOUSE
BLITES	BLOCKER	BLONDES	BLOOMIEST	BLOUSED
BLITHE	BLOCKERS	BLONDEST	BLOOMING	BLOUSES
BLITHEFUL	BLOCKHEAD	BLONDIE	BLOOMINGS	BLOUSIER
BLITHELY	BLOCKHOLE	BLONDIES	BLOOMLESS	BLOUSIEST
BLITHER	BLOCKIE	BLONDINE	BLOOMS	BLOUSILY
BLITHERED	BLOCKIER	BLONDINED	BLOOMY	BLOUSING
BLITHERS	BLOCKIES	BLONDINES	BLOOP	BLOUSON
BLITHEST	BLOCKIEST	BLONDING	BLOOPED	BLOUSONS
BLITS	BLOCKING	BLONDINGS	BLOOPER	BLOUSY
BLITTED	BLOCKINGS	BLONDISH	BLOOPERS	BLOVIATE
BLITTER	BLOCKISH	BLONDNESS	BLOOPIER	BLOVIATED
BLITTERS	BLOCKLIST	BLONDS	BLOOPIEST	BLOVIATES
BLITTING	BLOCKS	BLOOD	BLOOPING	BLOW
BLITZ	BLOCKSHIP	BLOODBATH	BLOOPS	BLOWBACK
BLITZED	BLOCKWORK	BLOODED	BLOOPY	BLOWBACKS
BLITZER	BLOCKY	BLOODFIN	BLOOSME	BLOWBALL
BLITZERS	BLOCS	BLOODFINS	BLOOSMED	BLOWBALLS
BLITZES	BLOG	BLOODIED	BLOOSMES	BLOWBY
BLITZING	BLOGGABLE	BLOODIER	BLOOSMING	BLOWBYS
BLIVE	BLOGGED	BLOODIES	BLOOTERED	BLOWDART
BLIZZARD	BLOGGER	BLOODIEST	BLOQUISTE	BLOWDARTS
BLIZZARDS	BLOGGERS	BLOODILY	BLORE	BLOWDOWN
BLIZZARDY	BLOGGIER	BLOODING	BLORES	BLOWDOWNS
BLOAT	BLOGGIEST	BLOODINGS	BLOSSOM	BLOWED
BLOATED	BLOGGING	BLOODLESS	BLOSSOMED	BLOWER
BLOATER	BLOGGINGS	BLOODLIKE	BLOSSOMS	BLOWERS
BLOATERS	BLOGGY	BLOODLINE	BLOSSOMY	BLOWFISH
BLOATING	BLOGPOST	BLOODLUST	BLOT	BLOWFLIES
BLOATINGS	BLOGPOSTS	BLOODRED	BLOTCH	BLOWFLY
BLOATS	BLOGRING	BLOODROOT	BLOTCHED	BLOWGUN
BLOATWARE	BLOGRINGS	BLOODS	BLOTCHES	BLOWGUNS
BLOB	BLOGROLL	BLOODSHED	BLOTCHIER	BLOWHARD
BLOBBED	BLOGROLLS	BLOODSHOT	BLOTCHILY	BLOWHARDS
BLOBBIER	BLOGS	BLOODWOOD	BLOTCHING	BLOWHOLE

BLOWHOLES	BLUBBING	BLUEFISH	BLUEWAY	BLUNKER
BLOWIE	BLUBS	BLUEGILL	BLUEWAYS	BLUNKERS
BLOWIER	BLUCHER	BLUEGILLS	BLUEWEED	BLUNKING
BLOWIES	BLUCHERS	BLUEGOWN	BLUEWEEDS	BLUNKS
BLOWIEST	BLUD	BLUEGOWNS	BLUEWING	BLUNT
BLOWINESS	BLUDE	BLUEGRASS	BLUEWINGS	BLUNTED
BLOWING	BLUDES	BLUEGUM	BLUEWOOD	BLUNTER
BLOWINGS	BLUDGE	BLUEGUMS	BLUEWOODS	BLUNTEST
BLOWJOB	BLUDGED	BLUEHEAD	BLUEY	BLUNTHEAD
BLOWJOBS	BLUDGEON	BLUEHEADS	BLUEYS	BLUNTING
BLOWKART	BLUDGEONS	BLUEING	BLUFF	BLUNTISH
BLOWKARTS	BLUDGER	BLUEINGS	BLUFFABLE	BLUNTLY
BLOWLAMP	BLUDGERS	BLUEISH	BLUFFED	BLUNTNESS
BLOWLAMPS	BLUDGES	BLUEJACK	BLUFFER	BLUNTS
BLOWN	BLUDGING	BLUEJACKS	BLUFFERS	BLUR
BLOWOFF	BLUDIE	BLUEJAY	BLUFFEST	BLURB
BLOWOFFS	BLUDIER	BLUEJAYS	BLUFFING	BLURBED
BLOWOUT	BLUDIEST	BLUEJEANS	BLUFFLY	BLURBING
BLOWOUTS	BLUDS	BLUELINE	BLUFFNESS	BLURBIST
BLOWPIPE	BLUDY	BLUELINER	BLUFFS	BLURBISTS
BLOWPIPES	BLUE	BLUELINES	BLUGGIER	BLURBS
BLOWS	BLUEBACK	BLUELY	BLUGGIEST	BLURRED
BLOWSE	BLUEBACKS	BLUEMOUTH	BLUGGY	BLURREDLY
BLOWSED	BLUEBALL	BLUENESS	BLUID	BLURRIER
BLOWSES	BLUEBALLS	BLUENOSE	BLUIDIER	BLURRIEST
BLOWSIER	BLUEBEARD	BLUENOSED	BLUIDIEST	BLURRILY
BLOWSIEST	BLUEBEAT	BLUENOSES	BLUIDS	BLURRING
BLOWSILY	BLUEBEATS	BLUEPOINT	BLUIDY	BLURRY
BLOWSY	BLUEBELL	BLUEPRINT	BLUIER	BLURS
BLOWTORCH	BLUEBELLS	BLUER	BLUIEST	BLURT
BLOWTUBE	BLUEBERRY	BLUES	BLUING	BLURTED
BLOWTUBES	BLUEBILL	BLUESHIFT	BLUINGS	BLURTER
BLOWUP	BLUEBILLS	BLUESIER	BLUISH	BLURTERS
BLOWUPS	BLUEBIRD	BLUESIEST	BLUME	BLURTING
BLOWY	BLUEBIRDS	BLUESMAN	BLUMED	BLURTINGS
BLOWZE	BLUEBLOOD	BLUESMEN	BLUMES	BLURTS
BLOWZED	BLUEBOOK	BLUEST	BLUMING	BLUSH
BLOWZES	BLUEBOOKS	BLUESTEM	BLUNDER	BLUSHED
BLOWZIER	BLUEBUCK	BLUESTEMS	BLUNDERED	BLUSHER
BLOWZIEST	BLUEBUCKS	BLUESTONE	BLUNDERER	BLUSHERS
BLOWZILY	BLUEBUSH	BLUESY	BLUNDERS	BLUSHES
BLOWZY	BLUECAP	BLUET	BLUNGE	BLUSHET
BLUB	BLUECAPS	BLUETICK	BLUNGED	BLUSHETS
BLUBBED	BLUECOAT	BLUETICKS	BLUNGER	BLUSHFUL
BLUBBER	BLUECOATS	BLUETIT	BLUNGERS	BLUSHING
BLUBBERED	BLUECURLS	BLUETITS	BLUNGES	BLUSHINGS
BLUBBERER	BLUED	BLUETS	BLUNGING	BLUSHLESS
BLUBBERS	BLUEFIN	BLUETTE	BLUNK	BLUSTER
BLUBBERY	BLUEFINS	BLUETTES	BLUNKED	BLUSTERED

BLUSTERER	BOATBILL	BOBBIN	BOBTAILS	BODGIER
BLUSTERS	BOATBILLS	BOBBINET	BOBWEIGHT	BODGIES
BLUSTERY	BOATED	BOBBINETS	BOBWHEEL	BODGIEST
BLUSTROUS	BOATEL	BOBBING	BOBWHEELS	BODGING
BLUTWURST	BOATELS	BOBBINS	BOBWHITE	BODHI
BLYPE	BOATER	BOBBISH	BOBWHITES	BODHIS
BLYPES	BOATERS	BOBBITT	BOBWIG	BODHRAN
BO	BOATFUL	BOBBITTED	BOBWIGS	BODHRANS
BOA	BOATFULS	BOBBITTS	BOCACCIO	BODICE
BOAB	BOATHOOK	BOBBLE	BOCACCIOS	BODICES
BOABS	BOATHOOKS	BOBBLED	BOCAGE	BODIED
BOAK	BOATHOUSE	BOBBLES	BOCAGES	BODIES
BOAKED	BOATIE	BOBBLIER	BOCCA	BODIKIN
BOAKING	BOATIES	BOBBLIEST	BOCCAS	BODIKINS
BOAKS	BOATING	BOBBLING	BOCCE	BODILESS
BOAR	BOATINGS	BOBBLY	BOCCES	BODILY
BOARD	BOATLIFT	BOBBY	BOCCI	BODING
BOARDABLE	BOATLIFTS	BOBBYSOCK	BOCCIA	BODINGLY
BOARDED	BOATLIKE	BOBBYSOX	BOCCIAS	BODINGS
BOARDER	BOATLOAD	BOBCAT	BOCCIE	BODKIN
BOARDERS	BOATLOADS	BOBCATS	BOCCIES	BODKINS
BOARDIES	BOATMAN	BOBECHE	BOCCIS	BODLE
BOARDING	BOATMEN	BOBECHES	BOCK	BODLES
BOARDINGS	BOATNECK	BOBFLOAT	BOCKED	BODRAG
BOARDLIKE	BOATNECKS	BOBFLOATS	BOCKEDY	BODRAGS
BOARDMAN	BOATPORT	BOBLET	BOCKING	BODS
BOARDMEN	BOATPORTS	BOBLETS	BOCKS	BODY
BOARDROOM	BOATS	BOBO	BOCONCINI	BODYBOARD
BOARDS	BOATSMAN	BOBOL	BOD	BODYBUILD
BOARDWALK	BOATSMEN	BOBOLINK	BODACH	BODYBUILT
BOARFISH	BOATSWAIN	BOBOLINKS	BODACHS	BODYCAM
BOARHOUND	BOATTAIL	BOBOLLED	BODACIOUS	BODYCAMS
BOARISH	BOATTAILS	BOBOLLING	BODDLE	BODYCHECK
BOARISHLY	BOATYARD	BOBOLS	BODDLES	BODYGUARD
BOARS	BOATYARDS	BOBOS	BODE	BODYING
BOART	BOB	BOBOTIE	BODED	BODYLINE
BOARTS	BOBA	BOBOTIES	BODEFUL	BODYLINES
BOAS	BOBAC	BOBOWLER	BODEGA	BODYMAN
BOAST	BOBACS	BOBOWLERS	BODEGAS	BODYMEN
BOASTED	BOBAK	BOBS	BODEGUERO	BODYSHELL
BOASTER	BOBAKS	BOBSKATE	BODEMENT	BODYSIDE
BOASTERS	BOBAS	BOBSKATES	BODEMENTS	BODYSIDES
BOASTFUL	BOBBED	BOBSLED	BODES	BODYSUIT
BOASTING	BOBBEJAAN	BOBSLEDS	BODGE	BODYSUITS
BOASTINGS	BOBBER	BOBSLEIGH	BODGED	BODYSURF
BOASTLESS	BOBBERIES	BOBSTAY	BODGER	BODYSURFS
BOASTS	BOBBERS	BOBSTAYS	BODGERS	BODYWASH
BOAT	BOBBERY	BOBTAIL	BODGES	BODYWORK
BOATABLE	BOBBIES	BOBTAILED	BODGIE	BODYWORKS

BOEHMITE	BOGGER	BOHEMIA	BOKO	BOLLED
BOEHMITES	BOGGERS	BOHEMIAN	BOKOS	BOLLEN
BOEP	BOGGIER	BOHEMIANS	BOKS	BOLLETRIE
BOEPS	BOGGIEST	BOHEMIAS	BOLA	BOLLING
BOERBUL	BOGGINESS	BOHO	BOLAR	BOLLIX
BOERBULL	BOGGING	BOHOS	BOLAS	BOLLIXED
BOERBULLS	BOGGISH	BOHRIUM	BOLASES	BOLLIXES
BOERBULS	BOGGLE	BOHRIUMS	BOLD	BOLLIXING
BOEREWORS	BOGGLED	BOHS	BOLDED	BOLLOCK
BOERTJIE	BOGGLER	BOI	BOLDEN	BOLLOCKED
BOERTJIES	BOGGLERS	BOIL	BOLDENED	BOLLOCKS
BOET	BOGGLES	BOILABLE	BOLDENING	BOLLOX
BOETS	BOGGLING	BOILED	BOLDENS	BOLLOXED
BOEUF	BOGGY	BOILER	BOLDER	BOLLOXES
BOEUFS	BOGHEAD	BOILERIES	BOLDEST	BOLLOXING
BOFF	BOGHOLE	BOILERMAN	BOLDFACE	BOLLS
BOFFED	BOGHOLES	BOILERMEN	BOLDFACED	BOLLWORM
BOFFIN	BOGIE	BOILERS	BOLDFACES	BOLLWORMS
BOFFING	BOGIED	BOILERY	BOLDING	BOLO
BOFFINIER	BOGIEING	BOILING	BOLDLY	BOLOGNA
BOFFINS	BOGIES	BOILINGLY	BOLDNESS	BOLOGNAS
BOFFINY	BOGLAND	BOILINGS	BOLDS	BOLOGNESE
BOFFO	BOGLANDS	BOILOFF	BOLE	BOLOGRAPH
BOFFOLA	BOGLE	BOILOFFS	BOLECTION	BOLOMETER
BOFFOLAS	BOGLED	BOILOVER	BOLERO	BOLOMETRY
BOFFOS	BOGLES	BOILOVERS	BOLEROS	BOLONEY
BOFFS	BOGLING	BOILS	BOLES	BOLONEYS
BOG	BOGMAN	BOING	BOLETE	BOLOS
BOGAN	BOGMEN	BOINGED	BOLETES	BOLSHEVIK
BOGANS	BOGOAK	BOINGING	BOLETI	BOLSHIE
BOGART	BOGOAKS	BOINGS	BOLETUS	BOLSHIER
BOGARTED	BOGONG	BOINK	BOLETUSES	BOLSHIES
BOGARTING	BOGONGS	BOINKED	BOLIDE	BOLSHIEST
BOGARTS	BOGS	BOINKING	BOLIDES	BOLSHY
BOGBEAN	BOGUE	BOINKS	BOLINE	BOLSON
BOGBEANS	BOGUES	BOIS	BOLINES	BOLSONS
BOGEY	BOGUS	BOISERIE	BOLIVAR	BOLSTER
BOGEYED	BOGUSLY	BOISERIES	BOLIVARES	BOLSTERED
BOGEYING	BOGUSNESS	BOITE	BOLIVARS	BOLSTERER
BOGEYISM	BOGWOOD	BOITES	BOLIVIA	BOLSTERS
BOGEYISMS	BOGWOODS	BOK	BOLIVIANO	BOLT
BOGEYMAN	BOGY	BOKE	BOLIVIAS	BOLTED
BOGEYMEN	BOGYISM	BOKED	BOLIX	BOLTER
BOGEYS	BOGYISMS	BOKEH	BOLIXED	BOLTERS
BOGGARD	BOGYMAN	BOKEHS	BOLIXES	BOLTHEAD
BOGGARDS	BOGYMEN	BOKES	BOLIXING	BOLTHEADS
BOGGART	BOH	BOKING	BOLL	BOLTHOLE
BOGGARTS	BOHEA	BOKKEN	BOLLARD	BOLTHOLES
BOGGED	BOHEAS	BOKKENS	BOLLARDS	BOLTING

BOLTINGS	BOMBPROOF	BONDSTONE	BONIBELL	BONSELLA
BOLTLESS	BOMBS	BONDUC	BONIBELLS	BONSELLAS
BOLTLIKE	BOMBSHELL	BONDUCS	BONIE	BONSOIR
BOLTONIA	BOMBSIGHT	BONDWOMAN	BONIER	BONSPELL
BOLTONIAS	BOMBSITE	BONDWOMEN	BONIEST	BONSPELLS
BOLTROPE	BOMBSITES	BONE	BONIFACE	BONSPIEL
BOLTROPES	BOMBYCID	BONEBED	BONIFACES	BONSPIELS
BOLTS	BOMBYCIDS	BONEBEDS	BONILASSE	BONTBOK
BOLUS	BOMBYCOID	BONEBLACK	BONINESS	BONTBOKS
BOLUSES	BOMBYX	BONED	BONING	BONTEBOK
BOMA	BOMBYXES	BONEFISH	BONINGS	BONTEBOKS
BOMAS	BOMMIE	BONEHEAD	BONISM	BONUS
BOMB	BOMMIES	BONEHEADS	BONISMS	BONUSED
BOMBABLE	BON	BONELESS	BONIST	BONUSES
BOMBARD	BONA	BONELIKE	BONISTS	BONUSING
BOMBARDE	BONACI	BONEMEAL	BONITA	BONUSINGS
BOMBARDED	BONACIS	BONEMEALS	BONITAS	BONUSSED
BOMBARDER	BONAMANI	BONER	BONITO	BONUSSES
BOMBARDES	BONAMANO	BONERS	BONITOES	BONUSSING
BOMBARDON	BONAMIA	BONES	BONITOS	BONXIE
BOMBARDS	BONAMIAS	BONESET	BONJOUR	BONXIES
BOMBASINE	BONANZA	BONESETS	BONK	BONY
BOMBAST	BONANZAS	BONETIRED	BONKED	BONZA
BOMBASTED	BONASSUS	BONEY	BONKERS	BONZE
BOMBASTER	BONASUS	BONEYARD	BONKING	BONZER
BOMBASTIC	BONASUSES	BONEYARDS	BONKINGS	BONZES
BOMBASTS	BONBON	BONEYER	BONKS	BOO
BOMBAX	BONBONS	BONEYEST	BONNE	BOOAI
BOMBAXES	BONCE	BONFIRE	BONNES	BOOAIS
BOMBAZINE	BONCES	BONFIRES	BONNET	BOOAY
BOMBE	BOND	BONG	BONNETED	BOOAYS
BOMBED	BONDABLE	BONGED	BONNETING	BOOB
BOMBER	BONDAGE	BONGING	BONNETS	BOOBED
BOMBERS	BONDAGER	BONGO	BONNIBELL	BOOBHEAD
BOMBES	BONDAGERS	BONGOES	BONNIE	BOOBHEADS
BOMBESIN	BONDAGES	BONGOIST	BONNIER	BOOBIALLA
BOMBESINS	BONDED	BONGOISTS	BONNIES	BOOBIE
BOMBILATE	BONDER	BONGOS	BONNIEST	BOOBIES
BOMBINATE	BONDERS	BONGRACE	BONNILY	BOOBING
BOMBING	BONDING	BONGRACES	BONNINESS	BOOBIRD
BOMBINGS	BONDINGS	BONGS	BONNOCK	BOOBIRDS
BOMBLET	BONDLESS	BONHAM	BONNOCKS	BOOBISH
BOMBLETS	BONDMAID	BONHAMS	BONNY	BOOBOISIE
BOMBLOAD	BONDMAIDS	BONHOMIE	BONOBO	BOOBOO
BOMBLOADS	BONDMAN	BONHOMIES	BONOBOS	BOOBOOK
BOMBO	BONDMEN	BONHOMMIE	BONSAI	BOOBOOKS
BOMBORA	BONDS	BONHOMOUS	BONSAIS	BOOBOOS
BOMBORAS	BONDSMAN	BONIATO	BONSELA	BOOBS
BOMBOS	BONDSMEN	BONIATOS	BONSELAS	BOOBY

B

BOOBYISH	BOOHOO	BOOKPLATE	BOON	BOOTIKINS
BOOBYISM	BOOHOOED	BOOKRACK	BOONDOCK	BOOTING
BOOBYISMS	BOOHOOING	BOOKRACKS	BOONDOCKS	BOOTJACK
BOOCOO	BOOHOOS	BOOKREST	BOONER	BOOTJACKS
BOOCOOS	BOOHS	BOOKRESTS	BOONERS	BOOTLACE
BOODIE	BOOING	BOOKS	BOONEST	BOOTLACES
BOODIED	BOOINGS	BOOKSHELF	BOONGARY	BOOTLAST
BOODIES	BOOJUM	BOOKSHOP	BOONIES	BOOTLASTS
BOODLE	BOOJUMS	BOOKSHOPS	BOONLESS	BOOTLEG
BOODLED	BOOK	BOOKSIE	BOONS	BOOTLEGS
BOODLER	BOOKABLE	BOOKSIER	BOOR	BOOTLESS
BOODLERS	BOOKBAG	BOOKSIEST	BOORD	BOOTLICK
BOODLES	BOOKBAGS	BOOKSTALL	BOORDE	BOOTLICKS
BOODLING	BOOKCASE	BOOKSTAND	BOORDES	BOOTMAKER
BOODY	BOOKCASES	BOOKSTORE	BOORDS	BOOTS
BOODYING	BOOKED	BOOKSY	BOORISH	BOOTSTRAP
BOOED	BOOKEND	BOOKWORK	BOORISHLY	BOOTY
BOOFHEAD	BOOKENDED	BOOKWORKS	BOORKA	BOOZE
BOOFHEADS	BOOKENDS	BOOKWORM	BOORKAS	BOOZED
BOOFIER	BOOKER	BOOKWORMS	BOORS	BOOZER
BOOFIEST	BOOKERS	BOOKY	BOORTREE	BOOZERS
BOOFY	BOOKFUL	BOOL	BOORTREES	BOOZES
BOOGALOO	BOOKFULS	BOOLED	BOOS	BOOZEY
BOOGALOOS	BOOKIE	BOOLING	BOOSE	BOOZIER
BOOGER	BOOKIER	BOOLS	BOOSED	BOOZIEST
BOOGERMAN	BOOKIES	BOOM	BOOSES	BOOZILY
BOOGERMEN	BOOKIEST	BOOMBOX	BOOSHIT	BOOZINESS
BOOGERS	BOOKING	BOOMBOXES	BOOSING	BOOZING
BOOGEY	BOOKINGS	BOOMBURB	BOOST	BOOZINGS
BOOGEYED	BOOKISH	BOOMBURBS	BOOSTED	BOOZY
BOOGEYING	BOOKISHLY	BOOMED	BOOSTER	BOP
BOOGEYMAN	BOOKLAND	BOOMER	BOOSTERS	BOPEEP
BOOGEYMEN	BOOKLANDS	BOOMERANG	BOOSTING	BOPEEPS
BOOGEYS	BOOKLESS	BOOMERS	BOOSTS	BOPO
BOOGIE	BOOKLET	BOOMIER	BOOT	BOPOS
BOOGIED	BOOKLETS	BOOMIEST	BOOTABLE	BOPPED
BOOGIEING	BOOKLICE	BOOMING	BOOTBLACK	BOPPER
BOOGIEMAN	BOOKLIGHT	BOOMINGLY	BOOTCUT	BOPPERS
BOOGIEMEN	BOOKLIKE	BOOMINGS	BOOTED	BOPPIER
BOOGIES	BOOKLORE	BOOMKIN	BOOTEE	BOPPIEST
BOOGY	BOOKLORES	BOOMKINS	BOOTEES	BOPPING
BOOGYING	BOOKLOUSE	BOOMLET	BOOTERIES	BOPPISH
BOOGYMAN	BOOKMAKER	BOOMLETS	BOOTERY	BOPPY
BOOGYMEN	BOOKMAN	BOOMS	BOOTH	BOPS
BOOH	BOOKMARK	BOOMSLANG	BOOTHOSE	BOR
BOOHAI	BOOKMARKS	BOOMSTICK	BOOTHS	BORA
BOOHAIS	BOOKMEN	BOOMTOWN	BOOTIE	BORACES
BOOHED	BOOKOO	BOOMTOWNS	BOOTIES	BORACHIO
BOOHING	BOOKOOS	BOOMY	BOOTIKIN	BORACHIOS

B

BORACIC	BOREDOMS	BORONIC	BOSCHVELD	BOSSINESS
BORACITE	BOREE	BORONS	BOSH	BOSSING
BORACITES	BOREEN	BOROUGH	BOSHBOK	BOSSINGS
BORAGE	BOREENS	BOROUGHS	BOSHBOKS	BOSSISM
BORAGES	BOREES	BORREL	BOSHES	BOSSISMS
BORAK	BOREHOLE	BORRELIA	BOSHTA	BOSSY
BORAKS	BOREHOLES	BORRELIAS	BOSHTER	BOSTANGI
BORAL	BOREL	BORRELL	BOSHVARK	BOSTANGIS
BORALS	BORELS	BORROW	BOSHVARKS	BOSTHOON
BORANE	BORER	BORROWED	BOSIE	BOSTHOONS
BORANES	BORERS	BORROWER	BOSIES	BOSTON
BORAS	BORES	BORROWERS	BOSK	BOSTONS
BORATE	BORESCOPE	BORROWING	BOSKAGE	BOSTRYX
BORATED	BORESOME	BORROWS	BOSKAGES	BOSTRYXES
BORATES	BORGHETTI	BORS	BOSKER	BOSUN
BORATING	BORGHETTO	BORSCH	BOSKET	BOSUNS
BORAX	BORGO	BORSCHES	BOSKETS	BOT
BORAXES	BORGOS	BORSCHT	BOSKIER	BOTA
BORAZON	BORIC	BORSCHTS	BOSKIEST	BOTANIC
BORAZONS	BORICUA	BORSHCH	BOSKINESS	BOTANICA
BORD	BORICUAS	BORSHCHES	BOSKS	BOTANICAL
BORDAR	BORIDE	BORSHT	BOSKY	BOTANICAS
BORDARS	BORIDES	BORSHTS	BOSOM	BOTANICS
BORDE	BORING	BORSIC	BOSOMED	BOTANIES
BORDEAUX	BORINGLY	BORSICS	BOSOMIER	BOTANISE
BORDEL	BORINGS	BORSTAL	BOSOMIEST	BOTANISED
BORDELLO	BORK	BORSTALL	BOSOMING	BOTANISER
BORDELLOS	BORKED	BORSTALLS	BOSOMS	BOTANISES
BORDELS	BORKING	BORSTALS	BOSOMY	BOTANIST
BORDER	BORKINGS	BORT	BOSON	BOTANISTS
BORDEREAU	BORKS	BORTIER	BOSONIC	BOTANIZE
BORDERED	BORLOTTI	BORTIEST	BOSONS	BOTANIZED
BORDERER	BORM	BORTS	BOSQUE	BOTANIZER
BORDERERS	BORMED	BORTSCH	BOSQUES	BOTANIZES
BORDERING	BORMING	BORTSCHES	BOSQUET	BOTANY
BORDERS	BORMS	BORTY	BOSQUETS	BOTARGO
BORDES	BORN	BORTZ	BOSS	BOTARGOES
BORDS	BORNA	BORTZES	BOSSDOM	BOTARGOS
BORDURE	BORNE	BORZOI	BOSSDOMS	BOTAS
BORDURES	BORNEOL	BORZOIS	BOSSED	BOTCH
BORE	BORNEOLS	BOS	BOSSER	BOTCHED
BOREAL	BORNITE	BOSBERAAD	BOSSES	BOTCHEDLY
BOREALIS	BORNITES	BOSBOK	BOSSEST	BOTCHER
BOREAS	BORNITIC	BOSBOKS	BOSSET	BOTCHERS
BOREASES	BORNYL	BOSCAGE	BOSSETS	BOTCHERY
BORECOLE	BORNYLS	BOSCAGES	BOSSIER	BOTCHES
BORECOLES	BORON	BOSCHBOK	BOSSIES	BOTCHIER
BORED	BORONIA	BOSCHBOKS	BOSSIEST	BOTCHIEST
BOREDOM	BORONIAS	BOSCHVARK	BOSSILY	BOTCHILY

BOTCHING	BOTTINES	BOUGED	BOUNCES	BOURGS
BOTCHINGS	BOTTING	BOUGES	BOUNCIER	BOURKHA
BOTCHY	BOTTLE	BOUGET	BOUNCIEST	BOURKHAS
BOTE	BOTTLED	BOUGETS	BOUNCILY	BOURLAW
BOTEL	BOTTLEFUL	BOUGH	BOUNCING	BOURLAWS
BOTELS	BOTTLER	BOUGHED	BOUNCY	BOURN
BOTES	BOTTLERS	BOUGHLESS	BOUND	BOURNE
BOTFLIES	BOTTLES	BOUGHPOT	BOUNDABLE	BOURNES
BOTFLY	BOTTLING	BOUGHPOTS	BOUNDARY	BOURNS
BOTH	BOTTLINGS	BOUGHS	BOUNDED	BOURREE
BOTHAN	BOTTOM	BOUGHT	BOUNDEN	BOURREES
BOTHANS	BOTTOMED	BOUGHTEN	BOUNDER	BOURRIDE
BOTHER	BOTTOMER	BOUGHTS	BOUNDERS	BOURRIDES
BOTHERED	BOTTOMERS	BOUGIE	BOUNDING	BOURSE
BOTHERING	BOTTOMING	BOUGIER	BOUNDLESS	BOURSES
BOTHERS	BOTTOMRY	BOUGIES	BOUNDNESS	BOURSIER
BOTHIE	BOTTOMS	BOUGIEST	BOUNDS	BOURSIERS
BOTHIES	BOTTOMSET	BOUGING	BOUNED	BOURSIN
BOTHOLE	BOTTONY	BOUILLI	BOUNING	BOURSINS
BOTHOLES	BOTTS	BOUILLIS	BOUNS	BOURTREE
BOTHRIA	BOTTY	BOUILLON	BOUNTEOUS	BOURTREES
BOTHRIUM	BOTULIN	BOUILLONS	BOUNTIED	BOUSE
BOTHRIUMS	BOTULINAL	BOUJEE	BOUNTIES	BOUSED
BOTHY	BOTULINS	BOUJIER	BOUNTIFUL	BOUSES
BOTHYMAN	BOTULINUM	BOUJIEST	BOUNTREE	BOUSIER
BOTHYMEN	BOTULINUS	BOUK	BOUNTREES	BOUSIEST
BOTNET	BOTULISM	BOUKS	BOUNTY	BOUSING
BOTNETS	BOTULISMS	BOULDER	BOUNTYHED	BOUSOUKI
BOTONE	BOUBOU	BOULDERED	BOUQUET	BOUSOUKIA
BOTONEE	BOUBOUS	BOULDERER	BOUQUETS	BOUSOUKIS
BOTONNEE	BOUCHE	BOULDERS	BOURASQUE	BOUSY
BOTOX	BOUCHEE	BOULDERY	BOURBON	BOUT
BOTOXED	BOUCHEES	BOULE	BOURBONS	BOUTADE
BOTOXES	BOUCHES	BOULES	BOURD	BOUTADES
BOTOXING	BOUCLE	BOULEVARD	BOURDED	BOUTIQUE
BOTRYOID	BOUCLEE	BOULLE	BOURDER	BOUTIQUES
BOTRYOSE	BOUCLEES	BOULLES	BOURDERS	BOUTIQUEY
BOTRYTIS	BOUCLES	BOULT	BOURDING	BOUTON
BOTS	BOUDERIE	BOULTED	BOURDON	BOUTONNE
BOTT	BOUDERIES	BOULTER	BOURDONS	BOUTONNEE
BOTTARGA	BOUDIN	BOULTERS	BOURDS	BOUTONS
BOTTARGAS	BOUDINS	BOULTING	BOURG	BOUTS
BOTTE	BOUDOIR	BOULTINGS	BOURGEOIS	BOUVARDIA
BOTTED	BOUDOIRS	BOULTS	BOURGEON	BOUVIER
BOTTEGA	BOUFFANT	BOUN	BOURGEONS	BOUVIERS
BOTTEGAS	BOUFFANTS	BOUNCE	BOURGIE	BOUZOUKI
BOTTES	BOUFFE	BOUNCED	BOURGIER	BOUZOUKIA
BOTTIES	BOUFFES	BOUNCER	BOURGIES	BOUZOUKIS
BOTTINE	BOUGE	BOUNCERS	BOURGIEST	BOVATE

BOVATES	BOWLDER	BOWWOOD	BOXWALLAH	BRAAIED
BOVID	BOWLDERS	BOWWOODS	BOXWOOD	BRAAIING
BOVIDS	BOWLED	BOWWOW	BOXWOODS	BRAAIS
BOVINE	BOWLEG	BOWWOWED	BOXY	BRAATA
BOVINELY	BOWLEGGED	BOWWOWING	BOY	BRAATAS
BOVINES	BOWLEGS	BOWWOWS	BOYAR	BRAATASES
BOVINITY	BOWLER	BOWYANG	BOYARD	BRABBLE
BOVVER	BOWLERS	BOWYANGS	BOYARDS	BRABBLED
BOVVERS	BOWLESS	BOWYER	BOYARISM	BRABBLER
BOW	BOWLFUL	BOWYERS	BOYARISMS	BRABBLERS
BOWAT	BOWLFULS	BOX	BOYARS	BRABBLES
BOWATS	BOWLIKE	BOXBALL	BOYAU	BRABBLING
BOWBENT	BOWLINE	BOXBALLS	BOYAUX	BRACCATE
BOWED	BOWLINES	BOXBERRY	BOYCHICK	BRACCIA
BOWEL	BOWLING	BOXBOARD	BOYCHICKS	BRACCIO
BOWELED	BOWLINGS	BOXBOARDS	BOYCHIK	BRACE
BOWELING	BOWLLIKE	BOXCAR	BOYCHIKS	BRACED
BOWELLED	BOWLS	BOXCARS	BOYCOTT	BRACELET
BOWELLESS	BOWMAN	BOXED	BOYCOTTED	BRACELETS
BOWELLING	BOWMEN	BOXEN	BOYCOTTER	BRACER
BOWELS	BOWNE	BOXER	BOYCOTTS	BRACERO
BOWER	BOWNED	BOXERCISE	BOYED	BRACEROS
BOWERBIRD	BOWNES	BOXERS	BOYF	BRACERS
BOWERED	BOWNING	BOXES	BOYFRIEND	BRACES
BOWERIES	BOWPOT	BOXFISH	BOYFS	BRACH
BOWERING	BOWPOTS	BOXFISHES	BOYG	BRACHAH
BOWERS	BOWR	BOXFUL	BOYGS	BRACHAHS
BOWERY	BOWRS	BOXFULS	BOYHOOD	BRACHES
BOWES	BOWS	BOXHAUL	BOYHOODS	BRACHET
BOWET	BOWSAW	BOXHAULED	BOYING	BRACHETS
BOWETS	BOWSAWS	BOXHAULS	BOYISH	BRACHIA
BOWFIN	BOWSE	BOXIER	BOYISHLY	BRACHIAL
BOWFINS	BOWSED	BOXIEST	BOYKIE	BRACHIALS
BOWFRONT	BOWSER	BOXILY	BOYKIES	BRACHIATE
BOWGET	BOWSERS	BOXINESS	BOYLA	BRACHIUM
BOWGETS	BOWSES	BOXING	BOYLAS	BRACHIUMS
BOWHEAD	BOWSEY	BOXINGS	BOYO	BRACHOT
BOWHEADS	BOWSEYS	BOXKEEPER	BOYOS	BRACHS
BOWHUNT	BOWSHOT	BOXLA	BOYS	BRACING
BOWHUNTED	BOWSHOTS	BOXLAS	BOYSHORTS	BRACINGLY
BOWHUNTER	BOWSIE	BOXLIKE	BOYSIER	BRACINGS
BOWHUNTS	BOWSIES	BOXPLOT	BOYSIEST	BRACIOLA
BOWIE	BOWSING	BOXPLOTS	BOYSY	BRACIOLAS
BOWING	BOWSMAN	BOXROOM	BOZO	BRACIOLE
BOWINGLY	BOWSMEN	BOXROOMS	BOZOS	BRACIOLES
BOWINGS	BOWSPRIT	BOXTHORN	BOZZETTI	BRACK
BOWKNOT	BOWSPRITS	BOXTHORNS	BOZZETTO	BRACKEN
BOWKNOTS	BOWSTRING	BOXTIES	BRA	BRACKENS
BOWL	BOWSTRUNG	BOXTY	BRAAI	BRACKET

BRACKETED	BRAID	BRAISED	BRAND	BRANTLE
BRACKETS	BRAIDE	BRAISES	BRANDADE	BRANTLES
BRACKISH	BRAIDED	BRAISING	BRANDADES	BRANTS
BRACKS	BRAIDER	BRAIZE	BRANDED	BRANZINI
BRACONID	BRAIDERS	BRAIZES	BRANDER	BRANZINO
BRACONIDS	BRAIDEST	BRAK	BRANDERED	BRANZINOS
BRACT	BRAIDING	BRAKE	BRANDERS	BRAP
BRACTEAL	BRAIDINGS	BRAKEAGE	BRANDIED	BRAS
BRACTEATE	BRAIDS	BRAKEAGES	BRANDIES	BRASCO
BRACTED	BRAIL	BRAKED	BRANDING	BRASCOS
BRACTEOLE	BRAILED	BRAKELESS	BRANDINGS	BRASERO
BRACTLESS	BRAILING	BRAKEMAN	BRANDISE	BRASEROS
BRACTLET	BRAILLE	BRAKEMEN	BRANDISES	BRASES
BRACTLETS	BRAILLED	BRAKES	BRANDISH	BRASH
BRACTS	BRAILLER	BRAKESMAN	BRANDLESS	BRASHED
BRAD	BRAILLERS	BRAKESMEN	BRANDLING	BRASHER
BRADAWL	BRAILLES	BRAKIER	BRANDRETH	BRASHES
BRADAWLS	BRAILLING	BRAKIEST	BRANDS	BRASHEST
BRADDED	BRAILLIST	BRAKING	BRANDY	BRASHIER
BRADDING	BRAILS	BRAKINGS	BRANDYING	BRASHIEST
BRADOON	BRAIN	BRAKS	BRANE	BRASHING
BRADOONS	BRAINBOX	BRAKY	BRANES	BRASHLY
BRADS	BRAINCASE	BRALESS	BRANGLE	BRASHNESS
BRAE	BRAINDEAD	BRALETTE	BRANGLED	BRASHY
BRAEHEID	BRAINED	BRALETTES	BRANGLES	BRASIER
BRAEHEIDS	BRAINFART	BRAMBLE	BRANGLING	BRASIERS
BRAES	BRAINFOOD	BRAMBLED	BRANK	BRASIL
BRAG	BRAINIAC	BRAMBLES	BRANKED	BRASILEIN
BRAGGART	BRAINIACS	BRAMBLIER	BRANKIER	BRASILIN
BRAGGARTS	BRAINIER	BRAMBLING	BRANKIEST	BRASILINS
BRAGGED	BRAINIEST	BRAMBLY	BRANKING	BRASILS
BRAGGER	BRAINILY	BRAME	BRANKS	BRASS
BRAGGERS	BRAINING	BRAMES	BRANKY	BRASSAGE
BRAGGEST	BRAINISH	BRAN	BRANLE	BRASSAGES
BRAGGIER	BRAINLESS	BRANCARD	BRANLES	BRASSARD
BRAGGIEST	BRAINPAN	BRANCARDS	BRANNED	BRASSARDS
BRAGGING	BRAINPANS	BRANCH	BRANNER	BRASSART
BRAGGINGS	BRAINS	BRANCHED	BRANNERS	BRASSARTS
BRAGGY	BRAINSICK	BRANCHER	BRANNIER	BRASSED
BRAGLY	BRAINSTEM	BRANCHERS	BRANNIEST	BRASSERIE
BRAGS	BRAINWASH	BRANCHERY	BRANNIGAN	BRASSES
BRAHMA	BRAINWAVE	BRANCHES	BRANNING	BRASSET
BRAHMAN	BRAINWORK	BRANCHIA	BRANNY	BRASSETS
BRAHMANI	BRAINY	BRANCHIAE	BRANS	BRASSICA
BRAHMANIS	BRAIRD	BRANCHIAL	BRANSLE	BRASSICAS
BRAHMANS	BRAIRDED	BRANCHIER	BRANSLES	BRASSIE
BRAHMAS	BRAIRDING	BRANCHING	BRANT	BRASSIER
BRAHMIN	BRAIRDS	BRANCHLET	BRANTAIL	BRASSIERE
BRAHMINS	BRAISE	BRANCHY	BRANTAILS	BRASSIES

B

BRASSIEST	BRAVEST	BRAZENLY	BREAKDOWN	BRECHAMS
BRASSILY	BRAVI	BRAZENRY	BREAKER	BRECHAN
BRASSING	BRAVING	BRAZENS	BREAKERS	BRECHANS
BRASSISH	BRAVO	BRAZER	BREAKEVEN	BRED
BRASSWARE	BRAVOED	BRAZERS	BREAKFAST	BREDE
BRASSY	BRAVOES	BRAZES	BREAKING	BREDED
BRAST	BRAVOING	BRAZIER	BREAKINGS	BREDES
BRASTING	BRAVOS	BRAZIERS	BREAKNECK	BREDIE
BRASTS	BRAVURA	BRAZIERY	BREAKOFF	BREDIES
BRAT	BRAVURAS	BRAZIL	BREAKOFFS	BREDING
BRATCHET	BRAVURE	BRAZILEIN	BREAKOUT	BREDREN
BRATCHETS	BRAW	BRAZILIN	BREAKOUTS	BREDRENS
BRATLING	BRAWER	BRAZILINS	BREAKROOM	BREDRIN
BRATLINGS	BRAWEST	BRAZILS	BREAKS	BREDRINS
BRATPACK	BRAWL	BRAZING	BREAKTIME	BREDS
BRATPACKS	BRAWLED	BREACH	BREAKUP	BREE
BRATS	BRAWLER	BREACHED	BREAKUPS	BREECH
BRATTICE	BRAWLERS	BREACHER	BREAKWALL	BREECHED
BRATTICED	BRAWLIE	BREACHERS	BREAM	BREECHES
BRATTICES	BRAWLIER	BREACHES	BREAMED	BREECHING
BRATTIER	BRAWLIEST	BREACHING	BREAMING	BREED
BRATTIEST	BRAWLING	BREAD	BREAMS	BREEDER
BRATTISH	BRAWLINGS	BREADBIN	BREARE	BREEDERS
BRATTLE	BRAWLS	BREADBINS	BREARES	BREEDING
BRATTLED	BRAWLY	BREADBOX	BREASKIT	BREEDINGS
BRATTLES	BRAWN	BREADED	BREASKITS	BREEDS
BRATTLING	BRAWNED	BREADHEAD	BREAST	BREEKS
BRATTY	BRAWNIER	BREADIER	BREASTED	BREEM
BRATWURST	BRAWNIEST	BREADIEST	BREASTFED	BREENGE
BRAUNCH	BRAWNILY	BREADING	BREASTING	BREENGED
BRAUNCHED	BRAWNS	BREADLESS	BREASTPIN	BREENGES
BRAUNCHES	BRAWNY	BREADLIKE	BREASTS	BREENGING
BRAUNITE	BRAWS	BREADLINE	BREATH	BREER
BRAUNITES	BRAXIES	BREADNUT	BREATHE	BREERED
BRAVA	BRAXY	BREADNUTS	BREATHED	BREERING
BRAVADO	BRAY	BREADROOM	BREATHER	BREERS
BRAVADOED	BRAYED	BREADROOT	BREATHERS	BREES
BRAVADOES	BRAYER	BREADS	BREATHES	BREESE
BRAVADOS	BRAYERS	BREADTH	BREATHFUL	BREESES
BRAVAS	BRAYING	BREADTHS	BREATHIER	BREEST
BRAVE	BRAYS	BREADY	BREATHILY	BREESTS
BRAVED	BRAZA	BREAK	BREATHING	BREEZE
BRAVELY	BRAZAS	BREAKABLE	BREATHS	BREEZED
BRAVENESS	BRAZE	BREAKAGE	BREATHY	BREEZES
BRAVER	BRAZED	BREAKAGES	BRECCIA	BREEZEWAY
BRAVERIES	BRAZELESS	BREAKAWAY	BRECCIAL	BREEZIER
BRAVERS	BRAZEN	BREAKBACK	BRECCIAS	BREEZIEST
BRAVERY	BRAZENED	BREAKBEAT	BRECCIATE	BREEZILY
BRAVES	BRAZENING	BREAKBONE	BRECHAM	BREEZING

BREEZY	BREVE	BRIARROOT	BRIDECAKE	BRIG
BREGMA	BREVES	BRIARS	BRIDED	BRIGADE
BREGMAS	BREVET	BRIARWOOD	BRIDEMAID	BRIGADED
BREGMATA	BREVETCY	BRIARY	BRIDEMAN	BRIGADES
BREGMATE	BREVETE	BRIBABLE	BRIDEMEN	BRIGADIER
BREGMATIC	BREVETED	BRIBE	BRIDES	BRIGADING
BREHON	BREVETING	BRIBEABLE	BRIDESMAN	BRIGALOW
BREHONS	BREVETS	BRIBED	BRIDESMEN	BRIGALOWS
BREI	BREVETTED	BRIBEE	BRIDEWELL	BRIGAND
BREID	BREVIARY	BRIBEES	BRIDGABLE	BRIGANDRY
BREIDS	BREVIATE	BRIBER	BRIDGE	BRIGANDS
BREIING	BREVIATES	BRIBERIES	BRIDGED	BRIGHT
BREINGE	BREVIER	BRIBERS	BRIDGES	BRIGHTEN
BREINGED	BREVIERS	BRIBERY	BRIDGING	BRIGHTENS
BREINGES	BREVIS	BRIBES	BRIDGINGS	BRIGHTER
BREINGING	BREVISES	BRIBING	BRIDIE	BRIGHTEST
BREIS	BREVITIES	BRICABRAC	BRIDIES	BRIGHTISH
BREIST	BREVITY	BRICHT	BRIDING	BRIGHTLY
BREISTS	BREW	BRICHTER	BRIDLE	BRIGHTS
BREKKIE	BREWAGE	BRICHTEST	BRIDLED	BRIGS
BREKKIES	BREWAGES	BRICK	BRIDLER	BRIGUE
BREKKY	BREWED	BRICKBAT	BRIDLERS	BRIGUED
BRELOQUE	BREWER	BRICKBATS	BRIDLES	BRIGUES
BRELOQUES	BREWERIES	BRICKCLAY	BRIDLEWAY	BRIGUING
BREME	BREWERS	BRICKED	BRIDLING	BRIGUINGS
BREN	BREWERY	BRICKEN	BRIDOON	BRIK
BRENNE	BREWHOUSE	BRICKIE	BRIDOONS	BRIKI
BRENNES	BREWING	BRICKIER	BRIE	BRIKIS
BRENNING	BREWINGS	BRICKIES	BRIEF	BRIKS
BRENS	BREWIS	BRICKIEST	BRIEFCASE	BRILL
BRENT	BREWISES	BRICKING	BRIEFED	BRILLER
BRENTER	BREWPUB	BRICKINGS	BRIEFER	BRILLEST
BRENTEST	BREWPUBS	BRICKKILN	BRIEFERS	BRILLIANT
BRENTS	BREWS	BRICKLE	BRIEFEST	BRILLO
BRER	BREWSKI	BRICKLES	BRIEFING	BRILLOS
BRERE	BREWSKIES	BRICKLIKE	BRIEFINGS	BRILLS
BRERES	BREWSKIS	BRICKS	BRIEFLESS	BRIM
BRERS	BREWSTER	BRICKWALL	BRIEFLY	BRIMFUL
BRESAOLA	BREWSTERS	BRICKWORK	BRIEFNESS	BRIMFULL
BRESAOLAS	BREY	BRICKY	BRIEFS	BRIMFULLY
BRETASCHE	BREYED	BRICKYARD	BRIER	BRIMING
BRETESSE	BREYING	BRICOLAGE	BRIERED	BRIMINGS
BRETESSES	BREYS	BRICOLE	BRIERIER	BRIMLESS
BRETHREN	BRIAR	BRICOLES	BRIERIEST	BRIMMED
BRETON	BRIARD	BRICOLEUR	BRIERROOT	BRIMMER
BRETONS	BRIARDS	BRIDAL	BRIERS	BRIMMERS
BRETTICE	BRIARED	BRIDALLY	BRIERWOOD	BRIMMING
BRETTICED	BRIARIER	BRIDALS	BRIERY	BRIMS
BRETTICES	BRIARIEST	BRIDE	BRIES	BRIMSTONE

BRIMSTONY	BRISANCE	BRITTLELY	BROASTING	BRODKINS
BRIN	BRISANCES	BRITTLER	BROASTS	BRODO
BRINDED	BRISANT	BRITTLES	BROCADE	BRODOS
BRINDISI	BRISE	BRITTLEST	BROCADED	BRODS
BRINDISIS	BRISES	BRITTLING	BROCADES	BROEKIES
BRINDLE	BRISK	BRITTLY	BROCADING	BROEY
BRINDLED	BRISKED	BRITTS	BROCAGE	BROG
BRINDLES	BRISKEN	BRITZKA	BROCAGES	BROGAN
BRINE	BRISKENED	BRITZKAS	BROCARD	BROGANS
BRINED	BRISKENS	BRITZSKA	BROCARDS	BROGGED
BRINELESS	BRISKER	BRITZSKAS	BROCATEL	BROGGING
BRINER	BRISKEST	BRIZE	BROCATELS	BROGH
BRINERS	BRISKET	BRIZES	BROCCOLI	BROGHS
BRINES	BRISKETS	BRO	BROCCOLIS	BROGS
BRING	BRISKIER	BROACH	BROCH	BROGUE
BRINGDOWN	BRISKIEST	BROACHED	BROCHAN	BROGUEISH
BRINGER	BRISKING	BROACHER	BROCHANS	BROGUERY
BRINGERS	BRISKISH	BROACHERS	BROCHE	BROGUES
BRINGING	BRISKLY	BROACHES	BROCHED	BROGUISH
BRINGINGS	BRISKNESS	BROACHING	BROCHES	BROIDER
BRINGS	BRISKS	BROAD	BROCHETTE	BROIDERED
BRINIER	BRISKY	BROADAX	BROCHING	BROIDERER
BRINIES	BRISLING	BROADAXE	BROCHO	BROIDERS
BRINIEST	BRISLINGS	BROADAXES	BROCHOS	BROIDERY
BRININESS	BRISS	BROADBAND	BROCHS	BROIER
BRINING	BRISSES	BROADBEAN	BROCHURE	BROIEST
BRINISH	BRISTLE	BROADBILL	BROCHURES	BROIGUS
BRINJAL	BRISTLED	BROADBRIM	BROCK	BROIGUSES
BRINJALS	BRISTLES	BROADCAST	BROCKAGE	BROIL
BRINJARRY	BRISTLIER	BROADEN	BROCKAGES	BROILED
BRINK	BRISTLING	BROADENED	BROCKED	BROILER
BRINKMAN	BRISTLY	BROADENER	BROCKET	BROILERS
BRINKMEN	BRISTOL	BROADENS	BROCKETS	BROILING
BRINKS	BRISTOLS	BROADER	BROCKIT	BROILS
BRINNIES	BRISURE	BROADEST	BROCKRAM	BROKAGE
BRINNY	BRISURES	BROADISH	BROCKRAMS	BROKAGES
BRINS	BRIT	BROADLEAF	BROCKS	BROKE
BRINY	BRITANNIA	BROADLINE	BROCOLI	BROKED
BRIO	BRITCHES	BROADLOOM	BROCOLIS	BROKEN
BRIOCHE	BRITH	BROADLY	BROD	BROKENLY
BRIOCHES	BRITHS	BROADNESS	BRODDED	BROKER
BRIOLETTE	BRITS	BROADS	BRODDING	BROKERAGE
BRIONIES	BRITSCHKA	BROADSIDE	BRODDLE	BROKERED
BRIONY	BRITSKA	BROADTAIL	BRODDLED	BROKERIES
BRIOS	BRITSKAS	BROADWAY	BRODDLES	BROKERING
BRIQUET	BRITT	BROADWAYS	BRODDLING	BROKERS
BRIQUETS	BRITTANIA	BROADWISE	BRODEKIN	BROKERY
BRIQUETTE	BRITTLE	BROAST	BRODEKINS	BROKES
BRIS	BRITTLED	BROASTED	BRODKIN	BROKING

BROKINGS	BROMOS	BROODS	BROTHY	BROWSES
BROLGA	BRONC	BROODY	BROUGH	BROWSIER
BROLGAS	BRONCHI	BROOK	BROUGHAM	BROWSIEST
BROLLIES	BRONCHIA	BROOKABLE	BROUGHAMS	BROWSING
BROLLY	BRONCHIAL	BROOKED	BROUGHS	BROWSINGS
BROMAL	BRONCHIUM	BROOKIE	BROUGHT	BROWST
BROMALS	BRONCHO	BROOKIES	BROUGHTA	BROWSTS
BROMANCE	BRONCHOS	BROOKING	BROUGHTAS	BROWSY
BROMANCES	BRONCHUS	BROOKITE	BROUHAHA	BRR
BROMANTIC	BRONCO	BROOKITES	BROUHAHAS	BRRR
BROMATE	BRONCOS	BROOKLET	BROUZE	BRU
BROMATED	BRONCS	BROOKLETS	BROUZES	BRUCELLA
BROMATES	BROND	BROOKLIKE	BROW	BRUCELLAE
BROMATING	BRONDE	BROOKLIME	BROWALLIA	BRUCELLAS
BROME	BRONDER	BROOKS	BROWBAND	BRUCHID
BROMELAIN	BRONDES	BROOKWEED	BROWBANDS	BRUCHIDS
BROMELIA	BRONDEST	BROOL	BROWBEAT	BRUCIN
BROMELIAD	BRONDS	BROOLS	BROWBEATS	BRUCINE
BROMELIAS	BRONDYRON	BROOM	BROWBONE	BRUCINES
BROMELIN	BRONZE	BROOMBALL	BROWBONES	BRUCINS
BROMELINS	BRONZED	BROOMCORN	BROWED	BRUCITE
BROMEOSIN	BRONZEN	BROOMED	BROWLESS	BRUCITES
BROMES	BRONZER	BROOMIER	BROWN	BRUCKLE
BROMIC	BRONZERS	BROOMIEST	BROWNED	BRUGH
BROMID	BRONZES	BROOMING	BROWNER	BRUGHS
BROMIDE	BRONZIER	BROOMRAPE	BROWNERS	BRUH
BROMIDES	BRONZIEST	BROOMS	BROWNEST	BRUHAHA
BROMIDIC	BRONZIFY	BROOMY	BROWNFACE	BRUHAHAS
BROMIDS	BRONZING	BROOS	BROWNIE	BRUHS
BROMIN	BRONZINGS	BROOSE	BROWNIER	BRUILZIE
BROMINATE	BRONZITE	BROOSES	BROWNIES	BRUILZIES
BROMINE	BRONZITES	BROS	BROWNIEST	BRUIN
BROMINES	BRONZY	BROSE	BROWNING	BRUINS
BROMINISM	BROO	BROSES	BROWNINGS	BRUISE
BROMINS	BROOCH	BROSIER	BROWNISH	BRUISED
BROMISE	BROOCHED	BROSIEST	BROWNNESS	BRUISER
BROMISED	BROOCHES	BROSY	BROWNNOSE	BRUISERS
BROMISES	BROOCHING	BROTH	BROWNOUT	BRUISES
BROMISING	BROOD	BROTHA	BROWNOUTS	BRUISING
BROMISM	BROODED	BROTHAS	BROWNS	BRUISINGS
BROMISMS	BROODER	BROTHEL	BROWNTAIL	BRUIT
BROMIZE	BROODERS	BROTHELS	BROWNY	BRUITED
BROMIZED	BROODIER	BROTHER	BROWRIDGE	BRUITER
BROMIZES	BROODIEST	BROTHERED	BROWS	BRUITERS
BROMIZING	BROODILY	BROTHERLY	BROWSABLE	BRUITING
BROMMER	BROODING	BROTHERS	BROWSE	BRUITS
BROMMERS	BROODINGS	BROTHIER	BROWSED	BRULE
BROMO	BROODLESS	BROTHIEST	BROWSER	BRULES
BROMOFORM	BROODMARE	BROTHS	BROWSERS	BRULOT

BRULOTS	BRUSHOFFS	BRUXES	BUBONIC	BUCKISH
BRULYIE	BRUSHUP	BRUXING	BUBS	BUCKISHLY
BRULYIES	BRUSHUPS	BRUXISM	BUBU	BUCKLE
BRULZIE	BRUSHWOOD	BRUXISMS	BUBUKLE	BUCKLED
BRULZIES	BRUSHWORK	BRYOLOGY	BUBUKLES	BUCKLER
BRUMAL	BRUSHY	BRYONIES	BUBUS	BUCKLERED
BRUMBIES	BRUSK	BRYONY	BUCARDO	BUCKLERS
BRUMBY	BRUSKER	BRYOPHYTE	BUCARDOS	BUCKLES
BRUME	BRUSKEST	BRYOZOAN	BUCATINI	BUCKLING
BRUMES	BRUSQUE	BRYOZOANS	BUCCAL	BUCKLINGS
BRUMMAGEM	BRUSQUELY	BUAT	BUCCALLY	BUCKO
BRUMMER	BRUSQUER	BUATS	BUCCANEER	BUCKOES
BRUMMERS	BRUSQUEST	BUAZE	BUCCANIER	BUCKOS
BRUMOUS	BRUSSELS	BUAZES	BUCCINA	BUCKRAKE
BRUNCH	BRUSSEN	BUB	BUCCINAS	BUCKRAKES
BRUNCHED	BRUST	BUBA	BUCELLAS	BUCKRAM
BRUNCHER	BRUSTING	BUBAL	BUCENTAUR	BUCKRAMED
BRUNCHERS	BRUSTS	BUBALE	BUCHU	BUCKRAMS
BRUNCHES	BRUT	BUBALES	BUCHUS	BUCKS
BRUNCHING	BRUTAL	BUBALINE	BUCK	BUCKSAW
BRUNET	BRUTALISE	BUBALIS	BUCKAROO	BUCKSAWS
BRUNETS	BRUTALISM	BUBALISES	BUCKAROOS	BUCKSHEE
BRUNETTE	BRUTALIST	BUBALS	BUCKAYRO	BUCKSHEES
BRUNETTES	BRUTALITY	BUBAS	BUCKAYROS	BUCKSHISH
BRUNG	BRUTALIZE	BUBBA	BUCKBEAN	BUCKSHOT
BRUNIZEM	BRUTALLY	BUBBAS	BUCKBEANS	BUCKSHOTS
BRUNIZEMS	BRUTE	BUBBE	BUCKBOARD	BUCKSKIN
BRUNT	BRUTED	BUBBES	BUCKBRUSH	BUCKSKINS
BRUNTED	BRUTELIKE	BUBBIE	BUCKED	BUCKSOM
BRUNTING	BRUTELY	BUBBIES	BUCKEEN	BUCKTAIL
BRUNTS	BRUTENESS	BUBBLE	BUCKEENS	BUCKTAILS
BRUS	BRUTER	BUBBLED	BUCKER	BUCKTEETH
BRUSH	BRUTERS	BUBBLEGUM	BUCKEROO	BUCKTHORN
BRUSHABLE	BRUTES	BUBBLER	BUCKEROOS	BUCKTOOTH
BRUSHBACK	BRUTEST	BUBBLERS	BUCKERS	BUCKU
BRUSHED	BRUTIFIED	BUBBLES	BUCKET	BUCKUS
BRUSHER	BRUTIFIES	BUBBLIER	BUCKETED	BUCKWHEAT
BRUSHERS	BRUTIFY	BUBBLIES	BUCKETFUL	BUCKYBALL
BRUSHES	BRUTING	BUBBLIEST	BUCKETING	BUCKYTUBE
BRUSHFIRE	BRUTINGS	BUBBLING	BUCKETS	BUCOLIC
BRUSHIER	BRUTISH	BUBBLY	BUCKEYE	BUCOLICAL
BRUSHIEST	BRUTISHLY	BUBBY	BUCKEYES	BUCOLICS
BRUSHING	BRUTISM	BUBINGA	BUCKHORN	BUD
BRUSHINGS	BRUTISMS	BUBINGAS	BUCKHORNS	BUDA
BRUSHLAND	BRUTS	BUBKES	BUCKHOUND	BUDAS
BRUSHLESS	BRUV	BUBKIS	BUCKIE	BUDDED
BRUSHLIKE	BRUVS	BUBO	BUCKIES	BUDDER
BRUSHMARK	BRUX	BUBOED	BUCKING	BUDDERS
BRUSHOFF	BRUXED	BUBOES	BUCKINGS	BUDDHA

B

BUDDHAS	BUDWORMS	BUGGANS	BUHUNDS	BULBS
BUDDIED	BUFF	BUGGED	BUIBUI	BULBUL
BUDDIER	BUFFA	BUGGER	BUIBUIS	BULBULS
BUDDIES	BUFFABLE	BUGGERED	BUIK	BULGAR
BUDDIEST	BUFFALO	BUGGERIES	BUIKS	BULGARS
BUDDING	BUFFALOED	BUGGERING	BUILD	BULGE
BUDDINGS	BUFFALOES	BUGGERS	BUILDABLE	BULGED
BUDDLE	BUFFALOS	BUGGERY	BUILDDOWN	BULGER
BUDDLED	BUFFAS	BUGGIER	BUILDED	BULGERS
BUDDLEIA	BUFFE	BUGGIES	BUILDER	BULGES
BUDDLEIAS	BUFFED	BUGGIEST	BUILDERS	BULGHUR
BUDDLES	BUFFEL	BUGGIN	BUILDING	BULGHURS
BUDDLING	BUFFER	BUGGINESS	BUILDINGS	BULGIER
BUDDY	BUFFERED	BUGGING	BUILDOUT	BULGIEST
BUDDYING	BUFFERING	BUGGINGS	BUILDOUTS	BULGINE
BUDGE	BUFFERS	BUGGINS	BUILDS	BULGINES
BUDGED	BUFFEST	BUGGY	BUILDUP	BULGINESS
BUDGER	BUFFET	BUGHOUSE	BUILDUPS	BULGING
BUDGEREE	BUFFETED	BUGHOUSES	BUILT	BULGINGLY
BUDGERO	BUFFETER	BUGLE	BUIRDLIER	BULGOGI
BUDGEROS	BUFFETERS	BUGLED	BUIRDLY	BULGOGIS
BUDGEROW	BUFFETING	BUGLER	BUIST	BULGUR
BUDGEROWS	BUFFETS	BUGLERS	BUISTED	BULGURS
BUDGERS	BUFFI	BUGLES	BUISTING	BULGY
BUDGES	BUFFIER	BUGLET	BUISTS	BULIMIA
BUDGET	BUFFIEST	BUGLETS	BUJO	BULIMIAC
BUDGETARY	BUFFING	BUGLEWEED	BUJOS	BULIMIACS
BUDGETED	BUFFINGS	BUGLING	BUKE	BULIMIAS
BUDGETEER	BUFFO	BUGLOSS	BUKES	BULIMIC
BUDGETER	BUFFOON	BUGLOSSES	BUKKAKE	BULIMICS
BUDGETERS	BUFFOONS	BUGONG	BUKKAKES	BULIMIES
BUDGETING	BUFFOS	BUGONGS	BUKSHEE	BULIMUS
BUDGETS	BUFFS	BUGOUT	BUKSHEES	BULIMUSES
BUDGIE	BUFFY	BUGOUTS	BUKSHI	BULIMY
BUDGIES	BUFO	BUGS	BUKSHIS	BULK
BUDGING	BUFOS	BUGSEED	BULB	BULKAGE
BUDI	BUFOTALIN	BUGSEEDS	BULBAR	BULKAGES
BUDIS	BUG	BUGSHA	BULBED	BULKED
BUDLESS	BUGABOO	BUGSHAS	BULBEL	BULKER
BUDLIKE	BUGABOOS	BUGWORT	BULBELS	BULKERS
BUDMASH	BUGBANE	BUGWORTS	BULBIL	BULKHEAD
BUDMASHES	BUGBANES	BUHL	BULBILS	BULKHEADS
BUDO	BUGBEAR	BUHLS	BULBING	BULKIER
BUDOS	BUGBEARS	BUHLWORK	BULBLET	BULKIEST
BUDS	BUGEYE	BUHLWORKS	BULBLETS	BULKILY
BUDTENDER	BUGEYES	BUHR	BULBLIKE	BULKINESS
BUDWOOD	BUGGAN	BUHRS	BULBOSITY	BULKING
BUDWOODS	BUGGANE	BUHRSTONE	BULBOUS	BULKINGS
BUDWORM	BUGGANES	BUHUND	BULBOUSLY	BULKS

BULKY	BULLIES	BULLYRAG	BUMMALOS	BUNBURY
BULL	BULLIEST	BULLYRAGS	BUMMALOTI	BUNCE
BULLA	BULLING	BULNBULN	BUMMAREE	BUNCED
BULLACE	BULLINGS	BULNBULNS	BUMMAREES	BUNCES
BULLACES	BULLION	BULRUSH	BUMMED	BUNCH
BULLAE	BULLIONS	BULRUSHES	BUMMEL	BUNCHED
BULLARIES	BULLISH	BULRUSHY	BUMMELS	BUNCHER
BULLARY	BULLISHLY	BULSE	BUMMER	BUNCHERS
BULLATE	BULLNECK	BULSES	BUMMERS	BUNCHES
BULLBARS	BULLNECKS	BULWADDEE	BUMMEST	BUNCHIER
BULLBAT	BULLNOSE	BULWADDY	BUMMING	BUNCHIEST
BULLBATS	BULLNOSED	BULWARK	BUMMLE	BUNCHILY
BULLBRIER	BULLNOSES	BULWARKED	BUMMLED	BUNCHING
BULLCOOK	BULLOCK	BULWARKS	BUMMLES	BUNCHINGS
BULLCOOKS	BULLOCKED	BUM	BUMMLING	BUNCHY
BULLDOG	BULLOCKS	BUMALO	BUMMOCK	BUNCING
BULLDOGS	BULLOCKY	BUMALOTI	BUMMOCKS	BUNCO
BULLDOZE	BULLOSA	BUMALOTIS	BUMP	BUNCOED
BULLDOZED	BULLOUS	BUMBAG	BUMPED	BUNCOES
BULLDOZER	BULLPEN	BUMBAGS	BUMPER	BUNCOING
BULLDOZES	BULLPENS	BUMBAZE	BUMPERED	BUNCOMBE
BULLDUST	BULLPOUT	BUMBAZED	BUMPERING	BUNCOMBES
BULLDUSTS	BULLPOUTS	BUMBAZES	BUMPERS	BUNCOS
BULLED	BULLRING	BUMBAZING	BUMPH	BUND
BULLER	BULLRINGS	BUMBLE	BUMPHS	BUNDE
BULLERED	BULLRUSH	BUMBLEBEE	BUMPIER	BUNDED
BULLERING	BULLS	BUMBLED	BUMPIEST	BUNDH
BULLERS	BULLSEYE	BUMBLEDOM	BUMPILY	BUNDHS
BULLET	BULLSEYES	BUMBLER	BUMPINESS	BUNDIED
BULLETED	BULLSHAT	BUMBLERS	BUMPING	BUNDIES
BULLETIN	BULLSHIT	BUMBLES	BUMPINGS	BUNDING
BULLETING	BULLSHITS	BUMBLING	BUMPKIN	BUNDIST
BULLETINS	BULLSHOT	BUMBLINGS	BUMPKINLY	BUNDISTS
BULLETRIE	BULLSHOTS	BUMBO	BUMPKINS	BUNDLE
BULLETS	BULLSNAKE	BUMBOAT	BUMPOLOGY	BUNDLED
BULLEY	BULLWADDY	BUMBOATS	BUMPS	BUNDLER
BULLEYS	BULLWEED	BUMBOS	BUMPTIOUS	BUNDLERS
BULLFIGHT	BULLWEEDS	BUMELIA	BUMPY	BUNDLES
BULLFINCH	BULLWHACK	BUMELIAS	BUMS	BUNDLING
BULLFROG	BULLWHIP	BUMF	BUMSTER	BUNDLINGS
BULLFROGS	BULLWHIPS	BUMFLUFF	BUMSTERS	BUNDOBUST
BULLGINE	BULLY	BUMFLUFFS	BUMSUCKER	BUNDOOK
BULLGINES	BULLYBOY	BUMFS	BUMWAD	BUNDOOKS
BULLHEAD	BULLYBOYS	BUMFUCK	BUMWADS	BUNDS
BULLHEADS	BULLYCIDE	BUMFUCKS	BUN	BUNDT
BULLHORN	BULLYING	BUMFUZZLE	BUNA	BUNDTS
BULLHORNS	BULLYINGS	BUMKIN	BUNAS	BUNDU
BULLIED	BULLYISM	BUMKINS	BUNBURIED	BUNDUS
BULLIER	BULLYISMS	BUMMALO	BUNBURIES	BUNDWALL

BUNDWALLS	BUNKERING	BUOYAGES	BURDENS	BURGOOS
BUNDY	BUNKERS	BUOYANCE	BURDIE	BURGOUT
BUNDYING	BUNKHOUSE	BUOYANCES	BURDIES	BURGOUTS
BUNFIGHT	BUNKIE	BUOYANCY	BURDIZZO	BURGRAVE
BUNFIGHTS	BUNKIES	BUOYANT	BURDIZZOS	BURGRAVES
BUNG	BUNKING	BUOYANTLY	BURDOCK	BURGS
BUNGALOID	BUNKMATE	BUOYED	BURDOCKS	BURGUNDY
BUNGALOW	BUNKMATES	BUOYING	BURDS	BURHEL
BUNGALOWS	BUNKO	BUOYS	BUREAU	BURHELS
BUNGED	BUNKOED	BUPKES	BUREAUS	BURIAL
BUNGEE	BUNKOING	BUPKIS	BUREAUX	BURIALS
BUNGEES	BUNKOS	BUPKUS	BURET	BURIED
BUNGER	BUNKS	BUPLEVER	BURETS	BURIER
BUNGERS	BUNKUM	BUPLEVERS	BURETTE	BURIERS
BUNGEY	BUNKUMS	BUPPIE	BURETTES	BURIES
BUNGEYS	BUNN	BUPPIES	BURFI	BURIN
BUNGHOLE	BUNNET	BUPPY	BURFIS	BURINIST
BUNGHOLES	BUNNETS	BUPRESTID	BURG	BURINISTS
BUNGIE	BUNNIA	BUPROPION	BURGAGE	BURINS
BUNGIES	BUNNIAS	BUQSHA	BURGAGES	BURITI
BUNGING	BUNNIES	BUQSHAS	BURGANET	BURITIS
BUNGLE	BUNNS	BUR	BURGANETS	BURK
BUNGLED	BUNNY	BURA	BURGEE	BURKA
BUNGLER	BUNODONT	BURAN	BURGEES	BURKAS
BUNGLERS	BUNRAKU	BURANS	BURGEON	BURKE
BUNGLES	BUNRAKUS	BURAS	BURGEONED	BURKED
BUNGLING	BUNS	BURB	BURGEONS	BURKER
BUNGLINGS	BUNSEN	BURBLE	BURGER	BURKERS
BUNGS	BUNSENS	BURBLED	BURGERS	BURKES
BUNGWALL	BUNT	BURBLER	BURGESS	BURKHA
BUNGWALLS	BUNTAL	BURBLERS	BURGESSES	BURKHAS
BUNGY	BUNTALS	BURBLES	BURGH	BURKING
BUNHEAD	BUNTED	BURBLIER	BURGHAL	BURKINI
BUNHEADS	BUNTER	BURBLIEST	BURGHER	BURKINIS
BUNIA	BUNTERS	BURBLING	BURGHERS	BURKITE
BUNIAS	BUNTIER	BURBLINGS	BURGHS	BURKITES
BUNION	BUNTIEST	BURBLY	BURGHUL	BURKS
BUNIONS	BUNTING	BURBOT	BURGHULS	BURL
BUNJE	BUNTINGS	BURBOTS	BURGLAR	BURLADERO
BUNJEE	BUNTLINE	BURBS	BURGLARED	BURLAP
BUNJEES	BUNTLINES	BURD	BURGLARS	BURLAPS
BUNJES	BUNTS	BURDASH	BURGLARY	BURLED
BUNJIE	BUNTY	BURDASHES	BURGLE	BURLER
BUNJIES	BUNYA	BURDEN	BURGLED	BURLERS
BUNJY	BUNYAS	BURDENED	BURGLES	BURLESK
BUNK	BUNYIP	BURDENER	BURGLING	BURLESKS
BUNKED	BUNYIPS	BURDENERS	BURGONET	BURLESQUE
BUNKER	BUOY	BURDENING	BURGONETS	BURLETTA
BUNKERED	BUOYAGE	BURDENOUS	BURGOO	BURLETTAS

BURLEY	BURPING	BURSEED	BUSHELED	BUSHWALKS
BURLEYCUE	BURPS	BURSEEDS	BUSHELER	BUSHWAS
BURLEYED	BURQA	BURSERA	BUSHELERS	BUSHWHACK
BURLEYING	BURQAS	BURSES	BUSHELFUL	BUSHWOMAN
BURLEYS	BURQUINI	BURSICON	BUSHELING	BUSHWOMEN
BURLIER	BURQUINIS	BURSICONS	BUSHELLED	BUSHY
BURLIEST	BURR	BURSIFORM	BUSHELLER	BUSIED
BURLIKE	BURRAMYS	BURSITIS	BUSHELMAN	BUSIER
BURLILY	BURRATA	BURST	BUSHELMEN	BUSIES
BURLINESS	BURRATAS	BURSTED	BUSHELS	BUSIEST
BURLING	BURRAWANG	BURSTEN	BUSHER	BUSILY
BURLS	BURRED	BURSTER	BUSHERS	BUSINESS
BURLY	BURREL	BURSTERS	BUSHES	BUSINESSY
BURN	BURRELL	BURSTIER	BUSHFIRE	BUSING
BURNABLE	BURRELLS	BURSTIEST	BUSHFIRES	BUSINGS
BURNABLES	BURRELS	BURSTING	BUSHFLIES	BUSK
BURNED	BURRER	BURSTONE	BUSHFLY	BUSKED
BURNER	BURRERS	BURSTONES	BUSHGOAT	BUSKER
BURNERS	BURRFISH	BURSTS	BUSHGOATS	BUSKERS
BURNET	BURRHEL	BURSTY	BUSHIDO	BUSKET
BURNETS	BURRHELS	BURTHEN	BUSHIDOS	BUSKETS
BURNIE	BURRIER	BURTHENED	BUSHIE	BUSKIN
BURNIES	BURRIEST	BURTHENS	BUSHIER	BUSKINED
BURNING	BURRING	BURTON	BUSHIES	BUSKING
BURNINGLY	BURRITO	BURTONS	BUSHIEST	BUSKINGS
BURNINGS	BURRITOS	BURWEED	BUSHILY	BUSKINS
BURNISH	BURRO	BURWEEDS	BUSHINESS	BUSKS
BURNISHED	BURROS	BURY	BUSHING	BUSKY
BURNISHER	BURROW	BURYING	BUSHINGS	BUSLOAD
BURNISHES	BURROWED	BUS	BUSHLAND	BUSLOADS
BURNOOSE	BURROWER	BUSBAR	BUSHLANDS	BUSMAN
BURNOOSED	BURROWERS	BUSBARS	BUSHLESS	BUSMEN
BURNOOSES	BURROWING	BUSBIES	BUSHLIKE	BUSS
BURNOUS	BURROWS	BUSBOY	BUSHLOT	BUSSED
BURNOUSE	BURRS	BUSBOYS	BUSHLOTS	BUSSES
BURNOUSED	BURRSTONE	BUSBY	BUSHMAN	BUSSING
BURNOUSES	BURRY	BUSED	BUSHMEAT	BUSSINGS
BURNOUT	BURS	BUSERA	BUSHMEATS	BUSSU
BURNOUTS	BURSA	BUSERAS	BUSHMEN	BUSSUS
BURNS	BURSAE	BUSES	BUSHPIG	BUST
BURNSIDE	BURSAL	BUSGIRL	BUSHPIGS	BUSTARD
BURNSIDES	BURSAR	BUSGIRLS	BUSHTIT	BUSTARDS
BURNT	BURSARIAL	BUSH	BUSHTITS	BUSTED
BUROO	BURSARIES	BUSHBABY	BUSHVELD	BUSTEE
BUROOS	BURSARS	BUSHBUCK	BUSHVELDS	BUSTEES
BURP	BURSARY	BUSHBUCKS	BUSHWA	BUSTER
BURPED	BURSAS	BUSHCRAFT	BUSHWAH	BUSTERS
BURPEE	BURSATE	BUSHED	BUSHWAHS	BUSTI
BURPEES	BURSE	BUSHEL	BUSHWALK	BUSTIC

BUSTICATE	BUTCHNESS	BUTTINSKI	BUY	BYCATCH
BUSTICS	BUTE	BUTTINSKY	BUYABLE	BYCATCHES
BUSTIER	BUTENE	BUTTLE	BUYABLES	BYCOKET
BUSTIERS	BUTENES	BUTTLED	BUYBACK	BYCOKETS
BUSTIEST	BUTEO	BUTTLES	BUYBACKS	BYDE
BUSTINESS	BUTEONINE	BUTTLING	BUYER	BYDED
BUSTING	BUTEOS	BUTTOCK	BUYERS	BYDES
BUSTINGS	BUTES	BUTTOCKED	BUYING	BYDING
BUSTIS	BUTLE	BUTTOCKS	BUYINGS	BYE
BUSTLE	BUTLED	BUTTON	BUYOFF	BYELAW
BUSTLED	BUTLER	BUTTONED	BUYOFFS	BYELAWS
BUSTLER	BUTLERAGE	BUTTONER	BUYOUT	BYES
BUSTLERS	BUTLERED	BUTTONERS	BUYOUTS	BYGONE
BUSTLES	BUTLERIES	BUTTONIER	BUYS	BYGONES
BUSTLINE	BUTLERING	BUTTONING	BUZKASHI	BYKE
BUSTLINES	BUTLERS	BUTTONS	BUZKASHIS	BYKED
BUSTLING	BUTLERY	BUTTONY	BUZUKI	BYKES
BUSTS	BUTLES	BUTTRESS	BUZUKIA	BYKING
BUSTY	BUTLING	BUTTS	BUZUKIS	BYLANDER
BUSULFAN	BUTMENT	BUTTSTOCK	BUZZ	BYLANDERS
BUSULFANS	BUTMENTS	BUTTY	BUZZARD	BYLANE
BUSUUTI	BUTOH	BUTTYMAN	BUZZARDS	BYLANES
BUSUUTIS	BUTOHS	BUTTYMEN	BUZZBAIT	BYLAW
BUSY	BUTS	BUTUT	BUZZBAITS	BYLAWS
BUSYBODY	BUTSUDAN	BUTUTS	BUZZCUT	BYLINE
BUSYING	BUTSUDANS	BUTYL	BUZZCUTS	BYLINED
BUSYNESS	BUTT	BUTYLATE	BUZZED	BYLINER
BUSYWORK	BUTTALS	BUTYLATED	BUZZER	BYLINERS
BUSYWORKS	BUTTE	BUTYLATES	BUZZERS	BYLINES
BUT	BUTTED	BUTYLENE	BUZZES	BYLINING
BUTADIENE	BUTTER	BUTYLENES	BUZZIER	BYLIVE
BUTANE	BUTTERBUR	BUTYLS	BUZZIEST	BYNAME
BUTANES	BUTTERCUP	BUTYRAL	BUZZING	BYNAMES
BUTANOIC	BUTTERED	BUTYRALS	BUZZINGLY	BYNEMPT
BUTANOL	BUTTERFAT	BUTYRATE	BUZZINGS	BYPASS
BUTANOLS	BUTTERFLY	BUTYRATES	BUZZKILL	BYPASSED
BUTANONE	BUTTERIER	BUTYRIC	BUZZKILLS	BYPASSES
BUTANONES	BUTTERIES	BUTYRIN	BUZZSAW	BYPASSING
BUTCH	BUTTERINE	BUTYRINS	BUZZSAWS	BYPAST
BUTCHER	BUTTERING	BUTYROUS	BUZZWIG	BYPATH
BUTCHERED	BUTTERNUT	BUTYRYL	BUZZWIGS	BYPATHS
BUTCHERER	BUTTERS	BUTYRYLS	BUZZWORD	BYPLACE
BUTCHERLY	BUTTERY	BUVETTE	BUZZWORDS	BYPLACES
BUTCHERS	BUTTES	BUVETTES	BUZZY	BYPLAY
BUTCHERY	BUTTHEAD	BUXOM	BWANA	BYPLAYS
BUTCHES	BUTTHEADS	BUXOMER	BWANAS	BYPRODUCT
BUTCHEST	BUTTHURT	BUXOMEST	BWAZI	BYRE
BUTCHING	BUTTIES	BUXOMLY	BWAZIS	BYREMAN
BUTCHINGS	BUTTING	BUXOMNESS	BY	BYREMEN

B

BYRES	BYRLING	BYSSAL	BYTALK	BYWONER
BYREWOMAN	BYRLS	BYSSI	BYTALKS	BYWONERS
BYREWOMEN	BYRNIE	BYSSINE	BYTE	BYWORD
BYRL	BYRNIES	BYSSOID	BYTECODE	BYWORDS
BYRLADY	BYROAD	BYSSUS	BYTECODES	BYWORK
BYRLAKIN	BYROADS	BYSSUSES	BYTES	BYWORKS
BYRLAW	BYROOM	BYSTANDER	BYTOWNITE	BYZANT
BYRLAWS	BYROOMS	BYSTREET	BYWAY	BYZANTINE
BYRLED	BYS	BYSTREETS	BYWAYS	BYZANTS

C

CAA	CABBIE	CABOBS	CACAFUEGO	CACKIEST
CAAED	CABBIES	CABOC	CACAO	CACKING
CAAING	CABBING	CABOCEER	CACAOS	CACKLE
CAAS	CABBY	CABOCEERS	CACAS	CACKLED
CAATINGA	CABDRIVER	CABOCHED	CACHACA	CACKLER
CAATINGAS	CABER	CABOCHON	CACHACAS	CACKLERS
CAB	CABERNET	CABOCHONS	CACHAEMIA	CACKLES
CABA	CABERNETS	CABOCS	CACHAEMIC	CACKLING
CABAL	CABERS	CABOMBA	CACHALOT	CACKS
CABALA	CABESTRO	CABOMBAS	CACHALOTS	CACKY
CABALAS	CABESTROS	CABOODLE	CACHE	CACODEMON
CABALETTA	CABEZON	CABOODLES	CACHECTIC	CACODOXY
CABALETTE	CABEZONE	CABOOSE	CACHED	CACODYL
CABALISM	CABEZONES	CABOOSES	CACHEMIA	CACODYLIC
CABALISMS	CABEZONS	CABOSHED	CACHEMIAS	CACODYLS
CABALIST	CABILDO	CABOTAGE	CACHEMIC	CACOEPIES
CABALISTS	CABILDOS	CABOTAGES	CACHEPOT	CACOEPY
CABALLED	CABIN	CABOVER	CACHEPOTS	CACOETHES
CABALLER	CABINED	CABOVERS	CACHES	CACOETHIC
CABALLERO	CABINET	CABRE	CACHET	CACOGENIC
CABALLERS	CABINETRY	CABRESTA	CACHETED	CACOLET
CABALLINE	CABINETS	CABRESTAS	CACHETING	CACOLETS
CABALLING	CABINING	CABRESTO	CACHETS	CACOLOGY
CABALS	CABINMATE	CABRESTOS	CACHEXIA	CACOMIXL
CABANA	CABINS	CABRETTA	CACHEXIAS	CACOMIXLE
CABANAS	CABLE	CABRETTAS	CACHEXIC	CACOMIXLS
CABARET	CABLECAST	CABRIE	CACHEXIES	CACONYM
CABARETS	CABLED	CABRIES	CACHEXY	CACONYMS
CABAS	CABLEGRAM	CABRILLA	CACHING	CACONYMY
CABBAGE	CABLER	CABRILLAS	CACHOLONG	CACOON
CABBAGED	CABLERS	CABRIO	CACHOLOT	CACOONS
CABBAGES	CABLES	CABRIOLE	CACHOLOTS	CACOPHONY
CABBAGEY	CABLET	CABRIOLES	CACHOU	CACOTOPIA
CABBAGIER	CABLETS	CABRIOLET	CACHOUS	CACTI
CABBAGING	CABLEWAY	CABRIOS	CACHUCHA	CACTIFORM
CABBAGY	CABLEWAYS	CABRIT	CACHUCHAS	CACTOID
CABBALA	CABLING	CABRITS	CACHUMBER	CACTUS
CABBALAH	CABLINGS	CABS	CACIQUE	CACTUSES
CABBALAHS	CABMAN	CABSTAND	CACIQUES	CACUMEN
CABBALAS	CABMEN	CABSTANDS	CACIQUISM	CACUMENS
CABBALISM	CABOB	CACA	CACK	CACUMINA
CABBALIST	CABOBBED	CACAFOGO	CACKED	CACUMINAL
CABBED	CABOBBING	CACAFOGOS	CACKIER	CAD

C

CADAGA	CADGED	CAESURAE	CAGINESS	CAISSON
CADAGAS	CADGER	CAESURAL	CAGING	CAISSONS
CADAGI	CADGERS	CAESURAS	CAGMAG	CAITIFF
CADAGIS	CADGES	CAESURIC	CAGMAGGED	CAITIFFS
CADASTER	CADGIER	CAF	CAGMAGS	CAITIVE
CADASTERS	CADGIEST	CAFARD	CAGOT	CAITIVES
CADASTRAL	CADGING	CAFARDS	CAGOTS	CAJAPUT
CADASTRE	CADGY	CAFE	CAGOUL	CAJAPUTS
CADASTRES	CADI	CAFES	CAGOULE	CAJEPUT
CADAVER	CADIE	CAFETERIA	CAGOULES	CAJEPUTS
CADAVERIC	CADIES	CAFETIERE	CAGOULS	CAJOLE
CADAVERS	CADIS	CAFETORIA	CAGS	CAJOLED
CADDICE	CADMIC	CAFF	CAGY	CAJOLER
CADDICES	CADMIUM	CAFFEIN	CAGYNESS	CAJOLERS
CADDIE	CADMIUMS	CAFFEINE	CAHIER	CAJOLERY
CADDIED	CADRANS	CAFFEINES	CAHIERS	CAJOLES
CADDIES	CADRANSES	CAFFEINIC	CAHOOT	CAJOLING
CADDIS	CADRE	CAFFEINS	CAHOOTS	CAJON
CADDISED	CADRES	CAFFEISM	CAHOUN	CAJONES
CADDISES	CADS	CAFFEISMS	CAHOUNS	CAJUN
CADDISFLY	CADUAC	CAFFILA	CAHOW	CAJUPUT
CADDISH	CADUACS	CAFFILAS	CAHOWS	CAJUPUTS
CADDISHLY	CADUCEAN	CAFFS	CAID	CAKE
CADDY	CADUCEI	CAFILA	CAIDS	CAKEAGE
CADDYING	CADUCEUS	CAFILAS	CAILLACH	CAKEAGES
CADDYSS	CADUCITY	CAFS	CAILLACHS	CAKEBOX
CADDYSSES	CADUCOUS	CAFTAN	CAILLE	CAKEBOXES
CADE	CAECA	CAFTANED	CAILLEACH	CAKED
CADEAU	CAECAL	CAFTANS	CAILLES	CAKEHOLE
CADEAUX	CAECALLY	CAG	CAILLIACH	CAKEHOLES
CADEE	CAECILIAN	CAGANER	CAIMAC	CAKES
CADEES	CAECITIS	CAGANERS	CAIMACAM	CAKEWALK
CADELLE	CAECUM	CAGE	CAIMACAMS	CAKEWALKS
CADELLES	CAEOMA	CAGED	CAIMACS	CAKEY
CADENCE	CAEOMAS	CAGEFUL	CAIMAN	CAKIER
CADENCED	CAERULE	CAGEFULS	CAIMANS	CAKIEST
CADENCES	CAERULEAN	CAGELIKE	CAIN	CAKINESS
CADENCIES	CAESAR	CAGELING	CAINS	CAKING
CADENCING	CAESAREAN	CAGELINGS	CAIQUE	CAKINGS
CADENCY	CAESARIAN	CAGER	CAIQUES	CAKY
CADENT	CAESARISM	CAGERS	CAIRD	CAL
CADENTIAL	CAESARS	CAGES	CAIRDS	CALABASH
CADENZA	CAESE	CAGEWORK	CAIRN	CALABAZA
CADENZAS	CAESIOUS	CAGEWORKS	CAIRNED	CALABAZAS
CADES	CAESIUM	CAGEY	CAIRNGORM	CALABOGUS
CADET	CAESIUMS	CAGEYNESS	CAIRNIER	CALABOOSE
CADETS	CAESTUS	CAGIER	CAIRNIEST	CALABRESE
CADETSHIP	CAESTUSES	CAGIEST	CAIRNS	CALADIUM
CADGE	CAESURA	CAGILY	CAIRNY	CALADIUMS

CALALOO	CALCEATES	CALENDAL	CALIFS	CALLBOARD
CALALOOS	CALCED	CALENDAR	CALIGO	CALLBOY
CALALU	CALCEDONY	CALENDARS	CALIGOES	CALLBOYS
CALALUS	CALCES	CALENDER	CALIGOS	CALLED
CALAMANCO	CALCIC	CALENDERS	CALIMA	CALLEE
CALAMANSI	CALCICOLE	CALENDRER	CALIMAS	CALLEES
CALAMAR	CALCIFIC	CALENDRIC	CALIMOCHO	CALLER
CALAMARI	CALCIFIED	CALENDRY	CALIOLOGY	CALLERS
CALAMARIS	CALCIFIES	CALENDS	CALIPASH	CALLET
CALAMARS	CALCIFUGE	CALENDULA	CALIPEE	CALLETS
CALAMARY	CALCIFY	CALENTURE	CALIPEES	CALLID
CALAMATA	CALCIMINE	CALESA	CALIPER	CALLIDITY
CALAMATAS	CALCINE	CALESAS	CALIPERED	CALLIGRAM
CALAMI	CALCINED	CALESCENT	CALIPERS	CALLING
CALAMINE	CALCINES	CALF	CALIPH	CALLINGS
CALAMINED	CALCINING	CALFDOZER	CALIPHAL	CALLIOPE
CALAMINES	CALCITE	CALFHOOD	CALIPHATE	CALLIOPES
CALAMINT	CALCITES	CALFHOODS	CALIPHS	CALLIPASH
CALAMINTS	CALCITIC	CALFLESS	CALISAYA	CALLIPEE
CALAMITE	CALCIUM	CALFLICK	CALISAYAS	CALLIPEES
CALAMITES	CALCIUMS	CALFLICKS	CALIVER	CALLIPER
CALAMITY	CALCRETE	CALFLIKE	CALIVERS	CALLIPERS
CALAMUS	CALCRETES	CALFS	CALIX	CALLOP
CALAMUSES	CALCSPAR	CALFSKIN	CALIXES	CALLOPS
CALANDO	CALCSPARS	CALFSKINS	CALK	CALLOSE
CALANDRIA	CALCTUFA	CALIATOUR	CALKED	CALLOSES
CALANTHE	CALCTUFAS	CALIBER	CALKER	CALLOSITY
CALANTHES	CALCTUFF	CALIBERED	CALKERS	CALLOUS
CALASH	CALCTUFFS	CALIBERS	CALKIN	CALLOUSED
CALASHES	CALCULAR	CALIBRATE	CALKING	CALLOUSES
CALATHEA	CALCULARY	CALIBRE	CALKINGS	CALLOUSLY
CALATHEAS	CALCULATE	CALIBRED	CALKINS	CALLOUT
CALATHI	CALCULI	CALIBRES	CALKS	CALLOUTS
CALATHOS	CALCULOSE	CALICES	CALL	CALLOW
CALATHUS	CALCULOUS	CALICHE	CALLA	CALLOWER
CALAVANCE	CALCULUS	CALICHES	CALLABLE	CALLOWEST
CALCANEA	CALDARIA	CALICLE	CALLAIDES	CALLOWLY
CALCANEAL	CALDARIUM	CALICLES	CALLAIS	CALLOWS
CALCANEAN	CALDERA	CALICO	CALLALOO	CALLS
CALCANEI	CALDERAS	CALICOES	CALLALOOS	CALLTIME
CALCANEUM	CALDRON	CALICOS	CALLALOU	CALLTIMES
CALCANEUS	CALDRONS	CALICULAR	CALLALOUS	CALLUNA
CALCAR	CALECHE	CALID	CALLAN	CALLUNAS
CALCARATE	CALECHES	CALIDITY	CALLANS	CALLUS
CALCARIA	CALEFIED	CALIF	CALLANT	CALLUSED
CALCARINE	CALEFIES	CALIFATE	CALLANTS	CALLUSES
CALCARS	CALEFY	CALIFATES	CALLAS	CALLUSING
CALCEATE	CALEFYING	CALIFONT	CALLBACK	CALM
CALCEATED	CALEMBOUR	CALIFONTS	CALLBACKS	CALMANT

C

CALMANTS	CALPS	CALYCLED	CAMBIST	CAMERAE
CALMATIVE	CALQUE	CALYCLES	CAMBISTRY	CAMERAL
CALMED	CALQUED	CALYCOID	CAMBISTS	CAMERAMAN
CALMER	CALQUES	CALYCULAR	CAMBIUM	CAMERAMEN
CALMEST	CALQUING	CALYCULE	CAMBIUMS	CAMERAS
CALMIER	CALS	CALYCULES	CAMBOGE	CAMERATED
CALMIEST	CALTHA	CALYCULI	CAMBOGES	CAMES
CALMING	CALTHAS	CALYCULUS	CAMBOGIA	CAMESE
CALMINGLY	CALTHROP	CALYPSO	CAMBOGIAS	CAMESES
CALMINGS	CALTHROPS	CALYPSOES	CAMBOOSE	CAMGIRL
CALMLY	CALTRAP	CALYPSOS	CAMBOOSES	CAMGIRLS
CALMNESS	CALTRAPS	CALYPTER	CAMBREL	CAMI
CALMS	CALTROP	CALYPTERA	CAMBRELS	CAMION
CALMSTANE	CALTROPS	CALYPTERS	CAMBRIC	CAMIONS
CALMSTONE	CALUMBA	CALYPTRA	CAMBRICS	CAMIS
CALMY	CALUMBAS	CALYPTRAS	CAMCORD	CAMISA
CALO	CALUMET	CALYX	CAMCORDED	CAMISADE
CALOMEL	CALUMETS	CALYXES	CAMCORDER	CAMISADES
CALOMELS	CALUMNIED	CALZONE	CAMCORDS	CAMISADO
CALORIC	CALUMNIES	CALZONES	CAME	CAMISADOS
CALORICS	CALUMNY	CALZONI	CAMEL	CAMISAS
CALORIE	CALUTRON	CAM	CAMELBACK	CAMISE
CALORIES	CALUTRONS	CAMA	CAMELEER	CAMISES
CALORIFIC	CALVADOS	CAMAIEU	CAMELEERS	CAMISIA
CALORISE	CALVARIA	CAMAIEUX	CAMELEON	CAMISIAS
CALORISED	CALVARIAE	CAMAIL	CAMELEONS	CAMISOLE
CALORISES	CALVARIAL	CAMAILED	CAMELHAIR	CAMISOLES
CALORIST	CALVARIAN	CAMAILS	CAMELIA	CAMLET
CALORISTS	CALVARIAS	CAMAN	CAMELIAS	CAMLETS
CALORIZE	CALVARIES	CAMANACHD	CAMELID	CAMMED
CALORIZED	CALVARIUM	CAMANS	CAMELIDS	CAMMER
CALORIZES	CALVARY	CAMARILLA	CAMELINE	CAMMERS
CALORY	CALVE	CAMARON	CAMELINES	CAMMIE
CALOS	CALVED	CAMARONS	CAMELISH	CAMMIES
CALOTTE	CALVER	CAMAS	CAMELLIA	CAMMING
CALOTTES	CALVERED	CAMASES	CAMELLIAS	CAMO
CALOTYPE	CALVERING	CAMASH	CAMELLIKE	CAMOGIE
CALOTYPES	CALVERS	CAMASHES	CAMELOID	CAMOGIES
CALOYER	CALVES	CAMASS	CAMELOIDS	CAMOMILE
CALOYERS	CALVING	CAMASSES	CAMELOT	CAMOMILES
CALP	CALVITIES	CAMBER	CAMELOTS	CAMOODI
CALPA	CALX	CAMBERED	CAMELRIES	CAMOODIS
CALPAC	CALXES	CAMBERING	CAMELRY	CAMORRA
CALPACK	CALYCATE	CAMBERS	CAMELS	CAMORRAS
CALPACKS	CALYCEAL	CAMBIA	CAMEO	CAMORRIST
CALPACS	CALYCES	CAMBIAL	CAMEOED	CAMOS
CALPAIN	CALYCINAL	CAMBIFORM	CAMEOING	CAMOTE
CALPAINS	CALYCINE	CAMBISM	CAMEOS	CAMOTES
CALPAS	CALYCLE	CAMBISMS	CAMERA	CAMOUFLET

CAMP	CAMPLE	CANAILLES	CANCEROUS	CANEFRUIT
CAMPAGNA	CAMPLED	CANAKIN	CANCERS	CANEGRUB
CAMPAGNAS	CAMPLES	CANAKINS	CANCHA	CANEGRUBS
CAMPAGNE	CAMPLING	CANAL	CANCHAS	CANEH
CAMPAIGN	CAMPLY	CANALBOAT	CANCRINE	CANEHS
CAMPAIGNS	CAMPNESS	CANALED	CANCROID	CANELLA
CAMPANA	CAMPO	CANALING	CANCROIDS	CANELLAS
CAMPANAS	CAMPODEID	CANALISE	CANDELA	CANELLINI
CAMPANERO	CAMPONG	CANALISED	CANDELAS	CANEPHOR
CAMPANILE	CAMPONGS	CANALISES	CANDENT	CANEPHORA
CAMPANILI	CAMPOREE	CANALIZE	CANDID	CANEPHORE
CAMPANIST	CAMPOREES	CANALIZED	CANDIDA	CANEPHORS
CAMPANULA	CAMPOS	CANALIZES	CANDIDACY	CANER
CAMPCRAFT	CAMPOUT	CANALLED	CANDIDAL	CANERS
CAMPEACHY	CAMPOUTS	CANALLER	CANDIDAS	CANES
CAMPEADOR	CAMPS	CANALLERS	CANDIDATE	CANESCENT
CAMPED	CAMPSHIRT	CANALLING	CANDIDER	CANEWARE
CAMPER	CAMPSITE	CANALS	CANDIDEST	CANEWARES
CAMPERIES	CAMPSITES	CANAPE	CANDIDLY	CANFIELD
CAMPERS	CAMPSTOOL	CANAPES	CANDIDS	CANFIELDS
CAMPERY	CAMPUS	CANARD	CANDIE	CANFUL
CAMPESINO	CAMPUSED	CANARDS	CANDIED	CANFULS
CAMPEST	CAMPUSES	CANARIED	CANDIES	CANG
CAMPFIRE	CAMPUSING	CANARIES	CANDIRU	CANGLE
CAMPFIRES	CAMPY	CANARY	CANDIRUS	CANGLED
CAMPHANE	CAMS	CANARYING	CANDLE	CANGLES
CAMPHANES	CAMSHAFT	CANASTA	CANDLED	CANGLING
CAMPHENE	CAMSHAFTS	CANASTAS	CANDLELIT	CANGS
CAMPHENES	CAMSHO	CANASTER	CANDLENUT	CANGUE
CAMPHINE	CAMSHOCH	CANASTERS	CANDLEPIN	CANGUES
CAMPHINES	CAMSTAIRY	CANBANK	CANDLER	CANICULAR
CAMPHIRE	CAMSTANE	CANBANKS	CANDLERS	CANID
CAMPHIRES	CAMSTANES	CANCAN	CANDLES	CANIDS
CAMPHOL	CAMSTEARY	CANCANS	CANDLING	CANIER
CAMPHOLS	CAMSTONE	CANCEL	CANDOCK	CANIEST
CAMPHONE	CAMSTONES	CANCELBOT	CANDOCKS	CANIKIN
CAMPHONES	CAMUS	CANCELED	CANDOR	CANIKINS
CAMPHOR	CAMUSES	CANCELEER	CANDORS	CANINE
CAMPHORIC	CAMWHORE	CANCELER	CANDOUR	CANINES
CAMPHORS	CAMWHORED	CANCELERS	CANDOURS	CANING
CAMPI	CAMWHORES	CANCELIER	CANDY	CANINGS
CAMPIER	CAMWOOD	CANCELING	CANDYGRAM	CANINITY
CAMPIEST	CAMWOODS	CANCELLED	CANDYING	CANISTEL
CAMPILY	CAN	CANCELLER	CANDYMAN	CANISTELS
CAMPINESS	CANADA	CANCELLI	CANDYMEN	CANISTER
CAMPING	CANADAS	CANCELS	CANDYTUFT	CANISTERS
CAMPINGS	CANAIGRE	CANCER	CANE	CANITIES
CAMPION	CANAIGRES	CANCERATE	CANEBRAKE	CANKER
CAMPIONS	CANAILLE	CANCERED	CANED	CANKERED

CANKERIER	CANNONS	CANOPYING	CANTICOS	CANTY
CANKERING	CANNOT	CANOROUS	CANTICOY	CANULA
CANKEROUS	CANNS	CANS	CANTICOYS	CANULAE
CANKERS	CANNULA	CANSFUL	CANTICUM	CANULAR
CANKERY	CANNULAE	CANSO	CANTICUMS	CANULAS
CANKLE	CANNULAR	CANSOS	CANTIER	CANULATE
CANKLES	CANNULAS	CANST	CANTIEST	CANULATED
CANN	CANNULATE	CANSTICK	CANTILENA	CANULATES
CANNA	CANNY	CANSTICKS	CANTILY	CANVAS
CANNABIC	CANOE	CANT	CANTINA	CANVASED
CANNABIN	CANOEABLE	CANTABANK	CANTINAS	CANVASER
CANNABINS	CANOED	CANTABILE	CANTINESS	CANVASERS
CANNABIS	CANOEING	CANTAL	CANTING	CANVASES
CANNACH	CANOEINGS	CANTALA	CANTINGLY	CANVASING
CANNACHS	CANOEIST	CANTALAS	CANTINGS	CANVASS
CANNAE	CANOEISTS	CANTALOUP	CANTION	CANVASSED
CANNAS	CANOEMAN	CANTALS	CANTIONS	CANVASSER
CANNED	CANOEMEN	CANTAR	CANTLE	CANVASSES
CANNEL	CANOER	CANTARS	CANTLED	CANY
CANNELON	CANOERS	CANTATA	CANTLES	CANYON
CANNELONI	CANOES	CANTATAS	CANTLET	CANYONEER
CANNELONS	CANOEWOOD	CANTATE	CANTLETS	CANYONING
CANNELS	CANOLA	CANTATES	CANTLING	CANYONS
CANNELURE	CANOLAS	CANTDOG	CANTO	CANZONA
CANNER	CANON	CANTDOGS	CANTON	CANZONAS
CANNERIES	CANONESS	CANTED	CANTONAL	CANZONE
CANNERS	CANONIC	CANTEEN	CANTONED	CANZONES
CANNERY	CANONICAL	CANTEENS	CANTONING	CANZONET
CANNIBAL	CANONISE	CANTER	CANTONISE	CANZONETS
CANNIBALS	CANONISED	CANTERED	CANTONIZE	CANZONI
CANNIE	CANONISER	CANTERING	CANTONS	CAP
CANNIER	CANONISES	CANTERS	CANTOR	CAPA
CANNIEST	CANONIST	CANTEST	CANTORIAL	CAPABLE
CANNIKIN	CANONISTS	CANTHAL	CANTORIS	CAPABLER
CANNIKINS	CANONIZE	CANTHARI	CANTORS	CAPABLEST
CANNILY	CANONIZED	CANTHARID	CANTOS	CAPABLY
CANNINESS	CANONIZER	CANTHARIS	CANTRAIP	CAPACIOUS
CANNING	CANONIZES	CANTHARUS	CANTRAIPS	CAPACITOR
CANNINGS	CANONRIES	CANTHI	CANTRAP	CAPACITY
CANNISTER	CANONRY	CANTHIC	CANTRAPS	CAPARISON
CANNOLI	CANONS	CANTHITIS	CANTRED	CAPAS
CANNOLIS	CANOODLE	CANTHOOK	CANTREDS	CAPCOM
CANNON	CANOODLED	CANTHOOKS	CANTREF	CAPCOMS
CANNONADE	CANOODLER	CANTHUS	CANTREFS	CAPE
CANNONED	CANOODLES	CANTIC	CANTRIP	CAPED
CANNONEER	CANOPIC	CANTICLE	CANTRIPS	CAPEESH
CANNONIER	CANOPIED	CANTICLES	CANTS	CAPELAN
CANNONING	CANOPIES	CANTICO	CANTUS	CAPELANS
CANNONRY	CANOPY	CANTICOED	CANTUSES	CAPELET

CAPELETS	CAPITAYN	CAPPED	CAPSIZED	CAPUCHE
CAPELIKE	CAPITAYNS	CAPPER	CAPSIZES	CAPUCHED
CAPELIN	CAPITELLA	CAPPERS	CAPSIZING	CAPUCHES
CAPELINE	CAPITOL	CAPPING	CAPSOMER	CAPUCHIN
CAPELINES	CAPITOLS	CAPPINGS	CAPSOMERE	CAPUCHINS
CAPELINS	CAPITULA	CAPRATE	CAPSOMERS	CAPUERA
CAPELLET	CAPITULAR	CAPRATES	CAPSTAN	CAPUERAS
CAPELLETS	CAPITULUM	CAPRESE	CAPSTANS	CAPUL
CAPELLINE	CAPIZ	CAPRESES	CAPSTONE	CAPULS
CAPELLINI	CAPIZES	CAPRI	CAPSTONES	CAPUT
CAPER	CAPLE	CAPRIC	CAPSULAR	CAPYBARA
CAPERED	CAPLES	CAPRICCI	CAPSULARY	CAPYBARAS
CAPERER	CAPLESS	CAPRICCIO	CAPSULATE	CAR
CAPERERS	CAPLET	CAPRICE	CAPSULE	CARABAO
CAPERING	CAPLETS	CAPRICES	CAPSULED	CARABAOS
CAPERS	CAPLIKE	CAPRID	CAPSULES	CARABID
CAPES	CAPLIN	CAPRIDS	CAPSULING	CARABIDS
CAPESKIN	CAPLINS	CAPRIFIED	CAPSULISE	CARABIN
CAPESKINS	CAPMAKER	CAPRIFIES	CAPSULIZE	CARABINE
CAPEWORK	CAPMAKERS	CAPRIFIG	CAPTAIN	CARABINER
CAPEWORKS	CAPO	CAPRIFIGS	CAPTAINCY	CARABINES
CAPEX	CAPOCCHIA	CAPRIFOIL	CAPTAINED	CARABINS
CAPEXES	CAPOEIRA	CAPRIFOLE	CAPTAINRY	CARACAL
CAPFUL	CAPOEIRAS	CAPRIFORM	CAPTAINS	CARACALS
CAPFULS	CAPON	CAPRIFY	CAPTAN	CARACARA
CAPH	CAPONATA	CAPRINE	CAPTANS	CARACARAS
CAPHS	CAPONATAS	CAPRIOLE	CAPTCHA	CARACK
CAPI	CAPONIER	CAPRIOLED	CAPTCHAS	CARACKS
CAPIAS	CAPONIERE	CAPRIOLES	CAPTION	CARACOL
CAPIASES	CAPONIERS	CAPRIS	CAPTIONED	CARACOLE
CAPICHE	CAPONISE	CAPROATE	CAPTIONS	CARACOLED
CAPICOLLA	CAPONISED	CAPROATES	CAPTIOUS	CARACOLER
CAPICOLLO	CAPONISES	CAPROCK	CAPTIVATE	CARACOLES
CAPILLARY	CAPONIZE	CAPROCKS	CAPTIVE	CARACOLS
CAPING	CAPONIZED	CAPROIC	CAPTIVED	CARACT
CAPISCE	CAPONIZES	CAPRYLATE	CAPTIVES	CARACTS
CAPISH	CAPONS	CAPRYLIC	CAPTIVING	CARACUL
CAPITA	CAPORAL	CAPS	CAPTIVITY	CARACULS
CAPITAL	CAPORALS	CAPSAICIN	CAPTOPRIL	CARAFE
CAPITALLY	CAPOS	CAPSICIN	CAPTOR	CARAFES
CAPITALS	CAPOT	CAPSICINS	CAPTORS	CARAGANA
CAPITAN	CAPOTASTO	CAPSICUM	CAPTURE	CARAGANAS
CAPITANI	CAPOTE	CAPSICUMS	CAPTURED	CARAGEEN
CAPITANO	CAPOTES	CAPSID	CAPTURER	CARAGEENS
CAPITANOS	CAPOTS	CAPSIDAL	CAPTURERS	CARAMBA
CAPITANS	CAPOTTED	CAPSIDS	CAPTURES	CARAMBOLA
CAPITATE	CAPOTTING	CAPSIZAL	CAPTURING	CARAMBOLE
CAPITATED	CAPOUCH	CAPSIZALS	CAPUCCIO	CARAMEL
CAPITATES	CAPOUCHES	CAPSIZE	CAPUCCIOS	CARAMELLY

C

CARAMELS	CARBENES	CARCAKES	CARDINGS	CARESSED
CARANGID	CARBIDE	CARCANET	CARDIO	CARESSER
CARANGIDS	CARBIDES	CARCANETS	CARDIOID	CARESSERS
CARANGOID	CARBIDOPA	CARCASE	CARDIOIDS	CARESSES
CARANNA	CARBIES	CARCASED	CARDIOS	CARESSING
CARANNAS	CARBINE	CARCASES	CARDIS	CARESSIVE
CARAP	CARBINEER	CARCASING	CARDITIC	CARET
CARAPACE	CARBINES	CARCASS	CARDITIS	CARETAKE
CARAPACED	CARBINIER	CARCASSED	CARDON	CARETAKEN
CARAPACES	CARBINOL	CARCASSES	CARDONS	CARETAKER
CARAPAX	CARBINOLS	CARCEL	CARDOON	CARETAKES
CARAPAXES	CARBO	CARCELS	CARDOONS	CARETOOK
CARAPS	CARBOLIC	CARCERAL	CARDPHONE	CARETS
CARASSOW	CARBOLICS	CARCINOID	CARDPUNCH	CAREWARE
CARASSOWS	CARBOLISE	CARCINOMA	CARDS	CAREWARES
CARAT	CARBOLIZE	CARD	CARDSHARP	CAREWORN
CARATE	CARBON	CARDAMINE	CARDUUS	CAREX
CARATES	CARBONADE	CARDAMOM	CARDUUSES	CARFARE
CARATS	CARBONADO	CARDAMOMS	CARDY	CARFARES
CARAUNA	CARBONARA	CARDAMON	CARE	CARFAX
CARAUNAS	CARBONATE	CARDAMONS	CARED	CARFAXES
CARAVAN	CARBONIC	CARDAMUM	CAREEN	CARFOX
CARAVANCE	CARBONISE	CARDAMUMS	CAREENAGE	CARFOXES
CARAVANED	CARBONIUM	CARDAN	CAREENED	CARFUFFLE
CARAVANER	CARBONIZE	CARDBOARD	CAREENER	CARFUL
CARAVANS	CARBONOUS	CARDCASE	CAREENERS	CARFULS
CARAVEL	CARBONS	CARDCASES	CAREENING	CARGEESE
CARAVELLE	CARBONYL	CARDECU	CAREENS	CARGO
CARAVELS	CARBONYLS	CARDECUE	CAREER	CARGOED
CARAWAY	CARBORA	CARDECUES	CAREERED	CARGOES
CARAWAYS	CARBORAS	CARDECUS	CAREERER	CARGOING
CARB	CARBORNE	CARDED	CAREERERS	CARGOOSE
CARBACHOL	CARBOS	CARDER	CAREERING	CARGOS
CARBAMATE	CARBOXYL	CARDERS	CAREERISM	CARHOP
CARBAMIC	CARBOXYLS	CARDI	CAREERIST	CARHOPPED
CARBAMIDE	CARBOY	CARDIA	CAREERS	CARHOPS
CARBAMINO	CARBOYED	CARDIAC	CAREFREE	CARIACOU
CARBAMOYL	CARBOYS	CARDIACAL	CAREFUL	CARIACOUS
CARBAMYL	CARBS	CARDIACS	CAREFULLY	CARIAMA
CARBAMYLS	CARBUNCLE	CARDIAE	CAREGIVER	CARIAMAS
CARBANION	CARBURATE	CARDIALGY	CARELESS	CARIBE
CARBARN	CARBURET	CARDIAS	CARELINE	CARIBES
CARBARNS	CARBURETS	CARDIE	CARELINES	CARIBOO
CARBARYL	CARBURISE	CARDIES	CAREME	CARIBOOS
CARBARYLS	CARBURIZE	CARDIGAN	CAREMES	CARIBOU
CARBAZOLE	CARBY	CARDIGANS	CARER	CARIBOUS
CARBEEN	CARCAJOU	CARDINAL	CARERS	CARICES
CARBEENS	CARCAJOUS	CARDINALS	CARES	CARIED
CARBENE	CARCAKE	CARDING	CARESS	CARIERE

CARIERES	CARLOTS	CARNIVORY	CAROUSED	CARRATS
CARIES	CARLS	CARNOSAUR	CAROUSEL	CARRAWAY
CARILLON	CARMAKER	CARNOSE	CAROUSELS	CARRAWAYS
CARILLONS	CARMAKERS	CARNOSITY	CAROUSER	CARRECT
CARINA	CARMAN	CARNOTITE	CAROUSERS	CARRECTS
CARINAE	CARMELITE	CARNS	CAROUSES	CARREFOUR
CARINAL	CARMEN	CARNY	CAROUSING	CARREL
CARINAS	CARMINE	CARNYING	CARP	CARRELL
CARINATE	CARMINES	CARNYX	CARPACCIO	CARRELLS
CARINATED	CARN	CARNYXES	CARPAL	CARRELS
CARING	CARNAGE	CAROACH	CARPALE	CARRIAGE
CARINGLY	CARNAGES	CAROACHES	CARPALES	CARRIAGES
CARINGS	CARNAHUBA	CAROB	CARPALIA	CARRICK
CARIOCA	CARNAL	CAROBS	CARPALS	CARRIED
CARIOCAS	CARNALISE	CAROCH	CARPED	CARRIER
CARIOLE	CARNALISM	CAROCHE	CARPEL	CARRIERS
CARIOLES	CARNALIST	CAROCHES	CARPELS	CARRIES
CARIOSE	CARNALITY	CAROL	CARPENTER	CARRIOLE
CARIOSITY	CARNALIZE	CAROLED	CARPENTRY	CARRIOLES
CARIOUS	CARNALLED	CAROLER	CARPER	CARRION
CARITAS	CARNALLY	CAROLERS	CARPERS	CARRIONS
CARITASES	CARNALS	CAROLI	CARPET	CARRITCH
CARITATES	CARNAROLI	CAROLING	CARPETBAG	CARROCH
CARJACK	CARNATION	CAROLINGS	CARPETED	CARROCHES
CARJACKED	CARNAUBA	CAROLLED	CARPETING	CARROM
CARJACKER	CARNAUBAS	CAROLLER	CARPETS	CARROMED
CARJACKS	CARNELIAN	CAROLLERS	CARPHONE	CARROMING
CARJACOU	CARNEOUS	CAROLLING	CARPHONES	CARROMS
CARJACOUS	CARNET	CAROLS	CARPI	CARRON
CARK	CARNETS	CAROLUS	CARPING	CARRONADE
CARKED	CARNEY	CAROLUSES	CARPINGLY	CARROT
CARKING	CARNEYED	CAROM	CARPINGS	CARROTIER
CARKS	CARNEYING	CAROMED	CARPLIKE	CARROTIN
CARL	CARNEYS	CAROMEL	CARPOLOGY	CARROTINS
CARLE	CARNIE	CAROMELS	CARPOOL	CARROTS
CARLES	CARNIED	CAROMING	CARPOOLED	CARROTTOP
CARLESS	CARNIER	CAROMS	CARPOOLER	CARROTY
CARLIN	CARNIES	CARON	CARPOOLS	CARROUSEL
CARLINE	CARNIEST	CARONS	CARPORT	CARRS
CARLINES	CARNIFEX	CAROTENE	CARPORTS	CARRY
CARLING	CARNIFIED	CAROTENES	CARPS	CARRYALL
CARLINGS	CARNIFIES	CAROTID	CARPUS	CARRYALLS
CARLINS	CARNIFY	CAROTIDAL	CARR	CARRYBACK
CARLISH	CARNITAS	CAROTIDS	CARRACK	CARRYCOT
CARLOAD	CARNITINE	CAROTIN	CARRACKS	CARRYCOTS
CARLOADS	CARNIVAL	CAROTINS	CARRACT	CARRYING
CARLOCK	CARNIVALS	CAROUSAL	CARRACTS	CARRYON
CARLOCKS	CARNIVORA	CAROUSALS	CARRAGEEN	CARRYONS
CARLOT	CARNIVORE	CAROUSE	CARRAT	CARRYOUT

CARRYOUTS	CARTOP	CASBAHS	CASEMIXES	CASINGS
CARRYOVER	CARTOPPER	CASCABEL	CASEOSE	CASINI
CARRYTALE	CARTOUCH	CASCABELS	CASEOSES	CASINO
CARS	CARTOUCHE	CASCABLE	CASEOUS	CASINOS
CARSE	CARTRIDGE	CASCABLES	CASERN	CASITA
CARSES	CARTROAD	CASCADE	CASERNE	CASITAS
CARSEY	CARTROADS	CASCADED	CASERNES	CASK
CARSEYS	CARTS	CASCADES	CASERNS	CASKED
CARSHARE	CARTULARY	CASCADING	CASES	CASKET
CARSHARED	CARTWAY	CASCADURA	CASETTE	CASKETED
CARSHARES	CARTWAYS	CASCARA	CASETTES	CASKETING
CARSICK	CARTWHEEL	CASCARAS	CASEVAC	CASKETS
CARSPIEL	CARUCAGE	CASCHROM	CASEVACED	CASKIER
CARSPIELS	CARUCAGES	CASCHROMS	CASEVACS	CASKIEST
CART	CARUCATE	CASCO	CASEWORK	CASKING
CARTA	CARUCATES	CASCOS	CASEWORKS	CASKS
CARTABLE	CARUNCLE	CASE	CASEWORM	CASKSTAND
CARTAGE	CARUNCLES	CASEASE	CASEWORMS	CASKY
CARTAGES	CARVACROL	CASEASES	CASH	CASPASE
CARTAS	CARVE	CASEATE	CASHABLE	CASPASES
CARTE	CARVED	CASEATED	CASHAW	CASQUE
CARTED	CARVEL	CASEATES	CASHAWS	CASQUED
CARTEL	CARVELS	CASEATING	CASHBACK	CASQUES
CARTELISE	CARVEN	CASEATION	CASHBACKS	CASSABA
CARTELISM	CARVER	CASEBOOK	CASHBOOK	CASSABAS
CARTELIST	CARVERIES	CASEBOOKS	CASHBOOKS	CASSAREEP
CARTELIZE	CARVERS	CASEBOUND	CASHBOX	CASSATA
CARTELS	CARVERY	CASED	CASHBOXES	CASSATAS
CARTER	CARVES	CASEFIED	CASHED	CASSATION
CARTERS	CARVIES	CASEFIES	CASHES	CASSAVA
CARTES	CARVING	CASEFY	CASHEW	CASSAVAS
CARTFUL	CARVINGS	CASEFYING	CASHEWS	CASSENA
CARTFULS	CARVY	CASEIC	CASHIER	CASSENAS
CARTHORSE	CARWASH	CASEIN	CASHIERED	CASSENE
CARTILAGE	CARWASHES	CASEINATE	CASHIERER	CASSENES
CARTING	CARYATIC	CASEINS	CASHIERS	CASSEROLE
CARTLOAD	CARYATID	CASELAW	CASHING	CASSETTE
CARTLOADS	CARYATIDS	CASELAWS	CASHLESS	CASSETTES
CARTOGRAM	CARYOPSES	CASELOAD	CASHMERE	CASSIA
CARTOLOGY	CARYOPSIS	CASELOADS	CASHMERES	CASSIAS
CARTON	CARYOTIN	CASEMAKER	CASHOO	CASSIE
CARTONAGE	CARYOTINS	CASEMAN	CASHOOS	CASSIES
CARTONED	CASA	CASEMATE	CASHPOINT	CASSIMERE
CARTONING	CASABA	CASEMATED	CASHSPIEL	CASSINA
CARTONS	CASABAS	CASEMATES	CASIMERE	CASSINAS
CARTOON	CASAS	CASEMEN	CASIMERES	CASSINE
CARTOONED	CASAVA	CASEMENT	CASIMIRE	CASSINES
CARTOONS	CASAVAS	CASEMENTS	CASIMIRES	CASSINGLE
CARTOONY	CASBAH	CASEMIX	CASING	CASSINO

CASSINOS	CASTORIES	CATALOGIC	CATBOAT	CATECHU
CASSIOPE	CASTORS	CATALOGNE	CATBOATS	CATECHUS
CASSIOPES	CASTORY	CATALOGS	CATBRIAR	CATEGORIC
CASSIS	CASTRAL	CATALOGUE	CATBRIARS	CATEGORY
CASSISES	CASTRATE	CATALOS	CATBRIER	CATELOG
CASSOCK	CASTRATED	CATALPA	CATBRIERS	CATELOGS
CASSOCKED	CASTRATER	CATALPAS	CATCALL	CATENA
CASSOCKS	CASTRATES	CATALYSE	CATCALLED	CATENAE
CASSONADE	CASTRATI	CATALYSED	CATCALLER	CATENANE
CASSONE	CASTRATO	CATALYSER	CATCALLS	CATENANES
CASSONES	CASTRATOR	CATALYSES	CATCH	CATENARY
CASSOULET	CASTRATOS	CATALYSIS	CATCHABLE	CATENAS
CASSOWARY	CASTS	CATALYST	CATCHALL	CATENATE
CASSPIR	CASUAL	CATALYSTS	CATCHALLS	CATENATED
CASSPIRS	CASUALISE	CATALYTIC	CATCHCRY	CATENATES
CAST	CASUALISM	CATALYZE	CATCHED	CATENOID
CASTABLE	CASUALIZE	CATALYZED	CATCHEN	CATENOIDS
CASTANET	CASUALLY	CATALYZER	CATCHER	CATER
CASTANETS	CASUALS	CATALYZES	CATCHERS	CATERAN
CASTAWAY	CASUALTY	CATAMARAN	CATCHES	CATERANS
CASTAWAYS	CASUARINA	CATAMENIA	CATCHFLY	CATERED
CASTE	CASUIST	CATAMITE	CATCHIER	CATERER
CASTED	CASUISTIC	CATAMITES	CATCHIEST	CATERERS
CASTEISM	CASUISTRY	CATAMOUNT	CATCHILY	CATERESS
CASTEISMS	CASUISTS	CATAPAN	CATCHING	CATERING
CASTELESS	CASUS	CATAPANS	CATCHINGS	CATERINGS
CASTELLA	CAT	CATAPHOR	CATCHLINE	CATERS
CASTELLAN	CATABASES	CATAPHORA	CATCHMENT	CATERWAUL
CASTELLUM	CATABASIS	CATAPHORS	CATCHPOLE	CATES
CASTER	CATABATIC	CATAPHYLL	CATCHPOLL	CATFACE
CASTERED	CATABOLIC	CATAPLASM	CATCHT	CATFACES
CASTERS	CATACLASM	CATAPLEXY	CATCHUP	CATFACING
CASTES	CATACLYSM	CATAPULT	CATCHUPS	CATFALL
CASTIGATE	CATACOMB	CATAPULTS	CATCHWEED	CATFALLS
CASTING	CATACOMBS	CATARACT	CATCHWORD	CATFIGHT
CASTINGS	CATAFALCO	CATARACTS	CATCHY	CATFIGHTS
CASTLE	CATAGEN	CATARHINE	CATCLAW	CATFISH
CASTLED	CATAGENS	CATARRH	CATCLAWS	CATFISHED
CASTLES	CATALASE	CATARRHAL	CATCON	CATFISHES
CASTLING	CATALASES	CATARRHS	CATCONS	CATFLAP
CASTLINGS	CATALATIC	CATASTA	CATE	CATFLAPS
CASTMATE	CATALEPSY	CATASTAS	CATECHIN	CATFOOD
CASTMATES	CATALEXES	CATATONIA	CATECHINS	CATFOODS
CASTOCK	CATALEXIS	CATATONIC	CATECHISE	CATGUT
CASTOCKS	CATALO	CATATONY	CATECHISM	CATGUTS
CASTOFF	CATALOES	CATAWBA	CATECHIST	CATH
CASTOFFS	CATALOG	CATAWBAS	CATECHIZE	CATHARISE
CASTOR	CATALOGED	CATBIRD	CATECHOL	CATHARIZE
CASTOREUM	CATALOGER	CATBIRDS	CATECHOLS	CATHARSES

CATHARSIS	CATLINGS	CATTLEMEN	CAULDRON	CAUSERS
CATHARTIC	CATLINITE	CATTLEYA	CAULDRONS	CAUSES
CATHEAD	CATLINS	CATTLEYAS	CAULDS	CAUSEWAY
CATHEADS	CATMINT	CATTY	CAULES	CAUSEWAYS
CATHECT	CATMINTS	CATWALK	CAULICLE	CAUSEY
CATHECTED	CATNAP	CATWALKS	CAULICLES	CAUSEYED
CATHECTIC	CATNAPER	CATWORKS	CAULICULI	CAUSEYS
CATHECTS	CATNAPERS	CATWORM	CAULIFORM	CAUSING
CATHED	CATNAPPED	CATWORMS	CAULINARY	CAUSTIC
CATHEDRA	CATNAPPER	CAUCHEMAR	CAULINE	CAUSTICAL
CATHEDRAE	CATNAPS	CAUCUS	CAULIS	CAUSTICS
CATHEDRAL	CATNEP	CAUCUSED	CAULK	CAUTEL
CATHEDRAS	CATNEPS	CAUCUSES	CAULKED	CAUTELOUS
CATHEPSIN	CATNIP	CAUCUSING	CAULKER	CAUTELS
CATHEPTIC	CATNIPS	CAUCUSSED	CAULKERS	CAUTER
CATHETER	CATOLYTE	CAUCUSSES	CAULKING	CAUTERANT
CATHETERS	CATOLYTES	CAUDA	CAULKINGS	CAUTERIES
CATHETUS	CATOPTRIC	CAUDAD	CAULKS	CAUTERISE
CATHEXES	CATRIGGED	CAUDAE	CAULOME	CAUTERISM
CATHEXIS	CATS	CAUDAL	CAULOMES	CAUTERIZE
CATHING	CATSKIN	CAUDALLY	CAULS	CAUTERS
CATHINONE	CATSKINS	CAUDATE	CAUM	CAUTERY
CATHISMA	CATSPAW	CAUDATED	CAUMED	CAUTION
CATHISMAS	CATSPAWS	CAUDATES	CAUMING	CAUTIONED
CATHODAL	CATSUIT	CAUDATION	CAUMS	CAUTIONER
CATHODE	CATSUITS	CAUDEX	CAUMSTANE	CAUTIONRY
CATHODES	CATSUP	CAUDEXES	CAUMSTONE	CAUTIONS
CATHODIC	CATSUPS	CAUDICES	CAUP	CAUTIOUS
CATHOLE	CATTABU	CAUDICLE	CAUPS	CAUVES
CATHOLES	CATTABUS	CAUDICLES	CAURI	CAVA
CATHOLIC	CATTAIL	CAUDILLO	CAURIS	CAVALCADE
CATHOLICS	CATTAILS	CAUDILLOS	CAUSA	CAVALERO
CATHOLYTE	CATTALO	CAUDLE	CAUSABLE	CAVALEROS
CATHOOD	CATTALOES	CAUDLED	CAUSAE	CAVALETTI
CATHOODS	CATTALOS	CAUDLES	CAUSAL	CAVALIER
CATHOUSE	CATTED	CAUDLING	CAUSALGIA	CAVALIERS
CATHOUSES	CATTERIES	CAUDRON	CAUSALGIC	CAVALLA
CATHS	CATTERY	CAUDRONS	CAUSALITY	CAVALLAS
CATION	CATTIE	CAUF	CAUSALLY	CAVALLIES
CATIONIC	CATTIER	CAUGHT	CAUSALS	CAVALLY
CATIONS	CATTIES	CAUK	CAUSATION	CAVALRIES
CATJANG	CATTIEST	CAUKER	CAUSATIVE	CAVALRY
CATJANGS	CATTILY	CAUKERS	CAUSE	CAVAS
CATKIN	CATTINESS	CAUKS	CAUSED	CAVASS
CATKINATE	CATTING	CAUL	CAUSELESS	CAVASSES
CATKINS	CATTISH	CAULD	CAUSEN	CAVATINA
CATLIKE	CATTISHLY	CAULDER	CAUSER	CAVATINAS
CATLIN	CATTLE	CAULDEST	CAUSERIE	CAVATINE
CATLING	CATTLEMAN	CAULDRIFE	CAUSERIES	CAVE

CAVEAT	CAVILLERS	CEASES	CEE	CELLAR
CAVEATED	CAVILLING	CEASING	CEES	CELLARAGE
CAVEATING	CAVILS	CEASINGS	CEIBA	CELLARED
CAVEATOR	CAVING	CEAZE	CEIBAS	CELLARER
CAVEATORS	CAVINGS	CEAZED	CEIL	CELLARERS
CAVEATS	CAVITARY	CEAZES	CEILED	CELLARET
CAVED	CAVITATE	CEAZING	CEILER	CELLARETS
CAVEFISH	CAVITATED	CEBADILLA	CEILERS	CELLARING
CAVEL	CAVITATES	CEBID	CEILI	CELLARIST
CAVELIKE	CAVITIED	CEBIDS	CEILIDH	CELLARMAN
CAVELS	CAVITIES	CEBOID	CEILIDHS	CELLARMEN
CAVEMAN	CAVITY	CEBOIDS	CEILING	CELLAROUS
CAVEMEN	CAVORT	CECA	CEILINGED	CELLARS
CAVENDISH	CAVORTED	CECAL	CEILINGS	CELLARWAY
CAVEOLA	CAVORTER	CECALLY	CEILIS	CELLBLOCK
CAVEOLAE	CAVORTERS	CECILS	CEILS	CELLED
CAVEOLAR	CAVORTING	CECITIES	CEINTURE	CELLI
CAVER	CAVORTS	CECITIS	CEINTURES	CELLIE
CAVERN	CAVY	CECITISES	CEL	CELLIES
CAVERNED	CAW	CECITY	CELADON	CELLING
CAVERNING	CAWED	CECROPIA	CELADONS	CELLINGS
CAVERNOUS	CAWING	CECROPIAS	CELANDINE	CELLIST
CAVERNS	CAWINGS	CECROPIN	CELEB	CELLISTS
CAVERS	CAWK	CECROPINS	CELEBRANT	CELLMATE
CAVES	CAWKER	CECUM	CELEBRATE	CELLMATES
CAVESSON	CAWKERS	CEDAR	CELEBRITY	CELLO
CAVESSONS	CAWKS	CEDARBIRD	CELEBS	CELLOIDIN
CAVETTI	CAWS	CEDARED	CELECOXIB	CELLOS
CAVETTO	CAXON	CEDARIER	CELERIAC	CELLOSE
CAVETTOS	CAXONS	CEDARIEST	CELERIACS	CELLOSES
CAVIAR	CAY	CEDARN	CELERIES	CELLPHONE
CAVIARE	CAYENNE	CEDARS	CELERITY	CELLS
CAVIARES	CAYENNED	CEDARWOOD	CELERY	CELLULAR
CAVIARIE	CAYENNES	CEDARY	CELESTA	CELLULARS
CAVIARIES	CAYMAN	CEDE	CELESTAS	CELLULASE
CAVIARS	CAYMANS	CEDED	CELESTE	CELLULE
CAVICORN	CAYS	CEDER	CELESTES	CELLULES
CAVICORNS	CAYUSE	CEDERS	CELESTIAL	CELLULITE
CAVIE	CAYUSES	CEDES	CELESTINE	CELLULOID
CAVIER	CAZ	CEDI	CELESTITE	CELLULOSE
CAVIERS	CAZH	CEDILLA	CELIAC	CELLULOUS
CAVIES	CAZIQUE	CEDILLAS	CELIACS	CELLY
CAVIL	CAZIQUES	CEDING	CELIBACY	CELOM
CAVILED	CEANOTHUS	CEDIS	CELIBATE	CELOMATA
CAVILER	CEAS	CEDRATE	CELIBATES	CELOMIC
CAVILERS	CEASE	CEDRATES	CELIBATIC	CELOMS
CAVILING	CEASED	CEDRINE	CELL	CELOSIA
CAVILLED	CEASEFIRE	CEDULA	CELLA	CELOSIAS
CAVILLER	CEASELESS	CEDULAS	CELLAE	CELOTEX

CELOTEXES	CENSURE	CENTINELS	CENTUPLES	CERCARIAE
CELS	CENSURED	CENTIPEDE	CENTURIAL	CERCARIAL
CELSITUDE	CENSURER	CENTNER	CENTURIES	CERCARIAN
CELT	CENSURERS	CENTNERS	CENTURION	CERCARIAS
CELTS	CENSURES	CENTO	CENTURY	CERCI
CEMBALI	CENSURING	CENTOIST	CEORL	CERCIS
CEMBALIST	CENSUS	CENTOISTS	CEORLISH	CERCISES
CEMBALO	CENSUSED	CENTONATE	CEORLS	CERCLAGE
CEMBALOS	CENSUSES	CENTONEL	CEP	CERCLAGES
CEMBRA	CENSUSING	CENTONELL	CEPACEOUS	CERCOPID
CEMBRAS	CENT	CENTONELS	CEPAGE	CERCOPIDS
CEMENT	CENTAGE	CENTONES	CEPAGES	CERCUS
CEMENTA	CENTAGES	CENTONIST	CEPE	CERE
CEMENTED	CENTAI	CENTOS	CEPES	CEREAL
CEMENTER	CENTAL	CENTRA	CEPHALAD	CEREALIST
CEMENTERS	CENTALS	CENTRAL	CEPHALATE	CEREALS
CEMENTING	CENTARE	CENTRALER	CEPHALIC	CEREBELLA
CEMENTITE	CENTARES	CENTRALLY	CEPHALICS	CEREBRA
CEMENTS	CENTAS	CENTRALS	CEPHALIN	CEREBRAL
CEMENTUM	CENTAUR	CENTRE	CEPHALINS	CEREBRALS
CEMENTUMS	CENTAUREA	CENTRED	CEPHALOUS	CEREBRATE
CEMETERY	CENTAURIC	CENTREING	CEPHEID	CEREBRIC
CEMITARE	CENTAURS	CENTREMAN	CEPHEIDS	CEREBROID
CEMITARES	CENTAURY	CENTREMEN	CEPS	CEREBRUM
CENACLE	CENTAVO	CENTRES	CERACEOUS	CEREBRUMS
CENACLES	CENTAVOS	CENTRIC	CERAMAL	CERECLOTH
CENDRE	CENTENARY	CENTRICAL	CERAMALS	CERED
CENOBITE	CENTENIER	CENTRIES	CERAMIC	CEREMENT
CENOBITES	CENTER	CENTRING	CERAMICS	CEREMENTS
CENOBITIC	CENTERED	CENTRINGS	CERAMIDE	CEREMONY
CENOTAPH	CENTERING	CENTRIOLE	CERAMIDES	CEREOUS
CENOTAPHS	CENTERMAN	CENTRISM	CERAMIST	CERES
CENOTE	CENTERMEN	CENTRISMS	CERAMISTS	CERESIN
CENOTES	CENTERS	CENTRIST	CERASIN	CERESINE
CENOZOIC	CENTESES	CENTRISTS	CERASINS	CERESINES
CENS	CENTESIMI	CENTRODE	CERASTES	CERESINS
CENSE	CENTESIMO	CENTRODES	CERASTIUM	CEREUS
CENSED	CENTESIS	CENTROID	CERATE	CEREUSES
CENSER	CENTIARE	CENTROIDS	CERATED	CERGE
CENSERS	CENTIARES	CENTRUM	CERATES	CERGES
CENSES	CENTIGRAM	CENTRUMS	CERATIN	CERIA
CENSING	CENTILE	CENTRY	CERATINS	CERIAS
CENSOR	CENTILES	CENTS	CERATITIS	CERIC
CENSORED	CENTIME	CENTU	CERATODUS	CERIMAN
CENSORIAL	CENTIMES	CENTUM	CERATOID	CERIMANS
CENSORIAN	CENTIMO	CENTUMS	CERBEREAN	CERING
CENSORING	CENTIMOS	CENTUMVIR	CERBERIAN	CERIPH
CENSORS	CENTINEL	CENTUPLE	CERCAL	CERIPHS
CENSUAL	CENTINELL	CENTUPLED	CERCARIA	CERISE

CERISES	CERUMEN	CESTOI	CHACED	CHAFFERS
CERITE	CERUMENS	CESTOID	CHACES	CHAFFERY
CERITES	CERUSE	CESTOIDS	CHACHKA	CHAFFIER
CERIUM	CERUSES	CESTOS	CHACHKAS	CHAFFIEST
CERIUMS	CERUSITE	CESTOSES	CHACING	CHAFFINCH
CERMET	CERUSITES	CESTUI	CHACK	CHAFFING
CERMETS	CERUSSITE	CESTUIS	CHACKED	CHAFFINGS
CERNE	CERVELAS	CESTUS	CHACKING	CHAFFRON
CERNED	CERVELAT	CESTUSES	CHACKS	CHAFFRONS
CERNES	CERVELATS	CESURA	CHACMA	CHAFFS
CERNING	CERVEZA	CESURAE	CHACMAS	CHAFFY
CERNUOUS	CERVEZAS	CESURAL	CHACO	CHAFING
CERO	CERVICAL	CESURAS	CHACOES	CHAFT
CEROC	CERVICES	CESURE	CHACONINE	CHAFTS
CEROCS	CERVICUM	CESURES	CHACONNE	CHAGA
CEROGRAPH	CERVICUMS	CETACEAN	CHACONNES	CHAGAN
CEROMANCY	CERVID	CETACEANS	CHACOS	CHAGANS
CEROON	CERVIDS	CETACEOUS	CHAD	CHAGAS
CEROONS	CERVINE	CETANE	CHADAR	CHAGRIN
CEROS	CERVIX	CETANES	CHADARIM	CHAGRINED
CEROTIC	CERVIXES	CETE	CHADARS	CHAGRINS
CEROTYPE	CESAREAN	CETERACH	CHADDAR	CHAI
CEROTYPES	CESAREANS	CETERACHS	CHADDARS	CHAIN
CEROUS	CESAREVNA	CETES	CHADDOR	CHAINE
CERRADO	CESARIAN	CETOLOGY	CHADDORS	CHAINED
CERRADOS	CESARIANS	CETRIMIDE	CHADLESS	CHAINER
CERRIAL	CESIOUS	CETUXIMAB	CHADO	CHAINERS
CERRIS	CESIUM	CETYL	CHADOR	CHAINES
CERRISES	CESIUMS	CETYLS	CHADORS	CHAINFALL
CERT	CESPITOSE	CETYWALL	CHADOS	CHAINING
CERTAIN	CESS	CETYWALLS	CHADRI	CHAINLESS
CERTAINER	CESSATION	CEVADILLA	CHADS	CHAINLET
CERTAINLY	CESSE	CEVAPCICI	CHAEBOL	CHAINLETS
CERTAINTY	CESSED	CEVICHE	CHAEBOLS	CHAINMAN
CERTES	CESSER	CEVICHES	CHAETA	CHAINMEN
CERTIE	CESSERS	CEVITAMIC	CHAETAE	CHAINS
CERTIFIED	CESSES	CEYLANITE	CHAETAL	CHAINSAW
CERTIFIER	CESSING	CEYLONITE	CHAETODON	CHAINSAWS
CERTIFIES	CESSION	CEZVE	CHAETOPOD	CHAINSHOT
CERTIFY	CESSIONS	CEZVES	CHAFE	CHAINWORK
CERTITUDE	CESSPIT	CH	CHAFED	CHAIR
CERTS	CESSPITS	CHA	CHAFER	CHAIRBACK
CERTY	CESSPOOL	CHABAZITE	CHAFERS	CHAIRDAYS
CERULE	CESSPOOLS	CHABLIS	CHAFES	CHAIRED
CERULEAN	CESTA	CHABOUK	CHAFF	CHAIRING
CERULEANS	CESTAS	CHABOUKS	CHAFFED	CHAIRLIFT
CERULEIN	CESTI	CHABUK	CHAFFER	CHAIRMAN
CERULEINS	CESTODE	CHABUKS	CHAFFERED	CHAIRMANS
CERULEOUS	CESTODES	CHACE	CHAFFERER	CHAIRMEN

CHAIRS	CHALLAH	CHAMISA	CHANCEL	CHANSON
CHAIS	CHALLAHS	CHAMISAL	CHANCELS	CHANSONS
CHAISE	CHALLAN	CHAMISALS	CHANCER	CHANT
CHAISES	CHALLANS	CHAMISAS	CHANCERS	CHANTABLE
CHAKALAKA	CHALLAS	CHAMISE	CHANCERY	CHANTAGE
CHAKRA	CHALLENGE	CHAMISES	CHANCES	CHANTAGES
CHAKRAS	CHALLIE	CHAMISO	CHANCEY	CHANTED
CHAL	CHALLIES	CHAMISOS	CHANCHITO	CHANTER
CHALAH	CHALLIS	CHAMLET	CHANCIER	CHANTERS
CHALAHS	CHALLISES	CHAMLETS	CHANCIEST	CHANTEUSE
CHALAN	CHALLOT	CHAMMIED	CHANCILY	CHANTEY
CHALANED	CHALLOTH	CHAMMIES	CHANCING	CHANTEYS
CHALANING	CHALLY	CHAMMY	CHANCRE	CHANTIE
CHALANNED	CHALONE	CHAMMYING	CHANCRES	CHANTIES
CHALANS	CHALONES	CHAMOIS	CHANCROID	CHANTILLY
CHALAZA	CHALONIC	CHAMOISED	CHANCROUS	CHANTING
CHALAZAE	CHALOT	CHAMOISES	CHANCY	CHANTINGS
CHALAZAL	CHALOTH	CHAMOIX	CHANDELLE	CHANTOR
CHALAZAS	CHALS	CHAMOMILE	CHANDLER	CHANTORS
CHALAZIA	CHALUMEAU	CHAMP	CHANDLERS	CHANTRESS
CHALAZION	CHALUPA	CHAMPAC	CHANDLERY	CHANTRIES
CHALCID	CHALUPAS	CHAMPACA	CHANFRON	CHANTRY
CHALCIDS	CHALUTZ	CHAMPACAS	CHANFRONS	CHANTS
CHALCOGEN	CHALUTZES	CHAMPACS	CHANG	CHANTY
CHALDER	CHALUTZIM	CHAMPAGNE	CHANGA	CHANUKIAH
CHALDERS	CHALYBEAN	CHAMPAIGN	CHANGE	CHAO
CHALDRON	CHALYBITE	CHAMPAK	CHANGED	CHAOLOGY
CHALDRONS	CHAM	CHAMPAKS	CHANGEFUL	CHAORDIC
CHALEH	CHAMADE	CHAMPART	CHANGER	CHAOS
CHALEHS	CHAMADES	CHAMPARTS	CHANGERS	CHAOSES
CHALET	CHAMBER	CHAMPAS	CHANGES	CHAOTIC
CHALETS	CHAMBERED	CHAMPED	CHANGEUP	CHAP
CHALICE	CHAMBERER	CHAMPER	CHANGEUPS	CHAPARRAL
CHALICED	CHAMBERS	CHAMPERS	CHANGING	CHAPATI
CHALICES	CHAMBRAY	CHAMPERTY	CHANGS	CHAPATIES
CHALK	CHAMBRAYS	CHAMPIER	CHANK	CHAPATIS
CHALKED	CHAMBRE	CHAMPIEST	CHANKS	CHAPATTI
CHALKFACE	CHAMELEON	CHAMPING	CHANNA	CHAPATTIS
CHALKIER	CHAMELOT	CHAMPION	CHANNAS	CHAPBOOK
CHALKIEST	CHAMELOTS	CHAMPIONS	CHANNEL	CHAPBOOKS
CHALKING	CHAMETZ	CHAMPLEVE	CHANNELED	CHAPE
CHALKLAND	CHAMETZES	CHAMPS	CHANNELER	CHAPEAU
CHALKLIKE	CHAMFER	CHAMPY	CHANNELS	CHAPEAUS
CHALKMARK	CHAMFERED	CHAMS	CHANNER	CHAPEAUX
CHALKPIT	CHAMFERER	CHANA	CHANNERS	CHAPEL
CHALKPITS	CHAMFERS	CHANAS	CHANOYO	CHAPELESS
CHALKS	CHAMFRAIN	CHANCE	CHANOYOS	CHAPELRY
CHALKY	CHAMFRON	CHANCED	CHANOYU	CHAPELS
CHALLA	CHAMFRONS	CHANCEFUL	CHANOYUS	CHAPERON

CHAPERONE	CHARACINS	CHARITY	CHARRIER	CHASSEED
CHAPERONS	CHARACT	CHARIVARI	CHARRIEST	CHASSEING
CHAPES	CHARACTER	CHARK	CHARRING	CHASSEPOT
CHAPESS	CHARACTS	CHARKA	CHARRO	CHASSES
CHAPESSES	CHARADE	CHARKAS	CHARROS	CHASSEUR
CHAPITER	CHARADES	CHARKED	CHARRS	CHASSEURS
CHAPITERS	CHARANGA	CHARKHA	CHARRY	CHASSIS
CHAPKA	CHARANGAS	CHARKHAS	CHARS	CHASTE
CHAPKAS	CHARANGO	CHARKING	CHART	CHASTELY
CHAPLAIN	CHARANGOS	CHARKS	CHARTA	CHASTEN
CHAPLAINS	CHARAS	CHARLADY	CHARTABLE	CHASTENED
CHAPLESS	CHARASES	CHARLATAN	CHARTAS	CHASTENER
CHAPLET	CHARBROIL	CHARLEY	CHARTED	CHASTENS
CHAPLETED	CHARCOAL	CHARLEYS	CHARTER	CHASTER
CHAPLETS	CHARCOALS	CHARLIE	CHARTERED	CHASTEST
CHAPMAN	CHARCOALY	CHARLIER	CHARTERER	CHASTISE
CHAPMEN	CHARD	CHARLIES	CHARTERS	CHASTISED
CHAPPAL	CHARDS	CHARLOCK	CHARTING	CHASTISER
CHAPPALS	CHARE	CHARLOCKS	CHARTISM	CHASTISES
CHAPPATI	CHARED	CHARLOTTE	CHARTISMS	CHASTITY
CHAPPATIS	CHARES	CHARM	CHARTIST	CHASUBLE
CHAPPED	CHARET	CHARMED	CHARTISTS	CHASUBLES
CHAPPESS	CHARETS	CHARMER	CHARTLESS	CHAT
CHAPPIE	CHARETTE	CHARMERS	CHARTS	CHATBOT
CHAPPIER	CHARETTES	CHARMEUSE	CHARVER	CHATBOTS
CHAPPIES	CHARGE	CHARMFUL	CHARVERS	CHATCHKA
CHAPPIEST	CHARGED	CHARMING	CHARWOMAN	CHATCHKAS
CHAPPING	CHARGEFUL	CHARMLESS	CHARWOMEN	CHATCHKE
CHAPPY	CHARGER	CHARMONIA	CHARY	CHATCHKES
CHAPRASI	CHARGERS	CHARMS	CHAS	CHATEAU
CHAPRASIS	CHARGES	CHARNECO	CHASE	CHATEAUS
CHAPRASSI	CHARGING	CHARNECOS	CHASEABLE	CHATEAUX
CHAPS	CHARGINGS	CHARNEL	CHASED	CHATELAIN
CHAPSTICK	CHARGRILL	CHARNELS	CHASEPORT	CHATLINE
CHAPT	CHARIDEE	CHAROSET	CHASER	CHATLINES
CHAPTER	CHARIDEES	CHAROSETH	CHASERS	CHATON
CHAPTERAL	CHARIER	CHAROSETS	CHASES	CHATONS
CHAPTERED	CHARIEST	CHARPAI	CHASING	CHATOYANT
CHAPTERS	CHARILY	CHARPAIS	CHASINGS	CHATROOM
CHAPTREL	CHARINESS	CHARPIE	CHASM	CHATROOMS
CHAPTRELS	CHARING	CHARPIES	CHASMAL	CHATS
CHAQUETA	CHARIOT	CHARPOY	CHASMED	CHATTA
CHAQUETAS	CHARIOTED	CHARPOYS	CHASMIC	CHATTAS
CHAR	CHARIOTS	CHARQUI	CHASMIER	CHATTED
CHARA	CHARISM	CHARQUID	CHASMIEST	CHATTEE
CHARABANC	CHARISMA	CHARQUIS	CHASMS	CHATTEES
CHARACID	CHARISMAS	CHARR	CHASMY	CHATTEL
CHARACIDS	CHARISMS	CHARREADA	CHASSE	CHATTELS
CHARACIN	CHARITIES	CHARRED	CHASSED	CHATTER

CHATTERED	CHAVETTE	CHEAPLY	CHECKSTOP	CHEERLESS
CHATTERER	CHAVETTES	CHEAPNESS	CHECKSUM	CHEERLY
CHATTERS	CHAVISH	CHEAPO	CHECKSUMS	CHEERO
CHATTERY	CHAVS	CHEAPOS	CHECKUP	CHEEROS
CHATTI	CHAVVIER	CHEAPS	CHECKUPS	CHEERS
CHATTIER	CHAVVIEST	CHEAPSHOT	CHECKY	CHEERY
CHATTIES	CHAVVY	CHEAPY	CHEDARIM	CHEESE
CHATTIEST	CHAW	CHEAT	CHEDDAR	CHEESED
CHATTILY	CHAWBACON	CHEATABLE	CHEDDARS	CHEESES
CHATTING	CHAWDRON	CHEATED	CHEDDARY	CHEESEVAT
CHATTIS	CHAWDRONS	CHEATER	CHEDDITE	CHEESIER
CHATTY	CHAWED	CHEATERS	CHEDDITES	CHEESIEST
CHAUFE	CHAWER	CHEATERY	CHEDER	CHEESILY
CHAUFED	CHAWERS	CHEATING	CHEDERS	CHEESING
CHAUFER	CHAWING	CHEATINGS	CHEDITE	CHEESY
CHAUFERS	CHAWK	CHEATS	CHEDITES	CHEETAH
CHAUFES	CHAWKS	CHEBEC	CHEECHAKO	CHEETAHS
CHAUFF	CHAWS	CHEBECS	CHEEK	CHEEWINK
CHAUFFED	CHAY	CHECHAKO	CHEEKBONE	CHEEWINKS
CHAUFFER	CHAYA	CHECHAKOS	CHEEKED	CHEF
CHAUFFERS	CHAYAS	CHECHAQUO	CHEEKFUL	CHEFDOM
CHAUFFEUR	CHAYOTE	CHECHIA	CHEEKFULS	CHEFDOMS
CHAUFFING	CHAYOTES	CHECHIAS	CHEEKIER	CHEFED
CHAUFFS	CHAYROOT	CHECK	CHEEKIEST	CHEFFED
CHAUFING	CHAYROOTS	CHECKABLE	CHEEKILY	CHEFFIER
CHAUMER	CHAYS	CHECKBOOK	CHEEKING	CHEFFIEST
CHAUMERS	CHAZAN	CHECKBOX	CHEEKLESS	CHEFFING
CHAUNCE	CHAZANIM	CHECKED	CHEEKS	CHEFFY
CHAUNCED	CHAZANS	CHECKER	CHEEKY	CHEFING
CHAUNCES	CHAZZAN	CHECKERED	CHEEP	CHEFS
CHAUNCING	CHAZZANIM	CHECKERS	CHEEPED	CHEGOE
CHAUNGE	CHAZZANS	CHECKIER	CHEEPER	CHEGOES
CHAUNGED	CHAZZEN	CHECKIEST	CHEEPERS	CHEILITIS
CHAUNGES	CHAZZENIM	CHECKING	CHEEPING	CHEKA
CHAUNGING	CHAZZENS	CHECKINGS	CHEEPS	CHEKAS
CHAUNT	CHE	CHECKLESS	CHEER	CHEKIST
CHAUNTED	CHEAP	CHECKLIST	CHEERED	CHEKISTS
CHAUNTER	CHEAPED	CHECKMARK	CHEERER	CHELA
CHAUNTERS	CHEAPEN	CHECKMATE	CHEERERS	CHELAE
CHAUNTING	CHEAPENED	CHECKOFF	CHEERFUL	CHELAS
CHAUNTRY	CHEAPENER	CHECKOFFS	CHEERIER	CHELASHIP
CHAUNTS	CHEAPENS	CHECKOUT	CHEERIEST	CHELATE
CHAUSSES	CHEAPER	CHECKOUTS	CHEERILY	CHELATED
CHAUSSURE	CHEAPEST	CHECKRAIL	CHEERING	CHELATES
CHAUVIN	CHEAPIE	CHECKREIN	CHEERINGS	CHELATING
CHAUVINS	CHEAPIES	CHECKROOM	CHEERIO	CHELATION
CHAV	CHEAPING	CHECKROW	CHEERIOS	CHELATOR
CHAVE	CHEAPISH	CHECKROWS	CHEERLEAD	CHELATORS
CHAVENDER	CHEAPJACK	CHECKS	CHEERLED	CHELICERA

CHELIFORM	CHENILLE	CHERUPS	CHEVERYES	CHIACKS
CHELIPED	CHENILLES	CHERVIL	CHEVET	CHIANTI
CHELIPEDS	CHENIX	CHERVILS	CHEVETS	CHIANTIS
CHELLUP	CHENIXES	CHESHIRE	CHEVIED	CHIAO
CHELLUPS	CHENOPOD	CHESHIRES	CHEVIES	CHIAOS
CHELOID	CHENOPODS	CHESIL	CHEVILLE	CHIAREZZA
CHELOIDAL	CHEONGSAM	CHESILS	CHEVILLES	CHIAREZZE
CHELOIDS	CHEQUE	CHESNUT	CHEVIN	CHIAS
CHELONE	CHEQUER	CHESNUTS	CHEVINS	CHIASM
CHELONES	CHEQUERED	CHESS	CHEVIOT	CHIASMA
CHELONIAN	CHEQUERS	CHESSEL	CHEVIOTS	CHIASMAL
CHELP	CHEQUES	CHESSELS	CHEVRE	CHIASMAS
CHELPED	CHEQUIER	CHESSES	CHEVRES	CHIASMATA
CHELPING	CHEQUIEST	CHESSMAN	CHEVRET	CHIASMI
CHELPS	CHEQUING	CHESSMEN	CHEVRETS	CHIASMIC
CHEM	CHEQUY	CHEST	CHEVRETTE	CHIASMS
CHEMIC	CHER	CHESTED	CHEVRON	CHIASMUS
CHEMICAL	CHERALITE	CHESTFUL	CHEVRONED	CHIASTIC
CHEMICALS	CHERE	CHESTFULS	CHEVRONS	CHIAUS
CHEMICKED	CHERIMOYA	CHESTIER	CHEVRONY	CHIAUSED
CHEMICS	CHERISH	CHESTIEST	CHEVROTIN	CHIAUSES
CHEMISE	CHERISHED	CHESTILY	CHEVY	CHIAUSING
CHEMISES	CHERISHER	CHESTING	CHEVYING	CHIB
CHEMISM	CHERISHES	CHESTNUT	CHEW	CHIBBED
CHEMISMS	CHERMOULA	CHESTNUTS	CHEWABLE	CHIBBING
CHEMISORB	CHERNOZEM	CHESTS	CHEWED	CHIBOL
CHEMIST	CHEROOT	CHESTY	CHEWER	CHIBOLS
CHEMISTRY	CHEROOTS	CHETAH	CHEWERS	CHIBOUK
CHEMISTS	CHERRIED	CHETAHS	CHEWET	CHIBOUKS
CHEMITYPE	CHERRIER	CHETH	CHEWETS	CHIBOUQUE
CHEMITYPY	CHERRIES	CHETHS	CHEWIE	CHIBS
CHEMMIES	CHERRIEST	CHETNIK	CHEWIER	CHIC
CHEMMY	CHERRY	CHETNIKS	CHEWIES	CHICA
CHEMO	CHERRYING	CHETRUM	CHEWIEST	CHICALOTE
CHEMOKINE	CHERT	CHETRUMS	CHEWINESS	CHICANA
CHEMOS	CHERTIER	CHEVAL	CHEWING	CHICANAS
CHEMOSORB	CHERTIEST	CHEVALET	CHEWINK	CHICANE
CHEMOSTAT	CHERTS	CHEVALETS	CHEWINKS	CHICANED
CHEMPADUK	CHERTY	CHEVALIER	CHEWS	CHICANER
CHEMS	CHERUB	CHEVELURE	CHEWY	CHICANERS
CHEMSEX	CHERUBIC	CHEVEN	CHEZ	CHICANERY
CHEMSEXES	CHERUBIM	CHEVENS	CHHATA	CHICANES
CHEMTRAIL	CHERUBIMS	CHEVEREL	CHHATAS	CHICANING
CHEMURGIC	CHERUBIN	CHEVERELS	CHHERTUM	CHICANO
CHEMURGY	CHERUBINS	CHEVERIL	CHI	CHICANOS
CHENAR	CHERUBS	CHEVERILS	CHIA	CHICAS
CHENARS	CHERUP	CHEVERON	CHIACK	CHICCORY
CHENET	CHERUPED	CHEVERONS	CHIACKED	CHICER
CHENETS	CHERUPING	CHEVERYE	CHIACKING	CHICEST

C

CHICH	CHIEFER	CHILDES	CHILLUMS	CHINAMPA
CHICHA	CHIEFERY	CHILDHOOD	CHILLWAVE	CHINAMPAS
CHICHAS	CHIEFESS	CHILDING	CHILLY	CHINAR
CHICHES	CHIEFEST	CHILDISH	CHILOPOD	CHINAROOT
CHICHI	CHIEFLESS	CHILDLESS	CHILOPODS	CHINARS
CHICHIER	CHIEFLING	CHILDLIER	CHILTEPIN	CHINAS
CHICHIEST	CHIEFLY	CHILDLIKE	CHIMAERA	CHINAWARE
CHICHIS	CHIEFRIES	CHILDLY	CHIMAERAS	CHINBONE
CHICK	CHIEFRY	CHILDNESS	CHIMAERIC	CHINBONES
CHICKADEE	CHIEFS	CHILDREN	CHIMAR	CHINCAPIN
CHICKAREE	CHIEFSHIP	CHILDS	CHIMARS	CHINCH
CHICKEE	CHIEFTAIN	CHILE	CHIMB	CHINCHED
CHICKEES	CHIEL	CHILES	CHIMBLEY	CHINCHES
CHICKEN	CHIELD	CHILI	CHIMBLEYS	CHINCHIER
CHICKENED	CHIELDS	CHILIAD	CHIMBLIES	CHINCHING
CHICKENS	CHIELS	CHILIADAL	CHIMBLY	CHINCHY
CHICKLING	CHIFFON	CHILIADIC	CHIMBS	CHINCOUGH
CHICKORY	CHIFFONS	CHILIADS	CHIME	CHINDIT
CHICKPEA	CHIFFONY	CHILIAGON	CHIMED	CHINDITS
CHICKPEAS	CHIGETAI	CHILIARCH	CHIMENEA	CHINE
CHICKS	CHIGETAIS	CHILIASM	CHIMENEAS	CHINED
CHICKWEED	CHIGGA	CHILIASMS	CHIMER	CHINES
CHICLE	CHIGGAS	CHILIAST	CHIMERA	CHINESE
CHICLES	CHIGGER	CHILIASTS	CHIMERAS	CHING
CHICLY	CHIGGERS	CHILIDOG	CHIMERE	CHINGS
CHICNESS	CHIGNON	CHILIDOGS	CHIMERES	CHINING
CHICO	CHIGNONED	CHILIES	CHIMERIC	CHINK
CHICON	CHIGNONS	CHILIS	CHIMERID	CHINKAPIN
CHICONS	CHIGOE	CHILL	CHIMERIDS	CHINKARA
CHICORIES	CHIGOES	CHILLADA	CHIMERISM	CHINKARAS
CHICORY	CHIGRE	CHILLADAS	CHIMERS	CHINKED
CHICOS	CHIGRES	CHILLAX	CHIMES	CHINKIER
CHICOT	CHIHUAHUA	CHILLAXED	CHIMINEA	CHINKIEST
CHICOTS	CHIK	CHILLAXES	CHIMINEAS	CHINKING
CHICS	CHIKARA	CHILLED	CHIMING	CHINKS
CHID	CHIKARAS	CHILLER	CHIMLA	CHINKY
CHIDDEN	CHIKHOR	CHILLERS	CHIMLAS	CHINLESS
CHIDE	CHIKHORS	CHILLEST	CHIMLEY	CHINNED
CHIDED	CHIKOR	CHILLI	CHIMLEYS	CHINNING
CHIDER	CHIKORS	CHILLIER	CHIMNEY	CHINO
CHIDERS	CHIKS	CHILLIES	CHIMNEYED	CHINOIS
CHIDES	CHILBLAIN	CHILLIEST	CHIMNEYS	CHINOISES
CHIDING	CHILD	CHILLILY	CHIMO	CHINONE
CHIDINGLY	CHILDBED	CHILLING	CHIMP	CHINONES
CHIDINGS	CHILDBEDS	CHILLINGS	CHIMPS	CHINOOK
CHIDLINGS	CHILDCARE	CHILLIS	CHIN	CHINOOKS
CHIEF	CHILDE	CHILLNESS	CHINA	CHINOS
CHIEFDOM	CHILDED	CHILLS	CHINAMAN	CHINOVNIK
CHIEFDOMS	CHILDER	CHILLUM	CHINAMEN	CHINS

CHINSE	CHIRK	CHIS	CHIVIES	CHLOROUS
CHINSED	CHIRKED	CHISEL	CHIVING	CHOANA
CHINSES	CHIRKER	CHISELED	CHIVS	CHOANAE
CHINSING	CHIRKEST	CHISELER	CHIVVED	CHOBDAR
CHINSTRAP	CHIRKING	CHISELERS	CHIVVIED	CHOBDARS
CHINTS	CHIRKS	CHISELING	CHIVVIES	CHOC
CHINTSES	CHIRL	CHISELLED	CHIVVING	CHOCCIER
CHINTZ	CHIRLED	CHISELLER	CHIVVY	CHOCCIES
CHINTZES	CHIRLING	CHISELS	CHIVVYING	CHOCCIEST
CHINTZIER	CHIRLS	CHIT	CHIVY	CHOCCY
CHINTZILY	CHIRM	CHITAL	CHIVYING	CHOCHO
CHINTZY	CHIRMED	CHITALS	CHIWEENIE	CHOCHOS
CHINWAG	CHIRMING	CHITCHAT	CHIYOGAMI	CHOCK
CHINWAGS	CHIRMS	CHITCHATS	CHIZ	CHOCKED
CHIP	CHIRO	CHITIN	CHIZZ	CHOCKER
CHIPBOARD	CHIROLOGY	CHITINOID	CHIZZED	CHOCKERS
CHIPLET	CHIRONOMY	CHITINOUS	CHIZZES	CHOCKFUL
CHIPLETS	CHIROPODY	CHITINS	CHIZZING	CHOCKFULL
CHIPMAKER	CHIROPTER	CHITLIN	CHLAMYDES	CHOCKIE
CHIPMUCK	CHIROS	CHITLING	CHLAMYDIA	CHOCKIER
CHIPMUCKS	CHIRP	CHITLINGS	CHLAMYS	CHOCKIES
CHIPMUNK	CHIRPED	CHITLINS	CHLAMYSES	CHOCKIEST
CHIPMUNKS	CHIRPER	CHITON	CHLOASMA	CHOCKING
CHIPOCHIA	CHIRPERS	CHITONS	CHLOASMAS	CHOCKO
CHIPOLATA	CHIRPIER	CHITOSAN	CHLORACNE	CHOCKOS
CHIPOTLE	CHIRPIEST	CHITOSANS	CHLORAL	CHOCKS
CHIPOTLES	CHIRPILY	CHITS	CHLORALS	CHOCKY
CHIPPABLE	CHIRPING	CHITTED	CHLORATE	CHOCO
CHIPPED	CHIRPINGS	CHITTER	CHLORATES	CHOCOLATE
CHIPPER	CHIRPS	CHITTERED	CHLORDAN	CHOCOLATY
CHIPPERED	CHIRPY	CHITTERS	CHLORDANE	CHOCOS
CHIPPERER	CHIRR	CHITTIER	CHLORDANS	CHOCS
CHIPPERS	CHIRRE	CHITTIES	CHLORELLA	CHOCTAW
CHIPPIE	CHIRRED	CHITTIEST	CHLORIC	CHOCTAWS
CHIPPIER	CHIRREN	CHITTING	CHLORID	CHODE
CHIPPIES	CHIRRES	CHITTY	CHLORIDE	CHOENIX
CHIPPIEST	CHIRRING	CHIV	CHLORIDES	CHOENIXES
CHIPPING	CHIRRS	CHIVALRIC	CHLORIDIC	CHOG
CHIPPINGS	CHIRRUP	CHIVALRY	CHLORIDS	CHOGS
CHIPPY	CHIRRUPED	CHIVAREE	CHLORIN	CHOICE
CHIPS	CHIRRUPER	CHIVAREED	CHLORINE	CHOICEFUL
CHIPSET	CHIRRUPS	CHIVAREES	CHLORINES	CHOICELY
CHIPSETS	CHIRRUPY	CHIVARI	CHLORINS	CHOICER
CHIRAGRA	CHIRT	CHIVARIED	CHLORITE	CHOICES
CHIRAGRAS	CHIRTED	CHIVARIES	CHLORITES	CHOICEST
CHIRAGRIC	CHIRTING	CHIVE	CHLORITIC	CHOIL
CHIRAL	CHIRTS	CHIVED	CHLOROSES	CHOILS
CHIRALITY	CHIRU	CHIVES	CHLOROSIS	CHOIR
CHIRIMOYA	CHIRUS	CHIVIED	CHLOROTIC	CHOIRBOY

CHOIRBOYS	CHOLER	CHONS	CHORALE	CHORIOIDS
CHOIRED	CHOLERA	CHOOF	CHORALES	CHORION
CHOIRGIRL	CHOLERAIC	CHOOFED	CHORALIST	CHORIONIC
CHOIRING	CHOLERAS	CHOOFING	CHORALLY	CHORIONS
CHOIRLIKE	CHOLERIC	CHOOFS	CHORALS	CHORISES
CHOIRMAN	CHOLEROID	CHOOK	CHORD	CHORISIS
CHOIRMEN	CHOLERS	CHOOKED	CHORDA	CHORISM
CHOIRS	CHOLI	CHOOKIE	CHORDAE	CHORISMS
CHOKE	CHOLIAMB	CHOOKIES	CHORDAL	CHORIST
CHOKEABLE	CHOLIAMBS	CHOOKING	CHORDATE	CHORISTER
CHOKEBORE	CHOLIC	CHOOKS	CHORDATES	CHORISTS
CHOKECOIL	CHOLINE	CHOOM	CHORDED	CHORIZO
CHOKED	CHOLINES	CHOOMS	CHORDEE	CHORIZONT
CHOKEDAMP	CHOLIS	CHOON	CHORDEES	CHORIZOS
CHOKEHOLD	CHOLLA	CHOONS	CHORDING	CHOROID
CHOKER	CHOLLAS	CHOOSE	CHORDINGS	CHOROIDAL
CHOKERMAN	CHOLLERS	CHOOSER	CHORDLIKE	CHOROIDS
CHOKERMEN	CHOLTRIES	CHOOSERS	CHORDS	CHOROLOGY
CHOKERS	CHOLTRY	CHOOSES	CHORDWISE	CHORRIE
CHOKES	CHOMETZ	CHOOSEY	CHORE	CHORRIES
CHOKEY	CHOMETZES	CHOOSIER	CHOREA	CHORTEN
CHOKEYS	CHOMMIE	CHOOSIEST	CHOREAL	CHORTENS
CHOKIDAR	CHOMMIES	CHOOSILY	CHOREAS	CHORTLE
CHOKIDARS	CHOMP	CHOOSING	CHOREATIC	CHORTLED
CHOKIER	CHOMPED	CHOOSY	CHOREBOY	CHORTLER
CHOKIES	CHOMPER	CHOP	CHOREBOYS	CHORTLERS
CHOKIEST	CHOMPERS	CHOPHOUSE	CHORED	CHORTLES
CHOKING	CHOMPING	CHOPIN	CHOREE	CHORTLING
CHOKINGLY	CHOMPS	CHOPINE	CHOREES	CHORUS
CHOKO	CHON	CHOPINES	CHOREGI	CHORUSED
CHOKOS	CHONDRAL	CHOPINS	CHOREGIC	CHORUSES
CHOKRA	CHONDRE	CHOPLOGIC	CHOREGUS	CHORUSING
CHOKRAS	CHONDRES	CHOPPED	CHOREIC	CHORUSSED
CHOKRI	CHONDRI	CHOPPER	CHOREMAN	CHORUSSES
CHOKRIS	CHONDRIFY	CHOPPERED	CHOREMEN	CHOSE
CHOKY	CHONDRIN	CHOPPERS	CHOREOID	CHOSEN
CHOLA	CHONDRINS	CHOPPIER	CHORES	CHOSES
CHOLAEMIA	CHONDRITE	CHOPPIEST	CHOREUS	CHOTA
CHOLAEMIC	CHONDROID	CHOPPILY	CHOREUSES	CHOTAS
CHOLAS	CHONDROMA	CHOPPING	CHORIA	CHOTT
CHOLATE	CHONDRULE	CHOPPINGS	CHORIAL	CHOTTS
CHOLATES	CHONDRUS	CHOPPY	CHORIAMB	CHOU
CHOLECYST	CHONK	CHOPS	CHORIAMBI	CHOUGH
CHOLELITH	CHONKER	CHOPSOCKY	CHORIAMBS	CHOUGHS
CHOLEMIA	CHONKEST	CHOPSTICK	CHORIC	CHOULTRY
CHOLEMIAS	CHONKIER	CHORAGI	CHORINE	CHOUNTER
CHOLEMIC	CHONKIEST	CHORAGIC	CHORINES	CHOUNTERS
CHOLENT	CHONKS	CHORAGUS	CHORING	CHOUSE
CHOLENTS	CHONKY	CHORAL	CHORIOID	CHOUSED

CHOUSER	CHRISTIES	CHRONIC	CHUFFIER	CHUNDERS
CHOUSERS	CHRISTOM	CHRONICAL	CHUFFIEST	CHUNGUS
CHOUSES	CHRISTOMS	CHRONICLE	CHUFFING	CHUNGUSES
CHOUSH	CHRISTY	CHRONICS	CHUFFS	CHUNK
CHOUSHES	CHROMA	CHRONON	CHUFFY	CHUNKED
CHOUSING	CHROMAKEY	CHRONONS	CHUG	CHUNKIER
CHOUT	CHROMAS	CHRYSALID	CHUGALUG	CHUNKIEST
CHOUTS	CHROMATE	CHRYSALIS	CHUGALUGS	CHUNKILY
CHOUX	CHROMATES	CHRYSANTH	CHUGGED	CHUNKING
CHOW	CHROMATIC	CHTHONIAN	CHUGGER	CHUNKINGS
CHOWCHOW	CHROMATID	CHTHONIC	CHUGGERS	CHUNKS
CHOWCHOWS	CHROMATIN	CHUB	CHUGGING	CHUNKY
CHOWDER	CHROME	CHUBASCO	CHUGGINGS	CHUNNEL
CHOWDERED	CHROMED	CHUBASCOS	CHUGS	CHUNNELS
CHOWDERS	CHROMEL	CHUBBIER	CHUKAR	CHUNNER
CHOWDOWN	CHROMELS	CHUBBIEST	CHUKARS	CHUNNERED
CHOWDOWNS	CHROMENE	CHUBBILY	CHUKKA	CHUNNERS
CHOWED	CHROMENES	CHUBBY	CHUKKAR	CHUNTER
CHOWHOUND	CHROMES	CHUBS	CHUKKARS	CHUNTERED
CHOWING	CHROMIC	CHUCK	CHUKKAS	CHUNTERS
CHOWK	CHROMIDE	CHUCKED	CHUKKER	CHUPATI
CHOWKIDAR	CHROMIDES	CHUCKER	CHUKKERS	CHUPATIS
CHOWKS	CHROMIDIA	CHUCKERS	CHUKOR	CHUPATTI
CHOWRI	CHROMIER	CHUCKHOLE	CHUKORS	CHUPATTIS
CHOWRIES	CHROMIEST	CHUCKIE	CHUM	CHUPATTY
CHOWRIS	CHROMING	CHUCKIES	CHUMASH	CHUPPA
CHOWRY	CHROMINGS	CHUCKING	CHUMASHES	CHUPPAH
CHOWS	CHROMIS	CHUCKLE	CHUMASHIM	CHUPPAHS
CHOWSE	CHROMISE	CHUCKLED	CHUMLEY	CHUPPAS
CHOWSED	CHROMISED	CHUCKLER	CHUMLEYS	CHUPPOT
CHOWSES	CHROMISES	CHUCKLERS	CHUMMAGE	CHUPPOTH
CHOWSING	CHROMITE	CHUCKLES	CHUMMAGES	CHUPRASSY
CHOWTIME	CHROMITES	CHUCKLING	CHUMMED	CHUR
CHOWTIMES	CHROMIUM	CHUCKS	CHUMMIER	CHURCH
CHRESARD	CHROMIUMS	CHUCKY	CHUMMIES	CHURCHED
CHRESARDS	CHROMIZE	CHUDDAH	CHUMMIEST	CHURCHES
CHRISM	CHROMIZED	CHUDDAHS	CHUMMILY	CHURCHIER
CHRISMA	CHROMIZES	CHUDDAR	CHUMMING	CHURCHING
CHRISMAL	CHROMO	CHUDDARS	CHUMMY	CHURCHISM
CHRISMALS	CHROMOGEN	CHUDDER	CHUMP	CHURCHLY
CHRISMON	CHROMOLY	CHUDDERS	CHUMPED	CHURCHMAN
CHRISMONS	CHROMOLYS	CHUDDIES	CHUMPING	CHURCHMEN
CHRISMS	CHROMOS	CHUDDY	CHUMPINGS	CHURCHWAY
CHRISOM	CHROMOUS	CHUFA	CHUMPS	CHURCHY
CHRISOMS	CHROMY	CHUFAS	CHUMS	CHURIDAR
CHRISTEN	CHROMYL	CHUFF	CHUMSHIP	CHURIDARS
CHRISTENS	CHROMYLS	CHUFFED	CHUMSHIPS	CHURINGA
CHRISTIAN	CHRONAXIE	CHUFFER	CHUNDER	CHURINGAS
CHRISTIE	CHRONAXY	CHUFFEST	CHUNDERED	CHURL

CHURLISH	CHYLURIA	CICERONED	CIGARILLO	CINCTURED
CHURLS	CHYLURIAS	CICERONES	CIGARLIKE	CINCTURES
CHURN	CHYME	CICERONI	CIGARS	CINDER
CHURNED	CHYMES	CICEROS	CIGGIE	CINDERED
CHURNER	CHYMIC	CICHLID	CIGGIES	CINDERIER
CHURNERS	CHYMICS	CICHLIDAE	CIGGY	CINDERING
CHURNING	CHYMIFIED	CICHLIDS	CIGS	CINDEROUS
CHURNINGS	CHYMIFIES	CICHLOID	CIGUATERA	CINDERS
CHURNMILK	CHYMIFY	CICINNUS	CILANTRO	CINDERY
CHURNS	CHYMIST	CICISBEI	CILANTROS	CINE
CHURR	CHYMISTRY	CICISBEO	CILIA	CINEAST
CHURRED	CHYMISTS	CICISBEOS	CILIARY	CINEASTE
CHURRING	CHYMOSIN	CICLATON	CILIATE	CINEASTES
CHURRO	CHYMOSINS	CICLATONS	CILIATED	CINEASTS
CHURROS	CHYMOUS	CICLATOUN	CILIATELY	CINEMA
CHURRS	CHYND	CICOREE	CILIATES	CINEMAS
CHURRUS	CHYPRE	CICOREES	CILIATION	CINEMATIC
CHURRUSES	CHYPRES	CICUTA	CILICE	CINEOL
CHUSE	CHYRON	CICUTAS	CILICES	CINEOLE
CHUSED	CHYRONS	CICUTINE	CILICIOUS	CINEOLES
CHUSES	CHYTRID	CICUTINES	CILIOLATE	CINEOLS
CHUSING	CHYTRIDS	CID	CILIUM	CINEPHILE
CHUT	CIABATTA	CIDARIS	CILL	CINEPLEX
CHUTE	CIABATTAS	CIDARISES	CILLS	CINERAMIC
CHUTED	CIABATTE	CIDE	CIMAR	CINERARIA
CHUTES	CIAO	CIDED	CIMARS	CINERARY
CHUTING	CIBATION	CIDER	CIMBALOM	CINERATOR
CHUTIST	CIBATIONS	CIDERIER	CIMBALOMS	CINEREA
CHUTISTS	CIBOL	CIDERIES	CIMELIA	CINEREAL
CHUTNEE	CIBOLS	CIDERIEST	CIMEX	CINEREAS
CHUTNEES	CIBORIA	CIDERKIN	CIMICES	CINEREOUS
CHUTNEY	CIBORIUM	CIDERKINS	CIMIER	CINERIN
CHUTNEYS	CIBORIUMS	CIDERS	CIMIERS	CINERINS
CHUTS	CIBOULE	CIDERY	CIMINITE	CINES
CHUTZPA	CIBOULES	CIDES	CIMINITES	CINGULA
CHUTZPAH	CICADA	CIDING	CIMMERIAN	CINGULAR
CHUTZPAHS	CICADAE	CIDS	CIMOLITE	CINGULATE
CHUTZPAS	CICADAS	CIEL	CIMOLITES	CINGULUM
CHYACK	CICALA	CIELED	CINCH	CINNABAR
CHYACKED	CICALAS	CIELING	CINCHED	CINNABARS
CHYACKING	CICALE	CIELINGS	CINCHES	CINNAMIC
CHYACKS	CICATRICE	CIELS	CINCHING	CINNAMON
CHYLDE	CICATRISE	CIERGE	CINCHINGS	CINNAMONS
CHYLE	CICATRIX	CIERGES	CINCHONA	CINNAMONY
CHYLES	CICATRIZE	CIG	CINCHONAS	CINNAMYL
CHYLIFIED	CICELIES	CIGAR	CINCHONIC	CINNAMYLS
CHYLIFIES	CICELY	CIGARET	CINCINNUS	CINQ
CHYLIFY	CICERO	CIGARETS	CINCT	CINQS
CHYLOUS	CICERONE	CIGARETTE	CINCTURE	CINQUAIN

CINQUAINS	CIRCUS	CISSUS	CITIFIED	CIVE
CINQUE	CIRCUSES	CISSUSES	CITIFIES	CIVES
CINQUES	CIRCUSIER	CISSY	CITIFY	CIVET
CION	CIRCUSSY	CIST	CITIFYING	CIVETLIKE
CIONS	CIRCUSY	CISTED	CITIGRADE	CIVETS
CIOPPINO	CIRE	CISTERN	CITING	CIVIC
CIOPPINOS	CIRES	CISTERNA	CITIZEN	CIVICALLY
CIPAILLE	CIRL	CISTERNAE	CITIZENLY	CIVICISM
CIPAILLES	CIRLS	CISTERNAL	CITIZENRY	CIVICISMS
CIPHER	CIRQUE	CISTERNS	CITIZENS	CIVICS
CIPHERED	CIRQUES	CISTIC	CITO	CIVIE
CIPHERER	CIRRATE	CISTRON	CITOLA	CIVIES
CIPHERERS	CIRRHOSED	CISTRONIC	CITOLAS	CIVIL
CIPHERING	CIRRHOSES	CISTRONS	CITOLE	CIVILIAN
CIPHERS	CIRRHOSIS	CISTS	CITOLES	CIVILIANS
CIPHONIES	CIRRHOTIC	CISTUS	CITRAL	CIVILISE
CIPHONY	CIRRI	CISTUSES	CITRALS	CIVILISED
CIPOLIN	CIRRIFORM	CISTVAEN	CITRANGE	CIVILISER
CIPOLINS	CIRRIPED	CISTVAENS	CITRANGES	CIVILISES
CIPOLLINO	CIRRIPEDE	CIT	CITRATE	CIVILIST
CIPPI	CIRRIPEDS	CITABLE	CITRATED	CIVILISTS
CIPPUS	CIRROSE	CITADEL	CITRATES	CIVILITY
CIRCA	CIRROUS	CITADELS	CITREOUS	CIVILIZE
CIRCADIAN	CIRRUS	CITAL	CITRIC	CIVILIZED
CIRCAR	CIRRUSES	CITALS	CITRIN	CIVILIZER
CIRCARS	CIRSOID	CITATION	CITRINE	CIVILIZES
CIRCINATE	CIS	CITATIONS	CITRINES	CIVILLY
CIRCITER	CISALPINE	CITATOR	CITRININ	CIVILNESS
CIRCLE	CISCO	CITATORS	CITRININS	CIVILS
CIRCLED	CISCOES	CITATORY	CITRINS	CIVISM
CIRCLER	CISCOS	CITE	CITRON	CIVISMS
CIRCLERS	CISELEUR	CITEABLE	CITRONS	CIVVIES
CIRCLES	CISELEURS	CITED	CITROUS	CIVVY
CIRCLET	CISELURE	CITER	CITRUS	CIZERS
CIRCLETS	CISELURES	CITERS	CITRUSES	CLABBER
CIRCLING	CISGENDER	CITES	CITRUSIER	CLABBERED
CIRCLINGS	CISHET	CITESS	CITRUSSY	CLABBERS
CIRCLIP	CISHETS	CITESSES	CITRUSY	CLACH
CIRCLIPS	CISLUNAR	CITHARA	CITS	CLACHAN
CIRCS	CISPADANE	CITHARAS	CITTERN	CLACHANS
CIRCUIT	CISPLATIN	CITHARIST	CITTERNS	CLACHED
CIRCUITAL	CISSIER	CITHER	CITY	CLACHES
CIRCUITED	CISSIES	CITHERN	CITYFIED	CLACHING
CIRCUITRY	CISSIEST	CITHERNS	CITYFIES	CLACHS
CIRCUITS	CISSIFIED	CITHERS	CITYFY	CLACK
CIRCUITY	CISSING	CITHREN	CITYFYING	CLACKBOX
CIRCULAR	CISSINGS	CITHRENS	CITYSCAPE	CLACKDISH
CIRCULARS	CISSOID	CITIED	CITYWARD	CLACKED
CIRCULATE	CISSOIDS	CITIES	CITYWIDE	CLACKER

CLACKERS	CLAMBAKES	CLANGOR	CLARET	CLASPS
CLACKING	CLAMBE	CLANGORED	CLARETED	CLASPT
CLACKS	CLAMBER	CLANGORS	CLARETING	CLASS
CLAD	CLAMBERED	CLANGOUR	CLARETS	CLASSABLE
CLADDAGH	CLAMBERER	CLANGOURS	CLARIES	CLASSED
CLADDAGHS	CLAMBERS	CLANGS	CLARIFIED	CLASSER
CLADDED	CLAME	CLANK	CLARIFIER	CLASSERS
CLADDER	CLAMES	CLANKED	CLARIFIES	CLASSES
CLADDERS	CLAMLIKE	CLANKIER	CLARIFY	CLASSIBLE
CLADDIE	CLAMMED	CLANKIEST	CLARINET	CLASSIC
CLADDIES	CLAMMER	CLANKING	CLARINETS	CLASSICAL
CLADDING	CLAMMERS	CLANKINGS	CLARINI	CLASSICO
CLADDINGS	CLAMMIER	CLANKS	CLARINO	CLASSICS
CLADE	CLAMMIEST	CLANKY	CLARINOS	CLASSIER
CLADES	CLAMMILY	CLANNISH	CLARION	CLASSIEST
CLADISM	CLAMMING	CLANS	CLARIONED	CLASSIFIC
CLADISMS	CLAMMY	CLANSHIP	CLARIONET	CLASSIFY
CLADIST	CLAMOR	CLANSHIPS	CLARIONS	CLASSILY
CLADISTIC	CLAMORED	CLANSMAN	CLARITIES	CLASSING
CLADISTS	CLAMORER	CLANSMEN	CLARITY	CLASSINGS
CLADODE	CLAMORERS	CLAP	CLARKIA	CLASSIS
CLADODES	CLAMORING	CLAPBACK	CLARKIAS	CLASSISM
CLADODIAL	CLAMOROUS	CLAPBACKS	CLARO	CLASSISMS
CLADOGRAM	CLAMORS	CLAPBOARD	CLAROES	CLASSIST
CLADS	CLAMOUR	CLAPBREAD	CLAROS	CLASSISTS
CLAES	CLAMOURED	CLAPDISH	CLARSACH	CLASSLESS
CLAFOUTI	CLAMOURER	CLAPNET	CLARSACHS	CLASSMAN
CLAFOUTIS	CLAMOURS	CLAPNETS	CLART	CLASSMATE
CLAG	CLAMP	CLAPPED	CLARTED	CLASSMEN
CLAGGED	CLAMPDOWN	CLAPPER	CLARTHEAD	CLASSON
CLAGGIER	CLAMPED	CLAPPERED	CLARTIER	CLASSONS
CLAGGIEST	CLAMPER	CLAPPERS	CLARTIEST	CLASSROOM
CLAGGING	CLAMPERED	CLAPPING	CLARTING	CLASSWORK
CLAGGY	CLAMPERS	CLAPPINGS	CLARTS	CLASSY
CLAGS	CLAMPING	CLAPS	CLARTY	CLAST
CLAIM	CLAMPINGS	CLAPT	CLARY	CLASTIC
CLAIMABLE	CLAMPS	CLAPTRAP	CLASH	CLASTICS
CLAIMANT	CLAMS	CLAPTRAPS	CLASHED	CLASTS
CLAIMANTS	CLAMSHELL	CLAQUE	CLASHER	CLAT
CLAIMED	CLAMWORM	CLAQUER	CLASHERS	CLATCH
CLAIMER	CLAMWORMS	CLAQUERS	CLASHES	CLATCHED
CLAIMERS	CLAN	CLAQUES	CLASHING	CLATCHES
CLAIMING	CLANG	CLAQUEUR	CLASHINGS	CLATCHING
CLAIMS	CLANGBOX	CLAQUEURS	CLASP	CLATHRATE
CLAM	CLANGED	CLARAIN	CLASPED	CLATS
CLAMANCY	CLANGER	CLARAINS	CLASPER	CLATTED
CLAMANT	CLANGERS	CLARENCE	CLASPERS	CLATTER
CLAMANTLY	CLANGING	CLARENCES	CLASPING	CLATTERED
CLAMBAKE	CLANGINGS	CLARENDON	CLASPINGS	CLATTERER

CLATTERS	CLAW	CLEANSER	CLECKED	CLEPES
CLATTERY	CLAWBACK	CLEANSERS	CLECKIER	CLEPING
CLATTING	CLAWBACKS	CLEANSES	CLECKIEST	CLEPSYDRA
CLAUCHT	CLAWED	CLEANSING	CLECKING	CLEPT
CLAUCHTED	CLAWER	CLEANSKIN	CLECKINGS	CLERGIES
CLAUCHTS	CLAWERS	CLEANTECH	CLECKS	CLERGY
CLAUGHT	CLAWING	CLEANUP	CLECKY	CLERGYMAN
CLAUGHTED	CLAWLESS	CLEANUPS	CLEEK	CLERGYMEN
CLAUGHTS	CLAWLIKE	CLEAR	CLEEKED	CLERIC
CLAUSAL	CLAWS	CLEARABLE	CLEEKING	CLERICAL
CLAUSE	CLAXON	CLEARAGE	CLEEKIT	CLERICALS
CLAUSES	CLAXONS	CLEARAGES	CLEEKS	CLERICATE
CLAUSTRA	CLAY	CLEARANCE	CLEEP	CLERICITY
CLAUSTRAL	CLAYBANK	CLEARCOLE	CLEEPED	CLERICS
CLAUSTRUM	CLAYBANKS	CLEARCUT	CLEEPING	CLERID
CLAUSULA	CLAYED	CLEARCUTS	CLEEPS	CLERIDS
CLAUSULAE	CLAYEY	CLEARED	CLEEVE	CLERIHEW
CLAUSULAR	CLAYIER	CLEARER	CLEEVES	CLERIHEWS
CLAUT	CLAYIEST	CLEARERS	CLEF	CLERISIES
CLAUTED	CLAYING	CLEAREST	CLEFS	CLERISY
CLAUTING	CLAYISH	CLEAREYED	CLEFT	CLERK
CLAUTS	CLAYLIKE	CLEARING	CLEFTED	CLERKDOM
CLAVATE	CLAYMORE	CLEARINGS	CLEFTING	CLERKDOMS
CLAVATED	CLAYMORES	CLEARLY	CLEFTS	CLERKED
CLAVATELY	CLAYPAN	CLEARNESS	CLEG	CLERKESS
CLAVATION	CLAYPANS	CLEAROUT	CLEGS	CLERKING
CLAVE	CLAYS	CLEAROUTS	CLEIDOIC	CLERKISH
CLAVECIN	CLAYSTONE	CLEARS	CLEIK	CLERKLIER
CLAVECINS	CLAYTONIA	CLEARSKIN	CLEIKS	CLERKLIKE
CLAVER	CLAYWARE	CLEARWAY	CLEITHRAL	CLERKLING
CLAVERED	CLAYWARES	CLEARWAYS	CLEM	CLERKLY
CLAVERING	CLEAN	CLEARWEED	CLEMATIS	CLERKS
CLAVERS	CLEANABLE	CLEARWING	CLEMENCY	CLERKSHIP
CLAVES	CLEANED	CLEAT	CLEMENT	CLERUCH
CLAVI	CLEANER	CLEATED	CLEMENTLY	CLERUCHIA
CLAVICLE	CLEANERS	CLEATING	CLEMMED	CLERUCHS
CLAVICLES	CLEANEST	CLEATS	CLEMMING	CLERUCHY
CLAVICORN	CLEANING	CLEAVABLE	CLEMS	CLEUCH
CLAVICULA	CLEANINGS	CLEAVAGE	CLENCH	CLEUCHS
CLAVIE	CLEANISH	CLEAVAGES	CLENCHED	CLEUGH
CLAVIER	CLEANLIER	CLEAVE	CLENCHER	CLEUGHS
CLAVIERS	CLEANLILY	CLEAVED	CLENCHERS	CLEVE
CLAVIES	CLEANLY	CLEAVER	CLENCHES	CLEVEITE
CLAVIFORM	CLEANNESS	CLEAVERS	CLENCHING	CLEVEITES
CLAVIGER	CLEANOUT	CLEAVES	CLEOME	CLEVER
CLAVIGERS	CLEANOUTS	CLEAVING	CLEOMES	CLEVERER
CLAVIS	CLEANS	CLEAVINGS	CLEOPATRA	CLEVEREST
CLAVULATE	CLEANSE	CLECHE	CLEPE	CLEVERISH
CLAVUS	CLEANSED	CLECK	CLEPED	CLEVERLY

CLEVES	CLIFTS	CLINGWRAP	CLIQUING	CLOCKING
CLEVIS	CLIFTY	CLINGY	CLIQUISH	CLOCKINGS
CLEVISES	CLIMACTIC	CLINIC	CLIQUISM	CLOCKLIKE
CLEW	CLIMATAL	CLINICAL	CLIQUISMS	CLOCKS
CLEWED	CLIMATE	CLINICIAN	CLIQUY	CLOCKWISE
CLEWING	CLIMATED	CLINICS	CLIT	CLOCKWORK
CLEWS	CLIMATES	CLINIQUE	CLITELLA	CLOD
CLIANTHUS	CLIMATIC	CLINIQUES	CLITELLAR	CLODDED
CLICHE	CLIMATING	CLINK	CLITELLUM	CLODDIER
CLICHED	CLIMATISE	CLINKED	CLITHRAL	CLODDIEST
CLICHEED	CLIMATIZE	CLINKER	CLITIC	CLODDING
CLICHES	CLIMATURE	CLINKERED	CLITICISE	CLODDISH
CLICK	CLIMAX	CLINKERS	CLITICIZE	CLODDY
CLICKABLE	CLIMAXED	CLINKING	CLITICS	CLODLY
CLICKBAIT	CLIMAXES	CLINKS	CLITORAL	CLODPATE
CLICKED	CLIMAXING	CLINOAXES	CLITORIC	CLODPATED
CLICKER	CLIMB	CLINOAXIS	CLITORIS	CLODPATES
CLICKERS	CLIMBABLE	CLINOSTAT	CLITS	CLODPOLE
CLICKET	CLIMBDOWN	CLINQUANT	CLITTER	CLODPOLES
CLICKETED	CLIMBED	CLINT	CLITTERED	CLODPOLL
CLICKETS	CLIMBER	CLINTONIA	CLITTERS	CLODPOLLS
CLICKING	CLIMBERS	CLINTS	CLIVERS	CLODS
CLICKINGS	CLIMBING	CLIOMETRY	CLIVIA	CLOFF
CLICKLESS	CLIMBINGS	CLIP	CLIVIAS	CLOFFS
CLICKS	CLIMBS	CLIPART	CLOACA	CLOG
CLICKWRAP	CLIME	CLIPARTS	CLOACAE	CLOGDANCE
CLIED	CLIMES	CLIPBOARD	CLOACAL	CLOGGED
CLIENT	CLINAL	CLIPE	CLOACAS	CLOGGER
CLIENTAGE	CLINALLY	CLIPED	CLOACINAL	CLOGGERS
CLIENTAL	CLINAMEN	CLIPES	CLOACITIS	CLOGGIER
CLIENTELE	CLINAMENS	CLIPING	CLOAK	CLOGGIEST
CLIENTS	CLINCH	CLIPPABLE	CLOAKED	CLOGGILY
CLIES	CLINCHED	CLIPPED	CLOAKING	CLOGGING
CLIFF	CLINCHER	CLIPPER	CLOAKROOM	CLOGGINGS
CLIFFED	CLINCHERS	CLIPPERS	CLOAKS	CLOGGY
CLIFFHANG	CLINCHES	CLIPPIE	CLOAM	CLOGMAKER
CLIFFHUNG	CLINCHING	CLIPPIES	CLOAMS	CLOGS
CLIFFIER	CLINE	CLIPPING	CLOBBER	CLOISON
CLIFFIEST	CLINES	CLIPPINGS	CLOBBERED	CLOISONNE
CLIFFLIKE	CLING	CLIPS	CLOBBERS	CLOISONS
CLIFFS	CLINGED	CLIPSHEAR	CLOCHARD	CLOISTER
CLIFFSIDE	CLINGER	CLIPSHEET	CLOCHARDS	CLOISTERS
CLIFFTOP	CLINGERS	CLIPT	CLOCHE	CLOISTRAL
CLIFFTOPS	CLINGFILM	CLIQUE	CLOCHES	CLOKE
CLIFFY	CLINGFISH	CLIQUED	CLOCK	CLOKED
CLIFT	CLINGIER	CLIQUES	CLOCKED	CLOKES
CLIFTED	CLINGIEST	CLIQUEY	CLOCKER	CLOKING
CLIFTIER	CLINGING	CLIQUIER	CLOCKERS	CLOMB
CLIFTIEST	CLINGS	CLIQUIEST	CLOCKFACE	CLOMP

CLOMPED	CLOSER	CLOU	CLOWNFISH	CLUBLANDS
CLOMPING	CLOSERS	CLOUD	CLOWNING	CLUBLIKE
CLOMPS	CLOSES	CLOUDAGE	CLOWNINGS	CLUBMAN
CLON	CLOSEST	CLOUDAGES	CLOWNISH	CLUBMATE
CLONAL	CLOSET	CLOUDED	CLOWNS	CLUBMATES
CLONALLY	CLOSETED	CLOUDIER	CLOWS	CLUBMEN
CLONE	CLOSETFUL	CLOUDIEST	CLOY	CLUBMOSS
CLONED	CLOSETING	CLOUDILY	CLOYE	CLUBROOM
CLONER	CLOSETS	CLOUDING	CLOYED	CLUBROOMS
CLONERS	CLOSEUP	CLOUDINGS	CLOYES	CLUBROOT
CLONES	CLOSEUPS	CLOUDLAND	CLOYING	CLUBROOTS
CLONIC	CLOSING	CLOUDLESS	CLOYINGLY	CLUBRUSH
CLONICITY	CLOSINGS	CLOUDLET	CLOYLESS	CLUBS
CLONIDINE	CLOSURE	CLOUDLETS	CLOYMENT	CLUBWOMAN
CLONING	CLOSURED	CLOUDLIKE	CLOYMENTS	CLUBWOMEN
CLONINGS	CLOSURES	CLOUDS	CLOYS	CLUCK
CLONISM	CLOSURING	CLOUDTOWN	CLOYSOME	CLUCKED
CLONISMS	CLOT	CLOUDY	CLOZAPINE	CLUCKER
CLONK	CLOTBUR	CLOUGH	CLOZE	CLUCKERS
CLONKED	CLOTBURS	CLOUGHS	CLOZES	CLUCKIER
CLONKIER	CLOTE	CLOUR	CLUB	CLUCKIEST
CLONKIEST	CLOTES	CLOURED	CLUBABLE	CLUCKING
CLONKING	CLOTH	CLOURING	CLUBBABLE	CLUCKS
CLONKS	CLOTHE	CLOURS	CLUBBED	CLUCKY
CLONKY	CLOTHED	CLOUS	CLUBBER	CLUDGIE
CLONS	CLOTHES	CLOUT	CLUBBERS	CLUDGIES
CLONUS	CLOTHIER	CLOUTED	CLUBBIER	CLUE
CLONUSES	CLOTHIERS	CLOUTER	CLUBBIEST	CLUED
CLOOP	CLOTHING	CLOUTERLY	CLUBBILY	CLUEING
CLOOPS	CLOTHINGS	CLOUTERS	CLUBBING	CLUELESS
CLOOT	CLOTHLIKE	CLOUTING	CLUBBINGS	CLUES
CLOOTIE	CLOTHS	CLOUTS	CLUBBISH	CLUEY
CLOOTS	CLOTPOLL	CLOVE	CLUBBISM	CLUIER
CLOP	CLOTPOLLS	CLOVEN	CLUBBISMS	CLUIEST
CLOPPED	CLOTS	CLOVER	CLUBBIST	CLUING
CLOPPING	CLOTTED	CLOVERED	CLUBBISTS	CLUMBER
CLOPS	CLOTTER	CLOVERIER	CLUBBY	CLUMBERS
CLOQUE	CLOTTERED	CLOVERS	CLUBFACE	CLUMP
CLOQUES	CLOTTERS	CLOVERY	CLUBFACES	CLUMPED
CLOSABLE	CLOTTIER	CLOVES	CLUBFEET	CLUMPER
CLOSE	CLOTTIEST	CLOVIS	CLUBFOOT	CLUMPERED
CLOSEABLE	CLOTTING	CLOW	CLUBHAND	CLUMPERS
CLOSED	CLOTTINGS	CLOWDER	CLUBHANDS	CLUMPET
CLOSEDOWN	CLOTTISH	CLOWDERS	CLUBHAUL	CLUMPETS
CLOSEHEAD	CLOTTY	CLOWED	CLUBHAULS	CLUMPIER
CLOSELY	CLOTURE	CLOWING	CLUBHEAD	CLUMPIEST
CLOSENESS	CLOTURED	CLOWN	CLUBHEADS	CLUMPING
CLOSEOUT	CLOTURES	CLOWNED	CLUBHOUSE	CLUMPISH
CLOSEOUTS	CLOTURING	CLOWNERY	CLUBLAND	CLUMPLIKE

CLUMPS	CLYSTERS	COADUNATE	COALISING	COASSUMED
CLUMPY	CNEMIAL	COADY	COALITION	COASSUMES
CLUMSIER	CNEMIDES	COAEVAL	COALIZE	COAST
CLUMSIEST	CNEMIS	COAEVALLY	COALIZED	COASTAL
CLUMSILY	CNIDA	COAEVALS	COALIZES	COASTALLY
CLUMSY	CNIDAE	COAGENCY	COALIZING	COASTED
CLUNCH	CNIDARIAN	COAGENT	COALLESS	COASTER
CLUNCHES	CNIDOCYST	COAGENTS	COALMAN	COASTERS
CLUNG	COACH	COAGULA	COALMEN	COASTING
CLUNK	COACHABLE	COAGULANT	COALMINE	COASTINGS
CLUNKED	COACHDOG	COAGULASE	COALMINER	COASTLAND
CLUNKER	COACHDOGS	COAGULATE	COALMINES	COASTLINE
CLUNKERS	COACHED	COAGULUM	COALPIT	COASTS
CLUNKIER	COACHEE	COAGULUMS	COALPITS	COASTWARD
CLUNKIEST	COACHEES	COAITA	COALS	COASTWISE
CLUNKING	COACHER	COAITAS	COALSACK	COAT
CLUNKS	COACHERS	COAL	COALSACKS	COATDRESS
CLUNKY	COACHES	COALA	COALSHED	COATE
CLUPEID	COACHIER	COALAS	COALSHEDS	COATED
CLUPEIDS	COACHIES	COALBALL	COALY	COATEE
CLUPEOID	COACHIEST	COALBALLS	COALYARD	COATEES
CLUPEOIDS	COACHING	COALBIN	COALYARDS	COATER
CLUSIA	COACHINGS	COALBINS	COAMING	COATERS
CLUSIAS	COACHLINE	COALBOX	COAMINGS	COATES
CLUSTER	COACHLOAD	COALBOXES	COANCHOR	COATI
CLUSTERED	COACHMAN	COALDUST	COANCHORS	COATING
CLUSTERS	COACHMEN	COALDUSTS	COANNEX	COATINGS
CLUSTERY	COACHROOF	COALED	COANNEXED	COATIS
CLUTCH	COACHWHIP	COALER	COANNEXES	COATLESS
CLUTCHED	COACHWOOD	COALERS	COAPPEAR	COATLIKE
CLUTCHES	COACHWORK	COALESCE	COAPPEARS	COATRACK
CLUTCHIER	COACHY	COALESCED	COAPT	COATRACKS
CLUTCHING	COACT	COALESCES	COAPTED	COATROOM
CLUTCHY	COACTED	COALFACE	COAPTING	COATROOMS
CLUTTER	COACTING	COALFACES	COAPTS	COATS
CLUTTERED	COACTION	COALFIELD	COARB	COATSTAND
CLUTTERS	COACTIONS	COALFISH	COARBS	COATTAIL
CLUTTERY	COACTIVE	COALHOLE	COARCTATE	COATTAILS
CLY	COACTOR	COALHOLES	COARSE	COATTEND
CLYING	COACTORS	COALHOUSE	COARSELY	COATTENDS
CLYPE	COACTS	COALIER	COARSEN	COATTEST
CLYPEAL	COADAPTED	COALIEST	COARSENED	COATTESTS
CLYPEATE	COADIES	COALIFIED	COARSENS	COAUTHOR
CLYPED	COADJUTOR	COALIFIES	COARSER	COAUTHORS
CLYPEI	COADMIRE	COALIFY	COARSEST	COAX
CLYPES	COADMIRED	COALING	COARSISH	COAXAL
CLYPEUS	COADMIRES	COALISE	COASSIST	COAXED
CLYPING	COADMIT	COALISED	COASSISTS	COAXER
CLYSTER	COADMITS	COALISES	COASSUME	COAXERS

COAXES	COBWEBBED	COCHLEARE	COCKLED	COCOBOLAS
COAXIAL	COBWEBBY	COCHLEARS	COCKLEERT	COCOBOLO
COAXIALLY	COBWEBS	COCHLEAS	COCKLEMAN	COCOBOLOS
COAXING	COBZA	COCHLEATE	COCKLEMEN	COCOMAT
COAXINGLY	COBZAS	COCINERA	COCKLER	COCOMATS
COAXINGS	COCA	COCINERAS	COCKLERS	COCONUT
COB	COCAIN	COCK	COCKLES	COCONUTS
COBAEA	COCAINE	COCKADE	COCKLIKE	COCONUTTY
COBAEAS	COCAINES	COCKADED	COCKLING	COCOON
COBALAMIN	COCAINISE	COCKADES	COCKLINGS	COCOONED
COBALT	COCAINISM	COCKAMAMY	COCKLOFT	COCOONER
COBALTIC	COCAINIST	COCKAPOO	COCKLOFTS	COCOONERS
COBALTINE	COCAINIZE	COCKAPOOS	COCKMATCH	COCOONERY
COBALTITE	COCAINS	COCKATEEL	COCKNEY	COCOONING
COBALTOUS	COCAPTAIN	COCKATIEL	COCKNEYFY	COCOONS
COBALTS	COCAS	COCKATOO	COCKNEYS	COCOPAN
COBB	COCCAL	COCKATOOS	COCKNIFY	COCOPANS
COBBED	COCCI	COCKBILL	COCKPIT	COCOPLUM
COBBER	COCCIC	COCKBILLS	COCKPITS	COCOPLUMS
COBBERS	COCCID	COCKBIRD	COCKROACH	COCOS
COBBIER	COCCIDIA	COCKBIRDS	COCKS	COCOTTE
COBBIEST	COCCIDIAN	COCKBLOCK	COCKSCOMB	COCOTTES
COBBING	COCCIDIUM	COCKBOAT	COCKSFOOT	COCOUNSEL
COBBLE	COCCIDS	COCKBOATS	COCKSHIES	COCOYAM
COBBLED	COCCO	COCKCROW	COCKSHOT	COCOYAMS
COBBLER	COCCOID	COCKCROWS	COCKSHOTS	COCOZELLE
COBBLERS	COCCOIDAL	COCKED	COCKSHUT	COCREATE
COBBLERY	COCCOIDS	COCKER	COCKSHUTS	COCREATED
COBBLES	COCCOLITE	COCKERED	COCKSHY	COCREATES
COBBLING	COCCOLITH	COCKEREL	COCKSIER	COCREATOR
COBBLINGS	COCCOS	COCKERELS	COCKSIEST	COCTILE
COBBS	COCCOUS	COCKERING	COCKSMAN	COCTION
COBBY	COCCUS	COCKERS	COCKSMEN	COCTIONS
COBIA	COCCYGEAL	COCKET	COCKSPUR	COCULTURE
COBIAS	COCCYGES	COCKETS	COCKSPURS	COCURATE
COBLE	COCCYGIAN	COCKEYE	COCKSURE	COCURATED
COBLES	COCCYX	COCKEYED	COCKSWAIN	COCURATES
COBLOAF	COCCYXES	COCKEYES	COCKSY	COCURATOR
COBLOAVES	COCH	COCKFIGHT	COCKTAIL	COCUSWOOD
COBNUT	COCHAIR	COCKHORSE	COCKTAILS	COD
COBNUTS	COCHAIRED	COCKIER	COCKUP	CODA
COBRA	COCHAIRS	COCKIES	COCKUPS	CODABLE
COBRAS	COCHES	COCKIEST	COCKY	CODAS
COBRIC	COCHIN	COCKILY	COCO	CODDED
COBRIFORM	COCHINEAL	COCKINESS	COCOA	CODDER
COBS	COCHINS	COCKING	COCOANUT	CODDERS
COBURG	COCHLEA	COCKISH	COCOANUTS	CODDING
COBURGS	COCHLEAE	COCKLE	COCOAS	CODDLE
COBWEB	COCHLEAR	COCKLEBUR	COCOBOLA	CODDLED

CODDLER	CODIFIED	COELIACS	COERCES	COFFLES
CODDLERS	CODIFIER	COELOM	COERCIBLE	COFFLING
CODDLES	CODIFIERS	COELOMATA	COERCIBLY	COFFRET
CODDLING	CODIFIES	COELOMATE	COERCING	COFFRETS
CODE	CODIFY	COELOME	COERCION	COFFS
CODEBASE	CODIFYING	COELOMES	COERCIONS	COFINANCE
CODEBASES	CODILLA	COELOMIC	COERCIVE	COFIRING
CODEBOOK	CODILLAS	COELOMS	COERECT	COFIRINGS
CODEBOOKS	CODILLE	COELOSTAT	COERECTED	COFOUND
CODEBTOR	CODILLES	COEMBODY	COERECTS	COFOUNDED
CODEBTORS	CODING	COEMPLOY	COESITE	COFOUNDER
CODEC	CODINGS	COEMPLOYS	COESITES	COFOUNDS
CODECS	CODIRECT	COEMPT	COETERNAL	COFT
CODED	CODIRECTS	COEMPTED	COEVAL	COG
CODEIA	CODIST	COEMPTING	COEVALITY	COGENCE
CODEIAS	CODISTS	COEMPTION	COEVALLY	COGENCES
CODEIN	CODLIN	COEMPTS	COEVALS	COGENCIES
CODEINA	CODLING	COENACLE	COEVOLVE	COGENCY
CODEINAS	CODLINGS	COENACLES	COEVOLVED	COGENER
CODEINE	CODLINS	COENACT	COEVOLVES	COGENERS
CODEINES	CODOLOGY	COENACTED	COEXERT	COGENT
CODEINS	CODOMAIN	COENACTS	COEXERTED	COGENTLY
CODELESS	CODOMAINS	COENAMOR	COEXERTS	COGGED
CODEN	CODON	COENAMORS	COEXIST	COGGER
CODENAME	CODONS	COENAMOUR	COEXISTED	COGGERS
CODENAMES	CODPIECE	COENDURE	COEXISTS	COGGIE
CODENS	CODPIECES	COENDURED	COEXTEND	COGGIES
CODER	CODRIVE	COENDURES	COEXTENDS	COGGING
CODERIVE	CODRIVEN	COENOBIA	COFACTOR	COGGINGS
CODERIVED	CODRIVER	COENOBITE	COFACTORS	COGGLE
CODERIVES	CODRIVERS	COENOBIUM	COFEATURE	COGGLED
CODERS	CODRIVES	COENOCYTE	COFF	COGGLES
CODES	CODRIVING	COENOSARC	COFFED	COGGLIER
CODESIGN	CODROVE	COENURE	COFFEE	COGGLIEST
CODESIGNS	CODS	COENURES	COFFEEPOT	COGGLING
CODETTA	COECILIAN	COENURI	COFFEES	COGGLY
CODETTAS	COED	COENURUS	COFFER	COGIE
CODEVELOP	COEDIT	COENZYME	COFFERDAM	COGIES
CODEWORD	COEDITED	COENZYMES	COFFERED	COGITABLE
CODEWORDS	COEDITING	COEQUAL	COFFERING	COGITATE
CODEX	COEDITOR	COEQUALLY	COFFERS	COGITATED
CODEXES	COEDITORS	COEQUALS	COFFIN	COGITATES
CODFISH	COEDITS	COEQUATE	COFFINED	COGITATOR
CODFISHES	COEDS	COEQUATED	COFFING	COGITO
CODGER	COEFFECT	COEQUATES	COFFINING	COGITOS
CODGERS	COEFFECTS	COERCE	COFFINITE	COGNAC
CODICES	COEHORN	COERCED	COFFINS	COGNACS
CODICIL	COEHORNS	COERCER	COFFLE	COGNATE
CODICILS	COELIAC	COERCERS	COFFLED	COGNATELY

COGNATES	COHEIRS	COIFED	COINSURED	COLAS
COGNATION	COHEN	COIFFE	COINSURER	COLBIES
COGNISANT	COHENS	COIFFED	COINSURES	COLBY
COGNISE	COHERE	COIFFES	COINTER	COLBYS
COGNISED	COHERED	COIFFEUR	COINTERS	COLCANNON
COGNISER	COHERENCE	COIFFEURS	COINTREAU	COLCHICA
COGNISERS	COHERENCY	COIFFEUSE	COINVENT	COLCHICUM
COGNISES	COHERENT	COIFFING	COINVENTS	COLCOTHAR
COGNISING	COHERER	COIFFURE	COINVEST	COLD
COGNITION	COHERERS	COIFFURED	COINVESTS	COLDBLOOD
COGNITIVE	COHERES	COIFFURES	COIR	COLDCOCK
COGNIZANT	COHERING	COIFING	COIRS	COLDCOCKS
COGNIZE	COHERITOR	COIFS	COISTREL	COLDER
COGNIZED	COHESIBLE	COIGN	COISTRELS	COLDEST
COGNIZER	COHESIN	COIGNE	COISTRIL	COLDHOUSE
COGNIZERS	COHESINS	COIGNED	COISTRILS	COLDIE
COGNIZES	COHESION	COIGNES	COIT	COLDIES
COGNIZING	COHESIONS	COIGNING	COITAL	COLDISH
COGNOMEN	COHESIVE	COIGNS	COITALLY	COLDLY
COGNOMENS	COHIBIT	COIL	COITION	COLDNESS
COGNOMINA	COHIBITED	COILED	COITIONAL	COLDS
COGNOSCE	COHIBITS	COILER	COITIONS	COLE
COGNOSCED	COHO	COILERS	COITS	COLEAD
COGNOSCES	COHOBATE	COILING	COITUS	COLEADER
COGNOVIT	COHOBATED	COILS	COITUSES	COLEADERS
COGNOVITS	COHOBATES	COIN	COJOIN	COLEADING
COGON	COHOE	COINABLE	COJOINED	COLEADS
COGONS	COHOES	COINAGE	COJOINING	COLECTOMY
COGS	COHOG	COINAGES	COJOINS	COLED
COGUE	COHOGS	COINCIDE	COJONES	COLEOPTER
COGUES	COHOLDER	COINCIDED	COKE	COLES
COGWAY	COHOLDERS	COINCIDES	COKED	COLESEED
COGWAYS	COHORN	COINED	COKEHEAD	COLESEEDS
COGWHEEL	COHORNS	COINER	COKEHEADS	COLESLAW
COGWHEELS	COHORT	COINERS	COKELIKE	COLESLAWS
COHAB	COHORTS	COINFECT	COKERNUT	COLESSEE
COHABIT	COHOS	COINFECTS	COKERNUTS	COLESSEES
COHABITED	COHOSH	COINFER	COKES	COLESSOR
COHABITEE	COHOSHES	COINFERS	COKESES	COLESSORS
COHABITER	COHOST	COINHERE	COKIER	COLETIT
COHABITOR	COHOSTED	COINHERED	COKIEST	COLETITS
COHABITS	COHOSTESS	COINHERES	COKING	COLEUS
COHABS	COHOSTING	COINING	COKINGS	COLEUSES
COHEAD	COHOSTS	COININGS	COKULORIS	COLEWORT
COHEADED	COHOUSING	COINMATE	COKY	COLEWORTS
COHEADING	COHUNE	COINMATES	COL	COLEY
COHEADS	COHUNES	COINOP	COLA	COLEYS
COHEIR	COHYPONYM	COINS	COLANDER	COLIBRI
COHEIRESS	COIF	COINSURE	COLANDERS	COLIBRIS

COLIC	COLLATING	COLLODIUM	COLOMBARD	COLORINGS
COLICIN	COLLATION	COLLOGUE	COLON	COLORISE
COLICINE	COLLATIVE	COLLOGUED	COLONE	COLORISED
COLICINES	COLLATOR	COLLOGUES	COLONEL	COLORISER
COLICINS	COLLATORS	COLLOID	COLONELCY	COLORISES
COLICKIER	COLLEAGUE	COLLOIDAL	COLONELS	COLORISM
COLICKY	COLLECT	COLLOIDS	COLONES	COLORISMS
COLICROOT	COLLECTED	COLLOP	COLONI	COLORIST
COLICS	COLLECTOR	COLLOPS	COLONIAL	COLORISTS
COLICWEED	COLLECTS	COLLOQUE	COLONIALS	COLORIZE
COLIES	COLLED	COLLOQUED	COLONIC	COLORIZED
COLIFORM	COLLEEN	COLLOQUES	COLONICS	COLORIZER
COLIFORMS	COLLEENS	COLLOQUIA	COLONIES	COLORIZES
COLIN	COLLEGE	COLLOQUY	COLONISE	COLORLESS
COLINEAR	COLLEGER	COLLOTYPE	COLONISED	COLORMAN
COLINS	COLLEGERS	COLLOTYPY	COLONISER	COLORMEN
COLIPHAGE	COLLEGES	COLLS	COLONISES	COLORS
COLISEUM	COLLEGIA	COLLUDE	COLONIST	COLORWASH
COLISEUMS	COLLEGIAL	COLLUDED	COLONISTS	COLORWAY
COLISTIN	COLLEGIAN	COLLUDER	COLONITIS	COLORWAYS
COLISTINS	COLLEGIUM	COLLUDERS	COLONIZE	COLORY
COLITIC	COLLET	COLLUDES	COLONIZED	COLOSSAL
COLITIS	COLLETED	COLLUDING	COLONIZER	COLOSSEUM
COLITISES	COLLETING	COLLUSION	COLONIZES	COLOSSI
COLL	COLLETS	COLLUSIVE	COLONNADE	COLOSSUS
COLLAB	COLLICULI	COLLUVIA	COLONS	COLOSTOMY
COLLABS	COLLIDE	COLLUVIAL	COLONUS	COLOSTRAL
COLLAGE	COLLIDED	COLLUVIES	COLONY	COLOSTRIC
COLLAGED	COLLIDER	COLLUVIUM	COLOPHON	COLOSTRUM
COLLAGEN	COLLIDERS	COLLY	COLOPHONS	COLOTOMY
COLLAGENS	COLLIDES	COLLYING	COLOPHONY	COLOUR
COLLAGES	COLLIDING	COLLYRIA	COLOR	COLOURANT
COLLAGING	COLLIE	COLLYRIUM	COLORABLE	COLOURED
COLLAGIST	COLLIED	COLOBI	COLORABLY	COLOUREDS
COLLAPSAR	COLLIER	COLOBID	COLORADO	COLOURER
COLLAPSE	COLLIERS	COLOBIDS	COLORANT	COLOURERS
COLLAPSED	COLLIERY	COLOBOMA	COLORANTS	COLOURFUL
COLLAPSES	COLLIES	COLOBOMAS	COLORBRED	COLOURIER
COLLAR	COLLIGATE	COLOBUS	COLORCAST	COLOURING
COLLARD	COLLIMATE	COLOBUSES	COLORED	COLOURISE
COLLARDS	COLLINEAR	COLOCATE	COLOREDS	COLOURISM
COLLARED	COLLING	COLOCATED	COLORER	COLOURIST
COLLARET	COLLINGS	COLOCATES	COLORERS	COLOURIZE
COLLARETS	COLLINS	COLOCYNTH	COLORFAST	COLOURMAN
COLLARING	COLLINSES	COLOG	COLORFUL	COLOURMEN
COLLARS	COLLINSIA	COLOGNE	COLORIER	COLOURS
COLLATE	COLLISION	COLOGNED	COLORIEST	COLOURWAY
COLLATED	COLLOCATE	COLOGNES	COLORIFIC	COLOURY
COLLATES	COLLODION	COLOGS	COLORING	COLPITIS

COLPOTOMY	COMAE	COMBINERS	COMERS	COMMANDER
COLS	COMAKE	COMBINES	COMES	COMMANDO
COLT	COMAKER	COMBING	COMET	COMMANDOS
COLTAN	COMAKERS	COMBINGS	COMETARY	COMMANDS
COLTANS	COMAKES	COMBINING	COMETH	COMMAS
COLTED	COMAKING	COMBIS	COMETHER	COMMATA
COLTER	COMAL	COMBLE	COMETHERS	COMMENCE
COLTERS	COMANAGE	COMBLES	COMETIC	COMMENCED
COLTHOOD	COMANAGED	COMBLESS	COMETS	COMMENCER
COLTHOODS	COMANAGER	COMBLIKE	COMFIER	COMMENCES
COLTING	COMANAGES	COMBO	COMFIEST	COMMEND
COLTISH	COMARB	COMBOS	COMFILY	COMMENDAM
COLTISHLY	COMARBS	COMBOVER	COMFINESS	COMMENDED
COLTS	COMART	COMBOVERS	COMFIT	COMMENDER
COLTSFOOT	COMARTS	COMBRETUM	COMFITS	COMMENDS
COLTWOOD	COMAS	COMBS	COMFITURE	COMMENSAL
COLTWOODS	COMATE	COMBUST	COMFORT	COMMENT
COLUBRIAD	COMATES	COMBUSTED	COMFORTED	COMMENTED
COLUBRID	COMATIC	COMBUSTOR	COMFORTER	COMMENTER
COLUBRIDS	COMATIK	COMBUSTS	COMFORTS	COMMENTOR
COLUBRINE	COMATIKS	COMBWISE	COMFREY	COMMENTS
COLUGO	COMATOSE	COMBY	COMFREYS	COMMER
COLUGOS	COMATULA	COME	COMFY	COMMERCE
COLUMBARY	COMATULAE	COMEBACK	COMIC	COMMERCED
COLUMBATE	COMATULID	COMEBACKS	COMICAL	COMMERCES
COLUMBIC	COMB	COMEDDLE	COMICALLY	COMMERE
COLUMBINE	COMBAT	COMEDDLED	COMICE	COMMERES
COLUMBITE	COMBATANT	COMEDDLES	COMICES	COMMERGE
COLUMBIUM	COMBATED	COMEDIAN	COMICS	COMMERGED
COLUMBOUS	COMBATER	COMEDIANS	COMING	COMMERGES
COLUMEL	COMBATERS	COMEDIC	COMINGLE	COMMERS
COLUMELLA	COMBATING	COMEDIES	COMINGLED	COMMIE
COLUMELS	COMBATIVE	COMEDIST	COMINGLES	COMMIES
COLUMN	COMBATS	COMEDISTS	COMINGS	COMMINATE
COLUMNAL	COMBATTED	COMEDO	COMIQUE	COMMINGLE
COLUMNALS	COMBE	COMEDONES	COMIQUES	COMMINUTE
COLUMNAR	COMBED	COMEDOS	COMITADJI	COMMIS
COLUMNEA	COMBER	COMEDOWN	COMITAL	COMMISH
COLUMNEAS	COMBERS	COMEDOWNS	COMITATUS	COMMISHES
COLUMNED	COMBES	COMEDY	COMITIA	COMMISSAR
COLUMNIST	COMBI	COMELIER	COMITIAL	COMMIT
COLUMNS	COMBIER	COMELIEST	COMITIAS	COMMITS
COLURE	COMBIES	COMELILY	COMITIES	COMMITTAL
COLURES	COMBIEST	COMELY	COMITY	COMMITTED
COLY	COMBINATE	COMEMBER	COMIX	COMMITTEE
COLZA	COMBINE	COMEMBERS	COMM	COMMITTER
COLZAS	COMBINED	COMEOVER	COMMA	COMMIX
COMA	COMBINEDS	COMEOVERS	COMMAND	COMMIXED
COMADE	COMBINER	COMER	COMMANDED	COMMIXES

COMMIXING	COMMUTER	COMPEARS	COMPLEXES	COMPRESS
COMMIXT	COMMUTERS	COMPED	COMPLEXLY	COMPRINT
COMMO	COMMUTES	COMPEER	COMPLEXUS	COMPRINTS
COMMODE	COMMUTING	COMPEERED	COMPLIANT	COMPRISAL
COMMODES	COMMUTUAL	COMPEERS	COMPLICE	COMPRISE
COMMODIFY	COMMY	COMPEL	COMPLICES	COMPRISED
COMMODITY	COMODO	COMPELLED	COMPLICIT	COMPRISES
COMMODO	COMONOMER	COMPELLER	COMPLIED	COMPRIZE
COMMODORE	COMORBID	COMPELS	COMPLIER	COMPRIZED
COMMON	COMOSE	COMPEND	COMPLIERS	COMPRIZES
COMMONAGE	COMOUS	COMPENDIA	COMPLIES	COMPS
COMMONED	COMP	COMPENDS	COMPLIN	COMPT
COMMONER	COMPACT	COMPER	COMPLINE	COMPTABLE
COMMONERS	COMPACTED	COMPERE	COMPLINES	COMPTED
COMMONEST	COMPACTER	COMPERED	COMPLINS	COMPTER
COMMONEY	COMPACTLY	COMPERES	COMPLISH	COMPTERS
COMMONEYS	COMPACTOR	COMPERING	COMPLOT	COMPTIBLE
COMMONING	COMPACTS	COMPERS	COMPLOTS	COMPTING
COMMONLY	COMPADRE	COMPESCE	COMPLUVIA	COMPTROLL
COMMONS	COMPADRES	COMPESCED	COMPLY	COMPTS
COMMORANT	COMPAGE	COMPESCES	COMPLYING	COMPULSE
COMMOS	COMPAGES	COMPETE	COMPO	COMPULSED
COMMOT	COMPAND	COMPETED	COMPONE	COMPULSES
COMMOTE	COMPANDED	COMPETENT	COMPONENT	COMPUTANT
COMMOTES	COMPANDER	COMPETES	COMPONY	COMPUTE
COMMOTION	COMPANDOR	COMPETING	COMPORT	COMPUTED
COMMOTS	COMPANDS	COMPILE	COMPORTED	COMPUTER
COMMOVE	COMPANIED	COMPILED	COMPORTS	COMPUTERS
COMMOVED	COMPANIES	COMPILER	COMPOS	COMPUTES
COMMOVES	COMPANING	COMPILERS	COMPOSE	COMPUTING
COMMOVING	COMPANION	COMPILES	COMPOSED	COMPUTIST
COMMS	COMPANY	COMPILING	COMPOSER	COMRADE
COMMUNAL	COMPARE	COMPING	COMPOSERS	COMRADELY
COMMUNARD	COMPARED	COMPINGS	COMPOSES	COMRADERY
COMMUNE	COMPARER	COMPITAL	COMPOSING	COMRADES
COMMUNED	COMPARERS	COMPLAIN	COMPOSITE	COMS
COMMUNER	COMPARES	COMPLAINS	COMPOST	COMSAT
COMMUNERS	COMPARING	COMPLAINT	COMPOSTED	COMSATS
COMMUNES	COMPART	COMPLEAT	COMPOSTER	COMSYMP
COMMUNING	COMPARTED	COMPLEATS	COMPOSTS	COMSYMPS
COMMUNION	COMPARTS	COMPLECT	COMPOSURE	COMTE
COMMUNISE	COMPAS	COMPLECTS	COMPOT	COMTES
COMMUNISM	COMPASES	COMPLETE	COMPOTE	COMUS
COMMUNIST	COMPASS	COMPLETED	COMPOTES	COMUSES
COMMUNITY	COMPASSED	COMPLETER	COMPOTIER	CON
COMMUNIZE	COMPASSES	COMPLETES	COMPOTS	CONACRE
COMMUTATE	COMPAST	COMPLEX	COMPOUND	CONACRED
COMMUTE	COMPEAR	COMPLEXED	COMPOUNDS	CONACRES
COMMUTED	COMPEARED	COMPLEXER	COMPRADOR	CONACRING

CONARIA	CONCERTED	CONCORDAL	CONDOLES	CONF
CONARIAL	CONCERTI	CONCORDAT	CONDOLING	CONFAB
CONARIUM	CONCERTO	CONCORDED	CONDOM	CONFABBED
CONATION	CONCERTOS	CONCORDS	CONDOMS	CONFABS
CONATIONS	CONCERTS	CONCOURS	CONDONE	CONFECT
CONATIVE	CONCETTI	CONCOURSE	CONDONED	CONFECTED
CONATUS	CONCETTO	CONCREATE	CONDONER	CONFECTS
CONCASSE	CONCH	CONCRETE	CONDONERS	CONFER
CONCASSES	CONCHA	CONCRETED	CONDONES	CONFEREE
CONCAUSE	CONCHAE	CONCRETES	CONDONING	CONFEREES
CONCAUSES	CONCHAL	CONCREW	CONDOR	CONFERRAL
CONCAVE	CONCHAS	CONCREWED	CONDORES	CONFERRED
CONCAVED	CONCHATE	CONCREWS	CONDORS	CONFERREE
CONCAVELY	CONCHE	CONCUBINE	CONDOS	CONFERRER
CONCAVES	CONCHED	CONCUPIES	CONDUCE	CONFERS
CONCAVING	CONCHES	CONCUPY	CONDUCED	CONFERVA
CONCAVITY	CONCHIE	CONCUR	CONDUCER	CONFERVAE
CONCEAL	CONCHIES	CONCURRED	CONDUCERS	CONFERVAL
CONCEALED	CONCHING	CONCURS	CONDUCES	CONFERVAS
CONCEALER	CONCHITIS	CONCUSS	CONDUCING	CONFESS
CONCEALS	CONCHO	CONCUSSED	CONDUCIVE	CONFESSED
CONCEDE	CONCHOID	CONCUSSES	CONDUCT	CONFESSES
CONCEDED	CONCHOIDS	CONCYCLIC	CONDUCTED	CONFESSOR
CONCEDER	CONCHOS	COND	CONDUCTI	CONFEST
CONCEDERS	CONCHS	CONDEMN	CONDUCTOR	CONFESTLY
CONCEDES	CONCHY	CONDEMNED	CONDUCTS	CONFETTI
CONCEDING	CONCIERGE	CONDEMNER	CONDUCTUS	CONFETTO
CONCEDO	CONCILIAR	CONDEMNOR	CONDUIT	CONFIDANT
CONCEIT	CONCISE	CONDEMNS	CONDUITS	CONFIDE
CONCEITED	CONCISED	CONDENSE	CONDYLAR	CONFIDED
CONCEITS	CONCISELY	CONDENSED	CONDYLE	CONFIDENT
CONCEITY	CONCISER	CONDENSER	CONDYLES	CONFIDER
CONCEIVE	CONCISES	CONDENSES	CONDYLOID	CONFIDERS
CONCEIVED	CONCISEST	CONDER	CONDYLOMA	CONFIDES
CONCEIVER	CONCISING	CONDERS	CONE	CONFIDING
CONCEIVES	CONCISION	CONDIDDLE	CONED	CONFIG
CONCENT	CONCLAVE	CONDIE	CONELESS	CONFIGS
CONCENTER	CONCLAVES	CONDIES	CONELIKE	CONFIGURE
CONCENTRE	CONCLUDE	CONDIGN	CONELRAD	CONFINE
CONCENTS	CONCLUDED	CONDIGNLY	CONELRADS	CONFINED
CONCENTUS	CONCLUDER	CONDIMENT	CONENOSE	CONFINER
CONCEPT	CONCLUDES	CONDITION	CONENOSES	CONFINERS
CONCEPTI	CONCOCT	CONDO	CONEPATE	CONFINES
CONCEPTS	CONCOCTED	CONDOES	CONEPATES	CONFINING
CONCEPTUS	CONCOCTER	CONDOLE	CONEPATL	CONFIRM
CONCERN	CONCOCTOR	CONDOLED	CONEPATLS	CONFIRMED
CONCERNED	CONCOCTS	CONDOLENT	CONES	CONFIRMEE
CONCERNS	CONCOLOR	CONDOLER	CONEY	CONFIRMER
CONCERT	CONCORD	CONDOLERS	CONEYS	CONFIRMOR

C

CONFIRMS	CONGEAL	CONIC	CONJURED	CONNIVER
CONFISEUR	CONGEALED	CONICAL	CONJURER	CONNIVERS
CONFIT	CONGEALER	CONICALLY	CONJURERS	CONNIVERY
CONFITEOR	CONGEALS	CONICINE	CONJURES	CONNIVES
CONFITS	CONGED	CONICINES	CONJURIES	CONNIVING
CONFITURE	CONGEE	CONICITY	CONJURING	CONNOR
CONFIX	CONGEED	CONICS	CONJUROR	CONNORS
CONFIXED	CONGEEING	CONIDIA	CONJURORS	CONNOTATE
CONFIXES	CONGEES	CONIDIAL	CONJURY	CONNOTE
CONFIXING	CONGEING	CONIDIAN	CONK	CONNOTED
CONFLATE	CONGENER	CONIDIUM	CONKED	CONNOTES
CONFLATED	CONGENERS	CONIES	CONKER	CONNOTING
CONFLATES	CONGENIAL	CONIFER	CONKERS	CONNOTIVE
CONFLICT	CONGENIC	CONIFERS	CONKIER	CONNS
CONFLICTS	CONGER	CONIFORM	CONKIEST	CONNUBIAL
CONFLUENT	CONGERIES	CONIINE	CONKING	CONODONT
CONFLUX	CONGERS	CONIINES	CONKOUT	CONODONTS
CONFLUXES	CONGES	CONIMA	CONKOUTS	CONOID
CONFOCAL	CONGEST	CONIMAS	CONKS	CONOIDAL
CONFORM	CONGESTED	CONIN	CONKY	CONOIDIC
CONFORMAL	CONGESTS	CONINE	CONLANG	CONOIDS
CONFORMED	CONGIARY	CONINES	CONLANGER	CONOMINEE
CONFORMER	CONGII	CONING	CONLANGS	CONQUER
CONFORMS	CONGIUS	CONINS	CONMAN	CONQUERED
CONFOUND	CONGLOBE	CONIOLOGY	CONMEN	CONQUERER
CONFOUNDS	CONGLOBED	CONIOSES	CONN	CONQUEROR
CONFRERE	CONGLOBES	CONIOSIS	CONNATE	CONQUERS
CONFRERES	CONGO	CONIUM	CONNATELY	CONQUEST
CONFRERIE	CONGOES	CONIUMS	CONNATION	CONQUESTS
CONFRONT	CONGOS	CONJECT	CONNATURE	CONQUIAN
CONFRONTE	CONGOU	CONJECTED	CONNE	CONQUIANS
CONFRONTS	CONGOUS	CONJECTS	CONNECT	CONS
CONFS	CONGRATS	CONJEE	CONNECTED	CONSCIENT
CONFUSE	CONGREE	CONJEED	CONNECTER	CONSCIOUS
CONFUSED	CONGREED	CONJEEING	CONNECTOR	CONSCRIBE
CONFUSES	CONGREES	CONJEES	CONNECTS	CONSCRIPT
CONFUSING	CONGREET	CONJOIN	CONNED	CONSEIL
CONFUSION	CONGREETS	CONJOINED	CONNER	CONSEILS
CONFUTE	CONGRESS	CONJOINER	CONNERS	CONSENSUS
CONFUTED	CONGRUE	CONJOINS	CONNES	CONSENT
CONFUTER	CONGRUED	CONJOINT	CONNEXION	CONSENTED
CONFUTERS	CONGRUENT	CONJUGAL	CONNEXIVE	CONSENTER
CONFUTES	CONGRUES	CONJUGANT	CONNIE	CONSENTS
CONFUTING	CONGRUING	CONJUGATE	CONNIES	CONSERVE
CONGA	CONGRUITY	CONJUNCT	CONNING	CONSERVED
CONGAED	CONGRUOUS	CONJUNCTS	CONNINGS	CONSERVER
CONGAING	CONI	CONJUNTO	CONNIVE	CONSERVES
CONGAS	CONIA	CONJUNTOS	CONNIVED	CONSIDER
CONGE	CONIAS	CONJURE	CONNIVENT	CONSIDERS

C

CONSIGN	CONSTRUAL	CONTEMN	CONTOURS	CONVECTOR
CONSIGNED	CONSTRUCT	CONTEMNED	CONTRA	CONVECTS
CONSIGNEE	CONSTRUE	CONTEMNER	CONTRACT	CONVENE
CONSIGNER	CONSTRUED	CONTEMNOR	CONTRACTS	CONVENED
CONSIGNOR	CONSTRUER	CONTEMNS	CONTRAIL	CONVENER
CONSIGNS	CONSTRUES	CONTEMPER	CONTRAILS	CONVENERS
CONSIST	CONSUL	CONTEMPO	CONTRAIR	CONVENES
CONSISTED	CONSULAGE	CONTEMPT	CONTRALTI	CONVENING
CONSISTS	CONSULAR	CONTEMPTS	CONTRALTO	CONVENOR
CONSOCIES	CONSULARS	CONTEND	CONTRARY	CONVENORS
CONSOL	CONSULATE	CONTENDED	CONTRAS	CONVENT
CONSOLATE	CONSULS	CONTENDER	CONTRAST	CONVENTED
CONSOLE	CONSULT	CONTENDS	CONTRASTS	CONVENTS
CONSOLED	CONSULTA	CONTENT	CONTRASTY	CONVERGE
CONSOLER	CONSULTAS	CONTENTED	CONTRAT	CONVERGED
CONSOLERS	CONSULTED	CONTENTLY	CONTRATE	CONVERGES
CONSOLES	CONSULTEE	CONTENTS	CONTRATS	CONVERSE
CONSOLING	CONSULTER	CONTES	CONTRIST	CONVERSED
CONSOLS	CONSULTOR	CONTESSA	CONTRISTS	CONVERSER
CONSOLUTE	CONSULTS	CONTESSAS	CONTRITE	CONVERSES
CONSOMME	CONSUME	CONTEST	CONTRIVE	CONVERSO
CONSOMMES	CONSUMED	CONTESTED	CONTRIVED	CONVERSOS
CONSONANT	CONSUMER	CONTESTER	CONTRIVER	CONVERT
CONSONOUS	CONSUMERS	CONTESTS	CONTRIVES	CONVERTED
CONSORT	CONSUMES	CONTEXT	CONTROL	CONVERTER
CONSORTED	CONSUMING	CONTEXTS	CONTROLE	CONVERTOR
CONSORTER	CONSUMPT	CONTICENT	CONTROLS	CONVERTS
CONSORTIA	CONSUMPTS	CONTINENT	CONTROUL	CONVEX
CONSORTS	CONTACT	CONTINUA	CONTROULS	CONVEXED
CONSPIRE	CONTACTED	CONTINUAL	CONTUMACY	CONVEXES
CONSPIRED	CONTACTEE	CONTINUE	CONTUMELY	CONVEXING
CONSPIRER	CONTACTOR	CONTINUED	CONTUND	CONVEXITY
CONSPIRES	CONTACTS	CONTINUER	CONTUNDED	CONVEXLY
CONSPUE	CONTADINA	CONTINUES	CONTUNDS	CONVEY
CONSPUED	CONTADINE	CONTINUO	CONTUSE	CONVEYAL
CONSPUES	CONTADINI	CONTINUOS	CONTUSED	CONVEYALS
CONSPUING	CONTADINO	CONTINUUM	CONTUSES	CONVEYED
CONSTABLE	CONTAGIA	CONTLINE	CONTUSING	CONVEYER
CONSTANCY	CONTAGION	CONTLINES	CONTUSION	CONVEYERS
CONSTANT	CONTAGIUM	CONTO	CONTUSIVE	CONVEYING
CONSTANTS	CONTAIN	CONTORNI	CONUNDRUM	CONVEYOR
CONSTATE	CONTAINED	CONTORNO	CONURBAN	CONVEYORS
CONSTATED	CONTAINER	CONTORNOS	CONURBIA	CONVEYS
CONSTATES	CONTAINS	CONTORT	CONURBIAS	CONVICT
CONSTER	CONTANGO	CONTORTED	CONURE	CONVICTED
CONSTERED	CONTANGOS	CONTORTS	CONURES	CONVICTS
CONSTERS	CONTE	CONTOS	CONUS	CONVINCE
CONSTRAIN	CONTECK	CONTOUR	CONVECT	CONVINCED
CONSTRICT	CONTECKS	CONTOURED	CONVECTED	CONVINCER

C

CONVINCES	COOK	COOLHOUSE	COOPERS	COPAL
CONVIVE	COOKABLE	COOLIBAH	COOPERY	COPALM
CONVIVED	COOKABLES	COOLIBAHS	COOPING	COPALMS
CONVIVES	COOKBOOK	COOLIBAR	COOPS	COPALS
CONVIVIAL	COOKBOOKS	COOLIBARS	COOPT	COPARCENY
CONVIVING	COOKED	COOLING	COOPTED	COPARENT
CONVO	COOKER	COOLINGLY	COOPTING	COPARENTS
CONVOCATE	COOKERIES	COOLINGS	COOPTION	COPARTNER
CONVOKE	COOKERS	COOLISH	COOPTIONS	COPASETIC
CONVOKED	COOKERY	COOLIST	COOPTS	COPASTOR
CONVOKER	COOKEY	COOLISTS	COORD	COPASTORS
CONVOKERS	COOKEYS	COOLLY	COORDINAL	COPATAINE
CONVOKES	COOKHOUSE	COOLNESS	COORDS	COPATRIOT
CONVOKING	COOKIE	COOLS	COORIE	COPATRON
CONVOLUTE	COOKIES	COOLTH	COORIED	COPATRONS
CONVOLVE	COOKING	COOLTHS	COORIEING	COPAY
CONVOLVED	COOKINGS	COOM	COORIES	COPAYMENT
CONVOLVES	COOKLESS	COOMB	COOS	COPAYS
CONVOS	COOKMAID	COOMBE	COOSEN	COPE
CONVOY	COOKMAIDS	COOMBES	COOSENED	COPECK
CONVOYED	COOKOFF	COOMBS	COOSENING	COPECKS
CONVOYING	COOKOFFS	COOMED	COOSENS	COPED
CONVOYS	COOKOUT	COOMIER	COOSER	COPEMATE
CONVULSE	COOKOUTS	COOMIEST	COOSERS	COPEMATES
CONVULSED	COOKROOM	COOMING	COOSIN	COPEN
CONVULSES	COOKROOMS	COOMS	COOSINED	COPENS
CONWOMAN	COOKS	COOMY	COOSINING	COPEPOD
CONWOMEN	COOKSHACK	COON	COOSINS	COPEPODS
CONY	COOKSHOP	COONCAN	COOST	COPER
COO	COOKSHOPS	COONCANS	COOT	COPERED
COOCH	COOKSTOVE	COONDOG	COOTCH	COPERING
COOCHES	COOKTOP	COONDOGS	COOTCHED	COPERS
COOCOO	COOKTOPS	COONHOUND	COOTCHES	COPES
COOED	COOKWARE	COONS	COOTCHING	COPESETIC
COOEE	COOKWARES	COONSHIT	COOTER	COPESTONE
COOEED	COOKY	COONSHITS	COOTERS	COPI
COOEEING	COOL	COONSKIN	COOTIE	COPIABLE
COOEES	COOLABAH	COONSKINS	COOTIES	COPIED
COOER	COOLABAHS	COONTIE	COOTIKIN	COPIER
COOERS	COOLAMON	COONTIES	COOTIKINS	COPIERS
COOEY	COOLAMONS	COONTY	COOTS	COPIES
COOEYED	COOLANT	COOP	COOZE	COPIHUE
COOEYING	COOLANTS	COOPED	COOZES	COPIHUES
COOEYS	COOLDOWN	COOPER	COP	COPILOT
COOF	COOLDOWNS	COOPERAGE	COPACETIC	COPILOTED
COOFS	COOLED	COOPERATE	COPAIBA	COPILOTS
COOING	COOLER	COOPERED	COPAIBAS	COPING
COOINGLY	COOLERS	COOPERIES	COPAIVA	COPINGS
COOINGS	COOLEST	COOPERING	COPAIVAS	COPIOUS

COPIOUSLY	COPROLITH	COPYIST	CORBANS	CORDONING
COPITA	COPROLOGY	COPYISTS	CORBE	CORDONNET
COPITAS	COPROSMA	COPYLEFT	CORBEAU	CORDONS
COPLANAR	COPROSMAS	COPYLEFTS	CORBEAUS	CORDOTOMY
COPLOT	COPROZOIC	COPYPASTA	CORBEIL	CORDOVAN
COPLOTS	COPS	COPYREAD	CORBEILLE	CORDOVANS
COPLOTTED	COPSE	COPYREADS	CORBEILS	CORDS
COPOLYMER	COPSED	COPYRIGHT	CORBEL	CORDUROY
COPOUT	COPSES	COPYTAKER	CORBELED	CORDUROYS
COPOUTS	COPSEWOOD	COQUET	CORBELING	CORDWAIN
COPPED	COPSHOP	COQUETRY	CORBELLED	CORDWAINS
COPPER	COPSHOPS	COQUETS	CORBELS	CORDWOOD
COPPERAH	COPSIER	COQUETTE	CORBES	CORDWOODS
COPPERAHS	COPSIEST	COQUETTED	CORBICULA	CORDYLINE
COPPERAS	COPSING	COQUETTES	CORBIE	CORE
COPPERED	COPSY	COQUI	CORBIES	CORED
COPPERIER	COPTER	COQUILLA	CORBINA	COREDEEM
COPPERING	COPTERS	COQUILLAS	CORBINAS	COREDEEMS
COPPERISH	COPUBLISH	COQUILLE	CORBY	COREGENT
COPPERS	COPULA	COQUILLES	CORCASS	COREGENTS
COPPERY	COPULAE	COQUINA	CORCASSES	COREIGN
COPPICE	COPULAR	COQUINAS	CORD	COREIGNS
COPPICED	COPULAS	COQUIS	CORDAGE	CORELATE
COPPICES	COPULATE	COQUITO	CORDAGES	CORELATED
COPPICING	COPULATED	COQUITOS	CORDATE	CORELATES
COPPIES	COPULATES	COR	CORDATELY	CORELESS
COPPIN	COPURIFY	CORACLE	CORDED	CORELLA
COPPING	COPY	CORACLES	CORDELLE	CORELLAS
COPPINS	COPYABLE	CORACOID	CORDELLED	COREMIA
COPPLE	COPYBOOK	CORACOIDS	CORDELLES	COREMIUM
COPPLES	COPYBOOKS	CORAGGIO	CORDER	COREOPSIS
COPPRA	COPYBOY	CORAL	CORDERS	CORER
COPPRAS	COPYBOYS	CORALLA	CORDGRASS	CORERS
COPPY	COPYCAT	CORALLINE	CORDIAL	CORES
COPRA	COPYCATS	CORALLITE	CORDIALLY	COREY
COPRAEMIA	COPYDESK	CORALLOID	CORDIALS	COREYS
COPRAEMIC	COPYDESKS	CORALLUM	CORDIFORM	CORF
COPRAH	COPYEDIT	CORALROOT	CORDINER	CORFHOUSE
COPRAHS	COPYEDITS	CORALS	CORDINERS	CORGI
COPRAS	COPYFIGHT	CORALWORT	CORDING	CORGIS
COPREMIA	COPYGIRL	CORAM	CORDINGS	CORIA
COPREMIAS	COPYGIRLS	CORAMINE	CORDITE	CORIANDER
COPREMIC	COPYGRAPH	CORAMINES	CORDITES	CORIES
COPRESENT	COPYHOLD	CORANACH	CORDLESS	CORING
COPRINCE	COPYHOLDS	CORANACHS	CORDLIKE	CORIOUS
COPRINCES	COPYING	CORANTO	CORDOBA	CORIUM
COPRODUCE	COPYINGS	CORANTOES	CORDOBAS	CORIUMS
COPRODUCT	COPYISM	CORANTOS	CORDON	CORIVAL
COPROLITE	COPYISMS	CORBAN	CORDONED	CORIVALRY

CORIVALS	CORNBRAID	CORNICE	CORNUA	COROTATE
CORIXID	CORNBRASH	CORNICED	CORNUAL	COROTATED
CORIXIDS	CORNBREAD	CORNICES	CORNUS	COROTATES
CORK	CORNCAKE	CORNICHE	CORNUSES	COROZO
CORKAGE	CORNCAKES	CORNICHES	CORNUTE	COROZOS
CORKAGES	CORNCOB	CORNICHON	CORNUTED	CORPORA
CORKBOARD	CORNCOBS	CORNICING	CORNUTES	CORPORAL
CORKBORER	CORNCRAKE	CORNICLE	CORNUTING	CORPORALE
CORKED	CORNCRIB	CORNICLES	CORNUTO	CORPORALS
CORKER	CORNCRIBS	CORNICULA	CORNUTOS	CORPORAS
CORKERS	CORNEA	CORNIER	CORNWORM	CORPORATE
CORKIER	CORNEAE	CORNIEST	CORNWORMS	CORPOREAL
CORKIEST	CORNEAL	CORNIFIC	CORNY	CORPORIFY
CORKINESS	CORNEAS	CORNIFIED	COROCORE	CORPOSANT
CORKING	CORNED	CORNIFIES	COROCORES	CORPS
CORKIR	CORNEITIS	CORNIFORM	COROCORO	CORPSE
CORKIRS	CORNEL	CORNIFY	COROCOROS	CORPSED
CORKLIKE	CORNELIAN	CORNILY	CORODIES	CORPSES
CORKS	CORNELS	CORNINESS	CORODY	CORPSING
CORKSCREW	CORNEMUSE	CORNING	COROLLA	CORPSMAN
CORKTREE	CORNEOUS	CORNIST	COROLLARY	CORPSMEN
CORKTREES	CORNER	CORNISTS	COROLLAS	CORPULENT
CORKWING	CORNERED	CORNLAND	COROLLATE	CORPUS
CORKWINGS	CORNERING	CORNLANDS	COROLLINE	CORPUSCLE
CORKWOOD	CORNERMAN	CORNLOFT	CORONA	CORPUSES
CORKWOODS	CORNERMEN	CORNLOFTS	CORONACH	CORRADE
CORKY	CORNERS	CORNMEAL	CORONACHS	CORRADED
CORM	CORNET	CORNMEALS	CORONAE	CORRADES
CORMEL	CORNETCY	CORNMILL	CORONAL	CORRADING
CORMELS	CORNETIST	CORNMILLS	CORONALLY	CORRAL
CORMIDIA	CORNETS	CORNMOTH	CORONALS	CORRALLED
CORMIDIUM	CORNETT	CORNMOTHS	CORONARY	CORRALS
CORMLET	CORNETTI	CORNO	CORONAS	CORRASION
CORMLETS	CORNETTO	CORNOPEAN	CORONATE	CORRASIVE
CORMLIKE	CORNETTOS	CORNPIPE	CORONATED	CORREA
CORMOID	CORNETTS	CORNPIPES	CORONATES	CORREAS
CORMORANT	CORNFED	CORNPONE	CORONEL	CORRECT
CORMOUS	CORNFIELD	CORNPONES	CORONELS	CORRECTED
CORMS	CORNFLAG	CORNRENT	CORONER	CORRECTER
CORMUS	CORNFLAGS	CORNRENTS	CORONERS	CORRECTLY
CORMUSES	CORNFLAKE	CORNROW	CORONET	CORRECTOR
CORN	CORNFLIES	CORNROWED	CORONETED	CORRECTS
CORNACRE	CORNFLOUR	CORNROWS	CORONETS	CORRELATE
CORNACRES	CORNFLY	CORNS	CORONIAL	CORRETTO
CORNAGE	CORNHOLE	CORNSILK	CORONIS	CORRETTOS
CORNAGES	CORNHOLES	CORNSILKS	CORONISES	CORRIDA
CORNBALL	CORNHUSK	CORNSTALK	CORONIUM	CORRIDAS
CORNBALLS	CORNHUSKS	CORNSTONE	CORONIUMS	CORRIDOR
CORNBORER	CORNI	CORNU	CORONOID	CORRIDORS

CORRIE	CORSLETS	CORYBANT	COSHES	COSPHERED
CORRIES	CORSNED	CORYBANTS	COSHING	COSPLAY
CORRIGENT	CORSNEDS	CORYDALIS	COSIE	COSPLAYED
CORRIVAL	CORSO	CORYDORAS	COSIED	COSPLAYER
CORRIVALS	CORSOS	CORYLUS	COSIER	COSPLAYS
CORRODANT	CORTADO	CORYLUSES	COSIERS	COSPONSOR
CORRODE	CORTADOS	CORYMB	COSIES	COSS
CORRODED	CORTEGE	CORYMBED	COSIEST	COSSACK
CORRODENT	CORTEGES	CORYMBOSE	COSIGN	COSSACKS
CORRODER	CORTEX	CORYMBOUS	COSIGNED	COSSES
CORRODERS	CORTEXES	CORYMBS	COSIGNER	COSSET
CORRODES	CORTICAL	CORYPHAEI	COSIGNERS	COSSETED
CORRODIES	CORTICATE	CORYPHE	COSIGNING	COSSETING
CORRODING	CORTICES	CORYPHEE	COSIGNS	COSSETS
CORRODY	CORTICOID	CORYPHEES	COSILY	COSSETTED
CORROSION	CORTICOSE	CORYPHENE	COSINE	COSSIE
CORROSIVE	CORTILE	CORYPHES	COSINES	COSSIES
CORRUGATE	CORTILI	CORYS	COSINESS	COST
CORRUPT	CORTIN	CORYZA	COSING	COSTA
CORRUPTED	CORTINA	CORYZAL	COSMEA	COSTAE
CORRUPTER	CORTINAS	CORYZAS	COSMEAS	COSTAL
CORRUPTLY	CORTINS	COS	COSMESES	COSTALGIA
CORRUPTOR	CORTISOL	COSCRIPT	COSMESIS	COSTALLY
CORRUPTS	CORTISOLS	COSCRIPTS	COSMETIC	COSTALS
CORS	CORTISONE	COSE	COSMETICS	COSTAR
CORSAC	CORULER	COSEC	COSMIC	COSTARD
CORSACS	CORULERS	COSECANT	COSMICAL	COSTARDS
CORSAGE	CORUNDUM	COSECANTS	COSMID	COSTARRED
CORSAGES	CORUNDUMS	COSECH	COSMIDS	COSTARS
CORSAIR	CORUSCANT	COSECHS	COSMIN	COSTATE
CORSAIRS	CORUSCATE	COSECS	COSMINE	COSTATED
CORSE	CORVEE	COSED	COSMINES	COSTE
CORSELET	CORVEES	COSEISMAL	COSMINS	COSTEAN
CORSELETS	CORVES	COSEISMIC	COSMISM	COSTEANED
CORSES	CORVET	COSES	COSMISMS	COSTEANS
CORSET	CORVETED	COSET	COSMIST	COSTED
CORSETED	CORVETING	COSETS	COSMISTS	COSTER
CORSETIER	CORVETS	COSEY	COSMO	COSTERS
CORSETING	CORVETTE	COSEYS	COSMOCRAT	COSTES
CORSETRY	CORVETTED	COSH	COSMOGENY	COSTING
CORSETS	CORVETTES	COSHED	COSMOGONY	COSTINGS
CORSEY	CORVID	COSHER	COSMOID	COSTIVE
CORSEYS	CORVIDS	COSHERED	COSMOLINE	COSTIVELY
CORSITE	CORVINA	COSHERER	COSMOLOGY	COSTLESS
CORSITES	CORVINAS	COSHERERS	COSMONAUT	COSTLIER
CORSIVE	CORVINE	COSHERIES	COSMORAMA	COSTLIEST
CORSIVES	CORVUS	COSHERING	COSMOS	COSTLY
CORSLET	CORVUSES	COSHERS	COSMOSES	COSTMARY
CORSLETED	CORY	COSHERY	COSMOTRON	COSTOTOMY

COSTREL	COTINGA	COTTONS	COULDEST	COUNTRY
COSTRELS	COTINGAS	COTTONY	COULDST	COUNTS
COSTS	COTININE	COTTOWN	COULEE	COUNTSHIP
COSTUME	COTININES	COTTOWNS	COULEES	COUNTY
COSTUMED	COTISE	COTTS	COULIBIAC	COUP
COSTUMER	COTISED	COTTUS	COULIS	COUPE
COSTUMERS	COTISES	COTTUSES	COULISSE	COUPED
COSTUMERY	COTISING	COTURNIX	COULISSES	COUPEE
COSTUMES	COTLAND	COTWAL	COULOIR	COUPEES
COSTUMEY	COTLANDS	COTWALS	COULOIRS	COUPER
COSTUMIER	COTQUEAN	COTYLAE	COULOMB	COUPERS
COSTUMING	COTQUEANS	COTYLE	COULOMBIC	COUPES
COSTUS	COTRUSTEE	COTYLEDON	COULOMBS	COUPING
COSTUSES	COTS	COTYLES	COULTER	COUPLE
COSY	COTT	COTYLOID	COULTERS	COUPLED
COSYING	COTTA	COTYLOIDS	COUMARIC	COUPLEDOM
COT	COTTABUS	COTYPE	COUMARIN	COUPLER
COTAN	COTTAE	COTYPES	COUMARINS	COUPLERS
COTANGENT	COTTAGE	COUCAL	COUMARONE	COUPLES
COTANS	COTTAGED	COUCALS	COUMAROU	COUPLET
COTE	COTTAGER	COUCH	COUMAROUS	COUPLETS
COTEAU	COTTAGERS	COUCHANT	COUNCIL	COUPLING
COTEAUS	COTTAGES	COUCHE	COUNCILOR	COUPLINGS
COTEAUX	COTTAGEY	COUCHED	COUNCILS	COUPON
COTED	COTTAGIER	COUCHEE	COUNSEL	COUPONING
COTELETTE	COTTAGING	COUCHEES	COUNSELED	COUPONS
COTELINE	COTTAR	COUCHER	COUNSELEE	COUPS
COTELINES	COTTARS	COUCHERS	COUNSELOR	COUPURE
COTENANCY	COTTAS	COUCHES	COUNSELS	COUPURES
COTENANT	COTTED	COUCHETTE	COUNT	COUR
COTENANTS	COTTER	COUCHING	COUNTABLE	COURAGE
COTERIE	COTTERED	COUCHINGS	COUNTABLY	COURAGES
COTERIES	COTTERING	COUDE	COUNTBACK	COURANT
COTES	COTTERS	COUDES	COUNTDOWN	COURANTE
COTH	COTTID	COUGAN	COUNTED	COURANTES
COTHS	COTTIDS	COUGANS	COUNTER	COURANTO
COTHURN	COTTIER	COUGAR	COUNTERED	COURANTOS
COTHURNAL	COTTIERS	COUGARS	COUNTERS	COURANTS
COTHURNI	COTTING	COUGH	COUNTESS	COURB
COTHURNS	COTTISE	COUGHED	COUNTIAN	COURBARIL
COTHURNUS	COTTISED	COUGHER	COUNTIANS	COURBED
COTICULAR	COTTISES	COUGHERS	COUNTIES	COURBETTE
COTIDAL	COTTISING	COUGHING	COUNTING	COURBING
COTIJA	COTTOID	COUGHINGS	COUNTINGS	COURBS
COTIJAS	COTTON	COUGHS	COUNTLESS	COURD
COTILLION	COTTONADE	COUGUAR	COUNTLINE	COURE
COTILLON	COTTONED	COUGUARS	COUNTRIES	COURED
COTILLONS	COTTONIER	COULD	COUNTROL	COURES
COTING	COTTONING	COULDA	COUNTROLS	COURGETTE

COURIE	COUTEAU	COVERAGES	COW	COWHEARDS
COURIED	COUTEAUX	COVERALL	COWABUNGA	COWHEEL
COURIEING	COUTER	COVERALLS	COWAGE	COWHEELS
COURIER	COUTERS	COVERED	COWAGES	COWHERB
COURIERED	COUTH	COVERER	COWAL	COWHERBS
COURIERS	COUTHER	COVERERS	COWALS	COWHERD
COURIES	COUTHEST	COVERING	COWAN	COWHERDS
COURING	COUTHIE	COVERINGS	COWANS	COWHIDE
COURLAN	COUTHIER	COVERLESS	COWARD	COWHIDED
COURLANS	COUTHIEST	COVERLET	COWARDED	COWHIDES
COURS	COUTHS	COVERLETS	COWARDICE	COWHIDING
COURSE	COUTHY	COVERLID	COWARDING	COWHOUSE
COURSED	COUTIL	COVERLIDS	COWARDLY	COWHOUSES
COURSER	COUTILLE	COVERS	COWARDRY	COWIER
COURSERS	COUTILLES	COVERSED	COWARDS	COWIEST
COURSES	COUTILS	COVERSINE	COWBANE	COWING
COURSING	COUTURE	COVERSLIP	COWBANES	COWINNER
COURSINGS	COUTURES	COVERT	COWBELL	COWINNERS
COURT	COUTURIER	COVERTER	COWBELLS	COWISH
COURTED	COUVADE	COVERTEST	COWBERRY	COWISHES
COURTEOUS	COUVADES	COVERTLY	COWBIND	COWITCH
COURTER	COUVERT	COVERTS	COWBINDS	COWITCHES
COURTERS	COUVERTS	COVERTURE	COWBIRD	COWK
COURTESAN	COUZIN	COVERUP	COWBIRDS	COWKED
COURTESY	COUZINS	COVERUPS	COWBOY	COWKING
COURTEZAN	COVALENCE	COVES	COWBOYED	COWKS
COURTIER	COVALENCY	COVET	COWBOYING	COWL
COURTIERS	COVALENT	COVETABLE	COWBOYS	COWLED
COURTING	COVARIANT	COVETED	COWED	COWLICK
COURTINGS	COVARIATE	COVETER	COWEDLY	COWLICKS
COURTLET	COVARIED	COVETERS	COWER	COWLIKE
COURTLETS	COVARIES	COVETING	COWERED	COWLING
COURTLIER	COVARY	COVETISE	COWERING	COWLINGS
COURTLIKE	COVARYING	COVETISES	COWERS	COWLS
COURTLING	COVE	COVETOUS	COWFEEDER	COWLSTAFF
COURTLY	COVED	COVETS	COWFISH	COWMAN
COURTROOM	COVELET	COVEY	COWFISHES	COWMEN
COURTS	COVELETS	COVEYS	COWFLAP	COWORKER
COURTSHIP	COVELLINE	COVID	COWFLAPS	COWORKERS
COURTSIDE	COVELLITE	COVIDS	COWFLOP	COWORKING
COURTYARD	COVEN	COVIN	COWFLOPS	COWP
COUSCOUS	COVENANT	COVINE	COWGIRL	COWPAT
COUSIN	COVENANTS	COVINES	COWGIRLS	COWPATS
COUSINAGE	COVENS	COVING	COWGRASS	COWPEA
COUSINLY	COVENT	COVINGS	COWHAGE	COWPEAS
COUSINRY	COVENTS	COVINOUS	COWHAGES	COWPED
COUSINS	COVER	COVINS	COWHAND	COWPIE
COUTA	COVERABLE	COVYNE	COWHANDS	COWPIES
COUTAS	COVERAGE	COVYNES	COWHEARD	COWPING

C

COWPLOP	COXIEST	COZEY	CRACKET	CRAFTY
COWPLOPS	COXINESS	COZEYS	CRACKETS	CRAG
COWPOKE	COXING	COZIE	CRACKHEAD	CRAGFAST
COWPOKES	COXITIDES	COZIED	CRACKIE	CRAGGED
COWPOX	COXITIS	COZIER	CRACKIER	CRAGGER
COWPOXES	COXITISES	COZIERS	CRACKIES	CRAGGERS
COWPS	COXLESS	COZIES	CRACKIEST	CRAGGIER
COWPUNK	COXSACKIE	COZIEST	CRACKING	CRAGGIEST
COWPUNKS	COXSWAIN	COZILY	CRACKINGS	CRAGGILY
COWRIE	COXSWAINS	COZINESS	CRACKJAW	CRAGGY
COWRIES	COXY	COZING	CRACKJAWS	CRAGS
COWRITE	COY	COZY	CRACKLE	CRAGSMAN
COWRITER	COYAU	COZYING	CRACKLED	CRAGSMEN
COWRITERS	COYAUS	COZZES	CRACKLES	CRAIC
COWRITES	COYDOG	COZZIE	CRACKLIER	CRAICS
COWRITING	COYDOGS	COZZIES	CRACKLING	CRAIG
COWRITTEN	COYED	CRAAL	CRACKLY	CRAIGS
COWROTE	COYER	CRAALED	CRACKNEL	CRAKE
COWRY	COYEST	CRAALING	CRACKNELS	CRAKED
COWS	COYING	CRAALS	CRACKPOT	CRAKES
COWSHED	COYISH	CRAB	CRACKPOTS	CRAKING
COWSHEDS	COYISHLY	CRABAPPLE	CRACKS	CRAM
COWSKIN	COYLY	CRABBED	CRACKSMAN	CRAMBE
COWSKINS	COYNESS	CRABBEDLY	CRACKSMEN	CRAMBES
COWSLIP	COYNESSES	CRABBER	CRACKUP	CRAMBO
COWSLIPS	COYOTE	CRABBERS	CRACKUPS	CRAMBOES
COWTOWN	COYOTES	CRABBIER	CRACKY	CRAMBOS
COWTOWNS	COYOTILLO	CRABBIEST	CRACOWE	CRAME
COWTREE	COYPOU	CRABBILY	CRACOWES	CRAMES
COWTREES	COYPOUS	CRABBING	CRADLE	CRAMESIES
COWY	COYPU	CRABBIT	CRADLED	CRAMESY
COX	COYPUS	CRABBY	CRADLER	CRAMFULL
COXA	COYS	CRABEATER	CRADLERS	CRAMMABLE
COXAE	COYSTREL	CRABGRASS	CRADLES	CRAMMED
COXAL	COYSTRELS	CRABLIKE	CRADLING	CRAMMER
COXALGIA	COYSTRIL	CRABMEAT	CRADLINGS	CRAMMERS
COXALGIAS	COYSTRILS	CRABMEATS	CRAFT	CRAMMING
COXALGIC	COZ	CRABS	CRAFTED	CRAMMINGS
COXALGIES	COZE	CRABSTICK	CRAFTER	CRAMOISIE
COXALGY	COZED	CRABWISE	CRAFTERS	CRAMOISY
COXCOMB	COZEN	CRABWOOD	CRAFTIER	CRAMP
COXCOMBIC	COZENAGE	CRABWOODS	CRAFTIEST	CRAMPBARK
COXCOMBRY	COZENAGES	CRACHACH	CRAFTILY	CRAMPED
COXCOMBS	COZENED	CRACK	CRAFTING	CRAMPER
COXED	COZENER	CRACKBACK	CRAFTLESS	CRAMPERS
COXES	COZENERS	CRACKDOWN	CRAFTS	CRAMPET
COXIB	COZENING	CRACKED	CRAFTSMAN	CRAMPETS
COXIBS	COZENS	CRACKER	CRAFTSMEN	CRAMPFISH
COXIER	COZES	CRACKERS	CRAFTWORK	CRAMPIER

CRAMPIEST	CRANKLING	CRARES	CRAVENED	CRAZIEST
CRAMPING	CRANKLY	CRASES	CRAVENER	CRAZILY
CRAMPIT	CRANKNESS	CRASH	CRAVENEST	CRAZINESS
CRAMPITS	CRANKOUS	CRASHED	CRAVENING	CRAZING
CRAMPON	CRANKPIN	CRASHER	CRAVENLY	CRAZINGS
CRAMPONED	CRANKPINS	CRASHERS	CRAVENS	CRAZY
CRAMPONS	CRANKS	CRASHES	CRAVER	CRAZYWEED
CRAMPOON	CRANKY	CRASHING	CRAVERS	CREACH
CRAMPOONS	CRANNIED	CRASHPAD	CRAVES	CREACHS
CRAMPS	CRANNIES	CRASHPADS	CRAVING	CREAGH
CRAMPY	CRANNOG	CRASIS	CRAVINGS	CREAGHS
CRAMS	CRANNOGE	CRASS	CRAW	CREAK
CRAN	CRANNOGES	CRASSER	CRAWDAD	CREAKED
CRANACHAN	CRANNOGS	CRASSEST	CRAWDADDY	CREAKIER
CRANAGE	CRANNY	CRASSLY	CRAWDADS	CREAKIEST
CRANAGES	CRANNYING	CRASSNESS	CRAWFISH	CREAKILY
CRANAPPLE	CRANREUCH	CRATCH	CRAWL	CREAKING
CRANBERRY	CRANS	CRATCHES	CRAWLED	CREAKS
CRANCH	CRANTS	CRATE	CRAWLER	CREAKY
CRANCHED	CRANTSES	CRATED	CRAWLERS	CREAM
CRANCHES	CRAP	CRATEFUL	CRAWLIER	CREAMCUPS
CRANCHING	CRAPAUD	CRATEFULS	CRAWLIEST	CREAMED
CRANE	CRAPAUDS	CRATER	CRAWLING	CREAMER
CRANED	CRAPE	CRATERED	CRAWLINGS	CREAMERS
CRANEFLY	CRAPED	CRATERING	CRAWLS	CREAMERY
CRANELIKE	CRAPELIKE	CRATERLET	CRAWLWAY	CREAMIER
CRANES	CRAPES	CRATEROUS	CRAWLWAYS	CREAMIEST
CRANIA	CRAPIER	CRATERS	CRAWLY	CREAMILY
CRANIAL	CRAPIEST	CRATES	CRAWS	CREAMING
CRANIALLY	CRAPING	CRATHUR	CRAY	CREAMLAID
CRANIATE	CRAPLE	CRATHURS	CRAYER	CREAMLIKE
CRANIATES	CRAPLES	CRATING	CRAYERS	CREAMPUFF
CRANING	CRAPOLA	CRATON	CRAYEST	CREAMS
CRANIUM	CRAPOLAS	CRATONIC	CRAYFISH	CREAMWARE
CRANIUMS	CRAPPED	CRATONS	CRAYON	CREAMWOVE
CRANK	CRAPPER	CRATUR	CRAYONED	CREAMY
CRANKBAIT	CRAPPERS	CRATURS	CRAYONER	CREANCE
CRANKCASE	CRAPPIE	CRAUNCH	CRAYONERS	CREANCES
CRANKED	CRAPPIER	CRAUNCHED	CRAYONING	CREANT
CRANKER	CRAPPIES	CRAUNCHES	CRAYONIST	CREASE
CRANKEST	CRAPPIEST	CRAUNCHY	CRAYONS	CREASED
CRANKIER	CRAPPING	CRAVAT	CRAYS	CREASER
CRANKIEST	CRAPPY	CRAVATE	CRAYTHUR	CREASERS
CRANKILY	CRAPS	CRAVATES	CRAYTHURS	CREASES
CRANKING	CRAPSHOOT	CRAVATS	CRAZE	CREASIER
CRANKISH	CRAPULENT	CRAVATTED	CRAZED	CREASIEST
CRANKLE	CRAPULOUS	CRAVE	CRAZES	CREASING
CRANKLED	CRAPY	CRAVED	CRAZIER	CREASOTE
CRANKLES	CRARE	CRAVEN	CRAZIES	CREASOTED

CREASOTES	CREEDAL	CREMATOR	CREOPHAGY	CRESTING
CREASY	CREEDS	CREMATORS	CREOSOL	CRESTINGS
CREATABLE	CREEING	CREMATORY	CREOSOLS	CRESTLESS
CREATE	CREEK	CREME	CREOSOTE	CRESTON
CREATED	CREEKIER	CREMES	CREOSOTED	CRESTONS
CREATES	CREEKIEST	CREMINI	CREOSOTES	CRESTS
CREATIC	CREEKS	CREMINIS	CREOSOTIC	CRESYL
CREATIN	CREEKSIDE	CREMOCARP	CREPANCE	CRESYLIC
CREATINE	CREEKY	CREMONA	CREPANCES	CRESYLS
CREATINES	CREEL	CREMONAS	CREPE	CRETIC
CREATING	CREELED	CREMOR	CREPED	CRETICS
CREATINS	CREELING	CREMORNE	CREPELIKE	CRETIN
CREATION	CREELS	CREMORNES	CREPERIE	CRETINISE
CREATIONS	CREEP	CREMORS	CREPERIES	CRETINISM
CREATIVE	CREEPAGE	CREMOSIN	CREPES	CRETINIZE
CREATIVES	CREEPAGES	CREMS	CREPEY	CRETINOID
CREATOR	CREEPED	CREMSIN	CREPIER	CRETINOUS
CREATORS	CREEPER	CRENA	CREPIEST	CRETINS
CREATRESS	CREEPERED	CRENAS	CREPINESS	CRETISM
CREATRIX	CREEPERS	CRENATE	CREPING	CRETISMS
CREATURAL	CREEPIE	CRENATED	CREPITANT	CRETONNE
CREATURE	CREEPIER	CRENATELY	CREPITATE	CRETONNES
CREATURES	CREEPIES	CRENATION	CREPITUS	CRETONS
CRECHE	CREEPIEST	CRENATURE	CREPOLINE	CREUTZER
CRECHES	CREEPILY	CRENEL	CREPON	CREUTZERS
CRED	CREEPING	CRENELATE	CREPONS	CREVALLE
CREDAL	CREEPMICE	CRENELED	CREPS	CREVALLES
CREDENCE	CREEPS	CRENELING	CREPT	CREVASSE
CREDENCES	CREEPY	CRENELLE	CREPUSCLE	CREVASSED
CREDENDA	CREES	CRENELLED	CREPY	CREVASSES
CREDENDUM	CREESE	CRENELLES	CRESCENDI	CREVETTE
CREDENT	CREESED	CRENELS	CRESCENDO	CREVETTES
CREDENZA	CREESES	CRENSHAW	CRESCENT	CREVICE
CREDENZAS	CREESH	CRENSHAWS	CRESCENTS	CREVICED
CREDIBLE	CREESHED	CRENULATE	CRESCIVE	CREVICES
CREDIBLY	CREESHES	CREODONT	CRESOL	CREW
CREDIT	CREESHIER	CREODONTS	CRESOLS	CREWCUT
CREDITED	CREESHING	CREOLE	CRESS	CREWCUTS
CREDITING	CREESHY	CREOLES	CRESSES	CREWE
CREDITOR	CREESING	CREOLIAN	CRESSET	CREWED
CREDITORS	CREM	CREOLIANS	CRESSETS	CREWEL
CREDITS	CREMAINS	CREOLISE	CRESSIER	CREWELIST
CREDO	CREMANT	CREOLISED	CRESSIEST	CREWELLED
CREDOS	CREMASTER	CREOLISES	CRESSY	CREWELS
CREDS	CREMATE	CREOLIST	CREST	CREWES
CREDULITY	CREMATED	CREOLISTS	CRESTA	CREWING
CREDULOUS	CREMATES	CREOLIZE	CRESTAL	CREWLESS
CREE	CREMATING	CREOLIZED	CRESTALS	CREWMAN
CREED	CREMATION	CREOLIZES	CRESTED	CREWMATE

CREWMATES	CRIKEY	CRINGEST	CRISPENS	CROAKERS
CREWMEN	CRIM	CRINGEY	CRISPER	CROAKIER
CREWNECK	CRIME	CRINGIER	CRISPERS	CROAKIEST
CREWNECKS	CRIMED	CRINGIEST	CRISPEST	CROAKILY
CREWS	CRIMEFUL	CRINGING	CRISPHEAD	CROAKING
CRIA	CRIMELESS	CRINGINGS	CRISPIER	CROAKINGS
CRIANT	CRIMEN	CRINGLE	CRISPIES	CROAKS
CRIAS	CRIMES	CRINGLES	CRISPIEST	CROAKY
CRIB	CRIMEWAVE	CRINGY	CRISPILY	CROC
CRIBBAGE	CRIMINA	CRINING	CRISPIN	CROCEATE
CRIBBAGES	CRIMINAL	CRINITE	CRISPING	CROCEIN
CRIBBED	CRIMINALS	CRINITES	CRISPINS	CROCEINE
CRIBBER	CRIMINATE	CRINKLE	CRISPLY	CROCEINES
CRIBBERS	CRIMINE	CRINKLED	CRISPNESS	CROCEINS
CRIBBING	CRIMING	CRINKLES	CRISPS	CROCEOUS
CRIBBINGS	CRIMINI	CRINKLIER	CRISPY	CROCHE
CRIBBLE	CRIMINIS	CRINKLIES	CRISSA	CROCHES
CRIBBLED	CRIMINOUS	CRINKLING	CRISSAL	CROCHET
CRIBBLES	CRIMINY	CRINKLY	CRISSUM	CROCHETED
CRIBBLING	CRIMMER	CRINOID	CRISTA	CROCHETER
CRIBELLA	CRIMMERS	CRINOIDAL	CRISTAE	CROCHETS
CRIBELLAR	CRIMP	CRINOIDS	CRISTATE	CROCI
CRIBELLUM	CRIMPED	CRINOLINE	CRISTATED	CROCINE
CRIBLE	CRIMPER	CRINOSE	CRIT	CROCK
CRIBLES	CRIMPERS	CRINUM	CRITERIA	CROCKED
CRIBRATE	CRIMPIER	CRINUMS	CRITERIAL	CROCKERY
CRIBROSE	CRIMPIEST	CRIOLLO	CRITERION	CROCKET
CRIBROUS	CRIMPING	CRIOLLOS	CRITERIUM	CROCKETED
CRIBS	CRIMPLE	CRIOS	CRITH	CROCKETS
CRIBWORK	CRIMPLED	CRIOSES	CRITHS	CROCKING
CRIBWORKS	CRIMPLES	CRIPE	CRITIC	CROCKPOT
CRICETID	CRIMPLING	CRIPES	CRITICAL	CROCKPOTS
CRICETIDS	CRIMPS	CRIPPLE	CRITICISE	CROCKS
CRICK	CRIMPY	CRIPPLED	CRITICISM	CROCODILE
CRICKED	CRIMS	CRIPPLER	CRITICIZE	CROCOITE
CRICKET	CRIMSON	CRIPPLERS	CRITICS	CROCOITES
CRICKETED	CRIMSONED	CRIPPLES	CRITIQUE	CROCOSMIA
CRICKETER	CRIMSONS	CRIPPLING	CRITIQUED	CROCS
CRICKETS	CRINAL	CRIS	CRITIQUES	CROCUS
CRICKEY	CRINATE	CRISE	CRITS	CROCUSES
CRICKING	CRINATED	CRISES	CRITTER	CROFT
CRICKS	CRINE	CRISIC	CRITTERS	CROFTED
CRICKY	CRINED	CRISIS	CRITTUR	CROFTER
CRICOID	CRINES	CRISP	CRITTURS	CROFTERS
CRICOIDS	CRINGE	CRISPATE	CRIVENS	CROFTING
CRIED	CRINGED	CRISPATED	CRIVVENS	CROFTINGS
CRIER	CRINGER	CRISPED	CROAK	CROFTS
CRIERS	CRINGERS	CRISPEN	CROAKED	CROG
CRIES	CRINGES	CRISPENED	CROAKER	CROGGED

CROGGIES	CROOKER	CRORES	CROSSTIES	CROUPIER
CROGGING	CROOKERY	CROSIER	CROSSTOWN	CROUPIERS
CROGGY	CROOKEST	CROSIERED	CROSSTREE	CROUPIEST
CROGS	CROOKING	CROSIERS	CROSSWALK	CROUPILY
CROISSANT	CROOKNECK	CROSS	CROSSWAY	CROUPING
CROJIK	CROOKS	CROSSABLE	CROSSWAYS	CROUPON
CROJIKS	CROOL	CROSSARM	CROSSWIND	CROUPONS
CROKINOLE	CROOLED	CROSSARMS	CROSSWIRE	CROUPOUS
CROMACK	CROOLING	CROSSBAND	CROSSWISE	CROUPS
CROMACKS	CROOLS	CROSSBAR	CROSSWORD	CROUPY
CROMB	CROON	CROSSBARS	CROSSWORT	CROUSE
CROMBEC	CROONED	CROSSBEAM	CROST	CROUSELY
CROMBECS	CROONER	CROSSBILL	CROSTATA	CROUSTADE
CROMBED	CROONERS	CROSSBIT	CROSTATAS	CROUT
CROMBING	CROONIER	CROSSBITE	CROSTINI	CROUTE
CROMBS	CROONIEST	CROSSBOW	CROSTINIS	CROUTES
CROME	CROONING	CROSSBOWS	CROSTINO	CROUTON
CROMED	CROONINGS	CROSSBRED	CROTAL	CROUTONS
CROMES	CROONS	CROSSBUCK	CROTALA	CROUTS
CROMING	CROONY	CROSSCUT	CROTALE	CROW
CROMLECH	CROOVE	CROSSCUTS	CROTALES	CROWBAIT
CROMLECHS	CROOVES	CROSSE	CROTALINE	CROWBAITS
CROMORNA	CROP	CROSSED	CROTALISM	CROWBAR
CROMORNAS	CROPBOUND	CROSSER	CROTALS	CROWBARS
CROMORNE	CROPFUL	CROSSERS	CROTALUM	CROWBERRY
CROMORNES	CROPFULL	CROSSES	CROTCH	CROWBOOT
CRON	CROPFULLS	CROSSEST	CROTCHED	CROWBOOTS
CRONE	CROPFULS	CROSSETTE	CROTCHES	CROWD
CRONES	CROPLAND	CROSSFALL	CROTCHET	CROWDED
CRONET	CROPLANDS	CROSSFIRE	CROTCHETS	CROWDEDLY
CRONETS	CROPLESS	CROSSFISH	CROTCHETY	CROWDER
CRONIES	CROPPED	CROSSHAIR	CROTON	CROWDERS
CRONISH	CROPPER	CROSSHEAD	CROTONBUG	CROWDFUND
CRONK	CROPPERS	CROSSING	CROTONIC	CROWDIE
CRONKER	CROPPIE	CROSSINGS	CROTONS	CROWDIES
CRONKEST	CROPPIES	CROSSISH	CROTTLE	CROWDING
CRONS	CROPPING	CROSSJACK	CROTTLES	CROWDS
CRONY	CROPPINGS	CROSSLET	CROUCH	CROWDY
CRONYISM	CROPPY	CROSSLETS	CROUCHED	CROWEA
CRONYISMS	CROPS	CROSSLIKE	CROUCHES	CROWEAS
CROODLE	CROPSICK	CROSSLY	CROUCHING	CROWED
CROODLED	CROQUANTE	CROSSNESS	CROUP	CROWER
CROODLES	CROQUET	CROSSOVER	CROUPADE	CROWERS
CROODLING	CROQUETED	CROSSPLY	CROUPADES	CROWFEET
CROOK	CROQUETS	CROSSROAD	CROUPE	CROWFOOT
CROOKBACK	CROQUETTE	CROSSRUFF	CROUPED	CROWFOOTS
CROOKED	CROQUIS	CROSSTALK	CROUPER	CROWING
CROOKEDER	CRORE	CROSSTIE	CROUPERS	CROWINGLY
CROOKEDLY	CROREPATI	CROSSTIED	CROUPES	CROWINGS

CROWLIKE	CRUCKS	CRUISER	CRUMMOCK	CRUSADE
CROWN	CRUD	CRUISERS	CRUMMOCKS	CRUSADED
CROWNED	CRUDDED	CRUISES	CRUMMY	CRUSADER
CROWNER	CRUDDIER	CRUISEWAY	CRUMP	CRUSADERS
CROWNERS	CRUDDIEST	CRUISEY	CRUMPED	CRUSADES
CROWNET	CRUDDING	CRUISIE	CRUMPER	CRUSADING
CROWNETS	CRUDDLE	CRUISIER	CRUMPEST	CRUSADO
CROWNING	CRUDDLED	CRUISIES	CRUMPET	CRUSADOES
CROWNINGS	CRUDDLES	CRUISIEST	CRUMPETS	CRUSADOS
CROWNLAND	CRUDDLING	CRUISING	CRUMPIER	CRUSE
CROWNLESS	CRUDDY	CRUISINGS	CRUMPIEST	CRUSES
CROWNLET	CRUDE	CRUISY	CRUMPING	CRUSET
CROWNLETS	CRUDELY	CRUIVE	CRUMPLE	CRUSETS
CROWNLIKE	CRUDENESS	CRUIVES	CRUMPLED	CRUSH
CROWNS	CRUDER	CRUIZIE	CRUMPLES	CRUSHABLE
CROWNWORK	CRUDES	CRUIZIES	CRUMPLIER	CRUSHED
CROWS	CRUDEST	CRULLER	CRUMPLING	CRUSHER
CROWSFEET	CRUDIER	CRULLERS	CRUMPLY	CRUSHERS
CROWSFOOT	CRUDIEST	CRUMB	CRUMPS	CRUSHES
CROWSTEP	CRUDITES	CRUMBED	CRUMPY	CRUSHING
CROWSTEPS	CRUDITIES	CRUMBER	CRUNCH	CRUSHINGS
CROZE	CRUDITY	CRUMBERS	CRUNCHED	CRUSIAN
CROZER	CRUDO	CRUMBIER	CRUNCHER	CRUSIANS
CROZERS	CRUDOS	CRUMBIEST	CRUNCHERS	CRUSIE
CROZES	CRUDS	CRUMBING	CRUNCHES	CRUSIES
CROZIER	CRUDY	CRUMBLE	CRUNCHIE	CRUSILY
CROZIERS	CRUE	CRUMBLED	CRUNCHIER	CRUST
CROZZLED	CRUEL	CRUMBLES	CRUNCHIES	CRUSTA
CRU	CRUELED	CRUMBLIER	CRUNCHILY	CRUSTACEA
CRUBEEN	CRUELER	CRUMBLIES	CRUNCHING	CRUSTAE
CRUBEENS	CRUELEST	CRUMBLING	CRUNCHY	CRUSTAL
CRUCES	CRUELING	CRUMBLY	CRUNK	CRUSTAS
CRUCIAL	CRUELLED	CRUMBS	CRUNKED	CRUSTATE
CRUCIALLY	CRUELLER	CRUMBUM	CRUNKLE	CRUSTATED
CRUCIAN	CRUELLEST	CRUMBUMS	CRUNKLED	CRUSTED
CRUCIANS	CRUELLING	CRUMBY	CRUNKLES	CRUSTIER
CRUCIATE	CRUELLS	CRUMEN	CRUNKLING	CRUSTIES
CRUCIATES	CRUELLY	CRUMENAL	CRUNKS	CRUSTIEST
CRUCIBLE	CRUELNESS	CRUMENALS	CRUNODAL	CRUSTILY
CRUCIBLES	CRUELS	CRUMENS	CRUNODE	CRUSTING
CRUCIFER	CRUELTIES	CRUMHORN	CRUNODES	CRUSTLESS
CRUCIFERS	CRUELTY	CRUMHORNS	CRUOR	CRUSTLIKE
CRUCIFIED	CRUES	CRUMMACK	CRUORES	CRUSTOSE
CRUCIFIER	CRUET	CRUMMACKS	CRUORS	CRUSTS
CRUCIFIES	CRUETS	CRUMMIE	CRUPPER	CRUSTY
CRUCIFIX	CRUFT	CRUMMIER	CRUPPERS	CRUSY
CRUCIFORM	CRUFTS	CRUMMIES	CRURA	CRUTCH
CRUCIFY	CRUISE	CRUMMIEST	CRURAL	CRUTCHED
CRUCK	CRUISED	CRUMMILY	CRUS	CRUTCHES

CRUTCHING	CRYPTAL	CUBERS	CUCKOOS	CUFFABLE
CRUVE	CRYPTIC	CUBES	CUCKS	CUFFED
CRUVES	CRYPTICAL	CUBESAT	CUCULLATE	CUFFIN
CRUX	CRYPTID	CUBESATS	CUCUMBER	CUFFING
CRUXES	CRYPTIDS	CUBHOOD	CUCUMBERS	CUFFINS
CRUZADO	CRYPTO	CUBHOODS	CUCURBIT	CUFFLE
CRUZADOES	CRYPTOGAM	CUBIC	CUCURBITS	CUFFLED
CRUZADOS	CRYPTON	CUBICA	CUD	CUFFLES
CRUZEIRO	CRYPTONS	CUBICAL	CUDBEAR	CUFFLESS
CRUZEIROS	CRYPTONYM	CUBICALLY	CUDBEARS	CUFFLING
CRUZIE	CRYPTOS	CUBICAS	CUDDEN	CUFFLINK
CRUZIES	CRYPTS	CUBICITY	CUDDENS	CUFFLINKS
CRWTH	CRYSTAL	CUBICLE	CUDDIE	CUFFO
CRWTHS	CRYSTALS	CUBICLES	CUDDIES	CUFFS
CRY	CSARDAS	CUBICLY	CUDDIN	CUFFUFFLE
CRYBABIES	CSARDASES	CUBICS	CUDDINS	CUIF
CRYBABY	CTENE	CUBICULA	CUDDLE	CUIFS
CRYBULLY	CTENES	CUBICULUM	CUDDLED	CUING
CRYER	CTENIDIA	CUBIFORM	CUDDLER	CUIRASS
CRYERS	CTENIDIUM	CUBING	CUDDLERS	CUIRASSED
CRYING	CTENIFORM	CUBISM	CUDDLES	CUIRASSES
CRYINGLY	CTENOID	CUBISMS	CUDDLIER	CUISH
CRYINGS	CUADRILLA	CUBIST	CUDDLIEST	CUISHES
CRYOBANK	CUATRO	CUBISTIC	CUDDLING	CUISINART
CRYOBANKS	CUATROS	CUBISTS	CUDDLY	CUISINE
CRYOCABLE	CUB	CUBIT	CUDDY	CUISINES
CRYOGEN	CUBAGE	CUBITAL	CUDGEL	CUISINIER
CRYOGENIC	CUBAGES	CUBITI	CUDGELED	CUISSE
CRYOGENS	CUBANE	CUBITS	CUDGELER	CUISSER
CRYOGENY	CUBANELLE	CUBITUS	CUDGELERS	CUISSERS
CRYOLITE	CUBANES	CUBITUSES	CUDGELING	CUISSES
CRYOLITES	CUBATURE	CUBLESS	CUDGELLED	CUIT
CRYOMETER	CUBATURES	CUBMASTER	CUDGELLER	CUITER
CRYOMETRY	CUBBED	CUBOID	CUDGELS	CUITERED
CRYONIC	CUBBIER	CUBOIDAL	CUDGERIE	CUITERING
CRYONICS	CUBBIES	CUBOIDS	CUDGERIES	CUITERS
CRYOPHYTE	CUBBIEST	CUBS	CUDS	CUITIKIN
CRYOPROBE	CUBBING	CUCK	CUDWEED	CUITIKINS
CRYOSCOPE	CUBBINGS	CUCKED	CUDWEEDS	CUITS
CRYOSCOPY	CUBBISH	CUCKING	CUE	CUITTLE
CRYOSLEEP	CUBBISHLY	CUCKOLD	CUED	CUITTLED
CRYOSTAT	CUBBY	CUCKOLDED	CUEING	CUITTLES
CRYOSTATS	CUBBYHOLE	CUCKOLDLY	CUEINGS	CUITTLING
CRYOTRON	CUBE	CUCKOLDOM	CUEIST	CUKE
CRYOTRONS	CUBEB	CUCKOLDRY	CUEISTS	CUKES
CRYPSES	CUBEBS	CUCKOLDS	CUES	CULCH
CRYPSIS	CUBED	CUCKOO	CUESTA	CULCHES
CRYPT	CUBELIKE	CUCKOOED	CUESTAS	CULCHIE
CRYPTADIA	CUBER	CUCKOOING	CUFF	CULCHIER

CULCHIES	CULPATORY	CUMACEAN	CUNDUMS	CUPHOLDER
CULCHIEST	CULPRIT	CUMACEANS	CUNDY	CUPID
CULET	CULPRITS	CUMARIC	CUNEAL	CUPIDITY
CULETS	CULSHIE	CUMARIN	CUNEATE	CUPIDS
CULEX	CULSHIER	CUMARINS	CUNEATED	CUPLIKE
CULEXES	CULSHIES	CUMARONE	CUNEATELY	CUPMAN
CULICES	CULSHIEST	CUMARONES	CUNEATIC	CUPMEN
CULICID	CULT	CUMBENT	CUNEI	CUPOLA
CULICIDS	CULTCH	CUMBER	CUNEIFORM	CUPOLAED
CULICINE	CULTCHES	CUMBERED	CUNETTE	CUPOLAING
CULICINES	CULTER	CUMBERER	CUNETTES	CUPOLAR
CULINARY	CULTERS	CUMBERERS	CUNEUS	CUPOLAS
CULL	CULTI	CUMBERING	CUNIFORM	CUPOLATED
CULLAY	CULTIC	CUMBERS	CUNIFORMS	CUPPA
CULLAYS	CULTIER	CUMBIA	CUNIT	CUPPAS
CULLED	CULTIEST	CUMBIAS	CUNITS	CUPPED
CULLENDER	CULTIGEN	CUMBRANCE	CUNJEVOI	CUPPER
CULLER	CULTIGENS	CUMBROUS	CUNJEVOIS	CUPPERS
CULLERS	CULTISH	CUMBUNGI	CUNNER	CUPPIER
CULLET	CULTISHLY	CUMBUNGIS	CUNNERS	CUPPIEST
CULLETS	CULTISM	CUMEC	CUNNING	CUPPING
CULLIED	CULTISMS	CUMECS	CUNNINGER	CUPPINGS
CULLIES	CULTIST	CUMIN	CUNNINGLY	CUPPY
CULLING	CULTISTS	CUMINS	CUNNINGS	CUPREOUS
CULLINGS	CULTIVAR	CUMMED	CUNT	CUPRESSUS
CULLION	CULTIVARS	CUMMER	CUNTS	CUPRIC
CULLIONLY	CULTIVATE	CUMMERS	CUP	CUPRITE
CULLIONS	CULTLIKE	CUMMIN	CUPBEARER	CUPRITES
CULLIS	CULTRATE	CUMMING	CUPBOARD	CUPROUS
CULLISES	CULTRATED	CUMMINS	CUPBOARDS	CUPRUM
CULLS	CULTS	CUMQUAT	CUPCAKE	CUPRUMS
CULLY	CULTURAL	CUMQUATS	CUPCAKES	CUPS
CULLYING	CULTURATI	CUMS	CUPEL	CUPSFUL
CULLYISM	CULTURE	CUMSHAW	CUPELED	CUPULA
CULLYISMS	CULTURED	CUMSHAWS	CUPELER	CUPULAE
CULM	CULTURES	CUMULATE	CUPELERS	CUPULAR
CULMED	CULTURING	CUMULATED	CUPELING	CUPULATE
CULMEN	CULTURIST	CUMULATES	CUPELLED	CUPULE
CULMINA	CULTUS	CUMULET	CUPELLER	CUPULES
CULMINANT	CULTUSES	CUMULETS	CUPELLERS	CUR
CULMINATE	CULTY	CUMULI	CUPELLING	CURABLE
CULMING	CULVER	CUMULOSE	CUPELS	CURABLY
CULMS	CULVERIN	CUMULOUS	CUPFERRON	CURACAO
CULOTTE	CULVERINS	CUMULUS	CUPFUL	CURACAOS
CULOTTES	CULVERS	CUMULUSES	CUPFULS	CURACIES
CULPA	CULVERT	CUNABULA	CUPGALL	CURACOA
CULPABLE	CULVERTED	CUNCTATOR	CUPGALLS	CURACOAS
CULPABLY	CULVERTS	CUNDIES	CUPHEAD	CURACY
CULPAE	CUM	CUNDUM	CUPHEADS	CURAGH

CURAGHS	CURCULIO	CURING	CURRAN	CURSIVE
CURANDERA	CURCULIOS	CURINGS	CURRANS	CURSIVELY
CURANDERO	CURCUMA	CURIO	CURRANT	CURSIVES
CURARA	CURCUMAS	CURIOS	CURRANTS	CURSOR
CURARAS	CURCUMIN	CURIOSA	CURRANTY	CURSORARY
CURARE	CURCUMINE	CURIOSITY	CURRAWONG	CURSORES
CURARES	CURCUMINS	CURIOUS	CURRED	CURSORIAL
CURARI	CURD	CURIOUSER	CURREJONG	CURSORILY
CURARINE	CURDED	CURIOUSLY	CURRENCY	CURSORS
CURARINES	CURDIER	CURITE	CURRENT	CURSORY
CURARIS	CURDIEST	CURITES	CURRENTLY	CURST
CURARISE	CURDINESS	CURIUM	CURRENTS	CURSTNESS
CURARISED	CURDING	CURIUMS	CURRICLE	CURSUS
CURARISES	CURDLE	CURL	CURRICLES	CURT
CURARIZE	CURDLED	CURLED	CURRICULA	CURTAIL
CURARIZED	CURDLER	CURLER	CURRIE	CURTAILED
CURARIZES	CURDLERS	CURLERS	CURRIED	CURTAILER
CURASSOW	CURDLES	CURLEW	CURRIER	CURTAILS
CURASSOWS	CURDLING	CURLEWS	CURRIERS	CURTAIN
CURAT	CURDS	CURLI	CURRIERY	CURTAINED
CURATE	CURDY	CURLICUE	CURRIES	CURTAINS
CURATED	CURE	CURLICUED	CURRIJONG	CURTAL
CURATES	CURED	CURLICUES	CURRING	CURTALAX
CURATING	CURELESS	CURLIER	CURRISH	CURTALAXE
CURATION	CURER	CURLIES	CURRISHLY	CURTALS
CURATIONS	CURERS	CURLIEST	CURRS	CURTANA
CURATIVE	CURES	CURLILY	CURRY	CURTANAS
CURATIVES	CURET	CURLINESS	CURRYCOMB	CURTATE
CURATOR	CURETS	CURLING	CURRYING	CURTATION
CURATORS	CURETTAGE	CURLINGS	CURRYINGS	CURTAXE
CURATORY	CURETTE	CURLPAPER	CURS	CURTAXES
CURATRIX	CURETTED	CURLS	CURSAL	CURTER
CURATS	CURETTES	CURLY	CURSE	CURTESIES
CURB	CURETTING	CURLYCUE	CURSED	CURTEST
CURBABLE	CURF	CURLYCUES	CURSEDER	CURTESY
CURBED	CURFEW	CURN	CURSEDEST	CURTILAGE
CURBER	CURFEWS	CURNEY	CURSEDLY	CURTLY
CURBERS	CURFS	CURNIER	CURSENARY	CURTNESS
CURBING	CURFUFFLE	CURNIEST	CURSER	CURTSEY
CURBINGS	CURIA	CURNS	CURSERS	CURTSEYED
CURBLESS	CURIAE	CURNY	CURSES	CURTSEYS
CURBS	CURIAL	CURPEL	CURSI	CURTSIED
CURBSIDE	CURIALISM	CURPELS	CURSILLO	CURTSIES
CURBSIDES	CURIALIST	CURR	CURSILLOS	CURTSY
CURBSTONE	CURIAS	CURRACH	CURSING	CURTSYING
CURCH	CURIE	CURRACHS	CURSINGS	CURULE
CURCHEF	CURIES	CURRAGH	CURSITOR	CURVATE
CURCHEFS	CURIET	CURRAGHS	CURSITORS	CURVATED
CURCHES	CURIETS	CURRAJONG	CURSITORY	CURVATION

CURVATIVE	CUSPAL	CUSTOS	CUTINISE	CUTTLING
CURVATURE	CUSPATE	CUSTREL	CUTINISED	CUTTO
CURVE	CUSPATED	CUSTRELS	CUTINISES	CUTTOE
CURVEBALL	CUSPED	CUSTUMAL	CUTINIZE	CUTTOES
CURVED	CUSPID	CUSTUMALS	CUTINIZED	CUTTY
CURVEDLY	CUSPIDAL	CUSTUMARY	CUTINIZES	CUTUP
CURVES	CUSPIDATE	CUSUM	CUTINS	CUTUPS
CURVESOME	CUSPIDES	CUSUMS	CUTIS	CUTWATER
CURVET	CUSPIDOR	CUT	CUTISES	CUTWATERS
CURVETED	CUSPIDORE	CUTANEOUS	CUTLAS	CUTWORK
CURVETING	CUSPIDORS	CUTAWAY	CUTLASES	CUTWORKS
CURVETS	CUSPIDS	CUTAWAYS	CUTLASS	CUTWORM
CURVETTED	CUSPIER	CUTBACK	CUTLASSES	CUTWORMS
CURVEY	CUSPIEST	CUTBACKS	CUTLER	CUVEE
CURVIER	CUSPIS	CUTBANK	CUTLERIES	CUVEES
CURVIEST	CUSPLIKE	CUTBANKS	CUTLERS	CUVETTE
CURVIFORM	CUSPS	CUTBLOCK	CUTLERY	CUVETTES
CURVINESS	CUSPY	CUTBLOCKS	CUTLET	CUZ
CURVING	CUSS	CUTCH	CUTLETS	CUZES
CURVITAL	CUSSED	CUTCHA	CUTLETTE	CUZZES
CURVITIES	CUSSEDLY	CUTCHERRY	CUTLETTES	CUZZIE
CURVITY	CUSSER	CUTCHERY	CUTLINE	CUZZIES
CURVY	CUSSERS	CUTCHES	CUTLINES	CWM
CUSCUS	CUSSES	CUTDOWN	CUTOFF	CWMS
CUSCUSES	CUSSING	CUTDOWNS	CUTOFFS	CWTCH
CUSEC	CUSSO	CUTE	CUTOUT	CWTCHED
CUSECS	CUSSOS	CUTELY	CUTOUTS	CWTCHES
CUSH	CUSSWORD	CUTENESS	CUTOVER	CWTCHING
CUSHAT	CUSSWORDS	CUTER	CUTOVERS	CYAN
CUSHATS	CUSTARD	CUTES	CUTPURSE	CYANAMID
CUSHAW	CUSTARDS	CUTESIE	CUTPURSES	CYANAMIDE
CUSHAWS	CUSTARDY	CUTESIER	CUTS	CYANAMIDS
CUSHES	CUSTOCK	CUTESIEST	CUTSCENE	CYANATE
CUSHIE	CUSTOCKS	CUTEST	CUTSCENES	CYANATES
CUSHIER	CUSTODE	CUTESY	CUTTABLE	CYANIC
CUSHIES	CUSTODES	CUTEY	CUTTAGE	CYANID
CUSHIEST	CUSTODIAL	CUTEYS	CUTTAGES	CYANIDE
CUSHILY	CUSTODIAN	CUTGLASS	CUTTER	CYANIDED
CUSHINESS	CUSTODIER	CUTGRASS	CUTTERS	CYANIDES
CUSHION	CUSTODIES	CUTICLE	CUTTHROAT	CYANIDING
CUSHIONED	CUSTODY	CUTICLES	CUTTIER	CYANIDS
CUSHIONET	CUSTOM	CUTICULA	CUTTIES	CYANIN
CUSHIONS	CUSTOMARY	CUTICULAE	CUTTIEST	CYANINE
CUSHIONY	CUSTOMED	CUTICULAR	CUTTING	CYANINES
CUSHTY	CUSTOMER	CUTIE	CUTTINGLY	CYANINS
CUSHY	CUSTOMERS	CUTIES	CUTTINGS	CYANISE
CUSK	CUSTOMISE	CUTIKIN	CUTTLE	CYANISED
CUSKS	CUSTOMIZE	CUTIKINS	CUTTLED	CYANISES
CUSP	CUSTOMS	CUTIN	CUTTLES	CYANISING

CYANITE	CYCLAMATE	CYCLONES	CYMBIFORM	CYPRIDS
CYANITES	CYCLAMEN	CYCLONIC	CYMBLING	CYPRINE
CYANITIC	CYCLAMENS	CYCLONITE	CYMBLINGS	CYPRINES
CYANIZE	CYCLAMIC	CYCLOPEAN	CYME	CYPRINID
CYANIZED	CYCLASE	CYCLOPES	CYMENE	CYPRINIDS
CYANIZES	CYCLASES	CYCLOPIAN	CYMENES	CYPRINOID
CYANIZING	CYCLE	CYCLOPIC	CYMES	CYPRIS
CYANO	CYCLECAR	CYCLOPS	CYMLIN	CYPRUS
CYANOGEN	CYCLECARS	CYCLORAMA	CYMLING	CYPRUSES
CYANOGENS	CYCLED	CYCLOS	CYMLINGS	CYPSELA
CYANOSE	CYCLEPATH	CYCLOSES	CYMLINS	CYPSELAE
CYANOSED	CYCLER	CYCLOSIS	CYMOGENE	CYST
CYANOSES	CYCLERIES	CYCLOTRON	CYMOGENES	CYSTEIN
CYANOSIS	CYCLERS	CYCLUS	CYMOGRAPH	CYSTEINE
CYANOTIC	CYCLERY	CYCLUSES	CYMOID	CYSTEINES
CYANOTYPE	CYCLES	CYDER	CYMOL	CYSTEINIC
CYANS	CYCLEWAY	CYDERS	CYMOLS	CYSTEINS
CYANURATE	CYCLEWAYS	CYESES	CYMOPHANE	CYSTIC
CYANURET	CYCLIC	CYESIS	CYMOSE	CYSTID
CYANURETS	CYCLICAL	CYGNET	CYMOSELY	CYSTIDEAN
CYANURIC	CYCLICALS	CYGNETS	CYMOUS	CYSTIDS
CYATHI	CYCLICISM	CYLICES	CYNANCHE	CYSTIFORM
CYATHIA	CYCLICITY	CYLIKES	CYNANCHES	CYSTINE
CYATHIUM	CYCLICLY	CYLINDER	CYNEGETIC	CYSTINES
CYATHUS	CYCLIN	CYLINDERS	CYNIC	CYSTITIS
CYBER	CYCLING	CYLINDRIC	CYNICAL	CYSTOCARP
CYBERCAFE	CYCLINGS	CYLIX	CYNICALLY	CYSTOCELE
CYBERCAST	CYCLINS	CYMA	CYNICISM	CYSTOID
CYBERNATE	CYCLISE	CYMAE	CYNICISMS	CYSTOIDS
CYBERNAUT	CYCLISED	CYMAGRAPH	CYNICS	CYSTOLITH
CYBERPET	CYCLISES	CYMAR	CYNODONT	CYSTOTOMY
CYBERPETS	CYCLISING	CYMARS	CYNODONTS	CYSTS
CYBERPORN	CYCLIST	CYMAS	CYNOMOLGI	CYTASE
CYBERPUNK	CYCLISTS	CYMATIA	CYNOPHOBE	CYTASES
CYBERSEX	CYCLITOL	CYMATICS	CYNOSURAL	CYTASTER
CYBERWAR	CYCLITOLS	CYMATIUM	CYNOSURE	CYTASTERS
CYBERWARS	CYCLIZE	CYMBAL	CYNOSURES	CYTE
CYBORG	CYCLIZED	CYMBALEER	CYPHER	CYTES
CYBORGS	CYCLIZES	CYMBALER	CYPHERED	CYTIDINE
CYBRARIAN	CYCLIZINE	CYMBALERS	CYPHERING	CYTIDINES
CYBRID	CYCLIZING	CYMBALIST	CYPHERS	CYTIDYLIC
CYBRIDS	CYCLO	CYMBALO	CYPRES	CYTISI
CYCAD	CYCLOGIRO	CYMBALOES	CYPRESES	CYTISINE
CYCADEOID	CYCLOID	CYMBALOM	CYPRESS	CYTISINES
CYCADS	CYCLOIDAL	CYMBALOMS	CYPRESSES	CYTISUS
CYCAS	CYCLOIDS	CYMBALOS	CYPRIAN	CYTODE
CYCASES	CYCLOLITH	CYMBALS	CYPRIANS	CYTODES
CYCASIN	CYCLONAL	CYMBIDIA	CYPRID	CYTOGENY
CYCASINS	CYCLONE	CYMBIDIUM	CYPRIDES	CYTOID

CYTOKINE	CYTOMETRY	CYTOSOLIC	CZAR	CZARISM
CYTOKINES	CYTON	CYTOSOLS	CZARDAS	CZARISMS
CYTOKININ	CYTONS	CYTOSOME	CZARDASES	CZARIST
CYTOLOGIC	CYTOPATHY	CYTOSOMES	CZARDOM	CZARISTS
CYTOLOGY	CYTOPENIA	CYTOTAXES	CZARDOMS	CZARITSA
CYTOLYSES	CYTOPLASM	CYTOTAXIS	CZAREVICH	CZARITSAS
CYTOLYSIN	CYTOPLAST	CYTOTOXIC	CZAREVNA	CZARITZA
CYTOLYSIS	CYTOSINE	CYTOTOXIN	CZAREVNAS	CZARITZAS
CYTOLYTIC	CYTOSINES	CZAPKA	CZARINA	CZARS
CYTOMETER	CYTOSOL	CZAPKAS	CZARINAS	

C

D

DA	DACOITS	DAE	DAGGIER	DAIKERING
DAAL	DACOITY	DAEDAL	DAGGIEST	DAIKERS
DAALS	DACQUOISE	DAEDALEAN	DAGGING	DAIKO
DAB	DACRON	DAEDALIAN	DAGGINGS	DAIKON
DABBA	DACRONS	DAEDALIC	DAGGLE	DAIKONS
DABBAS	DACTYL	DAEING	DAGGLED	DAIKOS
DABBED	DACTYLAR	DAEMON	DAGGLES	DAILIES
DABBER	DACTYLI	DAEMONES	DAGGLING	DAILINESS
DABBERS	DACTYLIC	DAEMONIC	DAGGY	DAILY
DABBING	DACTYLICS	DAEMONS	DAGLOCK	DAILYNESS
DABBINGS	DACTYLIST	DAES	DAGLOCKS	DAIMEN
DABBITIES	DACTYLS	DAFF	DAGOBA	DAIMIO
DABBITY	DACTYLUS	DAFFED	DAGOBAS	DAIMIOS
DABBLE	DAD	DAFFIER	DAGS	DAIMOKU
DABBLED	DADA	DAFFIES	DAGWOOD	DAIMOKUS
DABBLER	DADAH	DAFFIEST	DAGWOODS	DAIMON
DABBLERS	DADAHS	DAFFILY	DAH	DAIMONES
DABBLES	DADAISM	DAFFINESS	DAHABEAH	DAIMONIC
DABBLING	DADAISMS	DAFFING	DAHABEAHS	DAIMONS
DABBLINGS	DADAIST	DAFFINGS	DAHABEEAH	DAIMYO
DABCHICK	DADAISTIC	DAFFODIL	DAHABIAH	DAIMYOS
DABCHICKS	DADAISTS	DAFFODILS	DAHABIAHS	DAINE
DABS	DADAS	DAFFS	DAHABIEH	DAINED
DABSTER	DADBOD	DAFFY	DAHABIEHS	DAINES
DABSTERS	DADBODS	DAFT	DAHABIYA	DAINING
DACE	DADCHELOR	DAFTAR	DAHABIYAH	DAINT
DACES	DADDED	DAFTARS	DAHABIYAS	DAINTIER
DACHA	DADDIES	DAFTER	DAHABIYEH	DAINTIES
DACHAS	DADDING	DAFTEST	DAHL	DAINTIEST
DACHSHUND	DADDLE	DAFTIE	DAHLIA	DAINTILY
DACITE	DADDLED	DAFTIES	DAHLIAS	DAINTS
DACITES	DADDLES	DAFTLY	DAHLS	DAINTY
DACK	DADDLING	DAFTNESS	DAHOON	DAIQUIRI
DACKED	DADDOCK	DAG	DAHOONS	DAIQUIRIS
DACKER	DADDOCKS	DAGABA	DAHS	DAIRIES
DACKERED	DADDY	DAGABAS	DAIDLE	DAIRY
DACKERING	DADGUM	DAGGA	DAIDLED	DAIRYING
DACKERS	DADO	DAGGAS	DAIDLES	DAIRYINGS
DACKING	DADOED	DAGGED	DAIDLING	DAIRYMAID
DACKS	DADOES	DAGGER	DAIDZEIN	DAIRYMAN
DACOIT	DADOING	DAGGERED	DAIDZEINS	DAIRYMEN
DACOITAGE	DADOS	DAGGERING	DAIKER	DAIS
DACOITIES	DADS	DAGGERS	DAIKERED	DAISES

DAISHIKI	DALLIES	DAMEWORTS	DAMPEST	DANDIEST
DAISHIKIS	DALLOP	DAMFOOL	DAMPIER	DANDIFIED
DAISIED	DALLOPS	DAMFOOLS	DAMPIEST	DANDIFIES
DAISIES	DALLY	DAMIANA	DAMPING	DANDIFY
DAISY	DALLYING	DAMIANAS	DAMPINGS	DANDILY
DAISYLIKE	DALMAHOY	DAMMAR	DAMPISH	DANDIPRAT
DAITH	DALMAHOYS	DAMMARS	DAMPLY	DANDLE
DAITHS	DALMATIAN	DAMME	DAMPNESS	DANDLED
DAK	DALMATIC	DAMMED	DAMPS	DANDLER
DAKER	DALMATICS	DAMMER	DAMPY	DANDLERS
DAKERED	DALS	DAMMERS	DAMS	DANDLES
DAKERHEN	DALT	DAMMING	DAMSEL	DANDLING
DAKERHENS	DALTON	DAMMIT	DAMSELFLY	DANDRIFF
DAKERING	DALTONIAN	DAMN	DAMSELS	DANDRIFFS
DAKERS	DALTONIC	DAMNABLE	DAMSON	DANDRUFF
DAKOIT	DALTONISM	DAMNABLY	DAMSONS	DANDRUFFS
DAKOITI	DALTONS	DAMNATION	DAN	DANDRUFFY
DAKOITIES	DALTS	DAMNATORY	DANAZOL	DANDY
DAKOITIS	DAM	DAMNDEST	DANAZOLS	DANDYFUNK
DAKOITS	DAMAGE	DAMNDESTS	DANCE	DANDYISH
DAKOITY	DAMAGED	DAMNED	DANCEABLE	DANDYISM
DAKS	DAMAGER	DAMNEDER	DANCECORE	DANDYISMS
DAL	DAMAGERS	DAMNEDEST	DANCED	DANDYPRAT
DALAPON	DAMAGES	DAMNER	DANCEHALL	DANEGELD
DALAPONS	DAMAGING	DAMNERS	DANCELIKE	DANEGELDS
DALASI	DAMAN	DAMNEST	DANCER	DANEGELT
DALASIS	DAMANS	DAMNESTS	DANCERS	DANEGELTS
DALE	DAMAR	DAMNIFIED	DANCES	DANELAGH
DALED	DAMARS	DAMNIFIES	DANCETTE	DANELAGHS
DALEDH	DAMASCENE	DAMNIFY	DANCETTEE	DANELAW
DALEDHS	DAMASK	DAMNING	DANCETTES	DANELAWS
DALEDS	DAMASKED	DAMNINGLY	DANCETTY	DANEWEED
DALES	DAMASKEEN	DAMNS	DANCEWEAR	DANEWEEDS
DALESMAN	DAMASKIN	DAMOISEL	DANCEY	DANEWORT
DALESMEN	DAMASKING	DAMOISELS	DANCICAL	DANEWORTS
DALETH	DAMASKINS	DAMOSEL	DANCICALS	DANG
DALETHS	DAMASKS	DAMOSELS	DANCIER	DANGED
DALGONA	DAMASQUIN	DAMOZEL	DANCIEST	DANGER
DALGONAS	DAMASSIN	DAMOZELS	DANCING	DANGERED
DALGYTE	DAMASSINS	DAMP	DANCINGS	DANGERING
DALGYTES	DAMBOARD	DAMPED	DANCY	DANGEROUS
DALI	DAMBOARDS	DAMPEN	DANDELION	DANGERS
DALIS	DAMBROD	DAMPENED	DANDER	DANGEST
DALLE	DAMBRODS	DAMPENER	DANDERED	DANGING
DALLES	DAME	DAMPENERS	DANDERING	DANGLE
DALLIANCE	DAMEHOOD	DAMPENING	DANDERS	DANGLED
DALLIED	DAMEHOODS	DAMPENS	DANDIACAL	DANGLER
DALLIER	DAMES	DAMPER	DANDIER	DANGLERS
DALLIERS	DAMEWORT	DAMPERS	DANDIES	DANGLES

DANGLIER	DAPPING	DARKENER	DARRAIGNE	DASHIER
DANGLIEST	DAPPLE	DARKENERS	DARRAIGNS	DASHIEST
DANGLING	DAPPLED	DARKENING	DARRAIN	DASHIKI
DANGLINGS	DAPPLES	DARKENS	DARRAINE	DASHIKIS
DANGLY	DAPPLING	DARKER	DARRAINED	DASHING
DANGS	DAPS	DARKEST	DARRAINES	DASHINGLY
DANIO	DAPSONE	DARKFIELD	DARRAINS	DASHIS
DANIOS	DAPSONES	DARKING	DARRAYN	DASHLIGHT
DANISH	DAQUIRI	DARKISH	DARRAYNED	DASHPOT
DANISHES	DAQUIRIS	DARKLE	DARRAYNS	DASHPOTS
DANK	DARAF	DARKLED	DARRE	DASHY
DANKER	DARAFS	DARKLES	DARRED	DASSIE
DANKEST	DARB	DARKLIER	DARRES	DASSIES
DANKISH	DARBAR	DARKLIEST	DARRING	DASTARD
DANKLY	DARBARS	DARKLING	DARSHAN	DASTARDLY
DANKNESS	DARBIES	DARKLINGS	DARSHANS	DASTARDS
DANKS	DARBS	DARKLY	DART	DASTARDY
DANNEBROG	DARCIES	DARKMANS	DARTBOARD	DASYMETER
DANNIES	DARCY	DARKNESS	DARTED	DASYPOD
DANNY	DARCYS	DARKNET	DARTER	DASYPODS
DANS	DARE	DARKNETS	DARTERS	DASYURE
DANSAK	DARED	DARKROOM	DARTING	DASYURES
DANSAKS	DAREDEVIL	DARKROOMS	DARTINGLY	DATA
DANSEUR	DAREFUL	DARKS	DARTITIS	DATABANK
DANSEURS	DARER	DARKSOME	DARTLE	DATABANKS
DANSEUSE	DARERS	DARLING	DARTLED	DATABASE
DANSEUSES	DARES	DARLINGLY	DARTLES	DATABASED
DANT	DARESAY	DARLINGS	DARTLING	DATABASES
DANTED	DARG	DARN	DARTRE	DATABLE
DANTHONIA	DARGA	DARNATION	DARTRES	DATABUS
DANTING	DARGAH	DARNDEST	DARTROUS	DATABUSES
DANTON	DARGAHS	DARNDESTS	DARTS	DATACARD
DANTONED	DARGAS	DARNED	DARUNAVIR	DATACARDS
DANTONING	DARGLE	DARNEDER	DARZI	DATACOMMS
DANTONS	DARGLES	DARNEDEST	DARZIS	DATAFILE
DANTS	DARGS	DARNEL	DAS	DATAFILES
DAP	DARI	DARNELS	DASH	DATAFLOW
DAPHNE	DARIC	DARNER	DASHBOARD	DATAGLOVE
DAPHNES	DARICS	DARNERS	DASHCAM	DATAGRAM
DAPHNIA	DARING	DARNEST	DASHCAMS	DATAGRAMS
DAPHNIAS	DARINGLY	DARNESTS	DASHED	DATAL
DAPHNID	DARINGS	DARNING	DASHEEN	DATALLER
DAPHNIDS	DARIOLE	DARNINGS	DASHEENS	DATALLERS
DAPPED	DARIOLES	DARNS	DASHEKI	DATALS
DAPPER	DARIS	DAROGA	DASHEKIS	DATARIA
DAPPERER	DARK	DAROGAS	DASHER	DATARIAS
DAPPEREST	DARKED	DAROGHA	DASHERS	DATARIES
DAPPERLY	DARKEN	DAROGHAS	DASHES	DATARY
DAPPERS	DARKENED	DARRAIGN	DASHI	DATCHA

DATCHAS	DAUBS	DAVIT	DAYAN	DAYS
DATE	DAUBY	DAVITS	DAYANIM	DAYSACK
DATEABLE	DAUD	DAVY	DAYANS	DAYSACKS
DATEBOOK	DAUDED	DAW	DAYBED	DAYSAIL
DATEBOOKS	DAUDING	DAWAH	DAYBEDS	DAYSAILED
DATED	DAUDS	DAWAHS	DAYBOAT	DAYSAILER
DATEDLY	DAUGHTER	DAWBAKE	DAYBOATS	DAYSAILOR
DATEDNESS	DAUGHTERS	DAWBAKES	DAYBOOK	DAYSAILS
DATELESS	DAULT	DAWBRIES	DAYBOOKS	DAYSHELL
DATELINE	DAULTS	DAWBRY	DAYBOY	DAYSHELLS
DATELINED	DAUNDER	DAWCOCK	DAYBOYS	DAYSIDE
DATELINES	DAUNDERED	DAWCOCKS	DAYBREAK	DAYSIDES
DATER	DAUNDERS	DAWD	DAYBREAKS	DAYSMAN
DATERS	DAUNER	DAWDED	DAYCARE	DAYSMEN
DATES	DAUNERED	DAWDING	DAYCARES	DAYSPRING
DATING	DAUNERING	DAWDLE	DAYCATION	DAYSTAR
DATINGS	DAUNERS	DAWDLED	DAYCENTRE	DAYSTARS
DATIVAL	DAUNT	DAWDLER	DAYCH	DAYTALE
DATIVE	DAUNTED	DAWDLERS	DAYCHED	DAYTALER
DATIVELY	DAUNTER	DAWDLES	DAYCHES	DAYTALERS
DATIVES	DAUNTERS	DAWDLING	DAYCHING	DAYTALES
DATO	DAUNTING	DAWDLINGS	DAYDREAM	DAYTIME
DATOLITE	DAUNTLESS	DAWDS	DAYDREAMS	DAYTIMES
DATOLITES	DAUNTON	DAWED	DAYDREAMT	DAYWEAR
DATOS	DAUNTONED	DAWEN	DAYDREAMY	DAYWEARS
DATTO	DAUNTONS	DAWING	DAYFLIES	DAYWORK
DATTOS	DAUNTS	DAWISH	DAYFLOWER	DAYWORKER
DATUM	DAUPHIN	DAWK	DAYFLY	DAYWORKS
DATUMS	DAUPHINE	DAWKS	DAYGIRL	DAZE
DATURA	DAUPHINES	DAWN	DAYGIRLS	DAZED
DATURAS	DAUPHINS	DAWNED	DAYGLO	DAZEDLY
DATURIC	DAUR	DAWNER	DAYGLOW	DAZEDNESS
DATURINE	DAURED	DAWNERED	DAYGLOWS	DAZER
DATURINES	DAURING	DAWNERING	DAYLIGHT	DAZERS
DAUB	DAURS	DAWNERS	DAYLIGHTS	DAZES
DAUBE	DAUT	DAWNEY	DAYLILIES	DAZING
DAUBED	DAUTED	DAWNING	DAYLILY	DAZZLE
DAUBER	DAUTIE	DAWNINGS	DAYLIT	DAZZLED
DAUBERIES	DAUTIES	DAWNLIKE	DAYLONG	DAZZLER
DAUBERS	DAUTING	DAWNS	DAYMARE	DAZZLERS
DAUBERY	DAUTS	DAWS	DAYMARES	DAZZLES
DAUBES	DAVEN	DAWSONITE	DAYMARK	DAZZLING
DAUBIER	DAVENED	DAWT	DAYMARKS	DAZZLINGS
DAUBIEST	DAVENING	DAWTED	DAYNT	DE
DAUBING	DAVENPORT	DAWTIE	DAYNTS	DEACIDIFY
DAUBINGLY	DAVENS	DAWTIES	DAYPACK	DEACON
DAUBINGS	DAVIDIA	DAWTING	DAYPACKS	DEACONED
DAUBRIES	DAVIDIAS	DAWTS	DAYROOM	DEACONESS
DAUBRY	DAVIES	DAY	DAYROOMS	DEACONING

D

DEACONRY	DEADWATER	DEANING	DEATHLIER	DEBATER
DEACONS	DEADWOOD	DEANS	DEATHLIKE	DEBATERS
DEAD	DEADWOODS	DEANSHIP	DEATHLY	DEBATES
DEADASS	DEAERATE	DEANSHIPS	DEATHS	DEBATING
DEADBEAT	DEAERATED	DEAR	DEATHSMAN	DEBATINGS
DEADBEATS	DEAERATES	DEARE	DEATHSMEN	DEBAUCH
DEADBOLT	DEAERATOR	DEARED	DEATHTRAP	DEBAUCHED
DEADBOLTS	DEAF	DEARER	DEATHWARD	DEBAUCHEE
DEADBOY	DEAFBLIND	DEARES	DEATHY	DEBAUCHER
DEADBOYS	DEAFEN	DEAREST	DEAVE	DEBAUCHES
DEADED	DEAFENED	DEARESTS	DEAVED	DEBBIER
DEADEN	DEAFENING	DEARIE	DEAVES	DEBBIES
DEADENED	DEAFENS	DEARIES	DEAVING	DEBBIEST
DEADENER	DEAFER	DEARING	DEAW	DEBBY
DEADENERS	DEAFEST	DEARLING	DEAWED	DEBE
DEADENING	DEAFISH	DEARLINGS	DEAWIE	DEBEAK
DEADENS	DEAFLY	DEARLY	DEAWING	DEBEAKED
DEADER	DEAFNESS	DEARN	DEAWS	DEBEAKING
DEADERS	DEAIR	DEARNED	DEAWY	DEBEAKS
DEADEST	DEAIRED	DEARNESS	DEB	DEBEARD
DEADEYE	DEAIRING	DEARNFUL	DEBACLE	DEBEARDED
DEADEYES	DEAIRS	DEARNING	DEBACLES	DEBEARDS
DEADFALL	DEAL	DEARNLY	DEBAG	DEBEL
DEADFALLS	DEALATE	DEARNS	DEBAGGED	DEBELLED
DEADHEAD	DEALATED	DEARS	DEBAGGING	DEBELLING
DEADHEADS	DEALATES	DEARTH	DEBAGS	DEBELS
DEADHOUSE	DEALATION	DEARTHS	DEBAR	DEBENTURE
DEADING	DEALBATE	DEARY	DEBARK	DEBES
DEADLIER	DEALER	DEASH	DEBARKED	DEBILE
DEADLIEST	DEALERS	DEASHED	DEBARKER	DEBILITY
DEADLIFT	DEALFISH	DEASHES	DEBARKERS	DEBIT
DEADLIFTS	DEALIGN	DEASHING	DEBARKING	DEBITED
DEADLIGHT	DEALIGNED	DEASIL	DEBARKS	DEBITING
DEADLINE	DEALIGNS	DEASILS	DEBARMENT	DEBITOR
DEADLINED	DEALING	DEASIUL	DEBARRASS	DEBITORS
DEADLINES	DEALINGS	DEASIULS	DEBARRED	DEBITS
DEADLOCK	DEALMAKER	DEASOIL	DEBARRING	DEBOARD
DEADLOCKS	DEALS	DEASOILS	DEBARS	DEBOARDED
DEADLY	DEALT	DEATH	DEBASE	DEBOARDS
DEADMAN	DEAMINASE	DEATHBED	DEBASED	DEBONAIR
DEADMEN	DEAMINATE	DEATHBEDS	DEBASER	DEBONAIRE
DEADNAME	DEAMINISE	DEATHBLOW	DEBASERS	DEBONE
DEADNAMED	DEAMINIZE	DEATHCARE	DEBASES	DEBONED
DEADNAMES	DEAN	DEATHCUP	DEBASING	DEBONER
DEADNESS	DEANED	DEATHCUPS	DEBATABLE	DEBONERS
DEADPAN	DEANER	DEATHFUL	DEBATABLY	DEBONES
DEADPANS	DEANERIES	DEATHIER	DEBATE	DEBONING
DEADS	DEANERS	DEATHIEST	DEBATED	DEBOSH
DEADSTOCK	DEANERY	DEATHLESS	DEBATEFUL	DEBOSHED

DEBOSHES	DEBURRED	DECALOGS	DECEASE	DECIDABLE
DEBOSHING	DEBURRING	DECALOGUE	DECEASED	DECIDE
DEBOSS	DEBURRS	DECALS	DECEASEDS	DECIDED
DEBOSSED	DEBURS	DECAMETER	DECEASES	DECIDEDLY
DEBOSSES	DEBUS	DECAMETRE	DECEASING	DECIDER
DEBOSSING	DEBUSED	DECAMP	DECEDENT	DECIDERS
DEBOUCH	DEBUSES	DECAMPED	DECEDENTS	DECIDES
DEBOUCHE	DEBUSING	DECAMPING	DECEIT	DECIDING
DEBOUCHED	DEBUSSED	DECAMPS	DECEITFUL	DECIDUA
DEBOUCHES	DEBUSSES	DECAN	DECEITS	DECIDUAE
DEBRIDE	DEBUSSING	DECANAL	DECEIVE	DECIDUAL
DEBRIDED	DEBUT	DECANALLY	DECEIVED	DECIDUAS
DEBRIDES	DEBUTANT	DECANE	DECEIVER	DECIDUATE
DEBRIDING	DEBUTANTE	DECANES	DECEIVERS	DECIDUOUS
DEBRIEF	DEBUTANTS	DECANI	DECEIVES	DECIGRAM
DEBRIEFED	DEBUTED	DECANOIC	DECEIVING	DECIGRAMS
DEBRIEFER	DEBUTING	DECANS	DECELERON	DECILE
DEBRIEFS	DEBUTS	DECANT	DECEMVIR	DECILES
DEBRIS	DEBYE	DECANTATE	DECEMVIRI	DECILITER
DEBRUISE	DEBYES	DECANTED	DECEMVIRS	DECILITRE
DEBRUISED	DECACHORD	DECANTER	DECENARY	DECILLION
DEBRUISES	DECAD	DECANTERS	DECENCIES	DECIMAL
DEBS	DECADAL	DECANTING	DECENCY	DECIMALLY
DEBT	DECADE	DECANTS	DECENNARY	DECIMALS
DEBTED	DECADENCE	DECAPOD	DECENNIA	DECIMATE
DEBTEE	DECADENCY	DECAPODAL	DECENNIAL	DECIMATED
DEBTEES	DECADENT	DECAPODAN	DECENNIUM	DECIMATES
DEBTLESS	DECADENTS	DECAPODS	DECENT	DECIMATOR
DEBTOR	DECADES	DECARB	DECENTER	DECIME
DEBTORS	DECADS	DECARBED	DECENTERS	DECIMES
DEBTS	DECAF	DECARBING	DECENTEST	DECIMETER
DEBUD	DECAFF	DECARBS	DECENTLY	DECIMETRE
DEBUDDED	DECAFFS	DECARE	DECENTRE	DECIPHER
DEBUDDING	DECAFS	DECARES	DECENTRED	DECIPHERS
DEBUDS	DECAGON	DECASTERE	DECENTRES	DECISION
DEBUG	DECAGONAL	DECASTICH	DECEPTION	DECISIONS
DEBUGGED	DECAGONS	DECASTYLE	DECEPTIVE	DECISIVE
DEBUGGER	DECAGRAM	DECATHLON	DECEPTORY	DECISORY
DEBUGGERS	DECAGRAMS	DECAUDATE	DECERN	DECISTERE
DEBUGGING	DECAHEDRA	DECAY	DECERNED	DECK
DEBUGS	DECAL	DECAYABLE	DECERNING	DECKCHAIR
DEBUNK	DECALCIFY	DECAYED	DECERNS	DECKED
DEBUNKED	DECALED	DECAYER	DECERTIFY	DECKEL
DEBUNKER	DECALING	DECAYERS	DECESSION	DECKELS
DEBUNKERS	DECALITER	DECAYING	DECHEANCE	DECKER
DEBUNKING	DECALITRE	DECAYLESS	DECIARE	DECKERS
DEBUNKS	DECALLED	DECAYS	DECIARES	DECKHAND
DEBUR	DECALLING	DECCIE	DECIBEL	DECKHANDS
DEBURR	DECALOG	DECCIES	DECIBELS	DECKHOUSE

DECKING	DECOCTING	DECOYERS	DECUPLES	DEEDIER
DECKINGS	DECOCTION	DECOYING	DECUPLING	DEEDIEST
DECKLE	DECOCTIVE	DECOYS	DECURIA	DEEDILY
DECKLED	DECOCTS	DECREASE	DECURIAS	DEEDING
DECKLES	DECOCTURE	DECREASED	DECURIES	DEEDLESS
DECKLESS	DECODABLE	DECREASES	DECURION	DEEDS
DECKO	DECODE	DECREE	DECURIONS	DEEDY
DECKOED	DECODED	DECREED	DECURRENT	DEEING
DECKOING	DECODER	DECREEING	DECURSION	DEEJAY
DECKOS	DECODERS	DECREER	DECURSIVE	DEEJAYED
DECKS	DECODES	DECREERS	DECURVE	DEEJAYING
DECLAIM	DECODING	DECREES	DECURVED	DEEJAYS
DECLAIMED	DECODINGS	DECREET	DECURVES	DEEK
DECLAIMER	DECOHERER	DECREETS	DECURVING	DEELY
DECLAIMS	DECOKE	DECREMENT	DECURY	DEEM
DECLARANT	DECOKED	DECREPIT	DECUSSATE	DEEMED
DECLARE	DECOKES	DECRETAL	DEDAL	DEEMING
DECLARED	DECOKING	DECRETALS	DEDALIAN	DEEMS
DECLARER	DECOLLATE	DECRETIST	DEDANS	DEEMSTER
DECLARERS	DECOLLETE	DECRETIVE	DEDENDA	DEEMSTERS
DECLARES	DECOLOR	DECRETORY	DEDENDUM	DEEN
DECLARING	DECOLORED	DECREW	DEDENDUMS	DEENS
DECLASS	DECOLORS	DECREWED	DEDICANT	DEEP
DECLASSE	DECOLOUR	DECREWING	DEDICANTS	DEEPEN
DECLASSED	DECOLOURS	DECREWS	DEDICATE	DEEPENED
DECLASSEE	DECOMMIT	DECRIAL	DEDICATED	DEEPENER
DECLASSES	DECOMMITS	DECRIALS	DEDICATEE	DEEPENERS
DECLAW	DECOMPLEX	DECRIED	DEDICATES	DEEPENING
DECLAWED	DECOMPOSE	DECRIER	DEDICATOR	DEEPENS
DECLAWING	DECONGEST	DECRIERS	DEDIMUS	DEEPER
DECLAWS	DECONTROL	DECRIES	DEDIMUSES	DEEPEST
DECLINAL	DECOR	DECROWN	DEDUCE	DEEPFAKE
DECLINALS	DECORATE	DECROWNED	DEDUCED	DEEPFAKED
DECLINANT	DECORATED	DECROWNS	DEDUCES	DEEPFAKES
DECLINATE	DECORATES	DECRY	DEDUCIBLE	DEEPFELT
DECLINE	DECORATOR	DECRYING	DEDUCIBLY	DEEPFROZE
DECLINED	DECOROUS	DECRYPT	DEDUCING	DEEPIE
DECLINER	DECORS	DECRYPTED	DEDUCT	DEEPIES
DECLINERS	DECORUM	DECRYPTS	DEDUCTED	DEEPLY
DECLINES	DECORUMS	DECTET	DEDUCTING	DEEPMOST
DECLINING	DECOS	DECTETS	DEDUCTION	DEEPNESS
DECLINIST	DECOUPAGE	DECUBITAL	DEDUCTIVE	DEEPS
DECLIVITY	DECOUPLE	DECUBITI	DEDUCTS	DEEPWATER
DECLIVOUS	DECOUPLED	DECUBITUS	DEE	DEER
DECLUTCH	DECOUPLER	DECUMAN	DEED	DEERBERRY
DECLUTTER	DECOUPLES	DECUMANS	DEEDED	DEERE
DECO	DECOY	DECUMBENT	DEEDER	DEERES
DECOCT	DECOYED	DECUPLE	DEEDEST	DEERFLIES
DECOCTED	DECOYER	DECUPLED	DEEDFUL	DEERFLY

DEERGRASS	DEFAT	DEFERENTS	DEFLATERS	DEFOREST
DEERHORN	DEFATS	DEFERMENT	DEFLATES	DEFORESTS
DEERHORNS	DEFATTED	DEFERRAL	DEFLATING	DEFORM
DEERHOUND	DEFATTING	DEFERRALS	DEFLATION	DEFORMED
DEERLET	DEFAULT	DEFERRED	DEFLATOR	DEFORMER
DEERLETS	DEFAULTED	DEFERRER	DEFLATORS	DEFORMERS
DEERLIKE	DEFAULTER	DEFERRERS	DEFLEA	DEFORMING
DEERS	DEFAULTS	DEFERRING	DEFLEAED	DEFORMITY
DEERSKIN	DEFEAT	DEFERS	DEFLEAING	DEFORMS
DEERSKINS	DEFEATED	DEFFER	DEFLEAS	DEFOUL
DEERWEED	DEFEATER	DEFFEST	DEFLECT	DEFOULED
DEERWEEDS	DEFEATERS	DEFFLY	DEFLECTED	DEFOULING
DEERYARD	DEFEATING	DEFFO	DEFLECTOR	DEFOULS
DEERYARDS	DEFEATISM	DEFI	DEFLECTS	DEFRAG
DEES	DEFEATIST	DEFIANCE	DEFLEX	DEFRAGGED
DEET	DEFEATS	DEFIANCES	DEFLEXED	DEFRAGGER
DEETS	DEFEATURE	DEFIANT	DEFLEXES	DEFRAGS
DEEV	DEFECATE	DEFIANTLY	DEFLEXING	DEFRAUD
DEEVE	DEFECATED	DEFICIENT	DEFLEXION	DEFRAUDED
DEEVED	DEFECATES	DEFICIT	DEFLEXURE	DEFRAUDER
DEEVES	DEFECATOR	DEFICITS	DEFLORATE	DEFRAUDS
DEEVING	DEFECT	DEFIED	DEFLOWER	DEFRAY
DEEVS	DEFECTED	DEFIER	DEFLOWERS	DEFRAYAL
DEEWAN	DEFECTING	DEFIERS	DEFLUENT	DEFRAYALS
DEEWANS	DEFECTION	DEFIES	DEFLUXION	DEFRAYED
DEEYA	DEFECTIVE	DEFILADE	DEFO	DEFRAYER
DEEYAS	DEFECTOR	DEFILADED	DEFOAM	DEFRAYERS
DEF	DEFECTORS	DEFILADES	DEFOAMED	DEFRAYING
DEFACE	DEFECTS	DEFILE	DEFOAMER	DEFRAYS
DEFACED	DEFENCE	DEFILED	DEFOAMERS	DEFREEZE
DEFACER	DEFENCED	DEFILER	DEFOAMING	DEFREEZES
DEFACERS	DEFENCES	DEFILERS	DEFOAMS	DEFRIEND
DEFACES	DEFENCING	DEFILES	DEFOCUS	DEFRIENDS
DEFACING	DEFEND	DEFILING	DEFOCUSED	DEFROCK
DEFAECATE	DEFENDANT	DEFINABLE	DEFOCUSES	DEFROCKED
DEFALCATE	DEFENDED	DEFINABLY	DEFOG	DEFROCKS
DEFAME	DEFENDER	DEFINE	DEFOGGED	DEFROST
DEFAMED	DEFENDERS	DEFINED	DEFOGGER	DEFROSTED
DEFAMER	DEFENDING	DEFINER	DEFOGGERS	DEFROSTER
DEFAMERS	DEFENDS	DEFINERS	DEFOGGING	DEFROSTS
DEFAMES	DEFENSE	DEFINES	DEFOGS	DEFROZE
DEFAMING	DEFENSED	DEFINIENS	DEFOLIANT	DEFROZEN
DEFAMINGS	DEFENSES	DEFINING	DEFOLIATE	DEFT
DEFANG	DEFENSING	DEFINITE	DEFORCE	DEFTER
DEFANGED	DEFENSIVE	DEFINITES	DEFORCED	DEFTEST
DEFANGING	DEFER	DEFIS	DEFORCER	DEFTLY
DEFANGS	DEFERABLE	DEFLATE	DEFORCERS	DEFTNESS
DEFAST	DEFERENCE	DEFLATED	DEFORCES	DEFUEL
DEFASTE	DEFERENT	DEFLATER	DEFORCING	DEFUELED

DEFUELING	DEGLAZED	DEHORNED	DEINDEXES	DEKES
DEFUELLED	DEGLAZES	DEHORNER	DEINOSAUR	DEKING
DEFUELS	DEGLAZING	DEHORNERS	DEIONISE	DEKKO
DEFUNCT	DEGORGE	DEHORNING	DEIONISED	DEKKOED
DEFUNCTS	DEGORGED	DEHORNS	DEIONISER	DEKKOING
DEFUND	DEGORGES	DEHORS	DEIONISES	DEKKOS
DEFUNDED	DEGORGING	DEHORT	DEIONIZE	DEL
DEFUNDING	DEGOUT	DEHORTED	DEIONIZED	DELAINE
DEFUNDS	DEGOUTED	DEHORTER	DEIONIZER	DELAINES
DEFUSE	DEGOUTING	DEHORTERS	DEIONIZES	DELAPSE
DEFUSED	DEGOUTS	DEHORTING	DEIPAROUS	DELAPSED
DEFUSER	DEGRADE	DEHORTS	DEISEAL	DELAPSES
DEFUSERS	DEGRADED	DEHYDRATE	DEISEALS	DELAPSING
DEFUSES	DEGRADER	DEI	DEISHEAL	DELAPSION
DEFUSING	DEGRADERS	DEICE	DEISHEALS	DELATE
DEFUZE	DEGRADES	DEICED	DEISM	DELATED
DEFUZED	DEGRADING	DEICER	DEISMS	DELATES
DEFUZES	DEGRAS	DEICERS	DEIST	DELATING
DEFUZING	DEGREASE	DEICES	DEISTIC	DELATION
DEFY	DEGREASED	DEICIDAL	DEISTICAL	DELATIONS
DEFYING	DEGREASER	DEICIDE	DEISTS	DELATOR
DEG	DEGREASES	DEICIDES	DEITIES	DELATORS
DEGAGE	DEGREE	DEICING	DEITY	DELAY
DEGAME	DEGREED	DEICTIC	DEIXES	DELAYABLE
DEGAMES	DEGREES	DEICTICS	DEIXIS	DELAYED
DEGAMI	DEGROWTH	DEID	DEIXISES	DELAYER
DEGAMIS	DEGROWTHS	DEIDER	DEJECT	DELAYERS
DEGARNISH	DEGS	DEIDEST	DEJECTA	DELAYING
DEGAS	DEGU	DEIDS	DEJECTED	DELAYS
DEGASES	DEGUM	DEIF	DEJECTING	DELE
DEGASSED	DEGUMMED	DEIFER	DEJECTION	DELEAD
DEGASSER	DEGUMMING	DEIFEST	DEJECTORY	DELEADED
DEGASSERS	DEGUMS	DEIFIC	DEJECTS	DELEADING
DEGASSES	DEGUS	DEIFICAL	DEJEUNE	DELEADS
DEGASSING	DEGUST	DEIFIED	DEJEUNER	DELEAF
DEGAUSS	DEGUSTATE	DEIFIER	DEJEUNERS	DELEAFED
DEGAUSSED	DEGUSTED	DEIFIERS	DEJEUNES	DELEAFING
DEGAUSSER	DEGUSTING	DEIFIES	DEKAGRAM	DELEAFS
DEGAUSSES	DEGUSTS	DEIFORM	DEKAGRAMS	DELEAVE
DEGEARING	DEHAIR	DEIFY	DEKALITER	DELEAVED
DEGENDER	DEHAIRED	DEIFYING	DEKALITRE	DELEAVES
DEGENDERS	DEHAIRING	DEIGN	DEKALOGY	DELEAVING
DEGERM	DEHAIRS	DEIGNED	DEKAMETER	DELEBLE
DEGERMED	DEHISCE	DEIGNING	DEKAMETRE	DELECTATE
DEGERMING	DEHISCED	DEIGNS	DEKARE	DELED
DEGERMS	DEHISCENT	DEIL	DEKARES	DELEGABLE
DEGGED	DEHISCES	DEILS	DEKE	DELEGACY
DEGGING	DEHISCING	DEINDEX	DEKED	DELEGATE
DEGLAZE	DEHORN	DEINDEXED	DEKEING	DELEGATED

DELEGATEE	DELINKING	DELTIC	DEMANDED	DEMERGER
DELEGATES	DELINKS	DELTOID	DEMANDER	DEMERGERS
DELEGATOR	DELIQUIUM	DELTOIDEI	DEMANDERS	DEMERGES
DELEING	DELIRIA	DELTOIDS	DEMANDING	DEMERGING
DELENDA	DELIRIANT	DELTS	DEMANDS	DEMERIT
DELES	DELIRIOUS	DELUBRA	DEMANNED	DEMERITED
DELETABLE	DELIRIUM	DELUBRUM	DEMANNING	DEMERITS
DELETE	DELIRIUMS	DELUBRUMS	DEMANS	DEMERSAL
DELETED	DELIS	DELUDABLE	DEMANTOID	DEMERSE
DELETES	DELISH	DELUDE	DEMARCATE	DEMERSED
DELETING	DELIST	DELUDED	DEMARCHE	DEMERSES
DELETION	DELISTED	DELUDER	DEMARCHES	DEMERSING
DELETIONS	DELISTING	DELUDERS	DEMARK	DEMERSION
DELETIVE	DELISTS	DELUDES	DEMARKED	DEMES
DELETORY	DELIVER	DELUDING	DEMARKET	DEMESNE
DELF	DELIVERED	DELUGE	DEMARKETS	DEMESNES
DELFS	DELIVERER	DELUGED	DEMARKING	DEMETON
DELFT	DELIVERLY	DELUGES	DEMARKS	DEMETONS
DELFTS	DELIVERS	DELUGING	DEMAST	DEMIC
DELFTWARE	DELIVERY	DELUNDUNG	DEMASTED	DEMIES
DELI	DELL	DELUSION	DEMASTING	DEMIGOD
DELIBATE	DELLIER	DELUSIONS	DEMASTS	DEMIGODS
DELIBATED	DELLIES	DELUSIVE	DEMAYNE	DEMIJOHN
DELIBATES	DELLIEST	DELUSORY	DEMAYNES	DEMIJOHNS
DELIBLE	DELLS	DELUSTER	DEME	DEMILUNE
DELICACY	DELLY	DELUSTERS	DEMEAN	DEMILUNES
DELICATE	DELO	DELUSTRE	DEMEANE	DEMIMONDE
DELICATES	DELOPE	DELUSTRED	DEMEANED	DEMINER
DELICE	DELOPED	DELUSTRES	DEMEANES	DEMINERS
DELICENSE	DELOPES	DELUXE	DEMEANING	DEMINING
DELICES	DELOPING	DELVE	DEMEANOR	DEMININGS
DELICIOUS	DELOS	DELVED	DEMEANORS	DEMIPIQUE
DELICT	DELOUSE	DELVER	DEMEANOUR	DEMIREP
DELICTS	DELOUSED	DELVERS	DEMEANS	DEMIREPS
DELIGHT	DELOUSER	DELVES	DEMENT	DEMISABLE
DELIGHTED	DELOUSERS	DELVING	DEMENTATE	DEMISE
DELIGHTER	DELOUSES	DEMAGOG	DEMENTED	DEMISED
DELIGHTS	DELOUSING	DEMAGOGED	DEMENTI	DEMISES
DELIME	DELPH	DEMAGOGIC	DEMENTIA	DEMISING
DELIMED	DELPHIC	DEMAGOGS	DEMENTIAL	DEMISS
DELIMES	DELPHIN	DEMAGOGUE	DEMENTIAS	DEMISSION
DELIMING	DELPHINIA	DEMAGOGY	DEMENTING	DEMISSIVE
DELIMIT	DELPHINS	DEMAIN	DEMENTIS	DEMISSLY
DELIMITED	DELPHS	DEMAINE	DEMENTS	DEMIST
DELIMITER	DELS	DEMAINES	DEMERARA	DEMISTED
DELIMITS	DELT	DEMAINS	DEMERARAN	DEMISTER
DELINEATE	DELTA	DEMAN	DEMERARAS	DEMISTERS
DELINK	DELTAIC	DEMAND	DEMERGE	DEMISTING
DELINKED	DELTAS	DEMANDANT	DEMERGED	DEMISTS

DEMIT	DEMONIZES	DENAR	DENITRATE	DENTATED
DEMITASSE	DEMONRIES	DENARI	DENITRIFY	DENTATELY
DEMITS	DEMONRY	DENARIES	DENIZEN	DENTATION
DEMITTED	DEMONS	DENARII	DENIZENED	DENTED
DEMITTING	DEMONYM	DENARIUS	DENIZENS	DENTEL
DEMIURGE	DEMONYMS	DENARS	DENNED	DENTELLE
DEMIURGES	DEMOS	DENARY	DENNET	DENTELLES
DEMIURGIC	DEMOSCENE	DENATURE	DENNETS	DENTELS
DEMIURGUS	DEMOSES	DENATURED	DENNING	DENTEX
DEMIVEG	DEMOTE	DENATURES	DENOMINAL	DENTEXES
DEMIVEGES	DEMOTED	DENAY	DENOTABLE	DENTICARE
DEMIVOLT	DEMOTES	DENAYED	DENOTATE	DENTICLE
DEMIVOLTE	DEMOTIC	DENAYING	DENOTATED	DENTICLES
DEMIVOLTS	DEMOTICS	DENAYS	DENOTATES	DENTIFORM
DEMIWORLD	DEMOTING	DENAZIFY	DENOTE	DENTIL
DEMO	DEMOTION	DENCH	DENOTED	DENTILED
DEMOB	DEMOTIONS	DENDRIMER	DENOTES	DENTILS
DEMOBBED	DEMOTIST	DENDRITE	DENOTING	DENTIN
DEMOBBING	DEMOTISTS	DENDRITES	DENOTIVE	DENTINAL
DEMOBS	DEMOUNT	DENDRITIC	DENOUNCE	DENTINE
DEMOCIDE	DEMOUNTED	DENDROID	DENOUNCED	DENTINES
DEMOCIDES	DEMOUNTS	DENDROIDS	DENOUNCER	DENTING
DEMOCRACY	DEMPSTER	DENDRON	DENOUNCES	DENTINS
DEMOCRAT	DEMPSTERS	DENDRONS	DENS	DENTIST
DEMOCRATS	DEMPT	DENE	DENSE	DENTISTRY
DEMOCRATY	DEMULCENT	DENERVATE	DENSELY	DENTISTS
DEMODE	DEMULSIFY	DENES	DENSENESS	DENTITION
DEMODED	DEMUR	DENET	DENSER	DENTOID
DEMOED	DEMURE	DENETS	DENSEST	DENTS
DEMOI	DEMURED	DENETTED	DENSIFIED	DENTULOUS
DEMOING	DEMURELY	DENETTING	DENSIFIER	DENTURAL
DEMOLISH	DEMURER	DENGUE	DENSIFIES	DENTURE
DEMOLOGY	DEMURES	DENGUES	DENSIFY	DENTURES
DEMON	DEMUREST	DENI	DENSITIES	DENTURISM
DEMONESS	DEMURING	DENIABLE	DENSITY	DENTURIST
DEMONIAC	DEMURRAGE	DENIABLY	DENT	DENUDATE
DEMONIACS	DEMURRAL	DENIAL	DENTAL	DENUDATED
DEMONIAN	DEMURRALS	DENIALISM	DENTALIA	DENUDATES
DEMONIC	DEMURRED	DENIALIST	DENTALISE	DENUDE
DEMONICAL	DEMURRER	DENIALS	DENTALITY	DENUDED
DEMONISE	DEMURRERS	DENIED	DENTALIUM	DENUDER
DEMONISED	DEMURRING	DENIER	DENTALIZE	DENUDERS
DEMONISES	DEMURS	DENIERS	DENTALLY	DENUDES
DEMONISM	DEMY	DENIES	DENTALS	DENUDING
DEMONISMS	DEMYSHIP	DENIGRATE	DENTARIA	DENY
DEMONIST	DEMYSHIPS	DENIM	DENTARIAS	DENYING
DEMONISTS	DEMYSTIFY	DENIMED	DENTARIES	DENYINGLY
DEMONIZE	DEMYTHIFY	DENIMS	DENTARY	DEODAND
DEMONIZED	DEN	DENIS	DENTATE	DEODANDS

DEODAR	DEPERM	DEPLUMING	DEPRIMES	DERAILING
DEODARA	DEPERMED	DEPOLISH	DEPRIMING	DERAILS
DEODARAS	DEPERMING	DEPONE	DEPRIVAL	DERANGE
DEODARS	DEPERMS	DEPONED	DEPRIVALS	DERANGED
DEODATE	DEPICT	DEPONENT	DEPRIVE	DERANGER
DEODATES	DEPICTED	DEPONENTS	DEPRIVED	DERANGERS
DEODORANT	DEPICTER	DEPONES	DEPRIVER	DERANGES
DEODORISE	DEPICTERS	DEPONING	DEPRIVERS	DERANGING
DEODORIZE	DEPICTING	DEPORT	DEPRIVES	DERAT
DEONTIC	DEPICTION	DEPORTED	DEPRIVING	DERATE
DEONTICS	DEPICTIVE	DEPORTEE	DEPROGRAM	DERATED
DEORBIT	DEPICTOR	DEPORTEES	DEPS	DERATES
DEORBITED	DEPICTORS	DEPORTER	DEPSIDE	DERATING
DEORBITS	DEPICTS	DEPORTERS	DEPSIDES	DERATINGS
DEOXIDATE	DEPICTURE	DEPORTING	DEPTH	DERATION
DEOXIDISE	DEPIGMENT	DEPORTS	DEPTHLESS	DERATIONS
DEOXIDIZE	DEPILATE	DEPOSABLE	DEPTHS	DERATS
DEOXY	DEPILATED	DEPOSAL	DEPURANT	DERATTED
DEP	DEPILATES	DEPOSALS	DEPURANTS	DERATTING
DEPAINT	DEPILATOR	DEPOSE	DEPURATE	DERAY
DEPAINTED	DEPLANE	DEPOSED	DEPURATED	DERAYED
DEPAINTS	DEPLANED	DEPOSER	DEPURATES	DERAYING
DEPANNEUR	DEPLANES	DEPOSERS	DEPURATOR	DERAYS
DEPART	DEPLANING	DEPOSES	DEPUTABLE	DERBIES
DEPARTED	DEPLENISH	DEPOSING	DEPUTE	DERBY
DEPARTEDS	DEPLETE	DEPOSIT	DEPUTED	DERE
DEPARTEE	DEPLETED	DEPOSITED	DEPUTES	DERECHO
DEPARTEES	DEPLETER	DEPOSITOR	DEPUTIES	DERECHOS
DEPARTER	DEPLETERS	DEPOSITS	DEPUTING	DERED
DEPARTERS	DEPLETES	DEPOT	DEPUTISE	DERELICT
DEPARTING	DEPLETING	DEPOTS	DEPUTISED	DERELICTS
DEPARTS	DEPLETION	DEPRAVE	DEPUTISES	DEREPRESS
DEPARTURE	DEPLETIVE	DEPRAVED	DEPUTIZE	DERES
DEPASTURE	DEPLETORY	DEPRAVER	DEPUTIZED	DERHAM
DEPECHE	DEPLORE	DEPRAVERS	DEPUTIZES	DERHAMS
DEPECHED	DEPLORED	DEPRAVES	DEPUTY	DERIDE
DEPECHES	DEPLORER	DEPRAVING	DEQUEUE	DERIDED
DEPECHING	DEPLORERS	DEPRAVITY	DEQUEUED	DERIDER
DEPEINCT	DEPLORES	DEPRECATE	DEQUEUES	DERIDERS
DEPEINCTS	DEPLORING	DEPREDATE	DEQUEUING	DERIDES
DEPEND	DEPLOY	DEPREHEND	DERACINE	DERIDING
DEPENDANT	DEPLOYED	DEPRENYL	DERACINES	DERIG
DEPENDED	DEPLOYER	DEPRENYLS	DERAIGN	DERIGGED
DEPENDENT	DEPLOYERS	DEPRESS	DERAIGNED	DERIGGING
DEPENDING	DEPLOYING	DEPRESSED	DERAIGNS	DERIGS
DEPENDS	DEPLOYS	DEPRESSES	DERAIL	DERING
DEPEOPLE	DEPLUME	DEPRESSOR	DERAILED	DERINGER
DEPEOPLED	DEPLUMED	DEPRIME	DERAILER	DERINGERS
DEPEOPLES	DEPLUMES	DEPRIMED	DERAILERS	DERISIBLE

DERISION	DERRIERE	DESCRIERS	DESIGNS	DESMOIDS
DERISIONS	DERRIERES	DESCRIES	DESILVER	DESMOSOME
DERISIVE	DERRIES	DESCRIVE	DESILVERS	DESNOOD
DERISORY	DERRINGER	DESCRIVED	DESINE	DESNOODED
DERIVABLE	DERRIS	DESCRIVES	DESINED	DESNOODS
DERIVABLY	DERRISES	DESCRY	DESINENCE	DESOEUVRE
DERIVATE	DERRO	DESCRYING	DESINENT	DESOLATE
DERIVATED	DERROS	DESECRATE	DESINES	DESOLATED
DERIVATES	DERRY	DESEED	DESINING	DESOLATER
DERIVE	DERTH	DESEEDED	DESIPIENT	DESOLATES
DERIVED	DERTHS	DESEEDER	DESIRABLE	DESOLATOR
DERIVER	DERV	DESEEDERS	DESIRABLY	DESORB
DERIVERS	DERVISH	DESEEDING	DESIRE	DESORBED
DERIVES	DERVISHES	DESEEDS	DESIRED	DESORBER
DERIVING	DERVS	DESELECT	DESIRER	DESORBERS
DERM	DESALT	DESELECTS	DESIRERS	DESORBING
DERMA	DESALTED	DESERT	DESIRES	DESORBS
DERMAL	DESALTER	DESERTED	DESIRING	DESOXY
DERMAS	DESALTERS	DESERTER	DESIROUS	DESPAIR
DERMATIC	DESALTING	DESERTERS	DESIS	DESPAIRED
DERMATOID	DESALTS	DESERTIC	DESIST	DESPAIRER
DERMATOME	DESAND	DESERTIFY	DESISTED	DESPAIRS
DERMESTID	DESANDED	DESERTING	DESISTING	DESPATCH
DERMIC	DESANDING	DESERTION	DESISTS	DESPERADO
DERMIS	DESANDS	DESERTS	DESK	DESPERATE
DERMISES	DESCALE	DESERVE	DESKBOUND	DESPIGHT
DERMOID	DESCALED	DESERVED	DESKFAST	DESPIGHTS
DERMOIDS	DESCALER	DESERVER	DESKFASTS	DESPISAL
DERMS	DESCALERS	DESERVERS	DESKILL	DESPISALS
DERN	DESCALES	DESERVES	DESKILLED	DESPISE
DERNED	DESCALING	DESERVING	DESKILLS	DESPISED
DERNFUL	DESCANT	DESEX	DESKING	DESPISER
DERNIER	DESCANTED	DESEXED	DESKINGS	DESPISERS
DERNIES	DESCANTER	DESEXES	DESKMAN	DESPISES
DERNING	DESCANTS	DESEXING	DESKMEN	DESPISING
DERNLY	DESCEND	DESHI	DESKNOTE	DESPITE
DERNS	DESCENDED	DESHIS	DESKNOTES	DESPITED
DERNY	DESCENDER	DESI	DESKS	DESPITES
DERNYS	DESCENDS	DESICCANT	DESKTOP	DESPITING
DERO	DESCENT	DESICCATE	DESKTOPS	DESPOIL
DEROGATE	DESCENTS	DESIGN	DESMAN	DESPOILED
DEROGATED	DESCHOOL	DESIGNATE	DESMANS	DESPOILER
DEROGATES	DESCHOOLS	DESIGNED	DESMID	DESPOILS
DEROS	DESCRIBE	DESIGNEE	DESMIDIAN	DESPOND
DERP	DESCRIBED	DESIGNEES	DESMIDS	DESPONDED
DERPS	DESCRIBER	DESIGNER	DESMINE	DESPONDS
DERRICK	DESCRIBES	DESIGNERS	DESMINES	DESPOT
DERRICKED	DESCRIED	DESIGNFUL	DESMODIUM	DESPOTAT
DERRICKS	DESCRIER	DESIGNING	DESMOID	DESPOTATE

DESPOTATS	DESYNES	DETERGE	DETOURING	DEUTZIAS
DESPOTIC	DESYNING	DETERGED	DETOURS	DEV
DESPOTISM	DETACH	DETERGENT	DETOX	DEVA
DESPOTS	DETACHED	DETERGER	DETOXED	DEVALL
DESPUMATE	DETACHER	DETERGERS	DETOXES	DEVALLED
DESSE	DETACHERS	DETERGES	DETOXIFY	DEVALLING
DESSERT	DETACHES	DETERGING	DETOXING	DEVALLS
DESSERTS	DETACHING	DETERMENT	DETRACT	DEVALUATE
DESSES	DETAIL	DETERMINE	DETRACTED	DEVALUE
DESSYATIN	DETAILED	DETERRED	DETRACTOR	DEVALUED
DESTAIN	DETAILER	DETERRENT	DETRACTS	DEVALUES
DESTAINED	DETAILERS	DETERRER	DETRAIN	DEVALUING
DESTAINS	DETAILING	DETERRERS	DETRAINED	DEVAS
DESTEMPER	DETAILS	DETERRING	DETRAINS	DEVASTATE
DESTINATE	DETAIN	DETERS	DETRAQUE	DEVEIN
DESTINE	DETAINED	DETERSION	DETRAQUEE	DEVEINED
DESTINED	DETAINEE	DETERSIVE	DETRAQUES	DEVEINING
DESTINES	DETAINEES	DETEST	DETRIMENT	DEVEINS
DESTINIES	DETAINER	DETESTED	DETRITAL	DEVEL
DESTINING	DETAINERS	DETESTER	DETRITION	DEVELED
DESTINY	DETAINING	DETESTERS	DETRITUS	DEVELING
DESTITUTE	DETAINS	DETESTING	DETRUDE	DEVELLED
DESTOCK	DETANGLE	DETESTS	DETRUDED	DEVELLING
DESTOCKED	DETANGLED	DETHATCH	DETRUDES	DEVELOP
DESTOCKS	DETANGLER	DETHRONE	DETRUDING	DEVELOPE
DESTREAM	DETANGLES	DETHRONED	DETRUSION	DEVELOPED
DESTREAMS	DETASSEL	DETHRONER	DETRUSOR	DEVELOPER
DESTRESS	DETASSELS	DETHRONES	DETRUSORS	DEVELOPES
DESTRIER	DETECT	DETICK	DETUNE	DEVELOPPE
DESTRIERS	DETECTED	DETICKED	DETUNED	DEVELOPS
DESTROY	DETECTER	DETICKER	DETUNES	DEVELS
DESTROYED	DETECTERS	DETICKERS	DETUNING	DEVERBAL
DESTROYER	DETECTING	DETICKING	DEUCE	DEVERBALS
DESTROYS	DETECTION	DETICKS	DEUCED	DEVEST
DESTRUCT	DETECTIVE	DETINUE	DEUCEDLY	DEVESTED
DESTRUCTO	DETECTOR	DETINUES	DEUCES	DEVESTING
DESTRUCTS	DETECTORS	DETONABLE	DEUCING	DEVESTS
DESUETUDE	DETECTS	DETONATE	DEUDDARN	DEVI
DESUGAR	DETENT	DETONATED	DEUDDARNS	DEVIANCE
DESUGARED	DETENTE	DETONATES	DEUS	DEVIANCES
DESUGARS	DETENTES	DETONATOR	DEUTERATE	DEVIANCY
DESULFUR	DETENTION	DETORSION	DEUTERIC	DEVIANT
DESULFURS	DETENTIST	DETORT	DEUTERIDE	DEVIANTS
DESULPHUR	DETENTS	DETORTED	DEUTERIUM	DEVIATE
DESULTORY	DETENU	DETORTING	DEUTERON	DEVIATED
DESYATIN	DETENUE	DETORTION	DEUTERONS	DEVIATES
DESYATINS	DETENUES	DETORTS	DEUTON	DEVIATING
DESYNE	DETENUS	DETOUR	DEUTONS	DEVIATION
DESYNED	DETER	DETOURED	DEUTZIA	DEVIATIVE

D

DEVIATOR	DEVO	DEWANNY	DEWY	DHIMMI
DEVIATORS	DEVOICE	DEWANS	DEX	DHIMMIS
DEVIATORY	DEVOICED	DEWAR	DEXES	DHOBI
DEVICE	DEVOICES	DEWARS	DEXIE	DHOBIS
DEVICEFUL	DEVOICING	DEWATER	DEXIES	DHOL
DEVICES	DEVOID	DEWATERED	DEXTER	DHOLAK
DEVIL	DEVOIR	DEWATERER	DEXTERITY	DHOLAKS
DEVILDOM	DEVOIRS	DEWATERS	DEXTEROUS	DHOLE
DEVILDOMS	DEVOLVE	DEWAX	DEXTERS	DHOLES
DEVILED	DEVOLVED	DEWAXED	DEXTRAL	DHOLL
DEVILESS	DEVOLVES	DEWAXES	DEXTRALLY	DHOLLS
DEVILET	DEVOLVING	DEWAXING	DEXTRALS	DHOLS
DEVILETS	DEVON	DEWBERRY	DEXTRAN	DHOOLIES
DEVILFISH	DEVONIAN	DEWCLAW	DEXTRANS	DHOOLY
DEVILING	DEVONPORT	DEWCLAWED	DEXTRIN	DHOORA
DEVILINGS	DEVONS	DEWCLAWS	DEXTRINE	DHOORAS
DEVILISH	DEVORE	DEWDROP	DEXTRINES	DHOOTI
DEVILISM	DEVORES	DEWDROPS	DEXTRINS	DHOOTIE
DEVILISMS	DEVOS	DEWED	DEXTRO	DHOOTIES
DEVILKIN	DEVOT	DEWFALL	DEXTRORSE	DHOOTIS
DEVILKINS	DEVOTE	DEWFALLS	DEXTROSE	DHOTI
DEVILLED	DEVOTED	DEWFULL	DEXTROSES	DHOTIS
DEVILLING	DEVOTEDLY	DEWIER	DEXTROUS	DHOURRA
DEVILMENT	DEVOTEE	DEWIEST	DEXY	DHOURRAS
DEVILRIES	DEVOTEES	DEWILY	DEY	DHOW
DEVILRY	DEVOTES	DEWINESS	DEYS	DHOWS
DEVILS	DEVOTING	DEWING	DEZINC	DHURNA
DEVILSHIP	DEVOTION	DEWITT	DEZINCED	DHURNAS
DEVILTRY	DEVOTIONS	DEWITTED	DEZINCING	DHURRA
DEVILWOOD	DEVOTS	DEWITTING	DEZINCKED	DHURRAS
DEVIOUS	DEVOUR	DEWITTS	DEZINCS	DHURRIE
DEVIOUSLY	DEVOURED	DEWLAP	DHABA	DHURRIES
DEVIS	DEVOURER	DEWLAPPED	DHABAS	DHUTI
DEVISABLE	DEVOURERS	DEWLAPS	DHAK	DHUTIS
DEVISAL	DEVOURING	DEWLAPT	DHAKS	DHYANA
DEVISALS	DEVOURS	DEWLESS	DHAL	DHYANAS
DEVISE	DEVOUT	DEWOOL	DHALS	DI
DEVISED	DEVOUTER	DEWOOLED	DHAMMA	DIABASE
DEVISEE	DEVOUTEST	DEWOOLING	DHAMMAS	DIABASES
DEVISEES	DEVOUTLY	DEWOOLS	DHANSAK	DIABASIC
DEVISER	DEVS	DEWORM	DHANSAKS	DIABETES
DEVISERS	DEVVEL	DEWORMED	DHARMA	DIABETIC
DEVISES	DEVVELLED	DEWORMER	DHARMAS	DIABETICS
DEVISING	DEVVELS	DEWORMERS	DHARMIC	DIABLE
DEVISOR	DEW	DEWORMING	DHARMSALA	DIABLERIE
DEVISORS	DEWAN	DEWORMS	DHARNA	DIABLERY
DEVITRIFY	DEWANI	DEWPOINT	DHARNAS	DIABLES
DEVLING	DEWANIS	DEWPOINTS	DHIKR	DIABOLIC
DEVLINGS	DEWANNIES	DEWS	DHIKRS	DIABOLISE

DIABOLISM	DIAGRID	DIALYSING	DIAPHONE	DIASPORIC
DIABOLIST	DIAGRIDS	DIALYSIS	DIAPHONES	DIASTASE
DIABOLIZE	DIAL	DIALYTIC	DIAPHONIC	DIASTASES
DIABOLO	DIALECT	DIALYZATE	DIAPHONY	DIASTASIC
DIABOLOGY	DIALECTAL	DIALYZE	DIAPHRAGM	DIASTASIS
DIABOLOS	DIALECTIC	DIALYZED	DIAPHYSES	DIASTATIC
DIACETYL	DIALECTS	DIALYZER	DIAPHYSIS	DIASTEM
DIACETYLS	DIALED	DIALYZERS	DIAPIR	DIASTEMA
DIACHRONY	DIALER	DIALYZES	DIAPIRIC	DIASTEMAS
DIACHYLON	DIALERS	DIALYZING	DIAPIRISM	DIASTEMS
DIACHYLUM	DIALING	DIAMAGNET	DIAPIRS	DIASTER
DIACID	DIALINGS	DIAMANTE	DIAPSID	DIASTERS
DIACIDIC	DIALIST	DIAMANTES	DIAPSIDS	DIASTOLE
DIACIDS	DIALISTS	DIAMETER	DIAPYESES	DIASTOLES
DIACODION	DIALLAGE	DIAMETERS	DIAPYESIS	DIASTOLIC
DIACODIUM	DIALLAGES	DIAMETRAL	DIAPYETIC	DIASTRAL
DIACONAL	DIALLAGIC	DIAMETRIC	DIARCH	DIASTYLE
DIACONATE	DIALLED	DIAMIDE	DIARCHAL	DIASTYLES
DIACRITIC	DIALLEL	DIAMIDES	DIARCHIC	DIATHERMY
DIACT	DIALLELS	DIAMIN	DIARCHIES	DIATHESES
DIACTINAL	DIALLER	DIAMINE	DIARCHY	DIATHESIS
DIACTINE	DIALLERS	DIAMINES	DIARIAL	DIATHETIC
DIACTINES	DIALLING	DIAMINS	DIARIAN	DIATOM
DIACTINIC	DIALLINGS	DIAMOND	DIARIES	DIATOMIC
DIACTS	DIALLIST	DIAMONDED	DIARISE	DIATOMIST
DIADEM	DIALLISTS	DIAMONDS	DIARISED	DIATOMITE
DIADEMED	DIALOG	DIAMYL	DIARISES	DIATOMS
DIADEMING	DIALOGED	DIANDRIES	DIARISING	DIATONIC
DIADEMS	DIALOGER	DIANDROUS	DIARIST	DIATREME
DIADOCHI	DIALOGERS	DIANDRY	DIARISTIC	DIATREMES
DIADOCHY	DIALOGIC	DIANE	DIARISTS	DIATRETA
DIADROM	DIALOGING	DIANODAL	DIARIZE	DIATRETUM
DIADROMS	DIALOGISE	DIANOETIC	DIARIZED	DIATRIBE
DIAERESES	DIALOGISM	DIANOIA	DIARIZES	DIATRIBES
DIAERESIS	DIALOGIST	DIANOIAS	DIARIZING	DIATRON
DIAERETIC	DIALOGITE	DIANTHUS	DIARRHEA	DIATRONS
DIAGLYPH	DIALOGIZE	DIAPASE	DIARRHEAL	DIATROPIC
DIAGLYPHS	DIALOGS	DIAPASES	DIARRHEAS	DIAXON
DIAGNOSE	DIALOGUE	DIAPASON	DIARRHEIC	DIAXONS
DIAGNOSED	DIALOGUED	DIAPASONS	DIARRHOEA	DIAZEPAM
DIAGNOSES	DIALOGUER	DIAPAUSE	DIARY	DIAZEPAMS
DIAGNOSIS	DIALOGUES	DIAPAUSED	DIASCIA	DIAZEUXES
DIAGONAL	DIALS	DIAPAUSES	DIASCIAS	DIAZEUXIS
DIAGONALS	DIALYSATE	DIAPENTE	DIASCOPE	DIAZIN
DIAGRAM	DIALYSE	DIAPENTES	DIASCOPES	DIAZINE
DIAGRAMED	DIALYSED	DIAPER	DIASPORA	DIAZINES
DIAGRAMS	DIALYSER	DIAPERED	DIASPORAS	DIAZINON
DIAGRAPH	DIALYSERS	DIAPERING	DIASPORE	DIAZINONS
DIAGRAPHS	DIALYSES	DIAPERS	DIASPORES	DIAZINS

DIAZO	DICHASIA	DICLINIES	DIDAKEI	DIEB
DIAZOES	DICHASIAL	DICLINISM	DIDAKEIS	DIEBACK
DIAZOLE	DICHASIUM	DICLINOUS	DIDAPPER	DIEBACKS
DIAZOLES	DICHOGAMY	DICLINY	DIDAPPERS	DIEBS
DIAZONIUM	DICHONDRA	DICOT	DIDDER	DIECIOUS
DIAZOS	DICHOPTIC	DICOTS	DIDDERED	DIED
DIAZOTISE	DICHORD	DICOTYL	DIDDERING	DIEDRAL
DIAZOTIZE	DICHORDS	DICOTYLS	DIDDERS	DIEDRALS
DIB	DICHOTIC	DICROTAL	DIDDICOY	DIEDRE
DIBASIC	DICHOTOMY	DICROTIC	DIDDICOYS	DIEDRES
DIBBED	DICHROIC	DICROTISM	DIDDIER	DIEGESES
DIBBER	DICHROISM	DICROTOUS	DIDDIES	DIEGESIS
DIBBERS	DICHROITE	DICT	DIDDIEST	DIEGETIC
DIBBING	DICHROMAT	DICTA	DIDDLE	DIEHARD
DIBBLE	DICHROMIC	DICTATE	DIDDLED	DIEHARDS
DIBBLED	DICHT	DICTATED	DIDDLER	DIEING
DIBBLER	DICHTED	DICTATES	DIDDLERS	DIEL
DIBBLERS	DICHTING	DICTATING	DIDDLES	DIELDRIN
DIBBLES	DICHTS	DICTATION	DIDDLEY	DIELDRINS
DIBBLING	DICIER	DICTATOR	DIDDLEYS	DIELS
DIBBS	DICIEST	DICTATORS	DIDDLIES	DIELYTRA
DIBBUK	DICING	DICTATORY	DIDDLING	DIELYTRAS
DIBBUKIM	DICINGS	DICTATRIX	DIDDLY	DIEMAKER
DIBBUKKIM	DICK	DICTATURE	DIDDUMS	DIEMAKERS
DIBBUKS	DICKED	DICTED	DIDDY	DIENE
DIBROMIDE	DICKENS	DICTIER	DIDELPHIC	DIENES
DIBS	DICKENSES	DICTIEST	DIDELPHID	DIEOFF
DIBUTYL	DICKER	DICTING	DIDICOI	DIEOFFS
DICACIOUS	DICKERED	DICTION	DIDICOIS	DIERESES
DICACITY	DICKERER	DICTIONAL	DIDICOY	DIERESIS
DICACODYL	DICKERERS	DICTIONS	DIDICOYS	DIERETIC
DICALCIUM	DICKERING	DICTS	DIDIE	DIES
DICAMBA	DICKERS	DICTUM	DIDIES	DIESEL
DICAMBAS	DICKEY	DICTUMS	DIDJERIDU	DIESELED
DICAST	DICKEYS	DICTY	DIDO	DIESELING
DICASTERY	DICKHEAD	DICTYOGEN	DIDOES	DIESELISE
DICASTIC	DICKHEADS	DICUMAROL	DIDOS	DIESELIZE
DICASTS	DICKIE	DICYCLIC	DIDRACHM	DIESELS
DICE	DICKIER	DICYCLIES	DIDRACHMA	DIESES
DICED	DICKIES	DICYCLY	DIDRACHMS	DIESINKER
DICELIKE	DICKIEST	DID	DIDST	DIESIS
DICENTRA	DICKING	DIDACT	DIDY	DIESTER
DICENTRAS	DICKINGS	DIDACTIC	DIDYMIUM	DIESTERS
DICENTRIC	DICKS	DIDACTICS	DIDYMIUMS	DIESTOCK
DICER	DICKTIER	DIDACTS	DIDYMO	DIESTOCKS
DICERS	DICKTIEST	DIDACTYL	DIDYMOS	DIESTROUS
DICES	DICKTY	DIDACTYLS	DIDYMOUS	DIESTRUM
DICEY	DICKY	DIDAKAI	DIDYNAMY	DIESTRUMS
DICH	DICKYBIRD	DIDAKAIS	DIE	DIESTRUS

DIET	DIFS	DIGITISE	DIKA	DILLIER
DIETARIAN	DIG	DIGITISED	DIKAS	DILLIES
DIETARIES	DIGAMIES	DIGITISER	DIKAST	DILLIEST
DIETARILY	DIGAMIST	DIGITISES	DIKASTS	DILLING
DIETARY	DIGAMISTS	DIGITIZE	DIKDIK	DILLINGS
DIETED	DIGAMMA	DIGITIZED	DIKDIKS	DILLIS
DIETER	DIGAMMAS	DIGITIZER	DIKE	DILLS
DIETERS	DIGAMOUS	DIGITIZES	DIKED	DILLWEED
DIETETIC	DIGAMY	DIGITONIN	DIKER	DILLWEEDS
DIETETICS	DIGASTRIC	DIGITOXIN	DIKERS	DILLY
DIETHER	DIGENESES	DIGITRON	DIKES	DILSCOOP
DIETHERS	DIGENESIS	DIGITRONS	DIKETONE	DILSCOOPS
DIETHYL	DIGENETIC	DIGITS	DIKETONES	DILTIAZEM
DIETHYLS	DIGERATI	DIGITULE	DIKING	DILUENT
DIETICIAN	DIGEST	DIGITULES	DIKKOP	DILUENTS
DIETINE	DIGESTANT	DIGLOSSIA	DIKKOPS	DILUTABLE
DIETINES	DIGESTED	DIGLOSSIC	DIKTAT	DILUTE
DIETING	DIGESTER	DIGLOT	DIKTATS	DILUTED
DIETINGS	DIGESTERS	DIGLOTS	DILATABLE	DILUTEE
DIETIST	DIGESTIF	DIGLOTTIC	DILATABLY	DILUTEES
DIETISTS	DIGESTIFS	DIGLYPH	DILATANCY	DILUTER
DIETITIAN	DIGESTING	DIGLYPHS	DILATANT	DILUTERS
DIETS	DIGESTION	DIGNIFIED	DILATANTS	DILUTES
DIF	DIGESTIVE	DIGNIFIES	DILATATE	DILUTING
DIFF	DIGESTOR	DIGNIFY	DILATATOR	DILUTION
DIFFER	DIGESTORS	DIGNITARY	DILATE	DILUTIONS
DIFFERED	DIGESTS	DIGNITIES	DILATED	DILUTIVE
DIFFERENT	DIGGABLE	DIGNITY	DILATER	DILUTOR
DIFFERING	DIGGED	DIGONAL	DILATERS	DILUTORS
DIFFERS	DIGGER	DIGOXIN	DILATES	DILUVIA
DIFFICILE	DIGGERS	DIGOXINS	DILATING	DILUVIAL
DIFFICULT	DIGGING	DIGRAPH	DILATION	DILUVIAN
DIFFIDENT	DIGGINGS	DIGRAPHIC	DILATIONS	DILUVION
DIFFLUENT	DIGHT	DIGRAPHS	DILATIVE	DILUVIONS
DIFFORM	DIGHTED	DIGRESS	DILATOR	DILUVIUM
DIFFRACT	DIGHTING	DIGRESSED	DILATORS	DILUVIUMS
DIFFRACTS	DIGHTS	DIGRESSER	DILATORY	DIM
DIFFS	DIGICAM	DIGRESSES	DILDO	DIMBLE
DIFFUSE	DIGICAMS	DIGS	DILDOE	DIMBLES
DIFFUSED	DIGIPACK	DIGYNIAN	DILDOES	DIMBO
DIFFUSELY	DIGIPACKS	DIGYNOUS	DILDOS	DIMBOES
DIFFUSER	DIGIT	DIHEDRA	DILEMMA	DIMBOS
DIFFUSERS	DIGITAL	DIHEDRAL	DILEMMAS	DIME
DIFFUSES	DIGITALIN	DIHEDRALS	DILEMMIC	DIMENSION
DIFFUSING	DIGITALIS	DIHEDRON	DILIGENCE	DIMER
DIFFUSION	DIGITALLY	DIHEDRONS	DILIGENT	DIMERIC
DIFFUSIVE	DIGITALS	DIHYBRID	DILL	DIMERISE
DIFFUSOR	DIGITATE	DIHYBRIDS	DILLED	DIMERISED
DIFFUSORS	DIGITATED	DIHYDRIC	DILLI	DIMERISES

DIMERISM	DIMYARIAN	DINGOS	DINOTHERE	DIORITE
DIMERISMS	DIMYARY	DINGS	DINS	DIORITES
DIMERIZE	DIN	DINGUS	DINT	DIORITIC
DIMERIZED	DINAR	DINGUSES	DINTED	DIOSGENIN
DIMERIZES	DINARCHY	DINGY	DINTING	DIOTA
DIMEROUS	DINARS	DINGYING	DINTLESS	DIOTAS
DIMERS	DINDLE	DINIC	DINTS	DIOXAN
DIMES	DINDLED	DINICS	DIOBOL	DIOXANE
DIMETER	DINDLES	DINING	DIOBOLON	DIOXANES
DIMETERS	DINDLING	DININGS	DIOBOLONS	DIOXANS
DIMETHYL	DINE	DINITRO	DIOBOLS	DIOXID
DIMETHYLS	DINED	DINK	DIOCESAN	DIOXIDE
DIMETRIC	DINER	DINKED	DIOCESANS	DIOXIDES
DIMIDIATE	DINERIC	DINKER	DIOCESE	DIOXIDS
DIMINISH	DINERO	DINKEST	DIOCESES	DIOXIN
DIMISSORY	DINEROS	DINKEY	DIODE	DIOXINS
.DIMITIES	DINERS	DINKEYS	DIODES	DIP
DIMITY	DINES	DINKIE	DIOECIES	DIPCHICK
DIMLY	DINETTE	DINKIER	DIOECIOUS	DIPCHICKS
DIMMABLE	DINETTES	DINKIES	DIOECISM	DIPEPTIDE
DIMMED	DINFUL	DINKIEST	DIOECISMS	DIPHASE
DIMMER	DING	DINKING	DIOECY	DIPHASIC
DIMMERS	DINGBAT	DINKLIER	DIOESTRUS	DIPHENYL
DIMMEST	DINGBATS	DINKLIEST	DIOICOUS	DIPHENYLS
DIMMING	DINGDONG	DINKLY	DIOL	DIPHONE
DIMMINGS	DINGDONGS	DINKS	DIOLEFIN	DIPHONES
DIMMISH	DINGE	DINKUM	DIOLEFINS	DIPHTHONG
DIMNESS	DINGED	DINKUMS	DIOLS	DIPHYSITE
DIMNESSES	DINGER	DINKY	DIONYSIAC	DIPLEGIA
DIMORPH	DINGERS	DINMONT	DIONYSIAN	DIPLEGIAS
DIMORPHIC	DINGES	DINMONTS	DIOPSIDE	DIPLEGIC
DIMORPHS	DINGESES	DINNA	DIOPSIDES	DIPLEX
DIMOUT	DINGEY	DINNAE	DIOPSIDIC	DIPLEXER
DIMOUTS	DINGEYS	DINNED	DIOPTASE	DIPLEXERS
DIMP	DINGHIES	DINNER	DIOPTASES	DIPLOE
DIMPLE	DINGHY	DINNERED	DIOPTER	DIPLOES
DIMPLED	DINGIED	DINNERING	DIOPTERS	DIPLOGEN
DIMPLES	DINGIER	DINNERS	DIOPTRAL	DIPLOGENS
DIMPLIER	DINGIES	DINNING	DIOPTRATE	DIPLOIC
DIMPLIEST	DINGIEST	DINNLE	DIOPTRE	DIPLOID
DIMPLING	DINGILY	DINNLED	DIOPTRES	DIPLOIDIC
DIMPLY	DINGINESS	DINNLES	DIOPTRIC	DIPLOIDS
DIMPS	DINGING	DINNLING	DIOPTRICS	DIPLOIDY
DIMPSIES	DINGLE	DINO	DIORAMA	DIPLOMA
DIMPSY	DINGLES	DINOCERAS	DIORAMAS	DIPLOMACY
DIMS	DINGO	DINOMANIA	DIORAMIC	DIPLOMAED
DIMWIT	DINGOED	DINOS	DIORISM	DIPLOMAS
DIMWITS	DINGOES	DINOSAUR	DIORISMS	DIPLOMAT
DIMWITTED	DINGOING	DINOSAURS	DIORISTIC	DIPLOMATA

DIPLOMATE	DIPSOS	DIREMPT	DIRTY	DISAVOUCH
DIPLOMATS	DIPSTICK	DIREMPTED	DIRTYING	DISAVOW
DIPLON	DIPSTICKS	DIREMPTS	DIS	DISAVOWAL
DIPLONEMA	DIPSWITCH	DIRENESS	DISA	DISAVOWED
DIPLONS	DIPT	DIRER	DISABLE	DISAVOWER
DIPLONT	DIPTEL	DIREST	DISABLED	DISAVOWS
DIPLONTIC	DIPTELS	DIRGE	DISABLER	DISBAND
DIPLONTS	DIPTERA	DIRGEFUL	DISABLERS	DISBANDED
DIPLOPIA	DIPTERAL	DIRGELIKE	DISABLES	DISBANDS
DIPLOPIAS	DIPTERAN	DIRGES	DISABLING	DISBAR
DIPLOPIC	DIPTERANS	DIRHAM	DISABLISM	DISBARK
DIPLOPOD	DIPTERAS	DIRHAMS	DISABLIST	DISBARKED
DIPLOPODS	DIPTERIST	DIRHEM	DISABUSAL	DISBARKS
DIPLOSES	DIPTEROI	DIRHEMS	DISABUSE	DISBARRED
DIPLOSIS	DIPTERON	DIRIGE	DISABUSED	DISBARS
DIPLOTENE	DIPTERONS	DIRIGENT	DISABUSES	DISBELIEF
DIPLOZOA	DIPTEROS	DIRIGES	DISACCORD	DISBENCH
DIPLOZOIC	DIPTEROUS	DIRIGIBLE	DISADORN	DISBODIED
DIPLOZOON	DIPTYCA	DIRIGISM	DISADORNS	DISBOSOM
DIPNET	DIPTYCAS	DIRIGISME	DISAFFECT	DISBOSOMS
DIPNETS	DIPTYCH	DIRIGISMS	DISAFFIRM	DISBOUND
DIPNETTED	DIPTYCHS	DIRIGISTE	DISAGREE	DISBOWEL
DIPNOAN	DIQUARK	DIRIMENT	DISAGREED	DISBOWELS
DIPNOANS	DIQUARKS	DIRK	DISAGREES	DISBRANCH
DIPNOOUS	DIQUAT	DIRKE	DISALLIED	DISBUD
DIPODIC	DIQUATS	DIRKED	DISALLIES	DISBUDDED
DIPODIES	DIRAM	DIRKES	DISALLOW	DISBUDS
DIPODY	DIRAMS	DIRKING	DISALLOWS	DISBURDEN
DIPOLAR	DIRDAM	DIRKS	DISALLY	DISBURSAL
DIPOLE	DIRDAMS	DIRL	DISANCHOR	DISBURSE
DIPOLES	DIRDUM	DIRLED	DISANNEX	DISBURSED
DIPPABLE	DIRDUMS	DIRLING	DISANNUL	DISBURSER
DIPPED	DIRE	DIRLS	DISANNULS	DISBURSES
DIPPER	DIRECT	DIRNDL	DISANOINT	DISC
DIPPERFUL	DIRECTED	DIRNDLS	DISAPPEAR	DISCAGE
DIPPERS	DIRECTER	DIRT	DISAPPLY	DISCAGED
DIPPIER	DIRECTEST	DIRTBAG	DISARM	DISCAGES
DIPPIEST	DIRECTING	DIRTBAGS	DISARMED	DISCAGING
DIPPINESS	DIRECTION	DIRTBALL	DISARMER	DISCAL
DIPPING	DIRECTIVE	DIRTBALLS	DISARMERS	DISCALCED
DIPPINGS	DIRECTLY	DIRTED	DISARMING	DISCANDIE
DIPPY	DIRECTOR	DIRTIED	DISARMS	DISCANDY
DIPROTIC	DIRECTORS	DIRTIER	DISARRAY	DISCANT
DIPS	DIRECTORY	DIRTIES	DISARRAYS	DISCANTED
DIPSADES	DIRECTRIX	DIRTIEST	DISAS	DISCANTER
DIPSAS	DIRECTS	DIRTILY	DISASTER	DISCANTS
DIPSHIT	DIREFUL	DIRTINESS	DISASTERS	DISCARD
DIPSHITS	DIREFULLY	DIRTING	DISATTIRE	DISCARDED
DIPSO	DIRELY	DIRTS	DISATTUNE	DISCARDER

D

DISCARDS	DISCOLOGY	DISEDGING	DISGRACES	DISHONOUR
DISCASE	DISCOLOR	DISEMBARK	DISGRADE	DISHORN
DISCASED	DISCOLORS	DISEMBODY	DISGRADED	DISHORNED
DISCASES	DISCOLOUR	DISEMPLOY	DISGRADES	DISHORNS
DISCASING	DISCOMFIT	DISENABLE	DISGUISE	DISHORSE
DISCED	DISCOMMON	DISENDOW	DISGUISED	DISHORSED
DISCEPT	DISCORD	DISENDOWS	DISGUISER	DISHORSES
DISCEPTED	DISCORDED	DISENGAGE	DISGUISES	DISHOUSE
DISCEPTS	DISCORDS	DISENROL	DISGUST	DISHOUSED
DISCERN	DISCOS	DISENROLS	DISGUSTED	DISHOUSES
DISCERNED	DISCOUNT	DISENTAIL	DISGUSTS	DISHPAN
DISCERNER	DISCOUNTS	DISENTOMB	DISH	DISHPANS
DISCERNS	DISCOURE	DISESTEEM	DISHABIT	DISHRAG
DISCERP	DISCOURED	DISEUR	DISHABITS	DISHRAGS
DISCERPED	DISCOURES	DISEURS	DISHABLE	DISHTOWEL
DISCERPS	DISCOURSE	DISEUSE	DISHABLED	DISHUMOUR
DISCHARGE	DISCOVER	DISEUSES	DISHABLES	DISHWARE
DISCHURCH	DISCOVERS	DISFAME	DISHALLOW	DISHWARES
DISCI	DISCOVERT	DISFAMED	DISHCLOTH	DISHWATER
DISCIDE	DISCOVERY	DISFAMES	DISHCLOUT	DISHY
DISCIDED	DISCREDIT	DISFAMING	DISHDASH	DISILLUDE
DISCIDES	DISCREET	DISFAVOR	DISHDASHA	DISIMMURE
DISCIDING	DISCRETE	DISFAVORS	DISHED	DISINFECT
DISCIFORM	DISCRETER	DISFAVOUR	DISHELM	DISINFEST
DISCINCT	DISCROWN	DISFIGURE	DISHELMED	DISINFO
DISCING	DISCROWNS	DISFLESH	DISHELMS	DISINFORM
DISCIPLE	DISCS	DISFLUENT	DISHERIT	DISINFOS
DISCIPLED	DISCUMBER	DISFOREST	DISHERITS	DISINHUME
DISCIPLES	DISCURE	DISFORM	DISHES	DISINTER
DISCLAIM	DISCURED	DISFORMED	DISHEVEL	DISINTERS
DISCLAIMS	DISCURES	DISFORMS	DISHEVELS	DISINURE
DISCLESS	DISCURING	DISFROCK	DISHFUL	DISINURED
DISCLIKE	DISCURSUS	DISFROCKS	DISHFULS	DISINURES
DISCLIMAX	DISCUS	DISGAVEL	DISHIER	DISINVENT
DISCLOSE	DISCUSES	DISGAVELS	DISHIEST	DISINVEST
DISCLOSED	DISCUSS	DISGEST	DISHING	DISINVITE
DISCLOSER	DISCUSSED	DISGESTED	DISHINGS	DISJASKIT
DISCLOSES	DISCUSSER	DISGESTS	DISHLIKE	DISJECT
DISCLOST	DISCUSSES	DISGODDED	DISHMOP	DISJECTED
DISCO	DISDAIN	DISGORGE	DISHMOPS	DISJECTS
DISCOBOLI	DISDAINED	DISGORGED	DISHOARD	DISJOIN
DISCOED	DISDAINS	DISGORGER	DISHOARDS	DISJOINED
DISCOER	DISEASE	DISGORGES	DISHOME	DISJOINS
DISCOERS	DISEASED	DISGOWN	DISHOMED	DISJOINT
DISCOES	DISEASES	DISGOWNED	DISHOMES	DISJOINTS
DISCOID	DISEASING	DISGOWNS	DISHOMING	DISJUNCT
DISCOIDAL	DISEDGE	DISGRACE	DISHONEST	DISJUNCTS
DISCOIDS	DISEDGED	DISGRACED	DISHONOR	DISJUNE
DISCOING	DISEDGES	DISGRACER	DISHONORS	DISJUNED

DISJUNES	DISMALEST	DISORDERS	DISPLACED	DISPREAD
DISJUNING	DISMALITY	DISORIENT	DISPLACER	DISPREADS
DISK	DISMALLER	DISOWN	DISPLACES	DISPRED
DISKED	DISMALLY	DISOWNED	DISPLANT	DISPREDS
DISKER	DISMALS	DISOWNER	DISPLANTS	DISPRISON
DISKERS	DISMAN	DISOWNERS	DISPLAY	DISPRIZE
DISKETTE	DISMANNED	DISOWNING	DISPLAYED	DISPRIZED
DISKETTES	DISMANS	DISOWNS	DISPLAYER	DISPRIZES
DISKING	DISMANTLE	DISPACE	DISPLAYS	DISPROFIT
DISKLESS	DISMASK	DISPACED	DISPLE	DISPROOF
DISKLIKE	DISMASKED	DISPACES	DISPLEASE	DISPROOFS
DISKS	DISMASKS	DISPACING	DISPLED	DISPROOVE
DISLEAF	DISMAST	DISPARAGE	DISPLES	DISPROVAL
DISLEAFED	DISMASTED	DISPARATE	DISPLING	DISPROVE
DISLEAFS	DISMASTS	DISPARITY	DISPLODE	DISPROVED
DISLEAL	DISMAY	DISPARK	DISPLODED	DISPROVEN
DISLEAVE	DISMAYD	DISPARKED	DISPLODES	DISPROVER
DISLEAVED	DISMAYED	DISPARKS	DISPLUME	DISPROVES
DISLEAVES	DISMAYFUL	DISPART	DISPLUMED	DISPUNGE
DISLIKE	DISMAYING	DISPARTED	DISPLUMES	DISPUNGED
DISLIKED	DISMAYL	DISPARTS	DISPONDEE	DISPUNGES
DISLIKEN	DISMAYLED	DISPATCH	DISPONE	DISPURSE
DISLIKENS	DISMAYLS	DISPATHY	DISPONED	DISPURSED
DISLIKER	DISMAYS	DISPAUPER	DISPONEE	DISPURSES
DISLIKERS	DISME	DISPEACE	DISPONEES	DISPURVEY
DISLIKES	DISMEMBER	DISPEACES	DISPONER	DISPUTANT
DISLIKING	DISMES	DISPEL	DISPONERS	DISPUTE
DISLIMB	DISMISS	DISPELLED	DISPONES	DISPUTED
DISLIMBED	DISMISSAL	DISPELLER	DISPONGE	DISPUTER
DISLIMBS	DISMISSED	DISPELS	DISPONGED	DISPUTERS
DISLIMN	DISMISSES	DISPENCE	DISPONGES	DISPUTES
DISLIMNED	DISMODED	DISPENCED	DISPONING	DISPUTING
DISLIMNS	DISMOUNT	DISPENCES	DISPORT	DISQUIET
DISLINK	DISMOUNTS	DISPEND	DISPORTED	DISQUIETS
DISLINKED	DISNATURE	DISPENDED	DISPORTS	DISRANK
DISLINKS	DISNEST	DISPENDS	DISPOSAL	DISRANKED
DISLOAD	DISNESTED	DISPENSE	DISPOSALS	DISRANKS
DISLOADED	DISNESTS	DISPENSED	DISPOSE	DISRATE
DISLOADS	DISOBEY	DISPENSER	DISPOSED	DISRATED
DISLOCATE	DISOBEYED	DISPENSES	DISPOSER	DISRATES
DISLODGE	DISOBEYER	DISPEOPLE	DISPOSERS	DISRATING
DISLODGED	DISOBEYS	DISPERSAL	DISPOSES	DISREGARD
DISLODGES	DISOBLIGE	DISPERSE	DISPOSING	DISRELISH
DISLOIGN	DISODIUM	DISPERSED	DISPOST	DISREPAIR
DISLOIGNS	DISOMIC	DISPERSER	DISPOSTED	DISREPUTE
DISLOYAL	DISOMIES	DISPERSES	DISPOSTS	DISROBE
DISLUSTRE	DISOMY	DISPIRIT	DISPOSURE	DISROBED
DISMAL	DISORBED	DISPIRITS	DISPRAD	DISROBER
DISMALER	DISORDER	DISPLACE	DISPRAISE	DISROBERS

DISROBES	DISSERVES	DISTICH	DISUNION	DITHERING
DISROBING	DISSES	DISTICHAL	DISUNIONS	DITHERS
DISROOT	DISSEVER	DISTICHS	DISUNITE	DITHERY
DISROOTED	DISSEVERS	DISTIL	DISUNITED	DITHIOL
DISROOTS	DISSHIVER	DISTILL	DISUNITER	DITHIOLS
DISRUPT	DISSIDENT	DISTILLED	DISUNITES	DITHIONIC
DISRUPTED	DISSIGHT	DISTILLER	DISUNITY	DITHYRAMB
DISRUPTER	DISSIGHTS	DISTILLS	DISUSAGE	DITING
DISRUPTOR	DISSIMILE	DISTILS	DISUSAGES	DITOKOUS
DISRUPTS	DISSING	DISTINCT	DISUSE	DITONE
DISS	DISSIPATE	DISTINGUE	DISUSED	DITONES
DISSAVE	DISSOCIAL	DISTOME	DISUSES	DITROCHEE
DISSAVED	DISSOLUTE	DISTOMES	DISUSING	DITS
DISSAVER	DISSOLVE	DISTORT	DISVALUE	DITSIER
DISSAVERS	DISSOLVED	DISTORTED	DISVALUED	DITSIEST
DISSAVES	DISSOLVER	DISTORTER	DISVALUES	DITSINESS
DISSAVING	DISSOLVES	DISTORTS	DISVOUCH	DITSY
DISSEAT	DISSONANT	DISTRACT	DISYOKE	DITT
DISSEATED	DISSUADE	DISTRACTS	DISYOKED	DITTANDER
DISSEATS	DISSUADED	DISTRAIL	DISYOKES	DITTANIES
DISSECT	DISSUADER	DISTRAILS	DISYOKING	DITTANY
DISSECTED	DISSUADES	DISTRAIN	DIT	DITTAY
DISSECTOR	DISSUNDER	DISTRAINS	DITA	DITTAYS
DISSECTS	DISTAFF	DISTRAINT	DITAL	DITTED
DISSED	DISTAFFS	DISTRAIT	DITALS	DITTIED
DISSEISE	DISTAIN	DISTRAITE	DITAS	DITTIES
DISSEISED	DISTAINED	DISTRESS	DITCH	DITTING
DISSEISEE	DISTAINS	DISTRICT	DITCHED	DITTIT
DISSEISES	DISTAL	DISTRICTS	DITCHER	DITTO
DISSEISIN	DISTALLY	DISTRIX	DITCHERS	DITTOED
DISSEISOR	DISTANCE	DISTRIXES	DITCHES	DITTOING
DISSEIZE	DISTANCED	DISTRO	DITCHING	DITTOLOGY
DISSEIZED	DISTANCES	DISTROS	DITCHLESS	DITTOS
DISSEIZEE	DISTANT	DISTRUST	DITE	DITTS
DISSEIZES	DISTANTLY	DISTRUSTS	DITED	DITTY
DISSEIZIN	DISTASTE	DISTUNE	DITES	DITTYING
DISSEIZOR	DISTASTED	DISTUNED	DITHECAL	DITZ
DISSEMBLE	DISTASTES	DISTUNES	DITHECOUS	DITZES
DISSEMBLY	DISTAVES	DISTUNING	DITHEISM	DITZIER
DISSENSUS	DISTEMPER	DISTURB	DITHEISMS	DITZIEST
DISSENT	DISTEND	DISTURBED	DITHEIST	DITZINESS
DISSENTED	DISTENDED	DISTURBER	DITHEISTS	DITZY
DISSENTER	DISTENDER	DISTURBS	DITHELETE	DIURESES
DISSENTS	DISTENDS	DISTYLE	DITHELISM	DIURESIS
DISSERT	DISTENT	DISTYLES	DITHER	DIURETIC
DISSERTED	DISTENTS	DISULFATE	DITHERED	DIURETICS
DISSERTS	DISTHENE	DISULFID	DITHERER	DIURNAL
DISSERVE	DISTHENES	DISULFIDE	DITHERERS	DIURNALLY
DISSERVED	DISTHRONE	DISULFIDS	DITHERIER	DIURNALS

DIURON	DIVI	DIVORCE	DIZENS	DOBBINS
DIURONS	DIVIDABLE	DIVORCED	DIZYGOTIC	DOBBY
DIUTURNAL	DIVIDANT	DIVORCEE	DIZYGOUS	DOBCHICK
DIV	DIVIDE	DIVORCEES	DIZZARD	DOBCHICKS
DIVA	DIVIDED	DIVORCER	DIZZARDS	DOBE
DIVAGATE	DIVIDEDLY	DIVORCERS	DIZZIED	DOBES
DIVAGATED	DIVIDEND	DIVORCES	DIZZIER	DOBHASH
DIVAGATES	DIVIDENDS	DIVORCING	DIZZIES	DOBHASHES
DIVALENCE	DIVIDER	DIVORCIVE	DIZZIEST	DOBIE
DIVALENCY	DIVIDERS	DIVOS	DIZZILY	DOBIES
DIVALENT	DIVIDES	DIVOT	DIZZINESS	DOBLA
DIVALENTS	DIVIDING	DIVOTS	DIZZY	DOBLAS
DIVAN	DIVIDINGS	DIVS	DIZZYING	DOBLON
DIVANS	DIVIDIVI	DIVULGATE	DJEBEL	DOBLONES
DIVAS	DIVIDIVIS	DIVULGE	DJEBELS	DOBLONS
DIVE	DIVIDUAL	DIVULGED	DJELLABA	DOBRA
DIVEBOMB	DIVIDUOUS	DIVULGER	DJELLABAH	DOBRAS
DIVEBOMBS	DIVIED	DIVULGERS	DJELLABAS	DOBRO
DIVED	DIVINABLE	DIVULGES	DJEMBE	DOBROS
DIVELLENT	DIVINATOR	DIVULGING	DJEMBES	DOBS
DIVER	DIVINE	DIVULSE	DJIBBA	DOBSON
DIVERGE	DIVINED	DIVULSED	DJIBBAH	DOBSONFLY
DIVERGED	DIVINELY	DIVULSES	DJIBBAHS	DOBSONS
DIVERGENT	DIVINER	DIVULSING	DJIBBAS	DOBY
DIVERGES	DIVINERS	DIVULSION	DJIN	DOC
DIVERGING	DIVINES	DIVULSIVE	DJINN	DOCENT
DIVERS	DIVINEST	DIVVIED	DJINNI	DOCENTS
DIVERSE	DIVING	DIVVIER	DJINNS	DOCETIC
DIVERSED	DIVINGS	DIVVIES	DJINNY	DOCHMIAC
DIVERSELY	DIVINIFY	DIVVIEST	DJINS	DOCHMIACS
DIVERSES	DIVINING	DIVVY	DO	DOCHMII
DIVERSIFY	DIVINISE	DIVVYING	DOAB	DOCHMIUS
DIVERSING	DIVINISED	DIVYING	DOABLE	DOCHT
DIVERSION	DIVINISES	DIWAN	DOABS	DOCIBLE
DIVERSITY	DIVINITY	DIWANS	DOAT	DOCILE
DIVERSLY	DIVINIZE	DIXI	DOATED	DOCILELY
DIVERT	DIVINIZED	DIXIE	DOATER	DOCILER
DIVERTED	DIVINIZES	DIXIES	DOATERS	DOCILEST
DIVERTER	DIVIS	DIXIT	DOATING	DOCILITY
DIVERTERS	DIVISIBLE	DIXITS	DOATINGS	DOCIMASY
DIVERTING	DIVISIBLY	DIXY	DOATS	DOCK
DIVERTIVE	DIVISIM	DIYA	DOB	DOCKAGE
DIVERTS	DIVISION	DIYAS	DOBBED	DOCKAGES
DIVES	DIVISIONS	DIZAIN	DOBBER	DOCKED
DIVEST	DIVISIVE	DIZAINS	DOBBERS	DOCKEN
DIVESTED	DIVISOR	DIZEN	DOBBIE	DOCKENS
DIVESTING	DIVISORS	DIZENED	DOBBIES	DOCKER
DIVESTS	DIVNA	DIZENING	DOBBIN	DOCKERS
DIVESTURE	DIVO	DIZENMENT	DOBBING	DOCKET

DOCKETED	DOD	DOEK	DOGFISHES	DOGLIKE
DOCKETING	DODDARD	DOEKS	DOGFOOD	DOGMA
DOCKETS	DODDARDS	DOEN	DOGFOODS	DOGMAN
DOCKHAND	DODDED	DOER	DOGFOUGHT	DOGMAS
DOCKHANDS	DODDER	DOERS	DOGFOX	DOGMATA
DOCKING	DODDERED	DOES	DOGFOXES	DOGMATIC
DOCKINGS	DODDERER	DOESKIN	DOGGED	DOGMATICS
DOCKISE	DODDERERS	DOESKINS	DOGGEDER	DOGMATISE
DOCKISED	DODDERIER	DOEST	DOGGEDEST	DOGMATISM
DOCKISES	DODDERING	DOETH	DOGGEDLY	DOGMATIST
DOCKISING	DODDERS	DOF	DOGGER	DOGMATIZE
DOCKIZE	DODDERY	DOFF	DOGGEREL	DOGMATORY
DOCKIZED	DODDIER	DOFFED	DOGGERELS	DOGMEN
DOCKIZES	DODDIES	DOFFER	DOGGERIES	DOGNAP
DOCKIZING	DODDIEST	DOFFERS	DOGGERMAN	DOGNAPED
DOCKLAND	DODDING	DOFFING	DOGGERMEN	DOGNAPER
DOCKLANDS	DODDIPOLL	DOFFS	DOGGERS	DOGNAPERS
DOCKS	DODDLE	DOG	DOGGERY	DOGNAPING
DOCKSIDE	DODDLES	DOGARESSA	DOGGESS	DOGNAPPED
DOCKSIDES	DODDY	DOGATE	DOGGESSES	DOGNAPPER
DOCKYARD	DODDYPOLL	DOGATES	DOGGIE	DOGNAPS
DOCKYARDS	DODECAGON	DOGBANE	DOGGIER	DOGPILE
DOCO	DODGE	DOGBANES	DOGGIES	DOGPILED
DOCOS	DODGEBALL	DOGBERRY	DOGGIEST	DOGPILES
DOCQUET	DODGED	DOGBOLT	DOGGINESS	DOGPILING
DOCQUETED	DODGEM	DOGBOLTS	DOGGING	DOGREL
DOCQUETS	DODGEMS	DOGCART	DOGGINGS	DOGRELS
DOCS	DODGER	DOGCARTS	DOGGISH	DOGROBBER
DOCTOR	DODGERIES	DOGDOM	DOGGISHLY	DOGS
DOCTORAL	DODGERS	DOGDOMS	DOGGO	DOGSBODY
DOCTORAND	DODGERY	DOGE	DOGGONE	DOGSHIP
DOCTORATE	DODGES	DOGEAR	DOGGONED	DOGSHIPS
DOCTORED	DODGIER	DOGEARED	DOGGONER	DOGSHORES
DOCTORESS	DODGIEST	DOGEARING	DOGGONES	DOGSHOW
DOCTORIAL	DODGINESS	DOGEARS	DOGGONEST	DOGSHOWS
DOCTORING	DODGING	DOGEATE	DOGGONING	DOGSKIN
DOCTORLY	DODGINGS	DOGEATES	DOGGREL	DOGSKINS
DOCTORS	DODGY	DOGEDOM	DOGGRELS	DOGSLED
DOCTRESS	DODKIN	DOGEDOMS	DOGGY	DOGSLEDS
DOCTRINAL	DODKINS	DOGES	DOGHANGED	DOGSLEEP
DOCTRINE	DODMAN	DOGESHIP	DOGHOLE	DOGSLEEPS
DOCTRINES	DODMANS	DOGESHIPS	DOGHOLES	DOGSTAIL
DOCU	DODO	DOGEY	DOGHOUSE	DOGSTAILS
DOCUDRAMA	DODOES	DOGEYS	DOGHOUSES	DOGTAIL
DOCUMENT	DODOISM	DOGFACE	DOGIE	DOGTAILS
DOCUMENTS	DODOISMS	DOGFACES	DOGIES	DOGTEETH
DOCUS	DODOS	DOGFIGHT	DOGLEG	DOGTOOTH
DOCUSOAP	DODS	DOGFIGHTS	DOGLEGGED	DOGTOWN
DOCUSOAPS	DOE	DOGFISH	DOGLEGS	DOGTOWNS

DOGTROT	DOLIA	DOLORIFIC	DOMINANT	DONATOR
DOGTROTS	DOLICHOS	DOLOROSO	DOMINANTS	DONATORS
DOGVANE	DOLICHURI	DOLOROUS	DOMINATE	DONATORY
DOGVANES	DOLINA	DOLORS	DOMINATED	DONCHA
DOGWATCH	DOLINAS	DOLOS	DOMINATES	DONDER
DOGWOOD	DOLINE	DOLOSSE	DOMINATOR	DONDERED
DOGWOODS	DOLINES	DOLOSTONE	DOMINE	DONDERING
DOGY	DOLING	DOLOUR	DOMINEE	DONDERS
DOH	DOLIUM	DOLOURS	DOMINEER	DONE
DOHS	DOLL	DOLPHIN	DOMINEERS	DONEE
DOHYO	DOLLAR	DOLPHINET	DOMINEES	DONEES
DOHYOS	DOLLARED	DOLPHINS	DOMINES	DONEGAL
DOILED	DOLLARISE	DOLS	DOMING	DONEGALS
DOILIED	DOLLARIZE	DOLT	DOMINICAL	DONENESS
DOILIES	DOLLARS	DOLTISH	DOMINICK	DONEPEZIL
DOILT	DOLLDOM	DOLTISHLY	DOMINICKS	DONER
DOILTER	DOLLDOMS	DOLTS	DOMINIE	DONERS
DOILTEST	DOLLED	DOM	DOMINIES	DONG
DOILY	DOLLHOOD	DOMAIN	DOMINION	DONGA
DOING	DOLLHOODS	DOMAINAL	DOMINIONS	DONGAS
DOINGS	DOLLHOUSE	DOMAINE	DOMINIQUE	DONGED
DOIT	DOLLIED	DOMAINES	DOMINIUM	DONGING
DOITED	DOLLIER	DOMAINS	DOMINIUMS	DONGLE
DOITIT	DOLLIERS	DOMAL	DOMINO	DONGLES
DOITKIN	DOLLIES	DOMANIAL	DOMINOES	DONGOLA
DOITKINS	DOLLINESS	DOMATIA	DOMINOS	DONGOLAS
DOITS	DOLLING	DOMATIUM	DOMOIC	DONGS
DOJO	DOLLISH	DOME	DOMS	DONING
DOJOS	DOLLISHLY	DOMED	DOMY	DONINGS
DOL	DOLLOP	DOMELIKE	DON	DONJON
DOLABRATE	DOLLOPED	DOMES	DONA	DONJONS
DOLCE	DOLLOPING	DOMESDAY	DONAH	DONKEY
DOLCES	DOLLOPS	DOMESDAYS	DONAHS	DONKEYMAN
DOLCETTI	DOLLS	DOMESTIC	DONAIR	DONKEYMEN
DOLCETTO	DOLLY	DOMESTICS	DONAIRS	DONKEYS
DOLCETTOS	DOLLYBIRD	DOMETT	DONARIES	DONKO
DOLCI	DOLLYING	DOMETTS	DONARY	DONKOS
DOLDRUMS	DOLMA	DOMIC	DONAS	DONNA
DOLE	DOLMADES	DOMICAL	DONATARY	DONNARD
DOLED	DOLMAN	DOMICALLY	DONATE	DONNART
DOLEFUL	DOLMANS	DOMICIL	DONATED	DONNAS
DOLEFULLY	DOLMAS	DOMICILE	DONATES	DONNAT
DOLENT	DOLMEN	DOMICILED	DONATING	DONNATS
DOLENTE	DOLMENIC	DOMICILES	DONATION	DONNE
DOLERITE	DOLMENS	DOMICILS	DONATIONS	DONNED
DOLERITES	DOLOMITE	DOMIER	DONATISM	DONNEE
DOLERITIC	DOLOMITES	DOMIEST	DONATISMS	DONNEES
DOLES	DOLOMITIC	DOMINANCE	DONATIVE	DONNERD
DOLESOME	DOLOR	DOMINANCY	DONATIVES	DONNERED

D

DONNERT	DOODAHS	DOOMSMAN	DOORYARD	DOPPING
DONNES	DOODIES	DOOMSMEN	DOORYARDS	DOPPINGS
DONNICKER	DOODLE	DOOMSTER	DOOS	DOPPIO
DONNIES	DOODLEBUG	DOOMSTERS	DOOSES	DOPPIOS
DONNIKER	DOODLED	DOOMWATCH	DOOSRA	DOPS
DONNIKERS	DOODLER	DOOMY	DOOSRAS	DOPY
DONNING	DOODLERS	DOON	DOOWOP	DOR
DONNISH	DOODLES	DOONA	DOOWOPS	DORAD
DONNISHLY	DOODLING	DOONAS	DOOZER	DORADO
DONNISM	DOODOO	DOOR	DOOZERS	DORADOS
DONNISMS	DOODOOS	DOORBELL	DOOZIE	DORADS
DONNOT	DOODY	DOORBELLS	DOOZIES	DORB
DONNOTS	DOOFER	DOORCASE	DOOZY	DORBA
DONNY	DOOFERS	DOORCASES	DOP	DORBAS
DONOR	DOOFUS	DOORED	DOPA	DORBEETLE
DONORS	DOOFUSES	DOORFRAME	DOPAMINE	DORBS
DONORSHIP	DOOHICKEY	DOORJAMB	DOPAMINES	DORBUG
DONS	DOOK	DOORJAMBS	DOPANT	DORBUGS
DONSHIP	DOOKED	DOORKNOB	DOPANTS	DORE
DONSHIPS	DOOKET	DOORKNOBS	DOPAS	DOREE
DONSIE	DOOKETS	DOORKNOCK	DOPATTA	DOREES
DONSIER	DOOKING	DOORLESS	DOPATTAS	DORES
DONSIEST	DOOKS	DOORLIKE	DOPATTE	DORHAWK
DONSY	DOOL	DOORMAN	DOPE	DORHAWKS
DONUT	DOOLALLY	DOORMAT	DOPED	DORIC
DONUTS	DOOLAN	DOORMATS	DOPEHEAD	DORIDOID
DONUTTED	DOOLANS	DOORMEN	DOPEHEADS	DORIDOIDS
DONUTTING	DOOLE	DOORN	DOPER	DORIES
DONZEL	DOOLEE	DOORNAIL	DOPERS	DORIS
DONZELS	DOOLEES	DOORNAILS	DOPES	DORISE
DOO	DOOLES	DOORNBOOM	DOPESHEET	DORISED
DOOB	DOOLIE	DOORNS	DOPEST	DORISES
DOOBIE	DOOLIES	DOORPLATE	DOPESTER	DORISING
DOOBIES	DOOLS	DOORPOST	DOPESTERS	DORIZE
DOOBREY	DOOLY	DOORPOSTS	DOPEY	DORIZED
DOOBREYS	DOOM	DOORS	DOPEYNESS	DORIZES
DOOBRIE	DOOMED	DOORSILL	DOPIAZA	DORIZING
DOOBRIES	DOOMER	DOORSILLS	DOPIAZAS	DORK
DOOBRY	DOOMERS	DOORSMAN	DOPIER	DORKIER
DOOBS	DOOMFUL	DOORSMEN	DOPIEST	DORKIEST
DOOCE	DOOMFULLY	DOORSTEP	DOPILY	DORKINESS
DOOCED	DOOMIER	DOORSTEPS	DOPINESS	DORKISH
DOOCES	DOOMIEST	DOORSTONE	DOPING	DORKS
DOOCING	DOOMILY	DOORSTOP	DOPINGS	DORKY
DOOCOT	DOOMING	DOORSTOPS	DOPPED	DORLACH
DOOCOTS	DOOMS	DOORWAY	DOPPER	DORLACHS
DOODAD	DOOMSAYER	DOORWAYS	DOPPERS	DORM
DOODADS	DOOMSDAY	DOORWOMAN	DOPPIE	DORMANCY
DOODAH	DOOMSDAYS	DOORWOMEN	DOPPIES	DORMANT

DORMANTS	DORTIEST	DOSSING	DOTY	DOUCHING
DORMER	DORTINESS	DOST	DOUANE	DOUCHINGS
DORMERED	DORTING	DOT	DOUANES	DOUCINE
DORMERS	DORTOUR	DOTAGE	DOUANIER	DOUCINES
DORMICE	DORTOURS	DOTAGES	DOUANIERS	DOUCS
DORMIE	DORTS	DOTAL	DOUAR	DOUGH
DORMIENT	DORTY	DOTANT	DOUARS	DOUGHBALL
DORMIN	DORY	DOTANTS	DOUBLE	DOUGHBOY
DORMINS	DORYMAN	DOTARD	DOUBLED	DOUGHBOYS
DORMITION	DORYMEN	DOTARDLY	DOUBLER	DOUGHFACE
DORMITIVE	DOS	DOTARDS	DOUBLERS	DOUGHIER
DORMITORY	DOSA	DOTATION	DOUBLES	DOUGHIEST
DORMOUSE	DOSAGE	DOTATIONS	DOUBLET	DOUGHLIKE
DORMS	DOSAGES	DOTCOM	DOUBLETON	DOUGHNUT
DORMY	DOSAI	DOTCOMMER	DOUBLETS	DOUGHNUTS
DORNECK	DOSAS	DOTCOMS	DOUBLING	DOUGHS
DORNECKS	DOSE	DOTE	DOUBLINGS	DOUGHT
DORNICK	DOSED	DOTED	DOUBLOON	DOUGHTIER
DORNICKS	DOSEH	DOTER	DOUBLOONS	DOUGHTILY
DORNOCK	DOSEHS	DOTERS	DOUBLURE	DOUGHTY
DORNOCKS	DOSEMETER	DOTES	DOUBLURES	DOUGHY
DORONICUM	DOSER	DOTH	DOUBLY	DOUK
DORP	DOSERS	DOTIER	DOUBT	DOUKED
DORPER	DOSES	DOTIEST	DOUBTABLE	DOUKING
DORPERS	DOSH	DOTING	DOUBTABLY	DOUKS
DORPS	DOSHA	DOTINGLY	DOUBTED	DOULA
DORR	DOSHAS	DOTINGS	DOUBTER	DOULAS
DORRED	DOSHES	DOTISH	DOUBTERS	DOULEIA
DORRING	DOSIMETER	DOTS	DOUBTFUL	DOULEIAS
DORRS	DOSIMETRY	DOTTED	DOUBTFULS	DOUM
DORS	DOSING	DOTTEL	DOUBTING	DOUMA
DORSA	DOSIOLOGY	DOTTELS	DOUBTINGS	DOUMAS
DORSAD	DOSOLOGY	DOTTER	DOUBTLESS	DOUMS
DORSAL	DOSS	DOTTEREL	DOUBTS	DOUN
DORSALLY	DOSSAL	DOTTERELS	DOUC	DOUP
DORSALS	DOSSALS	DOTTERS	DOUCE	DOUPIONI
DORSE	DOSSED	DOTTIER	DOUCELY	DOUPIONIS
DORSEL	DOSSEL	DOTTIEST	DOUCENESS	DOUPPIONI
DORSELS	DOSSELS	DOTTILY	DOUCEPERE	DOUPS
DORSER	DOSSER	DOTTINESS	DOUCER	DOUR
DORSERS	DOSSERET	DOTTING	DOUCEST	DOURA
DORSES	DOSSERETS	DOTTLE	DOUCET	DOURAH
DORSIFLEX	DOSSERS	DOTTLED	DOUCETS	DOURAHS
DORSUM	DOSSES	DOTTLER	DOUCEUR	DOURAS
DORT	DOSSHOUSE	DOTTLES	DOUCEURS	DOURER
DORTED	DOSSIER	DOTTLEST	DOUCHE	DOUREST
DORTER	DOSSIERS	DOTTREL	DOUCHEBAG	DOURINE
DORTERS	DOSSIL	DOTTRELS	DOUCHED	DOURINES
DORTIER	DOSSILS	DOTTY	DOUCHES	DOURLY

DOURNESS	DOWABLE	DOWLY	DOWNLOW	DOWNWARD
DOUSE	DOWAGER	DOWN	DOWNLOWS	DOWNWARDS
DOUSED	DOWAGERS	DOWNA	DOWNMOST	DOWNWARP
DOUSER	DOWAR	DOWNBEAT	DOWNPIPE	DOWNWARPS
DOUSERS	DOWARS	DOWNBEATS	DOWNPIPES	DOWNWASH
DOUSES	DOWD	DOWNBOUND	DOWNPLAY	DOWNWIND
DOUSING	DOWDIER	DOWNBOW	DOWNPLAYS	DOWNY
DOUT	DOWDIES	DOWNBOWS	DOWNPOUR	DOWNZONE
DOUTED	DOWDIEST	DOWNBURST	DOWNPOURS	DOWNZONED
DOUTER	DOWDILY	DOWNCAST	DOWNRANGE	DOWNZONES
DOUTERS	DOWDINESS	DOWNCASTS	DOWNRATE	DOWP
DOUTING	DOWDS	DOWNCOME	DOWNRATED	DOWPS
DOUTS	DOWDY	DOWNCOMER	DOWNRATES	DOWRIES
DOUX	DOWDYISH	DOWNCOMES	DOWNRIGHT	DOWRY
DOUZEPER	DOWDYISM	DOWNCOURT	DOWNRIVER	DOWS
DOUZEPERS	DOWDYISMS	DOWNCRIED	DOWNRUSH	DOWSABEL
DOVE	DOWED	DOWNCRIES	DOWNS	DOWSABELS
DOVECOT	DOWEL	DOWNCRY	DOWNSCALE	DOWSE
DOVECOTE	DOWELED	DOWNDRAFT	DOWNSHIFT	DOWSED
DOVECOTES	DOWELING	DOWNED	DOWNSIDE	DOWSER
DOVECOTS	DOWELINGS	DOWNER	DOWNSIDES	DOWSERS
DOVED	DOWELLED	DOWNERS	DOWNSIZE	DOWSES
DOVEISH	DOWELLING	DOWNFALL	DOWNSIZED	DOWSET
DOVEISHLY	DOWELS	DOWNFALLS	DOWNSIZER	DOWSETS
DOVEKEY	DOWER	DOWNFIELD	DOWNSIZES	DOWSING
DOVEKEYS	DOWERED	DOWNFLOW	DOWNSLIDE	DOWSINGS
DOVEKIE	DOWERIES	DOWNFLOWS	DOWNSLOPE	DOWT
DOVEKIES	DOWERING	DOWNFORCE	DOWNSPIN	DOWTS
DOVELET	DOWERLESS	DOWNGRADE	DOWNSPINS	DOX
DOVELETS	DOWERS	DOWNHAUL	DOWNSPOUT	DOXAPRAM
DOVELIKE	DOWERY	DOWNHAULS	DOWNSTAGE	DOXAPRAMS
DOVEN	DOWF	DOWNHILL	DOWNSTAIR	DOXASTIC
DOVENED	DOWFNESS	DOWNHILLS	DOWNSTATE	DOXASTICS
DOVENING	DOWIE	DOWNHOLE	DOWNSWEPT	DOXED
DOVENS	DOWIER	DOWNIER	DOWNSWING	DOXES
DOVER	DOWIEST	DOWNIES	DOWNTHROW	DOXIE
DOVERED	DOWING	DOWNIEST	DOWNTICK	DOXIES
DOVERING	DOWITCHER	DOWNILY	DOWNTICKS	DOXING
DOVERS	DOWL	DOWNINESS	DOWNTIME	DOXINGS
DOVES	DOWLAS	DOWNING	DOWNTIMES	DOXOLOGY
DOVETAIL	DOWLASES	DOWNLAND	DOWNTOWN	DOXX
DOVETAILS	DOWLE	DOWNLANDS	DOWNTOWNS	DOXXED
DOVIE	DOWLES	DOWNLESS	DOWNTREND	DOXXES
DOVIER	DOWLIER	DOWNLIGHT	DOWNTROD	DOXXING
DOVIEST	DOWLIEST	DOWNLIKE	DOWNTURN	DOXXINGS
DOVING	DOWLNE	DOWNLINK	DOWNTURNS	DOXY
DOVISH	DOWLNES	DOWNLINKS	DOWNVOTE	DOY
DOVISHLY	DOWLNEY	DOWNLOAD	DOWNVOTED	DOYEN
DOW	DOWLS	DOWNLOADS	DOWNVOTES	DOYENNE

DOYENNES	DRABS	DRAGGIER	DRAINED	DRAPERS
DOYENS	DRAC	DRAGGIEST	DRAINER	DRAPERY
DOYLEY	DRACAENA	DRAGGING	DRAINERS	DRAPES
DOYLEYS	DRACAENAS	DRAGGINGS	DRAINING	DRAPET
DOYLIES	DRACENA	DRAGGLE	DRAINPIPE	DRAPETS
DOYLY	DRACENAS	DRAGGLED	DRAINS	DRAPEY
DOYS	DRACHM	DRAGGLES	DRAISENE	DRAPIER
DOZE	DRACHMA	DRAGGLING	DRAISENES	DRAPIERS
DOZED	DRACHMAE	DRAGGY	DRAISINE	DRAPIEST
DOZEN	DRACHMAI	DRAGHOUND	DRAISINES	DRAPING
DOZENED	DRACHMAS	DRAGLINE	DRAKE	DRAPPED
DOZENING	DRACHMS	DRAGLINES	DRAKES	DRAPPIE
DOZENS	DRACK	DRAGNET	DRAM	DRAPPIES
DOZENTH	DRACO	DRAGNETS	DRAMA	DRAPPING
DOZENTHS	DRACONE	DRAGOMAN	DRAMADIES	DRAPPY
DOZER	DRACONES	DRAGOMANS	DRAMADY	DRAPS
DOZERS	DRACONIAN	DRAGOMEN	DRAMAS	DRASTIC
DOZES	DRACONIC	DRAGON	DRAMATIC	DRASTICS
DOZIER	DRACONISM	DRAGONESS	DRAMATICS	DRAT
DOZIEST	DRACONTIC	DRAGONET	DRAMATISE	DRATCHELL
DOZILY	DRAD	DRAGONETS	DRAMATIST	DRATS
DOZINESS	DRAFF	DRAGONFLY	DRAMATIZE	DRATTED
DOZING	DRAFFIER	DRAGONISE	DRAMATURG	DRATTING
DOZINGS	DRAFFIEST	DRAGONISH	DRAMEDIES	DRAUGHT
DOZY	DRAFFISH	DRAGONISM	DRAMEDY	DRAUGHTED
DRAB	DRAFFS	DRAGONIZE	DRAMMACH	DRAUGHTER
DRABBED	DRAFFY	DRAGONNE	DRAMMACHS	DRAUGHTS
DRABBER	DRAFT	DRAGONS	DRAMMED	DRAUGHTY
DRABBERS	DRAFTABLE	DRAGOON	DRAMMING	DRAUNT
DRABBEST	DRAFTED	DRAGOONED	DRAMMOCK	DRAUNTED
DRABBET	DRAFTEE	DRAGOONS	DRAMMOCKS	DRAUNTING
DRABBETS	DRAFTEES	DRAGROPE	DRAMS	DRAUNTS
DRABBIER	DRAFTER	DRAGROPES	DRAMSHOP	DRAVE
DRABBIEST	DRAFTERS	DRAGS	DRAMSHOPS	DRAW
DRABBING	DRAFTIER	DRAGSMAN	DRANGWAY	DRAWABLE
DRABBISH	DRAFTIEST	DRAGSMEN	DRANGWAYS	DRAWBACK
DRABBLE	DRAFTILY	DRAGSTER	DRANK	DRAWBACKS
DRABBLED	DRAFTING	DRAGSTERS	DRANT	DRAWBAR
DRABBLER	DRAFTINGS	DRAGSTRIP	DRANTED	DRAWBARS
DRABBLERS	DRAFTS	DRAGWAY	DRANTING	DRAWBORE
DRABBLES	DRAFTSMAN	DRAGWAYS	DRANTS	DRAWBORES
DRABBLING	DRAFTSMEN	DRAIL	DRAP	DRAWCARD
DRABBY	DRAFTY	DRAILED	DRAPABLE	DRAWCARDS
DRABETTE	DRAG	DRAILING	DRAPE	DRAWCORD
DRABETTES	DRAGEE	DRAILS	DRAPEABLE	DRAWCORDS
DRABLER	DRAGEES	DRAIN	DRAPED	DRAWDOWN
DRABLERS	DRAGGED	DRAINABLE	DRAPER	DRAWDOWNS
DRABLY	DRAGGER	DRAINAGE	DRAPERIED	DRAWEE
DRABNESS	DRAGGERS	DRAINAGES	DRAPERIES	DRAWEES

DRAWER	DREAMERS	DREG	DREST	DRIFTS
DRAWERFUL	DREAMERY	DREGGIER	DREVILL	DRIFTWOOD
DRAWERS	DREAMFUL	DREGGIEST	DREVILLS	DRIFTY
DRAWING	DREAMHOLE	DREGGISH	DREW	DRILL
DRAWINGS	DREAMIER	DREGGY	DREY	DRILLABLE
DRAWKNIFE	DREAMIEST	DREGS	DREYS	DRILLED
DRAWL	DREAMILY	DREICH	DRIB	DRILLER
DRAWLED	DREAMING	DREICHER	DRIBBED	DRILLERS
DRAWLER	DREAMINGS	DREICHEST	DRIBBER	DRILLHOLE
DRAWLERS	DREAMLAND	DREIDEL	DRIBBERS	DRILLING
DRAWLIER	DREAMLESS	DREIDELS	DRIBBING	DRILLINGS
DRAWLIEST	DREAMLIKE	DREIDL	DRIBBLE	DRILLS
DRAWLING	DREAMS	DREIDLS	DRIBBLED	DRILLSHIP
DRAWLS	DREAMT	DREIGH	DRIBBLER	DRILY
DRAWLY	DREAMTIME	DREIGHER	DRIBBLERS	DRINK
DRAWN	DREAMY	DREIGHEST	DRIBBLES	DRINKABLE
DRAWNWORK	DREAR	DREK	DRIBBLET	DRINKABLY
DRAWPLATE	DREARE	DREKKIER	DRIBBLETS	DRINKER
DRAWS	DREARER	DREKKIEST	DRIBBLIER	DRINKERS
DRAWSHAVE	DREARES	DREKKY	DRIBBLING	DRINKING
DRAWTUBE	DREAREST	DREKS	DRIBBLY	DRINKINGS
DRAWTUBES	DREARIER	DRENCH	DRIBLET	DRINKS
DRAY	DREARIES	DRENCHED	DRIBLETS	DRIP
DRAYAGE	DREARIEST	DRENCHER	DRIBS	DRIPLESS
DRAYAGES	DREARILY	DRENCHERS	DRICE	DRIPPED
DRAYED	DREARING	DRENCHES	DRICES	DRIPPER
DRAYHORSE	DREARINGS	DRENCHING	DRICKSIE	DRIPPERS
DRAYING	DREARS	DRENT	DRICKSIER	DRIPPIER
DRAYMAN	DREARY	DREPANID	DRIED	DRIPPIEST
DRAYMEN	DRECK	DREPANIDS	DRIEGH	DRIPPILY
DRAYS	DRECKIER	DREPANIUM	DRIER	DRIPPING
DRAZEL	DRECKIEST	DRERE	DRIERS	DRIPPINGS
DRAZELS	DRECKISH	DRERES	DRIES	DRIPPY
DREAD	DRECKS	DRERIHEAD	DRIEST	DRIPS
DREADED	DRECKSILL	DRESS	DRIFT	DRIPSTONE
DREADER	DRECKY	DRESSAGE	DRIFTAGE	DRIPT
DREADERS	DREDGE	DRESSAGES	DRIFTAGES	DRISHEEN
DREADEST	DREDGED	DRESSED	DRIFTED	DRISHEENS
DREADFUL	DREDGER	DRESSER	DRIFTER	DRIVABLE
DREADFULS	DREDGERS	DRESSERS	DRIFTERS	DRIVE
DREADING	DREDGES	DRESSES	DRIFTIER	DRIVEABLE
DREADLESS	DREDGING	DRESSIER	DRIFTIEST	DRIVEL
DREADLOCK	DREDGINGS	DRESSIEST	DRIFTING	DRIVELED
DREADLY	DREE	DRESSILY	DRIFTINGS	DRIVELER
DREADS	DREED	DRESSING	DRIFTLESS	DRIVELERS
DREAM	DREEING	DRESSINGS	DRIFTNET	DRIVELINE
DREAMBOAT	DREER	DRESSMADE	DRIFTNETS	DRIVELING
DREAMED	DREES	DRESSMAKE	DRIFTPIN	DRIVELLED
DREAMER	DREEST	DRESSY	DRIFTPINS	DRIVELLER

DRIVELS	DROLLISH	DROOLS	DROPSY	DROWNERS
DRIVEN	DROLLNESS	DROOLY	DROPT	DROWNING
DRIVER	DROLLS	DROOME	DROPTOP	DROWNINGS
DRIVERS	DROLLY	DROOMES	DROPTOPS	DROWNS
DRIVES	DROME	DROOP	DROPWISE	DROWS
DRIVEWAY	DROMEDARE	DROOPED	DROPWORT	DROWSE
DRIVEWAYS	DROMEDARY	DROOPIER	DROPWORTS	DROWSED
DRIVING	DROMES	DROOPIEST	DROSERA	DROWSES
DRIVINGLY	DROMIC	DROOPILY	DROSERAS	DROWSIER
DRIVINGS	DROMICAL	DROOPING	DROSHKIES	DROWSIEST
DRIZZLE	DROMOI	DROOPS	DROSHKY	DROWSIHED
DRIZZLED	DROMON	DROOPY	DROSKIES	DROWSILY
DRIZZLES	DROMOND	DROP	DROSKY	DROWSING
DRIZZLIER	DROMONDS	DROPCLOTH	DROSS	DROWSY
DRIZZLING	DROMONS	DROPDOWN	DROSSES	DRUB
DRIZZLY	DROMOS	DROPDOWNS	DROSSIER	DRUBBED
DROGER	DRONE	DROPFLIES	DROSSIEST	DRUBBER
DROGERS	DRONED	DROPFLY	DROSSY	DRUBBERS
DROGHER	DRONER	DROPFORGE	DROSTDIES	DRUBBING
DROGHERS	DRONERS	DROPHEAD	DROSTDY	DRUBBINGS
DROGUE	DRONES	DROPHEADS	DROSTDYS	DRUBS
DROGUES	DRONGO	DROPKICK	DROUGHT	DRUCKEN
DROGUET	DRONGOES	DROPKICKS	DROUGHTS	DRUDGE
DROGUETS	DRONGOS	DROPLET	DROUGHTY	DRUDGED
DROICH	DRONIER	DROPLETS	DROUK	DRUDGER
DROICHIER	DRONIEST	DROPLIGHT	DROUKED	DRUDGERS
DROICHS	DRONING	DROPLIKE	DROUKING	DRUDGERY
DROICHY	DRONINGLY	DROPLOCK	DROUKINGS	DRUDGES
DROID	DRONISH	DROPLOCKS	DROUKIT	DRUDGING
DROIDS	DRONISHLY	DROPOUT	DROUKS	DRUDGISM
DROIL	DRONKLAP	DROPOUTS	DROUTH	DRUDGISMS
DROILED	DRONKLAPS	DROPPABLE	DROUTHIER	DRUG
DROILING	DRONY	DROPPED	DROUTHS	DRUGGED
DROILS	DROOB	DROPPER	DROUTHY	DRUGGER
DROIT	DROOBS	DROPPERS	DROVE	DRUGGERS
DROITS	DROOG	DROPPING	DROVED	DRUGGET
DROKE	DROOGISH	DROPPINGS	DROVER	DRUGGETS
DROKES	DROOGS	DROPPLE	DROVERS	DRUGGIE
DROLE	DROOK	DROPPLES	DROVES	DRUGGIER
DROLER	DROOKED	DROPS	DROVING	DRUGGIES
DROLES	DROOKING	DROPSEED	DROVINGS	DRUGGIEST
DROLEST	DROOKINGS	DROPSEEDS	DROW	DRUGGING
DROLL	DROOKIT	DROPSHOT	DROWN	DRUGGIST
DROLLED	DROOKS	DROPSHOTS	DROWND	DRUGGISTS
DROLLER	DROOL	DROPSICAL	DROWNDED	DRUGGY
DROLLERY	DROOLED	DROPSIED	DROWNDING	DRUGLESS
DROLLEST	DROOLIER	DROPSIES	DROWNDS	DRUGLORD
DROLLING	DROOLIEST	DROPSONDE	DROWNED	DRUGLORDS
DROLLINGS	DROOLING	DROPSTONE	DROWNER	DRUGMAKER

DRUGS	DRUNKER	DRYS	DUATHLETE	DUCK
DRUGSTER	DRUNKEST	DRYSALTER	DUATHLON	DUCKBILL
DRUGSTERS	DRUNKISH	DRYSTONE	DUATHLONS	DUCKBILLS
DRUGSTORE	DRUNKS	DRYSUIT	DUB	DUCKBOARD
DRUID	DRUPE	DRYSUITS	DUBBED	DUCKED
DRUIDESS	DRUPEL	DRYWALL	DUBBER	DUCKER
DRUIDIC	DRUPELET	DRYWALLED	DUBBERS	DUCKERS
DRUIDICAL	DRUPELETS	DRYWALLER	DUBBIN	DUCKFOOT
DRUIDISM	DRUPELS	DRYWALLS	DUBBINED	DUCKIE
DRUIDISMS	DRUPES	DRYWELL	DUBBING	DUCKIER
DRUIDRIES	DRUSE	DRYWELLS	DUBBINGS	DUCKIES
DRUIDRY	DRUSEN	DSO	DUBBINING	DUCKIEST
DRUIDS	DRUSES	DSOBO	DUBBINS	DUCKING
DRUM	DRUSIER	DSOBOS	DUBBO	DUCKINGS
DRUMBEAT	DRUSIEST	DSOMO	DUBBOS	DUCKISH
DRUMBEATS	DRUSY	DSOMOS	DUBIETIES	DUCKISHES
DRUMBLE	DRUTHER	DSOS	DUBIETY	DUCKLING
DRUMBLED	DRUTHERS	DUAD	DUBIOSITY	DUCKLINGS
DRUMBLES	DRUXIER	DUADS	DUBIOUS	DUCKMOLE
DRUMBLING	DRUXIEST	DUAL	DUBIOUSLY	DUCKMOLES
DRUMFIRE	DRUXY	DUALIN	DUBITABLE	DUCKPIN
DRUMFIRES	DRY	DUALINS	DUBITABLY	DUCKPINS
DRUMFISH	DRYABLE	DUALISE	DUBITANCY	DUCKS
DRUMHEAD	DRYAD	DUALISED	DUBITATE	DUCKSHOVE
DRUMHEADS	DRYADES	DUALISES	DUBITATED	DUCKTAIL
DRUMLIER	DRYADIC	DUALISING	DUBITATES	DUCKTAILS
DRUMLIEST	DRYADS	DUALISM	DUBNIUM	DUCKWALK
DRUMLIKE	DRYAS	DUALISMS	DUBNIUMS	DUCKWALKS
DRUMLIN	DRYASDUST	DUALIST	DUBONNET	DUCKWEED
DRUMLINS	DRYBEAT	DUALISTIC	DUBONNETS	DUCKWEEDS
DRUMLY	DRYBEATEN	DUALISTS	DUBS	DUCKY
DRUMMED	DRYBEATS	DUALITIES	DUBSTEP	DUCT
DRUMMER	DRYER	DUALITY	DUBSTEPS	DUCTAL
DRUMMERS	DRYERS	DUALIZE	DUCAL	DUCTED
DRUMMIES	DRYEST	DUALIZED	DUCALLY	DUCTILE
DRUMMING	DRYING	DUALIZES	DUCAT	DUCTILELY
DRUMMINGS	DRYINGS	DUALIZING	DUCATOON	DUCTILITY
DRUMMOCK	DRYISH	DUALLED	DUCATOONS	DUCTING
DRUMMOCKS	DRYLAND	DUALLIE	DUCATS	DUCTINGS
DRUMMY	DRYLANDS	DUALLIES	DUCDAME	DUCTLESS
DRUMROLL	DRYLOT	DUALLING	DUCE	DUCTS
DRUMROLLS	DRYLOTS	DUALLY	DUCES	DUCTULE
DRUMS	DRYLY	DUALS	DUCHESS	DUCTULES
DRUMSTICK	DRYMOUTH	DUAN	DUCHESSE	DUCTWORK
DRUNK	DRYMOUTHS	DUANS	DUCHESSED	DUCTWORKS
DRUNKARD	DRYNESS	DUAR	DUCHESSES	DUD
DRUNKARDS	DRYNESSES	DUARCHIES	DUCHIES	DUDDER
DRUNKEN	DRYPOINT	DUARCHY	DUCHY	DUDDERED
DRUNKENLY	DRYPOINTS	DUARS	DUCI	DUDDERIES

DUDDERING	DUELS	DUHKHA	DULCITOL	DUMBHEADS
DUDDERS	DUELSOME	DUHKHAS	DULCITOLS	DUMBING
DUDDERY	DUENDE	DUI	DULCITUDE	DUMBLY
DUDDIE	DUENDES	DUIKER	DULCOSE	DUMBNESS
DUDDIER	DUENESS	DUIKERBOK	DULCOSES	DUMBO
DUDDIES	DUENESSES	DUIKERS	DULE	DUMBOS
DUDDIEST	DUENNA	DUING	DULES	DUMBPHONE
DUDDY	DUENNAS	DUIT	DULIA	DUMBS
DUDE	DUES	DUITS	DULIAS	DUMBSHIT
DUDED	DUET	DUKA	DULL	DUMBSHITS
DUDEEN	DUETED	DUKAS	DULLARD	DUMBSHOW
DUDEENS	DUETING	DUKE	DULLARDS	DUMBSHOWS
DUDENESS	DUETS	DUKED	DULLED	DUMBSIZE
DUDES	DUETT	DUKEDOM	DULLER	DUMBSIZED
DUDETTE	DUETTED	DUKEDOMS	DULLEST	DUMBSIZES
DUDETTES	DUETTI	DUKELING	DULLIER	DUMDUM
DUDGEON	DUETTING	DUKELINGS	DULLIEST	DUMDUMS
DUDGEONS	DUETTINO	DUKERIES	DULLING	DUMELA
DUDHEEN	DUETTINOS	DUKERY	DULLISH	DUMFOUND
DUDHEENS	DUETTIST	DUKES	DULLISHLY	DUMFOUNDS
DUDING	DUETTISTS	DUKESHIP	DULLNESS	DUMKA
DUDISH	DUETTO	DUKESHIPS	DULLS	DUMKAS
DUDISHLY	DUETTOS	DUKING	DULLY	DUMKY
DUDISM	DUETTS	DUKKA	DULNESS	DUMMERER
DUDISMS	DUFF	DUKKAH	DULNESSES	DUMMERERS
DUDS	DUFFED	DUKKAHS	DULOCRACY	DUMMIED
DUE	DUFFEL	DUKKAS	DULOSES	DUMMIER
DUECENTO	DUFFELS	DUKKHA	DULOSIS	DUMMIES
DUECENTOS	DUFFER	DUKKHAS	DULOTIC	DUMMIEST
DUED	DUFFERDOM	DULCAMARA	DULSE	DUMMINESS
DUEFUL	DUFFERISM	DULCE	DULSES	DUMMKOPF
DUEL	DUFFERS	DULCES	DULY	DUMMKOPFS
DUELED	DUFFEST	DULCET	DUM	DUMMY
DUELER	DUFFING	DULCETLY	DUMA	DUMMYING
DUELERS	DUFFINGS	DULCETS	DUMAIST	DUMOSE
DUELING	DUFFLE	DULCIAN	DUMAISTS	DUMOSITY
DUELINGS	DUFFLES	DULCIANA	DUMAS	DUMOUS
DUELIST	DUFFS	DULCIANAS	DUMB	DUMP
DUELISTS	DUFUS	DULCIANS	DUMBASS	DUMPBIN
DUELLED	DUFUSES	DULCIFIED	DUMBASSES	DUMPBINS
DUELLER	DUG	DULCIFIES	DUMBBELL	DUMPCART
DUELLERS	DUGITE	DULCIFY	DUMBBELLS	DUMPCARTS
DUELLI	DUGITES	DULCIMER	DUMBCANE	DUMPED
DUELLING	DUGONG	DULCIMERS	DUMBCANES	DUMPEE
DUELLINGS	DUGONGS	DULCIMORE	DUMBED	DUMPEES
DUELLIST	DUGOUT	DULCINEA	DUMBER	DUMPER
DUELLISTS	DUGOUTS	DULCINEAS	DUMBEST	DUMPERS
DUELLO	DUGS	DULCITE	DUMBFOUND	DUMPIER
DUELLOS	DUH	DULCITES	DUMBHEAD	DUMPIES

D

DUMPIEST	DUNGEONED	DUNNOCKS	DUPLE	DURE
DUMPILY	DUNGEONER	DUNNY	DUPLET	DURED
DUMPINESS	DUNGEONS	DUNS	DUPLETS	DUREFUL
DUMPING	DUNGER	DUNSH	DUPLEX	DURES
DUMPINGS	DUNGERS	DUNSHED	DUPLEXED	DURESS
DUMPISH	DUNGHEAP	DUNSHES	DUPLEXER	DURESSE
DUMPISHLY	DUNGHEAPS	DUNSHING	DUPLEXERS	DURESSES
DUMPLE	DUNGHILL	DUNT	DUPLEXES	DURGAH
DUMPLED	DUNGHILLS	DUNTED	DUPLEXING	DURGAHS
DUMPLES	DUNGIER	DUNTING	DUPLEXITY	DURGAN
DUMPLING	DUNGIEST	DUNTS	DUPLICAND	DURGANS
DUMPLINGS	DUNGING	DUO	DUPLICATE	DURGIER
DUMPS	DUNGMERE	DUOBINARY	DUPLICITY	DURGIEST
DUMPSITE	DUNGMERES	DUODECIMO	DUPLIED	DURGY
DUMPSITES	DUNGS	DUODENA	DUPLIES	DURIAN
DUMPSTER	DUNGY	DUODENAL	DUPLY	DURIANS
DUMPSTERS	DUNITE	DUODENARY	DUPLYING	DURICRUST
DUMPTRUCK	DUNITES	DUODENUM	DUPONDII	DURING
DUMPY	DUNITIC	DUODENUMS	DUPONDIUS	DURION
DUN	DUNK	DUOLOG	DUPPED	DURIONS
DUNAM	DUNKED	DUOLOGS	DUPPIES	DURMAST
DUNAMS	DUNKER	DUOLOGUE	DUPPING	DURMASTS
DUNCE	DUNKERS	DUOLOGUES	DUPPY	DURN
DUNCEDOM	DUNKING	DUOMI	DUPS	DURNDEST
DUNCEDOMS	DUNKINGS	DUOMO	DUR	DURNED
DUNCELIKE	DUNKS	DUOMOS	DURA	DURNEDER
DUNCERIES	DUNLIN	DUOPOLIES	DURABLE	DURNEDEST
DUNCERY	DUNLINS	DUOPOLIST	DURABLES	DURNING
DUNCES	DUNNAGE	DUOPOLY	DURABLY	DURNS
DUNCH	DUNNAGES	DUOPSONY	DURAG	DURO
DUNCHED	DUNNAKIN	DUOS	DURAGS	DUROC
DUNCHES	DUNNAKINS	DUOTONE	DURAL	DUROCS
DUNCHING	DUNNART	DUOTONES	DURALS	DUROMETER
DUNCICAL	DUNNARTS	DUP	DURALUMIN	DUROS
DUNCISH	DUNNED	DUPABLE	DURAMEN	DUROY
DUNCISHLY	DUNNER	DUPATTA	DURAMENS	DUROYS
DUNDER	DUNNESS	DUPATTAS	DURANCE	DURR
DUNDERS	DUNNESSES	DUPATTE	DURANCES	DURRA
DUNE	DUNNEST	DUPE	DURANT	DURRAS
DUNELAND	DUNNIER	DUPED	DURANTS	DURRIE
DUNELANDS	DUNNIES	DUPER	DURAS	DURRIES
DUNELIKE	DUNNIEST	DUPERIES	DURATION	DURRS
DUNES	DUNNING	DUPERS	DURATIONS	DURRY
DUNG	DUNNINGS	DUPERY	DURATIVE	DURST
DUNGAREE	DUNNISH	DUPES	DURATIVES	DURUKULI
DUNGAREED	DUNNITE	DUPING	DURBAR	DURUKULIS
DUNGAREES	DUNNITES	DUPINGS	DURBARS	DURUM
DUNGED	DUNNO	DUPION	DURDUM	DURUMS
DUNGEON	DUNNOCK	DUPIONS	DURDUMS	DURZI

DURZIS	DUSTMEN	DWALE	DWINED	DYNAMISE
DUSH	DUSTOFF	DWALES	DWINES	DYNAMISED
DUSHED	DUSTOFFS	DWALM	DWINING	DYNAMISES
DUSHES	DUSTPAN	DWALMED	DYABLE	DYNAMISM
DUSHING	DUSTPANS	DWALMING	DYAD	DYNAMISMS
DUSK	DUSTPROOF	DWALMS	DYADIC	DYNAMIST
DUSKED	DUSTRAG	DWAM	DYADICS	DYNAMISTS
DUSKEN	DUSTRAGS	DWAMMED	DYADS	DYNAMITE
DUSKENED	DUSTS	DWAMMING	DYARCHAL	DYNAMITED
DUSKENING	DUSTSHEET	DWAMS	DYARCHIC	DYNAMITER
DUSKENS	DUSTSTORM	DWANG	DYARCHIES	DYNAMITES
DUSKER	DUSTUP	DWANGS	DYARCHY	DYNAMITIC
DUSKEST	DUSTUPS	DWARF	DYBBUK	DYNAMIZE
DUSKIER	DUSTY	DWARFED	DYBBUKIM	DYNAMIZED
DUSKIEST	DUTCH	DWARFER	DYBBUKKIM	DYNAMIZES
DUSKILY	DUTCHES	DWARFEST	DYBBUKS	DYNAMO
DUSKINESS	DUTCHMAN	DWARFING	DYE	DYNAMOS
DUSKING	DUTCHMEN	DWARFISH	DYEABLE	DYNAMOTOR
DUSKISH	DUTEOUS	DWARFISM	DYED	DYNAST
DUSKISHLY	DUTEOUSLY	DWARFISMS	DYEING	DYNASTIC
DUSKLY	DUTIABLE	DWARFLIKE	DYEINGS	DYNASTIES
DUSKNESS	DUTIED	DWARFNESS	DYELINE	DYNASTS
DUSKS	DUTIES	DWARFS	DYELINES	DYNASTY
DUSKY	DUTIFUL	DWARVES	DYER	DYNATRON
DUST	DUTIFULLY	DWAUM	DYERS	DYNATRONS
DUSTBALL	DUTY	DWAUMED	DYES	DYNE
DUSTBALLS	DUUMVIR	DWAUMING	DYESTER	DYNEIN
DUSTBIN	DUUMVIRAL	DWAUMS	DYESTERS	DYNEINS
DUSTBINS	DUUMVIRI	DWEEB	DYESTUFF	DYNEL
DUSTCART	DUUMVIRS	DWEEBIER	DYESTUFFS	DYNELS
DUSTCARTS	DUVET	DWEEBIEST	DYEWEED	DYNES
DUSTCLOTH	DUVETINE	DWEEBISH	DYEWEEDS	DYNODE
DUSTCOAT	DUVETINES	DWEEBS	DYEWOOD	DYNODES
DUSTCOATS	DUVETS	DWEEBY	DYEWOODS	DYNORPHIN
DUSTCOVER	DUVETYN	DWELL	DYEWORKS	DYSBINDIN
DUSTED	DUVETYNE	DWELLED	DYING	DYSCHROA
DUSTER	DUVETYNES	DWELLER	DYINGLY	DYSCHROAS
DUSTERS	DUVETYNS	DWELLERS	DYINGNESS	DYSCHROIA
DUSTHEAP	DUX	DWELLING	DYINGS	DYSCRASIA
DUSTHEAPS	DUXELLES	DWELLINGS	DYKE	DYSCRASIC
DUSTIER	DUXES	DWELLS	DYKED	DYSCRATIC
DUSTIEST	DUYKER	DWELT	DYKES	DYSENTERY
DUSTILY	DUYKERS	DWILE	DYKING	DYSFLUENT
DUSTINESS	DVANDVA	DWILES	DYKON	DYSGENIC
DUSTING	DVANDVAS	DWINDLE	DYKONS	DYSGENICS
DUSTINGS	DVORNIK	DWINDLED	DYNAMETER	DYSLALIA
DUSTLESS	DVORNIKS	DWINDLES	DYNAMIC	DYSLALIAS
DUSTLIKE	DWAAL	DWINDLING	DYNAMICAL	DYSLECTIC
DUSTMAN	DWAALS	DWINE	DYNAMICS	DYSLEXIA

DYSLEXIAS	DYSPEPSY	DYSPNOEA	DYSTOCIAL	DYTISCIDS
DYSLEXIC	DYSPEPTIC	DYSPNOEAL	DYSTOCIAS	DYVOUR
DYSLEXICS	DYSPHAGIA	DYSPNOEAS	DYSTONIA	DYVOURIES
DYSLOGIES	DYSPHAGIC	DYSPNOEIC	DYSTONIAS	DYVOURS
DYSLOGY	DYSPHAGY	DYSPNOIC	DYSTONIC	DYVOURY
DYSMELIA	DYSPHASIA	DYSPRAXIA	DYSTOPIA	DZEREN
DYSMELIAS	DYSPHASIC	DYSPRAXIC	DYSTOPIAN	DZERENS
DYSMELIC	DYSPHONIA	DYSTAXIA	DYSTOPIAS	DZHO
DYSODIL	DYSPHONIC	DYSTAXIAS	DYSTOPIC	DZHOS
DYSODILE	DYSPHORIA	DYSTAXIC	DYSTROPHY	DZIGGETAI
DYSODILES	DYSPHORIC	DYSTECTIC	DYSURIA	DZO
DYSODILS	DYSPLASIA	DYSTHESIA	DYSURIAS	DZOS
DYSODYLE	DYSPNEA	DYSTHETIC	DYSURIC	
DYSODYLES	DYSPNEAL	DYSTHYMIA	DYSURIES	
DYSPATHY	DYSPNEAS	DYSTHYMIC	DYSURY	
DYSPEPSIA	DYSPNEIC	DYSTOCIA	DYTISCID	

E

EA	EARBOBS	EARMARKED	EARTHLIER	EASES
EACH	EARBUD	EARMARKS	EARTHLIES	EASIED
EACHWHERE	EARBUDS	EARMUFF	EARTHLIKE	EASIER
EADISH	EARCON	EARMUFFS	EARTHLING	EASIES
EADISHES	EARCONS	EARN	EARTHLY	EASIEST
EAGER	EARD	EARNED	EARTHMAN	EASILY
EAGERER	EARDED	EARNER	EARTHMEN	EASINESS
EAGEREST	EARDING	EARNERS	EARTHNUT	EASING
EAGERLY	EARDROP	EARNEST	EARTHNUTS	EASINGS
EAGERNESS	EARDROPS	EARNESTLY	EARTHPEA	EASLE
EAGERS	EARDRUM	EARNESTS	EARTHPEAS	EASLES
EAGLE	EARDRUMS	EARNING	EARTHRISE	EASSEL
EAGLED	EARDS	EARNINGS	EARTHS	EASSIL
EAGLEHAWK	EARED	EARNS	EARTHSET	EAST
EAGLES	EARFLAP	EARNT	EARTHSETS	EASTABOUT
EAGLET	EARFLAPS	EARPHONE	EARTHSTAR	EASTBOUND
EAGLETS	EARFUL	EARPHONES	EARTHWARD	EASTED
EAGLEWOOD	EARFULS	EARPICK	EARTHWAX	EASTER
EAGLING	EARHOLE	EARPICKS	EARTHWOLF	EASTERLY
EAGRE	EARHOLES	EARPIECE	EARTHWORK	EASTERN
EAGRES	EARING	EARPIECES	EARTHWORM	EASTERNER
EALDORMAN	EARINGS	EARPLUG	EARTHY	EASTERS
EALDORMEN	EARL	EARPLUGS	EARWAX	EASTING
EALE	EARLAP	EARRING	EARWAXES	EASTINGS
EALED	EARLAPS	EARRINGED	EARWIG	EASTLAND
EALES	EARLDOM	EARRINGS	EARWIGGED	EASTLANDS
EALING	EARLDOMS	EARS	EARWIGGY	EASTLIN
EAN	EARLESS	EARSHOT	EARWIGS	EASTLING
EANED	EARLIER	EARSHOTS	EARWORM	EASTLINGS
EANING	EARLIES	EARST	EARWORMS	EASTLINS
EANLING	EARLIEST	EARSTONE	EAS	EASTMOST
EANLINGS	EARLIKE	EARSTONES	EASE	EASTS
EANS	EARLINESS	EARTH	EASED	EASTWARD
EAR	EARLOBE	EARTHBORN	EASEFUL	EASTWARDS
EARACHE	EARLOBES	EARTHED	EASEFULLY	EASY
EARACHES	EARLOCK	EARTHEN	EASEL	EASYGOING
EARBALL	EARLOCKS	EARTHFALL	EASELED	EASYING
EARBALLS	EARLS	EARTHFAST	EASELESS	EAT
EARBASH	EARLSHIP	EARTHFLAX	EASELS	EATABLE
EARBASHED	EARLSHIPS	EARTHIER	EASEMENT	EATABLES
EARBASHER	EARLY	EARTHIEST	EASEMENTS	EATAGE
EARBASHES	EARLYWOOD	EARTHILY	EASER	EATAGES
EARBOB	EARMARK	EARTHING	EASERS	EATCHE

EATCHES	EBONICS	ECDEMIC	ECHOES	ECLOSE
EATEN	EBONIES	ECDYSES	ECHOEY	ECLOSED
EATER	EBONISE	ECDYSIAL	ECHOGRAM	ECLOSES
EATERIE	EBONISED	ECDYSIAST	ECHOGRAMS	ECLOSING
EATERIES	EBONISES	ECDYSIS	ECHOGRAPH	ECLOSION
EATERS	EBONISING	ECDYSISES	ECHOIC	ECLOSIONS
EATERY	EBONIST	ECDYSON	ECHOIER	ECO
EATH	EBONISTS	ECDYSONE	ECHOIEST	ECOCIDAL
EATHE	EBONITE	ECDYSONES	ECHOING	ECOCIDE
EATHLY	EBONITES	ECDYSONS	ECHOISE	ECOCIDES
EATING	EBONIZE	ECESIC	ECHOISED	ECOD
EATINGS	EBONIZED	ECESIS	ECHOISES	ECOFREAK
EATS	EBONIZES	ECESISES	ECHOISING	ECOFREAKS
EAU	EBONIZING	ECH	ECHOISM	ECOGIFT
EAUS	EBONS	ECHAPPE	ECHOISMS	ECOGIFTS
EAUX	EBONY	ECHAPPES	ECHOIST	ECOLODGE
EAVE	EBOOK	ECHARD	ECHOISTS	ECOLODGES
EAVED	EBOOKS	ECHARDS	ECHOIZE	ECOLOGIC
EAVES	EBRIATE	ECHE	ECHOIZED	ECOLOGIES
EAVESDRIP	EBRIATED	ECHED	ECHOIZES	ECOLOGIST
EAVESDROP	EBRIETIES	ECHELLE	ECHOIZING	ECOLOGY
EAVING	EBRIETY	ECHELLES	ECHOLALIA	ECOMAP
EBAUCHE	EBRILLADE	ECHELON	ECHOLALIC	ECOMAPS
EBAUCHES	EBRIOSE	ECHELONED	ECHOLESS	ECOMM
EBAYER	EBRIOSITY	ECHELONS	ECHOS	ECOMMERCE
EBAYERS	EBULLIENT	ECHES	ECHOVIRUS	ECOMMS
EBAYING	EBURNEAN	ECHEVERIA	ECHT	ECOMUSEUM
EBAYINGS	EBURNEOUS	ECHIDNA	ECLAIR	ECONOBOX
EBB	ECAD	ECHIDNAE	ECLAIRS	ECONOMIC
EBBED	ECADS	ECHIDNAS	ECLAMPSIA	ECONOMICS
EBBET	ECARINATE	ECHIDNINE	ECLAMPSY	ECONOMIES
EBBETS	ECARTE	ECHINACEA	ECLAMPTIC	ECONOMISE
EBBING	ECARTES	ECHINATE	ECLAT	ECONOMISM
EBBLESS	ECAUDATE	ECHINATED	ECLATS	ECONOMIST
EBBS	ECBOLE	ECHING	ECLECTIC	ECONOMIZE
EBENEZER	ECBOLES	ECHINI	ECLECTICS	ECONOMY
EBENEZERS	ECBOLIC	ECHINOID	ECLIPSE	ECONUT
EBENISTE	ECBOLICS	ECHINOIDS	ECLIPSED	ECONUTS
EBENISTES	ECCE	ECHINUS	ECLIPSER	ECOPHOBIA
EBIONISE	ECCENTRIC	ECHINUSES	ECLIPSERS	ECORCHE
EBIONISED	ECCLESIA	ECHIUM	ECLIPSES	ECORCHES
EBIONISES	ECCLESIAE	ECHIUMS	ECLIPSING	ECOREGION
EBIONISM	ECCLESIAL	ECHIURAN	ECLIPSIS	ECOS
EBIONISMS	ECCO	ECHIURANS	ECLIPTIC	ECOSPHERE
EBIONITIC	ECCRINE	ECHIUROID	ECLIPTICS	ECOSSAISE
EBIONIZE	ECCRISES	ECHO	ECLOGITE	ECOSTATE
EBIONIZED	ECCRISIS	ECHOED	ECLOGITES	ECOSYSTEM
EBIONIZES	ECCRITIC	ECHOER	ECLOGUE	ECOTAGE
EBON	ECCRITICS	ECHOERS	ECLOGUES	ECOTAGES

ECOTARIAN	ECTOMERIC	EDDO	EDIFY	EECHING
ECOTONAL	ECTOMORPH	EDDOES	EDIFYING	EEEW
ECOTONE	ECTOPHYTE	EDDY	EDILE	EEJIT
ECOTONES	ECTOPIA	EDDYING	EDILES	EEJITS
ECOTOPIA	ECTOPIAS	EDELWEISS	EDIT	EEK
ECOTOPIAS	ECTOPIC	EDEMA	EDITABLE	EEL
ECOTOUR	ECTOPIES	EDEMAS	EDITED	EELED
ECOTOURED	ECTOPLASM	EDEMATA	EDITING	EELFARE
ECOTOURS	ECTOPROCT	EDEMATOSE	EDITINGS	EELFARES
ECOTOXIC	ECTOPY	EDEMATOUS	EDITION	EELGRASS
ECOTYPE	ECTOSARC	EDENIC	EDITIONED	EELIER
ECOTYPES	ECTOSARCS	EDENTAL	EDITIONS	EELIEST
ECOTYPIC	ECTOTHERM	EDENTATE	EDITOR	EELING
ECOZONE	ECTOZOA	EDENTATES	EDITORIAL	EELINGS
ECOZONES	ECTOZOAN	EDGE	EDITORS	EELLIKE
ECPHRASES	ECTOZOANS	EDGEBONE	EDITRESS	EELPOUT
ECPHRASIS	ECTOZOIC	EDGEBONES	EDITRICES	EELPOUTS
ECRASEUR	ECTOZOON	EDGED	EDITRIX	EELS
ECRASEURS	ECTROPIC	EDGELESS	EDITRIXES	EELWORM
ECRITOIRE	ECTROPION	EDGELORD	EDITS	EELWORMS
ECRU	ECTROPIUM	EDGELORDS	EDS	EELWRACK
ECRUS	ECTYPAL	EDGER	EDUCABLE	EELWRACKS
ECSTASES	ECTYPE	EDGERS	EDUCABLES	EELY
ECSTASIED	ECTYPES	EDGES	EDUCATE	EEN
ECSTASIES	ECU	EDGEWAYS	EDUCATED	EENSIER
ECSTASIS	ECUELLE	EDGEWISE	EDUCATES	EENSIEST
ECSTASISE	ECUELLES	EDGIER	EDUCATING	EENSY
ECSTASIZE	ECUMENE	EDGIEST	EDUCATION	EERIE
ECSTASY	ECUMENES	EDGILY	EDUCATIVE	EERIER
ECSTATIC	ECUMENIC	EDGINESS	EDUCATOR	EERIEST
ECSTATICS	ECUMENICS	EDGING	EDUCATORS	EERILY
ECTASES	ECUMENISM	EDGINGS	EDUCATORY	EERINESS
ECTASIA	ECUMENIST	EDGY	EDUCE	EERY
ECTASIAS	ECURIE	EDH	EDUCED	EEVEN
ECTASIS	ECURIES	EDHS	EDUCEMENT	EEVENS
ECTATIC	ECUS	EDIBILITY	EDUCES	EEVN
ECTHYMA	ECZEMA	EDIBLE	EDUCIBLE	EEVNING
ECTHYMAS	ECZEMAS	EDIBLES	EDUCING	EEVNINGS
ECTHYMATA	ED	EDICT	EDUCT	EEVNS
ECTOBLAST	EDACIOUS	EDICTAL	EDUCTION	EEW
ECTOCRINE	EDACITIES	EDICTALLY	EDUCTIONS	EF
ECTODERM	EDACITY	EDICTS	EDUCTIVE	EFF
ECTODERMS	EDAMAME	EDIFICE	EDUCTOR	EFFABLE
ECTOGENE	EDAMAMES	EDIFICES	EDUCTORS	EFFACE
ECTOGENES	EDAPHIC	EDIFICIAL	EDUCTS	EFFACED
ECTOGENIC	EDDIED	EDIFIED	EE	EFFACER
ECTOGENY	EDDIES	EDIFIER	EECH	EFFACERS
ECTOMERE	EDDISH	EDIFIERS	EECHED	EFFACES
ECTOMERES	EDDISHES	EDIFIES	EECHES	EFFACING

EFFECT	EFFORT	EGGAR	EGOISMS	EIDETICS
EFFECTED	EFFORTFUL	EGGARS	EGOIST	EIDOGRAPH
EFFECTER	EFFORTS	EGGBEATER	EGOISTIC	EIDOLA
EFFECTERS	EFFRAIDE	EGGCORN	EGOISTS	EIDOLIC
EFFECTING	EFFRAY	EGGCORNS	EGOITIES	EIDOLON
EFFECTIVE	EFFRAYS	EGGCUP	EGOITY	EIDOLONS
EFFECTOR	EFFS	EGGCUPS	EGOLESS	EIDOS
EFFECTORS	EFFULGE	EGGED	EGOMANIA	EIGENMODE
EFFECTS	EFFULGED	EGGER	EGOMANIAC	EIGENTONE
EFFECTUAL	EFFULGENT	EGGERIES	EGOMANIAS	EIGHT
EFFED	EFFULGES	EGGERS	EGOS	EIGHTBALL
EFFEIR	EFFULGING	EGGERY	EGOSURF	EIGHTEEN
EFFEIRED	EFFUSE	EGGFRUIT	EGOSURFED	EIGHTEENS
EFFEIRING	EFFUSED	EGGFRUITS	EGOSURFS	EIGHTFOIL
EFFEIRS	EFFUSES	EGGHEAD	EGOTHEISM	EIGHTFOLD
EFFENDI	EFFUSING	EGGHEADED	EGOTISE	EIGHTFOOT
EFFENDIS	EFFUSION	EGGHEADS	EGOTISED	EIGHTH
EFFERE	EFFUSIONS	EGGIER	EGOTISES	EIGHTHLY
EFFERED	EFFUSIVE	EGGIEST	EGOTISING	EIGHTHS
EFFERENCE	EFS	EGGING	EGOTISM	EIGHTIES
EFFERENT	EFT	EGGLER	EGOTISMS	EIGHTIETH
EFFERENTS	EFTEST	EGGLERS	EGOTIST	EIGHTS
EFFERES	EFTS	EGGLESS	EGOTISTIC	EIGHTSMAN
EFFERING	EFTSOON	EGGLIKE	EGOTISTS	EIGHTSMEN
EFFETE	EFTSOONS	EGGMASS	EGOTIZE	EIGHTSOME
EFFETELY	EGAD	EGGMASSES	EGOTIZED	EIGHTVO
EFFICACY	EGADS	EGGNOG	EGOTIZES	EIGHTVOS
EFFICIENT	EGAL	EGGNOGS	EGOTIZING	EIGHTY
EFFIERCE	EGALITE	EGGPLANT	EGREGIOUS	EIGNE
EFFIERCED	EGALITES	EGGPLANTS	EGRESS	EIK
EFFIERCES	EGALITIES	EGGS	EGRESSED	EIKED
EFFIGIAL	EGALITY	EGGSHELL	EGRESSES	EIKING
EFFIGIES	EGALLY	EGGSHELLS	EGRESSING	EIKON
EFFIGY	EGAREMENT	EGGWASH	EGRESSION	EIKONES
EFFING	EGENCE	EGGWASHES	EGRESSIVE	EIKONS
EFFINGS	EGENCES	EGGWHISK	EGRET	EIKS
EFFLUENCE	EGENCIES	EGGWHISKS	EGRETS	EILD
EFFLUENT	EGENCY	EGGY	EGYPTIAN	EILDING
EFFLUENTS	EGER	EGIS	EGYPTIANS	EILDINGS
EFFLUVIA	EGERS	EGISES	EH	EILDS
EFFLUVIAL	EGEST	EGLANTINE	EHED	EINA
EFFLUVIUM	EGESTA	EGLATERE	EHING	EINE
EFFLUX	EGESTED	EGLATERES	EHS	EINKORN
EFFLUXES	EGESTING	EGLOMISE	EIDE	EINKORNS
EFFLUXION	EGESTION	EGLOMISES	EIDENT	EINSTEIN
EFFORCE	EGESTIONS	EGMA	EIDER	EINSTEINS
EFFORCED	EGESTIVE	EGMAS	EIDERDOWN	EIRACK
EFFORCES	EGESTS	EGO	EIDERS	EIRACKS
EFFORCING	EGG	EGOISM	EIDETIC	EIRENIC

EIRENICAL	EKWELES	ELATION	ELECTRETS	ELENCHS
EIRENICON	EL	ELATIONS	ELECTRIC	ELENCHTIC
EIRENICS	ELABORATE	ELATIVE	ELECTRICS	ELENCHUS
EISEGESES	ELAEAGNUS	ELATIVES	ELECTRIFY	ELENCTIC
EISEGESIS	ELAEOLITE	ELBOW	ELECTRISE	ELEOPTENE
EISEL	ELAIN	ELBOWED	ELECTRIZE	ELEPHANT
EISELL	ELAINS	ELBOWING	ELECTRO	ELEPHANTS
EISELLS	ELAIOSOME	ELBOWINGS	ELECTRODE	ELEPIDOTE
EISELS	ELAN	ELBOWROOM	ELECTROED	ELEUTHERI
EISH	ELANCE	ELBOWS	ELECTRON	ELEVATE
EISWEIN	ELANCED	ELCHEE	ELECTRONS	ELEVATED
EISWEINS	ELANCES	ELCHEES	ELECTROS	ELEVATEDS
EITHER	ELANCING	ELCHI	ELECTRUM	ELEVATES
EJACULATE	ELAND	ELCHIS	ELECTRUMS	ELEVATING
EJECT	ELANDS	ELD	ELECTS	ELEVATION
EJECTA	ELANET	ELDER	ELECTUARY	ELEVATOR
EJECTABLE	ELANETS	ELDERCARE	ELEDOISIN	ELEVATORS
EJECTED	ELANS	ELDERLIES	ELEGANCE	ELEVATORY
EJECTING	ELAPHINE	ELDERLY	ELEGANCES	ELEVEN
EJECTION	ELAPID	ELDERS	ELEGANCY	ELEVENS
EJECTIONS	ELAPIDS	ELDERSHIP	ELEGANT	ELEVENSES
EJECTIVE	ELAPINE	ELDEST	ELEGANTLY	ELEVENTH
EJECTIVES	ELAPSE	ELDESTS	ELEGIAC	ELEVENTHS
EJECTMENT	ELAPSED	ELDIN	ELEGIACAL	ELEVON
EJECTOR	ELAPSES	ELDING	ELEGIACS	ELEVONS
EJECTORS	ELAPSING	ELDINGS	ELEGIAST	ELF
EJECTS	ELASTANCE	ELDINS	ELEGIASTS	ELFED
EJIDO	ELASTANE	ELDORADO	ELEGIES	ELFHOOD
EJIDOS	ELASTANES	ELDORADOS	ELEGISE	ELFHOODS
EKE	ELASTASE	ELDRESS	ELEGISED	ELFIN
EKED	ELASTASES	ELDRESSES	ELEGISES	ELFING
EKES	ELASTIC	ELDRICH	ELEGISING	ELFINS
EKING	ELASTICS	ELDRITCH	ELEGIST	ELFISH
EKISTIC	ELASTIN	ELDS	ELEGISTS	ELFISHES
EKISTICAL	ELASTINS	ELECT	ELEGIT	ELFISHLY
EKISTICS	ELASTOMER	ELECTABLE	ELEGITS	ELFLAND
EKKA	ELATE	ELECTED	ELEGIZE	ELFLANDS
EKKAS	ELATED	ELECTEE	ELEGIZED	ELFLIKE
EKLOGITE	ELATEDLY	ELECTEES	ELEGIZES	ELFLOCK
EKLOGITES	ELATER	ELECTING	ELEGIZING	ELFLOCKS
EKPHRASES	ELATERID	ELECTION	ELEGY	ELFS
EKPHRASIS	ELATERIDS	ELECTIONS	ELEMENT	ELHI
EKPWELE	ELATERIN	ELECTIVE	ELEMENTAL	ELIAD
EKPWELES	ELATERINS	ELECTIVES	ELEMENTS	ELIADS
EKTEXINE	ELATERITE	ELECTOR	ELEMI	ELICHE
EKTEXINES	ELATERIUM	ELECTORAL	ELEMIS	ELICHES
EKUELE	ELATERS	ELECTORS	ELENCH	ELICIT
EKUELES	ELATES	ELECTRESS	ELENCHI	ELICITED
EKWELE	ELATING	ELECTRET	ELENCHIC	ELICITING

E

ELICITOR	ELMY	ELSEWISE	ELVER	EMBALL
ELICITORS	ELOCUTE	ELSHIN	ELVERS	EMBALLED
ELICITS	ELOCUTED	ELSHINS	ELVES	EMBALLING
ELIDE	ELOCUTES	ELSIN	ELVISH	EMBALLS
ELIDED	ELOCUTING	ELSINS	ELVISHES	EMBALM
ELIDES	ELOCUTION	ELT	ELVISHLY	EMBALMED
ELIDIBLE	ELOCUTORY	ELTCHI	ELYSIAN	EMBALMER
ELIDING	ELODEA	ELTCHIS	ELYTRA	EMBALMERS
ELIGIBLE	ELODEAS	ELTS	ELYTRAL	EMBALMING
ELIGIBLES	ELOGE	ELUANT	ELYTROID	EMBALMS
ELIGIBLY	ELOGES	ELUANTS	ELYTRON	EMBANK
ELIMINANT	ELOGIES	ELUATE	ELYTROUS	EMBANKED
ELIMINATE	ELOGIST	ELUATES	ELYTRUM	EMBANKER
ELINT	ELOGISTS	ELUCIDATE	EM	EMBANKERS
ELINTS	ELOGIUM	ELUDE	EMACIATE	EMBANKING
ELISION	ELOGIUMS	ELUDED	EMACIATED	EMBANKS
ELISIONS	ELOGY	ELUDER	EMACIATES	EMBAR
ELITE	ELOIGN	ELUDERS	EMACS	EMBARGO
ELITES	ELOIGNED	ELUDES	EMACSEN	EMBARGOED
ELITISM	ELOIGNER	ELUDIBLE	EMAIL	EMBARGOES
ELITISMS	ELOIGNERS	ELUDING	EMAILABLE	EMBARK
ELITIST	ELOIGNING	ELUENT	EMAILED	EMBARKED
ELITISTS	ELOIGNS	ELUENTS	EMAILER	EMBARKING
ELIXIR	ELOIN	ELUSION	EMAILERS	EMBARKS
ELIXIRS	ELOINED	ELUSIONS	EMAILING	EMBARRAS
ELK	ELOINER	ELUSIVE	EMAILINGS	EMBARRASS
ELKHORN	ELOINERS	ELUSIVELY	EMAILS	EMBARRED
ELKHOUND	ELOINING	ELUSORY	EMANANT	EMBARRING
ELKHOUNDS	ELOINMENT	ELUTE	EMANATE	EMBARS
ELKS	ELOINS	ELUTED	EMANATED	EMBASE
ELL	ELONGATE	ELUTES	EMANATES	EMBASED
ELLAGIC	ELONGATED	ELUTING	EMANATING	EMBASES
ELLIPSE	ELONGATES	ELUTION	EMANATION	EMBASING
ELLIPSES	ELOPE	ELUTIONS	EMANATIST	EMBASSADE
ELLIPSIS	ELOPED	ELUTOR	EMANATIVE	EMBASSAGE
ELLIPSOID	ELOPEMENT	ELUTORS	EMANATOR	EMBASSIES
ELLIPTIC	ELOPER	ELUTRIATE	EMANATORS	EMBASSY
ELLOPS	ELOPERS	ELUVIA	EMANATORY	EMBASTE
ELLOPSES	ELOPES	ELUVIAL	EMBACE	EMBATHE
ELLS	ELOPING	ELUVIATE	EMBACES	EMBATHED
ELLWAND	ELOPS	ELUVIATED	EMBACING	EMBATHES
ELLWANDS	ELOPSES	ELUVIATES	EMBAIL	EMBATHING
ELM	ELOQUENCE	ELUVIUM	EMBAILED	EMBATTLE
ELMEN	ELOQUENT	ELUVIUMS	EMBAILING	EMBATTLED
ELMIER	ELPEE	ELVAN	EMBAILS	EMBATTLES
ELMIEST	ELPEES	ELVANITE	EMBALE	EMBAY
ELMS	ELS	ELVANITES	EMBALED	EMBAYED
ELMWOOD	ELSE	ELVANS	EMBALES	EMBAYING
ELMWOODS	ELSEWHERE	ELVEN	EMBALING	EMBAYLD

EMBAYMENT	EMBOGS	EMBOWELS	EMBRUES	EMENDING
EMBAYS	EMBOGUE	EMBOWER	EMBRUING	EMENDS
EMBED	EMBOGUED	EMBOWERED	EMBRUTE	EMERALD
EMBEDDED	EMBOGUES	EMBOWERS	EMBRUTED	EMERALDS
EMBEDDING	EMBOGUING	EMBOWING	EMBRUTES	EMERAUDE
EMBEDMENT	EMBOIL	EMBOWMENT	EMBRUTING	EMERAUDES
EMBEDS	EMBOILED	EMBOWS	EMBRYO	EMERG
EMBELLISH	EMBOILING	EMBOX	EMBRYOID	EMERGE
EMBER	EMBOILS	EMBOXED	EMBRYOIDS	EMERGED
EMBERS	EMBOLDEN	EMBOXES	EMBRYON	EMERGENCE
EMBEZZLE	EMBOLDENS	EMBOXING	EMBRYONAL	EMERGENCY
EMBEZZLED	EMBOLI	EMBRACE	EMBRYONIC	EMERGENT
EMBEZZLER	EMBOLIC	EMBRACED	EMBRYONS	EMERGENTS
EMBEZZLES	EMBOLIES	EMBRACEOR	EMBRYOS	EMERGES
EMBIGGEN	EMBOLISE	EMBRACER	EMBRYOTIC	EMERGING
EMBIGGENS	EMBOLISED	EMBRACERS	EMBUS	EMERGS
EMBITTER	EMBOLISES	EMBRACERY	EMBUSED	EMERIED
EMBITTERS	EMBOLISM	EMBRACES	EMBUSES	EMERIES
EMBLAZE	EMBOLISMS	EMBRACING	EMBUSIED	EMERITA
EMBLAZED	EMBOLIZE	EMBRACIVE	EMBUSIES	EMERITAE
EMBLAZER	EMBOLIZED	EMBRAID	EMBUSING	EMERITAS
EMBLAZERS	EMBOLIZES	EMBRAIDED	EMBUSQUE	EMERITI
EMBLAZES	EMBOLUS	EMBRAIDS	EMBUSQUES	EMERITUS
EMBLAZING	EMBOLUSES	EMBRANGLE	EMBUSSED	EMEROD
EMBLAZON	EMBOLY	EMBRASOR	EMBUSSES	EMERODS
EMBLAZONS	EMBORDER	EMBRASORS	EMBUSSING	EMEROID
EMBLEM	EMBORDERS	EMBRASURE	EMBUSY	EMEROIDS
EMBLEMA	EMBOSCATA	EMBRAVE	EMBUSYING	EMERSE
EMBLEMATA	EMBOSK	EMBRAVED	EMCEE	EMERSED
EMBLEMED	EMBOSKED	EMBRAVES	EMCEED	EMERSION
EMBLEMING	EMBOSKING	EMBRAVING	EMCEEING	EMERSIONS
EMBLEMISE	EMBOSKS	EMBRAZURE	EMCEES	EMERY
EMBLEMIZE	EMBOSOM	EMBREAD	EMDASH	EMERYING
EMBLEMS	EMBOSOMED	EMBREADED	EMDASHES	EMES
EMBLIC	EMBOSOMS	EMBREADS	EME	EMESES
EMBLICS	EMBOSS	EMBREATHE	EMEER	EMESIS
EMBLOOM	EMBOSSED	EMBRITTLE	EMEERATE	EMESISES
EMBLOOMED	EMBOSSER	EMBROCATE	EMEERATES	EMETIC
EMBLOOMS	EMBOSSERS	EMBROGLIO	EMEERS	EMETICAL
EMBLOSSOM	EMBOSSES	EMBROIDER	EMEND	EMETICS
EMBODIED	EMBOSSING	EMBROIL	EMENDABLE	EMETIN
EMBODIER	EMBOST	EMBROILED	EMENDALS	EMETINE
EMBODIERS	EMBOUND	EMBROILER	EMENDATE	EMETINES
EMBODIES	EMBOUNDED	EMBROILS	EMENDATED	EMETINS
EMBODY	EMBOUNDS	EMBROWN	EMENDATES	EMEU
EMBODYING	EMBOW	EMBROWNED	EMENDATOR	EMEUS
EMBOG	EMBOWED	EMBROWNS	EMENDED	EMEUTE
EMBOGGED	EMBOWEL	EMBRUE	EMENDER	EMEUTES
EMBOGGING	EMBOWELED	EMBRUED	EMENDERS	EMIC

EMICANT	EMMESHED	EMOVING	EMPENNAGE	EMPLASTER
EMICATE	EMMESHES	EMPACKET	EMPEOPLE	EMPLASTIC
EMICATED	EMMESHING	EMPACKETS	EMPEOPLED	EMPLASTRA
EMICATES	EMMET	EMPAESTIC	EMPEOPLES	EMPLEACH
EMICATING	EMMETROPE	EMPAIRE	EMPERCE	EMPLECTON
EMICATION	EMMETS	EMPAIRED	EMPERCED	EMPLECTUM
EMICS	EMMEW	EMPAIRES	EMPERCES	EMPLONGE
EMICTION	EMMEWED	EMPAIRING	EMPERCING	EMPLONGED
EMICTIONS	EMMEWING	EMPALE	EMPERIES	EMPLONGES
EMICTORY	EMMEWS	EMPALED	EMPERISE	EMPLOY
EMIGRANT	EMMOVE	EMPALER	EMPERISED	EMPLOYE
EMIGRANTS	EMMOVED	EMPALERS	EMPERISES	EMPLOYED
EMIGRATE	EMMOVES	EMPALES	EMPERISH	EMPLOYEE
EMIGRATED	EMMOVING	EMPALING	EMPERIZE	EMPLOYEES
EMIGRATES	EMMY	EMPANADA	EMPERIZED	EMPLOYER
EMIGRE	EMMYS	EMPANADAS	EMPERIZES	EMPLOYERS
EMIGREE	EMO	EMPANEL	EMPEROR	EMPLOYES
EMIGREES	EMOCORE	EMPANELED	EMPERORS	EMPLOYING
EMIGRES	EMOCORES	EMPANELS	EMPERY	EMPLOYS
EMINENCE	EMODIN	EMPANOPLY	EMPHASES	EMPLUME
EMINENCES	EMODINS	EMPARE	EMPHASIS	EMPLUMED
EMINENCY	EMOJI	EMPARED	EMPHASISE	EMPLUMES
EMINENT	EMOJIS	EMPARES	EMPHASIZE	EMPLUMING
EMINENTLY	EMOLLIATE	EMPARING	EMPHATIC	EMPOISON
EMIR	EMOLLIENT	EMPARL	EMPHATICS	EMPOISONS
EMIRATE	EMOLUMENT	EMPARLED	EMPHLYSES	EMPOLDER
EMIRATES	EMONG	EMPARLING	EMPHLYSIS	EMPOLDERS
EMIRS	EMONGES	EMPARLS	EMPHYSEMA	EMPORIA
EMISSARY	EMONGEST	EMPART	EMPIERCE	EMPORIUM
EMISSILE	EMONGST	EMPARTED	EMPIERCED	EMPORIUMS
EMISSION	EMOS	EMPARTING	EMPIERCES	EMPOWER
EMISSIONS	EMOTE	EMPARTS	EMPIGHT	EMPOWERED
EMISSIVE	EMOTED	EMPATH	EMPIGHTED	EMPOWERS
EMIT	EMOTER	EMPATHIC	EMPIGHTS	EMPRESS
EMITS	EMOTERS	EMPATHIES	EMPING	EMPRESSE
EMITTANCE	EMOTES	EMPATHISE	EMPINGS	EMPRESSES
EMITTED	EMOTICON	EMPATHIST	EMPIRE	EMPRISE
EMITTER	EMOTICONS	EMPATHIZE	EMPIRES	EMPRISES
EMITTERS	EMOTING	EMPATHS	EMPIRIC	EMPRIZE
EMITTING	EMOTION	EMPATHY	EMPIRICAL	EMPRIZES
EMLETS	EMOTIONAL	EMPATRON	EMPIRICS	EMPT
EMMA	EMOTIONS	EMPATRONS	EMPLACE	EMPTED
EMMARBLE	EMOTIVE	EMPAYRE	EMPLACED	EMPTIABLE
EMMARBLED	EMOTIVELY	EMPAYRED	EMPLACES	EMPTIED
EMMARBLES	EMOTIVISM	EMPAYRES	EMPLACING	EMPTIER
EMMAS	EMOTIVITY	EMPAYRING	EMPLANE	EMPTIERS
EMMER	EMOVE	EMPEACH	EMPLANED	EMPTIES
EMMERS	EMOVED	EMPEACHED	EMPLANES	EMPTIEST
EMMESH	EMOVES	EMPEACHES	EMPLANING	EMPTILY

EMPTINESS	EMULING	ENACTURE	ENCALMING	ENCHEASON
EMPTING	EMULOUS	ENACTURES	ENCALMS	ENCHEER
EMPTINGS	EMULOUSLY	ENALAPRIL	ENCAMP	ENCHEERED
EMPTINS	EMULSIBLE	ENALLAGE	ENCAMPED	ENCHEERS
EMPTION	EMULSIFY	ENALLAGES	ENCAMPING	ENCHILADA
EMPTIONAL	EMULSIN	ENAMEL	ENCAMPS	ENCHORIAL
EMPTIONS	EMULSINS	ENAMELED	ENCANTHIS	ENCHORIC
EMPTS	EMULSION	ENAMELER	ENCAPSULE	ENCIERRO
EMPTY	EMULSIONS	ENAMELERS	ENCARPUS	ENCIERROS
EMPTYING	EMULSIVE	ENAMELING	ENCASE	ENCINA
EMPTYINGS	EMULSOID	ENAMELIST	ENCASED	ENCINAL
EMPTYSES	EMULSOIDS	ENAMELLED	ENCASES	ENCINAS
EMPTYSIS	EMULSOR	ENAMELLER	ENCASH	ENCIPHER
EMPURPLE	EMULSORS	ENAMELS	ENCASHED	ENCIPHERS
EMPURPLED	EMUNCTION	ENAMINE	ENCASHES	ENCIRCLE
EMPURPLES	EMUNCTORY	ENAMINES	ENCASHING	ENCIRCLED
EMPUSA	EMUNGE	ENAMOR	ENCASING	ENCIRCLES
EMPUSAS	EMUNGED	ENAMORADO	ENCASTRE	ENCLASP
EMPUSE	EMUNGES	ENAMORED	ENCAUSTIC	ENCLASPED
EMPUSES	EMUNGING	ENAMORING	ENCAVE	ENCLASPS
EMPYEMA	EMURE	ENAMORS	ENCAVED	ENCLAVE
EMPYEMAS	EMURED	ENAMOUR	ENCAVES	ENCLAVED
EMPYEMATA	EMURES	ENAMOURED	ENCAVING	ENCLAVES
EMPYEMIC	EMURING	ENAMOURS	ENCEINTE	ENCLAVING
EMPYESES	EMUS	ENANTHEMA	ENCEINTES	ENCLISES
EMPYESIS	EMYD	ENARCH	ENCEPHALA	ENCLISIS
EMPYREAL	EMYDE	ENARCHED	ENCHAFE	ENCLITIC
EMPYREAN	EMYDES	ENARCHES	ENCHAFED	ENCLITICS
EMPYREANS	EMYDS	ENARCHING	ENCHAFES	ENCLOSE
EMPYREUMA	EMYS	ENARGITE	ENCHAFING	ENCLOSED
EMS	EN	ENARGITES	ENCHAIN	ENCLOSER
EMU	ENABLE	ENARM	ENCHAINED	ENCLOSERS
EMULATE	ENABLED	ENARMED	ENCHAINS	ENCLOSES
EMULATED	ENABLER	ENARMING	ENCHANT	ENCLOSING
EMULATES	ENABLERS	ENARMS	ENCHANTED	ENCLOSURE
EMULATING	ENABLES	ENATE	ENCHANTER	ENCLOTHE
EMULATION	ENABLING	ENATES	ENCHANTS	ENCLOTHED
EMULATIVE	ENACT	ENATIC	ENCHARGE	ENCLOTHES
EMULATOR	ENACTABLE	ENATION	ENCHARGED	ENCLOUD
EMULATORS	ENACTED	ENATIONS	ENCHARGES	ENCLOUDED
EMULE	ENACTING	ENAUNTER	ENCHARM	ENCLOUDS
EMULED	ENACTION	ENCAENIA	ENCHARMED	ENCODABLE
EMULES	ENACTIONS	ENCAENIAS	ENCHARMS	ENCODE
EMULGE	ENACTIVE	ENCAGE	ENCHASE	ENCODED
EMULGED	ENACTMENT	ENCAGED	ENCHASED	ENCODER
EMULGENCE	ENACTOR	ENCAGES	ENCHASER	ENCODERS
EMULGENT	ENACTORS	ENCAGING	ENCHASERS	ENCODES
EMULGES	ENACTORY	ENCALM	ENCHASES	ENCODING
EMULGING	ENACTS	ENCALMED	ENCHASING	ENCODINGS

ENCOLOR	ENCYSTS	ENDEWED	ENDOMORPH	ENDOZOA
ENCOLORED	END	ENDEWING	ENDONYM	ENDOZOIC
ENCOLORS	ENDAMAGE	ENDEWS	ENDONYMS	ENDOZOON
ENCOLOUR	ENDAMAGED	ENDEXINE	ENDOPHAGY	ENDPAPER
ENCOLOURS	ENDAMAGES	ENDEXINES	ENDOPHYTE	ENDPAPERS
ENCOLPIA	ENDAMEBA	ENDGAME	ENDOPLASM	ENDPLATE
ENCOLPION	ENDAMEBAE	ENDGAMES	ENDOPOD	ENDPLATES
ENCOLPIUM	ENDAMEBAS	ENDGATE	ENDOPODS	ENDPLAY
ENCOLURE	ENDAMEBIC	ENDGATES	ENDOPROCT	ENDPLAYED
ENCOLURES	ENDAMOEBA	ENDING	ENDORPHIN	ENDPLAYS
ENCOMIA	ENDANGER	ENDINGS	ENDORSE	ENDPOINT
ENCOMIAST	ENDANGERS	ENDIRON	ENDORSED	ENDPOINTS
ENCOMION	ENDARCH	ENDIRONS	ENDORSEE	ENDRIN
ENCOMIUM	ENDARCHY	ENDITE	ENDORSEES	ENDRINS
ENCOMIUMS	ENDART	ENDITED	ENDORSER	ENDS
ENCOMPASS	ENDARTED	ENDITES	ENDORSERS	ENDSHIP
ENCORE	ENDARTING	ENDITING	ENDORSES	ENDSHIPS
ENCORED	ENDARTS	ENDIVE	ENDORSING	ENDUE
ENCORES	ENDASH	ENDIVES	ENDORSIVE	ENDUED
ENCORING	ENDASHES	ENDLANG	ENDORSOR	ENDUES
ENCOUNTER	ENDBRAIN	ENDLEAF	ENDORSORS	ENDUING
ENCOURAGE	ENDBRAINS	ENDLEAFS	ENDOSARC	ENDUNGEON
ENCRADLE	ENDCAP	ENDLEAVES	ENDOSARCS	ENDURABLE
ENCRADLED	ENDCAPS	ENDLESS	ENDOSCOPE	ENDURABLY
ENCRADLES	ENDEAR	ENDLESSLY	ENDOSCOPY	ENDURANCE
ENCRATIES	ENDEARED	ENDLONG	ENDOSMOS	ENDURE
ENCRATY	ENDEARING	ENDMOST	ENDOSMOSE	ENDURED
ENCREASE	ENDEARS	ENDNOTE	ENDOSOME	ENDURER
ENCREASED	ENDEAVOR	ENDNOTES	ENDOSOMES	ENDURERS
ENCREASES	ENDEAVORS	ENDOBLAST	ENDOSPERM	ENDURES
ENCRIMSON	ENDEAVOUR	ENDOCARP	ENDOSPORE	ENDURING
ENCRINAL	ENDECAGON	ENDOCARPS	ENDOSS	ENDURO
ENCRINIC	ENDED	ENDOCAST	ENDOSSED	ENDUROS
ENCRINITE	ENDEICTIC	ENDOCASTS	ENDOSSES	ENDWAYS
ENCROACH	ENDEIXES	ENDOCRINE	ENDOSSING	ENDWISE
ENCRUST	ENDEIXIS	ENDOCYTIC	ENDOSTEA	ENDYSES
ENCRUSTED	ENDEMIAL	ENDODERM	ENDOSTEAL	ENDYSIS
ENCRUSTS	ENDEMIC	ENDODERMS	ENDOSTEUM	ENDZONE
ENCRYPT	ENDEMICAL	ENDODYNE	ENDOSTYLE	ENDZONES
ENCRYPTED	ENDEMICS	ENDOERGIC	ENDOTHERM	ENE
ENCRYPTS	ENDEMISM	ENDOGAMIC	ENDOTOXIC	ENEMA
ENCUMBER	ENDEMISMS	ENDOGAMY	ENDOTOXIN	ENEMAS
ENCUMBERS	ENDENIZEN	ENDOGEN	ENDOW	ENEMATA
ENCURTAIN	ENDER	ENDOGENIC	ENDOWED	ENEMIES
ENCYCLIC	ENDERMIC	ENDOGENS	ENDOWER	ENEMY
ENCYCLICS	ENDERON	ENDOGENY	ENDOWERS	ENERGETIC
ENCYST	ENDERONS	ENDOLYMPH	ENDOWING	ENERGIC
ENCYSTED	ENDERS	ENDOMIXES	ENDOWMENT	ENERGID
ENCYSTING	ENDEW	ENDOMIXIS	ENDOWS	ENERGIDS

ENERGIES	ENFILADE	ENFREEZES	ENGLOBED	ENGRAVED
ENERGISE	ENFILADED	ENFROSEN	ENGLOBES	ENGRAVEN
ENERGISED	ENFILADES	ENFROZE	ENGLOBING	ENGRAVER
ENERGISER	ENFILED	ENFROZEN	ENGLOOM	ENGRAVERS
ENERGISES	ENFIRE	ENG	ENGLOOMED	ENGRAVERY
ENERGIZE	ENFIRED	ENGAGE	ENGLOOMS	ENGRAVES
ENERGIZED	ENFIRES	ENGAGED	ENGLUT	ENGRAVING
ENERGIZER	ENFIRING	ENGAGEDLY	ENGLUTS	ENGRENAGE
ENERGIZES	ENFIX	ENGAGEE	ENGLUTTED	ENGRIEVE
ENERGUMEN	ENFIXED	ENGAGER	ENGOBE	ENGRIEVED
ENERGY	ENFIXES	ENGAGERS	ENGOBES	ENGRIEVES
ENERVATE	ENFIXING	ENGAGES	ENGORE	ENGROOVE
ENERVATED	ENFLAME	ENGAGING	ENGORED	ENGROOVED
ENERVATES	ENFLAMED	ENGAOL	ENGORES	ENGROOVES
ENERVATOR	ENFLAMES	ENGAOLED	ENGORGE	ENGROSS
ENERVE	ENFLAMING	ENGAOLING	ENGORGED	ENGROSSED
ENERVED	ENFLESH	ENGAOLS	ENGORGES	ENGROSSER
ENERVES	ENFLESHED	ENGARLAND	ENGORGING	ENGROSSES
ENERVING	ENFLESHES	ENGENDER	ENGORING	ENGS
ENES	ENFLOWER	ENGENDERS	ENGOULED	ENGUARD
ENEW	ENFLOWERS	ENGENDURE	ENGOUMENT	ENGUARDED
ENEWED	ENFOLD	ENGILD	ENGRACE	ENGUARDS
ENEWING	ENFOLDED	ENGILDED	ENGRACED	ENGULF
ENEWS	ENFOLDER	ENGILDING	ENGRACES	ENGULFED
ENFACE	ENFOLDERS	ENGILDS	ENGRACING	ENGULFING
ENFACED	ENFOLDING	ENGILT	ENGRAFF	ENGULFS
ENFACES	ENFOLDS	ENGINE	ENGRAFFED	ENGULPH
ENFACING	ENFORCE	ENGINED	ENGRAFFS	ENGULPHED
ENFANT	ENFORCED	ENGINEER	ENGRAFT	ENGULPHS
ENFANTS	ENFORCER	ENGINEERS	ENGRAFTED	ENGYSCOPE
ENFEEBLE	ENFORCERS	ENGINER	ENGRAFTS	ENHALO
ENFEEBLED	ENFORCES	ENGINERS	ENGRAIL	ENHALOED
ENFEEBLER	ENFORCING	ENGINERY	ENGRAILED	ENHALOES
ENFEEBLES	ENFOREST	ENGINES	ENGRAILS	ENHALOING
ENFELON	ENFORESTS	ENGINING	ENGRAIN	ENHALOS
ENFELONED	ENFORM	ENGINOUS	ENGRAINED	ENHANCE
ENFELONS	ENFORMED	ENGIRD	ENGRAINER	ENHANCED
ENFEOFF	ENFORMING	ENGIRDED	ENGRAINS	ENHANCER
ENFEOFFED	ENFORMS	ENGIRDING	ENGRAM	ENHANCERS
ENFEOFFS	ENFRAME	ENGIRDLE	ENGRAMMA	ENHANCES
ENFESTED	ENFRAMED	ENGIRDLED	ENGRAMMAS	ENHANCING
ENFETTER	ENFRAMES	ENGIRDLES	ENGRAMME	ENHANCIVE
ENFETTERS	ENFRAMING	ENGIRDS	ENGRAMMES	ENHEARSE
ENFEVER	ENFREE	ENGIRT	ENGRAMMIC	ENHEARSED
ENFEVERED	ENFREED	ENGLACIAL	ENGRAMS	ENHEARSES
ENFEVERS	ENFREEDOM	ENGLISH	ENGRASP	ENHEARTEN
ENFIERCE	ENFREEING	ENGLISHED	ENGRASPED	ENHUNGER
ENFIERCED	ENFREES	ENGLISHES	ENGRASPS	ENHUNGERS
ENFIERCES	ENFREEZE	ENGLOBE	ENGRAVE	ENHYDRITE

ENHYDROS	ENLARGENS	ENNAGE	ENOUNCED	ENRHEUMS
ENHYDROUS	ENLARGER	ENNAGES	ENOUNCES	ENRICH
ENIAC	ENLARGERS	ENNEAD	ENOUNCING	ENRICHED
ENIACS	ENLARGES	ENNEADIC	ENOW	ENRICHER
ENIGMA	ENLARGING	ENNEADS	ENOWS	ENRICHERS
ENIGMAS	ENLEVE	ENNEAGON	ENPLANE	ENRICHES
ENIGMATA	ENLIGHT	ENNEAGONS	ENPLANED	ENRICHING
ENIGMATIC	ENLIGHTED	ENNEAGRAM	ENPLANES	ENRIDGED
ENISLE	ENLIGHTEN	ENNOBLE	ENPLANING	ENRING
ENISLED	ENLIGHTS	ENNOBLED	ENPRINT	ENRINGED
ENISLES	ENLINK	ENNOBLER	ENPRINTS	ENRINGING
ENISLING	ENLINKED	ENNOBLERS	ENQUEUE	ENRINGS
ENJAMB	ENLINKING	ENNOBLES	ENQUEUED	ENRIVEN
ENJAMBED	ENLINKS	ENNOBLING	ENQUEUES	ENROBE
ENJAMBING	ENLIST	ENNOG	ENQUEUING	ENROBED
ENJAMBS	ENLISTED	ENNOGS	ENQUIRE	ENROBER
ENJOIN	ENLISTEE	ENNUI	ENQUIRED	ENROBERS
ENJOINDER	ENLISTEES	ENNUIED	ENQUIRER	ENROBES
ENJOINED	ENLISTER	ENNUIS	ENQUIRERS	ENROBING
ENJOINER	ENLISTERS	ENNUYE	ENQUIRES	ENROL
ENJOINERS	ENLISTING	ENNUYED	ENQUIRIES	ENROLL
ENJOINING	ENLISTS	ENNUYEE	ENQUIRING	ENROLLED
ENJOINS	ENLIT	ENNUYING	ENQUIRY	ENROLLEE
ENJOY	ENLIVEN	ENODAL	ENRACE	ENROLLEES
ENJOYABLE	ENLIVENED	ENOKI	ENRACED	ENROLLER
ENJOYABLY	ENLIVENER	ENOKIDAKE	ENRACES	ENROLLERS
ENJOYED	ENLIVENS	ENOKIS	ENRACING	ENROLLING
ENJOYER	ENLOCK	ENOKITAKE	ENRAGE	ENROLLS
ENJOYERS	ENLOCKED	ENOL	ENRAGED	ENROLMENT
ENJOYING	ENLOCKING	ENOLASE	ENRAGEDLY	ENROLS
ENJOYMENT	ENLOCKS	ENOLASES	ENRAGES	ENROOT
ENJOYS	ENLUMINE	ENOLIC	ENRAGING	ENROOTED
ENKERNEL	ENLUMINED	ENOLOGIES	ENRANCKLE	ENROOTING
ENKERNELS	ENLUMINES	ENOLOGIST	ENRANGE	ENROOTS
ENKINDLE	ENMESH	ENOLOGY	ENRANGED	ENROUGH
ENKINDLED	ENMESHED	ENOLS	ENRANGES	ENROUGHED
ENKINDLER	ENMESHES	ENOMOTIES	ENRANGING	ENROUGHS
ENKINDLES	ENMESHING	ENOMOTY	ENRANK	ENROUND
ENLACE	ENMEW	ENOPHILE	ENRANKED	ENROUNDED
ENLACED	ENMEWED	ENOPHILES	ENRANKING	ENROUNDS
ENLACES	ENMEWING	ENORM	ENRANKS	ENS
ENLACING	ENMEWS	ENORMITY	ENRAPT	ENSAMPLE
ENLARD	ENMITIES	ENORMOUS	ENRAPTURE	ENSAMPLED
ENLARDED	ENMITY	ENOSES	ENRAUNGE	ENSAMPLES
ENLARDING	ENMOSSED	ENOSIS	ENRAUNGED	ENSATE
ENLARDS	ENMOVE	ENOSISES	ENRAUNGES	ENSCONCE
ENLARGE	ENMOVED	ENOUGH	ENRAVISH	ENSCONCED
ENLARGED	ENMOVES	ENOUGHS	ENRHEUM	ENSCONCES
ENLARGEN	ENMOVING	ENOUNCE	ENRHEUMED	ENSCROLL

ENSCROLLS	ENSILES	ENSURE	ENTERALLY	ENTITLING
ENSEAL	ENSILING	ENSURED	ENTERATE	ENTITY
ENSEALED	ENSKIED	ENSURER	ENTERED	ENTOBLAST
ENSEALING	ENSKIES	ENSURERS	ENTERER	ENTODERM
ENSEALS	ENSKY	ENSURES	ENTERERS	ENTODERMS
ENSEAM	ENSKYED	ENSURING	ENTERIC	ENTOIL
ENSEAMED	ENSKYING	ENSWATHE	ENTERICS	ENTOILED
ENSEAMING	ENSLAVE	ENSWATHED	ENTERING	ENTOILING
ENSEAMS	ENSLAVED	ENSWATHES	ENTERINGS	ENTOILS
ENSEAR	ENSLAVER	ENSWEEP	ENTERITIS	ENTOMB
ENSEARED	ENSLAVERS	ENSWEEPS	ENTERON	ENTOMBED
ENSEARING	ENSLAVES	ENSWEPT	ENTERONS	ENTOMBING
ENSEARS	ENSLAVING	ENTAIL	ENTERS	ENTOMBS
ENSEMBLE	ENSNARE	ENTAILED	ENTERTAIN	ENTOMIC
ENSEMBLES	ENSNARED	ENTAILER	ENTERTAKE	ENTOPHYTE
ENSERF	ENSNARER	ENTAILERS	ENTERTOOK	ENTOPIC
ENSERFED	ENSNARERS	ENTAILING	ENTETE	ENTOPROCT
ENSERFING	ENSNARES	ENTAILS	ENTETEE	ENTOPTIC
ENSERFS	ENSNARING	ENTAME	ENTHALPY	ENTOPTICS
ENSEW	ENSNARL	ENTAMEBA	ENTHEOGEN	ENTOTIC
ENSEWED	ENSNARLED	ENTAMEBAE	ENTHETIC	ENTOURAGE
ENSEWING	ENSNARLS	ENTAMEBAS	ENTHRAL	ENTOZOA
ENSEWS	ENSORCEL	ENTAMED	ENTHRALL	ENTOZOAL
ENSHEATH	ENSORCELL	ENTAMES	ENTHRALLS	ENTOZOAN
ENSHEATHE	ENSORCELS	ENTAMING	ENTHRALS	ENTOZOANS
ENSHEATHS	ENSOUL	ENTAMOEBA	ENTHRONE	ENTOZOIC
ENSHELL	ENSOULED	ENTANGLE	ENTHRONED	ENTOZOON
ENSHELLED	ENSOULING	ENTANGLED	ENTHRONES	ENTRAIL
ENSHELLS	ENSOULS	ENTANGLER	ENTHUSE	ENTRAILED
ENSHELTER	ENSPHERE	ENTANGLES	ENTHUSED	ENTRAILS
ENSHIELD	ENSPHERED	ENTASES	ENTHUSES	ENTRAIN
ENSHIELDS	ENSPHERES	ENTASIA	ENTHUSING	ENTRAINED
ENSHRINE	ENSTAMP	ENTASIAS	ENTHYMEME	ENTRAINER
ENSHRINED	ENSTAMPED	ENTASIS	ENTIA	ENTRAINS
ENSHRINEE	ENSTAMPS	ENTASTIC	ENTICE	ENTRALL
ENSHRINES	ENSTATITE	ENTAYLE	ENTICED	ENTRALLES
ENSHROUD	ENSTEEP	ENTAYLED	ENTICER	ENTRAMMEL
ENSHROUDS	ENSTEEPED	ENTAYLES	ENTICERS	ENTRANCE
ENSIFORM	ENSTEEPS	ENTAYLING	ENTICES	ENTRANCED
ENSIGN	ENSTYLE	ENTELECHY	ENTICING	ENTRANCES
ENSIGNCY	ENSTYLED	ENTELLUS	ENTICINGS	ENTRANT
ENSIGNED	ENSTYLES	ENTENDER	ENTIRE	ENTRANTS
ENSIGNING	ENSTYLING	ENTENDERS	ENTIRELY	ENTRAP
ENSIGNS	ENSUE	ENTENTE	ENTIRES	ENTRAPPED
ENSILAGE	ENSUED	ENTENTES	ENTIRETY	ENTRAPPER
ENSILAGED	ENSUES	ENTER	ENTITIES	ENTRAPS
ENSILAGES	ENSUING	ENTERA	ENTITLE	ENTREAT
ENSILE	ENSUITE	ENTERABLE	ENTITLED	ENTREATED
ENSILED	ENSUITES	ENTERAL	ENTITLES	ENTREATS

ENTREATY	ENURES	ENVOYS	EOLIAN	EPAULETS
ENTRECHAT	ENURESES	ENVOYSHIP	EOLIENNE	EPAULETTE
ENTRECOTE	ENURESIS	ENVY	EOLIENNES	EPAXIAL
ENTREE	ENURETIC	ENVYING	EOLIPILE	EPAZOTE
ENTREES	ENURETICS	ENVYINGLY	EOLIPILES	EPAZOTES
ENTREMES	ENURING	ENVYINGS	EOLITH	EPEDAPHIC
ENTREMETS	ENURN	ENWALL	EOLITHIC	EPEE
ENTRENCH	ENURNED	ENWALLED	EOLITHS	EPEEIST
ENTREPOT	ENURNING	ENWALLING	EOLOPILE	EPEEISTS
ENTREPOTS	ENURNS	ENWALLOW	EOLOPILES	EPEES
ENTRESOL	ENVASSAL	ENWALLOWS	EON	EPEIRA
ENTRESOLS	ENVASSALS	ENWALLS	EONIAN	EPEIRAS
ENTREZ	ENVAULT	ENWHEEL	EONISM	EPEIRIC
ENTRIES	ENVAULTED	ENWHEELED	EONISMS	EPEIRID
ENTRISM	ENVAULTS	ENWHEELS	EONS	EPEIRIDS
ENTRISMS	ENVEIGLE	ENWIND	EORL	EPENDYMA
ENTRIST	ENVEIGLED	ENWINDING	EORLS	EPENDYMAL
ENTRISTS	ENVEIGLES	ENWINDS	EOSIN	EPENDYMAS
ENTROLD	ENVELOP	ENWOMB	EOSINE	EPEOLATRY
ENTROPIC	ENVELOPE	ENWOMBED	EOSINES	EPERDU
ENTROPIES	ENVELOPED	ENWOMBING	EOSINIC	EPERDUE
ENTROPION	ENVELOPER	ENWOMBS	EOSINS	EPERGNE
ENTROPIUM	ENVELOPES	ENWOUND	EOTHEN	EPERGNES
ENTROPY	ENVELOPS	ENWRAP	EPACRID	EPHA
ENTRUST	ENVENOM	ENWRAPPED	EPACRIDS	EPHAH
ENTRUSTED	ENVENOMED	ENWRAPS	EPACRIS	EPHAHS
ENTRUSTS	ENVENOMS	ENWRAPT	EPACRISES	EPHAS
ENTRY	ENVERMEIL	ENWREATH	EPACT	EPHEBE
ENTRYISM	ENVIABLE	ENWREATHE	EPACTS	EPHEBES
ENTRYISMS	ENVIABLY	ENWREATHS	EPAENETIC	EPHEBI
ENTRYIST	ENVIED	ENZIAN	EPAGOGE	EPHEBIC
ENTRYISTS	ENVIER	ENZIANS	EPAGOGES	EPHEBOI
ENTRYWAY	ENVIERS	ENZONE	EPAGOGIC	EPHEBOS
ENTRYWAYS	ENVIES	ENZONED	EPANODOS	EPHEBUS
ENTS	ENVIOUS	ENZONES	EPARCH	EPHEDRA
ENTWINE	ENVIOUSLY	ENZONING	EPARCHATE	EPHEDRAS
ENTWINED	ENVIRO	ENZOOTIC	EPARCHIAL	EPHEDRIN
ENTWINES	ENVIRON	ENZOOTICS	EPARCHIES	EPHEDRINE
ENTWINING	ENVIRONED	ENZYM	EPARCHS	EPHEDRINS
ENTWIST	ENVIRONS	ENZYMATIC	EPARCHY	EPHELIDES
ENTWISTED	ENVIROS	ENZYME	EPATANT	EPHELIS
ENTWISTS	ENVISAGE	ENZYMES	EPATER	EPHEMERA
ENUCLEATE	ENVISAGED	ENZYMIC	EPATERED	EPHEMERAE
ENUF	ENVISAGES	ENZYMS	EPATERING	EPHEMERAL
ENUMERATE	ENVISION	EOAN	EPATERS	EPHEMERAS
ENUNCIATE	ENVISIONS	EOBIONT	EPAULE	EPHEMERID
ENURE	ENVOI	EOBIONTS	EPAULES	EPHEMERIS
ENURED	ENVOIS	EOCENE	EPAULET	EPHEMERON
ENUREMENT	ENVOY	EOHIPPUS	EPAULETED	EPHIALTES

EPHOD	EPICOTYL	EPIGONE	EPIMERIZE	EPISPERMS
EPHODS	EPICOTYLS	EPIGONES	EPIMERS	EPISPORE
EPHOR	EPICRANIA	EPIGONI	EPIMYSIA	EPISPORES
EPHORAL	EPICRISES	EPIGONIC	EPIMYSIUM	EPISTASES
EPHORALTY	EPICRISIS	EPIGONISM	EPINAOI	EPISTASIS
EPHORATE	EPICRITIC	EPIGONOUS	EPINAOS	EPISTASY
EPHORATES	EPICS	EPIGONS	EPINASTIC	EPISTATIC
EPHORI	EPICURE	EPIGONUS	EPINASTY	EPISTAXES
EPHORS	EPICUREAN	EPIGRAM	EPINEURAL	EPISTAXIS
EPIBIOSES	EPICURES	EPIGRAMS	EPINEURIA	EPISTEMIC
EPIBIOSIS	EPICURISE	EPIGRAPH	EPINICIAN	EPISTERNA
EPIBIOTIC	EPICURISM	EPIGRAPHS	EPINICION	EPISTLE
EPIBLAST	EPICURIZE	EPIGRAPHY	EPINIKIAN	EPISTLED
EPIBLASTS	EPICYCLE	EPIGYNA	EPINIKION	EPISTLER
EPIBLEM	EPICYCLES	EPIGYNE	EPINOSIC	EPISTLERS
EPIBLEMS	EPICYCLIC	EPIGYNES	EPIPHANIC	EPISTLES
EPIBOLIC	EPIDEMIC	EPIGYNIES	EPIPHANY	EPISTLING
EPIBOLIES	EPIDEMICS	EPIGYNOUS	EPIPHRAGM	EPISTOLER
EPIBOLY	EPIDERM	EPIGYNUM	EPIPHYSES	EPISTOLET
EPIC	EPIDERMAL	EPIGYNUMS	EPIPHYSIS	EPISTOLIC
EPICAL	EPIDERMIC	EPIGYNY	EPIPHYTAL	EPISTOME
EPICALLY	EPIDERMIS	EPILATE	EPIPHYTE	EPISTOMES
EPICALYX	EPIDERMS	EPILATED	EPIPHYTES	EPISTYLE
EPICANTHI	EPIDICTIC	EPILATES	EPIPHYTIC	EPISTYLES
EPICARDIA	EPIDOSITE	EPILATING	EPIPLOA	EPITAPH
EPICARP	EPIDOTE	EPILATION	EPIPLOIC	EPITAPHED
EPICARPS	EPIDOTES	EPILATOR	EPIPLOON	EPITAPHER
EPICEDE	EPIDOTIC	EPILATORS	EPIPLOONS	EPITAPHIC
EPICEDES	EPIDURAL	EPILEPSY	EPIPOLIC	EPITAPHS
EPICEDIA	EPIDURALS	EPILEPTIC	EPIPOLISM	EPITASES
EPICEDIAL	EPIFAUNA	EPILIMNIA	EPIROGENY	EPITASIS
EPICEDIAN	EPIFAUNAE	EPILITHIC	EPIRRHEMA	EPITAXES
EPICEDIUM	EPIFAUNAL	EPILOBIUM	EPISCIA	EPITAXIAL
EPICENE	EPIFAUNAS	EPILOG	EPISCIAS	EPITAXIC
EPICENES	EPIFOCAL	EPILOGIC	EPISCOPAL	EPITAXIES
EPICENISM	EPIGAEAL	EPILOGISE	EPISCOPE	EPITAXIS
EPICENTER	EPIGAEAN	EPILOGIST	EPISCOPES	EPITAXY
EPICENTRA	EPIGAEOUS	EPILOGIZE	EPISCOPY	EPITHECA
EPICENTRE	EPIGAMIC	EPILOGS	EPISEMON	EPITHECAE
EPICIER	EPIGEAL	EPILOGUE	EPISEMONS	EPITHELIA
EPICIERS	EPIGEAN	EPILOGUED	EPISODAL	EPITHEM
EPICISM	EPIGEIC	EPILOGUES	EPISODE	EPITHEMA
EPICISMS	EPIGENE	EPIMER	EPISODES	EPITHEMS
EPICIST	EPIGENIC	EPIMERASE	EPISODIAL	EPITHESES
EPICISTS	EPIGENIST	EPIMERE	EPISODIC	EPITHESIS
EPICLESES	EPIGENOME	EPIMERES	EPISOMAL	EPITHET
EPICLESIS	EPIGENOUS	EPIMERIC	EPISOME	EPITHETED
EPICLIKE	EPIGEOUS	EPIMERISE	EPISOMES	EPITHETIC
EPICORMIC	EPIGON	EPIMERISM	EPISPERM	EPITHETON

EPITHETS	EPOXIDE	EQUALLING	EQUITABLE	ERECTNESS
EPITOME	EPOXIDES	EQUALLY	EQUITABLY	ERECTOR
EPITOMES	EPOXIDISE	EQUALNESS	EQUITANT	ERECTORS
EPITOMIC	EPOXIDIZE	EQUALS	EQUITES	ERECTS
EPITOMISE	EPOXIED	EQUANT	EQUITIES	ERED
EPITOMIST	EPOXIES	EQUANTS	EQUITY	ERELONG
EPITOMIZE	EPOXY	EQUATABLE	EQUIVALVE	EREMIC
EPITONIC	EPOXYED	EQUATE	EQUIVOCAL	EREMITAL
EPITOPE	EPOXYING	EQUATED	EQUIVOKE	EREMITE
EPITOPES	EPRIS	EQUATES	EQUIVOKES	EREMITES
EPITRITE	EPRISE	EQUATING	EQUIVOQUE	EREMITIC
EPITRITES	EPSILON	EQUATION	ER	EREMITISH
EPIZEUXES	EPSILONIC	EQUATIONS	ERA	EREMITISM
EPIZEUXIS	EPSILONS	EQUATIVE	ERADIATE	EREMURI
EPIZOA	EPSOMITE	EQUATOR	ERADIATED	EREMURUS
EPIZOAN	EPSOMITES	EQUATORS	ERADIATES	ERENOW
EPIZOANS	EPUISE	EQUERRIES	ERADICANT	EREPSIN
EPIZOIC	EPUISEE	EQUERRY	ERADICATE	EREPSINS
EPIZOISM	EPULARY	EQUES	ERAS	ERES
EPIZOISMS	EPULATION	EQUID	ERASABLE	ERETHIC
EPIZOITE	EPULIDES	EQUIDS	ERASE	ERETHISM
EPIZOITES	EPULIS	EQUIFINAL	ERASED	ERETHISMS
EPIZOON	EPULISES	EQUIMOLAL	ERASEMENT	ERETHITIC
EPIZOOTIC	EPULOTIC	EQUIMOLAR	ERASER	EREV
EPIZOOTY	EPULOTICS	EQUINAL	ERASERS	EREVS
EPKWELE	EPURATE	EQUINE	ERASES	EREWHILE
EPOCH	EPURATED	EQUINELY	ERASING	EREWHILES
EPOCHA	EPURATES	EQUINES	ERASION	ERF
EPOCHAL	EPURATING	EQUINIA	ERASIONS	ERG
EPOCHALLY	EPURATION	EQUINIAS	ERASURE	ERGASTIC
EPOCHAS	EPYLLIA	EQUINITY	ERASURES	ERGATANER
EPOCHS	EPYLLION	EQUINOX	ERATHEM	ERGATE
EPODE	EPYLLIONS	EQUINOXES	ERATHEMS	ERGATES
EPODES	EQUABLE	EQUIP	ERBIA	ERGATIVE
EPODIC	EQUABLY	EQUIPAGE	ERBIAS	ERGATIVES
EPONYM	EQUAL	EQUIPAGED	ERBIUM	ERGATOID
EPONYMIC	EQUALED	EQUIPAGES	ERBIUMS	ERGATOIDS
EPONYMIES	EQUALI	EQUIPE	ERE	ERGO
EPONYMOUS	EQUALING	EQUIPES	ERECT	ERGODIC
EPONYMS	EQUALISE	EQUIPMENT	ERECTABLE	ERGOGENIC
EPONYMY	EQUALISED	EQUIPOISE	ERECTED	ERGOGRAM
EPOPEE	EQUALISER	EQUIPPED	ERECTER	ERGOGRAMS
EPOPEES	EQUALISES	EQUIPPER	ERECTERS	ERGOGRAPH
EPOPOEIA	EQUALITY	EQUIPPERS	ERECTILE	ERGOMANIA
EPOPOEIAS	EQUALIZE	EQUIPPING	ERECTING	ERGOMETER
EPOPT	EQUALIZED	EQUIPS	ERECTION	ERGOMETRY
EPOPTS	EQUALIZER	EQUISETA	ERECTIONS	ERGON
EPOS	EQUALIZES	EQUISETIC	ERECTIVE	ERGONOMIC
EPOSES	EQUALLED	EQUISETUM	ERECTLY	ERGONS

ERGOS	ERMELINS	EROTISE	ERUCTATE	ESCALADER
ERGOT	ERMINE	EROTISED	ERUCTATED	ESCALADES
ERGOTIC	ERMINED	EROTISES	ERUCTATES	ESCALADO
ERGOTISE	ERMINES	EROTISING	ERUCTED	ESCALATE
ERGOTISED	ERN	EROTISM	ERUCTING	ESCALATED
ERGOTISES	ERNE	EROTISMS	ERUCTS	ESCALATES
ERGOTISM	ERNED	EROTIZE	ERUDITE	ESCALATOR
ERGOTISMS	ERNES	EROTIZED	ERUDITELY	ESCALIER
ERGOTIZE	ERNING	EROTIZES	ERUDITES	ESCALIERS
ERGOTIZED	ERNS	EROTIZING	ERUDITION	ESCALLOP
ERGOTIZES	ERODABLE	EROTOLOGY	ERUGO	ESCALLOPS
ERGOTS	ERODE	ERR	ERUGOS	ESCALOP
ERGS	ERODED	ERRABLE	ERUMPENT	ESCALOPE
ERHU	ERODENT	ERRANCIES	ERUPT	ESCALOPED
ERHUS	ERODENTS	ERRANCY	ERUPTED	ESCALOPES
ERIACH	ERODES	ERRAND	ERUPTIBLE	ESCALOPS
ERIACHS	ERODIBLE	ERRANDS	ERUPTING	ESCAPABLE
ERIC	ERODING	ERRANT	ERUPTION	ESCAPADE
ERICA	ERODIUM	ERRANTLY	ERUPTIONS	ESCAPADES
ERICAS	ERODIUMS	ERRANTRY	ERUPTIVE	ESCAPADO
ERICK	EROGENIC	ERRANTS	ERUPTIVES	ESCAPADOS
ERICKS	EROGENOUS	ERRATA	ERUPTS	ESCAPE
ERICOID	EROS	ERRATAS	ERUV	ESCAPED
ERICS	EROSE	ERRATIC	ERUVIM	ESCAPEE
ERIGERON	EROSELY	ERRATICAL	ERUVIN	ESCAPEES
ERIGERONS	EROSES	ERRATICS	ERUVS	ESCAPER
ERING	EROSIBLE	ERRATUM	ERVALENTA	ESCAPERS
ERINGO	EROSION	ERRED	ERVEN	ESCAPES
ERINGOES	EROSIONAL	ERRHINE	ERVIL	ESCAPING
ERINGOS	EROSIONS	ERRHINES	ERVILS	ESCAPISM
ERINITE	EROSIVE	ERRING	ERYNGIUM	ESCAPISMS
ERINITES	EROSIVITY	ERRINGLY	ERYNGIUMS	ESCAPIST
ERINUS	EROSTRATE	ERRINGS	ERYNGO	ESCAPISTS
ERINUSES	EROTEMA	ERRONEOUS	ERYNGOES	ESCAR
ERIOMETER	EROTEMAS	ERROR	ERYNGOS	ESCARGOT
ERIONITE	EROTEME	ERRORIST	ERYTHEMA	ESCARGOTS
ERIONITES	EROTEMES	ERRORISTS	ERYTHEMAL	ESCAROLE
ERIOPHYID	EROTESES	ERRORLESS	ERYTHEMAS	ESCAROLES
ERISTIC	EROTESIS	ERRORS	ERYTHEMIC	ESCARP
ERISTICAL	EROTETIC	ERRS	ERYTHRINA	ESCARPED
ERISTICS	EROTIC	ERS	ERYTHRISM	ESCARPING
ERK	EROTICA	ERSATZ	ERYTHRITE	ESCARPS
ERKS	EROTICAL	ERSATZES	ERYTHROID	ESCARS
ERLANG	EROTICAS	ERSES	ERYTHRON	ESCHALOT
ERLANGS	EROTICISE	ERST	ERYTHRONS	ESCHALOTS
ERLKING	EROTICISM	ERSTWHILE	ES	ESCHAR
ERLKINGS	EROTICIST	ERUCIC	ESCABECHE	ESCHARS
ERM	EROTICIZE	ERUCIFORM	ESCALADE	ESCHEAT
ERMELIN	EROTICS	ERUCT	ESCALADED	ESCHEATED

ESCHEATOR	ESES	ESPLANADE	ESSOINERS	ESTOILE
ESCHEATS	ESILE	ESPOIR	ESSOINING	ESTOILES
ESCHEW	ESILES	ESPOIRS	ESSOINS	ESTOP
ESCHEWAL	ESKAR	ESPORT	ESSONITE	ESTOPPAGE
ESCHEWALS	ESKARS	ESPORTS	ESSONITES	ESTOPPED
ESCHEWED	ESKER	ESPOUSAL	ESSOYNE	ESTOPPEL
ESCHEWER	ESKERS	ESPOUSALS	ESSOYNES	ESTOPPELS
ESCHEWERS	ESKIES	ESPOUSE	EST	ESTOPPING
ESCHEWING	ESKY	ESPOUSED	ESTABLISH	ESTOPS
ESCHEWS	ESLOIN	ESPOUSER	ESTACADE	ESTOVER
ESCLANDRE	ESLOINED	ESPOUSERS	ESTACADES	ESTOVERS
ESCOLAR	ESLOINING	ESPOUSES	ESTAFETTE	ESTRADE
ESCOLARS	ESLOINS	ESPOUSING	ESTAMINET	ESTRADES
ESCOPETTE	ESLOYNE	ESPRESSO	ESTANCIA	ESTRADIOL
ESCORT	ESLOYNED	ESPRESSOS	ESTANCIAS	ESTRAGON
ESCORTAGE	ESLOYNES	ESPRIT	ESTATE	ESTRAGONS
ESCORTED	ESLOYNING	ESPRITS	ESTATED	ESTRAL
ESCORTING	ESNE	ESPUMOSO	ESTATES	ESTRANGE
ESCORTS	ESNECIES	ESPUMOSOS	ESTATING	ESTRANGED
ESCOT	ESNECY	ESPY	ESTEEM	ESTRANGER
ESCOTED	ESNES	ESPYING	ESTEEMED	ESTRANGES
ESCOTING	ESOPHAGI	ESQUIRE	ESTEEMING	ESTRAPADE
ESCOTS	ESOPHAGUS	ESQUIRED	ESTEEMS	ESTRAY
ESCOTTED	ESOTERIC	ESQUIRES	ESTER	ESTRAYED
ESCOTTING	ESOTERICA	ESQUIRESS	ESTERASE	ESTRAYING
ESCRIBANO	ESOTERIES	ESQUIRING	ESTERASES	ESTRAYS
ESCRIBE	ESOTERISM	ESQUISSE	ESTERIFY	ESTREAT
ESCRIBED	ESOTERY	ESQUISSES	ESTERS	ESTREATED
ESCRIBES	ESOTROPIA	ESS	ESTHESES	ESTREATS
ESCRIBING	ESOTROPIC	ESSAY	ESTHESIA	ESTREPE
ESCROC	ESPADA	ESSAYED	ESTHESIAS	ESTREPED
ESCROCS	ESPADAS	ESSAYER	ESTHESIS	ESTREPES
ESCROL	ESPAGNOLE	ESSAYERS	ESTHETE	ESTREPING
ESCROLL	ESPALIER	ESSAYETTE	ESTHETES	ESTRICH
ESCROLLS	ESPALIERS	ESSAYING	ESTHETIC	ESTRICHES
ESCROLS	ESPANOL	ESSAYISH	ESTHETICS	ESTRIDGE
ESCROW	ESPANOLES	ESSAYIST	ESTIMABLE	ESTRIDGES
ESCROWED	ESPARTO	ESSAYISTS	ESTIMABLY	ESTRILDID
ESCROWING	ESPARTOS	ESSAYS	ESTIMATE	ESTRIN
ESCROWS	ESPECIAL	ESSE	ESTIMATED	ESTRINS
ESCUAGE	ESPERANCE	ESSENCE	ESTIMATES	ESTRIOL
ESCUAGES	ESPIAL	ESSENCES	ESTIMATOR	ESTRIOLS
ESCUDO	ESPIALS	ESSENTIAL	ESTIVAL	ESTRO
ESCUDOS	ESPIED	ESSES	ESTIVATE	ESTROGEN
ESCULENT	ESPIEGLE	ESSIVE	ESTIVATED	ESTROGENS
ESCULENTS	ESPIER	ESSIVES	ESTIVATES	ESTRONE
ESEMPLASY	ESPIERS	ESSOIN	ESTIVATOR	ESTRONES
ESERINE	ESPIES	ESSOINED	ESTOC	ESTROS
ESERINES	ESPIONAGE	ESSOINER	ESTOCS	ESTROUS

ESTRUAL	ETCHED	ETHERIONS	ETHNICITY	ETOILE
ESTRUM	ETCHER	ETHERISE	ETHNICS	ETOILES
ESTRUMS	ETCHERS	ETHERISED	ETHNOCIDE	ETOUFFEE
ESTRUS	ETCHES	ETHERISER	ETHNOGENY	ETOUFFEES
ESTRUSES	ETCHING	ETHERISES	ETHNOLOGY	ETOURDI
ESTS	ETCHINGS	ETHERISH	ETHNONYM	ETOURDIE
ESTUARIAL	ETEN	ETHERISM	ETHNONYMS	ETRANGER
ESTUARIAN	ETENS	ETHERISMS	ETHNOS	ETRANGERE
ESTUARIES	ETERNAL	ETHERIST	ETHNOSES	ETRANGERS
ESTUARINE	ETERNALLY	ETHERISTS	ETHOGRAM	ETRENNE
ESTUARY	ETERNALS	ETHERIZE	ETHOGRAMS	ETRENNES
ESURIENCE	ETERNE	ETHERIZED	ETHOLOGIC	ETRIER
ESURIENCY	ETERNISE	ETHERIZER	ETHOLOGY	ETRIERS
ESURIENT	ETERNISED	ETHERIZES	ETHONONE	ETTERCAP
ET	ETERNISES	ETHERS	ETHONONES	ETTERCAPS
ETA	ETERNITY	ETHIC	ETHOS	ETTIN
ETACISM	ETERNIZE	ETHICAL	ETHOSES	ETTINS
ETACISMS	ETERNIZED	ETHICALLY	ETHOXIDE	ETTLE
ETAERIO	ETERNIZES	ETHICALS	ETHOXIDES	ETTLED
ETAERIOS	ETESIAN	ETHICIAN	ETHOXIES	ETTLES
ETAGE	ETESIANS	ETHICIANS	ETHOXY	ETTLING
ETAGERE	ETH	ETHICISE	ETHOXYL	ETUDE
ETAGERES	ETHAL	ETHICISED	ETHOXYLS	ETUDES
ETAGES	ETHALS	ETHICISES	ETHS	ETUI
ETALAGE	ETHANAL	ETHICISM	ETHYL	ETUIS
ETALAGES	ETHANALS	ETHICISMS	ETHYLATE	ETWEE
ETALON	ETHANE	ETHICIST	ETHYLATED	ETWEES
ETALONS	ETHANES	ETHICISTS	ETHYLATES	ETYMA
ETAMIN	ETHANOATE	ETHICIZE	ETHYLENE	ETYMIC
ETAMINE	ETHANOIC	ETHICIZED	ETHYLENES	ETYMOLOGY
ETAMINES	ETHANOL	ETHICIZES	ETHYLENIC	ETYMON
ETAMINS	ETHANOLS	ETHICS	ETHYLIC	ETYMONS
ETAPE	ETHANOYL	ETHINYL	ETHYLS	ETYPIC
ETAPES	ETHANOYLS	ETHINYLS	ETHYNE	ETYPICAL
ETAS	ETHE	ETHION	ETHYNES	EUCAIN
ETAT	ETHENE	ETHIONINE	ETHYNYL	EUCAINE
ETATISM	ETHENES	ETHIONS	ETHYNYLS	EUCAINES
ETATISME	ETHEPHON	ETHIOPS	ETIC	EUCAINS
ETATISMES	ETHEPHONS	ETHIOPSES	ETICS	EUCALYPT
ETATISMS	ETHER	ETHMOID	ETIOLATE	EUCALYPTI
ETATIST	ETHERCAP	ETHMOIDAL	ETIOLATED	EUCALYPTS
ETATISTE	ETHERCAPS	ETHMOIDS	ETIOLATES	EUCARYON
ETATISTES	ETHEREAL	ETHNARCH	ETIOLIN	EUCARYONS
ETATS	ETHEREOUS	ETHNARCHS	ETIOLINS	EUCARYOT
ETCETERA	ETHERIAL	ETHNARCHY	ETIOLOGIC	EUCARYOTE
ETCETERAS	ETHERIC	ETHNE	ETIOLOGY	EUCARYOTS
ETCH	ETHERICAL	ETHNIC	ETIQUETTE	EUCHARIS
ETCHANT	ETHERIFY	ETHNICAL	ETNA	EUCHLORIC
ETCHANTS	ETHERION	ETHNICISM	ETNAS	EUCHLORIN

EUCHOLOGY	EUKARYOT	EUPATRIDS	EUPLOIDS	EUSTASIES
EUCHRE	EUKARYOTE	EUPEPSIA	EUPLOIDY	EUSTASY
EUCHRED	EUKARYOTS	EUPEPSIAS	EUPNEA	EUSTATIC
EUCHRES	EUKED	EUPEPSIES	EUPNEAS	EUSTELE
EUCHRING	EUKING	EUPEPSY	EUPNEIC	EUSTELES
EUCLASE	EUKS	EUPEPTIC	EUPNOEA	EUSTRESS
EUCLASES	EULACHAN	EUPHAUSID	EUPNOEAS	EUSTYLE
EUCLIDEAN	EULACHANS	EUPHEMISE	EUPNOEIC	EUSTYLES
EUCLIDIAN	EULACHON	EUPHEMISM	EUREKA	EUTAXIA
EUCRITE	EULACHONS	EUPHEMIST	EUREKAS	EUTAXIAS
EUCRITES	EULOGIA	EUPHEMIZE	EURHYTHMY	EUTAXIES
EUCRITIC	EULOGIAE	EUPHENIC	EURIPI	EUTAXITE
EUCRYPHIA	EULOGIAS	EUPHENICS	EURIPUS	EUTAXITES
EUCYCLIC	EULOGIES	EUPHOBIA	EURIPUSES	EUTAXITIC
EUDAEMON	EULOGISE	EUPHOBIAS	EURO	EUTAXY
EUDAEMONS	EULOGISED	EUPHON	EUROBOND	EUTECTIC
EUDAEMONY	EULOGISER	EUPHONIA	EUROBONDS	EUTECTICS
EUDAIMON	EULOGISES	EUPHONIAS	EUROCRAT	EUTECTOID
EUDAIMONS	EULOGIST	EUPHONIC	EUROCRATS	EUTEXIA
EUDEMON	EULOGISTS	EUPHONIES	EUROCREEP	EUTEXIAS
EUDEMONIA	EULOGIUM	EUPHONISE	EUROKIES	EUTHANASE
EUDEMONIC	EULOGIUMS	EUPHONISM	EUROKOUS	EUTHANASY
EUDEMONS	EULOGIZE	EUPHONIUM	EUROKY	EUTHANAZE
EUDIALYTE	EULOGIZED	EUPHONIZE	EUROLAND	EUTHANISE
EUGARIE	EULOGIZER	EUPHONS	EUROLANDS	EUTHANIZE
EUGARIES	EULOGIZES	EUPHONY	EURONOTE	EUTHENICS
EUGE	EULOGY	EUPHORBIA	EURONOTES	EUTHENIST
EUGENIA	EUMELANIN	EUPHORIA	EUROPHILE	EUTHERIAN
EUGENIAS	EUMERISM	EUPHORIAS	EUROPIUM	EUTHYMIA
EUGENIC	EUMERISMS	EUPHORIC	EUROPIUMS	EUTHYMIAS
EUGENICAL	EUMONG	EUPHORIES	EUROPOP	EUTHYROID
EUGENICS	EUMONGS	EUPHORY	EUROPOPS	EUTRAPELY
EUGENISM	EUMUNG	EUPHOTIC	EUROS	EUTROPHIC
EUGENISMS	EUMUNGS	EUPHRASIA	EUROZONE	EUTROPHY
EUGENIST	EUNUCH	EUPHRASY	EUROZONES	EUTROPIC
EUGENISTS	EUNUCHISE	EUPHROE	EURYBATH	EUTROPIES
EUGENOL	EUNUCHISM	EUPHROES	EURYBATHS	EUTROPOUS
EUGENOLS	EUNUCHIZE	EUPHUISE	EURYOKIES	EUTROPY
EUGH	EUNUCHOID	EUPHUISED	EURYOKOUS	EUXENITE
EUGHEN	EUNUCHS	EUPHUISES	EURYOKY	EUXENITES
EUGHS	EUOI	EUPHUISM	EURYTHERM	EVACUANT
EUGLENA	EUONYMIN	EUPHUISMS	EURYTHMIC	EVACUANTS
EUGLENAS	EUONYMINS	EUPHUIST	EURYTHMY	EVACUATE
EUGLENID	EUONYMUS	EUPHUISTS	EURYTOPIC	EVACUATED
EUGLENIDS	EUOUAE	EUPHUIZE	EUSOCIAL	EVACUATES
EUGLENOID	EUOUAES	EUPHUIZED	EUSOL	EVACUATOR
EUK	EUPAD	EUPHUIZES	EUSOLS	EVACUEE
EUKARYON	EUPADS	EUPLASTIC	EUSTACIES	EVACUEES
EUKARYONS	EUPATRID	EUPLOID	EUSTACY	EVADABLE

E

EVADE	EVENLY	EVHOE	EVITING	EVULSIONS
EVADED	EVENNESS	EVICT	EVO	EVZONE
EVADER	EVENS	EVICTED	EVOCABLE	EVZONES
EVADERS	EVENSONG	EVICTEE	EVOCATE	EW
EVADES	EVENSONGS	EVICTEES	EVOCATED	EWE
EVADIBLE	EVENT	EVICTING	EVOCATES	EWER
EVADING	EVENTED	EVICTION	EVOCATING	EWERS
EVADINGLY	EVENTER	EVICTIONS	EVOCATION	EWES
EVAGATION	EVENTERS	EVICTOR	EVOCATIVE	EWEST
EVAGINATE	EVENTFUL	EVICTORS	EVOCATOR	EWFTES
EVALUABLE	EVENTIDE	EVICTS	EVOCATORS	EWGHEN
EVALUATE	EVENTIDES	EVIDENCE	EVOCATORY	EWHOW
EVALUATED	EVENTING	EVIDENCED	EVOE	EWK
EVALUATES	EVENTINGS	EVIDENCES	EVOHE	EWKED
EVALUATOR	EVENTIVE	EVIDENT	EVOKE	EWKING
EVANESCE	EVENTLESS	EVIDENTLY	EVOKED	EWKS
EVANESCED	EVENTRATE	EVIDENTS	EVOKER	EWT
EVANESCES	EVENTS	EVIL	EVOKERS	EWTS
EVANGEL	EVENTUAL	EVILDOER	EVOKES	EWW
EVANGELIC	EVENTUATE	EVILDOERS	EVOKING	EX
EVANGELS	EVER	EVILDOING	EVOLUE	EXABYTE
EVANGELY	EVERGLADE	EVILER	EVOLUES	EXABYTES
EVANISH	EVERGREEN	EVILEST	EVOLUTE	EXACT
EVANISHED	EVERMORE	EVILLER	EVOLUTED	EXACTA
EVANISHES	EVERNET	EVILLEST	EVOLUTES	EXACTABLE
EVANITION	EVERNETS	EVILLY	EVOLUTING	EXACTAS
EVAPORATE	EVERSIBLE	EVILNESS	EVOLUTION	EXACTED
EVAPORITE	EVERSION	EVILS	EVOLUTIVE	EXACTER
EVASIBLE	EVERSIONS	EVINCE	EVOLVABLE	EXACTERS
EVASION	EVERT	EVINCED	EVOLVE	EXACTEST
EVASIONAL	EVERTED	EVINCES	EVOLVED	EXACTING
EVASIONS	EVERTING	EVINCIBLE	EVOLVENT	EXACTION
EVASIVE	EVERTOR	EVINCIBLY	EVOLVENTS	EXACTIONS
EVASIVELY	EVERTORS	EVINCING	EVOLVER	EXACTLY
EVE	EVERTS	EVINCIVE	EVOLVERS	EXACTMENT
EVECTION	EVERWHERE	EVIRATE	EVOLVES	EXACTNESS
EVECTIONS	EVERWHICH	EVIRATED	EVOLVING	EXACTOR
EVEJAR	EVERY	EVIRATES	EVONYMUS	EXACTORS
EVEJARS	EVERYBODY	EVIRATING	EVOS	EXACTRESS
EVEN	EVERYDAY	EVITABLE	EVOVAE	EXACTS
EVENED	EVERYDAYS	EVITATE	EVOVAES	EXACUM
EVENEMENT	EVERYMAN	EVITATED	EVULGATE	EXACUMS
EVENER	EVERYMEN	EVITATES	EVULGATED	EXAHERTZ
EVENERS	EVERYONE	EVITATING	EVULGATES	EXALT
EVENEST	EVERYWAY	EVITATION	EVULSE	EXALTED
EVENFALL	EVERYWHEN	EVITE	EVULSED	EXALTEDLY
EVENFALLS	EVES	EVITED	EVULSES	EXALTER
EVENING	EVET	EVITERNAL	EVULSING	EXALTERS
EVENINGS	EVETS	EVITES	EVULSION	EXALTING

EXALTS	EXCAVATOR	EXCIPLE	EXCRETAL	EXECUTING
EXAM	EXCEED	EXCIPLES	EXCRETE	EXECUTION
EXAMEN	EXCEEDED	EXCISABLE	EXCRETED	EXECUTIVE
EXAMENS	EXCEEDER	EXCISE	EXCRETER	EXECUTOR
EXAMETRE	EXCEEDERS	EXCISED	EXCRETERS	EXECUTORS
EXAMETRES	EXCEEDING	EXCISEMAN	EXCRETES	EXECUTORY
EXAMINANT	EXCEEDS	EXCISEMEN	EXCRETING	EXECUTRIX
EXAMINATE	EXCEL	EXCISES	EXCRETION	EXECUTRY
EXAMINE	EXCELLED	EXCISING	EXCRETIVE	EXED
EXAMINED	EXCELLENT	EXCISION	EXCRETORY	EXEDRA
EXAMINEE	EXCELLING	EXCISIONS	EXCUBANT	EXEDRAE
EXAMINEES	EXCELS	EXCITABLE	EXCUDIT	EXEDRAS
EXAMINER	EXCELSIOR	EXCITABLY	EXCULPATE	EXEEM
EXAMINERS	EXCENTRIC	EXCITANCY	EXCURRENT	EXEEMED
EXAMINES	EXCEPT	EXCITANT	EXCURSE	EXEEMING
EXAMINING	EXCEPTANT	EXCITANTS	EXCURSED	EXEEMS
EXAMPLAR	EXCEPTED	EXCITE	EXCURSES	EXEGESES
EXAMPLARS	EXCEPTING	EXCITED	EXCURSING	EXEGESIS
EXAMPLE	EXCEPTION	EXCITEDLY	EXCURSION	EXEGETE
EXAMPLED	EXCEPTIVE	EXCITER	EXCURSIVE	EXEGETES
EXAMPLES	EXCEPTOR	EXCITERS	EXCURSUS	EXEGETIC
EXAMPLING	EXCEPTORS	EXCITES	EXCUSABLE	EXEGETICS
EXAMS	EXCEPTS	EXCITING	EXCUSABLY	EXEGETIST
EXANIMATE	EXCERPT	EXCITON	EXCUSAL	EXEME
EXANTHEM	EXCERPTA	EXCITONIC	EXCUSALS	EXEMED
EXANTHEMA	EXCERPTED	EXCITONS	EXCUSE	EXEMES
EXANTHEMS	EXCERPTER	EXCITOR	EXCUSED	EXEMING
EXAPTED	EXCERPTOR	EXCITORS	EXCUSER	EXEMPLA
EXAPTIVE	EXCERPTS	EXCLAIM	EXCUSERS	EXEMPLAR
EXARATE	EXCERPTUM	EXCLAIMED	EXCUSES	EXEMPLARS
EXARATION	EXCESS	EXCLAIMER	EXCUSING	EXEMPLARY
EXARCH	EXCESSED	EXCLAIMS	EXCUSIVE	EXEMPLE
EXARCHAL	EXCESSES	EXCLAVE	EXEAT	EXEMPLES
EXARCHATE	EXCESSING	EXCLAVES	EXEATS	EXEMPLIFY
EXARCHIES	EXCESSIVE	EXCLOSURE	EXEC	EXEMPLUM
EXARCHIST	EXCHANGE	EXCLUDE	EXECRABLE	EXEMPT
EXARCHS	EXCHANGED	EXCLUDED	EXECRABLY	EXEMPTED
EXARCHY	EXCHANGER	EXCLUDEE	EXECRATE	EXEMPTING
EXCAMB	EXCHANGES	EXCLUDEES	EXECRATED	EXEMPTION
EXCAMBED	EXCHEAT	EXCLUDER	EXECRATES	EXEMPTIVE
EXCAMBING	EXCHEATS	EXCLUDERS	EXECRATOR	EXEMPTS
EXCAMBION	EXCHEQUER	EXCLUDES	EXECS	EXEQUATUR
EXCAMBIUM	EXCIDE	EXCLUDING	EXECUTANT	EXEQUIAL
EXCAMBS	EXCIDED	EXCLUSION	EXECUTARY	EXEQUIES
EXCARNATE	EXCIDES	EXCLUSIVE	EXECUTE	EXEQUY
EXCAUDATE	EXCIDING	EXCLUSORY	EXECUTED	EXERCISE
EXCAVATE	EXCIMER	EXCORIATE	EXECUTER	EXERCISED
EXCAVATED	EXCIMERS	EXCREMENT	EXECUTERS	EXERCISER
EXCAVATES	EXCIPIENT	EXCRETA	EXECUTES	EXERCISES

EXERCYCLE	EXHUMATED	EXITS	EXONYMS	EXOTOXIC
EXERGIES	EXHUMATES	EXO	EXOPHAGY	EXOTOXIN
EXERGONIC	EXHUME	EXOCARP	EXOPHORIC	EXOTOXINS
EXERGUAL	EXHUMED	EXOCARPS	EXOPLANET	EXOTROPIA
EXERGUE	EXHUMER	EXOCRINE	EXOPLASM	EXOTROPIC
EXERGUES	EXHUMERS	EXOCRINES	EXOPLASMS	EXPAND
EXERGY	EXHUMES	EXOCYCLIC	EXOPOD	EXPANDED
EXERT	EXHUMING	EXOCYTIC	EXOPODITE	EXPANDER
EXERTED	EXIES	EXOCYTOSE	EXOPODS	EXPANDERS
EXERTING	EXIGEANT	EXODE	EXORABLE	EXPANDING
EXERTION	EXIGEANTE	EXODERM	EXORATION	EXPANDOR
EXERTIONS	EXIGENCE	EXODERMAL	EXORCISE	EXPANDORS
EXERTIVE	EXIGENCES	EXODERMIS	EXORCISED	EXPANDS
EXERTS	EXIGENCY	EXODERMS	EXORCISER	EXPANSE
EXES	EXIGENT	EXODES	EXORCISES	EXPANSES
EXEUNT	EXIGENTLY	EXODIC	EXORCISM	EXPANSILE
EXFIL	EXIGENTS	EXODIST	EXORCISMS	EXPANSION
EXFILLED	EXIGIBLE	EXODISTS	EXORCIST	EXPANSIVE
EXFILLING	EXIGUITY	EXODOI	EXORCISTS	EXPAT
EXFILS	EXIGUOUS	EXODONTIA	EXORCIZE	EXPATIATE
EXFOLIANT	EXILABLE	EXODOS	EXORCIZED	EXPATS
EXFOLIATE	EXILE	EXODUS	EXORCIZER	EXPECT
EXHALABLE	EXILED	EXODUSES	EXORCIZES	EXPECTANT
EXHALANT	EXILEMENT	EXOENZYME	EXORDIA	EXPECTED
EXHALANTS	EXILER	EXOERGIC	EXORDIAL	EXPECTER
EXHALE	EXILERS	EXOGAMIC	EXORDIUM	EXPECTERS
EXHALED	EXILES	EXOGAMIES	EXORDIUMS	EXPECTING
EXHALENT	EXILIAN	EXOGAMOUS	EXOSMIC	EXPECTS
EXHALENTS	EXILIC	EXOGAMY	EXOSMOSE	EXPEDIENT
EXHALES	EXILING	EXOGEN	EXOSMOSES	EXPEDITE
EXHALING	EXILITIES	EXOGENIC	EXOSMOSIS	EXPEDITED
EXHAUST	EXILITY	EXOGENISM	EXOSMOTIC	EXPEDITER
EXHAUSTED	EXIMIOUS	EXOGENOUS	EXOSPHERE	EXPEDITES
EXHAUSTER	EXINE	EXOGENS	EXOSPORAL	EXPEDITOR
EXHAUSTS	EXINES	EXOME	EXOSPORE	EXPEL
EXHEDRA	EXING	EXOMES	EXOSPORES	EXPELLANT
EXHEDRAE	EXIST	EXOMION	EXOSPORIA	EXPELLED
EXHIBIT	EXISTED	EXOMIONS	EXOSTOSES	EXPELLEE
EXHIBITED	EXISTENCE	EXOMIS	EXOSTOSIS	EXPELLEES
EXHIBITER	EXISTENT	EXOMISES	EXOTERIC	EXPELLENT
EXHIBITOR	EXISTENTS	EXON	EXOTIC	EXPELLER
EXHIBITS	EXISTING	EXONERATE	EXOTICA	EXPELLERS
EXHORT	EXISTS	EXONEREE	EXOTICISE	EXPELLING
EXHORTED	EXIT	EXONEREES	EXOTICISM	EXPELS
EXHORTER	EXITANCE	EXONIC	EXOTICIST	EXPEND
EXHORTERS	EXITANCES	EXONS	EXOTICIZE	EXPENDED
EXHORTING	EXITED	EXONUMIA	EXOTICS	EXPENDER
EXHORTS	EXITING	EXONUMIST	EXOTISM	EXPENDERS
EXHUMATE	EXITLESS	EXONYM	EXOTISMS	EXPENDING

EXPENDS	EXPLODER	EXPRESS	EXSICCATE	EXTOLL
EXPENSE	EXPLODERS	EXPRESSED	EXSTROPHY	EXTOLLED
EXPENSED	EXPLODES	EXPRESSER	EXSUCCOUS	EXTOLLER
EXPENSES	EXPLODING	EXPRESSES	EXTANT	EXTOLLERS
EXPENSING	EXPLOIT	EXPRESSLY	EXTASIES	EXTOLLING
EXPENSIVE	EXPLOITED	EXPRESSO	EXTASY	EXTOLLS
EXPERT	EXPLOITER	EXPRESSOS	EXTATIC	EXTOLMENT
EXPERTED	EXPLOITS	EXPUGN	EXTEMPORE	EXTOLS
EXPERTING	EXPLORE	EXPUGNED	EXTEND	EXTORSIVE
EXPERTISE	EXPLORED	EXPUGNING	EXTENDANT	EXTORT
EXPERTISM	EXPLORER	EXPUGNS	EXTENDED	EXTORTED
EXPERTIZE	EXPLORERS	EXPULSE	EXTENDER	EXTORTER
EXPERTLY	EXPLORES	EXPULSED	EXTENDERS	EXTORTERS
EXPERTS	EXPLORING	EXPULSES	EXTENDING	EXTORTING
EXPIABLE	EXPLOSION	EXPULSING	EXTENDS	EXTORTION
EXPIATE	EXPLOSIVE	EXPULSION	EXTENSE	EXTORTIVE
EXPIATED	EXPO	EXPULSIVE	EXTENSES	EXTORTS
EXPIATES	EXPONENT	EXPUNCT	EXTENSILE	EXTRA
EXPIATING	EXPONENTS	EXPUNCTED	EXTENSION	EXTRABOLD
EXPIATION	EXPONIBLE	EXPUNCTS	EXTENSITY	EXTRACT
EXPIATOR	EXPORT	EXPUNGE	EXTENSIVE	EXTRACTED
EXPIATORS	EXPORTED	EXPUNGED	EXTENSOR	EXTRACTOR
EXPIATORY	EXPORTER	EXPUNGER	EXTENSORS	EXTRACTS
EXPIRABLE	EXPORTERS	EXPUNGERS	EXTENT	EXTRADITE
EXPIRANT	EXPORTING	EXPUNGES	EXTENTS	EXTRADOS
EXPIRANTS	EXPORTS	EXPUNGING	EXTENUATE	EXTRAIT
EXPIRE	EXPOS	EXPURGATE	EXTERIOR	EXTRAITS
EXPIRED	EXPOSABLE	EXPURGE	EXTERIORS	EXTRALITY
EXPIRER	EXPOSAL	EXPURGED	EXTERMINE	EXTRANET
EXPIRERS	EXPOSALS	EXPURGES	EXTERN	EXTRANETS
EXPIRES	EXPOSE	EXPURGING	EXTERNAL	EXTRAPOSE
EXPIRIES	EXPOSED	EXQUISITE	EXTERNALS	EXTRAS
EXPIRING	EXPOSER	EXSCIND	EXTERNAT	EXTRAUGHT
EXPIRY	EXPOSERS	EXSCINDED	EXTERNATS	EXTRAVERT
EXPISCATE	EXPOSES	EXSCINDS	EXTERNE	EXTREAT
EXPLAIN	EXPOSING	EXSECANT	EXTERNES	EXTREATED
EXPLAINED	EXPOSIT	EXSECANTS	EXTERNS	EXTREATS
EXPLAINER	EXPOSITED	EXSECT	EXTINCT	EXTREMA
EXPLAINS	EXPOSITOR	EXSECTED	EXTINCTED	EXTREMAL
EXPLANT	EXPOSITS	EXSECTING	EXTINCTS	EXTREMALS
EXPLANTED	EXPOSOME	EXSECTION	EXTINE	EXTREME
EXPLANTS	EXPOSOMES	EXSECTS	EXTINES	EXTREMELY
EXPLETIVE	EXPOSTURE	EXSERT	EXTIRP	EXTREMER
EXPLETORY	EXPOSURE	EXSERTED	EXTIRPATE	EXTREMES
EXPLICATE	EXPOSURES	EXSERTILE	EXTIRPED	EXTREMEST
EXPLICIT	EXPOUND	EXSERTING	EXTIRPING	EXTREMISM
EXPLICITS	EXPOUNDED	EXSERTION	EXTIRPS	EXTREMIST
EXPLODE	EXPOUNDER	EXSERTS	EXTOL	EXTREMITY
EXPLODED	EXPOUNDS	EXSICCANT	EXTOLD	EXTREMUM

EXTREMUMS	EXULT	EYEBEAM	EYELEVEL	EYESORES
EXTRICATE	EXULTANCE	EYEBEAMS	EYELIAD	EYESPOT
EXTRINSIC	EXULTANCY	EYEBLACK	EYELIADS	EYESPOTS
EXTROPIAN	EXULTANT	EYEBLACKS	EYELID	EYESTALK
EXTROPIES	EXULTED	EYEBLINK	EYELIDS	EYESTALKS
EXTROPY	EXULTING	EYEBLINKS	EYELIFT	EYESTONE
EXTRORSAL	EXULTS	EYEBOLT	EYELIFTS	EYESTONES
EXTRORSE	EXURB	EYEBOLTS	EYELIKE	EYESTRAIN
EXTROVERT	EXURBAN	EYEBRIGHT	EYELINE	EYETEETH
EXTRUDE	EXURBIA	EYEBROW	EYELINER	EYETOOTH
EXTRUDED	EXURBIAS	EYEBROWED	EYELINERS	EYEWALL
EXTRUDER	EXURBS	EYEBROWS	EYELINES	EYEWALLS
EXTRUDERS	EXUVIA	EYECUP	EYEN	EYEWASH
EXTRUDES	EXUVIAE	EYECUPS	EYEOPENER	EYEWASHES
EXTRUDING	EXUVIAL	EYED	EYEPATCH	EYEWATER
EXTRUSILE	EXUVIATE	EYEDNESS	EYEPIECE	EYEWATERS
EXTRUSION	EXUVIATED	EYEDROPS	EYEPIECES	EYEWEAR
EXTRUSIVE	EXUVIATES	EYEFOLD	EYEPOINT	EYEWEARS
EXTRUSORY	EXUVIUM	EYEFOLDS	EYEPOINTS	EYEWINK
EXTUBATE	EYALET	EYEFUL	EYEPOPPER	EYEWINKS
EXTUBATED	EYALETS	EYEFULS	EYER	EYING
EXTUBATES	EYAS	EYEGLASS	EYEROLL	EYLIAD
EXUBERANT	EYASES	EYEHOLE	EYEROLLS	EYLIADS
EXUBERATE	EYASS	EYEHOLES	EYERS	EYNE
EXUDATE	EYASSES	EYEHOOK	EYES	EYOT
EXUDATES	EYE	EYEHOOKS	EYESHADE	EYOTS
EXUDATION	EYEABLE	EYEING	EYESHADES	EYRA
EXUDATIVE	EYEBALL	EYELASH	EYESHADOW	EYRAS
EXUDE	EYEBALLED	EYELASHES	EYESHINE	EYRE
EXUDED	EYEBALLS	EYELESS	EYESHINES	EYRES
EXUDES	EYEBANK	EYELET	EYESHOT	EYRIE
EXUDING	EYEBANKS	EYELETED	EYESHOTS	EYRIES
EXUL	EYEBAR	EYELETEER	EYESIGHT	EYRIR
EXULLED	EYEBARS	EYELETING	EYESIGHTS	EYRY
EXULLING	EYEBATH	EYELETS	EYESOME	EZINE
EXULS	EYEBATHS	EYELETTED	EYESORE	EZINES

F

FA
FAA
FAAING
FAAN
FAAS
FAB
FABACEOUS
FABBER
FABBEST
FABBIER
FABBIEST
FABBY
FABLE
FABLED
FABLER
FABLERS
FABLES
FABLET
FABLETS
FABLIAU
FABLIAUX
FABLING
FABLINGS
FABRIC
FABRICANT
FABRICATE
FABRICKED
FABRICS
FABRIQUE
FABRIQUES
FABS
FABULAR
FABULATE
FABULATED
FABULATES
FABULATOR
FABULISE
FABULISED
FABULISES
FABULISM
FABULISMS
FABULIST
FABULISTS

FABULIZE
FABULIZED
FABULIZES
FABULOUS
FABURDEN
FABURDENS
FACADE
FACADES
FACE
FACEABLE
FACEBAR
FACEBARS
FACEBOOK
FACEBOOKS
FACECLOTH
FACED
FACEDOWN
FACEDOWNS
FACELESS
FACELIFT
FACELIFTS
FACEMAIL
FACEMAILS
FACEMAN
FACEMASK
FACEMASKS
FACEMEN
FACEOFF
FACEOFFS
FACEPALM
FACEPALMS
FACEPLANT
FACEPLATE
FACEPRINT
FACER
FACERS
FACES
FACET
FACETE
FACETED
FACETELY
FACETIAE
FACETIME

FACETIMED
FACETIMES
FACETING
FACETINGS
FACETIOUS
FACETS
FACETTED
FACETTING
FACEUP
FACIA
FACIAE
FACIAL
FACIALIST
FACIALLY
FACIALS
FACIAS
FACIEND
FACIENDS
FACIES
FACILE
FACILELY
FACILITY
FACING
FACINGS
FACONNE
FACONNES
FACSIMILE
FACT
FACTA
FACTFUL
FACTICE
FACTICES
FACTICITY
FACTION
FACTIONAL
FACTIONS
FACTIOUS
FACTIS
FACTISES
FACTITIVE
FACTIVE
FACTOID
FACTOIDAL

FACTOIDS
FACTOR
FACTORAGE
FACTORED
FACTORIAL
FACTORIES
FACTORING
FACTORISE
FACTORIZE
FACTORS
FACTORY
FACTOTUM
FACTOTUMS
FACTS
FACTSHEET
FACTUAL
FACTUALLY
FACTUM
FACTUMS
FACTURE
FACTURES
FACULA
FACULAE
FACULAR
FACULTIES
FACULTY
FACUNDITY
FAD
FADABLE
FADAISE
FADAISES
FADDIER
FADDIEST
FADDINESS
FADDISH
FADDISHLY
FADDISM
FADDISMS
FADDIST
FADDISTS
FADDLE
FADDLED
FADDLES

FADDLING
FADDY
FADE
FADEAWAY
FADEAWAYS
FADED
FADEDLY
FADEDNESS
FADEIN
FADEINS
FADELESS
FADEOUT
FADEOUTS
FADER
FADERS
FADES
FADEUR
FADEURS
FADGE
FADGED
FADGES
FADGING
FADIER
FADIEST
FADING
FADINGS
FADLIKE
FADO
FADOMETER
FADOS
FADS
FADY
FAE
FAECAL
FAECES
FAENA
FAENAS
FAERIE
FAERIES
FAERY
FAFF
FAFFED
FAFFIER

FAFFIEST	FAILLE	FAIRING	FAKEST	FALDSTOOL
FAFFING	FAILLES	FAIRINGS	FAKEY	FALL
FAFFS	FAILOVER	FAIRISH	FAKEYS	FALLACIES
FAFFY	FAILOVERS	FAIRISHLY	FAKIE	FALLACY
FAG	FAILS	FAIRLEAD	FAKIER	FALLAL
FAGACEOUS	FAILURE	FAIRLEADS	FAKIES	FALLALERY
FAGGED	FAILURES	FAIRLY	FAKIEST	FALLALISH
FAGGING	FAIN	FAIRNESS	FAKING	FALLALS
FAGGINGS	FAINE	FAIRS	FAKIR	FALLAWAY
FAGGOT	FAINEANCE	FAIRWAY	FAKIRISM	FALLAWAYS
FAGGOTED	FAINEANCY	FAIRWAYS	FAKIRISMS	FALLBACK
FAGGOTING	FAINEANT	FAIRY	FAKIRS	FALLBACKS
FAGGOTS	FAINEANTS	FAIRYDOM	FALAFEL	FALLBOARD
FAGIN	FAINED	FAIRYDOMS	FALAFELS	FALLEN
FAGINS	FAINER	FAIRYHOOD	FALAJ	FALLER
FAGOT	FAINES	FAIRYISM	FALANGISM	FALLERS
FAGOTED	FAINEST	FAIRYISMS	FALANGIST	FALLFISH
FAGOTER	FAINING	FAIRYLAND	FALBALA	FALLIBLE
FAGOTERS	FAINITES	FAIRYLIKE	FALBALAS	FALLIBLY
FAGOTING	FAINLY	FAIRYTALE	FALCADE	FALLING
FAGOTINGS	FAINNE	FAITH	FALCADES	FALLINGS
FAGOTS	FAINNES	FAITHCURE	FALCATE	FALLOFF
FAGOTTI	FAINNESS	FAITHED	FALCATED	FALLOFFS
FAGOTTIST	FAINS	FAITHER	FALCATION	FALLOUT
FAGOTTO	FAINT	FAITHERS	FALCES	FALLOUTS
FAGOTTOS	FAINTED	FAITHFUL	FALCHION	FALLOW
FAGS	FAINTER	FAITHFULS	FALCHIONS	FALLOWED
FAH	FAINTERS	FAITHING	FALCIFORM	FALLOWER
FAHLBAND	FAINTEST	FAITHINGS	FALCON	FALLOWEST
FAHLBANDS	FAINTIER	FAITHLESS	FALCONER	FALLOWING
FAHLERZ	FAINTIEST	FAITHS	FALCONERS	FALLOWS
FAHLERZES	FAINTING	FAITOR	FALCONET	FALLS
FAHLORE	FAINTINGS	FAITORS	FALCONETS	FALSE
FAHLORES	FAINTISH	FAITOUR	FALCONINE	FALSED
FAHS	FAINTLY	FAITOURS	FALCONOID	FALSEFACE
FAIBLE	FAINTNESS	FAIX	FALCONRY	FALSEHOOD
FAIBLES	FAINTS	FAJITA	FALCONS	FALSELY
FAIENCE	FAINTY	FAJITAS	FALCULA	FALSENESS
FAIENCES	FAIR	FAKE	FALCULAE	FALSER
FAIK	FAIRED	FAKED	FALCULAS	FALSERS
FAIKED	FAIRER	FAKEER	FALCULATE	FALSES
FAIKES	FAIREST	FAKEERS	FALDAGE	FALSEST
FAIKING	FAIRFACED	FAKEMENT	FALDAGES	FALSETTO
FAIKS	FAIRGOER	FAKEMENTS	FALDERAL	FALSETTOS
FAIL	FAIRGOERS	FAKER	FALDERALS	FALSEWORK
FAILED	FAIRIER	FAKERIES	FALDEROL	FALSIE
FAILING	FAIRIES	FAKERS	FALDEROLS	FALSIES
FAILINGLY	FAIRIEST	FAKERY	FALDETTA	FALSIFIED
FAILINGS	FAIRILY	FAKES	FALDETTAS	FALSIFIER

FALSIFIES	FANALS	FANFARONA	FANNINGS	FANZINE
FALSIFY	FANART	FANFARONS	FANNY	FANZINES
FALSING	FANARTS	FANFIC	FANNYING	FAP
FALSISH	FANATIC	FANFICS	FANO	FAPPED
FALSISM	FANATICAL	FANFOLD	FANON	FAPPING
FALSISMS	FANATICS	FANFOLDED	FANONS	FAPS
FALSITIES	FANBASE	FANFOLDS	FANOS	FAQIR
FALSITY	FANBASES	FANG	FANS	FAQIRS
FALTBOAT	FANBOY	FANGA	FANSITE	FAQUIR
FALTBOATS	FANBOYED	FANGAS	FANSITES	FAQUIRS
FALTER	FANBOYING	FANGED	FANSUB	FAR
FALTERED	FANBOYS	FANGING	FANSUBS	FARAD
FALTERER	FANCIABLE	FANGIRL	FANTAD	FARADAIC
FALTERERS	FANCIED	FANGIRLED	FANTADS	FARADAY
FALTERING	FANCIER	FANGIRLS	FANTAIL	FARADAYS
FALTERS	FANCIERS	FANGLE	FANTAILED	FARADIC
FALX	FANCIES	FANGLED	FANTAILS	FARADISE
FAM	FANCIEST	FANGLES	FANTASIA	FARADISED
FAME	FANCIFIED	FANGLESS	FANTASIAS	FARADISER
FAMED	FANCIFIES	FANGLIKE	FANTASIE	FARADISES
FAMELESS	FANCIFUL	FANGLING	FANTASIED	FARADISM
FAMES	FANCIFY	FANGO	FANTASIES	FARADISMS
FAMILIAL	FANCILESS	FANGOS	FANTASISE	FARADIZE
FAMILIAR	FANCILY	FANGS	FANTASIST	FARADIZED
FAMILIARS	FANCINESS	FANION	FANTASIZE	FARADIZER
FAMILIES	FANCY	FANIONS	FANTASM	FARADIZES
FAMILISM	FANCYING	FANJET	FANTASMAL	FARADS
FAMILISMS	FANCYWORK	FANJETS	FANTASMIC	FARAND
FAMILIST	FAND	FANK	FANTASMS	FARANDINE
FAMILLE	FANDANGLE	FANKED	FANTASQUE	FARANDOLE
FAMILLES	FANDANGO	FANKING	FANTAST	FARANG
FAMILY	FANDANGOS	FANKLE	FANTASTIC	FARANGS
FAMINE	FANDED	FANKLED	FANTASTRY	FARAWAY
FAMINES	FANDING	FANKLES	FANTASTS	FARAWAYS
FAMING	FANDOM	FANKLING	FANTASY	FARCE
FAMISH	FANDOMS	FANKS	FANTEEG	FARCED
FAMISHED	FANDS	FANLIGHT	FANTEEGS	FARCEMEAT
FAMISHES	FANE	FANLIGHTS	FANTIGUE	FARCER
FAMISHING	FANEGA	FANLIKE	FANTIGUES	FARCERS
FAMOUS	FANEGADA	FANNED	FANTOD	FARCES
FAMOUSED	FANEGADAS	FANNEL	FANTODS	FARCEUR
FAMOUSES	FANEGAS	FANNELL	FANTOM	FARCEURS
FAMOUSING	FANES	FANNELLS	FANTOMS	FARCEUSE
FAMOUSLY	FANFARADE	FANNELS	FANTOOSH	FARCEUSES
FAMS	FANFARE	FANNER	FANUM	FARCI
FAMULI	FANFARED	FANNERS	FANUMS	FARCICAL
FAMULUS	FANFARES	FANNIED	FANWISE	FARCIE
FAN	FANFARING	FANNIES	FANWORT	FARCIED
FANAL	FANFARON	FANNING	FANWORTS	FARCIES

FARCIFIED	FARMERESS	FARRUCAS	FASCIST	FATALISTS
FARCIFIES	FARMERIES	FARS	FASCISTA	FATALITY
FARCIFY	FARMERS	FARSE	FASCISTI	FATALLY
FARCIN	FARMERY	FARSED	FASCISTIC	FATALNESS
FARCING	FARMHAND	FARSEEING	FASCISTS	FATBACK
FARCINGS	FARMHANDS	FARSES	FASCITIS	FATBACKS
FARCINS	FARMHOUSE	FARSIDE	FASH	FATBERG
FARCY	FARMING	FARSIDES	FASHED	FATBERGS
FARD	FARMINGS	FARSING	FASHERIES	FATBIRD
FARDAGE	FARMLAND	FART	FASHERY	FATBIRDS
FARDAGES	FARMLANDS	FARTED	FASHES	FATE
FARDED	FARMOST	FARTHEL	FASHING	FATED
FARDEL	FARMS	FARTHELS	FASHION	FATEFUL
FARDELS	FARMSTEAD	FARTHER	FASHIONED	FATEFULLY
FARDEN	FARMWIFE	FARTHEST	FASHIONER	FATES
FARDENS	FARMWIVES	FARTHING	FASHIONS	FATHEAD
FARDING	FARMWORK	FARTHINGS	FASHIONY	FATHEADED
FARDINGS	FARMWORKS	FARTING	FASHIOUS	FATHEADS
FARDS	FARMYARD	FARTLEK	FAST	FATHER
FARE	FARMYARDS	FARTLEKS	FASTBACK	FATHERED
FAREBOX	FARNARKEL	FARTS	FASTBACKS	FATHERING
FAREBOXES	FARNESOL	FAS	FASTBALL	FATHERLY
FARED	FARNESOLS	FASCES	FASTBALLS	FATHERS
FARER	FARNESS	FASCI	FASTED	FATHOM
FARERS	FARNESSES	FASCIA	FASTEN	FATHOMED
FARES	FARO	FASCIAE	FASTENED	FATHOMER
FAREWELL	FAROLITO	FASCIAL	FASTENER	FATHOMERS
FAREWELLS	FAROLITOS	FASCIAS	FASTENERS	FATHOMING
FARFAL	FAROS	FASCIATE	FASTENING	FATHOMS
FARFALLE	FAROUCHE	FASCIATED	FASTENS	FATIDIC
FARFALLES	FARRAGO	FASCICLE	FASTER	FATIDICAL
FARFALS	FARRAGOES	FASCICLED	FASTERS	FATIGABLE
FARFEL	FARRAGOS	FASCICLES	FASTEST	FATIGATE
FARFELS	FARRAND	FASCICULE	FASTI	FATIGATED
FARFET	FARRANT	FASCICULI	FASTIE	FATIGATES
FARINA	FARRED	FASCIITIS	FASTIES	FATIGUE
FARINAS	FARREN	FASCINATE	FASTIGIUM	FATIGUED
FARING	FARRENS	FASCINE	FASTING	FATIGUES
FARINHA	FARRIER	FASCINES	FASTINGS	FATIGUING
FARINHAS	FARRIERS	FASCIO	FASTISH	FATING
FARINOSE	FARRIERY	FASCIOLA	FASTLY	FATISCENT
FARL	FARRING	FASCIOLAS	FASTNESS	FATLESS
FARLE	FARRO	FASCIOLE	FASTS	FATLIKE
FARLES	FARROS	FASCIOLES	FASTUOUS	FATLING
FARLS	FARROW	FASCIS	FAT	FATLINGS
FARM	FARROWED	FASCISM	FATAL	FATLY
FARMABLE	FARROWING	FASCISMI	FATALISM	FATNESS
FARMED	FARROWS	FASCISMO	FATALISMS	FATNESSES
FARMER	FARRUCA	FASCISMS	FATALIST	FATS

F

FATSIA	FAUCET	FAUTORS	FAVOURER	FAZENDAS
FATSIAS	FAUCETRY	FAUTS	FAVOURERS	FAZES
FATSO	FAUCETS	FAUVE	FAVOURING	FAZING
FATSOES	FAUCHION	FAUVES	FAVOURITE	FE
FATSOS	FAUCHIONS	FAUVETTE	FAVOURS	FEAGUE
FATSTOCK	FAUCHON	FAUVETTES	FAVOUS	FEAGUED
FATSTOCKS	FAUCHONS	FAUVISM	FAVRILE	FEAGUES
FATTED	FAUCIAL	FAUVISMS	FAVRILES	FEAGUING
FATTEN	FAUGH	FAUVIST	FAVS	FEAL
FATTENED	FAULCHION	FAUVISTS	FAVUS	FEALED
FATTENER	FAULD	FAUX	FAVUSES	FEALING
FATTENERS	FAULDS	FAUXHAWK	FAW	FEALS
FATTENING	FAULT	FAUXHAWKS	FAWN	FEALTIES
FATTENS	FAULTED	FAUXMANCE	FAWNED	FEALTY
FATTER	FAULTFUL	FAV	FAWNER	FEAR
FATTEST	FAULTIER	FAVA	FAWNERS	FEARE
FATTIER	FAULTIEST	FAVAS	FAWNIER	FEARED
FATTIES	FAULTILY	FAVE	FAWNIEST	FEARER
FATTIEST	FAULTING	FAVEL	FAWNING	FEARERS
FATTILY	FAULTLESS	FAVELA	FAWNINGLY	FEARES
FATTINESS	FAULTLINE	FAVELAS	FAWNINGS	FEARFUL
FATTING	FAULTS	FAVELL	FAWNLIKE	FEARFULLY
FATTISH	FAULTY	FAVELLA	FAWNS	FEARING
FATTISM	FAUN	FAVELLAS	FAWNY	FEARLESS
FATTISMS	FAUNA	FAVELS	FAWS	FEARS
FATTIST	FAUNAE	FAVEOLATE	FAX	FEARSOME
FATTISTS	FAUNAL	FAVER	FAXABLE	FEART
FATTRELS	FAUNALLY	FAVES	FAXED	FEASANCE
FATTY	FAUNAS	FAVEST	FAXES	FEASANCES
FATUITIES	FAUNIST	FAVICON	FAXING	FEASE
FATUITOUS	FAUNISTIC	FAVICONS	FAY	FEASED
FATUITY	FAUNISTS	FAVISM	FAYALITE	FEASES
FATUOUS	FAUNLIKE	FAVISMS	FAYALITES	FEASIBLE
FATUOUSLY	FAUNS	FAVONIAN	FAYED	FEASIBLY
FATWA	FAUNULA	FAVOR	FAYENCE	FEASING
FATWAED	FAUNULAE	FAVORABLE	FAYENCES	FEAST
FATWAH	FAUNULE	FAVORABLY	FAYER	FEASTED
FATWAHED	FAUNULES	FAVORED	FAYEST	FEASTER
FATWAHING	FAUR	FAVORER	FAYING	FEASTERS
FATWAHS	FAURD	FAVORERS	FAYNE	FEASTFUL
FATWAING	FAURER	FAVORING	FAYNED	FEASTING
FATWAS	FAUREST	FAVORITE	FAYNES	FEASTINGS
FATWOOD	FAUSTIAN	FAVORITED	FAYNING	FEASTLESS
FATWOODS	FAUT	FAVORITES	FAYRE	FEASTS
FAUBOURG	FAUTED	FAVORLESS	FAYRES	FEAT
FAUBOURGS	FAUTEUIL	FAVORS	FAYS	FEATED
FAUCAL	FAUTEUILS	FAVOSE	FAZE	FEATEOUS
FAUCALS	FAUTING	FAVOUR	FAZED	FEATER
FAUCES	FAUTOR	FAVOURED	FAZENDA	FEATEST

FEATHER	FECULENCE	FEEDER	FEEZES	FELDSCHER
FEATHERED	FECULENCY	FEEDERS	FEEZING	FELDSHER
FEATHERS	FECULENT	FEEDGRAIN	FEG	FELDSHERS
FEATHERY	FECUND	FEEDHOLE	FEGARIES	FELDSPAR
FEATING	FECUNDATE	FEEDHOLES	FEGARY	FELDSPARS
FEATLIER	FECUNDITY	FEEDING	FEGS	FELDSPATH
FEATLIEST	FED	FEEDINGS	FEH	FELICIA
FEATLY	FEDARIE	FEEDLOT	FEHM	FELICIAS
FEATOUS	FEDARIES	FEEDLOTS	FEHME	FELICIFIC
FEATS	FEDAYEE	FEEDPIPE	FEHMIC	FELICITER
FEATUOUS	FEDAYEEN	FEEDPIPES	FEHS	FELICITY
FEATURE	FEDELINI	FEEDS	FEIGN	FELID
FEATURED	FEDELINIS	FEEDSTOCK	FEIGNED	FELIDS
FEATURELY	FEDERACY	FEEDSTUFF	FEIGNEDLY	FELINE
FEATURES	FEDERAL	FEEDWATER	FEIGNER	FELINELY
FEATURING	FEDERALLY	FEEDYARD	FEIGNERS	FELINES
FEAZE	FEDERALS	FEEDYARDS	FEIGNING	FELINITY
FEAZED	FEDERARIE	FEEING	FEIGNINGS	FELL
FEAZES	FEDERARY	FEEL	FEIGNS	FELLA
FEAZING	FEDERATE	FEELBAD	FEIJOA	FELLABLE
FEBLESSE	FEDERATED	FEELER	FEIJOADA	FELLAH
FEBLESSES	FEDERATES	FEELERS	FEIJOADAS	FELLAHEEN
FEBRICITY	FEDERATOR	FEELESS	FEIJOAS	FELLAHIN
FEBRICULA	FEDEX	FEELGOOD	FEINT	FELLAHS
FEBRICULE	FEDEXED	FEELING	FEINTED	FELLAS
FEBRIFIC	FEDEXES	FEELINGLY	FEINTER	FELLATE
FEBRIFUGE	FEDEXING	FEELINGS	FEINTEST	FELLATED
FEBRILE	FEDORA	FEELS	FEINTING	FELLATES
FEBRILITY	FEDORAS	FEEN	FEINTS	FELLATING
FECAL	FEDS	FEENS	FEIRIE	FELLATIO
FECES	FEE	FEER	FEIRIER	FELLATION
FECHT	FEEB	FEERED	FEIRIEST	FELLATIOS
FECHTER	FEEBLE	FEERIE	FEIS	FELLATOR
FECHTERS	FEEBLED	FEERIES	FEISEANNA	FELLATORS
FECHTING	FEEBLER	FEERIN	FEIST	FELLATRIX
FECHTS	FEEBLES	FEERING	FEISTIER	FELLED
FECIAL	FEEBLEST	FEERINGS	FEISTIEST	FELLER
FECIALS	FEEBLING	FEERINS	FEISTILY	FELLERS
FECIT	FEEBLISH	FEERS	FEISTS	FELLEST
FECK	FEEBLY	FEES	FEISTY	FELLFIELD
FECKED	FEEBS	FEESE	FELAFEL	FELLIES
FECKIN	FEED	FEESED	FELAFELS	FELLING
FECKING	FEEDABLE	FEESES	FELCH	FELLINGS
FECKLESS	FEEDBACK	FEESING	FELCHED	FELLNESS
FECKLY	FEEDBACKS	FEET	FELCHES	FELLOE
FECKS	FEEDBAG	FEETFIRST	FELCHING	FELLOES
FECULA	FEEDBAGS	FEETLESS	FELDGRAU	FELLOW
FECULAE	FEEDBOX	FEEZE	FELDGRAUS	FELLOWED
FECULAS	FEEDBOXES	FEEZED	FELDSCHAR	FELLOWING

FELLOWLY	FEMERELL	FENCER	FENTANYLS	FERLY
FELLOWMAN	FEMERELLS	FENCEROW	FENTHION	FERLYING
FELLOWMEN	FEMES	FENCEROWS	FENTHIONS	FERM
FELLOWS	FEMETARY	FENCERS	FENTS	FERMATA
FELLS	FEMICIDAL	FENCES	FENUGREEK	FERMATAS
FELLY	FEMICIDE	FENCEWIRE	FENURON	FERMATE
FELON	FEMICIDES	FENCIBLE	FENURONS	FERMENT
FELONIES	FEMINACY	FENCIBLES	FEOD	FERMENTED
FELONIOUS	FEMINAL	FENCING	FEODAL	FERMENTER
FELONOUS	FEMINAZI	FENCINGS	FEODARIES	FERMENTOR
FELONRIES	FEMINAZIS	FEND	FEODARY	FERMENTS
FELONRY	FEMINEITY	FENDED	FEODS	FERMI
FELONS	FEMINIE	FENDER	FEOFF	FERMION
FELONY	FEMINIES	FENDERED	FEOFFED	FERMIONIC
FELQUISTE	FEMININE	FENDERS	FEOFFEE	FERMIONS
FELSIC	FEMININES	FENDIER	FEOFFEES	FERMIS
FELSITE	FEMINISE	FENDIEST	FEOFFER	FERMIUM
FELSITES	FEMINISED	FENDING	FEOFFERS	FERMIUMS
FELSITIC	FEMINISES	FENDS	FEOFFING	FERMS
FELSPAR	FEMINISM	FENDY	FEOFFMENT	FERN
FELSPARS	FEMINISMS	FENESTRA	FEOFFOR	FERNALLY
FELSTONE	FEMINIST	FENESTRAE	FEOFFORS	FERNBIRD
FELSTONES	FEMINISTS	FENESTRAL	FEOFFS	FERNBIRDS
FELT	FEMINITY	FENESTRAS	FER	FERNERIES
FELTED	FEMINIZE	FENI	FERACIOUS	FERNERY
FELTER	FEMINIZED	FENING	FERACITY	FERNIER
FELTERED	FEMINIZES	FENINGA	FERAL	FERNIEST
FELTERING	FEMITER	FENINGS	FERALISED	FERNING
FELTERS	FEMITERS	FENIS	FERALIZED	FERNINGS
FELTIER	FEMME	FENITAR	FERALS	FERNINST
FELTIEST	FEMMES	FENITARS	FERBAM	FERNLESS
FELTING	FEMMIER	FENKS	FERBAMS	FERNLIKE
FELTINGS	FEMMIEST	FENLAND	FERE	FERNS
FELTLIKE	FEMMY	FENLANDS	FERER	FERNSHAW
FELTS	FEMORA	FENMAN	FERES	FERNSHAWS
FELTY	FEMORAL	FENMEN	FEREST	FERNTICLE
FELUCCA	FEMS	FENNEC	FERETORY	FERNY
FELUCCAS	FEMUR	FENNECS	FERIA	FEROCIOUS
FELWORT	FEMURS	FENNEL	FERIAE	FEROCITY
FELWORTS	FEN	FENNELS	FERIAL	FERRATE
FEM	FENAGLE	FENNIER	FERIAS	FERRATES
FEMAL	FENAGLED	FENNIES	FERINE	FERREL
FEMALE	FENAGLES	FENNIEST	FERITIES	FERRELED
FEMALES	FENAGLING	FENNING	FERITY	FERRELING
FEMALITY	FENCE	FENNISH	FERLIE	FERRELLED
FEMALS	FENCED	FENNY	FERLIED	FERRELS
FEME	FENCELESS	FENS	FERLIER	FERREOUS
FEMERALL	FENCELIKE	FENT	FERLIES	FERRET
FEMERALLS	FENCELINE	FENTANYL	FERLIEST	FERRETED

FERRETER	FERVENT	FETA	FETOSCOPE	FEUILLETE
FERRETERS	FERVENTER	FETAL	FETOSCOPY	FEUING
FERRETIER	FERVENTLY	FETAS	FETS	FEUS
FERRETING	FERVID	FETATION	FETT	FEUTRE
FERRETS	FERVIDER	FETATIONS	FETTA	FEUTRED
FERRETY	FERVIDEST	FETCH	FETTAS	FEUTRES
FERRIAGE	FERVIDITY	FETCHED	FETTED	FEUTRING
FERRIAGES	FERVIDLY	FETCHER	FETTER	FEVER
FERRIC	FERVOR	FETCHERS	FETTERED	FEVERED
FERRIED	FERVOROUS	FETCHES	FETTERER	FEVERFEW
FERRIES	FERVORS	FETCHING	FETTERERS	FEVERFEWS
FERRITE	FERVOUR	FETE	FETTERING	FEVERING
FERRITES	FERVOURS	FETED	FETTERS	FEVERISH
FERRITIC	FES	FETERITA	FETTING	FEVERLESS
FERRITIN	FESCUE	FETERITAS	FETTLE	FEVEROUS
FERRITINS	FESCUES	FETES	FETTLED	FEVERROOT
FERROCENE	FESS	FETIAL	FETTLER	FEVERS
FERROGRAM	FESSE	FETIALES	FETTLERS	FEVERWEED
FERROTYPE	FESSED	FETIALIS	FETTLES	FEVERWORT
FERROUS	FESSES	FETIALS	FETTLING	FEW
FERRUGO	FESSING	FETICH	FETTLINGS	FEWER
FERRUGOS	FESSWISE	FETICHE	FETTS	FEWEST
FERRULE	FEST	FETICHES	FETTUCINE	FEWMET
FERRULED	FESTA	FETICHISE	FETTUCINI	FEWMETS
FERRULES	FESTAL	FETICHISM	FETUS	FEWNESS
FERRULING	FESTALLY	FETICHIST	FETUSES	FEWNESSES
FERRUM	FESTALS	FETICHIZE	FETWA	FEWS
FERRUMS	FESTAS	FETICIDAL	FETWAS	FEWTER
FERRY	FESTER	FETICIDE	FEU	FEWTERED
FERRYBOAT	FESTERED	FETICIDES	FEUAR	FEWTERING
FERRYING	FESTERING	FETID	FEUARS	FEWTERS
FERRYMAN	FESTERS	FETIDER	FEUD	FEWTRILS
FERRYMEN	FESTIER	FETIDEST	FEUDAL	FEY
FERTIGATE	FESTIEST	FETIDITY	FEUDALISE	FEYED
FERTILE	FESTILOGY	FETIDLY	FEUDALISM	FEYER
FERTILELY	FESTINATE	FETIDNESS	FEUDALIST	FEYEST
FERTILER	FESTIVAL	FETING	FEUDALITY	FEYING
FERTILEST	FESTIVALS	FETISH	FEUDALIZE	FEYLY
FERTILISE	FESTIVE	FETISHES	FEUDALLY	FEYNESS
FERTILITY	FESTIVELY	FETISHISE	FEUDARIES	FEYNESSES
FERTILIZE	FESTIVITY	FETISHISM	FEUDARY	FEYS
FERULA	FESTIVOUS	FETISHIST	FEUDATORY	FEZ
FERULAE	FESTOLOGY	FETISHIZE	FEUDED	FEZES
FERULAS	FESTOON	FETLOCK	FEUDING	FEZZED
FERULE	FESTOONED	FETLOCKED	FEUDINGS	FEZZES
FERULED	FESTOONS	FETLOCKS	FEUDIST	FEZZY
FERULES	FESTS	FETOLOGY	FEUDISTS	FIACRE
FERULING	FESTY	FETOR	FEUDS	FIACRES
FERVENCY	FET	FETORS	FEUED	FIANCE

FIANCEE	FIBRILLAR	FICKLING	FIDGING	FIESTAS
FIANCEES	FIBRILLIN	FICKLY	FIDIBUS	FIFE
FIANCES	FIBRILS	FICO	FIDIBUSES	FIFED
FIAR	FIBRIN	FICOES	FIDO	FIFER
FIARS	FIBRINOID	FICOS	FIDOS	FIFERS
FIASCHI	FIBRINOUS	FICTILE	FIDS	FIFES
FIASCO	FIBRINS	FICTION	FIDUCIAL	FIFI
FIASCOES	FIBRO	FICTIONAL	FIDUCIARY	FIFING
FIASCOS	FIBROCYTE	FICTIONS	FIE	FIFIS
FIAT	FIBROID	FICTIVE	FIEF	FIFTEEN
FIATED	FIBROIDS	FICTIVELY	FIEFDOM	FIFTEENER
FIATING	FIBROIN	FICTOR	FIEFDOMS	FIFTEENS
FIATS	FIBROINS	FICTORS	FIEFS	FIFTEENTH
FIAUNT	FIBROLINE	FICUS	FIELD	FIFTH
FIAUNTS	FIBROLITE	FICUSES	FIELDBOOT	FIFTHLY
FIB	FIBROMA	FID	FIELDED	FIFTHS
FIBBED	FIBROMAS	FIDDIOUS	FIELDER	FIFTIES
FIBBER	FIBROMATA	FIDDLE	FIELDERS	FIFTIETH
FIBBERIES	FIBROS	FIDDLED	FIELDFARE	FIFTIETHS
FIBBERS	FIBROSE	FIDDLER	FIELDING	FIFTY
FIBBERY	FIBROSED	FIDDLERS	FIELDINGS	FIFTYFOLD
FIBBING	FIBROSES	FIDDLES	FIELDMICE	FIFTYISH
FIBER	FIBROSING	FIDDLEY	FIELDS	FIG
FIBERED	FIBROSIS	FIDDLEYS	FIELDSMAN	FIGEATER
FIBERFILL	FIBROTIC	FIDDLIER	FIELDSMEN	FIGEATERS
FIBERISE	FIBROUS	FIDDLIEST	FIELDVOLE	FIGGED
FIBERISED	FIBROUSLY	FIDDLING	FIELDWARD	FIGGERIES
FIBERISES	FIBS	FIDDLINGS	FIELDWORK	FIGGERY
FIBERIZE	FIBSTER	FIDDLY	FIEND	FIGGIER
FIBERIZED	FIBSTERS	FIDEISM	FIENDISH	FIGGIEST
FIBERIZES	FIBULA	FIDEISMS	FIENDLIKE	FIGGING
FIBERLESS	FIBULAE	FIDEIST	FIENDS	FIGGY
FIBERLIKE	FIBULAR	FIDEISTIC	FIENT	FIGHT
FIBERS	FIBULAS	FIDEISTS	FIENTS	FIGHTABLE
FIBRANNE	FICAIN	FIDELISMO	FIER	FIGHTBACK
FIBRANNES	FICAINS	FIDELISTA	FIERCE	FIGHTER
FIBRATE	FICE	FIDELITY	FIERCELY	FIGHTERS
FIBRATES	FICES	FIDES	FIERCER	FIGHTING
FIBRE	FICHE	FIDGE	FIERCEST	FIGHTINGS
FIBRED	FICHES	FIDGED	FIERE	FIGHTS
FIBREFILL	FICHU	FIDGES	FIERES	FIGJAM
FIBRELESS	FICHUS	FIDGET	FIERIER	FIGJAMS
FIBRELIKE	FICIN	FIDGETED	FIERIEST	FIGLIKE
FIBRES	FICINS	FIDGETER	FIERILY	FIGMENT
FIBRIFORM	FICKLE	FIDGETERS	FIERINESS	FIGMENTS
FIBRIL	FICKLED	FIDGETIER	FIERS	FIGO
FIBRILAR	FICKLER	FIDGETING	FIERY	FIGOS
FIBRILLA	FICKLES	FIDGETS	FIEST	FIGS
FIBRILLAE	FICKLEST	FIDGETY	FIESTA	FIGTREE

FIGTREES	FILAREE	FILIATES	FILLISTER	FILTERER
FIGULINE	FILAREES	FILIATING	FILLO	FILTERERS
FIGULINES	FILARIA	FILIATION	FILLOS	FILTERING
FIGURABLE	FILARIAE	FILIBEG	FILLS	FILTERS
FIGURAL	FILARIAL	FILIBEGS	FILLY	FILTH
FIGURALLY	FILARIAN	FILICIDAL	FILM	FILTHIER
FIGURANT	FILARIID	FILICIDE	FILMABLE	FILTHIEST
FIGURANTE	FILARIIDS	FILICIDES	FILMCARD	FILTHILY
FIGURANTS	FILASSE	FILIFORM	FILMCARDS	FILTHS
FIGURATE	FILASSES	FILIGRAIN	FILMDOM	FILTHY
FIGURE	FILATORY	FILIGRANE	FILMDOMS	FILTRABLE
FIGURED	FILATURE	FILIGREE	FILMED	FILTRATE
FIGUREDLY	FILATURES	FILIGREED	FILMER	FILTRATED
FIGURER	FILAZER	FILIGREES	FILMERS	FILTRATES
FIGURERS	FILAZERS	FILII	FILMFEST	FILTRE
FIGURES	FILBERD	FILING	FILMFESTS	FILUM
FIGURINE	FILBERDS	FILINGS	FILMGOER	FIMBLE
FIGURINES	FILBERT	FILIOQUE	FILMGOERS	FIMBLES
FIGURING	FILBERTS	FILIOQUES	FILMGOING	FIMBRIA
FIGURIST	FILCH	FILISTER	FILMI	FIMBRIAE
FIGURISTS	FILCHED	FILISTERS	FILMIC	FIMBRIAL
FIGWORT	FILCHER	FILIUS	FILMIER	FIMBRIATE
FIGWORTS	FILCHERS	FILK	FILMIEST	FIN
FIKE	FILCHES	FILKS	FILMILY	FINABLE
FIKED	FILCHING	FILL	FILMINESS	FINAGLE
FIKERIES	FILCHINGS	FILLABLE	FILMING	FINAGLED
FIKERY	FILE	FILLAGREE	FILMINGS	FINAGLER
FIKES	FILEABLE	FILLE	FILMIS	FINAGLERS
FIKIER	FILECARD	FILLED	FILMISH	FINAGLES
FIKIEST	FILECARDS	FILLER	FILMLAND	FINAGLING
FIKING	FILED	FILLERS	FILMLANDS	FINAL
FIKISH	FILEFISH	FILLES	FILMLESS	FINALE
FIKY	FILEMOT	FILLESTER	FILMLIKE	FINALES
FIL	FILEMOTS	FILLET	FILMMAKER	FINALIS
FILA	FILENAME	FILLETED	FILMS	FINALISE
FILABEG	FILENAMES	FILLETER	FILMSET	FINALISED
FILABEGS	FILER	FILLETERS	FILMSETS	FINALISER
FILACEOUS	FILERS	FILLETING	FILMSTRIP	FINALISES
FILACER	FILES	FILLETS	FILMY	FINALISM
FILACERS	FILET	FILLIBEG	FILO	FINALISMS
FILAGGRIN	FILETED	FILLIBEGS	FILOPLUME	FINALIST
FILAGREE	FILETING	FILLIES	FILOPODIA	FINALISTS
FILAGREED	FILETS	FILLING	FILOS	FINALITY
FILAGREES	FILFOT	FILLINGS	FILOSE	FINALIZE
FILAMENT	FILFOTS	FILLIP	FILOSELLE	FINALIZED
FILAMENTS	FILIAL	FILLIPED	FILOVIRUS	FINALIZER
FILANDER	FILIALLY	FILLIPEEN	FILS	FINALIZES
FILANDERS	FILIATE	FILLIPING	FILTER	FINALLY
FILAR	FILIATED	FILLIPS	FILTERED	FINALS

FINANCE	FINFISHES	FINKING	FIPPLES	FIREFLOAT
FINANCED	FINFOOT	FINKS	FIQH	FIREFLOOD
FINANCES	FINFOOTS	FINLESS	FIQHS	FIREFLY
FINANCIAL	FINGAN	FINLIKE	FIQUE	FIREGUARD
FINANCIER	FINGANS	FINLIT	FIQUES	FIREHALL
FINANCING	FINGER	FINLITS	FIR	FIREHALLS
FINBACK	FINGERED	FINMARK	FIRE	FIREHOSE
FINBACKS	FINGERER	FINMARKS	FIREABLE	FIREHOSES
FINCA	FINGERERS	FINNA	FIREARM	FIREHOUSE
FINCAS	FINGERING	FINNAC	FIREARMED	FIRELESS
FINCH	FINGERS	FINNACK	FIREARMS	FIRELIGHT
FINCHED	FINGERTIP	FINNACKS	FIREBACK	FIRELIT
FINCHES	FINI	FINNACS	FIREBACKS	FIRELOCK
FINCHLIKE	FINIAL	FINNAN	FIREBALL	FIRELOCKS
FIND	FINIALED	FINNANS	FIREBALLS	FIREMAN
FINDABLE	FINIALS	FINNED	FIREBASE	FIREMANIC
FINDER	FINICAL	FINNER	FIREBASES	FIREMARK
FINDERS	FINICALLY	FINNERS	FIREBIRD	FIREMARKS
FINDING	FINICKETY	FINNESKO	FIREBIRDS	FIREMEN
FINDINGS	FINICKIER	FINNICKY	FIREBOARD	FIREPAN
FINDRAM	FINICKIN	FINNIER	FIREBOAT	FIREPANS
FINDRAMS	FINICKING	FINNIEST	FIREBOATS	FIREPINK
FINDS	FINICKY	FINNING	FIREBOMB	FIREPINKS
FINE	FINIKIN	FINNMARK	FIREBOMBS	FIREPIT
FINEABLE	FINIKING	FINNMARKS	FIREBOX	FIREPITS
FINED	FINING	FINNOCHIO	FIREBOXES	FIREPLACE
FINEER	FININGS	FINNOCK	FIREBRAND	FIREPLUG
FINEERED	FINIS	FINNOCKS	FIREBRAT	FIREPLUGS
FINEERING	FINISES	FINNSKO	FIREBRATS	FIREPOT
FINEERS	FINISH	FINNY	FIREBREAK	FIREPOTS
FINEISH	FINISHED	FINO	FIREBRICK	FIREPOWER
FINELESS	FINISHER	FINOCCHIO	FIREBUG	FIREPROOF
FINELY	FINISHERS	FINOCHIO	FIREBUGS	FIRER
FINENESS	FINISHES	FINOCHIOS	FIREBUSH	FIREREEL
FINER	FINISHING	FINOS	FIRECLAY	FIREREELS
FINERIES	FINITE	FINS	FIRECLAYS	FIREROOM
FINERS	FINITELY	FINSKO	FIRECREST	FIREROOMS
FINERY	FINITES	FINTECH	FIRED	FIRERS
FINES	FINITISM	FINTECHS	FIREDAMP	FIRES
FINESPUN	FINITISMS	FIORATURA	FIREDAMPS	FIRESCAPE
FINESSE	FINITIST	FIORD	FIREDOG	FIRESHIP
FINESSED	FINITISTS	FIORDS	FIREDOGS	FIRESHIPS
FINESSER	FINITO	FIORIN	FIREDRAKE	FIRESIDE
FINESSERS	FINITUDE	FIORINS	FIREE	FIRESIDES
FINESSES	FINITUDES	FIORITURA	FIREES	FIRESTONE
FINESSING	FINJAN	FIORITURE	FIREFANG	FIRESTORM
FINEST	FINJANS	FIPPENCE	FIREFANGS	FIRETHORN
FINESTS	FINK	FIPPENCES	FIREFIGHT	FIRETRAP
FINFISH	FINKED	FIPPLE	FIREFLIES	FIRETRAPS

FIRETRUCK	FIRST	FISHIEST	FISSIPEDE	FITFUL
FIREWALL	FIRSTBORN	FISHIFIED	FISSIPEDS	FITFULLY
FIREWALLS	FIRSTHAND	FISHIFIES	FISSIVE	FITLIER
FIREWATER	FIRSTLING	FISHIFY	FISSLE	FITLIEST
FIREWEED	FIRSTLY	FISHILY	FISSLED	FITLY
FIREWEEDS	FIRSTNESS	FISHINESS	FISSLES	FITMENT
FIREWOMAN	FIRSTS	FISHING	FISSLING	FITMENTS
FIREWOMEN	FIRTH	FISHINGS	FISSURAL	FITNA
FIREWOOD	FIRTHS	FISHKILL	FISSURE	FITNAS
FIREWOODS	FIRWOOD	FISHKILLS	FISSURED	FITNESS
FIREWORK	FIRWOODS	FISHLESS	FISSURES	FITNESSES
FIREWORKS	FISC	FISHLIKE	FISSURING	FITS
FIREWORM	FISCAL	FISHLINE	FIST	FITT
FIREWORMS	FISCALIST	FISHLINES	FISTED	FITTABLE
FIRIE	FISCALLY	FISHMEAL	FISTFIGHT	FITTE
FIRIES	FISCALS	FISHMEALS	FISTFUL	FITTED
FIRING	FISCS	FISHNET	FISTFULS	FITTER
FIRINGS	FISGIG	FISHNETS	FISTIANA	FITTERS
FIRK	FISGIGS	FISHPLATE	FISTIANAS	FITTES
FIRKED	FISH	FISHPOLE	FISTIC	FITTEST
FIRKIN	FISHABLE	FISHPOLES	FISTICAL	FITTING
FIRKING	FISHBALL	FISHPOND	FISTICUFF	FITTINGLY
FIRKINS	FISHBALLS	FISHPONDS	FISTIER	FITTINGS
FIRKS	FISHBOAT	FISHSKIN	FISTIEST	FITTS
FIRLOT	FISHBOATS	FISHSKINS	FISTING	FIVE
FIRLOTS	FISHBOLT	FISHTAIL	FISTINGS	FIVEFOLD
FIRM	FISHBOLTS	FISHTAILS	FISTMELE	FIVEPENCE
FIRMAMENT	FISHBONE	FISHWAY	FISTMELES	FIVEPENNY
FIRMAN	FISHBONES	FISHWAYS	FISTNOTE	FIVEPIN
FIRMANS	FISHBOWL	FISHWIFE	FISTNOTES	FIVEPINS
FIRMED	FISHBOWLS	FISHWIVES	FISTS	FIVER
FIRMER	FISHCAKE	FISHWORM	FISTULA	FIVERS
FIRMERS	FISHCAKES	FISHWORMS	FISTULAE	FIVES
FIRMEST	FISHED	FISHY	FISTULAR	FIX
FIRMING	FISHER	FISHYBACK	FISTULAS	FIXABLE
FIRMLESS	FISHERIES	FISK	FISTULATE	FIXATE
FIRMLY	FISHERMAN	FISKED	FISTULOSE	FIXATED
FIRMNESS	FISHERMEN	FISKING	FISTULOUS	FIXATES
FIRMS	FISHERS	FISKS	FISTY	FIXATIF
FIRMWARE	FISHERY	FISNOMIE	FIT	FIXATIFS
FIRMWARES	FISHES	FISNOMIES	FITCH	FIXATING
FIRN	FISHEYE	FISSATE	FITCHE	FIXATION
FIRNS	FISHEYES	FISSILE	FITCHEE	FIXATIONS
FIRRIER	FISHFUL	FISSILITY	FITCHES	FIXATIVE
FIRRIEST	FISHGIG	FISSION	FITCHET	FIXATIVES
FIRRING	FISHGIGS	FISSIONAL	FITCHETS	FIXATURE
FIRRINGS	FISHHOOK	FISSIONED	FITCHEW	FIXATURES
FIRRY	FISHHOOKS	FISSIONS	FITCHEWS	FIXED
FIRS	FISHIER	FISSIPED	FITCHY	FIXEDLY

F

FIXEDNESS	FLABBIER	FLAGONS	FLAMEN	FLANK
FIXER	FLABBIEST	FLAGPOLE	FLAMENCO	FLANKED
FIXERS	FLABBILY	FLAGPOLES	FLAMENCOS	FLANKEN
FIXES	FLABBY	FLAGRANCE	FLAMENS	FLANKENS
FIXING	FLABELLA	FLAGRANCY	FLAMEOUT	FLANKER
FIXINGS	FLABELLUM	FLAGRANT	FLAMEOUTS	FLANKERED
FIXIT	FLABS	FLAGS	FLAMER	FLANKERS
FIXITIES	FLACCID	FLAGSHIP	FLAMERS	FLANKING
FIXITS	FLACCIDER	FLAGSHIPS	FLAMES	FLANKS
FIXITY	FLACCIDLY	FLAGSTAFF	FLAMFEW	FLANNEL
FIXIVE	FLACK	FLAGSTICK	FLAMFEWS	FLANNELED
FIXT	FLACKED	FLAGSTONE	FLAMIER	FLANNELET
FIXTURE	FLACKER	FLAIL	FLAMIEST	FLANNELLY
FIXTURES	FLACKERED	FLAILED	FLAMINES	FLANNELS
FIXTURING	FLACKERS	FLAILING	FLAMING	FLANNEN
FIXURE	FLACKERY	FLAILS	FLAMINGLY	FLANNENS
FIXURES	FLACKET	FLAIR	FLAMINGO	FLANNIE
FIZ	FLACKETED	FLAIRS	FLAMINGOS	FLANNIES
FIZGIG	FLACKETS	FLAK	FLAMM	FLANNY
FIZGIGGED	FLACKING	FLAKE	FLAMMABLE	FLANS
FIZGIGS	FLACKS	FLAKED	FLAMMED	FLAP
FIZZ	FLACON	FLAKER	FLAMMING	FLAPERON
FIZZED	FLACONS	FLAKERS	FLAMMS	FLAPERONS
FIZZEN	FLAFF	FLAKES	FLAMMULE	FLAPJACK
FIZZENS	FLAFFED	FLAKEY	FLAMMULES	FLAPJACKS
FIZZER	FLAFFER	FLAKIER	FLAMS	FLAPLESS
FIZZERS	FLAFFERED	FLAKIES	FLAMY	FLAPLIKE
FIZZES	FLAFFERS	FLAKIEST	FLAN	FLAPPABLE
FIZZGIG	FLAFFING	FLAKILY	FLANCARD	FLAPPED
FIZZGIGS	FLAFFS	FLAKINESS	FLANCARDS	FLAPPER
FIZZIER	FLAG	FLAKING	FLANCH	FLAPPERS
FIZZIEST	FLAGELLA	FLAKS	FLANCHED	FLAPPIER
FIZZILY	FLAGELLAR	FLAKY	FLANCHES	FLAPPIEST
FIZZINESS	FLAGELLIN	FLAM	FLANCHING	FLAPPING
FIZZING	FLAGELLUM	FLAMBE	FLANE	FLAPPINGS
FIZZINGS	FLAGEOLET	FLAMBEAU	FLANED	FLAPPY
FIZZLE	FLAGGED	FLAMBEAUS	FLANERIE	FLAPS
FIZZLED	FLAGGER	FLAMBEAUX	FLANERIES	FLAPTRACK
FIZZLES	FLAGGERS	FLAMBEE	FLANES	FLARE
FIZZLING	FLAGGIER	FLAMBEED	FLANEUR	FLAREBACK
FIZZOG	FLAGGIEST	FLAMBEES	FLANEURS	FLARED
FIZZOGS	FLAGGING	FLAMBEING	FLANGE	FLARES
FIZZY	FLAGGINGS	FLAMBES	FLANGED	FLAREUP
FJELD	FLAGGY	FLAME	FLANGER	FLAREUPS
FJELDS	FLAGITATE	FLAMED	FLANGERS	FLARIER
FJORD	FLAGLESS	FLAMELESS	FLANGES	FLARIEST
FJORDIC	FLAGMAN	FLAMELET	FLANGING	FLARING
FJORDS	FLAGMEN	FLAMELETS	FLANGINGS	FLARINGLY
FLAB	FLAGON	FLAMELIKE	FLANING	FLARY

FLASER	FLATFORMS	FLATUSES	FLAVOR	FLEADH
FLASERS	FLATHEAD	FLATWARE	FLAVORED	FLEADHS
FLASH	FLATHEADS	FLATWARES	FLAVORER	FLEAM
FLASHBACK	FLATIRON	FLATWASH	FLAVORERS	FLEAMS
FLASHBANG	FLATIRONS	FLATWATER	FLAVORFUL	FLEAPIT
FLASHBULB	FLATLAND	FLATWAYS	FLAVORIER	FLEAPITS
FLASHCARD	FLATLANDS	FLATWISE	FLAVORING	FLEAS
FLASHCUBE	FLATLET	FLATWORK	FLAVORIST	FLEASOME
FLASHED	FLATLETS	FLATWORKS	FLAVOROUS	FLEAWORT
FLASHER	FLATLINE	FLATWORM	FLAVORS	FLEAWORTS
FLASHERS	FLATLINED	FLATWORMS	FLAVORY	FLECHE
FLASHES	FLATLINER	FLAUGHT	FLAVOUR	FLECHES
FLASHEST	FLATLINES	FLAUGHTED	FLAVOURED	FLECHETTE
FLASHGUN	FLATLING	FLAUGHTER	FLAVOURER	FLECK
FLASHGUNS	FLATLINGS	FLAUGHTS	FLAVOURS	FLECKED
FLASHIER	FLATLONG	FLAUNCH	FLAVOURY	FLECKER
FLASHIEST	FLATLY	FLAUNCHED	FLAW	FLECKERED
FLASHILY	FLATMATE	FLAUNCHES	FLAWED	FLECKERS
FLASHING	FLATMATES	FLAUNE	FLAWIER	FLECKIER
FLASHINGS	FLATNESS	FLAUNES	FLAWIEST	FLECKIEST
FLASHLAMP	FLATPACK	FLAUNT	FLAWING	FLECKING
FLASHOVER	FLATPACKS	FLAUNTED	FLAWLESS	FLECKLESS
FLASHTUBE	FLATPICK	FLAUNTER	FLAWN	FLECKS
FLASHY	FLATPICKS	FLAUNTERS	FLAWNS	FLECKY
FLASK	FLATS	FLAUNTIER	FLAWS	FLECTION
FLASKET	FLATSHARE	FLAUNTILY	FLAWY	FLECTIONS
FLASKETS	FLATSTICK	FLAUNTING	FLAX	FLED
FLASKS	FLATTED	FLAUNTS	FLAXEN	FLEDGE
FLAT	FLATTEN	FLAUNTY	FLAXES	FLEDGED
FLATBACK	FLATTENED	FLAUTA	FLAXIER	FLEDGES
FLATBACKS	FLATTENER	FLAUTAS	FLAXIEST	FLEDGIER
FLATBED	FLATTENS	FLAUTIST	FLAXLIKE	FLEDGIEST
FLATBEDS	FLATTER	FLAUTISTS	FLAXSEED	FLEDGING
FLATBOAT	FLATTERED	FLAVA	FLAXSEEDS	FLEDGLING
FLATBOATS	FLATTERER	FLAVANOL	FLAXY	FLEDGY
FLATBREAD	FLATTERS	FLAVANOLS	FLAY	FLEE
FLATBROD	FLATTERY	FLAVANONE	FLAYED	FLEECE
FLATBRODS	FLATTEST	FLAVAS	FLAYER	FLEECED
FLATCAP	FLATTIE	FLAVEDO	FLAYERS	FLEECER
FLATCAPS	FLATTIES	FLAVEDOS	FLAYING	FLEECERS
FLATCAR	FLATTING	FLAVIN	FLAYS	FLEECES
FLATCARS	FLATTINGS	FLAVINE	FLAYSOME	FLEECH
FLATETTE	FLATTISH	FLAVINES	FLEA	FLEECHED
FLATETTES	FLATTOP	FLAVINS	FLEABAG	FLEECHES
FLATFEET	FLATTOPS	FLAVONE	FLEABAGS	FLEECHING
FLATFISH	FLATTY	FLAVONES	FLEABANE	FLEECIE
FLATFOOT	FLATULENT	FLAVONOID	FLEABANES	FLEECIER
FLATFOOTS	FLATUOUS	FLAVONOL	FLEABITE	FLEECIES
FLATFORM	FLATUS	FLAVONOLS	FLEABITES	FLEECIEST

FLEECILY	FLENSERS	FLEXIBLE	FLIGHTIER	FLIPBOOKS
FLEECING	FLENSES	FLEXIBLY	FLIGHTILY	FLIPCHART
FLEECY	FLENSING	FLEXILE	FLIGHTING	FLIPFLOP
FLEEING	FLEROVIUM	FLEXING	FLIGHTS	FLIPFLOPS
FLEEK	FLESH	FLEXION	FLIGHTY	FLIPPANCY
FLEEKS	FLESHED	FLEXIONAL	FLIM	FLIPPANT
FLEER	FLESHER	FLEXIONS	FLIMFLAM	FLIPPED
FLEERED	FLESHERS	FLEXIS	FLIMFLAMS	FLIPPER
FLEERER	FLESHES	FLEXITIME	FLIMP	FLIPPERS
FLEERERS	FLESHHOOD	FLEXO	FLIMPED	FLIPPEST
FLEERING	FLESHIER	FLEXOR	FLIMPING	FLIPPIER
FLEERINGS	FLESHIEST	FLEXORS	FLIMPS	FLIPPIEST
FLEERS	FLESHILY	FLEXOS	FLIMS	FLIPPING
FLEES	FLESHING	FLEXTIME	FLIMSIER	FLIPPINGS
FLEET	FLESHINGS	FLEXTIMER	FLIMSIES	FLIPPY
FLEETED	FLESHLESS	FLEXTIMES	FLIMSIEST	FLIPS
FLEETER	FLESHLIER	FLEXUOSE	FLIMSILY	FLIPSIDE
FLEETERS	FLESHLING	FLEXUOUS	FLIMSY	FLIPSIDES
FLEETEST	FLESHLY	FLEXURAL	FLINCH	FLIR
FLEETING	FLESHMENT	FLEXURE	FLINCHED	FLIRS
FLEETLY	FLESHPOT	FLEXURES	FLINCHER	FLIRT
FLEETNESS	FLESHPOTS	FLEXWING	FLINCHERS	FLIRTED
FLEETS	FLESHWORM	FLEXWINGS	FLINCHES	FLIRTER
FLEG	FLESHY	FLEY	FLINCHING	FLIRTERS
FLEGGED	FLETCH	FLEYED	FLINDER	FLIRTIER
FLEGGING	FLETCHED	FLEYING	FLINDERED	FLIRTIEST
FLEGS	FLETCHER	FLEYS	FLINDERS	FLIRTING
FLEHMEN	FLETCHERS	FLIBBERT	FLING	FLIRTINGS
FLEHMENED	FLETCHES	FLIBBERTS	FLINGER	FLIRTISH
FLEHMENS	FLETCHING	FLIC	FLINGERS	FLIRTS
FLEISHIG	FLETTON	FLICHTER	FLINGING	FLIRTY
FLEISHIK	FLETTONS	FLICHTERS	FLINGS	FLISK
FLEME	FLEUR	FLICK	FLINKITE	FLISKED
FLEMED	FLEURET	FLICKABLE	FLINKITES	FLISKIER
FLEMES	FLEURETS	FLICKED	FLINT	FLISKIEST
FLEMING	FLEURETTE	FLICKER	FLINTED	FLISKING
FLEMISH	FLEURON	FLICKERED	FLINTHEAD	FLISKS
FLEMISHED	FLEURONS	FLICKERS	FLINTIER	FLISKY
FLEMISHES	FLEURS	FLICKERY	FLINTIEST	FLIT
FLEMIT	FLEURY	FLICKING	FLINTIFY	FLITCH
FLENCH	FLEW	FLICKS	FLINTILY	FLITCHED
FLENCHED	FLEWED	FLICS	FLINTING	FLITCHES
FLENCHER	FLEWS	FLIED	FLINTLIKE	FLITCHING
FLENCHERS	FLEX	FLIER	FLINTLOCK	FLITE
FLENCHES	FLEXAGON	FLIERS	FLINTS	FLITED
FLENCHING	FLEXAGONS	FLIES	FLINTY	FLITES
FLENSE	FLEXED	FLIEST	FLIP	FLITING
FLENSED	FLEXES	FLIGHT	FLIPBOARD	FLITS
FLENSER	FLEXI	FLIGHTED	FLIPBOOK	FLITT

FLITTED	FLOCCULI	FLOOIE	FLORETS	FLOTANT
FLITTER	FLOCCULUS	FLOOR	FLORIATED	FLOTAS
FLITTERED	FLOCCUS	FLOORAGE	FLORICANE	FLOTATION
FLITTERN	FLOCK	FLOORAGES	FLORID	FLOTE
FLITTERNS	FLOCKED	FLOORED	FLORIDEAN	FLOTED
FLITTERS	FLOCKIER	FLOORER	FLORIDER	FLOTEL
FLITTING	FLOCKIEST	FLOORERS	FLORIDEST	FLOTELS
FLITTINGS	FLOCKING	FLOORHEAD	FLORIDITY	FLOTES
FLITTS	FLOCKINGS	FLOORING	FLORIDLY	FLOTILLA
FLIVVER	FLOCKLESS	FLOORINGS	FLORIER	FLOTILLAS
FLIVVERS	FLOCKS	FLOORLESS	FLORIEST	FLOTING
FLIX	FLOCKY	FLOORPAN	FLORIFORM	FLOTSAM
FLIXED	FLOCS	FLOORPANS	FLORIGEN	FLOTSAMS
FLIXES	FLOE	FLOORS	FLORIGENS	FLOUNCE
FLIXING	FLOES	FLOORSHOW	FLORIN	FLOUNCED
FLIXWEED	FLOG	FLOOSIE	FLORINS	FLOUNCES
FLIXWEEDS	FLOGGABLE	FLOOSIES	FLORIST	FLOUNCIER
FLOAT	FLOGGED	FLOOSY	FLORISTIC	FLOUNCING
FLOATABLE	FLOGGER	FLOOZIE	FLORISTRY	FLOUNCY
FLOATAGE	FLOGGERS	FLOOZIES	FLORISTS	FLOUNDER
FLOATAGES	FLOGGING	FLOOZY	FLORS	FLOUNDERS
FLOATANT	FLOGGINGS	FLOP	FLORUIT	FLOUR
FLOATANTS	FLOGS	FLOPHOUSE	FLORUITS	FLOURED
FLOATBASE	FLOKATI	FLOPOVER	FLORULA	FLOURIER
FLOATCUT	FLOKATIS	FLOPOVERS	FLORULAE	FLOURIEST
FLOATED	FLONG	FLOPPED	FLORULE	FLOURING
FLOATEL	FLONGS	FLOPPER	FLORULES	FLOURISH
FLOATELS	FLOOD	FLOPPERS	FLORY	FLOURISHY
FLOATER	FLOODABLE	FLOPPIER	FLOSCULAR	FLOURLESS
FLOATERS	FLOODED	FLOPPIES	FLOSCULE	FLOURS
FLOATIER	FLOODER	FLOPPIEST	FLOSCULES	FLOURY
FLOATIES	FLOODERS	FLOPPILY	FLOSH	FLOUSE
FLOATIEST	FLOODGATE	FLOPPING	FLOSHES	FLOUSED
FLOATING	FLOODING	FLOPPY	FLOSS	FLOUSES
FLOATINGS	FLOODINGS	FLOPS	FLOSSED	FLOUSH
FLOATS	FLOODLESS	FLOPTICAL	FLOSSER	FLOUSHED
FLOATY	FLOODLIT	FLOR	FLOSSERS	FLOUSHES
FLOB	FLOODMARK	FLORA	FLOSSES	FLOUSHING
FLOBBED	FLOODS	FLORAE	FLOSSIE	FLOUSING
FLOBBING	FLOODTIDE	FLORAL	FLOSSIER	FLOUT
FLOBS	FLOODWALL	FLORALLY	FLOSSIES	FLOUTED
FLOC	FLOODWAY	FLORALS	FLOSSIEST	FLOUTER
FLOCCED	FLOODWAYS	FLORAS	FLOSSILY	FLOUTERS
FLOCCI	FLOOEY	FLOREANT	FLOSSING	FLOUTING
FLOCCING	FLOOF	FLOREAT	FLOSSINGS	FLOUTS
FLOCCOSE	FLOOFIER	FLOREATED	FLOSSY	FLOW
FLOCCULAR	FLOOFIEST	FLORENCE	FLOTA	FLOWABLE
FLOCCULE	FLOOFS	FLORENCES	FLOTAGE	FLOWAGE
FLOCCULES	FLOOFY	FLORET	FLOTAGES	FLOWAGES

FLOWBACK	FLUENT	FLUKED	FLUOROSES	FLUTISTS
FLOWBACKS	FLUENTLY	FLUKES	FLUOROSIS	FLUTTER
FLOWCHART	FLUENTS	FLUKEY	FLUOROTIC	FLUTTERED
FLOWED	FLUERIC	FLUKIER	FLUORS	FLUTTERER
FLOWER	FLUERICS	FLUKIEST	FLUORSPAR	FLUTTERS
FLOWERAGE	FLUES	FLUKILY	FLURR	FLUTTERY
FLOWERBED	FLUEWORK	FLUKINESS	FLURRED	FLUTY
FLOWERED	FLUEWORKS	FLUKING	FLURRIED	FLUVIAL
FLOWERER	FLUEY	FLUKY	FLURRIES	FLUVIATIC
FLOWERERS	FLUFF	FLUME	FLURRING	FLUX
FLOWERET	FLUFFBALL	FLUMED	FLURRS	FLUXED
FLOWERETS	FLUFFED	FLUMES	FLURRY	FLUXES
FLOWERFUL	FLUFFER	FLUMING	FLURRYING	FLUXGATE
FLOWERIER	FLUFFERS	FLUMMERY	FLUS	FLUXGATES
FLOWERILY	FLUFFIER	FLUMMOX	FLUSH	FLUXING
FLOWERING	FLUFFIEST	FLUMMOXED	FLUSHABLE	FLUXION
FLOWERPOT	FLUFFILY	FLUMMOXES	FLUSHED	FLUXIONAL
FLOWERS	FLUFFING	FLUMP	FLUSHER	FLUXIONS
FLOWERY	FLUFFS	FLUMPED	FLUSHERS	FLUXIVE
FLOWING	FLUFFY	FLUMPING	FLUSHES	FLUXMETER
FLOWINGLY	FLUGEL	FLUMPS	FLUSHEST	FLUYT
FLOWMETER	FLUGELMAN	FLUNG	FLUSHIER	FLUYTS
FLOWN	FLUGELMEN	FLUNK	FLUSHIEST	FLY
FLOWS	FLUGELS	FLUNKED	FLUSHING	FLYABLE
FLOWSTONE	FLUID	FLUNKER	FLUSHINGS	FLYAWAY
FLOX	FLUIDAL	FLUNKERS	FLUSHNESS	FLYAWAYS
FLU	FLUIDALLY	FLUNKEY	FLUSHWORK	FLYBACK
FLUATE	FLUIDIC	FLUNKEYS	FLUSHY	FLYBACKS
FLUATES	FLUIDICS	FLUNKIE	FLUSTER	FLYBANE
FLUB	FLUIDIFY	FLUNKIES	FLUSTERED	FLYBANES
FLUBBED	FLUIDISE	FLUNKING	FLUSTERS	FLYBELT
FLUBBER	FLUIDISED	FLUNKS	FLUSTERY	FLYBELTS
FLUBBERS	FLUIDISER	FLUNKY	FLUSTRATE	FLYBLEW
FLUBBING	FLUIDISES	FLUNKYISM	FLUTE	FLYBLOW
FLUBDUB	FLUIDITY	FLUOR	FLUTED	FLYBLOWN
FLUBDUBS	FLUIDIZE	FLUORENE	FLUTELIKE	FLYBLOWS
FLUBS	FLUIDIZED	FLUORENES	FLUTER	FLYBOAT
FLUCTUANT	FLUIDIZER	FLUORESCE	FLUTERS	FLYBOATS
FLUCTUATE	FLUIDIZES	FLUORIC	FLUTES	FLYBOOK
FLUE	FLUIDLIKE	FLUORID	FLUTEY	FLYBOOKS
FLUED	FLUIDLY	FLUORIDE	FLUTEYER	FLYBOY
FLUELLEN	FLUIDNESS	FLUORIDES	FLUTEYEST	FLYBOYS
FLUELLENS	FLUIDRAM	FLUORIDS	FLUTIER	FLYBRIDGE
FLUELLIN	FLUIDRAMS	FLUORIN	FLUTIEST	FLYBY
FLUELLINS	FLUIDS	FLUORINE	FLUTINA	FLYBYS
FLUENCE	FLUIER	FLUORINES	FLUTINAS	FLYER
FLUENCES	FLUIEST	FLUORINS	FLUTING	FLYERS
FLUENCIES	FLUISH	FLUORITE	FLUTINGS	FLYEST
FLUENCY	FLUKE	FLUORITES	FLUTIST	FLYFISHER

FLYHAND	FLYWEIGHT	FOCUSING	FOGEYS	FOILED
FLYHANDS	FLYWHEEL	FOCUSINGS	FOGFRUIT	FOILING
FLYING	FLYWHEELS	FOCUSLESS	FOGFRUITS	FOILINGS
FLYINGS	FOAL	FOCUSSED	FOGGAGE	FOILIST
FLYLEAF	FOALED	FOCUSSES	FOGGAGES	FOILISTS
FLYLEAVES	FOALFOOT	FOCUSSING	FOGGED	FOILS
FLYLESS	FOALFOOTS	FODDER	FOGGER	FOILSMAN
FLYLINE	FOALING	FODDERED	FOGGERS	FOILSMEN
FLYLINES	FOALINGS	FODDERER	FOGGIER	FOIN
FLYMAKER	FOALS	FODDERERS	FOGGIEST	FOINED
FLYMAKERS	FOAM	FODDERING	FOGGILY	FOINING
FLYMAN	FOAMABLE	FODDERS	FOGGINESS	FOININGLY
FLYMEN	FOAMED	FODGEL	FOGGING	FOINS
FLYOFF	FOAMER	FOE	FOGGINGS	FOISON
FLYOFFS	FOAMERS	FOEDARIE	FOGGY	FOISONS
FLYOVER	FOAMIER	FOEDARIES	FOGHORN	FOIST
FLYOVERS	FOAMIEST	FOEDERATI	FOGHORNS	FOISTED
FLYPAPER	FOAMILY	FOEFIE	FOGIE	FOISTER
FLYPAPERS	FOAMINESS	FOEHN	FOGIES	FOISTERS
FLYPAST	FOAMING	FOEHNS	FOGLE	FOISTING
FLYPASTS	FOAMINGLY	FOEMAN	FOGLES	FOISTS
FLYPE	FOAMINGS	FOEMEN	FOGLESS	FOLACIN
FLYPED	FOAMLESS	FOEN	FOGLIGHT	FOLACINS
FLYPES	FOAMLIKE	FOES	FOGLIGHTS	FOLATE
FLYPING	FOAMS	FOETAL	FOGMAN	FOLATES
FLYPITCH	FOAMY	FOETATION	FOGMEN	FOLD
FLYPOSTER	FOB	FOETICIDE	FOGOU	FOLDABLE
FLYRODDER	FOBBED	FOETID	FOGOUS	FOLDAWAY
FLYSCH	FOBBING	FOETIDER	FOGRAM	FOLDAWAYS
FLYSCHES	FOBS	FOETIDEST	FOGRAMITE	FOLDBACK
FLYSCREEN	FOCACCIA	FOETIDLY	FOGRAMITY	FOLDBACKS
FLYSHEET	FOCACCIAS	FOETOR	FOGRAMS	FOLDBOAT
FLYSHEETS	FOCAL	FOETORS	FOGS	FOLDBOATS
FLYSPECK	FOCALISE	FOETUS	FOGY	FOLDED
FLYSPECKS	FOCALISED	FOETUSES	FOGYDOM	FOLDER
FLYSPRAY	FOCALISES	FOG	FOGYDOMS	FOLDEROL
FLYSPRAYS	FOCALIZE	FOGASH	FOGYISH	FOLDEROLS
FLYSTRIKE	FOCALIZED	FOGASHES	FOGYISM	FOLDERS
FLYTE	FOCALIZES	FOGBOUND	FOGYISMS	FOLDING
FLYTED	FOCALLY	FOGBOW	FOH	FOLDINGS
FLYTES	FOCI	FOGBOWS	FOHN	FOLDOUT
FLYTIER	FOCIMETER	FOGDOG	FOHNS	FOLDOUTS
FLYTIERS	FOCOMETER	FOGDOGS	FOIBLE	FOLDS
FLYTING	FOCUS	FOGEY	FOIBLES	FOLDUP
FLYTINGS	FOCUSABLE	FOGEYDOM	FOID	FOLDUPS
FLYTRAP	FOCUSED	FOGEYDOMS	FOIDS	FOLEY
FLYTRAPS	FOCUSER	FOGEYISH	FOIL	FOLEYS
FLYWAY	FOCUSERS	FOGEYISM	FOILABLE	FOLIA
FLYWAYS	FOCUSES	FOGEYISMS	FOILBORNE	FOLIAGE

FOLIAGED	FOLKSILY	FONDLES	FOODOIR	FOOTERING
FOLIAGES	FOLKSONG	FONDLING	FOODOIRS	FOOTERS
FOLIAR	FOLKSONGS	FONDLINGS	FOODS	FOOTFALL
FOLIATE	FOLKSY	FONDLY	FOODSHED	FOOTFALLS
FOLIATED	FOLKTALE	FONDNESS	FOODSHEDS	FOOTFAULT
FOLIATES	FOLKTALES	FONDS	FOODSTUFF	FOOTGEAR
FOLIATING	FOLKWAY	FONDU	FOODWAYS	FOOTGEARS
FOLIATION	FOLKWAYS	FONDUE	FOODY	FOOTHILL
FOLIATURE	FOLKY	FONDUED	FOOFARAW	FOOTHILLS
FOLIC	FOLLES	FONDUEING	FOOFARAWS	FOOTHOLD
FOLIE	FOLLICLE	FONDUES	FOOL	FOOTHOLDS
FOLIES	FOLLICLES	FONDUING	FOOLED	FOOTIE
FOLIO	FOLLIED	FONDUS	FOOLERIES	FOOTIER
FOLIOED	FOLLIES	FONE	FOOLERY	FOOTIES
FOLIOING	FOLLIS	FONES	FOOLFISH	FOOTIEST
FOLIOLATE	FOLLOW	FONIO	FOOLHARDY	FOOTING
FOLIOLE	FOLLOWED	FONIOS	FOOLING	FOOTINGS
FOLIOLES	FOLLOWER	FONLY	FOOLINGS	FOOTLE
FOLIOLOSE	FOLLOWERS	FONNED	FOOLISH	FOOTLED
FOLIOS	FOLLOWING	FONNING	FOOLISHER	FOOTLER
FOLIOSE	FOLLOWS	FONS	FOOLISHLY	FOOTLERS
FOLIOUS	FOLLOWUP	FONT	FOOLPROOF	FOOTLES
FOLIUM	FOLLOWUPS	FONTAL	FOOLS	FOOTLESS
FOLIUMS	FOLLY	FONTANEL	FOOLSCAP	FOOTLIGHT
FOLK	FOLLYING	FONTANELS	FOOLSCAPS	FOOTLIKE
FOLKIE	FOLX	FONTANGE	FOOS	FOOTLING
FOLKIER	FOMENT	FONTANGES	FOOSBALL	FOOTLINGS
FOLKIES	FOMENTED	FONTICULI	FOOSBALLS	FOOTLONG
FOLKIEST	FOMENTER	FONTINA	FOOT	FOOTLONGS
FOLKINESS	FOMENTERS	FONTINAS	FOOTAGE	FOOTLOOSE
FOLKISH	FOMENTING	FONTLET	FOOTAGES	FOOTMAN
FOLKLAND	FOMENTS	FONTLETS	FOOTBAG	FOOTMARK
FOLKLANDS	FOMES	FONTS	FOOTBAGS	FOOTMARKS
FOLKLIFE	FOMITE	FOO	FOOTBALL	FOOTMEN
FOLKLIFES	FOMITES	FOOBAR	FOOTBALLS	FOOTMUFF
FOLKLIKE	FON	FOOD	FOOTBAR	FOOTMUFFS
FOLKLIVES	FOND	FOODBANK	FOOTBARS	FOOTNOTE
FOLKLORE	FONDA	FOODBANKS	FOOTBATH	FOOTNOTED
FOLKLORES	FONDANT	FOODBORNE	FOOTBATHS	FOOTNOTES
FOLKLORIC	FONDANTS	FOODERIES	FOOTBED	FOOTPACE
FOLKMOOT	FONDAS	FOODERY	FOOTBEDS	FOOTPACES
FOLKMOOTS	FONDED	FOODFUL	FOOTBOARD	FOOTPAD
FOLKMOT	FONDER	FOODIE	FOOTBOY	FOOTPADS
FOLKMOTE	FONDEST	FOODIES	FOOTBOYS	FOOTPAGE
FOLKMOTES	FONDING	FOODISM	FOOTBRAKE	FOOTPAGES
FOLKMOTS	FONDLE	FOODISMS	FOOTCLOTH	FOOTPATH
FOLKS	FONDLED	FOODLAND	FOOTED	FOOTPATHS
FOLKSIER	FONDLER	FOODLANDS	FOOTER	FOOTPLATE
FOLKSIEST	FONDLERS	FOODLESS	FOOTERED	FOOTPOST

FOOTPOSTS	FOOZLINGS	FORBODES	FOREBEAR	FOREGOERS
FOOTPRINT	FOP	FORBODING	FOREBEARS	FOREGOES
FOOTPUMP	FOPLING	FORBORE	FOREBITT	FOREGOING
FOOTPUMPS	FOPLINGS	FORBORNE	FOREBITTS	FOREGONE
FOOTRA	FOPPED	FORBS	FOREBODE	FOREGUT
FOOTRACE	FOPPERIES	FORBY	FOREBODED	FOREGUTS
FOOTRACES	FOPPERY	FORBYE	FOREBODER	FOREHAND
FOOTRAS	FOPPING	FORCAT	FOREBODES	FOREHANDS
FOOTREST	FOPPISH	FORCATS	FOREBODY	FOREHEAD
FOOTRESTS	FOPPISHLY	FORCE	FOREBOOM	FOREHEADS
FOOTROPE	FOPS	FORCEABLE	FOREBOOMS	FOREHENT
FOOTROPES	FOR	FORCEABLY	FOREBRAIN	FOREHENTS
FOOTRULE	FORA	FORCED	FOREBY	FOREHOCK
FOOTRULES	FORAGE	FORCEDLY	FOREBYE	FOREHOCKS
FOOTS	FORAGED	FORCEFUL	FORECABIN	FOREHOOF
FOOTSAL	FORAGER	FORCELESS	FORECADDY	FOREHOOFS
FOOTSALS	FORAGERS	FORCEMEAT	FORECAR	FOREIGN
FOOTSIE	FORAGES	FORCEOUT	FORECARS	FOREIGNER
FOOTSIES	FORAGING	FORCEOUTS	FORECAST	FOREIGNLY
FOOTSLOG	FORAM	FORCEPS	FORECASTS	FOREJUDGE
FOOTSLOGS	FORAMEN	FORCEPSES	FORECHECK	FOREKING
FOOTSORE	FORAMENS	FORCER	FORECLOSE	FOREKINGS
FOOTSTALK	FORAMINA	FORCERS	FORECLOTH	FOREKNEW
FOOTSTALL	FORAMINAL	FORCES	FORECOURT	FOREKNOW
FOOTSTEP	FORAMS	FORCIBLE	FOREDATE	FOREKNOWN
FOOTSTEPS	FORANE	FORCIBLY	FOREDATED	FOREKNOWS
FOOTSTOCK	FORASMUCH	FORCING	FOREDATES	FOREL
FOOTSTONE	FORAY	FORCINGLY	FOREDECK	FORELADY
FOOTSTOOL	FORAYED	FORCIPATE	FOREDECKS	FORELAID
FOOTSY	FORAYER	FORCIPES	FOREDID	FORELAIN
FOOTWALL	FORAYERS	FORD	FOREDO	FORELAND
FOOTWALLS	FORAYING	FORDABLE	FOREDOES	FORELANDS
FOOTWAY	FORAYS	FORDED	FOREDOING	FORELAY
FOOTWAYS	FORB	FORDID	FOREDONE	FORELAYS
FOOTWEAR	FORBAD	FORDING	FOREDOOM	FORELEG
FOOTWEARS	FORBADE	FORDLESS	FOREDOOMS	FORELEGS
FOOTWEARY	FORBARE	FORDO	FOREFACE	FORELEND
FOOTWELL	FORBEAR	FORDOES	FOREFACES	FORELENDS
FOOTWELLS	FORBEARER	FORDOING	FOREFEEL	FORELENT
FOOTWORK	FORBEARS	FORDONE	FOREFEELS	FORELIE
FOOTWORKS	FORBID	FORDONNE	FOREFEET	FORELIES
FOOTWORN	FORBIDAL	FORDS	FOREFELT	FORELIFT
FOOTY	FORBIDALS	FORE	FOREFEND	FORELIFTS
FOOZLE	FORBIDDAL	FOREANENT	FOREFENDS	FORELIMB
FOOZLED	FORBIDDEN	FOREARM	FOREFOOT	FORELIMBS
FOOZLER	FORBIDDER	FOREARMED	FOREFRONT	FORELLED
FOOZLERS	FORBIDS	FOREARMS	FOREGLEAM	FORELLING
FOOZLES	FORBODE	FOREBAY	FOREGO	FORELOCK
FOOZLING	FORBODED	FOREBAYS	FOREGOER	FORELOCKS

FORELS	FORESEER	FORETEACH	FORFICATE	FORHOWED
FORELYING	FORESEERS	FORETEETH	FORFOCHEN	FORHOWING
FOREMAN	FORESEES	FORETELL	FORGAT	FORHOWS
FOREMAST	FORESHANK	FORETELLS	FORGATHER	FORINSEC
FOREMASTS	FORESHEET	FORETHINK	FORGAVE	FORINT
FOREMEAN	FORESHEW	FORETIME	FORGE	FORINTS
FOREMEANS	FORESHEWN	FORETIMES	FORGEABLE	FORJASKIT
FOREMEANT	FORESHEWS	FORETOKEN	FORGED	FORJESKIT
FOREMEN	FORESHIP	FORETOLD	FORGEMAN	FORJUDGE
FOREMILK	FORESHIPS	FORETOOTH	FORGEMEN	FORJUDGED
FOREMILKS	FORESHOCK	FORETOP	FORGER	FORJUDGES
FOREMOST	FORESHORE	FORETOPS	FORGERIES	FORK
FORENAME	FORESHOW	FOREVER	FORGERS	FORKBALL
FORENAMED	FORESHOWN	FOREVERS	FORGERY	FORKBALLS
FORENAMES	FORESHOWS	FOREWARD	FORGES	FORKED
FORENIGHT	FORESIDE	FOREWARDS	FORGET	FORKEDLY
FORENOON	FORESIDES	FOREWARN	FORGETFUL	FORKER
FORENOONS	FORESIGHT	FOREWARNS	FORGETIVE	FORKERS
FORENSIC	FORESKIN	FOREWEIGH	FORGETS	FORKFUL
FORENSICS	FORESKINS	FOREWENT	FORGETTER	FORKFULS
FOREPART	FORESKIRT	FOREWIND	FORGING	FORKHEAD
FOREPARTS	FORESLACK	FOREWINDS	FORGINGS	FORKHEADS
FOREPAST	FORESLOW	FOREWING	FORGIVE	FORKIER
FOREPAW	FORESLOWS	FOREWINGS	FORGIVEN	FORKIEST
FOREPAWS	FORESPAKE	FOREWOMAN	FORGIVER	FORKINESS
FOREPEAK	FORESPEAK	FOREWOMEN	FORGIVERS	FORKING
FOREPEAKS	FORESPEND	FOREWORD	FORGIVES	FORKLESS
FOREPLAN	FORESPENT	FOREWORDS	FORGIVING	FORKLIFT
FOREPLANS	FORESPOKE	FOREWORN	FORGO	FORKLIFTS
FOREPLAY	FOREST	FOREX	FORGOER	FORKLIKE
FOREPLAYS	FORESTAGE	FOREXES	FORGOERS	FORKS
FOREPOINT	FORESTAIR	FOREYARD	FORGOES	FORKSFUL
FORERAN	FORESTAL	FOREYARDS	FORGOING	FORKTAIL
FORERANK	FORESTALL	FORFAIR	FORGONE	FORKTAILS
FORERANKS	FORESTAY	FORFAIRED	FORGOT	FORKY
FOREREACH	FORESTAYS	FORFAIRN	FORGOTTEN	FORLANA
FOREREAD	FORESTEAL	FORFAIRS	FORHAILE	FORLANAS
FOREREADS	FORESTED	FORFAITER	FORHAILED	FORLEND
FORERUN	FORESTER	FORFAULT	FORHAILES	FORLENDS
FORERUNS	FORESTERS	FORFAULTS	FORHENT	FORLENT
FORES	FORESTIAL	FORFEIT	FORHENTS	FORLESE
FORESAID	FORESTINE	FORFEITED	FORHOO	FORLESES
FORESAIL	FORESTING	FORFEITER	FORHOOED	FORLESING
FORESAILS	FORESTRY	FORFEITS	FORHOOIE	FORLORE
FORESAW	FORESTS	FORFEND	FORHOOIED	FORLORN
FORESAY	FORESWEAR	FORFENDED	FORHOOIES	FORLORNER
FORESAYS	FORESWORE	FORFENDS	FORHOOING	FORLORNLY
FORESEE	FORESWORN	FORFEX	FORHOOS	FORLORNS
FORESEEN	FORETASTE	FORFEXES	FORHOW	FORM

FORMABLE	FORMULA	FORSAYS	FORTIS	FOSSATE
FORMABLY	FORMULAE	FORSLACK	FORTITUDE	FOSSE
FORMAL	FORMULAIC	FORSLACKS	FORTLET	FOSSED
FORMALIN	FORMULAR	FORSLOE	FORTLETS	FOSSES
FORMALINE	FORMULARS	FORSLOED	FORTNIGHT	FOSSETTE
FORMALINS	FORMULARY	FORSLOES	FORTRESS	FOSSETTES
FORMALISE	FORMULAS	FORSLOW	FORTS	FOSSICK
FORMALISM	FORMULATE	FORSLOWED	FORTUITY	FOSSICKED
FORMALIST	FORMULISE	FORSLOWS	FORTUNATE	FOSSICKER
FORMALITY	FORMULISM	FORSOOK	FORTUNE	FOSSICKS
FORMALIZE	FORMULIST	FORSOOTH	FORTUNED	FOSSIL
FORMALLY	FORMULIZE	FORSPEAK	FORTUNES	FOSSILISE
FORMALS	FORMWORK	FORSPEAKS	FORTUNING	FOSSILIZE
FORMAMIDE	FORMWORKS	FORSPEND	FORTUNISE	FOSSILS
FORMANT	FORMYL	FORSPENDS	FORTUNIZE	FOSSOR
FORMANTS	FORMYLS	FORSPENT	FORTY	FOSSORIAL
FORMAT	FORNENST	FORSPOKE	FORTYFOLD	FOSSORS
FORMATE	FORNENT	FORSPOKEN	FORTYISH	FOSSULA
FORMATED	FORNICAL	FORSWATT	FORUM	FOSSULAE
FORMATES	FORNICATE	FORSWEAR	FORUMS	FOSSULATE
FORMATING	FORNICES	FORSWEARS	FORWANDER	FOSTER
FORMATION	FORNIX	FORSWINK	FORWARD	FOSTERAGE
FORMATIVE	FORPET	FORSWINKS	FORWARDED	FOSTERED
FORMATS	FORPETS	FORSWONCK	FORWARDER	FOSTERER
FORMATTED	FORPINE	FORSWORE	FORWARDLY	FOSTERERS
FORMATTER	FORPINED	FORSWORN	FORWARDS	FOSTERING
FORME	FORPINES	FORSWUNK	FORWARN	FOSTERS
FORMED	FORPINING	FORSYTHIA	FORWARNED	FOSTRESS
FORMEE	FORPIT	FORT	FORWARNS	FOTHER
FORMEES	FORPITS	FORTALICE	FORWASTE	FOTHERED
FORMER	FORRAD	FORTE	FORWASTED	FOTHERING
FORMERLY	FORRADER	FORTED	FORWASTES	FOTHERS
FORMERS	FORRADS	FORTES	FORWEARY	FOU
FORMES	FORRARDER	FORTH	FORWENT	FOUAT
FORMFUL	FORRAY	FORTHCAME	FORWHY	FOUATS
FORMIATE	FORRAYED	FORTHCOME	FORWORN	FOUD
FORMIATES	FORRAYING	FORTHINK	FORZA	FOUDRIE
FORMIC	FORRAYS	FORTHINKS	FORZANDI	FOUDRIES
FORMICA	FORREN	FORTHWITH	FORZANDO	FOUDS
FORMICANT	FORRIT	FORTHY	FORZANDOS	FOUER
FORMICARY	FORSAID	FORTIES	FORZATI	FOUEST
FORMICAS	FORSAKE	FORTIETH	FORZATO	FOUET
FORMICATE	FORSAKEN	FORTIETHS	FORZATOS	FOUETS
FORMING	FORSAKER	FORTIFIED	FORZE	FOUETTE
FORMINGS	FORSAKERS	FORTIFIER	FOSCARNET	FOUETTES
FORMLESS	FORSAKES	FORTIFIES	FOSS	FOUGADE
FORMOL	FORSAKING	FORTIFY	FOSSA	FOUGADES
FORMOLS	FORSAY	FORTILAGE	FOSSAE	FOUGASSE
FORMS	FORSAYING	FORTING	FOSSAS	FOUGASSES

FOUGHT	FOUREYED	FOVEOLE	FOXTAILS	FRACTURAL
FOUGHTEN	FOURFOLD	FOVEOLES	FOXTROT	FRACTURE
FOUGHTIER	FOURGON	FOVEOLET	FOXTROTS	FRACTURED
FOUGHTY	FOURGONS	FOVEOLETS	FOXY	FRACTURER
FOUL	FOURPENCE	FOWL	FOY	FRACTURES
FOULARD	FOURPENNY	FOWLED	FOYBOAT	FRACTURS
FOULARDS	FOURPLAY	FOWLER	FOYBOATS	FRACTUS
FOULBROOD	FOURPLAYS	FOWLERS	FOYER	FRAE
FOULDER	FOURPLEX	FOWLING	FOYERS	FRAENA
FOULDERED	FOURS	FOWLINGS	FOYLE	FRAENUM
FOULDERS	FOURSCORE	FOWLPOX	FOYLED	FRAENUMS
FOULE	FOURSES	FOWLPOXES	FOYLES	FRAG
FOULED	FOURSOME	FOWLS	FOYLING	FRAGGED
FOULER	FOURSOMES	FOWTH	FOYNE	FRAGGING
FOULES	FOURTEEN	FOWTHS	FOYNED	FRAGGINGS
FOULEST	FOURTEENS	FOX	FOYNES	FRAGILE
FOULIE	FOURTH	FOXBERRY	FOYNING	FRAGILELY
FOULIES	FOURTHLY	FOXED	FOYS	FRAGILER
FOULING	FOURTHS	FOXES	FOZIER	FRAGILEST
FOULINGS	FOUS	FOXFIRE	FOZIEST	FRAGILITY
FOULLY	FOUSSA	FOXFIRES	FOZINESS	FRAGMENT
FOULMART	FOUSSAS	FOXFISH	FOZY	FRAGMENTS
FOULMARTS	FOUSTIER	FOXFISHES	FRA	FRAGOR
FOULNESS	FOUSTIEST	FOXGLOVE	FRAB	FRAGORS
FOULS	FOUSTY	FOXGLOVES	FRABBED	FRAGRANCE
FOUMART	FOUTER	FOXHOLE	FRABBING	FRAGRANCY
FOUMARTS	FOUTERED	FOXHOLES	FRABBIT	FRAGRANT
FOUND	FOUTERING	FOXHOUND	FRABJOUS	FRAGS
FOUNDED	FOUTERS	FOXHOUNDS	FRABS	FRAICHEUR
FOUNDER	FOUTH	FOXHUNT	FRACAS	FRAIL
FOUNDERED	FOUTHS	FOXHUNTED	FRACASES	FRAILER
FOUNDERS	FOUTRA	FOXHUNTER	FRACK	FRAILEST
FOUNDING	FOUTRAS	FOXHUNTS	FRACKED	FRAILISH
FOUNDINGS	FOUTRE	FOXIE	FRACKER	FRAILLY
FOUNDLING	FOUTRED	FOXIER	FRACKERS	FRAILNESS
FOUNDRESS	FOUTRES	FOXIES	FRACKING	FRAILS
FOUNDRIES	FOUTRING	FOXIEST	FRACKINGS	FRAILTEE
FOUNDRY	FOVEA	FOXILY	FRACKS	FRAILTEES
FOUNDS	FOVEAE	FOXINESS	FRACT	FRAILTIES
FOUNT	FOVEAL	FOXING	FRACTAL	FRAILTY
FOUNTAIN	FOVEAS	FOXINGS	FRACTALS	FRAIM
FOUNTAINS	FOVEATE	FOXLIKE	FRACTED	FRAIMS
FOUNTFUL	FOVEATED	FOXSHARK	FRACTI	FRAISE
FOUNTS	FOVEIFORM	FOXSHARKS	FRACTING	FRAISED
FOUR	FOVEOLA	FOXSHIP	FRACTION	FRAISES
FOURBALL	FOVEOLAE	FOXSHIPS	FRACTIONS	FRAISING
FOURBALLS	FOVEOLAR	FOXSKIN	FRACTIOUS	FRAKTUR
FOURCHEE	FOVEOLAS	FOXSKINS	FRACTS	FRAKTURS
FOURCHEES	FOVEOLATE	FOXTAIL	FRACTUR	FRAMABLE

FRAMBESIA	FRANKS	FRAUDSMAN	FREEBASE	FREESIA
FRAMBOISE	FRANKUM	FRAUDSMEN	FREEBASED	FREESIAS
FRAME	FRANKUMS	FRAUDSTER	FREEBASER	FREEST
FRAMEABLE	FRANSERIA	FRAUGHAN	FREEBASES	FREESTONE
FRAMED	FRANTIC	FRAUGHANS	FREEBEE	FREESTYLE
FRAMELESS	FRANTICLY	FRAUGHT	FREEBEES	FREET
FRAMER	FRANZIER	FRAUGHTED	FREEBIE	FREETIER
FRAMERS	FRANZIEST	FRAUGHTER	FREEBIES	FREETIEST
FRAMES	FRANZY	FRAUGHTS	FREEBOARD	FREETS
FRAMEWORK	FRAP	FRAULEIN	FREEBOOT	FREETY
FRAMING	FRAPE	FRAULEINS	FREEBOOTS	FREEWARE
FRAMINGS	FRAPEAGE	FRAUS	FREEBOOTY	FREEWARES
FRAMPAL	FRAPEAGES	FRAUTAGE	FREEBORN	FREEWAY
FRAMPLER	FRAPED	FRAUTAGES	FREECYCLE	FREEWAYS
FRAMPLERS	FRAPES	FRAWZEY	FREED	FREEWHEEL
FRAMPOLD	FRAPING	FRAWZEYS	FREEDIVER	FREEWILL
FRANC	FRAPPANT	FRAY	FREEDMAN	FREEWOMAN
FRANCHISE	FRAPPE	FRAYED	FREEDMEN	FREEWOMEN
FRANCISE	FRAPPED	FRAYING	FREEDOM	FREEWRITE
FRANCISED	FRAPPEE	FRAYINGS	FREEDOMS	FREEWROTE
FRANCISES	FRAPPES	FRAYS	FREEFALL	FREEZABLE
FRANCIUM	FRAPPING	FRAZIL	FREEFORM	FREEZE
FRANCIUMS	FRAPS	FRAZILS	FREEGAN	FREEZER
FRANCIZE	FRAS	FRAZZLE	FREEGANS	FREEZERS
FRANCIZED	FRASCATI	FRAZZLED	FREEHAND	FREEZES
FRANCIZES	FRASCATIS	FRAZZLES	FREEHOLD	FREEZING
FRANCO	FRASS	FRAZZLING	FREEHOLDS	FREEZINGS
FRANCOLIN	FRASSES	FREAK	FREEING	FREIGHT
FRANCOS	FRAT	FREAKED	FREEKEH	FREIGHTED
FRANCS	FRATCH	FREAKERY	FREEKEHS	FREIGHTER
FRANGER	FRATCHES	FREAKFUL	FREELANCE	FREIGHTS
FRANGERS	FRATCHETY	FREAKIER	FREELOAD	FREIT
FRANGIBLE	FRATCHIER	FREAKIEST	FREELOADS	FREITIER
FRANGLAIS	FRATCHING	FREAKILY	FREELY	FREITIEST
FRANION	FRATCHY	FREAKING	FREEMAN	FREITS
FRANIONS	FRATE	FREAKISH	FREEMASON	FREITY
FRANK	FRATER	FREAKOUT	FREEMEN	FREMD
FRANKABLE	FRATERIES	FREAKOUTS	FREEMIUM	FREMDS
FRANKED	FRATERNAL	FREAKS	FREEMIUMS	FREMIT
FRANKER	FRATERS	FREAKY	FREENESS	FREMITS
FRANKERS	FRATERY	FRECKLE	FREEPHONE	FREMITUS
FRANKEST	FRATI	FRECKLED	FREEPOST	FRENA
FRANKFORT	FRATRIES	FRECKLES	FREEPOSTS	FRENCH
FRANKFURT	FRATRY	FRECKLIER	FREER	FRENCHED
FRANKING	FRATS	FRECKLING	FREERIDE	FRENCHES
FRANKLIN	FRAU	FRECKLY	FREERIDES	FRENCHIFY
FRANKLINS	FRAUD	FREDAINE	FREERS	FRENCHING
FRANKLY	FRAUDFUL	FREDAINES	FREES	FRENEMIES
FRANKNESS	FRAUDS	FREE	FREESHEET	FRENEMY

FRENETIC	FRESHISH	FRICASSEE	FRIGIDITY	FRISKA
FRENETICS	FRESHLY	FRICATIVE	FRIGIDLY	FRISKAS
FRENNE	FRESHMAN	FRICHT	FRIGOT	FRISKED
FRENNES	FRESHMEN	FRICHTED	FRIGOTS	FRISKER
FRENULA	FRESHNESS	FRICHTING	FRIGS	FRISKERS
FRENULAR	FRESNEL	FRICHTS	FRIJOL	FRISKET
FRENULUM	FRESNELS	FRICKING	FRIJOLE	FRISKETS
FRENULUMS	FRET	FRICOT	FRIJOLES	FRISKFUL
FRENUM	FRETBOARD	FRICOTS	FRIKKADEL	FRISKIER
FRENUMS	FRETFUL	FRICTION	FRILL	FRISKIEST
FRENZICAL	FRETFULLY	FRICTIONS	FRILLED	FRISKILY
FRENZIED	FRETLESS	FRIDGE	FRILLER	FRISKING
FRENZIES	FRETS	FRIDGED	FRILLERS	FRISKINGS
FRENZILY	FRETSAW	FRIDGES	FRILLERY	FRISKS
FRENZY	FRETSAWS	FRIDGING	FRILLIER	FRISKY
FRENZYING	FRETSOME	FRIED	FRILLIES	FRISSON
FREON	FRETTED	FRIEDCAKE	FRILLIEST	FRISSONS
FREONS	FRETTER	FRIEND	FRILLING	FRIST
FREQUENCE	FRETTERS	FRIENDED	FRILLINGS	FRISTED
FREQUENCY	FRETTIER	FRIENDING	FRILLS	FRISTING
FREQUENT	FRETTIEST	FRIENDLY	FRILLY	FRISTS
FREQUENTS	FRETTING	FRIENDS	FRINGE	FRISURE
FRERE	FRETTINGS	FRIER	FRINGED	FRISURES
FRERES	FRETTY	FRIERS	FRINGES	FRIT
FRESCADE	FRETWORK	FRIES	FRINGIER	FRITES
FRESCADES	FRETWORKS	FRIEZE	FRINGIEST	FRITFLIES
FRESCO	FRIABLE	FRIEZED	FRINGING	FRITFLY
FRESCOED	FRIAND	FRIEZES	FRINGINGS	FRITH
FRESCOER	FRIANDE	FRIEZING	FRINGY	FRITHBORH
FRESCOERS	FRIANDES	FRIG	FRIPON	FRITHS
FRESCOES	FRIANDS	FRIGATE	FRIPONS	FRITS
FRESCOING	FRIAR	FRIGATES	FRIPPER	FRITT
FRESCOIST	FRIARBIRD	FRIGATOON	FRIPPERER	FRITTATA
FRESCOS	FRIARIES	FRIGES	FRIPPERS	FRITTATAS
FRESH	FRIARLY	FRIGGED	FRIPPERY	FRITTED
FRESHED	FRIARS	FRIGGER	FRIPPET	FRITTER
FRESHEN	FRIARY	FRIGGERS	FRIPPETS	FRITTERED
FRESHENED	FRIB	FRIGGING	FRIS	FRITTERER
FRESHENER	FRIBBLE	FRIGGINGS	FRISBEE	FRITTERS
FRESHENS	FRIBBLED	FRIGHT	FRISBEES	FRITTING
FRESHER	FRIBBLER	FRIGHTED	FRISE	FRITTS
FRESHERS	FRIBBLERS	FRIGHTEN	FRISEE	FRITURE
FRESHES	FRIBBLES	FRIGHTENS	FRISEES	FRITURES
FRESHEST	FRIBBLING	FRIGHTFUL	FRISES	FRITZ
FRESHET	FRIBBLISH	FRIGHTING	FRISETTE	FRITZED
FRESHETS	FRIBS	FRIGHTS	FRISETTES	FRITZES
FRESHIE	FRICADEL	FRIGID	FRISEUR	FRITZING
FRESHIES	FRICADELS	FRIGIDER	FRISEURS	FRIULANO
FRESHING	FRICANDO	FRIGIDEST	FRISK	FRIULANOS

FRIVOL	FROES	FRONDOSE	FROSTFISH	FROWIEST
FRIVOLED	FROG	FRONDOUS	FROSTIER	FROWN
FRIVOLER	FROGBIT	FRONDS	FROSTIEST	FROWNED
FRIVOLERS	FROGBITS	FRONS	FROSTILY	FROWNER
FRIVOLING	FROGEYE	FRONT	FROSTING	FROWNERS
FRIVOLITY	FROGEYED	FRONTAGE	FROSTINGS	FROWNIER
FRIVOLLED	FROGEYES	FRONTAGER	FROSTLESS	FROWNIEST
FRIVOLLER	FROGFISH	FRONTAGES	FROSTLIKE	FROWNING
FRIVOLOUS	FROGGED	FRONTAL	FROSTLINE	FROWNS
FRIVOLS	FROGGERY	FRONTALLY	FROSTNIP	FROWNY
FRIZ	FROGGIER	FRONTALS	FROSTNIPS	FROWS
FRIZADO	FROGGIEST	FRONTED	FROSTS	FROWSIER
FRIZADOS	FROGGING	FRONTENIS	FROSTWORK	FROWSIEST
FRIZE	FROGGINGS	FRONTER	FROSTY	FROWSILY
FRIZED	FROGGY	FRONTERS	FROTH	FROWST
FRIZER	FROGLET	FRONTES	FROTHED	FROWSTED
FRIZERS	FROGLETS	FRONTEST	FROTHER	FROWSTER
FRIZES	FROGLIKE	FRONTIER	FROTHERS	FROWSTERS
FRIZETTE	FROGLING	FRONTIERS	FROTHERY	FROWSTIER
FRIZETTES	FROGLINGS	FRONTING	FROTHIER	FROWSTING
FRIZING	FROGMAN	FRONTLESS	FROTHIEST	FROWSTS
FRIZZ	FROGMARCH	FRONTLET	FROTHILY	FROWSTY
FRIZZANTE	FROGMEN	FRONTLETS	FROTHING	FROWSY
FRIZZED	FROGMOUTH	FRONTLINE	FROTHINGS	FROWY
FRIZZER	FROGS	FRONTLIST	FROTHLESS	FROWZIER
FRIZZERS	FROGSPAWN	FRONTMAN	FROTHS	FROWZIEST
FRIZZES	FROIDEUR	FRONTMEN	FROTHY	FROWZILY
FRIZZIER	FROIDEURS	FRONTON	FROTTAGE	FROWZY
FRIZZIES	FROING	FRONTONS	FROTTAGES	FROZE
FRIZZIEST	FROINGS	FRONTOON	FROTTEUR	FROZEN
FRIZZILY	FROISE	FRONTOONS	FROTTEURS	FROZENLY
FRIZZING	FROISES	FRONTPAGE	FROUFROU	FRUCTAN
FRIZZLE	FROLIC	FRONTS	FROUFROUS	FRUCTANS
FRIZZLED	FROLICKED	FRONTWARD	FROUGHIER	FRUCTED
FRIZZLER	FROLICKER	FRONTWAYS	FROUGHY	FRUCTIFY
FRIZZLERS	FROLICKY	FRONTWISE	FROUNCE	FRUCTIVE
FRIZZLES	FROLICS	FRORE	FROUNCED	FRUCTOSE
FRIZZLIER	FROM	FROREN	FROUNCES	FRUCTOSES
FRIZZLING	FROMAGE	FRORN	FROUNCING	FRUCTUARY
FRIZZLY	FROMAGES	FRORNE	FROUZIER	FRUCTUATE
FRIZZY	FROMENTY	FRORY	FROUZIEST	FRUCTUOUS
FRO	FROND	FROS	FROUZILY	FRUG
FROCK	FRONDAGE	FROSH	FROUZY	FRUGAL
FROCKED	FRONDAGES	FROSHES	FROW	FRUGALIST
FROCKING	FRONDED	FROST	FROWARD	FRUGALITY
FROCKINGS	FRONDENT	FROSTBIT	FROWARDLY	FRUGALLY
FROCKLESS	FRONDEUR	FROSTBITE	FROWARDS	FRUGGED
FROCKS	FRONDEURS	FROSTED	FROWIE	FRUGGING
FROE	FRONDLESS	FROSTEDS	FROWIER	FRUGIVORE

FRUGS	FRUSHING	FUCKER	FUELERS	FUGLING
FRUICT	FRUST	FUCKERS	FUELING	FUGLY
FRUICTS	FRUSTA	FUCKFACE	FUELLED	FUGS
FRUIT	FRUSTRATE	FUCKFACES	FUELLER	FUGU
FRUITAGE	FRUSTS	FUCKHEAD	FUELLERS	FUGUE
FRUITAGES	FRUSTULE	FUCKHEADS	FUELLING	FUGUED
FRUITCAKE	FRUSTULES	FUCKING	FUELS	FUGUELIKE
FRUITED	FRUSTUM	FUCKINGS	FUELWOOD	FUGUES
FRUITER	FRUSTUMS	FUCKOFF	FUELWOODS	FUGUING
FRUITERER	FRUTEX	FUCKOFFS	FUERO	FUGUIST
FRUITERS	FRUTICES	FUCKS	FUEROS	FUGUISTS
FRUITERY	FRUTICOSE	FUCKUP	FUFF	FUGUS
FRUITFUL	FRUTIFIED	FUCKUPS	FUFFED	FUHRER
FRUITIER	FRUTIFIES	FUCKWIT	FUFFIER	FUHRERS
FRUITIEST	FRUTIFY	FUCKWITS	FUFFIEST	FUJI
FRUITILY	FRY	FUCOID	FUFFING	FUJIS
FRUITING	FRYABLE	FUCOIDAL	FUFFS	FULCRA
FRUITINGS	FRYBREAD	FUCOIDS	FUFFY	FULCRATE
FRUITION	FRYBREADS	FUCOSE	FUG	FULCRUM
FRUITIONS	FRYER	FUCOSES	FUGACIOUS	FULCRUMS
FRUITIVE	FRYERS	FUCOUS	FUGACITY	FULFIL
FRUITLESS	FRYING	FUCUS	FUGAL	FULFILL
FRUITLET	FRYINGS	FUCUSED	FUGALLY	FULFILLED
FRUITLETS	FRYPAN	FUCUSES	FUGATO	FULFILLER
FRUITLIKE	FRYPANS	FUD	FUGATOS	FULFILLS
FRUITS	FUB	FUDDIER	FUGAZI	FULFILS
FRUITWOOD	FUBAR	FUDDIES	FUGAZIS	FULGENCY
FRUITWORM	FUBBED	FUDDIEST	FUGGED	FULGENT
FRUITY	FUBBERIES	FUDDLE	FUGGIER	FULGENTLY
FRUMENTY	FUBBERY	FUDDLED	FUGGIEST	FULGID
FRUMP	FUBBIER	FUDDLER	FUGGILY	FULGOR
FRUMPED	FUBBIEST	FUDDLERS	FUGGINESS	FULGOROUS
FRUMPIER	FUBBING	FUDDLES	FUGGING	FULGORS
FRUMPIEST	FUBBY	FUDDLING	FUGGY	FULGOUR
FRUMPILY	FUBS	FUDDLINGS	FUGHETTA	FULGOURS
FRUMPING	FUBSIER	FUDDY	FUGHETTAS	FULGURAL
FRUMPISH	FUBSIEST	FUDGE	FUGIE	FULGURANT
FRUMPLE	FUBSY	FUDGED	FUGIES	FULGURATE
FRUMPLED	FUCHSIA	FUDGES	FUGIO	FULGURITE
FRUMPLES	FUCHSIAS	FUDGIER	FUGIOS	FULGUROUS
FRUMPLING	FUCHSIN	FUDGIEST	FUGITIVE	FULHAM
FRUMPS	FUCHSINE	FUDGING	FUGITIVES	FULHAMS
FRUMPY	FUCHSINES	FUDGY	FUGLE	FULL
FRUNK	FUCHSINS	FUDS	FUGLED	FULLAGE
FRUNKS	FUCHSITE	FUEHRER	FUGLEMAN	FULLAGES
FRUSEMIDE	FUCHSITES	FUEHRERS	FUGLEMEN	FULLAM
FRUSH	FUCI	FUEL	FUGLES	FULLAMS
FRUSHED	FUCK	FUELED	FUGLIER	FULLAN
FRUSHES	FUCKED	FUELER	FUGLIEST	FULLANS

FULLBACK	FUMARIC	FUNCKIAS	FUNGOIDAL	FUNNYMEN
FULLBACKS	FUMAROLE	FUNCTION	FUNGOIDS	FUNPLEX
FULLBLOOD	FUMAROLES	FUNCTIONS	FUNGOING	FUNPLEXES
FULLED	FUMAROLIC	FUNCTOR	FUNGOS	FUNS
FULLER	FUMATORIA	FUNCTORS	FUNGOSITY	FUNSTER
FULLERED	FUMATORY	FUND	FUNGOUS	FUNSTERS
FULLERENE	FUMBLE	FUNDABLE	FUNGS	FUR
FULLERIDE	FUMBLED	FUNDAMENT	FUNGUS	FURACIOUS
FULLERIES	FUMBLER	FUNDED	FUNGUSES	FURACITY
FULLERING	FUMBLERS	FUNDER	FUNHOUSE	FURAL
FULLERITE	FUMBLES	FUNDERS	FUNHOUSES	FURALS
FULLERS	FUMBLING	FUNDI	FUNICLE	FURAN
FULLERY	FUME	FUNDIC	FUNICLES	FURANE
FULLEST	FUMED	FUNDIE	FUNICULAR	FURANES
FULLFACE	FUMELESS	FUNDIES	FUNICULI	FURANOSE
FULLFACES	FUMELIKE	FUNDING	FUNICULUS	FURANOSES
FULLING	FUMER	FUNDINGS	FUNK	FURANS
FULLISH	FUMEROLE	FUNDIS	FUNKED	FURBALL
FULLNESS	FUMEROLES	FUNDLESS	FUNKER	FURBALLS
FULLS	FUMERS	FUNDRAISE	FUNKERS	FURBEARER
FULLY	FUMES	FUNDS	FUNKHOLE	FURBELOW
FULMAR	FUMET	FUNDUS	FUNKHOLES	FURBELOWS
FULMARS	FUMETS	FUNDY	FUNKIA	FURBISH
FULMINANT	FUMETTE	FUNEBRAL	FUNKIAS	FURBISHED
FULMINATE	FUMETTES	FUNEBRE	FUNKIER	FURBISHER
FULMINE	FUMETTI	FUNEBRIAL	FUNKIEST	FURBISHES
FULMINED	FUMETTO	FUNERAL	FUNKILY	FURCA
FULMINES	FUMETTOS	FUNERALS	FUNKINESS	FURCAE
FULMINIC	FUMIER	FUNERARY	FUNKING	FURCAL
FULMINING	FUMIEST	FUNEREAL	FUNKS	FURCATE
FULMINOUS	FUMIGANT	FUNEST	FUNKSTER	FURCATED
FULNESS	FUMIGANTS	FUNFAIR	FUNKSTERS	FURCATELY
FULNESSES	FUMIGATE	FUNFAIRS	FUNKY	FURCATES
FULSOME	FUMIGATED	FUNFEST	FUNNED	FURCATING
FULSOMELY	FUMIGATES	FUNFESTS	FUNNEL	FURCATION
FULSOMER	FUMIGATOR	FUNG	FUNNELED	FURCRAEA
FULSOMEST	FUMING	FUNGAL	FUNNELING	FURCRAEAS
FULVID	FUMINGLY	FUNGALS	FUNNELLED	FURCULA
FULVOUS	FUMITORY	FUNGI	FUNNELS	FURCULAE
FUM	FUMOSITY	FUNGIBLE	FUNNER	FURCULAR
FUMADO	FUMOUS	FUNGIBLES	FUNNEST	FURCULUM
FUMADOES	FUMS	FUNGIC	FUNNIER	FURDER
FUMADOS	FUMULI	FUNGICIDE	FUNNIES	FUREUR
FUMAGE	FUMULUS	FUNGIFORM	FUNNIEST	FUREURS
FUMAGES	FUMY	FUNGISTAT	FUNNILY	FURFAIR
FUMARASE	FUN	FUNGO	FUNNINESS	FURFAIRS
FUMARASES	FUNBOARD	FUNGOED	FUNNING	FURFUR
FUMARATE	FUNBOARDS	FUNGOES	FUNNY	FURFURAL
FUMARATES	FUNCKIA	FUNGOID	FUNNYMAN	FURFURALS

FURFURAN	FUROLES	FURZY	FUSKER	FUTHORC
FURFURANS	FUROLS	FUSAIN	FUSKERED	FUTHORCS
FURFURES	FUROR	FUSAINS	FUSKERING	FUTHORK
FURFUROL	FURORE	FUSARIA	FUSKERS	FUTHORKS
FURFUROLE	FURORES	FUSARIUM	FUSKING	FUTILE
FURFUROLS	FURORS	FUSARIUMS	FUSKS	FUTILELY
FURFUROUS	FURPHIES	FUSAROL	FUSS	FUTILER
FURFURS	FURPHY	FUSAROLE	FUSSBALL	FUTILEST
FURIBUND	FURPIECE	FUSAROLES	FUSSBALLS	FUTILITY
FURIES	FURPIECES	FUSAROLS	FUSSED	FUTON
FURIOSITY	FURR	FUSBALL	FUSSER	FUTONS
FURIOSO	FURRED	FUSBALLS	FUSSERS	FUTSAL
FURIOSOS	FURRIER	FUSC	FUSSES	FUTSALS
FURIOUS	FURRIERS	FUSCOUS	FUSSIER	FUTTOCK
FURIOUSLY	FURRIERY	FUSE	FUSSIEST	FUTTOCKS
FURKID	FURRIES	FUSED	FUSSILY	FUTURAL
FURKIDS	FURRIEST	FUSEE	FUSSINESS	FUTURE
FURL	FURRILY	FUSEES	FUSSING	FUTURES
FURLABLE	FURRINER	FUSEL	FUSSPOT	FUTURISM
FURLANA	FURRINERS	FUSELAGE	FUSSPOTS	FUTURISMS
FURLANAS	FURRINESS	FUSELAGES	FUSSY	FUTURIST
FURLED	FURRING	FUSELESS	FUST	FUTURISTS
FURLER	FURRINGS	FUSELIKE	FUSTED	FUTURITY
FURLERS	FURROW	FUSELS	FUSTET	FUTZ
FURLESS	FURROWED	FUSES	FUSTETS	FUTZED
FURLIKE	FURROWER	FUSHION	FUSTIAN	FUTZES
FURLING	FURROWERS	FUSHIONS	FUSTIANS	FUTZING
FURLONG	FURROWIER	FUSIBLE	FUSTIC	FUZE
FURLONGS	FURROWING	FUSIBLY	FUSTICS	FUZED
FURLOUGH	FURROWS	FUSIDIC	FUSTIER	FUZEE
FURLOUGHS	FURROWY	FUSIFORM	FUSTIEST	FUZEES
FURLS	FURRS	FUSIL	FUSTIGATE	FUZELESS
FURMENTY	FURRY	FUSILE	FUSTILUGS	FUZES
FURMETIES	FURS	FUSILEER	FUSTILY	FUZIL
FURMETY	FURTH	FUSILEERS	FUSTINESS	FUZILS
FURMITIES	FURTHER	FUSILIER	FUSTING	FUZING
FURMITY	FURTHERED	FUSILIERS	FUSTOC	FUZZ
FURNACE	FURTHERER	FUSILLADE	FUSTOCS	FUZZBALL
FURNACED	FURTHERS	FUSILLI	FUSTS	FUZZBALLS
FURNACES	FURTHEST	FUSILLIS	FUSTY	FUZZBOX
FURNACING	FURTIVE	FUSILS	FUSULINID	FUZZBOXES
FURNIMENT	FURTIVELY	FUSING	FUSUMA	FUZZED
FURNISH	FURUNCLE	FUSION	FUSUMAS	FUZZES
FURNISHED	FURUNCLES	FUSIONAL	FUTCHEL	FUZZIER
FURNISHER	FURY	FUSIONISM	FUTCHELS	FUZZIEST
FURNISHES	FURZE	FUSIONIST	FUTHARC	FUZZILY
FURNITURE	FURZES	FUSIONS	FUTHARCS	FUZZINESS
FUROL	FURZIER	FUSK	FUTHARK	FUZZING
FUROLE	FURZIEST	FUSKED	FUTHARKS	FUZZLE

FUZZLED	FUZZY	FYKED	FYLFOT	FYRDS
FUZZLES	FY	FYKES	FYLFOTS	FYTTE
FUZZLING	FYCE	FYKING	FYNBOS	FYTTES
FUZZTONE	FYCES	FYLE	FYNBOSES	
FUZZTONES	FYKE	FYLES	FYRD	

G

GAB	GABLELIKE	GADIDS	GAGA	GAINFUL
GABARDINE	GABLES	GADIS	GAGAKU	GAINFULLY
GABBA	GABLET	GADJE	GAGAKUS	GAINING
GABBARD	GABLETS	GADJES	GAGE	GAININGS
GABBARDS	GABLING	GADJO	GAGEABLE	GAINLESS
GABBART	GABNASH	GADJOS	GAGEABLY	GAINLIER
GABBARTS	GABNASHES	GADLING	GAGED	GAINLIEST
GABBAS	GABOON	GADLINGS	GAGER	GAINLY
GABBED	GABOONS	GADMAN	GAGERS	GAINS
GABBER	GABS	GADMEN	GAGES	GAINSAID
GABBERS	GABY	GADOID	GAGGED	GAINSAY
GABBIER	GACH	GADOIDS	GAGGER	GAINSAYER
GABBIEST	GACHED	GADOLINIC	GAGGERIES	GAINSAYS
GABBINESS	GACHER	GADROON	GAGGERS	GAINST
GABBING	GACHERS	GADROONED	GAGGERY	GAIR
GABBLE	GACHES	GADROONS	GAGGING	GAIRFOWL
GABBLED	GACHING	GADS	GAGGLE	GAIRFOWLS
GABBLER	GAD	GADSMAN	GAGGLED	GAIRS
GABBLERS	GADABOUT	GADSMEN	GAGGLES	GAIT
GABBLES	GADABOUTS	GADSO	GAGGLING	GAITA
GABBLING	GADARENE	GADWALL	GAGGLINGS	GAITAS
GABBLINGS	GADDED	GADWALLS	GAGING	GAITED
GABBRO	GADDER	GADZOOKS	GAGMAN	GAITER
GABBROIC	GADDERS	GAE	GAGMEN	GAITERED
GABBROID	GADDI	GAED	GAGS	GAITERS
GABBROS	GADDING	GAEING	GAGSTER	GAITING
GABBY	GADDIS	GAELICISE	GAGSTERS	GAITS
GABELLE	GADE	GAELICISM	GAHNITE	GAITT
GABELLED	GADES	GAELICIZE	GAHNITES	GAITTS
GABELLER	GADFLIES	GAEN	GAID	GAJO
GABELLERS	GADFLY	GAES	GAIDS	GAJOS
GABELLES	GADGE	GAFF	GAIETIES	GAK
GABERDINE	GADGES	GAFFE	GAIETY	GAKS
GABFEST	GADGET	GAFFED	GAIJIN	GAL
GABFESTS	GADGETEER	GAFFER	GAILLARD	GALA
GABIES	GADGETIER	GAFFERS	GAILLARDE	GALABEA
GABION	GADGETRY	GAFFES	GAILY	GALABEAH
GABIONADE	GADGETS	GAFFING	GAIN	GALABEAHS
GABIONAGE	GADGETY	GAFFINGS	GAINABLE	GALABEAS
GABIONED	GADGIE	GAFFS	GAINED	GALABEYA
GABIONS	GADGIES	GAFFSAIL	GAINER	GALABEYAS
GABLE	GADI	GAFFSAILS	GAINERS	GALABIA
GABLED	GADID	GAG	GAINEST	GALABIAH

GALABIAHS	GALENIC	GALLERIST	GALLIZING	GALOPPED
GALABIAS	GALENICAL	GALLERY	GALLNUT	GALOPPING
GALABIEH	GALENITE	GALLET	GALLNUTS	GALOPS
GALABIEHS	GALENITES	GALLETA	GALLOCK	GALORE
GALABIYA	GALENOID	GALLETAS	GALLON	GALORES
GALABIYAH	GALERE	GALLETED	GALLONAGE	GALOSH
GALABIYAS	GALERES	GALLETING	GALLONS	GALOSHE
GALACTIC	GALES	GALLETS	GALLOON	GALOSHED
GALACTICO	GALETTE	GALLEY	GALLOONED	GALOSHES
GALACTOSE	GALETTES	GALLEYS	GALLOONS	GALOSHING
GALAGE	GALILEE	GALLFLIES	GALLOOT	GALOWSES
GALAGES	GALILEES	GALLFLY	GALLOOTS	GALRAVAGE
GALAGO	GALING	GALLIARD	GALLOP	GALS
GALAGOS	GALINGALE	GALLIARDS	GALLOPADE	GALTONIA
GALAH	GALIONGEE	GALLIASS	GALLOPED	GALTONIAS
GALAHS	GALIOT	GALLIC	GALLOPER	GALUMPH
GALANGA	GALIOTS	GALLICA	GALLOPERS	GALUMPHED
GALANGAL	GALIPOT	GALLICAN	GALLOPING	GALUMPHER
GALANGALS	GALIPOTS	GALLICAS	GALLOPS	GALUMPHS
GALANGAS	GALIVANT	GALLICISE	GALLOUS	GALUT
GALANT	GALIVANTS	GALLICISM	GALLOW	GALUTH
GALANTINE	GALL	GALLICIZE	GALLOWAY	GALUTHS
GALANTS	GALLABEA	GALLIED	GALLOWAYS	GALUTS
GALANTY	GALLABEAH	GALLIER	GALLOWED	GALVANIC
GALAPAGO	GALLABEAS	GALLIES	GALLOWING	GALVANISE
GALAPAGOS	GALLABIA	GALLIEST	GALLOWS	GALVANISM
GALAS	GALLABIAH	GALLINAZO	GALLOWSES	GALVANIST
GALATEA	GALLABIAS	GALLING	GALLS	GALVANIZE
GALATEAS	GALLABIEH	GALLINGLY	GALLSTONE	GALVO
GALAVANT	GALLABIYA	GALLINULE	GALLUMPH	GALVOS
GALAVANTS	GALLAMINE	GALLIOT	GALLUMPHS	GALYAC
GALAX	GALLANT	GALLIOTS	GALLUS	GALYACS
GALAXES	GALLANTED	GALLIPOT	GALLUSED	GALYAK
GALAXIES	GALLANTER	GALLIPOTS	GALLUSES	GALYAKS
GALAXY	GALLANTLY	GALLISE	GALLY	GAM
GALBANUM	GALLANTRY	GALLISED	GALLYING	GAMA
GALBANUMS	GALLANTS	GALLISES	GALOCHE	GAMAHUCHE
GALDRAGON	GALLATE	GALLISING	GALOCHED	GAMARUCHE
GALE	GALLATES	GALLISISE	GALOCHES	GAMAS
GALEA	GALLEASS	GALLISIZE	GALOCHING	GAMASH
GALEAE	GALLED	GALLIUM	GALOOT	GAMASHES
GALEAS	GALLEIN	GALLIUMS	GALOOTS	GAMAY
GALEATE	GALLEINS	GALLIVANT	GALOP	GAMAYS
GALEATED	GALLEON	GALLIVAT	GALOPADE	GAMB
GALED	GALLEONS	GALLIVATS	GALOPADES	GAMBA
GALEIFORM	GALLERIA	GALLIWASP	GALOPED	GAMBADE
GALENA	GALLERIAS	GALLIZE	GALOPIN	GAMBADES
GALENAS	GALLERIED	GALLIZED	GALOPING	GAMBADO
GALENGALE	GALLERIES	GALLIZES	GALOPINS	GAMBADOED

GAMBADOES	GAME	GAMIN	GANCHES	GANGSHAGS
GAMBADOS	GAMEBAG	GAMINE	GANCHING	GANGSMAN
GAMBAS	GAMEBAGS	GAMINERIE	GANDER	GANGSMEN
GAMBE	GAMEBOOK	GAMINES	GANDERED	GANGSTA
GAMBES	GAMEBOOKS	GAMINESS	GANDERING	GANGSTAS
GAMBESON	GAMECOCK	GAMING	GANDERISM	GANGSTER
GAMBESONS	GAMECOCKS	GAMINGS	GANDERS	GANGSTERS
GAMBET	GAMED	GAMINS	GANDY	GANGUE
GAMBETS	GAMEFISH	GAMMA	GANE	GANGUES
GAMBETTA	GAMEFOWL	GAMMADIA	GANEF	GANGWAY
GAMBETTAS	GAMEFOWLS	GAMMADION	GANEFS	GANGWAYS
GAMBIA	GAMELAN	GAMMAS	GANEV	GANISTER
GAMBIAS	GAMELANS	GAMMATIA	GANEVS	GANISTERS
GAMBIER	GAMELIKE	GAMMATION	GANG	GANJA
GAMBIERS	GAMELY	GAMME	GANGBANG	GANJAH
GAMBIR	GAMENESS	GAMMED	GANGBANGS	GANJAHS
GAMBIRS	GAMEPAD	GAMMER	GANGBO	GANJAS
GAMBIST	GAMEPADS	GAMMERS	GANGBOARD	GANK
GAMBISTS	GAMEPLAY	GAMMES	GANGBOS	GANKED
GAMBIT	GAMEPLAYS	GAMMIER	GANGED	GANKING
GAMBITED	GAMER	GAMMIEST	GANGER	GANKS
GAMBITING	GAMERS	GAMMING	GANGERS	GANNED
GAMBITS	GAMES	GAMMOCK	GANGING	GANNET
GAMBLE	GAMESHOW	GAMMOCKED	GANGINGS	GANNETRY
GAMBLED	GAMESHOWS	GAMMOCKS	GANGLAND	GANNETS
GAMBLER	GAMESIER	GAMMON	GANGLANDS	GANNING
GAMBLERS	GAMESIEST	GAMMONED	GANGLE	GANNISTER
GAMBLES	GAMESMAN	GAMMONER	GANGLED	GANOF
GAMBLING	GAMESMEN	GAMMONERS	GANGLES	GANOFS
GAMBLINGS	GAMESOME	GAMMONING	GANGLIA	GANOID
GAMBO	GAMEST	GAMMONS	GANGLIAL	GANOIDS
GAMBOES	GAMESTER	GAMMY	GANGLIAR	GANOIN
GAMBOGE	GAMESTERS	GAMODEME	GANGLIATE	GANOINE
GAMBOGES	GAMESY	GAMODEMES	GANGLIER	GANOINES
GAMBOGIAN	GAMETAL	GAMONE	GANGLIEST	GANOINS
GAMBOGIC	GAMETE	GAMONES	GANGLING	GANS
GAMBOL	GAMETES	GAMP	GANGLION	GANSEY
GAMBOLED	GAMETIC	GAMPISH	GANGLIONS	GANSEYS
GAMBOLING	GAMEY	GAMPS	GANGLY	GANT
GAMBOLLED	GAMEYNESS	GAMS	GANGPLANK	GANTED
GAMBOLS	GAMGEE	GAMUT	GANGPLOW	GANTELOPE
GAMBOS	GAMIC	GAMUTS	GANGPLOWS	GANTING
GAMBREL	GAMIER	GAMY	GANGREL	GANTLET
GAMBRELS	GAMIEST	GAMYNESS	GANGRELS	GANTLETED
GAMBROON	GAMIFIED	GAN	GANGRENE	GANTLETS
GAMBROONS	GAMIFIES	GANACHE	GANGRENED	GANTLINE
GAMBS	GAMIFY	GANACHES	GANGRENES	GANTLINES
GAMBUSIA	GAMIFYING	GANCH	GANGS	GANTLOPE
GAMBUSIAS	GAMILY	GANCHED	GANGSHAG	GANTLOPES

G

GANTRIES	GAR	GARDAI	GARISHING	GARRES
GANTRY	GARAGE	GARDANT	GARISHLY	GARRET
GANTS	GARAGED	GARDANTS	GARJAN	GARRETED
GANYMEDE	GARAGEMAN	GARDEN	GARJANS	GARRETEER
GANYMEDES	GARAGEMEN	GARDENED	GARLAND	GARRETS
GANZFELD	GARAGES	GARDENER	GARLANDED	GARRIGUE
GANZFELDS	GARAGEY	GARDENERS	GARLANDRY	GARRIGUES
GAOL	GARAGIER	GARDENFUL	GARLANDS	GARRING
GAOLBIRD	GARAGIEST	GARDENIA	GARLIC	GARRISON
GAOLBIRDS	GARAGING	GARDENIAS	GARLICKED	GARRISONS
GAOLBREAK	GARAGINGS	GARDENING	GARLICKY	GARRON
GAOLBROKE	GARAGIST	GARDENS	GARLICS	GARRONS
GAOLED	GARAGISTE	GARDEROBE	GARMENT	GARROT
GAOLER	GARAGISTS	GARDYLOO	GARMENTED	GARROTE
GAOLERESS	GARB	GARDYLOOS	GARMENTS	GARROTED
GAOLERS	GARBAGE	GARE	GARMS	GARROTER
GAOLING	GARBAGES	GAREFOWL	GARNER	GARROTERS
GAOLLESS	GARBAGEY	GAREFOWLS	GARNERED	GARROTES
GAOLS	GARBAGIER	GARES	GARNERING	GARROTING
GAP	GARBAGY	GARFISH	GARNERS	GARROTS
GAPE	GARBANZO	GARFISHES	GARNET	GARROTTE
GAPED	GARBANZOS	GARGANEY	GARNETS	GARROTTED
GAPER	GARBE	GARGANEYS	GARNI	GARROTTER
GAPERS	GARBED	GARGANTUA	GARNISH	GARROTTES
GAPES	GARBES	GARGARISE	GARNISHED	GARRULITY
GAPESEED	GARBING	GARGARISM	GARNISHEE	GARRULOUS
GAPESEEDS	GARBLE	GARGARIZE	GARNISHER	GARRYA
GAPEWORM	GARBLED	GARGET	GARNISHES	GARRYAS
GAPEWORMS	GARBLER	GARGETS	GARNISHOR	GARRYOWEN
GAPIER	GARBLERS	GARGETY	GARNISHRY	GARS
GAPIEST	GARBLES	GARGLE	GARNITURE	GART
GAPING	GARBLESS	GARGLED	GAROTE	GARTER
GAPINGLY	GARBLING	GARGLER	GAROTED	GARTERED
GAPINGS	GARBLINGS	GARGLERS	GAROTES	GARTERING
GAPLESS	GARBO	GARGLES	GAROTING	GARTERS
GAPO	GARBOARD	GARGLING	GAROTTE	GARTH
GAPOS	GARBOARDS	GARGOYLE	GAROTTED	GARTHS
GAPOSIS	GARBOIL	GARGOYLED	GAROTTER	GARUDA
GAPOSISES	GARBOILS	GARGOYLES	GAROTTERS	GARUDAS
GAPPED	GARBOLOGY	GARI	GAROTTES	GARUM
GAPPER	GARBOS	GARIAL	GAROTTING	GARUMS
GAPPERS	GARBS	GARIALS	GAROUPA	GARVEY
GAPPIER	GARBURE	GARIBALDI	GAROUPAS	GARVEYS
GAPPIEST	GARBURES	GARIGUE	GARPIKE	GARVIE
GAPPING	GARCINIA	GARIGUES	GARPIKES	GARVIES
GAPPINGS	GARCINIAS	GARIS	GARRAN	GARVOCK
GAPPY	GARCON	GARISH	GARRANS	GARVOCKS
GAPS	GARCONS	GARISHED	GARRE	GAS
GAPY	GARDA	GARISHES	GARRED	GASAHOL

GASAHOLS	GASMAN	GASTNESS	GATEPOSTS	GAUDILY
GASALIER	GASMEN	GASTNESSE	GATER	GAUDINESS
GASALIERS	GASOGENE	GASTRAEA	GATERS	GAUDING
GASBAG	GASOGENES	GASTRAEAS	GATES	GAUDS
GASBAGGED	GASOHOL	GASTRAEUM	GATEWAY	GAUDY
GASBAGS	GASOHOLS	GASTRAL	GATEWAYS	GAUFER
GASCON	GASOLENE	GASTREA	GATH	GAUFERS
GASCONADE	GASOLENES	GASTREAS	GATHER	GAUFFER
GASCONISM	GASOLIER	GASTRIC	GATHERED	GAUFFERED
GASCONS	GASOLIERS	GASTRIN	GATHERER	GAUFFERS
GASEITIES	GASOLINE	GASTRINS	GATHERERS	GAUFRE
GASEITY	GASOLINES	GASTRITIC	GATHERING	GAUFRES
GASELIER	GASOLINIC	GASTRITIS	GATHERS	GAUGE
GASELIERS	GASOMETER	GASTRO	GATHS	GAUGEABLE
GASEOUS	GASOMETRY	GASTROPOD	GATING	GAUGEABLY
GASES	GASP	GASTROPUB	GATINGS	GAUGED
GASFIELD	GASPED	GASTROS	GATLING	GAUGER
GASFIELDS	GASPER	GASTRULA	GATOR	GAUGERS
GASH	GASPEREAU	GASTRULAE	GATORS	GAUGES
GASHED	GASPERS	GASTRULAR	GATS	GAUGING
GASHER	GASPIER	GASTRULAS	GATVOL	GAUGINGS
GASHES	GASPIEST	GASTS	GAU	GAUJE
GASHEST	GASPINESS	GASWORKS	GAUCH	GAUJES
GASHFUL	GASPING	GAT	GAUCHE	GAULEITER
GASHING	GASPINGLY	GATCH	GAUCHED	GAULT
GASHLIER	GASPINGS	GATCHED	GAUCHELY	GAULTER
GASHLIEST	GASPS	GATCHER	GAUCHER	GAULTERS
GASHLY	GASPY	GATCHERS	GAUCHERIE	GAULTS
GASHOLDER	GASSED	GATCHES	GAUCHERS	GAUM
GASHOUSE	GASSER	GATCHING	GAUCHES	GAUMED
GASHOUSES	GASSERS	GATE	GAUCHESCO	GAUMIER
GASIFIED	GASSES	GATEAU	GAUCHEST	GAUMIEST
GASIFIER	GASSIER	GATEAUS	GAUCHING	GAUMING
GASIFIERS	GASSIEST	GATEAUX	GAUCHO	GAUMLESS
GASIFIES	GASSILY	GATECRASH	GAUCHOS	GAUMS
GASIFORM	GASSINESS	GATED	GAUCIE	GAUMY
GASIFY	GASSING	GATEFOLD	GAUCIER	GAUN
GASIFYING	GASSINGS	GATEFOLDS	GAUCIEST	GAUNCH
GASKET	GASSY	GATEHOUSE	GAUCY	GAUNCHED
GASKETED	GAST	GATEKEEP	GAUD	GAUNCHES
GASKETS	GASTED	GATEKEEPS	GAUDEAMUS	GAUNCHING
GASKIN	GASTER	GATEKEPT	GAUDED	GAUNT
GASKING	GASTERED	GATELEG	GAUDERIES	GAUNTED
GASKINGS	GASTERING	GATELEGS	GAUDERY	GAUNTER
GASKINS	GASTERS	GATELESS	GAUDGIE	GAUNTEST
GASLESS	GASTFULL	GATELIKE	GAUDGIES	GAUNTING
GASLIGHT	GASTHAUS	GATEMAN	GAUDIER	GAUNTLET
GASLIGHTS	GASTIGHT	GATEMEN	GAUDIES	GAUNTLETS
GASLIT	GASTING	GATEPOST	GAUDIEST	GAUNTLY

GAUNTNESS	GAVOTTES	GAYNESS	GAZOON	GECKOS
GAUNTREE	GAVOTTING	GAYNESSES	GAZOONS	GECKS
GAUNTREES	GAW	GAYS	GAZOOS	GED
GAUNTRIES	GAWCIER	GAYSOME	GAZPACHO	GEDACT
GAUNTRY	GAWCIEST	GAYWINGS	GAZPACHOS	GEDACTS
GAUNTS	GAWCY	GAZABO	GAZUMP	GEDDIT
GAUP	GAWD	GAZABOES	GAZUMPED	GEDECKT
GAUPED	GAWDS	GAZABOS	GAZUMPER	GEDECKTS
GAUPER	GAWK	GAZAL	GAZUMPERS	GEDS
GAUPERS	GAWKED	GAZALS	GAZUMPING	GEE
GAUPING	GAWKER	GAZANG	GAZUMPS	GEEBAG
GAUPS	GAWKERS	GAZANGED	GAZUNDER	GEEBAGS
GAUPUS	GAWKIER	GAZANGING	GAZUNDERS	GEEBUNG
GAUPUSES	GAWKIES	GAZANGS	GAZY	GEEBUNGS
GAUR	GAWKIEST	GAZANIA	GEAL	GEECHEE
GAURS	GAWKIHOOD	GAZANIAS	GEALED	GEECHEES
GAUS	GAWKILY	GAZAR	GEALING	GEED
GAUSS	GAWKINESS	GAZARS	GEALOUS	GEEGAW
GAUSSES	GAWKING	GAZE	GEALOUSY	GEEGAWS
GAUSSIAN	GAWKISH	GAZEBO	GEALS	GEEING
GAUZE	GAWKISHLY	GAZEBOES	GEAN	GEEK
GAUZELIKE	GAWKS	GAZEBOS	GEANS	GEEKDOM
GAUZES	GAWKY	GAZED	GEAR	GEEKDOMS
GAUZIER	GAWMOGE	GAZEFUL	GEARBOX	GEEKED
GAUZIEST	GAWMOGES	GAZEHOUND	GEARBOXES	GEEKERIES
GAUZILY	GAWP	GAZELLE	GEARCASE	GEEKERY
GAUZINESS	GAWPED	GAZELLES	GEARCASES	GEEKIER
GAUZY	GAWPER	GAZEMENT	GEARE	GEEKIEST
GAVAGE	GAWPERS	GAZEMENTS	GEARED	GEEKINESS
GAVAGES	GAWPING	GAZER	GEARES	GEEKISH
GAVE	GAWPS	GAZERS	GEARHEAD	GEEKISM
GAVEL	GAWPUS	GAZES	GEARHEADS	GEEKISMS
GAVELED	GAWPUSES	GAZETTE	GEARING	GEEKS
GAVELING	GAWS	GAZETTED	GEARINGS	GEEKSPEAK
GAVELKIND	GAWSIE	GAZETTEER	GEARLESS	GEEKY
GAVELLED	GAWSIER	GAZETTES	GEARS	GEELBEK
GAVELLING	GAWSIEST	GAZETTING	GEARSHIFT	GEELBEKS
GAVELMAN	GAWSY	GAZIER	GEARSTICK	GEEP
GAVELMEN	GAY	GAZIEST	GEARWHEEL	GEEPOUND
GAVELOCK	GAYAL	GAZILLION	GEASON	GEEPOUNDS
GAVELOCKS	GAYALS	GAZING	GEAT	GEEPS
GAVELS	GAYCATION	GAZINGS	GEATS	GEES
GAVIAL	GAYDAR	GAZOGENE	GEBUR	GEESE
GAVIALOID	GAYDARS	GAZOGENES	GEBURS	GEEST
GAVIALS	GAYER	GAZON	GECK	GEESTS
GAVOT	GAYEST	GAZONS	GECKED	GEEZ
GAVOTS	GAYETIES	GAZOO	GECKING	GEEZAH
GAVOTTE	GAYETY	GAZOOKA	GECKO	GEEZAHS
GAVOTTED	GAYLY	GAZOOKAS	GECKOES	GEEZER

G

GEEZERS	GELDS	GEMMATING	GENERA	GENISTAS
GEFILTE	GELEE	GEMMATION	GENERABLE	GENISTEIN
GEFUFFLE	GELEES	GEMMATIVE	GENERAL	GENITAL
GEFUFFLED	GELID	GEMMED	GENERALCY	GENITALIA
GEFUFFLES	GELIDER	GEMMEN	GENERALE	GENITALIC
GEFULLTE	GELIDEST	GEMMEOUS	GENERALIA	GENITALLY
GEGGIE	GELIDITY	GEMMERIES	GENERALLY	GENITALS
GEGGIES	GELIDLY	GEMMERY	GENERALS	GENITIVAL
GEHLENITE	GELIDNESS	GEMMIER	GENERANT	GENITIVE
GEISHA	GELIGNITE	GEMMIEST	GENERANTS	GENITIVES
GEISHAS	GELLANT	GEMMILY	GENERATE	GENITOR
GEIST	GELLANTS	GEMMINESS	GENERATED	GENITORS
GEISTS	GELLED	GEMMING	GENERATES	GENITRIX
GEIT	GELLIES	GEMMOLOGY	GENERATOR	GENITURE
GEITED	GELLING	GEMMULE	GENERIC	GENITURES
GEITING	GELLY	GEMMULES	GENERICAL	GENIUS
GEITS	GELOSIES	GEMMY	GENERICS	GENIUSES
GEL	GELOSY	GEMOLOGY	GENEROUS	GENIZAH
GELABLE	GELS	GEMONY	GENES	GENIZAHS
GELADA	GELSEMIA	GEMOT	GENESES	GENIZOT
GELADAS	GELSEMINE	GEMOTE	GENESIS	GENIZOTH
GELANDE	GELSEMIUM	GEMOTES	GENET	GENLOCK
GELANT	GELT	GEMOTS	GENETIC	GENLOCKED
GELANTS	GELTS	GEMS	GENETICAL	GENLOCKS
GELASTIC	GEM	GEMSBOK	GENETICS	GENNAKER
GELATE	GEMATRIA	GEMSBOKS	GENETRIX	GENNAKERS
GELATED	GEMATRIAS	GEMSBUCK	GENETS	GENNED
GELATES	GEMCLIP	GEMSBUCKS	GENETTE	GENNEL
GELATI	GEMCLIPS	GEMSHORN	GENETTES	GENNELS
GELATIN	GEMEL	GEMSHORNS	GENEVA	GENNET
GELATINE	GEMELS	GEMSTONE	GENEVAS	GENNETS
GELATINES	GEMFISH	GEMSTONES	GENIAL	GENNIES
GELATING	GEMFISHES	GEMUTLICH	GENIALISE	GENNING
GELATINS	GEMINAL	GEN	GENIALITY	GENNY
GELATION	GEMINALLY	GENA	GENIALIZE	GENOA
GELATIONS	GEMINATE	GENAL	GENIALLY	GENOAS
GELATIS	GEMINATED	GENAPPE	GENIC	GENOCIDAL
GELATO	GEMINATES	GENAPPES	GENICALLY	GENOCIDE
GELATOS	GEMINI	GENAS	GENICULAR	GENOCIDES
GELCAP	GEMINIES	GENDARME	GENIE	GENOGRAM
GELCAPS	GEMINOUS	GENDARMES	GENIES	GENOGRAMS
GELCOAT	GEMINY	GENDER	GENII	GENOISE
GELCOATS	GEMLIKE	GENDERED	GENIP	GENOISES
GELD	GEMMA	GENDERING	GENIPAP	GENOM
GELDED	GEMMAE	GENDERISE	GENIPAPO	GENOME
GELDER	GEMMAN	GENDERIZE	GENIPAPOS	GENOMES
GELDERS	GEMMATE	GENDERS	GENIPAPS	GENOMIC
GELDING	GEMMATED	GENE	GENIPS	GENOMICS
GELDINGS	GEMMATES	GENEALOGY	GENISTA	GENOMS

GENOTOXIC	GENUA	GEOIDAL	GEOTAG	GERMANISE
GENOTYPE	GENUFLECT	GEOIDS	GEOTAGGED	GERMANITE
GENOTYPED	GENUINE	GEOLATRY	GEOTAGS	GERMANIUM
GENOTYPES	GENUINELY	GEOLOGER	GEOTAXES	GERMANIZE
GENOTYPIC	GENUS	GEOLOGERS	GEOTAXIS	GERMANOUS
GENRE	GENUSES	GEOLOGIAN	GEOTHERM	GERMANS
GENRES	GEO	GEOLOGIC	GEOTHERMS	GERMED
GENRO	GEOBOTANY	GEOLOGIES	GEOTROPIC	GERMEN
GENROS	GEOCACHE	GEOLOGISE	GEPIK	GERMENS
GENS	GEOCACHED	GEOLOGIST	GEPIKS	GERMFREE
GENSENG	GEOCACHER	GEOLOGIZE	GER	GERMICIDE
GENSENGS	GEOCACHES	GEOLOGY	GERAH	GERMIER
GENT	GEOCARPIC	GEOMANCER	GERAHS	GERMIEST
GENTEEL	GEOCARPY	GEOMANCY	GERANIAL	GERMIN
GENTEELER	GEOCODE	GEOMANT	GERANIALS	GERMINA
GENTEELLY	GEOCODED	GEOMANTIC	GERANIOL	GERMINAL
GENTES	GEOCODES	GEOMANTS	GERANIOLS	GERMINANT
GENTIAN	GEOCODING	GEOMATICS	GERANIUM	GERMINATE
GENTIANS	GEOCORONA	GEOMETER	GERANIUMS	GERMINESS
GENTIER	GEODATA	GEOMETERS	GERARDIA	GERMING
GENTIEST	GEODE	GEOMETRIC	GERARDIAS	GERMINS
GENTIL	GEODES	GEOMETRID	GERBE	GERMLIKE
GENTILE	GEODESIC	GEOMETRY	GERBERA	GERMLINE
GENTILES	GEODESICS	GEOMYOID	GERBERAS	GERMLINES
GENTILIC	GEODESIES	GEONOMICS	GERBES	GERMPLASM
GENTILISE	GEODESIST	GEOPHAGIA	GERBIL	GERMPROOF
GENTILISH	GEODESY	GEOPHAGY	GERBILLE	GERMS
GENTILISM	GEODETIC	GEOPHILIC	GERBILLES	GERMY
GENTILITY	GEODETICS	GEOPHONE	GERBILS	GERNE
GENTILIZE	GEODIC	GEOPHONES	GERE	GERNED
GENTLE	GEODUCK	GEOPHYTE	GERENT	GERNES
GENTLED	GEODUCKS	GEOPHYTES	GERENTS	GERNING
GENTLEMAN	GEOFACT	GEOPHYTIC	GERENUK	GERONIMO
GENTLEMEN	GEOFACTS	GEOPONIC	GERENUKS	GERONTIC
GENTLER	GEOFENCE	GEOPONICS	GERES	GEROPIGA
GENTLES	GEOFENCED	GEOPROBE	GERFALCON	GEROPIGAS
GENTLEST	GEOFENCES	GEOPROBES	GERIATRIC	GERS
GENTLING	GEOGENIES	GEORGETTE	GERLE	GERT
GENTLY	GEOGENY	GEORGIC	GERLES	GERTCHA
GENTOO	GEOGNOSES	GEORGICAL	GERM	GERUND
GENTOOS	GEOGNOSIS	GEORGICS	GERMAIN	GERUNDIAL
GENTRICE	GEOGNOST	GEOS	GERMAINE	GERUNDIVE
GENTRICES	GEOGNOSTS	GEOSMIN	GERMAINES	GERUNDS
GENTRIES	GEOGNOSY	GEOSMINS	GERMAINS	GESNERIA
GENTRIFY	GEOGONIC	GEOSPACE	GERMAN	GESNERIAD
GENTRY	GEOGONIES	GEOSPACES	GERMANDER	GESNERIAS
GENTS	GEOGONY	GEOSPHERE	GERMANE	GESSAMINE
GENTY	GEOGRAPHY	GEOSTATIC	GERMANELY	GESSE
GENU	GEOID	GEOTACTIC	GERMANIC	GESSED

GESSES	GETUPS	GHESSE	GIANTISMS	GIBUS
GESSING	GEUM	GHESSED	GIANTLIER	GIBUSES
GESSO	GEUMS	GHESSES	GIANTLIKE	GID
GESSOED	GEWGAW	GHESSING	GIANTLY	GIDDAP
GESSOES	GEWGAWED	GHEST	GIANTRIES	GIDDAY
GEST	GEWGAWS	GHETTO	GIANTRY	GIDDIED
GESTALT	GEY	GHETTOED	GIANTS	GIDDIER
GESTALTEN	GEYAN	GHETTOES	GIANTSHIP	GIDDIES
GESTALTS	GEYER	GHETTOING	GIAOUR	GIDDIEST
GESTANT	GEYEST	GHETTOISE	GIAOURS	GIDDILY
GESTAPO	GEYSER	GHETTOIZE	GIARDIA	GIDDINESS
GESTAPOS	GEYSERED	GHETTOS	GIARDIAS	GIDDUP
GESTATE	GEYSERING	GHI	GIB	GIDDY
GESTATED	GEYSERITE	GHIBLI	GIBBED	GIDDYAP
GESTATES	GEYSERS	GHIBLIS	GIBBER	GIDDYING
GESTATING	GHARIAL	GHILGAI	GIBBERED	GIDDYUP
GESTATION	GHARIALS	GHILGAIS	GIBBERING	GIDGEE
GESTATIVE	GHARRI	GHILLIE	GIBBERISH	GIDGEES
GESTATORY	GHARRIES	GHILLIED	GIBBERS	GIDJEE
GESTE	GHARRIS	GHILLIES	GIBBET	GIDJEES
GESTES	GHARRY	GHILLYING	GIBBETED	GIDS
GESTIC	GHAST	GHIS	GIBBETING	GIE
GESTICAL	GHASTED	GHOST	GIBBETS	GIED
GESTS	GHASTFUL	GHOSTED	GIBBETTED	GIEING
GESTURAL	GHASTING	GHOSTIER	GIBBING	GIEN
GESTURE	GHASTLIER	GHOSTIEST	GIBBON	GIES
GESTURED	GHASTLY	GHOSTING	GIBBONS	GIF
GESTURER	GHASTNESS	GHOSTINGS	GIBBOSE	GIFS
GESTURERS	GHASTS	GHOSTLIER	GIBBOSITY	GIFT
GESTURES	GHAT	GHOSTLIKE	GIBBOUS	GIFTABLE
GESTURING	GHATS	GHOSTLY	GIBBOUSLY	GIFTABLES
GET	GHAUT	GHOSTS	GIBBSITE	GIFTED
GETA	GHAUTS	GHOSTY	GIBBSITES	GIFTEDLY
GETABLE	GHAZAL	GHOUL	GIBE	GIFTEE
GETAS	GHAZALS	GHOULIE	GIBED	GIFTEES
GETATABLE	GHAZEL	GHOULIES	GIBEL	GIFTING
GETAWAY	GHAZELS	GHOULISH	GIBELS	GIFTINGS
GETAWAYS	GHAZI	GHOULS	GIBER	GIFTLESS
GETOUT	GHAZIES	GHRELIN	GIBERS	GIFTS
GETOUTS	GHAZIS	GHRELINS	GIBES	GIFTSHOP
GETS	GHEE	GHUBAR	GIBING	GIFTSHOPS
GETTABLE	GHEES	GHYLL	GIBINGLY	GIFTWARE
GETTER	GHERAO	GHYLLS	GIBLET	GIFTWARES
GETTERED	GHERAOED	GI	GIBLETS	GIFTWRAP
GETTERING	GHERAOES	GIAMBEUX	GIBLI	GIFTWRAPS
GETTERS	GHERAOING	GIANT	GIBLIS	GIG
GETTING	GHERAOS	GIANTESS	GIBS	GIGA
GETTINGS	GHERKIN	GIANTHOOD	GIBSON	GIGABIT
GETUP	GHERKINS	GIANTISM	GIBSONS	GIGABITS

GIGABYTE	GILAS	GILRAVAGE	GINGAL	GINNED
GIGABYTES	GILBERT	GILSONITE	GINGALL	GINNEL
GIGACYCLE	GILBERTS	GILT	GINGALLS	GINNELS
GIGAFLOP	GILCUP	GILTCUP	GINGALS	GINNER
GIGAFLOPS	GILCUPS	GILTCUPS	GINGE	GINNERIES
GIGAHERTZ	GILD	GILTHEAD	GINGELEY	GINNERS
GIGANTEAN	GILDED	GILTHEADS	GINGELEYS	GINNERY
GIGANTIC	GILDEN	GILTS	GINGELI	GINNIER
GIGANTISM	GILDER	GILTWOOD	GINGELIES	GINNIEST
GIGAS	GILDERS	GIMBAL	GINGELIS	GINNING
GIGATON	GILDHALL	GIMBALED	GINGELLI	GINNINGS
GIGATONS	GILDHALLS	GIMBALING	GINGELLIS	GINNY
GIGAVOLT	GILDING	GIMBALLED	GINGELLY	GINORMOUS
GIGAVOLTS	GILDINGS	GIMBALS	GINGELY	GINS
GIGAWATT	GILDS	GIMCRACK	GINGER	GINSENG
GIGAWATTS	GILDSMAN	GIMCRACKS	GINGERADE	GINSENGS
GIGGED	GILDSMEN	GIMEL	GINGERED	GINSHOP
GIGGING	GILET	GIMELS	GINGERIER	GINSHOPS
GIGGIT	GILETS	GIMLET	GINGERING	GIO
GIGGITED	GILGAI	GIMLETED	GINGERLY	GIOCOSO
GIGGITING	GILGAIS	GIMLETING	GINGEROUS	GIOS
GIGGITS	GILGIE	GIMLETS	GINGERS	GIP
GIGGITY	GILGIES	GIMMAL	GINGERY	GIPON
GIGGLE	GILL	GIMMALLED	GINGES	GIPONS
GIGGLED	GILLAROO	GIMMALS	GINGHAM	GIPPED
GIGGLER	GILLAROOS	GIMME	GINGHAMS	GIPPER
GIGGLERS	GILLED	GIMMER	GINGILI	GIPPERS
GIGGLES	GILLER	GIMMERS	GINGILIS	GIPPIES
GIGGLIER	GILLERS	GIMMES	GINGILLI	GIPPING
GIGGLIEST	GILLET	GIMMICK	GINGILLIS	GIPPY
GIGGLING	GILLETS	GIMMICKED	GINGIVA	GIPS
GIGGLINGS	GILLFLIRT	GIMMICKRY	GINGIVAE	GIPSEN
GIGGLY	GILLIE	GIMMICKS	GINGIVAL	GIPSENS
GIGHE	GILLIED	GIMMICKY	GINGKO	GIPSIED
GIGLET	GILLIES	GIMMIE	GINGKOES	GIPSIES
GIGLETS	GILLING	GIMMIES	GINGKOS	GIPSY
GIGLOT	GILLION	GIMMOR	GINGLE	GIPSYDOM
GIGLOTS	GILLIONS	GIMMORS	GINGLES	GIPSYDOMS
GIGMAN	GILLNET	GIMP	GINGLYMI	GIPSYHOOD
GIGMANITY	GILLNETS	GIMPED	GINGLYMUS	GIPSYING
GIGMEN	GILLS	GIMPIER	GINGS	GIPSYISH
GIGOLO	GILLY	GIMPIEST	GINHOUSE	GIPSYISM
GIGOLOS	GILLYING	GIMPING	GINHOUSES	GIPSYISMS
GIGOT	GILLYVOR	GIMPS	GINK	GIPSYWORT
GIGOTS	GILLYVORS	GIMPY	GINKGO	GIRAFFE
GIGS	GILPEY	GIN	GINKGOES	GIRAFFES
GIGUE	GILPEYS	GINCH	GINKGOS	GIRAFFID
GIGUES	GILPIES	GINCHES	GINKS	GIRAFFIDS
GILA	GILPY	GING	GINN	GIRAFFINE

GIRAFFISH	GIROLLE	GITTIN	GLACIALLY	GLADWRAPS
GIRAFFOID	GIROLLES	GITTING	GLACIALS	GLADY
GIRANDOLA	GIRON	GIUST	GLACIATE	GLAIK
GIRANDOLE	GIRONIC	GIUSTED	GLACIATED	GLAIKET
GIRASOL	GIRONNY	GIUSTING	GLACIATES	GLAIKIT
GIRASOLE	GIRONS	GIUSTO	GLACIER	GLAIKS
GIRASOLES	GIROS	GIUSTS	GLACIERED	GLAIR
GIRASOLS	GIROSOL	GIVABLE	GLACIERS	GLAIRE
GIRD	GIROSOLS	GIVE	GLACIS	GLAIRED
GIRDED	GIRR	GIVEABLE	GLACISES	GLAIREOUS
GIRDER	GIRRS	GIVEAWAY	GLAD	GLAIRES
GIRDERS	GIRSH	GIVEAWAYS	GLADDED	GLAIRIER
GIRDING	GIRSHES	GIVEBACK	GLADDEN	GLAIRIEST
GIRDINGLY	GIRT	GIVEBACKS	GLADDENED	GLAIRIN
GIRDINGS	GIRTED	GIVED	GLADDENER	GLAIRING
GIRDLE	GIRTH	GIVEN	GLADDENS	GLAIRINS
GIRDLED	GIRTHED	GIVENNESS	GLADDER	GLAIRS
GIRDLER	GIRTHING	GIVENS	GLADDEST	GLAIRY
GIRDLERS	GIRTHLINE	GIVER	GLADDIE	GLAIVE
GIRDLES	GIRTHS	GIVERS	GLADDIES	GLAIVED
GIRDLING	GIRTING	GIVES	GLADDING	GLAIVES
GIRDS	GIRTLINE	GIVING	GLADDON	GLAM
GIRKIN	GIRTLINES	GIVINGS	GLADDONS	GLAMAZON
GIRKINS	GIRTS	GIZMO	GLADE	GLAMAZONS
GIRL	GIS	GIZMOLOGY	GLADELIKE	GLAMMED
GIRLHOOD	GISARME	GIZMOS	GLADES	GLAMMER
GIRLHOODS	GISARMES	GIZZ	GLADFUL	GLAMMEST
GIRLIE	GISM	GIZZARD	GLADIATE	GLAMMIER
GIRLIER	GISMO	GIZZARDS	GLADIATOR	GLAMMIEST
GIRLIES	GISMOLOGY	GIZZEN	GLADIER	GLAMMING
GIRLIEST	GISMOS	GIZZENED	GLADIEST	GLAMMY
GIRLISH	GISMS	GIZZENING	GLADIOLA	GLAMOR
GIRLISHLY	GIST	GIZZENS	GLADIOLAR	GLAMORED
GIRLOND	GISTS	GIZZES	GLADIOLAS	GLAMORING
GIRLONDS	GIT	GJETOST	GLADIOLE	GLAMORISE
GIRLS	GITANA	GJETOSTS	GLADIOLES	GLAMORIZE
GIRLY	GITANAS	GJU	GLADIOLI	GLAMOROUS
GIRN	GITANO	GJUS	GLADIOLUS	GLAMORS
GIRNED	GITANOS	GLABELLA	GLADIUS	GLAMOUR
GIRNEL	GITCH	GLABELLAE	GLADIUSES	GLAMOURED
GIRNELS	GITCHES	GLABELLAR	GLADLIER	GLAMOURS
GIRNER	GITE	GLABRATE	GLADLIEST	GLAMP
GIRNERS	GITES	GLABROUS	GLADLY	GLAMPED
GIRNIE	GITS	GLACE	GLADNESS	GLAMPER
GIRNIER	GITTARONE	GLACED	GLADS	GLAMPERS
GIRNIEST	GITTED	GLACEED	GLADSOME	GLAMPING
GIRNING	GITTERN	GLACEING	GLADSOMER	GLAMPINGS
GIRNS	GITTERNED	GLACES	GLADSTONE	GLAMPS
GIRO	GITTERNS	GLACIAL	GLADWRAP	GLAMPSITE

GLAMS	GLASSLIKE	GLEANERS	GLEGLY	GLIFF
GLANCE	GLASSMAN	GLEANING	GLEGNESS	GLIFFING
GLANCED	GLASSMEN	GLEANINGS	GLEI	GLIFFINGS
GLANCER	GLASSWARE	GLEANS	GLEIS	GLIFFS
GLANCERS	GLASSWORK	GLEAVE	GLEN	GLIFT
GLANCES	GLASSWORM	GLEAVES	GLENGARRY	GLIFTS
GLANCING	GLASSWORT	GLEBA	GLENLIKE	GLIKE
GLANCINGS	GLASSY	GLEBAE	GLENOID	GLIKES
GLAND	GLAUCOMA	GLEBE	GLENOIDAL	GLIM
GLANDERED	GLAUCOMAS	GLEBELESS	GLENOIDS	GLIME
GLANDERS	GLAUCOUS	GLEBES	GLENS	GLIMED
GLANDES	GLAUM	GLEBIER	GLENT	GLIMES
GLANDLESS	GLAUMED	GLEBIEST	GLENTED	GLIMING
GLANDLIKE	GLAUMING	GLEBOUS	GLENTING	GLIMMER
GLANDS	GLAUMS	GLEBY	GLENTS	GLIMMERED
GLANDULAR	GLAUR	GLED	GLEY	GLIMMERS
GLANDULE	GLAURIER	GLEDE	GLEYED	GLIMMERY
GLANDULES	GLAURIEST	GLEDES	GLEYING	GLIMPSE
GLANS	GLAURS	GLEDGE	GLEYINGS	GLIMPSED
GLARE	GLAURY	GLEDGED	GLEYS	GLIMPSER
GLAREAL	GLAZE	GLEDGES	GLIA	GLIMPSERS
GLARED	GLAZED	GLEDGING	GLIADIN	GLIMPSES
GLARELESS	GLAZEN	GLEDS	GLIADINE	GLIMPSING
GLAREOUS	GLAZER	GLEE	GLIADINES	GLIMS
GLARES	GLAZERS	GLEED	GLIADINS	GLINT
GLARIER	GLAZES	GLEEDS	GLIAL	GLINTED
GLARIEST	GLAZIER	GLEEFUL	GLIAS	GLINTIER
GLARINESS	GLAZIERS	GLEEFULLY	GLIB	GLINTIEST
GLARING	GLAZIERY	GLEEING	GLIBBED	GLINTING
GLARINGLY	GLAZIEST	GLEEK	GLIBBER	GLINTS
GLARY	GLAZILY	GLEEKED	GLIBBERY	GLINTY
GLASNOST	GLAZINESS	GLEEKING	GLIBBEST	GLIOMA
GLASNOSTS	GLAZING	GLEEKS	GLIBBING	GLIOMAS
GLASS	GLAZINGS	GLEEMAN	GLIBLY	GLIOMATA
GLASSED	GLAZY	GLEEMEN	GLIBNESS	GLIOSES
GLASSEN	GLEAM	GLEENIE	GLIBS	GLIOSIS
GLASSES	GLEAMED	GLEENIES	GLID	GLISK
GLASSFUL	GLEAMER	GLEES	GLIDDER	GLISKS
GLASSFULS	GLEAMERS	GLEESOME	GLIDDERY	GLISSADE
GLASSIE	GLEAMIER	GLEET	GLIDDEST	GLISSADED
GLASSIER	GLEAMIEST	GLEETED	GLIDE	GLISSADER
GLASSIES	GLEAMING	GLEETIER	GLIDED	GLISSADES
GLASSIEST	GLEAMINGS	GLEETIEST	GLIDEPATH	GLISSANDI
GLASSIFY	GLEAMS	GLEETING	GLIDER	GLISSANDO
GLASSILY	GLEAMY	GLEETS	GLIDERS	GLISSE
GLASSINE	GLEAN	GLEETY	GLIDES	GLISSES
GLASSINES	GLEANABLE	GLEG	GLIDING	GLISTEN
GLASSING	GLEANED	GLEGGER	GLIDINGLY	GLISTENED
GLASSLESS	GLEANER	GLEGGEST	GLIDINGS	GLISTENS

GLISTER	GLOBESITY	GLOOMIER	GLOSSERS	GLOWSTICK
GLISTERED	GLOBETROT	GLOOMIEST	GLOSSES	GLOWWORM
GLISTERS	GLOBI	GLOOMILY	GLOSSIER	GLOWWORMS
GLIT	GLOBIER	GLOOMING	GLOSSIES	GLOXINIA
GLITCH	GLOBIEST	GLOOMINGS	GLOSSIEST	GLOXINIAS
GLITCHES	GLOBIN	GLOOMLESS	GLOSSILY	GLOZE
GLITCHIER	GLOBING	GLOOMS	GLOSSINA	GLOZED
GLITCHY	GLOBINS	GLOOMSTER	GLOSSINAS	GLOZES
GLITS	GLOBOID	GLOOMY	GLOSSING	GLOZING
GLITTER	GLOBOIDS	GLOOP	GLOSSIST	GLOZINGS
GLITTERED	GLOBOSE	GLOOPED	GLOSSISTS	GLUCAGON
GLITTERS	GLOBOSELY	GLOOPIER	GLOSSITIC	GLUCAGONS
GLITTERY	GLOBOSITY	GLOOPIEST	GLOSSITIS	GLUCAN
GLITZ	GLOBOUS	GLOOPING	GLOSSLESS	GLUCANS
GLITZED	GLOBS	GLOOPS	GLOSSY	GLUCINA
GLITZES	GLOBULAR	GLOOPY	GLOST	GLUCINAS
GLITZIER	GLOBULARS	GLOP	GLOSTS	GLUCINIC
GLITZIEST	GLOBULE	GLOPPED	GLOTTAL	GLUCINIUM
GLITZILY	GLOBULES	GLOPPIER	GLOTTIC	GLUCINUM
GLITZING	GLOBULET	GLOPPIEST	GLOTTIDES	GLUCINUMS
GLITZY	GLOBULETS	GLOPPING	GLOTTIS	GLUCONATE
GLOAM	GLOBULIN	GLOPPY	GLOTTISES	GLUCONIC
GLOAMING	GLOBULINS	GLOPS	GLOUT	GLUCOSE
GLOAMINGS	GLOBULITE	GLORIA	GLOUTED	GLUCOSES
GLOAMS	GLOBULOUS	GLORIAS	GLOUTING	GLUCOSIC
GLOAT	GLOBUS	GLORIED	GLOUTS	GLUCOSIDE
GLOATED	GLOBY	GLORIES	GLOVE	GLUE
GLOATER	GLOCHID	GLORIFIED	GLOVEBOX	GLUEBALL
GLOATERS	GLOCHIDIA	GLORIFIER	GLOVED	GLUEBALLS
GLOATING	GLOCHIDS	GLORIFIES	GLOVELESS	GLUED
GLOATINGS	GLODE	GLORIFY	GLOVELIKE	GLUEING
GLOATS	GLOGG	GLORIOLE	GLOVER	GLUEISH
GLOB	GLOGGS	GLORIOLES	GLOVERS	GLUELIKE
GLOBAL	GLOIRE	GLORIOSA	GLOVES	GLUEPOT
GLOBALISE	GLOIRES	GLORIOSAS	GLOVING	GLUEPOTS
GLOBALISM	GLOM	GLORIOUS	GLOVINGS	GLUER
GLOBALIST	GLOMERA	GLORY	GLOW	GLUERS
GLOBALIZE	GLOMERATE	GLORYING	GLOWED	GLUES
GLOBALLY	GLOMERULE	GLOSS	GLOWER	GLUEY
GLOBATE	GLOMERULI	GLOSSA	GLOWERED	GLUEYNESS
GLOBATED	GLOMMED	GLOSSAE	GLOWERING	GLUG
GLOBBIER	GLOMMING	GLOSSAL	GLOWERS	GLUGGABLE
GLOBBIEST	GLOMS	GLOSSARY	GLOWFLIES	GLUGGED
GLOBBY	GLOMUS	GLOSSAS	GLOWFLY	GLUGGING
GLOBE	GLONOIN	GLOSSATOR	GLOWING	GLUGS
GLOBED	GLONOINS	GLOSSED	GLOWINGLY	GLUHWEIN
GLOBEFISH	GLOOM	GLOSSEME	GLOWLAMP	GLUHWEINS
GLOBELIKE	GLOOMED	GLOSSEMES	GLOWLAMPS	GLUIER
GLOBES	GLOOMFUL	GLOSSER	GLOWS	GLUIEST

GLUILY	GLUTENS	GLYPH	GNAWER	GOAF
GLUINESS	GLUTES	GLYPHIC	GNAWERS	GOAFS
GLUING	GLUTEUS	GLYPHS	GNAWING	GOAL
GLUISH	GLUTINOUS	GLYPTAL	GNAWINGLY	GOALBALL
GLUM	GLUTS	GLYPTALS	GNAWINGS	GOALBALLS
GLUME	GLUTTED	GLYPTIC	GNAWN	GOALED
GLUMELIKE	GLUTTING	GLYPTICS	GNAWS	GOALIE
GLUMELLA	GLUTTON	GMELINITE	GNEISS	GOALIES
GLUMELLAS	GLUTTONS	GNAMMA	GNEISSES	GOALING
GLUMES	GLUTTONY	GNAR	GNEISSIC	GOALLESS
GLUMLY	GLYCAEMIA	GNARL	GNEISSOID	GOALMOUTH
GLUMMER	GLYCAEMIC	GNARLED	GNEISSOSE	GOALPOST
GLUMMEST	GLYCAN	GNARLIER	GNETUM	GOALPOSTS
GLUMNESS	GLYCANS	GNARLIEST	GNETUMS	GOALS
GLUMPIER	GLYCATION	GNARLING	GNOCCHI	GOALWARD
GLUMPIEST	GLYCEMIA	GNARLS	GNOCCHIS	GOALWARDS
GLUMPILY	GLYCEMIAS	GNARLY	GNOMAE	GOANNA
GLUMPISH	GLYCEMIC	GNARR	GNOME	GOANNAS
GLUMPS	GLYCERIA	GNARRED	GNOMELIKE	GOARY
GLUMPY	GLYCERIAS	GNARRING	GNOMES	GOAS
GLUMS	GLYCERIC	GNARRS	GNOMIC	GOAT
GLUNCH	GLYCERIDE	GNARS	GNOMICAL	GOATEE
GLUNCHED	GLYCERIN	GNASH	GNOMISH	GOATEED
GLUNCHES	GLYCERINE	GNASHED	GNOMIST	GOATEES
GLUNCHING	GLYCERINS	GNASHER	GNOMISTS	GOATFISH
GLUON	GLYCEROL	GNASHERS	GNOMON	GOATHERD
GLUONS	GLYCEROLS	GNASHES	GNOMONIC	GOATHERDS
GLURGE	GLYCERYL	GNASHING	GNOMONICS	GOATIER
GLURGES	GLYCERYLS	GNASHINGS	GNOMONS	GOATIES
GLUT	GLYCIN	GNAT	GNOSES	GOATIEST
GLUTAEAL	GLYCINE	GNATHAL	GNOSIS	GOATISH
GLUTAEI	GLYCINES	GNATHIC	GNOSTIC	GOATISHLY
GLUTAEUS	GLYCINS	GNATHION	GNOSTICAL	GOATLIKE
GLUTAMATE	GLYCOCOLL	GNATHIONS	GNOSTICS	GOATLING
GLUTAMIC	GLYCOGEN	GNATHITE	GNOW	GOATLINGS
GLUTAMINE	GLYCOGENS	GNATHITES	GNOWS	GOATS
GLUTCH	GLYCOL	GNATHONIC	GNU	GOATSE
GLUTCHED	GLYCOLIC	GNATLIKE	GNUS	GOATSES
GLUTCHES	GLYCOLLIC	GNATLING	GO	GOATSKIN
GLUTCHING	GLYCOLS	GNATLINGS	GOA	GOATSKINS
GLUTE	GLYCONIC	GNATS	GOAD	GOATWEED
GLUTEAL	GLYCONICS	GNATTIER	GOADED	GOATWEEDS
GLUTEI	GLYCOSE	GNATTIEST	GOADING	GOATY
GLUTELIN	GLYCOSES	GNATTY	GOADLIKE	GOB
GLUTELINS	GLYCOSIDE	GNATWREN	GOADS	GOBAN
GLUTEN	GLYCOSYL	GNATWRENS	GOADSMAN	GOBANG
GLUTENIN	GLYCOSYLS	GNAW	GOADSMEN	GOBANGS
GLUTENINS	GLYCYL	GNAWABLE	GOADSTER	GOBANS
GLUTENOUS	GLYCYLS	GNAWED	GOADSTERS	GOBAR

G

GOBBED	GODDAMS	GODWIT	GOING	GOLDSMITH
GOBBELINE	GODDED	GODWITS	GOINGS	GOLDSPINK
GOBBET	GODDEN	GOE	GOITER	GOLDSTICK
GOBBETS	GODDENS	GOEL	GOITERED	GOLDSTONE
GOBBI	GODDESS	GOELS	GOITERS	GOLDTAIL
GOBBIER	GODDESSES	GOER	GOITRE	GOLDTONE
GOBBIEST	GODDING	GOERS	GOITRED	GOLDTONES
GOBBING	GODET	GOES	GOITRES	GOLDURN
GOBBLE	GODETIA	GOEST	GOITROGEN	GOLDURNS
GOBBLED	GODETIAS	GOETH	GOITROUS	GOLDWORK
GOBBLER	GODETS	GOETHITE	GOJI	GOLDWORKS
GOBBLERS	GODFATHER	GOETHITES	GOJIS	GOLDY
GOBBLES	GODHEAD	GOETIC	GOLCONDA	GOLE
GOBBLING	GODHEADS	GOETIES	GOLCONDAS	GOLEM
GOBBO	GODHOOD	GOETTA	GOLD	GOLEMS
GOBBY	GODHOODS	GOETTAS	GOLDARN	GOLES
GOBI	GODLESS	GOETY	GOLDARNED	GOLF
GOBIES	GODLESSLY	GOEY	GOLDARNS	GOLFED
GOBIID	GODLIER	GOFER	GOLDBRICK	GOLFER
GOBIIDS	GODLIEST	GOFERS	GOLDBUG	GOLFERS
GOBIOID	GODLIKE	GOFF	GOLDBUGS	GOLFIANA
GOBIOIDS	GODLILY	GOFFED	GOLDCREST	GOLFIANAS
GOBIS	GODLINESS	GOFFER	GOLDEN	GOLFING
GOBLET	GODLING	GOFFERED	GOLDENED	GOLFINGS
GOBLETS	GODLINGS	GOFFERING	GOLDENER	GOLFS
GOBLIN	GODLY	GOFFERS	GOLDENEST	GOLGOTHA
GOBLINS	GODMOTHER	GOFFING	GOLDENEYE	GOLGOTHAS
GOBO	GODOWN	GOFFS	GOLDENING	GOLIARD
GOBOES	GODOWNS	GOGGA	GOLDENLY	GOLIARDIC
GOBONEE	GODPARENT	GOGGAS	GOLDENROD	GOLIARDS
GOBONY	GODROON	GOGGLE	GOLDENS	GOLIARDY
GOBOS	GODROONED	GOGGLEBOX	GOLDER	GOLIAS
GOBS	GODROONS	GOGGLED	GOLDEST	GOLIASED
GOBSHITE	GODS	GOGGLER	GOLDEYE	GOLIASES
GOBSHITES	GODSEND	GOGGLERS	GOLDEYES	GOLIASING
GOBURRA	GODSENDS	GOGGLES	GOLDFIELD	GOLIATH
GOBURRAS	GODSHIP	GOGGLIER	GOLDFINCH	GOLIATHS
GOBY	GODSHIPS	GOGGLIEST	GOLDFINNY	GOLLAN
GOCHUJANG	GODSLOT	GOGGLING	GOLDFISH	GOLLAND
GOD	GODSLOTS	GOGGLINGS	GOLDIER	GOLLANDS
GODAWFUL	GODSO	GOGGLY	GOLDIES	GOLLANS
GODCHILD	GODSON	GOGLET	GOLDIEST	GOLLAR
GODDAM	GODSONS	GOGLETS	GOLDISH	GOLLARED
GODDAMMED	GODSPEED	GOGO	GOLDLESS	GOLLARING
GODDAMMIT	GODSPEEDS	GOGOS	GOLDMINER	GOLLARS
GODDAMN	GODSQUAD	GOHONZON	GOLDS	GOLLER
GODDAMNED	GODSQUADS	GOHONZONS	GOLDSINNY	GOLLERED
GODDAMNIT	GODWARD	GOIER	GOLDSIZE	GOLLERING
GODDAMNS	GODWARDS	GOIEST	GOLDSIZES	GOLLERS

GOLLIED	GONADAL	GONODUCTS	GOODWILLS	GOOMBAHS
GOLLIES	GONADIAL	GONOF	GOODWIVES	GOOMBAY
GOLLOP	GONADIC	GONOFS	GOODY	GOOMBAYS
GOLLOPED	GONADS	GONOPH	GOODYEAR	GOON
GOLLOPER	GONCH	GONOPHORE	GOODYEARS	GOONDA
GOLLOPERS	GONCHES	GONOPHS	GOOEY	GOONDAS
GOLLOPING	GONDELAY	GONOPOD	GOOEYNESS	GOONERIES
GOLLOPS	GONDELAYS	GONOPODS	GOOF	GOONERY
GOLLY	GONDOLA	GONOPORE	GOOFBALL	GOONEY
GOLLYING	GONDOLAS	GONOPORES	GOOFBALLS	GOONEYS
GOLOMYNKA	GONDOLIER	GONORRHEA	GOOFED	GOONIE
GOLOSH	GONE	GONOSOME	GOOFIER	GOONIER
GOLOSHE	GONEF	GONOSOMES	GOOFIEST	GOONIES
GOLOSHED	GONEFS	GONS	GOOFILY	GOONIEST
GOLOSHES	GONENESS	GONYS	GOOFINESS	GOONS
GOLOSHING	GONER	GONYSES	GOOFING	GOONY
GOLOSHOES	GONERS	GONZO	GOOFS	GOOP
GOLP	GONFALON	GONZOS	GOOFUS	GOOPED
GOLPE	GONFALONS	GOO	GOOFUSES	GOOPIER
GOLPES	GONFANON	GOOBER	GOOFY	GOOPIEST
GOLPS	GONFANONS	GOOBERS	GOOG	GOOPINESS
GOMBEEN	GONG	GOOBIES	GOOGLE	GOOPS
GOMBEENS	GONGED	GOOBY	GOOGLED	GOOPY
GOMBO	GONGING	GOOD	GOOGLES	GOOR
GOMBOS	GONGLIKE	GOODBY	GOOGLIES	GOORAL
GOMBRO	GONGS	GOODBYE	GOOGLING	GOORALS
GOMBROON	GONGSTER	GOODBYES	GOOGLY	GOORIE
GOMBROONS	GONGSTERS	GOODBYS	GOOGOL	GOORIES
GOMBROS	GONGYO	GOODFACED	GOOGOLS	GOOROO
GOMER	GONGYOS	GOODFELLA	GOOGS	GOOROOS
GOMERAL	GONIA	GOODIE	GOOIER	GOORS
GOMERALS	GONIATITE	GOODIER	GOOIEST	GOORY
GOMEREL	GONIDIA	GOODIES	GOOILY	GOOS
GOMERELS	GONIDIAL	GOODIEST	GOOINESS	GOOSANDER
GOMERIL	GONIDIC	GOODINESS	GOOK	GOOSE
GOMERILS	GONIDIUM	GOODISH	GOOKIER	GOOSED
GOMERS	GONIF	GOODLIER	GOOKIEST	GOOSEFISH
GOMOKU	GONIFF	GOODLIEST	GOOKS	GOOSEFOOT
GOMOKUS	GONIFFS	GOODLY	GOOKY	GOOSEGOB
GOMPA	GONIFS	GOODMAN	GOOL	GOOSEGOBS
GOMPAS	GONION	GOODMEN	GOOLD	GOOSEGOG
GOMPHOSES	GONIUM	GOODNESS	GOOLDS	GOOSEGOGS
GOMPHOSIS	GONK	GOODNIGHT	GOOLEY	GOOSEHERD
GOMUTI	GONKS	GOODS	GOOLEYS	GOOSELIKE
GOMUTIS	GONNA	GOODSIRE	GOOLIE	GOOSENECK
GOMUTO	GONOCOCCI	GOODSIRES	GOOLIES	GOOSERIES
GOMUTOS	GONOCYTE	GOODTIME	GOOLS	GOOSERY
GON	GONOCYTES	GOODWIFE	GOOLY	GOOSES
GONAD	GONODUCT	GOODWILL	GOOMBAH	GOOSEY

GOOSEYS	GORGERS	GORSES	GOSSIPIER	GOUGING
GOOSIER	GORGES	GORSIER	GOSSIPING	GOUJEERS
GOOSIES	GORGET	GORSIEST	GOSSIPPED	GOUJON
GOOSIEST	GORGETED	GORSOON	GOSSIPPER	GOUJONS
GOOSINESS	GORGETS	GORSOONS	GOSSIPRY	GOUK
GOOSING	GORGIA	GORSY	GOSSIPS	GOUKS
GOOSY	GORGIAS	GORY	GOSSIPY	GOULASH
GOPAK	GORGING	GOS	GOSSOON	GOULASHES
GOPAKS	GORGIO	GOSH	GOSSOONS	GOURA
GOPHER	GORGIOS	GOSHAWK	GOSSYPINE	GOURAMI
GOPHERED	GORGON	GOSHAWKS	GOSSYPOL	GOURAMIES
GOPHERING	GORGONEIA	GOSHT	GOSSYPOLS	GOURAMIS
GOPHERS	GORGONIAN	GOSHTS	GOSTER	GOURAS
GOPIK	GORGONISE	GOSLARITE	GOSTERED	GOURD
GOPIKS	GORGONIZE	GOSLET	GOSTERING	GOURDE
GOPURA	GORGONS	GOSLETS	GOSTERS	GOURDES
GOPURAM	GORHEN	GOSLING	GOT	GOURDFUL
GOPURAMS	GORHENS	GOSLINGS	GOTCH	GOURDFULS
GOPURAS	GORI	GOSPEL	GOTCHA	GOURDIER
GOR	GORIER	GOSPELER	GOTCHAS	GOURDIEST
GORA	GORIEST	GOSPELERS	GOTCHES	GOURDLIKE
GORAL	GORILLA	GOSPELISE	GOTCHIES	GOURDS
GORALS	GORILLAS	GOSPELIZE	GOTH	GOURDY
GORAMIES	GORILLIAN	GOSPELLED	GOTHIC	GOURMAND
GORAMY	GORILLINE	GOSPELLER	GOTHICISE	GOURMANDS
GORAS	GORILLOID	GOSPELLY	GOTHICISM	GOURMET
GORBELLY	GORILY	GOSPELS	GOTHICIZE	GOURMETS
GORBLIMEY	GORINESS	GOSPODA	GOTHICS	GOUSTIER
GORBLIMY	GORING	GOSPODAR	GOTHIER	GOUSTIEST
GORCOCK	GORINGS	GOSPODARS	GOTHIEST	GOUSTROUS
GORCOCKS	GORIS	GOSPODIN	GOTHITE	GOUSTY
GORCROW	GORM	GOSPORT	GOTHITES	GOUT
GORCROWS	GORMAND	GOSPORTS	GOTHS	GOUTFLIES
GORDITA	GORMANDS	GOSS	GOTHY	GOUTFLY
GORDITAS	GORMED	GOSSAMER	GOTTA	GOUTIER
GORE	GORMIER	GOSSAMERS	GOTTEN	GOUTIEST
GORED	GORMIEST	GOSSAMERY	GOUACHE	GOUTILY
GOREFEST	GORMING	GOSSAN	GOUACHES	GOUTINESS
GOREFESTS	GORMLESS	GOSSANS	GOUCH	GOUTS
GOREHOUND	GORMS	GOSSE	GOUCHED	GOUTTE
GORES	GORMY	GOSSED	GOUCHES	GOUTTES
GORGE	GORP	GOSSES	GOUCHING	GOUTWEED
GORGEABLE	GORPED	GOSSIB	GOUGE	GOUTWEEDS
GORGED	GORPING	GOSSIBS	GOUGED	GOUTWORT
GORGEDLY	GORPS	GOSSING	GOUGER	GOUTWORTS
GORGEOUS	GORS	GOSSIP	GOUGERE	GOUTY
GORGER	GORSE	GOSSIPED	GOUGERES	GOV
GORGERIN	GORSEDD	GOSSIPER	GOUGERS	GOVERN
GORGERINS	GORSEDDS	GOSSIPERS	GOUGES	GOVERNALL

GOVERNED	GOZZAN	GRADDANS	GRAFTERS	GRAMMABLE
GOVERNESS	GOZZANS	GRADE	GRAFTING	GRAMMAGE
GOVERNING	GRAAL	GRADED	GRAFTINGS	GRAMMAGES
GOVERNOR	GRAALS	GRADELESS	GRAFTS	GRAMMAR
GOVERNORS	GRAB	GRADELIER	GRAHAM	GRAMMARS
GOVERNS	GRABBABLE	GRADELY	GRAHAMS	GRAMMAS
GOVS	GRABBED	GRADER	GRAIL	GRAMMATIC
GOWAN	GRABBER	GRADERS	GRAILE	GRAMME
GOWANED	GRABBERS	GRADES	GRAILES	GRAMMES
GOWANS	GRABBIER	GRADIENT	GRAILS	GRAMOCHE
GOWANY	GRABBIEST	GRADIENTS	GRAIN	GRAMOCHES
GOWD	GRABBING	GRADIN	GRAINAGE	GRAMP
GOWDER	GRABBLE	GRADINE	GRAINAGES	GRAMPA
GOWDEST	GRABBLED	GRADINES	GRAINE	GRAMPAS
GOWDS	GRABBLER	GRADING	GRAINED	GRAMPIES
GOWDSPINK	GRABBLERS	GRADINGS	GRAINER	GRAMPS
GOWF	GRABBLES	GRADINI	GRAINERS	GRAMPUS
GOWFED	GRABBLING	GRADINO	GRAINES	GRAMPUSES
GOWFER	GRABBY	GRADINS	GRAINIER	GRAMPY
GOWFERS	GRABEN	GRADS	GRAINIEST	GRAMS
GOWFING	GRABENS	GRADUAL	GRAINING	GRAN
GOWFS	GRABS	GRADUALLY	GRAININGS	GRANA
GOWK	GRACE	GRADUALS	GRAINLESS	GRANARIES
GOWKS	GRACED	GRADUAND	GRAINS	GRANARY
GOWL	GRACEFUL	GRADUANDS	GRAINY	GRAND
GOWLAN	GRACELESS	GRADUATE	GRAIP	GRANDAD
GOWLAND	GRACES	GRADUATED	GRAIPS	GRANDADDY
GOWLANDS	GRACILE	GRADUATES	GRAITH	GRANDADS
GOWLANS	GRACILES	GRADUATOR	GRAITHED	GRANDAM
GOWLED	GRACILIS	GRADUS	GRAITHING	GRANDAME
GOWLING	GRACILITY	GRADUSES	GRAITHLY	GRANDAMES
GOWLS	GRACING	GRAECISE	GRAITHS	GRANDAMS
GOWN	GRACIOSO	GRAECISED	GRAKLE	GRANDAUNT
GOWNBOY	GRACIOSOS	GRAECISES	GRAKLES	GRANDBABY
GOWNBOYS	GRACIOUS	GRAECIZE	GRALLOCH	GRANDDAD
GOWNED	GRACKLE	GRAECIZED	GRALLOCHS	GRANDDADS
GOWNING	GRACKLES	GRAECIZES	GRAM	GRANDDAM
GOWNMAN	GRAD	GRAFF	GRAMA	GRANDDAMS
GOWNMEN	GRADABLE	GRAFFED	GRAMARIES	GRANDE
GOWNS	GRADABLES	GRAFFING	GRAMARY	GRANDEE
GOWNSMAN	GRADATE	GRAFFITI	GRAMARYE	GRANDEES
GOWNSMEN	GRADATED	GRAFFITIS	GRAMARYES	GRANDER
GOWPEN	GRADATES	GRAFFITO	GRAMAS	GRANDEST
GOWPENFUL	GRADATIM	GRAFFS	GRAMASH	GRANDEUR
GOWPENS	GRADATING	GRAFT	GRAMASHES	GRANDEURS
GOX	GRADATION	GRAFTAGE	GRAME	GRANDIOSE
GOXES	GRADATORY	GRAFTAGES	GRAMERCY	GRANDIOSO
GOYLE	GRADDAN	GRAFTED	GRAMES	GRANDKID
GOYLES	GRADDANED	GRAFTER	GRAMMA	GRANDKIDS

G

GRANDLY	GRANTER	GRAPHS	GRASSUM	GRAVELESS
GRANDMA	GRANTERS	GRAPIER	GRASSUMS	GRAVELIKE
GRANDMAMA	GRANTING	GRAPIEST	GRASSY	GRAVELING
GRANDMAS	GRANTOR	GRAPINESS	GRASTE	GRAVELISH
GRANDNESS	GRANTORS	GRAPING	GRAT	GRAVELLED
GRANDPA	GRANTS	GRAPLE	GRATE	GRAVELLY
GRANDPAPA	GRANTSMAN	GRAPLES	GRATED	GRAVELS
GRANDPAS	GRANTSMEN	GRAPLIN	GRATEFUL	GRAVELY
GRANDS	GRANULAR	GRAPLINE	GRATELESS	GRAVEN
GRANDSIR	GRANULARY	GRAPLINES	GRATER	GRAVENESS
GRANDSIRE	GRANULATE	GRAPLINS	GRATERS	GRAVER
GRANDSIRS	GRANULE	GRAPNEL	GRATES	GRAVERS
GRANDSON	GRANULES	GRAPNELS	GRATICULE	GRAVES
GRANDSONS	GRANULITE	GRAPPA	GRATIFIED	GRAVESIDE
GRANFER	GRANULOMA	GRAPPAS	GRATIFIER	GRAVESITE
GRANFERS	GRANULOSE	GRAPPLE	GRATIFIES	GRAVEST
GRANGE	GRANULOUS	GRAPPLED	GRATIFY	GRAVEWARD
GRANGER	GRANUM	GRAPPLER	GRATIN	GRAVEYARD
GRANGERS	GRANUMS	GRAPPLERS	GRATINATE	GRAVID
GRANGES	GRAPE	GRAPPLES	GRATINE	GRAVIDA
GRANITA	GRAPED	GRAPPLING	GRATINEE	GRAVIDAE
GRANITAS	GRAPELESS	GRAPY	GRATINEED	GRAVIDAS
GRANITE	GRAPELICE	GRASP	GRATINEES	GRAVIDITY
GRANITES	GRAPELIKE	GRASPABLE	GRATING	GRAVIDLY
GRANITIC	GRAPERIES	GRASPED	GRATINGLY	GRAVIES
GRANITISE	GRAPERY	GRASPER	GRATINGS	GRAVING
GRANITITE	GRAPES	GRASPERS	GRATINS	GRAVINGS
GRANITIZE	GRAPESEED	GRASPING	GRATIS	GRAVIS
GRANITOID	GRAPESHOT	GRASPLESS	GRATITUDE	GRAVITAS
GRANIVORE	GRAPETREE	GRASPS	GRATTOIR	GRAVITATE
GRANNAM	GRAPEVINE	GRASS	GRATTOIRS	GRAVITIES
GRANNAMS	GRAPEY	GRASSBIRD	GRATUITY	GRAVITINO
GRANNIE	GRAPH	GRASSED	GRATULANT	GRAVITON
GRANNIED	GRAPHED	GRASSER	GRATULATE	GRAVITONS
GRANNIES	GRAPHEME	GRASSERS	GRAUNCH	GRAVITY
GRANNOM	GRAPHEMES	GRASSES	GRAUNCHED	GRAVLAKS
GRANNOMS	GRAPHEMIC	GRASSFIRE	GRAUNCHER	GRAVLAX
GRANNY	GRAPHENE	GRASSHOOK	GRAUNCHES	GRAVLAXES
GRANNYING	GRAPHENES	GRASSIER	GRAUPEL	GRAVS
GRANNYISH	GRAPHIC	GRASSIEST	GRAUPELS	GRAVURE
GRANOLA	GRAPHICAL	GRASSILY	GRAV	GRAVURES
GRANOLAS	GRAPHICLY	GRASSING	GRAVADLAX	GRAVY
GRANOLITH	GRAPHICS	GRASSINGS	GRAVAMEN	GRAWLIX
GRANS	GRAPHING	GRASSLAND	GRAVAMENS	GRAWLIXES
GRANT	GRAPHITE	GRASSLESS	GRAVAMINA	GRAY
GRANTABLE	GRAPHITES	GRASSLIKE	GRAVE	GRAYBACK
GRANTED	GRAPHITIC	GRASSPLOT	GRAVED	GRAYBACKS
GRANTEE	GRAPHIUM	GRASSQUIT	GRAVEL	GRAYBEARD
GRANTEES	GRAPHIUMS	GRASSROOT	GRAVELED	GRAYED

GRAYER	GREASIER	GREEDIEST	GREENSICK	GREMLIN
GRAYEST	GREASIES	GREEDILY	GREENSOME	GREMLINS
GRAYFISH	GREASIEST	GREEDLESS	GREENTH	GREMMIE
GRAYFLIES	GREASILY	GREEDS	GREENTHS	GREMMIES
GRAYFLY	GREASING	GREEDSOME	GREENWASH	GREMMY
GRAYHEAD	GREASY	GREEDY	GREENWAY	GREMOLATA
GRAYHEADS	GREAT	GREEGREE	GREENWAYS	GREN
GRAYHEN	GREATCOAT	GREEGREES	GREENWEED	GRENACHE
GRAYHENS	GREATEN	GREEING	GREENWING	GRENACHES
GRAYHOUND	GREATENED	GREEK	GREENWOOD	GRENADE
GRAYING	GREATENS	GREEKED	GREENY	GRENADES
GRAYISH	GREATER	GREEKING	GREES	GRENADIER
GRAYLAG	GREATEST	GREEKINGS	GREESE	GRENADINE
GRAYLAGS	GREATESTS	GREEKS	GREESES	GRENNED
GRAYLE	GREATLY	GREEN	GREESING	GRENNING
GRAYLES	GREATNESS	GREENBACK	GREESINGS	GRENS
GRAYLING	GREATS	GREENBELT	GREET	GRESE
GRAYLINGS	GREAVE	GREENBONE	GREETE	GRESES
GRAYLIST	GREAVED	GREENBUG	GREETED	GRESSING
GRAYLISTS	GREAVES	GREENBUGS	GREETER	GRESSINGS
GRAYLY	GREAVING	GREENED	GREETERS	GREVE
GRAYMAIL	GREBE	GREENER	GREETES	GREVES
GRAYMAILS	GREBES	GREENERS	GREETING	GREVILLEA
GRAYNESS	GREBO	GREENERY	GREETINGS	GREW
GRAYOUT	GREBOES	GREENEST	GREETS	GREWED
GRAYOUTS	GREBOS	GREENEYE	GREFFIER	GREWHOUND
GRAYS	GRECE	GREENEYES	GREFFIERS	GREWING
GRAYSCALE	GRECES	GREENFLY	GREGALE	GREWS
GRAYSTONE	GRECIAN	GREENGAGE	GREGALES	GREWSOME
GRAYWACKE	GRECIANS	GREENHAND	GREGARIAN	GREWSOMER
GRAYWATER	GRECISE	GREENHEAD	GREGARINE	GREX
GRAZABLE	GRECISED	GREENHORN	GREGATIM	GREXES
GRAZE	GRECISES	GREENIE	GREGE	GREY
GRAZEABLE	GRECISING	GREENIER	GREGED	GREYBACK
GRAZED	GRECIZE	GREENIES	GREGES	GREYBACKS
GRAZER	GRECIZED	GREENIEST	GREGING	GREYBEARD
GRAZERS	GRECIZES	GREENING	GREGO	GREYED
GRAZES	GRECIZING	GREENINGS	GREGOS	GREYER
GRAZIER	GRECQUE	GREENISH	GREIGE	GREYEST
GRAZIERS	GRECQUES	GREENLET	GREIGES	GREYHEAD
GRAZING	GREE	GREENLETS	GREIN	GREYHEADS
GRAZINGLY	GREEBO	GREENLING	GREINED	GREYHEN
GRAZINGS	GREEBOES	GREENLIT	GREINING	GREYHENS
GRAZIOSO	GREEBOS	GREENLY	GREINS	GREYHOUND
GREASE	GREECE	GREENMAIL	GREISEN	GREYING
GREASED	GREECES	GREENNESS	GREISENS	GREYINGS
GREASER	GREED	GREENROOM	GREISLY	GREYISH
GREASERS	GREEDHEAD	GREENS	GREMIAL	GREYLAG
GREASES	GREEDIER	GREENSAND	GREMIALS	GREYLAGS

G

GREYLIST	GRIESLY	GRILLIONS	GRIOT	GRISLIER
GREYLISTS	GRIESY	GRILLROOM	GRIOTS	GRISLIES
GREYLY	GRIEVANCE	GRILLS	GRIP	GRISLIEST
GREYNESS	GRIEVANT	GRILLWORK	GRIPE	GRISLY
GREYOUT	GRIEVANTS	GRILSE	GRIPED	GRISON
GREYOUTS	GRIEVE	GRILSES	GRIPER	GRISONS
GREYS	GRIEVED	GRIM	GRIPERS	GRISSINI
GREYSCALE	GRIEVER	GRIMACE	GRIPES	GRISSINO
GREYSTONE	GRIEVERS	GRIMACED	GRIPEY	GRIST
GREYWACKE	GRIEVES	GRIMACER	GRIPIER	GRISTER
GRIBBLE	GRIEVING	GRIMACERS	GRIPIEST	GRISTERS
GRIBBLES	GRIEVINGS	GRIMACES	GRIPING	GRISTLE
GRICE	GRIEVOUS	GRIMACING	GRIPINGLY	GRISTLES
GRICED	GRIFF	GRIMALKIN	GRIPINGS	GRISTLIER
GRICER	GRIFFE	GRIMDARK	GRIPLE	GRISTLY
GRICERS	GRIFFES	GRIMDARKS	GRIPMAN	GRISTMILL
GRICES	GRIFFIN	GRIME	GRIPMEN	GRISTS
GRICING	GRIFFINS	GRIMED	GRIPPE	GRISY
GRICINGS	GRIFFON	GRIMES	GRIPPED	GRIT
GRID	GRIFFONS	GRIMIER	GRIPPER	GRITH
GRIDDED	GRIFFS	GRIMIEST	GRIPPERS	GRITHS
GRIDDER	GRIFT	GRIMILY	GRIPPES	GRITLESS
GRIDDERS	GRIFTED	GRIMINESS	GRIPPIER	GRITS
GRIDDING	GRIFTER	GRIMING	GRIPPIEST	GRITSTONE
GRIDDLE	GRIFTERS	GRIMLY	GRIPPING	GRITTED
GRIDDLED	GRIFTING	GRIMMER	GRIPPLE	GRITTER
GRIDDLES	GRIFTS	GRIMMEST	GRIPPLES	GRITTERS
GRIDDLING	GRIG	GRIMNESS	GRIPPY	GRITTEST
GRIDE	GRIGGED	GRIMOIRE	GRIPS	GRITTIER
GRIDED	GRIGGING	GRIMOIRES	GRIPSACK	GRITTIEST
GRIDELIN	GRIGRI	GRIMY	GRIPSACKS	GRITTILY
GRIDELINS	GRIGRIS	GRIN	GRIPT	GRITTING
GRIDES	GRIGS	GRINCH	GRIPTAPE	GRITTINGS
GRIDING	GRIKE	GRINCHES	GRIPTAPES	GRITTY
GRIDIRON	GRIKES	GRIND	GRIPY	GRIVATION
GRIDIRONS	GRILL	GRINDED	GRIS	GRIVET
GRIDLOCK	GRILLADE	GRINDELIA	GRISAILLE	GRIVETS
GRIDLOCKS	GRILLADES	GRINDER	GRISE	GRIZ
GRIDS	GRILLAGE	GRINDERS	GRISED	GRIZE
GRIECE	GRILLAGES	GRINDERY	GRISELY	GRIZES
GRIECED	GRILLE	GRINDING	GRISEOUS	GRIZZES
GRIECES	GRILLED	GRINDINGS	GRISES	GRIZZLE
GRIEF	GRILLER	GRINDS	GRISETTE	GRIZZLED
GRIEFER	GRILLERS	GRINNED	GRISETTES	GRIZZLER
GRIEFERS	GRILLERY	GRINNER	GRISGRIS	GRIZZLERS
GRIEFFUL	GRILLES	GRINNERS	GRISING	GRIZZLES
GRIEFLESS	GRILLING	GRINNING	GRISKIN	GRIZZLIER
GRIEFS	GRILLINGS	GRINNINGS	GRISKINS	GRIZZLIES
GRIESIE	GRILLION	GRINS	GRISLED	GRIZZLING

GRIZZLY	GROMETS	GROSERTS	GROUNDMEN	GROVELESS
GROAN	GROMMET	GROSET	GROUNDNUT	GROVELING
GROANED	GROMMETED	GROSETS	GROUNDOUT	GROVELLED
GROANER	GROMMETS	GROSGRAIN	GROUNDS	GROVELLER
GROANERS	GROMWELL	GROSS	GROUNDSEL	GROVELS
GROANFUL	GROMWELLS	GROSSART	GROUP	GROVES
GROANING	GRONE	GROSSARTS	GROUPABLE	GROVET
GROANINGS	GRONED	GROSSED	GROUPAGE	GROVETS
GROANS	GRONEFULL	GROSSER	GROUPAGES	GROVIER
GROAT	GRONES	GROSSERS	GROUPED	GROVIEST
GROATS	GRONING	GROSSES	GROUPER	GROVY
GROCER	GROOF	GROSSEST	GROUPERS	GROW
GROCERIES	GROOFS	GROSSING	GROUPIE	GROWABLE
GROCERS	GROOLIER	GROSSLY	GROUPIES	GROWER
GROCERY	GROOLIEST	GROSSNESS	GROUPING	GROWERS
GROCKED	GROOLY	GROSSULAR	GROUPINGS	GROWING
GROCKING	GROOM	GROSZ	GROUPIST	GROWINGLY
GROCKLE	GROOMED	GROSZE	GROUPISTS	GROWINGS
GROCKLES	GROOMER	GROSZY	GROUPLET	GROWL
GRODIER	GROOMERS	GROT	GROUPLETS	GROWLED
GRODIEST	GROOMING	GROTESQUE	GROUPOID	GROWLER
GRODY	GROOMINGS	GROTS	GROUPOIDS	GROWLERS
GROG	GROOMS	GROTTIER	GROUPS	GROWLERY
GROGGED	GROOMSMAN	GROTTIEST	GROUPWARE	GROWLIER
GROGGERY	GROOMSMEN	GROTTO	GROUPWORK	GROWLIEST
GROGGIER	GROOVE	GROTTOED	GROUPY	GROWLING
GROGGIEST	GROOVED	GROTTOES	GROUSE	GROWLINGS
GROGGILY	GROOVER	GROTTOS	GROUSED	GROWLS
GROGGING	GROOVERS	GROTTY	GROUSER	GROWLY
GROGGY	GROOVES	GROUCH	GROUSERS	GROWN
GROGRAM	GROOVIER	GROUCHED	GROUSES	GROWNUP
GROGRAMS	GROOVIEST	GROUCHES	GROUSEST	GROWNUPS
GROGS	GROOVILY	GROUCHIER	GROUSING	GROWS
GROGSHOP	GROOVING	GROUCHILY	GROUT	GROWTH
GROGSHOPS	GROOVY	GROUCHING	GROUTED	GROWTHIER
GROIN	GROPE	GROUCHY	GROUTER	GROWTHIST
GROINED	GROPED	GROUF	GROUTERS	GROWTHS
GROINING	GROPER	GROUFS	GROUTIER	GROWTHY
GROININGS	GROPERS	GROUGH	GROUTIEST	GROYNE
GROINS	GROPES	GROUGHS	GROUTING	GROYNES
GROK	GROPING	GROUND	GROUTINGS	GROZING
GROKED	GROPINGLY	GROUNDAGE	GROUTS	GRR
GROKING	GROSBEAK	GROUNDED	GROUTY	GRRL
GROKKED	GROSBEAKS	GROUNDEN	GROUTY	GRRLS
GROKKING	GROSCHEN	GROUNDER	GROVE	GRRRL
GROKS	GROSCHENS	GROUNDERS	GROVED	GRRRLS
GROMA	GROSER	GROUNDHOG	GROVEL	GRUB
GROMAS	GROSERS	GROUNDING	GROVELED	GRUBBED
GROMET	GROSERT	GROUNDMAN	GROVELER	GRUBBER

GRUBBERS	GRUFFISH	GRUNDLE	GRYSBOK	GUAR
GRUBBIER	GRUFFLY	GRUNDLES	GRYSBOKS	GUARACHA
GRUBBIEST	GRUFFNESS	GRUNGE	GRYSELY	GUARACHAS
GRUBBILY	GRUFFS	GRUNGER	GRYSIE	GUARACHE
GRUBBING	GRUFFY	GRUNGERS	GU	GUARACHES
GRUBBLE	GRUFTED	GRUNGES	GUAC	GUARACHI
GRUBBLED	GRUGRU	GRUNGEY	GUACAMOLE	GUARACHIS
GRUBBLES	GRUGRUS	GRUNGIER	GUACHARO	GUARANA
GRUBBLING	GRUIFORM	GRUNGIEST	GUACHAROS	GUARANAS
GRUBBY	GRUING	GRUNGY	GUACO	GUARANI
GRUBS	GRUM	GRUNION	GUACOS	GUARANIES
GRUBSTAKE	GRUMBLE	GRUNIONS	GUACS	GUARANIS
GRUBWORM	GRUMBLED	GRUNT	GUAIAC	GUARANTEE
GRUBWORMS	GRUMBLER	GRUNTED	GUAIACOL	GUARANTOR
GRUDGE	GRUMBLERS	GRUNTER	GUAIACOLS	GUARANTY
GRUDGED	GRUMBLES	GRUNTERS	GUAIACS	GUARD
GRUDGEFUL	GRUMBLIER	GRUNTING	GUAIACUM	GUARDABLE
GRUDGER	GRUMBLING	GRUNTINGS	GUAIACUMS	GUARDAGE
GRUDGERS	GRUMBLY	GRUNTLE	GUAIOCUM	GUARDAGES
GRUDGES	GRUME	GRUNTLED	GUAIOCUMS	GUARDANT
GRUDGING	GRUMES	GRUNTLES	GUAN	GUARDANTS
GRUDGINGS	GRUMLY	GRUNTLING	GUANA	GUARDDOG
GRUE	GRUMMER	GRUNTS	GUANABANA	GUARDDOGS
GRUED	GRUMMEST	GRUPPETTI	GUANACO	GUARDED
GRUEING	GRUMMET	GRUPPETTO	GUANACOS	GUARDEDLY
GRUEL	GRUMMETED	GRUSHIE	GUANAS	GUARDEE
GRUELED	GRUMMETS	GRUTCH	GUANASE	GUARDEES
GRUELER	GRUMNESS	GRUTCHED	GUANASES	GUARDER
GRUELERS	GRUMOSE	GRUTCHES	GUANAY	GUARDERS
GRUELING	GRUMOUS	GRUTCHING	GUANAYS	GUARDIAN
GRUELINGS	GRUMP	GRUTTEN	GUANAZOLO	GUARDIANS
GRUELLED	GRUMPED	GRUYERE	GUANCIALE	GUARDING
GRUELLER	GRUMPH	GRUYERES	GUANCIALI	GUARDLESS
GRUELLERS	GRUMPHED	GRYCE	GUANGO	GUARDLIKE
GRUELLING	GRUMPHIE	GRYCES	GUANGOS	GUARDRAIL
GRUELS	GRUMPHIES	GRYDE	GUANIDIN	GUARDROOM
GRUES	GRUMPHING	GRYDED	GUANIDINE	GUARDS
GRUESOME	GRUMPHS	GRYDES	GUANIDINS	GUARDSHIP
GRUESOMER	GRUMPHY	GRYDING	GUANIN	GUARDSMAN
GRUFE	GRUMPIER	GRYESY	GUANINE	GUARDSMEN
GRUFES	GRUMPIES	GRYFON	GUANINES	GUARISH
GRUFF	GRUMPIEST	GRYFONS	GUANINS	GUARISHED
GRUFFED	GRUMPILY	GRYKE	GUANO	GUARISHES
GRUFFER	GRUMPING	GRYKES	GUANOS	GUARS
GRUFFEST	GRUMPISH	GRYPE	GUANOSINE	GUAVA
GRUFFIER	GRUMPS	GRYPES	GUANS	GUAVAS
GRUFFIEST	GRUMPY	GRYPHON	GUANXI	GUAYABERA
GRUFFILY	GRUND	GRYPHONS	GUANXIS	GUAYULE
GRUFFING	GRUNDIES	GRYPT	GUANYLIC	GUAYULES

GUB	GUESS	GUIDERS	GUINEA	GULFWEED
GUBBAH	GUESSABLE	GUIDES	GUINEAS	GULFWEEDS
GUBBAHS	GUESSED	GUIDESHIP	GUINEP	GULFY
GUBBED	GUESSER	GUIDEWAY	GUINEPS	GULL
GUBBING	GUESSERS	GUIDEWAYS	GUIPURE	GULLABLE
GUBBINS	GUESSES	GUIDEWORD	GUIPURES	GULLABLY
GUBBINSES	GUESSING	GUIDING	GUIRO	GULLED
GUBERNIYA	GUESSINGS	GUIDINGS	GUIROS	GULLER
GUBS	GUESSWORK	GUIDON	GUISARD	GULLERIES
GUCK	GUEST	GUIDONS	GUISARDS	GULLERS
GUCKIER	GUESTBOOK	GUIDS	GUISE	GULLERY
GUCKIEST	GUESTED	GUILD	GUISED	GULLET
GUCKS	GUESTEN	GUILDER	GUISER	GULLETS
GUCKY	GUESTENED	GUILDERS	GUISERS	GULLEY
GUDDLE	GUESTENS	GUILDHALL	GUISES	GULLEYED
GUDDLED	GUESTING	GUILDRIES	GUISING	GULLEYING
GUDDLES	GUESTS	GUILDRY	GUISINGS	GULLEYS
GUDDLING	GUESTWISE	GUILDS	GUITAR	GULLIBLE
GUDE	GUFF	GUILDSHIP	GUITARIST	GULLIBLY
GUDEMAN	GUFFAW	GUILDSMAN	GUITARS	GULLIED
GUDEMEN	GUFFAWED	GUILDSMEN	GUITGUIT	GULLIES
GUDES	GUFFAWING	GUILE	GUITGUITS	GULLING
GUDESIRE	GUFFAWS	GUILED	GUIZER	GULLISH
GUDESIRES	GUFFIE	GUILEFUL	GUIZERS	GULLS
GUDEWIFE	GUFFIES	GUILELESS	GUL	GULLWING
GUDEWIVES	GUFFS	GUILER	GULA	GULLY
GUDGEON	GUGA	GUILERS	GULAG	GULLYING
GUDGEONED	GUGAS	GUILES	GULAGS	GULOSITY
GUDGEONS	GUGGLE	GUILING	GULAR	GULP
GUE	GUGGLED	GUILLEMET	GULARS	GULPED
GUELDER	GUGGLES	GUILLEMOT	GULAS	GULPER
GUENON	GUGGLING	GUILLOCHE	GULCH	GULPERS
GUENONS	GUGLET	GUILT	GULCHED	GULPH
GUERDON	GUGLETS	GUILTED	GULCHES	GULPHS
GUERDONED	GUICHET	GUILTIER	GULCHING	GULPIER
GUERDONER	GUICHETS	GUILTIEST	GULDEN	GULPIEST
GUERDONS	GUID	GUILTILY	GULDENS	GULPING
GUEREZA	GUIDABLE	GUILTING	GULE	GULPINGLY
GUEREZAS	GUIDAGE	GUILTLESS	GULES	GULPS
GUERIDON	GUIDAGES	GUILTS	GULESES	GULPY
GUERIDONS	GUIDANCE	GUILTY	GULET	GULS
GUERILLA	GUIDANCES	GUIMBARD	GULETS	GULY
GUERILLAS	GUIDE	GUIMBARDS	GULF	GUM
GUERITE	GUIDEBOOK	GUIMP	GULFED	GUMBALL
GUERITES	GUIDED	GUIMPE	GULFIER	GUMBALLS
GUERNSEY	GUIDELESS	GUIMPED	GULFIEST	GUMBO
GUERNSEYS	GUIDELINE	GUIMPES	GULFING	GUMBOIL
GUERRILLA	GUIDEPOST	GUIMPING	GULFLIKE	GUMBOILS
GUES	GUIDER	GUIMPS	GULFS	GUMBOOT

GUMBOOTS

GUMBOOTS
GUMBOS
GUMBOTIL
GUMBOTILS
GUMDROP
GUMDROPS
GUMLANDS
GUMLESS
GUMLIKE
GUMLINE
GUMLINES
GUMMA
GUMMAS
GUMMATA
GUMMATOUS
GUMMED
GUMMER
GUMMERS
GUMMI
GUMMIER
GUMMIES
GUMMIEST
GUMMILY
GUMMINESS
GUMMING
GUMMINGS
GUMMIS
GUMMITE
GUMMITES
GUMMOSE
GUMMOSES
GUMMOSIS
GUMMOSITY
GUMMOUS
GUMMY
GUMNUT
GUMNUTS
GUMP
GUMPED
GUMPHION
GUMPHIONS
GUMPING
GUMPS
GUMPTION
GUMPTIONS
GUMPTIOUS
GUMS
GUMSHIELD
GUMSHOE

GUMSHOED
GUMSHOES
GUMSUCKER
GUMTREE
GUMTREES
GUMWEED
GUMWEEDS
GUMWOOD
GUMWOODS
GUN
GUNBOAT
GUNBOATS
GUNCOTTON
GUNDIES
GUNDOG
GUNDOGS
GUNDY
GUNFIGHT
GUNFIGHTS
GUNFIRE
GUNFIRES
GUNFLINT
GUNFLINTS
GUNFOUGHT
GUNG
GUNGE
GUNGED
GUNGES
GUNGIER
GUNGIEST
GUNGING
GUNGY
GUNHOUSE
GUNHOUSES
GUNITE
GUNITES
GUNK
GUNKED
GUNKHOLE
GUNKHOLED
GUNKHOLES
GUNKIER
GUNKIEST
GUNKING
GUNKS
GUNKY
GUNLAYER
GUNLAYERS
GUNLESS

GUNLOCK
GUNLOCKS
GUNMAKER
GUNMAKERS
GUNMAN
GUNMEN
GUNMETAL
GUNMETALS
GUNNAGE
GUNNAGES
GUNNED
GUNNEL
GUNNELS
GUNNEN
GUNNER
GUNNERA
GUNNERAS
GUNNERIES
GUNNERS
GUNNERY
GUNNIES
GUNNING
GUNNINGS
GUNNY
GUNNYBAG
GUNNYBAGS
GUNNYSACK
GUNPAPER
GUNPAPERS
GUNPLAY
GUNPLAYS
GUNPOINT
GUNPOINTS
GUNPORT
GUNPORTS
GUNPOWDER
GUNROOM
GUNROOMS
GUNRUNNER
GUNS
GUNSEL
GUNSELS
GUNSHIP
GUNSHIPS
GUNSHOT
GUNSHOTS
GUNSIGHT
GUNSIGHTS
GUNSMITH

GUNSMITHS
GUNSTICK
GUNSTICKS
GUNSTOCK
GUNSTOCKS
GUNSTONE
GUNSTONES
GUNTER
GUNTERS
GUNWALE
GUNWALES
GUNYAH
GUNYAHS
GUP
GUPPIES
GUPPY
GUPS
GUQIN
GUQINS
GUR
GURAMI
GURAMIS
GURDIES
GURDWARA
GURDWARAS
GURDY
GURGE
GURGED
GURGES
GURGING
GURGLE
GURGLED
GURGLES
GURGLET
GURGLETS
GURGLIER
GURGLIEST
GURGLING
GURGLY
GURGOYLE
GURGOYLES
GURJUN
GURJUNS
GURL
GURLED
GURLET
GURLETS
GURLIER
GURLIEST

GURLING
GURLS
GURLY
GURN
GURNARD
GURNARDS
GURNED
GURNET
GURNETS
GURNEY
GURNEYS
GURNING
GURNS
GURRAH
GURRAHS
GURRIER
GURRIERS
GURRIES
GURRY
GURS
GURSH
GURSHES
GURU
GURUDOM
GURUDOMS
GURUISM
GURUISMS
GURUS
GURUSHIP
GURUSHIPS
GUS
GUSH
GUSHED
GUSHER
GUSHERS
GUSHES
GUSHIER
GUSHIEST
GUSHILY
GUSHINESS
GUSHING
GUSHINGLY
GUSHY
GUSLA
GUSLAR
GUSLARS
GUSLAS
GUSLE
GUSLES

GUSLI	GUTSIER	GUYLINES	GYMNASTS	GYPOS
GUSLIS	GUTSIEST	GUYLING	GYMNIC	GYPPIE
GUSSET	GUTSILY	GUYOT	GYMNOSOPH	GYPPIES
GUSSETED	GUTSINESS	GUYOTS	GYMP	GYPPY
GUSSETING	GUTSING	GUYS	GYMPED	GYPS
GUSSETS	GUTSY	GUYSE	GYMPIE	GYPSEIAN
GUSSIE	GUTTA	GUYSES	GYMPIES	GYPSEOUS
GUSSIED	GUTTAE	GUZZLE	GYMPING	GYPSIED
GUSSIES	GUTTAS	GUZZLED	GYMPS	GYPSIES
GUSSY	GUTTATE	GUZZLER	GYMS	GYPSUM
GUSSYING	GUTTATED	GUZZLERS	GYMSLIP	GYPSUMS
GUST	GUTTATES	GUZZLES	GYMSLIPS	GYPSY
GUSTABLE	GUTTATING	GUZZLING	GYMSUIT	GYPSYDOM
GUSTABLES	GUTTATION	GWEDUC	GYMSUITS	GYPSYDOMS
GUSTATION	GUTTED	GWEDUCK	GYNAE	GYPSYHOOD
GUSTATIVE	GUTTER	GWEDUCKS	GYNAECEA	GYPSYING
GUSTATORY	GUTTERED	GWEDUCS	GYNAECEUM	GYPSYISH
GUSTED	GUTTERIER	GWINE	GYNAECIA	GYPSYISM
GUSTFUL	GUTTERING	GWINIAD	GYNAECIUM	GYPSYISMS
GUSTIE	GUTTERS	GWINIADS	GYNAECOID	GYPSYWORT
GUSTIER	GUTTERY	GWYNIAD	GYNAES	GYRAL
GUSTIEST	GUTTIER	GWYNIADS	GYNANDRY	GYRALLY
GUSTILY	GUTTIES	GYAL	GYNARCHIC	GYRANT
GUSTINESS	GUTTIEST	GYALS	GYNARCHY	GYRASE
GUSTING	GUTTING	GYAN	GYNECIA	GYRASES
GUSTLESS	GUTTLE	GYANI	GYNECIC	GYRATE
GUSTO	GUTTLED	GYANIS	GYNECIUM	GYRATED
GUSTOES	GUTTLER	GYANS	GYNECOID	GYRATES
GUSTOS	GUTTLERS	GYBE	GYNIATRY	GYRATING
GUSTS	GUTTLES	GYBED	GYNIE	GYRATION
GUSTY	GUTTLING	GYBES	GYNIES	GYRATIONS
GUT	GUTTURAL	GYBING	GYNNEY	GYRATOR
GUTBUCKET	GUTTURALS	GYELD	GYNNEYS	GYRATORS
GUTCHER	GUTTY	GYELDS	GYNNIES	GYRATORY
GUTCHERS	GUTZER	GYLDEN	GYNNY	GYRE
GUTFUL	GUTZERS	GYM	GYNO	GYRED
GUTFULS	GUV	GYMBAL	GYNOCRACY	GYRENE
GUTLESS	GUVS	GYMBALS	GYNOECIA	GYRENES
GUTLESSLY	GUY	GYMKHANA	GYNOECIUM	GYRES
GUTLIKE	GUYED	GYMKHANAS	GYNOPHOBE	GYRFALCON
GUTROT	GUYING	GYMMAL	GYNOPHORE	GYRI
GUTROTS	GUYLE	GYMMALS	GYNOS	GYRING
GUTS	GUYLED	GYMNASIA	GYNY	GYRO
GUTSED	GUYLER	GYMNASIAL	GYOZA	GYROCAR
GUTSER	GUYLERS	GYMNASIC	GYOZAS	GYROCARS
GUTSERS	GUYLES	GYMNASIEN	GYP	GYRODYNE
GUTSES	GUYLINE	GYMNASIUM	GYPLURE	GYRODYNES
GUTSFUL	GUYLINER	GYMNAST	GYPLURES	GYROIDAL
GUTSFULS	GUYLINERS	GYMNASTIC	GYPO	GYROLITE

GYROLITES

GYROLITES	GYROPILOT	GYROSTATS	GYTES	GYVED
GYROMANCY	GYROPLANE	GYROUS	GYTRASH	GYVES
GYRON	GYROS	GYROVAGUE	GYTRASHES	GYVING
GYRONIC	GYROSCOPE	GYRUS	GYTTJA	
GYRONNY	GYROSE	GYRUSES	GYTTJAS	
GYRONS	GYROSTAT	GYTE	GYVE	

H

HA	HABU	HACKLING	HADRON	HAFFETS
HAAF	HABUS	HACKLY	HADRONIC	HAFFIT
HAAFS	HACEK	HACKMAN	HADRONS	HAFFITS
HAANEPOOT	HACEKS	HACKMEN	HADROSAUR	HAFFLIN
HAAR	HACENDADO	HACKNEY	HADS	HAFFLINS
HAARS	HACHIS	HACKNEYED	HADST	HAFFS
HABANERA	HACHURE	HACKNEYS	HAE	HAFIZ
HABANERAS	HACHURED	HACKS	HAECCEITY	HAFIZES
HABANERO	HACHURES	HACKSAW	HAED	HAFNIUM
HABANEROS	HACHURING	HACKSAWED	HAEING	HAFNIUMS
HABDABS	HACIENDA	HACKSAWN	HAEM	HAFT
HABDALAH	HACIENDAS	HACKSAWS	HAEMAL	HAFTARA
HABDALAHS	HACK	HACKWORK	HAEMATAL	HAFTARAH
HABENDUM	HACKABLE	HACKWORKS	HAEMATEIN	HAFTARAHS
HABENDUMS	HACKAMORE	HACQUETON	HAEMATIC	HAFTARAS
HABERDINE	HACKATHON	HAD	HAEMATICS	HAFTAROS
HABERGEON	HACKBERRY	HADAL	HAEMATIN	HAFTAROT
HABILABLE	HACKBOLT	HADARIM	HAEMATINS	HAFTAROTH
HABILE	HACKBOLTS	HADAWAY	HAEMATITE	HAFTED
HABIT	HACKBUT	HADDEN	HAEMATOID	HAFTER
HABITABLE	HACKBUTS	HADDEST	HAEMATOMA	HAFTERS
HABITABLY	HACKED	HADDIE	HAEMIC	HAFTING
HABITAN	HACKEE	HADDIES	HAEMIN	HAFTORAH
HABITANS	HACKEES	HADDING	HAEMINS	HAFTORAHS
HABITANT	HACKER	HADDOCK	HAEMOCOEL	HAFTOROS
HABITANTS	HACKERIES	HADDOCKS	HAEMOCYTE	HAFTOROT
HABITAT	HACKERS	HADE	HAEMOID	HAFTOROTH
HABITATS	HACKERY	HADEAN	HAEMOLYSE	HAFTS
HABITED	HACKETTE	HADED	HAEMOLYZE	HAG
HABITING	HACKETTES	HADEDAH	HAEMONIES	HAGADIC
HABITS	HACKIE	HADEDAHS	HAEMONY	HAGADIST
HABITUAL	HACKIES	HADES	HAEMOSTAT	HAGADISTS
HABITUALS	HACKING	HADING	HAEMS	HAGBERRY
HABITUATE	HACKINGS	HADITH	HAEN	HAGBOLT
HABITUDE	HACKLE	HADITHS	HAEREDES	HAGBOLTS
HABITUDES	HACKLED	HADJ	HAEREMAI	HAGBORN
HABITUE	HACKLER	HADJEE	HAEREMAIS	HAGBUSH
HABITUES	HACKLERS	HADJEES	HAERES	HAGBUSHES
HABITUS	HACKLES	HADJES	HAES	HAGBUT
HABITUSES	HACKLET	HADJI	HAET	HAGBUTEER
HABLE	HACKLETS	HADJIS	HAETS	HAGBUTS
HABOOB	HACKLIER	HADROME	HAFF	HAGBUTTER
HABOOBS	HACKLIEST	HADROMES	HAFFET	HAGDEN

HAGDENS	HAHNIUM	HAIRCAPS	HAJI	HALALLED
HAGDON	HAHNIUMS	HAIRCLOTH	HAJIS	HALALLING
HAGDONS	HAHS	HAIRCUT	HAJJ	HALALS
HAGDOWN	HAICK	HAIRCUTS	HAJJAH	HALATION
HAGDOWNS	HAICKS	HAIRDO	HAJJAHS	HALATIONS
HAGFISH	HAIDUK	HAIRDOS	HAJJES	HALAVAH
HAGFISHES	HAIDUKS	HAIRDRIER	HAJJI	HALAVAHS
HAGG	HAIK	HAIRDRYER	HAJJIS	HALAZONE
HAGGADA	HAIKA	HAIRED	HAKA	HALAZONES
HAGGADAH	HAIKAI	HAIRGRIP	HAKAM	HALBERD
HAGGADAHS	HAIKS	HAIRGRIPS	HAKAMS	HALBERDS
HAGGADAS	HAIKU	HAIRIER	HAKARI	HALBERT
HAGGADIC	HAIKUS	HAIRIEST	HAKARIS	HALBERTS
HAGGADIST	HAIL	HAIRIF	HAKAS	HALCYON
HAGGADOT	HAILED	HAIRIFS	HAKE	HALCYONIC
HAGGADOTH	HAILER	HAIRILY	HAKEA	HALCYONS
HAGGARD	HAILERS	HAIRINESS	HAKEAS	HALE
HAGGARDLY	HAILIER	HAIRING	HAKEEM	HALED
HAGGARDS	HAILIEST	HAIRLESS	HAKEEMS	HALENESS
HAGGED	HAILING	HAIRLIKE	HAKES	HALER
HAGGING	HAILS	HAIRLINE	HAKIM	HALERS
HAGGIS	HAILSHOT	HAIRLINES	HAKIMS	HALERU
HAGGISES	HAILSHOTS	HAIRLOCK	HAKU	HALES
HAGGISH	HAILSTONE	HAIRLOCKS	HAKUS	HALEST
HAGGISHLY	HAILSTORM	HAIRNET	HALACHA	HALF
HAGGLE	HAILY	HAIRNETS	HALACHAS	HALFA
HAGGLED	HAIMISH	HAIRPIECE	HALACHIC	HALFAS
HAGGLER	HAIN	HAIRPIN	HALACHIST	HALFBACK
HAGGLERS	HAINCH	HAIRPINS	HALACHOT	HALFBACKS
HAGGLES	HAINCHED	HAIRS	HALACHOTH	HALFBEAK
HAGGLING	HAINCHES	HAIRSPRAY	HALAKAH	HALFBEAKS
HAGGLINGS	HAINCHING	HAIRST	HALAKAHS	HALFEN
HAGGS	HAINED	HAIRSTED	HALAKHA	HALFLIFE
HAGIARCHY	HAINING	HAIRSTING	HALAKHAH	HALFLIFES
HAGIOLOGY	HAININGS	HAIRSTS	HALAKHAHS	HALFLIN
HAGLET	HAINS	HAIRSTYLE	HALAKHAS	HALFLING
HAGLETS	HAINT	HAIRTAIL	HALAKHIC	HALFLINGS
HAGLIKE	HAINTS	HAIRTAILS	HALAKHIST	HALFLINS
HAGRIDDEN	HAIQUE	HAIRWING	HALAKHOT	HALFLIVES
HAGRIDE	HAIQUES	HAIRWINGS	HALAKHOTH	HALFNESS
HAGRIDER	HAIR	HAIRWORK	HALAKIC	HALFPACE
HAGRIDERS	HAIRBALL	HAIRWORKS	HALAKIST	HALFPACES
HAGRIDES	HAIRBALLS	HAIRWORM	HALAKISTS	HALFPENCE
HAGRIDING	HAIRBAND	HAIRWORMS	HALAKOTH	HALFPENNY
HAGRODE	HAIRBANDS	HAIRY	HALAL	HALFPIPE
HAGS	HAIRBELL	HAIRYBACK	HALALA	HALFPIPES
HAH	HAIRBELLS	HAITH	HALALAH	HALFS
HAHA	HAIRBRUSH	HAJ	HALALAHS	HALFTIME
HAHAS	HAIRCAP	HAJES	HALALAS	HALFTIMES

HALFTONE	HALLELS	HALO	HALVAS	HAMLETS
HALFTONES	HALLIAN	HALOBIONT	HALVE	HAMMADA
HALFTRACK	HALLIANS	HALOCLINE	HALVED	HAMMADAS
HALFWAY	HALLIARD	HALOED	HALVER	HAMMAL
HALFWIT	HALLIARDS	HALOES	HALVERS	HAMMALS
HALFWITS	HALLING	HALOGEN	HALVES	HAMMAM
HALIBUT	HALLINGS	HALOGENIC	HALVING	HAMMAMS
HALIBUTS	HALLION	HALOGENS	HALVINGS	HAMMED
HALICORE	HALLIONS	HALOGETON	HALWA	HAMMER
HALICORES	HALLMARK	HALOID	HALWAS	HAMMERED
HALID	HALLMARKS	HALOIDS	HALYARD	HAMMERER
HALIDE	HALLO	HALOING	HALYARDS	HAMMERERS
HALIDES	HALLOA	HALOLIKE	HAM	HAMMERING
HALIDOM	HALLOAED	HALON	HAMADA	HAMMERKOP
HALIDOME	HALLOAING	HALONS	HAMADAS	HAMMERMAN
HALIDOMES	HALLOAS	HALOPHILE	HAMADRYAD	HAMMERMEN
HALIDOMS	HALLOED	HALOPHILY	HAMADRYAS	HAMMERS
HALIDS	HALLOES	HALOPHOBE	HAMAL	HAMMERTOE
HALIER	HALLOING	HALOPHYTE	HAMALS	HAMMIER
HALIEROV	HALLOO	HALOS	HAMAMELIS	HAMMIES
HALIERS	HALLOOED	HALOSERE	HAMARTIA	HAMMIEST
HALIEUTIC	HALLOOING	HALOSERES	HAMARTIAS	HAMMILY
HALIMOT	HALLOOS	HALOTHANE	HAMATE	HAMMINESS
HALIMOTE	HALLOS	HALOUMI	HAMATES	HAMMING
HALIMOTES	HALLOT	HALOUMIS	HAMATSA	HAMMOCK
HALIMOTS	HALLOTH	HALSE	HAMATSAS	HAMMOCKS
HALING	HALLOUMI	HALSED	HAMAUL	HAMMY
HALIOTIS	HALLOUMIS	HALSER	HAMAULS	HAMOSE
HALITE	HALLOW	HALSERS	HAMBA	HAMOUS
HALITES	HALLOWED	HALSES	HAMBLE	HAMPER
HALITOSES	HALLOWER	HALSING	HAMBLED	HAMPERED
HALITOSIS	HALLOWERS	HALT	HAMBLES	HAMPERER
HALITOTIC	HALLOWING	HALTED	HAMBLING	HAMPERERS
HALITOUS	HALLOWS	HALTER	HAMBONE	HAMPERING
HALITUS	HALLS	HALTERE	HAMBONED	HAMPERS
HALITUSES	HALLSTAND	HALTERED	HAMBONES	HAMPSTER
HALL	HALLUCAL	HALTERES	HAMBONING	HAMPSTERS
HALLAH	HALLUCES	HALTERING	HAMBURG	HAMS
HALLAHS	HALLUX	HALTERS	HAMBURGER	HAMSTER
HALLAL	HALLWAY	HALTING	HAMBURGS	HAMSTERS
HALLALI	HALLWAYS	HALTINGLY	HAME	HAMSTRING
HALLALIS	HALLYON	HALTINGS	HAMED	HAMSTRUNG
HALLALLED	HALLYONS	HALTLESS	HAMES	HAMULAR
HALLALOO	HALLYU	HALTS	HAMEWITH	HAMULATE
HALLALOOS	HALLYUS	HALUTZ	HAMFAT	HAMULI
HALLALS	HALM	HALUTZIM	HAMFATS	HAMULOSE
HALLAN	HALMA	HALVA	HAMFATTER	HAMULOUS
HALLANS	HALMAS	HALVAH	HAMING	HAMULUS
HALLEL	HALMS	HALVAHS	HAMLET	HAMZA

HAMZAH	HANDFED	HANDMAIDS	HANDY	HANJARS
HAMZAHS	HANDFEED	HANDOFF	HANDYMAN	HANK
HAMZAS	HANDFEEDS	HANDOFFS	HANDYMEN	HANKED
HAN	HANDFUL	HANDOUT	HANDYWORK	HANKER
HANAMI	HANDFULS	HANDOUTS	HANEPOOT	HANKERED
HANAMIS	HANDGLASS	HANDOVER	HANEPOOTS	HANKERER
HANAP	HANDGRIP	HANDOVERS	HANG	HANKERERS
HANAPER	HANDGRIPS	HANDPASS	HANGABLE	HANKERING
HANAPERS	HANDGUN	HANDPHONE	HANGAR	HANKERS
HANAPS	HANDGUNS	HANDPICK	HANGARAGE	HANKIE
HANBOK	HANDHELD	HANDPICKS	HANGARED	HANKIES
HANBOKS	HANDHELDS	HANDPLAY	HANGARING	HANKING
HANCE	HANDHOLD	HANDPLAYS	HANGARS	HANKS
HANCES	HANDHOLDS	HANDPRESS	HANGBIRD	HANKY
HANCH	HANDICAP	HANDPRINT	HANGBIRDS	HANSA
HANCHED	HANDICAPS	HANDRAIL	HANGDOG	HANSAS
HANCHES	HANDIER	HANDRAILS	HANGDOGS	HANSE
HANCHING	HANDIEST	HANDROLL	HANGED	HANSEATIC
HAND	HANDILY	HANDROLLS	HANGER	HANSEL
HANDAX	HANDINESS	HANDS	HANGERS	HANSELED
HANDAXE	HANDING	HANDSAW	HANGFIRE	HANSELING
HANDAXES	HANDISM	HANDSAWS	HANGFIRES	HANSELLED
HANDBAG	HANDISMS	HANDSEL	HANGI	HANSELS
HANDBAGS	HANDIWORK	HANDSELED	HANGING	HANSES
HANDBALL	HANDJAR	HANDSELS	HANGINGS	HANSOM
HANDBALLS	HANDJARS	HANDSET	HANGIS	HANSOMS
HANDBELL	HANDJOB	HANDSETS	HANGMAN	HANT
HANDBELLS	HANDJOBS	HANDSEWN	HANGMEN	HANTED
HANDBILL	HANDKNIT	HANDSFUL	HANGNAIL	HANTING
HANDBILLS	HANDKNITS	HANDSHAKE	HANGNAILS	HANTLE
HANDBLOWN	HANDLE	HANDSIER	HANGNEST	HANTLES
HANDBOOK	HANDLEBAR	HANDSIEST	HANGNESTS	HANTS
HANDBOOKS	HANDLED	HANDSOME	HANGOUT	HANUKIAH
HANDBRAKE	HANDLER	HANDSOMER	HANGOUTS	HANUKIAHS
HANDCAR	HANDLERS	HANDSOMES	HANGOVER	HANUMAN
HANDCARS	HANDLES	HANDSPIKE	HANGOVERS	HANUMANS
HANDCART	HANDLESS	HANDSTAFF	HANGRIER	HAO
HANDCARTS	HANDLIKE	HANDSTAMP	HANGRIEST	HAOMA
HANDCLAP	HANDLINE	HANDSTAND	HANGRY	HAOMAS
HANDCLAPS	HANDLINER	HANDSTURN	HANGS	HAOS
HANDCLASP	HANDLINES	HANDSY	HANGTAG	HAP
HANDCRAFT	HANDLING	HANDTOWEL	HANGTAGS	HAPAX
HANDCUFF	HANDLINGS	HANDWHEEL	HANGUL	HAPAXES
HANDCUFFS	HANDLIST	HANDWORK	HANGULS	HAPHAZARD
HANDED	HANDLISTS	HANDWORKS	HANGUP	HAPHTARA
HANDER	HANDLOOM	HANDWOVEN	HANGUPS	HAPHTARAH
HANDERS	HANDLOOMS	HANDWRIT	HANIWA	HAPHTARAS
HANDFAST	HANDMADE	HANDWRITE	HANIWAS	HAPHTAROT
HANDFASTS	HANDMAID	HANDWROTE	HANJAR	HAPKIDO

HAPKIDOS	HAPU	HARDBACKS	HARDLINE	HAREMS
HAPLESS	HAPUKA	HARDBAG	HARDLINER	HARES
HAPLESSLY	HAPUKAS	HARDBAGS	HARDLY	HARESTAIL
HAPLITE	HAPUKU	HARDBAKE	HARDMAN	HAREWOOD
HAPLITES	HAPUKUS	HARDBAKES	HARDMEN	HAREWOODS
HAPLITIC	HAPUS	HARDBALL	HARDNESS	HARIANA
HAPLOID	HAQUETON	HARDBALLS	HARDNOSE	HARIANAS
HAPLOIDIC	HAQUETONS	HARDBEAM	HARDNOSED	HARICOT
HAPLOIDS	HARAAM	HARDBEAMS	HARDNOSES	HARICOTS
HAPLOIDY	HARAKEKE	HARDBOARD	HARDOKE	HARIGALDS
HAPLOLOGY	HARAKEKES	HARDBODY	HARDOKES	HARIGALS
HAPLONT	HARAM	HARDBOOT	HARDPACK	HARIJAN
HAPLONTIC	HARAMBEE	HARDBOOTS	HARDPACKS	HARIJANS
HAPLONTS	HARAMBEES	HARDBOUND	HARDPAN	HARIM
HAPLOPIA	HARAMDA	HARDCASE	HARDPANS	HARIMS
HAPLOPIAS	HARAMDAS	HARDCASES	HARDPARTS	HARING
HAPLOSES	HARAMDI	HARDCORE	HARDROCK	HARIOLATE
HAPLOSIS	HARAMDIS	HARDCORES	HARDROCKS	HARIRA
HAPLOTYPE	HARAMS	HARDCOURT	HARDS	HARIRAS
HAPLY	HARAMZADA	HARDCOVER	HARDSCAPE	HARISH
HAPPED	HARAMZADI	HARDEDGE	HARDSET	HARISSA
HAPPEN	HARANGUE	HARDEDGES	HARDSHELL	HARISSAS
HAPPENED	HARANGUED	HARDEN	HARDSHIP	HARK
HAPPENING	HARANGUER	HARDENED	HARDSHIPS	HARKED
HAPPENS	HARANGUES	HARDENER	HARDSTAND	HARKEN
HAPPI	HARASS	HARDENERS	HARDTACK	HARKENED
HAPPIED	HARASSED	HARDENING	HARDTACKS	HARKENER
HAPPIER	HARASSER	HARDENS	HARDTAIL	HARKENERS
HAPPIES	HARASSERS	HARDER	HARDTAILS	HARKENING
HAPPIEST	HARASSES	HARDEST	HARDTOP	HARKENS
HAPPILY	HARASSING	HARDFACE	HARDTOPS	HARKING
HAPPINESS	HARBINGER	HARDFACES	HARDWARE	HARKS
HAPPING	HARBOR	HARDGOODS	HARDWARES	HARL
HAPPIS	HARBORAGE	HARDGRASS	HARDWIRE	HARLED
HAPPOSHU	HARBORED	HARDHACK	HARDWIRED	HARLEQUIN
HAPPOSHUS	HARBORER	HARDHACKS	HARDWIRES	HARLING
HAPPY	HARBORERS	HARDHAT	HARDWOOD	HARLINGS
HAPPYING	HARBORFUL	HARDHATS	HARDWOODS	HARLOT
HAPS	HARBORING	HARDHEAD	HARDY	HARLOTRY
HAPTEN	HARBOROUS	HARDHEADS	HARE	HARLOTS
HAPTENE	HARBORS	HARDIER	HAREBELL	HARLS
HAPTENES	HARBOUR	HARDIES	HAREBELLS	HARM
HAPTENIC	HARBOURED	HARDIEST	HARED	HARMALA
HAPTENS	HARBOURER	HARDIHEAD	HAREEM	HARMALAS
HAPTERON	HARBOURS	HARDIHOOD	HAREEMS	HARMALIN
HAPTERONS	HARD	HARDILY	HARELD	HARMALINE
HAPTIC	HARDASS	HARDIMENT	HARELDS	HARMALINS
HAPTICAL	HARDASSES	HARDINESS	HARELIKE	HARMAN
HAPTICS	HARDBACK	HARDISH	HAREM	HARMANS

HARMATTAN	HARPINS	HARTENS	HASSLES	HATCHETY
HARMDOING	HARPIST	HARTLESSE	HASSLING	HATCHING
HARMED	HARPISTS	HARTS	HASSOCK	HATCHINGS
HARMEL	HARPOON	HARTSHORN	HASSOCKS	HATCHLING
HARMELS	HARPOONED	HARUMPH	HASSOCKY	HATCHMENT
HARMER	HARPOONER	HARUMPHED	HAST	HATCHWAY
HARMERS	HARPOONS	HARUMPHS	HASTA	HATCHWAYS
HARMFUL	HARPS	HARUSPEX	HASTATE	HATE
HARMFULLY	HARPY	HARUSPICY	HASTATED	HATEABLE
HARMIN	HARPYLIKE	HARVEST	HASTATELY	HATED
HARMINE	HARQUEBUS	HARVESTED	HASTE	HATEFUL
HARMINES	HARRIDAN	HARVESTER	HASTED	HATEFULLY
HARMING	HARRIDANS	HARVESTS	HASTEFUL	HATELESS
HARMINS	HARRIED	HAS	HASTEN	HATER
HARMLESS	HARRIER	HASH	HASTENED	HATERENT
HARMONIC	HARRIERS	HASHED	HASTENER	HATERENTS
HARMONICA	HARRIES	HASHEESH	HASTENERS	HATERS
HARMONICS	HARROW	HASHES	HASTENING	HATES
HARMONIES	HARROWED	HASHHEAD	HASTENS	HATFUL
HARMONISE	HARROWER	HASHHEADS	HASTES	HATFULS
HARMONIST	HARROWERS	HASHIER	HASTIER	HATGUARD
HARMONIUM	HARROWING	HASHIEST	HASTIEST	HATGUARDS
HARMONIZE	HARROWS	HASHING	HASTILY	HATH
HARMONY	HARRUMPH	HASHINGS	HASTINESS	HATHA
HARMOST	HARRUMPHS	HASHISH	HASTING	HATINATOR
HARMOSTS	HARRY	HASHISHES	HASTINGS	HATING
HARMOSTY	HARRYING	HASHMARK	HASTY	HATLESS
HARMOTOME	HARSH	HASHMARKS	HAT	HATLIKE
HARMS	HARSHED	HASHTAG	HATABLE	HATMAKER
HARN	HARSHEN	HASHTAGS	HATBAND	HATMAKERS
HARNESS	HARSHENED	HASHY	HATBANDS	HATPEG
HARNESSED	HARSHENS	HASK	HATBOX	HATPEGS
HARNESSER	HARSHER	HASKS	HATBOXES	HATPIN
HARNESSES	HARSHES	HASLET	HATBRUSH	HATPINS
HARNS	HARSHEST	HASLETS	HATCH	HATRACK
HARO	HARSHING	HASP	HATCHABLE	HATRACKS
HAROS	HARSHLY	HASPED	HATCHBACK	HATRED
HAROSET	HARSHNESS	HASPING	HATCHECK	HATREDS
HAROSETH	HARSLET	HASPS	HATCHECKS	HATS
HAROSETHS	HARSLETS	HASS	HATCHED	HATSFUL
HAROSETS	HART	HASSAR	HATCHEL	HATSTAND
HARP	HARTAL	HASSARS	HATCHELED	HATSTANDS
HARPED	HARTALS	HASSEL	HATCHELS	HATTED
HARPER	HARTBEES	HASSELS	HATCHER	HATTER
HARPERS	HARTBEEST	HASSES	HATCHERS	HATTERED
HARPIES	HARTELY	HASSIUM	HATCHERY	HATTERIA
HARPIN	HARTEN	HASSIUMS	HATCHES	HATTERIAS
HARPING	HARTENED	HASSLE	HATCHET	HATTERING
HARPINGS	HARTENING	HASSLED	HATCHETS	HATTERS

HATTING	HAUNS	HAVEREL	HAWKISH	HAYINGS
HATTINGS	HAUNT	HAVERELS	HAWKISHLY	HAYLAGE
HATTOCK	HAUNTED	HAVERING	HAWKIT	HAYLAGES
HATTOCKS	HAUNTER	HAVERINGS	HAWKLIKE	HAYLE
HAUBERK	HAUNTERS	HAVERS	HAWKMOTH	HAYLES
HAUBERKS	HAUNTING	HAVERSACK	HAWKMOTHS	HAYLOFT
HAUBOIS	HAUNTINGS	HAVERSINE	HAWKNOSE	HAYLOFTS
HAUD	HAUNTS	HAVES	HAWKNOSES	HAYMAKER
HAUDING	HAURIANT	HAVILDAR	HAWKS	HAYMAKERS
HAUDS	HAURIENT	HAVILDARS	HAWKSBILL	HAYMAKING
HAUF	HAUSE	HAVING	HAWKSHAW	HAYMOW
HAUFS	HAUSED	HAVINGS	HAWKSHAWS	HAYMOWS
HAUGH	HAUSEN	HAVIOR	HAWKWEED	HAYRACK
HAUGHS	HAUSENS	HAVIORS	HAWKWEEDS	HAYRACKS
HAUGHT	HAUSES	HAVIOUR	HAWM	HAYRAKE
HAUGHTIER	HAUSFRAU	HAVIOURS	HAWMED	HAYRAKES
HAUGHTILY	HAUSFRAUS	HAVOC	HAWMING	HAYRICK
HAUGHTY	HAUSING	HAVOCKED	HAWMS	HAYRICKS
HAUL	HAUSTELLA	HAVOCKER	HAWS	HAYRIDE
HAULAGE	HAUSTORIA	HAVOCKERS	HAWSE	HAYRIDES
HAULAGES	HAUT	HAVOCKING	HAWSED	HAYS
HAULBACK	HAUTBOIS	HAVOCS	HAWSEHOLE	HAYSEED
HAULBACKS	HAUTBOY	HAW	HAWSEPIPE	HAYSEEDS
HAULD	HAUTBOYS	HAWALA	HAWSER	HAYSEL
HAULDS	HAUTE	HAWALAS	HAWSERS	HAYSELS
HAULED	HAUTER	HAWBUCK	HAWSES	HAYSTACK
HAULER	HAUTEST	HAWBUCKS	HAWSING	HAYSTACKS
HAULERS	HAUTEUR	HAWEATER	HAWTHORN	HAYWARD
HAULIER	HAUTEURS	HAWEATERS	HAWTHORNS	HAYWARDS
HAULIERS	HAUYNE	HAWED	HAWTHORNY	HAYWIRE
HAULING	HAUYNES	HAWFINCH	HAY	HAYWIRES
HAULINGS	HAVARTI	HAWING	HAYBAND	HAZAN
HAULM	HAVARTIS	HAWK	HAYBANDS	HAZANIM
HAULMIER	HAVDALAH	HAWKBELL	HAYBOX	HAZANS
HAULMIEST	HAVDALAHS	HAWKBELLS	HAYBOXES	HAZARD
HAULMS	HAVDOLOH	HAWKBILL	HAYCATION	HAZARDED
HAULMY	HAVDOLOHS	HAWKBILLS	HAYCOCK	HAZARDER
HAULOUT	HAVE	HAWKBIT	HAYCOCKS	HAZARDERS
HAULOUTS	HAVELOCK	HAWKBITS	HAYED	HAZARDING
HAULS	HAVELOCKS	HAWKED	HAYER	HAZARDIZE
HAULST	HAVEN	HAWKER	HAYERS	HAZARDOUS
HAULT	HAVENED	HAWKERS	HAYEY	HAZARDRY
HAULYARD	HAVENING	HAWKEY	HAYFIELD	HAZARDS
HAULYARDS	HAVENLESS	HAWKEYED	HAYFIELDS	HAZE
HAUN	HAVENS	HAWKEYS	HAYFORK	HAZED
HAUNCH	HAVEOUR	HAWKIE	HAYFORKS	HAZEL
HAUNCHED	HAVEOURS	HAWKIES	HAYIER	HAZELHEN
HAUNCHES	HAVER	HAWKING	HAYIEST	HAZELHENS
HAUNCHING	HAVERED	HAWKINGS	HAYING	HAZELLY

H

HAZELNUT	HEADFRAME	HEADRAIL	HEALABLE	HEARSAY
HAZELNUTS	HEADFUCK	HEADRAILS	HEALD	HEARSAYS
HAZELS	HEADFUCKS	HEADREACH	HEALDED	HEARSE
HAZELWOOD	HEADFUL	HEADREST	HEALDING	HEARSED
HAZER	HEADFULS	HEADRESTS	HEALDS	HEARSES
HAZERS	HEADGATE	HEADRIG	HEALED	HEARSIER
HAZES	HEADGATES	HEADRIGS	HEALEE	HEARSIEST
HAZIER	HEADGEAR	HEADRING	HEALEES	HEARSING
HAZIEST	HEADGEARS	HEADRINGS	HEALER	HEARSY
HAZILY	HEADGUARD	HEADROOM	HEALERS	HEART
HAZINESS	HEADHUNT	HEADROOMS	HEALING	HEARTACHE
HAZING	HEADHUNTS	HEADROPE	HEALINGLY	HEARTBEAT
HAZINGS	HEADIER	HEADROPES	HEALINGS	HEARTBURN
HAZMAT	HEADIEST	HEADS	HEALS	HEARTED
HAZMATS	HEADILY	HEADSAIL	HEALSOME	HEARTEN
HAZY	HEADINESS	HEADSAILS	HEALTH	HEARTENED
HAZZAN	HEADING	HEADSCARF	HEALTHFUL	HEARTENER
HAZZANIM	HEADINGS	HEADSET	HEALTHIER	HEARTENS
HAZZANS	HEADLAMP	HEADSETS	HEALTHILY	HEARTFELT
HE	HEADLAMPS	HEADSHAKE	HEALTHISM	HEARTFREE
HEAD	HEADLAND	HEADSHIP	HEALTHS	HEARTH
HEADACHE	HEADLANDS	HEADSHIPS	HEALTHY	HEARTHRUG
HEADACHES	HEADLEASE	HEADSHOT	HEAME	HEARTHS
HEADACHEY	HEADLESS	HEADSHOTS	HEAP	HEARTIER
HEADACHY	HEADLIGHT	HEADSMAN	HEAPED	HEARTIES
HEADAGE	HEADLIKE	HEADSMEN	HEAPER	HEARTIEST
HEADAGES	HEADLINE	HEADSPACE	HEAPERS	HEARTIKIN
HEADBAND	HEADLINED	HEADSTALL	HEAPIER	HEARTILY
HEADBANDS	HEADLINER	HEADSTAND	HEAPIEST	HEARTING
HEADBANG	HEADLINES	HEADSTAY	HEAPING	HEARTLAND
HEADBANGS	HEADLOCK	HEADSTAYS	HEAPS	HEARTLESS
HEADBOARD	HEADLOCKS	HEADSTICK	HEAPSTEAD	HEARTLET
HEADBUTT	HEADLONG	HEADSTOCK	HEAPY	HEARTLETS
HEADBUTTS	HEADMAN	HEADSTONE	HEAR	HEARTLING
HEADCASE	HEADMARK	HEADWALL	HEARABLE	HEARTLY
HEADCASES	HEADMARKS	HEADWALLS	HEARD	HEARTPEA
HEADCHAIR	HEADMEN	HEADWARD	HEARDS	HEARTPEAS
HEADCLOTH	HEADMOST	HEADWARDS	HEARE	HEARTS
HEADCOUNT	HEADNOTE	HEADWATER	HEARER	HEARTSEED
HEADDRESS	HEADNOTES	HEADWAY	HEARERS	HEARTSICK
HEADED	HEADPEACE	HEADWAYS	HEARES	HEARTSINK
HEADEND	HEADPHONE	HEADWIND	HEARIE	HEARTSOME
HEADENDS	HEADPIECE	HEADWINDS	HEARING	HEARTSORE
HEADER	HEADPIN	HEADWORD	HEARINGS	HEARTWOOD
HEADERS	HEADPINS	HEADWORDS	HEARKEN	HEARTWORM
HEADFAST	HEADPOND	HEADWORK	HEARKENED	HEARTY
HEADFASTS	HEADPONDS	HEADWORKS	HEARKENER	HEAST
HEADFIRST	HEADRACE	HEADY	HEARKENS	HEASTE
HEADFISH	HEADRACES	HEAL	HEARS	HEASTES

HEASTS	HEAVING	HECTICLY	HEDYSARUM	HEFTILY
HEAT	HEAVINGS	HECTICS	HEED	HEFTINESS
HEATABLE	HEAVY	HECTOGRAM	HEEDED	HEFTING
HEATED	HEAVYISH	HECTOR	HEEDER	HEFTS
HEATEDLY	HEAVYSET	HECTORED	HEEDERS	HEFTY
HEATER	HEBDOMAD	HECTORER	HEEDFUL	HEGARI
HEATERS	HEBDOMADS	HECTORERS	HEEDFULLY	HEGARIS
HEATH	HEBE	HECTORING	HEEDIER	HEGEMON
HEATHBIRD	HEBEN	HECTORISM	HEEDIEST	HEGEMONIC
HEATHCOCK	HEBENON	HECTORLY	HEEDINESS	HEGEMONS
HEATHEN	HEBENONS	HECTORS	HEEDING	HEGEMONY
HEATHENRY	HEBENS	HEDARIM	HEEDLESS	HEGIRA
HEATHENS	HEBES	HEDDLE	HEEDS	HEGIRAS
HEATHER	HEBETANT	HEDDLED	HEEDY	HEGUMEN
HEATHERED	HEBETATE	HEDDLES	HEEHAW	HEGUMENE
HEATHERS	HEBETATED	HEDDLING	HEEHAWED	HEGUMENES
HEATHERY	HEBETATES	HEDER	HEEHAWING	HEGUMENOI
HEATHFOWL	HEBETIC	HEDERA	HEEHAWS	HEGUMENOS
HEATHIER	HEBETUDE	HEDERAL	HEEL	HEGUMENS
HEATHIEST	HEBETUDES	HEDERAS	HEELBALL	HEGUMENY
HEATHLAND	HEBONA	HEDERATED	HEELBALLS	HEH
HEATHLESS	HEBONAS	HEDERS	HEELBAR	HEHS
HEATHLIKE	HEBRAISE	HEDGE	HEELBARS	HEID
HEATHS	HEBRAISED	HEDGEBILL	HEELED	HEIDS
HEATHY	HEBRAISES	HEDGED	HEELER	HEIDUC
HEATING	HEBRAIZE	HEDGEHOG	HEELERS	HEIDUCS
HEATINGS	HEBRAIZED	HEDGEHOGS	HEELING	HEIFER
HEATLESS	HEBRAIZES	HEDGEHOP	HEELINGS	HEIFERS
HEATPROOF	HECATOMB	HEDGEHOPS	HEELLESS	HEIGH
HEATS	HECATOMBS	HEDGEPIG	HEELPIECE	HEIGHT
HEATSPOT	HECH	HEDGEPIGS	HEELPLATE	HEIGHTEN
HEATSPOTS	HECHT	HEDGER	HEELPOST	HEIGHTENS
HEATWAVE	HECHTING	HEDGEROW	HEELPOSTS	HEIGHTH
HEATWAVES	HECHTS	HEDGEROWS	HEELS	HEIGHTHS
HEAUME	HECK	HEDGERS	HEELTAP	HEIGHTISM
HEAUMES	HECKLE	HEDGES	HEELTAPS	HEIGHTS
HEAVE	HECKLED	HEDGIER	HEEZE	HEIL
HEAVED	HECKLER	HEDGIEST	HEEZED	HEILED
HEAVEN	HECKLERS	HEDGING	HEEZES	HEILING
HEAVENLY	HECKLES	HEDGINGLY	HEEZIE	HEILS
HEAVENS	HECKLING	HEDGINGS	HEEZIES	HEIMISH
HEAVER	HECKLINGS	HEDGY	HEEZING	HEINIE
HEAVERS	HECKS	HEDONIC	HEFT	HEINIES
HEAVES	HECKUVA	HEDONICS	HEFTE	HEINOUS
HEAVIER	HECOGENIN	HEDONISM	HEFTED	HEINOUSLY
HEAVIES	HECTARE	HEDONISMS	HEFTER	HEIR
HEAVIEST	HECTARES	HEDONIST	HEFTERS	HEIRDOM
HEAVILY	HECTIC	HEDONISTS	HEFTIER	HEIRDOMS
HEAVINESS	HECTICAL	HEDYPHANE	HEFTIEST	HEIRED

H

HEIRESS	HELICASES	HELIX	HELMED	HEM
HEIRESSES	HELICES	HELIXES	HELMER	HEMAGOG
HEIRING	HELICITY	HELL	HELMERS	HEMAGOGS
HEIRLESS	HELICLINE	HELLA	HELMET	HEMAGOGUE
HEIRLOOM	HELICOID	HELLBENT	HELMETED	HEMAL
HEIRLOOMS	HELICOIDS	HELLBOX	HELMETING	HEMATAL
HEIRS	HELICON	HELLBOXES	HELMETS	HEMATEIN
HEIRSHIP	HELICONIA	HELLBROTH	HELMING	HEMATEINS
HEIRSHIPS	HELICONS	HELLCAT	HELMINTH	HEMATIC
HEISHE	HELICOPT	HELLCATS	HELMINTHS	HEMATICS
HEISHES	HELICOPTS	HELLDIVER	HELMLESS	HEMATIN
HEISHI	HELICTITE	HELLEBORE	HELMS	HEMATINE
HEISHIS	HELIDECK	HELLED	HELMSMAN	HEMATINES
HEIST	HELIDECKS	HELLENISE	HELMSMEN	HEMATINIC
HEISTED	HELIDROME	HELLENIZE	HELO	HEMATINS
HEISTER	HELILIFT	HELLER	HELOPHYTE	HEMATITE
HEISTERS	HELILIFTS	HELLERI	HELOS	HEMATITES
HEISTING	HELIMAN	HELLERIES	HELOT	HEMATITIC
HEISTS	HELIMEN	HELLERIS	HELOTAGE	HEMATOID
HEITIKI	HELING	HELLERS	HELOTAGES	HEMATOMA
HEITIKIS	HELIO	HELLERY	HELOTISM	HEMATOMAS
HEJAB	HELIODOR	HELLFIRE	HELOTISMS	HEMATOSES
HEJABS	HELIODORS	HELLFIRES	HELOTRIES	HEMATOSIS
HEJIRA	HELIOGRAM	HELLHOLE	HELOTRY	HEMATOZOA
HEJIRAS	HELIOLOGY	HELLHOLES	HELOTS	HEMATURIA
HEJRA	HELIOPSES	HELLHOUND	HELP	HEMATURIC
HEJRAS	HELIOPSIS	HELLICAT	HELPABLE	HEME
HEKETARA	HELIOS	HELLICATS	HELPDESK	HEMELYTRA
HEKETARAS	HELIOSES	HELLIER	HELPDESKS	HEMES
HEKTARE	HELIOSIS	HELLIERS	HELPED	HEMIALGIA
HEKTARES	HELIOSTAT	HELLING	HELPER	HEMIC
HEKTOGRAM	HELIOTYPE	HELLION	HELPERS	HEMICYCLE
HELCOID	HELIOTYPY	HELLIONS	HELPFUL	HEMIHEDRA
HELD	HELIOZOAN	HELLISH	HELPFULLY	HEMIHEDRY
HELE	HELIOZOIC	HELLISHLY	HELPING	HEMIN
HELED	HELIPAD	HELLKITE	HELPINGS	HEMINA
HELENIUM	HELIPADS	HELLKITES	HELPLESS	HEMINAS
HELENIUMS	HELIPILOT	HELLO	HELPLINE	HEMINS
HELES	HELIPORT	HELLOED	HELPLINES	HEMIOLA
HELIAC	HELIPORTS	HELLOES	HELPMATE	HEMIOLAS
HELIACAL	HELISKI	HELLOING	HELPMATES	HEMIOLIA
HELIAST	HELISKIED	HELLOS	HELPMEET	HEMIOLIAS
HELIASTS	HELISKIS	HELLOVA	HELPMEETS	HEMIOLIC
HELIBORNE	HELISTOP	HELLS	HELPS	HEMIONE
HELIBUS	HELISTOPS	HELLSCAPE	HELVE	HEMIONES
HELIBUSES	HELITACK	HELLUVA	HELVED	HEMIONUS
HELICAL	HELITACKS	HELLWARD	HELVES	HEMIOPIA
HELICALLY	HELIUM	HELLWARDS	HELVETIUM	HEMIOPIAS
HELICASE	HELIUMS	HELM	HELVING	HEMIOPIC

HEMIOPSIA	HEMPSEEDS	HENNIES	HEPSTER	HERBIVORE
HEMIPOD	HEMPWEED	HENNIEST	HEPSTERS	HERBIVORY
HEMIPODE	HEMPWEEDS	HENNIN	HEPT	HERBLESS
HEMIPODES	HEMPY	HENNING	HEPTAD	HERBLET
HEMIPODS	HEMS	HENNINS	HEPTADS	HERBLETS
HEMIPTER	HEMSTITCH	HENNISH	HEPTAGLOT	HERBLIKE
HEMIPTERS	HEN	HENNISHLY	HEPTAGON	HERBOLOGY
HEMISPACE	HENBANE	HENNY	HEPTAGONS	HERBORISE
HEMISTICH	HENBANES	HENOTIC	HEPTANE	HERBORIST
HEMITROPE	HENBIT	HENPECK	HEPTANES	HERBORIZE
HEMITROPY	HENBITS	HENPECKED	HEPTAPODY	HERBOSE
HEMLINE	HENCE	HENPECKS	HEPTARCH	HERBOUS
HEMLINES	HENCH	HENRIES	HEPTARCHS	HERBS
HEMLOCK	HENCHER	HENRY	HEPTARCHY	HERBY
HEMLOCKS	HENCHEST	HENRYS	HEPTOSE	HERCOGAMY
HEMMED	HENCHMAN	HENS	HEPTOSES	HERCULEAN
HEMMER	HENCHMEN	HENT	HER	HERCULES
HEMMERS	HENCOOP	HENTAI	HERALD	HERCYNITE
HEMMING	HENCOOPS	HENTAIS	HERALDED	HERD
HEMOCOEL	HEND	HENTED	HERALDIC	HERDBOY
HEMOCOELS	HENDED	HENTING	HERALDING	HERDBOYS
HEMOCONIA	HENDIADYS	HENTS	HERALDIST	HERDED
HEMOCYTE	HENDING	HEP	HERALDRY	HERDEN
HEMOCYTES	HENDS	HEPAR	HERALDS	HERDENS
HEMOID	HENEQUEN	HEPARIN	HERB	HERDER
HEMOLYMPH	HENEQUENS	HEPARINS	HERBAGE	HERDERS
HEMOLYSE	HENEQUIN	HEPARS	HERBAGED	HERDESS
HEMOLYSED	HENEQUINS	HEPATIC	HERBAGES	HERDESSES
HEMOLYSES	HENGE	HEPATICA	HERBAL	HERDIC
HEMOLYSIN	HENGES	HEPATICAE	HERBALISM	HERDICS
HEMOLYSIS	HENHOUSE	HEPATICAL	HERBALIST	HERDING
HEMOLYTIC	HENHOUSES	HEPATICAS	HERBALS	HERDINGS
HEMOLYZE	HENIQUEN	HEPATICS	HERBAR	HERDLIKE
HEMOLYZED	HENIQUENS	HEPATISE	HERBARIA	HERDMAN
HEMOLYZES	HENIQUIN	HEPATISED	HERBARIAL	HERDMEN
HEMOPHILE	HENIQUINS	HEPATISES	HERBARIAN	HERDS
HEMOSTAT	HENLEY	HEPATITE	HERBARIES	HERDSMAN
HEMOSTATS	HENLEYS	HEPATITES	HERBARIUM	HERDSMEN
HEMOTOXIC	HENLIKE	HEPATITIS	HERBARS	HERDWICK
HEMOTOXIN	HENNA	HEPATIZE	HERBARY	HERDWICKS
HEMP	HENNAED	HEPATIZED	HERBED	HERE
HEMPEN	HENNAING	HEPATIZES	HERBELET	HEREABOUT
HEMPIE	HENNAS	HEPATOMA	HERBELETS	HEREAFTER
HEMPIER	HENNED	HEPATOMAS	HERBICIDE	HEREAT
HEMPIES	HENNER	HEPCAT	HERBIER	HEREAWAY
HEMPIEST	HENNERIES	HEPCATS	HERBIEST	HEREAWAYS
HEMPLIKE	HENNERS	HEPPER	HERBIST	HEREBY
HEMPS	HENNERY	HEPPEST	HERBISTS	HEREDES
HEMPSEED	HENNIER	HEPS	HERBIVORA	HEREDITY

HEREFROM	HERMITAGE	HEROONS	HESPERID	HEUCHERA
HEREIN	HERMITESS	HEROS	HESPERIDS	HEUCHERAS
HEREINTO	HERMITIC	HEROSHIP	HESPING	HEUCHS
HERENESS	HERMITISM	HEROSHIPS	HESPS	HEUGH
HEREOF	HERMITRY	HERPES	HESSIAN	HEUGHS
HEREON	HERMITS	HERPESES	HESSIANS	HEUREKA
HERES	HERMS	HERPETIC	HESSITE	HEUREKAS
HERESIES	HERN	HERPETICS	HESSITES	HEURETIC
HERESY	HERNIA	HERPETOID	HESSONITE	HEURETICS
HERETIC	HERNIAE	HERPING	HEST	HEURISM
HERETICAL	HERNIAL	HERPINGS	HESTERNAL	HEURISMS
HERETICS	HERNIAS	HERPTILE	HESTS	HEURISTIC
HERETO	HERNIATE	HERRIED	HET	HEVEA
HERETRIX	HERNIATED	HERRIES	HETAERA	HEVEAS
HEREUNDER	HERNIATES	HERRIMENT	HETAERAE	HEW
HEREUNTO	HERNS	HERRING	HETAERAS	HEWABLE
HEREUPON	HERNSHAW	HERRINGER	HETAERIC	HEWED
HEREWITH	HERNSHAWS	HERRINGS	HETAERISM	HEWER
HERIED	HERO	HERRY	HETAERIST	HEWERS
HERIES	HEROES	HERRYING	HETAIRA	HEWGH
HERIOT	HEROIC	HERRYMENT	HETAIRAI	HEWING
HERIOTS	HEROICAL	HERS	HETAIRAS	HEWINGS
HERISSE	HEROICISE	HERSALL	HETAIRIA	HEWN
HERISSON	HEROICIZE	HERSALLS	HETAIRIAS	HEWS
HERISSONS	HEROICLY	HERSE	HETAIRIC	HEX
HERITABLE	HEROICS	HERSED	HETAIRISM	HEXACHORD
HERITABLY	HEROIN	HERSELF	HETAIRIST	HEXACT
HERITAGE	HEROINE	HERSES	HETE	HEXACTS
HERITAGES	HEROINES	HERSHIP	HETERO	HEXAD
HERITOR	HEROINISM	HERSHIPS	HETERODOX	HEXADE
HERITORS	HEROINS	HERSTORY	HETERONYM	HEXADECYL
HERITRESS	HEROISE	HERTZ	HETEROPOD	HEXADES
HERITRIX	HEROISED	HERTZES	HETEROS	HEXADIC
HERKOGAMY	HEROISES	HERY	HETEROSES	HEXADS
HERL	HEROISING	HERYE	HETEROSIS	HEXAFOIL
HERLING	HEROISM	HERYED	HETEROTIC	HEXAFOILS
HERLINGS	HEROISMS	HERYES	HETES	HEXAGLOT
HERLS	HEROIZE	HERYING	HETH	HEXAGLOTS
HERM	HEROIZED	HES	HETHER	HEXAGON
HERMA	HEROIZES	HESITANCE	HETHS	HEXAGONAL
HERMAE	HEROIZING	HESITANCY	HETING	HEXAGONS
HERMAEAN	HERON	HESITANT	HETMAN	HEXAGRAM
HERMAI	HERONRIES	HESITATE	HETMANATE	HEXAGRAMS
HERMANDAD	HERONRY	HESITATED	HETMANS	HEXAHEDRA
HERMETIC	HERONS	HESITATER	HETMEN	HEXAMERAL
HERMETICS	HERONSEW	HESITATES	HETS	HEXAMETER
HERMETISM	HERONSEWS	HESITATOR	HETTIE	HEXAMINE
HERMETIST	HERONSHAW	HESP	HETTIES	HEXAMINES
HERMIT	HEROON	HESPED	HEUCH	HEXANE

HEXANES	HIATAL	HIDDENITE	HIGGLE	HIGHT
HEXANOIC	HIATUS	HIDDENLY	HIGGLED	HIGHTAIL
HEXAPLA	HIATUSES	HIDDER	HIGGLER	HIGHTAILS
HEXAPLAR	HIBACHI	HIDDERS	HIGGLERS	HIGHTED
HEXAPLAS	HIBACHIS	HIDE	HIGGLES	HIGHTH
HEXAPLOID	HIBAKUSHA	HIDEAWAY	HIGGLING	HIGHTHS
HEXAPOD	HIBERNAL	HIDEAWAYS	HIGGLINGS	HIGHTING
HEXAPODAL	HIBERNATE	HIDEBOUND	HIGH	HIGHTINGS
HEXAPODIC	HIBERNISE	HIDED	HIGHBALL	HIGHTOP
HEXAPODS	HIBERNIZE	HIDELESS	HIGHBALLS	HIGHTOPS
HEXAPODY	HIBISCUS	HIDEOSITY	HIGHBORN	HIGHTS
HEXARCH	HIC	HIDEOUS	HIGHBOY	HIGHVELD
HEXARCHY	HICATEE	HIDEOUSLY	HIGHBOYS	HIGHVELDS
HEXASTICH	HICATEES	HIDEOUT	HIGHBRED	HIGHWAY
HEXASTYLE	HICCATEE	HIDEOUTS	HIGHBROW	HIGHWAYS
HEXATHLON	HICCATEES	HIDER	HIGHBROWS	HIJAB
HEXED	HICCOUGH	HIDERS	HIGHBUSH	HIJABS
HEXENE	HICCOUGHS	HIDES	HIGHCHAIR	HIJACK
HEXENES	HICCUP	HIDING	HIGHED	HIJACKED
HEXER	HICCUPED	HIDINGS	HIGHER	HIJACKER
HEXEREI	HICCUPIER	HIDLING	HIGHERED	HIJACKERS
HEXEREIS	HICCUPING	HIDLINGS	HIGHERING	HIJACKING
HEXERS	HICCUPPED	HIDLINS	HIGHERS	HIJACKS
HEXES	HICCUPS	HIDROSES	HIGHEST	HIJINKS
HEXING	HICCUPY	HIDROSIS	HIGHFLIER	HIJRA
HEXINGS	HICK	HIDROTIC	HIGHFLYER	HIJRAH
HEXONE	HICKER	HIDROTICS	HIGHING	HIJRAHS
HEXONES	HICKEST	HIE	HIGHISH	HIJRAS
HEXOSAN	HICKEY	HIED	HIGHJACK	HIKE
HEXOSANS	HICKEYS	HIEING	HIGHJACKS	HIKED
HEXOSE	HICKIE	HIELAMAN	HIGHJINKS	HIKER
HEXOSES	HICKIES	HIELAMANS	HIGHLAND	HIKERS
HEXYL	HICKISH	HIELAND	HIGHLANDS	HIKES
HEXYLENE	HICKORIES	HIEMAL	HIGHLIFE	HIKING
HEXYLENES	HICKORY	HIEMS	HIGHLIFES	HIKINGS
HEXYLIC	HICKS	HIERACIUM	HIGHLIGHT	HIKOI
HEXYLS	HICKWALL	HIERARCH	HIGHLINER	HIKOIED
HEY	HICKWALLS	HIERARCHS	HIGHLY	HIKOIING
HEYDAY	HICKYMAL	HIERARCHY	HIGHMAN	HIKOIS
HEYDAYS	HICKYMALS	HIERATIC	HIGHMEN	HILA
HEYDEY	HID	HIERATICA	HIGHMOST	HILAR
HEYDEYS	HIDABLE	HIERATICS	HIGHNESS	HILARIOUS
HEYDUCK	HIDAGE	HIEROCRAT	HIGHRISE	HILARITY
HEYDUCKS	HIDAGES	HIERODULE	HIGHRISES	HILCH
HEYED	HIDALGA	HIEROGRAM	HIGHROAD	HILCHED
HEYING	HIDALGAS	HIEROLOGY	HIGHROADS	HILCHES
HEYS	HIDALGO	HIERURGY	HIGHS	HILCHING
HI	HIDALGOS	HIES	HIGHSPOT	HILD
HIANT	HIDDEN	HIFALUTIN	HIGHSPOTS	HILDING

HILDINGS

HILDINGS	HIMBOS	HINKY	HIPPO	HIRSEL
HILI	HIMS	HINNIE	HIPPOCRAS	HIRSELED
HILL	HIMSELF	HINNIED	HIPPODAME	HIRSELING
HILLBILLY	HIN	HINNIES	HIPPOLOGY	HIRSELLED
HILLCREST	HINAHINA	HINNY	HIPPOS	HIRSELS
HILLED	HINAHINAS	HINNYING	HIPPURIC	HIRSLE
HILLER	HINAU	HINS	HIPPURITE	HIRSLED
HILLERS	HINAUS	HINT	HIPPUS	HIRSLES
HILLFOLK	HIND	HINTED	HIPPUSES	HIRSLING
HILLFORT	HINDBERRY	HINTER	HIPPY	HIRSTIE
HILLFORTS	HINDBRAIN	HINTERS	HIPPYDOM	HIRSUTE
HILLIER	HINDCAST	HINTING	HIPPYDOMS	HIRSUTISM
HILLIEST	HINDCASTS	HINTINGLY	HIPPYISH	HIRUDIN
HILLINESS	HINDER	HINTINGS	HIPS	HIRUDINS
HILLING	HINDERED	HINTS	HIPSHOT	HIRUNDINE
HILLINGS	HINDERER	HIOI	HIPSTER	HIS
HILLMEN	HINDERERS	HIOIS	HIPSTERS	HISH
HILLO	HINDERING	HIP	HIPT	HISHED
HILLOA	HINDERS	HIPBONE	HIRABLE	HISHES
HILLOAED	HINDFEET	HIPBONES	HIRAETH	HISHING
HILLOAING	HINDFOOT	HIPHUGGER	HIRAETHS	HISN
HILLOAS	HINDGUT	HIPLESS	HIRAGANA	HISPANISM
HILLOCK	HINDGUTS	HIPLIKE	HIRAGANAS	HISPI
HILLOCKED	HINDHEAD	HIPLINE	HIRAGE	HISPID
HILLOCKS	HINDHEADS	HIPLINES	HIRAGES	HISPIDITY
HILLOCKY	HINDLEG	HIPLY	HIRCINE	HISPIS
HILLOED	HINDLEGS	HIPNESS	HIRCOSITY	HISS
HILLOES	HINDMILK	HIPNESSES	HIRE	HISSED
HILLOING	HINDMILKS	HIPPARCH	HIREABLE	HISSELF
HILLOS	HINDMOST	HIPPARCHS	HIREAGE	HISSER
HILLS	HINDRANCE	HIPPED	HIREAGES	HISSERS
HILLSIDE	HINDS	HIPPEN	HIRED	HISSES
HILLSIDES	HINDSHANK	HIPPENS	HIREE	HISSIER
HILLSLOPE	HINDSIGHT	HIPPER	HIREES	HISSIES
HILLTOP	HINDWARD	HIPPEST	HIRELING	HISSIEST
HILLTOPS	HINDWING	HIPPIATRY	HIRELINGS	HISSING
HILLY	HINDWINGS	HIPPIC	HIRER	HISSINGLY
HILT	HING	HIPPIE	HIRERS	HISSINGS
HILTED	HINGE	HIPPIEDOM	HIRES	HISSY
HILTING	HINGED	HIPPIEISH	HIRING	HIST
HILTLESS	HINGELESS	HIPPIER	HIRINGS	HISTAMIN
HILTS	HINGELIKE	HIPPIES	HIRLING	HISTAMINE
HILUM	HINGER	HIPPIEST	HIRLINGS	HISTAMINS
HILUS	HINGERS	HIPPIN	HIRPLE	HISTED
HIM	HINGES	HIPPINESS	HIRPLED	HISTIDIN
HIMATIA	HINGING	HIPPING	HIRPLES	HISTIDINE
HIMATION	HINGS	HIPPINGS	HIRPLING	HISTIDINS
HIMATIONS	HINKIER	HIPPINS	HIRRIENT	HISTIE
HIMBO	HINKIEST	HIPPISH	HIRRIENTS	HISTING

272 | **two to nine letter words**

HISTIOID	HITTING	HOARILY	HOBBYISM	HOCUSED
HISTOGEN	HIVE	HOARINESS	HOBBYISMS	HOCUSES
HISTOGENS	HIVED	HOARING	HOBBYIST	HOCUSING
HISTOGENY	HIVELESS	HOARS	HOBBYISTS	HOCUSSED
HISTOGRAM	HIVELIKE	HOARSE	HOBBYLESS	HOCUSSES
HISTOID	HIVEMIND	HOARSELY	HOBDAY	HOCUSSING
HISTOLOGY	HIVEMINDS	HOARSEN	HOBDAYED	HOD
HISTONE	HIVER	HOARSENED	HOBDAYING	HODAD
HISTONES	HIVERS	HOARSENS	HOBDAYS	HODADDIES
HISTORIAN	HIVES	HOARSER	HOBGOBLIN	HODADDY
HISTORIC	HIVEWARD	HOARSEST	HOBJOB	HODADS
HISTORIED	HIVEWARDS	HOARY	HOBJOBBED	HODDED
HISTORIES	HIVING	HOAS	HOBJOBBER	HODDEN
HISTORIFY	HIYA	HOASCA	HOBJOBS	HODDENS
HISTORISM	HIZEN	HOASCAS	HOBLIKE	HODDIN
HISTORY	HIZENS	HOAST	HOBNAIL	HODDING
HISTRIO	HIZZ	HOASTED	HOBNAILED	HODDINS
HISTRION	HIZZED	HOASTING	HOBNAILS	HODDLE
HISTRIONS	HIZZES	HOASTMAN	HOBNOB	HODDLED
HISTRIOS	HIZZING	HOASTMEN	HOBNOBBED	HODDLES
HISTS	HIZZONER	HOASTS	HOBNOBBER	HODDLING
HIT	HIZZONERS	HOATCHING	HOBNOBBY	HODIERNAL
HITCH	HM	HOATZIN	HOBNOBS	HODJA
HITCHED	HMM	HOATZINES	HOBO	HODJAS
HITCHER	HMMM	HOATZINS	HOBODOM	HODMAN
HITCHERS	HO	HOAX	HOBODOMS	HODMANDOD
HITCHES	HOA	HOAXED	HOBOED	HODMEN
HITCHHIKE	HOACTZIN	HOAXER	HOBOES	HODOGRAPH
HITCHIER	HOACTZINS	HOAXERS	HOBOING	HODOMETER
HITCHIEST	HOAED	HOAXES	HOBOISM	HODOMETRY
HITCHILY	HOAGIE	HOAXING	HOBOISMS	HODOSCOPE
HITCHING	HOAGIES	HOB	HOBOS	HODS
HITCHY	HOAGY	HOBBED	HOBS	HOE
HITHE	HOAING	HOBBER	HOC	HOECAKE
HITHER	HOAR	HOBBERS	HOCK	HOECAKES
HITHERED	HOARD	HOBBIES	HOCKED	HOED
HITHERING	HOARDED	HOBBING	HOCKER	HOEDOWN
HITHERS	HOARDER	HOBBISH	HOCKERS	HOEDOWNS
HITHERTO	HOARDERS	HOBBIT	HOCKEY	HOEING
HITHES	HOARDING	HOBBITRY	HOCKEYS	HOELIKE
HITLESS	HOARDINGS	HOBBITS	HOCKING	HOER
HITMAKER	HOARDS	HOBBLE	HOCKLE	HOERS
HITMAKERS	HOARED	HOBBLED	HOCKLED	HOES
HITMAN	HOARFROST	HOBBLER	HOCKLES	HOG
HITMEN	HOARHEAD	HOBBLERS	HOCKLING	HOGAN
HITS	HOARHEADS	HOBBLES	HOCKS	HOGANS
HITTABLE	HOARHOUND	HOBBLING	HOCKSHOP	HOGBACK
HITTER	HOARIER	HOBBLINGS	HOCKSHOPS	HOGBACKS
HITTERS	HOARIEST	HOBBY	HOCUS	HOGEN

HOGENS	HOGWARDS	HOKAS	HOLELESS	HOLLOING
HOGFISH	HOGWASH	HOKE	HOLES	HOLLOO
HOGFISHES	HOGWASHES	HOKED	HOLESOM	HOLLOOED
HOGG	HOGWEED	HOKES	HOLESOME	HOLLOOING
HOGGED	HOGWEEDS	HOKEY	HOLEY	HOLLOOS
HOGGER	HOH	HOKEYNESS	HOLEYER	HOLLOS
HOGGEREL	HOHA	HOKI	HOLEYEST	HOLLOW
HOGGERELS	HOHED	HOKIER	HOLIBUT	HOLLOWARE
HOGGERIES	HOHING	HOKIEST	HOLIBUTS	HOLLOWED
HOGGERS	HOHS	HOKILY	HOLIDAY	HOLLOWER
HOGGERY	HOI	HOKINESS	HOLIDAYED	HOLLOWEST
HOGGET	HOICK	HOKING	HOLIDAYER	HOLLOWING
HOGGETS	HOICKED	HOKIS	HOLIDAYS	HOLLOWLY
HOGGIN	HOICKING	HOKKU	HOLIER	HOLLOWS
HOGGING	HOICKS	HOKKUS	HOLIES	HOLLY
HOGGINGS	HOICKSED	HOKONUI	HOLIEST	HOLLYHOCK
HOGGINS	HOICKSES	HOKONUIS	HOLILY	HOLM
HOGGISH	HOICKSING	HOKUM	HOLINESS	HOLME
HOGGISHLY	HOIDEN	HOKUMS	HOLING	HOLMES
HOGGS	HOIDENED	HOKYPOKY	HOLINGS	HOLMIA
HOGH	HOIDENING	HOLANDRIC	HOLISM	HOLMIAS
HOGHOOD	HOIDENISH	HOLARCHY	HOLISMS	HOLMIC
HOGHOODS	HOIDENS	HOLARD	HOLIST	HOLMIUM
HOGHS	HOIED	HOLARDS	HOLISTIC	HOLMIUMS
HOGLET	HOIING	HOLD	HOLISTS	HOLMS
HOGLETS	HOIK	HOLDABLE	HOLK	HOLO
HOGLIKE	HOIKED	HOLDALL	HOLKED	HOLOCAINE
HOGMANAY	HOIKING	HOLDALLS	HOLKING	HOLOCAUST
HOGMANAYS	HOIKS	HOLDBACK	HOLKS	HOLOCENE
HOGMANE	HOING	HOLDBACKS	HOLLA	HOLOCRINE
HOGMANES	HOIS	HOLDDOWN	HOLLAED	HOLOGAMY
HOGMENAY	HOISE	HOLDDOWNS	HOLLAING	HOLOGRAM
HOGMENAYS	HOISED	HOLDEN	HOLLAND	HOLOGRAMS
HOGNOSE	HOISES	HOLDER	HOLLANDS	HOLOGRAPH
HOGNOSED	HOISIN	HOLDERBAT	HOLLAS	HOLOGYNIC
HOGNOSES	HOISING	HOLDERS	HOLLER	HOLOGYNY
HOGNUT	HOISINS	HOLDFAST	HOLLERED	HOLOHEDRA
HOGNUTS	HOIST	HOLDFASTS	HOLLERING	HOLON
HOGS	HOISTED	HOLDING	HOLLERS	HOLONIC
HOGSBANE	HOISTER	HOLDINGS	HOLLIDAM	HOLONS
HOGSBANES	HOISTERS	HOLDOUT	HOLLIDAMS	HOLOPHOTE
HOGSHEAD	HOISTING	HOLDOUTS	HOLLIES	HOLOPHYTE
HOGSHEADS	HOISTINGS	HOLDOVER	HOLLO	HOLOPTIC
HOGTIE	HOISTMAN	HOLDOVERS	HOLLOA	HOLOS
HOGTIED	HOISTMEN	HOLDS	HOLLOAED	HOLOTYPE
HOGTIEING	HOISTS	HOLDUP	HOLLOAING	HOLOTYPES
HOGTIES	HOISTWAY	HOLDUPS	HOLLOAS	HOLOTYPIC
HOGTYING	HOISTWAYS	HOLE	HOLLOED	HOLOZOIC
HOGWARD	HOKA	HOLED	HOLLOES	HOLP

HOLPEN	HOMECOMER	HOMESTEAD	HOMMOCKS	HOMOTYPES
HOLS	HOMECRAFT	HOMESTYLE	HOMMOS	HOMOTYPIC
HOLSTEIN	HOMED	HOMETOWN	HOMMOSES	HOMOTYPY
HOLSTEINS	HOMEFELT	HOMETOWNS	HOMO	HOMOUSIAN
HOLSTER	HOMEGIRL	HOMEWARD	HOMOCERCY	HOMS
HOLSTERED	HOMEGIRLS	HOMEWARDS	HOMODONT	HOMUNCLE
HOLSTERS	HOMEGOING	HOMEWARE	HOMODYNE	HOMUNCLES
HOLT	HOMEGROWN	HOMEWARES	HOMOEOBOX	HOMUNCULE
HOLTS	HOMELAND	HOMEWORK	HOMOEOSES	HOMUNCULI
HOLUBTSI	HOMELANDS	HOMEWORKS	HOMOEOSIS	HOMY
HOLY	HOMELESS	HOMEY	HOMOEOTIC	HON
HOLYDAM	HOMELIER	HOMEYNESS	HOMOGAMIC	HONAN
HOLYDAME	HOMELIEST	HOMEYS	HOMOGAMY	HONANS
HOLYDAMES	HOMELIKE	HOMICIDAL	HOMOGENY	HONCHO
HOLYDAMS	HOMELILY	HOMICIDE	HOMOGONY	HONCHOED
HOLYDAY	HOMELY	HOMICIDES	HOMOGRAFT	HONCHOES
HOLYDAYS	HOMELYN	HOMIE	HOMOGRAPH	HONCHOING
HOLYSTONE	HOMELYNS	HOMIER	HOMOLOG	HONCHOS
HOLYTIDE	HOMEMADE	HOMIES	HOMOLOGIC	HOND
HOLYTIDES	HOMEMAKER	HOMIEST	HOMOLOGS	HONDA
HOM	HOMEOBOX	HOMILETIC	HOMOLOGUE	HONDAS
HOMA	HOMEOMERY	HOMILIES	HOMOLOGY	HONDLE
HOMAGE	HOMEOPATH	HOMILIST	HOMOLYSES	HONDLED
HOMAGED	HOMEOSES	HOMILISTS	HOMOLYSIS	HONDLES
HOMAGER	HOMEOSIS	HOMILY	HOMOLYTIC	HONDLING
HOMAGERS	HOMEOTIC	HOMINES	HOMOMORPH	HONDS
HOMAGES	HOMEOWNER	HOMINESS	HOMONYM	HONE
HOMAGING	HOMEPAGE	HOMING	HOMONYMIC	HONED
HOMALOID	HOMEPAGES	HOMINGS	HOMONYMS	HONER
HOMALOIDS	HOMEPLACE	HOMINIAN	HOMONYMY	HONERS
HOMAS	HOMEPORT	HOMINIANS	HOMOPHILE	HONES
HOMBRE	HOMEPORTS	HOMINID	HOMOPHOBE	HONEST
HOMBRES	HOMER	HOMINIDS	HOMOPHONE	HONESTER
HOMBURG	HOMERED	HOMINIES	HOMOPHONY	HONESTEST
HOMBURGS	HOMERIC	HOMININ	HOMOPHYLY	HONESTIES
HOME	HOMERING	HOMININE	HOMOPLASY	HONESTLY
HOMEBIRD	HOMEROOM	HOMININS	HOMOPOLAR	HONESTY
HOMEBIRDS	HOMEROOMS	HOMINISE	HOMOS	HONEWORT
HOMEBIRTH	HOMERS	HOMINISED	HOMOSEX	HONEWORTS
HOMEBODY	HOMES	HOMINISES	HOMOSEXES	HONEY
HOMEBOUND	HOMESICK	HOMINIZE	HOMOSPORY	HONEYBEE
HOMEBOY	HOMESITE	HOMINIZED	HOMOSTYLY	HONEYBEES
HOMEBOYS	HOMESITES	HOMINIZES	HOMOTAXES	HONEYBELL
HOMEBRED	HOMESPUN	HOMINOID	HOMOTAXIC	HONEYBUN
HOMEBREDS	HOMESPUNS	HOMINOIDS	HOMOTAXIS	HONEYBUNS
HOMEBREW	HOMESTALL	HOMINY	HOMOTONIC	HONEYCOMB
HOMEBREWS	HOMESTAND	HOMME	HOMOTONY	HONEYDEW
HOMEBUILT	HOMESTAY	HOMMES	HOMOTYPAL	HONEYDEWS
HOMEBUYER	HOMESTAYS	HOMMOCK	HOMOTYPE	HONEYED

H

HONEYEDLY	HONOURING	HOOFS	HOOPED	HOOTING
HONEYFUL	HONOURS	HOOK	HOOPER	HOOTNANNY
HONEYING	HONS	HOOKA	HOOPERS	HOOTS
HONEYLESS	HOO	HOOKAH	HOOPHOUSE	HOOTY
HONEYMOON	HOOCH	HOOKAHS	HOOPING	HOOVE
HONEYPOT	HOOCHES	HOOKAS	HOOPLA	HOOVED
HONEYPOTS	HOOCHIE	HOOKCHECK	HOOPLAS	HOOVEN
HONEYS	HOOCHIES	HOOKED	HOOPLESS	HOOVER
HONEYTRAP	HOOD	HOOKER	HOOPLIKE	HOOVERED
HONG	HOODED	HOOKERS	HOOPOE	HOOVERING
HONGI	HOODIA	HOOKEY	HOOPOES	HOOVERS
HONGIED	HOODIAS	HOOKEYS	HOOPOO	HOOVES
HONGIES	HOODIE	HOOKIER	HOOPOOS	HOOVING
HONGIING	HOODIER	HOOKIES	HOOPS	HOP
HONGING	HOODIES	HOOKIEST	HOOPSKIRT	HOPAK
HONGIS	HOODIEST	HOOKING	HOOPSTER	HOPAKS
HONGS	HOODING	HOOKINGS	HOOPSTERS	HOPBIND
HONIED	HOODLESS	HOOKLESS	HOOR	HOPBINDS
HONIEDLY	HOODLIKE	HOOKLET	HOORAH	HOPBINE
HONING	HOODLUM	HOOKLETS	HOORAHED	HOPBINES
HONK	HOODLUMS	HOOKLIKE	HOORAHING	HOPDOG
HONKED	HOODMAN	HOOKNOSE	HOORAHS	HOPDOGS
HONKER	HOODMEN	HOOKNOSED	HOORAY	HOPE
HONKERS	HOODMOLD	HOOKNOSES	HOORAYED	HOPED
HONKING	HOODMOLDS	HOOKS	HOORAYING	HOPEFUL
HONKS	HOODOO	HOOKUP	HOORAYS	HOPEFULLY
HONOR	HOODOOED	HOOKUPS	HOORD	HOPEFULS
HONORABLE	HOODOOING	HOOKWORM	HOORDS	HOPELESS
HONORABLY	HOODOOISM	HOOKWORMS	HOOROO	HOPEPUNK
HONORAND	HOODOOS	HOOKY	HOOROOED	HOPEPUNKS
HONORANDS	HOODS	HOOLACHAN	HOOROOING	HOPER
HONORARIA	HOODWINK	HOOLEY	HOOROOS	HOPERS
HONORARY	HOODWINKS	HOOLEYS	HOORS	HOPES
HONORED	HOODY	HOOLICAN	HOOSEGOW	HOPFIELD
HONOREE	HOOEY	HOOLICANS	HOOSEGOWS	HOPFIELDS
HONOREES	HOOEYS	HOOLIE	HOOSGOW	HOPHEAD
HONORER	HOOF	HOOLIER	HOOSGOWS	HOPHEADS
HONORERS	HOOFBEAT	HOOLIES	HOOSH	HOPING
HONORIFIC	HOOFBEATS	HOOLIEST	HOOSHED	HOPINGLY
HONORING	HOOFBOUND	HOOLIGAN	HOOSHES	HOPLITE
HONORLESS	HOOFED	HOOLIGANS	HOOSHING	HOPLITES
HONORS	HOOFER	HOOLOCK	HOOT	HOPLITIC
HONOUR	HOOFERS	HOOLOCKS	HOOTCH	HOPLOLOGY
HONOURARY	HOOFING	HOOLY	HOOTCHES	HOPPED
HONOURED	HOOFLESS	HOON	HOOTED	HOPPER
HONOUREE	HOOFLIKE	HOONED	HOOTER	HOPPERCAR
HONOUREES	HOOFPRINT	HOONING	HOOTERS	HOPPERS
HONOURER	HOOFROT	HOONS	HOOTIER	HOPPIER
HONOURERS	HOOFROTS	HOOP	HOOTIEST	HOPPIEST

HOPPINESS	HORMES	HORNLIKE	HORRORS	HORTATIVE
HOPPING	HORMESES	HORNPIPE	HORS	HORTATORY
HOPPINGS	HORMESIS	HORNPIPES	HORSE	HORTENSIA
HOPPLE	HORMETIC	HORNPOUT	HORSEBACK	HOS
HOPPLED	HORMIC	HORNPOUTS	HORSEBEAN	HOSANNA
HOPPLER	HORMONAL	HORNS	HORSEBOX	HOSANNAED
HOPPLERS	HORMONE	HORNSTONE	HORSECAR	HOSANNAH
HOPPLES	HORMONES	HORNTAIL	HORSECARS	HOSANNAHS
HOPPLING	HORMONIC	HORNTAILS	HORSED	HOSANNAS
HOPPUS	HORN	HORNWORK	HORSEFLY	HOSE
HOPPY	HORNBAG	HORNWORKS	HORSEHAIR	HOSED
HOPS	HORNBAGS	HORNWORM	HORSEHEAD	HOSEL
HOPSACK	HORNBEAK	HORNWORMS	HORSEHIDE	HOSELIKE
HOPSACKS	HORNBEAKS	HORNWORT	HORSELESS	HOSELS
HOPSCOTCH	HORNBEAM	HORNWORTS	HORSELIKE	HOSEMAN
HOPTOAD	HORNBEAMS	HORNWRACK	HORSEMAN	HOSEMEN
HOPTOADS	HORNBILL	HORNY	HORSEMEAT	HOSEN
HORA	HORNBILLS	HORNYHEAD	HORSEMEN	HOSEPIPE
HORAH	HORNBOOK	HORNYWINK	HORSEMINT	HOSEPIPES
HORAHS	HORNBOOKS	HOROEKA	HORSEPLAY	HOSER
HORAL	HORNBUG	HOROEKAS	HORSEPOND	HOSERS
HORARY	HORNBUGS	HOROKAKA	HORSEPOX	HOSES
HORAS	HORNDOG	HOROKAKAS	HORSERACE	HOSEY
HORCHATA	HORNDOGS	HOROLOGE	HORSES	HOSEYED
HORCHATAS	HORNED	HOROLOGER	HORSESHIT	HOSEYING
HORDE	HORNER	HOROLOGES	HORSESHOD	HOSEYS
HORDED	HORNERS	HOROLOGIA	HORSESHOE	HOSIER
HORDEIN	HORNET	HOROLOGIC	HORSETAIL	HOSIERIES
HORDEINS	HORNETS	HOROLOGY	HORSEWAY	HOSIERS
HORDEOLA	HORNFELS	HOROMETRY	HORSEWAYS	HOSIERY
HORDEOLUM	HORNFISH	HOROPITO	HORSEWEED	HOSING
HORDES	HORNFUL	HOROPITOS	HORSEWHIP	HOSPICE
HORDING	HORNFULS	HOROPTER	HORSEY	HOSPICES
HORDOCK	HORNGELD	HOROPTERS	HORSIE	HOSPITAGE
HORDOCKS	HORNGELDS	HOROSCOPE	HORSIER	HOSPITAL
HORE	HORNIER	HOROSCOPY	HORSIES	HOSPITALE
HOREHOUND	HORNIEST	HORRENT	HORSIEST	HOSPITALS
HORIATIKI	HORNILY	HORRIBLE	HORSILY	HOSPITIA
HORIZON	HORNINESS	HORRIBLES	HORSINESS	HOSPITIUM
HORIZONAL	HORNING	HORRIBLY	HORSING	HOSPODAR
HORIZONS	HORNINGS	HORRID	HORSINGS	HOSPODARS
HORK	HORNISH	HORRIDER	HORSON	HOSS
HORKED	HORNIST	HORRIDEST	HORSONS	HOSSES
HORKEY	HORNISTS	HORRIDLY	HORST	HOST
HORKEYS	HORNITO	HORRIFIC	HORSTE	HOSTA
HORKING	HORNITOS	HORRIFIED	HORSTES	HOSTAGE
HORKS	HORNLESS	HORRIFIES	HORSTS	HOSTAGES
HORLICKS	HORNLET	HORRIFY	HORSY	HOSTAS
HORME	HORNLETS	HORROR	HORTATION	HOSTED

HOSTEL	HOTE	HOTTERING	HOURPLATE	HOUTED
HOSTELED	HOTEL	HOTTERS	HOURS	HOUTING
HOSTELER	HOTELDOM	HOTTEST	HOUSE	HOUTINGS
HOSTELERS	HOTELDOMS	HOTTIE	HOUSEBOAT	HOUTS
HOSTELING	HOTELIER	HOTTIES	HOUSEBOY	HOVE
HOSTELLED	HOTELIERS	HOTTING	HOUSEBOYS	HOVEA
HOSTELLER	HOTELING	HOTTINGS	HOUSECARL	HOVEAS
HOSTELRY	HOTELINGS	HOTTISH	HOUSECOAT	HOVED
HOSTELS	HOTELLING	HOTTY	HOUSED	HOVEL
HOSTESS	HOTELMAN	HOUDAH	HOUSEFLY	HOVELED
HOSTESSED	HOTELMEN	HOUDAHS	HOUSEFUL	HOVELING
HOSTESSES	HOTELS	HOUDAN	HOUSEFULS	HOVELLED
HOSTIE	HOTEN	HOUDANS	HOUSEHOLD	HOVELLER
HOSTIES	HOTFOOT	HOUF	HOUSEKEEP	HOVELLERS
HOSTILE	HOTFOOTED	HOUFED	HOUSEKEPT	HOVELLING
HOSTILELY	HOTFOOTS	HOUFF	HOUSEL	HOVELS
HOSTILES	HOTHEAD	HOUFFED	HOUSELED	HOVEN
HOSTILITY	HOTHEADED	HOUFFING	HOUSELEEK	HOVER
HOSTING	HOTHEADS	HOUFFS	HOUSELESS	HOVERED
HOSTINGS	HOTHOUSE	HOUFING	HOUSELIKE	HOVERER
HOSTLER	HOTHOUSED	HOUFS	HOUSELINE	HOVERERS
HOSTLERS	HOTHOUSES	HOUGH	HOUSELING	HOVERFLY
HOSTLESS	HOTLINE	HOUGHED	HOUSELLED	HOVERING
HOSTLESSE	HOTLINER	HOUGHING	HOUSELS	HOVERPORT
HOSTLY	HOTLINERS	HOUGHS	HOUSEMAID	HOVERS
HOSTRIES	HOTLINES	HOUHERE	HOUSEMAN	HOVES
HOSTRY	HOTLINK	HOUHERES	HOUSEMATE	HOVING
HOSTS	HOTLINKS	HOUMMOS	HOUSEMEN	HOW
HOT	HOTLY	HOUMMOSES	HOUSER	HOWBE
HOTBED	HOTNESS	HOUMOUS	HOUSEROOM	HOWBEIT
HOTBEDS	HOTNESSES	HOUMOUSES	HOUSERS	HOWDAH
HOTBLOOD	HOTPLATE	HOUMUS	HOUSES	HOWDAHS
HOTBLOODS	HOTPLATES	HOUMUSES	HOUSESAT	HOWDIE
HOTBOX	HOTPOT	HOUND	HOUSESIT	HOWDIED
HOTBOXED	HOTPOTS	HOUNDED	HOUSESITS	HOWDIES
HOTBOXES	HOTPRESS	HOUNDER	HOUSETOP	HOWDY
HOTBOXING	HOTROD	HOUNDERS	HOUSETOPS	HOWDYING
HOTCAKE	HOTRODS	HOUNDFISH	HOUSEWIFE	HOWE
HOTCAKES	HOTS	HOUNDING	HOUSEWORK	HOWES
HOTCH	HOTSHOT	HOUNDS	HOUSEWRAP	HOWEVER
HOTCHED	HOTSHOTS	HOUNGAN	HOUSEY	HOWF
HOTCHES	HOTSPOT	HOUNGANS	HOUSIER	HOWFED
HOTCHING	HOTSPOTS	HOUR	HOUSIEST	HOWFF
HOTCHPOT	HOTSPUR	HOURGLASS	HOUSING	HOWFFED
HOTCHPOTS	HOTSPURS	HOURI	HOUSINGS	HOWFFING
HOTDOG	HOTTED	HOURIS	HOUSLING	HOWFFS
HOTDOGGED	HOTTENTOT	HOURLIES	HOUSLINGS	HOWFING
HOTDOGGER	HOTTER	HOURLONG	HOUSTONIA	HOWFS
HOTDOGS	HOTTERED	HOURLY	HOUT	HOWITZER

HOWITZERS	HRYVNIA	HUDDUP	HUIA	HUMANE
HOWK	HRYVNIAS	HUDNA	HUIAS	HUMANELY
HOWKED	HRYVNYA	HUDNAS	HUIC	HUMANER
HOWKER	HRYVNYAS	HUDUD	HUIPIL	HUMANEST
HOWKERS	HUANACO	HUDUDS	HUIPILES	HUMANHOOD
HOWKING	HUANACOS	HUE	HUIPILS	HUMANISE
HOWKS	HUAQUERO	HUED	HUIS	HUMANISED
HOWL	HUAQUEROS	HUELESS	HUISACHE	HUMANISER
HOWLBACK	HUARACHE	HUER	HUISACHES	HUMANISES
HOWLBACKS	HUARACHES	HUERS	HUISSIER	HUMANISM
HOWLED	HUARACHO	HUES	HUISSIERS	HUMANISMS
HOWLER	HUARACHOS	HUFF	HUITAIN	HUMANIST
HOWLERS	HUB	HUFFED	HUITAINS	HUMANISTS
HOWLET	HUBBIES	HUFFER	HULA	HUMANITY
HOWLETS	HUBBLIER	HUFFERS	HULAS	HUMANIZE
HOWLING	HUBBLIEST	HUFFIER	HULE	HUMANIZED
HOWLINGLY	HUBBLY	HUFFIEST	HULES	HUMANIZER
HOWLINGS	HUBBUB	HUFFILY	HULK	HUMANIZES
HOWLROUND	HUBBUBOO	HUFFINESS	HULKED	HUMANKIND
HOWLS	HUBBUBOOS	HUFFING	HULKIER	HUMANLIKE
HOWRE	HUBBUBS	HUFFINGS	HULKIEST	HUMANLY
HOWRES	HUBBY	HUFFISH	HULKING	HUMANNESS
HOWS	HUBCAP	HUFFISHLY	HULKS	HUMANOID
HOWSO	HUBCAPS	HUFFKIN	HULKY	HUMANOIDS
HOWSOEVER	HUBLESS	HUFFKINS	HULL	HUMANS
HOWTOWDIE	HUBRIS	HUFFS	HULLED	HUMAS
HOWZAT	HUBRISES	HUFFY	HULLER	HUMATE
HOWZIT	HUBRISTIC	HUG	HULLERS	HUMATES
HOX	HUBS	HUGE	HULLIER	HUMBLE
HOXED	HUCK	HUGELY	HULLIEST	HUMBLEBEE
HOXES	HUCKABACK	HUGENESS	HULLING	HUMBLED
HOXING	HUCKED	HUGEOUS	HULLO	HUMBLER
HOY	HUCKERY	HUGEOUSLY	HULLOA	HUMBLERS
HOYA	HUCKING	HUGER	HULLOAED	HUMBLES
HOYAS	HUCKLE	HUGEST	HULLOAING	HUMBLESSE
HOYDEN	HUCKLED	HUGGABLE	HULLOAS	HUMBLEST
HOYDENED	HUCKLES	HUGGED	HULLOED	HUMBLING
HOYDENING	HUCKLING	HUGGER	HULLOES	HUMBLINGS
HOYDENISH	HUCKS	HUGGERS	HULLOING	HUMBLY
HOYDENISM	HUCKSTER	HUGGIER	HULLOO	HUMBUCKER
HOYDENS	HUCKSTERS	HUGGIEST	HULLOOED	HUMBUG
HOYED	HUCKSTERY	HUGGING	HULLOOING	HUMBUGGED
HOYING	HUDDEN	HUGGY	HULLOOS	HUMBUGGER
HOYLE	HUDDLE	HUGS	HULLOS	HUMBUGS
HOYLES	HUDDLED	HUGY	HULLS	HUMBUZZ
HOYS	HUDDLER	HUH	HULLY	HUMBUZZES
HRYVNA	HUDDLERS	HUHU	HUM	HUMDINGER
HRYVNAS	HUDDLES	HUHUS	HUMA	HUMDRUM
HRYVNI	HUDDLING	HUI	HUMAN	HUMDRUMS

HUMECT	HUMLIE	HUMPBACKS	HUNGERED	HURDEN
HUMECTANT	HUMLIES	HUMPED	HUNGERFUL	HURDENS
HUMECTATE	HUMMABLE	HUMPEN	HUNGERING	HURDIES
HUMECTED	HUMMAUM	HUMPENS	HUNGERLY	HURDLE
HUMECTING	HUMMAUMS	HUMPER	HUNGERS	HURDLED
HUMECTIVE	HUMMED	HUMPERS	HUNGOVER	HURDLER
HUMECTS	HUMMEL	HUMPH	HUNGRIER	HURDLERS
HUMEFIED	HUMMELLED	HUMPHED	HUNGRIEST	HURDLES
HUMEFIES	HUMMELLER	HUMPHING	HUNGRILY	HURDLING
HUMEFY	HUMMELS	HUMPHS	HUNGRY	HURDLINGS
HUMEFYING	HUMMER	HUMPIER	HUNH	HURDS
HUMERAL	HUMMERS	HUMPIES	HUNK	HURL
HUMERALS	HUMMING	HUMPIEST	HUNKER	HURLBAT
HUMERI	HUMMINGS	HUMPINESS	HUNKERED	HURLBATS
HUMERUS	HUMMLE	HUMPING	HUNKERING	HURLED
HUMF	HUMMOCK	HUMPLESS	HUNKERS	HURLER
HUMFED	HUMMOCKED	HUMPLIKE	HUNKIER	HURLERS
HUMFING	HUMMOCKS	HUMPS	HUNKIEST	HURLEY
HUMFS	HUMMOCKY	HUMPTIES	HUNKS	HURLEYS
HUMHUM	HUMMUM	HUMPTY	HUNKSES	HURLIES
HUMHUMS	HUMMUMS	HUMPY	HUNKY	HURLING
HUMIC	HUMMUS	HUMS	HUNNISH	HURLINGS
HUMICOLE	HUMMUSES	HUMSTRUM	HUNS	HURLS
HUMICOLES	HUMOGEN	HUMSTRUMS	HUNT	HURLY
HUMID	HUMOGENS	HUMUNGOUS	HUNTABLE	HURRA
HUMIDER	HUMONGOUS	HUMUS	HUNTAWAY	HURRAED
HUMIDEST	HUMOR	HUMUSES	HUNTAWAYS	HURRAH
HUMIDEX	HUMORAL	HUMUSIER	HUNTED	HURRAHED
HUMIDEXES	HUMORALLY	HUMUSIEST	HUNTEDLY	HURRAHING
HUMIDICES	HUMORED	HUMUSY	HUNTER	HURRAHS
HUMIDIFY	HUMORESK	HUMVEE	HUNTERS	HURRAING
HUMIDITY	HUMORESKS	HUMVEES	HUNTING	HURRAS
HUMIDLY	HUMORFUL	HUN	HUNTINGS	HURRAY
HUMIDNESS	HUMORING	HUNCH	HUNTRESS	HURRAYED
HUMIDOR	HUMORIST	HUNCHBACK	HUNTS	HURRAYING
HUMIDORS	HUMORISTS	HUNCHED	HUNTSMAN	HURRAYS
HUMIFIED	HUMORLESS	HUNCHES	HUNTSMEN	HURRICANE
HUMIFIES	HUMOROUS	HUNCHING	HUP	HURRICANO
HUMIFY	HUMORS	HUNDO	HUPIRO	HURRIED
HUMIFYING	HUMORSOME	HUNDOS	HUPIROS	HURRIEDLY
HUMILIANT	HUMOUR	HUNDRED	HUPPAH	HURRIER
HUMILIATE	HUMOURED	HUNDREDER	HUPPAHS	HURRIERS
HUMILITY	HUMOURFUL	HUNDREDOR	HUPPED	HURRIES
HUMINT	HUMOURING	HUNDREDS	HUPPING	HURRY
HUMINTS	HUMOURS	HUNDREDTH	HUPPOT	HURRYING
HUMITE	HUMOUS	HUNG	HUPPOTH	HURRYINGS
HUMITES	HUMOUSES	HUNGAN	HUPS	HURST
HUMITURE	HUMP	HUNGANS	HURCHEON	HURSTS
HUMITURES	HUMPBACK	HUNGER	HURCHEONS	HURT

HURTER	HUSO	HUZZAING	HYDRAGOG	HYDROMA
HURTERS	HUSOS	HUZZAS	HYDRAGOGS	HYDROMAS
HURTFUL	HUSS	HUZZIES	HYDRANGEA	HYDROMATA
HURTFULLY	HUSSAR	HUZZY	HYDRANT	HYDROMEL
HURTING	HUSSARS	HWAN	HYDRANTH	HYDROMELS
HURTLE	HUSSES	HWYL	HYDRANTHS	HYDRONAUT
HURTLED	HUSSIES	HWYLS	HYDRANTS	HYDRONIC
HURTLES	HUSSIF	HYACINE	HYDRAS	HYDRONIUM
HURTLESS	HUSSIFS	HYACINES	HYDRASE	HYDROPATH
HURTLING	HUSSY	HYACINTH	HYDRASES	HYDROPIC
HURTS	HUSTINGS	HYACINTHS	HYDRASTIS	HYDROPS
HUSBAND	HUSTLE	HYAENA	HYDRATE	HYDROPSES
HUSBANDED	HUSTLED	HYAENAS	HYDRATED	HYDROPSY
HUSBANDER	HUSTLER	HYAENIC	HYDRATES	HYDROPTIC
HUSBANDLY	HUSTLERS	HYALIN	HYDRATING	HYDROPULT
HUSBANDRY	HUSTLES	HYALINE	HYDRATION	HYDROS
HUSBANDS	HUSTLING	HYALINES	HYDRATOR	HYDROSEED
HUSH	HUSTLINGS	HYALINISE	HYDRATORS	HYDROSERE
HUSHABIED	HUSWIFE	HYALINIZE	HYDRAULIC	HYDROSKI
HUSHABIES	HUSWIFES	HYALINS	HYDRAZIDE	HYDROSKIS
HUSHABY	HUSWIVES	HYALITE	HYDRAZINE	HYDROSOL
HUSHABYE	HUT	HYALITES	HYDRAZOIC	HYDROSOLS
HUSHED	HUTCH	HYALOGEN	HYDREMIA	HYDROSOMA
HUSHEDLY	HUTCHED	HYALOGENS	HYDREMIAS	HYDROSOME
HUSHER	HUTCHES	HYALOID	HYDRIA	HYDROSTAT
HUSHERED	HUTCHIE	HYALOIDS	HYDRIAE	HYDROUS
HUSHERING	HUTCHIES	HYALONEMA	HYDRIC	HYDROVANE
HUSHERS	HUTCHING	HYBRID	HYDRID	HYDROXIDE
HUSHES	HUTIA	HYBRIDISE	HYDRIDE	HYDROXIUM
HUSHFUL	HUTIAS	HYBRIDISM	HYDRIDES	HYDROXY
HUSHIER	HUTLIKE	HYBRIDIST	HYDRIDS	HYDROXYL
HUSHIEST	HUTMENT	HYBRIDITY	HYDRILLA	HYDROXYLS
HUSHING	HUTMENTS	HYBRIDIZE	HYDRILLAS	HYDROZOA
HUSHPUPPY	HUTS	HYBRIDOMA	HYDRIODIC	HYDROZOAN
HUSHY	HUTTED	HYBRIDOUS	HYDRO	HYDROZOON
HUSK	HUTTING	HYBRIDS	HYDROCAST	HYDYNE
HUSKED	HUTTINGS	HYBRIS	HYDROCELE	HYDYNES
HUSKER	HUTZPA	HYBRISES	HYDROFOIL	HYE
HUSKERS	HUTZPAH	HYBRISTIC	HYDROGEL	HYED
HUSKIER	HUTZPAHS	HYDANTOIN	HYDROGELS	HYEING
HUSKIES	HUTZPAS	HYDATHODE	HYDROGEN	HYEN
HUSKIEST	HUZOOR	HYDATID	HYDROGENS	HYENA
HUSKILY	HUZOORS	HYDATIDS	HYDROID	HYENAS
HUSKINESS	HUZZA	HYDATOID	HYDROIDS	HYENIC
HUSKING	HUZZAED	HYDRA	HYDROLASE	HYENINE
HUSKINGS	HUZZAH	HYDRACID	HYDROLOGY	HYENOID
HUSKLIKE	HUZZAHED	HYDRACIDS	HYDROLYSE	HYENS
HUSKS	HUZZAHING	HYDRAE	HYDROLYTE	HYES
HUSKY	HUZZAHS	HYDRAEMIA	HYDROLYZE	HYETAL

H

HYETOLOGY	HYMENAEAL	HYPERACID	HYPHENIZE	HYPOGEA
HYGEIST	HYMENAEAN	HYPERARID	HYPHENS	HYPOGEAL
HYGEISTS	HYMENAL	HYPERBOLA	HYPHIES	HYPOGEAN
HYGGE	HYMENEAL	HYPERBOLE	HYPHY	HYPOGENE
HYGGES	HYMENEALS	HYPERCUBE	HYPING	HYPOGENIC
HYGIEIST	HYMENEAN	HYPEREMIA	HYPINGS	HYPOGEOUS
HYGIEISTS	HYMENEANS	HYPEREMIC	HYPINOSES	HYPOGEUM
HYGIENE	HYMENIA	HYPERER	HYPINOSIS	HYPOGYNY
HYGIENES	HYMENIAL	HYPEREST	HYPNIC	HYPOID
HYGIENIC	HYMENIUM	HYPERFINE	HYPNICS	HYPOIDS
HYGIENICS	HYMENIUMS	HYPERGAMY	HYPNOGENY	HYPOING
HYGIENIST	HYMENS	HYPERGOL	HYPNOID	HYPOMANIA
HYGRISTOR	HYMN	HYPERGOLS	HYPNOIDAL	HYPOMANIC
HYGRODEIK	HYMNAL	HYPERICIN	HYPNOLOGY	HYPOMORPH
HYGROLOGY	HYMNALS	HYPERICUM	HYPNONE	HYPONASTY
HYGROMA	HYMNARIES	HYPERLINK	HYPNONES	HYPONEA
HYGROMAS	HYMNARY	HYPERMART	HYPNOSES	HYPONEAS
HYGROMATA	HYMNBOOK	HYPERNOVA	HYPNOSIS	HYPONOIA
HYGROPHIL	HYMNBOOKS	HYPERNYM	HYPNOTEE	HYPONOIAS
HYGROSTAT	HYMNED	HYPERNYMS	HYPNOTEES	HYPONYM
HYING	HYMNIC	HYPERNYMY	HYPNOTIC	HYPONYMS
HYKE	HYMNING	HYPERON	HYPNOTICS	HYPONYMY
HYKES	HYMNIST	HYPERONS	HYPNOTISE	HYPOPHYGE
HYLA	HYMNISTS	HYPEROPE	HYPNOTISM	HYPOPLOID
HYLAS	HYMNLESS	HYPEROPES	HYPNOTIST	HYPOPNEA
HYLDING	HYMNLIKE	HYPEROPIA	HYPNOTIZE	HYPOPNEAS
HYLDINGS	HYMNODIES	HYPEROPIC	HYPNOTOID	HYPOPNEIC
HYLE	HYMNODIST	HYPERPNEA	HYPNUM	HYPOPNOEA
HYLEG	HYMNODY	HYPERPURE	HYPNUMS	HYPOPYON
HYLEGS	HYMNOLOGY	HYPERREAL	HYPO	HYPOPYONS
HYLES	HYMNS	HYPERS	HYPOACID	HYPOS
HYLIC	HYNDE	HYPERTEXT	HYPOBARIC	HYPOSTOME
HYLICISM	HYNDES	HYPES	HYPOBLAST	HYPOSTYLE
HYLICISMS	HYOID	HYPESTER	HYPOBOLE	HYPOTAXES
HYLICIST	HYOIDAL	HYPESTERS	HYPOBOLES	HYPOTAXIS
HYLICISTS	HYOIDEAN	HYPETHRAL	HYPOCAUST	HYPOTHEC
HYLISM	HYOIDS	HYPHA	HYPOCIST	HYPOTHECA
HYLISMS	HYOSCINE	HYPHAE	HYPOCISTS	HYPOTHECS
HYLIST	HYOSCINES	HYPHAEMIA	HYPOCOTYL	HYPOTONIA
HYLISTS	HYP	HYPHAL	HYPOCRISY	HYPOTONIC
HYLOBATE	HYPALGIA	HYPHEMIA	HYPOCRITE	HYPOXEMIA
HYLOBATES	HYPALGIAS	HYPHEMIAS	HYPODERM	HYPOXEMIC
HYLOIST	HYPALLAGE	HYPHEN	HYPODERMA	HYPOXIA
HYLOISTS	HYPANTHIA	HYPHENATE	HYPODERMS	HYPOXIAS
HYLOPHYTE	HYPATE	HYPHENED	HYPOED	HYPOXIC
HYLOZOIC	HYPATES	HYPHENIC	HYPOGAEA	HYPPED
HYLOZOISM	HYPE	HYPHENING	HYPOGAEAL	HYPPING
HYLOZOIST	HYPED	HYPHENISE	HYPOGAEAN	HYPS
HYMEN	HYPER	HYPHENISM	HYPOGAEUM	HYPURAL

HYRACES	HYRAXES	HYSSOPS	HYSTERICS	HYTHES
HYRACOID	HYSON	HYSTERIA	HYSTEROID	
HYRACOIDS	HYSONS	HYSTERIAS	HYTE	
HYRAX	HYSSOP	HYSTERIC	HYTHE	

H

I

IAMB	ICECAPPED	ICHOR	ICONIZE	IDEALNESS
IAMBI	ICECAPS	ICHOROUS	ICONIZED	IDEALOGUE
IAMBIC	ICED	ICHORS	ICONIZES	IDEALOGY
IAMBICS	ICEFALL	ICHS	ICONIZING	IDEALS
IAMBIST	ICEFALLS	ICHTHIC	ICONOLOGY	IDEAS
IAMBISTS	ICEFIELD	ICHTHYIC	ICONOSTAS	IDEATA
IAMBS	ICEFIELDS	ICHTHYOID	ICONS	IDEATE
IAMBUS	ICEFISH	ICHTHYS	ICTAL	IDEATED
IAMBUSES	ICEFISHED	ICHTHYSES	ICTERIC	IDEATES
IANTHINE	ICEFISHES	ICICLE	ICTERICAL	IDEATING
IATRIC	ICEHOUSE	ICICLED	ICTERICS	IDEATION
IATRICAL	ICEHOUSES	ICICLES	ICTERID	IDEATIONS
IATROGENY	ICEKHANA	ICIER	ICTERIDS	IDEATIVE
IBADAH	ICEKHANAS	ICIEST	ICTERINE	IDEATUM
IBADAT	ICELESS	ICILY	ICTERUS	IDEE
IBERIS	ICELIKE	ICINESS	ICTERUSES	IDEES
IBERISES	ICEMAKER	ICINESSES	ICTIC	IDEM
IBEX	ICEMAKERS	ICING	ICTUS	IDENT
IBEXES	ICEMAN	ICINGS	ICTUSES	IDENTIC
IBICES	ICEMEN	ICK	ICY	IDENTICAL
IBIDEM	ICEPACK	ICKER	ID	IDENTIFY
IBIS	ICEPACKS	ICKERS	IDANT	IDENTIKIT
IBISES	ICER	ICKIER	IDANTS	IDENTITY
IBOGAINE	ICERS	ICKIEST	IDE	IDENTS
IBOGAINES	ICES	ICKILY	IDEA	IDEOGRAM
IBRIK	ICESCAPE	ICKINESS	IDEAED	IDEOGRAMS
IBRIKS	ICESCAPES	ICKLE	IDEAL	IDEOGRAPH
IBUPROFEN	ICESTONE	ICKLER	IDEALESS	IDEOLOGIC
ICE	ICESTONES	ICKLEST	IDEALISE	IDEOLOGUE
ICEBALL	ICEWINE	ICKS	IDEALISED	IDEOLOGY
ICEBALLS	ICEWINES	ICKY	IDEALISER	IDEOMOTOR
ICEBERG	ICEWORM	ICON	IDEALISES	IDEOPHONE
ICEBERGS	ICEWORMS	ICONES	IDEALISM	IDEOPOLIS
ICEBLINK	ICH	ICONIC	IDEALISMS	IDES
ICEBLINKS	ICHABOD	ICONICAL	IDEALIST	IDIOBLAST
ICEBOAT	ICHED	ICONICITY	IDEALISTS	IDIOCIES
ICEBOATED	ICHES	ICONIFIED	IDEALITY	IDIOCRACY
ICEBOATER	ICHING	ICONIFIES	IDEALIZE	IDIOCY
ICEBOATS	ICHNEUMON	ICONIFY	IDEALIZED	IDIOGRAM
ICEBOUND	ICHNITE	ICONISE	IDEALIZER	IDIOGRAMS
ICEBOX	ICHNITES	ICONISED	IDEALIZES	IDIOGRAPH
ICEBOXES	ICHNOLITE	ICONISES	IDEALLESS	IDIOLECT
ICECAP	ICHNOLOGY	ICONISING	IDEALLY	IDIOLECTS

IDIOM	IDOLISMS	IGLUS	IGUANID	ILLATIVE
IDIOMATIC	IDOLIST	IGNARO	IGUANIDS	ILLATIVES
IDIOMS	IDOLISTS	IGNAROES	IGUANODON	ILLAWARRA
IDIOPATHY	IDOLIZE	IGNAROS	IHRAM	ILLEGAL
IDIOPHONE	IDOLIZED	IGNATIA	IHRAMS	ILLEGALLY
IDIOPLASM	IDOLIZER	IGNATIAS	IJTIHAD	ILLEGALS
IDIOT	IDOLIZERS	IGNEOUS	IJTIHADS	ILLEGIBLE
IDIOTCIES	IDOLIZES	IGNESCENT	IKAN	ILLEGIBLY
IDIOTCY	IDOLIZING	IGNIFIED	IKANS	ILLER
IDIOTIC	IDOLON	IGNIFIES	IKAT	ILLEST
IDIOTICAL	IDOLS	IGNIFY	IKATS	ILLIAD
IDIOTICON	IDOLUM	IGNIFYING	IKEBANA	ILLIADS
IDIOTISH	IDONEITY	IGNITABLE	IKEBANAS	ILLIBERAL
IDIOTISM	IDONEOUS	IGNITE	IKON	ILLICIT
IDIOTISMS	IDPOL	IGNITED	IKONS	ILLICITLY
IDIOTS	IDPOLS	IGNITER	ILEA	ILLIMITED
IDIOTYPE	IDS	IGNITERS	ILEAC	ILLINIUM
IDIOTYPES	IDYL	IGNITES	ILEAL	ILLINIUMS
IDIOTYPIC	IDYLIST	IGNITIBLE	ILEITIDES	ILLIPE
IDLE	IDYLISTS	IGNITING	ILEITIS	ILLIPES
IDLED	IDYLL	IGNITION	ILEITISES	ILLIQUID
IDLEHOOD	IDYLLIAN	IGNITIONS	ILEOSTOMY	ILLISION
IDLEHOODS	IDYLLIC	IGNITOR	ILEUM	ILLISIONS
IDLENESS	IDYLLIST	IGNITORS	ILEUS	ILLITE
IDLER	IDYLLISTS	IGNITRON	ILEUSES	ILLITES
IDLERS	IDYLLS	IGNITRONS	ILEX	ILLITIC
IDLES	IDYLS	IGNOBLE	ILEXES	ILLNESS
IDLESSE	IF	IGNOBLER	ILIA	ILLNESSES
IDLESSES	IFF	IGNOBLEST	ILIAC	ILLOGIC
IDLEST	IFFIER	IGNOBLY	ILIACI	ILLOGICAL
IDLING	IFFIEST	IGNOMIES	ILIACUS	ILLOGICS
IDLINGS	IFFILY	IGNOMINY	ILIACUSES	ILLS
IDLY	IFFINESS	IGNOMY	ILIAD	ILLTH
IDOCRASE	IFFY	IGNORABLE	ILIADS	ILLTHS
IDOCRASES	IFS	IGNORAMI	ILIAL	ILLUDE
IDOL	IFTAR	IGNORAMUS	ILICES	ILLUDED
IDOLA	IFTARS	IGNORANCE	ILIUM	ILLUDES
IDOLATER	IGAD	IGNORANT	ILK	ILLUDING
IDOLATERS	IGAPO	IGNORANTS	ILKA	ILLUME
IDOLATOR	IGAPOS	IGNORE	ILKADAY	ILLUMED
IDOLATORS	IGARAPE	IGNORED	ILKADAYS	ILLUMES
IDOLATRY	IGARAPES	IGNORER	ILKS	ILLUMINE
IDOLISE	IGG	IGNORERS	ILL	ILLUMINED
IDOLISED	IGGED	IGNORES	ILLAPSE	ILLUMINER
IDOLISER	IGGING	IGNORING	ILLAPSED	ILLUMINES
IDOLISERS	IGGS	IGUANA	ILLAPSES	ILLUMING
IDOLISES	IGLOO	IGUANAS	ILLAPSING	ILLUPI
IDOLISING	IGLOOS	IGUANIAN	ILLATION	ILLUPIS
IDOLISM	IGLU	IGUANIANS	ILLATIONS	ILLUSION

ILLUSIONS	IMAUMS	IMBOLDEN	IMIDO	IMMERGING
ILLUSIVE	IMBALANCE	IMBOLDENS	IMIDS	IMMERSE
ILLUSORY	IMBALM	IMBORDER	IMINAZOLE	IMMERSED
ILLUVIA	IMBALMED	IMBORDERS	IMINE	IMMERSER
ILLUVIAL	IMBALMER	IMBOSK	IMINES	IMMERSERS
ILLUVIATE	IMBALMERS	IMBOSKED	IMINO	IMMERSES
ILLUVIUM	IMBALMING	IMBOSKING	IMINOUREA	IMMERSING
ILLUVIUMS	IMBALMS	IMBOSKS	IMIPENEM	IMMERSION
ILLY	IMBAR	IMBOSOM	IMIPENEMS	IMMERSIVE
ILMENITE	IMBARK	IMBOSOMED	IMITABLE	IMMESH
ILMENITES	IMBARKED	IMBOSOMS	IMITANCY	IMMESHED
IMAGE	IMBARKING	IMBOSS	IMITANT	IMMESHES
IMAGEABLE	IMBARKS	IMBOSSED	IMITANTS	IMMESHING
IMAGED	IMBARRED	IMBOSSES	IMITATE	IMMEW
IMAGELESS	IMBARRING	IMBOSSING	IMITATED	IMMEWED
IMAGER	IMBARS	IMBOWER	IMITATES	IMMEWING
IMAGERIES	IMBASE	IMBOWERED	IMITATING	IMMEWS
IMAGERS	IMBASED	IMBOWERS	IMITATION	IMMIES
IMAGERY	IMBASES	IMBRANGLE	IMITATIVE	IMMIGRANT
IMAGES	IMBASING	IMBRAST	IMITATOR	IMMIGRATE
IMAGINAL	IMBATHE	IMBREX	IMITATORS	IMMINENCE
IMAGINARY	IMBATHED	IMBRICATE	IMMA	IMMINENCY
IMAGINE	IMBATHES	IMBRICES	IMMANACLE	IMMINENT
IMAGINED	IMBATHING	IMBROGLIO	IMMANE	IMMINGLE
IMAGINEER	IMBECILE	IMBROWN	IMMANELY	IMMINGLED
IMAGINER	IMBECILES	IMBROWNED	IMMANENCE	IMMINGLES
IMAGINERS	IMBECILIC	IMBROWNS	IMMANENCY	IMMINUTE
IMAGINES	IMBED	IMBRUE	IMMANENT	IMMISSION
IMAGING	IMBEDDED	IMBRUED	IMMANITY	IMMIT
IMAGINGS	IMBEDDING	IMBRUES	IMMANTLE	IMMITS
IMAGINING	IMBEDS	IMBRUING	IMMANTLED	IMMITTED
IMAGINIST	IMBIBE	IMBRUTE	IMMANTLES	IMMITTING
IMAGISM	IMBIBED	IMBRUTED	IMMASK	IMMIX
IMAGISMS	IMBIBER	IMBRUTES	IMMASKED	IMMIXED
IMAGIST	IMBIBERS	IMBRUTING	IMMASKING	IMMIXES
IMAGISTIC	IMBIBES	IMBUE	IMMASKS	IMMIXING
IMAGISTS	IMBIBING	IMBUED	IMMATURE	IMMIXTURE
IMAGO	IMBITTER	IMBUEMENT	IMMATURER	IMMOBILE
IMAGOES	IMBITTERS	IMBUES	IMMATURES	IMMODEST
IMAGOS	IMBIZO	IMBUING	IMMEDIACY	IMMODESTY
IMAM	IMBIZOS	IMBURSE	IMMEDIATE	IMMOLATE
IMAMATE	IMBLAZE	IMBURSED	IMMENSE	IMMOLATED
IMAMATES	IMBLAZED	IMBURSES	IMMENSELY	IMMOLATES
IMAMS	IMBLAZES	IMBURSING	IMMENSER	IMMOLATOR
IMARET	IMBLAZING	IMID	IMMENSEST	IMMOMENT
IMARETS	IMBODIED	IMIDAZOLE	IMMENSITY	IMMORAL
IMARI	IMBODIES	IMIDE	IMMERGE	IMMORALLY
IMARIS	IMBODY	IMIDES	IMMERGED	IMMORTAL
IMAUM	IMBODYING	IMIDIC	IMMERGES	IMMORTALS

IMMOTILE	IMPALE	IMPAWNING	IMPETRATE	IMPLEXION
IMMOVABLE	IMPALED	IMPAWNS	IMPETUOUS	IMPLICATE
IMMOVABLY	IMPALER	IMPEACH	IMPETUS	IMPLICIT
IMMUNE	IMPALERS	IMPEACHED	IMPETUSES	IMPLICITY
IMMUNER	IMPALES	IMPEACHER	IMPHEE	IMPLIED
IMMUNES	IMPALING	IMPEACHES	IMPHEES	IMPLIEDLY
IMMUNEST	IMPANATE	IMPEARL	IMPI	IMPLIES
IMMUNISE	IMPANEL	IMPEARLED	IMPIES	IMPLODE
IMMUNISED	IMPANELED	IMPEARLS	IMPIETIES	IMPLODED
IMMUNISER	IMPANELS	IMPECCANT	IMPIETY	IMPLODENT
IMMUNISES	IMPANNEL	IMPED	IMPING	IMPLODES
IMMUNITY	IMPANNELS	IMPEDANCE	IMPINGE	IMPLODING
IMMUNIZE	IMPARITY	IMPEDE	IMPINGED	IMPLORE
IMMUNIZED	IMPARK	IMPEDED	IMPINGENT	IMPLORED
IMMUNIZER	IMPARKED	IMPEDER	IMPINGER	IMPLORER
IMMUNIZES	IMPARKING	IMPEDERS	IMPINGERS	IMPLORERS
IMMUNOGEN	IMPARKS	IMPEDES	IMPINGES	IMPLORES
IMMURE	IMPARL	IMPEDING	IMPINGING	IMPLORING
IMMURED	IMPARLED	IMPEDOR	IMPINGS	IMPLOSION
IMMURES	IMPARLING	IMPEDORS	IMPIOUS	IMPLOSIVE
IMMURING	IMPARLS	IMPEL	IMPIOUSLY	IMPLUNGE
IMMUTABLE	IMPART	IMPELLED	IMPIS	IMPLUNGED
IMMUTABLY	IMPARTED	IMPELLENT	IMPISH	IMPLUNGES
IMMY	IMPARTER	IMPELLER	IMPISHLY	IMPLUVIA
IMP	IMPARTERS	IMPELLERS	IMPLANT	IMPLUVIUM
IMPACABLE	IMPARTIAL	IMPELLING	IMPLANTED	IMPLY
IMPACT	IMPARTING	IMPELLOR	IMPLANTER	IMPLYING
IMPACTED	IMPARTS	IMPELLORS	IMPLANTS	IMPOCKET
IMPACTER	IMPASSE	IMPELS	IMPLATE	IMPOCKETS
IMPACTERS	IMPASSES	IMPEND	IMPLATED	IMPOLDER
IMPACTFUL	IMPASSION	IMPENDED	IMPLATES	IMPOLDERS
IMPACTING	IMPASSIVE	IMPENDENT	IMPLATING	IMPOLICY
IMPACTION	IMPASTE	IMPENDING	IMPLEACH	IMPOLITE
IMPACTITE	IMPASTED	IMPENDS	IMPLEAD	IMPOLITER
IMPACTIVE	IMPASTES	IMPENNATE	IMPLEADED	IMPOLITIC
IMPACTOR	IMPASTING	IMPERATOR	IMPLEADER	IMPONE
IMPACTORS	IMPASTO	IMPERFECT	IMPLEADS	IMPONED
IMPACTS	IMPASTOED	IMPERIA	IMPLED	IMPONENT
IMPAINT	IMPASTOS	IMPERIAL	IMPLEDGE	IMPONENTS
IMPAINTED	IMPATIENS	IMPERIALS	IMPLEDGED	IMPONES
IMPAINTS	IMPATIENT	IMPERIL	IMPLEDGES	IMPONING
IMPAIR	IMPAVE	IMPERILED	IMPLEMENT	IMPOROUS
IMPAIRED	IMPAVED	IMPERILS	IMPLETE	IMPORT
IMPAIRER	IMPAVES	IMPERIOUS	IMPLETED	IMPORTANT
IMPAIRERS	IMPAVID	IMPERIUM	IMPLETES	IMPORTED
IMPAIRING	IMPAVIDLY	IMPERIUMS	IMPLETING	IMPORTER
IMPAIRS	IMPAVING	IMPETICOS	IMPLETION	IMPORTERS
IMPALA	IMPAWN	IMPETIGO	IMPLEX	IMPORTING
IMPALAS	IMPAWNED	IMPETIGOS	IMPLEXES	IMPORTS

two to nine letter words | 287

IMPORTUNE	IMPRESTS	IMPURPLES	INAUGURAL	INCAVED
IMPOSABLE	IMPRIMIS	IMPUTABLE	INAURATE	INCAVES
IMPOSE	IMPRINT	IMPUTABLY	INAURATED	INCAVI
IMPOSED	IMPRINTED	IMPUTE	INAURATES	INCAVING
IMPOSER	IMPRINTER	IMPUTED	INBEING	INCAVO
IMPOSERS	IMPRINTS	IMPUTER	INBEINGS	INCEDE
IMPOSES	IMPRISON	IMPUTERS	INBENT	INCEDED
IMPOSEX	IMPRISONS	IMPUTES	INBOARD	INCEDES
IMPOSEXES	IMPRO	IMPUTING	INBOARDS	INCEDING
IMPOSING	IMPROBITY	IMSHI	INBORN	INCEL
IMPOST	IMPROMPTU	IMSHY	INBOUND	INCELS
IMPOSTED	IMPROPER	IN	INBOUNDED	INCENSE
IMPOSTER	IMPROS	INABILITY	INBOUNDS	INCENSED
IMPOSTERS	IMPROV	INACTION	INBOX	INCENSER
IMPOSTING	IMPROVE	INACTIONS	INBOXES	INCENSERS
IMPOSTOR	IMPROVED	INACTIVE	INBREAK	INCENSES
IMPOSTORS	IMPROVER	INAIDABLE	INBREAKS	INCENSING
IMPOSTS	IMPROVERS	INAMORATA	INBREATHE	INCENSOR
IMPOSTUME	IMPROVES	INAMORATI	INBRED	INCENSORS
IMPOSTURE	IMPROVING	INAMORATO	INBREDS	INCENSORY
IMPOT	IMPROVISE	INANE	INBREED	INCENT
IMPOTENCE	IMPROVS	INANELY	INBREEDER	INCENTED
IMPOTENCY	IMPRUDENT	INANENESS	INBREEDS	INCENTER
IMPOTENT	IMPS	INANER	INBRING	INCENTERS
IMPOTENTS	IMPSONITE	INANES	INBRINGS	INCENTING
IMPOTS	IMPUDENCE	INANEST	INBROUGHT	INCENTIVE
IMPOUND	IMPUDENCY	INANGA	INBUILT	INCENTRE
IMPOUNDED	IMPUDENT	INANGAS	INBURNING	INCENTRES
IMPOUNDER	IMPUGN	INANIMATE	INBURST	INCENTS
IMPOUNDS	IMPUGNED	INANITIES	INBURSTS	INCEPT
IMPOWER	IMPUGNER	INANITION	INBY	INCEPTED
IMPOWERED	IMPUGNERS	INANITY	INBYE	INCEPTING
IMPOWERS	IMPUGNING	INAPT	INCAGE	INCEPTION
IMPRECATE	IMPUGNS	INAPTER	INCAGED	INCEPTIVE
IMPRECISE	IMPULSE	INAPTEST	INCAGES	INCEPTOR
IMPREGN	IMPULSED	INAPTLY	INCAGING	INCEPTORS
IMPREGNED	IMPULSES	INAPTNESS	INCANT	INCEPTS
IMPREGNS	IMPULSING	INARABLE	INCANTED	INCERTAIN
IMPRESA	IMPULSION	INARCH	INCANTING	INCESSANT
IMPRESARI	IMPULSIVE	INARCHED	INCANTS	INCEST
IMPRESAS	IMPUNDULU	INARCHES	INCAPABLE	INCESTS
IMPRESE	IMPUNITY	INARCHING	INCAPABLY	INCH
IMPRESES	IMPURE	INARM	INCARNATE	INCHASE
IMPRESS	IMPURELY	INARMED	INCASE	INCHASED
IMPRESSE	IMPURER	INARMING	INCASED	INCHASES
IMPRESSED	IMPUREST	INARMS	INCASES	INCHASING
IMPRESSER	IMPURITY	INASMUCH	INCASING	INCHED
IMPRESSES	IMPURPLE	INAUDIBLE	INCAUTION	INCHER
IMPREST	IMPURPLED	INAUDIBLY	INCAVE	INCHERS

INCHES	INCLES	INCREASER	INCUSED	INDEXED
INCHING	INCLINE	INCREASES	INCUSES	INDEXER
INCHMEAL	INCLINED	INCREATE	INCUSING	INDEXERS
INCHOATE	INCLINER	INCREMATE	INCUT	INDEXES
INCHOATED	INCLINERS	INCREMENT	INCUTS	INDEXICAL
INCHOATES	INCLINES	INCRETION	INDABA	INDEXING
INCHPIN	INCLINING	INCRETORY	INDABAS	INDEXINGS
INCHPINS	INCLIP	INCROSS	INDAGATE	INDEXLESS
INCHTAPE	INCLIPPED	INCROSSED	INDAGATED	INDIA
INCHTAPES	INCLIPS	INCROSSES	INDAGATES	INDIAS
INCHWORM	INCLOSE	INCRUST	INDAGATOR	INDICAN
INCHWORMS	INCLOSED	INCRUSTED	INDAMIN	INDICANS
INCIDENCE	INCLOSER	INCRUSTS	INDAMINE	INDICANT
INCIDENT	INCLOSERS	INCUBATE	INDAMINES	INDICANTS
INCIDENTS	INCLOSES	INCUBATED	INDAMINS	INDICATE
INCIPIENT	INCLOSING	INCUBATES	INDART	INDICATED
INCIPIT	INCLOSURE	INCUBATOR	INDARTED	INDICATES
INCIPITS	INCLUDE	INCUBI	INDARTING	INDICATOR
INCISAL	INCLUDED	INCUBOUS	INDARTS	INDICES
INCISE	INCLUDES	INCUBUS	INDEBTED	INDICIA
INCISED	INCLUDING	INCUBUSES	INDECENCY	INDICIAL
INCISES	INCLUSION	INCUDAL	INDECENT	INDICIAS
INCISING	INCLUSIVE	INCUDATE	INDECORUM	INDICIUM
INCISION	INCOG	INCUDES	INDEED	INDICIUMS
INCISIONS	INCOGNITA	INCULCATE	INDEEDY	INDICT
INCISIVE	INCOGNITO	INCULPATE	INDELIBLE	INDICTED
INCISOR	INCOGS	INCULT	INDELIBLY	INDICTEE
INCISORS	INCOME	INCUMBENT	INDEMNIFY	INDICTEES
INCISORY	INCOMER	INCUMBER	INDEMNITY	INDICTER
INCISURAL	INCOMERS	INCUMBERS	INDENE	INDICTERS
INCISURE	INCOMES	INCUNABLE	INDENES	INDICTING
INCISURES	INCOMING	INCUR	INDENT	INDICTION
INCITABLE	INCOMINGS	INCURABLE	INDENTED	INDICTOR
INCITANT	INCOMMODE	INCURABLY	INDENTER	INDICTORS
INCITANTS	INCOMPACT	INCURIOUS	INDENTERS	INDICTS
INCITE	INCONDITE	INCURRED	INDENTING	INDIE
INCITED	INCONIE	INCURRENT	INDENTION	INDIES
INCITER	INCONNU	INCURRING	INDENTOR	INDIGEN
INCITERS	INCONNUE	INCURS	INDENTORS	INDIGENCE
INCITES	INCONNUES	INCURSION	INDENTS	INDIGENCY
INCITING	INCONNUS	INCURSIVE	INDENTURE	INDIGENE
INCIVIL	INCONY	INCURVATE	INDEVOUT	INDIGENES
INCIVISM	INCORPSE	INCURVE	INDEW	INDIGENS
INCIVISMS	INCORPSED	INCURVED	INDEWED	INDIGENT
INCLASP	INCORPSES	INCURVES	INDEWING	INDIGENTS
INCLASPED	INCORRECT	INCURVING	INDEWS	INDIGEST
INCLASPS	INCORRUPT	INCURVITY	INDEX	INDIGESTS
INCLE	INCREASE	INCUS	INDEXABLE	INDIGN
INCLEMENT	INCREASED	INCUSE	INDEXAL	INDIGNANT

INDIGNIFY	INDOXYLS	INDURATE	INERTEST	INFAUNA
INDIGNITY	INDRAFT	INDURATED	INERTIA	INFAUNAE
INDIGNLY	INDRAFTS	INDURATES	INERTIAE	INFAUNAL
INDIGO	INDRAUGHT	INDUSIA	INERTIAL	INFAUNAS
INDIGOES	INDRAWN	INDUSIAL	INERTIAS	INFAUST
INDIGOID	INDRENCH	INDUSIATE	INERTLY	INFECT
INDIGOIDS	INDRI	INDUSIUM	INERTNESS	INFECTANT
INDIGOS	INDRIS	INDUSTRY	INERTS	INFECTED
INDIGOTIC	INDRISES	INDUVIAE	INERUDITE	INFECTER
INDIGOTIN	INDUBIOUS	INDUVIAL	INESSIVE	INFECTERS
INDINAVIR	INDUCE	INDUVIATE	INESSIVES	INFECTING
INDIRECT	INDUCED	INDWELL	INEXACT	INFECTION
INDIRUBIN	INDUCER	INDWELLED	INEXACTLY	INFECTIVE
INDISPOSE	INDUCERS	INDWELLER	INEXPERT	INFECTOR
INDITE	INDUCES	INDWELLS	INEXPERTS	INFECTORS
INDITED	INDUCIAE	INDWELT	INFALL	INFECTS
INDITER	INDUCIBLE	INDY	INFALLING	INFECUND
INDITERS	INDUCING	INDYREF	INFALLS	INFEED
INDITES	INDUCT	INDYREFS	INFAME	INFEEDS
INDITING	INDUCTED	INEARTH	INFAMED	INFEFT
INDIUM	INDUCTEE	INEARTHED	INFAMES	INFEFTED
INDIUMS	INDUCTEES	INEARTHS	INFAMIES	INFEFTING
INDIVIDUA	INDUCTILE	INEBRIANT	INFAMING	INFEFTS
INDOCIBLE	INDUCTING	INEBRIATE	INFAMISE	INFELT
INDOCILE	INDUCTION	INEBRIETY	INFAMISED	INFEOFF
INDOL	INDUCTIVE	INEBRIOUS	INFAMISES	INFEOFFED
INDOLE	INDUCTOR	INEDIBLE	INFAMIZE	INFEOFFS
INDOLENCE	INDUCTORS	INEDIBLY	INFAMIZED	INFER
INDOLENCY	INDUCTS	INEDITA	INFAMIZES	INFERABLE
INDOLENT	INDUE	INEDITED	INFAMOUS	INFERABLY
INDOLES	INDUED	INEFFABLE	INFAMY	INFERE
INDOLS	INDUES	INEFFABLY	INFANCIES	INFERENCE
INDOOR	INDUING	INELASTIC	INFANCY	INFERIAE
INDOORS	INDULGE	INELEGANT	INFANT	INFERIBLE
INDORSE	INDULGED	INEPT	INFANTA	INFERIOR
INDORSED	INDULGENT	INEPTER	INFANTAS	INFERIORS
INDORSEE	INDULGER	INEPTEST	INFANTE	INFERNAL
INDORSEES	INDULGERS	INEPTLY	INFANTEER	INFERNO
INDORSER	INDULGES	INEPTNESS	INFANTES	INFERNOS
INDORSERS	INDULGING	INEQUABLE	INFANTILE	INFERRED
INDORSES	INDULIN	INEQUITY	INFANTINE	INFERRER
INDORSING	INDULINE	INERM	INFANTRY	INFERRERS
INDORSOR	INDULINES	INERMOUS	INFANTS	INFERRING
INDORSORS	INDULINS	INERRABLE	INFARCT	INFERS
INDOW	INDULT	INERRABLY	INFARCTED	INFERTILE
INDOWED	INDULTS	INERRANCY	INFARCTS	INFEST
INDOWING	INDUMENTA	INERRANT	INFARE	INFESTANT
INDOWS	INDUNA	INERT	INFARES	INFESTED
INDOXYL	INDUNAS	INERTER	INFATUATE	INFESTER

INFESTERS	INFLATING	INFORMER	INGENIUM	INGROOVE
INFESTING	INFLATION	INFORMERS	INGENIUMS	INGROOVED
INFESTS	INFLATIVE	INFORMING	INGENU	INGROOVES
INFICETE	INFLATOR	INFORMS	INGENUE	INGROSS
INFIDEL	INFLATORS	INFORTUNE	INGENUES	INGROSSED
INFIDELIC	INFLATUS	INFOS	INGENUITY	INGROSSES
INFIDELS	INFLECT	INFOSEC	INGENUOUS	INGROUND
INFIELD	INFLECTED	INFOSECS	INGENUS	INGROUNDS
INFIELDER	INFLECTOR	INFOTECH	INGEST	INGROUP
INFIELDS	INFLECTS	INFOTECHS	INGESTA	INGROUPS
INFIGHT	INFLEXED	INFOUGHT	INGESTED	INGROWING
INFIGHTER	INFLEXION	INFRA	INGESTING	INGROWN
INFIGHTS	INFLEXURE	INFRACT	INGESTION	INGROWTH
INFILL	INFLICT	INFRACTED	INGESTIVE	INGROWTHS
INFILLED	INFLICTED	INFRACTOR	INGESTS	INGRUM
INFILLING	INFLICTER	INFRACTS	INGINE	INGRUMS
INFILLS	INFLICTOR	INFRARED	INGINES	INGS
INFIMA	INFLICTS	INFRAREDS	INGLE	INGUINAL
INFIMUM	INFLIGHT	INFRINGE	INGLENEUK	INGULF
INFIMUMS	INFLOW	INFRINGED	INGLENOOK	INGULFED
INFINITE	INFLOWING	INFRINGER	INGLES	INGULFING
INFINITES	INFLOWS	INFRINGES	INGLOBE	INGULFS
INFINITY	INFLUENCE	INFRUGAL	INGLOBED	INGULPH
INFIRM	INFLUENT	INFULA	INGLOBES	INGULPHED
INFIRMARY	INFLUENTS	INFULAE	INGLOBING	INGULPHS
INFIRMED	INFLUENZA	INFURIATE	INGLUVIAL	INHABIT
INFIRMER	INFLUX	INFUSCATE	INGLUVIES	INHABITED
INFIRMEST	INFLUXES	INFUSE	INGO	INHABITER
INFIRMING	INFLUXION	INFUSED	INGOES	INHABITOR
INFIRMITY	INFO	INFUSER	INGOING	INHABITS
INFIRMLY	INFOBAHN	INFUSERS	INGOINGS	INHALABLE
INFIRMS	INFOBAHNS	INFUSES	INGOT	INHALANT
INFIX	INFODUMP	INFUSIBLE	INGOTED	INHALANTS
INFIXED	INFODUMPS	INFUSING	INGOTING	INHALATOR
INFIXES	INFOLD	INFUSION	INGOTS	INHALE
INFIXING	INFOLDED	INFUSIONS	INGRAFT	INHALED
INFIXION	INFOLDER	INFUSIVE	INGRAFTED	INHALER
INFIXIONS	INFOLDERS	INFUSORIA	INGRAFTS	INHALERS
INFLAME	INFOLDING	INFUSORY	INGRAIN	INHALES
INFLAMED	INFOLDS	ING	INGRAINED	INHALING
INFLAMER	INFOMANIA	INGAN	INGRAINER	INHARMONY
INFLAMERS	INFORCE	INGANS	INGRAINS	INHAUL
INFLAMES	INFORCED	INGATE	INGRAM	INHAULER
INFLAMING	INFORCES	INGATES	INGRAMS	INHAULERS
INFLATE	INFORCING	INGATHER	INGRATE	INHAULS
INFLATED	INFORM	INGATHERS	INGRATELY	INHAUST
INFLATER	INFORMAL	INGENER	INGRATES	INHAUSTED
INFLATERS	INFORMANT	INGENERS	INGRESS	INHAUSTS
INFLATES	INFORMED	INGENIOUS	INGRESSES	INHEARSE

INHEARSED	INIONS	INKBLOTS	INLANDER	INNIES
INHEARSES	INIQUITY	INKED	INLANDERS	INNING
INHERCE	INISLE	INKER	INLANDS	INNINGS
INHERCED	INISLED	INKERS	INLAY	INNINGSES
INHERCES	INISLES	INKHOLDER	INLAYER	INNIT
INHERCING	INISLING	INKHORN	INLAYERS	INNKEEPER
INHERE	INITIAL	INKHORNS	INLAYING	INNLESS
INHERED	INITIALED	INKHOSI	INLAYINGS	INNOCENCE
INHERENCE	INITIALER	INKHOSIS	INLAYS	INNOCENCY
INHERENCY	INITIALLY	INKIER	INLET	INNOCENT
INHERENT	INITIALS	INKIEST	INLETS	INNOCENTS
INHERES	INITIATE	INKINESS	INLETTING	INNOCUITY
INHERING	INITIATED	INKING	INLIER	INNOCUOUS
INHERIT	INITIATES	INKINGS	INLIERS	INNOVATE
INHERITED	INITIATOR	INKJET	INLOCK	INNOVATED
INHERITOR	INJECT	INKJETS	INLOCKED	INNOVATES
INHERITS	INJECTANT	INKLE	INLOCKING	INNOVATOR
INHESION	INJECTED	INKLED	INLOCKS	INNOXIOUS
INHESIONS	INJECTING	INKLES	INLY	INNS
INHIBIN	INJECTION	INKLESS	INLYING	INNUENDO
INHIBINS	INJECTIVE	INKLIKE	INMATE	INNUENDOS
INHIBIT	INJECTOR	INKLING	INMATES	INNYARD
INHIBITED	INJECTORS	INKLINGS	INMESH	INNYARDS
INHIBITER	INJECTS	INKOSI	INMESHED	INOCULA
INHIBITOR	INJELLIED	INKOSIS	INMESHES	INOCULANT
INHIBITS	INJELLIES	INKPAD	INMESHING	INOCULATE
INHOLDER	INJELLY	INKPADS	INMIGRANT	INOCULUM
INHOLDERS	INJERA	INKPOT	INMOST	INOCULUMS
INHOLDING	INJERAS	INKPOTS	INN	INODOROUS
INHOOP	INJOINT	INKS	INNAGE	INOPINATE
INHOOPED	INJOINTED	INKSPOT	INNAGES	INORB
INHOOPING	INJOINTS	INKSPOTS	INNARDS	INORBED
INHOOPS	INJUNCT	INKSTAIN	INNATE	INORBING
INHUMAN	INJUNCTED	INKSTAINS	INNATELY	INORBS
INHUMANE	INJUNCTS	INKSTAND	INNATIVE	INORGANIC
INHUMANER	INJURABLE	INKSTANDS	INNED	INORNATE
INHUMANLY	INJURE	INKSTONE	INNER	INOSINE
INHUMATE	INJURED	INKSTONES	INNERLY	INOSINES
INHUMATED	INJURER	INKWELL	INNERMOST	INOSITE
INHUMATES	INJURERS	INKWELLS	INNERNESS	INOSITES
INHUME	INJURES	INKWOOD	INNERS	INOSITOL
INHUMED	INJURIES	INKWOODS	INNERSOLE	INOSITOLS
INHUMER	INJURING	INKY	INNERVATE	INOTROPE
INHUMERS	INJURIOUS	INLACE	INNERVE	INOTROPES
INHUMES	INJURY	INLACED	INNERVED	INOTROPIC
INHUMING	INJUSTICE	INLACES	INNERVES	INPATIENT
INIA	INK	INLACING	INNERVING	INPAYMENT
INIMICAL	INKBERRY	INLAID	INNERWEAR	INPHASE
INION	INKBLOT	INLAND	INNIE	INPOUR

INPOURED	INSATIETY	INSETTING	INSOFAR	INSTALLER
INPOURING	INSCAPE	INSHALLAH	INSOLATE	INSTALLS
INPOURS	INSCAPES	INSHEATH	INSOLATED	INSTALS
INPUT	INSCIENCE	INSHEATHE	INSOLATES	INSTANCE
INPUTS	INSCIENT	INSHEATHS	INSOLE	INSTANCED
INPUTTED	INSCONCE	INSHELL	INSOLENCE	INSTANCES
INPUTTER	INSCONCED	INSHELLED	INSOLENT	INSTANCY
INPUTTERS	INSCONCES	INSHELLS	INSOLENTS	INSTANT
INPUTTING	INSCRIBE	INSHELTER	INSOLES	INSTANTER
INQILAB	INSCRIBED	INSHIP	INSOLUBLE	INSTANTLY
INQILABS	INSCRIBER	INSHIPPED	INSOLUBLY	INSTANTS
INQUERE	INSCRIBES	INSHIPS	INSOLVENT	INSTAR
INQUERED	INSCROLL	INSHORE	INSOMNIA	INSTARRED
INQUERES	INSCROLLS	INSHRINE	INSOMNIAC	INSTARS
INQUERING	INSCULP	INSHRINED	INSOMNIAS	INSTATE
INQUEST	INSCULPED	INSHRINEE	INSOMUCH	INSTATED
INQUESTS	INSCULPS	INSHRINES	INSOOTH	INSTATES
INQUIET	INSCULPT	INSIDE	INSOUL	INSTATING
INQUIETED	INSEAM	INSIDER	INSOULED	INSTEAD
INQUIETLY	INSEAMED	INSIDERS	INSOULING	INSTEP
INQUIETS	INSEAMING	INSIDES	INSOULS	INSTEPS
INQUILINE	INSEAMS	INSIDIOUS	INSOURCE	INSTIGATE
INQUINATE	INSECT	INSIGHT	INSOURCED	INSTIL
INQUIRE	INSECTAN	INSIGHTS	INSOURCES	INSTILL
INQUIRED	INSECTARY	INSIGNE	INSPAN	INSTILLED
INQUIRER	INSECTEAN	INSIGNIA	INSPANNED	INSTILLER
INQUIRERS	INSECTILE	INSIGNIAS	INSPANS	INSTILLS
INQUIRES	INSECTION	INSINCERE	INSPECT	INSTILS
INQUIRIES	INSECTS	INSINEW	INSPECTED	INSTINCT
INQUIRING	INSECURE	INSINEWED	INSPECTOR	INSTINCTS
INQUIRY	INSECURER	INSINEWS	INSPECTS	INSTITUTE
INQUORATE	INSEEM	INSINUATE	INSPHERE	INSTRESS
INRO	INSEEMED	INSIPID	INSPHERED	INSTROKE
INROAD	INSEEMING	INSIPIDER	INSPHERES	INSTROKES
INROADS	INSEEMS	INSIPIDLY	INSPIRE	INSTRUCT
INRUN	INSELBERG	INSIPIENT	INSPIRED	INSTRUCTS
INRUNS	INSENSATE	INSIST	INSPIRER	INSUCKEN
INRUSH	INSERT	INSISTED	INSPIRERS	INSULA
INRUSHES	INSERTED	INSISTENT	INSPIRES	INSULAE
INRUSHING	INSERTER	INSISTER	INSPIRING	INSULANT
INS	INSERTERS	INSISTERS	INSPIRIT	INSULANTS
INSANE	INSERTING	INSISTING	INSPIRITS	INSULAR
INSANELY	INSERTION	INSISTS	INSPO	INSULARLY
INSANER	INSERTS	INSNARE	INSPOS	INSULARS
INSANEST	INSET	INSNARED	INSTABLE	INSULATE
INSANIE	INSETS	INSNARER	INSTAGRAM	INSULATED
INSANIES	INSETTED	INSNARERS	INSTAL	INSULATES
INSANITY	INSETTER	INSNARES	INSTALL	INSULATOR
INSATIATE	INSETTERS	INSNARING	INSTALLED	INSULIN

INSULINS

INSULINS	INTEGRITY	INTERDASH	INTERMITS	INTERWEBS
INSULSE	INTEL	INTERDEAL	INTERMIX	INTERWIND
INSULSITY	INTELLECT	INTERDICT	INTERMONT	INTERWORD
INSULT	INTELS	INTERDINE	INTERMURE	INTERWORK
INSULTANT	INTENABLE	INTERESS	INTERN	INTERWOVE
INSULTED	INTEND	INTERESSE	INTERNAL	INTERZONE
INSULTER	INTENDANT	INTEREST	INTERNALS	INTESTACY
INSULTERS	INTENDED	INTERESTS	INTERNE	INTESTATE
INSULTING	INTENDEDS	INTERFACE	INTERNED	INTESTINE
INSULTS	INTENDER	INTERFERE	INTERNEE	INTHRAL
INSURABLE	INTENDERS	INTERFILE	INTERNEES	INTHRALL
INSURANCE	INTENDING	INTERFIRM	INTERNES	INTHRALLS
INSURANT	INTENDS	INTERFLOW	INTERNET	INTHRALS
INSURANTS	INTENIBLE	INTERFOLD	INTERNETS	INTHRONE
INSURE	INTENSATE	INTERFUSE	INTERNING	INTHRONED
INSURED	INTENSE	INTERGANG	INTERNIST	INTHRONES
INSUREDS	INTENSELY	INTERGREW	INTERNODE	INTI
INSURER	INTENSER	INTERGROW	INTERNS	INTIFADA
INSURERS	INTENSEST	INTERIM	INTERPAGE	INTIFADAH
INSURES	INTENSIFY	INTERIMS	INTERPLAY	INTIFADAS
INSURGENT	INTENSION	INTERIOR	INTERPLED	INTIFADEH
INSURING	INTENSITY	INTERIORS	INTERPONE	INTIL
INSWATHE	INTENSIVE	INTERJECT	INTERPOSE	INTIMA
INSWATHED	INTENT	INTERJOIN	INTERPRET	INTIMACY
INSWATHES	INTENTION	INTERKNIT	INTERRACE	INTIMAE
INSWEPT	INTENTIVE	INTERKNOT	INTERRAIL	INTIMAL
INSWING	INTENTLY	INTERLACE	INTERRED	INTIMAS
INSWINGER	INTENTS	INTERLAID	INTERREX	INTIMATE
INSWINGS	INTER	INTERLAP	INTERRING	INTIMATED
INT	INTERACT	INTERLAPS	INTERROW	INTIMATER
INTACT	INTERACTS	INTERLARD	INTERRUPT	INTIMATES
INTACTLY	INTERAGE	INTERLAY	INTERS	INTIME
INTAGLI	INTERARCH	INTERLAYS	INTERSECT	INTIMISM
INTAGLIO	INTERBANK	INTERLEAF	INTERSERT	INTIMISMS
INTAGLIOS	INTERBED	INTERLEND	INTERSEX	INTIMIST
INTAKE	INTERBEDS	INTERLENT	INTERTERM	INTIMISTE
INTAKES	INTERBRED	INTERLINE	INTERTEXT	INTIMISTS
INTARSIA	INTERCEDE	INTERLINK	INTERTIE	INTIMITY
INTARSIAS	INTERCELL	INTERLOAN	INTERTIES	INTINE
INTED	INTERCEPT	INTERLOCK	INTERTILL	INTINES
INTEGER	INTERCITY	INTERLOOP	INTERUNIT	INTING
INTEGERS	INTERCLAN	INTERLOPE	INTERVAL	INTIRE
INTEGRAL	INTERCLUB	INTERLUDE	INTERVALE	INTIS
INTEGRALS	INTERCOM	INTERMALE	INTERVALS	INTITLE
INTEGRAND	INTERCOMS	INTERMAT	INTERVEIN	INTITLED
INTEGRANT	INTERCOOL	INTERMATS	INTERVENE	INTITLES
INTEGRATE	INTERCROP	INTERMENT	INTERVIEW	INTITLING
INTEGRIN	INTERCUT	INTERMESH	INTERWAR	INTITULE
INTEGRINS	INTERCUTS	INTERMIT	INTERWEB	INTITULED

INTITULES	INTRINCE	INTWINED	INVADING	INVERTED
INTO	INTRINSIC	INTWINES	INVALID	INVERTER
INTOED	INTRO	INTWINING	INVALIDED	INVERTERS
INTOMB	INTRODUCE	INTWIST	INVALIDER	INVERTIN
INTOMBED	INTROFIED	INTWISTED	INVALIDLY	INVERTING
INTOMBING	INTROFIES	INTWISTS	INVALIDS	INVERTINS
INTOMBS	INTROFY	INUKSHUIT	INVAR	INVERTOR
INTONACO	INTROIT	INUKSHUK	INVARIANT	INVERTORS
INTONACOS	INTROITAL	INUKSHUKS	INVARS	INVERTS
INTONATE	INTROITS	INUKSUIT	INVASION	INVEST
INTONATED	INTROITUS	INUKSUK	INVASIONS	INVESTED
INTONATES	INTROJECT	INUKSUKS	INVASIVE	INVESTING
INTONATOR	INTROLD	INULA	INVEAGLE	INVESTOR
INTONE	INTROMIT	INULAS	INVEAGLED	INVESTORS
INTONED	INTROMITS	INULASE	INVEAGLES	INVESTS
INTONER	INTRON	INULASES	INVECKED	INVEXED
INTONERS	INTRONIC	INULIN	INVECTED	INVIABLE
INTONES	INTRONS	INULINS	INVECTIVE	INVIABLY
INTONING	INTRORSE	INUMBRATE	INVEIGH	INVIDIOUS
INTONINGS	INTROS	INUNCTION	INVEIGHED	INVIOLACY
INTORSION	INTROVERT	INUNDANT	INVEIGHER	INVIOLATE
INTORT	INTRUDE	INUNDATE	INVEIGHS	INVIOUS
INTORTED	INTRUDED	INUNDATED	INVEIGLE	INVIRILE
INTORTING	INTRUDER	INUNDATES	INVEIGLED	INVISCID
INTORTION	INTRUDERS	INUNDATOR	INVEIGLER	INVISIBLE
INTORTS	INTRUDES	INURBANE	INVEIGLES	INVISIBLY
INTOWN	INTRUDING	INURE	INVENIT	INVITAL
INTRA	INTRUSION	INURED	INVENT	INVITE
INTRACITY	INTRUSIVE	INUREMENT	INVENTED	INVITED
INTRADA	INTRUST	INURES	INVENTER	INVITEE
INTRADAS	INTRUSTED	INURING	INVENTERS	INVITEES
INTRADAY	INTRUSTS	INURN	INVENTING	INVITER
INTRADOS	INTS	INURNED	INVENTION	INVITERS
INTRANET	INTUBATE	INURNING	INVENTIVE	INVITES
INTRANETS	INTUBATED	INURNMENT	INVENTOR	INVITING
INTRANT	INTUBATES	INURNS	INVENTORS	INVITINGS
INTRANTS	INTUIT	INUSITATE	INVENTORY	INVOCABLE
INTREAT	INTUITED	INUST	INVENTS	INVOCATE
INTREATED	INTUITING	INUSTION	INVERITY	INVOCATED
INTREATS	INTUITION	INUSTIONS	INVERNESS	INVOCATES
INTRENCH	INTUITIVE	INUTILE	INVERSE	INVOCATOR
INTREPID	INTUITS	INUTILELY	INVERSED	INVOICE
INTRICACY	INTUMESCE	INUTILITY	INVERSELY	INVOICED
INTRICATE	INTURN	INVADABLE	INVERSES	INVOICES
INTRIGANT	INTURNED	INVADE	INVERSING	INVOICING
INTRIGUE	INTURNS	INVADED	INVERSION	INVOKE
INTRIGUED	INTUSE	INVADER	INVERSIVE	INVOKED
INTRIGUER	INTUSES	INVADERS	INVERT	INVOKER
INTRIGUES	INTWINE	INVADES	INVERTASE	INVOKERS

INVOKES	INYALA	IOLITES	IRADES	IRISCOPE
INVOKING	INYALAS	ION	IRASCIBLE	IRISCOPES
INVOLUCEL	IO	IONIC	IRASCIBLY	IRISED
INVOLUCRA	IODATE	IONICALLY	IRATE	IRISES
INVOLUCRE	IODATED	IONICITY	IRATELY	IRISING
INVOLUTE	IODATES	IONICS	IRATENESS	IRITIC
INVOLUTED	IODATING	IONISABLE	IRATER	IRITIDES
INVOLUTES	IODATION	IONISE	IRATEST	IRITIS
INVOLVE	IODATIONS	IONISED	IRE	IRITISES
INVOLVED	IODIC	IONISER	IRED	IRK
INVOLVER	IODID	IONISERS	IREFUL	IRKED
INVOLVERS	IODIDE	IONISES	IREFULLY	IRKING
INVOLVES	IODIDES	IONISING	IRELESS	IRKS
INVOLVING	IODIDS	IONIUM	IRENIC	IRKSOME
INWALL	IODIN	IONIUMS	IRENICAL	IRKSOMELY
INWALLED	IODINATE	IONIZABLE	IRENICISM	IROKO
INWALLING	IODINATED	IONIZE	IRENICON	IROKOS
INWALLS	IODINATES	IONIZED	IRENICONS	IRON
INWARD	IODINE	IONIZER	IRENICS	IRONBARK
INWARDLY	IODINES	IONIZERS	IRENOLOGY	IRONBARKS
INWARDS	IODINS	IONIZES	IRES	IRONBOUND
INWEAVE	IODISE	IONIZING	IRID	IRONCLAD
INWEAVED	IODISED	IONOGEN	IRIDAL	IRONCLADS
INWEAVES	IODISER	IONOGENIC	IRIDEAL	IRONE
INWEAVING	IODISERS	IONOGENS	IRIDES	IRONED
INWICK	IODISES	IONOMER	IRIDIAL	IRONER
INWICKED	IODISING	IONOMERS	IRIDIAN	IRONERS
INWICKING	IODISM	IONONE	IRIDIC	IRONES
INWICKS	IODISMS	IONONES	IRIDISE	IRONIC
INWIND	IODIZE	IONOPAUSE	IRIDISED	IRONICAL
INWINDING	IODIZED	IONOPHORE	IRIDISES	IRONIER
INWINDS	IODIZER	IONOSONDE	IRIDISING	IRONIES
INWIT	IODIZERS	IONOTROPY	IRIDIUM	IRONIEST
INWITH	IODIZES	IONS	IRIDIUMS	IRONING
INWITS	IODIZING	IOPANOIC	IRIDIZE	IRONINGS
INWORK	IODOFORM	IOS	IRIDIZED	IRONISE
INWORKED	IODOFORMS	IOTA	IRIDIZES	IRONISED
INWORKING	IODOMETRY	IOTACISM	IRIDIZING	IRONISES
INWORKS	IODOPHILE	IOTACISMS	IRIDOCYTE	IRONISING
INWORN	IODOPHOR	IOTAS	IRIDOLOGY	IRONIST
INWOUND	IODOPHORS	IPECAC	IRIDOTOMY	IRONISTS
INWOVE	IODOPSIN	IPECACS	IRIDS	IRONIZE
INWOVEN	IODOPSINS	IPOMOEA	IRING	IRONIZED
INWRAP	IODOUS	IPOMOEAS	IRIS	IRONIZES
INWRAPPED	IODURET	IPPON	IRISATE	IRONIZING
INWRAPS	IODURETS	IPPONS	IRISATED	IRONLESS
INWRAPT	IODYRITE	IPRINDOLE	IRISATES	IRONLIKE
INWREATHE	IODYRITES	IRACUND	IRISATING	IRONMAN
INWROUGHT	IOLITE	IRADE	IRISATION	IRONMEN

IRONNESS	IRRUPTS	ISLEMAN	ISOCHRONE	ISOGRAFT
IRONS	IRUKANDJI	ISLEMEN	ISOCHRONS	ISOGRAFTS
IRONSIDE	IS	ISLES	ISOCLINAL	ISOGRAM
IRONSIDES	ISABEL	ISLESMAN	ISOCLINE	ISOGRAMS
IRONSMITH	ISABELLA	ISLESMEN	ISOCLINES	ISOGRAPH
IRONSTONE	ISABELLAS	ISLET	ISOCLINIC	ISOGRAPHS
IRONWARE	ISABELS	ISLETED	ISOCRACY	ISOGRIV
IRONWARES	ISAGOGE	ISLETS	ISOCRATIC	ISOGRIVS
IRONWEED	ISAGOGES	ISLING	ISOCRYMAL	ISOHEL
IRONWEEDS	ISAGOGIC	ISLOMANIA	ISOCRYME	ISOHELS
IRONWOMAN	ISAGOGICS	ISM	ISOCRYMES	ISOHYDRIC
IRONWOMEN	ISALLOBAR	ISMATIC	ISOCYANIC	ISOHYET
IRONWOOD	ISARITHM	ISMATICAL	ISOCYCLIC	ISOHYETAL
IRONWOODS	ISARITHMS	ISMS	ISODICA	ISOHYETS
IRONWORK	ISATIN	ISNA	ISODICON	ISOKONT
IRONWORKS	ISATINE	ISNAE	ISODOMA	ISOKONTAN
IRONY	ISATINES	ISO	ISODOMON	ISOKONTS
IRRADIANT	ISATINIC	ISOAMYL	ISODOMOUS	ISOLABLE
IRRADIATE	ISATINS	ISOAMYLS	ISODOMUM	ISOLATE
IRREAL	ISBA	ISOBAR	ISODONT	ISOLATED
IRREALITY	ISBAS	ISOBARE	ISODONTAL	ISOLATES
IRREDENTA	ISCHAEMIA	ISOBARES	ISODONTS	ISOLATING
IRREGULAR	ISCHAEMIC	ISOBARIC	ISODOSE	ISOLATION
IRRELATED	ISCHEMIA	ISOBARISM	ISODOSES	ISOLATIVE
IRRIDENTA	ISCHEMIAS	ISOBARS	ISOENZYME	ISOLATOR
IRRIGABLE	ISCHEMIC	ISOBASE	ISOETES	ISOLATORS
IRRIGABLY	ISCHIA	ISOBASES	ISOFORM	ISOLEAD
IRRIGATE	ISCHIADIC	ISOBATH	ISOFORMS	ISOLEADS
IRRIGATED	ISCHIAL	ISOBATHIC	ISOGAMETE	ISOLEX
IRRIGATES	ISCHIATIC	ISOBATHS	ISOGAMIC	ISOLEXES
IRRIGATOR	ISCHIUM	ISOBRONT	ISOGAMIES	ISOLINE
IRRIGUOUS	ISCHURIA	ISOBRONTS	ISOGAMOUS	ISOLINES
IRRISION	ISCHURIAS	ISOBUTANE	ISOGAMY	ISOLOG
IRRISIONS	ISEIKONIA	ISOBUTENE	ISOGENEIC	ISOLOGOUS
IRRISORY	ISEIKONIC	ISOBUTYL	ISOGENIC	ISOLOGS
IRRITABLE	ISENERGIC	ISOBUTYLS	ISOGENIES	ISOLOGUE
IRRITABLY	ISH	ISOCHASM	ISOGENOUS	ISOLOGUES
IRRITANCY	ISHES	ISOCHASMS	ISOGENY	ISOMER
IRRITANT	ISINGLASS	ISOCHEIM	ISOGLOSS	ISOMERASE
IRRITANTS	ISIT	ISOCHEIMS	ISOGON	ISOMERE
IRRITATE	ISLAND	ISOCHIMAL	ISOGONAL	ISOMERES
IRRITATED	ISLANDED	ISOCHIME	ISOGONALS	ISOMERIC
IRRITATES	ISLANDER	ISOCHIMES	ISOGONE	ISOMERISE
IRRITATOR	ISLANDERS	ISOCHOR	ISOGONES	ISOMERISM
IRRUPT	ISLANDING	ISOCHORE	ISOGONIC	ISOMERIZE
IRRUPTED	ISLANDS	ISOCHORES	ISOGONICS	ISOMEROUS
IRRUPTING	ISLE	ISOCHORIC	ISOGONIES	ISOMERS
IRRUPTION	ISLED	ISOCHORS	ISOGONS	ISOMETRIC
IRRUPTIVE	ISLELESS	ISOCHRON	ISOGONY	ISOMETRY

ISOMORPH	ISOSTATIC	ISSUER	ITEMING	IVORISTS
ISOMORPHS	ISOSTERIC	ISSUERS	ITEMISE	IVORY
ISONIAZID	ISOTACH	ISSUES	ITEMISED	IVORYBILL
ISONOME	ISOTACHS	ISSUING	ITEMISER	IVORYLIKE
ISONOMES	ISOTACTIC	ISTANA	ITEMISERS	IVORYWOOD
ISONOMIC	ISOTHERAL	ISTANAS	ITEMISES	IVRESSE
ISONOMIES	ISOTHERE	ISTHMI	ITEMISING	IVRESSES
ISONOMOUS	ISOTHERES	ISTHMIAN	ITEMIZE	IVY
ISONOMY	ISOTHERM	ISTHMIANS	ITEMIZED	IVYLEAF
ISOOCTANE	ISOTHERMS	ISTHMIC	ITEMIZER	IVYLIKE
ISOPACH	ISOTONE	ISTHMOID	ITEMIZERS	IWI
ISOPACHS	ISOTONES	ISTHMUS	ITEMIZES	IWIS
ISOPHONE	ISOTONIC	ISTHMUSES	ITEMIZING	IXIA
ISOPHONES	ISOTOPE	ISTLE	ITEMS	IXIAS
ISOPHOTAL	ISOTOPES	ISTLES	ITERANCE	IXNAY
ISOPHOTE	ISOTOPIC	IT	ITERANCES	IXNAYED
ISOPHOTES	ISOTOPIES	ITA	ITERANT	IXNAYING
ISOPLETH	ISOTOPY	ITACISM	ITERATE	IXNAYS
ISOPLETHS	ISOTRON	ITACISMS	ITERATED	IXODIASES
ISOPOD	ISOTRONS	ITACONIC	ITERATES	IXODIASIS
ISOPODAN	ISOTROPIC	ITALIC	ITERATING	IXODID
ISOPODANS	ISOTROPY	ITALICISE	ITERATION	IXODIDS
ISOPODOUS	ISOTYPE	ITALICIZE	ITERATIVE	IXORA
ISOPODS	ISOTYPES	ITALICS	ITERUM	IXORAS
ISOPOLITY	ISOTYPIC	ITAS	ITHER	IXTLE
ISOPRENE	ISOZYME	ITCH	ITINERACY	IXTLES
ISOPRENES	ISOZYMES	ITCHED	ITINERANT	IZAR
ISOPROPYL	ISOZYMIC	ITCHES	ITINERARY	IZARD
ISOPTERAN	ISPAGHULA	ITCHIER	ITINERATE	IZARDS
ISOPYCNAL	ISSEI	ITCHIEST	ITS	IZARS
ISOPYCNIC	ISSEIS	ITCHILY	ITSELF	IZVESTIA
ISOS	ISSUABLE	ITCHINESS	IURE	IZVESTIAS
ISOSCELES	ISSUABLY	ITCHING	IVIED	IZVESTIYA
ISOSMOTIC	ISSUANCE	ITCHINGS	IVIES	IZZARD
ISOSPIN	ISSUANCES	ITCHWEED	IVORIED	IZZARDS
ISOSPINS	ISSUANT	ITCHWEEDS	IVORIER	IZZAT
ISOSPORY	ISSUE	ITCHY	IVORIES	IZZATS
ISOSTACY	ISSUED	ITEM	IVORIEST	
ISOSTASY	ISSUELESS	ITEMED	IVORIST	

J

JA	JACKALLED	JACKSIE	JAEGERS	JAGUARS
JAAP	JACKALOPE	JACKSIES	JAFA	JAI
JAAPS	JACKALS	JACKSMELT	JAFAS	JAIL
JAB	JACKAROO	JACKSMITH	JAFFA	JAILABLE
JABBED	JACKAROOS	JACKSNIPE	JAFFAS	JAILBAIT
JABBER	JACKASS	JACKSTAFF	JAG	JAILBAITS
JABBERED	JACKASSES	JACKSTAY	JAGA	JAILBIRD
JABBERER	JACKBOOT	JACKSTAYS	JAGAED	JAILBIRDS
JABBERERS	JACKBOOTS	JACKSTONE	JAGAING	JAILBREAK
JABBERING	JACKDAW	JACKSTRAW	JAGAS	JAILBROKE
JABBERS	JACKDAWS	JACKSY	JAGDWURST	JAILED
JABBING	JACKED	JACKY	JAGER	JAILER
JABBINGLY	JACKEEN	JACOBIN	JAGERS	JAILERESS
JABBLE	JACKEENS	JACOBINS	JAGG	JAILERS
JABBLED	JACKER	JACOBUS	JAGGARIES	JAILHOUSE
JABBLES	JACKEROO	JACOBUSES	JAGGARY	JAILING
JABBLING	JACKEROOS	JACONET	JAGGED	JAILLESS
JABERS	JACKERS	JACONETS	JAGGEDER	JAILOR
JABIRU	JACKET	JACQUARD	JAGGEDEST	JAILORESS
JABIRUS	JACKETED	JACQUARDS	JAGGEDLY	JAILORS
JABORANDI	JACKETING	JACQUERIE	JAGGER	JAILS
JABOT	JACKETS	JACTATION	JAGGERIES	JAK
JABOTS	JACKFISH	JACULATE	JAGGERS	JAKE
JABS	JACKFRUIT	JACULATED	JAGGERY	JAKER
JACAL	JACKIES	JACULATES	JAGGHERY	JAKES
JACALES	JACKING	JACULATOR	JAGGIER	JAKESES
JACALS	JACKINGS	JACUZZI	JAGGIES	JAKEST
JACAMAR	JACKKNIFE	JACUZZIS	JAGGIEST	JAKEY
JACAMARS	JACKLEG	JADE	JAGGING	JAKEYS
JACANA	JACKLEGS	JADED	JAGGS	JAKFRUIT
JACANAS	JACKLIGHT	JADEDLY	JAGGY	JAKFRUITS
JACARANDA	JACKLING	JADEDNESS	JAGHIR	JAKS
JACARE	JACKLINGS	JADEITE	JAGHIRDAR	JALABIB
JACARES	JACKMAN	JADEITES	JAGHIRE	JALAP
JACCHUS	JACKMEN	JADELIKE	JAGHIRES	JALAPENO
JACCHUSES	JACKPLANE	JADERIES	JAGHIRS	JALAPENOS
JACENT	JACKPOT	JADERY	JAGIR	JALAPIC
JACINTH	JACKPOTS	JADES	JAGIRS	JALAPIN
JACINTHE	JACKROLL	JADING	JAGLESS	JALAPINS
JACINTHES	JACKROLLS	JADISH	JAGRA	JALAPS
JACINTHS	JACKS	JADISHLY	JAGRAS	JALEBI
JACK	JACKSCREW	JADITIC	JAGS	JALEBIS
JACKAL	JACKSHAFT	JAEGER	JAGUAR	JALFREZI

JALFREZIS	JAMBOLANS	JANGLER	JAPANIZED	JARKMAN
JALLEBI	JAMBONE	JANGLERS	JAPANIZES	JARKMEN
JALLEBIS	JAMBONES	JANGLES	JAPANNED	JARKS
JALOP	JAMBOOL	JANGLIER	JAPANNER	JARL
JALOPIES	JAMBOOLS	JANGLIEST	JAPANNERS	JARLDOM
JALOPPIES	JAMBOREE	JANGLING	JAPANNING	JARLDOMS
JALOPPY	JAMBOREES	JANGLINGS	JAPANS	JARLS
JALOPS	JAMBS	JANGLY	JAPE	JARLSBERG
JALOPY	JAMBU	JANIFORM	JAPED	JAROOL
JALOUSE	JAMBUL	JANISARY	JAPER	JAROOLS
JALOUSED	JAMBULS	JANISSARY	JAPERIES	JAROSITE
JALOUSES	JAMBUS	JANITOR	JAPERS	JAROSITES
JALOUSIE	JAMBUSTER	JANITORS	JAPERY	JAROVISE
JALOUSIED	JAMDANI	JANITRESS	JAPES	JAROVISED
JALOUSIES	JAMDANIS	JANITRIX	JAPING	JAROVISES
JALOUSING	JAMES	JANIZAR	JAPINGLY	JAROVIZE
JAM	JAMESES	JANIZARS	JAPINGS	JAROVIZED
JAMAAT	JAMJAR	JANIZARY	JAPONICA	JAROVIZES
JAMAATS	JAMJARS	JANKER	JAPONICAS	JARP
JAMADAR	JAMLIKE	JANKERS	JAPPED	JARPED
JAMADARS	JAMMABLE	JANKIER	JAPPING	JARPING
JAMB	JAMMED	JANKIEST	JAPS	JARPS
JAMBALAYA	JAMMER	JANKY	JAR	JARRAH
JAMBART	JAMMERS	JANN	JARARACA	JARRAHS
JAMBARTS	JAMMIER	JANNEY	JARARACAS	JARRED
JAMBE	JAMMIES	JANNEYED	JARARAKA	JARRING
JAMBEAU	JAMMIEST	JANNEYING	JARARAKAS	JARRINGLY
JAMBEAUS	JAMMING	JANNEYS	JARFUL	JARRINGS
JAMBEAUX	JAMMINGS	JANNIED	JARFULS	JARS
JAMBED	JAMMY	JANNIES	JARGON	JARSFUL
JAMBEE	JAMOKE	JANNOCK	JARGONED	JARTA
JAMBEES	JAMOKES	JANNOCKS	JARGONEER	JARTAS
JAMBER	JAMON	JANNS	JARGONEL	JARUL
JAMBERS	JAMPACKED	JANNY	JARGONELS	JARULS
JAMBES	JAMPAN	JANNYING	JARGONIER	JARVEY
JAMBEUX	JAMPANEE	JANNYINGS	JARGONING	JARVEYS
JAMBIER	JAMPANEES	JANSKY	JARGONISE	JARVIE
JAMBIERS	JAMPANI	JANSKYS	JARGONISH	JARVIES
JAMBING	JAMPANIS	JANTEE	JARGONIST	JASEY
JAMBIYA	JAMPANS	JANTIER	JARGONIZE	JASEYS
JAMBIYAH	JAMPOT	JANTIES	JARGONS	JASIES
JAMBIYAHS	JAMPOTS	JANTIEST	JARGONY	JASMIN
JAMBIYAS	JAMS	JANTY	JARGOON	JASMINE
JAMBO	JANATA	JAP	JARGOONS	JASMINES
JAMBOK	JANATAS	JAPAN	JARHEAD	JASMINS
JAMBOKKED	JANE	JAPANISE	JARHEADS	JASMONATE
JAMBOKS	JANES	JAPANISED	JARINA	JASP
JAMBOLAN	JANGLE	JAPANISES	JARINAS	JASPE
JAMBOLANA	JANGLED	JAPANIZE	JARK	JASPER

JASPERIER	JAUP	JAYGEES	JEED	JEHADS
JASPERISE	JAUPED	JAYHAWKER	JEEING	JEHU
JASPERIZE	JAUPING	JAYS	JEEL	JEHUS
JASPEROUS	JAUPS	JAYVEE	JEELED	JEJUNA
JASPERS	JAVA	JAYVEES	JEELIE	JEJUNAL
JASPERY	JAVAS	JAYWALK	JEELIED	JEJUNE
JASPES	JAVEL	JAYWALKED	JEELIEING	JEJUNELY
JASPIDEAN	JAVELIN	JAYWALKER	JEELIES	JEJUNITY
JASPILITE	JAVELINA	JAYWALKS	JEELING	JEJUNUM
JASPIS	JAVELINAS	JAZERANT	JEELS	JEJUNUMS
JASPISES	JAVELINED	JAZERANTS	JEELY	JELAB
JASPS	JAVELINS	JAZIES	JEELYING	JELABS
JASS	JAVELLE	JAZY	JEEP	JELL
JASSES	JAVELS	JAZZ	JEEPED	JELLABA
JASSID	JAW	JAZZBO	JEEPERS	JELLABAH
JASSIDS	JAWAN	JAZZBOS	JEEPING	JELLABAHS
JASY	JAWANS	JAZZED	JEEPNEY	JELLABAS
JATAKA	JAWARI	JAZZER	JEEPNEYS	JELLED
JATAKAS	JAWARIS	JAZZERS	JEEPS	JELLIED
JATO	JAWBATION	JAZZES	JEER	JELLIES
JATOS	JAWBONE	JAZZIER	JEERED	JELLIFIED
JATROPHA	JAWBONED	JAZZIEST	JEERER	JELLIFIES
JATROPHAS	JAWBONER	JAZZILY	JEERERS	JELLIFY
JAUK	JAWBONERS	JAZZINESS	JEERING	JELLING
JAUKED	JAWBONES	JAZZING	JEERINGLY	JELLO
JAUKING	JAWBONING	JAZZLIKE	JEERINGS	JELLOS
JAUKS	JAWBOX	JAZZMAN	JEERS	JELLS
JAUNCE	JAWBOXES	JAZZMEN	JEES	JELLY
JAUNCED	JAWED	JAZZY	JEESLY	JELLYBEAN
JAUNCES	JAWFALL	JEALOUS	JEEZ	JELLYFISH
JAUNCING	JAWFALLS	JEALOUSE	JEEZE	JELLYING
JAUNDICE	JAWHOLE	JEALOUSED	JEEZELY	JELLYLIKE
JAUNDICED	JAWHOLES	JEALOUSER	JEEZLY	JELLYROLL
JAUNDICES	JAWING	JEALOUSES	JEFE	JELUTONG
JAUNSE	JAWINGS	JEALOUSLY	JEFES	JELUTONGS
JAUNSED	JAWLESS	JEALOUSY	JEFF	JEMADAR
JAUNSES	JAWLIKE	JEAN	JEFFED	JEMADARS
JAUNSING	JAWLINE	JEANED	JEFFING	JEMBE
JAUNT	JAWLINES	JEANETTE	JEFFS	JEMBES
JAUNTED	JAWS	JEANETTES	JEGGING	JEMIDAR
JAUNTEE	JAXIE	JEANS	JEGGINGS	JEMIDARS
JAUNTIE	JAXIES	JEANSWEAR	JEHAD	JEMIMA
JAUNTIER	JAXY	JEAT	JEHADEEN	JEMIMAS
JAUNTIES	JAY	JEATS	JEHADI	JEMMIED
JAUNTIEST	JAYBIRD	JEBEL	JEHADIS	JEMMIER
JAUNTILY	JAYBIRDS	JEBELS	JEHADISM	JEMMIES
JAUNTING	JAYCEE	JEDI	JEHADISMS	JEMMIEST
JAUNTS	JAYCEES	JEDIS	JEHADIST	JEMMINESS
JAUNTY	JAYGEE	JEE	JEHADISTS	JEMMY

JEMMYING	JERQUE	JETE	JEWELLER	JICAMAS
JENNET	JERQUED	JETES	JEWELLERS	JICKAJOG
JENNETING	JERQUER	JETFOIL	JEWELLERY	JICKAJOGS
JENNETS	JERQUERS	JETFOILS	JEWELLIKE	JIFF
JENNIES	JERQUES	JETLAG	JEWELLING	JIFFIES
JENNY	JERQUING	JETLAGS	JEWELRIES	JIFFS
JEOFAIL	JERQUINGS	JETLIKE	JEWELRY	JIFFY
JEOFAILS	JERREED	JETLINER	JEWELS	JIG
JEON	JERREEDS	JETLINERS	JEWELWEED	JIGAJIG
JEONS	JERRICAN	JETON	JEWFISH	JIGAJIGS
JEOPARD	JERRICANS	JETONS	JEWFISHES	JIGAJOG
JEOPARDED	JERRID	JETPACK	JEWIE	JIGAJOGS
JEOPARDER	JERRIDS	JETPACKS	JEWIES	JIGAMAREE
JEOPARDS	JERRIES	JETPORT	JEZAIL	JIGGED
JEOPARDY	JERRY	JETPORTS	JEZAILS	JIGGER
JEQUERITY	JERRYCAN	JETS	JEZEBEL	JIGGERED
JEQUIRITY	JERRYCANS	JETSAM	JEZEBELS	JIGGERING
JERBIL	JERSEY	JETSAMS	JHALA	JIGGERS
JERBILS	JERSEYED	JETSOM	JHALAS	JIGGIER
JERBOA	JERSEYS	JETSOMS	JHATKA	JIGGIEST
JERBOAS	JESS	JETSON	JHATKAS	JIGGING
JEREED	JESSAMIES	JETSONS	JIAO	JIGGINGS
JEREEDS	JESSAMINE	JETSTREAM	JIAOS	JIGGISH
JEREMIAD	JESSAMY	JETTATURA	JIB	JIGGLE
JEREMIADS	JESSANT	JETTED	JIBB	JIGGLED
JEREPIGO	JESSE	JETTIED	JIBBA	JIGGLES
JEREPIGOS	JESSED	JETTIER	JIBBAH	JIGGLIER
JERFALCON	JESSERANT	JETTIES	JIBBAHS	JIGGLIEST
JERID	JESSES	JETTIEST	JIBBAS	JIGGLING
JERIDS	JESSIE	JETTINESS	JIBBED	JIGGLY
JERK	JESSIES	JETTING	JIBBER	JIGGUMBOB
JERKED	JESSING	JETTISON	JIBBERED	JIGGY
JERKER	JEST	JETTISONS	JIBBERING	JIGJIG
JERKERS	JESTBOOK	JETTON	JIBBERS	JIGJIGS
JERKIER	JESTBOOKS	JETTONS	JIBBING	JIGLIKE
JERKIES	JESTED	JETTY	JIBBINGS	JIGOT
JERKIEST	JESTEE	JETTYING	JIBBONS	JIGOTS
JERKILY	JESTEES	JETWAY	JIBBOOM	JIGS
JERKIN	JESTER	JETWAYS	JIBBOOMS	JIGSAW
JERKINESS	JESTERS	JEU	JIBBS	JIGSAWED
JERKING	JESTFUL	JEUNE	JIBE	JIGSAWING
JERKINGLY	JESTING	JEUX	JIBED	JIGSAWN
JERKINGS	JESTINGLY	JEWEL	JIBER	JIGSAWS
JERKINS	JESTINGS	JEWELED	JIBERS	JIHAD
JERKS	JESTS	JEWELER	JIBES	JIHADEEN
JERKWATER	JESUS	JEWELERS	JIBING	JIHADI
JERKY	JET	JEWELFISH	JIBINGLY	JIHADIS
JEROBOAM	JETBEAD	JEWELING	JIBS	JIHADISM
JEROBOAMS	JETBEADS	JEWELLED	JICAMA	JIHADISMS

JIHADIST	JINGALL	JIPYAPA	JOANNA	JOCKS
JIHADISTS	JINGALLS	JIPYAPAS	JOANNAS	JOCKSTRAP
JIHADS	JINGALS	JIRBLE	JOANNES	JOCKTELEG
JILBAB	JINGBANG	JIRBLED	JOANNESES	JOCKY
JILBABS	JINGBANGS	JIRBLES	JOB	JOCO
JILEBI	JINGKO	JIRBLING	JOBATION	JOCOS
JILEBIS	JINGKOES	JIRD	JOBATIONS	JOCOSE
JILGIE	JINGLE	JIRDS	JOBBED	JOCOSELY
JILGIES	JINGLED	JIRGA	JOBBER	JOCOSER
JILL	JINGLER	JIRGAS	JOBBERIES	JOCOSEST
JILLAROO	JINGLERS	JIRKINET	JOBBERS	JOCOSITY
JILLAROOS	JINGLES	JIRKINETS	JOBBERY	JOCULAR
JILLET	JINGLET	JIRRE	JOBBIE	JOCULARLY
JILLETS	JINGLETS	JISM	JOBBIES	JOCULATOR
JILLFLIRT	JINGLIER	JISMS	JOBBING	JOCUND
JILLION	JINGLIEST	JISSOM	JOBBINGS	JOCUNDER
JILLIONS	JINGLING	JISSOMS	JOBCENTRE	JOCUNDEST
JILLIONTH	JINGLY	JITNEY	JOBE	JOCUNDITY
JILLS	JINGO	JITNEYS	JOBED	JOCUNDLY
JILT	JINGOES	JITTER	JOBERNOWL	JODEL
JILTED	JINGOISH	JITTERBUG	JOBES	JODELLED
JILTER	JINGOISM	JITTERED	JOBHOLDER	JODELLING
JILTERS	JINGOISMS	JITTERIER	JOBING	JODELS
JILTING	JINGOIST	JITTERING	JOBLESS	JODHPUR
JILTS	JINGOISTS	JITTERS	JOBNAME	JODHPURS
JIMCRACK	JINJILI	JITTERY	JOBNAMES	JOE
JIMCRACKS	JINJILIS	JIUJITSU	JOBS	JOES
JIMINY	JINK	JIUJITSUS	JOBSEEKER	JOEY
JIMJAM	JINKED	JIUJUTSU	JOBSHARE	JOEYS
JIMJAMS	JINKER	JIUJUTSUS	JOBSHARES	JOG
JIMMIE	JINKERED	JIVE	JOBSWORTH	JOGGED
JIMMIED	JINKERING	JIVEASS	JOCK	JOGGER
JIMMIES	JINKERS	JIVEASSES	JOCKDOM	JOGGERS
JIMMINY	JINKING	JIVED	JOCKDOMS	JOGGIES
JIMMY	JINKS	JIVER	JOCKETTE	JOGGING
JIMMYING	JINN	JIVERS	JOCKETTES	JOGGINGS
JIMP	JINNE	JIVES	JOCKEY	JOGGLE
JIMPER	JINNEE	JIVEST	JOCKEYED	JOGGLED
JIMPEST	JINNI	JIVEY	JOCKEYING	JOGGLER
JIMPIER	JINNIS	JIVIER	JOCKEYISH	JOGGLERS
JIMPIEST	JINNS	JIVIEST	JOCKEYISM	JOGGLES
JIMPLY	JINRIKSHA	JIVING	JOCKEYS	JOGGLING
JIMPNESS	JINS	JIVY	JOCKIER	JOGPANTS
JIMPSON	JINX	JIZ	JOCKIEST	JOGS
JIMPY	JINXED	JIZZ	JOCKISH	JOGTROT
JIMSON	JINXES	JIZZES	JOCKNEY	JOGTROTS
JIMSONS	JINXING	JNANA	JOCKNEYS	JOHANNES
JIN	JIPIJAPA	JNANAS	JOCKO	JOHN
JINGAL	JIPIJAPAS	JO	JOCKOS	JOHNBOAT

JOHNBOATS	JOKESTER	JOLLYERS	JORDANS	JOUK
JOHNNIE	JOKESTERS	JOLLYHEAD	JORDELOO	JOUKED
JOHNNIES	JOKEY	JOLLYING	JORDELOOS	JOUKERIES
JOHNNY	JOKIER	JOLLYINGS	JORS	JOUKERY
JOHNS	JOKIEST	JOLS	JORUM	JOUKING
JOHNSON	JOKILY	JOLT	JORUMS	JOUKS
JOHNSONS	JOKINESS	JOLTED	JOSEPH	JOULE
JOIN	JOKING	JOLTER	JOSEPHS	JOULED
JOINABLE	JOKINGLY	JOLTERS	JOSH	JOULES
JOINDER	JOKINGS	JOLTHEAD	JOSHED	JOULING
JOINDERS	JOKOL	JOLTHEADS	JOSHER	JOUNCE
JOINED	JOKY	JOLTIER	JOSHERS	JOUNCED
JOINER	JOL	JOLTIEST	JOSHES	JOUNCES
JOINERIES	JOLE	JOLTILY	JOSHING	JOUNCIER
JOINERS	JOLED	JOLTING	JOSHINGLY	JOUNCIEST
JOINERY	JOLES	JOLTINGLY	JOSHINGS	JOUNCING
JOINING	JOLING	JOLTINGS	JOSKIN	JOUNCINGS
JOININGS	JOLIOTIUM	JOLTS	JOSKINS	JOUNCY
JOINS	JOLL	JOLTY	JOSS	JOUR
JOINT	JOLLED	JOMO	JOSSER	JOURNAL
JOINTED	JOLLER	JOMON	JOSSERS	JOURNALED
JOINTEDLY	JOLLERS	JOMONS	JOSSES	JOURNALS
JOINTER	JOLLEY	JOMOS	JOSTLE	JOURNEY
JOINTERS	JOLLEYER	JONCANOE	JOSTLED	JOURNEYED
JOINTING	JOLLEYERS	JONCANOES	JOSTLER	JOURNEYER
JOINTINGS	JOLLEYING	JONES	JOSTLERS	JOURNEYS
JOINTLESS	JOLLEYS	JONESED	JOSTLES	JOURNO
JOINTLY	JOLLIED	JONESES	JOSTLING	JOURNOS
JOINTNESS	JOLLIER	JONESING	JOSTLINGS	JOURS
JOINTRESS	JOLLIERS	JONG	JOT	JOUSEI
JOINTS	JOLLIES	JONGLEUR	JOTA	JOUSEIS
JOINTURE	JOLLIEST	JONGLEURS	JOTAS	JOUST
JOINTURED	JOLLIFIED	JONGS	JOTS	JOUSTED
JOINTURES	JOLLIFIES	JONNOCK	JOTTED	JOUSTER
JOINTWEED	JOLLIFY	JONNYCAKE	JOTTER	JOUSTERS
JOINTWORM	JOLLILY	JONQUIL	JOTTERS	JOUSTING
JOIST	JOLLIMENT	JONQUILS	JOTTIER	JOUSTINGS
JOISTED	JOLLINESS	JONTIES	JOTTIEST	JOUSTS
JOISTING	JOLLING	JONTY	JOTTING	JOVIAL
JOISTS	JOLLITIES	JOOK	JOTTINGS	JOVIALITY
JOJOBA	JOLLITY	JOOKED	JOTTY	JOVIALLY
JOJOBAS	JOLLOF	JOOKERIES	JOTUN	JOVIALTY
JOKE	JOLLOFS	JOOKERY	JOTUNN	JOW
JOKED	JOLLOP	JOOKING	JOTUNNS	JOWAR
JOKER	JOLLOPS	JOOKS	JOTUNS	JOWARI
JOKERS	JOLLS	JOR	JOUAL	JOWARIS
JOKES	JOLLY	JORAM	JOUALS	JOWARS
JOKESMITH	JOLLYBOAT	JORAMS	JOUGS	JOWED
JOKESOME	JOLLYER	JORDAN	JOUISANCE	JOWING

JOWL	JUBHAHS	JUDIES	JUICED	JUMART
JOWLED	JUBILANCE	JUDO	JUICEHEAD	JUMARTS
JOWLER	JUBILANCY	JUDOGI	JUICELESS	JUMBAL
JOWLERS	JUBILANT	JUDOGIS	JUICER	JUMBALS
JOWLIER	JUBILATE	JUDOIST	JUICERIES	JUMBIE
JOWLIEST	JUBILATED	JUDOISTS	JUICERS	JUMBIES
JOWLINESS	JUBILATES	JUDOKA	JUICERY	JUMBLE
JOWLING	JUBILE	JUDOKAS	JUICES	JUMBLED
JOWLS	JUBILEE	JUDOS	JUICIER	JUMBLER
JOWLY	JUBILEES	JUDS	JUICIEST	JUMBLERS
JOWS	JUBILES	JUDY	JUICILY	JUMBLES
JOY	JUCO	JUG	JUICINESS	JUMBLIER
JOYANCE	JUCOS	JUGA	JUICING	JUMBLIEST
JOYANCES	JUD	JUGAAD	JUICY	JUMBLING
JOYED	JUDAS	JUGAADS	JUJITSU	JUMBLY
JOYFUL	JUDASES	JUGAL	JUJITSUS	JUMBO
JOYFULLER	JUDDER	JUGALS	JUJU	JUMBOISE
JOYFULLY	JUDDERED	JUGATE	JUJUBE	JUMBOISED
JOYING	JUDDERIER	JUGFUL	JUJUBES	JUMBOISES
JOYLESS	JUDDERING	JUGFULS	JUJUISM	JUMBOIZE
JOYLESSLY	JUDDERS	JUGGED	JUJUISMS	JUMBOIZED
JOYOUS	JUDDERY	JUGGING	JUJUIST	JUMBOIZES
JOYOUSLY	JUDGE	JUGGINGS	JUJUISTS	JUMBOS
JOYPAD	JUDGEABLE	JUGGINS	JUJUS	JUMBUCK
JOYPADS	JUDGED	JUGGINSES	JUJUTSU	JUMBUCKS
JOYPOP	JUDGELESS	JUGGLE	JUJUTSUS	JUMBY
JOYPOPPED	JUDGELIKE	JUGGLED	JUKE	JUMELLE
JOYPOPPER	JUDGEMENT	JUGGLER	JUKEBOX	JUMELLES
JOYPOPS	JUDGER	JUGGLERS	JUKEBOXES	JUMP
JOYRIDDEN	JUDGERS	JUGGLERY	JUKED	JUMPABLE
JOYRIDE	JUDGES	JUGGLES	JUKES	JUMPED
JOYRIDER	JUDGESHIP	JUGGLING	JUKING	JUMPER
JOYRIDERS	JUDGEY	JUGGLINGS	JUKSKEI	JUMPERS
JOYRIDES	JUDGIER	JUGHEAD	JUKSKEIS	JUMPIER
JOYRIDING	JUDGIEST	JUGHEADS	JUKU	JUMPIEST
JOYRODE	JUDGING	JUGLET	JUKUS	JUMPILY
JOYS	JUDGINGLY	JUGLETS	JULEP	JUMPINESS
JOYSTICK	JUDGINGS	JUGS	JULEPS	JUMPING
JOYSTICKS	JUDGMATIC	JUGSFUL	JULIENNE	JUMPINGLY
JUBA	JUDGMENT	JUGULA	JULIENNED	JUMPINGS
JUBAS	JUDGMENTS	JUGULAR	JULIENNES	JUMPOFF
JUBATE	JUDGY	JUGULARS	JULIET	JUMPOFFS
JUBBA	JUDICABLE	JUGULATE	JULIETS	JUMPROPE
JUBBAH	JUDICARE	JUGULATED	JUMAR	JUMPROPES
JUBBAHS	JUDICARES	JUGULATES	JUMARED	JUMPS
JUBBAS	JUDICATOR	JUGULUM	JUMARING	JUMPSCARE
JUBE	JUDICIAL	JUGUM	JUMARRED	JUMPSHOT
JUBES	JUDICIARY	JUGUMS	JUMARRING	JUMPSHOTS
JUBHAH	JUDICIOUS	JUICE	JUMARS	JUMPSIES

JUMPSUIT	JUNIORITY	JUNTA	JURY	JUSTNESS
JUMPSUITS	JUNIORS	JUNTAS	JURYING	JUSTS
JUMPY	JUNIPER	JUNTO	JURYLESS	JUT
JUN	JUNIPERS	JUNTOS	JURYMAN	JUTE
JUNCATE	JUNK	JUPATI	JURYMAST	JUTELIKE
JUNCATES	JUNKANOO	JUPATIS	JURYMASTS	JUTES
JUNCO	JUNKANOOS	JUPE	JURYMEN	JUTS
JUNCOES	JUNKED	JUPES	JURYWOMAN	JUTTED
JUNCOS	JUNKER	JUPON	JURYWOMEN	JUTTIED
JUNCTION	JUNKERDOM	JUPONS	JUS	JUTTIER
JUNCTIONS	JUNKERS	JURA	JUSSIVE	JUTTIES
JUNCTURAL	JUNKET	JURAL	JUSSIVES	JUTTIEST
JUNCTURE	JUNKETED	JURALLY	JUST	JUTTING
JUNCTURES	JUNKETEER	JURANT	JUSTED	JUTTINGLY
JUNCUS	JUNKETER	JURANTS	JUSTER	JUTTY
JUNCUSES	JUNKETERS	JURASSIC	JUSTERS	JUTTYING
JUNEATING	JUNKETING	JURAT	JUSTEST	JUVE
JUNGLE	JUNKETS	JURATORY	JUSTICE	JUVENAL
JUNGLED	JUNKETTED	JURATS	JUSTICER	JUVENALS
JUNGLEGYM	JUNKETTER	JURE	JUSTICERS	JUVENILE
JUNGLES	JUNKIE	JUREL	JUSTICES	JUVENILES
JUNGLI	JUNKIER	JURELS	JUSTICIAR	JUVENILIA
JUNGLIER	JUNKIES	JURES	JUSTIFIED	JUVES
JUNGLIEST	JUNKIEST	JURIDIC	JUSTIFIER	JUVIE
JUNGLIS	JUNKINESS	JURIDICAL	JUSTIFIES	JUVIES
JUNGLIST	JUNKING	JURIED	JUSTIFY	JUXTAPOSE
JUNGLISTS	JUNKMAN	JURIES	JUSTING	JYMOLD
JUNGLY	JUNKMEN	JURIST	JUSTLE	JYNX
JUNIOR	JUNKS	JURISTIC	JUSTLED	JYNXES
JUNIORATE	JUNKY	JURISTS	JUSTLES	
JUNIORED	JUNKYARD	JUROR	JUSTLING	
JUNIORING	JUNKYARDS	JURORS	JUSTLY	

K

KA	KABLOOIES	KAE	KAIF	KAKA
KAAL	KABLOONA	KAED	KAIFS	KAKAPO
KAAMA	KABLOONAS	KAEING	KAIK	KAKAPOS
KAAMAS	KABLOONAT	KAES	KAIKA	KAKARIKI
KAAMCHOR	KABOB	KAF	KAIKAI	KAKARIKIS
KAAMCHORS	KABOBBED	KAFFIYAH	KAIKAIS	KAKAS
KAAS	KABOBBING	KAFFIYAHS	KAIKAS	KAKEMONO
KAASES	KABOBS	KAFFIYEH	KAIKAWAKA	KAKEMONOS
KAB	KABOCHA	KAFFIYEHS	KAIKOMAKO	KAKI
KABAB	KABOCHAS	KAFILA	KAIKS	KAKIEMON
KABABBED	KABOODLE	KAFILAS	KAIL	KAKIEMONS
KABABBING	KABOODLES	KAFS	KAILS	KAKIS
KABABS	KABOOM	KAFTAN	KAILYAIRD	KAKIVAK
KABADDI	KABOOMS	KAFTANS	KAILYARD	KAKIVAKS
KABADDIS	KABS	KAFUFFLE	KAILYARDS	KAKODYL
KABAKA	KABUKI	KAFUFFLES	KAIM	KAKODYLS
KABAKAS	KABUKIS	KAGO	KAIMAKAM	KAKS
KABALA	KACCHA	KAGOOL	KAIMAKAMS	KAKURO
KABALAS	KACCHAS	KAGOOLS	KAIMS	KAKUROS
KABALISM	KACHA	KAGOS	KAIN	KALAM
KABALISMS	KACHAHARI	KAGOUL	KAING	KALAMANSI
KABALIST	KACHAHRI	KAGOULE	KAINGA	KALAMATA
KABALISTS	KACHAHRIS	KAGOULES	KAINGAS	KALAMATAS
KABAR	KACHCHA	KAGOULS	KAINIT	KALAMDAN
KABARS	KACHERI	KAGU	KAINITE	KALAMDANS
KABAYA	KACHERIS	KAGUS	KAINITES	KALAMKARI
KABAYAS	KACHINA	KAHAL	KAINITS	KALAMS
KABBALA	KACHINAS	KAHALS	KAINS	KALANCHOE
KABBALAH	KACHORI	KAHAWAI	KAIROMONE	KALE
KABBALAHS	KACHORIS	KAHAWAIS	KAIS	KALENDAR
KABBALAS	KACHUMBER	KAHIKATEA	KAISER	KALENDARS
KABBALISM	KACK	KAHIKATOA	KAISERDOM	KALENDS
KABBALIST	KACKS	KAHUNA	KAISERIN	KALES
KABELE	KADAI	KAHUNAS	KAISERINS	KALEWIFE
KABELES	KADAIS	KAI	KAISERISM	KALEWIVES
KABELJOU	KADAITCHA	KAIAK	KAISERS	KALEYARD
KABELJOUS	KADDISH	KAIAKED	KAIZEN	KALEYARDS
KABELJOUW	KADDISHES	KAIAKING	KAIZENS	KALI
KABIKI	KADDISHIM	KAIAKS	KAJAWAH	KALIAN
KABIKIS	KADE	KAID	KAJAWAHS	KALIANS
KABLOOEY	KADES	KAIDS	KAJEPUT	KALIF
KABLOOEYS	KADI	KAIE	KAJEPUTS	KALIFATE
KABLOOIE	KADIS	KAIES	KAK	KALIFATES

KALIFS	KAMAHI	KANDIES	KAOLINE	KARAS
KALIMBA	KAMAHIS	KANDY	KAOLINES	KARAT
KALIMBAS	KAMALA	KANE	KAOLINIC	KARATE
KALINITE	KAMALAS	KANEH	KAOLINISE	KARATEIST
KALINITES	KAMAS	KANEHS	KAOLINITE	KARATEKA
KALIPH	KAMCHOR	KANES	KAOLINIZE	KARATEKAS
KALIPHATE	KAMCHORS	KANG	KAOLINS	KARATES
KALIPHS	KAME	KANGA	KAON	KARATS
KALIS	KAMEES	KANGAROO	KAONIC	KAREAREA
KALIUM	KAMEESES	KANGAROOS	KAONS	KAREAREAS
KALIUMS	KAMEEZ	KANGAS	KAPA	KARENGO
KALLIDIN	KAMEEZES	KANGHA	KAPAS	KARENGOS
KALLIDINS	KAMELA	KANGHAS	KAPEEK	KARITE
KALLITYPE	KAMELAS	KANGS	KAPEYKA	KARITES
KALMIA	KAMERAD	KANJI	KAPH	KARK
KALMIAS	KAMERADED	KANJIS	KAPHS	KARKED
KALONG	KAMERADS	KANJOOS	KAPOK	KARKING
KALONGS	KAMES	KANJOOSES	KAPOKS	KARKS
KALONJI	KAMI	KANJUS	KAPOW	KARMA
KALONJIS	KAMICHI	KANJUSES	KAPOWS	KARMAS
KALOOKI	KAMICHIS	KANKAR	KAPPA	KARMIC
KALOOKIE	KAMIK	KANKARS	KAPPAS	KARN
KALOOKIES	KAMIKAZE	KANS	KAPU	KARNS
KALOOKIS	KAMIKAZES	KANSES	KAPUKA	KARO
KALOTYPE	KAMIKS	KANT	KAPUKAS	KAROO
KALOTYPES	KAMILA	KANTAR	KAPUS	KAROOS
KALPA	KAMILAS	KANTARS	KAPUT	KARORO
KALPAC	KAMIS	KANTED	KAPUTT	KAROROS
KALPACS	KAMISES	KANTELA	KARA	KAROS
KALPAK	KAMME	KANTELAS	KARABINER	KAROSHI
KALPAKS	KAMOKAMO	KANTELE	KARAHI	KAROSHIS
KALPAS	KAMOKAMOS	KANTELES	KARAHIS	KAROSS
KALPIS	KAMOTIK	KANTEN	KARAISM	KAROSSES
KALPISES	KAMOTIKS	KANTENS	KARAISMS	KARRI
KALSOMINE	KAMOTIQ	KANTHA	KARAIT	KARRIS
KALUKI	KAMOTIQS	KANTHAROI	KARAITS	KARROO
KALUKIS	KAMPONG	KANTHAROS	KARAKA	KARROOS
KALUMPIT	KAMPONGS	KANTHAS	KARAKAS	KARSEY
KALUMPITS	KAMSEEN	KANTIKOY	KARAKIA	KARSEYS
KALYPTRA	KAMSEENS	KANTIKOYS	KARAKIAS	KARSIES
KALYPTRAS	KAMSIN	KANTING	KARAKUL	KARST
KAM	KAMSINS	KANTS	KARAKULS	KARSTIC
KAMA	KANA	KANUKA	KARAMU	KARSTIFY
KAMAAINA	KANAE	KANUKAS	KARAMUS	KARSTS
KAMAAINAS	KANAES	KANZU	KARANGA	KARSY
KAMABOKO	KANAMYCIN	KANZUS	KARANGAED	KART
KAMABOKOS	KANAS	KAOLIANG	KARANGAS	KARTER
KAMACITE	KANBAN	KAOLIANGS	KARAOKE	KARTERS
KAMACITES	KANBANS	KAOLIN	KARAOKES	KARTING

KARTINGS	KATCINA	KAVASS	KBARS	KEDGEREE
KARTS	KATCINAS	KAVASSES	KEA	KEDGEREES
KARYOGAMY	KATHAK	KAW	KEAS	KEDGERS
KARYOGRAM	KATHAKALI	KAWA	KEASAR	KEDGES
KARYOLOGY	KATHAKS	KAWAII	KEASARS	KEDGIER
KARYON	KATHARSES	KAWAIIS	KEAVIE	KEDGIEST
KARYONS	KATHARSIS	KAWAKAWA	KEAVIES	KEDGING
KARYOSOME	KATHODAL	KAWAKAWAS	KEB	KEDGY
KARYOTIN	KATHODE	KAWAS	KEBAB	KEDS
KARYOTINS	KATHODES	KAWAU	KEBABBED	KEECH
KARYOTYPE	KATHODIC	KAWAUS	KEBABBING	KEECHES
KARZIES	KATHUMP	KAWED	KEBABS	KEEF
KARZY	KATHUMPS	KAWING	KEBAR	KEEFS
KAS	KATI	KAWS	KEBARS	KEEK
KASBAH	KATION	KAY	KEBBED	KEEKED
KASBAHS	KATIONS	KAYAK	KEBBIE	KEEKER
KASES	KATIPO	KAYAKED	KEBBIES	KEEKERS
KASHA	KATIPOS	KAYAKER	KEBBING	KEEKING
KASHAS	KATIS	KAYAKERS	KEBBOCK	KEEKS
KASHER	KATORGA	KAYAKING	KEBBOCKS	KEEL
KASHERED	KATORGAS	KAYAKINGS	KEBBUCK	KEELAGE
KASHERING	KATS	KAYAKS	KEBBUCKS	KEELAGES
KASHERS	KATSINA	KAYFABE	KEBELE	KEELBOAT
KASHMIR	KATSINAM	KAYFABES	KEBELES	KEELBOATS
KASHMIRS	KATSINAS	KAYLE	KEBLAH	KEELED
KASHRUS	KATSURA	KAYLES	KEBLAHS	KEELER
KASHRUSES	KATSURAS	KAYLIED	KEBOB	KEELERS
KASHRUT	KATTI	KAYO	KEBOBBED	KEELHALE
KASHRUTH	KATTIS	KAYOED	KEBOBBING	KEELHALED
KASHRUTHS	KATYDID	KAYOES	KEBOBS	KEELHALES
KASHRUTS	KATYDIDS	KAYOING	KEBS	KEELHAUL
KASME	KAUGH	KAYOINGS	KECK	KEELHAULS
KAT	KAUGHS	KAYOS	KECKED	KEELIE
KATA	KAUMATUA	KAYS	KECKING	KEELIES
KATABASES	KAUMATUAS	KAZACHKI	KECKLE	KEELING
KATABASIS	KAUPAPA	KAZACHOC	KECKLED	KEELINGS
KATABATIC	KAUPAPAS	KAZACHOCS	KECKLES	KEELIVINE
KATABOLIC	KAURI	KAZACHOK	KECKLING	KEELLESS
KATAKANA	KAURIES	KAZACHOKS	KECKLINGS	KEELMAN
KATAKANAS	KAURIS	KAZATSKI	KECKS	KEELMEN
KATAL	KAURU	KAZATSKY	KECKSES	KEELS
KATALS	KAURUS	KAZATZKA	KECKSIES	KEELSON
KATANA	KAURY	KAZATZKAS	KECKSY	KEELSONS
KATANAS	KAVA	KAZI	KED	KEELYVINE
KATAS	KAVAKAVA	KAZILLION	KEDDAH	KEEMA
KATCHINA	KAVAKAVAS	KAZIS	KEDDAHS	KEEMAS
KATCHINAS	KAVAL	KAZOO	KEDGE	KEEN
KATCHURI	KAVALS	KAZOOS	KEDGED	KEENED
KATCHURIS	KAVAS	KBAR	KEDGER	KEENER

KEENERS	KEGGING	KELPY	KENNELMAN	KERATIN
KEENEST	KEGLER	KELSON	KENNELMEN	KERATINS
KEENING	KEGLERS	KELSONS	KENNELS	KERATITIS
KEENINGS	KEGLING	KELT	KENNER	KERATOID
KEENLY	KEGLINGS	KELTER	KENNERS	KERATOMA
KEENNESS	KEGS	KELTERS	KENNET	KERATOMAS
KEENO	KEHUA	KELTIE	KENNETS	KERATOSE
KEENOS	KEHUAS	KELTIES	KENNETT	KERATOSES
KEENS	KEIGHT	KELTS	KENNETTED	KERATOSIC
KEEP	KEIR	KELTY	KENNETTS	KERATOSIS
KEEPABLE	KEIREN	KELVIN	KENNING	KERATOTIC
KEEPER	KEIRENS	KELVINS	KENNINGS	KERB
KEEPERS	KEIRETSU	KEMB	KENO	KERBAYA
KEEPING	KEIRETSUS	KEMBED	KENOS	KERBAYAS
KEEPINGS	KEIRIN	KEMBING	KENOSES	KERBED
KEEPNET	KEIRINS	KEMBLA	KENOSIS	KERBING
KEEPNETS	KEIRS	KEMBLAS	KENOSISES	KERBINGS
KEEPS	KEISTER	KEMBO	KENOTIC	KERBLOOEY
KEEPSAKE	KEISTERS	KEMBOED	KENOTICS	KERBS
KEEPSAKES	KEITLOA	KEMBOING	KENOTRON	KERBSIDE
KEEPSAKY	KEITLOAS	KEMBOS	KENOTRONS	KERBSIDES
KEESHOND	KEKENO	KEMBS	KENS	KERBSTONE
KEESHONDS	KEKENOS	KEMP	KENSPECK	KERCHIEF
KEESTER	KEKERENGU	KEMPED	KENT	KERCHIEFS
KEESTERS	KEKS	KEMPER	KENTE	KERCHOO
KEET	KEKSYE	KEMPERS	KENTED	KEREL
KEETS	KEKSYES	KEMPIER	KENTES	KERELS
KEEVE	KELEP	KEMPIEST	KENTIA	KERERU
KEEVES	KELEPS	KEMPING	KENTIAS	KERERUS
KEF	KELIM	KEMPINGS	KENTING	KERF
KEFFEL	KELIMS	KEMPLE	KENTLEDGE	KERFED
KEFFELS	KELL	KEMPLES	KENTS	KERFING
KEFFIYAH	KELLAUT	KEMPS	KEP	KERFLOOEY
KEFFIYAHS	KELLAUTS	KEMPT	KEPHALIC	KERFS
KEFFIYEH	KELLIES	KEMPY	KEPHALICS	KERFUFFLE
KEFFIYEHS	KELLS	KEN	KEPHALIN	KERKIER
KEFIR	KELLY	KENAF	KEPHALINS	KERKIEST
KEFIRS	KELOID	KENAFS	KEPHIR	KERKY
KEFS	KELOIDAL	KENCH	KEPHIRS	KERMA
KEFTEDES	KELOIDS	KENCHES	KEPI	KERMAS
KEFUFFLE	KELP	KENDO	KEPIS	KERMES
KEFUFFLED	KELPED	KENDOIST	KEPPED	KERMESES
KEFUFFLES	KELPER	KENDOISTS	KEPPEN	KERMESITE
KEG	KELPERS	KENDOS	KEPPING	KERMESS
KEGELER	KELPFISH	KENNED	KEPPIT	KERMESSE
KEGELERS	KELPIE	KENNEL	KEPS	KERMESSES
KEGGED	KELPIES	KENNELED	KEPT	KERMIS
KEGGER	KELPING	KENNELING	KERAMIC	KERMISES
KEGGERS	KELPS	KENNELLED	KERAMICS	KERMODE

KERMODES	KET	KEWLER	KEYSTONES	KHANUMS
KERN	KETA	KEWLEST	KEYSTROKE	KHAPH
KERNE	KETAINE	KEWPIE	KEYTAR	KHAPHS
KERNED	KETAMINE	KEWPIES	KEYTARS	KHARIF
KERNEL	KETAMINES	KEX	KEYWAY	KHARIFS
KERNELED	KETAS	KEXES	KEYWAYS	KHAT
KERNELING	KETCH	KEY	KEYWORD	KHATS
KERNELLED	KETCHES	KEYBOARD	KEYWORDS	KHAYA
KERNELLY	KETCHING	KEYBOARDS	KEYWORKER	KHAYAL
KERNELS	KETCHUP	KEYBUGLE	KGOTLA	KHAYALS
KERNES	KETCHUPS	KEYBUGLES	KGOTLAS	KHAYAS
KERNING	KETCHUPY	KEYBUTTON	KHADDAR	KHAZEN
KERNINGS	KETE	KEYCARD	KHADDARS	KHAZENIM
KERNISH	KETENE	KEYCARDS	KHADI	KHAZENS
KERNITE	KETENES	KEYED	KHADIS	KHAZI
KERNITES	KETES	KEYER	KHAF	KHAZIS
KERNS	KETMIA	KEYERS	KHAFS	KHEDA
KERO	KETMIAS	KEYEST	KHAKI	KHEDAH
KEROGEN	KETO	KEYFRAME	KHAKILIKE	KHEDAHS
KEROGENS	KETOGENIC	KEYFRAMES	KHAKIS	KHEDAS
KEROS	KETOL	KEYHOLE	KHALAT	KHEDIVA
KEROSENE	KETOLS	KEYHOLES	KHALATS	KHEDIVAL
KEROSENES	KETONE	KEYING	KHALIF	KHEDIVAS
KEROSINE	KETONEMIA	KEYINGS	KHALIFA	KHEDIVATE
KEROSINES	KETONES	KEYLESS	KHALIFAH	KHEDIVE
KERPLUNK	KETONIC	KEYLINE	KHALIFAHS	KHEDIVES
KERPLUNKS	KETONURIA	KEYLINES	KHALIFAS	KHEDIVIAL
KERRIA	KETOSE	KEYLOGGER	KHALIFAT	KHEEMA
KERRIAS	KETOSES	KEYNOTE	KHALIFATE	KHEEMAS
KERRIES	KETOSIS	KEYNOTED	KHALIFATS	KHET
KERRY	KETOTIC	KEYNOTER	KHALIFS	KHETH
KERSEY	KETOXIME	KEYNOTERS	KHAMSEEN	KHETHS
KERSEYS	KETOXIMES	KEYNOTES	KHAMSEENS	KHETS
KERVE	KETS	KEYNOTING	KHAMSIN	KHI
KERVED	KETTLE	KEYPAD	KHAMSINS	KHILAFAT
KERVES	KETTLED	KEYPADS	KHAN	KHILAFATS
KERVING	KETTLEFUL	KEYPAL	KHANATE	KHILAT
KERYGMA	KETTLES	KEYPALS	KHANATES	KHILATS
KERYGMAS	KETTLING	KEYPRESS	KHANDA	KHILIM
KERYGMATA	KETTLINGS	KEYPUNCH	KHANDAS	KHILIMS
KESAR	KETUBAH	KEYRING	KHANGA	KHIMAR
KESARS	KETUBAHS	KEYRINGS	KHANGAS	KHIMARS
KESH	KETUBOT	KEYS	KHANJAR	KHIRKAH
KESHES	KETUBOTH	KEYSET	KHANJARS	KHIRKAHS
KEST	KEVEL	KEYSETS	KHANS	KHIS
KESTING	KEVELS	KEYSTER	KHANSAMA	KHODJA
KESTREL	KEVIL	KEYSTERS	KHANSAMAH	KHODJAS
KESTRELS	KEVILS	KEYSTONE	KHANSAMAS	KHOJA
KESTS	KEWL	KEYSTONED	KHANUM	KHOJAS

K

KHOR	KIBIBYTES	KICKSTART	KIDNAPPEE	KILEY
KHORS	KIBITKA	KICKUP	KIDNAPPER	KILEYS
KHOTBAH	KIBITKAS	KICKUPS	KIDNAPS	KILIKITI
KHOTBAHS	KIBITZ	KICKY	KIDNEY	KILIKITIS
KHOTBEH	KIBITZED	KID	KIDNEYS	KILIM
KHOTBEHS	KIBITZER	KIDDED	KIDOLOGY	KILIMS
KHOUM	KIBITZERS	KIDDER	KIDS	KILL
KHOUMS	KIBITZES	KIDDERS	KIDSKIN	KILLABLE
KHUD	KIBITZING	KIDDIE	KIDSKINS	KILLADAR
KHUDS	KIBLA	KIDDIED	KIDSTAKES	KILLADARS
KHUKURI	KIBLAH	KIDDIER	KIDULT	KILLAS
KHUKURIS	KIBLAHS	KIDDIERS	KIDULTS	KILLASES
KHURTA	KIBLAS	KIDDIES	KIDVID	KILLCOW
KHURTAS	KIBOSH	KIDDING	KIDVIDS	KILLCOWS
KHUSKHUS	KIBOSHED	KIDDINGLY	KIEF	KILLCROP
KHUTBAH	KIBOSHES	KIDDINGS	KIEFS	KILLCROPS
KHUTBAHS	KIBOSHING	KIDDISH	KIEKIE	KILLDEE
KHYAL	KICK	KIDDLE	KIEKIES	KILLDEER
KHYALS	KICKABLE	KIDDLES	KIELBASA	KILLDEERS
KI	KICKABOUT	KIDDO	KIELBASAS	KILLDEES
KIAAT	KICKBACK	KIDDOES	KIELBASI	KILLED
KIAATS	KICKBACKS	KIDDOS	KIELBASY	KILLER
KIACK	KICKBALL	KIDDUSH	KIER	KILLERS
KIACKS	KICKBALLS	KIDDUSHES	KIERIE	KILLICK
KIANG	KICKBOARD	KIDDY	KIERIES	KILLICKS
KIANGS	KICKBOX	KIDDYING	KIERS	KILLIE
KIAUGH	KICKBOXED	KIDDYWINK	KIESELGUR	KILLIES
KIAUGHS	KICKBOXER	KIDEL	KIESERITE	KILLIFISH
KIBBE	KICKBOXES	KIDELS	KIESTER	KILLING
KIBBEH	KICKDOWN	KIDGE	KIESTERS	KILLINGLY
KIBBEHS	KICKDOWNS	KIDGIE	KIEV	KILLINGS
KIBBES	KICKED	KIDGIER	KIEVE	KILLJOY
KIBBI	KICKER	KIDGIEST	KIEVES	KILLJOYS
KIBBIS	KICKERS	KIDGLOVE	KIEVS	KILLOCK
KIBBITZ	KICKFLIP	KIDLET	KIF	KILLOCKS
KIBBITZED	KICKFLIPS	KIDLETS	KIFF	KILLOGIE
KIBBITZER	KICKIER	KIDLIKE	KIFS	KILLOGIES
KIBBITZES	KICKIEST	KIDLING	KIGHT	KILLS
KIBBLE	KICKING	KIDLINGS	KIGHTS	KILLUT
KIBBLED	KICKINGS	KIDLIT	KIKOI	KILLUTS
KIBBLES	KICKOFF	KIDLITS	KIKOIS	KILN
KIBBLING	KICKOFFS	KIDNAP	KIKUMON	KILNED
KIBBUTZ	KICKOUT	KIDNAPED	KIKUMONS	KILNING
KIBBUTZIM	KICKOUTS	KIDNAPEE	KIKUYU	KILNS
KIBE	KICKPLATE	KIDNAPEES	KIKUYUS	KILO
KIBEI	KICKS	KIDNAPER	KILD	KILOBAR
KIBEIS	KICKSHAW	KIDNAPERS	KILDERKIN	KILOBARS
KIBES	KICKSHAWS	KIDNAPING	KILERG	KILOBASE
KIBIBYTE	KICKSTAND	KIDNAPPED	KILERGS	KILOBASES

KILOBAUD	KIMBOS	KINE	KINGPINS	KIPES
KILOBAUDS	KIMCHEE	KINEMA	KINGPOST	KIPP
KILOBIT	KIMCHEES	KINEMAS	KINGPOSTS	KIPPA
KILOBITS	KIMCHI	KINEMATIC	KINGS	KIPPAGE
KILOBYTE	KIMCHIS	KINES	KINGSHIP	KIPPAGES
KILOBYTES	KIMMER	KINESCOPE	KINGSHIPS	KIPPAH
KILOCURIE	KIMMERS	KINESES	KINGSIDE	KIPPAHS
KILOCYCLE	KIMONO	KINESIC	KINGSIDES	KIPPAS
KILOGAUSS	KIMONOED	KINESICS	KINGSNAKE	KIPPED
KILOGRAM	KIMONOS	KINESIS	KINGWOOD	KIPPEN
KILOGRAMS	KIN	KINESISES	KINGWOODS	KIPPER
KILOGRAY	KINA	KINETIC	KININ	KIPPERED
KILOGRAYS	KINAKINA	KINETICAL	KININS	KIPPERER
KILOHERTZ	KINAKINAS	KINETICS	KINK	KIPPERERS
KILOJOULE	KINARA	KINETIN	KINKAJOU	KIPPERING
KILOLITER	KINARAS	KINETINS	KINKAJOUS	KIPPERS
KILOLITRE	KINAS	KINFOLK	KINKED	KIPPING
KILOMETER	KINASE	KINFOLKS	KINKIER	KIPPOT
KILOMETRE	KINASES	KING	KINKIEST	KIPPS
KILOMOLE	KINCHIN	KINGBIRD	KINKILY	KIPS
KILOMOLES	KINCHINS	KINGBIRDS	KINKINESS	KIPSKIN
KILOPOND	KINCOB	KINGBOLT	KINKING	KIPSKINS
KILOPONDS	KINCOBS	KINGBOLTS	KINKLE	KIPUNJI
KILORAD	KIND	KINGCRAFT	KINKLES	KIPUNJIS
KILORADS	KINDA	KINGCUP	KINKS	KIR
KILOS	KINDED	KINGCUPS	KINKY	KIRANA
KILOTON	KINDER	KINGDOM	KINLESS	KIRANAS
KILOTONNE	KINDERS	KINGDOMED	KINO	KIRBEH
KILOTONS	KINDEST	KINGDOMS	KINONE	KIRBEHS
KILOVOLT	KINDIE	KINGED	KINONES	KIRBIGRIP
KILOVOLTS	KINDIES	KINGFISH	KINOS	KIRBY
KILOWATT	KINDING	KINGHOOD	KINRED	KIRIGAMI
KILOWATTS	KINDLE	KINGHOODS	KINREDS	KIRIGAMIS
KILP	KINDLED	KINGING	KINS	KIRIMON
KILPS	KINDLER	KINGKLIP	KINSFOLK	KIRIMONS
KILT	KINDLERS	KINGKLIPS	KINSFOLKS	KIRK
KILTED	KINDLES	KINGLE	KINSHIP	KIRKED
KILTER	KINDLESS	KINGLES	KINSHIPS	KIRKING
KILTERS	KINDLIER	KINGLESS	KINSMAN	KIRKINGS
KILTIE	KINDLIEST	KINGLET	KINSMEN	KIRKMAN
KILTIES	KINDLILY	KINGLETS	KINSWOMAN	KIRKMEN
KILTING	KINDLING	KINGLIER	KINSWOMEN	KIRKS
KILTINGS	KINDLINGS	KINGLIEST	KINTLEDGE	KIRKTON
KILTLIKE	KINDLY	KINGLIKE	KIORE	KIRKTONS
KILTS	KINDNESS	KINGLING	KIORES	KIRKWARD
KILTY	KINDRED	KINGLINGS	KIOSK	KIRKYAIRD
KIMBO	KINDREDS	KINGLY	KIOSKS	KIRKYARD
KIMBOED	KINDS	KINGMAKER	KIP	KIRKYARDS
KIMBOING	KINDY	KINGPIN	KIPE	KIRMESS

KIRMESSES	KIST	KITTEN	KLEENEX	KLUDGES
KIRN	KISTED	KITTENED	KLEENEXES	KLUDGEY
KIRNED	KISTFUL	KITTENIER	KLEFTIKO	KLUDGIER
KIRNING	KISTFULS	KITTENING	KLEFTIKOS	KLUDGIEST
KIRNS	KISTING	KITTENISH	KLENDUSIC	KLUDGING
KIRPAN	KISTS	KITTENS	KLEPHT	KLUDGY
KIRPANS	KISTVAEN	KITTENY	KLEPHTIC	KLUGE
KIRRI	KISTVAENS	KITTIES	KLEPHTISM	KLUGED
KIRRIS	KIT	KITTING	KLEPHTS	KLUGES
KIRS	KITBAG	KITTIWAKE	KLEPTO	KLUGING
KIRSCH	KITBAGS	KITTLE	KLEPTOS	KLUTZ
KIRSCHES	KITCHEN	KITTLED	KLETT	KLUTZES
KIRTAN	KITCHENED	KITTLER	KLETTS	KLUTZIER
KIRTANS	KITCHENER	KITTLES	KLEZMER	KLUTZIEST
KIRTLE	KITCHENET	KITTLEST	KLEZMERS	KLUTZY
KIRTLED	KITCHENS	KITTLIER	KLEZMORIM	KLYSTRON
KIRTLES	KITE	KITTLIEST	KLICK	KLYSTRONS
KIS	KITEBOARD	KITTLING	KLICKS	KNACK
KISAN	KITED	KITTLY	KLIEG	KNACKED
KISANS	KITELIKE	KITTUL	KLIEGS	KNACKER
KISH	KITENGE	KITTULS	KLIK	KNACKERED
KISHES	KITENGES	KITTY	KLIKS	KNACKERS
KISHKA	KITER	KITUL	KLINKER	KNACKERY
KISHKAS	KITERS	KITULS	KLINKERS	KNACKIER
KISHKE	KITES	KIVA	KLINOSTAT	KNACKIEST
KISHKES	KITH	KIVAS	KLIPDAS	KNACKING
KISKADEE	KITHARA	KIWI	KLIPDASES	KNACKISH
KISKADEES	KITHARAS	KIWIFRUIT	KLISTER	KNACKS
KISMAT	KITHE	KIWIS	KLISTERS	KNACKY
KISMATS	KITHED	KLANG	KLONDIKE	KNAG
KISMET	KITHES	KLANGS	KLONDIKED	KNAGGIER
KISMETIC	KITHING	KLAP	KLONDIKER	KNAGGIEST
KISMETS	KITHS	KLAPPED	KLONDIKES	KNAGGY
KISS	KITING	KLAPPING	KLONDYKE	KNAGS
KISSABLE	KITINGS	KLAPS	KLONDYKED	KNAIDEL
KISSABLY	KITLING	KLATCH	KLONDYKER	KNAIDELS
KISSAGRAM	KITLINGS	KLATCHES	KLONDYKES	KNAIDLACH
KISSED	KITS	KLATSCH	KLONG	KNAP
KISSEL	KITSCH	KLATSCHES	KLONGS	KNAPPED
KISSELS	KITSCHES	KLAVERN	KLOOCH	KNAPPER
KISSER	KITSCHIER	KLAVERNS	KLOOCHES	KNAPPERS
KISSERS	KITSCHIFY	KLAVIER	KLOOCHMAN	KNAPPING
KISSES	KITSCHILY	KLAVIERS	KLOOCHMEN	KNAPPLE
KISSIER	KITSCHY	KLAXON	KLOOF	KNAPPLED
KISSIEST	KITSET	KLAXONED	KLOOFS	KNAPPLES
KISSING	KITSETS	KLAXONING	KLOOTCH	KNAPPLING
KISSINGS	KITTED	KLAXONS	KLOOTCHES	KNAPS
KISSOGRAM	KITTEL	KLEAGLE	KLUDGE	KNAPSACK
KISSY	KITTELS	KLEAGLES	KLUDGED	KNAPSACKS

KNAPWEED	KNEELS	KNISH	KNOCKLESS	KNOWER
KNAPWEEDS	KNEEPAD	KNISHES	KNOCKOFF	KNOWERS
KNAR	KNEEPADS	KNIT	KNOCKOFFS	KNOWES
KNARL	KNEEPAN	KNITBONE	KNOCKOUT	KNOWHOW
KNARLIER	KNEEPANS	KNITBONES	KNOCKOUTS	KNOWHOWS
KNARLIEST	KNEEPIECE	KNITCH	KNOCKS	KNOWING
KNARLS	KNEEROOM	KNITCHES	KNOLL	KNOWINGER
KNARLY	KNEEROOMS	KNITS	KNOLLED	KNOWINGLY
KNARRED	KNEES	KNITTABLE	KNOLLER	KNOWINGS
KNARRIER	KNEESIES	KNITTED	KNOLLERS	KNOWLEDGE
KNARRIEST	KNEESOCK	KNITTER	KNOLLIER	KNOWN
KNARRING	KNEESOCKS	KNITTERS	KNOLLIEST	KNOWNS
KNARRY	KNEIDEL	KNITTING	KNOLLING	KNOWS
KNARS	KNEIDELS	KNITTINGS	KNOLLS	KNUB
KNAUR	KNEIDLACH	KNITTLE	KNOLLY	KNUBBIER
KNAURS	KNELL	KNITTLES	KNOP	KNUBBIEST
KNAVE	KNELLED	KNITWEAR	KNOPPED	KNUBBLE
KNAVERIES	KNELLING	KNITWEARS	KNOPS	KNUBBLED
KNAVERY	KNELLS	KNIVE	KNOSP	KNUBBLES
KNAVES	KNELT	KNIVED	KNOSPS	KNUBBLIER
KNAVESHIP	KNESSET	KNIVES	KNOT	KNUBBLING
KNAVISH	KNESSETS	KNIVING	KNOTGRASS	KNUBBLY
KNAVISHLY	KNEVELL	KNOB	KNOTHEAD	KNUBBY
KNAWE	KNEVELLED	KNOBBED	KNOTHEADS	KNUBS
KNAWEL	KNEVELLS	KNOBBER	KNOTHOLE	KNUCKLE
KNAWELS	KNEW	KNOBBERS	KNOTHOLES	KNUCKLED
KNAWES	KNICKER	KNOBBIER	KNOTLESS	KNUCKLER
KNEAD	KNICKERED	KNOBBIEST	KNOTLIKE	KNUCKLERS
KNEADABLE	KNICKERS	KNOBBING	KNOTS	KNUCKLES
KNEADED	KNICKS	KNOBBLE	KNOTTED	KNUCKLIER
KNEADER	KNIFE	KNOBBLED	KNOTTER	KNUCKLING
KNEADERS	KNIFED	KNOBBLES	KNOTTERS	KNUCKLY
KNEADING	KNIFELESS	KNOBBLIER	KNOTTIER	KNUR
KNEADS	KNIFELIKE	KNOBBLING	KNOTTIEST	KNURL
KNEE	KNIFEMAN	KNOBBLY	KNOTTILY	KNURLED
KNEEBOARD	KNIFEMEN	KNOBBY	KNOTTING	KNURLIER
KNEECAP	KNIFER	KNOBHEAD	KNOTTINGS	KNURLIEST
KNEECAPS	KNIFEREST	KNOBHEADS	KNOTTY	KNURLING
KNEED	KNIFERS	KNOBLIKE	KNOTWEED	KNURLINGS
KNEEHOLE	KNIFES	KNOBS	KNOTWEEDS	KNURLS
KNEEHOLES	KNIFING	KNOBSTICK	KNOTWORK	KNURLY
KNEEING	KNIFINGS	KNOCK	KNOTWORKS	KNURR
KNEEJERK	KNIGHT	KNOCKBACK	KNOUT	KNURRS
KNEEL	KNIGHTAGE	KNOCKDOWN	KNOUTED	KNURS
KNEELED	KNIGHTED	KNOCKED	KNOUTING	KNUT
KNEELER	KNIGHTING	KNOCKER	KNOUTS	KNUTS
KNEELERS	KNIGHTLY	KNOCKERS	KNOW	KO
KNEELIKE	KNIGHTS	KNOCKING	KNOWABLE	KOA
KNEELING	KNIPHOFIA	KNOCKINGS	KNOWE	KOALA

K

KOALAS	KOIS	KOLOS	KOOKUM	KORKIR
KOAN	KOJI	KOMATIK	KOOKUMS	KORKIRS
KOANS	KOJIS	KOMATIKS	KOOKY	KORMA
KOAP	KOKA	KOMBU	KOOLAH	KORMAS
KOAPS	KOKAKO	KOMBUCHA	KOOLAHS	KORO
KOAS	KOKAKOS	KOMBUCHAS	KOORI	KOROMIKO
KOB	KOKAM	KOMBUS	KOORIES	KOROMIKOS
KOBAN	KOKAMS	KOMISSAR	KOORIS	KORORA
KOBANG	KOKANEE	KOMISSARS	KOP	KORORAS
KOBANGS	KOKANEES	KOMITAJI	KOPASETIC	KOROS
KOBANS	KOKAS	KOMITAJIS	KOPECK	KOROWAI
KOBO	KOKER	KOMONDOR	KOPECKS	KOROWAIS
KOBOCHA	KOKERS	KOMONDORS	KOPEK	KORS
KOBOCHAS	KOKIRI	KOMPROMAT	KOPEKS	KORU
KOBOLD	KOKIRIS	KON	KOPH	KORUN
KOBOLDS	KOKOBEH	KONAKI	KOPHS	KORUNA
KOBOS	KOKOPU	KONAKIS	KOPIAH	KORUNAS
KOBS	KOKOPUS	KONBU	KOPIAHS	KORUNY
KOCHIA	KOKOWAI	KONBUS	KOPIYKA	KORUS
KOCHIAS	KOKOWAIS	KOND	KOPIYKAS	KOS
KOEKOEA	KOKRA	KONDO	KOPIYKY	KOSES
KOEKOEAS	KOKRAS	KONDOS	KOPIYOK	KOSHER
KOEL	KOKUM	KONEKE	KOPJE	KOSHERED
KOELS	KOKUMS	KONEKES	KOPJES	KOSHERING
KOFF	KOLA	KONFYT	KOPPA	KOSHERS
KOFFS	KOLACKIES	KONFYTS	KOPPAS	KOSMOS
KOFTA	KOLACKY	KONGONI	KOPPIE	KOSMOSES
KOFTAS	KOLAS	KONIMETER	KOPPIES	KOSS
KOFTGAR	KOLBASI	KONINI	KOPS	KOSSES
KOFTGARI	KOLBASIS	KONINIS	KOR	KOTARE
KOFTGARIS	KOLBASSA	KONIOLOGY	KORA	KOTARES
KOFTGARS	KOLBASSAS	KONISCOPE	KORAI	KOTCH
KOFTWORK	KOLBASSI	KONK	KORARI	KOTCHED
KOFTWORKS	KOLBASSIS	KONKED	KORARIS	KOTCHES
KOGAL	KOLHOZ	KONKING	KORAS	KOTCHING
KOGALS	KOLHOZES	KONKS	KORAT	KOTO
KOHA	KOLHOZY	KONNING	KORATS	KOTOS
KOHANIM	KOLINSKI	KONS	KORE	KOTOW
KOHAS	KOLINSKY	KOODOO	KORERO	KOTOWED
KOHEKOHE	KOLKHOS	KOODOOS	KOREROED	KOTOWER
KOHEKOHES	KOLKHOSES	KOOK	KOREROING	KOTOWERS
KOHEN	KOLKHOSY	KOOKED	KOREROS	KOTOWING
KOHL	KOLKHOZ	KOOKIE	KORES	KOTOWS
KOHLRABI	KOLKHOZES	KOOKIER	KORFBALL	KOTTABOS
KOHLRABIS	KOLKHOZY	KOOKIEST	KORFBALLS	KOTUKU
KOHLS	KOLKOZ	KOOKILY	KORI	KOTUKUS
KOI	KOLKOZES	KOOKINESS	KORIMAKO	KOTWAL
KOINE	KOLKOZY	KOOKING	KORIMAKOS	KOTWALS
KOINES	KOLO	KOOKS	KORIS	KOULAN

KOULANS	KRANSES	KRISHI	KUCCHA	KUMBALOI
KOUMIS	KRANTZ	KRISHIS	KUCCHAS	KUMBAYA
KOUMISES	KRANTZES	KRISING	KUCHCHA	KUMERA
KOUMISS	KRANZ	KROMESKY	KUCHEN	KUMERAS
KOUMISSES	KRANZES	KRONA	KUCHENS	KUMIKUMI
KOUMYS	KRATER	KRONE	KUDLIK	KUMIKUMIS
KOUMYSES	KRATERS	KRONEN	KUDLIKS	KUMIS
KOUMYSS	KRATOM	KRONER	KUDO	KUMISES
KOUMYSSES	KRATOMS	KRONOR	KUDOS	KUMISS
KOUPREY	KRAUT	KRONUR	KUDOSES	KUMISSES
KOUPREYS	KRAUTROCK	KROON	KUDU	KUMITE
KOURA	KRAUTS	KROONI	KUDUS	KUMITES
KOURAS	KRAY	KROONS	KUDZU	KUMKUM
KOURBASH	KRAYS	KRUBI	KUDZUS	KUMKUMS
KOUROI	KREASOTE	KRUBIS	KUE	KUMMEL
KOUROS	KREASOTED	KRUBUT	KUEH	KUMMELS
KOUSKOUS	KREASOTES	KRUBUTS	KUES	KUMQUAT
KOUSSO	KREATINE	KRULLER	KUFI	KUMQUATS
KOUSSOS	KREATINES	KRULLERS	KUFIS	KUMYS
KOW	KREEP	KRUMHORN	KUFIYAH	KUMYSES
KOWHAI	KREEPS	KRUMHORNS	KUFIYAHS	KUNA
KOWHAIS	KREESE	KRUMKAKE	KUGEL	KUNDALINI
KOWS	KREESED	KRUMKAKES	KUGELS	KUNE
KOWTOW	KREESES	KRUMMHOLZ	KUIA	KUNEKUNE
KOWTOWED	KREESING	KRUMMHORN	KUIAS	KUNEKUNES
KOWTOWER	KREMLIN	KRUMPER	KUKRI	KUNJOOS
KOWTOWERS	KREMLINS	KRUMPERS	KUKRIS	KUNJOOSES
KOWTOWING	KRENG	KRUMPING	KUKU	KUNKAR
KOWTOWS	KRENGS	KRUMPINGS	KUKURI	KUNKARS
KRAAL	KREOSOTE	KRUNK	KUKURIS	KUNKUR
KRAALED	KREOSOTED	KRUNKED	KUKUS	KUNKURS
KRAALING	KREOSOTES	KRUNKS	KULA	KUNZITE
KRAALS	KREPLACH	KRYOLITE	KULAK	KUNZITES
KRAB	KREPLACHS	KRYOLITES	KULAKI	KURBASH
KRABS	KREPLECH	KRYOLITH	KULAKS	KURBASHED
KRAFT	KREPLECHS	KRYOLITHS	KULAN	KURBASHES
KRAFTS	KREUTZER	KRYOMETER	KULANS	KURFUFFLE
KRAI	KREUTZERS	KRYPSES	KULAS	KURGAN
KRAIS	KREUZER	KRYPSIS	KULBASA	KURGANS
KRAIT	KREUZERS	KRYPTON	KULBASAS	KURI
KRAITS	KREWE	KRYPTONS	KULFI	KURIS
KRAKEN	KREWES	KRYTRON	KULFIS	KURRAJONG
KRAKENS	KRILL	KRYTRONS	KULTUR	KURRE
KRAKOWIAK	KRILLS	KSAR	KULTURS	KURRES
KRAMERIA	KRIMMER	KSARS	KUMARA	KURSAAL
KRAMERIAS	KRIMMERS	KUBASA	KUMARAHOU	KURSAALS
KRANG	KRIS	KUBASAS	KUMARAS	KURTA
KRANGS	KRISED	KUBIE	KUMARI	KURTAS
KRANS	KRISES	KUBIES	KUMARIS	KURTOSES

K

KURTOSIS	KUZUS	KWELAS	KYBOSH	KYNDE
KURU	KVAS	KY	KYBOSHED	KYNDED
KURUS	KVASES	KYACK	KYBOSHES	KYNDES
KURUSH	KVASS	KYACKS	KYBOSHING	KYNDING
KURUSHES	KVASSES	KYAK	KYDST	KYNDS
KURVEY	KVELL	KYAKS	KYE	KYNE
KURVEYED	KVELLED	KYANG	KYES	KYOGEN
KURVEYING	KVELLING	KYANGS	KYLE	KYOGENS
KURVEYOR	KVELLS	KYANISE	KYLES	KYPE
KURVEYORS	KVETCH	KYANISED	KYLICES	KYPES
KURVEYS	KVETCHED	KYANISES	KYLIE	KYPHOSES
KUSSO	KVETCHER	KYANISING	KYLIES	KYPHOSIS
KUSSOS	KVETCHERS	KYANITE	KYLIKES	KYPHOTIC
KUTA	KVETCHES	KYANITES	KYLIN	KYRIE
KUTAS	KVETCHIER	KYANITIC	KYLINS	KYRIELLE
KUTCH	KVETCHILY	KYANIZE	KYLIX	KYRIELLES
KUTCHA	KVETCHING	KYANIZED	KYLIXES	KYRIES
KUTCHES	KVETCHY	KYANIZES	KYLLOSES	KYTE
KUTI	KWACHA	KYANIZING	KYLLOSIS	KYTES
KUTIS	KWACHAS	KYAR	KYLOE	KYTHE
KUTU	KWAITO	KYARS	KYLOES	KYTHED
KUTUS	KWAITOS	KYAT	KYMOGRAM	KYTHES
KUVASZ	KWANZA	KYATS	KYMOGRAMS	KYTHING
KUVASZOK	KWANZAS	KYBO	KYMOGRAPH	KYU
KUZU	KWELA	KYBOS	KYND	KYUS

L

LA	LABIATES	LABROIDS	LACHES	LACRIMOSO
LAAGER	LABILE	LABROSE	LACHESES	LACROSSE
LAAGERED	LABILITY	LABRUM	LACHRYMAL	LACROSSES
LAAGERING	LABIS	LABRUMS	LACIER	LACRYMAL
LAAGERS	LABISES	LABRUSCA	LACIEST	LACRYMALS
LAARI	LABIUM	LABRUSCAS	LACILY	LACS
LAARIS	LABLAB	LABRYS	LACINESS	LACTAM
LAB	LABLABS	LABRYSES	LACING	LACTAMS
LABARA	LABNEH	LABS	LACINGS	LACTARIAN
LABARUM	LABNEHS	LABURNUM	LACINIA	LACTARY
LABARUMS	LABOR	LABURNUMS	LACINIAE	LACTASE
LABDA	LABORED	LABYRINTH	LACINIATE	LACTASES
LABDACISM	LABOREDLY	LAC	LACK	LACTATE
LABDANUM	LABORER	LACCOLITE	LACKADAY	LACTATED
LABDANUMS	LABORERS	LACCOLITH	LACKED	LACTATES
LABDAS	LABORING	LACE	LACKER	LACTATING
LABEL	LABORIOUS	LACEBARK	LACKERED	LACTATION
LABELABLE	LABORISM	LACEBARKS	LACKERING	LACTEAL
LABELED	LABORISMS	LACED	LACKERS	LACTEALLY
LABELER	LABORIST	LACELESS	LACKEY	LACTEALS
LABELERS	LABORISTS	LACELIKE	LACKEYED	LACTEAN
LABELING	LABORITE	LACEMAKER	LACKEYING	LACTEOUS
LABELLA	LABORITES	LACER	LACKEYS	LACTIC
LABELLATE	LABORS	LACERABLE	LACKING	LACTIFIC
LABELLED	LABORSOME	LACERANT	LACKLAND	LACTITOL
LABELLER	LABOUR	LACERATE	LACKLANDS	LACTITOLS
LABELLERS	LABOURED	LACERATED	LACKS	LACTIVISM
LABELLING	LABOURER	LACERATES	LACMUS	LACTIVIST
LABELLIST	LABOURERS	LACERS	LACMUSES	LACTONE
LABELLOID	LABOURING	LACERTIAN	LACONIC	LACTONES
LABELLUM	LABOURISM	LACERTID	LACONICAL	LACTONIC
LABELMATE	LABOURIST	LACERTIDS	LACONISM	LACTOSE
LABELS	LABOURITE	LACERTINE	LACONISMS	LACTOSES
LABIA	LABOURS	LACES	LACQUER	LACTULOSE
LABIAL	LABRA	LACET	LACQUERED	LACUNA
LABIALISE	LABRADOR	LACETS	LACQUERER	LACUNAE
LABIALISM	LABRADORS	LACEWING	LACQUERS	LACUNAL
LABIALITY	LABRAL	LACEWINGS	LACQUEY	LACUNAR
LABIALIZE	LABRET	LACEWOOD	LACQUEYED	LACUNARIA
LABIALLY	LABRETS	LACEWOODS	LACQUEYS	LACUNARS
LABIALS	LABRID	LACEWORK	LACRIMAL	LACUNARY
LABIATE	LABRIDS	LACEWORKS	LACRIMALS	LACUNAS
LABIATED	LABROID	LACEY	LACRIMARY	LACUNATE

LACUNE	LADLERS	LAEVO	LAHARS	LAIRDLY
LACUNES	LADLES	LAEVOGYRE	LAHS	LAIRDS
LACUNOSE	LADLING	LAEVULIN	LAIC	LAIRDSHIP
LACY	LADRON	LAEVULINS	LAICAL	LAIRED
LAD	LADRONE	LAEVULOSE	LAICALLY	LAIRIER
LADANUM	LADRONES	LAG	LAICH	LAIRIEST
LADANUMS	LADRONS	LAGAN	LAICHS	LAIRING
LADDER	LADS	LAGANS	LAICISE	LAIRISE
LADDERED	LADY	LAGENA	LAICISED	LAIRISED
LADDERIER	LADYBIRD	LAGENAS	LAICISES	LAIRISES
LADDERING	LADYBIRDS	LAGEND	LAICISING	LAIRISING
LADDERS	LADYBOY	LAGENDS	LAICISM	LAIRIZE
LADDERY	LADYBOYS	LAGER	LAICISMS	LAIRIZED
LADDIE	LADYBUG	LAGERED	LAICITIES	LAIRIZES
LADDIER	LADYBUGS	LAGERING	LAICITY	LAIRIZING
LADDIES	LADYCOW	LAGERS	LAICIZE	LAIRS
LADDIEST	LADYCOWS	LAGGARD	LAICIZED	LAIRY
LADDISH	LADYFIED	LAGGARDLY	LAICIZES	LAISSE
LADDISHLY	LADYFIES	LAGGARDS	LAICIZING	LAISSES
LADDISM	LADYFISH	LAGGED	LAICS	LAITANCE
LADDISMS	LADYFLIES	LAGGEN	LAID	LAITANCES
LADDY	LADYFLY	LAGGENS	LAIDED	LAITH
LADE	LADYFY	LAGGER	LAIDING	LAITHLY
LADED	LADYFYING	LAGGERS	LAIDLIER	LAITIES
LADEN	LADYHOOD	LAGGIER	LAIDLIEST	LAITY
LADENED	LADYHOODS	LAGGIEST	LAIDLY	LAKE
LADENING	LADYISH	LAGGIN	LAIDS	LAKEBED
LADENS	LADYISM	LAGGING	LAIGH	LAKEBEDS
LADER	LADYISMS	LAGGINGLY	LAIGHER	LAKED
LADERS	LADYKIN	LAGGINGS	LAIGHEST	LAKEFILL
LADES	LADYKINS	LAGGINS	LAIGHS	LAKEFILLS
LADETTE	LADYLIKE	LAGGY	LAIK	LAKEFRONT
LADETTES	LADYLOVE	LAGNAPPE	LAIKA	LAKEHEAD
LADHOOD	LADYLOVES	LAGNAPPES	LAIKAS	LAKEHEADS
LADHOODS	LADYNESS	LAGNIAPPE	LAIKED	LAKELAND
LADIES	LADYPALM	LAGOMORPH	LAIKER	LAKELANDS
LADIFIED	LADYPALMS	LAGOON	LAIKERS	LAKELET
LADIFIES	LADYSHIP	LAGOONAL	LAIKING	LAKELETS
LADIFY	LADYSHIPS	LAGOONS	LAIKS	LAKELIKE
LADIFYING	LAER	LAGRIMOSO	LAIN	LAKEPORT
LADING	LAERED	LAGS	LAIPSE	LAKEPORTS
LADINGS	LAERING	LAGUNA	LAIPSED	LAKER
LADINO	LAERS	LAGUNAS	LAIPSES	LAKERS
LADINOS	LAESIE	LAGUNE	LAIPSING	LAKES
LADLE	LAETARE	LAGUNES	LAIR	LAKESHORE
LADLED	LAETARES	LAH	LAIRAGE	LAKESIDE
LADLEFUL	LAETRILE	LAHAL	LAIRAGES	LAKESIDES
LADLEFULS	LAETRILES	LAHALS	LAIRD	LAKEVIEW
LADLER	LAEVIGATE	LAHAR	LAIRDLIER	LAKEWARD

LAKEWARDS	LAMBDAS	LAMENTERS	LAMP	LANAIS
LAKH	LAMBDOID	LAMENTING	LAMPAD	LANAS
LAKHS	LAMBED	LAMENTS	LAMPADARY	LANATE
LAKIER	LAMBENCY	LAMER	LAMPADIST	LANATED
LAKIEST	LAMBENT	LAMES	LAMPADS	LANCE
LAKIN	LAMBENTLY	LAMEST	LAMPAS	LANCED
LAKING	LAMBER	LAMETER	LAMPASES	LANCEGAY
LAKINGS	LAMBERS	LAMETERS	LAMPASSE	LANCEGAYS
LAKINS	LAMBERT	LAMIA	LAMPASSES	LANCEJACK
LAKISH	LAMBERTS	LAMIAE	LAMPBLACK	LANCELET
LAKSA	LAMBIE	LAMIAS	LAMPBRUSH	LANCELETS
LAKSAS	LAMBIER	LAMIGER	LAMPED	LANCELIKE
LAKY	LAMBIES	LAMIGERS	LAMPER	LANCEOLAR
LALANG	LAMBIEST	LAMINA	LAMPERN	LANCER
LALANGS	LAMBING	LAMINABLE	LAMPERNS	LANCERS
LALDIE	LAMBINGS	LAMINAE	LAMPERS	LANCES
LALDIES	LAMBITIVE	LAMINAL	LAMPERSES	LANCET
LALDY	LAMBKILL	LAMINALS	LAMPHOLE	LANCETED
LALIQUE	LAMBKILLS	LAMINAR	LAMPHOLES	LANCETS
LALIQUES	LAMBKIN	LAMINARIA	LAMPING	LANCEWOOD
LALL	LAMBKINS	LAMINARIN	LAMPINGS	LANCH
LALLAN	LAMBLIKE	LAMINARY	LAMPION	LANCHED
LALLAND	LAMBLING	LAMINAS	LAMPIONS	LANCHES
LALLANDS	LAMBLINGS	LAMINATE	LAMPLESS	LANCHING
LALLANS	LAMBOYS	LAMINATED	LAMPLIGHT	LANCIERS
LALLATION	LAMBRUSCO	LAMINATES	LAMPLIT	LANCIFORM
LALLED	LAMBS	LAMINATOR	LAMPOON	LANCINATE
LALLING	LAMBSKIN	LAMING	LAMPOONED	LANCING
LALLINGS	LAMBSKINS	LAMINGTON	LAMPOONER	LAND
LALLS	LAMBSWOOL	LAMININ	LAMPOONS	LANDAMMAN
LALLYGAG	LAMBY	LAMININS	LAMPPOST	LANDAU
LALLYGAGS	LAME	LAMINITIS	LAMPPOSTS	LANDAULET
LAM	LAMEBRAIN	LAMINOSE	LAMPREY	LANDAUS
LAMA	LAMED	LAMINOUS	LAMPREYS	LANDBOARD
LAMAISTIC	LAMEDH	LAMISH	LAMPS	LANDDAMNE
LAMANTIN	LAMEDHS	LAMISTER	LAMPSHADE	LANDDROS
LAMANTINS	LAMEDS	LAMISTERS	LAMPSHELL	LANDDROST
LAMAS	LAMELLA	LAMITER	LAMPSTAND	LANDE
LAMASERAI	LAMELLAE	LAMITERS	LAMPUKA	LANDED
LAMASERY	LAMELLAR	LAMMED	LAMPUKAS	LANDER
LAMB	LAMELLAS	LAMMER	LAMPUKI	LANDERS
LAMBADA	LAMELLATE	LAMMERS	LAMPUKIS	LANDES
LAMBADAS	LAMELLOID	LAMMIE	LAMPYRID	LANDFALL
LAMBAST	LAMELLOSE	LAMMIES	LAMPYRIDS	LANDFALLS
LAMBASTE	LAMELY	LAMMIGER	LAMS	LANDFAST
LAMBASTED	LAMENESS	LAMMIGERS	LAMSTER	LANDFILL
LAMBASTES	LAMENT	LAMMING	LAMSTERS	LANDFILLS
LAMBASTS	LAMENTED	LAMMINGS	LANA	LANDFORCE
LAMBDA	LAMENTER	LAMMY	LANAI	LANDFORM

LANDFORMS	LANES	LANIARIES	LAOGAIS	LAPSE
LANDGRAB	LANEWAY	LANIARY	LAP	LAPSED
LANDGRABS	LANEWAYS	LANITAL	LAPBOARD	LAPSER
LANDGRAVE	LANG	LANITALS	LAPBOARDS	LAPSERS
LANDING	LANGAHA	LANK	LAPDOG	LAPSES
LANDINGS	LANGAHAS	LANKED	LAPDOGS	LAPSIBLE
LANDLADY	LANGAR	LANKER	LAPEL	LAPSING
LANDLER	LANGARS	LANKEST	LAPELED	LAPSTONE
LANDLERS	LANGER	LANKIER	LAPELLED	LAPSTONES
LANDLESS	LANGERED	LANKIEST	LAPELS	LAPSTRAKE
LANDLINE	LANGERS	LANKILY	LAPFUL	LAPSTREAK
LANDLINES	LANGEST	LANKINESS	LAPFULS	LAPSUS
LANDLOPER	LANGLAUF	LANKING	LAPHELD	LAPTOP
LANDLORD	LANGLAUFS	LANKLY	LAPIDARY	LAPTOPS
LANDLORDS	LANGLEY	LANKNESS	LAPIDATE	LAPTRAY
LANDMAN	LANGLEYS	LANKS	LAPIDATED	LAPTRAYS
LANDMARK	LANGOUSTE	LANKY	LAPIDATES	LAPWING
LANDMARKS	LANGRAGE	LANNER	LAPIDEOUS	LAPWINGS
LANDMASS	LANGRAGES	LANNERET	LAPIDES	LAPWORK
LANDMEN	LANGREL	LANNERETS	LAPIDIFIC	LAPWORKS
LANDMINE	LANGRELS	LANNERS	LAPIDIFY	LAQUEARIA
LANDMINED	LANGRIDGE	LANOLATED	LAPIDIST	LAR
LANDMINES	LANGSHAN	LANOLIN	LAPIDISTS	LARBOARD
LANDOWNER	LANGSHANS	LANOLINE	LAPILLI	LARBOARDS
LANDRACE	LANGSPEL	LANOLINES	LAPILLUS	LARCENER
LANDRACES	LANGSPELS	LANOLINS	LAPIN	LARCENERS
LANDRAIL	LANGSPIEL	LANOSE	LAPINS	LARCENIES
LANDRAILS	LANGSPIL	LANOSITY	LAPIS	LARCENIST
LANDS	LANGSPILS	LANT	LAPISES	LARCENOUS
LANDSCAPE	LANGSYNE	LANTANA	LAPJE	LARCENY
LANDSHARK	LANGSYNES	LANTANAS	LAPJES	LARCH
LANDSIDE	LANGUAGE	LANTERLOO	LAPPED	LARCHEN
LANDSIDES	LANGUAGED	LANTERN	LAPPEL	LARCHES
LANDSKIP	LANGUAGES	LANTERNED	LAPPELS	LARCHWOOD
LANDSKIPS	LANGUE	LANTERNS	LAPPER	LARD
LANDSLEIT	LANGUED	LANTHANON	LAPPERED	LARDALITE
LANDSLID	LANGUES	LANTHANUM	LAPPERING	LARDED
LANDSLIDE	LANGUET	LANTHORN	LAPPERS	LARDER
LANDSLIP	LANGUETS	LANTHORNS	LAPPET	LARDERER
LANDSLIPS	LANGUETTE	LANTS	LAPPETED	LARDERERS
LANDSMAN	LANGUID	LANTSKIP	LAPPETS	LARDERS
LANDSMEN	LANGUIDLY	LANTSKIPS	LAPPIE	LARDIER
LANDWARD	LANGUISH	LANUGO	LAPPIES	LARDIEST
LANDWARDS	LANGUOR	LANUGOS	LAPPING	LARDING
LANDWASH	LANGUORS	LANX	LAPPINGS	LARDLIKE
LANDWIND	LANGUR	LANYARD	LAPS	LARDON
LANDWINDS	LANGURS	LANYARDS	LAPSABLE	LARDONS
LANE	LANIARD	LAODICEAN	LAPSANG	LARDOON
LANELY	LANIARDS	LAOGAI	LAPSANGS	LARDOONS

L

LARDS	LARMIERS	LASED	LASTAGE	LATERALLY
LARDY	LARN	LASER	LASTAGES	LATERALS
LARE	LARNAKES	LASERDISC	LASTBORN	LATERBORN
LAREE	LARNAX	LASERDISK	LASTBORNS	LATERISE
LAREES	LARNED	LASERED	LASTED	LATERISED
LARES	LARNEY	LASERING	LASTER	LATERISES
LARGANDO	LARNEYS	LASERS	LASTERS	LATERITE
LARGE	LARNIER	LASERWORT	LASTING	LATERITES
LARGELY	LARNIEST	LASES	LASTINGLY	LATERITIC
LARGEN	LARNING	LASH	LASTINGS	LATERIZE
LARGENED	LARNS	LASHED	LASTLY	LATERIZED
LARGENESS	LARNT	LASHER	LASTS	LATERIZES
LARGENING	LAROID	LASHERS	LAT	LATERS
LARGENS	LARRIGAN	LASHES	LATAH	LATESCENT
LARGER	LARRIGANS	LASHING	LATAHS	LATEST
LARGES	LARRIKIN	LASHINGLY	LATAKIA	LATESTS
LARGESS	LARRIKINS	LASHINGS	LATAKIAS	LATEWAKE
LARGESSE	LARRUP	LASHINS	LATCH	LATEWAKES
LARGESSES	LARRUPED	LASHKAR	LATCHED	LATEWOOD
LARGEST	LARRUPER	LASHKARS	LATCHES	LATEWOODS
LARGHETTO	LARRUPERS	LASHLESS	LATCHET	LATEX
LARGISH	LARRUPING	LASING	LATCHETS	LATEXES
LARGITION	LARRUPS	LASINGS	LATCHING	LATH
LARGO	LARS	LASKET	LATCHKEY	LATHE
LARGOS	LARUM	LASKETS	LATCHKEYS	LATHED
LARI	LARUMS	LASQUE	LATE	LATHEE
LARIAT	LARVA	LASQUES	LATECOMER	LATHEES
LARIATED	LARVAE	LASS	LATED	LATHEN
LARIATING	LARVAL	LASSES	LATEEN	LATHER
LARIATS	LARVAS	LASSI	LATEENER	LATHERED
LARIGAN	LARVATE	LASSIE	LATEENERS	LATHERER
LARIGANS	LARVATED	LASSIES	LATEENS	LATHERERS
LARINE	LARVICIDE	LASSIS	LATELY	LATHERIER
LARIS	LARVIFORM	LASSITUDE	LATEN	LATHERING
LARK	LARVIKITE	LASSLORN	LATENCE	LATHERS
LARKED	LARYNGAL	LASSO	LATENCES	LATHERY
LARKER	LARYNGALS	LASSOCK	LATENCIES	LATHES
LARKERS	LARYNGEAL	LASSOCKS	LATENCY	LATHI
LARKIER	LARYNGES	LASSOED	LATENED	LATHIER
LARKIEST	LARYNX	LASSOER	LATENESS	LATHIEST
LARKINESS	LARYNXES	LASSOERS	LATENING	LATHING
LARKING	LAS	LASSOES	LATENS	LATHINGS
LARKISH	LASAGNA	LASSOING	LATENT	LATHIS
LARKS	LASAGNAS	LASSOINGS	LATENTLY	LATHLIKE
LARKSOME	LASAGNE	LASSOS	LATENTS	LATHS
LARKSPUR	LASAGNES	LASSU	LATER	LATHWORK
LARKSPURS	LASCAR	LASSUS	LATERAD	LATHWORKS
LARKY	LASCARS	LASSY	LATERAL	LATHY
LARMIER	LASE	LAST	LATERALED	LATHYRISM

LATHYRUS	LATTER	LAUGHSOME	LAVALAVA	LAVROCK
LATI	LATTERLY	LAUGHTER	LAVALAVAS	LAVROCKS
LATICES	LATTERS	LAUGHTERS	LAVALIER	LAVS
LATICIFER	LATTES	LAUGHY	LAVALIERE	LAVVIES
LATICLAVE	LATTICE	LAUNCE	LAVALIERS	LAVVY
LATIFONDI	LATTICED	LAUNCED	LAVALIKE	LAW
LATIFONDO	LATTICES	LAUNCES	LAVANDIN	LAWBOOK
LATIGO	LATTICING	LAUNCH	LAVANDINS	LAWBOOKS
LATIGOES	LATTICINI	LAUNCHED	LAVAS	LAWCOURT
LATIGOS	LATTICINO	LAUNCHER	LAVASH	LAWCOURTS
LATILLA	LATTIN	LAUNCHERS	LAVASHES	LAWED
LATILLAS	LATTINS	LAUNCHES	LAVATERA	LAWER
LATIMERIA	LATU	LAUNCHING	LAVATERAS	LAWEST
LATINA	LATUS	LAUNCHPAD	LAVATION	LAWFARE
LATINAS	LAUAN	LAUNCING	LAVATIONS	LAWFARES
LATINISE	LAUANS	LAUND	LAVATORY	LAWFUL
LATINISED	LAUCH	LAUNDER	LAVE	LAWFULLY
LATINISES	LAUCHING	LAUNDERED	LAVED	LAWGIVER
LATINITY	LAUCHS	LAUNDERER	LAVEER	LAWGIVERS
LATINIZE	LAUD	LAUNDERS	LAVEERED	LAWGIVING
LATINIZED	LAUDABLE	LAUNDRESS	LAVEERING	LAWIN
LATINIZES	LAUDABLY	LAUNDRIES	LAVEERS	LAWINE
LATINO	LAUDANUM	LAUNDRY	LAVEMENT	LAWINES
LATINOS	LAUDANUMS	LAUNDS	LAVEMENTS	LAWING
LATISH	LAUDATION	LAURA	LAVENDER	LAWINGS
LATITANCY	LAUDATIVE	LAURAE	LAVENDERS	LAWINS
LATITANT	LAUDATOR	LAURAS	LAVER	LAWK
LATITAT	LAUDATORS	LAUREATE	LAVEROCK	LAWKS
LATITATS	LAUDATORY	LAUREATED	LAVEROCKS	LAWLAND
LATITUDE	LAUDED	LAUREATES	LAVERS	LAWLANDS
LATITUDES	LAUDER	LAUREL	LAVES	LAWLESS
LATKE	LAUDERS	LAURELED	LAVING	LAWLESSLY
LATKES	LAUDING	LAURELING	LAVISH	LAWLIKE
LATOSOL	LAUDS	LAURELLED	LAVISHED	LAWMAKER
LATOSOLIC	LAUF	LAURELS	LAVISHER	LAWMAKERS
LATOSOLS	LAUFS	LAURIC	LAVISHERS	LAWMAKING
LATRANT	LAUGH	LAURYL	LAVISHES	LAWMAN
LATRATION	LAUGHABLE	LAURYLS	LAVISHEST	LAWMEN
LATRIA	LAUGHABLY	LAUWINE	LAVISHING	LAWMONGER
LATRIAS	LAUGHED	LAUWINES	LAVISHLY	LAWN
LATRINE	LAUGHER	LAV	LAVOLT	LAWNED
LATRINES	LAUGHERS	LAVA	LAVOLTA	LAWNIER
LATROCINY	LAUGHFUL	LAVABO	LAVOLTAED	LAWNIEST
LATRON	LAUGHIER	LAVABOES	LAVOLTAS	LAWNING
LATRONS	LAUGHIEST	LAVABOS	LAVOLTED	LAWNMOWER
LATS	LAUGHING	LAVAFORM	LAVOLTING	LAWNS
LATTE	LAUGHINGS	LAVAGE	LAVOLTS	LAWNY
LATTEN	LAUGHLINE	LAVAGES	LAVRA	LAWS
LATTENS	LAUGHS	LAVAL	LAVRAS	LAWSUIT

LAWSUITS	LAYINS	LAZULITE	LEADPLANT	LEAKED
LAWYER	LAYLOCK	LAZULITES	LEADS	LEAKER
LAWYERED	LAYLOCKS	LAZURITE	LEADSCREW	LEAKERS
LAWYERING	LAYMAN	LAZURITES	LEADSMAN	LEAKIER
LAWYERLY	LAYMANISE	LAZY	LEADSMEN	LEAKIEST
LAWYERS	LAYMANIZE	LAZYBONES	LEADWORK	LEAKILY
LAX	LAYMEN	LAZYING	LEADWORKS	LEAKINESS
LAXATION	LAYOFF	LAZYISH	LEADWORT	LEAKING
LAXATIONS	LAYOFFS	LAZZARONE	LEADWORTS	LEAKLESS
LAXATIVE	LAYOUT	LAZZARONI	LEADY	LEAKPROOF
LAXATIVES	LAYOUTS	LAZZI	LEAF	LEAKS
LAXATOR	LAYOVER	LAZZO	LEAFAGE	LEAKY
LAXATORS	LAYOVERS	LEA	LEAFAGES	LEAL
LAXED	LAYPEOPLE	LEACH	LEAFBUD	LEALER
LAXER	LAYPERSON	LEACHABLE	LEAFBUDS	LEALEST
LAXES	LAYS	LEACHATE	LEAFED	LEALLY
LAXEST	LAYSHAFT	LEACHATES	LEAFER	LEALTIES
LAXING	LAYSHAFTS	LEACHED	LEAFERIES	LEALTY
LAXISM	LAYSTALL	LEACHER	LEAFERS	LEAM
LAXISMS	LAYSTALLS	LEACHERS	LEAFERY	LEAMED
LAXIST	LAYTIME	LEACHES	LEAFIER	LEAMING
LAXISTS	LAYTIMES	LEACHIER	LEAFIEST	LEAMS
LAXITIES	LAYUP	LEACHIEST	LEAFINESS	LEAN
LAXITY	LAYUPS	LEACHING	LEAFING	LEANED
LAXLY	LAYWOMAN	LEACHINGS	LEAFLESS	LEANER
LAXNESS	LAYWOMEN	LEACHOUR	LEAFLET	LEANERS
LAXNESSES	LAZAR	LEACHOURS	LEAFLETED	LEANEST
LAY	LAZARET	LEACHY	LEAFLETER	LEANING
LAYABOUT	LAZARETS	LEAD	LEAFLETS	LEANINGS
LAYABOUTS	LAZARETTE	LEADABLE	LEAFLIKE	LEANLY
LAYAWAY	LAZARETTO	LEADED	LEAFMOLD	LEANNESS
LAYAWAYS	LAZARS	LEADEN	LEAFMOLDS	LEANS
LAYBACK	LAZE	LEADENED	LEAFROLL	LEANT
LAYBACKED	LAZED	LEADENING	LEAFROLLS	LEANY
LAYBACKS	LAZES	LEADENLY	LEAFS	LEAP
LAYDEEZ	LAZIED	LEADENS	LEAFSTALK	LEAPED
LAYED	LAZIER	LEADER	LEAFWORM	LEAPER
LAYER	LAZIES	LEADERENE	LEAFWORMS	LEAPEROUS
LAYERAGE	LAZIEST	LEADERS	LEAFY	LEAPERS
LAYERAGES	LAZILY	LEADIER	LEAGUE	LEAPFROG
LAYERED	LAZINESS	LEADIEST	LEAGUED	LEAPFROGS
LAYERING	LAZING	LEADING	LEAGUER	LEAPING
LAYERINGS	LAZO	LEADINGLY	LEAGUERED	LEAPOROUS
LAYERS	LAZOED	LEADINGS	LEAGUERS	LEAPROUS
LAYETTE	LAZOES	LEADLESS	LEAGUES	LEAPS
LAYETTES	LAZOING	LEADMAN	LEAGUING	LEAPT
LAYIN	LAZOS	LEADMEN	LEAK	LEAR
LAYING	LAZULI	LEADOFF	LEAKAGE	LEARE
LAYINGS	LAZULIS	LEADOFFS	LEAKAGES	LEARED

LEARES	LEATHERS	LECITHINS	LEECHEE	LEFTMOST
LEARIER	LEATHERY	LECTERN	LEECHEES	LEFTMOSTS
LEARIEST	LEATS	LECTERNS	LEECHES	LEFTOVER
LEARILY	LEAVE	LECTIN	LEECHING	LEFTOVERS
LEARINESS	LEAVED	LECTINS	LEECHLIKE	LEFTS
LEARING	LEAVEN	LECTION	LEED	LEFTWARD
LEARN	LEAVENED	LECTIONS	LEEING	LEFTWARDS
LEARNABLE	LEAVENER	LECTOR	LEEK	LEFTWING
LEARNED	LEAVENERS	LECTORATE	LEEKS	LEFTY
LEARNEDLY	LEAVENING	LECTORS	LEEP	LEG
LEARNER	LEAVENOUS	LECTOTYPE	LEEPED	LEGACIES
LEARNERS	LEAVENS	LECTRESS	LEEPING	LEGACY
LEARNING	LEAVER	LECTURE	LEEPS	LEGAL
LEARNINGS	LEAVERS	LECTURED	LEER	LEGALESE
LEARNS	LEAVES	LECTURER	LEERED	LEGALESES
LEARNT	LEAVIER	LECTURERS	LEERIER	LEGALISE
LEARS	LEAVIEST	LECTURES	LEERIEST	LEGALISED
LEARY	LEAVING	LECTURING	LEERILY	LEGALISER
LEAS	LEAVINGS	LECTURN	LEERINESS	LEGALISES
LEASABLE	LEAVY	LECTURNS	LEERING	LEGALISM
LEASE	LEAZE	LECYTHI	LEERINGLY	LEGALISMS
LEASEBACK	LEAZES	LECYTHIS	LEERINGS	LEGALIST
LEASED	LEBBEK	LECYTHUS	LEERS	LEGALISTS
LEASEHOLD	LEBBEKS	LED	LEERY	LEGALITY
LEASER	LEBEN	LEDDEN	LEES	LEGALIZE
LEASERS	LEBENS	LEDDENS	LEESE	LEGALIZED
LEASES	LEBKUCHEN	LEDE	LEESES	LEGALIZER
LEASH	LECANORA	LEDES	LEESING	LEGALIZES
LEASHED	LECANORAS	LEDGE	LEET	LEGALLY
LEASHES	LECCIES	LEDGED	LEETLE	LEGALS
LEASHING	LECCY	LEDGER	LEETS	LEGATARY
LEASING	LECH	LEDGERED	LEETSPEAK	LEGATE
LEASINGS	LECHAIM	LEDGERING	LEEWARD	LEGATED
LEASOW	LECHAIMS	LEDGERS	LEEWARDLY	LEGATEE
LEASOWE	LECHAYIM	LEDGES	LEEWARDS	LEGATEES
LEASOWED	LECHAYIMS	LEDGIER	LEEWAY	LEGATES
LEASOWES	LECHED	LEDGIEST	LEEWAYS	LEGATINE
LEASOWING	LECHER	LEDGY	LEEZE	LEGATING
LEASOWS	LECHERED	LEDUM	LEFT	LEGATION
LEAST	LECHERIES	LEDUMS	LEFTE	LEGATIONS
LEASTS	LECHERING	LEE	LEFTER	LEGATO
LEASTWAYS	LECHEROUS	LEEAR	LEFTEST	LEGATOR
LEASTWISE	LECHERS	LEEARS	LEFTIE	LEGATORS
LEASURE	LECHERY	LEEBOARD	LEFTIES	LEGATOS
LEASURES	LECHES	LEEBOARDS	LEFTISH	LEGEND
LEAT	LECHING	LEECH	LEFTISM	LEGENDARY
LEATHER	LECHWE	LEECHDOM	LEFTISMS	LEGENDISE
LEATHERED	LECHWES	LEECHDOMS	LEFTIST	LEGENDIST
LEATHERN	LECITHIN	LEECHED	LEFTISTS	LEGENDIZE

LEGENDRY	LEGLESS	LEIS	LEMNISCI	LENGTHS
LEGENDS	LEGLET	LEISH	LEMNISCUS	LENGTHY
LEGER	LEGLETS	LEISHER	LEMON	LENIENCE
LEGERING	LEGLIKE	LEISHEST	LEMONADE	LENIENCES
LEGERINGS	LEGLIN	LEISLER	LEMONADES	LENIENCY
LEGERITY	LEGLINS	LEISLERS	LEMONED	LENIENT
LEGERS	LEGMAN	LEISTER	LEMONFISH	LENIENTLY
LEGES	LEGMEN	LEISTERED	LEMONIER	LENIENTS
LEGGE	LEGONG	LEISTERS	LEMONIEST	LENIFIED
LEGGED	LEGONGS	LEISURE	LEMONING	LENIFIES
LEGGER	LEGROOM	LEISURED	LEMONISH	LENIFY
LEGGERS	LEGROOMS	LEISURELY	LEMONLIKE	LENIFYING
LEGGES	LEGS	LEISURES	LEMONS	LENIS
LEGGIE	LEGSIDE	LEISURING	LEMONWOOD	LENITE
LEGGIER	LEGSIDES	LEITMOTIF	LEMONY	LENITED
LEGGIERO	LEGUAAN	LEITMOTIV	LEMPIRA	LENITES
LEGGIES	LEGUAANS	LEK	LEMPIRAS	LENITIES
LEGGIEST	LEGUAN	LEKE	LEMUR	LENITING
LEGGIN	LEGUANS	LEKGOTLA	LEMURES	LENITION
LEGGINESS	LEGUME	LEKGOTLAS	LEMURIAN	LENITIONS
LEGGING	LEGUMES	LEKKED	LEMURIANS	LENITIVE
LEGGINGED	LEGUMIN	LEKKER	LEMURINE	LENITIVES
LEGGINGS	LEGUMINS	LEKKING	LEMURINES	LENITY
LEGGINS	LEGWARMER	LEKKINGS	LEMURLIKE	LENO
LEGGISM	LEGWEAR	LEKS	LEMUROID	LENOS
LEGGISMS	LEGWEARS	LEKU	LEMUROIDS	LENS
LEGGO	LEGWORK	LEKVAR	LEMURS	LENSE
LEGGY	LEGWORKS	LEKVARS	LEND	LENSED
LEGHOLD	LEHAIM	LEKYTHI	LENDABLE	LENSES
LEGHOLDS	LEHAIMS	LEKYTHOI	LENDER	LENSING
LEGHORN	LEHAYIM	LEKYTHOS	LENDERS	LENSINGS
LEGHORNS	LEHAYIMS	LEKYTHUS	LENDING	LENSLESS
LEGIBLE	LEHR	LEMAN	LENDINGS	LENSLIKE
LEGIBLY	LEHRJAHRE	LEMANS	LENDS	LENSMAN
LEGION	LEHRS	LEME	LENES	LENSMEN
LEGIONARY	LEHUA	LEMED	LENG	LENT
LEGIONED	LEHUAS	LEMEL	LENGED	LENTANDO
LEGIONS	LEI	LEMELS	LENGER	LENTEN
LEGISLATE	LEIDGER	LEMES	LENGEST	LENTI
LEGIST	LEIDGERS	LEMING	LENGING	LENTIC
LEGISTS	LEIGER	LEMMA	LENGS	LENTICEL
LEGIT	LEIGERS	LEMMAS	LENGTH	LENTICELS
LEGITIM	LEIOMYOMA	LEMMATA	LENGTHEN	LENTICLE
LEGITIMS	LEIPOA	LEMMATISE	LENGTHENS	LENTICLES
LEGITS	LEIPOAS	LEMMATIZE	LENGTHFUL	LENTICULE
LEGLAN	LEIR	LEMME	LENGTHIER	LENTIFORM
LEGLANS	LEIRED	LEMMING	LENGTHILY	LENTIGO
LEGLEN	LEIRING	LEMMINGS	LENGTHMAN	LENTIL
LEGLENS	LEIRS	LEMNISCAL	LENGTHMEN	LENTILS

L

LENTISC	LEPTOMES	LETCHED	LEUCEMIC	LEVA
LENTISCS	LEPTON	LETCHES	LEUCH	LEVANT
LENTISK	LEPTONIC	LETCHING	LEUCHEN	LEVANTED
LENTISKS	LEPTONS	LETCHINGS	LEUCIN	LEVANTER
LENTO	LEPTOPHOS	LETDOWN	LEUCINE	LEVANTERS
LENTOID	LEPTOSOME	LETDOWNS	LEUCINES	LEVANTINE
LENTOIDS	LEPTOTENE	LETHAL	LEUCINS	LEVANTING
LENTOR	LEQUEAR	LETHALITY	LEUCISM	LEVANTS
LENTORS	LEQUEARS	LETHALLY	LEUCISMS	LEVAS
LENTOS	LERE	LETHALS	LEUCISTIC	LEVATOR
LENTOUS	LERED	LETHARGIC	LEUCITE	LEVATORES
LENVOY	LERES	LETHARGY	LEUCITES	LEVATORS
LENVOYS	LERING	LETHE	LEUCITIC	LEVE
LEONE	LERNAEAN	LETHEAN	LEUCO	LEVEE
LEONES	LERP	LETHEE	LEUCOCYTE	LEVEED
LEONINE	LERPS	LETHEES	LEUCOMA	LEVEEING
LEOPARD	LESBIAN	LETHES	LEUCOMAS	LEVEES
LEOPARDS	LESBIANS	LETHIED	LEUCON	LEVEL
LEOTARD	LESBIC	LETOUT	LEUCONS	LEVELED
LEOTARDED	LESBIGAY	LETOUTS	LEUCOSES	LEVELER
LEOTARDS	LESBIGAYS	LETROZOLE	LEUCOSIN	LEVELERS
LEP	LESION	LETS	LEUCOSINS	LEVELING
LEPER	LESIONED	LETTABLE	LEUCOSIS	LEVELLED
LEPERS	LESIONING	LETTED	LEUCOTIC	LEVELLER
LEPID	LESIONS	LETTER	LEUCOTOME	LEVELLERS
LEPIDOTE	LESPEDEZA	LETTERBOX	LEUCOTOMY	LEVELLEST
LEPIDOTES	LESS	LETTERED	LEUD	LEVELLING
LEPORID	LESSEE	LETTERER	LEUDES	LEVELLY
LEPORIDAE	LESSEES	LETTERERS	LEUDS	LEVELNESS
LEPORIDS	LESSEN	LETTERING	LEUGH	LEVELS
LEPORINE	LESSENED	LETTERMAN	LEUGHEN	LEVER
LEPPED	LESSENING	LETTERMEN	LEUKAEMIA	LEVERAGE
LEPPING	LESSENS	LETTERN	LEUKAEMIC	LEVERAGED
LEPRA	LESSER	LETTERNS	LEUKEMIA	LEVERAGES
LEPRAS	LESSES	LETTERS	LEUKEMIAS	LEVERED
LEPROSE	LESSON	LETTERSET	LEUKEMIC	LEVERET
LEPROSERY	LESSONED	LETTING	LEUKEMICS	LEVERETS
LEPROSIES	LESSONING	LETTINGS	LEUKEMOID	LEVERING
LEPROSITY	LESSONS	LETTRE	LEUKOCYTE	LEVERS
LEPROSY	LESSOR	LETTRES	LEUKOMA	LEVES
LEPROTIC	LESSORS	LETTUCE	LEUKOMAS	LEVIABLE
LEPROUS	LEST	LETTUCES	LEUKON	LEVIATHAN
LEPROUSLY	LESTED	LETUP	LEUKONS	LEVIED
LEPS	LESTING	LETUPS	LEUKOSES	LEVIER
LEPT	LESTS	LEU	LEUKOSIS	LEVIERS
LEPTA	LESULA	LEUCAEMIA	LEUKOTIC	LEVIES
LEPTIN	LESULAS	LEUCAEMIC	LEUKOTOME	LEVIGABLE
LEPTINS	LET	LEUCEMIA	LEUKOTOMY	LEVIGATE
LEPTOME	LETCH	LEUCEMIAS	LEV	LEVIGATED

LEVIGATES	LEWKS	LIBATED	LIBERTINE	LICENSURE
LEVIGATOR	LEX	LIBATES	LIBERTY	LICENTE
LEVIN	LEXEME	LIBATING	LIBIDINAL	LICH
LEVINS	LEXEMES	LIBATION	LIBIDO	LICHANOI
LEVIRATE	LEXEMIC	LIBATIONS	LIBIDOS	LICHANOS
LEVIRATES	LEXES	LIBATORY	LIBKEN	LICHEE
LEVIRATIC	LEXICA	LIBBARD	LIBKENS	LICHEES
LEVIS	LEXICAL	LIBBARDS	LIBLAB	LICHEN
LEVITATE	LEXICALLY	LIBBED	LIBLABS	LICHENED
LEVITATED	LEXICON	LIBBER	LIBRA	LICHENIN
LEVITATES	LEXICONS	LIBBERS	LIBRAE	LICHENING
LEVITATOR	LEXIGRAM	LIBBING	LIBRAIRE	LICHENINS
LEVITE	LEXIGRAMS	LIBECCHIO	LIBRAIRES	LICHENISM
LEVITES	LEXIS	LIBECCIO	LIBRAIRIE	LICHENIST
LEVITIC	LEXISES	LIBECCIOS	LIBRARIAN	LICHENOID
LEVITICAL	LEY	LIBEL	LIBRARIES	LICHENOSE
LEVITIES	LEYLANDI	LIBELANT	LIBRARY	LICHENOUS
LEVITY	LEYLANDII	LIBELANTS	LIBRAS	LICHENS
LEVO	LEYLANDIS	LIBELED	LIBRATE	LICHES
LEVODOPA	LEYS	LIBELEE	LIBRATED	LICHGATE
LEVODOPAS	LI	LIBELEES	LIBRATES	LICHGATES
LEVOGYRE	LIABILITY	LIBELER	LIBRATING	LICHI
LEVOGYRES	LIABLE	LIBELERS	LIBRATION	LICHIS
LEVS	LIAISE	LIBELING	LIBRATORY	LICHT
LEVULIN	LIAISED	LIBELINGS	LIBRETTI	LICHTED
LEVULINS	LIAISES	LIBELIST	LIBRETTO	LICHTER
LEVULOSE	LIAISING	LIBELISTS	LIBRETTOS	LICHTEST
LEVULOSES	LIAISON	LIBELLANT	LIBRI	LICHTING
LEVY	LIAISONS	LIBELLED	LIBRIFORM	LICHTLIED
LEVYING	LIANA	LIBELLEE	LIBS	LICHTLIES
LEW	LIANAS	LIBELLEES	LICE	LICHTLY
LEWD	LIANE	LIBELLER	LICENCE	LICHTS
LEWDER	LIANES	LIBELLERS	LICENCED	LICHWAKE
LEWDEST	LIANG	LIBELLING	LICENCEE	LICHWAKES
LEWDLY	LIANGS	LIBELLOUS	LICENCEES	LICHWAY
LEWDNESS	LIANOID	LIBELOUS	LICENCER	LICHWAYS
LEWDSBIES	LIAR	LIBELS	LICENCERS	LICIT
LEWDSBY	LIARD	LIBER	LICENCES	LICITLY
LEWDSTER	LIARDS	LIBERAL	LICENCING	LICITNESS
LEWDSTERS	LIARS	LIBERALLY	LICENSE	LICK
LEWIS	LIART	LIBERALS	LICENSED	LICKED
LEWISES	LIAS	LIBERATE	LICENSEE	LICKER
LEWISIA	LIASES	LIBERATED	LICENSEES	LICKERISH
LEWISIAS	LIASSIC	LIBERATES	LICENSER	LICKERS
LEWISITE	LIATRIS	LIBERATOR	LICENSERS	LICKING
LEWISITES	LIATRISES	LIBERO	LICENSES	LICKINGS
LEWISSON	LIB	LIBEROS	LICENSING	LICKPENNY
LEWISSONS	LIBANT	LIBERS	LICENSOR	LICKS
LEWK	LIBATE	LIBERTIES	LICENSORS	LICKSPIT

LICKSPITS	LIERS	LIFTED	LIGHTERS	LIGULAS
LICORICE	LIES	LIFTER	LIGHTEST	LIGULATE
LICORICES	LIEU	LIFTERS	LIGHTFACE	LIGULATED
LICTOR	LIEUS	LIFTGATE	LIGHTFAST	LIGULE
LICTORIAN	LIEVE	LIFTGATES	LIGHTFUL	LIGULES
LICTORS	LIEVER	LIFTING	LIGHTING	LIGULOID
LID	LIEVES	LIFTMAN	LIGHTINGS	LIGURE
LIDAR	LIEVEST	LIFTMEN	LIGHTISH	LIGURES
LIDARS	LIFE	LIFTOFF	LIGHTLESS	LIGUSTRUM
LIDDED	LIFEBELT	LIFTOFFS	LIGHTLIED	LIKABLE
LIDDING	LIFEBELTS	LIFTS	LIGHTLIES	LIKABLY
LIDDINGS	LIFEBLOOD	LIFULL	LIGHTLY	LIKE
LIDGER	LIFEBOAT	LIG	LIGHTNESS	LIKEABLE
LIDGERS	LIFEBOATS	LIGAMENT	LIGHTNING	LIKEABLY
LIDLESS	LIFEBUOY	LIGAMENTS	LIGHTS	LIKED
LIDO	LIFEBUOYS	LIGAN	LIGHTSHIP	LIKELIER
LIDOCAINE	LIFECARE	LIGAND	LIGHTSOME	LIKELIEST
LIDOS	LIFECARES	LIGANDS	LIGHTWAVE	LIKELY
LIDS	LIFEFUL	LIGANS	LIGHTWOOD	LIKEN
LIE	LIFEGUARD	LIGASE	LIGNAGE	LIKENED
LIED	LIFEHACK	LIGASES	LIGNAGES	LIKENESS
LIEDER	LIFEHACKS	LIGATE	LIGNALOES	LIKENING
LIEF	LIFEHOLD	LIGATED	LIGNAN	LIKENS
LIEFER	LIFELESS	LIGATES	LIGNANS	LIKER
LIEFEST	LIFELIKE	LIGATING	LIGNE	LIKERS
LIEFLY	LIFELINE	LIGATION	LIGNEOUS	LIKES
LIEFS	LIFELINES	LIGATIONS	LIGNES	LIKEST
LIEGE	LIFELONG	LIGATIVE	LIGNICOLE	LIKEWAKE
LIEGEDOM	LIFER	LIGATURE	LIGNIFIED	LIKEWAKES
LIEGEDOMS	LIFERS	LIGATURED	LIGNIFIES	LIKEWALK
LIEGELESS	LIFES	LIGATURES	LIGNIFORM	LIKEWALKS
LIEGEMAN	LIFESAVER	LIGER	LIGNIFY	LIKEWISE
LIEGEMEN	LIFESOME	LIGERS	LIGNIN	LIKIN
LIEGER	LIFESPAN	LIGGE	LIGNINS	LIKING
LIEGERS	LIFESPANS	LIGGED	LIGNITE	LIKINGS
LIEGES	LIFESTYLE	LIGGER	LIGNITES	LIKINS
LIEN	LIFETIME	LIGGERS	LIGNITIC	LIKUTA
LIENABLE	LIFETIMES	LIGGES	LIGNOSE	LILAC
LIENAL	LIFEWAY	LIGGING	LIGNOSES	LILACS
LIENEE	LIFEWAYS	LIGGINGS	LIGNUM	LILANGENI
LIENEES	LIFEWORK	LIGHT	LIGNUMS	LILIED
LIENOR	LIFEWORKS	LIGHTBULB	LIGROIN	LILIES
LIENORS	LIFEWORLD	LIGHTED	LIGROINE	LILL
LIENS	LIFT	LIGHTEN	LIGROINES	LILLED
LIENTERIC	LIFTABLE	LIGHTENED	LIGROINS	LILLING
LIENTERY	LIFTBACK	LIGHTENER	LIGS	LILLIPUT
LIER	LIFTBACKS	LIGHTENS	LIGULA	LILLIPUTS
LIERNE	LIFTBOY	LIGHTER	LIGULAE	LILLS
LIERNES	LIFTBOYS	LIGHTERED	LIGULAR	LILO

LILOS	LIMBOES	LIMITLESS	LIMPS	LINEALITY
LILT	LIMBOING	LIMITS	LIMPSEY	LINEALLY
LILTED	LIMBOS	LIMMA	LIMPSIER	LINEAMENT
LILTING	LIMBOUS	LIMMAS	LIMPSIEST	LINEAR
LILTINGLY	LIMBS	LIMMER	LIMPSY	LINEARISE
LILTS	LIMBUS	LIMMERS	LIMULI	LINEARITY
LILY	LIMBUSES	LIMN	LIMULOID	LINEARIZE
LILYLIKE	LIMBY	LIMNAEID	LIMULOIDS	LINEARLY
LIMA	LIME	LIMNAEIDS	LIMULUS	LINEATE
LIMACEL	LIMEADE	LIMNED	LIMULUSES	LINEATED
LIMACELS	LIMEADES	LIMNER	LIMY	LINEATION
LIMACEOUS	LIMED	LIMNERS	LIN	LINEBRED
LIMACES	LIMEKILN	LIMNETIC	LINABLE	LINECUT
LIMACINE	LIMEKILNS	LIMNIC	LINAC	LINECUTS
LIMACON	LIMELESS	LIMNING	LINACS	LINED
LIMACONS	LIMELIGHT	LIMNOLOGY	LINAGE	LINELESS
LIMAIL	LIMELIT	LIMNS	LINAGES	LINELIKE
LIMAILS	LIMEN	LIMO	LINALOL	LINEMAN
LIMAN	LIMENS	LIMONENE	LINALOLS	LINEMATE
LIMANS	LIMEPIT	LIMONENES	LINALOOL	LINEMATES
LIMAS	LIMEPITS	LIMONITE	LINALOOLS	LINEMEN
LIMATION	LIMERENCE	LIMONITES	LINCH	LINEN
LIMATIONS	LIMERICK	LIMONITIC	LINCHES	LINENFOLD
LIMAX	LIMERICKS	LIMONIUM	LINCHET	LINENIER
LIMB	LIMES	LIMONIUMS	LINCHETS	LINENIEST
LIMBA	LIMESCALE	LIMOS	LINCHPIN	LINENS
LIMBAS	LIMESTONE	LIMOSES	LINCHPINS	LINENY
LIMBATE	LIMEWASH	LIMOSIS	LINCRUSTA	LINEOLATE
LIMBEC	LIMEWATER	LIMOUS	LINCTURE	LINER
LIMBECK	LIMEY	LIMOUSINE	LINCTURES	LINERLESS
LIMBECKS	LIMEYS	LIMP	LINCTUS	LINERS
LIMBECS	LIMIER	LIMPA	LINCTUSES	LINES
LIMBED	LIMIEST	LIMPAS	LIND	LINESCORE
LIMBER	LIMINA	LIMPED	LINDANE	LINESMAN
LIMBERED	LIMINAL	LIMPER	LINDANES	LINESMEN
LIMBERER	LIMINESS	LIMPERS	LINDEN	LINEUP
LIMBEREST	LIMING	LIMPEST	LINDENS	LINEUPS
LIMBERING	LIMINGS	LIMPET	LINDIED	LINEY
LIMBERLY	LIMIT	LIMPETS	LINDIES	LING
LIMBERS	LIMITABLE	LIMPID	LINDS	LINGA
LIMBI	LIMITARY	LIMPIDITY	LINDWORM	LINGAM
LIMBIC	LIMITED	LIMPIDLY	LINDWORMS	LINGAMS
LIMBIER	LIMITEDLY	LIMPING	LINDY	LINGAS
LIMBIEST	LIMITEDS	LIMPINGLY	LINDYING	LINGBERRY
LIMBING	LIMITER	LIMPINGS	LINE	LINGCOD
LIMBLESS	LIMITERS	LIMPKIN	LINEABLE	LINGCODS
LIMBMEAL	LIMITES	LIMPKINS	LINEAGE	LINGEL
LIMBO	LIMITING	LIMPLY	LINEAGES	LINGELS
LIMBOED	LIMITINGS	LIMPNESS	LINEAL	LINGER

LINGERED	LININGS	LINOCUTS	LINY	LIPIDE
LINGERER	LININS	LINOLEATE	LION	LIPIDES
LINGERERS	LINISH	LINOLEIC	LIONCEL	LIPIDIC
LINGERIE	LINISHED	LINOLENIC	LIONCELLE	LIPIDOSES
LINGERIES	LINISHER	LINOLEUM	LIONCELS	LIPIDOSIS
LINGERING	LINISHERS	LINOLEUMS	LIONEL	LIPIDS
LINGERS	LINISHES	LINOS	LIONELS	LIPIN
LINGIER	LINISHING	LINOTYPE	LIONESS	LIPINS
LINGIEST	LINK	LINOTYPED	LIONESSES	LIPLESS
LINGLE	LINKABLE	LINOTYPER	LIONET	LIPLIKE
LINGLES	LINKAGE	LINOTYPES	LIONETS	LIPLINER
LINGO	LINKAGES	LINS	LIONFISH	LIPLINERS
LINGOES	LINKBOY	LINSANG	LIONHEAD	LIPO
LINGOS	LINKBOYS	LINSANGS	LIONHEADS	LIPOCYTE
LINGOT	LINKED	LINSEED	LIONISE	LIPOCYTES
LINGOTS	LINKER	LINSEEDS	LIONISED	LIPOED
LINGS	LINKERS	LINSEY	LIONISER	LIPOGRAM
LINGSTER	LINKIER	LINSEYS	LIONISERS	LIPOGRAMS
LINGSTERS	LINKIEST	LINSTOCK	LIONISES	LIPOIC
LINGUA	LINKING	LINSTOCKS	LIONISING	LIPOID
LINGUAE	LINKMAN	LINT	LIONISM	LIPOIDAL
LINGUAL	LINKMEN	LINTED	LIONISMS	LIPOIDS
LINGUALLY	LINKROT	LINTEL	LIONIZE	LIPOING
LINGUALS	LINKROTS	LINTELED	LIONIZED	LIPOLITIC
LINGUAS	LINKS	LINTELLED	LIONIZER	LIPOLYSES
LINGUICA	LINKSLAND	LINTELS	LIONIZERS	LIPOLYSIS
LINGUICAS	LINKSMAN	LINTER	LIONIZES	LIPOLYTIC
LINGUINE	LINKSMEN	LINTERS	LIONIZING	LIPOMA
LINGUINES	LINKSPAN	LINTIE	LIONLIER	LIPOMAS
LINGUINI	LINKSPANS	LINTIER	LIONLIEST	LIPOMATA
LINGUINIS	LINKSTER	LINTIES	LIONLIKE	LIPOPLAST
LINGUISA	LINKSTERS	LINTIEST	LIONLY	LIPOS
LINGUISAS	LINKUP	LINTING	LIONS	LIPOSOMAL
LINGUIST	LINKUPS	LINTINGS	LIP	LIPOSOME
LINGUISTS	LINKWORK	LINTLESS	LIPA	LIPOSOMES
LINGULA	LINKWORKS	LINTOL	LIPAEMIA	LIPOSUCK
LINGULAE	LINKY	LINTOLS	LIPAEMIAS	LIPOSUCKS
LINGULAR	LINN	LINTS	LIPARITE	LIPOTROPY
LINGULAS	LINNED	LINTSEED	LIPARITES	LIPPED
LINGULATE	LINNET	LINTSEEDS	LIPAS	LIPPEN
LINGY	LINNETS	LINTSTOCK	LIPASE	LIPPENED
LINHAY	LINNEY	LINTWHITE	LIPASES	LIPPENING
LINHAYS	LINNEYS	LINTY	LIPE	LIPPENS
LINIER	LINNIES	LINUM	LIPECTOMY	LIPPER
LINIEST	LINNING	LINUMS	LIPEMIA	LIPPERED
LINIMENT	LINNS	LINURON	LIPEMIAS	LIPPERING
LINIMENTS	LINNY	LINURONS	LIPES	LIPPERS
LININ	LINO	LINUX	LIPGLOSS	LIPPIE
LINING	LINOCUT	LINUXES	LIPID	LIPPIER

LIPPIES	LIQUOR	LISTED	LITEROSE	LITHOSOL
LIPPIEST	LIQUORED	LISTEE	LITERS	LITHOSOLS
LIPPINESS	LIQUORICE	LISTEES	LITES	LITHOTOME
LIPPING	LIQUORING	LISTEL	LITEST	LITHOTOMY
LIPPINGS	LIQUORISH	LISTELS	LITH	LITHOTYPE
LIPPITUDE	LIQUORS	LISTEN	LITHAEMIA	LITHS
LIPPY	LIRA	LISTENED	LITHAEMIC	LITIGABLE
LIPREAD	LIRAS	LISTENER	LITHARGE	LITIGANT
LIPREADER	LIRE	LISTENERS	LITHARGES	LITIGANTS
LIPREADS	LIRI	LISTENING	LITHATE	LITIGATE
LIPS	LIRIOPE	LISTENS	LITHATES	LITIGATED
LIPSALVE	LIRIOPES	LISTER	LITHE	LITIGATES
LIPSALVES	LIRIPIPE	LISTERIA	LITHED	LITIGATOR
LIPSTICK	LIRIPIPES	LISTERIAL	LITHELY	LITIGIOUS
LIPSTICKS	LIRIPOOP	LISTERIAS	LITHEMIA	LITING
LIPURIA	LIRIPOOPS	LISTERS	LITHEMIAS	LITMUS
LIPURIAS	LIRK	LISTETH	LITHEMIC	LITMUSES
LIQUABLE	LIRKED	LISTFUL	LITHENESS	LITORAL
LIQUATE	LIRKING	LISTICLE	LITHER	LITOTES
LIQUATED	LIRKS	LISTICLES	LITHERLY	LITOTIC
LIQUATES	LIROT	LISTING	LITHES	LITRE
LIQUATING	LIROTH	LISTINGS	LITHESOME	LITREAGE
LIQUATION	LIS	LISTLESS	LITHEST	LITREAGES
LIQUEFIED	LISENTE	LISTS	LITHIA	LITRES
LIQUEFIER	LISK	LISTSERV	LITHIAS	LITS
LIQUEFIES	LISKS	LISTSERVS	LITHIASES	LITTEN
LIQUEFY	LISLE	LIT	LITHIASIS	LITTER
LIQUESCE	LISLES	LITAI	LITHIC	LITTERBAG
LIQUESCED	LISP	LITANIES	LITHIFIED	LITTERBUG
LIQUESCES	LISPED	LITANY	LITHIFIES	LITTERED
LIQUEUR	LISPER	LITAS	LITHIFY	LITTERER
LIQUEURED	LISPERS	LITCHI	LITHING	LITTERERS
LIQUEURS	LISPING	LITCHIS	LITHISTID	LITTERIER
LIQUID	LISPINGLY	LITE	LITHITE	LITTERING
LIQUIDATE	LISPINGS	LITED	LITHITES	LITTERS
LIQUIDIER	LISPOUND	LITENESS	LITHIUM	LITTERY
LIQUIDISE	LISPOUNDS	LITER	LITHIUMS	LITTLE
LIQUIDITY	LISPS	LITERACY	LITHO	LITTLER
LIQUIDIZE	LISPUND	LITERAL	LITHOCYST	LITTLES
LIQUIDLY	LISPUNDS	LITERALLY	LITHOED	LITTLEST
LIQUIDS	LISSES	LITERALS	LITHOES	LITTLIE
LIQUIDUS	LISSOM	LITERARY	LITHOID	LITTLIES
LIQUIDY	LISSOME	LITERATE	LITHOIDAL	LITTLIN
LIQUIFIED	LISSOMELY	LITERATES	LITHOING	LITTLING
LIQUIFIER	LISSOMLY	LITERATI	LITHOLOGY	LITTLINGS
LIQUIFIES	LIST	LITERATIM	LITHOPONE	LITTLINS
LIQUIFY	LISTABLE	LITERATO	LITHOPS	LITTLISH
LIQUITAB	LISTBOX	LITERATOR	LITHOPSES	LITTORAL
LIQUITABS	LISTBOXES	LITERATUS	LITHOS	LITTORALS

LITU	LIVEST	LOAD	LOANWORDS	LOBEFINS
LITURGIC	LIVESTOCK	LOADABLE	LOAST	LOBELESS
LITURGICS	LIVETRAP	LOADED	LOATH	LOBELET
LITURGIES	LIVETRAPS	LOADEN	LOATHE	LOBELETS
LITURGISM	LIVEWARE	LOADENED	LOATHED	LOBELIA
LITURGIST	LIVEWARES	LOADENING	LOATHER	LOBELIAS
LITURGY	LIVEWELL	LOADENS	LOATHERS	LOBELIKE
LITUUS	LIVEWELLS	LOADER	LOATHES	LOBELINE
LITUUSES	LIVEYER	LOADERS	LOATHEST	LOBELINES
LIVABLE	LIVEYERE	LOADING	LOATHFUL	LOBES
LIVE	LIVEYERES	LOADINGS	LOATHING	LOBI
LIVEABLE	LIVEYERS	LOADOUT	LOATHINGS	LOBING
LIVEBLOG	LIVID	LOADOUTS	LOATHLIER	LOBINGS
LIVEBLOGS	LIVIDER	LOADS	LOATHLY	LOBIPED
LIVED	LIVIDEST	LOADSPACE	LOATHNESS	LOBLOLLY
LIVEDO	LIVIDITY	LOADSTAR	LOATHSOME	LOBO
LIVEDOS	LIVIDLY	LOADSTARS	LOATHY	LOBOLA
LIVELIER	LIVIDNESS	LOADSTONE	LOAVE	LOBOLAS
LIVELIEST	LIVIER	LOAF	LOAVED	LOBOLO
LIVELILY	LIVIERS	LOAFED	LOAVES	LOBOLOS
LIVELOD	LIVING	LOAFER	LOAVING	LOBOS
LIVELODS	LIVINGLY	LOAFERISH	LOB	LOBOSE
LIVELONG	LIVINGS	LOAFERS	LOBAR	LOBOTOMY
LIVELONGS	LIVOR	LOAFING	LOBATE	LOBS
LIVELOOD	LIVORS	LOAFINGS	LOBATED	LOBSCOUSE
LIVELOODS	LIVRAISON	LOAFS	LOBATELY	LOBSTER
LIVELY	LIVRE	LOAM	LOBATION	LOBSTERED
LIVEN	LIVRES	LOAMED	LOBATIONS	LOBSTERER
LIVENED	LIVYER	LOAMIER	LOBBED	LOBSTERS
LIVENER	LIVYERS	LOAMIEST	LOBBER	LOBSTICK
LIVENERS	LIXIVIA	LOAMINESS	LOBBERS	LOBSTICKS
LIVENESS	LIXIVIAL	LOAMING	LOBBIED	LOBTAIL
LIVENING	LIXIVIATE	LOAMLESS	LOBBIES	LOBTAILED
LIVENS	LIXIVIOUS	LOAMS	LOBBING	LOBTAILS
LIVER	LIXIVIUM	LOAMY	LOBBY	LOBULAR
LIVERED	LIXIVIUMS	LOAN	LOBBYER	LOBULARLY
LIVERIED	LIZARD	LOANABLE	LOBBYERS	LOBULATE
LIVERIES	LIZARDS	LOANBACK	LOBBYGOW	LOBULATED
LIVERING	LIZZIE	LOANBACKS	LOBBYGOWS	LOBULE
LIVERINGS	LIZZIES	LOANED	LOBBYING	LOBULES
LIVERISH	LLAMA	LOANEE	LOBBYINGS	LOBULI
LIVERLEAF	LLAMAS	LOANEES	LOBBYISM	LOBULOSE
LIVERLESS	LLANERO	LOANER	LOBBYISMS	LOBULUS
LIVERS	LLANEROS	LOANERS	LOBBYIST	LOBUS
LIVERWORT	LLANO	LOANING	LOBBYISTS	LOBWORM
LIVERY	LLANOS	LOANINGS	LOBE	LOBWORMS
LIVERYMAN	LO	LOANS	LOBECTOMY	LOC
LIVERYMEN	LOACH	LOANSHIFT	LOBED	LOCA
LIVES	LOACHES	LOANWORD	LOBEFIN	LOCAL

LOCALE	LOCIS	LOCOFOCO	LODGE	LOGBOOKS
LOCALES	LOCK	LOCOFOCOS	LODGEABLE	LOGE
LOCALISE	LOCKABLE	LOCOING	LODGED	LOGES
LOCALISED	LOCKAGE	LOCOISM	LODGEMENT	LOGGAT
LOCALISER	LOCKAGES	LOCOISMS	LODGEPOLE	LOGGATS
LOCALISES	LOCKAWAY	LOCOMAN	LODGER	LOGGED
LOCALISM	LOCKAWAYS	LOCOMEN	LODGERS	LOGGER
LOCALISMS	LOCKBOX	LOCOMOTE	LODGES	LOGGERS
LOCALIST	LOCKBOXES	LOCOMOTED	LODGING	LOGGETS
LOCALISTS	LOCKDOWN	LOCOMOTES	LODGINGS	LOGGIA
LOCALITE	LOCKDOWNS	LOCOMOTOR	LODGMENT	LOGGIAS
LOCALITES	LOCKED	LOCOPLANT	LODGMENTS	LOGGIE
LOCALITY	LOCKER	LOCOS	LODICULA	LOGGIER
LOCALIZE	LOCKERS	LOCOWEED	LODICULAE	LOGGIEST
LOCALIZED	LOCKET	LOCOWEEDS	LODICULE	LOGGING
LOCALIZER	LOCKETS	LOCS	LODICULES	LOGGINGS
LOCALIZES	LOCKFAST	LOCTICIAN	LODS	LOGGISH
LOCALLY	LOCKFUL	LOCULAR	LOERIE	LOGGY
LOCALNESS	LOCKFULS	LOCULATE	LOERIES	LOGIA
LOCALS	LOCKHOUSE	LOCULATED	LOESS	LOGIC
LOCATABLE	LOCKING	LOCULE	LOESSAL	LOGICAL
LOCATE	LOCKINGS	LOCULED	LOESSES	LOGICALLY
LOCATED	LOCKJAW	LOCULES	LOESSIAL	LOGICIAN
LOCATER	LOCKJAWS	LOCULI	LOESSIC	LOGICIANS
LOCATERS	LOCKLESS	LOCULUS	LOFT	LOGICISE
LOCATES	LOCKMAKER	LOCUM	LOFTED	LOGICISED
LOCATING	LOCKMAN	LOCUMS	LOFTER	LOGICISES
LOCATION	LOCKMEN	LOCUPLETE	LOFTERS	LOGICISM
LOCATIONS	LOCKNUT	LOCUS	LOFTIER	LOGICISMS
LOCATIVE	LOCKNUTS	LOCUST	LOFTIEST	LOGICIST
LOCATIVES	LOCKOUT	LOCUSTA	LOFTILY	LOGICISTS
LOCATOR	LOCKOUTS	LOCUSTAE	LOFTINESS	LOGICIZE
LOCATORS	LOCKPICK	LOCUSTAL	LOFTING	LOGICIZED
LOCAVORE	LOCKPICKS	LOCUSTED	LOFTLESS	LOGICIZES
LOCAVORES	LOCKRAM	LOCUSTING	LOFTLIKE	LOGICLESS
LOCELLATE	LOCKRAMS	LOCUSTS	LOFTS	LOGICS
LOCH	LOCKS	LOCUTION	LOFTSMAN	LOGIE
LOCHAN	LOCKSET	LOCUTIONS	LOFTSMEN	LOGIER
LOCHANS	LOCKSETS	LOCUTORY	LOFTY	LOGIES
LOCHE	LOCKSMAN	LOD	LOG	LOGIEST
LOCHES	LOCKSMEN	LODE	LOGAN	LOGILY
LOCHIA	LOCKSMITH	LODEN	LOGANIA	LOGIN
LOCHIAL	LOCKSTEP	LODENS	LOGANIAS	LOGINESS
LOCHIAS	LOCKSTEPS	LODES	LOGANS	LOGINS
LOCHS	LOCKUP	LODESMAN	LOGAOEDIC	LOGION
LOCI	LOCKUPS	LODESMEN	LOGARITHM	LOGIONS
LOCIE	LOCO	LODESTAR	LOGBOARD	LOGISTIC
LOCIES	LOCOED	LODESTARS	LOGBOARDS	LOGISTICS
LOCING	LOCOES	LODESTONE	LOGBOOK	LOGJAM

LOGJAMMED	LOIDED	LOMATA	LONGHAIR	LOOBIEST
LOGJAMS	LOIDING	LOME	LONGHAIRS	LOOBILY
LOGJUICE	LOIDS	LOMED	LONGHAND	LOOBY
LOGJUICES	LOIN	LOMEIN	LONGHANDS	LOOED
LOGLINE	LOINCLOTH	LOMEINS	LONGHEAD	LOOEY
LOGLINES	LOINS	LOMENT	LONGHEADS	LOOEYS
LOGLOG	LOIPE	LOMENTA	LONGHORN	LOOF
LOGLOGS	LOIPEN	LOMENTS	LONGHORNS	LOOFA
LOGNORMAL	LOIR	LOMENTUM	LONGHOUSE	LOOFAH
LOGO	LOIRS	LOMENTUMS	LONGICORN	LOOFAHS
LOGOED	LOITER	LOMES	LONGIES	LOOFAS
LOGOFF	LOITERED	LOMING	LONGING	LOOFFUL
LOGOFFS	LOITERER	LOMPISH	LONGINGLY	LOOFFULS
LOGOGRAM	LOITERERS	LONE	LONGINGS	LOOFS
LOGOGRAMS	LOITERING	LONELIER	LONGISH	LOOGIE
LOGOGRAPH	LOITERS	LONELIEST	LONGITUDE	LOOGIES
LOGOGRIPH	LOKE	LONELILY	LONGJUMP	LOOIE
LOGOI	LOKES	LONELY	LONGJUMPS	LOOIES
LOGOMACH	LOKSHEN	LONENESS	LONGLEAF	LOOING
LOGOMACHS	LOLIGO	LONER	LONGLINE	LOOK
LOGOMACHY	LOLIGOS	LONERS	LONGLINER	LOOKALIKE
LOGON	LOLIUM	LONESOME	LONGLINES	LOOKDOWN
LOGONS	LOLIUMS	LONESOMES	LONGLIST	LOOKDOWNS
LOGOPEDIC	LOLL	LONG	LONGLISTS	LOOKED
LOGOPHILE	LOLLED	LONGA	LONGLY	LOOKER
LOGORRHEA	LOLLER	LONGAEVAL	LONGNECK	LOOKERS
LOGOS	LOLLERS	LONGAN	LONGNECKS	LOOKIE
LOGOTHETE	LOLLIES	LONGANS	LONGNESS	LOOKING
LOGOTYPE	LOLLING	LONGAS	LONGS	LOOKISM
LOGOTYPES	LOLLINGLY	LONGBOARD	LONGSHIP	LOOKISMS
LOGOTYPY	LOLLIPOP	LONGBOAT	LONGSHIPS	LOOKIST
LOGOUT	LOLLIPOPS	LONGBOATS	LONGSHORE	LOOKISTS
LOGOUTS	LOLLOP	LONGBOW	LONGSOME	LOOKIT
LOGROLL	LOLLOPED	LONGBOWS	LONGSPUR	LOOKOUT
LOGROLLED	LOLLOPIER	LONGCASE	LONGSPURS	LOOKOUTS
LOGROLLER	LOLLOPING	LONGCLOTH	LONGTIME	LOOKOVER
LOGROLLS	LOLLOPS	LONGE	LONGUEUR	LOOKOVERS
LOGS	LOLLOPY	LONGED	LONGUEURS	LOOKS
LOGWAY	LOLLS	LONGEING	LONGWALL	LOOKSISM
LOGWAYS	LOLLY	LONGER	LONGWALLS	LOOKSISMS
LOGWOOD	LOLLYGAG	LONGERON	LONGWAYS	LOOKUP
LOGWOODS	LOLLYGAGS	LONGERONS	LONGWISE	LOOKUPS
LOGY	LOLLYPOP	LONGERS	LONGWORM	LOOKY
LOHAN	LOLLYPOPS	LONGES	LONGWORMS	LOOM
LOHANS	LOLOG	LONGEST	LONICERA	LOOMED
LOIASES	LOLOGS	LONGEVAL	LONICERAS	LOOMING
LOIASIS	LOLZ	LONGEVITY	LOO	LOOMS
LOIASISES	LOMA	LONGEVOUS	LOOBIER	LOON
LOID	LOMAS	LONGFORM	LOOBIES	LOONEY

LOONEYS	LOOT	LORCHA	LORING	LOTES
LOONIE	LOOTED	LORCHAS	LORINGS	LOTH
LOONIER	LOOTEN	LORD	LORIOT	LOTHARIO
LOONIES	LOOTER	LORDED	LORIOTS	LOTHARIOS
LOONIEST	LOOTERS	LORDING	LORIS	LOTHEFULL
LOONILY	LOOTING	LORDINGS	LORISES	LOTHER
LOONINESS	LOOTINGS	LORDKIN	LORN	LOTHEST
LOONING	LOOTS	LORDKINS	LORNER	LOTHFULL
LOONINGS	LOOVES	LORDLESS	LORNEST	LOTHNESS
LOONS	LOP	LORDLIER	LORNNESS	LOTHSOME
LOONY	LOPE	LORDLIEST	LORREL	LOTI
LOOP	LOPED	LORDLIKE	LORRELLS	LOTIC
LOOPED	LOPER	LORDLING	LORRIES	LOTION
LOOPER	LOPERS	LORDLINGS	LORRY	LOTIONS
LOOPERS	LOPES	LORDLY	LORY	LOTO
LOOPHOLE	LOPGRASS	LORDOMA	LOS	LOTOS
LOOPHOLED	LOPHODONT	LORDOMAS	LOSABLE	LOTOSES
LOOPHOLES	LOPINAVIR	LORDOSES	LOSARTAN	LOTS
LOOPIER	LOPING	LORDOSIS	LOSARTANS	LOTSA
LOOPIEST	LOPINGLY	LORDOTIC	LOSE	LOTTA
LOOPILY	LOPOLITH	LORDS	LOSED	LOTTE
LOOPINESS	LOPOLITHS	LORDSHIP	LOSEL	LOTTED
LOOPING	LOPPED	LORDSHIPS	LOSELS	LOTTER
LOOPINGS	LOPPER	LORDY	LOSEN	LOTTERIES
LOOPLIKE	LOPPERED	LORE	LOSER	LOTTERS
LOOPS	LOPPERING	LOREAL	LOSERS	LOTTERY
LOOPY	LOPPERS	LOREL	LOSES	LOTTES
LOOR	LOPPET	LORELS	LOSH	LOTTING
LOORD	LOPPETS	LORES	LOSING	LOTTO
LOORDS	LOPPIER	LORETTE	LOSINGEST	LOTTOS
LOOS	LOPPIES	LORETTES	LOSINGLY	LOTUS
LOOSE	LOPPIEST	LORGNETTE	LOSINGS	LOTUSES
LOOSEBOX	LOPPING	LORGNON	LOSLYF	LOTUSLAND
LOOSED	LOPPINGS	LORGNONS	LOSLYFS	LOU
LOOSELY	LOPPY	LORIC	LOSS	LOUCHE
LOOSEN	LOPS	LORICA	LOSSES	LOUCHELY
LOOSENED	LOPSIDED	LORICAE	LOSSIER	LOUCHER
LOOSENER	LOPSTICK	LORICAS	LOSSIEST	LOUCHEST
LOOSENERS	LOPSTICKS	LORICATE	LOSSLESS	LOUD
LOOSENESS	LOQUACITY	LORICATED	LOSSMAKER	LOUDEN
LOOSENING	LOQUAT	LORICATES	LOSSY	LOUDENED
LOOSENS	LOQUATS	LORICS	LOST	LOUDENING
LOOSER	LOQUITUR	LORIES	LOSTNESS	LOUDENS
LOOSES	LOR	LORIKEET	LOT	LOUDER
LOOSEST	LORAL	LORIKEETS	LOTA	LOUDEST
LOOSIE	LORAN	LORIMER	LOTAH	LOUDISH
LOOSIES	LORANS	LORIMERS	LOTAHS	LOUDLIER
LOOSING	LORATE	LORINER	LOTAS	LOUDLIEST
LOOSINGS	LORAZEPAM	LORINERS	LOTE	LOUDLY

LOUDMOUTH	LOURING	LOVEBUGS	LOWBUSH	LOWNS
LOUDNESS	LOURINGLY	LOVED	LOWBUSHES	LOWP
LOUED	LOURINGS	LOVEFEST	LOWDOWN	LOWPASS
LOUGH	LOURS	LOVEFESTS	LOWDOWNS	LOWPED
LOUGHS	LOURY	LOVELESS	LOWE	LOWPING
LOUIE	LOUS	LOVELIER	LOWED	LOWPS
LOUIES	LOUSE	LOVELIES	LOWER	LOWRIDER
LOUING	LOUSED	LOVELIEST	LOWERABLE	LOWRIDERS
LOUIS	LOUSER	LOVELIGHT	LOWERCASE	LOWRIE
LOUMA	LOUSERS	LOVELILY	LOWERED	LOWRIES
LOUMAS	LOUSES	LOVELOCK	LOWERIER	LOWRY
LOUN	LOUSEWORT	LOVELOCKS	LOWERIEST	LOWS
LOUND	LOUSIER	LOVELORN	LOWERING	LOWSE
LOUNDED	LOUSIEST	LOVELY	LOWERINGS	LOWSED
LOUNDER	LOUSILY	LOVEMAKER	LOWERMOST	LOWSENING
LOUNDERED	LOUSINESS	LOVER	LOWERS	LOWSER
LOUNDERS	LOUSING	LOVERED	LOWERY	LOWSES
LOUNDING	LOUSINGS	LOVERLESS	LOWES	LOWSEST
LOUNDS	LOUSY	LOVERLY	LOWEST	LOWSING
LOUNED	LOUT	LOVERS	LOWING	LOWSIT
LOUNGE	LOUTED	LOVES	LOWINGS	LOWT
LOUNGED	LOUTERIES	LOVESEAT	LOWISH	LOWTED
LOUNGER	LOUTERY	LOVESEATS	LOWLAND	LOWTING
LOUNGERS	LOUTING	LOVESICK	LOWLANDER	LOWTS
LOUNGES	LOUTISH	LOVESOME	LOWLANDS	LOWVELD
LOUNGEY	LOUTISHLY	LOVEVINE	LOWLIER	LOWVELDS
LOUNGIER	LOUTS	LOVEVINES	LOWLIEST	LOX
LOUNGIEST	LOUVAR	LOVEY	LOWLIFE	LOXED
LOUNGING	LOUVARS	LOVEYS	LOWLIFER	LOXES
LOUNGINGS	LOUVER	LOVIE	LOWLIFERS	LOXING
LOUNGY	LOUVERED	LOVIER	LOWLIFES	LOXODROME
LOUNING	LOUVERS	LOVIES	LOWLIGHT	LOXODROMY
LOUNS	LOUVRE	LOVIEST	LOWLIGHTS	LOXYGEN
LOUP	LOUVRED	LOVING	LOWLIHEAD	LOXYGENS
LOUPE	LOUVRES	LOVINGLY	LOWLILY	LOY
LOUPED	LOVABLE	LOVINGS	LOWLINESS	LOYAL
LOUPEN	LOVABLY	LOW	LOWLIVES	LOYALER
LOUPES	LOVAGE	LOWAN	LOWLY	LOYALEST
LOUPING	LOVAGES	LOWANS	LOWN	LOYALISM
LOUPIT	LOVAT	LOWBALL	LOWND	LOYALISMS
LOUPS	LOVATS	LOWBALLED	LOWNDED	LOYALIST
LOUR	LOVE	LOWBALLS	LOWNDING	LOYALISTS
LOURE	LOVEABLE	LOWBORN	LOWNDS	LOYALLER
LOURED	LOVEABLY	LOWBOY	LOWNE	LOYALLEST
LOURES	LOVEBIRD	LOWBOYS	LOWNED	LOYALLY
LOURIE	LOVEBIRDS	LOWBRED	LOWNES	LOYALNESS
LOURIER	LOVEBITE	LOWBROW	LOWNESS	LOYALTIES
LOURIES	LOVEBITES	LOWBROWED	LOWNESSES	LOYALTY
LOURIEST	LOVEBUG	LOWBROWS	LOWNING	LOYS

LOZELL	LUCIDLY	LUETICS	LULLS	LUMMIER
LOZELLS	LUCIDNESS	LUFF	LULU	LUMMIEST
LOZEN	LUCIFER	LUFFA	LULUS	LUMMOX
LOZENGE	LUCIFERIN	LUFFAS	LULZ	LUMMOXES
LOZENGED	LUCIFERS	LUFFED	LUM	LUMMY
LOZENGES	LUCIGEN	LUFFING	LUMA	LUMP
LOZENGIER	LUCIGENS	LUFFS	LUMAS	LUMPED
LOZENGY	LUCITE	LUG	LUMBAGO	LUMPEN
LOZENS	LUCITES	LUGE	LUMBAGOS	LUMPENLY
LUACH	LUCK	LUGED	LUMBANG	LUMPENS
LUAU	LUCKED	LUGEING	LUMBANGS	LUMPER
LUAUS	LUCKEN	LUGEINGS	LUMBAR	LUMPERS
LUBBARD	LUCKIE	LUGER	LUMBARS	LUMPFISH
LUBBARDS	LUCKIER	LUGERS	LUMBER	LUMPIA
LUBBER	LUCKIES	LUGES	LUMBERED	LUMPIAS
LUBBERLY	LUCKIEST	LUGGABLE	LUMBERER	LUMPIER
LUBBERS	LUCKILY	LUGGABLES	LUMBERERS	LUMPIEST
LUBE	LUCKINESS	LUGGAGE	LUMBERING	LUMPILY
LUBED	LUCKING	LUGGAGES	LUMBERLY	LUMPINESS
LUBES	LUCKLESS	LUGGED	LUMBERMAN	LUMPING
LUBFISH	LUCKPENNY	LUGGER	LUMBERMEN	LUMPINGLY
LUBFISHES	LUCKS	LUGGERS	LUMBERS	LUMPISH
LUBING	LUCKY	LUGGIE	LUMBI	LUMPISHLY
LUBRIC	LUCRATIVE	LUGGIES	LUMBRICAL	LUMPKIN
LUBRICAL	LUCRE	LUGGING	LUMBRICI	LUMPKINS
LUBRICANT	LUCRES	LUGHOLE	LUMBRICUS	LUMPS
LUBRICATE	LUCTATION	LUGHOLES	LUMBUS	LUMPY
LUBRICITY	LUCUBRATE	LUGING	LUMEN	LUMS
LUBRICOUS	LUCULENT	LUGINGS	LUMENAL	LUN
LUCARNE	LUCUMA	LUGS	LUMENS	LUNA
LUCARNES	LUCUMAS	LUGSAIL	LUMINA	LUNACIES
LUCE	LUCUMO	LUGSAILS	LUMINAIRE	LUNACY
LUCENCE	LUCUMONES	LUGWORM	LUMINAL	LUNANAUT
LUCENCES	LUCUMOS	LUGWORMS	LUMINANCE	LUNANAUTS
LUCENCIES	LUD	LUIT	LUMINANT	LUNAR
LUCENCY	LUDE	LUITEN	LUMINANTS	LUNARIAN
LUCENT	LUDERICK	LUKE	LUMINARIA	LUNARIANS
LUCENTLY	LUDERICKS	LUKEWARM	LUMINARY	LUNARIES
LUCERN	LUDES	LULIBUB	LUMINE	LUNARIST
LUCERNE	LUDIC	LULIBUBS	LUMINED	LUNARISTS
LUCERNES	LUDICALLY	LULL	LUMINES	LUNARNAUT
LUCERNS	LUDICROUS	LULLABIED	LUMINESCE	LUNARS
LUCES	LUDO	LULLABIES	LUMINING	LUNARY
LUCHOT	LUDOS	LULLABY	LUMINISM	LUNAS
LUCHOTH	LUDS	LULLED	LUMINISMS	LUNATE
LUCID	LUDSHIP	LULLER	LUMINIST	LUNATED
LUCIDER	LUDSHIPS	LULLERS	LUMINISTS	LUNATELY
LUCIDEST	LUES	LULLING	LUMINOUS	LUNATES
LUCIDITY	LUETIC	LULLINGLY	LUMME	LUNATIC

L

LUNATICAL	LUNGYI	LURCHES	LUSHIER	LUTANIST
LUNATICS	LUNGYIS	LURCHING	LUSHIES	LUTANISTS
LUNATION	LUNIER	LURDAN	LUSHIEST	LUTE
LUNATIONS	LUNIES	LURDANE	LUSHING	LUTEA
LUNCH	LUNIEST	LURDANES	LUSHLY	LUTEAL
LUNCHBOX	LUNINESS	LURDANS	LUSHNESS	LUTECIUM
LUNCHED	LUNISOLAR	LURDEN	LUSHY	LUTECIUMS
LUNCHEON	LUNITIDAL	LURDENS	LUSK	LUTED
LUNCHEONS	LUNK	LURE	LUSKED	LUTEFISK
LUNCHER	LUNKER	LURED	LUSKING	LUTEFISKS
LUNCHERS	LUNKERS	LURER	LUSKISH	LUTEIN
LUNCHES	LUNKHEAD	LURERS	LUSKS	LUTEINISE
LUNCHING	LUNKHEADS	LURES	LUST	LUTEINIZE
LUNCHMEAT	LUNKS	LUREX	LUSTED	LUTEINS
LUNCHPAIL	LUNS	LUREXES	LUSTER	LUTELIKE
LUNCHROOM	LUNT	LURGI	LUSTERED	LUTENIST
LUNCHTIME	LUNTED	LURGIES	LUSTERING	LUTENISTS
LUNE	LUNTING	LURGIS	LUSTERS	LUTEOLIN
LUNES	LUNTS	LURGY	LUSTFUL	LUTEOLINS
LUNET	LUNULA	LURID	LUSTFULLY	LUTEOLOUS
LUNETS	LUNULAE	LURIDER	LUSTICK	LUTEOUS
LUNETTE	LUNULAR	LURIDEST	LUSTIER	LUTER
LUNETTES	LUNULATE	LURIDLY	LUSTIEST	LUTERS
LUNG	LUNULATED	LURIDNESS	LUSTIHEAD	LUTES
LUNGAN	LUNULE	LURING	LUSTIHOOD	LUTESCENT
LUNGANS	LUNULES	LURINGLY	LUSTILY	LUTETIUM
LUNGE	LUNY	LURINGS	LUSTINESS	LUTETIUMS
LUNGED	LUNYIE	LURK	LUSTING	LUTEUM
LUNGEE	LUNYIES	LURKED	LUSTIQUE	LUTFISK
LUNGEES	LUPANAR	LURKER	LUSTLESS	LUTFISKS
LUNGEING	LUPANARS	LURKERS	LUSTRA	LUTHERN
LUNGER	LUPIN	LURKING	LUSTRAL	LUTHERNS
LUNGERS	LUPINE	LURKINGLY	LUSTRATE	LUTHIER
LUNGES	LUPINES	LURKINGS	LUSTRATED	LUTHIERS
LUNGFISH	LUPINS	LURKS	LUSTRATES	LUTING
LUNGFUL	LUPOID	LURRIES	LUSTRE	LUTINGS
LUNGFULS	LUPOUS	LURRY	LUSTRED	LUTIST
LUNGI	LUPPEN	LURS	LUSTRES	LUTISTS
LUNGIE	LUPULIN	LURVE	LUSTRINE	LUTITE
LUNGIES	LUPULINE	LURVES	LUSTRINES	LUTITES
LUNGING	LUPULINIC	LUSCIOUS	LUSTRING	LUTTEN
LUNGIS	LUPULINS	LUSER	LUSTRINGS	LUTZ
LUNGLESS	LUPUS	LUSERS	LUSTROUS	LUTZES
LUNGLIKE	LUPUSES	LUSH	LUSTRUM	LUV
LUNGS	LUR	LUSHED	LUSTRUMS	LUVS
LUNGWORM	LURCH	LUSHER	LUSTS	LUVVED
LUNGWORMS	LURCHED	LUSHERS	LUSTY	LUVVIE
LUNGWORT	LURCHER	LUSHES	LUSUS	LUVVIEDOM
LUNGWORTS	LURCHERS	LUSHEST	LUSUSES	LUVVIES

LUVVING	LYCAENIDS	LYMITER	LYOPHILED	LYSERGIC
LUVVY	LYCEA	LYMITERS	LYOPHILIC	LYSERGIDE
LUX	LYCEE	LYMPH	LYOPHOBE	LYSES
LUXATE	LYCEES	LYMPHAD	LYOPHOBIC	LYSIGENIC
LUXATED	LYCEUM	LYMPHADS	LYRA	LYSIMETER
LUXATES	LYCEUMS	LYMPHATIC	LYRATE	LYSIN
LUXATING	LYCH	LYMPHOID	LYRATED	LYSINE
LUXATION	LYCHEE	LYMPHOMA	LYRATELY	LYSINES
LUXATIONS	LYCHEES	LYMPHOMAS	LYRE	LYSING
LUXE	LYCHES	LYMPHOUS	LYREBIRD	LYSINS
LUXED	LYCHGATE	LYMPHS	LYREBIRDS	LYSIS
LUXER	LYCHGATES	LYMS	LYRES	LYSOGEN
LUXES	LYCHNIS	LYNAGE	LYRIC	LYSOGENIC
LUXEST	LYCHNISES	LYNAGES	LYRICAL	LYSOGENS
LUXING	LYCOPENE	LYNCEAN	LYRICALLY	LYSOGENY
LUXMETER	LYCOPENES	LYNCH	LYRICISE	LYSOL
LUXMETERS	LYCOPOD	LYNCHED	LYRICISED	LYSOLS
LUXURIANT	LYCOPODS	LYNCHER	LYRICISES	LYSOSOMAL
LUXURIATE	LYCOPSID	LYNCHERS	LYRICISM	LYSOSOME
LUXURIES	LYCOPSIDS	LYNCHES	LYRICISMS	LYSOSOMES
LUXURIOUS	LYCRA	LYNCHET	LYRICIST	LYSOZYME
LUXURIST	LYCRAS	LYNCHETS	LYRICISTS	LYSOZYMES
LUXURISTS	LYDDITE	LYNCHING	LYRICIZE	LYSSA
LUXURY	LYDDITES	LYNCHINGS	LYRICIZED	LYSSAS
LUZ	LYE	LYNCHPIN	LYRICIZES	LYTE
LUZERN	LYES	LYNCHPINS	LYRICON	LYTED
LUZERNS	LYFULL	LYNE	LYRICONS	LYTES
LUZZES	LYING	LYNES	LYRICS	LYTHE
LWEI	LYINGLY	LYNX	LYRIFORM	LYTHES
LWEIS	LYINGS	LYNXES	LYRISM	LYTHRUM
LYAM	LYKEWAKE	LYNXLIKE	LYRISMS	LYTHRUMS
LYAMS	LYKEWAKES	LYOLYSES	LYRIST	LYTIC
LYARD	LYKEWALK	LYOLYSIS	LYRISTS	LYTICALLY
LYART	LYKEWALKS	LYOMEROUS	LYSATE	LYTING
LYASE	LYM	LYONNAISE	LYSATES	LYTTA
LYASES	LYME	LYOPHIL	LYSE	LYTTAE
LYCAENID	LYMES	LYOPHILE	LYSED	LYTTAS

M

MA	MACARONIC	MACHES	MACOYAS	MACULING
MAA	MACARONIS	MACHETE	MACRAME	MACULOSE
MAAED	MACARONS	MACHETES	MACRAMES	MACUMBA
MAAING	MACAROON	MACHI	MACRAMI	MACUMBAS
MAAR	MACAROONS	MACHINATE	MACRAMIS	MAD
MAARE	MACAS	MACHINE	MACRO	MADAFU
MAARS	MACASSAR	MACHINED	MACROBIAN	MADAFUS
MAAS	MACASSARS	MACHINERY	MACROCODE	MADAM
MAASES	MACAW	MACHINES	MACROCOPY	MADAME
MAATJES	MACAWS	MACHINIMA	MACROCOSM	MADAMED
MABE	MACCABAW	MACHINING	MACROCYST	MADAMES
MABELA	MACCABAWS	MACHINIST	MACROCYTE	MADAMING
MABELAS	MACCABOY	MACHISMO	MACRODOME	MADAMS
MABES	MACCABOYS	MACHISMOS	MACRODONT	MADAROSES
MAC	MACCARONI	MACHMETER	MACROGLIA	MADAROSIS
MACA	MACCHIA	MACHO	MACROLIDE	MADBRAIN
MACABER	MACCHIATO	MACHOISM	MACROLOGY	MADBRAINS
MACABRE	MACCHIE	MACHOISMS	MACROMERE	MADCAP
MACABRELY	MACCOBOY	MACHOS	MACROMOLE	MADCAPS
MACABRER	MACCOBOYS	MACHREE	MACRON	MADDED
MACABREST	MACE	MACHREES	MACRONS	MADDEN
MACACO	MACED	MACHS	MACROPOD	MADDENED
MACACOS	MACEDOINE	MACHZOR	MACROPODS	MADDENING
MACADAM	MACER	MACHZORIM	MACROPSIA	MADDENS
MACADAMED	MACERAL	MACHZORS	MACROS	MADDER
MACADAMIA	MACERALS	MACING	MACROTOUS	MADDERS
MACADAMS	MACERATE	MACINTOSH	MACRURAL	MADDEST
MACAHUBA	MACERATED	MACK	MACRURAN	MADDING
MACAHUBAS	MACERATER	MACKEREL	MACRURANS	MADDINGLY
MACALLUM	MACERATES	MACKERELS	MACRUROID	MADDISH
MACALLUMS	MACERATOR	MACKINAW	MACRUROUS	MADDOCK
MACAQUE	MACERS	MACKINAWS	MACS	MADDOCKS
MACAQUES	MACES	MACKLE	MACTATION	MADE
MACARISE	MACH	MACKLED	MACULA	MADEFIED
MACARISED	MACHACA	MACKLES	MACULAE	MADEFIES
MACARISES	MACHACAS	MACKLING	MACULAR	MADEFY
MACARISM	MACHAIR	MACKS	MACULAS	MADEFYING
MACARISMS	MACHAIRS	MACLE	MACULATE	MADEIRA
MACARIZE	MACHAN	MACLED	MACULATED	MADEIRAS
MACARIZED	MACHANS	MACLES	MACULATES	MADELEINE
MACARIZES	MACHE	MACON	MACULE	MADERISE
MACARON	MACHER	MACONS	MACULED	MADERISED
MACARONI	MACHERS	MACOYA	MACULES	MADERISES

MADERIZE	MADWOMEN	MAGAZINE	MAGNATE	MAGSMEN
MADERIZED	MADWORT	MAGAZINES	MAGNATES	MAGSTRIPE
MADERIZES	MADWORTS	MAGDALEN	MAGNES	MAGUEY
MADEUPPY	MADZOON	MAGDALENE	MAGNESES	MAGUEYS
MADGE	MADZOONS	MAGDALENS	MAGNESIA	MAGUS
MADGES	MAE	MAGE	MAGNESIAL	MAGYAR
MADHOUSE	MAELID	MAGENTA	MAGNESIAN	MAHA
MADHOUSES	MAELIDS	MAGENTAS	MAGNESIAS	MAHANT
MADID	MAELSTROM	MAGES	MAGNESIC	MAHANTS
MADISON	MAENAD	MAGESHIP	MAGNESITE	MAHARAJA
MADISONS	MAENADES	MAGESHIPS	MAGNESIUM	MAHARAJAH
MADLING	MAENADIC	MAGG	MAGNET	MAHARAJAS
MADLINGS	MAENADISM	MAGGED	MAGNETAR	MAHARANEE
MADLY	MAENADS	MAGGIE	MAGNETARS	MAHARANI
MADMAN	MAERL	MAGGIES	MAGNETIC	MAHARANIS
MADMEN	MAERLS	MAGGING	MAGNETICS	MAHARISHI
MADNESS	MAES	MAGGOT	MAGNETISE	MAHATMA
MADNESSES	MAESTOSO	MAGGOTIER	MAGNETISM	MAHATMAS
MADONNA	MAESTOSOS	MAGGOTS	MAGNETIST	MAHEWU
MADONNAS	MAESTRI	MAGGOTY	MAGNETITE	MAHEWUS
MADOQUA	MAESTRO	MAGGS	MAGNETIZE	MAHIMAHI
MADOQUAS	MAESTROS	MAGI	MAGNETO	MAHIMAHIS
MADRAS	MAFFIA	MAGIAN	MAGNETON	MAHJONG
MADRASA	MAFFIAS	MAGIANISM	MAGNETONS	MAHJONGG
MADRASAH	MAFFICK	MAGIANS	MAGNETOS	MAHJONGGS
MADRASAHS	MAFFICKED	MAGIC	MAGNETRON	MAHJONGS
MADRASAS	MAFFICKER	MAGICAL	MAGNETS	MAHLSTICK
MADRASES	MAFFICKS	MAGICALLY	MAGNIFIC	MAHMAL
MADRASSA	MAFFLED	MAGICIAN	MAGNIFICO	MAHMALS
MADRASSAH	MAFFLIN	MAGICIANS	MAGNIFIED	MAHOE
MADRASSAS	MAFFLING	MAGICKED	MAGNIFIER	MAHOES
MADRE	MAFFLINGS	MAGICKING	MAGNIFIES	MAHOGANY
MADREPORE	MAFFLINS	MAGICS	MAGNIFY	MAHONIA
MADRES	MAFIA	MAGILP	MAGNITUDE	MAHONIAS
MADRIGAL	MAFIAS	MAGILPS	MAGNOLIA	MAHOOSIVE
MADRIGALS	MAFIC	MAGISM	MAGNOLIAS	MAHOUT
MADRILENE	MAFICS	MAGISMS	MAGNON	MAHOUTS
MADRONA	MAFIOSI	MAGISTER	MAGNONS	MAHSEER
MADRONAS	MAFIOSO	MAGISTERS	MAGNOX	MAHSEERS
MADRONE	MAFIOSOS	MAGISTERY	MAGNOXES	MAHSIR
MADRONES	MAFTED	MAGISTRAL	MAGNUM	MAHSIRS
MADRONO	MAFTIR	MAGLEV	MAGNUMS	MAHUA
MADRONOS	MAFTIRS	MAGLEVS	MAGNUS	MAHUANG
MADS	MAG	MAGMA	MAGOT	MAHUANGS
MADTOM	MAGAININ	MAGMAS	MAGOTS	MAHUAS
MADTOMS	MAGAININS	MAGMATA	MAGPIE	MAHWA
MADURO	MAGALOG	MAGMATIC	MAGPIES	MAHWAS
MADUROS	MAGALOGS	MAGMATISM	MAGS	MAHZOR
MADWOMAN	MAGALOGUE	MAGNALIUM	MAGSMAN	MAHZORIM

M

MAHZORS	MAILINGS	MAINOURS	MAJORDOMO	MAL
MAIASAUR	MAILL	MAINPRISE	MAJORED	MALA
MAIASAURA	MAILLESS	MAINS	MAJORETTE	MALACCA
MAIASAURS	MAILLOT	MAINSAIL	MAJORING	MALACCAS
MAID	MAILLOTS	MAINSAILS	MAJORITY	MALACHITE
MAIDAN	MAILLS	MAINSHEET	MAJORLY	MALACIA
MAIDANS	MAILMAN	MAINSTAGE	MAJORS	MALACIAS
MAIDED	MAILMEN	MAINSTAY	MAJORSHIP	MALADIES
MAIDEN	MAILMERGE	MAINSTAYS	MAJUSCULE	MALADROIT
MAIDENISH	MAILPOUCH	MAINTAIN	MAK	MALADY
MAIDENLY	MAILROOM	MAINTAINS	MAKABLE	MALAGUENA
MAIDENS	MAILROOMS	MAINTOP	MAKABLES	MALAISE
MAIDHOOD	MAILS	MAINTOPS	MAKAR	MALAISES
MAIDHOODS	MAILSACK	MAINYARD	MAKARS	MALAM
MAIDING	MAILSACKS	MAINYARDS	MAKE	MALAMS
MAIDISH	MAILSHOT	MAIOLICA	MAKEABLE	MALAMUTE
MAIDISM	MAILSHOTS	MAIOLICAS	MAKEABLES	MALAMUTES
MAIDISMS	MAILVAN	MAIR	MAKEBATE	MALANDER
MAIDLESS	MAILVANS	MAIRE	MAKEBATES	MALANDERS
MAIDS	MAIM	MAIREHAU	MAKEFAST	MALANGA
MAIEUTIC	MAIMED	MAIREHAUS	MAKEFASTS	MALANGAS
MAIEUTICS	MAIMER	MAIRES	MAKELESS	MALAPERT
MAIGRE	MAIMERS	MAIRS	MAKEOVER	MALAPERTS
MAIGRES	MAIMING	MAISE	MAKEOVERS	MALAPROP
MAIHEM	MAIMINGS	MAISES	MAKER	MALAPROPS
MAIHEMS	MAIMS	MAIST	MAKEREADY	MALAR
MAIK	MAIN	MAISTER	MAKERS	MALARIA
MAIKO	MAINBOOM	MAISTERED	MAKES	MALARIAL
MAIKOS	MAINBOOMS	MAISTERS	MAKESHIFT	MALARIAN
MAIKS	MAINBRACE	MAISTRIES	MAKEUP	MALARIAS
MAIL	MAINDOOR	MAISTRING	MAKEUPS	MALARIOUS
MAILABLE	MAINDOORS	MAISTRY	MAKHANI	MALARKEY
MAILBAG	MAINED	MAISTS	MAKHANIS	MALARKEYS
MAILBAGS	MAINER	MAITAKE	MAKHNI	MALARKIES
MAILBOAT	MAINEST	MAITAKES	MAKHNIS	MALARKY
MAILBOATS	MAINFRAME	MAIZE	MAKI	MALAROMA
MAILBOX	MAINING	MAIZES	MAKIMONO	MALAROMAS
MAILBOXES	MAINLAND	MAJAGUA	MAKIMONOS	MALARS
MAILCAR	MAINLANDS	MAJAGUAS	MAKING	MALAS
MAILCARS	MAINLINE	MAJESTIC	MAKINGS	MALATE
MAILCOACH	MAINLINED	MAJESTIES	MAKIS	MALATES
MAILE	MAINLINER	MAJESTY	MAKO	MALATHION
MAILED	MAINLINES	MAJLIS	MAKOS	MALAX
MAILER	MAINLY	MAJLISES	MAKS	MALAXAGE
MAILERS	MAINMAST	MAJOLICA	MAKUTA	MALAXAGES
MAILES	MAINMASTS	MAJOLICAS	MAKUTU	MALAXATE
MAILGRAM	MAINOR	MAJOR	MAKUTUED	MALAXATED
MAILGRAMS	MAINORS	MAJORAT	MAKUTUING	MALAXATES
MAILING	MAINOUR	MAJORATS	MAKUTUS	MALAXATOR

MALAXED	MALIKS	MALMAGS	MALTWORMS	MAMEY
MALAXES	MALINE	MALMIER	MALTY	MAMEYES
MALAXING	MALINES	MALMIEST	MALUS	MAMEYS
MALE	MALINGER	MALMS	MALUSES	MAMIE
MALEATE	MALINGERS	MALMSEY	MALVA	MAMIES
MALEATES	MALINGERY	MALMSEYS	MALVAS	MAMILLA
MALEDICT	MALIS	MALMSTONE	MALVASIA	MAMILLAE
MALEDICTS	MALISM	MALMY	MALVASIAN	MAMILLAR
MALEFFECT	MALISMS	MALODOR	MALVASIAS	MAMILLARY
MALEFIC	MALISON	MALODORS	MALVESIE	MAMILLATE
MALEFICE	MALISONS	MALODOUR	MALVESIES	MAMLUK
MALEFICES	MALIST	MALODOURS	MALVOISIE	MAMLUKS
MALEIC	MALKIN	MALONATE	MALWA	MAMMA
MALEMIUT	MALKINS	MALONATES	MALWARE	MAMMAE
MALEMIUTS	MALL	MALONIC	MALWARES	MAMMAL
MALEMUTE	MALLAM	MALOTI	MALWAS	MAMMALIAN
MALEMUTES	MALLAMS	MALPIGHIA	MAM	MAMMALITY
MALENESS	MALLANDER	MALPOSED	MAMA	MAMMALOGY
MALENGINE	MALLARD	MALS	MAMAGUY	MAMMALS
MALES	MALLARDS	MALSTICK	MAMAGUYED	MAMMARIES
MALFED	MALLCORE	MALSTICKS	MAMAGUYS	MAMMARY
MALFORMED	MALLCORES	MALT	MAMAKAU	MAMMAS
MALGRADO	MALLEABLE	MALTALENT	MAMAKAUS	MAMMATE
MALGRE	MALLEABLY	MALTASE	MAMAKO	MAMMATI
MALGRED	MALLEATE	MALTASES	MAMAKOS	MAMMATUS
MALGRES	MALLEATED	MALTED	MAMAKU	MAMMEE
MALGRING	MALLEATES	MALTEDS	MAMAKUS	MAMMEES
MALI	MALLECHO	MALTESE	MAMALIGA	MAMMER
MALIBU	MALLECHOS	MALTHA	MAMALIGAS	MAMMERED
MALIC	MALLED	MALTHAS	MAMAS	MAMMERING
MALICE	MALLEE	MALTIER	MAMASAN	MAMMERS
MALICED	MALLEES	MALTIEST	MAMASANS	MAMMET
MALICES	MALLEI	MALTINESS	MAMATEEK	MAMMETRY
MALICHO	MALLEMUCK	MALTING	MAMATEEKS	MAMMETS
MALICHOS	MALLENDER	MALTINGS	MAMBA	MAMMEY
MALICING	MALLEOLAR	MALTIPOO	MAMBAS	MAMMEYS
MALICIOUS	MALLEOLI	MALTIPOOS	MAMBO	MAMMIE
MALIGN	MALLEOLUS	MALTMAN	MAMBOED	MAMMIES
MALIGNANT	MALLET	MALTMEN	MAMBOES	MAMMIFER
MALIGNED	MALLETS	MALTOL	MAMBOING	MAMMIFERS
MALIGNER	MALLEUS	MALTOLS	MAMBOS	MAMMIFORM
MALIGNERS	MALLEUSES	MALTOSE	MAMEE	MAMMILLA
MALIGNING	MALLING	MALTOSES	MAMEES	MAMMILLAE
MALIGNITY	MALLINGS	MALTREAT	MAMELON	MAMMILLAR
MALIGNLY	MALLOW	MALTREATS	MAMELONS	MAMMITIS
MALIGNS	MALLOWS	MALTS	MAMELUCO	MAMMOCK
MALIHINI	MALLS	MALTSTER	MAMELUCOS	MAMMOCKED
MALIHINIS	MALM	MALTSTERS	MAMELUKE	MAMMOCKS
MALIK	MALMAG	MALTWORM	MAMELUKES	MAMMOGRAM

M

MAMMON	MANBAG	MANDIS	MANGANATE	MANHOODS
MAMMONISH	MANBAGS	MANDOLA	MANGANESE	MANHUNT
MAMMONISM	MANBAND	MANDOLAS	MANGANIC	MANHUNTER
MAMMONIST	MANBANDS	MANDOLIN	MANGANIN	MANHUNTS
MAMMONITE	MANCALA	MANDOLINE	MANGANINS	MANI
MAMMONS	MANCALAS	MANDOLINS	MANGANITE	MANIA
MAMMOTH	MANCANDO	MANDOM	MANGANOUS	MANIAC
MAMMOTHS	MANCHE	MANDOMS	MANGAS	MANIACAL
MAMMY	MANCHEGO	MANDORA	MANGE	MANIACS
MAMPARA	MANCHEGOS	MANDORAS	MANGEAO	MANIAS
MAMPARAS	MANCHES	MANDORLA	MANGEAOS	MANIC
MAMPOER	MANCHET	MANDORLAS	MANGED	MANICALLY
MAMPOERS	MANCHETS	MANDRAKE	MANGEL	MANICOTTI
MAMS	MANCIPATE	MANDRAKES	MANGELS	MANICS
MAMSELLE	MANCIPLE	MANDREL	MANGER	MANICURE
MAMSELLES	MANCIPLES	MANDRELS	MANGERS	MANICURED
MAMZER	MANCUS	MANDRIL	MANGES	MANICURES
MAMZERIM	MANCUSES	MANDRILL	MANGETOUT	MANIES
MAMZERS	MAND	MANDRILLS	MANGEY	MANIFEST
MAN	MANDALA	MANDRILS	MANGIER	MANIFESTO
MANA	MANDALAS	MANDUCATE	MANGIEST	MANIFESTS
MANACLE	MANDALIC	MANDYLION	MANGILY	MANIFOLD
MANACLED	MANDAMUS	MANE	MANGINESS	MANIFOLDS
MANACLES	MANDARIN	MANEB	MANGING	MANIFORM
MANACLING	MANDARINE	MANEBS	MANGLE	MANIHOC
MANAGE	MANDARINS	MANED	MANGLED	MANIHOCS
MANAGED	MANDATARY	MANEGE	MANGLER	MANIHOT
MANAGER	MANDATE	MANEGED	MANGLERS	MANIHOTS
MANAGERS	MANDATED	MANEGES	MANGLES	MANIKIN
MANAGES	MANDATES	MANEGING	MANGLING	MANIKINS
MANAGING	MANDATING	MANEH	MANGO	MANILA
MANAIA	MANDATOR	MANEHS	MANGOES	MANILAS
MANAIAS	MANDATORS	MANELESS	MANGOLD	MANILLA
MANAKIN	MANDATORY	MANENT	MANGOLDS	MANILLAS
MANAKINS	MANDEM	MANES	MANGONEL	MANILLE
MANANA	MANDEMS	MANET	MANGONELS	MANILLES
MANANAS	MANDI	MANEUVER	MANGOS	MANIOC
MANAS	MANDIBLE	MANEUVERS	MANGOSTAN	MANIOCA
MANAT	MANDIBLES	MANFUL	MANGOUSTE	MANIOCAS
MANATEE	MANDILION	MANFULLER	MANGROVE	MANIOCS
MANATEES	MANDIOC	MANFULLY	MANGROVES	MANIPLE
MANATI	MANDIOCA	MANG	MANGS	MANIPLES
MANATIS	MANDIOCAS	MANGA	MANGULATE	MANIPLIES
MANATOID	MANDIOCCA	MANGABEY	MANGY	MANIPULAR
MANATS	MANDIOCS	MANGABEYS	MANHANDLE	MANIS
MANATU	MANDIR	MANGABIES	MANHATTAN	MANISES
MANATUS	MANDIRA	MANGABY	MANHOLE	MANITO
MANAWA	MANDIRAS	MANGAL	MANHOLES	MANITOS
MANAWAS	MANDIRS	MANGALS	MANHOOD	MANITOU

MANITOUS	MANOEUVER	MANTEEL	MANUHIRI	MAPPABLE
MANITU	MANOEUVRE	MANTEELS	MANUHIRIS	MAPPED
MANITUS	MANOMETER	MANTEL	MANUKA	MAPPEMOND
MANJACK	MANOMETRY	MANTELET	MANUKAS	MAPPER
MANJACKS	MANOR	MANTELETS	MANUL	MAPPERIES
MANKIER	MANORIAL	MANTELS	MANULS	MAPPERS
MANKIEST	MANORS	MANTES	MANUMATIC	MAPPERY
MANKIND	MANOS	MANTIC	MANUMEA	MAPPING
MANKINDS	MANOSCOPY	MANTICORA	MANUMEAS	MAPPINGS
MANKINI	MANPACK	MANTICORE	MANUMIT	MAPPIST
MANKINIS	MANPACKS	MANTID	MANUMITS	MAPPISTS
MANKY	MANPOWER	MANTIDS	MANURANCE	MAPS
MANLESS	MANPOWERS	MANTIES	MANURE	MAPSTICK
MANLIER	MANQUE	MANTILLA	MANURED	MAPSTICKS
MANLIEST	MANQUES	MANTILLAS	MANURER	MAPWISE
MANLIKE	MANRED	MANTIS	MANURERS	MAQUETTE
MANLIKELY	MANREDS	MANTISES	MANURES	MAQUETTES
MANLILY	MANRENT	MANTISSA	MANURIAL	MAQUI
MANLINESS	MANRENTS	MANTISSAS	MANURING	MAQUILA
MANLY	MANRIDER	MANTLE	MANURINGS	MAQUILAS
MANMADE	MANRIDERS	MANTLED	MANUS	MAQUIS
MANNA	MANRIDING	MANTLES	MANWARD	MAQUISARD
MANNAN	MANROPE	MANTLET	MANWARDS	MAR
MANNANS	MANROPES	MANTLETS	MANWISE	MARA
MANNAS	MANS	MANTLING	MANY	MARABI
MANNED	MANSARD	MANTLINGS	MANYATA	MARABIS
MANNEQUIN	MANSARDED	MANTO	MANYATAS	MARABOU
MANNER	MANSARDS	MANTOES	MANYATTA	MARABOUS
MANNERED	MANSCAPE	MANTOS	MANYATTAS	MARABOUT
MANNERISM	MANSCAPED	MANTRA	MANYFOLD	MARABOUTS
MANNERIST	MANSCAPES	MANTRAM	MANYPLIES	MARABUNTA
MANNERLY	MANSE	MANTRAMS	MANZANITA	MARACA
MANNERS	MANSES	MANTRAP	MANZELLO	MARACAS
MANNIKIN	MANSHIFT	MANTRAPS	MANZELLOS	MARAE
MANNIKINS	MANSHIFTS	MANTRAS	MAOMAO	MARAES
MANNING	MANSION	MANTRIC	MAOMAOS	MARAGING
MANNISH	MANSIONS	MANTUA	MAORMOR	MARAGINGS
MANNISHLY	MANSLAYER	MANTUAS	MAORMORS	MARAH
MANNITE	MANSONRY	MANTY	MAP	MARAHS
MANNITES	MANSPLAIN	MANTYHOSE	MAPAU	MARAKA
MANNITIC	MANSPREAD	MANUAL	MAPAUS	MARANATHA
MANNITOL	MANSUETE	MANUALLY	MAPLE	MARANTA
MANNITOLS	MANSWORN	MANUALS	MAPLELIKE	MARANTAS
MANNOSE	MANSWORNS	MANUARY	MAPLES	MARARI
MANNOSES	MANTA	MANUBRIA	MAPLESS	MARARIS
MANO	MANTAS	MANUBRIAL	MAPLIKE	MARAS
MANOAO	MANTEAU	MANUBRIUM	MAPMAKER	MARASCA
MANOAOS	MANTEAUS	MANUCODE	MAPMAKERS	MARASCAS
MANOES	MANTEAUX	MANUCODES	MAPMAKING	MARASMIC

M

MARASMOID	MARCHMAN	MARGRAVES	MARKA	MARLSTONE
MARASMUS	MARCHMEN	MARGS	MARKAS	MARLY
MARATHON	MARCHPANE	MARIA	MARKDOWN	MARM
MARATHONS	MARCONI	MARIACHI	MARKDOWNS	MARMALADE
MARAUD	MARCONIED	MARIACHIS	MARKED	MARMALISE
MARAUDED	MARCONIS	MARIALITE	MARKEDLY	MARMALIZE
MARAUDER	MARCS	MARID	MARKER	MARMARISE
MARAUDERS	MARD	MARIDS	MARKERS	MARMARIZE
MARAUDING	MARDIED	MARIES	MARKET	MARMELISE
MARAUDS	MARDIER	MARIGOLD	MARKETED	MARMELIZE
MARAVEDI	MARDIES	MARIGOLDS	MARKETEER	MARMEM
MARAVEDIS	MARDIEST	MARIGRAM	MARKETER	MARMITE
MARBELISE	MARDY	MARIGRAMS	MARKETERS	MARMITES
MARBELIZE	MARDYING	MARIGRAPH	MARKETING	MARMOREAL
MARBLE	MARE	MARIHUANA	MARKETISE	MARMOREAN
MARBLED	MAREMMA	MARIJUANA	MARKETIZE	MARMOSE
MARBLEISE	MAREMMAS	MARIMBA	MARKETS	MARMOSES
MARBLEIZE	MAREMME	MARIMBAS	MARKHOOR	MARMOSET
MARBLER	MARENGO	MARIMBIST	MARKHOORS	MARMOSETS
MARBLERS	MARERO	MARINA	MARKHOR	MARMOT
MARBLES	MAREROS	MARINADE	MARKHORS	MARMOTS
MARBLIER	MARES	MARINADED	MARKING	MARMS
MARBLIEST	MARESCHAL	MARINADES	MARKINGS	MAROCAIN
MARBLING	MARG	MARINARA	MARKKA	MAROCAINS
MARBLINGS	MARGARIC	MARINARAS	MARKKAA	MARON
MARBLY	MARGARIN	MARINAS	MARKKAS	MARONS
MARC	MARGARINE	MARINATE	MARKMAN	MAROON
MARCASITE	MARGARINS	MARINATED	MARKMEN	MAROONED
MARCATO	MARGARITA	MARINATES	MARKS	MAROONER
MARCATOS	MARGARITE	MARINE	MARKSMAN	MAROONERS
MARCEL	MARGATE	MARINER	MARKSMEN	MAROONING
MARCELLA	MARGATES	MARINERA	MARKUP	MAROONS
MARCELLAS	MARGAY	MARINERAS	MARKUPS	MAROQUIN
MARCELLED	MARGAYS	MARINERS	MARL	MAROQUINS
MARCELLER	MARGE	MARINES	MARLE	MAROR
MARCELS	MARGENT	MARINIERE	MARLED	MARORS
MARCH	MARGENTED	MARIPOSA	MARLES	MARPLOT
MARCHED	MARGENTS	MARIPOSAS	MARLIER	MARPLOTS
MARCHEN	MARGES	MARISCHAL	MARLIEST	MARQUE
MARCHER	MARGIN	MARISH	MARLIN	MARQUEE
MARCHERS	MARGINAL	MARISHES	MARLINE	MARQUEES
MARCHES	MARGINALS	MARITAGE	MARLINES	MARQUES
MARCHESA	MARGINATE	MARITAGES	MARLING	MARQUESS
MARCHESAS	MARGINED	MARITAL	MARLINGS	MARQUETRY
MARCHESE	MARGINING	MARITALLY	MARLINS	MARQUIS
MARCHESI	MARGINS	MARITIME	MARLITE	MARQUISE
MARCHING	MARGOSA	MARJORAM	MARLITES	MARQUISES
MARCHLAND	MARGOSAS	MARJORAMS	MARLITIC	MARRA
MARCHLIKE	MARGRAVE	MARK	MARLS	MARRAM

MARRAMS	MARSHED	MARTYRING	MASCULINE	MASKEG
MARRANO	MARSHES	MARTYRISE	MASCULISM	MASKEGS
MARRANOS	MARSHIER	MARTYRISH	MASCULIST	MASKER
MARRAS	MARSHIEST	MARTYRIUM	MASCULY	MASKERS
MARRED	MARSHLAND	MARTYRIZE	MASE	MASKING
MARRELS	MARSHLIKE	MARTYRLY	MASED	MASKINGS
MARRER	MARSHWORT	MARTYRS	MASER	MASKLESS
MARRERS	MARSHY	MARTYRY	MASERS	MASKLIKE
MARRI	MARSPORT	MARVEL	MASES	MASKNE
MARRIAGE	MARSPORTS	MARVELED	MASH	MASKNES
MARRIAGES	MARSQUAKE	MARVELER	MASHALLAH	MASKS
MARRIED	MARSUPIA	MARVELERS	MASHED	MASLIN
MARRIEDS	MARSUPIAL	MARVELING	MASHER	MASLINS
MARRIER	MARSUPIAN	MARVELLED	MASHERS	MASOCHISM
MARRIERS	MARSUPIUM	MARVELLER	MASHES	MASOCHIST
MARRIES	MART	MARVELOUS	MASHGIACH	MASON
MARRING	MARTAGON	MARVELS	MASHGIAH	MASONED
MARRIS	MARTAGONS	MARVER	MASHGIHIM	MASONIC
MARRON	MARTED	MARVERED	MASHIACH	MASONING
MARRONS	MARTEL	MARVERING	MASHIACHS	MASONITE
MARROW	MARTELLED	MARVERS	MASHIE	MASONITES
MARROWED	MARTELLO	MARVIER	MASHIER	MASONRIED
MARROWFAT	MARTELLOS	MARVIEST	MASHIES	MASONRIES
MARROWIER	MARTELS	MARVY	MASHIEST	MASONRY
MARROWING	MARTEN	MARXISANT	MASHING	MASONS
MARROWISH	MARTENS	MARY	MASHINGS	MASOOLA
MARROWS	MARTEXT	MARYBUD	MASHLAM	MASOOLAH
MARROWSKY	MARTEXTS	MARYBUDS	MASHLAMS	MASOOLAHS
MARROWY	MARTIAL	MARYJANE	MASHLIM	MASOOLAS
MARRUM	MARTIALLY	MARYJANES	MASHLIMS	MASQUE
MARRUMS	MARTIALS	MARZIPAN	MASHLIN	MASQUER
MARRY	MARTIAN	MARZIPANS	MASHLINS	MASQUERS
MARRYING	MARTIANS	MAS	MASHLOCH	MASQUES
MARRYINGS	MARTIN	MASA	MASHLOCHS	MASS
MARS	MARTINET	MASALA	MASHLUM	MASSA
MARSALA	MARTINETS	MASALAS	MASHLUMS	MASSACRE
MARSALAS	MARTING	MASAS	MASHMAN	MASSACRED
MARSE	MARTINGAL	MASCARA	MASHMEN	MASSACRER
MARSEILLE	MARTINI	MASCARAED	MASHUA	MASSACRES
MARSES	MARTINIS	MASCARAS	MASHUAS	MASSAGE
MARSH	MARTINS	MASCARON	MASHUP	MASSAGED
MARSHAL	MARTLET	MASCARONS	MASHUPS	MASSAGER
MARSHALCY	MARTLETS	MASCLE	MASHY	MASSAGERS
MARSHALED	MARTS	MASCLED	MASING	MASSAGES
MARSHALER	MARTYR	MASCLES	MASJID	MASSAGING
MARSHALL	MARTYRDOM	MASCON	MASJIDS	MASSAGIST
MARSHALLS	MARTYRED	MASCONS	MASK	MASSAS
MARSHALS	MARTYRIA	MASCOT	MASKABLE	MASSCULT
MARSHBUCK	MARTYRIES	MASCOTS	MASKED	MASSCULTS

MASSE	MASTICATE	MATAIS	MATESHIPS	MATRICULA
MASSED	MASTICH	MATAMATA	MATEY	MATRILINY
MASSEDLY	MASTICHE	MATAMATAS	MATEYNESS	MATRIMONY
MASSES	MASTICHES	MATAMBALA	MATEYS	MATRIX
MASSETER	MASTICHS	MATATA	MATFELLON	MATRIXES
MASSETERS	MASTICOT	MATATAS	MATFELON	MATRON
MASSEUR	MASTICOTS	MATATU	MATFELONS	MATRONAGE
MASSEURS	MASTICS	MATATUS	MATGRASS	MATRONAL
MASSEUSE	MASTIER	MATCH	MATH	MATRONISE
MASSEUSES	MASTIEST	MATCHA	MATHESES	MATRONIZE
MASSICOT	MASTIFF	MATCHABLE	MATHESIS	MATRONLY
MASSICOTS	MASTIFFS	MATCHAS	MATHS	MATRONS
MASSIER	MASTING	MATCHBOOK	MATICO	MATROSS
MASSIEST	MASTITIC	MATCHBOX	MATICOS	MATROSSES
MASSIF	MASTITIS	MATCHED	MATIER	MATS
MASSIFS	MASTIX	MATCHER	MATIES	MATSAH
MASSINESS	MASTIXES	MATCHERS	MATIEST	MATSAHS
MASSING	MASTLESS	MATCHES	MATILDA	MATSURI
MASSIVE	MASTLIKE	MATCHET	MATILDAS	MATSURIS
MASSIVELY	MASTODON	MATCHETS	MATILY	MATSUTAKE
MASSIVES	MASTODONS	MATCHING	MATIN	MATT
MASSLESS	MASTODONT	MATCHLESS	MATINAL	MATTAMORE
MASSOOLA	MASTOID	MATCHLOCK	MATINEE	MATTE
MASSOOLAS	MASTOIDAL	MATCHMADE	MATINEES	MATTED
MASSTIGE	MASTOIDS	MATCHMAKE	MATINESS	MATTEDLY
MASSTIGES	MASTOPEXY	MATCHMARK	MATING	MATTER
MASSY	MASTS	MATCHPLAY	MATINGS	MATTERED
MASSYMORE	MASTY	MATCHUP	MATINS	MATTERFUL
MAST	MASU	MATCHUPS	MATIPO	MATTERIER
MASTABA	MASULA	MATCHWOOD	MATIPOS	MATTERING
MASTABAH	MASULAH	MATE	MATJES	MATTERS
MASTABAHS	MASULAHS	MATED	MATLESS	MATTERY
MASTABAS	MASULAS	MATELASSE	MATLO	MATTES
MASTED	MASURIUM	MATELESS	MATLOS	MATTIE
MASTER	MASURIUMS	MATELOT	MATLOW	MATTIES
MASTERATE	MASUS	MATELOTE	MATLOWS	MATTIFIED
MASTERDOM	MAT	MATELOTES	MATOKE	MATTIFIES
MASTERED	MATACHIN	MATELOTS	MATOKES	MATTIFY
MASTERFUL	MATACHINA	MATELOTTE	MATOOKE	MATTIN
MASTERIES	MATACHINI	MATER	MATOOKES	MATTING
MASTERING	MATACHINS	MATERIAL	MATRASS	MATTINGS
MASTERLY	MATADOR	MATERIALS	MATRASSES	MATTINS
MASTERS	MATADORA	MATERIEL	MATRES	MATTOCK
MASTERY	MATADORAS	MATERIELS	MATRIARCH	MATTOCKS
MASTFUL	MATADORE	MATERNAL	MATRIC	MATTOID
MASTHEAD	MATADORES	MATERNITY	MATRICE	MATTOIDS
MASTHEADS	MATADORS	MATERS	MATRICES	MATTRASS
MASTHOUSE	MATAGOURI	MATES	MATRICIDE	MATTRESS
MASTIC	MATAI	MATESHIP	MATRICS	MATTS

MATURABLE	MAULING	MAUVINS	MAXICOAT	MAYBES
MATURATE	MAULINGS	MAUZIER	MAXICOATS	MAYBIRD
MATURATED	MAULS	MAUZIEST	MAXIDRESS	MAYBIRDS
MATURATES	MAULSTICK	MAUZY	MAXILLA	MAYBUSH
MATURE	MAULVI	MAVEN	MAXILLAE	MAYBUSHES
MATURED	MAULVIS	MAVENS	MAXILLAR	MAYDAY
MATURELY	MAUMET	MAVERICK	MAXILLARY	MAYDAYS
MATURER	MAUMETRY	MAVERICKS	MAXILLAS	MAYED
MATURERS	MAUMETS	MAVIE	MAXILLULA	MAYEST
MATURES	MAUN	MAVIES	MAXIM	MAYFISH
MATUREST	MAUND	MAVIN	MAXIMA	MAYFISHES
MATURING	MAUNDED	MAVINS	MAXIMAL	MAYFLIES
MATURITY	MAUNDER	MAVIS	MAXIMALLY	MAYFLOWER
MATUTINAL	MAUNDERED	MAVISES	MAXIMALS	MAYFLY
MATUTINE	MAUNDERER	MAVOURNIN	MAXIMAND	MAYHAP
MATWEED	MAUNDERS	MAW	MAXIMANDS	MAYHAPPEN
MATWEEDS	MAUNDIES	MAWBOUND	MAXIMIN	MAYHEM
MATY	MAUNDING	MAWED	MAXIMINS	MAYHEMS
MATZA	MAUNDS	MAWGER	MAXIMISE	MAYING
MATZAH	MAUNDY	MAWING	MAXIMISED	MAYINGS
MATZAHS	MAUNGIER	MAWK	MAXIMISER	MAYO
MATZAS	MAUNGIEST	MAWKIER	MAXIMISES	MAYOR
MATZO	MAUNGY	MAWKIEST	MAXIMIST	MAYORAL
MATZOH	MAUNNA	MAWKIN	MAXIMISTS	MAYORALTY
MATZOHS	MAURI	MAWKINS	MAXIMITE	MAYORESS
MATZOON	MAURIS	MAWKISH	MAXIMITES	MAYORS
MATZOONS	MAUSIER	MAWKISHLY	MAXIMIZE	MAYORSHIP
MATZOS	MAUSIEST	MAWKS	MAXIMIZED	MAYOS
MATZOT	MAUSOLEA	MAWKY	MAXIMIZER	MAYPOLE
MATZOTH	MAUSOLEAN	MAWMET	MAXIMIZES	MAYPOLES
MAUBIES	MAUSOLEUM	MAWMETRY	MAXIMS	MAYPOP
MAUBY	MAUSY	MAWMETS	MAXIMUM	MAYPOPS
MAUD	MAUT	MAWN	MAXIMUMLY	MAYS
MAUDLIN	MAUTHER	MAWNS	MAXIMUMS	MAYST
MAUDLINLY	MAUTHERS	MAWPUS	MAXIMUS	MAYSTER
MAUDS	MAUTS	MAWPUSES	MAXIMUSES	MAYSTERS
MAUGER	MAUVAIS	MAWR	MAXING	MAYVIN
MAUGRE	MAUVAISE	MAWRS	MAXIS	MAYVINS
MAUGRED	MAUVE	MAWS	MAXIXE	MAYWEED
MAUGRES	MAUVEIN	MAWSEED	MAXIXES	MAYWEEDS
MAUGRING	MAUVEINE	MAWSEEDS	MAXWELL	MAZAEDIA
MAUL	MAUVEINES	MAWTHER	MAXWELLS	MAZAEDIUM
MAULED	MAUVEINS	MAWTHERS	MAY	MAZARD
MAULER	MAUVER	MAX	MAYA	MAZARDS
MAULERS	MAUVES	MAXED	MAYAN	MAZARINE
MAULGRE	MAUVEST	MAXES	MAYAPPLE	MAZARINES
MAULGRED	MAUVIN	MAXI	MAYAPPLES	MAZE
MAULGRES	MAUVINE	MAXIBOAT	MAYAS	MAZED
MAULGRING	MAUVINES	MAXIBOATS	MAYBE	MAZEDLY

MAZEDNESS	MEAGRE	MEANY	MEAWES	MEDALLIST
MAZEFUL	MEAGRELY	MEARE	MEAZEL	MEDALPLAY
MAZELIKE	MEAGRER	MEARES	MEAZELS	MEDALS
MAZELTOV	MEAGRES	MEARING	MEBIBYTE	MEDCINAL
MAZEMENT	MEAGREST	MEASE	MEBIBYTES	MEDDLE
MAZEMENTS	MEAL	MEASED	MEBOS	MEDDLED
MAZER	MEALED	MEASES	MEBOSES	MEDDLER
MAZERS	MEALER	MEASING	MECCA	MEDDLERS
MAZES	MEALERS	MEASLE	MECCAS	MEDDLES
MAZEY	MEALIE	MEASLED	MECH	MEDDLING
MAZHBI	MEALIER	MEASLES	MECHANIC	MEDDLINGS
MAZHBIS	MEALIES	MEASLIER	MECHANICS	MEDEVAC
MAZIER	MEALIEST	MEASLIEST	MECHANISE	MEDEVACED
MAZIEST	MEALINESS	MEASLING	MECHANISM	MEDEVACS
MAZILY	MEALING	MEASLY	MECHANIST	MEDFLIES
MAZINESS	MEALLESS	MEASURE	MECHANIZE	MEDFLY
MAZING	MEALS	MEASURED	MECHITZA	MEDIA
MAZOURKA	MEALTIME	MEASURER	MECHITZAS	MEDIACIES
MAZOURKAS	MEALTIMES	MEASURERS	MECHITZOT	MEDIACY
MAZOUT	MEALWORM	MEASURES	MECHOUI	MEDIAD
MAZOUTS	MEALWORMS	MEASURING	MECHOUIS	MEDIAE
MAZUMA	MEALY	MEAT	MECHS	MEDIAEVAL
MAZUMAS	MEALYBUG	MEATAL	MECK	MEDIAL
MAZURKA	MEALYBUGS	MEATAXE	MECKS	MEDIALLY
MAZURKAS	MEAN	MEATAXES	MECLIZINE	MEDIALS
MAZUT	MEANDER	MEATBALL	MECONATE	MEDIAN
MAZUTS	MEANDERED	MEATBALLS	MECONATES	MEDIANLY
MAZY	MEANDERER	MEATED	MECONIC	MEDIANS
MAZZARD	MEANDERS	MEATH	MECONIN	MEDIANT
MAZZARDS	MEANDRIAN	MEATHE	MECONINS	MEDIANTS
MBAQANGA	MEANDROUS	MEATHEAD	MECONIUM	MEDIAS
MBAQANGAS	MEANE	MEATHEADS	MECONIUMS	MEDIATE
MBIRA	MEANED	MEATHES	MED	MEDIATED
MBIRAS	MEANER	MEATHOOK	MEDACCA	MEDIATELY
ME	MEANERS	MEATHOOKS	MEDACCAS	MEDIATES
MEACOCK	MEANES	MEATHS	MEDAILLON	MEDIATING
MEACOCKS	MEANEST	MEATIER	MEDAKA	MEDIATION
MEAD	MEANIE	MEATIEST	MEDAKAS	MEDIATISE
MEADERIES	MEANIES	MEATILY	MEDAL	MEDIATIVE
MEADERY	MEANING	MEATINESS	MEDALED	MEDIATIZE
MEADOW	MEANINGLY	MEATLESS	MEDALET	MEDIATOR
MEADOWIER	MEANINGS	MEATLOAF	MEDALETS	MEDIATORS
MEADOWS	MEANLY	MEATMAN	MEDALING	MEDIATORY
MEADOWY	MEANNESS	MEATMEN	MEDALIST	MEDIATRIX
MEADS	MEANS	MEATS	MEDALISTS	MEDIC
MEAGER	MEANT	MEATSPACE	MEDALLED	MEDICABLE
MEAGERER	MEANTIME	MEATUS	MEDALLIC	MEDICABLY
MEAGEREST	MEANTIMES	MEATUSES	MEDALLING	MEDICAID
MEAGERLY	MEANWHILE	MEATY	MEDALLION	MEDICAIDS

MEDICAL	MEDRESA	MEETLY	MEGAMALLS	MEHENDIS
MEDICALLY	MEDRESAS	MEETNESS	MEGAPHONE	MEHNDI
MEDICALS	MEDRESE	MEETS	MEGAPHYLL	MEHNDIS
MEDICANT	MEDRESES	MEETUP	MEGAPIXEL	MEIBOMIAN
MEDICANTS	MEDRESSEH	MEETUPS	MEGAPLEX	MEIKLE
MEDICARE	MEDS	MEFF	MEGAPOD	MEIKLER
MEDICARES	MEDULLA	MEFFS	MEGAPODE	MEIKLEST
MEDICATE	MEDULLAE	MEG	MEGAPODES	MEIN
MEDICATED	MEDULLAR	MEGA	MEGAPODS	MEINED
MEDICATES	MEDULLARY	MEGABAR	MEGAPOLIS	MEINEY
MEDICIDE	MEDULLAS	MEGABARS	MEGAQUAKE	MEINEYS
MEDICIDES	MEDULLATE	MEGABIT	MEGARA	MEINIE
MEDICINAL	MEDUSA	MEGABITS	MEGARAD	MEINIES
MEDICINE	MEDUSAE	MEGABUCK	MEGARADS	MEINING
MEDICINED	MEDUSAL	MEGABUCKS	MEGARON	MEINS
MEDICINER	MEDUSAN	MEGABYTE	MEGARONS	MEINT
MEDICINES	MEDUSANS	MEGABYTES	MEGASCOPE	MEINY
MEDICK	MEDUSAS	MEGACITY	MEGASPORE	MEIOCYTE
MEDICKS	MEDUSOID	MEGACURIE	MEGASS	MEIOCYTES
MEDICO	MEDUSOIDS	MEGACYCLE	MEGASSE	MEIOFAUNA
MEDICOS	MEE	MEGADEAL	MEGASSES	MEIONITE
MEDICS	MEED	MEGADEALS	MEGASTAR	MEIONITES
MEDIEVAL	MEEDS	MEGADEATH	MEGASTARS	MEIOSES
MEDIEVALS	MEEK	MEGADOSE	MEGASTORE	MEIOSIS
MEDIGAP	MEEKEN	MEGADOSES	MEGASTORM	MEIOSPORE
MEDIGAPS	MEEKENED	MEGADYNE	MEGATHERE	MEIOTIC
MEDII	MEEKENING	MEGADYNES	MEGATON	MEISHI
MEDINA	MEEKENS	MEGAFARAD	MEGATONIC	MEISHIS
MEDINAS	MEEKER	MEGAFAUNA	MEGATONS	MEISTER
MEDIOCRE	MEEKEST	MEGAFIRE	MEGAVOLT	MEISTERS
MEDITATE	MEEKLY	MEGAFIRES	MEGAVOLTS	MEITH
MEDITATED	MEEKNESS	MEGAFLOP	MEGAWATT	MEITHS
MEDITATES	MEEMIE	MEGAFLOPS	MEGAWATTS	MEJLIS
MEDITATOR	MEEMIES	MEGAFLORA	MEGILLA	MEJLISES
MEDIUM	MEER	MEGAFOG	MEGILLAH	MEKKA
MEDIUMS	MEERCAT	MEGAFOGS	MEGILLAHS	MEKKAS
MEDIUS	MEERCATS	MEGAGAUSS	MEGILLAS	MEKOMETER
MEDIUSES	MEERED	MEGAHERTZ	MEGILLOTH	MEL
MEDIVAC	MEERING	MEGAHIT	MEGILP	MELA
MEDIVACED	MEERKAT	MEGAHITS	MEGILPH	MELAENA
MEDIVACS	MEERKATS	MEGAJOULE	MEGILPHS	MELAENAS
MEDLAR	MEERS	MEGALITER	MEGILPS	MELALEUCA
MEDLARS	MEES	MEGALITH	MEGOHM	MELAMDIM
MEDLE	MEET	MEGALITHS	MEGOHMS	MELAMED
MEDLED	MEETER	MEGALITRE	MEGRIM	MELAMINE
MEDLES	MEETERS	MEGALODON	MEGRIMS	MELAMINES
MEDLEY	MEETEST	MEGALOPIC	MEGS	MELAMPODE
MEDLEYS	MEETING	MEGALOPS	MEH	MELANATED
MEDLING	MEETINGS	MEGAMALL	MEHENDI	MELANEMIA

M

MELANGE	MELICK	MELODICAS	MELTITHS	MEN
MELANGES	MELICKS	MELODICS	MELTON	MENACE
MELANIAN	MELICS	MELODIES	MELTONS	MENACED
MELANIANS	MELIK	MELODION	MELTS	MENACER
MELANIC	MELIKS	MELODIONS	MELTWATER	MENACERS
MELANICS	MELILITE	MELODIOUS	MELTY	MENACES
MELANIN	MELILITES	MELODISE	MELUNGEON	MENACING
MELANINS	MELILOT	MELODISED	MEM	MENAD
MELANISE	MELILOTS	MELODISER	MEMBER	MENADIONE
MELANISED	MELINITE	MELODISES	MEMBERED	MENADS
MELANISES	MELINITES	MELODIST	MEMBERS	MENAGE
MELANISM	MELINJO	MELODISTS	MEMBRAL	MENAGED
MELANISMS	MELINJOS	MELODIZE	MEMBRANAL	MENAGERIE
MELANIST	MELIORATE	MELODIZED	MEMBRANE	MENAGES
MELANISTS	MELIORISM	MELODIZER	MEMBRANED	MENAGING
MELANITE	MELIORIST	MELODIZES	MEMBRANES	MENARCHE
MELANITES	MELIORITY	MELODRAMA	MEMBRILLO	MENARCHES
MELANITIC	MELISMA	MELODRAME	MEME	MENAZON
MELANIZE	MELISMAS	MELODY	MEMENTO	MENAZONS
MELANIZED	MELISMATA	MELOID	MEMENTOES	MEND
MELANIZES	MELITTIN	MELOIDS	MEMENTOS	MENDABLE
MELANO	MELITTINS	MELOMANIA	MEMES	MENDACITY
MELANOID	MELL	MELOMANIC	MEMETIC	MENDED
MELANOIDS	MELLAY	MELON	MEMETICS	MENDER
MELANOMA	MELLAYS	MELONGENE	MEMO	MENDERS
MELANOMAS	MELLED	MELONIER	MEMOIR	MENDICANT
MELANOS	MELLIFIC	MELONIEST	MEMOIRISM	MENDICITY
MELANOSES	MELLING	MELONS	MEMOIRIST	MENDIGO
MELANOSIS	MELLITE	MELONY	MEMOIRS	MENDIGOS
MELANOTIC	MELLITES	MELOXICAM	MEMORABLE	MENDING
MELANOUS	MELLITIC	MELPHALAN	MEMORABLY	MENDINGS
MELANURIA	MELLOTRON	MELS	MEMORANDA	MENDS
MELANURIC	MELLOW	MELT	MEMORIAL	MENE
MELAPHYRE	MELLOWED	MELTABLE	MEMORIALS	MENED
MELAS	MELLOWER	MELTAGE	MEMORIES	MENEER
MELASTOME	MELLOWEST	MELTAGES	MEMORISE	MENEERS
MELATONIN	MELLOWIER	MELTDOWN	MEMORISED	MENES
MELBA	MELLOWING	MELTDOWNS	MEMORISER	MENFOLK
MELD	MELLOWLY	MELTED	MEMORISES	MENFOLKS
MELDED	MELLOWS	MELTEMI	MEMORITER	MENG
MELDER	MELLOWY	MELTEMIS	MEMORIZE	MENGE
MELDERS	MELLS	MELTER	MEMORIZED	MENGED
MELDING	MELOCOTON	MELTERS	MEMORIZER	MENGES
MELDS	MELODEON	MELTIER	MEMORIZES	MENGING
MELEE	MELODEONS	MELTIEST	MEMORY	MENGS
MELEES	MELODIA	MELTING	MEMOS	MENHADEN
MELENA	MELODIAS	MELTINGLY	MEMS	MENHADENS
MELENAS	MELODIC	MELTINGS	MEMSAHIB	MENHIR
MELIC	MELODICA	MELTITH	MEMSAHIBS	MENHIRS

MENIAL	MENSUAL	MEPHITIS	MEREL	MERISMS
MENIALLY	MENSURAL	MEPHITISM	MERELL	MERISTEM
MENIALS	MENSWEAR	MERANTI	MERELLS	MERISTEMS
MENILITE	MENSWEARS	MERANTIS	MERELS	MERISTIC
MENILITES	MENT	MERBROMIN	MERELY	MERIT
MENING	MENTA	MERC	MERENGUE	MERITED
MENINGEAL	MENTAL	MERCADO	MERENGUES	MERITING
MENINGES	MENTALESE	MERCADOS	MEREOLOGY	MERITLESS
MENINX	MENTALISM	MERCAPTAN	MERER	MERITS
MENISCAL	MENTALIST	MERCAPTO	MERES	MERK
MENISCATE	MENTALITY	MERCAT	MERESMAN	MERKIN
MENISCI	MENTALLY	MERCATS	MERESMEN	MERKINS
MENISCOID	MENTATION	MERCENARY	MEREST	MERKS
MENISCUS	MENTEE	MERCER	MERESTONE	MERL
MENO	MENTEES	MERCERIES	MERFOLK	MERLE
MENOLOGY	MENTHENE	MERCERISE	MERFOLKS	MERLES
MENOMINEE	MENTHENES	MERCERIZE	MERGANSER	MERLIN
MENOMINI	MENTHOL	MERCERS	MERGE	MERLING
MENOMINIS	MENTHOLS	MERCERY	MERGED	MERLINGS
MENOPAUSE	MENTICIDE	MERCES	MERGEE	MERLINS
MENOPOLIS	MENTION	MERCH	MERGEES	MERLON
MENOPOME	MENTIONED	MERCHANT	MERGENCE	MERLONS
MENOPOMES	MENTIONER	MERCHANTS	MERGENCES	MERLOT
MENORAH	MENTIONS	MERCHES	MERGER	MERLOTS
MENORAHS	MENTO	MERCHET	MERGERS	MERLS
MENORRHEA	MENTOR	MERCHETS	MERGES	MERMAID
MENSA	MENTORED	MERCHILD	MERGING	MERMAIDEN
MENSAE	MENTORIAL	MERCIABLE	MERGINGS	MERMAIDS
MENSAL	MENTORING	MERCIES	MERGUEZ	MERMAN
MENSAS	MENTORS	MERCIFIDE	MERGUEZES	MERMEN
MENSCH	MENTOS	MERCIFIED	MERI	MEROCRINE
MENSCHEN	MENTUM	MERCIFIES	MERICARP	MEROGONY
MENSCHES	MENU	MERCIFUL	MERICARPS	MEROISTIC
MENSCHIER	MENUDO	MERCIFY	MERIDIAN	MEROME
MENSCHY	MENUDOS	MERCILESS	MERIDIANS	MEROMES
MENSE	MENUISIER	MERCS	MERIL	MERONYM
MENSED	MENUS	MERCURATE	MERILS	MERONYMS
MENSEFUL	MENYIE	MERCURIAL	MERIMAKE	MERONYMY
MENSELESS	MENYIES	MERCURIC	MERIMAKES	MEROPIA
MENSES	MEOU	MERCURIES	MERING	MEROPIAS
MENSH	MEOUED	MERCURISE	MERINGS	MEROPIC
MENSHED	MEOUING	MERCURIZE	MERINGUE	MEROPIDAN
MENSHEN	MEOUS	MERCUROUS	MERINGUES	MEROSOME
MENSHES	MEOW	MERCURY	MERINO	MEROSOMES
MENSHING	MEOWED	MERCY	MERINOS	MEROZOITE
MENSING	MEOWING	MERDE	MERIS	MERPEOPLE
MENSTRUA	MEOWS	MERDES	MERISES	MERRIE
MENSTRUAL	MEPACRINE	MERE	MERISIS	MERRIER
MENSTRUUM	MEPHITIC	MERED	MERISM	MERRIES

MERRIEST	MESHES	MESOPHYL	MESSMATE	METALISE
MERRILY	MESHIER	MESOPHYLL	MESSMATES	METALISED
MERRIMENT	MESHIEST	MESOPHYLS	MESSMEN	METALISES
MERRINESS	MESHING	MESOPHYTE	MESSUAGE	METALIST
MERRY	MESHINGS	MESOSAUR	MESSUAGES	METALISTS
MERRYMAN	MESHUGA	MESOSAURS	MESSY	METALIZE
MERRYMEN	MESHUGAAS	MESOSCALE	MESTEE	METALIZED
MERSALYL	MESHUGAH	MESOSOME	MESTEES	METALIZES
MERSALYLS	MESHUGAS	MESOSOMES	MESTER	METALLED
MERSE	MESHUGGA	MESOTRON	MESTERS	METALLIC
MERSES	MESHUGGAH	MESOTRONS	MESTESO	METALLICS
MERSION	MESHUGGE	MESOZOAN	MESTESOES	METALLIKE
MERSIONS	MESHWORK	MESOZOANS	MESTESOS	METALLINE
MERYCISM	MESHWORKS	MESOZOIC	MESTINO	METALLING
MERYCISMS	MESHY	MESPIL	MESTINOES	METALLISE
MES	MESIAD	MESPILS	MESTINOS	METALLIST
MESA	MESIAL	MESPRISE	MESTIZA	METALLIZE
MESAIL	MESIALLY	MESPRISES	MESTIZAS	METALLOID
MESAILS	MESIAN	MESPRIZE	MESTIZO	METALLY
MESAL	MESIC	MESPRIZES	MESTIZOES	METALMARK
MESALLY	MESICALLY	MESQUIN	MESTIZOS	METALS
MESARAIC	MESMERIC	MESQUINE	MESTO	METALWARE
MESARCH	MESMERISE	MESQUIT	MESTOM	METALWORK
MESAS	MESMERISM	MESQUITE	MESTOME	METAMALE
MESCAL	MESMERIST	MESQUITES	MESTOMES	METAMALES
MESCALIN	MESMERIZE	MESQUITS	MESTOMS	METAMER
MESCALINE	MESNALTY	MESS	MESTRANOL	METAMERAL
MESCALINS	MESNE	MESSAGE	MET	METAMERE
MESCALISM	MESNES	MESSAGED	META	METAMERES
MESCALS	MESOBLAST	MESSAGES	METABASES	METAMERIC
MESCLUM	MESOCARP	MESSAGING	METABASIS	METAMERS
MESCLUMS	MESOCARPS	MESSALINE	METABATIC	METAMICT
MESCLUN	MESOCRANY	MESSAN	METABOLIC	METANOIA
MESCLUNS	MESODERM	MESSANS	METABOLY	METANOIAS
MESDAMES	MESODERMS	MESSED	METACARPI	METAPELET
MESE	MESOGLEA	MESSENGER	METADATA	METAPHASE
MESEEMED	MESOGLEAL	MESSES	METADATAS	METAPHONY
MESEEMETH	MESOGLEAS	MESSIAH	METAFILE	METAPHOR
MESEEMS	MESOGLOEA	MESSIAHS	METAFILES	METAPHORS
MESEL	MESOLITE	MESSIANIC	METAGE	METAPLASM
MESELED	MESOLITES	MESSIAS	METAGENIC	METAPLOT
MESELS	MESOMERE	MESSIASES	METAGES	METARCHON
MESENTERA	MESOMERES	MESSIER	METAIRIE	METASOMA
MESENTERY	MESOMORPH	MESSIEST	METAIRIES	METASOMAS
MESES	MESON	MESSIEURS	METAL	METATAG
MESETA	MESONIC	MESSILY	METALCORE	METATAGS
MESETAS	MESONS	MESSINESS	METALED	METATARSI
MESH	MESOPAUSE	MESSING	METALHEAD	METATE
MESHED	MESOPHILE	MESSMAN	METALING	METATES

METAVERSE	METHANOL	METOLS	MEU	MEZZALUNA
METAXYLEM	METHANOLS	METONYM	MEUNIERE	MEZZANINE
METAYAGE	METHANOYL	METONYMIC	MEUS	MEZZE
METAYAGES	METHEGLIN	METONYMS	MEUSE	MEZZES
METAYER	METHINK	METONYMY	MEUSED	MEZZO
METAYERS	METHINKS	METOPAE	MEUSES	MEZZOS
METAZOA	METHO	METOPE	MEUSING	MEZZOTINT
METAZOAL	METHOD	METOPES	MEVE	MGANGA
METAZOAN	METHODIC	METOPIC	MEVED	MGANGAS
METAZOANS	METHODISE	METOPISM	MEVES	MHO
METAZOIC	METHODISM	METOPISMS	MEVING	MHORR
METAZOON	METHODIST	METOPON	MEVROU	MHORRS
METCAST	METHODIZE	METOPONS	MEVROUS	MHOS
METCASTS	METHODS	METOPRYL	MEW	MI
METE	METHOS	METOPRYLS	MEWED	MIAOU
METED	METHOUGHT	METRALGIA	MEWING	MIAOUED
METEOR	METHOXIDE	METRAZOL	MEWL	MIAOUING
METEORIC	METHOXIES	METRAZOLS	MEWLED	MIAOUS
METEORISM	METHOXY	METRE	MEWLER	MIAOW
METEORIST	METHOXYL	METRED	MEWLERS	MIAOWED
METEORITE	METHOXYLS	METRES	MEWLING	MIAOWING
METEOROID	METHS	METRIC	MEWLS	MIAOWS
METEOROUS	METHYL	METRICAL	MEWS	MIASM
METEORS	METHYLAL	METRICATE	MEWSED	MIASMA
METEPA	METHYLALS	METRICIAN	MEWSES	MIASMAL
METEPAS	METHYLASE	METRICISE	MEWSING	MIASMAS
METER	METHYLATE	METRICISM	MEYNT	MIASMATA
METERAGE	METHYLENE	METRICIST	MEZAIL	MIASMATIC
METERAGES	METHYLIC	METRICIZE	MEZAILS	MIASMIC
METERED	METHYLS	METRICS	MEZCAL	MIASMOUS
METERING	METHYSES	METRIFIED	MEZCALINE	MIASMS
METERS	METHYSIS	METRIFIER	MEZCALS	MIAUL
METES	METHYSTIC	METRIFIES	MEZE	MIAULED
METESTICK	METIC	METRIFY	MEZEREON	MIAULING
METESTRUS	METICA	METRING	MEZEREONS	MIAULS
METEWAND	METICAIS	METRIST	MEZEREUM	MIB
METEWANDS	METICAL	METRISTS	MEZEREUMS	MIBS
METEYARD	METICALS	METRITIS	MEZES	MIBUNA
METEYARDS	METICAS	METRO	MEZQUIT	MIBUNAS
METFORMIN	METICS	METROLOGY	MEZQUITE	MIC
METH	METIER	METRONOME	MEZQUITES	MICA
METHADON	METIERS	METROPLEX	MEZQUITS	MICACEOUS
METHADONE	METIF	METROS	MEZUZA	MICAS
METHADONS	METIFS	METS	MEZUZAH	MICATE
METHANAL	METING	METTLE	MEZUZAHS	MICATED
METHANALS	METIS	METTLED	MEZUZAS	MICATES
METHANE	METISSE	METTLES	MEZUZOT	MICATING
METHANES	METISSES	METUMP	MEZUZOTH	MICAWBER
METHANOIC	METOL	METUMPS	MEZZ	MICAWBERS

MICE	MICROBIAN	MICROPYLE	MIDFIELDS	MIDRASHIM
MICELL	MICROBIC	MICROS	MIDGE	MIDRASHOT
MICELLA	MICROBLOG	MICROSITE	MIDGES	MIDRIB
MICELLAE	MICROBREW	MICROSOME	MIDGET	MIDRIBS
MICELLAR	MICROBUS	MICROTOME	MIDGETS	MIDRIFF
MICELLAS	MICROCAP	MICROTOMY	MIDGIE	MIDRIFFS
MICELLE	MICROCAR	MICROTONE	MIDGIER	MIDROLL
MICELLES	MICROCARD	MICROTUBE	MIDGIES	MIDROLLS
MICELLS	MICROCARS	MICROVOLT	MIDGIEST	MIDS
MICH	MICROCHIP	MICROWATT	MIDGUT	MIDSEASON
MICHAEL	MICROCODE	MICROWAVE	MIDGUTS	MIDSHIP
MICHAELS	MICROCOPY	MICROWIRE	MIDGY	MIDSHIPS
MICHE	MICROCOSM	MICRURGY	MIDI	MIDSHORE
MICHED	MICROCYTE	MICS	MIDIBUS	MIDSIZE
MICHER	MICRODONT	MICTION	MIDIBUSES	MIDSIZED
MICHERS	MICRODOSE	MICTIONS	MIDINETTE	MIDSOLE
MICHES	MICRODOT	MICTURATE	MIDIRON	MIDSOLES
MICHIGAN	MICRODOTS	MID	MIDIRONS	MIDSPACE
MICHIGANS	MICROFILM	MIDAIR	MIDIS	MIDSPACES
MICHING	MICROFINE	MIDAIRS	MIDISKIRT	MIDST
MICHINGS	MICROFORM	MIDBAND	MIDLAND	MIDSTORY
MICHT	MICROGLIA	MIDBRAIN	MIDLANDER	MIDSTREAM
MICHTS	MICROGRAM	MIDBRAINS	MIDLANDS	MIDSTS
MICKERIES	MICROGRID	MIDCALF	MIDLEG	MIDSUMMER
MICKERY	MICROHERB	MIDCALVES	MIDLEGS	MIDTERM
MICKEY	MICROHM	MIDCAP	MIDLIFE	MIDTERMS
MICKEYED	MICROHMS	MIDCOURSE	MIDLIFER	MIDTHIGH
MICKEYING	MICROINCH	MIDCULT	MIDLIFERS	MIDTHIGHS
MICKEYS	MICROJET	MIDCULTS	MIDLIFES	MIDTOWN
MICKIES	MICROJETS	MIDDAY	MIDLINE	MIDTOWNS
MICKLE	MICROLITE	MIDDAYS	MIDLINES	MIDWATCH
MICKLER	MICROLITH	MIDDEN	MIDLIST	MIDWATER
MICKLES	MICROLOAN	MIDDENS	MIDLISTS	MIDWATERS
MICKLEST	MICROLOGY	MIDDER	MIDLIVES	MIDWAY
MICKY	MICROLUX	MIDDEST	MIDMONTH	MIDWAYS
MICO	MICROMERE	MIDDIE	MIDMONTHS	MIDWEEK
MICOS	MICROMESH	MIDDIES	MIDMOST	MIDWEEKLY
MICRA	MICROMHO	MIDDLE	MIDMOSTS	MIDWEEKS
MICRIFIED	MICROMHOS	MIDDLED	MIDNIGHT	MIDWIFE
MICRIFIES	MICROMINI	MIDDLEMAN	MIDNIGHTS	MIDWIFED
MICRIFY	MICROMOLE	MIDDLEMEN	MIDNOON	MIDWIFERY
MICRO	MICROMORT	MIDDLER	MIDNOONS	MIDWIFES
MICROBAR	MICRON	MIDDLERS	MIDPAY	MIDWIFING
MICROBARS	MICRONISE	MIDDLES	MIDPOINT	MIDWINTER
MICROBE	MICRONIZE	MIDDLING	MIDPOINTS	MIDWIVE
MICROBEAD	MICRONS	MIDDLINGS	MIDRANGE	MIDWIVED
MICROBEAM	MICROPORE	MIDDORSAL	MIDRANGES	MIDWIVES
MICROBES	MICROPSIA	MIDDY	MIDRASH	MIDWIVING
MICROBIAL	MICROPUMP	MIDFIELD	MIDRASHIC	MIDYEAR

MIDYEARS	MIGRATORS	MILDEW	MILIUM	MILLEPED
MIELIE	MIGRATORY	MILDEWED	MILK	MILLEPEDE
MIELIES	MIGS	MILDEWIER	MILKED	MILLEPEDS
MIEN	MIHA	MILDEWING	MILKEN	MILLEPORE
MIENS	MIHAS	MILDEWS	MILKER	MILLER
MIEVE	MIHI	MILDEWY	MILKERS	MILLERITE
MIEVED	MIHIED	MILDING	MILKFISH	MILLERS
MIEVES	MIHIING	MILDISH	MILKIER	MILLES
MIEVING	MIHIS	MILDLY	MILKIEST	MILLET
MIFF	MIHRAB	MILDNESS	MILKILY	MILLETS
MIFFED	MIHRABS	MILDS	MILKINESS	MILLHAND
MIFFIER	MIJNHEER	MILE	MILKING	MILLHANDS
MIFFIEST	MIJNHEERS	MILEAGE	MILKINGS	MILLHOUSE
MIFFILY	MIKADO	MILEAGES	MILKLESS	MILLIAMP
MIFFINESS	MIKADOS	MILEPOST	MILKLIKE	MILLIAMPS
MIFFING	MIKE	MILEPOSTS	MILKMAID	MILLIARD
MIFFS	MIKED	MILER	MILKMAIDS	MILLIARDS
MIFFY	MIKES	MILERS	MILKMAN	MILLIARE
MIFTY	MIKING	MILES	MILKMEN	MILLIARES
MIG	MIKRA	MILESIAN	MILKO	MILLIARY
MIGAWD	MIKRON	MILESIMO	MILKOS	MILLIBAR
MIGG	MIKRONS	MILESIMOS	MILKS	MILLIBARS
MIGGLE	MIKVA	MILESTONE	MILKSHAKE	MILLIE
MIGGLES	MIKVAH	MILF	MILKSHED	MILLIEME
MIGGS	MIKVAHS	MILFOIL	MILKSHEDS	MILLIEMES
MIGHT	MIKVAS	MILFOILS	MILKSOP	MILLIER
MIGHTEST	MIKVEH	MILFS	MILKSOPPY	MILLIERS
MIGHTFUL	MIKVEHS	MILIA	MILKSOPS	MILLIES
MIGHTIER	MIKVOS	MILIARIA	MILKTOAST	MILLIGAL
MIGHTIEST	MIKVOT	MILIARIAL	MILKWEED	MILLIGALS
MIGHTILY	MIKVOTH	MILIARIAS	MILKWEEDS	MILLIGRAM
MIGHTS	MIL	MILIARY	MILKWOOD	MILLILUX
MIGHTST	MILADI	MILIEU	MILKWOODS	MILLIME
MIGHTY	MILADIES	MILIEUS	MILKWORT	MILLIMES
MIGMATITE	MILADIS	MILIEUX	MILKWORTS	MILLIMHO
MIGNON	MILADY	MILING	MILKY	MILLIMHOS
MIGNONNE	MILAGE	MILINGS	MILL	MILLIMOLE
MIGNONNES	MILAGES	MILITANCE	MILLABLE	MILLINE
MIGNONS	MILCH	MILITANCY	MILLAGE	MILLINER
MIGRAINE	MILCHIG	MILITANT	MILLAGES	MILLINERS
MIGRAINES	MILCHIK	MILITANTS	MILLBOARD	MILLINERY
MIGRANT	MILD	MILITAR	MILLCAKE	MILLINES
MIGRANTS	MILDED	MILITARIA	MILLCAKES	MILLING
MIGRATE	MILDEN	MILITARY	MILLDAM	MILLINGS
MIGRATED	MILDENED	MILITATE	MILLDAMS	MILLIOHM
MIGRATES	MILDENING	MILITATED	MILLE	MILLIOHMS
MIGRATING	MILDENS	MILITATES	MILLED	MILLION
MIGRATION	MILDER	MILITIA	MILLENARY	MILLIONS
MIGRATOR	MILDEST	MILITIAS	MILLENNIA	MILLIONTH

M

MILLIPED	MILTY	MIMULUSES	MINEOLA	MINICAB
MILLIPEDE	MILTZ	MINA	MINEOLAS	MINICABS
MILLIPEDS	MILTZES	MINABLE	MINER	MINICAM
MILLIREM	MILVINE	MINACIOUS	MINERAL	MINICAMP
MILLIREMS	MIM	MINACITY	MINERALS	MINICAMPS
MILLIVOLT	MIMBAR	MINAE	MINERS	MINICAMS
MILLIWATT	MIMBARS	MINAR	MINES	MINICAR
MILLOCRAT	MIME	MINARET	MINESHAFT	MINICARS
MILLPOND	MIMED	MINARETED	MINESTONE	MINICOM
MILLPONDS	MIMEO	MINARETS	MINETTE	MINICOMS
MILLRACE	MIMEOED	MINARS	MINETTES	MINIDISC
MILLRACES	MIMEOING	MINAS	MINEVER	MINIDISCS
MILLRIND	MIMEOS	MINATORY	MINEVERS	MINIDISH
MILLRINDS	MIMER	MINBAR	MING	MINIDISK
MILLRUN	MIMERS	MINBARS	MINGE	MINIDISKS
MILLRUNS	MIMES	MINCE	MINGED	MINIDRESS
MILLS	MIMESES	MINCED	MINGER	MINIER
MILLSCALE	MIMESIS	MINCEMEAT	MINGERS	MINIEST
MILLSTONE	MIMESISES	MINCER	MINGES	MINIFIED
MILLTAIL	MIMESTER	MINCERS	MINGIER	MINIFIES
MILLTAILS	MIMESTERS	MINCES	MINGIEST	MINIFY
MILLWHEEL	MIMETIC	MINCEUR	MINGILY	MINIFYING
MILLWORK	MIMETICAL	MINCIER	MINGINESS	MINIGOLF
MILLWORKS	MIMETITE	MINCIEST	MINGING	MINIGOLFS
MILNEB	MIMETITES	MINCING	MINGLE	MINIKIN
MILNEBS	MIMIC	MINCINGLY	MINGLED	MINIKINS
MILO	MIMICAL	MINCY	MINGLER	MINILAB
MILOMETER	MIMICKED	MIND	MINGLERS	MINILABS
MILOR	MIMICKER	MINDED	MINGLES	MINIM
MILORD	MIMICKERS	MINDEDLY	MINGLING	MINIMA
MILORDS	MIMICKING	MINDER	MINGLINGS	MINIMAL
MILORS	MIMICRIES	MINDERS	MINGS	MINIMALLY
MILOS	MIMICRY	MINDFUCK	MINGY	MINIMALS
MILPA	MIMICS	MINDFUCKS	MINI	MINIMART
MILPAS	MIMING	MINDFUL	MINIATE	MINIMARTS
MILREIS	MIMIVIRUS	MINDFULLY	MINIATED	MINIMAX
MILS	MIMMER	MINDING	MINIATES	MINIMAXED
MILSEY	MIMMEST	MINDINGS	MINIATING	MINIMAXES
MILSEYS	MIMMICK	MINDLESS	MINIATION	MINIMENT
MILT	MIMMICKED	MINDS	MINIATURE	MINIMENTS
MILTED	MIMMICKS	MINDSCAPE	MINIBAR	MINIMILL
MILTER	MIMOSA	MINDSET	MINIBARS	MINIMILLS
MILTERS	MIMOSAE	MINDSETS	MINIBEAST	MINIMISE
MILTIER	MIMOSAS	MINDSHARE	MINIBIKE	MINIMISED
MILTIEST	MIMSEY	MINE	MINIBIKER	MINIMISER
MILTING	MIMSIER	MINEABLE	MINIBIKES	MINIMISES
MILTONIA	MIMSIEST	MINED	MINIBREAK	MINIMISM
MILTONIAS	MIMSY	MINEFIELD	MINIBUS	MINIMISMS
MILTS	MIMULUS	MINELAYER	MINIBUSES	MINIMIST

MINIMISTS	MINKS	MINUETS	MIRBANE	MIRTHS
MINIMIZE	MINNEOLA	MINUS	MIRBANES	MIRV
MINIMIZED	MINNEOLAS	MINUSCULE	MIRCHI	MIRVED
MINIMIZER	MINNICK	MINUSES	MIRE	MIRVING
MINIMIZES	MINNICKED	MINUTE	MIRED	MIRVS
MINIMOTO	MINNICKS	MINUTED	MIREPOIX	MIRY
MINIMOTOS	MINNIE	MINUTELY	MIRES	MIRZA
MINIMS	MINNIES	MINUTEMAN	MIREX	MIRZAS
MINIMUM	MINNOCK	MINUTEMEN	MIREXES	MIS
MINIMUMS	MINNOCKED	MINUTER	MIRI	MISACT
MINIMUS	MINNOCKS	MINUTES	MIRID	MISACTED
MINIMUSES	MINNOW	MINUTEST	MIRIDS	MISACTING
MINING	MINNOWS	MINUTIA	MIRIER	MISACTS
MININGS	MINNY	MINUTIAE	MIRIEST	MISADAPT
MINION	MINO	MINUTIAL	MIRIFIC	MISADAPTS
MINIONS	MINOR	MINUTING	MIRIFICAL	MISADD
MINIPARK	MINORCA	MINUTIOSE	MIRIN	MISADDED
MINIPARKS	MINORCAS	MINX	MIRINESS	MISADDING
MINIPILL	MINORED	MINXES	MIRING	MISADDS
MINIPILLS	MINORING	MINXISH	MIRINS	MISADJUST
MINIRUGBY	MINORITY	MINY	MIRITI	MISADVICE
MINIS	MINORS	MINYAN	MIRITIS	MISADVISE
MINISCULE	MINORSHIP	MINYANIM	MIRK	MISAGENT
MINISH	MINOS	MINYANS	MIRKER	MISAGENTS
MINISHED	MINOTAUR	MIOCENE	MIRKEST	MISAIM
MINISHES	MINOXIDIL	MIOMBO	MIRKIER	MISAIMED
MINISHING	MINSHUKU	MIOMBOS	MIRKIEST	MISAIMING
MINISKI	MINSHUKUS	MIOSES	MIRKILY	MISAIMS
MINISKIRT	MINSTER	MIOSIS	MIRKINESS	MISALIGN
MINISKIS	MINSTERS	MIOSISES	MIRKS	MISALIGNS
MINISODE	MINSTREL	MIOTIC	MIRKY	MISALLEGE
MINISODES	MINSTRELS	MIOTICS	MIRLIER	MISALLIED
MINISTATE	MINT	MIPS	MIRLIEST	MISALLIES
MINISTER	MINTAGE	MIQUELET	MIRLIGOES	MISALLOT
MINISTERS	MINTAGES	MIQUELETS	MIRLITON	MISALLOTS
MINISTRY	MINTED	MIR	MIRLITONS	MISALLY
MINITOWER	MINTER	MIRABELLE	MIRLY	MISALTER
MINITRACK	MINTERS	MIRABILIA	MIRO	MISALTERS
MINIUM	MINTIER	MIRABILIS	MIROMIRO	MISANDRY
MINIUMS	MINTIEST	MIRABLE	MIROMIROS	MISAPPLY
MINIVAN	MINTING	MIRACIDIA	MIROS	MISARRAY
MINIVANS	MINTLIKE	MIRACLE	MIRROR	MISARRAYS
MINIVER	MINTS	MIRACLES	MIRRORED	MISASSAY
MINIVERS	MINTY	MIRADOR	MIRRORING	MISASSAYS
MINIVET	MINUEND	MIRADORS	MIRRORS	MISASSIGN
MINIVETS	MINUENDS	MIRAGE	MIRS	MISASSUME
MINK	MINUET	MIRAGES	MIRTH	MISATE
MINKE	MINUETED	MIRANDISE	MIRTHFUL	MISATONE
MINKES	MINUETING	MIRANDIZE	MIRTHLESS	MISATONED

MISATONES	MISCHANCY	MISDATING	MISEATEN	MISFILED
MISAUNTER	MISCHARGE	MISDEAL	MISEATING	MISFILES
MISAVER	MISCHIEF	MISDEALER	MISEATS	MISFILING
MISAVERS	MISCHIEFS	MISDEALS	MISEDIT	MISFIRE
MISAVISED	MISCHOICE	MISDEALT	MISEDITED	MISFIRED
MISAWARD	MISCHOOSE	MISDEED	MISEDITS	MISFIRES
MISAWARDS	MISCHOSE	MISDEEDS	MISEMPLOY	MISFIRING
MISBECAME	MISCHOSEN	MISDEEM	MISENROL	MISFIT
MISBECOME	MISCIBLE	MISDEEMED	MISENROLL	MISFITS
MISBEGAN	MISCITE	MISDEEMS	MISENROLS	MISFITTED
MISBEGIN	MISCITED	MISDEFINE	MISENTER	MISFOCUS
MISBEGINS	MISCITES	MISDEMEAN	MISENTERS	MISFOLD
MISBEGOT	MISCITING	MISDEMPT	MISENTRY	MISFOLDED
MISBEGUN	MISCLAIM	MISDESERT	MISER	MISFOLDS
MISBEHAVE	MISCLAIMS	MISDIAL	MISERABLE	MISFORM
MISBELIEF	MISCLASS	MISDIALED	MISERABLY	MISFORMED
MISBESEEM	MISCODE	MISDIALS	MISERE	MISFORMS
MISBESTOW	MISCODED	MISDID	MISERERE	MISFRAME
MISBIAS	MISCODES	MISDIET	MISERERES	MISFRAMED
MISBIASED	MISCODING	MISDIETED	MISERES	MISFRAMES
MISBIASES	MISCOIN	MISDIETS	MISERIES	MISGAGE
MISBILL	MISCOINED	MISDIGHT	MISERLIER	MISGAGED
MISBILLED	MISCOINS	MISDIGHTS	MISERLY	MISGAGES
MISBILLS	MISCOLOR	MISDIRECT	MISERS	MISGAGING
MISBIND	MISCOLORS	MISDIVIDE	MISERY	MISGAUGE
MISBINDS	MISCOLOUR	MISDO	MISES	MISGAUGED
MISBIRTH	MISCOOK	MISDOER	MISESTEEM	MISGAUGES
MISBIRTHS	MISCOOKED	MISDOERS	MISEVENT	MISGAVE
MISBORN	MISCOOKS	MISDOES	MISEVENTS	MISGENDER
MISBOUND	MISCOPIED	MISDOING	MISFAITH	MISGIVE
MISBRAND	MISCOPIES	MISDOINGS	MISFAITHS	MISGIVEN
MISBRANDS	MISCOPY	MISDONE	MISFALL	MISGIVES
MISBUILD	MISCOUNT	MISDONNE	MISFALLEN	MISGIVING
MISBUILDS	MISCOUNTS	MISDOUBT	MISFALLS	MISGO
MISBUILT	MISCREANT	MISDOUBTS	MISFALNE	MISGOES
MISBUTTON	MISCREATE	MISDRAW	MISFARE	MISGOING
MISCALL	MISCREDIT	MISDRAWN	MISFARED	MISGONE
MISCALLED	MISCREED	MISDRAWS	MISFARES	MISGOTTEN
MISCALLER	MISCREEDS	MISDREAD	MISFARING	MISGOVERN
MISCALLS	MISCUE	MISDREADS	MISFEASOR	MISGRADE
MISCARRY	MISCUED	MISDREW	MISFED	MISGRADED
MISCAST	MISCUEING	MISDRIVE	MISFEED	MISGRADES
MISCASTS	MISCUES	MISDRIVEN	MISFEEDS	MISGRAFF
MISCEGEN	MISCUING	MISDRIVES	MISFEIGN	MISGRAFT
MISCEGENE	MISCUT	MISDROVE	MISFEIGNS	MISGRAFTS
MISCEGENS	MISCUTS	MISE	MISFELL	MISGREW
MISCEGINE	MISDATE	MISEASE	MISFIELD	MISGROW
MISCH	MISDATED	MISEASES	MISFIELDS	MISGROWN
MISCHANCE	MISDATES	MISEAT	MISFILE	MISGROWS

MISGROWTH	MISKEPT	MISLIVE	MISOGYNIC	MISPRICES
MISGUESS	MISKEY	MISLIVED	MISOGYNY	MISPRINT
MISGUGGLE	MISKEYED	MISLIVES	MISOLOGY	MISPRINTS
MISGUIDE	MISKEYING	MISLIVING	MISONEISM	MISPRISE
MISGUIDED	MISKEYS	MISLOCATE	MISONEIST	MISPRISED
MISGUIDER	MISKICK	MISLODGE	MISORDER	MISPRISES
MISGUIDES	MISKICKED	MISLODGED	MISORDERS	MISPRIZE
MISHANDLE	MISKICKS	MISLODGES	MISORIENT	MISPRIZED
MISHANTER	MISKNEW	MISLUCK	MISOS	MISPRIZER
MISHAP	MISKNOW	MISLUCKED	MISPAGE	MISPRIZES
MISHAPPED	MISKNOWN	MISLUCKS	MISPAGED	MISPROUD
MISHAPPEN	MISKNOWS	MISLYING	MISPAGES	MISQUOTE
MISHAPS	MISLABEL	MISMADE	MISPAGING	MISQUOTED
MISHAPT	MISLABELS	MISMAKE	MISPAINT	MISQUOTER
MISHEAR	MISLABOR	MISMAKES	MISPAINTS	MISQUOTES
MISHEARD	MISLABORS	MISMAKING	MISPARSE	MISRAISE
MISHEARS	MISLABOUR	MISMANAGE	MISPARSED	MISRAISED
MISHEGAAS	MISLAID	MISMARK	MISPARSES	MISRAISES
MISHEGOSS	MISLAIN	MISMARKED	MISPART	MISRATE
MISHIT	MISLAY	MISMARKS	MISPARTED	MISRATED
MISHITS	MISLAYER	MISMARRY	MISPARTS	MISRATES
MISHMASH	MISLAYERS	MISMATCH	MISPATCH	MISRATING
MISHMEE	MISLAYING	MISMATE	MISPEN	MISREAD
MISHMEES	MISLAYS	MISMATED	MISPENNED	MISREADS
MISHMI	MISLEAD	MISMATES	MISPENS	MISRECKON
MISHMIS	MISLEADER	MISMATING	MISPHRASE	MISRECORD
MISHMOSH	MISLEADS	MISMEET	MISPICKEL	MISREFER
MISHUGAS	MISLEARED	MISMEETS	MISPLACE	MISREFERS
MISINFER	MISLEARN	MISMET	MISPLACED	MISREGARD
MISINFERS	MISLEARNS	MISMETER	MISPLACES	MISRELATE
MISINFORM	MISLEARNT	MISMETERS	MISPLAN	MISRELIED
MISINTEND	MISLED	MISMETRE	MISPLANS	MISRELIES
MISINTER	MISLEEKE	MISMETRED	MISPLANT	MISRELY
MISINTERS	MISLEEKED	MISMETRES	MISPLANTS	MISRENDER
MISJOIN	MISLEEKES	MISMOVE	MISPLAY	MISREPORT
MISJOINED	MISLETOE	MISMOVED	MISPLAYED	MISRHYMED
MISJOINS	MISLETOES	MISMOVES	MISPLAYS	MISROUTE
MISJUDGE	MISLIE	MISMOVING	MISPLEAD	MISROUTED
MISJUDGED	MISLIES	MISNAME	MISPLEADS	MISROUTES
MISJUDGER	MISLIGHT	MISNAMED	MISPLEASE	MISRULE
MISJUDGES	MISLIGHTS	MISNAMES	MISPLED	MISRULED
MISKAL	MISLIKE	MISNAMING	MISPOINT	MISRULES
MISKALS	MISLIKED	MISNOMER	MISPOINTS	MISRULING
MISKEEP	MISLIKER	MISNOMERS	MISPOISE	MISS
MISKEEPS	MISLIKERS	MISNUMBER	MISPOISED	MISSA
MISKEN	MISLIKES	MISO	MISPOISES	MISSABLE
MISKENNED	MISLIKING	MISOCLERE	MISPRAISE	MISSAE
MISKENS	MISLIPPEN	MISOGAMIC	MISPRICE	MISSAID
MISKENT	MISLIT	MISOGAMY	MISPRICED	MISSAL

MISSALS	MISSIONED	MISSUITS	MISTIMES	MISUSAGES
MISSAW	MISSIONER	MISSUS	MISTIMING	MISUSE
MISSAY	MISSIONS	MISSUSES	MISTINESS	MISUSED
MISSAYING	MISSIS	MISSY	MISTING	MISUSER
MISSAYS	MISSISES	MIST	MISTINGS	MISUSERS
MISSEAT	MISSISH	MISTAKE	MISTITLE	MISUSES
MISSEATED	MISSIVE	MISTAKEN	MISTITLED	MISUSING
MISSEATS	MISSIVES	MISTAKER	MISTITLES	MISUST
MISSED	MISSOLD	MISTAKERS	MISTLE	MISVALUE
MISSEE	MISSORT	MISTAKES	MISTLED	MISVALUED
MISSEEING	MISSORTED	MISTAKING	MISTLES	MISVALUES
MISSEEM	MISSORTS	MISTAL	MISTLETOE	MISWEEN
MISSEEMED	MISSOUND	MISTALS	MISTLING	MISWEENED
MISSEEMS	MISSOUNDS	MISTAUGHT	MISTOLD	MISWEENS
MISSEEN	MISSOUT	MISTBOW	MISTOOK	MISWEND
MISSEES	MISSOUTS	MISTBOWS	MISTOUCH	MISWENDS
MISSEL	MISSPACE	MISTEACH	MISTRACE	MISWENT
MISSELL	MISSPACED	MISTED	MISTRACED	MISWORD
MISSELLS	MISSPACES	MISTELL	MISTRACES	MISWORDED
MISSELS	MISSPEAK	MISTELLS	MISTRAIN	MISWORDS
MISSEND	MISSPEAKS	MISTEMPER	MISTRAINS	MISWRIT
MISSENDS	MISSPELL	MISTEND	MISTRAL	MISWRITE
MISSENSE	MISSPELLS	MISTENDED	MISTRALS	MISWRITES
MISSENSED	MISSPELT	MISTENDS	MISTREAT	MISWROTE
MISSENSES	MISSPEND	MISTER	MISTREATS	MISYOKE
MISSENT	MISSPENDS	MISTERED	MISTRESS	MISYOKED
MISSES	MISSPENT	MISTERIES	MISTRIAL	MISYOKES
MISSET	MISSPOKE	MISTERING	MISTRIALS	MISYOKING
MISSETS	MISSPOKEN	MISTERM	MISTRUST	MITCH
MISSHAPE	MISSTAMP	MISTERMED	MISTRUSTS	MITCHED
MISSHAPED	MISSTAMPS	MISTERMS	MISTRUTH	MITCHES
MISSHAPEN	MISSTART	MISTERS	MISTRUTHS	MITCHING
MISSHAPER	MISSTARTS	MISTERY	MISTRYST	MITE
MISSHAPES	MISSTATE	MISTEUK	MISTRYSTS	MITER
MISSHOD	MISSTATED	MISTFUL	MISTS	MITERED
MISSHOOD	MISSTATES	MISTHINK	MISTUNE	MITERER
MISSHOODS	MISSTEER	MISTHINKS	MISTUNED	MITERERS
MISSIER	MISSTEERS	MISTHREW	MISTUNES	MITERING
MISSIES	MISSTEP	MISTHROW	MISTUNING	MITERS
MISSIEST	MISSTEPS	MISTHROWN	MISTUTOR	MITERWORT
MISSILE	MISSTOP	MISTHROWS	MISTUTORS	MITES
MISSILEER	MISSTOPS	MISTICO	MISTY	MITHER
MISSILERY	MISSTRIKE	MISTICOS	MISTYPE	MITHERED
MISSILES	MISSTRUCK	MISTIER	MISTYPED	MITHERING
MISSILRY	MISSTYLE	MISTIEST	MISTYPES	MITHERS
MISSING	MISSTYLED	MISTIGRIS	MISTYPING	MITICIDAL
MISSINGLY	MISSTYLES	MISTILY	MISUNION	MITICIDE
MISSION	MISSUIT	MISTIME	MISUNIONS	MITICIDES
MISSIONAL	MISSUITED	MISTIMED	MISUSAGE	MITIER

MITIEST	MIXEN	MNEME	MOBE	MOCHELL
MITIGABLE	MIXENS	MNEMES	MOBES	MOCHELLS
MITIGANT	MIXER	MNEMIC	MOBEY	MOCHI
MITIGANTS	MIXERS	MNEMON	MOBEYS	MOCHIE
MITIGATE	MIXES	MNEMONIC	MOBIE	MOCHIER
MITIGATED	MIXIBLE	MNEMONICS	MOBIES	MOCHIEST
MITIGATES	MIXIER	MNEMONIST	MOBILE	MOCHILA
MITIGATOR	MIXIEST	MNEMONS	MOBILES	MOCHILAS
MITIS	MIXING	MO	MOBILISE	MOCHINESS
MITISES	MIXINGS	MOA	MOBILISED	MOCHING
MITOGEN	MIXMASTER	MOAI	MOBILISER	MOCHIS
MITOGENIC	MIXOLOGY	MOAN	MOBILISES	MOCHS
MITOGENS	MIXT	MOANED	MOBILITY	MOCHY
MITOMYCIN	MIXTAPE	MOANER	MOBILIZE	MOCK
MITOSES	MIXTAPES	MOANERS	MOBILIZED	MOCKABLE
MITOSIS	MIXTE	MOANFUL	MOBILIZER	MOCKADO
MITOTIC	MIXTION	MOANFULLY	MOBILIZES	MOCKADOES
MITRAILLE	MIXTIONS	MOANING	MOBISODE	MOCKAGE
MITRAL	MIXTURE	MOANINGLY	MOBISODES	MOCKAGES
MITRE	MIXTURES	MOANINGS	MOBLE	MOCKED
MITRED	MIXUP	MOANS	MOBLED	MOCKER
MITRES	MIXUPS	MOAS	MOBLES	MOCKERED
MITREWORT	MIXY	MOAT	MOBLING	MOCKERIES
MITRIFORM	MIZ	MOATED	MOBLOG	MOCKERING
MITRING	MIZEN	MOATING	MOBLOGGER	MOCKERNUT
MITSVAH	MIZENMAST	MOATLIKE	MOBLOGS	MOCKERS
MITSVAHS	MIZENS	MOATS	MOBO	MOCKERY
MITSVOTH	MIZMAZE	MOB	MOBOCRACY	MOCKING
MITT	MIZMAZES	MOBBED	MOBOCRAT	MOCKINGLY
MITTEN	MIZUNA	MOBBER	MOBOCRATS	MOCKINGS
MITTENED	MIZUNAS	MOBBERS	MOBOS	MOCKNEY
MITTENS	MIZZ	MOBBIE	MOBS	MOCKNEYS
MITTIMUS	MIZZEN	MOBBIES	MOBSMAN	MOCKS
MITTS	MIZZENS	MOBBING	MOBSMEN	MOCKTAIL
MITUMBA	MIZZES	MOBBINGS	MOBSTER	MOCKTAILS
MITUMBAS	MIZZLE	MOBBISH	MOBSTERS	MOCKUP
MITY	MIZZLED	MOBBISHLY	MOBY	MOCKUPS
MITZVAH	MIZZLES	MOBBISM	MOC	MOCOCK
MITZVAHS	MIZZLIER	MOBBISMS	MOCAP	MOCOCKS
MITZVOTH	MIZZLIEST	MOBBLE	MOCAPS	MOCS
MIURUS	MIZZLING	MOBBLED	MOCASSIN	MOCUCK
MIURUSES	MIZZLINGS	MOBBLES	MOCASSINS	MOCUCKS
MIX	MIZZLY	MOBBLING	MOCCASIN	MOCUDDUM
MIXABLE	MIZZONITE	MOBBY	MOCCASINS	MOCUDDUMS
MIXDOWN	MIZZY	MOBCAP	MOCCIES	MOD
MIXDOWNS	MM	MOBCAPS	MOCH	MODAFINIL
MIXED	MMM	MOBCAST	MOCHA	MODAL
MIXEDLY	MNA	MOBCASTED	MOCHAS	MODALISM
MIXEDNESS	MNAS	MOBCASTS	MOCHED	MODALISMS

M

MODALIST	MODERNIST	MODULE	MOHOS	MOIT
MODALISTS	MODERNITY	MODULES	MOHR	MOITHER
MODALITY	MODERNIZE	MODULI	MOHRS	MOITHERED
MODALLY	MODERNLY	MODULO	MOHUA	MOITHERS
MODALS	MODERNS	MODULUS	MOHUAS	MOITS
MODDED	MODERS	MODUS	MOHUR	MOJAHEDIN
MODDER	MODES	MOE	MOHURS	MOJARRA
MODDERS	MODEST	MOELLON	MOI	MOJARRAS
MODDEST	MODESTER	MOELLONS	MOIDER	MOJITO
MODDING	MODESTEST	MOER	MOIDERED	MOJITOS
MODDINGS	MODESTIES	MOERED	MOIDERING	MOJO
MODE	MODESTLY	MOERING	MOIDERS	MOJOES
MODEL	MODESTY	MOERS	MOIDORE	MOJOS
MODELED	MODGE	MOES	MOIDORES	MOKADDAM
MODELER	MODGED	MOFETTE	MOIETIES	MOKADDAMS
MODELERS	MODGES	MOFETTES	MOIETY	MOKE
MODELING	MODGING	MOFFETTE	MOIL	MOKES
MODELINGS	MODI	MOFFETTES	MOILE	MOKI
MODELIST	MODICA	MOFO	MOILED	MOKIHI
MODELISTS	MODICUM	MOFONGO	MOILER	MOKIHIS
MODELLED	MODICUMS	MOFONGOS	MOILERS	MOKIS
MODELLER	MODIFIED	MOFOS	MOILES	MOKO
MODELLERS	MODIFIER	MOFUSSIL	MOILING	MOKOMOKO
MODELLI	MODIFIERS	MOFUSSILS	MOILINGLY	MOKOMOKOS
MODELLING	MODIFIES	MOG	MOILS	MOKOPUNA
MODELLIST	MODIFY	MOGGAN	MOINEAU	MOKOPUNAS
MODELLO	MODIFYING	MOGGANS	MOINEAUS	MOKORO
MODELLOS	MODII	MOGGED	MOIRA	MOKOROS
MODELS	MODILLION	MOGGIE	MOIRAI	MOKOS
MODEM	MODIOLAR	MOGGIES	MOIRE	MOKSHA
MODEMED	MODIOLI	MOGGING	MOIRES	MOKSHAS
MODEMING	MODIOLUS	MOGGY	MOISER	MOL
MODEMS	MODISH	MOGHUL	MOISERS	MOLA
MODENA	MODISHLY	MOGHULS	MOIST	MOLAL
MODENAS	MODIST	MOGS	MOISTED	MOLALITY
MODER	MODISTE	MOGUL	MOISTEN	MOLAR
MODERATE	MODISTES	MOGULED	MOISTENED	MOLARITY
MODERATED	MODISTS	MOGULS	MOISTENER	MOLARS
MODERATES	MODIUS	MOHAIR	MOISTENS	MOLAS
MODERATO	MODIWORT	MOHAIRS	MOISTER	MOLASSE
MODERATOR	MODIWORTS	MOHALIM	MOISTEST	MOLASSES
MODERATOS	MODS	MOHAWK	MOISTFUL	MOLD
MODERN	MODULAR	MOHAWKS	MOISTIFY	MOLDABLE
MODERNE	MODULARLY	MOHEL	MOISTING	MOLDAVITE
MODERNER	MODULARS	MOHELIM	MOISTLY	MOLDBOARD
MODERNES	MODULATE	MOHELS	MOISTNESS	MOLDED
MODERNEST	MODULATED	MOHICAN	MOISTS	MOLDER
MODERNISE	MODULATES	MOHICANS	MOISTURE	MOLDERED
MODERNISM	MODULATOR	MOHO	MOISTURES	MOLDERING

MOLDERS	MOLLIFIES	MOMENTUM	MONARCHIC	MONETIZES
MOLDIER	MOLLIFY	MOMENTUMS	MONARCHS	MONEY
MOLDIEST	MOLLITIES	MOMES	MONARCHY	MONEYBAG
MOLDINESS	MOLLS	MOMI	MONARDA	MONEYBAGS
MOLDING	MOLLUSC	MOMISM	MONARDAS	MONEYBELT
MOLDINGS	MOLLUSCA	MOMISMS	MONAS	MONEYBOX
MOLDS	MOLLUSCAN	MOMMA	MONASES	MONEYED
MOLDWARP	MOLLUSCS	MOMMAS	MONASTERY	MONEYER
MOLDWARPS	MOLLUSCUM	MOMMET	MONASTIC	MONEYERS
MOLDY	MOLLUSK	MOMMETS	MONASTICS	MONEYLESS
MOLE	MOLLUSKAN	MOMMIES	MONATOMIC	MONEYMAN
MOLECAST	MOLLUSKS	MOMMY	MONAUL	MONEYMEN
MOLECASTS	MOLLY	MOMOIR	MONAULS	MONEYS
MOLECULAR	MOLLYHAWK	MOMOIRS	MONAURAL	MONEYWORT
MOLECULE	MOLLYMAWK	MOMS	MONAXIAL	MONG
MOLECULES	MOLOCH	MOMSER	MONAXON	MONGCORN
MOLED	MOLOCHISE	MOMSERS	MONAXONIC	MONGCORNS
MOLEHILL	MOLOCHIZE	MOMUS	MONAXONS	MONGEESE
MOLEHILLS	MOLOCHS	MOMUSES	MONAZITE	MONGER
MOLEHUNT	MOLOSSI	MOMZER	MONAZITES	MONGERED
MOLEHUNTS	MOLOSSUS	MOMZERIM	MONDAIN	MONGERIES
MOLELIKE	MOLS	MOMZERS	MONDAINE	MONGERING
MOLES	MOLT	MON	MONDAINES	MONGERS
MOLESKIN	MOLTED	MONA	MONDAINS	MONGERY
MOLESKINS	MOLTEN	MONACHAL	MONDE	MONGO
MOLEST	MOLTENLY	MONACHISM	MONDES	MONGOE
MOLESTED	MOLTER	MONACHIST	MONDIAL	MONGOES
MOLESTER	MOLTERS	MONACID	MONDO	MONGOOSE
MOLESTERS	MOLTING	MONACIDIC	MONDOS	MONGOOSES
MOLESTFUL	MOLTINGS	MONACIDS	MONECIAN	MONGOS
MOLESTING	MOLTO	MONACT	MONECIOUS	MONGREL
MOLESTS	MOLTS	MONACTINE	MONELLIN	MONGRELLY
MOLIES	MOLY	MONACTS	MONELLINS	MONGRELS
MOLIMEN	MOLYBDATE	MONAD	MONEME	MONGS
MOLIMENS	MOLYBDIC	MONADAL	MONEMES	MONGST
MOLINE	MOLYBDOUS	MONADES	MONER	MONIAL
MOLINES	MOLYS	MONADIC	MONERA	MONIALS
MOLINET	MOM	MONADICAL	MONERAN	MONIC
MOLINETS	MOME	MONADISM	MONERANS	MONICKER
MOLING	MOMENT	MONADISMS	MONERGISM	MONICKERS
MOLL	MOMENTA	MONADNOCK	MONERON	MONIE
MOLLA	MOMENTANY	MONADS	MONETARY	MONIED
MOLLAH	MOMENTARY	MONAL	MONETH	MONIES
MOLLAHS	MOMENTLY	MONALS	MONETHS	MONIKER
MOLLAS	MOMENTO	MONAMINE	MONETISE	MONIKERED
MOLLIE	MOMENTOES	MONAMINES	MONETISED	MONIKERS
MOLLIES	MOMENTOS	MONANDRY	MONETISES	MONILIA
MOLLIFIED	MOMENTOUS	MONARCH	MONETIZE	MONILIAE
MOLLIFIER	MOMENTS	MONARCHAL	MONETIZED	MONILIAL

MONILIAS	MONOBROWS	MONOGRAPH	MONOPOLES	MONOXYLON
MONIMENT	MONOCARP	MONOGYNY	MONOPOLY	MONS
MONIMENTS	MONOCARPS	MONOHULL	MONOPRINT	MONSIEUR
MONIPLIES	MONOCEROS	MONOHULLS	MONOPSONY	MONSIGNOR
MONISH	MONOCHORD	MONOICOUS	MONOPTERA	MONSOON
MONISHED	MONOCLE	MONOKINE	MONOPTOTE	MONSOONAL
MONISHES	MONOCLED	MONOKINES	MONOPULSE	MONSOONS
MONISHING	MONOCLES	MONOKINI	MONORAIL	MONSTER
MONISM	MONOCLINE	MONOKINIS	MONORAILS	MONSTERA
MONISMS	MONOCOQUE	MONOLATER	MONORCHID	MONSTERAS
MONIST	MONOCOT	MONOLATRY	MONORHINE	MONSTERED
MONISTIC	MONOCOTS	MONOLAYER	MONORHYME	MONSTERS
MONISTS	MONOCOTYL	MONOLINE	MONOS	MONSTROUS
MONITION	MONOCRACY	MONOLITH	MONOSEMIC	MONTADALE
MONITIONS	MONOCRAT	MONOLITHS	MONOSEMY	MONTAGE
MONITIVE	MONOCRATS	MONOLOG	MONOSES	MONTAGED
MONITOR	MONOCROP	MONOLOGIC	MONOSIES	MONTAGES
MONITORED	MONOCROPS	MONOLOGS	MONOSIS	MONTAGING
MONITORS	MONOCULAR	MONOLOGUE	MONOSKI	MONTAN
MONITORY	MONOCYCLE	MONOLOGY	MONOSKIED	MONTANE
MONITRESS	MONOCYTE	MONOMACHY	MONOSKIER	MONTANES
MONK	MONOCYTES	MONOMANIA	MONOSKIS	MONTANT
MONKERIES	MONOCYTIC	MONOMARK	MONOSOME	MONTANTO
MONKERY	MONODIC	MONOMARKS	MONOSOMES	MONTANTOS
MONKEY	MONODICAL	MONOMER	MONOSOMIC	MONTANTS
MONKEYED	MONODIES	MONOMERIC	MONOSOMY	MONTARIA
MONKEYING	MONODIST	MONOMERS	MONOSTELE	MONTARIAS
MONKEYISH	MONODISTS	MONOMETER	MONOSTELY	MONTE
MONKEYISM	MONODONT	MONOMIAL	MONOSTICH	MONTEITH
MONKEYPOD	MONODRAMA	MONOMIALS	MONOSTOME	MONTEITHS
MONKEYPOT	MONODY	MONOMODE	MONOSTYLE	MONTEM
MONKEYPOX	MONOECIES	MONOMYTH	MONOSY	MONTEMS
MONKEYS	MONOECISM	MONOMYTHS	MONOTASK	MONTERO
MONKFISH	MONOECY	MONONYM	MONOTASKS	MONTEROS
MONKHOOD	MONOESTER	MONONYMS	MONOTINT	MONTES
MONKHOODS	MONOFIL	MONOPHAGY	MONOTINTS	MONTH
MONKISH	MONOFILS	MONOPHASE	MONOTONE	MONTHLIES
MONKISHLY	MONOFUEL	MONOPHONY	MONOTONED	MONTHLING
MONKS	MONOFUELS	MONOPHYLY	MONOTONES	MONTHLONG
MONKSHOOD	MONOGAMIC	MONOPITCH	MONOTONIC	MONTHLY
MONO	MONOGAMY	MONOPLANE	MONOTONY	MONTHS
MONOACID	MONOGENIC	MONOPLOID	MONOTREME	MONTICLE
MONOACIDS	MONOGENY	MONOPOD	MONOTROCH	MONTICLES
MONOAMINE	MONOGERM	MONOPODE	MONOTYPE	MONTICULE
MONOAO	MONOGLOT	MONOPODES	MONOTYPES	MONTIES
MONOAOS	MONOGLOTS	MONOPODIA	MONOTYPIC	MONTRE
MONOBASIC	MONOGONY	MONOPODS	MONOVULAR	MONTRES
MONOBLOC	MONOGRAM	MONOPODY	MONOXIDE	MONTURE
MONOBROW	MONOGRAMS	MONOPOLE	MONOXIDES	MONTURES

MONTY	MOOLVI	MOONPORTS	MOORIER	MOPE
MONUMENT	MOOLVIE	MOONQUAKE	MOORIEST	MOPED
MONUMENTS	MOOLVIES	MOONRAKER	MOORILL	MOPEDS
MONURON	MOOLVIS	MOONRISE	MOORILLS	MOPEHAWK
MONURONS	MOOLY	MOONRISES	MOORING	MOPEHAWKS
MONY	MOON	MOONROCK	MOORINGS	MOPER
MONYPLIES	MOONBEAM	MOONROCKS	MOORISH	MOPERIES
MONZONITE	MOONBEAMS	MOONROOF	MOORLAND	MOPERS
MOO	MOONBLIND	MOONROOFS	MOORLANDS	MOPERY
MOOBIES	MOONBOOTS	MOONS	MOORLOG	MOPES
MOOBS	MOONBOW	MOONSAIL	MOORLOGS	MOPEY
MOOCH	MOONBOWS	MOONSAILS	MOORMAN	MOPHEAD
MOOCHED	MOONCAKE	MOONSCAPE	MOORMEN	MOPHEADED
MOOCHER	MOONCAKES	MOONSEED	MOORS	MOPHEADS
MOOCHERS	MOONCALF	MOONSEEDS	MOORVA	MOPIER
MOOCHES	MOONCHILD	MOONSET	MOORVAS	MOPIEST
MOOCHING	MOONCRAFT	MOONSETS	MOORWORT	MOPILY
MOOD	MOONDOG	MOONSHEE	MOORWORTS	MOPINESS
MOODIED	MOONDOGS	MOONSHEES	MOORY	MOPING
MOODIER	MOONDUST	MOONSHINE	MOOS	MOPINGLY
MOODIES	MOONDUSTS	MOONSHINY	MOOSE	MOPISH
MOODIEST	MOONED	MOONSHIP	MOOSEBIRD	MOPISHLY
MOODILY	MOONER	MOONSHIPS	MOOSEHAIR	MOPOKE
MOODINESS	MOONERS	MOONSHOT	MOOSEHIDE	MOPOKES
MOODS	MOONEYE	MOONSHOTS	MOOSEWOOD	MOPPED
MOODY	MOONEYES	MOONSTONE	MOOSEYARD	MOPPER
MOODYING	MOONFACE	MOONWALK	MOOT	MOPPERS
MOOED	MOONFACED	MOONWALKS	MOOTABLE	MOPPET
MOOI	MOONFACES	MOONWARD	MOOTED	MOPPETS
MOOING	MOONFISH	MOONWARDS	MOOTER	MOPPIER
MOOK	MOONG	MOONWORT	MOOTERS	MOPPIEST
MOOKS	MOONGATE	MOONWORTS	MOOTEST	MOPPING
MOOKTAR	MOONGATES	MOONY	MOOTING	MOPPY
MOOKTARS	MOONIER	MOOP	MOOTINGS	MOPS
MOOL	MOONIES	MOOPED	MOOTMAN	MOPSIES
MOOLA	MOONIEST	MOOPING	MOOTMEN	MOPSTICK
MOOLAH	MOONILY	MOOPS	MOOTNESS	MOPSTICKS
MOOLAHS	MOONINESS	MOOR	MOOTS	MOPSY
MOOLAS	MOONING	MOORAGE	MOOVE	MOPUS
MOOLED	MOONISH	MOORAGES	MOOVED	MOPUSES
MOOLEY	MOONISHLY	MOORBURN	MOOVES	MOPY
MOOLEYS	MOONLESS	MOORBURNS	MOOVING	MOQUETTE
MOOLI	MOONLET	MOORCOCK	MOP	MOQUETTES
MOOLIES	MOONLETS	MOORCOCKS	MOPANE	MOR
MOOLING	MOONLIGHT	MOORED	MOPANES	MORA
MOOLIS	MOONLIKE	MOORFOWL	MOPANI	MORACEOUS
MOOLOO	MOONLIT	MOORFOWLS	MOPANIS	MORAE
MOOLOOS	MOONPHASE	MOORHEN	MOPBOARD	MORAINAL
MOOLS	MOONPORT	MOORHENS	MOPBOARDS	MORAINE

MORAINES	MORCHAS	MORKINS	MORPHOSES	MORTBELL
MORAINIC	MORDACITY	MORLING	MORPHOSIS	MORTBELLS
MORAL	MORDANCY	MORLINGS	MORPHOTIC	MORTCLOTH
MORALE	MORDANT	MORMAOR	MORPHS	MORTGAGE
MORALES	MORDANTED	MORMAORS	MORRA	MORTGAGED
MORALISE	MORDANTLY	MORN	MORRAS	MORTGAGEE
MORALISED	MORDANTS	MORNAY	MORRELL	MORTGAGER
MORALISER	MORDENT	MORNAYS	MORRELLS	MORTGAGES
MORALISES	MORDENTS	MORNE	MORRHUA	MORTGAGOR
MORALISM	MORE	MORNED	MORRHUAS	MORTICE
MORALISMS	MOREEN	MORNES	MORRICE	MORTICED
MORALIST	MOREENS	MORNING	MORRICES	MORTICER
MORALISTS	MOREISH	MORNINGS	MORRION	MORTICERS
MORALITY	MOREL	MORNS	MORRIONS	MORTICES
MORALIZE	MORELLE	MOROCCO	MORRIS	MORTICIAN
MORALIZED	MORELLES	MOROCCOS	MORRISED	MORTICING
MORALIZER	MORELLO	MORON	MORRISES	MORTIFIC
MORALIZES	MORELLOS	MORONIC	MORRISING	MORTIFIED
MORALL	MORELS	MORONISM	MORRO	MORTIFIER
MORALLED	MORENDO	MORONISMS	MORROS	MORTIFIES
MORALLER	MORENDOS	MORONITY	MORROW	MORTIFY
MORALLERS	MORENESS	MORONS	MORROWS	MORTISE
MORALLING	MOREOVER	MOROSE	MORS	MORTISED
MORALLS	MOREPORK	MOROSELY	MORSAL	MORTISER
MORALLY	MOREPORKS	MOROSER	MORSALS	MORTISERS
MORALS	MORES	MOROSEST	MORSE	MORTISES
MORAS	MORESQUE	MOROSITY	MORSEL	MORTISING
MORASS	MORESQUES	MORPH	MORSELED	MORTLING
MORASSES	MORGAN	MORPHEAN	MORSELING	MORTLINGS
MORASSIER	MORGANITE	MORPHED	MORSELLED	MORTMAIN
MORASSY	MORGANS	MORPHEME	MORSELS	MORTMAINS
MORAT	MORGAY	MORPHEMES	MORSES	MORTS
MORATORIA	MORGAYS	MORPHEMIC	MORSURE	MORTSAFE
MORATORY	MORGEN	MORPHEMIC	MORSURES	MORTSAFES
MORATS	MORGENS	MORPHETIC	MORT	MORTUARY
MORAY	MORGUE	MORPHEW	MORTAL	MORULA
MORAYS	MORGUES	MORPHEWS	MORTALISE	MORULAE
MORBID	MORIA	MORPHIA	MORTALITY	MORULAR
MORBIDER	MORIAS	MORPHIAS	MORTALIZE	MORULAS
MORBIDEST	MORIBUND	MORPHIC	MORTALLY	MORWONG
MORBIDITY	MORICHE	MORPHIN	MORTALS	MORWONGS
MORBIDLY	MORICHES	MORPHINE	MORTAR	MORYAH
MORBIFIC	MORION	MORPHINES	MORTARED	MOS
MORBILLI	MORIONS	MORPHING	MORTARIER	MOSAIC
MORBUS	MORISCO	MORPHINGS	MORTARING	MOSAICISM
MORBUSES	MORISCOES	MORPHINIC	MORTARMAN	MOSAICIST
MORCEAU	MORISCOS	MORPHINS	MORTARMEN	MOSAICKED
MORCEAUX	MORISH	MORPHO	MORTARS	MOSAICS
MORCHA	MORKIN	MORPHOS	MORTARY	MOSASAUR

MOSASAURI	MOSSLANDS	MOTIF	MOTORIC	MOTUS
MOSASAURS	MOSSLIKE	MOTIFIC	MOTORICS	MOTZA
MOSCATO	MOSSO	MOTIFS	MOTORING	MOTZAS
MOSCATOS	MOSSPLANT	MOTILE	MOTORINGS	MOU
MOSCHATE	MOSSY	MOTILES	MOTORISE	MOUCH
MOSCHATEL	MOST	MOTILITY	MOTORISED	MOUCHARD
MOSCOVIUM	MOSTE	MOTION	MOTORISES	MOUCHARDS
MOSE	MOSTEST	MOTIONAL	MOTORIST	MOUCHED
MOSED	MOSTESTS	MOTIONED	MOTORISTS	MOUCHER
MOSELLE	MOSTLY	MOTIONER	MOTORIUM	MOUCHERS
MOSELLES	MOSTS	MOTIONERS	MOTORIUMS	MOUCHES
MOSES	MOSTWHAT	MOTIONING	MOTORIZE	MOUCHING
MOSEY	MOT	MOTIONIST	MOTORIZED	MOUCHOIR
MOSEYED	MOTE	MOTIONS	MOTORIZES	MOUCHOIRS
MOSEYING	MOTED	MOTIS	MOTORLESS	MOUDIWART
MOSEYS	MOTEL	MOTIVATE	MOTORMAN	MOUDIWORT
MOSH	MOTELIER	MOTIVATED	MOTORMEN	MOUE
MOSHAV	MOTELIERS	MOTIVATES	MOTORS	MOUES
MOSHAVIM	MOTELS	MOTIVATOR	MOTORSHIP	MOUFFLON
MOSHED	MOTEN	MOTIVE	MOTORWAY	MOUFFLONS
MOSHER	MOTES	MOTIVED	MOTORWAYS	MOUFLON
MOSHERS	MOTET	MOTIVES	MOTORY	MOUFLONS
MOSHES	MOTETS	MOTIVIC	MOTOSCAFI	MOUGHT
MOSHING	MOTETT	MOTIVING	MOTOSCAFO	MOUILLE
MOSHINGS	MOTETTIST	MOTIVITY	MOTS	MOUJIK
MOSING	MOTETTS	MOTLEY	MOTSER	MOUJIKS
MOSK	MOTEY	MOTLEYER	MOTSERS	MOULAGE
MOSKONFYT	MOTEYS	MOTLEYEST	MOTT	MOULAGES
MOSKS	MOTH	MOTLEYS	MOTTE	MOULD
MOSLINGS	MOTHBALL	MOTLIER	MOTTES	MOULDABLE
MOSQUE	MOTHBALLS	MOTLIEST	MOTTIER	MOULDED
MOSQUES	MOTHED	MOTMOT	MOTTIES	MOULDER
MOSQUITO	MOTHER	MOTMOTS	MOTTIEST	MOULDERED
MOSQUITOS	MOTHERED	MOTOCROSS	MOTTLE	MOULDERS
MOSS	MOTHERESE	MOTOR	MOTTLED	MOULDIER
MOSSBACK	MOTHERIER	MOTORABLE	MOTTLER	MOULDIEST
MOSSBACKS	MOTHERING	MOTORAIL	MOTTLERS	MOULDING
MOSSED	MOTHERLY	MOTORAILS	MOTTLES	MOULDINGS
MOSSER	MOTHERS	MOTORBIKE	MOTTLING	MOULDS
MOSSERS	MOTHERY	MOTORBOAT	MOTTLINGS	MOULDWARP
MOSSES	MOTHIER	MOTORBUS	MOTTO	MOULDY
MOSSGROWN	MOTHIEST	MOTORCADE	MOTTOED	MOULIN
MOSSIE	MOTHLIKE	MOTORCAR	MOTTOES	MOULINET
MOSSIER	MOTHPROOF	MOTORCARS	MOTTOS	MOULINETS
MOSSIES	MOTHS	MOTORDOM	MOTTS	MOULINS
MOSSIEST	MOTHY	MOTORDOMS	MOTTY	MOULS
MOSSINESS	MOTI	MOTORED	MOTU	MOULT
MOSSING	MOTIER	MOTORHOME	MOTUCA	MOULTED
MOSSLAND	MOTIEST	MOTORIAL	MOTUCAS	MOULTEN

M

MOULTER	MOUSEMATS	MOUTH	MOVIOLA	MOZZETTA
MOULTERS	MOUSEOVER	MOUTHABLE	MOVIOLAS	MOZZETTAS
MOULTING	MOUSEPAD	MOUTHED	MOW	MOZZETTE
MOULTINGS	MOUSEPADS	MOUTHER	MOWA	MOZZIE
MOULTS	MOUSER	MOUTHERS	MOWAS	MOZZIES
MOUND	MOUSERIES	MOUTHFEEL	MOWBURN	MOZZLE
MOUNDBIRD	MOUSERS	MOUTHFUL	MOWBURNED	MOZZLED
MOUNDED	MOUSERY	MOUTHFULS	MOWBURNS	MOZZLES
MOUNDING	MOUSES	MOUTHIER	MOWBURNT	MOZZLING
MOUNDS	MOUSETAIL	MOUTHIEST	MOWDIE	MPOX
MOUNSEER	MOUSETRAP	MOUTHILY	MOWDIES	MPOXES
MOUNSEERS	MOUSEY	MOUTHING	MOWED	MPRET
MOUNT	MOUSIE	MOUTHLESS	MOWER	MPRETS
MOUNTABLE	MOUSIER	MOUTHLIKE	MOWERS	MRIDAMGAM
MOUNTAIN	MOUSIES	MOUTHPART	MOWING	MRIDANG
MOUNTAINS	MOUSIEST	MOUTHS	MOWINGS	MRIDANGA
MOUNTAINY	MOUSILY	MOUTHWASH	MOWN	MRIDANGAM
MOUNTANT	MOUSINESS	MOUTHY	MOWRA	MRIDANGAS
MOUNTANTS	MOUSING	MOUTON	MOWRAS	MRIDANGS
MOUNTED	MOUSINGS	MOUTONNEE	MOWS	MU
MOUNTER	MOUSLE	MOUTONS	MOXA	MUCATE
MOUNTERS	MOUSLED	MOVABLE	MOXAS	MUCATES
MOUNTING	MOUSLES	MOVABLES	MOXIE	MUCH
MOUNTINGS	MOUSLING	MOVABLY	MOXIES	MUCHACHA
MOUNTS	MOUSME	MOVANT	MOY	MUCHACHAS
MOUP	MOUSMEE	MOVANTS	MOYA	MUCHACHO
MOUPED	MOUSMEES	MOVE	MOYAS	MUCHACHOS
MOUPING	MOUSMES	MOVEABLE	MOYGASHEL	MUCHEL
MOUPS	MOUSSAKA	MOVEABLES	MOYITIES	MUCHELL
MOURN	MOUSSAKAS	MOVEABLY	MOYITY	MUCHELLS
MOURNED	MOUSSE	MOVED	MOYL	MUCHELS
MOURNER	MOUSSED	MOVELESS	MOYLE	MUCHES
MOURNERS	MOUSSES	MOVEMENT	MOYLED	MUCHLY
MOURNFUL	MOUSSEUX	MOVEMENTS	MOYLES	MUCHNESS
MOURNING	MOUSSING	MOVER	MOYLING	MUCHO
MOURNINGS	MOUST	MOVERS	MOYLS	MUCIC
MOURNIVAL	MOUSTACHE	MOVES	MOYS	MUCID
MOURNS	MOUSTED	MOVIE	MOZ	MUCIDITY
MOURVEDRE	MOUSTING	MOVIEDOM	MOZE	MUCIDNESS
MOUS	MOUSTS	MOVIEDOMS	MOZED	MUCIGEN
MOUSAKA	MOUSY	MOVIEGOER	MOZES	MUCIGENS
MOUSAKAS	MOUTAN	MOVIELAND	MOZETTA	MUCILAGE
MOUSE	MOUTANS	MOVIEOKE	MOZETTAS	MUCILAGES
MOUSEBIRD	MOUTER	MOVIEOKES	MOZETTE	MUCIN
MOUSED	MOUTERED	MOVIEOLA	MOZING	MUCINOGEN
MOUSEKIN	MOUTERER	MOVIEOLAS	MOZO	MUCINOID
MOUSEKINS	MOUTERERS	MOVIES	MOZOS	MUCINOUS
MOUSELIKE	MOUTERING	MOVING	MOZZ	MUCINS
MOUSEMAT	MOUTERS	MOVINGLY	MOZZES	MUCK

MUCKAMUCK	MUCROS	MUDFLOWS	MUDWORT	MUGGINGS
MUCKED	MUCULENT	MUDGE	MUDWORTS	MUGGINS
MUCKENDER	MUCUS	MUDGED	MUEDDIN	MUGGINSES
MUCKER	MUCUSES	MUDGER	MUEDDINS	MUGGISH
MUCKERED	MUD	MUDGERS	MUENSTER	MUGGLE
MUCKERING	MUDBANK	MUDGES	MUENSTERS	MUGGLES
MUCKERISH	MUDBANKS	MUDGING	MUESLI	MUGGS
MUCKERS	MUDBATH	MUDGUARD	MUESLIS	MUGGUR
MUCKHEAP	MUDBATHS	MUDGUARDS	MUEZZIN	MUGGURS
MUCKHEAPS	MUDBUG	MUDHEN	MUEZZINS	MUGGY
MUCKIER	MUDBUGS	MUDHENS	MUFF	MUGHAL
MUCKIEST	MUDCAP	MUDHOLE	MUFFED	MUGHALS
MUCKILY	MUDCAPPED	MUDHOLES	MUFFETTEE	MUGS
MUCKINESS	MUDCAPS	MUDHOOK	MUFFIN	MUGSHOT
MUCKING	MUDCAT	MUDHOOKS	MUFFINEER	MUGSHOTS
MUCKLE	MUDCATS	MUDHOPPER	MUFFING	MUGWORT
MUCKLER	MUDDED	MUDIR	MUFFINS	MUGWORTS
MUCKLES	MUDDER	MUDIRIA	MUFFISH	MUGWUMP
MUCKLEST	MUDDERS	MUDIRIAS	MUFFLE	MUGWUMPS
MUCKLUCK	MUDDIED	MUDIRIEH	MUFFLED	MUHLIES
MUCKLUCKS	MUDDIER	MUDIRIEHS	MUFFLER	MUHLY
MUCKRAKE	MUDDIES	MUDIRS	MUFFLERED	MUID
MUCKRAKED	MUDDIEST	MUDLARK	MUFFLERS	MUIDS
MUCKRAKER	MUDDILY	MUDLARKED	MUFFLES	MUIL
MUCKRAKES	MUDDINESS	MUDLARKS	MUFFLING	MUILS
MUCKS	MUDDING	MUDLOGGER	MUFFS	MUIR
MUCKSWEAT	MUDDLE	MUDPACK	MUFLON	MUIRBURN
MUCKWORM	MUDDLED	MUDPACKS	MUFLONS	MUIRBURNS
MUCKWORMS	MUDDLER	MUDPIE	MUFTI	MUIRS
MUCKY	MUDDLERS	MUDPIES	MUFTIS	MUIST
MUCKYMUCK	MUDDLES	MUDPUPPY	MUG	MUISTED
MUCLUC	MUDDLIER	MUDRA	MUGEARITE	MUISTING
MUCLUCS	MUDDLIEST	MUDRAS	MUGFUL	MUISTS
MUCOID	MUDDLING	MUDROCK	MUGFULS	MUJAHEDIN
MUCOIDAL	MUDDLINGS	MUDROCKS	MUGG	MUJAHIDIN
MUCOIDS	MUDDLY	MUDROOM	MUGGA	MUJIK
MUCOLYTIC	MUDDY	MUDROOMS	MUGGAR	MUJIKS
MUCOR	MUDDYING	MUDS	MUGGARS	MUKHTAR
MUCORS	MUDEJAR	MUDSCOW	MUGGAS	MUKHTARS
MUCOSA	MUDEJARES	MUDSCOWS	MUGGED	MUKLUK
MUCOSAE	MUDEYE	MUDSILL	MUGGEE	MUKLUKS
MUCOSAL	MUDEYES	MUDSILLS	MUGGEES	MUKTUK
MUCOSAS	MUDFISH	MUDSLIDE	MUGGER	MUKTUKS
MUCOSE	MUDFISHES	MUDSLIDES	MUGGERS	MULBERRY
MUCOSITY	MUDFLAP	MUDSLING	MUGGIER	MULCH
MUCOUS	MUDFLAPS	MUDSLINGS	MUGGIEST	MULCHED
MUCRO	MUDFLAT	MUDSLUNG	MUGGILY	MULCHES
MUCRONATE	MUDFLATS	MUDSTONE	MUGGINESS	MULCHING
MUCRONES	MUDFLOW	MUDSTONES	MUGGING	MULCT

M

MULCTED	MULLION	MULTIHIT	MULTURING	MUMSIEST
MULCTING	MULLIONED	MULTIHUED	MUM	MUMSINESS
MULCTS	MULLIONS	MULTIHULL	MUMBLE	MUMSY
MULE	MULLITE	MULTIJET	MUMBLED	MUMU
MULED	MULLITES	MULTILANE	MUMBLER	MUMUS
MULES	MULLOCK	MULTILINE	MUMBLERS	MUN
MULESED	MULLOCKS	MULTILOBE	MUMBLES	MUNCH
MULESES	MULLOCKY	MULTIMODE	MUMBLIER	MUNCHABLE
MULESING	MULLOWAY	MULTIPACK	MUMBLIEST	MUNCHED
MULESINGS	MULLOWAYS	MULTIPAGE	MUMBLING	MUNCHER
MULETA	MULLS	MULTIPARA	MUMBLINGS	MUNCHERS
MULETAS	MULMUL	MULTIPART	MUMBLY	MUNCHES
MULETEER	MULMULL	MULTIPATH	MUMCHANCE	MUNCHIE
MULETEERS	MULMULLS	MULTIPED	MUMM	MUNCHIER
MULEY	MULMULS	MULTIPEDE	MUMMED	MUNCHIES
MULEYS	MULSE	MULTIPEDS	MUMMER	MUNCHIEST
MULGA	MULSES	MULTIPION	MUMMERED	MUNCHING
MULGAS	MULSH	MULTIPLE	MUMMERIES	MUNCHKIN
MULIE	MULSHED	MULTIPLES	MUMMERING	MUNCHKINS
MULIES	MULSHES	MULTIPLET	MUMMERS	MUNCHY
MULING	MULSHING	MULTIPLEX	MUMMERY	MUNDANE
MULISH	MULTEITY	MULTIPLY	MUMMIA	MUNDANELY
MULISHLY	MULTIAGE	MULTIPOLE	MUMMIAS	MUNDANER
MULL	MULTIATOM	MULTIPORT	MUMMICHOG	MUNDANEST
MULLA	MULTIBAND	MULTIRISK	MUMMIED	MUNDANITY
MULLAH	MULTIBANK	MULTIROLE	MUMMIES	MUNDIC
MULLAHED	MULTICAR	MULTIROOM	MUMMIFIED	MUNDICS
MULLAHING	MULTICAST	MULTISITE	MUMMIFIES	MUNDIFIED
MULLAHISM	MULTICELL	MULTISIZE	MUMMIFORM	MUNDIFIES
MULLAHS	MULTICIDE	MULTISTEP	MUMMIFY	MUNDIFY
MULLARKY	MULTICITY	MULTITASK	MUMMING	MUNDUNGO
MULLAS	MULTICOPY	MULTITIER	MUMMINGS	MUNDUNGOS
MULLED	MULTICORE	MULTITON	MUMMOCK	MUNDUNGUS
MULLEIN	MULTICULT	MULTITONE	MUMMOCKS	MUNG
MULLEINS	MULTIDAY	MULTITOOL	MUMMS	MUNGA
MULLEN	MULTIDISC	MULTITUDE	MUMMY	MUNGAS
MULLENS	MULTIDISK	MULTIUNIT	MUMMYING	MUNGCORN
MULLER	MULTIDRUG	MULTIUSE	MUMP	MUNGCORNS
MULLERED	MULTIFID	MULTIUSER	MUMPED	MUNGE
MULLERIAN	MULTIFIL	MULTIWALL	MUMPER	MUNGED
MULLERING	MULTIFILS	MULTIWAY	MUMPERS	MUNGES
MULLERS	MULTIFOIL	MULTIYEAR	MUMPING	MUNGING
MULLET	MULTIFOLD	MULTUM	MUMPISH	MUNGO
MULLETS	MULTIFORM	MULTUMS	MUMPISHLY	MUNGOES
MULLEY	MULTIGENE	MULTURE	MUMPS	MUNGOOSE
MULLEYS	MULTIGERM	MULTURED	MUMPSIMUS	MUNGOOSES
MULLIGAN	MULTIGRID	MULTURER	MUMS	MUNGOS
MULLIGANS	MULTIGYM	MULTURERS	MUMSIER	MUNGS
MULLING	MULTIGYMS	MULTURES	MUMSIES	MUNI

MUNICIPAL	MURAGE	MURKIER	MURREN	MUSCATS
MUNIFIED	MURAGES	MURKIEST	MURRENS	MUSCAVADO
MUNIFIES	MURAL	MURKILY	MURRES	MUSCID
MUNIFY	MURALED	MURKINESS	MURREY	MUSCIDS
MUNIFYING	MURALIST	MURKING	MURREYS	MUSCLE
MUNIMENT	MURALISTS	MURKISH	MURRHA	MUSCLED
MUNIMENTS	MURALLED	MURKLY	MURRHAS	MUSCLEMAN
MUNIS	MURALS	MURKS	MURRHINE	MUSCLEMEN
MUNITE	MURAS	MURKSOME	MURRHINES	MUSCLES
MUNITED	MURDABAD	MURKY	MURRI	MUSCLEY
MUNITES	MURDER	MURL	MURRIES	MUSCLIER
MUNITING	MURDERED	MURLAIN	MURRIN	MUSCLIEST
MUNITION	MURDEREE	MURLAINS	MURRINE	MUSCLING
MUNITIONS	MURDEREES	MURLAN	MURRINES	MUSCLINGS
MUNNION	MURDERER	MURLANS	MURRINS	MUSCLY
MUNNIONS	MURDERERS	MURLED	MURRION	MUSCOID
MUNS	MURDERESS	MURLIER	MURRIONS	MUSCOIDS
MUNSHI	MURDERING	MURLIEST	MURRIS	MUSCOLOGY
MUNSHIS	MURDEROUS	MURLIN	MURRS	MUSCONE
MUNSTER	MURDERS	MURLING	MURRY	MUSCONES
MUNSTERS	MURE	MURLINS	MURSHID	MUSCOSE
MUNTED	MURED	MURLS	MURSHIDS	MUSCOVADO
MUNTER	MUREIN	MURLY	MURTHER	MUSCOVITE
MUNTERS	MUREINS	MURMUR	MURTHERED	MUSCOVY
MUNTIN	MURENA	MURMURED	MURTHERER	MUSCULAR
MUNTINED	MURENAS	MURMURER	MURTHERS	MUSCULOUS
MUNTING	MURES	MURMURERS	MURTI	MUSE
MUNTINGS	MUREX	MURMURING	MURTIS	MUSED
MUNTINS	MUREXES	MURMUROUS	MURVA	MUSEFUL
MUNTJAC	MURGEON	MURMURS	MURVAS	MUSEFULLY
MUNTJACS	MURGEONED	MURPHIES	MUS	MUSEOLOGY
MUNTJAK	MURGEONS	MURPHY	MUSACEOUS	MUSER
MUNTJAKS	MURIATE	MURR	MUSANG	MUSERS
MUNTRIE	MURIATED	MURRA	MUSANGS	MUSES
MUNTRIES	MURIATES	MURRAGH	MUSAR	MUSET
MUON	MURIATIC	MURRAGHS	MUSARS	MUSETS
MUONIC	MURICATE	MURRAIN	MUSCA	MUSETTE
MUONIUM	MURICATED	MURRAINED	MUSCADEL	MUSETTES
MUONIUMS	MURICES	MURRAINS	MUSCADELS	MUSEUM
MUONS	MURID	MURRAM	MUSCADET	MUSEUMS
MUPPET	MURIDS	MURRAMS	MUSCADETS	MUSH
MUPPETS	MURIFORM	MURRAS	MUSCADIN	MUSHA
MUQADDAM	MURINE	MURRAY	MUSCADINE	MUSHED
MUQADDAMS	MURINES	MURRAYS	MUSCADINS	MUSHER
MURA	MURING	MURRE	MUSCAE	MUSHERS
MURAENA	MURK	MURREE	MUSCARINE	MUSHES
MURAENAS	MURKED	MURREES	MUSCAT	MUSHIE
MURAENID	MURKER	MURRELET	MUSCATEL	MUSHIER
MURAENIDS	MURKEST	MURRELETS	MUSCATELS	MUSHIES

MUSHIEST	MUSKIES	MUSTACHE	MUTATOR	MUTTERERS
MUSHILY	MUSKIEST	MUSTACHED	MUTATORS	MUTTERING
MUSHINESS	MUSKILY	MUSTACHES	MUTATORY	MUTTERS
MUSHING	MUSKINESS	MUSTACHIO	MUTCH	MUTTON
MUSHINGS	MUSKING	MUSTANG	MUTCHED	MUTTONIER
MUSHMOUTH	MUSKIT	MUSTANGS	MUTCHES	MUTTONS
MUSHRAT	MUSKITS	MUSTARD	MUTCHING	MUTTONY
MUSHRATS	MUSKLE	MUSTARDS	MUTCHKIN	MUTTS
MUSHROOM	MUSKLES	MUSTARDY	MUTCHKINS	MUTUAL
MUSHROOMS	MUSKMELON	MUSTED	MUTE	MUTUALISE
MUSHROOMY	MUSKONE	MUSTEE	MUTED	MUTUALISM
MUSHY	MUSKONES	MUSTEES	MUTEDLY	MUTUALIST
MUSIC	MUSKOX	MUSTELID	MUTELY	MUTUALITY
MUSICAL	MUSKOXEN	MUSTELIDS	MUTENESS	MUTUALIZE
MUSICALE	MUSKRAT	MUSTELINE	MUTER	MUTUALLY
MUSICALES	MUSKRATS	MUSTER	MUTES	MUTUALS
MUSICALLY	MUSKROOT	MUSTERED	MUTEST	MUTUCA
MUSICALS	MUSKROOTS	MUSTERER	MUTHA	MUTUCAS
MUSICIAN	MUSKS	MUSTERERS	MUTHAS	MUTUEL
MUSICIANS	MUSKY	MUSTERING	MUTI	MUTUELS
MUSICK	MUSLIN	MUSTERS	MUTICATE	MUTULAR
MUSICKED	MUSLINED	MUSTH	MUTICOUS	MUTULE
MUSICKER	MUSLINET	MUSTHS	MUTILATE	MUTULES
MUSICKERS	MUSLINETS	MUSTIER	MUTILATED	MUTUUM
MUSICKING	MUSLINS	MUSTIEST	MUTILATES	MUTUUMS
MUSICKS	MUSMON	MUSTILY	MUTILATOR	MUUMUU
MUSICLESS	MUSMONS	MUSTINESS	MUTINE	MUUMUUS
MUSICS	MUSO	MUSTING	MUTINED	MUX
MUSIMON	MUSOS	MUSTS	MUTINEER	MUXED
MUSIMONS	MUSPIKE	MUSTY	MUTINEERS	MUXES
MUSING	MUSPIKES	MUT	MUTINES	MUXING
MUSINGLY	MUSQUASH	MUTABLE	MUTING	MUZAK
MUSINGS	MUSROL	MUTABLY	MUTINIED	MUZAKIER
MUSIT	MUSROLS	MUTAGEN	MUTINIES	MUZAKIEST
MUSITS	MUSS	MUTAGENIC	MUTINING	MUZAKS
MUSIVE	MUSSE	MUTAGENS	MUTINOUS	MUZAKY
MUSJID	MUSSED	MUTANDA	MUTINY	MUZHIK
MUSJIDS	MUSSEL	MUTANDUM	MUTINYING	MUZHIKS
MUSK	MUSSELLED	MUTANT	MUTIS	MUZJIK
MUSKED	MUSSELS	MUTANTS	MUTISM	MUZJIKS
MUSKEG	MUSSES	MUTASE	MUTISMS	MUZZ
MUSKEGS	MUSSIER	MUTASES	MUTON	MUZZED
MUSKET	MUSSIEST	MUTATE	MUTONS	MUZZES
MUSKETEER	MUSSILY	MUTATED	MUTOSCOPE	MUZZIER
MUSKETOON	MUSSINESS	MUTATES	MUTS	MUZZIEST
MUSKETRY	MUSSING	MUTATING	MUTT	MUZZILY
MUSKETS	MUSSITATE	MUTATION	MUTTER	MUZZINESS
MUSKIE	MUSSY	MUTATIONS	MUTTERED	MUZZING
MUSKIER	MUST	MUTATIVE	MUTTERER	MUZZLE

MUZZLED	MYCS	MYOGLOBIN	MYOTOMES	MYSTAGOGY
MUZZLER	MYDRIASES	MYOGRAM	MYOTONIA	MYSTERIES
MUZZLERS	MYDRIASIS	MYOGRAMS	MYOTONIAS	MYSTERY
MUZZLES	MYDRIATIC	MYOGRAPH	MYOTONIC	MYSTIC
MUZZLING	MYELIN	MYOGRAPHS	MYOTUBE	MYSTICAL
MUZZY	MYELINE	MYOGRAPHY	MYOTUBES	MYSTICETE
MVULE	MYELINES	MYOID	MYRBANE	MYSTICISM
MVULES	MYELINIC	MYOIDS	MYRBANES	MYSTICLY
MWAH	MYELINS	MYOLOGIC	MYRIAD	MYSTICS
MWALIMU	MYELITES	MYOLOGIES	MYRIADS	MYSTIFIED
MWALIMUS	MYELITIS	MYOLOGIST	MYRIADTH	MYSTIFIER
MY	MYELOCYTE	MYOLOGY	MYRIADTHS	MYSTIFIES
MYAL	MYELOGRAM	MYOMA	MYRIAPOD	MYSTIFY
MYALGIA	MYELOID	MYOMANCY	MYRIAPODS	MYSTIQUE
MYALGIAS	MYELOMA	MYOMANTIC	MYRICA	MYSTIQUES
MYALGIC	MYELOMAS	MYOMAS	MYRICAS	MYTH
MYALISM	MYELOMATA	MYOMATA	MYRINGA	MYTHI
MYALISMS	MYELON	MYOMATOUS	MYRINGAS	MYTHIC
MYALIST	MYELONS	MYOMERE	MYRIOPOD	MYTHICAL
MYALISTS	MYGALE	MYOMERES	MYRIOPODS	MYTHICISE
MYALL	MYGALES	MYONEURAL	MYRIORAMA	MYTHICISM
MYALLS	MYIASES	MYOPATHIC	MYRISTIC	MYTHICIST
MYASES	MYIASIS	MYOPATHY	MYRMECOID	MYTHICIZE
MYASIS	MYIOPHILY	MYOPE	MYRMIDON	MYTHIER
MYC	MYLAR	MYOPES	MYRMIDONS	MYTHIEST
MYCELE	MYLARS	MYOPHILY	MYROBALAN	MYTHISE
MYCELES	MYLODON	MYOPIA	MYRRH	MYTHISED
MYCELIA	MYLODONS	MYOPIAS	MYRRHIC	MYTHISES
MYCELIAL	MYLODONT	MYOPIC	MYRRHIER	MYTHISING
MYCELIAN	MYLODONTS	MYOPICS	MYRRHIEST	MYTHISM
MYCELIUM	MYLOHYOID	MYOPIES	MYRRHINE	MYTHISMS
MYCELLA	MYLONITE	MYOPS	MYRRHOL	MYTHIST
MYCELLAS	MYLONITES	MYOPSES	MYRRHOLS	MYTHISTS
MYCELOID	MYLONITIC	MYOPY	MYRRHS	MYTHIZE
MYCETES	MYNA	MYOSCOPE	MYRRHY	MYTHIZED
MYCETOMA	MYNAH	MYOSCOPES	MYRTLE	MYTHIZES
MYCETOMAS	MYNAHS	MYOSES	MYRTLES	MYTHIZING
MYCOBIONT	MYNAS	MYOSIN	MYSELF	MYTHMAKER
MYCOFLORA	MYNHEER	MYOSINS	MYSID	MYTHOI
MYCOLOGIC	MYNHEERS	MYOSIS	MYSIDS	MYTHOLOGY
MYCOLOGY	MYOBLAST	MYOSISES	MYSOPHOBE	MYTHOMANE
MYCOPHAGY	MYOBLASTS	MYOSITIS	MYSOST	MYTHOPEIC
MYCOPHILE	MYOCARDIA	MYOSOTE	MYSOSTS	MYTHOPOET
MYCORHIZA	MYOCLONIC	MYOSOTES	MYSPACE	MYTHOS
MYCOSES	MYOCLONUS	MYOSOTIS	MYSPACED	MYTHS
MYCOSIS	MYOFIBRIL	MYOSTATIN	MYSPACES	MYTHUS
MYCOTIC	MYOGEN	MYOTIC	MYSPACING	MYTHY
MYCOTOXIN	MYOGENIC	MYOTICS	MYSTAGOG	MYTILOID
MYCOVIRUS	MYOGENS	MYOTOME	MYSTAGOGS	MYXAMEBA

MYXAMEBAE	MYXEDEMIC	MYXOID	MYXOVIRAL	MZUNGUS
MYXAMEBAS	MYXO	MYXOMA	MYXOVIRUS	
MYXAMOEBA	MYXOCYTE	MYXOMAS	MZEE	
MYXEDEMA	MYXOCYTES	MYXOMATA	MZEES	
MYXEDEMAS	MYXOEDEMA	MYXOS	MZUNGU	

M

N

NA	NACKETS	NAGGED	NAILHEAD	NALIDIXIC
NAAM	NACRE	NAGGER	NAILHEADS	NALLA
NAAMS	NACRED	NAGGERS	NAILING	NALLAH
NAAN	NACREOUS	NAGGIER	NAILINGS	NALLAHS
NAANS	NACRES	NAGGIEST	NAILLESS	NALLAS
NAARTJE	NACRITE	NAGGING	NAILS	NALOXONE
NAARTJES	NACRITES	NAGGINGLY	NAILSET	NALOXONES
NAARTJIE	NACROUS	NAGGINGS	NAILSETS	NAM
NAARTJIES	NADA	NAGGY	NAIN	NAMABLE
NAB	NADAS	NAGMAAL	NAINSELL	NAMASKAR
NABBED	NADIR	NAGMAALS	NAINSELLS	NAMASKARS
NABBER	NADIRAL	NAGOR	NAINSOOK	NAMASTE
NABBERS	NADIRS	NAGORS	NAINSOOKS	NAMASTES
NABBING	NADORS	NAGS	NAIRA	NAMAYCUSH
NABE	NADS	NAGWARE	NAIRAS	NAME
NABES	NAE	NAGWARES	NAIRU	NAMEABLE
NABIS	NAEBODIES	NAH	NAIRUS	NAMECHECK
NABK	NAEBODY	NAHAL	NAISSANCE	NAMED
NABKS	NAES	NAHALS	NAISSANT	NAMELESS
NABLA	NAETHING	NAIAD	NAIVE	NAMELY
NABLAS	NAETHINGS	NAIADES	NAIVELY	NAMEPLATE
NABOB	NAEVE	NAIADS	NAIVENESS	NAMER
NABOBERY	NAEVES	NAIANT	NAIVER	NAMERS
NABOBESS	NAEVI	NAIF	NAIVES	NAMES
NABOBISH	NAEVOID	NAIFER	NAIVEST	NAMESAKE
NABOBISM	NAEVUS	NAIFEST	NAIVETE	NAMESAKES
NABOBISMS	NAFF	NAIFLY	NAIVETES	NAMETAG
NABOBS	NAFFED	NAIFNESS	NAIVETIES	NAMETAGS
NABS	NAFFER	NAIFS	NAIVETY	NAMETAPE
NACARAT	NAFFEST	NAIK	NAIVIST	NAMETAPES
NACARATS	NAFFING	NAIKS	NAKED	NAMING
NACELLE	NAFFLY	NAIL	NAKEDER	NAMINGS
NACELLES	NAFFNESS	NAILBITER	NAKEDEST	NAMMA
NACH	NAFFS	NAILBRUSH	NAKEDLY	NAMS
NACHAS	NAG	NAILED	NAKEDNESS	NAMU
NACHASES	NAGA	NAILER	NAKER	NAMUS
NACHE	NAGANA	NAILERIES	NAKERS	NAN
NACHES	NAGANAS	NAILERS	NAKFA	NANA
NACHESES	NAGAPIE	NAILERY	NAKFAS	NANAS
NACHO	NAGAPIES	NAILFILE	NALA	NANDIN
NACHOS	NAGARI	NAILFILES	NALAS	NANDINA
NACHTMAAL	NAGARIS	NAILFOLD	NALED	NANDINAS
NACKET	NAGAS	NAILFOLDS	NALEDS	NANDINE

NANDINES	NANOTESLA	NAPPE	NARD	NARROWED
NANDINS	NANOTUBE	NAPPED	NARDED	NARROWER
NANDOO	NANOTUBES	NAPPER	NARDINE	NARROWEST
NANDOOS	NANOWATT	NAPPERS	NARDING	NARROWING
NANDU	NANOWATTS	NAPPES	NARDOO	NARROWISH
NANDUS	NANOWIRE	NAPPIE	NARDOOS	NARROWLY
NANE	NANOWIRES	NAPPIER	NARDS	NARROWS
NANG	NANOWORLD	NAPPIES	NARE	NARTHEX
NANISM	NANS	NAPPIEST	NARES	NARTHEXES
NANISMS	NANUA	NAPPINESS	NARGHILE	NARTJIE
NANITE	NANUAS	NAPPING	NARGHILES	NARTJIES
NANITES	NAOI	NAPPY	NARGHILLY	NARWAL
NANKEEN	NAOS	NAPRON	NARGHILY	NARWALS
NANKEENS	NAOSES	NAPRONS	NARGILE	NARWHAL
NANKIN	NAP	NAPROXEN	NARGILEH	NARWHALE
NANKINS	NAPA	NAPROXENS	NARGILEHS	NARWHALES
NANNA	NAPALM	NAPS	NARGILES	NARWHALS
NANNAS	NAPALMED	NARAS	NARGILIES	NARY
NANNIE	NAPALMING	NARASES	NARGILY	NAS
NANNIED	NAPALMS	NARC	NARGUILEH	NASAL
NANNIES	NAPAS	NARCEEN	NARIAL	NASALISE
NANNY	NAPE	NARCEENS	NARIC	NASALISED
NANNYGAI	NAPED	NARCEIN	NARICORN	NASALISES
NANNYGAIS	NAPERIES	NARCEINE	NARICORNS	NASALISM
NANNYING	NAPERY	NARCEINES	NARINE	NASALISMS
NANNYINGS	NAPES	NARCEINS	NARIS	NASALITY
NANNYISH	NAPHTHA	NARCISM	NARK	NASALIZE
NANO	NAPHTHAS	NARCISMS	NARKED	NASALIZED
NANOBE	NAPHTHENE	NARCISSI	NARKIER	NASALIZES
NANOBEE	NAPHTHOL	NARCISSUS	NARKIEST	NASALLY
NANOBEES	NAPHTHOLS	NARCIST	NARKING	NASALS
NANOBES	NAPHTHOUS	NARCISTIC	NARKS	NASARD
NANOBOT	NAPHTHYL	NARCISTS	NARKY	NASARDS
NANOBOTS	NAPHTHYLS	NARCO	NARQUOIS	NASCENCE
NANODOT	NAPHTOL	NARCOMA	NARRAS	NASCENCES
NANODOTS	NAPHTOLS	NARCOMAS	NARRASES	NASCENCY
NANOGRAM	NAPIFORM	NARCOMATA	NARRATE	NASCENT
NANOGRAMS	NAPING	NARCOS	NARRATED	NASEBERRY
NANOGRASS	NAPKIN	NARCOSE	NARRATER	NASHGAB
NANOMETER	NAPKINS	NARCOSES	NARRATERS	NASHGABS
NANOMETRE	NAPLESS	NARCOSIS	NARRATES	NASHI
NANOOK	NAPOLEON	NARCOTIC	NARRATING	NASHIS
NANOOKS	NAPOLEONS	NARCOTICS	NARRATION	NASIAL
NANOPORE	NAPOO	NARCOTINE	NARRATIVE	NASION
NANOPORES	NAPOOED	NARCOTISE	NARRATOR	NASIONS
NANOS	NAPOOING	NARCOTISM	NARRATORS	NASSELLA
NANOSCALE	NAPOOS	NARCOTIST	NARRATORY	NASTALIK
NANOTECH	NAPPA	NARCOTIZE	NARRE	NASTALIKS
NANOTECHS	NAPPAS	NARCS	NARROW	NASTIC

NASTIER	NATTERERS	NAUSEOUS	NAVVY	NEAREST
NASTIES	NATTERIER	NAUTCH	NAVVYING	NEARING
NASTIEST	NATTERING	NAUTCHES	NAVY	NEARISH
NASTILY	NATTERS	NAUTIC	NAW	NEARLIER
NASTINESS	NATTERY	NAUTICAL	NAWAB	NEARLIEST
NASTY	NATTIER	NAUTICS	NAWABS	NEARLY
NASUTE	NATTIEST	NAUTILI	NAY	NEARNESS
NASUTES	NATTILY	NAUTILOID	NAYS	NEARS
NAT	NATTINESS	NAUTILUS	NAYSAID	NEARSHORE
NATAK	NATTO	NAV	NAYSAY	NEARSIDE
NATAKS	NATTOS	NAVAID	NAYSAYER	NEARSIDES
NATAL	NATTY	NAVAIDS	NAYSAYERS	NEAT
NATALITY	NATURA	NAVAL	NAYSAYING	NEATEN
NATANT	NATURAE	NAVALISM	NAYSAYS	NEATENED
NATANTLY	NATURAL	NAVALISMS	NAYTHLES	NEATENING
NATATION	NATURALLY	NAVALLY	NAYWARD	NEATENS
NATATIONS	NATURALS	NAVAR	NAYWARDS	NEATER
NATATORIA	NATURE	NAVARCH	NAYWORD	NEATEST
NATATORY	NATURED	NAVARCHS	NAYWORDS	NEATH
NATCH	NATURES	NAVARCHY	NAZE	NEATHERD
NATCHES	NATURING	NAVARHO	NAZES	NEATHERDS
NATES	NATURISM	NAVARHOS	NAZI	NEATLY
NATHELESS	NATURISMS	NAVARIN	NAZIFIED	NEATNESS
NATHEMO	NATURIST	NAVARINS	NAZIFIES	NEATNIK
NATHEMORE	NATURISTS	NAVARS	NAZIFY	NEATNIKS
NATHLESS	NAUCH	NAVE	NAZIFYING	NEATS
NATIFORM	NAUCHES	NAVEL	NAZIR	NEB
NATION	NAUGAHYDE	NAVELS	NAZIRS	NEBBED
NATIONAL	NAUGHT	NAVELWORT	NAZIS	NEBBICH
NATIONALS	NAUGHTIER	NAVES	NDUJA	NEBBICHS
NATIONS	NAUGHTIES	NAVETTE	NDUJAS	NEBBING
NATIS	NAUGHTILY	NAVETTES	NE	NEBBISH
NATIVE	NAUGHTS	NAVEW	NEAFE	NEBBISHE
NATIVELY	NAUGHTY	NAVEWS	NEAFES	NEBBISHER
NATIVES	NAUMACHIA	NAVICERT	NEAFFE	NEBBISHES
NATIVISM	NAUMACHY	NAVICERTS	NEAFFES	NEBBISHY
NATIVISMS	NAUNT	NAVICULA	NEAL	NEBBUK
NATIVIST	NAUNTS	NAVICULAR	NEALED	NEBBUKS
NATIVISTS	NAUPLIAL	NAVICULAS	NEALING	NEBECK
NATIVITY	NAUPLII	NAVIES	NEALS	NEBECKS
NATRIUM	NAUPLIOID	NAVIGABLE	NEANIC	NEBEK
NATRIUMS	NAUPLIUS	NAVIGABLY	NEAP	NEBEKS
NATROLITE	NAUSEA	NAVIGATE	NEAPED	NEBEL
NATRON	NAUSEANT	NAVIGATED	NEAPING	NEBELS
NATRONS	NAUSEANTS	NAVIGATES	NEAPS	NEBENKERN
NATS	NAUSEAS	NAVIGATOR	NEAR	NEBISH
NATTER	NAUSEATE	NAVS	NEARBY	NEBISHES
NATTERED	NAUSEATED	NAVVIED	NEARED	NEBRIS
NATTERER	NAUSEATES	NAVVIES	NEARER	NEBRISES

NEBS	NECKSHOTS	NEEDFULLY	NEGATED	NEINEIS
NEBULA	NECKTIE	NEEDFULS	NEGATER	NEIST
NEBULAE	NECKTIES	NEEDIER	NEGATERS	NEITHER
NEBULAR	NECKVERSE	NEEDIEST	NEGATES	NEIVE
NEBULAS	NECKWEAR	NEEDILY	NEGATING	NEIVES
NEBULE	NECKWEARS	NEEDINESS	NEGATION	NEK
NEBULES	NECKWEED	NEEDING	NEGATIONS	NEKS
NEBULISE	NECKWEEDS	NEEDLE	NEGATIVE	NEKTON
NEBULISED	NECROLOGY	NEEDLED	NEGATIVED	NEKTONIC
NEBULISER	NECROPHIL	NEEDLEFUL	NEGATIVES	NEKTONS
NEBULISES	NECROPOLI	NEEDLER	NEGATON	NELIES
NEBULIUM	NECROPSY	NEEDLERS	NEGATONS	NELIS
NEBULIUMS	NECROSE	NEEDLES	NEGATOR	NELLIE
NEBULIZE	NECROSED	NEEDLESS	NEGATORS	NELLIES
NEBULIZED	NECROSES	NEEDLIER	NEGATORY	NELLY
NEBULIZER	NECROSING	NEEDLIEST	NEGATRON	NELSON
NEBULIZES	NECROSIS	NEEDLING	NEGATRONS	NELSONS
NEBULOSE	NECROTIC	NEEDLINGS	NEGGED	NELUMBIUM
NEBULOUS	NECROTISE	NEEDLY	NEGGING	NELUMBO
NEBULY	NECROTIZE	NEEDMENT	NEGLECT	NELUMBOS
NECESSARY	NECROTOMY	NEEDMENTS	NEGLECTED	NEMA
NECESSITY	NECTAR	NEEDS	NEGLECTER	NEMAS
NECK	NECTAREAL	NEEDY	NEGLECTOR	NEMATIC
NECKATEE	NECTAREAN	NEELD	NEGLECTS	NEMATICS
NECKATEES	NECTARED	NEELDS	NEGLIGE	NEMATODE
NECKBAND	NECTARIAL	NEELE	NEGLIGEE	NEMATODES
NECKBANDS	NECTARIED	NEELES	NEGLIGEES	NEMATOID
NECKBEEF	NECTARIES	NEEM	NEGLIGENT	NEMERTEAN
NECKBEEFS	NECTARINE	NEEMB	NEGLIGES	NEMERTIAN
NECKCLOTH	NECTAROUS	NEEMBS	NEGOCIANT	NEMERTINE
NECKED	NECTARS	NEEMS	NEGOTIANT	NEMESES
NECKER	NECTARY	NEEP	NEGOTIATE	NEMESIA
NECKERS	NED	NEEPS	NEGRITUDE	NEMESIAS
NECKGEAR	NEDDIER	NEESBERRY	NEGRONI	NEMESIS
NECKGEARS	NEDDIES	NEESE	NEGRONIS	NEMN
NECKING	NEDDIEST	NEESED	NEGS	NEMNED
NECKINGS	NEDDISH	NEESES	NEGUS	NEMNING
NECKLACE	NEDDY	NEESING	NEGUSES	NEMNS
NECKLACED	NEDETTE	NEEZE	NEIF	NEMOPHILA
NECKLACES	NEDETTES	NEEZED	NEIFS	NEMORAL
NECKLESS	NEDS	NEEZES	NEIGH	NEMOROUS
NECKLET	NEE	NEEZING	NEIGHBOR	NEMPT
NECKLETS	NEED	NEF	NEIGHBORS	NENE
NECKLIKE	NEEDED	NEFANDOUS	NEIGHBOUR	NENES
NECKLINE	NEEDER	NEFARIOUS	NEIGHED	NENNIGAI
NECKLINES	NEEDERS	NEFAST	NEIGHING	NENNIGAIS
NECKPIECE	NEEDFIRE	NEFS	NEIGHINGS	NENUPHAR
NECKS	NEEDFIRES	NEG	NEIGHS	NENUPHARS
NECKSHOT	NEEDFUL	NEGATE	NEINEI	NEOBLAST

NEOBLASTS	NEOPRENES	NEPIONIC	NERVED	NESTLINGS
NEOCON	NEOSOUL	NEPIT	NERVELESS	NESTMATE
NEOCONS	NEOSOULS	NEPITS	NERVELET	NESTMATES
NEOCORTEX	NEOTEINIA	NEPOTIC	NERVELETS	NESTOR
NEODYMIUM	NEOTENIC	NEPOTISM	NERVER	NESTORS
NEOGENE	NEOTENIES	NEPOTISMS	NERVERS	NESTS
NEOGOTHIC	NEOTENOUS	NEPOTIST	NERVES	NET
NEOLITH	NEOTENY	NEPOTISTS	NERVIER	NETBALL
NEOLITHIC	NEOTERIC	NEPS	NERVIEST	NETBALLER
NEOLITHS	NEOTERICS	NEPTUNIUM	NERVILY	NETBALLS
NEOLOGIAN	NEOTERISE	NERAL	NERVINE	NETBOOK
NEOLOGIC	NEOTERISM	NERALS	NERVINES	NETBOOKS
NEOLOGIES	NEOTERIST	NERD	NERVINESS	NETE
NEOLOGISE	NEOTERIZE	NERDIC	NERVING	NETES
NEOLOGISM	NEOTOXIN	NERDICS	NERVINGS	NETFUL
NEOLOGIST	NEOTOXINS	NERDIER	NERVOSITY	NETFULS
NEOLOGIZE	NEOTROPIC	NERDIEST	NERVOUS	NETHEAD
NEOLOGY	NEOTYPE	NERDINESS	NERVOUSLY	NETHEADS
NEOMORPH	NEOTYPES	NERDISH	NERVULAR	NETHELESS
NEOMORPHS	NEP	NERDS	NERVULE	NETHER
NEOMYCIN	NEPENTHE	NERDY	NERVULES	NETIZEN
NEOMYCINS	NEPENTHES	NEREID	NERVURE	NETIZENS
NEON	NEPER	NEREIDES	NERVURES	NETLESS
NEONATAL	NEPERS	NEREIDS	NERVY	NETLIKE
NEONATE	NEPETA	NEREIS	NESCIENCE	NETMINDER
NEONATES	NEPETAS	NERF	NESCIENT	NETOP
NEONED	NEPHALISM	NERFED	NESCIENTS	NETOPS
NEONIC	NEPHALIST	NERFING	NESH	NETROOT
NEONICS	NEPHELINE	NERFS	NESHER	NETROOTS
NEONOMIAN	NEPHELITE	NERINE	NESHEST	NETS
NEONS	NEPHEW	NERINES	NESHNESS	NETSPEAK
NEOPAGAN	NEPHEWS	NERITE	NESS	NETSPEAKS
NEOPAGANS	NEPHOGRAM	NERITES	NESSES	NETSUKE
NEOPHILE	NEPHOLOGY	NERITIC	NEST	NETSUKES
NEOPHILES	NEPHRALGY	NERK	NESTABLE	NETSURF
NEOPHILIA	NEPHRIC	NERKA	NESTED	NETSURFED
NEOPHOBE	NEPHRIDIA	NERKAS	NESTER	NETSURFER
NEOPHOBES	NEPHRISM	NERKS	NESTERS	NETSURFS
NEOPHOBIA	NEPHRISMS	NEROL	NESTFUL	NETT
NEOPHOBIC	NEPHRITE	NEROLI	NESTFULS	NETTABLE
NEOPHYTE	NEPHRITES	NEROLIS	NESTING	NETTED
NEOPHYTES	NEPHRITIC	NEROLS	NESTINGS	NETTER
NEOPHYTIC	NEPHRITIS	NERTS	NESTLE	NETTERS
NEOPILINA	NEPHROID	NERTZ	NESTLED	NETTIE
NEOPLASIA	NEPHRON	NERVAL	NESTLER	NETTIER
NEOPLASM	NEPHRONS	NERVATE	NESTLERS	NETTIES
NEOPLASMS	NEPHROSES	NERVATION	NESTLES	NETTIEST
NEOPLASTY	NEPHROSIS	NERVATURE	NESTLIKE	NETTING
NEOPRENE	NEPHROTIC	NERVE	NESTLING	NETTINGS

NETTLE	NEUROMAST	NEVOID	NEWSFEED	NGAIO
NETTLED	NEUROMATA	NEVUS	NEWSFEEDS	NGAIOS
NETTLER	NEURON	NEW	NEWSFLASH	NGANA
NETTLERS	NEURONAL	NEWB	NEWSGIRL	NGANAS
NETTLES	NEURONE	NEWBIE	NEWSGIRLS	NGARARA
NETTLIER	NEURONES	NEWBIES	NEWSGROUP	NGARARAS
NETTLIEST	NEURONIC	NEWBORN	NEWSHAWK	NGATI
NETTLING	NEURONS	NEWBORNS	NEWSHAWKS	NGATIS
NETTLY	NEUROPATH	NEWBS	NEWSHOUND	NGOMA
NETTS	NEUROPIL	NEWCOME	NEWSIE	NGOMAS
NETTY	NEUROPILS	NEWCOMER	NEWSIER	NGRAM
NETWORK	NEUROSAL	NEWCOMERS	NEWSIES	NGRAMS
NETWORKED	NEUROSES	NEWED	NEWSIEST	NGULTRUM
NETWORKER	NEUROSIS	NEWEL	NEWSINESS	NGULTRUMS
NETWORKS	NEUROTIC	NEWELL	NEWSING	NGWEE
NEUK	NEUROTICS	NEWELLED	NEWSLESS	NGWEES
NEUKS	NEUROTOMY	NEWELLS	NEWSMAKER	NHANDU
NEUM	NEURULA	NEWELS	NEWSMAN	NHANDUS
NEUMATIC	NEURULAE	NEWER	NEWSMEN	NIACIN
NEUME	NEURULAR	NEWEST	NEWSPAPER	NIACINS
NEUMES	NEURULAS	NEWFANGLE	NEWSPEAK	NIAGARA
NEUMIC	NEUSTIC	NEWFOUND	NEWSPEAKS	NIAGARAS
NEUMS	NEUSTICS	NEWIE	NEWSPRINT	NIAISERIE
NEURAL	NEUSTON	NEWIES	NEWSREEL	NIALAMIDE
NEURALGIA	NEUSTONIC	NEWING	NEWSREELS	NIB
NEURALGIC	NEUSTONS	NEWISH	NEWSROOM	NIBBED
NEURALLY	NEUTER	NEWISHLY	NEWSROOMS	NIBBING
NEURATION	NEUTERED	NEWLY	NEWSSHEET	NIBBLE
NEURAXON	NEUTERING	NEWLYWED	NEWSSTAND	NIBBLED
NEURAXONS	NEUTERS	NEWLYWEDS	NEWSTRADE	NIBBLER
NEURILITY	NEUTRAL	NEWMARKET	NEWSWIRE	NIBBLERS
NEURINE	NEUTRALLY	NEWMOWN	NEWSWIRES	NIBBLES
NEURINES	NEUTRALS	NEWNESS	NEWSWOMAN	NIBBLIES
NEURISM	NEUTRETTO	NEWNESSES	NEWSWOMEN	NIBBLING
NEURISMS	NEUTRINO	NEWS	NEWSY	NIBBLINGS
NEURITE	NEUTRINOS	NEWSAGENT	NEWT	NIBBLY
NEURITES	NEUTRON	NEWSBEAT	NEWTON	NIBLET
NEURITIC	NEUTRONIC	NEWSBEATS	NEWTONS	NIBLETS
NEURITICS	NEUTRONS	NEWSBOY	NEWTS	NIBLICK
NEURITIS	NEVE	NEWSBOYS	NEWWAVER	NIBLICKS
NEUROCHIP	NEVEL	NEWSBREAK	NEWWAVERS	NIBLIKE
NEUROCOEL	NEVELLED	NEWSCAST	NEXT	NIBLING
NEUROGLIA	NEVELLING	NEWSCASTS	NEXTDOOR	NIBLINGS
NEUROGRAM	NEVELS	NEWSCLIP	NEXTLY	NIBS
NEUROID	NEVER	NEWSCLIPS	NEXTNESS	NICAD
NEUROIDS	NEVERMIND	NEWSDESK	NEXTS	NICADS
NEUROLOGY	NEVERMORE	NEWSDESKS	NEXUS	NICCOLITE
NEUROMA	NEVES	NEWSED	NEXUSES	NICE
NEUROMAS	NEVI	NEWSES	NGAI	NICEISH

NICELY	NICKPOINT	NIDIFIES	NIFTILY	NIGHTMARY
NICENESS	NICKS	NIDIFY	NIFTINESS	NIGHTS
NICER	NICKSTICK	NIDIFYING	NIFTY	NIGHTSIDE
NICEST	NICKUM	NIDING	NIGELLA	NIGHTSPOT
NICETIES	NICKUMS	NIDINGS	NIGELLAS	NIGHTTIDE
NICETY	NICOISE	NIDOR	NIGGARD	NIGHTTIME
NICHE	NICOL	NIDOROUS	NIGGARDED	NIGHTWARD
NICHED	NICOLS	NIDORS	NIGGARDLY	NIGHTWEAR
NICHER	NICOMPOOP	NIDS	NIGGARDS	NIGHTY
NICHERED	NICOTIAN	NIDUS	NIGGLE	NIGIRI
NICHERING	NICOTIANA	NIDUSES	NIGGLED	NIGIRIS
NICHERS	NICOTIANS	NIE	NIGGLER	NIGRICANT
NICHES	NICOTIN	NIECE	NIGGLERS	NIGRIFIED
NICHING	NICOTINE	NIECES	NIGGLES	NIGRIFIES
NICHROME	NICOTINED	NIED	NIGGLIER	NIGRIFY
NICHROMES	NICOTINES	NIEF	NIGGLIEST	NIGRITUDE
NICHT	NICOTINIC	NIEFS	NIGGLING	NIGROSIN
NICHTS	NICOTINS	NIELLATED	NIGGLINGS	NIGROSINE
NICISH	NICTATE	NIELLI	NIGGLY	NIGROSINS
NICK	NICTATED	NIELLIST	NIGH	NIHIL
NICKAR	NICTATES	NIELLISTS	NIGHED	NIHILISM
NICKARS	NICTATING	NIELLO	NIGHER	NIHILISMS
NICKED	NICTATION	NIELLOED	NIGHEST	NIHILIST
NICKEL	NICTITANT	NIELLOING	NIGHING	NIHILISTS
NICKELED	NICTITATE	NIELLOS	NIGHLY	NIHILITY
NICKELIC	NID	NIENTE	NIGHNESS	NIHILS
NICKELINE	NIDAL	NIES	NIGHS	NIHONGA
NICKELING	NIDAMENTA	NIEVE	NIGHT	NIHONGAS
NICKELISE	NIDATE	NIEVEFUL	NIGHTBIRD	NIHONIUM
NICKELIZE	NIDATED	NIEVEFULS	NIGHTCAP	NIHONIUMS
NICKELLED	NIDATES	NIEVES	NIGHTCAPS	NIKAB
NICKELOUS	NIDATING	NIFE	NIGHTCLUB	NIKABS
NICKELS	NIDATION	NIFES	NIGHTED	NIKAH
NICKER	NIDATIONS	NIFF	NIGHTFALL	NIKAHS
NICKERED	NIDDERING	NIFFED	NIGHTFIRE	NIKAU
NICKERING	NIDDICK	NIFFER	NIGHTGEAR	NIKAUS
NICKERNUT	NIDDICKS	NIFFERED	NIGHTGLOW	NIL
NICKERS	NIDE	NIFFERING	NIGHTGOWN	NILGAI
NICKING	NIDED	NIFFERS	NIGHTHAWK	NILGAIS
NICKLE	NIDERING	NIFFIER	NIGHTIE	NILGAU
NICKLED	NIDERINGS	NIFFIEST	NIGHTIES	NILGAUS
NICKLES	NIDERLING	NIFFING	NIGHTJAR	NILGHAI
NICKLING	NIDES	NIFFNAFF	NIGHTJARS	NILGHAIS
NICKNACK	NIDGET	NIFFNAFFS	NIGHTLESS	NILGHAU
NICKNACKS	NIDGETED	NIFFS	NIGHTLIFE	NILGHAUS
NICKNAME	NIDGETING	NIFFY	NIGHTLIKE	NILL
NICKNAMED	NIDGETS	NIFTIER	NIGHTLONG	NILLED
NICKNAMER	NIDI	NIFTIES	NIGHTLY	NILLING
NICKNAMES	NIDIFIED	NIFTIEST	NIGHTMARE	NILLS

NILPOTENT	NINETEENS	NIPTER	NITINOL	NITROXYL
NILS	NINETIES	NIPTERS	NITINOLS	NITROXYLS
NIM	NINETIETH	NIQAAB	NITON	NITRY
NIMB	NINETY	NIQAABS	NITONS	NITRYL
NIMBED	NINHYDRIN	NIQAB	NITPICK	NITRYLS
NIMBI	NINJA	NIQABS	NITPICKED	NITS
NIMBLE	NINJAS	NIRAMIAI	NITPICKER	NITTIER
NIMBLER	NINJITSU	NIRAMIAIS	NITPICKS	NITTIEST
NIMBLESSE	NINJITSUS	NIRL	NITPICKY	NITTY
NIMBLEST	NINJUTSU	NIRLED	NITRAMINE	NITWIT
NIMBLEWIT	NINJUTSUS	NIRLIE	NITRATE	NITWITS
NIMBLY	NINNIES	NIRLIER	NITRATED	NITWITTED
NIMBS	NINNY	NIRLIEST	NITRATES	NIVAL
NIMBUS	NINNYISH	NIRLING	NITRATINE	NIVATION
NIMBUSED	NINON	NIRLIT	NITRATING	NIVATIONS
NIMBUSES	NINONS	NIRLS	NITRATION	NIVEOUS
NIMBYISM	NINTH	NIRLY	NITRATOR	NIX
NIMBYISMS	NINTHLY	NIRVANA	NITRATORS	NIXE
NIMBYNESS	NINTHS	NIRVANAS	NITRE	NIXED
NIMIETIES	NIOBATE	NIRVANIC	NITREOUS	NIXER
NIMIETY	NIOBATES	NIS	NITRES	NIXERS
NIMIOUS	NIOBIC	NISBERRY	NITRIC	NIXES
NIMMED	NIOBITE	NISEI	NITRID	NIXIE
NIMMER	NIOBITES	NISEIS	NITRIDE	NIXIES
NIMMERS	NIOBIUM	NISGUL	NITRIDED	NIXING
NIMMING	NIOBIUMS	NISGULS	NITRIDES	NIXY
NIMONIC	NIOBOUS	NISH	NITRIDING	NIZAM
NIMPS	NIP	NISHES	NITRIDS	NIZAMATE
NIMROD	NIPA	NISI	NITRIFIED	NIZAMATES
NIMRODS	NIPAS	NISIN	NITRIFIER	NIZAMS
NIMS	NIPCHEESE	NISINS	NITRIFIES	NKOSI
NINCOM	NIPPED	NISSE	NITRIFY	NKOSIS
NINCOMS	NIPPER	NISSES	NITRIL	NO
NINCUM	NIPPERED	NISUS	NITRILE	NOAH
NINCUMS	NIPPERING	NIT	NITRILES	NOAHS
NINE	NIPPERKIN	NITE	NITRILS	NOB
NINEBARK	NIPPERS	NITER	NITRITE	NOBBIER
NINEBARKS	NIPPIER	NITERIE	NITRITES	NOBBIEST
NINEFOLD	NIPPIEST	NITERIES	NITRO	NOBBILY
NINEHOLES	NIPPILY	NITERS	NITROGEN	NOBBINESS
NINEPENCE	NIPPINESS	NITERY	NITROGENS	NOBBLE
NINEPENNY	NIPPING	NITES	NITROLIC	NOBBLED
NINEPIN	NIPPINGLY	NITHER	NITROS	NOBBLER
NINEPINS	NIPPLE	NITHERED	NITROSO	NOBBLERS
NINER	NIPPLED	NITHERING	NITROSYL	NOBBLES
NINERS	NIPPLES	NITHERS	NITROSYLS	NOBBLING
NINES	NIPPLING	NITHING	NITROUS	NOBBUT
NINESCORE	NIPPY	NITHINGS	NITROX	NOBBY
NINETEEN	NIPS	NITID	NITROXES	NOBELIUM

NOBELIUMS	NOCTURN	NODUS	NOISILY	NOMINATED
NOBILESSE	NOCTURNAL	NOEL	NOISINESS	NOMINATES
NOBILIARY	NOCTURNE	NOELS	NOISING	NOMINATOR
NOBILITY	NOCTURNES	NOES	NOISOME	NOMINEE
NOBLE	NOCTURNS	NOESES	NOISOMELY	NOMINEES
NOBLEMAN	NOCUOUS	NOESIS	NOISY	NOMISM
NOBLEMEN	NOCUOUSLY	NOESISES	NOLE	NOMISMS
NOBLENESS	NOD	NOETIC	NOLES	NOMISTIC
NOBLER	NODAL	NOG	NOLITION	NOMOCRACY
NOBLES	NODALISE	NOGAKU	NOLITIONS	NOMOGENY
NOBLESSE	NODALISED	NOGG	NOLL	NOMOGRAM
NOBLESSES	NODALISES	NOGGED	NOLLS	NOMOGRAMS
NOBLEST	NODALITY	NOGGIN	NOLO	NOMOGRAPH
NOBLY	NODALIZE	NOGGING	NOLOS	NOMOI
NOBODIES	NODALIZED	NOGGINGS	NOM	NOMOLOGIC
NOBODY	NODALIZES	NOGGINS	NOMA	NOMOLOGY
NOBS	NODALLY	NOGGS	NOMAD	NOMOS
NOCAKE	NODATED	NOGOODNIK	NOMADE	NOMOTHETE
NOCAKES	NODATION	NOGS	NOMADES	NOMS
NOCEBO	NODATIONS	NOH	NOMADIC	NON
NOCEBOS	NODDED	NOHOW	NOMADIES	NONA
NOCENT	NODDER	NOHOWISH	NOMADISE	NONACID
NOCENTLY	NODDERS	NOICE	NOMADISED	NONACIDIC
NOCENTS	NODDIER	NOIL	NOMADISES	NONACIDS
NOCHEL	NODDIES	NOILIER	NOMADISM	NONACTING
NOCHELED	NODDIEST	NOILIES	NOMADISMS	NONACTION
NOCHELING	NODDING	NOILIEST	NOMADIZE	NONACTIVE
NOCHELLED	NODDINGLY	NOILS	NOMADIZED	NONACTOR
NOCHELS	NODDINGS	NOILY	NOMADIZES	NONACTORS
NOCK	NODDLE	NOINT	NOMADS	NONADDICT
NOCKED	NODDLED	NOINTED	NOMADY	NONADULT
NOCKET	NODDLES	NOINTER	NOMARCH	NONADULTS
NOCKETS	NODDLING	NOINTERS	NOMARCHS	NONAGE
NOCKING	NODDY	NOINTING	NOMARCHY	NONAGED
NOCKS	NODE	NOINTS	NOMAS	NONAGES
NOCTILIO	NODES	NOIR	NOMBLES	NONAGON
NOCTILIOS	NODI	NOIRISH	NOMBRIL	NONAGONAL
NOCTILUCA	NODICAL	NOIRS	NOMBRILS	NONAGONS
NOCTUA	NODOSE	NOISE	NOME	NONANE
NOCTUARY	NODOSITY	NOISED	NOMEN	NONANES
NOCTUAS	NODOUS	NOISEFUL	NOMENS	NONANIMAL
NOCTUID	NODS	NOISELESS	NOMES	NONANOIC
NOCTUIDS	NODULAR	NOISENIK	NOMIC	NONANSWER
NOCTULE	NODULATED	NOISENIKS	NOMINA	NONARABLE
NOCTULES	NODULE	NOISES	NOMINABLE	NONARIES
NOCTUOID	NODULED	NOISETTE	NOMINAL	NONART
NOCTUOIDS	NODULES	NOISETTES	NOMINALLY	NONARTIST
NOCTURIA	NODULOSE	NOISIER	NOMINALS	NONARTS
NOCTURIAS	NODULOUS	NOISIEST	NOMINATE	NONARY

N

NONAS	NONCRIME	NONEXTANT	NONHARDY	NONLIVING
NONATOMIC	NONCRIMES	NONFACT	NONHEME	NONLOCAL
NONAUTHOR	NONCRISES	NONFACTOR	NONHERO	NONLOCALS
NONAVIAN	NONCRISIS	NONFACTS	NONHEROES	NONLOVING
NONBANK	NONCYCLIC	NONFADING	NONHEROIC	NONLOYAL
NONBANKS	NONDAIRY	NONFAMILY	NONHOME	NONLYRIC
NONBASIC	NONDANCE	NONFAN	NONHUMAN	NONMAJOR
NONBEING	NONDANCER	NONFANS	NONHUMANS	NONMAJORS
NONBEINGS	NONDANCES	NONFARM	NONHUNTER	NONMAN
NONBELIEF	NONDEALER	NONFARMER	NONI	NONMANUAL
NONBINARY	NONDEGREE	NONFAT	NONIDEAL	NONMARKET
NONBITING	NONDEMAND	NONFATAL	NONILLION	NONMATURE
NONBLACK	NONDESERT	NONFATTY	NONIMAGE	NONMEAT
NONBLACKS	NONDOCTOR	NONFEUDAL	NONIMAGES	NONMEATS
NONBODIES	NONDOLLAR	NONFILIAL	NONIMMUNE	NONMEMBER
NONBODY	NONDRIP	NONFINAL	NONIMPACT	NONMEN
NONBONDED	NONDRIVER	NONFINITE	NONINERT	NONMENTAL
NONBOOK	NONDRUG	NONFISCAL	NONINJURY	NONMETAL
NONBOOKS	NONDRYING	NONFLUID	NONINSECT	NONMETALS
NONBRAND	NONE	NONFLUIDS	NONIONIC	NONMETRIC
NONBUYING	NONEDIBLE	NONFLYING	NONIRON	NONMETRO
NONCAKING	NONEGO	NONFOCAL	NONIS	NONMOBILE
NONCAMPUS	NONEGOS	NONFOOD	NONISSUE	NONMODAL
NONCAREER	NONELECT	NONFOODS	NONISSUES	NONMODERN
NONCASH	NONELECTS	NONFORMAL	NONJOINER	NONMONEY
NONCASUAL	NONELITE	NONFOSSIL	NONJURIES	NONMORAL
NONCAUSAL	NONEMPTY	NONFROZEN	NONJURING	NONMORTAL
NONCE	NONENDING	NONFUEL	NONJUROR	NONMOTILE
NONCEREAL	NONENERGY	NONFUELS	NONJURORS	NONMOVING
NONCES	NONENTITY	NONFUNDED	NONJURY	NONMUSIC
NONCHURCH	NONENTRY	NONG	NONKIN	NONMUSICS
NONCLASS	NONEQUAL	NONGAME	NONKINS	NONMUTANT
NONCLING	NONEQUALS	NONGAY	NONKOSHER	NONMUTUAL
NONCODING	NONEROTIC	NONGAYS	NONLABOR	NONNASAL
NONCOITAL	NONES	NONGHETTO	NONLABOUR	NONNATIVE
NONCOKING	NONESUCH	NONGLARE	NONLAWYER	NONNAVAL
NONCOLA	NONET	NONGLARES	NONLEADED	NONNEURAL
NONCOLAS	NONETHNIC	NONGLAZED	NONLEAFY	NONNEWS
NONCOLOR	NONETS	NONGLOSSY	NONLEAGUE	NONNIES
NONCOLORS	NONETTE	NONGOLFER	NONLEGAL	NONNOBLE
NONCOLOUR	NONETTES	NONGRADED	NONLEGUME	NONNORMAL
NONCOM	NONETTI	NONGREASY	NONLETHAL	NONNOVEL
NONCOMBAT	NONETTO	NONGREEN	NONLEVEL	NONNOVELS
NONCOMS	NONETTOS	NONGROWTH	NONLIABLE	NONNY
NONCONCUR	NONEVENT	NONGS	NONLIFE	NONOBESE
NONCORE	NONEVENTS	NONGUEST	NONLINEAL	NONOHMIC
NONCOUNT	NONEXEMPT	NONGUESTS	NONLINEAR	NONOILY
NONCOUNTY	NONEXOTIC	NONGUILT	NONLIQUID	NONORAL
NONCREDIT	NONEXPERT	NONGUILTS	NONLIVES	NONORALLY

NONOWNER	NONRIVAL	NONSUGAR	NONVIRILE	NOOKIER
NONOWNERS	NONRIVALS	NONSUGARS	NONVISUAL	NOOKIES
NONPAGAN	NONROYAL	NONSUIT	NONVITAL	NOOKIEST
NONPAGANS	NONROYALS	NONSUITED	NONVOCAL	NOOKLIKE
NONPAID	NONRUBBER	NONSUITS	NONVOCALS	NOOKS
NONPAPAL	NONRULING	NONSYSTEM	NONVOTER	NOOKY
NONPAR	NONRUN	NONTALKER	NONVOTERS	NOOLOGIES
NONPAREIL	NONRUNNER	NONTARGET	NONVOTING	NOOLOGY
NONPARENT	NONRURAL	NONTARIFF	NONWAGE	NOOMETRY
NONPARITY	NONSACRED	NONTAX	NONWAR	NOON
NONPAROUS	NONSALINE	NONTAXES	NONWARS	NOONDAY
NONPARTY	NONSCHOOL	NONTHEISM	NONWHITE	NOONDAYS
NONPAST	NONSECRET	NONTHEIST	NONWHITES	NOONED
NONPASTS	NONSECURE	NONTIDAL	NONWINGED	NOONER
NONPAYING	NONSELF	NONTITLE	NONWOODY	NOONERS
NONPEAK	NONSELVES	NONTONAL	NONWOOL	NOONING
NONPEAKS	NONSENSE	NONTONIC	NONWORD	NOONINGS
NONPERSON	NONSENSES	NONTOXIC	NONWORDS	NOONS
NONPLANAR	NONSERIAL	NONTOXICS	NONWORK	NOONTIDE
NONPLAY	NONSEXIST	NONTRAGIC	NONWORKER	NOONTIDES
NONPLAYER	NONSEXUAL	NONTRIBAL	NONWORKS	NOONTIME
NONPLAYS	NONSHRINK	NONTRUMP	NONWOVEN	NOONTIMES
NONPLIANT	NONSIGNER	NONTRUTH	NONWOVENS	NOOP
NONPLUS	NONSKATER	NONTRUTHS	NONWRITER	NOOPS
NONPLUSED	NONSKED	NONUNION	NONYL	NOOSE
NONPLUSES	NONSKEDS	NONUNIONS	NONYLS	NOOSED
NONPOETIC	NONSKID	NONUNIQUE	NONZERO	NOOSELIKE
NONPOINT	NONSKIER	NONUPLE	NOO	NOOSER
NONPOLAR	NONSKIERS	NONUPLES	NOOB	NOOSERS
NONPOLICE	NONSLIP	NONUPLET	NOOBIE	NOOSES
NONPOOR	NONSMOKER	NONUPLETS	NOOBIES	NOOSING
NONPOORS	NONSOCIAL	NONURBAN	NOOBS	NOOSPHERE
NONPOROUS	NONSOLAR	NONURGENT	NOOCH	NOOTROPIC
NONPOSTAL	NONSOLID	NONUSABLE	NOOCHES	NOPAL
NONPRINT	NONSOLIDS	NONUSE	NOODGE	NOPALES
NONPROFIT	NONSPEECH	NONUSER	NOODGED	NOPALITO
NONPROS	NONSTAPLE	NONUSERS	NOODGES	NOPALITOS
NONPROVEN	NONSTATE	NONUSES	NOODGING	NOPALS
NONPUBLIC	NONSTATIC	NONUSING	NOODLE	NOPE
NONQUOTA	NONSTEADY	NONVACANT	NOODLED	NOPLACE
NONRACIAL	NONSTICK	NONVALID	NOODLEDOM	NOR
NONRACISM	NONSTICKY	NONVECTOR	NOODLES	NORDIC
NONRANDOM	NONSTOP	NONVENOUS	NOODLING	NORDICITY
NONRATED	NONSTOPS	NONVERBAL	NOODLINGS	NORI
NONREADER	NONSTORY	NONVESTED	NOOGIE	NORIA
NONRETURN	NONSTYLE	NONVIABLE	NOOGIES	NORIAS
NONRHOTIC	NONSTYLES	NONVIEWER	NOOIT	NORIMON
NONRIGID	NONSUCH	NONVIRAL	NOOK	NORIMONS
NONRIOTER	NONSUCHES	NONVIRGIN	NOOKIE	NORIS

NORITE	NORTHLAND	NOSING	NOTATORS	NOTIFYING
NORITES	NORTHMOST	NOSINGS	NOTCH	NOTING
NORITIC	NORTHS	NOSODE	NOTCHBACK	NOTION
NORK	NORTHWARD	NOSODES	NOTCHED	NOTIONAL
NORKS	NORTHWEST	NOSOLOGIC	NOTCHEL	NOTIONIST
NORLAND	NORWARD	NOSOLOGY	NOTCHELED	NOTIONS
NORLANDS	NORWARDS	NOSTALGIA	NOTCHELS	NOTITIA
NORM	NOS	NOSTALGIC	NOTCHER	NOTITIAE
NORMA	NOSE	NOSTOC	NOTCHERS	NOTITIAS
NORMAL	NOSEAN	NOSTOCS	NOTCHES	NOTOCHORD
NORMALCY	NOSEANS	NOSTOI	NOTCHIER	NOTORIETY
NORMALISE	NOSEBAG	NOSTOLOGY	NOTCHIEST	NOTORIOUS
NORMALITY	NOSEBAGS	NOSTOS	NOTCHING	NOTORNIS
NORMALIZE	NOSEBAND	NOSTRIL	NOTCHINGS	NOTOUR
NORMALLY	NOSEBANDS	NOSTRILS	NOTCHY	NOTT
NORMALS	NOSEBLEED	NOSTRO	NOTE	NOTTURNI
NORMAN	NOSED	NOSTRUM	NOTEBANDI	NOTTURNO
NORMANDE	NOSEDIVE	NOSTRUMS	NOTEBOOK	NOTUM
NORMANDES	NOSEDIVED	NOSY	NOTEBOOKS	NOUGAT
NORMANS	NOSEDIVES	NOT	NOTECARD	NOUGATINE
NORMAS	NOSEDOVE	NOTA	NOTECARDS	NOUGATS
NORMATIVE	NOSEGAY	NOTABILIA	NOTECASE	NOUGHT
NORMCORE	NOSEGAYS	NOTABLE	NOTECASES	NOUGHTIES
NORMCORES	NOSEGUARD	NOTABLES	NOTED	NOUGHTS
NORMED	NOSELESS	NOTABLY	NOTEDLY	NOUL
NORMIE	NOSELIKE	NOTAEUM	NOTEDNESS	NOULD
NORMIES	NOSELITE	NOTAEUMS	NOTELESS	NOULDE
NORMLESS	NOSELITES	NOTAIRE	NOTELET	NOULE
NORMS	NOSEPIECE	NOTAIRES	NOTELETS	NOULES
NOROVIRUS	NOSER	NOTAL	NOTEPAD	NOULS
NORSEL	NOSERS	NOTANDA	NOTEPADS	NOUMENA
NORSELLED	NOSES	NOTANDUM	NOTEPAPER	NOUMENAL
NORSELLER	NOSEWHEEL	NOTAPHILY	NOTER	NOUMENON
NORSELS	NOSEY	NOTARIAL	NOTERS	NOUN
NORTENA	NOSEYS	NOTARIES	NOTES	NOUNAL
NORTENAS	NOSH	NOTARISE	NOTHER	NOUNALLY
NORTENO	NOSHED	NOTARISED	NOTHING	NOUNIER
NORTENOS	NOSHER	NOTARISES	NOTHINGS	NOUNIEST
NORTH	NOSHERIE	NOTARIZE	NOTICE	NOUNLESS
NORTHEAST	NOSHERIES	NOTARIZED	NOTICED	NOUNS
NORTHED	NOSHERS	NOTARIZES	NOTICER	NOUNY
NORTHER	NOSHERY	NOTARY	NOTICERS	NOUP
NORTHERED	NOSHES	NOTATE	NOTICES	NOUPS
NORTHERLY	NOSHING	NOTATED	NOTICING	NOURICE
NORTHERN	NOSIER	NOTATES	NOTIFIED	NOURICES
NORTHERNS	NOSIES	NOTATING	NOTIFIER	NOURISH
NORTHERS	NOSIEST	NOTATION	NOTIFIERS	NOURISHED
NORTHING	NOSILY	NOTATIONS	NOTIFIES	NOURISHER
NORTHINGS	NOSINESS	NOTATOR	NOTIFY	NOURISHES

NOURITURE	NOVELLA	NOWTIER	NUBBLIER	NUCLEUS
NOURSLE	NOVELLAE	NOWTIEST	NUBBLIEST	NUCLEUSES
NOURSLED	NOVELLAS	NOWTS	NUBBLING	NUCLIDE
NOURSLES	NOVELLE	NOWTY	NUBBLY	NUCLIDES
NOURSLING	NOVELLY	NOWY	NUBBY	NUCLIDIC
NOUS	NOVELS	NOX	NUBECULA	NUCULE
NOUSELL	NOVELTIES	NOXAL	NUBECULAE	NUCULES
NOUSELLED	NOVELTY	NOXES	NUBIA	NUDATION
NOUSELLS	NOVEMBER	NOXIOUS	NUBIAS	NUDATIONS
NOUSES	NOVEMBERS	NOXIOUSLY	NUBIFORM	NUDDIES
NOUSLE	NOVENA	NOY	NUBILE	NUDDY
NOUSLED	NOVENAE	NOYADE	NUBILITY	NUDE
NOUSLES	NOVENARY	NOYADES	NUBILOSE	NUDELY
NOUSLING	NOVENAS	NOYANCE	NUBILOUS	NUDENESS
NOUT	NOVENNIAL	NOYANCES	NUBS	NUDER
NOUVEAU	NOVERCAL	NOYAU	NUBUCK	NUDES
NOUVEAUX	NOVERINT	NOYAUS	NUBUCKS	NUDEST
NOUVELLE	NOVERINTS	NOYAUX	NUCELLAR	NUDGE
NOUVELLES	NOVICE	NOYED	NUCELLI	NUDGED
NOVA	NOVICES	NOYES	NUCELLUS	NUDGER
NOVAE	NOVICHOK	NOYESES	NUCHA	NUDGERS
NOVALIA	NOVICHOKS	NOYING	NUCHAE	NUDGES
NOVALIKE	NOVICIATE	NOYOUS	NUCHAL	NUDGING
NOVAS	NOVITIATE	NOYS	NUCHALS	NUDICAUL
NOVATE	NOVITIES	NOYSOME	NUCLEAL	NUDIE
NOVATED	NOVITY	NOZZER	NUCLEAR	NUDIES
NOVATES	NOVOCAINE	NOZZERS	NUCLEASE	NUDISM
NOVATING	NOVODAMUS	NOZZLE	NUCLEASES	NUDISMS
NOVATION	NOVUM	NOZZLES	NUCLEATE	NUDIST
NOVATIONS	NOVUMS	NTH	NUCLEATED	NUDISTS
NOVEL	NOW	NU	NUCLEATES	NUDITIES
NOVELDOM	NOWADAYS	NUANCE	NUCLEATOR	NUDITY
NOVELDOMS	NOWAY	NUANCED	NUCLEI	NUDNICK
NOVELESE	NOWAYS	NUANCES	NUCLEIC	NUDNICKS
NOVELESES	NOWCAST	NUANCING	NUCLEIDE	NUDNIK
NOVELETTE	NOWCASTS	NUB	NUCLEIDES	NUDNIKS
NOVELISE	NOWED	NUBBED	NUCLEIN	NUDZH
NOVELISED	NOWHENCE	NUBBER	NUCLEINIC	NUDZHED
NOVELISER	NOWHERE	NUBBERS	NUCLEINS	NUDZHES
NOVELISES	NOWHERES	NUBBIER	NUCLEOID	NUDZHING
NOVELISH	NOWHITHER	NUBBIEST	NUCLEOIDS	NUFF
NOVELISM	NOWISE	NUBBIN	NUCLEOLAR	NUFFIN
NOVELISMS	NOWL	NUBBINESS	NUCLEOLE	NUFFINS
NOVELIST	NOWLS	NUBBING	NUCLEOLES	NUFFS
NOVELISTS	NOWN	NUBBINGS	NUCLEOLI	NUG
NOVELIZE	NOWNESS	NUBBINS	NUCLEOLUS	NUGAE
NOVELIZED	NOWNESSES	NUBBLE	NUCLEON	NUGATORY
NOVELIZER	NOWS	NUBBLED	NUCLEONIC	NUGGAR
NOVELIZES	NOWT	NUBBLES	NUCLEONS	NUGGARS

N

NUGGET	NUMBLES	NUNATAKS	NURLED	NUTCASES
NUGGETED	NUMBLY	NUNCHAKU	NURLING	NUTGALL
NUGGETIER	NUMBNESS	NUNCHAKUS	NURLS	NUTGALLS
NUGGETING	NUMBNUT	NUNCHEON	NURR	NUTGRASS
NUGGETS	NUMBNUTS	NUNCHEONS	NURRS	NUTHATCH
NUGGETTED	NUMBS	NUNCHUCK	NURS	NUTHIN
NUGGETY	NUMBSKULL	NUNCHUCKS	NURSE	NUTHOUSE
NUGS	NUMCHUCK	NUNCHUK	NURSED	NUTHOUSES
NUISANCE	NUMCHUCKS	NUNCHUKS	NURSELIKE	NUTJOB
NUISANCER	NUMDAH	NUNCIO	NURSELING	NUTJOBBER
NUISANCES	NUMDAHS	NUNCIOS	NURSEMAID	NUTJOBS
NUKE	NUMEN	NUNCLE	NURSER	NUTLET
NUKED	NUMERABLE	NUNCLES	NURSERIES	NUTLETS
NUKES	NUMERABLY	NUNCUPATE	NURSERS	NUTLIKE
NUKING	NUMERACY	NUNDINAL	NURSERY	NUTLOAF
NULL	NUMERAIRE	NUNDINALS	NURSES	NUTLOAVES
NULLA	NUMERAL	NUNDINE	NURSING	NUTMEAL
NULLAH	NUMERALLY	NUNDINES	NURSINGS	NUTMEALS
NULLAHS	NUMERALS	NUNHOOD	NURSLE	NUTMEAT
NULLAS	NUMERARY	NUNHOODS	NURSLED	NUTMEATS
NULLED	NUMERATE	NUNLIKE	NURSLES	NUTMEG
NULLIFIED	NUMERATED	NUNNATION	NURSLING	NUTMEGGED
NULLIFIER	NUMERATES	NUNNERIES	NURSLINGS	NUTMEGGY
NULLIFIES	NUMERATOR	NUNNERY	NURTURAL	NUTMEGS
NULLIFY	NUMERIC	NUNNISH	NURTURANT	NUTPECKER
NULLING	NUMERICAL	NUNNY	NURTURE	NUTPICK
NULLINGS	NUMERICS	NUNS	NURTURED	NUTPICKS
NULLIPARA	NUMEROUS	NUNSHIP	NURTURER	NUTRIA
NULLIPORE	NUMINA	NUNSHIPS	NURTURERS	NUTRIAS
NULLITIES	NUMINOUS	NUPTIAL	NURTURES	NUTRIENT
NULLITY	NUMMARY	NUPTIALLY	NURTURING	NUTRIENTS
NULLNESS	NUMMIER	NUPTIALS	NUS	NUTRIMENT
NULLS	NUMMIEST	NUR	NUT	NUTRITION
NUMB	NUMMULAR	NURAGHE	NUTANT	NUTRITIVE
NUMBAT	NUMMULARY	NURAGHI	NUTARIAN	NUTS
NUMBATS	NUMMULINE	NURAGHIC	NUTARIANS	NUTSACK
NUMBED	NUMMULITE	NURD	NUTATE	NUTSACKS
NUMBER	NUMMY	NURDIER	NUTATED	NUTSEDGE
NUMBERED	NUMNAH	NURDIEST	NUTATES	NUTSEDGES
NUMBERER	NUMNAHS	NURDISH	NUTATING	NUTSHELL
NUMBERERS	NUMPKIN	NURDLE	NUTATION	NUTSHELLS
NUMBERING	NUMPKINS	NURDLED	NUTATIONS	NUTSIER
NUMBERS	NUMPTIES	NURDLES	NUTBALL	NUTSIEST
NUMBEST	NUMPTY	NURDLING	NUTBALLS	NUTSO
NUMBFISH	NUMSKULL	NURDS	NUTBAR	NUTSOS
NUMBHEAD	NUMSKULLS	NURDY	NUTBARS	NUTSY
NUMBHEADS	NUN	NURHAG	NUTBROWN	NUTTED
NUMBING	NUNATAK	NURHAGS	NUTBUTTER	NUTTER
NUMBINGLY	NUNATAKER	NURL	NUTCASE	NUTTERIES

NUTTERS	NUZZLERS	NYASES	NYM	NYMPHICAL
NUTTERY	NUZZLES	NYBBLE	NYMPH	NYMPHING
NUTTIER	NUZZLING	NYBBLES	NYMPHA	NYMPHISH
NUTTIEST	NY	NYCTALOPE	NYMPHAE	NYMPHLIER
NUTTILY	NYAFF	NYCTALOPS	NYMPHAEA	NYMPHLIKE
NUTTINESS	NYAFFED	NYE	NYMPHAEAS	NYMPHLY
NUTTING	NYAFFING	NYED	NYMPHAEUM	NYMPHO
NUTTINGS	NYAFFS	NYES	NYMPHAL	NYMPHOS
NUTTY	NYAH	NYING	NYMPHALID	NYMPHS
NUTWOOD	NYALA	NYLGHAI	NYMPHEAN	NYS
NUTWOODS	NYALAS	NYLGHAIS	NYMPHED	NYSSA
NUZZER	NYANZA	NYLGHAU	NYMPHET	NYSSAS
NUZZERS	NYANZAS	NYLGHAUS	NYMPHETIC	NYSTAGMIC
NUZZLE	NYAOPE	NYLON	NYMPHETS	NYSTAGMUS
NUZZLED	NYAOPES	NYLONED	NYMPHETTE	NYSTATIN
NUZZLER	NYAS	NYLONS	NYMPHIC	NYSTATINS

N

O

OAF	OARSMAN	OBDURE	OBESER	OBJURGATE
OAFISH	OARSMEN	OBDURED	OBESEST	OBJURING
OAFISHLY	OARSWOMAN	OBDURES	OBESITIES	OBLAST
OAFS	OARSWOMEN	OBDURING	OBESITY	OBLASTI
OAK	OARWEED	OBE	OBESOGEN	OBLASTS
OAKED	OARWEEDS	OBEAH	OBESOGENS	OBLATE
OAKEN	OARY	OBEAHED	OBEY	OBLATELY
OAKENSHAW	OASES	OBEAHING	OBEYABLE	OBLATES
OAKER	OASIS	OBEAHISM	OBEYED	OBLATION
OAKERS	OAST	OBEAHISMS	OBEYER	OBLATIONS
OAKIER	OASTHOUSE	OBEAHS	OBEYERS	OBLATORY
OAKIES	OASTS	OBECHE	OBEYING	OBLIGABLE
OAKIEST	OAT	OBECHES	OBEYS	OBLIGANT
OAKINESS	OATCAKE	OBEDIENCE	OBFUSCATE	OBLIGANTS
OAKLEAF	OATCAKES	OBEDIENT	OBI	OBLIGATE
OAKLEAVES	OATEN	OBEISANCE	OBIA	OBLIGATED
OAKLIKE	OATER	OBEISANT	OBIAS	OBLIGATES
OAKLING	OATERS	OBEISM	OBIED	OBLIGATI
OAKLINGS	OATH	OBEISMS	OBIING	OBLIGATO
OAKMOSS	OATHABLE	OBELI	OBIISM	OBLIGATOR
OAKMOSSES	OATHS	OBELIA	OBIISMS	OBLIGATOS
OAKS	OATIER	OBELIAS	OBIIT	OBLIGE
OAKUM	OATIEST	OBELION	OBIS	OBLIGED
OAKUMS	OATLIKE	OBELISCAL	OBIT	OBLIGEE
OAKWOOD	OATMEAL	OBELISE	OBITAL	OBLIGEES
OAKWOODS	OATMEALS	OBELISED	OBITER	OBLIGER
OAKY	OATS	OBELISES	OBITS	OBLIGERS
OANSHAGH	OATY	OBELISING	OBITUAL	OBLIGES
OANSHAGHS	OAVES	OBELISK	OBITUARY	OBLIGING
OAR	OB	OBELISKS	OBJECT	OBLIGOR
OARAGE	OBA	OBELISM	OBJECTED	OBLIGORS
OARAGES	OBANG	OBELISMS	OBJECTIFY	OBLIQUE
OARED	OBANGS	OBELIZE	OBJECTING	OBLIQUED
OARFISH	OBAS	OBELIZED	OBJECTION	OBLIQUELY
OARFISHES	OBBLIGATI	OBELIZES	OBJECTIVE	OBLIQUER
OARIER	OBBLIGATO	OBELIZING	OBJECTOR	OBLIQUES
OARIEST	OBCONIC	OBELUS	OBJECTORS	OBLIQUEST
OARING	OBCONICAL	OBENTO	OBJECTS	OBLIQUID
OARLESS	OBCORDATE	OBENTOS	OBJET	OBLIQUING
OARLIKE	OBDURACY	OBES	OBJETS	OBLIQUITY
OARLOCK	OBDURATE	OBESE	OBJURE	OBLIVION
OARLOCKS	OBDURATED	OBESELY	OBJURED	OBLIVIONS
OARS	OBDURATES	OBESENESS	OBJURES	OBLIVIOUS

OBLONG	OBSERVER	OBTESTS	OCARINA	OCCUPYING
OBLONGLY	OBSERVERS	OBTRUDE	OCARINAS	OCCUR
OBLONGS	OBSERVES	OBTRUDED	OCAS	OCCURRED
OBLOQUIAL	OBSERVING	OBTRUDER	OCCAM	OCCURRENT
OBLOQUIES	OBSESS	OBTRUDERS	OCCAMIES	OCCURRING
OBLOQUY	OBSESSED	OBTRUDES	OCCAMS	OCCURS
OBNOXIOUS	OBSESSES	OBTRUDING	OCCAMY	OCCY
OBO	OBSESSING	OBTRUSION	OCCASION	OCEAN
OBOE	OBSESSION	OBTRUSIVE	OCCASIONS	OCEANARIA
OBOES	OBSESSIVE	OBTUND	OCCIDENT	OCEANAUT
OBOIST	OBSESSOR	OBTUNDED	OCCIDENTS	OCEANAUTS
OBOISTS	OBSESSORS	OBTUNDENT	OCCIES	OCEANIC
OBOL	OBSIDIAN	OBTUNDING	OCCIPITA	OCEANID
OBOLARY	OBSIDIANS	OBTUNDITY	OCCIPITAL	OCEANIDES
OBOLE	OBSIGN	OBTUNDS	OCCIPUT	OCEANIDS
OBOLES	OBSIGNATE	OBTURATE	OCCIPUTS	OCEANS
OBOLI	OBSIGNED	OBTURATED	OCCLUDE	OCEANSIDE
OBOLS	OBSIGNING	OBTURATES	OCCLUDED	OCEANVIEW
OBOLUS	OBSIGNS	OBTURATOR	OCCLUDENT	OCEANWARD
OBOS	OBSOLESCE	OBTUSE	OCCLUDER	OCELLAR
OBOVATE	OBSOLETE	OBTUSELY	OCCLUDERS	OCELLATE
OBOVATELY	OBSOLETED	OBTUSER	OCCLUDES	OCELLATED
OBOVOID	OBSOLETES	OBTUSEST	OCCLUDING	OCELLI
OBREPTION	OBSTACLE	OBTUSITY	OCCLUSAL	OCELLUS
OBS	OBSTACLES	OBUMBRATE	OCCLUSION	OCELOID
OBSCENE	OBSTETRIC	OBVENTION	OCCLUSIVE	OCELOT
OBSCENELY	OBSTINACY	OBVERSE	OCCLUSOR	OCELOTS
OBSCENER	OBSTINATE	OBVERSELY	OCCLUSORS	OCH
OBSCENEST	OBSTRUCT	OBVERSES	OCCULT	OCHE
OBSCENITY	OBSTRUCTS	OBVERSION	OCCULTED	OCHER
OBSCURANT	OBSTRUENT	OBVERT	OCCULTER	OCHERED
OBSCURE	OBTAIN	OBVERTED	OCCULTERS	OCHERIER
OBSCURED	OBTAINED	OBVERTING	OCCULTING	OCHERIEST
OBSCURELY	OBTAINER	OBVERTS	OCCULTISM	OCHERING
OBSCURER	OBTAINERS	OBVIABLE	OCCULTIST	OCHERISH
OBSCURERS	OBTAINING	OBVIATE	OCCULTLY	OCHEROID
OBSCURES	OBTAINS	OBVIATED	OCCULTS	OCHEROUS
OBSCUREST	OBTECT	OBVIATES	OCCUPANCE	OCHERS
OBSCURING	OBTECTED	OBVIATING	OCCUPANCY	OCHERY
OBSCURITY	OBTEMPER	OBVIATION	OCCUPANT	OCHES
OBSECRATE	OBTEMPERS	OBVIATOR	OCCUPANTS	OCHIDORE
OBSEQUENT	OBTEND	OBVIATORS	OCCUPATE	OCHIDORES
OBSEQUIAL	OBTENDED	OBVIOUS	OCCUPATED	OCHLOCRAT
OBSEQUIE	OBTENDING	OBVIOUSLY	OCCUPATES	OCHONE
OBSEQUIES	OBTENDS	OBVOLUTE	OCCUPIED	OCHRE
OBSEQUY	OBTENTION	OBVOLUTED	OCCUPIER	OCHREA
OBSERVANT	OBTEST	OBVOLVENT	OCCUPIERS	OCHREAE
OBSERVE	OBTESTED	OBVS	OCCUPIES	OCHREAS
OBSERVED	OBTESTING	OCA	OCCUPY	OCHREATE

OCHRED	OCTAPODIC	OCULAR	ODIFEROUS	ODOURED
OCHREOUS	OCTAPODY	OCULARIST	ODIOUS	ODOURFUL
OCHRES	OCTARCHY	OCULARLY	ODIOUSLY	ODOURLESS
OCHREY	OCTAS	OCULARS	ODISM	ODOURS
OCHRIER	OCTASTICH	OCULATE	ODISMS	ODS
OCHRIEST	OCTASTYLE	OCULATED	ODIST	ODSO
OCHRING	OCTAVAL	OCULI	ODISTS	ODYL
OCHROID	OCTAVE	OCULIST	ODIUM	ODYLE
OCHROUS	OCTAVES	OCULISTS	ODIUMS	ODYLES
OCHRY	OCTAVO	OCULUS	ODOGRAPH	ODYLISM
OCICAT	OCTAVOS	OD	ODOGRAPHS	ODYLISMS
OCICATS	OCTENNIAL	ODA	ODOMETER	ODYLS
OCKER	OCTET	ODAH	ODOMETERS	ODYSSEAN
OCKERISM	OCTETS	ODAHS	ODOMETRY	ODYSSEY
OCKERISMS	OCTETT	ODAL	ODONATA	ODYSSEYS
OCKERS	OCTETTE	ODALIQUE	ODONATE	ODZOOKS
OCKODOLS	OCTETTES	ODALIQUES	ODONATES	OE
OCOTILLO	OCTETTS	ODALISK	ODONATIST	OECIST
OCOTILLOS	OCTILLION	ODALISKS	ODONTALGY	OECISTS
OCREA	OCTOFID	ODALISQUE	ODONTIC	OECOLOGIC
OCREAE	OCTOHEDRA	ODALLER	ODONTIST	OECOLOGY
OCREAS	OCTONARII	ODALLERS	ODONTISTS	OECUMENIC
OCREATE	OCTONARY	ODALS	ODONTOID	OEDEMA
OCTA	OCTOPI	ODAS	ODONTOIDS	OEDEMAS
OCTACHORD	OCTOPLOID	ODD	ODONTOMA	OEDEMATA
OCTAD	OCTOPOD	ODDBALL	ODONTOMAS	OEDIPAL
OCTADIC	OCTOPODAN	ODDBALLS	ODOR	OEDIPALLY
OCTADS	OCTOPODES	ODDER	ODORANT	OEDIPEAN
OCTAGON	OCTOPODS	ODDEST	ODORANTS	OEDOMETER
OCTAGONAL	OCTOPOID	ODDISH	ODORATE	OEILLADE
OCTAGONS	OCTOPUS	ODDITIES	ODORED	OEILLADES
OCTAHEDRA	OCTOPUSES	ODDITY	ODORFUL	OENANTHIC
OCTAL	OCTOPUSH	ODDLY	ODORISE	OENOLOGY
OCTALS	OCTOSTYLE	ODDMENT	ODORISED	OENOMANCY
OCTAMETER	OCTOTHORP	ODDMENTS	ODORISER	OENOMANIA
OCTAN	OCTROI	ODDNESS	ODORISERS	OENOMEL
OCTANE	OCTROIS	ODDNESSES	ODORISES	OENOMELS
OCTANES	OCTUOR	ODDS	ODORISING	OENOMETER
OCTANGLE	OCTUORS	ODDSMAKER	ODORIZE	OENOPHIL
OCTANGLES	OCTUPLE	ODDSMAN	ODORIZED	OENOPHILE
OCTANOL	OCTUPLED	ODDSMEN	ODORIZER	OENOPHILS
OCTANOLS	OCTUPLES	ODE	ODORIZERS	OENOPHILY
OCTANS	OCTUPLET	ODEA	ODORIZES	OENOTHERA
OCTANT	OCTUPLETS	ODEON	ODORIZING	OERLIKON
OCTANTAL	OCTUPLEX	ODEONS	ODORLESS	OERLIKONS
OCTANTS	OCTUPLING	ODES	ODOROUS	OERSTED
OCTAPLA	OCTUPLY	ODEUM	ODOROUSLY	OERSTEDS
OCTAPLAS	OCTYL	ODEUMS	ODORS	OES
OCTAPLOID	OCTYLS	ODIC	ODOUR	OESOPHAGI

OESTRAL	OFFERORS	OFFSIDER	OGREISHLY	OILERY
OESTRIN	OFFERS	OFFSIDERS	OGREISM	OILFIELD
OESTRINS	OFFERTORY	OFFSIDES	OGREISMS	OILFIELDS
OESTRIOL	OFFHAND	OFFSPRING	OGRES	OILFIRED
OESTRIOLS	OFFHANDED	OFFSTAGE	OGRESS	OILGAS
OESTROGEN	OFFICE	OFFSTAGES	OGRESSES	OILGASES
OESTRONE	OFFICER	OFFTAKE	OGRISH	OILHOLE
OESTRONES	OFFICERED	OFFTAKES	OGRISHLY	OILHOLES
OESTROUS	OFFICERS	OFFTRACK	OGRISM	OILIER
OESTRUAL	OFFICES	OFFY	OGRISMS	OILIEST
OESTRUM	OFFICIAL	OFLAG	OH	OILILY
OESTRUMS	OFFICIALS	OFLAGS	OHED	OILINESS
OESTRUS	OFFICIANT	OFT	OHIA	OILING
OESTRUSES	OFFICIARY	OFTEN	OHIAS	OILLET
OEUVRE	OFFICIATE	OFTENER	OHING	OILLETS
OEUVRES	OFFICINAL	OFTENEST	OHM	OILMAN
OF	OFFICIOUS	OFTENNESS	OHMAGE	OILMEN
OFF	OFFIE	OFTER	OHMAGES	OILNUT
OFFA	OFFIES	OFTEST	OHMIC	OILNUTS
OFFAL	OFFING	OFTTIMES	OHMICALLY	OILPAN
OFFALS	OFFINGS	OGAM	OHMMETER	OILPANS
OFFBEAT	OFFISH	OGAMIC	OHMMETERS	OILPAPER
OFFBEATS	OFFISHLY	OGAMS	OHMS	OILPAPERS
OFFCAST	OFFKEY	OGANESSON	OHO	OILPROOF
OFFCASTS	OFFLINE	OGDOAD	OHONE	OILS
OFFCUT	OFFLOAD	OGDOADS	OHS	OILSEED
OFFCUTS	OFFLOADED	OGEE	OI	OILSEEDS
OFFED	OFFLOADS	OGEED	OIDIA	OILSKIN
OFFENCE	OFFPEAK	OGEES	OIDIOID	OILSKINS
OFFENCES	OFFPRINT	OGGIN	OIDIUM	OILSTONE
OFFEND	OFFPRINTS	OGGINS	OIK	OILSTONES
OFFENDED	OFFPUT	OGHAM	OIKIST	OILTIGHT
OFFENDER	OFFPUTS	OGHAMIC	OIKISTS	OILWAY
OFFENDERS	OFFRAMP	OGHAMIST	OIKS	OILWAYS
OFFENDING	OFFRAMPS	OGHAMISTS	OIL	OILY
OFFENDS	OFFS	OGHAMS	OILBIRD	OINK
OFFENSE	OFFSADDLE	OGIVAL	OILBIRDS	OINKED
OFFENSES	OFFSCREEN	OGIVE	OILCAMP	OINKING
OFFENSIVE	OFFSCUM	OGIVES	OILCAMPS	OINKS
OFFER	OFFSCUMS	OGLE	OILCAN	OINOLOGY
OFFERABLE	OFFSEASON	OGLED	OILCANS	OINOMEL
OFFERED	OFFSET	OGLER	OILCLOTH	OINOMELS
OFFEREE	OFFSETS	OGLERS	OILCLOTHS	OINT
OFFEREES	OFFSHOOT	OGLES	OILCUP	OINTED
OFFERER	OFFSHOOTS	OGLING	OILCUPS	OINTING
OFFERERS	OFFSHORE	OGLINGS	OILED	OINTMENT
OFFERING	OFFSHORED	OGMIC	OILER	OINTMENTS
OFFERINGS	OFFSHORES	OGRE	OILERIES	OINTS
OFFEROR	OFFSIDE	OGREISH	OILERS	OIS

O

OITICICA	OLDY	OLIGARCH	OLM	OMEN
OITICICAS	OLE	OLIGARCHS	OLMS	OMENED
OJIME	OLEA	OLIGARCHY	OLOGIES	OMENING
OJIMES	OLEACEOUS	OLIGEMIA	OLOGIST	OMENS
OK	OLEANDER	OLIGEMIAS	OLOGISTS	OMENTA
OKA	OLEANDERS	OLIGEMIC	OLOGOAN	OMENTAL
OKAPI	OLEARIA	OLIGIST	OLOGOANED	OMENTUM
OKAPIS	OLEARIAS	OLIGISTS	OLOGOANS	OMENTUMS
OKARA	OLEASTER	OLIGOCENE	OLOGY	OMER
OKARAS	OLEASTERS	OLIGOGENE	OLOLIUQUI	OMERS
OKAS	OLEATE	OLIGOMER	OLOROSO	OMERTA
OKAY	OLEATES	OLIGOMERS	OLOROSOS	OMERTAS
OKAYED	OLECRANAL	OLIGOPOLY	OLPAE	OMICRON
OKAYING	OLECRANON	OLIGURIA	OLPE	OMICRONS
OKAYS	OLEFIANT	OLIGURIAS	OLPES	OMIGOD
OKE	OLEFIN	OLIGURIC	OLYCOOK	OMIKRON
OKEH	OLEFINE	OLINGO	OLYCOOKS	OMIKRONS
OKEHS	OLEFINES	OLINGOS	OLYKOEK	OMINOUS
OKES	OLEFINIC	OLINGUITO	OLYKOEKS	OMINOUSLY
OKEYDOKE	OLEFINS	OLIO	OLYMPIAD	OMISSIBLE
OKEYDOKEY	OLEIC	OLIOS	OLYMPIADS	OMISSION
OKIMONO	OLEIN	OLIPHANT	OLYMPICS	OMISSIONS
OKIMONOS	OLEINE	OLIPHANTS	OM	OMISSIVE
OKRA	OLEINES	OLITORIES	OMA	OMIT
OKRAS	OLEINS	OLITORY	OMADHAUN	OMITS
OKTA	OLENT	OLIVARY	OMADHAUNS	OMITTANCE
OKTAS	OLEO	OLIVE	OMAKASE	OMITTED
OLD	OLEOGRAPH	OLIVENITE	OMAKASES	OMITTER
OLDE	OLEORESIN	OLIVER	OMAS	OMITTERS
OLDEN	OLEOS	OLIVERS	OMASA	OMITTING
OLDENED	OLES	OLIVES	OMASAL	OMLAH
OLDENING	OLESTRA	OLIVET	OMASUM	OMLAHS
OLDENS	OLESTRAS	OLIVETS	OMBER	OMMATEA
OLDER	OLEUM	OLIVEWOOD	OMBERS	OMMATEUM
OLDEST	OLEUMS	OLIVINE	OMBRE	OMMATIDIA
OLDIE	OLFACT	OLIVINES	OMBRELLA	OMNEITIES
OLDIES	OLFACTED	OLIVINIC	OMBRELLAS	OMNEITY
OLDISH	OLFACTING	OLLA	OMBRES	OMNIANA
OLDNESS	OLFACTION	OLLAMH	OMBROPHIL	OMNIANAS
OLDNESSES	OLFACTIVE	OLLAMHS	OMBU	OMNIARCH
OLDS	OLFACTORY	OLLAS	OMBUDSMAN	OMNIARCHS
OLDSQUAW	OLFACTS	OLLAV	OMBUDSMEN	OMNIBUS
OLDSQUAWS	OLIBANUM	OLLAVS	OMBUS	OMNIBUSES
OLDSTER	OLIBANUMS	OLLER	OMEGA	OMNICIDAL
OLDSTERS	OLICOOK	OLLERS	OMEGAS	OMNICIDE
OLDSTYLE	OLICOOKS	OLLIE	OMELET	OMNICIDES
OLDSTYLES	OLID	OLLIED	OMELETS	OMNIETIES
OLDWIFE	OLIGAEMIA	OLLIEING	OMELETTE	OMNIETY
OLDWIVES	OLIGAEMIC	OLLIES	OMELETTES	OMNIFIC

OMNIFIED	ONCES	ONERY	ONLY	ONYCHIUMS
OMNIFIES	ONCET	ONES	ONNED	ONYMOUS
OMNIFORM	ONCIDIUM	ONESELF	ONNING	ONYX
OMNIFY	ONCIDIUMS	ONESIE	ONO	ONYXES
OMNIFYING	ONCOGEN	ONESIES	ONOMAST	OO
OMNIMODE	ONCOGENE	ONETIME	ONOMASTIC	OOBIT
OMNIRANGE	ONCOGENES	ONEYER	ONOMASTS	OOBITS
OMNIUM	ONCOGENIC	ONEYERS	ONOS	OOBLECK
OMNIUMS	ONCOGENS	ONEYRE	ONRUSH	OOBLECKS
OMNIVORA	ONCOLOGIC	ONEYRES	ONRUSHES	OOCYST
OMNIVORE	ONCOLOGY	ONFALL	ONRUSHING	OOCYSTS
OMNIVORES	ONCOLYSES	ONFALLS	ONS	OOCYTE
OMNIVORY	ONCOLYSIS	ONFLOW	ONSCREEN	OOCYTES
OMOHYOID	ONCOLYTIC	ONFLOWS	ONSET	OODLES
OMOHYOIDS	ONCOME	ONGAONGA	ONSETS	OODLINS
OMOPHAGIA	ONCOMES	ONGAONGAS	ONSETTER	OOF
OMOPHAGIC	ONCOMETER	ONGLET	ONSETTERS	OOFIER
OMOPHAGY	ONCOMICE	ONGLETS	ONSETTING	OOFIEST
OMOPHORIA	ONCOMING	ONGOING	ONSHORE	OOFS
OMOPLATE	ONCOMINGS	ONGOINGS	ONSHORING	OOFTISH
OMOPLATES	ONCOMOUSE	ONIE	ONSIDE	OOFTISHES
OMOV	ONCOST	ONIGIRI	ONSIDES	OOFY
OMOVS	ONCOSTMAN	ONIGIRIS	ONSLAUGHT	OOGAMETE
OMPHACITE	ONCOSTMEN	ONION	ONST	OOGAMETES
OMPHALI	ONCOSTS	ONIONED	ONSTAGE	OOGAMIES
OMPHALIC	ONCOTOMY	ONIONIER	ONSTEAD	OOGAMOUS
OMPHALOI	ONCOVIRUS	ONIONIEST	ONSTEADS	OOGAMY
OMPHALOID	ONCUS	ONIONING	ONSTREAM	OOGENESES
OMPHALOS	ONDATRA	ONIONS	ONTIC	OOGENESIS
OMRAH	ONDATRAS	ONIONSKIN	ONTICALLY	OOGENETIC
OMRAHS	ONDINE	ONIONY	ONTO	OOGENIES
OMS	ONDINES	ONIRIC	ONTOGENIC	OOGENY
ON	ONDING	ONISCOID	ONTOGENY	OOGONIA
ONAGER	ONDINGS	ONIUM	ONTOLOGIC	OOGONIAL
ONAGERS	ONDOGRAM	ONIUMS	ONTOLOGY	OOGONIUM
ONAGRI	ONDOGRAMS	ONKUS	ONUS	OOGONIUMS
ONANISM	ONDOGRAPH	ONLAY	ONUSES	OOH
ONANISMS	ONE	ONLAYS	ONWARD	OOHED
ONANIST	ONEFOLD	ONLIEST	ONWARDLY	OOHING
ONANISTIC	ONEIRIC	ONLINE	ONWARDS	OOHINGS
ONANISTS	ONELY	ONLINER	ONY	OOHS
ONBEAT	ONENESS	ONLINERS	ONYCHA	OOIDAL
ONBEATS	ONENESSES	ONLOAD	ONYCHAS	OOLACHAN
ONBOARD	ONER	ONLOADED	ONYCHIA	OOLACHANS
ONBOARDED	ONERIER	ONLOADING	ONYCHIAS	OOLAKAN
ONBOARDS	ONERIEST	ONLOADS	ONYCHITE	OOLAKANS
ONCE	ONEROUS	ONLOOKER	ONYCHITES	OOLICHAN
ONCER	ONEROUSLY	ONLOOKERS	ONYCHITIS	OOLICHANS
ONCERS	ONERS	ONLOOKING	ONYCHIUM	OOLITE

O

OOLITES	OORIEST	OPALISED	OPERATION	OPINION
OOLITH	OOS	OPALIZED	OPERATISE	OPINIONED
OOLITHS	OOSE	OPALS	OPERATIVE	OPINIONS
OOLITIC	OOSES	OPAQUE	OPERATIZE	OPIOID
OOLOGIC	OOSIER	OPAQUED	OPERATOR	OPIOIDS
OOLOGICAL	OOSIEST	OPAQUELY	OPERATORS	OPIUM
OOLOGIES	OOSPERM	OPAQUER	OPERCELE	OPIUMISM
OOLOGIST	OOSPERMS	OPAQUES	OPERCELES	OPIUMISMS
OOLOGISTS	OOSPHERE	OPAQUEST	OPERCULA	OPIUMS
OOLOGY	OOSPHERES	OPAQUING	OPERCULAR	OPOBALSAM
OOLONG	OOSPORE	OPAS	OPERCULE	OPODELDOC
OOLONGS	OOSPORES	OPCODE	OPERCULES	OPOPANAX
OOM	OOSPORIC	OPCODES	OPERCULUM	OPORICE
OOMIAC	OOSPOROUS	OPE	OPERETTA	OPORICES
OOMIACK	OOSY	OPED	OPERETTAS	OPOSSUM
OOMIACKS	OOT	OPEN	OPERON	OPOSSUMS
OOMIACS	OOTHECA	OPENABLE	OPERONS	OPPIDAN
OOMIAK	OOTHECAE	OPENCAST	OPEROSE	OPPIDANS
OOMIAKS	OOTHECAL	OPENED	OPEROSELY	OPPILANT
OOMPAH	OOTID	OPENER	OPEROSITY	OPPILATE
OOMPAHED	OOTIDS	OPENERS	OPES	OPPILATED
OOMPAHING	OOTS	OPENEST	OPGEFOK	OPPILATES
OOMPAHPAH	OOZE	OPENING	OPHIDIAN	OPPO
OOMPAHS	OOZED	OPENINGS	OPHIDIANS	OPPONENCY
OOMPH	OOZES	OPENLY	OPHIOLITE	OPPONENS
OOMPHS	OOZIER	OPENNESS	OPHIOLOGY	OPPONENT
OOMS	OOZIEST	OPENS	OPHITE	OPPONENTS
OOMYCETE	OOZILY	OPENSIDE	OPHITES	OPPORTUNE
OOMYCETES	OOZINESS	OPENSIDES	OPHITIC	OPPOS
OON	OOZING	OPENWORK	OPHIURA	OPPOSABLE
OONS	OOZY	OPENWORKS	OPHIURAN	OPPOSABLY
OONT	OP	OPEPE	OPHIURANS	OPPOSE
OONTS	OPA	OPEPES	OPHIURAS	OPPOSED
OOP	OPACIFIED	OPERA	OPHIURID	OPPOSER
OOPED	OPACIFIER	OPERABLE	OPHIURIDS	OPPOSERS
OOPHORON	OPACIFIES	OPERABLY	OPHIUROID	OPPOSES
OOPHORONS	OPACIFY	OPERAGOER	OPIATE	OPPOSING
OOPHYTE	OPACITIES	OPERAND	OPIATED	OPPOSITE
OOPHYTES	OPACITY	OPERANDS	OPIATES	OPPOSITES
OOPHYTIC	OPACOUS	OPERANT	OPIATING	OPPRESS
OOPING	OPAH	OPERANTLY	OPIFICER	OPPRESSED
OOPS	OPAHS	OPERANTS	OPIFICERS	OPPRESSES
OOR	OPAL	OPERAS	OPINABLE	OPPRESSOR
OORALI	OPALED	OPERATE	OPINE	OPPUGN
OORALIS	OPALESCE	OPERATED	OPINED	OPPUGNANT
OORIAL	OPALESCED	OPERATES	OPINES	OPPUGNED
OORIALS	OPALESCES	OPERATIC	OPING	OPPUGNER
OORIE	OPALINE	OPERATICS	OPINICUS	OPPUGNERS
OORIER	OPALINES	OPERATING	OPINING	OPPUGNING

OPPUGNS	OPTIMIST	ORACIES	ORATORIAL	ORCHESES
OPS	OPTIMISTS	ORACLE	ORATORIAN	ORCHESIS
OPSIMATH	OPTIMIZE	ORACLED	ORATORIES	ORCHESTIC
OPSIMATHS	OPTIMIZED	ORACLES	ORATORIO	ORCHESTRA
OPSIMATHY	OPTIMIZER	ORACLING	ORATORIOS	ORCHID
OPSIN	OPTIMIZES	ORACULAR	ORATORS	ORCHIDIST
OPSINS	OPTIMUM	ORACULOUS	ORATORY	ORCHIDS
OPSOMANIA	OPTIMUMS	ORACY	ORATRESS	ORCHIL
OPSONIC	OPTING	ORAD	ORATRICES	ORCHILLA
OPSONIFY	OPTION	ORAGIOUS	ORATRIX	ORCHILLAS
OPSONIN	OPTIONAL	ORAL	ORATRIXES	ORCHILS
OPSONINS	OPTIONALS	ORALISM	ORATURE	ORCHIS
OPSONISE	OPTIONED	ORALISMS	ORATURES	ORCHISES
OPSONISED	OPTIONEE	ORALIST	ORB	ORCHITIC
OPSONISES	OPTIONEES	ORALISTS	ORBED	ORCHITIS
OPSONIUM	OPTIONING	ORALITIES	ORBICULAR	ORCIN
OPSONIUMS	OPTIONS	ORALITY	ORBIER	ORCINE
OPSONIZE	OPTOLOGY	ORALLY	ORBIEST	ORCINES
OPSONIZED	OPTOMETER	ORALS	ORBING	ORCINOL
OPSONIZES	OPTOMETRY	ORANG	ORBIT	ORCINOLS
OPT	OPTOPHONE	ORANGE	ORBITA	ORCINS
OPTANT	OPTRONIC	ORANGEADE	ORBITAL	ORCS
OPTANTS	OPTRONICS	ORANGER	ORBITALLY	ORD
OPTATIVE	OPTS	ORANGERIE	ORBITALS	ORDAIN
OPTATIVES	OPULENCE	ORANGERY	ORBITAS	ORDAINED
OPTED	OPULENCES	ORANGES	ORBITED	ORDAINER
OPTER	OPULENCY	ORANGEST	ORBITER	ORDAINERS
OPTERS	OPULENT	ORANGEY	ORBITERS	ORDAINING
OPTIC	OPULENTLY	ORANGIER	ORBITIES	ORDAINS
OPTICAL	OPULUS	ORANGIEST	ORBITING	ORDALIAN
OPTICALLY	OPULUSES	ORANGISH	ORBITS	ORDALIUM
OPTICIAN	OPUNTIA	ORANGS	ORBITY	ORDALIUMS
OPTICIANS	OPUNTIAS	ORANGUTAN	ORBLESS	ORDEAL
OPTICIST	OPUS	ORANGY	ORBLIKE	ORDEALS
OPTICISTS	OPUSCLE	ORANT	ORBS	ORDER
OPTICS	OPUSCLES	ORANTS	ORBY	ORDERABLE
OPTIMA	OPUSCULA	ORARIA	ORC	ORDERED
OPTIMAL	OPUSCULAR	ORARIAN	ORCA	ORDERER
OPTIMALLY	OPUSCULE	ORARIANS	ORCAS	ORDERERS
OPTIMATE	OPUSCULES	ORARION	ORCEIN	ORDERING
OPTIMATES	OPUSCULUM	ORARIONS	ORCEINS	ORDERINGS
OPTIME	OPUSES	ORARIUM	ORCHARD	ORDERLESS
OPTIMES	OQUASSA	ORATE	ORCHARDS	ORDERLIES
OPTIMISE	OQUASSAS	ORATED	ORCHAT	ORDERLY
OPTIMISED	OR	ORATES	ORCHATS	ORDERS
OPTIMISER	ORA	ORATING	ORCHEL	ORDINAIRE
OPTIMISES	ORACH	ORATION	ORCHELLA	ORDINAL
OPTIMISM	ORACHE	ORATIONS	ORCHELLAS	ORDINALLY
OPTIMISMS	ORACHES	ORATOR	ORCHELS	ORDINALS

O

ORDINANCE	ORFRAY	ORGIAST	ORIGIN	OROGEN
ORDINAND	ORFRAYS	ORGIASTIC	ORIGINAL	OROGENIC
ORDINANDS	ORFS	ORGIASTS	ORIGINALS	OROGENIES
ORDINANT	ORG	ORGIC	ORIGINARY	OROGENS
ORDINANTS	ORGAN	ORGIES	ORIGINATE	OROGENY
ORDINAR	ORGANA	ORGILLOUS	ORIGINS	OROGRAPHY
ORDINARS	ORGANDIE	ORGONE	ORIHOU	OROIDE
ORDINARY	ORGANDIES	ORGONES	ORIHOUS	OROIDES
ORDINATE	ORGANDY	ORGS	ORILLION	OROLOGIES
ORDINATED	ORGANELLE	ORGUE	ORILLIONS	OROLOGIST
ORDINATES	ORGANIC	ORGUES	ORINASAL	OROLOGY
ORDINEE	ORGANICAL	ORGULOUS	ORINASALS	OROMETER
ORDINEES	ORGANICS	ORGY	ORIOLE	OROMETERS
ORDINES	ORGANISE	ORIBATID	ORIOLES	ORONASAL
ORDNANCE	ORGANISED	ORIBATIDS	ORISHA	OROPESA
ORDNANCES	ORGANISER	ORIBI	ORISHAS	OROPESAS
ORDO	ORGANISES	ORIBIS	ORISON	OROTUND
ORDOS	ORGANISM	ORICALCHE	ORISONS	OROTUNDLY
ORDS	ORGANISMS	ORICHALC	ORIXA	ORPHAN
ORDURE	ORGANIST	ORICHALCS	ORIXAS	ORPHANAGE
ORDURES	ORGANISTS	ORIEL	ORLE	ORPHANED
ORDUROUS	ORGANITY	ORIELLED	ORLEANS	ORPHANING
ORE	ORGANIZE	ORIELS	ORLEANSES	ORPHANISM
OREAD	ORGANIZED	ORIENCIES	ORLES	ORPHANS
OREADES	ORGANIZER	ORIENCY	ORLISTAT	ORPHARION
OREADS	ORGANIZES	ORIENT	ORLISTATS	ORPHIC
OREBODIES	ORGANOID	ORIENTAL	ORLON	ORPHICAL
OREBODY	ORGANOIDS	ORIENTALS	ORLONS	ORPHISM
ORECTIC	ORGANON	ORIENTATE	ORLOP	ORPHISMS
ORECTIVE	ORGANONS	ORIENTED	ORLOPS	ORPHREY
OREGANO	ORGANOSOL	ORIENTEER	ORMER	ORPHREYED
OREGANOS	ORGANOTIN	ORIENTER	ORMERS	ORPHREYS
OREIDE	ORGANS	ORIENTERS	ORMOLU	ORPIMENT
OREIDES	ORGANUM	ORIENTING	ORMOLUS	ORPIMENTS
OREODONT	ORGANUMS	ORIENTS	ORNAMENT	ORPIN
OREODONTS	ORGANZA	ORIFEX	ORNAMENTS	ORPINE
OREOLOGY	ORGANZAS	ORIFEXES	ORNATE	ORPINES
OREPEARCH	ORGANZINE	ORIFICE	ORNATELY	ORPINS
ORES	ORGASM	ORIFICES	ORNATER	ORRA
ORESTUNCK	ORGASMED	ORIFICIAL	ORNATEST	ORRAMAN
OREWEED	ORGASMIC	ORIFLAMME	ORNERIER	ORRAMEN
OREWEEDS	ORGASMING	ORIGAMI	ORNERIEST	ORRERIES
OREXIN	ORGASMS	ORIGAMIS	ORNERY	ORRERY
OREXINS	ORGASTIC	ORIGAN	ORNIS	ORRICE
OREXIS	ORGEAT	ORIGANE	ORNISES	ORRICES
OREXISES	ORGEATS	ORIGANES	ORNITHES	ORRIS
ORF	ORGIA	ORIGANS	ORNITHIC	ORRISES
ORFE	ORGIAC	ORIGANUM	ORNITHINE	ORRISROOT
ORFES	ORGIAS	ORIGANUMS	ORNITHOID	ORS

ORSEILLE	OSCITANCY	OSMOSIS	OSTEITIS	OSTRACEAN
ORSEILLES	OSCITANT	OSMOTIC	OSTENSIVE	OSTRACISE
ORSELLIC	OSCITATE	OSMOUS	OSTENSORY	OSTRACISM
ORT	OSCITATED	OSMUND	OSTENT	OSTRACIZE
ORTANIQUE	OSCITATES	OSMUNDA	OSTENTED	OSTRACOD
ORTHIAN	OSCULA	OSMUNDAS	OSTENTING	OSTRACODE
ORTHICON	OSCULANT	OSMUNDINE	OSTENTS	OSTRACODS
ORTHICONS	OSCULAR	OSMUNDS	OSTEOCYTE	OSTRACON
ORTHO	OSCULATE	OSNABURG	OSTEODERM	OSTRAKA
ORTHOAXES	OSCULATED	OSNABURGS	OSTEOGEN	OSTRAKON
ORTHOAXIS	OSCULATES	OSPREY	OSTEOGENS	OSTREGER
ORTHODOX	OSCULE	OSPREYS	OSTEOGENY	OSTREGERS
ORTHODOXY	OSCULES	OSSA	OSTEOID	OSTRICH
ORTHOEPIC	OSCULUM	OSSARIUM	OSTEOIDS	OSTRICHES
ORTHOEPY	OSE	OSSARIUMS	OSTEOLOGY	OTAKU
ORTHOPEDY	OSES	OSSATURE	OSTEOMA	OTAKUS
ORTHOPOD	OSETRA	OSSATURES	OSTEOMAS	OTALGIA
ORTHOPODS	OSETRAS	OSSEIN	OSTEOMATA	OTALGIAS
ORTHOPTER	OSHAC	OSSEINS	OSTEOPATH	OTALGIC
ORTHOPTIC	OSHACS	OSSELET	OSTEOSES	OTALGIES
ORTHOS	OSIER	OSSELETS	OSTEOSIS	OTALGY
ORTHOSES	OSIERED	OSSEOUS	OSTEOTOME	OTARID
ORTHOSIS	OSIERIES	OSSEOUSLY	OSTEOTOMY	OTARIES
ORTHOTIC	OSIERS	OSSETER	OSTIA	OTARINE
ORTHOTICS	OSIERY	OSSETERS	OSTIAL	OTARY
ORTHOTIST	OSMATE	OSSETRA	OSTIARIES	OTHER
ORTHOTONE	OSMATES	OSSETRAS	OSTIARY	OTHERED
ORTHROI	OSMATIC	OSSIA	OSTIATE	OTHERING
ORTHROS	OSMETERIA	OSSIAS	OSTINATI	OTHERINGS
ORTHROSES	OSMIATE	OSSICLE	OSTINATO	OTHERNESS
ORTOLAN	OSMIATES	OSSICLES	OSTINATOS	OTHERS
ORTOLANS	OSMIC	OSSICONE	OSTIOLAR	OTHERWISE
ORTS	OSMICALLY	OSSICONES	OSTIOLATE	OTIC
ORVAL	OSMICS	OSSICULAR	OSTIOLE	OTIOSE
ORVALS	OSMIOUS	OSSIFIC	OSTIOLES	OTIOSELY
ORYX	OSMIUM	OSSIFIED	OSTIUM	OTIOSITY
ORYXES	OSMIUMS	OSSIFIER	OSTLER	OTITIC
ORZO	OSMOL	OSSIFIERS	OSTLERESS	OTITIDES
ORZOS	OSMOLAL	OSSIFIES	OSTLERS	OTITIS
OS	OSMOLAR	OSSIFRAGA	OSTMARK	OTITISES
OSAR	OSMOLE	OSSIFRAGE	OSTMARKS	OTOCYST
OSCAR	OSMOLES	OSSIFY	OSTOMATE	OTOCYSTIC
OSCARS	OSMOLS	OSSIFYING	OSTOMATES	OTOCYSTS
OSCHEAL	OSMOMETER	OSSOBUCO	OSTOMIES	OTOLITH
OSCILLATE	OSMOMETRY	OSSOBUCOS	OSTOMY	OTOLITHIC
OSCINE	OSMOSE	OSSUARIES	OSTOSES	OTOLITHS
OSCINES	OSMOSED	OSSUARY	OSTOSIS	OTOLOGIC
OSCININE	OSMOSES	OSTEAL	OSTOSISES	OTOLOGIES
OSCITANCE	OSMOSING	OSTEITIC	OSTRACA	OTOLOGIST

OTOLOGY	OUGHTLINS	OURALIS	OUTASKS	OUTBOXES
OTOPLASTY	OUGHTNESS	OURANG	OUTATE	OUTBOXING
OTORRHOEA	OUGHTS	OURANGS	OUTBACK	OUTBRAG
OTOSCOPE	OUGIYA	OURARI	OUTBACKER	OUTBRAGS
OTOSCOPES	OUGIYAS	OURARIS	OUTBACKS	OUTBRAVE
OTOSCOPIC	OUGLIE	OUREBI	OUTBAKE	OUTBRAVED
OTOSCOPY	OUGLIED	OUREBIS	OUTBAKED	OUTBRAVES
OTOTOXIC	OUGLIEING	OURIE	OUTBAKES	OUTBRAWL
OTTAR	OUGLIES	OURIER	OUTBAKING	OUTBRAWLS
OTTARS	OUGUIYA	OURIEST	OUTBAR	OUTBRAZEN
OTTAVA	OUGUIYAS	OURN	OUTBARK	OUTBREAK
OTTAVAS	OUIJA	OUROBOROI	OUTBARKED	OUTBREAKS
OTTAVINO	OUIJAS	OUROBOROS	OUTBARKS ·	OUTBRED
OTTAVINOS	OUISTITI	OUROLOGY	OUTBARRED	OUTBREED
OTTER	OUISTITIS	OUROSCOPY	OUTBARS	OUTBREEDS
OTTERED	OUK	OURS	OUTBAWL	OUTBRIBE
OTTERING	OUKS	OURSELF	OUTBAWLED	OUTBRIBED
OTTERS	OULACHON	OURSELVES	OUTBAWLS	OUTBRIBES
OTTO	OULACHONS	OUS	OUTBEAM	OUTBROKE
OTTOMAN	OULAKAN	OUSEL	OUTBEAMED	OUTBROKEN
OTTOMANS	OULAKANS	OUSELS	OUTBEAMS	OUTBUILD
OTTOS	OULD	OUST	OUTBEG	OUTBUILDS
OTTRELITE	OULDER	OUSTED	OUTBEGGED	OUTBUILT
OU	OULDEST	OUSTER	OUTBEGS	OUTBULGE
OUABAIN	OULK	OUSTERS	OUTBID	OUTBULGED
OUABAINS	OULKS	OUSTING	OUTBIDDEN	OUTBULGES
OUAKARI	OULONG	OUSTITI	OUTBIDDER	OUTBULK
OUAKARIS	OULONGS	OUSTITIS	OUTBIDS	OUTBULKED
OUBAAS	OUMA	OUSTS	OUTBITCH	OUTBULKS
OUBAASES	OUMAS	OUT	OUTBLAZE	OUTBULLY
OUBIT	OUNCE	OUTA	OUTBLAZED	OUTBURN
OUBITS	OUNCER	OUTACT	OUTBLAZES	OUTBURNED
OUBLIETTE	OUNCERS	OUTACTED	OUTBLEAT	OUTBURNS
OUCH	OUNCES	OUTACTING	OUTBLEATS	OUTBURNT
OUCHED	OUNDIER	OUTACTS	OUTBLESS	OUTBURST
OUCHES	OUNDIEST	OUTADD	OUTBLOOM	OUTBURSTS
OUCHING	OUNDY	OUTADDED	OUTBLOOMS	OUTBUY
OUCHT	OUP	OUTADDING	OUTBLUFF	OUTBUYING
OUCHTS	OUPA	OUTADDS	OUTBLUFFS	OUTBUYS
OUD	OUPAS	OUTAGE	OUTBLUSH	OUTBY
OUDS	OUPED	OUTAGES	OUTBOARD	OUTBYE
OUENS	OUPH	OUTARGUE	OUTBOARDS	OUTCALL
OUGHLIED	OUPHE	OUTARGUED	OUTBOAST	OUTCALLED
OUGHLIES	OUPHES	OUTARGUES	OUTBOASTS	OUTCALLS
OUGHLY	OUPHS	OUTASIGHT	OUTBOUGHT	OUTCAPER
OUGHLYING	OUPING	OUTASITE	OUTBOUND	OUTCAPERS
OUGHT	OUPS	OUTASK	OUTBOUNDS	OUTCAST
OUGHTED	OUR	OUTASKED	OUTBOX	OUTCASTE
OUGHTING	OURALI	OUTASKING	OUTBOXED	OUTCASTED

OUTCASTES	OUTDANCE	OUTDUELS	OUTFIELD	OUTFUMBLE
OUTCASTS	OUTDANCED	OUTDURE	OUTFIELDS	OUTGAIN
OUTCATCH	OUTDANCES	OUTDURED	OUTFIGHT	OUTGAINED
OUTCAUGHT	OUTDARE	OUTDURES	OUTFIGHTS	OUTGAINS
OUTCAVIL	OUTDARED	OUTDURING	OUTFIGURE	OUTGALLOP
OUTCAVILS	OUTDARES	OUTDWELL	OUTFIND	OUTGAMBLE
OUTCHARGE	OUTDARING	OUTDWELLS	OUTFINDS	OUTGAS
OUTCHARM	OUTDATE	OUTDWELT	OUTFIRE	OUTGASES
OUTCHARMS	OUTDATED	OUTEARN	OUTFIRED	OUTGASSED
OUTCHEAT	OUTDATES	OUTEARNED	OUTFIRES	OUTGASSES
OUTCHEATS	OUTDATING	OUTEARNS	OUTFIRING	OUTGATE
OUTCHID	OUTDAZZLE	OUTEAT	OUTFISH	OUTGATES
OUTCHIDE	OUTDEBATE	OUTEATEN	OUTFISHED	OUTGAVE
OUTCHIDED	OUTDESIGN	OUTEATING	OUTFISHES	OUTGAZE
OUTCHIDES	OUTDID	OUTEATS	OUTFIT	OUTGAZED
OUTCITIES	OUTDO	OUTECHO	OUTFITS	OUTGAZES
OUTCITY	OUTDODGE	OUTECHOED	OUTFITTED	OUTGAZING
OUTCLASS	OUTDODGED	OUTECHOES	OUTFITTER	OUTGIVE
OUTCLIMB	OUTDODGES	OUTED	OUTFLANK	OUTGIVEN
OUTCLIMBS	OUTDOER	OUTEDGE	OUTFLANKS	OUTGIVES
OUTCLOMB	OUTDOERS	OUTEDGES	OUTFLASH	OUTGIVING
OUTCOACH	OUTDOES	OUTER	OUTFLEW	OUTGLARE
OUTCOME	OUTDOING	OUTERCOAT	OUTFLIES	OUTGLARED
OUTCOMES	OUTDONE	OUTERMOST	OUTFLING	OUTGLARES
OUTCOOK	OUTDOOR	OUTERS	OUTFLINGS	OUTGLEAM
OUTCOOKED	OUTDOORS	OUTERWEAR	OUTFLOAT	OUTGLEAMS
OUTCOOKS	OUTDOORSY	OUTFABLE	OUTFLOATS	OUTGLOW
OUTCOUNT	OUTDRAG	OUTFABLED	OUTFLOW	OUTGLOWED
OUTCOUNTS	OUTDRAGS	OUTFABLES	OUTFLOWED	OUTGLOWS
OUTCRAFTY	OUTDRANK	OUTFACE	OUTFLOWN	OUTGNAW
OUTCRAWL	OUTDRAW	OUTFACED	OUTFLOWS	OUTGNAWED
OUTCRAWLS	OUTDRAWN	OUTFACES	OUTFLUNG	OUTGNAWN
OUTCRIED	OUTDRAWS	OUTFACING	OUTFLUSH	OUTGNAWS
OUTCRIES	OUTDREAM	OUTFALL	OUTFLY	OUTGO
OUTCROP	OUTDREAMS	OUTFALLS	OUTFLYING	OUTGOER
OUTCROPS	OUTDREAMT	OUTFAST	OUTFOOL	OUTGOERS
OUTCROSS	OUTDRESS	OUTFASTED	OUTFOOLED	OUTGOES
OUTCROW	OUTDREW	OUTFASTS	OUTFOOLS	OUTGOING
OUTCROWD	OUTDRINK	OUTFAWN	OUTFOOT	OUTGOINGS
OUTCROWDS	OUTDRINKS	OUTFAWNED	OUTFOOTED	OUTGONE
OUTCROWED	OUTDRIVE	OUTFAWNS	OUTFOOTS	OUTGREW
OUTCROWS	OUTDRIVEN	OUTFEAST	OUTFOUGHT	OUTGRIN
OUTCRY	OUTDRIVES	OUTFEASTS	OUTFOUND	OUTGRINS
OUTCRYING	OUTDROP	OUTFEEL	OUTFOX	OUTGROSS
OUTCURSE	OUTDROPS	OUTFEELS	OUTFOXED	OUTGROUP
OUTCURSED	OUTDROVE	OUTFELT	OUTFOXES	OUTGROUPS
OUTCURSES	OUTDRUNK	OUTFENCE	OUTFOXING	OUTGROW
OUTCURVE	OUTDUEL	OUTFENCED	OUTFROWN	OUTGROWN
OUTCURVES	OUTDUELED	OUTFENCES	OUTFROWNS	OUTGROWS

OUTGROWTH	OUTINGS	OUTLAY	OUTMARCH	OUTPLAN
OUTGUARD	OUTJEST	OUTLAYING	OUTMASTER	OUTPLANS
OUTGUARDS	OUTJESTED	OUTLAYS	OUTMATCH	OUTPLAY
OUTGUESS	OUTJESTS	OUTLEAD	OUTMODE	OUTPLAYED
OUTGUIDE	OUTJET	OUTLEADS	OUTMODED	OUTPLAYS
OUTGUIDED	OUTJETS	OUTLEAP	OUTMODES	OUTPLOD
OUTGUIDES	OUTJINX	OUTLEAPED	OUTMODING	OUTPLODS
OUTGUN	OUTJINXED	OUTLEAPS	OUTMOST	OUTPLOT
OUTGUNNED	OUTJINXES	OUTLEAPT	OUTMOVE	OUTPLOTS
OUTGUNS	OUTJOCKEY	OUTLEARN	OUTMOVED	OUTPOINT
OUTGUSH	OUTJUGGLE	OUTLEARNS	OUTMOVES	OUTPOINTS
OUTGUSHED	OUTJUMP	OUTLEARNT	OUTMOVING	OUTPOLL
OUTGUSHES	OUTJUMPED	OUTLED	OUTMUSCLE	OUTPOLLED
OUTHANDLE	OUTJUMPS	OUTLER	OUTNAME	OUTPOLLS
OUTHARBOR	OUTJUT	OUTLERS	OUTNAMED	OUTPORT
OUTHAUL	OUTJUTS	OUTLET	OUTNAMES	OUTPORTER
OUTHAULER	OUTJUTTED	OUTLETS	OUTNAMING	OUTPORTS
OUTHAULS	OUTKEEP	OUTLIE	OUTNESS	OUTPOST
OUTHEAR	OUTKEEPS	OUTLIED	OUTNESSES	OUTPOSTS
OUTHEARD	OUTKEPT	OUTLIER	OUTNIGHT	OUTPOUR
OUTHEARS	OUTKICK	OUTLIERS	OUTNIGHTS	OUTPOURED
OUTHER	OUTKICKED	OUTLIES	OUTNUMBER	OUTPOURER
OUTHIRE	OUTKICKS	OUTLINE	OUTOFFICE	OUTPOURS
OUTHIRED	OUTKILL	OUTLINEAR	OUTPACE	OUTPOWER
OUTHIRES	OUTKILLED	OUTLINED	OUTPACED	OUTPOWERS
OUTHIRING	OUTKILLS	OUTLINER	OUTPACES	OUTPRAY
OUTHIT	OUTKISS	OUTLINERS	OUTPACING	OUTPRAYED
OUTHITS	OUTKISSED	OUTLINES	OUTPAINT	OUTPRAYS
OUTHOMER	OUTKISSES	OUTLINING	OUTPAINTS	OUTPREACH
OUTHOMERS	OUTLAID	OUTLIVE	OUTPART	OUTPREEN
OUTHOUSE	OUTLAIN	OUTLIVED	OUTPARTS	OUTPREENS
OUTHOUSES	OUTLAND	OUTLIVER	OUTPASS	OUTPRESS
OUTHOWL	OUTLANDER	OUTLIVERS	OUTPASSED	OUTPRICE
OUTHOWLED	OUTLANDS	OUTLIVES	OUTPASSES	OUTPRICED
OUTHOWLS	OUTLASH	OUTLIVING	OUTPEEP	OUTPRICES
OUTHUMOR	OUTLASHED	OUTLOOK	OUTPEEPED	OUTPRIZE
OUTHUMORS	OUTLASHES	OUTLOOKED	OUTPEEPS	OUTPRIZED
OUTHUMOUR	OUTLAST	OUTLOOKS	OUTPEER	OUTPRIZES
OUTHUNT	OUTLASTED	OUTLOVE	OUTPEERED	OUTPSYCH
OUTHUNTED	OUTLASTS	OUTLOVED	OUTPEERS	OUTPSYCHS
OUTHUNTS	OUTLAUGH	OUTLOVES	OUTPEOPLE	OUTPULL
OUTHUSTLE	OUTLAUGHS	OUTLOVING	OUTPITCH	OUTPULLED
OUTHYRE	OUTLAUNCE	OUTLUSTER	OUTPITIED	OUTPULLS
OUTHYRED	OUTLAUNCH	OUTLUSTRE	OUTPITIES	OUTPUNCH
OUTHYRES	OUTLAW	OUTLYING	OUTPITY	OUTPUPIL
OUTHYRING	OUTLAWED	OUTMAN	OUTPLACE	OUTPUPILS
OUTIE	OUTLAWING	OUTMANNED	OUTPLACED	OUTPURSUE
OUTIES	OUTLAWRY	OUTMANS	OUTPLACER	OUTPUSH
OUTING	OUTLAWS	OUTMANTLE	OUTPLACES	OUTPUSHED

OUTPUSHES	OUTREMER	OUTRUSHES	OUTSHOTS	OUTSOURCE
OUTPUT	OUTREMERS	OUTS	OUTSHOUT	OUTSPAN
OUTPUTS	OUTRIDDEN	OUTSAID	OUTSHOUTS	OUTSPANS
OUTPUTTED	OUTRIDE	OUTSAIL	OUTSIDE	OUTSPEAK
OUTQUOTE	OUTRIDER	OUTSAILED	OUTSIDER	OUTSPEAKS
OUTQUOTED	OUTRIDERS	OUTSAILS	OUTSIDERS	OUTSPED
OUTQUOTES	OUTRIDES	OUTSANG	OUTSIDES	OUTSPEED
OUTRACE	OUTRIDING	OUTSAT	OUTSIGHT	OUTSPEEDS
OUTRACED	OUTRIG	OUTSAVOR	OUTSIGHTS	OUTSPELL
OUTRACES	OUTRIGGED	OUTSAVORS	OUTSIN	OUTSPELLS
OUTRACING	OUTRIGGER	OUTSAVOUR	OUTSING	OUTSPELT
OUTRAGE	OUTRIGHT	OUTSAW	OUTSINGS	OUTSPEND
OUTRAGED	OUTRIGS	OUTSAY	OUTSINNED	OUTSPENDS
OUTRAGES	OUTRING	OUTSAYING	OUTSINS	OUTSPENT
OUTRAGING	OUTRINGS	OUTSAYS	OUTSIT	OUTSPOKE
OUTRAISE	OUTRIVAL	OUTSCHEME	OUTSITS	OUTSPOKEN
OUTRAISED	OUTRIVALS	OUTSCOLD	OUTSIZE	OUTSPORT
OUTRAISES	OUTRO	OUTSCOLDS	OUTSIZED	OUTSPORTS
OUTRAN	OUTROAR	OUTSCOOP	OUTSIZES	OUTSPRANG
OUTRANCE	OUTROARED	OUTSCOOPS	OUTSKATE	OUTSPREAD
OUTRANCES	OUTROARS	OUTSCORE	OUTSKATED	OUTSPRING
OUTRANG	OUTROCK	OUTSCORED	OUTSKATES	OUTSPRINT
OUTRANGE	OUTROCKED	OUTSCORES	OUTSKIRT	OUTSPRUNG
OUTRANGED	OUTROCKS	OUTSCORN	OUTSKIRTS	OUTSTAND
OUTRANGES	OUTRODE	OUTSCORNS	OUTSLEEP	OUTSTANDS
OUTRANK	OUTROLL	OUTSCREAM	OUTSLEEPS	OUTSTARE
OUTRANKED	OUTROLLED	OUTSEE	OUTSLEPT	OUTSTARED
OUTRANKS	OUTROLLS	OUTSEEING	OUTSLICK	OUTSTARES
OUTRATE	OUTROOP	OUTSEEN	OUTSLICKS	OUTSTART
OUTRATED	OUTROOPER	OUTSEES	OUTSMART	OUTSTARTS
OUTRATES	OUTROOPS	OUTSELL	OUTSMARTS	OUTSTATE
OUTRATING	OUTROOT	OUTSELLS	OUTSMELL	OUTSTATED
OUTRAVE	OUTROOTED	OUTSERT	OUTSMELLS	OUTSTATES
OUTRAVED	OUTROOTS	OUTSERTS	OUTSMELT	OUTSTAY
OUTRAVES	OUTROPE	OUTSERVE	OUTSMILE	OUTSTAYED
OUTRAVING	OUTROPER	OUTSERVED	OUTSMILED	OUTSTAYS
OUTRE	OUTROPERS	OUTSERVES	OUTSMILES	OUTSTEER
OUTREACH	OUTROPES	OUTSET	OUTSMOKE	OUTSTEERS
OUTREAD	OUTROS	OUTSETS	OUTSMOKED	OUTSTEP
OUTREADS	OUTROW	OUTSHAME	OUTSMOKES	OUTSTEPS
OUTREASON	OUTROWED	OUTSHAMED	OUTSNORE	OUTSTOOD
OUTRECKON	OUTROWING	OUTSHAMES	OUTSNORED	OUTSTRAIN
OUTRED	OUTROWS	OUTSHINE	OUTSNORES	OUTSTRIDE
OUTREDDED	OUTRUN	OUTSHINED	OUTSOAR	OUTSTRIKE
OUTREDDEN	OUTRUNG	OUTSHINES	OUTSOARED	OUTSTRIP
OUTREDS	OUTRUNNER	OUTSHONE	OUTSOARS	OUTSTRIPS
OUTREIGN	OUTRUNS	OUTSHOOT	OUTSOLD	OUTSTRIVE
OUTREIGNS	OUTRUSH	OUTSHOOTS	OUTSOLE	OUTSTRODE
OUTRELIEF	OUTRUSHED	OUTSHOT	OUTSOLES	OUTSTROKE

OUTSTROVE	OUTTHROBS	OUTWALKED	OUTWISH	OVALNESS
OUTSTRUCK	OUTTHROW	OUTWALKS	OUTWISHED	OVALS
OUTSTUDY	OUTTHROWN	OUTWAR	OUTWISHES	OVARIAL
OUTSTUNT	OUTTHROWS	OUTWARD	OUTWIT	OVARIAN
OUTSTUNTS	OUTTHRUST	OUTWARDLY	OUTWITH	OVARIES
OUTSULK	OUTTOLD	OUTWARDS	OUTWITS	OVARIOLE
OUTSULKED	OUTTONGUE	OUTWARRED	OUTWITTED	OVARIOLES
OUTSULKS	OUTTOOK	OUTWARS	OUTWON	OVARIOUS
OUTSUM	OUTTOP	OUTWASH	OUTWORE	OVARITIS
OUTSUMMED	OUTTOPPED	OUTWASHES	OUTWORK	OVARY
OUTSUMS	OUTTOPS	OUTWASTE	OUTWORKED	OVATE
OUTSUNG	OUTTOWER	OUTWASTED	OUTWORKER	OVATED
OUTSWAM	OUTTOWERS	OUTWASTES	OUTWORKS	OVATELY
OUTSWARE	OUTTRADE	OUTWATCH	OUTWORN	OVATES
OUTSWEAR	OUTTRADED	OUTWEAR	OUTWORTH	OVATING
OUTSWEARS	OUTTRADES	OUTWEARS	OUTWORTHS	OVATION
OUTSWEEP	OUTTRAVEL	OUTWEARY	OUTWOUND	OVATIONAL
OUTSWEEPS	OUTTRICK	OUTWEED	OUTWREST	OVATIONS
OUTSWELL	OUTTRICKS	OUTWEEDED	OUTWRESTS	OVATOR
OUTSWELLS	OUTTROT	OUTWEEDS	OUTWRIT	OVATORS
OUTSWEPT	OUTTROTS	OUTWEEP	OUTWRITE	OVEL
OUTSWIM	OUTTRUMP	OUTWEEPS	OUTWRITES	OVELS
OUTSWIMS	OUTTRUMPS	OUTWEIGH	OUTWROTE	OVEN
OUTSWING	OUTTURN	OUTWEIGHS	OUTYELL	OVENABLE
OUTSWINGS	OUTTURNS	OUTWELL	OUTYELLED	OVENBIRD
OUTSWORE	OUTVALUE	OUTWELLED	OUTYELLS	OVENBIRDS
OUTSWORN	OUTVALUED	OUTWELLS	OUTYELP	OVENED
OUTSWUM	OUTVALUES	OUTWENT	OUTYELPED	OVENING
OUTSWUNG	OUTVAUNT	OUTWEPT	OUTYELPS	OVENLIKE
OUTTA	OUTVAUNTS	OUTWHIRL	OUTYIELD	OVENPROOF
OUTTAKE	OUTVENOM	OUTWHIRLS	OUTYIELDS	OVENS
OUTTAKEN	OUTVENOMS	OUTWICK	OUVERT	OVENWARE
OUTTAKES	OUTVIE	OUTWICKED	OUVERTE	OVENWARES
OUTTAKING	OUTVIED	OUTWICKS	OUVRAGE	OVENWOOD
OUTTALK	OUTVIES	OUTWILE	OUVRAGES	OVENWOODS
OUTTALKED	OUTVOICE	OUTWILED	OUVRIER	OVER
OUTTALKS	OUTVOICED	OUTWILES	OUVRIERE	OVERABLE
OUTTASK	OUTVOICES	OUTWILING	OUVRIERES	OVERACT
OUTTASKED	OUTVOTE	OUTWILL	OUVRIERS	OVERACTED
OUTTASKS	OUTVOTED	OUTWILLED	OUZEL	OVERACTS
OUTTELL	OUTVOTER	OUTWILLS	OUZELS	OVERACUTE
OUTTELLS	OUTVOTERS	OUTWIN	OUZO	OVERAGE
OUTTHANK	OUTVOTES	OUTWIND	OUZOS	OVERAGED
OUTTHANKS	OUTVOTING	OUTWINDED	OVA	OVERAGES
OUTTHIEVE	OUTVYING	OUTWINDS	OVAL	OVERALERT
OUTTHINK	OUTWAIT	OUTWING	OVALBUMIN	OVERALL
OUTTHINKS	OUTWAITED	OUTWINGED	OVALITIES	OVERALLED
OUTTHREW	OUTWAITS	OUTWINGS	OVALITY	OVERALLS
OUTTHROB	OUTWALK	OUTWINS	OVALLY	OVERAPT

OVERARCH	OVERBRIMS	OVERCOOLS	OVERDROVE	OVERFLEW
OVERARM	OVERBROAD	OVERCOUNT	OVERDRUNK	OVERFLIES
OVERARMED	OVERBROW	OVERCOVER	OVERDRY	OVERFLOOD
OVERARMS	OVERBROWS	OVERCOY	OVERDUB	OVERFLOW
OVERATE	OVERBUILD	OVERCRAM	OVERDUBS	OVERFLOWN
OVERAWE	OVERBUILT	OVERCRAMS	OVERDUE	OVERFLOWS
OVERAWED	OVERBULK	OVERCRAW	OVERDUST	OVERFLUSH
OVERAWES	OVERBULKS	OVERCRAWS	OVERDUSTS	OVERFLY
OVERAWING	OVERBURN	OVERCROP	OVERDYE	OVERFOCUS
OVERBAKE	OVERBURNS	OVERCROPS	OVERDYED	OVERFOLD
OVERBAKED	OVERBURNT	OVERCROW	OVERDYER	OVERFOLDS
OVERBAKES	OVERBUSY	OVERCROWD	OVERDYERS	OVERFOND
OVERBANK	OVERBUY	OVERCROWS	OVERDYES	OVERFOUL
OVERBANKS	OVERBUYS	OVERCURE	OVEREAGER	OVERFRANK
OVERBEAR	OVERBY	OVERCURED	OVEREASY	OVERFREE
OVERBEARS	OVERCALL	OVERCURES	OVEREAT	OVERFULL
OVERBEAT	OVERCALLS	OVERCUT	OVEREATEN	OVERFUND
OVERBEATS	OVERCAME	OVERCUTS	OVEREATER	OVERFUNDS
OVERBED	OVERCARRY	OVERDARE	OVEREATS	OVERFUSSY
OVERBET	OVERCAST	OVERDARED	OVERED	OVERGALL
OVERBETS	OVERCASTS	OVERDARES	OVEREDIT	OVERGALLS
OVERBID	OVERCATCH	OVERDATED	OVEREDITS	OVERGANG
OVERBIDS	OVERCHEAP	OVERDEAR	OVEREGG	OVERGANGS
OVERBIG	OVERCHECK	OVERDECK	OVEREGGED	OVERGAVE
OVERBILL	OVERCHILL	OVERDECKS	OVEREGGS	OVERGEAR
OVERBILLS	OVERCIVIL	OVERDID	OVEREMOTE	OVERGEARS
OVERBITE	OVERCLAD	OVERDIGHT	OVEREQUIP	OVERGET
OVERBITES	OVERCLAIM	OVERDO	OVEREXERT	OVERGETS
OVERBLEW	OVERCLASS	OVERDOER	OVEREYE	OVERGILD
OVERBLOW	OVERCLEAN	OVERDOERS	OVEREYED	OVERGILDS
OVERBLOWN	OVERCLEAR	OVERDOES	OVEREYES	OVERGILT
OVERBLOWS	OVERCLOCK	OVERDOG	OVEREYING	OVERGIRD
OVERBOARD	OVERCLOSE	OVERDOGS	OVERFALL	OVERGIRDS
OVERBOIL	OVERCLOUD	OVERDOING	OVERFALLS	OVERGIRT
OVERBOILS	OVERCLOY	OVERDONE	OVERFAR	OVERGIVE
OVERBOLD	OVERCLOYS	OVERDOSE	OVERFAST	OVERGIVEN
OVERBOOK	OVERCLUB	OVERDOSED	OVERFAT	OVERGIVES
OVERBOOKS	OVERCLUBS	OVERDOSES	OVERFAVOR	OVERGLAD
OVERBOOT	OVERCOACH	OVERDRAFT	OVERFEAR	OVERGLAZE
OVERBOOTS	OVERCOAT	OVERDRANK	OVERFEARS	OVERGLOOM
OVERBORE	OVERCOATS	OVERDRAW	OVERFED	OVERGO
OVERBORN	OVERCOLD	OVERDRAWN	OVERFEED	OVERGOAD
OVERBORNE	OVERCOLOR	OVERDRAWS	OVERFEEDS	OVERGOADS
OVERBOUND	OVERCOME	OVERDRESS	OVERFELL	OVERGOES
OVERBRAKE	OVERCOMER	OVERDREW	OVERFILL	OVERGOING
OVERBRED	OVERCOMES	OVERDRIED	OVERFILLS	OVERGONE
OVERBREED	OVERCOOK	OVERDRIES	OVERFINE	OVERGORGE
OVERBRIEF	OVERCOOKS	OVERDRINK	OVERFISH	OVERGOT
OVERBRIM	OVERCOOL	OVERDRIVE	OVERFIT	OVERGRADE

OVERGRAIN	OVERHOPES	OVERLEAPS	OVERMINE	OVERPOST
OVERGRASS	OVERHOT	OVERLEAPT	OVERMINED	OVERPOSTS
OVERGRAZE	OVERHUNG	OVERLEARN	OVERMINES	OVERPOWER
OVERGREAT	OVERHUNT	OVERLEND	OVERMIX	OVERPRESS
OVERGREEN	OVERHUNTS	OVERLENDS	OVERMIXED	OVERPRICE
OVERGREW	OVERHYPE	OVERLENT	OVERMIXES	OVERPRINT
OVERGROW	OVERHYPED	OVERLET	OVERMOUNT	OVERPRIZE
OVERGROWN	OVERHYPES	OVERLETS	OVERMUCH	OVERPROOF
OVERGROWS	OVERIDLE	OVERLEWD	OVERNAME	OVERPROUD
OVERHAILE	OVERING	OVERLIE	OVERNAMED	OVERPUMP
OVERHAIR	OVERINKED	OVERLIER	OVERNAMES	OVERPUMPS
OVERHAIRS	OVERISSUE	OVERLIERS	OVERNEAR	OVERQUICK
OVERHALE	OVERJOY	OVERLIES	OVERNEAT	OVERRACK
OVERHALED	OVERJOYED	OVERLIGHT	OVERNET	OVERRACKS
OVERHALES	OVERJOYS	OVERLIT	OVERNETS	OVERRAKE
OVERHAND	OVERJUMP	OVERLIVE	OVERNEW	OVERRAKED
OVERHANDS	OVERJUMPS	OVERLIVED	OVERNICE	OVERRAKES
OVERHANG	OVERJUST	OVERLIVES	OVERNIGHT	OVERRAN
OVERHANGS	OVERKEEN	OVERLOAD	OVERPACK	OVERRANK
OVERHAPPY	OVERKEEP	OVERLOADS	OVERPACKS	OVERRANKS
OVERHARD	OVERKEEPS	OVERLOCK	OVERPAGE	OVERRASH
OVERHASTE	OVERKEPT	OVERLOCKS	OVERPAID	OVERRATE
OVERHASTY	OVERKEST	OVERLONG	OVERPAINT	OVERRATED
OVERHATE	OVERKILL	OVERLOOK	OVERPART	OVERRATES
OVERHATED	OVERKILLS	OVERLOOKS	OVERPARTS	OVERREACH
OVERHATES	OVERKIND	OVERLORD	OVERPASS	OVERREACT
OVERHAUL	OVERKING	OVERLORDS	OVERPAST	OVERREAD
OVERHAULS	OVERKINGS	OVERLOUD	OVERPAY	OVERREADS
OVERHEAD	OVERKNEE	OVERLOVE	OVERPAYS	OVERRED
OVERHEADS	OVERLABOR	OVERLOVED	OVERPEDAL	OVERREDS
OVERHEAP	OVERLADE	OVERLOVES	OVERPEER	OVERREN
OVERHEAPS	OVERLADED	OVERLUSH	OVERPEERS	OVERRENS
OVERHEAR	OVERLADEN	OVERLUSTY	OVERPERCH	OVERRICH
OVERHEARD	OVERLADES	OVERLY	OVERPERT	OVERRIDE
OVERHEARS	OVERLAID	OVERLYING	OVERPITCH	OVERRIDER
OVERHEAT	OVERLAIN	OVERMAN	OVERPLAID	OVERRIDES
OVERHEATS	OVERLAND	OVERMANS	OVERPLAN	OVERRIFE
OVERHELD	OVERLANDS	OVERMANY	OVERPLANS	OVERRIGID
OVERHENT	OVERLAP	OVERMAST	OVERPLANT	OVERRIPE
OVERHENTS	OVERLAPS	OVERMASTS	OVERPLAST	OVERRIPEN
OVERHIGH	OVERLARD	OVERMATCH	OVERPLAY	OVERROAST
OVERHIT	OVERLARDS	OVERMEEK	OVERPLAYS	OVERRODE
OVERHITS	OVERLARGE	OVERMELT	OVERPLIED	OVERRUDE
OVERHOLD	OVERLATE	OVERMELTS	OVERPLIES	OVERRUFF
OVERHOLDS	OVERLAX	OVERMEN	OVERPLOT	OVERRUFFS
OVERHOLY	OVERLAY	OVERMERRY	OVERPLOTS	OVERRULE
OVERHONOR	OVERLAYS	OVERMILD	OVERPLUS	OVERRULED
OVERHOPE	OVERLEAF	OVERMILK	OVERPLY	OVERRULER
OVERHOPED	OVERLEAP	OVERMILKS	OVERPOISE	OVERRULES

OVERRUN	OVERSIDES	OVERSTIRS	OVERTIMED	OVERVIVID
OVERRUNS	OVERSIGHT	OVERSTOCK	OVERTIMER	OVERVOTE
OVERS	OVERSIZE	OVERSTOOD	OVERTIMES	OVERVOTED
OVERSAD	OVERSIZED	OVERSTORY	OVERTIMID	OVERVOTES
OVERSAIL	OVERSIZES	OVERSTREW	OVERTIP	OVERWARM
OVERSAILS	OVERSKATE	OVERSTUDY	OVERTIPS	OVERWARMS
OVERSALE	OVERSKIP	OVERSTUFF	OVERTIRE	OVERWARY
OVERSALES	OVERSKIPS	OVERSTUNK	OVERTIRED	OVERWASH
OVERSALT	OVERSKIRT	OVERSUDS	OVERTIRES	OVERWATCH
OVERSALTS	OVERSLEEP	OVERSUP	OVERTLY	OVERWATER
OVERSAUCE	OVERSLEPT	OVERSUPS	OVERTNESS	OVERWEAK
OVERSAVE	OVERSLIP	OVERSURE	OVERTOIL	OVERWEAR
OVERSAVED	OVERSLIPS	OVERSWAM	OVERTOILS	OVERWEARS
OVERSAVES	OVERSLIPT	OVERSWAY	OVERTONE	OVERWEARY
OVERSAW	OVERSLOW	OVERSWAYS	OVERTONES	OVERWEEN
OVERSCALE	OVERSMAN	OVERSWEAR	OVERTOOK	OVERWEENS
OVERSCORE	OVERSMEN	OVERSWEET	OVERTOP	OVERWEIGH
OVERSEA	OVERSMOKE	OVERSWELL	OVERTOPS	OVERWENT
OVERSEAS	OVERSOAK	OVERSWIM	OVERTOWER	OVERWET
OVERSEE	OVERSOAKS	OVERSWIMS	OVERTRADE	OVERWETS
OVERSEED	OVERSOFT	OVERSWING	OVERTRAIN	OVERWHELM
OVERSEEDS	OVERSOLD	OVERSWORE	OVERTREAT	OVERWIDE
OVERSEEN	OVERSOON	OVERSWORN	OVERTRICK	OVERWILY
OVERSEER	OVERSOUL	OVERSWUM	OVERTRIM	OVERWIND
OVERSEERS	OVERSOULS	OVERSWUNG	OVERTRIMS	OVERWINDS
OVERSEES	OVERSOW	OVERT	OVERTRIP	OVERWING
OVERSELL	OVERSOWED	OVERTAKE	OVERTRIPS	OVERWINGS
OVERSELLS	OVERSOWN	OVERTAKEN	OVERTRUMP	OVERWISE
OVERSERVE	OVERSOWS	OVERTAKES	OVERTRUST	OVERWORD
OVERSET	OVERSPEND	OVERTALK	OVERTURE	OVERWORDS
OVERSETS	OVERSPENT	OVERTALKS	OVERTURED	OVERWORE
OVERSEW	OVERSPICE	OVERTAME	OVERTURES	OVERWORK
OVERSEWED	OVERSPILL	OVERTART	OVERTURN	OVERWORKS
OVERSEWN	OVERSPILT	OVERTASK	OVERTURNS	OVERWORN
OVERSEWS	OVERSPIN	OVERTASKS	OVERTYPE	OVERWOUND
OVERSEXED	OVERSPINS	OVERTAX	OVERTYPED	OVERWRAP
OVERSHADE	OVERSTAFF	OVERTAXED	OVERTYPES	OVERWRAPS
OVERSHARE	OVERSTAIN	OVERTAXES	OVERURGE	OVERWRAPT
OVERSHARP	OVERSTAND	OVERTEACH	OVERURGED	OVERWREST
OVERSHINE	OVERSTANK	OVERTEEM	OVERURGES	OVERWRITE
OVERSHIRT	OVERSTARE	OVERTEEMS	OVERUSE	OVERWROTE
OVERSHOE	OVERSTATE	OVERTHICK	OVERUSED	OVERYEAR
OVERSHOES	OVERSTAY	OVERTHIN	OVERUSES	OVERYEARS
OVERSHONE	OVERSTAYS	OVERTHINK	OVERUSING	OVERZEAL
OVERSHOOT	OVERSTEER	OVERTHINS	OVERVALUE	OVERZEALS
OVERSHOT	OVERSTEP	OVERTHREW	OVERVEIL	OVIBOS
OVERSHOTS	OVERSTEPS	OVERTHROW	OVERVEILS	OVIBOSES
OVERSICK	OVERSTINK	OVERTIGHT	OVERVIEW	OVIBOVINE
OVERSIDE	OVERSTIR	OVERTIME	OVERVIEWS	OVICIDAL

OVICIDE	OWELTY	OWSE	OXIDABLE	OXTAILS
OVICIDES	OWER	OWSEN	OXIDANT	OXTER
OVIDUCAL	OWERBY	OWT	OXIDANTS	OXTERED
OVIDUCT	OWERLOUP	OWTS	OXIDASE	OXTERING
OVIDUCTAL	OWERLOUPS	OX	OXIDASES	OXTERS
OVIDUCTS	OWES	OXACILLIN	OXIDASIC	OXTONGUE
OVIFEROUS	OWIE	OXALATE	OXIDATE	OXTONGUES
OVIFORM	OWIES	OXALATED	OXIDATED	OXY
OVIGEROUS	OWING	OXALATES	OXIDATES	OXYACID
OVINE	OWL	OXALATING	OXIDATING	OXYACIDS
OVINES	OWLED	OXALIC	OXIDATION	OXYANION
OVIPARA	OWLER	OXALIS	OXIDATIVE	OXYANIONS
OVIPARITY	OWLERIES	OXALISES	OXIDE	OXYCODONE
OVIPAROUS	OWLERS	OXAZEPAM	OXIDES	OXYGEN
OVIPOSIT	OWLERY	OXAZEPAMS	OXIDIC	OXYGENASE
OVIPOSITS	OWLET	OXAZINE	OXIDISE	OXYGENATE
OVIRAPTOR	OWLETS	OXAZINES	OXIDISED	OXYGENIC
OVISAC	OWLIER	OXAZOLE	OXIDISER	OXYGENISE
OVISACS	OWLIEST	OXAZOLES	OXIDISERS	OXYGENIZE
OVIST	OWLING	OXBLOOD	OXIDISES	OXYGENOUS
OVISTS	OWLISH	OXBLOODS	OXIDISING	OXYGENS
OVOID	OWLISHLY	OXBOW	OXIDIZE	OXYMEL
OVOIDAL	OWLLIKE	OXBOWS	OXIDIZED	OXYMELS
OVOIDALS	OWLS	OXCART	OXIDIZER	OXYMORA
OVOIDS	OWLY	OXCARTS	OXIDIZERS	OXYMORON
OVOLI	OWN	OXEN	OXIDIZES	OXYMORONS
OVOLO	OWNABLE	OXER	OXIDIZING	OXYNTIC
OVOLOS	OWNED	OXERS	OXIDS	OXYPHIL
OVONIC	OWNER	OXES	OXIES	OXYPHILE
OVONICS	OWNERLESS	OXEYE	OXIM	OXYPHILES
OVOTESTES	OWNERS	OXEYES	OXIME	OXYPHILIC
OVOTESTIS	OWNERSHIP	OXFORD	OXIMES	OXYPHILS
OVULAR	OWNING	OXFORDS	OXIMETER	OXYSALT
OVULARY	OWNS	OXGALL	OXIMETERS	OXYSALTS
OVULATE	OWNSOME	OXGALLS	OXIMETRY	OXYSOME
OVULATED	OWNSOMES	OXGANG	OXIMS	OXYSOMES
OVULATES	OWO	OXGANGS	OXLAND	OXYTOCIC
OVULATING	OWRE	OXGATE	OXLANDS	OXYTOCICS
OVULATION	OWRECAME	OXGATES	OXLIKE	OXYTOCIN
OVULATORY	OWRECOME	OXHEAD	OXLIP	OXYTOCINS
OVULE	OWRECOMES	OXHEADS	OXLIPS	OXYTONE
OVULES	OWRELAY	OXHEART	OXO	OXYTONES
OVUM	OWRELAYS	OXHEARTS	OXONIUM	OXYTONIC
OW	OWRES	OXHERD	OXONIUMS	OXYTROPE
OWCHE	OWREWORD	OXHERDS	OXPECKER	OXYTROPES
OWCHES	OWREWORDS	OXHIDE	OXPECKERS	OY
OWE	OWRIE	OXHIDES	OXSLIP	OYE
OWED	OWRIER	OXIC	OXSLIPS	OYER
OWELTIES	OWRIEST	OXID	OXTAIL	OYERS

OYES	OYSTERING	OZEKI	OZONES	OZONIZE
OYESES	OYSTERMAN	OZEKIS	OZONIC	OZONIZED
OYESSES	OYSTERMEN	OZOCERITE	OZONIDE	OZONIZER
OYEZ	OYSTERS	OZOKERITE	OZONIDES	OZONIZERS
OYEZES	OYSTRIGE	OZONATE	OZONISE	OZONIZES
OYS	OYSTRIGES	OZONATED	OZONISED	OZONIZING
OYSTER	OZAENA	OZONATES	OZONISER	OZONOUS
OYSTERED	OZAENAS	OZONATING	OZONISERS	OZZIE
OYSTERER	OZALID	OZONATION	OZONISES	OZZIES
OYSTERERS	OZALIDS	OZONE	OZONISING	

P

PA	PACHOULIS	PACKFRAME	PADDINGS	PADS
PAAL	PACHUCO	PACKHORSE	PADDLE	PADSAW
PAALS	PACHUCOS	PACKING	PADDLED	PADSAWS
PAAN	PACHYDERM	PACKINGS	PADDLER	PADSHAH
PAANS	PACHYTENE	PACKLY	PADDLERS	PADSHAHS
PABLUM	PACIER	PACKMAN	PADDLES	PADUASOY
PABLUMS	PACIEST	PACKMEN	PADDLING	PADUASOYS
PABOUCHE	PACIFIC	PACKMULE	PADDLINGS	PADYMELON
PABOUCHES	PACIFICAE	PACKMULES	PADDOCK	PAEAN
PABULAR	PACIFICAL	PACKNESS	PADDOCKED	PAEANISM
PABULOUS	PACIFIED	PACKS	PADDOCKS	PAEANISMS
PABULUM	PACIFIER	PACKSACK	PADDY	PAEANS
PABULUMS	PACIFIERS	PACKSACKS	PADDYWACK	PAEDERAST
PAC	PACIFIES	PACKSHEET	PADELLA	PAEDEUTIC
PACA	PACIFISM	PACKSTAFF	PADELLAS	PAEDIATRY
PACABLE	PACIFISMS	PACKWAX	PADEMELON	PAEDO
PACAS	PACIFIST	PACKWAXES	PADERERO	PAEDOLOGY
PACATION	PACIFISTS	PACKWAY	PADEREROS	PAEDOS
PACATIONS	PACIFY	PACKWAYS	PADI	PAELLA
PACE	PACIFYING	PACO	PADIS	PAELLAS
PACED	PACING	PACOS	PADISHAH	PAENULA
PACEMAKER	PACINGS	PACS	PADISHAHS	PAENULAE
PACEMAN	PACK	PACT	PADKOS	PAENULAS
PACEMEN	PACKABLE	PACTA	PADLE	PAEON
PACER	PACKAGE	PACTION	PADLES	PAEONIC
PACERS	PACKAGED	PACTIONAL	PADLOCK	PAEONICS
PACES	PACKAGER	PACTIONED	PADLOCKED	PAEONIES
PACEWAY	PACKAGERS	PACTIONS	PADLOCKS	PAEONS
PACEWAYS	PACKAGES	PACTS	PADMA	PAEONY
PACEY	PACKAGING	PACTUM	PADMAS	PAESAN
PACHA	PACKBOARD	PACY	PADNAG	PAESANI
PACHADOM	PACKCLOTH	PACZKI	PADNAGS	PAESANO
PACHADOMS	PACKED	PACZKIS	PADOUK	PAESANOS
PACHAK	PACKER	PAD	PADOUKS	PAESANS
PACHAKS	PACKERS	PADANG	PADRE	PAGAN
PACHALIC	PACKET	PADANGS	PADRES	PAGANDOM
PACHALICS	PACKETED	PADAUK	PADRI	PAGANDOMS
PACHAS	PACKETING	PADAUKS	PADRONA	PAGANISE
PACHINKO	PACKETISE	PADDED	PADRONAS	PAGANISED
PACHINKOS	PACKETIZE	PADDER	PADRONE	PAGANISER
PACHISI	PACKETS	PADDERS	PADRONES	PAGANISES
PACHISIS	PACKFONG	PADDIES	PADRONI	PAGANISH
PACHOULI	PACKFONGS	PADDING	PADRONISM	PAGANISM

PAGANISMS	PAHOEHOE	PAINTRESS	PAKEHA	PALATALLY
PAGANIST	PAHOEHOES	PAINTS	PAKEHAS	PALATALS
PAGANISTS	PAHS	PAINTURE	PAKFONG	PALATE
PAGANIZE	PAID	PAINTURES	PAKFONGS	PALATED
PAGANIZED	PAIDEUTIC	PAINTWORK	PAKIHI	PALATES
PAGANIZER	PAIDLE	PAINTY	PAKIHIS	PALATIAL
PAGANIZES	PAIDLES	PAIOCK	PAKKA	PALATINE
PAGANS	PAIGLE	PAIOCKE	PAKOKO	PALATINES
PAGE	PAIGLES	PAIOCKES	PAKOKOS	PALATING
PAGEANT	PAIK	PAIOCKS	PAKORA	PALAVER
PAGEANTRY	PAIKED	PAIR	PAKORAS	PALAVERED
PAGEANTS	PAIKING	PAIRABLE	PAKS	PALAVERER
PAGEBOY	PAIKS	PAIRE	PAKTHONG	PALAVERS
PAGEBOYS	PAIL	PAIRED	PAKTHONGS	PALAY
PAGED	PAILFUL	PAIRER	PAKTONG	PALAYS
PAGEFUL	PAILFULS	PAIRES	PAKTONGS	PALAZZI
PAGEFULS	PAILLARD	PAIREST	PAL	PALAZZO
PAGEHOOD	PAILLARDS	PAIRIAL	PALABRA	PALAZZOS
PAGEHOODS	PAILLASSE	PAIRIALS	PALABRAS	PALE
PAGER	PAILLETTE	PAIRING	PALACE	PALEA
PAGERS	PAILLON	PAIRINGS	PALACED	PALEAE
PAGES	PAILLONS	PAIRS	PALACES	PALEAL
PAGEVIEW	PAILS	PAIRWISE	PALACINKE	PALEATE
PAGEVIEWS	PAILSFUL	PAIS	PALADIN	PALEBUCK
PAGINAL	PAIN	PAISA	PALADINS	PALEBUCKS
PAGINATE	PAINCH	PAISAN	PALAEO	PALED
PAGINATED	PAINCHES	PAISANA	PALAEOART	PALEFACE
PAGINATES	PAINED	PAISANAS	PALAEOS	PALEFACES
PAGING	PAINFUL	PAISANO	PALAEOSOL	PALELY
PAGINGS	PAINFULLY	PAISANOS	PALAESTRA	PALEMPORE
PAGLE	PAINIM	PAISANS	PALAFITTE	PALENESS
PAGLES	PAINIMS	PAISAS	PALAGI	PALEO
PAGOD	PAINING	PAISE	PALAGIS	PALEOART
PAGODA	PAINLESS	PAISLEY	PALAIS	PALEOARTS
PAGODAS	PAINS	PAISLEYS	PALAMA	PALEOCENE
PAGODITE	PAINT	PAITRICK	PALAMAE	PALEOCON
PAGODITES	PAINTABLE	PAITRICKS	PALAMATE	PALEOCONS
PAGODS	PAINTBALL	PAJAMA	PALAMINO	PALEOGENE
PAGRI	PAINTBOX	PAJAMAED	PALAMINOS	PALEOLITH
PAGRIS	PAINTED	PAJAMAS	PALAMPORE	PALEOLOGY
PAGURIAN	PAINTER	PAJOCK	PALANKEEN	PALEOS
PAGURIANS	PAINTERLY	PAJOCKE	PALANQUIN	PALEOSOL
PAGURID	PAINTERS	PAJOCKES	PALAPA	PALEOSOLS
PAGURIDS	PAINTIER	PAJOCKS	PALAPAS	PALEOZOIC
PAH	PAINTIEST	PAK	PALAS	PALER
PAHAUTEA	PAINTING	PAKAHI	PALASES	PALES
PAHAUTEAS	PAINTINGS	PAKAHIS	PALATABLE	PALEST
PAHLAVI	PAINTPOT	PAKAPOO	PALATABLY	PALESTRA
PAHLAVIS	PAINTPOTS	PAKAPOOS	PALATAL	PALESTRAE

PALESTRAL	PALLASITE	PALMER	PALPATES	PALUDISM
PALESTRAS	PALLED	PALMERS	PALPATING	PALUDISMS
PALET	PALLET	PALMETTE	PALPATION	PALUDOSE
PALETOT	PALLETED	PALMETTES	PALPATOR	PALUDOUS
PALETOTS	PALLETING	PALMETTO	PALPATORS	PALUSTRAL
PALETS	PALLETISE	PALMETTOS	PALPATORY	PALY
PALETTE	PALLETIZE	PALMFUL	PALPEBRA	PAM
PALETTES	PALLETS	PALMFULS	PALPEBRAE	PAMPA
PALEWAYS	PALLETTE	PALMHOUSE	PALPEBRAL	PAMPAS
PALEWISE	PALLETTES	PALMIE	PALPEBRAS	PAMPASES
PALFREY	PALLIA	PALMIER	PALPED	PAMPEAN
PALFREYED	PALLIAL	PALMIERS	PALPI	PAMPEANS
PALFREYS	PALLIARD	PALMIES	PALPING	PAMPER
PALI	PALLIARDS	PALMIEST	PALPITANT	PAMPERED
PALIER	PALLIASSE	PALMIET	PALPITATE	PAMPERER
PALIEST	PALLIATE	PALMIETS	PALPS	PAMPERERS
PALIFORM	PALLIATED	PALMING	PALPUS	PAMPERING
PALIKAR	PALLIATES	PALMIPED	PALPUSES	PAMPERO
PALIKARS	PALLIATOR	PALMIPEDE	PALS	PAMPEROS
PALILALIA	PALLID	PALMIPEDS	PALSA	PAMPERS
PALILLOGY	PALLIDER	PALMIST	PALSAS	PAMPHLET
PALIMONY	PALLIDEST	PALMISTER	PALSGRAVE	PAMPHLETS
PALING	PALLIDITY	PALMISTRY	PALSHIP	PAMPHREY
PALINGS	PALLIDLY	PALMISTS	PALSHIPS	PAMPHREYS
PALINKA	PALLIED	PALMITATE	PALSIED	PAMPOEN
PALINKAS	PALLIER	PALMITIC	PALSIER	PAMPOENS
PALINODE	PALLIES	PALMITIN	PALSIES	PAMPOOTIE
PALINODES	PALLIEST	PALMITINS	PALSIEST	PAMS
PALINODY	PALLING	PALMLIKE	PALSTAFF	PAN
PALINOPIA	PALLIUM	PALMPRINT	PALSTAFFS	PANACEA
PALIS	PALLIUMS	PALMS	PALSTAVE	PANACEAN
PALISADE	PALLONE	PALMTOP	PALSTAVES	PANACEAS
PALISADED	PALLONES	PALMTOPS	PALSY	PANACHAEA
PALISADES	PALLOR	PALMY	PALSYING	PANACHE
PALISADO	PALLORS	PALMYRA	PALSYLIKE	PANACHES
PALISH	PALLS	PALMYRAS	PALTER	PANADA
PALKEE	PALLY	PALOLO	PALTERED	PANADAS
PALKEES	PALLYING	PALOLOS	PALTERER	PANAMA
PALKI	PALM	PALOMINO	PALTERERS	PANAMAS
PALKIS	PALMAR	PALOMINOS	PALTERING	PANARIES
PALL	PALMARIAN	PALOOKA	PALTERS	PANARY
PALLA	PALMARY	PALOOKAS	PALTRIER	PANATELA
PALLADIA	PALMATE	PALOVERDE	PALTRIEST	PANATELAS
PALLADIC	PALMATED	PALP	PALTRILY	PANATELLA
PALLADIUM	PALMATELY	PALPABLE	PALTRY	PANAX
PALLADOUS	PALMATION	PALPABLY	PALUDAL	PANAXES
PALLAE	PALMBALL	PALPAL	PALUDIC	PANBROIL
PALLAH	PALMBALLS	PALPATE	PALUDINAL	PANBROILS
PALLAHS	PALMED	PALPATED	PALUDINE	PANCAKE

PANCAKED	PANDERS	PANETTONI	PANIMS	PANNUS
PANCAKES	PANDIED	PANFISH	PANING	PANNUSES
PANCAKING	PANDIES	PANFISHED	PANINI	PANOCHA
PANCE	PANDIT	PANFISHES	PANINIS	PANOCHAS
PANCES	PANDITS	PANFORTE	PANINO	PANOCHE
PANCETTA	PANDOOR	PANFORTES	PANISC	PANOCHES
PANCETTAS	PANDOORS	PANFRIED	PANISCS	PANOISTIC
PANCHAX	PANDORA	PANFRIES	PANISK	PANOPLIED
PANCHAXES	PANDORAS	PANFRY	PANISKS	PANOPLIES
PANCHAYAT	PANDORE	PANFRYING	PANISLAM	PANOPLY
PANCHEON	PANDORES	PANFUL	PANISLAMS	PANOPTIC
PANCHEONS	PANDOUR	PANFULS	PANISSE	PANORAMA
PANCHION	PANDOURS	PANG	PANISSES	PANORAMAS
PANCHIONS	PANDOWDY	PANGA	PANJANDRA	PANORAMIC
PANCOSMIC	PANDROP	PANGAMIC	PANKO	PANPIPE
PANCRATIA	PANDROPS	PANGAMIES	PANKOS	PANPIPES
PANCRATIC	PANDS	PANGAMY	PANLIKE	PANS
PANCREAS	PANDURA	PANGAS	PANLOGISM	PANSEXUAL
PAND	PANDURAS	PANGED	PANMICTIC	PANSIED
PANDA	PANDURATE	PANGEN	PANMIXES	PANSIES
PANDAN	PANDY	PANGENE	PANMIXIA	PANSOPHIC
PANDANI	PANDYING	PANGENES	PANMIXIAS	PANSOPHY
PANDANIS	PANE	PANGENS	PANMIXIS	PANSPERMY
PANDANS	PANED	PANGING	PANNAGE	PANSTICK
PANDANUS	PANEER	PANGLESS	PANNAGES	PANSTICKS
PANDAR	PANEERS	PANGOLIN	PANNE	PANSY
PANDARED	PANEGOISM	PANGOLINS	PANNED	PANT
PANDARING	PANEGYRIC	PANGRAM	PANNELLED	PANTABLE
PANDARS	PANEGYRY	PANGRAMS	PANNER	PANTABLES
PANDAS	PANEITIES	PANGS	PANNERS	PANTAGAMY
PANDATION	PANEITY	PANHANDLE	PANNES	PANTALEON
PANDECT	PANEL	PANHUMAN	PANNI	PANTALET
PANDECTS	PANELED	PANIC	PANNICK	PANTALETS
PANDEIRO	PANELESS	PANICALLY	PANNICKS	PANTALON
PANDEIROS	PANELING	PANICK	PANNICLE	PANTALONE
PANDEMIA	PANELINGS	PANICKED	PANNICLES	PANTALONS
PANDEMIAN	PANELISED	PANICKIER	PANNIER	PANTALOON
PANDEMIAS	PANELIST	PANICKING	PANNIERED	PANTDRESS
PANDEMIC	PANELISTS	PANICKS	PANNIERS	PANTED
PANDEMICS	PANELIZED	PANICKY	PANNIKEL	PANTER
PANDER	PANELLED	PANICLE	PANNIKELL	PANTERS
PANDERED	PANELLING	PANICLED	PANNIKELS	PANTHEISM
PANDERER	PANELLIST	PANICLES	PANNIKIN	PANTHEIST
PANDERERS	PANELS	PANICS	PANNIKINS	PANTHENOL
PANDERESS	PANES	PANICUM	PANNING	PANTHEON
PANDERING	PANETELA	PANICUMS	PANNINGS	PANTHEONS
PANDERISM	PANETELAS	PANIER	PANNIST	PANTHER
PANDERLY	PANETELLA	PANIERS	PANNISTS	PANTHERS
PANDEROUS	PANETTONE	PANIM	PANNOSE	PANTIE

PANTIES	PAPACIES	PAPERING	PAPRIKAS	PARADES
PANTIHOSE	PAPACY	PAPERINGS	PAPRIKASH	PARADIGM
PANTILE	PAPADAM	PAPERLESS	PAPS	PARADIGMS
PANTILED	PAPADAMS	PAPERS	PAPULA	PARADING
PANTILES	PAPADOM	PAPERWARE	PAPULAE	PARADISAL
PANTILING	PAPADOMS	PAPERWORK	PAPULAR	PARADISE
PANTINE	PAPADUM	PAPERY	PAPULAS	PARADISES
PANTINES	PAPADUMS	PAPES	PAPULE	PARADISIC
PANTING	PAPAIN	PAPETERIE	PAPULES	PARADOR
PANTINGLY	PAPAINS	PAPHIAN	PAPULOSE	PARADORES
PANTINGS	PAPAL	PAPHIANS	PAPULOUS	PARADORS
PANTLEG	PAPALISE	PAPILIO	PAPYRAL	PARADOS
PANTLEGS	PAPALISED	PAPILIOS	PAPYRI	PARADOSES
PANTLER	PAPALISES	PAPILLA	PAPYRIAN	PARADOX
PANTLERS	PAPALISM	PAPILLAE	PAPYRINE	PARADOXAL
PANTO	PAPALISMS	PAPILLAR	PAPYRUS	PARADOXER
PANTOFFLE	PAPALIST	PAPILLARY	PAPYRUSES	PARADOXES
PANTOFLE	PAPALISTS	PAPILLATE	PAR	PARADOXY
PANTOFLES	PAPALIZE	PAPILLOMA	PARA	PARADROP
PANTOMIME	PAPALIZED	PAPILLON	PARABASES	PARADROPS
PANTON	PAPALIZES	PAPILLONS	PARABASIS	PARAE
PANTONS	PAPALLY	PAPILLOSE	PARABEMA	PARAFFIN
PANTOS	PAPARAZZI	PAPILLOTE	PARABEN	PARAFFINE
PANTOUFLE	PAPARAZZO	PAPILLOUS	PARABENS	PARAFFINS
PANTOUM	PAPAS	PAPILLULE	PARABLAST	PARAFFINY
PANTOUMS	PAPASAN	PAPOOSE	PARABLE	PARAFFLE
PANTRIES	PAPASANS	PAPOOSES	PARABLED	PARAFFLES
PANTROPIC	PAPAUMA	PAPPADAM	PARABLES	PARAFLE
PANTRY	PAPAUMAS	PAPPADAMS	PARABLING	PARAFLES
PANTRYMAN	PAPAVER	PAPPADOM	PARABOLA	PARAFOIL
PANTRYMEN	PAPAVERS	PAPPADOMS	PARABOLAE	PARAFOILS
PANTS	PAPAW	PAPPADUM	PARABOLAS	PARAFORM
PANTSED	PAPAWS	PAPPADUMS	PARABOLE	PARAFORMS
PANTSES	PAPAYA	PAPPED	PARABOLES	PARAGE
PANTSING	PAPAYAN	PAPPI	PARABOLIC	PARAGES
PANTSUIT	PAPAYAS	PAPPIER	PARABRAKE	PARAGLIDE
PANTSUITS	PAPE	PAPPIES	PARACHOR	PARAGOGE
PANTUN	PAPER	PAPPIEST	PARACHORS	PARAGOGES
PANTUNS	PAPERBACK	PAPPING	PARACHUTE	PARAGOGIC
PANTY	PAPERBARK	PAPPOOSE	PARACLETE	PARAGOGUE
PANTYHOSE	PAPERBOY	PAPPOOSES	PARACME	PARAGON
PANZER	PAPERBOYS	PAPPOSE	PARACMES	PARAGONED
PANZERS	PAPERCLIP	PAPPOUS	PARACRINE	PARAGONS
PANZOOTIC	PAPERED	PAPPUS	PARACUSES	PARAGRAM
PAOLI	PAPERER	PAPPUSES	PARACUSIS	PARAGRAMS
PAOLO	PAPERERS	PAPPY	PARADE	PARAGRAPH
PAP	PAPERGIRL	PAPRICA	PARADED	PARAKEET
PAPA	PAPERIER	PAPRICAS	PARADER	PARAKEETS
PAPABLE	PAPERIEST	PAPRIKA	PARADERS	PARAKELIA

PARAKITE	PARANOICS	PARAVANT	PARDALOTE	PARESIS
PARAKITES	PARANOID	PARAVANTS	PARDALS	PARETIC
PARALALIA	PARANOIDS	PARAVAUNT	PARDED	PARETICS
PARALEGAL	PARANYM	PARAWING	PARDEE	PAREU
PARALEXIA	PARANYMPH	PARAWINGS	PARDI	PAREUS
PARALEXIC	PARANYMS	PARAXIAL	PARDIE	PAREV
PARALLAX	PARAPARA	PARAZOA	PARDINE	PAREVE
PARALLEL	PARAPARAS	PARAZOAN	PARDNER	PARFAIT
PARALLELS	PARAPENTE	PARAZOANS	PARDNERS	PARFAITS
PARALOGIA	PARAPET	PARAZOON	PARDON	PARFLECHE
PARALOGUE	PARAPETED	PARBAKE	PARDONED	PARFLESH
PARALOGY	PARAPETS	PARBAKED	PARDONER	PARFOCAL
PARALYSE	PARAPH	PARBAKES	PARDONERS	PARGANA
PARALYSED	PARAPHED	PARBAKING	PARDONING	PARGANAS
PARALYSER	PARAPHING	PARBOIL	PARDONS	PARGASITE
PARALYSES	PARAPHS	PARBOILED	PARDS	PARGE
PARALYSIS	PARAPODIA	PARBOILS	PARDY	PARGED
PARALYTIC	PARAQUAT	PARBREAK	PARE	PARGES
PARALYZE	PARAQUATS	PARBREAKS	PARECIOUS	PARGET
PARALYZED	PARAQUET	PARBUCKLE	PARECISM	PARGETED
PARALYZER	PARAQUETS	PARCEL	PARECISMS	PARGETER
PARALYZES	PARAQUITO	PARCELED	PARED	PARGETERS
PARAMATTA	PARARHYME	PARCELING	PAREGORIC	PARGETING
PARAMECIA	PARAS	PARCELLED	PAREIRA	PARGETS
PARAMEDIC	PARASAIL	PARCELS	PAREIRAS	PARGETTED
PARAMENT	PARASAILS	PARCENARY	PARELLA	PARGETTER
PARAMENTA	PARASANG	PARCENER	PARELLAS	PARGING
PARAMENTS	PARASANGS	PARCENERS	PARELLE	PARGINGS
PARAMESE	PARASCEVE	PARCH	PARELLES	PARGO
PARAMESES	PARASHAH	PARCHED	PAREN	PARGOES
PARAMETER	PARASHAHS	PARCHEDLY	PARENESES	PARGOS
PARAMO	PARASHOT	PARCHEESI	PARENESIS	PARGYLINE
PARAMORPH	PARASHOTH	PARCHES	PARENS	PARHELIA
PARAMOS	PARASITE	PARCHESI	PARENT	PARHELIC
PARAMOUNT	PARASITES	PARCHESIS	PARENTAGE	PARHELION
PARAMOUR	PARASITIC	PARCHING	PARENTAL	PARHYPATE
PARAMOURS	PARASOL	PARCHISI	PARENTED	PARIAH
PARAMYLUM	PARASOLED	PARCHISIS	PARENTING	PARIAHS
PARANETE	PARASOLS	PARCHMENT	PARENTS	PARIAL
PARANETES	PARATAXES	PARCIMONY	PAREO	PARIALS
PARANG	PARATAXIS	PARCLOSE	PAREOS	PARIAN
PARANGS	PARATHA	PARCLOSES	PARER	PARIANS
PARANOEA	PARATHAS	PARD	PARERA	PARIES
PARANOEAS	PARATHION	PARDAH	PARERAS	PARIETAL
PARANOEIC	PARATONIC	PARDAHS	PARERGA	PARIETALS
PARANOIA	PARATROOP	PARDAL	PARERGON	PARIETES
PARANOIAC	PARAVAIL	PARDALE	PARERS	PARING
PARANOIAS	PARAVANE	PARDALES	PARES	PARINGS
PARANOIC	PARAVANES	PARDALIS	PARESES	PARIS

two to nine letter words | 419

PARISCHAN	PARLANCE	PAROEMIA	PARPING	PARSECS
PARISES	PARLANCES	PAROEMIAC	PARPOINT	PARSED
PARISH	PARLANDO	PAROEMIAL	PARPOINTS	PARSER
PARISHAD	PARLANTE	PAROEMIAS	PARPS	PARSERS
PARISHADS	PARLAY	PAROICOUS	PARQUET	PARSES
PARISHEN	PARLAYED	PAROL	PARQUETED	PARSIMONY
PARISHENS	PARLAYING	PAROLABLE	PARQUETRY	PARSING
PARISHES	PARLAYS	PAROLE	PARQUETS	PARSINGS
PARISON	PARLE	PAROLED	PARR	PARSLEY
PARISONS	PARLED	PAROLEE	PARRA	PARSLEYED
PARITIES	PARLEMENT	PAROLEES	PARRAKEET	PARSLEYS
PARITOR	PARLES	PAROLES	PARRAL	PARSLIED
PARITORS	PARLEY	PAROLING	PARRALS	PARSNEP
PARITY	PARLEYED	PAROLS	PARRAS	PARSNEPS
PARK	PARLEYER	PARONYM	PARRED	PARSNIP
PARKA	PARLEYERS	PARONYMIC	PARREL	PARSNIPS
PARKADE	PARLEYING	PARONYMS	PARRELS	PARSON
PARKADES	PARLEYS	PARONYMY	PARRHESIA	PARSONAGE
PARKAS	PARLEYVOO	PAROQUET	PARRICIDE	PARSONIC
PARKED	PARLIES	PAROQUETS	PARRIDGE	PARSONISH
PARKEE	PARLING	PARORE	PARRIDGES	PARSONS
PARKEES	PARLOR	PARORES	PARRIED	PART
PARKER	PARLORS	PAROSMIA	PARRIER	PARTAKE
PARKERS	PARLOUR	PAROSMIAS	PARRIERS	PARTAKEN
PARKETTE	PARLOURS	PAROTIC	PARRIES	PARTAKER
PARKETTES	PARLOUS	PAROTID	PARRING	PARTAKERS
PARKI	PARLOUSLY	PAROTIDES	PARRITCH	PARTAKES
PARKIE	PARLY	PAROTIDS	PARROCK	PARTAKING
PARKIER	PARM	PAROTIS	PARROCKED	PARTAN
PARKIES	PARMA	PAROTISES	PARROCKS	PARTANS
PARKIEST	PARMAS	PAROTITIC	PARROKET	PARTED
PARKIN	PARMESAN	PAROTITIS	PARROKETS	PARTER
PARKING	PARMESANS	PAROTOID	PARROQUET	PARTERRE
PARKINGS	PARMS	PAROTOIDS	PARROT	PARTERRES
PARKINS	PAROCHIAL	PAROUS	PARROTED	PARTERS
PARKIS	PAROCHIN	PAROUSIA	PARROTER	PARTI
PARKISH	PAROCHINE	PAROUSIAS	PARROTERS	PARTIAL
PARKLAND	PAROCHINS	PAROXYSM	PARROTIER	PARTIALLY
PARKLANDS	PARODIC	PAROXYSMS	PARROTING	PARTIALS
PARKLIKE	PARODICAL	PARP	PARROTRY	PARTIBLE
PARKLY	PARODIED	PARPANE	PARROTS	PARTICLE
PARKOUR	PARODIES	PARPANES	PARROTY	PARTICLES
PARKOURS	PARODIST	PARPED	PARRS	PARTIED
PARKS	PARODISTS	PARPEN	PARRY	PARTIER
PARKWARD	PARODOI	PARPEND	PARRYING	PARTIERS
PARKWARDS	PARODOS	PARPENDS	PARS	PARTIES
PARKWAY	PARODY	PARPENS	PARSABLE	PARTIEST
PARKWAYS	PARODYING	PARPENT	PARSE	PARTIM
PARKY	PAROECISM	PARPENTS	PARSEC	PARTING

PARTINGS	PARVENUES	PASKHA	PASSIBLY	PASTERS
PARTIS	PARVENUS	PASKHAS	PASSIM	PASTES
PARTISAN	PARVIS	PASODOBLE	PASSING	PASTEUP
PARTISANS	PARVISE	PASPALUM	PASSINGLY	PASTEUPS
PARTITA	PARVISES	PASPALUMS	PASSINGS	PASTICCI
PARTITAS	PARVO	PASPIES	PASSION	PASTICCIO
PARTITE	PARVOLIN	PASPY	PASSIONAL	PASTICHE
PARTITION	PARVOLINE	PASQUIL	PASSIONED	PASTICHES
PARTITIVE	PARVOLINS	PASQUILER	PASSIONS	PASTIE
PARTITURA	PARVOS	PASQUILS	PASSIVATE	PASTIER
PARTIZAN	PAS	PASS	PASSIVE	PASTIES
PARTIZANS	PASCAL	PASSABLE	PASSIVELY	PASTIEST
PARTLET	PASCALS	PASSABLY	PASSIVES	PASTIL
PARTLETS	PASCHAL	PASSADE	PASSIVISM	PASTILLE
PARTLY	PASCHALS	PASSADES	PASSIVIST	PASTILLES
PARTNER	PASCUAL	PASSADO	PASSIVITY	PASTILS
PARTNERED	PASCUALS	PASSADOES	PASSKEY	PASTILY
PARTNERS	PASE	PASSADOS	PASSKEYS	PASTIME
PARTON	PASEAR	PASSAGE	PASSLESS	PASTIMES
PARTONS	PASEARED	PASSAGED	PASSMAN	PASTINA
PARTOOK	PASEARING	PASSAGER	PASSMEN	PASTINAS
PARTRIDGE	PASEARS	PASSAGES	PASSMENT	PASTINESS
PARTS	PASELA	PASSAGING	PASSMENTS	PASTING
PARTURE	PASELAS	PASSALONG	PASSOUT	PASTINGS
PARTURES	PASEO	PASSAMENT	PASSOUTS	PASTIS
PARTWAY	PASEOS	PASSANT	PASSOVER	PASTISES
PARTWORK	PASES	PASSATA	PASSOVERS	PASTITSIO
PARTWORKS	PASH	PASSATAS	PASSPORT	PASTITSO
PARTY	PASHA	PASSBAND	PASSPORTS	PASTITSOS
PARTYER	PASHADOM	PASSBANDS	PASSUS	PASTLESS
PARTYERS	PASHADOMS	PASSBOOK	PASSUSES	PASTNESS
PARTYGOER	PASHALIC	PASSBOOKS	PASSWORD	PASTOR
PARTYING	PASHALICS	PASSCODE	PASSWORDS	PASTORAL
PARTYINGS	PASHALIK	PASSCODES	PAST	PASTORALE
PARTYISM	PASHALIKS	PASSE	PASTA	PASTORALI
PARTYISMS	PASHAS	PASSED	PASTALIKE	PASTORALS
PARULIDES	PASHED	PASSEE	PASTANCE	PASTORATE
PARULIS	PASHES	PASSEL	PASTANCES	PASTORED
PARULISES	PASHIM	PASSELS	PASTAS	PASTORING
PARURA	PASHIMS	PASSEMENT	PASTE	PASTORIUM
PARURAS	PASHING	PASSENGER	PASTED	PASTORLY
PARURE	PASHKA	PASSEPIED	PASTEDOWN	PASTORS
PARURES	PASHKAS	PASSER	PASTEL	PASTRAMI
PARURESES	PASHM	PASSERBY	PASTELIKE	PASTRAMIS
PARURESIS	PASHMINA	PASSERINE	PASTELIST	PASTRIES
PARURETIC	PASHMINAS	PASSERS	PASTELS	PASTROMI
PARVE	PASHMS	PASSERSBY	PASTER	PASTROMIS
PARVENU	PASKA	PASSES	PASTERN	PASTRY
PARVENUE	PASKAS	PASSIBLE	PASTERNS	PASTS

P

PASTURAGE	PATENT	PATIKIS	PATRIOT	PATTLE
PASTURAL	PATENTED	PATIN	PATRIOTIC	PATTLES
PASTURE	PATENTEE	PATINA	PATRIOTS	PATTRESS
PASTURED	PATENTEES	PATINAE	PATRISTIC	PATTY
PASTURER	PATENTING	PATINAED	PATROL	PATTYPAN
PASTURERS	PATENTLY	PATINAS	PATROLLED	PATTYPANS
PASTURES	PATENTOR	PATINATE	PATROLLER	PATU
PASTURING	PATENTORS	PATINATED	PATROLMAN	PATULENT
PASTY	PATENTS	PATINATES	PATROLMEN	PATULIN
PAT	PATER	PATINE	PATROLOGY	PATULINS
PATACA	PATERA	PATINED	PATROLS	PATULOUS
PATACAS	PATERAE	PATINES	PATRON	PATUS
PATAGIA	PATERCOVE	PATINING	PATRONAGE	PATUTUKI
PATAGIAL	PATERERO	PATINISE	PATRONAL	PATUTUKIS
PATAGIUM	PATEREROS	PATINISED	PATRONESS	PATY
PATAKA	PATERNAL	PATINISES	PATRONISE	PATZER
PATAKAS	PATERNITY	PATINIZE	PATRONIZE	PATZERS
PATAMAR	PATERS	PATINIZED	PATRONLY	PAUA
PATAMARS	PATES	PATINIZES	PATRONNE	PAUAS
PATBALL	PATH	PATINS	PATRONNES	PAUCAL
PATBALLS	PATHED	PATIO	PATRONS	PAUCALS
PATCH	PATHETIC	PATIOS	PATROON	PAUCITIES
PATCHABLE	PATHETICS	PATISSIER	PATROONS	PAUCITY
PATCHED	PATHIC	PATKA	PATS	PAUGHTIER
PATCHER	PATHICS	PATKAS	PATSIES	PAUGHTY
PATCHERS	PATHING	PATLY	PATSY	PAUL
PATCHERY	PATHINGS	PATNESS	PATTAMAR	PAULDRON
PATCHES	PATHLESS	PATNESSES	PATTAMARS	PAULDRONS
PATCHIER	PATHNAME	PATOIS	PATTE	PAULIN
PATCHIEST	PATHNAMES	PATONCE	PATTED	PAULINS
PATCHILY	PATHOGEN	PATOOT	PATTEE	PAULOWNIA
PATCHING	PATHOGENE	PATOOTIE	PATTEN	PAULS
PATCHINGS	PATHOGENS	PATOOTIES	PATTENED	PAUNCE
PATCHOCKE	PATHOGENY	PATOOTS	PATTENING	PAUNCES
PATCHOULI	PATHOLOGY	PATRIAL	PATTENS	PAUNCH
PATCHOULY	PATHOS	PATRIALS	PATTER	PAUNCHED
PATCHWORK	PATHOSES	PATRIARCH	PATTERED	PAUNCHES
PATCHY	PATHS	PATRIATE	PATTERER	PAUNCHIER
PATE	PATHWAY	PATRIATED	PATTERERS	PAUNCHING
PATED	PATHWAYS	PATRIATES	PATTERING	PAUNCHY
PATELLA	PATIBLE	PATRICIAN	PATTERN	PAUPER
PATELLAE	PATIENCE	PATRICIDE	PATTERNED	PAUPERDOM
PATELLAR	PATIENCES	PATRICK	PATTERNS	PAUPERED
PATELLAS	PATIENT	PATRICKS	PATTERS	PAUPERESS
PATELLATE	PATIENTED	PATRICO	PATTES	PAUPERING
PATEN	PATIENTER	PATRICOES	PATTEST	PAUPERISE
PATENCIES	PATIENTLY	PATRICOS	PATTIE	PAUPERISM
PATENCY	PATIENTS	PATRILINY	PATTIES	PAUPERIZE
PATENS	PATIKI	PATRIMONY	PATTING	PAUPERS

PAUPIETTE	PAVISERS	PAWPAW	PAYOLAS	PEACHING
PAURAQUE	PAVISES	PAWPAWS	PAYOR	PEACHY
PAURAQUES	PAVISSE	PAWPRINT	PAYORS	PEACING
PAUROPOD	PAVISSES	PAWPRINTS	PAYOUT	PEACOAT
PAUROPODS	PAVLOVA	PAWS	PAYOUTS	PEACOATS
PAUSAL	PAVLOVAS	PAX	PAYPHONE	PEACOCK
PAUSE	PAVONAZZO	PAXES	PAYPHONES	PEACOCKED
PAUSED	PAVONE	PAXIUBA	PAYROLL	PEACOCKS
PAUSEFUL	PAVONES	PAXIUBAS	PAYROLLS	PEACOCKY
PAUSELESS	PAVONIAN	PAXWAX	PAYS	PEACOD
PAUSER	PAVONINE	PAXWAXES	PAYSAGE	PEACODS
PAUSERS	PAVS	PAY	PAYSAGES	PEAFOWL
PAUSES	PAW	PAYABLE	PAYSAGIST	PEAFOWLS
PAUSING	PAWA	PAYABLES	PAYSD	PEAG
PAUSINGLY	PAWAS	PAYABLY	PAYSLIP	PEAGE
PAUSINGS	PAWAW	PAYBACK	PAYSLIPS	PEAGES
PAV	PAWAWED	PAYBACKS	PAYWALL	PEAGS
PAVAGE	PAWAWING	PAYCHECK	PAYWALLED	PEAHEN
PAVAGES	PAWAWS	PAYCHECKS	PAYWALLS	PEAHENS
PAVAN	PAWED	PAYCHEQUE	PAZAZZ	PEAK
PAVANE	PAWER	PAYDAY	PAZAZZES	PEAKED
PAVANES	PAWERS	PAYDAYS	PAZZAZZ	PEAKIER
PAVANS	PAWING	PAYDOWN	PAZZAZZES	PEAKIEST
PAVE	PAWK	PAYDOWNS	PE	PEAKINESS
PAVED	PAWKIER	PAYED	PEA	PEAKING
PAVEED	PAWKIEST	PAYEE	PEABERRY	PEAKINGS
PAVEMENT	PAWKILY	PAYEES	PEABRAIN	PEAKISH
PAVEMENTS	PAWKINESS	PAYER	PEABRAINS	PEAKLESS
PAVEN	PAWKS	PAYERS	PEACE	PEAKLIKE
PAVENS	PAWKY	PAYESS	PEACEABLE	PEAKS
PAVER	PAWL	PAYFONE	PEACEABLY	PEAKY
PAVERS	PAWLS	PAYFONES	PEACED	PEAL
PAVES	PAWN	PAYGRADE	PEACEFUL	PEALED
PAVID	PAWNABLE	PAYGRADES	PEACELESS	PEALIKE
PAVILION	PAWNAGE	PAYING	PEACENIK	PEALING
PAVILIONS	PAWNAGES	PAYINGS	PEACENIKS	PEALS
PAVILLON	PAWNCE	PAYLIST	PEACES	PEAN
PAVILLONS	PAWNCES	PAYLISTS	PEACETIME	PEANED
PAVIN	PAWNED	PAYLOAD	PEACH	PEANING
PAVING	PAWNEE	PAYLOADS	PEACHBLOW	PEANS
PAVINGS	PAWNEES	PAYMASTER	PEACHED	PEANUT
PAVINS	PAWNER	PAYMENT	PEACHER	PEANUTS
PAVIOR	PAWNERS	PAYMENTS	PEACHERS	PEANUTTY
PAVIORS	PAWNING	PAYNIM	PEACHES	PEAPOD
PAVIOUR	PAWNOR	PAYNIMRY	PEACHICK	PEAPODS
PAVIOURS	PAWNORS	PAYNIMS	PEACHICKS	PEAR
PAVIS	PAWNS	PAYOFF	PEACHIER	PEARCE
PAVISE	PAWNSHOP	PAYOFFS	PEACHIEST	PEARCED
PAVISER	PAWNSHOPS	PAYOLA	PEACHILY	PEARCES

PEARCING	PEASON	PECCAVI	PECTIZES	PEDANTS
PEARE	PEASOUPER	PECCAVIS	PECTIZING	PEDATE
PEARES	PEAT	PECH	PECTOLITE	PEDATELY
PEARL	PEATARIES	PECHAN	PECTORAL	PEDATIFID
PEARLASH	PEATARY	PECHANS	PECTORALS	PEDDER
PEARLED	PEATED	PECHED	PECTOSE	PEDDERS
PEARLER	PEATERIES	PECHING	PECTOSES	PEDDLE
PEARLERS	PEATERY	PECHS	PECULATE	PEDDLED
PEARLIER	PEATIER	PECK	PECULATED	PEDDLER
PEARLIES	PEATIEST	PECKE	PECULATES	PEDDLERS
PEARLIEST	PEATLAND	PECKED	PECULATOR	PEDDLERY
PEARLIN	PEATLANDS	PECKER	PECULIA	PEDDLES
PEARLING	PEATMAN	PECKERS	PECULIAR	PEDDLING
PEARLINGS	PEATMEN	PECKES	PECULIARS	PEDDLINGS
PEARLINS	PEATS	PECKIER	PECULIUM	PEDERAST
PEARLISED	PEATSHIP	PECKIEST	PECUNIARY	PEDERASTS
PEARLITE	PEATSHIPS	PECKING	PECUNIOUS	PEDERASTY
PEARLITES	PEATY	PECKINGS	PED	PEDERERO
PEARLITIC	PEAVEY	PECKISH	PEDAGOG	PEDEREROS
PEARLIZED	PEAVEYS	PECKISHLY	PEDAGOGIC	PEDES
PEARLS	PEAVIES	PECKS	PEDAGOGS	PEDESES
PEARLWARE	PEAVY	PECKY	PEDAGOGUE	PEDESIS
PEARLWORT	PEAZE	PECORINI	PEDAGOGY	PEDESTAL
PEARLY	PEAZED	PECORINO	PEDAL	PEDESTALS
PEARMAIN	PEAZES	PECORINOS	PEDALBOAT	PEDETIC
PEARMAINS	PEAZING	PECS	PEDALCAR	PEDI
PEARS	PEBA	PECTASE	PEDALCARS	PEDIATRIC
PEARST	PEBAS	PECTASES	PEDALED	PEDICAB
PEART	PEBBLE	PECTATE	PEDALER	PEDICABS
PEARTER	PEBBLED	PECTATES	PEDALERS	PEDICEL
PEARTEST	PEBBLES	PECTEN	PEDALFER	PEDICELS
PEARTLY	PEBBLIER	PECTENS	PEDALFERS	PEDICLE
PEARTNESS	PEBBLIEST	PECTIC	PEDALIER	PEDICLED
PEARWOOD	PEBBLING	PECTIN	PEDALIERS	PEDICLES
PEARWOODS	PEBBLINGS	PECTINAL	PEDALING	PEDICULAR
PEAS	PEBBLY	PECTINALS	PEDALLED	PEDICULI
PEASANT	PEBIBYTE	PECTINATE	PEDALLER	PEDICULUS
PEASANTRY	PEBIBYTES	PECTINEAL	PEDALLERS	PEDICURE
PEASANTS	PEBRINE	PECTINEI	PEDALLING	PEDICURED
PEASANTY	PEBRINES	PECTINES	PEDALO	PEDICURES
PEASCOD	PEC	PECTINEUS	PEDALOES	PEDIFORM
PEASCODS	PECAN	PECTINOUS	PEDALOS	PEDIGREE
PEASE	PECANS	PECTINS	PEDALS	PEDIGREED
PEASECOD	PECCABLE	PECTISE	PEDANT	PEDIGREES
PEASECODS	PECCANCY	PECTISED	PEDANTIC	PEDIMENT
PEASED	PECCANT	PECTISES	PEDANTISE	PEDIMENTS
PEASEN	PECCANTLY	PECTISING	PEDANTISM	PEDIPALP
PEASES	PECCARIES	PECTIZE	PEDANTIZE	PEDIPALPI
PEASING	PECCARY	PECTIZED	PEDANTRY	PEDIPALPS

PEDIS	PEELABLE	PEERLESS	PEIN	PELERINE
PEDLAR	PEELED	PEERS	PEINCT	PELERINES
PEDLARIES	PEELER	PEERY	PEINCTED	PELES
PEDLARS	PEELERS	PEES	PEINCTING	PELF
PEDLARY	PEELING	PEESWEEP	PEINCTS	PELFS
PEDLER	PEELINGS	PEESWEEPS	PEINED	PELHAM
PEDLERIES	PEELS	PEETWEET	PEINING	PELHAMS
PEDLERS	PEEN	PEETWEETS	PEINS	PELICAN
PEDLERY	PEENED	PEEVE	PEIRASTIC	PELICANS
PEDOCAL	PEENGE	PEEVED	PEISE	PELISSE
PEDOCALIC	PEENGED	PEEVER	PEISED	PELISSES
PEDOCALS	PEENGEING	PEEVERS	PEISES	PELITE
PEDOGENIC	PEENGES	PEEVES	PEISHWA	PELITES
PEDOLOGIC	PEENGING	PEEVING	PEISHWAH	PELITIC
PEDOLOGY	PEENING	PEEVISH	PEISHWAHS	PELL
PEDOMETER	PEENINGS	PEEVISHLY	PEISHWAS	PELLACH
PEDOPHILE	PEENS	PEEWEE	PEISING	PELLACHS
PEDORTHIC	PEEOY	PEEWEES	PEIZE	PELLACK
PEDRAIL	PEEOYS	PEEWIT	PEIZED	PELLACKS
PEDRAILS	PEEP	PEEWITS	PEIZES	PELLAGRA
PEDRERO	PEEPAL	PEG	PEIZING	PELLAGRAS
PEDREROES	PEEPALS	PEGASUS	PEJORATE	PELLAGRIN
PEDREROS	PEEPBO	PEGASUSES	PEJORATED	PELLED
PEDRO	PEEPBOS	PEGBOARD	PEJORATES	PELLET
PEDROS	PEEPE	PEGBOARDS	PEKAN	PELLETAL
PEDS	PEEPED	PEGBOX	PEKANS	PELLETED
PEDUNCLE	PEEPER	PEGBOXES	PEKE	PELLETIFY
PEDUNCLED	PEEPERS	PEGGED	PEKEPOO	PELLETING
PEDUNCLES	PEEPES	PEGGIER	PEKEPOOS	PELLETISE
PEDWAY	PEEPHOLE	PEGGIES	PEKES	PELLETIZE
PEDWAYS	PEEPHOLES	PEGGIEST	PEKIN	PELLETS
PEE	PEEPING	PEGGING	PEKINS	PELLICLE
PEEBEEN	PEEPS	PEGGINGS	PEKOE	PELLICLES
PEEBEENS	PEEPSHOW	PEGGY	PEKOES	PELLING
PEECE	PEEPSHOWS	PEGH	PEL	PELLITORY
PEECES	PEEPTOE	PEGHED	PELA	PELLMELL
PEED	PEEPUL	PEGHING	PELAGE	PELLMELLS
PEEING	PEEPULS	PEGHS	PELAGES	PELLOCK
PEEK	PEER	PEGLEGGED	PELAGIAL	PELLOCKS
PEEKABO	PEERAGE	PEGLESS	PELAGIALS	PELLS
PEEKABOO	PEERAGES	PEGLIKE	PELAGIAN	PELLUCID
PEEKABOOS	PEERED	PEGMATITE	PELAGIANS	PELLUM
PEEKABOS	PEERESS	PEGS	PELAGIC	PELLUMS
PEEKAPOO	PEERESSES	PEGTOP	PELAGICS	PELMA
PEEKAPOOS	PEERIE	PEGTOPS	PELAS	PELMANISM
PEEKED	PEERIER	PEH	PELAU	PELMAS
PEEKING	PEERIES	PEHS	PELAUS	PELMATIC
PEEKS	PEERIEST	PEIGNOIR	PELE	PELMET
PEEL	PEERING	PEIGNOIRS	PELECYPOD	PELMETS

P

PELOID	PEMBINA	PEND	PENICILS	PENNIED
PELOIDS	PEMBINAS	PENDANT	PENIE	PENNIES
PELOLOGY	PEMBROKE	PENDANTLY	PENIES	PENNIFORM
PELON	PEMBROKES	PENDANTS	PENILE	PENNILESS
PELONS	PEMICAN	PENDED	PENILL	PENNILL
PELORIA	PEMICANS	PENDENCY	PENILLION	PENNINE
PELORIAN	PEMMICAN	PENDENT	PENING	PENNINES
PELORIAS	PEMMICANS	PENDENTLY	PENINSULA	PENNING
PELORIC	PEMOLINE	PENDENTS	PENIS	PENNINITE
PELORIES	PEMOLINES	PENDICLE	PENISES	PENNIS
PELORISED	PEMPHIGI	PENDICLER	PENISTONE	PENNON
PELORISM	PEMPHIGUS	PENDICLES	PENITENCE	PENNONCEL
PELORISMS	PEMPHIX	PENDING	PENITENCY	PENNONED
PELORIZED	PEMPHIXES	PENDRAGON	PENITENT	PENNONS
PELORUS	PEN	PENDS	PENITENTS	PENNY
PELORUSES	PENAL	PENDU	PENK	PENNYBOY
PELORY	PENALISE	PENDULAR	PENKNIFE	PENNYBOYS
PELOTA	PENALISED	PENDULATE	PENKNIVES	PENNYFEE
PELOTAS	PENALISES	PENDULE	PENKS	PENNYFEES
PELOTON	PENALITY	PENDULES	PENLIGHT	PENNYLAND
PELOTONS	PENALIZE	PENDULINE	PENLIGHTS	PENNYWISE
PELS	PENALIZED	PENDULOUS	PENLIKE	PENNYWORT
PELT	PENALIZES	PENDULUM	PENLITE	PENOCHE
PELTA	PENALLY	PENDULUMS	PENLITES	PENOCHES
PELTAE	PENALTIES	PENE	PENMAN	PENOLOGY
PELTAS	PENALTY	PENED	PENMEN	PENONCEL
PELTAST	PENANCE	PENEPLAIN	PENNA	PENONCELS
PELTASTS	PENANCED	PENEPLANE	PENNAE	PENPOINT
PELTATE	PENANCES	PENES	PENNAL	PENPOINTS
PELTATELY	PENANCING	PENETRANT	PENNALISM	PENPUSHER
PELTATION	PENANG	PENETRATE	PENNALS	PENS
PELTED	PENANGS	PENFOLD	PENNAME	PENSEE
PELTER	PENATES	PENFOLDS	PENNAMES	PENSEES
PELTERED	PENCE	PENFRIEND	PENNANT	PENSEL
PELTERING	PENCEL	PENFUL	PENNANTS	PENSELS
PELTERS	PENCELS	PENFULS	PENNATE	PENSEROSO
PELTING	PENCES	PENG	PENNATED	PENSIL
PELTINGLY	PENCHANT	PENGER	PENNATULA	PENSILE
PELTINGS	PENCHANTS	PENGEST	PENNE	PENSILITY
PELTLESS	PENCIL	PENGO	PENNED	PENSILS
PELTRIES	PENCILED	PENGOS	PENNEECH	PENSION
PELTRY	PENCILER	PENGUIN	PENNEECHS	PENSIONE
PELTS	PENCILERS	PENGUINRY	PENNEECK	PENSIONED
PELVES	PENCILING	PENGUINS	PENNEECKS	PENSIONER
PELVIC	PENCILLED	PENHOLDER	PENNER	PENSIONES
PELVICS	PENCILLER	PENI	PENNERS	PENSIONI
PELVIFORM	PENCILS	PENIAL	PENNES	PENSIONS
PELVIS	PENCRAFT	PENICIL	PENNI	PENSIVE
PELVISES	PENCRAFTS	PENICILLI	PENNIA	PENSIVELY

PENSTEMON	PENTODE	PEOPLER	PEPSINATE	PERCALE
PENSTER	PENTODES	PEOPLERS	PEPSINE	PERCALES
PENSTERS	PENTOMIC	PEOPLES	PEPSINES	PERCALINE
PENSTOCK	PENTOSAN	PEOPLING	PEPSINS	PERCASE
PENSTOCKS	PENTOSANE	PEP	PEPSIS	PERCE
PENSUM	PENTOSANS	PEPERINO	PEPTALK	PERCEABLE
PENSUMS	PENTOSE	PEPERINOS	PEPTALKED	PERCEANT
PENT	PENTOSES	PEPEROMIA	PEPTALKS	PERCED
PENTACLE	PENTOSIDE	PEPERONI	PEPTIC	PERCEIVE
PENTACLES	PENTOXIDE	PEPERONIS	PEPTICITY	PERCEIVED
PENTACT	PENTROOF	PEPFUL	PEPTICS	PERCEIVER
PENTACTS	PENTROOFS	PEPINO	PEPTID	PERCEIVES
PENTAD	PENTS	PEPINOS	PEPTIDASE	PERCEN
PENTADIC	PENTYL	PEPITA	PEPTIDE	PERCENT
PENTADS	PENTYLENE	PEPITAS	PEPTIDES	PERCENTAL
PENTAGON	PENTYLS	PEPLA	PEPTIDIC	PERCENTS
PENTAGONS	PENUCHE	PEPLOS	PEPTIDS	PERCEPT
PENTAGRAM	PENUCHES	PEPLOSES	PEPTISE	PERCEPTS
PENTALOGY	PENUCHI	PEPLUM	PEPTISED	PERCES
PENTALPHA	PENUCHIS	PEPLUMED	PEPTISER	PERCH
PENTAMERY	PENUCHLE	PEPLUMS	PEPTISERS	PERCHANCE
PENTANE	PENUCHLES	PEPLUS	PEPTISES	PERCHED
PENTANES	PENUCKLE	PEPLUSES	PEPTISING	PERCHER
PENTANGLE	PENUCKLES	PEPO	PEPTIZE	PERCHERON
PENTANOIC	PENULT	PEPONIDA	PEPTIZED	PERCHERS
PENTANOL	PENULTIMA	PEPONIDAS	PEPTIZER	PERCHERY
PENTANOLS	PENULTS	PEPONIUM	PEPTIZERS	PERCHES
PENTAPODY	PENUMBRA	PEPONIUMS	PEPTIZES	PERCHING
PENTARCH	PENUMBRAE	PEPOS	PEPTIZING	PERCHINGS
PENTARCHS	PENUMBRAL	PEPPED	PEPTONE	PERCID
PENTARCHY	PENUMBRAS	PEPPER	PEPTONES	PERCIDS
PENTATHLA	PENURIES	PEPPERBOX	PEPTONIC	PERCIFORM
PENTEL	PENURIOUS	PEPPERED	PEPTONISE	PERCINE
PENTELS	PENURY	PEPPERER	PEPTONIZE	PERCINES
PENTENE	PENWIPER	PEPPERERS	PEQUISTE	PERCING
PENTENES	PENWIPERS	PEPPERIER	PEQUISTES	PERCOCT
PENTHIA	PENWOMAN	PEPPERING	PER	PERCOCTED
PENTHIAS	PENWOMEN	PEPPERONI	PERACID	PERCOCTS
PENTHOUSE	PEON	PEPPERS	PERACIDS	PERCOID
PENTICE	PEONAGE	PEPPERY	PERACUTE	PERCOIDS
PENTICED	PEONAGES	PEPPIER	PERAEA	PERCOLATE
PENTICES	PEONES	PEPPIEST	PERAEON	PERCOLIN
PENTICING	PEONIES	PEPPILY	PERAEONS	PERCOLINS
PENTISE	PEONISM	PEPPINESS	PERAEOPOD	PERCS
PENTISED	PEONISMS	PEPPING	PERAI	PERCUSS
PENTISES	PEONS	PEPPY	PERAIS	PERCUSSED
PENTISING	PEONY	PEPS	PERBORATE	PERCUSSES
PENTITI	PEOPLE	PEPSI	PERBORIC	PERCUSSOR
PENTITO	PEOPLED	PEPSIN	PERC	PERDENDO

P

PERDIE	PERFET	PERIBLEMS	PERILOUS	PERISH
PERDITION	PERFIDIES	PERIBOLI	PERILS	PERISHED
PERDU	PERFIDY	PERIBOLOI	PERILUNE	PERISHER
PERDUE	PERFIN	PERIBOLOS	PERILUNES	PERISHERS
PERDUES	PERFING	PERIBOLUS	PERILYMPH	PERISHES
PERDURE	PERFINGS	PERICARP	PERIMETER	PERISHING
PERDURED	PERFINS	PERICARPS	PERIMETRY	PERISPERM
PERDURES	PERFORANS	PERICLASE	PERIMORPH	PERISTOME
PERDURING	PERFORANT	PERICLINE	PERIMYSIA	PERISTYLE
PERDUS	PERFORATE	PERICON	PERINAEUM	PERITI
PERDY	PERFORCE	PERICONES	PERINATAL	PERITONEA
PERE	PERFORM	PERICOPAE	PERINEA	PERITRACK
PEREA	PERFORMED	PERICOPAL	PERINEAL	PERITRICH
PEREGAL	PERFORMER	PERICOPE	PERINEUM	PERITUS
PEREGALS	PERFORMS	PERICOPES	PERINEUMS	PERIURBAN
PEREGRIN	PERFUME	PERICOPIC	PERIOD	PERIWIG
PEREGRINE	PERFUMED	PERICYCLE	PERIODATE	PERIWIGS
PEREGRINS	PERFUMER	PERIDERM	PERIODED	PERJINK
PEREIA	PERFUMERS	PERIDERMS	PERIODIC	PERJURE
PEREION	PERFUMERY	PERIDIA	PERIODID	PERJURED
PEREIONS	PERFUMES	PERIDIAL	PERIODIDE	PERJURER
PEREIOPOD	PERFUMIER	PERIDINIA	PERIODIDS	PERJURERS
PEREIRA	PERFUMING	PERIDIUM	PERIODING	PERJURES
PEREIRAS	PERFUMY	PERIDIUMS	PERIODISE	PERJURIES
PERENNATE	PERFUSATE	PERIDOT	PERIODIZE	PERJURING
PERENNIAL	PERFUSE	PERIDOTE	PERIODS	PERJUROUS
PERENNITY	PERFUSED	PERIDOTES	PERIOST	PERJURY
PERENTIE	PERFUSES	PERIDOTIC	PERIOSTEA	PERK
PERENTIES	PERFUSING	PERIDOTS	PERIOSTS	PERKED
PERENTY	PERFUSION	PERIDROME	PERIOTIC	PERKIER
PEREON	PERFUSIVE	PERIGEAL	PERIOTICS	PERKIEST
PEREONS	PERGOLA	PERIGEAN	PERIPATUS	PERKILY
PEREOPOD	PERGOLAS	PERIGEE	PERIPETIA	PERKIN
PEREOPODS	PERGUNNAH	PERIGEES	PERIPETY	PERKINESS
PERES	PERHAPS	PERIGON	PERIPHERY	PERKING
PERFAY	PERHAPSES	PERIGONE	PERIPLASM	PERKINS
PERFECT	PERI	PERIGONES	PERIPLAST	PERKISH
PERFECTA	PERIAGUA	PERIGONIA	PERIPLUS	PERKS
PERFECTAS	PERIAGUAS	PERIGONS	PERIPROCT	PERKY
PERFECTED	PERIAKTOI	PERIGYNY	PERIPTER	PERLEMOEN
PERFECTER	PERIAKTOS	PERIHELIA	PERIPTERS	PERLITE
PERFECTI	PERIANTH	PERIKARYA	PERIPTERY	PERLITES
PERFECTLY	PERIANTHS	PERIL	PERIQUE	PERLITIC
PERFECTO	PERIAPSES	PERILED	PERIQUES	PERLOUS
PERFECTOR	PERIAPSIS	PERILING	PERIS	PERM
PERFECTOS	PERIAPT	PERILLA	PERISARC	PERMABEAR
PERFECTS	PERIAPTS	PERILLAS	PERISARCS	PERMABULL
PERFERVID	PERIBLAST	PERILLED	PERISCIAN	PERMALINK
PERFERVOR	PERIBLEM	PERILLING	PERISCOPE	PERMALLOY

PERMANENT	PERONEI	PERSES	PERTAKE	PERVERSER
PERMATAN	PERONES	PERSEVERE	PERTAKEN	PERVERT
PERMATANS	PERONEUS	PERSICO	PERTAKES	PERVERTED
PERMEABLE	PERORAL	PERSICOS	PERTAKING	PERVERTER
PERMEABLY	PERORALLY	PERSICOT	PERTER	PERVERTS
PERMEANCE	PERORATE	PERSICOTS	PERTEST	PERVES
PERMEANT	PERORATED	PERSIENNE	PERTHITE	PERVIATE
PERMEANTS	PERORATES	PERSIMMON	PERTHITES	PERVIATED
PERMEASE	PERORATOR	PERSING	PERTHITIC	PERVIATES
PERMEASES	PEROVSKIA	PERSIST	PERTINENT	PERVICACY
PERMEATE	PEROXID	PERSISTED	PERTLY	PERVIER
PERMEATED	PEROXIDE	PERSISTER	PERTNESS	PERVIEST
PERMEATES	PEROXIDED	PERSISTS	PERTOOK	PERVING
PERMEATOR	PEROXIDES	PERSON	PERTS	PERVIOUS
PERMED	PEROXIDIC	PERSONA	PERTURB	PERVO
PERMIAN	PEROXIDS	PERSONAE	PERTURBED	PERVOS
PERMIE	PEROXO	PERSONAGE	PERTURBER	PERVS
PERMIES	PEROXY	PERSONAL	PERTURBS	PERVY
PERMING	PERP	PERSONALS	PERTUSATE	PES
PERMIT	PERPEND	PERSONAS	PERTUSE	PESADE
PERMITS	PERPENDED	PERSONATE	PERTUSED	PESADES
PERMITTED	PERPENDS	PERSONIFY	PERTUSION	PESANT
PERMITTEE	PERPENT	PERSONISE	PERTUSSAL	PESANTE
PERMITTER	PERPENTS	PERSONIZE	PERTUSSES	PESANTS
PERMS	PERPETUAL	PERSONNED	PERTUSSIS	PESAUNT
PERMUTATE	PERPLEX	PERSONNEL	PERUKE	PESAUNTS
PERMUTE	PERPLEXED	PERSONS	PERUKED	PESETA
PERMUTED	PERPLEXER	PERSPEX	PERUKES	PESETAS
PERMUTES	PERPLEXES	PERSPEXES	PERUSABLE	PESEWA
PERMUTING	PERPS	PERSPIRE	PERUSAL	PESEWAS
PERN	PERRADIAL	PERSPIRED	PERUSALS	PESHMERGA
PERNANCY	PERRADII	PERSPIRES	PERUSE	PESHWA
PERNED	PERRADIUS	PERSPIRY	PERUSED	PESHWAS
PERNING	PERRIER	PERST	PERUSER	PESKIER
PERNIO	PERRIERS	PERSUADE	PERUSERS	PESKIEST
PERNIONES	PERRIES	PERSUADED	PERUSES	PESKILY
PERNOD	PERRON	PERSUADER	PERUSING	PESKINESS
PERNODS	PERRONS	PERSUADES	PERV	PESKY
PERNS	PERRUQUE	PERSUE	PERVADE	PESO
PEROG	PERRUQUES	PERSUED	PERVADED	PESOS
PEROGEN	PERRY	PERSUES	PERVADER	PESSARIES
PEROGI	PERSALT	PERSUING	PERVADERS	PESSARY
PEROGIE	PERSALTS	PERSWADE	PERVADES	PESSIMA
PEROGIES	PERSANT	PERSWADED	PERVADING	PESSIMAL
PEROGIS	PERSAUNT	PERSWADES	PERVASION	PESSIMISM
PEROGS	PERSE	PERT	PERVASIVE	PESSIMIST
PEROGY	PERSECUTE	PERTAIN	PERVE	PESSIMUM
PERONE	PERSEITY	PERTAINED	PERVED	PEST
PERONEAL	PERSELINE	PERTAINS	PERVERSE	PESTER

P

PESTERED	PETARDS	PETRALES	PETTISH	PEZIZOID
PESTERER	PETARIES	PETRARIES	PETTISHLY	PFENNIG
PESTERERS	PETARS	PETRARY	PETTITOES	PFENNIGE
PESTERING	PETARY	PETRE	PETTLE	PFENNIGS
PESTEROUS	PETASOS	PETREL	PETTLED	PFENNING
PESTERS	PETASOSES	PETRELS	PETTLES	PFENNINGS
PESTFUL	PETASUS	PETRES	PETTLING	PFFT
PESTHOLE	PETASUSES	PETRI	PETTO	PFUI
PESTHOLES	PETAURINE	PETRICHOR	PETTY	PHABLET
PESTHOUSE	PETAURIST	PETRIFIC	PETULANCE	PHABLETS
PESTICIDE	PETCHARY	PETRIFIED	PETULANCY	PHACELIA
PESTIER	PETCOCK	PETRIFIER	PETULANT	PHACELIAS
PESTIEST	PETCOCKS	PETRIFIES	PETUNIA	PHACOID
PESTILENT	PETECHIA	PETRIFY	PETUNIAS	PHACOIDAL
PESTLE	PETECHIAE	PETROGENY	PETUNTSE	PHACOLITE
PESTLED	PETECHIAL	PETROGRAM	PETUNTSES	PHACOLITH
PESTLES	PETER	PETROL	PETUNTZE	PHAEIC
PESTLING	PETERED	PETROLAGE	PETUNTZES	PHAEISM
PESTO	PETERING	PETROLEUM	PEW	PHAEISMS
PESTOLOGY	PETERMAN	PETROLEUR	PEWEE	PHAENOGAM
PESTOS	PETERMEN	PETROLIC	PEWEES	PHAETON
PESTS	PETERS	PETROLLED	PEWHOLDER	PHAETONS
PESTY	PETERSHAM	PETROLOGY	PEWIT	PHAGE
PET	PETHER	PETROLS	PEWITS	PHAGEDENA
PETABYTE	PETHERS	PETRONEL	PEWS	PHAGES
PETABYTES	PETHIDINE	PETRONELS	PEWTER	PHAGOCYTE
PETAFLOP	PETILLANT	PETROSAL	PEWTERER	PHAGOSOME
PETAFLOPS	PETIOLAR	PETROSALS	PEWTERERS	PHALANGAL
PETAHERTZ	PETIOLATE	PETROUS	PEWTERIER	PHALANGE
PETAL	PETIOLE	PETS	PEWTERS	PHALANGER
PETALED	PETIOLED	PETSAI	PEWTERY	PHALANGES
PETALINE	PETIOLES	PETSAIS	PEYOTE	PHALANGID
PETALISM	PETIOLULE	PETTABLE	PEYOTES	PHALANX
PETALISMS	PETIT	PETTED	PEYOTISM	PHALANXES
PETALLED	PETITE	PETTEDLY	PEYOTISMS	PHALAROPE
PETALLIKE	PETITES	PETTER	PEYOTIST	PHALLI
PETALODIC	PETITIO	PETTERS	PEYOTISTS	PHALLIC
PETALODY	PETITION	PETTI	PEYOTL	PHALLIN
PETALOID	PETITIONS	PETTICOAT	PEYOTLS	PHALLINS
PETALOUS	PETITIOS	PETTIER	PEYSE	PHALLISM
PETALS	PETITORY	PETTIES	PEYSED	PHALLISMS
PETAMETER	PETNAP	PETTIEST	PEYSES	PHALLIST
PETAMETRE	PETNAPER	PETTIFOG	PEYSING	PHALLISTS
PETANQUE	PETNAPERS	PETTIFOGS	PEYTRAL	PHALLOID
PETANQUES	PETNAPING	PETTILY	PEYTRALS	PHALLUS
PETAR	PETNAPPED	PETTINESS	PEYTREL	PHALLUSES
PETARA	PETNAPPER	PETTING	PEYTRELS	PHANG
PETARAS	PETNAPS	PETTINGS	PEZANT	PHANGED
PETARD	PETRALE	PETTIS	PEZANTS	PHANGING

PHANGS	PHASING	PHENGITES	PHILATELY	PHLEGM
PHANSIGAR	PHASINGS	PHENIC	PHILAVERY	PHLEGMIER
PHANTASIM	PHASIS	PHENIX	PHILHORSE	PHLEGMON
PHANTASM	PHASMID	PHENIXES	PHILIBEG	PHLEGMONS
PHANTASMA	PHASMIDS	PHENOBARB	PHILIBEGS	PHLEGMS
PHANTASMS	PHASOR	PHENOCOPY	PHILIPPIC	PHLEGMY
PHANTAST	PHASORS	PHENOGAM	PHILISTIA	PHLOEM
PHANTASTS	PHAT	PHENOGAMS	PHILLABEG	PHLOEMS
PHANTASY	PHATIC	PHENOL	PHILLIBEG	PHLOMIS
PHANTOM	PHATTER	PHENOLATE	PHILOGYNY	PHLOMISES
PHANTOMS	PHATTEST	PHENOLIC	PHILOLOGY	PHLORIZIN
PHANTOMY	PHEASANT	PHENOLICS	PHILOMATH	PHLOX
PHANTOSME	PHEASANTS	PHENOLOGY	PHILOMEL	PHLOXES
PHARAOH	PHEAZAR	PHENOLS	PHILOMELA	PHLYCTENA
PHARAOHS	PHEAZARS	PHENOM	PHILOMELS	PHO
PHARAONIC	PHEER	PHENOME	PHILOMOT	PHOBIA
PHARE	PHEERE	PHENOMENA	PHILOMOTS	PHOBIAS
PHARES	PHEERES	PHENOMES	PHILOPENA	PHOBIC
PHARISAIC	PHEERS	PHENOMS	PHILTER	PHOBICS
PHARISEE	PHEESE	PHENOTYPE	PHILTERED	PHOBISM
PHARISEES	PHEESED	PHENOXIDE	PHILTERS	PHOBISMS
PHARM	PHEESES	PHENOXY	PHILTRA	PHOBIST
PHARMA	PHEESING	PHENYL	PHILTRE	PHOBISTS
PHARMACY	PHEEZE	PHENYLENE	PHILTRED	PHOCA
PHARMAS	PHEEZED	PHENYLIC	PHILTRES	PHOCAE
PHARMED	PHEEZES	PHENYLS	PHILTRING	PHOCAS
PHARMER	PHEEZING	PHENYTOIN	PHILTRUM	PHOCINE
PHARMERS	PHELLEM	PHEO	PHIMOSES	PHOCOMELY
PHARMING	PHELLEMS	PHEON	PHIMOSIS	PHOEBE
PHARMINGS	PHELLOGEN	PHEONS	PHIMOTIC	PHOEBES
PHARMS	PHELLOID	PHEOS	PHINNOCK	PHOEBUS
PHAROS	PHELONIA	PHERESES	PHINNOCKS	PHOEBUSES
PHAROSES	PHELONION	PHERESIS	PHIS	PHOENIX
PHARYNGAL	PHENACITE	PHEROMONE	PHISH	PHOENIXES
PHARYNGES	PHENAKISM	PHESE	PHISHED	PHOH
PHARYNX	PHENAKITE	PHESED	PHISHER	PHOLADES
PHARYNXES	PHENATE	PHESES	PHISHERS	PHOLAS
PHASE	PHENATES	PHESING	PHISHES	PHON
PHASEAL	PHENAZIN	PHEW	PHISHING	PHONAL
PHASED	PHENAZINE	PHI	PHISHINGS	PHONATE
PHASEDOWN	PHENAZINS	PHIAL	PHISNOMY	PHONATED
PHASELESS	PHENE	PHIALLED	PHIZ	PHONATES
PHASEOLIN	PHENES	PHIALLING	PHIZES	PHONATHON
PHASEOUT	PHENETIC	PHIALS	PHIZOG	PHONATING
PHASEOUTS	PHENETICS	PHILABEG	PHIZOGS	PHONATION
PHASER	PHENETOL	PHILABEGS	PHIZZ	PHONATORY
PHASERS	PHENETOLE	PHILAMOT	PHIZZES	PHONE
PHASES	PHENETOLS	PHILAMOTS	PHLEBITIC	PHONECAM
PHASIC	PHENGITE	PHILANDER	PHLEBITIS	PHONECAMS

PHONECARD	PHORMIUM	PHOTOLYSE	PHREAKERS	PHYLETICS
PHONED	PHORMIUMS	PHOTOLYZE	PHREAKING	PHYLIC
PHONEME	PHORONID	PHOTOMAP	PHREAKS	PHYLLARY
PHONEMES	PHORONIDS	PHOTOMAPS	PHREATIC	PHYLLID
PHONEMIC	PHOS	PHOTOMASK	PHRENESES	PHYLLIDS
PHONEMICS	PHOSGENE	PHOTON	PHRENESIS	PHYLLITE
PHONER	PHOSGENES	PHOTONIC	PHRENETIC	PHYLLITES
PHONERS	PHOSPHATE	PHOTONICS	PHRENIC	PHYLLITIC
PHONES	PHOSPHENE	PHOTONS	PHRENICS	PHYLLO
PHONETIC	PHOSPHID	PHOTOPHIL	PHRENISM	PHYLLODE
PHONETICS	PHOSPHIDE	PHOTOPIA	PHRENISMS	PHYLLODES
PHONETISE	PHOSPHIDS	PHOTOPIAS	PHRENITIC	PHYLLODIA
PHONETISM	PHOSPHIN	PHOTOPIC	PHRENITIS	PHYLLODY
PHONETIST	PHOSPHINE	PHOTOPLAY	PHRENSIED	PHYLLOID
PHONETIZE	PHOSPHINS	PHOTOPSIA	PHRENSIES	PHYLLOIDS
PHONEY	PHOSPHITE	PHOTOPSY	PHRENSY	PHYLLOME
PHONEYED	PHOSPHOR	PHOTOS	PHRENTICK	PHYLLOMES
PHONEYING	PHOSPHORE	PHOTOSCAN	PHRYGANA	PHYLLOMIC
PHONEYS	PHOSPHORI	PHOTOSET	PHRYGANAS	PHYLLOPOD
PHONIC	PHOSPHORS	PHOTOSETS	PHT	PHYLLOS
PHONICS	PHOSSY	PHOTOSHOP	PHTHALATE	PHYLOGENY
PHONIED	PHOT	PHOTOSTAT	PHTHALEIN	PHYLON
PHONIER	PHOTIC	PHOTOTAXY	PHTHALIC	PHYLUM
PHONIES	PHOTICS	PHOTOTUBE	PHTHALIN	PHYSALIA
PHONIEST	PHOTINIA	PHOTOTYPE	PHTHALINS	PHYSALIAS
PHONILY	PHOTINIAS	PHOTOTYPY	PHTHISES	PHYSALIS
PHONINESS	PHOTINO	PHOTS	PHTHISIC	PHYSED
PHONING	PHOTINOS	PHPHT	PHTHISICS	PHYSEDS
PHONMETER	PHOTISM	PHRASAL	PHTHISIS	PHYSES
PHONO	PHOTISMS	PHRASALLY	PHUT	PHYSETER
PHONOGRAM	PHOTO	PHRASE	PHUTS	PHYSETERS
PHONOLITE	PHOTOBLOG	PHRASED	PHUTTED	PHYSIATRY
PHONOLOGY	PHOTOBOMB	PHRASEMAN	PHUTTING	PHYSIC
PHONON	PHOTOCALL	PHRASEMEN	PHWOAH	PHYSICAL
PHONONS	PHOTOCARD	PHRASER	PHWOAR	PHYSICALS
PHONOPORE	PHOTOCELL	PHRASERS	PHYCOCYAN	PHYSICIAN
PHONOS	PHOTOCOPY	PHRASES	PHYCOLOGY	PHYSICISM
PHONOTYPE	PHOTODISK	PHRASIER	PHYLA	PHYSICIST
PHONOTYPY	PHOTOED	PHRASIEST	PHYLACTIC	PHYSICKED
PHONS	PHOTOFIT	PHRASING	PHYLAE	PHYSICKY
PHONY	PHOTOFITS	PHRASINGS	PHYLAR	PHYSICS
PHONYING	PHOTOG	PHRASY	PHYLARCH	PHYSIO
PHOOEY	PHOTOGEN	PHRATRAL	PHYLARCHS	PHYSIOS
PHORATE	PHOTOGENE	PHRATRIC	PHYLARCHY	PHYSIQUE
PHORATES	PHOTOGENS	PHRATRIES	PHYLAXIS	PHYSIQUED
PHORESIES	PHOTOGENY	PHRATRY	PHYLE	PHYSIQUES
PHORESY	PHOTOGRAM	PHREAK	PHYLESES	PHYSIS
PHORETIC	PHOTOGS	PHREAKED	PHYLESIS	PHYTANE
PHORMINX	PHOTOING	PHREAKER	PHYLETIC	PHYTANES

PHYTIN	PIAS	PICCOLOS	PICKINGS	PICOTING
PHYTINS	PIASABA	PICCY	PICKINS	PICOTITE
PHYTOGENY	PIASABAS	PICE	PICKLE	PICOTITES
PHYTOID	PIASAVA	PICENE	PICKLED	PICOTS
PHYTOL	PIASAVAS	PICENES	PICKLER	PICOWAVE
PHYTOLITH	PIASSABA	PICEOUS	PICKLERS	PICOWAVED
PHYTOLOGY	PIASSABAS	PICHOLINE	PICKLES	PICOWAVES
PHYTOLS	PIASSAVA	PICHURIM	PICKLING	PICQUET
PHYTON	PIASSAVAS	PICHURIMS	PICKLOCK	PICQUETED
PHYTONIC	PIASTER	PICIFORM	PICKLOCKS	PICQUETS
PHYTONS	PIASTERS	PICINE	PICKMAW	PICRA
PHYTOSES	PIASTRE	PICK	PICKMAWS	PICRAS
PHYTOSIS	PIASTRES	PICKABACK	PICKOFF	PICRATE
PHYTOTOMY	PIAZZA	PICKABLE	PICKOFFS	PICRATED
PHYTOTRON	PIAZZAS	PICKADIL	PICKPROOF	PICRATES
PI	PIAZZE	PICKADILL	PICKS	PICRIC
PIA	PIAZZIAN	PICKADILS	PICKTHANK	PICRITE
PIACEVOLE	PIBAL	PICKAPACK	PICKUP	PICRITES
PIACULAR	PIBALS	PICKAROON	PICKUPS	PICRITIC
PIAFFE	PIBROCH	PICKAX	PICKWICK	PICS
PIAFFED	PIBROCHS	PICKAXE	PICKWICKS	PICTARNIE
PIAFFER	PIC	PICKAXED	PICKY	PICTOGRAM
PIAFFERS	PICA	PICKAXES	PICLORAM	PICTORIAL
PIAFFES	PICACHO	PICKAXING	PICLORAMS	PICTURAL
PIAFFING	PICACHOS	PICKBACK	PICNIC	PICTURALS
PIAL	PICADILLO	PICKBACKS	PICNICKED	PICTURE
PIAN	PICADOR	PICKED	PICNICKER	PICTURED
PIANETTE	PICADORES	PICKEER	PICNICKY	PICTURES
PIANETTES	PICADORS	PICKEERED	PICNICS	PICTURING
PIANI	PICAL	PICKEERER	PICOCURIE	PICTURISE
PIANIC	PICAMAR	PICKEERS	PICOFARAD	PICTURIZE
PIANINO	PICAMARS	PICKER	PICOGRAM	PICUL
PIANINOS	PICANTE	PICKEREL	PICOGRAMS	PICULET
PIANISM	PICARA	PICKERELS	PICOLIN	PICULETS
PIANISMS	PICARAS	PICKERIES	PICOLINE	PICULS
PIANIST	PICARIAN	PICKERS	PICOLINES	PIDDLE
PIANISTE	PICARIANS	PICKERY	PICOLINIC	PIDDLED
PIANISTES	PICARO	PICKET	PICOLINS	PIDDLER
PIANISTIC	PICAROON	PICKETED	PICOMETER	PIDDLERS
PIANISTS	PICAROONS	PICKETER	PICOMETRE	PIDDLES
PIANO	PICAROS	PICKETERS	PICOMOLE	PIDDLIER
PIANOLA	PICAS	PICKETING	PICOMOLES	PIDDLIEST
PIANOLAS	PICAYUNE	PICKETS	PICONG	PIDDLING
PIANOLESS	PICAYUNES	PICKIER	PICONGS	PIDDLY
PIANOLIST	PICCADILL	PICKIEST	PICOT	PIDDOCK
PIANOS	PICCATA	PICKILY	PICOTE	PIDDOCKS
PIANS	PICCATAS	PICKIN	PICOTED	PIDGEON
PIARIST	PICCIES	PICKINESS	PICOTEE	PIDGEONS
PIARISTS	PICCOLO	PICKING	PICOTEES	PIDGIN

PIDGINISE	PIERCE	PIFFLERS	PIGMEAT	PIHOIHOIS
PIDGINIZE	PIERCED	PIFFLES	PIGMEATS	PIING
PIDGINS	PIERCER	PIFFLING	PIGMEN	PIKA
PIE	PIERCERS	PIG	PIGMENT	PIKAKE
PIEBALD	PIERCES	PIGBOAT	PIGMENTAL	PIKAKES
PIEBALDS	PIERCING	PIGBOATS	PIGMENTED	PIKAS
PIECE	PIERCINGS	PIGEON	PIGMENTS	PIKAU
PIECED	PIERHEAD	PIGEONED	PIGMIES	PIKAUS
PIECELESS	PIERHEADS	PIGEONING	PIGMOID	PIKE
PIECEMEAL	PIERID	PIGEONITE	PIGMOIDS	PIKED
PIECEN	PIERIDINE	PIGEONRY	PIGMY	PIKELET
PIECENED	PIERIDS	PIGEONS	PIGNERATE	PIKELETS
PIECENER	PIERIS	PIGFACE	PIGNOLI	PIKELIKE
PIECENERS	PIERISES	PIGFACES	PIGNOLIA	PIKEMAN
PIECENING	PIEROG	PIGFEED	PIGNOLIAS	PIKEMEN
PIECENS	PIEROGEN	PIGFEEDS	PIGNOLIS	PIKEPERCH
PIECER	PIEROGI	PIGFISH	PIGNORA	PIKER
PIECERS	PIEROGIE	PIGFISHES	PIGNORATE	PIKERS
PIECES	PIEROGIES	PIGGED	PIGNUS	PIKES
PIECEWISE	PIEROGIS	PIGGERIES	PIGNUT	PIKESTAFF
PIECEWORK	PIEROGS	PIGGERY	PIGNUTS	PIKI
PIECING	PIEROGY	PIGGIE	PIGOUT	PIKING
PIECINGS	PIERRETTE	PIGGIER	PIGOUTS	PIKINGS
PIECRUST	PIERROT	PIGGIES	PIGPEN	PIKIS
PIECRUSTS	PIERROTS	PIGGIEST	PIGPENS	PIKUL
PIED	PIERS	PIGGIN	PIGS	PIKULS
PIEDFORT	PIERST	PIGGINESS	PIGSCONCE	PILA
PIEDFORTS	PIERT	PIGGING	PIGSKIN	PILAE
PIEDISH	PIERTS	PIGGINGS	PIGSKINS	PILAF
PIEDISHES	PIES	PIGGINS	PIGSNEY	PILAFF
PIEDMONT	PIET	PIGGISH	PIGSNEYS	PILAFFS
PIEDMONTS	PIETA	PIGGISHLY	PIGSNIE	PILAFS
PIEDNESS	PIETAS	PIGGY	PIGSNIES	PILAO
PIEFORT	PIETIES	PIGGYBACK	PIGSNY	PILAOS
PIEFORTS	PIETISM	PIGHEADED	PIGSTICK	PILAR
PIEHOLE	PIETISMS	PIGHT	PIGSTICKS	PILASTER
PIEHOLES	PIETIST	PIGHTED	PIGSTIES	PILASTERS
PIEING	PIETISTIC	PIGHTING	PIGSTUCK	PILAU
PIEINGS	PIETISTS	PIGHTLE	PIGSTY	PILAUS
PIEMAN	PIETS	PIGHTLES	PIGSWILL	PILAW
PIEMEN	PIETY	PIGHTS	PIGSWILLS	PILAWS
PIEND	PIEZO	PIGLET	PIGTAIL	PILCH
PIENDS	PIFFERARI	PIGLETS	PIGTAILED	PILCHARD
PIEPLANT	PIFFERARO	PIGLIKE	PIGTAILS	PILCHARDS
PIEPLANTS	PIFFERO	PIGLING	PIGWASH	PILCHER
PIEPOWDER	PIFFEROS	PIGLINGS	PIGWASHES	PILCHERS
PIER	PIFFLE	PIGMAEAN	PIGWEED	PILCHES
PIERAGE	PIFFLED	PIGMAN	PIGWEEDS	PILCORN
PIERAGES	PIFFLER	PIGMEAN	PIHOIHOI	PILCORNS

P

PILCROW	PILLAGERS	PILOTAGES	PINA	PINDAREE
PILCROWS	PILLAGES	PILOTED	PINACEOUS	PINDAREES
PILE	PILLAGING	PILOTFISH	PINACOID	PINDARI
PILEA	PILLAR	PILOTING	PINACOIDS	PINDARIS
PILEAS	PILLARED	PILOTINGS	PINAFORE	PINDER
PILEATE	PILLARING	PILOTIS	PINAFORED	PINDERS
PILEATED	PILLARIST	PILOTLESS	PINAFORES	PINDLING
PILED	PILLARS	PILOTMAN	PINAKOID	PINDOWN
PILEI	PILLAU	PILOTMEN	PINAKOIDS	PINDOWNS
PILELESS	PILLAUS	PILOTS	PINANG	PINE
PILEOUS	PILLBOX	PILOUS	PINANGS	PINEAL
PILER	PILLBOXES	PILOW	PINAS	PINEALS
PILERS	PILLBUG	PILOWS	PINASTER	PINEAPPLE
PILES	PILLBUGS	PILSENER	PINASTERS	PINECONE
PILEUM	PILLED	PILSENERS	PINATA	PINECONES
PILEUP	PILLHEAD	PILSNER	PINATAS	PINED
PILEUPS	PILLHEADS	PILSNERS	PINBALL	PINEDROPS
PILEUS	PILLICOCK	PILULA	PINBALLED	PINELAND
PILEWORK	PILLIE	PILULAE	PINBALLS	PINELANDS
PILEWORKS	PILLIES	PILULAR	PINBOARD	PINELIKE
PILEWORT	PILLING	PILULAS	PINBOARDS	PINENE
PILEWORTS	PILLINGS	PILULE	PINBONE	PINENES
PILFER	PILLION	PILULES	PINBONES	PINERIES
PILFERAGE	PILLIONED	PILUM	PINCASE	PINERY
PILFERED	PILLIONS	PILUS	PINCASES	PINES
PILFERER	PILLOCK	PILY	PINCER	PINESAP
PILFERERS	PILLOCKS	PIMA	PINCERED	PINESAPS
PILFERIES	PILLORIED	PIMAS	PINCERING	PINETA
PILFERING	PILLORIES	PIMENT	PINCERS	PINETUM
PILFERS	PILLORISE	PIMENTO	PINCH	PINEWOOD
PILFERY	PILLORIZE	PIMENTON	PINCHBECK	PINEWOODS
PILGARLIC	PILLORY	PIMENTONS	PINCHBUG	PINEY
PILGRIM	PILLOW	PIMENTOS	PINCHBUGS	PINFALL
PILGRIMED	PILLOWED	PIMENTS	PINCHCOCK	PINFALLS
PILGRIMER	PILLOWIER	PIMIENTO	PINCHECK	PINFISH
PILGRIMS	PILLOWING	PIMIENTOS	PINCHECKS	PINFISHES
PILI	PILLOWS	PIMP	PINCHED	PINFOLD
PILIER	PILLOWY	PIMPED	PINCHER	PINFOLDED
PILIEST	PILLS	PIMPERNEL	PINCHERS	PINFOLDS
PILIFORM	PILLWORM	PIMPING	PINCHES	PING
PILING	PILLWORMS	PIMPINGS	PINCHFIST	PINGED
PILINGS	PILLWORT	PIMPLE	PINCHGUT	PINGER
PILINUT	PILLWORTS	PIMPLED	PINCHGUTS	PINGERS
PILINUTS	PILOMOTOR	PIMPLES	PINCHING	PINGING
PILIS	PILONIDAL	PIMPLIER	PINCHINGS	PINGLE
PILL	PILOSE	PIMPLIEST	PINCURL	PINGLED
PILLAGE	PILOSITY	PIMPLY	PINCURLS	PINGLER
PILLAGED	PILOT	PIMPS	PINDAN	PINGLERS
PILLAGER	PILOTAGE	PIN	PINDANS	PINGLES

P

PINGLING	PINKING	PINNY	PINTS	PIOUSNESS
PINGO	PINKINGS	PINOCHLE	PINTSIZE	PIOY
PINGOES	PINKISH	PINOCHLES	PINTSIZED	PIOYE
PINGOS	PINKLY	PINOCLE	PINTUCK	PIOYES
PINGPONG	PINKNESS	PINOCLES	PINTUCKED	PIOYS
PINGPONGS	PINKO	PINOCYTIC	PINTUCKS	PIP
PINGRASS	PINKOES	PINOLE	PINUP	PIPA
PINGS	PINKOS	PINOLES	PINUPS	PIPAGE
PINGUEFY	PINKROOT	PINON	PINWALE	PIPAGES
PINGUID	PINKROOTS	PINONES	PINWALES	PIPAL
PINGUIN	PINKS	PINONS	PINWEED	PIPALS
PINGUINS	PINKWASH	PINOT	PINWEEDS	PIPAS
PINHEAD	PINKY	PINOTAGE	PINWHEEL	PIPE
PINHEADED	PINLESS	PINOTAGES	PINWHEELS	PIPEAGE
PINHEADS	PINNA	PINOTS	PINWORK	PIPEAGES
PINHOLE	PINNACE	PINPOINT	PINWORKS	PIPECLAY
PINHOLES	PINNACES	PINPOINTS	PINWORM	PIPECLAYS
PINHOOKER	PINNACLE	PINPRICK	PINWORMS	PIPED
PINIER	PINNACLED	PINPRICKS	PINWRENCH	PIPEFISH
PINIES	PINNACLES	PINS	PINXIT	PIPEFUL
PINIEST	PINNAE	PINSCHER	PINY	PIPEFULS
PINING	PINNAL	PINSCHERS	PINYIN	PIPELESS
PINION	PINNAS	PINSETTER	PINYINS	PIPELIKE
PINIONED	PINNATE	PINSPOT	PINYON	PIPELINE
PINIONING	PINNATED	PINSPOTS	PINYONS	PIPELINED
PINIONS	PINNATELY	PINSTRIPE	PIOLET	PIPELINES
PINITE	PINNATION	PINSWELL	PIOLETS	PIPER
PINITES	PINNED	PINSWELLS	PION	PIPERIC
PINITOL	PINNER	PINT	PIONED	PIPERINE
PINITOLS	PINNERS	PINTA	PIONEER	PIPERINES
PINK	PINNET	PINTABLE	PIONEERED	PIPERONAL
PINKED	PINNETS	PINTABLES	PIONEERS	PIPERS
PINKEN	PINNIE	PINTADA	PIONER	PIPES
PINKENED	PINNIES	PINTADAS	PIONERS	PIPESTEM
PINKENING	PINNING	PINTADERA	PIONEY	PIPESTEMS
PINKENS	PINNINGS	PINTADO	PIONEYS	PIPESTONE
PINKER	PINNIPED	PINTADOES	PIONIC	PIPET
PINKERS	PINNIPEDE	PINTADOS	PIONIES	PIPETS
PINKERTON	PINNIPEDS	PINTAIL	PIONING	PIPETTE
PINKEST	PINNOCK	PINTAILED	PIONINGS	PIPETTED
PINKEY	PINNOCKS	PINTAILS	PIONS	PIPETTES
PINKEYE	PINNOED	PINTANO	PIONY	PIPETTING
PINKEYES	PINNULA	PINTANOS	PIOPIO	PIPEWORK
PINKEYS	PINNULAE	PINTAS	PIOPIOS	PIPEWORKS
PINKIE	PINNULAR	PINTLE	PIOSITIES	PIPEWORT
PINKIER	PINNULAS	PINTLES	PIOSITY	PIPEWORTS
PINKIES	PINNULATE	PINTO	PIOTED	PIPI
PINKIEST	PINNULE	PINTOES	PIOUS	PIPIER
PINKINESS	PINNULES	PINTOS	PIOUSLY	PIPIEST

PIPINESS	PIRANHAS	PISCATORY	PISSHOLES	PITCHER
PIPING	PIRARUCU	PISCATRIX	PISSIER	PITCHERS
PIPINGLY	PIRARUCUS	PISCIFORM	PISSIEST	PITCHES
PIPINGS	PIRATE	PISCINA	PISSING	PITCHFORK
PIPIS	PIRATED	PISCINAE	PISSOIR	PITCHIER
PIPISTREL	PIRATES	PISCINAL	PISSOIRS	PITCHIEST
PIPIT	PIRATIC	PISCINAS	PISSY	PITCHILY
PIPITS	PIRATICAL	PISCINE	PISTACHE	PITCHING
PIPKIN	PIRATING	PISCINES	PISTACHES	PITCHINGS
PIPKINS	PIRATINGS	PISCIVORE	PISTACHIO	PITCHMAN
PIPLESS	PIRAYA	PISCO	PISTAREEN	PITCHMEN
PIPPED	PIRAYAS	PISCOS	PISTE	PITCHOUT
PIPPIER	PIRIFORM	PISE	PISTED	PITCHOUTS
PIPPIEST	PIRL	PISES	PISTES	PITCHPINE
PIPPIN	PIRLICUE	PISH	PISTIL	PITCHPIPE
PIPPING	PIRLICUED	PISHED	PISTILLAR	PITCHPOLE
PIPPINS	PIRLICUES	PISHEOG	PISTILS	PITCHY
PIPPY	PIRLS	PISHEOGS	PISTOL	PITEOUS
PIPS	PIRN	PISHER	PISTOLE	PITEOUSLY
PIPSQUEAK	PIRNIE	PISHERS	PISTOLED	PITFALL
PIPUL	PIRNIES	PISHES	PISTOLEER	PITFALLS
PIPULS	PIRNIT	PISHING	PISTOLERO	PITH
PIPY	PIRNS	PISHOGE	PISTOLES	PITHBALL
PIQUANCE	PIROG	PISHOGES	PISTOLET	PITHBALLS
PIQUANCES	PIROGEN	PISHOGUE	PISTOLETS	PITHEAD
PIQUANCY	PIROGHI	PISHOGUES	PISTOLIER	PITHEADS
PIQUANT	PIROGI	PISIFORM	PISTOLING	PITHECOID
PIQUANTLY	PIROGIE	PISIFORMS	PISTOLLED	PITHED
PIQUE	PIROGIES	PISKIES	PISTOLS	PITHFUL
PIQUED	PIROGIS	PISKY	PISTON	PITHIER
PIQUES	PIROGS	PISMIRE	PISTONS	PITHIEST
PIQUET	PIROGUE	PISMIRES	PISTOU	PITHILY
PIQUETED	PIROGUES	PISO	PISTOUS	PITHINESS
PIQUETING	PIROGY	PISOLITE	PIT	PITHING
PIQUETS	PIROJKI	PISOLITES	PITA	PITHIVIER
PIQUILLO	PIROPLASM	PISOLITH	PITAHAYA	PITHLESS
PIQUILLOS	PIROQUE	PISOLITHS	PITAHAYAS	PITHLIKE
PIQUING	PIROQUES	PISOLITIC	PITAPAT	PITHOI
PIR	PIROSHKI	PISOS	PITAPATS	PITHOS
PIRACETAM	PIROSHOK	PISS	PITARA	PITHS
PIRACIES	PIROUETTE	PISSANT	PITARAH	PITHY
PIRACY	PIROZHKI	PISSANTS	PITARAHS	PITIABLE
PIRAGUA	PIROZHOK	PISSED	PITARAS	PITIABLY
PIRAGUAS	PIRS	PISSER	PITAS	PITIED
PIRAI	PIS	PISSERS	PITAYA	PITIER
PIRAIS	PISCARIES	PISSES	PITAYAS	PITIERS
PIRANA	PISCARY	PISSHEAD	PITCH	PITIES
PIRANAS	PISCATOR	PISSHEADS	PITCHBEND	PITIETH
PIRANHA	PISCATORS	PISSHOLE	PITCHED	PITIFUL

PITIFULLY	PIVOTABLE	PIZZELLE	PLACETS	PLAIN
PITIKINS	PIVOTAL	PIZZELLES	PLACID	PLAINANT
PITILESS	PIVOTALLY	PIZZERIA	PLACIDER	PLAINANTS
PITLIKE	PIVOTED	PIZZERIAS	PLACIDEST	PLAINED
PITMAN	PIVOTER	PIZZICATI	PLACIDITY	PLAINER
PITMANS	PIVOTERS	PIZZICATO	PLACIDLY	PLAINEST
PITMASTER	PIVOTING	PIZZLE	PLACING	PLAINFUL
PITMEN	PIVOTINGS	PIZZLES	PLACINGS	PLAINING
PITON	PIVOTMAN	PLAAS	PLACIT	PLAININGS
PITONS	PIVOTMEN	PLAASES	PLACITA	PLAINISH
PITOT	PIVOTS	PLACABLE	PLACITORY	PLAINLY
PITOTS	PIX	PLACABLY	PLACITS	PLAINNESS
PITPROP	PIXEL	PLACARD	PLACITUM	PLAINS
PITPROPS	PIXELATE	PLACARDED	PLACK	PLAINSMAN
PITS	PIXELATED	PLACARDS	PLACKET	PLAINSMEN
PITSAW	PIXELATES	PLACATE	PLACKETS	PLAINSONG
PITSAWS	PIXELLATE	PLACATED	PLACKLESS	PLAINT
PITTA	PIXELS	PLACATER	PLACKS	PLAINTEXT
PITTANCE	PIXES	PLACATERS	PLACODERM	PLAINTFUL
PITTANCES	PIXIE	PLACATES	PLACOID	PLAINTIFF
PITTAS	PIXIEISH	PLACATING	PLACOIDS	PLAINTIVE
PITTED	PIXIES	PLACATION	PLAFOND	PLAINTS
PITTEN	PIXILATE	PLACATIVE	PLAFONDS	PLAINWORK
PITTER	PIXILATED	PLACATORY	PLAGAL	PLAISTER
PITTERED	PIXILATES	PLACCAT	PLAGE	PLAISTERS
PITTERING	PIXILLATE	PLACCATE	PLAGES	PLAIT
PITTERS	PIXINESS	PLACCATES	PLAGIARY	PLAITED
PITTING	PIXY	PLACCATS	PLAGIUM	PLAITER
PITTINGS	PIXYISH	PLACE	PLAGIUMS	PLAITERS
PITTITE	PIZAZZ	PLACEABLE	PLAGUE	PLAITING
PITTITES	PIZAZZES	PLACEBO	PLAGUED	PLAITINGS
PITUITA	PIZAZZIER	PLACEBOES	PLAGUER	PLAITS
PITUITARY	PIZAZZY	PLACEBOS	PLAGUERS	PLAN
PITUITAS	PIZE	PLACED	PLAGUES	PLANAR
PITUITE	PIZED	PLACEKICK	PLAGUEY	PLANARIA
PITUITES	PIZES	PLACELESS	PLAGUIER	PLANARIAN
PITUITRIN	PIZING	PLACEMAN	PLAGUIEST	PLANARIAS
PITURI	PIZZA	PLACEMAT	PLAGUILY	PLANARITY
PITURIS	PIZZAIOLA	PLACEMATS	PLAGUING	PLANATE
PITY	PIZZAIOLE	PLACEMEN	PLAGUY	PLANATION
PITYING	PIZZAIOLI	PLACEMENT	PLAICE	PLANCH
PITYINGLY	PIZZAIOLO	PLACENTA	PLAICES	PLANCHE
PITYROID	PIZZALIKE	PLACENTAE	PLAID	PLANCHED
PIU	PIZZAS	PLACENTAL	PLAIDED	PLANCHES
PIUM	PIZZAZ	PLACENTAS	PLAIDING	PLANCHET
PIUMS	PIZZAZES	PLACER	PLAIDINGS	PLANCHETS
PIUPIU	PIZZAZZ	PLACERS	PLAIDMAN	PLANCHING
PIUPIUS	PIZZAZZES	PLACES	PLAIDMEN	PLANE
PIVOT	PIZZAZZY	PLACET	PLAIDS	PLANED

PLANELOAD	PLANTAINS	PLASMA	PLATEAUED	PLATY
PLANENESS	PLANTAR	PLASMAGEL	PLATEAUS	PLATYFISH
PLANER	PLANTAS	PLASMAS	PLATEAUX	PLATYPI
PLANERS	PLANTED	PLASMASOL	PLATED	PLATYPUS
PLANES	PLANTER	PLASMATIC	PLATEFUL	PLATYS
PLANESIDE	PLANTERS	PLASMIC	PLATEFULS	PLATYSMA
PLANET	PLANTING	PLASMID	PLATELESS	PLATYSMAS
PLANETARY	PLANTINGS	PLASMIDS	PLATELET	PLAUDIT
PLANETIC	PLANTLESS	PLASMIN	PLATELETS	PLAUDITE
PLANETOID	PLANTLET	PLASMINS	PLATELIKE	PLAUDITS
PLANETS	PLANTLETS	PLASMODIA	PLATEMAN	PLAUSIBLE
PLANFORM	PLANTLIKE	PLASMOID	PLATEMARK	PLAUSIBLY
PLANFORMS	PLANTLING	PLASMOIDS	PLATEMEN	PLAUSIVE
PLANGENCY	PLANTS	PLASMON	PLATEN	PLAUSTRAL
PLANGENT	PLANTSMAN	PLASMONS	PLATENS	PLAY
PLANIGRAM	PLANTSMEN	PLASMS	PLATER	PLAYA
PLANING	PLANTULE	PLAST	PLATERS	PLAYABLE
PLANISH	PLANTULES	PLASTE	PLATES	PLAYABLES
PLANISHED	PLANULA	PLASTER	PLATESFUL	PLAYACT
PLANISHER	PLANULAE	PLASTERED	PLATFORM	PLAYACTED
PLANISHES	PLANULAR	PLASTERER	PLATFORMS	PLAYACTOR
PLANK	PLANULATE	PLASTERS	PLATIER	PLAYACTS
PLANKED	PLANULOID	PLASTERY	PLATIES	PLAYAS
PLANKING	PLANURIA	PLASTIC	PLATIEST	PLAYBACK
PLANKINGS	PLANURIAS	PLASTICKY	PLATINA	PLAYBACKS
PLANKLIKE	PLANURIES	PLASTICLY	PLATINAS	PLAYBILL
PLANKS	PLANURY	PLASTICS	PLATING	PLAYBILLS
PLANKTER	PLANXTIES	PLASTID	PLATINGS	PLAYBOOK
PLANKTERS	PLANXTY	PLASTIDS	PLATINIC	PLAYBOOKS
PLANKTIC	PLAP	PLASTIQUE	PLATINISE	PLAYBOY
PLANKTON	PLAPPED	PLASTISOL	PLATINIZE	PLAYBOYS
PLANKTONS	PLAPPING	PLASTRAL	PLATINOID	PLAYBUS
PLANLESS	PLAPS	PLASTRON	PLATINOUS	PLAYBUSES
PLANNED	PLAQUE	PLASTRONS	PLATINUM	PLAYDATE
PLANNER	PLAQUES	PLASTRUM	PLATINUMS	PLAYDATES
PLANNERS	PLAQUETTE	PLASTRUMS	PLATITUDE	PLAYDAY
PLANNING	PLASH	PLAT	PLATONIC	PLAYDAYS
PLANNINGS	PLASHED	PLATAN	PLATONICS	PLAYDOUGH
PLANOGRAM	PLASHER	PLATANE	PLATONISM	PLAYDOWN
PLANOSOL	PLASHERS	PLATANES	PLATOON	PLAYDOWNS
PLANOSOLS	PLASHES	PLATANNA	PLATOONED	PLAYED
PLANS	PLASHET	PLATANNAS	PLATOONS	PLAYER
PLANT	PLASHETS	PLATANS	PLATS	PLAYERS
PLANTA	PLASHIER	PLATBAND	PLATT	PLAYFIELD
PLANTABLE	PLASHIEST	PLATBANDS	PLATTED	PLAYFUL
PLANTAE	PLASHING	PLATE	PLATTER	PLAYFULLY
PLANTAGE	PLASHINGS	PLATEASM	PLATTERS	PLAYGIRL
PLANTAGES	PLASHY	PLATEASMS	PLATTING	PLAYGIRLS
PLANTAIN	PLASM	PLATEAU	PLATTINGS	PLAYGOER

P

PLAYGOERS	PLEADING	PLECTRES	PLENTIFUL	PLEWS
PLAYGOING	PLEADINGS	PLECTRON	PLENTY	PLEX
PLAYGROUP	PLEADS	PLECTRONS	PLENUM	PLEXAL
PLAYHOUSE	PLEAED	PLECTRUM	PLENUMS	PLEXED
PLAYING	PLEAING	PLECTRUMS	PLEON	PLEXES
PLAYINGS	PLEAS	PLED	PLEONAL	PLEXIFORM
PLAYLAND	PLEASABLE	PLEDGABLE	PLEONASM	PLEXING
PLAYLANDS	PLEASANCE	PLEDGE	PLEONASMS	PLEXOR
PLAYLESS	PLEASANT	PLEDGED	PLEONAST	PLEXORS
PLAYLET	PLEASE	PLEDGEE	PLEONASTE	PLEXURE
PLAYLETS	PLEASED	PLEDGEES	PLEONASTS	PLEXURES
PLAYLIKE	PLEASEDLY	PLEDGEOR	PLEONEXIA	PLEXUS
PLAYLIST	PLEASEMAN	PLEDGEORS	PLEONIC	PLEXUSES
PLAYLISTS	PLEASEMEN	PLEDGER	PLEONS	PLIABLE
PLAYMAKER	PLEASER	PLEDGERS	PLEOPOD	PLIABLY
PLAYMATE	PLEASERS	PLEDGES	PLEOPODS	PLIANCIES
PLAYMATES	PLEASES	PLEDGET	PLERION	PLIANCY
PLAYOFF	PLEASETH	PLEDGETS	PLERIONS	PLIANT
PLAYOFFS	PLEASING	PLEDGING	PLEROMA	PLIANTLY
PLAYPEN	PLEASINGS	PLEDGOR	PLEROMAS	PLICA
PLAYPENS	PLEASURE	PLEDGORS	PLEROME	PLICAE
PLAYROOM	PLEASURED	PLEIAD	PLEROMES	PLICAL
PLAYROOMS	PLEASURER	PLEIADES	PLESH	PLICAS
PLAYS	PLEASURES	PLEIADS	PLESHES	PLICATE
PLAYSCAPE	PLEAT	PLEIOCENE	PLESSOR	PLICATED
PLAYSET	PLEATED	PLEIOMERY	PLESSORS	PLICATELY
PLAYSETS	PLEATER	PLEIOTAXY	PLETHORA	PLICATES
PLAYSLIP	PLEATERS	PLENA	PLETHORAS	PLICATING
PLAYSLIPS	PLEATHER	PLENARIES	PLETHORIC	PLICATION
PLAYSOME	PLEATHERS	PLENARILY	PLEUCH	PLICATURE
PLAYSUIT	PLEATING	PLENARTY	PLEUCHED	PLIE
PLAYSUITS	PLEATINGS	PLENARY	PLEUCHING	PLIED
PLAYTHING	PLEATLESS	PLENCH	PLEUCHS	PLIER
PLAYTIME	PLEATS	PLENCHES	PLEUGH	PLIERS
PLAYTIMES	PLEB	PLENILUNE	PLEUGHED	PLIES
PLAYWEAR	PLEBBIER	PLENIPO	PLEUGHING	PLIGHT
PLAYWEARS	PLEBBIEST	PLENIPOES	PLEUGHS	PLIGHTED
PLAZA	PLEBBY	PLENIPOS	PLEURA	PLIGHTER
PLAZAS	PLEBE	PLENISH	PLEURAE	PLIGHTERS
PLEA	PLEBEAN	PLENISHED	PLEURAL	PLIGHTFUL
PLEACH	PLEBEIAN	PLENISHER	PLEURAS	PLIGHTING
PLEACHED	PLEBEIANS	PLENISHES	PLEURISY	PLIGHTS
PLEACHES	PLEBES	PLENISM	PLEURITIC	PLIM
PLEACHING	PLEBIFIED	PLENISMS	PLEURITIS	PLIMMED
PLEAD	PLEBIFIES	PLENIST	PLEURON	PLIMMING
PLEADABLE	PLEBIFY	PLENISTS	PLEURONIA	PLIMS
PLEADED	PLEBS	PLENITUDE	PLEUSTON	PLIMSOL
PLEADER	PLECTRA	PLENTEOUS	PLEUSTONS	PLIMSOLE
PLEADERS	PLECTRE	PLENTIES	PLEW	PLIMSOLES

PLIMSOLL	PLOGGINGS	PLOTTIER	PLOWS	PLUM
PLIMSOLLS	PLOIDIES	PLOTTIES	PLOWSHARE	PLUMAGE
PLIMSOLS	PLOIDY	PLOTTIEST	PLOWSTAFF	PLUMAGED
PLING	PLONG	PLOTTING	PLOWTAIL	PLUMAGES
PLINGED	PLONGD	PLOTTINGS	PLOWTAILS	PLUMATE
PLINGING	PLONGE	PLOTTY	PLOWTER	PLUMB
PLINGS	PLONGED	PLOTZ	PLOWTERED	PLUMBABLE
PLINK	PLONGES	PLOTZED	PLOWTERS	PLUMBAGO
PLINKED	PLONGING	PLOTZES	PLOWWISE	PLUMBAGOS
PLINKER	PLONGS	PLOTZING	PLOY	PLUMBATE
PLINKERS	PLONK	PLOUGH	PLOYE	PLUMBATES
PLINKIER	PLONKED	PLOUGHBOY	PLOYED	PLUMBED
PLINKIEST	PLONKER	PLOUGHED	PLOYES	PLUMBEOUS
PLINKING	PLONKERS	PLOUGHER	PLOYING	PLUMBER
PLINKINGS	PLONKIER	PLOUGHERS	PLOYS	PLUMBERS
PLINKS	PLONKIEST	PLOUGHING	PLU	PLUMBERY
PLINKY	PLONKING	PLOUGHMAN	PLUCK	PLUMBIC
PLINTH	PLONKINGS	PLOUGHMEN	PLUCKED	PLUMBING
PLINTHS	PLONKO	PLOUGHS	PLUCKER	PLUMBINGS
PLIOCENE	PLONKOS	PLOUK	PLUCKERS	PLUMBISM
PLIOFILM	PLONKS	PLOUKIE	PLUCKIER	PLUMBISMS
PLIOFILMS	PLONKY	PLOUKIER	PLUCKIEST	PLUMBITE
PLIOSAUR	PLOOK	PLOUKIEST	PLUCKILY	PLUMBITES
PLIOSAURS	PLOOKIE	PLOUKS	PLUCKING	PLUMBLESS
PLIOTRON	PLOOKIER	PLOUKY	PLUCKS	PLUMBNESS
PLIOTRONS	PLOOKIEST	PLOUTER	PLUCKY	PLUMBOUS
PLISKIE	PLOOKS	PLOUTERED	PLUE	PLUMBS
PLISKIER	PLOOKY	PLOUTERS	PLUES	PLUMBUM
PLISKIES	PLOP	PLOVER	PLUFF	PLUMBUMS
PLISKIEST	PLOPPED	PLOVERIER	PLUFFED	PLUMCAKE
PLISKY	PLOPPING	PLOVERS	PLUFFIER	PLUMCAKES
PLISSE	PLOPS	PLOVERY	PLUFFIEST	PLUMCOT
PLISSES	PLOSION	PLOW	PLUFFING	PLUMCOTS
PLOAT	PLOSIONS	PLOWABLE	PLUFFS	PLUMDAMAS
PLOATED	PLOSIVE	PLOWBACK	PLUFFY	PLUME
PLOATING	PLOSIVES	PLOWBACKS	PLUG	PLUMED
PLOATS	PLOT	PLOWBOY	PLUGBOARD	PLUMELESS
PLOD	PLOTFUL	PLOWBOYS	PLUGGED	PLUMELET
PLODDED	PLOTLESS	PLOWED	PLUGGER	PLUMELETS
PLODDER	PLOTLINE	PLOWER	PLUGGERS	PLUMELIKE
PLODDERS	PLOTLINES	PLOWERS	PLUGGING	PLUMERIA
PLODDING	PLOTS	PLOWHEAD	PLUGGINGS	PLUMERIAS
PLODDINGS	PLOTTAGE	PLOWHEADS	PLUGHOLE	PLUMERIES
PLODGE	PLOTTAGES	PLOWING	PLUGHOLES	PLUMERY
PLODGED	PLOTTED	PLOWINGS	PLUGLESS	PLUMES
PLODGES	PLOTTER	PLOWLAND	PLUGOLA	PLUMIER
PLODGING	PLOTTERED	PLOWLANDS	PLUGOLAS	PLUMIEST
PLODS	PLOTTERS	PLOWMAN	PLUGS	PLUMING
PLOGGING	PLOTTIE	PLOWMEN	PLUGUGLY	PLUMIPED

P

PLUMIPEDS	PLUNGERS	PLUSSES	POACHABLE	POCKPITS
PLUMIST	PLUNGES	PLUSSING	POACHED	POCKS
PLUMISTS	PLUNGING	PLUTEAL	POACHER	POCKY
PLUMLIKE	PLUNGINGS	PLUTEI	POACHERS	POCO
PLUMMER	PLUNK	PLUTEUS	POACHES	POCOSEN
PLUMMEST	PLUNKED	PLUTEUSES	POACHIER	POCOSENS
PLUMMET	PLUNKER	PLUTO	POACHIEST	POCOSIN
PLUMMETED	PLUNKERS	PLUTOCRAT	POACHING	POCOSINS
PLUMMETS	PLUNKIER	PLUTOED	POACHINGS	POCOSON
PLUMMIER	PLUNKIEST	PLUTOES	POACHY	POCOSONS
PLUMMIEST	PLUNKING	PLUTOID	POAKA	POD
PLUMMY	PLUNKS	PLUTOIDS	POAKAS	PODAGRA
PLUMOSE	PLUNKY	PLUTOING	POAKE	PODAGRAL
PLUMOSELY	PLUOT	PLUTOLOGY	POAKES	PODAGRAS
PLUMOSITY	PLUOTS	PLUTON	POAS	PODAGRIC
PLUMOUS	PLURAL	PLUTONIAN	POBLANO	PODAGROUS
PLUMP	PLURALISE	PLUTONIC	POBLANOS	PODAL
PLUMPED	PLURALISM	PLUTONISM	POBOY	PODALIC
PLUMPEN	PLURALIST	PLUTONIUM	POBOYS	PODARGUS
PLUMPENED	PLURALITY	PLUTONOMY	POCHARD	PODCAST
PLUMPENS	PLURALIZE	PLUTONS	POCHARDS	PODCASTED
PLUMPER	PLURALLY	PLUTOS	POCHAY	PODCASTER
PLUMPERS	PLURALS	PLUVIAL	POCHAYED	PODCASTS
PLUMPEST	PLURIPARA	PLUVIALS	POCHAYING	PODDED
PLUMPIE	PLURISIE	PLUVIAN	POCHAYS	PODDIE
PLUMPIER	PLURISIES	PLUVIANS	POCHETTE	PODDIER
PLUMPIEST	PLURRY	PLUVIOSE	POCHETTES	PODDIES
PLUMPING	PLUS	PLUVIOUS	POCHOIR	PODDIEST
PLUMPISH	PLUSAGE	PLUVIUS	POCHOIRS	PODDING
PLUMPLY	PLUSAGES	PLY	POCK	PODDLE
PLUMPNESS	PLUSED	PLYER	POCKARD	PODDLED
PLUMPS	PLUSES	PLYERS	POCKARDS	PODDLES
PLUMPY	PLUSH	PLYING	POCKED	PODDLING
PLUMS	PLUSHED	PLYINGLY	POCKET	PODDY
PLUMULA	PLUSHER	PLYWOOD	POCKETED	PODESTA
PLUMULAE	PLUSHES	PLYWOODS	POCKETER	PODESTAS
PLUMULAR	PLUSHEST	PNEUMA	POCKETERS	PODEX
PLUMULATE	PLUSHIE	PNEUMAS	POCKETFUL	PODEXES
PLUMULE	PLUSHIER	PNEUMATA	POCKETING	PODGE
PLUMULES	PLUSHIES	PNEUMATIC	POCKETS	PODGES
PLUMULOSE	PLUSHIEST	PNEUMONIA	POCKIER	PODGIER
PLUMY	PLUSHILY	PNEUMONIC	POCKIES	PODGIEST
PLUNDER	PLUSHLY	PNICOGEN	POCKIEST	PODGILY
PLUNDERED	PLUSHNESS	PNICOGENS	POCKILY	PODGINESS
PLUNDERER	PLUSHY	PNICTOGEN	POCKING	PODGY
PLUNDERS	PLUSING	PO	POCKMANKY	PODIA
PLUNGE	PLUSSAGE	POA	POCKMARK	PODIAL
PLUNGED	PLUSSAGES	POACEOUS	POCKMARKS	PODIATRIC
PLUNGER	PLUSSED	POACH	POCKPIT	PODIATRY

PODITE	POETIC	POGROMIST	POINTY	POKILY
PODITES	POETICAL	POGROMS	POIS	POKINESS
PODITIC	POETICALS	POGY	POISE	POKING
PODIUM	POETICISE	POH	POISED	POKY
PODIUMED	POETICISM	POHED	POISER	POL
PODIUMING	POETICIZE	POHING	POISERS	POLACCA
PODIUMS	POETICS	POHIRI	POISES	POLACCAS
PODLEY	POETICULE	POHIRIS	POISHA	POLACRE
PODLEYS	POETISE	POHS	POISHAS	POLACRES
PODLIKE	POETISED	POI	POISING	POLAR
PODOCARP	POETISER	POIGNADO	POISON	POLARISE
PODOCARPS	POETISERS	POIGNANCE	POISONED	POLARISED
PODOLOGY	POETISES	POIGNANCY	POISONER	POLARISER
PODOMERE	POETISING	POIGNANT	POISONERS	POLARISES
PODOMERES	POETIZE	POILU	POISONING	POLARITY
PODS	POETIZED	POILUS	POISONOUS	POLARIZE
PODSOL	POETIZER	POINADO	POISONS	POLARIZED
PODSOLIC	POETIZERS	POINADOES	POISSON	POLARIZER
PODSOLISE	POETIZES	POINCIANA	POISSONS	POLARIZES
PODSOLIZE	POETIZING	POIND	POITIN	POLARON
PODSOLS	POETLESS	POINDED	POITINS	POLARONS
PODUNK	POETLIKE	POINDER	POITREL	POLARS
PODUNKS	POETRESSE	POINDERS	POITRELS	POLDER
PODZOL	POETRIES	POINDING	POITRINE	POLDERED
PODZOLIC	POETRY	POINDINGS	POITRINES	POLDERING
PODZOLISE	POETS	POINDS	POKABLE	POLDERS
PODZOLIZE	POETSHIP	POINT	POKAL	POLE
PODZOLS	POETSHIPS	POINTABLE	POKALS	POLEAX
POECHORE	POFFLE	POINTE	POKE	POLEAXE
POECHORES	POFFLES	POINTED	POKEBERRY	POLEAXED
POEM	POGEY	POINTEDLY	POKED	POLEAXES
POEMATIC	POGEYS	POINTEL	POKEFUL	POLEAXING
POEMS	POGGE	POINTELLE	POKEFULS	POLECAT
POENOLOGY	POGGES	POINTELS	POKELOGAN	POLECATS
POEP	POGIES	POINTER	POKER	POLED
POEPED	POGO	POINTERS	POKERISH	POLEIS
POEPING	POGOED	POINTES	POKEROOT	POLELESS
POEPOL	POGOER	POINTIER	POKEROOTS	POLEMARCH
POEPOLS	POGOERS	POINTIEST	POKERS	POLEMIC
POEPS	POGOES	POINTILLE	POKERWORK	POLEMICAL
POESIED	POGOING	POINTING	POKES	POLEMICS
POESIES	POGONIA	POINTINGS	POKEWEED	POLEMISE
POESY	POGONIAS	POINTLESS	POKEWEEDS	POLEMISED
POESYING	POGONIP	POINTLIKE	POKEY	POLEMISES
POET	POGONIPS	POINTMAN	POKEYS	POLEMIST
POETASTER	POGOS	POINTMEN	POKIE	POLEMISTS
POETASTRY	POGROM	POINTS	POKIER	POLEMIZE
POETESS	POGROMED	POINTSMAN	POKIES	POLEMIZED
POETESSES	POGROMING	POINTSMEN	POKIEST	POLEMIZES

POLENTA	POLITICLY	POLLINGS	POLONIUM	POLYGALA
POLENTAS	POLITICO	POLLINIA	POLONIUMS	POLYGALAS
POLER	POLITICOS	POLLINIC	POLONIZE	POLYGAM
POLERS	POLITICS	POLLINISE	POLONIZED	POLYGAMIC
POLES	POLITIES	POLLINIUM	POLONIZES	POLYGAMS
POLESTAR	POLITIQUE	POLLINIZE	POLONY	POLYGAMY
POLESTARS	POLITY	POLLIST	POLOS	POLYGENE
POLEWARD	POLJE	POLLISTS	POLS	POLYGENES
POLEY	POLJES	POLLIWIG	POLT	POLYGENIC
POLEYN	POLK	POLLIWIGS	POLTED	POLYGENY
POLEYNS	POLKA	POLLIWOG	POLTFEET	POLYGLOT
POLEYS	POLKAED	POLLIWOGS	POLTFOOT	POLYGLOTS
POLIANITE	POLKAING	POLLMAN	POLTING	POLYGLOTT
POLICE	POLKAS	POLLMEN	POLTROON	POLYGON
POLICED	POLKED	POLLOCK	POLTROONS	POLYGONAL
POLICEMAN	POLKING	POLLOCKS	POLTS	POLYGONS
POLICEMEN	POLKS	POLLS	POLVERINE	POLYGONUM
POLICER	POLL	POLLSTER	POLY	POLYGONY
POLICERS	POLLACK	POLLSTERS	POLYACID	POLYGRAPH
POLICES	POLLACKS	POLLTAKER	POLYACIDS	POLYGYNE
POLICIER	POLLAN	POLLUCITE	POLYACT	POLYGYNY
POLICIERS	POLLANS	POLLUSION	POLYADIC	POLYHEDRA
POLICIES	POLLARD	POLLUTANT	POLYAMIDE	POLYIMIDE
POLICING	POLLARDED	POLLUTE	POLYAMINE	POLYLEMMA
POLICINGS	POLLARDS	POLLUTED	POLYAMORY	POLYMASTY
POLICY	POLLAXE	POLLUTER	POLYANDRY	POLYMATH
POLIES	POLLAXED	POLLUTERS	POLYANTHA	POLYMATHS
POLING	POLLAXES	POLLUTES	POLYANTHI	POLYMATHY
POLINGS	POLLAXING	POLLUTING	POLYARCH	POLYMER
POLIO	POLLED	POLLUTION	POLYARCHY	POLYMERIC
POLIOS	POLLEE	POLLUTIVE	POLYAXIAL	POLYMERS
POLIS	POLLEES	POLLY	POLYAXON	POLYMERY
POLISES	POLLEN	POLLYANNA	POLYAXONS	POLYMORPH
POLISH	POLLENATE	POLLYWIG	POLYBAG	POLYMYXIN
POLISHED	POLLENED	POLLYWIGS	POLYBAGS	POLYNIA
POLISHER	POLLENING	POLLYWOG	POLYBASIC	POLYNIAS
POLISHERS	POLLENS	POLLYWOGS	POLYBRID	POLYNYA
POLISHES	POLLENT	POLO	POLYBRIDS	POLYNYAS
POLISHING	POLLER	POLOIDAL	POLYCARPY	POLYNYI
POLITBURO	POLLERS	POLOIST	POLYCHETE	POLYOL
POLITE	POLLEX	POLOISTS	POLYCONIC	POLYOLS
POLITELY	POLLICAL	POLONAISE	POLYCOT	POLYOMA
POLITER	POLLICES	POLONIE	POLYCOTS	POLYOMAS
POLITESSE	POLLICIE	POLONIES	POLYDEMIC	POLYOMINO
POLITEST	POLLICIES	POLONISE	POLYDRUG	POLYONYM
POLITIC	POLLICY	POLONISED	POLYENE	POLYONYMS
POLITICAL	POLLIES	POLONISES	POLYENES	POLYONYMY
POLITICK	POLLINATE	POLONISM	POLYENIC	POLYP
POLITICKS	POLLING	POLONISMS	POLYESTER	POLYPARIA

POLYPARY	POLYTHENE	POMMELING	PONCED	PONGING
POLYPE	POLYTONAL	POMMELLED	PONCES	PONGO
POLYPED	POLYTYPE	POMMELS	PONCEY	PONGOES
POLYPEDS	POLYTYPED	POMMETTY	PONCHO	PONGOS
POLYPES	POLYTYPES	POMMIE	PONCHOED	PONGS
POLYPHAGY	POLYTYPIC	POMMIES	PONCHOS	PONGY
POLYPHASE	POLYURIA	POMMY	PONCIER	PONIARD
POLYPHON	POLYURIAS	POMO	PONCIEST	PONIARDED
POLYPHONE	POLYURIC	POMOERIUM	PONCING	PONIARDS
POLYPHONS	POLYVINYL	POMOLOGY	PONCY	PONIED
POLYPHONY	POLYWATER	POMOS	POND	PONIES
POLYPI	POLYZOA	POMP	PONDAGE	PONK
POLYPIDE	POLYZOAN	POMPADOUR	PONDAGES	PONKED
POLYPIDES	POLYZOANS	POMPANO	PONDED	PONKING
POLYPIDOM	POLYZOARY	POMPANOS	PONDER	PONKS
POLYPILL	POLYZOIC	POMPELO	PONDERAL	PONS
POLYPILLS	POLYZONAL	POMPELOS	PONDERATE	PONT
POLYPINE	POLYZOOID	POMPEY	PONDERED	PONTAGE
POLYPITE	POLYZOON	POMPEYED	PONDERER	PONTAGES
POLYPITES	POM	POMPEYING	PONDERERS	PONTAL
POLYPLOID	POMACE	POMPEYS	PONDERING	PONTES
POLYPNEA	POMACEOUS	POMPHOLYX	PONDEROSA	PONTIANAC
POLYPNEAS	POMACES	POMPIER	PONDEROUS	PONTIANAK
POLYPNEIC	POMADE	POMPIERS	PONDERS	PONTIC
POLYPOD	POMADED	POMPILID	PONDING	PONTIE
POLYPODS	POMADES	POMPILIDS	PONDOK	PONTIES
POLYPODY	POMADING	POMPION	PONDOKKIE	PONTIFEX
POLYPOID	POMANDER	POMPIONS	PONDOKS	PONTIFF
POLYPORE	POMANDERS	POMPOM	PONDS	PONTIFFS
POLYPORES	POMATO	POMPOMMED	PONDWEED	PONTIFIC
POLYPOSES	POMATOES	POMPOMS	PONDWEEDS	PONTIFICE
POLYPOSIS	POMATUM	POMPON	PONE	PONTIFIED
POLYPOUS	POMATUMED	POMPONS	PONENT	PONTIFIES
POLYPS	POMATUMS	POMPOON	PONENTS	PONTIFY
POLYPTYCH	POMBE	POMPOONS	PONES	PONTIL
POLYPUS	POMBES	POMPOSITY	PONEY	PONTILE
POLYPUSES	POME	POMPOSO	PONEYS	PONTILES
POLYS	POMELIKE	POMPOUS	PONG	PONTILS
POLYSEME	POMELO	POMPOUSLY	PONGA	PONTINE
POLYSEMES	POMELOS	POMPS	PONGAL	PONTLEVIS
POLYSEMIC	POMEROY	POMROY	PONGALS	PONTON
POLYSEMY	POMEROYS	POMROYS	PONGAS	PONTONEER
POLYSOME	POMES	POMS	PONGED	PONTONIER
POLYSOMES	POMFRET	POMWATER	PONGEE	PONTONS
POLYSOMIC	POMFRETS	POMWATERS	PONGEES	PONTOON
POLYSOMY	POMMEE	PONCE	PONGID	PONTOONED
POLYSTYLE	POMMEL	PONCEAU	PONGIDS	PONTOONER
POLYTENE	POMMELE	PONCEAUS	PONGIER	PONTOONS
POLYTENY	POMMELED	PONCEAUX	PONGIEST	PONTS

PONTY	POOLSIDE	POOTLE	POPLITIC	POPTASTIC
PONY	POOLSIDES	POOTLED	POPOUT	POPULACE
PONYING	POON	POOTLES	POPOUTS	POPULACES
PONYSKIN	POONAC	POOTLING	POPOVER	POPULAR
PONYSKINS	POONACS	POOTS	POPOVERS	POPULARLY
PONYTAIL	POONCE	POP	POPPA	POPULARS
PONYTAILS	POONCED	POPADUM	POPPADOM	POPULATE
PONZU	POONCES	POPADUMS	POPPADOMS	POPULATED
PONZUS	POONCING	POPCORN	POPPADUM	POPULATES
POO	POONS	POPCORNS	POPPADUMS	POPULISM
POOBAH	POONTANG	POPE	POPPAS	POPULISMS
POOBAHS	POONTANGS	POPEDOM	POPPED	POPULIST
POOCH	POOP	POPEDOMS	POPPER	POPULISTS
POOCHED	POOPED	POPEHOOD	POPPERING	POPULOUS
POOCHES	POOPER	POPEHOODS	POPPERS	PORAE
POOCHING	POOPERS	POPELESS	POPPET	PORAES
POOD	POOPIER	POPELIKE	POPPETS	PORAL
POODLE	POOPIEST	POPELING	POPPIED	PORANGI
POODLES	POOPING	POPELINGS	POPPIER	PORBEAGLE
POODS	POOPS	POPERA	POPPIES	PORCELAIN
POOED	POOPY	POPERAS	POPPIEST	PORCH
POOF	POOR	POPERIN	POPPING	PORCHED
POOGYE	POORBOX	POPERINS	POPPISH	PORCHES
POOGYES	POORBOXES	POPES	POPPIT	PORCHETTA
POOH	POORER	POPESEYE	POPPITS	PORCHLESS
POOHED	POOREST	POPESHIP	POPPLE	PORCINE
POOHING	POORHOUSE	POPESHIPS	POPPLED	PORCINI
POOHS	POORI	POPETTE	POPPLES	PORCINIS
POOING	POORIS	POPETTES	POPPLIER	PORCINO
POOJA	POORISH	POPEYED	POPPLIEST	PORCUPINE
POOJAH	POORLIER	POPGUN	POPPLING	PORCUPINY
POOJAHS	POORLIEST	POPGUNS	POPPLY	PORE
POOJAS	POORLY	POPINAC	POPPY	PORED
POOK	POORMOUTH	POPINACK	POPPYCOCK	PORER
POOKA	POORNESS	POPINACKS	POPPYHEAD	PORERS
POOKAS	POORT	POPINACS	POPPYSEED	PORES
POOKING	POORTITH	POPINJAY	POPRIN	PORGE
POOKIT	POORTITHS	POPINJAYS	POPS	PORGED
POOKS	POORTS	POPJOY	POPSICLE	PORGES
POOL	POORWILL	POPJOYED	POPSICLES	PORGIE
POOLED	POORWILLS	POPJOYING	POPSIE	PORGIES
POOLER	POOS	POPJOYS	POPSIES	PORGING
POOLERS	POOT	POPLAR	POPSOCK	PORGY
POOLHALL	POOTED	POPLARS	POPSOCKS	PORIER
POOLHALLS	POOTER	POPLIN	POPSTER	PORIEST
POOLING	POOTERED	POPLINS	POPSTERS	PORIFER
POOLROOM	POOTERING	POPLITEAL	POPSTREL	PORIFERAL
POOLROOMS	POOTERS	POPLITEI	POPSTRELS	PORIFERAN
POOLS	POOTING	POPLITEUS	POPSY	PORIFERS

PORIN	PORPESS	PORTENDS	PORTOISE	POSHLY
PORINA	PORPESSE	PORTENT	PORTOISES	POSHNESS
PORINAS	PORPESSES	PORTENTS	PORTOLAN	POSHO
PORINESS	PORPHYRIA	PORTEOUS	PORTOLANI	POSHOS
PORING	PORPHYRIC	PORTER	PORTOLANO	POSHTEEN
PORINS	PORPHYRIN	PORTERAGE	PORTOLANS	POSHTEENS
PORISM	PORPHYRIO	PORTERED	PORTOUS	POSIDRIVE
PORISMS	PORPHYRY	PORTERESS	PORTOUSES	POSIER
PORISTIC	PORPOISE	PORTERING	PORTRAIT	POSIES
PORK	PORPOISED	PORTERLY	PORTRAITS	POSIEST
PORKED	PORPOISES	PORTERS	PORTRAY	POSIGRADE
PORKER	PORPORATE	PORTESS	PORTRAYAL	POSING
PORKERS	PORRECT	PORTESSE	PORTRAYED	POSINGLY
PORKIER	PORRECTED	PORTESSES	PORTRAYER	POSINGS
PORKIES	PORRECTS	PORTFIRE	PORTRAYS	POSIT
PORKIEST	PORRENGER	PORTFIRES	PORTREEVE	POSITED
PORKINESS	PORRIDGE	PORTFOLIO	PORTRESS	POSITIF
PORKING	PORRIDGES	PORTHOLE	PORTS	POSITIFS
PORKLING	PORRIDGY	PORTHOLES	PORTSIDE	POSITING
PORKLINGS	PORRIGO	PORTHORS	PORTULACA	POSITION
PORKPIE	PORRIGOS	PORTHOS	PORTULAN	POSITIONS
PORKPIES	PORRINGER	PORTHOSES	PORTULANS	POSITIVE
PORKS	PORT	PORTHOUSE	PORTY	POSITIVER
PORKWOOD	PORTA	PORTICO	PORWIGGLE	POSITIVES
PORKWOODS	PORTABLE	PORTICOED	PORY	POSITON
PORKY	PORTABLES	PORTICOES	POS	POSITONS
PORLOCK	PORTABLY	PORTICOS	POSABLE	POSITRON
PORLOCKED	PORTAGE	PORTIER	POSADA	POSITRONS
PORLOCKS	PORTAGED	PORTIERE	POSADAS	POSITS
PORN	PORTAGES	PORTIERED	POSAUNE	POSNET
PORNIER	PORTAGING	PORTIERES	POSAUNES	POSNETS
PORNIEST	PORTAGUE	PORTIEST	POSE	POSOLE
PORNO	PORTAGUES	PORTIGUE	POSEABLE	POSOLES
PORNOMAG	PORTAL	PORTIGUES	POSED	POSOLOGIC
PORNOMAGS	PORTALED	PORTING	POSER	POSOLOGY
PORNOS	PORTALS	PORTION	POSERISH	POSS
PORNS	PORTANCE	PORTIONED	POSERS	POSSE
PORNY	PORTANCES	PORTIONER	POSES	POSSED
POROGAMIC	PORTAPACK	PORTIONS	POSEUR	POSSER
POROGAMY	PORTAPAK	PORTLAND	POSEURS	POSSERS
POROMERIC	PORTAPAKS	PORTLANDS	POSEUSE	POSSES
POROSCOPE	PORTAS	PORTLAST	POSEUSES	POSSESS
POROSCOPY	PORTASES	PORTLASTS	POSEY	POSSESSED
POROSE	PORTATE	PORTLESS	POSH	POSSESSES
POROSES	PORTATILE	PORTLIER	POSHED	POSSESSOR
POROSIS	PORTATIVE	PORTLIEST	POSHER	POSSET
POROSITY	PORTED	PORTLY	POSHES	POSSETED
POROUS	PORTEND	PORTMAN	POSHEST	POSSETING
POROUSLY	PORTENDED	PORTMEN	POSHING	POSSETS

POSSIBLE	POSTEEN	POSTINS	POSTURERS	POTCHED
POSSIBLER	POSTEENS	POSTIQUE	POSTURES	POTCHER
POSSIBLES	POSTER	POSTIQUES	POSTURING	POTCHERS
POSSIBLY	POSTERED	POSTLIKE	POSTURISE	POTCHES
POSSIE	POSTERING	POSTLUDE	POSTURIST	POTCHING
POSSIES	POSTERIOR	POSTLUDES	POSTURIZE	POTE
POSSING	POSTERISE	POSTMAN	POSTVIRAL	POTED
POSSUM	POSTERITY	POSTMARK	POSTWAR	POTEEN
POSSUMED	POSTERIZE	POSTMARKS	POSTWOMAN	POTEENS
POSSUMING	POSTERN	POSTMEN	POSTWOMEN	POTENCE
POSSUMS	POSTERNS	POSTNASAL	POSY	POTENCES
POST	POSTERS	POSTNATAL	POT	POTENCIES
POSTAGE	POSTFACE	POSTNATI	POTABLE	POTENCY
POSTAGES	POSTFACES	POSTOP	POTABLES	POTENT
POSTAL	POSTFACT	POSTOPS	POTAE	POTENTATE
POSTALLY	POSTFAULT	POSTORAL	POTAES	POTENTIAL
POSTALS	POSTFIRE	POSTPAID	POTAGE	POTENTISE
POSTANAL	POSTFIX	POSTPONE	POTAGER	POTENTIZE
POSTAXIAL	POSTFIXAL	POSTPONED	POTAGERS	POTENTLY
POSTBAG	POSTFIXED	POSTPONER	POTAGES	POTENTS
POSTBAGS	POSTFIXES	POSTPONES	POTALE	POTES
POSTBASE	POSTFORM	POSTPOSE	POTALES	POTFUL
POSTBASES	POSTFORMS	POSTPOSED	POTAMIC	POTFULS
POSTBOX	POSTGAME	POSTPOSES	POTASH	POTGUN
POSTBOXES	POSTGRAD	POSTPUNK	POTASHED	POTGUNS
POSTBOY	POSTGRADS	POSTPUNKS	POTASHES	POTHEAD
POSTBOYS	POSTHASTE	POSTRACE	POTASHING	POTHEADS
POSTBURN	POSTHEAT	POSTRIDER	POTASS	POTHECARY
POSTBUS	POSTHEATS	POSTRIOT	POTASSA	POTHEEN
POSTBUSES	POSTHOLE	POSTROLL	POTASSAS	POTHEENS
POSTCARD	POSTHOLES	POSTROLLS	POTASSES	POTHER
POSTCARDS	POSTHORSE	POSTS	POTASSIC	POTHERB
POSTCAVA	POSTHOUSE	POSTSHOW	POTASSIUM	POTHERBS
POSTCAVAE	POSTICAL	POSTSYNC	POTATION	POTHERED
POSTCAVAL	POSTICHE	POSTSYNCS	POTATIONS	POTHERIER
POSTCAVAS	POSTICHES	POSTTAX	POTATO	POTHERING
POSTCODE	POSTICOUS	POSTTEEN	POTATOBUG	POTHERS
POSTCODED	POSTIE	POSTTEENS	POTATOES	POTHERY
POSTCODES	POSTIES	POSTTEST	POTATORY	POTHOLDER
POSTCOUP	POSTIL	POSTTESTS	POTBELLY	POTHOLE
POSTCRASH	POSTILED	POSTTRIAL	POTBOIL	POTHOLED
POSTDATE	POSTILING	POSTTRUTH	POTBOILED	POTHOLER
POSTDATED	POSTILION	POSTULANT	POTBOILER	POTHOLERS
POSTDATES	POSTILLED	POSTULATA	POTBOILS	POTHOLES
POSTDIVE	POSTILLER	POSTULATE	POTBOUND	POTHOLING
POSTDOC	POSTILS	POSTURAL	POTBOY	POTHOOK
POSTDOCS	POSTIN	POSTURE	POTBOYS	POTHOOKS
POSTDRUG	POSTING	POSTURED	POTCH	POTHOS
POSTED	POSTINGS	POSTURER	POTCHE	POTHOSES

POTHOUSE POTTABLE POUFFES POUNCHING POUSSES
POTHOUSES POTTAGE POUFFIER POUNCING POUSSETTE
POTHUNTER POTTAGES POUFFIEST POUND POUSSIE
POTICARY POTTED POUFFING POUNDAGE POUSSIES
POTICHE POTTEEN POUFFS POUNDAGES POUSSIN
POTICHES POTTEENS POUFFY POUNDAL POUSSINS
POTIN POTTER POUFING POUNDALS POUT
POTING POTTERED POUFS POUNDCAKE POUTASSOU
POTINS POTTERER POUK POUNDED POUTED
POTION POTTERERS POUKE POUNDER POUTER
POTIONS POTTERIES POUKES POUNDERS POUTERS
POTJIE POTTERING POUKING POUNDING POUTFUL
POTJIES POTTERS POUKIT POUNDINGS POUTHER
POTLACH POTTERY POUKS POUNDS POUTHERED
POTLACHE POTTIER POULAINE POUNDSHOP POUTHERS
POTLACHES POTTIES POULAINES POUPE POUTIER
POTLATCH POTTIEST POULARD POUPED POUTIEST
POTLIKE POTTINESS POULARDE POUPES POUTINE
POTLINE POTTING POULARDES POUPING POUTINES
POTLINES POTTINGAR POULARDS POUPT POUTING
POTLUCK POTTINGER POULDER POUR POUTINGLY
POTLUCKS POTTLE POULDERS POURABLE POUTINGS
POTMAN POTTLES POULDRE POURBOIRE POUTS
POTMEN POTTO POULDRES POURED POUTY
POTOMETER POTTOS POULDRON POURER POVERTIES
POTOO POTTS POULDRONS POURERS POVERTY
POTOOS POTTY POULE POURIE POW
POTOROO POTWALLER POULES POURIES POWAN
POTOROOS POTZER POULP POURING POWANS
POTPIE POTZERS POULPE POURINGLY POWDER
POTPIES POUCH POULPES POURINGS POWDERED
POTPOURRI POUCHED POULPS POURPOINT POWDERER
POTS POUCHES POULT POURS POWDERERS
POTSHARD POUCHFUL POULTER POURSEW POWDERIER
POTSHARDS POUCHFULS POULTERER POURSEWED POWDERING
POTSHARE POUCHIER POULTERS POURSEWS POWDERMAN
POTSHARES POUCHIEST POULTICE POURSUE POWDERMEN
POTSHERD POUCHING POULTICED POURSUED POWDERS
POTSHERDS POUCHLIKE POULTICES POURSUES POWDERY
POTSHOP POUCHY POULTRIES POURSUING POWELLISE
POTSHOPS POUDER POULTRY POURSUIT POWELLITE
POTSHOT POUDERS POULTS POURSUITS POWELLIZE
POTSHOTS POUDRE POUNCE POURTRAY POWER
POTSIE POUDRES POUNCED POURTRAYD POWERBAND
POTSIES POUF POUNCER POURTRAYS POWERBOAT
POTSTONE POUFED POUNCERS POUSADA POWERED
POTSTONES POUFF POUNCES POUSADAS POWERFUL
POTSY POUFFE POUNCET POUSOWDIE POWERING
POTT POUFFED POUNCETS POUSSE POWERLESS

POWERPLAY	POYOUS	PRAEDIAL	PRANCKING	PRATTLER
POWERS	POYSE	PRAEDIALS	PRANCKS	PRATTLERS
POWERSLID	POYSED	PRAEFECT	PRANDIAL	PRATTLES
POWERWASH	POYSES	PRAEFECTS	PRANG	PRATTLING
POWFAGGED	POYSING	PRAELECT	PRANGED	PRATTS
POWHIRI	POYSON	PRAELECTS	PRANGING	PRATY
POWHIRIS	POYSONED	PRAELUDIA	PRANGS	PRAU
POWIN	POYSONING	PRAENOMEN	PRANK	PRAUNCE
POWINS	POYSONS	PRAESES	PRANKED	PRAUNCED
POWN	POZ	PRAESIDIA	PRANKFUL	PRAUNCES
POWND	POZIDRIVE	PRAETOR	PRANKIER	PRAUNCING
POWNDED	POZOLE	PRAETORS	PRANKIEST	PRAUS
POWNDING	POZOLES	PRAGMATIC	PRANKING	PRAVITIES
POWNDS	POZZ	PRAHU	PRANKINGS	PRAVITY
POWNEY	POZZIES	PRAHUS	PRANKISH	PRAWLE
POWNEYS	POZZOLAN	PRAIRIE	PRANKLE	PRAWLES
POWNIE	POZZOLANA	PRAIRIED	PRANKLED	PRAWLIN
POWNIES	POZZOLANS	PRAIRIES	PRANKLES	PRAWLINS
POWNS	POZZY	PRAISE	PRANKLING	PRAWN
POWNY	PRAAM	PRAISEACH	PRANKS	PRAWNED
POWRE	PRAAMS	PRAISED	PRANKSOME	PRAWNER
POWRED	PRABBLE	PRAISEFUL	PRANKSTER	PRAWNERS
POWRES	PRABBLES	PRAISER	PRANKY	PRAWNING
POWRING	PRACHARAK	PRAISERS	PRAO	PRAWNS
POWS	PRACTIC	PRAISES	PRAOS	PRAXES
POWSOWDY	PRACTICAL	PRAISING	PRASE	PRAXIS
POWTER	PRACTICE	PRAISINGS	PRASES	PRAXISES
POWTERED	PRACTICED	PRAJNA	PRAT	PRAY
POWTERING	PRACTICER	PRAJNAS	PRATE	PRAYED
POWTERS	PRACTICES	PRALINE	PRATED	PRAYER
POWWAW	PRACTICK	PRALINES	PRATER	PRAYERFUL
POWWOW	PRACTICKS	PRAM	PRATERS	PRAYERS
POWWOWED	PRACTICS	PRAMS	PRATES	PRAYING
POWWOWING	PRACTICUM	PRANA	PRATFALL	PRAYINGLY
POWWOWS	PRACTIQUE	PRANAS	PRATFALLS	PRAYINGS
POX	PRACTISE	PRANAYAM	PRATFELL	PRAYS
POXED	PRACTISED	PRANAYAMA	PRATIE	PRE
POXES	PRACTISER	PRANAYAMS	PRATIES	PREABSORB
POXIER	PRACTISES	PRANCE	PRATING	PREACCUSE
POXIEST	PRACTIVE	PRANCED	PRATINGLY	PREACE
POXING	PRACTOLOL	PRANCER	PRATINGS	PREACED
POXVIRUS	PRAD	PRANCERS	PRATIQUE	PREACES
POXY	PRADHAN	PRANCES	PRATIQUES	PREACH
POYNANT	PRADHANS	PRANCING	PRATS	PREACHED
POYNT	PRADS	PRANCINGS	PRATT	PREACHER
POYNTED	PRAEAMBLE	PRANCK	PRATTED	PREACHERS
POYNTING	PRAECIPE	PRANCKE	PRATTING	PREACHES
POYNTS	PRAECIPES	PRANCKED	PRATTLE	PREACHIER
POYOU	PRAECOCES	PRANCKES	PRATTLED	PREACHIFY

PREACHILY	PREAVERS	PRECASTS	PRECISELY	PRECYCLES
PREACHING	PREAXIAL	PRECATIVE	PRECISER	PREDACITY
PREACHY	PREBADE	PRECATORY	PRECISES	PREDATE
PREACING	PREBAKE	PRECAUDAL	PRECISEST	PREDATED
PREACT	PREBAKED	PRECAVA	PRECISIAN	PREDATES
PREACTED	PREBAKES	PRECAVAE	PRECISING	PREDATING
PREACTING	PREBAKING	PRECAVAL	PRECISION	PREDATION
PREACTS	PREBASAL	PRECAVALS	PRECISIVE	PREDATISM
PREADAMIC	PREBATTLE	PRECEDE	PRECITED	PREDATIVE
PREADAPT	PREBEND	PRECEDED	PRECLEAN	PREDATOR
PREADAPTS	PREBENDAL	PRECEDENT	PRECLEANS	PREDATORS
PREADJUST	PREBENDS	PRECEDES	PRECLEAR	PREDATORY
PREADMIT	PREBID	PRECEDING	PRECLEARS	PREDAWN
PREADMITS	PREBIDDEN	PRECEESE	PRECLUDE	PREDAWNS
PREADOPT	PREBIDS	PRECENSOR	PRECLUDED	PREDEATH
PREADOPTS	PREBILL	PRECENT	PRECLUDES	PREDEATHS
PREADULT	PREBILLED	PRECENTED	PRECOCIAL	PREDEBATE
PREADULTS	PREBILLS	PRECENTOR	PRECOCITY	PREDEDUCT
PREAGED	PREBIND	PRECENTS	PRECODE	PREDEFINE
PREALLOT	PREBINDS	PRECEPIT	PRECODED	PREDELLA
PREALLOTS	PREBIOTIC	PRECEPITS	PRECODES	PREDELLAS
PREALTER	PREBIRTH	PRECEPT	PRECODING	PREDELLE
PREALTERS	PREBIRTHS	PRECEPTOR	PRECOITAL	PREDESIGN
PREAMBLE	PREBLESS	PRECEPTS	PRECONISE	PREDEVOTE
PREAMBLED	PREBOARD	PRECES	PRECONIZE	PREDIAL
PREAMBLES	PREBOARDS	PRECESS	PRECOOK	PREDIALS
PREAMP	PREBOIL	PRECESSED	PRECOOKED	PREDICANT
PREAMPS	PREBOILED	PRECESSES	PRECOOKER	PREDICATE
PREANAL	PREBOILS	PRECHARGE	PRECOOKS	PREDICT
PREAPPLY	PREBOOK	PRECHECK	PRECOOL	PREDICTED
PREARM	PREBOOKED	PRECHECKS	PRECOOLED	PREDICTER
PREARMED	PREBOOKS	PRECHILL	PRECOOLS	PREDICTOR
PREARMING	PREBOOM	PRECHILLS	PRECOUP	PREDICTS
PREARMS	PREBORN	PRECHOOSE	PRECRASH	PREDIED
PREASE	PREBOUGHT	PRECHOSE	PRECREASE	PREDIES
PREASED	PREBOUND	PRECHOSEN	PRECRISIS	PREDIGEST
PREASES	PREBUDGET	PRECIEUSE	PRECURE	PREDIKANT
PREASING	PREBUILD	PRECIEUX	PRECURED	PREDILECT
PREASSE	PREBUILDS	PRECINCT	PRECURES	PREDINNER
PREASSED	PREBUILT	PRECINCTS	PRECURING	PREDIVE
PREASSES	PREBUTTAL	PRECIOUS	PRECURRER	PREDOOM
PREASSIGN	PREBUY	PRECIP	PRECURSE	PREDOOMED
PREASSING	PREBUYING	PRECIPE	PRECURSED	PREDOOMS
PREASSURE	PREBUYS	PRECIPES	PRECURSES	PREDRAFT
PREATOMIC	PRECANCEL	PRECIPICE	PRECURSOR	PREDRAFTS
PREATTUNE	PRECANCER	PRECIPS	PRECUT	PREDRIED
PREAUDIT	PRECARIAT	PRECIS	PRECUTS	PREDRIES
PREAUDITS	PRECARITY	PRECISE	PRECYCLE	PREDRILL
PREAVER	PRECAST	PRECISED	PRECYCLED	PREDRILLS

P

PREDRY	PREFACIAL	PREGAMES	PRELACIES	PREMADE
PREDRYING	PREFACING	PREGAMING	PRELACY	PREMAKE
PREDUSK	PREFADE	PREGGERS	PRELATE	PREMAKES
PREDUSKS	PREFADED	PREGGIER	PRELATES	PREMAKING
PREDY	PREFADES	PREGGIEST	PRELATESS	PREMAN
PREDYING	PREFADING	PREGGO	PRELATIAL	PREMARKET
PREE	PREFARD	PREGGY	PRELATIC	PREMATURE
PREED	PREFATORY	PREGNABLE	PRELATIES	PREMEAL
PREEDIT	PREFECT	PREGNANCE	PRELATION	PREMED
PREEDITED	PREFECTS	PREGNANCY	PRELATISE	PREMEDIC
PREEDITS	PREFER	PREGNANT	PRELATISH	PREMEDICS
PREEING	PREFERRED	PREGROWTH	PRELATISM	PREMEDS
PREELECT	PREFERRER	PREGUIDE	PRELATIST	PREMEET
PREELECTS	PREFERS	PREGUIDED	PRELATIZE	PREMEN
PREEMIE	PREFEUDAL	PREGUIDES	PRELATURE	PREMERGER
PREEMIES	PREFIGHT	PREHAB	PRELATY	PREMIA
PREEMPT	PREFIGURE	PREHABS	PRELAUNCH	PREMIE
PREEMPTED	PREFILE	PREHALLUX	PRELAW	PREMIER
PREEMPTOR	PREFILED	PREHANDLE	PRELECT	PREMIERE
PREEMPTS	PREFILES	PREHARDEN	PRELECTED	PREMIERED
PREEN	PREFILING	PREHEAT	PRELECTOR	PREMIERES
PREENACT	PREFILLED	PREHEATED	PRELECTS	PREMIERS
PREENACTS	PREFIRE	PREHEATER	PRELEGAL	PREMIES
PREENED	PREFIRED	PREHEATS	PRELIFE	PREMISE
PREENER	PREFIRES	PREHEND	PRELIM	PREMISED
PREENERS	PREFIRING	PREHENDED	PRELIMIT	PREMISES
PREENING	PREFIX	PREHENDS	PRELIMITS	PREMISING
PREENS	PREFIXAL	PREHENSOR	PRELIMS	PREMISS
PREERECT	PREFIXED	PREHIRE	PRELIVES	PREMISSED
PREERECTS	PREFIXES	PREHIRING	PRELOAD	PREMISSES
PREES	PREFIXING	PREHNITE	PRELOADED	PREMIUM
PREEVE	PREFIXION	PREHNITES	PRELOADS	PREMIUMS
PREEVED	PREFLAME	PREHUMAN	PRELOCATE	PREMIX
PREEVES	PREFLIGHT	PREHUMANS	PRELOVED	PREMIXED
PREEVING	PREFOCUS	PREIF	PRELUDE	PREMIXES
PREEXCITE	PREFORM	PREIFE	PRELUDED	PREMIXING
PREEXEMPT	PREFORMAT	PREIFES	PRELUDER	PREMIXT
PREEXILIC	PREFORMED	PREIFS	PRELUDERS	PREMODERN
PREEXIST	PREFORMS	PREIMPOSE	PRELUDES	PREMODIFY
PREEXISTS	PREFRANK	PREINFORM	PRELUDI	PREMOLAR
PREEXPOSE	PREFRANKS	PREINSERT	PRELUDIAL	PREMOLARS
PREFAB	PREFREEZE	PREINVITE	PRELUDING	PREMOLD
PREFABBED	PREFROZE	PREJINK	PRELUDIO	PREMOLDED
PREFABS	PREFROZEN	PREJUDGE	PRELUDIOS	PREMOLDS
PREFACE	PREFUND	PREJUDGED	PRELUNCH	PREMOLT
PREFACED	PREFUNDED	PREJUDGER	PRELUSION	PREMONISH
PREFACER	PREFUNDS	PREJUDGES	PRELUSIVE	PREMORAL
PREFACERS	PREGAME	PREJUDICE	PRELUSORY	PREMORSE
PREFACES	PREGAMED	PREJUDIZE	PREM	PREMOSAIC

PREMOTION	PREOWNED	PREPPIEST	PRESAGING	PRESHOW
PREMOTOR	PREP	PREPPILY	PRESALE	PRESHOWED
PREMOULD	PREPACK	PREPPING	PRESALES	PRESHOWN
PREMOULDS	PREPACKED	PREPPY	PRESBYOPE	PRESHOWS
PREMOULT	PREPACKS	PREPREG	PRESBYOPY	PRESHRANK
PREMOVE	PREPAID	PREPREGS	PRESBYTE	PRESHRINK
PREMOVED	PREPARE	PREPRESS	PRESBYTER	PRESHRUNK
PREMOVES	PREPARED	PREPRICE	PRESBYTES	PRESIDE
PREMOVING	PREPARER	PREPRICED	PRESBYTIC	PRESIDED
PREMS	PREPARERS	PREPRICES	PRESCHOOL	PRESIDENT
PREMUNE	PREPARES	PREPRINT	PRESCIENT	PRESIDER
PREMY	PREPARING	PREPRINTS	PRESCIND	PRESIDERS
PRENAME	PREPASTE	PREPS	PRESCINDS	PRESIDES
PRENAMES	PREPASTED	PREPUBES	PRESCIOUS	PRESIDIA
PRENASAL	PREPASTES	PREPUBIS	PRESCORE	PRESIDIAL
PRENASALS	PREPAVE	PREPUCE	PRESCORED	PRESIDING
PRENATAL	PREPAVED	PREPUCES	PRESCORES	PRESIDIO
PRENATALS	PREPAVES	PREPUEBLO	PRESCREEN	PRESIDIOS
PRENEED	PREPAVING	PREPUNCH	PRESCRIBE	PRESIDIUM
PRENOMEN	PREPAY	PREPUPA	PRESCRIPT	PRESIFT
PRENOMENS	PREPAYING	PREPUPAE	PRESCUTA	PRESIFTED
PRENOMINA	PREPAYS	PREPUPAL	PRESCUTUM	PRESIFTS
PRENOON	PREPENSE	PREPUPAS	PRESE	PRESIGNAL
PRENOTIFY	PREPENSED	PREPUTIAL	PRESEASON	PRESLEEP
PRENOTION	PREPENSES	PREQUEL	PRESELECT	PRESLICE
PRENT	PREPILL	PREQUELS	PRESELL	PRESLICED
PRENTED	PREPLACE	PRERACE	PRESELLS	PRESLICES
PRENTICE	PREPLACED	PRERADIO	PRESENCE	PRESOAK
PRENTICED	PREPLACES	PRERECORD	PRESENCES	PRESOAKED
PRENTICES	PREPLAN	PRERECTAL	PRESENILE	PRESOAKS
PRENTING	PREPLANS	PREREFORM	PRESENT	PRESOLD
PRENTS	PREPLANT	PRERENAL	PRESENTED	PRESOLVE
PRENUBILE	PREPOLLEX	PRERETURN	PRESENTEE	PRESOLVED
PRENUMBER	PREPONE	PREREVIEW	PRESENTER	PRESOLVES
PRENUP	PREPONED	PRERINSE	PRESENTLY	PRESONG
PRENUPS	PREPONES	PRERINSED	PRESENTS	PRESORT
PRENZIE	PREPONING	PRERINSES	PRESERVE	PRESORTED
PREOBTAIN	PREPOSE	PRERIOT	PRESERVED	PRESORTS
PREOCCUPY	PREPOSED	PREROCK	PRESERVER	PRESPLIT
PREOCULAR	PREPOSES	PREROLL	PRESERVES	PRESS
PREON	PREPOSING	PREROLLED	PRESES	PRESSBACK
PREONS	PREPOSTOR	PREROLLS	PRESET	PRESSED
PREOP	PREPOTENT	PRERUPT	PRESETS	PRESSER
PREOPS	PREPPED	PRESA	PRESETTLE	PRESSERS
PREOPTION	PREPPER	PRESAGE	PRESHAPE	PRESSES
PREORAL	PREPPERS	PRESAGED	PRESHAPED	PRESSFAT
PREORDAIN	PREPPIE	PRESAGER	PRESHAPES	PRESSFATS
PREORDER	PREPPIER	PRESAGERS	PRESHIP	PRESSFUL
PREORDERS	PREPPIES	PRESAGES	PRESHIPS	PRESSFULS

P

PRESSGANG	PRETAPING	PRETTIFY	PREVISING	PREYS
PRESSIE	PRETASTE	PRETTILY	PREVISION	PREZ
PRESSIES	PRETASTED	PRETTY	PREVISIT	PREZES
PRESSING	PRETASTES	PRETTYING	PREVISITS	PREZZIE
PRESSINGS	PRETAX	PRETTYISH	PREVISOR	PREZZIES
PRESSION	PRETEEN	PRETTYISM	PREVISORS	PRIAL
PRESSIONS	PRETEENS	PRETYPE	PREVUE	PRIALS
PRESSMAN	PRETELL	PRETYPED	PREVUED	PRIAPEAN
PRESSMARK	PRETELLS	PRETYPES	PREVUES	PRIAPI
PRESSMEN	PRETENCE	PRETYPING	PREVUING	PRIAPIC
PRESSOR	PRETENCES	PRETZEL	PREWAR	PRIAPISM
PRESSORS	PRETEND	PRETZELS	PREWARM	PRIAPISMS
PRESSROOM	PRETENDED	PREUNION	PREWARMED	PRIAPUS
PRESSRUN	PRETENDER	PREUNIONS	PREWARMS	PRIAPUSES
PRESSRUNS	PRETENDS	PREUNITE	PREWARN	PRIBBLE
PRESSURE	PRETENSE	PREUNITED	PREWARNED	PRIBBLES
PRESSURED	PRETENSES	PREUNITES	PREWARNS	PRICE
PRESSURES	PRETERIST	PREVAIL	PREWASH	PRICEABLE
PRESSWORK	PRETERIT	PREVAILED	PREWASHED	PRICED
PRESSY	PRETERITE	PREVAILER	PREWASHES	PRICELESS
PREST	PRETERITS	PREVAILS	PREWEANED	PRICER
PRESTAMP	PRETERM	PREVALENT	PREWEIGH	PRICERS
PRESTAMPS	PRETERMIT	PREVALUE	PREWEIGHS	PRICES
PRESTED	PRETERMS	PREVALUED	PREWIRE	PRICEY
PRESTER	PRETEST	PREVALUES	PREWIRED	PRICIER
PRESTERNA	PRETESTED	PREVE	PREWIRES	PRICIEST
PRESTERS	PRETESTS	PREVED	PREWIRING	PRICILY
PRESTIGE	PRETEXT	PREVENE	PREWORK	PRICINESS
PRESTIGES	PRETEXTED	PREVENED	PREWORKED	PRICING
PRESTING	PRETEXTS	PREVENES	PREWORKS	PRICINGS
PRESTO	PRETOLD	PREVENING	PREWORN	PRICK
PRESTORE	PRETONIC	PREVENT	PREWRAP	PRICKED
PRESTORED	PRETOR	PREVENTED	PREWRAPS	PRICKER
PRESTORES	PRETORIAL	PREVENTER	PREWRITE	PRICKERS
PRESTOS	PRETORIAN	PREVENTS	PREWRITES	PRICKET
PRESTRESS	PRETORS	PREVERB	PREWROTE	PRICKETS
PRESTRIKE	PRETRAIN	PREVERBAL	PREWYN	PRICKIER
PRESTS	PRETRAINS	PREVERBS	PREWYNS	PRICKIEST
PRESUME	PRETRAVEL	PREVES	PREX	PRICKING
PRESUMED	PRETREAT	PREVIABLE	PREXES	PRICKINGS
PRESUMER	PRETREATS	PREVIEW	PREXIE	PRICKLE
PRESUMERS	PRETRIAL	PREVIEWED	PREXIES	PRICKLED
PRESUMES	PRETRIALS	PREVIEWER	PREXY	PRICKLES
PRESUMING	PRETRIM	PREVIEWS	PREY	PRICKLIER
PRESUMMIT	PRETRIMS	PREVING	PREYED	PRICKLING
PRESURVEY	PRETTIED	PREVIOUS	PREYER	PRICKLY
PRETAPE	PRETTIER	PREVISE	PREYERS	PRICKS
PRETAPED	PRETTIES	PREVISED	PREYFUL	PRICKWOOD
PRETAPES	PRETTIEST	PREVISES	PREYING	PRICKY

PRICY	PRIMAGE	PRIMOS	PRINTERY	PRISSILY
PRIDE	PRIMAGES	PRIMP	PRINTHEAD	PRISSING
PRIDED	PRIMAL	PRIMPED	PRINTING	PRISSY
PRIDEFUL	PRIMALITY	PRIMPING	PRINTINGS	PRISTANE
PRIDELESS	PRIMALLY	PRIMPS	PRINTLESS	PRISTANES
PRIDES	PRIMARIED	PRIMROSE	PRINTOUT	PRISTINE
PRIDIAN	PRIMARIES	PRIMROSED	PRINTOUTS	PRITHEE
PRIDING	PRIMARILY	PRIMROSES	PRINTS	PRIVACIES
PRIED	PRIMARY	PRIMROSY	PRION	PRIVACY
PRIEDIEU	PRIMAS	PRIMS	PRIONS	PRIVADO
PRIEDIEUS	PRIMATAL	PRIMSIE	PRIOR	PRIVADOES
PRIEDIEUX	PRIMATALS	PRIMSIER	PRIORATE	PRIVADOS
PRIEF	PRIMATE	PRIMSIEST	PRIORATES	PRIVATE
PRIEFE	PRIMATES	PRIMULA	PRIORESS	PRIVATEER
PRIEFES	PRIMATIAL	PRIMULAS	PRIORIES	PRIVATELY
PRIEFS	PRIMATIC	PRIMULINE	PRIORITY	PRIVATER
PRIER	PRIMAVERA	PRIMUS	PRIORLY	PRIVATES
PRIERS	PRIME	PRIMUSES	PRIORS	PRIVATEST
PRIES	PRIMED	PRIMY	PRIORSHIP	PRIVATION
PRIEST	PRIMELY	PRINCE	PRIORY	PRIVATISE
PRIESTED	PRIMENESS	PRINCED	PRISAGE	PRIVATISM
PRIESTESS	PRIMER	PRINCEDOM	PRISAGES	PRIVATIST
PRIESTING	PRIMERO	PRINCEKIN	PRISE	PRIVATIVE
PRIESTLY	PRIMEROS	PRINCELET	PRISED	PRIVATIZE
PRIESTS	PRIMERS	PRINCELY	PRISER	PRIVET
PRIEVE	PRIMES	PRINCES	PRISERE	PRIVETS
PRIEVED	PRIMETIME	PRINCESS	PRISERES	PRIVIER
PRIEVES	PRIMEUR	PRINCESSE	PRISERS	PRIVIES
PRIEVING	PRIMEURS	PRINCING	PRISES	PRIVIEST
PRIG	PRIMEVAL	PRINCIPAL	PRISING	PRIVILEGE
PRIGGED	PRIMI	PRINCIPE	PRISM	PRIVILY
PRIGGER	PRIMINE	PRINCIPI	PRISMATIC	PRIVITIES
PRIGGERS	PRIMINES	PRINCIPIA	PRISMOID	PRIVITY
PRIGGERY	PRIMING	PRINCIPLE	PRISMOIDS	PRIVY
PRIGGING	PRIMINGS	PRINCOCK	PRISMS	PRIZABLE
PRIGGINGS	PRIMIPARA	PRINCOCKS	PRISMY	PRIZE
PRIGGISH	PRIMITIAE	PRINCOX	PRISON	PRIZED
PRIGGISM	PRIMITIAL	PRINCOXES	PRISONED	PRIZEMAN
PRIGGISMS	PRIMITIAS	PRINK	PRISONER	PRIZEMEN
PRIGS	PRIMITIVE	PRINKED	PRISONERS	PRIZER
PRILL	PRIMLY	PRINKER	PRISONING	PRIZERS
PRILLED	PRIMMED	PRINKERS	PRISONOUS	PRIZES
PRILLING	PRIMMER	PRINKING	PRISONS	PRIZING
PRILLS	PRIMMERS	PRINKS	PRISS	PRO
PRIM	PRIMMEST	PRINT	PRISSED	PROA
PRIMA	PRIMMING	PRINTABLE	PRISSES	PROACTION
PRIMACIES	PRIMNESS	PRINTED	PRISSIER	PROACTIVE
PRIMACY	PRIMO	PRINTER	PRISSIES	PROAS
PRIMAEVAL	PRIMORDIA	PRINTERS	PRISSIEST	PROB

P

PROBABLE	PROCESSES	PRODNOSE	PROFILED	PROGS
PROBABLES	PROCESSOR	PRODNOSED	PROFILER	PROGUN
PROBABLY	PROCHAIN	PRODNOSES	PROFILERS	PROHIBIT
PROBALL	PROCHEIN	PRODROMA	PROFILES	PROHIBITS
PROBAND	PROCHOICE	PRODROMAL	PROFILING	PROIGN
PROBANDS	PROCHURCH	PRODROME	PROFILIST	PROIGNED
PROBANG	PROCIDENT	PRODROMES	PROFIT	PROIGNING
PROBANGS	PROCINCT	PRODROMI	PROFITED	PROIGNS
PROBATE	PROCINCTS	PRODROMIC	PROFITEER	PROIN
PROBATED	PROCLAIM	PRODROMUS	PROFITER	PROINE
PROBATES	PROCLAIMS	PRODRUG	PROFITERS	PROINED
PROBATING	PROCLISES	PRODRUGS	PROFITING	PROINES
PROBATION	PROCLISIS	PRODS	PROFITS	PROINING
PROBATIVE	PROCLITIC	PRODUCE	PROFLUENT	PROINS
PROBATORY	PROCLIVE	PRODUCED	PROFORMA	PROJECT
PROBE	PROCONSUL	PRODUCER	PROFORMAS	PROJECTED
PROBEABLE	PROCREANT	PRODUCERS	PROFOUND	PROJECTOR
PROBED	PROCREATE	PRODUCES	PROFOUNDS	PROJECTS
PROBER	PROCTAL	PRODUCING	PROFS	PROJET
PROBERS	PROCTITIS	PRODUCT	PROFUSE	PROJETS
PROBES	PROCTODEA	PRODUCTS	PROFUSELY	PROKARYON
PROBING	PROCTOR	PROEM	PROFUSER	PROKARYOT
PROBINGLY	PROCTORED	PROEMBRYO	PROFUSERS	PROKE
PROBINGS	PROCTORS	PROEMIAL	PROFUSION	PROKED
PROBIOTIC	PROCURACY	PROEMS	PROFUSIVE	PROKER
PROBIT	PROCURAL	PROENZYME	PROG	PROKERS
PROBITIES	PROCURALS	PROESTRUS	PROGENIES	PROKES
PROBITS	PROCURE	PROETTE	PROGENY	PROKING
PROBITY	PROCURED	PROETTES	PROGERIA	PROLABOR
PROBLEM	PROCURER	PROF	PROGERIAS	PROLABOUR
PROBLEMS	PROCURERS	PROFACE	PROGESTIN	PROLACTIN
PROBOSCIS	PROCURES	PROFAMILY	PROGGED	PROLAMIN
PROBS	PROCURESS	PROFANE	PROGGER	PROLAMINE
PROCACITY	PROCUREUR	PROFANED	PROGGERS	PROLAMINS
PROCAINE	PROCURING	PROFANELY	PROGGING	PROLAN
PROCAINES	PROCYONID	PROFANER	PROGGINS	PROLANS
PROCAMBIA	PROD	PROFANERS	PROGNOSE	PROLAPSE
PROCARP	PRODDED	PROFANES	PROGNOSED	PROLAPSED
PROCARPS	PRODDER	PROFANING	PROGNOSES	PROLAPSES
PROCARYON	PRODDERS	PROFANITY	PROGNOSIS	PROLAPSUS
PROCEDURE	PRODDING	PROFESS	PROGRADE	PROLATE
PROCEED	PRODDINGS	PROFESSED	PROGRADED	PROLATED
PROCEEDED	PRODIGAL	PROFESSES	PROGRADES	PROLATELY
PROCEEDER	PRODIGALS	PROFESSOR	PROGRAM	PROLATES
PROCEEDS	PRODIGIES	PROFFER	PROGRAMED	PROLATING
PROCERITY	PRODIGY	PROFFERED	PROGRAMER	PROLATION
PROCESS	PRODITOR	PROFFERER	PROGRAMME	PROLATIVE
PROCESSED	PRODITORS	PROFFERS	PROGRAMS	PROLE
PROCESSER	PRODITORY	PROFILE	PROGRESS	PROLED

PROLEG	PROMINE	PRONATED	PROOFS	PROPHASES
PROLEGS	PROMINENT	PRONATES	PROOTIC	PROPHASIC
PROLEPSES	PROMINES	PRONATING	PROOTICS	PROPHECY
PROLEPSIS	PROMISE	PRONATION	PROP	PROPHESY
PROLEPTIC	PROMISED	PRONATOR	PROPAGATE	PROPHET
PROLER	PROMISEE	PRONATORS	PROPAGE	PROPHETIC
PROLERS	PROMISEES	PRONE	PROPAGED	PROPHETS
PROLES	PROMISER	PRONED	PROPAGES	PROPHYLL
PROLETARY	PROMISERS	PRONELY	PROPAGING	PROPHYLLS
PROLICIDE	PROMISES	PRONENESS	PROPAGULA	PROPINE
PROLIFIC	PROMISING	PRONEPHRA	PROPAGULE	PROPINED
PROLINE	PROMISOR	PRONER	PROPALE	PROPINES
PROLINES	PROMISORS	PRONES	PROPALED	PROPINING
PROLING	PROMISSOR	PRONEST	PROPALES	PROPIONIC
PROLIX	PROMMER	PRONEUR	PROPALING	PROPJET
PROLIXITY	PROMMERS	PRONEURS	PROPANE	PROPJETS
PROLIXLY	PROMO	PRONG	PROPANES	PROPMAN
PROLL	PROMODERN	PRONGBUCK	PROPANOIC	PROPMEN
PROLLED	PROMOED	PRONGED	PROPANOL	PROPODEON
PROLLER	PROMOING	PRONGHORN	PROPANOLS	PROPODEUM
PROLLERS	PROMOS	PRONGING	PROPANONE	PROPOLIS
PROLLING	PROMOTE	PRONGS	PROPEL	PROPONE
PROLLS	PROMOTED	PRONING	PROPELLED	PROPONED
PROLLY	PROMOTER	PRONK	PROPELLER	PROPONENT
PROLOG	PROMOTERS	PRONKED	PROPELLOR	PROPONES
PROLOGED	PROMOTES	PRONKING	PROPELS	PROPONING
PROLOGING	PROMOTING	PRONKINGS	PROPENAL	PROPOSAL
PROLOGISE	PROMOTION	PRONKS	PROPENALS	PROPOSALS
PROLOGIST	PROMOTIVE	PRONOTA	PROPEND	PROPOSE
PROLOGIZE	PROMOTOR	PRONOTAL	PROPENDED	PROPOSED
PROLOGS	PROMOTORS	PRONOTUM	PROPENDS	PROPOSER
PROLOGUE	PROMPT	PRONOUN	PROPENE	PROPOSERS
PROLOGUED	PROMPTED	PRONOUNCE	PROPENES	PROPOSES
PROLOGUES	PROMPTER	PRONOUNS	PROPENOIC	PROPOSING
PROLONG	PROMPTERS	PRONTO	PROPENOL	PROPOSITA
PROLONGE	PROMPTEST	PRONUCLEI	PROPENOLS	PROPOSITI
PROLONGED	PROMPTING	PRONUNCIO	PROPENSE	PROPOUND
PROLONGER	PROMPTLY	PROO	PROPENYL	PROPOUNDS
PROLONGES	PROMPTS	PROOEMION	PROPENYLS	PROPPANT
PROLONGS	PROMPTURE	PROOEMIUM	PROPER	PROPPANTS
PROLUSION	PROMS	PROOF	PROPERDIN	PROPPED
PROLUSORY	PROMULGE	PROOFED	PROPERER	PROPPING
PROM	PROMULGED	PROOFER	PROPEREST	PROPRETOR
PROMACHOI	PROMULGES	PROOFERS	PROPERLY	PROPRIA
PROMACHOS	PROMUSCES	PROOFING	PROPERS	PROPRIETY
PROMENADE	PROMUSCIS	PROOFINGS	PROPERTY	PROPRIUM
PROMETAL	PRONAOI	PROOFLESS	PROPHAGE	PROPS
PROMETALS	PRONAOS	PROOFREAD	PROPHAGES	PROPTOSES
PROMETRIC	PRONATE	PROOFROOM	PROPHASE	PROPTOSIS

PROPULSOR	PROSER	PROSTYLE	PROTESTOR	PROTURAN
PROPYL	PROSERS	PROSTYLES	PROTESTS	PROTURANS
PROPYLA	PROSES	PROSUMER	PROTEUS	PROTYL
PROPYLAEA	PROSEUCHA	PROSUMERS	PROTEUSES	PROTYLE
PROPYLENE	PROSEUCHE	PROSY	PROTHALLI	PROTYLES
PROPYLIC	PROSIER	PROTAMIN	PROTHESES	PROTYLS
PROPYLITE	PROSIEST	PROTAMINE	PROTHESIS	PROUD
PROPYLON	PROSIFIED	PROTAMINS	PROTHETIC	PROUDER
PROPYLONS	PROSIFIES	PROTANDRY	PROTHORAX	PROUDEST
PROPYLS	PROSIFY	PROTANOPE	PROTHYL	PROUDFUL
PROPYNE	PROSILY	PROTASES	PROTHYLS	PROUDISH
PROPYNES	PROSIMIAN	PROTASIS	PROTIST	PROUDLY
PRORATE	PROSINESS	PROTATIC	PROTISTAN	PROUDNESS
PRORATED	PROSING	PROTEA	PROTISTIC	PROUL
PRORATES	PROSINGS	PROTEAN	PROTISTS	PROULED
PRORATING	PROSIT	PROTEANS	PROTIUM	PROULER
PRORATION	PROSO	PROTEAS	PROTIUMS	PROULERS
PRORE	PROSOCIAL	PROTEASE	PROTO	PROULING
PRORECTOR	PROSODIAL	PROTEASES	PROTOAVIS	PROULS
PROREFORM	PROSODIAN	PROTECT	PROTOCOL	PROUNION
PRORES	PROSODIC	PROTECTED	PROTOCOLS	PROUSTITE
PROROGATE	PROSODIES	PROTECTER	PROTODERM	PROVABLE
PROROGUE	PROSODIST	PROTECTOR	PROTOGINE	PROVABLY
PROROGUED	PROSODY	PROTECTS	PROTOGYNY	PROVAND
PROROGUES	PROSOMA	PROTEGE	PROTON	PROVANDS
PROS	PROSOMAL	PROTEGEE	PROTONATE	PROVANT
PROSAIC	PROSOMAS	PROTEGEES	PROTONEMA	PROVANTED
PROSAICAL	PROSOMATA	PROTEGES	PROTONIC	PROVANTS
PROSAISM	PROSOPON	PROTEI	PROTONS	PROVE
PROSAISMS	PROSOPONS	PROTEID	PROTOPOD	PROVEABLE
PROSAIST	PROSOS	PROTEIDE	PROTOPODS	PROVEABLY
PROSAISTS	PROSPECT	PROTEIDES	PROTORE	PROVED
PROSATEUR	PROSPECTS	PROTEIDS	PROTORES	PROVEDOR
PROSCENIA	PROSPER	PROTEIN	PROTOSTAR	PROVEDORE
PROSCRIBE	PROSPERED	PROTEINIC	PROTOTYPE	PROVEDORS
PROSCRIPT	PROSPERS	PROTEINS	PROTOXID	PROVEN
PROSE	PROSS	PROTEND	PROTOXIDE	PROVEND
PROSECCO	PROSSES	PROTENDED	PROTOXIDS	PROVENDER
PROSECCOS	PROSSIE	PROTENDS	PROTOZOA	PROVENDS
PROSECT	PROSSIES	PROTENSE	PROTOZOAL	PROVENLY
PROSECTED	PROST	PROTENSES	PROTOZOAN	PROVER
PROSECTOR	PROSTATE	PROTEOME	PROTOZOIC	PROVERB
PROSECTS	PROSTATES	PROTEOMES	PROTOZOON	PROVERBED
PROSECUTE	PROSTATIC	PROTEOMIC	PROTRACT	PROVERBS
PROSED	PROSTERNA	PROTEOSE	PROTRACTS	PROVERS
PROSELIKE	PROSTIE	PROTEOSES	PROTRADE	PROVES
PROSELYTE	PROSTIES	PROTEST	PROTRUDE	PROVIANT
PROSEMAN	PROSTOMIA	PROTESTED	PROTRUDED	PROVIANTS
PROSEMEN	PROSTRATE	PROTESTER	PROTRUDES	PROVIDE

PROVIDED	PROWLS	PRUNIEST	PSALMS	PSOAI
PROVIDENT	PROWS	PRUNING	PSALTER	PSOAS
PROVIDER	PROXEMIC	PRUNINGS	PSALTERER	PSOASES
PROVIDERS	PROXEMICS	PRUNT	PSALTERIA	PSOATIC
PROVIDES	PROXIES	PRUNTED	PSALTERS	PSOCID
PROVIDING	PROXIMAL	PRUNTS	PSALTERY	PSOCIDS
PROVIDOR	PROXIMATE	PRUNUS	PSALTRESS	PSORA
PROVIDORS	PROXIMITY	PRUNUSES	PSALTRIES	PSORALEA
PROVINCE	PROXIMO	PRURIENCE	PSALTRY	PSORALEAS
PROVINCES	PROXY	PRURIENCY	PSAMMITE	PSORALEN
PROVINE	PROYN	PRURIENT	PSAMMITES	PSORALENS
PROVINED	PROYNE	PRURIGO	PSAMMITIC	PSORAS
PROVINES	PROYNED	PRURIGOS	PSAMMON	PSORIASES
PROVING	PROYNES	PRURITIC	PSAMMONS	PSORIASIS
PROVINGS	PROYNING	PRURITUS	PSCHENT	PSORIATIC
PROVINING	PROYNS	PRUSIK	PSCHENTS	PSORIC
PROVIRAL	PROZYMITE	PRUSIKED	PSELLISM	PSST
PROVIRUS	PROZZIE	PRUSIKING	PSELLISMS	PST
PROVISION	PROZZIES	PRUSIKS	PSEPHISM	PSYCH
PROVISO	PRUDE	PRUSSIAN	PSEPHISMS	PSYCHE
PROVISOES	PRUDENCE	PRUSSIATE	PSEPHITE	PSYCHED
PROVISOR	PRUDENCES	PRUSSIC	PSEPHITES	PSYCHES
PROVISORS	PRUDENT	PRUTA	PSEPHITIC	PSYCHIC
PROVISORY	PRUDENTLY	PRUTAH	PSEUD	PSYCHICAL
PROVISOS	PRUDERIES	PRUTOT	PSEUDAXES	PSYCHICS
PROVOCANT	PRUDERY	PRUTOTH	PSEUDAXIS	PSYCHING
PROVOKE	PRUDES	PRY	PSEUDERY	PSYCHISM
PROVOKED	PRUDISH	PRYER	PSEUDISH	PSYCHISMS
PROVOKER	PRUDISHLY	PRYERS	PSEUDO	PSYCHIST
PROVOKERS	PRUH	PRYING	PSEUDONYM	PSYCHISTS
PROVOKES	PRUINA	PRYINGLY	PSEUDOPOD	PSYCHO
PROVOKING	PRUINAS	PRYINGS	PSEUDOS	PSYCHOGAS
PROVOLONE	PRUINE	PRYS	PSEUDS	PSYCHOID
PROVOST	PRUINES	PRYSE	PSHAW	PSYCHOIDS
PROVOSTRY	PRUINOSE	PRYSED	PSHAWED	PSYCHOS
PROVOSTS	PRUNABLE	PRYSES	PSHAWING	PSYCHOSES
PROW	PRUNE	PRYSING	PSHAWS	PSYCHOSIS
PROWAR	PRUNED	PRYTANEA	PSI	PSYCHOTIC
PROWER	PRUNELLA	PRYTANEUM	PSILOCIN	PSYCHS
PROWESS	PRUNELLAS	PRYTHEE	PSILOCINS	PSYLLA
PROWESSED	PRUNELLE	PSALM	PSILOSES	PSYLLAS
PROWESSES	PRUNELLES	PSALMBOOK	PSILOSIS	PSYLLID
PROWEST	PRUNELLO	PSALMED	PSILOTIC	PSYLLIDS
PROWL	PRUNELLOS	PSALMIC	PSION	PSYLLIUM
PROWLED	PRUNER	PSALMING	PSIONIC	PSYLLIUMS
PROWLER	PRUNERS	PSALMIST	PSIONICS	PSYOP
PROWLERS	PRUNES	PSALMISTS	PSIONS	PSYOPS
PROWLING	PRUNEY	PSALMODIC	PSIS	PSYWAR
PROWLINGS	PRUNIER	PSALMODY	PSOAE	PSYWARS

PTARMIC	PUBCO	PUCKERS	PUDEURS	PUFFIEST
PTARMICS	PUBCOS	PUCKERY	PUDGE	PUFFILY
PTARMIGAN	PUBE	PUCKFIST	PUDGES	PUFFIN
PTERIA	PUBERAL	PUCKFISTS	PUDGIER	PUFFINESS
PTERIDINE	PUBERTAL	PUCKING	PUDGIEST	PUFFING
PTERIN	PUBERTIES	PUCKISH	PUDGILY	PUFFINGLY
PTERINS	PUBERTY	PUCKISHLY	PUDGINESS	PUFFINGS
PTERION	PUBES	PUCKLE	PUDGY	PUFFINS
PTEROIC	PUBESCENT	PUCKLES	PUDIBUND	PUFFS
PTEROPOD	PUBIC	PUCKOUT	PUDIC	PUFFY
PTEROPODS	PUBIS	PUCKOUTS	PUDICITY	PUFTALOON
PTEROSAUR	PUBISES	PUCKS	PUDOR	PUG
PTERYGIA	PUBLIC	PUCKSTER	PUDORS	PUGAREE
PTERYGIAL	PUBLICAN	PUCKSTERS	PUDS	PUGAREES
PTERYGIUM	PUBLICANS	PUD	PUDSEY	PUGGAREE
PTERYGOID	PUBLICISE	PUDDEN	PUDSIER	PUGGAREES
PTERYLA	PUBLICIST	PUDDENING	PUDSIES	PUGGED
PTERYLAE	PUBLICITY	PUDDENS	PUDSIEST	PUGGERIES
PTILOSES	PUBLICIZE	PUDDER	PUDSY	PUGGERY
PTILOSIS	PUBLICLY	PUDDERED	PUDU	PUGGIE
PTISAN	PUBLICS	PUDDERING	PUDUS	PUGGIER
PTISANS	PUBLISH	PUDDERS	PUEBLO	PUGGIES
PTOMAIN	PUBLISHED	PUDDIER	PUEBLOS	PUGGIEST
PTOMAINE	PUBLISHER	PUDDIES	PUER	PUGGINESS
PTOMAINES	PUBLISHES	PUDDIEST	PUERED	PUGGING
PTOMAINIC	PUBS	PUDDING	PUERILE	PUGGINGS
PTOMAINS	PUCAN	PUDDINGS	PUERILELY	PUGGISH
PTOOEY	PUCANS	PUDDINGY	PUERILISM	PUGGLE
PTOSES	PUCCOON	PUDDLE	PUERILITY	PUGGLED
PTOSIS	PUCCOONS	PUDDLED	PUERING	PUGGLES
PTOTIC	PUCE	PUDDLER	PUERPERA	PUGGLING
PTUI	PUCELAGE	PUDDLERS	PUERPERAE	PUGGREE
PTYALIN	PUCELAGES	PUDDLES	PUERPERAL	PUGGREES
PTYALINS	PUCELLE	PUDDLIER	PUERPERIA	PUGGRIES
PTYALISE	PUCELLES	PUDDLIEST	PUERS	PUGGRY
PTYALISED	PUCER	PUDDLING	PUFF	PUGGY
PTYALISES	PUCES	PUDDLINGS	PUFFA	PUGH
PTYALISM	PUCEST	PUDDLY	PUFFBACK	PUGIL
PTYALISMS	PUCK	PUDDOCK	PUFFBACKS	PUGILISM
PTYALIZE	PUCKA	PUDDOCKS	PUFFBALL	PUGILISMS
PTYALIZED	PUCKED	PUDDY	PUFFBALLS	PUGILIST
PTYALIZES	PUCKER	PUDENCIES	PUFFBIRD	PUGILISTS
PTYXES	PUCKERED	PUDENCY	PUFFBIRDS	PUGILS
PTYXIS	PUCKERER	PUDENDA	PUFFED	PUGMARK
PTYXISES	PUCKERERS	PUDENDAL	PUFFER	PUGMARKS
PUB	PUCKERIER	PUDENDOUS	PUFFERIES	PUGNACITY
PUBBED	PUCKERIES	PUDENDUM	PUFFERS	PUGREE
PUBBING	PUCKERING	PUDENT	PUFFERY	PUGREES
PUBBINGS	PUCKEROOD	PUDEUR	PUFFIER	PUGS

PUH	PULER	PULMONARY	PULSATED	PULVIL
PUHA	PULERS	PULMONATE	PULSATES	PULVILIO
PUHAS	PULES	PULMONES	PULSATILE	PULVILIOS
PUIR	PULI	PULMONIC	PULSATING	PULVILLAR
PUIRER	PULICENE	PULMONICS	PULSATION	PULVILLE
PUIREST	PULICIDE	PULMOTOR	PULSATIVE	PULVILLED
PUIRTITH	PULICIDES	PULMOTORS	PULSATOR	PULVILLES
PUIRTITHS	PULIER	PULP	PULSATORS	PULVILLI
PUISNE	PULIEST	PULPAL	PULSATORY	PULVILLIO
PUISNES	PULIK	PULPALLY	PULSE	PULVILLUS
PUISNY	PULING	PULPBOARD	PULSEBEAT	PULVILS
PUISSANCE	PULINGLY	PULPED	PULSED	PULVINAR
PUISSANT	PULINGS	PULPER	PULSEJET	PULVINARS
PUISSAUNT	PULIS	PULPERS	PULSEJETS	PULVINATE
PUJA	PULK	PULPIER	PULSELESS	PULVINI
PUJAH	PULKA	PULPIEST	PULSER	PULVINULE
PUJAHS	PULKAS	PULPIFIED	PULSERS	PULVINUS
PUJARI	PULKHA	PULPIFIES	PULSES	PULWAR
PUJARIS	PULKHAS	PULPIFY	PULSIDGE	PULWARS
PUJAS	PULKS	PULPILY	PULSIDGES	PULY
PUKA	PULL	PULPINESS	PULSIFIC	PUMA
PUKAS	PULLBACK	PULPING	PULSING	PUMAS
PUKATEA	PULLBACKS	PULPINGS	PULSION	PUMELO
PUKATEAS	PULLED	PULPIT	PULSIONS	PUMELOS
PUKE	PULLER	PULPITAL	PULSOJET	PUMICATE
PUKED	PULLERS	PULPITED	PULSOJETS	PUMICATED
PUKEKO	PULLET	PULPITEER	PULTAN	PUMICATES
PUKEKOS	PULLETS	PULPITER	PULTANS	PUMICE
PUKER	PULLEY	PULPITERS	PULTON	PUMICED
PUKERS	PULLEYED	PULPITRY	PULTONS	PUMICEOUS
PUKES	PULLEYING	PULPITS	PULTOON	PUMICER
PUKEY	PULLEYS	PULPITUM	PULTOONS	PUMICERS
PUKIER	PULLI	PULPITUMS	PULTRUDE	PUMICES
PUKIEST	PULLIES	PULPLESS	PULTRUDED	PUMICING
PUKING	PULLING	PULPMILL	PULTRUDES	PUMICITE
PUKKA	PULLMAN	PULPMILLS	PULTUN	PUMICITES
PUKKAH	PULLMANS	PULPOUS	PULTUNS	PUMIE
PUKU	PULLORUM	PULPS	PULTURE	PUMIES
PUKUS	PULLOUT	PULPSTONE	PULTURES	PUMMEL
PUKY	PULLOUTS	PULPWOOD	PULU	PUMMELED
PUL	PULLOVER	PULPWOODS	PULUS	PUMMELING
PULA	PULLOVERS	PULPY	PULVER	PUMMELLED
PULAO	PULLS	PULQUE	PULVERED	PUMMELO
PULAOS	PULLULATE	PULQUES	PULVERINE	PUMMELOS
PULAS	PULLUP	PULS	PULVERING	PUMMELS
PULDRON	PULLUPS	PULSANT	PULVERISE	PUMP
PULDRONS	PULLUS	PULSAR	PULVERIZE	PUMPABLE
PULE	PULLY	PULSARS	PULVEROUS	PUMPED
PULED	PULMO	PULSATE	PULVERS	PUMPER

P

PUMPERS	PUNCHOUT	PUNITION	PUNTER	PUPPYDOM
PUMPHOOD	PUNCHOUTS	PUNITIONS	PUNTERS	PUPPYDOMS
PUMPHOODS	PUNCHY	PUNITIVE	PUNTIES	PUPPYHOOD
PUMPHOUSE	PUNCING	PUNITORY	PUNTING	PUPPYING
PUMPING	PUNCTA	PUNJI	PUNTO	PUPPYISH
PUMPINGS	PUNCTATE	PUNJIED	PUNTOS	PUPPYISM
PUMPION	PUNCTATED	PUNJIES	PUNTS	PUPPYISMS
PUMPIONS	PUNCTATOR	PUNJIING	PUNTSMAN	PUPPYLIKE
PUMPJACK	PUNCTILIO	PUNJIS	PUNTSMEN	PUPS
PUMPJACKS	PUNCTO	PUNK	PUNTY	PUPU
PUMPKIN	PUNCTOS	PUNKA	PUNY	PUPUNHA
PUMPKING	PUNCTUAL	PUNKAH	PUP	PUPUNHAS
PUMPKINGS	PUNCTUATE	PUNKAHS	PUPA	PUPUS
PUMPKINS	PUNCTULE	PUNKAS	PUPAE	PUR
PUMPLESS	PUNCTULES	PUNKER	PUPAL	PURANA
PUMPLIKE	PUNCTUM	PUNKERS	PUPARIA	PURANAS
PUMPS	PUNCTUMS	PUNKEST	PUPARIAL	PURANIC
PUMY	PUNCTURE	PUNKETTE	PUPARIUM	PURBLIND
PUN	PUNCTURED	PUNKETTES	PUPAS	PURCHASE
PUNA	PUNCTURER	PUNKEY	PUPATE	PURCHASED
PUNAANI	PUNCTURES	PUNKEYS	PUPATED	PURCHASER
PUNAANY	PUNDIT	PUNKIE	PUPATES	PURCHASES
PUNALUA	PUNDITIC	PUNKIER	PUPATING	PURDA
PUNALUAN	PUNDITRY	PUNKIES	PUPATION	PURDAH
PUNALUAS	PUNDITS	PUNKIEST	PUPATIONS	PURDAHED
PUNANI	PUNDONOR	PUNKIN	PUPFISH	PURDAHS
PUNANY	PUNG	PUNKINESS	PUPFISHES	PURDAS
PUNAS	PUNGA	PUNKINS	PUPIL	PURDONIUM
PUNCE	PUNGAS	PUNKISH	PUPILAGE	PURE
PUNCED	PUNGENCE	PUNKS	PUPILAGES	PUREBLOOD
PUNCES	PUNGENCES	PUNKY	PUPILAR	PUREBRED
PUNCH	PUNGENCY	PUNNED	PUPILARY	PUREBREDS
PUNCHABLE	PUNGENT	PUNNER	PUPILLAGE	PURED
PUNCHBAG	PUNGENTLY	PUNNERS	PUPILLAR	PUREE
PUNCHBAGS	PUNGLE	PUNNET	PUPILLARY	PUREED
PUNCHBALL	PUNGLED	PUNNETS	PUPILLATE	PUREEING
PUNCHBOWL	PUNGLES	PUNNIER	PUPILS	PUREES
PUNCHED	PUNGLING	PUNNIEST	PUPILSHIP	PURELY
PUNCHEON	PUNGS	PUNNING	PUPPED	PURENESS
PUNCHEONS	PUNIER	PUNNINGLY	PUPPET	PURER
PUNCHER	PUNIEST	PUNNINGS	PUPPETEER	PURES
PUNCHERS	PUNILY	PUNNY	PUPPETRY	PUREST
PUNCHES	PUNINESS	PUNS	PUPPETS	PURFLE
PUNCHIER	PUNISH	PUNSTER	PUPPIED	PURFLED
PUNCHIEST	PUNISHED	PUNSTERS	PUPPIES	PURFLER
PUNCHILY	PUNISHER	PUNT	PUPPING	PURFLERS
PUNCHING	PUNISHERS	PUNTED	PUPPODUM	PURFLES
PUNCHLESS	PUNISHES	PUNTEE	PUPPODUMS	PURFLING
PUNCHLINE	PUNISHING	PUNTEES	PUPPY	PURFLINGS

PURFLY	PURLINES	PURSEFUL	PURVIEWS	PUSSERS
PURGATION	PURLING	PURSEFULS	PUS	PUSSES
PURGATIVE	PURLINGS	PURSELIKE	PUSES	PUSSIER
PURGATORY	PURLINS	PURSER	PUSH	PUSSIES
PURGE	PURLOIN	PURSERS	PUSHBACK	PUSSIEST
PURGEABLE	PURLOINED	PURSES	PUSHBACKS	PUSSLEY
PURGED	PURLOINER	PURSEW	PUSHBALL	PUSSLEYS
PURGER	PURLOINS	PURSEWED	PUSHBALLS	PUSSLIES
PURGERS	PURLS	PURSEWING	PUSHBIKE	PUSSLIKE
PURGES	PUROMYCIN	PURSEWS	PUSHBIKES	PUSSLY
PURGING	PURPIE	PURSIER	PUSHCART	PUSSY
PURGINGS	PURPIES	PURSIEST	PUSHCARTS	PUSSYCAT
PURI	PURPLE	PURSILY	PUSHCHAIR	PUSSYCATS
PURIFIED	PURPLED	PURSINESS	PUSHDOWN	PUSSYFOOT
PURIFIER	PURPLER	PURSING	PUSHDOWNS	PUSSYTOES
PURIFIERS	PURPLES	PURSLAIN	PUSHED	PUSTULANT
PURIFIES	PURPLEST	PURSLAINS	PUSHER	PUSTULAR
PURIFY	PURPLIER	PURSLANE	PUSHERS	PUSTULATE
PURIFYING	PURPLIEST	PURSLANES	PUSHES	PUSTULE
PURIN	PURPLING	PURSUABLE	PUSHFUL	PUSTULED
PURINE	PURPLISH	PURSUAL	PUSHFULLY	PUSTULES
PURINES	PURPLY	PURSUALS	PUSHIER	PUSTULOUS
PURING	PURPORT	PURSUANCE	PUSHIEST	PUT
PURINS	PURPORTED	PURSUANT	PUSHILY	PUTAMEN
PURIRI	PURPORTS	PURSUE	PUSHINESS	PUTAMENS
PURIRIS	PURPOSE	PURSUED	PUSHING	PUTAMINA
PURIS	PURPOSED	PURSUER	PUSHINGLY	PUTATIVE
PURISM	PURPOSELY	PURSUERS	PUSHOVER	PUTCHEON
PURISMS	PURPOSES	PURSUES	PUSHOVERS	PUTCHEONS
PURIST	PURPOSING	PURSUING	PUSHPIN	PUTCHER
PURISTIC	PURPOSIVE	PURSUINGS	PUSHPINS	PUTCHERS
PURISTS	PURPURA	PURSUIT	PUSHPIT	PUTCHOCK
PURITAN	PURPURAS	PURSUITS	PUSHPITS	PUTCHOCKS
PURITANIC	PURPURE	PURSY	PUSHROD	PUTCHUK
PURITANS	PURPUREAL	PURTIER	PUSHRODS	PUTCHUKS
PURITIES	PURPURES	PURTIEST	PUSHUP	PUTDOWN
PURITY	PURPURIC	PURTRAID	PUSHUPS	PUTDOWNS
PURL	PURPURIN	PURTRAYD	PUSHY	PUTEAL
PURLED	PURPURINS	PURTY	PUSLE	PUTEALS
PURLER	PURPY	PURULENCE	PUSLED	PUTELI
PURLERS	PURR	PURULENCY	PUSLES	PUTELIS
PURLICUE	PURRED	PURULENT	PUSLEY	PUTID
PURLICUED	PURRING	PURVEY	PUSLEYS	PUTLOCK
PURLICUES	PURRINGLY	PURVEYED	PUSLIKE	PUTLOCKS
PURLIEU	PURRINGS	PURVEYING	PUSLING	PUTLOG
PURLIEUS	PURRS	PURVEYOR	PUSS	PUTLOGS
PURLIEUX	PURS	PURVEYORS	PUSSEL	PUTOFF
PURLIN	PURSE	PURVEYS	PUSSELS	PUTOFFS
PURLINE	PURSED	PURVIEW	PUSSER	PUTOIS

P

PUTON	PUTZED	PYEMIAS	PYODERMA	PYRETHRUM
PUTONGHUA	PUTZES	PYEMIC	PYODERMAS	PYRETIC
PUTONS	PUTZING	PYENGADU	PYODERMIC	PYREX
PUTOUT	PUY	PYENGADUS	PYOGENIC	PYREXES
PUTOUTS	PUYS	PYES	PYOID	PYREXIA
PUTREFIED	PUZEL	PYET	PYONER	PYREXIAL
PUTREFIER	PUZELS	PYETS	PYONERS	PYREXIAS
PUTREFIES	PUZZEL	PYGAL	PYONINGS	PYREXIC
PUTREFY	PUZZELS	PYGALS	PYORRHEA	PYRIC
PUTRID	PUZZLE	PYGARG	PYORRHEAL	PYRIDIC
PUTRIDER	PUZZLED	PYGARGS	PYORRHEAS	PYRIDINE
PUTRIDEST	PUZZLEDLY	PYGARGUS	PYORRHEIC	PYRIDINES
PUTRIDITY	PUZZLEDOM	PYGIDIA	PYORRHOEA	PYRIDOXAL
PUTRIDLY	PUZZLER	PYGIDIAL	PYOSES	PYRIDOXIN
PUTS	PUZZLERS	PYGIDIUM	PYOSIS	PYRIFORM
PUTSCH	PUZZLES	PYGMAEAN	PYOT	PYRITE
PUTSCHES	PUZZLING	PYGMEAN	PYOTS	PYRITES
PUTSCHIST	PUZZOLANA	PYGMIES	PYRACANTH	PYRITIC
PUTT	PWN	PYGMOID	PYRAL	PYRITICAL
PUTTED	PWNED	PYGMOIDS	PYRALID	PYRITISE
PUTTEE	PWNING	PYGMY	PYRALIDID	PYRITISED
PUTTEES	PWNS	PYGMYISH	PYRALIDS	PYRITISES
PUTTEN	PYA	PYGMYISM	PYRALIS	PYRITIZE
PUTTER	PYAEMIA	PYGMYISMS	PYRALISES	PYRITIZED
PUTTERED	PYAEMIAS	PYGOSTYLE	PYRAMID	PYRITIZES
PUTTERER	PYAEMIC	PYIC	PYRAMIDAL	PYRITOUS
PUTTERERS	PYAS	PYIN	PYRAMIDED	PYRO
PUTTERING	PYAT	PYINKADO	PYRAMIDES	PYROBORIC
PUTTERS	PYATS	PYINKADOS	PYRAMIDIA	PYROCERAM
PUTTI	PYCNIC	PYINS	PYRAMIDIC	PYROCLAST
PUTTIE	PYCNIDIA	PYJAMA	PYRAMIDON	PYROGEN
PUTTIED	PYCNIDIAL	PYJAMAED	PYRAMIDS	PYROGENIC
PUTTIER	PYCNIDIUM	PYJAMAS	PYRAMIS	PYROGENS
PUTTIERS	PYCNITE	PYKNIC	PYRAMISES	PYROGIES
PUTTIES	PYCNITES	PYKNICS	PYRAN	PYROGY
PUTTING	PYCNON	PYKNOSES	PYRANOID	PYROHIES
PUTTINGS	PYCNONS	PYKNOSIS	PYRANOSE	PYROHY
PUTTO	PYCNOSES	PYKNOSOME	PYRANOSES	PYROLA
PUTTOCK	PYCNOSIS	PYKNOTIC	PYRANS	PYROLAS
PUTTOCKS	PYCNOSOME	PYLON	PYRAZOLE	PYROLATER
PUTTS	PYCNOTIC	PYLONS	PYRAZOLES	PYROLATRY
PUTTY	PYE	PYLORI	PYRE	PYROLISE
PUTTYING	PYEBALD	PYLORIC	PYRENE	PYROLISED
PUTTYLESS	PYEBALDS	PYLORUS	PYRENEITE	PYROLISES
PUTTYLIKE	PYEING	PYLORUSES	PYRENES	PYROLIZE
PUTTYROOT	PYELITIC	PYNE	PYRENOID	PYROLIZED
PUTURE	PYELITIS	PYNED	PYRENOIDS	PYROLIZES
PUTURES	PYELOGRAM	PYNES	PYRES	PYROLOGY
PUTZ	PYEMIA	PYNING	PYRETHRIN	PYROLYSE

PYROLYSED	PYRONIN	PYROSOMES	PYRROLES	PYURIAS
PYROLYSER	PYRONINE	PYROSTAT	PYRROLIC	PYX
PYROLYSES	PYRONINES	PYROSTATS	PYRROLS	PYXED
PYROLYSIS	PYRONINS	PYROXENE	PYRUVATE	PYXES
PYROLYTIC	PYROPE	PYROXENES	PYRUVATES	PYXIDES
PYROLYZE	PYROPES	PYROXENIC	PYRUVIC	PYXIDIA
PYROLYZED	PYROPHONE	PYROXYLE	PYSANKA	PYXIDIUM
PYROLYZER	PYROPUS	PYROXYLES	PYSANKY	PYXIE
PYROLYZES	PYROPUSES	PYROXYLIC	PYTHIUM	PYXIES
PYROMANCY	PYROS	PYROXYLIN	PYTHIUMS	PYXING
PYROMANIA	PYROSCOPE	PYRRHIC	PYTHON	PYXIS
PYROMETER	PYROSES	PYRRHICS	PYTHONESS	PZAZZ
PYROMETRY	PYROSIS	PYRRHOUS	PYTHONIC	PZAZZES
PYRONE	PYROSISES	PYRROL	PYTHONS	
PYRONES	PYROSOME	PYRROLE	PYURIA	

P

QABALA	QINDARKA	QUADRANTS	QUAGGIER	QUALE
QABALAH	QINDARS	QUADRAT	QUAGGIEST	QUALIA
QABALAHS	QINGHAOSU	QUADRATE	QUAGGY	QUALIFIED
QABALAS	QINS	QUADRATED	QUAGMIRE	QUALIFIER
QABALISM	QINTAR	QUADRATES	QUAGMIRED	QUALIFIES
QABALISMS	QINTARKA	QUADRATI	QUAGMIRES	QUALIFY
QABALIST	QINTARS	QUADRATIC	QUAGMIRY	QUALITIED
QABALISTS	QIS	QUADRATS	QUAGS	QUALITIES
QADI	QIVIUT	QUADRATUS	QUAHAUG	QUALITY
QADIS	QIVIUTS	QUADRELLA	QUAHAUGS	QUALM
QAID	QOPH	QUADRIC	QUAHOG	QUALMIER
QAIDS	QOPHS	QUADRICEP	QUAHOGS	QUALMIEST
QAIMAQAM	QORMA	QUADRICS	QUAI	QUALMING
QAIMAQAMS	QORMAS	QUADRIFID	QUAICH	QUALMINGS
QAJAQ	QUA	QUADRIGA	QUAICHES	QUALMISH
QAJAQS	QUAALUDE	QUADRIGAE	QUAICHS	QUALMLESS
QALAMDAN	QUAALUDES	QUADRIGAS	QUAIGH	QUALMS
QALAMDANS	QUACK	QUADRILLE	QUAIGHS	QUALMY
QAMEEZ	QUACKED	QUADRIVIA	QUAIL	QUAMASH
QAMEEZES	QUACKER	QUADROTOR	QUAILED	QUAMASHES
QAMUTIK	QUACKERS	QUADRUMAN	QUAILING	QUANDANG
QAMUTIKS	QUACKERY	QUADRUPED	QUAILINGS	QUANDANGS
QANAT	QUACKIER	QUADRUPLE	QUAILS	QUANDARY
QANATS	QUACKIEST	QUADRUPLY	QUAINT	QUANDONG
QAPIK	QUACKING	QUADS	QUAINTER	QUANDONGS
QAPIKS	QUACKISH	QUAERE	QUAINTEST	QUANGO
QASIDA	QUACKISM	QUAERED	QUAINTLY	QUANGOS
QASIDAS	QUACKISMS	QUAEREING	QUAIR	QUANNET
QAT	QUACKLE	QUAERES	QUAIRS	QUANNETS
QATS	QUACKLED	QUAERITUR	QUAIS	QUANT
QAWWAL	QUACKLES	QUAESITUM	QUAKE	QUANTA
QAWWALI	QUACKLING	QUAESTOR	QUAKED	QUANTAL
QAWWALIS	QUACKS	QUAESTORS	QUAKER	QUANTALLY
QAWWALS	QUACKY	QUAFF	QUAKERS	QUANTED
QEEMA	QUAD	QUAFFABLE	QUAKES	QUANTIC
QEEMAS	QUADDED	QUAFFED	QUAKIER	QUANTICAL
QI	QUADDING	QUAFFER	QUAKIEST	QUANTICS
QIBLA	QUADDINGS	QUAFFERS	QUAKILY	QUANTIFY
QIBLAS	QUADPLAY	QUAFFING	QUAKINESS	QUANTILE
QIGONG	QUADPLAYS	QUAFFS	QUAKING	QUANTILES
QIGONGS	QUADPLEX	QUAG	QUAKINGLY	QUANTING
QIN	QUADRANS	QUAGGA	QUAKINGS	QUANTISE
QINDAR	QUADRANT	QUAGGAS	QUAKY	QUANTISED

QUANTISER	QUARTETT	QUATS	QUEENDOMS	QUEME
QUANTISES	QUARTETTE	QUATTED	QUEENED	QUEMED
QUANTITY	QUARTETTI	QUATTING	QUEENFISH	QUEMES
QUANTIZE	QUARTETTO	QUAVER	QUEENHOOD	QUEMING
QUANTIZED	QUARTETTS	QUAVERED	QUEENIE	QUENA
QUANTIZER	QUARTIC	QUAVERER	QUEENIER	QUENAS
QUANTIZES	QUARTICS	QUAVERERS	QUEENIES	QUENCH
QUANTONG	QUARTIER	QUAVERIER	QUEENIEST	QUENCHED
QUANTONGS	QUARTIERS	QUAVERING	QUEENING	QUENCHER
QUANTS	QUARTILE	QUAVERS	QUEENINGS	QUENCHERS
QUANTUM	QUARTILES	QUAVERY	QUEENITE	QUENCHES
QUANTUMS	QUARTO	QUAY	QUEENITES	QUENCHING
QUARE	QUARTOS	QUAYAGE	QUEENLESS	QUENELLE
QUARENDEN	QUARTS	QUAYAGES	QUEENLET	QUENELLES
QUARENDER	QUARTZ	QUAYD	QUEENLETS	QUEP
QUARER	QUARTZES	QUAYLIKE	QUEENLIER	QUERCETIC
QUAREST	QUARTZIER	QUAYS	QUEENLIKE	QUERCETIN
QUARK	QUARTZITE	QUAYSIDE	QUEENLY	QUERCETUM
QUARKS	QUARTZOSE	QUAYSIDES	QUEENS	QUERCINE
QUARREL	QUARTZOUS	QUAZZIER	QUEENSHIP	QUERCITIN
QUARRELED	QUARTZY	QUAZZIEST	QUEENSIDE	QUERIDA
QUARRELER	QUASAR	QUAZZY	QUEENY	QUERIDAS
QUARRELS	QUASARS	QUBIT	QUEER	QUERIED
QUARRIAN	QUASH	QUBITS	QUEERCORE	QUERIER
QUARRIANS	QUASHED	QUBYTE	QUEERED	QUERIERS
QUARRIED	QUASHER	QUBYTES	QUEERER	QUERIES
QUARRIER	QUASHERS	QUEACH	QUEEREST	QUERIMONY
QUARRIERS	QUASHES	QUEACHES	QUEERING	QUERIST
QUARRIES	QUASHING	QUEACHIER	QUEERISH	QUERISTS
QUARRION	QUASI	QUEACHY	QUEERITY	QUERN
QUARRIONS	QUASS	QUEAN	QUEERLY	QUERNS
QUARRY	QUASSES	QUEANS	QUEERNESS	QUERULOUS
QUARRYING	QUASSIA	QUEASIER	QUEERS	QUERY
QUARRYMAN	QUASSIAS	QUEASIEST	QUEEST	QUERYING
QUARRYMEN	QUASSIN	QUEASILY	QUEESTS	QUERYINGS
QUART	QUASSINS	QUEASY	QUEINT	QUESO
QUARTAN	QUAT	QUEAZIER	QUELCH	QUESOS
QUARTANS	QUATCH	QUEAZIEST	QUELCHED	QUEST
QUARTE	QUATCHED	QUEAZY	QUELCHES	QUESTANT
QUARTER	QUATCHES	QUEBEC	QUELCHING	QUESTANTS
QUARTERED	QUATCHING	QUEBECS	QUELEA	QUESTED
QUARTERER	QUATE	QUEBRACHO	QUELEAS	QUESTER
QUARTERLY	QUATES	QUEECHIER	QUELL	QUESTERS
QUARTERN	QUATORZE	QUEECHY	QUELLABLE	QUESTING
QUARTERNS	QUATORZES	QUEEN	QUELLED	QUESTINGS
QUARTERS	QUATRAIN	QUEENCAKE	QUELLER	QUESTION
QUARTES	QUATRAINS	QUEENCUP	QUELLERS	QUESTIONS
QUARTET	QUATRE	QUEENCUPS	QUELLING	QUESTOR
QUARTETS	QUATRES	QUEENDOM	QUELLS	QUESTORS

QUESTRIST	QUICKENER	QUIETISM	QUILTS	QUINONE
QUESTS	QUICKENS	QUIETISMS	QUIM	QUINONES
QUETCH	QUICKER	QUIETIST	QUIMS	QUINONOID
QUETCHED	QUICKEST	QUIETISTS	QUIN	QUINOS
QUETCHES	QUICKFIRE	QUIETIVE	QUINA	QUINQUINA
QUETCHING	QUICKIE	QUIETIVES	QUINARIES	QUINS
QUETHE	QUICKIES	QUIETLY	QUINARY	QUINSIED
QUETHES	QUICKLIME	QUIETNESS	QUINAS	QUINSIES
QUETHING	QUICKLY	QUIETS	QUINATE	QUINSY
QUETSCH	QUICKNESS	QUIETSOME	QUINCE	QUINT
QUETSCHES	QUICKS	QUIETUDE	QUINCES	QUINTA
QUETZAL	QUICKSAND	QUIETUDES	QUINCH	QUINTAIN
QUETZALES	QUICKSET	QUIETUS	QUINCHE	QUINTAINS
QUETZALS	QUICKSETS	QUIETUSES	QUINCHED	QUINTAL
QUEUE	QUICKSTEP	QUIFF	QUINCHES	QUINTALS
QUEUED	QUICKY	QUIFFED	QUINCHING	QUINTAN
QUEUEING	QUID	QUIFFS	QUINCUNX	QUINTANS
QUEUEINGS	QUIDAM	QUIGHT	QUINE	QUINTAR
QUEUER	QUIDAMS	QUIGHTED	QUINELA	QUINTARS
QUEUERS	QUIDDANY	QUIGHTING	QUINELAS	QUINTAS
QUEUES	QUIDDIT	QUIGHTS	QUINELLA	QUINTE
QUEUING	QUIDDITCH	QUILL	QUINELLAS	QUINTES
QUEUINGS	QUIDDITS	QUILLAI	QUINES	QUINTET
QUEY	QUIDDITY	QUILLAIA	QUINIC	QUINTETS
QUEYN	QUIDDLE	QUILLAIAS	QUINIDINE	QUINTETT
QUEYNIE	QUIDDLED	QUILLAIS	QUINIE	QUINTETTE
QUEYNIES	QUIDDLER	QUILLAJA	QUINIELA	QUINTETTI
QUEYNS	QUIDDLERS	QUILLAJAS	QUINIELAS	QUINTETTO
QUEYS	QUIDDLES	QUILLBACK	QUINIES	QUINTETTS
QUEZAL	QUIDDLING	QUILLED	QUININ	QUINTIC
QUEZALES	QUIDNUNC	QUILLET	QUININA	QUINTICS
QUEZALS	QUIDNUNCS	QUILLETS	QUININAS	QUINTILE
QUIBBLE	QUIDS	QUILLING	QUININE	QUINTILES
QUIBBLED	QUIESCE	QUILLINGS	QUININES	QUINTIN
QUIBBLER	QUIESCED	QUILLMAN	QUININS	QUINTINS
QUIBBLERS	QUIESCENT	QUILLMEN	QUINNAT	QUINTS
QUIBBLES	QUIESCES	QUILLON	QUINNATS	QUINTUPLE
QUIBBLING	QUIESCING	QUILLONS	QUINO	QUINTUPLY
QUIBLIN	QUIET	QUILLOW	QUINOA	QUINZE
QUIBLINS	QUIETED	QUILLOWS	QUINOAS	QUINZES
QUICH	QUIETEN	QUILLS	QUINOID	QUINZHEE
QUICHE	QUIETENED	QUILLWORK	QUINOIDAL	QUINZHEES
QUICHED	QUIETENER	QUILLWORT	QUINOIDS	QUINZIE
QUICHES	QUIETENS	QUILT	QUINOL	QUINZIES
QUICHING	QUIETER	QUILTED	QUINOLIN	QUIP
QUICK	QUIETERS	QUILTER	QUINOLINE	QUIPO
QUICKBEAM	QUIETEST	QUILTERS	QUINOLINS	QUIPOS
QUICKEN	QUIETING	QUILTING	QUINOLONE	QUIPPED
QUICKENED	QUIETINGS	QUILTINGS	QUINOLS	QUIPPER

QUIPPERS	QUIST	QUIVERY	QUOINED	QUOTABLY
QUIPPIER	QUISTS	QUIXOTE	QUOINING	QUOTAS
QUIPPIEST	QUIT	QUIXOTES	QUOININGS	QUOTATION
QUIPPING	QUITCH	QUIXOTIC	QUOINS	QUOTATIVE
QUIPPISH	QUITCHED	QUIXOTISM	QUOIST	QUOTE
QUIPPU	QUITCHES	QUIXOTRY	QUOISTS	QUOTED
QUIPPUS	QUITCHING	QUIZ	QUOIT	QUOTER
QUIPPY	QUITCLAIM	QUIZZED	QUOITED	QUOTERS
QUIPS	QUITE	QUIZZER	QUOITER	QUOTES
QUIPSTER	QUITED	QUIZZERS	QUOITERS	QUOTH
QUIPSTERS	QUITES	QUIZZERY	QUOITING	QUOTHA
QUIPU	QUITING	QUIZZES	QUOITS	QUOTIDIAN
QUIPUS	QUITRENT	QUIZZICAL	QUOKKA	QUOTIENT
QUIRE	QUITRENTS	QUIZZIFY	QUOKKAS	QUOTIENTS
QUIRED	QUITS	QUIZZING	QUOLL	QUOTING
QUIRES	QUITTAL	QUIZZINGS	QUOLLS	QUOTITION
QUIRING	QUITTALS	QULLIQ	QUOMODO	QUOTUM
QUIRISTER	QUITTANCE	QULLIQS	QUOMODOS	QUOTUMS
QUIRK	QUITTED	QUOAD	QUONDAM	QURSH
QUIRKED	QUITTER	QUOD	QUONK	QURSHES
QUIRKIER	QUITTERS	QUODDED	QUONKED	QURUSH
QUIRKIEST	QUITTING	QUODDING	QUONKING	QURUSHES
QUIRKILY	QUITTOR	QUODLIBET	QUONKS	QUYTE
QUIRKING	QUITTORS	QUODLIN	QUOOKE	QUYTED
QUIRKISH	QUIVER	QUODLINS	QUOP	QUYTES
QUIRKS	QUIVERED	QUODS	QUOPPED	QUYTING
QUIRKY	QUIVERER	QUOHOG	QUOPPING	QWERTIES
QUIRT	QUIVERERS	QUOHOGS	QUOPS	QWERTY
QUIRTED	QUIVERFUL	QUOIF	QUORATE	QWERTYS
QUIRTING	QUIVERIER	QUOIFED	QUORUM	
QUIRTS	QUIVERING	QUOIFING	QUORUMS	
QUISLING	QUIVERISH	QUOIFS	QUOTA	
QUISLINGS	QUIVERS	QUOIN	QUOTABLE	

Q

R

RABANNA	RABBITY	RACEMIC	RACIALIST	RACLETTES
RABANNAS	RABBLE	RACEMISE	RACIALIZE	RACLOIR
RABASKA	RABBLED	RACEMISED	RACIALLY	RACLOIRS
RABASKAS	RABBLER	RACEMISES	RACIATION	RACON
RABAT	RABBLERS	RACEMISM	RACIER	RACONS
RABATINE	RABBLES	RACEMISMS	RACIEST	RACONTEUR
RABATINES	RABBLING	RACEMIZE	RACILY	RACOON
RABATMENT	RABBLINGS	RACEMIZED	RACINESS	RACOONS
RABATO	RABBONI	RACEMIZES	RACING	RACQUET
RABATOES	RABBONIS	RACEMOID	RACINGS	RACQUETED
RABATOS	RABI	RACEMOSE	RACINO	RACQUETS
RABATS	RABIC	RACEMOUS	RACINOS	RACY
RABATTE	RABID	RACEPATH	RACISM	RAD
RABATTED	RABIDER	RACEPATHS	RACISMS	RADAR
RABATTES	RABIDEST	RACER	RACIST	RADARS
RABATTING	RABIDITY	RACERS	RACISTS	RADDED
RABBET	RABIDLY	RACES	RACK	RADDER
RABBETED	RABIDNESS	RACETRACK	RACKED	RADDEST
RABBETING	RABIES	RACEWALK	RACKER	RADDING
RABBETS	RABIETIC	RACEWALKS	RACKERS	RADDLE
RABBI	RABIS	RACEWAY	RACKET	RADDLED
RABBIES	RABONA	RACEWAYS	RACKETED	RADDLEMAN
RABBIN	RABONAS	RACH	RACKETEER	RADDLEMEN
RABBINATE	RACA	RACHE	RACKETER	RADDLES
RABBINIC	RACAHOUT	RACHES	RACKETERS	RADDLING
RABBINICS	RACAHOUTS	RACHET	RACKETIER	RADDOCKE
RABBINISM	RACCAHOUT	RACHETED	RACKETING	RADDOCKES
RABBINIST	RACCOON	RACHETING	RACKETRY	RADE
RABBINITE	RACCOONS	RACHETS	RACKETS	RADGE
RABBINS	RACE	RACHIAL	RACKETT	RADGER
RABBIS	RACEABLE	RACHIDES	RACKETTS	RADGES
RABBIT	RACECARD	RACHIDIAL	RACKETY	RADGEST
RABBITED	RACECARDS	RACHIDIAN	RACKFUL	RADIABLE
RABBITER	RACED	RACHILLA	RACKFULS	RADIAL
RABBITERS	RACEGOER	RACHILLAE	RACKING	RADIALE
RABBITIER	RACEGOERS	RACHILLAS	RACKINGLY	RADIALIA
RABBITING	RACEGOING	RACHIS	RACKINGS	RADIALISE
RABBITO	RACEHORSE	RACHISES	RACKLE	RADIALITY
RABBITOH	RACEMATE	RACHITIC	RACKLES	RADIALIZE
RABBITOHS	RACEMATES	RACHITIS	RACKS	RADIALLY
RABBITOS	RACEME	RACIAL	RACKWORK	RADIALS
RABBITRY	RACEMED	RACIALISE	RACKWORKS	RADIAN
RABBITS	RACEMES	RACIALISM	RACLETTE	RADIANCE

RADIANCES	RADISH	RAFTMEN	RAGINGS	RAIA
RADIANCY	RADISHES	RAFTS	RAGINI	RAIAS
RADIANS	RADIUM	RAFTSMAN	RAGINIS	RAID
RADIANT	RADIUMS	RAFTSMEN	RAGIS	RAIDED
RADIANTLY	RADIUS	RAG	RAGLAN	RAIDER
RADIANTS	RADIUSED	RAGA	RAGLANS	RAIDERS
RADIATA	RADIUSES	RAGAS	RAGMAN	RAIDING
RADIATAS	RADIUSING	RAGBAG	RAGMANS	RAIDINGS
RADIATE	RADIX	RAGBAGS	RAGMEN	RAIDS
RADIATED	RADIXES	RAGBOLT	RAGMENT	RAIK
RADIATELY	RADOME	RAGBOLTS	RAGMENTS	RAIKED
RADIATES	RADOMES	RAGDE	RAGOUT	RAIKING
RADIATING	RADON	RAGDOLL	RAGOUTED	RAIKS
RADIATION	RADONS	RAGDOLLS	RAGOUTING	RAIL
RADIATIVE	RADS	RAGE	RAGOUTS	RAILAGE
RADIATOR	RADULA	RAGED	RAGPICKER	RAILAGES
RADIATORS	RADULAE	RAGEE	RAGS	RAILBED
RADIATORY	RADULAR	RAGEES	RAGSTONE	RAILBEDS
RADICAL	RADULAS	RAGEFUL	RAGSTONES	RAILBIRD
RADICALLY	RADULATE	RAGER	RAGTAG	RAILBIRDS
RADICALS	RADWASTE	RAGERS	RAGTAGS	RAILBUS
RADICAND	RADWASTES	RAGES	RAGTAIL	RAILBUSES
RADICANDS	RAFALE	RAGG	RAGTIME	RAILCAR
RADICANT	RAFALES	RAGGA	RAGTIMER	RAILCARD
RADICATE	RAFF	RAGGAS	RAGTIMERS	RAILCARDS
RADICATED	RAFFIA	RAGGED	RAGTIMES	RAILCARS
RADICATES	RAFFIAS	RAGGEDER	RAGTOP	RAILE
RADICCHIO	RAFFINATE	RAGGEDEST	RAGTOPS	RAILED
RADICEL	RAFFINOSE	RAGGEDIER	RAGU	RAILER
RADICELS	RAFFISH	RAGGEDLY	RAGULED	RAILERS
RADICES	RAFFISHLY	RAGGEDY	RAGULY	RAILES
RADICLE	RAFFLE	RAGGEE	RAGUS	RAILGUN
RADICLES	RAFFLED	RAGGEES	RAGWEED	RAILGUNS
RADICULAR	RAFFLER	RAGGERIES	RAGWEEDS	RAILHEAD
RADICULE	RAFFLERS	RAGGERY	RAGWHEEL	RAILHEADS
RADICULES	RAFFLES	RAGGIER	RAGWHEELS	RAILING
RADII	RAFFLESIA	RAGGIES	RAGWORK	RAILINGLY
RADIO	RAFFLING	RAGGIEST	RAGWORKS	RAILINGS
RADIOED	RAFFS	RAGGING	RAGWORM	RAILLERY
RADIOES	RAFT	RAGGINGS	RAGWORMS	RAILLESS
RADIOGOLD	RAFTABLE	RAGGLE	RAGWORT	RAILLIES
RADIOGRAM	RAFTED	RAGGLED	RAGWORTS	RAILLY
RADIOING	RAFTER	RAGGLES	RAH	RAILMAN
RADIOLOGY	RAFTERED	RAGGLING	RAHED	RAILMEN
RADIOMAN	RAFTERING	RAGGS	RAHING	RAILROAD
RADIOMEN	RAFTERS	RAGGY	RAHS	RAILROADS
RADIONICS	RAFTING	RAGI	RAHUI	RAILS
RADIOS	RAFTINGS	RAGING	RAHUIS	RAILWAY
RADIOTHON	RAFTMAN	RAGINGLY	RAI	RAILWAYS

R

RAILWOMAN	RAIRDS	RAKI	RAMBLING	RAMMLES
RAILWOMEN	RAIS	RAKIA	RAMBLINGS	RAMMY
RAIMENT	RAISABLE	RAKIAS	RAMBUTAN	RAMONA
RAIMENTS	RAISE	RAKIJA	RAMBUTANS	RAMONAS
RAIN	RAISEABLE	RAKIJAS	RAMCAT	RAMOSE
RAINBAND	RAISED	RAKING	RAMCATS	RAMOSELY
RAINBANDS	RAISER	RAKINGS	RAMEAL	RAMOSITY
RAINBIRD	RAISERS	RAKIS	RAMEE	RAMOUS
RAINBIRDS	RAISES	RAKISH	RAMEES	RAMOUSLY
RAINBOW	RAISIN	RAKISHLY	RAMEKIN	RAMP
RAINBOWED	RAISING	RAKSHAS	RAMEKINS	RAMPAGE
RAINBOWS	RAISINGS	RAKSHASA	RAMEN	RAMPAGED
RAINBOWY	RAISINIER	RAKSHASAS	RAMENS	RAMPAGER
RAINCHECK	RAISINS	RAKSHASES	RAMENTA	RAMPAGERS
RAINCOAT	RAISINY	RAKU	RAMENTUM	RAMPAGES
RAINCOATS	RAISONNE	RAKUS	RAMEOUS	RAMPAGING
RAINDATE	RAIT	RALE	RAMEQUIN	RAMPANCY
RAINDATES	RAITA	RALES	RAMEQUINS	RAMPANT
RAINDROP	RAITAS	RALLIED	RAMET	RAMPANTLY
RAINDROPS	RAITED	RALLIER	RAMETS	RAMPART
RAINE	RAITING	RALLIERS	RAMI	RAMPARTED
RAINED	RAITS	RALLIES	RAMIE	RAMPARTS
RAINES	RAIYAT	RALLIFORM	RAMIES	RAMPAUGE
RAINFALL	RAIYATS	RALLINE	RAMIFIED	RAMPAUGED
RAINFALLS	RAJ	RALLY	RAMIFIES	RAMPAUGES
RAINIER	RAJA	RALLYE	RAMIFORM	RAMPED
RAINIEST	RAJAH	RALLYES	RAMIFY	RAMPER
RAINILY	RAJAHS	RALLYING	RAMIFYING	RAMPERS
RAININESS	RAJAHSHIP	RALLYINGS	RAMILIE	RAMPICK
RAINING	RAJAS	RALLYIST	RAMILIES	RAMPICKED
RAINLESS	RAJASHIP	RALLYISTS	RAMILLIE	RAMPICKS
RAINMAKER	RAJASHIPS	RALPH	RAMILLIES	RAMPIKE
RAINOUT	RAJES	RALPHED	RAMIN	RAMPIKES
RAINOUTS	RAKE	RALPHING	RAMINS	RAMPING
RAINPROOF	RAKED	RALPHS	RAMIS	RAMPINGS
RAINS	RAKEE	RAM	RAMJET	RAMPION
RAINSPOUT	RAKEES	RAMADA	RAMJETS	RAMPIONS
RAINSTICK	RAKEHELL	RAMADAS	RAMMED	RAMPIRE
RAINSTORM	RAKEHELLS	RAMAKIN	RAMMEL	RAMPIRED
RAINSUIT	RAKEHELLY	RAMAKINS	RAMMELS	RAMPIRES
RAINSUITS	RAKELIKE	RAMAL	RAMMER	RAMPOLE
RAINSWEPT	RAKEOFF	RAMATE	RAMMERS	RAMPOLES
RAINTIGHT	RAKEOFFS	RAMBLA	RAMMIER	RAMPS
RAINWASH	RAKER	RAMBLAS	RAMMIES	RAMPSMAN
RAINWATER	RAKERIES	RAMBLE	RAMMIEST	RAMPSMEN
RAINWEAR	RAKERS	RAMBLED	RAMMING	RAMROD
RAINWEARS	RAKERY	RAMBLER	RAMMISH	RAMRODDED
RAINY	RAKES	RAMBLERS	RAMMISHLY	RAMRODS
RAIRD	RAKESHAME	RAMBLES	RAMMLE	RAMS

RAMSHORN	RANCID	RANGERS	RANSACKER	RAPHIDE
RAMSHORNS	RANCIDER	RANGES	RANSACKS	RAPHIDES
RAMSON	RANCIDEST	RANGI	RANSEL	RAPHIS
RAMSONS	RANCIDITY	RANGIER	RANSELS	RAPID
RAMSTAM	RANCIDLY	RANGIEST	RANSHAKLE	RAPIDER
RAMTIL	RANCING	RANGILY	RANSOM	RAPIDEST
RAMTILLA	RANCOR	RANGINESS	RANSOMED	RAPIDITY
RAMTILLAS	RANCORED	RANGING	RANSOMER	RAPIDLY
RAMTILS	RANCOROUS	RANGINGS	RANSOMERS	RAPIDNESS
RAMULAR	RANCORS	RANGIORA	RANSOMING	RAPIDS
RAMULI	RANCOUR	RANGIORAS	RANSOMS	RAPIER
RAMULOSE	RANCOURED	RANGIS	RANT	RAPIERED
RAMULOUS	RANCOURS	RANGOLI	RANTED	RAPIERS
RAMULUS	RAND	RANGOLIS	RANTER	RAPIEST
RAMUS	RANDAN	RANGS	RANTERISM	RAPINE
RAN	RANDANS	RANGY	RANTERS	RAPINES
RANA	RANDED	RANI	RANTING	RAPING
RANARIA	RANDEM	RANID	RANTINGLY	RAPINI
RANARIAN	RANDEMS	RANIDS	RANTINGS	RAPINIS
RANARIUM	RANDIE	RANIFORM	RANTIPOLE	RAPIST
RANARIUMS	RANDIER	RANINE	RANTS	RAPISTS
RANAS	RANDIES	RANIS	RANULA	RAPLOCH
RANCE	RANDIEST	RANK	RANULAR	RAPLOCHS
RANCED	RANDILY	RANKE	RANULAS	RAPPAREE
RANCEL	RANDINESS	RANKED	RANUNCULI	RAPPAREES
RANCELLED	RANDING	RANKER	RANZEL	RAPPE
RANCELS	RANDLORD	RANKERS	RANZELMAN	RAPPED
RANCES	RANDLORDS	RANKES	RANZELMEN	RAPPEE
RANCH	RANDO	RANKEST	RANZELS	RAPPEES
RANCHED	RANDOM	RANKING	RAOULIA	RAPPEL
RANCHER	RANDOMISE	RANKINGS	RAOULIAS	RAPPELED
RANCHERA	RANDOMIZE	RANKISH	RAP	RAPPELING
RANCHERAS	RANDOMLY	RANKISM	RAPACIOUS	RAPPELLED
RANCHERIA	RANDOMS	RANKISMS	RAPACITY	RAPPELS
RANCHERIE	RANDON	RANKIST	RAPE	RAPPEN
RANCHERO	RANDONS	RANKISTS	RAPED	RAPPER
RANCHEROS	RANDOS	RANKLE	RAPER	RAPPERS
RANCHERS	RANDS	RANKLED	RAPERS	RAPPES
RANCHES	RANDY	RANKLES	RAPES	RAPPING
RANCHETTE	RANEE	RANKLESS	RAPESEED	RAPPINGS
RANCHING	RANEES	RANKLING	RAPESEEDS	RAPPINI
RANCHINGS	RANG	RANKLY	RAPEY	RAPPINIS
RANCHLAND	RANGA	RANKNESS	RAPHAE	RAPPORT
RANCHLESS	RANGAS	RANKS	RAPHANIA	RAPPORTS
RANCHLIKE	RANGATIRA	RANKSHIFT	RAPHANIAS	RAPS
RANCHMAN	RANGE	RANPIKE	RAPHE	RAPT
RANCHMEN	RANGED	RANPIKES	RAPHES	RAPTLY
RANCHO	RANGELAND	RANSACK	RAPHIA	RAPTNESS
RANCHOS	RANGER	RANSACKED	RAPHIAS	RAPTOR

R

RAPTORIAL	RASCASSE	RASTA	RATEL	RATIOS
RAPTORS	RASCASSES	RASTAFARI	RATELS	RATITE
RAPTURE	RASCHEL	RASTER	RATEMETER	RATITES
RAPTURED	RASCHELS	RASTERED	RATEPAYER	RATLIKE
RAPTURES	RASE	RASTERING	RATER	RATLIN
RAPTURING	RASED	RASTERISE	RATERS	RATLINE
RAPTURISE	RASER	RASTERIZE	RATES	RATLINES
RAPTURIST	RASERS	RASTERS	RATFINK	RATLING
RAPTURIZE	RASES	RASTRUM	RATFINKS	RATLINGS
RAPTUROUS	RASH	RASTRUMS	RATFISH	RATLINS
RARE	RASHED	RASURE	RATFISHES	RATO
RAREBIT	RASHER	RASURES	RATFUCK	RATOO
RAREBITS	RASHERS	RAT	RATFUCKS	RATOON
RARED	RASHES	RATA	RATH	RATOONED
RAREE	RASHEST	RATABLE	RATHA	RATOONER
RAREFIED	RASHIE	RATABLES	RATHAS	RATOONERS
RAREFIER	RASHIES	RATABLY	RATHE	RATOONING
RAREFIERS	RASHING	RATAFEE	RATHER	RATOONS
RAREFIES	RASHLIKE	RATAFEES	RATHEREST	RATOOS
RAREFY	RASHLY	RATAFIA	RATHERIPE	RATOS
RAREFYING	RASHNESS	RATAFIAS	RATHERISH	RATPACK
RARELY	RASING	RATAL	RATHEST	RATPACKS
RARENESS	RASMALAI	RATALS	RATHOLE	RATPROOF
RARER	RASMALAIS	RATAN	RATHOLES	RATS
RARERIPE	RASORIAL	RATANIES	RATHOUSE	RATSBANE
RARERIPES	RASP	RATANS	RATHOUSES	RATSBANES
RARES	RASPATORY	RATANY	RATHRIPE	RATTAIL
RAREST	RASPBERRY	RATAPLAN	RATHRIPES	RATTAILED
RARIFIED	RASPED	RATAPLANS	RATHS	RATTAILS
RARIFIES	RASPER	RATAS	RATICIDE	RATTAN
RARIFY	RASPERS	RATATAT	RATICIDES	RATTANS
RARIFYING	RASPIER	RATATATS	RATIFIED	RATTED
RARING	RASPIEST	RATBAG	RATIFIER	RATTEEN
RARITIES	RASPINESS	RATBAGS	RATIFIERS	RATTEENS
RARITY	RASPING	RATBITE	RATIFIES	RATTEN
RARK	RASPINGLY	RATCH	RATIFY	RATTENED
RARKED	RASPINGS	RATCHED	RATIFYING	RATTENER
RARKING	RASPISH	RATCHES	RATINE	RATTENERS
RARKS	RASPS	RATCHET	RATINES	RATTENING
RAS	RASPY	RATCHETED	RATING	RATTENS
RASBORA	RASSE	RATCHETS	RATINGS	RATTER
RASBORAS	RASSES	RATCHING	RATIO	RATTERIES
RASCAILLE	RASSLE	RATE	RATION	RATTERS
RASCAL	RASSLED	RATEABLE	RATIONAL	RATTERY
RASCALDOM	RASSLER	RATEABLES	RATIONALE	RATTIER
RASCALISM	RASSLERS	RATEABLY	RATIONALS	RATTIEST
RASCALITY	RASSLES	RATED	RATIONED	RATTILY
RASCALLY	RASSLING	RATEEN	RATIONING	RATTINESS
RASCALS	RAST	RATEENS	RATIONS	RATTING

R

RATTINGS	RAUNS	RAVIGOTE	RAXING	RAZZED
RATTISH	RAUPATU	RAVIGOTES	RAY	RAZZES
RATTLE	RAUPATUS	RAVIGOTTE	RAYA	RAZZIA
RATTLEBAG	RAUPO	RAVIN	RAYAH	RAZZIAS
RATTLEBOX	RAUPOS	RAVINE	RAYAHS	RAZZING
RATTLED	RAURIKI	RAVINED	RAYAS	RAZZINGS
RATTLER	RAURIKIS	RAVINES	RAYED	RAZZLE
RATTLERS	RAUWOLFIA	RAVING	RAYGRASS	RAZZLES
RATTLES	RAV	RAVINGLY	RAYING	RE
RATTLIER	RAVAGE	RAVINGS	RAYLE	REABSORB
RATTLIEST	RAVAGED	RAVINING	RAYLED	REABSORBS
RATTLIN	RAVAGER	RAVINS	RAYLES	REACCEDE
RATTLINE	RAVAGERS	RAVIOLI	RAYLESS	REACCEDED
RATTLINES	RAVAGES	RAVIOLIS	RAYLESSLY	REACCEDES
RATTLING	RAVAGING	RAVISH	RAYLET	REACCENT
RATTLINGS	RAVE	RAVISHED	RAYLETS	REACCENTS
RATTLINS	RAVED	RAVISHER	RAYLIKE	REACCEPT
RATTLY	RAVEL	RAVISHERS	RAYLING	REACCEPTS
RATTON	RAVELED	RAVISHES	RAYNE	REACCLAIM
RATTONS	RAVELER	RAVISHING	RAYNES	REACCUSE
RATTOON	RAVELERS	RAVS	RAYON	REACCUSED
RATTOONED	RAVELIN	RAW	RAYONS	REACCUSES
RATTOONS	RAVELING	RAWARU	RAYS	REACH
RATTRAP	RAVELINGS	RAWARUS	RAZE	REACHABLE
RATTRAPS	RAVELINS	RAWBONE	RAZED	REACHED
RATTY	RAVELLED	RAWBONED	RAZEE	REACHER
RATU	RAVELLER	RAWER	RAZEED	REACHERS
RATUS	RAVELLERS	RAWEST	RAZEEING	REACHES
RAUCID	RAVELLIER	RAWHEAD	RAZEES	REACHING
RAUCITIES	RAVELLING	RAWHEADS	RAZER	REACHLESS
RAUCITY	RAVELLY	RAWHIDE	RAZERS	REACQUIRE
RAUCLE	RAVELMENT	RAWHIDED	RAZES	REACT
RAUCLER	RAVELS	RAWHIDES	RAZING	REACTANCE
RAUCLEST	RAVEN	RAWHIDING	RAZMATAZ	REACTANT
RAUCOUS	RAVENED	RAWIN	RAZOO	REACTANTS
RAUCOUSLY	RAVENER	RAWING	RAZOOS	REACTED
RAUGHT	RAVENERS	RAWINGS	RAZOR	REACTING
RAUN	RAVENEST	RAWINS	RAZORABLE	REACTION
RAUNCH	RAVENING	RAWISH	RAZORBACK	REACTIONS
RAUNCHED	RAVENINGS	RAWLY	RAZORBILL	REACTIVE
RAUNCHES	RAVENLIKE	RAWMAISH	RAZORCLAM	REACTOR
RAUNCHIER	RAVENOUS	RAWN	RAZORED	REACTORS
RAUNCHILY	RAVENS	RAWNESS	RAZORFISH	REACTS
RAUNCHING	RAVER	RAWNESSES	RAZORING	REACTUATE
RAUNCHY	RAVERS	RAWNS	RAZORS	READ
RAUNGE	RAVES	RAWS	RAZURE	READABLE
RAUNGED	RAVEY	RAX	RAZURES	READABLY
RAUNGES	RAVIER	RAXED	RAZZ	READAPT
RAUNGING	RAVIEST	RAXES	RAZZBERRY	READAPTED

READAPTS	REAGENT	REALNESS	REAPINGS	REASON
READD	REAGENTS	REALO	REAPPAREL	REASONED
READDED	REAGIN	REALOS	REAPPEAR	REASONER
READDICT	REAGINIC	REALS	REAPPEARS	REASONERS
READDICTS	REAGINS	REALTER	REAPPLIED	REASONING
READDING	REAIS	REALTERED	REAPPLIES	REASONS
READDRESS	REAK	REALTERS	REAPPLY	REASSAIL
READDS	REAKED	REALTIE	REAPPOINT	REASSAILS
READER	REAKING	REALTIES	REAPPROVE	REASSERT
READERLY	REAKS	REALTIME	REAPS	REASSERTS
READERS	REAL	REALTONE	REAR	REASSESS
READIED	REALER	REALTONES	REARED	REASSIGN
READIER	REALES	REALTOR	REARER	REASSIGNS
READIES	REALEST	REALTORS	REARERS	REASSORT
READIEST	REALGAR	REALTY	REARGUARD	REASSORTS
READILY	REALGARS	REAM	REARGUE	REASSUME
READINESS	REALIA	REAME	REARGUED	REASSUMED
READING	REALIGN	REAMED	REARGUES	REASSUMES
READINGS	REALIGNED	REAMEND	REARGUING	REASSURE
READJUST	REALIGNS	REAMENDED	REARHORSE	REASSURED
READJUSTS	REALISE	REAMENDS	REARING	REASSURER
README	REALISED	REAMER	REARINGS	REASSURES
READMES	REALISER	REAMERS	REARISE	REAST
READMIT	REALISERS	REAMES	REARISEN	REASTED
READMITS	REALISES	REAMIER	REARISES	REASTIER
READOPT	REALISING	REAMIEST	REARISING	REASTIEST
READOPTED	REALISM	REAMING	REARLY	REASTING
READOPTS	REALISMS	REAMS	REARM	REASTS
READORN	REALIST	REAMY	REARMED	REASTY
READORNED	REALISTIC	REAN	REARMICE	REATA
READORNS	REALISTS	REANALYSE	REARMING	REATAS
READOUT	REALITIES	REANALYZE	REARMOST	REATE
READOUTS	REALITY	REANIMATE	REARMOUSE	REATES
READS	REALIZE	REANNEX	REARMS	REATTACH
READVANCE	REALIZED	REANNEXED	REAROSE	REATTACK
READVISE	REALIZER	REANNEXES	REAROUSAL	REATTACKS
READVISED	REALIZERS	REANOINT	REAROUSE	REATTAIN
READVISES	REALIZES	REANOINTS	REAROUSED	REATTAINS
READY	REALIZING	REANS	REAROUSES	REATTEMPT
READYING	REALLIE	REANSWER	REARRANGE	REAVAIL
READYMADE	REALLIED	REANSWERS	REARREST	REAVAILED
REAEDIFY	REALLIES	REAP	REARRESTS	REAVAILS
REAEDIFYE	REALLOT	REAPABLE	REARS	REAVE
REAFFIRM	REALLOTS	REAPED	REARWARD	REAVED
REAFFIRMS	REALLY	REAPER	REARWARDS	REAVER
REAFFIX	REALLYING	REAPERS	REASCEND	REAVERS
REAFFIXED	REALM	REAPHOOK	REASCENDS	REAVES
REAFFIXES	REALMLESS	REAPHOOKS	REASCENT	REAVING
REAGENCY	REALMS	REAPING	REASCENTS	REAVOW

R

REAVOWED	REBECKS	REBOARDS	REBUFF	RECAMIER
REAVOWING	REBECS	REBOATION	REBUFFED	RECAMIERS
REAVOWS	REBEGAN	REBODIED	REBUFFING	RECANE
REAWAKE	REBEGIN	REBODIES	REBUFFS	RECANED
REAWAKED	REBEGINS	REBODY	REBUILD	RECANES
REAWAKEN	REBEGUN	REBODYING	REBUILDED	RECANING
REAWAKENS	REBEL	REBOIL	REBUILDS	RECANT
REAWAKES	REBELDOM	REBOILED	REBUILT	RECANTED
REAWAKING	REBELDOMS	REBOILING	REBUKABLE	RECANTER
REAWOKE	REBELLED	REBOILS	REBUKE	RECANTERS
REAWOKEN	REBELLER	REBOOK	REBUKED	RECANTING
REB	REBELLERS	REBOOKED	REBUKEFUL	RECANTS
REBACK	REBELLING	REBOOKING	REBUKER	RECAP
REBACKED	REBELLION	REBOOKS	REBUKERS	RECAPPED
REBACKING	REBELLOW	REBOOT	REBUKES	RECAPPING
REBACKS	REBELLOWS	REBOOTED	REBUKING	RECAPS
REBADGE	REBELS	REBOOTING	REBURIAL	RECAPTION
REBADGED	REBID	REBOOTS	REBURIALS	RECAPTOR
REBADGES	REBIDDEN	REBOP	REBURIED	RECAPTORS
REBADGING	REBIDDING	REBOPS	REBURIES	RECAPTURE
REBAIT	REBIDS	REBORE	REBURY	RECARPET
REBAITED	REBILL	REBORED	REBURYING	RECARPETS
REBAITING	REBILLED	REBORES	REBUS	RECARRIED
REBAITS	REBILLING	REBORING	REBUSES	RECARRIES
REBALANCE	REBILLS	REBORN	REBUT	RECARRY
REBAPTISE	REBIND	REBORROW	REBUTMENT	RECAST
REBAPTISM	REBINDING	REBORROWS	REBUTS	RECASTING
REBAPTIZE	REBINDS	REBOTTLE	REBUTTAL	RECASTS
REBAR	REBIRTH	REBOTTLED	REBUTTALS	RECATALOG
REBARS	REBIRTHER	REBOTTLES	REBUTTED	RECATCH
REBASE	REBIRTHS	REBOUGHT	REBUTTER	RECATCHES
REBASED	REBIT	REBOUND	REBUTTERS	RECAUGHT
REBASES	REBITE	REBOUNDED	REBUTTING	RECAUTION
REBASING	REBITES	REBOUNDER	REBUTTON	RECCE
REBATABLE	REBITING	REBOUNDS	REBUTTONS	RECCED
REBATE	REBITTEN	REBOZO	REBUY	RECCEED
REBATED	REBLEND	REBOZOS	REBUYING	RECCEING
REBATER	REBLENDED	REBRACE	REBUYS	RECCES
REBATERS	REBLENDS	REBRACED	REC	RECCIED
REBATES	REBLENT	REBRACES	RECAL	RECCIES
REBATING	REBLOCHON	REBRACING	RECALESCE	RECCO
REBATO	REBLOOM	REBRANCH	RECALL	RECCOS
REBATOES	REBLOOMED	REBRAND	RECALLED	RECCY
REBATOS	REBLOOMER	REBRANDED	RECALLER	RECCYING
REBBE	REBLOOMS	REBRANDS	RECALLERS	RECEDE
REBBES	REBLOSSOM	REBRED	RECALLING	RECEDED
REBBETZIN	REBOANT	REBREED	RECALLS	RECEDES
REBEC	REBOARD	REBREEDS	RECALMENT	RECEDING
REBECK	REBOARDED	REBS	RECALS	RECEIPT

RECEIPTED	RECHARGES	RECKANS	RECLUSIVE	RECOMPACT
RECEIPTOR	RECHART	RECKED	RECLUSORY	RECOMPILE
RECEIPTS	RECHARTED	RECKING	RECOAL	RECOMPOSE
RECEIVAL	RECHARTER	RECKLESS	RECOALED	RECOMPUTE
RECEIVALS	RECHARTS	RECKLING	RECOALING	RECON
RECEIVE	RECHATE	RECKLINGS	RECOALS	RECONCILE
RECEIVED	RECHATES	RECKON	RECOAT	RECONDITE
RECEIVER	RECHAUFFE	RECKONED	RECOATED	RECONDUCT
RECEIVERS	RECHEAT	RECKONER	RECOATING	RECONFER
RECEIVES	RECHEATED	RECKONERS	RECOATS	RECONFERS
RECEIVING	RECHEATS	RECKONING	RECOCK	RECONFINE
RECEMENT	RECHECK	RECKONS	RECOCKED	RECONFIRM
RECEMENTS	RECHECKED	RECKS	RECOCKING	RECONNECT
RECENCIES	RECHECKS	RECLAD	RECOCKS	RECONNED
RECENCY	RECHERCHE	RECLADDED	RECODE	RECONNING
RECENSE	RECHEW	RECLADS	RECODED	RECONQUER
RECENSED	RECHEWED	RECLAIM	RECODES	RECONS
RECENSES	RECHEWING	RECLAIMED	RECODIFY	RECONSIGN
RECENSING	RECHEWS	RECLAIMER	RECODING	RECONSOLE
RECENSION	RECHIE	RECLAIMS	RECOGNISE	RECONSULT
RECENSOR	RECHIP	RECLAME	RECOGNIZE	RECONTACT
RECENSORS	RECHIPPED	RECLAMES	RECOIL	RECONTOUR
RECENT	RECHIPS	RECLASP	RECOILED	RECONVENE
RECENTER	RECHLESSE	RECLASPED	RECOILER	RECONVERT
RECENTEST	RECHOOSE	RECLASPS	RECOILERS	RECONVEY
RECENTLY	RECHOOSES	RECLEAN	RECOILING	RECONVEYS
RECENTRE	RECHOSE	RECLEANED	RECOILS	RECONVICT
RECENTRED	RECHOSEN	RECLEANS	RECOIN	RECOOK
RECENTRES	RECIPE	RECLIMB	RECOINAGE	RECOOKED
RECEPT	RECIPES	RECLIMBED	RECOINED	RECOOKING
RECEPTION	RECIPIENT	RECLIMBS	RECOINING	RECOOKS
RECEPTIVE	RECIRCLE	RECLINATE	RECOINS	RECOPIED
RECEPTOR	RECIRCLED	RECLINE	RECOLLECT	RECOPIES
RECEPTORS	RECIRCLES	RECLINED	RECOLLET	RECOPY
RECEPTS	RECISION	RECLINER	RECOLLETS	RECOPYING
RECERTIFY	RECISIONS	RECLINERS	RECOLOR	RECORD
RECESS	RECIT	RECLINES	RECOLORED	RECORDED
RECESSED	RECITABLE	RECLINING	RECOLORS	RECORDER
RECESSES	RECITAL	RECLOSE	RECOLOUR	RECORDERS
RECESSING	RECITALS	RECLOSED	RECOLOURS	RECORDING
RECESSION	RECITE	RECLOSES	RECOMB	RECORDIST
RECESSIVE	RECITED	RECLOSING	RECOMBED	RECORDS
RECHANGE	RECITER	RECLOTHE	RECOMBINE	RECORK
RECHANGED	RECITERS	RECLOTHED	RECOMBING	RECORKED
RECHANGES	RECITES	RECLOTHES	RECOMBS	RECORKING
RECHANNEL	RECITING	RECLUSE	RECOMFORT	RECORKS
RECHARGE	RECITS	RECLUSELY	RECOMMEND	RECOUNT
RECHARGED	RECK	RECLUSES	RECOMMIT	RECOUNTAL
RECHARGER	RECKAN	RECLUSION	RECOMMITS	RECOUNTED

R

RECOUNTER	RECROWNED	RECURE	REDARGUE	REDDINGS
RECOUNTS	RECROWNS	RECURED	REDARGUED	REDDISH
RECOUP	RECRUIT	RECURES	REDARGUES	REDDISHLY
RECOUPE	RECRUITAL	RECURING	REDATE	REDDLE
RECOUPED	RECRUITED	RECURRED	REDATED	REDDLED
RECOUPES	RECRUITER	RECURRENT	REDATES	REDDLEMAN
RECOUPING	RECRUITS	RECURRING	REDATING	REDDLEMEN
RECOUPLE	RECS	RECURS	REDBACK	REDDLES
RECOUPLED	RECTA	RECURSION	REDBACKS	REDDLING
RECOUPLES	RECTAL	RECURSIVE	REDBAIT	REDDS
RECOUPS	RECTALLY	RECURVATE	REDBAITED	REDDY
RECOURE	RECTANGLE	RECURVE	REDBAITER	REDE
RECOURED	RECTI	RECURVED	REDBAITS	REDEAL
RECOURES	RECTIFIED	RECURVES	REDBAY	REDEALING
RECOURING	RECTIFIER	RECURVING	REDBAYS	REDEALS
RECOURSE	RECTIFIES	RECUSAL	REDBELLY	REDEALT
RECOURSED	RECTIFY	RECUSALS	REDBIRD	REDEAR
RECOURSES	RECTION	RECUSANCE	REDBIRDS	REDEARS
RECOVER	RECTIONS	RECUSANCY	REDBONE	REDECIDE
RECOVERED	RECTITIC	RECUSANT	REDBONES	REDECIDED
RECOVEREE	RECTITIS	RECUSANTS	REDBREAST	REDECIDES
RECOVERER	RECTITUDE	RECUSE	REDBRICK	REDECRAFT
RECOVEROR	RECTO	RECUSED	REDBRICKS	REDED
RECOVERS	RECTOCELE	RECUSES	REDBUD	REDEEM
RECOVERY	RECTOR	RECUSING	REDBUDS	REDEEMED
RECOWER	RECTORAL	RECUT	REDBUG	REDEEMER
RECOWERED	RECTORATE	RECUTS	REDBUGS	REDEEMERS
RECOWERS	RECTORESS	RECUTTING	REDBUSH	REDEEMING
RECOYLE	RECTORIAL	RECYCLATE	REDBUSHES	REDEEMS
RECOYLED	RECTORIES	RECYCLE	REDCAP	REDEFEAT
RECOYLES	RECTORS	RECYCLED	REDCAPS	REDEFEATS
RECOYLING	RECTORY	RECYCLER	REDCOAT	REDEFECT
RECRATE	RECTOS	RECYCLERS	REDCOATS	REDEFECTS
RECRATED	RECTRESS	RECYCLES	REDD	REDEFIED
RECRATES	RECTRICES	RECYCLING	REDDED	REDEFIES
RECRATING	RECTRIX	RECYCLIST	REDDEN	REDEFINE
RECREANCE	RECTUM	RED	REDDENDA	REDEFINED
RECREANCY	RECTUMS	REDACT	REDDENDO	REDEFINES
RECREANT	RECTUS	REDACTED	REDDENDOS	REDEFY
RECREANTS	RECUILE	REDACTING	REDDENDUM	REDEFYING
RECREATE	RECUILED	REDACTION	REDDENED	REDELESS
RECREATED	RECUILES	REDACTOR	REDDENING	REDELIVER
RECREATES	RECUILING	REDACTORS	REDDENS	REDEMAND
RECREATOR	RECULE	REDACTS	REDDER	REDEMANDS
RECREMENT	RECULED	REDAMAGE	REDDERS	REDENIED
RECROSS	RECULES	REDAMAGED	REDDEST	REDENIES
RECROSSED	RECULING	REDAMAGES	REDDIER	REDENY
RECROSSES	RECUMBENT	REDAN	REDDIEST	REDENYING
RECROWN	RECUR	REDANS	REDDING	REDEPLOY

R

REDEPLOYS	REDIVIDE	REDPOLLS	REDTAIL	REECHES
REDEPOSIT	REDIVIDED	REDRAFT	REDTAILS	REECHIE
REDES	REDIVIDES	REDRAFTED	REDTOP	REECHIER
REDESCEND	REDIVIVUS	REDRAFTS	REDTOPS	REECHIEST
REDESIGN	REDIVORCE	REDRAW	REDUB	REECHING
REDESIGNS	REDLEG	REDRAWER	REDUBBED	REECHO
REDEVELOP	REDLEGS	REDRAWERS	REDUBBING	REECHOED
REDEYE	REDLINE	REDRAWING	REDUBS	REECHOES
REDEYES	REDLINED	REDRAWN	REDUCE	REECHOING
REDFIN	REDLINER	REDRAWS	REDUCED	REECHY
REDFINS	REDLINERS	REDREAM	REDUCER	REED
REDFISH	REDLINES	REDREAMED	REDUCERS	REEDBED
REDFISHES	REDLINING	REDREAMS	REDUCES	REEDBEDS
REDFOOT	REDLY	REDREAMT	REDUCIBLE	REEDBIRD
REDFOOTS	REDNESS	REDRESS	REDUCIBLY	REEDBIRDS
REDHANDED	REDNESSES	REDRESSAL	REDUCING	REEDBUCK
REDHEAD	REDO	REDRESSED	REDUCTANT	REEDBUCKS
REDHEADED	REDOCK	REDRESSER	REDUCTASE	REEDE
REDHEADS	REDOCKED	REDRESSES	REDUCTION	REEDED
REDHORSE	REDOCKING	REDRESSOR	REDUCTIVE	REEDEN
REDHORSES	REDOCKS	REDREW	REDUCTOR	REEDER
REDIA	REDOES	REDRIED	REDUCTORS	REEDERS
REDIAE	REDOING	REDRIES	REDUIT	REEDES
REDIAL	REDOLENCE	REDRILL	REDUITS	REEDIER
REDIALED	REDOLENCY	REDRILLED	REDUNDANT	REEDIEST
REDIALING	REDOLENT	REDRILLS	REDUVIID	REEDIFIED
REDIALLED	REDON	REDRIVE	REDUVIIDS	REEDIFIES
REDIALS	REDONE	REDRIVEN	REDUX	REEDIFY
REDIAS	REDONNED	REDRIVES	REDWARE	REEDILY
REDICTATE	REDONNING	REDRIVING	REDWARES	REEDINESS
REDID	REDONS	REDROOT	REDWATER	REEDING
REDIGEST	REDOS	REDROOTS	REDWATERS	REEDINGS
REDIGESTS	REDOUBLE	REDROVE	REDWING	REEDIT
REDIGRESS	REDOUBLED	REDRY	REDWINGS	REEDITED
REDING	REDOUBLER	REDRYING	REDWOOD	REEDITING
REDINGOTE	REDOUBLES	REDS	REDWOODS	REEDITION
REDIP	REDOUBT	REDSEAR	REDYE	REEDITS
REDIPPED	REDOUBTED	REDSHANK	REDYED	REEDLIKE
REDIPPING	REDOUBTS	REDSHANKS	REDYEING	REEDLING
REDIPS	REDOUND	REDSHARE	REDYES	REEDLINGS
REDIPT	REDOUNDED	REDSHIFT	REE	REEDMAN
REDIRECT	REDOUNDS	REDSHIFTS	REEARN	REEDMEN
REDIRECTS	REDOUT	REDSHIRE	REEARNED	REEDS
REDISCUSS	REDOUTS	REDSHIRT	REEARNING	REEDSTOP
REDISPLAY	REDOWA	REDSHIRTS	REEARNS	REEDSTOPS
REDISPOSE	REDOWAS	REDSHORT	REEBOK	REEDUCATE
REDISTIL	REDOX	REDSTART	REEBOKS	REEDY
REDISTILL	REDOXES	REDSTARTS	REECH	REEF
REDISTILS	REDPOLL	REDSTREAK	REECHED	REEFABLE

REEFED	REEMPLOY	REEVOKE	REFENCE	REFINED
REEFER	REEMPLOYS	REEVOKED	REFENCED	REFINEDLY
REEFERS	REEN	REEVOKES	REFENCES	REFINER
REEFIER	REENACT	REEVOKING	REFENCING	REFINERS
REEFIEST	REENACTED	REEXAMINE	REFER	REFINERY
REEFING	REENACTOR	REEXECUTE	REFERABLE	REFINES
REEFINGS	REENACTS	REEXHIBIT	REFEREE	REFINING
REEFPOINT	REENDOW	REEXPEL	REFEREED	REFININGS
REEFS	REENDOWED	REEXPELS	REFEREES	REFINISH
REEFY	REENDOWS	REEXPLAIN	REFERENCE	REFIRE
REEJECT	REENFORCE	REEXPLORE	REFERENDA	REFIRED
REEJECTED	REENGAGE	REEXPORT	REFERENT	REFIRES
REEJECTS	REENGAGED	REEXPORTS	REFERENTS	REFIRING
REEK	REENGAGES	REEXPOSE	REFERRAL	REFIS
REEKED	REENGRAVE	REEXPOSED	REFERRALS	REFIT
REEKER	REENJOY	REEXPOSES	REFERRED	REFITMENT
REEKERS	REENJOYED	REEXPRESS	REFERRER	REFITS
REEKIE	REENJOYS	REF	REFERRERS	REFITTED
REEKIER	REENLARGE	REFACE	REFERRING	REFITTING
REEKIEST	REENLIST	REFACED	REFERS	REFIX
REEKING	REENLISTS	REFACES	REFFED	REFIXED
REEKINGLY	REENROLL	REFACING	REFFING	REFIXES
REEKS	REENROLLS	REFALL	REFFINGS	REFIXING
REEKY	REENS	REFALLEN	REFI	REFLAG
REEL	REENSLAVE	REFALLING	REFIGHT	REFLAGGED
REELABLE	REENTER	REFALLS	REFIGHTS	REFLAGS
REELECT	REENTERED	REFASHION	REFIGURE	REFLATE
REELECTED	REENTERS	REFASTEN	REFIGURED	REFLATED
REELECTS	REENTRANT	REFASTENS	REFIGURES	REFLATES
REELED	REENTRIES	REFECT	REFILE	REFLATING
REELER	REENTRY	REFECTED	REFILED	REFLATION
REELERS	REEQUIP	REFECTING	REFILES	REFLECT
REELEVATE	REEQUIPS	REFECTION	REFILING	REFLECTED
REELING	REERECT	REFECTIVE	REFILL	REFLECTER
REELINGLY	REERECTED	REFECTORY	REFILLED	REFLECTOR
REELINGS	REERECTS	REFECTS	REFILLING	REFLECTS
REELMAN	REES	REFED	REFILLS	REFLET
REELMEN	REEST	REFEED	REFILM	REFLETS
REELS	REESTED	REFEEDING	REFILMED	REFLEW
REEMBARK	REESTIER	REFEEDS	REFILMING	REFLEX
REEMBARKS	REESTIEST	REFEEL	REFILMS	REFLEXED
REEMBODY	REESTING	REFEELING	REFILTER	REFLEXES
REEMBRACE	REESTS	REFEELS	REFILTERS	REFLEXING
REEMERGE	REESTY	REFEL	REFINABLE	REFLEXION
REEMERGED	REEVE	REFELL	REFINANCE	REFLEXIVE
REEMERGES	REEVED	REFELLED	REFIND	REFLEXLY
REEMIT	REEVES	REFELLING	REFINDING	REFLIES
REEMITS	REEVESHIP	REFELS	REFINDS	REFLOAT
REEMITTED	REEVING	REFELT	REFINE	REFLOATED

REFLOATS	REFORTIFY	REFUGIA	REGALED	REGES
REFLOOD	REFOUGHT	REFUGING	REGALER	REGEST
REFLOODED	REFOUND	REFUGIUM	REGALERS	REGESTED
REFLOODS	REFOUNDED	REFULGENT	REGALES	REGESTING
REFLOW	REFOUNDER	REFUND	REGALIA	REGESTS
REFLOWED	REFOUNDS	REFUNDED	REGALIAN	REGEX
REFLOWER	REFRACT	REFUNDER	REGALIAS	REGEXES
REFLOWERS	REFRACTED	REFUNDERS	REGALING	REGGAE
REFLOWING	REFRACTOR	REFUNDING	REGALISM	REGGAES
REFLOWN	REFRACTS	REFUNDS	REGALISMS	REGGAETON
REFLOWS	REFRAIN	REFURB	REGALIST	REGGO
REFLUENCE	REFRAINED	REFURBED	REGALISTS	REGGOS
REFLUENT	REFRAINER	REFURBING	REGALITY	REGICIDAL
REFLUX	REFRAINS	REFURBISH	REGALLY	REGICIDE
REFLUXED	REFRAME	REFURBS	REGALNESS	REGICIDES
REFLUXES	REFRAMED	REFURNISH	REGALS	REGIE
REFLUXING	REFRAMES	REFUSABLE	REGAR	REGIES
REFLY	REFRAMING	REFUSAL	REGARD	REGIFT
REFLYING	REFREEZE	REFUSALS	REGARDANT	REGIFTED
REFOCUS	REFREEZES	REFUSE	REGARDED	REGIFTER
REFOCUSED	REFRESH	REFUSED	REGARDER	REGIFTERS
REFOCUSES	REFRESHED	REFUSENIK	REGARDERS	REGIFTING
REFOLD	REFRESHEN	REFUSER	REGARDFUL	REGIFTS
REFOLDED	REFRESHER	REFUSERS	REGARDING	REGILD
REFOLDING	REFRESHES	REFUSES	REGARDS	REGILDED
REFOLDS	REFRIED	REFUSING	REGARS	REGILDING
REFOOT	REFRIES	REFUSION	REGATHER	REGILDS
REFOOTED	REFRINGE	REFUSIONS	REGATHERS	REGILT
REFOOTING	REFRINGED	REFUSNIK	REGATTA	REGIME
REFOOTS	REFRINGES	REFUSNIKS	REGATTAS	REGIMEN
REFOREST	REFRONT	REFUTABLE	REGAUGE	REGIMENS
REFORESTS	REFRONTED	REFUTABLY	REGAUGED	REGIMENT
REFORGE	REFRONTS	REFUTAL	REGAUGES	REGIMENTS
REFORGED	REFROZE	REFUTALS	REGAUGING	REGIMES
REFORGES	REFROZEN	REFUTE	REGAVE	REGIMINAL
REFORGING	REFRY	REFUTED	REGEAR	REGINA
REFORM	REFRYING	REFUTER	REGEARED	REGINAE
REFORMADE	REFS	REFUTERS	REGEARING	REGINAL
REFORMADO	REFT	REFUTES	REGEARS	REGINAS
REFORMAT	REFUEL	REFUTING	REGELATE	REGION
REFORMATE	REFUELED	REG	REGELATED	REGIONAL
REFORMATS	REFUELING	REGAIN	REGELATES	REGIONALS
REFORMED	REFUELLED	REGAINED	REGENCE	REGIONARY
REFORMER	REFUELS	REGAINER	REGENCES	REGIONS
REFORMERS	REFUGE	REGAINERS	REGENCIES	REGISSEUR
REFORMING	REFUGED	REGAINING	REGENCY	REGISTER
REFORMISM	REFUGEE	REGAINS	REGENT	REGISTERS
REFORMIST	REFUGEES	REGAL	REGENTAL	REGISTRAR
REFORMS	REFUGES	REGALE	REGENTS	REGISTRY

REGIUS	REGRANT	REGS	REHEARD	REIFIES
REGIVE	REGRANTED	REGUERDON	REHEARING	REIFS
REGIVEN	REGRANTS	REGULA	REHEARS	REIFY
REGIVES	REGRATE	REGULABLE	REHEARSAL	REIFYING
REGIVING	REGRATED	REGULAE	REHEARSE	REIGN
REGLAZE	REGRATER	REGULAR	REHEARSED	REIGNED
REGLAZED	REGRATERS	REGULARLY	REHEARSER	REIGNING
REGLAZES	REGRATES	REGULARS	REHEARSES	REIGNITE
REGLAZING	REGRATING	REGULATE	REHEAT	REIGNITED
REGLET	REGRATOR	REGULATED	REHEATED	REIGNITES
REGLETS	REGRATORS	REGULATES	REHEATER	REIGNS
REGLORIFY	REGREDE	REGULATOR	REHEATERS	REIK
REGLOSS	REGREDED	REGULI	REHEATING	REIKI
REGLOSSED	REGREDES	REGULINE	REHEATS	REIKIS
REGLOSSES	REGREDING	REGULISE	REHEEL	REIKS
REGLOW	REGREEN	REGULISED	REHEELED	REILLUME
REGLOWED	REGREENED	REGULISES	REHEELING	REILLUMED
REGLOWING	REGREENS	REGULIZE	REHEELS	REILLUMES
REGLOWS	REGREET	REGULIZED	REHEM	REIMAGE
REGLUE	REGREETED	REGULIZES	REHEMMED	REIMAGED
REGLUED	REGREETS	REGULO	REHEMMING	REIMAGES
REGLUES	REGRESS	REGULOS	REHEMS	REIMAGINE
REGLUING	REGRESSED	REGULUS	REHINGE	REIMAGING
REGMA	REGRESSES	REGULUSES	REHINGED	REIMBURSE
REGMAKER	REGRESSOR	REGUR	REHINGES	REIMMERSE
REGMAKERS	REGRET	REGURS	REHINGING	REIMPLANT
REGMATA	REGRETFUL	REH	REHIRE	REIMPORT
REGNA	REGRETS	REHAB	REHIRED	REIMPORTS
REGNAL	REGRETTED	REHABBED	REHIRES	REIMPOSE
REGNANCY	REGRETTER	REHABBER	REHIRING	REIMPOSED
REGNANT	REGREW	REHABBERS	REHOBOAM	REIMPOSES
REGNUM	REGRIND	REHABBING	REHOBOAMS	REIN
REGO	REGRINDS	REHABS	REHOME	REINCITE
REGOLITH	REGROOM	REHAMMER	REHOMED	REINCITED
REGOLITHS	REGROOMED	REHAMMERS	REHOMES	REINCITES
REGORGE	REGROOMS	REHANDLE	REHOMING	REINCUR
REGORGED	REGROOVE	REHANDLED	REHOMINGS	REINCURS
REGORGES	REGROOVED	REHANDLES	REHOUSE	REINDEER
REGORGING	REGROOVES	REHANG	REHOUSED	REINDEERS
REGOS	REGROUND	REHANGED	REHOUSES	REINDEX
REGOSOL	REGROUP	REHANGING	REHOUSING	REINDEXED
REGOSOLS	REGROUPED	REHANGS	REHS	REINDEXES
REGRADE	REGROUPS	REHARDEN	REHUNG	REINDICT
REGRADED	REGROW	REHARDENS	REHYDRATE	REINDICTS
REGRADES	REGROWING	REHASH	REI	REINDUCE
REGRADING	REGROWN	REHASHED	REIF	REINDUCED
REGRAFT	REGROWS	REHASHES	REIFIED	REINDUCES
REGRAFTED	REGROWTH	REHASHING	REIFIER	REINDUCT
REGRAFTS	REGROWTHS	REHEAR	REIFIERS	REINDUCTS

R

REINED	REINVENTS	REJECTERS	REKING	RELAXABLE
REINETTE	REINVEST	REJECTING	REKNIT	RELAXANT
REINETTES	REINVESTS	REJECTION	REKNITS	RELAXANTS
REINFECT	REINVITE	REJECTIVE	REKNITTED	RELAXED
REINFECTS	REINVITED	REJECTOR	REKNOT	RELAXEDLY
REINFLAME	REINVITES	REJECTORS	REKNOTS	RELAXER
REINFLATE	REINVOKE	REJECTS	REKNOTTED	RELAXERS
REINFORCE	REINVOKED	REJIG	RELABEL	RELAXES
REINFORM	REINVOKES	REJIGGED	RELABELED	RELAXIN
REINFORMS	REINVOLVE	REJIGGER	RELABELS	RELAXING
REINFUND	REIRD	REJIGGERS	RELACE	RELAXINS
REINFUNDS	REIRDS	REJIGGING	RELACED	RELAY
REINFUSE	REIS	REJIGS	RELACES	RELAYED
REINFUSED	REISES	REJOICE	RELACHE	RELAYING
REINFUSES	REISHI	REJOICED	RELACHES	RELAYS
REINHABIT	REISHIS	REJOICER	RELACING	RELEARN
REINING	REISSUE	REJOICERS	RELACQUER	RELEARNED
REINJECT	REISSUED	REJOICES	RELAID	RELEARNS
REINJECTS	REISSUER	REJOICING	RELAND	RELEARNT
REINJURE	REISSUERS	REJOIN	RELANDED	RELEASE
REINJURED	REISSUES	REJOINDER	RELANDING	RELEASED
REINJURES	REISSUING	REJOINED	RELANDS	RELEASEE
REINJURY	REIST	REJOINING	RELAPSE	RELEASEES
REINK	REISTAFEL	REJOINS	RELAPSED	RELEASER
REINKED	REISTED	REJON	RELAPSER	RELEASERS
REINKING	REISTING	REJONEO	RELAPSERS	RELEASES
REINKS	REISTS	REJONEOS	RELAPSES	RELEASING
REINLESS	REITBOK	REJONES	RELAPSING	RELEASOR
REINS	REITBOKS	REJOURN	RELATA	RELEASORS
REINSERT	REITER	REJOURNED	RELATABLE	RELEGABLE
REINSERTS	REITERANT	REJOURNS	RELATABLY	RELEGATE
REINSMAN	REITERATE	REJUDGE	RELATE	RELEGATED
REINSMEN	REITERED	REJUDGED	RELATED	RELEGATES
REINSPECT	REITERING	REJUDGES	RELATEDLY	RELEND
REINSPIRE	REITERS	REJUDGING	RELATER	RELENDING
REINSTAL	REIVE	REJUGGLE	RELATERS	RELENDS
REINSTALL	REIVED	REJUGGLED	RELATES	RELENT
REINSTALS	REIVER	REJUGGLES	RELATING	RELENTED
REINSTATE	REIVERS	REJUSTIFY	RELATION	RELENTING
REINSURE	REIVES	REKE	RELATIONS	RELENTS
REINSURED	REIVING	REKED	RELATIVAL	RELET
REINSURER	REIVINGS	REKES	RELATIVE	RELETS
REINSURES	REJACKET	REKEY	RELATIVES	RELETTER
REINTER	REJACKETS	REKEYED	RELATOR	RELETTERS
REINTERS	REJECT	REKEYING	RELATORS	RELETTING
REINVADE	REJECTED	REKEYS	RELATUM	RELEVANCE
REINVADED	REJECTEE	REKINDLE	RELAUNCH	RELEVANCY
REINVADES	REJECTEES	REKINDLED	RELAUNDER	RELEVANT
REINVENT	REJECTER	REKINDLES	RELAX	RELEVE

RELEVES	RELIQUEFY	RELOCKING	REMANENCY	REMEDED
RELIABLE	RELIQUES	RELOCKS	REMANENT	REMEDES
RELIABLES	RELIQUIAE	RELOOK	REMANENTS	REMEDIAL
RELIABLY	RELIQUIFY	RELOOKED	REMANET	REMEDIAT
RELIANCE	RELISH	RELOOKING	REMANETS	REMEDIATE
RELIANCES	RELISHED	RELOOKS	REMANIE	REMEDIED
RELIANT	RELISHES	RELUCENT	REMANIES	REMEDIES
RELIANTLY	RELISHING	RELUCT	REMANNED	REMEDING
RELIC	RELIST	RELUCTANT	REMANNING	REMEDY
RELICENSE	RELISTED	RELUCTATE	REMANS	REMEDYING
RELICS	RELISTEN	RELUCTED	REMAP	REMEET
RELICT	RELISTENS	RELUCTING	REMAPPED	REMEETING
RELICTION	RELISTING	RELUCTS	REMAPPING	REMEETS
RELICTS	RELISTS	RELUME	REMAPS	REMEID
RELIDE	RELIT	RELUMED	REMARK	REMEIDED
RELIE	RELIVABLE	RELUMES	REMARKED	REMEIDING
RELIED	RELIVE	RELUMINE	REMARKER	REMEIDS
RELIEF	RELIVED	RELUMINED	REMARKERS	REMELT
RELIEFS	RELIVER	RELUMINES	REMARKET	REMELTED
RELIER	RELIVERED	RELUMING	REMARKETS	REMELTING
RELIERS	RELIVERS	RELY	REMARKING	REMELTS
RELIES	RELIVES	RELYING	REMARKS	REMEMBER
RELIEVE	RELIVING	REM	REMARQUE	REMEMBERS
RELIEVED	RELLENO	REMADE	REMARQUED	REMEN
RELIEVER	RELLENOS	REMADES	REMARQUES	REMEND
RELIEVERS	RELLIE	REMAIL	REMARRIED	REMENDED
RELIEVES	RELLIES	REMAILED	REMARRIES	REMENDING
RELIEVING	RELLISH	REMAILER	REMARRY	REMENDS
RELIEVO	RELLISHED	REMAILERS	REMASTER	REMENS
RELIEVOS	RELLISHES	REMAILING	REMASTERS	REMERCIED
RELIGHT	RELLO	REMAILS	REMATCH	REMERCIES
RELIGHTED	RELLOS	REMAIN	REMATCHED	REMERCY
RELIGHTS	RELOAD	REMAINDER	REMATCHES	REMERGE
RELIGIEUX	RELOADED	REMAINED	REMATE	REMERGED
RELIGION	RELOADER	REMAINER	REMATED	REMERGES
RELIGIONS	RELOADERS	REMAINERS	REMATES	REMERGING
RELIGIOSE	RELOADING	REMAINING	REMATING	REMET
RELIGIOSO	RELOADS	REMAINS	REMBLAI	REMEX
RELIGIOUS	RELOAN	REMAKE	REMBLAIS	REMIGATE
RELINE	RELOANED	REMAKER	REMBLE	REMIGATED
RELINED	RELOANING	REMAKERS	REMBLED	REMIGATES
RELINES	RELOANS	REMAKES	REMBLES	REMIGES
RELINING	RELOCATE	REMAKING	REMBLING	REMIGIAL
RELINK	RELOCATED	REMAN	REMEAD	REMIGRATE
RELINKED	RELOCATEE	REMAND	REMEADED	REMIND
RELINKING	RELOCATES	REMANDED	REMEADING	REMINDED
RELINKS	RELOCATOR	REMANDING	REMEADS	REMINDER
RELIQUARY	RELOCK	REMANDS	REMEASURE	REMINDERS
RELIQUE	RELOCKED	REMANENCE	REMEDE	REMINDFUL

R

REMINDING	REMOLADE	RENAGUE	RENEGED	RENITENT
REMINDS	REMOLADES	RENAGUED	RENEGER	RENK
REMINISCE	REMOLD	RENAGUES	RENEGERS	RENKER
REMINT	REMOLDED	RENAGUING	RENEGES	RENKEST
REMINTED	REMOLDING	RENAIL	RENEGING	RENMINBI
REMINTING	REMOLDS	RENAILED	RENEGUE	RENMINBIS
REMINTS	REMONTANT	RENAILING	RENEGUED	RENNASE
REMISE	REMONTOIR	RENAILS	RENEGUER	RENNASES
REMISED	REMORA	RENAL	RENEGUERS	RENNE
REMISES	REMORAS	RENAME	RENEGUES	RENNED
REMISING	REMORID	RENAMED	RENEGUING	RENNES
REMISS	REMORSE	RENAMES	RENEST	RENNET
REMISSION	REMORSES	RENAMING	RENESTED	RENNETS
REMISSIVE	REMOTE	RENASCENT	RENESTING	RENNIN
REMISSLY	REMOTELY	RENATURE	RENESTS	RENNING
REMISSORY	REMOTER	RENATURED	RENEW	RENNINGS
REMIT	REMOTES	RENATURES	RENEWABLE	RENNINS
REMITMENT	REMOTEST	RENAY	RENEWABLY	RENO
REMITS	REMOTION	RENAYED	RENEWAL	RENOGRAM
REMITTAL	REMOTIONS	RENAYING	RENEWALS	RENOGRAMS
REMITTALS	REMOUD	RENAYS	RENEWED	RENOS
REMITTED	REMOULADE	RENCONTRE	RENEWEDLY	RENOTIFY
REMITTEE	REMOULD	REND	RENEWER	RENOUNCE
REMITTEES	REMOULDED	RENDANG	RENEWERS	RENOUNCED
REMITTENT	REMOULDS	RENDANGS	RENEWING	RENOUNCER
REMITTER	REMOUNT	RENDED	RENEWINGS	RENOUNCES
REMITTERS	REMOUNTED	RENDER	RENEWS	RENOVATE
REMITTING	REMOUNTS	RENDERED	RENEY	RENOVATED
REMITTOR	REMOVABLE	RENDERER	RENEYED	RENOVATES
REMITTORS	REMOVABLY	RENDERERS	RENEYING	RENOVATOR
REMIX	REMOVAL	RENDERING	RENEYS	RENOWN
REMIXED	REMOVALS	RENDERS	RENFIERST	RENOWNED
REMIXER	REMOVE	RENDIBLE	RENFORCE	RENOWNER
REMIXERS	REMOVED	RENDING	RENFORCED	RENOWNERS
REMIXES	REMOVEDLY	RENDITION	RENFORCES	RENOWNING
REMIXING	REMOVER	RENDS	RENFORST	RENOWNS
REMIXT	REMOVERS	RENDZINA	RENGA	RENS
REMIXTURE	REMOVES	RENDZINAS	RENGAS	RENT
REMNANT	REMOVING	RENEAGUE	RENIED	RENTABLE
REMNANTAL	REMS	RENEAGUED	RENIES	RENTAL
REMNANTS	REMUAGE	RENEAGUES	RENIFORM	RENTALLER
REMOANER	REMUAGES	RENEGADE	RENIG	RENTALS
REMOANERS	REMUDA	RENEGADED	RENIGGED	RENTE
REMODEL	REMUDAS	RENEGADES	RENIGGING	RENTED
REMODELED	REMUEUR	RENEGADO	RENIGS	RENTER
REMODELER	REMUEURS	RENEGADOS	RENIN	RENTERS
REMODELS	REMURMUR	RENEGATE	RENINS	RENTES
REMODIFY	REMURMURS	RENEGATES	RENITENCE	RENTIER
REMOISTEN	REN	RENEGE	RENITENCY	RENTIERS

RENTING	REORGED	REPASSED	REPENTER	REPLANS
RENTINGS	REORGING	REPASSES	REPENTERS	REPLANT
RENTS	REORGS	REPASSING	REPENTING	REPLANTED
RENUMBER	REORIENT	REPAST	REPENTS	REPLANTS
RENUMBERS	REORIENTS	REPASTED	REPEOPLE	REPLASTER
RENVERSE	REOS	REPASTING	REPEOPLED	REPLATE
RENVERSED	REOUTFIT	REPASTS	REPEOPLES	REPLATED
RENVERSES	REOUTFITS	REPASTURE	REPERCUSS	REPLATES
RENVERST	REOVIRUS	REPATCH	REPEREPE	REPLATING
RENVOI	REOXIDISE	REPATCHED	REPEREPES	REPLAY
RENVOIS	REOXIDIZE	REPATCHES	REPERK	REPLAYED
RENVOY	REP	REPATTERN	REPERKED	REPLAYING
RENVOYS	REPACIFY	REPAVE	REPERKING	REPLAYS
RENY	REPACK	REPAVED	REPERKS	REPLEAD
RENYING	REPACKAGE	REPAVES	REPERTORY	REPLEADED
REO	REPACKED	REPAVING	REPERUSAL	REPLEADER
REOBJECT	REPACKING	REPAY	REPERUSE	REPLEADS
REOBJECTS	REPACKS	REPAYABLE	REPERUSED	REPLED
REOBSERVE	REPAID	REPAYING	REPERUSES	REPLEDGE
REOBTAIN	REPAINT	REPAYMENT	REPETEND	REPLEDGED
REOBTAINS	REPAINTED	REPAYS	REPETENDS	REPLEDGES
REOCCUPY	REPAINTS	REPEAL	REPHRASE	REPLENISH
REOCCUR	REPAIR	REPEALED	REPHRASED	REPLETE
REOCCURS	REPAIRED	REPEALER	REPHRASES	REPLETED
REOFFEND	REPAIRER	REPEALERS	REPIGMENT	REPLETELY
REOFFENDS	REPAIRERS	REPEALING	REPIN	REPLETES
REOFFER	REPAIRING	REPEALS	REPINE	REPLETING
REOFFERED	REPAIRMAN	REPEAT	REPINED	REPLETION
REOFFERS	REPAIRMEN	REPEATED	REPINER	REPLEVIED
REOIL	REPAIRS	REPEATER	REPINERS	REPLEVIES
REOILED	REPAND	REPEATERS	REPINES	REPLEVIN
REOILING	REPANDLY	REPEATING	REPINING	REPLEVINS
REOILS	REPANEL	REPEATS	REPININGS	REPLEVY
REOPEN	REPANELED	REPECHAGE	REPINNED	REPLICA
REOPENED	REPANELS	REPEG	REPINNING	REPLICANT
REOPENER	REPAPER	REPEGGED	REPINS	REPLICAS
REOPENERS	REPAPERED	REPEGGING	REPIQUE	REPLICASE
REOPENING	REPAPERS	REPEGS	REPIQUED	REPLICATE
REOPENS	REPARABLE	REPEL	REPIQUES	REPLICON
REOPERATE	REPARABLY	REPELLANT	REPIQUING	REPLICONS
REOPPOSE	REPARK	REPELLED	REPLA	REPLIED
REOPPOSED	REPARKED	REPELLENT	REPLACE	REPLIER
REOPPOSES	REPARKING	REPELLER	REPLACED	REPLIERS
REORDAIN	REPARKS	REPELLERS	REPLACER	REPLIES
REORDAINS	REPARTEE	REPELLING	REPLACERS	REPLOT
REORDER	REPARTEED	REPELS	REPLACES	REPLOTS
REORDERED	REPARTEES	REPENT	REPLACING	REPLOTTED
REORDERS	REPASS	REPENTANT	REPLAN	REPLOUGH
REORG	REPASSAGE	REPENTED	REPLANNED	REPLOUGHS

R

REPLOW	REPOSITED	REPRIMAND	REPRYVING	REPUTED
REPLOWED	REPOSITOR	REPRIME	REPS	REPUTEDLY
REPLOWING	REPOSITS	REPRIMED	REPTANT	REPUTES
REPLOWS	REPOSSESS	REPRIMES	REPTATION	REPUTING
REPLUM	REPOST	REPRIMING	REPTILE	REPUTINGS
REPLUMB	REPOSTED	REPRINT	REPTILES	REQUALIFY
REPLUMBED	REPOSTING	REPRINTED	REPTILIA	REQUERE
REPLUMBS	REPOSTS	REPRINTER	REPTILIAN	REQUERED
REPLUNGE	REPOSURE	REPRINTS	REPTILIUM	REQUERES
REPLUNGED	REPOSURES	REPRISAL	REPTILOID	REQUERING
REPLUNGES	REPOT	REPRISALS	REPUBLIC	REQUEST
REPLY	REPOTS	REPRISE	REPUBLICS	REQUESTED
REPLYING	REPOTTED	REPRISED	REPUBLISH	REQUESTER
REPO	REPOTTING	REPRISES	REPUDIATE	REQUESTOR
REPOINT	REPOUR	REPRISING	REPUGN	REQUESTS
REPOINTED	REPOURED	REPRIVE	REPUGNANT	REQUICKEN
REPOINTS	REPOURING	REPRIVED	REPUGNED	REQUIEM
REPOLISH	REPOURS	REPRIVES	REPUGNING	REQUIEMS
REPOLL	REPOUSSE	REPRIVING	REPUGNS	REQUIGHT
REPOLLED	REPOUSSES	REPRIZE	REPULP	REQUIGHTS
REPOLLING	REPOWER	REPRIZED	REPULPED	REQUIN
REPOLLS	REPOWERED	REPRIZES	REPULPING	REQUINS
REPOMAN	REPOWERS	REPRIZING	REPULPS	REQUINTO
REPOMEN	REPP	REPRO	REPULSE	REQUINTOS
REPONE	REPPED	REPROACH	REPULSED	REQUIRE
REPONED	REPPING	REPROBACY	REPULSER	REQUIRED
REPONES	REPPINGS	REPROBATE	REPULSERS	REQUIRER
REPONING	REPPS	REPROBE	REPULSES	REQUIRERS
REPORT	REPREEVE	REPROBED	REPULSING	REQUIRES
REPORTAGE	REPREEVED	REPROBES	REPULSION	REQUIRING
REPORTED	REPREEVES	REPROBING	REPULSIVE	REQUISITE
REPORTER	REPREHEND	REPROCESS	REPUMP	REQUIT
REPORTERS	REPRESENT	REPRODUCE	REPUMPED	REQUITAL
REPORTING	REPRESS	REPROGRAM	REPUMPING	REQUITALS
REPORTS	REPRESSED	REPROOF	REPUMPS	REQUITE
REPOS	REPRESSER	REPROOFED	REPUNIT	REQUITED
REPOSAL	REPRESSES	REPROOFS	REPUNITS	REQUITER
REPOSALL	REPRESSOR	REPROS	REPURE	REQUITERS
REPOSALLS	REPRICE	REPROVAL	REPURED	REQUITES
REPOSALS	REPRICED	REPROVALS	REPURES	REQUITING
REPOSE	REPRICES	REPROVE	REPURIFY	REQUITS
REPOSED	REPRICING	REPROVED	REPURING	REQUITTED
REPOSEDLY	REPRIEFE	REPROVER	REPURPOSE	REQUOTE
REPOSEFUL	REPRIEFES	REPROVERS	REPURSUE	REQUOTED
REPOSER	REPRIEVAL	REPROVES	REPURSUED	REQUOTES
REPOSERS	REPRIEVE	REPROVING	REPURSUES	REQUOTING
REPOSES	REPRIEVED	REPRYVE	REPUTABLE	REQUOYLE
REPOSING	REPRIEVER	REPRYVED	REPUTABLY	REQUOYLED
REPOSIT	REPRIEVES	REPRYVES	REPUTE	REQUOYLES

RERACK	RERISES	RESCALE	RESECURED	RESERVING
RERACKED	RERISING	RESCALED	RESECURES	RESERVIST
RERACKING	REROLL	RESCALES	RESEDA	RESERVOIR
RERACKS	REROLLED	RESCALING	RESEDAS	RESES
RERADIATE	REROLLER	RESCHOOL	RESEE	RESET
RERAIL	REROLLERS	RESCHOOLS	RESEED	RESETS
RERAILED	REROLLING	RESCIND	RESEEDED	RESETTED
RERAILING	REROLLS	RESCINDED	RESEEDING	RESETTER
RERAILS	REROOF	RESCINDER	RESEEDS	RESETTERS
RERAISE	REROOFED	RESCINDS	RESEEING	RESETTING
RERAISED	REROOFING	RESCORE	RESEEK	RESETTLE
RERAISES	REROOFS	RESCORED	RESEEKING	RESETTLED
RERAISING	REROSE	RESCORES	RESEEKS	RESETTLES
RERAN	REROUTE	RESCORING	RESEEN	RESEW
REREAD	REROUTED	RESCREEN	RESEES	RESEWED
REREADING	REROUTES	RESCREENS	RESEIZE	RESEWING
REREADS	REROUTING	RESCRIPT	RESEIZED	RESEWN
REREBRACE	RERUN	RESCRIPTS	RESEIZES	RESEWS
RERECORD	RERUNNING	RESCUABLE	RESEIZING	RESH
RERECORDS	RERUNS	RESCUE	RESEIZURE	RESHAPE
REREDOS	RES	RESCUED	RESELECT	RESHAPED
REREDOSES	RESADDLE	RESCUEE	RESELECTS	RESHAPER
REREDOSSE	RESADDLED	RESCUEES	RESELL	RESHAPERS
RERELEASE	RESADDLES	RESCUER	RESELLER	RESHAPES
REREMAI	RESAID	RESCUERS	RESELLERS	RESHAPING
REREMAIS	RESAIL	RESCUES	RESELLING	RESHARPEN
REREMICE	RESAILED	RESCUING	RESELLS	RESHAVE
REREMIND	RESAILING	RESCULPT	RESEMBLE	RESHAVED
REREMINDS	RESAILS	RESCULPTS	RESEMBLED	RESHAVEN
REREMOUSE	RESALABLE	RESEAL	RESEMBLER	RESHAVES
RERENT	RESALE	RESEALED	RESEMBLES	RESHAVING
RERENTED	RESALES	RESEALING	RESEND	RESHES
RERENTING	RESALGAR	RESEALS	RESENDING	RESHINE
RERENTS	RESALGARS	RESEARCH	RESENDS	RESHINED
REREPEAT	RESALUTE	RESEASON	RESENT	RESHINES
REREPEATS	RESALUTED	RESEASONS	RESENTED	RESHINGLE
REREVIEW	RESALUTES	RESEAT	RESENTER	RESHINING
REREVIEWS	RESAMPLE	RESEATED	RESENTERS	RESHIP
REREVISE	RESAMPLED	RESEATING	RESENTFUL	RESHIPPED
REREVISED	RESAMPLES	RESEATS	RESENTING	RESHIPPER
REREVISES	RESAT	RESEAU	RESENTIVE	RESHIPS
REREWARD	RESAW	RESEAUS	RESENTS	RESHOD
REREWARDS	RESAWED	RESEAUX	RESERPINE	RESHOE
RERIG	RESAWING	RESECT	RESERVE	RESHOED
RERIGGED	RESAWN	RESECTED	RESERVED	RESHOEING
RERIGGING	RESAWS	RESECTING	RESERVER	RESHOES
RERIGS	RESAY	RESECTION	RESERVERS	RESHONE
RERISE	RESAYING	RESECTS	RESERVES	RESHOOT
RERISEN	RESAYS	RESECURE	RESERVICE	RESHOOTS

R

RESHORING	RESILED	RESITES	RESOLDERS	RESPACED
RESHOT	RESILES	RESITING	RESOLE	RESPACES
RESHOW	RESILIENT	RESITS	RESOLED	RESPACING
RESHOWED	RESILIN	RESITTING	RESOLES	RESPADE
RESHOWER	RESILING	RESITUATE	RESOLING	RESPADED
RESHOWERS	RESILINS	RESIZABLE	RESOLUBLE	RESPADES
RESHOWING	RESILVER	RESIZE	RESOLUTE	RESPADING
RESHOWN	RESILVERS	RESIZED	RESOLUTER	RESPAWN
RESHOWS	RESIN	RESIZES	RESOLUTES	RESPAWNED
RESHUFFLE	RESINATA	RESIZING	RESOLVE	RESPAWNS
RESIANCE	RESINATAS	RESKETCH	RESOLVED	RESPEAK
RESIANCES	RESINATE	RESKEW	RESOLVENT	RESPEAKS
RESIANT	RESINATED	RESKEWED	RESOLVER	RESPECIFY
RESIANTS	RESINATES	RESKEWING	RESOLVERS	RESPECT
RESID	RESINED	RESKEWS	RESOLVES	RESPECTED
RESIDE	RESINER	RESKILL	RESOLVING	RESPECTER
RESIDED	RESINERS	RESKILLED	RESONANCE	RESPECTS
RESIDENCE	RESINIER	RESKILLS	RESONANT	RESPELL
RESIDENCY	RESINIEST	RESKIN	RESONANTS	RESPELLED
RESIDENT	RESINIFY	RESKINNED	RESONATE	RESPELLS
RESIDENTS	RESINING	RESKINS	RESONATED	RESPELT
RESIDER	RESINISE	RESKUE	RESONATES	RESPIRE
RESIDERS	RESINISED	RESKUED	RESONATOR	RESPIRED
RESIDES	RESINISES	RESKUES	RESORB	RESPIRES
RESIDING	RESINIZE	RESKUING	RESORBED	RESPIRING
RESIDS	RESINIZED	RESLATE	RESORBENT	RESPITE
RESIDUA	RESINIZES	RESLATED	RESORBING	RESPITED
RESIDUAL	RESINLIKE	RESLATES	RESORBS	RESPITES
RESIDUALS	RESINOID	RESLATING	RESORCIN	RESPITING
RESIDUARY	RESINOIDS	RESMELT	RESORCINS	RESPLEND
RESIDUE	RESINOSES	RESMELTED	RESORT	RESPLENDS
RESIDUES	RESINOSIS	RESMELTS	RESORTED	RESPLICE
RESIDUOUS	RESINOUS	RESMOOTH	RESORTER	RESPLICED
RESIDUUM	RESINS	RESMOOTHS	RESORTERS	RESPLICES
RESIDUUMS	RESINY	RESNATRON	RESORTING	RESPLIT
RESIFT	RESIST	RESOAK	RESORTS	RESPLITS
RESIFTED	RESISTANT	RESOAKED	RESOUGHT	RESPOKE
RESIFTING	RESISTED	RESOAKING	RESOUND	RESPOKEN
RESIFTS	RESISTENT	RESOAKS	RESOUNDED	RESPOND
RESIGHT	RESISTER	RESOD	RESOUNDS	RESPONDED
RESIGHTED	RESISTERS	RESODDED	RESOURCE	RESPONDER
RESIGHTS	RESISTING	RESODDING	RESOURCED	RESPONDS
RESIGN	RESISTIVE	RESODS	RESOURCES	RESPONSA
RESIGNED	RESISTOR	RESOFTEN	RESOW	RESPONSE
RESIGNER	RESISTORS	RESOFTENS	RESOWED	RESPONSER
RESIGNERS	RESISTS	RESOJET	RESOWING	RESPONSES
RESIGNING	RESIT	RESOJETS	RESOWN	RESPONSOR
RESIGNS	RESITE	RESOLD	RESOWS	RESPONSUM
RESILE	RESITED	RESOLDER	RESPACE	RESPOOL

RESPOOLED	RESTFUL	RESTRUNG	RESWALLOW	RETARDANT
RESPOOLS	RESTFULLY	RESTS	RET	RETARDED
RESPOT	RESTIER	RESTUDIED	RETABLE	RETARDER
RESPOTS	RESTIEST	RESTUDIES	RETABLES	RETARDERS
RESPOTTED	RESTIFF	RESTUDY	RETABLO	RETARDING
RESPRANG	RESTIFORM	RESTUFF	RETABLOS	RETARDS
RESPRAY	RESTING	RESTUFFED	RETACK	RETARGET
RESPRAYED	RESTINGS	RESTUFFS	RETACKED	RETARGETS
RESPRAYS	RESTITCH	RESTUMP	RETACKING	RETASTE
RESPREAD	RESTITUTE	RESTUMPED	RETACKLE	RETASTED
RESPREADS	RESTIVE	RESTUMPS	RETACKLED	RETASTES
RESPRING	RESTIVELY	RESTY	RETACKLES	RETASTING
RESPRINGS	RESTLESS	RESTYLE	RETACKS	RETAUGHT
RESPROUT	RESTO	RESTYLED	RETAG	RETAX
RESPROUTS	RESTOCK	RESTYLES	RETAGGED	RETAXED
RESPRUNG	RESTOCKED	RESTYLING	RETAGGING	RETAXES
RESSALDAR	RESTOCKS	RESUBJECT	RETAGS	RETAXING
REST	RESTOKE	RESUBMIT	RETAIL	RETCH
RESTABLE	RESTOKED	RESUBMITS	RETAILED	RETCHED
RESTABLED	RESTOKES	RESULT	RETAILER	RETCHES
RESTABLES	RESTOKING	RESULTANT	RETAILERS	RETCHING
RESTACK	RESTORAL	RESULTED	RETAILING	RETCHINGS
RESTACKED	RESTORALS	RESULTFUL	RETAILOR	RETCHLESS
RESTACKS	RESTORE	RESULTING	RETAILORS	RETCON
RESTAFF	RESTORED	RESULTS	RETAILS	RETCONNED
RESTAFFED	RESTORER	RESUMABLE	RETAIN	RETCONS
RESTAFFS	RESTORERS	RESUME	RETAINED	RETE
RESTAGE	RESTORES	RESUMED	RETAINER	RETEACH
RESTAGED	RESTORING	RESUMER	RETAINERS	RETEACHES
RESTAGES	RESTOS	RESUMERS	RETAINING	RETEAM
RESTAGING	RESTRAIN	RESUMES	RETAINS	RETEAMED
RESTAMP	RESTRAINS	RESUMING	RETAKE	RETEAMING
RESTAMPED	RESTRAINT	RESUMMON	RETAKEN	RETEAMS
RESTAMPS	RESTRESS	RESUMMONS	RETAKER	RETEAR
RESTART	RESTRETCH	RESUPINE	RETAKERS	RETEARING
RESTARTED	RESTRICT	RESUPPLY	RETAKES	RETEARS
RESTARTER	RESTRICTS	RESURFACE	RETAKING	RETELL
RESTARTS	RESTRIKE	RESURGE	RETAKINGS	RETELLER
RESTATE	RESTRIKES	RESURGED	RETALIATE	RETELLERS
RESTATED	RESTRING	RESURGENT	RETALLIED	RETELLING
RESTATES	RESTRINGE	RESURGES	RETALLIES	RETELLS
RESTATING	RESTRINGS	RESURGING	RETALLY	RETEM
RESTATION	RESTRIVE	RESURRECT	RETAMA	RETEMPER
RESTED	RESTRIVEN	RESURVEY	RETAMAS	RETEMPERS
RESTEM	RESTRIVES	RESURVEYS	RETAPE	RETEMS
RESTEMMED	RESTROOM	RESUS	RETAPED	RETENE
RESTEMS	RESTROOMS	RESUSES	RETAPES	RETENES
RESTER	RESTROVE	RESUSPEND	RETAPING	RETENTION
RESTERS	RESTRUCK	RESUSSES	RETARD	RETENTIVE

RETEST	RETINENES	RETORTED	RETRATE	RETSINA
RETESTED	RETINES	RETORTER	RETRATED	RETSINAS
RETESTIFY	RETINITE	RETORTERS	RETRATES	RETTED
RETESTING	RETINITES	RETORTING	RETRATING	RETTERIES
RETESTS	RETINITIS	RETORTION	RETREAD	RETTERY
RETEXTURE	RETINOIC	RETORTIVE	RETREADED	RETTING
RETHINK	RETINOID	RETORTS	RETREADS	RETUND
RETHINKER	RETINOIDS	RETOTAL	RETREAT	RETUNDED
RETHINKS	RETINOL	RETOTALED	RETREATED	RETUNDING
RETHOUGHT	RETINOLS	RETOTALS	RETREATER	RETUNDS
RETHREAD	RETINT	RETOUCH	RETREATS	RETUNE
RETHREADS	RETINTED	RETOUCHED	RETREE	RETUNED
RETIA	RETINTING	RETOUCHER	RETREES	RETUNES
RETIAL	RETINTS	RETOUCHES	RETRENCH	RETUNING
RETIARII	RETINUE	RETOUR	RETRIAL	RETURF
RETIARIUS	RETINUED	RETOURED	RETRIALS	RETURFED
RETIARY	RETINUES	RETOURING	RETRIBUTE	RETURFING
RETICELLA	RETINULA	RETOURS	RETRIED	RETURFS
RETICENCE	RETINULAE	RETOX	RETRIES	RETURN
RETICENCY	RETINULAR	RETOXED	RETRIEVAL	RETURNED
RETICENT	RETINULAS	RETOXES	RETRIEVE	RETURNEE
RETICLE	RETIRACY	RETOXING	RETRIEVED	RETURNEES
RETICLES	RETIRAL	RETRACE	RETRIEVER	RETURNER
RETICULA	RETIRALS	RETRACED	RETRIEVES	RETURNERS
RETICULAR	RETIRANT	RETRACER	RETRIM	RETURNIK
RETICULE	RETIRANTS	RETRACERS	RETRIMMED	RETURNIKS
RETICULES	RETIRE	RETRACES	RETRIMS	RETURNING
RETICULUM	RETIRED	RETRACING	RETRO	RETURNS
RETIE	RETIREDLY	RETRACK	RETROACT	RETUSE
RETIED	RETIREE	RETRACKED	RETROACTS	RETWEET
RETIEING	RETIREES	RETRACKS	RETROCEDE	RETWEETED
RETIES	RETIRER	RETRACT	RETROD	RETWEETS
RETIFORM	RETIRERS	RETRACTED	RETRODDEN	RETWIST
RETIGHTEN	RETIRES	RETRACTOR	RETRODICT	RETWISTED
RETILE	RETIRING	RETRACTS	RETROFIRE	RETWISTS
RETILED	RETITLE	RETRAICT	RETROFIT	RETYING
RETILES	RETITLED	RETRAICTS	RETROFITS	RETYPE
RETILING	RETITLES	RETRAIN	RETROFLEX	RETYPED
RETIME	RETITLING	RETRAINED	RETROJECT	RETYPES
RETIMED	RETOLD	RETRAINEE	RETRONYM	RETYPING
RETIMES	RETOOK	RETRAINS	RETRONYMS	REUNIFIED
RETIMING	RETOOL	RETRAIT	RETROPACK	REUNIFIES
RETINA	RETOOLED	RETRAITE	RETRORSE	REUNIFY
RETINAE	RETOOLING	RETRAITES	RETROS	REUNION
RETINAL	RETOOLS	RETRAITS	RETROUSSE	REUNIONS
RETINALS	RETORE	RETRAITT	RETROVERT	REUNITE
RETINAS	RETORN	RETRAITTS	RETRY	REUNITED
RETINE	RETORSION	RETRAL	RETRYING	REUNITER
RETINENE	RETORT	RETRALLY	RETS	REUNITERS

REUNITES	REVELER	REVERSALS	REVILE	REVOKER
REUNITING	REVELERS	REVERSE	REVILED	REVOKERS
REUPTAKE	REVELING	REVERSED	REVILER	REVOKES
REUPTAKEN	REVELLED	REVERSELY	REVILERS	REVOKING
REUPTAKES	REVELLER	REVERSER	REVILES	REVOLT
REUPTOOK	REVELLERS	REVERSERS	REVILING	REVOLTED
REURGE	REVELLING	REVERSES	REVILINGS	REVOLTER
REURGED	REVELMENT	REVERSI	REVIOLATE	REVOLTERS
REURGES	REVELRIES	REVERSING	REVISABLE	REVOLTING
REURGING	REVELROUS	REVERSION	REVISAL	REVOLTS
REUSABLE	REVELRY	REVERSIS	REVISALS	REVOLUTE
REUSABLES	REVELS	REVERSO	REVISE	REVOLVE
REUSE	REVENANT	REVERSOS	REVISED	REVOLVED
REUSED	REVENANTS	REVERT	REVISER	REVOLVER
REUSES	REVENGE	REVERTANT	REVISERS	REVOLVERS
REUSING	REVENGED	REVERTED	REVISES	REVOLVES
REUTILISE	REVENGER	REVERTER	REVISING	REVOLVING
REUTILIZE	REVENGERS	REVERTERS	REVISION	REVOTE
REUTTER	REVENGES	REVERTING	REVISIONS	REVOTED
REUTTERED	REVENGING	REVERTIVE	REVISIT	REVOTES
REUTTERS	REVENGIVE	REVERTS	REVISITED	REVOTING
REV	REVENUAL	REVERY	REVISITS	REVS
REVALENTA	REVENUE	REVEST	REVISOR	REVUE
REVALUATE	REVENUED	REVESTED	REVISORS	REVUES
REVALUE	REVENUER	REVESTING	REVISORY	REVUIST
REVALUED	REVENUERS	REVESTRY	REVIVABLE	REVUISTS
REVALUES	REVENUES	REVESTS	REVIVABLY	REVULSED
REVALUING	REVERABLE	REVET	REVIVAL	REVULSION
REVAMP	REVERB	REVETMENT	REVIVALS	REVULSIVE
REVAMPED	REVERBED	REVETS	REVIVE	REVVED
REVAMPER	REVERBING	REVETTED	REVIVED	REVVING
REVAMPERS	REVERBS	REVETTING	REVIVER	REVYING
REVAMPING	REVERE	REVEUR	REVIVERS	REW
REVAMPS	REVERED	REVEURS	REVIVES	REWAKE
REVANCHE	REVERENCE	REVEUSE	REVIVIFY	REWAKED
REVANCHES	REVEREND	REVEUSES	REVIVING	REWAKEN
REVARNISH	REVERENDS	REVIBRATE	REVIVINGS	REWAKENED
REVEAL	REVERENT	REVICTUAL	REVIVOR	REWAKENS
REVEALED	REVERER	REVIE	REVIVORS	REWAKES
REVEALER	REVERERS	REVIED	REVOCABLE	REWAKING
REVEALERS	REVERES	REVIES	REVOCABLY	REWAN
REVEALING	REVERIE	REVIEW	REVOICE	REWARD
REVEALS	REVERIES	REVIEWAL	REVOICED	REWARDED
REVEHENT	REVERIFY	REVIEWALS	REVOICES	REWARDER
REVEILLE	REVERING	REVIEWED	REVOICING	REWARDERS
REVEILLES	REVERIST	REVIEWER	REVOKABLE	REWARDFUL
REVEL	REVERISTS	REVIEWERS	REVOKABLY	REWARDING
REVELATOR	REVERS	REVIEWING	REVOKE	REWARDS
REVELED	REVERSAL	REVIEWS	REVOKED	REWAREWA

R

REWAREWAS	REWIND	REYNARD	RHATANIES	RHEXIS
REWARM	REWINDED	REYNARDS	RHATANY	RHEXISES
REWARMED	REWINDER	REZ	RHEA	RHIES
REWARMING	REWINDERS	REZERO	RHEAS	RHIGOLENE
REWARMS	REWINDING	REZEROED	RHEBOK	RHIME
REWASH	REWINDS	REZEROES	RHEBOKS	RHIMES
REWASHED	REWINNING	REZEROING	RHEMATIC	RHINAL
REWASHES	REWINS	REZEROS	RHEME	RHINE
REWASHING	REWIRABLE	REZES	RHEMES	RHINES
REWATCH	REWIRE	REZONE	RHENIUM	RHINITIC
REWATCHED	REWIRED	REZONED	RHENIUMS	RHINITIS
REWATCHES	REWIRES	REZONES	RHEOBASE	RHINO
REWATER	REWIRING	REZONING	RHEOBASES	RHINOCERI
REWATERED	REWIRINGS	REZONINGS	RHEOBASIC	RHINOLITH
REWATERS	REWOKE	REZZES	RHEOCHORD	RHINOLOGY
REWAX	REWOKEN	RHABDOID	RHEOCORD	RHINOS
REWAXED	REWON	RHABDOIDS	RHEOCORDS	RHIPIDATE
REWAXES	REWORD	RHABDOM	RHEOLOGIC	RHIPIDION
REWAXING	REWORDED	RHABDOMAL	RHEOLOGY	RHIPIDIUM
REWEAR	REWORDING	RHABDOME	RHEOMETER	RHIZIC
REWEARING	REWORDS	RHABDOMES	RHEOMETRY	RHIZINE
REWEARS	REWORE	RHABDOMS	RHEOPHIL	RHIZINES
REWEAVE	REWORK	RHABDUS	RHEOPHILE	RHIZOBIA
REWEAVED	REWORKED	RHABDUSES	RHEOSCOPE	RHIZOBIAL
REWEAVES	REWORKING	RHACHIAL	RHEOSTAT	RHIZOBIUM
REWEAVING	REWORKS	RHACHIDES	RHEOSTATS	RHIZOCARP
REWED	REWORN	RHACHILLA	RHEOTAXES	RHIZOCAUL
REWEDDED	REWOUND	RHACHIS	RHEOTAXIS	RHIZOID
REWEDDING	REWOVE	RHACHISES	RHEOTOME	RHIZOIDAL
REWEDS	REWOVEN	RHACHITIS	RHEOTOMES	RHIZOIDS
REWEIGH	REWRAP	RHAGADES	RHEOTROPE	RHIZOMA
REWEIGHED	REWRAPPED	RHAMNOSE	RHESUS	RHIZOMATA
REWEIGHS	REWRAPS	RHAMNOSES	RHESUSES	RHIZOME
REWELD	REWRAPT	RHAMNUS	RHETOR	RHIZOMES
REWELDED	REWRITE	RHAMNUSES	RHETORIC	RHIZOMIC
REWELDING	REWRITER	RHAMPHOID	RHETORICS	RHIZOPI
REWELDS	REWRITERS	RHANJA	RHETORISE	RHIZOPOD
REWET	REWRITES	RHANJAS	RHETORIZE	RHIZOPODS
REWETS	REWRITING	RHAPHAE	RHETORS	RHIZOPUS
REWETTED	REWRITTEN	RHAPHE	RHEUM	RHIZOTOMY
REWETTING	REWROTE	RHAPHES	RHEUMATIC	RHO
REWIDEN	REWROUGHT	RHAPHIDE	RHEUMATIZ	RHODAMIN
REWIDENED	REWS	RHAPHIDES	RHEUMED	RHODAMINE
REWIDENS	REWTH	RHAPHIS	RHEUMIC	RHODAMINS
REWILD	REWTHS	RHAPONTIC	RHEUMIER	RHODANATE
REWILDED	REX	RHAPSODE	RHEUMIEST	RHODANIC
REWILDING	REXES	RHAPSODES	RHEUMS	RHODANISE
REWILDS	REXINE	RHAPSODIC	RHEUMY	RHODANIZE
REWIN	REXINES	RHAPSODY	RHEXES	RHODIC

R

RHODIE	RHUMBAING	RIAS	RIBIBLE	RICHES
RHODIES	RHUMBAS	RIATA	RIBIBLES	RICHESSE
RHODINAL	RHUMBS	RIATAS	RIBIER	RICHESSES
RHODINALS	RHUS	RIB	RIBIERS	RICHEST
RHODIUM	RHUSES	RIBA	RIBLESS	RICHING
RHODIUMS	RHY	RIBALD	RIBLET	RICHLY
RHODOLITE	RHYME	RIBALDER	RIBLETS	RICHNESS
RHODONITE	RHYMED	RIBALDEST	RIBLIKE	RICHT
RHODOPSIN	RHYMELESS	RIBALDLY	RIBOSE	RICHTED
RHODORA	RHYMER	RIBALDRY	RIBOSES	RICHTER
RHODORAS	RHYMERS	RIBALDS	RIBOSOMAL	RICHTEST
RHODOUS	RHYMES	RIBAND	RIBOSOME	RICHTING
RHODY	RHYMESTER	RIBANDS	RIBOSOMES	RICHTS
RHOEADINE	RHYMING	RIBAS	RIBOZYMAL	RICHWEED
RHOMB	RHYMIST	RIBATTUTA	RIBOZYME	RICHWEEDS
RHOMBI	RHYMISTS	RIBAUD	RIBOZYMES	RICIER
RHOMBIC	RHYNE	RIBAUDRED	RIBS	RICIEST
RHOMBICAL	RHYNES	RIBAUDRY	RIBSTON	RICIN
RHOMBOI	RHYOLITE	RIBAUDS	RIBSTONE	RICING
RHOMBOID	RHYOLITES	RIBAVIRIN	RIBSTONES	RICINS
RHOMBOIDS	RHYOLITIC	RIBBAND	RIBSTONS	RICINUS
RHOMBOS	RHYTA	RIBBANDS	RIBULOSE	RICINUSES
RHOMBS	RHYTHM	RIBBED	RIBULOSES	RICK
RHOMBUS	RHYTHMAL	RIBBER	RIBWORK	RICKED
RHOMBUSES	RHYTHMED	RIBBERS	RIBWORKS	RICKER
RHONCHAL	RHYTHMI	RIBBIE	RIBWORT	RICKERS
RHONCHI	RHYTHMIC	RIBBIER	RIBWORTS	RICKET
RHONCHIAL	RHYTHMICS	RIBBIES	RICE	RICKETIER
RHONCHUS	RHYTHMISE	RIBBIEST	RICEBIRD	RICKETILY
RHONCUS	RHYTHMIST	RIBBING	RICEBIRDS	RICKETS
RHONCUSES	RHYTHMIZE	RIBBINGS	RICED	RICKETTY
RHONE	RHYTHMS	RIBBIT	RICEFIELD	RICKETY
RHONES	RHYTHMUS	RIBBITS	RICEGRASS	RICKEY
RHOPALIC	RHYTIDOME	RIBBON	RICER	RICKEYS
RHOPALISM	RHYTINA	RIBBONED	RICERCAR	RICKING
RHOS	RHYTINAS	RIBBONIER	RICERCARE	RICKLE
RHOTACISE	RHYTON	RIBBONING	RICERCARI	RICKLES
RHOTACISM	RHYTONS	RIBBONRY	RICERCARS	RICKLIER
RHOTACIST	RIA	RIBBONS	RICERCATA	RICKLIEST
RHOTACIZE	RIAD	RIBBONY	RICERS	RICKLY
RHOTIC	RIADS	RIBBY	RICES	RICKRACK
RHOTICITY	RIAL	RIBCAGE	RICEY	RICKRACKS
RHUBARB	RIALS	RIBCAGES	RICH	RICKS
RHUBARBED	RIALTO	RIBES	RICHED	RICKSHA
RHUBARBS	RIALTOS	RIBEYE	RICHEN	RICKSHAS
RHUBARBY	RIANCIES	RIBEYES	RICHENED	RICKSHAW
RHUMB	RIANCY	RIBGRASS	RICHENING	RICKSHAWS
RHUMBA	RIANT	RIBIBE	RICHENS	RICKSTAND
RHUMBAED	RIANTLY	RIBIBES	RICHER	RICKSTICK

R

RICKYARD	RIDGES	RIFEST	RIGGALD	RIGIDIZED
RICKYARDS	RIDGETOP	RIFF	RIGGALDS	RIGIDIZES
RICOCHET	RIDGETOPS	RIFFAGE	RIGGED	RIGIDLY
RICOCHETS	RIDGETREE	RIFFAGES	RIGGER	RIGIDNESS
RICOTTA	RIDGEWAY	RIFFED	RIGGERS	RIGIDS
RICOTTAS	RIDGEWAYS	RIFFING	RIGGING	RIGLIN
RICRAC	RIDGIER	RIFFLE	RIGGINGS	RIGLING
RICRACS	RIDGIEST	RIFFLED	RIGGISH	RIGLINGS
RICTAL	RIDGIL	RIFFLER	RIGGS	RIGLINS
RICTUS	RIDGILS	RIFFLERS	RIGHT	RIGMAROLE
RICTUSES	RIDGING	RIFFLES	RIGHTABLE	RIGOL
RICY	RIDGINGS	RIFFLING	RIGHTABLY	RIGOLL
RID	RIDGLING	RIFFOLA	RIGHTED	RIGOLLS
RIDABLE	RIDGLINGS	RIFFOLAS	RIGHTEN	RIGOLS
RIDDANCE	RIDGY	RIFFRAFF	RIGHTENED	RIGOR
RIDDANCES	RIDIC	RIFFRAFFS	RIGHTENS	RIGORISM
RIDDED	RIDICULE	RIFFS	RIGHTEOUS	RIGORISMS
RIDDEN	RIDICULED	RIFLE	RIGHTER	RIGORIST
RIDDER	RIDICULER	RIFLEBIRD	RIGHTERS	RIGORISTS
RIDDERS	RIDICULES	RIFLED	RIGHTEST	RIGOROUS
RIDDING	RIDING	RIFLEMAN	RIGHTFUL	RIGORS
RIDDLE	RIDINGS	RIFLEMEN	RIGHTIER	RIGOUR
RIDDLED	RIDLEY	RIFLER	RIGHTIES	RIGOURS
RIDDLER	RIDLEYS	RIFLERIES	RIGHTIEST	RIGOUT
RIDDLERS	RIDOTTO	RIFLERS	RIGHTING	RIGOUTS
RIDDLES	RIDOTTOS	RIFLERY	RIGHTINGS	RIGS
RIDDLING	RIDS	RIFLES	RIGHTISH	RIGSDALER
RIDDLINGS	RIEL	RIFLING	RIGHTISM	RIGWIDDIE
RIDE	RIELS	RIFLINGS	RIGHTISMS	RIGWOODIE
RIDEABLE	RIEM	RIFLIP	RIGHTIST	RIJSTAFEL
RIDENT	RIEMPIE	RIFLIPS	RIGHTISTS	RIKISHA
RIDER	RIEMPIES	RIFS	RIGHTLESS	RIKISHAS
RIDERED	RIEMS	RIFT	RIGHTLY	RIKISHI
RIDERLESS	RIESLING	RIFTE	RIGHTMOST	RIKSHAW
RIDERS	RIESLINGS	RIFTED	RIGHTNESS	RIKSHAWS
RIDERSHIP	RIEVE	RIFTIER	RIGHTO	RILE
RIDES	RIEVED	RIFTIEST	RIGHTS	RILED
RIDESHARE	RIEVER	RIFTING	RIGHTSIZE	RILES
RIDGE	RIEVERS	RIFTLESS	RIGHTWARD	RILEY
RIDGEBACK	RIEVES	RIFTS	RIGHTY	RILIER
RIDGED	RIEVING	RIFTY	RIGID	RILIEST
RIDGEL	RIF	RIG	RIGIDER	RILIEVI
RIDGELIKE	RIFAMPIN	RIGADOON	RIGIDEST	RILIEVO
RIDGELINE	RIFAMPINS	RIGADOONS	RIGIDIFY	RILING
RIDGELING	RIFAMYCIN	RIGATONI	RIGIDISE	RILL
RIDGELS	RIFE	RIGATONIS	RIGIDISED	RILLE
RIDGEPOLE	RIFELY	RIGAUDON	RIGIDISES	RILLED
RIDGER	RIFENESS	RIGAUDONS	RIGIDITY	RILLES
RIDGERS	RIFER	RIGG	RIGIDIZE	RILLET

RILLETS	RIN	RINGSTER	RIOTOUS	RIPPINGLY
RILLETTES	RIND	RINGSTERS	RIOTOUSLY	RIPPINGS
RILLING	RINDED	RINGTAIL	RIOTRIES	RIPPLE
RILLMARK	RINDIER	RINGTAILS	RIOTRY	RIPPLED
RILLMARKS	RINDIEST	RINGTAW	RIOTS	RIPPLER
RILLS	RINDING	RINGTAWS	RIP	RIPPLERS
RIM	RINDLESS	RINGTONE	RIPARIAL	RIPPLES
RIMA	RINDS	RINGTONES	RIPARIALS	RIPPLET
RIMAE	RINDY	RINGTOSS	RIPARIAN	RIPPLETS
RIMAYE	RINE	RINGWAY	RIPARIANS	RIPPLIER
RIMAYES	RINES	RINGWAYS	RIPCORD	RIPPLIEST
RIME	RING	RINGWISE	RIPCORDS	RIPPLING
RIMED	RINGBARK	RINGWOMB	RIPE	RIPPLINGS
RIMELESS	RINGBARKS	RINGWOMBS	RIPECK	RIPPLY
RIMER	RINGBIT	RINGWORK	RIPECKS	RIPPS
RIMERS	RINGBITS	RINGWORKS	RIPED	RIPRAP
RIMES	RINGBOLT	RINGWORM	RIPELY	RIPRAPPED
RIMESTER	RINGBOLTS	RINGWORMS	RIPEN	RIPRAPS
RIMESTERS	RINGBONE	RINK	RIPENED	RIPS
RIMFIRE	RINGBONES	RINKED	RIPENER	RIPSAW
RIMFIRES	RINGDOVE	RINKHALS	RIPENERS	RIPSAWED
RIMIER	RINGDOVES	RINKING	RIPENESS	RIPSAWING
RIMIEST	RINGED	RINKS	RIPENING	RIPSAWN
RIMINESS	RINGENT	RINKSIDE	RIPENS	RIPSAWS
RIMING	RINGER	RINKSIDES	RIPER	RIPSTOP
RIMLAND	RINGERS	RINNING	RIPERS	RIPSTOPS
RIMLANDS	RINGETTE	RINS	RIPES	RIPT
RIMLESS	RINGETTES	RINSABLE	RIPEST	RIPTIDE
RIMMED	RINGGIT	RINSE	RIPIENI	RIPTIDES
RIMMER	RINGGITS	RINSEABLE	RIPIENIST	RIRORIRO
RIMMERS	RINGHALS	RINSED	RIPIENO	RIRORIROS
RIMMING	RINGING	RINSER	RIPIENOS	RISALDAR
RIMMINGS	RINGINGLY	RINSERS	RIPING	RISALDARS
RIMOSE	RINGINGS	RINSES	RIPOFF	RISE
RIMOSELY	RINGLESS	RINSIBLE	RIPOFFS	RISEN
RIMOSITY	RINGLET	RINSING	RIPOST	RISER
RIMOUS	RINGLETED	RINSINGS	RIPOSTE	RISERS
RIMPLE	RINGLETS	RIOJA	RIPOSTED	RISES
RIMPLED	RINGLETY	RIOJAS	RIPOSTES	RISHI
RIMPLES	RINGLIKE	RIOT	RIPOSTING	RISHIS
RIMPLING	RINGMAN	RIOTED	RIPOSTS	RISIBLE
RIMROCK	RINGMEN	RIOTER	RIPP	RISIBLES
RIMROCKS	RINGNECK	RIOTERS	RIPPABLE	RISIBLY
RIMS	RINGNECKS	RIOTING	RIPPED	RISING
RIMSHOT	RINGS	RIOTINGS	RIPPER	RISINGS
RIMSHOTS	RINGSIDE	RIOTISE	RIPPERS	RISK
RIMU	RINGSIDER	RIOTISES	RIPPIER	RISKED
RIMUS	RINGSIDES	RIOTIZE	RIPPIERS	RISKER
RIMY	RINGSTAND	RIOTIZES	RIPPING	RISKERS

R

RISKFUL	RITUAL	RIVERBED	RIZARD	ROADSTERS
RISKIER	RITUALISE	RIVERBEDS	RIZARDS	ROADWAY
RISKIEST	RITUALISM	RIVERBOAT	RIZAS	ROADWAYS
RISKILY	RITUALIST	RIVERED	RIZZAR	ROADWORK
RISKINESS	RITUALIZE	RIVERET	RIZZARED	ROADWORKS
RISKING	RITUALLY	RIVERETS	RIZZARING	ROAM
RISKLESS	RITUALS	RIVERHEAD	RIZZARS	ROAMED
RISKS	RITUXIMAB	RIVERIER	RIZZART	ROAMER
RISKY	RITZ	RIVERIEST	RIZZARTS	ROAMERS
RISOLUTO	RITZES	RIVERINE	RIZZER	ROAMING
RISORII	RITZIER	RIVERLESS	RIZZERED	ROAMINGS
RISORIUS	RITZIEST	RIVERLIKE	RIZZERING	ROAMS
RISOTTO	RITZILY	RIVERMAN	RIZZERS	ROAN
RISOTTOS	RITZINESS	RIVERMEN	RIZZOR	ROANPIPE
RISP	RITZY	RIVERS	RIZZORED	ROANPIPES
RISPED	RIVA	RIVERSIDE	RIZZORING	ROANS
RISPETTI	RIVAGE	RIVERWALK	RIZZORS	ROAR
RISPETTO	RIVAGES	RIVERWARD	ROACH	ROARED
RISPING	RIVAL	RIVERWAY	ROACHED	ROARER
RISPINGS	RIVALED	RIVERWAYS	ROACHES	ROARERS
RISPS	RIVALESS	RIVERWEED	ROACHING	ROARIE
RISQUE	RIVALING	RIVERY	ROAD	ROARIER
RISQUES	RIVALISE	RIVES	ROADBED	ROARIEST
RISSOLE	RIVALISED	RIVET	ROADBEDS	ROARING
RISSOLES	RIVALISES	RIVETED	ROADBLOCK	ROARINGLY
RISTRA	RIVALITY	RIVETER	ROADCRAFT	ROARINGS
RISTRAS	RIVALIZE	RIVETERS	ROADEO	ROARMING
RISTRETTO	RIVALIZED	RIVETING	ROADEOS	ROARS
RISUS	RIVALIZES	RIVETINGS	ROADHOG	ROARY
RISUSES	RIVALLED	RIVETS	ROADHOGS	ROAST
RIT	RIVALLESS	RIVETTED	ROADHOUSE	ROASTED
RITARD	RIVALLING	RIVETTING	ROADIE	ROASTER
RITARDS	RIVALRIES	RIVIERA	ROADIES	ROASTERS
RITE	RIVALROUS	RIVIERAS	ROADING	ROASTERY
RITELESS	RIVALRY	RIVIERE	ROADINGS	ROASTIE
RITENUTO	RIVALS	RIVIERES	ROADKILL	ROASTIES
RITENUTOS	RIVALSHIP	RIVING	ROADKILLS	ROASTING
RITES	RIVAS	RIVLIN	ROADLESS	ROASTINGS
RITONAVIR	RIVE	RIVLINS	ROADMAN	ROASTS
RITORNEL	RIVED	RIVO	ROADMEN	ROATE
RITORNELL	RIVEL	RIVULET	ROADS	ROATED
RITORNELS	RIVELLED	RIVULETS	ROADSHOW	ROATES
RITS	RIVELLING	RIVULOSE	ROADSHOWS	ROATING
RITT	RIVELS	RIVULUS	ROADSIDE	ROB
RITTED	RIVEN	RIVULUSES	ROADSIDES	ROBALO
RITTER	RIVER	RIYAL	ROADSMAN	ROBALOS
RITTERS	RIVERAIN	RIYALS	ROADSMEN	ROBAND
RITTING	RIVERAINS	RIZ	ROADSTEAD	ROBANDS
RITTS	RIVERBANK	RIZA	ROADSTER	ROBATA

ROBATAS	ROCAILLE	ROCKOON	RODSTER	ROILIEST
ROBBED	ROCAILLES	ROCKOONS	RODSTERS	ROILING
ROBBER	ROCAMBOLE	ROCKROSE	ROE	ROILS
ROBBERIES	ROCH	ROCKROSES	ROEBUCK	ROILY
ROBBERS	ROCHES	ROCKS	ROEBUCKS	ROIN
ROBBERY	ROCHET	ROCKSHAFT	ROED	ROINED
ROBBIN	ROCHETS	ROCKSLIDE	ROEMER	ROINING
ROBBING	ROCK	ROCKWATER	ROEMERS	ROINISH
ROBBINS	ROCKABIES	ROCKWEED	ROENTGEN	ROINS
ROBE	ROCKABLE	ROCKWEEDS	ROENTGENS	ROIST
ROBED	ROCKABY	ROCKWOOL	ROES	ROISTED
ROBELIKE	ROCKABYE	ROCKWOOLS	ROESTI	ROISTER
ROBES	ROCKABYES	ROCKWORK	ROESTIS	ROISTERED
ROBIN	ROCKAWAY	ROCKWORKS	ROESTONE	ROISTERER
ROBING	ROCKAWAYS	ROCKY	ROESTONES	ROISTERS
ROBINGS	ROCKBOUND	ROCOCO	ROGALLO	ROISTING
ROBINIA	ROCKBURST	ROCOCOS	ROGALLOS	ROISTS
ROBINIAS	ROCKCRESS	ROCQUET	ROGATION	ROJAK
ROBINS	ROCKED	ROCQUETS	ROGATIONS	ROJAKS
ROBLE	ROCKER	ROCS	ROGATORY	ROJI
ROBLES	ROCKERIES	ROD	ROGER	ROJIS
ROBOCALL	ROCKERS	RODDED	ROGERED	ROK
ROBOCALLS	ROCKERY	RODDING	ROGERING	ROKE
ROBORANT	ROCKET	RODDINGS	ROGERINGS	ROKED
ROBORANTS	ROCKETED	RODE	ROGERS	ROKELAY
ROBOT	ROCKETEER	RODED	ROGNON	ROKELAYS
ROBOTIC	ROCKETER	RODENT	ROGNONS	ROKER
ROBOTICS	ROCKETERS	RODENTIAL	ROGUE	ROKERS
ROBOTISE	ROCKETING	RODENTS	ROGUED	ROKES
ROBOTISED	ROCKETRY	RODEO	ROGUEING	ROKIER
ROBOTISES	ROCKETS	RODEOED	ROGUER	ROKIEST
ROBOTISM	ROCKFALL	RODEOING	ROGUERIES	ROKING
ROBOTISMS	ROCKFALLS	RODEOS	ROGUERS	ROKKAKU
ROBOTIZE	ROCKFISH	RODES	ROGUERY	ROKS
ROBOTIZED	ROCKHOUND	RODEWAY	ROGUES	ROKY
ROBOTIZES	ROCKIER	RODEWAYS	ROGUESHIP	ROLAG
ROBOTRIES	ROCKIERS	RODFISHER	ROGUIER	ROLAGS
ROBOTRY	ROCKIEST	RODGERSIA	ROGUIEST	ROLAMITE
ROBOTS	ROCKILY	RODING	ROGUING	ROLAMITES
ROBS	ROCKINESS	RODINGS	ROGUISH	ROLE
ROBURITE	ROCKING	RODLESS	ROGUISHLY	ROLES
ROBURITES	ROCKINGLY	RODLIKE	ROGUY	ROLF
ROBUST	ROCKINGS	RODMAN	ROHE	ROLFED
ROBUSTA	ROCKLAY	RODMEN	ROHES	ROLFER
ROBUSTAS	ROCKLAYS	RODNEY	ROID	ROLFERS
ROBUSTER	ROCKLESS	RODNEYS	ROIDS	ROLFING
ROBUSTEST	ROCKLIKE	RODS	ROIL	ROLFINGS
ROBUSTLY	ROCKLING	RODSMAN	ROILED	ROLFS
ROC	ROCKLINGS	RODSMEN	ROILIER	ROLL

R

ROLLABLE
ROLLAWAY
ROLLAWAYS
ROLLBACK
ROLLBACKS
ROLLBAR
ROLLBARS
ROLLED
ROLLER
ROLLERS
ROLLICK
ROLLICKED
ROLLICKS
ROLLICKY
ROLLIE
ROLLIES
ROLLING
ROLLINGS
ROLLMOP
ROLLMOPS
ROLLNECK
ROLLNECKS
ROLLOCK
ROLLOCKS
ROLLOUT
ROLLOUTS
ROLLOVER
ROLLOVERS
ROLLS
ROLLTOP
ROLLUP
ROLLUPS
ROLLWAY
ROLLWAYS
ROM
ROMA
ROMAGE
ROMAGES
ROMAIKA
ROMAIKAS
ROMAINE
ROMAINES
ROMAJI
ROMAJIS
ROMAL
ROMALS
ROMAN
ROMANCE
ROMANCED

ROMANCER
ROMANCERS
ROMANCES
ROMANCING
ROMANESCO
ROMANISE
ROMANISED
ROMANISES
ROMANIZE
ROMANIZED
ROMANIZES
ROMANO
ROMANOS
ROMANS
ROMANTIC
ROMANTICS
ROMANZA
ROMANZAS
ROMAUNT
ROMAUNTS
ROMCOM
ROMCOMS
ROMELDALE
ROMEO
ROMEOS
ROMNEYA
ROMNEYAS
ROMP
ROMPED
ROMPER
ROMPERS
ROMPING
ROMPINGLY
ROMPISH
ROMPISHLY
ROMPS
ROMS
RONA
RONAS
RONCADOR
RONCADORS
RONDACHE
RONDACHES
RONDAVEL
RONDAVELS
RONDE
RONDEAU
RONDEAUX
RONDEL

RONDELET
RONDELETS
RONDELLE
RONDELLES
RONDELS
RONDES
RONDINO
RONDINOS
RONDO
RONDOS
RONDURE
RONDURES
RONE
RONEO
RONEOED
RONEOING
RONEOS
RONEPIPE
RONEPIPES
RONES
RONG
RONGGENG
RONGGENGS
RONIN
RONINS
RONION
RONIONS
RONNE
RONNEL
RONNELS
RONNIE
RONNIES
RONNING
RONT
RONTE
RONTES
RONTGEN
RONTGENS
RONTS
RONYON
RONYONS
RONZ
RONZER
RONZERS
ROO
ROOD
ROODS
ROOF
ROOFED

ROOFER
ROOFERS
ROOFIE
ROOFIER
ROOFIES
ROOFIEST
ROOFING
ROOFINGS
ROOFLESS
ROOFLIKE
ROOFLINE
ROOFLINES
ROOFS
ROOFSCAPE
ROOFTOP
ROOFTOPS
ROOFTREE
ROOFTREES
ROOFY
ROOIBOS
ROOIBOSES
ROOIKAT
ROOIKATS
ROOINEK
ROOINEKS
ROOK
ROOKED
ROOKERIES
ROOKERY
ROOKIE
ROOKIER
ROOKIES
ROOKIEST
ROOKING
ROOKISH
ROOKS
ROOKY
ROOM
ROOMED
ROOMER
ROOMERS
ROOMETTE
ROOMETTES
ROOMFUL
ROOMFULS
ROOMIE
ROOMIER
ROOMIES
ROOMIEST

ROOMILY
ROOMINESS
ROOMING
ROOMMATE
ROOMMATES
ROOMS
ROOMSFUL
ROOMSOME
ROOMY
ROON
ROONS
ROOP
ROOPED
ROOPIER
ROOPIEST
ROOPING
ROOPIT
ROOPS
ROOPY
ROORBACH
ROORBACHS
ROORBACK
ROORBACKS
ROOS
ROOSA
ROOSAS
ROOSE
ROOSED
ROOSER
ROOSERS
ROOSES
ROOSING
ROOST
ROOSTED
ROOSTER
ROOSTERS
ROOSTING
ROOSTS
ROOT
ROOTAGE
ROOTAGES
ROOTBALL
ROOTBALLS
ROOTBOUND
ROOTCAP
ROOTCAPS
ROOTED
ROOTEDLY
ROOTER

ROOTERS	ROPING	ROSARY	ROSETTY	ROSTELLUM
ROOTHOLD	ROPINGS	ROSBIF	ROSETY	ROSTER
ROOTHOLDS	ROPY	ROSBIFS	ROSEWATER	ROSTERED
ROOTIER	ROQUE	ROSCID	ROSEWOOD	ROSTERING
ROOTIES	ROQUEFORT	ROSCOE	ROSEWOODS	ROSTERS
ROOTIEST	ROQUES	ROSCOES	ROSHAMBO	ROSTI
ROOTINESS	ROQUET	ROSE	ROSHAMBOS	ROSTING
ROOTING	ROQUETED	ROSEAL	ROSHI	ROSTIS
ROOTINGS	ROQUETING	ROSEATE	ROSHIS	ROSTRA
ROOTKIT	ROQUETS	ROSEATELY	ROSIED	ROSTRAL
ROOTKITS	ROQUETTE	ROSEBAY	ROSIER	ROSTRALLY
ROOTLE	ROQUETTES	ROSEBAYS	ROSIERE	ROSTRATE
ROOTLED	RORAL	ROSEBED	ROSIERES	ROSTRATED
ROOTLES	RORE	ROSEBEDS	ROSIERS	ROSTRUM
ROOTLESS	RORES	ROSEBOWL	ROSIES	ROSTRUMS
ROOTLET	RORIC	ROSEBOWLS	ROSIEST	ROSTS
ROOTLETS	RORID	ROSEBUD	ROSILY	ROSULA
ROOTLIKE	RORIE	ROSEBUDS	ROSIN	ROSULAS
ROOTLING	RORIER	ROSEBUSH	ROSINATE	ROSULATE
ROOTS	RORIEST	ROSED	ROSINATES	ROSY
ROOTSIER	RORQUAL	ROSEFINCH	ROSINED	ROSYING
ROOTSIEST	RORQUALS	ROSEFISH	ROSINER	ROT
ROOTSTALK	RORT	ROSEHIP	ROSINERS	ROTA
ROOTSTOCK	RORTED	ROSEHIPS	ROSINESS	ROTACHUTE
ROOTSY	RORTER	ROSELESS	ROSING	ROTAL
ROOTWORM	RORTERS	ROSELIKE	ROSINIER	ROTAMETER
ROOTWORMS	RORTIER	ROSELLA	ROSINIEST	ROTAN
ROOTY	RORTIEST	ROSELLAS	ROSINING	ROTANS
ROOPABLE	RORTING	ROSELLE	ROSINOL	ROTAPLANE
ROPE	RORTINGS	ROSELLES	ROSINOLS	ROTARIES
ROPEABLE	RORTS	ROSEMARY	ROSINOUS	ROTARY
ROPED	RORTY	ROSEOLA	ROSINS	ROTAS
ROPELIKE	RORY	ROSEOLAR	ROSINWEED	ROTATABLE
ROPER	ROSACE	ROSEOLAS	ROSINY	ROTATE
ROPERIES	ROSACEA	ROSERIES	ROSIT	ROTATED
ROPERS	ROSACEAS	ROSEROOT	ROSITED	ROTATES
ROPERY	ROSACEOUS	ROSEROOTS	ROSITING	ROTATING
ROPES	ROSACES	ROSERY	ROSITS	ROTATION
ROPEWALK	ROSAKER	ROSES	ROSMARINE	ROTATIONS
ROPEWALKS	ROSAKERS	ROSESLUG	ROSOGLIO	ROTATIVE
ROPEWAY	ROSALIA	ROSESLUGS	ROSOGLIOS	ROTATOR
ROPEWAYS	ROSALIAS	ROSET	ROSOLIO	ROTATORES
ROPEWORK	ROSANILIN	ROSETED	ROSOLIOS	ROTATORS
ROPEWORKS	ROSARIA	ROSETING	ROSSER	ROTATORY
ROPEY	ROSARIAN	ROSETS	ROSSERS	ROTAVATE
ROPIER	ROSARIANS	ROSETTE	ROST	ROTAVATED
ROPIEST	ROSARIES	ROSETTED	ROSTED	ROTAVATES
ROPILY	ROSARIUM	ROSETTES	ROSTELLA	ROTAVATOR
ROPINESS	ROSARIUMS	ROSETTING	ROSTELLAR	ROTAVIRAL

R

ROTAVIRUS	ROTTANS	ROUGHDRY	ROUNCIES	ROUSER
ROTCH	ROTTE	ROUGHED	ROUNCY	ROUSERS
ROTCHE	ROTTED	ROUGHEN	ROUND	ROUSES
ROTCHES	ROTTEN	ROUGHENED	ROUNDARCH	ROUSING
ROTCHIE	ROTTENER	ROUGHENS	ROUNDBALL	ROUSINGLY
ROTCHIES	ROTTENEST	ROUGHER	ROUNDED	ROUSSEAU
ROTE	ROTTENLY	ROUGHERS	ROUNDEDLY	ROUSSEAUS
ROTED	ROTTENS	ROUGHEST	ROUNDEL	ROUSSETTE
ROTELY	ROTTER	ROUGHHEW	ROUNDELAY	ROUST
ROTENONE	ROTTERS	ROUGHHEWN	ROUNDELS	ROUSTED
ROTENONES	ROTTES	ROUGHHEWS	ROUNDER	ROUSTER
ROTES	ROTTING	ROUGHIE	ROUNDERS	ROUSTERS
ROTGRASS	ROTULA	ROUGHIES	ROUNDEST	ROUSTING
ROTGUT	ROTULAE	ROUGHING	ROUNDHAND	ROUSTS
ROTGUTS	ROTULAS	ROUGHINGS	ROUNDHEEL	ROUT
ROTHER	ROTUND	ROUGHISH	ROUNDING	ROUTABLE
ROTHERS	ROTUNDA	ROUGHLEG	ROUNDINGS	ROUTE
ROTI	ROTUNDAS	ROUGHLEGS	ROUNDISH	ROUTEABLE
ROTIFER	ROTUNDATE	ROUGHLY	ROUNDLE	ROUTED
ROTIFERAL	ROTUNDED	ROUGHNECK	ROUNDLES	ROUTEING
ROTIFERAN	ROTUNDER	ROUGHNESS	ROUNDLET	ROUTEMAN
ROTIFERS	ROTUNDEST	ROUGHOUT	ROUNDLETS	ROUTEMEN
ROTIFORM	ROTUNDING	ROUGHOUTS	ROUNDLY	ROUTER
ROTING	ROTUNDITY	ROUGHS	ROUNDNESS	ROUTERS
ROTINI	ROTUNDLY	ROUGHSHOD	ROUNDS	ROUTES
ROTINIS	ROTUNDS	ROUGHT	ROUNDSMAN	ROUTEWAY
ROTIS	ROTURIER	ROUGHY	ROUNDSMEN	ROUTEWAYS
ROTL	ROTURIERS	ROUGING	ROUNDTRIP	ROUTH
ROTLS	ROUBLE	ROUILLE	ROUNDUP	ROUTHIE
ROTO	ROUBLES	ROUILLES	ROUNDUPS	ROUTHIER
ROTOGRAPH	ROUCHE	ROUL	ROUNDURE	ROUTHIEST
ROTOLI	ROUCHED	ROULADE	ROUNDURES	ROUTHS
ROTOLO	ROUCHES	ROULADES	ROUNDWOOD	ROUTINE
ROTOLOS	ROUCHING	ROULE	ROUNDWORM	ROUTINEER
ROTON	ROUCHINGS	ROULEAU	ROUP	ROUTINELY
ROTONS	ROUCOU	ROULEAUS	ROUPED	ROUTINES
ROTOR	ROUCOUS	ROULEAUX	ROUPET	ROUTING
ROTORS	ROUE	ROULES	ROUPIER	ROUTINGS
ROTOS	ROUEN	ROULETTE	ROUPIEST	ROUTINISE
ROTOSCOPE	ROUENS	ROULETTED	ROUPILY	ROUTINISM
ROTOTILL	ROUES	ROULETTES	ROUPING	ROUTINIST
ROTOTILLS	ROUGE	ROULS	ROUPIT	ROUTINIZE
ROTOVATE	ROUGED	ROUM	ROUPS	ROUTOUS
ROTOVATED	ROUGES	ROUMING	ROUPY	ROUTOUSLY
ROTOVATES	ROUGH	ROUMINGS	ROUSABLE	ROUTS
ROTOVATOR	ROUGHAGE	ROUMS	ROUSANT	ROUX
ROTPROOF	ROUGHAGES	ROUNCE	ROUSE	ROVE
ROTS	ROUGHBACK	ROUNCES	ROUSED	ROVED
ROTTAN	ROUGHCAST	ROUNCEVAL	ROUSEMENT	ROVEN

ROVER	ROWNDELLS	ROZETING	RUBBLE	RUBIN
ROVERS	ROWNDING	ROZETS	RUBBLED	RUBINE
ROVES	ROWNDS	ROZIT	RUBBLES	RUBINEOUS
ROVING	ROWOVER	ROZITED	RUBBLIER	RUBINES
ROVINGLY	ROWOVERS	ROZITING	RUBBLIEST	RUBINS
ROVINGS	ROWS	ROZITS	RUBBLING	RUBIOUS
ROW	ROWT	ROZZER	RUBBLY	RUBLE
ROWABLE	ROWTED	ROZZERS	RUBBOARD	RUBLES
ROWAN	ROWTH	RUANA	RUBBOARDS	RUBLI
ROWANS	ROWTHS	RUANAS	RUBBY	RUBOFF
ROWBOAT	ROWTING	RUB	RUBBYDUB	RUBOFFS
ROWBOATS	ROWTS	RUBABOO	RUBBYDUBS	RUBOUT
ROWDEDOW	ROYAL	RUBABOOS	RUBDOWN	RUBOUTS
ROWDEDOWS	ROYALET	RUBACE	RUBDOWNS	RUBRIC
ROWDIER	ROYALETS	RUBACES	RUBE	RUBRICAL
ROWDIES	ROYALISE	RUBAI	RUBEFIED	RUBRICATE
ROWDIEST	ROYALISED	RUBAIS	RUBEFIES	RUBRICIAN
ROWDILY	ROYALISES	RUBAIYAT	RUBEFY	RUBRICS
ROWDINESS	ROYALISM	RUBAIYATS	RUBEFYING	RUBS
ROWDY	ROYALISMS	RUBASSE	RUBEL	RUBSTONE
ROWDYDOW	ROYALIST	RUBASSES	RUBELLA	RUBSTONES
ROWDYDOWS	ROYALISTS	RUBATI	RUBELLAN	RUBUS
ROWDYISH	ROYALIZE	RUBATO	RUBELLANS	RUBUSES
ROWDYISM	ROYALIZED	RUBATOS	RUBELLAS	RUBY
ROWDYISMS	ROYALIZES	RUBBABOO	RUBELLITE	RUBYING
ROWED	ROYALLER	RUBBABOOS	RUBELS	RUBYLIKE
ROWEL	ROYALLEST	RUBBED	RUBEOLA	RUC
ROWELED	ROYALLY	RUBBER	RUBEOLAR	RUCHE
ROWELING	ROYALMAST	RUBBERED	RUBEOLAS	RUCHED
ROWELLED	ROYALS	RUBBERIER	RUBES	RUCHES
ROWELLING	ROYALTIES	RUBBERING	RUBESCENT	RUCHING
ROWELS	ROYALTY	RUBBERISE	RUBICELLE	RUCHINGS
ROWEN	ROYNE	RUBBERIZE	RUBICON	RUCK
ROWENS	ROYNED	RUBBERS	RUBICONED	RUCKED
ROWER	ROYNES	RUBBERY	RUBICONS	RUCKING
ROWERS	ROYNING	RUBBET	RUBICUND	RUCKLE
ROWHOUSE	ROYNISH	RUBBIDIES	RUBIDIC	RUCKLED
ROWHOUSES	ROYST	RUBBIDY	RUBIDIUM	RUCKLES
ROWIE	ROYSTED	RUBBIES	RUBIDIUMS	RUCKLING
ROWIES	ROYSTER	RUBBING	RUBIED	RUCKMAN
ROWING	ROYSTERED	RUBBINGS	RUBIER	RUCKMEN
ROWINGS	ROYSTERER	RUBBISH	RUBIES	RUCKS
ROWLOCK	ROYSTERS	RUBBISHED	RUBIEST	RUCKSACK
ROWLOCKS	ROYSTING	RUBBISHES	RUBIFIED	RUCKSACKS
ROWME	ROYSTS	RUBBISHLY	RUBIFIES	RUCKSEAT
ROWMES	ROZELLE	RUBBISHY	RUBIFY	RUCKSEATS
ROWND	ROZELLES	RUBBIT	RUBIFYING	RUCKUS
ROWNDED	ROZET	RUBBITIES	RUBIGO	RUCKUSES
ROWNDELL	ROZETED	RUBBITY	RUBIGOS	RUCOLA

RUCOLAS	RUDIMENTS	RUFIYAAS	RUINER	RUMBLIER
RUCS	RUDIS	RUFOUS	RUINERS	RUMBLIEST
RUCTATION	RUDISH	RUFOUSES	RUING	RUMBLING
RUCTION	RUDIST	RUG	RUINGS	RUMBLINGS
RUCTIONS	RUDISTID	RUGA	RUINING	RUMBLY
RUCTIOUS	RUDISTIDS	RUGAE	RUININGS	RUMBO
RUD	RUDISTS	RUGAL	RUINOUS	RUMBOS
RUDACEOUS	RUDS	RUGALACH	RUINOUSLY	RUMDUM
RUDAS	RUDY	RUGALACHS	RUINS	RUMDUMS
RUDASES	RUE	RUGATE	RUKH	RUME
RUDBECKIA	RUED	RUGBIES	RUKHS	RUMEN
RUDD	RUEDA	RUGBY	RULABLE	RUMENS
RUDDED	RUEDAS	RUGELACH	RULE	RUMES
RUDDER	RUEFUL	RUGELACHS	RULED	RUMINA
RUDDERS	RUEFULLY	RUGGED	RULELESS	RUMINAL
RUDDIED	RUEING	RUGGEDER	RULER	RUMINANT
RUDDIER	RUEINGS	RUGGEDEST	RULERED	RUMINANTS
RUDDIES	RUELLE	RUGGEDISE	RULERING	RUMINATE
RUDDIEST	RUELLES	RUGGEDIZE	RULERS	RUMINATED
RUDDILY	RUELLIA	RUGGEDLY	RULERSHIP	RUMINATES
RUDDINESS	RUELLIAS	RUGGELACH	RULES	RUMINATOR
RUDDING	RUER	RUGGER	RULESET	RUMKIN
RUDDLE	RUERS	RUGGERS	RULESETS	RUMKINS
RUDDLED	RUES	RUGGIER	RULESSE	RUMLY
RUDDLEMAN	RUFESCENT	RUGGIEST	RULIER	RUMMAGE
RUDDLEMEN	RUFF	RUGGING	RULIEST	RUMMAGED
RUDDLES	RUFFE	RUGGINGS	RULING	RUMMAGER
RUDDLING	RUFFED	RUGGY	RULINGS	RUMMAGERS
RUDDOCK	RUFFES	RUGLIKE	RULLION	RUMMAGES
RUDDOCKS	RUFFIAN	RUGOLA	RULLIONS	RUMMAGING
RUDDS	RUFFIANED	RUGOLAS	RULLOCK	RUMMER
RUDDY	RUFFIANLY	RUGOSA	RULLOCKS	RUMMERS
RUDDYING	RUFFIANS	RUGOSAS	RULY	RUMMEST
RUDE	RUFFIN	RUGOSE	RUM	RUMMIER
RUDELY	RUFFING	RUGOSELY	RUMAKI	RUMMIES
RUDENESS	RUFFINS	RUGOSITY	RUMAKIS	RUMMIEST
RUDER	RUFFLE	RUGOUS	RUMAL	RUMMILY
RUDERAL	RUFFLED	RUGRAT	RUMALS	RUMMINESS
RUDERALS	RUFFLER	RUGRATS	RUMBA	RUMMISH
RUDERIES	RUFFLERS	RUGS	RUMBAED	RUMMISHED
RUDERY	RUFFLES	RUGULOSE	RUMBAING	RUMMISHES
RUDES	RUFFLIER	RUIN	RUMBAS	RUMMY
RUDESBIES	RUFFLIEST	RUINABLE	RUMBELOW	RUMNESS
RUDESBY	RUFFLIKE	RUINATE	RUMBELOWS	RUMNESSES
RUDEST	RUFFLING	RUINATED	RUMBLE	RUMOR
RUDI	RUFFLINGS	RUINATES	RUMBLED	RUMORED
RUDIE	RUFFLY	RUINATING	RUMBLER	RUMORER
RUDIES	RUFFS	RUINATION	RUMBLERS	RUMORERS
RUDIMENT	RUFIYAA	RUINED	RUMBLES	RUMORING

RUMOROUS	RUNDALE	RUNOVER	RURU	RUSTABLE
RUMORS	RUNDALES	RUNOVERS	RURUS	RUSTED
RUMOUR	RUNDLE	RUNPROOF	RUSA	RUSTIC
RUMOURED	RUNDLED	RUNRIG	RUSALKA	RUSTICAL
RUMOURER	RUNDLES	RUNRIGS	RUSALKAS	RUSTICALS
RUMOURERS	RUNDLET	RUNROUND	RUSAS	RUSTICANA
RUMOURING	RUNDLETS	RUNROUNDS	RUSCUS	RUSTICATE
RUMOURS	RUNDOWN	RUNS	RUSCUSES	RUSTICIAL
RUMP	RUNDOWNS	RUNT	RUSE	RUSTICISE
RUMPED	RUNDS	RUNTED	RUSES	RUSTICISM
RUMPIER	RUNE	RUNTIER	RUSH	RUSTICITY
RUMPIES	RUNECRAFT	RUNTIEST	RUSHED	RUSTICIZE
RUMPIEST	RUNED	RUNTINESS	RUSHEE	RUSTICLY
RUMPING	RUNELIKE	RUNTISH	RUSHEES	RUSTICS
RUMPLE	RUNES	RUNTISHLY	RUSHEN	RUSTIER
RUMPLED	RUNFLAT	RUNTS	RUSHER	RUSTIEST
RUMPLES	RUNFLATS	RUNTY	RUSHERS	RUSTILY
RUMPLESS	RUNG	RUNWAY	RUSHES	RUSTINESS
RUMPLIER	RUNGED	RUNWAYS	RUSHIER	RUSTING
RUMPLIEST	RUNGLESS	RUPEE	RUSHIEST	RUSTINGS
RUMPLING	RUNGS	RUPEES	RUSHINESS	RUSTLE
RUMPLY	RUNIC	RUPIA	RUSHING	RUSTLED
RUMPO	RUNKLE	RUPIAH	RUSHINGS	RUSTLER
RUMPOS	RUNKLED	RUPIAHS	RUSHLIGHT	RUSTLERS
RUMPOT	RUNKLES	RUPIAS	RUSHLIKE	RUSTLES
RUMPOTS	RUNKLING	RUPTURE	RUSHY	RUSTLESS
RUMPS	RUNLESS	RUPTURED	RUSINE	RUSTLING
RUMPUS	RUNLET	RUPTURES	RUSK	RUSTLINGS
RUMPUSES	RUNLETS	RUPTURING	RUSKS	RUSTPROOF
RUMPY	RUNNABLE	RURAL	RUSMA	RUSTRE
RUMRUNNER	RUNNEL	RURALISE	RUSMAS	RUSTRED
RUMS	RUNNELS	RURALISED	RUSSE	RUSTRES
RUN	RUNNER	RURALISES	RUSSEL	RUSTS
RUNABOUT	RUNNERS	RURALISM	RUSSELS	RUSTY
RUNABOUTS	RUNNET	RURALISMS	RUSSET	RUT
RUNAGATE	RUNNETS	RURALIST	RUSSETED	RUTABAGA
RUNAGATES	RUNNIER	RURALISTS	RUSSETIER	RUTABAGAS
RUNANGA	RUNNIEST	RURALITE	RUSSETING	RUTACEOUS
RUNANGAS	RUNNINESS	RURALITES	RUSSETS	RUTH
RUNAROUND	RUNNING	RURALITY	RUSSETY	RUTHENIC
RUNAWAY	RUNNINGLY	RURALIZE	RUSSIA	RUTHENIUM
RUNAWAYS	RUNNINGS	RURALIZED	RUSSIAS	RUTHER
RUNBACK	RUNNION	RURALIZES	RUSSIFIED	RUTHFUL
RUNBACKS	RUNNIONS	RURALLY	RUSSIFIES	RUTHFULLY
RUNCH	RUNNY	RURALNESS	RUSSIFY	RUTHLESS
RUNCHES	RUNOFF	RURALS	RUSSULA	RUTHS
RUNCIBLE	RUNOFFS	RURBAN	RUSSULAE	RUTILANT
RUNCINATE	RUNOUT	RURP	RUSSULAS	RUTILATED
RUND	RUNOUTS	RURPS	RUST	RUTILE

R

RUTILES	RUTTING	RYBAUDRYE	RYKE	RYOKANS
RUTIN	RUTTINGS	RYE	RYKED	RYOT
RUTINS	RUTTISH	RYEBREAD	RYKES	RYOTS
RUTS	RUTTISHLY	RYEBREADS	RYKING	RYOTWARI
RUTTED	RUTTY	RYEFLOUR	RYMME	RYOTWARIS
RUTTER	RYA	RYEFLOURS	RYMMED	RYPE
RUTTERS	RYAL	RYEGRASS	RYMMES	RYPECK
RUTTIER	RYALS	RYEPECK	RYMMING	RYPECKS
RUTTIEST	RYAS	RYEPECKS	RYND	RYPER
RUTTILY	RYBAT	RYES	RYNDS	RYU
RUTTINESS	RYBATS	RYFE	RYOKAN	RYUS

R

S

SAAG
SAAGS
SAB
SABADILLA
SABAL
SABALS
SABATON
SABATONS
SABAYON
SABAYONS
SABBAT
SABBATH
SABBATHS
SABBATIC
SABBATICS
SABBATINE
SABBATISE
SABBATISM
SABBATIZE
SABBATS
SABBED
SABBING
SABBINGS
SABE
SABED
SABEING
SABELLA
SABELLAS
SABER
SABERED
SABERING
SABERLIKE
SABERS
SABES
SABHA
SABHAS
SABICU
SABICUS
SABIN
SABINE
SABINES
SABINS
SABIR

SABIRS
SABKHA
SABKHAH
SABKHAHS
SABKHAS
SABKHAT
SABKHATS
SABLE
SABLED
SABLEFISH
SABLER
SABLES
SABLEST
SABLING
SABOT
SABOTAGE
SABOTAGED
SABOTAGES
SABOTED
SABOTEUR
SABOTEURS
SABOTIER
SABOTIERS
SABOTS
SABRA
SABRAS
SABRE
SABRED
SABRELIKE
SABRES
SABREUR
SABREURS
SABREWING
SABRING
SABS
SABULINE
SABULOSE
SABULOUS
SABURRA
SABURRAL
SABURRAS
SAC
SACATON

SACATONS
SACBUT
SACBUTS
SACCADE
SACCADES
SACCADIC
SACCATE
SACCHARIC
SACCHARIN
SACCHARUM
SACCIFORM
SACCOI
SACCOS
SACCOSES
SACCULAR
SACCULATE
SACCULE
SACCULES
SACCULI
SACCULUS
SACELLA
SACELLUM
SACHEM
SACHEMDOM
SACHEMIC
SACHEMS
SACHET
SACHETED
SACHETS
SACK
SACKABLE
SACKAGE
SACKAGED
SACKAGES
SACKAGING
SACKBUT
SACKBUTS
SACKCLOTH
SACKED
SACKER
SACKERS
SACKFUL
SACKFULS

SACKING
SACKINGS
SACKLESS
SACKLIKE
SACKLOAD
SACKLOADS
SACKS
SACKSFUL
SACLESS
SACLIKE
SACQUE
SACQUES
SACRA
SACRAL
SACRALGIA
SACRALISE
SACRALITY
SACRALIZE
SACRALS
SACRAMENT
SACRARIA
SACRARIAL
SACRARIUM
SACRED
SACREDER
SACREDEST
SACREDLY
SACRIFICE
SACRIFIDE
SACRIFIED
SACRIFIES
SACRIFY
SACRILEGE
SACRING
SACRINGS
SACRIST
SACRISTAN
SACRISTS
SACRISTY
SACRUM
SACRUMS
SACS
SAD

SADDED
SADDEN
SADDENED
SADDENING
SADDENS
SADDER
SADDEST
SADDHU
SADDHUS
SADDIE
SADDIES
SADDING
SADDISH
SADDLE
SADDLEBAG
SADDLEBOW
SADDLED
SADDLER
SADDLERS
SADDLERY
SADDLES
SADDLING
SADDO
SADDOES
SADDOS
SADE
SADES
SADHANA
SADHANAS
SADHE
SADHES
SADHU
SADHUS
SADI
SADIRON
SADIRONS
SADIS
SADISM
SADISMS
SADIST
SADISTIC
SADISTS
SADLY

S

SADNESS	SAFRONAL	SAGGY	SAIDST	SAINTHOOD
SADNESSES	SAFRONALS	SAGIER	SAIGA	SAINTING
SADO	SAFT	SAGIEST	SAIGAS	SAINTISH
SADOS	SAFTER	SAGINATE	SAIKEI	SAINTISM
SADS	SAFTEST	SAGINATED	SAIKEIS	SAINTISMS
SADZA	SAG	SAGINATES	SAIKLESS	SAINTLESS
SADZAS	SAGA	SAGITTA	SAIL	SAINTLIER
SAE	SAGACIOUS	SAGITTAL	SAILABLE	SAINTLIKE
SAECULA	SAGACITY	SAGITTARY	SAILBOARD	SAINTLILY
SAECULUM	SAGAMAN	SAGITTAS	SAILBOAT	SAINTLING
SAECULUMS	SAGAMEN	SAGITTATE	SAILBOATS	SAINTLY
SAETER	SAGAMORE	SAGO	SAILCLOTH	SAINTS
SAETERS	SAGAMORES	SAGOIN	SAILED	SAINTSHIP
SAFARI	SAGANASH	SAGOINS	SAILER	SAIQUE
SAFARIED	SAGAPENUM	SAGOS	SAILERS	SAIQUES
SAFARIING	SAGAS	SAGOUIN	SAILFISH	SAIR
SAFARIS	SAGATHIES	SAGOUINS	SAILING	SAIRED
SAFARIST	SAGATHY	SAGRADA	SAILINGS	SAIRER
SAFARISTS	SAGBUT	SAGS	SAILLESS	SAIREST
SAFE	SAGBUTS	SAGUARO	SAILMAKER	SAIRING
SAFED	SAGE	SAGUAROS	SAILOR	SAIRS
SAFEGUARD	SAGEBRUSH	SAGUIN	SAILORING	SAIS
SAFELIGHT	SAGEHOOD	SAGUINS	SAILORLY	SAIST
SAFELY	SAGEHOODS	SAGUM	SAILORS	SAITH
SAFENESS	SAGELY	SAGY	SAILPAST	SAITHE
SAFER	SAGENE	SAHEB	SAILPASTS	SAITHES
SAFES	SAGENES	SAHEBS	SAILPLANE	SAITHS
SAFEST	SAGENESS	SAHIB	SAILROOM	SAIYID
SAFETIED	SAGENITE	SAHIBA	SAILROOMS	SAIYIDS
SAFETIES	SAGENITES	SAHIBAH	SAILS	SAJOU
SAFETY	SAGENITIC	SAHIBAHS	SAIM	SAJOUS
SAFETYING	SAGER	SAHIBAS	SAIMIN	SAKE
SAFETYMAN	SAGES	SAHIBS	SAIMINS	SAKER
SAFETYMEN	SAGEST	SAHIWAL	SAIMIRI	SAKERET
SAFFIAN	SAGGAR	SAHIWALS	SAIMIRIS	SAKERETS
SAFFIANS	SAGGARD	SAHUARO	SAIMS	SAKERS
SAFFLOWER	SAGGARDS	SAHUAROS	SAIN	SAKES
SAFFRON	SAGGARED	SAI	SAINE	SAKI
SAFFRONED	SAGGARING	SAIBLING	SAINED	SAKIA
SAFFRONS	SAGGARS	SAIBLINGS	SAINFOIN	SAKIAS
SAFFRONY	SAGGED	SAIC	SAINFOINS	SAKIEH
SAFING	SAGGER	SAICE	SAINING	SAKIEHS
SAFRANIN	SAGGERED	SAICES	SAINS	SAKIS
SAFRANINE	SAGGERING	SAICK	SAINT	SAKIYEH
SAFRANINS	SAGGERS	SAICKS	SAINTDOM	SAKIYEHS
SAFROL	SAGGIER	SAICS	SAINTDOMS	SAKKOI
SAFROLE	SAGGIEST	SAID	SAINTED	SAKKOS
SAFROLES	SAGGING	SAIDEST	SAINTESS	SAKKOSES
SAFROLS	SAGGINGS	SAIDS	SAINTFOIN	SAKSAUL

S

SAKSAULS	SALEROOM	SALINISED	SALMONIDS	SALTATED
SAKTI	SALEROOMS	SALINISES	SALMONIER	SALTATES
SAKTIS	SALES	SALINITY	SALMONOID	SALTATING
SAL	SALESGIRL	SALINIZE	SALMONS	SALTATION
SALAAM	SALESLADY	SALINIZED	SALMONY	SALTATO
SALAAMED	SALESMAN	SALINIZES	SALOL	SALTATORY
SALAAMING	SALESMEN	SALIVA	SALOLS	SALTATOS
SALAAMS	SALESROOM	SALIVAL	SALOMETER	SALTBOX
SALABLE	SALET	SALIVARY	SALON	SALTBOXES
SALABLY	SALETS	SALIVAS	SALONS	SALTBUSH
SALACIOUS	SALEWD	SALIVATE	SALOON	SALTCAT
SALACITY	SALEYARD	SALIVATED	SALOONS	SALTCATS
SALAD	SALEYARDS	SALIVATES	SALOOP	SALTCHUCK
SALADANG	SALFERN	SALIVATOR	SALOOPS	SALTED
SALADANGS	SALFERNS	SALIX	SALOP	SALTER
SALADE	SALIAUNCE	SALL	SALOPIAN	SALTERIES
SALADES	SALIC	SALLAD	SALOPS	SALTERN
SALADING	SALICES	SALLADS	SALP	SALTERNS
SALADINGS	SALICET	SALLAL	SALPA	SALTERS
SALADS	SALICETA	SALLALS	SALPAE	SALTERY
SALAL	SALICETS	SALLE	SALPAS	SALTEST
SALALS	SALICETUM	SALLEE	SALPIAN	SALTFISH
SALAMI	SALICIN	SALLEES	SALPIANS	SALTIE
SALAMIS	SALICINE	SALLES	SALPICON	SALTIER
SALAMON	SALICINES	SALLET	SALPICONS	SALTIERS
SALAMONS	SALICINS	SALLETS	SALPID	SALTIES
SALANGANE	SALICYLIC	SALLIED	SALPIDS	SALTIEST
SALARIAT	SALIENCE	SALLIER	SALPIFORM	SALTILY
SALARIATS	SALIENCES	SALLIERS	SALPINGES	SALTINE
SALARIED	SALIENCY	SALLIES	SALPINX	SALTINES
SALARIES	SALIENT	SALLOW	SALPINXES	SALTINESS
SALARY	SALIENTLY	SALLOWED	SALPS	SALTING
SALARYING	SALIENTS	SALLOWER	SALS	SALTINGS
SALARYMAN	SALIFIED	SALLOWEST	SALSA	SALTIRE
SALARYMEN	SALIFIES	SALLOWIER	SALSAED	SALTIRES
SALAT	SALIFY	SALLOWING	SALSAING	SALTISH
SALATS	SALIFYING	SALLOWISH	SALSAS	SALTISHLY
SALBAND	SALIGOT	SALLOWLY	SALSE	SALTLESS
SALBANDS	SALIGOTS	SALLOWS	SALSES	SALTLIKE
SALCHOW	SALIMETER	SALLOWY	SALSIFIES	SALTLY
SALCHOWS	SALIMETRY	SALLY	SALSIFY	SALTNESS
SALE	SALINA	SALLYING	SALSILLA	SALTO
SALEABLE	SALINAS	SALLYPORT	SALSILLAS	SALTOED
SALEABLY	SALINATE	SALMI	SALT	SALTOING
SALEP	SALINATED	SALMIS	SALTANDO	SALTOS
SALEPS	SALINATES	SALMON	SALTANDOS	SALTPAN
SALERATUS	SALINE	SALMONET	SALTANT	SALTPANS
SALERING	SALINES	SALMONETS	SALTANTS	SALTPETER
SALERINGS	SALINISE	SALMONID	SALTATE	SALTPETRE

S

SALTS	SALVIFIC	SAME	SAMPAN	SANDALED
SALTUS	SALVING	SAMECH	SAMPANS	SANDALING
SALTUSES	SALVINGS	SAMECHS	SAMPHIRE	SANDALLED
SALTWATER	SALVO	SAMEK	SAMPHIRES	SANDALS
SALTWORK	SALVOED	SAMEKH	SAMPI	SANDARAC
SALTWORKS	SALVOES	SAMEKHS	SAMPIRE	SANDARACH
SALTWORT	SALVOING	SAMEKS	SAMPIRES	SANDARACS
SALTWORTS	SALVOR	SAMEL	SAMPIS	SANDBAG
SALTY	SALVORS	SAMELY	SAMPLE	SANDBAGS
SALUBRITY	SALVOS	SAMEN	SAMPLED	SANDBANK
SALUE	SALWAR	SAMENESS	SAMPLER	SANDBANKS
SALUED	SALWARS	SAMES	SAMPLERS	SANDBAR
SALUES	SAM	SAMEY	SAMPLERY	SANDBARS
SALUING	SAMA	SAMEYNESS	SAMPLES	SANDBLAST
SALUKI	SAMAAN	SAMFOO	SAMPLING	SANDBOX
SALUKIS	SAMAANS	SAMFOOS	SAMPLINGS	SANDBOXES
SALUME	SAMADHI	SAMFU	SAMPS	SANDBOY
SALUMI	SAMADHIS	SAMFUS	SAMS	SANDBOYS
SALURETIC	SAMAJ	SAMIEL	SAMSARA	SANDBUR
SALUT	SAMAJES	SAMIELS	SAMSARAS	SANDBURR
SALUTARY	SAMAN	SAMIER	SAMSARIC	SANDBURRS
SALUTE	SAMANS	SAMIEST	SAMSHOO	SANDBURS
SALUTED	SAMARA	SAMISEN	SAMSHOOS	SANDCRACK
SALUTER	SAMARAS	SAMISENS	SAMSHU	SANDDAB
SALUTERS	SAMARITAN	SAMITE	SAMSHUS	SANDDABS
SALUTES	SAMARIUM	SAMITES	SAMSKARA	SANDED
SALUTING	SAMARIUMS	SAMITHI	SAMSKARAS	SANDEK
SALVABLE	SAMAS	SAMITHIS	SAMURAI	SANDEKS
SALVABLY	SAMBA	SAMITI	SAMURAIS	SANDER
SALVAGE	SAMBAED	SAMITIS	SAN	SANDERS
SALVAGED	SAMBAING	SAMIZDAT	SANATIVE	SANDERSES
SALVAGEE	SAMBAL	SAMIZDATS	SANATORIA	SANDFISH
SALVAGEES	SAMBALS	SAMLET	SANATORY	SANDFLIES
SALVAGER	SAMBAR	SAMLETS	SANBENITO	SANDFLY
SALVAGERS	SAMBARS	SAMLOR	SANCAI	SANDGLASS
SALVAGES	SAMBAS	SAMLORS	SANCAIS	SANDHEAP
SALVAGING	SAMBHAR	SAMMED	SANCHO	SANDHEAPS
SALVARSAN	SAMBHARS	SAMMIE	SANCHOS	SANDHI
SALVATION	SAMBHUR	SAMMIES	SANCTA	SANDHILL
SALVATORY	SAMBHURS	SAMMING	SANCTIFY	SANDHILLS
SALVE	SAMBO	SAMMY	SANCTION	SANDHIS
SALVED	SAMBOES	SAMNITIS	SANCTIONS	SANDHOG
SALVER	SAMBOS	SAMOSA	SANCTITY	SANDHOGS
SALVERS	SAMBUCA	SAMOSAS	SANCTUARY	SANDIER
SALVES	SAMBUCAS	SAMOVAR	SANCTUM	SANDIEST
SALVETE	SAMBUKE	SAMOVARS	SANCTUMS	SANDINESS
SALVETES	SAMBUKES	SAMOYED	SAND	SANDING
SALVIA	SAMBUR	SAMOYEDS	SANDABLE	SANDINGS
SALVIAS	SAMBURS	SAMP	SANDAL	SANDIVER

S

SANDIVERS	SANGAREES	SANITIES	SANTERIA	SAPHENA
SANDLESS	SANGARS	SANITISE	SANTERIAS	SAPHENAE
SANDLIKE	SANGAS	SANITISED	SANTERO	SAPHENAS
SANDLING	SANGAT	SANITISER	SANTEROS	SAPHENOUS
SANDLINGS	SANGATS	SANITISES	SANTIM	SAPID
SANDLOT	SANGEET	SANITIZE	SANTIMI	SAPIDER
SANDLOTS	SANGEETS	SANITIZED	SANTIMS	SAPIDEST
SANDMAN	SANGER	SANITIZER	SANTIMU	SAPIDITY
SANDMEN	SANGERS	SANITIZES	SANTIR	SAPIDLESS
SANDPAPER	SANGFROID	SANITORIA	SANTIRS	SAPIDNESS
SANDPEEP	SANGH	SANITY	SANTO	SAPIENCE
SANDPEEPS	SANGHA	SANJAK	SANTOKU	SAPIENCES
SANDPILE	SANGHAS	SANJAKS	SANTOKUS	SAPIENCY
SANDPILES	SANGHAT	SANK	SANTOL	SAPIENS
SANDPIPER	SANGHATS	SANKO	SANTOLINA	SAPIENT
SANDPIT	SANGHS	SANKOS	SANTOLS	SAPIENTLY
SANDPITS	SANGLIER	SANNIE	SANTON	SAPIENTS
SANDPUMP	SANGLIERS	SANNIES	SANTONICA	SAPLESS
SANDPUMPS	SANGO	SANNOP	SANTONIN	SAPLING
SANDS	SANGOMA	SANNOPS	SANTONINS	SAPLINGS
SANDSHOE	SANGOMAS	SANNUP	SANTONS	SAPODILLA
SANDSHOES	SANGOS	SANNUPS	SANTOOR	SAPOGENIN
SANDSOAP	SANGRAIL	SANNY	SANTOORS	SAPONARIA
SANDSOAPS	SANGRAILS	SANNYASI	SANTOS	SAPONATED
SANDSPIT	SANGREAL	SANNYASIN	SANTOUR	SAPONIFY
SANDSPITS	SANGREALS	SANNYASIS	SANTOURS	SAPONIN
SANDSPOUT	SANGRIA	SANPAN	SANTS	SAPONINE
SANDSPUR	SANGRIAS	SANPANS	SANTUR	SAPONINES
SANDSPURS	SANGS	SANPRO	SANTURS	SAPONINS
SANDSTONE	SANGUIFY	SANPROS	SANYASI	SAPONITE
SANDSTORM	SANGUINE	SANS	SANYASIS	SAPONITES
SANDWICH	SANGUINED	SANSA	SAOLA	SAPOR
SANDWORM	SANGUINES	SANSAR	SAOLAS	SAPORIFIC
SANDWORMS	SANICLE	SANSARS	SAOUARI	SAPOROUS
SANDWORT	SANICLES	SANSAS	SAOUARIS	SAPORS
SANDWORTS	SANIDINE	SANSEI	SAP	SAPOTA
SANDY	SANIDINES	SANSEIS	SAPAJOU	SAPOTAS
SANDYISH	SANIES	SANSERIF	SAPAJOUS	SAPOTE
SANE	SANIFIED	SANSERIFS	SAPAN	SAPOTES
SANED	SANIFIES	SANT	SAPANS	SAPOUR
SANELY	SANIFY	SANTAL	SAPANWOOD	SAPOURS
SANENESS	SANIFYING	SANTALIC	SAPEGO	SAPPAN
SANER	SANING	SANTALIN	SAPEGOES	SAPPANS
SANES	SANIOUS	SANTALINS	SAPELE	SAPPED
SANEST	SANITARIA	SANTALOL	SAPELES	SAPPER
SANG	SANITARY	SANTALOLS	SAPFUL	SAPPERS
SANGA	SANITATE	SANTALS	SAPHEAD	SAPPHIC
SANGAR	SANITATED	SANTERA	SAPHEADED	SAPPHICS
SANGAREE	SANITATES	SANTERAS	SAPHEADS	SAPPHIRE

S

SAPPHIRED	SARAPE	SAREES	SARRASINS	SASSARARA
SAPPHIRES	SARAPES	SARGASSA	SARRAZIN	SASSE
SAPPHISM	SARBACANE	SARGASSO	SARRAZINS	SASSED
SAPPHISMS	SARCASM	SARGASSOS	SARS	SASSES
SAPPHIST	SARCASMS	SARGASSUM	SARSAR	SASSIER
SAPPHISTS	SARCASTIC	SARGE	SARSARS	SASSIES
SAPPIER	SARCENET	SARGES	SARSDEN	SASSIEST
SAPPIEST	SARCENETS	SARGO	SARSDENS	SASSILY
SAPPILY	SARCINA	SARGOS	SARSEN	SASSINESS
SAPPINESS	SARCINAE	SARGOSES	SARSENET	SASSING
SAPPING	SARCINAS	SARGUS	SARSENETS	SASSOLIN
SAPPINGS	SARCOCARP	SARGUSES	SARSENS	SASSOLINS
SAPPLE	SARCODE	SARI	SARSNET	SASSOLITE
SAPPLED	SARCODES	SARIN	SARSNETS	SASSWOOD
SAPPLES	SARCODIC	SARING	SARTOR	SASSWOODS
SAPPLING	SARCODINE	SARINS	SARTORIAL	SASSY
SAPPY	SARCOID	SARIS	SARTORIAN	SASSYWOOD
SAPRAEMIA	SARCOIDS	SARK	SARTORII	SASTRA
SAPRAEMIC	SARCOLOGY	SARKIER	SARTORIUS	SASTRAS
SAPREMIA	SARCOMA	SARKIEST	SARTORS	SASTRUGA
SAPREMIAS	SARCOMAS	SARKILY	SARUS	SASTRUGI
SAPREMIC	SARCOMATA	SARKINESS	SARUSES	SAT
SAPROBE	SARCOMERE	SARKING	SASANQUA	SATAI
SAPROBES	SARCONET	SARKINGS	SASANQUAS	SATAIS
SAPROBIAL	SARCONETS	SARKS	SASARARA	SATANG
SAPROBIC	SARCOPTIC	SARKY	SASARARAS	SATANGS
SAPROBITY	SARCOSOME	SARMENT	SASER	SATANIC
SAPROLITE	SARCOUS	SARMENTA	SASERS	SATANICAL
SAPROPEL	SARD	SARMENTS	SASH	SATANISM
SAPROPELS	SARDANA	SARMENTUM	SASHAY	SATANISMS
SAPROZOIC	SARDANAS	SARMIE	SASHAYED	SATANIST
SAPS	SARDAR	SARMIES	SASHAYING	SATANISTS
SAPSAGO	SARDARS	SARNEY	SASHAYS	SATANITY
SAPSAGOS	SARDEL	SARNEYS	SASHED	SATARA
SAPSUCKER	SARDELLE	SARNIE	SASHES	SATARAS
SAPUCAIA	SARDELLES	SARNIES	SASHIMI	SATAY
SAPUCAIAS	SARDELS	SAROD	SASHIMIS	SATAYS
SAPWOOD	SARDINE	SARODE	SASHING	SATCHEL
SAPWOODS	SARDINED	SARODES	SASHLESS	SATCHELED
SAR	SARDINES	SARODIST	SASIN	SATCHELS
SARABAND	SARDINING	SARODISTS	SASINE	SATCOM
SARABANDE	SARDIUS	SARODS	SASINES	SATCOMS
SARABANDS	SARDIUSES	SARONG	SASINS	SATE
SARAFAN	SARDONIAN	SARONGS	SASKATOON	SATED
SARAFANS	SARDONIC	SARONIC	SASQUATCH	SATEDNESS
SARAN	SARDONYX	SAROS	SASS	SATEEN
SARANGI	SARDS	SAROSES	SASSABIES	SATEENS
SARANGIS	SARED	SARPANCH	SASSABY	SATELESS
SARANS	SAREE	SARRASIN	SASSAFRAS	SATELLES

SATELLITE	SATNAV	SAUCEBOX	SAUNTS	SAVARI
SATEM	SATNAVS	SAUCED	SAUREL	SAVARIN
SATES	SATORI	SAUCELESS	SAURELS	SAVARINS
SATI	SATORIS	SAUCEPAN	SAURIAN	SAVARIS
SATIABLE	SATOSHI	SAUCEPANS	SAURIANS	SAVASANA
SATIABLY	SATOSHIS	SAUCEPOT	SAURIES	SAVASANAS
SATIATE	SATRAP	SAUCEPOTS	SAUROID	SAVATE
SATIATED	SATRAPAL	SAUCER	SAUROIDS	SAVATES
SATIATES	SATRAPIES	SAUCERFUL	SAUROPOD	SAVE
SATIATING	SATRAPS	SAUCERS	SAUROPODS	SAVEABLE
SATIATION	SATRAPY	SAUCES	SAURY	SAVED
SATIETIES	SATSANG	SAUCH	SAUSAGE	SAVEGARD
SATIETY	SATSANGS	SAUCHS	SAUSAGES	SAVEGARDS
SATIN	SATSUMA	SAUCIER	SAUT	SAVELOY
SATINED	SATSUMAS	SAUCIERS	SAUTE	SAVELOYS
SATINET	SATURABLE	SAUCIEST	SAUTED	SAVER
SATINETS	SATURANT	SAUCILY	SAUTEED	SAVERS
SATINETTA	SATURANTS	SAUCINESS	SAUTEEING	SAVES
SATINETTE	SATURATE	SAUCING	SAUTEING	SAVEY
SATING	SATURATED	SAUCISSE	SAUTERNE	SAVEYED
SATINIER	SATURATER	SAUCISSES	SAUTERNES	SAVEYING
SATINIEST	SATURATES	SAUCISSON	SAUTES	SAVEYS
SATINING	SATURATOR	SAUCY	SAUTING	SAVIN
SATINPOD	SATURNIC	SAUFGARD	SAUTOIR	SAVINE
SATINPODS	SATURNIID	SAUFGARDS	SAUTOIRE	SAVINES
SATINS	SATURNINE	SAUGER	SAUTOIRES	SAVING
SATINWOOD	SATURNISM	SAUGERS	SAUTOIRS	SAVINGLY
SATINY	SATURNIST	SAUGH	SAUTS	SAVINGS
SATIRE	SATYR	SAUGHS	SAV	SAVINS
SATIRES	SATYRA	SAUGHY	SAVABLE	SAVIOR
SATIRIC	SATYRAL	SAUL	SAVAGE	SAVIORS
SATIRICAL	SATYRALS	SAULGE	SAVAGED	SAVIOUR
SATIRISE	SATYRAS	SAULGES	SAVAGEDOM	SAVIOURS
SATIRISED	SATYRE	SAULIE	SAVAGELY	SAVOR
SATIRISER	SATYRES	SAULIES	SAVAGER	SAVORED
SATIRISES	SATYRESS	SAULS	SAVAGERY	SAVORER
SATIRIST	SATYRIC	SAULT	SAVAGES	SAVORERS
SATIRISTS	SATYRICAL	SAULTS	SAVAGEST	SAVORIER
SATIRIZE	SATYRID	SAUNA	SAVAGING	SAVORIES
SATIRIZED	SATYRIDS	SAUNAED	SAVAGISM	SAVORIEST
SATIRIZER	SATYRISK	SAUNAING	SAVAGISMS	SAVORILY
SATIRIZES	SATYRISKS	SAUNAS	SAVANNA	SAVORING
SATIS	SATYRLIKE	SAUNT	SAVANNAH	SAVORLESS
SATISFICE	SATYRS	SAUNTED	SAVANNAHS	SAVOROUS
SATISFIED	SAU	SAUNTER	SAVANNAS	SAVORS
SATISFIER	SAUBA	SAUNTERED	SAVANT	SAVORY
SATISFIES	SAUBAS	SAUNTERER	SAVANTE	SAVOUR
SATISFY	SAUCE	SAUNTERS	SAVANTES	SAVOURED
SATIVE	SAUCEBOAT	SAUNTING	SAVANTS	SAVOURER

S

SAVOURERS	SAWFLY	SAYABLES	SCABRID	SCALDED
SAVOURIER	SAWGRASS	SAYED	SCABROUS	SCALDER
SAVOURIES	SAWHORSE	SAYEDS	SCABS	SCALDERS
SAVOURILY	SAWHORSES	SAYER	SCAD	SCALDFISH
SAVOURING	SAWING	SAYERS	SCADS	SCALDHEAD
SAVOURLY	SAWINGS	SAYEST	SCAFF	SCALDIC
SAVOURS	SAWLIKE	SAYID	SCAFFED	SCALDING
SAVOURY	SAWLOG	SAYIDS	SCAFFIE	SCALDINGS
SAVOY	SAWLOGS	SAYING	SCAFFIER	SCALDINI
SAVOYARD	SAWMILL	SAYINGS	SCAFFIES	SCALDINO
SAVOYARDS	SAWMILLER	SAYNE	SCAFFIEST	SCALDS
SAVOYS	SAWMILLS	SAYON	SCAFFING	SCALDSHIP
SAVS	SAWN	SAYONARA	SCAFFOLD	SCALE
SAVVEY	SAWNEY	SAYONARAS	SCAFFOLDS	SCALEABLE
SAVVEYED	SAWNEYS	SAYONS	SCAFFS	SCALEABLY
SAVVEYING	SAWPIT	SAYS	SCAFFY	SCALED
SAVVEYS	SAWPITS	SAYST	SCAG	SCALELESS
SAVVIED	SAWS	SAYYID	SCAGGED	SCALELIKE
SAVVIER	SAWSHARK	SAYYIDS	SCAGGING	SCALENE
SAVVIES	SAWSHARKS	SAZ	SCAGLIA	SCALENES
SAVVIEST	SAWTEETH	SAZERAC	SCAGLIAS	SCALENI
SAVVILY	SAWTIMBER	SAZERACS	SCAGLIOLA	SCALENUS
SAVVINESS	SAWTOOTH	SAZES	SCAGS	SCALEPAN
SAVVY	SAWYER	SAZHEN	SCAIL	SCALEPANS
SAVVYING	SAWYERS	SAZHENS	SCAILED	SCALER
SAW	SAX	SAZZES	SCAILING	SCALERS
SAWAH	SAXATILE	SBIRRI	SCAILS	SCALES
SAWAHS	SAXAUL	SBIRRO	SCAITH	SCALETAIL
SAWBILL	SAXAULS	SCAB	SCAITHED	SCALEUP
SAWBILLS	SAXE	SCABBARD	SCAITHING	SCALEUPS
SAWBLADE	SAXES	SCABBARDS	SCAITHS	SCALEWORK
SAWBLADES	SAXHORN	SCABBED	SCALA	SCALIER
SAWBONES	SAXHORNS	SCABBIER	SCALABLE	SCALIEST
SAWBUCK	SAXICOLE	SCABBIEST	SCALABLY	SCALINESS
SAWBUCKS	SAXIFRAGE	SCABBILY	SCALADE	SCALING
SAWDER	SAXIST	SCABBING	SCALADES	SCALINGS
SAWDERED	SAXISTS	SCABBLE	SCALADO	SCALL
SAWDERING	SAXITOXIN	SCABBLED	SCALADOS	SCALLAWAG
SAWDERS	SAXMAN	SCABBLES	SCALAE	SCALLED
SAWDUST	SAXMEN	SCABBLING	SCALAGE	SCALLIES
SAWDUSTED	SAXONIES	SCABBY	SCALAGES	SCALLION
SAWDUSTS	SAXONITE	SCABIES	SCALAR	SCALLIONS
SAWDUSTY	SAXONITES	SCABIETIC	SCALARE	SCALLOP
SAWED	SAXONY	SCABIOSA	SCALARES	SCALLOPED
SAWER	SAXOPHONE	SCABIOSAS	SCALARS	SCALLOPER
SAWERS	SAXTUBA	SCABIOUS	SCALATION	SCALLOPS
SAWFISH	SAXTUBAS	SCABLAND	SCALAWAG	SCALLS
SAWFISHES	SAY	SCABLANDS	SCALAWAGS	SCALLY
SAWFLIES	SAYABLE	SCABLIKE	SCALD	SCALLYWAG

S

SCALOGRAM	SCAMTOS	SCAPHOID	SCARFISH	SCARRY
SCALP	SCAN	SCAPHOIDS	SCARFPIN	SCARS
SCALPED	SCAND	SCAPHOPOD	SCARFPINS	SCART
SCALPEL	SCANDAL	SCAPI	SCARFS	SCARTED
SCALPELS	SCANDALED	SCAPING	SCARFSKIN	SCARTH
SCALPER	SCANDALS	SCAPOLITE	SCARFWISE	SCARTHS
SCALPERS	SCANDENT	SCAPOSE	SCARIER	SCARTING
SCALPING	SCANDIA	SCAPPLE	SCARIEST	SCARTS
SCALPINGS	SCANDIAS	SCAPPLED	SCARIFIED	SCARVED
SCALPINS	SCANDIC	SCAPPLES	SCARIFIER	SCARVES
SCALPLESS	SCANDIUM	SCAPPLING	SCARIFIES	SCARY
SCALPRUM	SCANDIUMS	SCAPULA	SCARIFY	SCAT
SCALPRUMS	SCANNABLE	SCAPULAE	SCARILY	SCATBACK
SCALPS	SCANNED	SCAPULAR	SCARINESS	SCATBACKS
SCALY	SCANNER	SCAPULARS	SCARING	SCATCH
SCAM	SCANNERS	SCAPULARY	SCARIOSE	SCATCHES
SCAMBLE	SCANNING	SCAPULAS	SCARIOUS	SCATH
SCAMBLED	SCANNINGS	SCAPUS	SCARLESS	SCATHE
SCAMBLER	SCANS	SCAR	SCARLET	SCATHED
SCAMBLERS	SCANSION	SCARAB	SCARLETED	SCATHEFUL
SCAMBLES	SCANSIONS	SCARABAEI	SCARLETS	SCATHES
SCAMBLING	SCANT	SCARABEE	SCARMOGE	SCATHING
SCAMEL	SCANTED	SCARABEES	SCARMOGES	SCATHS
SCAMELS	SCANTER	SCARABOID	SCARP	SCATOLE
SCAMMED	SCANTEST	SCARABS	SCARPA	SCATOLES
SCAMMER	SCANTIER	SCARCE	SCARPAED	SCATOLOGY
SCAMMERS	SCANTIES	SCARCELY	SCARPAING	SCATS
SCAMMIER	SCANTIEST	SCARCER	SCARPAS	SCATT
SCAMMIEST	SCANTILY	SCARCEST	SCARPED	SCATTED
SCAMMING	SCANTING	SCARCITY	SCARPER	SCATTER
SCAMMONY	SCANTITY	SCARE	SCARPERED	SCATTERED
SCAMMY	SCANTLE	SCARECROW	SCARPERS	SCATTERER
SCAMP	SCANTLED	SCARED	SCARPETTI	SCATTERS
SCAMPED	SCANTLES	SCAREDER	SCARPETTO	SCATTERY
SCAMPER	SCANTLING	SCAREDEST	SCARPH	SCATTIER
SCAMPERED	SCANTLY	SCAREDIES	SCARPHED	SCATTIEST
SCAMPERER	SCANTNESS	SCAREDY	SCARPHING	SCATTILY
SCAMPERS	SCANTS	SCAREHEAD	SCARPHS	SCATTING
SCAMPI	SCANTY	SCARER	SCARPINES	SCATTINGS
SCAMPIES	SCAPA	SCARERS	SCARPING	SCATTS
SCAMPING	SCAPAED	SCARES	SCARPINGS	SCATTY
SCAMPINGS	SCAPAING	SCAREWARE	SCARPS	SCAUD
SCAMPIS	SCAPAS	SCAREY	SCARRE	SCAUDED
SCAMPISH	SCAPE	SCARF	SCARRED	SCAUDING
SCAMPS	SCAPED	SCARFED	SCARRES	SCAUDS
SCAMS	SCAPEGOAT	SCARFER	SCARRIER	SCAUP
SCAMSTER	SCAPELESS	SCARFERS	SCARRIEST	SCAUPED
SCAMSTERS	SCAPEMENT	SCARFING	SCARRING	SCAUPER
SCAMTO	SCAPES	SCARFINGS	SCARRINGS	SCAUPERS

S

SCAUPING	SCENDING	SCHAPSKAS	SCHIZOID	SCHMECKS
SCAUPS	SCENDS	SCHATCHEN	SCHIZOIDS	SCHMEER
SCAUR	SCENE	SCHAV	SCHIZONT	SCHMEERED
SCAURED	SCENED	SCHAVS	SCHIZONTS	SCHMEERS
SCAURIES	SCENEMAN	SCHECHITA	SCHIZOPOD	SCHMELZ
SCAURING	SCENEMEN	SCHEDULAR	SCHLAGER	SCHMELZE
SCAURS	SCENERIES	SCHEDULE	SCHLAGERS	SCHMELZES
SCAURY	SCENERY	SCHEDULED	SCHLEMIEL	SCHMICK
SCAVAGE	SCENES	SCHEDULER	SCHLEMIHL	SCHMICKER
SCAVAGED	SCENESTER	SCHEDULES	SCHLEP	SCHMO
SCAVAGER	SCENIC	SCHEELITE	SCHLEPP	SCHMOCK
SCAVAGERS	SCENICAL	SCHELLIES	SCHLEPPED	SCHMOCKS
SCAVAGES	SCENICS	SCHELLUM	SCHLEPPER	SCHMOE
SCAVAGING	SCENING	SCHELLUMS	SCHLEPPS	SCHMOES
SCAVENGE	SCENT	SCHELLY	SCHLEPPY	SCHMOOS
SCAVENGED	SCENTED	SCHELM	SCHLEPS	SCHMOOSE
SCAVENGER	SCENTFUL	SCHELMS	SCHLICH	SCHMOOSED
SCAVENGES	SCENTING	SCHEMA	SCHLICHS	SCHMOOSES
SCAW	SCENTINGS	SCHEMAS	SCHLIERE	SCHMOOZ
SCAWS	SCENTLESS	SCHEMATA	SCHLIEREN	SCHMOOZE
SCAWTITE	SCENTS	SCHEMATIC	SCHLIERIC	SCHMOOZED
SCAWTITES	SCEPSIS	SCHEME	SCHLOCK	SCHMOOZER
SCAZON	SCEPSISES	SCHEMED	SCHLOCKER	SCHMOOZES
SCAZONS	SCEPTER	SCHEMER	SCHLOCKEY	SCHMOOZY
SCAZONTES	SCEPTERED	SCHEMERS	SCHLOCKS	SCHMOS
SCAZONTIC	SCEPTERS	SCHEMES	SCHLOCKY	SCHMUCK
SCEAT	SCEPTIC	SCHEMIE	SCHLONG	SCHMUCKED
SCEATS	SCEPTICAL	SCHEMIES	SCHLONGS	SCHMUCKS
SCEATT	SCEPTICS	SCHEMING	SCHLOSS	SCHMUCKY
SCEATTAS	SCEPTRAL	SCHEMINGS	SCHLOSSES	SCHMUTTER
SCEATTS	SCEPTRE	SCHERZI	SCHLUB	SCHMUTZ
SCEDULE	SCEPTRED	SCHERZO	SCHLUBS	SCHMUTZES
SCEDULED	SCEPTRES	SCHERZOS	SCHLUMP	SCHNAPPER
SCEDULES	SCEPTRING	SCHIAVONE	SCHLUMPED	SCHNAPPS
SCEDULING	SCEPTRY	SCHIEDAM	SCHLUMPS	SCHNAPS
SCELERAT	SCERNE	SCHIEDAMS	SCHLUMPY	SCHNAPSES
SCELERATE	SCERNED	SCHILLER	SCHMALTZ	SCHNAUZER
SCELERATS	SCERNES	SCHILLERS	SCHMALTZY	SCHNECKE
SCENA	SCERNING	SCHILLING	SCHMALZ	SCHNECKEN
SCENARIES	SCHANSE	SCHIMMEL	SCHMALZES	SCHNEID
SCENARIO	SCHANSES	SCHIMMELS	SCHMALZY	SCHNEIDS
SCENARIOS	SCHANTZE	SCHISM	SCHMATTE	SCHNELL
SCENARISE	SCHANTZES	SCHISMA	SCHMATTES	SCHNITZEL
SCENARIST	SCHANZE	SCHISMAS	SCHMEAR	SCHNOODLE
SCENARIZE	SCHANZES	SCHISMS	SCHMEARED	SCHNOOK
SCENARY	SCHAPPE	SCHIST	SCHMEARS	SCHNOOKS
SCENAS	SCHAPPED	SCHISTOSE	SCHMECK	SCHNORKEL
SCEND	SCHAPPES	SCHISTOUS	SCHMECKED	SCHNORR
SCENDED	SCHAPSKA	SCHISTS	SCHMECKER	SCHNORRED

SCHNORRER	SCHTOOM	SCILICET	SCIUROID	SCOBY
SCHNORRS	SCHTUCK	SCILLA	SCLAFF	SCODIER
SCHNOZ	SCHTUCKS	SCILLAS	SCLAFFED	SCODIEST
SCHNOZES	SCHTUM	SCIMETAR	SCLAFFER	SCODY
SCHNOZZ	SCHTUMMER	SCIMETARS	SCLAFFERS	SCOFF
SCHNOZZES	SCHTUP	SCIMITAR	SCLAFFING	SCOFFED
SCHNOZZLE	SCHTUPPED	SCIMITARS	SCLAFFS	SCOFFER
SCHOLAR	SCHTUPS	SCIMITER	SCLATE	SCOFFERS
SCHOLARCH	SCHUIT	SCIMITERS	SCLATED	SCOFFING
SCHOLARLY	SCHUITS	SCINCOID	SCLATES	SCOFFINGS
SCHOLARS	SCHUL	SCINCOIDS	SCLATING	SCOFFLAW
SCHOLIA	SCHULN	SCINTILLA	SCLAUNDER	SCOFFLAWS
SCHOLIAST	SCHULS	SCIOLISM	SCLAVE	SCOFFS
SCHOLION	SCHUSS	SCIOLISMS	SCLAVES	SCOG
SCHOLIUM	SCHUSSED	SCIOLIST	SCLERA	SCOGGED
SCHOLIUMS	SCHUSSER	SCIOLISTS	SCLERAE	SCOGGING
SCHOOL	SCHUSSERS	SCIOLOUS	SCLERAL	SCOGS
SCHOOLBAG	SCHUSSES	SCIOLTO	SCLERAS	SCOINSON
SCHOOLBOY	SCHUSSING	SCIOMACHY	SCLERE	SCOINSONS
SCHOOLDAY	SCHUYT	SCIOMANCY	SCLEREID	SCOLD
SCHOOLE	SCHUYTS	SCION	SCLEREIDE	SCOLDABLE
SCHOOLED	SCHVITZ	SCIONS	SCLEREIDS	SCOLDED
SCHOOLER	SCHVITZED	SCIOPHYTE	SCLEREMA	SCOLDER
SCHOOLERS	SCHVITZES	SCIOSOPHY	SCLEREMAS	SCOLDERS
SCHOOLERY	SCHWA	SCIROC	SCLERES	SCOLDING
SCHOOLES	SCHWAG	SCIROCCO	SCLERITE	SCOLDINGS
SCHOOLIE	SCHWAGS	SCIROCCOS	SCLERITES	SCOLDS
SCHOOLIES	SCHWAS	SCIROCS	SCLERITIC	SCOLECES
SCHOOLING	SCIAENID	SCIRRHI	SCLERITIS	SCOLECID
SCHOOLKID	SCIAENIDS	SCIRRHOID	SCLEROID	SCOLECIDS
SCHOOLMAN	SCIAENOID	SCIRRHOUS	SCLEROMA	SCOLECITE
SCHOOLMEN	SCIAMACHY	SCIRRHUS	SCLEROMAS	SCOLECOID
SCHOOLS	SCIARID	SCISSEL	SCLEROSAL	SCOLEX
SCHOONER	SCIARIDS	SCISSELS	SCLEROSE	SCOLIA
SCHOONERS	SCIATIC	SCISSIL	SCLEROSED	SCOLICES
SCHORL	SCIATICA	SCISSILE	SCLEROSES	SCOLIOMA
SCHORLS	SCIATICAL	SCISSILS	SCLEROSIS	SCOLIOMAS
SCHOUT	SCIATICAS	SCISSION	SCLEROTAL	SCOLION
SCHOUTS	SCIATICS	SCISSIONS	SCLEROTIA	SCOLIOSES
SCHRIK	SCIENCE	SCISSOR	SCLEROTIC	SCOLIOSIS
SCHRIKS	SCIENCED	SCISSORED	SCLEROTIN	SCOLIOTIC
SCHROD	SCIENCES	SCISSORER	SCLEROUS	SCOLLOP
SCHRODS	SCIENT	SCISSORS	SCLIFF	SCOLLOPED
SCHTICK	SCIENTER	SCISSURE	SCLIFFS	SCOLLOPS
SCHTICKS	SCIENTIAL	SCISSURES	SCLIM	SCOLYTID
SCHTIK	SCIENTISE	SCIURID	SCLIMMED	SCOLYTIDS
SCHTIKS	SCIENTISM	SCIURIDS	SCLIMMING	SCOLYTOID
SCHTOOK	SCIENTIST	SCIURINE	SCLIMS	SCOMBRID
SCHTOOKS	SCIENTIZE	SCIURINES	SCOBIES	SCOMBRIDS

S

SCOMBROID	SCOPAS	SCORNINGS	SCOURER	SCOWRER
SCOMFISH	SCOPATE	SCORNS	SCOURERS	SCOWRERS
SCONCE	SCOPE	SCORODITE	SCOURGE	SCOWRIE
SCONCED	SCOPED	SCORPER	SCOURGED	SCOWRIES
SCONCES	SCOPELID	SCORPERS	SCOURGER	SCOWS
SCONCHEON	SCOPELIDS	SCORPIOID	SCOURGERS	SCOWTH
SCONCING	SCOPELOID	SCORPION	SCOURGES	SCOWTHER
SCONE	SCOPES	SCORPIONS	SCOURGING	SCOWTHERS
SCONES	SCOPING	SCORRENDO	SCOURIE	SCOWTHS
SCONTION	SCOPOLINE	SCORSE	SCOURIES	SCOZZA
SCONTIONS	SCOPS	SCORSED	SCOURING	SCOZZAS
SCOOBIES	SCOPULA	SCORSER	SCOURINGS	SCRAB
SCOOBY	SCOPULAE	SCORSERS	SCOURS	SCRABBED
SCOOCH	SCOPULAS	SCORSES	SCOURSE	SCRABBING
SCOOCHED	SCOPULATE	SCORSING	SCOURSED	SCRABBLE
SCOOCHES	SCORBUTIC	SCOT	SCOURSES	SCRABBLED
SCOOCHING	SCORCH	SCOTCH	SCOURSING	SCRABBLER
SCOOG	SCORCHED	SCOTCHED	SCOUSE	SCRABBLES
SCOOGED	SCORCHER	SCOTCHES	SCOUSER	SCRABBLY
SCOOGING	SCORCHERS	SCOTCHING	SCOUSERS	SCRABS
SCOOGS	SCORCHES	SCOTER	SCOUSES	SCRAE
SCOOP	SCORCHING	SCOTERS	SCOUT	SCRAES
SCOOPABLE	SCORDATO	SCOTIA	SCOUTED	SCRAG
SCOOPED	SCORE	SCOTIAS	SCOUTER	SCRAGGED
SCOOPER	SCORECARD	SCOTOMA	SCOUTERS	SCRAGGIER
SCOOPERS	SCORED	SCOTOMAS	SCOUTH	SCRAGGILY
SCOOPFUL	SCORELESS	SCOTOMATA	SCOUTHER	SCRAGGING
SCOOPFULS	SCORELINE	SCOTOMIA	SCOUTHERS	SCRAGGLY
SCOOPING	SCOREPAD	SCOTOMIAS	SCOUTHERY	SCRAGGY
SCOOPINGS	SCOREPADS	SCOTOMIES	SCOUTHS	SCRAGS
SCOOPS	SCORER	SCOTOMY	SCOUTING	SCRAICH
SCOOPSFUL	SCORERS	SCOTOPHIL	SCOUTINGS	SCRAICHED
SCOOSH	SCORES	SCOTOPIA	SCOUTS	SCRAICHS
SCOOSHED	SCORIA	SCOTOPIAS	SCOW	SCRAIGH
SCOOSHES	SCORIAC	SCOTOPIC	SCOWDER	SCRAIGHED
SCOOSHING	SCORIAE	SCOTS	SCOWDERED	SCRAIGHS
SCOOT	SCORIFIED	SCOTTIE	SCOWDERS	SCRAM
SCOOTCH	SCORIFIER	SCOTTIES	SCOWED	SCRAMB
SCOOTCHED	SCORIFIES	SCOUG	SCOWING	SCRAMBED
SCOOTCHES	SCORIFY	SCOUGED	SCOWL	SCRAMBING
SCOOTED	SCORING	SCOUGING	SCOWLED	SCRAMBLE
SCOOTER	SCORINGS	SCOUGS	SCOWLER	SCRAMBLED
SCOOTERED	SCORIOUS	SCOUNDREL	SCOWLERS	SCRAMBLER
SCOOTERS	SCORN	SCOUP	SCOWLING	SCRAMBLES
SCOOTING	SCORNED	SCOUPED	SCOWLS	SCRAMBS
SCOOTS	SCORNER	SCOUPING	SCOWP	SCRAMJET
SCOP	SCORNERS	SCOUPS	SCOWPED	SCRAMJETS
SCOPA	SCORNFUL	SCOUR	SCOWPING	SCRAMMED
SCOPAE	SCORNING	SCOURED	SCOWPS	SCRAMMING

SCRAMS	SCRAUCH	SCREAMO	SCREWIER	SCRIMP
SCRAN	SCRAUCHED	SCREAMOS	SCREWIEST	SCRIMPED
SCRANCH	SCRAUCHS	SCREAMS	SCREWING	SCRIMPER
SCRANCHED	SCRAUGH	SCREE	SCREWINGS	SCRIMPERS
SCRANCHES	SCRAUGHED	SCREECH	SCREWLIKE	SCRIMPIER
SCRANNEL	SCRAUGHS	SCREECHED	SCREWS	SCRIMPILY
SCRANNELS	SCRAVEL	SCREECHER	SCREWTOP	SCRIMPING
SCRANNIER	SCRAVELED	SCREECHES	SCREWTOPS	SCRIMPIT
SCRANNY	SCRAVELS	SCREECHY	SCREWUP	SCRIMPLY
SCRANS	SCRAW	SCREED	SCREWUPS	SCRIMPS
SCRAP	SCRAWB	SCREEDED	SCREWWORM	SCRIMPY
SCRAPABLE	SCRAWBED	SCREEDER	SCREWY	SCRIMS
SCRAPBOOK	SCRAWBING	SCREEDERS	SCRIBABLE	SCRIMSHAW
SCRAPE	SCRAWBS	SCREEDING	SCRIBAL	SCRIMURE
SCRAPED	SCRAWL	SCREEDS	SCRIBBLE	SCRIMURES
SCRAPEGUT	SCRAWLED	SCREEN	SCRIBBLED	SCRINE
SCRAPER	SCRAWLER	SCREENED	SCRIBBLER	SCRINES
SCRAPERS	SCRAWLERS	SCREENER	SCRIBBLES	SCRIP
SCRAPES	SCRAWLIER	SCREENERS	SCRIBBLY	SCRIPPAGE
SCRAPHEAP	SCRAWLING	SCREENFUL	SCRIBE	SCRIPS
SCRAPIE	SCRAWLS	SCREENIE	SCRIBED	SCRIPT
SCRAPIES	SCRAWLY	SCREENIES	SCRIBER	SCRIPTED
SCRAPING	SCRAWM	SCREENING	SCRIBERS	SCRIPTER
SCRAPINGS	SCRAWMED	SCREENS	SCRIBES	SCRIPTERS
SCRAPPAGE	SCRAWMING	SCREES	SCRIBING	SCRIPTING
SCRAPPED	SCRAWMS	SCREET	SCRIBINGS	SCRIPTORY
SCRAPPER	SCRAWNIER	SCREETED	SCRIBISM	SCRIPTS
SCRAPPERS	SCRAWNILY	SCREETING	SCRIBISMS	SCRIPTURE
SCRAPPIER	SCRAWNY	SCREETS	SCRIECH	SCRITCH
SCRAPPILY	SCRAWP	SCREEVE	SCRIECHED	SCRITCHED
SCRAPPING	SCRAWPED	SCREEVED	SCRIECHS	SCRITCHES
SCRAPPLE	SCRAWPING	SCREEVER	SCRIED	SCRIVE
SCRAPPLES	SCRAWPS	SCREEVERS	SCRIENE	SCRIVED
SCRAPPY	SCRAWS	SCREEVES	SCRIENES	SCRIVENER
SCRAPS	SCRAY	SCREEVING	SCRIES	SCRIVES
SCRAPYARD	SCRAYE	SCREICH	SCRIEVE	SCRIVING
SCRAT	SCRAYES	SCREICHED	SCRIEVED	SCROB
SCRATCH	SCRAYS	SCREICHS	SCRIEVES	SCROBBED
SCRATCHED	SCREAK	SCREIGH	SCRIEVING	SCROBBING
SCRATCHER	SCREAKED	SCREIGHED	SCRIGGLE	SCROBBLE
SCRATCHES	SCREAKIER	SCREIGHS	SCRIGGLED	SCROBBLED
SCRATCHIE	SCREAKING	SCREW	SCRIGGLES	SCROBBLES
SCRATCHY	SCREAKS	SCREWABLE	SCRIGGLY	SCROBE
SCRATS	SCREAKY	SCREWBALL	SCRIKE	SCROBES
SCRATTED	SCREAM	SCREWBEAN	SCRIKED	SCROBS
SCRATTING	SCREAMED	SCREWED	SCRIKES	SCROD
SCRATTLE	SCREAMER	SCREWER	SCRIKING	SCRODDLED
SCRATTLED	SCREAMERS	SCREWERS	SCRIM	SCRODS
SCRATTLES	SCREAMING	SCREWHEAD	SCRIMMAGE	SCROFULA

S

SCROFULAS	SCROW	SCRUMS	SCUDDLES	SCULPING
SCROG	SCROWDGE	SCRUNCH	SCUDDLING	SCULPINS
SCROGGIE	SCROWDGED	SCRUNCHED	SCUDI	SCULPS
SCROGGIER	SCROWDGES	SCRUNCHES	SCUDLER	SCULPSIT
SCROGGIN	SCROWL	SCRUNCHIE	SCUDLERS	SCULPT
SCROGGINS	SCROWLE	SCRUNCHIN	SCUDO	SCULPTED
SCROGGY	SCROWLED	SCRUNCHY	SCUDS	SCULPTING
SCROGS	SCROWLES	SCRUNT	SCUFF	SCULPTOR
SCROLL	SCROWLING	SCRUNTIER	SCUFFED	SCULPTORS
SCROLLED	SCROWLS	SCRUNTS	SCUFFER	SCULPTS
SCROLLER	SCROWS	SCRUNTY	SCUFFERS	SCULPTURE
SCROLLERS	SCROYLE	SCRUPLE	SCUFFING	SCULS
SCROLLING	SCROYLES	SCRUPLED	SCUFFLE	SCULTCH
SCROLLS	SCRUB	SCRUPLER	SCUFFLED	SCULTCHES
SCROME	SCRUBBED	SCRUPLERS	SCUFFLER	SCUM
SCROMED	SCRUBBER	SCRUPLES	SCUFFLERS	SCUMBAG
SCROMES	SCRUBBERS	SCRUPLING	SCUFFLES	SCUMBAGS
SCROMING	SCRUBBIER	SCRUTABLE	SCUFFLING	SCUMBALL
SCROOCH	SCRUBBILY	SCRUTATOR	SCUFFS	SCUMBALLS
SCROOCHED	SCRUBBING	SCRUTINY	SCUFT	SCUMBER
SCROOCHES	SCRUBBY	SCRUTO	SCUFTS	SCUMBERED
SCROOGE	SCRUBLAND	SCRUTOIRE	SCUG	SCUMBERS
SCROOGED	SCRUBS	SCRUTOS	SCUGGED	SCUMBLE
SCROOGES	SCRUFF	SCRUZE	SCUGGING	SCUMBLED
SCROOGING	SCRUFFED	SCRUZED	SCUGS	SCUMBLES
SCROOP	SCRUFFIER	SCRUZES	SCUL	SCUMBLING
SCROOPED	SCRUFFILY	SCRUZING	SCULCH	SCUMBRO
SCROOPING	SCRUFFING	SCRY	SCULCHES	SCUMBROS
SCROOPS	SCRUFFS	SCRYDE	SCULK	SCUMFISH
SCROOTCH	SCRUFFY	SCRYER	SCULKED	SCUMLESS
SCRORP	SCRUM	SCRYERS	SCULKER	SCUMLIKE
SCRORPS	SCRUMDOWN	SCRYING	SCULKERS	SCUMMED
SCROTA	SCRUMMAGE	SCRYINGS	SCULKING	SCUMMER
SCROTAL	SCRUMMED	SCRYNE	SCULKS	SCUMMERS
SCROTE	SCRUMMIE	SCRYNES	SCULL	SCUMMIER
SCROTES	SCRUMMIER	SCUBA	SCULLE	SCUMMIEST
SCROTUM	SCRUMMIES	SCUBAED	SCULLED	SCUMMILY
SCROTUMS	SCRUMMING	SCUBAING	SCULLER	SCUMMING
SCROUGE	SCRUMMY	SCUBAS	SCULLERS	SCUMMINGS
SCROUGED	SCRUMP	SCUCHIN	SCULLERY	SCUMMY
SCROUGER	SCRUMPED	SCUCHINS	SCULLES	SCUMS
SCROUGERS	SCRUMPIES	SCUD	SCULLING	SCUNCHEON
SCROUGES	SCRUMPING	SCUDDALER	SCULLINGS	SCUNDERED
SCROUGING	SCRUMPLE	SCUDDED	SCULLION	SCUNGE
SCROUNGE	SCRUMPLED	SCUDDER	SCULLIONS	SCUNGED
SCROUNGED	SCRUMPLES	SCUDDERS	SCULLS	SCUNGES
SCROUNGER	SCRUMPOX	SCUDDING	SCULP	SCUNGIER
SCROUNGES	SCRUMPS	SCUDDLE	SCULPED	SCUNGIEST
SCROUNGY	SCRUMPY	SCUDDLED	SCULPIN	SCUNGILE

SCUNGILI	SCUTCH	SCYTHEMEN	SEACUNNY	SEALIFT
SCUNGILLE	SCUTCHED	SCYTHER	SEADOG	SEALIFTED
SCUNGILLI	SCUTCHEON	SCYTHERS	SEADOGS	SEALIFTS
SCUNGING	SCUTCHER	SCYTHES	SEADROME	SEALINE
SCUNGY	SCUTCHERS	SCYTHING	SEADROMES	SEALINES
SCUNNER	SCUTCHES	SDAINE	SEAFARER	SEALING
SCUNNERED	SCUTCHING	SDAINED	SEAFARERS	SEALINGS
SCUNNERS	SCUTE	SDAINES	SEAFARING	SEALION
SCUP	SCUTELLA	SDAINING	SEAFLOOR	SEALIONED
SCUPPAUG	SCUTELLAR	SDAYN	SEAFLOORS	SEALIONS
SCUPPAUGS	SCUTELLUM	SDAYNED	SEAFOAM	SEALLIKE
SCUPPER	SCUTES	SDAYNING	SEAFOAMS	SEALPOINT
SCUPPERED	SCUTIFORM	SDAYNS	SEAFOLK	SEALS
SCUPPERS	SCUTIGER	SDEIGN	SEAFOLKS	SEALSKIN
SCUPS	SCUTIGERS	SDEIGNE	SEAFOOD	SEALSKINS
SCUR	SCUTS	SDEIGNED	SEAFOODS	SEALWAX
SCURF	SCUTTER	SDEIGNES	SEAFOWL	SEALWAXES
SCURFIER	SCUTTERED	SDEIGNING	SEAFOWLS	SEALYHAM
SCURFIEST	SCUTTERS	SDEIGNS	SEAFRONT	SEALYHAMS
SCURFS	SCUTTLE	SDEIN	SEAFRONTS	SEAM
SCURFY	SCUTTLED	SDEINED	SEAGIRT	SEAMAID
SCURRED	SCUTTLER	SDEINING	SEAGOING	SEAMAIDS
SCURRIED	SCUTTLERS	SDEINS	SEAGRASS	SEAMAN
SCURRIER	SCUTTLES	SEA	SEAGULL	SEAMANLY
SCURRIERS	SCUTTLING	SEABAG	SEAGULLS	SEAMARK
SCURRIES	SCUTUM	SEABAGS	SEAHAWK	SEAMARKS
SCURRIL	SCUTWORK	SEABANK	SEAHAWKS	SEAME
SCURRILE	SCUTWORKS	SEABANKS	SEAHOG	SEAMED
SCURRING	SCUZZ	SEABEACH	SEAHOGS	SEAMEN
SCURRIOUR	SCUZZBAG	SEABED	SEAHORSE	SEAMER
SCURRY	SCUZZBAGS	SEABEDS	SEAHORSES	SEAMERS
SCURRYING	SCUZZBALL	SEABIRD	SEAHOUND	SEAMES
SCURS	SCUZZES	SEABIRDS	SEAHOUNDS	SEAMFREE
SCURVIER	SCUZZIER	SEABLITE	SEAKALE	SEAMIER
SCURVIES	SCUZZIEST	SEABLITES	SEAKALES	SEAMIEST
SCURVIEST	SCUZZY	SEABOARD	SEAKINDLY	SEAMINESS
SCURVILY	SCYBALA	SEABOARDS	SEAL	SEAMING
SCURVY	SCYBALOUS	SEABOOT	SEALABLE	SEAMINGS
SCUSE	SCYBALUM	SEABOOTS	SEALANT	SEAMLESS
SCUSED	SCYE	SEABORNE	SEALANTS	SEAMLIKE
SCUSES	SCYES	SEABOTTLE	SEALCH	SEAMOUNT
SCUSING	SCYPHATE	SEABREAM	SEALCHS	SEAMOUNTS
SCUT	SCYPHI	SEABREAMS	SEALED	SEAMS
SCUTA	SCYPHUS	SEACOAST	SEALER	SEAMSET
SCUTAGE	SCYTALE	SEACOASTS	SEALERIES	SEAMSETS
SCUTAGES	SCYTALES	SEACOCK	SEALERS	SEAMSTER
SCUTAL	SCYTHE	SEACOCKS	SEALERY	SEAMSTERS
SCUTATE	SCYTHED	SEACRAFT	SEALGH	SEAMY
SCUTATION	SCYTHEMAN	SEACRAFTS	SEALGHS	SEAN

SEANCE	SEASHORE	SEAWARDS	SECEDERS	SECRETA
SEANCES	SEASHORES	SEAWARE	SECEDES	SECRETAGE
SEANED	SEASICK	SEAWARES	SECEDING	SECRETARY
SEANING	SEASICKER	SEAWATER	SECERN	SECRETE
SEANNACHY	SEASIDE	SEAWATERS	SECERNED	SECRETED
SEANS	SEASIDES	SEAWAY	SECERNENT	SECRETER
SEAPIECE	SEASING	SEAWAYS	SECERNING	SECRETES
SEAPIECES	SEASON	SEAWEED	SECERNS	SECRETEST
SEAPLANE	SEASONAL	SEAWEEDS	SECESH	SECRETIN
SEAPLANES	SEASONALS	SEAWEEDY	SECESHER	SECRETING
SEAPORT	SEASONED	SEAWIFE	SECESHERS	SECRETINS
SEAPORTS	SEASONER	SEAWIVES	SECESHES	SECRETION
SEAQUAKE	SEASONERS	SEAWOMAN	SECESSION	SECRETIVE
SEAQUAKES	SEASONING	SEAWOMEN	SECH	SECRETLY
SEAQUARIA	SEASONS	SEAWORM	SECHS	SECRETOR
SEAR	SEASPEAK	SEAWORMS	SECKEL	SECRETORS
SEARAT	SEASPEAKS	SEAWORTHY	SECKELS	SECRETORY
SEARATS	SEASTRAND	SEAX	SECKLE	SECRETS
SEARCE	SEASURE	SEAXES	SECKLES	SECS
SEARCED	SEASURES	SEAZE	SECLUDE	SECT
SEARCES	SEAT	SEAZED	SECLUDED	SECTARIAL
SEARCH	SEATBACK	SEAZES	SECLUDES	SECTARIAN
SEARCHED	SEATBACKS	SEAZING	SECLUDING	SECTARIES
SEARCHER	SEATBELT	SEBACEOUS	SECLUSION	SECTARY
SEARCHERS	SEATBELTS	SEBACIC	SECLUSIVE	SECTATOR
SEARCHES	SEATED	SEBASIC	SECO	SECTATORS
SEARCHING	SEATER	SEBATE	SECODONT	SECTILE
SEARCING	SEATERS	SEBATES	SECODONTS	SECTILITY
SEARE	SEATING	SEBESTEN	SECONAL	SECTION
SEARED	SEATINGS	SEBESTENS	SECONALS	SECTIONAL
SEARER	SEATLESS	SEBIFIC	SECOND	SECTIONED
SEAREST	SEATMATE	SEBORRHEA	SECONDARY	SECTIONS
SEARING	SEATMATES	SEBUM	SECONDE	SECTOR
SEARINGLY	SEATRAIN	SEBUMS	SECONDED	SECTORAL
SEARINGS	SEATRAINS	SEBUNDIES	SECONDEE	SECTORED
SEARNESS	SEATROUT	SEBUNDY	SECONDEES	SECTORIAL
SEAROBIN	SEATROUTS	SEC	SECONDER	SECTORING
SEAROBINS	SEATS	SECALOSE	SECONDERS	SECTORISE
SEARS	SEATWORK	SECALOSES	SECONDES	SECTORIZE
SEAS	SEATWORKS	SECANT	SECONDI	SECTORS
SEASCAPE	SEAWALL	SECANTLY	SECONDING	SECTS
SEASCAPES	SEAWALLED	SECANTS	SECONDLY	SECULA
SEASCOUT	SEAWALLS	SECATEUR	SECONDO	SECULAR
SEASCOUTS	SEAWAN	SECATEURS	SECONDS	SECULARLY
SEASE	SEAWANS	SECCO	SECPAR	SECULARS
SEASED	SEAWANT	SECCOS	SECPARS	SECULUM
SEASES	SEAWANTS	SECEDE	SECRECIES	SECULUMS
SEASHELL	SEAWARD	SECEDED	SECRECY	SECUND
SEASHELLS	SEAWARDLY	SECEDER	SECRET	SECUNDINE

S

SECUNDLY	SEDITIONS	SEEDMAN	SEEPIEST	SEGUE
SECUNDUM	SEDITIOUS	SEEDMEN	SEEPING	SEGUED
SECURABLE	SEDUCE	SEEDNESS	SEEPS	SEGUEING
SECURANCE	SEDUCED	SEEDPOD	SEEPY	SEGUES
SECURE	SEDUCER	SEEDPODS	SEER	SEGUGIO
SECURED	SEDUCERS	SEEDS	SEERESS	SEGUGIOS
SECURELY	SEDUCES	SEEDSMAN	SEERESSES	SEHRI
SECURER	SEDUCIBLE	SEEDSMEN	SEERS	SEHRIS
SECURERS	SEDUCING	SEEDSTOCK	SEES	SEI
SECURES	SEDUCINGS	SEEDTIME	SEESAW	SEICENTO
SECUREST	SEDUCIVE	SEEDTIMES	SEESAWED	SEICENTOS
SECURING	SEDUCTION	SEEDY	SEESAWING	SEICHE
SECURITAN	SEDUCTIVE	SEEING	SEESAWS	SEICHES
SECURITY	SEDUCTOR	SEEINGS	SEETHE	SEIDEL
SED	SEDUCTORS	SEEK	SEETHED	SEIDELS
SEDAN	SEDULITY	SEEKER	SEETHER	SEIF
SEDANS	SEDULOUS	SEEKERS	SEETHERS	SEIFS
SEDARIM	SEDUM	SEEKING	SEETHES	SEIGNEUR
SEDATE	SEDUMS	SEEKS	SEETHING	SEIGNEURS
SEDATED	SEE	SEEL	SEETHINGS	SEIGNEURY
SEDATELY	SEEABLE	SEELD	SEEWING	SEIGNIOR
SEDATER	SEECATCH	SEELED	SEEWINGS	SEIGNIORS
SEDATES	SEED	SEELIE	SEFER	SEIGNIORY
SEDATEST	SEEDBED	SEELIER	SEG	SEIGNORAL
SEDATING	SEEDBEDS	SEELIEST	SEGAR	SEIGNORY
SEDATION	SEEDBOX	SEELING	SEGARS	SEIK
SEDATIONS	SEEDBOXES	SEELINGS	SEGETAL	SEIKER
SEDATIVE	SEEDCAKE	SEELS	SEGGAR	SEIKEST
SEDATIVES	SEEDCAKES	SEELY	SEGGARS	SEIL
SEDENT	SEEDCASE	SEEM	SEGHOL	SEILED
SEDENTARY	SEEDCASES	SEEMED	SEGHOLATE	SEILING
SEDER	SEEDEATER	SEEMER	SEGHOLS	SEILS
SEDERS	SEEDED	SEEMERS	SEGMENT	SEINE
SEDERUNT	SEEDER	SEEMING	SEGMENTAL	SEINED
SEDERUNTS	SEEDERS	SEEMINGLY	SEGMENTED	SEINEN
SEDES	SEEDHEAD	SEEMINGS	SEGMENTS	SEINENS
SEDGE	SEEDHEADS	SEEMLESS	SEGNI	SEINER
SEDGED	SEEDIER	SEEMLIER	SEGNO	SEINERS
SEDGELAND	SEEDIEST	SEEMLIEST	SEGNOS	SEINES
SEDGES	SEEDILY	SEEMLIHED	SEGO	SEINING
SEDGIER	SEEDINESS	SEEMLY	SEGOL	SEININGS
SEDGIEST	SEEDING	SEEMLYHED	SEGOLATE	SEIR
SEDGY	SEEDINGS	SEEMS	SEGOLATES	SEIRS
SEDILE	SEEDLESS	SEEN	SEGOLS	SEIS
SEDILIA	SEEDLIKE	SEEP	SEGOS	SEISABLE
SEDILIUM	SEEDLING	SEEPAGE	SEGREANT	SEISE
SEDIMENT	SEEDLINGS	SEEPAGES	SEGREGANT	SEISED
SEDIMENTS	SEEDLIP	SEEPED	SEGREGATE	SEISER
SEDITION	SEEDLIPS	SEEPIER	SEGS	SEISERS

SEISES	SELAH	SELFHOODS	SELVAGING	SEMICOMA
SEISIN	SELAHS	SELFIE	SELVAS	SEMICOMAS
SEISING	SELAMLIK	SELFIES	SELVEDGE	SEMICURED
SEISINGS	SELAMLIKS	SELFING	SELVEDGED	SEMIDEAF
SEISINS	SELCOUTH	SELFINGS	SELVEDGES	SEMIDEIFY
SEISM	SELD	SELFISH	SELVES	SEMIDOME
SEISMAL	SELDOM	SELFISHLY	SEMAINIER	SEMIDOMED
SEISMIC	SELDOMLY	SELFISM	SEMANTEME	SEMIDOMES
SEISMICAL	SELDSEEN	SELFISMS	SEMANTIC	SEMIDRIER
SEISMISM	SELDSHOWN	SELFIST	SEMANTICS	SEMIDRY
SEISMISMS	SELE	SELFISTS	SEMANTIDE	SEMIDWARF
SEISMS	SELECT	SELFLESS	SEMANTRA	SEMIE
SEISOR	SELECTA	SELFNESS	SEMANTRON	SEMIERECT
SEISORS	SELECTAS	SELFS	SEMAPHORE	SEMIES
SEISURE	SELECTED	SELFSAME	SEMATIC	SEMIFINAL
SEISURES	SELECTEE	SELFWARD	SEMBLABLE	SEMIFIT
SEITAN	SELECTEES	SELFWARDS	SEMBLABLY	SEMIFLUID
SEITANS	SELECTING	SELICTAR	SEMBLANCE	SEMIGALA
SEITEN	SELECTION	SELICTARS	SEMBLANT	SEMIGALAS
SEITENS	SELECTIVE	SELKIE	SEMBLANTS	SEMIGLOBE
SEITIES	SELECTLY	SELKIES	SEMBLE	SEMIGLOSS
SEITY	SELECTMAN	SELL	SEMBLED	SEMIGROUP
SEIZA	SELECTMEN	SELLA	SEMBLES	SEMIHARD
SEIZABLE	SELECTOR	SELLABLE	SEMBLING	SEMIHIGH
SEIZAS	SELECTORS	SELLAE	SEME	SEMIHOBO
SEIZE	SELECTS	SELLAS	SEMEE	SEMIHOBOS
SEIZED	SELENATE	SELLE	SEMEED	SEMILLON
SEIZER	SELENATES	SELLER	SEMEIA	SEMILLONS
SEIZERS	SELENIAN	SELLERS	SEMEION	SEMILOG
SEIZES	SELENIC	SELLES	SEMEIOTIC	SEMILUNAR
SEIZIN	SELENIDE	SELLING	SEMEME	SEMILUNE
SEIZING	SELENIDES	SELLINGS	SEMEMES	SEMILUNES
SEIZINGS	SELENIOUS	SELLOFF	SEMEMIC	SEMIMAT
SEIZINS	SELENITE	SELLOFFS	SEMEN	SEMIMATT
SEIZOR	SELENITES	SELLOTAPE	SEMENS	SEMIMATTE
SEIZORS	SELENITIC	SELLOUT	SEMES	SEMIMETAL
SEIZURE	SELENIUM	SELLOUTS	SEMESTER	SEMIMICRO
SEIZURES	SELENIUMS	SELLS	SEMESTERS	SEMIMILD
SEJANT	SELENOSES	SELS	SEMESTRAL	SEMIMOIST
SEJEANT	SELENOSIS	SELSYN	SEMI	SEMINA
SEKOI	SELENOUS	SELSYNS	SEMIANGLE	SEMINAL
SEKOS	SELES	SELTZER	SEMIARID	SEMINALLY
SEKOSES	SELF	SELTZERS	SEMIBALD	SEMINAR
SEKT	SELFDOM	SELVA	SEMIBOLD	SEMINARS
SEKTS	SELFDOMS	SELVAGE	SEMIBOLDS	SEMINARY
SEL	SELFED	SELVAGED	SEMIBREVE	SEMINATE
SELACHIAN	SELFHEAL	SELVAGEE	SEMIBULL	SEMINATED
SELADANG	SELFHEALS	SELVAGEES	SEMIBULLS	SEMINATES
SELADANGS	SELFHOOD	SELVAGES	SEMICOLON	SEMINOMA

S

SEMINOMAD	SEMPER	SENESCENT	SENSATING	SENTIENCY
SEMINOMAS	SEMPLE	SENESCES	SENSATION	SENTIENT
SEMINUDE	SEMPLER	SENESCHAL	SENSE	SENTIENTS
SEMIOLOGY	SEMPLEST	SENESCING	SENSED	SENTIMENT
SEMIOPEN	SEMPLICE	SENGI	SENSEFUL	SENTIMO
SEMIOSES	SEMPRE	SENGIS	SENSEI	SENTIMOS
SEMIOSIS	SEMPSTER	SENGREEN	SENSEIS	SENTINEL
SEMIOTIC	SEMPSTERS	SENGREENS	SENSELESS	SENTINELS
SEMIOTICS	SEMSEM	SENHOR	SENSES	SENTING
SEMIOVAL	SEMSEMS	SENHORA	SENSI	SENTRIES
SEMIPED	SEMUNCIA	SENHORAS	SENSIBLE	SENTRY
SEMIPEDS	SEMUNCIAE	SENHORES	SENSIBLER	SENTS
SEMIPIOUS	SEMUNCIAL	SENHORITA	SENSIBLES	SENVIES
SEMIPLUME	SEMUNCIAS	SENHORS	SENSIBLY	SENVY
SEMIPOLAR	SEN	SENILE	SENSILE	SENZA
SEMIPRO	SENA	SENILELY	SENSILLA	SEPAD
SEMIPROS	SENARIES	SENILES	SENSILLAE	SEPADDED
SEMIRAW	SENARII	SENILITY	SENSILLUM	SEPADDING
SEMIRIGID	SENARIUS	SENIOR	SENSING	SEPADS
SEMIROUND	SENARY	SENIORITY	SENSINGS	SEPAL
SEMIRURAL	SENAS	SENIORS	SENSIS	SEPALED
SEMIS	SENATE	SENITI	SENSISM	SEPALINE
SEMISES	SENATES	SENITIS	SENSISMS	SEPALLED
SEMISOFT	SENATOR	SENNA	SENSIST	SEPALODY
SEMISOLID	SENATORS	SENNACHIE	SENSISTS	SEPALOID
SEMISOLUS	SEND	SENNAS	SENSITISE	SEPALOUS
SEMISTIFF	SENDABLE	SENNET	SENSITIVE	SEPALS
SEMISWEET	SENDAL	SENNETS	SENSITIZE	SEPARABLE
SEMITAR	SENDALS	SENNIGHT	SENSOR	SEPARABLY
SEMITARS	SENDED	SENNIGHTS	SENSORIA	SEPARATA
SEMITAUR	SENDER	SENNIT	SENSORIAL	SEPARATE
SEMITAURS	SENDERS	SENNITS	SENSORILY	SEPARATED
SEMITIST	SENDING	SENOPIA	SENSORIUM	SEPARATES
SEMITISTS	SENDINGS	SENOPIAS	SENSORS	SEPARATOR
SEMITONAL	SENDOFF	SENOR	SENSORY	SEPARATUM
SEMITONE	SENDOFFS	SENORA	SENSUAL	SEPHEN
SEMITONES	SENDS	SENORAS	SENSUALLY	SEPHENS
SEMITONIC	SENDUP	SENORES	SENSUM	SEPIA
SEMITRUCK	SENDUPS	SENORITA	SENSUOUS	SEPIAS
SEMIURBAN	SENE	SENORITAS	SENT	SEPIC
SEMIVOCAL	SENECA	SENORS	SENTE	SEPIMENT
SEMIVOWEL	SENECAS	SENRYU	SENTED	SEPIMENTS
SEMIWATER	SENECIO	SENRYUS	SENTENCE	SEPIOLITE
SEMIWILD	SENECIOS	SENS	SENTENCED	SEPIOST
SEMIWORKS	SENEGA	SENSA	SENTENCER	SEPIOSTS
SEMMIT	SENEGAS	SENSATE	SENTENCES	SEPIUM
SEMMITS	SENES	SENSATED	SENTENTIA	SEPIUMS
SEMOLINA	SENESCE	SENSATELY	SENTI	SEPMAG
SEMOLINAS	SENESCED	SENSATES	SENTIENCE	SEPOY

S

two to nine letter words | 525

SEPOYS	SEQUACITY	SERAPHIN	SERGER	SERJEANCY
SEPPUKU	SEQUEL	SERAPHINE	SERGERS	SERJEANT
SEPPUKUS	SEQUELA	SERAPHINS	SERGES	SERJEANTS
SEPS	SEQUELAE	SERAPHS	SERGING	SERJEANTY
SEPSES	SEQUELISE	SERASKIER	SERGINGS	SERK
SEPSIS	SEQUELIZE	SERDAB	SERIAL	SERKALI
SEPT	SEQUELS	SERDABS	SERIALISE	SERKALIS
SEPTA	SEQUENCE	SERE	SERIALISM	SERKS
SEPTAGE	SEQUENCED	SERED	SERIALIST	SERMON
SEPTAGES	SEQUENCER	SEREIN	SERIALITY	SERMONED
SEPTAL	SEQUENCES	SEREINS	SERIALIZE	SERMONEER
SEPTARIA	SEQUENCY	SERENADE	SERIALLY	SERMONER
SEPTARIAN	SEQUENT	SERENADED	SERIALS	SERMONERS
SEPTARIUM	SEQUENTLY	SERENADER	SERIATE	SERMONET
SEPTATE	SEQUENTS	SERENADES	SERIATED	SERMONETS
SEPTATION	SEQUESTER	SERENATA	SERIATELY	SERMONIC
SEPTEMFID	SEQUESTRA	SERENATAS	SERIATES	SERMONING
SEPTEMVIR	SEQUIN	SERENATE	SERIATIM	SERMONISE
SEPTENARY	SEQUINED	SERENATED	SERIATING	SERMONIZE
SEPTENNIA	SEQUINING	SERENATES	SERIATION	SERMONS
SEPTET	SEQUINNED	SERENE	SERIC	SEROGROUP
SEPTETS	SEQUINS	SERENED	SERICEOUS	SEROLOGIC
SEPTETTE	SEQUITUR	SERENELY	SERICIN	SEROLOGY
SEPTETTES	SEQUITURS	SERENER	SERICINS	SEROMA
SEPTIC	SEQUOIA	SERENES	SERICITE	SEROMAS
SEPTICAL	SEQUOIAS	SERENEST	SERICITES	SERON
SEPTICITY	SER	SERENING	SERICITIC	SERONS
SEPTICS	SERA	SERENITY	SERICON	SEROON
SEPTIFORM	SERAC	SERER	SERICONS	SEROONS
SEPTIMAL	SERACS	SERES	SERIEMA	SEROPUS
SEPTIME	SERAFILE	SEREST	SERIEMAS	SEROPUSES
SEPTIMES	SERAFILES	SERF	SERIES	SEROSA
SEPTIMOLE	SERAFIN	SERFAGE	SERIF	SEROSAE
SEPTLEVA	SERAFINS	SERFAGES	SERIFED	SEROSAL
SEPTLEVAS	SERAGLIO	SERFDOM	SERIFFED	SEROSAS
SEPTORIA	SERAGLIOS	SERFDOMS	SERIFS	SEROSITY
SEPTORIAS	SERAI	SERFHOOD	SERIGRAPH	SEROTINAL
SEPTS	SERAIL	SERFHOODS	SERIN	SEROTINE
SEPTUM	SERAILS	SERFISH	SERINE	SEROTINES
SEPTUMS	SERAIS	SERFLIKE	SERINES	SEROTINY
SEPTUOR	SERAL	SERFS	SERINETTE	SEROTONIN
SEPTUORS	SERANG	SERFSHIP	SERING	SEROTYPE
SEPTUPLE	SERANGS	SERFSHIPS	SERINGA	SEROTYPED
SEPTUPLED	SERAPE	SERGE	SERINGAS	SEROTYPES
SEPTUPLES	SERAPES	SERGEANCY	SERINS	SEROTYPIC
SEPTUPLET	SERAPH	SERGEANT	SERIOUS	SEROUS
SEPULCHER	SERAPHIC	SERGEANTS	SERIOUSLY	SEROVAR
SEPULCHRE	SERAPHIM	SERGEANTY	SERIPH	SEROVARS
SEPULTURE	SERAPHIMS	SERGED	SERIPHS	SEROW

S

SEROWS	SERUEWES	SESAME	SETENANTS	SEVENISH
SERPENT	SERUEWING	SESAMES	SETIFORM	SEVENS
SERPENTRY	SERUM	SESAMOID	SETLINE	SEVENTEEN
SERPENTS	SERUMAL	SESAMOIDS	SETLINES	SEVENTH
SERPIGO	SERUMS	SESE	SETNESS	SEVENTHLY
SERPIGOES	SERVABLE	SESELI	SETNESSES	SEVENTHS
SERPIGOS	SERVAL	SESELIS	SETOFF	SEVENTIES
SERPULA	SERVALS	SESEY	SETOFFS	SEVENTY
SERPULAE	SERVANT	SESH	SETON	SEVER
SERPULAS	SERVANTED	SESHES	SETONS	SEVERABLE
SERPULID	SERVANTRY	SESS	SETOSE	SEVERAL
SERPULIDS	SERVANTS	SESSA	SETOUS	SEVERALLY
SERPULITE	SERVE	SESSED	SETOUT	SEVERALS
SERR	SERVEABLE	SESSES	SETOUTS	SEVERALTY
SERRA	SERVED	SESSILE	SETS	SEVERANCE
SERRAE	SERVER	SESSILITY	SETSCREW	SEVERE
SERRAN	SERVERIES	SESSING	SETSCREWS	SEVERED
SERRANID	SERVERS	SESSION	SETT	SEVERELY
SERRANIDS	SERVERY	SESSIONAL	SETTEE	SEVERER
SERRANO	SERVES	SESSIONS	SETTEES	SEVEREST
SERRANOID	SERVEWARE	SESSPOOL	SETTER	SEVERIES
SERRANOS	SERVEWE	SESSPOOLS	SETTERED	SEVERING
SERRANS	SERVEWED	SESTERCE	SETTERING	SEVERITY
SERRAS	SERVEWES	SESTERCES	SETTERS	SEVERS
SERRATE	SERVEWING	SESTERTIA	SETTING	SEVERY
SERRATED	SERVICE	SESTERTII	SETTINGS	SEVICHE
SERRATES	SERVICED	SESTET	SETTLE	SEVICHES
SERRATI	SERVICER	SESTETS	SETTLED	SEVRUGA
SERRATING	SERVICERS	SESTETT	SETTLER	SEVRUGAS
SERRATION	SERVICES	SESTETTE	SETTLERS	SEVS
SERRATURE	SERVICING	SESTETTES	SETTLES	SEW
SERRATUS	SERVIENT	SESTETTI	SETTLING	SEWABLE
SERRE	SERVIETTE	SESTETTO	SETTLINGS	SEWAGE
SERRED	SERVILE	SESTETTOS	SETTLOR	SEWAGES
SERREFILE	SERVILELY	SESTETTS	SETTLORS	SEWAN
SERRES	SERVILES	SESTINA	SETTS	SEWANS
SERRICORN	SERVILISM	SESTINAS	SETUALE	SEWAR
SERRIED	SERVILITY	SESTINE	SETUALES	SEWARS
SERRIEDLY	SERVING	SESTINES	SETULE	SEWED
SERRIES	SERVINGS	SESTON	SETULES	SEWEL
SERRIFORM	SERVITOR	SESTONS	SETULOSE	SEWELLEL
SERRING	SERVITORS	SET	SETULOUS	SEWELLELS
SERRS	SERVITUDE	SETA	SETUP	SEWELS
SERRULATE	SERVLET	SETACEOUS	SETUPS	SEWEN
SERRY	SERVLETS	SETAE	SETWALL	SEWENS
SERRYING	SERVO	SETAL	SETWALLS	SEWER
SERS	SERVOS	SETBACK	SEV	SEWERAGE
SERUEWE	SERVQUAL	SETBACKS	SEVEN	SEWERAGES
SERUEWED	SERVQUALS	SETENANT	SEVENFOLD	SEWERED

SEWERING	SEXTANTAL	SFORZATI	SHADER	SHAGGILY
SEWERINGS	SEXTANTS	SFORZATO	SHADERS	SHAGGING
SEWERLESS	SEXTARII	SFORZATOS	SHADES	SHAGGY
SEWERLIKE	SEXTARIUS	SFUMATO	SHADFLIES	SHAGPILE
SEWERS	SEXTED	SFUMATOS	SHADFLY	SHAGREEN
SEWIN	SEXTET	SGRAFFITI	SHADIER	SHAGREENS
SEWING	SEXTETS	SGRAFFITO	SHADIEST	SHAGROON
SEWINGS	SEXTETT	SH	SHADILY	SHAGROONS
SEWINS	SEXTETTE	SHA	SHADINESS	SHAGS
SEWN	SEXTETTES	SHABASH	SHADING	SHAH
SEWS	SEXTETTS	SHABBATOT	SHADINGS	SHAHADA
SEX	SEXTILE	SHABBIER	SHADKHAN	SHAHADAH
SEXAHOLIC	SEXTILES	SHABBIEST	SHADKHANS	SHAHADAHS
SEXCAPADE	SEXTING	SHABBILY	SHADOOF	SHAHADAS
SEXED	SEXTINGS	SHABBLE	SHADOOFS	SHAHDOM
SEXENNIAL	SEXTO	SHABBLES	SHADOW	SHAHDOMS
SEXER	SEXTOLET	SHABBY	SHADOWBAN	SHAHEED
SEXERCISE	SEXTOLETS	SHABRACK	SHADOWBOX	SHAHEEDS
SEXERS	SEXTON	SHABRACKS	SHADOWED	SHAHID
SEXES	SEXTONESS	SHACK	SHADOWER	SHAHIDS
SEXFID	SEXTONS	SHACKED	SHADOWERS	SHAHS
SEXFOIL	SEXTOS	SHACKIER	SHADOWIER	SHAHTOOSH
SEXFOILS	SEXTS	SHACKIEST	SHADOWILY	SHAIKH
SEXIER	SEXTUOR	SHACKING	SHADOWING	SHAIKHS
SEXIEST	SEXTUORS	SHACKLE	SHADOWS	SHAIRD
SEXILY	SEXTUPLE	SHACKLED	SHADOWY	SHAIRDS
SEXINESS	SEXTUPLED	SHACKLER	SHADRACH	SHAIRN
SEXING	SEXTUPLES	SHACKLERS	SHADRACHS	SHAIRNS
SEXINGS	SEXTUPLET	SHACKLES	SHADS	SHAITAN
SEXISM	SEXTUPLY	SHACKLING	SHADUF	SHAITANS
SEXISMS	SEXUAL	SHACKO	SHADUFS	SHAKABLE
SEXIST	SEXUALISE	SHACKOES	SHADY	SHAKE
SEXISTS	SEXUALISM	SHACKOS	SHAFT	SHAKEABLE
SEXLESS	SEXUALIST	SHACKS	SHAFTED	SHAKED
SEXLESSLY	SEXUALITY	SHACKTOWN	SHAFTER	SHAKEDOWN
SEXLINKED	SEXUALIZE	SHACKY	SHAFTERS	SHAKEN
SEXOLOGIC	SEXUALLY	SHAD	SHAFTING	SHAKEOUT
SEXOLOGY	SEXVALENT	SHADBERRY	SHAFTINGS	SHAKEOUTS
SEXPERT	SEXY	SHADBLOW	SHAFTLESS	SHAKER
SEXPERTS	SEY	SHADBLOWS	SHAFTS	SHAKERS
SEXPOT	SEYEN	SHADBUSH	SHAG	SHAKES
SEXPOTS	SEYENS	SHADCHAN	SHAGBARK	SHAKEUP
SEXT	SEYS	SHADCHANS	SHAGBARKS	SHAKEUPS
SEXTAIN	SEYSURE	SHADDOCK	SHAGGABLE	SHAKIER
SEXTAINS	SEYSURES	SHADDOCKS	SHAGGED	SHAKIEST
SEXTAN	SEZ	SHADDUP	SHAGGER	SHAKILY
SEXTANS	SFERICS	SHADE	SHAGGERS	SHAKINESS
SEXTANSES	SFORZANDI	SHADED	SHAGGIER	SHAKING
SEXTANT	SFORZANDO	SHADELESS	SHAGGIEST	SHAKINGS

SHAKO	SHAMANIC	SHAMOIS	SHAPE	SHARKERS
SHAKOES	SHAMANISM	SHAMOISED	SHAPEABLE	SHARKING
SHAKOS	SHAMANIST	SHAMOISES	SHAPED	SHARKINGS
SHAKSHUKA	SHAMANS	SHAMOS	SHAPELESS	SHARKISH
SHAKT	SHAMAS	SHAMOSIM	SHAPELIER	SHARKLIKE
SHAKUDO	SHAMATEUR	SHAMOY	SHAPELY	SHARKS
SHAKUDOS	SHAMBA	SHAMOYED	SHAPEN	SHARKSKIN
SHAKY	SHAMBAS	SHAMOYING	SHAPENED	SHARN
SHALE	SHAMBLE	SHAMOYS	SHAPENING	SHARNIER
SHALED	SHAMBLED	SHAMPOO	SHAPENS	SHARNIES
SHALELIKE	SHAMBLES	SHAMPOOED	SHAPER	SHARNIEST
SHALES	SHAMBLIER	SHAMPOOER	SHAPERS	SHARNS
SHALEY	SHAMBLING	SHAMPOOS	SHAPES	SHARNY
SHALIER	SHAMBLY	SHAMROCK	SHAPEUP	SHARON
SHALIEST	SHAMBOLIC	SHAMROCKS	SHAPEUPS	SHARP
SHALING	SHAME	SHAMS	SHAPEWEAR	SHARPED
SHALL	SHAMEABLE	SHAMUS	SHAPING	SHARPEN
SHALLI	SHAMEABLY	SHAMUSES	SHAPINGS	SHARPENED
SHALLIS	SHAMED	SHAN	SHAPS	SHARPENER
SHALLON	SHAMEFAST	SHANACHIE	SHARABLE	SHARPENS
SHALLONS	SHAMEFUL	SHAND	SHARD	SHARPER
SHALLOON	SHAMELESS	SHANDIES	SHARDED	SHARPERS
SHALLOONS	SHAMER	SHANDRIES	SHARDS	SHARPEST
SHALLOP	SHAMERS	SHANDRY	SHARE	SHARPIE
SHALLOPS	SHAMES	SHANDS	SHAREABLE	SHARPIES
SHALLOT	SHAMIANA	SHANDY	SHARECROP	SHARPING
SHALLOTS	SHAMIANAH	SHANGHAI	SHARED	SHARPINGS
SHALLOW	SHAMIANAS	SHANGHAIS	SHAREMAN	SHARPISH
SHALLOWED	SHAMINA	SHANK	SHAREMEN	SHARPLY
SHALLOWER	SHAMINAS	SHANKBONE	SHARER	SHARPNESS
SHALLOWLY	SHAMING	SHANKED	SHARERS	SHARPS
SHALLOWS	SHAMINGLY	SHANKING	SHARES	SHARPTAIL
SHALM	SHAMINGS	SHANKS	SHARESMAN	SHARPY
SHALMS	SHAMISEN	SHANNIES	SHARESMEN	SHART
SHALOM	SHAMISENS	SHANNY	SHAREWARE	SHARTED
SHALOMS	SHAMMAS	SHANS	SHARIA	SHARTING
SHALOT	SHAMMASH	SHANTEY	SHARIAH	SHARTS
SHALOTS	SHAMMASIM	SHANTEYS	SHARIAHS	SHASH
SHALT	SHAMMED	SHANTI	SHARIAS	SHASHED
SHALWAR	SHAMMER	SHANTIES	SHARIAT	SHASHES
SHALWARS	SHAMMERS	SHANTIH	SHARIATS	SHASHING
SHALY	SHAMMES	SHANTIHS	SHARIF	SHASHLICK
SHAM	SHAMMIED	SHANTIS	SHARIFIAN	SHASHLIK
SHAMA	SHAMMIES	SHANTUNG	SHARIFS	SHASHLIKS
SHAMABLE	SHAMMING	SHANTUNGS	SHARING	SHASLIK
SHAMABLY	SHAMMOS	SHANTY	SHARINGS	SHASLIKS
SHAMAL	SHAMMOSIM	SHANTYMAN	SHARK	SHASTA
SHAMALS	SHAMMY	SHANTYMEN	SHARKED	SHASTAS
SHAMAN	SHAMMYING	SHAPABLE	SHARKER	SHASTER

SHASTERS	SHAWLS	SHEATHERS	SHEEP	SHEEVES
SHASTRA	SHAWM	SHEATHES	SHEEPCOT	SHEHITA
SHASTRAS	SHAWMS	SHEATHIER	SHEEPCOTE	SHEHITAH
SHAT	SHAWN	SHEATHING	SHEEPCOTS	SHEHITAHS
SHATOOSH	SHAWS	SHEATHS	SHEEPDOG	SHEHITAS
SHATTER	SHAY	SHEATHY	SHEEPDOGS	SHEHNAI
SHATTERED	SHAYA	SHEAVE	SHEEPFOLD	SHEHNAIS
SHATTERER	SHAYAS	SHEAVED	SHEEPHEAD	SHEIK
SHATTERS	SHAYKH	SHEAVES	SHEEPIER	SHEIKDOM
SHATTERY	SHAYKHS	SHEAVING	SHEEPIEST	SHEIKDOMS
SHAUCHLE	SHAYS	SHEBANG	SHEEPISH	SHEIKH
SHAUCHLED	SHAZAM	SHEBANGS	SHEEPLE	SHEIKHA
SHAUCHLES	SHCHI	SHEBEAN	SHEEPLES	SHEIKHAS
SHAUCHLY	SHCHIS	SHEBEANS	SHEEPLIKE	SHEIKHDOM
SHAUGH	SHE	SHEBEEN	SHEEPMAN	SHEIKHS
SHAUGHS	SHEA	SHEBEENED	SHEEPMEN	SHEIKS
SHAUL	SHEADING	SHEBEENER	SHEEPO	SHEILA
SHAULED	SHEADINGS	SHEBEENS	SHEEPOS	SHEILAS
SHAULING	SHEAF	SHECHITA	SHEEPSKIN	SHEILING
SHAULS	SHEAFED	SHECHITAH	SHEEPWALK	SHEILINGS
SHAVABLE	SHEAFIER	SHECHITAS	SHEEPY	SHEITAN
SHAVASANA	SHEAFIEST	SHED	SHEER	SHEITANS
SHAVE	SHEAFING	SHEDABLE	SHEERED	SHEITEL
SHAVEABLE	SHEAFLIKE	SHEDDABLE	SHEERER	SHEITELS
SHAVED	SHEAFS	SHEDDED	SHEEREST	SHEKALIM
SHAVELING	SHEAFY	SHEDDER	SHEERING	SHEKEL
SHAVEN	SHEAL	SHEDDERS	SHEERLEG	SHEKELIM
SHAVER	SHEALED	SHEDDING	SHEERLEGS	SHEKELS
SHAVERS	SHEALING	SHEDDINGS	SHEERLY	SHELDDUCK
SHAVES	SHEALINGS	SHEDFUL	SHEERNESS	SHELDRAKE
SHAVETAIL	SHEALS	SHEDFULS	SHEERS	SHELDUCK
SHAVIE	SHEAR	SHEDHAND	SHEESH	SHELDUCKS
SHAVIES	SHEARED	SHEDHANDS	SHEESHA	SHELF
SHAVING	SHEARER	SHEDLIKE	SHEESHAS	SHELFED
SHAVINGS	SHEARERS	SHEDLOAD	SHEET	SHELFFUL
SHAW	SHEARING	SHEDLOADS	SHEETED	SHELFFULS
SHAWARMA	SHEARINGS	SHEDS	SHEETER	SHELFIER
SHAWARMAS	SHEARLEG	SHEEL	SHEETERS	SHELFIEST
SHAWED	SHEARLEGS	SHEELED	SHEETFED	SHELFING
SHAWING	SHEARLING	SHEELING	SHEETIER	SHELFLIKE
SHAWL	SHEARMAN	SHEELS	SHEETIEST	SHELFROOM
SHAWLED	SHEARMEN	SHEEN	SHEETING	SHELFS
SHAWLEY	SHEARS	SHEENED	SHEETINGS	SHELFY
SHAWLEYS	SHEAS	SHEENFUL	SHEETLESS	SHELL
SHAWLIE	SHEATFISH	SHEENIER	SHEETLIKE	SHELLAC
SHAWLIES	SHEATH	SHEENIEST	SHEETROCK	SHELLACK
SHAWLING	SHEATHE	SHEENING	SHEETS	SHELLACKS
SHAWLINGS	SHEATHED	SHEENS	SHEETY	SHELLACS
SHAWLLESS	SHEATHER	SHEENY	SHEEVE	SHELLBACK

S

SHELLBARK	SHEQEL	SHEUGHING	SHIFTED	SHIMMER
SHELLDUCK	SHEQELS	SHEUGHS	SHIFTER	SHIMMERED
SHELLED	SHERANG	SHEVA	SHIFTERS	SHIMMERS
SHELLER	SHERANGS	SHEVAS	SHIFTIER	SHIMMERY
SHELLERS	SHERBERT	SHEW	SHIFTIEST	SHIMMEY
SHELLFIRE	SHERBERTS	SHEWBREAD	SHIFTILY	SHIMMEYS
SHELLFISH	SHERBET	SHEWED	SHIFTING	SHIMMIED
SHELLFUL	SHERBETS	SHEWEL	SHIFTINGS	SHIMMIES
SHELLFULS	SHERD	SHEWELS	SHIFTLESS	SHIMMING
SHELLIER	SHERDS	SHEWER	SHIFTS	SHIMMY
SHELLIEST	SHERE	SHEWERS	SHIFTWORK	SHIMMYING
SHELLING	SHEREEF	SHEWING	SHIFTY	SHIMOZZLE
SHELLINGS	SHEREEFS	SHEWN	SHIGELLA	SHIMS
SHELLS	SHERIA	SHEWS	SHIGELLAE	SHIN
SHELLWORK	SHERIAS	SHH	SHIGELLAS	SHINBONE
SHELLY	SHERIAT	SHHH	SHIITAKE	SHINBONES
SHELTA	SHERIATS	SHIAI	SHIITAKES	SHINDIES
SHELTAS	SHERIF	SHIAIS	SHIKAR	SHINDIG
SHELTER	SHERIFF	SHIATSU	SHIKARA	SHINDIGS
SHELTERED	SHERIFFS	SHIATSUS	SHIKARAS	SHINDY
SHELTERER	SHERIFIAN	SHIATZU	SHIKAREE	SHINDYS
SHELTERS	SHERIFS	SHIATZUS	SHIKAREES	SHINE
SHELTERY	SHERLOCK	SHIBAH	SHIKARI	SHINED
SHELTIE	SHERLOCKS	SHIBAHS	SHIKARIS	SHINELESS
SHELTIES	SHERO	SHIBUICHI	SHIKARRED	SHINER
SHELTY	SHEROES	SHICKER	SHIKARS	SHINERS
SHELVE	SHEROOT	SHICKERED	SHIKKER	SHINES
SHELVED	SHEROOTS	SHICKERS	SHIKKERED	SHINESS
SHELVER	SHERPA	SHIDDER	SHIKKERS	SHINESSES
SHELVERS	SHERPAS	SHIDDERS	SHIKRA	SHINGLE
SHELVES	SHERRIED	SHIDDUCH	SHIKRAS	SHINGLED
SHELVIER	SHERRIES	SHIED	SHILINGI	SHINGLER
SHELVIEST	SHERRIS	SHIEL	SHILINGIS	SHINGLERS
SHELVING	SHERRISES	SHIELD	SHILL	SHINGLES
SHELVINGS	SHERRY	SHIELDED	SHILLABER	SHINGLIER
SHELVY	SHERWANI	SHIELDER	SHILLALA	SHINGLING
SHEMOZZLE	SHERWANIS	SHIELDERS	SHILLALAH	SHINGLY
SHEN	SHES	SHIELDING	SHILLALAS	SHINGUARD
SHENAI	SHET	SHIELDS	SHILLED	SHINIER
SHENAIS	SHETLAND	SHIELED	SHILLELAH	SHINIES
SHEND	SHETLANDS	SHIELING	SHILLING	SHINIEST
SHENDING	SHETS	SHIELINGS	SHILLINGS	SHINILY
SHENDS	SHETTING	SHIELS	SHILLS	SHININESS
SHENT	SHEUCH	SHIER	SHILPIT	SHINING
SHEOL	SHEUCHED	SHIERS	SHILY	SHININGLY
SHEOLS	SHEUCHING	SHIES	SHIM	SHINJU
SHEPHERD	SHEUCHS	SHIEST	SHIMAAL	SHINJUS
SHEPHERDS	SHEUGH	SHIFT	SHIMAALS	SHINKIN
SHEQALIM	SHEUGHED	SHIFTABLE	SHIMMED	SHINKINS

SHINLEAF	SHIPPO	SHIRTIEST	SHITTAHS	SHLEP
SHINLEAFS	SHIPPON	SHIRTILY	SHITTED	SHLEPP
SHINNE	SHIPPONS	SHIRTING	SHITTER	SHLEPPED
SHINNED	SHIPPOS	SHIRTINGS	SHITTERS	SHLEPPER
SHINNERY	SHIPPOUND	SHIRTLESS	SHITTIER	SHLEPPERS
SHINNES	SHIPS	SHIRTLIKE	SHITTIEST	SHLEPPIER
SHINNEY	SHIPSHAPE	SHIRTS	SHITTILY	SHLEPPING
SHINNEYED	SHIPSIDE	SHIRTTAIL	SHITTIM	SHLEPPS
SHINNEYS	SHIPSIDES	SHIRTY	SHITTIMS	SHLEPPY
SHINNIED	SHIPTIME	SHISH	SHITTING	SHLEPS
SHINNIES	SHIPTIMES	SHISHA	SHITTY	SHLIMAZEL
SHINNING	SHIPWAY	SHISHAS	SHITWORK	SHLOCK
SHINNY	SHIPWAYS	SHISO	SHITWORKS	SHLOCKIER
SHINNYING	SHIPWORM	SHISOS	SHITZU	SHLOCKS
SHINOLA	SHIPWORMS	SHIST	SHITZUS	SHLOCKY
SHINOLAS	SHIPWRECK	SHISTS	SHIUR	SHLONG
SHINS	SHIPYARD	SHIT	SHIURIM	SHLONGS
SHINTIED	SHIPYARDS	SHITAKE	SHIV	SHLOSHIM
SHINTIES	SHIR	SHITAKES	SHIVA	SHLOSHIMS
SHINTY	SHIRALEE	SHITBAG	SHIVAH	SHLUB
SHINTYING	SHIRALEES	SHITBAGS	SHIVAHS	SHLUBS
SHINY	SHIRAZ	SHITCAN	SHIVAREE	SHLUMP
SHIP	SHIRAZES	SHITCANS	SHIVAREED	SHLUMPED
SHIPBOARD	SHIRE	SHITE	SHIVAREES	SHLUMPIER
SHIPBORNE	SHIRED	SHITED	SHIVAS	SHLUMPING
SHIPFUL	SHIREMAN	SHITES	SHIVE	SHLUMPS
SHIPFULS	SHIREMEN	SHITFACE	SHIVED	SHLUMPY
SHIPLAP	SHIRES	SHITFACED	SHIVER	SHMALTZ
SHIPLAPS	SHIRETOWN	SHITFACES	SHIVERED	SHMALTZES
SHIPLESS	SHIRING	SHITHEAD	SHIVERER	SHMALTZY
SHIPLOAD	SHIRK	SHITHEADS	SHIVERERS	SHMATTE
SHIPLOADS	SHIRKED	SHITHEEL	SHIVERIER	SHMATTES
SHIPMAN	SHIRKER	SHITHEELS	SHIVERING	SHMEAR
SHIPMATE	SHIRKERS	SHITHOLE	SHIVERS	SHMEARED
SHIPMATES	SHIRKING	SHITHOLES	SHIVERY	SHMEARING
SHIPMEN	SHIRKS	SHITHOUSE	SHIVES	SHMEARS
SHIPMENT	SHIRR	SHITING	SHIVING	SHMEER
SHIPMENTS	SHIRRA	SHITLESS	SHIVITI	SHMEERED
SHIPOWNER	SHIRRALEE	SHITLIST	SHIVITIS	SHMEERING
SHIPPABLE	SHIRRAS	SHITLISTS	SHIVOO	SHMEERS
SHIPPED	SHIRRED	SHITLOAD	SHIVOOS	SHMEK
SHIPPEN	SHIRRING	SHITLOADS	SHIVS	SHMEKS
SHIPPENS	SHIRRINGS	SHITPOST	SHIVVED	SHMO
SHIPPER	SHIRRS	SHITPOSTS	SHIVVING	SHMOCK
SHIPPERS	SHIRS	SHITS	SHIZZLE	SHMOCKS
SHIPPIE	SHIRT	SHITSHOW	SHIZZLES	SHMOE
SHIPPIES	SHIRTBAND	SHITSHOWS	SHLEMIEHL	SHMOES
SHIPPING	SHIRTED	SHITSTORM	SHLEMIEL	SHMOOSE
SHIPPINGS	SHIRTIER	SHITTAH	SHLEMIELS	SHMOOSED

SHMOOSES	SHODDIER	SHOGS	SHOOSHES	SHOPTALK
SHMOOSING	SHODDIES	SHOGUN	SHOOSHING	SHOPTALKS
SHMOOZE	SHODDIEST	SHOGUNAL	SHOOT	SHOPWOMAN
SHMOOZED	SHODDILY	SHOGUNATE	SHOOTABLE	SHOPWOMEN
SHMOOZER	SHODDY	SHOGUNS	SHOOTDOWN	SHOPWORN
SHMOOZERS	SHODER	SHOJI	SHOOTER	SHORAN
SHMOOZES	SHODERS	SHOJIS	SHOOTERS	SHORANS
SHMOOZIER	SHOE	SHOJO	SHOOTIE	SHORE
SHMOOZING	SHOEBILL	SHOJOS	SHOOTIES	SHOREBIRD
SHMOOZY	SHOEBILLS	SHOLA	SHOOTING	SHORED
SHMUCK	SHOEBLACK	SHOLAS	SHOOTINGS	SHOREFAST
SHMUCKIER	SHOEBOX	SHOLOM	SHOOTIST	SHORELESS
SHMUCKS	SHOEBOXES	SHOLOMS	SHOOTISTS	SHORELINE
SHMUCKY	SHOEBRUSH	SHONE	SHOOTOUT	SHOREMAN
SHNAPPS	SHOED	SHONEEN	SHOOTOUTS	SHOREMEN
SHNAPS	SHOEGAZE	SHONEENS	SHOOTS	SHORER
SHNOOK	SHOEGAZES	SHONEN	SHOP	SHORERS
SHNOOKS	SHOEHORN	SHONENS	SHOPBOARD	SHORES
SHNORRER	SHOEHORNS	SHONKIER	SHOPBOT	SHORESIDE
SHNORRERS	SHOEING	SHONKIEST	SHOPBOTS	SHORESMAN
SHO	SHOEINGS	SHONKY	SHOPBOY	SHORESMEN
SHOAL	SHOELACE	SHOO	SHOPBOYS	SHOREWARD
SHOALED	SHOELACES	SHOOED	SHOPE	SHOREWEED
SHOALER	SHOELESS	SHOOFLIES	SHOPFRONT	SHORING
SHOALEST	SHOEMAKER	SHOOFLY	SHOPFUL	SHORINGS
SHOALIER	SHOEPAC	SHOOGIE	SHOPFULS	SHORL
SHOALIEST	SHOEPACK	SHOOGIED	SHOPGIRL	SHORLS
SHOALING	SHOEPACKS	SHOOGIES	SHOPGIRLS	SHORN
SHOALINGS	SHOEPACS	SHOOGLE	SHOPHAR	SHORT
SHOALNESS	SHOER	SHOOGLED	SHOPHARS	SHORTAGE
SHOALS	SHOERS	SHOOGLES	SHOPHOUSE	SHORTAGES
SHOALWISE	SHOES	SHOOGLIER	SHOPHROTH	SHORTARM
SHOALY	SHOESHINE	SHOOGLING	SHOPLESS	SHORTARSE
SHOAT	SHOETREE	SHOOGLY	SHOPLIFT	SHORTCAKE
SHOATS	SHOETREES	SHOOING	SHOPLIFTS	SHORTCUT
SHOCHET	SHOFAR	SHOOK	SHOPMAN	SHORTCUTS
SHOCHETIM	SHOFARS	SHOOKS	SHOPMEN	SHORTED
SHOCHETS	SHOFROTH	SHOOL	SHOPPE	SHORTEN
SHOCHU	SHOG	SHOOLE	SHOPPED	SHORTENED
SHOCHUS	SHOGGED	SHOOLED	SHOPPER	SHORTENER
SHOCK	SHOGGING	SHOOLES	SHOPPERS	SHORTENS
SHOCKABLE	SHOGGLE	SHOOLING	SHOPPES	SHORTER
SHOCKED	SHOGGLED	SHOOLS	SHOPPIER	SHORTEST
SHOCKER	SHOGGLES	SHOON	SHOPPIES	SHORTFALL
SHOCKERS	SHOGGLIER	SHOORA	SHOPPIEST	SHORTGOWN
SHOCKING	SHOGGLING	SHOORAS	SHOPPING	SHORTHAIR
SHOCKS	SHOGGLY	SHOOS	SHOPPINGS	SHORTHAND
SHOD	SHOGI	SHOOSH	SHOPPY	SHORTHEAD
SHODDEN	SHOGIS	SHOOSHED	SHOPS	SHORTHOLD

S

SHORTHORN	SHOUSES	SHOWDS	SHRADDHAS	SHRIEVES
SHORTIA	SHOUT	SHOWED	SHRANK	SHRIEVING
SHORTIAS	SHOUTED	SHOWER	SHRAPNEL	SHRIFT
SHORTIE	SHOUTER	SHOWERED	SHRAPNELS	SHRIFTS
SHORTIES	SHOUTERS	SHOWERER	SHRED	SHRIGHT
SHORTING	SHOUTHER	SHOWERERS	SHREDDED	SHRIGHTS
SHORTISH	SHOUTHERS	SHOWERFUL	SHREDDER	SHRIKE
SHORTLIST	SHOUTIER	SHOWERIER	SHREDDERS	SHRIKED
SHORTLY	SHOUTIEST	SHOWERING	SHREDDIER	SHRIKES
SHORTNESS	SHOUTING	SHOWERS	SHREDDING	SHRIKING
SHORTS	SHOUTINGS	SHOWERY	SHREDDY	SHRILL
SHORTSTOP	SHOUTLINE	SHOWGHE	SHREDLESS	SHRILLED
SHORTWAVE	SHOUTOUT	SHOWGHES	SHREDS	SHRILLER
SHORTY	SHOUTOUTS	SHOWGIRL	SHREEK	SHRILLEST
SHOT	SHOUTS	SHOWGIRLS	SHREEKED	SHRILLIER
SHOTCRETE	SHOUTY	SHOWGOER	SHREEKING	SHRILLING
SHOTE	SHOVE	SHOWGOERS	SHREEKS	SHRILLS
SHOTES	SHOVED	SHOWIER	SHREIK	SHRILLY
SHOTFIRER	SHOVEL	SHOWIEST	SHREIKED	SHRIMP
SHOTGUN	SHOVELED	SHOWILY	SHREIKING	SHRIMPED
SHOTGUNS	SHOVELER	SHOWINESS	SHREIKS	SHRIMPER
SHOTHOLE	SHOVELERS	SHOWING	SHREW	SHRIMPERS
SHOTHOLES	SHOVELFUL	SHOWINGS	SHREWD	SHRIMPIER
SHOTMAKER	SHOVELING	SHOWJUMP	SHREWDER	SHRIMPING
SHOTPROOF	SHOVELLED	SHOWJUMPS	SHREWDEST	SHRIMPS
SHOTS	SHOVELLER	SHOWMAN	SHREWDIE	SHRIMPY
SHOTT	SHOVELS	SHOWMANCE	SHREWDIES	SHRINAL
SHOTTE	SHOVER	SHOWMANLY	SHREWDLY	SHRINE
SHOTTED	SHOVERS	SHOWMEN	SHREWED	SHRINED
SHOTTEN	SHOVES	SHOWN	SHREWING	SHRINES
SHOTTES	SHOVING	SHOWOFF	SHREWISH	SHRINING
SHOTTING	SHOVINGS	SHOWOFFS	SHREWLIKE	SHRINK
SHOTTLE	SHOW	SHOWPIECE	SHREWMICE	SHRINKAGE
SHOTTLES	SHOWABLE	SHOWPLACE	SHREWS	SHRINKER
SHOTTS	SHOWBIZ	SHOWRING	SHRI	SHRINKERS
SHOUGH	SHOWBIZZY	SHOWRINGS	SHRIECH	SHRINKING
SHOUGHS	SHOWBOAT	SHOWROOM	SHRIECHED	SHRINKS
SHOUJO	SHOWBOATS	SHOWROOMS	SHRIECHES	SHRIS
SHOUJOS	SHOWBOX	SHOWS	SHRIEK	SHRITCH
SHOULD	SHOWBOXES	SHOWTIME	SHRIEKED	SHRITCHED
SHOULDA	SHOWBREAD	SHOWTIMES	SHRIEKER	SHRITCHES
SHOULDER	SHOWCASE	SHOWWOMAN	SHRIEKERS	SHRIVE
SHOULDERS	SHOWCASED	SHOWWOMEN	SHRIEKIER	SHRIVED
SHOULDEST	SHOWCASES	SHOWY	SHRIEKING	SHRIVEL
SHOULDNA	SHOWD	SHOWYARD	SHRIEKS	SHRIVELED
SHOULDST	SHOWDED	SHOWYARDS	SHRIEKY	SHRIVELS
SHOUNEN	SHOWDING	SHOYU	SHRIEVAL	SHRIVEN
SHOUNENS	SHOWDOWN	SHOYUS	SHRIEVE	SHRIVER
SHOUSE	SHOWDOWNS	SHRADDHA	SHRIEVED	SHRIVERS

SHRIVES	SHTETL	SHUL	SHUTOUTS	SIALONS
SHRIVING	SHTETLACH	SHULE	SHUTS	SIALS
SHRIVINGS	SHTETLS	SHULED	SHUTTER	SIAMANG
SHROFF	SHTICK	SHULES	SHUTTERED	SIAMANGS
SHROFFAGE	SHTICKIER	SHULING	SHUTTERS	SIAMESE
SHROFFED	SHTICKS	SHULN	SHUTTING	SIAMESED
SHROFFING	SHTICKY	SHULS	SHUTTLE	SIAMESES
SHROFFS	SHTIK	SHUMAI	SHUTTLED	SIAMESING
SHROOM	SHTIKS	SHUN	SHUTTLER	SIAMEZE
SHROOMED	SHTOOK	SHUNLESS	SHUTTLERS	SIAMEZED
SHROOMER	SHTOOKS	SHUNNABLE	SHUTTLES	SIAMEZES
SHROOMERS	SHTOOM	SHUNNED	SHUTTLING	SIAMEZING
SHROOMING	SHTOOMER	SHUNNER	SHVITZ	SIB
SHROOMS	SHTOOMEST	SHUNNERS	SHVITZED	SIBB
SHROUD	SHTREIMEL	SHUNNING	SHVITZES	SIBBS
SHROUDED	SHTUCK	SHUNPIKE	SHVITZING	SIBILANCE
SHROUDIER	SHTUCKS	SHUNPIKED	SHWA	SIBILANCY
SHROUDING	SHTUM	SHUNPIKER	SHWANPAN	SIBILANT
SHROUDS	SHTUMM	SHUNPIKES	SHWANPANS	SIBILANTS
SHROUDY	SHTUMMER	SHUNS	SHWAS	SIBILATE
SHROVE	SHTUMMEST	SHUNT	SHWESHWE	SIBILATED
SHROVED	SHTUP	SHUNTED	SHWESHWES	SIBILATES
SHROVES	SHTUPPED	SHUNTER	SHY	SIBILATOR
SHROVING	SHTUPPING	SHUNTERS	SHYER	SIBILOUS
SHROW	SHTUPS	SHUNTING	SHYERS	SIBLING
SHROWD	SHUBUNKIN	SHUNTINGS	SHYEST	SIBLINGS
SHROWED	SHUCK	SHUNTS	SHYING	SIBS
SHROWING	SHUCKED	SHURA	SHYISH	SIBSHIP
SHROWS	SHUCKER	SHURAS	SHYLOCK	SIBSHIPS
SHRUB	SHUCKERS	SHURIKEN	SHYLOCKED	SIBYL
SHRUBBED	SHUCKING	SHURIKENS	SHYLOCKS	SIBYLIC
SHRUBBERY	SHUCKINGS	SHUSH	SHYLY	SIBYLLIC
SHRUBBIER	SHUCKS	SHUSHED	SHYNESS	SIBYLLINE
SHRUBBING	SHUDDER	SHUSHER	SHYNESSES	SIBYLS
SHRUBBY	SHUDDERED	SHUSHERS	SHYPOO	SIC
SHRUBLAND	SHUDDERS	SHUSHES	SHYPOOS	SICARIO
SHRUBLESS	SHUDDERY	SHUSHING	SHYSTER	SICARIOS
SHRUBLIKE	SHUFFLE	SHUT	SHYSTERS	SICCAN
SHRUBS	SHUFFLED	SHUTDOWN	SI	SICCAR
SHRUG	SHUFFLER	SHUTDOWNS	SIAL	SICCATIVE
SHRUGGED	SHUFFLERS	SHUTE	SIALIC	SICCED
SHRUGGING	SHUFFLES	SHUTED	SIALID	SICCING
SHRUGS	SHUFFLING	SHUTES	SIALIDAN	SICCITIES
SHRUNK	SHUFTI	SHUTEYE	SIALIDANS	SICCITY
SHRUNKEN	SHUFTIES	SHUTEYES	SIALIDS	SICE
SHTCHI	SHUFTIS	SHUTING	SIALOGRAM	SICES
SHTCHIS	SHUFTY	SHUTOFF	SIALOID	SICH
SHTETEL	SHUGGIES	SHUTOFFS	SIALOLITH	SICHT
SHTETELS	SHUGGY	SHUTOUT	SIALON	SICHTED

S

SICHTING	SICKROOMS	SIDELINER	SIDEWALL	SIESTAS
SICHTS	SICKS	SIDELINES	SIDEWALLS	SIETH
SICILIANA	SICKY	SIDELING	SIDEWARD	SIETHS
SICILIANE	SICLIKE	SIDELINGS	SIDEWARDS	SIEUR
SICILIANO	SICS	SIDELOCK	SIDEWAY	SIEURS
SICK	SIDA	SIDELOCKS	SIDEWAYS	SIEVE
SICKBAY	SIDALCEA	SIDELONG	SIDEWHEEL	SIEVED
SICKBAYS	SIDALCEAS	SIDEMAN	SIDEWISE	SIEVELIKE
SICKBED	SIDAS	SIDEMEAT	SIDH	SIEVERT
SICKBEDS	SIDDHA	SIDEMEATS	SIDHA	SIEVERTS
SICKED	SIDDHAS	SIDEMEN	SIDHAS	SIEVES
SICKEE	SIDDHI	SIDENOTE	SIDHE	SIEVING
SICKEES	SIDDHIS	SIDENOTES	SIDHUISM	SIF
SICKEN	SIDDHUISM	SIDEPATH	SIDHUISMS	SIFAKA
SICKENED	SIDDUR	SIDEPATHS	SIDING	SIFAKAS
SICKENER	SIDDURIM	SIDEPIECE	SIDINGS	SIFFLE
SICKENERS	SIDDURS	SIDER	SIDLE	SIFFLED
SICKENING	SIDE	SIDERAL	SIDLED	SIFFLES
SICKENS	SIDEARM	SIDERATE	SIDLER	SIFFLEUR
SICKER	SIDEARMED	SIDERATED	SIDLERS	SIFFLEURS
SICKERLY	SIDEARMER	SIDERATES	SIDLES	SIFFLEUSE
SICKEST	SIDEARMS	SIDEREAL	SIDLING	SIFFLING
SICKIE	SIDEBAND	SIDERITE	SIDLINGLY	SIFREI
SICKIES	SIDEBANDS	SIDERITES	SIECLE	SIFT
SICKING	SIDEBAR	SIDERITIC	SIECLES	SIFTED
SICKISH	SIDEBARS	SIDEROAD	SIEGE	SIFTER
SICKISHLY	SIDEBOARD	SIDEROADS	SIEGED	SIFTERS
SICKLE	SIDEBONE	SIDEROSES	SIEGER	SIFTING
SICKLED	SIDEBONES	SIDEROSIS	SIEGERS	SIFTINGLY
SICKLEMAN	SIDEBOOB	SIDEROTIC	SIEGES	SIFTINGS
SICKLEMEN	SIDEBOOBS	SIDERS	SIEGING	SIFTS
SICKLEMIA	SIDEBURN	SIDES	SIELD	SIG
SICKLEMIC	SIDEBURNS	SIDESHOOT	SIEMENS	SIGANID
SICKLES	SIDECAR	SIDESHOW	SIEMENSES	SIGANIDS
SICKLIED	SIDECARS	SIDESHOWS	SIEN	SIGH
SICKLIER	SIDECHAIR	SIDESLIP	SIENITE	SIGHED
SICKLIES	SIDECHECK	SIDESLIPS	SIENITES	SIGHER
SICKLIEST	SIDED	SIDESMAN	SIENNA	SIGHERS
SICKLILY	SIDEDLY	SIDESMEN	SIENNAS	SIGHFUL
SICKLING	SIDEDNESS	SIDESPIN	SIENS	SIGHING
SICKLY	SIDEDRESS	SIDESPINS	SIENT	SIGHINGLY
SICKLYING	SIDEHILL	SIDESPLIT	SIENTS	SIGHINGS
SICKNESS	SIDEHILLS	SIDESTEP	SIEROZEM	SIGHLESS
SICKNURSE	SIDEKICK	SIDESTEPS	SIEROZEMS	SIGHLIKE
SICKO	SIDEKICKS	SIDESWIPE	SIERRA	SIGHS
SICKOS	SIDELESS	SIDETABLE	SIERRAN	SIGHT
SICKOUT	SIDELIGHT	SIDETRACK	SIERRAS	SIGHTABLE
SICKOUTS	SIDELINE	SIDEWALK	SIES	SIGHTED
SICKROOM	SIDELINED	SIDEWALKS	SIESTA	SIGHTER

SIGHTERS	SIGNALISE	SIGNORINE	SILENUS	SILKENING
SIGHTING	SIGNALIZE	SIGNORINI	SILER	SILKENS
SIGHTINGS	SIGNALLED	SIGNORINO	SILERS	SILKIE
SIGHTLESS	SIGNALLER	SIGNORS	SILES	SILKIER
SIGHTLIER	SIGNALLY	SIGNORY	SILESIA	SILKIES
SIGHTLINE	SIGNALMAN	SIGNPOST	SILESIAS	SILKIEST
SIGHTLY	SIGNALMEN	SIGNPOSTS	SILEX	SILKILY
SIGHTS	SIGNALS	SIGNS	SILEXES	SILKINESS
SIGHTSAW	SIGNARIES	SIGS	SILICA	SILKING
SIGHTSEE	SIGNARY	SIJO	SILICAS	SILKLIKE
SIGHTSEEN	SIGNATORY	SIJOS	SILICATE	SILKOLINE
SIGHTSEER	SIGNATURE	SIK	SILICATED	SILKS
SIGHTSEES	SIGNBOARD	SIKA	SILICATES	SILKTAIL
SIGHTSMAN	SIGNED	SIKAS	SILICEOUS	SILKTAILS
SIGHTSMEN	SIGNEE	SIKE	SILICIC	SILKWEED
SIGIL	SIGNEES	SIKER	SILICIDE	SILKWEEDS
SIGILLARY	SIGNER	SIKES	SILICIDES	SILKWORM
SIGILLATE	SIGNERS	SIKORSKY	SILICIFY	SILKWORMS
SIGILS	SIGNET	SIKSIK	SILICIOUS	SILKY
SIGISBEI	SIGNETED	SIKSIKS	SILICIUM	SILL
SIGISBEO	SIGNETING	SILAGE	SILICIUMS	SILLABUB
SIGLA	SIGNETS	SILAGED	SILICLE	SILLABUBS
SIGLAS	SIGNEUR	SILAGEING	SILICLES	SILLADAR
SIGLOI	SIGNEURIE	SILAGES	SILICON	SILLADARS
SIGLOS	SIGNIEUR	SILAGING	SILICONE	SILLER
SIGLUM	SIGNIEURS	SILANE	SILICONES	SILLERS
SIGMA	SIGNIFICS	SILANES	SILICONS	SILLIBUB
SIGMAS	SIGNIFIED	SILASTIC	SILICOSES	SILLIBUBS
SIGMATE	SIGNIFIER	SILASTICS	SILICOSIS	SILLIER
SIGMATED	SIGNIFIES	SILD	SILICOTIC	SILLIES
SIGMATES	SIGNIFY	SILDS	SILICULA	SILLIEST
SIGMATIC	SIGNING	SILE	SILICULAE	SILLILY
SIGMATING	SIGNINGS	SILED	SILICULAS	SILLINESS
SIGMATION	SIGNIOR	SILEN	SILICULE	SILLOCK
SIGMATISM	SIGNIORI	SILENCE	SILICULES	SILLOCKS
SIGMATRON	SIGNIORS	SILENCED	SILING	SILLS
SIGMOID	SIGNIORY	SILENCER	SILIQUA	SILLY
SIGMOIDAL	SIGNLESS	SILENCERS	SILIQUAE	SILO
SIGMOIDS	SIGNOR	SILENCES	SILIQUAS	SILOED
SIGN	SIGNORA	SILENCING	SILIQUE	SILOES
SIGNA	SIGNORAS	SILENE	SILIQUES	SILOING
SIGNABLE	SIGNORE	SILENES	SILIQUOSE	SILOS
SIGNAGE	SIGNORES	SILENI	SILIQUOUS	SILOVIK
SIGNAGES	SIGNORI	SILENS	SILK	SILOVIKI
SIGNAL	SIGNORIA	SILENT	SILKALENE	SILOXANE
SIGNALED	SIGNORIAL	SILENTER	SILKALINE	SILOXANES
SIGNALER	SIGNORIAS	SILENTEST	SILKED	SILPHIA
SIGNALERS	SIGNORIES	SILENTLY	SILKEN	SILPHIUM
SIGNALING	SIGNORINA	SILENTS	SILKENED	SILPHIUMS

S

SILT	SIMARUBAS	SIMONISED	SIMUL	SINEWS
SILTATION	SIMAS	SIMONISES	SIMULACRA	SINEWY
SILTED	SIMATIC	SIMONIST	SIMULACRE	SINFONIA
SILTIER	SIMAZINE	SIMONISTS	SIMULANT	SINFONIAS
SILTIEST	SIMAZINES	SIMONIZE	SIMULANTS	SINFONIE
SILTING	SIMBA	SIMONIZED	SIMULAR	SINFUL
SILTS	SIMBAS	SIMONIZES	SIMULARS	SINFULLY
SILTSTONE	SIMCHA	SIMONY	SIMULATE	SING
SILTY	SIMCHAS	SIMOOM	SIMULATED	SINGABLE
SILURIAN	SIMI	SIMOOMS	SIMULATES	SINGALONG
SILURID	SIMIAL	SIMOON	SIMULATOR	SINGE
SILURIDS	SIMIAN	SIMOONS	SIMULCAST	SINGED
SILURIST	SIMIANS	SIMORG	SIMULIUM	SINGEING
SILURISTS	SIMILAR	SIMORGS	SIMULIUMS	SINGER
SILUROID	SIMILARLY	SIMP	SIMULS	SINGERS
SILUROIDS	SIMILE	SIMPAI	SIMURG	SINGES
SILVA	SIMILES	SIMPAIS	SIMURGH	SINGING
SILVAE	SIMILISE	SIMPATICO	SIMURGHS	SINGINGLY
SILVAN	SIMILISED	SIMPER	SIMURGS	SINGINGS
SILVANS	SIMILISES	SIMPERED	SIN	SINGLE
SILVAS	SIMILIZE	SIMPERER	SINAPISM	SINGLED
SILVATIC	SIMILIZED	SIMPERERS	SINAPISMS	SINGLEDOM
SILVER	SIMILIZES	SIMPERING	SINCE	SINGLES
SILVERED	SIMILOR	SIMPERS	SINCERE	SINGLET
SILVERER	SIMILORS	SIMPKIN	SINCERELY	SINGLETON
SILVERERS	SIMIOID	SIMPKINS	SINCERER	SINGLETS
SILVEREYE	SIMIOUS	SIMPLE	SINCEREST	SINGLING
SILVERIER	SIMIS	SIMPLED	SINCERITY	SINGLINGS
SILVERING	SIMIT	SIMPLER	SINCIPITA	SINGLY
SILVERISE	SIMITAR	SIMPLERS	SINCIPUT	SINGS
SILVERIZE	SIMITARS	SIMPLES	SINCIPUTS	SINGSONG
SILVERLY	SIMITS	SIMPLESSE	SIND	SINGSONGS
SILVERN	SIMKIN	SIMPLEST	SINDED	SINGSONGY
SILVERS	SIMKINS	SIMPLETON	SINDING	SINGSPIEL
SILVERTIP	SIMLIN	SIMPLEX	SINDINGS	SINGULAR
SILVERY	SIMLINS	SIMPLEXES	SINDON	SINGULARS
SILVEX	SIMMER	SIMPLICES	SINDONS	SINGULARY
SILVEXES	SIMMERED	SIMPLICIA	SINDS	SINGULT
SILVICAL	SIMMERING	SIMPLIFY	SINE	SINGULTS
SILVICS	SIMMERS	SIMPLING	SINECURE	SINGULTUS
SILYMARIN	SIMNEL	SIMPLINGS	SINECURES	SINH
SIM	SIMNELS	SIMPLISM	SINED	SINHS
SIMA	SIMOLEON	SIMPLISMS	SINES	SINICAL
SIMAR	SIMOLEONS	SIMPLIST	SINEW	SINICISE
SIMAROUBA	SIMONIAC	SIMPLISTE	SINEWED	SINICISED
SIMARRE	SIMONIACS	SIMPLISTS	SINEWIER	SINICISES
SIMARRES	SIMONIES	SIMPLY	SINEWIEST	SINICIZE
SIMARS	SIMONIOUS	SIMPS	SINEWING	SINICIZED
SIMARUBA	SIMONISE	SIMS	SINEWLESS	SINICIZES

S

SINING	SINUATELY	SIRE	SIRRED	SISTS
SINISTER	SINUATES	SIRED	SIRREE	SIT
SINISTRAL	SINUATING	SIREE	SIRREES	SITAR
SINK	SINUATION	SIREES	SIRRING	SITARIST
SINKABLE	SINUITIS	SIREN	SIRS	SITARISTS
SINKAGE	SINUOSE	SIRENIAN	SIRTUIN	SITARS
SINKAGES	SINUOSITY	SIRENIANS	SIRTUINS	SITATUNGA
SINKER	SINUOUS	SIRENIC	SIRUP	SITCH
SINKERS	SINUOUSLY	SIRENISE	SIRUPED	SITCHES
SINKFUL	SINUS	SIRENISED	SIRUPIER	SITCOM
SINKFULS	SINUSES	SIRENISES	SIRUPIEST	SITCOMS
SINKHOLE	SINUSITIS	SIRENIZE	SIRUPING	SITE
SINKHOLES	SINUSLIKE	SIRENIZED	SIRUPS	SITED
SINKIER	SINUSOID	SIRENIZES	SIRUPY	SITELLA
SINKIEST	SINUSOIDS	SIRENS	SIRVENTE	SITELLAS
SINKING	SIP	SIRES	SIRVENTES	SITES
SINKINGS	SIPE	SIRGANG	SIS	SITFAST
SINKS	SIPED	SIRGANGS	SISAL	SITFASTS
SINKY	SIPES	SIRI	SISALS	SITH
SINLESS	SIPHON	SIRIASES	SISERARY	SITHE
SINLESSLY	SIPHONAGE	SIRIASIS	SISES	SITHED
SINNED	SIPHONAL	SIRIH	SISKIN	SITHEE
SINNER	SIPHONATE	SIRIHS	SISKINS	SITHEN
SINNERED	SIPHONED	SIRING	SISS	SITHENCE
SINNERING	SIPHONET	SIRINGS	SISSES	SITHENS
SINNERS	SIPHONETS	SIRIS	SISSIER	SITHES
SINNET	SIPHONIC	SIRKAR	SISSIES	SITHING
SINNETS	SIPHONING	SIRKARS	SISSIEST	SITING
SINNING	SIPHONS	SIRLOIN	SISSIFIED	SITINGS
SINNINGIA	SIPHUNCLE	SIRLOINS	SISSINESS	SITIOLOGY
SINOLOGUE	SIPING	SIRNAME	SISSOO	SITKA
SINOLOGY	SIPPABLE	SIRNAMED	SISSOOS	SITKAMER
SINOPIA	SIPPED	SIRNAMES	SISSY	SITKAMERS
SINOPIAS	SIPPER	SIRNAMING	SISSYISH	SITOLOGY
SINOPIE	SIPPERS	SIROC	SISSYNESS	SITREP
SINOPIS	SIPPET	SIROCCO	SIST	SITREPS
SINOPISES	SIPPETS	SIROCCOS	SISTA	SITS
SINOPITE	SIPPING	SIROCS	SISTAS	SITTAR
SINOPITES	SIPPLE	SIRONISE	SISTED	SITTARS
SINS	SIPPLED	SIRONISED	SISTER	SITTELLA
SINSYNE	SIPPLES	SIRONISES	SISTERED	SITTELLAS
SINTER	SIPPLING	SIRONIZE	SISTERING	SITTEN
SINTERED	SIPPY	SIRONIZED	SISTERLY	SITTER
SINTERIER	SIPS	SIRONIZES	SISTERS	SITTERS
SINTERING	SIR	SIROSET	SISTING	SITTINE
SINTERS	SIRCAR	SIRRA	SISTRA	SITTINES
SINTERY	SIRCARS	SIRRAH	SISTROID	SITTING
SINUATE	SIRDAR	SIRRAHS	SISTRUM	SITTINGS
SINUATED	SIRDARS	SIRRAS	SISTRUMS	SITUATE

S

SITUATED	SIXTIETH	SKAILING	SKEANS	SKEIGH
SITUATES	SIXTIETHS	SKAILS	SKEAR	SKEIGHER
SITUATING	SIXTY	SKAITH	SKEARED	SKEIGHEST
SITUATION	SIXTYFOLD	SKAITHED	SKEARIER	SKEIN
SITULA	SIXTYISH	SKAITHING	SKEARIEST	SKEINED
SITULAE	SIZABLE	SKAITHS	SKEARING	SKEINING
SITUP	SIZABLY	SKALD	SKEARS	SKEINS
SITUPS	SIZAR	SKALDIC	SKEARY	SKELDER
SITUS	SIZARS	SKALDS	SKED	SKELDERED
SITUSES	SIZARSHIP	SKALDSHIP	SKEDADDLE	SKELDERS
SITUTUNGA	SIZE	SKANGER	SKEDDED	SKELETAL
SITZ	SIZEABLE	SKANGERS	SKEDDING	SKELETON
SITZKRIEG	SIZEABLY	SKANK	SKEDS	SKELETONS
SITZMARK	SIZED	SKANKED	SKEE	SKELF
SITZMARKS	SIZEISM	SKANKER	SKEECHAN	SKELFS
SIVER	SIZEISMS	SKANKERS	SKEECHANS	SKELL
SIVERS	SIZEIST	SKANKIER	SKEED	SKELLIE
SIWASH	SIZEISTS	SKANKIEST	SKEEF	SKELLIED
SIWASHED	SIZEL	SKANKING	SKEEING	SKELLIER
SIWASHES	SIZELS	SKANKINGS	SKEELIER	SKELLIES
SIWASHING	SIZER	SKANKS	SKEELIEST	SKELLIEST
SIX	SIZERS	SKANKY	SKEELY	SKELLOCH
SIXAIN	SIZES	SKART	SKEEN	SKELLOCHS
SIXAINE	SIZIER	SKARTH	SKEENS	SKELLS
SIXAINES	SIZIEST	SKARTHS	SKEER	SKELLUM
SIXAINS	SIZINESS	SKARTS	SKEERED	SKELLUMS
SIXER	SIZING	SKAS	SKEERIER	SKELLY
SIXERS	SIZINGS	SKAT	SKEERIEST	SKELLYING
SIXES	SIZISM	SKATE	SKEERING	SKELM
SIXFOLD	SIZISMS	SKATED	SKEERS	SKELMS
SIXISH	SIZIST	SKATEPARK	SKEERY	SKELP
SIXMO	SIZISTS	SKATEPUNK	SKEES	SKELPED
SIXMOS	SIZY	SKATER	SKEESICKS	SKELPING
SIXPENCE	SIZZLE	SKATERS	SKEET	SKELPINGS
SIXPENCES	SIZZLED	SKATES	SKEETER	SKELPIT
SIXPENNY	SIZZLER	SKATING	SKEETERS	SKELPS
SIXSCORE	SIZZLERS	SKATINGS	SKEETS	SKELTER
SIXSCORES	SIZZLES	SKATOL	SKEEVIER	SKELTERED
SIXTE	SIZZLING	SKATOLE	SKEEVIEST	SKELTERS
SIXTEEN	SIZZLINGS	SKATOLES	SKEEVY	SKELUM
SIXTEENER	SJAMBOK	SKATOLS	SKEEZIER	SKELUMS
SIXTEENMO	SJAMBOKED	SKATS	SKEEZIEST	SKEN
SIXTEENS	SJAMBOKS	SKATT	SKEEZY	SKENE
SIXTEENTH	SJOE	SKATTS	SKEG	SKENES
SIXTES	SKA	SKAW	SKEGG	SKENNED
SIXTH	SKAG	SKAWS	SKEGGER	SKENNING
SIXTHLY	SKAGS	SKEAN	SKEGGERS	SKENS
SIXTHS	SKAIL	SKEANE	SKEGGS	SKEO
SIXTIES	SKAILED	SKEANES	SKEGS	SKEOES

SKITTER

SKEOS	SKI	SKIEYER	SKIMPIEST	SKIPJACKS
SKEP	SKIABLE	SKIEYEST	SKIMPILY	SKIPLANE
SKEPFUL	SKIAGRAM	SKIFF	SKIMPING	SKIPLANES
SKEPFULS	SKIAGRAMS	SKIFFED	SKIMPS	SKIPPABLE
SKEPPED	SKIAGRAPH	SKIFFING	SKIMPY	SKIPPED
SKEPPING	SKIAMACHY	SKIFFLE	SKIMS	SKIPPER
SKEPS	SKIASCOPE	SKIFFLED	SKIN	SKIPPERED
SKEPSIS	SKIASCOPY	SKIFFLES	SKINCARE	SKIPPERS
SKEPSISES	SKIATRON	SKIFFLESS	SKINCARES	SKIPPET
SKEPTIC	SKIATRONS	SKIFFLING	SKINFLICK	SKIPPETS
SKEPTICAL	SKIBOB	SKIFFS	SKINFLINT	SKIPPIER
SKEPTICS	SKIBOBBED	SKIING	SKINFOOD	SKIPPIEST
SKER	SKIBOBBER	SKIINGS	SKINFOODS	SKIPPING
SKERRED	SKIBOBS	SKIJORER	SKINFUL	SKIPPINGS
SKERRICK	SKID	SKIJORERS	SKINFULS	SKIPPY
SKERRICKS	SKIDDED	SKIJORING	SKINHEAD	SKIPS
SKERRIES	SKIDDER	SKIJUMPER	SKINHEADS	SKIRL
SKERRING	SKIDDERS	SKIKJORER	SKINK	SKIRLED
SKERRY	SKIDDIER	SKILFUL	SKINKED	SKIRLING
SKERS	SKIDDIEST	SKILFULL	SKINKER	SKIRLINGS
SKET	SKIDDING	SKILFULLY	SKINKERS	SKIRLS
SKETCH	SKIDDINGS	SKILL	SKINKING	SKIRMISH
SKETCHED	SKIDDOO	SKILLED	SKINKS	SKIRR
SKETCHER	SKIDDOOED	SKILLESS	SKINLESS	SKIRRED
SKETCHERS	SKIDDOOS	SKILLET	SKINLIKE	SKIRRET
SKETCHES	SKIDDY	SKILLETS	SKINNED	SKIRRETS
SKETCHIER	SKIDLID	SKILLFUL	SKINNER	SKIRRING
SKETCHILY	SKIDLIDS	SKILLIER	SKINNERS	SKIRRS
SKETCHING	SKIDMARK	SKILLIES	SKINNIER	SKIRT
SKETCHPAD	SKIDMARKS	SKILLIEST	SKINNIES	SKIRTED
SKETCHY	SKIDOO	SKILLING	SKINNIEST	SKIRTER
SKETS	SKIDOOED	SKILLINGS	SKINNING	SKIRTERS
SKETTED	SKIDOOER	SKILLION	SKINNY	SKIRTING
SKETTING	SKIDOOERS	SKILLIONS	SKINS	SKIRTINGS
SKEW	SKIDOOING	SKILLS	SKINSUIT	SKIRTLESS
SKEWBACK	SKIDOOS	SKILLY	SKINSUITS	SKIRTLIKE
SKEWBACKS	SKIDPAD	SKIM	SKINT	SKIRTS
SKEWBALD	SKIDPADS	SKIMBOARD	SKINTER	SKIS
SKEWBALDS	SKIDPAN	SKIMMED	SKINTEST	SKIT
SKEWED	SKIDPANS	SKIMMER	SKINTIGHT	SKITCH
SKEWER	SKIDPROOF	SKIMMERS	SKIO	SKITCHED
SKEWERED	SKIDS	SKIMMIA	SKIOES	SKITCHES
SKEWERING	SKIDWAY	SKIMMIAS	SKIORER	SKITCHING
SKEWERS	SKIDWAYS	SKIMMING	SKIORERS	SKITE
SKEWEST	SKIED	SKIMMINGS	SKIORING	SKITED
SKEWING	SKIER	SKIMOBILE	SKIORINGS	SKITES
SKEWNESS	SKIERS	SKIMP	SKIOS	SKITING
SKEWS	SKIES	SKIMPED	SKIP	SKITS
SKEWWHIFF	SKIEY	SKIMPIER	SKIPJACK	SKITTER

two to nine letter words | 541

SKITTERED	SKODY	SKRIEGH	SKUMMERED	SKYGLOWS
SKITTERS	SKOFF	SKRIEGHED	SKUMMERS	SKYHOME
SKITTERY	SKOFFED	SKRIEGHS	SKUNK	SKYHOMES
SKITTISH	SKOFFING	SKRIES	SKUNKBIRD	SKYHOOK
SKITTLE	SKOFFS	SKRIK	SKUNKBUSH	SKYHOOKS
SKITTLED	SKOG	SKRIKE	SKUNKED	SKYIER
SKITTLES	SKOGGED	SKRIKED	SKUNKIER	SKYIEST
SKITTLING	SKOGGING	SKRIKES	SKUNKIEST	SKYING
SKIVE	SKOGS	SKRIKING	SKUNKING	SKYISH
SKIVED	SKOKIAAN	SKRIKS	SKUNKS	SKYJACK
SKIVER	SKOKIAANS	SKRIMMAGE	SKUNKWEED	SKYJACKED
SKIVERED	SKOL	SKRIMP	SKUNKY	SKYJACKER
SKIVERING	SKOLED	SKRIMPED	SKURRIED	SKYJACKS
SKIVERS	SKOLIA	SKRIMPING	SKURRIES	SKYLAB
SKIVES	SKOLING	SKRIMPS	SKURRY	SKYLABS
SKIVIE	SKOLION	SKRONK	SKURRYING	SKYLARK
SKIVIER	SKOLLED	SKRONKS	SKUTTLE	SKYLARKED
SKIVIEST	SKOLLIE	SKRUMP	SKUTTLED	SKYLARKER
SKIVING	SKOLLIES	SKRUMPED	SKUTTLES	SKYLARKS
SKIVINGS	SKOLLING	SKRUMPING	SKUTTLING	SKYLESS
SKIVVIED	SKOLLY	SKRUMPS	SKY	SKYLIGHT
SKIVVIES	SKOLS	SKRY	SKYBOARD	SKYLIGHTS
SKIVVY	SKOOKUM	SKRYER	SKYBOARDS	SKYLIKE
SKIVVYING	SKOOKUMS	SKRYERS	SKYBORN	SKYLINE
SKIVY	SKOOL	SKRYING	SKYBORNE	SKYLINES
SKIWEAR	SKOOLS	SKUA	SKYBOX	SKYLIT
SKIWEARS	SKOOSH	SKUAS	SKYBOXES	SKYMAN
SKLATE	SKOOSHED	SKUDLER	SKYBRIDGE	SKYMEN
SKLATED	SKOOSHES	SKUDLERS	SKYCAP	SKYPHOI
SKLATES	SKOOSHING	SKUG	SKYCAPS	SKYPHOS
SKLATING	SKORDALIA	SKUGGED	SKYCLAD	SKYR
SKLENT	SKORT	SKUGGING	SKYDIVE	SKYRE
SKLENTED	SKORTS	SKUGS	SKYDIVED	SKYRED
SKLENTING	SKOSH	SKULK	SKYDIVER	SKYRES
SKLENTS	SKOSHES	SKULKED	SKYDIVERS	SKYRING
SKLIFF	SKRAN	SKULKER	SKYDIVES	SKYRMION
SKLIFFED	SKRANS	SKULKERS	SKYDIVING	SKYRMIONS
SKLIFFING	SKREEGH	SKULKING	SKYDOVE	SKYROCKET
SKLIFFS	SKREEGHED	SKULKINGS	SKYED	SKYRS
SKLIM	SKREEGHS	SKULKS	SKYER	SKYSAIL
SKLIMMED	SKREEN	SKULL	SKYERS	SKYSAILS
SKLIMMING	SKREENS	SKULLCAP	SKYEY	SKYSCAPE
SKLIMS	SKREIGH	SKULLCAPS	SKYEYER	SKYSCAPES
SKOAL	SKREIGHED	SKULLED	SKYEYEST	SKYSURF
SKOALED	SKREIGHS	SKULLING	SKYF	SKYSURFED
SKOALING	SKRIECH	SKULLS	SKYFED	SKYSURFER
SKOALS	SKRIECHED	SKULPIN	SKYFING	SKYSURFS
SKODIER	SKRIECHS	SKULPINS	SKYFS	SKYTE
SKODIEST	SKRIED	SKUMMER	SKYGLOW	SKYTED

S

SKYTES	SLAGGED	SLANDERER	SLARTING	SLAVERING
SKYTING	SLAGGIER	SLANDERS	SLARTS	SLAVERS
SKYWALK	SLAGGIEST	SLANE	SLASH	SLAVERY
SKYWALKS	SLAGGING	SLANES	SLASHED	SLAVES
SKYWARD	SLAGGINGS	SLANG	SLASHER	SLAVEY
SKYWARDS	SLAGGY	SLANGED	SLASHERS	SLAVEYS
SKYWATCH	SLAGHEAP	SLANGER	SLASHES	SLAVING
SKYWAY	SLAGHEAPS	SLANGERS	SLASHFEST	SLAVISH
SKYWAYS	SLAGS	SLANGIER	SLASHIE	SLAVISHLY
SKYWRITE	SLAHAL	SLANGIEST	SLASHIES	SLAVOCRAT
SKYWRITER	SLAHALS	SLANGILY	SLASHING	SLAVOPHIL
SKYWRITES	SLAID	SLANGING	SLASHINGS	SLAW
SKYWROTE	SLAIDS	SLANGINGS	SLAT	SLAWS
SLAB	SLAIN	SLANGISH	SLATCH	SLAY
SLABBED	SLAINTE	SLANGS	SLATCHES	SLAYABLE
SLABBER	SLAIRG	SLANGUAGE	SLATE	SLAYED
SLABBERED	SLAIRGED	SLANGULAR	SLATED	SLAYER
SLABBERER	SLAIRGING	SLANGY	SLATELIKE	SLAYERS
SLABBERS	SLAIRGS	SLANK	SLATER	SLAYING
SLABBERY	SLAISTER	SLANT	SLATERS	SLAYINGS
SLABBIER	SLAISTERS	SLANTED	SLATES	SLAYS
SLABBIES	SLAISTERY	SLANTER	SLATEY	SLEAVE
SLABBIEST	SLAKABLE	SLANTERS	SLATHER	SLEAVED
SLABBING	SLAKE	SLANTIER	SLATHERED	SLEAVES
SLABBINGS	SLAKEABLE	SLANTIEST	SLATHERS	SLEAVING
SLABBY	SLAKED	SLANTING	SLATIER	SLEAZE
SLABLIKE	SLAKELESS	SLANTLY	SLATIEST	SLEAZEBAG
SLABS	SLAKER	SLANTS	SLATINESS	SLEAZED
SLABSTONE	SLAKERS	SLANTWAYS	SLATING	SLEAZES
SLACK	SLAKES	SLANTWISE	SLATINGS	SLEAZIER
SLACKED	SLAKING	SLANTY	SLATS	SLEAZIEST
SLACKEN	SLALOM	SLAP	SLATTED	SLEAZILY
SLACKENED	SLALOMED	SLAPDASH	SLATTER	SLEAZING
SLACKENER	SLALOMER	SLAPHAPPY	SLATTERED	SLEAZO
SLACKENS	SLALOMERS	SLAPHEAD	SLATTERN	SLEAZOID
SLACKER	SLALOMING	SLAPHEADS	SLATTERNS	SLEAZOIDS
SLACKERS	SLALOMIST	SLAPJACK	SLATTERS	SLEAZOS
SLACKEST	SLALOMS	SLAPJACKS	SLATTERY	SLEAZY
SLACKING	SLAM	SLAPPED	SLATTING	SLEB
SLACKLY	SLAMDANCE	SLAPPER	SLATTINGS	SLEBS
SLACKNESS	SLAMMAKIN	SLAPPERS	SLATY	SLED
SLACKS	SLAMMED	SLAPPING	SLAUGHTER	SLEDDED
SLADANG	SLAMMER	SLAPPINGS	SLAVE	SLEDDER
SLADANGS	SLAMMERS	SLAPS	SLAVED	SLEDDERS
SLADE	SLAMMING	SLAPSHOT	SLAVER	SLEDDING
SLADES	SLAMMINGS	SLAPSHOTS	SLAVERED	SLEDDINGS
SLAE	SLAMS	SLAPSTICK	SLAVERER	SLEDED
SLAES	SLANDER	SLART	SLAVERERS	SLEDGE
SLAG	SLANDERED	SLARTED	SLAVERIES	SLEDGED

SLEDGER	SLEER	SLICED	SLIGHTEST	SLINKER
SLEDGERS	SLEEST	SLICER	SLIGHTING	SLINKERS
SLEDGES	SLEET	SLICERS	SLIGHTISH	SLINKIER
SLEDGING	SLEETED	SLICES	SLIGHTLY	SLINKIEST
SLEDGINGS	SLEETIER	SLICING	SLIGHTS	SLINKILY
SLEDS	SLEETIEST	SLICINGS	SLILY	SLINKING
SLEE	SLEETING	SLICK	SLIM	SLINKS
SLEECH	SLEETS	SLICKED	SLIMDOWN	SLINKSKIN
SLEECHES	SLEETY	SLICKEN	SLIMDOWNS	SLINKWEED
SLEECHIER	SLEEVE	SLICKENED	SLIME	SLINKY
SLEECHY	SLEEVED	SLICKENER	SLIMEBAG	SLINTER
SLEEK	SLEEVEEN	SLICKENS	SLIMEBAGS	SLINTERS
SLEEKED	SLEEVEENS	SLICKER	SLIMEBALL	SLIOTAR
SLEEKEN	SLEEVELET	SLICKERED	SLIMED	SLIOTARS
SLEEKENED	SLEEVER	SLICKERS	SLIMES	SLIP
SLEEKENS	SLEEVERS	SLICKEST	SLIMIER	SLIPCASE
SLEEKER	SLEEVES	SLICKING	SLIMIEST	SLIPCASED
SLEEKERS	SLEEVING	SLICKINGS	SLIMILY	SLIPCASES
SLEEKEST	SLEEVINGS	SLICKLY	SLIMINESS	SLIPCOVER
SLEEKIER	SLEEZIER	SLICKNESS	SLIMING	SLIPDRESS
SLEEKIEST	SLEEZIEST	SLICKROCK	SLIMLINE	SLIPE
SLEEKING	SLEEZY	SLICKS	SLIMLY	SLIPED
SLEEKINGS	SLEIDED	SLICKSTER	SLIMMED	SLIPES
SLEEKIT	SLEIGH	SLID	SLIMMER	SLIPFORM
SLEEKLY	SLEIGHED	SLIDABLE	SLIMMERS	SLIPFORMS
SLEEKNESS	SLEIGHER	SLIDDEN	SLIMMEST	SLIPING
SLEEKS	SLEIGHERS	SLIDDER	SLIMMING	SLIPKNOT
SLEEKY	SLEIGHING	SLIDDERED	SLIMMINGS	SLIPKNOTS
SLEEP	SLEIGHS	SLIDDERS	SLIMMISH	SLIPLESS
SLEEPAWAY	SLEIGHT	SLIDDERY	SLIMNESS	SLIPNOOSE
SLEEPER	SLEIGHTS	SLIDE	SLIMPSIER	SLIPOUT
SLEEPERS	SLENDER	SLIDED	SLIMPSY	SLIPOUTS
SLEEPERY	SLENDERER	SLIDER	SLIMS	SLIPOVER
SLEEPIER	SLENDERLY	SLIDERS	SLIMSIER	SLIPOVERS
SLEEPIEST	SLENTER	SLIDES	SLIMSIEST	SLIPPAGE
SLEEPILY	SLENTERS	SLIDESHOW	SLIMSY	SLIPPAGES
SLEEPING	SLEPT	SLIDEWAY	SLIMY	SLIPPED
SLEEPINGS	SLEUTH	SLIDEWAYS	SLING	SLIPPER
SLEEPLESS	SLEUTHED	SLIDING	SLINGBACK	SLIPPERED
SLEEPLIKE	SLEUTHING	SLIDINGLY	SLINGER	SLIPPERS
SLEEPOUT	SLEUTHS	SLIDINGS	SLINGERS	SLIPPERY
SLEEPOUTS	SLEW	SLIER	SLINGIER	SLIPPIER
SLEEPOVER	SLEWED	SLIEST	SLINGIEST	SLIPPIEST
SLEEPRY	SLEWING	SLIEVE	SLINGING	SLIPPILY
SLEEPS	SLEWS	SLIEVES	SLINGS	SLIPPING
SLEEPSUIT	SLEY	SLIGHT	SLINGSHOT	SLIPPY
SLEEPWALK	SLEYS	SLIGHTED	SLINGY	SLIPRAIL
SLEEPWEAR	SLICE	SLIGHTER	SLINK	SLIPRAILS
SLEEPY	SLICEABLE	SLIGHTERS	SLINKED	SLIPS

S

SLIPSHEET	SLOBBER	SLOOMIEST	SLOTH	SLOWWORM
SLIPSHOD	SLOBBERED	SLOOMING	SLOTHED	SLOWWORMS
SLIPSLOP	SLOBBERER	SLOOMS	SLOTHFUL	SLOYD
SLIPSLOPS	SLOBBERS	SLOOMY	SLOTHING	SLOYDS
SLIPSOLE	SLOBBERY	SLOOP	SLOTHS	SLUB
SLIPSOLES	SLOBBIER	SLOOPS	SLOTS	SLUBB
SLIPT	SLOBBIEST	SLOOSH	SLOTTED	SLUBBED
SLIPUP	SLOBBING	SLOOSHED	SLOTTER	SLUBBER
SLIPUPS	SLOBBISH	SLOOSHES	SLOTTERS	SLUBBERED
SLIPWARE	SLOBBY	SLOOSHING	SLOTTING	SLUBBERS
SLIPWARES	SLOBLAND	SLOOT	SLOUCH	SLUBBEST
SLIPWAY	SLOBLANDS	SLOOTS	SLOUCHED	SLUBBIER
SLIPWAYS	SLOBS	SLOP	SLOUCHER	SLUBBIEST
SLISH	SLOCKEN	SLOPE	SLOUCHERS	SLUBBING
SLISHES	SLOCKENED	SLOPED	SLOUCHES	SLUBBINGS
SLIT	SLOCKENS	SLOPER	SLOUCHIER	SLUBBS
SLITHER	SLOE	SLOPERS	SLOUCHILY	SLUBBY
SLITHERED	SLOEBUSH	SLOPES	SLOUCHING	SLUBS
SLITHERS	SLOES	SLOPESIDE	SLOUCHY	SLUDGE
SLITHERY	SLOETHORN	SLOPEWISE	SLOUGH	SLUDGED
SLITLESS	SLOETREE	SLOPIER	SLOUGHED	SLUDGES
SLITLIKE	SLOETREES	SLOPIEST	SLOUGHI	SLUDGIER
SLITS	SLOG	SLOPING	SLOUGHIER	SLUDGIEST
SLITTED	SLOGAN	SLOPINGLY	SLOUGHING	SLUDGING
SLITTER	SLOGANED	SLOPPED	SLOUGHIS	SLUDGY
SLITTERS	SLOGANEER	SLOPPIER	SLOUGHS	SLUE
SLITTIER	SLOGANISE	SLOPPIEST	SLOUGHY	SLUED
SLITTIEST	SLOGANIZE	SLOPPILY	SLOVE	SLUEING
SLITTING	SLOGANS	SLOPPING	SLOVEN	SLUES
SLITTY	SLOGGED	SLOPPY	SLOVENLY	SLUFF
SLIVE	SLOGGER	SLOPS	SLOVENRY	SLUFFED
SLIVED	SLOGGERS	SLOPWORK	SLOVENS	SLUFFING
SLIVEN	SLOGGING	SLOPWORKS	SLOW	SLUFFS
SLIVER	SLOGS	SLOPY	SLOWBACK	SLUG
SLIVERED	SLOID	SLORM	SLOWBACKS	SLUGABED
SLIVERER	SLOIDS	SLORMED	SLOWCOACH	SLUGABEDS
SLIVERERS	SLOJD	SLORMING	SLOWDOWN	SLUGFEST
SLIVERING	SLOJDS	SLORMS	SLOWDOWNS	SLUGFESTS
SLIVERS	SLOKEN	SLOSH	SLOWED	SLUGGABED
SLIVES	SLOKENED	SLOSHED	SLOWER	SLUGGARD
SLIVING	SLOKENING	SLOSHES	SLOWEST	SLUGGARDS
SLIVOVIC	SLOKENS	SLOSHIER	SLOWING	SLUGGED
SLIVOVICA	SLOMMOCK	SLOSHIEST	SLOWINGS	SLUGGER
SLIVOVITZ	SLOMMOCKS	SLOSHING	SLOWISH	SLUGGERS
SLIVOWITZ	SLOMO	SLOSHINGS	SLOWLY	SLUGGING
SLOAN	SLOMOS	SLOSHY	SLOWNESS	SLUGGISH
SLOANS	SLOOM	SLOT	SLOWPOKE	SLUGHORN
SLOB	SLOOMED	SLOTBACK	SLOWPOKES	SLUGHORNE
SLOBBED	SLOOMIER	SLOTBACKS	SLOWS	SLUGHORNS

S

SLUGLIKE	SLURB	SLYER	SMALT	SMASHUPS
SLUGS	SLURBAN	SLYEST	SMALTI	SMATCH
SLUICE	SLURBS	SLYISH	SMALTINE	SMATCHED
SLUICED	SLURP	SLYLY	SMALTINES	SMATCHES
SLUICES	SLURPED	SLYNESS	SMALTITE	SMATCHING
SLUICEWAY	SLURPER	SLYNESSES	SMALTITES	SMATTER
SLUICIER	SLURPERS	SLYPE	SMALTO	SMATTERED
SLUICIEST	SLURPIER	SLYPES	SMALTOS	SMATTERER
SLUICING	SLURPIEST	SMA	SMALTS	SMATTERS
SLUICY	SLURPING	SMAAK	SMARAGD	SMAZE
SLUING	SLURPS	SMAAKED	SMARAGDE	SMAZES
SLUIT	SLURPY	SMAAKING	SMARAGDES	SMEAR
SLUITS	SLURRED	SMAAKS	SMARAGDS	SMEARCASE
SLUM	SLURRIED	SMACK	SMARM	SMEARED
SLUMBER	SLURRIES	SMACKDOWN	SMARMED	SMEARER
SLUMBERED	SLURRING	SMACKED	SMARMIER	SMEARERS
SLUMBERER	SLURRY	SMACKER	SMARMIEST	SMEARIER
SLUMBERS	SLURRYING	SMACKEROO	SMARMILY	SMEARIEST
SLUMBERY	SLURS	SMACKERS	SMARMING	SMEARILY
SLUMBROUS	SLURVE	SMACKHEAD	SMARMS	SMEARING
SLUMBRY	SLURVES	SMACKING	SMARMY	SMEARS
SLUMGUM	SLUSE	SMACKINGS	SMART	SMEARY
SLUMGUMS	SLUSES	SMACKS	SMARTARSE	SMEATH
SLUMISM	SLUSH	SMAIK	SMARTASS	SMEATHS
SLUMISMS	SLUSHED	SMAIKS	SMARTED	SMECTIC
SLUMLORD	SLUSHEE	SMALL	SMARTEN	SMECTITE
SLUMLORDS	SLUSHEES	SMALLAGE	SMARTENED	SMECTITES
SLUMMED	SLUSHES	SMALLAGES	SMARTENS	SMECTITIC
SLUMMER	SLUSHIE	SMALLBOY	SMARTER	SMEDDUM
SLUMMERS	SLUSHIER	SMALLBOYS	SMARTEST	SMEDDUMS
SLUMMIER	SLUSHIES	SMALLED	SMARTIE	SMEE
SLUMMIEST	SLUSHIEST	SMALLER	SMARTIES	SMEECH
SLUMMING	SLUSHILY	SMALLEST	SMARTING	SMEECHED
SLUMMINGS	SLUSHING	SMALLING	SMARTISH	SMEECHES
SLUMMOCK	SLUSHY	SMALLISH	SMARTLY	SMEECHING
SLUMMOCKS	SLUT	SMALLNESS	SMARTNESS	SMEEK
SLUMMY	SLUTCH	SMALLPOX	SMARTS	SMEEKED
SLUMP	SLUTCHES	SMALLS	SMARTWEED	SMEEKING
SLUMPED	SLUTCHIER	SMALLSAT	SMARTY	SMEEKS
SLUMPIER	SLUTCHY	SMALLSATS	SMASH	SMEES
SLUMPIEST	SLUTS	SMALLTIME	SMASHABLE	SMEETH
SLUMPING	SLUTTERY	SMALM	SMASHED	SMEETHED
SLUMPS	SLUTTIER	SMALMED	SMASHER	SMEETHING
SLUMPY	SLUTTIEST	SMALMIER	SMASHEROO	SMEETHS
SLUMS	SLUTTILY	SMALMIEST	SMASHERS	SMEGMA
SLUNG	SLUTTISH	SMALMILY	SMASHES	SMEGMAS
SLUNGSHOT	SLUTTY	SMALMING	SMASHING	SMEIK
SLUNK	SLY	SMALMS	SMASHINGS	SMEIKED
SLUR	SLYBOOTS	SMALMY	SMASHUP	SMEIKING

SMEIKS	SMIDGIN	SMIRRS	SMOKEBUSH	SMOORING
SMEKE	SMIDGINS	SMIRRY	SMOKED	SMOORS
SMEKED	SMIERCASE	SMIRS	SMOKEHO	SMOOSH
SMEKES	SMIGHT	SMIRTING	SMOKEHOOD	SMOOSHED
SMEKING	SMIGHTING	SMIRTINGS	SMOKEHOS	SMOOSHES
SMELL	SMIGHTS	SMISHING	SMOKEJACK	SMOOSHING
SMELLABLE	SMILAX	SMISHINGS	SMOKELESS	SMOOT
SMELLED	SMILAXES	SMIT	SMOKELIKE	SMOOTED
SMELLER	SMILE	SMITE	SMOKEPOT	SMOOTH
SMELLERS	SMILED	SMITER	SMOKEPOTS	SMOOTHE
SMELLIER	SMILEFUL	SMITERS	SMOKER	SMOOTHED
SMELLIES	SMILELESS	SMITES	SMOKERS	SMOOTHEN
SMELLIEST	SMILER	SMITH	SMOKES	SMOOTHENS
SMELLING	SMILERS	SMITHED	SMOKEY	SMOOTHER
SMELLINGS	SMILES	SMITHERS	SMOKEYS	SMOOTHERS
SMELLS	SMILET	SMITHERY	SMOKIE	SMOOTHES
SMELLY	SMILETS	SMITHIED	SMOKIER	SMOOTHEST
SMELT	SMILEY	SMITHIES	SMOKIES	SMOOTHIE
SMELTED	SMILEYS	SMITHING	SMOKIEST	SMOOTHIES
SMELTER	SMILIER	SMITHINGS	SMOKILY	SMOOTHING
SMELTERS	SMILIES	SMITHS	SMOKINESS	SMOOTHISH
SMELTERY	SMILIEST	SMITHY	SMOKING	SMOOTHLY
SMELTING	SMILING	SMITHYING	SMOKINGS	SMOOTHS
SMELTINGS	SMILINGLY	SMITING	SMOKO	SMOOTHY
SMELTS	SMILINGS	SMITS	SMOKOS	SMOOTING
SMERK	SMILODON	SMITTED	SMOKY	SMOOTS
SMERKED	SMILODONS	SMITTEN	SMOLDER	SMORBROD
SMERKING	SMIR	SMITTING	SMOLDERED	SMORBRODS
SMERKS	SMIRCH	SMITTLE	SMOLDERS	SMORE
SMEUSE	SMIRCHED	SMOCK	SMOLT	SMORED
SMEUSES	SMIRCHER	SMOCKED	SMOLTS	SMORES
SMEW	SMIRCHERS	SMOCKING	SMOOCH	SMORG
SMEWS	SMIRCHES	SMOCKINGS	SMOOCHED	SMORGS
SMICKER	SMIRCHING	SMOCKLIKE	SMOOCHER	SMORING
SMICKERED	SMIRK	SMOCKS	SMOOCHERS	SMORZANDO
SMICKERS	SMIRKED	SMOG	SMOOCHES	SMORZATO
SMICKET	SMIRKER	SMOGGIER	SMOOCHIER	SMOTE
SMICKETS	SMIRKERS	SMOGGIEST	SMOOCHING	SMOTHER
SMICKLY	SMIRKIER	SMOGGY	SMOOCHY	SMOTHERED
SMIDDIED	SMIRKIEST	SMOGLESS	SMOODGE	SMOTHERER
SMIDDIES	SMIRKILY	SMOGS	SMOODGED	SMOTHERS
SMIDDY	SMIRKING	SMOILE	SMOODGES	SMOTHERY
SMIDDYING	SMIRKS	SMOILED	SMOODGING	SMOUCH
SMIDGE	SMIRKY	SMOILES	SMOOGE	SMOUCHED
SMIDGEN	SMIRR	SMOILING	SMOOGED	SMOUCHES
SMIDGENS	SMIRRED	SMOKABLE	SMOOGES	SMOUCHING
SMIDGEON	SMIRRIER	SMOKE	SMOOGING	SMOULDER
SMIDGEONS	SMIRRIEST	SMOKEABLE	SMOOR	SMOULDERS
SMIDGES	SMIRRING	SMOKEBOX	SMOORED	SMOULDRY

SMOUSE	SMURRIER	SNAFUS	SNAPBACKS	SNARKS
SMOUSED	SMURRIEST	SNAG	SNAPHANCE	SNARKY
SMOUSER	SMURRING	SNAGGED	SNAPLESS	SNARL
SMOUSERS	SMURRY	SNAGGER	SNAPLINK	SNARLED
SMOUSES	SMURS	SNAGGERS	SNAPLINKS	SNARLER
SMOUSING	SMUSH	SNAGGIER	SNAPPABLE	SNARLERS
SMOUT	SMUSHED	SNAGGIEST	SNAPPED	SNARLIER
SMOUTED	SMUSHES	SNAGGING	SNAPPER	SNARLIEST
SMOUTING	SMUSHING	SNAGGLE	SNAPPERED	SNARLING
SMOUTS	SMUT	SNAGGLES	SNAPPERS	SNARLINGS
SMOWT	SMUTCH	SNAGGY	SNAPPIER	SNARLS
SMOWTS	SMUTCHED	SNAGLIKE	SNAPPIEST	SNARLY
SMOYLE	SMUTCHES	SNAGS	SNAPPILY	SNARRED
SMOYLED	SMUTCHIER	SNAIL	SNAPPING	SNARRING
SMOYLES	SMUTCHING	SNAILED	SNAPPINGS	SNARS
SMOYLING	SMUTCHY	SNAILERY	SNAPPISH	SNARY
SMRITI	SMUTS	SNAILFISH	SNAPPY	SNASH
SMRITIS	SMUTTED	SNAILIER	SNAPS	SNASHED
SMUDGE	SMUTTIER	SNAILIEST	SNAPSHOT	SNASHES
SMUDGED	SMUTTIEST	SNAILING	SNAPSHOTS	SNASHING
SMUDGEDLY	SMUTTILY	SNAILLIKE	SNAPTIN	SNASTE
SMUDGER	SMUTTING	SNAILS	SNAPTINS	SNASTES
SMUDGERS	SMUTTY	SNAILY	SNAPWEED	SNATCH
SMUDGES	SMYTRIE	SNAKE	SNAPWEEDS	SNATCHED
SMUDGIER	SMYTRIES	SNAKEBIRD	SNAR	SNATCHER
SMUDGIEST	SNAB	SNAKEBIT	SNARE	SNATCHERS
SMUDGILY	SNABBLE	SNAKEBITE	SNARED	SNATCHES
SMUDGING	SNABBLED	SNAKED	SNARELESS	SNATCHIER
SMUDGINGS	SNABBLES	SNAKEFISH	SNARER	SNATCHILY
SMUDGY	SNABBLING	SNAKEHEAD	SNARERS	SNATCHING
SMUG	SNABS	SNAKELIKE	SNARES	SNATCHY
SMUGGED	SNACK	SNAKEPIT	SNARF	SNATH
SMUGGER	SNACKABLE	SNAKEPITS	SNARFED	SNATHE
SMUGGERY	SNACKED	SNAKEROOT	SNARFING	SNATHES
SMUGGEST	SNACKER	SNAKES	SNARFLE	SNATHS
SMUGGING	SNACKERS	SNAKESKIN	SNARFLED	SNAW
SMUGGLE	SNACKETTE	SNAKEWEED	SNARFLES	SNAWED
SMUGGLED	SNACKIER	SNAKEWISE	SNARFLING	SNAWING
SMUGGLER	SNACKIEST	SNAKEWOOD	SNARFS	SNAWS
SMUGGLERS	SNACKING	SNAKEY	SNARIER	SNAZZIER
SMUGGLES	SNACKS	SNAKIER	SNARIEST	SNAZZIEST
SMUGGLING	SNACKY	SNAKIEST	SNARING	SNAZZILY
SMUGLY	SNAFFLE	SNAKILY	SNARINGS	SNAZZY
SMUGNESS	SNAFFLED	SNAKINESS	SNARK	SNEAD
SMUGS	SNAFFLES	SNAKING	SNARKED	SNEADS
SMUR	SNAFFLING	SNAKISH	SNARKIER	SNEAK
SMURFING	SNAFU	SNAKY	SNARKIEST	SNEAKBOX
SMURFINGS	SNAFUED	SNAP	SNARKILY	SNEAKED
SMURRED	SNAFUING	SNAPBACK	SNARKING	SNEAKER

SNEAKERED	SNEESHANS	SNIES	SNIPE	SNIVELERS
SNEAKERS	SNEESHED	SNIFF	SNIPED	SNIVELIER
SNEAKEUP	SNEESHES	SNIFFABLE	SNIPEFISH	SNIVELING
SNEAKEUPS	SNEESHIN	SNIFFED	SNIPELIKE	SNIVELLED
SNEAKIER	SNEESHING	SNIFFER	SNIPER	SNIVELLER
SNEAKIEST	SNEESHINS	SNIFFERS	SNIPERS	SNIVELLY
SNEAKILY	SNEEZE	SNIFFIER	SNIPES	SNIVELS
SNEAKING	SNEEZED	SNIFFIEST	SNIPIER	SNIVELY
SNEAKISH	SNEEZER	SNIFFILY	SNIPIEST	SNOB
SNEAKS	SNEEZERS	SNIFFING	SNIPING	SNOBBERY
SNEAKSBY	SNEEZES	SNIFFINGS	SNIPINGS	SNOBBIER
SNEAKY	SNEEZIER	SNIFFISH	SNIPPED	SNOBBIEST
SNEAP	SNEEZIEST	SNIFFLE	SNIPPER	SNOBBILY
SNEAPED	SNEEZING	SNIFFLED	SNIPPERS	SNOBBISH
SNEAPING	SNEEZINGS	SNIFFLER	SNIPPET	SNOBBISM
SNEAPS	SNEEZY	SNIFFLERS	SNIPPETS	SNOBBISMS
SNEATH	SNELL	SNIFFLES	SNIPPETY	SNOBBY
SNEATHS	SNELLED	SNIFFLIER	SNIPPIER	SNOBLING
SNEB	SNELLER	SNIFFLING	SNIPPIEST	SNOBLINGS
SNEBBE	SNELLEST	SNIFFLY	SNIPPILY	SNOBS
SNEBBED	SNELLING	SNIFFS	SNIPPING	SNOCOACH
SNEBBES	SNELLS	SNIFFY	SNIPPINGS	SNOD
SNEBBING	SNELLY	SNIFT	SNIPPY	SNODDED
SNEBS	SNIB	SNIFTED	SNIPS	SNODDER
SNECK	SNIBBED	SNIFTER	SNIPY	SNODDEST
SNECKED	SNIBBING	SNIFTERED	SNIRT	SNODDING
SNECKING	SNIBS	SNIFTERS	SNIRTED	SNODDIT
SNECKS	SNICK	SNIFTIER	SNIRTING	SNODS
SNED	SNICKED	SNIFTIEST	SNIRTLE	SNOEK
SNEDDED	SNICKER	SNIFTING	SNIRTLED	SNOEKS
SNEDDING	SNICKERED	SNIFTS	SNIRTLES	SNOEP
SNEDS	SNICKERER	SNIFTY	SNIRTLING	SNOG
SNEE	SNICKERS	SNIG	SNIRTS	SNOGGED
SNEED	SNICKERY	SNIGGED	SNIT	SNOGGER
SNEEING	SNICKET	SNIGGER	SNITCH	SNOGGERS
SNEER	SNICKETS	SNIGGERED	SNITCHED	SNOGGING
SNEERED	SNICKING	SNIGGERER	SNITCHER	SNOGS
SNEERER	SNICKS	SNIGGERS	SNITCHERS	SNOKE
SNEERERS	SNIDE	SNIGGING	SNITCHES	SNOKED
SNEERFUL	SNIDED	SNIGGLE	SNITCHIER	SNOKES
SNEERIER	SNIDELY	SNIGGLED	SNITCHING	SNOKING
SNEERIEST	SNIDENESS	SNIGGLER	SNITCHY	SNOOD
SNEERING	SNIDER	SNIGGLERS	SNITS	SNOODED
SNEERINGS	SNIDES	SNIGGLES	SNITTIER	SNOODING
SNEERS	SNIDEST	SNIGGLING	SNITTIEST	SNOODS
SNEERY	SNIDEY	SNIGLET	SNITTY	SNOOK
SNEES	SNIDIER	SNIGLETS	SNIVEL	SNOOKED
SNEESH	SNIDIEST	SNIGS	SNIVELED	SNOOKER
SNEESHAN	SNIDING	SNIP	SNIVELER	SNOOKERED

SNOOKERS	SNORKEL	SNOWBERRY	SNOWMELT	SNUFFBOX
SNOOKING	SNORKELED	SNOWBIRD	SNOWMELTS	SNUFFED
SNOOKS	SNORKELER	SNOWBIRDS	SNOWMEN	SNUFFER
SNOOL	SNORKELS	SNOWBLINK	SNOWMOLD	SNUFFERS
SNOOLED	SNORT	SNOWBOARD	SNOWMOLDS	SNUFFIER
SNOOLING	SNORTED	SNOWBOOT	SNOWMOULD	SNUFFIEST
SNOOLS	SNORTER	SNOWBOOTS	SNOWPACK	SNUFFILY
SNOOP	SNORTERS	SNOWBOUND	SNOWPACKS	SNUFFING
SNOOPED	SNORTIER	SNOWBRUSH	SNOWPANTS	SNUFFINGS
SNOOPER	SNORTIEST	SNOWBUSH	SNOWPLOW	SNUFFLE
SNOOPERS	SNORTING	SNOWCAP	SNOWPLOWS	SNUFFLED
SNOOPIER	SNORTINGS	SNOWCAPS	SNOWS	SNUFFLER
SNOOPIEST	SNORTS	SNOWCAT	SNOWSCAPE	SNUFFLERS
SNOOPILY	SNORTY	SNOWCATS	SNOWSHED	SNUFFLES
SNOOPING	SNOT	SNOWCLONE	SNOWSHEDS	SNUFFLIER
SNOOPS	SNOTRAG	SNOWCOACH	SNOWSHOE	SNUFFLING
SNOOPY	SNOTRAGS	SNOWDOME	SNOWSHOED	SNUFFLY
SNOOSE	SNOTS	SNOWDOMES	SNOWSHOER	SNUFFS
SNOOSES	SNOTTED	SNOWDRIFT	SNOWSHOES	SNUFFY
SNOOT	SNOTTER	SNOWDROP	SNOWSLIDE	SNUG
SNOOTED	SNOTTERED	SNOWDROPS	SNOWSLIP	SNUGGED
SNOOTFUL	SNOTTERS	SNOWED	SNOWSLIPS	SNUGGER
SNOOTFULS	SNOTTERY	SNOWFALL	SNOWSNAKE	SNUGGERIE
SNOOTIER	SNOTTIE	SNOWFALLS	SNOWSTORM	SNUGGERY
SNOOTIEST	SNOTTIER	SNOWFIELD	SNOWSUIT	SNUGGEST
SNOOTILY	SNOTTIES	SNOWFLAKE	SNOWSUITS	SNUGGIES
SNOOTING	SNOTTIEST	SNOWFLEA	SNOWY	SNUGGING
SNOOTS	SNOTTILY	SNOWFLEAS	SNUB	SNUGGLE
SNOOTY	SNOTTING	SNOWFLECK	SNUBBE	SNUGGLED
SNOOZE	SNOTTY	SNOWFLICK	SNUBBED	SNUGGLES
SNOOZED	SNOUT	SNOWGLOBE	SNUBBER	SNUGGLIER
SNOOZER	SNOUTED	SNOWIER	SNUBBERS	SNUGGLING
SNOOZERS	SNOUTIER	SNOWIEST	SNUBBES	SNUGGLY
SNOOZES	SNOUTIEST	SNOWILY	SNUBBEST	SNUGLY
SNOOZIER	SNOUTING	SNOWINESS	SNUBBIER	SNUGNESS
SNOOZIEST	SNOUTISH	SNOWING	SNUBBIEST	SNUGS
SNOOZING	SNOUTLESS	SNOWISH	SNUBBING	SNUSH
SNOOZLE	SNOUTLIKE	SNOWK	SNUBBINGS	SNUSHED
SNOOZLED	SNOUTS	SNOWKED	SNUBBISH	SNUSHES
SNOOZLES	SNOUTY	SNOWKING	SNUBBY	SNUSHING
SNOOZLING	SNOW	SNOWKS	SNUBFIN	SNUZZLE
SNOOZY	SNOWBALL	SNOWLAND	SNUBNESS	SNUZZLED
SNORE	SNOWBALLS	SNOWLANDS	SNUBS	SNUZZLES
SNORED	SNOWBANK	SNOWLESS	SNUCK	SNUZZLING
SNORER	SNOWBANKS	SNOWLIKE	SNUDGE	SNY
SNORERS	SNOWBELL	SNOWLINE	SNUDGED	SNYE
SNORES	SNOWBELLS	SNOWLINES	SNUDGES	SNYES
SNORING	SNOWBELT	SNOWMAKER	SNUDGING	SO
SNORINGS	SNOWBELTS	SNOWMAN	SNUFF	SOAK

SOAKAGE	SOARERS	SOCES	SODAINE	SOFABED
SOAKAGES	SOARES	SOCIABLE	SODALESS	SOFABEDS
SOAKAWAY	SOARING	SOCIABLES	SODALIST	SOFAR
SOAKAWAYS	SOARINGLY	SOCIABLY	SODALISTS	SOFARS
SOAKED	SOARINGS	SOCIAL	SODALITE	SOFAS
SOAKEN	SOARS	SOCIALISE	SODALITES	SOFFIONI
SOAKER	SOAVE	SOCIALISM	SODALITY	SOFFIT
SOAKERS	SOAVES	SOCIALIST	SODAMIDE	SOFFITS
SOAKING	SOB	SOCIALITE	SODAMIDES	SOFRITO
SOAKINGLY	SOBA	SOCIALITY	SODAS	SOFRITOS
SOAKINGS	SOBAS	SOCIALIZE	SODBUSTER	SOFT
SOAKS	SOBBED	SOCIALLY	SODDED	SOFTA
SOAP	SOBBER	SOCIALS	SODDEN	SOFTAS
SOAPBARK	SOBBERS	SOCIATE	SODDENED	SOFTBACK
SOAPBARKS	SOBBING	SOCIATES	SODDENING	SOFTBACKS
SOAPBERRY	SOBBINGLY	SOCIATION	SODDENLY	SOFTBALL
SOAPBOX	SOBBINGS	SOCIATIVE	SODDENS	SOFTBALLS
SOAPBOXED	SOBEIT	SOCIETAL	SODDIE	SOFTBOUND
SOAPBOXES	SOBER	SOCIETIES	SODDIER	SOFTCORE
SOAPDISH	SOBERED	SOCIETY	SODDIES	SOFTCOVER
SOAPED	SOBERER	SOCIOGRAM	SODDIEST	SOFTED
SOAPER	SOBEREST	SOCIOLECT	SODDING	SOFTEN
SOAPERS	SOBERING	SOCIOLOGY	SODDY	SOFTENED
SOAPFISH	SOBERISE	SOCIOPATH	SODGER	SOFTENER
SOAPIE	SOBERISED	SOCK	SODGERED	SOFTENERS
SOAPIER	SOBERISES	SOCKED	SODGERING	SOFTENING
SOAPIES	SOBERIZE	SOCKET	SODGERS	SOFTENS
SOAPIEST	SOBERIZED	SOCKETED	SODIC	SOFTER
SOAPILY	SOBERIZES	SOCKETING	SODICITY	SOFTEST
SOAPINESS	SOBERLY	SOCKETS	SODIUM	SOFTGOODS
SOAPING	SOBERNESS	SOCKETTE	SODIUMS	SOFTHEAD
SOAPLAND	SOBERS	SOCKETTES	SODOM	SOFTHEADS
SOAPLANDS	SOBFUL	SOCKEYE	SODOMIES	SOFTIE
SOAPLESS	SOBOLE	SOCKEYES	SODOMISE	SOFTIES
SOAPLIKE	SOBOLES	SOCKING	SODOMISED	SOFTING
SOAPROOT	SOBRIETY	SOCKLESS	SODOMISES	SOFTISH
SOAPROOTS	SOBRIQUET	SOCKMAN	SODOMIST	SOFTLING
SOAPS	SOBS	SOCKMEN	SODOMISTS	SOFTLINGS
SOAPSTONE	SOC	SOCKO	SODOMITE	SOFTLY
SOAPSUDS	SOCA	SOCKS	SODOMITES	SOFTNESS
SOAPSUDSY	SOCAGE	SOCLE	SODOMITIC	SOFTPASTE
SOAPWORT	SOCAGER	SOCLES	SODOMIZE	SOFTS
SOAPWORTS	SOCAGERS	SOCMAN	SODOMIZED	SOFTSCAPE
SOAPY	SOCAGES	SOCMEN	SODOMIZES	SOFTSHELL
SOAR	SOCAS	SOCS	SODOMS	SOFTWARE
SOARAWAY	SOCCAGE	SOD	SODOMY	SOFTWARES
SOARE	SOCCAGES	SODA	SODS	SOFTWOOD
SOARED	SOCCER	SODAIC	SOEVER	SOFTWOODS
SOARER	SOCCERS	SODAIN	SOFA	SOFTY

S

SOG	SOKEMANRY	SOLATED	SOLEMNIFY	SOLIDISMS
SOGER	SOKEMEN	SOLATES	SOLEMNISE	SOLIDIST
SOGERS	SOKEN	SOLATIA	SOLEMNITY	SOLIDISTS
SOGGED	SOKENS	SOLATING	SOLEMNIZE	SOLIDITY
SOGGIER	SOKES	SOLATION	SOLEMNLY	SOLIDLY
SOGGIEST	SOKOL	SOLATIONS	SOLENESS	SOLIDNESS
SOGGILY	SOKOLS	SOLATIUM	SOLENETTE	SOLIDS
SOGGINESS	SOL	SOLD	SOLENODON	SOLIDUM
SOGGING	SOLA	SOLDADO	SOLENOID	SOLIDUMS
SOGGINGS	SOLACE	SOLDADOES	SOLENOIDS	SOLIDUS
SOGGY	SOLACED	SOLDADOS	SOLEPLATE	SOLILOQUY
SOGS	SOLACER	SOLDAN	SOLEPRINT	SOLING
SOH	SOLACERS	SOLDANS	SOLER	SOLION
SOHO	SOLACES	SOLDE	SOLERA	SOLIONS
SOHS	SOLACING	SOLDER	SOLERAS	SOLIPED
SOHUR	SOLACIOUS	SOLDERED	SOLERET	SOLIPEDS
SOHURS	SOLAH	SOLDERER	SOLERETS	SOLIPSISM
SOIGNE	SOLAHS	SOLDERERS	SOLERS	SOLIPSIST
SOIGNEE	SOLAN	SOLDERING	SOLES	SOLIQUID
SOIL	SOLAND	SOLDERS	SOLEUS	SOLIQUIDS
SOILAGE	SOLANDER	SOLDES	SOLEUSES	SOLITAIRE
SOILAGES	SOLANDERS	SOLDI	SOLFATARA	SOLITARY
SOILBORNE	SOLANDS	SOLDIER	SOLFEGE	SOLITO
SOILED	SOLANIN	SOLDIERED	SOLFEGES	SOLITON
SOILIER	SOLANINE	SOLDIERLY	SOLFEGGI	SOLITONS
SOILIEST	SOLANINES	SOLDIERS	SOLFEGGIO	SOLITUDE
SOILINESS	SOLANINS	SOLDIERY	SOLFERINO	SOLITUDES
SOILING	SOLANO	SOLDO	SOLGEL	SOLIVE
SOILINGS	SOLANOS	SOLDS	SOLI	SOLIVES
SOILLESS	SOLANS	SOLE	SOLICIT	SOLLAR
SOILS	SOLANUM	SOLECISE	SOLICITED	SOLLARED
SOILURE	SOLANUMS	SOLECISED	SOLICITOR	SOLLARING
SOILURES	SOLAR	SOLECISES	SOLICITS	SOLLARS
SOILY	SOLARIA	SOLECISM	SOLICITY	SOLLER
SOIREE	SOLARISE	SOLECISMS	SOLID	SOLLERET
SOIREES	SOLARISED	SOLECIST	SOLIDAGO	SOLLERETS
SOJA	SOLARISES	SOLECISTS	SOLIDAGOS	SOLLERS
SOJAS	SOLARISM	SOLECIZE	SOLIDARE	SOLLICKER
SOJOURN	SOLARISMS	SOLECIZED	SOLIDARES	SOLO
SOJOURNED	SOLARIST	SOLECIZES	SOLIDARY	SOLOED
SOJOURNER	SOLARISTS	SOLED	SOLIDATE	SOLOES
SOJOURNS	SOLARIUM	SOLEI	SOLIDATED	SOLOING
SOJU	SOLARIUMS	SOLEIN	SOLIDATES	SOLOIST
SOJUS	SOLARIZE	SOLELESS	SOLIDER	SOLOISTIC
SOKAH	SOLARIZED	SOLELY	SOLIDEST	SOLOISTS
SOKAHS	SOLARIZES	SOLEMN	SOLIDI	SOLON
SOKAIYA	SOLARS	SOLEMNER	SOLIDIFY	SOLONCHAK
SOKE	SOLAS	SOLEMNESS	SOLIDISH	SOLONETS
SOKEMAN	SOLATE	SOLEMNEST	SOLIDISM	SOLONETZ

SOLONS	SOMATISTS	SOMNIATE	SONGFUL	SONORITY
SOLOS	SOMBER	SOMNIATED	SONGFULLY	SONOROUS
SOLPUGID	SOMBERED	SOMNIATES	SONGKOK	SONOVOX
SOLPUGIDS	SOMBERER	SOMNIFIC	SONGKOKS	SONOVOXES
SOLS	SOMBEREST	SOMNOLENT	SONGLESS	SONS
SOLSTICE	SOMBERING	SOMONI	SONGLIKE	SONSE
SOLSTICES	SOMBERLY	SOMONIS	SONGMAN	SONSES
SOLUBLE	SOMBERS	SOMS	SONGMEN	SONSHIP
SOLUBLES	SOMBRE	SOMY	SONGOLOLO	SONSHIPS
SOLUBLY	SOMBRED	SON	SONGS	SONSIE
SOLUM	SOMBRELY	SONANCE	SONGSHEET	SONSIER
SOLUMS	SOMBRER	SONANCES	SONGSMITH	SONSIEST
SOLUNAR	SOMBRERO	SONANCIES	SONGSTER	SONSY
SOLUS	SOMBREROS	SONANCY	SONGSTERS	SONTAG
SOLUSES	SOMBRES	SONANT	SONHOOD	SONTAGS
SOLUTAL	SOMBREST	SONANTAL	SONHOODS	SONTIES
SOLUTE	SOMBRING	SONANTIC	SONIC	SOOCHONG
SOLUTES	SOMBROUS	SONANTS	SONICALLY	SOOCHONGS
SOLUTION	SOME	SONAR	SONICATE	SOOEY
SOLUTIONS	SOMEBODY	SONARMAN	SONICATED	SOOGEE
SOLUTIVE	SOMEDAY	SONARMEN	SONICATES	SOOGEED
SOLUTIVES	SOMEDEAL	SONARS	SONICATOR	SOOGEEING
SOLVABLE	SOMEDEALS	SONATA	SONICS	SOOGEES
SOLVATE	SOMEDELE	SONATAS	SONLESS	SOOGIE
SOLVATED	SOMEGATE	SONATINA	SONLIER	SOOGIED
SOLVATES	SOMEHOW	SONATINAS	SONLIEST	SOOGIEING
SOLVATING	SOMEONE	SONATINE	SONLIKE	SOOGIES
SOLVATION	SOMEONES	SONCE	SONLY	SOOJEY
SOLVE	SOMEPLACE	SONCES	SONNE	SOOJEYS
SOLVED	SOMERSET	SONDAGE	SONNES	SOOK
SOLVENCY	SOMERSETS	SONDAGES	SONNET	SOOKED
SOLVENT	SOMETHING	SONDE	SONNETARY	SOOKIER
SOLVENTLY	SOMETIME	SONDELI	SONNETED	SOOKIEST
SOLVENTS	SOMETIMES	SONDELIS	SONNETEER	SOOKING
SOLVER	SOMEWAY	SONDER	SONNETING	SOOKS
SOLVERS	SOMEWAYS	SONDERS	SONNETISE	SOOKY
SOLVES	SOMEWHAT	SONDES	SONNETIZE	SOOL
SOLVING	SOMEWHATS	SONE	SONNETS	SOOLE
SOM	SOMEWHEN	SONERI	SONNETTED	SOOLED
SOMA	SOMEWHERE	SONERIS	SONNIES	SOOLER
SOMAN	SOMEWHILE	SONES	SONNY	SOOLERS
SOMANS	SOMEWHY	SONG	SONOBUOY	SOOLES
SOMAS	SOMEWISE	SONGBIRD	SONOBUOYS	SOOLING
SOMASCOPE	SOMITAL	SONGBIRDS	SONOGRAM	SOOLS
SOMATA	SOMITE	SONGBOOK	SONOGRAMS	SOOM
SOMATIC	SOMITES	SONGBOOKS	SONOGRAPH	SOOMED
SOMATISM	SOMITIC	SONGCRAFT	SONOMETER	SOOMING
SOMATISMS	SOMMELIER	SONGFEST	SONORANT	SOOMS
SOMATIST	SOMNIAL	SONGFESTS	SONORANTS	SOON

SOONER	SOPHISM	SORBET	SOREES	SORORITY
SOONERS	SOPHISMS	SORBETS	SOREHEAD	SORORIZE
SOONEST	SOPHIST	SORBIC	SOREHEADS	SORORIZED
SOONISH	SOPHISTER	SORBING	SOREHON	SORORIZES
SOOP	SOPHISTIC	SORBITAN	SOREHONS	SOROSES
SOOPED	SOPHISTRY	SORBITANS	SOREL	SOROSIS
SOOPING	SOPHISTS	SORBITE	SORELL	SOROSISES
SOOPINGS	SOPHOMORE	SORBITES	SORELLS	SORPTION
SOOPS	SOPHS	SORBITIC	SORELS	SORPTIONS
SOOPSTAKE	SOPHY	SORBITISE	SORELY	SORPTIVE
SOOT	SOPITE	SORBITIZE	SORENESS	SORRA
SOOTE	SOPITED	SORBITOL	SORER	SORRAS
SOOTED	SOPITES	SORBITOLS	SORES	SORREL
SOOTERKIN	SOPITING	SORBO	SOREST	SORRELS
SOOTES	SOPOR	SORBOSE	SOREX	SORRIER
SOOTFLAKE	SOPORIFIC	SORBOSES	SOREXES	SORRIEST
SOOTH	SOPOROSE	SORBS	SORGHO	SORRILY
SOOTHE	SOPOROUS	SORBUS	SORGHOS	SORRINESS
SOOTHED	SOPORS	SORBUSES	SORGHUM	SORROW
SOOTHER	SOPPED	SORCERER	SORGHUMS	SORROWED
SOOTHERED	SOPPIER	SORCERERS	SORGO	SORROWER
SOOTHERS	SOPPIEST	SORCERESS	SORGOS	SORROWERS
SOOTHES	SOPPILY	SORCERIES	SORI	SORROWFUL
SOOTHEST	SOPPINESS	SORCEROUS	SORICINE	SORROWING
SOOTHFAST	SOPPING	SORCERY	SORICOID	SORROWS
SOOTHFUL	SOPPINGS	SORD	SORING	SORRY
SOOTHING	SOPPY	SORDA	SORINGS	SORRYISH
SOOTHINGS	SOPRA	SORDED	SORITES	SORT
SOOTHLICH	SOPRANI	SORDES	SORITIC	SORTA
SOOTHLY	SOPRANINI	SORDID	SORITICAL	SORTABLE
SOOTHS	SOPRANINO	SORDIDER	SORN	SORTABLY
SOOTHSAID	SOPRANIST	SORDIDEST	SORNED	SORTAL
SOOTHSAY	SOPRANO	SORDIDLY	SORNER	SORTALS
SOOTHSAYS	SOPRANOS	SORDINE	SORNERS	SORTANCE
SOOTIER	SOPS	SORDINES	SORNING	SORTANCES
SOOTIEST	SORA	SORDING	SORNINGS	SORTATION
SOOTILY	SORAGE	SORDINI	SORNS	SORTED
SOOTINESS	SORAGES	SORDINO	SOROBAN	SORTER
SOOTING	SORAL	SORDO	SOROBANS	SORTERS
SOOTINGS	SORAS	SORDOR	SOROCHE	SORTES
SOOTLESS	SORB	SORDORS	SOROCHES	SORTIE
SOOTS	SORBABLE	SORDS	SORORAL	SORTIED
SOOTY	SORBARIA	SORE	SORORALLY	SORTIEING
SOP	SORBARIAS	SORED	SORORATE	SORTIES
SOPAPILLA	SORBATE	SOREDIA	SORORATES	SORTILEGE
SOPH	SORBATES	SOREDIAL	SORORIAL	SORTILEGY
SOPHERIC	SORBED	SOREDIATE	SORORISE	SORTING
SOPHERIM	SORBENT	SOREDIUM	SORORISED	SORTINGS
SOPHIES	SORBENTS	SOREE	SORORISES	SORTITION

SORTMENT	SOUGH	SOUNDPOST	SOURPUSS	SOUTHSAID
SORTMENTS	SOUGHED	SOUNDS	SOURS	SOUTHSAY
SORTS	SOUGHING	SOUP	SOURSE	SOUTHSAYS
SORUS	SOUGHS	SOUPCON	SOURSES	SOUTHWARD
SOS	SOUGHT	SOUPCONS	SOURSOP	SOUTHWEST
SOSATIE	SOUK	SOUPED	SOURSOPS	SOUTIE
SOSATIES	SOUKED	SOUPER	SOURVELD	SOUTIES
SOSS	SOUKING	SOUPERS	SOURVELDS	SOUTPIEL
SOSSED	SOUKOUS	SOUPFIN	SOURWOOD	SOUTPIELS
SOSSES	SOUKOUSES	SOUPFINS	SOURWOODS	SOUTS
SOSSING	SOUKS	SOUPIER	SOUS	SOUVENIR
SOSSINGS	SOUL	SOUPIEST	SOUSE	SOUVENIRS
SOSTENUTI	SOULDAN	SOUPILY	SOUSED	SOUVLAKI
SOSTENUTO	SOULDANS	SOUPINESS	SOUSER	SOUVLAKIA
SOT	SOULDIER	SOUPING	SOUSERS	SOUVLAKIS
SOTERIAL	SOULDIERS	SOUPLE	SOUSES	SOV
SOTH	SOULED	SOUPLED	SOUSING	SOVENANCE
SOTHS	SOULFUL	SOUPLES	SOUSINGS	SOVEREIGN
SOTOL	SOULFULLY	SOUPLESS	SOUSLIK	SOVIET
SOTOLS	SOULLESS	SOUPLIKE	SOUSLIKS	SOVIETIC
SOTS	SOULLIKE	SOUPLING	SOUT	SOVIETISE
SOTTED	SOULMATE	SOUPS	SOUTACHE	SOVIETISM
SOTTEDLY	SOULMATES	SOUPSPOON	SOUTACHES	SOVIETIST
SOTTING	SOULS	SOUPY	SOUTANE	SOVIETIZE
SOTTINGS	SOULSTER	SOUR	SOUTANES	SOVIETS
SOTTISH	SOULSTERS	SOURBALL	SOUTAR	SOVKHOZ
SOTTISHLY	SOUM	SOURBALLS	SOUTARS	SOVKHOZES
SOTTISIER	SOUMED	SOURCE	SOUTENEUR	SOVKHOZY
SOU	SOUMING	SOURCED	SOUTER	SOVRAN
SOUARI	SOUMINGS	SOURCEFUL	SOUTERLY	SOVRANLY
SOUARIS	SOUMS	SOURCES	SOUTERS	SOVRANS
SOUBISE	SOUND	SOURCING	SOUTH	SOVRANTY
SOUBISES	SOUNDABLE	SOURCINGS	SOUTHEAST	SOVS
SOUBRETTE	SOUNDBAR	SOURDINE	SOUTHED	SOW
SOUCAR	SOUNDBARS	SOURDINES	SOUTHER	SOWABLE
SOUCARS	SOUNDBITE	SOURDOUGH	SOUTHERED	SOWANS
SOUCE	SOUNDBOX	SOURED	SOUTHERLY	SOWAR
SOUCED	SOUNDCARD	SOURER	SOUTHERN	SOWARREE
SOUCES	SOUNDED	SOUREST	SOUTHERNS	SOWARREES
SOUCHONG	SOUNDER	SOURGUM	SOUTHERS	SOWARRIES
SOUCHONGS	SOUNDERS	SOURGUMS	SOUTHING	SOWARRY
SOUCING	SOUNDEST	SOURING	SOUTHINGS	SOWARS
SOUCT	SOUNDING	SOURINGS	SOUTHLAND	SOWBACK
SOUDAN	SOUNDINGS	SOURISH	SOUTHMOST	SOWBACKS
SOUDANS	SOUNDLESS	SOURISHLY	SOUTHPAW	SOWBELLY
SOUFFLE	SOUNDLY	SOURLY	SOUTHPAWS	SOWBREAD
SOUFFLED	SOUNDMAN	SOURNESS	SOUTHRON	SOWBREADS
SOUFFLEED	SOUNDMEN	SOUROCK	SOUTHRONS	SOWBUG
SOUFFLES	SOUNDNESS	SOUROCKS	SOUTHS	SOWBUGS

S

SOWCAR	SOWSSED	SPACER	SPADIXES	SPAIRGES
SOWCARS	SOWSSES	SPACERS	SPADO	SPAIRGING
SOWCE	SOWSSING	SPACES	SPADOES	SPAIT
SOWCED	SOWTER	SPACESHIP	SPADONES	SPAITS
SOWCES	SOWTERS	SPACESUIT	SPADOS	SPAKE
SOWCING	SOWTH	SPACETIME	SPADROON	SPALD
SOWDER	SOWTHED	SPACEWALK	SPADROONS	SPALDEEN
SOWDERS	SOWTHING	SPACEWARD	SPAE	SPALDEENS
SOWED	SOWTHS	SPACEY	SPAED	SPALDS
SOWENS	SOX	SPACIAL	SPAEING	SPALE
SOWER	SOY	SPACIALLY	SPAEINGS	SPALES
SOWERS	SOYA	SPACIER	SPAEMAN	SPALL
SOWF	SOYAS	SPACIEST	SPAEMEN	SPALLABLE
SOWFED	SOYBEAN	SPACINESS	SPAER	SPALLE
SOWFF	SOYBEANS	SPACING	SPAERS	SPALLED
SOWFFED	SOYBURGER	SPACINGS	SPAES	SPALLER
SOWFFING	SOYLE	SPACIOUS	SPAETZLE	SPALLERS
SOWFFS	SOYLED	SPACKLE	SPAETZLES	SPALLES
SOWFING	SOYLES	SPACKLED	SPAEWIFE	SPALLING
SOWFS	SOYLING	SPACKLES	SPAEWIVES	SPALLINGS
SOWING	SOYMEAL	SPACKLING	SPAFF	SPALLS
SOWINGS	SOYMEALS	SPACY	SPAFFED	SPALPEEN
SOWL	SOYMILK	SPADASSIN	SPAFFING	SPALPEENS
SOWLE	SOYMILKS	SPADE	SPAFFS	SPALT
SOWLED	SOYS	SPADED	SPAG	SPALTED
SOWLES	SOYUZ	SPADEFEET	SPAGERIC	SPALTING
SOWLING	SOYUZES	SPADEFISH	SPAGGED	SPALTS
SOWLS	SOZ	SPADEFOOT	SPAGGING	SPAM
SOWM	SOZIN	SPADEFUL	SPAGHETTI	SPAMBOT
SOWMED	SOZINE	SPADEFULS	SPAGIRIC	SPAMBOTS
SOWMING	SOZINES	SPADELIKE	SPAGIRIST	SPAMMED
SOWMS	SOZINS	SPADEMAN	SPAGS	SPAMMER
SOWN	SOZZLE	SPADEMEN	SPAGYRIC	SPAMMERS
SOWND	SOZZLED	SPADER	SPAGYRICS	SPAMMIE
SOWNDED	SOZZLES	SPADERS	SPAGYRIST	SPAMMIER
SOWNDING	SOZZLIER	SPADES	SPAHEE	SPAMMIES
SOWNDS	SOZZLIEST	SPADESMAN	SPAHEES	SPAMMIEST
SOWNE	SOZZLING	SPADESMEN	SPAHI	SPAMMING
SOWNES	SOZZLY	SPADEWORK	SPAHIS	SPAMMINGS
SOWP	SPA	SPADGER	SPAIL	SPAMMY
SOWPED	SPACE	SPADGERS	SPAILS	SPAMS
SOWPING	SPACEBAND	SPADICES	SPAIN	SPAN
SOWPS	SPACED	SPADILLE	SPAINED	SPANAEMIA
SOWS	SPACELAB	SPADILLES	SPAING	SPANAEMIC
SOWSE	SPACELABS	SPADILLIO	SPAINGS	SPANCEL
SOWSED	SPACELESS	SPADILLO	SPAINING	SPANCELED
SOWSES	SPACEMAN	SPADILLOS	SPAINS	SPANCELS
SOWSING	SPACEMEN	SPADING	SPAIRGE	SPANDEX
SOWSSE	SPACEPORT	SPADIX	SPAIRGED	SPANDEXED

S

SPANDEXES	SPAR	SPARKLIES	SPASMODIC	SPAWLS
SPANDREL	SPARABLE	SPARKLING	SPASMS	SPAWN
SPANDRELS	SPARABLES	SPARKLY	SPASTIC	SPAWNED
SPANDRIL	SPARAXIS	SPARKPLUG	SPAT	SPAWNER
SPANDRILS	SPARD	SPARKS	SPATE	SPAWNERS
SPANE	SPARE	SPARKY	SPATES	SPAWNIER
SPANED	SPAREABLE	SPARLIKE	SPATFALL	SPAWNIEST
SPANEMIA	SPARED	SPARLING	SPATFALLS	SPAWNING
SPANEMIAS	SPARELESS	SPARLINGS	SPATHAL	SPAWNINGS
SPANEMIC	SPARELY	SPAROID	SPATHE	SPAWNS
SPANES	SPARENESS	SPAROIDS	SPATHED	SPAWNY
SPANG	SPARER	SPARRE	SPATHES	SPAWS
SPANGED	SPARERIB	SPARRED	SPATHIC	SPAY
SPANGHEW	SPARERIBS	SPARRER	SPATHOSE	SPAYAD
SPANGHEWS	SPARERS	SPARRERS	SPATIAL	SPAYADS
SPANGING	SPARES	SPARRES	SPATIALLY	SPAYD
SPANGLE	SPAREST	SPARRIER	SPATLESE	SPAYDS
SPANGLED	SPARGE	SPARRIEST	SPATLESEN	SPAYED
SPANGLER	SPARGED	SPARRING	SPATLESES	SPAYING
SPANGLERS	SPARGER	SPARRINGS	SPATS	SPAYS
SPANGLES	SPARGERS	SPARROW	SPATTED	SPAZA
SPANGLET	SPARGES	SPARROWS	SPATTEE	SPEAK
SPANGLETS	SPARGING	SPARRY	SPATTEES	SPEAKABLE
SPANGLIER	SPARID	SPARS	SPATTER	SPEAKEASY
SPANGLING	SPARIDS	SPARSE	SPATTERED	SPEAKER
SPANGLY	SPARING	SPARSEDLY	SPATTERS	SPEAKERS
SPANGS	SPARINGLY	SPARSELY	SPATTING	SPEAKING
SPANIEL	SPARK	SPARSER	SPATULA	SPEAKINGS
SPANIELS	SPARKE	SPARSEST	SPATULAR	SPEAKOUT
SPANING	SPARKED	SPARSITY	SPATULAS	SPEAKOUTS
SPANK	SPARKER	SPART	SPATULATE	SPEAKS
SPANKED	SPARKERS	SPARTAN	SPATULE	SPEAL
SPANKER	SPARKES	SPARTANS	SPATULES	SPEALS
SPANKERS	SPARKIE	SPARTEINE	SPATZLE	SPEAN
SPANKING	SPARKIER	SPARTERIE	SPATZLES	SPEANED
SPANKINGS	SPARKIES	SPARTH	SPAUL	SPEANING
SPANKS	SPARKIEST	SPARTHE	SPAULD	SPEANS
SPANLESS	SPARKILY	SPARTHES	SPAULDS	SPEAR
SPANNED	SPARKING	SPARTHS	SPAULS	SPEARED
SPANNER	SPARKISH	SPARTICLE	SPAVIE	SPEARER
SPANNERS	SPARKLE	SPARTINA	SPAVIES	SPEARERS
SPANNING	SPARKLED	SPARTINAS	SPAVIET	SPEARFISH
SPANS	SPARKLER	SPARTS	SPAVIN	SPEARGUN
SPANSPEK	SPARKLERS	SPAS	SPAVINED	SPEARGUNS
SPANSPEKS	SPARKLES	SPASM	SPAVINS	SPEARHEAD
SPANSULE	SPARKLESS	SPASMATIC	SPAW	SPEARIER
SPANSULES	SPARKLET	SPASMED	SPAWL	SPEARIEST
SPANWORM	SPARKLETS	SPASMIC	SPAWLED	SPEARING
SPANWORMS	SPARKLIER	SPASMING	SPAWLING	SPEARINGS

S

SPEARLIKE	SPECS	SPEEDRUN	SPELDRIN	SPEOSES
SPEARMAN	SPECT	SPEEDRUNS	SPELDRING	SPERLING
SPEARMEN	SPECTACLE	SPEEDS	SPELDRINS	SPERLINGS
SPEARMINT	SPECTATE	SPEEDSTER	SPELDS	SPERM
SPEARS	SPECTATED	SPEEDUP	SPELEAN	SPERMARIA
SPEARWORT	SPECTATES	SPEEDUPS	SPELK	SPERMARY
SPEARY	SPECTATOR	SPEEDWALK	SPELKS	SPERMATIA
SPEAT	SPECTED	SPEEDWAY	SPELL	SPERMATIC
SPEATS	SPECTER	SPEEDWAYS	SPELLABLE	SPERMATID
SPEC	SPECTERS	SPEEDWELL	SPELLBIND	SPERMIC
SPECCED	SPECTING	SPEEDY	SPELLDOWN	SPERMINE
SPECCIER	SPECTRA	SPEEL	SPELLED	SPERMINES
SPECCIES	SPECTRAL	SPEELED	SPELLER	SPERMOUS
SPECCIEST	SPECTRE	SPEELER	SPELLERS	SPERMS
SPECCING	SPECTRES	SPEELERS	SPELLFUL	SPERRE
SPECCY	SPECTRIN	SPEELING	SPELLICAN	SPERRED
SPECIAL	SPECTRINS	SPEELS	SPELLING	SPERRES
SPECIALER	SPECTRUM	SPEER	SPELLINGS	SPERRING
SPECIALLY	SPECTRUMS	SPEERED	SPELLS	SPERSE
SPECIALOG	SPECTS	SPEERING	SPELT	SPERSED
SPECIALS	SPECULA	SPEERINGS	SPELTER	SPERSES
SPECIALTY	SPECULAR	SPEERS	SPELTERS	SPERSING
SPECIATE	SPECULATE	SPEIL	SPELTS	SPERST
SPECIATED	SPECULUM	SPEILED	SPELTZ	SPERTHE
SPECIATES	SPECULUMS	SPEILING	SPELTZES	SPERTHES
SPECIE	SPED	SPEILS	SPELUNK	SPET
SPECIES	SPEECH	SPEIR	SPELUNKED	SPETCH
SPECIFIC	SPEECHED	SPEIRED	SPELUNKER	SPETCHED
SPECIFICS	SPEECHES	SPEIRING	SPELUNKS	SPETCHES
SPECIFIED	SPEECHFUL	SPEIRINGS	SPENCE	SPETCHING
SPECIFIER	SPEECHIFY	SPEIRS	SPENCER	SPETS
SPECIFIES	SPEECHING	SPEISE	SPENCERS	SPETSNAZ
SPECIFY	SPEED	SPEISES	SPENCES	SPETTING
SPECIMEN	SPEEDBALL	SPEISS	SPEND	SPETZNAZ
SPECIMENS	SPEEDBOAT	SPEISSES	SPENDABLE	SPEUG
SPECIOUS	SPEEDED	SPEK	SPENDALL	SPEUGS
SPECK	SPEEDER	SPEKBOOM	SPENDALLS	SPEW
SPECKED	SPEEDERS	SPEKBOOMS	SPENDER	SPEWED
SPECKIER	SPEEDFUL	SPEKS	SPENDERS	SPEWER
SPECKIES	SPEEDIER	SPELAEAN	SPENDIER	SPEWERS
SPECKIEST	SPEEDIEST	SPELD	SPENDIEST	SPEWIER
SPECKING	SPEEDILY	SPELDED	SPENDING	SPEWIEST
SPECKLE	SPEEDING	SPELDER	SPENDINGS	SPEWINESS
SPECKLED	SPEEDINGS	SPELDERED	SPENDS	SPEWING
SPECKLES	SPEEDLESS	SPELDERS	SPENDY	SPEWS
SPECKLESS	SPEEDO	SPELDIN	SPENSE	SPEWY
SPECKLING	SPEEDOS	SPELDING	SPENSES	SPHACELUS
SPECKS	SPEEDRAN	SPELDINGS	SPENT	SPHAER
SPECKY	SPEEDREAD	SPELDINS	SPEOS	SPHAERE

S

SPHAERES	SPICAE	SPIEGEL	SPIKILY	SPINALS
SPHAERITE	SPICAS	SPIEGELS	SPIKINESS	SPINAR
SPHAERS	SPICATE	SPIEL	SPIKING	SPINARAMA
SPHAGNOUS	SPICATED	SPIELED	SPIKY	SPINARS
SPHAGNUM	SPICCATO	SPIELER	SPILE	SPINAS
SPHAGNUMS	SPICCATOS	SPIELERS	SPILED	SPINATE
SPHAIREE	SPICE	SPIELING	SPILES	SPINDLE
SPHAIREES	SPICEBUSH	SPIELS	SPILIKIN	SPINDLED
SPHEAR	SPICED	SPIER	SPILIKINS	SPINDLER
SPHEARE	SPICELESS	SPIERED	SPILING	SPINDLERS
SPHEARES	SPICER	SPIERING	SPILINGS	SPINDLES
SPHEARS	SPICERIES	SPIERS	SPILITE	SPINDLIER
SPHENDONE	SPICERS	SPIES	SPILITES	SPINDLING
SPHENE	SPICERY	SPIF	SPILITIC	SPINDLY
SPHENES	SPICES	SPIFF	SPILL	SPINDRIFT
SPHENIC	SPICEY	SPIFFED	SPILLABLE	SPINE
SPHENODON	SPICIER	SPIFFIED	SPILLAGE	SPINED
SPHENOID	SPICIEST	SPIFFIER	SPILLAGES	SPINEL
SPHENOIDS	SPICILEGE	SPIFFIES	SPILLED	SPINELESS
SPHERAL	SPICILY	SPIFFIEST	SPILLER	SPINELIKE
SPHERE	SPICINESS	SPIFFILY	SPILLERS	SPINELLE
SPHERED	SPICING	SPIFFING	SPILLIKIN	SPINELLES
SPHERES	SPICK	SPIFFS	SPILLING	SPINELS
SPHERIC	SPICKER	SPIFFY	SPILLINGS	SPINES
SPHERICAL	SPICKEST	SPIFFYING	SPILLOVER	SPINET
SPHERICS	SPICKNEL	SPIFS	SPILLS	SPINETS
SPHERIER	SPICKNELS	SPIGHT	SPILLWAY	SPINETTE
SPHERIEST	SPICULA	SPIGHTED	SPILLWAYS	SPINETTES
SPHERING	SPICULAE	SPIGHTING	SPILOSITE	SPINIER
SPHEROID	SPICULAR	SPIGHTS	SPILT	SPINIEST
SPHEROIDS	SPICULATE	SPIGNEL	SPILTH	SPINIFEX
SPHERULAR	SPICULE	SPIGNELS	SPILTHS	SPINIFORM
SPHERULE	SPICULES	SPIGOT	SPIM	SPININESS
SPHERULES	SPICULUM	SPIGOTS	SPIMMER	SPINK
SPHERY	SPICY	SPIKE	SPIMMERS	SPINKED
SPHINCTER	SPIDE	SPIKED	SPIMMING	SPINKING
SPHINGES	SPIDER	SPIKEFISH	SPIMMINGS	SPINKS
SPHINGID	SPIDERED	SPIKELET	SPIMS	SPINLESS
SPHINGIDS	SPIDERIER	SPIKELETS	SPIN	SPINNAKER
SPHINX	SPIDERING	SPIKELIKE	SPINA	SPINNER
SPHINXES	SPIDERISH	SPIKENARD	SPINACENE	SPINNERET
SPHYGMIC	SPIDERMAN	SPIKER	SPINACH	SPINNERS
SPHYGMOID	SPIDERMEN	SPIKERIES	SPINACHES	SPINNERY
SPHYGMUS	SPIDERS	SPIKERS	SPINACHY	SPINNET
SPHYNX	SPIDERWEB	SPIKERY	SPINAE	SPINNETS
SPHYNXES	SPIDERY	SPIKES	SPINAGE	SPINNEY
SPIAL	SPIDES	SPIKEY	SPINAGES	SPINNEYS
SPIALS	SPIE	SPIKIER	SPINAL	SPINNIER
SPICA	SPIED	SPIKIEST	SPINALLY	SPINNIES

S

SPINNIEST	SPIRASTER	SPIRULAE	SPLASHES	SPLICINGS
SPINNING	SPIRATED	SPIRULAS	SPLASHIER	SPLIFF
SPINNINGS	SPIRATION	SPIRULINA	SPLASHILY	SPLIFFS
SPINNY	SPIRE	SPIRY	SPLASHING	SPLINE
SPINODE	SPIREA	SPIT	SPLASHY	SPLINED
SPINODES	SPIREAS	SPITAL	SPLAT	SPLINES
SPINOFF	SPIRED	SPITALS	SPLATCH	SPLINING
SPINOFFS	SPIRELESS	SPITBALL	SPLATCHED	SPLINT
SPINONE	SPIRELET	SPITBALLS	SPLATCHES	SPLINTED
SPINONI	SPIRELETS	SPITCHER	SPLATS	SPLINTER
SPINOR	SPIREM	SPITCHERS	SPLATTED	SPLINTERS
SPINORS	SPIREME	SPITE	SPLATTER	SPLINTERY
SPINOSE	SPIREMES	SPITED	SPLATTERS	SPLINTING
SPINOSELY	SPIREMS	SPITEFUL	SPLATTING	SPLINTS
SPINOSITY	SPIRES	SPITES	SPLAY	SPLISH
SPINOUS	SPIREWISE	SPITFIRE	SPLAYED	SPLISHED
SPINOUT	SPIRIC	SPITFIRES	SPLAYFEET	SPLISHES
SPINOUTS	SPIRICS	SPITING	SPLAYFOOT	SPLISHING
SPINS	SPIRIER	SPITS	SPLAYING	SPLIT
SPINSTER	SPIRIEST	SPITTED	SPLAYS	SPLITS
SPINSTERS	SPIRILLA	SPITTEN	SPLEEN	SPLITTED
SPINTEXT	SPIRILLAR	SPITTER	SPLEENFUL	SPLITTER
SPINTEXTS	SPIRILLUM	SPITTERS	SPLEENIER	SPLITTERS
SPINTO	SPIRING	SPITTIER	SPLEENISH	SPLITTING
SPINTOS	SPIRIT	SPITTIEST	SPLEENS	SPLITTISM
SPINULA	SPIRITED	SPITTING	SPLEENY	SPLITTIST
SPINULAE	SPIRITFUL	SPITTINGS	SPLENDENT	SPLODGE
SPINULATE	SPIRITING	SPITTLE	SPLENDID	SPLODGED
SPINULE	SPIRITISM	SPITTLES	SPLENDOR	SPLODGES
SPINULES	SPIRITIST	SPITTLIER	SPLENDORS	SPLODGIER
SPINULOSE	SPIRITOSO	SPITTLY	SPLENDOUR	SPLODGILY
SPINULOUS	SPIRITOUS	SPITTOON	SPLENETIC	SPLODGING
SPINY	SPIRITS	SPITTOONS	SPLENIA	SPLODGY
SPIRACLE	SPIRITUAL	SPITTY	SPLENIAL	SPLOG
SPIRACLES	SPIRITUEL	SPITZ	SPLENIC	SPLOGS
SPIRACULA	SPIRITUS	SPITZES	SPLENII	SPLOOSH
SPIRAEA	SPIRITY	SPIV	SPLENITIS	SPLOOSHED
SPIRAEAS	SPIRLING	SPIVS	SPLENIUM	SPLOOSHES
SPIRAL	SPIRLINGS	SPIVVERY	SPLENIUMS	SPLOOT
SPIRALED	SPIROGRAM	SPIVVIER	SPLENIUS	SPLOOTED
SPIRALING	SPIROGYRA	SPIVVIEST	SPLENT	SPLOOTING
SPIRALISM	SPIROID	SPIVVISH	SPLENTS	SPLOOTS
SPIRALIST	SPIRT	SPIVVY	SPLEUCHAN	SPLORE
SPIRALITY	SPIRTED	SPLAKE	SPLICE	SPLORES
SPIRALLED	SPIRTING	SPLAKES	SPLICED	SPLOSH
SPIRALLY	SPIRTLE	SPLASH	SPLICER	SPLOSHED
SPIRALS	SPIRTLES	SPLASHED	SPLICERS	SPLOSHES
SPIRANT	SPIRTS	SPLASHER	SPLICES	SPLOSHING
SPIRANTS	SPIRULA	SPLASHERS	SPLICING	SPLOTCH

S

SPLOTCHED	SPOKEN	SPONTOON	SPOONILY	SPORTBIKE
SPLOTCHES	SPOKES	SPONTOONS	SPOONING	SPORTCOAT
SPLOTCHY	SPOKESMAN	SPOOF	SPOONLIKE	SPORTED
SPLURGE	SPOKESMEN	SPOOFED	SPOONS	SPORTER
SPLURGED	SPOKEWISE	SPOOFER	SPOONSFUL	SPORTERS
SPLURGER	SPOKING	SPOOFERS	SPOONWAYS	SPORTFUL
SPLURGERS	SPOLIATE	SPOOFERY	SPOONWISE	SPORTIER
SPLURGES	SPOLIATED	SPOOFIER	SPOONWORM	SPORTIES
SPLURGIER	SPOLIATES	SPOOFIEST	SPOONY	SPORTIEST
SPLURGING	SPOLIATOR	SPOOFING	SPOOR	SPORTIF
SPLURGY	SPONCON	SPOOFINGS	SPOORED	SPORTIFS
SPLURT	SPONCONS	SPOOFS	SPOORER	SPORTILY
SPLURTED	SPONDAIC	SPOOFY	SPOORERS	SPORTING
SPLURTING	SPONDAICS	SPOOK	SPOORING	SPORTIVE
SPLURTS	SPONDEE	SPOOKED	SPOORS	SPORTLESS
SPLUTTER	SPONDEES	SPOOKERY	SPOOT	SPORTS
SPLUTTERS	SPONDULIX	SPOOKIER	SPOOTS	SPORTSMAN
SPLUTTERY	SPONDYL	SPOOKIEST	SPORADIC	SPORTSMEN
SPOD	SPONDYLS	SPOOKILY	SPORAL	SPORTY
SPODDIER	SPONGE	SPOOKING	SPORANGIA	SPORULAR
SPODDIEST	SPONGEBAG	SPOOKISH	SPORE	SPORULATE
SPODDY	SPONGED	SPOOKS	SPORED	SPORULE
SPODE	SPONGEING	SPOOKY	SPORELIKE	SPORULES
SPODES	SPONGEOUS	SPOOL	SPORES	SPOSE
SPODIUM	SPONGER	SPOOLED	SPORICIDE	SPOSED
SPODIUMS	SPONGERS	SPOOLER	SPORIDESM	SPOSES
SPODOGRAM	SPONGES	SPOOLERS	SPORIDIA	SPOSH
SPODOSOL	SPONGIER	SPOOLING	SPORIDIAL	SPOSHES
SPODOSOLS	SPONGIEST	SPOOLINGS	SPORIDIUM	SPOSHIER
SPODS	SPONGILY	SPOOLS	SPORING	SPOSHIEST
SPODUMENE	SPONGIN	SPOOM	SPORK	SPOSHY
SPOFFISH	SPONGING	SPOOMED	SPORKS	SPOSING
SPOFFY	SPONGINS	SPOOMING	SPOROCARP	SPOT
SPOIL	SPONGIOSE	SPOOMS	SPOROCYST	SPOTLESS
SPOILABLE	SPONGIOUS	SPOON	SPOROCYTE	SPOTLIGHT
SPOILAGE	SPONGOID	SPOONBAIT	SPOROGENY	SPOTLIT
SPOILAGES	SPONGY	SPOONBILL	SPOROGONY	SPOTS
SPOILED	SPONSAL	SPOONED	SPOROID	SPOTTABLE
SPOILER	SPONSALIA	SPOONER	SPOROPHYL	SPOTTED
SPOILERS	SPONSIBLE	SPOONERS	SPOROZOA	SPOTTER
SPOILFIVE	SPONSING	SPOONEY	SPOROZOAL	SPOTTERS
SPOILFUL	SPONSINGS	SPOONEYS	SPOROZOAN	SPOTTIE
SPOILING	SPONSION	SPOONFED	SPOROZOIC	SPOTTIER
SPOILS	SPONSIONS	SPOONFUL	SPOROZOON	SPOTTIES
SPOILSMAN	SPONSON	SPOONFULS	SPORRAN	SPOTTIEST
SPOILSMEN	SPONSONS	SPOONHOOK	SPORRANS	SPOTTILY
SPOILT	SPONSOR	SPOONIER	SPORT	SPOTTING
SPOKE	SPONSORED	SPOONIES	SPORTABLE	SPOTTINGS
SPOKED	SPONSORS	SPOONIEST	SPORTANCE	SPOTTY

SPOUSAGE	SPRAUCHLE	SPREETHED	SPRINKLES	SPRUG
SPOUSAGES	SPRAUNCY	SPREETHES	SPRINT	SPRUGS
SPOUSAL	SPRAWL	SPREEZE	SPRINTED	SPRUIK
SPOUSALLY	SPRAWLED	SPREEZED	SPRINTER	SPRUIKED
SPOUSALS	SPRAWLER	SPREEZES	SPRINTERS	SPRUIKER
SPOUSE	SPRAWLERS	SPREEZING	SPRINTING	SPRUIKERS
SPOUSED	SPRAWLIER	SPREKELIA	SPRINTS	SPRUIKING
SPOUSES	SPRAWLING	SPRENT	SPRIT	SPRUIKS
SPOUSING	SPRAWLS	SPRENTED	SPRITE	SPRUIT
SPOUT	SPRAWLY	SPRENTING	SPRITEFUL	SPRUITS
SPOUTED	SPRAY	SPRENTS	SPRITELY	SPRUNG
SPOUTER	SPRAYED	SPREW	SPRITES	SPRUSH
SPOUTERS	SPRAYER	SPREWS	SPRITS	SPRUSHED
SPOUTIER	SPRAYERS	SPRIER	SPRITSAIL	SPRUSHES
SPOUTIEST	SPRAYEY	SPRIEST	SPRITZ	SPRUSHING
SPOUTING	SPRAYIER	SPRIG	SPRITZED	SPRY
SPOUTINGS	SPRAYIEST	SPRIGGED	SPRITZER	SPRYER
SPOUTLESS	SPRAYING	SPRIGGER	SPRITZERS	SPRYEST
SPOUTS	SPRAYINGS	SPRIGGERS	SPRITZES	SPRYLY
SPOUTY	SPRAYS	SPRIGGIER	SPRITZIER	SPRYNESS
SPRACK	SPREAD	SPRIGGING	SPRITZIG	SPUD
SPRACKLE	SPREADER	SPRIGGY	SPRITZIGS	SPUDDED
SPRACKLED	SPREADERS	SPRIGHT	SPRITZING	SPUDDER
SPRACKLES	SPREADING	SPRIGHTED	SPRITZY	SPUDDERS
SPRAD	SPREADS	SPRIGHTLY	SPROCKET	SPUDDIER
SPRADDLE	SPREAGH	SPRIGHTS	SPROCKETS	SPUDDIEST
SPRADDLED	SPREAGHS	SPRIGS	SPROD	SPUDDING
SPRADDLES	SPREATHE	SPRIGTAIL	SPRODS	SPUDDINGS
SPRAG	SPREATHED	SPRING	SPROG	SPUDDLE
SPRAGGED	SPREATHES	SPRINGAL	SPROGLET	SPUDDLES
SPRAGGING	SPREAZE	SPRINGALD	SPROGLETS	SPUDDY
SPRAGS	SPREAZED	SPRINGALS	SPROGS	SPUDGEL
SPRAID	SPREAZES	SPRINGBOK	SPRONG	SPUDGELS
SPRAIN	SPREAZING	SPRINGE	SPROUT	SPUDS
SPRAINED	SPRECHERY	SPRINGED	SPROUTED	SPUE
SPRAINING	SPRECKLED	SPRINGER	SPROUTING	SPUED
SPRAINS	SPRED	SPRINGERS	SPROUTS	SPUEING
SPRAINT	SPREDD	SPRINGES	SPRUCE	SPUER
SPRAINTS	SPREDDE	SPRINGIER	SPRUCED	SPUERS
SPRANG	SPREDDEN	SPRINGILY	SPRUCELY	SPUES
SPRANGLE	SPREDDES	SPRINGING	SPRUCER	SPUG
SPRANGLED	SPREDDING	SPRINGLE	SPRUCES	SPUGGIES
SPRANGLES	SPREDDS	SPRINGLES	SPRUCEST	SPUGGY
SPRANGS	SPREDS	SPRINGLET	SPRUCIER	SPUGS
SPRAT	SPREE	SPRINGS	SPRUCIEST	SPUILZIE
SPRATS	SPREED	SPRINGY	SPRUCING	SPUILZIED
SPRATTLE	SPREEING	SPRINKLE	SPRUCY	SPUILZIES
SPRATTLED	SPREES	SPRINKLED	SPRUE	SPUING
SPRATTLES	SPREETHE	SPRINKLER	SPRUES	SPULE

SPULES	SPURLESS	SPYCAM	SQUALID	SQUASHED
SPULYE	SPURLIKE	SPYCAMS	SQUALIDER	SQUASHER
SPULYED	SPURLING	SPYGLASS	SQUALIDLY	SQUASHERS
SPULYEING	SPURLINGS	SPYHOLE	SQUALL	SQUASHES
SPULYES	SPURN	SPYHOLES	SQUALLED	SQUASHIER
SPULYIE	SPURNE	SPYING	SQUALLER	SQUASHILY
SPULYIED	SPURNED	SPYINGS	SQUALLERS	SQUASHING
SPULYIES	SPURNER	SPYMASTER	SQUALLIER	SQUASHY
SPULZIE	SPURNERS	SPYPLANE	SQUALLING	SQUAT
SPULZIED	SPURNES	SPYPLANES	SQUALLISH	SQUATLY
SPULZIES	SPURNING	SPYRE	SQUALLS	SQUATNESS
SPUMANTE	SPURNINGS	SPYRES	SQUALLY	SQUATS
SPUMANTES	SPURNS	SPYWARE	SQUALOID	SQUATTED
SPUME	SPURRED	SPYWARES	SQUALOR	SQUATTER
SPUMED	SPURRER	SQUAB	SQUALORS	SQUATTERS
SPUMES	SPURRERS	SQUABASH	SQUAMA	SQUATTEST
SPUMIER	SPURREY	SQUABBED	SQUAMAE	SQUATTIER
SPUMIEST	SPURREYS	SQUABBER	SQUAMATE	SQUATTILY
SPUMING	SPURRIER	SQUABBEST	SQUAMATES	SQUATTING
SPUMONE	SPURRIERS	SQUABBIER	SQUAME	SQUATTLE
SPUMONES	SPURRIES	SQUABBING	SQUAMELLA	SQUATTLED
SPUMONI	SPURRIEST	SQUABBISH	SQUAMES	SQUATTLES
SPUMONIS	SPURRING	SQUABBLE	SQUAMOSAL	SQUATTY
SPUMOUS	SPURRINGS	SQUABBLED	SQUAMOSE	SQUAWBUSH
SPUMY	SPURRY	SQUABBLER	SQUAMOUS	SQUAWFISH
SPUN	SPURS	SQUABBLES	SQUAMULA	SQUAWK
SPUNGE	SPURT	SQUABBY	SQUAMULAS	SQUAWKED
SPUNGES	SPURTED	SQUABS	SQUAMULE	SQUAWKER
SPUNK	SPURTER	SQUACCO	SQUAMULES	SQUAWKERS
SPUNKED	SPURTERS	SQUACCOS	SQUANDER	SQUAWKIER
SPUNKIE	SPURTING	SQUAD	SQUANDERS	SQUAWKING
SPUNKIER	SPURTLE	SQUADDED	SQUARE	SQUAWKS
SPUNKIES	SPURTLES	SQUADDIE	SQUARED	SQUAWKY
SPUNKIEST	SPURTS	SQUADDIES	SQUARELY	SQUAWROOT
SPUNKILY	SPURWAY	SQUADDING	SQUARER	SQUEAK
SPUNKING	SPURWAYS	SQUADDY	SQUARERS	SQUEAKED
SPUNKS	SPUTA	SQUADOOSH	SQUARES	SQUEAKER
SPUNKY	SPUTNIK	SQUADRON	SQUAREST	SQUEAKERS
SPUNYARN	SPUTNIKS	SQUADRONE	SQUARIAL	SQUEAKERY
SPUNYARNS	SPUTTER	SQUADRONS	SQUARIALS	SQUEAKIER
SPUR	SPUTTERED	SQUADS	SQUARING	SQUEAKILY
SPURDOG	SPUTTERER	SQUAIL	SQUARINGS	SQUEAKING
SPURDOGS	SPUTTERS	SQUAILED	SQUARISH	SQUEAKS
SPURGALL	SPUTTERY	SQUAILER	SQUARK	SQUEAKY
SPURGALLS	SPUTUM	SQUAILERS	SQUARKS	SQUEAL
SPURGE	SPUTUMS	SQUAILING	SQUARROSE	SQUEALED
SPURGES	SPY	SQUAILS	SQUARSON	SQUEALER
SPURIAE	SPYAL	SQUALENE	SQUARSONS	SQUEALERS
SPURIOUS	SPYALS	SQUALENES	SQUASH	SQUEALING

S

SQUEALS	SQUIGGLE	SQUIRISH	SRI	STACKET
SQUEAMISH	SQUIGGLED	SQUIRL	SRIRACHA	STACKETS
SQUEEGEE	SQUIGGLER	SQUIRLS	SRIRACHAS	STACKING
SQUEEGEED	SQUIGGLES	SQUIRM	SRIS	STACKINGS
SQUEEGEES	SQUIGGLY	SQUIRMED	SRUTI	STACKLESS
SQUEEZE	SQUILGEE	SQUIRMER	SRUTIS	STACKROOM
SQUEEZED	SQUILGEED	SQUIRMERS	ST	STACKS
SQUEEZER	SQUILGEES	SQUIRMIER	STAB	STACKUP
SQUEEZERS	SQUILL	SQUIRMING	STABBED	STACKUPS
SQUEEZES	SQUILLA	SQUIRMS	STABBER	STACKYARD
SQUEEZIER	SQUILLAE	SQUIRMY	STABBERS	STACTE
SQUEEZING	SQUILLAS	SQUIRR	STABBIER	STACTES
SQUEEZY	SQUILLION	SQUIRRED	STABBIEST	STADDA
SQUEG	SQUILLS	SQUIRREL	STABBING	STADDAS
SQUEGGED	SQUINANCY	SQUIRRELS	STABBINGS	STADDLE
SQUEGGER	SQUINCH	SQUIRRELY	STABBY	STADDLES
SQUEGGERS	SQUINCHED	SQUIRRING	STABILATE	STADE
SQUEGGING	SQUINCHES	SQUIRRS	STABILE	STADES
SQUEGS	SQUINIED	SQUIRT	STABILES	STADIA
SQUELCH	SQUINIES	SQUIRTED	STABILISE	STADIAL
SQUELCHED	SQUINNIED	SQUIRTER	STABILITY	STADIALS
SQUELCHER	SQUINNIER	SQUIRTERS	STABILIZE	STADIAS
SQUELCHES	SQUINNIES	SQUIRTING	STABLE	STADIUM
SQUELCHY	SQUINNY	SQUIRTS	STABLEBOY	STADIUMS
SQUIB	SQUINT	SQUISH	STABLED	STAFF
SQUIBBED	SQUINTED	SQUISHED	STABLEMAN	STAFFAGE
SQUIBBER	SQUINTER	SQUISHES	STABLEMEN	STAFFAGES
SQUIBBERS	SQUINTERS	SQUISHIER	STABLER	STAFFED
SQUIBBING	SQUINTEST	SQUISHING	STABLERS	STAFFER
SQUIBS	SQUINTIER	SQUISHY	STABLES	STAFFERS
SQUID	SQUINTING	SQUIT	STABLEST	STAFFING
SQUIDDED	SQUINTS	SQUITCH	STABLING	STAFFINGS
SQUIDDING	SQUINTY	SQUITCHES	STABLINGS	STAFFMAN
SQUIDGE	SQUINY	SQUITS	STABLISH	STAFFMEN
SQUIDGED	SQUINYING	SQUITTERS	STABLY	STAFFROOM
SQUIDGES	SQUIRAGE	SQUIZ	STABS	STAFFS
SQUIDGIER	SQUIRAGES	SQUIZZES	STACATION	STAG
SQUIDGING	SQUIRALTY	SQUOOSH	STACCATI	STAGE
SQUIDGY	SQUIRARCH	SQUOOSHED	STACCATO	STAGEABLE
SQUIDLIKE	SQUIRE	SQUOOSHES	STACCATOS	STAGED
SQUIDS	SQUIREAGE	SQUOOSHY	STACHE	STAGEFUL
SQUIER	SQUIRED	SQUUSH	STACHES	STAGEFULS
SQUIERS	SQUIREDOM	SQUUSHED	STACHYS	STAGEHAND
SQUIFF	SQUIREEN	SQUUSHES	STACHYSES	STAGEHEAD
SQUIFFED	SQUIREENS	SQUUSHING	STACK	STAGELIKE
SQUIFFER	SQUIRELY	SRADDHA	STACKABLE	STAGER
SQUIFFERS	SQUIRES	SRADDHAS	STACKED	STAGERIES
SQUIFFIER	SQUIRESS	SRADHA	STACKER	STAGERS
SQUIFFY	SQUIRING	SRADHAS	STACKERS	STAGERY

S

STAGES	STAINING	STALKIER	STAMPEDER	STANDS
STAGETTE	STAININGS	STALKIEST	STAMPEDES	STANDUP
STAGETTES	STAINLESS	STALKILY	STAMPEDO	STANDUPS
STAGEY	STAINS	STALKING	STAMPEDOS	STANE
STAGGARD	STAIR	STALKINGS	STAMPER	STANED
STAGGARDS	STAIRCASE	STALKLESS	STAMPERS	STANES
STAGGART	STAIRED	STALKLIKE	STAMPING	STANG
STAGGARTS	STAIRFOOT	STALKO	STAMPINGS	STANGED
STAGGED	STAIRHEAD	STALKOES	STAMPLESS	STANGING
STAGGER	STAIRLESS	STALKOS	STAMPS	STANGS
STAGGERED	STAIRLIFT	STALKS	STAN	STANHOPE
STAGGERER	STAIRLIKE	STALKY	STANCE	STANHOPES
STAGGERS	STAIRS	STALL	STANCES	STANIEL
STAGGERY	STAIRSTEP	STALLAGE	STANCH	STANIELS
STAGGIE	STAIRWAY	STALLAGES	STANCHED	STANINE
STAGGIER	STAIRWAYS	STALLED	STANCHEL	STANINES
STAGGIES	STAIRWELL	STALLING	STANCHELS	STANING
STAGGIEST	STAIRWISE	STALLINGS	STANCHER	STANK
STAGGING	STAIRWORK	STALLION	STANCHERS	STANKED
STAGGY	STAITH	STALLIONS	STANCHES	STANKING
STAGHORN	STAITHE	STALLMAN	STANCHEST	STANKS
STAGHORNS	STAITHES	STALLMEN	STANCHING	STANNARY
STAGHOUND	STAITHS	STALLS	STANCHION	STANNATE
STAGIER	STAKE	STALWART	STANCHLY	STANNATES
STAGIEST	STAKED	STALWARTS	STANCK	STANNATOR
STAGILY	STAKEOUT	STALWORTH	STAND	STANNED
STAGINESS	STAKEOUTS	STAMEN	STANDARD	STANNEL
STAGING	STAKER	STAMENED	STANDARDS	STANNELS
STAGINGS	STAKERS	STAMENS	STANDAWAY	STANNIC
STAGNANCE	STAKES	STAMINA	STANDBY	STANNING
STAGNANCY	STAKING	STAMINAL	STANDBYS	STANNITE
STAGNANT	STALACTIC	STAMINAS	STANDDOWN	STANNITES
STAGNATE	STALAG	STAMINATE	STANDEE	STANNOUS
STAGNATED	STALAGMA	STAMINEAL	STANDEES	STANNUM
STAGNATES	STALAGMAS	STAMINEÀL	STANDEN	STANNUMS
STAGS	STALAGS	STAMINODE	STANDER	STANOL
STAGY	STALE	STAMINODY	STANDERS	STANOLS
STAID	STALED	STAMINOID	STANDFAST	STANS
STAIDER	STALELY	STAMMEL	STANDGALE	STANYEL
STAIDEST	STALEMATE	STAMMELS	STANDING	STANYELS
STAIDLY	STALENESS	STAMMER	STANDINGS	STANZA
STAIDNESS	STALER	STAMMERED	STANDISH	STANZAED
STAIG	STALES	STAMMERER	STANDOFF	STANZAIC
STAIGS	STALEST	STAMMERS	STANDOFFS	STANZAS
STAIN	STALING	STAMNOI	STANDOUT	STANZE
STAINABLE	STALK	STAMNOS	STANDOUTS	STANZES
STAINED	STALKED	STAMP	STANDOVER	STANZO
STAINER	STALKER	STAMPED	STANDPAT	STANZOES
STAINERS	STALKERS	STAMPEDE	STANDPIPE	STANZOS
		STAMPEDED		

S

STAP	STARETZES	STARRS	STASIS	STATOR
STAPEDES	STARFISH	STARRY	STAT	STATORS
STAPEDIAL	STARFRUIT	STARS	STATABLE	STATS
STAPEDII	STARGAZE	STARSHINE	STATAL	STATTO
STAPEDIUS	STARGAZED	STARSHIP	STATANT	STATTOS
STAPELIA	STARGAZER	STARSHIPS	STATE	STATUA
STAPELIAS	STARGAZES	STARSPOT	STATEABLE	STATUARY
STAPES	STARGAZEY	STARSPOTS	STATED	STATUAS
STAPH	STARING	STARSTONE	STATEDLY	STATUE
STAPHS	STARINGLY	START	STATEHOOD	STATUED
STAPLE	STARINGS	STARTED	STATELESS	STATUES
STAPLED	STARK	STARTER	STATELET	STATUETTE
STAPLER	STARKED	STARTERS	STATELETS	STATURE
STAPLERS	STARKEN	STARTFUL	STATELIER	STATURED
STAPLES	STARKENED	STARTING	STATELILY	STATURES
STAPLING	STARKENS	STARTINGS	STATELY	STATUS
STAPLINGS	STARKER	STARTISH	STATEMENT	STATUSES
STAPPED	STARKERS	STARTLE	STATER	STATUSIER
STAPPING	STARKEST	STARTLED	STATEROOM	STATUSY
STAPPLE	STARKING	STARTLER	STATERS	STATUTE
STAPPLES	STARKLY	STARTLERS	STATES	STATUTES
STAPS	STARKNESS	STARTLES	STATESIDE	STATUTORY
STAR	STARKS	STARTLIER	STATESMAN	STAUMREL
STARAGEN	STARLESS	STARTLING	STATESMEN	STAUMRELS
STARAGENS	STARLET	STARTLISH	STATEWIDE	STAUN
STARBOARD	STARLETS	STARTLY	STATIC	STAUNCH
STARBURST	STARLIGHT	STARTS	STATICAL	STAUNCHED
STARCH	STARLIKE	STARTSY	STATICE	STAUNCHER
STARCHED	STARLING	STARTUP	STATICES	STAUNCHES
STARCHER	STARLINGS	STARTUPS	STATICKY	STAUNCHLY
STARCHERS	STARLIT	STARVE	STATICS	STAUNING
STARCHES	STARN	STARVED	STATIM	STAUNS
STARCHIER	STARNED	STARVER	STATIN	STAVE
STARCHILY	STARNIE	STARVERS	STATING	STAVED
STARCHING	STARNIES	STARVES	STATINS	STAVES
STARCHY	STARNING	STARVING	STATION	STAVING
STARDOM	STARNOSE	STARVINGS	STATIONAL	STAVUDINE
STARDOMS	STARNOSES	STARWORT	STATIONED	STAW
STARDRIFT	STARNS	STARWORTS	STATIONER	STAWED
STARDUST	STAROSTA	STASES	STATIONS	STAWING
STARDUSTS	STAROSTAS	STASH	STATISM	STAWS
STARE	STAROSTY	STASHED	STATISMS	STAY
STARED	STARR	STASHES	STATIST	STAYAWAY
STARER	STARRED	STASHIE	STATISTIC	STAYAWAYS
STARERS	STARRIER	STASHIES	STATISTS	STAYED
STARES	STARRIEST	STASHING	STATIVE	STAYER
STARETS	STARRILY	STASIDION	STATIVES	STAYERS
STARETSES	STARRING	STASIMA	STATOCYST	STAYING
STARETZ	STARRINGS	STASIMON	STATOLITH	STAYLESS

STAYMAKER	STEAMERS	STEDDE	STEEMED	STEERSMAN
STAYNE	STEAMIE	STEDDED	STEEMING	STEERSMEN
STAYNED	STEAMIER	STEDDES	STEEMS	STEERY
STAYNES	STEAMIES	STEDDIED	STEEN	STEEVE
STAYNING	STEAMIEST	STEDDIES	STEENBOK	STEEVED
STAYRE	STEAMILY	STEDDING	STEENBOKS	STEEVELY
STAYRES	STEAMING	STEDDS	STEENBRAS	STEEVER
STAYS	STEAMINGS	STEDDY	STEENBUCK	STEEVES
STAYSAIL	STEAMPUNK	STEDDYING	STEENED	STEEVEST
STAYSAILS	STEAMROLL	STEDE	STEENING	STEEVING
STEAD	STEAMS	STEDED	STEENINGS	STEEVINGS
STEADED	STEAMSHIP	STEDES	STEENKIRK	STEGNOSES
STEADFAST	STEAMY	STEDFAST	STEENS	STEGNOSIS
STEADIED	STEAN	STEDING	STEEP	STEGNOTIC
STEADIER	STEANE	STEDS	STEEPED	STEGODON
STEADIERS	STEANED	STEED	STEEPEN	STEGODONS
STEADIES	STEANES	STEEDED	STEEPENED	STEGODONT
STEADIEST	STEANING	STEEDIED	STEEPENS	STEGOMYIA
STEADILY	STEANINGS	STEEDIES	STEEPER	STEGOSAUR
STEADING	STEANS	STEEDING	STEEPERS	STEIL
STEADINGS	STEAPSIN	STEEDLIKE	STEEPEST	STEILS
STEADS	STEAPSINS	STEEDS	STEEPEUP	STEIN
STEADY	STEAR	STEEDY	STEEPIER	STEINBOCK
STEADYING	STEARAGE	STEEDYING	STEEPIEST	STEINBOK
STEAK	STEARAGES	STEEK	STEEPING	STEINBOKS
STEAKETTE	STEARATE	STEEKED	STEEPISH	STEINED
STEAKS	STEARATES	STEEKING	STEEPLE	STEINING
STEAL	STEARD	STEEKIT	STEEPLED	STEININGS
STEALABLE	STEARE	STEEKS	STEEPLES	STEINKIRK
STEALAGE	STEARED	STEEL	STEEPLING	STEINS
STEALAGES	STEARES	STEELBOW	STEEPLY	STELA
STEALE	STEARIC	STEELBOWS	STEEPNESS	STELAE
STEALED	STEARIN	STEELD	STEEPS	STELAI
STEALER	STEARINE	STEELED	STEEPUP	STELAR
STEALERS	STEARINES	STEELHEAD	STEEPY	STELE
STEALES	STEARING	STEELIE	STEER	STELENE
STEALING	STEARINS	STEELIER	STEERABLE	STELES
STEALINGS	STEARS	STEELIES	STEERAGE	STELIC
STEALS	STEARSMAN	STEELIEST	STEERAGES	STELL
STEALT	STEARSMEN	STEELING	STEERED	STELLA
STEALTH	STEATITE	STEELINGS	STEERER	STELLAR
STEALTHED	STEATITES	STEELMAN	STEERERS	STELLAS
STEALTHS	STEATITIC	STEELMEN	STEERIER	STELLATE
STEALTHY	STEATOMA	STEELS	STEERIES	STELLATED
STEAM	STEATOMAS	STEELWARE	STEERIEST	STELLED
STEAMBOAT	STEATOSES	STEELWORK	STEERING	STELLERID
STEAMED	STEATOSIS	STEELY	STEERINGS	STELLIFY
STEAMER	STED	STEELYARD	STEERLING	STELLING
STEAMERED	STEDD	STEEM	STEERS	STELLIO

STELLION	STENCHFUL	STEPDOWNS	STERLINGS	STEVIAS
STELLIONS	STENCHIER	STEPHANE	STERN	STEW
STELLITE	STENCHING	STEPHANES	STERNA	STEWABLE
STELLITES	STENCHY	STEPLESS	STERNAGE	STEWARD
STELLS	STENCIL	STEPLIKE	STERNAGES	STEWARDED
STELLULAR	STENCILED	STEPMOM	STERNAL	STEWARDRY
STEM	STENCILER	STEPMOMS	STERNEBRA	STEWARDS
STEMBOK	STENCILS	STEPNEY	STERNED	STEWARTRY
STEMBOKS	STEND	STEPNEYS	STERNER	STEWBUM
STEMBUCK	STENDED	STEPOVER	STERNEST	STEWBUMS
STEMBUCKS	STENDING	STEPOVERS	STERNFAST	STEWED
STEME	STENDS	STEPPE	STERNING	STEWER
STEMED	STENGAH	STEPPED	STERNITE	STEWERS
STEMES	STENGAHS	STEPPER	STERNITES	STEWIER
STEMHEAD	STENLOCK	STEPPERS	STERNITIC	STEWIEST
STEMHEADS	STENLOCKS	STEPPES	STERNLY	STEWING
STEMING	STENNED	STEPPING	STERNMOST	STEWINGS
STEMLESS	STENNING	STEPS	STERNNESS	STEWPAN
STEMLET	STENO	STEPSON	STERNPORT	STEWPANS
STEMLETS	STENOBATH	STEPSONS	STERNPOST	STEWPOND
STEMLIKE	STENOKIES	STEPSTOOL	STERNS	STEWPONDS
STEMMA	STENOKOUS	STEPT	STERNSON	STEWPOT
STEMMAS	STENOKY	STEPWISE	STERNSONS	STEWPOTS
STEMMATA	STENOPAIC	STERADIAN	STERNUM	STEWS
STEMMATIC	STENOS	STERANE	STERNUMS	STEWY
STEMME	STENOSED	STERANES	STERNWARD	STEY
STEMMED	STENOSES	STERCORAL	STERNWAY	STEYER
STEMMER	STENOSING	STERCULIA	STERNWAYS	STEYEST
STEMMERS	STENOSIS	STERE	STEROID	STEYS
STEMMERY	STENOTIC	STEREO	STEROIDAL	STHENIA
STEMMES	STENOTYPE	STEREOED	STEROIDS	STHENIAS
STEMMIER	STENOTYPY	STEREOING	STEROL	STHENIC
STEMMIEST	STENS	STEREOME	STEROLS	STIBBLE
STEMMING	STENT	STEREOMES	STERTOR	STIBBLER
STEMMINGS	STENTED	STEREOS	STERTORS	STIBBLERS
STEMMY	STENTING	STERES	STERVE	STIBBLES
STEMPEL	STENTOR	STERIC	STERVED	STIBIAL
STEMPELS	STENTORS	STERICAL	STERVES	STIBINE
STEMPLE	STENTOUR	STERIGMA	STERVING	STIBINES
STEMPLES	STENTOURS	STERIGMAS	STET	STIBIUM
STEMS	STENTS	STERILANT	STETS	STIBIUMS
STEMSON	STEP	STERILE	STETSON	STIBNITE
STEMSONS	STEPBAIRN	STERILELY	STETSONS	STIBNITES
STEMWARE	STEPCHILD	STERILISE	STETTED	STICCADO
STEMWARES	STEPDAD	STERILITY	STETTING	STICCADOS
STEN	STEPDADS	STERILIZE	STEVEDORE	STICCATO
STENCH	STEPDAME	STERLET	STEVEN	STICCATOS
STENCHED	STEPDAMES	STERLETS	STEVENS	STICH
STENCHES	STEPDOWN	STERLING	STEVIA	STICHARIA

STICHERA	STICKYING	STILBITE	STIMED	STINKIEST
STICHERON	STICTION	STILBITES	STIMES	STINKING
STICHIC	STICTIONS	STILBS	STIMIE	STINKO
STICHIDIA	STIDDIE	STILE	STIMIED	STINKPOT
STICHOI	STIDDIED	STILED	STIMIES	STINKPOTS
STICHOS	STIDDIES	STILES	STIMING	STINKS
STICHS	STIE	STILET	STIMMED	STINKWEED
STICK	STIED	STILETS	STIMMING	STINKWOOD
STICKABLE	STIES	STILETTO	STIMS	STINKY
STICKBALL	STIEVE	STILETTOS	STIMULANT	STINT
STICKED	STIEVELY	STILING	STIMULATE	STINTED
STICKER	STIEVER	STILL	STIMULI	STINTEDLY
STICKERED	STIEVEST	STILLAGE	STIMULUS	STINTER
STICKERS	STIFADO	STILLAGES	STIMY	STINTERS
STICKFUL	STIFADOS	STILLBORN	STIMYING	STINTIER
STICKFULS	STIFF	STILLED	STING	STINTIEST
STICKIE	STIFFED	STILLER	STINGAREE	STINTING
STICKIED	STIFFEN	STILLERS	STINGBULL	STINTINGS
STICKIER	STIFFENED	STILLEST	STINGE	STINTLESS
STICKIES	STIFFENER	STILLIER	STINGED	STINTS
STICKIEST	STIFFENS	STILLIEST	STINGER	STINTY
STICKILY	STIFFER	STILLING	STINGERS	STIPA
STICKING	STIFFEST	STILLINGS	STINGES	STIPAS
STICKINGS	STIFFIE	STILLION	STINGFISH	STIPE
STICKIT	STIFFIES	STILLIONS	STINGIER	STIPED
STICKJAW	STIFFING	STILLMAN	STINGIES	STIPEL
STICKJAWS	STIFFISH	STILLMEN	STINGIEST	STIPELS
STICKLE	STIFFLY	STILLNESS	STINGILY	STIPEND
STICKLED	STIFFNESS	STILLROOM	STINGING	STIPENDS
STICKLER	STIFFS	STILLS	STINGINGS	STIPES
STICKLERS	STIFFWARE	STILLSON	STINGLESS	STIPIFORM
STICKLES	STIFFY	STILLSONS	STINGO	STIPITATE
STICKLIKE	STIFLE	STILLY	STINGOS	STIPITES
STICKLING	STIFLED	STILT	STINGRAY	STIPPLE
STICKMAN	STIFLER	STILTBIRD	STINGRAYS	STIPPLED
STICKMEN	STIFLERS	STILTED	STINGS	STIPPLER
STICKOUT	STIFLES	STILTEDLY	STINGY	STIPPLERS
STICKOUTS	STIFLING	STILTER	STINK	STIPPLES
STICKPIN	STIFLINGS	STILTERS	STINKARD	STIPPLING
STICKPINS	STIGMA	STILTIER	STINKARDS	STIPULAR
STICKS	STIGMAL	STILTIEST	STINKBIRD	STIPULARY
STICKSEED	STIGMAS	STILTING	STINKBUG	STIPULATE
STICKUM	STIGMATA	STILTINGS	STINKBUGS	STIPULE
STICKUMS	STIGMATIC	STILTISH	STINKER	STIPULED
STICKUP	STIGME	STILTLIKE	STINKEROO	STIPULES
STICKUPS	STIGMES	STILTS	STINKERS	STIR
STICKWEED	STILB	STILTY	STINKHORN	STIRABOUT
STICKWORK	STILBENE	STIM	STINKIER	STIRE
STICKY	STILBENES	STIME	STINKIER	STIRED

S

STIRES	STOAT	STODGE	STOLIDITY	STONDS
STIRING	STOATS	STODGED	STOLIDLY	STONE
STIRK	STOB	STODGER	STOLLEN	STONEABLE
STIRKS	STOBBED	STODGERS	STOLLENS	STONEBOAT
STIRLESS	STOBBING	STODGES	STOLN	STONECAST
STIRP	STOBIE	STODGIER	STOLON	STONECHAT
STIRPES	STOBS	STODGIEST	STOLONATE	STONECROP
STIRPS	STOCCADO	STODGILY	STOLONIC	STONECUT
STIRRA	STOCCADOS	STODGING	STOLONS	STONECUTS
STIRRABLE	STOCCATA	STODGY	STOLPORT	STONED
STIRRAH	STOCCATAS	STOEP	STOLPORTS	STONEFISH
STIRRAHS	STOCIOUS	STOEPS	STOMA	STONEFLY
STIRRAS	STOCK	STOGEY	STOMACH	STONEHAND
STIRRE	STOCKADE	STOGEYS	STOMACHAL	STONELESS
STIRRED	STOCKADED	STOGIE	STOMACHED	STONELIKE
STIRRER	STOCKADES	STOGIES	STOMACHER	STONEN
STIRRERS	STOCKAGE	STOGY	STOMACHIC	STONER
STIRRES	STOCKAGES	STOIC	STOMACHS	STONERAG
STIRRING	STOCKCAR	STOICAL	STOMACHY	STONERAGS
STIRRINGS	STOCKCARS	STOICALLY	STOMACK	STONERAW
STIRRUP	STOCKED	STOICISM	STOMACKS	STONERAWS
STIRRUPS	STOCKER	STOICISMS	STOMAL	STONERN
STIRS	STOCKERS	STOICS	STOMAS	STONERS
STISHIE	STOCKFISH	STOIT	STOMATA	STONES
STISHIES	STOCKHORN	STOITED	STOMATAL	STONESHOT
STITCH	STOCKIER	STOITER	STOMATE	STONEWALL
STITCHED	STOCKIEST	STOITERED	STOMATES	STONEWARE
STITCHER	STOCKILY	STOITERS	STOMATIC	STONEWASH
STITCHERS	STOCKINET	STOITING	STOMATOUS	STONEWORK
STITCHERY	STOCKING	STOITS	STOMIA	STONEWORT
STITCHES	STOCKINGS	STOKE	STOMIUM	STONEY
STITCHING	STOCKISH	STOKED	STOMIUMS	STONG
STITHIED	STOCKIST	STOKEHOLD	STOMODAEA	STONIED
STITHIES	STOCKISTS	STOKEHOLE	STOMODEA	STONIER
STITHY	STOCKLESS	STOKER	STOMODEAL	STONIES
STITHYING	STOCKLIST	STOKERS	STOMODEUM	STONIEST
STIVE	STOCKLOCK	STOKES	STOMP	STONILY
STIVED	STOCKMAN	STOKESIA	STOMPED	STONINESS
STIVER	STOCKMEN	STOKESIAS	STOMPER	STONING
STIVERS	STOCKPILE	STOKING	STOMPERS	STONINGS
STIVES	STOCKPOT	STOKVEL	STOMPIE	STONISH
STIVIER	STOCKPOTS	STOKVELS	STOMPIER	STONISHED
STIVIEST	STOCKROOM	STOLE	STOMPIES	STONISHES
STIVING	STOCKS	STOLED	STOMPIEST	STONK
STIVY	STOCKTAKE	STOLEN	STOMPING	STONKED
STOA	STOCKTOOK	STOLES	STOMPS	STONKER
STOAE	STOCKWORK	STOLID	STOMPY	STONKERED
STOAI	STOCKY	STOLIDER	STONABLE	STONKERS
STOAS	STOCKYARD	STOLIDEST	STOND	STONKING

S

STONKS	STOOZES	STORE	STOSS	STOUTEST
STONN	STOOZING	STORECARD	STOSSES	STOUTH
STONNE	STOOZINGS	STORED	STOT	STOUTHS
STONNED	STOP	STOREMAN	STOTIN	STOUTISH
STONNES	STOPBAND	STOREMEN	STOTINKA	STOUTLY
STONNING	STOPBANDS	STORER	STOTINKAS	STOUTNESS
STONNS	STOPBANK	STOREROOM	STOTINKI	STOUTS
STONY	STOPBANKS	STORERS	STOTINOV	STOVAINE
STONYING	STOPCOCK	STORES	STOTINS	STOVAINES
STOOD	STOPCOCKS	STORESHIP	STOTIOUS	STOVE
STOODEN	STOPE	STOREWIDE	STOTS	STOVED
STOOGE	STOPED	STOREY	STOTT	STOVEPIPE
STOOGED	STOPER	STOREYED	STOTTED	STOVER
STOOGES	STOPERS	STOREYS	STOTTER	STOVERS
STOOGING	STOPES	STORGE	STOTTERED	STOVES
STOOK	STOPGAP	STORGES	STOTTERS	STOVETOP
STOOKED	STOPGAPS	STORIATED	STOTTIE	STOVETOPS
STOOKER	STOPING	STORIED	STOTTIES	STOVEWOOD
STOOKERS	STOPINGS	STORIES	STOTTING	STOVIES
STOOKIE	STOPLESS	STORIETTE	STOTTS	STOVING
STOOKIES	STOPLIGHT	STORING	STOTTY	STOVINGS
STOOKING	STOPOFF	STORK	STOUN	STOW
STOOKINGS	STOPOFFS	STORKS	STOUND	STOWABLE
STOOKS	STOPOVER	STORM	STOUNDED	STOWAGE
STOOL	STOPOVERS	STORMBIRD	STOUNDING	STOWAGES
STOOLBALL	STOPPABLE	STORMCOCK	STOUNDS	STOWAWAY
STOOLED	STOPPAGE	STORMED	STOUNING	STOWAWAYS
STOOLIE	STOPPAGES	STORMER	STOUNS	STOWDOWN
STOOLIES	STOPPED	STORMERS	STOUP	STOWDOWNS
STOOLING	STOPPER	STORMFUL	STOUPS	STOWED
STOOLS	STOPPERED	STORMIER	STOUR	STOWER
STOOLY	STOPPERS	STORMIEST	STOURE	STOWERS
STOOP	STOPPING	STORMILY	STOURES	STOWING
STOOPBALL	STOPPINGS	STORMING	STOURIE	STOWINGS
STOOPE	STOPPLE	STORMINGS	STOURIER	STOWLINS
STOOPED	STOPPLED	STORMLESS	STOURIEST	STOWN
STOOPER	STOPPLES	STORMLIKE	STOURS	STOWND
STOOPERS	STOPPLING	STORMS	STOURY	STOWNDED
STOOPES	STOPS	STORMY	STOUSH	STOWNDING
STOOPING	STOPT	STORNELLI	STOUSHED	STOWNDS
STOOPS	STOPWATCH	STORNELLO	STOUSHES	STOWNLINS
STOOR	STOPWORD	STORY	STOUSHIE	STOWP
STOORS	STOPWORDS	STORYBOOK	STOUSHIES	STOWPS
STOOSHIE	STORABLE	STORYETTE	STOUSHING	STOWRE
STOOSHIES	STORABLES	STORYING	STOUT	STOWRES
STOOZE	STORAGE	STORYINGS	STOUTEN	STOWS
STOOZED	STORAGES	STORYLESS	STOUTENED	STRABISM
STOOZER	STORAX	STORYLINE	STOUTENS	STRABISMS
STOOZERS	STORAXES	STORYTIME	STOUTER	STRACK

S

STRAD	STRAITING	STRAPWORT	STRAYLING	STREIGNES
STRADDLE	STRAITLY	STRASS	STRAYS	STRELITZ
STRADDLED	STRAITS	STRASSES	STRAYVE	STRELITZI
STRADDLER	STRAK	STRATA	STRAYVED	STRENE
STRADDLES	STRAKE	STRATAGEM	STRAYVES	STRENES
STRADIOT	STRAKED	STRATAL	STRAYVING	STRENGTH
STRADIOTS	STRAKES	STRATAS	STREAK	STRENGTHS
STRADS	STRAMACON	STRATEGIC	STREAKED	STRENUITY
STRAE	STRAMASH	STRATEGY	STREAKER	STRENUOUS
STRAES	STRAMAZON	STRATH	STREAKERS	STREP
STRAFE	STRAMMEL	STRATHS	STREAKIER	STREPENT
STRAFED	STRAMMELS	STRATI	STREAKILY	STREPS
STRAFER	STRAMONY	STRATIFY	STREAKING	STRESS
STRAFERS	STRAMP	STRATONIC	STREAKS	STRESSED
STRAFES	STRAMPED	STRATOSE	STREAKY	STRESSES
STRAFF	STRAMPING	STRATOUS	STREAM	STRESSFUL
STRAFFED	STRAMPS	STRATUM	STREAMBED	STRESSIER
STRAFFING	STRAND	STRATUMS	STREAMED	STRESSING
STRAFFS	STRANDED	STRATUS	STREAMER	STRESSOR
STRAFING	STRANDER	STRATUSES	STREAMERS	STRESSORS
STRAFINGS	STRANDERS	STRAUCHT	STREAMIER	STRESSY
STRAG	STRANDING	STRAUCHTS	STREAMING	STRETCH
STRAGGLE	STRANDS	STRAUGHT	STREAMLET	STRETCHED
STRAGGLED	STRANG	STRAUGHTS	STREAMS	STRETCHER
STRAGGLER	STRANGE	STRAUNGE	STREAMY	STRETCHES
STRAGGLES	STRANGELY	STRAVAGE	STREEK	STRETCHY
STRAGGLY	STRANGER	STRAVAGED	STREEKED	STRETTA
STRAGS	STRANGERS	STRAVAGES	STREEKER	STRETTAS
STRAICHT	STRANGES	STRAVAIG	STREEKERS	STRETTE
STRAIGHT	STRANGEST	STRAVAIGS	STREEKING	STRETTI
STRAIGHTS	STRANGLE	STRAW	STREEKS	STRETTO
STRAIK	STRANGLED	STRAWED	STREEL	STRETTOS
STRAIKED	STRANGLER	STRAWEN	STREELED	STREUSEL
STRAIKING	STRANGLES	STRAWHAT	STREELING	STREUSELS
STRAIKS	STRANGURY	STRAWIER	STREELS	STREW
STRAIN	STRAP	STRAWIEST	STREET	STREWAGE
STRAINED	STRAPHANG	STRAWING	STREETAGE	STREWAGES
STRAINER	STRAPHUNG	STRAWLESS	STREETBOY	STREWED
STRAINERS	STRAPLESS	STRAWLIKE	STREETCAR	STREWER
STRAINING	STRAPLIKE	STRAWN	STREETED	STREWERS
STRAINS	STRAPLINE	STRAWS	STREETFUL	STREWING
STRAINT	STRAPPADO	STRAWWORM	STREETIER	STREWINGS
STRAINTS	STRAPPED	STRAWY	STREETING	STREWMENT
STRAIT	STRAPPER	STRAY	STREETS	STREWN
STRAITED	STRAPPERS	STRAYED	STREETY	STREWS
STRAITEN	STRAPPIER	STRAYER	STREIGHT	STREWTH
STRAITENS	STRAPPING	STRAYERS	STREIGHTS	STRIA
STRAITER	STRAPPY	STRAYING	STREIGNE	STRIAE
STRAITEST	STRAPS	STRAYINGS	STREIGNED	STRIATA

STRIATAL	STRIGGING	STRIPS	STROLLER	STROSSERS
STRIATE	STRIGIL	STRIPT	STROLLERS	STROUD
STRIATED	STRIGILS	STRIPY	STROLLING	STROUDING
STRIATES	STRIGINE	STRIVE	STROLLS	STROUDS
STRIATING	STRIGOSE	STRIVED	STROMA	STROUP
STRIATION	STRIGS	STRIVEN	STROMAL	STROUPACH
STRIATUM	STRIKABLE	STRIVER	STROMATA	STROUPAN
STRIATUMS	STRIKE	STRIVERS	STROMATIC	STROUPANS
STRIATURE	STRIKEOUT	STRIVES	STROMB	STROUPS
STRICH	STRIKER	STRIVING	STROMBOLI	STROUT
STRICHES	STRIKERS	STRIVINGS	STROMBS	STROUTED
STRICK	STRIKES	STROAM	STROMBUS	STROUTING
STRICKEN	STRIKING	STROAMED	STROND	STROUTS
STRICKLE	STRIKINGS	STROAMING	STRONDS	STROVE
STRICKLED	STRIM	STROAMS	STRONG	STROW
STRICKLES	STRIMMED	STROBE	STRONGARM	STROWED
STRICKS	STRIMMING	STROBED	STRONGBOX	STROWER
STRICT	STRIMS	STROBES	STRONGER	STROWERS
STRICTER	STRINE	STROBIC	STRONGEST	STROWING
STRICTEST	STRINES	STROBIL	STRONGISH	STROWINGS
STRICTION	STRING	STROBILA	STRONGLY	STROWN
STRICTISH	STRINGED	STROBILAE	STRONGMAN	STROWS
STRICTLY	STRINGENT	STROBILAR	STRONGMEN	STROY
STRICTURE	STRINGER	STROBILE	STRONGYL	STROYED
STRIDDEN	STRINGERS	STROBILES	STRONGYLE	STROYER
STRIDDLE	STRINGIER	STROBILI	STRONGYLS	STROYERS
STRIDDLED	STRINGILY	STROBILS	STRONTIA	STROYING
STRIDDLES	STRINGING	STROBILUS	STRONTIAN	STROYS
STRIDE	STRINGS	STROBING	STRONTIAS	STRUCK
STRIDENCE	STRINGY	STROBINGS	STRONTIC	STRUCKEN
STRIDENCY	STRINKLE	STRODDLE	STRONTIUM	STRUCTURE
STRIDENT	STRINKLED	STRODDLED	STROOK	STRUDEL
STRIDER	STRINKLES	STRODDLES	STROOKE	STRUDELS
STRIDERS	STRIP	STRODE	STROOKEN	STRUGGLE
STRIDES	STRIPE	STRODLE	STROOKES	STRUGGLED
STRIDING	STRIPED	STRODLED	STROP	STRUGGLER
STRIDLING	STRIPER	STRODLES	STROPHE	STRUGGLES
STRIDOR	STRIPERS	STRODLING	STROPHES	STRUM
STRIDORS	STRIPES	STROKABLE	STROPHIC	STRUMA
STRIFE	STRIPEY	STROKE	STROPHOID	STRUMAE
STRIFEFUL	STRIPIER	STROKED	STROPHULI	STRUMAS
STRIFES	STRIPIEST	STROKEN	STROPPED	STRUMATIC
STRIFT	STRIPING	STROKER	STROPPER	STRUMITIS
STRIFTS	STRIPINGS	STROKERS	STROPPERS	STRUMMED
STRIG	STRIPLING	STROKES	STROPPIER	STRUMMEL
STRIGA	STRIPPED	STROKING	STROPPILY	STRUMMELS
STRIGAE	STRIPPER	STROKINGS	STROPPING	STRUMMER
STRIGATE	STRIPPERS	STROLL	STROPPY	STRUMMERS
STRIGGED	STRIPPING	STROLLED	STROPS	STRUMMING

STRUMOSE	STUDDIE	STUIVER	STUNS	STURTING
STRUMOUS	STUDDIES	STUIVERS	STUNSAIL	STURTS
STRUMPET	STUDDING	STUKKEND	STUNSAILS	STUSHIE
STRUMPETS	STUDDINGS	STULL	STUNT	STUSHIES
STRUMS	STUDDLE	STULLS	STUNTED	STUTTER
STRUNG	STUDDLES	STULM	STUNTING	STUTTERED
STRUNT	STUDE	STULMS	STUNTMAN	STUTTERER
STRUNTED	STUDENT	STULTIFY	STUNTMEN	STUTTERS
STRUNTING	STUDENTRY	STUM	STUNTS	STY
STRUNTS	STUDENTS	STUMBLE	STUPA	STYE
STRUT	STUDENTY	STUMBLED	STUPAS	STYED
STRUTS	STUDFARM	STUMBLER	STUPE	STYES
STRUTTED	STUDFARMS	STUMBLERS	STUPED	STYGIAN
STRUTTER	STUDFISH	STUMBLES	STUPEFIED	STYING
STRUTTERS	STUDHORSE	STUMBLIER	STUPEFIER	STYLAR
STRUTTING	STUDIED	STUMBLING	STUPEFIES	STYLATE
STRYCHNIA	STUDIEDLY	STUMBLY	STUPEFY	STYLE
STRYCHNIC	STUDIER	STUMER	STUPENT	STYLEBOOK
STUB	STUDIERS	STUMERS	STUPES	STYLED
STUBBED	STUDIES	STUMM	STUPID	STYLEE
STUBBIE	STUDIO	STUMMED	STUPIDER	STYLEES
STUBBIER	STUDIOS	STUMMEL	STUPIDEST	STYLELESS
STUBBIES	STUDIOUS	STUMMELS	STUPIDITY	STYLER
STUBBIEST	STUDLIER	STUMMING	STUPIDLY	STYLERS
STUBBILY	STUDLIEST	STUMP	STUPIDS	STYLES
STUBBING	STUDLIKE	STUMPAGE	STUPING	STYLET
STUBBLE	STUDLY	STUMPAGES	STUPOR	STYLETS
STUBBLED	STUDS	STUMPED	STUPOROUS	STYLI
STUBBLES	STUDWORK	STUMPER	STUPORS	STYLIE
STUBBLIER	STUDWORKS	STUMPERS	STUPRATE	STYLIER
STUBBLY	STUDY	STUMPIER	STUPRATED	STYLIEST
STUBBORN	STUDYING	STUMPIES	STUPRATES	STYLIFORM
STUBBORNS	STUFF	STUMPIEST	STURDIED	STYLING
STUBBY	STUFFED	STUMPILY	STURDIER	STYLINGS
STUBS	STUFFER	STUMPING	STURDIES	STYLISE
STUCCO	STUFFERS	STUMPINGS	STURDIEST	STYLISED
STUCCOED	STUFFIE	STUMPS	STURDILY	STYLISER
STUCCOER	STUFFIER	STUMPWORK	STURDY	STYLISERS
STUCCOERS	STUFFIES	STUMPY	STURE	STYLISES
STUCCOES	STUFFIEST	STUMS	STURGEON	STYLISH
STUCCOING	STUFFILY	STUN	STURGEONS	STYLISHLY
STUCCOS	STUFFING	STUNG	STURMER	STYLISING
STUCK	STUFFINGS	STUNK	STURMERS	STYLIST
STUCKS	STUFFLESS	STUNKARD	STURNINE	STYLISTIC
STUD	STUFFS	STUNNED	STURNOID	STYLISTS
STUDBOOK	STUFFY	STUNNER	STURNUS	STYLITE
STUDBOOKS	STUGGIER	STUNNERS	STURNUSES	STYLITES
STUDDED	STUGGIEST	STUNNING	STURT	STYLITIC
STUDDEN	STUGGY	STUNNINGS	STURTED	STYLITISM

STYLIZE	SUABLE	SUBAREAS	SUBCLANS	SUBDUCT
STYLIZED	SUABLY	SUBARID	SUBCLASS	SUBDUCTED
STYLIZER	SUASIBLE	SUBAS	SUBCLAUSE	SUBDUCTS
STYLIZERS	SUASION	SUBASTRAL	SUBCLERK	SUBDUE
STYLIZES	SUASIONS	SUBATOM	SUBCLERKS	SUBDUED
STYLIZING	SUASIVE	SUBATOMIC	SUBCLIMAX	SUBDUEDLY
STYLO	SUASIVELY	SUBATOMS	SUBCODE	SUBDUER
STYLOBATE	SUASORY	SUBAUDIO	SUBCODES	SUBDUERS
STYLOID	SUAVE	SUBAURAL	SUBCOLONY	SUBDUES
STYLOIDS	SUAVELY	SUBAXIAL	SUBCONSUL	SUBDUING
STYLOLITE	SUAVENESS	SUBBASAL	SUBCOOL	SUBDUPLE
STYLOPES	SUAVER	SUBBASE	SUBCOOLED	SUBDURAL
STYLOPID	SUAVEST	SUBBASES	SUBCOOLS	SUBDWARF
STYLOPIDS	SUAVITIES	SUBBASIN	SUBCORTEX	SUBDWARFS
STYLOPISE	SUAVITY	SUBBASINS	SUBCOSTA	SUBECHO
STYLOPIZE	SUB	SUBBASS	SUBCOSTAE	SUBECHOES
STYLOPS	SUBA	SUBBASSES	SUBCOSTAL	SUBEDAR
STYLOS	SUBABBOT	SUBBED	SUBCOUNTY	SUBEDARS
STYLUS	SUBABBOTS	SUBBIE	SUBCRUST	SUBEDIT
STYLUSES	SUBACID	SUBBIES	SUBCRUSTS	SUBEDITED
STYME	SUBACIDLY	SUBBING	SUBCULT	SUBEDITOR
STYMED	SUBACRID	SUBBINGS	SUBCULTS	SUBEDITS
STYMES	SUBACT	SUBBLOCK	SUBCUTES	SUBENTIRE
STYMIE	SUBACTED	SUBBLOCKS	SUBCUTIS	SUBENTRY
STYMIED	SUBACTING	SUBBRANCH	SUBDEACON	SUBEPOCH
STYMIEING	SUBACTION	SUBBREED	SUBDEALER	SUBEPOCHS
STYMIES	SUBACTS	SUBBREEDS	SUBDEAN	SUBEQUAL
STYMING	SUBACUTE	SUBBUREAU	SUBDEANS	SUBER
STYMY	SUBADAR	SUBBY	SUBDEB	SUBERATE
STYMYING	SUBADARS	SUBCANTOR	SUBDEBS	SUBERATES
STYPSIS	SUBADULT	SUBCASTE	SUBDEPOT	SUBERECT
STYPSISES	SUBADULTS	SUBCASTES	SUBDEPOTS	SUBEREOUS
STYPTIC	SUBAERIAL	SUBCAUDAL	SUBDEPUTY	SUBERIC
STYPTICAL	SUBAGENCY	SUBCAUSE	SUBDERMAL	SUBERIN
STYPTICS	SUBAGENT	SUBCAUSES	SUBDEW	SUBERINS
STYRAX	SUBAGENTS	SUBCAVITY	SUBDEWED	SUBERISE
STYRAXES	SUBAH	SUBCELL	SUBDEWING	SUBERISED
STYRE	SUBAHDAR	SUBCELLAR	SUBDEWS	SUBERISES
STYRED	SUBAHDARS	SUBCELLS	SUBDIVIDE	SUBERIZE
STYRENE	SUBAHDARY	SUBCENTER	SUBDOLOUS	SUBERIZED
STYRENES	SUBAHS	SUBCENTRE	SUBDORSAL	SUBERIZES
STYRES	SUBAHSHIP	SUBCHASER	SUBDUABLE	SUBEROSE
STYRING	SUBALAR	SUBCHIEF	SUBDUABLY	SUBEROUS
STYROFOAM	SUBALPINE	SUBCHIEFS	SUBDUAL	SUBERS
STYTE	SUBALTERN	SUBCHORD	SUBDUALS	SUBFAMILY
STYTED	SUBAPICAL	SUBCHORDS	SUBDUCE	SUBFEU
STYTES	SUBAQUA	SUBCLAIM	SUBDUCED	SUBFEUED
STYTING	SUBARCTIC	SUBCLAIMS	SUBDUCES	SUBFEUING
SUABILITY	SUBAREA	SUBCLAN	SUBDUCING	SUBFEUS

S

SUBFIELD	SUBITISED	SUBLUNAR	SUBORN	SUBSALE
SUBFIELDS	SUBITISES	SUBLUNARY	SUBORNED	SUBSALES
SUBFILE	SUBITIZE	SUBLUNATE	SUBORNER	SUBSAMPLE
SUBFILES	SUBITIZED	SUBLUXATE	SUBORNERS	SUBSCALE
SUBFIX	SUBITIZES	SUBMAN	SUBORNING	SUBSCALES
SUBFIXES	SUBITO	SUBMARINE	SUBORNS	SUBSCHEMA
SUBFLOOR	SUBJACENT	SUBMARKET	SUBOSCINE	SUBSCRIBE
SUBFLOORS	SUBJECT	SUBMATRIX	SUBOVAL	SUBSCRIPT
SUBFLUID	SUBJECTED	SUBMEN	SUBOVATE	SUBSEA
SUBFOLDER	SUBJECTS	SUBMENTA	SUBOXIDE	SUBSECIVE
SUBFOSSIL	SUBJOIN	SUBMENTAL	SUBOXIDES	SUBSECT
SUBFRAME	SUBJOINED	SUBMENTUM	SUBPANEL	SUBSECTOR
SUBFRAMES	SUBJOINS	SUBMENU	SUBPANELS	SUBSECTS
SUBFUSC	SUBJUGATE	SUBMENUS	SUBPAR	SUBSELLIA
SUBFUSCS	SUBLATE	SUBMERGE	SUBPART	SUBSENSE
SUBFUSK	SUBLATED	SUBMERGED	SUBPARTS	SUBSENSES
SUBFUSKS	SUBLATES	SUBMERGES	SUBPENA	SUBSERE
SUBGENERA	SUBLATING	SUBMERSE	SUBPENAED	SUBSERES
SUBGENRE	SUBLATION	SUBMERSED	SUBPENAS	SUBSERIES
SUBGENRES	SUBLEASE	SUBMERSES	SUBPERIOD	SUBSERVE
SUBGENUS	SUBLEASED	SUBMICRON	SUBPHASE	SUBSERVED
SUBGOAL	SUBLEASES	SUBMISS	SUBPHASES	SUBSERVES
SUBGOALS	SUBLESSEE	SUBMISSLY	SUBPHYLA	SUBSET
SUBGRADE	SUBLESSOR	SUBMIT	SUBPHYLAR	SUBSETS
SUBGRADES	SUBLET	SUBMITS	SUBPHYLUM	SUBSHAFT
SUBGRAPH	SUBLETHAL	SUBMITTAL	SUBPLOT	SUBSHAFTS
SUBGRAPHS	SUBLETS	SUBMITTED	SUBPLOTS	SUBSHELL
SUBGROUP	SUBLETTER	SUBMITTER	SUBPOENA	SUBSHELLS
SUBGROUPS	SUBLEVEL	SUBMUCOSA	SUBPOENAS	SUBSHRUB
SUBGUM	SUBLEVELS	SUBMUCOUS	SUBPOLAR	SUBSHRUBS
SUBGUMS	SUBLIMATE	SUBNASAL	SUBPOTENT	SUBSIDE
SUBHA	SUBLIME	SUBNET	SUBPRIME	SUBSIDED
SUBHAS	SUBLIMED	SUBNETS	SUBPRIMES	SUBSIDER
SUBHEAD	SUBLIMELY	SUBNEURAL	SUBPRIOR	SUBSIDERS
SUBHEADS	SUBLIMER	SUBNICHE	SUBPRIORS	SUBSIDES
SUBHEDRAL	SUBLIMERS	SUBNICHES	SUBPUBIC	SUBSIDIES
SUBHUMAN	SUBLIMES	SUBNIVEAL	SUBRACE	SUBSIDING
SUBHUMANS	SUBLIMEST	SUBNIVEAN	SUBRACES	SUBSIDISE
SUBHUMID	SUBLIMING	SUBNODAL	SUBREGION	SUBSIDIZE
SUBIDEA	SUBLIMISE	SUBNORMAL	SUBRENT	SUBSIDY
SUBIDEAS	SUBLIMIT	SUBNUCLEI	SUBRENTED	SUBSIST
SUBIMAGO	SUBLIMITS	SUBOCEAN	SUBRENTS	SUBSISTED
SUBIMAGOS	SUBLIMITY	SUBOCTAVE	SUBRING	SUBSISTER
SUBINCISE	SUBLIMIZE	SUBOCULAR	SUBRINGS	SUBSISTS
SUBINDEX	SUBLINE	SUBOFFICE	SUBROGATE	SUBSITE
SUBINFEUD	SUBLINEAR	SUBOPTIC	SUBRULE	SUBSITES
SUBITEM	SUBLINES	SUBORAL	SUBRULES	SUBSIZAR
SUBITEMS	SUBLOT	SUBORDER	SUBS	SUBSIZARS
SUBITISE	SUBLOTS	SUBORDERS	SUBSACRAL	SUBSKILL

SUBSKILLS	SUBTEST	SUBTRUDED	SUBWRITER	SUCCUBINE
SUBSOCIAL	SUBTESTS	SUBTRUDES	SUBZERO	SUCCUBOUS
SUBSOIL	SUBTEXT	SUBTUNIC	SUBZONAL	SUCCUBUS
SUBSOILED	SUBTEXTS	SUBTUNICS	SUBZONE	SUCCULENT
SUBSOILER	SUBTHEME	SUBTWEET	SUBZONES	SUCCUMB
SUBSOILS	SUBTHEMES	SUBTWEETS	SUCCADE	SUCCUMBED
SUBSOLAR	SUBTIDAL	SUBTYPE	SUCCADES	SUCCUMBER
SUBSONG	SUBTIL	SUBTYPES	SUCCAH	SUCCUMBS
SUBSONGS	SUBTILE	SUBUCULA	SUCCAHS	SUCCURSAL
SUBSONIC	SUBTILELY	SUBUCULAS	SUCCEDENT	SUCCUS
SUBSPACE	SUBTILER	SUBULATE	SUCCEED	SUCCUSS
SUBSPACES	SUBTILEST	SUBUNIT	SUCCEEDED	SUCCUSSED
SUBSTAGE	SUBTILIN	SUBUNITS	SUCCEEDER	SUCCUSSES
SUBSTAGES	SUBTILINS	SUBURB	SUCCEEDS	SUCH
SUBSTANCE	SUBTILISE	SUBURBAN	SUCCENTOR	SUCHLIKE
SUBSTATE	SUBTILITY	SUBURBANS	SUCCES	SUCHLIKES
SUBSTATES	SUBTILIZE	SUBURBED	SUCCESS	SUCHNESS
SUBSTORM	SUBTILTY	SUBURBIA	SUCCESSES	SUCHWISE
SUBSTORMS	SUBTITLE	SUBURBIAS	SUCCESSOR	SUCK
SUBSTRACT	SUBTITLED	SUBURBS	SUCCI	SUCKED
SUBSTRATA	SUBTITLES	SUBURSINE	SUCCINATE	SUCKEN
SUBSTRATE	SUBTLE	SUBVASSAL	SUCCINCT	SUCKENER
SUBSTRUCT	SUBTLER	SUBVENE	SUCCINIC	SUCKENERS
SUBSTYLAR	SUBTLEST	SUBVENED	SUCCINITE	SUCKENS
SUBSTYLE	SUBTLETY	SUBVENES	SUCCINYL	SUCKER
SUBSTYLES	SUBTLY	SUBVENING	SUCCINYLS	SUCKERED
SUBSULTUS	SUBTONE	SUBVERSAL	SUCCISE	SUCKERING
SUBSUME	SUBTONES	SUBVERSE	SUCCOR	SUCKERS
SUBSUMED	SUBTONIC	SUBVERSED	SUCCORED	SUCKET
SUBSUMES	SUBTONICS	SUBVERSES	SUCCORER	SUCKETS
SUBSUMING	SUBTOPIA	SUBVERST	SUCCORERS	SUCKFISH
SUBSYSTEM	SUBTOPIAN	SUBVERT	SUCCORIES	SUCKHOLE
SUBTACK	SUBTOPIAS	SUBVERTED	SUCCORING	SUCKHOLED
SUBTACKS	SUBTOPIC	SUBVERTER	SUCCORS	SUCKHOLES
SUBTALAR	SUBTOPICS	SUBVERTS	SUCCORY	SUCKIER
SUBTASK	SUBTORRID	SUBVICAR	SUCCOS	SUCKIEST
SUBTASKS	SUBTOTAL	SUBVICARS	SUCCOSE	SUCKINESS
SUBTAXA	SUBTOTALS	SUBVIRAL	SUCCOT	SUCKING
SUBTAXON	SUBTRACT	SUBVIRUS	SUCCOTASH	SUCKINGS
SUBTAXONS	SUBTRACTS	SUBVISUAL	SUCCOTH	SUCKLE
SUBTEEN	SUBTRADE	SUBVOCAL	SUCCOUR	SUCKLED
SUBTEENS	SUBTRADES	SUBWARDEN	SUCCOURED	SUCKLER
SUBTENANT	SUBTREND	SUBWAY	SUCCOURER	SUCKLERS
SUBTEND	SUBTRENDS	SUBWAYED	SUCCOURS	SUCKLES
SUBTENDED	SUBTRIBE	SUBWAYING	SUCCOUS	SUCKLESS
SUBTENDS	SUBTRIBES	SUBWAYS	SUCCUBA	SUCKLING
SUBTENSE	SUBTRIST	SUBWOOFER	SUCCUBAE	SUCKLINGS
SUBTENSES	SUBTROPIC	SUBWORLD	SUCCUBAS	SUCKS
SUBTENURE	SUBTRUDE	SUBWORLDS	SUCCUBI	SUCKY

S

SUCRALOSE	SUDS	SUFFICER	SUGGING	SUIVEZ
SUCRASE	SUDSED	SUFFICERS	SUGGINGS	SUJEE
SUCRASES	SUDSER	SUFFICES	SUGH	SUJEES
SUCRE	SUDSERS	SUFFICING	SUGHED	SUK
SUCRES	SUDSES	SUFFIX	SUGHING	SUKH
SUCRIER	SUDSIER	SUFFIXAL	SUGHS	SUKHS
SUCRIERS	SUDSIEST	SUFFIXED	SUGO	SUKIYAKI
SUCROSE	SUDSING	SUFFIXES	SUGOS	SUKIYAKIS
SUCROSES	SUDSLESS	SUFFIXING	SUGS	SUKKAH
SUCTION	SUDSY	SUFFIXION	SUHUR	SUKKAHS
SUCTIONAL	SUE	SUFFLATE	SUHURS	SUKKOS
SUCTIONED	SUEABLE	SUFFLATED	SUI	SUKKOT
SUCTIONS	SUEABLY	SUFFLATES	SUICIDAL	SUKKOTH
SUCTORIAL	SUED	SUFFOCATE	SUICIDE	SUKS
SUCTORIAN	SUEDE	SUFFRAGAN	SUICIDED	SUKUK
SUCURUJU	SUEDED	SUFFRAGE	SUICIDES	SUKUKS
SUCURUJUS	SUEDELIKE	SUFFRAGES	SUICIDING	SULCAL
SUD	SUEDES	SUFFUSE	SUID	SULCALISE
SUDAMEN	SUEDETTE	SUFFUSED	SUIDIAN	SULCALIZE
SUDAMENS	SUEDETTES	SUFFUSES	SUIDIANS	SULCATE
SUDAMINA	SUEDING	SUFFUSING	SUIDS	SULCATED
SUDAMINAL	SUENT	SUFFUSION	SUILLINE	SULCATION
SUDARIA	SUER	SUFFUSIVE	SUING	SULCI
SUDARIES	SUERS	SUG	SUINGS	SULCUS
SUDARIUM	SUES	SUGAN	SUINT	SULDAN
SUDARY	SUET	SUGANS	SUINTS	SULDANS
SUDATE	SUETE	SUGAR	SUIPLAP	SULFA
SUDATED	SUETES	SUGARALLY	SUIPLAPS	SULFAMATE
SUDATES	SUETIER	SUGARBUSH	SUIT	SULFAS
SUDATING	SUETIEST	SUGARCANE	SUITABLE	SULFATASE
SUDATION	SUETS	SUGARCOAT	SUITABLY	SULFATE
SUDATIONS	SUETTIER	SUGARED	SUITCASE	SULFATED
SUDATORIA	SUETTIEST	SUGARER	SUITCASES	SULFATES
SUDATORY	SUETTY	SUGARERS	SUITE	SULFATIC
SUDD	SUETY	SUGARIER	SUITED	SULFATING
SUDDEN	SUFFARI	SUGARIEST	SUITER	SULFATION
SUDDENLY	SUFFARIS	SUGARING	SUITERS	SULFID
SUDDENS	SUFFECT	SUGARINGS	SUITES	SULFIDE
SUDDENTY	SUFFECTS	SUGARLESS	SUITING	SULFIDES
SUDDER	SUFFER	SUGARLIKE	SUITINGS	SULFIDS
SUDDERS	SUFFERED	SUGARLOAF	SUITLIKE	SULFINYL
SUDDS	SUFFERER	SUGARPLUM	SUITOR	SULFINYLS
SUDOKU	SUFFERERS	SUGARS	SUITORED	SULFITE
SUDOKUS	SUFFERING	SUGARY	SUITORING	SULFITES
SUDOR	SUFFERS	SUGGED	SUITORS	SULFITIC
SUDORAL	SUFFETE	SUGGEST	SUITRESS	SULFO
SUDORIFIC	SUFFETES	SUGGESTED	SUITS	SULFONATE
SUDOROUS	SUFFICE	SUGGESTER	SUIVANTE	SULFONE
SUDORS	SUFFICED	SUGGESTS	SUIVANTES	SULFONES

S

SULFONIC	SULPHATES	SUMMAND	SUMOS	SUNBLOCKS
SULFONIUM	SULPHATIC	SUMMANDS	SUMOTORI	SUNBONNET
SULFONYL	SULPHID	SUMMAR	SUMOTORIS	SUNBOW
SULFONYLS	SULPHIDE	SUMMARIES	SUMP	SUNBOWS
SULFOXIDE	SULPHIDES	SUMMARILY	SUMPH	SUNBRIGHT
SULFUR	SULPHIDS	SUMMARISE	SUMPHISH	SUNBURN
SULFURATE	SULPHINYL	SUMMARIST	SUMPHS	SUNBURNED
SULFURED	SULPHITE	SUMMARIZE	SUMPIT	SUNBURNS
SULFURET	SULPHITES	SUMMARY	SUMPITAN	SUNBURNT
SULFURETS	SULPHITIC	SUMMAS	SUMPITANS	SUNBURST
SULFURIC	SULPHONE	SUMMAT	SUMPITS	SUNBURSTS
SULFURIER	SULPHONES	SUMMATE	SUMPS	SUNCARE
SULFURING	SULPHONIC	SUMMATED	SUMPSIMUS	SUNCARES
SULFURISE	SULPHONYL	SUMMATES	SUMPTER	SUNCHOKE
SULFURIZE	SULPHS	SUMMATING	SUMPTERS	SUNCHOKES
SULFUROUS	SULPHUR	SUMMATION	SUMPTUARY	SUNDAE
SULFURS	SULPHURED	SUMMATIVE	SUMPTUOUS	SUNDAES
SULFURY	SULPHURET	SUMMATS	SUMPWEED	SUNDARI
SULFURYL	SULPHURIC	SUMMED	SUMPWEEDS	SUNDARIS
SULFURYLS	SULPHURS	SUMMER	SUMS	SUNDECK
SULK	SULPHURY	SUMMERED	SUMY	SUNDECKS
SULKED	SULPHURYL	SUMMERIER	SUN	SUNDER
SULKER	SULTAN	SUMMERING	SUNBACK	SUNDERED
SULKERS	SULTANA	SUMMERLY	SUNBAKE	SUNDERER
SULKIER	SULTANAS	SUMMERS	SUNBAKED	SUNDERERS
SULKIES	SULTANATE	SUMMERSET	SUNBAKES	SUNDERING
SULKIEST	SULTANESS	SUMMERY	SUNBAKING	SUNDERS
SULKILY	SULTANIC	SUMMING	SUNBATH	SUNDEW
SULKINESS	SULTANS	SUMMINGS	SUNBATHE	SUNDEWS
SULKING	SULTRIER	SUMMIST	SUNBATHED	SUNDIAL
SULKS	SULTRIEST	SUMMISTS	SUNBATHER	SUNDIALS
SULKY	SULTRILY	SUMMIT	SUNBATHES	SUNDOG
SULLAGE	SULTRY	SUMMITAL	SUNBATHS	SUNDOGS
SULLAGES	SULU	SUMMITED	SUNBEAM	SUNDOWN
SULLEN	SULUS	SUMMITEER	SUNBEAMED	SUNDOWNED
SULLENER	SUM	SUMMITING	SUNBEAMS	SUNDOWNER
SULLENEST	SUMAC	SUMMITRY	SUNBEAMY	SUNDOWNS
SULLENLY	SUMACH	SUMMITS	SUNBEAT	SUNDRA
SULLENS	SUMACHS	SUMMON	SUNBEATEN	SUNDRAS
SULLIABLE	SUMACS	SUMMONED	SUNBED	SUNDRESS
SULLIED	SUMATRA	SUMMONER	SUNBEDS	SUNDRI
SULLIES	SUMATRAS	SUMMONERS	SUNBELT	SUNDRIES
SULLY	SUMBITCH	SUMMONING	SUNBELTS	SUNDRILY
SULLYING	SUMI	SUMMONS	SUNBERRY	SUNDRIS
SULPH	SUMIS	SUMMONSED	SUNBIRD	SUNDROPS
SULPHA	SUMLESS	SUMMONSES	SUNBIRDS	SUNDRY
SULPHAS	SUMMA	SUMO	SUNBLIND	SUNFAST
SULPHATE	SUMMABLE	SUMOIST	SUNBLINDS	SUNFISH
SULPHATED	SUMMAE	SUMOISTS	SUNBLOCK	SUNFISHES

S

SUNFLOWER	SUNPORCH	SUPER	SUPERFLUX	SUPERPIMP
SUNG	SUNPROOF	SUPERABLE	SUPERFLY	SUPERPLUS
SUNGAR	SUNRAY	SUPERABLY	SUPERFOOD	SUPERPORT
SUNGARS	SUNRAYS	SUPERADD	SUPERFUND	SUPERPOSE
SUNGAZER	SUNRISE	SUPERADDS	SUPERFUSE	SUPERPRO
SUNGAZERS	SUNRISES	SUPERATE	SUPERGENE	SUPERPROS
SUNGAZING	SUNRISING	SUPERATED	SUPERGLUE	SUPERRACE
SUNGLASS	SUNROOF	SUPERATES	SUPERGOOD	SUPERREAL
SUNGLOW	SUNROOFS	SUPERATOM	SUPERGUN	SUPERRICH
SUNGLOWS	SUNROOM	SUPERB	SUPERGUNS	SUPERROAD
SUNGREBE	SUNROOMS	SUPERBAD	SUPERHARD	SUPERS
SUNGREBES	SUNS	SUPERBANK	SUPERHEAT	SUPERSAFE
SUNHAT	SUNSCALD	SUPERBER	SUPERHERO	SUPERSALE
SUNHATS	SUNSCALDS	SUPERBEST	SUPERHET	SUPERSALT
SUNI	SUNSCREEN	SUPERBIKE	SUPERHETS	SUPERSAUR
SUNIS	SUNSEEKER	SUPERBITY	SUPERHIGH	SUPERSEDE
SUNK	SUNSET	SUPERBLY	SUPERHIT	SUPERSELL
SUNKEN	SUNSETS	SUPERBOLD	SUPERHITS	SUPERSET
SUNKER	SUNSETTED	SUPERBOMB	SUPERHIVE	SUPERSETS
SUNKERS	SUNSHADE	SUPERBRAT	SUPERHOT	SUPERSEX
SUNKET	SUNSHADES	SUPERBUG	SUPERHYPE	SUPERSHOW
SUNKETS	SUNSHINE	SUPERBUGS	SUPERING	SUPERSIZE
SUNKIE	SUNSHINES	SUPERCAR	SUPERIOR	SUPERSOFT
SUNKIES	SUNSHINY	SUPERCARS	SUPERIORS	SUPERSOLD
SUNKS	SUNSPECS	SUPERCEDE	SUPERJET	SUPERSPY
SUNLAMP	SUNSPOT	SUPERCELL	SUPERJETS	SUPERSTAR
SUNLAMPS	SUNSPOTS	SUPERCHIC	SUPERJOCK	SUPERSTUD
SUNLAND	SUNSTAR	SUPERCITY	SUPERLAIN	SUPERTASK
SUNLANDS	SUNSTARS	SUPERCLUB	SUPERLAY	SUPERTAX
SUNLESS	SUNSTONE	SUPERCOIL	SUPERLIE	SUPERTHIN
SUNLESSLY	SUNSTONES	SUPERCOLD	SUPERLIES	SUPERTRAM
SUNLIGHT	SUNSTROKE	SUPERCOOL	SUPERLOAD	SUPERUSER
SUNLIGHTS	SUNSTRUCK	SUPERCOP	SUPERLONG	SUPERVENE
SUNLIKE	SUNSUIT	SUPERCOPS	SUPERLOO	SUPERVISE
SUNLIT	SUNSUITS	SUPERCOW	SUPERLOOS	SUPERWAIF
SUNN	SUNTAN	SUPERCOWS	SUPERMALE	SUPERWAVE
SUNNA	SUNTANNED	SUPERCUTE	SUPERMAN	SUPERWEED
SUNNAH	SUNTANS	SUPERED	SUPERMART	SUPERWIDE
SUNNAHS	SUNTRAP	SUPEREGO	SUPERMAX	SUPERWIFE
SUNNAS	SUNTRAPS	SUPEREGOS	SUPERMEN	SUPES
SUNNED	SUNUP	SUPERETTE	SUPERMIND	SUPINATE
SUNNIER	SUNUPS	SUPERFAN	SUPERMINI	SUPINATED
SUNNIES	SUNWARD	SUPERFANS	SUPERMOM	SUPINATES
SUNNIEST	SUNWARDS	SUPERFARM	SUPERMOMS	SUPINATOR
SUNNILY	SUNWISE	SUPERFAST	SUPERMOON	SUPINE
SUNNINESS	SUP	SUPERFINE	SUPERMOTO	SUPINELY
SUNNING	SUPAWN	SUPERFIRM	SUPERNAL	SUPINES
SUNNS	SUPAWNS	SUPERFIT	SUPERNATE	SUPLEX
SUNNY	SUPE	SUPERFIX	SUPERNOVA	SUPLEXES

S

SUPPAWN	SUPREMEST	SURED	SURFY	SURNAMING
SUPPAWNS	SUPREMITY	SUREFIRE	SURGE	SURPASS
SUPPEAGO	SUPREMO	SURELY	SURGED	SURPASSED
SUPPED	SUPREMOS	SURENESS	SURGEFUL	SURPASSER
SUPPER	SUPREMUM	SURER	SURGELESS	SURPASSES
SUPPERED	SUPREMUMS	SURES	SURGENT	SURPLICE
SUPPERING	SUPS	SUREST	SURGEON	SURPLICED
SUPPERS	SUQ	SURETIED	SURGEONCY	SURPLICES
SUPPING	SUQS	SURETIES	SURGEONS	SURPLUS
SUPPLANT	SUR	SURETY	SURGER	SURPLUSED
SUPPLANTS	SURA	SURETYING	SURGERIES	SURPLUSES
SUPPLE	SURAH	SURF	SURGERS	SURPRINT
SUPPLED	SURAHS	SURFABLE	SURGERY	SURPRINTS
SUPPLELY	SURAL	SURFACE	SURGES	SURPRISAL
SUPPLER	SURAMIN	SURFACED	SURGICAL	SURPRISE
SUPPLES	SURAMINS	SURFACER	SURGIER	SURPRISED
SUPPLEST	SURANCE	SURFACERS	SURGIEST	SURPRISER
SUPPLIAL	SURANCES	SURFACES	SURGING	SURPRISES
SUPPLIALS	SURAS	SURFACING	SURGINGS	SURPRIZE
SUPPLIANT	SURAT	SURFBIRD	SURGY	SURPRIZED
SUPPLICAT	SURATS	SURFBIRDS	SURICATE	SURPRIZES
SUPPLIED	SURBAHAR	SURFBOARD	SURICATES	SURQUEDRY
SUPPLIER	SURBAHARS	SURFBOAT	SURIMI	SURQUEDY
SUPPLIERS	SURBASE	SURFBOATS	SURIMIS	SURRA
SUPPLIES	SURBASED	SURFED	SURING	SURRAS
SUPPLING	SURBASES	SURFEIT	SURLIER	SURREAL
SUPPLY	SURBATE	SURFEITED	SURLIEST	SURREALLY
SUPPLYING	SURBATED	SURFEITER	SURLILY	SURREALS
SUPPORT	SURBATES	SURFEITS	SURLINESS	SURREBUT
SUPPORTED	SURBATING	SURFER	SURLOIN	SURREBUTS
SUPPORTER	SURBED	SURFERS	SURLOINS	SURREINED
SUPPORTS	SURBEDDED	SURFFISH	SURLY	SURREJOIN
SUPPOSAL	SURBEDS	SURFICIAL	SURMASTER	SURRENDER
SUPPOSALS	SURBET	SURFIE	SURMISAL	SURRENDRY
SUPPOSE	SURCEASE	SURFIER	SURMISALS	SURREY
SUPPOSED	SURCEASED	SURFIES	SURMISE	SURREYS
SUPPOSER	SURCEASES	SURFIEST	SURMISED	SURROGACY
SUPPOSERS	SURCHARGE	SURFING	SURMISER	SURROGATE
SUPPOSES	SURCINGLE	SURFINGS	SURMISERS	SURROUND
SUPPOSING	SURCOAT	SURFLIKE	SURMISES	SURROUNDS
SUPPRESS	SURCOATS	SURFMAN	SURMISING	SURROYAL
SUPPURATE	SURCULI	SURFMEN	SURMOUNT	SURROYALS
SUPRA	SURCULOSE	SURFPERCH	SURMOUNTS	SURTAX
SUPREMA	SURCULUS	SURFRIDE	SURMULLET	SURTAXED
SUPREMACY	SURD	SURFRIDER	SURNAME	SURTAXES
SUPREME	SURDITIES	SURFRIDES	SURNAMED	SURTAXING
SUPREMELY	SURDITY	SURFRODE	SURNAMER	SURTITLE
SUPREMER	SURDS	SURFS	SURNAMERS	SURTITLES
SUPREMES	SURE	SURFSIDE	SURNAMES	SURTOUT

S

SURTOUTS	SUSPENSER	SUTURES	SWAGGERS	SWAMPS
SURUCUCU	SUSPENSES	SUTURING	SWAGGIE	SWAMPY
SURUCUCUS	SUSPENSOR	SUZERAIN	SWAGGIES	SWAMY
SURVEIL	SUSPICION	SUZERAINS	SWAGGING	SWAN
SURVEILED	SUSPIRE	SVARAJ	SWAGING	SWANG
SURVEILLE	SUSPIRED	SVARAJES	SWAGMAN	SWANHERD
SURVEILS	SUSPIRES	SVASTIKA	SWAGMEN	SWANHERDS
SURVEY	SUSPIRING	SVASTIKAS	SWAGS	SWANK
SURVEYAL	SUSS	SVEDBERG	SWAGSHOP	SWANKED
SURVEYALS	SUSSED	SVEDBERGS	SWAGSHOPS	SWANKER
SURVEYED	SUSSES	SVELTE	SWAGSMAN	SWANKERS
SURVEYING	SUSSING	SVELTELY	SWAGSMEN	SWANKEST
SURVEYOR	SUSTAIN	SVELTER	SWAIL	SWANKEY
SURVEYORS	SUSTAINED	SVELTEST	SWAILS	SWANKEYS
SURVEYS	SUSTAINER	SWAB	SWAIN	SWANKIE
SURVIEW	SUSTAINS	SWABBED	SWAINING	SWANKIER
SURVIEWED	SUSTINENT	SWABBER	SWAININGS	SWANKIES
SURVIEWS	SUSU	SWABBERS	SWAINISH	SWANKIEST
SURVIVAL	SUSURRANT	SWABBIE	SWAINS	SWANKILY
SURVIVALS	SUSURRATE	SWABBIES	SWALE	SWANKING
SURVIVE	SUSURROUS	SWABBING	SWALED	SWANKPOT
SURVIVED	SUSURRUS	SWABBY	SWALES	SWANKPOTS
SURVIVER	SUSUS	SWABS	SWALIER	SWANKS
SURVIVERS	SUTILE	SWACHH	SWALIEST	SWANKY
SURVIVES	SUTLER	SWACK	SWALING	SWANLIKE
SURVIVING	SUTLERIES	SWACKED	SWALINGS	SWANNED
SURVIVOR	SUTLERS	SWACKING	SWALLET	SWANNERY
SURVIVORS	SUTLERY	SWACKS	SWALLETS	SWANNIE
SUS	SUTOR	SWAD	SWALLIES	SWANNIER
SUSCEPTOR	SUTORIAL	SWADDIE	SWALLOW	SWANNIES
SUSCITATE	SUTORIAN	SWADDIES	SWALLOWED	SWANNIEST
SUSED	SUTORS	SWADDLE	SWALLOWER	SWANNING
SUSES	SUTRA	SWADDLED	SWALLOWS	SWANNINGS
SUSHI	SUTRAS	SWADDLER	SWALLY	SWANNY
SUSHIS	SUTTA	SWADDLERS	SWALY	SWANPAN
SUSING	SUTTAS	SWADDLES	SWAM	SWANPANS
SUSLIK	SUTTEE	SWADDLING	SWAMI	SWANS
SUSLIKS	SUTTEEISM	SWADDY	SWAMIES	SWANSDOWN
SUSPECT	SUTTEES	SWADS	SWAMIS	SWANSKIN
SUSPECTED	SUTTLE	SWAG	SWAMP	SWANSKINS
SUSPECTER	SUTTLED	SWAGE	SWAMPED	SWANSONG
SUSPECTS	SUTTLES	SWAGED	SWAMPER	SWANSONGS
SUSPENCE	SUTTLETIE	SWAGER	SWAMPERS	SWAP
SUSPEND	SUTTLING	SWAGERS	SWAMPIER	SWAPFILE
SUSPENDED	SUTTLY	SWAGES	SWAMPIEST	SWAPFILES
SUSPENDER	SUTURAL	SWAGGED	SWAMPING	SWAPPABLE
SUSPENDS	SUTURALLY	SWAGGER	SWAMPISH	SWAPPED
SUSPENS	SUTURE	SWAGGERED	SWAMPLAND	SWAPPER
SUSPENSE	SUTURED	SWAGGERER	SWAMPLESS	SWAPPERS

SWAPPING	SWASHIEST	SWAYLING	SWEELING	SWEETVELD
SWAPPINGS	SWASHING	SWAYLINGS	SWEELS	SWEETWOOD
SWAPS	SWASHINGS	SWAYLS	SWEENEY	SWEETY
SWAPT	SWASHWORK	SWAYS	SWEENEYS	SWEIR
SWAPTION	SWASHY	SWAZZLE	SWEENIES	SWEIRED
SWAPTIONS	SWASTICA	SWAZZLES	SWEENY	SWEIRER
SWARAJ	SWASTICAS	SWEAL	SWEEP	SWEIREST
SWARAJES	SWASTIKA	SWEALED	SWEEPBACK	SWEIRING
SWARAJISM	SWASTIKAS	SWEALING	SWEEPER	SWEIRNESS
SWARAJIST	SWAT	SWEALINGS	SWEEPERS	SWEIRS
SWARD	SWATCH	SWEALS	SWEEPIER	SWEIRT
SWARDED	SWATCHES	SWEAR	SWEEPIEST	SWELCHIE
SWARDIER	SWATH	SWEARD	SWEEPING	SWELCHIES
SWARDIEST	SWATHABLE	SWEARDS	SWEEPINGS	SWELL
SWARDING	SWATHE	SWEARER	SWEEPS	SWELLDOM
SWARDS	SWATHED	SWEARERS	SWEEPY	SWELLDOMS
SWARDY	SWATHER	SWEARIER	SWEER	SWELLED
SWARE	SWATHERS	SWEARIEST	SWEERED	SWELLER
SWARF	SWATHES	SWEARING	SWEERING	SWELLERS
SWARFED	SWATHIER	SWEARINGS	SWEERS	SWELLEST
SWARFING	SWATHIEST	SWEARS	SWEERT	SWELLFISH
SWARFS	SWATHING	SWEARWORD	SWEES	SWELLHEAD
SWARM	SWATHINGS	SWEARY	SWEET	SWELLING
SWARMED	SWATHS	SWEAT	SWEETCORN	SWELLINGS
SWARMER	SWATHY	SWEATBAND	SWEETED	SWELLISH
SWARMERS	SWATS	SWEATBOX	SWEETEN	SWELLS
SWARMING	SWATTED	SWEATED	SWEETENED	SWELT
SWARMINGS	SWATTER	SWEATER	SWEETENER	SWELTED
SWARMS	SWATTERED	SWEATERED	SWEETENS	SWELTER
SWART	SWATTERS	SWEATERS	SWEETER	SWELTERED
SWARTH	SWATTIER	SWEATIER	SWEETEST	SWELTERS
SWARTHIER	SWATTIEST	SWEATIEST	SWEETFISH	SWELTING
SWARTHILY	SWATTING	SWEATILY	SWEETIE	SWELTRIER
SWARTHS	SWATTINGS	SWEATING	SWEETIES	SWELTRY
SWARTHY	SWATTY	SWEATINGS	SWEETING	SWELTS
SWARTIER	SWAY	SWEATLESS	SWEETINGS	SWEPT
SWARTIEST	SWAYABLE	SWEATS	SWEETISH	SWEPTBACK
SWARTNESS	SWAYBACK	SWEATSHOP	SWEETLIP	SWEPTWING
SWARTY	SWAYBACKS	SWEATSUIT	SWEETLIPS	SWERF
SWARVE	SWAYBAR	SWEATY	SWEETLY	SWERFED
SWARVED	SWAYBARS	SWEDE	SWEETMAN	SWERFING
SWARVES	SWAYED	SWEDES	SWEETMEAL	SWERFS
SWARVING	SWAYER	SWEDGER	SWEETMEAT	SWERVABLE
SWASH	SWAYERS	SWEDGERS	SWEETMEN	SWERVE
SWASHED	SWAYFUL	SWEE	SWEETNESS	SWERVED
SWASHER	SWAYING	SWEED	SWEETS	SWERVER
SWASHERS	SWAYINGS	SWEEING	SWEETSHOP	SWERVERS
SWASHES	SWAYL	SWEEL	SWEETSOP	SWERVES
SWASHIER	SWAYLED	SWEELED	SWEETSOPS	SWERVING

SWERVINGS	SWIMMIEST	SWINGLE	SWISHIEST	SWIZZLING
SWEVEN	SWIMMILY	SWINGLED	SWISHING	SWOB
SWEVENS	SWIMMING	SWINGLES	SWISHINGS	SWOBBED
SWEY	SWIMMINGS	SWINGLING	SWISHY	SWOBBER
SWEYED	SWIMMY	SWINGMAN	SWISS	SWOBBERS
SWEYING	SWIMS	SWINGMEN	SWISSES	SWOBBING
SWEYS	SWIMSUIT	SWINGS	SWISSING	SWOBS
SWIDDEN	SWIMSUITS	SWINGTAIL	SWISSINGS	SWOFFER
SWIDDENS	SWIMWEAR	SWINGTREE	SWITCH	SWOFFERS
SWIES	SWIMWEARS	SWINGY	SWITCHED	SWOFFING
SWIFT	SWINDGE	SWINISH	SWITCHEL	SWOFFINGS
SWIFTED	SWINDGED	SWINISHLY	SWITCHELS	SWOLE
SWIFTER	SWINDGES	SWINK	SWITCHER	SWOLER
SWIFTERS	SWINDGING	SWINKED	SWITCHERS	SWOLEST
SWIFTEST	SWINDLE	SWINKER	SWITCHES	SWOLLEN
SWIFTIE	SWINDLED	SWINKERS	SWITCHIER	SWOLLENLY
SWIFTIES	SWINDLER	SWINKING	SWITCHING	SWOLN
SWIFTING	SWINDLERS	SWINKS	SWITCHMAN	SWOON
SWIFTLET	SWINDLES	SWINNEY	SWITCHMEN	SWOONED
SWIFTLETS	SWINDLING	SWINNEYS	SWITCHY	SWOONER
SWIFTLY	SWINE	SWIPE	SWITH	SWOONERS
SWIFTNESS	SWINEHERD	SWIPED	SWITHE	SWOONIER
SWIFTS	SWINEHOOD	SWIPER	SWITHER	SWOONIEST
SWIFTY	SWINELIKE	SWIPERS	SWITHERED	SWOONING
SWIG	SWINEPOX	SWIPES	SWITHERS	SWOONINGS
SWIGGED	SWINERIES	SWIPEY	SWITHLY	SWOONS
SWIGGER	SWINERY	SWIPIER	SWITS	SWOONY
SWIGGERS	SWINES	SWIPIEST	SWITSES	SWOOP
SWIGGING	SWING	SWIPING	SWIVE	SWOOPED
SWIGS	SWINGARM	SWIPLE	SWIVED	SWOOPER
SWILE	SWINGARMS	SWIPLES	SWIVEL	SWOOPERS
SWILER	SWINGBEAT	SWIPPLE	SWIVELED	SWOOPIER
SWILERS	SWINGBIN	SWIPPLES	SWIVELING	SWOOPIEST
SWILES	SWINGBINS	SWIRE	SWIVELLED	SWOOPING
SWILING	SWINGBOAT	SWIRES	SWIVELS	SWOOPS
SWILINGS	SWINGBY	SWIRL	SWIVES	SWOOPY
SWILL	SWINGBYS	SWIRLED	SWIVET	SWOOSH
SWILLED	SWINGE	SWIRLIER	SWIVETS	SWOOSHED
SWILLER	SWINGED	SWIRLIEST	SWIVING	SWOOSHES
SWILLERS	SWINGEING	SWIRLING	SWIZ	SWOOSHING
SWILLING	SWINGER	SWIRLS	SWIZZ	SWOP
SWILLINGS	SWINGERS	SWIRLY	SWIZZED	SWOPPABLE
SWILLS	SWINGES	SWISH	SWIZZES	SWOPPED
SWIM	SWINGIER	SWISHED	SWIZZING	SWOPPER
SWIMMABLE	SWINGIEST	SWISHER	SWIZZLE	SWOPPERS
SWIMMER	SWINGING	SWISHERS	SWIZZLED	SWOPPING
SWIMMERET	SWINGINGS	SWISHES	SWIZZLER	SWOPPINGS
SWIMMERS	SWINGISM	SWISHEST	SWIZZLERS	SWOPS
SWIMMIER	SWINGISMS	SWISHIER	SWIZZLES	SWOPT

SWORD	SYBARITES	SYLLABICS	SYLVINS	SYMPHYSIS
SWORDBILL	SYBARITIC	SYLLABIFY	SYLVITE	SYMPHYTIC
SWORDED	SYBBE	SYLLABISE	SYLVITES	SYMPLAST
SWORDER	SYBBES	SYLLABISM	SYMAR	SYMPLASTS
SWORDERS	SYBIL	SYLLABIZE	SYMARS	SYMPLOCE
SWORDFERN	SYBILS	SYLLABLE	SYMBION	SYMPLOCES
SWORDFISH	SYBO	SYLLABLED	SYMBIONS	SYMPODIA
SWORDING	SYBOE	SYLLABLES	SYMBIONT	SYMPODIAL
SWORDLESS	SYBOES	SYLLABUB	SYMBIONTS	SYMPODIUM
SWORDLIKE	SYBOTIC	SYLLABUBS	SYMBIOSES	SYMPOSIA
SWORDMAN	SYBOTISM	SYLLABUS	SYMBIOSIS	SYMPOSIAC
SWORDMEN	SYBOTISMS	SYLLEPSES	SYMBIOT	SYMPOSIAL
SWORDPLAY	SYBOW	SYLLEPSIS	SYMBIOTE	SYMPOSIUM
SWORDS	SYBOWS	SYLLEPTIC	SYMBIOTES	SYMPTOM
SWORDSMAN	SYCAMINE	SYLLOGE	SYMBIOTIC	SYMPTOMS
SWORDSMEN	SYCAMINES	SYLLOGES	SYMBIOTS	SYMPTOSES
SWORDTAIL	SYCAMORE	SYLLOGISE	SYMBOL	SYMPTOSIS
SWORE	SYCAMORES	SYLLOGISM	SYMBOLE	SYMPTOTIC
SWORN	SYCE	SYLLOGIST	SYMBOLED	SYN
SWOT	SYCEE	SYLLOGIZE	SYMBOLES	SYNAGOG
SWOTS	SYCEES	SYLPH	SYMBOLIC	SYNAGOGAL
SWOTTED	SYCES	SYLPHIC	SYMBOLICS	SYNAGOGS
SWOTTER	SYCOMORE	SYLPHID	SYMBOLING	SYNAGOGUE
SWOTTERS	SYCOMORES	SYLPHIDE	SYMBOLISE	SYNALEPHA
SWOTTIER	SYCON	SYLPHIDES	SYMBOLISM	SYNANDRIA
SWOTTIEST	SYCONIA	SYLPHIDS	SYMBOLIST	SYNANGIA
SWOTTING	SYCONIUM	SYLPHIER	SYMBOLIZE	SYNANGIUM
SWOTTINGS	SYCONOID	SYLPHIEST	SYMBOLLED	SYNANON
SWOTTY	SYCONS	SYLPHINE	SYMBOLOGY	SYNANONS
SWOUN	SYCOPHANT	SYLPHISH	SYMBOLS	SYNANTHIC
SWOUND	SYCOSES	SYLPHLIKE	SYMITAR	SYNANTHY
SWOUNDED	SYCOSIS	SYLPHS	SYMITARE	SYNAPHEA
SWOUNDING	SYE	SYLPHY	SYMITARES	SYNAPHEAS
SWOUNDS	SYED	SYLVA	SYMITARS	SYNAPHEIA
SWOUNE	SYEING	SYLVAE	SYMMETRAL	SYNAPSE
SWOUNED	SYEN	SYLVAN	SYMMETRIC	SYNAPSED
SWOUNES	SYENITE	SYLVANER	SYMMETRY	SYNAPSES
SWOUNING	SYENITES	SYLVANERS	SYMPATHIN	SYNAPSID
SWOUNS	SYENITIC	SYLVANITE	SYMPATHY	SYNAPSIDS
SWOWND	SYENS	SYLVANS	SYMPATICO	SYNAPSING
SWOWNDS	SYES	SYLVAS	SYMPATRIC	SYNAPSIS
SWOWNE	SYKE	SYLVATIC	SYMPATRY	SYNAPTASE
SWOWNES	SYKER	SYLVIA	SYMPETALY	SYNAPTE
SWOZZLE	SYKES	SYLVIAS	SYMPHILE	SYNAPTES
SWOZZLES	SYLI	SYLVIINE	SYMPHILES	SYNAPTIC
SWUM	SYLIS	SYLVIN	SYMPHILY	SYNARCHY
SWUNG	SYLLABARY	SYLVINE	SYMPHONIC	SYNASTRY
SWY	SYLLABI	SYLVINES	SYMPHONY	SYNAXARIA
SYBARITE	SYLLABIC	SYLVINITE	SYMPHYSES	SYNAXES

S

SYNAXIS	SYNDROME	SYNKARYON	SYNTEXIS	SYRAH
SYNBIOTIC	SYNDROMES	SYNOD	SYNTH	SYRAHS
SYNC	SYNDROMIC	SYNODAL	SYNTHASE	SYREN
SYNCARP	SYNDS	SYNODALS	SYNTHASES	SYRENS
SYNCARPS	SYNE	SYNODIC	SYNTHESES	SYRETTE
SYNCARPY	SYNECHIA	SYNODICAL	SYNTHESIS	SYRETTES
SYNCED	SYNECHIAS	SYNODS	SYNTHETIC	SYRINGA
SYNCH	SYNECIOUS	SYNODSMAN	SYNTHON	SYRINGAS
SYNCHED	SYNECTIC	SYNODSMEN	SYNTHONS	SYRINGE
SYNCHING	SYNECTICS	SYNOECETE	SYNTHPOP	SYRINGEAL
SYNCHRO	SYNED	SYNOECISE	SYNTHPOPS	SYRINGED
SYNCHRONY	SYNEDRIA	SYNOECISM	SYNTHRONI	SYRINGES
SYNCHROS	SYNEDRIAL	SYNOECIZE	SYNTHS	SYRINGING
SYNCHS	SYNEDRION	SYNOEKETE	SYNTONE	SYRINX
SYNCHYSES	SYNEDRIUM	SYNOICOUS	SYNTONES	SYRINXES
SYNCHYSIS	SYNERESES	SYNONYM	SYNTONIC	SYRPHIAN
SYNCING	SYNERESIS	SYNONYME	SYNTONIES	SYRPHIANS
SYNCLINAL	SYNERGIA	SYNONYMES	SYNTONIN	SYRPHID
SYNCLINE	SYNERGIAS	SYNONYMIC	SYNTONINS	SYRPHIDS
SYNCLINES	SYNERGIC	SYNONYMS	SYNTONISE	SYRTES
SYNCOM	SYNERGID	SYNONYMY	SYNTONIZE	SYRTIS
SYNCOMS	SYNERGIDS	SYNOPSES	SYNTONOUS	SYRUP
SYNCOPAL	SYNERGIES	SYNOPSIS	SYNTONY	SYRUPED
SYNCOPATE	SYNERGISE	SYNOPSISE	SYNTYPE	SYRUPIER
SYNCOPE	SYNERGISM	SYNOPSIZE	SYNTYPES	SYRUPIEST
SYNCOPES	SYNERGIST	SYNOPTIC	SYNURA	SYRUPING
SYNCOPIC	SYNERGIZE	SYNOPTICS	SYNURAE	SYRUPLIKE
SYNCOPTIC	SYNERGY	SYNOPTIST	SYPE	SYRUPS
SYNCRETIC	SYNES	SYNOVIA	SYPED	SYRUPY
SYNCS	SYNESES	SYNOVIAL	SYPES	SYSADMIN
SYNCYTIA	SYNESIS	SYNOVIAS	SYPH	SYSADMINS
SYNCYTIAL	SYNESISES	SYNOVITIC	SYPHER	SYSOP
SYNCYTIUM	SYNFUEL	SYNOVITIS	SYPHERED	SYSOPS
SYND	SYNFUELS	SYNROC	SYPHERING	SYSSITIA
SYNDACTYL	SYNGAMIC	SYNROCS	SYPHERS	SYSSITIAS
SYNDED	SYNGAMIES	SYNTACTIC	SYPHILIS	SYSTALTIC
SYNDESES	SYNGAMOUS	SYNTAGM	SYPHILISE	SYSTEM
SYNDESIS	SYNGAMY	SYNTAGMA	SYPHILIZE	SYSTEMED
SYNDET	SYNGAS	SYNTAGMAS	SYPHILOID	SYSTEMIC
SYNDETIC	SYNGASES	SYNTAGMIC	SYPHILOMA	SYSTEMICS
SYNDETON	SYNGASSES	SYNTAGMS	SYPHON	SYSTEMISE
SYNDETONS	SYNGENEIC	SYNTAN	SYPHONAGE	SYSTEMIZE
SYNDETS	SYNGENIC	SYNTANS	SYPHONAL	SYSTEMS
SYNDIC	SYNGRAPH	SYNTAX	SYPHONED	SYSTOLE
SYNDICAL	SYNGRAPHS	SYNTAXES	SYPHONIC	SYSTOLES
SYNDICATE	SYNING	SYNTECTIC	SYPHONING	SYSTOLIC
SYNDICS	SYNIZESES	SYNTENIC	SYPHONS	SYSTYLE
SYNDING	SYNIZESIS	SYNTENIES	SYPHS	SYSTYLES
SYNDINGS	SYNKARYA	SYNTENY	SYPING	SYTHE

SYTHES	SYVERS	SYZYGETIC	SYZYGIES
SYVER	SYZYGAL	SYZYGIAL	SYZYGY

S

T

TA	TABERED	TABLOID	TABUED	TACHYLYTE
TAAL	TABERING	TABLOIDS	TABUING	TACHYON
TAALS	TABERS	TABLOIDY	TABULA	TACHYONIC
TAATA	TABES	TABOGGAN	TABULABLE	TACHYONS
TAATAS	TABESCENT	TABOGGANS	TABULAE	TACHYPNEA
TAB	TABETIC	TABOO	TABULAR	TACIT
TABANID	TABETICS	TABOOED	TABULARLY	TACITLY
TABANIDS	TABI	TABOOING	TABULATE	TACITNESS
TABARD	TABID	TABOOLEY	TABULATED	TACITURN
TABARDED	TABINET	TABOOLEYS	TABULATES	TACK
TABARDS	TABINETS	TABOOS	TABULATOR	TACKBOARD
TABARET	TABIS	TABOR	TABULI	TACKED
TABARETS	TABLA	TABORED	TABULIS	TACKER
TABASHEER	TABLAS	TABORER	TABUN	TACKERS
TABASHIR	TABLATURE	TABORERS	TABUNS	TACKET
TABASHIRS	TABLE	TABORET	TABUS	TACKETIER
TABBED	TABLEAU	TABORETS	TACAHOUT	TACKETS
TABBIED	TABLEAUS	TABORIN	TACAHOUTS	TACKETY
TABBIER	TABLEAUX	TABORINE	TACAMAHAC	TACKEY
TABBIES	TABLED	TABORINES	TACAN	TACKIER
TABBIEST	TABLEFUL	TABORING	TACANS	TACKIES
TABBINET	TABLEFULS	TABORINS	TACE	TACKIEST
TABBINETS	TABLELAND	TABORS	TACES	TACKIFIED
TABBING	TABLELESS	TABOULEH	TACET	TACKIFIER
TABBINGS	TABLEMAT	TABOULEHS	TACH	TACKIFIES
TABBIS	TABLEMATE	TABOULI	TACHE	TACKIFY
TABBISES	TABLEMATS	TABOULIS	TACHES	TACKILY
TABBOULEH	TABLES	TABOUR	TACHINA	TACKINESS
TABBOULI	TABLESFUL	TABOURED	TACHINID	TACKING
TABBOULIS	TABLESIDE	TABOURER	TACHINIDS	TACKINGS
TABBY	TABLET	TABOURERS	TACHISM	TACKLE
TABBYHOOD	TABLETED	TABOURET	TACHISME	TACKLED
TABBYING	TABLETING	TABOURETS	TACHISMES	TACKLER
TABEFIED	TABLETOP	TABOURIN	TACHISMS	TACKLERS
TABEFIES	TABLETOPS	TABOURING	TACHIST	TACKLES
TABEFY	TABLETS	TABOURINS	TACHISTE	TACKLESS
TABEFYING	TABLETTED	TABOURS	TACHISTES	TACKLING
TABELLION	TABLEWARE	TABRERE	TACHISTS	TACKLINGS
TABER	TABLEWISE	TABRERES	TACHO	TACKS
TABERD	TABLIER	TABRET	TACHOGRAM	TACKSMAN
TABERDAR	TABLIERS	TABRETS	TACHOS	TACKSMEN
TABERDARS	TABLING	TABS	TACHS	TACKY
TABERDS	TABLINGS	TABU	TACHYLITE	TACMAHACK

TACNODE	TAENIOID	TAGLIONIS	TAILCOATS	TAILSPINS
TACNODES	TAENITE	TAGMA	TAILED	TAILSPUN
TACO	TAENITES	TAGMATA	TAILENDER	TAILSTOCK
TACONITE	TAES	TAGMEME	TAILER	TAILWATER
TACONITES	TAFFAREL	TAGMEMES	TAILERON	TAILWHEEL
TACOS	TAFFARELS	TAGMEMIC	TAILERONS	TAILWIND
TACRINE	TAFFEREL	TAGMEMICS	TAILERS	TAILWINDS
TACRINES	TAFFERELS	TAGRAG	TAILFAN	TAILYE
TACT	TAFFETA	TAGRAGS	TAILFANS	TAILYES
TACTFUL	TAFFETAS	TAGS	TAILFIN	TAILZIE
TACTFULLY	TAFFETIER	TAGUAN	TAILFINS	TAILZIES
TACTIC	TAFFETY	TAGUANS	TAILFLIES	TAIN
TACTICAL	TAFFIA	TAHA	TAILFLY	TAINS
TACTICIAN	TAFFIAS	TAHAS	TAILGATE	TAINT
TACTICITY	TAFFIES	TAHINA	TAILGATED	TAINTED
TACTICS	TAFFRAIL	TAHINAS	TAILGATER	TAINTING
TACTILE	TAFFRAILS	TAHINI	TAILGATES	TAINTLESS
TACTILELY	TAFFY	TAHINIS	TAILHOOK	TAINTS
TACTILIST	TAFIA	TAHR	TAILHOOKS	TAINTURE
TACTILITY	TAFIAS	TAHRS	TAILING	TAINTURES
TACTION	TAG	TAHSIL	TAILINGS	TAIPAN
TACTIONS	TAGALONG	TAHSILDAR	TAILLAMP	TAIPANS
TACTISM	TAGALONGS	TAHSILS	TAILLAMPS	TAIRA
TACTISMS	TAGAREEN	TAI	TAILLE	TAIRAS
TACTLESS	TAGAREENS	TAIAHA	TAILLES	TAIS
TACTS	TAGBOARD	TAIAHAS	TAILLESS	TAISCH
TACTUAL	TAGBOARDS	TAIGA	TAILLEUR	TAISCHES
TACTUALLY	TAGETES	TAIGAS	TAILLEURS	TAISH
TAD	TAGGANT	TAIGLACH	TAILLIE	TAISHES
TADALAFIL	TAGGANTS	TAIGLE	TAILLIES	TAIT
TADDIE	TAGGED	TAIGLED	TAILLIGHT	TAITS
TADDIES	TAGGEE	TAIGLES	TAILLIKE	TAIVER
TADPOLE	TAGGEES	TAIGLING	TAILOR	TAIVERED
TADPOLES	TAGGER	TAIHOA	TAILORED	TAIVERING
TADS	TAGGERS	TAIHOAED	TAILORESS	TAIVERS
TAE	TAGGIER	TAIHOAING	TAILORING	TAIVERT
TAED	TAGGIEST	TAIHOAS	TAILORS	TAJ
TAEDIUM	TAGGING	TAIKO	TAILPIECE	TAJES
TAEDIUMS	TAGGINGS	TAIKONAUT	TAILPIPE	TAJINE
TAEING	TAGGY	TAIKOS	TAILPIPED	TAJINES
TAEKWONDO	TAGHAIRM	TAIL	TAILPIPES	TAK
TAEL	TAGHAIRMS	TAILARD	TAILPLANE	TAKA
TAELS	TAGINE	TAILARDS	TAILRACE	TAKABLE
TAENIA	TAGINES	TAILBACK	TAILRACES	TAKAHE
TAENIAE	TAGLESS	TAILBACKS	TAILS	TAKAHES
TAENIAS	TAGLIKE	TAILBOARD	TAILSKID	TAKAMAKA
TAENIASES	TAGLINE	TAILBONE	TAILSKIDS	TAKAMAKAS
TAENIASIS	TAGLINES	TAILBONES	TAILSLIDE	TAKAS
TAENIATE	TAGLIONI	TAILCOAT	TAILSPIN	TAKE

TAKEABLE	TALBOT	TALIPOTS	TALLIER	TALOOKAS
TAKEAWAY	TALBOTS	TALISMAN	TALLIERS	TALPA
TAKEAWAYS	TALBOTYPE	TALISMANS	TALLIES	TALPAE
TAKEDOWN	TALC	TALK	TALLIS	TALPAS
TAKEDOWNS	TALCED	TALKABLE	TALLISES	TALUK
TAKEN	TALCIER	TALKATHON	TALLISH	TALUKA
TAKEOFF	TALCIEST	TALKATIVE	TALLISIM	TALUKAS
TAKEOFFS	TALCING	TALKBACK	TALLIT	TALUKDAR
TAKEOUT	TALCKED	TALKBACKS	TALLITES	TALUKDARS
TAKEOUTS	TALCKIER	TALKBOX	TALLITH	TALUKS
TAKEOVER	TALCKIEST	TALKBOXES	TALLITHES	TALUS
TAKEOVERS	TALCKING	TALKED	TALLITHIM	TALUSES
TAKER	TALCKY	TALKER	TALLITHS	TALWEG
TAKERS	TALCOSE	TALKERS	TALLITIM	TALWEGS
TAKES	TALCOUS	TALKFEST	TALLITOT	TAM
TAKEUP	TALCS	TALKFESTS	TALLITOTH	TAMABLE
TAKEUPS	TALCUM	TALKIE	TALLITS	TAMAL
TAKHI	TALCUMED	TALKIER	TALLNESS	TAMALE
TAKHIS	TALCUMING	TALKIES	TALLOL	TAMALES
TAKI	TALCUMS	TALKIEST	TALLOLS	TAMALS
TAKIER	TALCY	TALKINESS	TALLOT	TAMANDU
TAKIEST	TALE	TALKING	TALLOTS	TAMANDUA
TAKIN	TALEA	TALKINGS	TALLOW	TAMANDUAS
TAKING	TALEAE	TALKS	TALLOWED	TAMANDUS
TAKINGLY	TALEFUL	TALKTIME	TALLOWIER	TAMANOIR
TAKINGS	TALEGALLA	TALKTIMES	TALLOWING	TAMANOIRS
TAKINS	TALEGGIO	TALKY	TALLOWISH	TAMANU
TAKIS	TALEGGIOS	TALL	TALLOWS	TAMANUS
TAKKIES	TALENT	TALLAGE	TALLOWY	TAMARA
TAKKY	TALENTED	TALLAGED	TALLS	TAMARACK
TAKS	TALENTS	TALLAGES	TALLY	TAMARACKS
TAKY	TALER	TALLAGING	TALLYHO	TAMARAO
TALA	TALERS	TALLAISIM	TALLYHOED	TAMARAOS
TALAK	TALES	TALLAT	TALLYHOES	TAMARAS
TALAKS	TALESMAN	TALLATS	TALLYHOS	TAMARAU
TALANT	TALESMEN	TALLBOY	TALLYING	TAMARAUS
TALANTS	TALEYSIM	TALLBOYS	TALLYMAN	TAMARI
TALAPOIN	TALI	TALLENT	TALLYMEN	TAMARILLO
TALAPOINS	TALIGRADE	TALLENTS	TALLYSHOP	TAMARIN
TALAQ	TALION	TALLER	TALMA	TAMARIND
TALAQS	TALIONIC	TALLEST	TALMAS	TAMARINDS
TALAR	TALIONS	TALLET	TALMUD	TAMARINS
TALARIA	TALIPAT	TALLETS	TALMUDIC	TAMARIS
TALARS	TALIPATS	TALLGRASS	TALMUDISM	TAMARISK
TALAS	TALIPED	TALLIABLE	TALMUDS	TAMARISKS
TALAUNT	TALIPEDS	TALLIATE	TALON	TAMASHA
TALAUNTS	TALIPES	TALLIATED	TALONED	TAMASHAS
TALAYOT	TALIPESES	TALLIATES	TALONS	TAMBAC
TALAYOTS	TALIPOT	TALLIED	TALOOKA	TAMBACS

TAMBAK	TAMPALA	TANGA	TANGY	TANNERS
TAMBAKS	TAMPALAS	TANGAS	TANH	TANNERY
TAMBALA	TAMPAN	TANGED	TANHS	TANNEST
TAMBALAS	TAMPANS	TANGELO	TANIST	TANNIC
TAMBER	TAMPED	TANGELOS	TANISTRY	TANNIE
TAMBERS	TAMPER	TANGENCE	TANISTS	TANNIES
TAMBOUR	TAMPERED	TANGENCES	TANIWHA	TANNIN
TAMBOURA	TAMPERER	TANGENCY	TANIWHAS	TANNING
TAMBOURAS	TAMPERERS	TANGENT	TANK	TANNINGS
TAMBOURED	TAMPERING	TANGENTAL	TANKA	TANNINS
TAMBOURER	TAMPERS	TANGENTS	TANKAGE	TANNISH
TAMBOURIN	TAMPING	TANGERINE	TANKAGES	TANNOY
TAMBOURS	TAMPINGS	TANGHIN	TANKARD	TANNOYED
TAMBUR	TAMPION	TANGHININ	TANKARDS	TANNOYING
TAMBURA	TAMPIONS	TANGHINS	TANKAS	TANNOYS
TAMBURAS	TAMPON	TANGI	TANKED	TANOREXIC
TAMBURIN	TAMPONADE	TANGIBLE	TANKER	TANREC
TAMBURINS	TAMPONAGE	TANGIBLES	TANKERED	TANRECS
TAMBURS	TAMPONED	TANGIBLY	TANKERING	TANS
TAME	TAMPONING	TANGIE	TANKERS	TANSIES
TAMEABLE	TAMPONS	TANGIER	TANKFUL	TANSY
TAMED	TAMPS	TANGIES	TANKFULS	TANTALATE
TAMEIN	TAMS	TANGIEST	TANKIA	TANTALIC
TAMEINS	TAMWORTH	TANGINESS	TANKIAS	TANTALISE
TAMELESS	TAMWORTHS	TANGING	TANKIES	TANTALISM
TAMELY	TAN	TANGIS	TANKING	TANTALITE
TAMENESS	TANA	TANGLE	TANKINGS	TANTALIZE
TAMER	TANADAR	TANGLED	TANKINI	TANTALOUS
TAMERS	TANADARS	TANGLER	TANKINIS	TANTALUM
TAMES	TANAGER	TANGLERS	TANKLESS	TANTALUMS
TAMEST	TANAGERS	TANGLES	TANKLIKE	TANTALUS
TAMIN	TANAGRA	TANGLIER	TANKS	TANTARA
TAMINE	TANAGRAS	TANGLIEST	TANKSHIP	TANTARARA
TAMINES	TANAGRINE	TANGLING	TANKSHIPS	TANTARAS
TAMING	TANAISTE	TANGLINGS	TANKY	TANTI
TAMINGS	TANAISTES	TANGLY	TANLING	TANTIES
TAMINS	TANALISED	TANGO	TANLINGS	TANTIVIES
TAMIS	TANALIZED	TANGOED	TANNA	TANTIVY
TAMISE	TANAS	TANGOES	TANNABLE	TANTO
TAMISES	TANBARK	TANGOING	TANNAGE	TANTONIES
TAMMAR	TANBARKS	TANGOIST	TANNAGES	TANTONY
TAMMARS	TANDEM	TANGOISTS	TANNAH	TANTOS
TAMMIE	TANDEMS	TANGOLIKE	TANNAHS	TANTRA
TAMMIED	TANDOOR	TANGOS	TANNAS	TANTRAS
TAMMIES	TANDOORI	TANGRAM	TANNATE	TANTRIC
TAMMY	TANDOORIS	TANGRAMS	TANNATES	TANTRISM
TAMMYING	TANDOORS	TANGS	TANNED	TANTRISMS
TAMOXIFEN	TANE	TANGUN	TANNER	TANTRIST
TAMP	TANG	TANGUNS	TANNERIES	TANTRISTS

T

TANTRUM	TAPETED	TAPS	TARDILY	TAROS
TANTRUMS	TAPETI	TAPSMAN	TARDINESS	TAROT
TANTY	TAPETING	TAPSMEN	TARDIVE	TAROTS
TANUKI	TAPETIS	TAPSTER	TARDO	TARP
TANUKIS	TAPETS	TAPSTERS	TARDY	TARPAN
TANYARD	TAPETUM	TAPSTRESS	TARDYING	TARPANS
TANYARDS	TAPETUMS	TAPSTRIES	TARDYON	TARPAPER
TANZANITE	TAPEWORM	TAPSTRY	TARDYONS	TARPAPERS
TAO	TAPEWORMS	TAPU	TARE	TARPAULIN
TAONGA	TAPHOLE	TAPUED	TARED	TARPON
TAONGAS	TAPHOLES	TAPUING	TARES	TARPONS
TAOS	TAPHONOMY	TAPUS	TARGA	TARPS
TAP	TAPHOUSE	TAQUERIA	TARGAS	TARRAGON
TAPA	TAPHOUSES	TAQUERIAS	TARGE	TARRAGONS
TAPACOLO	TAPING	TAR	TARGED	TARRAS
TAPACOLOS	TAPINGS	TARA	TARGES	TARRASES
TAPACULO	TAPIOCA	TARABISH	TARGET	TARRE
TAPACULOS	TAPIOCAS	TARAIRE	TARGETED	TARRED
TAPADERA	TAPIR	TARAIRES	TARGETEER	TARRES
TAPADERAS	TAPIROID	TARAKIHI	TARGETING	TARRIANCE
TAPADERO	TAPIROIDS	TARAKIHIS	TARGETS	TARRIED
TAPADEROS	TAPIRS	TARAMA	TARGING	TARRIER
TAPALO	TAPIS	TARAMAS	TARIFF	TARRIERS
TAPALOS	TAPISES	TARAMEA	TARIFFED	TARRIES
TAPAS	TAPIST	TARAMEAS	TARIFFING	TARRIEST
TAPE	TAPISTS	TARAND	TARIFFS	TARRINESS
TAPEABLE	TAPLASH	TARANDS	TARING	TARRING
TAPED	TAPLASHES	TARANTARA	TARINGS	TARRINGS
TAPELESS	TAPLESS	TARANTAS	TARLATAN	TARROCK
TAPELIKE	TAPPA	TARANTASS	TARLATANS	TARROCKS
TAPELINE	TAPPABLE	TARANTISM	TARLETAN	TARROW
TAPELINES	TAPPAS	TARANTIST	TARLETANS	TARROWED
TAPEN	TAPPED	TARANTULA	TARMAC	TARROWING
TAPENADE	TAPPER	TARAS	TARMACKED	TARROWS
TAPENADES	TAPPERS	TARAXACUM	TARMACS	TARRY
TAPER	TAPPET	TARBOGGIN	TARN	TARRYING
TAPERED	TAPPETS	TARBOOSH	TARNAL	TARS
TAPERER	TAPPICE	TARBOUCHE	TARNALLY	TARSAL
TAPERERS	TAPPICED	TARBOUSH	TARNATION	TARSALGIA
TAPERING	TAPPICES	TARBOY	TARNISH	TARSALS
TAPERINGS	TAPPICING	TARBOYS	TARNISHED	TARSEAL
TAPERNESS	TAPPING	TARBUSH	TARNISHER	TARSEALS
TAPERS	TAPPINGS	TARBUSHES	TARNISHES	TARSEL
TAPERWISE	TAPPIT	TARCEL	TARNS	TARSELS
TAPES	TAPROOM	TARCELS	TARO	TARSI
TAPESTRY	TAPROOMS	TARDIED	TAROC	TARSIA
TAPET	TAPROOT	TARDIER	TAROCS	TARSIAS
TAPETA	TAPROOTED	TARDIES	TAROK	TARSIER
TAPETAL	TAPROOTS	TARDIEST	TAROKS	TARSIERS

TAUTOGS

TARSIOID	TARTUFOS	TASSELL	TATIES	TATUS
TARSIOIDS	TARTY	TASSELLED	TATLER	TAU
TARSIPED	TARWEED	TASSELLS	TATLERS	TAUBE
TARSIPEDS	TARWEEDS	TASSELLY	TATOU	TAUBES
TARSUS	TARWHINE	TASSELS	TATOUAY	TAUGHT
TART	TARWHINES	TASSELY	TATOUAYS	TAUHINU
TARTAN	TARZAN	TASSES	TATOUS	TAUHINUS
TARTANA	TARZANS	TASSET	TATS	TAUHOU
TARTANAS	TAS	TASSETS	TATSOI	TAUHOUS
TARTANE	TASAR	TASSIE	TATSOIS	TAUIWI
TARTANED	TASARS	TASSIES	TATT	TAUIWIS
TARTANES	TASBIH	TASSO	TATTED	TAULD
TARTANRY	TASBIHS	TASSOS	TATTER	TAUNT
TARTANS	TASE	TASSWAGE	TATTERED	TAUNTED
TARTAR	TASED	TASTABLE	TATTERIER	TAUNTER
TARTARE	TASER	TASTE	TATTERING	TAUNTERS
TARTARES	TASERED	TASTEABLE	TATTERS	TAUNTING
TARTARIC	TASERING	TASTED	TATTERY	TAUNTINGS
TARTARISE	TASERS	TASTEFUL	TATTIE	TAUNTS
TARTARIZE	TASES	TASTELESS	TATTIER	TAUON
TARTARLY	TASH	TASTER	TATTIES	TAUONS
TARTAROUS	TASHED	TASTERS	TATTIEST	TAUPATA
TARTARS	TASHES	TASTES	TATTILY	TAUPATAS
TARTED	TASHING	TASTEVIN	TATTINESS	TAUPE
TARTER	TASIMETER	TASTEVINS	TATTING	TAUPES
TARTEST	TASIMETRY	TASTIER	TATTINGS	TAUPIE
TARTIER	TASING	TASTIEST	TATTLE	TAUPIES
TARTIEST	TASK	TASTILY	TATTLED	TAUREAN
TARTILY	TASKBAR	TASTINESS	TATTLER	TAURIC
TARTINE	TASKBARS	TASTING	TATTLERS	TAURIFORM
TARTINES	TASKED	TASTINGS	TATTLES	TAURINE
TARTINESS	TASKER	TASTY	TATTLING	TAURINES
TARTING	TASKERS	TAT	TATTLINGS	TAUS
TARTISH	TASKING	TATAHASH	TATTOO	TAUT
TARTISHLY	TASKINGS	TATAMI	TATTOOED	TAUTAUG
TARTLET	TASKLESS	TATAMIS	TATTOOER	TAUTAUGS
TARTLETS	TASKS	TATAR	TATTOOERS	TAUTED
TARTLY	TASKWORK	TATARS	TATTOOING	TAUTEN
TARTNESS	TASKWORKS	TATE	TATTOOIST	TAUTENED
TARTRATE	TASLET	TATER	TATTOOS	TAUTENING
TARTRATED	TASLETS	TATERS	TATTOW	TAUTENS
TARTRATES	TASS	TATES	TATTOWED	TAUTER
TARTS	TASSA	TATH	TATTOWING	TAUTEST
TARTUFE	TASSAS	TATHATA	TATTOWS	TAUTING
TARTUFES	TASSE	TATHATAS	TATTS	TAUTIT
TARTUFFE	TASSEL	TATHED	TATTY	TAUTLY
TARTUFFES	TASSELED	TATHING	TATU	TAUTNESS
TARTUFI	TASSELIER	TATHS	TATUED	TAUTOG
TARTUFO	TASSELING	TATIE	TATUING	TAUTOGS

TAUTOLOGY	TAWNEYS	TAXIMETER	TEABERRY	TEAM
TAUTOMER	TAWNIER	TAXING	TEABOARD	TEAMAKER
TAUTOMERS	TAWNIES	TAXINGLY	TEABOARDS	TEAMAKERS
TAUTONYM	TAWNIEST	TAXINGS	TEABOWL	TEAMED
TAUTONYMS	TAWNILY	TAXIPLANE	TEABOWLS	TEAMER
TAUTONYMY	TAWNINESS	TAXIS	TEABOX	TEAMERS
TAUTS	TAWNY	TAXISES	TEABOXES	TEAMING
TAV	TAWPIE	TAXITE	TEABREAD	TEAMINGS
TAVA	TAWPIES	TAXITES	TEABREADS	TEAMMATE
TAVAH	TAWS	TAXITIC	TEACAKE	TEAMMATES
TAVAHS	TAWSE	TAXIWAY	TEACAKES	TEAMS
TAVAS	TAWSED	TAXIWAYS	TEACART	TEAMSTER
TAVER	TAWSES	TAXLESS	TEACARTS	TEAMSTERS
TAVERED	TAWSING	TAXMAN	TEACH	TEAMWISE
TAVERING	TAWT	TAXMEN	TEACHABLE	TEAMWORK
TAVERN	TAWTED	TAXOL	TEACHABLY	TEAMWORKS
TAVERNA	TAWTIE	TAXOLS	TEACHER	TEAPOT
TAVERNAS	TAWTIER	TAXON	TEACHERLY	TEAPOTS
TAVERNER	TAWTIEST	TAXONOMER	TEACHERS	TEAPOY
TAVERNERS	TAWTING	TAXONOMIC	TEACHES	TEAPOYS
TAVERNS	TAWTS	TAXONOMY	TEACHIE	TEAR
TAVERS	TAX	TAXONS	TEACHING	TEARABLE
TAVERT	TAXA	TAXOR	TEACHINGS	TEARAWAY
TAVS	TAXABLE	TAXORS	TEACHLESS	TEARAWAYS
TAW	TAXABLES	TAXPAID	TEACUP	TEARDOWN
TAWA	TAXABLY	TAXPAYER	TEACUPFUL	TEARDOWNS
TAWAI	TAXACEOUS	TAXPAYERS	TEACUPS	TEARDROP
TAWAIS	TAXAMETER	TAXPAYING	TEAD	TEARDROPS
TAWAS	TAXATION	TAXUS	TEADE	TEARED
TAWDRIER	TAXATIONS	TAXWISE	TEADES	TEARER
TAWDRIES	TAXATIVE	TAXYING	TEADS	TEARERS
TAWDRIEST	TAXED	TAY	TEAED	TEARFUL
TAWDRILY	TAXEME	TAYASSUID	TEAGLE	TEARFULLY
TAWDRY	TAXEMES	TAYBERRY	TEAGLED	TEARGAS
TAWED	TAXEMIC	TAYRA	TEAGLES	TEARGASES
TAWER	TAXER	TAYRAS	TEAGLING	TEARIER
TAWERIES	TAXERS	TAYS	TEAHOUSE	TEARIEST
TAWERS	TAXES	TAZZA	TEAHOUSES	TEARILY
TAWERY	TAXI	TAZZAS	TEAING	TEARINESS
TAWHAI	TAXIARCH	TAZZE	TEAK	TEARING
TAWHAIS	TAXIARCHS	TCHICK	TEAKETTLE	TEARLESS
TAWHIRI	TAXICAB	TCHICKED	TEAKS	TEARLIKE
TAWHIRIS	TAXICABS	TCHICKING	TEAKWOOD	TEAROOM
TAWIE	TAXIDERMY	TCHICKS	TEAKWOODS	TEAROOMS
TAWIER	TAXIED	TCHOTCHKE	TEAL	TEARS
TAWIEST	TAXIES	TE	TEALIGHT	TEARSHEET
TAWING	TAXIING	TEA	TEALIGHTS	TEARSTAIN
TAWINGS	TAXIMAN	TEABAG	TEALIKE	TEARSTRIP
TAWNEY	TAXIMEN	TEABAGS	TEALS	TEARY

TEAS	TECHED	TEDIOUSLY	TEENTSY	TEGUA
TEASABLE	TECHIE	TEDISOME	TEENTY	TEGUAS
TEASE	TECHIER	TEDIUM	TEENY	TEGUEXIN
TEASED	TECHIES	TEDIUMS	TEENYBOP	TEGUEXINS
TEASEL	TECHIEST	TEDS	TEEPEE	TEGULA
TEASELED	TECHILY	TEDY	TEEPEES	TEGULAE
TEASELER	TECHINESS	TEE	TEER	TEGULAR
TEASELERS	TECHNIC	TEED	TEERED	TEGULARLY
TEASELING	TECHNICAL	TEEING	TEERING	TEGULATED
TEASELLED	TECHNICS	TEEK	TEERS	TEGUMEN
TEASELLER	TECHNIKON	TEEL	TEES	TEGUMENT
TEASELS	TECHNIQUE	TEELS	TEETER	TEGUMENTS
TEASER	TECHNO	TEEM	TEETERED	TEGUMINA
TEASERS	TECHNOID	TEEMED	TEETERING	TEGUS
TEASES	TECHNOIDS	TEEMER	TEETERS	TEHR
TEASHOP	TECHNOPOP	TEEMERS	TEETH	TEHRS
TEASHOPS	TECHNOS	TEEMFUL	TEETHE	TEHSIL
TEASING	TECHS	TEEMING	TEETHED	TEHSILDAR
TEASINGLY	TECHY	TEEMINGLY	TEETHER	TEHSILS
TEASINGS	TECKEL	TEEMLESS	TEETHERS	TEIGLACH
TEASPOON	TECKELS	TEEMS	TEETHES	TEIID
TEASPOONS	TECS	TEEN	TEETHING	TEIIDS
TEAT	TECTA	TEENAGE	TEETHINGS	TEIL
TEATASTER	TECTAL	TEENAGED	TEETHLESS	TEILS
TEATED	TECTIFORM	TEENAGER	TEETOTAL	TEIN
TEATIME	TECTITE	TEENAGERS	TEETOTALS	TEIND
TEATIMES	TECTITES	TEENAGES	TEETOTUM	TEINDED
TEATS	TECTONIC	TEEND	TEETOTUMS	TEINDING
TEAWARE	TECTONICS	TEENDED	TEEVEE	TEINDS
TEAWARES	TECTONISM	TEENDING	TEEVEES	TEINS
TEAZE	TECTORIAL	TEENDOM	TEF	TEKKIE
TEAZED	TECTRICES	TEENDOMS	TEFF	TEKKIES
TEAZEL	TECTRIX	TEENDS	TEFFS	TEKNONYMY
TEAZELED	TECTUM	TEENE	TEFILLAH	TEKTITE
TEAZELING	TECTUMS	TEENED	TEFILLIN	TEKTITES
TEAZELLED	TED	TEENER	TEFLON	TEKTITIC
TEAZELS	TEDDED	TEENERS	TEFLONS	TEL
TEAZES	TEDDER	TEENES	TEFS	TELA
TEAZING	TEDDERED	TEENFUL	TEG	TELAE
TEAZLE	TEDDERING	TEENIER	TEGG	TELAMON
TEAZLED	TEDDERS	TEENIEST	TEGGS	TELAMONES
TEAZLES	TEDDIE	TEENING	TEGMEN	TELAMONS
TEAZLING	TEDDIES	TEENS	TEGMENTA	TELARY
TEBBAD	TEDDING	TEENSIER	TEGMENTAL	TELCO
TEBBADS	TEDDY	TEENSIEST	TEGMENTUM	TELCOS
TEBIBYTE	TEDIER	TEENSY	TEGMINA	TELD
TEBIBYTES	TEDIEST	TEENTIER	TEGMINAL	TELE
TEC	TEDIOSITY	TEENTIEST	TEGS	TELEA
TECH	TEDIOUS	TEENTSIER	TEGU	TELECAST

TELECASTS	TELEPLAYS	TELEXES	TELLUS	TEMPERATE
TELECHIR	TELEPOINT	TELEXING	TELLUSES	TEMPERED
TELECHIRS	TELEPORT	TELFER	TELLY	TEMPERER
TELECINE	TELEPORTS	TELFERAGE	TELLYS	TEMPERERS
TELECINES	TELEPRINT	TELFERED	TELNET	TEMPERING
TELECOM	TELERAN	TELFERIC	TELNETED	TEMPERS
TELECOMM	TELERANS	TELFERING	TELNETING	TEMPEST
TELECOMMS	TELERGIC	TELFERS	TELNETS	TEMPESTED
TELECOMS	TELERGIES	TELFORD	TELNETTED	TEMPESTS
TELECON	TELERGY	TELFORDS	TELOGEN	TEMPI
TELECONS	TELEROBOT	TELIA	TELOGENS	TEMPING
TELECOPY	TELES	TELIAL	TELOI	TEMPINGS
TELEDU	TELESALE	TELIC	TELOME	TEMPLAR
TELEDUS	TELESALES	TELICALLY	TELOMERE	TEMPLARS
TELEFAX	TELESCOPE	TELICITY	TELOMERES	TEMPLATE
TELEFAXED	TELESCOPY	TELIUM	TELOMES	TEMPLATES
TELEFAXES	TELESEME	TELL	TELOMIC	TEMPLE
TELEFILM	TELESEMES	TELLABLE	TELOPHASE	TEMPLED
TELEFILMS	TELESES	TELLAR	TELOS	TEMPLES
TELEGA	TELESHOP	TELLARED	TELOSES	TEMPLET
TELEGAS	TELESHOPS	TELLARING	TELOTAXES	TEMPLETS
TELEGENIC	TELESIS	TELLARS	TELOTAXIS	TEMPO
TELEGONIC	TELESM	TELLEN	TELPHER	TEMPORAL
TELEGONY	TELESMS	TELLENS	TELPHERED	TEMPORALS
TELEGRAM	TELESTIC	TELLER	TELPHERIC	TEMPORARY
TELEGRAMS	TELESTICH	TELLERED	TELPHERS	TEMPORE
TELEGRAPH	TELESTICS	TELLERING	TELS	TEMPORISE
TELEMAN	TELETEX	TELLERS	TELSON	TEMPORIZE
TELEMARK	TELETEXES	TELLIES	TELSONIC	TEMPOS
TELEMARKS	TELETEXT	TELLIN	TELSONS	TEMPS
TELEMATIC	TELETEXTS	TELLING	TELT	TEMPT
TELEMEN	TELETHON	TELLINGLY	TEMAZEPAM	TEMPTABLE
TELEMETER	TELETHONS	TELLINGS	TEMBLOR	TEMPTED
TELEMETRY	TELETRON	TELLINOID	TEMBLORES	TEMPTER
TELEOLOGY	TELETRONS	TELLINS	TEMBLORS	TEMPTERS
TELEONOMY	TELETYPE	TELLS	TEME	TEMPTING
TELEOSAUR	TELETYPED	TELLTALE	TEMED	TEMPTINGS
TELEOST	TELETYPES	TELLTALES	TEMENE	TEMPTRESS
TELEOSTS	TELEVIEW	TELLURAL	TEMENOS	TEMPTS
TELEPATH	TELEVIEWS	TELLURATE	TEMERITY	TEMPURA
TELEPATHS	TELEVISE	TELLURIAN	TEMEROUS	TEMPURAS
TELEPATHY	TELEVISED	TELLURIC	TEMES	TEMS
TELEPHEME	TELEVISER	TELLURIDE	TEMP	TEMSE
TELEPHONE	TELEVISES	TELLURION	TEMPED	TEMSED
TELEPHONY	TELEVISOR	TELLURISE	TEMPEH	TEMSES
TELEPHOTO	TELEWORK	TELLURITE	TEMPEHS	TEMSING
TELEPIC	TELEWORKS	TELLURIUM	TEMPER	TEMULENCE
TELEPICS	TELEX	TELLURIZE	TEMPERA	TEMULENCY
TELEPLAY	TELEXED	TELLUROUS	TEMPERAS	TEMULENT

TEN	TENDRIL	TENNISES	TENSILITY	TENTS
TENABLE	TENDRILED	TENNIST	TENSING	TENTWISE
TENABLY	TENDRILLY	TENNISTS	TENSION	TENTY
TENACE	TENDRILS	TENNO	TENSIONAL	TENUE
TENACES	TENDRON	TENNOS	TENSIONED	TENUES
TENACIOUS	TENDRONS	TENNY	TENSIONER	TENUIOUS
TENACITY	TENDS	TENON	TENSIONS	TENUIS
TENACULA	TENDU	TENONED	TENSITIES	TENUITIES
TENACULUM	TENDUS	TENONER	TENSITY	TENUITY
TENAIL	TENE	TENONERS	TENSIVE	TENUOUS
TENAILLE	TENEBRAE	TENONING	TENSON	TENUOUSLY
TENAILLES	TENEBRIO	TENONS	TENSONS	TENURABLE
TENAILLON	TENEBRIOS	TENOR	TENSOR	TENURE
TENAILS	TENEBRISM	TENORINI	TENSORIAL	TENURED
TENANCIES	TENEBRIST	TENORINO	TENSORS	TENURES
TENANCY	TENEBRITY	TENORIST	TENT	TENURIAL
TENANT	TENEBROSE	TENORISTS	TENTACLE	TENURING
TENANTED	TENEBROUS	TENORITE	TENTACLED	TENUTI
TENANTING	TENEMENT	TENORITES	TENTACLES	TENUTO
TENANTRY	TENEMENTS	TENORLESS	TENTACULA	TENUTOS
TENANTS	TENENDA	TENORMAN	TENTAGE	TENZON
TENCH	TENENDUM	TENORMEN	TENTAGES	TENZONS
TENCHES	TENENDUMS	TENOROON	TENTATION	TEOCALLI
TEND	TENES	TENOROONS	TENTATIVE	TEOCALLIS
TENDANCE	TENESI	TENORS	TENTED	TEOPAN
TENDANCES	TENESMIC	TENOTOMY	TENTER	TEOPANS
TENDED	TENESMUS	TENOUR	TENTERED	TEOSINTE
TENDENCE	TENET	TENOURS	TENTERING	TEOSINTES
TENDENCES	TENETS	TENPENCE	TENTERS	TEPA
TENDENCY	TENFOLD	TENPENCES	TENTFUL	TEPACHE
TENDENZ	TENFOLDS	TENPENNY	TENTFULS	TEPACHES
TENDENZEN	TENGE	TENPIN	TENTH	TEPAL
TENDER	TENGES	TENPINNER	TENTHLY	TEPALS
TENDERED	TENIA	TENPINS	TENTHS	TEPAS
TENDERER	TENIACIDE	TENREC	TENTIE	TEPEE
TENDERERS	TENIAE	TENRECS	TENTIER	TEPEES
TENDEREST	TENIAFUGE	TENS	TENTIEST	TEPEFIED
TENDERING	TENIAS	TENSE	TENTIGO	TEPEFIES
TENDERISE	TENIASES	TENSED	TENTIGOS	TEPEFY
TENDERIZE	TENIASIS	TENSELESS	TENTING	TEPEFYING
TENDERLY	TENIATE	TENSELY	TENTINGS	TEPHIGRAM
TENDERS	TENIOID	TENSENESS	TENTLESS	TEPHILLAH
TENDING	TENNE	TENSER	TENTLIKE	TEPHILLIN
TENDINOUS	TENNER	TENSES	TENTMAKER	TEPHRA
TENDON	TENNERS	TENSEST	TENTORIA	TEPHRAS
TENDONS	TENNES	TENSIBLE	TENTORIAL	TEPHRITE
TENDRE	TENNESI	TENSIBLY	TENTORIUM	TEPHRITES
TENDRES	TENNIES	TENSILE	TENTPOLE	TEPHRITIC
TENDRESSE	TENNIS	TENSILELY	TENTPOLES	TEPHROITE

TEPID	TERCELS	TERMINISM	TERRANES	TERSENESS
TEPIDARIA	TERCES	TERMINIST	TERRAPIN	TERSER
TEPIDER	TERCET	TERMINUS	TERRAPINS	TERSEST
TEPIDEST	TERCETS	TERMITARY	TERRARIA	TERSION
TEPIDITY	TERCIO	TERMITE	TERRARIUM	TERSIONS
TEPIDLY	TERCIOS	TERMITES	TERRAS	TERTIA
TEPIDNESS	TEREBENE	TERMITIC	TERRASES	TERTIAL
TEPOY	TEREBENES	TERMLESS	TERRASSE	TERTIALS
TEPOYS	TEREBIC	TERMLIES	TERRASSES	TERTIAN
TEQUILA	TEREBINTH	TERMLY	TERRAZZO	TERTIANS
TEQUILAS	TEREBRA	TERMOR	TERRAZZOS	TERTIARY
TEQUILLA	TEREBRAE	TERMORS	TERREEN	TERTIAS
TEQUILLAS	TEREBRANT	TERMS	TERREENS	TERTIUM
TERABYTE	TEREBRAS	TERMTIME	TERRELLA	TERTIUS
TERABYTES	TEREBRATE	TERMTIMES	TERRELLAS	TERTIUSES
TERAFLOP	TEREDINES	TERN	TERRENE	TERTS
TERAFLOPS	TEREDO	TERNAL	TERRENELY	TERVALENT
TERAGLIN	TEREDOS	TERNARIES	TERRENES	TERYLENE
TERAGLINS	TEREFA	TERNARY	TERRET	TERYLENES
TERAHERTZ	TEREFAH	TERNATE	TERRETS	TERZETTA
TERAI	TEREK	TERNATELY	TERRIBLE	TERZETTAS
TERAIS	TEREKS	TERNE	TERRIBLES	TERZETTI
TERAKIHI	TERES	TERNED	TERRIBLY	TERZETTO
TERAKIHIS	TERESES	TERNES	TERRICOLE	TERZETTOS
TERAMETER	TERETE	TERNING	TERRIER	TES
TERAOHM	TERETES	TERNION	TERRIERS	TESLA
TERAOHMS	TERF	TERNIONS	TERRIES	TESLAS
TERAPH	TERFE	TERNS	TERRIFIC	TESSELATE
TERAPHIM	TERFES	TERPENE	TERRIFIED	TESSELLA
TERAPHIMS	TERFS	TERPENES	TERRIFIER	TESSELLAE
TERAS	TERGA	TERPENIC	TERRIFIES	TESSELLAR
TERATA	TERGAL	TERPENOID	TERRIFY	TESSERA
TERATISM	TERGITE	TERPINE	TERRINE	TESSERACT
TERATISMS	TERGITES	TERPINEOL	TERRINES	TESSERAE
TERATOGEN	TERGUM	TERPINES	TERRIT	TESSERAL
TERATOID	TERIYAKI	TERPINOL	TERRITORY	TESSITURA
TERATOMA	TERIYAKIS	TERPINOLS	TERRITS	TESSITURE
TERATOMAS	TERM	TERRA	TERROIR	TEST
TERAWATT	TERMAGANT	TERRACE	TERROIRS	TESTA
TERAWATTS	TERMED	TERRACED	TERROR	TESTABLE
TERBIA	TERMER	TERRACES	TERRORFUL	TESTACEAN
TERBIAS	TERMERS	TERRACING	TERRORISE	TESTACIES
TERBIC	TERMINAL	TERRAE	TERRORISM	TESTACY
TERBIUM	TERMINALS	TERRAFORM	TERRORIST	TESTAE
TERBIUMS	TERMINATE	TERRAIN	TERRORIZE	TESTAMENT
TERCE	TERMINER	TERRAINS	TERRORS	TESTAMUR
TERCEL	TERMINERS	TERRAMARA	TERRY	TESTAMURS
TERCELET	TERMING	TERRAMARE	TERSE	TESTATA
TERCELETS	TERMINI	TERRANE	TERSELY	TESTATE

TESTATES	TETANIES	TETRAS	TEWITS	THALASSIC
TESTATION	TETANISE	TETRAXON	TEWS	THALE
TESTATOR	TETANISED	TETRAXONS	TEX	THALER
TESTATORS	TETANISES	TETRI	TEXAS	THALERS
TESTATRIX	TETANIZE	TETRIS	TEXASES	THALI
TESTATUM	TETANIZED	TETRODE	TEXES	THALIAN
TESTATUMS	TETANIZES	TETRODES	TEXT	THALIS
TESTCROSS	TETANOID	TETRONAL	TEXTBOOK	THALLI
TESTE	TETANUS	TETRONALS	TEXTBOOKS	THALLIC
TESTED	TETANUSES	TETROSE	TEXTED	THALLINE
TESTEE	TETANY	TETROSES	TEXTER	THALLINES
TESTEES	TETCHED	TETROXID	TEXTERS	THALLIOUS
TESTER	TETCHIER	TETROXIDE	TEXTILE	THALLIUM
TESTERN	TETCHIEST	TETROXIDS	TEXTILES	THALLIUMS
TESTERNED	TETCHILY	TETRYL	TEXTING	THALLOID
TESTERNS	TETCHY	TETRYLS	TEXTINGS	THALLOUS
TESTERS	TETE	TETS	TEXTISM	THALLUS
TESTES	TETES	TETTER	TEXTISMS	THALLUSES
TESTICLE	TETH	TETTERED	TEXTLESS	THALWEG
TESTICLES	TETHER	TETTERING	TEXTONYM	THALWEGS
TESTIER	TETHERED	TETTEROUS	TEXTONYMS	THAN
TESTIEST	TETHERING	TETTERS	TEXTORIAL	THANA
TESTIFIED	TETHERS	TETTIX	TEXTPHONE	THANADAR
TESTIFIER	TETHS	TETTIXES	TEXTS	THANADARS
TESTIFIES	TETOTUM	TEUCH	TEXTSPEAK	THANAGE
TESTIFY	TETOTUMS	TEUCHAT	TEXTUAL	THANAGES
TESTILY	TETRA	TEUCHATS	TEXTUALLY	THANAH
TESTIMONY	TETRACID	TEUCHER	TEXTUARY	THANAHS
TESTINESS	TETRACIDS	TEUCHEST	TEXTURAL	THANAS
TESTING	TETRACT	TEUCHTER	TEXTURE	THANATISM
TESTINGS	TETRACTS	TEUCHTERS	TEXTURED	THANATIST
TESTIS	TETRAD	TEUGH	TEXTURES	THANATOID
TESTON	TETRADIC	TEUGHER	TEXTURING	THANATOS
TESTONS	TETRADITE	TEUGHEST	TEXTURISE	THANE
TESTOON	TETRADS	TEUGHLY	TEXTURIZE	THANEDOM
TESTOONS	TETRAGON	TEUTONISE	TEXTUROUS	THANEDOMS
TESTRIL	TETRAGONS	TEUTONIZE	THACK	THANEHOOD
TESTRILL	TETRAGRAM	TEVATRON	THACKED	THANES
TESTRILLS	TETRALOGY	TEVATRONS	THACKING	THANESHIP
TESTRILS	TETRAMER	TEW	THACKS	THANG
TESTS	TETRAMERS	TEWART	THAE	THANGKA
TESTUDO	TETRAPLA	TEWARTS	THAGI	THANGKAS
TESTUDOS	TETRAPLAS	TEWED	THAGIS	THANGS
TESTY	TETRAPOD	TEWEL	THAIM	THANK
TET	TETRAPODS	TEWELS	THAIRM	THANKED
TETANAL	TETRAPODY	TEWHIT	THAIRMS	THANKEE
TETANIC	TETRARCH	TEWHITS	THALAMI	THANKER
TETANICAL	TETRARCHS	TEWING	THALAMIC	THANKERS
TETANICS	TETRARCHY	TEWIT	THALAMUS	THANKFUL

THANKING	THEATERS	THEIST	THEOPATHY	THEREINTO
THANKINGS	THEATRAL	THEISTIC	THEOPHAGY	THEREMIN
THANKIT	THEATRE	THEISTS	THEOPHANY	THEREMINS
THANKLESS	THEATRES	THELEMENT	THEORBIST	THERENESS
THANKS	THEATRIC	THELF	THEORBO	THEREOF
THANKYOU	THEATRICS	THELITIS	THEORBOS	THEREON
THANKYOUS	THEAVE	THELVES	THEOREM	THEREOUT
THANNA	THEAVES	THELYTOKY	THEOREMIC	THERES
THANNAH	THEBAINE	THEM	THEOREMS	THERETO
THANNAHS	THEBAINES	THEMA	THEORETIC	THEREUNTO
THANNAS	THEBE	THEMATA	THEORIC	THEREUPON
THANS	THEBES	THEMATIC	THEORICS	THEREWITH
THANX	THECA	THEMATICS	THEORIES	THERIAC
THAR	THECAE	THEMATISE	THEORIQUE	THERIACA
THARM	THECAL	THEMATIZE	THEORISE	THERIACAL
THARMS	THECATE	THEME	THEORISED	THERIACAS
THARS	THECODONT	THEMED	THEORISER	THERIACS
THAT	THEE	THEMELESS	THEORISES	THERIAN
THATAWAY	THEED	THEMES	THEORIST	THERIANS
THATCH	THEEING	THEMING	THEORISTS	THERM
THATCHED	THEEK	THEMSELF	THEORIZE	THERMAE
THATCHER	THEEKED	THEN	THEORIZED	THERMAL
THATCHERS	THEEKING	THENABOUT	THEORIZER	THERMALLY
THATCHES	THEEKS	THENAGE	THEORIZES	THERMALS
THATCHIER	THEELIN	THENAGES	THEORY	THERME
THATCHING	THEELINS	THENAL	THEOSOPH	THERMEL
THATCHT	THEELOL	THENAR	THEOSOPHS	THERMELS
THATCHY	THEELOLS	THENARS	THEOSOPHY	THERMES
THATNESS	THEES	THENCE	THEOTOKOI	THERMETTE
THAUMATIN	THEFT	THENS	THEOTOKOS	THERMIC
THAW	THEFTLESS	THEOCON	THEOW	THERMICAL
THAWED	THEFTS	THEOCONS	THEOWS	THERMIDOR
THAWER	THEFTUOUS	THEOCRACY	THERALITE	THERMION
THAWERS	THEGITHER	THEOCRASY	THERAPIES	THERMIONS
THAWIER	THEGN	THEOCRAT	THERAPISE	THERMIT
THAWIEST	THEGNLIER	THEOCRATS	THERAPIST	THERMITE
THAWING	THEGNLY	THEODICY	THERAPIZE	THERMITES
THAWINGS	THEGNS	THEOGONIC	THERAPSID	THERMITS
THAWLESS	THEIC	THEOGONY	THERAPY	THERMOS
THAWS	THEICS	THEOLOG	THERBLIG	THERMOSES
THAWY	THEIN	THEOLOGER	THERBLIGS	THERMOSET
THE	THEINE	THEOLOGIC	THERE	THERMOTIC
THEACEOUS	THEINES	THEOLOGS	THEREAT	THERMS
THEANDRIC	THEINS	THEOLOGUE	THEREAWAY	THEROID
THEANINE	THEIR	THEOLOGY	THEREBY	THEROLOGY
THEANINES	THEIRS	THEOMACHY	THEREFOR	THEROPOD
THEARCHIC	THEIRSELF	THEOMANCY	THEREFORE	THEROPODS
THEARCHY	THEISM	THEOMANIA	THEREFROM	THESAURAL
THEATER	THEISMS	THEONOMY	THEREIN	THESAURI

THESAURUS	THIAZOLS	THIGH	THINNISH	THIRSTING
THESE	THIBET	THIGHBONE	THINS	THIRSTS
THESES	THIBETS	THIGHED	THIO	THIRSTY
THESIS	THIBLE	THIGHS	THIOFURAN	THIRTEEN
THESP	THIBLES	THIGS	THIOL	THIRTEENS
THESPIAN	THICK	THILK	THIOLIC	THIRTIES
THESPIANS	THICKED	THILL	THIOLS	THIRTIETH
THESPS	THICKEN	THILLER	THIONATE	THIRTY
THETA	THICKENED	THILLERS	THIONATES	THIRTYISH
THETAS	THICKENER	THILLS	THIONIC	THIS
THETCH	THICKENS	THIMBLE	THIONIN	THISAWAY
THETCHED	THICKER	THIMBLED	THIONINE	THISNESS
THETCHES	THICKEST	THIMBLES	THIONINES	THISTLE
THETCHING	THICKET	THIMBLING	THIONINS	THISTLES
THETE	THICKETED	THIN	THIONYL	THISTLIER
THETES	THICKETS	THINCLAD	THIONYLS	THISTLY
THETHER	THICKETY	THINCLADS	THIOPHEN	THITHER
THETIC	THICKHEAD	THINDOWN	THIOPHENE	THITHERTO
THETICAL	THICKIE	THINDOWNS	THIOPHENS	THIVEL
THETRI	THICKIES	THINE	THIOPHIL	THIVELS
THETRIS	THICKING	THING	THIOTEPA	THLIPSES
THEURGIC	THICKISH	THINGAMY	THIOTEPAS	THLIPSIS
THEURGIES	THICKLEAF	THINGHOOD	THIOUREA	THO
THEURGIST	THICKLY	THINGIE	THIOUREAS	THOFT
THEURGY	THICKNESS	THINGIER	THIR	THOFTS
THEW	THICKO	THINGIES	THIRAM	THOLE
THEWED	THICKOES	THINGIEST	THIRAMS	THOLED
THEWES	THICKOS	THINGNESS	THIRD	THOLEIITE
THEWIER	THICKS	THINGO	THIRDED	THOLEPIN
THEWIEST	THICKSET	THINGOS	THIRDHAND	THOLEPINS
THEWLESS	THICKSETS	THINGS	THIRDING	THOLES
THEWS	THICKSKIN	THINGUMMY	THIRDINGS	THOLI
THEWY	THICKY	THINGY	THIRDLY	THOLING
THEY	THIEF	THINK	THIRDS	THOLOBATE
THIAMIN	THIEFLIKE	THINKABLE	THIRDSMAN	THOLOI
THIAMINE	THIEVE	THINKABLY	THIRDSMEN	THOLOS
THIAMINES	THIEVED	THINKER	THIRL	THOLUS
THIAMINS	THIEVERY	THINKERS	THIRLAGE	THON
THIASUS	THIEVES	THINKING	THIRLAGES	THONDER
THIASUSES	THIEVING	THINKINGS	THIRLED	THONG
THIAZIDE	THIEVINGS	THINKS	THIRLING	THONGED
THIAZIDES	THIEVISH	THINLY	THIRLS	THONGIER
THIAZIN	THIG	THINNED	THIRST	THONGIEST
THIAZINE	THIGGED	THINNER	THIRSTED	THONGING
THIAZINES	THIGGER	THINNERS	THIRSTER	THONGS
THIAZINS	THIGGERS	THINNESS	THIRSTERS	THONGY
THIAZOL	THIGGING	THINNEST	THIRSTFUL	THORACAL
THIAZOLE	THIGGINGS	THINNING	THIRSTIER	THORACES
THIAZOLES	THIGGIT	THINNINGS	THIRSTILY	THORACIC

T

THORAX	THOWELS	THREAP	THRESHOLD	THROATED
THORAXES	THOWL	THREAPED	THRETTIES	THROATIER
THORIA	THOWLESS	THREAPER	THRETTY	THROATILY
THORIAS	THOWLS	THREAPERS	THREW	THROATING
THORIC	THRAE	THREAPING	THRICE	THROATS
THORITE	THRAIPING	THREAPIT	THRID	THROATY
THORITES	THRALDOM	THREAPS	THRIDACE	THROB
THORIUM	THRALDOMS	THREAT	THRIDACES	THROBBED
THORIUMS	THRALL	THREATED	THRIDDED	THROBBER
THORN	THRALLDOM	THREATEN	THRIDDING	THROBBERS
THORNBACK	THRALLED	THREATENS	THRIDS	THROBBING
THORNBILL	THRALLING	THREATFUL	THRIFT	THROBLESS
THORNBIRD	THRALLS	THREATING	THRIFTIER	THROBS
THORNBUSH	THRANG	THREATS	THRIFTILY	THROE
THORNED	THRANGED	THREAVE	THRIFTS	THROED
THORNIER	THRANGING	THREAVES	THRIFTY	THROEING
THORNIEST	THRANGS	THREE	THRILL	THROES
THORNILY	THRAPPLE	THREEFOLD	THRILLANT	THROMBI
THORNING	THRAPPLED	THREENESS	THRILLED	THROMBIN
THORNLESS	THRAPPLES	THREEP	THRILLER	THROMBINS
THORNLIKE	THRASH	THREEPEAT	THRILLERS	THROMBOSE
THORNS	THRASHED	THREEPED	THRILLIER	THROMBUS
THORNSET	THRASHER	THREEPER	THRILLING	THRONE
THORNTAIL	THRASHERS	THREEPERS	THRILLS	THRONED
THORNTREE	THRASHES	THREEPING	THRILLY	THRONES
THORNY	THRASHIER	THREEPIT	THRIMSA	THRONG
THORO	THRASHING	THREEPS	THRIMSAS	THRONGED
THORON	THRASHY	THREEQUEL	THRIP	THRONGFUL
THORONS	THRASONIC	THREES	THRIPS	THRONGING
THOROUGH	THRAVE	THREESOME	THRIPSES	THRONGS
THOROUGHS	THRAVES	THRENE	THRISSEL	THRONING
THORP	THRAW	THRENES	THRISSELS	THRONNER
THORPE	THRAWARD	THRENETIC	THRIST	THRONNERS
THORPES	THRAWART	THRENODE	THRISTED	THROPPLE
THORPS	THRAWED	THRENODES	THRISTING	THROPPLED
THOSE	THRAWING	THRENODIC	THRISTLE	THROPPLES
THOTHER	THRAWN	THRENODY	THRISTLES	THROSTLE
THOU	THRAWNLY	THRENOI	THRISTS	THROSTLES
THOUED	THRAWS	THRENOS	THRISTY	THROTTLE
THOUGH	THREAD	THRENOSES	THRIVE	THROTTLED
THOUGHT	THREADED	THREONINE	THRIVED	THROTTLER
THOUGHTED	THREADEN	THRESH	THRIVEN	THROTTLES
THOUGHTEN	THREADER	THRESHED	THRIVER	THROUGH
THOUGHTS	THREADERS	THRESHEL	THRIVERS	THROUGHLY
THOUING	THREADFIN	THRESHELS	THRIVES	THROVE
THOUS	THREADIER	THRESHER	THRIVING	THROW
THOUSAND	THREADING	THRESHERS	THRIVINGS	THROWABLE
THOUSANDS	THREADS	THRESHES	THRO	THROWAWAY
THOWEL	THREADY	THRESHING	THROAT	THROWBACK

THROWDOWN	THUGGERY	THUNDERY	THYMES	TIBIAS
THROWE	THUGGISH	THUNDROUS	THYMEY	TIC
THROWER	THUGGISM	THUNK	THYMI	TICAL
THROWERS	THUGGISMS	THUNKED	THYMIC	TICALS
THROWES	THUGGO	THUNKING	THYMIDINE	TICCA
THROWING	THUGGOS	THUNKS	THYMIER	TICCED
THROWINGS	THUGLIFE	THURIBLE	THYMIEST	TICCING
THROWN	THUGLIFES	THURIBLES	THYMINE	TICE
THROWOVER	THUGLIVES	THURIFER	THYMINES	TICED
THROWS	THUGS	THURIFERS	THYMOCYTE	TICES
THROWSTER	THUJA	THURIFIED	THYMOL	TICH
THRU	THUJAS	THURIFIES	THYMOLS	TICHES
THRUM	THULIA	THURIFY	THYMOMA	TICHIER
THRUMMED	THULIAS	THURL	THYMOMAS	TICHIEST
THRUMMER	THULITE	THURLS	THYMOMATA	TICHY
THRUMMERS	THULITES	THUS	THYMOSIN	TICING
THRUMMIER	THULIUM	THUSES	THYMOSINS	TICK
THRUMMING	THULIUMS	THUSLY	THYMUS	TICKED
THRUMMY	THUMB	THUSNESS	THYMUSES	TICKEN
THRUMS	THUMBED	THUSWISE	THYMY	TICKENS
THRUPENNY	THUMBHOLE	THUYA	THYRATRON	TICKER
THRUPUT	THUMBIER	THUYAS	THYREOID	TICKERS
THRUPUTS	THUMBIEST	THWACK	THYREOIDS	TICKET
THRUSH	THUMBING	THWACKED	THYRISTOR	TICKETED
THRUSHES	THUMBKIN	THWACKER	THYROID	TICKETING
THRUST	THUMBKINS	THWACKERS	THYROIDAL	TICKETS
THRUSTED	THUMBLESS	THWACKING	THYROIDS	TICKEY
THRUSTER	THUMBLIKE	THWACKS	THYROXIN	TICKEYS
THRUSTERS	THUMBLING	THWAITE	THYROXINE	TICKIES
THRUSTFUL	THUMBNAIL	THWAITES	THYROXINS	TICKING
THRUSTING	THUMBNUT	THWAP	THYRSE	TICKINGS
THRUSTOR	THUMBNUTS	THWAPPED	THYRSES	TICKLACE
THRUSTORS	THUMBPAD	THWAPPING	THYRSI	TICKLACES
THRUSTS	THUMBPADS	THWAPS	THYRSOID	TICKLE
THRUTCH	THUMBPOT	THWART	THYRSUS	TICKLEASS
THRUTCHED	THUMBPOTS	THWARTED	THYSELF	TICKLED
THRUTCHES	THUMBS	THWARTER	TI	TICKLER
THRUWAY	THUMBTACK	THWARTERS	TIAN	TICKLERS
THRUWAYS	THUMBY	THWARTING	TIANS	TICKLES
THRYMSA	THUMP	THWARTLY	TIAR	TICKLIER
THRYMSAS	THUMPED	THWARTS	TIARA	TICKLIEST
THUD	THUMPER	THY	TIARAED	TICKLING
THUDDED	THUMPERS	THYINE	TIARAS	TICKLINGS
THUDDING	THUMPING	THYLACINE	TIARS	TICKLISH
THUDDINGS	THUMPS	THYLAKOID	TIBIA	TICKLY
THUDS	THUNDER	THYLOSE	TIBIAE	TICKS
THUG	THUNDERED	THYLOSES	TIBIAL	TICKSEED
THUGGEE	THUNDERER	THYLOSIS	TIBIALES	TICKSEEDS
THUGGEES	THUNDERS	THYME	TIBIALIS	TICKTACK

TICKTACKS	TIDEWATER	TIETACKS	TIGHTENER	TILAPIA
TICKTOCK	TIDEWAVE	TIETACS	TIGHTENS	TILAPIAS
TICKTOCKS	TIDEWAVES	TIFF	TIGHTER	TILBURIES
TICKY	TIDEWAY	TIFFANIES	TIGHTEST	TILBURY
TICS	TIDEWAYS	TIFFANY	TIGHTISH	TILDE
TICTAC	TIDIED	TIFFED	TIGHTKNIT	TILDES
TICTACKED	TIDIER	TIFFIN	TIGHTLY	TILE
TICTACS	TIDIERS	TIFFINED	TIGHTNESS	TILED
TICTOC	TIDIES	TIFFING	TIGHTROPE	TILEFISH
TICTOCKED	TIDIEST	TIFFINGS	TIGHTS	TILELIKE
TICTOCS	TIDILY	TIFFINING	TIGHTWAD	TILER
TID	TIDINESS	TIFFINS	TIGHTWADS	TILERIES
TIDAL	TIDING	TIFFS	TIGHTWIRE	TILERS
TIDALLY	TIDINGS	TIFO	TIGLIC	TILERY
TIDBIT	TIDIVATE	TIFOS	TIGLON	TILES
TIDBITS	TIDIVATED	TIFOSI	TIGLONS	TILING
TIDDIER	TIDIVATES	TIFOSO	TIGNON	TILINGS
TIDDIES	TIDS	TIFOSOS	TIGNONS	TILL
TIDDIEST	TIDY	TIFT	TIGON	TILLABLE
TIDDLE	TIDYING	TIFTED	TIGONS	TILLAGE
TIDDLED	TIDYTIPS	TIFTING	TIGRESS	TILLAGES
TIDDLER	TIE	TIFTS	TIGRESSES	TILLED
TIDDLERS	TIEBACK	TIG	TIGRIDIA	TILLER
TIDDLES	TIEBACKS	TIGE	TIGRIDIAS	TILLERED
TIDDLEY	TIEBREAK	TIGER	TIGRINE	TILLERING
TIDDLEYS	TIEBREAKS	TIGEREYE	TIGRISH	TILLERMAN
TIDDLIER	TIECLASP	TIGEREYES	TIGRISHLY	TILLERMEN
TIDDLIES	TIECLASPS	TIGERIER	TIGROID	TILLERS
TIDDLIEST	TIED	TIGERIEST	TIGS	TILLICUM
TIDDLING	TIEING	TIGERISH	TIK	TILLICUMS
TIDDLY	TIELESS	TIGERISM	TIKA	TILLIER
TIDDY	TIEPIN	TIGERISMS	TIKANGA	TILLIEST
TIDE	TIEPINS	TIGERLIER	TIKANGAS	TILLING
TIDED	TIER	TIGERLIKE	TIKAS	TILLINGS
TIDELAND	TIERCE	TIGERLY	TIKE	TILLITE
TIDELANDS	TIERCED	TIGERS	TIKES	TILLITES
TIDELESS	TIERCEL	TIGERWOOD	TIKI	TILLS
TIDELIKE	TIERCELET	TIGERY	TIKIED	TILLY
TIDELINE	TIERCELS	TIGES	TIKIING	TILS
TIDELINES	TIERCERON	TIGGED	TIKINAGAN	TILT
TIDEMARK	TIERCES	TIGGER	TIKIS	TILTABLE
TIDEMARKS	TIERCET	TIGGERED	TIKKA	TILTED
TIDEMILL	TIERCETS	TIGGERING	TIKKAS	TILTER
TIDEMILLS	TIERED	TIGGERS	TIKOLOSHE	TILTERS
TIDERIP	TIERING	TIGGING	TIKS	TILTH
TIDERIPS	TIERS	TIGHT	TIKTAALIK	TILTHS
TIDES	TIES	TIGHTASS	TIL	TILTING
TIDESMAN	TIETAC	TIGHTEN	TILAK	TILTINGS
TIDESMEN	TIETACK	TIGHTENED	TILAKS	TILTMETER

TILTROTOR	TIMES	TINCALS	TINGLY	TINNY
TILTS	TIMESAVER	TINCHEL	TINGS	TINPLATE
TILTYARD	TIMESCALE	TINCHELS	TINGUAITE	TINPLATED
TILTYARDS	TIMESHARE	TINCT	TINHORN	TINPLATES
TIMARAU	TIMESHIFT	TINCTED	TINHORNS	TINPOT
TIMARAUS	TIMESTAMP	TINCTING	TINIER	TINPOTS
TIMARIOT	TIMETABLE	TINCTS	TINIES	TINS
TIMARIOTS	TIMEWORK	TINCTURE	TINIEST	TINSEL
TIMBAL	TIMEWORKS	TINCTURED	TINILY	TINSELED
TIMBALE	TIMEWORN	TINCTURES	TININESS	TINSELIER
TIMBALES	TIMID	TIND	TINING	TINSELING
TIMBALS	TIMIDER	TINDAL	TINK	TINSELLED
TIMBER	TIMIDEST	TINDALS	TINKED	TINSELLY
TIMBERED	TIMIDITY	TINDED	TINKER	TINSELRY
TIMBERIER	TIMIDLY	TINDER	TINKERED	TINSELS
TIMBERING	TIMIDNESS	TINDERBOX	TINKERER	TINSELY
TIMBERMAN	TIMING	TINDERIER	TINKERERS	TINSEY
TIMBERMEN	TIMINGS	TINDERS	TINKERING	TINSEYS
TIMBERS	TIMIST	TINDERY	TINKERMAN	TINSMITH
TIMBERY	TIMISTS	TINDING	TINKERMEN	TINSMITHS
TIMBO	TIMOCRACY	TINDS	TINKERS	TINSNIPS
TIMBOS	TIMOLOL	TINE	TINKERTOY	TINSTONE
TIMBRAL	TIMOLOLS	TINEA	TINKING	TINSTONES
TIMBRE	TIMON	TINEAL	TINKLE	TINT
TIMBREL	TIMONEER	TINEAS	TINKLED	TINTACK
TIMBRELS	TIMONEERS	TINED	TINKLER	TINTACKS
TIMBRES	TIMONS	TINEID	TINKLERS	TINTED
TIME	TIMOROUS	TINEIDS	TINKLES	TINTER
TIMEBOMB	TIMORSOME	TINES	TINKLIER	TINTERS
TIMEBOMBS	TIMOTHIES	TINFOIL	TINKLIEST	TINTIER
TIMECARD	TIMOTHY	TINFOILS	TINKLING	TINTIEST
TIMECARDS	TIMOUS	TINFUL	TINKLINGS	TINTINESS
TIMED	TIMOUSLY	TINFULS	TINKLY	TINTING
TIMEFRAME	TIMPANA	TING	TINKS	TINTINGS
TIMELESS	TIMPANAS	TINGE	TINLIKE	TINTLESS
TIMELIER	TIMPANI	TINGED	TINMAN	TINTOOKIE
TIMELIEST	TIMPANIST	TINGEING	TINMEN	TINTS
TIMELINE	TIMPANO	TINGES	TINNED	TINTY
TIMELINES	TIMPANUM	TINGING	TINNER	TINTYPE
TIMELY	TIMPANUMS	TINGLE	TINNERS	TINTYPES
TIMENOGUY	TIMPS	TINGLED	TINNIE	TINWARE
TIMEOUS	TIN	TINGLER	TINNIER	TINWARES
TIMEOUSLY	TINA	TINGLERS	TINNIES	TINWORK
TIMEOUT	TINAJA	TINGLES	TINNIEST	TINWORKS
TIMEOUTS	TINAJAS	TINGLIER	TINNILY	TINY
TIMEPASS	TINAMOU	TINGLIEST	TINNINESS	TIP
TIMEPIECE	TINAMOUS	TINGLING	TINNING	TIPCART
TIMER	TINAS	TINGLINGS	TINNINGS	TIPCARTS
TIMERS	TINCAL	TINGLISH	TINNITUS	TIPCAT

TIPCATS	TIPTOEING	TIRRIVEE	TITER	TITRATING
TIPI	TIPTOES	TIRRIVEES	TITERS	TITRATION
TIPIS	TIPTOP	TIRRIVIE	TITFER	TITRATOR
TIPLESS	TIPTOPS	TIRRIVIES	TITFERS	TITRATORS
TIPOFF	TIPTRONIC	TIRRS	TITHABLE	TITRE
TIPOFFS	TIPULA	TIS	TITHE	TITRES
TIPPABLE	TIPULAS	TISANE	TITHED	TITS
TIPPED	TIPUNA	TISANES	TITHER	TITTED
TIPPEE	TIPUNAS	TISICK	TITHERS	TITTER
TIPPEES	TIRADE	TISICKS	TITHES	TITTERED
TIPPER	TIRADES	TISSUAL	TITHING	TITTERER
TIPPERS	TIRAGE	TISSUE	TITHINGS	TITTERERS
TIPPET	TIRAGES	TISSUED	TITHONIA	TITTERING
TIPPETS	TIRAMISU	TISSUES	TITHONIAS	TITTERS
TIPPIER	TIRAMISUS	TISSUEY	TITI	TITTIE
TIPPIEST	TIRASSE	TISSUIER	TITIAN	TITTIES
TIPPING	TIRASSES	TISSUIEST	TITIANS	TITTING
TIPPINGS	TIRE	TISSUING	TITILLATE	TITTISH
TIPPLE	TIRED	TISSULAR	TITIS	TITTIVATE
TIPPLED	TIREDER	TISWAS	TITIVATE	TITTLE
TIPPLER	TIREDEST	TISWASES	TITIVATED	TITTLEBAT
TIPPLERS	TIREDLY	TIT	TITIVATES	TITTLED
TIPPLES	TIREDNESS	TITAN	TITIVATOR	TITTLES
TIPPLING	TIRELESS	TITANATE	TITLARK	TITTLING
TIPPY	TIRELING	TITANATES	TITLARKS	TITTUP
TIPPYTOE	TIRELINGS	TITANESS	TITLE	TITTUPED
TIPPYTOED	TIREMAKER	TITANIA	TITLED	TITTUPIER
TIPPYTOES	TIRES	TITANIAS	TITLELESS	TITTUPING
TIPS	TIRESOME	TITANIC	TITLER	TITTUPPED
TIPSHEET	TIREWOMAN	TITANIS	TITLERS	TITTUPPY
TIPSHEETS	TIREWOMEN	TITANISES	TITLES	TITTUPS
TIPSIER	TIRING	TITANISM	TITLIKE	TITTUPY
TIPSIEST	TIRINGLY	TITANISMS	TITLING	TITTY
TIPSIFIED	TIRINGS	TITANITE	TITLINGS	TITUBANCY
TIPSIFIES	TIRITI	TITANITES	TITLIST	TITUBANT
TIPSIFY	TIRITIS	TITANIUM	TITLISTS	TITUBATE
TIPSILY	TIRL	TITANIUMS	TITMAN	TITUBATED
TIPSINESS	TIRLED	TITANOUS	TITMEN	TITUBATES
TIPSTAFF	TIRLING	TITANS	TITMICE	TITULAR
TIPSTAFFS	TIRLS	TITBIT	TITMOSE	TITULARLY
TIPSTAVES	TIRO	TITBITS	TITMOUSE	TITULARS
TIPSTER	TIROES	TITCH	TITOKI	TITULARY
TIPSTERS	TIRONIC	TITCHES	TITOKIS	TITULE
TIPSTOCK	TIROS	TITCHIE	TITRABLE	TITULED
TIPSTOCKS	TIRR	TITCHIER	TITRANT	TITULES
TIPSY	TIRRED	TITCHIEST	TITRANTS	TITULI
TIPT	TIRRING	TITCHY	TITRATE	TITULING
TIPTOE	TIRRIT	TITE	TITRATED	TITULUS
TIPTOED	TIRRITS	TITELY	TITRATES	TITUP

TITUPED	TOAST	TOD	TOESHOES	TOGUE
TITUPIER	TOASTED	TODAY	TOETOE	TOGUES
TITUPIEST	TOASTER	TODAYS	TOETOES	TOHEROA
TITUPING	TOASTERS	TODDE	TOEY	TOHEROAS
TITUPPED	TOASTIE	TODDED	TOFF	TOHO
TITUPPING	TOASTIER	TODDES	TOFFEE	TOHOS
TITUPS	TOASTIES	TODDIES	TOFFEES	TOHUNGA
TITUPY	TOASTIEST	TODDING	TOFFIER	TOHUNGAS
TIVY	TOASTING	TODDLE	TOFFIES	TOIL
TIX	TOASTINGS	TODDLED	TOFFIEST	TOILE
TIYIN	TOASTS	TODDLER	TOFFISH	TOILED
TIYINS	TOASTY	TODDLERS	TOFFS	TOILER
TIYN	TOAZE	TODDLES	TOFFY	TOILERS
TIYNS	TOAZED	TODDLING	TOFORE	TOILES
TIZ	TOAZES	TODDY	TOFT	TOILET
TIZES	TOAZING	TODGER	TOFTS	TOILETED
TIZWAS	TOBACCO	TODGERS	TOFU	TOILETING
TIZWASES	TOBACCOES	TODIES	TOFUS	TOILETRY
TIZZ	TOBACCOS	TODS	TOFUTTI	TOILETS
TIZZES	TOBIES	TODY	TOFUTTIS	TOILETTE
TIZZIES	TOBOGGAN	TOE	TOG	TOILETTES
TIZZY	TOBOGGANS	TOEA	TOGA	TOILFUL
TJANTING	TOBOGGIN	TOEAS	TOGAE	TOILFULLY
TJANTINGS	TOBOGGINS	TOEBIE	TOGAED	TOILINET
TMESES	TOBY	TOEBIES	TOGAS	TOILINETS
TMESIS	TOC	TOECAP	TOGATE	TOILING
TO	TOCCATA	TOECAPS	TOGATED	TOILINGS
TOAD	TOCCATAS	TOECLIP	TOGAVIRUS	TOILLESS
TOADEATER	TOCCATE	TOECLIPS	TOGE	TOILS
TOADFISH	TOCCATINA	TOED	TOGED	TOILSOME
TOADFLAX	TOCHER	TOEHOLD	TOGES	TOILWORN
TOADGRASS	TOCHERED	TOEHOLDS	TOGETHER	TOING
TOADIED	TOCHERING	TOEIER	TOGGED	TOINGS
TOADIES	TOCHERS	TOEIEST	TOGGER	TOISE
TOADISH	TOCK	TOEING	TOGGERED	TOISEACH
TOADLESS	TOCKED	TOELESS	TOGGERIES	TOISEACHS
TOADLET	TOCKIER	TOELIKE	TOGGERING	TOISECH
TOADLETS	TOCKIEST	TOENAIL	TOGGERS	TOISECHS
TOADLIKE	TOCKING	TOENAILED	TOGGERY	TOISES
TOADRUSH	TOCKLEY	TOENAILS	TOGGING	TOISON
TOADS	TOCKLEYS	TOEPIECE	TOGGLE	TOISONS
TOADSTONE	TOCKS	TOEPIECES	TOGGLED	TOIT
TOADSTOOL	TOCKY	TOEPLATE	TOGGLER	TOITED
TOADY	TOCO	TOEPLATES	TOGGLERS	TOITING
TOADYING	TOCOLOGY	TOERAG	TOGGLES	TOITOI
TOADYINGS	TOCOS	TOERAGGER	TOGGLING	TOITOIS
TOADYISH	TOCS	TOERAGS	TOGROG	TOITS
TOADYISM	TOCSIN	TOES	TOGROGS	TOKAMAK
TOADYISMS	TOCSINS	TOESHOE	TOGS	TOKAMAKS

TOKAY	TOLERATES	TOLUATE	TOMBOC	TOMPON
TOKAYS	TOLERATOR	TOLUATES	TOMBOCS	TOMPONED
TOKE	TOLES	TOLUENE	TOMBOLA	TOMPONING
TOKED	TOLEWARE	TOLUENES	TOMBOLAS	TOMPONS
TOKEN	TOLEWARES	TOLUIC	TOMBOLO	TOMPOT
TOKENED	TOLIDIN	TOLUID	TOMBOLOS	TOMS
TOKENING	TOLIDINE	TOLUIDE	TOMBOY	TOMTIT
TOKENISM	TOLIDINES	TOLUIDES	TOMBOYISH	TOMTITS
TOKENISMS	TOLIDINS	TOLUIDIDE	TOMBOYS	TON
TOKENS	TOLING	TOLUIDIN	TOMBS	TONAL
TOKER	TOLINGS	TOLUIDINE	TOMBSTONE	TONALITE
TOKERS	TOLL	TOLUIDINS	TOMCAT	TONALITES
TOKES	TOLLABLE	TOLUIDS	TOMCATS	TONALITIC
TOKING	TOLLAGE	TOLUOL	TOMCATTED	TONALITY
TOKO	TOLLAGES	TOLUOLE	TOMCOD	TONALLY
TOKOLOGY	TOLLBAR	TOLUOLES	TOMCODS	TONANT
TOKOLOSHE	TOLLBARS	TOLUOLS	TOME	TONDI
TOKOLOSHI	TOLLBOOTH	TOLUS	TOMENTA	TONDINI
TOKOMAK	TOLLDISH	TOLUYL	TOMENTOSE	TONDINO
TOKOMAKS	TOLLED	TOLUYLS	TOMENTOUS	TONDINOS
TOKONOMA	TOLLER	TOLYL	TOMENTUM	TONDO
TOKONOMAS	TOLLERS	TOLYLS	TOMES	TONDOS
TOKOS	TOLLEY	TOLZEY	TOMFOOL	TONE
TOKOTOKO	TOLLEYS	TOLZEYS	TOMFOOLED	TONEARM
TOKOTOKOS	TOLLGATE	TOM	TOMFOOLS	TONEARMS
TOKTOKKIE	TOLLGATED	TOMAHAWK	TOMIA	TONED
TOLA	TOLLGATES	TOMAHAWKS	TOMIAL	TONELESS
TOLAN	TOLLHOUSE	TOMALLEY	TOMIUM	TONEME
TOLANE	TOLLIE	TOMALLEYS	TOMMED	TONEMES
TOLANES	TOLLIES	TOMAN	TOMMIED	TONEMIC
TOLANS	TOLLING	TOMANS	TOMMIES	TONEPAD
TOLAR	TOLLINGS	TOMATILLO	TOMMING	TONEPADS
TOLARJEV	TOLLMAN	TOMATO	TOMMY	TONER
TOLARJI	TOLLMEN	TOMATOES	TOMMYCOD	TONERS
TOLARS	TOLLS	TOMATOEY	TOMMYCODS	TONES
TOLAS	TOLLWAY	TOMATOIER	TOMMYING	TONETIC
TOLBOOTH	TOLLWAYS	TOMB	TOMMYROT	TONETICS
TOLBOOTHS	TOLLY	TOMBAC	TOMMYROTS	TONETTE
TOLD	TOLSEL	TOMBACK	TOMO	TONETTES
TOLE	TOLSELS	TOMBACKS	TOMOGRAM	TONEY
TOLED	TOLSEY	TOMBACS	TOMOGRAMS	TONG
TOLEDO	TOLSEYS	TOMBAK	TOMOGRAPH	TONGA
TOLEDOS	TOLT	TOMBAKS	TOMOPHOBE	TONGAS
TOLERABLE	TOLTER	TOMBAL	TOMORROW	TONGED
TOLERABLY	TOLTERED	TOMBED	TOMORROWS	TONGER
TOLERANCE	TOLTERING	TOMBIC	TOMOS	TONGERS
TOLERANT	TOLTERS	TOMBING	TOMOZ	TONGING
TOLERATE	TOLTS	TOMBLESS	TOMPION	TONGMAN
TOLERATED	TOLU	TOMBLIKE	TOMPIONS	TONGMEN

TONGS	TONNES	TOOLIE	TOOTHING	TOPFULL
TONGSTER	TONNISH	TOOLIES	TOOTHINGS	TOPH
TONGSTERS	TONNISHLY	TOOLING	TOOTHLESS	TOPHE
TONGUE	TONOMETER	TOOLINGS	TOOTHLIKE	TOPHES
TONGUED	TONOMETRY	TOOLKIT	TOOTHPICK	TOPHI
TONGUELET	TONOPLAST	TOOLKITS	TOOTHS	TOPHS
TONGUES	TONS	TOOLLESS	TOOTHSOME	TOPHUS
TONGUING	TONSIL	TOOLMAKER	TOOTHWASH	TOPI
TONGUINGS	TONSILAR	TOOLMAN	TOOTHWORT	TOPIARIAN
TONIC	TONSILLAR	TOOLMEN	TOOTHY	TOPIARIES
TONICALLY	TONSILS	TOOLPUSH	TOOTING	TOPIARIST
TONICITY	TONSOR	TOOLROOM	TOOTLE	TOPIARY
TONICS	TONSORIAL	TOOLROOMS	TOOTLED	TOPIC
TONIER	TONSORS	TOOLS	TOOTLER	TOPICAL
TONIES	TONSURE	TOOLSET	TOOTLERS	TOPICALLY
TONIEST	TONSURED	TOOLSETS	TOOTLES	TOPICALS
TONIFIED	TONSURES	TOOLSHED	TOOTLING	TOPICS
TONIFIES	TONSURING	TOOLSHEDS	TOOTS	TOPING
TONIFY	TONTINE	TOOLTIP	TOOTSED	TOPIS
TONIFYING	TONTINER	TOOLTIPS	TOOTSES	TOPKICK
TONIGHT	TONTINERS	TOOM	TOOTSIE	TOPKICKS
TONIGHTS	TONTINES	TOOMED	TOOTSIES	TOPKNOT
TONING	TONUS	TOOMER	TOOTSING	TOPKNOTS
TONINGS	TONUSES	TOOMEST	TOOTSY	TOPLESS
TONISH	TONY	TOOMING	TOP	TOPLINE
TONISHLY	TOO	TOOMS	TOPALGIA	TOPLINED
TONITE	TOOART	TOON	TOPALGIAS	TOPLINER
TONITES	TOOARTS	TOONIE	TOPARCH	TOPLINERS
TONK	TOODLE	TOONIES	TOPARCHS	TOPLINES
TONKA	TOODLED	TOONS	TOPARCHY	TOPLINING
TONKED	TOODLES	TOORIE	TOPAZ	TOPLOFTY
TONKER	TOODLING	TOORIES	TOPAZES	TOPMAKER
TONKERS	TOOK	TOOSHIE	TOPAZINE	TOPMAKERS
TONKING	TOOL	TOOSHIER	TOPCOAT	TOPMAKING
TONKS	TOOLBAG	TOOSHIEST	TOPCOATS	TOPMAN
TONLET	TOOLBAGS	TOOT	TOPCROSS	TOPMAST
TONLETS	TOOLBAR	TOOTED	TOPDRESS	TOPMASTS
TONNAG	TOOLBARS	TOOTER	TOPE	TOPMEN
TONNAGE	TOOLBOX	TOOTERS	TOPECTOMY	TOPMINNOW
TONNAGES	TOOLBOXES	TOOTH	TOPED	TOPMOST
TONNAGS	TOOLCASE	TOOTHACHE	TOPEE	TOPNOTCH
TONNE	TOOLCASES	TOOTHCOMB	TOPEES	TOPO
TONNEAU	TOOLCHEST	TOOTHED	TOPEK	TOPOGRAPH
TONNEAUS	TOOLED	TOOTHFISH	TOPEKS	TOPOI
TONNEAUX	TOOLER	TOOTHFUL	TOPER	TOPOLOGIC
TONNELL	TOOLERS	TOOTHFULS	TOPERS	TOPOLOGY
TONNELLS	TOOLHEAD	TOOTHIER	TOPES	TOPOMETRY
TONNER	TOOLHEADS	TOOTHIEST	TOPFLIGHT	TOPONYM
TONNERS	TOOLHOUSE	TOOTHILY	TOPFUL	TOPONYMAL

TOPONYMIC	TOQUILLA	TORIC	TORQUATE	TORTE
TOPONYMS	TOQUILLAS	TORICS	TORQUATED	TORTELLI
TOPONYMY	TOR	TORIES	TORQUE	TORTELLIS
TOPOS	TORA	TORII	TORQUED	TORTEN
TOPOTYPE	TORAH	TORMENT	TORQUER	TORTES
TOPOTYPES	TORAHS	TORMENTA	TORQUERS	TORTIE
TOPPED	TORAN	TORMENTED	TORQUES	TORTIERE
TOPPER	TORANA	TORMENTER	TORQUESES	TORTIERES
TOPPERS	TORANAS	TORMENTIL	TORQUEY	TORTIES
TOPPIER	TORANS	TORMENTOR	TORQUIER	TORTILE
TOPPIEST	TORAS	TORMENTS	TORQUIEST	TORTILITY
TOPPING	TORBANITE	TORMENTUM	TORQUING	TORTILLA
TOPPINGLY	TORC	TORMINA	TORR	TORTILLAS
TOPPINGS	TORCH	TORMINAL	TORREFIED	TORTILLON
TOPPLE	TORCHABLE	TORMINOUS	TORREFIES	TORTIOUS
TOPPLED	TORCHED	TORN	TORREFY	TORTIVE
TOPPLES	TORCHER	TORNADE	TORRENT	TORTOISE
TOPPLING	TORCHERE	TORNADES	TORRENTED	TORTOISES
TOPPY	TORCHERES	TORNADIC	TORRENTS	TORTONI
TOPRAIL	TORCHERS	TORNADO	TORRET	TORTONIS
TOPRAILS	TORCHES	TORNADOES	TORRETS	TORTRICES
TOPS	TORCHIER	TORNADOS	TORRID	TORTRICID
TOPSAIL	TORCHIERE	TORNILLO	TORRIDER	TORTRIX
TOPSAILS	TORCHIERS	TORNILLOS	TORRIDEST	TORTRIXES
TOPSCORE	TORCHIEST	TORO	TORRIDITY	TORTS
TOPSCORED	TORCHING	TOROID	TORRIDLY	TORTUOUS
TOPSCORES	TORCHINGS	TOROIDAL	TORRIFIED	TORTURE
TOPSIDE	TORCHLIKE	TOROIDS	TORRIFIES	TORTURED
TOPSIDER	TORCHLIT	TOROS	TORRIFY	TORTURER
TOPSIDERS	TORCHON	TOROSE	TORRS	TORTURERS
TOPSIDES	TORCHONS	TOROSITY	TORS	TORTURES
TOPSMAN	TORCHWOOD	TOROT	TORSADE	TORTURING
TOPSMEN	TORCHY	TOROTH	TORSADES	TORTUROUS
TOPSOIL	TORCS	TOROUS	TORSE	TORULA
TOPSOILED	TORCULAR	TORPEDO	TORSEL	TORULAE
TOPSOILS	TORCULARS	TORPEDOED	TORSELS	TORULAS
TOPSPIN	TORDION	TORPEDOER	TORSES	TORULI
TOPSPINS	TORDIONS	TORPEDOES	TORSI	TORULIN
TOPSTITCH	TORE	TORPEDOS	TORSION	TORULINS
TOPSTONE	TOREADOR	TORPEFIED	TORSIONAL	TORULOSE
TOPSTONES	TOREADORS	TORPEFIES	TORSIONS	TORULOSES
TOPWATER	TORERO	TORPEFY	TORSIVE	TORULOSIS
TOPWORK	TOREROS	TORPID	TORSK	TORULUS
TOPWORKED	TORES	TORPIDITY	TORSKS	TORUS
TOPWORKS	TOREUTIC	TORPIDLY	TORSO	TORUSES
TOQUE	TOREUTICS	TORPIDS	TORSOS	TORY
TOQUES	TORGOCH	TORPITUDE	TORT	TOSA
TOQUET	TORGOCHS	TORPOR	TORTA	TOSAS
TOQUETS	TORI	TORPORS	TORTAS	TOSE

TOSED	TOTALISTS	TOTTIES	TOUGHNESS	TOUSERS
TOSES	TOTALITY	TOTTIEST	TOUGHS	TOUSES
TOSH	TOTALIZE	TOTTING	TOUGHY	TOUSIER
TOSHACH	TOTALIZED	TOTTINGS	TOUK	TOUSIEST
TOSHACHS	TOTALIZER	TOTTRING	TOUKED	TOUSING
TOSHED	TOTALIZES	TOTTY	TOUKING	TOUSINGS
TOSHER	TOTALLED	TOUCAN	TOUKS	TOUSLE
TOSHERS	TOTALLING	TOUCANET	TOULADI	TOUSLED
TOSHES	TOTALLY	TOUCANETS	TOULADIS	TOUSLES
TOSHIER	TOTALS	TOUCANS	TOUN	TOUSLING
TOSHIEST	TOTANUS	TOUCH	TOUNS	TOUSTIE
TOSHING	TOTANUSES	TOUCHABLE	TOUPEE	TOUSTIER
TOSHY	TOTAQUINE	TOUCHABLY	TOUPEED	TOUSTIEST
TOSING	TOTARA	TOUCHBACK	TOUPEES	TOUSY
TOSS	TOTARAS	TOUCHDOWN	TOUPET	TOUT
TOSSED	TOTE	TOUCHE	TOUPETS	TOUTED
TOSSEN	TOTEABLE	TOUCHED	TOUPIE	TOUTER
TOSSER	TOTED	TOUCHER	TOUPIES	TOUTERS
TOSSERS	TOTEM	TOUCHERS	TOUR	TOUTIE
TOSSES	TOTEMIC	TOUCHES	TOURACO	TOUTIER
TOSSIER	TOTEMISM	TOUCHHOLE	TOURACOS	TOUTIEST
TOSSIEST	TOTEMISMS	TOUCHIER	TOURED	TOUTING
TOSSILY	TOTEMIST	TOUCHIEST	TOURER	TOUTON
TOSSING	TOTEMISTS	TOUCHILY	TOURERS	TOUTONS
TOSSINGS	TOTEMITE	TOUCHING	TOURIE	TOUTS
TOSSPOT	TOTEMITES	TOUCHINGS	TOURIES	TOUZE
TOSSPOTS	TOTEMS	TOUCHLESS	TOURING	TOUZED
TOSSUP	TOTER	TOUCHLINE	TOURINGS	TOUZES
TOSSUPS	TOTERS	TOUCHMARK	TOURISM	TOUZIER
TOSSY	TOTES	TOUCHPAD	TOURISMS	TOUZIEST
TOST	TOTHER	TOUCHPADS	TOURIST	TOUZING
TOSTADA	TOTHERS	TOUCHTONE	TOURISTA	TOUZLE
TOSTADAS	TOTIENT	TOUCHUP	TOURISTAS	TOUZLED
TOSTADO	TOTIENTS	TOUCHUPS	TOURISTED	TOUZLES
TOSTADOS	TOTING	TOUCHWOOD	TOURISTIC	TOUZLING
TOSTONE	TOTITIVE	TOUCHY	TOURISTS	TOUZY
TOSTONES	TOTITIVES	TOUGH	TOURISTY	TOVARICH
TOT	TOTS	TOUGHED	TOURNEDOS	TOVARISCH
TOTABLE	TOTTED	TOUGHEN	TOURNEY	TOVARISH
TOTAL	TOTTER	TOUGHENED	TOURNEYED	TOW
TOTALED	TOTTERED	TOUGHENER	TOURNEYER	TOWABLE
TOTALING	TOTTERER	TOUGHENS	TOURNEYS	TOWAGE
TOTALISE	TOTTERERS	TOUGHER	TOURNURE	TOWAGES
TOTALISED	TOTTERIER	TOUGHEST	TOURNURES	TOWARD
TOTALISER	TOTTERING	TOUGHIE	TOURS	TOWARDLY
TOTALISES	TOTTERS	TOUGHIES	TOURTIERE	TOWARDS
TOTALISM	TOTTERY	TOUGHING	TOUSE	TOWAWAY
TOTALISMS	TOTTIE	TOUGHISH	TOUSED	TOWAWAYS
TOTALIST	TOTTIER	TOUGHLY	TOUSER	TOWBAR

TOWBARS	TOWNHOUSE	TOWSY	TOYING	TRACHEAL
TOWBOAT	TOWNIE	TOWT	TOYINGS	TRACHEARY
TOWBOATS	TOWNIER	TOWTED	TOYISH	TRACHEAS
TOWED	TOWNIES	TOWTING	TOYISHLY	TRACHEATE
TOWEL	TOWNIEST	TOWTS	TOYLAND	TRACHEID
TOWELED	TOWNISH	TOWY	TOYLANDS	TRACHEIDE
TOWELETTE	TOWNLAND	TOWZE	TOYLESOME	TRACHEIDS
TOWELING	TOWNLANDS	TOWZED	TOYLESS	TRACHEOLE
TOWELINGS	TOWNLESS	TOWZES	TOYLIKE	TRACHINUS
TOWELLED	TOWNLET	TOWZIER	TOYLSOM	TRACHITIS
TOWELLING	TOWNLETS	TOWZIEST	TOYMAN	TRACHLE
TOWELS	TOWNLIER	TOWZING	TOYMEN	TRACHLED
TOWER	TOWNLIEST	TOWZY	TOYO	TRACHLES
TOWERED	TOWNLING	TOXAEMIA	TOYON	TRACHLING
TOWERIER	TOWNLINGS	TOXAEMIAS	TOYONS	TRACHOMA
TOWERIEST	TOWNLY	TOXAEMIC	TOYOS	TRACHOMAS
TOWERING	TOWNS	TOXAPHENE	TOYS	TRACHYTE
TOWERLESS	TOWNSCAPE	TOXEMIA	TOYSHOP	TRACHYTES
TOWERLIKE	TOWNSFOLK	TOXEMIAS	TOYSHOPS	TRACHYTIC
TOWERS	TOWNSHIP	TOXEMIC	TOYSOME	TRACING
TOWERY	TOWNSHIPS	TOXIC	TOYTOWN	TRACINGS
TOWHEAD	TOWNSITE	TOXICAL	TOYTOWNS	TRACK
TOWHEADED	TOWNSITES	TOXICALLY	TOYWOMAN	TRACKABLE
TOWHEADS	TOWNSKIP	TOXICANT	TOYWOMEN	TRACKAGE
TOWHEE	TOWNSKIPS	TOXICANTS	TOZE	TRACKAGES
TOWHEES	TOWNSMAN	TOXICITY	TOZED	TRACKBALL
TOWIE	TOWNSMEN	TOXICOSES	TOZES	TRACKBED
TOWIER	TOWNWARD	TOXICOSIS	TOZIE	TRACKBEDS
TOWIES	TOWNWARDS	TOXICS	TOZIES	TRACKED
TOWIEST	TOWNWEAR	TOXIGENIC	TOZING	TRACKER
TOWING	TOWNWEARS	TOXIN	TRABEATE	TRACKERS
TOWINGS	TOWNY	TOXINE	TRABEATED	TRACKIE
TOWKAY	TOWPATH	TOXINES	TRABECULA	TRACKIES
TOWKAYS	TOWPATHS	TOXINS	TRABS	TRACKING
TOWLINE	TOWPLANE	TOXOCARA	TRACE	TRACKINGS
TOWLINES	TOWPLANES	TOXOCARAL	TRACEABLE	TRACKLESS
TOWMON	TOWROPE	TOXOCARAS	TRACEABLY	TRACKMAN
TOWMOND	TOWROPES	TOXOID	TRACED	TRACKMEN
TOWMONDS	TOWS	TOXOIDS	TRACELESS	TRACKPAD
TOWMONS	TOWSACK	TOXOPHILY	TRACER	TRACKPADS
TOWMONT	TOWSACKS	TOY	TRACERIED	TRACKROAD
TOWMONTS	TOWSE	TOYBOX	TRACERIES	TRACKS
TOWN	TOWSED	TOYBOXES	TRACERS	TRACKSIDE
TOWNEE	TOWSER	TOYCHEST	TRACERY	TRACKSUIT
TOWNEES	TOWSERS	TOYCHESTS	TRACES	TRACKWAY
TOWNFOLK	TOWSES	TOYED	TRACEUR	TRACKWAYS
TOWNHALL	TOWSIER	TOYER	TRACEURS	TRACKY
TOWNHOME	TOWSIEST	TOYERS	TRACHEA	TRACT
TOWNHOMES	TOWSING	TOYETIC	TRACHEAE	TRACTABLE

TRACTABLY	TRAFFICKY	TRAINMAN	TRAMPIER	TRANS
TRACTATE	TRAFFICS	TRAINMEN	TRAMPIEST	TRANSACT
TRACTATES	TRAGAL	TRAINS	TRAMPING	TRANSACTS
TRACTATOR	TRAGEDIAN	TRAINWAY	TRAMPINGS	TRANSAXLE
TRACTED	TRAGEDIES	TRAINWAYS	TRAMPISH	TRANSCEND
TRACTILE	TRAGEDY	TRAIPSE	TRAMPLE	TRANSCODE
TRACTING	TRAGELAPH	TRAIPSED	TRAMPLED	TRANSDUCE
TRACTION	TRAGI	TRAIPSES	TRAMPLER	TRANSE
TRACTIONS	TRAGIC	TRAIPSING	TRAMPLERS	TRANSECT
TRACTIVE	TRAGICAL	TRAIT	TRAMPLES	TRANSECTS
TRACTOR	TRAGICS	TRAITOR	TRAMPLING	TRANSENNA
TRACTORS	TRAGOPAN	TRAITORLY	TRAMPOLIN	TRANSEPT
TRACTRIX	TRAGOPANS	TRAITORS	TRAMPS	TRANSEPTS
TRACTS	TRAGULE	TRAITRESS	TRAMPY	TRANSES
TRACTUS	TRAGULES	TRAITS	TRAMROAD	TRANSEUNT
TRACTUSES	TRAGULINE	TRAJECT	TRAMROADS	TRANSFARD
TRAD	TRAGUS	TRAJECTED	TRAMS	TRANSFECT
TRADABLE	TRAHISON	TRAJECTS	TRAMWAY	TRANSFEM
TRADE	TRAHISONS	TRAM	TRAMWAYS	TRANSFER
TRADEABLE	TRAIK	TRAMADOL	TRANCE	TRANSFERS
TRADED	TRAIKED	TRAMADOLS	TRANCED	TRANSFIX
TRADEFUL	TRAIKING	TRAMCAR	TRANCEDLY	TRANSFIXT
TRADELESS	TRAIKIT	TRAMCARS	TRANCES	TRANSFORM
TRADEMARK	TRAIKS	TRAMEL	TRANCEY	TRANSFUSE
TRADENAME	TRAIL	TRAMELED	TRANCHE	TRANSGENE
TRADEOFF	TRAILABLE	TRAMELING	TRANCHES	TRANSHIP
TRADEOFFS	TRAILED	TRAMELL	TRANCHET	TRANSHIPS
TRADER	TRAILER	TRAMELLED	TRANCHETS	TRANSHUME
TRADERS	TRAILERED	TRAMELLS	TRANCIER	TRANSIENT
TRADES	TRAILERS	TRAMELS	TRANCIEST	TRANSIRE
TRADESMAN	TRAILHEAD	TRAMLESS	TRANCING	TRANSIRES
TRADESMEN	TRAILING	TRAMLINE	TRANECT	TRANSIT
TRADIE	TRAILLESS	TRAMLINED	TRANECTS	TRANSITED
TRADIES	TRAILS	TRAMLINES	TRANGAM	TRANSITS
TRADING	TRAILSIDE	TRAMMED	TRANGAMS	TRANSLATE
TRADINGS	TRAIN	TRAMMEL	TRANGLE	TRANSMASC
TRADITION	TRAINABLE	TRAMMELED	TRANGLES	TRANSMEW
TRADITIVE	TRAINBAND	TRAMMELER	TRANK	TRANSMEWS
TRADITOR	TRAINED	TRAMMELS	TRANKED	TRANSMIT
TRADITORS	TRAINEE	TRAMMIE	TRANKING	TRANSMITS
TRADS	TRAINEES	TRAMMIES	TRANKS	TRANSMOVE
TRADUCE	TRAINER	TRAMMING	TRANKUM	TRANSMUTE
TRADUCED	TRAINERS	TRAMP	TRANKUMS	TRANSNESS
TRADUCER	TRAINFUL	TRAMPED	TRANNIE	TRANSOM
TRADUCERS	TRAINFULS	TRAMPER	TRANNIES	TRANSOMED
TRADUCES	TRAINING	TRAMPERS	TRANNY	TRANSOMS
TRADUCIAN	TRAININGS	TRAMPET	TRANQ	TRANSONIC
TRADUCING	TRAINLESS	TRAMPETS	TRANQS	TRANSPIRE
TRAFFIC	TRAINLOAD	TRAMPETTE	TRANQUIL	TRANSPORT

TRANSPOSE	TRAPNESTS	TRAUMA	TRAYFUL	TREATINGS
TRANSSHIP	TRAPPEAN	TRAUMAS	TRAYFULS	TREATISE
TRANSUDE	TRAPPED	TRAUMATA	TRAYNE	TREATISES
TRANSUDED	TRAPPER	TRAUMATIC	TRAYNED	TREATMENT
TRANSUDES	TRAPPERS	TRAVAIL	TRAYNES	TREATS
TRANSUME	TRAPPIER	TRAVAILED	TRAYNING	TREATY
TRANSUMED	TRAPPIEST	TRAVAILS	TRAYS	TREBBIANO
TRANSUMES	TRAPPING	TRAVE	TRAZODONE	TREBLE
TRANSUMPT	TRAPPINGS	TRAVEL	TREACHER	TREBLED
TRANSVEST	TRAPPOSE	TRAVELED	TREACHERS	TREBLES
TRANT	TRAPPOUS	TRAVELER	TREACHERY	TREBLIER
TRANTED	TRAPPY	TRAVELERS	TREACHOUR	TREBLIEST
TRANTER	TRAPROCK	TRAVELING	TREACLE	TREBLING
TRANTERS	TRAPROCKS	TRAVELLED	TREACLED	TREBLINGS
TRANTING	TRAPS	TRAVELLER	TREACLES	TREBLY
TRANTS	TRAPSE	TRAVELOG	TREACLIER	TREBUCHET
TRAP	TRAPSED	TRAVELOGS	TREACLING	TREBUCKET
TRAPAN	TRAPSES	TRAVELS	TREACLY	TRECENTO
TRAPANNED	TRAPSING	TRAVERSAL	TREAD	TRECENTOS
TRAPANNER	TRAPT	TRAVERSE	TREADED	TRECK
TRAPANS	TRAPUNTO	TRAVERSED	TREADER	TRECKED
TRAPBALL	TRAPUNTOS	TRAVERSER	TREADERS	TRECKING
TRAPBALLS	TRASH	TRAVERSES	TREADING	TRECKS
TRAPDOOR	TRASHCAN	TRAVERTIN	TREADINGS	TREDDLE
TRAPDOORS	TRASHCANS	TRAVES	TREADLE	TREDDLED
TRAPE	TRASHED	TRAVESTY	TREADLED	TREDDLES
TRAPED	TRASHER	TRAVIS	TREADLER	TREDDLING
TRAPES	TRASHERS	TRAVISES	TREADLERS	TREDILLE
TRAPESED	TRASHERY	TRAVOIS	TREADLES	TREDILLES
TRAPESES	TRASHES	TRAVOISE	TREADLESS	TREDRILLE
TRAPESING	TRASHIER	TRAVOISES	TREADLING	TREE
TRAPEZE	TRASHIEST	TRAWL	TREADMILL	TREED
TRAPEZED	TRASHILY	TRAWLED	TREADS	TREEHOUSE
TRAPEZES	TRASHING	TRAWLER	TREAGUE	TREEING
TRAPEZIA	TRASHMAN	TRAWLERS	TREAGUES	TREELAWN
TRAPEZIAL	TRASHMEN	TRAWLEY	TREASON	TREELAWNS
TRAPEZII	TRASHTRIE	TRAWLEYS	TREASONS	TREELESS
TRAPEZING	TRASHY	TRAWLING	TREASURE	TREELIKE
TRAPEZIST	TRASS	TRAWLINGS	TREASURED	TREELINE
TRAPEZIUM	TRASSES	TRAWLNET	TREASURER	TREELINES
TRAPEZIUS	TRAT	TRAWLNETS	TREASURES	TREEN
TRAPEZOID	TRATS	TRAWLS	TREASURY	TREENAIL
TRAPFALL	TRATT	TRAY	TREAT	TREENAILS
TRAPFALLS	TRATTORIA	TRAYBAKE	TREATABLE	TREENS
TRAPING	TRATTORIE	TRAYBAKES	TREATED	TREENWARE
TRAPLIKE	TRATTS	TRAYBIT	TREATER	TREES
TRAPLINE	TRAUCHLE	TRAYBITS	TREATERS	TREESHIP
TRAPLINES	TRAUCHLED	TRAYCLOTH	TREATIES	TREESHIPS
TRAPNEST	TRAUCHLES	TRAYF	TREATING	TREETOP

TREETOPS	TREMIES	TREPHINED	TREZES	TRIAXIAL
TREEWARE	TREMOLANT	TREPHINER	TRIABLE	TRIAXIALS
TREEWARES	TREMOLITE	TREPHINES	TRIAC	TRIAXON
TREEWAX	TREMOLO	TREPID	TRIACID	TRIAXONS
TREEWAXES	TREMOLOS	TREPIDANT	TRIACIDS	TRIAZIN
TREF	TREMOR	TREPONEMA	TRIACS	TRIAZINE
TREFA	TREMORED	TREPONEME	TRIACT	TRIAZINES
TREFAH	TREMORING	TRES	TRIACTINE	TRIAZINS
TREFOIL	TREMOROUS	TRESPASS	TRIACTOR	TRIAZOLE
TREFOILED	TREMORS	TRESS	TRIACTORS	TRIAZOLES
TREFOILS	TREMS	TRESSED	TRIACTS	TRIAZOLIC
TREGETOUR	TREMULANT	TRESSEL	TRIAD	TRIBADE
TREGGINGS	TREMULATE	TRESSELS	TRIADIC	TRIBADES
TREHALA	TREMULOUS	TRESSES	TRIADICS	TRIBADIC
TREHALAS	TRENAIL	TRESSIER	TRIADISM	TRIBADIES
TREHALOSE	TRENAILS	TRESSIEST	TRIADISMS	TRIBADISM
TREIF	TRENCH	TRESSING	TRIADIST	TRIBADY
TREIFA	TRENCHAND	TRESSOUR	TRIADISTS	TRIBAL
TREILLAGE	TRENCHANT	TRESSOURS	TRIADS	TRIBALISM
TREILLE	TRENCHARD	TRESSURE	TRIAGE	TRIBALIST
TREILLES	TRENCHED	TRESSURED	TRIAGED	TRIBALLY
TREK	TRENCHER	TRESSURES	TRIAGES	TRIBALS
TREKKED	TRENCHERS	TRESSY	TRIAGING	TRIBASIC
TREKKER	TRENCHES	TREST	TRIAL	TRIBBLE
TREKKERS	TRENCHING	TRESTLE	TRIALED	TRIBBLES
TREKKING	TREND	TRESTLES	TRIALING	TRIBE
TREKKINGS	TRENDED	TRESTS	TRIALISM	TRIBELESS
TREKS	TRENDIER	TRET	TRIALISMS	TRIBES
TRELLIS	TRENDIES	TRETINOIN	TRIALIST	TRIBESMAN
TRELLISED	TRENDIEST	TRETS	TRIALISTS	TRIBESMEN
TRELLISES	TRENDIFY	TREVALLY	TRIALITY	TRIBLET
TREM	TRENDILY	TREVALLYS	TRIALLED	TRIBLETS
TREMA	TRENDING	TREVET	TRIALLING	TRIBOLOGY
TREMAS	TRENDOID	TREVETS	TRIALLIST	TRIBRACH
TREMATIC	TRENDOIDS	TREVIS	TRIALOGUE	TRIBRACHS
TREMATODE	TRENDS	TREVISES	TRIALS	TRIBULATE
TREMATOID	TRENDY	TREVISS	TRIALWARE	TRIBUNAL
TREMBLANT	TRENDYISM	TREVISSES	TRIANGLE	TRIBUNALS
TREMBLE	TRENISE	TREW	TRIANGLED	TRIBUNARY
TREMBLED	TRENISES	TREWS	TRIANGLES	TRIBUNATE
TREMBLER	TRENTAL	TREWSMAN	TRIAPSAL	TRIBUNE
TREMBLERS	TRENTALS	TREWSMEN	TRIARCH	TRIBUNES
TREMBLES	TREPAN	TREY	TRIARCHS	TRIBUTARY
TREMBLIER	TREPANG	TREYBIT	TRIARCHY	TRIBUTE
TREMBLING	TREPANGS	TREYBITS	TRIASSIC	TRIBUTER
TREMBLOR	TREPANNED	TREYF	TRIATHLON	TRIBUTERS
TREMBLORS	TREPANNER	TREYFA	TRIATIC	TRIBUTES
TREMBLY	TREPANS	TREYS	TRIATICS	TRICAR
TREMIE	TREPHINE	TREZ	TRIATOMIC	TRICARS

TRICE	TRICKSIER	TRIENE	TRIGGED	TRILL
TRICED	TRICKSILY	TRIENES	TRIGGER	TRILLED
TRICEP	TRICKSOME	TRIENNIA	TRIGGERED	TRILLER
TRICEPS	TRICKSTER	TRIENNIAL	TRIGGERS	TRILLERS
TRICEPSES	TRICKSY	TRIENNIUM	TRIGGEST	TRILLING
TRICERION	TRICKY	TRIENS	TRIGGING	TRILLINGS
TRICES	TRICLAD	TRIENTES	TRIGLOT	TRILLION
TRICHINA	TRICLADS	TRIER	TRIGLOTS	TRILLIONS
TRICHINAE	TRICLINIA	TRIERARCH	TRIGLY	TRILLIUM
TRICHINAL	TRICLINIC	TRIERS	TRIGLYPH	TRILLIUMS
TRICHINAS	TRICLOSAN	TRIES	TRIGLYPHS	TRILLO
TRICHITE	TRICOLOR	TRIETERIC	TRIGNESS	TRILLOES
TRICHITES	TRICOLORS	TRIETHYL	TRIGO	TRILLS
TRICHITIC	TRICOLOUR	TRIFACIAL	TRIGON	TRILOBAL
TRICHOID	TRICORN	TRIFECTA	TRIGONAL	TRILOBATE
TRICHOME	TRICORNE	TRIFECTAS	TRIGONIC	TRILOBE
TRICHOMES	TRICORNES	TRIFF	TRIGONOUS	TRILOBED
TRICHOMIC	TRICORNS	TRIFFER	TRIGONS	TRILOBES
TRICHORD	TRICOT	TRIFFEST	TRIGOS	TRILOBITE
TRICHORDS	TRICOTINE	TRIFFIC	TRIGRAM	TRILOGIES
TRICHOSES	TRICOTS	TRIFFID	TRIGRAMS	TRILOGY
TRICHOSIS	TRICROTIC	TRIFFIDS	TRIGRAPH	TRIM
TRICHROIC	TRICTRAC	TRIFFIDY	TRIGRAPHS	TRIMARAN
TRICHROME	TRICTRACS	TRIFID	TRIGS	TRIMARANS
TRICING	TRICUSPID	TRIFLE	TRIGYNIAN	TRIMER
TRICITIES	TRICYCLE	TRIFLED	TRIGYNOUS	TRIMERIC
TRICITY	TRICYCLED	TRIFLER	TRIHEDRA	TRIMERISM
TRICK	TRICYCLER	TRIFLERS	TRIHEDRAL	TRIMEROUS
TRICKED	TRICYCLES	TRIFLES	TRIHEDRON	TRIMERS
TRICKER	TRICYCLIC	TRIFLING	TRIHYBRID	TRIMESTER
TRICKERS	TRIDACNA	TRIFLINGS	TRIHYDRIC	TRIMETER
TRICKERY	TRIDACNAS	TRIFOCAL	TRIJET	TRIMETERS
TRICKIE	TRIDACTYL	TRIFOCALS	TRIJETS	TRIMETHYL
TRICKIER	TRIDARN	TRIFOLD	TRIJUGATE	TRIMETRIC
TRICKIEST	TRIDARNS	TRIFOLIA	TRIJUGOUS	TRIMIX
TRICKILY	TRIDE	TRIFOLIES	TRIKE	TRIMIXES
TRICKING	TRIDENT	TRIFOLIUM	TRIKES	TRIMLY
TRICKINGS	TRIDENTAL	TRIFOLY	TRILBIED	TRIMMED
TRICKISH	TRIDENTED	TRIFORIA	TRILBIES	TRIMMER
TRICKLE	TRIDENTS	TRIFORIAL	TRILBY	TRIMMERS
TRICKLED	TRIDUAN	TRIFORIUM	TRILBYS	TRIMMEST
TRICKLES	TRIDUUM	TRIFORM	TRILD	TRIMMING
TRICKLESS	TRIDUUMS	TRIFORMED	TRILEMMA	TRIMMINGS
TRICKLET	TRIDYMITE	TRIG	TRILEMMAS	TRIMNESS
TRICKLETS	TRIE	TRIGAMIES	TRILINEAR	TRIMORPH
TRICKLIER	TRIECIOUS	TRIGAMIST	TRILITH	TRIMORPHS
TRICKLING	TRIED	TRIGAMOUS	TRILITHIC	TRIMOTOR
TRICKLY	TRIELLA	TRIGAMY	TRILITHON	TRIMOTORS
TRICKS	TRIELLAS	TRIGEMINI	TRILITHS	TRIMPHONE

TRIMPOT	TRIOXID	TRIPODS	TRISCELES	TRITIATED
TRIMPOTS	TRIOXIDE	TRIPODY	TRISECT	TRITIATES
TRIMS	TRIOXIDES	TRIPOLI	TRISECTED	TRITICAL
TRIMTAB	TRIOXIDS	TRIPOLIS	TRISECTOR	TRITICALE
TRIMTABS	TRIOXYGEN	TRIPOS	TRISECTS	TRITICISM
TRIN	TRIP	TRIPOSES	TRISEME	TRITICUM
TRINAL	TRIPACK	TRIPPANT	TRISEMES	TRITICUMS
TRINARY	TRIPACKS	TRIPPED	TRISEMIC	TRITIDE
TRINDLE	TRIPART	TRIPPER	TRISERIAL	TRITIDES
TRINDLED	TRIPE	TRIPPERS	TRISHAW	TRITIUM
TRINDLES	TRIPEDAL	TRIPPERY	TRISHAWS	TRITIUMS
TRINDLING	TRIPERIES	TRIPPET	TRISKELE	TRITOMA
TRINE	TRIPERY	TRIPPETS	TRISKELES	TRITOMAS
TRINED	TRIPES	TRIPPIER	TRISKELIA	TRITON
TRINES	TRIPEY	TRIPPIEST	TRISMIC	TRITONE
TRINGLE	TRIPHASE	TRIPPING	TRISMUS	TRITONES
TRINGLES	TRIPHONE	TRIPPINGS	TRISMUSES	TRITONIA
TRINING	TRIPHONES	TRIPPLE	TRISODIUM	TRITONIAS
TRINITIES	TRIPIER	TRIPPLED	TRISOME	TRITONS
TRINITRIN	TRIPIEST	TRIPPLER	TRISOMES	TRITURATE
TRINITY	TRIPITAKA	TRIPPLERS	TRISOMIC	TRIUMPH
TRINKET	TRIPLANE	TRIPPLES	TRISOMICS	TRIUMPHAL
TRINKETED	TRIPLANES	TRIPPLING	TRISOMIES	TRIUMPHED
TRINKETER	TRIPLE	TRIPPY	TRISOMY	TRIUMPHER
TRINKETRY	TRIPLED	TRIPS	TRIST	TRIUMPHS
TRINKETS	TRIPLES	TRIPSES	TRISTATE	TRIUMVIR
TRINKUM	TRIPLET	TRIPSIS	TRISTE	TRIUMVIRI
TRINKUMS	TRIPLETS	TRIPTAN	TRISTESSE	TRIUMVIRS
TRINODAL	TRIPLEX	TRIPTANE	TRISTEZA	TRIUMVIRY
TRINOMIAL	TRIPLEXED	TRIPTANES	TRISTEZAS	TRIUNE
TRINS	TRIPLEXES	TRIPTANS	TRISTFUL	TRIUNES
TRIO	TRIPLIED	TRIPTOTE	TRISTICH	TRIUNITY
TRIODE	TRIPLIES	TRIPTOTES	TRISTICHS	TRIVALENT
TRIODES	TRIPLING	TRIPTYCA	TRISUL	TRIVALVE
TRIOL	TRIPLINGS	TRIPTYCAS	TRISULA	TRIVALVED
TRIOLEIN	TRIPLITE	TRIPTYCH	TRISULAS	TRIVALVES
TRIOLEINS	TRIPLITES	TRIPTYCHS	TRISULS	TRIVET
TRIOLET	TRIPLOID	TRIPTYQUE	TRITANOPE	TRIVETS
TRIOLETS	TRIPLOIDS	TRIPUDIA	TRITE	TRIVIA
TRIOLS	TRIPLOIDY	TRIPUDIUM	TRITELY	TRIVIAL
TRIONES	TRIPLY	TRIPWIRE	TRITENESS	TRIVIALLY
TRIONYM	TRIPLYING	TRIPWIRES	TRITER	TRIVIUM
TRIONYMAL	TRIPMAN	TRIPY	TRITES	TRIVIUMS
TRIONYMS	TRIPMEN	TRIQUETRA	TRITEST	TRIWEEKLY
TRIOR	TRIPMETER	TRIRADIAL	TRITHEISM	TRIZONAL
TRIORS	TRIPOD	TRIREME	TRITHEIST	TRIZONE
TRIOS	TRIPODAL	TRIREMES	TRITHING	TRIZONES
TRIOSE	TRIPODIC	TRISAGION	TRITHINGS	TROAD
TRIOSES	TRIPODIES	TRISCELE	TRITIATE	TROADE

TROADES	TRODS	TROLLOPEE	TROPES	TROUBLER
TROADS	TROELIE	TROLLOPS	TROPHESY	TROUBLERS
TROAK	TROELIES	TROLLOPY	TROPHI	TROUBLES
TROAKED	TROELY	TROLLS	TROPHIC	TROUBLING
TROAKING	TROFFER	TROLLY	TROPHIED	TROUBLOUS
TROAKS	TROFFERS	TROLLYING	TROPHIES	TROUCH
TROAT	TROFIE	TROMBONE	TROPHY	TROUCHES
TROATED	TROFIES	TROMBONES	TROPHYING	TROUGH
TROATING	TROG	TROMINO	TROPIC	TROUGHED
TROATS	TROGGED	TROMINOES	TROPICAL	TROUGHING
TROCAR	TROGGING	TROMINOS	TROPICALS	TROUGHS
TROCARS	TROGGS	TROMMEL	TROPICS	TROULE
TROCHAIC	TROGON	TROMMELS	TROPIN	TROULED
TROCHAICS	TROGONS	TROMP	TROPINE	TROULES
TROCHAL	TROGS	TROMPE	TROPINES	TROULING
TROCHAR	TROIKA	TROMPED	TROPING	TROUNCE
TROCHARS	TROIKAS	TROMPES	TROPINS	TROUNCED
TROCHE	TROILISM	TROMPING	TROPISM	TROUNCER
TROCHEE	TROILISMS	TROMPS	TROPISMS	TROUNCERS
TROCHEES	TROILIST	TRON	TROPIST	TROUNCES
TROCHES	TROILISTS	TRONA	TROPISTIC	TROUNCING
TROCHI	TROILITE	TRONAS	TROPISTS	TROUPE
TROCHIL	TROILITES	TRONC	TROPOLOGY	TROUPED
TROCHILI	TROILUS	TRONCS	TROPONIN	TROUPER
TROCHILIC	TROILUSES	TRONE	TROPONINS	TROUPERS
TROCHILS	TROIS	TRONES	TROPPO	TROUPES
TROCHILUS	TROJAN	TRONK	TROSSERS	TROUPIAL
TROCHISCI	TROJANS	TRONKS	TROT	TROUPIALS
TROCHISK	TROKE	TRONS	TROTH	TROUPING
TROCHISKS	TROKED	TROOLIE	TROTHED	TROUSE
TROCHITE	TROKES	TROOLIES	TROTHFUL	TROUSER
TROCHITES	TROKING	TROOP	TROTHING	TROUSERED
TROCHLEA	TROLAND	TROOPED	TROTHLESS	TROUSERS
TROCHLEAE	TROLANDS	TROOPER	TROTHS	TROUSES
TROCHLEAR	TROLL	TROOPERS	TROTLINE	TROUSSEAU
TROCHLEAS	TROLLED	TROOPIAL	TROTLINES	TROUT
TROCHOID	TROLLER	TROOPIALS	TROTS	TROUTER
TROCHOIDS	TROLLERS	TROOPING	TROTTED	TROUTERS
TROCHUS	TROLLEY	TROOPS	TROTTER	TROUTFUL
TROCHUSES	TROLLEYED	TROOPSHIP	TROTTERS	TROUTIER
TROCK	TROLLEYS	TROOSTITE	TROTTING	TROUTIEST
TROCKED	TROLLIED	TROOZ	TROTTINGS	TROUTING
TROCKEN	TROLLIES	TROP	TROTTOIR	TROUTINGS
TROCKING	TROLLING	TROPAEOLA	TROTTOIRS	TROUTLESS
TROCKS	TROLLINGS	TROPARIA	TROTYL	TROUTLET
TROD	TROLLISH	TROPARION	TROTYLS	TROUTLETS
TRODDEN	TROLLIUS	TROPE	TROU	TROUTLIKE
TRODE	TROLLOP	TROPED	TROUBLE	TROUTLING
TRODES	TROLLOPED	TROPEOLIN	TROUBLED	TROUTS

TROUTY	TRUCKED	TRUFFE	TRUNKLIKE	TRYER
TROUVERE	TRUCKER	TRUFFES	TRUNKS	TRYERS
TROUVERES	TRUCKERS	TRUFFLE	TRUNKWORK	TRYING
TROUVEUR	TRUCKFUL	TRUFFLED	TRUNNEL	TRYINGLY
TROUVEURS	TRUCKFULS	TRUFFLES	TRUNNELS	TRYINGS
TROVE	TRUCKIE	TRUFFLING	TRUNNION	TRYKE
TROVER	TRUCKIES	TRUG	TRUNNIONS	TRYKES
TROVERS	TRUCKING	TRUGO	TRUQUAGE	TRYMA
TROVES	TRUCKINGS	TRUGOS	TRUQUAGES	TRYMATA
TROW	TRUCKLE	TRUGS	TRUQUEUR	TRYNA
TROWED	TRUCKLED	TRUING	TRUQUEURS	TRYOUT
TROWEL	TRUCKLER	TRUISM	TRUSS	TRYOUTS
TROWELED	TRUCKLERS	TRUISMS	TRUSSED	TRYP
TROWELER	TRUCKLES	TRUISTIC	TRUSSER	TRYPAN
TROWELERS	TRUCKLINE	TRULL	TRUSSERS	TRYPS
TROWELING	TRUCKLING	TRULLS	TRUSSES	TRYPSIN
TROWELLED	TRUCKLOAD	TRULY	TRUSSING	TRYPSINS
TROWELLER	TRUCKMAN	TRUMEAU	TRUSSINGS	TRYPTIC
TROWELS	TRUCKMEN	TRUMEAUX	TRUST	TRYSAIL
TROWING	TRUCKS	TRUMP	TRUSTABLE	TRYSAILS
TROWS	TRUCKSTOP	TRUMPED	TRUSTED	TRYST
TROWSERS	TRUCULENT	TRUMPERY	TRUSTEE	TRYSTE
TROWTH	TRUDGE	TRUMPET	TRUSTEED	TRYSTED
TROWTHS	TRUDGED	TRUMPETED	TRUSTEES	TRYSTER
TROY	TRUDGEN	TRUMPETER	TRUSTER	TRYSTERS
TROYS	TRUDGENS	TRUMPETS	TRUSTERS	TRYSTES
TRUANCIES	TRUDGEON	TRUMPING	TRUSTFUL	TRYSTING
TRUANCY	TRUDGEONS	TRUMPINGS	TRUSTIER	TRYSTS
TRUANT	TRUDGER	TRUMPLESS	TRUSTIES	TRYWORKS
TRUANTED	TRUDGERS	TRUMPS	TRUSTIEST	TSADDIK
TRUANTING	TRUDGES	TRUNCAL	TRUSTILY	TSADDIKIM
TRUANTLY	TRUDGING	TRUNCATE	TRUSTING	TSADDIKS
TRUANTRY	TRUDGINGS	TRUNCATED	TRUSTLESS	TSADDIQ
TRUANTS	TRUE	TRUNCATES	TRUSTOR	TSADDIQIM
TRUCAGE	TRUEBLUE	TRUNCHEON	TRUSTORS	TSADDIQS
TRUCAGES	TRUEBLUES	TRUNDLE	TRUSTS	TSADE
TRUCE	TRUEBORN	TRUNDLED	TRUSTY	TSADES
TRUCED	TRUEBRED	TRUNDLER	TRUTH	TSADI
TRUCELESS	TRUED	TRUNDLERS	TRUTHER	TSADIK
TRUCES	TRUEING	TRUNDLES	TRUTHERS	TSADIKS
TRUCHMAN	TRUELOVE	TRUNDLING	TRUTHFUL	TSADIS
TRUCHMANS	TRUELOVES	TRUNK	TRUTHIER	TSAMBA
TRUCHMEN	TRUEMAN	TRUNKED	TRUTHIEST	TSAMBAS
TRUCIAL	TRUEMEN	TRUNKFISH	TRUTHLESS	TSANTSA
TRUCING	TRUENESS	TRUNKFUL	TRUTHLIKE	TSANTSAS
TRUCK	TRUEPENNY	TRUNKFULS	TRUTHS	TSAR
TRUCKABLE	TRUER	TRUNKING	TRUTHY	TSARDOM
TRUCKAGE	TRUES	TRUNKINGS	TRY	TSARDOMS
TRUCKAGES	TRUEST	TRUNKLESS	TRYE	TSAREVICH

T

TSAREVNA	TSUNAMIS	TUBERCLE	TUBULOUS	TUFTERS
TSAREVNAS	TSURIS	TUBERCLED	TUBULURE	TUFTIER
TSARINA	TSURISES	TUBERCLES	TUBULURES	TUFTIEST
TSARINAS	TSUTSUMU	TUBERCULA	TUCHIS	TUFTILY
TSARISM	TSUTSUMUS	TUBERCULE	TUCHISES	TUFTING
TSARISMS	TUAN	TUBEROID	TUCHUN	TUFTINGS
TSARIST	TUANS	TUBEROIDS	TUCHUNS	TUFTS
TSARISTS	TUART	TUBEROSE	TUCHUS	TUFTY
TSARITSA	TUARTS	TUBEROSES	TUCHUSES	TUG
TSARITSAS	TUATARA	TUBEROUS	TUCK	TUGBOAT
TSARITZA	TUATARAS	TUBERS	TUCKAHOE	TUGBOATS
TSARITZAS	TUATERA	TUBES	TUCKAHOES	TUGGED
TSARS	TUATERAS	TUBEWELL	TUCKAMORE	TUGGER
TSATSKE	TUATH	TUBEWELLS	TUCKBOX	TUGGERS
TSATSKES	TUATHS	TUBEWORK	TUCKBOXES	TUGGING
TSESSEBE	TUATUA	TUBEWORKS	TUCKED	TUGGINGLY
TSESSEBES	TUATUAS	TUBEWORM	TUCKER	TUGGINGS
TSETSE	TUB	TUBEWORMS	TUCKERBAG	TUGHRA
TSETSES	TUBA	TUBFAST	TUCKERBOX	TUGHRAS
TSIGANE	TUBAE	TUBFASTS	TUCKERED	TUGHRIK
TSIGANES	TUBAGE	TUBFISH	TUCKERING	TUGHRIKS
TSIMMES	TUBAGES	TUBFISHES	TUCKERS	TUGLESS
TSIMMESES	TUBAIST	TUBFUL	TUCKET	TUGRA
TSITSITH	TUBAISTS	TUBFULS	TUCKETS	TUGRAS
TSK	TUBAL	TUBICOLAR	TUCKING	TUGRIK
TSKED	TUBAR	TUBICOLE	TUCKINGS	TUGRIKS
TSKING	TUBAS	TUBICOLES	TUCKS	TUGS
TSKS	TUBATE	TUBIFEX	TUCKSHOP	TUI
TSKTSK	TUBBABLE	TUBIFEXES	TUCKSHOPS	TUILE
TSKTSKED	TUBBED	TUBIFICID	TUCOTUCO	TUILES
TSKTSKING	TUBBER	TUBIFORM	TUCOTUCOS	TUILLE
TSKTSKS	TUBBERS	TUBING	TUCUTUCO	TUILLES
TSOORIS	TUBBIER	TUBINGS	TUCUTUCOS	TUILLETTE
TSOORISES	TUBBIEST	TUBIST	TUCUTUCU	TUILYIE
TSORES	TUBBINESS	TUBISTS	TUCUTUCUS	TUILYIED
TSORESES	TUBBING	TUBLIKE	TUFA	TUILYIES
TSORIS	TUBBINGS	TUBS	TUFACEOUS	TUILZIE
TSORISES	TUBBISH	TUBULAR	TUFAS	TUILZIED
TSORRISS	TUBBY	TUBULARLY	TUFF	TUILZIES
TSOTSI	TUBE	TUBULARS	TUFFE	TUINA
TSOTSIS	TUBECTOMY	TUBULATE	TUFFES	TUINAS
TSOURIS	TUBED	TUBULATED	TUFFET	TUIS
TSOURISES	TUBEFUL	TUBULATES	TUFFETS	TUISM
TSUBA	TUBEFULS	TUBULATOR	TUFFS	TUISMS
TSUBAS	TUBELESS	TUBULE	TUFOLI	TUITION
TSUBO	TUBELIKE	TUBULES	TUFOLIS	TUITIONAL
TSUBOS	TUBENOSE	TUBULIN	TUFT	TUITIONS
TSUNAMI	TUBENOSES	TUBULINS	TUFTED	TUKTOO
TSUNAMIC	TUBER	TUBULOSE	TUFTER	TUKTOOS

TUKTU	TUMESCES	TUNDED	TUNKETS	TURBANNED
TUKTUS	TUMESCING	TUNDING	TUNNAGE	TURBANS
TULADI	TUMID	TUNDISH	TUNNAGES	TURBANT
TULADIS	TUMIDITY	TUNDISHES	TUNNED	TURBANTS
TULAREMIA	TUMIDLY	TUNDRA	TUNNEL	TURBARIES
TULAREMIC	TUMIDNESS	TUNDRAS	TUNNELED	TURBARY
TULBAN	TUMMIES	TUNDS	TUNNELER	TURBETH
TULBANS	TUMMLER	TUNDUN	TUNNELERS	TURBETHS
TULCHAN	TUMMLERS	TUNDUNS	TUNNELING	TURBID
TULCHANS	TUMMY	TUNE	TUNNELLED	TURBIDITE
TULE	TUMOR	TUNEABLE	TUNNELLER	TURBIDITY
TULES	TUMORAL	TUNEABLY	TUNNELS	TURBIDLY
TULIP	TUMORLIKE	TUNEAGE	TUNNIES	TURBINAL
TULIPANT	TUMOROUS	TUNEAGES	TUNNING	TURBINALS
TULIPANTS	TUMORS	TUNED	TUNNINGS	TURBINATE
TULIPLIKE	TUMOUR	TUNEFUL	TUNNY	TURBINE
TULIPS	TUMOURS	TUNEFULLY	TUNS	TURBINED
TULIPWOOD	TUMP	TUNELESS	TUNY	TURBINES
TULLE	TUMPED	TUNER	TUP	TURBIT
TULLES	TUMPHIES	TUNERS	TUPEK	TURBITH
TULLIBEE	TUMPHY	TUNES	TUPEKS	TURBITHS
TULLIBEES	TUMPIER	TUNESMITH	TUPELO	TURBITS
TULPA	TUMPIEST	TUNEUP	TUPELOS	TURBO
TULPAS	TUMPING	TUNEUPS	TUPIK	TURBOCAR
TULSI	TUMPLINE	TUNG	TUPIKS	TURBOCARS
TULSIS	TUMPLINES	TUNGS	TUPLE	TURBOFAN
TULWAR	TUMPS	TUNGSTATE	TUPLES	TURBOFANS
TULWARS	TUMPY	TUNGSTEN	TUPPED	TURBOJET
TUM	TUMS	TUNGSTENS	TUPPENCE	TURBOJETS
TUMBLE	TUMSHIE	TUNGSTIC	TUPPENCES	TURBOND
TUMBLEBUG	TUMSHIES	TUNGSTITE	TUPPENNY	TURBONDS
TUMBLED	TUMULAR	TUNGSTOUS	TUPPING	TURBOPROP
TUMBLER	TUMULARY	TUNIC	TUPPINGS	TURBOS
TUMBLERS	TUMULI	TUNICA	TUPS	TURBOT
TUMBLES	TUMULOSE	TUNICAE	TUPTOWING	TURBOTS
TUMBLESET	TUMULOUS	TUNICATE	TUPUNA	TURBULENT
TUMBLING	TUMULT	TUNICATED	TUPUNAS	TURCOPOLE
TUMBLINGS	TUMULTED	TUNICATES	TUQUE	TURD
TUMBREL	TUMULTING	TUNICIN	TUQUES	TURDINE
TUMBRELS	TUMULTS	TUNICINS	TURACIN	TURDION
TUMBRIL	TUMULUS	TUNICKED	TURACINS	TURDIONS
TUMBRILS	TUMULUSES	TUNICLE	TURACO	TURDOID
TUMEFIED	TUN	TUNICLES	TURACOS	TURDS
TUMEFIES	TUNA	TUNICS	TURACOU	TURDUCKEN
TUMEFY	TUNABLE	TUNIER	TURACOUS	TUREEN
TUMEFYING	TUNABLY	TUNIEST	TURBAN	TUREENS
TUMESCE	TUNAS	TUNING	TURBAND	TURF
TUMESCED	TUNBELLY	TUNINGS	TURBANDS	TURFED
TUMESCENT	TUND	TUNKET	TURBANED	TURFEN

T

TURFGRASS	TURMOIL	TURNSOLE	TUSKARS	TUTELAR
TURFIER	TURMOILED	TURNSOLES	TUSKED	TUTELARS
TURFIEST	TURMOILS	TURNSPIT	TUSKER	TUTELARY
TURFINESS	TURMS	TURNSPITS	TUSKERS	TUTENAG
TURFING	TURN	TURNSTILE	TUSKIER	TUTENAGS
TURFINGS	TURNABLE	TURNSTONE	TUSKIEST	TUTIORISM
TURFITE	TURNABOUT	TURNT	TUSKING	TUTIORIST
TURFITES	TURNAGAIN	TURNTABLE	TUSKINGS	TUTMAN
TURFLESS	TURNBACK	TURNUP	TUSKLESS	TUTMEN
TURFLIKE	TURNBACKS	TURNUPS	TUSKLIKE	TUTOR
TURFMAN	TURNCOAT	TUROPHILE	TUSKS	TUTORAGE
TURFMEN	TURNCOATS	TURPETH	TUSKY	TUTORAGES
TURFS	TURNCOCK	TURPETHS	TUSSAC	TUTORED
TURFSKI	TURNCOCKS	TURPITUDE	TUSSAH	TUTORESS
TURFSKIS	TURNDOWN	TURPS	TUSSAHS	TUTORIAL
TURFY	TURNDOWNS	TURQUOIS	TUSSAL	TUTORIALS
TURGENCY	TURNDUN	TURQUOISE	TUSSAR	TUTORING
TURGENT	TURNDUNS	TURR	TUSSARS	TUTORINGS
TURGENTLY	TURNED	TURRET	TUSSEH	TUTORISE
TURGID	TURNER	TURRETED	TUSSEHS	TUTORISED
TURGIDER	TURNERIES	TURRETS	TUSSER	TUTORISES
TURGIDEST	TURNERS	TURRIBANT	TUSSERS	TUTORISM
TURGIDITY	TURNERY	TURRICAL	TUSSES	TUTORISMS
TURGIDLY	TURNHALL	TURRS	TUSSIS	TUTORIZE
TURGITE	TURNHALLS	TURTLE	TUSSISES	TUTORIZED
TURGITES	TURNING	TURTLED	TUSSIVE	TUTORIZES
TURGOR	TURNINGS	TURTLER	TUSSLE	TUTORS
TURGORS	TURNIP	TURTLERS	TUSSLED	TUTORSHIP
TURION	TURNIPED	TURTLES	TUSSLES	TUTOYED
TURIONS	TURNIPIER	TURTLING	TUSSLING	TUTOYER
TURISTA	TURNIPING	TURTLINGS	TUSSOCK	TUTOYERED
TURISTAS	TURNIPS	TURVES	TUSSOCKED	TUTOYERS
TURK	TURNIPY	TUSCHE	TUSSOCKS	TUTRESS
TURKEY	TURNKEY	TUSCHES	TUSSOCKY	TUTRESSES
TURKEYS	TURNKEYS	TUSH	TUSSOR	TUTRICES
TURKIES	TURNOFF	TUSHED	TUSSORE	TUTRIX
TURKIESES	TURNOFFS	TUSHERIES	TUSSORES	TUTRIXES
TURKIS	TURNON	TUSHERY	TUSSORS	TUTS
TURKISES	TURNONS	TUSHES	TUSSUCK	TUTSAN
TURKOIS	TURNOUT	TUSHIE	TUSSUCKS	TUTSANS
TURKOISES	TURNOUTS	TUSHIES	TUSSUR	TUTSED
TURKS	TURNOVER	TUSHING	TUSSURS	TUTSES
TURLOUGH	TURNOVERS	TUSHKAR	TUT	TUTSING
TURLOUGHS	TURNPIKE	TUSHKARS	TUTANIA	TUTTED
TURM	TURNPIKES	TUSHKER	TUTANIAS	TUTTI
TURME	TURNROUND	TUSHKERS	TUTEE	TUTTIES
TURMERIC	TURNS	TUSHY	TUTEES	TUTTING
TURMERICS	TURNSKIN	TUSK	TUTELAGE	TUTTINGS
TURMES	TURNSKINS	TUSKAR	TUTELAGES	TUTTIS

TUTTY	TWANGLERS	TWEEDLING	TWENTIETH	TWIGLETS
TUTU	TWANGLES	TWEEDS	TWENTY	TWIGLIKE
TUTUED	TWANGLING	TWEEDY	TWENTYISH	TWIGLOO
TUTUS	TWANGS	TWEEL	TWERK	TWIGLOOS
TUTWORK	TWANGY	TWEELED	TWERKED	TWIGS
TUTWORKER	TWANK	TWEELING	TWERKING	TWIGSOME
TUTWORKS	TWANKAY	TWEELS	TWERKINGS	TWILIGHT
TUX	TWANKAYS	TWEELY	TWERKS	TWILIGHTS
TUXEDO	TWANKED	TWEEN	TWERP	TWILIT
TUXEDOED	TWANKIES	TWEENAGE	TWERPIER	TWILL
TUXEDOES	TWANKING	TWEENAGER	TWERPIEST	TWILLED
TUXEDOS	TWANKS	TWEENER	TWERPS	TWILLIES
TUXES	TWANKY	TWEENERS	TWERPY	TWILLING
TUYER	TWAS	TWEENESS	TWIBIL	TWILLINGS
TUYERE	TWASOME	TWEENIE	TWIBILL	TWILLS
TUYERES	TWASOMES	TWEENIES	TWIBILLS	TWILLY
TUYERS	TWAT	TWEENS	TWIBILS	TWILT
TUZZ	TWATS	TWEENY	TWICE	TWILTED
TUZZES	TWATTED	TWEEP	TWICER	TWILTING
TWA	TWATTING	TWEEPLE	TWICERS	TWILTS
TWADDLE	TWATTLE	TWEEPS	TWICHILD	TWIN
TWADDLED	TWATTLED	TWEER	TWIDDLE	TWINBERRY
TWADDLER	TWATTLER	TWEERED	TWIDDLED	TWINBORN
TWADDLERS	TWATTLERS	TWEERING	TWIDDLER	TWINE
TWADDLES	TWATTLES	TWEERS	TWIDDLERS	TWINED
TWADDLIER	TWATTLING	TWEEST	TWIDDLES	TWINER
TWADDLING	TWAY	TWEET	TWIDDLIER	TWINERS
TWADDLY	TWAYBLADE	TWEETABLE	TWIDDLING	TWINES
TWAE	TWAYS	TWEETED	TWIDDLY	TWINGE
TWAES	TWEAK	TWEETER	TWIER	TWINGED
TWAFALD	TWEAKED	TWEETERS	TWIERS	TWINGEING
TWAIN	TWEAKER	TWEETING	TWIFOLD	TWINGES
TWAINS	TWEAKERS	TWEETS	TWIFORKED	TWINGING
TWAITE	TWEAKIER	TWEETUP	TWIFORMED	TWINIER
TWAITES	TWEAKIEST	TWEETUPS	TWIG	TWINIEST
TWAL	TWEAKING	TWEEZE	TWIGGED	TWINIGHT
TWALPENNY	TWEAKINGS	TWEEZED	TWIGGEN	TWINING
TWALS	TWEAKS	TWEEZER	TWIGGER	TWININGLY
TWANG	TWEAKY	TWEEZERS	TWIGGERS	TWININGS
TWANGED	TWEE	TWEEZES	TWIGGIER	TWINJET
TWANGER	TWEED	TWEEZING	TWIGGIEST	TWINJETS
TWANGERS	TWEEDIER	TWELFTH	TWIGGING	TWINK
TWANGIER	TWEEDIEST	TWELFTHLY	TWIGGY	TWINKED
TWANGIEST	TWEEDILY	TWELFTHS	TWIGHT	TWINKIE
TWANGING	TWEEDLE	TWELVE	TWIGHTED	TWINKIES
TWANGINGS	TWEEDLED	TWELVEMO	TWIGHTING	TWINKING
TWANGLE	TWEEDLER	TWELVEMOS	TWIGHTS	TWINKLE
TWANGLED	TWEEDLERS	TWELVES	TWIGLESS	TWINKLED
TWANGLER	TWEEDLES	TWENTIES	TWIGLET	TWINKLER

T

TWINKLERS	TWISTOR	TWONESSES	TYLOSES	TYPHLITIC
TWINKLES	TWISTORS	TWONIE	TYLOSIN	TYPHLITIS
TWINKLIER	TWISTS	TWONIES	TYLOSINS	TYPHOID
TWINKLING	TWISTY	TWOONIE	TYLOSIS	TYPHOIDAL
TWINKLY	TWIT	TWOONIES	TYLOTE	TYPHOIDIN
TWINKS	TWITCH	TWOPENCE	TYLOTES	TYPHOIDS
TWINKY	TWITCHED	TWOPENCES	TYMBAL	TYPHON
TWINLING	TWITCHER	TWOPENNY	TYMBALS	TYPHONIAN
TWINLINGS	TWITCHERS	TWOS	TYMP	TYPHONIC
TWINNED	TWITCHES	TWOSEATER	TYMPAN	TYPHONS
TWINNING	TWITCHIER	TWOSOME	TYMPANA	TYPHOON
TWINNINGS	TWITCHILY	TWOSOMES	TYMPANAL	TYPHOONS
TWINS	TWITCHING	TWOSTROKE	TYMPANI	TYPHOSE
TWINSET	TWITCHY	TWP	TYMPANIC	TYPHOUS
TWINSETS	TWITE	TWYER	TYMPANICS	TYPHUS
TWINSHIP	TWITES	TWYERE	TYMPANIES	TYPHUSES
TWINSHIPS	TWITS	TWYERES	TYMPANIST	TYPIC
TWINTER	TWITTED	TWYERS	TYMPANO	TYPICAL
TWINTERS	TWITTEN	TWYFOLD	TYMPANS	TYPICALLY
TWINY	TWITTENS	TYCHISM	TYMPANUM	TYPIER
TWIRE	TWITTER	TYCHISMS	TYMPANUMS	TYPIEST
TWIRED	TWITTERED	TYCOON	TYMPANY	TYPIFIED
TWIRES	TWITTERER	TYCOONATE	TYMPS	TYPIFIER
TWIRING	TWITTERS	TYCOONERY	TYND	TYPIFIERS
TWIRL	TWITTERY	TYCOONS	TYNDE	TYPIFIES
TWIRLED	TWITTING	TYDE	TYNE	TYPIFY
TWIRLER	TWITTINGS	TYE	TYNED	TYPIFYING
TWIRLERS	TWITTISH	TYED	TYNES	TYPING
TWIRLIER	TWIXT	TYEE	TYNING	TYPINGS
TWIRLIEST	TWIZZLE	TYEES	TYPABLE	TYPIST
TWIRLING	TWIZZLED	TYEING	TYPAL	TYPISTS
TWIRLS	TWIZZLES	TYER	TYPE	TYPO
TWIRLY	TWIZZLING	TYERS	TYPEABLE	TYPOGRAPH
TWIRP	TWO	TYES	TYPEBAR	TYPOLOGIC
TWIRPIER	TWOCCER	TYG	TYPEBARS	TYPOLOGY
TWIRPIEST	TWOCCERS	TYGS	TYPECASE	TYPOMANIA
TWIRPS	TWOCCING	TYIN	TYPECASES	TYPOS
TWIRPY	TWOCCINGS	TYING	TYPECAST	TYPP
TWISCAR	TWOCKER	TYINS	TYPECASTS	TYPPS
TWISCARS	TWOCKERS	TYIYN	TYPED	TYPTO
TWIST	TWOCKING	TYIYNS	TYPEFACE	TYPTOED
TWISTABLE	TWOCKINGS	TYKE	TYPEFACES	TYPTOING
TWISTED	TWOER	TYKES	TYPES	TYPTOS
TWISTER	TWOERS	TYKISH	TYPESET	TYPY
TWISTERS	TWOFER	TYLECTOMY	TYPESETS	TYRAMINE
TWISTIER	TWOFERS	TYLER	TYPESTYLE	TYRAMINES
TWISTIEST	TWOFOLD	TYLERS	TYPEWRITE	TYRAN
TWISTING	TWOFOLDS	TYLOPOD	TYPEWROTE	TYRANED
TWISTINGS	TWONESS	TYLOPODS	TYPEY	TYRANING

TYRANNE	TYRE	TYSTIE	TZAR	TZEDAKAHS
TYRANNED	TYRED	TYSTIES	TZARDOM	TZETSE
TYRANNES	TYRELESS	TYTE	TZARDOMS	TZETSES
TYRANNESS	TYREMAKER	TYTHE	TZAREVNA	TZETZE
TYRANNIC	TYRES	TYTHED	TZAREVNAS	TZETZES
TYRANNIES	TYRING	TYTHES	TZARINA	TZIGANE
TYRANNING	TYRO	TYTHING	TZARINAS	TZIGANES
TYRANNIS	TYROCIDIN	TZADDI	TZARISM	TZIGANIES
TYRANNISE	TYROES	TZADDIK	TZARISMS	TZIGANY
TYRANNIZE	TYRONES	TZADDIKIM	TZARIST	TZIMMES
TYRANNOUS	TYRONIC	TZADDIKS	TZARISTS	TZIMMESES
TYRANNY	TYROPITA	TZADDIQ	TZARITZA	TZITZIS
TYRANS	TYROPITAS	TZADDIQIM	TZARITZAS	TZITZIT
TYRANT	TYROPITTA	TZADDIQS	TZARS	TZITZITH
TYRANTED	TYROS	TZADDIS	TZATZIKI	TZURIS
TYRANTING	TYROSINE	TZADIK	TZATZIKIS	TZURISES
TYRANTS	TYROSINES	TZADIKS	TZEDAKAH	

U

UAKARI	UGGING	ULANS	ULOSIS	ULTRARICH
UAKARIS	UGH	ULCER	ULOTRICHY	ULTRAS
UBEROUS	UGHS	ULCERATE	ULPAN	ULTRASAFE
UBERTIES	UGLIED	ULCERATED	ULPANIM	ULTRASLOW
UBERTY	UGLIER	ULCERATES	ULSTER	ULTRASOFT
UBIETIES	UGLIES	ULCERED	ULSTERED	ULTRATHIN
UBIETY	UGLIEST	ULCERING	ULSTERS	ULTRATINY
UBIQUE	UGLIFIED	ULCEROUS	ULTERIOR	ULTRAWIDE
UBIQUITIN	UGLIFIER	ULCERS	ULTIMA	ULU
UBIQUITY	UGLIFIERS	ULE	ULTIMACY	ULULANT
UBUNTU	UGLIFIES	ULEMA	ULTIMAS	ULULATE
UBUNTUS	UGLIFY	ULEMAS	ULTIMATA	ULULATED
UCKERS	UGLIFYING	ULES	ULTIMATE	ULULATES
UDAL	UGLILY	ULEX	ULTIMATED	ULULATING
UDALLER	UGLINESS	ULEXES	ULTIMATES	ULULATION
UDALLERS	UGLY	ULEXITE	ULTIMATUM	ULUS
UDALS	UGLYING	ULEXITES	ULTIMO	ULVA
UDDER	UGS	ULICES	ULTION	ULVAS
UDDERED	UGSOME	ULICON	ULTIONS	ULYIE
UDDERFUL	UH	ULICONS	ULTISOL	ULYIES
UDDERFULS	UHLAN	ULIGINOSE	ULTISOLS	ULZIE
UDDERLESS	UHLANS	ULIGINOUS	ULTRA	ULZIES
UDDERS	UHURU	ULIKON	ULTRACHIC	UM
UDO	UHURUS	ULIKONS	ULTRACOLD	UMAMI
UDOMETER	UILLEAN	ULITIS	ULTRACOOL	UMAMIS
UDOMETERS	UILLEANN	ULITISES	ULTRADRY	UMANGITE
UDOMETRIC	UINTAHITE	ULLAGE	ULTRAFAST	UMANGITES
UDOMETRY	UINTAITE	ULLAGED	ULTRAFINE	UMBEL
UDON	UINTAITES	ULLAGES	ULTRAHEAT	UMBELED
UDONS	UITLANDER	ULLAGING	ULTRAHIGH	UMBELLAR
UDOS	UJAMAA	ULLING	ULTRAHIP	UMBELLATE
UDS	UJAMAAS	ULLINGS	ULTRAHOT	UMBELLED
UEY	UKASE	ULMACEOUS	ULTRAISM	UMBELLET
UEYS	UKASES	ULMIN	ULTRAISMS	UMBELLETS
UFO	UKE	ULMINS	ULTRAIST	UMBELLULE
UFOLOGIES	UKELELE	ULNA	ULTRAISTS	UMBELS
UFOLOGIST	UKELELES	ULNAD	ULTRALEFT	UMBELULE
UFOLOGY	UKES	ULNAE	ULTRALOW	UMBELULES
UFOS	UKULELE	ULNAR	ULTRAPOSH	UMBER
UG	UKULELES	ULNARE	ULTRAPURE	UMBERED
UGALI	ULAMA	ULNARIA	ULTRARARE	UMBERIER
UGALIS	ULAMAS	ULNAS	ULTRARED	UMBERIEST
UGGED	ULAN	ULOSES	ULTRAREDS	UMBERING

UMBERS	UMIAC	UMWELT	UNAKIN	UNASHAMED
UMBERY	UMIACK	UMWELTS	UNAKING	UNASKED
UMBILICAL	UMIACKS	UMWHILE	UNAKITE	UNASSAYED
UMBILICI	UMIACS	UN	UNAKITES	UNASSUMED
UMBILICUS	UMIAK	UNABASHED	UNALARMED	UNASSURED
UMBLE	UMIAKS	UNABATED	UNALERTED	UNATONED
UMBLES	UMIAQ	UNABATING	UNALIGNED	UNATTIRED
UMBO	UMIAQS	UNABETTED	UNALIKE	UNATTUNED
UMBONAL	UMLAUT	UNABIDING	UNALIST	UNAU
UMBONATE	UMLAUTED	UNABJURED	UNALISTS	UNAUDITED
UMBONES	UMLAUTING	UNABLE	UNALIVE	UNAUS
UMBONIC	UMLAUTS	UNABORTED	UNALLAYED	UNAVENGED
UMBOS	UMM	UNABRADED	UNALLEGED	UNAVERAGE
UMBRA	UMMA	UNABUSED	UNALLIED	UNAVERTED
UMBRACULA	UMMAH	UNABUSIVE	UNALLOWED	UNAVOIDED
UMBRAE	UMMAHS	UNACCRUED	UNALLOYED	UNAVOWED
UMBRAGE	UMMAS	UNACCUSED	UNALTERED	UNAWAKE
UMBRAGED	UMMED	UNACERBIC	UNAMASSED	UNAWAKED
UMBRAGES	UMMING	UNACHING	UNAMAZED	UNAWARDED
UMBRAGING	UMP	UNACIDIC	UNAMENDED	UNAWARE
UMBRAL	UMPED	UNACTABLE	UNAMERCED	UNAWARELY
UMBRAS	UMPH	UNACTED	UNAMIABLE	UNAWARES
UMBRATED	UMPHS	UNACTIVE	UNAMUSED	UNAWED
UMBRATIC	UMPIE	UNACTIVED	UNAMUSING	UNAWESOME
UMBRATILE	UMPIES	UNACTIVES	UNANCHOR	UNAXED
UMBRE	UMPING	UNADAPTED	UNANCHORS	UNBACKED
UMBREL	UMPIRAGE	UNADDED	UNANELED	UNBAFFLED
UMBRELLA	UMPIRAGES	UNADEPT	UNANIMITY	UNBAG
UMBRELLAS	UMPIRE	UNADEPTLY	UNANIMOUS	UNBAGGED
UMBRELLO	UMPIRED	UNADEPTS	UNANNEXED	UNBAGGING
UMBRELLOS	UMPIRES	UNADMIRED	UNANNOYED	UNBAGS
UMBRELS	UMPIRING	UNADOPTED	UNANXIOUS	UNBAITED
UMBRERE	UMPS	UNADORED	UNAPPAREL	UNBAKED
UMBRERES	UMPTEEN	UNADORNED	UNAPPLIED	UNBALANCE
UMBRES	UMPTEENTH	UNADULT	UNAPT	UNBALE
UMBRETTE	UMPTIER	UNADVISED	UNAPTLY	UNBALED
UMBRETTES	UMPTIEST	UNAFRAID	UNAPTNESS	UNBALES
UMBRIERE	UMPTIETH	UNAGED	UNARCHED	UNBALING
UMBRIERES	UMPTY	UNAGEING	UNARGUED	UNBAN
UMBRIL	UMPY	UNAGILE	UNARISEN	UNBANDAGE
UMBRILS	UMQUHILE	UNAGING	UNARM	UNBANDED
UMBROSE	UMRA	UNAGREED	UNARMED	UNBANKED
UMBROUS	UMRAH	UNAI	UNARMING	UNBANKEDS
UME	UMRAHS	UNAIDABLE	UNARMORED	UNBANNED
UMEBOSHI	UMRAS	UNAIDED	UNARMS	UNBANNING
UMEBOSHIS	UMS	UNAIDEDLY	UNAROUSED	UNBANS
UMES	UMTEENTH	UNAIMED	UNARRAYED	UNBAPTISE
UMFAZI	UMU	UNAIRED	UNARTFUL	UNBAPTIZE
UMFAZIS	UMUS	UNAIS	UNARY	UNBAR

UNBARBED	UNBENDING	UNBLUNTED	UNBRAID	UNBURYING
UNBARE	UNBENDS	UNBLURRED	UNBRAIDED	UNBUSIED
UNBARED	UNBENIGN	UNBOARDED	UNBRAIDS	UNBUSIER
UNBARES	UNBENT	UNBOBBED	UNBRAKE	UNBUSIES
UNBARING	UNBEREFT	UNBODIED	UNBRAKED	UNBUSIEST
UNBARK	UNBERUFEN	UNBODING	UNBRAKES	UNBUSTED
UNBARKED	UNBESEEM	UNBOILED	UNBRAKING	UNBUSY
UNBARKING	UNBESEEMS	UNBOLT	UNBRANDED	UNBUSYING
UNBARKS	UNBESPEAK	UNBOLTED	UNBRASTE	UNBUTTON
UNBARRED	UNBESPOKE	UNBOLTING	UNBRED	UNBUTTONS
UNBARRING	UNBIAS	UNBOLTS	UNBREECH	UNCAGE
UNBARS	UNBIASED	UNBONDED	UNBRIDGED	UNCAGED
UNBASED	UNBIASES	UNBONE	UNBRIDLE	UNCAGES
UNBASHFUL	UNBIASING	UNBONED	UNBRIDLED	UNCAGING
UNBASTED	UNBIASSED	UNBONES	UNBRIDLES	UNCAKE
UNBATED	UNBIASSES	UNBONING	UNBRIEFED	UNCAKED
UNBATHED	UNBID	UNBONNET	UNBRIGHT	UNCAKES
UNBE	UNBIDDEN	UNBONNETS	UNBRIZZED	UNCAKING
UNBEAR	UNBIGOTED	UNBOOKED	UNBROILED	UNCALLED
UNBEARDED	UNBILLED	UNBOOKISH	UNBROKE	UNCANCEL
UNBEARED	UNBIND	UNBOOT	UNBROKEN	UNCANCELS
UNBEARING	UNBINDING	UNBOOTED	UNBROWNED	UNCANDID
UNBEARS	UNBINDS	UNBOOTING	UNBRUISED	UNCANDLED
UNBEATEN	UNBISHOP	UNBOOTS	UNBRUSED	UNCANDOR
UNBED	UNBISHOPS	UNBORE	UNBRUSHED	UNCANDORS
UNBEDDED	UNBITT	UNBORN	UNBUCKLE	UNCANDOUR
UNBEDDING	UNBITTED	UNBORNE	UNBUCKLED	UNCANNED
UNBEDS	UNBITTEN	UNBOSOM	UNBUCKLES	UNCANNIER
UNBEEN	UNBITTER	UNBOSOMED	UNBUDDED	UNCANNILY
UNBEGET	UNBITTING	UNBOSOMER	UNBUDGING	UNCANNY
UNBEGETS	UNBITTS	UNBOSOMS	UNBUILD	UNCANONIC
UNBEGGED	UNBLAMED	UNBOTTLE	UNBUILDS	UNCAP
UNBEGOT	UNBLENDED	UNBOTTLED	UNBUILT	UNCAPABLE
UNBEGUILE	UNBLENT	UNBOTTLES	UNBULKIER	UNCAPE
UNBEGUN	UNBLESS	UNBOUGHT	UNBULKY	UNCAPED
UNBEING	UNBLESSED	UNBOUNCY	UNBUNDLE	UNCAPES
UNBEINGS	UNBLESSES	UNBOUND	UNBUNDLED	UNCAPING
UNBEKNOWN	UNBLEST	UNBOUNDED	UNBUNDLER	UNCAPPED
UNBELIEF	UNBLIND	UNBOWED	UNBUNDLES	UNCAPPING
UNBELIEFS	UNBLINDED	UNBOWING	UNBURDEN	UNCAPS
UNBELIEVE	UNBLINDS	UNBOX	UNBURDENS	UNCARDED
UNBELOVED	UNBLOCK	UNBOXED	UNBURIED	UNCARED
UNBELT	UNBLOCKED	UNBOXES	UNBURIES	UNCAREFUL
UNBELTED	UNBLOCKS	UNBOXING	UNBURNED	UNCARING
UNBELTING	UNBLOODED	UNBOXINGS	UNBURNT	UNCART
UNBELTS	UNBLOODY	UNBRACE	UNBURROW	UNCARTED
UNBEMUSED	UNBLOTTED	UNBRACED	UNBURROWS	UNCARTING
UNBEND	UNBLOWED	UNBRACES	UNBURTHEN	UNCARTS
UNBENDED	UNBLOWN	UNBRACING	UNBURY	UNCARVED

UNCASE	UNCHICLY	UNCLEARED	UNCOCKING	UNCOSTLY
UNCASED	UNCHILD	UNCLEARER	UNCOCKS	UNCOUNTED
UNCASES	UNCHILDED	UNCLEARLY	UNCODED	UNCOUPLE
UNCASHED	UNCHILDS	UNCLED	UNCOER	UNCOUPLED
UNCASING	UNCHILLED	UNCLEFT	UNCOERCED	UNCOUPLER
UNCASKED	UNCHOKE	UNCLENCH	UNCOES	UNCOUPLES
UNCAST	UNCHOKED	UNCLES	UNCOEST	UNCOURTLY
UNCASTED	UNCHOKES	UNCLESHIP	UNCOFFIN	UNCOUTH
UNCASTING	UNCHOKING	UNCLEW	UNCOFFINS	UNCOUTHER
UNCASTS	UNCHOSEN	UNCLEWED	UNCOIL	UNCOUTHLY
UNCATCHY	UNCHRISOM	UNCLEWING	UNCOILED	UNCOVER
UNCATE	UNCHURCH	UNCLEWS	UNCOILING	UNCOVERED
UNCATERED	UNCI	UNCLICHED	UNCOILS	UNCOVERS
UNCAUGHT	UNCIA	UNCLIMBED	UNCOINED	UNCOWL
UNCAUSED	UNCIAE	UNCLINCH	UNCOLORED	UNCOWLED
UNCE	UNCIAL	UNCLING	UNCOLT	UNCOWLING
UNCEASING	UNCIALLY	UNCLIP	UNCOLTED	UNCOWLS
UNCEDED	UNCIALS	UNCLIPPED	UNCOLTING	UNCOY
UNCERTAIN	UNCIFORM	UNCLIPS	UNCOLTS	UNCOYNED
UNCES	UNCIFORMS	UNCLIPT	UNCOMBED	UNCRACKED
UNCESSANT	UNCINAL	UNCLOAK	UNCOMBINE	UNCRATE
UNCHAIN	UNCINARIA	UNCLOAKED	UNCOMELY	UNCRATED
UNCHAINED	UNCINATE	UNCLOAKS	UNCOMFIER	UNCRATES
UNCHAINS	UNCINATED	UNCLOG	UNCOMFY	UNCRATING
UNCHAIR	UNCINI	UNCLOGGED	UNCOMIC	UNCRAZIER
UNCHAIRED	UNCINUS	UNCLOGS	UNCOMMON	UNCRAZY
UNCHAIRS	UNCIPHER	UNCLONED	UNCONCERN	UNCREASED
UNCHANCY	UNCIPHERS	UNCLOSE	UNCONFINE	UNCREATE
UNCHANGED	UNCITED	UNCLOSED	UNCONFORM	UNCREATED
UNCHARGE	UNCIVIL	UNCLOSES	UNCONFUSE	UNCREATES
UNCHARGED	UNCIVILLY	UNCLOSING	UNCONGEAL	UNCREWED
UNCHARGES	UNCLAD	UNCLOTHE	UNCOOKED	UNCROPPED
UNCHARIER	UNCLAIMED	UNCLOTHED	UNCOOL	UNCROSS
UNCHARITY	UNCLAMP	UNCLOTHES	UNCOOLED	UNCROSSED
UNCHARM	UNCLAMPED	UNCLOUD	UNCOPE	UNCROSSES
UNCHARMED	UNCLAMPS	UNCLOUDED	UNCOPED	UNCROWDED
UNCHARMS	UNCLARITY	UNCLOUDS	UNCOPES	UNCROWN
UNCHARNEL	UNCLASP	UNCLOUDY	UNCOPING	UNCROWNED
UNCHARRED	UNCLASPED	UNCLOVEN	UNCORD	UNCROWNS
UNCHARTED	UNCLASPS	UNCLOYED	UNCORDED	UNCRUDDED
UNCHARY	UNCLASSED	UNCLOYING	UNCORDIAL	UNCRUMPLE
UNCHASTE	UNCLASSY	UNCLUTCH	UNCORDING	UNCRUSHED
UNCHASTER	UNCLAWED	UNCLUTTER	UNCORDS	UNCTION
UNCHECK	UNCLE	UNCO	UNCORK	UNCTIONS
UNCHECKED	UNCLEAN	UNCOATED	UNCORKED	UNCTUOUS
UNCHECKS	UNCLEANED	UNCOATING	UNCORKING	UNCUFF
UNCHEERED	UNCLEANER	UNCOBBLED	UNCORKS	UNCUFFED
UNCHEWED	UNCLEANLY	UNCOCK	UNCORRUPT	UNCUFFING
UNCHIC	UNCLEAR	UNCOCKED	UNCOS	UNCUFFS

U

UNCULLED	UNDEAFS	UNDERBOOB	UNDERGOD	UNDERPART
UNCURABLE	UNDEALT	UNDERBORE	UNDERGODS	UNDERPASS
UNCURABLY	UNDEAR	UNDERBOSS	UNDERGOER	UNDERPAY
UNCURB	UNDEBASED	UNDERBRED	UNDERGOES	UNDERPAYS
UNCURBED	UNDEBATED	UNDERBRIM	UNDERGONE	UNDERPEEP
UNCURBING	UNDECAGON	UNDERBUD	UNDERGOWN	UNDERPIN
UNCURBS	UNDECAYED	UNDERBUDS	UNDERGRAD	UNDERPINS
UNCURDLED	UNDECEIVE	UNDERBUSH	UNDERHAIR	UNDERPLAY
UNCURED	UNDECENT	UNDERBUY	UNDERHAND	UNDERPLOT
UNCURIOUS	UNDECIDED	UNDERBUYS	UNDERHEAT	UNDERPROP
UNCURL	UNDECIMAL	UNDERCARD	UNDERHIT	UNDERRAN
UNCURLED	UNDECK	UNDERCART	UNDERHITS	UNDERRATE
UNCURLING	UNDECKED	UNDERCAST	UNDERHUNG	UNDERRIPE
UNCURLS	UNDECKING	UNDERCLAD	UNDERIVED	UNDERRUN
UNCURRENT	UNDECKS	UNDERCLAY	UNDERJAW	UNDERRUNS
UNCURSE	UNDEE	UNDERCLUB	UNDERJAWS	UNDERSAID
UNCURSED	UNDEEDED	UNDERCOAT	UNDERKEEP	UNDERSAY
UNCURSES	UNDEFACED	UNDERCOOK	UNDERKEPT	UNDERSAYS
UNCURSING	UNDEFIDE	UNDERCOOL	UNDERKILL	UNDERSEA
UNCURTAIN	UNDEFIED	UNDERCUT	UNDERKING	UNDERSEAL
UNCURVED	UNDEFILED	UNDERCUTS	UNDERLAID	UNDERSEAS
UNCUS	UNDEFINED	UNDERDAKS	UNDERLAIN	UNDERSELF
UNCUT	UNDEIFIED	UNDERDECK	UNDERLAP	UNDERSELL
UNCUTE	UNDEIFIES	UNDERDID	UNDERLAPS	UNDERSET
UNCYNICAL	UNDEIFY	UNDERDO	UNDERLAY	UNDERSETS
UNDAM	UNDELAYED	UNDERDOER	UNDERLAYS	UNDERSHOT
UNDAMAGED	UNDELETE	UNDERDOES	UNDERLEAF	UNDERSIDE
UNDAMMED	UNDELETED	UNDERDOG	UNDERLET	UNDERSIGN
UNDAMMING	UNDELETES	UNDERDOGS	UNDERLETS	UNDERSIZE
UNDAMNED	UNDELIGHT	UNDERDONE	UNDERLIE	UNDERSKY
UNDAMPED	UNDELUDED	UNDERDOSE	UNDERLIER	UNDERSOIL
UNDAMS	UNDENIED	UNDERDRAW	UNDERLIES	UNDERSOLD
UNDARING	UNDENTED	UNDERDREW	UNDERLINE	UNDERSONG
UNDASHED	UNDER	UNDEREAT	UNDERLING	UNDERSOW
UNDATABLE	UNDERACT	UNDEREATS	UNDERLIP	UNDERSOWN
UNDATE	UNDERACTS	UNDERFED	UNDERLIPS	UNDERSOWS
UNDATED	UNDERAGE	UNDERFEED	UNDERLIT	UNDERSPIN
UNDATES	UNDERAGED	UNDERFELT	UNDERLOAD	UNDERTAKE
UNDATING	UNDERAGES	UNDERFIRE	UNDERMAN	UNDERTANE
UNDAUNTED	UNDERARM	UNDERFISH	UNDERMANS	UNDERTAX
UNDAWNING	UNDERARMS	UNDERFLOW	UNDERMEN	UNDERTIME
UNDAZZLE	UNDERATE	UNDERFONG	UNDERMINE	UNDERTINT
UNDAZZLED	UNDERBAKE	UNDERFOOT	UNDERMOST	UNDERTONE
UNDAZZLES	UNDERBEAR	UNDERFUND	UNDERN	UNDERTOOK
UNDE	UNDERBID	UNDERFUR	UNDERNOTE	UNDERTOW
UNDEAD	UNDERBIDS	UNDERFURS	UNDERNS	UNDERTOWS
UNDEAF	UNDERBIT	UNDERGIRD	UNDERPAD	UNDERUSE
UNDEAFED	UNDERBITE	UNDERGIRT	UNDERPADS	UNDERUSED
UNDEAFING	UNDERBODY	UNDERGO	UNDERPAID	UNDERUSES

UNDERVEST	UNDOUBLED	UNEAGER	UNESSENCE	UNFAZED
UNDERVOTE	UNDOUBLES	UNEAGERLY	UNETH	UNFEARED
UNDERWAY	UNDOUBTED	UNEARED	UNETHICAL	UNFEARFUL
UNDERWEAR	UNDOWERED	UNEARNED	UNEVADED	UNFEARING
UNDERWENT	UNDRAINED	UNEARTH	UNEVEN	UNFED
UNDERWING	UNDRAPE	UNEARTHED	UNEVENER	UNFEED
UNDERWIRE	UNDRAPED	UNEARTHLY	UNEVENEST	UNFEELING
UNDERWIT	UNDRAPES	UNEARTHS	UNEVENLY	UNFEIGNED
UNDERWITS	UNDRAPING	UNEASE	UNEVOLVED	UNFELLED
UNDERWOOD	UNDRAW	UNEASES	UNEXALTED	UNFELT
UNDERWOOL	UNDRAWING	UNEASIER	UNEXCITED	UNFELTED
UNDERWORK	UNDRAWN	UNEASIEST	UNEXCUSED	UNFENCE
UNDESERT	UNDRAWS	UNEASILY	UNEXOTIC	UNFENCED
UNDESERTS	UNDREADED	UNEASY	UNEXPERT	UNFENCES
UNDESERVE	UNDREAMED	UNEATABLE	UNEXPIRED	UNFENCING
UNDESIRED	UNDREAMT	UNEATEN	UNEXPOSED	UNFERTILE
UNDEVOUT	UNDRESS	UNEATH	UNEXTINCT	UNFETTER
UNDID	UNDRESSED	UNEATHES	UNEXTREME	UNFETTERS
UNDIES	UNDRESSES	UNEDGE	UNEYED	UNFEUDAL
UNDIGHT	UNDREST	UNEDGED	UNFABLED	UNFEUED
UNDIGHTS	UNDREW	UNEDGES	UNFACETED	UNFIGURED
UNDIGNIFY	UNDRIED	UNEDGING	UNFACT	UNFILDE
UNDILUTED	UNDRILLED	UNEDIBLE	UNFACTS	UNFILED
UNDIMMED	UNDRIVEN	UNEDITED	UNFADABLE	UNFILIAL
UNDINE	UNDROSSY	UNEFFACED	UNFADED	UNFILLED
UNDINES	UNDROWNED	UNELATED	UNFADING	UNFILMED
UNDINISM	UNDRUNK	UNELECTED	UNFAILING	UNFINE
UNDINISMS	UNDUBBED	UNEMPTIED	UNFAIR	UNFIRED
UNDINTED	UNDUE	UNENDED	UNFAIRED	UNFIRM
UNDIPPED	UNDUG	UNENDING	UNFAIRER	UNFISHED
UNDIVIDED	UNDULANCE	UNENDOWED	UNFAIREST	UNFIT
UNDIVINE	UNDULANCY	UNENGAGED	UNFAIRING	UNFITLY
UNDO	UNDULANT	UNENJOYED	UNFAIRLY	UNFITNESS
UNDOABLE	UNDULAR	UNENSURED	UNFAIRS	UNFITS
UNDOCILE	UNDULATE	UNENTERED	UNFAITH	UNFITTED
UNDOCK	UNDULATED	UNENVIED	UNFAITHS	UNFITTER
UNDOCKED	UNDULATES	UNENVIOUS	UNFAKED	UNFITTEST
UNDOCKING	UNDULATOR	UNENVYING	UNFALLEN	UNFITTING
UNDOCKS	UNDULLED	UNEQUABLE	UNFAMED	UNFIX
UNDOER	UNDULOSE	UNEQUAL	UNFAMOUS	UNFIXED
UNDOERS	UNDULOUS	UNEQUALED	UNFANCIED	UNFIXES
UNDOES	UNDULY	UNEQUALLY	UNFANCIER	UNFIXING
UNDOING	UNDUTEOUS	UNEQUALS	UNFANCY	UNFIXITY
UNDOINGS	UNDUTIFUL	UNERASED	UNFANNED	UNFIXT
UNDONE	UNDY	UNEROTIC	UNFASTEN	UNFLAPPED
UNDOOMED	UNDYED	UNERRING	UNFASTENS	UNFLASHY
UNDOS	UNDYING	UNERUPTED	UNFAULTY	UNFLAWED
UNDOTTED	UNDYINGLY	UNESPIED	UNFAVORED	UNFLEDGED
UNDOUBLE	UNDYNAMIC	UNESSAYED	UNFAZABLE	UNFLESH

UNFLESHED	UNFREEMEN	UNGENIAL	UNGORGED	UNGYVED
UNFLESHES	UNFREES	UNGENTEEL	UNGOT	UNGYVES
UNFLESHLY	UNFREEZE	UNGENTLE	UNGOTTEN	UNGYVING
UNFLEXED	UNFREEZES	UNGENTLER	UNGOWN	UNHABLE
UNFLOORED	UNFRETTED	UNGENTLY	UNGOWNED	UNHACKED
UNFLUSH	UNFRIEND	UNGENUINE	UNGOWNING	UNHAILED
UNFLUSHED	UNFRIENDS	UNGERMANE	UNGOWNS	UNHAIR
UNFLUSHES	UNFROCK	UNGET	UNGRACED	UNHAIRED
UNFLUTED	UNFROCKED	UNGETS	UNGRADED	UNHAIRER
UNFLYABLE	UNFROCKS	UNGETTING	UNGRASSED	UNHAIRERS
UNFOCUSED	UNFROZE	UNGHOSTED	UNGRAVELY	UNHAIRING
UNFOILED	UNFROZEN	UNGHOSTLY	UNGRAZED	UNHAIRS
UNFOLD	UNFUELLED	UNGIFTED	UNGREASED	UNHALLOW
UNFOLDED	UNFUMED	UNGILD	UNGREEDY	UNHALLOWS
UNFOLDER	UNFUNDED	UNGILDED	UNGREEN	UNHALSED
UNFOLDERS	UNFUNNIER	UNGILDING	UNGREENER	UNHALVED
UNFOLDING	UNFUNNILY	UNGILDS	UNGROOMED	UNHAND
UNFOLDS	UNFUNNY	UNGILT	UNGROUND	UNHANDED
UNFOLLOW	UNFURL	UNGIRD	UNGROUP	UNHANDIER
UNFOLLOWS	UNFURLED	UNGIRDED	UNGROUPED	UNHANDILY
UNFOND	UNFURLING	UNGIRDING	UNGROUPS	UNHANDING
UNFONDLY	UNFURLS	UNGIRDS	UNGROWN	UNHANDLED
UNFOOL	UNFURNISH	UNGIRT	UNGRUDGED	UNHANDS
UNFOOLED	UNFURRED	UNGIRTH	UNGUAL	UNHANDY
UNFOOLING	UNFUSED	UNGIRTHED	UNGUARD	UNHANG
UNFOOLS	UNFUSSED	UNGIRTHS	UNGUARDED	UNHANGED
UNFOOTED	UNFUSSIER	UNGIVING	UNGUARDS	UNHANGING
UNFORBID	UNFUSSILY	UNGLAD	UNGUENT	UNHANGS
UNFORCED	UNFUSSY	UNGLAZED	UNGUENTA	UNHAPPEN
UNFORGED	UNGAG	UNGLITZY	UNGUENTS	UNHAPPENS
UNFORGOT	UNGAGGED	UNGLOSSED	UNGUENTUM	UNHAPPIED
UNFORKED	UNGAGGING	UNGLOVE	UNGUES	UNHAPPIER
UNFORM	UNGAGS	UNGLOVED	UNGUESSED	UNHAPPIES
UNFORMAL	UNGAIN	UNGLOVES	UNGUIDED	UNHAPPILY
UNFORMED	UNGAINFUL	UNGLOVING	UNGUIFORM	UNHAPPY
UNFORMING	UNGAINLY	UNGLUE	UNGUILTY	UNHARBOUR
UNFORMS	UNGALLANT	UNGLUED	UNGUINOUS	UNHARDIER
UNFORTUNE	UNGALLED	UNGLUES	UNGUIS	UNHARDY
UNFOUGHT	UNGARBED	UNGLUING	UNGULA	UNHARMED
UNFOUND	UNGARBLED	UNGOD	UNGULAE	UNHARMFUL
UNFOUNDED	UNGATED	UNGODDED	UNGULAR	UNHARMING
UNFRAMED	UNGAUGED	UNGODDING	UNGULATE	UNHARNESS
UNFRANKED	UNGAZED	UNGODLIER	UNGULATES	UNHARRIED
UNFRAUGHT	UNGAZING	UNGODLIKE	UNGULED	UNHASP
UNFREE	UNGEAR	UNGODLILY	UNGUM	UNHASPED
UNFREED	UNGEARED	UNGODLY	UNGUMMED	UNHASPING
UNFREEDOM	UNGEARING	UNGODS	UNGUMMING	UNHASPS
UNFREEING	UNGEARS	UNGORD	UNGUMS	UNHASTIER
UNFREEMAN	UNGELDED	UNGORED	UNGYVE	UNHASTING

UNHASTY	UNHINGE	UNHOUSES	UNIFORMLY	UNIQUELY
UNHAT	UNHINGED	UNHOUSING	UNIFORMS	UNIQUER
UNHATCHED	UNHINGES	UNHUMAN	UNIFY	UNIQUES
UNHATS	UNHINGING	UNHUMANLY	UNIFYING	UNIQUEST
UNHATTED	UNHIP	UNHUMBLED	UNIFYINGS	UNIRAMOSE
UNHATTING	UNHIPPER	UNHUNG	UNIGNITED	UNIRAMOUS
UNHAUNTED	UNHIPPEST	UNHUNTED	UNIJUGATE	UNIRONED
UNHEAD	UNHIRABLE	UNHURRIED	UNILINEAL	UNIRONIC
UNHEADED	UNHIRED	UNHURT	UNILINEAR	UNIS
UNHEADING	UNHITCH	UNHURTFUL	UNILLUMED	UNISERIAL
UNHEADS	UNHITCHED	UNHUSK	UNILOBAR	UNISEX
UNHEAL	UNHITCHES	UNHUSKED	UNILOBED	UNISEXES
UNHEALED	UNHIVE	UNHUSKING	UNIMBUED	UNISEXUAL
UNHEALING	UNHIVED	UNHUSKS	UNIMODAL	UNISIZE
UNHEALS	UNHIVES	UNI	UNIMPEDED	UNISON
UNHEALTH	UNHIVING	UNIALGAL	UNIMPOSED	UNISONAL
UNHEALTHS	UNHOARD	UNIAXIAL	UNINCITED	UNISONANT
UNHEALTHY	UNHOARDED	UNIBODIES	UNINDEXED	UNISONOUS
UNHEARD	UNHOARDS	UNIBODY	UNINJURED	UNISONS
UNHEARSE	UNHOLIER	UNIBROW	UNINSTAL	UNISSUED
UNHEARSED	UNHOLIEST	UNIBROWS	UNINSTALL	UNIT
UNHEARSES	UNHOLILY	UNICA	UNINSTALS	UNITAGE
UNHEART	UNHOLPEN	UNICED	UNINSURED	UNITAGES
UNHEARTED	UNHOLSTER	UNICITIES	UNINURED	UNITAL
UNHEARTS	UNHOLY	UNICITY	UNINVITED	UNITARD
UNHEATED	UNHOMELY	UNICOLOR	UNINVOKED	UNITARDS
UNHEDGED	UNHONEST	UNICOLOUR	UNION	UNITARIAN
UNHEEDED	UNHONORED	UNICOM	UNIONISE	UNITARILY
UNHEEDFUL	UNHOOD	UNICOMS	UNIONISED	UNITARITY
UNHEEDIER	UNHOODED	UNICORN	UNIONISER	UNITARY
UNHEEDILY	UNHOODING	UNICORNS	UNIONISES	UNITE
UNHEEDING	UNHOODS	UNICUM	UNIONISM	UNITED
UNHEEDY	UNHOOK	UNICYCLE	UNIONISMS	UNITEDLY
UNHELE	UNHOOKED	UNICYCLED	UNIONIST	UNITER
UNHELED	UNHOOKING	UNICYCLES	UNIONISTS	UNITERS
UNHELES	UNHOOKS	UNIDEAED	UNIONIZE	UNITES
UNHELING	UNHOOP	UNIDEAL	UNIONIZED	UNITIES
UNHELM	UNHOOPED	UNIFACE	UNIONIZER	UNITING
UNHELMED	UNHOOPING	UNIFACES	UNIONIZES	UNITINGS
UNHELMING	UNHOOPS	UNIFIABLE	UNIONS	.UNITION
UNHELMS	UNHOPED	UNIFIC	UNIPAROUS	UNITIONS
UNHELPED	UNHOPEFUL	UNIFIED	UNIPED	UNITISE
UNHELPFUL	UNHORSE	UNIFIER	UNIPEDS	UNITISED
UNHEMMED	UNHORSED	UNIFIERS	UNIPLANAR	UNITISER
UNHEPPEN	UNHORSES	UNIFIES	UNIPOD	UNITISERS
UNHEROIC	UNHORSING	UNIFILAR	UNIPODS	UNITISES
UNHERST	UNHOSTILE	UNIFORM	UNIPOLAR	UNITISING
UNHEWN	UNHOUSE	UNIFORMED	UNIPOTENT	UNITIVE
UNHIDDEN	UNHOUSED	UNIFORMER	UNIQUE	UNITIVELY

U

UNITIZE	UNKINDER	UNLATCH	UNLIME	UNLOST
UNITIZED	UNKINDEST	UNLATCHED	UNLIMED	UNLOVABLE
UNITIZER	UNKINDLED	UNLATCHES	UNLIMES	UNLOVE
UNITIZERS	UNKINDLY	UNLAW	UNLIMING	UNLOVED
UNITIZES	UNKING	UNLAWED	UNLIMITED	UNLOVELY
UNITIZING	UNKINGED	UNLAWFUL	UNLINE	UNLOVES
UNITRUST	UNKINGING	UNLAWING	UNLINEAL	UNLOVING
UNITRUSTS	UNKINGLY	UNLAWS	UNLINED	UNLUCKIER
UNITS	UNKINGS	UNLAY	UNLINES	UNLUCKILY
UNITY	UNKINK	UNLAYING	UNLINING	UNLUCKY
UNIVALENT	UNKINKED	UNLAYS	UNLINK	UNLYRICAL
UNIVALVE	UNKINKING	UNLEAD	UNLINKED	UNMACHO
UNIVALVED	UNKINKS	UNLEADED	UNLINKING	UNMADE
UNIVALVES	UNKISS	UNLEADEDS	UNLINKS	UNMAILED
UNIVERSAL	UNKISSED	UNLEADING	UNLISTED	UNMAIMED
UNIVERSE	UNKISSES	UNLEADS	UNLIT	UNMAKABLE
UNIVERSES	UNKISSING	UNLEAL	UNLIVABLE	UNMAKE
UNIVOCAL	UNKNELLED	UNLEARN	UNLIVE	UNMAKER
UNIVOCALS	UNKNIGHT	UNLEARNED	UNLIVED	UNMAKERS
UNJADED	UNKNIGHTS	UNLEARNS	UNLIVELY	UNMAKES
UNJAM	UNKNIT	UNLEARNT	UNLIVES	UNMAKING
UNJAMMED	UNKNITS	UNLEASED	UNLIVING	UNMAKINGS
UNJAMMING	UNKNITTED	UNLEASH	UNLOAD	UNMALTED
UNJAMS	UNKNOT	UNLEASHED	UNLOADED	UNMAN
UNJEALOUS	UNKNOTS	UNLEASHES	UNLOADER	UNMANACLE
UNJOINED	UNKNOTTED	UNLED	UNLOADERS	UNMANAGED
UNJOINT	UNKNOWING	UNLESS	UNLOADING	UNMANFUL
UNJOINTED	UNKNOWN	UNLET	UNLOADS	UNMANLIER
UNJOINTS	UNKNOWNS	UNLETHAL	UNLOBED	UNMANLIKE
UNJOYFUL	UNKOSHER	UNLETTED	UNLOCATED	UNMANLY
UNJOYOUS	UNLABELED	UNLEVEL	UNLOCK	UNMANNED
UNJUDGED	UNLABORED	UNLEVELED	UNLOCKED	UNMANNING
UNJUST	UNLACE	UNLEVELS	UNLOCKING	UNMANNISH
UNJUSTER	UNLACED	UNLEVIED	UNLOCKS	UNMANS
UNJUSTEST	UNLACES	UNLICH	UNLOGICAL	UNMANTLE
UNJUSTLY	UNLACING	UNLICKED	UNLOOKED	UNMANTLED
UNKED	UNLADE	UNLID	UNLOOSE	UNMANTLES
UNKEELED	UNLADED	UNLIDDED	UNLOOSED	UNMANURED
UNKEMPT	UNLADEN	UNLIDDING	UNLOOSEN	UNMAPPED
UNKEMPTLY	UNLADES	UNLIDS	UNLOOSENS	UNMARD
UNKEND	UNLADING	UNLIGHTED	UNLOOSES	UNMARKED
UNKENNED	UNLADINGS	UNLIKABLE	UNLOOSING	UNMARRED
UNKENNEL	UNLAID	UNLIKE	UNLOPPED	UNMARRIED
UNKENNELS	UNLASH	UNLIKED	UNLORD	UNMARRIES
UNKENT	UNLASHED	UNLIKELY	UNLORDED	UNMARRY
UNKEPT	UNLASHES	UNLIKES	UNLORDING	UNMASK
UNKET	UNLASHING	UNLIKING	UNLORDLY	UNMASKED
UNKID	UNLAST	UNLIMBER	UNLORDS	UNMASKER
UNKIND	UNLASTE	UNLIMBERS	UNLOSABLE	UNMASKERS

UNMASKING	UNMIXED	UNNAILS	UNPACKER	UNPEOPLES
UNMASKS	UNMIXEDLY	UNNAMABLE	UNPACKERS	UNPERCH
UNMATCHED	UNMIXES	UNNAMED	UNPACKING	UNPERCHED
UNMATED	UNMIXING	UNNANELD	UNPACKS	UNPERCHES
UNMATTED	UNMIXT	UNNATIVE	UNPADDED	UNPERFECT
UNMATURED	UNMOANED	UNNATIVED	UNPAGED	UNPERPLEX
UNMEANING	UNMODISH	UNNATIVES	UNPAID	UNPERSON
UNMEANT	UNMOLD	UNNATURAL	UNPAINED	UNPERSONS
UNMEEK	UNMOLDED	UNNEATH	UNPAINFUL	UNPERVERT
UNMEET	UNMOLDING	UNNEEDED	UNPAINT	UNPICK
UNMEETLY	UNMOLDS	UNNEEDFUL	UNPAINTED	UNPICKED
UNMELLOW	UNMOLTEN	UNNERVE	UNPAINTS	UNPICKING
UNMELTED	UNMONEYED	UNNERVED	UNPAIR	UNPICKS
UNMENDED	UNMONIED	UNNERVES	UNPAIRED	UNPIERCED
UNMERITED	UNMOOR	UNNERVING	UNPAIRING	UNPILE
UNMERRIER	UNMOORED	UNNEST	UNPAIRS	UNPILED
UNMERRY	UNMOORING	UNNESTED	UNPALSIED	UNPILES
UNMESH	UNMOORS	UNNESTING	UNPANEL	UNPILING
UNMESHED	UNMORAL	UNNESTS	UNPANELS	UNPILOTED
UNMESHES	UNMORALLY	UNNETHES	UNPANGED	UNPIN
UNMESHING	UNMORTISE	UNNETTED	UNPANNEL	UNPINKED
UNMET	UNMOTIVED	UNNOBLE	UNPANNELS	UNPINKT
UNMETED	UNMOULD	UNNOBLED	UNPAPER	UNPINNED
UNMETERED	UNMOULDED	UNNOBLES	UNPAPERED	UNPINNING
UNMEW	UNMOULDS	UNNOBLING	UNPAPERS	UNPINS
UNMEWED	UNMOUNT	UNNOISIER	UNPARED	UNPITIED
UNMEWING	UNMOUNTED	UNNOISY	UNPARTED	UNPITIFUL
UNMEWS	UNMOUNTS	UNNOTED	UNPARTIAL	UNPITTED
UNMILKED	UNMOURNED	UNNOTICED	UNPATCHED	UNPITYING
UNMILLED	UNMOVABLE	UNNUANCED	UNPATHED	UNPLACE
UNMINDED	UNMOVABLY	UNOAKED	UNPAVED	UNPLACED
UNMINDFUL	UNMOVED	UNOBEYED	UNPAY	UNPLACES
UNMINED	UNMOVEDLY	UNOBVIOUS	UNPAYABLE	UNPLACING
UNMINGLE	UNMOVING	UNOFFERED	UNPAYING	UNPLAGUED
UNMINGLED	UNMOWN	UNOFTEN	UNPAYS	UNPLAINED
UNMINGLES	UNMUFFLE	UNOILED	UNPEELED	UNPLAIT
UNMIRIER	UNMUFFLED	UNOPEN	UNPEERED	UNPLAITED
UNMIRIEST	UNMUFFLES	UNOPENED	UNPEG	UNPLAITS
UNMIRY	UNMUSICAL	UNOPPOSED	UNPEGGED	UNPLANKED
UNMISSED	UNMUTE	UNORDER	UNPEGGING	UNPLANNED
UNMITER	UNMUTED	UNORDERED	UNPEGS	UNPLANTED
UNMITERED	UNMUTES	UNORDERLY	UNPEN	UNPLAYED
UNMITERS	UNMUTING	UNORDERS	UNPENNED	UNPLEASED
UNMITRE	UNMUZZLE	UNORNATE	UNPENNIED	UNPLEATED
UNMITRED	UNMUZZLED	UNOWED	UNPENNING	UNPLEDGED
UNMITRES	UNMUZZLES	UNOWNED	UNPENS	UNPLIABLE
UNMITRING	UNNAIL	UNPACED	UNPENT	UNPLIABLY
UNMIX	UNNAILED	UNPACK	UNPEOPLE	UNPLIANT
UNMIXABLE	UNNAILING	UNPACKED	UNPEOPLED	UNPLOWED

UNPLUCKED

UNPLUCKED	UNPRINTED	UNRAKES	UNREINING	UNRIPPED
UNPLUG	UNPRISON	UNRAKING	UNREINS	UNRIPPING
UNPLUGGED	UNPRISONS	UNRANKED	UNRELATED	UNRIPS
UNPLUGS	UNPRIZED	UNRATED	UNRELAXED	UNRISEN
UNPLUMB	UNPROBED	UNRAVAGED	UNREMOVED	UNRIVALED
UNPLUMBED	UNPROP	UNRAVEL	UNRENEWED	UNRIVEN
UNPLUMBS	UNPROPER	UNRAVELED	UNRENT	UNRIVET
UNPLUME	UNPROPPED	UNRAVELS	UNRENTED	UNRIVETED
UNPLUMED	UNPROPS	UNRAZED	UNREPAID	UNRIVETS
UNPLUMES	UNPROVED	UNRAZORED	UNREPAIR	UNROASTED
UNPLUMING	UNPROVEN	UNREACHED	UNREPAIRS	UNROBE
UNPOETIC	UNPROVIDE	UNREAD	UNRESERVE	UNROBED
UNPOINTED	UNPROVOKE	UNREADIER	UNREST	UNROBES
UNPOISED	UNPRUNED	UNREADILY	UNRESTED	UNROBING
UNPOISON	UNPUCKER	UNREADY	UNRESTFUL	UNROLL
UNPOISONS	UNPUCKERS	UNREAL	UNRESTING	UNROLLED
UNPOLICED	UNPULLED	UNREALISE	UNRESTS	UNROLLING
UNPOLISH	UNPURE	UNREALISM	UNRETIRE	UNROLLS
UNPOLITE	UNPURELY	UNREALITY	UNRETIRED	UNROOF
UNPOLITIC	UNPURGED	UNREALIZE	UNRETIRES	UNROOFED
UNPOLLED	UNPURSE	UNREALLY	UNREVISED	UNROOFING
UNPOPE	UNPURSED	UNREAPED	UNREVOKED	UNROOFS
UNPOPED	UNPURSES	UNREASON	UNRHYMED	UNROOST
UNPOPES	UNPURSING	UNREASONS	UNRIBBED	UNROOSTED
UNPOPING	UNPURSUED	UNREAVE	UNRID	UNROOSTS
UNPOPULAR	UNPUZZLE	UNREAVED	UNRIDABLE	UNROOT
UNPOSED	UNPUZZLED	UNREAVES	UNRIDDEN	UNROOTED
UNPOSTED	UNPUZZLES	UNREAVING	UNRIDDLE	UNROOTING
UNPOTABLE	UNQUAKING	UNREBATED	UNRIDDLED	UNROOTS
UNPOTTED	UNQUALIFY	UNREBUKED	UNRIDDLER	UNROPE
UNPOURED	UNQUEEN	UNRECKED	UNRIDDLES	UNROPED
UNPOWERED	UNQUEENED	UNRED	UNRIDGED	UNROPES
UNPRAISE	UNQUEENLY	UNREDREST	UNRIFLED	UNROPING
UNPRAISED	UNQUEENS	UNREDUCED	UNRIG	UNROSINED
UNPRAISES	UNQUELLED	UNREDY	UNRIGGED	UNROTTED
UNPRAY	UNQUIET	UNREEL	UNRIGGING	UNROTTEN
UNPRAYED	UNQUIETED	UNREELED	UNRIGHT	UNROUGED
UNPRAYING	UNQUIETER	UNREELER	UNRIGHTED	UNROUGH
UNPRAYS	UNQUIETLY	UNREELERS	UNRIGHTS	UNROUND
UNPREACH	UNQUIETS	UNREELING	UNRIGS	UNROUNDED
UNPRECISE	UNQUOTE	UNREELS	UNRIMED	UNROUNDS
UNPREDICT	UNQUOTED	UNREEVE	UNRINGED	UNROUSED
UNPREPARE	UNQUOTES	UNREEVED	UNRINSED	UNROVE
UNPRESSED	UNQUOTING	UNREEVES	UNRIP	UNROVEN
UNPRETTY	UNRACED	UNREEVING	UNRIPE	UNROYAL
UNPRICED	UNRACKED	UNREFINED	UNRIPELY	UNROYALLY
UNPRIEST	UNRAISED	UNREFUTED	UNRIPENED	UNRUBBED
UNPRIESTS	UNRAKE	UNREIN	UNRIPER	UNRUDE
UNPRIMED	UNRAKED	UNREINED	UNRIPEST	UNRUFFE

636 | **two to nine letter words**

UNRUFFLE	UNSCALE	UNSEIZED	UNSHALING	UNSHRUBD
UNRUFFLED	UNSCALED	UNSELDOM	UNSHAMED	UNSHRUNK
UNRUFFLES	UNSCALES	UNSELF	UNSHAPE	UNSHUNNED
UNRULE	UNSCALING	UNSELFED	UNSHAPED	UNSHUT
UNRULED	UNSCANNED	UNSELFING	UNSHAPELY	UNSHUTS
UNRULES	UNSCARIER	UNSELFISH	UNSHAPEN	UNSHUTTER
UNRULIER	UNSCARRED	UNSELFS	UNSHAPES	UNSICKER
UNRULIEST	UNSCARY	UNSELL	UNSHAPING	UNSICKLED
UNRULY	UNSCATHED	UNSELLING	UNSHARED	UNSIFTED
UNRUMPLED	UNSCENTED	UNSELLS	UNSHARP	UNSIGHING
UNRUSHED	UNSCOURED	UNSELVES	UNSHAVED	UNSIGHT
UNRUSTED	UNSCREW	UNSENSE	UNSHAVEN	UNSIGHTED
UNS	UNSCREWED	UNSENSED	UNSHEATHE	UNSIGHTLY
UNSADDLE	UNSCREWS	UNSENSES	UNSHED	UNSIGHTS
UNSADDLED	UNSCYTHED	UNSENSING	UNSHELL	UNSIGNED
UNSADDLES	UNSEAL	UNSENT	UNSHELLED	UNSILENT
UNSAFE	UNSEALED	UNSERIOUS	UNSHELLS	UNSIMILAR
UNSAFELY	UNSEALING	UNSERVED	UNSHENT	UNSINEW
UNSAFER	UNSEALS	UNSET	UNSHEWN	UNSINEWED
UNSAFEST	UNSEAM	UNSETS	UNSHIFT	UNSINEWS
UNSAFETY	UNSEAMED	UNSETTING	UNSHIFTED	UNSINFUL
UNSAID	UNSEAMING	UNSETTLE	UNSHIFTS	UNSISTING
UNSAILED	UNSEAMS	UNSETTLED	UNSHIP	UNSIZABLE
UNSAINED	UNSEARED	UNSETTLES	UNSHIPPED	UNSIZED
UNSAINT	UNSEASON	UNSEVERED	UNSHIPS	UNSKILFUL
UNSAINTED	UNSEASONS	UNSEW	UNSHIRTED	UNSKILLED
UNSAINTLY	UNSEAT	UNSEWED	UNSHOCKED	UNSKIMMED
UNSAINTS	UNSEATED	UNSEWING	UNSHOD	UNSKINNED
UNSALABLE	UNSEATING	UNSEWN	UNSHOE	UNSLAIN
UNSALABLY	UNSEATS	UNSEWS	UNSHOED	UNSLAKED
UNSALTED	UNSECRET	UNSEX	UNSHOEING	UNSLICED
UNSALUTED	UNSECRETS	UNSEXED	UNSHOES	UNSLICK
UNSAMPLED	UNSECULAR	UNSEXES	UNSHOOT	UNSLING
UNSAPPED	UNSECURED	UNSEXIER	UNSHOOTED	UNSLINGS
UNSASHED	UNSEDUCED	UNSEXIEST	UNSHOOTS	UNSLUICE
UNSATABLE	UNSEE	UNSEXILY	UNSHORN	UNSLUICED
UNSATED	UNSEEABLE	UNSEXING	UNSHOT	UNSLUICES
UNSATIATE	UNSEEDED	UNSEXIST	UNSHOTS	UNSLUNG
UNSATING	UNSEEING	UNSEXUAL	UNSHOTTED	UNSMART
UNSAVED	UNSEEL	UNSEXY	UNSHOUT	UNSMILING
UNSAVORY	UNSEELED	UNSHACKLE	UNSHOUTED	UNSMITTEN
UNSAVOURY	UNSEELIE	UNSHADED	UNSHOUTS	UNSMOKED
UNSAW	UNSEELING	UNSHADOW	UNSHOWIER	UNSMOOTH
UNSAWED	UNSEELS	UNSHADOWS	UNSHOWN	UNSMOOTHS
UNSAWN	UNSEEMING	UNSHAKED	UNSHOWY	UNSMOTE
UNSAY	UNSEEMLY	UNSHAKEN	UNSHRIVED	UNSNAG
UNSAYABLE	UNSEEN	UNSHALE	UNSHRIVEN	UNSNAGGED
UNSAYING	UNSEENS	UNSHALED	UNSHROUD	UNSNAGS
UNSAYS	UNSEES	UNSHALES	UNSHROUDS	UNSNAP

U

UNSNAPPED	UNSOWN	UNSTATES	UNSTYLISH	UNTAILED
UNSNAPS	UNSPAR	UNSTATING	UNSUB	UNTAINTED
UNSNARL	UNSPARED	UNSTAYED	UNSUBDUED	UNTAKEN
UNSNARLED	UNSPARING	UNSTAYING	UNSUBJECT	UNTAMABLE
UNSNARLS	UNSPARRED	UNSTEADY	UNSUBS	UNTAMABLY
UNSNECK	UNSPARS	UNSTEEL	UNSUBTLE	UNTAME
UNSNECKED	UNSPEAK	UNSTEELED	UNSUBTLER	UNTAMED
UNSNECKS	UNSPEAKS	UNSTEELS	UNSUBTLY	UNTAMES
UNSNUFFED	UNSPED	UNSTEMMED	UNSUCCESS	UNTAMING
UNSOAKED	UNSPELL	UNSTEP	UNSUCKED	UNTANGLE
UNSOAPED	UNSPELLED	UNSTEPPED	UNSUIT	UNTANGLED
UNSOBER	UNSPELLS	UNSTEPS	UNSUITED	UNTANGLES
UNSOBERED	UNSPENT	UNSTERILE	UNSUITING	UNTANNED
UNSOBERLY	UNSPHERE	UNSTICK	UNSUITS	UNTAPPED
UNSOBERS	UNSPHERED	UNSTICKS	UNSULLIED	UNTARRED
UNSOCIAL	UNSPHERES	UNSTIFFEN	UNSUMMED	UNTASTED
UNSOCKET	UNSPIDE	UNSTIFLED	UNSUNG	UNTAUGHT
UNSOCKETS	UNSPIED	UNSTILLED	UNSUNK	UNTAX
UNSOD	UNSPILLED	UNSTINTED	UNSUNNED	UNTAXABLE
UNSODDEN	UNSPILT	UNSTIRRED	UNSUNNIER	UNTAXED
UNSOFT	UNSPLIT	UNSTITCH	UNSUNNY	UNTAXES
UNSOILED	UNSPOILED	UNSTOCK	UNSUPPLE	UNTAXING
UNSOLACED	UNSPOILT	UNSTOCKED	UNSURE	UNTEACH
UNSOLD	UNSPOKE	UNSTOCKS	UNSURED	UNTEACHES
UNSOLDER	UNSPOKEN	UNSTONED	UNSURELY	UNTEAM
UNSOLDERS	UNSPOOL	UNSTOP	UNSURER	UNTEAMED
UNSOLEMN	UNSPOOLED	UNSTOPPED	UNSUREST	UNTEAMING
UNSOLID	UNSPOOLS	UNSTOPPER	UNSUSPECT	UNTEAMS
UNSOLIDLY	UNSPOTTED	UNSTOPS	UNSWADDLE	UNTEMPER
UNSOLVED	UNSPRAYED	UNSTOW	UNSWATHE	UNTEMPERS
UNSONCY	UNSPRUNG	UNSTOWED	UNSWATHED	UNTEMPTED
UNSONSIE	UNSPUN	UNSTOWING	UNSWATHES	UNTENABLE
UNSONSIER	UNSQUARED	UNSTOWS	UNSWAYED	UNTENABLY
UNSONSY	UNSTABLE	UNSTRAP	UNSWEAR	UNTENANT
UNSOOTE	UNSTABLER	UNSTRAPS	UNSWEARS	UNTENANTS
UNSOOTHED	UNSTABLY	UNSTRESS	UNSWEET	UNTENDED
UNSORTED	UNSTACK	UNSTRING	UNSWEPT	UNTENDER
UNSOUGHT	UNSTACKED	UNSTRINGS	UNSWOLLEN	UNTENT
UNSOUL	UNSTACKS	UNSTRIP	UNSWORE	UNTENTED
UNSOULED	UNSTAGED	UNSTRIPED	UNSWORN	UNTENTIER
UNSOULING	UNSTAID	UNSTRIPS	UNTACK	UNTENTING
UNSOULS	UNSTAINED	UNSTRUCK	UNTACKED	UNTENTS
UNSOUND	UNSTALKED	UNSTRUNG	UNTACKING	UNTENTY
UNSOUNDED	UNSTAMPED	UNSTUCK	UNTACKLE	UNTENURED
UNSOUNDER	UNSTARCH	UNSTUDIED	UNTACKLED	UNTESTED
UNSOUNDLY	UNSTARRED	UNSTUFFED	UNTACKLES	UNTETHER
UNSOURCED	UNSTARRY	UNSTUFFY	UNTACKS	UNTETHERS
UNSOURED	UNSTATE	UNSTUFT	UNTACTFUL	UNTHANKED
UNSOWED	UNSTATED	UNSTUNG	UNTAGGED	UNTHATCH

UNTHAW	UNTOMB	UNTUCK	UNVAILE	UNWARELY
UNTHAWED	UNTOMBED	UNTUCKED	UNVAILED	UNWARES
UNTHAWING	UNTOMBING	UNTUCKING	UNVAILES	UNWARIE
UNTHAWS	UNTOMBS	UNTUCKS	UNVAILING	UNWARIER
UNTHINK	UNTONED	UNTUFTED	UNVAILS	UNWARIEST
UNTHINKS	UNTOOLED	UNTUMBLED	UNVALUED	UNWARILY
UNTHOUGHT	UNTOOTHED	UNTUNABLE	UNVARIED	UNWARLIKE
UNTHREAD	UNTORN	UNTUNABLY	UNVARYING	UNWARMED
UNTHREADS	UNTOUCHED	UNTUNE	UNVAXED	UNWARNED
UNTHRIFT	UNTOWARD	UNTUNED	UNVAXXED	UNWARPED
UNTHRIFTS	UNTRACE	UNTUNEFUL	UNVEIL	UNWARY
UNTHRIFTY	UNTRACED	UNTUNES	UNVEILED	UNWASHED
UNTHRONE	UNTRACES	UNTUNING	UNVEILER	UNWASHEDS
UNTHRONED	UNTRACING	UNTURBID	UNVEILERS	UNWASHEN
UNTHRONES	UNTRACK	UNTURF	UNVEILING	UNWASTED
UNTIDIED	UNTRACKED	UNTURFED	UNVEILS	UNWASTING
UNTIDIER	UNTRACKS	UNTURFING	UNVEINED	UNWATCHED
UNTIDIES	UNTRADED	UNTURFS	UNVENTED	UNWATER
UNTIDIEST	UNTRAINED	UNTURN	UNVERSED	UNWATERED
UNTIDILY	UNTRAPPED	UNTURNED	UNVESTED	UNWATERS
UNTIDY	UNTREAD	UNTURNING	UNVETTED	UNWATERY
UNTIDYING	UNTREADED	UNTURNS	UNVEXED	UNWAXED
UNTIE	UNTREADS	UNTUTORED	UNVEXT	UNWAYED
UNTIED	UNTREATED	UNTWILLED	UNVIABLE	UNWEAL
UNTIEING	UNTRENDY	UNTWINE	UNVIEWED	UNWEALS
UNTIES	UNTRESSED	UNTWINED	UNVIRTUE	UNWEANED
UNTIL	UNTRIDE	UNTWINES	UNVIRTUES	UNWEAPON
UNTILE	UNTRIED	UNTWINING	UNVISITED	UNWEAPONS
UNTILED	UNTRIM	UNTWIST	UNVISOR	UNWEARIED
UNTILES	UNTRIMMED	UNTWISTED	UNVISORED	UNWEARIER
UNTILING	UNTRIMS	UNTWISTS	UNVISORS	UNWEARIES
UNTILLED	UNTROD	UNTYING	UNVITAL	UNWEARY
UNTILTED	UNTRODDEN	UNTYINGS	UNVIZARD	UNWEAVE
UNTIMED	UNTRUE	UNTYPABLE	UNVIZARDS	UNWEAVES
UNTIMELY	UNTRUER	UNTYPICAL	UNVOCAL	UNWEAVING
UNTIMEOUS	UNTRUEST	UNUNBIUM	UNVOICE	UNWEBBED
UNTIN	UNTRUISM	UNUNBIUMS	UNVOICED	UNWED
UNTINGED	UNTRUISMS	UNUNITED	UNVOICES	UNWEDDED
UNTINNED	UNTRULY	UNUNUNIUM	UNVOICING	UNWEEDED
UNTINNING	UNTRUSS	UNURGED	UNVULGAR	UNWEENED
UNTINS	UNTRUSSED	UNUSABLE	UNWAGED	UNWEETING
UNTIPPED	UNTRUSSER	UNUSABLY	UNWAISTED	UNWEIGHED
UNTIRABLE	UNTRUSSES	UNUSED	UNWAKED	UNWEIGHT
UNTIRED	UNTRUST	UNUSEFUL	UNWAKENED	UNWEIGHTS
UNTIRING	UNTRUSTED	UNUSHERED	UNWALLED	UNWELCOME
UNTITLED	UNTRUSTS	UNUSUAL	UNWANING	UNWELDED
UNTO	UNTRUSTY	UNUSUALLY	UNWANTED	UNWELDY
UNTOILING	UNTRUTH	UNUTTERED	UNWARDED	UNWELL
UNTOLD	UNTRUTHS	UNVAIL	UNWARE	UNWEPT

UNWET	UNWIVED	UNZIP	UPBRINGS	UPCURVES
UNWETTED	UNWIVES	UNZIPPED	UPBROKE	UPCURVING
UNWHIPPED	UNWIVING	UNZIPPING	UPBROKEN	UPCYCLE
UNWHIPT	UNWOMAN	UNZIPS	UPBROUGHT	UPCYCLED
UNWHITE	UNWOMANED	UNZONED	UPBUILD	UPCYCLES
UNWIELDLY	UNWOMANLY	UP	UPBUILDER	UPCYCLING
UNWIELDY	UNWOMANS	UPADAISY	UPBUILDS	UPDART
UNWIFELY	UNWON	UPAITHRIC	UPBUILT	UPDARTED
UNWIGGED	UNWONT	UPALONG	UPBURNING	UPDARTING
UNWILFUL	UNWONTED	UPALONGS	UPBURST	UPDARTS
UNWILL	UNWOODED	UPAS	UPBURSTS	UPDATABLE
UNWILLED	UNWOOED	UPASES	UPBY	UPDATE
UNWILLING	UNWORDED	UPBEAR	UPBYE	UPDATED
UNWILLS	UNWORK	UPBEARER	UPCAST	UPDATER
UNWIND	UNWORKED	UPBEARERS	UPCASTING	UPDATERS
UNWINDER	UNWORKING	UPBEARING	UPCASTS	UPDATES
UNWINDERS	UNWORKS	UPBEARS	UPCATCH	UPDATING
UNWINDING	UNWORLDLY	UPBEAT	UPCATCHES	UPDIVE
UNWINDS	UNWORMED	UPBEATS	UPCAUGHT	UPDIVED
UNWINGED	UNWORN	UPBIND	UPCHEER	UPDIVES
UNWINKING	UNWORRIED	UPBINDING	UPCHEERED	UPDIVING
UNWIPED	UNWORTH	UPBINDS	UPCHEERS	UPDO
UNWIRE	UNWORTHS	UPBLEW	UPCHUCK	UPDOMING
UNWIRED	UNWORTHY	UPBLOW	UPCHUCKED	UPDOMINGS
UNWIRES	UNWOUND	UPBLOWING	UPCHUCKS	UPDOS
UNWIRING	UNWOUNDED	UPBLOWN	UPCLIMB	UPDOVE
UNWISDOM	UNWOVE	UPBLOWS	UPCLIMBED	UPDRAFT
UNWISDOMS	UNWOVEN	UPBOIL	UPCLIMBS	UPDRAFTS
UNWISE	UNWRAP	UPBOILED	UPCLOSE	UPDRAG
UNWISELY	UNWRAPPED	UPBOILING	UPCLOSED	UPDRAGGED
UNWISER	UNWRAPS	UPBOILS	UPCLOSES	UPDRAGS
UNWISEST	UNWREAKED	UPBORE	UPCLOSING	UPDRAUGHT
UNWISH	UNWREATHE	UPBORNE	UPCOAST	UPDRAW
UNWISHED	UNWRINKLE	UPBOUND	UPCOIL	UPDRAWING
UNWISHES	UNWRITE	UPBOUNDEN	UPCOILED	UPDRAWN
UNWISHFUL	UNWRITES	UPBOW	UPCOILING	UPDRAWS
UNWISHING	UNWRITING	UPBOWS	UPCOILS	UPDREW
UNWIST	UNWRITTEN	UPBRAID	UPCOME	UPDRIED
UNWIT	UNWROTE	UPBRAIDED	UPCOMES	UPDRIES
UNWITCH	UNWROUGHT	UPBRAIDER	UPCOMING	UPDRY
UNWITCHED	UNWRUNG	UPBRAIDS	UPCOUNTRY	UPDRYING
UNWITCHES	UNYEANED	UPBRAST	UPCOURT	UPEND
UNWITS	UNYIELDED	UPBRAY	UPCURL	UPENDED
UNWITTED	UNYOKE	UPBRAYED	UPCURLED	UPENDING
UNWITTIER	UNYOKED	UPBRAYING	UPCURLING	UPENDS
UNWITTILY	UNYOKES	UPBRAYS	UPCURLS	UPFIELD
UNWITTING	UNYOKING	UPBREAK	UPCURRENT	UPFILL
UNWITTY	UNYOUNG	UPBREAKS	UPCURVE	UPFILLED
UNWIVE	UNZEALOUS	UPBRING	UPCURVED	UPFILLING

UPFILLS	UPGROWN	UPHUDDEN	UPLINKED	UPPROP
UPFLING	UPGROWS	UPHUNG	UPLINKING	UPPROPPED
UPFLINGS	UPGROWTH	UPHURL	UPLINKS	UPPROPS
UPFLOW	UPGROWTHS	UPHURLED	UPLIT	UPRAISE
UPFLOWED	UPGUSH	UPHURLING	UPLOAD	UPRAISED
UPFLOWING	UPGUSHED	UPHURLS	UPLOADED	UPRAISER
UPFLOWS	UPGUSHES	UPJET	UPLOADING	UPRAISERS
UPFLUNG	UPGUSHING	UPJETS	UPLOADS	UPRAISES
UPFOLD	UPHAND	UPJETTED	UPLOCK	UPRAISING
UPFOLDED	UPHANG	UPJETTING	UPLOCKED	UPRAN
UPFOLDING	UPHANGING	UPKEEP	UPLOCKING	UPRATE
UPFOLDS	UPHANGS	UPKEEPS	UPLOCKS	UPRATED
UPFOLLOW	UPHAUD	UPKNIT	UPLOOK	UPRATES
UPFOLLOWS	UPHAUDING	UPKNITS	UPLOOKED	UPRATING
UPFRONT	UPHAUDS	UPKNITTED	UPLOOKING	UPREACH
UPFURL	UPHEAP	UPLAID	UPLOOKS	UPREACHED
UPFURLED	UPHEAPED	UPLAND	UPLYING	UPREACHES
UPFURLING	UPHEAPING	UPLANDER	UPMADE	UPREAR
UPFURLS	UPHEAPS	UPLANDERS	UPMAKE	UPREARED
UPGANG	UPHEAVAL	UPLANDISH	UPMAKER	UPREARING
UPGANGS	UPHEAVALS	UPLANDS	UPMAKERS	UPREARS
UPGATHER	UPHEAVE	UPLAY	UPMAKES	UPREST
UPGATHERS	UPHEAVED	UPLAYING	UPMAKING	UPRESTS
UPGAZE	UPHEAVER	UPLAYS	UPMAKINGS	UPRIGHT
UPGAZED	UPHEAVERS	UPLEAD	UPMANSHIP	UPRIGHTED
UPGAZES	UPHEAVES	UPLEADING	UPMARKET	UPRIGHTLY
UPGAZING	UPHEAVING	UPLEADS	UPMARKETS	UPRIGHTS
UPGIRD	UPHELD	UPLEAN	UPMOST	UPRISAL
UPGIRDED	UPHILD	UPLEANED	UPO	UPRISALS
UPGIRDING	UPHILL	UPLEANING	UPON	UPRISE
UPGIRDS	UPHILLS	UPLEANS	UPPED	UPRISEN
UPGIRT	UPHOARD	UPLEANT	UPPER	UPRISER
UPGIRTED	UPHOARDED	UPLEAP	UPPERCASE	UPRISERS
UPGIRTING	UPHOARDS	UPLEAPED	UPPERCUT	UPRISES
UPGIRTS	UPHOIST	UPLEAPING	UPPERCUTS	UPRISING
UPGO	UPHOISTED	UPLEAPS	UPPERMOST	UPRISINGS
UPGOES	UPHOISTS	UPLEAPT	UPPERPART	UPRIST
UPGOING	UPHOLD	UPLED	UPPERS	UPRISTS
UPGOINGS	UPHOLDER	UPLIFT	UPPILE	UPRIVER
UPGONE	UPHOLDERS	UPLIFTED	UPPILED	UPRIVERS
UPGRADE	UPHOLDING	UPLIFTER	UPPILES	UPROAR
UPGRADED	UPHOLDS	UPLIFTERS	UPPILING	UPROARED
UPGRADER	UPHOLSTER	UPLIFTING	UPPING	UPROARING
UPGRADERS	UPHOORD	UPLIFTS	UPPINGS	UPROARS
UPGRADES	UPHOORDED	UPLIGHT	UPPISH	UPROLL
UPGRADING	UPHOORDS	UPLIGHTED	UPPISHLY	UPROLLED
UPGREW	UPHOVE	UPLIGHTER	UPPITIER	UPROLLING
UPGROW	UPHROE	UPLIGHTS	UPPITIEST	UPROLLS
UPGROWING	UPHROES	UPLINK	UPPITY	UPROOT

UPROOTAL	UPSIDE	UPSTARTED	UPTAKES	UPTREND
UPROOTALS	UPSIDES	UPSTARTS	UPTAKING	UPTRENDS
UPROOTED	UPSIES	UPSTATE	UPTAKS	UPTRILLED
UPROOTER	UPSILON	UPSTATER	UPTALK	UPTURN
UPROOTERS	UPSILONS	UPSTATERS	UPTALKED	UPTURNED
UPROOTING	UPSITTING	UPSTATES	UPTALKING	UPTURNING
UPROOTS	UPSIZE	UPSTAY	UPTALKS	UPTURNS
UPROSE	UPSIZED	UPSTAYED	UPTEAR	UPTYING
UPROUSE	UPSIZES	UPSTAYING	UPTEARING	UPVALUE
UPROUSED	UPSIZING	UPSTAYS	UPTEARS	UPVALUED
UPROUSES	UPSKILL	UPSTEP	UPTEMPO	UPVALUES
UPROUSING	UPSKILLED	UPSTEPPED	UPTEMPOS	UPVALUING
UPRUN	UPSKILLS	UPSTEPS	UPTER	UPVOTE
UPRUNNING	UPSKIRT	UPSTIR	UPTHREAD	UPVOTED
UPRUNS	UPSKIRTS	UPSTIRRED	UPTHREW	UPVOTES
UPRUSH	UPSLOPE	UPSTIRS	UPTHROW	UPVOTING
UPRUSHED	UPSLOPES	UPSTOOD	UPTHROWN	UPWAFT
UPRUSHES	UPSOAR	UPSTREAM	UPTHROWS	UPWAFTED
UPRUSHING	UPSOARED	UPSTREAMS	UPTHRUST	UPWAFTING
UPRYST	UPSOARING	UPSTROKE	UPTHRUSTS	UPWAFTS
UPS	UPSOARS	UPSTROKES	UPTHUNDER	UPWARD
UPSADAISY	UPSOLD	UPSUM	UPTICK	UPWARDLY
UPSCALE	UPSPAKE	UPSUMS	UPTICKS	UPWARDS
UPSCALED	UPSPEAK	UPSURGE	UPTIE	UPWELL
UPSCALES	UPSPEAKS	UPSURGED	UPTIED	UPWELLED
UPSCALING	UPSPEAR	UPSURGES	UPTIES	UPWELLING
UPSEE	UPSPEARED	UPSURGING	UPTIGHT	UPWELLS
UPSEES	UPSPEARS	UPSWARM	UPTIGHTER	UPWENT
UPSELL	UPSPOKE	UPSWARMED	UPTILT	UPWHIRL
UPSELLING	UPSPOKEN	UPSWARMS	UPTILTED	UPWHIRLED
UPSELLS	UPSPRANG	UPSWAY	UPTILTING	UPWHIRLS
UPSEND	UPSPRING	UPSWAYED	UPTILTS	UPWIND
UPSENDING	UPSPRINGS	UPSWAYING	UPTIME	UPWINDING
UPSENDS	UPSPRUNG	UPSWAYS	UPTIMES	UPWINDS
UPSENT	UPSTAGE	UPSWEEP	UPTITLING	UPWOUND
UPSET	UPSTAGED	UPSWEEPS	UPTOOK	UPWRAP
UPSETS	UPSTAGER	UPSWELL	UPTORE	UPWRAPS
UPSETTER	UPSTAGERS	UPSWELLED	UPTORN	UPWROUGHT
UPSETTERS	UPSTAGES	UPSWELLS	UPTOSS	UR
UPSETTING	UPSTAGING	UPSWEPT	UPTOSSED	URACHI
UPSEY	UPSTAIR	UPSWING	UPTOSSES	URACHUS
UPSEYS	UPSTAIRS	UPSWINGS	UPTOSSING	URACHUSES
UPSHIFT	UPSTAND	UPSWOLLEN	UPTOWN	URACIL
UPSHIFTED	UPSTANDS	UPSWUNG	UPTOWNER	URACILS
UPSHIFTS	UPSTARE	UPSY	UPTOWNERS	URAEI
UPSHOOT	UPSTARED	UPTA	UPTOWNS	URAEMIA
UPSHOOTS	UPSTARES	UPTAK	UPTRAIN	URAEMIAS
UPSHOT	UPSTARING	UPTAKE	UPTRAINED	URAEMIC
UPSHOTS	UPSTART	UPTAKEN	UPTRAINS	URAEUS

URAEUSES
URALI
URALIS
URALITE
URALITES
URALITIC
URALITISE
URALITIZE
URANIA
URANIAN
URANIAS
URANIC
URANIDE
URANIDES
URANIN
URANINITE
URANINS
URANISCI
URANISCUS
URANISM
URANISMS
URANITE
URANITES
URANITIC
URANIUM
URANIUMS
URANOLOGY
URANOUS
URANYL
URANYLIC
URANYLS
URAO
URAOS
URARE
URARES
URARI
URARIS
URASE
URASES
URATE
URATES
URATIC
URB
URBAN
URBANE
URBANELY
URBANER
URBANEST
URBANISE

URBANISED
URBANISES
URBANISM
URBANISMS
URBANIST
URBANISTS
URBANITE
URBANITES
URBANITY
URBANIZE
URBANIZED
URBANIZES
URBEX
URBEXES
URBIA
URBIAS
URBS
URCEOLATE
URCEOLI
URCEOLUS
URCHIN
URCHINS
URD
URDE
URDEE
URDS
URDY
URE
UREA
UREAL
UREAS
UREASE
UREASES
UREDIA
UREDIAL
UREDINE
UREDINES
UREDINIA
UREDINIAL
UREDINIUM
UREDINOUS
UREDIUM
UREDO
UREDOS
UREDOSORI
UREIC
UREIDE
UREIDES
UREMIA

UREMIAS
UREMIC
URENA
URENAS
URENT
UREOTELIC
URES
URESES
URESIS
URETER
URETERAL
URETERIC
URETERS
URETHAN
URETHANE
URETHANED
URETHANES
URETHANS
URETHRA
URETHRAE
URETHRAL
URETHRAS
URETIC
URGE
URGED
URGENCE
URGENCES
URGENCIES
URGENCY
URGENT
URGENTLY
URGER
URGERS
URGES
URGING
URGINGLY
URGINGS
URIAL
URIALS
URIC
URICASE
URICASES
URIDINE
URIDINES
URIDYLIC
URINAEMIA
URINAEMIC
URINAL
URINALS

URINANT
URINARIES
URINARY
URINATE
URINATED
URINATES
URINATING
URINATION
URINATIVE
URINATOR
URINATORS
URINE
URINED
URINEMIA
URINEMIAS
URINEMIC
URINES
URINING
URINOLOGY
URINOSE
URINOUS
URITE
URITES
URMAN
URMANS
URN
URNAL
URNED
URNFIELD
URNFIELDS
URNFUL
URNFULS
URNING
URNINGS
URNLIKE
URNS
UROBILIN
UROBILINS
UROBORIC
UROBOROS
UROCHORD
UROCHORDS
UROCHROME
URODELAN
URODELANS
URODELE
URODELES
URODELOUS
UROGENOUS

UROGRAM
UROGRAMS
UROGRAPHY
UROKINASE
UROLAGNIA
UROLITH
UROLITHIC
UROLITHS
UROLOGIC
UROLOGIES
UROLOGIST
UROLOGY
UROMERE
UROMERES
UROPOD
UROPODAL
UROPODOUS
UROPODS
UROPYGIA
UROPYGIAL
UROPYGIUM
UROSCOPIC
UROSCOPY
UROSES
UROSIS
UROSOME
UROSOMES
UROSTEGE
UROSTEGES
UROSTOMY
UROSTYLE
UROSTYLES
URP
URPED
URPING
URPS
URSA
URSAE
URSID
URSIDS
URSIFORM
URSINE
URSON
URSONS
URTEXT
URTEXTE
URTEXTS
URTICA
URTICANT

U

URTICANTS	USERS	USURES	UTILISER	UTTERERS
URTICARIA	USES	USURESS	UTILISERS	UTTEREST
URTICAS	USHER	USURESSES	UTILISES	UTTERING
URTICATE	USHERED	USURIES	UTILISING	UTTERINGS
URTICATED	USHERESS	USURING	UTILITIES	UTTERLESS
URTICATES	USHERETTE	USURIOUS	UTILITY	UTTERLY
URUBU	USHERING	USUROUS	UTILIZE	UTTERMOST
URUBUS	USHERINGS	USURP	UTILIZED	UTTERNESS
URUS	USHERS	USURPED	UTILIZER	UTTERS
URUSES	USHERSHIP	USURPEDLY	UTILIZERS	UTU
URUSHIOL	USING	USURPER	UTILIZES	UTUS
URUSHIOLS	USNEA	USURPERS	UTILIZING	UVA
URVA	USNEAS	USURPING	UTIS	UVAE
URVAS	USQUABAE	USURPINGS	UTISES	UVAROVITE
US	USQUABAES	USURPS	UTMOST	UVAS
USABILITY	USQUE	USURY	UTMOSTS	UVEA
USABLE	USQUEBAE	USWARD	UTOPIA	UVEAL
USABLY	USQUEBAES	USWARDS	UTOPIAN	UVEAS
USAGE	USQUES	UT	UTOPIANS	UVEITIC
USAGER	USTION	UTA	UTOPIAS	UVEITIDES
USAGERS	USTIONS	UTAS	UTOPIAST	UVEITIS
USAGES	USTULATE	UTASES	UTOPIASTS	UVEITISES
USANCE	USTULATED	UTE	UTOPISM	UVEOUS
USANCES	USTULATES	UTENSIL	UTOPISMS	UVULA
USAUNCE	USUAL	UTENSILS	UTOPIST	UVULAE
USAUNCES	USUALLY	UTERI	UTOPISTIC	UVULAR
USE	USUALNESS	UTERINE	UTOPISTS	UVULARLY
USEABLE	USUALS	UTERITIS	UTRICLE	UVULARS
USEABLY	USUCAPION	UTEROTOMY	UTRICLES	UVULAS
USED	USUCAPT	UTERUS	UTRICULAR	UVULITIS
USEFUL	USUCAPTED	UTERUSES	UTRICULI	UWU
USEFULLY	USUCAPTS	UTES	UTRICULUS	UXORIAL
USEFULS	USUFRUCT	UTILE	UTS	UXORIALLY
USELESS	USUFRUCTS	UTILES	UTTER	UXORICIDE
USELESSLY	USURE	UTILIDOR	UTTERABLE	UXORIOUS
USER	USURED	UTILIDORS	UTTERANCE	
USERNAME	USURER	UTILISE	UTTERED	
USERNAMES	USURERS	UTILISED	UTTERER	

U

V

VAC	VACUIST	VAGINITIS	VAINNESS	VALETES
VACANCE	VACUISTS	VAGINOSES	VAIR	VALETING
VACANCES	VACUITIES	VAGINOSIS	VAIRE	VALETINGS
VACANCIES	VACUITY	VAGINULA	VAIRIER	VALETS
VACANCY	VACUOLAR	VAGINULAE	VAIRIEST	VALGOID
VACANT	VACUOLATE	VAGINULE	VAIRS	VALGOUS
VACANTLY	VACUOLE	VAGINULES	VAIRY	VALGUS
VACATABLE	VACUOLES	VAGITUS	VAIVODE	VALGUSES
VACATE	VACUOUS	VAGITUSES	VAIVODES	VALI
VACATED	VACUOUSLY	VAGOTOMY	VAJAZZLE	VALIANCE
VACATES	VACUUM	VAGOTONIA	VAJAZZLED	VALIANCES
VACATING	VACUUMED	VAGOTONIC	VAJAZZLES	VALIANCY
VACATION	VACUUMING	VAGRANCY	VAKAS	VALIANT
VACATIONS	VACUUMS	VAGRANT	VAKASES	VALIANTLY
VACATUR	VADE	VAGRANTLY	VAKASS	VALIANTS
VACATURS	VADED	VAGRANTS	VAKASSES	VALID
VACAY	VADES	VAGROM	VAKEEL	VALIDATE
VACAYS	VADING	VAGS	VAKEELS	VALIDATED
VACCINA	VADOSE	VAGUE	VAKIL	VALIDATES
VACCINAL	VAE	VAGUED	VAKILS	VALIDATOR
VACCINAS	VAES	VAGUELY	VALANCE	VALIDER
VACCINATE	VAG	VAGUENESS	VALANCED	VALIDEST
VACCINE	VAGABOND	VAGUER	VALANCES	VALIDITY
VACCINEE	VAGABONDS	VAGUES	VALANCING	VALIDLY
VACCINEES	VAGAL	VAGUEST	VALE	VALIDNESS
VACCINES	VAGALLY	VAGUING	VALENCE	VALINE
VACCINIA	VAGARIES	VAGUISH	VALENCES	VALINES
VACCINIAL	VAGARIOUS	VAGUS	VALENCIA	VALIS
VACCINIAS	VAGARISH	VAHANA	VALENCIAS	VALISE
VACCINIUM	VAGARY	VAHANAS	VALENCIES	VALISES
VACHERIN	VAGGED	VAHINE	VALENCY	VALIUM
VACHERINS	VAGGING	VAHINES	VALENTINE	VALIUMS
VACILLANT	VAGI	VAIL	VALERATE	VALKYR
VACILLATE	VAGILE	VAILED	VALERATES	VALKYRIE
VACKED	VAGILITY	VAILING	VALERIAN	VALKYRIES
VACKING	VAGINA	VAILS	VALERIANS	VALKYRS
VACS	VAGINAE	VAIN	VALERIC	VALLAR
VACUA	VAGINAL	VAINER	VALES	VALLARIES
VACUATE	VAGINALLY	VAINESSE	VALET	VALLARS
VACUATED	VAGINANT	VAINESSES	VALETA	VALLARY
VACUATES	VAGINAS	VAINEST	VALETAS	VALLATE
VACUATING	VAGINATE	VAINGLORY	VALETE	VALLATION
VACUATION	VAGINATED	VAINLY	VALETED	VALLECULA

VALLEY	VALVAL	VAMPS	VANITIED	VAPORIFIC
VALLEYED	VALVAR	VAMPY	VANITIES	VAPORING
VALLEYS	VALVASSOR	VAN	VANITORY	VAPORINGS
VALLHUND	VALVATE	VANADATE	VANITY	VAPORISE
VALLHUNDS	VALVE	VANADATES	VANLIKE	VAPORISED
VALLONIA	VALVED	VANADIATE	VANLOAD	VAPORISER
VALLONIAS	VALVELESS	VANADIC	VANLOADS	VAPORISES
VALLUM	VALVELET	VANADIUM	VANMAN	VAPORISH
VALLUMS	VALVELETS	VANADIUMS	VANMEN	VAPORIZE
VALONEA	VALVELIKE	VANADOUS	VANNED	VAPORIZED
VALONEAS	VALVES	VANASPATI	VANNER	VAPORIZER
VALONIA	VALVING	VANDA	VANNERS	VAPORIZES
VALONIAS	VALVULA	VANDAL	VANNING	VAPORLESS
VALOR	VALVULAE	VANDALIC	VANNINGS	VAPORLIKE
VALORISE	VALVULAR	VANDALISE	VANPOOL	VAPOROUS
VALORISED	VALVULE	VANDALISH	VANPOOLS	VAPORS
VALORISES	VALVULES	VANDALISM	VANQUISH	VAPORWARE
VALORIZE	VAMBRACE	VANDALIZE	VANS	VAPORWAVE
VALORIZED	VAMBRACED	VANDALS	VANT	VAPORY
VALORIZES	VAMBRACES	VANDAS	VANTAGE	VAPOUR
VALOROUS	VAMOOSE	VANDYKE	VANTAGED	VAPOURED
VALORS	VAMOOSED	VANDYKED	VANTAGES	VAPOURER
VALOUR	VAMOOSES	VANDYKES	VANTAGING	VAPOURERS
VALOURS	VAMOOSING	VANDYKING	VANTBRACE	VAPOURIER
VALPROATE	VAMOSE	VANE	VANTBRASS	VAPOURING
VALPROIC	VAMOSED	VANED	VANTS	VAPOURISH
VALSE	VAMOSES	VANELESS	VANWARD	VAPOUROUS
VALSED	VAMOSING	VANES	VAPE	VAPOURS
VALSES	VAMP	VANESSA	VAPED	VAPOURY
VALSING	VAMPED	VANESSAS	VAPER	VAPULATE
VALUABLE	VAMPER	VANESSID	VAPERS	VAPULATED
VALUABLES	VAMPERS	VANESSIDS	VAPES	VAPULATES
VALUABLY	VAMPIER	VANG	VAPID	VAQUERO
VALUATE	VAMPIEST	VANGS	VAPIDER	VAQUEROS
VALUATED	VAMPING	VANGUARD	VAPIDEST	VAQUITA
VALUATES	VAMPINGS	VANGUARDS	VAPIDITY	VAQUITAS
VALUATING	VAMPIRE	VANILLA	VAPIDLY	VAR
VALUATION	VAMPIRED	VANILLAS	VAPIDNESS	VARA
VALUATOR	VAMPIRES	VANILLIC	VAPING	VARACTOR
VALUATORS	VAMPIRIC	VANILLIN	VAPINGS	VARACTORS
VALUE	VAMPIRING	VANILLINS	VAPOR	VARAN
VALUED	VAMPIRISE	VANISH	VAPORABLE	VARANS
VALUELESS	VAMPIRISH	VANISHED	VAPORED	VARAS
VALUER	VAMPIRISM	VANISHER	VAPORER	VARDIES
VALUERS	VAMPIRIZE	VANISHERS	VAPORERS	VARDY
VALUES	VAMPISH	VANISHES	VAPORETTI	VARE
VALUING	VAMPISHLY	VANISHING	VAPORETTO	VAREC
VALUTA	VAMPLATE	VANITAS	VAPORIER	VARECH
VALUTAS	VAMPLATES	VANITASES	VAPORIEST	VARECHS

VARECS	VARIOLOID	VARVELS	VASTS	VAUNTER
VARENYKY	VARIOLOUS	VARVES	VASTY	VAUNTERS
VARES	VARIORUM	VARY	VAT	VAUNTERY
VAREUSE	VARIORUMS	VARYING	VATABLE	VAUNTFUL
VAREUSES	VARIOUS	VARYINGLY	VATFUL	VAUNTIE
VARGUENO	VARIOUSLY	VARYINGS	VATFULS	VAUNTIER
VARGUENOS	VARISCITE	VAS	VATIC	VAUNTIEST
VARIA	VARISIZED	VASA	VATICAL	VAUNTING
VARIABLE	VARISTOR	VASAL	VATICIDE	VAUNTINGS
VARIABLES	VARISTORS	VASCULA	VATICIDES	VAUNTS
VARIABLY	VARITYPE	VASCULAR	VATICINAL	VAUNTY
VARIANCE	VARITYPED	VASCULUM	VATMAN	VAURIEN
VARIANCES	VARITYPES	VASCULUMS	VATMEN	VAURIENS
VARIANT	VARIX	VASE	VATS	VAUS
VARIANTS	VARLET	VASECTOMY	VATTED	VAUT
VARIAS	VARLETESS	VASEFUL	VATTER	VAUTE
VARIATE	VARLETRY	VASEFULS	VATTERS	VAUTED
VARIATED	VARLETS	VASELIKE	VATTING	VAUTES
VARIATES	VARLETTO	VASELINE	VATU	VAUTING
VARIATING	VARLETTOS	VASELINED	VATUS	VAUTS
VARIATION	VARMENT	VASELINES	VAU	VAV
VARIATIVE	VARMENTS	VASES	VAUCH	VAVASOR
VARICEAL	VARMINT	VASIFORM	VAUCHED	VAVASORS
VARICELLA	VARMINTS	VASOMOTOR	VAUCHES	VAVASORY
VARICES	VARNA	VASOSPASM	VAUCHING	VAVASOUR
VARICOID	VARNAS	VASOTOCIN	VAUDOO	VAVASOURS
VARICOSE	VARNISH	VASOTOMY	VAUDOOS	VAVASSOR
VARICOSED	VARNISHED	VASOVAGAL	VAUDOUX	VAVASSORS
VARICOSES	VARNISHER	VASSAIL	VAULT	VAVS
VARICOSIS	VARNISHES	VASSAILS	VAULTAGE	VAW
VARIED	VARNISHY	VASSAL	VAULTAGES	VAWARD
VARIEDLY	VAROOM	VASSALAGE	VAULTED	VAWARDS
VARIEGATE	VAROOMED	VASSALESS	VAULTER	VAWNTIE
VARIER	VAROOMING	VASSALISE	VAULTERS	VAWNTIER
VARIERS	VAROOMS	VASSALIZE	VAULTIER	VAWNTIEST
VARIES	VARROA	VASSALLED	VAULTIEST	VAWS
VARIETAL	VARROAS	VASSALRY	VAULTING	VAWTE
VARIETALS	VARS	VASSALS	VAULTINGS	VAWTED
VARIETIES	VARSAL	VAST	VAULTLIKE	VAWTES
VARIETY	VARSITIES	VASTER	VAULTS	VAWTING
VARIFOCAL	VARSITY	VASTEST	VAULTY	VAX
VARIFORM	VARTABED	VASTIDITY	VAUNCE	VAXED
VARIOLA	VARTABEDS	VASTIER	VAUNCED	VAXES
VARIOLAR	VARUS	VASTIEST	VAUNCES	VAXING
VARIOLAS	VARUSES	VASTITIES	VAUNCING	VAXX
VARIOLATE	VARVE	VASTITUDE	VAUNT	VAXXED
VARIOLE	VARVED	VASTITY	VAUNTAGE	VAXXES
VARIOLES	VARVEL	VASTLY	VAUNTAGES	VAXXING
VARIOLITE	VARVELLED	VASTNESS	VAUNTED	VEAL

VEALE	VEGANISE	VEHME	VELARIZE	VELVERET
VEALED	VEGANISED	VEHMIC	VELARIZED	VELVERETS
VEALER	VEGANISES	VEHMIQUE	VELARIZES	VELVET
VEALERS	VEGANISM	VEIL	VELARS	VELVETED
VEALES	VEGANISMS	VEILED	VELATE	VELVETEEN
VEALIER	VEGANIZE	VEILEDLY	VELATED	VELVETIER
VEALIEST	VEGANIZED	VEILER	VELATURA	VELVETING
VEALING	VEGANIZES	VEILERS	VELATURAS	VELVETS
VEALS	VEGANS	VEILIER	VELCRO	VELVETY
VEALY	VEGAS	VEILIEST	VELCROS	VENA
VECTOR	VEGELATE	VEILING	VELD	VENAE
VECTORED	VEGELATES	VEILINGS	VELDS	VENAL
VECTORIAL	VEGEMITE	VEILLESS	VELDSKOEN	VENALITY
VECTORING	VEGEMITES	VEILLEUSE	VELDT	VENALLY
VECTORISE	VEGES	VEILLIKE	VELDTS	VENATIC
VECTORIZE	VEGETABLE	VEILS	VELE	VENATICAL
VECTORS	VEGETABLY	VEILY	VELES	VENATION
VEDALIA	VEGETAL	VEIN	VELETA	VENATIONS
VEDALIAS	VEGETALLY	VEINAL	VELETAS	VENATOR
VEDETTE	VEGETALS	VEINED	VELIGER	VENATORS
VEDETTES	VEGETANT	VEINER	VELIGERS	VEND
VEDUTA	VEGETATE	VEINERS	VELITES	VENDABLE
VEDUTAS	VEGETATED	VEINIER	VELL	VENDABLES
VEDUTE	VEGETATES	VEINIEST	VELLEITY	VENDACE
VEDUTISTA	VEGETE	VEINING	VELLENAGE	VENDACES
VEDUTISTE	VEGETIST	VEININGS	VELLET	VENDAGE
VEDUTISTI	VEGETISTS	VEINLESS	VELLETS	VENDAGES
VEE	VEGETIVE	VEINLET	VELLICATE	VENDANGE
VEEJAY	VEGETIVES	VEINLETS	VELLON	VENDANGES
VEEJAYS	VEGGED	VEINLIKE	VELLONS	VENDED
VEENA	VEGGES	VEINOUS	VELLS	VENDEE
VEENAS	VEGGIE	VEINS	VELLUM	VENDEES
VEEP	VEGGIER	VEINSTONE	VELLUMS	VENDER
VEEPEE	VEGGIES	VEINSTUFF	VELLUS	VENDERS
VEEPEES	VEGGIEST	VEINULE	VELOCE	VENDETTA
VEEPS	VEGGING	VEINULES	VELOCITY	VENDETTAS
VEER	VEGIE	VEINULET	VELODROME	VENDEUSE
VEERED	VEGIER	VEINULETS	VELOUR	VENDEUSES
VEERIES	VEGIES	VEINY	VELOURS	VENDIBLE
VEERING	VEGIEST	VELA	VELOUTE	VENDIBLES
VEERINGLY	VEGO	VELAMEN	VELOUTES	VENDIBLY
VEERINGS	VEGOS	VELAMINA	VELOUTINE	VENDING
VEERS	VEHEMENCE	VELAR	VELSKOEN	VENDINGS
VEERY	VEHEMENCY	VELARIA	VELSKOENS	VENDIS
VEES	VEHEMENT	VELARIC	VELUM	VENDISES
VEG	VEHICLE	VELARISE	VELURE	VENDISS
VEGA	VEHICLES	VELARISED	VELURED	VENDISSES
VEGAN	VEHICULAR	VELARISES	VELURES	VENDITION
VEGANIC	VEHM	VELARIUM	VELURING	VENDOR

VENDORS	VENIAL	VENTIFACT	VERANDAED	VERD
VENDS	VENIALITY	VENTIGE	VERANDAH	VERDANCY
VENDUE	VENIALLY	VENTIGES	VERANDAHS	VERDANT
VENDUES	VENIDIUM	VENTIL	VERANDAS	VERDANTLY
VENEER	VENIDIUMS	VENTILATE	VERAPAMIL	VERDELHO
VENEERED	VENIN	VENTILS	VERATRIA	VERDELHÒS
VENEERER	VENINE	VENTING	VERATRIAS	VERDERER
VENEERERS	VENINES	VENTINGS	VERATRIN	VERDERERS
VENEERING	VENINS	VENTLESS	VERATRINE	VERDEROR
VENEERS	VENIRE	VENTOSE	VERATRINS	VERDERORS
VENEFIC	VENIREMAN	VENTOSES	VERATRUM	VERDET
VENEFICAL	VENIREMEN	VENTOSITY	VERATRUMS	VERDETS
VENENATE	VENIRES	VENTOUSE	VERB	VERDICT
VENENATED	VENISON	VENTOUSES	VERBAL	VERDICTS
VENENATES	VENISONS	VENTRAL	VERBALISE	VERDIGRIS
VENENE	VENITE	VENTRALLY	VERBALISM	VERDIN
VENENES	VENITES	VENTRALS	VERBALIST	VERDINS
VENENOSE	VENNEL	VENTRE	VERBALITY	VERDIT
VENERABLE	VENNELS	VENTRED	VERBALIZE	VERDITE
VENERABLY	VENOGRAM	VENTRES	VERBALLED	VERDITER
VENERATE	VENOGRAMS	VENTRICLE	VERBALLY	VERDITERS
VENERATED	VENOLOGY	VENTRING	VERBALS	VERDITES
VENERATES	VENOM	VENTRINGS	VERBARIAN	VERDITS
VENERATOR	VENOMED	VENTROUS	VERBASCUM	VERDOY
VENEREAL	VENOMER	VENTS	VERBATIM	VERDOYS
VENEREAN	VENOMERS	VENTURE	VERBED	VERDURE
VENEREANS	VENOMING	VENTURED	VERBENA	VERDURED
VENEREOUS	VENOMLESS	VENTURER	VERBENAS	VERDURES
VENERER	VENOMOUS	VENTURERS	VERBERATE	VERDUROUS
VENERERS	VENOMS	VENTURES	VERBIAGE	VERECUND
VENERIES	VENOSE	VENTURI	VERBIAGES	VERGE
VENERY	VENOSITY	VENTURING	VERBICIDE	VERGED
VENETIAN	VENOUS	VENTURIS	VERBID	VERGENCE
VENETIANS	VENOUSLY	VENTUROUS	VERBIDS	VERGENCES
VENEWE	VENT	VENUE	VERBIFIED	VERGENCY
VENEWES	VENTAGE	VENUES	VERBIFIES	VERGER
VENEY	VENTAGES	VENULAR	VERBIFY	VERGERS
VENEYS	VENTAIL	VENULE	VERBILE	VERGES
VENGE	VENTAILE	VENULES	VERBILES	VERGING
VENGEABLE	VENTAILES	VENULOSE	VERBING	VERGLAS
VENGEABLY	VENTAILS	VENULOUS	VERBINGS	VERGLASES
VENGEANCE	VENTANA	VENUS	VERBLESS	VERIDIC
VENGED	VENTANAS	VENUSES	VERBOSE	VERIDICAL
VENGEFUL	VENTAYLE	VENVILLE	VERBOSELY	VERIER
VENGEMENT	VENTAYLES	VENVILLES	VERBOSER	VERIEST
VENGER	VENTED	VERA	VERBOSEST	VERIFIED
VENGERS	VENTER	VERACIOUS	VERBOSITY	VERIFIER
VENGES	VENTERS	VERACITY	VERBOTEN	VERIFIERS
VENGING	VENTIDUCT	VERANDA	VERBS	VERIFIES

VERIFY	VERMIN	VERRUGAS	VERTEBRAS	VESPA
VERIFYING	VERMINATE	VERRY	VERTED	VESPAS
VERILY	VERMINED	VERS	VERTEX	VESPER
VERISM	VERMINIER	VERSAL	VERTEXES	VESPERAL
VERISMO	VERMINOUS	VERSALS	VERTICAL	VESPERALS
VERISMOS	VERMINS	VERSANT	VERTICALS	VESPERS
VERISMS	VERMINY	VERSANTS	VERTICES	VESPIARY
VERIST	VERMIS	VERSATILE	VERTICIL	VESPID
VERISTIC	VERMOULU	VERSE	VERTICILS	VESPIDS
VERISTS	VERMOUTH	VERSED	VERTICITY	VESPINE
VERITABLE	VERMOUTHS	VERSELET	VERTIGO	VESPOID
VERITABLY	VERMUTH	VERSELETS	VERTIGOES	VESSAIL
VERITAS	VERMUTHS	VERSEMAN	VERTIGOS	VESSAILS
VERITATES	VERNACLE	VERSEMEN	VERTING	VESSEL
VERITE	VERNACLES	VERSER	VERTIPORT	VESSELED
VERITES	VERNAL	VERSERS	VERTISOL	VESSELS
VERITIES	VERNALISE	VERSES	VERTISOLS	VEST
VERITY	VERNALITY	VERSET	VERTS	VESTA
VERJUICE	VERNALIZE	VERSETS	VERTU	VESTAL
VERJUICED	VERNALLY	VERSICLE	VERTUE	VESTALLY
VERJUICES	VERNANT	VERSICLES	VERTUES	VESTALS
VERJUS	VERNATION	VERSIFIED	VERTUOUS	VESTAS
VERJUSES	VERNICLE	VERSIFIER	VERTUS	VESTED
VERKLEMPT	VERNICLES	VERSIFIES	VERVAIN	VESTEE
VERKRAMP	VERNIER	VERSIFORM	VERVAINS	VESTEES
VERLAN	VERNIERS	VERSIFY	VERVE	VESTIARY
VERLANS	VERNIX	VERSIN	VERVEL	VESTIBULA
VERLIG	VERNIXES	VERSINE	VERVELLED	VESTIBULE
VERLIGTE	VERONAL	VERSINES	VERVELS	VESTIGE
VERLIGTES	VERONALS	VERSING	VERVEN	VESTIGES
VERMAL	VERONICA	VERSINGS	VERVENS	VESTIGIA
VERMEIL	VERONICAS	VERSINS	VERVES	VESTIGIAL
VERMEILED	VERONIQUE	VERSION	VERVET	VESTIGIUM
VERMEILLE	VERQUERE	VERSIONAL	VERVETS	VESTIMENT
VERMEILS	VERQUERES	VERSIONED	VERY	VESTING
VERMELL	VERQUIRE	VERSIONER	VESICA	VESTINGS
VERMELLS	VERQUIRES	VERSIONS	VESICAE	VESTITURE
VERMES	VERRA	VERSO	VESICAL	VESTLESS
VERMIAN	VERREL	VERSOS	VESICANT	VESTLIKE
VERMICIDE	VERRELS	VERST	VESICANTS	VESTMENT
VERMICULE	VERREY	VERSTE	VESICAS	VESTMENTS
VERMIFORM	VERRINE	VERSTES	VESICATE	VESTRAL
VERMIFUGE	VERRINES	VERSTS	VESICATED	VESTRIES
VERMIL	VERRUCA	VERSUS	VESICATES	VESTRY
VERMILIES	VERRUCAE	VERSUTE	VESICLE	VESTRYMAN
VERMILION	VERRUCAS	VERT	VESICLES	VESTRYMEN
VERMILLED	VERRUCOSE	VERTEBRA	VESICULA	VESTS
VERMILS	VERRUCOUS	VERTEBRAE	VESICULAE	VESTURAL
VERMILY	VERRUGA	VERTEBRAL	VESICULAR	VESTURE

VESTURED	VEXES	VIBICES	VICARIATE	VICTRESS
VESTURER	VEXIL	VIBIER	VICARIES	VICTRIX
VESTURERS	VEXILLA	VIBIEST	VICARIOUS	VICTRIXES
VESTURES	VEXILLAR	VIBING	VICARLIER	VICTROLA
VESTURING	VEXILLARY	VIBIST	VICARLY	VICTROLAS
VESUVIAN	VEXILLATE	VIBISTS	VICARS	VICTUAL
VESUVIANS	VEXILLUM	VIBRACULA	VICARSHIP	VICTUALED
VET	VEXILS	VIBRAHARP	VICARY	VICTUALER
VETCH	VEXING	VIBRANCE	VICE	VICTUALS
VETCHES	VEXINGLY	VIBRANCES	VICED	VICUGNA
VETCHIER	VEXINGS	VIBRANCY	VICEGERAL	VICUGNAS
VETCHIEST	VEXT	VIBRANT	VICELESS	VICUNA
VETCHLING	VEZIR	VIBRANTLY	VICELIKE	VICUNAS
VETCHY	VEZIRS	VIBRANTS	VICENARY	VID
VETERAN	VIA	VIBRATE	VICENNIAL	VIDALIA
VETERANS	VIABILITY	VIBRATED	VICEREGAL	VIDALIAS
VETIVER	VIABLE	VIBRATES	VICEREINE	VIDAME
VETIVERS	VIABLY	VIBRATILE	VICEROY	VIDAMES
VETIVERT	VIADUCT	VIBRATING	VICEROYS	VIDE
VETIVERTS	VIADUCTS	VIBRATION	VICES	VIDELICET
VETKOEK	VIAE	VIBRATIVE	VICESIMAL	VIDENDA
VETKOEKS	VIAL	VIBRATO	VICHIES	VIDENDUM
VETO	VIALED	VIBRATOR	VICHY	VIDEO
VETOED	VIALFUL	VIBRATORS	VICIATE	VIDEOCAM
VETOER	VIALFULS	VIBRATORY	VICIATED	VIDEOCAMS
VETOERS	VIALING	VIBRATOS	VICIATES	VIDEODISC
VETOES	VIALLED	VIBRIO	VICIATING	VIDEODISK
VETOING	VIALLING	VIBRIOID	VICINAGE	VIDEOED
VETOLESS	VIALS	VIBRION	VICINAGES	VIDEOFIT
VETS	VIAMETER	VIBRIONIC	VICINAL	VIDEOFITS
VETTED	VIAMETERS	VIBRIONS	VICING	VIDEOGRAM
VETTER	VIAND	VIBRIOS	VICINITY	VIDEOING
VETTERS	VIANDS	VIBRIOSES	VICIOSITY	VIDEOLAND
VETTING	VIAS	VIBRIOSIS	VICIOUS	VIDEOS
VETTINGS	VIATIC	VIBRISSA	VICIOUSLY	VIDEOTAPE
VETTURA	VIATICA	VIBRISSAE	VICOMTE	VIDEOTEX
VETTURAS	VIATICAL	VIBRISSAL	VICOMTES	VIDEOTEXT
VETTURINI	VIATICALS	VIBRONIC	VICTIM	VIDETTE
VETTURINO	VIATICUM	VIBS	VICTIMISE	VIDETTES
VEX	VIATICUMS	VIBURNUM	VICTIMIZE	VIDICON
VEXATION	VIATOR	VIBURNUMS	VICTIMS	VIDICONS
VEXATIONS	VIATORES	VICAR	VICTOR	VIDIMUS
VEXATIOUS	VIATORIAL	VICARAGE	VICTORESS	VIDIMUSES
VEXATORY	VIATORS	VICARAGES	VICTORIA	VIDIOT
VEXED	VIBE	VICARATE	VICTORIAS	VIDIOTS
VEXEDLY	VIBED	VICARATES	VICTORIES	VIDS
VEXEDNESS	VIBES	VICARESS	VICTORINE	VIDSCREEN
VEXER	VIBEX	VICARIAL	VICTORS	VIDUAGE
VEXERS	VIBEY	VICARIANT	VICTORY	VIDUAGES

VIDUAL	VIGILANCE	VILIFYING	VIMINA	VINIFIED
VIDUITIES	VIGILANT	VILIPEND	VIMINAL	VINIFIES
VIDUITY	VIGILANTE	VILIPENDS	VIMINEOUS	VINIFY
VIDUOUS	VIGILS	VILL	VIMS	VINIFYING
VIE	VIGNERON	VILLA	VIN	VINING
VIED	VIGNERONS	VILLADOM	VINA	VINO
VIELLE	VIGNETTE	VILLADOMS	VINACEOUS	VINOLENT
VIELLES	VIGNETTED	VILLAE	VINAL	VINOLOGY
VIENNA	VIGNETTER	VILLAGE	VINALS	VINOS
VIER	VIGNETTES	VILLAGER	VINAS	VINOSITY
VIERS	VIGOR	VILLAGERS	VINASSE	VINOUS
VIES	VIGORISH	VILLAGERY	VINASSES	VINOUSLY
VIEW	VIGORO	VILLAGES	VINCA	VINS
VIEWABLE	VIGOROS	VILLAGEY	VINCAS	VINT
VIEWBOOK	VIGOROSO	VILLAGIER	VINCIBLE	VINTAGE
VIEWBOOKS	VIGOROUS	VILLAGIO	VINCIBLY	VINTAGED
VIEWDATA	VIGORS	VILLAGIOS	VINCULA	VINTAGER
VIEWDATAS	VIGOUR	VILLAGREE	VINCULAR	VINTAGERS
VIEWED	VIGOURS	VILLAIN	VINCULUM	VINTAGES
VIEWER	VIGS	VILLAINS	VINCULUMS	VINTAGING
VIEWERS	VIHARA	VILLAINY	VINDALOO	VINTED
VIEWIER	VIHARAS	VILLAN	VINDALOOS	VINTING
VIEWIEST	VIHUELA	VILLANAGE	VINDEMIAL	VINTNER
VIEWINESS	VIHUELAS	VILLANIES	VINDICATE	VINTNERS
VIEWING	VIKING	VILLANOUS	VINE	VINTRIES
VIEWINGS	VIKINGISM	VILLANS	VINEAL	VINTRY
VIEWLESS	VIKINGS	VILLANY	VINED	VINTS
VIEWLY	VILAYET	VILLAR	VINEGAR	VINY
VIEWPHONE	VILAYETS	VILLAS	VINEGARED	VINYL
VIEWPOINT	VILD	VILLATIC	VINEGARS	VINYLIC
VIEWPORT	VILDE	VILLEIN	VINEGARY	VINYLS
VIEWPORTS	VILDLY	VILLEINS	VINELESS	VIOL
VIEWS	VILDNESS	VILLENAGE	VINELIKE	VIOLA
VIEWSHED	VILE	VILLI	VINER	VIOLABLE
VIEWSHEDS	VILELY	VILLIACO	VINERIES	VIOLABLY
VIEWY	VILENESS	VILLIACOS	VINERS	VIOLAS
VIFDA	VILER	VILLIAGO	VINERY	VIOLATE
VIFDAS	VILEST	VILLIAGOS	VINES	VIOLATED
VIFF	VILIACO	VILLIFORM	VINEW	VIOLATER
VIFFED	VILIACOES	VILLOSE	VINEWED	VIOLATERS
VIFFING	VILIACOS	VILLOSITY	VINEWING	VIOLATES
VIFFS	VILIAGO	VILLOUS	VINEWS	VIOLATING
VIG	VILIAGOES	VILLOUSLY	VINEYARD	VIOLATION
VIGA	VILIAGOS	VILLS	VINEYARDS	VIOLATIVE
VIGAS	VILIFIED	VILLUS	VINIC	VIOLATOR
VIGESIMAL	VILIFIER	VIM	VINIER	VIOLATORS
VIGIA	VILIFIERS	VIMANA	VINIEST	VIOLD
VIGIAS	VILIFIES	VIMANAS	VINIFERA	VIOLENCE
VIGIL	VILIFY	VIMEN	VINIFERAS	VIOLENCES

VIOLENT	VIREMENTS	VIRILISM	VIS	VISIE
VIOLENTED	VIREMIA	VIRILISMS	VISA	VISIED
VIOLENTLY	VIREMIAS	VIRILITY	VISAED	VISIEING
VIOLENTS	VIREMIC	VIRILIZE	VISAGE	VISIER
VIOLER	VIRENT	VIRILIZED	VISAGED	VISIERS
VIOLERS	VIREO	VIRILIZES	VISAGES	VISIES
VIOLET	VIREONINE	VIRILOCAL	VISAGIST	VISILE
VIOLETS	VIREOS	VIRING	VISAGISTE	VISILES
VIOLIN	VIRES	VIRINO	VISAGISTS	VISING
VIOLINIST	VIRESCENT	VIRINOS	VISAING	VISION
VIOLINS	VIRETOT	VIRION	VISARD	VISIONAL
VIOLIST	VIRETOTS	VIRIONS	VISARDS	VISIONARY
VIOLISTS	VIRGA	VIRL	VISAS	VISIONED
VIOLONE	VIRGAE	VIRLS	VISCACHA	VISIONER
VIOLONES	VIRGAS	VIROGENE	VISCACHAS	VISIONERS
VIOLS	VIRGATE	VIROGENES	VISCARIA	VISIONING
VIOMYCIN	VIRGATES	VIROID	VISCARIAS	VISIONIST
VIOMYCINS	VIRGE	VIROIDS	VISCERA	VISIONS
VIOSTEROL	VIRGER	VIROLOGIC	VISCERAL	VISIT
VIPASSANA	VIRGERS	VIROLOGY	VISCERATE	VISITABLE
VIPER	VIRGES	VIROSE	VISCID	VISITANT
VIPERFISH	VIRGIN	VIROSES	VISCIDITY	VISITANTS
VIPERINE	VIRGINAL	VIROSIS	VISCIDLY	VISITATOR
VIPERISH	VIRGINALS	VIROUS	VISCIN	VISITE
VIPERLIKE	VIRGINED	VIRTU	VISCINS	VISITED
VIPEROUS	VIRGINIA	VIRTUAL	VISCOID	VISITEE
VIPERS	VIRGINIAS	VIRTUALLY	VISCOIDAL	VISITEES
VIRAEMIA	VIRGINING	VIRTUE	VISCOSE	VISITER
VIRAEMIAS	VIRGINITY	VIRTUES	VISCOSES	VISITERS
VIRAEMIC	VIRGINIUM	VIRTUOSA	VISCOSITY	VISITES
VIRAGO	VIRGINLY	VIRTUOSAS	VISCOUNT	VISITING
VIRAGOES	VIRGINS	VIRTUOSE	VISCOUNTS	VISITINGS
VIRAGOISH	VIRGULATE	VIRTUOSI	VISCOUNTY	VISITOR
VIRAGOS	VIRGULE	VIRTUOSIC	VISCOUS	VISITORS
VIRAL	VIRGULES	VIRTUOSO	VISCOUSLY	VISITRESS
VIRALITY	VIRICIDAL	VIRTUOSOS	VISCUM	VISITS
VIRALLY	VIRICIDE	VIRTUOUS	VISCUMS	VISIVE
VIRALS	VIRICIDES	VIRTUS	VISCUS	VISNE
VIRANDA	VIRID	VIRUCIDAL	VISE	VISNES
VIRANDAS	VIRIDIAN	VIRUCIDE	VISED	VISNOMIE
VIRANDO	VIRIDIANS	VIRUCIDES	VISEED	VISNOMIES
VIRANDOS	VIRIDITE	VIRULENCE	VISEING	VISNOMY
VIRE	VIRIDITES	VIRULENCY	VISELIKE	VISON
VIRED	VIRIDITY	VIRULENT	VISES	VISONS
VIRELAI	VIRILE	VIRUS	VISHING	VISOR
VIRELAIS	VIRILELY	VIRUSES	VISHINGS	VISORED
VIRELAY	VIRILISE	VIRUSLIKE	VISIBLE	VISORING
VIRELAYS	VIRILISED	VIRUSOID	VISIBLES	VISORLESS
VIREMENT	VIRILISES	VIRUSOIDS	VISIBLY	VISORS

VISTA	VITELLINE	VITTLED	VIVIFYING	VLOGGER
VISTAED	VITELLINS	VITTLES	VIVIPARA	VLOGGERS
VISTAING	VITELLUS	VITTLING	VIVIPARY	VLOGGING
VISTAL	VITESSE	VITULAR	VIVISECT	VLOGGINGS
VISTALESS	VITESSES	VITULINE	VIVISECTS	VLOGS
VISTAS	VITEX	VIVA	VIVO	VLY
VISTO	VITEXES	VIVACE	VIVRES	VOAR
VISTOS	VITIABLE	VIVACES	VIXEN	VOARS
VISUAL	VITIATE	VIVACIOUS	VIXENISH	VOCAB
VISUALISE	VITIATED	VIVACITY	VIXENLY	VOCABLE
VISUALIST	VITIATES	VIVAED	VIXENS	VOCABLES
VISUALITY	VITIATING	VIVAING	VIZAMENT	VOCABLY
VISUALIZE	VITIATION	VIVAMENTE	VIZAMENTS	VOCABS
VISUALLY	VITIATOR	VIVANDIER	VIZARD	VOCABULAR
VISUALS	VITIATORS	VIVARIA	VIZARDED	VOCAL
VITA	VITICETA	VIVARIES	VIZARDING	VOCALESE
VITACEOUS	VITICETUM	VIVARIUM	VIZARDS	VOCALESES
VITAE	VITICIDE	VIVARIUMS	VIZCACHA	VOCALIC
VITAL	VITICIDES	VIVARY	VIZCACHAS	VOCALICS
VITALISE	VITILIGO	VIVAS	VIZIED	VOCALION
VITALISED	VITILIGOS	VIVAT	VIZIER	VOCALIONS
VITALISER	VITIOSITY	VIVATS	VIZIERATE	VOCALISE
VITALISES	VITIOUS	VIVDA	VIZIERIAL	VOCALISED
VITALISM	VITRAGE	VIVDAS	VIZIERS	VOCALISER
VITALISMS	VITRAGES	VIVE	VIZIES	VOCALISES
VITALIST	VITRAIL	VIVELY	VIZIR	VOCALISM
VITALISTS	VITRAIN	VIVENCIES	VIZIRATE	VOCALISMS
VITALITY	VITRAINS	VIVENCY	VIZIRATES	VOCALIST
VITALIZE	VITRAUX	VIVER	VIZIRIAL	VOCALISTS
VITALIZED	VITREOUS	VIVERRA	VIZIRS	VOCALITY
VITALIZER	VITREUM	VIVERRAS	VIZIRSHIP	VOCALIZE
VITALIZES	VITREUMS	VIVERRID	VIZOR	VOCALIZED
VITALLY	VITRIC	VIVERRIDS	VIZORED	VOCALIZER
VITALNESS	VITRICS	VIVERRINE	VIZORING	VOCALIZES
VITALS	VITRIFIED	VIVERS	VIZORLESS	VOCALLY
VITAMER	VITRIFIES	VIVES	VIZORS	VOCALNESS
VITAMERS	VITRIFORM	VIVIANITE	VIZSLA	VOCALS
VITAMIN	VITRIFY	VIVID	VIZSLAS	VOCATION
VITAMINE	VITRINE	VIVIDER	VIZY	VOCATIONS
VITAMINES	VITRINES	VIVIDEST	VIZYING	VOCATIVE
VITAMINIC	VITRIOL	VIVIDITY	VIZZIE	VOCATIVES
VITAMINS	VITRIOLED	VIVIDLY	VIZZIED	VOCES
VITAS	VITRIOLIC	VIVIDNESS	VIZZIEING	VOCODER
VITASCOPE	VITRIOLS	VIVIFIC	VIZZIES	VOCODERED
VITATIVE	VITRO	VIVIFIED	VLEI	VOCODERS
VITE	VITTA	VIVIFIER	VLEIS	VOCULAR
VITELLARY	VITTAE	VIVIFIERS	VLIES	VOCULE
VITELLI	VITTATE	VIVIFIES	VLOG	VOCULES
VITELLIN	VITTLE	VIVIFY	VLOGGED	VODCAST

VODCASTED	VOICING	VOLCANOES	VOLTI	VOLVOXES
VODCASTER	VOICINGS	VOLCANOS	VOLTIGEUR	VOLVULI
VODCASTS	VOID	VOLE	VOLTING	VOLVULUS
VODDIES	VOIDABLE	VOLED	VOLTINISM	VOM
VODDY	VOIDANCE	VOLELIKE	VOLTIS	VOMER
VODKA	VOIDANCES	VOLENS	VOLTMETER	VOMERINE
VODKAS	VOIDED	VOLERIES	VOLTS	VOMERS
VODOU	VOIDEE	VOLERY	VOLUBIL	VOMICA
VODOUN	VOIDEES	VOLES	VOLUBLE	VOMICAE
VODOUNS	VOIDER	VOLET	VOLUBLY	VOMICAS
VODOUS	VOIDERS	VOLETS	VOLUCRINE	VOMIT
VODUN	VOIDING	VOLING	VOLUME	VOMITED
VODUNS	VOIDINGS	VOLITANT	VOLUMED	VOMITER
VOE	VOIDNESS	VOLITATE	VOLUMES	VOMITERS
VOEMA	VOIDS	VOLITATED	VOLUMETER	VOMITIER
VOEMAS	VOILA	VOLITATES	VOLUMETRY	VOMITIEST
VOERTSAK	VOILE	VOLITIENT	VOLUMINAL	VOMITING
VOERTSEK	VOILES	VOLITION	VOLUMING	VOMITINGS
VOES	VOIP	VOLITIONS	VOLUMISE	VOMITIVE
VOETSAK	VOIPS	VOLITIVE	VOLUMISED	VOMITIVES
VOETSEK	VOISINAGE	VOLITIVES	VOLUMISER	VOMITO
VOG	VOITURE	VOLK	VOLUMISES	VOMITORIA
VOGIE	VOITURES	VOLKS	VOLUMIST	VOMITORY
VOGIER	VOITURIER	VOLKSLIED	VOLUMISTS	VOMITOS
VOGIEST	VOIVODE	VOLKSRAAD	VOLUMIZE	VOMITOUS
VOGS	VOIVODES	VOLLEY	VOLUMIZED	VOMITS
VOGUE	VOL	VOLLEYED	VOLUMIZER	VOMITUS
VOGUED	VOLA	VOLLEYER	VOLUMIZES	VOMITUSES
VOGUEING	VOLABLE	VOLLEYERS	VOLUNTARY	VOMITY
VOGUEINGS	VOLAE	VOLLEYING	VOLUNTEER	VOMMED
VOGUER	VOLAGE	VOLLEYS	VOLUSPA	VOMMING
VOGUERS	VOLANT	VOLOST	VOLUSPAS	VOMS
VOGUES	VOLANTE	VOLOSTS	VOLUTE	VONGOLE
VOGUEY	VOLANTES	VOLPINO	VOLUTED	VOODOO
VOGUIER	VOLAR	VOLPINOS	VOLUTES	VOODOOED
VOGUIEST	VOLARIES	VOLPLANE	VOLUTIN	VOODOOING
VOGUING	VOLARY	VOLPLANED	VOLUTINS	VOODOOISM
VOGUINGS	VOLATIC	VOLPLANES	VOLUTION	VOODOOIST
VOGUISH	VOLATICS	VOLS	VOLUTIONS	VOODOOS
VOGUISHLY	VOLATILE	VOLT	VOLUTOID	VOORKAMER
VOICE	VOLATILES	VOLTA	VOLVA	VOORSKOT
VOICED	VOLCANIAN	VOLTAGE	VOLVAE	VOORSKOTS
VOICEFUL	VOLCANIC	VOLTAGES	VOLVAS	VOR
VOICELESS	VOLCANICS	VOLTAIC	VOLVATE	VORACIOUS
VOICEMAIL	VOLCANISE	VOLTAISM	VOLVE	VORACITY
VOICEOVER	VOLCANISM	VOLTAISMS	VOLVED	VORAGO
VOICER	VOLCANIST	VOLTE	VOLVES	VORAGOES
VOICERS	VOLCANIZE	VOLTED	VOLVING	VORAGOS
VOICES	VOLCANO	VOLTES	VOLVOX	VORANT

VORLAGE	VOUCHER	VOWELS	VROW	VULNED
VORLAGES	VOUCHERED	VOWER	VROWS	VULNERARY
VORPAL	VOUCHERS	VOWERS	VRYSTATER	VULNERATE
VORRED	VOUCHES	VOWESS	VUG	VULNING
VORRING	VOUCHING	VOWESSES	VUGG	VULNS
VORS	VOUCHSAFE	VOWING	VUGGIER	VULPICIDE
VORTEX	VOUDON	VOWLESS	VUGGIEST	VULPINE
VORTEXES	VOUDONS	VOWS	VUGGS	VULPINISM
VORTICAL	VOUDOU	VOX	VUGGY	VULPINITE
VORTICES	VOUDOUED	VOXEL	VUGH	VULSELLA
VORTICISM	VOUDOUING	VOXELS	VUGHIER	VULSELLAE
VORTICIST	VOUDOUN	VOYAGE	VUGHIEST	VULSELLUM
VORTICITY	VOUDOUNS	VOYAGED	VUGHS	VULTURE
VORTICOSE	VOUDOUS	VOYAGER	VUGHY	VULTURES
VOSTRO	VOUGE	VOYAGERS	VUGS	VULTURINE
VOTABLE	VOUGES	VOYAGES	VUGULAR	VULTURISH
VOTARESS	VOULGE	VOYAGEUR	VULCAN	VULTURISM
VOTARIES	VOULGES	VOYAGEURS	VULCANIAN	VULTURN
VOTARIST	VOULU	VOYAGING	VULCANIC	VULTURNS
VOTARISTS	VOUSSOIR	VOYAGINGS	VULCANISE	VULTUROUS
VOTARY	VOUSSOIRS	VOYEUR	VULCANISM	VULVA
VOTE	VOUTSAFE	VOYEURISM	VULCANIST	VULVAE
VOTEABLE	VOUTSAFED	VOYEURS	VULCANITE	VULVAL
VOTED	VOUTSAFES	VOZHD	VULCANIZE	VULVAR
VOTEEN	VOUVRAY	VOZHDS	VULCANS	VULVAS
VOTEENS	VOUVRAYS	VRAIC	VULGAR	VULVATE
VOTELESS	VOW	VRAICKER	VULGARER	VULVIFORM
VOTER	VOWED	VRAICKERS	VULGAREST	VULVITIS
VOTERS	VOWEL	VRAICKING	VULGARIAN	VUM
VOTES	VOWELED	VRAICS	VULGARISE	VUMMED
VOTING	VOWELISE	VRIL	VULGARISM	VUMMING
VOTINGS	VOWELISED	VRILS	VULGARITY	VUMS
VOTIVE	VOWELISES	VROOM	VULGARIZE	VUTTIER
VOTIVELY	VOWELIZE	VROOMED	VULGARLY	VUTTIEST
VOTIVES	VOWELIZED	VROOMING	VULGARS	VUTTY
VOTRESS	VOWELIZES	VROOMS	VULGATE	VUVUZELA
VOTRESSES	VOWELLED	VROT	VULGATES	VUVUZELAS
VOUCH	VOWELLESS	VROU	VULGO	VYING
VOUCHED	VOWELLIER	VROUS	VULGUS	VYINGLY
VOUCHEE	VOWELLING	VROUW	VULGUSES	VYINGS
VOUCHEES	VOWELLY	VROUWS	VULN	

W

WAAC	WADDER	WADSET	WAFTED	WAGGONERS
WAACS	WADDERS	WADSETS	WAFTER	WAGGONING
WAAH	WADDIE	WADSETT	WAFTERS	WAGGONS
WAB	WADDIED	WADSETTED	WAFTING	WAGHALTER
WABAIN	WADDIES	WADSETTER	WAFTINGS	WAGING
WABAINS	WADDING	WADSETTS	WAFTS	WAGMOIRE
WABBIT	WADDINGS	WADT	WAFTURE	WAGMOIRES
WABBLE	WADDLE	WADTS	WAFTURES	WAGON
WABBLED	WADDLED	WADY	WAG	WAGONAGE
WABBLER	WADDLER	WAE	WAGE	WAGONAGES
WABBLERS	WADDLERS	WAEFUL	WAGED	WAGONED
WABBLES	WADDLES	WAENESS	WAGELESS	WAGONER
WABBLIER	WADDLIER	WAENESSES	WAGENBOOM	WAGONERS
WABBLIEST	WADDLIEST	WAES	WAGER	WAGONETTE
WABBLING	WADDLING	WAESOME	WAGERED	WAGONFUL
WABBLY	WADDLY	WAESUCK	WAGERER	WAGONFULS
WABOOM	WADDS	WAESUCKS	WAGERERS	WAGONING
WABOOMS	WADDY	WAFER	WAGERING	WAGONLESS
WABS	WADDYING	WAFERED	WAGERINGS	WAGONLOAD
WABSTER	WADE	WAFERIER	WAGERS	WAGONS
WABSTERS	WADEABLE	WAFERIEST	WAGES	WAGS
WACK	WADED	WAFERING	WAGGA	WAGSOME
WACKE	WADER	WAFERS	WAGGAS	WAGTAIL
WACKED	WADERS	WAFERY	WAGGED	WAGTAILS
WACKER	WADES	WAFF	WAGGER	WAGWAN
WACKERS	WADGE	WAFFED	WAGGERIES	WAGYU
WACKES	WADGES	WAFFIE	WAGGERS	WAGYUS
WACKEST	WADI	WAFFIES	WAGGERY	WAHCONDA
WACKIER	WADIES	WAFFING	WAGGING	WAHCONDAS
WACKIEST	WADING	WAFFLE	WAGGISH	WAHINE
WACKILY	WADINGS	WAFFLED	WAGGISHLY	WAHINES
WACKINESS	WADIS	WAFFLER	WAGGLE	WAHOO
WACKO	WADMAAL	WAFFLERS	WAGGLED	WAHOOS
WACKOES	WADMAALS	WAFFLES	WAGGLER	WAI
WACKOS	WADMAL	WAFFLIER	WAGGLERS	WAIATA
WACKS	WADMALS	WAFFLIEST	WAGGLES	WAIATAS
WACKY	WADMEL	WAFFLING	WAGGLIER	WAID
WACONDA	WADMELS	WAFFLINGS	WAGGLIEST	WAIDE
WACONDAS	WADMOL	WAFFLY	WAGGLING	WAIF
WAD	WADMOLL	WAFFS	WAGGLY	WAIFED
WADABLE	WADMOLLS	WAFT	WAGGON	WAIFING
WADD	WADMOLS	WAFTAGE	WAGGONED	WAIFISH
WADDED	WADS	WAFTAGES	WAGGONER	WAIFLIKE

WAIFS	WAITER	WAKER	WALKOUT	WALLOWER
WAIFT	WAITERAGE	WAKERIFE	WALKOUTS	WALLOWERS
WAIFTS	WAITERED	WAKERS	WALKOVER	WALLOWING
WAIFU	WAITERING	WAKES	WALKOVERS	WALLOWS
WAIFUS	WAITERS	WAKF	WALKS	WALLPAPER
WAIL	WAITES	WAKFS	WALKUP	WALLS
WAILED	WAITING	WAKIKI	WALKUPS	WALLSEND
WAILER	WAITINGLY	WAKIKIS	WALKWAY	WALLSENDS
WAILERS	WAITINGS	WAKING	WALKWAYS	WALLWORT
WAILFUL	WAITLIST	WAKINGS	WALKYRIE	WALLWORTS
WAILFULLY	WAITLISTS	WALD	WALKYRIES	WALLY
WAILING	WAITRESS	WALDFLUTE	WALL	WALLYBALL
WAILINGLY	WAITRON	WALDGRAVE	WALLA	WALLYDRAG
WAILINGS	WAITRONS	WALDHORN	WALLABA	WALNUT
WAILS	WAITS	WALDHORNS	WALLABAS	WALNUTS
WAILSOME	WAITSTAFF	WALDO	WALLABIES	WALRUS
WAIN	WAIVE	WALDOES	WALLABY	WALRUSES
WAINAGE	WAIVED	WALDOS	WALLAH	WALTIER
WAINAGES	WAIVER	WALDRAPP	WALLAHS	WALTIEST
WAINED	WAIVERS	WALDRAPPS	WALLAROO	WALTY
WAINING	WAIVES	WALDS	WALLAROOS	WALTZ
WAINS	WAIVING	WALE	WALLAS	WALTZED
WAINSCOT	WAIVODE	WALED	WALLBOARD	WALTZER
WAINSCOTS	WAIVODES	WALER	WALLCHART	WALTZERS
WAIR	WAIWODE	WALERS	WALLED	WALTZES
WAIRED	WAIWODES	WALES	WALLER	WALTZING
WAIRING	WAKA	WALI	WALLERS	WALTZINGS
WAIRS	WAKAME	WALIE	WALLET	WALTZLIKE
WAIRSH	WAKAMES	WALIER	WALLETS	WALY
WAIRSHER	WAKANDA	WALIES	WALLEY	WAMBENGER
WAIRSHEST	WAKANDAS	WALIEST	WALLEYE	WAMBLE
WAIRUA	WAKANE	WALING	WALLEYED	WAMBLED
WAIRUAS	WAKANES	WALIS	WALLEYES	WAMBLES
WAIS	WAKAS	WALISE	WALLEYS	WAMBLIER
WAIST	WAKE	WALISES	WALLFISH	WAMBLIEST
WAISTBAND	WAKEBOARD	WALK	WALLIE	WAMBLING
WAISTBELT	WAKED	WALKABLE	WALLIER	WAMBLINGS
WAISTCOAT	WAKEFUL	WALKABOUT	WALLIES	WAMBLY
WAISTED	WAKEFULLY	WALKATHON	WALLIEST	WAME
WAISTER	WAKELESS	WALKAWAY	WALLING	WAMED
WAISTERS	WAKEMAN	WALKAWAYS	WALLINGS	WAMEFOU
WAISTING	WAKEMEN	WALKED	WALLOP	WAMEFOUS
WAISTINGS	WAKEN	WALKER	WALLOPED	WAMEFUL
WAISTLESS	WAKENED	WALKERS	WALLOPER	WAMEFULS
WAISTLINE	WAKENER	WALKIES	WALLOPERS	WAMES
WAISTS	WAKENERS	WALKING	WALLOPING	WAMMUL
WAIT	WAKENING	WALKINGS	WALLOPS	WAMMULS
WAITE	WAKENINGS	WALKMILL	WALLOW	WAMMUS
WAITED	WAKENS	WALKMILLS	WALLOWED	WAMMUSES

WAMPEE	WANIER	WANTHILLS	WARBLE	WARDSHIPS
WAMPEES	WANIEST	WANTIES	WARBLED	WARE
WAMPISH	WANIGAN	WANTING	WARBLER	WARED
WAMPISHED	WANIGANS	WANTON	WARBLERS	WAREHOU
WAMPISHES	WANING	WANTONED	WARBLES	WAREHOUS
WAMPUM	WANINGS	WANTONER	WARBLIER	WAREHOUSE
WAMPUMS	WANION	WANTONERS	WARBLIEST	WARELESS
WAMPUS	WANIONS	WANTONEST	WARBLING	WAREROOM
WAMPUSES	WANK	WANTONING	WARBLINGS	WAREROOMS
WAMUS	WANKED	WANTONISE	WARBLY	WARES
WAMUSES	WANKER	WANTONIZE	WARBONNET	WAREZ
WAN	WANKERS	WANTONLY	WARBOT	WARFARE
WANCHANCY	WANKIER	WANTONS	WARBOTS	WARFARED
WAND	WANKIEST	WANTS	WARBS	WARFARER
WANDER	WANKING	WANTY	WARBY	WARFARERS
WANDERED	WANKLE	WANWORDY	WARCRAFT	WARFARES
WANDERER	WANKS	WANWORTH	WARCRAFTS	WARFARIN
WANDERERS	WANKSTA	WANWORTHS	WARD	WARFARING
WANDERING	WANKSTAS	WANY	WARDCORN	WARFARINS
WANDEROO	WANKY	WANZE	WARDCORNS	WARGAME
WANDEROOS	WANLE	WANZED	WARDED	WARGAMED
WANDERS	WANLY	WANZES	WARDEN	WARGAMER
WANDLE	WANNA	WANZING	WARDENED	WARGAMERS
WANDLED	WANNABE	WAP	WARDENING	WARGAMES
WANDLES	WANNABEE	WAPENSHAW	WARDENRY	WARGAMING
WANDLIKE	WANNABEES	WAPENTAKE	WARDENS	WARHABLE
WANDLING	WANNABES	WAPINSHAW	WARDER	WARHEAD
WANDOO	WANNED	WAPITI	WARDERED	WARHEADS
WANDOOS	WANNEL	WAPITIS	WARDERING	WARHORSE
WANDS	WANNER	WAPPED	WARDERS	WARHORSES
WANE	WANNESS	WAPPEND	WARDIAN	WARIBASHI
WANED	WANNESSES	WAPPER	WARDING	WARIER
WANES	WANNEST	WAPPERED	WARDINGS	WARIEST
WANEY	WANNIGAN	WAPPERING	WARDLESS	WARILY
WANG	WANNIGANS	WAPPERS	WARDMOTE	WARIMENT
WANGAN	WANNING	WAPPING	WARDMOTES	WARIMENTS
WANGANS	WANNION	WAPS	WARDOG	WARINESS
WANGLE	WANNIONS	WAQF	WARDOGS	WARING
WANGLED	WANNISH	WAQFS	WARDRESS	WARISON
WANGLER	WANS	WAR	WARDROBE	WARISONS
WANGLERS	WANT	WARAGI	WARDROBED	WARK
WANGLES	WANTAGE	WARAGIS	WARDROBER	WARKED
WANGLING	WANTAGES	WARATAH	WARDROBES	WARKING
WANGLINGS	WANTAWAY	WARATAHS	WARDROOM	WARKS
WANGS	WANTAWAYS	WARB	WARDROOMS	WARLESS
WANGUN	WANTED	WARBIER	WARDROP	WARLIKE
WANGUNS	WANTER	WARBIEST	WARDROPS	WARLING
WANHOPE	WANTERS	WARBIRD	WARDS	WARLINGS
WANHOPES	WANTHILL	WARBIRDS	WARDSHIP	WARLOCK

W

WARLOCKRY	WARPLANE	WARSAWS	WASHAWAYS	WASHTUB
WARLOCKS	WARPLANES	WARSHIP	WASHBAG	WASHTUBS
WARLORD	WARPOWER	WARSHIPS	WASHBAGS	WASHUP
WARLORDS	WARPOWERS	WARSLE	WASHBALL	WASHUPS
WARM	WARPS	WARSLED	WASHBALLS	WASHWIPE
WARMAKER	WARPWISE	WARSLER	WASHBASIN	WASHWIPES
WARMAKERS	WARRAGAL	WARSLERS	WASHBOARD	WASHWOMAN
WARMAN	WARRAGALS	WARSLES	WASHBOWL	WASHWOMEN
WARMBLOOD	WARRAGLE	WARSLING	WASHBOWLS	WASHY
WARMED	WARRAGLES	WARST	WASHCLOTH	WASM
WARMEN	WARRAGUL	WARSTLE	WASHDAY	WASMS
WARMER	WARRAGULS	WARSTLED	WASHDAYS	WASP
WARMERS	WARRAN	WARSTLER	WASHDOWN	WASPIE
WARMEST	WARRAND	WARSTLERS	WASHDOWNS	WASPIER
WARMING	WARRANDED	WARSTLES	WASHED	WASPIES
WARMINGS	WARRANDS	WARSTLING	WASHEN	WASPIEST
WARMISH	WARRANED	WART	WASHER	WASPILY
WARMIST	WARRANING	WARTED	WASHERED	WASPINESS
WARMISTS	WARRANS	WARTHOG	WASHERIES	WASPISH
WARMLY	WARRANT	WARTHOGS	WASHERING	WASPISHLY
WARMNESS	WARRANTED	WARTIER	WASHERMAN	WASPLIKE
WARMONGER	WARRANTEE	WARTIEST	WASHERMEN	WASPNEST
WARMOUTH	WARRANTER	WARTIME	WASHERS	WASPNESTS
WARMOUTHS	WARRANTOR	WARTIMES	WASHERY	WASPS
WARMS	WARRANTS	WARTLESS	WASHES	WASPY
WARMTH	WARRANTY	WARTLIKE	WASHFAST	WASSAIL
WARMTHS	WARRAY	WARTS	WASHHAND	WASSAILED
WARMUP	WARRAYED	WARTWEED	WASHHOUSE	WASSAILER
WARMUPS	WARRAYING	WARTWEEDS	WASHI	WASSAILRY
WARN	WARRAYS	WARTWORT	WASHIER	WASSAILS
WARNED	WARRE	WARTWORTS	WASHIEST	WASSERMAN
WARNER	WARRED	WARTY	WASHILY	WASSERMEN
WARNERS	WARREN	WARWOLF	WASHIN	WASSUP
WARNING	WARRENER	WARWOLVES	WASHINESS	WAST
WARNINGLY	WARRENERS	WARWORK	WASHING	WASTABLE
WARNINGS	WARRENS	WARWORKS	WASHINGS	WASTAGE
WARNS	WARREY	WARWORN	WASHINS	WASTAGES
WARP	WARREYED	WARY	WASHIS	WASTE
WARPAGE	WARREYING	WARZONE	WASHLAND	WASTEBIN
WARPAGES	WARREYS	WARZONES	WASHLANDS	WASTEBINS
WARPAINT	WARRIGAL	WAS	WASHOUT	WASTED
WARPAINTS	WARRIGALS	WASABI	WASHOUTS	WASTEFUL
WARPATH	WARRING	WASABIS	WASHPOT	WASTEL
WARPATHS	WARRIOR	WASE	WASHPOTS	WASTELAND
WARPED	WARRIORS	WASES	WASHRAG	WASTELOT
WARPER	WARRISON	WASH	WASHRAGS	WASTELOTS
WARPERS	WARRISONS	WASHABLE	WASHROOM	WASTELS
WARPING	WARS	WASHABLES	WASHROOMS	WASTENESS
WARPINGS	WARSAW	WASHAWAY	WASHSTAND	WASTER

W

WASTERED	WATCHMAN	WATERSHED	WAUKING	WAVES
WASTERFUL	WATCHMEN	WATERSIDE	WAUKMILL	WAVESHAPE
WASTERIE	WATCHOUT	WATERSKI	WAUKMILLS	WAVESON
WASTERIES	WATCHOUTS	WATERSKIS	WAUKRIFE	WAVESONS
WASTERING	WATCHWORD	WATERWAY	WAUKS	WAVETABLE
WASTERS	WATE	WATERWAYS	WAUL	WAVEY
WASTERY	WATER	WATERWEED	WAULED	WAVEYS
WASTES	WATERAGE	WATERWORK	WAULING	WAVICLE
WASTEWAY	WATERAGES	WATERWORN	WAULINGS	WAVICLES
WASTEWAYS	WATERBED	WATERY	WAULK	WAVIER
WASTEWEIR	WATERBEDS	WATERZOOI	WAULKED	WAVIES
WASTFULL	WATERBIRD	WATS	WAULKER	WAVIEST
WASTING	WATERBUCK	WATT	WAULKERS	WAVILY
WASTINGLY	WATERBUS	WATTAGE	WAULKING	WAVINESS
WASTINGS	WATERDOG	WATTAGES	WAULKMILL	WAVING
WASTNESS	WATERDOGS	WATTAPE	WAULKS	WAVINGS
WASTREL	WATERED	WATTAPES	WAULS	WAVY
WASTRELS	WATERER	WATTER	WAUR	WAW
WASTRIE	WATERERS	WATTEST	WAURED	WAWA
WASTRIES	WATERFALL	WATTHOUR	WAURING	WAWAED
WASTRIFE	WATERFOWL	WATTHOURS	WAURS	WAWAING
WASTRIFES	WATERGATE	WATTLE	WAURST	WAWAS
WASTRY	WATERHEAD	WATTLED	WAVE	WAWE
WASTS	WATERHEN	WATTLES	WAVEBAND	WAWES
WAT	WATERHENS	WATTLESS	WAVEBANDS	WAWL
WATAP	WATERHOLE	WATTLING	WAVED	WAWLED
WATAPE	WATERIER	WATTLINGS	WAVEFORM	WAWLING
WATAPES	WATERIEST	WATTMETER	WAVEFORMS	WAWLINGS
WATAPS	WATERILY	WATTS	WAVEFRONT	WAWLS
WATCH	WATERING	WAUCHT	WAVEGUIDE	WAWS
WATCHA	WATERINGS	WAUCHTED	WAVELESS	WAX
WATCHABLE	WATERISH	WAUCHTING	WAVELET	WAXABLE
WATCHBAND	WATERJET	WAUCHTS	WAVELETS	WAXBERRY
WATCHBOX	WATERJETS	WAUFF	WAVELIKE	WAXBILL
WATCHCASE	WATERLEAF	WAUFFED	WAVELLITE	WAXBILLS
WATCHCRY	WATERLESS	WAUFFING	WAVEMETER	WAXCLOTH
WATCHDOG	WATERLILY	WAUFFS	WAVEOFF	WAXCLOTHS
WATCHDOGS	WATERLINE	WAUGH	WAVEOFFS	WAXED
WATCHED	WATERLOG	WAUGHED	WAVER	WAXEN
WATCHER	WATERLOGS	WAUGHING	WAVERED	WAXER
WATCHERS	WATERLOO	WAUGHS	WAVERER	WAXERS
WATCHES	WATERLOOS	WAUGHT	WAVERERS	WAXES
WATCHET	WATERMAN	WAUGHTED	WAVERIER	WAXEYE
WATCHETS	WATERMARK	WAUGHTING	WAVERIEST	WAXEYES
WATCHEYE	WATERMEN	WAUGHTS	WAVERING	WAXFLOWER
WATCHEYES	WATERMILL	WAUK	WAVERINGS	WAXIER
WATCHFUL	WATERPARK	WAUKED	WAVEROUS	WAXIEST
WATCHING	WATERPOX	WAUKER	WAVERS	WAXILY
WATCHLIST	WATERS	WAUKERS	WAVERY	WAXINESS

W

WAXING	WAYMARK	WEAKLY	WEARILESS	WEBBIE
WAXINGS	WAYMARKED	WEAKNESS	WEARILY	WEBBIER
WAXLIKE	WAYMARKS	WEAKON	WEARINESS	WEBBIES
WAXPLANT	WAYMENT	WEAKONS	WEARING	WEBBIEST
WAXPLANTS	WAYMENTED	WEAKSIDE	WEARINGLY	WEBBING
WAXWEED	WAYMENTS	WEAKSIDES	WEARINGS	WEBBINGS
WAXWEEDS	WAYPOINT	WEAL	WEARISH	WEBBY
WAXWING	WAYPOINTS	WEALD	WEARISOME	WEBCAM
WAXWINGS	WAYPOST	WEALDS	WEARPROOF	WEBCAMS
WAXWORK	WAYPOSTS	WEALS	WEARS	WEBCAST
WAXWORKER	WAYS	WEALSMAN	WEARY	WEBCASTED
WAXWORKS	WAYSIDE	WEALSMEN	WEARYING	WEBCASTER
WAXWORM	WAYSIDES	WEALTH	WEASAND	WEBCASTS
WAXWORMS	WAYWARD	WEALTHIER	WEASANDS	WEBCHAT
WAXY	WAYWARDLY	WEALTHILY	WEASEL	WEBCHATS
WAY	WAYWISER	WEALTHS	WEASELED	WEBCOMIC
WAYANG	WAYWISERS	WEALTHY	WEASELER	WEBCOMICS
WAYANGS	WAYWODE	WEAMB	WEASELERS	WEBER
WAYBACK	WAYWODES	WEAMBS	WEASELIER	WEBERS
WAYBACKS	WAYWORN	WEAN	WEASELING	WEBFED
WAYBILL	WAYZGOOSE	WEANED	WEASELLED	WEBFEET
WAYBILLS	WAZ	WEANEL	WEASELLER	WEBFOOT
WAYBOARD	WAZIR	WEANELS	WEASELLY	WEBFOOTED
WAYBOARDS	WAZIRS	WEANER	WEASELS	WEBHEAD
WAYBREAD	WAZOO	WEANERS	WEASELY	WEBHEADS
WAYBREADS	WAZOOS	WEANING	WEASON	WEBIFIED
WAYED	WAZZ	WEANINGS	WEASONS	WEBIFIES
WAYFARE	WAZZED	WEANLING	WEATHER	WEBIFY
WAYFARED	WAZZES	WEANLINGS	WEATHERED	WEBIFYING
WAYFARER	WAZZING	WEANS	WEATHERER	WEBINAR
WAYFARERS	WAZZOCK	WEAPON	WEATHERLY	WEBINARS
WAYFARES	WAZZOCKS	WEAPONED	WEATHERS	WEBISODE
WAYFARING	WE	WEAPONEER	WEAVE	WEBISODES
WAYGOING	WEAK	WEAPONING	WEAVED	WEBLESS
WAYGOINGS	WEAKEN	WEAPONISE	WEAVER	WEBLIKE
WAYGONE	WEAKENED	WEAPONIZE	WEAVERS	WEBLISH
WAYGOOSE	WEAKENER	WEAPONRY	WEAVES	WEBLISHES
WAYGOOSES	WEAKENERS	WEAPONS	WEAVING	WEBLOG
WAYING	WEAKENING	WEAR	WEAVINGS	WEBLOGGER
WAYLAID	WEAKENS	WEARABLE	WEAZAND	WEBLOGS
WAYLAY	WEAKER	WEARABLES	WEAZANDS	WEBMAIL
WAYLAYER	WEAKEST	WEARED	WEAZEN	WEBMAILS
WAYLAYERS	WEAKFISH	WEARER	WEAZENED	WEBMASTER
WAYLAYING	WEAKISH	WEARERS	WEAZENING	WEBPAGE
WAYLAYS	WEAKISHLY	WEARIED	WEAZENS	WEBPAGES
WAYLEAVE	WEAKLIER	WEARIER	WEB	WEBRING
WAYLEAVES	WEAKLIEST	WEARIES	WEBAPP	WEBRINGS
WAYLEGGO	WEAKLING	WEARIEST	WEBAPPS	WEBS
WAYLESS	WEAKLINGS	WEARIFUL	WEBBED	WEBSITE

W

WEBSITES	WEED	WEENING	WEFTAGE	WEIRDNESS
WEBSPACE	WEEDBED	WEENS	WEFTAGES	WEIRDO
WEBSPACES	WEEDBEDS	WEENSIER	WEFTE	WEIRDOES
WEBSTER	WEEDED	WEENSIEST	WEFTED	WEIRDOS
WEBSTERS	WEEDER	WEENSY	WEFTES	WEIRDS
WEBWHEEL	WEEDERIES	WEENY	WEFTING	WEIRDY
WEBWHEELS	WEEDERS	WEEP	WEFTS	WEIRED
WEBWORK	WEEDERY	WEEPER	WEFTWISE	WEIRING
WEBWORKS	WEEDHEAD	WEEPERS	WEID	WEIRS
WEBWORM	WEEDHEADS	WEEPHOLE	WEIDS	WEISE
WEBWORMS	WEEDICIDE	WEEPHOLES	WEIGELA	WEISED
WEBZINE	WEEDIER	WEEPIE	WEIGELAS	WEISES
WEBZINES	WEEDIEST	WEEPIER	WEIGELIA	WEISING
WECHT	WEEDILY	WEEPIES	WEIGELIAS	WEIZE
WECHTED	WEEDINESS	WEEPIEST	WEIGH	WEIZED
WECHTING	WEEDING	WEEPILY	WEIGHABLE	WEIZES
WECHTS	WEEDINGS	WEEPINESS	WEIGHAGE	WEIZING
WED	WEEDLESS	WEEPING	WEIGHAGES	WEKA
WEDDED	WEEDLIKE	WEEPINGLY	WEIGHED	WEKAS
WEDDER	WEEDLINE	WEEPINGS	WEIGHER	WELAWAY
WEDDERED	WEEDLINES	WEEPS	WEIGHERS	WELCH
WEDDERING	WEEDS	WEEPY	WEIGHING	WELCHED
WEDDERS	WEEDY	WEER	WEIGHINGS	WELCHER
WEDDING	WEEING	WEES	WEIGHMAN	WELCHERS
WEDDINGS	WEEJUNS	WEEST	WEIGHMEN	WELCHES
WEDEL	WEEK	WEET	WEIGHS	WELCHING
WEDELED	WEEKDAY	WEETE	WEIGHT	WELCOME
WEDELING	WEEKDAYS	WEETED	WEIGHTAGE	WELCOMED
WEDELN	WEEKE	WEETEN	WEIGHTED	WELCOMELY
WEDELNED	WEEKEND	WEETER	WEIGHTER	WELCOMER
WEDELNING	WEEKENDED	WEETEST	WEIGHTERS	WELCOMERS
WEDELNS	WEEKENDER	WEETING	WEIGHTIER	WELCOMES
WEDELS	WEEKENDS	WEETINGLY	WEIGHTILY	WELCOMING
WEDGE	WEEKES	WEETLESS	WEIGHTING	WELD
WEDGED	WEEKLIES	WEETS	WEIGHTS	WELDABLE
WEDGELIKE	WEEKLONG	WEEVER	WEIGHTY	WELDED
WEDGES	WEEKLY	WEEVERS	WEIL	WELDER
WEDGEWISE	WEEKNIGHT	WEEVIL	WEILS	WELDERS
WEDGIE	WEEKS	WEEVILED	WEINER	WELDING
WEDGIER	WEEL	WEEVILIER	WEINERS	WELDINGS
WEDGIES	WEELS	WEEVILLED	WEIR	WELDLESS
WEDGIEST	WEEM	WEEVILLY	WEIRD	WELDMENT
WEDGING	WEEMS	WEEVILS	WEIRDED	WELDMENTS
WEDGINGS	WEEN	WEEVILY	WEIRDER	WELDMESH
WEDGY	WEENED	WEEWEE	WEIRDEST	WELDOR
WEDLOCK	WEENIE	WEEWEED	WEIRDIE	WELDORS
WEDLOCKS	WEENIER	WEEWEEING	WEIRDIES	WELDS
WEDS	WEENIES	WEEWEES	WEIRDING	WELFARE
WEE	WEENIEST	WEFT	WEIRDLY	WELFARES

WELFARISM	WELTER	WERRIS	WETSUITS	WHAKAPAPA
WELFARIST	WELTERED	WERRISES	WETTABLE	WHALE
WELFARITE	WELTERING	WERSH	WETTED	WHALEBACK
WELK	WELTERS	WERSHER	WETTER	WHALEBOAT
WELKE	WELTING	WERSHEST	WETTERS	WHALEBONE
WELKED	WELTINGS	WERT	WETTEST	WHALED
WELKES	WELTS	WERWOLF	WETTIE	WHALELIKE
WELKIN	WEM	WERWOLVES	WETTIES	WHALEMAN
WELKING	WEMB	WESAND	WETTING	WHALEMEN
WELKINS	WEMBS	WESANDS	WETTINGS	WHALER
WELKS	WEMS	WESKIT	WETTISH	WHALERIES
WELKT	WEN	WESKITS	WETWARE	WHALERS
WELL	WENA	WESSAND	WETWARES	WHALERY
WELLADAY	WENCH	WESSANDS	WEX	WHALES
WELLADAYS	WENCHED	WEST	WEXE	WHALING
WELLANEAR	WENCHER	WESTABOUT	WEXED	WHALINGS
WELLAWAY	WENCHERS	WESTBOUND	WEXES	WHALLY
WELLAWAYS	WENCHES	WESTED	WEXING	WHAM
WELLBEING	WENCHING	WESTER	WEY	WHAMMED
WELLBORN	WEND	WESTERED	WEYARD	WHAMMIES
WELLCURB	WENDED	WESTERING	WEYS	WHAMMING
WELLCURBS	WENDIGO	WESTERLY	WEYWARD	WHAMMO
WELLDOER	WENDIGOES	WESTERN	WEZAND	WHAMMOS
WELLDOERS	WENDIGOS	WESTERNER	WEZANDS	WHAMMY
WELLED	WENDING	WESTERNS	WHA	WHAMO
WELLHEAD	WENDS	WESTERS	WHACK	WHAMPLE
WELLHEADS	WENGE	WESTIE	WHACKED	WHAMPLES
WELLHOLE	WENGES	WESTIES	WHACKER	WHAMS
WELLHOLES	WENNIER	WESTING	WHACKERS	WHANAU
WELLHOUSE	WENNIEST	WESTINGS	WHACKIER	WHANAUS
WELLIE	WENNISH	WESTLIN	WHACKIEST	WHANG
WELLIES	WENNY	WESTLINS	WHACKING	WHANGAM
WELLING	WENS	WESTMOST	WHACKINGS	WHANGAMS
WELLINGS	WENT	WESTS	WHACKO	WHANGED
WELLNESS	WENTS	WESTWARD	WHACKOES	WHANGEE
WELLS	WEPT	WESTWARDS	WHACKOS	WHANGEES
WELLSITE	WERE	WET	WHACKS	WHANGING
WELLSITES	WEREGILD	WETA	WHACKY	WHANGS
WELLY	WEREGILDS	WETAS	WHAE	WHAP
WELP	WEREWOLF	WETHER	WHAISLE	WHAPPED
WELS	WERGELD	WETHERS	WHAISLED	WHAPPER
WELSH	WERGELDS	WETLAND	WHAISLES	WHAPPERS
WELSHED	WERGELT	WETLANDS	WHAISLING	WHAPPING
WELSHER	WERGELTS	WETLY	WHAIZLE	WHAPS
WELSHERS	WERGILD	WETNESS	WHAIZLED	WHARE
WELSHES	WERGILDS	WETNESSES	WHAIZLES	WHARENUI
WELSHING	WERNERITE	WETPROOF	WHAIZLING	WHARENUIS
WELT	WERO	WETS	WHAKAIRO	WHAREPUNI
WELTED	WEROS	WETSUIT	WHAKAIROS	WHARES

WHARF	WHEATS	WHEESHED	WHENUA	WHEUGHED
WHARFAGE	WHEATWORM	WHEESHES	WHENUAS	WHEUGHING
WHARFAGES	WHEATY	WHEESHING	WHENWE	WHEUGHS
WHARFED	WHEE	WHEESHT	WHENWES	WHEW
WHARFIE	WHEECH	WHEESHTED	WHERE	WHEWED
WHARFIES	WHEECHED	WHEESHTS	WHEREAS	WHEWING
WHARFING	WHEECHING	WHEEZE	WHEREASES	WHEWS
WHARFINGS	WHEECHS	WHEEZED	WHEREAT	WHEY
WHARFS	WHEEDLE	WHEEZER	WHEREBY	WHEYEY
WHARVE	WHEEDLED	WHEEZERS	WHEREFOR	WHEYFACE
WHARVES	WHEEDLER	WHEEZES	WHEREFORE	WHEYFACED
WHAT	WHEEDLERS	WHEEZIER	WHEREFORS	WHEYFACES
WHATA	WHEEDLES	WHEEZIEST	WHEREFROM	WHEYIER
WHATAS	WHEEDLING	WHEEZILY	WHEREIN	WHEYIEST
WHATCHA	WHEEL	WHEEZING	WHEREINTO	WHEYISH
WHATEN	WHEELBASE	WHEEZINGS	WHERENESS	WHEYLIKE
WHATEVER	WHEELED	WHEEZLE	WHEREOF	WHEYS
WHATEVS	WHEELER	WHEEZLED	WHEREON	WHICH
WHATNA	WHEELERS	WHEEZLES	WHEREOUT	WHICHEVER
WHATNESS	WHEELIE	WHEEZLING	WHERES	WHICKER
WHATNOT	WHEELIER	WHEEZY	WHERESO	WHICKERED
WHATNOTS	WHEELIES	WHEFT	WHERETO	WHICKERS
WHATS	WHEELIEST	WHEFTS	WHEREUNTO	WHID
WHATSIS	WHEELING	WHELK	WHEREUPON	WHIDAH
WHATSISES	WHEELINGS	WHELKED	WHEREVER	WHIDAHS
WHATSIT	WHEELLESS	WHELKIER	WHEREWITH	WHIDDED
WHATSITS	WHEELMAN	WHELKIEST	WHERRET	WHIDDER
WHATSO	WHEELMEN	WHELKS	WHERRETED	WHIDDERED
WHATTEN	WHEELS	WHELKY	WHERRETS	WHIDDERS
WHAUP	WHEELSMAN	WHELM	WHERRIED	WHIDDING
WHAUPS	WHEELSMEN	WHELMED	WHERRIES	WHIDS
WHAUR	WHEELSPIN	WHELMING	WHERRIT	WHIFF
WHAURS	WHEELWORK	WHELMS	WHERRITED	WHIFFED
WHEAL	WHEELY	WHELP	WHERRITS	WHIFFER
WHEALS	WHEEN	WHELPED	WHERRY	WHIFFERS
WHEAR	WHEENGE	WHELPING	WHERRYING	WHIFFET
WHEARE	WHEENGED	WHELPLESS	WHERRYMAN	WHIFFETS
WHEAT	WHEENGES	WHELPS	WHERRYMEN	WHIFFIER
WHEATEAR	WHEENGING	WHEMMLE	WHERVE	WHIFFIEST
WHEATEARS	WHEENS	WHEMMLED	WHERVES	WHIFFING
WHEATEN	WHEEP	WHEMMLES	WHET	WHIFFINGS
WHEATENS	WHEEPED	WHEMMLING	WHETHER	WHIFFLE
WHEATGERM	WHEEPING	WHEN	WHETS	WHIFFLED
WHEATIER	WHEEPLE	WHENAS	WHETSTONE	WHIFFLER
WHEATIEST	WHEEPLED	WHENCE	WHETTED	WHIFFLERS
WHEATLAND	WHEEPLES	WHENCES	WHETTER	WHIFFLERY
WHEATLESS	WHEEPLING	WHENCEVER	WHETTERS	WHIFFLES
WHEATLIKE	WHEEPS	WHENEVER	WHETTING	WHIFFLING
WHEATMEAL	WHEESH	WHENS	WHEUGH	WHIFFS

W

WHIFFY	WHINBERRY	WHIPCRACK	WHIRLPOOL	WHISS
WHIFT	WHINCHAT	WHIPJACK	WHIRLS	WHISSED
WHIFTS	WHINCHATS	WHIPJACKS	WHIRLWIND	WHISSES
WHIG	WHINE	WHIPLASH	WHIRLY	WHISSING
WHIGGED	WHINED	WHIPLESS	WHIRR	WHIST
WHIGGING	WHINER	WHIPLIKE	WHIRRA	WHISTED
WHIGS	WHINERS	WHIPPED	WHIRRED	WHISTING
WHILE	WHINES	WHIPPER	WHIRRET	WHISTLE
WHILED	WHINEY	WHIPPERS	WHIRRETED	WHISTLED
WHILERE	WHINGDING	WHIPPET	WHIRRETS	WHISTLER
WHILES	WHINGE	WHIPPETS	WHIRRIED	WHISTLERS
WHILEVER	WHINGED	WHIPPIER	WHIRRIER	WHISTLES
WHILING	WHINGEING	WHIPPIEST	WHIRRIES	WHISTLING
WHILK	WHINGER	WHIPPING	WHIRRIEST	WHISTS
WHILLIED	WHINGERS	WHIPPINGS	WHIRRING	WHIT
WHILLIES	WHINGES	WHIPPIT	WHIRRINGS	WHITE
WHILLY	WHINGIER	WHIPPITS	WHIRRS	WHITEBAIT
WHILLYING	WHINGIEST	WHIPPY	WHIRRY	WHITEBASS
WHILLYWHA	WHINGING	WHIPRAY	WHIRRYING	WHITEBEAM
WHILOM	WHINGY	WHIPRAYS	WHIRS	WHITECAP
WHILST	WHINIARD	WHIPS	WHIRTLE	WHITECAPS
WHIM	WHINIARDS	WHIPSAW	WHIRTLES	WHITECOAT
WHIMBERRY	WHINIER	WHIPSAWED	WHISH	WHITECOMB
WHIMBREL	WHINIEST	WHIPSAWN	WHISHED	WHITED
WHIMBRELS	WHININESS	WHIPSAWS	WHISHES	WHITEDAMP
WHIMMED	WHINING	WHIPSNAKE	WHISHING	WHITEFACE
WHIMMIER	WHININGLY	WHIPSTAFF	WHISHT	WHITEFISH
WHIMMIEST	WHININGS	WHIPSTALL	WHISHTED	WHITEFLY
WHIMMING	WHINNIED	WHIPSTER	WHISHTING	WHITEHEAD
WHIMMY	WHINNIER	WHIPSTERS	WHISHTS	WHITELIST
WHIMPER	WHINNIES	WHIPSTOCK	WHISK	WHITELY
WHIMPERED	WHINNIEST	WHIPT	WHISKED	WHITEN
WHIMPERER	WHINNY	WHIPTAIL	WHISKER	WHITENED
WHIMPERS	WHINNYING	WHIPTAILS	WHISKERED	WHITENER
WHIMPLE	WHINS	WHIPWORM	WHISKERS	WHITENERS
WHIMPLED	WHINSTONE	WHIPWORMS	WHISKERY	WHITENESS
WHIMPLES	WHINY	WHIR	WHISKET	WHITENING
WHIMPLING	WHINYARD	WHIRL	WHISKETS	WHITENS
WHIMS	WHINYARDS	WHIRLBAT	WHISKEY	WHITEOUT
WHIMSEY	WHIO	WHIRLBATS	WHISKEYS	WHITEOUTS
WHIMSEYS	WHIOS	WHIRLED	WHISKIES	WHITEPOT
WHIMSICAL	WHIP	WHIRLER	WHISKING	WHITEPOTS
WHIMSIED	WHIPBIRD	WHIRLERS	WHISKS	WHITER
WHIMSIER	WHIPBIRDS	WHIRLIER	WHISKY	WHITES
WHIMSIES	WHIPCAT	WHIRLIES	WHISPER	WHITEST
WHIMSIEST	WHIPCATS	WHIRLIEST	WHISPERED	WHITETAIL
WHIMSILY	WHIPCORD	WHIRLIGIG	WHISPERER	WHITETIP
WHIMSY	WHIPCORDS	WHIRLING	WHISPERS	WHITETIPS
WHIN	WHIPCORDY	WHIRLINGS	WHISPERY	WHITEWALL

W

WHITEWARE	WHIZZES	WHOOMP	WHORL	WIBBLED
WHITEWASH	WHIZZIER	WHOOMPH	WHORLBAT	WIBBLES
WHITEWING	WHIZZIEST	WHOOMPHS	WHORLBATS	WIBBLING
WHITEWOOD	WHIZZING	WHOOMPS	WHORLED	WICCA
WHITEY	WHIZZINGS	WHOONGA	WHORLING	WICCAN
WHITHER	WHIZZO	WHOONGAS	WHORLS	WICCANS
WHITHERED	WHIZZY	WHOOP	WHORT	WICCAS
WHITHERS	WHO	WHOOPED	WHORTLE	WICE
WHITIER	WHOA	WHOOPEE	WHORTLES	WICH
WHITIEST	WHODUNIT	WHOOPEES	WHORTS	WICHES
WHITING	WHODUNITS	WHOOPER	WHOSE	WICK
WHITINGS	WHODUNNIT	WHOOPERS	WHOSESO	WICKAPE
WHITISH	WHOEVER	WHOOPIE	WHOSEVER	WICKAPES
WHITLING	WHOLE	WHOOPIES	WHOSIS	WICKED
WHITLINGS	WHOLEFOOD	WHOOPING	WHOSISES	WICKEDER
WHITLOW	WHOLEMEAL	WHOOPINGS	WHOSIT	WICKEDEST
WHITLOWS	WHOLENESS	WHOOPLA	WHOSITS	WICKEDLY
WHITRACK	WHOLES	WHOOPLAS	WHOSO	WICKEDS
WHITRACKS	WHOLESALE	WHOOPS	WHOSOEVER	WICKEN
WHITRET	WHOLESOME	WHOOPSIE	WHOT	WICKENS
WHITRETS	WHOLISM	WHOOPSIES	WHOW	WICKER
WHITRICK	WHOLISMS	WHOOSH	WHOWED	WICKERED
WHITRICKS	WHOLIST	WHOOSHED	WHOWING	WICKERS
WHITS	WHOLISTIC	WHOOSHES	WHOWS	WICKET
WHITSTER	WHOLISTS	WHOOSHING	WHUMMLE	WICKETS
WHITSTERS	WHOLLY	WHOOSIS	WHUMMLED	WICKIES
WHITTAW	WHOLPHIN	WHOOSISES	WHUMMLES	WICKING
WHITTAWER	WHOLPHINS	WHOOT	WHUMMLING	WICKINGS
WHITTAWS	WHOM	WHOOTED	WHUMP	WICKIUP
WHITTER	WHOMBLE	WHOOTING	WHUMPED	WICKIUPS
WHITTERED	WHOMBLED	WHOOTS	WHUMPING	WICKLESS
WHITTERS	WHOMBLES	WHOP	WHUMPS	WICKS
WHITTLE	WHOMBLING	WHOPPED	WHUNSTANE	WICKTHING
WHITTLED	WHOMEVER	WHOPPER	WHUP	WICKY
WHITTLER	WHOMMLE	WHOPPERS	WHUPPED	WICKYUP
WHITTLERS	WHOMMLED	WHOPPING	WHUPPING	WICKYUPS
WHITTLES	WHOMMLES	WHOPPINGS	WHUPPINGS	WICOPIES
WHITTLING	WHOMMLING	WHOPS	WHUPS	WICOPY
WHITTRET	WHOMP	WHORE	WHY	WIDDER
WHITTRETS	WHOMPED	WHORED	WHYDA	WIDDERS
WHITY	WHOMPING	WHOREDOM	WHYDAH	WIDDIE
WHIZ	WHOMPS	WHOREDOMS	WHYDAHS	WIDDIES
WHIZBANG	WHOMSO	WHORES	WHYDAS	WIDDLE
WHIZBANGS	WHOOBUB	WHORESON	WHYDUNIT	WIDDLED
WHIZZ	WHOOBUBS	WHORESONS	WHYDUNITS	WIDDLES
WHIZZBANG	WHOOF	WHORING	WHYDUNNIT	WIDDLING
WHIZZED	WHOOFED	WHORINGS	WHYEVER	WIDDY
WHIZZER	WHOOFING	WHORISH	WHYS	WIDE
WHIZZERS	WHOOFS	WHORISHLY	WIBBLE	WIDEAWAKE

WIDEBAND	WIELDLESS	WIGGY	WILDLINGS	WILLIWAUS
WIDEBANDS	WIELDS	WIGHT	WILDLY	WILLIWAW
WIDEBODY	WIELDY	WIGHTED	WILDMAN	WILLIWAWS
WIDELY	WIELS	WIGHTING	WILDMEN	WILLOW
WIDEN	WIENER	WIGHTLY	WILDNESS	WILLOWED
WIDENED	WIENERS	WIGHTS	WILDS	WILLOWER
WIDENER	WIENIE	WIGLESS	WILDWOOD	WILLOWERS
WIDENERS	WIENIES	WIGLET	WILDWOODS	WILLOWIER
WIDENESS	WIFE	WIGLETS	WILE	WILLOWING
WIDENING	WIFED	WIGLIKE	WILED	WILLOWISH
WIDENINGS	WIFEDOM	WIGMAKER	WILEFUL	WILLOWS
WIDENS	WIFEDOMS	WIGMAKERS	WILES	WILLOWY
WIDEOUT	WIFEHOOD	WIGS	WILFUL	WILLPOWER
WIDEOUTS	WIFEHOODS	WIGWAG	WILFULLY	WILLS
WIDER	WIFELESS	WIGWAGGED	WILGA	WILLY
WIDES	WIFELIER	WIGWAGGER	WILGAS	WILLYARD
WIDEST	WIFELIEST	WIGWAGS	WILI	WILLYART
WIDGEON	WIFELIKE	WIGWAM	WILIER	WILLYING
WIDGEONS	WIFELY	WIGWAMS	WILIEST	WILLYWAW
WIDGET	WIFES	WIKI	WILILY	WILLYWAWS
WIDGETS	WIFEY	WIKIALITY	WILINESS	WILT
WIDGIE	WIFEYS	WIKIS	WILING	WILTED
WIDGIES	WIFIE	WIKIUP	WILIS	WILTING
WIDISH	WIFIES	WIKIUPS	WILJA	WILTJA
WIDOW	WIFING	WILCO	WILJAS	WILTJAS
WIDOWBIRD	WIFTIER	WILD	WILL	WILTS
WIDOWED	WIFTIEST	WILDCARD	WILLABLE	WILY
WIDOWER	WIFTY	WILDCARDS	WILLED	WIMBLE
WIDOWERED	WIG	WILDCAT	WILLEMITE	WIMBLED
WIDOWERS	WIGAN	WILDCATS	WILLER	WIMBLES
WIDOWHOOD	WIGANS	WILDED	WILLERS	WIMBLING
WIDOWING	WIGEON	WILDER	WILLEST	WIMBREL
WIDOWMAN	WIGEONS	WILDERED	WILLET	WIMBRELS
WIDOWMEN	WIGGED	WILDERING	WILLETS	WIMMIN
WIDOWS	WIGGERIES	WILDERS	WILLEY	WIMP
WIDTH	WIGGERY	WILDEST	WILLEYED	WIMPED
WIDTHS	WIGGIER	WILDFIRE	WILLEYING	WIMPIER
WIDTHWAY	WIGGIEST	WILDFIRES	WILLEYS	WIMPIEST
WIDTHWAYS	WIGGING	WILDFOWL	WILLFUL	WIMPINESS
WIDTHWISE	WIGGINGS	WILDFOWLS	WILLFULLY	WIMPING
WIEL	WIGGLE	WILDGRAVE	WILLIAM	WIMPISH
WIELD	WIGGLED	WILDING	WILLIAMS	WIMPISHLY
WIELDABLE	WIGGLER	WILDINGS	WILLIE	WIMPLE
WIELDED	WIGGLERS	WILDISH	WILLIED	WIMPLED
WIELDER	WIGGLES	WILDLAND	WILLIES	WIMPLES
WIELDERS	WIGGLIER	WILDLANDS	WILLING	WIMPLING
WIELDIER	WIGGLIEST	WILDLIFE	WILLINGER	WIMPS
WIELDIEST	WIGGLING	WILDLIFES	WILLINGLY	WIMPY
WIELDING	WIGGLY	WILDLING	WILLIWAU	WIN

WINCE	WINDFLAW	WINDSAIL	WINGCHAIR	WINLESS
WINCED	WINDFLAWS	WINDSAILS	WINGDING	WINN
WINCER	WINDGALL	WINDSES	WINGDINGS	WINNA
WINCERS	WINDGALLS	WINDSHAKE	WINGE	WINNABLE
WINCES	WINDGUN	WINDSHIP	WINGED	WINNARD
WINCEY	WINDGUNS	WINDSHIPS	WINGEDLY	WINNARDS
WINCEYS	WINDHOVER	WINDSLAB	WINGEING	WINNED
WINCH	WINDIER	WINDSLABS	WINGER	WINNER
WINCHED	WINDIEST	WINDSOCK	WINGERS	WINNERS
WINCHER	WINDIGO	WINDSOCKS	WINGES	WINNING
WINCHERS	WINDIGOES	WINDSTORM	WINGIER	WINNINGLY
WINCHES	WINDIGOS	WINDSURF	WINGIEST	WINNINGS
WINCHING	WINDILY	WINDSURFS	WINGING	WINNLE
WINCHMAN	WINDINESS	WINDSWEPT	WINGLESS	WINNLES
WINCHMEN	WINDING	WINDTHROW	WINGLET	WINNOCK
WINCING	WINDINGLY	WINDTIGHT	WINGLETS	WINNOCKS
WINCINGLY	WINDINGS	WINDUP	WINGLIKE	WINNOW
WINCINGS	WINDLASS	WINDUPS	WINGMAN	WINNOWED
WINCOPIPE	WINDLE	WINDWARD	WINGMEN	WINNOWER
WIND	WINDLED	WINDWARDS	WINGNUT	WINNOWERS
WINDABLE	WINDLES	WINDWAY	WINGNUTS	WINNOWING
WINDAC	WINDLESS	WINDWAYS	WINGOVER	WINNOWS
WINDACS	WINDLING	WINDY	WINGOVERS	WINNS
WINDAGE	WINDLINGS	WINE	WINGS	WINO
WINDAGES	WINDLOAD	WINEBERRY	WINGSPAN	WINOES
WINDAS	WINDLOADS	WINED	WINGSPANS	WINOS
WINDASES	WINDMILL	WINEGLASS	WINGSUIT	WINS
WINDBAG	WINDMILLS	WINELESS	WINGSUITS	WINSEY
WINDBAGS	WINDOCK	WINEMAKER	WINGTIP	WINSEYS
WINDBELL	WINDOCKS	WINEPRESS	WINGTIPS	WINSOME
WINDBELLS	WINDORE	WINERIES	WINGY	WINSOMELY
WINDBILL	WINDORES	WINERY	WINIER	WINSOMER
WINDBILLS	WINDOW	WINES	WINIEST	WINSOMEST
WINDBLAST	WINDOWED	WINESAP	WINING	WINTER
WINDBLOW	WINDOWIER	WINESAPS	WINISH	WINTERED
WINDBLOWN	WINDOWING	WINESHOP	WINK	WINTERER
WINDBLOWS	WINDOWS	WINESHOPS	WINKED	WINTERERS
WINDBORNE	WINDOWY	WINESKIN	WINKER	WINTERFED
WINDBOUND	WINDPACK	WINESKINS	WINKERS	WINTERIER
WINDBREAK	WINDPACKS	WINESOP	WINKING	WINTERING
WINDBURN	WINDPIPE	WINESOPS	WINKINGLY	WINTERISE
WINDBURNS	WINDPIPES	WINEY	WINKINGS	WINTERISH
WINDBURNT	WINDPROOF	WING	WINKLE	WINTERIZE
WINDCHILL	WINDRING	WINGBACK	WINKLED	WINTERLY
WINDED	WINDROW	WINGBACKS	WINKLER	WINTERS
WINDER	WINDROWED	WINGBEAT	WINKLERS	WINTERY
WINDERS	WINDROWER	WINGBEATS	WINKLES	WINTLE
WINDFALL	WINDROWS	WINGBOW	WINKLING	WINTLED
WINDFALLS	WINDS	WINGBOWS	WINKS	WINTLES

W

WINTLING	WIREWOVE	WISHES	WITCHHOOD	WITHWIND
WINTRIER	WIRIER	WISHFUL	WITCHIER	WITHWINDS
WINTRIEST	WIRIEST	WISHFULLY	WITCHIEST	WITHY
WINTRILY	WIRILDA	WISHING	WITCHING	WITHYWIND
WINTRY	WIRILDAS	WISHINGS	WITCHINGS	WITING
WINY	WIRILY	WISHLESS	WITCHKNOT	WITLESS
WINZE	WIRINESS	WISHT	WITCHLIKE	WITLESSLY
WINZES	WIRING	WISING	WITCHWEED	WITLING
WIPE	WIRINGS	WISKET	WITCHY	WITLINGS
WIPEABLE	WIRRA	WISKETS	WITE	WITLOOF
WIPED	WIRRAH	WISP	WITED	WITLOOFS
WIPEOUT	WIRRAHS	WISPED	WITELESS	WITNESS
WIPEOUTS	WIRRICOW	WISPIER	WITES	WITNESSED
WIPER	WIRRICOWS	WISPIEST	WITGAT	WITNESSER
WIPERS	WIRY	WISPILY	WITGATS	WITNESSES
WIPES	WIS	WISPINESS	WITH	WITNEY
WIPING	WISARD	WISPING	WITHAL	WITNEYS
WIPINGS	WISARDS	WISPISH	WITHDRAW	WITS
WIPPEN	WISDOM	WISPLIKE	WITHDRAWN	WITTED
WIPPENS	WISDOMS	WISPS	WITHDRAWS	WITTER
WIRABLE	WISE	WISPY	WITHDREW	WITTERED
WIRE	WISEACRE	WISS	WITHE	WITTERING
WIRED	WISEACRES	WISSED	WITHED	WITTERS
WIREDRAW	WISEASS	WISSES	WITHER	WITTICISM
WIREDRAWN	WISEASSES	WISSING	WITHERED	WITTIER
WIREDRAWS	WISECRACK	WIST	WITHERER	WITTIEST
WIREDREW	WISED	WISTARIA	WITHERERS	WITTILY
WIREFRAME	WISEGUY	WISTARIAS	WITHERING	WITTINESS
WIREGRASS	WISEGUYS	WISTED	WITHERITE	WITTING
WIREHAIR	WISELIER	WISTERIA	WITHEROD	WITTINGLY
WIREHAIRS	WISELIEST	WISTERIAS	WITHERODS	WITTINGS
WIRELESS	WISELING	WISTFUL	WITHERS	WITTOL
WIRELIKE	WISELINGS	WISTFULLY	WITHES	WITTOLLY
WIRELINE	WISELY	WISTING	WITHHAULT	WITTOLS
WIRELINES	WISENESS	WISTITI	WITHHELD	WITTY
WIREMAN	WISENT	WISTITIS	WITHHOLD	WITWALL
WIREMEN	WISENTS	WISTLY	WITHHOLDS	WITWALLS
WIREPHOTO	WISER	WISTS	WITHIER	WITWANTON
WIRER	WISES	WIT	WITHIES	WIVE
WIRERS	WISEST	WITAN	WITHIEST	WIVED
WIRES	WISEWOMAN	WITANS	WITHIN	WIVEHOOD
WIRETAP	WISEWOMEN	WITBLITS	WITHING	WIVEHOODS
WIRETAPS	WISH	WITCH	WITHINS	WIVER
WIREWAY	WISHA	WITCHED	WITHOUT	WIVERN
WIREWAYS	WISHBONE	WITCHEN	WITHOUTEN	WIVERNS
WIREWORK	WISHBONES	WITCHENS	WITHOUTS	WIVERS
WIREWORKS	WISHED	WITCHERY	WITHS	WIVES
WIREWORM	WISHER	WITCHES	WITHSTAND	WIVING
WIREWORMS	WISHERS	WITCHETTY	WITHSTOOD	WIZ

W

WIZARD	WOEFULLY	WOLFS	WOMBING	WONS
WIZARDER	WOENESS	WOLFSBANE	WOMBLIKE	WONT
WIZARDEST	WOENESSES	WOLFSKIN	WOMBS	WONTED
WIZARDLY	WOES	WOLFSKINS	WOMBY	WONTEDLY
WIZARDRY	WOESOME	WOLLIES	WOMEN	WONTING
WIZARDS	WOF	WOLLY	WOMENFOLK	WONTLESS
WIZEN	WOFS	WOLVE	WOMENKIND	WONTON
WIZENED	WOFUL	WOLVED	WOMERA	WONTONS
WIZENER	WOFULLER	WOLVER	WOMERAS	WONTS
WIZENEST	WOFULLEST	WOLVERENE	WOMMERA	WOO
WIZENING	WOFULLY	WOLVERINE	WOMMERAS	WOOABLE
WIZENS	WOFULNESS	WOLVERS	WOMMIT	WOOBUT
WIZES	WOGGLE	WOLVES	WOMMITS	WOOBUTS
WIZIER	WOGGLES	WOLVING	WOMYN	WOOD
WIZIERS	WOIWODE	WOLVINGS	WON	WOODBIN
WIZZEN	WOIWODES	WOLVISH	WONDER	WOODBIND
WIZZENS	WOJUS	WOLVISHLY	WONDERED	WOODBINDS
WIZZES	WOK	WOMAN	WONDERER	WOODBINE
WO	WOKE	WOMANED	WONDERERS	WOODBINES
WOAD	WOKEISM	WOMANHOOD	WONDERFUL	WOODBINS
WOADED	WOKEISMS	WOMANING	WONDERING	WOODBLOCK
WOADS	WOKEN	WOMANISE	WONDERKID	WOODBORER
WOADWAX	WOKENESS	WOMANISED	WONDEROUS	WOODBOX
WOADWAXEN	WOKER	WOMANISER	WONDERS	WOODBOXES
WOADWAXES	WOKERIES	WOMANISES	WONDRED	WOODCHAT
WOAH	WOKERY	WOMANISH	WONDROUS	WOODCHATS
WOALD	WOKEST	WOMANISM	WONGA	WOODCHIP
WOALDS	WOKKA	WOMANISMS	WONGAS	WOODCHIPS
WOBBEGONG	WOKS	WOMANIST	WONGI	WOODCHOP
WOBBLE	WOLD	WOMANISTS	WONGIED	WOODCHOPS
WOBBLED	WOLDS	WOMANIZE	WONGIING	WOODCHUCK
WOBBLER	WOLF	WOMANIZED	WONGIS	WOODCOCK
WOBBLERS	WOLFBERRY	WOMANIZER	WONING	WOODCOCKS
WOBBLES	WOLFED	WOMANIZES	WONINGS	WOODCRAFT
WOBBLIER	WOLFER	WOMANKIND	WONK	WOODCUT
WOBBLIES	WOLFERS	WOMANLESS	WONKERIES	WOODCUTS
WOBBLIEST	WOLFFISH	WOMANLIER	WONKERY	WOODED
WOBBLING	WOLFHOUND	WOMANLIKE	WONKIER	WOODEN
WOBBLINGS	WOLFING	WOMANLY	WONKIEST	WOODENED
WOBBLY	WOLFINGS	WOMANNED	WONKILY	WOODENER
WOBEGONE	WOLFISH	WOMANNESS	WONKINESS	WOODENEST
WOCK	WOLFISHLY	WOMANNING	WONKISH	WOODENING
WOCKS	WOLFKIN	WOMANS	WONKS	WOODENLY
WODGE	WOLFKINS	WOMB	WONKY	WOODENS
WODGES	WOLFLIKE	WOMBAT	WONNED	WOODENTOP
WOE	WOLFLING	WOMBATS	WONNER	WOODFERN
WOEBEGONE	WOLFLINGS	WOMBED	WONNERS	WOODFERNS
WOEFUL	WOLFRAM	WOMBIER	WONNING	WOODFREE
WOEFULLER	WOLFRAMS	WOMBIEST	WONNINGS	WOODGRAIN

WOODHEN	WOODSIAS	WOOINGS	WOOLWORK	WORD
WOODHENS	WOODSIER	WOOL	WOOLWORKS	WORDAGE
WOODHOLE	WOODSIEST	WOOLD	WOOLY	WORDAGES
WOODHOLES	WOODSKIN	WOOLDED	WOOMERA	WORDBOOK
WOODHORSE	WOODSKINS	WOOLDER	WOOMERANG	WORDBOOKS
WOODHOUSE	WOODSMAN	WOOLDERS	WOOMERAS	WORDBOUND
WOODIE	WOODSMEN	WOOLDING	WOON	WORDBREAK
WOODIER	WOODSMOKE	WOOLDINGS	WOONED	WORDCOUNT
WOODIES	WOODSPITE	WOOLDS	WOONERF	WORDED
WOODIEST	WOODSTONE	WOOLED	WOONERFS	WORDGAME
WOODINESS	WOODSTOVE	WOOLEN	WOONING	WORDGAMES
WOODING	WOODSY	WOOLENS	WOONS	WORDIE
WOODLAND	WOODTONE	WOOLER	WOOPIE	WORDIER
WOODLANDS	WOODTONES	WOOLERS	WOOPIES	WORDIES
WOODLARK	WOODWALE	WOOLFAT	WOOPS	WORDIEST
WOODLARKS	WOODWALES	WOOLFATS	WOOPSED	WORDILY
WOODLESS	WOODWARD	WOOLFELL	WOOPSES	WORDINESS
WOODLICE	WOODWARDS	WOOLFELLS	WOOPSING	WORDING
WOODLORE	WOODWASP	WOOLHAT	WOOPY	WORDINGS
WOODLORES	WOODWASPS	WOOLHATS	WOORALI	WORDISH
WOODLOT	WOODWAX	WOOLIE	WOORALIS	WORDLESS
WOODLOTS	WOODWAXEN	WOOLIER	WOORARA	WORDLORE
WOODLOUSE	WOODWAXES	WOOLIES	WOORARAS	WORDLORES
WOODMAN	WOODWIND	WOOLIEST	WOORARI	WORDPLAY
WOODMEAL	WOODWINDS	WOOLILY	WOORARIS	WORDPLAYS
WOODMEALS	WOODWORK	WOOLINESS	WOOS	WORDS
WOODMEN	WOODWORKS	WOOLLED	WOOSE	WORDSMITH
WOODMICE	WOODWORM	WOOLLEN	WOOSEL	WORDWRAP
WOODMOUSE	WOODWORMS	WOOLLENS	WOOSELL	WORDWRAPS
WOODNESS	WOODWOSE	WOOLLIER	WOOSELLS	WORDY
WOODNOTE	WOODWOSES	WOOLLIES	WOOSELS	WORE
WOODNOTES	WOODY	WOOLLIEST	WOOSES	WORK
WOODPILE	WOODYARD	WOOLLIKE	WOOSH	WORKABLE
WOODPILES	WOODYARDS	WOOLLILY	WOOSHED	WORKABLY
WOODPRINT	WOOED	WOOLLY	WOOSHES	WORKADAY
WOODRAT	WOOER	WOOLMAN	WOOSHING	WORKADAYS
WOODRATS	WOOERS	WOOLMEN	WOOT	WORKBAG
WOODREEVE	WOOF	WOOLPACK	WOOTZ	WORKBAGS
WOODROOF	WOOFED	WOOLPACKS	WOOTZES	WORKBENCH
WOODROOFS	WOOFER	WOOLS	WOOZIER	WORKBOAT
WOODRUFF	WOOFERS	WOOLSACK	WOOZIEST	WORKBOATS
WOODRUFFS	WOOFIER	WOOLSACKS	WOOZILY	WORKBOOK
WOODRUSH	WOOFIEST	WOOLSEY	WOOZINESS	WORKBOOKS
WOODS	WOOFING	WOOLSEYS	WOOZY	WORKBOOT
WOODSCREW	WOOFS	WOOLSHED	WOP	WORKBOOTS
WOODSHED	WOOFY	WOOLSHEDS	WOPPED	WORKBOX
WOODSHEDS	WOOHOO	WOOLSKIN	WOPPING	WORKBOXES
WOODSHOCK	WOOING	WOOLSKINS	WOPS	WORKDAY
WOODSIA	WOOINGLY	WOOLWARD	WORCESTER	WORKDAYS

WORKED	WORKTOP	WORMSEED	WORSTED	WOUNDING
WORKER	WORKTOPS	WORMSEEDS	WORSTEDS	WOUNDINGS
WORKERIST	WORKUP	WORMWHEEL	WORSTING	WOUNDLESS
WORKERS	WORKUPS	WORMWOOD	WORSTS	WOUNDS
WORKFARE	WORKWEAR	WORMWOODS	WORT	WOUNDWORT
WORKFARES	WORKWEARS	WORMY	WORTH	WOUNDY
WORKFLOW	WORKWEEK	WORN	WORTHED	WOURALI
WORKFLOWS	WORKWEEKS	WORNNESS	WORTHFUL	WOURALIS
WORKFOLK	WORKWOMAN	WORRAL	WORTHIED	WOVE
WORKFOLKS	WORKWOMEN	WORRALS	WORTHIER	WOVEN
WORKFORCE	WORLD	WORREL	WORTHIES	WOVENS
WORKFUL	WORLDBEAT	WORRELS	WORTHIEST	WOW
WORKGIRL	WORLDED	WORRICOW	WORTHILY	WOWED
WORKGIRLS	WORLDER	WORRICOWS	WORTHING	WOWEE
WORKGROUP	WORLDERS	WORRIED	WORTHLESS	WOWF
WORKHORSE	WORLDIE	WORRIEDLY	WORTHS	WOWFER
WORKHOUR	WORLDIES	WORRIER	WORTHY	WOWFEST
WORKHOURS	WORLDLIER	WORRIERS	WORTHYING	WOWING
WORKHOUSE	WORLDLING	WORRIES	WORTLE	WOWS
WORKING	WORLDLY	WORRIMENT	WORTLES	WOWSER
WORKINGS	WORLDS	WORRISOME	WORTS	WOWSERS
WORKLESS	WORLDVIEW	WORRIT	WOS	WOX
WORKLOAD	WORLDWIDE	WORRITED	WOSBIRD	WOXEN
WORKLOADS	WORM	WORRITING	WOSBIRDS	WRACK
WORKMAN	WORMCAST	WORRITS	WOST	WRACKED
WORKMANLY	WORMCASTS	WORRY	WOT	WRACKFUL
WORKMATE	WORMED	WORRYCOW	WOTCHA	WRACKING
WORKMATES	WORMER	WORRYCOWS	WOTCHER	WRACKS
WORKMEN	WORMERIES	WORRYGUTS	WOTS	WRAITH
WORKOUT	WORMERS	WORRYING	WOTTED	WRAITHS
WORKOUTS	WORMERY	WORRYINGS	WOTTEST	WRANG
WORKPIECE	WORMFLIES	WORRYWART	WOTTETH	WRANGED
WORKPLACE	WORMFLY	WORSE	WOTTING	WRANGING
WORKPRINT	WORMGEAR	WORSED	WOUBIT	WRANGLE
WORKROOM	WORMGEARS	WORSEN	WOUBITS	WRANGLED
WORKROOMS	WORMHOLE	WORSENED	WOULD	WRANGLER
WORKS	WORMHOLED	WORSENESS	WOULDA	WRANGLERS
WORKSAFE	WORMHOLES	WORSENING	WOULDEST	WRANGLES
WORKSHEET	WORMIER	WORSENS	WOULDS	WRANGLING
WORKSHOP	WORMIEST	WORSER	WOULDST	WRANGS
WORKSHOPS	WORMIL	WORSES	WOUND	WRAP
WORKSHY	WORMILS	WORSET	WOUNDABLE	WRAPOVER
WORKSITE	WORMINESS	WORSETS	WOUNDED	WRAPOVERS
WORKSITES	WORMING	WORSHIP	WOUNDEDLY	WRAPPAGE
WORKSOME	WORMISH	WORSHIPED	WOUNDER	WRAPPAGES
WORKSONG	WORMLIKE	WORSHIPER	WOUNDERS	WRAPPED
WORKSONGS	WORMROOT	WORSHIPS	WOUNDIER	WRAPPER
WORKSPACE	WORMROOTS	WORSING	WOUNDIEST	WRAPPERED
WORKTABLE	WORMS	WORST	WOUNDILY	WRAPPERS

W

WRAPPING	WREATHED	WRICK	WRITEABLE	WRYBILL
WRAPPINGS	WREATHEN	WRICKED	WRITEDOWN	WRYBILLS
WRAPROUND	WREATHER	WRICKING	WRITEOFF	WRYER
WRAPS	WREATHERS	WRICKS	WRITEOFFS	WRYEST
WRAPT	WREATHES	WRIED	WRITER	WRYING
WRASSE	WREATHIER	WRIER	WRITERESS	WRYLY
WRASSES	WREATHING	WRIES	WRITERLY	WRYNECK
WRASSLE	WREATHS	WRIEST	WRITERS	WRYNECKS
WRASSLED	WREATHY	WRIGGLE	WRITES	WRYNESS
WRASSLES	WRECK	WRIGGLED	WRITHE	WRYNESSES
WRASSLING	WRECKAGE	WRIGGLER	WRITHED	WRYTHEN
WRAST	WRECKAGES	WRIGGLERS	WRITHEN	WUD
WRASTED	WRECKED	WRIGGLES	WRITHER	WUDDED
WRASTING	WRECKER	WRIGGLIER	WRITHERS	WUDDIES
WRASTLE	WRECKERS	WRIGGLING	WRITHES	WUDDING
WRASTLED	WRECKFISH	WRIGGLY	WRITHING	WUDDY
WRASTLES	WRECKFUL	WRIGHT	WRITHINGS	WUDJULA
WRASTLING	WRECKING	WRIGHTS	WRITHLED	WUDJULAS
WRASTS	WRECKINGS	WRING	WRITING	WUDS
WRATE	WRECKS	WRINGED	WRITINGS	WUDU
WRATH	WREN	WRINGER	WRITS	WUDUS
WRATHED	WRENCH	WRINGERS	WRITTEN	WUKKAS
WRATHFUL	WRENCHED	WRINGING	WRIZLED	WULFENITE
WRATHIER	WRENCHER	WRINGS	WROATH	WULL
WRATHIEST	WRENCHERS	WRINKLE	WROATHS	WULLED
WRATHILY	WRENCHES	WRINKLED	WROKE	WULLING
WRATHING	WRENCHING	WRINKLES	WROKEN	WULLS
WRATHLESS	WRENS	WRINKLIE	WRONG	WUNNER
WRATHS	WRENTIT	WRINKLIER	WRONGDOER	WUNNERS
WRATHY	WRENTITS	WRINKLIES	WRONGED	WURLEY
WRAWL	WREST	WRINKLING	WRONGER	WURLEYS
WRAWLED	WRESTED	WRINKLY	WRONGERS	WURLIE
WRAWLING	WRESTER	WRIST	WRONGEST	WURLIES
WRAWLS	WRESTERS	WRISTBAND	WRONGFUL	WURST
WRAXLE	WRESTING	WRISTED	WRONGING	WURSTS
WRAXLED	WRESTLE	WRISTER	WRONGLY	WURTZITE
WRAXLES	WRESTLED	WRISTERS	WRONGNESS	WURTZITES
WRAXLING	WRESTLER	WRISTIER	WRONGOUS	WURZEL
WRAXLINGS	WRESTLERS	WRISTIEST	WRONGS	WURZELS
WREAK	WRESTLES	WRISTING	WROOT	WUS
WREAKED	WRESTLING	WRISTLET	WROOTED	WUSES
WREAKER	WRESTS	WRISTLETS	WROOTING	WUSHU
WREAKERS	WRETCH	WRISTLOCK	WROOTS	WUSHUS
WREAKFUL	WRETCHED	WRISTS	WROTE	WUSS
WREAKING	WRETCHES	WRISTY	WROTH	WUSSES
WREAKLESS	WRETHE	WRIT	WROTHFUL	WUSSIER
WREAKS	WRETHED	WRITABLE	WROUGHT	WUSSIES
WREATH	WRETHES	WRITATIVE	WRUNG	WUSSIEST
WREATHE	WRETHING	WRITE	WRY	WUSSY

W

WUTHER	WUZZLE	WYE	WYN	WYTE
WUTHERED	WUZZLED	WYES	WYND	WYTED
WUTHERING	WUZZLES	WYLE	WYNDS	WYTES
WUTHERS	WUZZLING	WYLED	WYNN	WYTING
WUXIA	WYANDOTTE	WYLES	WYNNS	WYVERN
WUXIAS	WYCH	WYLIECOAT	WYNS	WYVERNS
WUZ	WYCHES	WYLING	WYSIWYG	

X

XANTHAM	XENNIAL	XERARCH	XIPHOIDAL	XYLOIDINE
XANTHAMS	XENNIALS	XERASIA	XIPHOIDS	XYLOIDINS
XANTHAN	XENOBLAST	XERASIAS	XIPHOPAGI	XYLOL
XANTHANS	XENOCRYST	XERIC	XIS	XYLOLOGY
XANTHATE	XENOGAMY	XERICALLY	XOANA	XYLOLS
XANTHATES	XENOGENIC	XERISCAPE	XOANON	XYLOMA
XANTHEIN	XENOGENY	XEROCHASY	XRAY	XYLOMAS
XANTHEINS	XENOGRAFT	XERODERMA	XRAYS	XYLOMATA
XANTHENE	XENOLITH	XEROMA	XU	XYLOMETER
XANTHENES	XENOLITHS	XEROMAS	XYLAN	XYLONIC
XANTHIC	XENOMANIA	XEROMATA	XYLANS	XYLONITE
XANTHIN	XENOMENIA	XEROMORPH	XYLEM	XYLONITES
XANTHINE	XENON	XEROPHAGY	XYLEMS	XYLOPHAGE
XANTHINES	XENONS	XEROPHILE	XYLENE	XYLOPHONE
XANTHINS	XENOPHILE	XEROPHILY	XYLENES	XYLORIMBA
XANTHISM	XENOPHOBE	XEROPHYTE	XYLENOL	XYLOSE
XANTHISMS	XENOPHOBY	XEROSERE	XYLENOLS	XYLOSES
XANTHOMA	XENOPHYA	XEROSERES	XYLIC	XYLOTOMY
XANTHOMAS	XENOPUS	XEROSES	XYLIDIN	XYLYL
XANTHONE	XENOPUSES	XEROSIS	XYLIDINE	XYLYLS
XANTHONES	XENOTIME	XEROSTOMA	XYLIDINES	XYST
XANTHOUS	XENOTIMES	XEROTES	XYLIDINS	XYSTER
XANTHOXYL	XENURINE	XEROTIC	XYLITOL	XYSTERS
XEBEC	XENURINES	XEROX	XYLITOLS	XYSTI
XEBECS	XERAFIN	XEROXED	XYLOCARP	XYSTOI
XED	XERAFINS	XEROXES	XYLOCARPS	XYSTOS
XENIA	XERANSES	XEROXING	XYLOGEN	XYSTS
XENIAL	XERANSIS	XERUS	XYLOGENS	XYSTUS
XENIAS	XERANTIC	XERUSES	XYLOGRAPH	
XENIC	XERAPHIN	XI	XYLOID	
XENIUM	XERAPHINS	XIPHOID	XYLOIDIN	

Y

YA	YAFFED	YAKUZA	YAPOK	YARDLIGHT
YAAR	YAFFING	YALD	YAPOKS	YARDMAN
YAARS	YAFFLE	YALE	YAPON	YARDMEN
YABA	YAFFLES	YALES	YAPONS	YARDS
YABAS	YAFFS	YAM	YAPP	YARDSTICK
YABBA	YAG	YAMALKA	YAPPED	YARDWAND
YABBAS	YAGE	YAMALKAS	YAPPER	YARDWANDS
YABBER	YAGER	YAMEN	YAPPERS	YARDWORK
YABBERED	YAGERS	YAMENS	YAPPIE	YARDWORKS
YABBERING	YAGES	YAMMER	YAPPIER	YARE
YABBERS	YAGGER	YAMMERED	YAPPIES	YARELY
YABBIE	YAGGERS	YAMMERER	YAPPIEST	YARER
YABBIED	YAGI	YAMMERERS	YAPPING	YAREST
YABBIES	YAGIS	YAMMERING	YAPPINGLY	YARFA
YABBY	YAGS	YAMMERS	YAPPINGS	YARFAS
YABBYING	YAH	YAMPIES	YAPPS	YARK
YACCA	YAHOO	YAMPY	YAPPY	YARKED
YACCAS	YAHOOISM	YAMS	YAPS	YARKING
YACHT	YAHOOISMS	YAMULKA	YAPSTER	YARKS
YACHTED	YAHOOS	YAMULKAS	YAPSTERS	YARMELKE
YACHTER	YAHRZEIT	YAMUN	YAQONA	YARMELKES
YACHTERS	YAHRZEITS	YAMUNS	YAQONAS	YARMULKA
YACHTIE	YAHS	YANG	YAR	YARMULKAS
YACHTIES	YAIRD	YANGS	YARAK	YARMULKE
YACHTING	YAIRDS	YANK	YARAKS	YARMULKES
YACHTINGS	YAJE	YANKED	YARCO	YARN
YACHTMAN	YAJES	YANKEE	YARCOS	YARNED
YACHTMEN	YAK	YANKEES	YARD	YARNER
YACHTS	YAKHDAN	YANKER	YARDAGE	YARNERS
YACHTSMAN	YAKHDANS	YANKERS	YARDAGES	YARNING
YACHTSMEN	YAKIMONO	YANKIE	YARDANG	YARNS
YACK	YAKIMONOS	YANKIES	YARDANGS	YARPHA
YACKA	YAKITORI	YANKING	YARDARM	YARPHAS
YACKAS	YAKITORIS	YANKS	YARDARMS	YARR
YACKED	YAKKA	YANQUI	YARDBIRD	YARRAMAN
YACKER	YAKKAS	YANQUIS	YARDBIRDS	YARRAMANS
YACKERS	YAKKED	YANTRA	YARDED	YARRAMEN
YACKING	YAKKER	YANTRAS	YARDER	YARRAN
YACKS	YAKKERS	YAOURT	YARDERS	YARRANS
YAD	YAKKING	YAOURTS	YARDING	YARRED
YADS	YAKOW	YAP	YARDINGS	YARRING
YAE	YAKOWS	YAPOCK	YARDLAND	YARROW
YAFF	YAKS	YAPOCKS	YARDLANDS	YARROWS

YARRS	YAWNER	YEALM	YECH	YELLOWS
YARTA	YAWNERS	YEALMED	YECHIER	YELLOWY
YARTAS	YAWNIER	YEALMING	YECHIEST	YELLS
YARTO	YAWNIEST	YEALMS	YECHS	YELM
YARTOS	YAWNING	YEAN	YECHY	YELMED
YAS	YAWNINGLY	YEANED	YEDE	YELMING
YASHMAC	YAWNINGS	YEANING	YEDES	YELMS
YASHMACS	YAWNS	YEANLING	YEDING	YELP
YASHMAK	YAWNSOME	YEANLINGS	YEED	YELPED
YASHMAKS	YAWNY	YEANS	YEEDING	YELPER
YASMAK	YAWP	YEAR	YEEDS	YELPERS
YASMAKS	YAWPED	YEARBOOK	YEEHAW	YELPING
YATAGAN	YAWPER	YEARBOOKS	YEELIN	YELPINGS
YATAGANS	YAWPERS	YEARD	YEELINS	YELPS
YATAGHAN	YAWPING	YEARDED	YEESH	YELT
YATAGHANS	YAWPINGS	YEARDING	YEET	YELTS
YATE	YAWPS	YEARDS	YEETED	YEMMER
YATES	YAWS	YEAREND	YEETING	YEMMERS
YATTER	YAWY	YEARENDS	YEETS	YEN
YATTERED	YAY	YEARLIES	YEGG	YENNED
YATTERING	YAYS	YEARLING	YEGGMAN	YENNING
YATTERS	YBET	YEARLINGS	YEGGMEN	YENS
YAUD	YBLENT	YEARLONG	YEGGS	YENTA
YAUDS	YBORE	YEARLY	YEH	YENTAS
YAULD	YBOUND	YEARN	YELD	YENTE
YAUP	YBOUNDEN	YEARNED	YELDRING	YENTES
YAUPED	YBRENT	YEARNER	YELDRINGS	YEOMAN
YAUPER	YCLAD	YEARNERS	YELDROCK	YEOMANLY
YAUPERS	YCLED	YEARNING	YELDROCKS	YEOMANRY
YAUPING	YCLEEPE	YEARNINGS	YELK	YEOMEN
YAUPON	YCLEEPED	YEARNS	YELKS	YEOW
YAUPONS	YCLEEPES	YEARS	YELL	YEP
YAUPS	YCLEEPING	YEARSLONG	YELLED	YEPS
YAUTIA	YCLEPED	YEAS	YELLER	YER
YAUTIAS	YCLEPT	YEASAYER	YELLERS	YERBA
YAW	YCOND	YEASAYERS	YELLING	YERBAS
YAWED	YDRAD	YEAST	YELLINGS	YERD
YAWEY	YDRED	YEASTED	YELLOCH	YERDED
YAWIER	YE	YEASTIER	YELLOCHED	YERDING
YAWIEST	YEA	YEASTIEST	YELLOCHS	YERDS
YAWING	YEAD	YEASTILY	YELLOW	YERK
YAWL	YEADING	YEASTING	YELLOWED	YERKED
YAWLED	YEADS	YEASTLESS	YELLOWER	YERKING
YAWLING	YEAH	YEASTLIKE	YELLOWEST	YERKS
YAWLS	YEAHS	YEASTS	YELLOWFIN	YERSINIA
YAWMETER	YEALDON	YEASTY	YELLOWIER	YERSINIAE
YAWMETERS	YEALDONS	YEBO	YELLOWING	YERSINIAS
YAWN	YEALING	YECCH	YELLOWISH	YES
YAWNED	YEALINGS	YECCHS	YELLOWLY	YESES

Y

YESHIVA	YEXING	YIPPIES	YOBBY	YOGURT
YESHIVAH	YEZ	YIPPING	YOBS	YOGURTS
YESHIVAHS	YFERE	YIPPY	YOCK	YOHIMBE
YESHIVAS	YFERES	YIPS	YOCKED	YOHIMBES
YESHIVOT	YGLAUNST	YIRD	YOCKING	YOHIMBINE
YESHIVOTH	YGO	YIRDED	YOCKS	YOICK
YESK	YGOE	YIRDING	YOD	YOICKED
YESKED	YIBBLES	YIRDS	YODE	YOICKING
YESKING	YICKER	YIRK	YODEL	YOICKS
YESKS	YICKERED	YIRKED	YODELED	YOICKSED
YESSED	YICKERING	YIRKING	YODELER	YOICKSES
YESSES	YICKERS	YIRKS	YODELERS	YOICKSING
YESSING	YIDAKI	YIRR	YODELING	YOJAN
YESSIR	YIDAKIS	YIRRED	YODELINGS	YOJANA
YESSIREE	YIELD	YIRRING	YODELLED	YOJANAS
YESSUM	YIELDABLE	YIRRS	YODELLER	YOJANS
YEST	YIELDED	YIRTH	YODELLERS	YOK
YESTER	YIELDER	YIRTHS	YODELLING	YOKE
YESTERDAY	YIELDERS	YITE	YODELS	YOKED
YESTEREVE	YIELDING	YITES	YODH	YOKEL
YESTERN	YIELDINGS	YITIE	YODHS	YOKELESS
YESTREEN	YIELDS	YITIES	YODLE	YOKELISH
YESTREENS	YIKE	YITTEN	YODLED	YOKELS
YESTS	YIKED	YLEM	YODLER	YOKEMATE
YESTY	YIKES	YLEMS	YODLERS	YOKEMATES
YET	YIKING	YLIKE	YODLES	YOKER
YETI	YIKKER	YLKE	YODLING	YOKERED
YETIS	YIKKERED	YLKES	YODS	YOKERING
YETT	YIKKERING	YMOLT	YOGA	YOKERS
YETTIE	YIKKERS	YMOLTEN	YOGAS	YOKES
YETTIES	YILL	YMPE	YOGEE	YOKING
YETTS	YILLED	YMPES	YOGEES	YOKINGS
YEUK	YILLING	YMPING	YOGH	YOKKED
YEUKED	YILLS	YMPT	YOGHOURT	YOKKING
YEUKIER	YIN	YNAMBU	YOGHOURTS	YOKOZUNA
YEUKIEST	YINCE	YNAMBUS	YOGHS	YOKOZUNAS
YEUKING	YINDIE	YO	YOGHURT	YOKS
YEUKS	YINDIES	YOB	YOGHURTS	YOKUL
YEUKY	YINGYANG	YOBBERIES	YOGI	YOLD
YEVE	YINGYANGS	YOBBERY	YOGIC	YOLDRING
YEVEN	YINS	YOBBIER	YOGIN	YOLDRINGS
YEVES	YIP	YOBBIEST	YOGINI	YOLK
YEVING	YIPE	YOBBISH	YOGINIS	YOLKED
YEW	YIPES	YOBBISHLY	YOGINS	YOLKIER
YEWEN	YIPPED	YOBBISM	YOGIS	YOLKIEST
YEWS	YIPPEE	YOBBISMS	YOGISM	YOLKLESS
YEX	YIPPER	YOBBO	YOGISMS	YOLKS
YEXED	YIPPERS	YOBBOES	YOGOURT	YOLKY
YEXES	YIPPIE	YOBBOS	YOGOURTS	YOM

Y

YOMIM	YOUKS	YOWL	YUCA	YULETIDE
YOMP	YOUNG	YOWLED	YUCAS	YULETIDES
YOMPED	YOUNGER	YOWLER	YUCCA	YUM
YOMPING	YOUNGERS	YOWLERS	YUCCAS	YUMBERRY
YOMPS	YOUNGEST	YOWLEY	YUCCH	YUMMIER
YON	YOUNGISH	YOWLEYS	YUCH	YUMMIES
YOND	YOUNGLING	YOWLING	YUCK	YUMMIEST
YONDER	YOUNGLY	YOWLINGS	YUCKED	YUMMINESS
YONDERLY	YOUNGNESS	YOWLS	YUCKER	YUMMO
YONDERS	YOUNGS	YOWS	YUCKERS	YUMMY
YONI	YOUNGSTER	YOWZA	YUCKIER	YUMP
YONIC	YOUNGTH	YPERITE	YUCKIEST	YUMPED
YONIS	YOUNGTHLY	YPERITES	YUCKINESS	YUMPIE
YONKER	YOUNGTHS	YPIGHT	YUCKING	YUMPIES
YONKERS	YOUNKER	YPLAST	YUCKO	YUMPING
YONKS	YOUNKERS	YPLIGHT	YUCKS	YUMPS
YONNIE	YOUPON	YPSILOID	YUCKY	YUNX
YONNIES	YOUPONS	YPSILON	YUFT	YUNXES
YONT	YOUR	YPSILONS	YUFTS	YUP
YOOF	YOURN	YRAPT	YUG	YUPON
YOOFS	YOURS	YRAVISHED	YUGA	YUPONS
YOOP	YOURSELF	YRENT	YUGARIE	YUPPIE
YOOPS	YOURT	YRIVD	YUGARIES	YUPPIEDOM
YOPPER	YOURTS	YRNEH	YUGAS	YUPPIEISH
YOPPERS	YOUS	YRNEHS	YUGS	YUPPIES
YORE	YOUSE	YSAME	YUK	YUPPIFIED
YORES	YOUTH	YSHEND	YUKATA	YUPPIFIES
YORK	YOUTHEN	YSHENDING	YUKATAS	YUPPIFY
YORKED	YOUTHENED	YSHENDS	YUKE	YUPPY
YORKER	YOUTHENS	YSHENT	YUKED	YUPPYDOM
YORKERS	YOUTHFUL	YSLAKED	YUKES	YUPPYDOMS
YORKIE	YOUTHHEAD	YTOST	YUKIER	YUPS
YORKIES	YOUTHHOOD	YTTERBIA	YUKIEST	YUPSTER
YORKING	YOUTHIER	YTTERBIAS	YUKING	YUPSTERS
YORKS	YOUTHIEST	YTTERBIC	YUKKED	YURT
YORLING	YOUTHLESS	YTTERBITE	YUKKIER	YURTA
YORLINGS	YOUTHLY	YTTERBIUM	YUKKIEST	YURTAS
YORP	YOUTHS	YTTERBOUS	YUKKING	YURTS
YORPED	YOUTHSOME	YTTRIA	YUKKY	YUS
YORPING	YOUTHY	YTTRIAS	YUKO	YUTZ
YORPS	YOW	YTTRIC	YUKOS	YUTZES
YOTE	YOWE	YTTRIOUS	YUKS	YUZU
YOTTABYTE	YOWED	YTTRIUM	YUKY	YUZUS
YOU	YOWES	YTTRIUMS	YULAN	YWIS
YOUK	YOWIE	YU	YULANS	YWROKE
YOUKED	YOWIES	YUAN	YULE	
YOUKING	YOWING	YUANS	YULES	

Z

ZA	ZAIKAI	ZANDER	ZAPTIEH	ZEALOTS
ZAATAR	ZAIKAIS	ZANDERS	ZAPTIEHS	ZEALOUS
ZAATARS	ZAIRE	ZANELLA	ZARAPE	ZEALOUSLY
ZABAIONE	ZAIRES	ZANELLAS	ZARAPES	ZEALS
ZABAIONES	ZAITECH	ZANIED	ZARATITE	ZEAS
ZABAJONE	ZAITECHS	ZANIER	ZARATITES	ZEATIN
ZABAJONES	ZAKAT	ZANIES	ZAREBA	ZEATINS
ZABETA	ZAKATS	ZANIEST	ZAREBAS	ZEBEC
ZABETAS	ZAKOUSKA	ZANILY	ZAREEBA	ZEBECK
ZABRA	ZAKOUSKI	ZANINESS	ZAREEBAS	ZEBECKS
ZABRAS	ZAKUSKA	ZANJA	ZARF	ZEBECS
ZABTIEH	ZAKUSKI	ZANJAS	ZARFS	ZEBRA
ZABTIEHS	ZAMAN	ZANJERO	ZARI	ZEBRAFISH
ZACATON	ZAMANG	ZANJEROS	ZARIBA	ZEBRAIC
ZACATONS	ZAMANGS	ZANTE	ZARIBAS	ZEBRANO
ZACK	ZAMANS	ZANTES	ZARIS	ZEBRANOS
ZACKS	ZAMARRA	ZANTEWOOD	ZARNEC	ZEBRAS
ZADDICK	ZAMARRAS	ZANTHOXYL	ZARNECS	ZEBRASS
ZADDICKS	ZAMARRO	ZANY	ZARNICH	ZEBRASSES
ZADDIK	ZAMARROS	ZANYING	ZARNICHS	ZEBRAWOOD
ZADDIKIM	ZAMBOMBA	ZANYISH	ZARZUELA	ZEBRINA
ZADDIKS	ZAMBOMBAS	ZANYISM	ZARZUELAS	ZEBRINAS
ZAFFAR	ZAMBOORAK	ZANYISMS	ZAS	ZEBRINE
ZAFFARS	ZAMBUCK	ZANZA	ZASTRUGA	ZEBRINES
ZAFFER	ZAMBUCKS	ZANZAS	ZASTRUGI	ZEBRINNY
ZAFFERS	ZAMBUK	ZANZE	ZATI	ZEBROID
ZAFFIR	ZAMBUKS	ZANZES	ZATIS	ZEBRULA
ZAFFIRS	ZAMIA	ZAP	ZAX	ZEBRULAS
ZAFFRE	ZAMIAS	ZAPATA	ZAXES	ZEBRULE
ZAFFRES	ZAMINDAR	ZAPATEADO	ZAYIN	ZEBRULES
ZAFTIG	ZAMINDARI	ZAPATEO	ZAYINS	ZEBU
ZAG	ZAMINDARS	ZAPATEOS	ZAZEN	ZEBUB
ZAGGED	ZAMINDARY	ZAPOTILLA	ZAZENS	ZEBUBS
ZAGGING	ZAMOUSE	ZAPPED	ZE	ZEBUS
ZAGS	ZAMOUSES	ZAPPER	ZEA	ZECCHIN
ZAIBATSU	ZAMPOGNA	ZAPPERS	ZEAL	ZECCHINE
ZAIBATSUS	ZAMPOGNAS	ZAPPIER	ZEALANT	ZECCHINES
ZAIDA	ZAMPONE	ZAPPIEST	ZEALANTS	ZECCHINI
ZAIDAS	ZAMPONI	ZAPPING	ZEALFUL	ZECCHINO
ZAIDEH	ZAMZAWED	ZAPPY	ZEALLESS	ZECCHINOS
ZAIDEHS	ZANAMIVIR	ZAPS	ZEALOT	ZECCHINS
ZAIDIES	ZANANA	ZAPTIAH	ZEALOTISM	ZECHIN
ZAIDY	ZANANAS	ZAPTIAHS	ZEALOTRY	ZECHINS

ZED	ZENS	ZEUGMA	ZIKURAT	ZINDABAD
ZEDA	ZEOLITE	ZEUGMAS	ZIKURATS	ZINE
ZEDAS	ZEOLITES	ZEUGMATIC	ZILA	ZINEB
ZEDOARIES	ZEOLITIC	ZEUXITE	ZILAS	ZINEBS
ZEDOARY	ZEP	ZEUXITES	ZILCH	ZINES
ZEDONK	ZEPHYR	ZEX	ZILCHES	ZINFANDEL
ZEDONKS	ZEPHYRS	ZEXES	ZILL	ZING
ZEDS	ZEPPELIN	ZEZE	ZILLA	ZINGANI
ZEE	ZEPPELINS	ZEZES	ZILLAH	ZINGANO
ZEEDONK	ZEPPOLE	ZHO	ZILLAHS	ZINGARA
ZEEDONKS	ZEPPOLES	ZHOMO	ZILLAS	ZINGARE
ZEES	ZEPPOLI	ZHOMOS	ZILLION	ZINGARI
ZEIN	ZEPPOLIS	ZHOOSH	ZILLIONS	ZINGARO
ZEINS	ZEPS	ZHOOSHED	ZILLIONTH	ZINGED
ZEITGEBER	ZERDA	ZHOOSHES	ZILLS	ZINGEL
ZEITGEIST	ZERDAS	ZHOOSHING	ZIMB	ZINGELS
ZEK	ZEREBA	ZHOS	ZIMBI	ZINGER
ZEKS	ZEREBAS	ZHUZH	ZIMBIS	ZINGERS
ZEL	ZERIBA	ZHUZHED	ZIMBS	ZINGIBER
ZELANT	ZERIBAS	ZHUZHES	ZIMOCCA	ZINGIBERS
ZELANTS	ZERK	ZHUZHING	ZIMOCCAS	ZINGIER
ZELATOR	ZERKS	ZIBELINE	ZIN	ZINGIEST
ZELATORS	ZERO	ZIBELINES	ZINC	ZINGING
ZELATRICE	ZEROED	ZIBELLINE	ZINCATE	ZINGS
ZELATRIX	ZEROES	ZIBET	ZINCATES	ZINGY
ZELKOVA	ZEROING	ZIBETH	ZINCED	ZINKE
ZELKOVAS	ZEROS	ZIBETHS	ZINCIC	ZINKED
ZELOSO	ZEROTH	ZIBETS	ZINCIER	ZINKENITE
ZELOTYPIA	ZERUMBET	ZIFF	ZINCIEST	ZINKES
ZELS	ZERUMBETS	ZIFFIUS	ZINCIFIED	ZINKIER
ZEMINDAR	ZEST	ZIFFIUSES	ZINCIFIES	ZINKIEST
ZEMINDARI	ZESTED	ZIFFS	ZINCIFY	ZINKIFIED
ZEMINDARS	ZESTER	ZIG	ZINCING	ZINKIFIES
ZEMINDARY	ZESTERS	ZIGAN	ZINCITE	ZINKIFY
ZEMSTVA	ZESTFUL	ZIGANKA	ZINCITES	ZINKING
ZEMSTVO	ZESTFULLY	ZIGANKAS	ZINCKED	ZINKY
ZEMSTVOS	ZESTIER	ZIGANS	ZINCKIER	ZINNIA
ZEN	ZESTIEST	ZIGGED	ZINCKIEST	ZINNIAS
ZENAIDA	ZESTILY	ZIGGING	ZINCKIFY	ZINS
ZENAIDAS	ZESTINESS	ZIGGURAT	ZINCKING	ZIP
ZENANA	ZESTING	ZIGGURATS	ZINCKY	ZIPLESS
ZENANAS	ZESTLESS	ZIGS	ZINCO	ZIPLINE
ZENDIK	ZESTS	ZIGZAG	ZINCODE	ZIPLINED
ZENDIKS	ZESTY	ZIGZAGGED	ZINCODES	ZIPLINES
ZENDO	ZETA	ZIGZAGGER	ZINCOID	ZIPLINING
ZENDOS	ZETAS	ZIGZAGGY	ZINCOS	ZIPLOCK
ZENITH	ZETETIC	ZIGZAGS	ZINCOUS	ZIPLOCKED
ZENITHAL	ZETETICS	ZIKKURAT	ZINCS	ZIPLOCKS
ZENITHS	ZETTABYTE	ZIKKURATS	ZINCY	ZIPOLA

ZIPOLAS	ZIZZ	ZOIATRICS	ZONKING	ZOOGONIES
ZIPPED	ZIZZED	ZOIC	ZONKS	ZOOGONOUS
ZIPPER	ZIZZES	ZOISITE	ZONOID	ZOOGONY
ZIPPERED	ZIZZING	ZOISITES	ZONOIDS	ZOOGRAFT
ZIPPERING	ZIZZLE	ZOISM	ZONULA	ZOOGRAFTS
ZIPPERS	ZIZZLED	ZOISMS	ZONULAE	ZOOGRAPHY
ZIPPIER	ZIZZLES	ZOIST	ZONULAR	ZOOID
ZIPPIEST	ZIZZLING	ZOISTS	ZONULAS	ZOOIDAL
ZIPPILY	ZLOTE	ZOL	ZONULE	ZOOIDS
ZIPPINESS	ZLOTIES	ZOLPIDEM	ZONULES	ZOOIER
ZIPPING	ZLOTY	ZOLPIDEMS	ZONULET	ZOOIEST
ZIPPO	ZLOTYCH	ZOLS	ZONULETS	ZOOKEEPER
ZIPPOS	ZLOTYS	ZOMBI	ZONURE	ZOOKS
ZIPPY	ZO	ZOMBIE	ZONURES	ZOOLATER
ZIPS	ZOA	ZOMBIES	ZOO	ZOOLATERS
ZIPTOP	ZOAEA	ZOMBIFIED	ZOOBIOTIC	ZOOLATRIA
ZIPWIRE	ZOAEAE	ZOMBIFIES	ZOOBLAST	ZOOLATRY
ZIPWIRES	ZOAEAS	ZOMBIFY	ZOOBLASTS	ZOOLITE
ZIRAM	ZOARIA	ZOMBIISM	ZOOCHORE	ZOOLITES
ZIRAMS	ZOARIAL	ZOMBIISMS	ZOOCHORES	ZOOLITH
ZIRCALLOY	ZOARIUM	ZOMBIS	ZOOCHORY	ZOOLITHIC
ZIRCALOY	ZOBO	ZOMBOID	ZOOCYTIA	ZOOLITHS
ZIRCALOYS	ZOBOS	ZOMBORUK	ZOOCYTIUM	ZOOLITIC
ZIRCON	ZOBU	ZOMBORUKS	ZOODLE	ZOOLOGIC
ZIRCONIA	ZOBUS	ZONA	ZOODLES	ZOOLOGIES
ZIRCONIAS	ZOCALO	ZONAE	ZOOEA	ZOOLOGIST
ZIRCONIC	ZOCALOS	ZONAL	ZOOEAE	ZOOLOGY
ZIRCONIUM	ZOCCO	ZONALLY	ZOOEAL	ZOOM
ZIRCONS	ZOCCOLO	ZONARY	ZOOEAS	ZOOMABLE
ZIRICOTE	ZOCCOLOS	ZONATE	ZOOECIA	ZOOMANCY
ZIRICOTES	ZOCCOS	ZONATED	ZOOECIUM	ZOOMANIA
ZIT	ZODIAC	ZONATION	ZOOEY	ZOOMANIAS
ZITE	ZODIACAL	ZONATIONS	ZOOGAMETE	ZOOMANTIC
ZITHER	ZODIACS	ZONDA	ZOOGAMIES	ZOOMED
ZITHERIST	ZOEA	ZONDAS	ZOOGAMOUS	ZOOMER
ZITHERN	ZOEAE	ZONE	ZOOGAMY	ZOOMERS
ZITHERNS	ZOEAL	ZONED	ZOOGENIC	ZOOMETRIC
ZITHERS	ZOEAS	ZONELESS	ZOOGENIES	ZOOMETRY
ZITI	ZOECHROME	ZONER	ZOOGENOUS	ZOOMING
ZITIS	ZOECIA	ZONERS	ZOOGENY	ZOOMORPH
ZITS	ZOECIUM	ZONES	ZOOGLEA	ZOOMORPHS
ZIZ	ZOEFORM	ZONETIME	ZOOGLEAE	ZOOMORPHY
ZIZANIA	ZOETIC	ZONETIMES	ZOOGLEAL	ZOOMS
ZIZANIAS	ZOETROPE	ZONING	ZOOGLEAS	ZOON
ZIZEL	ZOETROPES	ZONINGS	ZOOGLOEA	ZOONAL
ZIZELS	ZOETROPIC	ZONK	ZOOGLOEAE	ZOONED
ZIZIT	ZOFTIG	ZONKED	ZOOGLOEAL	ZOONIC
ZIZITH	ZOIATRIA	ZONKEY	ZOOGLOEAS	ZOONING
ZIZYPHUS	ZOIATRIAS	ZONKEYS	ZOOGLOEIC	ZOONITE

Z

ZOONITES	ZOOSPORIC	ZORILLE	ZUMBOORUK	ZYGOTES
ZOONITIC	ZOOSTEROL	ZORILLES	ZUPA	ZYGOTIC
ZOONOMIA	ZOOT	ZORILLO	ZUPAN	ZYLONITE
ZOONOMIAS	ZOOTAXIES	ZORILLOS	ZUPANS	ZYLONITES
ZOONOMIC	ZOOTAXY	ZORILS	ZUPAS	ZYMASE
ZOONOMIES	ZOOTECHNY	ZORINO	ZUPPA	ZYMASES
ZOONOMIST	ZOOTHECIA	ZORINOS	ZUPPAS	ZYME
ZOONOMY	ZOOTHEISM	ZORIS	ZURF	ZYMES
ZOONOSES	ZOOTHOME	ZORRO	ZURFS	ZYMIC
ZOONOSIS	ZOOTHOMES	ZORROS	ZUZ	ZYMITE
ZOONOTIC	ZOOTIER	ZOS	ZUZIM	ZYMITES
ZOONS	ZOOTIEST	ZOSTER	ZUZZIM	ZYMOGEN
ZOOPATHY	ZOOTOMIC	ZOSTERS	ZWANZIGER	ZYMOGENE
ZOOPERAL	ZOOTOMIES	ZOUAVE	ZWIEBACK	ZYMOGENES
ZOOPERIES	ZOOTOMIST	ZOUAVES	ZWIEBACKS	ZYMOGENIC
ZOOPERIST	ZOOTOMY	ZOUK	ZYDECO	ZYMOGENS
ZOOPERY	ZOOTOXIC	ZOUKS	ZYDECOS	ZYMOGRAM
ZOOPHAGAN	ZOOTOXIN	ZOUNDS	ZYGA	ZYMOGRAMS
ZOOPHAGY	ZOOTOXINS	ZOWEE	ZYGAENID	ZYMOID
ZOOPHILE	ZOOTROPE	ZOWIE	ZYGAENOID	ZYMOLOGIC
ZOOPHILES	ZOOTROPES	ZOYSIA	ZYGAL	ZYMOLOGY
ZOOPHILIA	ZOOTROPHY	ZOYSIAS	ZYGANTRA	ZYMOLYSES
ZOOPHILIC	ZOOTY	ZUCCHETTI	ZYGANTRUM	ZYMOLYSIS
ZOOPHILY	ZOOTYPE	ZUCCHETTO	ZYGOCACTI	ZYMOLYTIC
ZOOPHOBE	ZOOTYPES	ZUCCHINI	ZYGODONT	ZYMOME
ZOOPHOBES	ZOOTYPIC	ZUCCHINIS	ZYGOID	ZYMOMES
ZOOPHOBIA	ZOOZOO	ZUCHETTA	ZYGOMA	ZYMOMETER
ZOOPHORI	ZOOZOOS	ZUCHETTAS	ZYGOMAS	ZYMOSAN
ZOOPHORIC	ZOPILOTE	ZUCHETTO	ZYGOMATA	ZYMOSANS
ZOOPHORUS	ZOPILOTES	ZUCHETTOS	ZYGOMATIC	ZYMOSES
ZOOPHYTE	ZOPPA	ZUFFOLI	ZYGON	ZYMOSIS
ZOOPHYTES	ZOPPO	ZUFFOLO	ZYGOPHYTE	ZYMOTIC
ZOOPHYTIC	ZORBING	ZUFOLI	ZYGOSE	ZYMOTICS
ZOOPLASTY	ZORBINGS	ZUFOLO	ZYGOSES	ZYMURGIES
ZOOS	ZORBONAUT	ZUFOLOS	ZYGOSIS	ZYMURGY
ZOOSCOPIC	ZORGITE	ZUGZWANG	ZYGOSITY	ZYTHUM
ZOOSCOPY	ZORGITES	ZUGZWANGS	ZYGOSPERM	ZYTHUMS
ZOOSPERM	ZORI	ZUKE	ZYGOSPORE	ZYZZYVA
ZOOSPERMS	ZORIL	ZUKES	ZYGOTE	ZYZZYVAS
ZOOSPORE	ZORILLA	ZULU	ZYGOTENE	ZZZ
ZOOSPORES	ZORILLAS	ZULUS	ZYGOTENES	ZZZS

Z

TEN TO FIFTEEN LETTER WORDS

A

AARDWOLVES	ABERNETHIES	ABJURATIONS	ABONNEMENTS	ABROGATORS
ABACTERIAL	ABERRANCES	ABLACTATION	ABORIGINAL	ABRUPTIONS
ABACTINALLY	ABERRANCIES	ABLACTATIONS	ABORIGINALISM	ABRUPTNESS
ABANDONEDLY	ABERRANTLY	ABLATITIOUS	ABORIGINALISMS	ABRUPTNESSES
ABANDONEES	ABERRATING	ABLATIVELY	ABORIGINALITIES	ABSCESSING
ABANDONERS	ABERRATION	ABLUTIONARY	ABORIGINALITY	ABSCINDING
ABANDONING	ABERRATIONAL	ABLUTOMANE	ABORIGINALLY	ABSCISSINS
ABANDONMENT	ABERRATIONS	ABLUTOMANES	ABORIGINALS	ABSCISSION
ABANDONMENTS	ABEYANCIES	ABNEGATING	ABORIGINES	ABSCISSIONS
ABANDONWARE	ABHOMINABLE	ABNEGATION	ABORTICIDE	ABSCONDENCE
ABANDONWARES	ABHORRENCE	ABNEGATIONS	ABORTICIDES	ABSCONDENCES
ABASEMENTS	ABHORRENCES	ABNEGATORS	ABORTIFACIENT	ABSCONDERS
ABASHMENTS	ABHORRENCIES	ABNORMALISM	ABORTIFACIENTS	ABSCONDING
ABATEMENTS	ABHORRENCY	ABNORMALISMS	ABORTIONAL	ABSCONDINGS
ABBOTSHIPS	ABHORRENTLY	ABNORMALITIES	ABORTIONIST	ABSEILINGS
ABBREVIATE	ABHORRINGS	ABNORMALITY	ABORTIONISTS	ABSENTEEISM
ABBREVIATED	ABIOGENESES	ABNORMALLY	ABORTIVELY	ABSENTEEISMS
ABBREVIATES	ABIOGENESIS	ABNORMITIES	ABORTIVENESS	ABSENTMINDED
ABBREVIATING	ABIOGENETIC	ABODEMENTS	ABORTIVENESSES	ABSENTMINDEDLY
ABBREVIATION	ABIOGENETICALLY	ABOLISHABLE	ABORTUARIES	ABSINTHIATED
ABBREVIATIONS	ABIOGENICALLY	ABOLISHERS	ABOVEBOARD	ABSINTHISM
ABBREVIATOR	ABIOGENIST	ABOLISHING	ABOVEGROUND	ABSINTHISMS
ABBREVIATORS	ABIOGENISTS	ABOLISHMENT	ABRACADABRA	ABSOLUTELY
ABBREVIATORY	ABIOLOGICAL	ABOLISHMENTS	ABRACADABRAS	ABSOLUTENESS
ABBREVIATURE	ABIOTICALLY	ABOLITIONAL	ABRANCHIAL	ABSOLUTENESSES
ABBREVIATURES	ABIOTROPHIC	ABOLITIONARY	ABRANCHIATE	ABSOLUTEST
ABCOULOMBS	ABIOTROPHIES	ABOLITIONISM	ABRASIVELY	ABSOLUTION
ABDICATING	ABIOTROPHY	ABOLITIONISMS	ABRASIVENESS	ABSOLUTIONS
ABDICATION	ABIRRITANT	ABOLITIONIST	ABRASIVENESSES	ABSOLUTISE
ABDICATIONS	ABIRRITANTS	ABOLITIONISTS	ABREACTING	ABSOLUTISED
ABDICATIVE	ABIRRITATE	ABOLITIONS	ABREACTION	ABSOLUTISES
ABDICATORS	ABIRRITATED	ABOMINABLE	ABREACTIONS	ABSOLUTISING
ABDOMINALLY	ABIRRITATES	ABOMINABLENESS	ABREACTIVE	ABSOLUTISM
ABDOMINALS	ABIRRITATING	ABOMINABLY	ABRIDGABLE	ABSOLUTISMS
ABDOMINOPLASTY	ABITURIENT	ABOMINATED	ABRIDGEABLE	ABSOLUTIST
ABDOMINOUS	ABITURIENTS	ABOMINATES	ABRIDGEMENT	ABSOLUTISTIC
ABDUCENTES	ABJECTIONS	ABOMINATING	ABRIDGEMENTS	ABSOLUTISTS
ABDUCTIONS	ABJECTNESS	ABOMINATION	ABRIDGMENT	ABSOLUTIVE
ABDUCTORES	ABJECTNESSES	ABOMINATIONS	ABRIDGMENTS	ABSOLUTIVES
ABECEDARIAN	ABJOINTING	ABOMINATOR	ABROGATING	ABSOLUTIZE
ABECEDARIANS	ABJUNCTION	ABOMINATORS	ABROGATION	ABSOLUTIZED
ABERDEVINE	ABJUNCTIONS	ABONDANCES	ABROGATIONS	ABSOLUTIZES
ABERDEVINES	ABJURATION	ABONNEMENT	ABROGATIVE	ABSOLUTIZING

ABSOLUTORY	ABSTERGING	ABUNDANCIES	ACCELERANDO	ACCESSARILY
ABSOLVABLE	ABSTERSION	ABUNDANTLY	ACCELERANDOS	ACCESSARINESS
ABSOLVENTS	ABSTERSIONS	ABUSIVENESS	ACCELERANT	ACCESSARINESSES
ABSOLVITOR	ABSTERSIVE	ABUSIVENESSES	ACCELERANTS	ACCESSIBILITIES
ABSOLVITORS	ABSTERSIVES	ABYSSOPELAGIC	ACCELERATE	ACCESSIBILITY
ABSORBABILITIES	ABSTINENCE	ACADEMICAL	ACCELERATED	ACCESSIBLE
ABSORBABILITY	ABSTINENCES	ACADEMICALISM	ACCELERATES	ACCESSIBLENESS
ABSORBABLE	ABSTINENCIES	ACADEMICALISMS	ACCELERATING	ACCESSIBLY
ABSORBANCE	ABSTINENCY	ACADEMICALLY	ACCELERATINGLY	ACCESSIONAL
ABSORBANCES	ABSTINENTLY	ACADEMICALS	ACCELERATION	ACCESSIONED
ABSORBANCIES	ABSTRACTABLE	ACADEMICIAN	ACCELERATIONS	ACCESSIONING
ABSORBANCY	ABSTRACTED	ACADEMICIANS	ACCELERATIVE	ACCESSIONS
ABSORBANTS	ABSTRACTEDLY	ACADEMICISM	ACCELERATOR	ACCESSORIAL
ABSORBATES	ABSTRACTEDNESS	ACADEMICISMS	ACCELERATORS	ACCESSORIES
ABSORBEDLY	ABSTRACTER	ACADEMISMS	ACCELERATORY	ACCESSORII
ABSORBEFACIENT	ABSTRACTERS	ACADEMISTS	ACCELEROMETER	ACCESSORILY
ABSORBEFACIENTS	ABSTRACTEST	ACALCULIAS	ACCELEROMETERS	ACCESSORINESS
ABSORBENCIES	ABSTRACTING	ACALEPHANS	ACCENSIONS	ACCESSORINESSES
ABSORBENCY	ABSTRACTION	ACANACEOUS	ACCENTLESS	ACCESSORISE
ABSORBENTS	ABSTRACTIONAL	ACANTHACEOUS	ACCENTUALITIES	ACCESSORISED
ABSORBINGLY	ABSTRACTIONISM	ACANTHOCEPHALAN	ACCENTUALITY	ACCESSORISES
ABSORPTANCE	ABSTRACTIONISMS	ACANTHUSES	ACCENTUALLY	ACCESSORISING
ABSORPTANCES	ABSTRACTIONIST	ACARICIDAL	ACCENTUATE	ACCESSORIUS
ABSORPTIOMETER	ABSTRACTIONISTS	ACARICIDES	ACCENTUATED	ACCESSORIZE
ABSORPTIOMETERS	ABSTRACTIONS	ACARIDEANS	ACCENTUATES	ACCESSORIZED
ABSORPTION	ABSTRACTIVE	ACARIDIANS	ACCENTUATING	ACCESSORIZES
ABSORPTIONS	ABSTRACTIVELY	ACARIDOMATIA	ACCENTUATION	ACCESSORIZING
ABSORPTIVE	ABSTRACTIVES	ACARIDOMATIUM	ACCENTUATIONS	ACCIACCATURA
ABSORPTIVENESS	ABSTRACTLY	ACARODOMATIA	ACCEPTABILITIES	ACCIACCATURAS
ABSORPTIVITIES	ABSTRACTNESS	ACARODOMATIUM	ACCEPTABILITY	ACCIACCATURE
ABSORPTIVITY	ABSTRACTNESSES	ACAROLOGIES	ACCEPTABLE	ACCIDENCES
ABSQUATULATE	ABSTRACTOR	ACAROLOGIST	ACCEPTABLENESS	ACCIDENTAL
ABSQUATULATED	ABSTRACTORS	ACAROLOGISTS	ACCEPTABLY	ACCIDENTALISM
ABSQUATULATES	ABSTRICTED	ACAROPHILIES	ACCEPTANCE	ACCIDENTALISMS
ABSQUATULATING	ABSTRICTING	ACAROPHILY	ACCEPTANCES	ACCIDENTALITIES
ABSTAINERS	ABSTRICTION	ACARPELLOUS	ACCEPTANCIES	ACCIDENTALITY
ABSTAINING	ABSTRICTIONS	ACARPELOUS	ACCEPTANCY	ACCIDENTALLY
ABSTEMIOUS	ABSTRUSELY	ACATALECTIC	ACCEPTANTS	ACCIDENTALNESS
ABSTEMIOUSLY	ABSTRUSENESS	ACATALECTICS	ACCEPTATION	ACCIDENTALS
ABSTEMIOUSNESS	ABSTRUSENESSES	ACATALEPSIES	ACCEPTATIONS	ACCIDENTED
ABSTENTION	ABSTRUSEST	ACATALEPSY	ACCEPTEDLY	ACCIDENTLY
ABSTENTIONISM	ABSTRUSITIES	ACATALEPTIC	ACCEPTILATION	ACCIDENTOLOGIES
ABSTENTIONISMS	ABSTRUSITY	ACATALEPTICS	ACCEPTILATIONS	ACCIDENTOLOGY
ABSTENTIONIST	ABSURDISMS	ACATAMATHESIA	ACCEPTINGLY	ACCIPITERS
ABSTENTIONISTS	ABSURDISTS	ACATAMATHESIAS	ACCEPTINGNESS	ACCIPITRAL
ABSTENTIONS	ABSURDITIES	ACATHISIAS	ACCEPTINGNESSES	ACCIPITRINE
ABSTENTIOUS	ABSURDNESS	ACAULESCENT	ACCEPTIVITIES	ACCIPITRINES
ABSTERGENT	ABSURDNESSES	ACCEDENCES	ACCEPTIVITY	ACCLAIMERS
ABSTERGENTS	ABUNDANCES	ACCELERABLE	ACCESSARIES	ACCLAIMING

ACCLAMATION	ACCOMPANIST	ACCOUNTINGS	ACCUMULATIVELY	ACETANILIDES
ACCLAMATIONS	ACCOMPANISTS	ACCOUPLEMENT	ACCUMULATOR	ACETANILIDS
ACCLAMATORY	ACCOMPANYING	ACCOUPLEMENTS	ACCUMULATORS	ACETAZOLAMIDE
ACCLIMATABLE	ACCOMPANYIST	ACCOURAGED	ACCURACIES	ACETAZOLAMIDES
ACCLIMATATION	ACCOMPANYISTS	ACCOURAGES	ACCURATELY	ACETIFICATION
ACCLIMATATIONS	ACCOMPLICE	ACCOURAGING	ACCURATENESS	ACETIFICATIONS
ACCLIMATED	ACCOMPLICES	ACCOURTING	ACCURATENESSES	ACETIFIERS
ACCLIMATES	ACCOMPLISH	ACCOUSTREMENT	ACCURSEDLY	ACETIFYING
ACCLIMATING	ACCOMPLISHABLE	ACCOUSTREMENTS	ACCURSEDNESS	ACETOACETIC
ACCLIMATION	ACCOMPLISHED	ACCOUTERED	ACCURSEDNESSES	ACETOMETER
ACCLIMATIONS	ACCOMPLISHER	ACCOUTERING	ACCUSATION	ACETOMETERS
ACCLIMATISABLE	ACCOMPLISHERS	ACCOUTERMENT	ACCUSATIONS	ACETONAEMIA
ACCLIMATISATION	ACCOMPLISHES	ACCOUTERMENTS	ACCUSATIVAL	ACETONAEMIAS
ACCLIMATISE	ACCOMPLISHING	ACCOUTREMENT	ACCUSATIVE	ACETONEMIA
ACCLIMATISED	ACCOMPLISHMENT	ACCOUTREMENTS	ACCUSATIVELY	ACETONEMIAS
ACCLIMATISER	ACCOMPLISHMENTS	ACCOUTRING	ACCUSATIVES	ACETONITRILE
ACCLIMATISERS	ACCOMPTABLE	ACCREDITABLE	ACCUSATORIAL	ACETONITRILES
ACCLIMATISES	ACCOMPTANT	ACCREDITATION	ACCUSATORY	ACETONURIA
ACCLIMATISING	ACCOMPTANTS	ACCREDITATIONS	ACCUSEMENT	ACETONURIAS
ACCLIMATIZABLE	ACCOMPTING	ACCREDITED	ACCUSEMENTS	ACETOPHENETIDIN
ACCLIMATIZATION	ACCORAGING	ACCREDITING	ACCUSINGLY	ACETYLATED
ACCLIMATIZE	ACCORDABLE	ACCRESCENCE	ACCUSTOMARY	ACETYLATES
ACCLIMATIZED	ACCORDANCE	ACCRESCENCES	ACCUSTOMATION	ACETYLATING
ACCLIMATIZER	ACCORDANCES	ACCRESCENT	ACCUSTOMATIONS	ACETYLATION
ACCLIMATIZERS	ACCORDANCIES	ACCRETIONARY	ACCUSTOMED	ACETYLATIONS
ACCLIMATIZES	ACCORDANCY	ACCRETIONS	ACCUSTOMEDNESS	ACETYLATIVE
ACCLIMATIZING	ACCORDANTLY	ACCRUEMENT	ACCUSTOMING	ACETYLCHOLINE
ACCLIVITIES	ACCORDINGLY	ACCRUEMENTS	ACCUSTREMENT	ACETYLCHOLINES
ACCLIVITOUS	ACCORDIONIST	ACCUBATION	ACCUSTREMENTS	ACETYLENES
ACCOASTING	ACCORDIONISTS	ACCUBATIONS	ACEPHALOUS	ACETYLENIC
ACCOLADING	ACCORDIONS	ACCULTURAL	ACERACEOUS	ACETYLIDES
ACCOMMODABLE	ACCOSTABLE	ACCULTURATE	ACERBATING	ACETYLSALICYLIC
ACCOMMODATE	ACCOUCHEMENT	ACCULTURATED	ACERBICALLY	ACHAENIUMS
ACCOMMODATED	ACCOUCHEMENTS	ACCULTURATES	ACERBITIES	ACHAENOCARP
ACCOMMODATES	ACCOUCHEUR	ACCULTURATING	ACERVATELY	ACHAENOCARPS
ACCOMMODATING	ACCOUCHEURS	ACCULTURATION	ACERVATION	ACHALASIAS
ACCOMMODATINGLY	ACCOUCHEUSE	ACCULTURATIONAL	ACERVATIONS	ACHIEVABLE
ACCOMMODATION	ACCOUCHEUSES	ACCULTURATIONS	ACESCENCES	ACHIEVEMENT
ACCOMMODATIONAL	ACCOUNTABILITY	ACCULTURATIVE	ACESCENCIES	ACHIEVEMENTS
ACCOMMODATIONS	ACCOUNTABLE	ACCUMBENCIES	ACETABULAR	ACHINESSES
ACCOMMODATIVE	ACCOUNTABLENESS	ACCUMBENCY	ACETABULUM	ACHLAMYDEOUS
ACCOMMODATOR	ACCOUNTABLY	ACCUMULABLE	ACETABULUMS	ACHLORHYDRIA
ACCOMMODATORS	ACCOUNTANCIES	ACCUMULATE	ACETALDEHYDE	ACHLORHYDRIAS
ACCOMPANIED	ACCOUNTANCY	ACCUMULATED	ACETALDEHYDES	ACHLORHYDRIC
ACCOMPANIER	ACCOUNTANT	ACCUMULATES	ACETAMIDES	ACHONDRITE
ACCOMPANIERS	ACCOUNTANTS	ACCUMULATING	ACETAMINOPHEN	ACHONDRITES
ACCOMPANIES	ACCOUNTANTSHIP	ACCUMULATION	ACETAMINOPHENS	ACHONDRITIC
ACCOMPANIMENT	ACCOUNTANTSHIPS	ACCUMULATIONS	ACETANILID	ACHONDROPLASIA
ACCOMPANIMENTS	ACCOUNTING	ACCUMULATIVE	ACETANILIDE	ACHONDROPLASIAS

A

ACHONDROPLASTIC	ACIDOPHILUSES	ACQUIESCENTLY	ACROCYANOSIS	ACTINOMERE
ACHROMATIC	ACIDULATED	ACQUIESCENTS	ACRODROMOUS	ACTINOMERES
ACHROMATICALLY	ACIDULATES	ACQUIESCES	ACROGENOUS	ACTINOMETER
ACHROMATICITIES	ACIDULATING	ACQUIESCING	ACROGENOUSLY	ACTINOMETERS
ACHROMATICITY	ACIDULATION	ACQUIESCINGLY	ACROLITHIC	ACTINOMETRIC
ACHROMATIN	ACIDULATIONS	ACQUIGHTING	ACROMEGALIC	ACTINOMETRICAL
ACHROMATINS	ACIERATING	ACQUIRABILITIES	ACROMEGALICS	ACTINOMETRIES
ACHROMATISATION	ACIERATION	ACQUIRABILITY	ACROMEGALIES	ACTINOMETRY
ACHROMATISE	ACIERATIONS	ACQUIRABLE	ACROMEGALY	ACTINOMORPHIC
ACHROMATISED	ACINACEOUS	ACQUIREMENT	ACRONICALLY	ACTINOMORPHIES
ACHROMATISES	ACINACIFORM	ACQUIREMENTS	ACRONYCALLY	ACTINOMORPHOUS
ACHROMATISING	ACINETOBACTER	ACQUISITION	ACRONYCHAL	ACTINOMORPHY
ACHROMATISM	ACINETOBACTERS	ACQUISITIONAL	ACRONYCHALLY	ACTINOMYCES
ACHROMATISMS	ACKNOWLEDGE	ACQUISITIONS	ACRONYMANIA	ACTINOMYCETE
ACHROMATIZATION	ACKNOWLEDGEABLE	ACQUISITIVE	ACRONYMANIAS	ACTINOMYCETES
ACHROMATIZE	ACKNOWLEDGEABLY	ACQUISITIVELY	ACRONYMICALLY	ACTINOMYCETOUS
ACHROMATIZED	ACKNOWLEDGED	ACQUISITIVENESS	ACRONYMOUS	ACTINOMYCIN
ACHROMATIZES	ACKNOWLEDGEDLY	ACQUISITOR	ACROPARESTHESIA	ACTINOMYCINS
ACHROMATIZING	ACKNOWLEDGEMENT	ACQUISITORS	ACROPETALLY	ACTINOMYCOSES
ACHROMATOPSIA	ACKNOWLEDGER	ACQUITMENT	ACROPHOBES	ACTINOMYCOSIS
ACHROMATOPSIAS	ACKNOWLEDGERS	ACQUITMENTS	ACROPHOBIA	ACTINOMYCOTIC
ACHROMATOUS	ACKNOWLEDGES	ACQUITTALS	ACROPHOBIAS	ACTINOPODS
ACICLOVIRS	ACKNOWLEDGING	ACQUITTANCE	ACROPHOBIC	ACTINOTHERAPIES
ACICULATED	ACKNOWLEDGMENT	ACQUITTANCED	ACROPHOBICS	ACTINOTHERAPY
ACIDAEMIAS	ACKNOWLEDGMENTS	ACQUITTANCES	ACROPHONETIC	ACTINOURANIUM
ACIDANTHERA	ACOELOMATE	ACQUITTANCING	ACROPHONIC	ACTINOURANIUMS
ACIDANTHERAS	ACOELOMATES	ACQUITTERS	ACROPHONIES	ACTINOZOAN
ACIDICALLY	ACOLOUTHIC	ACQUITTING	ACROPOLISES	ACTINOZOANS
ACIDIFIABLE	ACOLOUTHITE	ACRIDITIES	ACROSPIRES	ACTIONABLE
ACIDIFICATION	ACOLOUTHITES	ACRIDNESSES	ACROSTICAL	ACTIONABLY
ACIDIFICATIONS	ACOLOUTHOI	ACRIFLAVIN	ACROSTICALLY	ACTIONISTS
ACIDIFIERS	ACOLOUTHOS	ACRIFLAVINE	ACROTERIAL	ACTIONLESS
ACIDIFYING	ACOLOUTHOSES	ACRIFLAVINES	ACROTERION	ACTIVATING
ACIDIMETER	ACONITINES	ACRIFLAVINS	ACROTERIUM	ACTIVATION
ACIDIMETERS	ACOTYLEDON	ACRIMONIES	ACRYLAMIDE	ACTIVATIONS
ACIDIMETRIC	ACOTYLEDONOUS	ACRIMONIOUS	ACRYLAMIDES	ACTIVATORS
ACIDIMETRICAL	ACOTYLEDONS	ACRIMONIOUSLY	ACRYLONITRILE	ACTIVENESS
ACIDIMETRICALLY	ACOUSTICAL	ACRIMONIOUSNESS	ACRYLONITRILES	ACTIVENESSES
ACIDIMETRIES	ACOUSTICALLY	ACRITARCHS	ACTABILITIES	ACTIVISING
ACIDIMETRY	ACOUSTICIAN	ACROAMATIC	ACTABILITY	ACTIVISTIC
ACIDNESSES	ACOUSTICIANS	ACROAMATICAL	ACTINICALLY	ACTIVITIES
ACIDOMETER	ACQUAINTANCE	ACROBATICALLY	ACTINIFORM	ACTIVIZING
ACIDOMETERS	ACQUAINTANCES	ACROBATICS	ACTINOBACILLI	ACTOMYOSIN
ACIDOPHILE	ACQUAINTED	ACROBATISM	ACTINOBACILLUS	ACTOMYOSINS
ACIDOPHILES	ACQUAINTING	ACROBATISMS	ACTINOBIOLOGIES	ACTORLIEST
ACIDOPHILIC	ACQUIESCED	ACROCARPOUS	ACTINOBIOLOGY	ACTRESSIER
ACIDOPHILOUS	ACQUIESCENCE	ACROCENTRIC	ACTINOCHEMISTRY	ACTRESSIEST
ACIDOPHILS	ACQUIESCENCES	ACROCENTRICS	ACTINOLITE	ACTUALISATION
ACIDOPHILUS	ACQUIESCENT	ACROCYANOSES	ACTINOLITES	ACTUALISATIONS

ACTUALISED	ADAPTOGENS	ADENOVIRUS	ADJUDGMENT	ADMINISTRATING
ACTUALISES	ADBLOCKERS	ADENOVIRUSES	ADJUDGMENTS	ADMINISTRATION
ACTUALISING	ADDERBEADS	ADENYLATES	ADJUDICATE	ADMINISTRATIONS
ACTUALISTS	ADDERSTONE	ADEPTNESSES	ADJUDICATED	ADMINISTRATIVE
ACTUALITES	ADDERSTONES	ADEQUACIES	ADJUDICATES	ADMINISTRATOR
ACTUALITIES	ADDERWORTS	ADEQUATELY	ADJUDICATING	ADMINISTRATORS
ACTUALIZATION	ADDICTEDNESS	ADEQUATENESS	ADJUDICATION	ADMINISTRATRIX
ACTUALIZATIONS	ADDICTEDNESSES	ADEQUATENESSES	ADJUDICATIONS	ADMIRABILITIES
ACTUALIZED	ADDICTIONS	ADEQUATIVE	ADJUDICATIVE	ADMIRABILITY
ACTUALIZES	ADDICTIVENESS	ADHERENCES	ADJUDICATOR	ADMIRABLENESS
ACTUALIZING	ADDICTIVENESSES	ADHERENTLY	ADJUDICATORS	ADMIRABLENESSES
ACTUARIALLY	ADDITAMENT	ADHESIONAL	ADJUDICATORY	ADMIRALSHIP
ACTUATIONS	ADDITAMENTS	ADHESIVELY	ADJUNCTION	ADMIRALSHIPS
ACUMINATED	ADDITIONAL	ADHESIVENESS	ADJUNCTIONS	ADMIRALTIES
ACUMINATES	ADDITIONALITIES	ADHESIVENESSES	ADJUNCTIVE	ADMIRANCES
ACUMINATING	ADDITIONALITY	ADHIBITING	ADJUNCTIVELY	ADMIRATION
ACUMINATION	ADDITIONALLY	ADHIBITION	ADJURATION	ADMIRATIONS
ACUMINATIONS	ADDITITIOUS	ADHIBITIONS	ADJURATIONS	ADMIRATIVE
ACUPRESSURE	ADDITIVELY	ADHOCRACIES	ADJURATORY	ADMIRAUNCE
ACUPRESSURES	ADDITIVITIES	ADIABATICALLY	ADJUSTABILITIES	ADMIRAUNCES
ACUPUNCTURAL	ADDITIVITY	ADIABATICS	ADJUSTABILITY	ADMIRINGLY
ACUPUNCTURE	ADDLEMENTS	ADIACTINIC	ADJUSTABLE	ADMISSIBILITIES
ACUPUNCTURES	ADDLEPATED	ADIAPHORISM	ADJUSTABLY	ADMISSIBILITY
ACUPUNCTURIST	ADDRESSABILITY	ADIAPHORISMS	ADJUSTMENT	ADMISSIBLE
ACUPUNCTURISTS	ADDRESSABLE	ADIAPHORIST	ADJUSTMENTAL	ADMISSIBLENESS
ACUTENESSES	ADDRESSEES	ADIAPHORISTIC	ADJUSTMENTS	ADMISSIONS
ACYCLOVIRS	ADDRESSERS	ADIAPHORISTS	ADJUTANCIES	ADMITTABLE
ACYLATIONS	ADDRESSING	ADIAPHORON	ADJUVANCIES	ADMITTANCE
ADACTYLOUS	ADDRESSINGS	ADIAPHOROUS	ADMEASURED	ADMITTANCES
ADAMANCIES	ADDRESSORS	ADIATHERMANCIES	ADMEASUREMENT	ADMITTEDLY
ADAMANTEAN	ADDUCEABLE	ADIATHERMANCY	ADMEASUREMENTS	ADMIXTURES
ADAMANTINE	ADDUCTIONS	ADIATHERMANOUS	ADMEASURES	ADMONISHED
ADAPTABILITIES	ADELANTADO	ADIATHERMIC	ADMEASURING	ADMONISHER
ADAPTABILITY	ADELANTADOS	ADIPOCERES	ADMINICLES	ADMONISHERS
ADAPTABLENESS	ADEMPTIONS	ADIPOCEROUS	ADMINICULAR	ADMONISHES
ADAPTABLENESSES	ADENECTOMIES	ADIPOCYTES	ADMINICULATE	ADMONISHING
ADAPTATION	ADENECTOMY	ADIPOSITIES	ADMINICULATED	ADMONISHINGLY
ADAPTATIONAL	ADENITISES	ADJACENCES	ADMINICULATES	ADMONISHMENT
ADAPTATIONALLY	ADENOCARCINOMA	ADJACENCIES	ADMINICULATING	ADMONISHMENTS
ADAPTATIONS	ADENOCARCINOMAS	ADJACENTLY	ADMINISTER	ADMONITION
ADAPTATIVE	ADENOHYPOPHYSES	ADJECTIVAL	ADMINISTERED	ADMONITIONS
ADAPTEDNESS	ADENOHYPOPHYSIS	ADJECTIVALLY	ADMINISTERING	ADMONITIVE
ADAPTEDNESSES	ADENOIDECTOMIES	ADJECTIVELY	ADMINISTERS	ADMONITORILY
ADAPTIVELY	ADENOIDECTOMY	ADJECTIVES	ADMINISTRABLE	ADMONITORS
ADAPTIVENESS	ADENOMATOUS	ADJOURNING	ADMINISTRANT	ADMONITORY
ADAPTIVENESSES	ADENOPATHIES	ADJOURNMENT	ADMINISTRANTS	ADNOMINALS
ADAPTIVITIES	ADENOPATHY	ADJOURNMENTS	ADMINISTRATE	ADOLESCENCE
ADAPTIVITY	ADENOSINES	ADJUDGEMENT	ADMINISTRATED	ADOLESCENCES
ADAPTOGENIC	ADENOVIRAL	ADJUDGEMENTS	ADMINISTRATES	ADOLESCENT

A

ADOLESCENTLY	ADSORPTIVE	ADVANTAGEOUS	ADVERSENESS	AECIDIOSPORE
ADOLESCENTS	ADULARESCENCE	ADVANTAGEOUSLY	ADVERSENESSES	AECIDIOSPORES
ADOPTABILITIES	ADULARESCENCES	ADVANTAGES	ADVERSITIES	AECIDOSPORE
ADOPTABILITY	ADULARESCENT	ADVANTAGING	ADVERTENCE	AECIDOSPORES
ADOPTIANISM	ADULATIONS	ADVECTIONS	ADVERTENCES	AECIOSPORE
ADOPTIANISMS	ADULTERANT	ADVENTITIA	ADVERTENCIES	AECIOSPORES
ADOPTIANIST	ADULTERANTS	ADVENTITIAL	ADVERTENCY	AEDILESHIP
ADOPTIANISTS	ADULTERATE	ADVENTITIAS	ADVERTENTLY	AEDILESHIPS
ADOPTIONISM	ADULTERATED	ADVENTITIOUS	ADVERTISED	AEOLIPILES
ADOPTIONISMS	ADULTERATES	ADVENTITIOUSLY	ADVERTISEMENT	AEOLIPYLES
ADOPTIONIST	ADULTERATING	ADVENTIVES	ADVERTISEMENTS	AEOLOTROPIC
ADOPTIONISTS	ADULTERATION	ADVENTURED	ADVERTISER	AEOLOTROPIES
ADOPTIVELY	ADULTERATIONS	ADVENTUREFUL	ADVERTISERS	AEOLOTROPY
ADORABILITIES	ADULTERATOR	ADVENTURER	ADVERTISES	AEPYORNISES
ADORABILITY	ADULTERATORS	ADVENTURERS	ADVERTISING	AERENCHYMA
ADORABLENESS	ADULTERERS	ADVENTURES	ADVERTISINGS	AERENCHYMAS
ADORABLENESSES	ADULTERESS	ADVENTURESOME	ADVERTIZED	AERENCHYMATOUS
ADORATIONS	ADULTERESSES	ADVENTURESS	ADVERTIZEMENT	AERIALISTS
ADORNMENTS	ADULTERIES	ADVENTURESSES	ADVERTIZEMENTS	AERIALITIES
ADPRESSING	ADULTERINE	ADVENTURING	ADVERTIZER	AERIFICATION
ADRENALECTOMIES	ADULTERINES	ADVENTURINGS	ADVERTIZERS	AERIFICATIONS
ADRENALECTOMY	ADULTERISE	ADVENTURISM	ADVERTIZES	AEROACOUSTICS
ADRENALINE	ADULTERISED	ADVENTURISMS	ADVERTIZING	AEROBALLISTICS
ADRENALINES	ADULTERISES	ADVENTURIST	ADVERTIZINGS	AEROBATICS
ADRENALINS	ADULTERISING	ADVENTURISTIC	ADVERTORIAL	AEROBICALLY
ADRENALISED	ADULTERIZE	ADVENTURISTS	ADVERTORIALS	AEROBICISE
ADRENALIZED	ADULTERIZED	ADVENTUROUS	ADVISABILITIES	AEROBICISED
ADRENERGIC	ADULTERIZES	ADVENTUROUSLY	ADVISABILITY	AEROBICISES
ADRENERGICALLY	ADULTERIZING	ADVENTUROUSNESS	ADVISABLENESS	AEROBICISING
ADRENOCEPTOR	ADULTEROUS	ADVERBIALISE	ADVISABLENESSES	AEROBICIST
ADRENOCEPTORS	ADULTEROUSLY	ADVERBIALISED	ADVISATORY	AEROBICISTS
ADRENOCHROME	ADULTESCENT	ADVERBIALISES	ADVISEDNESS	AEROBICIZE
ADRENOCHROMES	ADULTESCENTS	ADVERBIALISING	ADVISEDNESSES	AEROBICIZED
ADRENOCORTICAL	ADULTHOODS	ADVERBIALIZE	ADVISEMENT	AEROBICIZES
ADRIAMYCIN	ADULTNESSES	ADVERBIALIZED	ADVISEMENTS	AEROBICIZING
ADRIAMYCINS	ADULTRESSES	ADVERBIALIZES	ADVISERSHIP	AEROBIOLOGICAL
ADROITNESS	ADUMBRATED	ADVERBIALIZING	ADVISERSHIPS	AEROBIOLOGIES
ADROITNESSES	ADUMBRATES	ADVERBIALLY	ADVISORATE	AEROBIOLOGIST
ADSCITITIOUS	ADUMBRATING	ADVERBIALS	ADVISORATES	AEROBIOLOGISTS
ADSCITITIOUSLY	ADUMBRATION	ADVERGAMING	ADVISORIES	AEROBIOLOGY
ADSCRIPTION	ADUMBRATIONS	ADVERGAMINGS	ADVOCACIES	AEROBIONTS
ADSCRIPTIONS	ADUMBRATIVE	ADVERSARIA	ADVOCATING	AEROBIOSES
ADSORBABILITIES	ADUMBRATIVELY	ADVERSARIAL	ADVOCATION	AEROBIOSIS
ADSORBABILITY	ADUNCITIES	ADVERSARIES	ADVOCATIONS	AEROBIOTIC
ADSORBABLE	ADVANCEMENT	ADVERSARINESS	ADVOCATIVE	AEROBIOTICALLY
ADSORBATES	ADVANCEMENTS	ADVERSARINESSES	ADVOCATORS	AEROBRAKED
ADSORBENTS	ADVANCINGLY	ADVERSATIVE	ADVOCATORY	AEROBRAKES
ADSORPTION	ADVANTAGEABLE	ADVERSATIVELY	ADVOUTRERS	AEROBRAKING
ADSORPTIONS	ADVANTAGED	ADVERSATIVES	ADVOUTRIES	AEROBRAKINGS

AEROBUSSES
AERODIGESTIVE
AERODONETICS
AERODROMES
AERODYNAMIC
AERODYNAMICAL
AERODYNAMICALLY
AERODYNAMICIST
AERODYNAMICISTS
AERODYNAMICS
AEROELASTIC
AEROELASTICIAN
AEROELASTICIANS
AEROELASTICITY
AEROEMBOLISM
AEROEMBOLISMS
AEROGENERATOR
AEROGENERATORS
AEROGRAMME
AEROGRAMMES
AEROGRAPHIES
AEROGRAPHS
AEROGRAPHY
AEROHYDROPLANE
AEROHYDROPLANES
AEROLITHOLOGIES
AEROLITHOLOGY
AEROLOGICAL
AEROLOGIES
AEROLOGIST
AEROLOGISTS
AEROMAGNETIC
AEROMANCIES
AEROMECHANIC
AEROMECHANICAL
AEROMECHANICS
AEROMEDICAL
AEROMEDICINE
AEROMEDICINES
AEROMETERS
AEROMETRIC
AEROMETRIES
AEROMODELING
AEROMODELINGS
AEROMODELLING
AEROMODELLINGS
AEROMOTORS
AERONAUTIC
AERONAUTICAL

AERONAUTICALLY
AERONAUTICS
AERONEUROSES
AERONEUROSIS
AERONOMERS
AERONOMICAL
AERONOMIES
AERONOMIST
AERONOMISTS
AEROPAUSES
AEROPHAGIA
AEROPHAGIAS
AEROPHAGIES
AEROPHOBES
AEROPHOBIA
AEROPHOBIAS
AEROPHOBIC
AEROPHONES
AEROPHORES
AEROPHYTES
AEROPLANES
AEROPLANKTON
AEROPLANKTONS
AEROPULSES
AEROSCOPES
AEROSHELLS
AEROSIDERITE
AEROSIDERITES
AEROSOLISATION
AEROSOLISATIONS
AEROSOLISE
AEROSOLISED
AEROSOLISES
AEROSOLISING
AEROSOLIZATION
AEROSOLIZATIONS
AEROSOLIZE
AEROSOLIZED
AEROSOLIZES
AEROSOLIZING
AEROSPACES
AEROSPHERE
AEROSPHERES
AEROSPIKES
AEROSTATIC
AEROSTATICAL
AEROSTATICS
AEROSTATION
AEROSTATIONS

AEROSTRUCTURE
AEROSTRUCTURES
AEROTACTIC
AEROTRAINS
AEROTROPIC
AEROTROPISM
AEROTROPISMS
AERUGINOUS
AESTHESIAS
AESTHESIOGEN
AESTHESIOGENIC
AESTHESIOGENS
AESTHETICAL
AESTHETICALLY
AESTHETICIAN
AESTHETICIANS
AESTHETICISE
AESTHETICISED
AESTHETICISES
AESTHETICISING
AESTHETICISM
AESTHETICISMS
AESTHETICIST
AESTHETICISTS
AESTHETICIZE
AESTHETICIZED
AESTHETICIZES
AESTHETICIZING
AESTHETICS
AESTIVATED
AESTIVATES
AESTIVATING
AESTIVATION
AESTIVATIONS
AESTIVATOR
AESTIVATORS
AETHEREALITIES
AETHEREALITY
AETHEREALLY
AETHRIOSCOPE
AETHRIOSCOPES
AETIOLOGICAL
AETIOLOGICALLY
AETIOLOGIES
AETIOLOGIST
AETIOLOGISTS
AFFABILITIES
AFFABILITY
AFFECTABILITIES

AFFECTABILITY
AFFECTABLE
AFFECTATION
AFFECTATIONS
AFFECTEDLY
AFFECTEDNESS
AFFECTEDNESSES
AFFECTINGLY
AFFECTIONAL
AFFECTIONALLY
AFFECTIONATE
AFFECTIONATELY
AFFECTIONED
AFFECTIONING
AFFECTIONLESS
AFFECTIONS
AFFECTIVELY
AFFECTIVENESS
AFFECTIVENESSES
AFFECTIVITIES
AFFECTIVITY
AFFECTLESS
AFFECTLESSNESS
AFFEERMENT
AFFEERMENTS
AFFENPINSCHER
AFFENPINSCHERS
AFFERENTLY
AFFETTUOSO
AFFIANCING
AFFICIONADO
AFFICIONADOS
AFFIDAVITS
AFFILIABLE
AFFILIATED
AFFILIATES
AFFILIATING
AFFILIATION
AFFILIATIONS
AFFINITIES
AFFINITIVE
AFFIRMABLE
AFFIRMANCE
AFFIRMANCES
AFFIRMANTS
AFFIRMATION
AFFIRMATIONS
AFFIRMATIVE
AFFIRMATIVELY

AFFIRMATIVES
AFFIRMATORY
AFFIRMINGLY
AFFIXATION
AFFIXATIONS
AFFIXMENTS
AFFIXTURES
AFFLATIONS
AFFLATUSES
AFFLICTERS
AFFLICTING
AFFLICTINGS
AFFLICTION
AFFLICTIONS
AFFLICTIVE
AFFLICTIVELY
AFFLUENCES
AFFLUENCIES
AFFLUENTIAL
AFFLUENTIALS
AFFLUENTLY
AFFLUENTNESS
AFFLUENTNESSES
AFFLUENZAS
AFFLUXIONS
AFFOORDING
AFFORCEMENT
AFFORCEMENTS
AFFORDABILITIES
AFFORDABILITY
AFFORDABLE
AFFORDABLY
AFFORESTABLE
AFFORESTATION
AFFORESTATIONS
AFFORESTED
AFFORESTING
AFFRANCHISE
AFFRANCHISED
AFFRANCHISEMENT
AFFRANCHISES
AFFRANCHISING
AFFRAPPING
AFFREIGHTMENT
AFFREIGHTMENTS
AFFRICATED
AFFRICATES
AFFRICATING
AFFRICATION

AFFRICATIONS	AFTERGROWTH	AGAMOGENESES	AGGRANDISEMENT	AGITATIONAL
AFFRICATIVE	AFTERGROWTHS	AGAMOGENESIS	AGGRANDISEMENTS	AGITATIONS
AFFRICATIVES	AFTERGUARD	AGAMOGENETIC	AGGRANDISER	AGNATICALLY
AFFRIGHTED	AFTERGUARDS	AGAMOGONIES	AGGRANDISERS	AGNOIOLOGIES
AFFRIGHTEDLY	AFTERHEATS	AGAMOSPERMIES	AGGRANDISES	AGNOIOLOGY
AFFRIGHTEN	AFTERIMAGE	AGAMOSPERMY	AGGRANDISING	AGNOLOTTIS
AFFRIGHTENED	AFTERIMAGES	AGAPANTHUS	AGGRANDIZE	AGNOSTICISM
AFFRIGHTENING	AFTERLIFES	AGAPANTHUSES	AGGRANDIZED	AGNOSTICISMS
AFFRIGHTENS	AFTERLIVES	AGARICACEOUS	AGGRANDIZEMENT	AGONISEDLY
AFFRIGHTFUL	AFTERMARKET	AGATEWARES	AGGRANDIZEMENTS	AGONISINGLY
AFFRIGHTING	AFTERMARKETS	AGATHODAIMON	AGGRANDIZER	AGONISTICAL
AFFRIGHTMENT	AFTERMASTS	AGATHODAIMONS	AGGRANDIZERS	AGONISTICALLY
AFFRIGHTMENTS	AFTERMATHS	AGEDNESSES	AGGRANDIZES	AGONISTICS
AFFRONTING	AFTERNOONS	AGELESSNESS	AGGRANDIZING	AGONIZEDLY
AFFRONTINGLY	AFTERPAINS	AGELESSNESSES	AGGRAVATED	AGONIZINGLY
AFFRONTINGS	AFTERPARTIES	AGENDALESS	AGGRAVATES	AGONOTHETES
AFFRONTIVE	AFTERPARTY	AGENTIVITIES	AGGRAVATING	AGORAPHOBE
AFICIONADA	AFTERPEAKS	AGENTIVITY	AGGRAVATINGLY	AGORAPHOBES
AFICIONADAS	AFTERPIECE	AGFLATIONS	AGGRAVATION	AGORAPHOBIA
AFICIONADO	AFTERPIECES	AGGIORNAMENTI	AGGRAVATIONS	AGORAPHOBIAS
AFICIONADOS	AFTERSALES	AGGIORNAMENTO	AGGREGATED	AGORAPHOBIC
AFLATOXINS	AFTERSENSATION	AGGIORNAMENTOS	AGGREGATELY	AGORAPHOBICS
AFOREMENTIONED	AFTERSENSATIONS	AGGLOMERATE	AGGREGATENESS	AGRAMMATICAL
AFORETHOUGHT	AFTERSHAFT	AGGLOMERATED	AGGREGATENESSES	AGRANULOCYTE
AFORETHOUGHTS	AFTERSHAFTS	AGGLOMERATES	AGGREGATES	AGRANULOCYTES
AFRORMOSIA	AFTERSHAVE	AGGLOMERATING	AGGREGATING	AGRANULOCYTOSES
AFRORMOSIAS	AFTERSHAVES	AGGLOMERATION	AGGREGATION	AGRANULOCYTOSIS
AFTERBIRTH	AFTERSHOCK	AGGLOMERATIONS	AGGREGATIONAL	AGRANULOSES
AFTERBIRTHS	AFTERSHOCKS	AGGLOMERATIVE	AGGREGATIONS	AGRANULOSIS
AFTERBODIES	AFTERSHOWS	AGGLUTINABILITY	AGGREGATIVE	AGRARIANISM
AFTERBRAIN	AFTERSUPPER	AGGLUTINABLE	AGGREGATIVELY	AGRARIANISMS
AFTERBRAINS	AFTERSUPPERS	AGGLUTINANT	AGGREGATOR	AGREEABILITIES
AFTERBURNER	AFTERSWARM	AGGLUTINANTS	AGGREGATORS	AGREEABILITY
AFTERBURNERS	AFTERSWARMS	AGGLUTINATE	AGGRESSING	AGREEABLENESS
AFTERBURNING	AFTERTASTE	AGGLUTINATED	AGGRESSION	AGREEABLENESSES
AFTERBURNINGS	AFTERTASTES	AGGLUTINATES	AGGRESSIONS	AGREEMENTS
AFTERBURNS	AFTERTHOUGHT	AGGLUTINATING	AGGRESSIVE	AGREGATION
AFTERCARES	AFTERTHOUGHTS	AGGLUTINATION	AGGRESSIVELY	AGREGATIONS
AFTERCLAPS	AFTERTIMES	AGGLUTINATIONS	AGGRESSIVENESS	AGRIBUSINESS
AFTERDAMPS	AFTERTREATMENT	AGGLUTINATIVE	AGGRESSIVITIES	AGRIBUSINESSES
AFTERDECKS	AFTERTREATMENTS	AGGLUTININ	AGGRESSIVITY	AGRIBUSINESSMAN
AFTEREFFECT	AFTERWARDS	AGGLUTININS	AGGRESSORS	AGRIBUSINESSMEN
AFTEREFFECTS	AFTERWORDS	AGGLUTINOGEN	AGGRIEVEDLY	AGRICHEMICAL
AFTEREYEING	AFTERWORLD	AGGLUTINOGENIC	AGGRIEVEMENT	AGRICHEMICALS
AFTEREYING	AFTERWORLDS	AGGLUTINOGENS	AGGRIEVEMENTS	AGRICULTURAL
AFTERGAMES	AGALACTIAS	AGGRADATION	AGGRIEVING	AGRICULTURALIST
AFTERGLOWS	AGALMATOLITE	AGGRADATIONS	AGILENESSES	AGRICULTURALLY
AFTERGRASS	AGALMATOLITES	AGGRANDISE	AGISTMENTS	AGRICULTURE
AFTERGRASSES	AGAMICALLY	AGGRANDISED	AGITATEDLY	AGRICULTURES

AGRICULTURIST	AGROSTOLOGY	AIRBURSTING	ALABLASTERS	ALCHEMICAL
AGRICULTURISTS	AGROTERRORISM	AIRCOACHES	ALACRITIES	ALCHEMICALLY
AGRIFOODSTUFFS	AGROTERRORISMS	AIRCRAFTMAN	ALACRITOUS	ALCHEMISED
AGRIMONIES	AGROTOURISM	AIRCRAFTMEN	ALARMINGLY	ALCHEMISES
AGRIOLOGIES	AGROTOURISMS	AIRCRAFTSMAN	ALBARELLOS	ALCHEMISING
AGRIPRODUCT	AGROTOURIST	AIRCRAFTSMEN	ALBATROSSES	ALCHEMISTIC
AGRIPRODUCTS	AGROTOURISTS	AIRCRAFTSWOMAN	ALBERTITES	ALCHEMISTICAL
AGRITOURISM	AGRYPNOTIC	AIRCRAFTSWOMEN	ALBESCENCE	ALCHEMISTS
AGRITOURISMS	AGRYPNOTICS	AIRCRAFTWOMAN	ALBESCENCES	ALCHEMIZED
AGRITOURIST	AGTERSKOTS	AIRCRAFTWOMEN	ALBESPINES	ALCHEMIZES
AGRITOURISTS	AGUARDIENTE	AIRDASHING	ALBESPYNES	ALCHEMIZING
AGROBIOLOGICAL	AGUARDIENTES	AIRDROPPED	ALBINESSES	ALCHERINGA
AGROBIOLOGIES	AHISTORICAL	AIRDROPPING	ALBINISTIC	ALCHERINGAS
AGROBIOLOGIST	AHORSEBACK	AIRFREIGHT	ALBINOISMS	ALCOHOLICALLY
AGROBIOLOGISTS	AHURUHURUS	AIRFREIGHTED	ALBITISING	ALCOHOLICITIES
AGROBIOLOGY	AICHMOPHOBIA	AIRFREIGHTING	ALBITIZING	ALCOHOLICITY
AGROBUSINESS	AICHMOPHOBIAS	AIRFREIGHTS	ALBUGINEOUS	ALCOHOLICS
AGROBUSINESSES	AIGUILLETTE	AIRINESSES	ALBUMBLATT	ALCOHOLISATION
AGROCHEMICAL	AIGUILLETTES	AIRLESSNESS	ALBUMBLATTER	ALCOHOLISATIONS
AGROCHEMICALS	AILANTHUSES	AIRLESSNESSES	ALBUMBLATTS	ALCOHOLISE
AGRODOLCES	AILOUROPHILE	AIRLIFTING	ALBUMENISE	ALCOHOLISED
AGROECOLOGIES	AILOUROPHILES	AIRMAILING	ALBUMENISED	ALCOHOLISES
AGROECOLOGY	AILOUROPHILIA	AIRMANSHIP	ALBUMENISES	ALCOHOLISING
AGROFORESTER	AILOUROPHILIAS	AIRMANSHIPS	ALBUMENISING	ALCOHOLISM
AGROFORESTERS	AILOUROPHILIC	AIRPROOFED	ALBUMENIZE	ALCOHOLISMS
AGROFORESTRIES	AILOUROPHOBE	AIRPROOFING	ALBUMENIZED	ALCOHOLIZATION
AGROFORESTRY	AILOUROPHOBES	AIRSICKNESS	ALBUMENIZES	ALCOHOLIZATIONS
AGROINDUSTRIAL	AILOUROPHOBIA	AIRSICKNESSES	ALBUMENIZING	ALCOHOLIZE
AGROINDUSTRIES	AILOUROPHOBIAS	AIRSTREAMS	ALBUMINATE	ALCOHOLIZED
AGROINDUSTRY	AILOUROPHOBIC	AIRSTRIKES	ALBUMINATES	ALCOHOLIZES
AGROLOGICAL	AILUROPHILE	AIRTIGHTNESS	ALBUMINISE	ALCOHOLIZING
AGROLOGIES	AILUROPHILES	AIRTIGHTNESSES	ALBUMINISED	ALCOHOLOMETER
AGROLOGIST	AILUROPHILIA	AIRWORTHIER	ALBUMINISES	ALCOHOLOMETERS
AGROLOGISTS	AILUROPHILIAS	AIRWORTHIEST	ALBUMINISING	ALCOHOLOMETRIES
AGRONOMIAL	AILUROPHILIC	AIRWORTHINESS	ALBUMINIZE	ALCOHOLOMETRY
AGRONOMICAL	AILUROPHOBE	AIRWORTHINESSES	ALBUMINIZED	ALCYONARIAN
AGRONOMICALLY	AILUROPHOBES	AITCHBONES	ALBUMINIZES	ALCYONARIANS
AGRONOMICS	AILUROPHOBIA	AKATHISIAS	ALBUMINIZING	ALDERFLIES
AGRONOMIES	AILUROPHOBIAS	AKOLOUTHOS	ALBUMINOID	ALDERMANIC
AGRONOMIST	AILUROPHOBIC	AKOLOUTHOSES	ALBUMINOIDS	ALDERMANITIES
AGRONOMISTS	AIMLESSNESS	AKOLUTHOSES	ALBUMINOUS	ALDERMANITY
AGROSTEMMA	AIMLESSNESSES	ALABAMINES	ALBUMINURIA	ALDERMANLIER
AGROSTEMMAS	AIRBALLING	ALABANDINE	ALBUMINURIAS	ALDERMANLIEST
AGROSTEMMATA	AIRBOARDING	ALABANDINES	ALBUMINURIC	ALDERMANLIKE
AGROSTOLOGIC	AIRBOARDINGS	ALABANDITE	ALBUTEROLS	ALDERMANLY
AGROSTOLOGICAL	AIRBRUSHED	ALABANDITES	ALCAICERIA	ALDERMANRIES
AGROSTOLOGIES	AIRBRUSHES	ALABASTERS	ALCAICERIAS	ALDERMANRY
AGROSTOLOGIST	AIRBRUSHING	ALABASTRINE	ALCARRAZAS	ALDERMANSHIP
AGROSTOLOGISTS	AIRBURSTED	ALABLASTER	ALCATRASES	ALDERMANSHIPS

ALDERWOMAN	ALGOLAGNIACS	ALKALESCENT	ALLEGORICALNESS	ALLHALLOWN
ALDERWOMEN	ALGOLAGNIAS	ALKALIFIED	ALLEGORIES	ALLHOLLOWN
ALDOHEXOSE	ALGOLAGNIC	ALKALIFIES	ALLEGORISATION	ALLIACEOUS
ALDOHEXOSES	ALGOLAGNIST	ALKALIFYING	ALLEGORISATIONS	ALLICHOLIES
ALDOLISATION	ALGOLAGNISTS	ALKALIMETER	ALLEGORISE	ALLIGARTAS
ALDOLISATIONS	ALGOLOGICAL	ALKALIMETERS	ALLEGORISED	ALLIGATING
ALDOLIZATION	ALGOLOGICALLY	ALKALIMETRIC	ALLEGORISER	ALLIGATION
ALDOLIZATIONS	ALGOLOGIES	ALKALIMETRIES	ALLEGORISERS	ALLIGATIONS
ALDOPENTOSE	ALGOLOGIST	ALKALIMETRY	ALLEGORISES	ALLIGATORS
ALDOPENTOSES	ALGOLOGISTS	ALKALINISATION	ALLEGORISING	ALLINEATION
ALDOSTERONE	ALGOMETERS	ALKALINISATIONS	ALLEGORIST	ALLINEATIONS
ALDOSTERONES	ALGOMETRIES	ALKALINISE	ALLEGORISTS	ALLITERATE
ALDOSTERONISM	ALGOPHOBIA	ALKALINISED	ALLEGORIZATION	ALLITERATED
ALDOSTERONISMS	ALGOPHOBIAS	ALKALINISES	ALLEGORIZATIONS	ALLITERATES
ALEATORIES	ALGORISMIC	ALKALINISING	ALLEGORIZE	ALLITERATING
ALEBENCHES	ALGORITHMIC	ALKALINITIES	ALLEGORIZED	ALLITERATION
ALECTRYONS	ALGORITHMICALLY	ALKALINITY	ALLEGORIZER	ALLITERATIONS
ALEGGEAUNCE	ALGORITHMS	ALKALINIZATION	ALLEGORIZERS	ALLITERATIVE
ALEGGEAUNCES	ALIENABILITIES	ALKALINIZATIONS	ALLEGORIZES	ALLITERATIVELY
ALEMBICATED	ALIENABILITY	ALKALINIZE	ALLEGORIZING	ALLNIGHTER
ALEMBICATION	ALIENATING	ALKALINIZED	ALLEGRETTO	ALLNIGHTERS
ALEMBICATIONS	ALIENATION	ALKALINIZES	ALLEGRETTOS	ALLOANTIBODIES
ALEMBROTHS	ALIENATIONS	ALKALINIZING	ALLELOMORPH	ALLOANTIBODY
ALERTNESSES	ALIENATORS	ALKALISABLE	ALLELOMORPHIC	ALLOANTIGEN
ALEXANDERS	ALIENNESSES	ALKALISERS	ALLELOMORPHISM	ALLOANTIGENS
ALEXANDERSES	ALIGHTMENT	ALKALISING	ALLELOMORPHISMS	ALLOCARPIES
ALEXANDRINE	ALIGHTMENTS	ALKALIZABLE	ALLELOMORPHS	ALLOCATABLE
ALEXANDRINES	ALIGNMENTS	ALKALIZERS	ALLELOPATHIC	ALLOCATING
ALEXANDRITE	ALIKENESSES	ALKALIZING	ALLELOPATHIES	ALLOCATION
ALEXANDRITES	ALIMENTARY	ALKALOIDAL	ALLELOPATHY	ALLOCATIONS
ALEXIPHARMAKON	ALIMENTATION	ALKYLATING	ALLELUIAHS	ALLOCATORS
ALEXIPHARMAKONS	ALIMENTATIONS	ALKYLATION	ALLEMANDES	ALLOCHEIRIA
ALEXIPHARMIC	ALIMENTATIVE	ALKYLATIONS	ALLERGENIC	ALLOCHEIRIAS
ALEXIPHARMICS	ALIMENTING	ALLANTOIDAL	ALLERGENICITIES	ALLOCHIRIA
ALEXITHYMIA	ALIMENTIVE	ALLANTOIDES	ALLERGENICITY	ALLOCHIRIAS
ALEXITHYMIAS	ALIMENTIVENESS	ALLANTOIDS	ALLERGISTS	ALLOCHTHONOUS
ALFILARIAS	ALINEATION	ALLANTOINS	ALLETHRINS	ALLOCUTION
ALFILERIAS	ALINEATIONS	ALLANTOISES	ALLEVIANTS	ALLOCUTIONS
ALGAECIDES	ALINEMENTS	ALLARGANDO	ALLEVIATED	ALLODYNIAS
ALGARROBAS	ALISMACEOUS	ALLAYMENTS	ALLEVIATES	ALLOGAMIES
ALGARROBOS	ALITERACIES	ALLEGATION	ALLEVIATING	ALLOGAMOUS
ALGEBRAICAL	ALITERATES	ALLEGATIONS	ALLEVIATION	ALLOGENEIC
ALGEBRAICALLY	ALIVENESSES	ALLEGEANCE	ALLEVIATIONS	ALLOGRAFTED
ALGEBRAIST	ALIZARINES	ALLEGEANCES	ALLEVIATIVE	ALLOGRAFTING
ALGEBRAISTS	ALKAHESTIC	ALLEGIANCE	ALLEVIATOR	ALLOGRAFTS
ALGIDITIES	ALKALESCENCE	ALLEGIANCES	ALLEVIATORS	ALLOGRAPHIC
ALGIDNESSES	ALKALESCENCES	ALLEGIANTS	ALLEVIATORY	ALLOGRAPHS
ALGOLAGNIA	ALKALESCENCIES	ALLEGORICAL	ALLHALLOND	ALLOIOSTROPHOS
ALGOLAGNIAC	ALKALESCENCY	ALLEGORICALLY	ALLHALLOWEN	ALLOMERISM

ALLOMERISMS	ALLOTYPIES	ALPESTRINE	ALTERATIONS	ALUMINATES
ALLOMEROUS	ALLOWABILITIES	ALPHABETARIAN	ALTERATIVE	ALUMINIDES
ALLOMETRIC	ALLOWABILITY	ALPHABETARIANS	ALTERATIVES	ALUMINIFEROUS
ALLOMETRIES	ALLOWABLENESS	ALPHABETED	ALTERCATED	ALUMINISED
ALLOMORPHIC	ALLOWABLENESSES	ALPHABETIC	ALTERCATES	ALUMINISES
ALLOMORPHISM	ALLOWABLES	ALPHABETICAL	ALTERCATING	ALUMINISING
ALLOMORPHISMS	ALLOWANCED	ALPHABETICALLY	ALTERCATION	ALUMINIUMS
ALLOMORPHS	ALLOWANCES	ALPHABETIFORM	ALTERCATIONS	ALUMINIZED
ALLONYMOUS	ALLOWANCING	ALPHABETING	ALTERCATIVE	ALUMINIZES
ALLOPATHIC	ALLUREMENT	ALPHABETISATION	ALTERITIES	ALUMINIZING
ALLOPATHICALLY	ALLUREMENTS	ALPHABETISE	ALTERNANCE	ALUMINOSILICATE
ALLOPATHIES	ALLURINGLY	ALPHABETISED	ALTERNANCES	ALUMINOSITIES
ALLOPATHIST	ALLUSIVELY	ALPHABETISER	ALTERNANTS	ALUMINOSITY
ALLOPATHISTS	ALLUSIVENESS	ALPHABETISERS	ALTERNATED	ALUMINOTHERMIES
ALLOPATRIC	ALLUSIVENESSES	ALPHABETISES	ALTERNATELY	ALUMINOTHERMY
ALLOPATRICALLY	ALLWEATHER	ALPHABETISING	ALTERNATES	ALUMSTONES
ALLOPATRIES	ALLWEATHERS	ALPHABETIZATION	ALTERNATIM	ALVEOLARLY
ALLOPHANES	ALLYCHOLLIES	ALPHABETIZE	ALTERNATING	ALVEOLATION
ALLOPHONES	ALLYCHOLLY	ALPHABETIZED	ALTERNATION	ALVEOLATIONS
ALLOPHONIC	ALMACANTAR	ALPHABETIZER	ALTERNATIONS	ALVEOLITIS
ALLOPLASMIC	ALMACANTARS	ALPHABETIZERS	ALTERNATIVE	ALVEOLITISES
ALLOPLASMS	ALMANDINES	ALPHABETIZES	ALTERNATIVELY	ALYCOMPAINE
ALLOPLASTIC	ALMANDITES	ALPHABETIZING	ALTERNATIVENESS	ALYCOMPAINES
ALLOPOLYPLOID	ALMIGHTIER	ALPHAMERIC	ALTERNATIVES	AMALGAMATE
ALLOPOLYPLOIDS	ALMIGHTIEST	ALPHAMERICAL	ALTERNATOR	AMALGAMATED
ALLOPOLYPLOIDY	ALMIGHTILY	ALPHAMERICALLY	ALTERNATORS	AMALGAMATES
ALLOPURINOL	ALMIGHTINESS	ALPHAMETIC	ALTIGRAPHS	AMALGAMATING
ALLOPURINOLS	ALMIGHTINESSES	ALPHAMETICS	ALTIMETERS	AMALGAMATION
ALLOSAURUS	ALMONDIEST	ALPHANUMERIC	ALTIMETRICAL	AMALGAMATIONS
ALLOSAURUSES	ALMONDITES	ALPHANUMERICAL	ALTIMETRICALLY	AMALGAMATIVE
ALLOSTERIC	ALMSGIVERS	ALPHANUMERICS	ALTIMETRIES	AMALGAMATOR
ALLOSTERICALLY	ALMSGIVING	ALPHASORTED	ALTIPLANOS	AMALGAMATORS
ALLOSTERIES	ALMSGIVINGS	ALPHASORTING	ALTISONANT	AMANTADINE
ALLOTETRAPLOID	ALMSHOUSES	ALPHASORTS	ALTISSIMOS	AMANTADINES
ALLOTETRAPLOIDS	ALMUCANTAR	ALPHATESTED	ALTITONANT	AMANUENSES
ALLOTETRAPLOIDY	ALMUCANTARS	ALPHATESTING	ALTITUDINAL	AMANUENSIS
ALLOTHEISM	ALOESWOODS	ALPHATESTS	ALTITUDINARIAN	AMARACUSES
ALLOTHEISMS	ALOGICALLY	ALPHOSISES	ALTITUDINARIANS	AMARANTACEOUS
ALLOTMENTS	ALONENESSES	ALSTROEMERIA	ALTITUDINOUS	AMARANTHACEOUS
ALLOTRIOMORPHIC	ALONGSHORE	ALSTROEMERIAS	ALTOCUMULI	AMARANTHINE
ALLOTROPES	ALONGSHOREMAN	ALTALTISSIMO	ALTOCUMULUS	AMARANTINE
ALLOTROPIC	ALONGSHOREMEN	ALTALTISSIMOS	ALTOGETHER	AMARANTINS
ALLOTROPICALLY	ALOOFNESSES	ALTARPIECE	ALTOGETHERS	AMARYLLIDACEOUS
ALLOTROPIES	ALOPECOIDS	ALTARPIECES	ALTORUFFLED	AMARYLLIDS
ALLOTROPISM	ALPARGATAS	ALTAZIMUTH	ALTOSTRATI	AMARYLLISES
ALLOTROPISMS	ALPENGLOWS	ALTAZIMUTHS	ALTOSTRATUS	AMASSMENTS
ALLOTROPOUS	ALPENHORNS	ALTERABILITIES	ALTRICIALS	AMATEURISH
ALLOTTERIES	ALPENSTOCK	ALTERABILITY	ALTRUISTIC	AMATEURISHLY
ALLOTYPICALLY	ALPENSTOCKS	ALTERATION	ALTRUISTICALLY	AMATEURISHNESS

AMATEURISM	AMBITIONING	AMELIORABLE	AMIANTHOID	AMMONOLYSES
AMATEURISMS	AMBITIONLESS	AMELIORANT	AMIANTHOIDAL	AMMONOLYSIS
AMATEURSHIP	AMBITIOUSLY	AMELIORANTS	AMIANTHUSES	AMMOPHILOUS
AMATEURSHIPS	AMBITIOUSNESS	AMELIORATE	AMIANTUSES	AMMUNITION
AMATIVENESS	AMBITIOUSNESSES	AMELIORATED	AMICABILITIES	AMMUNITIONED
AMATIVENESSES	AMBIVALENCE	AMELIORATES	AMICABILITY	AMMUNITIONING
AMATORIALLY	AMBIVALENCES	AMELIORATING	AMICABLENESS	AMMUNITIONS
AMATORIOUS	AMBIVALENCIES	AMELIORATION	AMICABLENESSES	AMNESTYING
AMAZEBALLS	AMBIVALENCY	AMELIORATIONS	AMINOACETIC	AMNIOCENTESES
AMAZEDNESS	AMBIVALENT	AMELIORATIVE	AMINOACIDURIA	AMNIOCENTESIS
AMAZEDNESSES	AMBIVALENTLY	AMELIORATOR	AMINOACIDURIAS	AMNIOTOMIES
AMAZEMENTS	AMBIVERSION	AMELIORATORS	AMINOBENZOIC	AMOBARBITAL
AMAZONIANS	AMBIVERSIONS	AMELIORATORY	AMINOBUTENE	AMOBARBITALS
AMAZONITES	AMBLYGONITE	AMELOBLAST	AMINOBUTENES	AMOEBIASES
AMAZONSTONE	AMBLYGONITES	AMELOBLASTS	AMINOPEPTIDASE	AMOEBIASIS
AMAZONSTONES	AMBLYOPIAS	AMELOGENESES	AMINOPEPTIDASES	AMOEBIFORM
AMBAGITORY	AMBOCEPTOR	AMELOGENESIS	AMINOPHENAZONE	AMOEBOCYTE
AMBASSADOR	AMBOCEPTORS	AMENABILITIES	AMINOPHENAZONES	AMOEBOCYTES
AMBASSADORIAL	AMBOSEXUAL	AMENABILITY	AMINOPHENOL	AMONTILLADO
AMBASSADORS	AMBOSEXUALITIES	AMENABLENESS	AMINOPHENOLS	AMONTILLADOS
AMBASSADORSHIP	AMBOSEXUALITY	AMENABLENESSES	AMINOPHYLLINE	AMORALISMS
AMBASSADORSHIPS	AMBOSEXUALLY	AMENAUNCES	AMINOPHYLLINES	AMORALISTS
AMBASSADRESS	AMBROSIALLY	AMENDATORY	AMINOPTERIN	AMORALITIES
AMBASSADRESSES	AMBROTYPES	AMENDMENTS	AMINOPTERINS	AMOROSITIES
AMBASSAGES	AMBULACRAL	AMENORRHEA	AMINOPYRINE	AMOROUSNESS
AMBERGRISES	AMBULACRUM	AMENORRHEAS	AMINOPYRINES	AMOROUSNESSES
AMBERJACKS	AMBULANCEMAN	AMENORRHEIC	AMINOTOLUENE	AMORPHISMS
AMBIDENTATE	AMBULANCEMEN	AMENORRHOEA	AMINOTOLUENES	AMORPHOUSLY
AMBIDEXTER	AMBULANCES	AMENORRHOEAS	AMISSIBILITIES	AMORPHOUSNESS
AMBIDEXTERITIES	AMBULANCEWOMAN	AMENTACEOUS	AMISSIBILITY	AMORPHOUSNESSES
AMBIDEXTERITY	AMBULANCEWOMEN	AMENTIFEROUS	AMITOTICALLY	AMORTISABLE
AMBIDEXTEROUS	AMBULATING	AMERCEABLE	AMITRIPTYLINE	AMORTISATION
AMBIDEXTERS	AMBULATION	AMERCEMENT	AMITRIPTYLINES	AMORTISATIONS
AMBIDEXTROUS	AMBULATIONS	AMERCEMENTS	AMITRYPTYLINE	AMORTISEMENT
AMBIDEXTROUSLY	AMBULATORIES	AMERCIABLE	AMITRYPTYLINES	AMORTISEMENTS
AMBIGUITIES	AMBULATORILY	AMERCIAMENT	AMMOCOETES	AMORTISING
AMBIGUOUSLY	AMBULATORS	AMERCIAMENTS	AMMONIACAL	AMORTIZABLE
AMBIGUOUSNESS	AMBULATORY	AMERICIUMS	AMMONIACUM	AMORTIZATION
AMBIGUOUSNESSES	AMBULETTES	AMETABOLIC	AMMONIACUMS	AMORTIZATIONS
AMBILATERAL	AMBUSCADED	AMETABOLISM	AMMONIATED	AMORTIZEMENT
AMBIOPHONIES	AMBUSCADER	AMETABOLISMS	AMMONIATES	AMORTIZEMENTS
AMBIOPHONY	AMBUSCADERS	AMETABOLOUS	AMMONIATING	AMORTIZING
AMBISEXUAL	AMBUSCADES	AMETHYSTINE	AMMONIATION	AMOURETTES
AMBISEXUALITIES	AMBUSCADING	AMETROPIAS	AMMONIATIONS	AMOXICILLIN
AMBISEXUALITY	AMBUSCADOES	AMIABILITIES	AMMONIFICATION	AMOXICILLINS
AMBISEXUALLY	AMBUSCADOS	AMIABILITY	AMMONIFICATIONS	AMOXYCILLIN
AMBISEXUALS	AMBUSHMENT	AMIABLENESS	AMMONIFIED	AMOXYCILLINS
AMBISONICS	AMBUSHMENTS	AMIABLENESSES	AMMONIFIES	AMPACITIES
AMBITIONED	AMEBOCYTES	AMIANTHINE	AMMONIFYING	AMPELOGRAPHIES

AMPELOGRAPHY	AMPHIGORIES	AMPLENESSES	AMYLOPLASTS	ANACOLUTHON
AMPELOPSES	AMPHIGOURI	AMPLEXICAUL	AMYLOPSINS	ANACOLUTHONS
AMPELOPSIS	AMPHIGOURIS	AMPLEXUSES	AMYOTONIAS	ANACOUSTIC
AMPELOPSISES	AMPHIMACER	AMPLIATION	AMYOTROPHIC	ANACREONTIC
AMPEROMETRIC	AMPHIMACERS	AMPLIATIONS	AMYOTROPHIES	ANACREONTICALLY
AMPERSANDS	AMPHIMICTIC	AMPLIATIVE	AMYOTROPHY	ANACREONTICS
AMPERZANDS	AMPHIMIXES	AMPLIDYNES	ANABANTIDS	ANACRUSTIC
AMPHETAMINE	AMPHIMIXIS	AMPLIFIABLE	ANABAPTISE	ANADIPLOSES
AMPHETAMINES	AMPHIOXUSES	AMPLIFICATION	ANABAPTISED	ANADIPLOSIS
AMPHIARTHROSES	AMPHIPATHIC	AMPLIFICATIONS	ANABAPTISES	ANADROMOUS
AMPHIARTHROSIS	AMPHIPHILE	AMPLIFIERS	ANABAPTISING	ANADYOMENE
AMPHIASTER	AMPHIPHILES	AMPLIFYING	ANABAPTISM	ANAEMICALLY
AMPHIASTERS	AMPHIPHILIC	AMPLITUDES	ANABAPTISMS	ANAEROBICALLY
AMPHIBIANS	AMPHIPLOID	AMPLOSOMES	ANABAPTIST	ANAEROBIONT
AMPHIBIOTIC	AMPHIPLOIDIES	AMPULLACEAL	ANABAPTISTIC	ANAEROBIONTS
AMPHIBIOUS	AMPHIPLOIDS	AMPULLACEOUS	ANABAPTISTS	ANAEROBIOSES
AMPHIBIOUSLY	AMPHIPLOIDY	AMPULLOSITIES	ANABAPTIZE	ANAEROBIOSIS
AMPHIBIOUSNESS	AMPHIPODOUS	AMPULLOSITY	ANABAPTIZED	ANAEROBIOTIC
AMPHIBLASTIC	AMPHIPROSTYLAR	AMPUTATING	ANABAPTIZES	ANAEROBIUM
AMPHIBLASTULA	AMPHIPROSTYLE	AMPUTATION	ANABAPTIZING	ANAESTHESES
AMPHIBLASTULAE	AMPHIPROSTYLES	AMPUTATIONS	ANABLEPSES	ANAESTHESIA
AMPHIBOLES	AMPHIPROTIC	AMPUTATORS	ANABOLISMS	ANAESTHESIAS
AMPHIBOLIC	AMPHISBAENA	AMRITATTVA	ANABOLITES	ANAESTHESIOLOGY
AMPHIBOLIES	AMPHISBAENAE	AMRITATTVAS	ANABOLITIC	ANAESTHESIS
AMPHIBOLITE	AMPHISBAENAS	AMRITATVAS	ANABRANCHES	ANAESTHETIC
AMPHIBOLITES	AMPHISBAENIC	AMSINCKIAS	ANACARDIACEOUS	ANAESTHETICALLY
AMPHIBOLOGICAL	AMPHISCIAN	AMUSEMENTS	ANACARDIUM	ANAESTHETICS
AMPHIBOLOGIES	AMPHISCIANS	AMUSINGNESS	ANACARDIUMS	ANAESTHETISE
AMPHIBOLOGY	AMPHISTOMATAL	AMUSINGNESSES	ANACATHARSES	ANAESTHETISED
AMPHIBOLOUS	AMPHISTOMATIC	AMUSIVENESS	ANACATHARSIS	ANAESTHETISES
AMPHIBRACH	AMPHISTOMOUS	AMUSIVENESSES	ANACATHARTIC	ANAESTHETISING
AMPHIBRACHIC	AMPHISTYLAR	AMYGDALACEOUS	ANACATHARTICS	ANAESTHETIST
AMPHIBRACHS	AMPHISTYLARS	AMYGDALATE	ANACHARISES	ANAESTHETISTS
AMPHICHROIC	AMPHITHEATER	AMYGDALINE	ANACHORISM	ANAESTHETIZE
AMPHICHROMATIC	AMPHITHEATERS	AMYGDALINS	ANACHORISMS	ANAESTHETIZED
AMPHICOELOUS	AMPHITHEATRAL	AMYGDALOID	ANACHRONIC	ANAESTHETIZES
AMPHICTYON	AMPHITHEATRE	AMYGDALOIDAL	ANACHRONICAL	ANAESTHETIZING
AMPHICTYONIC	AMPHITHEATRES	AMYGDALOIDS	ANACHRONICALLY	ANAGENESES
AMPHICTYONIES	AMPHITHEATRIC	AMYLACEOUS	ANACHRONISM	ANAGENESIS
AMPHICTYONS	AMPHITHEATRICAL	AMYLOBARBITONE	ANACHRONISMS	ANAGLYPHIC
AMPHICTYONY	AMPHITHECIA	AMYLOBARBITONES	ANACHRONISTIC	ANAGLYPHICAL
AMPHIDENTATE	AMPHITHECIUM	AMYLOIDOSES	ANACHRONOUS	ANAGLYPHIES
AMPHIDIPLOID	AMPHITRICHA	AMYLOIDOSIS	ANACHRONOUSLY	ANAGLYPTIC
AMPHIDIPLOIDIES	AMPHITRICHOUS	AMYLOLYSES	ANACLASTIC	ANAGLYPTICAL
AMPHIDIPLOIDS	AMPHITROPOUS	AMYLOLYSIS	ANACOLUTHA	ANAGNORISES
AMPHIDIPLOIDY	AMPHOLYTES	AMYLOLYTIC	ANACOLUTHIA	ANAGNORISIS
AMPHIGASTRIA	AMPHOTERIC	AMYLOPECTIN	ANACOLUTHIAS	ANAGOGICAL
AMPHIGASTRIUM	AMPICILLIN	AMYLOPECTINS	ANACOLUTHIC	ANAGOGICALLY
AMPHIGORIC	AMPICILLINS	AMYLOPLAST	ANACOLUTHICALLY	ANAGRAMMATIC

ANAGRAMMATICAL	ANALYSATIONS	ANAPLEROSIS	ANATOMISATION	ANCIENTEST
ANAGRAMMATISE	ANALYTICAL	ANAPLEROTIC	ANATOMISATIONS	ANCIENTNESS
ANAGRAMMATISED	ANALYTICALLY	ANAPTYCTIC	ANATOMISED	ANCIENTNESSES
ANAGRAMMATISES	ANALYTICITIES	ANAPTYCTICAL	ANATOMISER	ANCIENTRIES
ANAGRAMMATISING	ANALYTICITY	ANARCHICAL	ANATOMISERS	ANCILLARIES
ANAGRAMMATISM	ANALYZABILITIES	ANARCHICALLY	ANATOMISES	ANCIPITOUS
ANAGRAMMATISMS	ANALYZABILITY	ANARCHISED	ANATOMISING	ANCYLOSTOMIASES
ANAGRAMMATIST	ANALYZABLE	ANARCHISES	ANATOMISTS	ANCYLOSTOMIASIS
ANAGRAMMATISTS	ANALYZATION	ANARCHISING	ANATOMIZATION	ANDALUSITE
ANAGRAMMATIZE	ANALYZATIONS	ANARCHISMS	ANATOMIZATIONS	ANDALUSITES
ANAGRAMMATIZED	ANAMNESTIC	ANARCHISTIC	ANATOMIZED	ANDANTINOS
ANAGRAMMATIZES	ANAMNESTICALLY	ANARCHISTICALLY	ANATOMIZER	ANDOUILLES
ANAGRAMMATIZING	ANAMNIOTES	ANARCHISTS	ANATOMIZERS	ANDOUILLETTE
ANAGRAMMED	ANAMNIOTIC	ANARCHIZED	ANATOMIZES	ANDOUILLETTES
ANAGRAMMER	ANAMORPHIC	ANARCHIZES	ANATOMIZING	ANDRADITES
ANAGRAMMERS	ANAMORPHISM	ANARCHIZING	ANATROPIES	ANDROCENTRIC
ANAGRAMMING	ANAMORPHISMS	ANARTHRIAS	ANATROPOUS	ANDROCENTRISM
ANALEMMATA	ANAMORPHOSCOPE	ANARTHROUS	ANCESTORED	ANDROCENTRISMS
ANALEMMATIC	ANAMORPHOSCOPES	ANARTHROUSLY	ANCESTORIAL	ANDROCEPHALOUS
ANALEPTICS	ANAMORPHOSES	ANARTHROUSNESS	ANCESTORING	ANDROCLINIA
ANALGESIAS	ANAMORPHOSIS	ANASARCOUS	ANCESTRALLY	ANDROCLINIUM
ANALGESICS	ANAMORPHOUS	ANASTIGMAT	ANCESTRALS	ANDRODIOECIOUS
ANALGETICS	ANANDAMIDE	ANASTIGMATIC	ANCESTRESS	ANDRODIOECISM
ANALOGICAL	ANANDAMIDES	ANASTIGMATISM	ANCESTRESSES	ANDRODIOECISMS
ANALOGICALLY	ANAPAESTIC	ANASTIGMATISMS	ANCESTRIES	ANDROECIAL
ANALOGISED	ANAPAESTICAL	ANASTIGMATS	ANCHORAGES	ANDROECIUM
ANALOGISES	ANAPESTICS	ANASTOMOSE	ANCHORESSES	ANDROGENESES
ANALOGISING	ANAPHORESES	ANASTOMOSED	ANCHORETIC	ANDROGENESIS
ANALOGISMS	ANAPHORESIS	ANASTOMOSES	ANCHORETICAL	ANDROGENETIC
ANALOGISTS	ANAPHORICAL	ANASTOMOSING	ANCHORETTE	ANDROGENIC
ANALOGIZED	ANAPHORICALLY	ANASTOMOSIS	ANCHORETTES	ANDROGENOUS
ANALOGIZES	ANAPHRODISIA	ANASTOMOTIC	ANCHORITES	ANDROGYNES
ANALOGIZING	ANAPHRODISIAC	ANASTROPHE	ANCHORITIC	ANDROGYNIES
ANALOGOUSLY	ANAPHRODISIACS	ANASTROPHES	ANCHORITICAL	ANDROGYNOPHORE
ANALOGOUSNESS	ANAPHRODISIAS	ANASTROZOLE	ANCHORITICALLY	ANDROGYNOPHORES
ANALOGOUSNESSES	ANAPHYLACTIC	ANASTROZOLES	ANCHORLESS	ANDROGYNOUS
ANALPHABET	ANAPHYLACTOID	ANATHEMATA	ANCHORPEOPLE	ANDROLOGIES
ANALPHABETE	ANAPHYLAXES	ANATHEMATICAL	ANCHORPERSON	ANDROLOGIST
ANALPHABETES	ANAPHYLAXIES	ANATHEMATICALS	ANCHORPERSONS	ANDROLOGISTS
ANALPHABETIC	ANAPHYLAXIS	ANATHEMATISE	ANCHORWOMAN	ANDROMEDAS
ANALPHABETICS	ANAPHYLAXY	ANATHEMATISED	ANCHORWOMEN	ANDROMEDOTOXIN
ANALPHABETISM	ANAPLASIAS	ANATHEMATISES	ANCHOVETAS	ANDROMEDOTOXINS
ANALPHABETISMS	ANAPLASMAS	ANATHEMATISING	ANCHOVETTA	ANDROMONOECIOUS
ANALPHABETS	ANAPLASMATA	ANATHEMATIZE	ANCHOVETTAS	ANDROMONOECISM
ANALYSABILITIES	ANAPLASMOSES	ANATHEMATIZED	ANCHYLOSED	ANDROMONOECISMS
ANALYSABILITY	ANAPLASMOSIS	ANATHEMATIZES	ANCHYLOSES	ANDROPAUSE
ANALYSABLE	ANAPLASTIC	ANATHEMATIZING	ANCHYLOSING	ANDROPAUSES
ANALYSANDS	ANAPLASTIES	ANATOMICAL	ANCHYLOSIS	ANDROPHORE
ANALYSATION	ANAPLEROSES	ANATOMICALLY	ANCHYLOTIC	ANDROPHORES

ANDROSPHINGES	ANESTHESIOLOGY	ANGIOGRAPHIC	ANGLOMANIAS	ANICONISMS
ANDROSPHINX	ANESTHETIC	ANGIOGRAPHIES	ANGLOPHILE	ANICONISTS
ANDROSPHINXES	ANESTHETICALLY	ANGIOGRAPHY	ANGLOPHILES	ANILINCTUS
ANDROSTERONE	ANESTHETICS	ANGIOLOGIES	ANGLOPHILIA	ANILINCTUSES
ANDROSTERONES	ANESTHETISATION	ANGIOMATOUS	ANGLOPHILIAS	ANILINGUSES
ANECDOTAGE	ANESTHETISE	ANGIOOEDEMA	ANGLOPHILIC	ANIMADVERSION
ANECDOTAGES	ANESTHETISED	ANGIOOEDEMAS	ANGLOPHILS	ANIMADVERSIONS
ANECDOTALISM	ANESTHETISES	ANGIOOEDEMATA	ANGLOPHOBE	ANIMADVERT
ANECDOTALISMS	ANESTHETISING	ANGIOPLASTIES	ANGLOPHOBES	ANIMADVERTED
ANECDOTALIST	ANESTHETIST	ANGIOPLASTY	ANGLOPHOBIA	ANIMADVERTER
ANECDOTALISTS	ANESTHETISTS	ANGIOSARCOMA	ANGLOPHOBIAC	ANIMADVERTERS
ANECDOTALLY	ANESTHETIZATION	ANGIOSARCOMAS	ANGLOPHOBIACS	ANIMADVERTING
ANECDOTICAL	ANESTHETIZE	ANGIOSARCOMATA	ANGLOPHOBIAS	ANIMADVERTS
ANECDOTICALLY	ANESTHETIZED	ANGIOSPERM	ANGLOPHOBIC	ANIMALCULA
ANECDOTIST	ANESTHETIZES	ANGIOSPERMAL	ANGLOPHONE	ANIMALCULAR
ANECDOTISTS	ANESTHETIZING	ANGIOSPERMOUS	ANGLOPHONES	ANIMALCULE
ANELASTICITIES	ANEUPLOIDIES	ANGIOSPERMS	ANGLOPHONIC	ANIMALCULES
ANELASTICITY	ANEUPLOIDS	ANGIOSTOMATOUS	ANGOPHORAS	ANIMALCULISM
ANEMICALLY	ANEUPLOIDY	ANGIOSTOMOUS	ANGOSTURAS	ANIMALCULISMS
ANEMOCHORE	ANEURISMAL	ANGIOTENSIN	ANGRINESSES	ANIMALCULIST
ANEMOCHORES	ANEURISMALLY	ANGIOTENSINS	ANGUIFAUNA	ANIMALCULISTS
ANEMOCHOROUS	ANEURISMATIC	ANGISHORES	ANGUIFAUNAE	ANIMALCULUM
ANEMOGRAMS	ANEURYSMAL	ANGLEBERRIES	ANGUIFAUNAS	ANIMALIERS
ANEMOGRAPH	ANEURYSMALLY	ANGLEBERRY	ANGUILLIFORM	ANIMALISATION
ANEMOGRAPHIC	ANEURYSMATIC	ANGLEDOZER	ANGUIPEDES	ANIMALISATIONS
ANEMOGRAPHIES	ANFRACTUOSITIES	ANGLEDOZERS	ANGUISHING	ANIMALISED
ANEMOGRAPHS	ANFRACTUOSITY	ANGLERFISH	ANGULARITIES	ANIMALISES
ANEMOGRAPHY	ANFRACTUOUS	ANGLERFISHES	ANGULARITY	ANIMALISING
ANEMOLOGIES	ANGANWADIS	ANGLESITES	ANGULARNESS	ANIMALISMS
ANEMOMETER	ANGASHORES	ANGLETWITCH	ANGULARNESSES	ANIMALISTIC
ANEMOMETERS	ANGELFISHES	ANGLETWITCHES	ANGULATING	ANIMALISTS
ANEMOMETRIC	ANGELHOODS	ANGLEWORMS	ANGULATION	ANIMALITIES
ANEMOMETRICAL	ANGELICALLY	ANGLICISATION	ANGULATIONS	ANIMALIZATION
ANEMOMETRIES	ANGELOLATRIES	ANGLICISATIONS	ANGUSTIFOLIATE	ANIMALIZATIONS
ANEMOMETRY	ANGELOLATRY	ANGLICISED	ANGUSTIROSTRATE	ANIMALIZED
ANEMOPHILIES	ANGELOLOGIES	ANGLICISES	ANGWANTIBO	ANIMALIZES
ANEMOPHILOUS	ANGELOLOGIST	ANGLICISING	ANGWANTIBOS	ANIMALIZING
ANEMOPHILY	ANGELOLOGISTS	ANGLICISMS	ANHARMONIC	ANIMALLIKE
ANEMOPHOBIA	ANGELOLOGY	ANGLICISTS	ANHEDONIAS	ANIMATEDLY
ANEMOPHOBIAS	ANGELOPHANIES	ANGLICIZATION	ANHELATION	ANIMATENESS
ANEMOSCOPE	ANGELOPHANY	ANGLICIZATIONS	ANHELATIONS	ANIMATENESSES
ANEMOSCOPES	ANGIOCARPOUS	ANGLICIZED	ANHIDROSES	ANIMATEURS
ANENCEPHALIA	ANGIOEDEMA	ANGLICIZES	ANHIDROSIS	ANIMATINGLY
ANENCEPHALIAS	ANGIOEDEMAS	ANGLICIZING	ANHIDROTIC	ANIMATIONS
ANENCEPHALIC	ANGIOEDEMATA	ANGLIFYING	ANHIDROTICS	ANIMATISMS
ANENCEPHALIES	ANGIOGENESES	ANGLISTICS	ANHUNGERED	ANIMATISTS
ANENCEPHALY	ANGIOGENESIS	ANGLOMANIA	ANHYDRASES	ANIMATRONIC
ANESTHESIA	ANGIOGENIC	ANGLOMANIAC	ANHYDRIDES	ANIMATRONICALLY
ANESTHESIAS	ANGIOGRAMS	ANGLOMANIACS	ANHYDRITES	ANIMATRONICS

ANIMOSITIES	ANNIHILABLE	ANNUNCIATION	ANORTHOSITIC	ANTECEDENTLY
ANISEIKONIA	ANNIHILATE	ANNUNCIATIONS	ANOTHERGUESS	ANTECEDENTS
ANISEIKONIAS	ANNIHILATED	ANNUNCIATIVE	ANOVULANTS	ANTECEDING
ANISEIKONIC	ANNIHILATES	ANNUNCIATOR	ANOVULATION	ANTECESSOR
ANISOCERCAL	ANNIHILATING	ANNUNCIATORS	ANOVULATIONS	ANTECESSORS
ANISODACTYL	ANNIHILATION	ANNUNCIATORY	ANOVULATORY	ANTECHAMBER
ANISODACTYLOUS	ANNIHILATIONISM	ANNUNTIATE	ANOXAEMIAS	ANTECHAMBERS
ANISODACTYLS	ANNIHILATIONS	ANNUNTIATED	ANSAPHONES	ANTECHAPEL
ANISOGAMIES	ANNIHILATIVE	ANNUNTIATES	ANSWERABILITIES	ANTECHAPELS
ANISOGAMOUS	ANNIHILATOR	ANNUNTIATING	ANSWERABILITY	ANTECHOIRS
ANISOMERIC	ANNIHILATORS	ANODICALLY	ANSWERABLE	ANTEDATING
ANISOMEROUS	ANNIHILATORY	ANODISATION	ANSWERABLENESS	ANTEDATINGS
ANISOMETRIC	ANNIVERSARIES	ANODISATIONS	ANSWERABLY	ANTEDILUVIAL
ANISOMETROPIA	ANNIVERSARY	ANODIZATION	ANSWERLESS	ANTEDILUVIALLY
ANISOMETROPIAS	ANNOTATABLE	ANODIZATIONS	ANSWERPHONE	ANTEDILUVIAN
ANISOMETROPIC	ANNOTATING	ANODONTIAS	ANSWERPHONES	ANTEDILUVIANS
ANISOMORPHIC	ANNOTATION	ANOESTROUS	ANTAGONISABLE	ANTEMERIDIAN
ANISOPHYLLIES	ANNOTATIONS	ANOINTINGS	ANTAGONISATION	ANTEMORTEM
ANISOPHYLLOUS	ANNOTATIVE	ANOINTMENT	ANTAGONISATIONS	ANTEMUNDANE
ANISOPHYLLY	ANNOTATORS	ANOINTMENTS	ANTAGONISE	ANTENATALLY
ANISOTROPIC	ANNOUNCEMENT	ANOMALISTIC	ANTAGONISED	ANTENATALS
ANISOTROPICALLY	ANNOUNCEMENTS	ANOMALISTICAL	ANTAGONISES	ANTENNIFEROUS
ANISOTROPIES	ANNOUNCERS	ANOMALISTICALLY	ANTAGONISING	ANTENNIFORM
ANISOTROPISM	ANNOUNCING	ANOMALOUSLY	ANTAGONISM	ANTENNULAR
ANISOTROPISMS	ANNOYANCES	ANOMALOUSNESS	ANTAGONISMS	ANTENNULES
ANISOTROPY	ANNOYINGLY	ANOMALOUSNESSES	ANTAGONIST	ANTENUPTIAL
ANKLEBONES	ANNUALISED	ANONACEOUS	ANTAGONISTIC	ANTENUPTIALS
ANKYLOSAUR	ANNUALISES	ANONYMISED	ANTAGONISTS	ANTEORBITAL
ANKYLOSAURS	ANNUALISING	ANONYMISER	ANTAGONIZABLE	ANTEPENDIA
ANKYLOSAURUS	ANNUALIZED	ANONYMISERS	ANTAGONIZATION	ANTEPENDIUM
ANKYLOSAURUSES	ANNUALIZES	ANONYMISES	ANTAGONIZATIONS	ANTEPENDIUMS
ANKYLOSING	ANNUALIZING	ANONYMISING	ANTAGONIZE	ANTEPENULT
ANKYLOSTOMIASES	ANNUITANTS	ANONYMITIES	ANTAGONIZED	ANTEPENULTIMA
ANKYLOSTOMIASIS	ANNUITISED	ANONYMIZED	ANTAGONIZES	ANTEPENULTIMAS
ANNABERGITE	ANNUITISES	ANONYMIZER	ANTAGONIZING	ANTEPENULTIMATE
ANNABERGITES	ANNUITISING	ANONYMIZERS	ANTALKALIES	ANTEPENULTS
ANNALISING	ANNUITIZED	ANONYMIZES	ANTALKALINE	ANTEPOSITION
ANNALISTIC	ANNUITIZES	ANONYMIZING	ANTALKALINES	ANTEPOSITIONS
ANNALIZING	ANNUITIZING	ANONYMOUSLY	ANTALKALIS	ANTEPRANDIAL
ANNEALINGS	ANNULARITIES	ANONYMOUSNESS	ANTAPHRODISIAC	ANTERIORITIES
ANNELIDANS	ANNULARITY	ANONYMOUSNESSES	ANTAPHRODISIACS	ANTERIORITY
ANNEXATION	ANNULATION	ANOPHELINE	ANTARTHRITIC	ANTERIORLY
ANNEXATIONAL	ANNULATIONS	ANOPHELINES	ANTARTHRITICS	ANTEROGRADE
ANNEXATIONISM	ANNULLABLE	ANORECTICS	ANTASTHMATIC	ANTEVERSION
ANNEXATIONISMS	ANNULMENTS	ANOREXIGENIC	ANTASTHMATICS	ANTEVERSIONS
ANNEXATIONIST	ANNUNCIATE	ANORTHITES	ANTEBELLUM	ANTEVERTED
ANNEXATIONISTS	ANNUNCIATED	ANORTHITIC	ANTECEDENCE	ANTEVERTING
ANNEXATIONS	ANNUNCIATES	ANORTHOSITE	ANTECEDENCES	ANTHELICES
ANNEXMENTS	ANNUNCIATING	ANORTHOSITES	ANTECEDENT	ANTHELIONS

ANTHELIXES	ANTHOXANTHIN	ANTHROPOPATHIC	ANTIARTHRITIC	ANTICELLULITE
ANTHELMINTHIC	ANTHOXANTHINS	ANTHROPOPATHIES	ANTIARTHRITICS	ANTICENSORSHIP
ANTHELMINTHICS	ANTHOZOANS	ANTHROPOPATHISM	ANTIARTHRITIS	ANTICHLORISTIC
ANTHELMINTIC	ANTHRACENE	ANTHROPOPATHY	ANTIASTHMA	ANTICHLORS
ANTHELMINTICS	ANTHRACENES	ANTHROPOPHAGI	ANTIASTHMATIC	ANTICHOICE
ANTHEMISES	ANTHRACITE	ANTHROPOPHAGIC	ANTIASTHMATICS	ANTICHOICER
ANTHEMWISE	ANTHRACITES	ANTHROPOPHAGIES	ANTIAUTHORITY	ANTICHOICERS
ANTHERIDIA	ANTHRACITIC	ANTHROPOPHAGITE	ANTIAUXINS	ANTICHOLESTEROL
ANTHERIDIAL	ANTHRACNOSE	ANTHROPOPHAGOUS	ANTIBACCHII	ANTICHOLINERGIC
ANTHERIDIUM	ANTHRACNOSES	ANTHROPOPHAGUS	ANTIBACCHIUS	ANTICHRIST
ANTHEROZOID	ANTHRACOID	ANTHROPOPHAGY	ANTIBACKLASH	ANTICHRISTIAN
ANTHEROZOIDS	ANTHRACOSES	ANTHROPOPHOBIA	ANTIBACTERIAL	ANTICHRISTIANLY
ANTHEROZOOID	ANTHRACOSIS	ANTHROPOPHOBIAS	ANTIBACTERIALS	ANTICHRISTS
ANTHEROZOOIDS	ANTHRACYCLINE	ANTHROPOPHOBIC	ANTIBALLISTIC	ANTICHTHONES
ANTHERSMUT	ANTHRACYCLINES	ANTHROPOPHOBICS	ANTIBARBARUS	ANTICHURCH
ANTHERSMUTS	ANTHRANILATE	ANTHROPOPHUISM	ANTIBARBARUSES	ANTICIGARETTE
ANTHOCARPOUS	ANTHRANILATES	ANTHROPOPHUISMS	ANTIBARYON	ANTICIPANT
ANTHOCARPS	ANTHRANILIC	ANTHROPOPHYTE	ANTIBARYONS	ANTICIPANTS
ANTHOCHLORE	ANTHRAQUINONE	ANTHROPOPHYTES	ANTIBILIOUS	ANTICIPATABLE
ANTHOCHLORES	ANTHRAQUINONES	ANTHROPOPSYCHIC	ANTIBILLBOARD	ANTICIPATE
ANTHOCYANIN	ANTHROPICAL	ANTHROPOSOPHIC	ANTIBIOSES	ANTICIPATED
ANTHOCYANINS	ANTHROPOBIOLOGY	ANTHROPOSOPHIES	ANTIBIOSIS	ANTICIPATES
ANTHOCYANS	ANTHROPOCENTRIC	ANTHROPOSOPHIST	ANTIBIOTIC	ANTICIPATING
ANTHOLOGICAL	ANTHROPOGENESES	ANTHROPOSOPHY	ANTIBIOTICALLY	ANTICIPATION
ANTHOLOGIES	ANTHROPOGENESIS	ANTHROPOTOMIES	ANTIBIOTICS	ANTICIPATIONS
ANTHOLOGISE	ANTHROPOGENETIC	ANTHROPOTOMY	ANTIBLACKISM	ANTICIPATIVE
ANTHOLOGISED	ANTHROPOGENIC	ANTHURIUMS	ANTIBLACKISMS	ANTICIPATIVELY
ANTHOLOGISER	ANTHROPOGENIES	ANTIABORTION	ANTIBODIES	ANTICIPATOR
ANTHOLOGISERS	ANTHROPOGENY	ANTIABORTIONIST	ANTIBOURGEOIS	ANTICIPATORILY
ANTHOLOGISES	ANTHROPOGONIES	ANTIACADEMIC	ANTIBOYCOTT	ANTICIPATORS
ANTHOLOGISING	ANTHROPOGONY	ANTIADITIS	ANTIBURGLAR	ANTICIPATORY
ANTHOLOGIST	ANTHROPOGRAPHY	ANTIADITISES	ANTIBURGLARY	ANTICISING
ANTHOLOGISTS	ANTHROPOID	ANTIAGGRESSION	ANTIBUSERS	ANTICIVISM
ANTHOLOGIZE	ANTHROPOIDAL	ANTIAIRCRAFT	ANTIBUSINESS	ANTICIVISMS
ANTHOLOGIZED	ANTHROPOIDS	ANTIAIRCRAFTS	ANTIBUSING	ANTICIZING
ANTHOLOGIZER	ANTHROPOLATRIES	ANTIALCOHOL	ANTICAKING	ANTICLASSICAL
ANTHOLOGIZERS	ANTHROPOLATRY	ANTIALCOHOLISM	ANTICANCER	ANTICLASTIC
ANTHOLOGIZES	ANTHROPOLOGICAL	ANTIALCOHOLISMS	ANTICAPITALISM	ANTICLERICAL
ANTHOLOGIZING	ANTHROPOLOGIES	ANTIALLERGENIC	ANTICAPITALISMS	ANTICLERICALISM
ANTHOMANIA	ANTHROPOLOGIST	ANTIANAEMIA	ANTICAPITALIST	ANTICLERICALS
ANTHOMANIAC	ANTHROPOLOGISTS	ANTIANDROGEN	ANTICAPITALISTS	ANTICLIMACTIC
ANTHOMANIACS	ANTHROPOLOGY	ANTIANDROGENS	ANTICARCINOGEN	ANTICLIMACTICAL
ANTHOMANIAS	ANTHROPOMETRIC	ANTIANEMIA	ANTICARCINOGENS	ANTICLIMAX
ANTHOPHILOUS	ANTHROPOMETRIES	ANTIANXIETY	ANTICARIES	ANTICLIMAXES
ANTHOPHORE	ANTHROPOMETRIST	ANTIAPARTHEID	ANTICATALYST	ANTICLINAL
ANTHOPHORES	ANTHROPOMETRY	ANTIAPHRODISIAC	ANTICATALYSTS	ANTICLINALS
ANTHOPHYLLITE	ANTHROPOMORPH	ANTIARMOUR	ANTICATHODE	ANTICLINES
ANTHOPHYLLITES	ANTHROPOMORPHIC	ANTIARRHYTHMIC	ANTICATHODES	ANTICLINORIA
ANTHOTAXIES	ANTHROPOMORPHS	ANTIARRHYTHMICS	ANTICATHOLIC	ANTICLINORIUM

A

ANTICLOCKWISE	ANTIDIARRHEALS	ANTIFEMINISM	ANTIHISTAMINICS	ANTIMARIJUANA
ANTICLOTTING	ANTIDIARRHOEAL	ANTIFEMINISMS	ANTIHISTORICAL	ANTIMARKET
ANTICOAGULANT	ANTIDIARRHOEALS	ANTIFEMINIST	ANTIHOMOSEXUAL	ANTIMARKETEER
ANTICOAGULANTS	ANTIDILUTION	ANTIFEMINISTS	ANTIHUMANISM	ANTIMARKETEERS
ANTICODONS	ANTIDIURETIC	ANTIFERROMAGNET	ANTIHUMANISMS	ANTIMASQUE
ANTICOINCIDENCE	ANTIDIURETICS	ANTIFERTILITY	ANTIHUMANISTIC	ANTIMASQUES
ANTICOLLISION	ANTIDOGMATIC	ANTIFILIBUSTER	ANTIHUNTER	ANTIMATERIALISM
ANTICOLONIAL	ANTIDOTALLY	ANTIFILIBUSTERS	ANTIHUNTERS	ANTIMATERIALIST
ANTICOLONIALISM	ANTIDOTING	ANTIFOAMING	ANTIHUNTING	ANTIMATTER
ANTICOLONIALIST	ANTIDROMIC	ANTIFOGGING	ANTIHYDROGEN	ANTIMATTERS
ANTICOLONIALS	ANTIDROMICALLY	ANTIFORECLOSURE	ANTIHYDROGENS	ANTIMECHANIST
ANTICOMMERCIAL	ANTIDUMPING	ANTIFOREIGN	ANTIHYSTERIC	ANTIMECHANISTS
ANTICOMMUNISM	ANTIDUMPINGS	ANTIFOREIGNER	ANTIHYSTERICS	ANTIMERGER
ANTICOMMUNISMS	ANTIECONOMIC	ANTIFORMALIST	ANTIJACOBIN	ANTIMERISM
ANTICOMMUNIST	ANTIEDUCATIONAL	ANTIFOULING	ANTIJACOBINS	ANTIMERISMS
ANTICOMMUNISTS	ANTIEGALITARIAN	ANTIFOULINGS	ANTIJAMMING	ANTIMETABOLE
ANTICOMPETITIVE	ANTIELECTRON	ANTIFREEZE	ANTIJAMMINGS	ANTIMETABOLES
ANTICONSUMER	ANTIELECTRONS	ANTIFREEZES	ANTIKICKBACK	ANTIMETABOLIC
ANTICONVULSANT	ANTIELITES	ANTIFRICTION	ANTIKNOCKS	ANTIMETABOLITE
ANTICONVULSANTS	ANTIELITISM	ANTIFUNGAL	ANTILEGOMENA	ANTIMETABOLITES
ANTICONVULSIVE	ANTIELITISMS	ANTIFUNGALS	ANTILEPROSY	ANTIMETATHESES
ANTICONVULSIVES	ANTIELITIST	ANTIGAMBLING	ANTILEPTON	ANTIMETATHESIS
ANTICORPORATE	ANTIELITISTS	ANTIGENICALLY	ANTILEPTONS	ANTIMICROBIAL
ANTICORROSION	ANTIEMETIC	ANTIGENICITIES	ANTILEUKAEMIC	ANTIMICROBIALS
ANTICORROSIONS	ANTIEMETICS	ANTIGENICITY	ANTILEUKEMIC	ANTIMILITARISM
ANTICORROSIVE	ANTIENTROPIC	ANTIGLOBULIN	ANTILIBERAL	ANTIMILITARISMS
ANTICORROSIVES	ANTIEPILEPSY	ANTIGLOBULINS	ANTILIBERALISM	ANTIMILITARIST
ANTICORRUPTION	ANTIEPILEPTIC	ANTIGOVERNMENT	ANTILIBERALISMS	ANTIMILITARISTS
ANTICREATIVE	ANTIEPILEPTICS	ANTIGRAVITIES	ANTILIBERALS	ANTIMILITARY
ANTICRUELTY	ANTIEROTIC	ANTIGRAVITY	ANTILIBERTARIAN	ANTIMISSILE
ANTICULTURAL	ANTIESTROGEN	ANTIGROPELOES	ANTILIFERS	ANTIMISSILES
ANTICYCLONE	ANTIESTROGENS	ANTIGROPELOS	ANTILITERATE	ANTIMITOTIC
ANTICYCLONES	ANTIEVOLUTION	ANTIGROWTH	ANTILITTER	ANTIMITOTICS
ANTICYCLONIC	ANTIEVOLUTIONS	ANTIGUERRILLA	ANTILITTERING	ANTIMNEMONIC
ANTIDANDRUFF	ANTIFAMILY	ANTIHALATION	ANTILOGARITHM	ANTIMNEMONICS
ANTIDAZZLE	ANTIFASCISM	ANTIHALATIONS	ANTILOGARITHMIC	ANTIMODERN
ANTIDEFAMATION	ANTIFASCISMS	ANTIHELICES	ANTILOGARITHMS	ANTIMODERNIST
ANTIDEMOCRATIC	ANTIFASCIST	ANTIHELIXES	ANTILOGICAL	ANTIMODERNISTS
ANTIDEPRESSANT	ANTIFASCISTS	ANTIHELMINTHIC	ANTILOGIES	ANTIMONARCHICAL
ANTIDEPRESSANTS	ANTIFASHION	ANTIHELMINTHICS	ANTILOGOUS	ANTIMONARCHIST
ANTIDEPRESSION	ANTIFASHIONABLE	ANTIHEROES	ANTILOPINE	ANTIMONARCHISTS
ANTIDERIVATIVE	ANTIFASHIONS	ANTIHEROIC	ANTILYNCHING	ANTIMONATE
ANTIDERIVATIVES	ANTIFATIGUE	ANTIHEROINE	ANTIMACASSAR	ANTIMONATES
ANTIDESICCANT	ANTIFEBRILE	ANTIHEROINES	ANTIMACASSARS	ANTIMONIAL
ANTIDESICCANTS	ANTIFEBRILES	ANTIHERPES	ANTIMAGNETIC	ANTIMONIALS
ANTIDEVELOPMENT	ANTIFEDERALIST	ANTIHIJACK	ANTIMALARIA	ANTIMONIATE
ANTIDIABETIC	ANTIFEDERALISTS	ANTIHISTAMINE	ANTIMALARIAL	ANTIMONIATES
ANTIDIABETICS	ANTIFEMALE	ANTIHISTAMINES	ANTIMALARIALS	ANTIMONIDE
ANTIDIARRHEAL	ANTIFEMININE	ANTIHISTAMINIC	ANTIMANAGEMENT	ANTIMONIDES

ANTIMONIES	ANTIOBESITY	ANTIPHRASES	ANTIQUATION	ANTIRRHINUM
ANTIMONIOUS	ANTIOBSCENITY	ANTIPHRASIS	ANTIQUATIONS	ANTIRRHINUMS
ANTIMONITE	ANTIODONTALGIC	ANTIPHRASTIC	ANTIQUENESS	ANTISATELLITE
ANTIMONITES	ANTIODONTALGICS	ANTIPHRASTICAL	ANTIQUENESSES	ANTISCIANS
ANTIMONOPOLIST	ANTIOESTROGEN	ANTIPIRACY	ANTIQUIEST	ANTISCIENCE
ANTIMONOPOLISTS	ANTIOESTROGENS	ANTIPLAGUE	ANTIQUITARIAN	ANTISCIENCES
ANTIMONOPOLY	ANTIOXIDANT	ANTIPLAQUE	ANTIQUITARIANS	ANTISCIENTIFIC
ANTIMONOUS	ANTIOXIDANTS	ANTIPLEASURE	ANTIQUITIES	ANTISCORBUTIC
ANTIMONYLS	ANTIOZONANT	ANTIPOACHING	ANTIRABIES	ANTISCORBUTICS
ANTIMOSQUITO	ANTIOZONANTS	ANTIPODALS	ANTIRACHITIC	ANTISCRIPTURAL
ANTIMUSICAL	ANTIPARALLEL	ANTIPODEAN	ANTIRACHITICS	ANTISECRECY
ANTIMUSICS	ANTIPARALLELS	ANTIPODEANS	ANTIRACISM	ANTISEGREGATION
ANTIMUTAGEN	ANTIPARASITIC	ANTIPOETIC	ANTIRACISMS	ANTISEIZURE
ANTIMUTAGENS	ANTIPARASITICS	ANTIPOLICE	ANTIRACIST	ANTISEMITE
ANTIMYCINS	ANTIPARTICLE	ANTIPOLITICAL	ANTIRACISTS	ANTISEMITES
ANTIMYCOTIC	ANTIPARTICLES	ANTIPOLITICS	ANTIRADARS	ANTISEMITIC
ANTINARRATIVE	ANTIPARTIES	ANTIPOLLUTION	ANTIRADICAL	ANTISEMITICALLY
ANTINARRATIVES	ANTIPASTOS	ANTIPOLLUTIONS	ANTIRADICALISM	ANTISEMITISM
ANTINATIONAL	ANTIPATHETIC	ANTIPOPULAR	ANTIRADICALISMS	ANTISEMITISMS
ANTINATIONALIST	ANTIPATHETICAL	ANTIPORNOGRAPHY	ANTIRATIONAL	ANTISENTIMENTAL
ANTINATURAL	ANTIPATHIC	ANTIPORTER	ANTIRATIONALISM	ANTISEPALOUS
ANTINATURE	ANTIPATHIES	ANTIPORTERS	ANTIRATIONALIST	ANTISEPARATIST
ANTINAUSEA	ANTIPATHIST	ANTIPOVERTY	ANTIRATIONALITY	ANTISEPARATISTS
ANTINEOPLASTIC	ANTIPATHISTS	ANTIPREDATOR	ANTIREALISM	ANTISEPSES
ANTINEOPLASTICS	ANTIPERIODIC	ANTIPRIESTLY	ANTIREALISMS	ANTISEPSIS
ANTINEPHRITIC	ANTIPERIODICS	ANTIPROGRESSIVE	ANTIREALIST	ANTISEPTIC
ANTINEPHRITICS	ANTIPERISTALSES	ANTIPROTON	ANTIREALISTS	ANTISEPTICALLY
ANTINEPOTISM	ANTIPERISTALSIS	ANTIPROTONS	ANTIRECESSION	ANTISEPTICISE
ANTINEUTRINO	ANTIPERISTALTIC	ANTIPRURITIC	ANTIREFLECTION	ANTISEPTICISED
ANTINEUTRINOS	ANTIPERISTASES	ANTIPRURITICS	ANTIREFLECTIVE	ANTISEPTICISES
ANTINEUTRON	ANTIPERISTASIS	ANTIPSYCHIATRY	ANTIREFORM	ANTISEPTICISING
ANTINEUTRONS	ANTIPERSONNEL	ANTIPSYCHOTIC	ANTIREGULATORY	ANTISEPTICISM
ANTINOISES	ANTIPERSPIRANT	ANTIPSYCHOTICS	ANTIREJECTION	ANTISEPTICISMS
ANTINOMIAN	ANTIPERSPIRANTS	ANTIPYRESES	ANTIRELIGION	ANTISEPTICIZE
ANTINOMIANISM	ANTIPESTICIDE	ANTIPYRESIS	ANTIRELIGIONS	ANTISEPTICIZED
ANTINOMIANISMS	ANTIPETALOUS	ANTIPYRETIC	ANTIRELIGIOUS	ANTISEPTICIZES
ANTINOMIANS	ANTIPHLOGISTIC	ANTIPYRETICS	ANTIREPUBLICAN	ANTISEPTICIZING
ANTINOMICAL	ANTIPHLOGISTICS	ANTIPYRINE	ANTIREPUBLICANS	ANTISEPTICS
ANTINOMICALLY	ANTIPHONAL	ANTIPYRINES	ANTIRETROVIRAL	ANTISERUMS
ANTINOMIES	ANTIPHONALLY	ANTIQUARIAN	ANTIRETROVIRALS	ANTISEXIST
ANTINOVELIST	ANTIPHONALS	ANTIQUARIANISM	ANTIRHEUMATIC	ANTISEXISTS
ANTINOVELISTS	ANTIPHONARIES	ANTIQUARIANISMS	ANTIRHEUMATICS	ANTISEXUAL
ANTINOVELS	ANTIPHONARY	ANTIQUARIANS	ANTIRITUALISM	ANTISEXUALITIES
ANTINUCLEAR	ANTIPHONER	ANTIQUARIES	ANTIRITUALISMS	ANTISEXUALITY
ANTINUCLEARIST	ANTIPHONERS	ANTIQUARKS	ANTIROMANTIC	ANTISEXUALS
ANTINUCLEARISTS	ANTIPHONIC	ANTIQUATED	ANTIROMANTICISM	ANTISHAKES
ANTINUCLEON	ANTIPHONICAL	ANTIQUATEDNESS	ANTIROMANTICS	ANTISHOCKS
ANTINUCLEONS	ANTIPHONICALLY	ANTIQUATES	ANTIROYALIST	ANTISHOPLIFTING
ANTINUKERS	ANTIPHONIES	ANTIQUATING	ANTIROYALISTS	ANTISLAVERY

ANTISMOKER	ANTITERRORISTS	ANTIVITAMIN	APFELSTRUDELS	APOCALYPSE
ANTISMOKERS	ANTITHALIAN	ANTIVITAMINS	APHAERESES	APOCALYPSES
ANTISMOKING	ANTITHEISM	ANTIVIVISECTION	APHAERESIS	APOCALYPTIC
ANTISMUGGLING	ANTITHEISMS	ANTIWELFARE	APHAERETIC	APOCALYPTICAL
ANTISOCIAL	ANTITHEIST	ANTIWHALING	APHANIPTEROUS	APOCALYPTICALLY
ANTISOCIALISM	ANTITHEISTIC	ANTIWORLDS	APHANTASIA	APOCALYPTICISM
ANTISOCIALISMS	ANTITHEISTS	ANTIWRINKLE	APHANTASIAS	APOCALYPTICISMS
ANTISOCIALIST	ANTITHEORETICAL	ANTONINIANUS	APHELANDRA	APOCALYPTISM
ANTISOCIALISTS	ANTITHESES	ANTONINIANUSES	APHELANDRAS	APOCALYPTISMS
ANTISOCIALITIES	ANTITHESIS	ANTONOMASIA	APHELIOTROPIC	APOCALYPTIST
ANTISOCIALITY	ANTITHETIC	ANTONOMASIAS	APHELIOTROPISM	APOCALYPTISTS
ANTISOCIALLY	ANTITHETICAL	ANTONOMASTIC	APHELIOTROPISMS	APOCARPIES
ANTISOCIALS	ANTITHETICALLY	ANTONYMIES	APHETICALLY	APOCARPOUS
ANTISPASMODIC	ANTITHROMBIN	ANTONYMOUS	APHETISING	APOCATASTASES
ANTISPASMODICS	ANTITHROMBINS	ANTRORSELY	APHETIZING	APOCATASTASIS
ANTISPASTIC	ANTITHROMBOTIC	ANTSINESSES	APHIDICIDE	APOCHROMAT
ANTISPASTICS	ANTITHROMBOTICS	ANUCLEATED	APHIDICIDES	APOCHROMATIC
ANTISPASTS	ANTITHYROID	ANXIOLYTIC	APHORISERS	APOCHROMATISM
ANTISPECULATION	ANTITOBACCO	ANXIOLYTICS	APHORISING	APOCHROMATISMS
ANTISPECULATIVE	ANTITOXINS	ANXIOUSNESS	APHORISTIC	APOCHROMATS
ANTISPENDING	ANTITRADES	ANXIOUSNESSES	APHORISTICALLY	APOCOPATED
ANTISTATIC	ANTITRADITIONAL	ANYTHINGARIAN	APHORIZERS	APOCOPATES
ANTISTATICS	ANTITRAGUS	ANYTHINGARIANS	APHORIZING	APOCOPATING
ANTISTORIES	ANTITRANSPIRANT	ANYWHITHER	APHRODISIA	APOCOPATION
ANTISTRESS	ANTITRINITARIAN	AORISTICALLY	APHRODISIAC	APOCOPATIONS
ANTISTRIKE	ANTITRUSTER	AORTITISES	APHRODISIACAL	APOCRYPHAL
ANTISTROPHE	ANTITRUSTERS	AORTOGRAPHIC	APHRODISIACS	APOCRYPHALLY
ANTISTROPHES	ANTITUBERCULAR	AORTOGRAPHIES	APHRODISIAS	APOCRYPHALNESS
ANTISTROPHIC	ANTITUBERCULOUS	AORTOGRAPHY	APHRODITES	APOCRYPHON
ANTISTROPHON	ANTITUMORAL	APAGOGICAL	APICULTURAL	APOCYNACEOUS
ANTISTROPHONS	ANTITUMORS	APAGOGICALLY	APICULTURE	APOCYNTHION
ANTISTUDENT	ANTITUMOUR	APARTHEIDS	APICULTURES	APOCYNTHIONS
ANTISTYLES	ANTITUMOURAL	APARTHOTEL	APICULTURIST	APODEICTIC
ANTISUBMARINE	ANTITUSSIVE	APARTHOTELS	APICULTURISTS	APODEICTICAL
ANTISUBSIDY	ANTITUSSIVES	APARTMENTAL	APIOLOGIES	APODEICTICALLY
ANTISUBVERSION	ANTITYPHOID	APARTMENTS	APIPHOBIAS	APODICTICAL
ANTISUBVERSIVE	ANTITYPICAL	APARTNESSES	APIPHOBICS	APODICTICALLY
ANTISUICIDE	ANTITYPICALLY	APATHATONS	APISHNESSES	APODYTERIUM
ANTISYMMETRIC	ANTIUNIVERSITY	APATHETICAL	APITHERAPIES	APODYTERIUMS
ANTISYPHILITIC	ANTIVAXERS	APATHETICALLY	APITHERAPY	APOENZYMES
ANTISYPHILITICS	ANTIVAXXER	APATOSAURS	APLACENTAL	APOGAMOUSLY
ANTISYZYGIES	ANTIVAXXERS	APATOSAURUS	APLANATICALLY	APOGEOTROPIC
ANTISYZYGY	ANTIVENENE	APATOSAURUSES	APLANATISM	APOGEOTROPISM
ANTITAKEOVER	ANTIVENENES	APERIODICALLY	APLANATISMS	APOGEOTROPISMS
ANTITARNISH	ANTIVENINS	APERIODICITIES	APLANOGAMETE	APOLAUSTIC
ANTITECHNOLOGY	ANTIVENOMS	APERIODICITY	APLANOGAMETES	APOLAUSTICS
ANTITERRORISM	ANTIVIOLENCE	APERITIVES	APLANOSPORE	APOLIPOPROTEIN
ANTITERRORISMS	ANTIVIRALS	APERTNESSES	APLANOSPORES	APOLIPOPROTEINS
ANTITERRORIST	ANTIVIRUSES	APFELSTRUDEL	APOAPSIDES	APOLITICAL

A

APOLITICALITIES	APOPLECTIC	APOSTROPHISED	APPARELMENT	APPENDIXES
APOLITICALITY	APOPLECTICAL	APOSTROPHISES	APPARELMENTS	APPERCEIVE
APOLITICALLY	APOPLECTICALLY	APOSTROPHISING	APPARENCIES	APPERCEIVED
APOLITICISM	APOPLECTICS	APOSTROPHIZE	APPARENTLY	APPERCEIVES
APOLITICISMS	APOPLEXIES	APOSTROPHIZED	APPARENTNESS	APPERCEIVING
APOLLONIAN	APOPLEXING	APOSTROPHIZES	APPARENTNESSES	APPERCEPTION
APOLLONICON	APOPROTEIN	APOSTROPHIZING	APPARITION	APPERCEPTIONS
APOLLONICONS	APOPROTEINS	APOSTROPHUS	APPARITIONAL	APPERCEPTIVE
APOLOGETIC	APOSEMATIC	APOSTROPHUSES	APPARITIONS	APPERCIPIENT
APOLOGETICAL	APOSEMATICALLY	APOTHECARIES	APPARITORS	APPERTAINANCE
APOLOGETICALLY	APOSIOPESES	APOTHECARY	APPARTEMENT	APPERTAINANCES
APOLOGETICS	APOSIOPESIS	APOTHECIAL	APPARTEMENTS	APPERTAINED
APOLOGISED	APOSIOPETIC	APOTHECIUM	APPASSIONATO	APPERTAINING
APOLOGISER	APOSPORIES	APOTHEGMATIC	APPEACHING	APPERTAINMENT
APOLOGISERS	APOSPOROUS	APOTHEGMATICAL	APPEACHMENT	APPERTAINMENTS
APOLOGISES	APOSTACIES	APOTHEGMATISE	APPEACHMENTS	APPERTAINS
APOLOGISING	APOSTASIES	APOTHEGMATISED	APPEALABILITIES	APPERTINENT
APOLOGISTS	APOSTATICAL	APOTHEGMATISES	APPEALABILITY	APPERTINENTS
APOLOGIZED	APOSTATISE	APOTHEGMATISING	APPEALABLE	APPETEEZEMENT
APOLOGIZER	APOSTATISED	APOTHEGMATIST	APPEALINGLY	APPETEEZEMENTS
APOLOGIZERS	APOSTATISES	APOTHEGMATISTS	APPEALINGNESS	APPETENCES
APOLOGIZES	APOSTATISING	APOTHEGMATIZE	APPEALINGNESSES	APPETENCIES
APOLOGIZING	APOSTATIZE	APOTHEGMATIZED	APPEARANCE	APPETISEMENT
APOMICTICAL	APOSTATIZED	APOTHEGMATIZES	APPEARANCES	APPETISEMENTS
APOMICTICALLY	APOSTATIZES	APOTHEGMATIZING	APPEASABLE	APPETISERS
APOMORPHIA	APOSTATIZING	APOTHEOSES	APPEASEMENT	APPETISING
APOMORPHIAS	APOSTILLES	APOTHEOSIS	APPEASEMENTS	APPETISINGLY
APOMORPHINE	APOSTLESHIP	APOTHEOSISE	APPEASINGLY	APPETITION
APOMORPHINES	APOSTLESHIPS	APOTHEOSISED	APPELLANTS	APPETITIONS
APONEUROSES	APOSTOLATE	APOTHEOSISES	APPELLATION	APPETITIVE
APONEUROSIS	APOSTOLATES	APOTHEOSISING	APPELLATIONAL	APPETIZERS
APONEUROTIC	APOSTOLICAL	APOTHEOSIZE	APPELLATIONS	APPETIZING
APOPEMPTIC	APOSTOLICALLY	APOTHEOSIZED	APPELLATIVE	APPETIZINGLY
APOPEMPTICS	APOSTOLICISM	APOTHEOSIZES	APPELLATIVELY	APPLAUDABLE
APOPHENIAS	APOSTOLICISMS	APOTHEOSIZING	APPELLATIVES	APPLAUDABLY
APOPHLEGMATIC	APOSTOLICITIES	APOTROPAIC	APPENDAGES	APPLAUDERS
APOPHLEGMATICS	APOSTOLICITY	APOTROPAICALLY	APPENDANTS	APPLAUDING
APOPHONIES	APOSTOLISE	APOTROPAISM	APPENDECTOMIES	APPLAUDINGLY
APOPHTHEGM	APOSTOLISED	APOTROPAISMS	APPENDECTOMY	APPLAUSIVE
APOPHTHEGMATIC	APOSTOLISES	APOTROPOUS	APPENDENTS	APPLAUSIVELY
APOPHTHEGMATISE	APOSTOLISING	APPALLINGLY	APPENDICECTOMY	APPLECARTS
APOPHTHEGMATIST	APOSTOLIZE	APPALOOSAS	APPENDICES	APPLEDRAIN
APOPHTHEGMATIZE	APOSTOLIZED	APPARATCHIK	APPENDICITIS	APPLEDRAINS
APOPHTHEGMS	APOSTOLIZES	APPARATCHIKI	APPENDICITISES	APPLEJACKS
APOPHYLLITE	APOSTOLIZING	APPARATCHIKS	APPENDICLE	APPLERINGIE
APOPHYLLITES	APOSTROPHE	APPARATUSES	APPENDICLES	APPLERINGIES
APOPHYSATE	APOSTROPHES	APPARELING	APPENDICULAR	APPLESAUCE
APOPHYSEAL	APOSTROPHIC	APPARELLED	APPENDICULARIAN	APPLESAUCES
APOPHYSIAL	APOSTROPHISE	APPARELLING	APPENDICULATE	APPLETINIS

APPLIANCES	APPRAISINGLY	APPROBATION	APPURTENANTS	AQUAPLANES
APPLICABILITIES	APPRAISIVE	APPROBATIONS	APRICATING	AQUAPLANING
APPLICABILITY	APPRAISIVELY	APPROBATIVE	APRICATION	AQUAPLANINGS
APPLICABLE	APPRECIABLE	APPROBATORY	APRICATIONS	AQUAPONICS
APPLICABLENESS	APPRECIABLY	APPROPINQUATE	APRIORISMS	AQUAPORINS
APPLICABLY	APPRECIATE	APPROPINQUATED	APRIORISTS	AQUARELLES
APPLICANTS	APPRECIATED	APPROPINQUATES	APRIORITIES	AQUARELLIST
APPLICATION	APPRECIATES	APPROPINQUATING	APSIDIOLES	AQUARELLISTS
APPLICATIONS	APPRECIATING	APPROPINQUATION	APTERYGIAL	AQUARIISTS
APPLICATIVE	APPRECIATION	APPROPINQUE	APTITUDINAL	AQUAROBICS
APPLICATIVELY	APPRECIATIONS	APPROPINQUED	APTITUDINALLY	AQUASCAPES
APPLICATOR	APPRECIATIVE	APPROPINQUES	AQUABATICS	AQUATICALLY
APPLICATORS	APPRECIATIVELY	APPROPINQUING	AQUABOARDS	AQUATINTAS
APPLICATORY	APPRECIATOR	APPROPINQUITIES	AQUACEUTICAL	AQUATINTED
APPLIQUEING	APPRECIATORILY	APPROPINQUITY	AQUACEUTICALS	AQUATINTER
APPOGGIATURA	APPRECIATORS	APPROPRIABLE	AQUACULTURAL	AQUATINTERS
APPOGGIATURAS	APPRECIATORY	APPROPRIACIES	AQUACULTURE	AQUATINTING
APPOGGIATURE	APPREHENDED	APPROPRIACY	AQUACULTURES	AQUATINTIST
APPOINTEES	APPREHENDING	APPROPRIATE	AQUACULTURIST	AQUATINTISTS
APPOINTERS	APPREHENDS	APPROPRIATED	AQUACULTURISTS	AQUICULTURAL
APPOINTING	APPREHENSIBLE	APPROPRIATELY	AQUADROMES	AQUICULTURE
APPOINTIVE	APPREHENSIBLY	APPROPRIATENESS	AQUAEROBIC	AQUICULTURES
APPOINTMENT	APPREHENSION	APPROPRIATES	AQUAEROBICS	AQUICULTURIST
APPOINTMENTS	APPREHENSIONS	APPROPRIATING	AQUAFARMED	AQUICULTURISTS
APPOINTORS	APPREHENSIVE	APPROPRIATION	AQUAFARMING	AQUIFEROUS
APPORTIONABLE	APPREHENSIVELY	APPROPRIATIONS	AQUAFARMINGS	AQUIFOLIACEOUS
APPORTIONED	APPRENTICE	APPROPRIATIVE	AQUAFITNESS	AQUILEGIAS
APPORTIONER	APPRENTICED	APPROPRIATOR	AQUAFITNESSES	AQUILINITIES
APPORTIONERS	APPRENTICEHOOD	APPROPRIATORS	AQUAFORTIS	AQUILINITY
APPORTIONING	APPRENTICEHOODS	APPROVABLE	AQUAFORTISES	ARABESQUED
APPORTIONMENT	APPRENTICEMENT	APPROVABLY	AQUAFORTIST	ARABESQUES
APPORTIONMENTS	APPRENTICEMENTS	APPROVANCE	AQUAFORTISTS	ARABICISATION
APPORTIONS	APPRENTICES	APPROVANCES	AQUALEATHER	ARABICISATIONS
APPOSITELY	APPRENTICESHIP	APPROVINGLY	AQUALEATHERS	ARABICISED
APPOSITENESS	APPRENTICESHIPS	APPROXIMAL	AQUAMANALE	ARABICISES
APPOSITENESSES	APPRENTICING	APPROXIMATE	AQUAMANALES	ARABICISING
APPOSITION	APPRESSING	APPROXIMATED	AQUAMANILE	ARABICIZATION
APPOSITIONAL	APPRESSORIA	APPROXIMATELY	AQUAMANILES	ARABICIZATIONS
APPOSITIONS	APPRESSORIUM	APPROXIMATES	AQUAMARINE	ARABICIZED
APPOSITIVE	APPRISINGS	APPROXIMATING	AQUAMARINES	ARABICIZES
APPOSITIVELY	APPRIZINGS	APPROXIMATION	AQUANAUTICS	ARABICIZING
APPOSITIVES	APPROACHABILITY	APPROXIMATIONS	AQUAPHOBES	ARABILITIES
APPRAISABLE	APPROACHABLE	APPROXIMATIVE	AQUAPHOBIA	ARABINOSES
APPRAISALS	APPROACHED	APPROXIMEETING	AQUAPHOBIAS	ARABINOSIDE
APPRAISEES	APPROACHES	APPROXIMEETINGS	AQUAPHOBIC	ARABINOSIDES
APPRAISEMENT	APPROACHING	APPULSIVELY	AQUAPHOBICS	ARABISATION
APPRAISEMENTS	APPROBATED	APPURTENANCE	AQUAPLANED	ARABISATIONS
APPRAISERS	APPROBATES	APPURTENANCES	AQUAPLANER	ARABIZATION
APPRAISING	APPROBATING	APPURTENANT	AQUAPLANERS	ARABIZATIONS

A

ARACHIDONIC	ARBITRARINESSES	ARCHAEOLOGISTS	ARCHENTERON	ARCHIPELAGOES
ARACHNIDAN	ARBITRATED	ARCHAEOLOGY	ARCHENTERONS	ARCHIPELAGOS
ARACHNIDANS	ARBITRATES	ARCHAEOMETRIC	ARCHEOASTRONOMY	ARCHIPHONEME
ARACHNOIDAL	ARBITRATING	ARCHAEOMETRIES	ARCHEOBOTANIES	ARCHIPHONEMES
ARACHNOIDITIS	ARBITRATION	ARCHAEOMETRIST	ARCHEOBOTANIST	ARCHIPLASM
ARACHNOIDITISES	ARBITRATIONAL	ARCHAEOMETRISTS	ARCHEOBOTANISTS	ARCHIPLASMIC
ARACHNOIDS	ARBITRATIONS	ARCHAEOMETRY	ARCHEOBOTANY	ARCHIPLASMS
ARACHNOLOGICAL	ARBITRATIVE	ARCHAEOPTERYX	ARCHEOLOGICAL	ARCHITECTED
ARACHNOLOGIES	ARBITRATOR	ARCHAEOPTERYXES	ARCHEOLOGICALLY	ARCHITECTING
ARACHNOLOGIST	ARBITRATORS	ARCHAEORNIS	ARCHEOLOGIES	ARCHITECTONIC
ARACHNOLOGISTS	ARBITRATRICES	ARCHAEORNISES	ARCHEOLOGIST	ARCHITECTONICS
ARACHNOLOGY	ARBITRATRIX	ARCHAEOZOOLOGY	ARCHEOLOGISTS	ARCHITECTS
ARACHNOPHOBE	ARBITRATRIXES	ARCHAEZOOLOGIES	ARCHEOLOGY	ARCHITECTURAL
ARACHNOPHOBES	ARBITREMENT	ARCHAEZOOLOGY	ARCHEOMAGNETISM	ARCHITECTURALLY
ARACHNOPHOBIA	ARBITREMENTS	ARCHAICALLY	ARCHEOMETRIES	ARCHITECTURE
ARACHNOPHOBIAS	ARBITRESSES	ARCHAICISM	ARCHEOMETRY	ARCHITECTURES
ARACHNOPHOBIC	ARBITRIUMS	ARCHAICISMS	ARCHEOZOOLOGIES	ARCHITRAVE
ARACHNOPHOBICS	ARBLASTERS	ARCHAISERS	ARCHEOZOOLOGIST	ARCHITRAVED
ARAEOMETER	ARBORACEOUS	ARCHAISING	ARCHEOZOOLOGY	ARCHITRAVES
ARAEOMETERS	ARBOREALLY	ARCHAISTIC	ARCHERESSES	ARCHITYPES
ARAEOMETRIC	ARBORESCENCE	ARCHAIZERS	ARCHERFISH	ARCHIVISTS
ARAEOMETRICAL	ARBORESCENCES	ARCHAIZING	ARCHERFISHES	ARCHIVOLTS
ARAEOMETRIES	ARBORESCENT	ARCHANGELIC	ARCHESPORE	ARCHNESSES
ARAEOMETRY	ARBORETUMS	ARCHANGELS	ARCHESPORES	ARCHOLOGIES
ARAEOSTYLE	ARBORICULTURAL	ARCHBISHOP	ARCHESPORIA	ARCHONSHIP
ARAEOSTYLES	ARBORICULTURE	ARCHBISHOPRIC	ARCHESPORIAL	ARCHONSHIPS
ARAEOSYSTYLE	ARBORICULTURES	ARCHBISHOPRICS	ARCHESPORIUM	ARCHONTATE
ARAEOSYSTYLES	ARBORICULTURIST	ARCHBISHOPS	ARCHETYPAL	ARCHONTATES
ARAGONITES	ARBORISATION	ARCHDEACON	ARCHETYPALLY	ARCHOPLASM
ARAGONITIC	ARBORISATIONS	ARCHDEACONRIES	ARCHETYPES	ARCHOPLASMIC
ARALIACEOUS	ARBORISING	ARCHDEACONRY	ARCHETYPICAL	ARCHOPLASMS
ARAUCARIAN	ARBORIZATION	ARCHDEACONS	ARCHETYPICALLY	ARCHOSAURIAN
ARAUCARIAS	ARBORIZATIONS	ARCHDIOCESAN	ARCHFIENDS	ARCHOSAURIANS
ARBALESTER	ARBORIZING	ARCHDIOCESE	ARCHGENETHLIAC	ARCHOSAURS
ARBALESTERS	ARBORVITAE	ARCHDIOCESES	ARCHGENETHLIACS	ARCHPRIEST
ARBALISTER	ARBORVITAES	ARCHDRUIDS	ARCHICARPS	ARCHPRIESTHOOD
ARBALISTERS	ARBOVIRUSES	ARCHDUCHESS	ARCHIDIACONAL	ARCHPRIESTHOODS
ARBITRABLE	ARBUSCULAR	ARCHDUCHESSES	ARCHIDIACONATE	ARCHPRIESTS
ARBITRAGED	ARCANENESS	ARCHDUCHIES	ARCHIDIACONATES	ARCHPRIESTSHIP
ARBITRAGER	ARCANENESSES	ARCHDUKEDOM	ARCHIEPISCOPACY	ARCHPRIESTSHIPS
ARBITRAGERS	ARCCOSINES	ARCHDUKEDOMS	ARCHIEPISCOPAL	ARCHRIVALS
ARBITRAGES	ARCHAEBACTERIA	ARCHEGONIA	ARCHIEPISCOPATE	ARCHSTONES
ARBITRAGEUR	ARCHAEBACTERIUM	ARCHEGONIAL	ARCHILOWES	ARCMINUTES
ARBITRAGEURS	ARCHAEOBOTANIES	ARCHEGONIATE	ARCHIMAGES	ARCOGRAPHS
ARBITRAGING	ARCHAEOBOTANIST	ARCHEGONIATES	ARCHIMANDRITE	ARCOLOGIES
ARBITRAMENT	ARCHAEOBOTANY	ARCHEGONIUM	ARCHIMANDRITES	ARCSECONDS
ARBITRAMENTS	ARCHAEOLOGICAL	ARCHENEMIES	ARCHIPELAGIAN	ARCTANGENT
ARBITRARILY	ARCHAEOLOGIES	ARCHENTERA	ARCHIPELAGIC	ARCTANGENTS
ARBITRARINESS	ARCHAEOLOGIST	ARCHENTERIC	ARCHIPELAGO	ARCTICALLY

ARCTOPHILE	ARGUMENTUM	ARMORIALLY	ARRANGEMENTS	ARTEMISININS
ARCTOPHILES	ARGUMENTUMS	ARMOURLESS	ARRAYMENTS	ARTERIALISATION
ARCTOPHILIA	ARGUTENESS	AROMANTICS	ARREARAGES	ARTERIALISE
ARCTOPHILIAS	ARGUTENESSES	AROMATASES	ARRESTABLE	ARTERIALISED
ARCTOPHILIES	ARGYRODITE	AROMATHERAPIES	ARRESTANTS	ARTERIALISES
ARCTOPHILIST	ARGYRODITES	AROMATHERAPIST	ARRESTATION	ARTERIALISING
ARCTOPHILISTS	ARHATSHIPS	AROMATHERAPISTS	ARRESTATIONS	ARTERIALIZATION
ARCTOPHILS	ARHYTHMIAS	AROMATHERAPY	ARRESTINGLY	ARTERIALIZE
ARCTOPHILY	ARIBOFLAVINOSES	AROMATICALLY	ARRESTMENT	ARTERIALIZED
ARCUATIONS	ARIBOFLAVINOSIS	AROMATICITIES	ARRESTMENTS	ARTERIALIZES
ARCUBALIST	ARIDNESSES	AROMATICITY	ARRHENOTOKIES	ARTERIALIZING
ARCUBALISTS	ARISTOCRACIES	AROMATISATION	ARRHENOTOKY	ARTERIALLY
ARDUOUSNESS	ARISTOCRACY	AROMATISATIONS	ARRHYTHMIA	ARTERIOGRAM
ARDUOUSNESSES	ARISTOCRAT	AROMATISED	ARRHYTHMIAS	ARTERIOGRAMS
ARECOLINES	ARISTOCRATIC	AROMATISES	ARRHYTHMIC	ARTERIOGRAPHIC
AREFACTION	ARISTOCRATICAL	AROMATISING	ARRIVANCES	ARTERIOGRAPHIES
AREFACTIONS	ARISTOCRATISM	AROMATIZATION	ARRIVANCIES	ARTERIOGRAPHY
ARENACEOUS	ARISTOCRATISMS	AROMATIZATIONS	ARRIVEDERCI	ARTERIOLAR
ARENATIONS	ARISTOCRATS	AROMATIZED	ARRIVISMES	ARTERIOLES
ARENICOLOUS	ARISTOLOCHIA	AROMATIZES	ARRIVISTES	ARTERIOTOMIES
AREOCENTRIC	ARISTOLOCHIAS	AROMATIZING	ARROGANCES	ARTERIOTOMY
AREOGRAPHIC	ARISTOLOGIES	ARPEGGIATE	ARROGANCIES	ARTERIOVENOUS
AREOGRAPHIES	ARISTOLOGY	ARPEGGIATED	ARROGANTLY	ARTERITIDES
AREOGRAPHY	ARISTOTLES	ARPEGGIATES	ARROGATING	ARTERITISES
AREOLATION	ARITHMETIC	ARPEGGIATING	ARROGATION	ARTFULNESS
AREOLATIONS	ARITHMETICAL	ARPEGGIATION	ARROGATIONS	ARTFULNESSES
AREOLOGIES	ARITHMETICALLY	ARPEGGIATIONS	ARROGATIVE	ARTHRALGIA
AREOMETERS	ARITHMETICIAN	ARPEGGIONE	ARROGATORS	ARTHRALGIAS
AREOMETRIC	ARITHMETICIANS	ARPEGGIONES	ARRONDISSEMENT	ARTHRALGIC
AREOMETRICAL	ARITHMETICS	ARPILLERAS	ARRONDISSEMENTS	ARTHRECTOMIES
AREOMETRIES	ARITHMOMANIA	ARQUEBUSADE	ARROWGRASS	ARTHRECTOMY
AREOSTYLES	ARITHMOMANIAS	ARQUEBUSADES	ARROWGRASSES	ARTHRITICALLY
AREOSYSTILE	ARITHMOMETER	ARQUEBUSES	ARROWHEADS	ARTHRITICS
AREOSYSTILES	ARITHMOMETERS	ARQUEBUSIER	ARROWROOTS	ARTHRITIDES
ARFVEDSONITE	ARITHMOPHOBIA	ARQUEBUSIERS	ARROWWOODS	ARTHRITISES
ARFVEDSONITES	ARITHMOPHOBIAS	ARRABBIATA	ARROWWORMS	ARTHRODESES
ARGENTIFEROUS	ARMADILLOS	ARRABBIATAS	ARSENIATES	ARTHRODESIS
ARGENTINES	ARMAMENTARIA	ARRABIATAS	ARSENICALS	ARTHRODIAE
ARGENTITES	ARMAMENTARIUM	ARRACACHAS	ARSENOPYRITE	ARTHRODIAL
ARGILLACEOUS	ARMAMENTARIUMS	ARRAGONITE	ARSENOPYRITES	ARTHROGRAPHIES
ARGILLIFEROUS	ARMATURING	ARRAGONITES	ARSMETRICK	ARTHROGRAPHY
ARGILLITES	ARMIGEROUS	ARRAGONITIC	ARSMETRICKS	ARTHROMERE
ARGILLITIC	ARMILLARIA	ARRAIGNERS	ARSPHENAMINE	ARTHROMERES
ARGONAUTIC	ARMILLARIAS	ARRAIGNING	ARSPHENAMINES	ARTHROMERIC
ARGUMENTATION	ARMIPOTENCE	ARRAIGNINGS	ARTEFACTING	ARTHROPATHIES
ARGUMENTATIONS	ARMIPOTENCES	ARRAIGNMENT	ARTEFACTINGS	ARTHROPATHY
ARGUMENTATIVE	ARMIPOTENT	ARRAIGNMENTS	ARTEFACTUAL	ARTHROPLASTIES
ARGUMENTATIVELY	ARMISTICES	ARRANGEABLE	ARTEMISIAS	ARTHROPLASTY
ARGUMENTIVE	ARMLOCKING	ARRANGEMENT	ARTEMISININ	ARTHROPODAL

ARTHROPODAN	ARTILLERYMEN	ASCENDIBLE	ASHRAMITES	ASPHYXIATED
ARTHROPODOUS	ARTINESSES	ASCENSIONAL	ASININITIES	ASPHYXIATES
ARTHROPODS	ARTIODACTYL	ASCENSIONIST	ASKEWNESSES	ASPHYXIATING
ARTHROSCOPE	ARTIODACTYLOUS	ASCENSIONISTS	ASPARAGINASE	ASPHYXIATION
ARTHROSCOPES	ARTIODACTYLS	ASCENSIONS	ASPARAGINASES	ASPHYXIATIONS
ARTHROSCOPIC	ARTISANSHIP	ASCERTAINABLE	ASPARAGINE	ASPHYXIATOR
ARTHROSCOPIES	ARTISANSHIPS	ASCERTAINABLY	ASPARAGINES	ASPHYXIATORS
ARTHROSCOPY	ARTISTICAL	ASCERTAINED	ASPARAGUSES	ASPHYXYING
ARTHROSPORE	ARTISTICALLY	ASCERTAINING	ASPARTAMES	ASPIDISTRA
ARTHROSPORES	ARTISTRIES	ASCERTAINMENT	ASPARTATES	ASPIDISTRAS
ARTHROSPORIC	ARTLESSNESS	ASCERTAINMENTS	ASPECTABLE	ASPIRATING
ARTHROSPOROUS	ARTLESSNESSES	ASCERTAINS	ASPERATING	ASPIRATION
ARTICHOKES	ARTMAKINGS	ASCETICALLY	ASPERGATION	ASPIRATIONAL
ARTICULABLE	ARTOCARPUS	ASCETICISM	ASPERGATIONS	ASPIRATIONS
ARTICULACIES	ARTOCARPUSES	ASCETICISMS	ASPERGILLA	ASPIRATORS
ARTICULACY	ARTSINESSES	ASCITITIOUS	ASPERGILLI	ASPIRATORY
ARTICULATE	ARUNDINACEOUS	ASCLEPIADACEOUS	ASPERGILLOSES	ASPIRINGLY
ARTICULATED	ARVICOLINE	ASCLEPIADS	ASPERGILLOSIS	ASPIRINGNESS
ARTICULATELY	ARYBALLOID	ASCLEPIASES	ASPERGILLS	ASPIRINGNESSES
ARTICULATENESS	ARYBALLOSES	ASCOCARPIC	ASPERGILLUM	ASPLANCHNIC
ARTICULATES	ARYTAENOID	ASCOGONIUM	ASPERGILLUMS	ASPLENIUMS
ARTICULATING	ARYTAENOIDS	ASCOMYCETE	ASPERGILLUS	ASPORTATION
ARTICULATION	ARYTENOIDAL	ASCOMYCETES	ASPERITIES	ASPORTATIONS
ARTICULATIONS	ARYTENOIDS	ASCOMYCETOUS	ASPERSIONS	ASSAFETIDA
ARTICULATIVE	ASAFETIDAS	ASCORBATES	ASPERSIVELY	ASSAFETIDAS
ARTICULATOR	ASAFOETIDA	ASCOSPORES	ASPERSOIRS	ASSAFOETIDA
ARTICULATORS	ASAFOETIDAS	ASCOSPORIC	ASPERSORIA	ASSAFOETIDAS
ARTICULATORY	ASARABACCA	ASCRIBABLE	ASPERSORIES	ASSAGAIING
ARTIFACTING	ASARABACCAS	ASCRIPTION	ASPERSORIUM	ASSAILABLE
ARTIFACTINGS	ASBESTIFORM	ASCRIPTIONS	ASPERSORIUMS	ASSAILANTS
ARTIFACTUAL	ASBESTOSES	ASCRIPTIVE	ASPHALTERS	ASSAILMENT
ARTIFICERS	ASBESTOSIS	ASEPTICALLY	ASPHALTING	ASSAILMENTS
ARTIFICIAL	ASBESTUSES	ASEPTICISE	ASPHALTITE	ASSASSINATE
ARTIFICIALISE	ASCARIASES	ASEPTICISED	ASPHALTITES	ASSASSINATED
ARTIFICIALISED	ASCARIASIS	ASEPTICISES	ASPHALTUMS	ASSASSINATES
ARTIFICIALISES	ASCENDABLE	ASEPTICISING	ASPHERICAL	ASSASSINATING
ARTIFICIALISING	ASCENDANCE	ASEPTICISM	ASPHETERISE	ASSASSINATION
ARTIFICIALITIES	ASCENDANCES	ASEPTICISMS	ASPHETERISED	ASSASSINATIONS
ARTIFICIALITY	ASCENDANCIES	ASEPTICIZE	ASPHETERISES	ASSASSINATOR
ARTIFICIALIZE	ASCENDANCY	ASEPTICIZED	ASPHETERISING	ASSASSINATORS
ARTIFICIALIZED	ASCENDANTLY	ASEPTICIZES	ASPHETERISM	ASSAULTERS
ARTIFICIALIZES	ASCENDANTS	ASEPTICIZING	ASPHETERISMS	ASSAULTING
ARTIFICIALIZING	ASCENDENCE	ASEXUALITIES	ASPHETERIZE	ASSAULTIVE
ARTIFICIALLY	ASCENDENCES	ASEXUALITY	ASPHETERIZED	ASSAULTIVELY
ARTIFICIALNESS	ASCENDENCIES	ASHAMEDNESS	ASPHETERIZES	ASSAULTIVENESS
ARTILLERIES	ASCENDENCY	ASHAMEDNESSES	ASPHETERIZING	ASSEGAAIED
ARTILLERIST	ASCENDENTLY	ASHINESSES	ASPHYXIANT	ASSEGAAIING
ARTILLERISTS	ASCENDENTS	ASHLARINGS	ASPHYXIANTS	ASSEGAIING
ARTILLERYMAN	ASCENDEURS	ASHLERINGS	ASPHYXIATE	ASSEMBLAGE

ASSEMBLAGES

ASSEMBLAGES
ASSEMBLAGIST
ASSEMBLAGISTS
ASSEMBLANCE
ASSEMBLANCES
ASSEMBLAUNCE
ASSEMBLAUNCES
ASSEMBLERS
ASSEMBLIES
ASSEMBLING
ASSEMBLYMAN
ASSEMBLYMEN
ASSEMBLYWOMAN
ASSEMBLYWOMEN
ASSENTANEOUS
ASSENTATION
ASSENTATIONS
ASSENTATOR
ASSENTATORS
ASSENTIENT
ASSENTIENTS
ASSENTINGLY
ASSENTIVENESS
ASSENTIVENESSES
ASSERTABLE
ASSERTEDLY
ASSERTIBLE
ASSERTIONS
ASSERTIVELY
ASSERTIVENESS
ASSERTIVENESSES
ASSERTORIC
ASSESSABLE
ASSESSMENT
ASSESSMENTS
ASSESSORIAL
ASSESSORSHIP
ASSESSORSHIPS
ASSEVERATE
ASSEVERATED
ASSEVERATES
ASSEVERATING
ASSEVERATINGLY
ASSEVERATION
ASSEVERATIONS
ASSEVERATIVE
ASSEVERING
ASSIBILATE
ASSIBILATED

ASSIBILATES
ASSIBILATING
ASSIBILATION
ASSIBILATIONS
ASSIDUITIES
ASSIDUOUSLY
ASSIDUOUSNESS
ASSIDUOUSNESSES
ASSIGNABILITIES
ASSIGNABILITY
ASSIGNABLE
ASSIGNABLY
ASSIGNATION
ASSIGNATIONS
ASSIGNMENT
ASSIGNMENTS
ASSIMILABILITY
ASSIMILABLE
ASSIMILABLY
ASSIMILATE
ASSIMILATED
ASSIMILATES
ASSIMILATING
ASSIMILATION
ASSIMILATIONISM
ASSIMILATIONIST
ASSIMILATIONS
ASSIMILATIVE
ASSIMILATIVELY
ASSIMILATOR
ASSIMILATORS
ASSIMILATORY
ASSISTANCE
ASSISTANCES
ASSISTANTS
ASSISTANTSHIP
ASSISTANTSHIPS
ASSOCIABILITIES
ASSOCIABILITY
ASSOCIABLE
ASSOCIATED
ASSOCIATES
ASSOCIATESHIP
ASSOCIATESHIPS
ASSOCIATING
ASSOCIATION
ASSOCIATIONAL
ASSOCIATIONISM
ASSOCIATIONISMS

ASSOCIATIONIST
ASSOCIATIONISTS
ASSOCIATIONS
ASSOCIATIVE
ASSOCIATIVELY
ASSOCIATIVITIES
ASSOCIATIVITY
ASSOCIATOR
ASSOCIATORS
ASSOCIATORY
ASSOILMENT
ASSOILMENTS
ASSOILZIED
ASSOILZIEING
ASSOILZIES
ASSONANCES
ASSONANTAL
ASSONATING
ASSORTATIVE
ASSORTATIVELY
ASSORTEDNESS
ASSORTEDNESSES
ASSORTIVELY
ASSORTMENT
ASSORTMENTS
ASSUAGEMENT
ASSUAGEMENTS
ASSUAGINGS
ASSUBJUGATE
ASSUBJUGATED
ASSUBJUGATES
ASSUBJUGATING
ASSUEFACTION
ASSUEFACTIONS
ASSUETUDES
ASSUMABILITIES
ASSUMABILITY
ASSUMINGLY
ASSUMPSITS
ASSUMPTION
ASSUMPTIONS
ASSUMPTIVE
ASSUMPTIVELY
ASSURANCES
ASSUREDNESS
ASSUREDNESSES
ASSURGENCIES
ASSURGENCY
ASSYTHMENT

ASSYTHMENTS
ASTACOLOGICAL
ASTACOLOGIES
ASTACOLOGIST
ASTACOLOGISTS
ASTACOLOGY
ASTARBOARD
ASTATICALLY
ASTATICISM
ASTATICISMS
ASTEREOGNOSES
ASTEREOGNOSIS
ASTERIATED
ASTERIDIAN
ASTERIDIANS
ASTERISKED
ASTERISKING
ASTERISKLESS
ASTEROIDAL
ASTEROIDEAN
ASTEROIDEANS
ASTHENOPIA
ASTHENOPIAS
ASTHENOPIC
ASTHENOSPHERE
ASTHENOSPHERES
ASTHENOSPHERIC
ASTHMATICAL
ASTHMATICALLY
ASTHMATICS
ASTIGMATIC
ASTIGMATICALLY
ASTIGMATICS
ASTIGMATISM
ASTIGMATISMS
ASTOMATOUS
ASTONISHED
ASTONISHES
ASTONISHING
ASTONISHINGLY
ASTONISHMENT
ASTONISHMENTS
ASTOUNDING
ASTOUNDINGLY
ASTOUNDMENT
ASTOUNDMENTS
ASTRACHANS
ASTRAGALUS
ASTRAKHANS

ASTRANTIAS
ASTRAPHOBIA
ASTRAPHOBIAS
ASTRAPHOBIC
ASTRAPOPHOBIA
ASTRAPOPHOBIAS
ASTRICTING
ASTRICTION
ASTRICTIONS
ASTRICTIVE
ASTRICTIVELY
ASTRINGENCE
ASTRINGENCES
ASTRINGENCIES
ASTRINGENCY
ASTRINGENT
ASTRINGENTLY
ASTRINGENTS
ASTRINGERS
ASTRINGING
ASTROBIOLOGIES
ASTROBIOLOGIST
ASTROBIOLOGISTS
ASTROBIOLOGY
ASTROBLEME
ASTROBLEMES
ASTROBOTANIES
ASTROBOTANY
ASTROCHEMISTRY
ASTROCOMPASS
ASTROCOMPASSES
ASTROCYTES
ASTROCYTIC
ASTROCYTOMA
ASTROCYTOMAS
ASTROCYTOMATA
ASTRODOMES
ASTRODYNAMICIST
ASTRODYNAMICS
ASTROFELLS
ASTROGEOLOGIES
ASTROGEOLOGIST
ASTROGEOLOGISTS
ASTROGEOLOGY
ASTROHATCH
ASTROHATCHES
ASTROLABES
ASTROLATRIES
ASTROLATRY

ASTROLOGER	ASTROTOURISTS	ATHEOLOGIES	ATONALITIES	ATTENDMENT
ASTROLOGERS	ASTROTURFER	ATHEORETICAL	ATONEMENTS	ATTENDMENTS
ASTROLOGIC	ASTROTURFERS	ATHERMANCIES	ATONICITIES	ATTENTIONAL
ASTROLOGICAL	ASTROTURFING	ATHERMANCY	ATORVASTATIN	ATTENTIONS
ASTROLOGICALLY	ASTROTURFINGS	ATHERMANOUS	ATORVASTATINS	ATTENTIVELY
ASTROLOGIES	ASTUCIOUSLY	ATHEROGENESES	ATRABILIAR	ATTENTIVENESS
ASTROLOGIST	ASTUCITIES	ATHEROGENESIS	ATRABILIOUS	ATTENTIVENESSES
ASTROLOGISTS	ASTUTENESS	ATHEROGENIC	ATRABILIOUSNESS	ATTENUANTS
ASTROMETRIC	ASTUTENESSES	ATHEROMATA	ATRACURIUM	ATTENUATED
ASTROMETRICAL	ASYMMETRIC	ATHEROMATOUS	ATRACURIUMS	ATTENUATES
ASTROMETRIES	ASYMMETRICAL	ATHEROSCLEROSES	ATRAMENTAL	ATTENUATING
ASTROMETRY	ASYMMETRICALLY	ATHEROSCLEROSIS	ATRAMENTOUS	ATTENUATION
ASTRONAUTIC	ASYMMETRIES	ATHEROSCLEROTIC	ATROCIOUSLY	ATTENUATIONS
ASTRONAUTICAL	ASYMPTOMATIC	ATHETISING	ATROCIOUSNESS	ATTENUATOR
ASTRONAUTICALLY	ASYMPTOTES	ATHETIZING	ATROCIOUSNESSES	ATTENUATORS
ASTRONAUTICS	ASYMPTOTIC	ATHLEISURE	ATROCITIES	ATTESTABLE
ASTRONAUTS	ASYMPTOTICAL	ATHLEISURES	ATROPHYING	ATTESTANTS
ASTRONAVIGATION	ASYMPTOTICALLY	ATHLETICALLY	ATTACHABLE	ATTESTATION
ASTRONAVIGATOR	ASYNARTETE	ATHLETICISM	ATTACHMENT	ATTESTATIONS
ASTRONAVIGATORS	ASYNARTETES	ATHLETICISMS	ATTACHMENTS	ATTESTATIVE
ASTRONOMER	ASYNARTETIC	ATHROCYTES	ATTACKABLE	ATTESTATOR
ASTRONOMERS	ASYNCHRONIES	ATHROCYTOSES	ATTAINABILITIES	ATTESTATORS
ASTRONOMIC	ASYNCHRONISM	ATHROCYTOSIS	ATTAINABILITY	ATTICISING
ASTRONOMICAL	ASYNCHRONISMS	ATHWARTSHIP	ATTAINABLE	ATTICIZING
ASTRONOMICALLY	ASYNCHRONOUS	ATHWARTSHIPS	ATTAINABLENESS	ATTIREMENT
ASTRONOMIES	ASYNCHRONOUSLY	ATMOLOGIES	ATTAINDERS	ATTIREMENTS
ASTRONOMISE	ASYNCHRONY	ATMOLOGIST	ATTAINMENT	ATTITUDINAL
ASTRONOMISED	ASYNDETICALLY	ATMOLOGISTS	ATTAINMENTS	ATTITUDINALLY
ASTRONOMISES	ASYNDETONS	ATMOLYSING	ATTAINTING	ATTITUDINARIAN
ASTRONOMISING	ASYNERGIAS	ATMOLYZING	ATTAINTMENT	ATTITUDINARIANS
ASTRONOMIZE	ASYNERGIES	ATMOMETERS	ATTAINTMENTS	ATTITUDINISE
ASTRONOMIZED	ASYNTACTIC	ATMOMETRIES	ATTAINTURE	ATTITUDINISED
ASTRONOMIZES	ASYSTOLISM	ATMOSPHERE	ATTAINTURES	ATTITUDINISER
ASTRONOMIZING	ASYSTOLISMS	ATMOSPHERED	ATTEMPERED	ATTITUDINISERS
ASTROPHELS	ATACAMITES	ATMOSPHERES	ATTEMPERING	ATTITUDINISES
ASTROPHOBIA	ATARACTICS	ATMOSPHERIC	ATTEMPERMENT	ATTITUDINISING
ASTROPHOBIAS	ATAVISTICALLY	ATMOSPHERICAL	ATTEMPERMENTS	ATTITUDINISINGS
ASTROPHOBIC	ATCHIEVING	ATMOSPHERICALLY	ATTEMPTABILITY	ATTITUDINIZE
ASTROPHOTOGRAPH	ATELECTASES	ATMOSPHERICS	ATTEMPTABLE	ATTITUDINIZED
ASTROPHYSICAL	ATELECTASIS	ATOMICALLY	ATTEMPTERS	ATTITUDINIZER
ASTROPHYSICALLY	ATELECTATIC	ATOMICITIES	ATTEMPTING	ATTITUDINIZERS
ASTROPHYSICIST	ATELEIOSES	ATOMISATION	ATTENDANCE	ATTITUDINIZES
ASTROPHYSICISTS	ATELEIOSIS	ATOMISATIONS	ATTENDANCES	ATTITUDINIZING
ASTROPHYSICS	ATHANASIES	ATOMISTICAL	ATTENDANCIES	ATTITUDINIZINGS
ASTROSPHERE	ATHEISTICAL	ATOMISTICALLY	ATTENDANCY	ATTOLASERS
ASTROSPHERES	ATHEISTICALLY	ATOMIZATION	ATTENDANTS	ATTOLLENTS
ASTROTOURISM	ATHEMATICALLY	ATOMIZATIONS	ATTENDEMENT	ATTOMETERS
ASTROTOURISMS	ATHENAEUMS	ATONALISMS	ATTENDEMENTS	ATTOMETRES
ASTROTOURIST	ATHEOLOGICAL	ATONALISTS	ATTENDINGS	ATTOPHYSICS

ATTORNEYDOM	ATTRITTING	AUDIOMETRISTS	AURISCOPES	AUTHENTICATIONS
ATTORNEYDOMS	ATTUITIONAL	AUDIOMETRY	AURISCOPIC	AUTHENTICATOR
ATTORNEYED	ATTUITIONS	AUDIOPHILE	AUSCULTATE	AUTHENTICATORS
ATTORNEYING	ATTUITIVELY	AUDIOPHILES	AUSCULTATED	AUTHENTICITIES
ATTORNEYISM	ATTUNEMENT	AUDIOPHILS	AUSCULTATES	AUTHENTICITY
ATTORNEYISMS	ATTUNEMENTS	AUDIOTAPED	AUSCULTATING	AUTHIGENIC
ATTORNEYSHIP	ATYPICALITIES	AUDIOTAPES	AUSCULTATION	AUTHORCRAFT
ATTORNEYSHIPS	ATYPICALITY	AUDIOTAPING	AUSCULTATIONS	AUTHORCRAFTS
ATTORNMENT	ATYPICALLY	AUDIOTYPING	AUSCULTATIVE	AUTHORESSES
ATTORNMENTS	AUBERGINES	AUDIOTYPINGS	AUSCULTATOR	AUTHORINGS
ATTOSECOND	AUBERGISTE	AUDIOTYPIST	AUSCULTATORS	AUTHORISABLE
ATTOSECONDS	AUBERGISTES	AUDIOTYPISTS	AUSCULTATORY	AUTHORISATION
ATTOTESLAS	AUBRIETIAS	AUDIOVISUAL	AUSFORMING	AUTHORISATIONS
ATTRACTABLE	AUCTIONARY	AUDIOVISUALLY	AUSFORMINGS	AUTHORISED
ATTRACTANCE	AUCTIONEER	AUDIOVISUALS	AUSLANDERS	AUTHORISER
ATTRACTANCES	AUCTIONEERED	AUDIPHONES	AUSPICATED	AUTHORISERS
ATTRACTANCIES	AUCTIONEERING	AUDITIONED	AUSPICATES	AUTHORISES
ATTRACTANCY	AUCTIONEERS	AUDITIONER	AUSPICATING	AUTHORISING
ATTRACTANT	AUCTIONING	AUDITIONERS	AUSPICIOUS	AUTHORISMS
ATTRACTANTS	AUDACIOUSLY	AUDITIONING	AUSPICIOUSLY	AUTHORITARIAN
ATTRACTERS	AUDACIOUSNESS	AUDITORIAL	AUSPICIOUSNESS	AUTHORITARIANS
ATTRACTING	AUDACIOUSNESSES	AUDITORIES	AUSTENITES	AUTHORITATIVE
ATTRACTINGLY	AUDACITIES	AUDITORILY	AUSTENITIC	AUTHORITATIVELY
ATTRACTION	AUDIBILITIES	AUDITORIUM	AUSTERENESS	AUTHORITIES
ATTRACTIONS	AUDIBILITY	AUDITORIUMS	AUSTERENESSES	AUTHORIZABLE
ATTRACTIVE	AUDIBLENESS	AUDITORSHIP	AUSTERITIES	AUTHORIZATION
ATTRACTIVELY	AUDIBLENESSES	AUDITORSHIPS	AUSTRALITE	AUTHORIZATIONS
ATTRACTIVENESS	AUDIENCIAS	AUDITRESSES	AUSTRALITES	AUTHORIZED
ATTRACTORS	AUDIOBOOKS	AUGMENTABLE	AUSTRINGER	AUTHORIZER
ATTRAHENTS	AUDIOCASSETTE	AUGMENTATION	AUSTRINGERS	AUTHORIZERS
ATTRAPPING	AUDIOCASSETTES	AUGMENTATIONS	AUTARCHICAL	AUTHORIZES
ATTRIBUTABLE	AUDIOGENIC	AUGMENTATIVE	AUTARCHIES	AUTHORIZING
ATTRIBUTED	AUDIOGRAMS	AUGMENTATIVELY	AUTARCHIST	AUTHORLESS
ATTRIBUTER	AUDIOGRAPH	AUGMENTATIVES	AUTARCHISTS	AUTHORSHIP
ATTRIBUTERS	AUDIOGRAPHS	AUGMENTERS	AUTARKICAL	AUTHORSHIPS
ATTRIBUTES	AUDIOLOGIC	AUGMENTING	AUTARKISTS	AUTISTICALLY
ATTRIBUTING	AUDIOLOGICAL	AUGMENTORS	AUTECOLOGIC	AUTOALLOGAMIES
ATTRIBUTION	AUDIOLOGICALLY	AUGURSHIPS	AUTECOLOGICAL	AUTOALLOGAMY
ATTRIBUTIONAL	AUDIOLOGIES	AUGUSTNESS	AUTECOLOGIES	AUTOANTIBODIES
ATTRIBUTIONS	AUDIOLOGIST	AUGUSTNESSES	AUTECOLOGY	AUTOANTIBODY
ATTRIBUTIVE	AUDIOLOGISTS	AURALITIES	AUTEURISMS	AUTOBAHNEN
ATTRIBUTIVELY	AUDIOMETER	AUREATENESS	AUTEURISTS	AUTOBIOGRAPHER
ATTRIBUTIVENESS	AUDIOMETERS	AUREATENESSES	AUTHENTICAL	AUTOBIOGRAPHERS
ATTRIBUTIVES	AUDIOMETRIC	AURICULARLY	AUTHENTICALLY	AUTOBIOGRAPHIC
ATTRIBUTOR	AUDIOMETRICALLY	AURICULARS	AUTHENTICATE	AUTOBIOGRAPHIES
ATTRIBUTORS	AUDIOMETRICIAN	AURICULATE	AUTHENTICATED	AUTOBIOGRAPHY
ATTRISTING	AUDIOMETRICIANS	AURICULATED	AUTHENTICATES	AUTOBODIES
ATTRITIONAL	AUDIOMETRIES	AURICULATELY	AUTHENTICATING	AUTOBUSSES
ATTRITIONS	AUDIOMETRIST	AURIFEROUS	AUTHENTICATION	AUTOCATALYSE

AUTOCATALYSED AUTODESTRUCTS AUTOGRAPHS AUTOMATISED AUTOPHONIES
AUTOCATALYSES AUTODIALED AUTOGRAPHY AUTOMATISES AUTOPHYTES
AUTOCATALYSING AUTODIALING AUTOGRAVURE AUTOMATISING AUTOPHYTIC
AUTOCATALYSIS AUTODIALLED AUTOGRAVURES AUTOMATISM AUTOPHYTICALLY
AUTOCATALYTIC AUTODIALLING AUTOGUIDES AUTOMATISMS AUTOPILOTS
AUTOCATALYZE AUTODIDACT AUTOHYPNOSES AUTOMATIST AUTOPISTAS
AUTOCATALYZED AUTODIDACTIC AUTOHYPNOSIS AUTOMATISTS AUTOPLASTIC
AUTOCATALYZES AUTODIDACTICISM AUTOHYPNOTIC AUTOMATIZATION AUTOPLASTIES
AUTOCATALYZING AUTODIDACTS AUTOIMMUNE AUTOMATIZATIONS AUTOPLASTY
AUTOCEPHALIC AUTODROMES AUTOIMMUNITIES AUTOMATIZE AUTOPOINTS
AUTOCEPHALIES AUTOECIOUS AUTOIMMUNITY AUTOMATIZED AUTOPOLYPLOID
AUTOCEPHALOUS AUTOECIOUSLY AUTOINFECTION AUTOMATIZES AUTOPOLYPLOIDS
AUTOCEPHALY AUTOECISMS AUTOINFECTIONS AUTOMATIZING AUTOPOLYPLOIDY
AUTOCHANGER AUTOEROTIC AUTOINOCULATION AUTOMATONS AUTOPSISTS
AUTOCHANGERS AUTOEROTICISM AUTOIONISATION AUTOMATOUS AUTOPSYING
AUTOCHTHON AUTOEROTICISMS AUTOIONISATIONS AUTOMETERS AUTOPTICAL
AUTOCHTHONAL AUTOEROTISM AUTOIONIZATION AUTOMOBILE AUTOPTICALLY
AUTOCHTHONES AUTOEROTISMS AUTOIONIZATIONS AUTOMOBILED AUTORADIOGRAM
AUTOCHTHONIC AUTOEXPOSURE AUTOJUMBLE AUTOMOBILES AUTORADIOGRAMS
AUTOCHTHONIES AUTOEXPOSURES AUTOJUMBLES AUTOMOBILIA AUTORADIOGRAPH
AUTOCHTHONISM AUTOFICTION AUTOKINESES AUTOMOBILING AUTORADIOGRAPHS
AUTOCHTHONISMS AUTOFICTIONS AUTOKINESIS AUTOMOBILISM AUTORADIOGRAPHY
AUTOCHTHONOUS AUTOFILLED AUTOKINETIC AUTOMOBILISMS AUTOREPLIES
AUTOCHTHONOUSLY AUTOFILLING AUTOLATRIES AUTOMOBILIST AUTOREVERSE
AUTOCHTHONS AUTOFLARES AUTOLOADED AUTOMOBILISTS AUTOREVERSES
AUTOCHTHONY AUTOFOCUSED AUTOLOADING AUTOMOBILITIES AUTORICKSHAW
AUTOCLAVED AUTOFOCUSES AUTOLOGIES AUTOMOBILITY AUTORICKSHAWS
AUTOCLAVES AUTOFOCUSING AUTOLOGOUS AUTOMORPHIC AUTOROTATE
AUTOCLAVING AUTOFOCUSSED AUTOLYSATE AUTOMORPHICALLY AUTOROTATED
AUTOCOMPLETE AUTOFOCUSSES AUTOLYSATES AUTOMORPHISM AUTOROTATES
AUTOCOMPLETES AUTOFOCUSSING AUTOLYSING AUTOMORPHISMS AUTOROTATING
AUTOCOPROPHAGY AUTOGAMIES AUTOLYSINS AUTOMOTIVE AUTOROTATION
AUTOCORRECT AUTOGAMOUS AUTOLYZATE AUTONOMICAL AUTOROTATIONS
AUTOCORRECTS AUTOGENESES AUTOLYZATES AUTONOMICALLY AUTOROUTES
AUTOCORRELATION AUTOGENESIS AUTOLYZING AUTONOMICS AUTOSAVING
AUTOCRACIES AUTOGENETIC AUTOMAGICALLY AUTONOMIES AUTOSCHEDIASM
AUTOCRATIC AUTOGENICS AUTOMAKERS AUTONOMIST AUTOSCHEDIASMS
AUTOCRATICAL AUTOGENIES AUTOMATABLE AUTONOMISTS AUTOSCHEDIASTIC
AUTOCRATICALLY AUTOGENOUS AUTOMATICAL AUTONOMOUS AUTOSCHEDIAZE
AUTOCRIMES AUTOGENOUSLY AUTOMATICALLY AUTONOMOUSLY AUTOSCHEDIAZED
AUTOCRITIQUE AUTOGRAFTED AUTOMATICITIES AUTONYMOUS AUTOSCHEDIAZES
AUTOCRITIQUES AUTOGRAFTING AUTOMATICITY AUTOPHAGIA AUTOSCHEDIAZING
AUTOCROSSES AUTOGRAFTS AUTOMATICS AUTOPHAGIAS AUTOSCOPIC
AUTOCUTIES AUTOGRAPHED AUTOMATING AUTOPHAGIES AUTOSCOPIES
AUTOCYCLES AUTOGRAPHIC AUTOMATION AUTOPHAGOUS AUTOSEXING
AUTODESTRUCT AUTOGRAPHICAL AUTOMATIONS AUTOPHANOUS AUTOSEXINGS
AUTODESTRUCTED AUTOGRAPHICALLY AUTOMATISATION AUTOPHOBIA AUTOSOMALLY
AUTODESTRUCTING AUTOGRAPHIES AUTOMATISATIONS AUTOPHOBIAS AUTOSPORES
AUTODESTRUCTIVE AUTOGRAPHING AUTOMATISE AUTOPHOBIES AUTOSPORTS

A

AUTOSTABILITIES	AUTOWINDER	AVERRUNCATE	AVOIRDUPOIS	AXIOMATICS
AUTOSTABILITY	AUTOWINDERS	AVERRUNCATED	AVOIRDUPOISES	AXIOMATISATION
AUTOSTRADA	AUTOWORKER	AVERRUNCATES	AVOPARCINS	AXIOMATISATIONS
AUTOSTRADAS	AUTOWORKERS	AVERRUNCATING	AVOUCHABLE	AXIOMATISE
AUTOSTRADE	AUTOXIDATION	AVERRUNCATION	AVOUCHMENT	AXIOMATISED
AUTOSUGGEST	AUTOXIDATIONS	AVERRUNCATIONS	AVOUCHMENTS	AXIOMATISES
AUTOSUGGESTED	AUTUMNALLY	AVERRUNCATOR	AVOUTERERS	AXIOMATISING
AUTOSUGGESTING	AUTUMNIEST	AVERRUNCATORS	AVOWABLENESS	AXIOMATIZATION
AUTOSUGGESTION	AUXANOMETER	AVERSENESS	AVOWABLENESSES	AXIOMATIZATIONS
AUTOSUGGESTIONS	AUXANOMETERS	AVERSENESSES	AVUNCULARITIES	AXIOMATIZE
AUTOSUGGESTIVE	AUXILIARIES	AVERSIVELY	AVUNCULARITY	AXIOMATIZED
AUTOSUGGESTS	AUXOCHROME	AVERSIVENESS	AVUNCULARLY	AXIOMATIZES
AUTOTELLER	AUXOCHROMES	AVERSIVENESSES	AVUNCULATE	AXIOMATIZING
AUTOTELLERS	AUXOMETERS	AVERTIMENT	AVUNCULATES	AXISYMMETRIC
AUTOTETRAPLOID	AUXOSPORES	AVERTIMENTS	AVVOGADORE	AXISYMMETRICAL
AUTOTETRAPLOIDS	AUXOTROPHIC	AVGOLEMONO	AVVOGADORES	AXISYMMETRIES
AUTOTETRAPLOIDY	AUXOTROPHIES	AVGOLEMONOS	AWAKENINGS	AXISYMMETRY
AUTOTHEISM	AUXOTROPHS	AVIANISING	AWARENESSES	AXOLEMMATA
AUTOTHEISMS	AUXOTROPHY	AVIANIZING	AWAYNESSES	AXONOMETRIC
AUTOTHEIST	AVAILABILITIES	AVIAPHOBES	AWELESSNESS	AXONOMETRIES
AUTOTHEISTS	AVAILABILITY	AVIAPHOBIA	AWELESSNESSES	AXONOMETRY
AUTOTIMERS	AVAILABLENESS	AVIAPHOBIAS	AWESOMENESS	AXOPLASMIC
AUTOTOMIES	AVAILABLENESSES	AVIAPHOBIC	AWESOMENESSES	AYAHUASCAS
AUTOTOMISE	AVAILINGLY	AVIAPHOBICS	AWESTRICKEN	AYAHUASCOS
AUTOTOMISED	AVALANCHED	AVIATRESSES	AWESTRIKES	AYATOLLAHS
AUTOTOMISES	AVALANCHES	AVIATRICES	AWESTRIKING	AYUNTAMIENTO
AUTOTOMISING	AVALANCHING	AVIATRIXES	AWFULNESSES	AYUNTAMIENTOS
AUTOTOMIZE	AVALEMENTS	AVICULTURE	AWKWARDEST	AYURVEDICS
AUTOTOMIZED	AVANTURINE	AVICULTURES	AWKWARDISH	AZATHIOPRINE
AUTOTOMIZES	AVANTURINES	AVICULTURIST	AWKWARDNESS	AZATHIOPRINES
AUTOTOMIZING	AVARICIOUS	AVICULTURISTS	AWKWARDNESSES	AZEDARACHS
AUTOTOMOUS	AVARICIOUSLY	AVIDNESSES	AWLESSNESS	AZEOTROPES
AUTOTOXAEMIA	AVARICIOUSNESS	AVIOPHOBES	AWLESSNESSES	AZEOTROPIC
AUTOTOXAEMIAS	AVASCULARITIES	AVIOPHOBIA	AXENICALLY	AZEOTROPIES
AUTOTOXEMIA	AVASCULARITY	AVIOPHOBIAS	AXEROPHTHOL	AZIDOTHYMIDINE
AUTOTOXEMIAS	AVENACEOUS	AVIOPHOBIC	AXEROPHTHOLS	AZIDOTHYMIDINES
AUTOTOXINS	AVENGEMENT	AVIOPHOBICS	AXIALITIES	AZIMUTHALLY
AUTOTRANSFORMER	AVENGEMENTS	AVISANDUMS	AXILLARIES	AZOBENZENE
AUTOTRANSFUSION	AVENGERESS	AVISEMENTS	AXINOMANCIES	AZOBENZENES
AUTOTROPHIC	AVENGERESSES	AVITAMINOSES	AXINOMANCY	AZOOSPERMIA
AUTOTROPHICALLY	AVENTAILES	AVITAMINOSIS	AXIOLOGICAL	AZOOSPERMIAS
AUTOTROPHIES	AVENTURINE	AVITAMINOTIC	AXIOLOGICALLY	AZOOSPERMIC
AUTOTROPHS	AVENTURINES	AVIZANDUMS	AXIOLOGIES	AZOTAEMIAS
AUTOTROPHY	AVENTURINS	AVOCATIONAL	AXIOLOGIST	AZOTOBACTER
AUTOTYPIES	AVERAGENESS	AVOCATIONALLY	AXIOLOGISTS	AZOTOBACTERS
AUTOTYPING	AVERAGENESSES	AVOCATIONS	AXIOMATICAL	AZYGOSPORE
AUTOTYPOGRAPHY	AVERAGINGS	AVOIDANCES	AXIOMATICALLY	AZYGOSPORES

B

BAALEBATIM
BABACOOTES
BABBITRIES
BABBITTING
BABBITTRIES
BABBLATIVE
BABBLEMENT
BABBLEMENTS
BABELESQUE
BABESIASES
BABESIASIS
BABESIOSES
BABESIOSIS
BABINGTONITE
BABINGTONITES
BABIROUSSA
BABIROUSSAS
BABIRUSSAS
BABOONERIES
BABYCCINOS
BABYDADDIES
BABYISHNESS
BABYISHNESSES
BABYPROOFED
BABYPROOFING
BABYPROOFS
BABYSITTING
BACCALAUREAN
BACCALAUREATE
BACCALAUREATES
BACCHANALIA
BACCHANALIAN
BACCHANALIANISM
BACCHANALIANS
BACCHANALS
BACCHANTES
BACCIFEROUS
BACCIVOROUS
BACHARACHS
BACHELORDOM
BACHELORDOMS
BACHELORETTE
BACHELORETTES

BACHELORHOOD
BACHELORHOODS
BACHELORISM
BACHELORISMS
BACHELORSHIP
BACHELORSHIPS
BACILLAEMIA
BACILLAEMIAS
BACILLEMIA
BACILLEMIAS
BACILLICIDE
BACILLICIDES
BACILLIFORM
BACILLURIA
BACILLURIAS
BACITRACIN
BACITRACINS
BACKACTERS
BACKBENCHER
BACKBENCHERS
BACKBENCHES
BACKBITERS
BACKBITING
BACKBITINGS
BACKBITTEN
BACKBLOCKER
BACKBLOCKERS
BACKBLOCKS
BACKBOARDS
BACKBONELESS
BACKBREAKER
BACKBREAKERS
BACKBREAKING
BACKBURNED
BACKBURNING
BACKCASTING
BACKCHANNEL
BACKCHANNELS
BACKCHATTED
BACKCHATTING
BACKCHECKED
BACKCHECKING
BACKCHECKS

BACKCLOTHS
BACKCOMBED
BACKCOMBING
BACKCOUNTRIES
BACKCOUNTRY
BACKCOURTMAN
BACKCOURTMEN
BACKCOURTS
BACKCROSSED
BACKCROSSES
BACKCROSSING
BACKDATING
BACKDRAFTS
BACKDRAUGHT
BACKDRAUGHTS
BACKDROPPED
BACKDROPPING
BACKFIELDS
BACKFILLED
BACKFILLING
BACKFILLINGS
BACKFIRING
BACKFISCHES
BACKFITTED
BACKFITTING
BACKFITTINGS
BACKFLIPPED
BACKFLIPPING
BACKFLIPPINGS
BACKGAMMON
BACKGAMMONED
BACKGAMMONING
BACKGAMMONS
BACKGROUND
BACKGROUNDED
BACKGROUNDER
BACKGROUNDERS
BACKGROUNDING
BACKGROUNDS
BACKHANDED
BACKHANDEDLY
BACKHANDEDNESS
BACKHANDER

BACKHANDERS
BACKHANDING
BACKHAULED
BACKHAULING
BACKHOEING
BACKHOUSES
BACKLASHED
BACKLASHER
BACKLASHERS
BACKLASHES
BACKLASHING
BACKLIGHTED
BACKLIGHTING
BACKLIGHTINGS
BACKLIGHTS
BACKLINERS
BACKLISTED
BACKLISTING
BACKLOADED
BACKLOADING
BACKLOGGED
BACKLOGGING
BACKMARKER
BACKMARKERS
BACKPACKED
BACKPACKER
BACKPACKERS
BACKPACKING
BACKPACKINGS
BACKPEDALED
BACKPEDALING
BACKPEDALLED
BACKPEDALLING
BACKPEDALS
BACKPIECES
BACKPLANES
BACKPLATES
BACKRONYMS
BACKRUSHES
BACKSCATTER
BACKSCATTERED
BACKSCATTERING
BACKSCATTERINGS

BACKSCATTERS
BACKSCRATCH
BACKSCRATCHED
BACKSCRATCHER
BACKSCRATCHERS
BACKSCRATCHES
BACKSCRATCHING
BACKSCRATCHINGS
BACKSETTING
BACKSHEESH
BACKSHEESHED
BACKSHEESHES
BACKSHEESHING
BACKSHISHED
BACKSHISHES
BACKSHISHING
BACKSHORES
BACKSIGHTS
BACKSLAPPED
BACKSLAPPER
BACKSLAPPERS
BACKSLAPPING
BACKSLASHES
BACKSLIDDEN
BACKSLIDER
BACKSLIDERS
BACKSLIDES
BACKSLIDING
BACKSLIDINGS
BACKSPACED
BACKSPACER
BACKSPACERS
BACKSPACES
BACKSPACING
BACKSPEERED
BACKSPEERING
BACKSPEERS
BACKSPEIRED
BACKSPEIRING
BACKSPEIRS
BACKSPLASH
BACKSPLASHES
BACKSPLITS

BACKSTABBED	BACKWARDNESSES	BACTERIOSTASES	BAIGNOIRES	BALDNESSES
BACKSTABBER	BACKWASHED	BACTERIOSTASIS	BAILIESHIP	BALECTIONS
BACKSTABBERS	BACKWASHES	BACTERIOSTAT	BAILIESHIPS	BALEFULNESS
BACKSTABBING	BACKWASHING	BACTERIOSTATIC	BAILIFFSHIP	BALEFULNESSES
BACKSTABBINGS	BACKWATERS	BACTERIOSTATS	BAILIFFSHIPS	BALIBUNTAL
BACKSTAGES	BACKWINDED	BACTERIOTOXIN	BAILIWICKS	BALIBUNTALS
BACKSTAIRS	BACKWINDING	BACTERIOTOXINS	BAILLIAGES	BALKANISATION
BACKSTALLED	BACKWOODSIER	BACTERISATION	BAILLIESHIP	BALKANISATIONS
BACKSTALLING	BACKWOODSIEST	BACTERISATIONS	BAILLIESHIPS	BALKANISED
BACKSTALLS	BACKWOODSMAN	BACTERISED	BAIRNLIEST	BALKANISES
BACKSTAMPED	BACKWOODSMEN	BACTERISES	BAISEMAINS	BALKANISING
BACKSTAMPING	BACKWOODSY	BACTERISING	BAITFISHES	BALKANIZATION
BACKSTAMPS	BACKWORKER	BACTERIURIA	BAJILLIONS	BALKANIZATIONS
BACKSTARTING	BACKWORKERS	BACTERIURIAS	BAKEAPPLES	BALKANIZED
BACKSTARTINGS	BACTERAEMIA	BACTERIZATION	BAKEBOARDS	BALKANIZES
BACKSTITCH	BACTERAEMIAS	BACTERIZATIONS	BAKEHOUSES	BALKANIZING
BACKSTITCHED	BACTERAEMIC	BACTERIZED	BAKESTONES	BALKINESSES
BACKSTITCHES	BACTEREMIA	BACTERIZES	BAKHSHISHED	BALLABILES
BACKSTITCHING	BACTEREMIAS	BACTERIZING	BAKHSHISHES	BALLADEERED
BACKSTOPPED	BACTEREMIC	BACTEROIDS	BAKHSHISHING	BALLADEERING
BACKSTOPPING	BACTERIALLY	BACTERURIA	BAKSHEESHED	BALLADEERS
BACKSTORIES	BACTERIALS	BACTERURIAS	BAKSHEESHES	BALLADINES
BACKSTRAPS	BACTERICIDAL	BACULIFORM	BAKSHEESHING	BALLADISTS
BACKSTREET	BACTERICIDALLY	BACULOVIRUS	BAKSHISHED	BALLADMONGER
BACKSTREETS	BACTERICIDE	BACULOVIRUSES	BAKSHISHES	BALLADMONGERS
BACKSTRETCH	BACTERICIDES	BADAMASHES	BAKSHISHING	BALLADRIES
BACKSTRETCHES	BACTERIOCIN	BADDELEYITE	BALACLAVAS	BALLANTING
BACKSTROKE	BACTERIOCINS	BADDELEYITES	BALALAIKAS	BALLANWRASSE
BACKSTROKED	BACTERIOID	BADDERLOCK	BALANCEABLE	BALLANWRASSES
BACKSTROKES	BACTERIOIDS	BADDERLOCKS	BALANCINGS	BALLASTERS
BACKSTROKING	BACTERIOLOGIC	BADGERLIER	BALANITISES	BALLASTING
BACKSWIMMER	BACTERIOLOGICAL	BADGERLIEST	BALAYAGING	BALLBREAKER
BACKSWIMMERS	BACTERIOLOGIES	BADINAGING	BALBRIGGAN	BALLBREAKERS
BACKSWINGS	BACTERIOLOGIST	BADINERIES	BALBRIGGANS	BALLCARRIER
BACKSWORDMAN	BACTERIOLOGISTS	BADMINTONS	BALBUTIENT	BALLCARRIERS
BACKSWORDMEN	BACTERIOLOGY	BADMOUTHED	BALCONETTE	BALLERINAS
BACKSWORDS	BACTERIOLYSES	BADMOUTHING	BALCONETTES	BALLETICALLY
BACKSWORDSMAN	BACTERIOLYSIN	BAFFLEGABS	BALCONINGS	BALLETOMANE
BACKSWORDSMEN	BACTERIOLYSINS	BAFFLEMENT	BALDACHINO	BALLETOMANES
BACKTRACKED	BACTERIOLYSIS	BAFFLEMENTS	BALDACHINOS	BALLETOMANIA
BACKTRACKING	BACTERIOLYTIC	BAFFLINGLY	BALDACHINS	BALLETOMANIAS
BACKTRACKINGS	BACTERIOPHAGE	BAGASSOSES	BALDAQUINS	BALLFIELDS
BACKTRACKS	BACTERIOPHAGES	BAGASSOSIS	BALDERDASH	BALLFLOWER
BACKVELDER	BACTERIOPHAGIC	BAGATELLES	BALDERDASHES	BALLFLOWERS
BACKVELDERS	BACTERIOPHAGIES	BAGGINESSES	BALDERLOCKS	BALLHANDLING
BACKWARDATION	BACTERIOPHAGOUS	BAGPIPINGS	BALDERLOCKSES	BALLHANDLINGS
BACKWARDATIONS	BACTERIOPHAGY	BAGSWINGER	BALDHEADED	BALLHAWKED
BACKWARDLY	BACTERIOSES	BAGSWINGERS	BALDICOOTS	BALLHAWKING
BACKWARDNESS	BACTERIOSIS	BAHUVRIHIS	BALDMONEYS	BALLICATTER

BALLICATTERS	BALUSTRADE	BANDOLEERS	BANQUETERS	BARBELLATE
BALLISTICALLY	BALUSTRADED	BANDOLEONS	BANQUETING	BARBEQUING
BALLISTICS	BALUSTRADES	BANDOLEROS	BANQUETINGS	BARBERRIES
BALLISTITE	BALZARINES	BANDOLIERED	BANQUETTES	BARBERSHOP
BALLISTITES	BAMBOOZLED	BANDOLIERS	BANTAMWEIGHT	BARBERSHOPS
BALLISTOSPORE	BAMBOOZLEMENT	BANDOLINED	BANTAMWEIGHTS	BARBITONES
BALLISTOSPORES	BAMBOOZLEMENTS	BANDOLINES	BANTERINGLY	BARBITURATE
BALLOCKSED	BAMBOOZLER	BANDOLINING	BANTERINGS	BARBITURATES
BALLOCKSES	BAMBOOZLERS	BANDONEONS	BANTINGISM	BARBITURIC
BALLOCKSING	BAMBOOZLES	BANDONIONS	BANTINGISMS	BARBOTINES
BALLOONING	BAMBOOZLING	BANDPASSES	BAPHOMETIC	BARCAROLES
BALLOONINGS	BANALISATION	BANDSAWING	BAPTISMALLY	BARCAROLLE
BALLOONIST	BANALISATIONS	BANDSHELLS	BAPTISTERIES	BARCAROLLES
BALLOONISTS	BANALISING	BANDSPREADING	BAPTISTERY	BARDOLATER
BALLOTINGS	BANALITIES	BANDSPREADINGS	BAPTISTRIES	BARDOLATERS
BALLOTTEMENT	BANALIZATION	BANDSTANDS	BARACHOISES	BARDOLATRIES
BALLOTTEMENTS	BANALIZATIONS	BANDURISTS	BARAESTHESIA	BARDOLATROUS
BALLPARKED	BANALIZING	BANDWAGONED	BARAESTHESIAS	BARDOLATRY
BALLPARKING	BANCASSURANCE	BANDWAGONING	BARAGOUINS	BAREBACKED
BALLPLAYER	BANCASSURANCES	BANDWAGONS	BARASINGAS	BAREBACKING
BALLPLAYERS	BANCASSURER	BANDWIDTHS	BARASINGHA	BAREBACKINGS
BALLPOINTS	BANCASSURERS	BANEBERRIES	BARASINGHAS	BAREFACEDLY
BALLSINESS	BANDAGINGS	BANEFULNESS	BARATHRUMS	BAREFACEDNESS
BALLSINESSES	BANDALORES	BANEFULNESSES	BARBARESQUE	BAREFACEDNESSES
BALLYHOOED	BANDARIYAS	BANGBELLIES	BARBARIANISM	BAREFOOTED
BALLYHOOING	BANDBRAKES	BANGSRINGS	BARBARIANISMS	BAREHANDED
BALLYRAGGED	BANDEIRANTE	BANISHMENT	BARBARIANS	BAREHANDING
BALLYRAGGING	BANDEIRANTES	BANISHMENTS	BARBARICALLY	BAREHEADED
BALMACAANS	BANDELIERS	BANISTERED	BARBARISATION	BARELEGGED
BALMINESSES	BANDERILLA	BANJOLELES	BARBARISATIONS	BARENESSES
BALMORALITIES	BANDERILLAS	BANJULELES	BARBARISED	BARESTHESIA
BALMORALITY	BANDERILLERO	BANKABILITIES	BARBARISES	BARESTHESIAS
BALNEARIES	BANDERILLEROS	BANKABILITY	BARBARISING	BARGAINERS
BALNEATION	BANDEROLES	BANKERLIER	BARBARISMS	BARGAINING
BALNEATIONS	BANDERSNATCH	BANKERLIEST	BARBARITIES	BARGAININGS
BALNEOLOGICAL	BANDERSNATCHES	BANKROLLED	BARBARIZATION	BARGANDERS
BALNEOLOGIES	BANDFISHES	BANKROLLER	BARBARIZATIONS	BARGEBOARD
BALNEOLOGIST	BANDICOOTED	BANKROLLERS	BARBARIZED	BARGEBOARDS
BALNEOLOGISTS	BANDICOOTING	BANKROLLING	BARBARIZES	BARGEMASTER
BALNEOLOGY	BANDICOOTS	BANKRUPTCIES	BARBARIZING	BARGEMASTERS
BALNEOTHERAPIES	BANDINESSES	BANKRUPTCY	BARBAROUSLY	BARGEPOLES
BALNEOTHERAPY	BANDITRIES	BANKRUPTED	BARBAROUSNESS	BARHOPPING
BALSAMIEST	BANDLEADER	BANKRUPTING	BARBAROUSNESSES	BARIATRICS
BALSAMIFEROUS	BANDLEADERS	BANNERALLS	BARBASCOES	BARKANTINE
BALSAMINACEOUS	BANDMASTER	BANNERETTE	BARBASTELLE	BARKANTINES
BALSAWOODS	BANDMASTERS	BANNERETTES	BARBASTELLES	BARKEEPERS
BALTHASARS	BANDOBASTS	BANNISTERS	BARBASTELS	BARKENTINE
BALTHAZARS	BANDOBUSTS	BANQUETEER	BARBECUERS	BARKENTINES
BALUSTERED	BANDOLEERED	BANQUETEERS	BARBECUING	BARLEYCORN

BARLEYCORNS	BARPERSONS	BARRISTERS	BASIDIOSPORES	BASTINADOED
BARMBRACKS	BARQUANTINE	BARRISTERSHIP	BASIDIOSPOROUS	BASTINADOES
BARMINESSES	BARQUANTINES	BARRISTERSHIPS	BASIFICATION	BASTINADOING
BARMITSVAH	BARQUENTINE	BARROWFULS	BASIFICATIONS	BASTNAESITE
BARMITSVAHS	BARQUENTINES	BARTENDERS	BASILICONS	BASTNAESITES
BARMITZVAH	BARQUETTES	BARTENDING	BASIPETALLY	BASTNASITE
BARMITZVAHS	BARRACKERS	BARTENDINGS	BASKETBALL	BASTNASITES
BARNBOARDS	BARRACKING	BARTIZANED	BASKETBALLS	BATFOWLERS
BARNBRACKS	BARRACKINGS	BARYCENTRE	BASKETFULS	BATFOWLING
BARNSBREAKING	BARRACOONS	BARYCENTRES	BASKETLIKE	BATFOWLINGS
BARNSBREAKINGS	BARRACOUTA	BARYCENTRIC	BASKETRIES	BATHETICALLY
BARNSTORMED	BARRACOUTAS	BARYSPHERE	BASKETSFUL	BATHHOUSES
BARNSTORMER	BARRACUDAS	BARYSPHERES	BASKETWEAVE	BATHMITSVAH
BARNSTORMERS	BARRAMUNDA	BASALTINES	BASKETWEAVER	BATHMITSVAHS
BARNSTORMING	BARRAMUNDAS	BASALTWARE	BASKETWEAVERS	BATHMITZVAH
BARNSTORMINGS	BARRAMUNDI	BASALTWARES	BASKETWEAVES	BATHMITZVAHS
BARNSTORMS	BARRAMUNDIES	BASEBALLER	BASKETWORK	BATHMIZVAH
BAROCEPTOR	BARRAMUNDIS	BASEBALLERS	BASKETWORKS	BATHMIZVAHS
BAROCEPTORS	BARRASWAYS	BASEBOARDS	BASMITZVAH	BATHMOPHOBIA
BARODYNAMICS	BARRATRIES	BASEBURNER	BASMITZVAHS	BATHMOPHOBIAS
BAROGNOSES	BARRATROUS	BASEBURNERS	BASOPHILES	BATHOCHROME
BAROGNOSIS	BARRATROUSLY	BASELESSLY	BASOPHILIA	BATHOCHROMES
BAROGRAPHIC	BARRELAGES	BASELESSNESS	BASOPHILIAS	BATHOCHROMIC
BAROGRAPHS	BARRELFULS	BASELESSNESSES	BASOPHILIC	BATHOLITES
BAROMETERS	BARRELHEAD	BASELINERS	BASSETTING	BATHOLITHIC
BAROMETRIC	BARRELHEADS	BASEMENTLESS	BASSNESSES	BATHOLITHS
BAROMETRICAL	BARRELHOUSE	BASENESSES	BASSOONIST	BATHOLITIC
BAROMETRICALLY	BARRELHOUSES	BASEPLATES	BASSOONISTS	BATHOMETER
BAROMETRIES	BARRELLING	BASERUNNER	BASTARDIES	BATHOMETERS
BAROMETZES	BARRELSFUL	BASERUNNERS	BASTARDISATION	BATHOMETRIC
BARONESSES	BARRENNESS	BASERUNNING	BASTARDISATIONS	BATHOMETRICALLY
BARONETAGE	BARRENNESSES	BASERUNNINGS	BASTARDISE	BATHOMETRIES
BARONETAGES	BARRENWORT	BASHAWISMS	BASTARDISED	BATHOMETRY
BARONETCIES	BARRENWORTS	BASHAWSHIP	BASTARDISES	BATHOPHILOUS
BARONETESS	BARRETRIES	BASHAWSHIPS	BASTARDISING	BATHOPHOBIA
BARONETESSES	BARRETROUS	BASHFULLER	BASTARDISM	BATHOPHOBIAS
BARONETICAL	BARRETROUSLY	BASHFULLEST	BASTARDISMS	BATHWATERS
BAROPHILES	BARRETTERS	BASHFULNESS	BASTARDIZATION	BATHYBIUSES
BAROPHILIC	BARRICADED	BASHFULNESSES	BASTARDIZATIONS	BATHYGRAPHIC
BAROPHORESES	BARRICADER	BASHIBAZOUK	BASTARDIZE	BATHYGRAPHICAL
BAROPHORESIS	BARRICADERS	BASHIBAZOUKS	BASTARDIZED	BATHYLIMNETIC
BARORECEPTOR	BARRICADES	BASICITIES	BASTARDIZES	BATHYLITES
BARORECEPTORS	BARRICADING	BASICRANIAL	BASTARDIZING	BATHYLITHIC
BAROSCOPES	BARRICADOED	BASIDIOCARP	BASTARDLIER	BATHYLITHS
BAROSCOPIC	BARRICADOES	BASIDIOCARPS	BASTARDLIEST	BATHYLITIC
BAROTITISES	BARRICADOING	BASIDIOMYCETE	BASTARDRIES	BATHYMETER
BAROTRAUMA	BARRICADOS	BASIDIOMYCETES	BASTINADED	BATHYMETERS
BAROTRAUMAS	BARRIERING	BASIDIOMYCETOUS	BASTINADES	BATHYMETRIC
BAROTRAUMATA	BARRISTERIAL	BASIDIOSPORE	BASTINADING	BATHYMETRICAL

BATHYMETRICALLY	BATTLEGROUNDS	BEADBLASTS	BEAUJOLAIS	BECOMINGNESS
BATHYMETRIES	BATTLEMENT	BEADHOUSES	BEAUJOLAISES	BECOMINGNESSES
BATHYMETRY	BATTLEMENTED	BEADINESSES	BEAUMONTAGE	BECOWARDED
BATHYPELAGIC	BATTLEMENTS	BEADLEDOMS	BEAUMONTAGES	BECOWARDING
BATHYSCAPE	BATTLEPIECE	BEADLEHOOD	BEAUMONTAGUE	BECQUERELS
BATHYSCAPES	BATTLEPIECES	BEADLEHOODS	BEAUMONTAGUES	BECRAWLING
BATHYSCAPH	BATTLEPLANE	BEADLESHIP	BEAUTEOUSLY	BECROWDING
BATHYSCAPHE	BATTLEPLANES	BEADLESHIPS	BEAUTEOUSNESS	BECRUSTING
BATHYSCAPHES	BATTLESHIP	BEADSWOMAN	BEAUTEOUSNESSES	BECUDGELED
BATHYSCAPHS	BATTLESHIPS	BEADSWOMEN	BEAUTICIAN	BECUDGELING
BATHYSPHERE	BATTLESPACE	BEAKERFULS	BEAUTICIANS	BECUDGELLED
BATHYSPHERES	BATTLESPACES	BEAMINESSES	BEAUTIFICATION	BECUDGELLING
BATMITZVAH	BATTLEWAGON	BEANFEASTS	BEAUTIFICATIONS	BEDABBLING
BATMITZVAHS	BATTLEWAGONS	BEANINESSES	BEAUTIFIED	BEDAGGLING
BATOLOGICAL	BATTOLOGICAL	BEANSPROUT	BEAUTIFIER	BEDARKENED
BATOLOGIES	BATTOLOGIES	BEANSPROUTS	BEAUTIFIERS	BEDARKENING
BATOLOGIST	BAUDRICKES	BEANSTALKS	BEAUTIFIES	BEDAZZLEMENT
BATOLOGISTS	BAUDRONSES	BEARABILITIES	BEAUTIFULLER	BEDAZZLEMENTS
BATONNIERS	BAULKINESS	BEARABILITY	BEAUTIFULLEST	BEDAZZLING
BATRACHIAN	BAULKINESSES	BEARABLENESS	BEAUTIFULLY	BEDCHAMBER
BATRACHIANS	BAULKINGLY	BEARABLENESSES	BEAUTIFULNESS	BEDCHAMBERS
BATRACHOPHOBIA	BAULKLINES	BEARBAITING	BEAUTIFULNESSES	BEDCLOTHES
BATRACHOPHOBIAS	BAVARDAGES	BEARBAITINGS	BEAUTIFYING	BEDCOVERING
BATRACHOPHOBIC	BAVAROISES	BEARBERRIES	BEAVERBOARD	BEDCOVERINGS
BATSMANSHIP	BAWDINESSES	BEARDEDNESS	BEAVERBOARDS	BEDEAFENED
BATSMANSHIPS	BAWDYHOUSE	BEARDEDNESSES	BEBEERINES	BEDEAFENING
BATTAILOUS	BAWDYHOUSES	BEARDLESSNESS	BEBLOODING	BEDEHOUSES
BATTALIONS	BAYBERRIES	BEARDLESSNESSES	BEBLUBBERED	BEDELLSHIP
BATTEILANT	BAYNODDIES	BEARDTONGUE	BECARPETED	BEDELLSHIPS
BATTELLING	BAYONETING	BEARDTONGUES	BECARPETING	BEDELSHIPS
BATTEMENTS	BAYONETTED	BEARGRASSES	BECCACCIAS	BEDEVILING
BATTENINGS	BAYONETTING	BEARHUGGED	BECCAFICOS	BEDEVILLED
BATTERINGS	BAZILLIONS	BEARHUGGING	BECHALKING	BEDEVILLING
BATTILLING	BEACHBALLS	BEARISHNESS	BECHANCING	BEDEVILMENT
BATTINESSES	BEACHCOMBED	BEARISHNESSES	BECHARMING	BEDEVILMENTS
BATTLEAXES	BEACHCOMBER	BEARNAISES	BECKONINGLY	BEDFELLOWS
BATTLEBUSES	BEACHCOMBERS	BEASTHOODS	BECKONINGS	BEDIAPERED
BATTLEBUSSES	BEACHCOMBING	BEASTLIEST	BECLAMORED	BEDIAPERING
BATTLEDOOR	BEACHCOMBINGS	BEASTLINESS	BECLAMORING	BEDIGHTING
BATTLEDOORS	BEACHCOMBS	BEASTLINESSES	BECLAMOURED	BEDIMMINGS
BATTLEDORE	BEACHFRONT	BEATBOXERS	BECLAMOURING	BEDIMPLING
BATTLEDORES	BEACHFRONTS	BEATBOXING	BECLAMOURS	BEDIRTYING
BATTLEDRESS	BEACHGOERS	BEATBOXINGS	BECLASPING	BEDIZENING
BATTLEDRESSES	BEACHHEADS	BEATIFICAL	BECLOAKING	BEDIZENMENT
BATTLEFIELD	BEACHWEARS	BEATIFICALLY	BECLOGGING	BEDIZENMENTS
BATTLEFIELDS	BEADBLASTED	BEATIFICATION	BECLOTHING	BEDLAMISMS
BATTLEFRONT	BEADBLASTER	BEATIFICATIONS	BECLOUDING	BEDLAMITES
BATTLEFRONTS	BEADBLASTERS	BEATIFYING	BECLOWNING	BEDPRESSER
BATTLEGROUND	BEADBLASTING	BEATITUDES	BECOMINGLY	BEDPRESSERS

BEDRAGGLED	BEFLOWERING	BEHAPPENED	BELIEVABILITIES	BELLWETHER
BEDRAGGLES	BEFLUMMING	BEHAPPENING	BELIEVABILITY	BELLWETHERS
BEDRAGGLING	BEFOREHAND	BEHAVIORAL	BELIEVABLE	BELLYACHED
BEDRENCHED	BEFORETIME	BEHAVIORALLY	BELIEVABLY	BELLYACHER
BEDRENCHES	BEFORTUNED	BEHAVIORISM	BELIEVINGLY	BELLYACHERS
BEDRENCHING	BEFORTUNES	BEHAVIORISMS	BELIEVINGS	BELLYACHES
BEDRIVELED	BEFORTUNING	BEHAVIORIST	BELIQUORED	BELLYACHING
BEDRIVELING	BEFOULMENT	BEHAVIORISTIC	BELIQUORING	BELLYACHINGS
BEDRIVELLED	BEFOULMENTS	BEHAVIORISTS	BELITTLEMENT	BELLYBANDS
BEDRIVELLING	BEFRETTING	BEHAVIOURAL	BELITTLEMENTS	BELLYBOATS
BEDROPPING	BEFRIENDED	BEHAVIOURALLY	BELITTLERS	BELLYBUTTON
BEDRUGGING	BEFRIENDER	BEHAVIOURISM	BELITTLING	BELLYBUTTONS
BEDSITTERS	BEFRIENDERS	BEHAVIOURISMS	BELITTLINGLY	BELLYFLOPPED
BEDSITTING	BEFRIENDING	BEHAVIOURIST	BELLADONNA	BELLYFLOPPING
BEDSPREADS	BEFRINGING	BEHAVIOURISTIC	BELLADONNAS	BELLYFLOPS
BEDSPRINGS	BEFUDDLEMENT	BEHAVIOURISTS	BELLAMOURE	BELOMANCIES
BEDWARFING	BEFUDDLEMENTS	BEHAVIOURS	BELLAMOURES	BELONGINGNESS
BEDWARMERS	BEFUDDLING	BEHEADINGS	BELLARMINE	BELONGINGNESSES
BEDWETTERS	BEGGARDOMS	BEHIGHTING	BELLARMINES	BELONGINGS
BEECHDROPS	BEGGARHOOD	BEHINDHAND	BELLETRISM	BELOWDECKS
BEECHMASTS	BEGGARHOODS	BEHOLDINGS	BELLETRISMS	BELOWGROUND
BEECHWOODS	BEGGARLIER	BEIGELLING	BELLETRIST	BELOWSTAIRS
BEEFBURGER	BEGGARLIEST	BEINGNESSES	BELLETRISTIC	BELSHAZZAR
BEEFBURGERS	BEGGARLINESS	BEINNESSES	BELLETRISTICAL	BELSHAZZARS
BEEFEATERS	BEGGARLINESSES	BEJABERSES	BELLETRISTS	BELTCOURSE
BEEFINESSES	BEGGARWEED	BEJEEZUSES	BELLETTRIST	BELTCOURSES
BEEFSTEAKS	BEGGARWEEDS	BEJESUITED	BELLETTRISTS	BELVEDERES
BEEKEEPERS	BEGINNINGLESS	BEJESUITING	BELLFLOWER	BEMADAMING
BEEKEEPING	BEGINNINGS	BEJEWELING	BELLFLOWERS	BEMADDENED
BEEKEEPINGS	BEGIRDLING	BEJEWELLED	BELLFOUNDER	BEMADDENING
BEERINESSES	BEGLADDING	BEJEWELLING	BELLFOUNDERS	BEMEDALING
BEESWAXING	BEGLAMORED	BEJUMBLING	BELLFOUNDRIES	BEMEDALLED
BEESWINGED	BEGLAMORING	BEKNIGHTED	BELLFOUNDRY	BEMEDALLING
BEETLEBRAIN	BEGLAMOURED	BEKNIGHTING	BELLHANGER	BEMINGLING
BEETLEBRAINED	BEGLAMOURING	BEKNOTTING	BELLHANGERS	BEMOANINGS
BEETLEBRAINS	BEGLAMOURS	BELABORING	BELLIBONES	BEMONSTERED
BEETLEHEAD	BEGLERBEGS	BELABOURED	BELLICOSELY	BEMONSTERING
BEETLEHEADED	BEGLOOMING	BELABOURING	BELLICOSITIES	BEMONSTERS
BEETLEHEADS	BEGRIMMING	BELAMOURES	BELLICOSITY	BEMOUTHING
BEETMASTER	BEGROANING	BELATEDNESS	BELLIGERATI	BEMUDDLING
BEETMASTERS	BEGRUDGERIES	BELATEDNESSES	BELLIGERENCE	BEMUFFLING
BEETMISTER	BEGRUDGERS	BELEAGUERED	BELLIGERENCES	BEMURMURED
BEETMISTERS	BEGRUDGERY	BELEAGUERING	BELLIGERENCIES	BEMURMURING
BEFINGERED	BEGRUDGING	BELEAGUERMENT	BELLIGERENCY	BEMUSEMENT
BEFINGERING	BEGRUDGINGLY	BELEAGUERMENTS	BELLIGERENT	BEMUSEMENTS
BEFITTINGLY	BEGUILEMENT	BELEAGUERS	BELLIGERENTLY	BEMUZZLING
BEFLAGGING	BEGUILEMENTS	BELEMNITES	BELLIGERENTS	BENCHERSHIP
BEFLECKING	BEGUILINGLY	BELGICISMS	BELLOCKING	BENCHERSHIPS
BEFLOWERED	BEGUINAGES	BELIEFLESS	BELLOWINGS	BENCHLANDS

B

BENCHMARKED	BENEVOLENCE	BENZOFURANS	BERKELIUMS	BESIEGINGLY
BENCHMARKING	BENEVOLENCES	BENZOLINES	BERRYFRUIT	BESIEGINGS
BENCHMARKINGS	BENEVOLENT	BENZOPHENONE	BERRYFRUITS	BESLAVERED
BENCHMARKS	BENEVOLENTLY	BENZOPHENONES	BERSAGLIERE	BESLAVERING
BENCHWARMER	BENEVOLENTNESS	BENZOQUINONE	BERSAGLIERI	BESLOBBERED
BENCHWARMERS	BENGALINES	BENZOQUINONES	BERSERKERS	BESLOBBERING
BENDINESSES	BENIGHTEDLY	BENZPYRENE	BERTILLONAGE	BESLOBBERS
BENEDICITE	BENIGHTEDNESS	BENZPYRENES	BERTILLONAGES	BESLUBBERED
BENEDICITES	BENIGHTEDNESSES	BENZYLIDINE	BERYLLIOSES	BESLUBBERING
BENEDICTION	BENIGHTENED	BENZYLIDINES	BERYLLIOSIS	BESLUBBERS
BENEDICTIONAL	BENIGHTENING	BEPAINTING	BERYLLIUMS	BESMEARERS
BENEDICTIONALS	BENIGHTENINGS	BEPEARLING	BESAINTING	BESMEARING
BENEDICTIONS	BENIGHTENS	BEPEPPERED	BESCATTERED	BESMIRCHED
BENEDICTIVE	BENIGHTERS	BEPEPPERING	BESCATTERING	BESMIRCHES
BENEDICTORY	BENIGHTING	BEPESTERED	BESCATTERS	BESMIRCHING
BENEDICTUS	BENIGHTINGS	BEPESTERING	BESCORCHED	BESMOOTHED
BENEDICTUSES	BENIGHTMENT	BEPIMPLING	BESCORCHES	BESMOOTHING
BENEFACTED	BENIGHTMENTS	BEPLASTERED	BESCORCHING	BESMUDGING
BENEFACTING	BENIGNANCIES	BEPLASTERING	BESCOURING	BESMUTCHED
BENEFACTION	BENIGNANCY	BEPLASTERS	BESCRAWLED	BESMUTCHES
BENEFACTIONS	BENIGNANTLY	BEPOMMELLED	BESCRAWLING	BESMUTCHING
BENEFACTOR	BENIGNITIES	BEPOMMELLING	BESCREENED	BESMUTTING
BENEFACTORS	BENTGRASSES	BEPOWDERED	BESCREENING	BESOOTHING
BENEFACTORY	BENTHOPELAGIC	BEPOWDERING	BESCRIBBLE	BESOTTEDLY
BENEFACTRESS	BENTHOSCOPE	BEPRAISING	BESCRIBBLED	BESOTTEDNESS
BENEFACTRESSES	BENTHOSCOPES	BEQUEATHABLE	BESCRIBBLES	BESOTTEDNESSES
BENEFICENCE	BENTONITES	BEQUEATHAL	BESCRIBBLING	BESPANGLED
BENEFICENCES	BENTONITIC	BEQUEATHALS	BESEECHERS	BESPANGLES
BENEFICENT	BENUMBEDNESS	BEQUEATHED	BESEECHING	BESPANGLING
BENEFICENTIAL	BENUMBEDNESSES	BEQUEATHER	BESEECHINGLY	BESPATTERED
BENEFICENTLY	BENUMBINGLY	BEQUEATHERS	BESEECHINGNESS	BESPATTERING
BENEFICIAL	BENUMBMENT	BEQUEATHING	BESEECHINGS	BESPATTERS
BENEFICIALLY	BENUMBMENTS	BEQUEATHMENT	BESEEMINGLY	BESPEAKING
BENEFICIALNESS	BENZALDEHYDE	BEQUEATHMENTS	BESEEMINGNESS	BESPECKLED
BENEFICIALS	BENZALDEHYDES	BERASCALED	BESEEMINGNESSES	BESPECKLES
BENEFICIARIES	BENZANTHRACENE	BERASCALING	BESEEMINGS	BESPECKLING
BENEFICIARY	BENZANTHRACENES	BERBERIDACEOUS	BESEEMLIER	BESPECTACLED
BENEFICIATE	BENZENECARBONYL	BERBERINES	BESEEMLIEST	BESPEEDING
BENEFICIATED	BENZENOIDS	BERBERISES	BESETMENTS	BESPITTING
BENEFICIATES	BENZIDINES	BEREAVEMENT	BESHADOWED	BESPORTING
BENEFICIATING	BENZIMIDAZOLE	BEREAVEMENTS	BESHADOWING	BESPOTTEDNESS
BENEFICIATION	BENZIMIDAZOLES	BERGAMASKO	BESHIVERED	BESPOTTEDNESSES
BENEFICIATIONS	BENZOAPYRENE	BERGAMASKOS	BESHIVERING	BESPOTTING
BENEFICING	BENZOAPYRENES	BERGAMASKS	BESHOUTING	BESPOUSING
BENEFITERS	BENZOCAINE	BERGANDERS	BESHREWING	BESPOUTING
BENEFITING	BENZOCAINES	BERGOMASKS	BESHROUDED	BESPREADING
BENEFITTED	BENZODIAZEPINE	BERGSCHRUND	BESHROUDING	BESPRINKLE
BENEFITTING	BENZODIAZEPINES	BERGSCHRUNDS	BESIEGEMENT	BESPRINKLED
BENEPLACITO	BENZOFURAN	BERIBBONED	BESIEGEMENTS	BESPRINKLES

ten to fifteen letter words | 721

BESPRINKLING	BETHANKITS	BEWITCHERS	BIBLIOPEGIST	BICENTENARIES
BESTAINING	BETHINKING	BEWITCHERY	BIBLIOPEGISTS	BICENTENARY
BESTARRING	BETHORNING	BEWITCHING	BIBLIOPEGY	BICENTENNIAL
BESTEADING	BETHRALLED	BEWITCHINGLY	BIBLIOPHAGIST	BICENTENNIALS
BESTIALISE	BETHRALLING	BEWITCHMENT	BIBLIOPHAGISTS	BICEPHALOUS
BESTIALISED	BETHUMBING	BEWITCHMENTS	BIBLIOPHIL	BICHLORIDE
BESTIALISES	BETHUMPING	BEWORRYING	BIBLIOPHILE	BICHLORIDES
BESTIALISING	BETHWACKED	BEWRAPPING	BIBLIOPHILES	BICHROMATE
BESTIALISM	BETHWACKING	BHIKKHUNIS	BIBLIOPHILIC	BICHROMATED
BESTIALISMS	BETOKENING	BIANNUALLY	BIBLIOPHILIES	BICHROMATES
BESTIALITIES	BETREADING	BIANNULATE	BIBLIOPHILISM	BICKERINGS
BESTIALITY	BETRIMMING	BIASNESSES	BIBLIOPHILISMS	BICOLLATERAL
BESTIALIZE	BETROTHALS	BIATHLETES	BIBLIOPHILIST	BICOLOURED
BESTIALIZED	BETROTHEDS	BIAURICULAR	BIBLIOPHILISTIC	BICOMPONENT
BESTIALIZES	BETROTHING	BIAURICULATE	BIBLIOPHILISTS	BICOMPONENTS
BESTIALIZING	BETROTHMENT	BIBLICALLY	BIBLIOPHILS	BICONCAVITIES
BESTIARIES	BETROTHMENTS	BIBLICISMS	BIBLIOPHILY	BICONCAVITY
BESTICKING	BETTERINGS	BIBLICISTS	BIBLIOPHOBIA	BICONDITIONAL
BESTILLING	BETTERMENT	BIBLIOGRAPHER	BIBLIOPHOBIAS	BICONDITIONALS
BESTIRRING	BETTERMENTS	BIBLIOGRAPHERS	BIBLIOPOLE	BICONVEXITIES
BESTORMING	BETTERMOST	BIBLIOGRAPHIC	BIBLIOPOLES	BICONVEXITY
BESTOWMENT	BETTERNESS	BIBLIOGRAPHICAL	BIBLIOPOLIC	BICORNUATE
BESTOWMENTS	BETTERNESSES	BIBLIOGRAPHIES	BIBLIOPOLICAL	BICORPORATE
BESTRADDLE	BETULACEOUS	BIBLIOGRAPHY	BIBLIOPOLIES	BICULTURAL
BESTRADDLED	BETWEENBRAIN	BIBLIOLATER	BIBLIOPOLIST	BICULTURALISM
BESTRADDLES	BETWEENBRAINS	BIBLIOLATERS	BIBLIOPOLISTS	BICULTURALISMS
BESTRADDLING	BETWEENITIES	BIBLIOLATRIES	BIBLIOPOLY	BICUSPIDATE
BESTRAUGHT	BETWEENITY	BIBLIOLATRIST	BIBLIOTHECA	BICUSPIDATES
BESTREAKED	BETWEENNESS	BIBLIOLATRISTS	BIBLIOTHECAE	BICYCLICAL
BESTREAKING	BETWEENNESSES	BIBLIOLATROUS	BIBLIOTHECAL	BICYCLISTS
BESTREWING	BETWEENTIME	BIBLIOLATRY	BIBLIOTHECARIES	BIDDABILITIES
BESTRIDABLE	BETWEENTIMES	BIBLIOLOGICAL	BIBLIOTHECARY	BIDDABILITY
BESTRIDDEN	BETWEENWHILES	BIBLIOLOGIES	BIBLIOTHECAS	BIDDABLENESS
BESTRIDING	BEVELLINGS	BIBLIOLOGIST	BIBLIOTHERAPIES	BIDDABLENESSES
BESTROWING	BEVELMENTS	BIBLIOLOGISTS	BIBLIOTHERAPY	BIDENTATED
BESTSELLER	BEVOMITING	BIBLIOLOGY	BIBLIOTICS	BIDIALECTAL
BESTSELLERDOM	BEWAILINGLY	BIBLIOMANCIES	BIBLIOTIST	BIDIALECTALISM
BESTSELLERDOMS	BEWAILINGS	BIBLIOMANCY	BIBLIOTISTS	BIDIALECTALISMS
BESTSELLERS	BEWEARYING	BIBLIOMANE	BIBULOUSLY	BIDIRECTIONAL
BESTSELLING	BEWELTERED	BIBLIOMANES	BIBULOUSNESS	BIDIRECTIONALLY
BESTUDDING	BEWHISKERED	BIBLIOMANIA	BIBULOUSNESSES	BIDONVILLE
BESWARMING	BEWILDERED	BIBLIOMANIAC	BICAMERALISM	BIDONVILLES
BETACAROTENE	BEWILDEREDLY	BIBLIOMANIACAL	BICAMERALISMS	BIENNIALLY
BETACAROTENES	BEWILDEREDNESS	BIBLIOMANIACS	BICAMERALIST	BIENSEANCE
BETACYANIN	BEWILDERING	BIBLIOMANIAS	BICAMERALISTS	BIENSEANCES
BETACYANINS	BEWILDERINGLY	BIBLIOMETRIC	BICAPSULAR	BIERKELLER
BETATTERED	BEWILDERMENT	BIBLIOMETRICS	BICARBONATE	BIERKELLERS
BETATTERING	BEWILDERMENTS	BIBLIOPEGIC	BICARBONATES	BIERWURSTS
BETHANKING	BEWITCHERIES	BIBLIOPEGIES	BICARPELLARY	BIFACIALLY

BIFARIOUSLY	BILINGUALS	BIMILLENNIAL	BIOCELLATE	BIOECOLOGIST
BIFIDITIES	BILINGUIST	BIMILLENNIALS	BIOCENOLOGIES	BIOECOLOGISTS
BIFLAGELLATE	BILINGUISTS	BIMILLENNIUM	BIOCENOLOGY	BIOECOLOGY
BIFOLIOLATE	BILIOUSNESS	BIMILLENNIUMS	BIOCENOSES	BIOELECTRIC
BIFUNCTIONAL	BILIOUSNESSES	BIMODALITIES	BIOCENOSIS	BIOELECTRICAL
BIFURCATED	BILIRUBINS	BIMODALITY	BIOCENOTIC	BIOELECTRICITY
BIFURCATES	BILIVERDIN	BIMOLECULAR	BIOCHEMICAL	BIOENERGETIC
BIFURCATING	BILIVERDINS	BIMOLECULARLY	BIOCHEMICALLY	BIOENERGETICS
BIFURCATION	BILLABONGS	BIMONTHLIES	BIOCHEMICALS	BIOENERGIES
BIFURCATIONS	BILLBOARDED	BIMORPHEMIC	BIOCHEMIST	BIOENGINEER
BIGAMOUSLY	BILLBOARDING	BINATIONAL	BIOCHEMISTRIES	BIOENGINEERED
BIGARREAUS	BILLBOARDS	BINAURALLY	BIOCHEMISTRY	BIOENGINEERING
BIGEMINIES	BILLETINGS	BINDINGNESS	BIOCHEMISTS	BIOENGINEERINGS
BIGENDERED	BILLFISHES	BINDINGNESSES	BIOCLASTIC	BIOENGINEERS
BIGFOOTING	BILLINGSGATE	BINOCULARITIES	BIOCLIMATIC	BIOETHANOL
BIGGETIEST	BILLINGSGATES	BINOCULARITY	BIOCLIMATOLOGY	BIOETHANOLS
BIGGITIEST	BILLIONAIRE	BINOCULARLY	BIOCOENOLOGIES	BIOETHICAL
BIGHEADEDLY	BILLIONAIRES	BINOCULARS	BIOCOENOLOGY	BIOETHICIST
BIGHEADEDNESS	BILLIONTHS	BINOMIALLY	BIOCOENOSES	BIOETHICISTS
BIGHEADEDNESSES	BILLOWIEST	BINOMINALS	BIOCOENOSIS	BIOFEEDBACK
BIGHEARTED	BILLOWINESS	BINTURONGS	BIOCOENOTIC	BIOFEEDBACKS
BIGHEARTEDLY	BILLOWINESSES	BINUCLEATE	BIOCOMPATIBLE	BIOFLAVONOID
BIGHEARTEDNESS	BILLOWINGS	BINUCLEATED	BIOCOMPUTING	BIOFLAVONOIDS
BIGMOUTHED	BILLPOSTER	BIOACCUMULATE	BIOCOMPUTINGS	BIOFOULERS
BIGNONIACEOUS	BILLPOSTERS	BIOACCUMULATED	BIOCONTROL	BIOFOULING
BIGUANIDES	BILLPOSTING	BIOACCUMULATES	BIOCONTROLS	BIOFOULINGS
BIJECTIONS	BILLPOSTINGS	BIOACCUMULATING	BIOCONVERSION	BIOFUELLED
BIJOUTERIE	BILLSTICKER	BIOACCUMULATION	BIOCONVERSIONS	BIOGENESES
BIJOUTERIES	BILLSTICKERS	BIOACOUSTICS	BIODEGRADABLE	BIOGENESIS
BILATERALISM	BILLSTICKING	BIOACTIVITIES	BIODEGRADABLES	BIOGENETIC
BILATERALISMS	BILLSTICKINGS	BIOACTIVITY	BIODEGRADATION	BIOGENETICAL
BILATERALLY	BILLYCOCKS	BIOAERATION	BIODEGRADATIONS	BIOGENETICALLY
BILBERRIES	BILOCATION	BIOAERATIONS	BIODEGRADE	BIOGENETICS
BILDUNGSROMAN	BILOCATIONS	BIOAERONAUTICS	BIODEGRADED	BIOGEOCHEMICAL
BILDUNGSROMANS	BILOCULATE	BIOARCHAEOLOGY	BIODEGRADES	BIOGEOCHEMICALS
BILECTIONS	BIMANUALLY	BIOASSAYED	BIODEGRADING	BIOGEOCHEMISTRY
BILESTONES	BIMATERNAL	BIOASSAYING	BIODESTRUCTIBLE	BIOGEOGRAPHER
BILGEWATER	BIMESTRIAL	BIOASTRONAUTICS	BIODETECTION	BIOGEOGRAPHERS
BILGEWATERS	BIMESTRIALLY	BIOASTRONOMIES	BIODETECTIONS	BIOGEOGRAPHIC
BILHARZIAL	BIMETALLIC	BIOASTRONOMY	BIODIESELS	BIOGEOGRAPHICAL
BILHARZIAS	BIMETALLICS	BIOAVAILABILITY	BIODIVERSE	BIOGEOGRAPHIES
BILHARZIASES	BIMETALLISM	BIOAVAILABLE	BIODIVERSITIES	BIOGEOGRAPHY
BILHARZIASIS	BIMETALLISMS	BIOBANDING	BIODIVERSITY	BIOGRAPHED
BILHARZIOSES	BIMETALLIST	BIOBANDINGS	BIODYNAMIC	BIOGRAPHEE
BILHARZIOSIS	BIMETALLISTIC	BIOBANKING	BIODYNAMICAL	BIOGRAPHEES
BILIMBINGS	BIMETALLISTS	BIOBANKINGS	BIODYNAMICS	BIOGRAPHER
BILINGUALISM	BIMILLENARIES	BIOCATALYST	BIOECOLOGICAL	BIOGRAPHERS
BILINGUALISMS	BIMILLENARY	BIOCATALYSTS	BIOECOLOGICALLY	BIOGRAPHIC
BILINGUALLY	BIMILLENNIA	BIOCATALYTIC	BIOECOLOGIES	BIOGRAPHICAL

BIOGRAPHICALLY	BIOMIMETICS	BIOREGIONALISTS	BIOTELEMETRY	BIQUINTILES
BIOGRAPHIES	BIOMIMICRIES	BIOREGIONS	BIOTERRORS	BIRACIALISM
BIOGRAPHING	BIOMIMICRY	BIOREMEDIATION	BIOTICALLY	BIRACIALISMS
BIOGRAPHISE	BIOMININGS	BIOREMEDIATIONS	BIOTURBATION	BIRACIALLY
BIOGRAPHISED	BIOMOLECULAR	BIORHYTHMIC	BIOTURBATIONS	BIRADICALS
BIOGRAPHISES	BIOMOLECULE	BIORHYTHMICALLY	BIOWEAPONS	BIRCHBARKS
BIOGRAPHISING	BIOMOLECULES	BIORHYTHMICS	BIPARENTAL	BIRCHWOODS
BIOGRAPHIZE	BIOMORPHIC	BIORHYTHMS	BIPARENTALLY	BIRDBRAINED
BIOGRAPHIZED	BIONOMICALLY	BIOSAFETIES	BIPARIETAL	BIRDBRAINS
BIOGRAPHIZES	BIONOMISTS	BIOSATELLITE	BIPARTISAN	BIRDDOGGED
BIOGRAPHIZING	BIOPARENTS	BIOSATELLITES	BIPARTISANISM	BIRDDOGGING
BIOHACKERS	BIOPESTICIDAL	BIOSCIENCE	BIPARTISANISMS	BIRDDOGGINGS
BIOHACKING	BIOPESTICIDE	BIOSCIENCES	BIPARTISANSHIP	BIRDHOUSES
BIOHACKINGS	BIOPESTICIDES	BIOSCIENTIFIC	BIPARTISANSHIPS	BIRDLIMING
BIOHAZARDOUS	BIOPHILIAS	BIOSCIENTIST	BIPARTITELY	BIRDSFOOTS
BIOHAZARDS	BIOPHYSICAL	BIOSCIENTISTS	BIPARTITION	BIRDWATCHED
BIOINDICATOR	BIOPHYSICALLY	BIOSCOPIES	BIPARTITIONS	BIRDWATCHER
BIOINDICATORS	BIOPHYSICIST	BIOSECURITIES	BIPEDALISM	BIRDWATCHERS
BIOINDUSTRIES	BIOPHYSICISTS	BIOSECURITY	BIPEDALISMS	BIRDWATCHES
BIOINDUSTRY	BIOPHYSICS	BIOSENSING	BIPEDALITIES	BIRDWATCHING
BIOINFORMATICS	BIOPIRACIES	BIOSENSINGS	BIPEDALITY	BIRDWATCHINGS
BIOLOGICAL	BIOPIRATES	BIOSENSORS	BIPETALOUS	BIREFRINGENCE
BIOLOGICALLY	BIOPLASMIC	BIOSIGNATURE	BIPINNARIA	BIREFRINGENCES
BIOLOGICALS	BIOPLASTIC	BIOSIGNATURES	BIPINNARIAS	BIREFRINGENT
BIOLOGISMS	BIOPLASTICS	BIOSOCIALLY	BIPINNATELY	BIROSTRATE
BIOLOGISTIC	BIOPOIESES	BIOSPHERES	BIPOLARISATION	BIRTHDATES
BIOLOGISTS	BIOPOIESIS	BIOSPHERIC	BIPOLARISATIONS	BIRTHMARKS
BIOLUMINESCENCE	BIOPOLYMER	BIOSTATICALLY	BIPOLARISE	BIRTHNAMES
BIOLUMINESCENT	BIOPOLYMERS	BIOSTATICS	BIPOLARISED	BIRTHNIGHT
BIOMAGNETICS	BIOPRINTER	BIOSTATISTICAL	BIPOLARISES	BIRTHNIGHTS
BIOMARKERS	BIOPRINTERS	BIOSTATISTICIAN	BIPOLARISING	BIRTHPLACE
BIOMATERIAL	BIOPRINTING	BIOSTATISTICS	BIPOLARITIES	BIRTHPLACES
BIOMATERIALS	BIOPRINTINGS	BIOSTRATIGRAPHY	BIPOLARITY	BIRTHRATES
BIOMATHEMATICAL	BIOPRIVACIES	BIOSTROMES	BIPOLARIZATION	BIRTHRIGHT
BIOMATHEMATICS	BIOPRIVACY	BIOSURGERIES	BIPOLARIZATIONS	BIRTHRIGHTS
BIOMECHANICAL	BIOPROSPECTING	BIOSURGERY	BIPOLARIZE	BIRTHROOTS
BIOMECHANICALLY	BIOPROSPECTINGS	BIOSYNTHESES	BIPOLARIZED	BIRTHSTONE
BIOMECHANICS	BIOPSYCHOLOGIES	BIOSYNTHESIS	BIPOLARIZES	BIRTHSTONES
BIOMEDICAL	BIOPSYCHOLOGY	BIOSYNTHETIC	BIPOLARIZING	BIRTHWORTS
BIOMEDICINE	BIOREACTOR	BIOSYSTEMATIC	BIPROPELLANT	BISCUITIER
BIOMEDICINES	BIOREACTORS	BIOSYSTEMATICS	BIPROPELLANTS	BISCUITIEST
BIOMETEOROLOGY	BIOREAGENT	BIOSYSTEMATIST	BIPYRAMIDAL	BISECTIONAL
BIOMETRICAL	BIOREAGENTS	BIOSYSTEMATISTS	BIPYRAMIDS	BISECTIONALLY
BIOMETRICALLY	BIOREFINERIES	BIOTECHNICAL	BIQUADRATE	BISECTIONS
BIOMETRICIAN	BIOREFINERY	BIOTECHNOLOGIES	BIQUADRATES	BISECTRICES
BIOMETRICIANS	BIOREGIONAL	BIOTECHNOLOGIST	BIQUADRATIC	BISEXUALISM
BIOMETRICS	BIOREGIONALISM	BIOTECHNOLOGY	BIQUADRATICS	BISEXUALISMS
BIOMETRIES	BIOREGIONALISMS	BIOTELEMETRIC	BIQUARTERLY	BISEXUALITIES
BIOMIMETIC	BIOREGIONALIST	BIOTELEMETRIES	BIQUINTILE	BISEXUALITY

BISEXUALLY	BITTERCRESS	BLABBERING	BLACKHEART	BLADDERNOSES
BISHOPBIRD	BITTERCRESSES	BLABBERMOUTH	BLACKHEARTS	BLADDERNUT
BISHOPBIRDS	BITTERLING	BLABBERMOUTHS	BLACKISHLY	BLADDERNUTS
BISHOPDOMS	BITTERLINGS	BLACKBALLED	BLACKJACKED	BLADDERWORT
BISHOPESSES	BITTERNESS	BLACKBALLING	BLACKJACKING	BLADDERWORTS
BISHOPRICS	BITTERNESSES	BLACKBALLINGS	BLACKJACKS	BLADDERWRACK
BISHOPWEED	BITTERNUTS	BLACKBALLS	BLACKLANDS	BLADDERWRACKS
BISHOPWEEDS	BITTERROOT	BLACKBANDS	BLACKLEADED	BLADEWORKS
BISMUTHINITE	BITTERROOTS	BLACKBERRIED	BLACKLEADING	BLAEBERRIES
BISMUTHINITES	BITTERSWEET	BLACKBERRIES	BLACKLEADS	BLAMABLENESS
BISMUTHOUS	BITTERSWEETLY	BLACKBERRY	BLACKLEGGED	BLAMABLENESSES
BISOCIATION	BITTERSWEETNESS	BLACKBERRYING	BLACKLEGGING	BLAMEABLENESS
BISOCIATIONS	BITTERSWEETS	BLACKBERRYINGS	BLACKLISTED	BLAMEABLENESSES
BISOCIATIVE	BITTERWEED	BLACKBIRDED	BLACKLISTER	BLAMEFULLY
BISPHENOLS	BITTERWEEDS	BLACKBIRDER	BLACKLISTERS	BLAMEFULNESS
BISPHOSPHONATE	BITTERWOOD	BLACKBIRDERS	BLACKLISTING	BLAMEFULNESSES
BISPHOSPHONATES	BITTERWOODS	BLACKBIRDING	BLACKLISTINGS	BLAMELESSLY
BISSEXTILE	BITTINESSES	BLACKBIRDINGS	BLACKLISTS	BLAMELESSNESS
BISSEXTILES	BITUMINATE	BLACKBIRDS	BLACKMAILED	BLAMELESSNESSES
BISTOURIES	BITUMINATED	BLACKBOARD	BLACKMAILER	BLAMESTORM
BISULFATES	BITUMINATES	BLACKBOARDS	BLACKMAILERS	BLAMESTORMED
BISULFIDES	BITUMINATING	BLACKBODIES	BLACKMAILING	BLAMESTORMING
BISULFITES	BITUMINISATION	BLACKBUCKS	BLACKMAILS	BLAMESTORMINGS
BISULPHATE	BITUMINISATIONS	BLACKBUTTS	BLACKNESSES	BLAMESTORMS
BISULPHATES	BITUMINISE	BLACKCOCKS	BLACKPOLLS	BLAMEWORTHIER
BISULPHIDE	BITUMINISED	BLACKCURRANT	BLACKSMITH	BLAMEWORTHIEST
BISULPHIDES	BITUMINISES	BLACKCURRANTS	BLACKSMITHING	BLAMEWORTHINESS
BISULPHITE	BITUMINISING	BLACKDAMPS	BLACKSMITHINGS	BLAMEWORTHY
BISULPHITES	BITUMINIZATION	BLACKENERS	BLACKSMITHS	BLANCHISSEUSE
BISYMMETRIC	BITUMINIZATIONS	BLACKENING	BLACKSNAKE	BLANCHISSEUSES
BISYMMETRICAL	BITUMINIZE	BLACKENINGS	BLACKSNAKES	BLANCMANGE
BISYMMETRICALLY	BITUMINIZED	BLACKFACED	BLACKSPOTS	BLANCMANGES
BISYMMETRIES	BITUMINIZES	BLACKFACES	BLACKSTRAP	BLANDISHED
BISYMMETRY	BITUMINIZING	BLACKFISHES	BLACKSTRAPS	BLANDISHER
BITARTRATE	BITUMINOUS	BLACKFLIES	BLACKTAILS	BLANDISHERS
BITARTRATES	BIUNIQUENESS	BLACKGAMES	BLACKTHORN	BLANDISHES
BITCHERIES	BIUNIQUENESSES	BLACKGUARD	BLACKTHORNS	BLANDISHING
BITCHFESTS	BIVALENCES	BLACKGUARDED	BLACKTOPPED	BLANDISHMENT
BITCHINESS	BIVALENCIES	BLACKGUARDING	BLACKTOPPING	BLANDISHMENTS
BITCHINESSES	BIVALVULAR	BLACKGUARDISM	BLACKWASHED	BLANDNESSES
BITEPLATES	BIVARIANTS	BLACKGUARDISMS	BLACKWASHES	BLANKETFLOWER
BITMAPPING	BIVARIATES	BLACKGUARDLIER	BLACKWASHING	BLANKETFLOWERS
BITONALITIES	BIVOUACKED	BLACKGUARDLIEST	BLACKWATER	BLANKETIES
BITONALITY	BIVOUACKING	BLACKGUARDLY	BLACKWATERS	BLANKETING
BITSTREAMS	BIWEEKLIES	BLACKGUARDS	BLACKWOODS	BLANKETINGS
BITTERBARK	BIZARRENESS	BLACKHANDER	BLADDERIER	BLANKETLIKE
BITTERBARKS	BIZARRENESSES	BLACKHANDERS	BLADDERIEST	BLANKETWEED
BITTERBRUSH	BIZARRERIE	BLACKHEADED	BLADDERLIKE	BLANKETWEEDS
BITTERBRUSHES	BIZARRERIES	BLACKHEADS	BLADDERNOSE	BLANKNESSES

BLANQUETTE	BLASTULATION	BLETHERING	BLOATEDNESSES	BLOODGUILT
BLANQUETTES	BLASTULATIONS	BLETHERINGS	BLOATWARES	BLOODGUILTIER
BLARNEYING	BLATANCIES	BLETHERSKATE	BLOCKADERS	BLOODGUILTIEST
BLASPHEMED	BLATHERERS	BLETHERSKATES	BLOCKADING	BLOODGUILTINESS
BLASPHEMER	BLATHERING	BLIGHTINGLY	BLOCKBOARD	BLOODGUILTS
BLASPHEMERS	BLATHERINGS	BLIGHTINGS	BLOCKBOARDS	BLOODGUILTY
BLASPHEMES	BLATHERSKITE	BLIMPERIES	BLOCKBUSTED	BLOODHOUND
BLASPHEMIES	BLATHERSKITES	BLIMPISHLY	BLOCKBUSTER	BLOODHOUNDS
BLASPHEMING	BLATTERING	BLIMPISHNESS	BLOCKBUSTERS	BLOODINESS
BLASPHEMOUS	BLAXPLOITATION	BLIMPISHNESSES	BLOCKBUSTING	BLOODINESSES
BLASPHEMOUSLY	BLAXPLOITATIONS	BLINDFISHES	BLOCKBUSTINGS	BLOODLESSLY
BLASPHEMOUSNESS	BLAZONINGS	BLINDFOLDED	BLOCKBUSTS	BLOODLESSNESS
BLASTEMATA	BLAZONRIES	BLINDFOLDING	BLOCKCHAIN	BLOODLESSNESSES
BLASTEMATIC	BLEACHABLE	BLINDFOLDS	BLOCKCHAINS	BLOODLETTER
BLASTHOLES	BLEACHERIES	BLINDINGLY	BLOCKHEADED	BLOODLETTERS
BLASTMENTS	BLEACHERITE	BLINDNESSES	BLOCKHEADEDLY	BLOODLETTING
BLASTOCHYLE	BLEACHERITES	BLINDSIDED	BLOCKHEADEDNESS	BLOODLETTINGS
BLASTOCHYLES	BLEACHINGS	BLINDSIDES	BLOCKHEADS	BLOODLINES
BLASTOCOEL	BLEAKNESSES	BLINDSIDING	BLOCKHOLES	BLOODLUSTS
BLASTOCOELE	BLEARINESS	BLINDSIGHT	BLOCKHOUSE	BLOODMOBILE
BLASTOCOELES	BLEARINESSES	BLINDSIGHTS	BLOCKHOUSES	BLOODMOBILES
BLASTOCOELIC	BLEMISHERS	BLINDSTOREY	BLOCKINESS	BLOODROOTS
BLASTOCOELS	BLEMISHING	BLINDSTOREYS	BLOCKINESSES	BLOODSHEDS
BLASTOCYST	BLEMISHMENT	BLINDSTORIES	BLOCKISHLY	BLOODSPRENT
BLASTOCYSTS	BLEMISHMENTS	BLINDSTORY	BLOCKISHNESS	BLOODSTAIN
BLASTODERM	BLENNIOIDS	BLINDWORMS	BLOCKISHNESSES	BLOODSTAINED
BLASTODERMIC	BLENNORRHEA	BLINGLISHES	BLOCKLISTS	BLOODSTAINS
BLASTODERMS	BLENNORRHEAS	BLINKERING	BLOCKSHIPS	BLOODSTOCK
BLASTODISC	BLENNORRHOEA	BLISSFULLY	BLOCKWORKS	BLOODSTOCKS
BLASTODISCS	BLENNORRHOEAS	BLISSFULNESS	BLOGGERATI	BLOODSTONE
BLASTOGENESES	BLEOMYCINS	BLISSFULNESSES	BLOGJACKING	BLOODSTONES
BLASTOGENESIS	BLEPHARISM	BLISTERIER	BLOGJACKINGS	BLOODSTREAM
BLASTOGENETIC	BLEPHARISMS	BLISTERIEST	BLOGOSPHERE	BLOODSTREAMS
BLASTOGENIC	BLEPHARITIC	BLISTERING	BLOGOSPHERES	BLOODSUCKER
BLASTOMATA	BLEPHARITIS	BLISTERINGLY	BLOGSTREAM	BLOODSUCKERS
BLASTOMERE	BLEPHARITISES	BLITHENESS	BLOGSTREAMS	BLOODSUCKING
BLASTOMERES	BLEPHAROPLAST	BLITHENESSES	BLOKARTING	BLOODTHIRSTIER
BLASTOMERIC	BLEPHAROPLASTS	BLITHERING	BLOKARTINGS	BLOODTHIRSTIEST
BLASTOMYCOSES	BLEPHAROPLASTY	BLITHESOME	BLOKEISHNESS	BLOODTHIRSTILY
BLASTOMYCOSIS	BLEPHAROSPASM	BLITHESOMELY	BLOKEISHNESSES	BLOODTHIRSTY
BLASTOPORAL	BLEPHAROSPASMS	BLITHESOMENESS	BLOKISHNESS	BLOODWOODS
BLASTOPORE	BLESSEDEST	BLITZKRIEG	BLOKISHNESSES	BLOODWORKS
BLASTOPORES	BLESSEDNESS	BLITZKRIEGS	BLONDENESS	BLOODWORMS
BLASTOPORIC	BLESSEDNESSES	BLIZZARDED	BLONDENESSES	BLOODWORTS
BLASTOPORS	BLETHERANSKATE	BLIZZARDIER	BLONDINING	BLOOMERIES
BLASTOSPHERE	BLETHERANSKATES	BLIZZARDIEST	BLONDNESSES	BLOQUISTES
BLASTOSPHERES	BLETHERATION	BLIZZARDING	BLOODBATHS	BLOSSOMIER
BLASTOSPORE	BLETHERATIONS	BLIZZARDLY	BLOODCURDLING	BLOSSOMIEST
BLASTOSPORES	BLETHERERS	BLOATEDNESS	BLOODCURDLINGLY	BLOSSOMING

BLOSSOMINGS	BLUEPOINTS	BOARDWALKS	BODYBUILDINGS	BOLIVIANOS
BLOSSOMLESS	BLUEPRINTED	BOARFISHES	BODYBUILDS	BOLLETRIES
BLOTCHIEST	BLUEPRINTING	BOARHOUNDS	BODYCHECKED	BOLLOCKING
BLOTCHINESS	BLUEPRINTS	BOARISHNESS	BODYCHECKING	BOLLOCKINGS
BLOTCHINESSES	BLUESHIFTED	BOARISHNESSES	BODYCHECKS	BOLLOCKSED
BLOTCHINGS	BLUESHIFTS	BOASTFULLY	BODYGUARDED	BOLLOCKSES
BLOTTESQUE	BLUESNARFING	BOASTFULNESS	BODYGUARDING	BOLLOCKSING
BLOTTESQUES	BLUESNARFINGS	BOASTFULNESSES	BODYGUARDS	BOLOGNESES
BLOVIATING	BLUESTOCKING	BOASTINGLY	BODYSHAPER	BOLOGRAPHS
BLOVIATION	BLUESTOCKINGS	BOATBUILDER	BODYSHAPERS	BOLOMETERS
BLOVIATIONS	BLUESTONES	BOATBUILDERS	BODYSHELLS	BOLOMETRIC
BLOWFISHES	BLUETHROAT	BOATBUILDING	BODYSNATCHER	BOLOMETRICALLY
BLOWINESSES	BLUETHROATS	BOATBUILDINGS	BODYSNATCHERS	BOLOMETRIES
BLOWSINESS	BLUETONGUE	BOATHOUSES	BODYSURFED	BOLSHEVIKI
BLOWSINESSES	BLUETONGUES	BOATLIFTED	BODYSURFER	BOLSHEVIKS
BLOWTORCHED	BLUFFNESSES	BOATLIFTING	BODYSURFERS	BOLSHEVISE
BLOWTORCHES	BLUISHNESS	BOATSWAINS	BODYSURFING	BOLSHEVISED
BLOWTORCHING	BLUISHNESSES	BOBBEJAANS	BODYSURFINGS	BOLSHEVISES
BLOWZINESS	BLUNDERBUSS	BOBBITTING	BODYWASHES	BOLSHEVISING
BLOWZINESSES	BLUNDERBUSSES	BOBBLEHEAD	BODYWORKER	BOLSHEVISM
BLUBBERERS	BLUNDERERS	BOBBLEHEADS	BODYWORKERS	BOLSHEVISMS
BLUBBERIER	BLUNDERING	BOBBYSOCKS	BOEREMUSIEK	BOLSHEVIZE
BLUBBERIEST	BLUNDERINGLY	BOBBYSOXER	BOEREMUSIEKS	BOLSHEVIZED
BLUBBERING	BLUNDERINGS	BOBBYSOXERS	BOEREWORSES	BOLSHEVIZES
BLUDGEONED	BLUNTHEADS	BOBSLEDDED	BOFFINIEST	BOLSHEVIZING
BLUDGEONER	BLUNTNESSES	BOBSLEDDER	BOGGINESSES	BOLSTERERS
BLUDGEONERS	BLURREDNESS	BOBSLEDDERS	BOGTROTTING	BOLSTERING
BLUDGEONING	BLURREDNESSES	BOBSLEDDING	BOGTROTTINGS	BOLSTERINGS
BLUEBEARDS	BLURRINESS	BOBSLEDDINGS	BOGUSNESSES	BOMBACACEOUS
BLUEBERRIES	BLURRINESSES	BOBSLEIGHED	BOHEMIANISM	BOMBARDERS
BLUEBLOODS	BLURRINGLY	BOBSLEIGHING	BOHEMIANISMS	BOMBARDIER
BLUEBONNET	BLUSHINGLY	BOBSLEIGHINGS	BOILERMAKER	BOMBARDIERS
BLUEBONNETS	BLUSHLESSLY	BOBSLEIGHS	BOILERMAKERS	BOMBARDING
BLUEBOTTLE	BLUSTERERS	BOBTAILING	BOILERMAKING	BOMBARDMENT
BLUEBOTTLES	BLUSTERIER	BOBWEIGHTS	BOILERMAKINGS	BOMBARDMENTS
BLUEBREAST	BLUSTERIEST	BOCCONCINI	BOILERPLATE	BOMBARDONS
BLUEBREASTS	BLUSTERING	BODACIOUSLY	BOILERPLATED	BOMBASINES
BLUEBUSHES	BLUSTERINGLY	BODDHISATTVA	BOILERPLATES	BOMBASTERS
BLUEFISHES	BLUSTERINGS	BODDHISATTVAS	BOILERPLATING	BOMBASTICALLY
BLUEGRASSES	BLUSTEROUS	BODEGUEROS	BOILERSUIT	BOMBASTING
BLUEISHNESS	BLUSTEROUSLY	BODHISATTVA	BOILERSUITS	BOMBAZINES
BLUEISHNESSES	BLUTWURSTS	BODHISATTVAS	BOISTEROUS	BOMBILATED
BLUEJACKET	BOARDINGHOUSE	BODYBOARDED	BOISTEROUSLY	BOMBILATES
BLUEJACKETS	BOARDINGHOUSES	BODYBOARDING	BOISTEROUSNESS	BOMBILATING
BLUEJACKING	BOARDROOMS	BODYBOARDINGS	BOKMAKIERIE	BOMBILATION
BLUEJACKINGS	BOARDSAILING	BODYBOARDS	BOKMAKIERIES	BOMBILATIONS
BLUELINERS	BOARDSAILINGS	BODYBUILDER	BOLDFACING	BOMBINATED
BLUEMOUTHS	BOARDSAILOR	BODYBUILDERS	BOLDNESSES	BOMBINATES
BLUENESSES	BOARDSAILORS	BODYBUILDING	BOLECTIONS	BOMBINATING

BOMBINATION	BOOKBINDERY	BOOTLEGGED	BOSCHVELDS	BOUILLABAISSE
BOMBINATIONS	BOOKBINDING	BOOTLEGGER	BOSKINESSES	BOUILLABAISSES
BOMBPROOFED	BOOKBINDINGS	BOOTLEGGERS	BOSSINESSES	BOUILLOTTE
BOMBPROOFING	BOOKCROSSING	BOOTLEGGING	BOSSNAPPING	BOUILLOTTES
BOMBPROOFS	BOOKCROSSINGS	BOOTLEGGINGS	BOSSNAPPINGS	BOULDERERS
BOMBSHELLS	BOOKENDING	BOOTLESSLY	BOSSYBOOTS	BOULDERIER
BOMBSIGHTS	BOOKISHNESS	BOOTLESSNESS	BOTANICALLY	BOULDERIEST
BONAMIASES	BOOKISHNESSES	BOOTLESSNESSES	BOTANICALS	BOULDERING
BONAMIASIS	BOOKKEEPER	BOOTLICKED	BOTANISERS	BOULDERINGS
BONASSUSES	BOOKKEEPERS	BOOTLICKER	BOTANISING	BOULEVARDIER
BONBONNIERE	BOOKKEEPING	BOOTLICKERS	BOTANIZERS	BOULEVARDIERS
BONBONNIERES	BOOKKEEPINGS	BOOTLICKING	BOTANIZING	BOULEVARDS
BONDHOLDER	BOOKLIGHTS	BOOTLICKINGS	BOTANOMANCIES	BOULEVERSEMENT
BONDHOLDERS	BOOKMAKERS	BOOTLOADER	BOTANOMANCY	BOULEVERSEMENTS
BONDMANSHIP	BOOKMAKING	BOOTLOADERS	BOTCHERIES	BOULLEWORK
BONDMANSHIPS	BOOKMAKINGS	BOOTMAKERS	BOTCHINESS	BOULLEWORKS
BONDSERVANT	BOOKMARKED	BOOTMAKING	BOTCHINESSES	BOUNCEDOWN
BONDSERVANTS	BOOKMARKER	BOOTMAKINGS	BOTHERATION	BOUNCEDOWNS
BONDSTONES	BOOKMARKERS	BOOTSTRAPPED	BOTHERATIONS	BOUNCINESS
BONDSWOMAN	BOOKMARKING	BOOTSTRAPPING	BOTHERSOME	BOUNCINESSES
BONDSWOMEN	BOOKMOBILE	BOOTSTRAPS	BOTRYOIDAL	BOUNCINGLY
BONEBLACKS	BOOKMOBILES	BOOTYLICIOUS	BOTRYTISES	BOUNDARIES
BONEFISHES	BOOKPLATES	BOOZEHOUND	BOTTLEBRUSH	BOUNDEDNESS
BONEFISHING	BOOKSELLER	BOOZEHOUNDS	BOTTLEBRUSHES	BOUNDEDNESSES
BONEFISHINGS	BOOKSELLERS	BOOZINESSES	BOTTLEFULS	BOUNDERISH
BONEHEADED	BOOKSELLING	BORAGINACEOUS	BOTTLENECK	BOUNDLESSLY
BONEHEADEDNESS	BOOKSELLINGS	BORBORYGMAL	BOTTLENECKED	BOUNDLESSNESS
BONESETTER	BOOKSHELVES	BORBORYGMI	BOTTLENECKING	BOUNDLESSNESSES
BONESETTERS	BOOKSTALLS	BORBORYGMIC	BOTTLENECKS	BOUNDNESSES
BONESHAKER	BOOKSTANDS	BORBORYGMUS	BOTTLENOSE	BOUNTEOUSLY
BONESHAKERS	BOOKSTORES	BORDEREAUX	BOTTLENOSES	BOUNTEOUSNESS
BONHOMMIES	BOOMERANGED	BORDERLAND	BOTTOMINGS	BOUNTEOUSNESSES
BONILASSES	BOOMERANGING	BORDERLANDS	BOTTOMLAND	BOUNTIFULLY
BONINESSES	BOOMERANGS	BORDERLESS	BOTTOMLANDS	BOUNTIFULNESS
BONKBUSTER	BOOMSLANGS	BORDERLINE	BOTTOMLESS	BOUNTIFULNESSES
BONKBUSTERS	BOOMSTICKS	BORDERLINES	BOTTOMLESSLY	BOUNTYHEDS
BONNIBELLS	BOONDOGGLE	BORDRAGING	BOTTOMLESSNESS	BOUQUETIERE
BONNILASSE	BOONDOGGLED	BORDRAGINGS	BOTTOMMOST	BOUQUETIERES
BONNILASSES	BOONDOGGLER	BORESCOPES	BOTTOMNESS	BOURASQUES
BONNINESSES	BOONDOGGLERS	BORGHETTOS	BOTTOMNESSES	BOURBONISM
BONNYCLABBER	BOONDOGGLES	BORINGNESS	BOTTOMRIES	BOURBONISMS
BONNYCLABBERS	BOONDOGGLING	BORINGNESSES	BOTULINUMS	BOURGEOISE
BOOBIALLAS	BOONGARIES	BOROHYDRIDE	BOTULINUSES	BOURGEOISES
BOOBOISIES	BOORISHNESS	BOROHYDRIDES	BOUGAINVILIA	BOURGEOISIE
BOOGALOOED	BOORISHNESSES	BOROSILICATE	BOUGAINVILIAS	BOURGEOISIES
BOOGALOOING	BOOSTERISH	BOROSILICATES	BOUGAINVILLAEA	BOURGEOISIFIED
BOOKBINDER	BOOSTERISM	BORROWINGS	BOUGAINVILLAEAS	BOURGEOISIFIES
BOOKBINDERIES	BOOSTERISMS	BOSBERAADS	BOUGAINVILLEA	BOURGEOISIFY
BOOKBINDERS	BOOTBLACKS	BOSCHVARKS	BOUGAINVILLEAS	BOURGEOISIFYING

BOURGEONED	BOXINESSES	BRACHYGRAPHY	BRAHMANIST	BRANCHIOPOD
BOURGEONING	BOXKEEPERS	BRACHYLOGIES	BRAHMANISTS	BRANCHIOPODS
BOURGUIGNON	BOXWALLAHS	BRACHYLOGOUS	BRAHMINISM	BRANCHIOSTEGAL
BOURGUIGNONNE	BOYCOTTERS	BRACHYLOGY	BRAHMINISMS	BRANCHLESS
BOURGUIGNONNES	BOYCOTTING	BRACHYODONT	BRAHMINIST	BRANCHLETS
BOURGUIGNONS	BOYFRIENDS	BRACHYPINAKOID	BRAHMINISTS	BRANCHLIKE
BOUSINGKEN	BOYISHNESS	BRACHYPINAKOIDS	BRAILLEWRITER	BRANCHLINE
BOUSINGKENS	BOYISHNESSES	BRACHYPRISM	BRAILLEWRITERS	BRANCHLINES
BOUSTROPHEDON	BOYSENBERRIES	BRACHYPRISMS	BRAILLISTS	BRANDERING
BOUSTROPHEDONIC	BOYSENBERRY	BRACHYPTERISM	BRAINBOXES	BRANDISHED
BOUSTROPHEDONS	BRAAIVLEIS	BRACHYPTERISMS	BRAINCASES	BRANDISHER
BOUTIQUIER	BRAAIVLEISES	BRACHYPTEROUS	BRAINCHILD	BRANDISHERS
BOUTIQUIEST	BRABBLEMENT	BRACHYTHERAPIES	BRAINCHILDREN	BRANDISHES
BOUTONNIERE	BRABBLEMENTS	BRACHYTHERAPY	BRAINFARTS	BRANDISHING
BOUTONNIERES	BRACHIATED	BRACHYURAL	BRAINFOODS	BRANDLINGS
BOUVARDIAS	BRACHIATES	BRACHYURAN	BRAININESS	BRANDRETHS
BOVINITIES	BRACHIATING	BRACHYURANS	BRAININESSES	BRANFULNESS
BOWDLERISATION	BRACHIATION	BRACHYUROUS	BRAINLESSLY	BRANFULNESSES
BOWDLERISATIONS	BRACHIATIONS	BRACKETING	BRAINLESSNESS	BRANGLINGS
BOWDLERISE	BRACHIATOR	BRACKETINGS	BRAINLESSNESSES	BRANKURSINE
BOWDLERISED	BRACHIATORS	BRACKISHNESS	BRAINPOWER	BRANKURSINES
BOWDLERISER	BRACHIOCEPHALIC	BRACKISHNESSES	BRAINPOWERS	BRANNIGANS
BOWDLERISERS	BRACHIOPOD	BRACTEATES	BRAINSICKLY	BRASHINESS
BOWDLERISES	BRACHIOPODS	BRACTEOLATE	BRAINSICKNESS	BRASHINESSES
BOWDLERISING	BRACHIOSAURUS	BRACTEOLES	BRAINSICKNESSES	BRASHNESSES
BOWDLERISM	BRACHIOSAURUSES	BRADYCARDIA	BRAINSTEMS	BRASILEINS
BOWDLERISMS	BRACHISTOCHRONE	BRADYCARDIAC	BRAINSTORM	BRASSBOUND
BOWDLERIZATION	BRACHYAXES	BRADYCARDIAS	BRAINSTORMED	BRASSERIES
BOWDLERIZATIONS	BRACHYAXIS	BRADYKINESIA	BRAINSTORMER	BRASSFOUNDER
BOWDLERIZE	BRACHYCEPHAL	BRADYKINESIAS	BRAINSTORMERS	BRASSFOUNDERS
BOWDLERIZED	BRACHYCEPHALIC	BRADYKININ	BRAINSTORMING	BRASSFOUNDING
BOWDLERIZER	BRACHYCEPHALICS	BRADYKININS	BRAINSTORMINGS	BRASSFOUNDINGS
BOWDLERIZERS	BRACHYCEPHALIES	BRADYPEPTIC	BRAINSTORMS	BRASSICACEOUS
BOWDLERIZES	BRACHYCEPHALISM	BRADYPEPTICS	BRAINTEASER	BRASSIERES
BOWDLERIZING	BRACHYCEPHALOUS	BRADYSEISM	BRAINTEASERS	BRASSINESS
BOWERBIRDS	BRACHYCEPHALS	BRADYSEISMS	BRAINWASHED	BRASSINESSES
BOWERWOMAN	BRACHYCEPHALY	BRAGADISME	BRAINWASHER	BRASSWARES
BOWERWOMEN	BRACHYCEROUS	BRAGADISMES	BRAINWASHERS	BRATPACKER
BOWHUNTERS	BRACHYDACTYL	BRAGGADOCIO	BRAINWASHES	BRATPACKERS
BOWHUNTING	BRACHYDACTYLIC	BRAGGADOCIOS	BRAINWASHING	BRATTICING
BOWHUNTINGS	BRACHYDACTYLIES	BRAGGADOCIOUS	BRAINWASHINGS	BRATTICINGS
BOWLINGUAL	BRACHYDACTYLISM	BRAGGARTISM	BRAINWAVES	BRATTINESS
BOWLINGUALS	BRACHYDACTYLOUS	BRAGGARTISMS	BRAINWORKS	BRATTINESSES
BOWSTRINGED	BRACHYDACTYLY	BRAGGARTLIER	BRAMBLIEST	BRATTISHED
BOWSTRINGING	BRACHYDIAGONAL	BRAGGARTLIEST	BRAMBLINGS	BRATTISHES
BOWSTRINGS	BRACHYDIAGONALS	BRAGGARTLY	BRANCHERIES	BRATTISHING
BOXBERRIES	BRACHYDOME	BRAGGINGLY	BRANCHIATE	BRATTISHINGS
BOXERCISES	BRACHYDOMES	BRAHMANISM	BRANCHIEST	BRATTLINGS
BOXHAULING	BRACHYGRAPHIES	BRAHMANISMS	BRANCHINGS	BRATWURSTS

BRAUNCHING	BREAKAWAYS	BREATHABILITY	BRESSUMMERS	BRIDEZILLAS
BRAUNSCHWEIGER	BREAKBEATS	BREATHABLE	BRETASCHES	BRIDGEABLE
BRAUNSCHWEIGERS	BREAKDANCE	BREATHALYSE	BRETTICING	BRIDGEBOARD
BRAVADOING	BREAKDANCED	BREATHALYSED	BREUNNERITE	BRIDGEBOARDS
BRAVENESSES	BREAKDANCER	BREATHALYSER	BREUNNERITES	BRIDGEHEAD
BRAVISSIMO	BREAKDANCERS	BREATHALYSERS	BREVETCIES	BRIDGEHEADS
BRAWNINESS	BREAKDANCES	BREATHALYSES	BREVETTING	BRIDGELESS
BRAWNINESSES	BREAKDANCING	BREATHALYSING	BREVIARIES	BRIDGELIKE
BRAZENNESS	BREAKDANCINGS	BREATHALYZE	BREVIPENNATE	BRIDGEWORK
BRAZENNESSES	BREAKDOWNS	BREATHALYZED	BREWHOUSES	BRIDGEWORKS
BRAZENRIES	BREAKEVENS	BREATHALYZER	BREWMASTER	BRIDLEWAYS
BRAZIERIES	BREAKFASTED	BREATHALYZERS	BREWMASTERS	BRIDLEWISE
BRAZILEINS	BREAKFASTER	BREATHALYZES	BRIARROOTS	BRIEFCASES
BRAZILWOOD	BREAKFASTERS	BREATHALYZING	BRIARWOODS	BRIEFNESSES
BRAZILWOODS	BREAKFASTING	BREATHARIAN	BRICABRACS	BRIERROOTS
BREADBASKET	BREAKFASTS	BREATHARIANISM	BRICKCLAYS	BRIERWOODS
BREADBASKETS	BREAKFRONT	BREATHARIANISMS	BRICKEARTH	BRIGADIERS
BREADBERRIES	BREAKFRONTS	BREATHARIANS	BRICKEARTHS	BRIGANDAGE
BREADBERRY	BREAKPOINT	BREATHIEST	BRICKFIELD	BRIGANDAGES
BREADBOARD	BREAKPOINTS	BREATHINESS	BRICKFIELDER	BRIGANDINE
BREADBOARDED	BREAKROOMS	BREATHINESSES	BRICKFIELDERS	BRIGANDINES
BREADBOARDING	BREAKTHROUGH	BREATHINGS	BRICKFIELDS	BRIGANDRIES
BREADBOARDS	BREAKTHROUGHS	BREATHLESS	BRICKKILNS	BRIGANTINE
BREADBOXES	BREAKTIMES	BREATHLESSLY	BRICKLAYER	BRIGANTINES
BREADCRUMB	BREAKWALLS	BREATHLESSNESS	BRICKLAYERS	BRIGHTENED
BREADCRUMBED	BREAKWATER	BREATHTAKING	BRICKLAYING	BRIGHTENER
BREADCRUMBING	BREAKWATERS	BREATHTAKINGLY	BRICKLAYINGS	BRIGHTENERS
BREADCRUMBS	BREASTBONE	BRECCIATED	BRICKMAKER	BRIGHTENING
BREADFRUIT	BREASTBONES	BRECCIATES	BRICKMAKERS	BRIGHTNESS
BREADFRUITS	BREASTFEED	BRECCIATING	BRICKMAKING	BRIGHTNESSES
BREADHEADS	BREASTFEEDING	BRECCIATION	BRICKMAKINGS	BRIGHTSOME
BREADKNIFE	BREASTFEEDINGS	BRECCIATIONS	BRICKSHAPED	BRIGHTWORK
BREADKNIVES	BREASTFEEDS	BREECHBLOCK	BRICKWALLS	BRIGHTWORKS
BREADLINES	BREASTPINS	BREECHBLOCKS	BRICKWORKS	BRILLIANCE
BREADROOMS	BREASTPLATE	BREECHCLOTH	BRICKYARDS	BRILLIANCES
BREADROOTS	BREASTPLATES	BREECHCLOTHS	BRICOLAGES	BRILLIANCIES
BREADSTICK	BREASTPLOUGH	BREECHCLOUT	BRICOLEURS	BRILLIANCY
BREADSTICKS	BREASTPLOUGHS	BREECHCLOUTS	BRIDECAKES	BRILLIANTE
BREADSTUFF	BREASTRAIL	BREECHINGS	BRIDEGROOM	BRILLIANTED
BREADSTUFFS	BREASTRAILS	BREECHLESS	BRIDEGROOMS	BRILLIANTINE
BREADTHWAYS	BREASTSTROKE	BREECHLOADER	BRIDEMAIDEN	BRILLIANTINED
BREADTHWISE	BREASTSTROKER	BREECHLOADERS	BRIDEMAIDENS	BRILLIANTINES
BREADWINNER	BREASTSTROKERS	BREEZELESS	BRIDEMAIDS	BRILLIANTING
BREADWINNERS	BREASTSTROKES	BREEZEWAYS	BRIDESMAID	BRILLIANTLY
BREADWINNING	BREASTSUMMER	BREEZINESS	BRIDESMAIDS	BRILLIANTNESS
BREADWINNINGS	BREASTSUMMERS	BREEZINESSES	BRIDEWEALTH	BRILLIANTNESSES
BREAKABLENESS	BREASTWORK	BREMSSTRAHLUNG	BRIDEWEALTHS	BRILLIANTS
BREAKABLENESSES	BREASTWORKS	BREMSSTRAHLUNGS	BRIDEWELLS	BRIMFULLNESS
BREAKABLES	BREATHABILITIES	BRESSUMMER	BRIDEZILLA	BRIMFULLNESSES

BRIMFULNESS
BRIMFULNESSES
BRIMSTONES
BRIMSTONIER
BRIMSTONIEST
BRINELLING
BRINELLINGS
BRINGDOWNS
BRININESSES
BRINJARRIES
BRINKMANSHIP
BRINKMANSHIPS
BRINKSMANSHIP
BRINKSMANSHIPS
BRIOLETTES
BRIQUETTED
BRIQUETTES
BRIQUETTING
BRISKENING
BRISKNESSES
BRISTLECONE
BRISTLECONES
BRISTLELIKE
BRISTLETAIL
BRISTLETAILS
BRISTLIEST
BRISTLINESS
BRISTLINESSES
BRITANNIAS
BRITSCHKAS
BRITTANIAS
BRITTLENESS
BRITTLENESSES
BROADBANDS
BROADBEANS
BROADBILLS
BROADBRIMS
BROADBRUSH
BROADCASTED
BROADCASTER
BROADCASTERS
BROADCASTING
BROADCASTINGS
BROADCASTS
BROADCLOTH
BROADCLOTHS
BROADENERS
BROADENING
BROADLEAVED

BROADLEAVES
BROADLINES
BROADLOOMS
BROADNESSES
BROADPIECE
BROADPIECES
BROADSCALE
BROADSHEET
BROADSHEETS
BROADSIDED
BROADSIDES
BROADSIDING
BROADSWORD
BROADSWORDS
BROADTAILS
BROBDINGNAGIAN
BROCATELLE
BROCATELLES
BROCCOLINI
BROCCOLINIS
BROCHETTES
BROGUERIES
BROIDERERS
BROIDERIES
BROIDERING
BROIDERINGS
BROKENHEARTED
BROKENHEARTEDLY
BROKENNESS
BROKENNESSES
BROKERAGES
BROKERINGS
BROMEGRASS
BROMEGRASSES
BROMELAINS
BROMELIACEOUS
BROMELIADS
BROMEOSINS
BROMHIDROSES
BROMHIDROSIS
BROMIDROSES
BROMIDROSIS
BROMINATED
BROMINATES
BROMINATING
BROMINATION
BROMINATIONS
BROMINISMS
BROMOCRIPTINE

BROMOCRIPTINES
BROMOFORMS
BROMOURACIL
BROMOURACILS
BRONCHIALLY
BRONCHIECTASES
BRONCHIECTASIS
BRONCHIOLAR
BRONCHIOLE
BRONCHIOLES
BRONCHIOLITIS
BRONCHIOLITISES
BRONCHITIC
BRONCHITICS
BRONCHITIS
BRONCHITISES
BRONCHODILATOR
BRONCHODILATORS
BRONCHOGENIC
BRONCHOGRAPHIES
BRONCHOGRAPHY
BRONCHOSCOPE
BRONCHOSCOPES
BRONCHOSCOPIC
BRONCHOSCOPICAL
BRONCHOSCOPIES
BRONCHOSCOPIST
BRONCHOSCOPISTS
BRONCHOSCOPY
BRONCHOSPASM
BRONCHOSPASMS
BRONCHOSPASTIC
BRONCOBUSTER
BRONCOBUSTERS
BRONDYRONS
BRONTOBYTE
BRONTOBYTES
BRONTOSAUR
BRONTOSAURS
BRONTOSAURUS
BRONTOSAURUSES
BRONZIFIED
BRONZIFIES
BRONZIFYING
BROODINESS
BROODINESSES
BROODINGLY
BROODMARES
BROOKLIMES

BROOKWEEDS
BROOMBALLER
BROOMBALLERS
BROOMBALLS
BROOMCORNS
BROOMRAPES
BROOMSTAFF
BROOMSTAFFS
BROOMSTICK
BROOMSTICKS
BROTHERHOOD
BROTHERHOODS
BROTHERING
BROTHERLIER
BROTHERLIEST
BROTHERLIKE
BROTHERLINESS
BROTHERLINESSES
BROUGHTASES
BROWALLIAS
BROWBEATEN
BROWBEATER
BROWBEATERS
BROWBEATING
BROWBEATINGS
BROWNFACES
BROWNFIELD
BROWNFIELDS
BROWNNESSES
BROWNNOSED
BROWNNOSER
BROWNNOSERS
BROWNNOSES
BROWNNOSING
BROWNSHIRT
BROWNSHIRTS
BROWNSTONE
BROWNSTONES
BROWRIDGES
BROWSABLES
BRUCELLOSES
BRUCELLOSIS
BRUGMANSIA
BRUGMANSIAS
BRUMMAGEMS
BRUSCHETTA
BRUSCHETTAS
BRUSCHETTE
BRUSHABILITIES

BRUSHABILITY
BRUSHBACKS
BRUSHFIRES
BRUSHLANDS
BRUSHMARKS
BRUSHSTROKE
BRUSHSTROKES
BRUSHWHEEL
BRUSHWHEELS
BRUSHWOODS
BRUSHWORKS
BRUSQUENESS
BRUSQUENESSES
BRUSQUERIE
BRUSQUERIES
BRUTALISATION
BRUTALISATIONS
BRUTALISED
BRUTALISES
BRUTALISING
BRUTALISMS
BRUTALISTS
BRUTALITIES
BRUTALIZATION
BRUTALIZATIONS
BRUTALIZED
BRUTALIZES
BRUTALIZING
BRUTENESSES
BRUTIFYING
BRUTISHNESS
BRUTISHNESSES
BRYOLOGICAL
BRYOLOGIES
BRYOLOGIST
BRYOLOGISTS
BRYOPHYLLUM
BRYOPHYLLUMS
BRYOPHYTES
BRYOPHYTIC
BUBBLEGUMS
BUBBLEHEAD
BUBBLEHEADED
BUBBLEHEADS
BUBONOCELE
BUBONOCELES
BUCCANEERED
BUCCANEERING
BUCCANEERINGS

B

BUCCANEERISH	BUFOTALINS	BULLNECKED	BUMPKINLIEST	BUREAUCRATS
BUCCANEERS	BUFOTENINE	BULLOCKIER	BUMPOLOGIES	BURGEONING
BUCCANIERED	BUFOTENINES	BULLOCKIES	BUMPSADAISY	BURGLARIES
BUCCANIERING	BUGGINESSES	BULLOCKIEST	BUMPTIOUSLY	BURGLARING
BUCCANIERS	BUGLEWEEDS	BULLOCKING	BUMPTIOUSNESS	BURGLARIOUS
BUCCINATOR	BUHRSTONES	BULLROARER	BUMPTIOUSNESSES	BURGLARIOUSLY
BUCCINATORS	BUILDDOWNS	BULLROARERS	BUMSUCKERS	BURGLARISE
BUCCINATORY	BUIRDLIEST	BULLRUSHES	BUMSUCKING	BURGLARISED
BUCELLASES	BULBIFEROUS	BULLSHITTED	BUMSUCKINGS	BURGLARISES
BUCENTAURS	BULBOSITIES	BULLSHITTER	BUNBURYING	BURGLARISING
BUCKBOARDS	BULBOUSNESS	BULLSHITTERS	BUNCHBERRIES	BURGLARIZE
BUCKBRUSHES	BULBOUSNESSES	BULLSHITTING	BUNCHBERRY	BURGLARIZED
BUCKETFULS	BULGINESSES	BULLSHITTINGS	BUNCHGRASS	BURGLARIZES
BUCKETINGS	BULKHEADED	BULLSNAKES	BUNCHGRASSES	BURGLARIZING
BUCKETSFUL	BULKINESSES	BULLTERRIER	BUNCHINESS	BURGLARPROOF
BUCKHOUNDS	BULLBAITING	BULLTERRIERS	BUNCHINESSES	BURGOMASTER
BUCKJUMPER	BULLBAITINGS	BULLWADDIE	BUNDOBUSTS	BURGOMASTERS
BUCKJUMPERS	BULLBRIERS	BULLWADDIES	BUNGALOIDS	BURGUNDIES
BUCKJUMPING	BULLDOGGED	BULLWHACKED	BUNGLESOME	BURLADEROS
BUCKJUMPINGS	BULLDOGGER	BULLWHACKING	BUNGLINGLY	BURLESQUED
BUCKLERING	BULLDOGGERS	BULLWHACKS	BUNKHOUSES	BURLESQUELY
BUCKRAMING	BULLDOGGING	BULLWHIPPED	BUOYANCIES	BURLESQUER
BUCKSHISHED	BULLDOGGINGS	BULLWHIPPING	BUOYANTNESS	BURLESQUERS
BUCKSHISHES	BULLDOZERS	BULLYCIDES	BUOYANTNESSES	BURLESQUES
BUCKSHISHING	BULLDOZING	BULLYRAGGED	BUPIVACAINE	BURLESQUING
BUCKSKINNED	BULLETINED	BULLYRAGGING	BUPIVACAINES	BURLEYCUES
BUCKTHORNS	BULLETINING	BULRUSHIER	BUPRENORPHINE	BURLINESSES
BUCKTOOTHED	BULLETPROOF	BULRUSHIEST	BUPRENORPHINES	BURNETTISE
BUCKWHEATS	BULLETPROOFED	BULWADDEES	BUPRESTIDS	BURNETTISED
BUCKYBALLS	BULLETPROOFING	BULWADDIES	BUPROPIONS	BURNETTISES
BUCKYTUBES	BULLETPROOFS	BULWARKING	BURDENSOME	BURNETTISING
BUCOLICALLY	BULLETRIES	BUMBAILIFF	BUREAUCRACIES	BURNETTIZE
BUDGERIGAR	BULLETWOOD	BUMBAILIFFS	BUREAUCRACY	BURNETTIZED
BUDGERIGARS	BULLETWOODS	BUMBERSHOOT	BUREAUCRAT	BURNETTIZES
BUDGETEERS	BULLFIGHTER	BUMBERSHOOTS	BUREAUCRATESE	BURNETTIZING
BUDGETINGS	BULLFIGHTERS	BUMBLEBEES	BUREAUCRATESES	BURNISHABLE
BUDTENDERS	BULLFIGHTING	BUMBLEBERRIES	BUREAUCRATIC	BURNISHERS
BUFFALOBERRIES	BULLFIGHTINGS	BUMBLEBERRY	BUREAUCRATISE	BURNISHING
BUFFALOBERRY	BULLFIGHTS	BUMBLEDOMS	BUREAUCRATISED	BURNISHINGS
BUFFALOFISH	BULLFINCHES	BUMBLINGLY	BUREAUCRATISES	BURNISHMENT
BUFFALOFISHES	BULLHEADED	BUMFREEZER	BUREAUCRATISING	BURNISHMENTS
BUFFALOING	BULLHEADEDLY	BUMFREEZERS	BUREAUCRATISM	BURRAMUNDI
BUFFERINGS	BULLHEADEDNESS	BUMFUZZLED	BUREAUCRATISMS	BURRAMUNDIS
BUFFETINGS	BULLIONIST	BUMFUZZLES	BUREAUCRATIST	BURRAMYSES
BUFFLEHEAD	BULLIONISTS	BUMFUZZLING	BUREAUCRATISTS	BURRAWANGS
BUFFLEHEADS	BULLISHNESS	BUMMALOTIS	BUREAUCRATIZE	BURRFISHES
BUFFOONERIES	BULLISHNESSES	BUMPINESSES	BUREAUCRATIZED	BURROWSTOWN
BUFFOONERY	BULLMASTIFF	BUMPKINISH	BUREAUCRATIZES	BURROWSTOWNS
BUFFOONISH	BULLMASTIFFS	BUMPKINLIER	BUREAUCRATIZING	BURRSTONES

BURSARSHIP	BUSHWALKERS	BUTCHERBIRDS	BUTTERFLYING	BUTTONHOOK
BURSARSHIPS	BUSHWALKING	BUTCHERERS	BUTTERIEST	BUTTONHOOKED
BURSERACEOUS	BUSHWALKINGS	BUTCHERIES	BUTTERINES	BUTTONHOOKING
BURSICULATE	BUSHWHACKED	BUTCHERING	BUTTERINESS	BUTTONHOOKS
BURSITISES	BUSHWHACKER	BUTCHERINGS	BUTTERINESSES	BUTTONIEST
BURTHENING	BUSHWHACKERS	BUTCHERLIER	BUTTERLESS	BUTTONLESS
BURTHENSOME	BUSHWHACKING	BUTCHERLIEST	BUTTERMILK	BUTTONMOULD
BUSHBABIES	BUSHWHACKINGS	BUTCHNESSES	BUTTERMILKS	BUTTONMOULDS
BUSHBASHING	BUSHWHACKS	BUTENEDIOIC	BUTTERNUTS	BUTTONWOOD
BUSHBASHINGS	BUSINESSES	BUTEONINES	BUTTERSCOTCH	BUTTONWOODS
BUSHCRAFTS	BUSINESSIER	BUTLERAGES	BUTTERSCOTCHES	BUTTRESSED
BUSHELFULS	BUSINESSIEST	BUTLERSHIP	BUTTERWEED	BUTTRESSES
BUSHELLERS	BUSINESSLIKE	BUTLERSHIPS	BUTTERWEEDS	BUTTRESSING
BUSHELLING	BUSINESSMAN	BUTTERBALL	BUTTERWORT	BUTTSTOCKS
BUSHELLINGS	BUSINESSMEN	BUTTERBALLS	BUTTERWORTS	BUTYLATING
BUSHELWOMAN	BUSINESSPEOPLE	BUTTERBURS	BUTTINSKIES	BUTYLATION
BUSHELWOMEN	BUSINESSPERSON	BUTTERCREAM	BUTTINSKIS	BUTYLATIONS
BUSHFIGHTING	BUSINESSPERSONS	BUTTERCREAMS	BUTTOCKING	BUTYRACEOUS
BUSHFIGHTINGS	BUSINESSWOMAN	BUTTERCUPS	BUTTONBALL	BUTYRALDEHYDE
BUSHHAMMER	BUSINESSWOMEN	BUTTERDOCK	BUTTONBALLS	BUTYRALDEHYDES
BUSHHAMMERS	BUSTICATED	BUTTERDOCKS	BUTTONBUSH	BUTYROPHENONE
BUSHINESSES	BUSTICATES	BUTTERFATS	BUTTONBUSHES	BUTYROPHENONES
BUSHMANSHIP	BUSTICATING	BUTTERFINGERED	BUTTONHELD	BUXOMNESSES
BUSHMANSHIPS	BUSTINESSES	BUTTERFINGERS	BUTTONHOLD	BUZZKILLER
BUSHMASTER	BUSTLINGLY	BUTTERFISH	BUTTONHOLDING	BUZZKILLERS
BUSHMASTERS	BUSYBODIED	BUTTERFISHES	BUTTONHOLDS	BYPRODUCTS
BUSHRANGER	BUSYBODIES	BUTTERFLIED	BUTTONHOLE	BYSSACEOUS
BUSHRANGERS	BUSYBODYING	BUTTERFLIES	BUTTONHOLED	BYSSINOSES
BUSHRANGING	BUSYBODYINGS	BUTTERFLYER	BUTTONHOLER	BYSSINOSIS
BUSHRANGINGS	BUSYNESSES	BUTTERFLYERS	BUTTONHOLERS	BYSTANDERS
BUSHWALKED	BUTADIENES	BUTTERFLYFISH	BUTTONHOLES	BYTOWNITES
BUSHWALKER	BUTCHERBIRD	BUTTERFLYFISHES	BUTTONHOLING	

C

CABALETTAS	CACIQUISMS	CADAVEROUS	CAJOLINGLY	CALCIFEROLS
CABALISTIC	CACKERMANDER	CADAVEROUSLY	CAKEWALKED	CALCIFEROUS
CABALISTICAL	CACKERMANDERS	CADAVEROUSNESS	CAKEWALKER	CALCIFICATION
CABALLEROS	CACKLEBERRIES	CADDISFLIES	CAKEWALKERS	CALCIFICATIONS
CABBAGETOWN	CACKLEBERRY	CADDISHNESS	CAKEWALKING	CALCIFUGAL
CABBAGETOWNS	CACODAEMON	CADDISHNESSES	CAKINESSES	CALCIFUGES
CABBAGEWORM	CACODAEMONS	CADDISWORM	CALABASHES	CALCIFUGOUS
CABBAGEWORMS	CACODEMONIC	CADDISWORMS	CALABOGUSES	CALCIFYING
CABBAGIEST	CACODEMONS	CADETSHIPS	CALABOOSES	CALCIGEROUS
CABBALISMS	CACODOXIES	CADUCITIES	CALABRESES	CALCIMINED
CABBALISTIC	CACOEPISTIC	CAECILIANS	CALAMANCOES	CALCIMINES
CABBALISTICAL	CACOGASTRIC	CAECITISES	CALAMANCOS	CALCIMINING
CABBALISTS	CACOGENICS	CAENOGENESES	CALAMANDER	CALCINABLE
CABDRIVERS	CACOGRAPHER	CAENOGENESIS	CALAMANDERS	CALCINATION
CABINETMAKER	CACOGRAPHERS	CAENOGENETIC	CALAMARIES	CALCINATIONS
CABINETMAKERS	CACOGRAPHIC	CAESALPINOID	CALAMINING	CALCINOSES
CABINETMAKING	CACOGRAPHICAL	CAESAREANS	CALAMITIES	CALCINOSIS
CABINETMAKINGS	CACOGRAPHIES	CAESARIANS	CALAMITOUS	CALCITONIN
CABINETRIES	CACOGRAPHY	CAESARISMS	CALAMITOUSLY	CALCITONINS
CABINETWORK	CACOLOGIES	CAESAROPAPISM	CALAMITOUSNESS	CALCSINTER
CABINETWORKS	CACOMISTLE	CAESAROPAPISMS	CALAMONDIN	CALCSINTERS
CABINMATES	CACOMISTLES	CAESPITOSE	CALAMONDINS	CALCULABILITIES
CABLECASTED	CACOMIXLES	CAESPITOSELY	CALANDRIAS	CALCULABILITY
CABLECASTING	CACONYMIES	CAFETERIAS	CALAVANCES	CALCULABLE
CABLECASTS	CACOPHONIC	CAFETIERES	CALAVERITE	CALCULABLY
CABLEGRAMS	CACOPHONICAL	CAFETORIUM	CALAVERITES	CALCULATED
CABLEVISION	CACOPHONICALLY	CAFETORIUMS	CALCAREOUS	CALCULATEDLY
CABLEVISIONS	CACOPHONIES	CAFFEINATED	CALCAREOUSLY	CALCULATEDNESS
CABRIOLETS	CACOPHONIOUS	CAFFEINISM	CALCARIFEROUS	CALCULATES
CACAFUEGOS	CACOPHONOUS	CAFFEINISMS	CALCARIFORM	CALCULATING
CACCIATORA	CACOPHONOUSLY	CAGEYNESSES	CALCEAMENTA	CALCULATINGLY
CACCIATORE	CACOTOPIAN	CAGINESSES	CALCEAMENTUM	CALCULATION
CACHAEMIAS	CACOTOPIAS	CAGMAGGING	CALCEATING	CALCULATIONAL
CACHECTICAL	CACOTROPHIES	CAGYNESSES	CALCEDONIES	CALCULATIONS
CACHINNATE	CACOTROPHY	CAILLEACHS	CALCEDONIO	CALCULATIVE
CACHINNATED	CACTACEOUS	CAILLIACHS	CALCEDONIOS	CALCULATOR
CACHINNATES	CACTOBLASTES	CAINOGENESES	CALCEIFORM	CALCULATORS
CACHINNATING	CACTOBLASTIS	CAINOGENESIS	CALCEOLARIA	CALCULUSES
CACHINNATION	CACUMINALS	CAINOGENETIC	CALCEOLARIAS	CALEFACIENT
CACHINNATIONS	CACUMINOUS	CAIRNGORMS	CALCEOLATE	CALEFACIENTS
CACHINNATORY	CADASTRALLY	CAJOLEMENT	CALCICOLES	CALEFACTION
CACHOLONGS	CADAVERINE	CAJOLEMENTS	CALCICOLOUS	CALEFACTIONS
CACHUMBERS	CADAVERINES	CAJOLERIES	CALCIFEROL	CALEFACTIVE

CALEFACTOR	CALIGINOUS	CALORESCENCE	CAMANACHDS	CAMPANILES
CALEFACTORIES	CALIMOCHOS	CALORESCENCES	CAMARADERIE	CAMPANISTS
CALEFACTORS	CALIOLOGIES	CALORESCENT	CAMARADERIES	CAMPANOLOGER
CALEFACTORY	CALIPASHES	CALORICALLY	CAMARILLAS	CAMPANOLOGERS
CALEMBOURS	CALIPERING	CALORICITIES	CAMBERINGS	CAMPANOLOGICAL
CALENDARED	CALIPHATES	CALORICITY	CAMBISTRIES	CAMPANOLOGIES
CALENDARER	CALISTHENIC	CALORIFICALLY	CAMCORDERS	CAMPANOLOGIST
CALENDARERS	CALISTHENICS	CALORIFICATION	CAMCORDING	CAMPANOLOGISTS
CALENDARING	CALLBOARDS	CALORIFICATIONS	CAMELBACKS	CAMPANOLOGY
CALENDARISATION	CALLIATURE	CALORIFIER	CAMELEOPARD	CAMPANULACEOUS
CALENDARISE	CALLIATURES	CALORIFIERS	CAMELEOPARDS	CAMPANULAR
CALENDARISED	CALLIDITIES	CALORIMETER	CAMELHAIRS	CAMPANULAS
CALENDARISES	CALLIGRAMME	CALORIMETERS	CAMELOPARD	CAMPANULATE
CALENDARISING	CALLIGRAMMES	CALORIMETRIC	CAMELOPARDS	CAMPCRAFTS
CALENDARIST	CALLIGRAMS	CALORIMETRICAL	CAMERAPERSON	CAMPEADORS
CALENDARISTS	CALLIGRAPHER	CALORIMETRIES	CAMERAPERSONS	CAMPESINOS
CALENDARIZATION	CALLIGRAPHERS	CALORIMETRY	CAMERAPHONE	CAMPESTRAL
CALENDARIZE	CALLIGRAPHIC	CALORISING	CAMERAPHONES	CAMPESTRIAN
CALENDARIZED	CALLIGRAPHICAL	CALORIZING	CAMERATION	CAMPGROUND
CALENDARIZES	CALLIGRAPHIES	CALOTYPIST	CAMERATIONS	CAMPGROUNDS
CALENDARIZING	CALLIGRAPHIST	CALOTYPISTS	CAMERAWOMAN	CAMPHORACEOUS
CALENDERED	CALLIGRAPHISTS	CALUMNIABLE	CAMERAWOMEN	CAMPHORATE
CALENDERER	CALLIGRAPHY	CALUMNIATE	CAMERAWORK	CAMPHORATED
CALENDERERS	CALLIOPSIS	CALUMNIATED	CAMERAWORKS	CAMPHORATES
CALENDERING	CALLIPASHES	CALUMNIATES	CAMERLENGO	CAMPHORATING
CALENDERINGS	CALLIPERED	CALUMNIATING	CAMERLENGOS	CAMPIMETRIES
CALENDRERS	CALLIPERING	CALUMNIATION	CAMERLINGO	CAMPIMETRY
CALENDRICAL	CALLIPYGEAN	CALUMNIATIONS	CAMERLINGOS	CAMPINESSES
CALENDRIES	CALLIPYGIAN	CALUMNIATOR	CAMIKNICKERS	CAMPNESSES
CALENDULAS	CALLIPYGOUS	CALUMNIATORS	CAMIKNICKS	CAMPODEIDS
CALENTURES	CALLISTEMON	CALUMNIATORY	CAMISADOES	CAMPODEIFORM
CALESCENCE	CALLISTEMONS	CALUMNIOUS	CAMORRISTA	CAMPSHIRTS
CALESCENCES	CALLISTHENIC	CALUMNIOUSLY	CAMORRISTI	CAMPSTOOLS
CALFDOZERS	CALLISTHENICS	CALUMNYING	CAMORRISTS	CAMPYLOBACTER
CALIATOURS	CALLITHUMP	CALVADOSES	CAMOUFLAGE	CAMPYLOBACTERS
CALIBRATED	CALLITHUMPIAN	CALVARIUMS	CAMOUFLAGEABLE	CAMPYLOTROPOUS
CALIBRATER	CALLITHUMPS	CALYCANTHEMIES	CAMOUFLAGED	CAMSTEERIE
CALIBRATERS	CALLOSITIES	CALYCANTHEMY	CAMOUFLAGES	CAMWHORING
CALIBRATES	CALLOUSING	CALYCANTHUS	CAMOUFLAGIC	CANALBOATS
CALIBRATING	CALLOUSNESS	CALYCANTHUSES	CAMOUFLAGING	CANALICULAR
CALIBRATION	CALLOUSNESSES	CALYCIFORM	CAMOUFLETS	CANALICULATE
CALIBRATIONS	CALLOWNESS	CALYCOIDEOUS	CAMOUFLEUR	CANALICULATED
CALIBRATOR	CALLOWNESSES	CALYCULATE	CAMOUFLEURS	CANALICULI
CALIBRATORS	CALMATIVES	CALYPSONIAN	CAMPAIGNED	CANALICULUS
CALIDITIES	CALMNESSES	CALYPSONIANS	CAMPAIGNER	CANALISATION
CALIFORNIUM	CALMODULIN	CALYPTERAS	CAMPAIGNERS	CANALISATIONS
CALIFORNIUMS	CALMODULINS	CALYPTRATE	CAMPAIGNING	CANALISING
CALIGINOSITIES	CALMSTANES	CALYPTROGEN	CAMPANEROS	CANALIZATION
CALIGINOSITY	CALMSTONES	CALYPTROGENS	CAMPANIFORM	CANALIZATIONS

C

CANALIZING	CANDIDATESHIP	CANISTERISES	CANNONRIES	CANTHARIDIAN
CANCELABLE	CANDIDATESHIPS	CANISTERISING	CANNULATED	CANTHARIDIC
CANCELATION	CANDIDATURE	CANISTERIZATION	CANNULATES	CANTHARIDIN
CANCELATIONS	CANDIDATURES	CANISTERIZE	CANNULATING	CANTHARIDINS
CANCELBOTS	CANDIDIASES	CANISTERIZED	CANNULATION	CANTHARIDS
CANCELEERED	CANDIDIASIS	CANISTERIZES	CANNULATIONS	CANTHAXANTHIN
CANCELEERING	CANDIDNESS	CANISTERIZING	CANOEWOODS	CANTHAXANTHINE
CANCELEERS	CANDIDNESSES	CANKEREDLY	CANONESSES	CANTHAXANTHINES
CANCELIERED	CANDLEBERRIES	CANKEREDNESS	CANONICALLY	CANTHAXANTHINS
CANCELIERING	CANDLEBERRY	CANKEREDNESSES	CANONICALS	CANTHITISES
CANCELIERS	CANDLEFISH	CANKERIEST	CANONICATE	CANTICOING
CANCELLABLE	CANDLEFISHES	CANKERWORM	CANONICATES	CANTICOYED
CANCELLARIAL	CANDLEHOLDER	CANKERWORMS	CANONICITIES	CANTICOYING
CANCELLARIAN	CANDLEHOLDERS	CANNABIDIOL	CANONICITY	CANTILENAS
CANCELLARIATE	CANDLELIGHT	CANNABIDIOLS	CANONISATION	CANTILEVER
CANCELLARIATES	CANDLELIGHTED	CANNABINOID	CANONISATIONS	CANTILEVERED
CANCELLATE	CANDLELIGHTER	CANNABINOIDS	CANONISERS	CANTILEVERING
CANCELLATED	CANDLELIGHTERS	CANNABINOL	CANONISING	CANTILEVERS
CANCELLATION	CANDLELIGHTS	CANNABINOLS	CANONISTIC	CANTILLATE
CANCELLATIONS	CANDLENUTS	CANNABISES	CANONIZATION	CANTILLATED
CANCELLERS	CANDLEPINS	CANNELLINI	CANONIZATIONS	CANTILLATES
CANCELLING	CANDLEPOWER	CANNELLINIS	CANONIZERS	CANTILLATING
CANCELLOUS	CANDLEPOWERS	CANNELLONI	CANONIZING	CANTILLATION
CANCERATED	CANDLESNUFFER	CANNELURES	CANOODLERS	CANTILLATIONS
CANCERATES	CANDLESNUFFERS	CANNIBALISATION	CANOODLING	CANTILLATORY
CANCERATING	CANDLESTICK	CANNIBALISE	CANOPHILIA	CANTINESSES
CANCERATION	CANDLESTICKS	CANNIBALISED	CANOPHILIAS	CANTONISATION
CANCERATIONS	CANDLEWICK	CANNIBALISES	CANOPHILIST	CANTONISATIONS
CANCEROPHOBIA	CANDLEWICKS	CANNIBALISING	CANOPHILISTS	CANTONISED
CANCEROPHOBIAS	CANDLEWOOD	CANNIBALISM	CANOPHOBIA	CANTONISES
CANCEROUSLY	CANDLEWOODS	CANNIBALISMS	CANOPHOBIAS	CANTONISING
CANCERPHOBIA	CANDYFLOSS	CANNIBALISTIC	CANOROUSLY	CANTONIZATION
CANCERPHOBIAS	CANDYFLOSSES	CANNIBALIZATION	CANOROUSNESS	CANTONIZATIONS
CANCIONERO	CANDYGRAMS	CANNIBALIZE	CANOROUSNESSES	CANTONIZED
CANCIONEROS	CANDYTUFTS	CANNIBALIZED	CANTABANKS	CANTONIZES
CANCRIFORM	CANEBRAKES	CANNIBALIZES	CANTABILES	CANTONIZING
CANCRIZANS	CANEFRUITS	CANNIBALIZING	CANTALOUPE	CANTONMENT
CANDELABRA	CANEPHORAS	CANNIBALLY	CANTALOUPES	CANTONMENTS
CANDELABRAS	CANEPHORES	CANNINESSES	CANTALOUPS	CANULATING
CANDELABRUM	CANEPHORUS	CANNISTERS	CANTANKEROUS	CANULATION
CANDELABRUMS	CANEPHORUSES	CANNONADED	CANTANKEROUSLY	CANULATIONS
CANDELILLA	CANESCENCE	CANNONADES	CANTATRICE	CANVASBACK
CANDELILLAS	CANESCENCES	CANNONADING	CANTATRICES	CANVASBACKS
CANDESCENCE	CANINITIES	CANNONBALL	CANTATRICI	CANVASLIKE
CANDESCENCES	CANISTERED	CANNONBALLED	CANTERBURIES	CANVASSERS
CANDESCENT	CANISTERING	CANNONBALLING	CANTERBURY	CANVASSING
CANDESCENTLY	CANISTERISATION	CANNONBALLS	CANTERBURYS	CANVASSINGS
CANDIDACIES	CANISTERISE	CANNONEERS	CANTHARIDAL	CANYONEERS
CANDIDATES	CANISTERISED	CANNONIERS	CANTHARIDES	CANYONINGS

CANZONETTA	CAPILLITIUM	CAPPELLETTI	CAPTIVATINGLY	CARAVANERS
CANZONETTAS	CAPITALISATION	CAPPERNOITIES	CAPTIVATION	CARAVANETTE
CANZONETTE	CAPITALISATIONS	CAPPERNOITY	CAPTIVATIONS	CARAVANETTES
CAOUTCHOUC	CAPITALISE	CAPPUCCINI	CAPTIVATOR	CARAVANING
CAOUTCHOUCS	CAPITALISED	CAPPUCCINO	CAPTIVATORS	CARAVANINGS
CAPABILITIES	CAPITALISES	CAPPUCCINOS	CAPTIVAUNCE	CARAVANNED
CAPABILITY	CAPITALISING	CAPREOLATE	CAPTIVAUNCES	CARAVANNER
CAPABLENESS	CAPITALISM	CAPRICCIOS	CAPTIVITIES	CARAVANNERS
CAPABLENESSES	CAPITALISMS	CAPRICCIOSO	CAPTOPRILS	CARAVANNING
CAPACIOUSLY	CAPITALIST	CAPRICIOUS	CARABINEER	CARAVANNINGS
CAPACIOUSNESS	CAPITALISTIC	CAPRICIOUSLY	CARABINEERS	CARAVANSARAI
CAPACIOUSNESSES	CAPITALISTS	CAPRICIOUSNESS	CARABINERO	CARAVANSARAIS
CAPACITANCE	CAPITALIZATION	CAPRIFICATION	CARABINEROS	CARAVANSARIES
CAPACITANCES	CAPITALIZATIONS	CAPRIFICATIONS	CARABINERS	CARAVANSARY
CAPACITATE	CAPITALIZE	CAPRIFOILS	CARABINIER	CARAVANSERAI
CAPACITATED	CAPITALIZED	CAPRIFOLES	CARABINIERE	CARAVANSERAIS
CAPACITATES	CAPITALIZES	CAPRIFOLIACEOUS	CARABINIERI	CARAVELLES
CAPACITATING	CAPITALIZING	CAPRIFYING	CARABINIERS	CARBACHOLS
CAPACITATION	CAPITATION	CAPRIOLING	CARACOLERS	CARBAMATES
CAPACITATIONS	CAPITATIONS	CAPROLACTAM	CARACOLING	CARBAMAZEPINE
CAPACITIES	CAPITATIVE	CAPROLACTAMS	CARACOLLED	CARBAMAZEPINES
CAPACITIVE	CAPITELLUM	CAPRYLATES	CARACOLLING	CARBAMIDES
CAPACITIVELY	CAPITOLIAN	CAPSAICINS	CARAGEENAN	CARBAMIDINE
CAPACITORS	CAPITOLINE	CAPSIZABLE	CARAGEENANS	CARBAMIDINES
CAPARISONED	CAPITULANT	CAPSOMERES	CARAMBOLAS	CARBAMOYLS
CAPARISONING	CAPITULANTS	CAPSULATED	CARAMBOLED	CARBANIONS
CAPARISONS	CAPITULARIES	CAPSULATION	CARAMBOLES	CARBAZOLES
CAPELLINES	CAPITULARLY	CAPSULATIONS	CARAMBOLING	CARBIDOPAS
CAPELLINIS	CAPITULARS	CAPSULISED	CARAMELISATION	CARBIMAZOLE
CAPELLMEISTER	CAPITULARY	CAPSULISES	CARAMELISATIONS	CARBIMAZOLES
CAPELLMEISTERS	CAPITULATE	CAPSULISING	CARAMELISE	CARBINEERS
CAPERCAILLIE	CAPITULATED	CAPSULIZED	CARAMELISED	CARBINIERS
CAPERCAILLIES	CAPITULATES	CAPSULIZES	CARAMELISES	CARBOCYCLIC
CAPERCAILZIE	CAPITULATING	CAPSULIZING	CARAMELISING	CARBOHYDRASE
CAPERCAILZIES	CAPITULATION	CAPTAINCIES	CARAMELIZATION	CARBOHYDRASES
CAPERINGLY	CAPITULATIONS	CAPTAINING	CARAMELIZATIONS	CARBOHYDRATE
CAPERNOITED	CAPITULATOR	CAPTAINRIES	CARAMELIZE	CARBOHYDRATES
CAPERNOITIE	CAPITULATORS	CAPTAINSHIP	CARAMELIZED	CARBOLATED
CAPERNOITIES	CAPITULATORY	CAPTAINSHIPS	CARAMELIZES	CARBOLISED
CAPERNOITY	CAPNOMANCIES	CAPTIONING	CARAMELIZING	CARBOLISES
CAPICOLLAS	CAPNOMANCY	CAPTIONLESS	CARAMELLED	CARBOLISING
CAPICOLLOS	CAPOCCHIAS	CAPTIOUSLY	CARAMELLIER	CARBOLIZED
CAPILLACEOUS	CAPODASTRO	CAPTIOUSNESS	CARAMELLIEST	CARBOLIZES
CAPILLAIRE	CAPODASTROS	CAPTIOUSNESSES	CARAMELLING	CARBOLIZING
CAPILLAIRES	CAPONIERES	CAPTIVANCE	CARANGOIDS	CARBONACEOUS
CAPILLARIES	CAPONISING	CAPTIVANCES	CARAPACIAL	CARBONADES
CAPILLARITIES	CAPONIZING	CAPTIVATED	CARAVANCES	CARBONADOED
CAPILLARITY	CAPOTASTOS	CAPTIVATES	CARAVANEER	CARBONADOES
CAPILLITIA	CAPPARIDACEOUS	CAPTIVATING	CARAVANEERS	CARBONADOING

C

CARBONADOS	CARBUNCLES	CARCINOMATOSES	CARDIOMEGALY	CARETAKINGS
CARBONARAS	CARBUNCULAR	CARCINOMATOSIS	CARDIOMOTOR	CAREWORKER
CARBONATED	CARBURATED	CARCINOMATOUS	CARDIOMYOPATHY	CAREWORKERS
CARBONATES	CARBURATES	CARCINOSARCOMA	CARDIOPATHIES	CARFUFFLED
CARBONATING	CARBURATING	CARCINOSARCOMAS	CARDIOPATHY	CARFUFFLES
CARBONATION	CARBURATION	CARCINOSES	CARDIOPLEGIA	CARFUFFLING
CARBONATIONS	CARBURATIONS	CARCINOSIS	CARDIOPLEGIAS	CARHOPPING
CARBONATITE	CARBURETED	CARDAMINES	CARDIOPULMONARY	CARHOPPINGS
CARBONATITES	CARBURETER	CARDBOARDIER	CARDIOTHORACIC	CARICATURA
CARBONETTE	CARBURETERS	CARDBOARDIEST	CARDIOTONIC	CARICATURAL
CARBONETTES	CARBURETING	CARDBOARDS	CARDIOTONICS	CARICATURAS
CARBONIFEROUS	CARBURETION	CARDBOARDY	CARDIOVASCULAR	CARICATURE
CARBONISATION	CARBURETIONS	CARDCASTLE	CARDITISES	CARICATURED
CARBONISATIONS	CARBURETOR	CARDCASTLES	CARDOPHAGI	CARICATURES
CARBONISED	CARBURETORS	CARDHOLDER	CARDOPHAGUS	CARICATURING
CARBONISER	CARBURETTED	CARDHOLDERS	CARDPHONES	CARICATURIST
CARBONISERS	CARBURETTER	CARDIALGIA	CARDPLAYER	CARICATURISTS
CARBONISES	CARBURETTERS	CARDIALGIAS	CARDPLAYERS	CARILLONED
CARBONISING	CARBURETTING	CARDIALGIC	CARDPUNCHES	CARILLONING
CARBONIUMS	CARBURETTOR	CARDIALGIES	CARDSHARPER	CARILLONIST
CARBONIZATION	CARBURETTORS	CARDIGANED	CARDSHARPERS	CARILLONISTS
CARBONIZATIONS	CARBURISATION	CARDINALATE	CARDSHARPING	CARILLONNED
CARBONIZED	CARBURISATIONS	CARDINALATES	CARDSHARPINGS	CARILLONNEUR
CARBONIZER	CARBURISED	CARDINALATIAL	CARDSHARPS	CARILLONNEURS
CARBONIZERS	CARBURISES	CARDINALITIAL	CARDUACEOUS	CARILLONNING
CARBONIZES	CARBURISING	CARDINALITIES	CAREENAGES	CARIOGENIC
CARBONIZING	CARBURIZATION	CARDINALITY	CAREERISMS	CARIOSITIES
CARBONLESS	CARBURIZATIONS	CARDINALLY	CAREERISTS	CARIOUSNESS
CARBONNADE	CARBURIZED	CARDINALSHIP	CAREFREENESS	CARIOUSNESSES
CARBONNADES	CARBURIZES	CARDINALSHIPS	CAREFREENESSES	CARJACKERS
CARBONYLATE	CARBURIZING	CARDIOCENTESES	CAREFULLER	CARJACKING
CARBONYLATED	CARBYLAMINE	CARDIOCENTESIS	CAREFULLEST	CARJACKINGS
CARBONYLATES	CARBYLAMINES	CARDIOGENIC	CAREFULNESS	CARMAGNOLE
CARBONYLATING	CARCASSING	CARDIOGRAM	CAREFULNESSES	CARMAGNOLES
CARBONYLATION	CARCINOGEN	CARDIOGRAMS	CAREGIVERS	CARMELITES
CARBONYLATIONS	CARCINOGENESES	CARDIOGRAPH	CAREGIVING	CARMINATIVE
CARBONYLIC	CARCINOGENESIS	CARDIOGRAPHER	CAREGIVINGS	CARMINATIVES
CARBOREXIC	CARCINOGENIC	CARDIOGRAPHERS	CARELESSLY	CARNAHUBAS
CARBOREXICS	CARCINOGENICITY	CARDIOGRAPHIC	CARELESSNESS	CARNALISED
CARBOXYLASE	CARCINOGENS	CARDIOGRAPHICAL	CARELESSNESSES	CARNALISES
CARBOXYLASES	CARCINOIDS	CARDIOGRAPHIES	CAREMONGER	CARNALISING
CARBOXYLATE	CARCINOLOGICAL	CARDIOGRAPHS	CAREMONGERING	CARNALISMS
CARBOXYLATED	CARCINOLOGIES	CARDIOGRAPHY	CAREMONGERINGS	CARNALISTS
CARBOXYLATES	CARCINOLOGIST	CARDIOLOGICAL	CAREMONGERS	CARNALITIES
CARBOXYLATING	CARCINOLOGISTS	CARDIOLOGIES	CARESSINGLY	CARNALIZED
CARBOXYLATION	CARCINOLOGY	CARDIOLOGIST	CARESSINGS	CARNALIZES
CARBOXYLATIONS	CARCINOMAS	CARDIOLOGISTS	CARESSIVELY	CARNALIZING
CARBOXYLIC	CARCINOMATA	CARDIOLOGY	CARETAKERS	CARNALLING
CARBUNCLED	CARCINOMATOID	CARDIOMEGALIES	CARETAKING	CARNALLITE

CARNALLITES	CARPETBAGS	CARRYBACKS	CARTOPHILE	CASHIERMENTS
CARNAPTIOUS	CARPETINGS	CARRYFORWARD	CARTOPHILES	CASHMOBBING
CARNAROLIS	CARPETLIKE	CARRYFORWARDS	CARTOPHILIC	CASHMOBBINGS
CARNASSIAL	CARPETMONGER	CARRYOVERS	CARTOPHILIES	CASHPOINTS
CARNASSIALS	CARPETMONGERS	CARRYTALES	CARTOPHILIST	CASHSPIELS
CARNATIONED	CARPETWEED	CARSHARING	CARTOPHILISTS	CASINGHEAD
CARNATIONS	CARPETWEEDS	CARSHARINGS	CARTOPHILY	CASINGHEADS
CARNELIANS	CARPHOLOGIES	CARSICKNESS	CARTOPPERS	CASKSTANDS
CARNIFEXES	CARPHOLOGY	CARSICKNESSES	CARTOUCHES	CASSAREEPS
CARNIFICATION	CARPOGONIA	CARTELISATION	CARTRIDGES	CASSATIONS
CARNIFICATIONS	CARPOGONIAL	CARTELISATIONS	CARTULARIES	CASSEROLED
CARNIFICIAL	CARPOGONIUM	CARTELISED	CARTWHEELED	CASSEROLES
CARNIFYING	CARPOLOGICAL	CARTELISES	CARTWHEELER	CASSEROLING
CARNITINES	CARPOLOGIES	CARTELISING	CARTWHEELERS	CASSIMERES
CARNIVALESQUE	CARPOLOGIST	CARTELISMS	CARTWHEELING	CASSINGLES
CARNIVORES	CARPOLOGISTS	CARTELISTS	CARTWHEELS	CASSIOPEIUM
CARNIVORIES	CARPOMETACARPI	CARTELIZATION	CARTWRIGHT	CASSIOPEIUMS
CARNIVOROUS	CARPOMETACARPUS	CARTELIZATIONS	CARTWRIGHTS	CASSITERITE
CARNIVOROUSLY	CARPOOLERS	CARTELIZED	CARUNCULAR	CASSITERITES
CARNIVOROUSNESS	CARPOOLING	CARTELIZES	CARUNCULATE	CASSOLETTE
CARNOSAURS	CARPOOLINGS	CARTELIZING	CARUNCULATED	CASSOLETTES
CARNOSITIES	CARPOPHAGOUS	CARTHAMINE	CARUNCULOUS	CASSONADES
CARNOTITES	CARPOPHORE	CARTHAMINES	CARVACROLS	CASSOULETS
CAROLLINGS	CARPOPHORES	CARTHORSES	CARYATIDAL	CASSOWARIES
CAROMELLED	CARPOSPORE	CARTILAGES	CARYATIDEAN	CASSUMUNAR
CAROMELLING	CARPOSPORES	CARTILAGINOUS	CARYATIDES	CASSUMUNARS
CAROTENOID	CARRAGEENAN	CARTOGRAMS	CARYATIDIC	CASTABILITIES
CAROTENOIDS	CARRAGEENANS	CARTOGRAPHER	CARYOPSIDES	CASTABILITY
CAROTINOID	CARRAGEENIN	CARTOGRAPHERS	CARYOPTERIS	CASTANOSPERMINE
CAROTINOIDS	CARRAGEENINS	CARTOGRAPHIC	CARYOPTERISES	CASTELLANS
CAROUSINGLY	CARRAGEENS	CARTOGRAPHICAL	CASCADURAS	CASTELLATED
CAROUSINGS	CARRAGHEEN	CARTOGRAPHIES	CASCARILLA	CASTELLATION
CARPACCIOS	CARRAGHEENAN	CARTOGRAPHY	CASCARILLAS	CASTELLATIONS
CARPELLARY	CARRAGHEENANS	CARTOLOGICAL	CASEATIONS	CASTELLUMS
CARPELLATE	CARRAGHEENIN	CARTOLOGIES	CASEBEARER	CASTIGATED
CARPELLATES	CARRAGHEENINS	CARTOMANCIES	CASEBEARERS	CASTIGATES
CARPENTARIA	CARRAGHEENS	CARTOMANCY	CASEINATES	CASTIGATING
CARPENTARIAS	CARREFOURS	CARTONAGES	CASEINOGEN	CASTIGATION
CARPENTERED	CARRIAGEABLE	CARTONNAGE	CASEINOGENS	CASTIGATIONS
CARPENTERING	CARRIAGEWAY	CARTONNAGES	CASEMAKERS	CASTIGATOR
CARPENTERS	CARRIAGEWAYS	CARTOONIER	CASEMENTED	CASTIGATORS
CARPENTRIES	CARRITCHES	CARTOONIEST	CASEVACING	CASTIGATORY
CARPETBAGGED	CARRIWITCHET	CARTOONING	CASEWORKER	CASTOREUMS
CARPETBAGGER	CARRIWITCHETS	CARTOONINGS	CASEWORKERS	CASTRAMETATION
CARPETBAGGERIES	CARRONADES	CARTOONISH	CASHIERERS	CASTRAMETATIONS
CARPETBAGGERS	CARROTIEST	CARTOONISHLY	CASHIERING	CASTRATERS
CARPETBAGGERY	CARROTTOPPED	CARTOONIST	CASHIERINGS	CASTRATING
CARPETBAGGING	CARROTTOPS	CARTOONISTS	CASHIERLESS	CASTRATION
CARPETBAGGINGS	CARROUSELS	CARTOONLIKE	CASHIERMENT	CASTRATIONS

CASTRATORS	CATACOUSTICS	CATAMARANS	CATASTROPHIST	CATECHISTICAL
CASTRATORY	CATACUMBAL	CATAMENIAL	CATASTROPHISTS	CATECHISTICALLY
CASUALISATION	CATADIOPTRIC	CATAMOUNTAIN	CATASTROPHIZE	CATECHISTS
CASUALISATIONS	CATADIOPTRICAL	CATAMOUNTAINS	CATASTROPHIZED	CATECHIZATION
CASUALISED	CATADROMOUS	CATAMOUNTS	CATASTROPHIZES	CATECHIZATIONS
CASUALISES	CATAFALCOES	CATANANCHE	CATASTROPHIZING	CATECHIZED
CASUALISING	CATAFALQUE	CATANANCHES	CATATONIAS	CATECHIZER
CASUALISMS	CATAFALQUES	CATAPHONIC	CATATONICALLY	CATECHIZERS
CASUALIZATION	CATALECTIC	CATAPHONICS	CATATONICS	CATECHIZES
CASUALIZATIONS	CATALECTICS	CATAPHORAS	CATATONIES	CATECHIZING
CASUALIZED	CATALEPSIES	CATAPHORESES	CATCALLERS	CATECHIZINGS
CASUALIZES	CATALEPTIC	CATAPHORESIS	CATCALLING	CATECHOLAMINE
CASUALIZING	CATALEPTICALLY	CATAPHORETIC	CATCHCRIES	CATECHOLAMINES
CASUALNESS	CATALEPTICS	CATAPHORIC	CATCHFLIES	CATECHUMEN
CASUALNESSES	CATALLACTIC	CATAPHORICALLY	CATCHINESS	CATECHUMENAL
CASUALTIES	CATALLACTICALLY	CATAPHRACT	CATCHINESSES	CATECHUMENATE
CASUARINAS	CATALLACTICS	CATAPHRACTIC	CATCHLIGHT	CATECHUMENATES
CASUISTICAL	CATALOGERS	CATAPHRACTS	CATCHLIGHTS	CATECHUMENICAL
CASUISTICALLY	CATALOGING	CATAPHYLLARY	CATCHLINES	CATECHUMENISM
CASUISTRIES	CATALOGISE	CATAPHYLLS	CATCHMENTS	CATECHUMENISMS
CATABOLICALLY	CATALOGISED	CATAPHYSICAL	CATCHPENNIES	CATECHUMENS
CATABOLISE	CATALOGISES	CATAPLASIA	CATCHPENNY	CATECHUMENSHIP
CATABOLISED	CATALOGISING	CATAPLASIAS	CATCHPHRASE	CATECHUMENSHIPS
CATABOLISES	CATALOGIZE	CATAPLASMS	CATCHPHRASES	CATEGOREMATIC
CATABOLISING	CATALOGIZED	CATAPLASTIC	CATCHPOLES	CATEGORIAL
CATABOLISM	CATALOGIZES	CATAPLECTIC	CATCHPOLLS	CATEGORIALLY
CATABOLISMS	CATALOGIZING	CATAPLEXIES	CATCHWATER	CATEGORICAL
CATABOLITE	CATALOGNES	CATAPULTED	CATCHWATERS	CATEGORICALLY
CATABOLITES	CATALOGUED	CATAPULTIC	CATCHWEEDS	CATEGORICALNESS
CATABOLIZE	CATALOGUER	CATAPULTIER	CATCHWEIGHT	CATEGORIES
CATABOLIZED	CATALOGUERS	CATAPULTIERS	CATCHWORDS	CATEGORISATION
CATABOLIZES	CATALOGUES	CATAPULTING	CATECHESES	CATEGORISATIONS
CATABOLIZING	CATALOGUING	CATARACTOUS	CATECHESIS	CATEGORISE
CATACAUSTIC	CATALOGUISE	CATARHINES	CATECHESISES	CATEGORISED
CATACAUSTICS	CATALOGUISED	CATARRHALLY	CATECHETIC	CATEGORISES
CATACHRESES	CATALOGUISES	CATARRHINE	CATECHETICAL	CATEGORISING
CATACHRESIS	CATALOGUISING	CATARRHINES	CATECHETICALLY	CATEGORIST
CATACHRESTIC	CATALOGUIST	CATARRHOUS	CATECHETICS	CATEGORISTS
CATACHRESTICAL	CATALOGUISTS	CATASTASES	CATECHISATION	CATEGORIZATION
CATACLASES	CATALOGUIZE	CATASTASIS	CATECHISATIONS	CATEGORIZATIONS
CATACLASIS	CATALOGUIZED	CATASTROPHE	CATECHISED	CATEGORIZE
CATACLASMIC	CATALOGUIZES	CATASTROPHES	CATECHISER	CATEGORIZED
CATACLASMS	CATALOGUIZING	CATASTROPHIC	CATECHISERS	CATEGORIZES
CATACLASTIC	CATALYSERS	CATASTROPHISE	CATECHISES	CATEGORIZING
CATACLINAL	CATALYSING	CATASTROPHISED	CATECHISING	CATENACCIO
CATACLYSMAL	CATALYTICAL	CATASTROPHISES	CATECHISINGS	CATENACCIOS
CATACLYSMIC	CATALYTICALLY	CATASTROPHISING	CATECHISMAL	CATENARIAN
CATACLYSMICALLY	CATALYZERS	CATASTROPHISM	CATECHISMS	CATENARIES
CATACLYSMS	CATALYZING	CATASTROPHISMS	CATECHISTIC	CATENATING

CATENATION	CATHODICALLY	CAULICULUS	CAUTIONERS	CELEBRATION
CATENATIONS	CATHODOGRAPH	CAULICULUSES	CAUTIONING	CELEBRATIONS
CATENULATE	CATHODOGRAPHER	CAULIFLORIES	CAUTIONRIES	CELEBRATIVE
CATERCORNER	CATHODOGRAPHERS	CAULIFLOROUS	CAUTIOUSLY	CELEBRATOR
CATERCORNERED	CATHODOGRAPHIES	CAULIFLORY	CAUTIOUSNESS	CELEBRATORS
CATERESSES	CATHODOGRAPHS	CAULIFLOWER	CAUTIOUSNESSES	CELEBRATORY
CATERPILLAR	CATHODOGRAPHY	CAULIFLOWERET	CAVALCADED	CELEBREALITIES
CATERPILLARS	CATHOLICALLY	CAULIFLOWERETS	CAVALCADES	CELEBREALITY
CATERWAULED	CATHOLICATE	CAULIFLOWERS	CAVALCADING	CELEBRITIES
CATERWAULER	CATHOLICATES	CAULIGENOUS	CAVALIERED	CELEBUTANTE
CATERWAULERS	CATHOLICISATION	CAUMSTANES	CAVALIERING	CELEBUTANTES
CATERWAULING	CATHOLICISE	CAUMSTONES	CAVALIERISH	CELECOXIBS
CATERWAULINGS	CATHOLICISED	CAUSABILITIES	CAVALIERISM	CELERITIES
CATERWAULS	CATHOLICISES	CAUSABILITY	CAVALIERISMS	CELERYLIKE
CATFACINGS	CATHOLICISING	CAUSALGIAS	CAVALIERLY	CELESTIALLY
CATFISHING	CATHOLICISM	CAUSALITIES	CAVALLETTI	CELESTIALS
CATHARISED	CATHOLICISMS	CAUSATIONAL	CAVALRYMAN	CELESTINES
CATHARISES	CATHOLICITIES	CAUSATIONISM	CAVALRYMEN	CELESTITES
CATHARISING	CATHOLICITY	CAUSATIONISMS	CAVEFISHES	CELIBACIES
CATHARIZED	CATHOLICIZATION	CAUSATIONIST	CAVENDISHES	CELIBATARIAN
CATHARIZES	CATHOLICIZE	CAUSATIONISTS	CAVERNICOLOUS	CELIBATARIANS
CATHARIZING	CATHOLICIZED	CAUSATIONS	CAVERNOUSLY	CELLARAGES
CATHARTICAL	CATHOLICIZES	CAUSATIVELY	CAVERNULOUS	CELLARETTE
CATHARTICALLY	CATHOLICIZING	CAUSATIVENESS	CAVILLATION	CELLARETTES
CATHARTICS	CATHOLICLY	CAUSATIVENESSES	CAVILLATIONS	CELLARISTS
CATHECTING	CATHOLICOI	CAUSATIVES	CAVILLINGS	CELLARWAYS
CATHEDRALS	CATHOLICON	CAUSELESSLY	CAVITATING	CELLBLOCKS
CATHEDRATIC	CATHOLICONS	CAUSELESSNESS	CAVITATION	CELLENTANI
CATHEPSINS	CATHOLICOS	CAUSELESSNESSES	CAVITATIONS	CELLENTANIS
CATHETERISATION	CATHOLICOSES	CAUSEWAYED	CAVORTINGS	CELLIFEROUS
CATHETERISE	CATHOLYTES	CAUSEWAYING	CEANOTHUSES	CELLOBIOSE
CATHETERISED	CATIONICALLY	CAUSTICALLY	CEASEFIRES	CELLOBIOSES
CATHETERISES	CATLINITES	CAUSTICITIES	CEASELESSLY	CELLOIDINS
CATHETERISING	CATNAPPERS	CAUSTICITY	CEASELESSNESS	CELLOPHANE
CATHETERISM	CATNAPPING	CAUSTICNESS	CEASELESSNESSES	CELLOPHANES
CATHETERISMS	CATOPTRICAL	CAUSTICNESSES	CEBADILLAS	CELLPHONES
CATHETERIZATION	CATOPTRICS	CAUTERANTS	CECUTIENCIES	CELLULARITIES
CATHETERIZE	CATTINESSES	CAUTERISATION	CECUTIENCY	CELLULARITY
CATHETERIZED	CATTISHNESS	CAUTERISATIONS	CEDARBIRDS	CELLULASES
CATHETERIZES	CATTISHNESSES	CAUTERISED	CEDARWOODS	CELLULATED
CATHETERIZING	CAUCHEMARS	CAUTERISES	CEDRELACEOUS	CELLULIFEROUS
CATHETOMETER	CAUCUSSING	CAUTERISING	CEILOMETER	CELLULITES
CATHETOMETERS	CAUCUSSINGS	CAUTERISMS	CEILOMETERS	CELLULITIS
CATHETUSES	CAUDATIONS	CAUTERIZATION	CELANDINES	CELLULITISES
CATHINONES	CAUDILLISMO	CAUTERIZATIONS	CELEBRANTS	CELLULOIDS
CATHIODERMIE	CAUDILLISMOS	CAUTERIZED	CELEBRATED	CELLULOLYTIC
CATHIODERMIES	CAULESCENT	CAUTERIZES	CELEBRATEDNESS	CELLULOSES
CATHODALLY	CAULICOLOUS	CAUTERIZING	CELEBRATES	CELLULOSIC
CATHODICAL	CAULICULATE	CAUTIONARY	CELEBRATING	CELLULOSICS

CELSITUDES	CENTERFOLD	CENTRALISMS	CENTRIPETAL	CEPHALOCELES
CEMBALISTS	CENTERFOLDS	CENTRALIST	CENTRIPETALISM	CEPHALOCHORDATE
CEMENTATION	CENTERINGS	CENTRALISTIC	CENTRIPETALISMS	CEPHALOMETER
CEMENTATIONS	CENTERLESS	CENTRALISTS	CENTRIPETALLY	CEPHALOMETERS
CEMENTATORY	CENTERLINE	CENTRALITIES	CENTROBARIC	CEPHALOMETRIC
CEMENTITES	CENTERLINES	CENTRALITY	CENTROCLINAL	CEPHALOMETRIES
CEMENTITIOUS	CENTERPIECE	CENTRALIZATION	CENTROIDAL	CEPHALOMETRY
CEMETERIES	CENTERPIECES	CENTRALIZATIONS	CENTROLECITHAL	CEPHALOPOD
CENESTHESES	CENTESIMAL	CENTRALIZE	CENTROMERE	CEPHALOPODAN
CENESTHESIA	CENTESIMALLY	CENTRALIZED	CENTROMERES	CEPHALOPODANS
CENESTHESIAS	CENTESIMALS	CENTRALIZER	CENTROMERIC	CEPHALOPODIC
CENESTHESIS	CENTESIMOS	CENTRALIZERS	CENTROSOME	CEPHALOPODOUS
CENESTHETIC	CENTIGRADE	CENTRALIZES	CENTROSOMES	CEPHALOPODS
CENOBITICAL	CENTIGRADES	CENTRALIZING	CENTROSOMIC	CEPHALORIDINE
CENOBITISM	CENTIGRAMME	CENTREBOARD	CENTROSPHERE	CEPHALORIDINES
CENOBITISMS	CENTIGRAMMES	CENTREBOARDS	CENTROSPHERES	CEPHALOSPORIN
CENOGENESES	CENTIGRAMS	CENTREDNESS	CENTROSYMMETRIC	CEPHALOSPORINS
CENOGENESIS	CENTILITER	CENTREDNESSES	CENTUMVIRATE	CEPHALOTHIN
CENOGENETIC	CENTILITERS	CENTREFOLD	CENTUMVIRATES	CEPHALOTHINS
CENOGENETICALLY	CENTILITRE	CENTREFOLDS	CENTUMVIRI	CEPHALOTHORACES
CENOSPECIES	CENTILITRES	CENTREINGS	CENTUMVIRS	CEPHALOTHORACIC
CENOTAPHIC	CENTILLION	CENTRELESS	CENTUPLICATE	CEPHALOTHORAX
CENSORABLE	CENTILLIONS	CENTRELINE	CENTUPLICATED	CEPHALOTHORAXES
CENSORIOUS	CENTILLIONTH	CENTRELINES	CENTUPLICATES	CEPHALOTOMIES
CENSORIOUSLY	CENTILLIONTHS	CENTREPIECE	CENTUPLICATING	CEPHALOTOMY
CENSORIOUSNESS	CENTIMETER	CENTREPIECES	CENTUPLICATION	CERAMICIST
CENSORSHIP	CENTIMETERS	CENTRICALLY	CENTUPLICATIONS	CERAMICISTS
CENSORSHIPS	CENTIMETRE	CENTRICALNESS	CENTUPLING	CERAMOGRAPHIES
CENSURABILITIES	CENTIMETRES	CENTRICALNESSES	CENTURIATION	CERAMOGRAPHY
CENSURABILITY	CENTIMETRIC	CENTRICITIES	CENTURIATIONS	CERARGYRITE
CENSURABLE	CENTIMORGAN	CENTRICITY	CENTURIATOR	CERARGYRITES
CENSURABLENESS	CENTIMORGANS	CENTRIFUGAL	CENTURIATORS	CERASTIUMS
CENSURABLY	CENTINELLS	CENTRIFUGALISE	CENTURIONS	CERATITISES
CENTAUREAS	CENTIPEDES	CENTRIFUGALISED	CEPHALAGRA	CERATODUSES
CENTAURIAN	CENTIPOISE	CENTRIFUGALISES	CEPHALAGRAS	CERATOPSIAN
CENTAURIES	CENTIPOISES	CENTRIFUGALIZE	CEPHALALGIA	CERATOPSIANS
CENTENARIAN	CENTONATES	CENTRIFUGALIZED	CEPHALALGIAS	CERATOPSID
CENTENARIANISM	CENTONELLS	CENTRIFUGALIZES	CEPHALALGIC	CERATOPSIDS
CENTENARIANISMS	CENTONISTS	CENTRIFUGALLY	CEPHALALGICS	CERAUNOGRAPH
CENTENARIANS	CENTRALEST	CENTRIFUGALS	CEPHALEXIN	CERAUNOGRAPHS
CENTENARIES	CENTRALISATION	CENTRIFUGATION	CEPHALEXINS	CERCARIANS
CENTENIERS	CENTRALISATIONS	CENTRIFUGATIONS	CEPHALICALLY	CERCOPITHECID
CENTENNIAL	CENTRALISE	CENTRIFUGE	CEPHALISATION	CERCOPITHECIDS
CENTENNIALLY	CENTRALISED	CENTRIFUGED	CEPHALISATIONS	CERCOPITHECOID
CENTENNIALS	CENTRALISER	CENTRIFUGENCE	CEPHALITIS	CERCOPITHECOIDS
CENTERBOARD	CENTRALISERS	CENTRIFUGENCES	CEPHALITISES	CEREALISTS
CENTERBOARDS	CENTRALISES	CENTRIFUGES	CEPHALIZATION	CEREBELLAR
CENTEREDNESS	CENTRALISING	CENTRIFUGING	CEPHALIZATIONS	CEREBELLIC
CENTEREDNESSES	CENTRALISM	CENTRIOLES	CEPHALOCELE	CEREBELLOUS

CEREBELLUM	CERTIFIABLY	CHABAZITES	CHALANNING	CHALUMEAUX
CEREBELLUMS	CERTIFICATE	CHACONINES	CHALAZIONS	CHALYBEATE
CEREBRALISM	CERTIFICATED	CHAENOMELES	CHALAZOGAMIC	CHALYBEATES
CEREBRALISMS	CERTIFICATES	CHAENOMELESES	CHALAZOGAMIES	CHALYBITES
CEREBRALIST	CERTIFICATING	CHAETIFEROUS	CHALAZOGAMY	CHAMAELEON
CEREBRALISTS	CERTIFICATION	CHAETODONS	CHALCANTHITE	CHAMAELEONS
CEREBRALLY	CERTIFICATIONS	CHAETOGNATH	CHALCANTHITES	CHAMAEPHYTE
CEREBRATED	CERTIFICATORIES	CHAETOGNATHS	CHALCEDONIC	CHAMAEPHYTES
CEREBRATES	CERTIFICATORY	CHAETOPODS	CHALCEDONIES	CHAMBERERS
CEREBRATING	CERTIFIERS	CHAFFERERS	CHALCEDONY	CHAMBERHAND
CEREBRATION	CERTIFYING	CHAFFERIES	CHALCEDONYX	CHAMBERHANDS
CEREBRATIONS	CERTIORARI	CHAFFERING	CHALCEDONYXES	CHAMBERING
CEREBRIFORM	CERTIORARIS	CHAFFINCHES	CHALCOCITE	CHAMBERINGS
CEREBRITIS	CERTITUDES	CHAFFINGLY	CHALCOCITES	CHAMBERLAIN
CEREBRITISES	CERULOPLASMIN	CHAGRINING	CHALCOGENIDE	CHAMBERLAINS
CEREBROSIDE	CERULOPLASMINS	CHAGRINNED	CHALCOGENIDES	CHAMBERLAINSHIP
CEREBROSIDES	CERUMINOUS	CHAGRINNING	CHALCOGENS	CHAMBERMAID
CEREBROSPINAL	CERUSSITES	CHAINBRAKE	CHALCOGRAPHER	CHAMBERMAIDS
CEREBROTONIA	CERVELASES	CHAINBRAKES	CHALCOGRAPHERS	CHAMBERPOT
CEREBROTONIAS	CERVICITIS	CHAINFALLS	CHALCOGRAPHIC	CHAMBERPOTS
CEREBROTONIC	CERVICITISES	CHAINPLATE	CHALCOGRAPHICAL	CHAMBRANLE
CEREBROTONICS	CERVICOGRAPHIES	CHAINPLATES	CHALCOGRAPHIES	CHAMBRANLES
CEREBROVASCULAR	CERVICOGRAPHY	CHAINSAWED	CHALCOGRAPHIST	CHAMELEONIC
CERECLOTHS	CESAREVICH	CHAINSAWING	CHALCOGRAPHISTS	CHAMELEONLIKE
CEREMONIAL	CESAREVICHES	CHAINSHOTS	CHALCOGRAPHY	CHAMELEONS
CEREMONIALISM	CESAREVITCH	CHAINSTITCH	CHALCOLITHIC	CHAMFERERS
CEREMONIALISMS	CESAREVITCHES	CHAINSTITCHES	CHALCOPYRITE	CHAMFERING
CEREMONIALIST	CESAREVNAS	CHAINWHEEL	CHALCOPYRITES	CHAMFRAINS
CEREMONIALISTS	CESAREWICH	CHAINWHEELS	CHALICOTHERE	CHAMOISING
CEREMONIALLY	CESAREWICHES	CHAINWORKS	CHALICOTHERES	CHAMOMILES
CEREMONIALS	CESAREWITCH	CHAIRBACKS	CHALKBOARD	CHAMPAGNES
CEREMONIES	CESAREWITCHES	CHAIRBORNE	CHALKBOARDS	CHAMPAIGNS
CEREMONIOUS	CESPITOSELY	CHAIRBOUND	CHALKFACES	CHAMPERTIES
CEREMONIOUSLY	CESSATIONS	CHAIRLIFTS	CHALKINESS	CHAMPERTOUS
CEREMONIOUSNESS	CESSIONARIES	CHAIRMANED	CHALKINESSES	CHAMPIGNON
CERIFEROUS	CESSIONARY	CHAIRMANING	CHALKLANDS	CHAMPIGNONS
CEROGRAPHIC	CESTOIDEAN	CHAIRMANNED	CHALKMARKS	CHAMPIONED
CEROGRAPHICAL	CESTOIDEANS	CHAIRMANNING	CHALKSTONE	CHAMPIONESS
CEROGRAPHIES	CETEOSAURUS	CHAIRMANSHIP	CHALKSTONES	CHAMPIONESSES
CEROGRAPHIST	CETEOSAURUSES	CHAIRMANSHIPS	CHALKSTRIPE	CHAMPIONING
CEROGRAPHISTS	CETOLOGICAL	CHAIRPEOPLE	CHALKSTRIPES	CHAMPIONSHIP
CEROGRAPHS	CETOLOGIES	CHAIRPERSON	CHALLENGEABLE	CHAMPIONSHIPS
CEROGRAPHY	CETOLOGIST	CHAIRPERSONS	CHALLENGED	CHAMPLEVES
CEROMANCIES	CETOLOGISTS	CHAIRWARMER	CHALLENGER	CHANCELESS
CEROPLASTIC	CETRIMIDES	CHAIRWARMERS	CHALLENGERS	CHANCELLERIES
CEROPLASTICS	CETUXIMABS	CHAIRWOMAN	CHALLENGES	CHANCELLERY
CERTAINEST	CEVADILLAS	CHAIRWOMEN	CHALLENGING	CHANCELLOR
CERTAINTIES	CEYLANITES	CHAISELESS	CHALLENGINGLY	CHANCELLORIES
CERTIFIABLE	CEYLONITES	CHAKALAKAS	CHALUMEAUS	CHANCELLORS

C

CHANCELLORSHIP	CHANNELIZED	CHAPSTICKS	CHARCOALED	CHARLESTONED
CHANCELLORSHIPS	CHANNELIZES	CHAPTALISATION	CHARCOALIER	CHARLESTONING
CHANCELLORY	CHANNELIZING	CHAPTALISATIONS	CHARCOALIEST	CHARLESTONS
CHANCERIES	CHANNELLED	CHAPTALISE	CHARCOALING	CHARLOTTES
CHANCHITOS	CHANNELLER	CHAPTALISED	CHARCUTERIE	CHARMEUSES
CHANCINESS	CHANNELLERS	CHAPTALISES	CHARCUTERIES	CHARMINGER
CHANCINESSES	CHANNELLING	CHAPTALISING	CHARDONNAY	CHARMINGEST
CHANCROIDAL	CHANSONETTE	CHAPTALIZATION	CHARDONNAYS	CHARMINGLY
CHANCROIDS	CHANSONETTES	CHAPTALIZATIONS	CHARGEABILITIES	CHARMLESSLY
CHANDELIER	CHANSONNIER	CHAPTALIZE	CHARGEABILITY	CHARMONIUM
CHANDELIERED	CHANSONNIERS	CHAPTALIZED	CHARGEABLE	CHAROSETHS
CHANDELIERS	CHANTARELLE	CHAPTALIZES	CHARGEABLENESS	CHARREADAS
CHANDELLED	CHANTARELLES	CHAPTALIZING	CHARGEABLY	CHARTACEOUS
CHANDELLES	CHANTECLER	CHAPTERHOUSE	CHARGEBACK	CHARTERERS
CHANDELLING	CHANTECLERS	CHAPTERHOUSES	CHARGEBACKS	CHARTERING
CHANDLERIES	CHANTERELLE	CHAPTERING	CHARGEHAND	CHARTERPARTIES
CHANDLERING	CHANTERELLES	CHARABANCS	CHARGEHANDS	CHARTERPARTY
CHANDLERINGS	CHANTEUSES	CHARACINOID	CHARGELESS	CHARTHOUSE
CHANDLERLY	CHANTICLEER	CHARACTERED	CHARGESHEET	CHARTHOUSES
CHANGEABILITIES	CHANTICLEERS	CHARACTERFUL	CHARGESHEETS	CHARTOGRAPHER
CHANGEABILITY	CHANTINGLY	CHARACTERIES	CHARGRILLED	CHARTOGRAPHERS
CHANGEABLE	CHANTRESSES	CHARACTERING	CHARGRILLING	CHARTOGRAPHIC
CHANGEABLENESS	CHANUKIAHS	CHARACTERISABLE	CHARGRILLS	CHARTOGRAPHICAL
CHANGEABLY	CHAOLOGIES	CHARACTERISE	CHARINESSES	CHARTOGRAPHIES
CHANGEAROUND	CHAOLOGIST	CHARACTERISED	CHARIOTEER	CHARTOGRAPHY
CHANGEAROUNDS	CHAOLOGISTS	CHARACTERISER	CHARIOTEERED	CHARTREUSE
CHANGEFULLY	CHAOTICALLY	CHARACTERISERS	CHARIOTEERING	CHARTREUSES
CHANGEFULNESS	CHAPARAJOS	CHARACTERISES	CHARIOTEERS	CHARTULARIES
CHANGEFULNESSES	CHAPAREJOS	CHARACTERISING	CHARIOTING	CHARTULARY
CHANGELESS	CHAPARRALS	CHARACTERISM	CHARISMATA	CHASEPORTS
CHANGELESSLY	CHAPATTIES	CHARACTERISMS	CHARISMATIC	CHASMOGAMIC
CHANGELESSNESS	CHAPELRIES	CHARACTERISTIC	CHARISMATICALLY	CHASMOGAMIES
CHANGELING	CHAPERONAGE	CHARACTERISTICS	CHARISMATICS	CHASMOGAMOUS
CHANGELINGS	CHAPERONAGES	CHARACTERIZABLE	CHARITABLE	CHASMOGAMY
CHANGEOVER	CHAPERONED	CHARACTERIZE	CHARITABLENESS	CHASSEPOTS
CHANGEOVERS	CHAPERONES	CHARACTERIZED	CHARITABLY	CHASTENERS
CHANGEROUND	CHAPERONING	CHARACTERIZER	CHARIVARIED	CHASTENESS
CHANGEROUNDS	CHAPFALLEN	CHARACTERIZERS	CHARIVARIING	CHASTENESSES
CHANNELERS	CHAPLAINCIES	CHARACTERIZES	CHARIVARIS	CHASTENING
CHANNELING	CHAPLAINCY	CHARACTERIZING	CHARLADIES	CHASTENINGLY
CHANNELISATION	CHAPLAINRIES	CHARACTERLESS	CHARLATANIC	CHASTENMENT
CHANNELISATIONS	CHAPLAINRY	CHARACTEROLOGY	CHARLATANICAL	CHASTENMENTS
CHANNELISE	CHAPLAINSHIP	CHARACTERS	CHARLATANISM	CHASTISABLE
CHANNELISED	CHAPLAINSHIPS	CHARACTERY	CHARLATANISMS	CHASTISEMENT
CHANNELISES	CHAPMANSHIP	CHARBROILED	CHARLATANISTIC	CHASTISEMENTS
CHANNELISING	CHAPMANSHIPS	CHARBROILER	CHARLATANRIES	CHASTISERS
CHANNELIZATION	CHAPPESSES	CHARBROILERS	CHARLATANRY	CHASTISING
CHANNELIZATIONS	CHAPRASSIES	CHARBROILING	CHARLATANS	CHASTITIES
CHANNELIZE	CHAPRASSIS	CHARBROILS	CHARLESTON	CHATEAUBRIAND

CHATEAUBRIANDS	CHEAPJACKS	CHEEKINESS	CHEESESTEAK	CHEMITYPIES
CHATELAINE	CHEAPNESSES	CHEEKINESSES	CHEESESTEAKS	CHEMOATTRACTANT
CHATELAINES	CHEAPSHOTS	CHEEKPIECE	CHEESETASTER	CHEMOAUTOTROPH
CHATELAINS	CHEAPSKATE	CHEEKPIECES	CHEESETASTERS	CHEMOAUTOTROPHS
CHATOYANCE	CHEAPSKATES	CHEEKPOUCH	CHEESEVATS	CHEMOAUTOTROPHY
CHATOYANCES	CHEATERIES	CHEEKPOUCHES	CHEESEWIRE	CHEMOAUTROPH
CHATOYANCIES	CHEATINGLY	CHEEKTEETH	CHEESEWIRES	CHEMOAUTROPHS
CHATOYANCY	CHECHAKOES	CHEEKTOOTH	CHEESEWOOD	CHEMOCEPTOR
CHATOYANTS	CHECHAQUOS	CHEERFULLER	CHEESEWOODS	CHEMOCEPTORS
CHATTERATI	CHECKBOOKS	CHEERFULLEST	CHEESEWRING	CHEMOKINES
CHATTERBOX	CHECKBOXES	CHEERFULLY	CHEESEWRINGS	CHEMOKINESES
CHATTERBOXES	CHECKCLERK	CHEERFULNESS	CHEESINESS	CHEMOKINESIS
CHATTERERS	CHECKCLERKS	CHEERFULNESSES	CHEESINESSES	CHEMOLITHOTROPH
CHATTERIER	CHECKERBERRIES	CHEERINESS	CHEILITISES	CHEMONASTIES
CHATTERIEST	CHECKERBERRY	CHEERINESSES	CHEIROMANCER	CHEMONASTY
CHATTERING	CHECKERBLOOM	CHEERINGLY	CHEIROMANCERS	CHEMOPREVENTION
CHATTERINGS	CHECKERBLOOMS	CHEERISHNESS	CHEIROMANCIES	CHEMOPSYCHIATRY
CHATTINESS	CHECKERBOARD	CHEERISHNESSES	CHEIROMANCY	CHEMORECEPTION
CHATTINESSES	CHECKERBOARDS	CHEERLEADER	CHELASHIPS	CHEMORECEPTIONS
CHAUDFROID	CHECKERING	CHEERLEADERS	CHELATABLE	CHEMORECEPTIVE
CHAUDFROIDS	CHECKLATON	CHEERLEADING	CHELATIONS	CHEMORECEPTOR
CHAUFFEURED	CHECKLATONS	CHEERLEADINGS	CHELICERAE	CHEMORECEPTORS
CHAUFFEURING	CHECKLISTED	CHEERLEADS	CHELICERAL	CHEMOSMOSES
CHAUFFEURS	CHECKLISTING	CHEERLESSLY	CHELICERATE	CHEMOSMOSIS
CHAUFFEUSE	CHECKLISTS	CHEERLESSNESS	CHELICERATES	CHEMOSMOTIC
CHAUFFEUSED	CHECKMARKED	CHEERLESSNESSES	CHELIFEROUS	CHEMOSORBED
CHAUFFEUSES	CHECKMARKING	CHEESEBOARD	CHELONIANS	CHEMOSORBING
CHAUFFEUSING	CHECKMARKS	CHEESEBOARDS	CHELUVIATION	CHEMOSORBS
CHAULMOOGRA	CHECKMATED	CHEESEBURGER	CHELUVIATIONS	CHEMOSPHERE
CHAULMOOGRAS	CHECKMATES	CHEESEBURGERS	CHEMAUTOTROPH	CHEMOSPHERES
CHAULMUGRA	CHECKMATING	CHEESECAKE	CHEMAUTOTROPHIC	CHEMOSPHERIC
CHAULMUGRAS	CHECKPOINT	CHEESECAKES	CHEMAUTOTROPHS	CHEMOSTATS
CHAUNTRESS	CHECKPOINTS	CHEESECLOTH	CHEMIATRIC	CHEMOSURGERIES
CHAUNTRESSES	CHECKRAILS	CHEESECLOTHS	CHEMICALLY	CHEMOSURGERY
CHAUNTRIES	CHECKREINS	CHEESECUTTER	CHEMICKING	CHEMOSURGICAL
CHAUSSURES	CHECKROOMS	CHEESECUTTERS	CHEMICKINGS	CHEMOSYNTHESES
CHAUTAUQUA	CHECKROWED	CHEESEHOPPER	CHEMICOPHYSICAL	CHEMOSYNTHESIS
CHAUTAUQUAS	CHECKROWING	CHEESEHOPPERS	CHEMIOSMOSES	CHEMOSYNTHETIC
CHAUVINISM	CHECKSTOPS	CHEESELIKE	CHEMIOSMOSIS	CHEMOTACTIC
CHAUVINISMS	CHECKWEIGHER	CHEESEMITE	CHEMIOSMOTIC	CHEMOTACTICALLY
CHAUVINIST	CHECKWEIGHERS	CHEESEMITES	CHEMISETTE	CHEMOTAXES
CHAUVINISTIC	CHEDDARIER	CHEESEMONGER	CHEMISETTES	CHEMOTAXIS
CHAUVINISTS	CHEDDARIEST	CHEESEMONGERS	CHEMISORBED	CHEMOTAXISES
CHAVENDERS	CHEECHAKOES	CHEESEPARER	CHEMISORBING	CHEMOTAXONOMIC
CHAVTASTIC	CHEECHAKOS	CHEESEPARERS	CHEMISORBS	CHEMOTAXONOMIES
CHAWBACONS	CHEECHALKO	CHEESEPARING	CHEMISORPTION	CHEMOTAXONOMIST
CHEAPENERS	CHEECHALKOES	CHEESEPARINGS	CHEMISORPTIONS	CHEMOTAXONOMY
CHEAPENING	CHEECHALKOS	CHEESEPRESS	CHEMISTRIES	CHEMOTHERAPIES
CHEAPISHLY	CHEEKBONES	CHEESEPRESSES	CHEMITYPES	CHEMOTHERAPIST

CHEMOTHERAPISTS	CHESSPLAYER	CHICNESSES	CHILDMINDERS	CHINABERRY
CHEMOTHERAPY	CHESSPLAYERS	CHIEFERIES	CHILDMINDING	CHINACHINA
CHEMOTROPIC	CHESSYLITE	CHIEFESSES	CHILDMINDINGS	CHINACHINAS
CHEMOTROPICALLY	CHESSYLITES	CHIEFLINGS	CHILDNESSES	CHINAROOTS
CHEMOTROPISM	CHESTERFIELD	CHIEFSHIPS	CHILDPROOF	CHINAWARES
CHEMOTROPISMS	CHESTERFIELDS	CHIEFTAINCIES	CHILDPROOFED	CHINCAPINS
CHEMPADUKS	CHESTINESS	CHIEFTAINCY	CHILDPROOFING	CHINCHERINCHEE
CHEMTRAILS	CHESTINESSES	CHIEFTAINESS	CHILDPROOFS	CHINCHERINCHEES
CHEMURGICAL	CHEVALIERS	CHIEFTAINESSES	CHILDRENSWEAR	CHINCHIEST
CHEMURGIES	CHEVELURES	CHIEFTAINRIES	CHILDRENSWEARS	CHINCHILLA
CHENOPODIACEOUS	CHEVESAILE	CHIEFTAINRY	CHILIAGONS	CHINCHILLAS
CHEONGSAMS	CHEVESAILES	CHIEFTAINS	CHILIAHEDRA	CHINCOUGHS
CHEQUEBOOK	CHEVISANCE	CHIEFTAINSHIP	CHILIAHEDRON	CHINKAPINS
CHEQUEBOOKS	CHEVISANCES	CHIEFTAINSHIPS	CHILIAHEDRONS	CHINKERINCHEE
CHEQUERBOARD	CHEVRETTES	CHIFFCHAFF	CHILIARCHIES	CHINKERINCHEES
CHEQUERBOARDS	CHEVROTAIN	CHIFFCHAFFS	CHILIARCHS	CHINOISERIE
CHEQUERING	CHEVROTAINS	CHIFFONADE	CHILIARCHY	CHINOISERIES
CHEQUERWISE	CHEVROTINS	CHIFFONADES	CHILIASTIC	CHINOVNIKS
CHEQUERWORK	CHEWINESSES	CHIFFONIER	CHILLAXING	CHINQUAPIN
CHEQUERWORKS	CHIACKINGS	CHIFFONIERS	CHILLINESS	CHINQUAPINS
CHERALITES	CHIAREZZAS	CHIFFONNIER	CHILLINESSES	CHINSTRAPS
CHERIMOYAS	CHIAROSCURISM	CHIFFONNIERS	CHILLINGLY	CHINTZIEST
CHERIMOYER	CHIAROSCURISMS	CHIFFONNIEST	CHILLNESSES	CHINWAGGED
CHERIMOYERS	CHIAROSCURIST	CHIFFOROBE	CHILLWAVES	CHINWAGGING
CHERISHABLE	CHIAROSCURISTS	CHIFFOROBES	CHILOPODAN	CHIONODOXA
CHERISHERS	CHIAROSCURO	CHIHUAHUAS	CHILOPODANS	CHIONODOXAS
CHERISHING	CHIAROSCUROS	CHIKUNGUNYA	CHILOPODOUS	CHIPBOARDS
CHERISHINGLY	CHIASMATIC	CHIKUNGUNYAS	CHILTEPINS	CHIPMAKERS
CHERISHMENT	CHIASMUSES	CHILBLAINED	CHIMAERISM	CHIPOCHIAS
CHERISHMENTS	CHIASTOLITE	CHILBLAINS	CHIMAERISMS	CHIPOLATAS
CHERMOULAS	CHIASTOLITES	CHILDBEARING	CHIMERICAL	CHIPPEREST
CHERNOZEMIC	CHIBOUQUES	CHILDBEARINGS	CHIMERICALLY	CHIPPERING
CHERNOZEMS	CHICALOTES	CHILDBIRTH	CHIMERICALNESS	CHIPPINESS
CHERRYLIKE	CHICANERIES	CHILDBIRTHS	CHIMERISMS	CHIPPINESSES
CHERRYSTONE	CHICANINGS	CHILDCARES	CHIMICHANGA	CHIQUICHIQUI
CHERRYSTONES	CHICCORIES	CHILDCROWING	CHIMICHANGAS	CHIQUICHIQUIS
CHERSONESE	CHICKABIDDIES	CHILDCROWINGS	CHIMNEYBOARD	CHIRAGRICAL
CHERSONESES	CHICKABIDDY	CHILDERMAS	CHIMNEYBOARDS	CHIRALITIES
CHERUBICAL	CHICKADEES	CHILDERMASES	CHIMNEYBREAST	CHIRIMOYAS
CHERUBICALLY	CHICKAREES	CHILDHOODS	CHIMNEYBREASTS	CHIROGNOMIES
CHERUBIMIC	CHICKENHEARTED	CHILDISHLY	CHIMNEYING	CHIROGNOMIST
CHERUBLIKE	CHICKENING	CHILDISHNESS	CHIMNEYLIKE	CHIROGNOMISTS
CHERVONETS	CHICKENPOX	CHILDISHNESSES	CHIMNEYPIECE	CHIROGNOMY
CHESSBOARD	CHICKENPOXES	CHILDLESSNESS	CHIMNEYPIECES	CHIROGRAPH
CHESSBOARDS	CHICKENSHIT	CHILDLESSNESSES	CHIMNEYPOT	CHIROGRAPHER
CHESSBOXING	CHICKENSHITS	CHILDLIEST	CHIMNEYPOTS	CHIROGRAPHERS
CHESSBOXINGS	CHICKLINGS	CHILDLIKENESS	CHIMPANZEE	CHIROGRAPHIC
CHESSPIECE	CHICKORIES	CHILDLIKENESSES	CHIMPANZEES	CHIROGRAPHICAL
CHESSPIECES	CHICKWEEDS	CHILDMINDER	CHINABERRIES	CHIROGRAPHIES

CHIROGRAPHIST
CHIROGRAPHISTS
CHIROGRAPHS
CHIROGRAPHY
CHIROLOGIES
CHIROLOGIST
CHIROLOGISTS
CHIROMANCER
CHIROMANCERS
CHIROMANCIES
CHIROMANCY
CHIROMANTIC
CHIROMANTICAL
CHIRONOMER
CHIRONOMERS
CHIRONOMIC
CHIRONOMID
CHIRONOMIDS
CHIRONOMIES
CHIROPODIAL
CHIROPODIES
CHIROPODIST
CHIROPODISTS
CHIROPRACTIC
CHIROPRACTICS
CHIROPRACTOR
CHIROPRACTORS
CHIROPTERAN
CHIROPTERANS
CHIROPTEROUS
CHIROPTERS
CHIRPINESS
CHIRPINESSES
CHIRRUPERS
CHIRRUPIER
CHIRRUPIEST
CHIRRUPING
CHIRURGEON
CHIRURGEONLY
CHIRURGEONS
CHIRURGERIES
CHIRURGERY
CHIRURGICAL
CHISELLERS
CHISELLING
CHISELLINGS
CHITARRONE
CHITARRONI
CHITCHATTED

CHITCHATTING
CHITTAGONG
CHITTAGONGS
CHITTERING
CHITTERINGS
CHITTERLING
CHITTERLINGS
CHIVALRESQUE
CHIVALRIES
CHIVALROUS
CHIVALROUSLY
CHIVALROUSNESS
CHIVAREEING
CHIVARIING
CHIWEENIES
CHIYOGAMIS
CHLAMYDATE
CHLAMYDEOUS
CHLAMYDIAE
CHLAMYDIAL
CHLAMYDIAS
CHLAMYDOMONADES
CHLAMYDOMONAS
CHLAMYDOSPORE
CHLAMYDOSPORES
CHLOANTHITE
CHLOANTHITES
CHLOASMATA
CHLORACETIC
CHLORACNES
CHLORALISM
CHLORALISMS
CHLORALOSE
CHLORALOSED
CHLORALOSES
CHLORAMBUCIL
CHLORAMBUCILS
CHLORAMINE
CHLORAMINES
CHLORAMPHENICOL
CHLORARGYRITE
CHLORARGYRITES
CHLORDANES
CHLORELLAS
CHLORENCHYMA
CHLORENCHYMAS
CHLORHEXIDINE
CHLORHEXIDINES
CHLORIDATE

CHLORIDATED
CHLORIDATES
CHLORIDATING
CHLORIDISE
CHLORIDISED
CHLORIDISES
CHLORIDISING
CHLORIDIZE
CHLORIDIZED
CHLORIDIZES
CHLORIDIZING
CHLORIMETER
CHLORIMETERS
CHLORIMETRIC
CHLORIMETRIES
CHLORIMETRY
CHLORINATE
CHLORINATED
CHLORINATES
CHLORINATING
CHLORINATION
CHLORINATIONS
CHLORINATOR
CHLORINATORS
CHLORINISE
CHLORINISED
CHLORINISES
CHLORINISING
CHLORINITIES
CHLORINITY
CHLORINIZE
CHLORINIZED
CHLORINIZES
CHLORINIZING
CHLORITISATION
CHLORITISATIONS
CHLORITIZATION
CHLORITIZATIONS
CHLOROACETIC
CHLOROARGYRITE
CHLOROBENZENE
CHLOROBENZENES
CHLOROBROMIDE
CHLOROBROMIDES
CHLOROCALCITE
CHLOROCALCITES
CHLOROCRUORIN
CHLOROCRUORINS
CHLORODYNE

CHLORODYNES
CHLOROETHENE
CHLOROETHENES
CHLOROETHYLENE
CHLOROETHYLENES
CHLOROFORM
CHLOROFORMED
CHLOROFORMER
CHLOROFORMERS
CHLOROFORMING
CHLOROFORMIST
CHLOROFORMISTS
CHLOROFORMS
CHLOROHYDRIN
CHLOROHYDRINS
CHLOROMETER
CHLOROMETERS
CHLOROMETHANE
CHLOROMETHANES
CHLOROMETRIC
CHLOROMETRIES
CHLOROMETRY
CHLOROPHYL
CHLOROPHYLL
CHLOROPHYLLOID
CHLOROPHYLLOUS
CHLOROPHYLLS
CHLOROPHYLS
CHLOROPHYTUM
CHLOROPHYTUMS
CHLOROPICRIN
CHLOROPICRINS
CHLOROPLAST
CHLOROPLASTAL
CHLOROPLASTIC
CHLOROPLASTS
CHLOROPRENE
CHLOROPRENES
CHLOROQUIN
CHLOROQUINE
CHLOROQUINES
CHLOROQUINS
CHLOROSISES
CHLOROTHIAZIDE
CHLOROTHIAZIDES
CHLORPICRIN
CHLORPICRINS
CHLORPROMAZINE
CHLORPROMAZINES

CHLORPROPAMIDE
CHLORPROPAMIDES
CHLORTHALIDONE
CHLORTHALIDONES
CHOANOCYTE
CHOANOCYTES
CHOCAHOLIC
CHOCAHOLICS
CHOCKABLOCK
CHOCKSTONE
CHOCKSTONES
CHOCOHOLIC
CHOCOHOLICS
CHOCOLATES
CHOCOLATEY
CHOCOLATIER
CHOCOLATIERS
CHOCOLATIEST
CHOICENESS
CHOICENESSES
CHOIRGIRLS
CHOIRMASTER
CHOIRMASTERS
CHOIRSCREEN
CHOIRSCREENS
CHOIRSTALL
CHOIRSTALLS
CHOKEBERRIES
CHOKEBERRY
CHOKEBORES
CHOKECHERRIES
CHOKECHERRY
CHOKECOILS
CHOKEDAMPS
CHOKEHOLDS
CHOLAEMIAS
CHOLAGOGIC
CHOLAGOGUE
CHOLAGOGUES
CHOLANGIOGRAM
CHOLANGIOGRAMS
CHOLANGIOGRAPHY
CHOLECALCIFEROL
CHOLECYSTECTOMY
CHOLECYSTITIDES
CHOLECYSTITIS
CHOLECYSTITISES
CHOLECYSTOKININ
CHOLECYSTOSTOMY

C

CHOLECYSTOTOMY	CHONDROGENESIS	CHOREOGRAPHED	CHOUNTERING	CHROMATOGRAPHER
CHOLECYSTS	CHONDROITIN	CHOREOGRAPHER	CHOWDERHEAD	CHROMATOGRAPHIC
CHOLELITHIASES	CHONDROITINS	CHOREOGRAPHERS	CHOWDERHEADED	CHROMATOGRAPHS
CHOLELITHIASIS	CHONDROMAS	CHOREOGRAPHIC	CHOWDERHEADS	CHROMATOGRAPHY
CHOLELITHS	CHONDROMATA	CHOREOGRAPHIES	CHOWDERING	CHROMATOID
CHOLERICALLY	CHONDROMATOSES	CHOREOGRAPHING	CHOWHOUNDS	CHROMATOLOGIES
CHOLERICLY	CHONDROMATOSIS	CHOREOGRAPHS	CHOWKIDARS	CHROMATOLOGIST
CHOLESTASES	CHONDROMATOUS	CHOREOGRAPHY	CHREMATIST	CHROMATOLOGISTS
CHOLESTASIS	CHONDROPHORE	CHOREOLOGIES	CHREMATISTIC	CHROMATOLOGY
CHOLESTATIC	CHONDROPHORES	CHOREOLOGIST	CHREMATISTICS	CHROMATOLYSES
CHOLESTERATE	CHONDROPHORINE	CHOREOLOGISTS	CHREMATISTS	CHROMATOLYSIS
CHOLESTERATES	CHONDROPHORINES	CHOREOLOGY	CHRESTOMATHIC	CHROMATOLYTIC
CHOLESTERIC	CHONDROSAMINE	CHOREPISCOPAL	CHRESTOMATHICAL	CHROMATOPHORE
CHOLESTERIN	CHONDROSAMINES	CHORIAMBIC	CHRESTOMATHIES	CHROMATOPHORES
CHOLESTERINS	CHONDROSKELETON	CHORIAMBICS	CHRESTOMATHY	CHROMATOPHORIC
CHOLESTEROL	CHONDROSTIAN	CHORIAMBUS	CHRISMATION	CHROMATOPHOROUS
CHOLESTEROLEMIA	CHONDROSTIANS	CHORIAMBUSES	CHRISMATIONS	CHROMATOPSIA
CHOLESTEROLS	CHONDRULES	CHORIOALLANTOIC	CHRISMATORIES	CHROMATOPSIAS
CHOLESTYRAMINE	CHOPFALLEN	CHORIOALLANTOIS	CHRISMATORY	CHROMATOSPHERE
CHOLESTYRAMINES	CHOPHOUSES	CHORIOCARCINOMA	CHRISTCROSS	CHROMATOSPHERES
CHOLIAMBIC	CHOPLOGICS	CHORISATION	CHRISTCROSSES	CHROMATYPE
CHOLIAMBICS	CHOPPERING	CHORISATIONS	CHRISTENED	CHROMATYPES
CHOLINERGIC	CHOPPINESS	CHORISTERS	CHRISTENER	CHROMIDIUM
CHOLINERGICALLY	CHOPPINESSES	CHORIZATION	CHRISTENERS	CHROMINANCE
CHOLINESTERASE	CHOPSOCKIES	CHORIZATIONS	CHRISTENING	CHROMINANCES
CHOLINESTERASES	CHOPSTICKS	CHORIZONTIST	CHRISTENINGS	CHROMISING
CHOMOPHYTE	CHORAGUSES	CHORIZONTISTS	CHRISTIANIA	CHROMIZING
CHOMOPHYTES	CHORALISTS	CHORIZONTS	CHRISTIANIAS	CHROMOCENTER
CHONDRICHTHYAN	CHORDAMESODERM	CHOROGRAPHER	CHRISTOPHANIES	CHROMOCENTERS
CHONDRICHTHYANS	CHORDAMESODERMS	CHOROGRAPHERS	CHRISTOPHANY	CHROMOCENTRE
CHONDRIFICATION	CHORDOPHONE	CHOROGRAPHIC	CHROMAFFIN	CHROMOCENTRES
CHONDRIFIED	CHORDOPHONES	CHOROGRAPHICAL	CHROMAKEYS	CHROMODYNAMICS
CHONDRIFIES	CHORDOPHONIC	CHOROGRAPHIES	CHROMATICALLY	CHROMOGENIC
CHONDRIFYING	CHORDOTOMIES	CHOROGRAPHY	CHROMATICISM	CHROMOGENS
CHONDRIOSOMAL	CHORDOTOMY	CHOROIDITIS	CHROMATICISMS	CHROMOGRAM
CHONDRIOSOME	CHOREGRAPH	CHOROIDITISES	CHROMATICITIES	CHROMOGRAMS
CHONDRIOSOMES	CHOREGRAPHED	CHOROLOGICAL	CHROMATICITY	CHROMOLIES
CHONDRITES	CHOREGRAPHER	CHOROLOGIES	CHROMATICNESS	CHROMOMERE
CHONDRITIC	CHOREGRAPHERS	CHOROLOGIST	CHROMATICNESSES	CHROMOMERES
CHONDRITIS	CHOREGRAPHIC	CHOROLOGISTS	CHROMATICS	CHROMOMERIC
CHONDRITISES	CHOREGRAPHIES	CHOROPLETH	CHROMATIDS	CHROMONEMA
CHONDROBLAST	CHOREGRAPHING	CHOROPLETHS	CHROMATINIC	CHROMONEMAL
CHONDROBLASTS	CHOREGRAPHS	CHORUSMASTER	CHROMATINS	CHROMONEMATA
CHONDROCRANIA	CHOREGRAPHY	CHORUSMASTERS	CHROMATIST	CHROMONEMATIC
CHONDROCRANIUM	CHOREGUSES	CHORUSSING	CHROMATISTS	CHROMONEMIC
CHONDROCRANIUMS	CHOREIFORM	CHOUCROUTE	CHROMATOGRAM	CHROMOPHIL
CHONDROCYTE	CHOREODRAMA	CHOUCROUTES	CHROMATOGRAMS	CHROMOPHILIC
CHONDROCYTES	CHOREODRAMAS	CHOULTRIES	CHROMATOGRAPH	CHROMOPHILS
CHONDROGENESES	CHOREOGRAPH	CHOUNTERED	CHROMATOGRAPHED	CHROMOPHOBE

CHROMOPHOBES	CHRONOLOGICAL	CHRYSOPHILITE	CHURCHLINESS	CICATRICLES
CHROMOPHORE	CHRONOLOGICALLY	CHRYSOPHILITES	CHURCHLINESSES	CICATRICOSE
CHROMOPHORES	CHRONOLOGIES	CHRYSOPHYTE	CHURCHMANLIER	CICATRICULA
CHROMOPHORIC	CHRONOLOGISE	CHRYSOPHYTES	CHURCHMANLIEST	CICATRICULAS
CHROMOPHOROUS	CHRONOLOGISED	CHRYSOPRASE	CHURCHMANLY	CICATRISANT
CHROMOPLAST	CHRONOLOGISES	CHRYSOPRASES	CHURCHMANSHIP	CICATRISATION
CHROMOPLASTS	CHRONOLOGISING	CHRYSOTILE	CHURCHMANSHIPS	CICATRISATIONS
CHROMOPROTEIN	CHRONOLOGIST	CHRYSOTILES	CHURCHPEOPLE	CICATRISED
CHROMOPROTEINS	CHRONOLOGISTS	CHUBBINESS	CHURCHWARD	CICATRISER
CHROMOSCOPE	CHRONOLOGIZE	CHUBBINESSES	CHURCHWARDEN	CICATRISERS
CHROMOSCOPES	CHRONOLOGIZED	CHUCKAWALLA	CHURCHWARDENS	CICATRISES
CHROMOSOMAL	CHRONOLOGIZES	CHUCKAWALLAS	CHURCHWARDS	CICATRISING
CHROMOSOMALLY	CHRONOLOGIZING	CHUCKHOLES	CHURCHWAYS	CICATRIXES
CHROMOSOME	CHRONOLOGY	CHUCKLEHEAD	CHURCHWOMAN	CICATRIZANT
CHROMOSOMES	CHRONOMETER	CHUCKLEHEADED	CHURCHWOMEN	CICATRIZATION
CHROMOSPHERE	CHRONOMETERS	CHUCKLEHEADS	CHURCHYARD	CICATRIZATIONS
CHROMOSPHERES	CHRONOMETRIC	CHUCKLESOME	CHURCHYARDS	CICATRIZED
CHROMOSPHERIC	CHRONOMETRICAL	CHUCKLINGLY	CHURLISHLY	CICATRIZER
CHROMOTHERAPIES	CHRONOMETRIES	CHUCKLINGS	CHURLISHNESS	CICATRIZERS
CHROMOTHERAPY	CHRONOMETRY	CHUCKWALLA	CHURLISHNESSES	CICATRIZES
CHROMOTYPE	CHRONOSCOPE	CHUCKWALLAS	CHURNALISM	CICATRIZING
CHROMOTYPES	CHRONOSCOPES	CHUFFINESS	CHURNALISMS	CICERONEING
CHROMOXYLOGRAPH	CHRONOSCOPIC	CHUFFINESSES	CHURNMILKS	CICHORACEOUS
CHRONAXIES	CHRONOTHERAPIES	CHUGALUGGED	CHURRIGUERESCO	CICINNUSES
CHRONICALLY	CHRONOTHERAPY	CHUGALUGGING	CHURRIGUERESQUE	CICISBEISM
CHRONICITIES	CHRONOTRON	CHUMMINESS	CHYLACEOUS	CICISBEISMS
CHRONICITY	CHRONOTRONS	CHUMMINESSES	CHYLIFEROUS	CICLATOUNS
CHRONICLED	CHRYSALIDAL	CHUNDERING	CHYLIFICATION	CICLOSPORIN
CHRONICLER	CHRYSALIDES	CHUNDEROUS	CHYLIFICATIONS	CICLOSPORINS
CHRONICLERS	CHRYSALIDS	CHUNKINESS	CHYLIFYING	CIGARETTES
CHRONICLES	CHRYSALISES	CHUNKINESSES	CHYLOMICRON	CIGARILLOS
CHRONICLING	CHRYSANTHEMUM	CHUNNERING	CHYLOMICRONS	CIGUATERAS
CHRONOBIOLOGIC	CHRYSANTHEMUMS	CHUNTERING	CHYMIFEROUS	CIGUATOXIN
CHRONOBIOLOGIES	CHRYSANTHS	CHUPATTIES	CHYMIFICATION	CIGUATOXINS
CHRONOBIOLOGIST	CHRYSAROBIN	CHUPRASSIES	CHYMIFICATIONS	CILIATIONS
CHRONOBIOLOGY	CHRYSAROBINS	CHURCHGOER	CHYMIFYING	CIMETIDINE
CHRONOGRAM	CHRYSOBERYL	CHURCHGOERS	CHYMISTRIES	CIMETIDINES
CHRONOGRAMMATIC	CHRYSOBERYLS	CHURCHGOING	CHYMOTRYPSIN	CINCHONACEOUS
CHRONOGRAMS	CHRYSOCOLLA	CHURCHGOINGS	CHYMOTRYPSINS	CINCHONIDINE
CHRONOGRAPH	CHRYSOCOLLAS	CHURCHIANITIES	CHYMOTRYPTIC	CINCHONIDINES
CHRONOGRAPHER	CHRYSOCRACIES	CHURCHIANITY	CIBACHROME	CINCHONINE
CHRONOGRAPHERS	CHRYSOCRACY	CHURCHIEST	CIBACHROMES	CINCHONINES
CHRONOGRAPHIC	CHRYSOLITE	CHURCHINESS	CICADELLID	CINCHONINIC
CHRONOGRAPHIES	CHRYSOLITES	CHURCHINESSES	CICADELLIDS	CINCHONISATION
CHRONOGRAPHS	CHRYSOLITIC	CHURCHINGS	CICATRICES	CINCHONISATIONS
CHRONOGRAPHY	CHRYSOMELID	CHURCHISMS	CICATRICHULE	CINCHONISE
CHRONOLOGER	CHRYSOMELIDS	CHURCHLESS	CICATRICHULES	CINCHONISED
CHRONOLOGERS	CHRYSOPHAN	CHURCHLIER	CICATRICIAL	CINCHONISES
CHRONOLOGIC	CHRYSOPHANS	CHURCHLIEST	CICATRICLE	CINCHONISING

CINCHONISM	CINNARIZINES	CIRCULARNESSES	CIRCUMFERENCE	CIRCUMMURES
CINCHONISMS	CINQUECENTIST	CIRCULATABLE	CIRCUMFERENCES	CIRCUMMURING
CINCHONIZATION	CINQUECENTISTS	CIRCULATED	CIRCUMFERENTIAL	CIRCUMNAVIGABLE
CINCHONIZATIONS	CINQUECENTO	CIRCULATES	CIRCUMFERENTOR	CIRCUMNAVIGATE
CINCHONIZE	CINQUECENTOS	CIRCULATING	CIRCUMFERENTORS	CIRCUMNAVIGATED
CINCHONIZED	CINQUEFOIL	CIRCULATINGS	CIRCUMFLECT	CIRCUMNAVIGATES
CINCHONIZES	CINQUEFOILS	CIRCULATION	CIRCUMFLECTED	CIRCUMNAVIGATOR
CINCHONIZING	CIPHERINGS	CIRCULATIONS	CIRCUMFLECTING	CIRCUMNUTATE
CINCINNATE	CIPHERTEXT	CIRCULATIVE	CIRCUMFLECTS	CIRCUMNUTATED
CINCINNUSES	CIPHERTEXTS	CIRCULATOR	CIRCUMFLEX	CIRCUMNUTATES
CINCTURING	CIPOLLINOS	CIRCULATORS	CIRCUMFLEXES	CIRCUMNUTATING
CINDERIEST	CIPROFLOXACIN	CIRCULATORY	CIRCUMFLEXION	CIRCUMNUTATION
CINEANGIOGRAPHY	CIPROFLOXACINS	CIRCUMAMBAGES	CIRCUMFLEXIONS	CIRCUMNUTATIONS
CINEMAGOER	CIRCASSIAN	CIRCUMAMBAGIOUS	CIRCUMFLUENCE	CIRCUMNUTATORY
CINEMAGOERS	CIRCASSIANS	CIRCUMAMBIENCE	CIRCUMFLUENCES	CIRCUMPOLAR
CINEMATHEQUE	CIRCASSIENNE	CIRCUMAMBIENCES	CIRCUMFLUENT	CIRCUMPOSE
CINEMATHEQUES	CIRCASSIENNES	CIRCUMAMBIENCY	CIRCUMFLUOUS	CIRCUMPOSED
CINEMATICALLY	CIRCENSIAL	CIRCUMAMBIENT	CIRCUMFORANEAN	CIRCUMPOSES
CINEMATISE	CIRCENSIAN	CIRCUMAMBIENTLY	CIRCUMFORANEOUS	CIRCUMPOSING
CINEMATISED	CIRCINATELY	CIRCUMAMBULATE	CIRCUMFUSE	CIRCUMPOSITION
CINEMATISES	CIRCUITEER	CIRCUMAMBULATED	CIRCUMFUSED	CIRCUMPOSITIONS
CINEMATISING	CIRCUITEERED	CIRCUMAMBULATES	CIRCUMFUSES	CIRCUMROTATE
CINEMATIZE	CIRCUITEERING	CIRCUMAMBULATOR	CIRCUMFUSILE	CIRCUMROTATED
CINEMATIZED	CIRCUITEERS	CIRCUMBENDIBUS	CIRCUMFUSING	CIRCUMROTATES
CINEMATIZES	CIRCUITIES	CIRCUMCENTER	CIRCUMFUSION	CIRCUMROTATING
CINEMATIZING	CIRCUITING	CIRCUMCENTERS	CIRCUMFUSIONS	CIRCUMSCISSILE
CINEMATOGRAPH	CIRCUITOUS	CIRCUMCENTRE	CIRCUMGYRATE	CIRCUMSCRIBABLE
CINEMATOGRAPHED	CIRCUITOUSLY	CIRCUMCENTRES	CIRCUMGYRATED	CIRCUMSCRIBE
CINEMATOGRAPHER	CIRCUITOUSNESS	CIRCUMCIRCLE	CIRCUMGYRATES	CIRCUMSCRIBED
CINEMATOGRAPHIC	CIRCUITRIES	CIRCUMCIRCLES	CIRCUMGYRATING	CIRCUMSCRIBER
CINEMATOGRAPHS	CIRCULABLE	CIRCUMCISE	CIRCUMGYRATION	CIRCUMSCRIBERS
CINEMATOGRAPHY	CIRCULARISATION	CIRCUMCISED	CIRCUMGYRATIONS	CIRCUMSCRIBES
CINEMICROGRAPHY	CIRCULARISE	CIRCUMCISER	CIRCUMGYRATORY	CIRCUMSCRIBING
CINEPHILES	CIRCULARISED	CIRCUMCISERS	CIRCUMINCESSION	CIRCUMSCRIPTION
CINEPLEXES	CIRCULARISER	CIRCUMCISES	CIRCUMINSESSION	CIRCUMSCRIPTIVE
CINERARIAS	CIRCULARISERS	CIRCUMCISING	CIRCUMJACENCIES	CIRCUMSOLAR
CINERARIUM	CIRCULARISES	CIRCUMCISION	CIRCUMJACENCY	CIRCUMSPECT
CINERARIUMS	CIRCULARISING	CIRCUMCISIONS	CIRCUMJACENT	CIRCUMSPECTION
CINERATION	CIRCULARITIES	CIRCUMDUCE	CIRCUMLITTORAL	CIRCUMSPECTIONS
CINERATIONS	CIRCULARITY	CIRCUMDUCED	CIRCUMLOCUTE	CIRCUMSPECTIVE
CINERATORS	CIRCULARIZATION	CIRCUMDUCES	CIRCUMLOCUTED	CIRCUMSPECTLY
CINERITIOUS	CIRCULARIZE	CIRCUMDUCING	CIRCUMLOCUTES	CIRCUMSPECTNESS
CINGULATED	CIRCULARIZED	CIRCUMDUCT	CIRCUMLOCUTING	CIRCUMSTANCE
CINNABARIC	CIRCULARIZER	CIRCUMDUCTED	CIRCUMLOCUTION	CIRCUMSTANCED
CINNABARINE	CIRCULARIZERS	CIRCUMDUCTING	CIRCUMLOCUTIONS	CIRCUMSTANCES
CINNAMONIC	CIRCULARIZES	CIRCUMDUCTION	CIRCUMLOCUTORY	CIRCUMSTANCING
CINNAMONIER	CIRCULARIZING	CIRCUMDUCTIONS	CIRCUMLUNAR	CIRCUMSTANTIAL
CINNAMONIEST	CIRCULARLY	CIRCUMDUCTORY	CIRCUMMURE	CIRCUMSTANTIALS
CINNARIZINE	CIRCULARNESS	CIRCUMDUCTS	CIRCUMMURED	CIRCUMSTANTIATE

CIRCUMSTELLAR
CIRCUMVALLATE
CIRCUMVALLATED
CIRCUMVALLATES
CIRCUMVALLATING
CIRCUMVALLATION
CIRCUMVENT
CIRCUMVENTED
CIRCUMVENTER
CIRCUMVENTERS
CIRCUMVENTING
CIRCUMVENTION
CIRCUMVENTIONS
CIRCUMVENTIVE
CIRCUMVENTOR
CIRCUMVENTORS
CIRCUMVENTS
CIRCUMVOLUTION
CIRCUMVOLUTIONS
CIRCUMVOLUTORY
CIRCUMVOLVE
CIRCUMVOLVED
CIRCUMVOLVES
CIRCUMVOLVING
CIRCUSIEST
CIRCUSSIER
CIRCUSSIEST
CIRRHIPEDE
CIRRHIPEDES
CIRRHOTICS
CIRRIGRADE
CIRRIPEDES
CIRROCUMULI
CIRROCUMULUS
CIRROSTRATI
CIRROSTRATIVE
CIRROSTRATUS
CISGENDERED
CISMONTANE
CISPLATINS
CISPONTINE
CISTACEOUS
CITATIONAL
CITHARISTIC
CITHARISTS
CITIFICATION
CITIFICATIONS
CITIZENESS
CITIZENESSES

CITIZENISE
CITIZENISED
CITIZENISES
CITIZENISING
CITIZENIZE
CITIZENIZED
CITIZENIZES
CITIZENIZING
CITIZENLIER
CITIZENLIEST
CITIZENRIES
CITIZENSHIP
CITIZENSHIPS
CITRICULTURE
CITRICULTURES
CITRICULTURIST
CITRICULTURISTS
CITRONELLA
CITRONELLAL
CITRONELLALS
CITRONELLAS
CITRONELLOL
CITRONELLOLS
CITRULLINE
CITRULLINES
CITRUSIEST
CITRUSSIER
CITRUSSIEST
CITYFICATION
CITYFICATIONS
CITYSCAPES
CIVILIANISATION
CIVILIANISE
CIVILIANISED
CIVILIANISES
CIVILIANISING
CIVILIANIZATION
CIVILIANIZE
CIVILIANIZED
CIVILIANIZES
CIVILIANIZING
CIVILISABLE
CIVILISATION
CIVILISATIONAL
CIVILISATIONS
CIVILISERS
CIVILISING
CIVILITIES
CIVILIZABLE

CIVILIZATION
CIVILIZATIONAL
CIVILIZATIONS
CIVILIZERS
CIVILIZING
CIVILNESSES
CLABBERING
CLACKBOXES
CLACKDISHES
CLADISTICALLY
CLADISTICS
CLADOCERAN
CLADOCERANS
CLADOGENESES
CLADOGENESIS
CLADOGENETIC
CLADOGRAMS
CLADOPHYLL
CLADOPHYLLS
CLADOSPORIA
CLADOSPORIUM
CLAIRAUDIENCE
CLAIRAUDIENCES
CLAIRAUDIENT
CLAIRAUDIENTLY
CLAIRAUDIENTS
CLAIRCOLLE
CLAIRCOLLES
CLAIRSCHACH
CLAIRSCHACHS
CLAIRVOYANCE
CLAIRVOYANCES
CLAIRVOYANCIES
CLAIRVOYANCY
CLAIRVOYANT
CLAIRVOYANTLY
CLAIRVOYANTS
CLAMANCIES
CLAMATORIAL
CLAMBERERS
CLAMBERING
CLAMJAMFRIES
CLAMJAMFRY
CLAMJAMPHRIE
CLAMJAMPHRIES
CLAMMINESS
CLAMMINESSES
CLAMOROUSLY
CLAMOROUSNESS

CLAMOROUSNESSES
CLAMOURERS
CLAMOURING
CLAMPDOWNS
CLAMPERING
CLAMSHELLS
CLANDESTINE
CLANDESTINELY
CLANDESTINENESS
CLANDESTINITIES
CLANDESTINITY
CLANGBOXES
CLANGORING
CLANGOROUS
CLANGOROUSLY
CLANGOURED
CLANGOURING
CLANJAMFRAY
CLANJAMFRAYS
CLANKINGLY
CLANNISHLY
CLANNISHNESS
CLANNISHNESSES
CLANSWOMAN
CLANSWOMEN
CLAPBOARDED
CLAPBOARDING
CLAPBOARDS
CLAPBREADS
CLAPDISHES
CLAPOMETER
CLAPOMETERS
CLAPPERBOARD
CLAPPERBOARDS
CLAPPERBOY
CLAPPERBOYS
CLAPPERCLAW
CLAPPERCLAWED
CLAPPERCLAWER
CLAPPERCLAWERS
CLAPPERCLAWING
CLAPPERCLAWS
CLAPPERING
CLAPPERINGS
CLAPTRAPPERIES
CLAPTRAPPERY
CLARABELLA
CLARABELLAS
CLARENDONS

CLARIBELLA
CLARIBELLAS
CLARICHORD
CLARICHORDS
CLARIFICATION
CLARIFICATIONS
CLARIFIERS
CLARIFYING
CLARINETIST
CLARINETISTS
CLARINETTIST
CLARINETTISTS
CLARIONETS
CLARIONING
CLARTHEADS
CLASHINGLY
CLASSICALISM
CLASSICALISMS
CLASSICALIST
CLASSICALISTS
CLASSICALITIES
CLASSICALITY
CLASSICALLY
CLASSICALNESS
CLASSICALNESSES
CLASSICALS
CLASSICISE
CLASSICISED
CLASSICISES
CLASSICISING
CLASSICISM
CLASSICISMS
CLASSICIST
CLASSICISTIC
CLASSICISTS
CLASSICIZE
CLASSICIZED
CLASSICIZES
CLASSICIZING
CLASSIFIABLE
CLASSIFICATION
CLASSIFICATIONS
CLASSIFICATORY
CLASSIFIED
CLASSIFIEDS
CLASSIFIER
CLASSIFIERS
CLASSIFIES
CLASSIFYING

CLASSINESS	CLAYSTONES	CLEPTOCRACIES	CLICKTIVIST	CLINGINGNESS
CLASSINESSES	CLAYTONIAS	CLEPTOCRACY	CLICKTIVISTS	CLINGINGNESSES
CLASSLESSNESS	CLEANABILITIES	CLEPTOMANIA	CLICKWRAPS	CLINGSTONE
CLASSLESSNESSES	CLEANABILITY	CLEPTOMANIAC	CLIENTAGES	CLINGSTONES
CLASSMATES	CLEANHANDED	CLEPTOMANIACS	CLIENTELES	CLINGWRAPS
CLASSROOMS	CLEANLIEST	CLEPTOMANIAS	CLIENTLESS	CLINICALLY
CLASSWORKS	CLEANLINESS	CLERESTORIED	CLIENTSHIP	CLINICALNESS
CLATHRATES	CLEANLINESSES	CLERESTORIES	CLIENTSHIPS	CLINICALNESSES
CLATTERERS	CLEANNESSES	CLERESTORY	CLIFFHANGER	CLINICIANS
CLATTERIER	CLEANSABLE	CLERGIABLE	CLIFFHANGERS	CLINKERING
CLATTERIEST	CLEANSINGS	CLERGYABLE	CLIFFHANGING	CLINKSTONE
CLATTERING	CLEANSKINS	CLERGYWOMAN	CLIFFHANGINGS	CLINKSTONES
CLATTERINGLY	CLEANTECHS	CLERGYWOMEN	CLIFFHANGS	CLINOCHLORE
CLAUCHTING	CLEARANCES	CLERICALISM	CLIFFSIDES	CLINOCHLORES
CLAUDICATION	CLEARCOLED	CLERICALISMS	CLIMACTERIC	CLINODIAGONAL
CLAUDICATIONS	CLEARCOLES	CLERICALIST	CLIMACTERICAL	CLINODIAGONALS
CLAUGHTING	CLEARCOLING	CLERICALISTS	CLIMACTERICALLY	CLINOMETER
CLAUSTRATION	CLEARCUTTING	CLERICALLY	CLIMACTERICS	CLINOMETERS
CLAUSTRATIONS	CLEARCUTTINGS	CLERICATES	CLIMACTICAL	CLINOMETRIC
CLAUSTROPHILIA	CLEARHEADED	CLERICITIES	CLIMACTICALLY	CLINOMETRICAL
CLAUSTROPHILIAS	CLEARHEADEDLY	CLERKESSES	CLIMATICAL	CLINOMETRIES
CLAUSTROPHOBE	CLEARHEADEDNESS	CLERKLIEST	CLIMATICALLY	CLINOMETRY
CLAUSTROPHOBES	CLEARINGHOUSE	CLERKLINESS	CLIMATISED	CLINOPINACOID
CLAUSTROPHOBIA	CLEARINGHOUSES	CLERKLINESSES	CLIMATISES	CLINOPINACOIDS
CLAUSTROPHOBIAS	CLEARNESSES	CLERKLINGS	CLIMATISING	CLINOPINAKOID
CLAUSTROPHOBIC	CLEARSKINS	CLERKSHIPS	CLIMATIZED	CLINOPINAKOIDS
CLAVATIONS	CLEARSTORIED	CLEROMANCIES	CLIMATIZES	CLINOPYROXENE
CLAVECINIST	CLEARSTORIES	CLEROMANCY	CLIMATIZING	CLINOPYROXENES
CLAVECINISTS	CLEARSTORY	CLERUCHIAL	CLIMATOGRAPHIES	CLINOSTATS
CLAVICEMBALO	CLEARWEEDS	CLERUCHIAS	CLIMATOGRAPHY	CLINQUANTS
CLAVICEMBALOS	CLEARWINGS	CLERUCHIES	CLIMATOLOGIC	CLINTONIAS
CLAVICHORD	CLEAVABILITIES	CLEVERALITIES	CLIMATOLOGICAL	CLIOMETRIC
CLAVICHORDIST	CLEAVABILITY	CLEVERALITY	CLIMATOLOGIES	CLIOMETRICAL
CLAVICHORDISTS	CLEAVABLENESS	CLEVERDICK	CLIMATOLOGIST	CLIOMETRICIAN
CLAVICHORDS	CLEAVABLENESSES	CLEVERDICKS	CLIMATOLOGISTS	CLIOMETRICIANS
CLAVICORNS	CLEISTOGAMIC	CLEVERNESS	CLIMATOLOGY	CLIOMETRICS
CLAVICULAE	CLEISTOGAMIES	CLEVERNESSES	CLIMATURES	CLIOMETRIES
CLAVICULAR	CLEISTOGAMOUS	CLIANTHUSES	CLIMAXLESS	CLIPBOARDS
CLAVICULATE	CLEISTOGAMOUSLY	CLICKBAITED	CLIMBDOWNS	CLIPSHEARS
CLAVICYTHERIA	CLEISTOGAMY	CLICKBAITING	CLINANDRIA	CLIPSHEETS
CLAVICYTHERIUM	CLEMATISES	CLICKBAITINGS	CLINANDRIUM	CLIQUINESS
CLAVIERIST	CLEMENCIES	CLICKBAITS	CLINCHINGLY	CLIQUINESSES
CLAVIERISTIC	CLEMENTINE	CLICKETING	CLINDAMYCIN	CLIQUISHLY
CLAVIERISTS	CLEMENTINES	CLICKJACKING	CLINDAMYCINS	CLIQUISHNESS
CLAVIGEROUS	CLENBUTEROL	CLICKJACKINGS	CLINGFILMS	CLIQUISHNESSES
CLAWHAMMER	CLENBUTEROLS	CLICKSTREAM	CLINGFISHES	CLISHMACLAVER
CLAWHAMMERS	CLEOPATRAS	CLICKSTREAMS	CLINGINESS	CLISHMACLAVERS
CLAYMATION	CLEPSYDRAE	CLICKTIVISM	CLINGINESSES	CLISTOGAMIES
CLAYMATIONS	CLEPSYDRAS	CLICKTIVISMS	CLINGINGLY	CLISTOGAMY

C

CLITICISED	CLOSEHEADS	CLOWNISHNESSES	COACHLINES	COAGULATORS
CLITICISES	CLOSEMOUTHED	CLOXACILLIN	COACHLOADS	COAGULATORY
CLITICISING	CLOSENESSES	CLOXACILLINS	COACHROOFS	COALESCENCE
CLITICIZED	CLOSESTOOL	CLOZAPINES	COACHWHIPS	COALESCENCES
CLITICIZES	CLOSESTOOLS	CLUBABILITIES	COACHWOODS	COALESCENT
CLITICIZING	CLOSETFULS	CLUBABILITY	COACHWORKS	COALESCING
CLITORECTOMIES	CLOSTRIDIA	CLUBBABILITIES	COACTIVELY	COALFIELDS
CLITORECTOMY	CLOSTRIDIAL	CLUBBABILITY	COACTIVITIES	COALFISHES
CLITORIDECTOMY	CLOSTRIDIAN	CLUBBINESS	COACTIVITY	COALHOUSES
CLITORIDES	CLOSTRIDIUM	CLUBBINESSES	COADAPTATION	COALIFICATION
CLITORISES	CLOSTRIDIUMS	CLUBFOOTED	COADAPTATIONS	COALIFICATIONS
CLITTERING	CLOTHBOUND	CLUBHAULED	COADJACENCIES	COALIFYING
CLOACALINE	CLOTHESHORSE	CLUBHAULING	COADJACENCY	COALITIONAL
CLOACITISES	CLOTHESHORSES	CLUBHOUSES	COADJACENT	COALITIONER
CLOAKROOMS	CLOTHESLINE	CLUBMANSHIP	COADJACENTS	COALITIONERS
CLOBBERING	CLOTHESLINED	CLUBMANSHIPS	COADJUTANT	COALITIONISM
CLOCKFACES	CLOTHESLINES	CLUBMASTER	COADJUTANTS	COALITIONISMS
CLOCKMAKER	CLOTHESLINING	CLUBMASTERS	COADJUTORS	COALITIONIST
CLOCKMAKERS	CLOTHESPIN	CLUBMOSSES	COADJUTORSHIP	COALITIONISTS
CLOCKWORKS	CLOTHESPINS	CLUBRUSHES	COADJUTORSHIPS	COALITIONS
CLODDISHLY	CLOTHESPRESS	CLUMPERING	COADJUTRESS	COALMASTER
CLODDISHNESS	CLOTHESPRESSES	CLUMPINESS	COADJUTRESSES	COALMASTERS
CLODDISHNESSES	CLOTTERING	CLUMPINESSES	COADJUTRICES	COALMINERS
CLODHOPPER	CLOTTINESS	CLUMSINESS	COADJUTRIX	COANCHORED
CLODHOPPERS	CLOTTINESSES	CLUMSINESSES	COADJUTRIXES	COANCHORING
CLODHOPPING	CLOUDBERRIES	CLUSTERIER	COADMIRING	COANNEXING
CLOFIBRATE	CLOUDBERRY	CLUSTERIEST	COADMITTED	COAPPEARED
CLOFIBRATES	CLOUDBURST	CLUSTERING	COADMITTING	COAPPEARING
CLOGDANCES	CLOUDBURSTS	CLUSTERINGLY	COADUNATED	COAPTATION
CLOGGINESS	CLOUDINESS	CLUTCHIEST	COADUNATES	COAPTATIONS
CLOGGINESSES	CLOUDINESSES	CLUTTERIER	COADUNATING	COARCTATED
CLOGMAKERS	CLOUDLANDS	CLUTTERIEST	COADUNATION	COARCTATES
CLOISONNAGE	CLOUDLESSLY	CLUTTERING	COADUNATIONS	COARCTATING
CLOISONNAGES	CLOUDLESSNESS	CLYPEIFORM	COADUNATIVE	COARCTATION
CLOISONNES	CLOUDLESSNESSES	CNIDARIANS	COAEVALITIES	COARCTATIONS
CLOISTERED	CLOUDSCAPE	CNIDOBLAST	COAEVALITY	COARSENESS
CLOISTERER	CLOUDSCAPES	CNIDOBLASTS	COAGENCIES	COARSENESSES
CLOISTERERS	CLOUDTOWNS	CNIDOCYSTS	COAGULABILITIES	COARSENING
CLOISTERING	CLOVERGRASS	COACERVATE	COAGULABILITY	COASSISTED
CLOISTRESS	CLOVERGRASSES	COACERVATED	COAGULABLE	COASSISTING
CLOISTRESSES	CLOVERIEST	COACERVATES	COAGULANTS	COASSUMING
CLOMIPHENE	CLOVERLEAF	COACERVATING	COAGULASES	COASTEERING
CLOMIPHENES	CLOVERLEAFS	COACERVATION	COAGULATED	COASTEERINGS
CLONAZEPAM	CLOVERLEAVES	COACERVATIONS	COAGULATES	COASTGUARD
CLONAZEPAMS	CLOVERLIKE	COACHBUILDER	COAGULATING	COASTGUARDMAN
CLONICITIES	CLOWNERIES	COACHBUILDERS	COAGULATION	COASTGUARDMEN
CLONIDINES	CLOWNFISHES	COACHBUILDING	COAGULATIONS	COASTGUARDS
CLOSEDOWNS	CLOWNISHLY	COACHBUILDINGS	COAGULATIVE	COASTGUARDSMAN
CLOSEFISTED	CLOWNISHNESS	COACHBUILT	COAGULATOR	COASTGUARDSMEN

COASTLANDS	COCARCINOGENIC	COCKCHAFER	COCKTAILING	CODEPENDENT
COASTLINES	COCARCINOGENS	COCKCHAFERS	COCKTEASER	CODEPENDENTS
COASTWARDS	COCATALYST	COCKCROWING	COCKTEASERS	CODERIVING
COATDRESSES	COCATALYSTS	COCKCROWINGS	COCKTHROWING	CODESIGNED
COATIMUNDI	COCCIDIANS	COCKERNONIES	COCKTHROWINGS	CODESIGNING
COATIMUNDIS	COCCIDIOSES	COCKERNONY	COCKYLEEKIES	CODETERMINATION
COATSTANDS	COCCIDIOSIS	COCKEYEDLY	COCKYLEEKY	CODEVELOPED
COATTENDED	COCCIDIOSTAT	COCKEYEDNESS	COCOMPOSER	CODEVELOPER
COATTENDING	COCCIDIOSTATS	COCKEYEDNESSES	COCOMPOSERS	CODEVELOPERS
COATTESTED	COCCIFEROUS	COCKFIGHTING	COCONSCIOUS	CODEVELOPING
COATTESTING	COCCINEOUS	COCKFIGHTINGS	COCONSCIOUSES	CODEVELOPS
COAUTHORED	COCCOLITES	COCKFIGHTS	COCONSCIOUSNESS	CODICILLARY
COAUTHORING	COCCOLITHS	COCKHORSES	COCONSPIRATOR	CODICOLOGICAL
COAUTHORSHIP	COCHAIRING	COCKIELEEKIE	COCONSPIRATORS	CODICOLOGIES
COAUTHORSHIPS	COCHAIRMAN	COCKIELEEKIES	COCONUTTIER	CODICOLOGY
COBALAMINS	COCHAIRMANSHIP	COCKINESSES	COCONUTTIEST	CODIFIABILITIES
COBALTIFEROUS	COCHAIRMANSHIPS	COCKLEBOAT	COCOONERIES	CODIFIABILITY
COBALTINES	COCHAIRMEN	COCKLEBOATS	COCOONINGS	CODIFIABLE
COBALTITES	COCHAIRPERSON	COCKLEBURS	COCOUNSELED	CODIFICATION
COBBLERIES	COCHAIRPERSONS	COCKLEERTS	COCOUNSELING	CODIFICATIONS
COBBLESTONE	COCHAIRWOMAN	COCKLESHELL	COCOUNSELLED	CODIRECTED
COBBLESTONED	COCHAIRWOMEN	COCKLESHELLS	COCOUNSELLING	CODIRECTING
COBBLESTONES	COCHAMPION	COCKMATCHES	COCOUNSELS	CODIRECTION
COBBLESTONING	COCHAMPIONS	COCKNEYDOM	COCOZELLES	CODIRECTIONS
COBELLIGERENT	COCHINEALS	COCKNEYDOMS	COCREATING	CODIRECTOR
COBELLIGERENTS	COCHLEARES	COCKNEYFICATION	COCREATORS	CODIRECTORS
COBWEBBERIES	COCHLEARIFORM	COCKNEYFIED	COCULTIVATE	CODISCOVER
COBWEBBERY	COCHLEATED	COCKNEYFIES	COCULTIVATED	CODISCOVERED
COBWEBBIER	COCKABULLIES	COCKNEYFYING	COCULTIVATES	CODISCOVERER
COBWEBBIEST	COCKABULLY	COCKNEYISH	COCULTIVATING	CODISCOVERERS
COBWEBBING	COCKALEEKIE	COCKNEYISM	COCULTIVATION	CODISCOVERING
COCAINISATION	COCKALEEKIES	COCKNEYISMS	COCULTIVATIONS	CODISCOVERS
COCAINISATIONS	COCKALORUM	COCKNIFICATION	COCULTURED	CODOLOGIES
COCAINISED	COCKALORUMS	COCKNIFICATIONS	COCULTURES	CODOMINANCE
COCAINISES	COCKAMAMIE	COCKNIFIED	COCULTURING	CODOMINANCES
COCAINISING	COCKAMAMIER	COCKNIFIES	COCURATING	CODOMINANT
COCAINISMS	COCKAMAMIEST	COCKNIFYING	COCURATORS	CODOMINANTS
COCAINISTS	COCKATEELS	COCKROACHES	COCURRICULAR	CODSWALLOP
COCAINIZATION	COCKATIELS	COCKSCOMBS	COCUSWOODS	CODSWALLOPS
COCAINIZATIONS	COCKATRICE	COCKSFOOTS	CODEBREAKER	COECILIANS
COCAINIZED	COCKATRICES	COCKSINESS	CODEBREAKERS	COEDUCATION
COCAINIZES	COCKBILLED	COCKSINESSES	CODECLINATION	COEDUCATIONAL
COCAINIZING	COCKBILLING	COCKSURELY	CODECLINATIONS	COEDUCATIONALLY
COCAPTAINED	COCKBLOCKED	COCKSURENESS	CODEFENDANT	COEDUCATIONS
COCAPTAINING	COCKBLOCKER	COCKSURENESSES	CODEFENDANTS	COEFFICIENT
COCAPTAINS	COCKBLOCKERS	COCKSWAINED	CODEPENDENCE	COEFFICIENTS
COCARBOXYLASE	COCKBLOCKING	COCKSWAINING	CODEPENDENCES	COELACANTH
COCARBOXYLASES	COCKBLOCKINGS	COCKSWAINS	CODEPENDENCIES	COELACANTHIC
COCARCINOGEN	COCKBLOCKS	COCKTAILED	CODEPENDENCY	COELACANTHS

COELANAGLYPHIC	COENOSPECIES	COEXTENSIVE	COGNIZANCE	COIFFURING
COELENTERA	COENOSTEUM	COEXTENSIVELY	COGNIZANCES	COILABILITIES
COELENTERATE	COENOSTEUMS	COFAVORITE	COGNOMINAL	COILABILITY
COELENTERATES	COENZYMATIC	COFAVORITES	COGNOMINALLY	COINCIDENCE
COELENTERIC	COENZYMATICALLY	COFEATURED	COGNOMINATE	COINCIDENCES
COELENTERON	COEQUALITIES	COFEATURES	COGNOMINATED	COINCIDENCIES
COELENTERONS	COEQUALITY	COFEATURING	COGNOMINATES	COINCIDENCY
COELIOSCOPIES	COEQUALNESS	COFFEEHOUSE	COGNOMINATING	COINCIDENT
COELIOSCOPY	COEQUALNESSES	COFFEEHOUSES	COGNOMINATION	COINCIDENTAL
COELOMATES	COEQUATING	COFFEEMAKER	COGNOMINATIONS	COINCIDENTALLY
COELOMATIC	COERCIMETER	COFFEEMAKERS	COGNOSCENTE	COINCIDENTLY
COELOSTATS	COERCIMETERS	COFFEEPOTS	COGNOSCENTI	COINCIDING
COELUROSAUR	COERCIONIST	COFFERDAMS	COGNOSCIBLE	COINFECTED
COELUROSAURS	COERCIONISTS	COFFINITES	COGNOSCING	COINFECTING
COEMBODIED	COERCIVELY	COFINANCED	COHABITANT	COINFERRED
COEMBODIES	COERCIVENESS	COFINANCES	COHABITANTS	COINFERRING
COEMBODYING	COERCIVENESSES	COFINANCING	COHABITATION	COINHERENCE
COEMPLOYED	COERCIVITIES	COFOUNDERS	COHABITATIONS	COINHERENCES
COEMPLOYING	COERCIVITY	COFOUNDING	COHABITEES	COINHERING
COEMPTIONS	COERECTING	COFUNCTION	COHABITERS	COINHERITANCE
COENACTING	COESSENTIAL	COFUNCTIONS	COHABITING	COINHERITANCES
COENAESTHESES	COESSENTIALITY	COGENERATION	COHABITORS	COINHERITOR
COENAESTHESIA	COESSENTIALLY	COGENERATIONS	COHEIRESSES	COINHERITORS
COENAESTHESIAS	COESSENTIALNESS	COGENERATOR	COHERENCES	COINSTANTANEITY
COENAESTHESIS	COETANEOUS	COGENERATORS	COHERENCIES	COINSTANTANEOUS
COENAMORED	COETANEOUSLY	COGITATING	COHERENTLY	COINSURANCE
COENAMORING	COETANEOUSNESS	COGITATINGLY	COHERITORS	COINSURANCES
COENAMOURED	COETERNALLY	COGITATION	COHESIBILITIES	COINSURERS
COENAMOURING	COETERNITIES	COGITATIONS	COHESIBILITY	COINSURING
COENAMOURS	COETERNITY	COGITATIVE	COHESIONLESS	COINTERRED
COENDURING	COEVALITIES	COGITATIVELY	COHESIVELY	COINTERRING
COENENCHYMA	COEVOLUTION	COGITATIVENESS	COHESIVENESS	COINTREAUS
COENENCHYMAS	COEVOLUTIONARY	COGITATORS	COHESIVENESSES	COINVENTED
COENENCHYMATA	COEVOLUTIONS	COGNATENESS	COHIBITING	COINVENTING
COENENCHYME	COEVOLVING	COGNATENESSES	COHIBITION	COINVENTOR
COENENCHYMES	COEXECUTOR	COGNATIONS	COHIBITIONS	COINVENTORS
COENESTHESES	COEXECUTORS	COGNISABLE	COHIBITIVE	COINVESTED
COENESTHESIA	COEXECUTRICES	COGNISABLY	COHOBATING	COINVESTIGATOR
COENESTHESIAS	COEXECUTRIX	COGNISANCE	COHOMOLOGICAL	COINVESTIGATORS
COENESTHESIS	COEXECUTRIXES	COGNISANCES	COHOMOLOGIES	COINVESTING
COENESTHETIC	COEXERTING	COGNITIONAL	COHOMOLOGY	COINVESTOR
COENOBITES	COEXISTENCE	COGNITIONS	COHORTATIVE	COINVESTORS
COENOBITIC	COEXISTENCES	COGNITIVELY	COHORTATIVES	COKULORISES
COENOBITICAL	COEXISTENT	COGNITIVISM	COHOSTESSED	COLATITUDE
COENOBITISM	COEXISTING	COGNITIVISMS	COHOSTESSES	COLATITUDES
COENOBITISMS	COEXTENDED	COGNITIVITIES	COHOSTESSING	COLCANNONS
COENOCYTES	COEXTENDING	COGNITIVITY	COHOUSINGS	COLCHICINE
COENOCYTIC	COEXTENSION	COGNIZABLE	COHYPONYMS	COLCHICINES
COENOSARCS	COEXTENSIONS	COGNIZABLY	COIFFEUSES	COLCHICUMS

COLCOTHARS	COLLAGENIC	COLLECTIVELY	COLLIGATING	COLLOQUIALITIES
COLDBLOODS	COLLAGENOUS	COLLECTIVENESS	COLLIGATION	COLLOQUIALITY
COLDCOCKED	COLLAGISTS	COLLECTIVES	COLLIGATIONS	COLLOQUIALLY
COLDCOCKING	COLLAPSABILITY	COLLECTIVISE	COLLIGATIVE	COLLOQUIALNESS
COLDHEARTED	COLLAPSABLE	COLLECTIVISED	COLLIMATED	COLLOQUIALS
COLDHEARTEDLY	COLLAPSARS	COLLECTIVISES	COLLIMATES	COLLOQUIED
COLDHEARTEDNESS	COLLAPSIBILITY	COLLECTIVISING	COLLIMATING	COLLOQUIES
COLDHOUSES	COLLAPSIBLE	COLLECTIVISM	COLLIMATION	COLLOQUING
COLDNESSES	COLLAPSING	COLLECTIVISMS	COLLIMATIONS	COLLOQUISE
COLECTOMIES	COLLARBONE	COLLECTIVIST	COLLIMATOR	COLLOQUISED
COLEMANITE	COLLARBONES	COLLECTIVISTIC	COLLIMATORS	COLLOQUISES
COLEMANITES	COLLARETTE	COLLECTIVISTS	COLLINEARITIES	COLLOQUISING
COLEOPTERA	COLLARETTES	COLLECTIVITIES	COLLINEARITY	COLLOQUIST
COLEOPTERAL	COLLARLESS	COLLECTIVITY	COLLINEARLY	COLLOQUISTS
COLEOPTERAN	COLLARSTUD	COLLECTIVIZE	COLLINSIAS	COLLOQUIUM
COLEOPTERANS	COLLARSTUDS	COLLECTIVIZED	COLLIQUABLE	COLLOQUIUMS
COLEOPTERIST	COLLATABLE	COLLECTIVIZES	COLLIQUANT	COLLOQUIZE
COLEOPTERISTS	COLLATERAL	COLLECTIVIZING	COLLIQUATE	COLLOQUIZED
COLEOPTERON	COLLATERALISE	COLLECTORATE	COLLIQUATED	COLLOQUIZES
COLEOPTERONS	COLLATERALISED	COLLECTORATES	COLLIQUATES	COLLOQUIZING
COLEOPTEROUS	COLLATERALISES	COLLECTORS	COLLIQUATING	COLLOQUYING
COLEOPTERS	COLLATERALISING	COLLECTORSHIP	COLLIQUATION	COLLOTYPES
COLEOPTILE	COLLATERALITIES	COLLECTORSHIPS	COLLIQUATIONS	COLLOTYPIC
COLEOPTILES	COLLATERALITY	COLLEGIALISM	COLLIQUATIVE	COLLOTYPIES
COLEORHIZA	COLLATERALIZE	COLLEGIALISMS	COLLIQUESCENCE	COLLUCTATION
COLEORHIZAE	COLLATERALIZED	COLLEGIALITIES	COLLIQUESCENCES	COLLUCTATIONS
COLEORRHIZA	COLLATERALIZES	COLLEGIALITY	COLLISIONAL	COLLUSIONS
COLEORRHIZAE	COLLATERALIZING	COLLEGIALLY	COLLISIONALLY	COLLUSIVELY
COLESTIPOL	COLLATERALLY	COLLEGIANER	COLLISIONS	COLLUVIUMS
COLESTIPOLS	COLLATERALS	COLLEGIANERS	COLLOCATED	COLLYRIUMS
COLICKIEST	COLLATIONS	COLLEGIANS	COLLOCATES	COLLYWOBBLES
COLICROOTS	COLLEAGUED	COLLEGIATE	COLLOCATING	COLOBOMATA
COLICWEEDS	COLLEAGUES	COLLEGIATELY	COLLOCATION	COLOCATING
COLINEARITIES	COLLEAGUESHIP	COLLEGIATES	COLLOCATIONAL	COLOCYNTHS
COLINEARITY	COLLEAGUESHIPS	COLLEGIUMS	COLLOCATIONS	COLOGARITHM
COLIPHAGES	COLLEAGUING	COLLEMBOLAN	COLLOCUTOR	COLOGARITHMS
COLLABORATE	COLLECTABLE	COLLEMBOLANS	COLLOCUTORS	COLOMBARDS
COLLABORATED	COLLECTABLES	COLLEMBOLOUS	COLLOCUTORY	COLONELCIES
COLLABORATES	COLLECTANEA	COLLENCHYMA	COLLODIONS	COLONELLING
COLLABORATING	COLLECTEDLY	COLLENCHYMAS	COLLODIUMS	COLONELLINGS
COLLABORATION	COLLECTEDNESS	COLLENCHYMATA	COLLOGUING	COLONELSHIP
COLLABORATIONS	COLLECTEDNESSES	COLLENCHYMATOUS	COLLOIDALITIES	COLONELSHIPS
COLLABORATIVE	COLLECTIBLE	COLLETERIAL	COLLOIDALITY	COLONIALISE
COLLABORATIVELY	COLLECTIBLES	COLLICULUS	COLLOIDALLY	COLONIALISED
COLLABORATIVES	COLLECTING	COLLIERIES	COLLOQUIAL	COLONIALISES
COLLABORATOR	COLLECTINGS	COLLIESHANGIE	COLLOQUIALISM	COLONIALISING
COLLABORATORS	COLLECTION	COLLIESHANGIES	COLLOQUIALISMS	COLONIALISM
COLLAGENASE	COLLECTIONS	COLLIGATED	COLLOQUIALIST	COLONIALISMS
COLLAGENASES	COLLECTIVE	COLLIGATES	COLLOQUIALISTS	COLONIALIST

COLONIALISTIC	COLORFASTNESSES	COLOURCASTING	COLTISHNESS	COMBURGESS
COLONIALISTS	COLORFULLY	COLOURCASTS	COLTISHNESSES	COMBURGESSES
COLONIALIZE	COLORFULNESS	COLOURFAST	COLTSFOOTS	COMBUSTIBILITY
COLONIALIZED	COLORFULNESSES	COLOURFASTNESS	COLUBRIADS	COMBUSTIBLE
COLONIALIZES	COLORIMETER	COLOURFULLY	COLUBRIFORM	COMBUSTIBLENESS
COLONIALIZING	COLORIMETERS	COLOURFULNESS	COLUMBARIA	COMBUSTIBLES
COLONIALLY	COLORIMETRIC	COLOURFULNESSES	COLUMBARIES	COMBUSTIBLY
COLONIALNESS	COLORIMETRICAL	COLOURIEST	COLUMBARIUM	COMBUSTING
COLONIALNESSES	COLORIMETRIES	COLOURINGS	COLUMBATES	COMBUSTION
COLONISABLE	COLORIMETRY	COLOURISATION	COLUMBINES	COMBUSTIONS
COLONISATION	COLORISATION	COLOURISATIONS	COLUMBITES	COMBUSTIOUS
COLONISATIONIST	COLORISATIONS	COLOURISED	COLUMBIUMS	COMBUSTIVE
COLONISATIONS	COLORISERS	COLOURISER	COLUMELLAE	COMBUSTIVES
COLONISERS	COLORISING	COLOURISERS	COLUMELLAR	COMBUSTORS
COLONISING	COLORISTIC	COLOURISES	COLUMNARITIES	COMEDDLING
COLONITISES	COLORISTICALLY	COLOURISING	COLUMNARITY	COMEDICALLY
COLONIZABLE	COLORIZATION	COLOURISMS	COLUMNATED	COMEDIENNE
COLONIZATION	COLORIZATIONS	COLOURISTIC	COLUMNIATED	COMEDIENNES
COLONIZATIONIST	COLORIZERS	COLOURISTICALLY	COLUMNIATION	COMEDIETTA
COLONIZATIONS	COLORIZING	COLOURISTS	COLUMNIATIONS	COMEDIETTAS
COLONIZERS	COLORLESSLY	COLOURIZATION	COLUMNISTIC	COMEDOGENIC
COLONIZING	COLORLESSNESS	COLOURIZATIONS	COLUMNISTS	COMELINESS
COLONNADED	COLORLESSNESSES	COLOURIZED	COMANAGEMENT	COMELINESSES
COLONNADES	COLORPOINT	COLOURIZER	COMANAGEMENTS	COMESTIBLE
COLONOSCOPE	COLORPOINTS	COLOURIZERS	COMANAGERS	COMESTIBLES
COLONOSCOPES	COLORWASHED	COLOURIZES	COMANAGING	COMETOGRAPHIES
COLONOSCOPIES	COLORWASHES	COLOURIZING	COMANCHERO	COMETOGRAPHY
COLONOSCOPY	COLORWASHING	COLOURLESS	COMANCHEROS	COMETOLOGIES
COLOPHONIES	COLOSSALLY	COLOURLESSLY	COMATOSELY	COMETOLOGY
COLOQUINTIDA	COLOSSEUMS	COLOURLESSNESS	COMATULIDS	COMEUPPANCE
COLOQUINTIDAS	COLOSSUSES	COLOURPOINT	COMBATABLE	COMEUPPANCES
COLORABILITIES	COLOSTOMIES	COLOURPOINTS	COMBATANTS	COMFINESSES
COLORABILITY	COLOSTROUS	COLOURWASH	COMBATIVELY	COMFITURES
COLORABLENESS	COLOSTRUMS	COLOURWASHED	COMBATIVENESS	COMFORTABLE
COLORABLENESSES	COLOTOMIES	COLOURWASHES	COMBATIVENESSES	COMFORTABLENESS
COLORATION	COLOURABILITIES	COLOURWASHING	COMBATTING	COMFORTABLY
COLORATIONS	COLOURABILITY	COLOURWAYS	COMBINABILITIES	COMFORTERS
COLORATURA	COLOURABLE	COLPITISES	COMBINABILITY	COMFORTING
COLORATURAS	COLOURABLENESS	COLPORTAGE	COMBINABLE	COMFORTINGLY
COLORATURE	COLOURABLY	COLPORTAGES	COMBINATION	COMFORTLESS
COLORATURES	COLOURANTS	COLPORTEUR	COMBINATIONAL	COMFORTLESSLY
COLORBREED	COLOURATION	COLPORTEURS	COMBINATIONS	COMFORTLESSNESS
COLORBREEDING	COLOURATIONS	COLPOSCOPE	COMBINATIVE	COMICALITIES
COLORBREEDS	COLOURBRED	COLPOSCOPES	COMBINATORIAL	COMICALITY
COLORCASTED	COLOURBREED	COLPOSCOPICAL	COMBINATORIALLY	COMICALNESS
COLORCASTING	COLOURBREEDING	COLPOSCOPICALLY	COMBINATORICS	COMICALNESSES
COLORCASTS	COLOURBREEDS	COLPOSCOPIES	COMBINATORY	COMINGLING
COLORECTAL	COLOURCAST	COLPOSCOPY	COMBININGS	COMITADJIS
COLORFASTNESS	COLOURCASTED	COLPOTOMIES	COMBRETUMS	COMITATIVE

COMITATIVES	COMMENDATIONS	COMMERCIALIZE	COMMISSIONARY	COMMONALTIES
COMITATUSES	COMMENDATOR	COMMERCIALIZED	COMMISSIONED	COMMONALTY
COMMANDABLE	COMMENDATORS	COMMERCIALIZES	COMMISSIONER	COMMONHOLD
COMMANDANT	COMMENDATORY	COMMERCIALIZING	COMMISSIONERS	COMMONHOLDS
COMMANDANTS	COMMENDERS	COMMERCIALLY	COMMISSIONING	COMMONINGS
COMMANDANTSHIP	COMMENDING	COMMERCIALS	COMMISSIONS	COMMONNESS
COMMANDANTSHIPS	COMMENSALISM	COMMERCING	COMMISSURAL	COMMONNESSES
COMMANDEER	COMMENSALISMS	COMMERGING	COMMISSURE	COMMONPLACE
COMMANDEERED	COMMENSALITIES	COMMINATED	COMMISSURES	COMMONPLACED
COMMANDEERING	COMMENSALITY	COMMINATES	COMMITMENT	COMMONPLACENESS
COMMANDEERS	COMMENSALLY	COMMINATING	COMMITMENTS	COMMONPLACES
COMMANDERIES	COMMENSALS	COMMINATION	COMMITTABLE	COMMONPLACING
COMMANDERS	COMMENSURABLE	COMMINATIONS	COMMITTALS	COMMONSENSE
COMMANDERSHIP	COMMENSURABLY	COMMINATIVE	COMMITTEEMAN	COMMONSENSIBLE
COMMANDERSHIPS	COMMENSURATE	COMMINATORY	COMMITTEEMEN	COMMONSENSICAL
COMMANDERY	COMMENSURATELY	COMMINGLED	COMMITTEES	COMMONWEAL
COMMANDING	COMMENSURATION	COMMINGLES	COMMITTEESHIP	COMMONWEALS
COMMANDINGLY	COMMENSURATIONS	COMMINGLING	COMMITTEESHIPS	COMMONWEALTH
COMMANDMENT	COMMENTARIAL	COMMINUTED	COMMITTEEWOMAN	COMMONWEALTHS
COMMANDMENTS	COMMENTARIAT	COMMINUTES	COMMITTEEWOMEN	COMMORANTS
COMMANDOES	COMMENTARIATS	COMMINUTING	COMMITTERS	COMMORIENTES
COMMEASURABLE	COMMENTARIES	COMMINUTION	COMMITTING	COMMOTIONAL
COMMEASURE	COMMENTARY	COMMINUTIONS	COMMIXTION	COMMOTIONS
COMMEASURED	COMMENTATE	COMMISERABLE	COMMIXTIONS	COMMUNALISATION
COMMEASURES	COMMENTATED	COMMISERATE	COMMIXTURE	COMMUNALISE
COMMEASURING	COMMENTATES	COMMISERATED	COMMIXTURES	COMMUNALISED
COMMEMORABLE	COMMENTATING	COMMISERATES	COMMODIFICATION	COMMUNALISER
COMMEMORATE	COMMENTATION	COMMISERATING	COMMODIFIED	COMMUNALISERS
COMMEMORATED	COMMENTATIONS	COMMISERATINGLY	COMMODIFIES	COMMUNALISES
COMMEMORATES	COMMENTATOR	COMMISERATION	COMMODIFYING	COMMUNALISING
COMMEMORATING	COMMENTATORIAL	COMMISERATIONS	COMMODIOUS	COMMUNALISM
COMMEMORATION	COMMENTATORS	COMMISERATIVE	COMMODIOUSLY	COMMUNALISMS
COMMEMORATIONAL	COMMENTERS	COMMISERATIVELY	COMMODIOUSNESS	COMMUNALIST
COMMEMORATIONS	COMMENTING	COMMISERATOR	COMMODITIES	COMMUNALISTIC
COMMEMORATIVE	COMMENTORS	COMMISERATORS	COMMODITISATION	COMMUNALISTS
COMMEMORATIVELY	COMMERCIAL	COMMISSAIRE	COMMODITISE	COMMUNALITIES
COMMEMORATIVES	COMMERCIALESE	COMMISSAIRES	COMMODITISED	COMMUNALITY
COMMEMORATOR	COMMERCIALESES	COMMISSARIAL	COMMODITISES	COMMUNALIZATION
COMMEMORATORS	COMMERCIALISE	COMMISSARIAT	COMMODITISING	COMMUNALIZE
COMMEMORATORY	COMMERCIALISED	COMMISSARIATS	COMMODITIZATION	COMMUNALIZED
COMMENCEMENT	COMMERCIALISES	COMMISSARIES	COMMODITIZE	COMMUNALIZER
COMMENCEMENTS	COMMERCIALISING	COMMISSARS	COMMODITIZED	COMMUNALIZERS
COMMENCERS	COMMERCIALISM	COMMISSARY	COMMODITIZES	COMMUNALIZES
COMMENCING	COMMERCIALISMS	COMMISSARYSHIP	COMMODITIZING	COMMUNALIZING
COMMENDABLE	COMMERCIALIST	COMMISSARYSHIPS	COMMODORES	COMMUNALLY
COMMENDABLENESS	COMMERCIALISTIC	COMMISSION	COMMONABLE	COMMUNARDS
COMMENDABLY	COMMERCIALISTS	COMMISSIONAIRE	COMMONAGES	COMMUNAUTAIRE
COMMENDAMS	COMMERCIALITIES	COMMISSIONAIRES	COMMONALITIES	COMMUNAUTAIRES
COMMENDATION	COMMERCIALITY	COMMISSIONAL	COMMONALITY	COMMUNICABILITY

COMMUNICABLE
COMMUNICABLY
COMMUNICANT
COMMUNICANTS
COMMUNICATE
COMMUNICATED
COMMUNICATEE
COMMUNICATEES
COMMUNICATES
COMMUNICATING
COMMUNICATION
COMMUNICATIONAL
COMMUNICATIONS
COMMUNICATIVE
COMMUNICATIVELY
COMMUNICATOR
COMMUNICATORS
COMMUNICATORY
COMMUNINGS
COMMUNIONAL
COMMUNIONALLY
COMMUNIONS
COMMUNIQUE
COMMUNIQUES
COMMUNISATION
COMMUNISATIONS
COMMUNISED
COMMUNISES
COMMUNISING
COMMUNISMS
COMMUNISTIC
COMMUNISTICALLY
COMMUNISTS
COMMUNITAIRE
COMMUNITAIRES
COMMUNITARIAN
COMMUNITARIANS
COMMUNITIES
COMMUNIZATION
COMMUNIZATIONS
COMMUNIZED
COMMUNIZES
COMMUNIZING
COMMUTABILITIES
COMMUTABILITY
COMMUTABLE
COMMUTABLENESS
COMMUTATED
COMMUTATES

COMMUTATING
COMMUTATION
COMMUTATIONS
COMMUTATIVE
COMMUTATIVELY
COMMUTATIVITIES
COMMUTATIVITY
COMMUTATOR
COMMUTATORS
COMMUTINGS
COMONOMERS
COMORBIDITIES
COMORBIDITY
COMPACTEDLY
COMPACTEDNESS
COMPACTEDNESSES
COMPACTERS
COMPACTEST
COMPACTIBLE
COMPACTIFIED
COMPACTIFIES
COMPACTIFY
COMPACTIFYING
COMPACTING
COMPACTION
COMPACTIONS
COMPACTNESS
COMPACTNESSES
COMPACTORS
COMPACTURE
COMPACTURES
COMPAGINATE
COMPAGINATED
COMPAGINATES
COMPAGINATING
COMPAGINATION
COMPAGINATIONS
COMPANDERS
COMPANDING
COMPANDORS
COMPANIABLE
COMPANIONABLE
COMPANIONABLY
COMPANIONATE
COMPANIONED
COMPANIONHOOD
COMPANIONHOODS
COMPANIONING
COMPANIONLESS

COMPANIONS
COMPANIONSHIP
COMPANIONSHIPS
COMPANIONWAY
COMPANIONWAYS
COMPANYING
COMPARABILITIES
COMPARABILITY
COMPARABLE
COMPARABLENESS
COMPARABLY
COMPARATIST
COMPARATISTS
COMPARATIVE
COMPARATIVELY
COMPARATIVENESS
COMPARATIVES
COMPARATIVIST
COMPARATIVISTS
COMPARATOR
COMPARATORS
COMPARISON
COMPARISONS
COMPARTING
COMPARTMENT
COMPARTMENTAL
COMPARTMENTALLY
COMPARTMENTED
COMPARTMENTING
COMPARTMENTS
COMPASSABLE
COMPASSING
COMPASSINGS
COMPASSION
COMPASSIONABLE
COMPASSIONATE
COMPASSIONATED
COMPASSIONATELY
COMPASSIONATES
COMPASSIONATING
COMPASSIONED
COMPASSIONING
COMPASSIONLESS
COMPASSIONS
COMPATIBILITIES
COMPATIBILITY
COMPATIBLE
COMPATIBLENESS
COMPATIBLES

COMPATIBLY
COMPATRIOT
COMPATRIOTIC
COMPATRIOTISM
COMPATRIOTISMS
COMPATRIOTS
COMPEARANCE
COMPEARANCES
COMPEARANT
COMPEARANTS
COMPEARING
COMPEERING
COMPELLABLE
COMPELLABLY
COMPELLATION
COMPELLATIONS
COMPELLATIVE
COMPELLATIVES
COMPELLERS
COMPELLING
COMPELLINGLY
COMPENDIOUS
COMPENDIOUSLY
COMPENDIOUSNESS
COMPENDIUM
COMPENDIUMS
COMPENSABILITY
COMPENSABLE
COMPENSATE
COMPENSATED
COMPENSATES
COMPENSATING
COMPENSATION
COMPENSATIONAL
COMPENSATIONS
COMPENSATIVE
COMPENSATOR
COMPENSATORS
COMPENSATORY
COMPESCING
COMPETENCE
COMPETENCES
COMPETENCIES
COMPETENCY
COMPETENTLY
COMPETENTNESS
COMPETENTNESSES
COMPETITION
COMPETITIONS

COMPETITIVE
COMPETITIVELY
COMPETITIVENESS
COMPETITOR
COMPETITORS
COMPILATION
COMPILATIONS
COMPILATOR
COMPILATORS
COMPILATORY
COMPILEMENT
COMPILEMENTS
COMPLACENCE
COMPLACENCES
COMPLACENCIES
COMPLACENCY
COMPLACENT
COMPLACENTLY
COMPLAINANT
COMPLAINANTS
COMPLAINED
COMPLAINER
COMPLAINERS
COMPLAINING
COMPLAININGLY
COMPLAININGS
COMPLAINTS
COMPLAISANCE
COMPLAISANCES
COMPLAISANT
COMPLAISANTLY
COMPLANATE
COMPLANATION
COMPLANATIONS
COMPLEATED
COMPLEATING
COMPLECTED
COMPLECTING
COMPLEMENT
COMPLEMENTAL
COMPLEMENTALLY
COMPLEMENTARIES
COMPLEMENTARILY
COMPLEMENTARITY
COMPLEMENTARY
COMPLEMENTATION
COMPLEMENTED
COMPLEMENTING
COMPLEMENTISER

COMPLEMENTISERS

COMPLEMENTISERS	COMPLIANCY	COMPOSEDNESS	COMPREHENSIBLE	COMPULSING
COMPLEMENTIZER	COMPLIANTLY	COMPOSEDNESSES	COMPREHENSIBLY	COMPULSION
COMPLEMENTIZERS	COMPLIANTNESS	COMPOSITED	COMPREHENSION	COMPULSIONIST
COMPLEMENTS	COMPLIANTNESSES	COMPOSITELY	COMPREHENSIONS	COMPULSIONISTS
COMPLETABLE	COMPLICACIES	COMPOSITENESS	COMPREHENSIVE	COMPULSIONS
COMPLETEDNESS	COMPLICACY	COMPOSITENESSES	COMPREHENSIVELY	COMPULSITOR
COMPLETEDNESSES	COMPLICANT	COMPOSITES	COMPREHENSIVES	COMPULSITORS
COMPLETELY	COMPLICATE	COMPOSITING	COMPREHENSIVISE	COMPULSIVE
COMPLETENESS	COMPLICATED	COMPOSITION	COMPREHENSIVIZE	COMPULSIVELY
COMPLETENESSES	COMPLICATEDLY	COMPOSITIONAL	COMPRESSED	COMPULSIVENESS
COMPLETERS	COMPLICATEDNESS	COMPOSITIONALLY	COMPRESSEDLY	COMPULSIVES
COMPLETEST	COMPLICATES	COMPOSITIONS	COMPRESSES	COMPULSIVITIES
COMPLETING	COMPLICATING	COMPOSITIVE	COMPRESSIBILITY	COMPULSIVITY
COMPLETION	COMPLICATION	COMPOSITOR	COMPRESSIBLE	COMPULSORIES
COMPLETIONS	COMPLICATIONS	COMPOSITORIAL	COMPRESSIBLY	COMPULSORILY
COMPLETIST	COMPLICATIVE	COMPOSITORS	COMPRESSING	COMPULSORINESS
COMPLETISTS	COMPLICITIES	COMPOSITOUS	COMPRESSION	COMPULSORY
COMPLETIVE	COMPLICITLY	COMPOSSIBILITY	COMPRESSIONAL	COMPUNCTION
COMPLETORIES	COMPLICITOUS	COMPOSSIBLE	COMPRESSIONS	COMPUNCTIONS
COMPLETORY	COMPLICITY	COMPOSTABLE	COMPRESSIVE	COMPUNCTIOUS
COMPLEXATION	COMPLIMENT	COMPOSTERS	COMPRESSIVELY	COMPUNCTIOUSLY
COMPLEXATIONS	COMPLIMENTAL	COMPOSTING	COMPRESSOR	COMPURGATION
COMPLEXEDNESS	COMPLIMENTARILY	COMPOSTINGS	COMPRESSORS	COMPURGATIONS
COMPLEXEDNESSES	COMPLIMENTARY	COMPOSTURE	COMPRESSURE	COMPURGATOR
COMPLEXEST	COMPLIMENTED	COMPOSTURED	COMPRESSURES	COMPURGATORIAL
COMPLEXIFIED	COMPLIMENTER	COMPOSTURES	COMPRIMARIO	COMPURGATORS
COMPLEXIFIES	COMPLIMENTERS	COMPOSTURING	COMPRIMARIOS	COMPURGATORY
COMPLEXIFY	COMPLIMENTING	COMPOSURES	COMPRINTED	COMPURSION
COMPLEXIFYING	COMPLIMENTS	COMPOTATION	COMPRINTING	COMPURSIONS
COMPLEXING	COMPLISHED	COMPOTATIONS	COMPRISABLE	COMPUTABILITIES
COMPLEXION	COMPLISHES	COMPOTATIONSHIP	COMPRISALS	COMPUTABILITY
COMPLEXIONAL	COMPLISHING	COMPOTATOR	COMPRISING	COMPUTABLE
COMPLEXIONED	COMPLOTTED	COMPOTATORS	COMPRIZING	COMPUTANTS
COMPLEXIONLESS	COMPLOTTER	COMPOTATORY	COMPROMISE	COMPUTATION
COMPLEXIONS	COMPLOTTERS	COMPOTIERS	COMPROMISED	COMPUTATIONAL
COMPLEXITIES	COMPLOTTING	COMPOUNDABLE	COMPROMISER	COMPUTATIONALLY
COMPLEXITY	COMPLUVIUM	COMPOUNDED	COMPROMISERS	COMPUTATIONS
COMPLEXNESS	COMPLUVIUMS	COMPOUNDER	COMPROMISES	COMPUTATIVE
COMPLEXNESSES	COMPONENCIES	COMPOUNDERS	COMPROMISING	COMPUTATOR
COMPLEXOMETRIC	COMPONENCY	COMPOUNDING	COMPROMISINGLY	COMPUTATORS
COMPLEXONE	COMPONENTAL	COMPOUNDINGS	COMPROVINCIAL	COMPUTERATE
COMPLEXONES	COMPONENTIAL	COMPRADORE	COMPTROLLED	COMPUTERDOM
COMPLEXUSES	COMPONENTS	COMPRADORES	COMPTROLLER	COMPUTERDOMS
COMPLIABLE	COMPORTANCE	COMPRADORS	COMPTROLLERS	COMPUTERESE
COMPLIABLENESS	COMPORTANCES	COMPREHEND	COMPTROLLERSHIP	COMPUTERESES
COMPLIABLY	COMPORTING	COMPREHENDED	COMPTROLLING	COMPUTERISABLE
COMPLIANCE	COMPORTMENT	COMPREHENDIBLE	COMPTROLLS	COMPUTERISATION
COMPLIANCES	COMPORTMENTS	COMPREHENDING	COMPULSATIVE	COMPUTERISE
COMPLIANCIES	COMPOSEDLY	COMPREHENDS	COMPULSATORY	COMPUTERISED

COMPUTERISES	CONCAVENESSES	CONCENTRICITY	CONCERTINA	CONCHITISES
COMPUTERISING	CONCAVITIES	CONCENTRING	CONCERTINAED	CONCHOIDAL
COMPUTERIST	CONCEALABLE	CONCEPTACLE	CONCERTINAING	CONCHOIDALLY
COMPUTERISTS	CONCEALERS	CONCEPTACLES	CONCERTINAS	CONCHOLOGICAL
COMPUTERITIS	CONCEALING	CONCEPTION	CONCERTING	CONCHOLOGIES
COMPUTERITISES	CONCEALINGLY	CONCEPTIONAL	CONCERTINI	CONCHOLOGIST
COMPUTERIZABLE	CONCEALMENT	CONCEPTIONS	CONCERTINIST	CONCHOLOGISTS
COMPUTERIZATION	CONCEALMENTS	CONCEPTIOUS	CONCERTINISTS	CONCHOLOGY
COMPUTERIZE	CONCEDEDLY	CONCEPTIVE	CONCERTINO	CONCIERGES
COMPUTERIZED	CONCEITEDLY	CONCEPTUAL	CONCERTINOS	CONCILIABLE
COMPUTERIZES	CONCEITEDNESS	CONCEPTUALISE	CONCERTISE	CONCILIARLY
COMPUTERIZING	CONCEITEDNESSES	CONCEPTUALISED	CONCERTISED	CONCILIARY
COMPUTERLESS	CONCEITFUL	CONCEPTUALISER	CONCERTISES	CONCILIATE
COMPUTERLIKE	CONCEITING	CONCEPTUALISERS	CONCERTISING	CONCILIATED
COMPUTERNIK	CONCEITLESS	CONCEPTUALISES	CONCERTIZE	CONCILIATES
COMPUTERNIKS	CONCEIVABILITY	CONCEPTUALISING	CONCERTIZED	CONCILIATING
COMPUTERPHOBE	CONCEIVABLE	CONCEPTUALISM	CONCERTIZES	CONCILIATION
COMPUTERPHOBES	CONCEIVABLENESS	CONCEPTUALISMS	CONCERTIZING	CONCILIATIONS
COMPUTERPHOBIA	CONCEIVABLY	CONCEPTUALIST	CONCERTMASTER	CONCILIATIVE
COMPUTERPHOBIAS	CONCEIVERS	CONCEPTUALISTIC	CONCERTMASTERS	CONCILIATOR
COMPUTERPHOBIC	CONCEIVING	CONCEPTUALISTS	CONCERTMEISTER	CONCILIATORILY
COMPUTERPHOBICS	CONCELEBRANT	CONCEPTUALITIES	CONCERTMEISTERS	CONCILIATORS
COMPUTINGS	CONCELEBRANTS	CONCEPTUALITY	CONCERTMISTRESS	CONCILIATORY
COMPUTISTS	CONCELEBRATE	CONCEPTUALIZE	CONCERTSTUCK	CONCINNITIES
COMRADELIER	CONCELEBRATED	CONCEPTUALIZED	CONCERTSTUCKS	CONCINNITY
COMRADELIEST	CONCELEBRATES	CONCEPTUALIZER	CONCESSIBLE	CONCINNOUS
COMRADELINESS	CONCELEBRATING	CONCEPTUALIZERS	CONCESSION	CONCIPIENCIES
COMRADELINESSES	CONCELEBRATION	CONCEPTUALIZES	CONCESSIONAIRE	CONCIPIENCY
COMRADERIES	CONCELEBRATIONS	CONCEPTUALIZING	CONCESSIONAIRES	CONCIPIENT
COMRADESHIP	CONCENTERED	CONCEPTUALLY	CONCESSIONAL	CONCISENESS
COMRADESHIPS	CONCENTERING	CONCEPTUSES	CONCESSIONARIES	CONCISENESSES
COMSTOCKER	CONCENTERS	CONCERNANCIES	CONCESSIONARY	CONCISIONS
COMSTOCKERIES	CONCENTRATE	CONCERNANCY	CONCESSIONER	CONCLAMATION
COMSTOCKERS	CONCENTRATED	CONCERNEDLY	CONCESSIONERS	CONCLAMATIONS
COMSTOCKERY	CONCENTRATEDLY	CONCERNEDNESS	CONCESSIONIST	CONCLAVISM
COMSTOCKISM	CONCENTRATES	CONCERNEDNESSES	CONCESSIONISTS	CONCLAVISMS
COMSTOCKISMS	CONCENTRATING	CONCERNING	CONCESSIONNAIRE	CONCLAVIST
CONACREISM	CONCENTRATION	CONCERNMENT	CONCESSIONS	CONCLAVISTS
CONACREISMS	CONCENTRATIONS	CONCERNMENTS	CONCESSIVE	CONCLUDERS
CONATIONAL	CONCENTRATIVE	CONCERTANTE	CONCESSIVELY	CONCLUDING
CONCANAVALIN	CONCENTRATIVELY	CONCERTANTES	CONCETTISM	CONCLUSION
CONCANAVALINS	CONCENTRATOR	CONCERTANTI	CONCETTISMS	CONCLUSIONARY
CONCATENATE	CONCENTRATORS	CONCERTEDLY	CONCETTIST	CONCLUSIONS
CONCATENATED	CONCENTRED	CONCERTEDNESS	CONCETTISTS	CONCLUSIVE
CONCATENATES	CONCENTRES	CONCERTEDNESSES	CONCHIFEROUS	CONCLUSIVELY
CONCATENATING	CONCENTRIC	CONCERTGOER	CONCHIFORM	CONCLUSIVENESS
CONCATENATION	CONCENTRICAL	CONCERTGOERS	CONCHIGLIE	CONCLUSORY
CONCATENATIONS	CONCENTRICALLY	CONCERTGOING	CONCHIOLIN	CONCOCTERS
CONCAVENESS	CONCENTRICITIES	CONCERTGOINGS	CONCHIOLINS	CONCOCTING

CONCOCTION	CONCRETISTS	CONDENSATED	CONDOLEMENTS	CONFABULATE
CONCOCTIONS	CONCRETIVE	CONDENSATES	CONDOLENCE	CONFABULATED
CONCOCTIVE	CONCRETIVELY	CONDENSATING	CONDOLENCES	CONFABULATES
CONCOCTORS	CONCRETIZATION	CONDENSATION	CONDOLINGLY	CONFABULATING
CONCOLORATE	CONCRETIZATIONS	CONDENSATIONAL	CONDOMINIA	CONFABULATION
CONCOLOROUS	CONCRETIZE	CONDENSATIONS	CONDOMINIUM	CONFABULATIONS
CONCOMITANCE	CONCRETIZED	CONDENSERIES	CONDOMINIUMS	CONFABULATOR
CONCOMITANCES	CONCRETIZES	CONDENSERS	CONDONABLE	CONFABULATORS
CONCOMITANCIES	CONCRETIZING	CONDENSERY	CONDONATION	CONFABULATORY
CONCOMITANCY	CONCREWING	CONDENSIBILITY	CONDONATIONS	CONFARREATE
CONCOMITANT	CONCUBINAGE	CONDENSIBLE	CONDOTTIERE	CONFARREATION
CONCOMITANTLY	CONCUBINAGES	CONDENSING	CONDOTTIERI	CONFARREATIONS
CONCOMITANTS	CONCUBINARIES	CONDESCEND	CONDUCEMENT	CONFECTING
CONCORDANCE	CONCUBINARY	CONDESCENDED	CONDUCEMENTS	CONFECTION
CONCORDANCES	CONCUBINES	CONDESCENDENCE	CONDUCIBLE	CONFECTIONARIES
CONCORDANT	CONCUBITANCIES	CONDESCENDENCES	CONDUCINGLY	CONFECTIONARY
CONCORDANTLY	CONCUBITANCY	CONDESCENDING	CONDUCIVENESS	CONFECTIONER
CONCORDATS	CONCUBITANT	CONDESCENDINGLY	CONDUCIVENESSES	CONFECTIONERIES
CONCORDIAL	CONCUBITANTS	CONDESCENDS	CONDUCTANCE	CONFECTIONERS
CONCORDING	CONCUPISCENCE	CONDESCENSION	CONDUCTANCES	CONFECTIONERY
CONCORPORATE	CONCUPISCENCES	CONDESCENSIONS	CONDUCTIBILITY	CONFECTIONS
CONCORPORATED	CONCUPISCENT	CONDIDDLED	CONDUCTIBLE	CONFEDERACIES
CONCORPORATES	CONCUPISCIBLE	CONDIDDLES	CONDUCTIMETRIC	CONFEDERACY
CONCORPORATING	CONCURRENCE	CONDIDDLING	CONDUCTING	CONFEDERAL
CONCOURSES	CONCURRENCES	CONDIGNNESS	CONDUCTIOMETRIC	CONFEDERATE
CONCREATED	CONCURRENCIES	CONDIGNNESSES	CONDUCTION	CONFEDERATED
CONCREATES	CONCURRENCY	CONDIMENTAL	CONDUCTIONAL	CONFEDERATES
CONCREATING	CONCURRENT	CONDIMENTED	CONDUCTIONS	CONFEDERATING
CONCREMATION	CONCURRENTLY	CONDIMENTING	CONDUCTIVE	CONFEDERATION
CONCREMATIONS	CONCURRENTS	CONDIMENTS	CONDUCTIVELY	CONFEDERATIONS
CONCRESCENCE	CONCURRING	CONDISCIPLE	CONDUCTIVITIES	CONFEDERATIVE
CONCRESCENCES	CONCURRINGLY	CONDISCIPLES	CONDUCTIVITY	CONFERENCE
CONCRESCENT	CONCUSSING	CONDITIONABLE	CONDUCTOMETRIC	CONFERENCES
CONCRETELY	CONCUSSION	CONDITIONAL	CONDUCTORIAL	CONFERENCIER
CONCRETENESS	CONCUSSIONS	CONDITIONALITY	CONDUCTORS	CONFERENCIERS
CONCRETENESSES	CONCUSSIVE	CONDITIONALLY	CONDUCTORSHIP	CONFERENCING
CONCRETING	CONCYCLICALLY	CONDITIONALS	CONDUCTORSHIPS	CONFERENCINGS
CONCRETION	CONDEMNABLE	CONDITIONATE	CONDUCTRESS	CONFERENTIAL
CONCRETIONARY	CONDEMNABLY	CONDITIONATED	CONDUCTRESSES	CONFERMENT
CONCRETIONS	CONDEMNATION	CONDITIONATES	CONDUPLICATE	CONFERMENTS
CONCRETISATION	CONDEMNATIONS	CONDITIONATING	CONDUPLICATION	CONFERRABLE
CONCRETISATIONS	CONDEMNATORY	CONDITIONED	CONDUPLICATIONS	CONFERRALS
CONCRETISE	CONDEMNERS	CONDITIONER	CONDYLOMAS	CONFERREES
CONCRETISED	CONDEMNING	CONDITIONERS	CONDYLOMATA	CONFERRENCE
CONCRETISES	CONDEMNINGLY	CONDITIONING	CONDYLOMATOUS	CONFERRENCES
CONCRETISING	CONDEMNORS	CONDITIONINGS	CONEFLOWER	CONFERRERS
CONCRETISM	CONDENSABILITY	CONDITIONS	CONEFLOWERS	CONFERRING
CONCRETISMS	CONDENSABLE	CONDOLATORY	CONFABBING	CONFERVOID
CONCRETIST	CONDENSATE	CONDOLEMENT	CONFABULAR	CONFERVOIDS

CONFESSABLE	CONFINABLE	CONFLAGRATIONS	CONFRONTAL	CONGENITALNESS
CONFESSANT	CONFINEABLE	CONFLAGRATIVE	CONFRONTALS	CONGESTIBLE
CONFESSANTS	CONFINEDLY	CONFLATING	CONFRONTATION	CONGESTING
CONFESSEDLY	CONFINEDNESS	CONFLATION	CONFRONTATIONAL	CONGESTION
CONFESSING	CONFINEDNESSES	CONFLATIONS	CONFRONTATIONS	CONGESTIONS
CONFESSION	CONFINELESS	CONFLICTED	CONFRONTED	CONGESTIVE
CONFESSIONAL	CONFINEMENT	CONFLICTFUL	CONFRONTER	CONGIARIES
CONFESSIONALISM	CONFINEMENTS	CONFLICTING	CONFRONTERS	CONGLOBATE
CONFESSIONALIST	CONFIRMABILITY	CONFLICTINGLY	CONFRONTING	CONGLOBATED
CONFESSIONALLY	CONFIRMABLE	CONFLICTION	CONFRONTMENT	CONGLOBATES
CONFESSIONALS	CONFIRMAND	CONFLICTIONS	CONFRONTMENTS	CONGLOBATING
CONFESSIONARIES	CONFIRMANDS	CONFLICTIVE	CONFUSABILITIES	CONGLOBATION
CONFESSIONARY	CONFIRMATION	CONFLICTORY	CONFUSABILITY	CONGLOBATIONS
CONFESSIONS	CONFIRMATIONAL	CONFLICTUAL	CONFUSABLE	CONGLOBING
CONFESSORESS	CONFIRMATIONS	CONFLUENCE	CONFUSABLES	CONGLOBULATE
CONFESSORESSES	CONFIRMATIVE	CONFLUENCES	CONFUSEDLY	CONGLOBULATED
CONFESSORS	CONFIRMATOR	CONFLUENTLY	CONFUSEDNESS	CONGLOBULATES
CONFESSORSHIP	CONFIRMATORS	CONFLUENTS	CONFUSEDNESSES	CONGLOBULATING
CONFESSORSHIPS	CONFIRMATORY	CONFOCALLY	CONFUSIBLE	CONGLOBULATION
CONFIDANTE	CONFIRMEDLY	CONFORMABILITY	CONFUSIBLES	CONGLOBULATIONS
CONFIDANTES	CONFIRMEDNESS	CONFORMABLE	CONFUSINGLY	CONGLOMERATE
CONFIDANTS	CONFIRMEDNESSES	CONFORMABLENESS	CONFUSIONAL	CONGLOMERATED
CONFIDENCE	CONFIRMEES	CONFORMABLY	CONFUSIONS	CONGLOMERATES
CONFIDENCES	CONFIRMERS	CONFORMANCE	CONFUTABLE	CONGLOMERATEUR
CONFIDENCIES	CONFIRMING	CONFORMANCES	CONFUTATION	CONGLOMERATEURS
CONFIDENCY	CONFIRMINGS	CONFORMATION	CONFUTATIONS	CONGLOMERATIC
CONFIDENTIAL	CONFIRMORS	CONFORMATIONAL	CONFUTATIVE	CONGLOMERATING
CONFIDENTIALITY	CONFISCABLE	CONFORMATIONS	CONFUTEMENT	CONGLOMERATION
CONFIDENTIALLY	CONFISCATABLE	CONFORMERS	CONFUTEMENTS	CONGLOMERATIONS
CONFIDENTLY	CONFISCATE	CONFORMING	CONGEALABLE	CONGLOMERATIVE
CONFIDENTS	CONFISCATED	CONFORMINGLY	CONGEALABLENESS	CONGLOMERATOR
CONFIDINGLY	CONFISCATES	CONFORMISM	CONGEALERS	CONGLOMERATORS
CONFIDINGNESS	CONFISCATING	CONFORMISMS	CONGEALING	CONGLUTINANT
CONFIDINGNESSES	CONFISCATION	CONFORMIST	CONGEALMENT	CONGLUTINATE
CONFIGURABILITY	CONFISCATIONS	CONFORMISTS	CONGEALMENTS	CONGLUTINATED
CONFIGURABLE	CONFISCATOR	CONFORMITIES	CONGELATION	CONGLUTINATES
CONFIGURATE	CONFISCATORS	CONFORMITY	CONGELATIONS	CONGLUTINATING
CONFIGURATED	CONFISCATORY	CONFOUNDABLE	CONGENERIC	CONGLUTINATION
CONFIGURATES	CONFISERIE	CONFOUNDED	CONGENERICAL	CONGLUTINATIONS
CONFIGURATING	CONFISERIES	CONFOUNDEDLY	CONGENERICS	CONGLUTINATIVE
CONFIGURATION	CONFISEURS	CONFOUNDEDNESS	CONGENEROUS	CONGLUTINATOR
CONFIGURATIONAL	CONFITEORS	CONFOUNDER	CONGENETIC	CONGLUTINATORS
CONFIGURATIONS	CONFITURES	CONFOUNDERS	CONGENIALITIES	CONGRATTERS
CONFIGURATIVE	CONFLAGRANT	CONFOUNDING	CONGENIALITY	CONGRATULABLE
CONFIGURATOR	CONFLAGRATE	CONFOUNDINGLY	CONGENIALLY	CONGRATULANT
CONFIGURATORS	CONFLAGRATED	CONFRATERNAL	CONGENIALNESS	CONGRATULANTS
CONFIGURED	CONFLAGRATES	CONFRATERNITIES	CONGENIALNESSES	CONGRATULATE
CONFIGURES	CONFLAGRATING	CONFRATERNITY	CONGENITAL	CONGRATULATED
CONFIGURING	CONFLAGRATION	CONFRERIES	CONGENITALLY	CONGRATULATES

C

CONGRATULATING	CONIFEROUS	CONJUNCTLY	CONNECTIVITIES	CONQUERABLENESS
CONGRATULATION	CONIOLOGIES	CONJUNCTURAL	CONNECTIVITY	CONQUERERS
CONGRATULATIONS	CONIROSTRAL	CONJUNCTURE	CONNECTORS	CONQUERESS
CONGRATULATIVE	CONJECTING	CONJUNCTURES	CONNEXIONAL	CONQUERESSES
CONGRATULATOR	CONJECTURABLE	CONJURATION	CONNEXIONS	CONQUERING
CONGRATULATORS	CONJECTURABLY	CONJURATIONS	CONNIPTION	CONQUERINGLY
CONGRATULATORY	CONJECTURAL	CONJURATOR	CONNIPTIONS	CONQUERORS
CONGREEING	CONJECTURALLY	CONJURATORS	CONNIVANCE	CONQUISTADOR
CONGREETED	CONJECTURE	CONJUREMENT	CONNIVANCES	CONQUISTADORES
CONGREETING	CONJECTURED	CONJUREMENTS	CONNIVANCIES	CONQUISTADORS
CONGREGANT	CONJECTURER	CONJURINGS	CONNIVANCY	CONSANGUINE
CONGREGANTS	CONJECTURERS	CONLANGERS	CONNIVENCE	CONSANGUINEOUS
CONGREGATE	CONJECTURES	CONNASCENCE	CONNIVENCES	CONSANGUINITIES
CONGREGATED	CONJECTURING	CONNASCENCES	CONNIVENCIES	CONSANGUINITY
CONGREGATES	CONJOINERS	CONNASCENCIES	CONNIVENCY	CONSCIENCE
CONGREGATING	CONJOINING	CONNASCENCY	CONNIVENTLY	CONSCIENCELESS
CONGREGATION	CONJOINTLY	CONNASCENT	CONNIVERIES	CONSCIENCES
CONGREGATIONAL	CONJUGABLE	CONNATENESS	CONNIVINGLY	CONSCIENTIOUS
CONGREGATIONS	CONJUGALITIES	CONNATENESSES	CONNIVINGS	CONSCIENTIOUSLY
CONGREGATIVE	CONJUGALITY	CONNATIONS	CONNOISSEUR	CONSCIENTISE
CONGREGATOR	CONJUGALLY	CONNATURAL	CONNOISSEURS	CONSCIENTISED
CONGREGATORS	CONJUGANTS	CONNATURALISE	CONNOISSEURSHIP	CONSCIENTISES
CONGRESSED	CONJUGATED	CONNATURALISED	CONNOTATED	CONSCIENTISING
CONGRESSES	CONJUGATELY	CONNATURALISES	CONNOTATES	CONSCIENTIZE
CONGRESSING	CONJUGATENESS	CONNATURALISING	CONNOTATING	CONSCIENTIZED
CONGRESSIONAL	CONJUGATENESSES	CONNATURALITIES	CONNOTATION	CONSCIENTIZES
CONGRESSIONALLY	CONJUGATES	CONNATURALITY	CONNOTATIONAL	CONSCIENTIZING
CONGRESSMAN	CONJUGATING	CONNATURALIZE	CONNOTATIONS	CONSCIONABILITY
CONGRESSMEN	CONJUGATINGS	CONNATURALIZED	CONNOTATIVE	CONSCIONABLE
CONGRESSPEOPLE	CONJUGATION	CONNATURALIZES	CONNOTATIVELY	CONSCIONABLY
CONGRESSPERSON	CONJUGATIONAL	CONNATURALIZING	CONNOTIVELY	CONSCIOUSES
CONGRESSPERSONS	CONJUGATIONALLY	CONNATURALLY	CONNUBIALISM	CONSCIOUSLY
CONGRESSWOMAN	CONJUGATIONS	CONNATURALNESS	CONNUBIALISMS	CONSCIOUSNESS
CONGRESSWOMEN	CONJUGATIVE	CONNATURES	CONNUBIALITIES	CONSCIOUSNESSES
CONGRUENCE	CONJUGATOR	CONNECTABLE	CONNUBIALITY	CONSCRIBED
CONGRUENCES	CONJUGATORS	CONNECTEDLY	CONNUBIALLY	CONSCRIBES
CONGRUENCIES	CONJUNCTION	CONNECTEDNESS	CONNUMERATE	CONSCRIBING
CONGRUENCY	CONJUNCTIONAL	CONNECTEDNESSES	CONNUMERATED	CONSCRIPTED
CONGRUENTLY	CONJUNCTIONALLY	CONNECTERS	CONNUMERATES	CONSCRIPTING
CONGRUITIES	CONJUNCTIONS	CONNECTIBLE	CONNUMERATING	CONSCRIPTION
CONGRUOUSLY	CONJUNCTIVA	CONNECTING	CONNUMERATION	CONSCRIPTIONAL
CONGRUOUSNESS	CONJUNCTIVAE	CONNECTION	CONNUMERATIONS	CONSCRIPTIONIST
CONGRUOUSNESSES	CONJUNCTIVAL	CONNECTIONAL	CONOIDALLY	CONSCRIPTIONS
CONICITIES	CONJUNCTIVAS	CONNECTIONISM	CONOIDICAL	CONSCRIPTS
CONIDIOPHORE	CONJUNCTIVE	CONNECTIONISMS	CONOMINEES	CONSECRATE
CONIDIOPHORES	CONJUNCTIVELY	CONNECTIONS	CONOSCENTE	CONSECRATED
CONIDIOPHOROUS	CONJUNCTIVENESS	CONNECTIVE	CONOSCENTI	CONSECRATEDNESS
CONIDIOSPORE	CONJUNCTIVES	CONNECTIVELY	CONQUERABILITY	CONSECRATES
CONIDIOSPORES	CONJUNCTIVITIS	CONNECTIVES	CONQUERABLE	CONSECRATING

CONSECRATION	CONSERVATIONS	CONSIGLIERI	CONSOLATIONS	CONSPIRATION
CONSECRATIONS	CONSERVATISE	CONSIGNABLE	CONSOLATORIES	CONSPIRATIONAL
CONSECRATIVE	CONSERVATISED	CONSIGNATION	CONSOLATORY	CONSPIRATIONS
CONSECRATOR	CONSERVATISES	CONSIGNATIONS	CONSOLATRICES	CONSPIRATOR
CONSECRATORS	CONSERVATISING	CONSIGNATORIES	CONSOLATRIX	CONSPIRATORIAL
CONSECRATORY	CONSERVATISM	CONSIGNATORY	CONSOLATRIXES	CONSPIRATORS
CONSECTANEOUS	CONSERVATISMS	CONSIGNEES	CONSOLEMENT	CONSPIRATORY
CONSECTARIES	CONSERVATIVE	CONSIGNERS	CONSOLEMENTS	CONSPIRATRESS
CONSECTARY	CONSERVATIVELY	CONSIGNIFIED	CONSOLIDATE	CONSPIRATRESSES
CONSECUTION	CONSERVATIVES	CONSIGNIFIES	CONSOLIDATED	CONSPIRERS
CONSECUTIONS	CONSERVATIZE	CONSIGNIFY	CONSOLIDATES	CONSPIRING
CONSECUTIVE	CONSERVATIZED	CONSIGNIFYING	CONSOLIDATING	CONSPIRINGLY
CONSECUTIVELY	CONSERVATIZES	CONSIGNING	CONSOLIDATION	CONSPURCATION
CONSECUTIVENESS	CONSERVATIZING	CONSIGNMENT	CONSOLIDATIONS	CONSPURCATIONS
CONSENESCENCE	CONSERVATOIRE	CONSIGNMENTS	CONSOLIDATIVE	CONSTABLES
CONSENESCENCES	CONSERVATOIRES	CONSIGNORS	CONSOLIDATOR	CONSTABLESHIP
CONSENESCENCIES	CONSERVATOR	CONSILIENCE	CONSOLIDATORS	CONSTABLESHIPS
CONSENESCENCY	CONSERVATORIA	CONSILIENCES	CONSOLINGLY	CONSTABLEWICK
CONSENSION	CONSERVATORIAL	CONSILIENT	CONSONANCE	CONSTABLEWICKS
CONSENSIONS	CONSERVATORIES	CONSIMILAR	CONSONANCES	CONSTABULARIES
CONSENSUAL	CONSERVATORIUM	CONSIMILARITIES	CONSONANCIES	CONSTABULARY
CONSENSUALLY	CONSERVATORIUMS	CONSIMILARITY	CONSONANCY	CONSTANCIES
CONSENSUSES	CONSERVATORS	CONSIMILITIES	CONSONANTAL	CONSTANTAN
CONSENTANEITIES	CONSERVATORSHIP	CONSIMILITUDE	CONSONANTALLY	CONSTANTANS
CONSENTANEITY	CONSERVATORY	CONSIMILITUDES	CONSONANTLY	CONSTANTLY
CONSENTANEOUS	CONSERVATRICES	CONSIMILITY	CONSONANTS	CONSTATATION
CONSENTANEOUSLY	CONSERVATRIX	CONSISTENCE	CONSORTABLE	CONSTATATIONS
CONSENTERS	CONSERVATRIXES	CONSISTENCES	CONSORTERS	CONSTATING
CONSENTIENCE	CONSERVERS	CONSISTENCIES	CONSORTIAL	CONSTATIVE
CONSENTIENCES	CONSERVING	CONSISTENCY	CONSORTING	CONSTATIVES
CONSENTIENT	CONSIDERABLE	CONSISTENT	CONSORTISM	CONSTELLATE
CONSENTING	CONSIDERABLES	CONSISTENTLY	CONSORTISMS	CONSTELLATED
CONSENTINGLY	CONSIDERABLY	CONSISTING	CONSORTIUM	CONSTELLATES
CONSEQUENCE	CONSIDERANCE	CONSISTORIAL	CONSORTIUMS	CONSTELLATING
CONSEQUENCED	CONSIDERANCES	CONSISTORIAN	CONSPECIFIC	CONSTELLATION
CONSEQUENCES	CONSIDERATE	CONSISTORIES	CONSPECIFICS	CONSTELLATIONAL
CONSEQUENCING	CONSIDERATELY	CONSISTORY	CONSPECTUITIES	CONSTELLATIONS
CONSEQUENT	CONSIDERATENESS	CONSOCIATE	CONSPECTUITY	CONSTELLATORY
CONSEQUENTIAL	CONSIDERATION	CONSOCIATED	CONSPECTUS	CONSTERING
CONSEQUENTIALLY	CONSIDERATIONS	CONSOCIATES	CONSPECTUSES	CONSTERNATE
CONSEQUENTLY	CONSIDERATIVE	CONSOCIATING	CONSPICUITIES	CONSTERNATED
CONSEQUENTS	CONSIDERATIVELY	CONSOCIATION	CONSPICUITY	CONSTERNATES
CONSERVABLE	CONSIDERED	CONSOCIATIONAL	CONSPICUOUS	CONSTERNATING
CONSERVANCIES	CONSIDERER	CONSOCIATIONS	CONSPICUOUSLY	CONSTERNATION
CONSERVANCY	CONSIDERERS	CONSOLABLE	CONSPICUOUSNESS	CONSTERNATIONS
CONSERVANT	CONSIDERING	CONSOLATED	CONSPIRACIES	CONSTIPATE
CONSERVATION	CONSIDERINGLY	CONSOLATES	CONSPIRACY	CONSTIPATED
CONSERVATIONAL	CONSIGLIERE	CONSOLATING	CONSPIRANT	CONSTIPATES
CONSERVATIONIST	CONSIGLIERES	CONSOLATION	CONSPIRANTS	CONSTIPATING

CONSTIPATION	CONSTRUABILITY	CONSULTANT	CONTABESCENT	CONTANGOES
CONSTIPATIONS	CONSTRUABLE	CONSULTANTS	CONTACTABLE	CONTANGOING
CONSTITUENCIES	CONSTRUALS	CONSULTANTSHIP	CONTACTEES	CONTEMNERS
CONSTITUENCY	CONSTRUCTABLE	CONSULTANTSHIPS	CONTACTING	CONTEMNIBLE
CONSTITUENT	CONSTRUCTED	CONSULTATION	CONTACTLESS	CONTEMNIBLY
CONSTITUENTLY	CONSTRUCTER	CONSULTATIONS	CONTACTORS	CONTEMNING
CONSTITUENTS	CONSTRUCTERS	CONSULTATIVE	CONTACTUAL	CONTEMNORS
CONSTITUTE	CONSTRUCTIBLE	CONSULTATIVELY	CONTACTUALLY	CONTEMPERATION
CONSTITUTED	CONSTRUCTING	CONSULTATORY	CONTADINAS	CONTEMPERATIONS
CONSTITUTER	CONSTRUCTION	CONSULTEES	CONTADINOS	CONTEMPERATURE
CONSTITUTERS	CONSTRUCTIONAL	CONSULTERS	CONTAGIONIST	CONTEMPERATURES
CONSTITUTES	CONSTRUCTIONISM	CONSULTING	CONTAGIONISTS	CONTEMPERED
CONSTITUTING	CONSTRUCTIONIST	CONSULTINGS	CONTAGIONS	CONTEMPERING
CONSTITUTION	CONSTRUCTIONS	CONSULTIVE	CONTAGIOUS	CONTEMPERS
CONSTITUTIONAL	CONSTRUCTIVE	CONSULTORS	CONTAGIOUSLY	CONTEMPLABLE
CONSTITUTIONALS	CONSTRUCTIVELY	CONSULTORY	CONTAGIOUSNESS	CONTEMPLANT
CONSTITUTIONIST	CONSTRUCTIVISM	CONSUMABLE	CONTAINABLE	CONTEMPLANTS
CONSTITUTIONS	CONSTRUCTIVISMS	CONSUMABLES	CONTAINERBOARD	CONTEMPLATE
CONSTITUTIVE	CONSTRUCTIVIST	CONSUMEDLY	CONTAINERBOARDS	CONTEMPLATED
CONSTITUTIVELY	CONSTRUCTIVISTS	CONSUMERISM	CONTAINERISE	CONTEMPLATES
CONSTITUTOR	CONSTRUCTOR	CONSUMERISMS	CONTAINERISED	CONTEMPLATING
CONSTITUTORS	CONSTRUCTORS	CONSUMERIST	CONTAINERISES	CONTEMPLATION
CONSTRAINABLE	CONSTRUCTS	CONSUMERISTIC	CONTAINERISING	CONTEMPLATIONS
CONSTRAINED	CONSTRUCTURE	CONSUMERISTS	CONTAINERIZE	CONTEMPLATIST
CONSTRAINEDLY	CONSTRUCTURES	CONSUMERSHIP	CONTAINERIZED	CONTEMPLATISTS
CONSTRAINER	CONSTRUERS	CONSUMERSHIPS	CONTAINERIZES	CONTEMPLATIVE
CONSTRAINERS	CONSTRUING	CONSUMINGLY	CONTAINERIZING	CONTEMPLATIVELY
CONSTRAINING	CONSTUPRATE	CONSUMINGS	CONTAINERLESS	CONTEMPLATIVES
CONSTRAINS	CONSTUPRATED	CONSUMMATE	CONTAINERPORT	CONTEMPLATOR
CONSTRAINT	CONSTUPRATES	CONSUMMATED	CONTAINERPORTS	CONTEMPLATORS
CONSTRAINTS	CONSTUPRATING	CONSUMMATELY	CONTAINERS	CONTEMPORANEAN
CONSTRICTED	CONSTUPRATION	CONSUMMATES	CONTAINERSHIP	CONTEMPORANEANS
CONSTRICTING	CONSTUPRATIONS	CONSUMMATING	CONTAINERSHIPS	CONTEMPORANEITY
CONSTRICTION	CONSUBSIST	CONSUMMATION	CONTAINING	CONTEMPORANEOUS
CONSTRICTIONS	CONSUBSISTED	CONSUMMATIONS	CONTAINMENT	CONTEMPORARIES
CONSTRICTIVE	CONSUBSISTING	CONSUMMATIVE	CONTAINMENTS	CONTEMPORARILY
CONSTRICTIVELY	CONSUBSISTS	CONSUMMATOR	CONTAMINABLE	CONTEMPORARY
CONSTRICTOR	CONSUBSTANTIAL	CONSUMMATORS	CONTAMINANT	CONTEMPORISE
CONSTRICTORS	CONSUBSTANTIATE	CONSUMMATORY	CONTAMINANTS	CONTEMPORISED
CONSTRICTS	CONSUETUDE	CONSUMPTION	CONTAMINATE	CONTEMPORISES
CONSTRINGE	CONSUETUDES	CONSUMPTIONS	CONTAMINATED	CONTEMPORISING
CONSTRINGED	CONSUETUDINARY	CONSUMPTIVE	CONTAMINATES	CONTEMPORIZE
CONSTRINGENCE	CONSULAGES	CONSUMPTIVELY	CONTAMINATING	CONTEMPORIZED
CONSTRINGENCES	CONSULATES	CONSUMPTIVENESS	CONTAMINATION	CONTEMPORIZES
CONSTRINGENCIES	CONSULSHIP	CONSUMPTIVES	CONTAMINATIONS	CONTEMPORIZING
CONSTRINGENCY	CONSULSHIPS	CONSUMPTIVITIES	CONTAMINATIVE	CONTEMPTIBILITY
CONSTRINGENT	CONSULTABLE	CONSUMPTIVITY	CONTAMINATOR	CONTEMPTIBLE
CONSTRINGES	CONSULTANCIES	CONTABESCENCE	CONTAMINATORS	CONTEMPTIBLY
CONSTRINGING	CONSULTANCY	CONTABESCENCES	CONTANGOED	CONTEMPTUOUS

CONTEMPTUOUSLY	CONTEXTUALIZED	CONTINUATIVES	CONTRABBASSO	CONTRADICTORIES
CONTENDENT	CONTEXTUALIZES	CONTINUATOR	CONTRABBASSOS	CONTRADICTORILY
CONTENDENTS	CONTEXTUALIZING	CONTINUATORS	CONTRACEPTION	CONTRADICTORS
CONTENDERS	CONTEXTUALLY	CONTINUEDLY	CONTRACEPTIONS	CONTRADICTORY
CONTENDING	CONTEXTURAL	CONTINUEDNESS	CONTRACEPTIVE	CONTRADICTS
CONTENDINGLY	CONTEXTURE	CONTINUEDNESSES	CONTRACEPTIVES	CONTRAFAGOTTI
CONTENDINGS	CONTEXTURES	CONTINUERS	CONTRACLOCKWISE	CONTRAFAGOTTO
CONTENEMENT	CONTIGNATION	CONTINUING	CONTRACTABILITY	CONTRAFAGOTTOS
CONTENEMENTS	CONTIGNATIONS	CONTINUINGLY	CONTRACTABLE	CONTRAFLOW
CONTENTATION	CONTIGUITIES	CONTINUITIES	CONTRACTABLY	CONTRAFLOWS
CONTENTATIONS	CONTIGUITY	CONTINUITY	CONTRACTED	CONTRAGESTION
CONTENTEDLY	CONTIGUOUS	CONTINUOUS	CONTRACTEDLY	CONTRAGESTIONS
CONTENTEDNESS	CONTIGUOUSLY	CONTINUOUSLY	CONTRACTEDNESS	CONTRAGESTIVE
CONTENTEDNESSES	CONTIGUOUSNESS	CONTINUOUSNESS	CONTRACTIBILITY	CONTRAGESTIVES
CONTENTING	CONTINENCE	CONTINUUMS	CONTRACTIBLE	CONTRAHENT
CONTENTION	CONTINENCES	CONTORNIATE	CONTRACTIBLY	CONTRAHENTS
CONTENTIONS	CONTINENCIES	CONTORNIATES	CONTRACTILE	CONTRAINDICANT
CONTENTIOUS	CONTINENCY	CONTORTEDLY	CONTRACTILITIES	CONTRAINDICANTS
CONTENTIOUSLY	CONTINENTAL	CONTORTEDNESS	CONTRACTILITY	CONTRAINDICATE
CONTENTIOUSNESS	CONTINENTALISM	CONTORTEDNESSES	CONTRACTING	CONTRAINDICATED
CONTENTLESS	CONTINENTALISMS	CONTORTING	CONTRACTION	CONTRAINDICATES
CONTENTMENT	CONTINENTALIST	CONTORTION	CONTRACTIONAL	CONTRALATERAL
CONTENTMENTS	CONTINENTALISTS	CONTORTIONAL	CONTRACTIONARY	CONTRALTOS
CONTERMINAL	CONTINENTALLY	CONTORTIONATE	CONTRACTIONS	CONTRANATANT
CONTERMINALLY	CONTINENTALS	CONTORTIONED	CONTRACTIVE	CONTRAOCTAVE
CONTERMINANT	CONTINENTLY	CONTORTIONISM	CONTRACTIVELY	CONTRAOCTAVES
CONTERMINATE	CONTINENTS	CONTORTIONISMS	CONTRACTIVENESS	CONTRAPLEX
CONTERMINOUS	CONTINGENCE	CONTORTIONIST	CONTRACTOR	CONTRAPOSITION
CONTERMINOUSLY	CONTINGENCES	CONTORTIONISTIC	CONTRACTORS	CONTRAPOSITIONS
CONTESSERATION	CONTINGENCIES	CONTORTIONISTS	CONTRACTUAL	CONTRAPOSITIVE
CONTESSERATIONS	CONTINGENCY	CONTORTIONS	CONTRACTUALLY	CONTRAPOSITIVES
CONTESTABILITY	CONTINGENT	CONTORTIVE	CONTRACTURAL	CONTRAPPOSTO
CONTESTABLE	CONTINGENTLY	CONTOURING	CONTRACTURE	CONTRAPPOSTOS
CONTESTABLENESS	CONTINGENTS	CONTRABAND	CONTRACTURES	CONTRAPROP
CONTESTABLY	CONTINUABLE	CONTRABANDISM	CONTRACYCLICAL	CONTRAPROPELLER
CONTESTANT	CONTINUALITIES	CONTRABANDISMS	CONTRADANCE	CONTRAPROPS
CONTESTANTS	CONTINUALITY	CONTRABANDIST	CONTRADANCES	CONTRAPTION
CONTESTATION	CONTINUALLY	CONTRABANDISTS	CONTRADICT	CONTRAPTIONS
CONTESTATIONS	CONTINUALNESS	CONTRABANDS	CONTRADICTABLE	CONTRAPUNTAL
CONTESTERS	CONTINUALNESSES	CONTRABASS	CONTRADICTED	CONTRAPUNTALIST
CONTESTING	CONTINUANCE	CONTRABASSES	CONTRADICTER	CONTRAPUNTALLY
CONTESTINGLY	CONTINUANCES	CONTRABASSI	CONTRADICTERS	CONTRAPUNTIST
CONTEXTLESS	CONTINUANT	CONTRABASSIST	CONTRADICTING	CONTRAPUNTISTS
CONTEXTUAL	CONTINUANTS	CONTRABASSISTS	CONTRADICTION	CONTRARIAN
CONTEXTUALISE	CONTINUATE	CONTRABASSO	CONTRADICTIONS	CONTRARIANS
CONTEXTUALISED	CONTINUATION	CONTRABASSOON	CONTRADICTIOUS	CONTRARIED
CONTEXTUALISES	CONTINUATIONS	CONTRABASSOONS	CONTRADICTIVE	CONTRARIES
CONTEXTUALISING	CONTINUATIVE	CONTRABASSOS	CONTRADICTIVELY	CONTRARIETIES
CONTEXTUALIZE	CONTINUATIVELY	CONTRABBASSI	CONTRADICTOR	CONTRARIETY

CONTRARILY	CONTRIBUTOR	CONTROVERTING	CONVENORSHIP	CONVERSATIONAL
CONTRARINESS	CONTRIBUTORIES	CONTROVERTIST	CONVENORSHIPS	CONVERSATIONISM
CONTRARINESSES	CONTRIBUTORS	CONTROVERTISTS	CONVENTICLE	CONVERSATIONIST
CONTRARIOUS	CONTRIBUTORY	CONTROVERTS	CONVENTICLED	CONVERSATIONS
CONTRARIOUSLY	CONTRISTATION	CONTUBERNAL	CONVENTICLER	CONVERSATIVE
CONTRARIOUSNESS	CONTRISTATIONS	CONTUBERNYAL	CONVENTICLERS	CONVERSAZIONE
CONTRARIWISE	CONTRISTED	CONTUMACIES	CONVENTICLES	CONVERSAZIONES
CONTRARYING	CONTRISTING	CONTUMACIOUS	CONVENTICLING	CONVERSAZIONI
CONTRASEXUAL	CONTRITELY	CONTUMACIOUSLY	CONVENTING	CONVERSELY
CONTRASEXUALS	CONTRITENESS	CONTUMACITIES	CONVENTION	CONVERSERS
CONTRASTABLE	CONTRITENESSES	CONTUMACITY	CONVENTIONAL	CONVERSING
CONTRASTABLY	CONTRITION	CONTUMELIES	CONVENTIONALISE	CONVERSION
CONTRASTED	CONTRITIONS	CONTUMELIOUS	CONVENTIONALISM	CONVERSIONAL
CONTRASTIER	CONTRITURATE	CONTUMELIOUSLY	CONVENTIONALIST	CONVERSIONARY
CONTRASTIEST	CONTRITURATED	CONTUNDING	CONVENTIONALITY	CONVERSIONS
CONTRASTING	CONTRITURATES	CONTUSIONED	CONVENTIONALIZE	CONVERTAPLANE
CONTRASTINGLY	CONTRITURATING	CONTUSIONS	CONVENTIONALLY	CONVERTAPLANES
CONTRASTIVE	CONTRIVABLE	CONUNDRUMS	CONVENTIONALS	CONVERTEND
CONTRASTIVELY	CONTRIVANCE	CONURBATION	CONVENTIONARY	CONVERTENDS
CONTRATERRENE	CONTRIVANCES	CONURBATIONS	CONVENTIONEER	CONVERTERS
CONTRAVALLATION	CONTRIVEMENT	CONVALESCE	CONVENTIONEERS	CONVERTIBILITY
CONTRAVENE	CONTRIVEMENTS	CONVALESCED	CONVENTIONER	CONVERTIBLE
CONTRAVENED	CONTRIVERS	CONVALESCENCE	CONVENTIONERS	CONVERTIBLENESS
CONTRAVENER	CONTRIVING	CONVALESCENCES	CONVENTIONIST	CONVERTIBLES
CONTRAVENERS	CONTROLLABILITY	CONVALESCENCIES	CONVENTIONISTS	CONVERTIBLY
CONTRAVENES	CONTROLLABLE	CONVALESCENCY	CONVENTIONS	CONVERTING
CONTRAVENING	CONTROLLABLY	CONVALESCENT	CONVENTUAL	CONVERTIPLANE
CONTRAVENTION	CONTROLLED	CONVALESCENTLY	CONVENTUALLY	CONVERTIPLANES
CONTRAVENTIONS	CONTROLLER	CONVALESCENTS	CONVENTUALS	CONVERTITE
CONTRAYERVA	CONTROLLERS	CONVALESCES	CONVERGENCE	CONVERTITES
CONTRAYERVAS	CONTROLLERSHIP	CONVALESCING	CONVERGENCES	CONVERTIVE
CONTRECOUP	CONTROLLERSHIPS	CONVECTING	CONVERGENCIES	CONVERTOPLANE
CONTRECOUPS	CONTROLLING	CONVECTION	CONVERGENCY	CONVERTOPLANES
CONTREDANCE	CONTROLMENT	CONVECTIONAL	CONVERGENT	CONVERTORS
CONTREDANCES	CONTROLMENTS	CONVECTIONS	CONVERGING	CONVEXEDLY
CONTREDANSE	CONTROULED	CONVECTIVE	CONVERSABLE	CONVEXITIES
CONTREDANSES	CONTROULING	CONVECTORS	CONVERSABLENESS	CONVEXNESS
CONTRETEMPS	CONTROVERSE	CONVENABLE	CONVERSABLY	CONVEXNESSES
CONTRIBUTABLE	CONTROVERSES	CONVENANCE	CONVERSANCE	CONVEYABLE
CONTRIBUTARIES	CONTROVERSIAL	CONVENANCES	CONVERSANCES	CONVEYANCE
CONTRIBUTARY	CONTROVERSIALLY	CONVENERSHIP	CONVERSANCIES	CONVEYANCER
CONTRIBUTE	CONTROVERSIES	CONVENERSHIPS	CONVERSANCY	CONVEYANCERS
CONTRIBUTED	CONTROVERSY	CONVENIENCE	CONVERSANT	CONVEYANCES
CONTRIBUTES	CONTROVERT	CONVENIENCES	CONVERSANTLY	CONVEYANCING
CONTRIBUTING	CONTROVERTED	CONVENIENCIES	CONVERSATE	CONVEYANCINGS
CONTRIBUTION	CONTROVERTER	CONVENIENCY	CONVERSATED	CONVEYORISATION
CONTRIBUTIONS	CONTROVERTERS	CONVENIENT	CONVERSATES	CONVEYORISE
CONTRIBUTIVE	CONTROVERTIBLE	CONVENIENTLY	CONVERSATING	CONVEYORISED
CONTRIBUTIVELY	CONTROVERTIBLY	CONVENINGS	CONVERSATION	CONVEYORISES

CONVEYORISING	CONVOLUTIONARY	COOPTATIONS	COPOLYMERISE	COPROLALIAS
CONVEYORIZATION	CONVOLUTIONS	COOPTATIVE	COPOLYMERISED	COPROLITES
CONVEYORIZE	CONVOLVING	COORDINANCE	COPOLYMERISES	COPROLITHS
CONVEYORIZED	CONVOLVULACEOUS	COORDINANCES	COPOLYMERISING	COPROLITIC
CONVEYORIZES	CONVOLVULI	COORDINATE	COPOLYMERIZE	COPROLOGIES
CONVEYORIZING	CONVOLVULUS	COORDINATED	COPOLYMERIZED	COPROMOTER
CONVICINITIES	CONVOLVULUSES	COORDINATELY	COPOLYMERIZES	COPROMOTERS
CONVICINITY	CONVULSANT	COORDINATENESS	COPOLYMERIZING	COPROPHAGAN
CONVICTABLE	CONVULSANTS	COORDINATES	COPOLYMERS	COPROPHAGANS
CONVICTIBLE	CONVULSIBLE	COORDINATING	COPPERASES	COPROPHAGIC
CONVICTING	CONVULSING	COORDINATION	COPPERHEAD	COPROPHAGIES
CONVICTION	CONVULSION	COORDINATIONS	COPPERHEADS	COPROPHAGIST
CONVICTIONAL	CONVULSIONAL	COORDINATIVE	COPPERIEST	COPROPHAGISTS
CONVICTIONS	CONVULSIONARIES	COORDINATOR	COPPERINGS	COPROPHAGOUS
CONVICTISM	CONVULSIONARY	COORDINATORS	COPPERPLATE	COPROPHAGY
CONVICTISMS	CONVULSIONIST	COPARCENARIES	COPPERPLATES	COPROPHILIA
CONVICTIVE	CONVULSIONISTS	COPARCENARY	COPPERSMITH	COPROPHILIAC
CONVICTIVELY	CONVULSIONS	COPARCENER	COPPERSMITHS	COPROPHILIACS
CONVINCEMENT	CONVULSIVE	COPARCENERIES	COPPERWORK	COPROPHILIAS
CONVINCEMENTS	CONVULSIVELY	COPARCENERS	COPPERWORKS	COPROPHILIC
CONVINCERS	CONVULSIVENESS	COPARCENERY	COPPERWORM	COPROPHILOUS
CONVINCIBLE	COOKHOUSES	COPARCENIES	COPPERWORMS	COPROPRIETOR
CONVINCING	COOKSHACKS	COPARENTED	COPPICINGS	COPROPRIETORS
CONVINCINGLY	COOKSTOVES	COPARENTING	COPRAEMIAS	COPROSPERITIES
CONVINCINGNESS	COOLHEADED	COPARTNERED	COPRESENCE	COPROSPERITY
CONVIVIALIST	COOLHOUSES	COPARTNERIES	COPRESENCES	COPROSTEROL
CONVIVIALISTS	COOLINGNESS	COPARTNERING	COPRESENTED	COPROSTEROLS
CONVIVIALITIES	COOLINGNESSES	COPARTNERS	COPRESENTING	COPSEWOODS
CONVIVIALITY	COOLNESSES	COPARTNERSHIP	COPRESENTS	COPUBLISHED
CONVIVIALLY	COOMCEILED	COPARTNERSHIPS	COPRESIDENT	COPUBLISHER
CONVOCATED	COONHOUNDS	COPARTNERY	COPRESIDENTS	COPUBLISHERS
CONVOCATES	COOPERAGES	COPATRIOTS	COPRINCIPAL	COPUBLISHES
CONVOCATING	COOPERATED	COPAYMENTS	COPRINCIPALS	COPUBLISHING
CONVOCATION	COOPERATES	COPERNICIUM	COPRISONER	COPULATING
CONVOCATIONAL	COOPERATING	COPERNICIUMS	COPRISONERS	COPULATION
CONVOCATIONIST	COOPERATION	COPESETTIC	COPROCESSING	COPULATIONS
CONVOCATIONISTS	COOPERATIONIST	COPESTONES	COPROCESSINGS	COPULATIVE
CONVOCATIONS	COOPERATIONISTS	COPILOTING	COPROCESSOR	COPULATIVELY
CONVOCATIVE	COOPERATIONS	COPINGSTONE	COPROCESSORS	COPULATIVES
CONVOCATOR	COOPERATIVE	COPINGSTONES	COPRODUCED	COPULATORY
CONVOCATORS	COOPERATIVELY	COPIOUSNESS	COPRODUCER	COPURIFIED
CONVOLUTED	COOPERATIVENESS	COPIOUSNESSES	COPRODUCERS	COPURIFIES
CONVOLUTEDLY	COOPERATIVES	COPLAINTIFF	COPRODUCES	COPURIFYING
CONVOLUTEDNESS	COOPERATIVITIES	COPLAINTIFFS	COPRODUCING	COPYCATTED
CONVOLUTELY	COOPERATIVITY	COPLANARITIES	COPRODUCTION	COPYCATTING
CONVOLUTES	COOPERATOR	COPLANARITY	COPRODUCTIONS	COPYEDITED
CONVOLUTING	COOPERATORS	COPLOTTING	COPRODUCTS	COPYEDITING
CONVOLUTION	COOPERINGS	COPLOTTINGS	COPROLALIA	COPYFIGHTS
CONVOLUTIONAL	COOPTATION	COPOLYMERIC	COPROLALIAC	COPYGRAPHS

COPYHOLDER	CORBICULATE	COREPRESSORS	CORNELIANS	COROLLIFORM
COPYHOLDERS	CORDECTOMIES	COREQUISITE	CORNEMUSES	COROMANDEL
COPYLEFTED	CORDECTOMY	COREQUISITES	CORNERBACK	COROMANDELS
COPYLEFTING	CORDELLING	CORESEARCHER	CORNERBACKS	CORONAGRAPH
COPYPASTAS	CORDGRASSES	CORESEARCHERS	CORNERINGS	CORONAGRAPHS
COPYREADER	CORDIALISE	CORESIDENT	CORNERSTONE	CORONARIES
COPYREADERS	CORDIALISED	CORESIDENTIAL	CORNERSTONES	CORONATING
COPYREADING	CORDIALISES	CORESIDENTS	CORNERWAYS	CORONATION
COPYREADINGS	CORDIALISING	CORESPONDENT	CORNERWISE	CORONATIONS
COPYRIGHTABLE	CORDIALITIES	CORESPONDENTS	CORNETCIES	CORONAVIRUS
COPYRIGHTED	CORDIALITY	CORFHOUSES	CORNETISTS	CORONAVIRUSES
COPYRIGHTER	CORDIALIZE	CORIACEOUS	CORNETTINI	CORONERSHIP
COPYRIGHTERS	CORDIALIZED	CORIANDERS	CORNETTINO	CORONERSHIPS
COPYRIGHTING	CORDIALIZES	CORINTHIANISE	CORNETTINOS	CORONOGRAPH
COPYRIGHTS	CORDIALIZING	CORINTHIANISED	CORNETTIST	CORONOGRAPHS
COPYTAKERS	CORDIALNESS	CORINTHIANISES	CORNETTISTS	COROTATING
COPYWRITER	CORDIALNESSES	CORINTHIANISING	CORNFIELDS	COROTATION
COPYWRITERS	CORDIERITE	CORINTHIANIZE	CORNFLAKES	COROTATIONS
COPYWRITING	CORDIERITES	CORINTHIANIZED	CORNFLOURS	CORPORALES
COPYWRITINGS	CORDILLERA	CORINTHIANIZES	CORNFLOWER	CORPORALITIES
COQUELICOT	CORDILLERAN	CORINTHIANIZING	CORNFLOWERS	CORPORALITY
COQUELICOTS	CORDILLERAS	CORIVALLED	CORNHUSKER	CORPORALLY
COQUETRIES	CORDLESSES	CORIVALLING	CORNHUSKERS	CORPORALSHIP
COQUETTING	CORDOCENTESES	CORIVALRIES	CORNHUSKING	CORPORALSHIPS
COQUETTISH	CORDOCENTESIS	CORIVALSHIP	CORNHUSKINGS	CORPORASES
COQUETTISHLY	CORDONNETS	CORIVALSHIPS	CORNICHONS	CORPORATELY
COQUETTISHNESS	CORDOTOMIES	CORKBOARDS	CORNICINGS	CORPORATENESS
COQUIMBITE	CORDUROYED	CORKBORERS	CORNICULATE	CORPORATENESSES
COQUIMBITES	CORDUROYING	CORKINESSES	CORNICULUM	CORPORATES
CORACIIFORM	CORDWAINER	CORKSCREWED	CORNICULUMS	CORPORATION
CORADICATE	CORDWAINERIES	CORKSCREWING	CORNIFEROUS	CORPORATIONS
CORALBELLS	CORDWAINERS	CORKSCREWS	CORNIFICATION	CORPORATISE
CORALBERRIES	CORDWAINERY	CORMOPHYTE	CORNIFICATIONS	CORPORATISED
CORALBERRY	CORDYLINES	CORMOPHYTES	CORNIFYING	CORPORATISES
CORALLACEOUS	CORECIPIENT	CORMOPHYTIC	CORNIGEROUS	CORPORATISING
CORALLIFEROUS	CORECIPIENTS	CORMORANTS	CORNINESSES	CORPORATISM
CORALLIFORM	COREDEEMED	CORNACEOUS	CORNOPEANS	CORPORATISMS
CORALLIGENOUS	COREDEEMING	CORNBORERS	CORNROWING	CORPORATIST
CORALLINES	COREFERENTIAL	CORNBRAIDED	CORNSTALKS	CORPORATISTS
CORALLITES	COREGONINE	CORNBRAIDING	CORNSTARCH	CORPORATIVE
CORALLOIDAL	CORELATING	CORNBRAIDS	CORNSTARCHES	CORPORATIVISM
CORALLOIDS	CORELATION	CORNBRANDIES	CORNSTONES	CORPORATIVISMS
CORALROOTS	CORELATIONS	CORNBRANDY	CORNUCOPIA	CORPORATIZE
CORALWORTS	CORELATIVE	CORNBRASHES	CORNUCOPIAN	CORPORATIZED
CORBEILLES	CORELATIVES	CORNBREADS	CORNUCOPIAS	CORPORATIZES
CORBELINGS	CORELIGIONIST	CORNCOCKLE	COROLLACEOUS	CORPORATIZING
CORBELLING	CORELIGIONISTS	CORNCOCKLES	COROLLARIES	CORPORATOR
CORBELLINGS	COREOPSISES	CORNCRAKES	COROLLIFLORAL	CORPORATORS
CORBICULAE	COREPRESSOR	CORNEITISES	COROLLIFLOROUS	CORPOREALISE

CORPOREALISED	CORRECTIVE	CORRIVALRIES	CORRUPTION	CORYNEBACTERIAL
CORPOREALISES	CORRECTIVELY	CORRIVALRY	CORRUPTIONIST	CORYNEBACTERIUM
CORPOREALISING	CORRECTIVES	CORRIVALSHIP	CORRUPTIONISTS	CORYNEFORM
CORPOREALISM	CORRECTNESS	CORRIVALSHIPS	CORRUPTIONS	CORYPHAEUS
CORPOREALISMS	CORRECTNESSES	CORROBORABLE	CORRUPTIVE	CORYPHENES
CORPOREALIST	CORRECTORS	CORROBORANT	CORRUPTIVELY	COSCINOMANCIES
CORPOREALISTS	CORRECTORY	CORROBORATE	CORRUPTNESS	COSCINOMANCY
CORPOREALITIES	CORREGIDOR	CORROBORATED	CORRUPTNESSES	COSCRIPTED
CORPOREALITY	CORREGIDORS	CORROBORATES	CORRUPTORS	COSCRIPTING
CORPOREALIZE	CORRELATABLE	CORROBORATING	CORSELETTE	COSEISMALS
CORPOREALIZED	CORRELATED	CORROBORATION	CORSELETTES	COSEISMICS
CORPOREALIZES	CORRELATES	CORROBORATIONS	CORSETIERE	COSENTIENT
CORPOREALIZING	CORRELATING	CORROBORATIVE	CORSETIERES	COSHERINGS
CORPOREALLY	CORRELATION	CORROBORATIVELY	CORSETIERS	COSIGNATORIES
CORPOREALNESS	CORRELATIONAL	CORROBORATIVES	CORSETRIES	COSIGNATORY
CORPOREALNESSES	CORRELATIONS	CORROBORATOR	CORTICALLY	COSIGNIFICATIVE
CORPOREITIES	CORRELATIVE	CORROBORATORS	CORTICATED	COSINESSES
CORPOREITY	CORRELATIVELY	CORROBORATORY	CORTICATION	COSMECEUTICAL
CORPORIFICATION	CORRELATIVENESS	CORROBOREE	CORTICATIONS	COSMECEUTICALS
CORPORIFIED	CORRELATIVES	CORROBOREED	CORTICOIDS	COSMETICAL
CORPORIFIES	CORRELATIVITIES	CORROBOREEING	CORTICOLOUS	COSMETICALLY
CORPORIFYING	CORRELATIVITY	CORROBOREES	CORTICOSTEROID	COSMETICIAN
CORPOSANTS	CORRELATOR	CORRODANTS	CORTICOSTEROIDS	COSMETICIANS
CORPSELIKE	CORRELATORS	CORRODENTS	CORTICOSTERONE	COSMETICISE
CORPULENCE	CORRELIGIONIST	CORRODIBILITIES	CORTICOSTERONES	COSMETICISED
CORPULENCES	CORRELIGIONISTS	CORRODIBILITY	CORTICOTROPHIC	COSMETICISES
CORPULENCIES	CORREPTION	CORRODIBLE	CORTICOTROPHIN	COSMETICISING
CORPULENCY	CORREPTIONS	CORROSIBILITIES	CORTICOTROPHINS	COSMETICISM
CORPULENTLY	CORRESPOND	CORROSIBILITY	CORTICOTROPIC	COSMETICISMS
CORPUSCLES	CORRESPONDED	CORROSIBLE	CORTICOTROPIN	COSMETICIZE
CORPUSCULAR	CORRESPONDENCE	CORROSIONS	CORTICOTROPINS	COSMETICIZED
CORPUSCULARIAN	CORRESPONDENCES	CORROSIVELY	CORTISONES	COSMETICIZES
CORPUSCULARIANS	CORRESPONDENCY	CORROSIVENESS	CORUSCATED	COSMETICIZING
CORPUSCULARITY	CORRESPONDENT	CORROSIVENESSES	CORUSCATES	COSMETICOLOGIES
CORPUSCULE	CORRESPONDENTLY	CORROSIVES	CORUSCATING	COSMETICOLOGY
CORPUSCULES	CORRESPONDENTS	CORRUGATED	CORUSCATION	COSMETOLOGIES
CORRALLING	CORRESPONDING	CORRUGATES	CORUSCATIONS	COSMETOLOGIST
CORRASIONS	CORRESPONDINGLY	CORRUGATING	CORVETTING	COSMETOLOGISTS
CORRECTABLE	CORRESPONDS	CORRUGATION	CORYBANTES	COSMETOLOGY
CORRECTEST	CORRESPONSIVE	CORRUGATIONS	CORYBANTIC	COSMICALLY
CORRECTIBLE	CORRIGENDA	CORRUGATOR	CORYBANTISM	COSMOCHEMICAL
CORRECTING	CORRIGENDUM	CORRUGATORS	CORYBANTISMS	COSMOCHEMIST
CORRECTION	CORRIGENTS	CORRUPTERS	CORYDALINE	COSMOCHEMISTRY
CORRECTIONAL	CORRIGIBILITIES	CORRUPTEST	CORYDALINES	COSMOCHEMISTS
CORRECTIONER	CORRIGIBILITY	CORRUPTIBILITY	CORYDALISES	COSMOCRATIC
CORRECTIONERS	CORRIGIBLE	CORRUPTIBLE	CORYLOPSES	COSMOCRATS
CORRECTIONS	CORRIGIBLY	CORRUPTIBLENESS	CORYLOPSIS	COSMODROME
CORRECTITUDE	CORRIVALLED	CORRUPTIBLY	CORYMBOSELY	COSMODROMES
CORRECTITUDES	CORRIVALLING	CORRUPTING	CORYNEBACTERIA	COSMOGENIC

COSMOGENIES	COSMOTRONS	COTRANSPORT	COULOMETRY	COUNTERACTS
COSMOGONAL	COSPLAYERS	COTRANSPORTED	COUMARILIC	COUNTERAGENT
COSMOGONIC	COSPLAYING	COTRANSPORTING	COUMARONES	COUNTERAGENTS
COSMOGONICAL	COSPLAYINGS	COTRANSPORTS	COUNCILLOR	COUNTERARGUE
COSMOGONIES	COSPONSORED	COTRUSTEES	COUNCILLORS	COUNTERARGUED
COSMOGONIST	COSPONSORING	COTTABUSES	COUNCILLORSHIP	COUNTERARGUES
COSMOGONISTS	COSPONSORS	COTTAGIEST	COUNCILLORSHIPS	COUNTERARGUING
COSMOGRAPHER	COSPONSORSHIP	COTTAGINGS	COUNCILMAN	COUNTERARGUMENT
COSMOGRAPHERS	COSPONSORSHIPS	COTTERLESS	COUNCILMANIC	COUNTERASSAULT
COSMOGRAPHIC	COSSETTING	COTTIERISM	COUNCILMEN	COUNTERASSAULTS
COSMOGRAPHICAL	COSTALGIAS	COTTIERISMS	COUNCILORS	COUNTERATTACK
COSMOGRAPHIES	COSTARDMONGER	COTTONADES	COUNCILORSHIP	COUNTERATTACKED
COSMOGRAPHIST	COSTARDMONGERS	COTTONIEST	COUNCILORSHIPS	COUNTERATTACKER
COSMOGRAPHISTS	COSTARRING	COTTONMOUTH	COUNCILWOMAN	COUNTERATTACKS
COSMOGRAPHY	COSTEANING	COTTONMOUTHS	COUNCILWOMEN	COUNTERBALANCE
COSMOLATRIES	COSTEANINGS	COTTONOCRACIES	COUNSELABLE	COUNTERBALANCED
COSMOLATRY	COSTERMONGER	COTTONOCRACY	COUNSELEES	COUNTERBALANCES
COSMOLINED	COSTERMONGERS	COTTONSEED	COUNSELING	COUNTERBASE
COSMOLINES	COSTIVENESS	COTTONSEEDS	COUNSELINGS	COUNTERBASES
COSMOLINING	COSTIVENESSES	COTTONTAIL	COUNSELLABLE	COUNTERBID
COSMOLOGIC	COSTLESSLY	COTTONTAILS	COUNSELLED	COUNTERBIDDER
COSMOLOGICAL	COSTLINESS	COTTONWEED	COUNSELLEE	COUNTERBIDDERS
COSMOLOGICALLY	COSTLINESSES	COTTONWEEDS	COUNSELLEES	COUNTERBIDS
COSMOLOGIES	COSTMARIES	COTTONWOOD	COUNSELLING	COUNTERBLAST
COSMOLOGIST	COSTOTOMIES	COTTONWOODS	COUNSELLINGS	COUNTERBLASTS
COSMOLOGISTS	COSTUMERIES	COTURNIXES	COUNSELLOR	COUNTERBLOCKADE
COSMONAUTICS	COSTUMIERS	COTYLEDONAL	COUNSELLORS	COUNTERBLOW
COSMONAUTS	COSTUMINGS	COTYLEDONARY	COUNSELLORSHIP	COUNTERBLOWS
COSMOPLASTIC	COSURFACTANT	COTYLEDONOID	COUNSELLORSHIPS	COUNTERBLUFF
COSMOPOLIS	COSURFACTANTS	COTYLEDONOUS	COUNSELORS	COUNTERBLUFFS
COSMOPOLISES	COTANGENTIAL	COTYLEDONS	COUNSELORSHIP	COUNTERBOND
COSMOPOLITAN	COTANGENTS	COTYLIFORM	COUNSELORSHIPS	COUNTERBONDS
COSMOPOLITANISM	COTELETTES	COTYLOIDAL	COUNTABILITIES	COUNTERBORE
COSMOPOLITANS	COTEMPORANEOUS	COTYLOIDALS	COUNTABILITY	COUNTERBORED
COSMOPOLITE	COTEMPORARY	COTYLOSAUR	COUNTBACKS	COUNTERBORES
COSMOPOLITES	COTENANCIES	COTYLOSAURS	COUNTDOWNS	COUNTERBORING
COSMOPOLITIC	COTERMINOUS	COUCHETTES	COUNTENANCE	COUNTERBRACE
COSMOPOLITICAL	COTERMINOUSLY	COUCHSURFING	COUNTENANCED	COUNTERBRACED
COSMOPOLITICS	COTILLIONS	COUCHSURFINGS	COUNTENANCER	COUNTERBRACES
COSMOPOLITISM	COTONEASTER	COULIBIACA	COUNTENANCERS	COUNTERBRACING
COSMOPOLITISMS	COTONEASTERS	COULIBIACAS	COUNTENANCES	COUNTERBUFF
COSMORAMAS	COTRANSDUCE	COULIBIACS	COUNTENANCING	COUNTERBUFFED
COSMORAMIC	COTRANSDUCED	COULOMBMETER	COUNTERACT	COUNTERBUFFING
COSMOSPHERE	COTRANSDUCES	COULOMBMETERS	COUNTERACTED	COUNTERBUFFS
COSMOSPHERES	COTRANSDUCING	COULOMETER	COUNTERACTING	COUNTERCAMPAIGN
COSMOTHEISM	COTRANSDUCTION	COULOMETERS	COUNTERACTION	COUNTERCHANGE
COSMOTHEISMS	COTRANSDUCTIONS	COULOMETRIC	COUNTERACTIONS	COUNTERCHANGED
COSMOTHETIC	COTRANSFER	COULOMETRICALLY	COUNTERACTIVE	COUNTERCHANGES
COSMOTHETICAL	COTRANSFERS	COULOMETRIES	COUNTERACTIVELY	COUNTERCHANGING

COUNTERCHARGE	COUNTERFEITLY	COUNTERMOTIONS	COUNTERPLEAS	COUNTERREFORMS
COUNTERCHARGED	COUNTERFEITS	COUNTERMOVE	COUNTERPLED	COUNTERRESPONSE
COUNTERCHARGES	COUNTERFESAUNCE	COUNTERMOVED	COUNTERPLOT	COUNTERSANK
COUNTERCHARGING	COUNTERFIRE	COUNTERMOVEMENT	COUNTERPLOTS	COUNTERSCARP
COUNTERCHARM	COUNTERFIRES	COUNTERMOVES	COUNTERPLOTTED	COUNTERSCARPS
COUNTERCHARMED	COUNTERFLOW	COUNTERMOVING	COUNTERPLOTTING	COUNTERSEAL
COUNTERCHARMING	COUNTERFLOWS	COUNTERMURE	COUNTERPLOY	COUNTERSEALED
COUNTERCHARMS	COUNTERFOIL	COUNTERMURED	COUNTERPLOYS	COUNTERSEALING
COUNTERCHECK	COUNTERFOILS	COUNTERMURES	COUNTERPOINT	COUNTERSEALS
COUNTERCHECKED	COUNTERFORCE	COUNTERMURING	COUNTERPOINTED	COUNTERSHADING
COUNTERCHECKING	COUNTERFORCES	COUNTERMYTH	COUNTERPOINTING	COUNTERSHADINGS
COUNTERCHECKS	COUNTERFORT	COUNTERMYTHS	COUNTERPOINTS	COUNTERSHAFT
COUNTERCLAIM	COUNTERFORTS	COUNTEROFFER	COUNTERPOISE	COUNTERSHAFTS
COUNTERCLAIMANT	COUNTERGLOW	COUNTEROFFERS	COUNTERPOISED	COUNTERSHOT
COUNTERCLAIMED	COUNTERGLOWS	COUNTERORDER	COUNTERPOISES	COUNTERSHOTS
COUNTERCLAIMING	COUNTERGUERILLA	COUNTERORDERED	COUNTERPOISING	COUNTERSIGN
COUNTERCLAIMS	COUNTERIMAGE	COUNTERORDERING	COUNTERPOSE	COUNTERSIGNED
COUNTERCOUP	COUNTERIMAGES	COUNTERORDERS	COUNTERPOSED	COUNTERSIGNING
COUNTERCOUPS	COUNTERING	COUNTERPACE	COUNTERPOSES	COUNTERSIGNS
COUNTERCRIES	COUNTERINSTANCE	COUNTERPACES	COUNTERPOSING	COUNTERSINK
COUNTERCRY	COUNTERION	COUNTERPANE	COUNTERPOWER	COUNTERSINKING
COUNTERCULTURAL	COUNTERIONS	COUNTERPANES	COUNTERPOWERS	COUNTERSINKS
COUNTERCULTURE	COUNTERIRRITANT	COUNTERPART	COUNTERPRESSURE	COUNTERSNIPER
COUNTERCULTURES	COUNTERLIGHT	COUNTERPARTIES	COUNTERPROJECT	COUNTERSNIPERS
COUNTERCURRENT	COUNTERLIGHTS	COUNTERPARTS	COUNTERPROJECTS	COUNTERSPELL
COUNTERCURRENTS	COUNTERMAN	COUNTERPARTY	COUNTERPROOF	COUNTERSPELLS
COUNTERCYCLICAL	COUNTERMAND	COUNTERPEISE	COUNTERPROOFS	COUNTERSPIES
COUNTERDEMAND	COUNTERMANDABLE	COUNTERPEISED	COUNTERPROPOSAL	COUNTERSPY
COUNTERDEMANDS	COUNTERMANDED	COUNTERPEISES	COUNTERPROTEST	COUNTERSPYING
COUNTERDRAW	COUNTERMANDING	COUNTERPEISING	COUNTERPROTESTS	COUNTERSPYINGS
COUNTERDRAWING	COUNTERMANDS	COUNTERPETITION	COUNTERPUNCH	COUNTERSTAIN
COUNTERDRAWN	COUNTERMARCH	COUNTERPICKET	COUNTERPUNCHED	COUNTERSTAINED
COUNTERDRAWS	COUNTERMARCHED	COUNTERPICKETED	COUNTERPUNCHER	COUNTERSTAINING
COUNTERDREW	COUNTERMARCHES	COUNTERPICKETS	COUNTERPUNCHERS	COUNTERSTAINS
COUNTEREFFORT	COUNTERMARCHING	COUNTERPLAN	COUNTERPUNCHES	COUNTERSTATE
COUNTEREFFORTS	COUNTERMARK	COUNTERPLANNED	COUNTERPUNCHING	COUNTERSTATED
COUNTEREVIDENCE	COUNTERMARKS	COUNTERPLANNING	COUNTERQUESTION	COUNTERSTATES
COUNTEREXAMPLE	COUNTERMEASURE	COUNTERPLANS	COUNTERRAID	COUNTERSTATING
COUNTEREXAMPLES	COUNTERMEASURES	COUNTERPLAY	COUNTERRAIDED	COUNTERSTEP
COUNTERFACTUAL	COUNTERMELODIES	COUNTERPLAYED	COUNTERRAIDING	COUNTERSTEPS
COUNTERFACTUALS	COUNTERMELODY	COUNTERPLAYER	COUNTERRAIDS	COUNTERSTRATEGY
COUNTERFECT	COUNTERMEMO	COUNTERPLAYERS	COUNTERRALLIED	COUNTERSTREAM
COUNTERFEISANCE	COUNTERMEMOS	COUNTERPLAYING	COUNTERRALLIES	COUNTERSTREAMS
COUNTERFEIT	COUNTERMEN	COUNTERPLAYS	COUNTERRALLY	COUNTERSTRICKEN
COUNTERFEITED	COUNTERMINE	COUNTERPLEA	COUNTERRALLYING	COUNTERSTRIKE
COUNTERFEITER	COUNTERMINED	COUNTERPLEAD	COUNTERREACTION	COUNTERSTRIKES
COUNTERFEITERS	COUNTERMINES	COUNTERPLEADED	COUNTERREFORM	COUNTERSTRIKING
COUNTERFEITING	COUNTERMINING	COUNTERPLEADING	COUNTERREFORMED	COUNTERSTROKE
COUNTERFEITINGS	COUNTERMOTION	COUNTERPLEADS	COUNTERREFORMER	COUNTERSTROKES

ten to fifteen letter words | 773

COUNTERSTRUCK

COUNTERSTRUCK	COUNTERWORDS	COURTCRAFTS	COVENANTEE	COXCOMICAL
COUNTERSTYLE	COUNTERWORK	COURTEOUSLY	COVENANTEES	COXINESSES
COUNTERSTYLES	COUNTERWORKED	COURTEOUSNESS	COVENANTER	COXSWAINED
COUNTERSUBJECT	COUNTERWORKER	COURTEOUSNESSES	COVENANTERS	COXSWAINING
COUNTERSUBJECTS	COUNTERWORKERS	COURTESANS	COVENANTING	COYISHNESS
COUNTERSUE	COUNTERWORKING	COURTESIED	COVENANTOR	COYISHNESSES
COUNTERSUED	COUNTERWORKS	COURTESIES	COVENANTORS	COYOTILLOS
COUNTERSUES	COUNTERWORLD	COURTESYING	COVERALLED	COZINESSES
COUNTERSUING	COUNTERWORLDS	COURTEZANS	COVERMOUNT	CRABAPPLES
COUNTERSUIT	COUNTESSES	COURTHOUSE	COVERMOUNTED	CRABBEDNESS
COUNTERSUITS	COUNTINGHOUSE	COURTHOUSES	COVERMOUNTING	CRABBEDNESSES
COUNTERSUNK	COUNTINGHOUSES	COURTIERISM	COVERMOUNTS	CRABBINESS
COUNTERTACTIC	COUNTLESSLY	COURTIERISMS	COVERSINES	CRABBINESSES
COUNTERTACTICS	COUNTLINES	COURTIERLIKE	COVERSLIPS	CRABEATERS
COUNTERTENDENCY	COUNTRIFIED	COURTIERLY	COVERTNESS	CRABGRASSES
COUNTERTENOR	COUNTROLLED	COURTLIEST	COVERTNESSES	CRABSTICKS
COUNTERTENORS	COUNTROLLING	COURTLINESS	COVERTURES	CRACKAJACK
COUNTERTERROR	COUNTRYFIED	COURTLINESSES	COVETINGLY	CRACKAJACKS
COUNTERTERRORS	COUNTRYISH	COURTLINGS	COVETIVENESS	CRACKBACKS
COUNTERTHREAT	COUNTRYMAN	COURTROOMS	COVETIVENESSES	CRACKBERRIES
COUNTERTHREATS	COUNTRYMEN	COURTSHIPS	COVETOUSLY	CRACKBERRY
COUNTERTHRUST	COUNTRYSEAT	COURTSIDES	COVETOUSNESS	CRACKBRAIN
COUNTERTHRUSTS	COUNTRYSEATS	COURTYARDS	COVETOUSNESSES	CRACKBRAINED
COUNTERTOP	COUNTRYSIDE	COUSCOUSES	COWARDICES	CRACKBRAINS
COUNTERTOPS	COUNTRYSIDES	COUSCOUSOU	COWARDLIER	CRACKDOWNS
COUNTERTRADE	COUNTRYWIDE	COUSCOUSOUS	COWARDLIEST	CRACKERJACK
COUNTERTRADED	COUNTRYWOMAN	COUSINAGES	COWARDLINESS	CRACKERJACKS
COUNTERTRADES	COUNTRYWOMEN	COUSINHOOD	COWARDLINESSES	CRACKHEADS
COUNTERTRADING	COUNTSHIPS	COUSINHOODS	COWARDRIES	CRACKLEWARE
COUNTERTREND	COUPLEDOMS	COUSINRIES	COWARDSHIP	CRACKLEWARES
COUNTERTRENDS	COUPLEMENT	COUSINSHIP	COWARDSHIPS	CRACKLIEST
COUNTERTYPE	COUPLEMENTS	COUSINSHIPS	COWBERRIES	CRACKLINGS
COUNTERTYPES	COUPONINGS	COUTURIERE	COWBOYINGS	CRACOVIENNE
COUNTERVAIL	COURAGEFUL	COUTURIERES	COWCATCHER	CRACOVIENNES
COUNTERVAILABLE	COURAGEOUS	COUTURIERS	COWCATCHERS	CRADLESONG
COUNTERVAILED	COURAGEOUSLY	COVALENCES	COWERINGLY	CRADLESONGS
COUNTERVAILING	COURAGEOUSNESS	COVALENCIES	COWFEEDERS	CRADLEWALK
COUNTERVAILS	COURANTOES	COVALENTLY	COWFETERIA	CRADLEWALKS
COUNTERVIEW	COURBARILS	COVARIANCE	COWFETERIAS	CRAFTINESS
COUNTERVIEWS	COURBETTES	COVARIANCES	COWGRASSES	CRAFTINESSES
COUNTERVIOLENCE	COURGETTES	COVARIANTS	COWLSTAFFS	CRAFTMANSHIP
COUNTERWEIGH	COURIERING	COVARIATES	COWLSTAVES	CRAFTMANSHIPS
COUNTERWEIGHED	COURSEBOOK	COVARIATION	COWORKINGS	CRAFTSMANLIKE
COUNTERWEIGHING	COURSEBOOKS	COVARIATIONS	COWPUNCHER	CRAFTSMANLY
COUNTERWEIGHS	COURSEWARE	COVELLINES	COWPUNCHERS	CRAFTSMANSHIP
COUNTERWEIGHT	COURSEWARES	COVELLITES	COXCOMBICAL	CRAFTSMANSHIPS
COUNTERWEIGHTED	COURSEWORK	COVENANTAL	COXCOMBICALITY	CRAFTSPEOPLE
COUNTERWEIGHTS	COURSEWORKS	COVENANTALLY	COXCOMBICALLY	CRAFTSPERSON
COUNTERWORD	COURTCRAFT	COVENANTED	COXCOMBRIES	CRAFTSPERSONS

CRAFTSWOMAN	CRANIOSCOPIST	CRAUNCHABLE	CREATURELINESS	CREMATORIAL
CRAFTSWOMEN	CRANIOSCOPISTS	CRAUNCHIER	CREATURELY	CREMATORIES
CRAFTWORKS	CRANIOSCOPY	CRAUNCHIEST	CREATURESHIP	CREMATORIUM
CRAGGEDNESS	CRANIOTOMIES	CRAUNCHINESS	CREATURESHIPS	CREMATORIUMS
CRAGGEDNESSES	CRANIOTOMY	CRAUNCHINESSES	CREDENTIAL	CREMOCARPS
CRAGGINESS	CRANKBAITS	CRAUNCHING	CREDENTIALED	CRENATIONS
CRAGGINESSES	CRANKCASES	CRAVATTING	CREDENTIALING	CRENATURES
CRAIGFLUKE	CRANKHANDLE	CRAVENNESS	CREDENTIALINGS	CRENELATED
CRAIGFLUKES	CRANKHANDLES	CRAVENNESSES	CREDENTIALISM	CRENELATES
CRAKEBERRIES	CRANKINESS	CRAWDADDIES	CREDENTIALISMS	CRENELATING
CRAKEBERRY	CRANKINESSES	CRAWFISHED	CREDENTIALLED	CRENELATION
CRAMBOCLINK	CRANKNESSES	CRAWFISHES	CREDENTIALLING	CRENELATIONS
CRAMBOCLINKS	CRANKSHAFT	CRAWFISHING	CREDENTIALLINGS	CRENELLATE
CRAMOISIES	CRANKSHAFTS	CRAWLINGLY	CREDENTIALS	CRENELLATED
CRAMPBARKS	CRANREUCHS	CRAYFISHES	CREDIBILITIES	CRENELLATES
CRAMPFISHES	CRAPEHANGER	CRAYONISTS	CREDIBILITY	CRENELLATING
CRAMPONING	CRAPEHANGERS	CRAZINESSES	CREDIBLENESS	CRENELLATION
CRAMPONNED	CRAPEHANGING	CRAZYWEEDS	CREDIBLENESSES	CRENELLATIONS
CRAMPONNING	CRAPEHANGINGS	CREAKINESS	CREDITABILITIES	CRENELLING
CRAMPONNINGS	CRAPSHOOTER	CREAKINESSES	CREDITABILITY	CRENULATED
CRANACHANS	CRAPSHOOTERS	CREAKINGLY	CREDITABLE	CRENULATION
CRANBERRIES	CRAPSHOOTS	CREAMERIES	CREDITABLENESS	CRENULATIONS
CRANEFLIES	CRAPULENCE	CREAMINESS	CREDITABLY	CREOLISATION
CRANESBILL	CRAPULENCES	CREAMINESSES	CREDITLESS	CREOLISATIONS
CRANESBILLS	CRAPULENTLY	CREAMPUFFS	CREDITORSHIP	CREOLISING
CRANIECTOMIES	CRAPULOSITIES	CREAMWARES	CREDITORSHIPS	CREOLIZATION
CRANIECTOMY	CRAPULOSITY	CREASELESS	CREDITWORTHIER	CREOLIZATIONS
CRANIOCEREBRAL	CRAPULOUSLY	CREASOTING	CREDITWORTHIEST	CREOLIZING
CRANIOFACIAL	CRAPULOUSNESS	CREATIANISM	CREDITWORTHY	CREOPHAGIES
CRANIOGNOMIES	CRAPULOUSNESSES	CREATIANISMS	CREDULITIES	CREOPHAGOUS
CRANIOGNOMY	CRAQUELURE	CREATININE	CREDULOUSLY	CREOSOTING
CRANIOLOGICAL	CRAQUELURES	CREATININES	CREDULOUSNESS	CREPEHANGER
CRANIOLOGICALLY	CRASHINGLY	CREATIONAL	CREDULOUSNESSES	CREPEHANGERS
CRANIOLOGIES	CRASHWORTHIER	CREATIONISM	CREEKSIDES	CREPEHANGING
CRANIOLOGIST	CRASHWORTHIEST	CREATIONISMS	CREEPINESS	CREPEHANGINGS
CRANIOLOGISTS	CRASHWORTHINESS	CREATIONIST	CREEPINESSES	CREPINESSES
CRANIOLOGY	CRASHWORTHY	CREATIONISTIC	CREEPINGLY	CREPITATED
CRANIOMETER	CRASSAMENTA	CREATIONISTS	CREEPMOUSE	CREPITATES
CRANIOMETERS	CRASSAMENTUM	CREATIVELY	CREEPMOUSES	CREPITATING
CRANIOMETRIC	CRASSITUDE	CREATIVENESS	CREESHIEST	CREPITATION
CRANIOMETRICAL	CRASSITUDES	CREATIVENESSES	CREMAILLERE	CREPITATIONS
CRANIOMETRIES	CRASSNESSES	CREATIVITIES	CREMAILLERES	CREPITATIVE
CRANIOMETRIST	CRASSULACEAN	CREATIVITY	CREMASTERS	CREPITUSES
CRANIOMETRISTS	CRASSULACEOUS	CREATORSHIP	CREMATIONISM	CREPOLINES
CRANIOMETRY	CRATERIFORM	CREATORSHIPS	CREMATIONISMS	CREPUSCLES
CRANIOPAGI	CRATERINGS	CREATRESSES	CREMATIONIST	CREPUSCULAR
CRANIOPAGUS	CRATERLESS	CREATRIXES	CREMATIONISTS	CREPUSCULE
CRANIOSACRAL	CRATERLETS	CREATUREHOOD	CREMATIONS	CREPUSCULES
CRANIOSCOPIES	CRATERLIKE	CREATUREHOODS	CREMATORIA	CREPUSCULOUS

CRESCENDOED	CRIMINALISTS	CRIPPLINGLY	CROAKINESSES	CROSSBENCHES
CRESCENDOES	CRIMINALITIES	CRIPPLINGS	CROCHETERS	CROSSBILLS
CRESCENDOING	CRIMINALITY	CRISPATION	CROCHETING	CROSSBIRTH
CRESCENDOS	CRIMINALIZATION	CRISPATIONS	CROCHETINGS	CROSSBIRTHS
CRESCENTADE	CRIMINALIZE	CRISPATURE	CROCIDOLITE	CROSSBITES
CRESCENTADES	CRIMINALIZED	CRISPATURES	CROCIDOLITES	CROSSBITING
CRESCENTED	CRIMINALIZES	CRISPBREAD	CROCKERIES	CROSSBITTEN
CRESCENTIC	CRIMINALIZING	CRISPBREADS	CROCODILES	CROSSBONES
CRESCIVELY	CRIMINALLY	CRISPENING	CROCODILIAN	CROSSBOWER
CRESCOGRAPH	CRIMINATED	CRISPHEADS	CROCODILIANS	CROSSBOWERS
CRESCOGRAPHS	CRIMINATES	CRISPINESS	CROCOISITE	CROSSBOWMAN
CRESTFALLEN	CRIMINATING	CRISPINESSES	CROCOISITES	CROSSBOWMEN
CRESTFALLENLY	CRIMINATION	CRISPNESSES	CROCOSMIAS	CROSSBREDS
CRESTFALLENNESS	CRIMINATIONS	CRISSCROSS	CROISSANTS	CROSSBREED
CRETACEOUS	CRIMINATIVE	CRISSCROSSED	CROKINOLES	CROSSBREEDING
CRETACEOUSES	CRIMINATOR	CRISSCROSSES	CROOKBACKED	CROSSBREEDINGS
CRETACEOUSLY	CRIMINATORS	CRISSCROSSING	CROOKBACKS	CROSSBREEDS
CRETINISED	CRIMINATORY	CRISTIFORM	CROOKEDEST	CROSSBUCKS
CRETINISES	CRIMINOGENIC	CRISTOBALITE	CROOKEDNESS	CROSSCHECK
CRETINISING	CRIMINOLOGIC	CRISTOBALITES	CROOKEDNESSES	CROSSCHECKED
CRETINISMS	CRIMINOLOGICAL	CRITERIONS	CROOKERIES	CROSSCHECKING
CRETINIZED	CRIMINOLOGIES	CRITERIUMS	CROOKNECKS	CROSSCHECKS
CRETINIZES	CRIMINOLOGIST	CRITHIDIAL	CROPDUSTER	CROSSCLAIM
CRETINIZING	CRIMINOLOGISTS	CRITHOMANCIES	CROPDUSTERS	CROSSCLAIMS
CRETINOIDS	CRIMINOLOGY	CRITHOMANCY	CROPDUSTING	CROSSCOURT
CREVASSING	CRIMINOUSNESS	CRITICALITIES	CROPDUSTINGS	CROSSCURRENT
CREWELISTS	CRIMINOUSNESSES	CRITICALITY	CROQUANTES	CROSSCURRENTS
CREWELLERIES	CRIMSONING	CRITICALLY	CROQUETING	CROSSCUTTING
CREWELLERY	CRIMSONNESS	CRITICALNESS	CROQUETTES	CROSSCUTTINGS
CREWELLING	CRIMSONNESSES	CRITICALNESSES	CROQUIGNOLE	CROSSETTES
CREWELLINGS	CRINGELING	CRITICASTER	CROQUIGNOLES	CROSSFALLS
CREWELWORK	CRINGELINGS	CRITICASTERS	CROREPATIS	CROSSFIELD
CREWELWORKS	CRINGEWORTHIER	CRITICISABLE	CROSSABILITIES	CROSSFIRES
CRIBRATION	CRINGEWORTHIEST	CRITICISED	CROSSABILITY	CROSSFISHES
CRIBRATIONS	CRINGEWORTHY	CRITICISER	CROSSANDRA	CROSSHAIRS
CRIBRIFORM	CRINGINGLY	CRITICISERS	CROSSANDRAS	CROSSHATCH
CRICKETERS	CRINICULTURAL	CRITICISES	CROSSBANDED	CROSSHATCHED
CRICKETING	CRINIGEROUS	CRITICISING	CROSSBANDING	CROSSHATCHES
CRICKETINGS	CRINKLEROOT	CRITICISINGLY	CROSSBANDINGS	CROSSHATCHING
CRIMEWAVES	CRINKLEROOTS	CRITICISMS	CROSSBANDS	CROSSHATCHINGS
CRIMINALESE	CRINKLIEST	CRITICIZABLE	CROSSBARRED	CROSSHEADS
CRIMINALESES	CRINOIDEAN	CRITICIZED	CROSSBARRING	CROSSJACKS
CRIMINALISATION	CRINOIDEANS	CRITICIZER	CROSSBARRINGS	CROSSLIGHT
CRIMINALISE	CRINOLETTE	CRITICIZERS	CROSSBEAMS	CROSSLIGHTS
CRIMINALISED	CRINOLETTES	CRITICIZES	CROSSBEARER	CROSSLINGUISTIC
CRIMINALISES	CRINOLINED	CRITICIZING	CROSSBEARERS	CROSSNESSES
CRIMINALISING	CRINOLINES	CRITICIZINGLY	CROSSBENCH	CROSSOPTERYGIAN
CRIMINALIST	CRIPPLEWARE	CRITIQUING	CROSSBENCHER	CROSSOVERS
CRIMINALISTICS	CRIPPLEWARES	CROAKINESS	CROSSBENCHERS	CROSSPATCH

CROSSPATCHES	CROWNPIECE	CRUSTINESS	CRYOSURGERY	CRYPTOGRAPHS
CROSSPIECE	CROWNPIECES	CRUSTINESSES	CRYOSURGICAL	CRYPTOGRAPHY
CROSSPIECES	CROWNWORKS	CRUTCHINGS	CRYOTHERAPIES	CRYPTOLOGIC
CROSSROADS	CROWSTEPPED	CRYBULLIES	CRYOTHERAPY	CRYPTOLOGICAL
CROSSRUFFED	CRUCIATELY	CRYMOTHERAPIES	CRYPTAESTHESIA	CRYPTOLOGIES
CROSSRUFFING	CRUCIFEROUS	CRYMOTHERAPY	CRYPTAESTHESIAS	CRYPTOLOGIST
CROSSRUFFS	CRUCIFIERS	CRYOBIOLOGICAL	CRYPTAESTHETIC	CRYPTOLOGISTS
CROSSTALKS	CRUCIFIXES	CRYOBIOLOGIES	CRYPTANALYSES	CRYPTOLOGY
CROSSTREES	CRUCIFIXION	CRYOBIOLOGIST	CRYPTANALYSIS	CRYPTOMERIA
CROSSWALKS	CRUCIFIXIONS	CRYOBIOLOGISTS	CRYPTANALYST	CRYPTOMERIAS
CROSSWINDS	CRUCIFORMLY	CRYOBIOLOGY	CRYPTANALYSTS	CRYPTOMETER
CROSSWIRES	CRUCIFORMS	CRYOCABLES	CRYPTANALYTIC	CRYPTOMETERS
CROSSWORDS	CRUCIFYING	CRYOCONITE	CRYPTANALYTICAL	CRYPTOMNESIA
CROSSWORTS	CRUCIVERBAL	CRYOCONITES	CRYPTARITHM	CRYPTOMNESIAS
CROTALARIA	CRUCIVERBALISM	CRYOGENICALLY	CRYPTARITHMS	CRYPTOMNESIC
CROTALARIAS	CRUCIVERBALISMS	CRYOGENICS	CRYPTESTHESIA	CRYPTONYMOUS
CROTALISMS	CRUCIVERBALIST	CRYOGENIES	CRYPTESTHESIAS	CRYPTONYMS
CROTCHETED	CRUCIVERBALISTS	CRYOGLOBULIN	CRYPTESTHETIC	CRYPTOPHYTE
CROTCHETEER	CRUDENESSES	CRYOGLOBULINS	CRYPTICALLY	CRYPTOPHYTES
CROTCHETEERS	CRUELNESSES	CRYOHYDRATE	CRYPTOBIONT	CRYPTOPHYTIC
CROTCHETIER	CRUISERWEIGHT	CRYOHYDRATES	CRYPTOBIONTS	CRYPTORCHID
CROTCHETIEST	CRUISERWEIGHTS	CRYOMETERS	CRYPTOBIOSES	CRYPTORCHIDISM
CROTCHETINESS	CRUISEWAYS	CRYOMETRIC	CRYPTOBIOSIS	CRYPTORCHIDISMS
CROTCHETINESSES	CRUISEWEAR	CRYOMETRIES	CRYPTOCLASTIC	CRYPTORCHIDS
CROTONALDEHYDE	CRUISEWEARS	CRYONICALLY	CRYPTOCOCCAL	CRYPTORCHISM
CROTONALDEHYDES	CRUMBCLOTH	CRYOPHILIC	CRYPTOCOCCI	CRYPTORCHISMS
CROTONBUGS	CRUMBCLOTHS	CRYOPHORUS	CRYPTOCOCCOSES	CRYPTOSPORIDIA
CROUPINESS	CRUMBLIEST	CRYOPHORUSES	CRYPTOCOCCOSIS	CRYPTOSPORIDIUM
CROUPINESSES	CRUMBLINESS	CRYOPHYSICS	CRYPTOCOCCUS	CRYPTOZOIC
CROUSTADES	CRUMBLINESSES	CRYOPHYTES	CRYPTOCURRENCY	CRYPTOZOITE
CROWBARRED	CRUMBLINGS	CRYOPLANKTON	CRYPTOGAMIAN	CRYPTOZOITES
CROWBARRING	CRUMMINESS	CRYOPLANKTONS	CRYPTOGAMIC	CRYPTOZOOLOGIES
CROWBERRIES	CRUMMINESSES	CRYOPRECIPITATE	CRYPTOGAMIES	CRYPTOZOOLOGIST
CROWDEDNESS	CRUMPLIEST	CRYOPRESERVE	CRYPTOGAMIST	CRYPTOZOOLOGY
CROWDEDNESSES	CRUMPLINGS	CRYOPRESERVED	CRYPTOGAMISTS	CRYSTALISABLE
CROWDFUNDED	CRUNCHABLE	CRYOPRESERVES	CRYPTOGAMOUS	CRYSTALISATION
CROWDFUNDING	CRUNCHIEST	CRYOPRESERVING	CRYPTOGAMS	CRYSTALISATIONS
CROWDFUNDINGS	CRUNCHINESS	CRYOPROBES	CRYPTOGAMY	CRYSTALISE
CROWDFUNDS	CRUNCHINESSES	CRYOPROTECTANT	CRYPTOGENIC	CRYSTALISED
CROWDSOURCE	CRUNCHINGS	CRYOPROTECTANTS	CRYPTOGRAM	CRYSTALISER
CROWDSOURCED	CRUSHABILITIES	CRYOPROTECTIVE	CRYPTOGRAMS	CRYSTALISERS
CROWDSOURCES	CRUSHABILITY	CRYOSCOPES	CRYPTOGRAPH	CRYSTALISES
CROWDSOURCING	CRUSHINGLY	CRYOSCOPIC	CRYPTOGRAPHER	CRYSTALISING
CROWDSOURCINGS	CRUSHPROOF	CRYOSCOPIES	CRYPTOGRAPHERS	CRYSTALIZABLE
CROWDWORKING	CRUSTACEAN	CRYOSLEEPS	CRYPTOGRAPHIC	CRYSTALIZATION
CROWDWORKINGS	CRUSTACEANS	CRYOSTATIC	CRYPTOGRAPHICAL	CRYSTALIZATIONS
CROWKEEPER	CRUSTACEOUS	CRYOSURGEON	CRYPTOGRAPHIES	CRYSTALIZE
CROWKEEPERS	CRUSTATION	CRYOSURGEONS	CRYPTOGRAPHIST	CRYSTALIZED
CROWNLANDS	CRUSTATIONS	CRYOSURGERIES	CRYPTOGRAPHISTS	CRYSTALIZER

CRYSTALIZERS	CUCKOLDISING	CULTIVATED	CUNCTATION	CURATORSHIPS
CRYSTALIZES	CUCKOLDIZE	CULTIVATES	CUNCTATIONS	CURATRICES
CRYSTALIZING	CUCKOLDIZED	CULTIVATING	CUNCTATIOUS	CURATRIXES
CRYSTALLINE	CUCKOLDIZES	CULTIVATION	CUNCTATIVE	CURBSTONES
CRYSTALLINES	CUCKOLDIZING	CULTIVATIONS	CUNCTATORS	CURCUMINES
CRYSTALLINITIES	CUCKOLDOMS	CULTIVATOR	CUNCTATORY	CURDINESSES
CRYSTALLINITY	CUCKOLDRIES	CULTIVATORS	CUNEIFORMS	CURETTAGES
CRYSTALLISABLE	CUCKOOFLOWER	CULTRIFORM	CUNNILINCTUS	CURETTEMENT
CRYSTALLISATION	CUCKOOFLOWERS	CULTURABLE	CUNNILINCTUSES	CURETTEMENTS
CRYSTALLISE	CUCKOOPINT	CULTURALLY	CUNNILINGUS	CURFUFFLED
CRYSTALLISED	CUCKOOPINTS	CULTURELESS	CUNNILINGUSES	CURFUFFLES
CRYSTALLISER	CUCULIFORM	CULTURISTS	CUNNINGEST	CURFUFFLING
CRYSTALLISERS	CUCULLATED	CULVERINEER	CUNNINGNESS	CURIALISMS
CRYSTALLISES	CUCULLATELY	CULVERINEERS	CUNNINGNESSES	CURIALISTIC
CRYSTALLISING	CUCUMIFORM	CULVERTAGE	CUPBEARERS	CURIALISTS
CRYSTALLITE	CUCURBITACEOUS	CULVERTAGES	CUPBOARDED	CURIETHERAPIES
CRYSTALLITES	CUCURBITAL	CULVERTAILED	CUPBOARDING	CURIETHERAPY
CRYSTALLITIC	CUDDLESOME	CULVERTING	CUPELLATION	CURIOSITIES
CRYSTALLITIS	CUDGELINGS	CUMBERBUND	CUPELLATIONS	CURIOUSEST
CRYSTALLITISES	CUDGELLERS	CUMBERBUNDS	CUPFERRONS	CURIOUSNESS
CRYSTALLIZABLE	CUDGELLING	CUMBERLESS	CUPHOLDERS	CURIOUSNESSES
CRYSTALLIZATION	CUDGELLINGS	CUMBERMENT	CUPIDINOUS	CURLICUING
CRYSTALLIZE	CUFFUFFLES	CUMBERMENTS	CUPIDITIES	CURLIEWURLIE
CRYSTALLIZED	CUIRASSIER	CUMBERSOME	CUPRAMMONIUM	CURLIEWURLIES
CRYSTALLIZER	CUIRASSIERS	CUMBERSOMELY	CUPRAMMONIUMS	CURLINESSES
CRYSTALLIZERS	CUIRASSING	CUMBERSOMENESS	CUPRESSUSES	CURLPAPERS
CRYSTALLIZES	CUISINARTS	CUMBRANCES	CUPRIFEROUS	CURMUDGEON
CRYSTALLIZING	CUISINIERS	CUMBROUSLY	CUPRONICKEL	CURMUDGEONLIER
CRYSTALLOGRAPHY	CULICIFORM	CUMBROUSNESS	CUPRONICKELS	CURMUDGEONLIEST
CRYSTALLOID	CULINARIAN	CUMBROUSNESSES	CUPULIFEROUS	CURMUDGEONLY
CRYSTALLOIDAL	CULINARIANS	CUMMERBUND	CURABILITIES	CURMUDGEONS
CRYSTALLOIDS	CULINARILY	CUMMERBUNDS	CURABILITY	CURMURRING
CRYSTALLOMANCY	CULLENDERS	CUMMINGTONITE	CURABLENESS	CURMURRINGS
CTENOPHORAN	CULMIFEROUS	CUMMINGTONITES	CURABLENESSES	CURNAPTIOUS
CTENOPHORANS	CULMINATED	CUMULATELY	CURANDERAS	CURRAJONGS
CTENOPHORE	CULMINATES	CUMULATING	CURANDEROS	CURRANTIER
CTENOPHORES	CULMINATING	CUMULATION	CURARISATION	CURRANTIEST
CUADRILLAS	CULMINATION	CUMULATIONS	CURARISATIONS	CURRAWONGS
CUBANELLES	CULMINATIONS	CUMULATIVE	CURARISING	CURREJONGS
CUBBYHOLES	CULPABILITIES	CUMULATIVELY	CURARIZATION	CURRENCIES
CUBICALNESS	CULPABILITY	CUMULATIVENESS	CURARIZATIONS	CURRENTNESS
CUBICALNESSES	CULPABLENESS	CUMULIFORM	CURARIZING	CURRENTNESSES
CUBICITIES	CULPABLENESSES	CUMULOCIRRI	CURATESHIP	CURRICULAR
CUBISTICALLY	CULTISHNESS	CUMULOCIRRUS	CURATESHIPS	CURRICULUM
CUBMASTERS	CULTISHNESSES	CUMULONIMBI	CURATIVELY	CURRICULUMS
CUCKOLDING	CULTIVABILITIES	CUMULONIMBUS	CURATIVENESS	CURRIERIES
CUCKOLDISE	CULTIVABILITY	CUMULONIMBUSES	CURATIVENESSES	CURRIJONGS
CUCKOLDISED	CULTIVABLE	CUMULOSTRATI	CURATORIAL	CURRISHNESS
CUCKOLDISES	CULTIVATABLE	CUMULOSTRATUS	CURATORSHIP	CURRISIINESSES

CURRYCOMBED	CUSHIONIEST	CUTINISING	CYBERBULLYING	CYCADACEOUS
CURRYCOMBING	CUSHIONING	CUTINIZATION	CYBERBULLYINGS	CYCADEOIDS
CURRYCOMBS	CUSHIONINGS	CUTINIZATIONS	CYBERCAFES	CYCADOPHYTE
CURSEDNESS	CUSHIONLESS	CUTINIZING	CYBERCASTS	CYCADOPHYTES
CURSEDNESSES	CUSPIDATED	CUTTHROATS	CYBERCHONDRIA	CYCLAMATES
CURSELARIE	CUSPIDATION	CUTTLEBONE	CYBERCHONDRIAC	CYCLANDELATE
CURSIVENESS	CUSPIDATIONS	CUTTLEBONES	CYBERCHONDRIACS	CYCLANDELATES
CURSIVENESSES	CUSPIDORES	CUTTLEFISH	CYBERCHONDRIAS	CYCLANTHACEOUS
CURSORINESS	CUSSEDNESS	CUTTLEFISHES	CYBERCRIME	CYCLAZOCINE
CURSORINESSES	CUSSEDNESSES	CYANAMIDES	CYBERCRIMES	CYCLAZOCINES
CURSTNESSES	CUSTARDIER	CYANIDATION	CYBERCRIMINAL	CYCLEPATHS
CURTAILERS	CUSTARDIEST	CYANIDATIONS	CYBERCRIMINALS	CYCLICALITIES
CURTAILING	CUSTODIANS	CYANIDINGS	CYBERNATED	CYCLICALITY
CURTAILMENT	CUSTODIANSHIP	CYANOACETYLENE	CYBERNATES	CYCLICALLY
CURTAILMENTS	CUSTODIANSHIPS	CYANOACETYLENES	CYBERNATING	CYCLICISMS
CURTAINING	CUSTODIERS	CYANOACRYLATE	CYBERNATION	CYCLICITIES
CURTAINLESS	CUSTOMABLE	CYANOACRYLATES	CYBERNATIONS	CYCLISATION
CURTALAXES	CUSTOMARIES	CYANOBACTERIA	CYBERNAUTS	CYCLISATIONS
CURTATIONS	CUSTOMARILY	CYANOBACTERIUM	CYBERNETIC	CYCLIZATION
CURTILAGES	CUSTOMARINESS	CYANOCOBALAMIN	CYBERNETICAL	CYCLIZATIONS
CURTNESSES	CUSTOMARINESSES	CYANOCOBALAMINE	CYBERNETICALLY	CYCLIZINES
CURTSEYING	CUSTOMHOUSE	CYANOCOBALAMINS	CYBERNETICIAN	CYCLOADDITION
CURVACEOUS	CUSTOMHOUSES	CYANOETHYLATE	CYBERNETICIANS	CYCLOADDITIONS
CURVACEOUSLY	CUSTOMISATION	CYANOETHYLATED	CYBERNETICIST	CYCLOALIPHATIC
CURVACEOUSNESS	CUSTOMISATIONS	CYANOETHYLATES	CYBERNETICISTS	CYCLOALKANE
CURVACIOUS	CUSTOMISED	CYANOETHYLATING	CYBERNETICS	CYCLOALKANES
CURVACIOUSLY	CUSTOMISER	CYANOETHYLATION	CYBERPHOBIA	CYCLOBARBITONE
CURVACIOUSNESS	CUSTOMISERS	CYANOGENAMIDE	CYBERPHOBIAS	CYCLOBARBITONES
CURVATIONS	CUSTOMISES	CYANOGENAMIDES	CYBERPHOBIC	CYCLODEXTRIN
CURVATURES	CUSTOMISING	CYANOGENESES	CYBERPORNS	CYCLODEXTRINS
CURVEBALLED	CUSTOMIZATION	CYANOGENESIS	CYBERPUNKS	CYCLODIALYSES
CURVEBALLING	CUSTOMIZATIONS	CYANOGENETIC	CYBERSECURITIES	CYCLODIALYSIS
CURVEBALLS	CUSTOMIZED	CYANOGENIC	CYBERSECURITY	CYCLODIENE
CURVEDNESS	CUSTOMIZER	CYANOHYDRIN	CYBERSEXES	CYCLODIENES
CURVEDNESSES	CUSTOMIZERS	CYANOHYDRINS	CYBERSPACE	CYCLOGENESES
CURVETTING	CUSTOMIZES	CYANOMETER	CYBERSPACES	CYCLOGENESIS
CURVICAUDATE	CUSTOMIZING	CYANOMETERS	CYBERSQUATTER	CYCLOGIROS
CURVICOSTATE	CUSTOMSHOUSE	CYANOPHYTE	CYBERSQUATTERS	CYCLOGRAPH
CURVIFOLIATE	CUSTOMSHOUSES	CYANOPHYTES	CYBERSQUATTING	CYCLOGRAPHIC
CURVILINEAL	CUSTUMARIES	CYANOTYPES	CYBERSQUATTINGS	CYCLOGRAPHS
CURVILINEALLY	CUTABILITIES	CYANURATES	CYBERSTALKER	CYCLOHEXANE
CURVILINEAR	CUTABILITY	CYATHIFORM	CYBERSTALKERS	CYCLOHEXANES
CURVILINEARITY	CUTANEOUSLY	CYBERATHLETE	CYBERSTALKING	CYCLOHEXANONE
CURVILINEARLY	CUTCHERIES	CYBERATHLETES	CYBERSTALKINGS	CYCLOHEXANONES
CURVINESSES	CUTCHERRIES	CYBERATHLETICS	CYBERTERRORISM	CYCLOHEXIMIDE
CURVIROSTRAL	CUTENESSES	CYBERATTACK	CYBERTERRORISMS	CYCLOHEXIMIDES
CUSHINESSES	CUTGRASSES	CYBERATTACKS	CYBERTERRORIST	CYCLOHEXYLAMINE
CUSHIONETS	CUTINISATION	CYBERBULLIES	CYBERTERRORISTS	CYCLOIDALLY
CUSHIONIER	CUTINISATIONS	CYBERBULLY	CYBRARIANS	CYCLOIDIAN

C

CYCLOIDIANS	CYCLOSTOMATOUS	CYNGHANEDD	CYSTOCARPIC	CYTOLYSINS
CYCLOLITHS	CYCLOSTOME	CYNGHANEDDS	CYSTOCARPS	CYTOMEGALIC
CYCLOMETER	CYCLOSTOMES	CYNICALNESS	CYSTOCELES	CYTOMEGALOVIRUS
CYCLOMETERS	CYCLOSTOMOUS	CYNICALNESSES	CYSTOGENOUS	CYTOMEMBRANE
CYCLOMETRIES	CYCLOSTYLE	CYNOMOLGUS	CYSTOGRAPHIES	CYTOMEMBRANES
CYCLOMETRY	CYCLOSTYLED	CYNOMOLGUSES	CYSTOGRAPHY	CYTOMETERS
CYCLONICAL	CYCLOSTYLES	CYNOPHILIA	CYSTOLITHIASES	CYTOMETRIC
CYCLONICALLY	CYCLOSTYLING	CYNOPHILIAS	CYSTOLITHIASIS	CYTOMETRIES
CYCLONITES	CYCLOTHYME	CYNOPHILIST	CYSTOLITHS	CYTOPATHIC
CYCLOOLEFIN	CYCLOTHYMES	CYNOPHILISTS	CYSTOSCOPE	CYTOPATHIES
CYCLOOLEFINIC	CYCLOTHYMIA	CYNOPHOBES	CYSTOSCOPES	CYTOPATHOGENIC
CYCLOOLEFINS	CYCLOTHYMIAC	CYNOPHOBIA	CYSTOSCOPIC	CYTOPATHOLOGIES
CYCLOPAEDIA	CYCLOTHYMIACS	CYNOPHOBIAS	CYSTOSCOPIES	CYTOPATHOLOGY
CYCLOPAEDIAS	CYCLOTHYMIAS	CYNOPHOBIC	CYSTOSCOPY	CYTOPENIAS
CYCLOPAEDIC	CYCLOTHYMIC	CYNOPHOBICS	CYSTOSTOMIES	CYTOPHILIC
CYCLOPAEDIST	CYCLOTHYMICS	CYNOPODOUS	CYSTOSTOMY	CYTOPHOTOMETRIC
CYCLOPAEDISTS	CYCLOTOMIC	CYPERACEOUS	CYSTOTOMIES	CYTOPHOTOMETRY
CYCLOPARAFFIN	CYCLOTRONS	CYPRINODONT	CYTOCHALASIN	CYTOPLASMIC
CYCLOPARAFFINS	CYLINDERED	CYPRINODONTS	CYTOCHALASINS	CYTOPLASMICALLY
CYCLOPEDIA	CYLINDERING	CYPRINOIDS	CYTOCHEMICAL	CYTOPLASMS
CYCLOPEDIAS	CYLINDRACEOUS	CYPRIPEDIA	CYTOCHEMISTRIES	CYTOPLASTIC
CYCLOPEDIC	CYLINDRICAL	CYPRIPEDIUM	CYTOCHEMISTRY	CYTOPLASTS
CYCLOPEDIST	CYLINDRICALITY	CYPRIPEDIUMS	CYTOCHROME	CYTOSKELETAL
CYCLOPEDISTS	CYLINDRICALLY	CYPROHEPTADINE	CYTOCHROMES	CYTOSKELETON
CYCLOPENTADIENE	CYLINDRICALNESS	CYPROHEPTADINES	CYTODIAGNOSES	CYTOSKELETONS
CYCLOPENTANE	CYLINDRICITIES	CYPROTERONE	CYTODIAGNOSIS	CYTOSTATIC
CYCLOPENTANES	CYLINDRICITY	CYPROTERONES	CYTOGENESES	CYTOSTATICALLY
CYCLOPENTOLATE	CYLINDRIFORM	CYSTEAMINE	CYTOGENESIS	CYTOSTATICS
CYCLOPENTOLATES	CYLINDRITE	CYSTEAMINES	CYTOGENETIC	CYTOTAXONOMIC
CYCLOPLEGIA	CYLINDRITES	CYSTECTOMIES	CYTOGENETICAL	CYTOTAXONOMIES
CYCLOPLEGIAS	CYLINDROID	CYSTECTOMY	CYTOGENETICALLY	CYTOTAXONOMIST
CYCLOPLEGIC	CYLINDROIDS	CYSTICERCI	CYTOGENETICIST	CYTOTAXONOMISTS
CYCLOPROPANE	CYMAGRAPHS	CYSTICERCOID	CYTOGENETICISTS	CYTOTAXONOMY
CYCLOPROPANES	CYMBALEERS	CYSTICERCOIDS	CYTOGENETICS	CYTOTECHNOLOGY
CYCLORAMAS	CYMBALISTS	CYSTICERCOSES	CYTOGENIES	CYTOTOXICITIES
CYCLORAMIC	CYMBIDIUMS	CYSTICERCOSIS	CYTOKINESES	CYTOTOXICITY
CYCLOSERINE	CYMIFEROUS	CYSTICERCUS	CYTOKINESIS	CYTOTOXINS
CYCLOSERINES	CYMOGRAPHIC	CYSTIDEANS	CYTOKINETIC	CZAREVICHES
CYCLOSPERMOUS	CYMOGRAPHS	CYSTINOSES	CYTOKININS	CZAREVITCH
CYCLOSPORIN	CYMOPHANES	CYSTINOSIS	CYTOLOGICAL	CZAREVITCHES
CYCLOSPORINE	CYMOPHANOUS	CYSTINURIA	CYTOLOGICALLY	
CYCLOSPORINES	CYMOTRICHIES	CYSTINURIAS	CYTOLOGIES	
CYCLOSPORINS	CYMOTRICHOUS	CYSTITIDES	CYTOLOGIST	
CYCLOSTOMATE	CYMOTRICHY	CYSTITISES	CYTOLOGISTS	

D

DABBLINGLY	DAHABIYAHS	DAMNIFYING	DARKNESSES	DAUGHTERLIER
DACHSHUNDS	DAHABIYEHS	DAMOISELLE	DARLINGNESS	DAUGHTERLIEST
DACOITAGES	DAILINESSES	DAMOISELLES	DARLINGNESSES	DAUGHTERLINESS
DACQUOISES	DAILYNESSES	DAMPCOURSE	DARMSTADTIUM	DAUGHTERLING
DACTYLICALLY	DAINTINESS	DAMPCOURSES	DARMSTADTIUMS	DAUGHTERLINGS
DACTYLIOGRAPHY	DAINTINESSES	DAMPISHNESS	DARNATIONS	DAUGHTERLY
DACTYLIOLOGIES	DAIRYMAIDS	DAMPISHNESSES	DARNEDESTS	DAUNDERING
DACTYLIOLOGY	DAISYWHEEL	DAMPNESSES	DARRAIGNED	DAUNOMYCIN
DACTYLIOMANCIES	DAISYWHEELS	DAMSELFISH	DARRAIGNES	DAUNOMYCINS
DACTYLIOMANCY	DALLIANCES	DAMSELFISHES	DARRAIGNING	DAUNORUBICIN
DACTYLISTS	DALMATIANS	DAMSELFLIES	DARRAIGNMENT	DAUNORUBICINS
DACTYLOGRAM	DALTONIANS	DANCECORES	DARRAIGNMENTS	DAUNTINGLY
DACTYLOGRAMS	DALTONISMS	DANCEHALLS	DARRAINING	DAUNTLESSLY
DACTYLOGRAPHER	DAMAGEABILITIES	DANCEWEARS	DARRAYNING	DAUNTLESSNESS
DACTYLOGRAPHERS	DAMAGEABILITY	DANDELIONS	DARTBOARDS	DAUNTLESSNESSES
DACTYLOGRAPHIC	DAMAGEABLE	DANDIFICATION	DARTITISES	DAUNTONING
DACTYLOGRAPHIES	DAMAGINGLY	DANDIFICATIONS	DARUNAVIRS	DAUPHINESS
DACTYLOGRAPHY	DAMASCEENE	DANDIFYING	DASHBOARDS	DAUPHINESSES
DACTYLOLOGIES	DAMASCEENED	DANDIPRATS	DASHLIGHTS	DAVENPORTS
DACTYLOLOGY	DAMASCEENES	DANDRUFFIER	DASTARDIES	DAWDLINGLY
DACTYLOSCOPIES	DAMASCEENING	DANDRUFFIEST	DASTARDLIER	DAWSONITES
DACTYLOSCOPY	DAMASCENED	DANDYFUNKS	DASTARDLIEST	DAYCATIONS
DAFFADOWNDILLY	DAMASCENES	DANDYISHLY	DASTARDLINESS	DAYCENTRES
DAFFINESSES	DAMASCENING	DANDYPRATS	DASTARDLINESSES	DAYDREAMED
DAFFODILLIES	DAMASCENINGS	DANGERLESS	DASTARDNESS	DAYDREAMER
DAFFODILLY	DAMASKEENED	DANGEROUSLY	DASTARDNESSES	DAYDREAMERS
DAFTNESSES	DAMASKEENING	DANGEROUSNESS	DASYMETERS	DAYDREAMIER
DAGGERBOARD	DAMASKEENS	DANGEROUSNESSES	DASYPAEDAL	DAYDREAMIEST
DAGGERBOARDS	DAMASKINED	DANGLINGLY	DASYPHYLLOUS	DAYDREAMING
DAGGERLIKE	DAMASKINING	DANKNESSES	DATABASING	DAYDREAMINGS
DAGUERREAN	DAMASQUINED	DANNEBROGS	DATABUSSES	DAYDREAMLIKE
DAGUERREOTYPE	DAMASQUINING	DANTHONIAS	DATAGLOVES	DAYFLOWERS
DAGUERREOTYPED	DAMASQUINS	DAPPERLING	DATAMATION	DAYLIGHTED
DAGUERREOTYPER	DAMINOZIDE	DAPPERLINGS	DATAMATIONS	DAYLIGHTING
DAGUERREOTYPERS	DAMINOZIDES	DAPPERNESS	DATAVEILLANCE	DAYLIGHTINGS
DAGUERREOTYPES	DAMNABILITIES	DAPPERNESSES	DATAVEILLANCES	DAYSAILERS
DAGUERREOTYPIES	DAMNABILITY	DAREDEVILRIES	DATEDNESSES	DAYSAILING
DAGUERREOTYPING	DAMNABLENESS	DAREDEVILRY	DATELINING	DAYSAILORS
DAGUERREOTYPIST	DAMNABLENESSES	DAREDEVILS	DAUGHTERBOARD	DAYSPRINGS
DAGUERREOTYPY	DAMNATIONS	DAREDEVILTRIES	DAUGHTERBOARDS	DAYWORKERS
DAHABEEAHS	DAMNEDESTS	DAREDEVILTRY	DAUGHTERHOOD	DAZEDNESSES
DAHABEEYAH	DAMNIFICATION	DARINGNESS	DAUGHTERHOODS	DAZZLEMENT
DAHABEEYAHS	DAMNIFICATIONS	DARINGNESSES	DAUGHTERLESS	DAZZLEMENTS

DAZZLINGLY	DEAFNESSES	DEATHBLOWS	DEBILITATING	DECALESCENCE
DEACIDIFICATION	DEALATIONS	DEATHLESSLY	DEBILITATION	DECALESCENCES
DEACIDIFIED	DEALBATION	DEATHLESSNESS	DEBILITATIONS	DECALESCENT
DEACIDIFIES	DEALBATIONS	DEATHLESSNESSES	DEBILITATIVE	DECALITERS
DEACIDIFYING	DEALBREAKER	DEATHLIEST	DEBILITIES	DECALITRES
DEACONESSES	DEALBREAKERS	DEATHLINESS	DEBOARDING	DECALOGIST
DEACONHOOD	DEALCOHOLISE	DEATHLINESSES	DEBONAIRLY	DECALOGISTS
DEACONHOODS	DEALCOHOLISED	DEATHTRAPS	DEBONAIRNESS	DECALOGUES
DEACONRIES	DEALCOHOLISES	DEATHWARDS	DEBONAIRNESSES	DECAMERONIC
DEACONSHIP	DEALCOHOLISING	DEATHWATCH	DEBONNAIRE	DECAMEROUS
DEACONSHIPS	DEALCOHOLIZE	DEATHWATCHES	DEBOUCHING	DECAMETERS
DEACTIVATE	DEALCOHOLIZED	DEATTRIBUTE	DEBOUCHMENT	DECAMETHONIUM
DEACTIVATED	DEALCOHOLIZES	DEATTRIBUTED	DEBOUCHMENTS	DECAMETHONIUMS
DEACTIVATES	DEALCOHOLIZING	DEATTRIBUTES	DEBOUCHURE	DECAMETRES
DEACTIVATING	DEALERSHIP	DEATTRIBUTING	DEBOUCHURES	DECAMETRIC
DEACTIVATION	DEALERSHIPS	DEBAGGINGS	DEBRIDEMENT	DECAMPMENT
DEACTIVATIONS	DEALFISHES	DEBARCATION	DEBRIDEMENTS	DECAMPMENTS
DEACTIVATOR	DEALIGNING	DEBARCATIONS	DEBRIEFERS	DECANDRIAN
DEACTIVATORS	DEALMAKERS	DEBARKATION	DEBRIEFING	DECANDROUS
DEADENINGLY	DEAMBULATORIES	DEBARKATIONS	DEBRIEFINGS	DECANEDIOIC
DEADENINGS	DEAMBULATORY	DEBARMENTS	DEBRUISING	DECANICALLY
DEADHEADED	DEAMINASES	DEBARRASSED	DEBUGGINGS	DECANTATED
DEADHEADING	DEAMINATED	DEBARRASSES	DEBUTANTES	DECANTATES
DEADHOUSES	DEAMINATES	DEBARRASSING	DECACHORDS	DECANTATING
DEADLIFTED	DEAMINATING	DEBASEDNESS	DECADENCES	DECANTATION
DEADLIFTING	DEAMINATION	DEBASEDNESSES	DECADENCIES	DECANTATIONS
DEADLIGHTS	DEAMINATIONS	DEBASEMENT	DECADENTLY	DECAPITALISE
DEADLINESS	DEAMINISATION	DEBASEMENTS	DECAFFEINATE	DECAPITALISED
DEADLINESSES	DEAMINISATIONS	DEBASINGLY	DECAFFEINATED	DECAPITALISES
DEADLINING	DEAMINISED	DEBATEABLE	DECAFFEINATES	DECAPITALISING
DEADLOCKED	DEAMINISES	DEBATEMENT	DECAFFEINATING	DECAPITALIZE
DEADLOCKING	DEAMINISING	DEBATEMENTS	DECAGONALLY	DECAPITALIZED
DEADNAMING	DEAMINIZATION	DEBATINGLY	DECAGRAMME	DECAPITALIZES
DEADNESSES	DEAMINIZATIONS	DEBAUCHEDLY	DECAGRAMMES	DECAPITALIZING
DEADPANNED	DEAMINIZED	DEBAUCHEDNESS	DECAGYNIAN	DECAPITATE
DEADPANNER	DEAMINIZES	DEBAUCHEDNESSES	DECAGYNOUS	DECAPITATED
DEADPANNERS	DEAMINIZING	DEBAUCHEES	DECAHEDRAL	DECAPITATES
DEADPANNING	DEARBOUGHT	DEBAUCHERIES	DECAHEDRON	DECAPITATING
DEADSTOCKS	DEARNESSES	DEBAUCHERS	DECAHEDRONS	DECAPITATION
DEADSTROKE	DEARTICULATE	DEBAUCHERY	DECAHYDRATE	DECAPITATIONS
DEADWATERS	DEARTICULATED	DEBAUCHING	DECAHYDRATES	DECAPITATOR
DEADWEIGHT	DEARTICULATES	DEBAUCHMENT	DECALCIFICATION	DECAPITATORS
DEADWEIGHTS	DEARTICULATING	DEBAUCHMENTS	DECALCIFIED	DECAPODANS
DEAERATING	DEASPIRATE	DEBEARDING	DECALCIFIER	DECAPODOUS
DEAERATION	DEASPIRATED	DEBENTURED	DECALCIFIERS	DECAPSULATE
DEAERATIONS	DEASPIRATES	DEBENTURES	DECALCIFIES	DECAPSULATED
DEAERATORS	DEASPIRATING	DEBILITATE	DECALCIFYING	DECAPSULATES
DEAFENINGLY	DEASPIRATION	DEBILITATED	DECALCOMANIA	DECAPSULATING
DEAFENINGS	DEASPIRATIONS	DEBILITATES	DECALCOMANIAS	DECAPSULATION

DECAPSULATIONS	DECARTELIZING	DECENNARIES	DECHEANCES	DECIMETRIC
DECARBONATE	DECASTERES	DECENNIALLY	DECHLORINATE	DECINORMAL
DECARBONATED	DECASTICHS	DECENNIALS	DECHLORINATED	DECIPHERABILITY
DECARBONATES	DECASTYLES	DECENNIUMS	DECHLORINATES	DECIPHERABLE
DECARBONATING	DECASUALISATION	DECENNOVAL	DECHLORINATING	DECIPHERED
DECARBONATION	DECASUALISE	DECENTERED	DECHLORINATION	DECIPHERER
DECARBONATIONS	DECASUALISED	DECENTERING	DECHLORINATIONS	DECIPHERERS
DECARBONATOR	DECASUALISES	DECENTERINGS	DECHRISTIANISE	DECIPHERING
DECARBONATORS	DECASUALISING	DECENTNESS	DECHRISTIANISED	DECIPHERMENT
DECARBONISATION	DECASUALIZATION	DECENTNESSES	DECHRISTIANISES	DECIPHERMENTS
DECARBONISE	DECASUALIZE	DECENTRALISE	DECHRISTIANIZE	DECISIONAL
DECARBONISED	DECASUALIZED	DECENTRALISED	DECHRISTIANIZED	DECISIONED
DECARBONISER	DECASUALIZES	DECENTRALISES	DECHRISTIANIZES	DECISIONING
DECARBONISERS	DECASUALIZING	DECENTRALISING	DECIDABILITIES	DECISIVELY
DECARBONISES	DECASYLLABIC	DECENTRALIST	DECIDABILITY	DECISIVENESS
DECARBONISING	DECASYLLABICS	DECENTRALISTS	DECIDEDNESS	DECISIVENESSES
DECARBONIZATION	DECASYLLABLE	DECENTRALIZE	DECIDEDNESSES	DECISTERES
DECARBONIZE	DECASYLLABLES	DECENTRALIZED	DECIDUOUSLY	DECITIZENISE
DECARBONIZED	DECATHLETE	DECENTRALIZES	DECIDUOUSNESS	DECITIZENISED
DECARBONIZER	DECATHLETES	DECENTRALIZING	DECIDUOUSNESSES	DECITIZENISES
DECARBONIZERS	DECATHLONS	DECENTRING	DECIGRAMME	DECITIZENISING
DECARBONIZES	DECAUDATED	DECEPTIBILITIES	DECIGRAMMES	DECITIZENIZE
DECARBONIZING	DECAUDATES	DECEPTIBILITY	DECILITERS	DECITIZENIZED
DECARBOXYLASE	DECAUDATING	DECEPTIBLE	DECILITRES	DECITIZENIZES
DECARBOXYLASES	DECEITFULLY	DECEPTIONAL	DECILLIONS	DECITIZENIZING
DECARBOXYLATE	DECEITFULNESS	DECEPTIONS	DECILLIONTH	DECIVILISE
DECARBOXYLATED	DECEITFULNESSES	DECEPTIOUS	DECILLIONTHS	DECIVILISED
DECARBOXYLATES	DECEIVABILITIES	DECEPTIVELY	DECIMALISATION	DECIVILISES
DECARBOXYLATING	DECEIVABILITY	DECEPTIVENESS	DECIMALISATIONS	DECIVILISING
DECARBOXYLATION	DECEIVABLE	DECEPTIVENESSES	DECIMALISE	DECIVILIZE
DECARBURATION	DECEIVABLENESS	DECEREBRATE	DECIMALISED	DECIVILIZED
DECARBURATIONS	DECEIVABLY	DECEREBRATED	DECIMALISES	DECIVILIZES
DECARBURISATION	DECEIVINGLY	DECEREBRATES	DECIMALISING	DECIVILIZING
DECARBURISE	DECEIVINGS	DECEREBRATING	DECIMALISM	DECKCHAIRS
DECARBURISED	DECELERATE	DECEREBRATION	DECIMALISMS	DECKHOUSES
DECARBURISES	DECELERATED	DECEREBRATIONS	DECIMALIST	DECLAIMANT
DECARBURISING	DECELERATES	DECEREBRISE	DECIMALISTS	DECLAIMANTS
DECARBURIZATION	DECELERATING	DECEREBRISED	DECIMALIZATION	DECLAIMERS
DECARBURIZE	DECELERATION	DECEREBRISES	DECIMALIZATIONS	DECLAIMING
DECARBURIZED	DECELERATIONS	DECEREBRISING	DECIMALIZE	DECLAIMINGS
DECARBURIZES	DECELERATOR	DECEREBRIZE	DECIMALIZED	DECLAMATION
DECARBURIZING	DECELERATORS	DECEREBRIZED	DECIMALIZES	DECLAMATIONS
DECARTELISE	DECELEROMETER	DECEREBRIZES	DECIMALIZING	DECLAMATORILY
DECARTELISED	DECELEROMETERS	DECEREBRIZING	DECIMATING	DECLAMATORY
DECARTELISES	DECELERONS	DECERTIFICATION	DECIMATION	DECLARABLE
DECARTELISING	DECEMVIRAL	DECERTIFIED	DECIMATIONS	DECLARANTS
DECARTELIZE	DECEMVIRATE	DECERTIFIES	DECIMATORS	DECLARATION
DECARTELIZED	DECEMVIRATES	DECERTIFYING	DECIMETERS	DECLARATIONS
DECARTELIZES	DECENARIES	DECESSIONS	DECIMETRES	DECLARATIVE

DECLARATIVELY	DECOLLATOR	DECOLOURISES	DECOMPRESS	DECONTAMINATOR
DECLARATOR	DECOLLATORS	DECOLOURISING	DECOMPRESSED	DECONTAMINATORS
DECLARATORILY	DECOLLETAGE	DECOLOURIZATION	DECOMPRESSES	DECONTEXTUALISE
DECLARATORS	DECOLLETAGES	DECOLOURIZE	DECOMPRESSING	DECONTEXTUALIZE
DECLARATORY	DECOLLETES	DECOLOURIZED	DECOMPRESSION	DECONTROLLED
DECLAREDLY	DECOLONISATION	DECOLOURIZER	DECOMPRESSIONS	DECONTROLLING
DECLASSIFIABLE	DECOLONISATIONS	DECOLOURIZERS	DECOMPRESSIVE	DECONTROLS
DECLASSIFIED	DECOLONISE	DECOLOURIZES	DECOMPRESSOR	DECORATING
DECLASSIFIES	DECOLONISED	DECOLOURIZING	DECOMPRESSORS	DECORATINGS
DECLASSIFY	DECOLONISES	DECOMMISSION	DECONCENTRATE	DECORATION
DECLASSIFYING	DECOLONISING	DECOMMISSIONED	DECONCENTRATED	DECORATIONS
DECLASSING	DECOLONIZATION	DECOMMISSIONER	DECONCENTRATES	DECORATIVE
DECLENSION	DECOLONIZATIONS	DECOMMISSIONERS	DECONCENTRATING	DECORATIVELY
DECLENSIONAL	DECOLONIZE	DECOMMISSIONING	DECONCENTRATION	DECORATIVENESS
DECLENSIONALLY	DECOLONIZED	DECOMMISSIONS	DECONDITION	DECORATORS
DECLENSIONS	DECOLONIZES	DECOMMITTED	DECONDITIONED	DECOROUSLY
DECLINABLE	DECOLONIZING	DECOMMITTING	DECONDITIONING	DECOROUSNESS
DECLINANTS	DECOLORANT	DECOMMUNISATION	DECONDITIONS	DECOROUSNESSES
DECLINATION	DECOLORANTS	DECOMMUNISE	DECONGESTANT	DECORTICATE
DECLINATIONAL	DECOLORATE	DECOMMUNISED	DECONGESTANTS	DECORTICATED
DECLINATIONS	DECOLORATED	DECOMMUNISES	DECONGESTED	DECORTICATES
DECLINATOR	DECOLORATES	DECOMMUNISING	DECONGESTING	DECORTICATING
DECLINATORIES	DECOLORATING	DECOMMUNIZATION	DECONGESTION	DECORTICATION
DECLINATORS	DECOLORATION	DECOMMUNIZE	DECONGESTIONS	DECORTICATIONS
DECLINATORY	DECOLORATIONS	DECOMMUNIZED	DECONGESTIVE	DECORTICATOR
DECLINATURE	DECOLORING	DECOMMUNIZES	DECONGESTS	DECORTICATORS
DECLINATURES	DECOLORISATION	DECOMMUNIZING	DECONSECRATE	DECOUPAGED
DECLINISTS	DECOLORISATIONS	DECOMPENSATE	DECONSECRATED	DECOUPAGES
DECLINOMETER	DECOLORISE	DECOMPENSATED	DECONSECRATES	DECOUPAGING
DECLINOMETERS	DECOLORISED	DECOMPENSATES	DECONSECRATING	DECOUPLERS
DECLIVITIES	DECOLORISER	DECOMPENSATING	DECONSECRATION	DECOUPLING
DECLIVITOUS	DECOLORISERS	DECOMPENSATION	DECONSECRATIONS	DECOUPLINGS
DECLUTCHED	DECOLORISES	DECOMPENSATIONS	DECONSTRUCT	DECRASSIFIED
DECLUTCHES	DECOLORISING	DECOMPOSABILITY	DECONSTRUCTED	DECRASSIFIES
DECLUTCHING	DECOLORIZATION	DECOMPOSABLE	DECONSTRUCTING	DECRASSIFY
DECLUTTERED	DECOLORIZATIONS	DECOMPOSED	DECONSTRUCTION	DECRASSIFYING
DECLUTTERING	DECOLORIZE	DECOMPOSER	DECONSTRUCTIONS	DECREASING
DECLUTTERS	DECOLORIZED	DECOMPOSERS	DECONSTRUCTIVE	DECREASINGLY
DECOCTIBLE	DECOLORIZER	DECOMPOSES	DECONSTRUCTOR	DECREASINGS
DECOCTIONS	DECOLORIZERS	DECOMPOSING	DECONSTRUCTORS	DECREEABLE
DECOCTURES	DECOLORIZES	DECOMPOSITE	DECONSTRUCTS	DECREMENTAL
DECOHERENCE	DECOLORIZING	DECOMPOSITES	DECONTAMINANT	DECREMENTED
DECOHERENCES	DECOLOURED	DECOMPOSITION	DECONTAMINANTS	DECREMENTING
DECOHERERS	DECOLOURING	DECOMPOSITIONS	DECONTAMINATE	DECREMENTS
DECOLLATED	DECOLOURISATION	DECOMPOUND	DECONTAMINATED	DECREPITATE
DECOLLATES	DECOLOURISE	DECOMPOUNDABLE	DECONTAMINATES	DECREPITATED
DECOLLATING	DECOLOURISED	DECOMPOUNDED	DECONTAMINATING	DECREPITATES
DECOLLATION	DECOLOURISER	DECOMPOUNDING	DECONTAMINATION	DECREPITATING
DECOLLATIONS	DECOLOURISERS	DECOMPOUNDS	DECONTAMINATIVE	DECREPITATION

D

DECREPITATIONS	DECUSSATING	DEEPNESSES	DEFECATORS	DEFENSIVENESS
DECREPITLY	DECUSSATION	DEEPWATERMAN	DEFECTIBILITIES	DEFENSIVENESSES
DECREPITNESS	DECUSSATIONS	DEEPWATERMEN	DEFECTIBILITY	DEFENSIVES
DECREPITNESSES	DEDICATEDLY	DEERBERRIES	DEFECTIBLE	DEFERENCES
DECREPITUDE	DEDICATEES	DEERGRASSES	DEFECTIONIST	DEFERENTIAL
DECREPITUDES	DEDICATING	DEERHOUNDS	DEFECTIONISTS	DEFERENTIALLY
DECRESCENCE	DEDICATION	DEERSTALKER	DEFECTIONS	DEFERMENTS
DECRESCENCES	DEDICATIONAL	DEERSTALKERS	DEFECTIVELY	DEFERRABLE
DECRESCENDO	DEDICATIONS	DEERSTALKING	DEFECTIVENESS	DEFERRABLES
DECRESCENDOS	DEDICATIVE	DEERSTALKINGS	DEFECTIVENESSES	DEFERVESCENCE
DECRESCENT	DEDICATORIAL	DEFACEABLE	DEFECTIVES	DEFERVESCENCES
DECRETALIST	DEDICATORS	DEFACEMENT	DEFEMINISATION	DEFERVESCENCIES
DECRETALISTS	DEDICATORY	DEFACEMENTS	DEFEMINISATIONS	DEFERVESCENCY
DECRETISTS	DEDIFFERENTIATE	DEFACINGLY	DEFEMINISE	DEFEUDALISE
DECRIMINALISE	DEDRAMATISE	DEFAECATED	DEFEMINISED	DEFEUDALISED
DECRIMINALISED	DEDRAMATISED	DEFAECATES	DEFEMINISES	DEFEUDALISES
DECRIMINALISES	DEDRAMATISES	DEFAECATING	DEFEMINISING	DEFEUDALISING
DECRIMINALISING	DEDRAMATISING	DEFAECATION	DEFEMINIZATION	DEFEUDALIZE
DECRIMINALIZE	DEDRAMATIZE	DEFAECATIONS	DEFEMINIZATIONS	DEFEUDALIZED
DECRIMINALIZED	DEDRAMATIZED	DEFAECATOR	DEFEMINIZE	DEFEUDALIZES
DECRIMINALIZES	DEDRAMATIZES	DEFAECATORS	DEFEMINIZED	DEFEUDALIZING
DECRIMINALIZING	DEDRAMATIZING	DEFALCATED	DEFEMINIZES	DEFIANTNESS
DECROWNING	DEDUCEMENT	DEFALCATES	DEFEMINIZING	DEFIANTNESSES
DECRUSTATION	DEDUCEMENTS	DEFALCATING	DEFENCELESS	DEFIBRILLATE
DECRUSTATIONS	DEDUCIBILITIES	DEFALCATION	DEFENCELESSLY	DEFIBRILLATED
DECRYPTING	DEDUCIBILITY	DEFALCATIONS	DEFENCELESSNESS	DEFIBRILLATES
DECRYPTION	DEDUCIBLENESS	DEFALCATOR	DEFENCEMAN	DEFIBRILLATING
DECRYPTIONS	DEDUCIBLENESSES	DEFALCATORS	DEFENCEMEN	DEFIBRILLATION
DECUMBENCE	DEDUCTIBILITIES	DEFAMATION	DEFENDABLE	DEFIBRILLATIONS
DECUMBENCES	DEDUCTIBILITY	DEFAMATIONS	DEFENDANTS	DEFIBRILLATOR
DECUMBENCIES	DEDUCTIBLE	DEFAMATORILY	DEFENESTRATE	DEFIBRILLATORS
DECUMBENCY	DEDUCTIBLES	DEFAMATORY	DEFENESTRATED	DEFIBRINATE
DECUMBENTLY	DEDUCTIONS	DEFAULTERS	DEFENESTRATES	DEFIBRINATED
DECUMBITURE	DEDUCTIVELY	DEFAULTING	DEFENESTRATING	DEFIBRINATES
DECUMBITURES	DEDUPLICATE	DEFEASANCE	DEFENESTRATION	DEFIBRINATING
DECUMULATION	DEDUPLICATED	DEFEASANCED	DEFENESTRATIONS	DEFIBRINATION
DECUMULATIONS	DEDUPLICATES	DEFEASANCES	DEFENSATIVE	DEFIBRINATIONS
DECURIONATE	DEDUPLICATING	DEFEASIBILITIES	DEFENSATIVES	DEFIBRINISE
DECURIONATES	DEDUPLICATION	DEFEASIBILITY	DEFENSELESS	DEFIBRINISED
DECURRENCIES	DEDUPLICATIONS	DEFEASIBLE	DEFENSELESSLY	DEFIBRINISES
DECURRENCY	DEEJAYINGS	DEFEASIBLENESS	DEFENSELESSNESS	DEFIBRINISING
DECURRENTLY	DEEMSTERSHIP	DEFEATISMS	DEFENSEMAN	DEFIBRINIZE
DECURSIONS	DEEMSTERSHIPS	DEFEATISTS	DEFENSEMEN	DEFIBRINIZED
DECURSIVELY	DEEPENINGS	DEFEATURED	DEFENSIBILITIES	DEFIBRINIZES
DECURVATION	DEEPFAKING	DEFEATURES	DEFENSIBILITY	DEFIBRINIZING
DECURVATIONS	DEEPFREEZE	DEFEATURING	DEFENSIBLE	DEFICIENCE
DECUSSATED	DEEPFREEZES	DEFECATING	DEFENSIBLENESS	DEFICIENCES
DECUSSATELY	DEEPFREEZING	DEFECATION	DEFENSIBLY	DEFICIENCIES
DECUSSATES	DEEPFROZEN	DEFECATIONS	DEFENSIVELY	DEFICIENCY

DEFICIENTLY	DEFLATIONS	DEFORESTED	DEFUNCTIONS	DEGRADABILITIES
DEFICIENTNESS	DEFLECTABLE	DEFORESTER	DEFUNCTIVE	DEGRADABILITY
DEFICIENTNESSES	DEFLECTING	DEFORESTERS	DEFUNCTNESS	DEGRADABLE
DEFICIENTS	DEFLECTION	DEFORESTING	DEFUNCTNESSES	DEGRADATION
DEFILADING	DEFLECTIONAL	DEFORMABILITIES	DEGARNISHED	DEGRADATIONS
DEFILEMENT	DEFLECTIONS	DEFORMABILITY	DEGARNISHES	DEGRADATIVE
DEFILEMENTS	DEFLECTIVE	DEFORMABLE	DEGARNISHING	DEGRADEDLY
DEFILIATION	DEFLECTORS	DEFORMALISE	DEGAUSSERS	DEGRADINGLY
DEFILIATIONS	DEFLEXIONAL	DEFORMALISED	DEGAUSSING	DEGRADINGNESS
DEFINABILITIES	DEFLEXIONS	DEFORMALISES	DEGAUSSINGS	DEGRADINGNESSES
DEFINABILITY	DEFLEXURES	DEFORMALISING	DEGEARINGS	DEGRANULATION
DEFINEMENT	DEFLOCCULANT	DEFORMALIZE	DEGENDERED	DEGRANULATIONS
DEFINEMENTS	DEFLOCCULANTS	DEFORMALIZED	DEGENDERING	DEGREASANT
DEFINIENDA	DEFLOCCULATE	DEFORMALIZES	DEGENERACIES	DEGREASANTS
DEFINIENDUM	DEFLOCCULATED	DEFORMALIZING	DEGENERACY	DEGREASERS
DEFINIENTIA	DEFLOCCULATES	DEFORMATION	DEGENERATE	DEGREASING
DEFINITELY	DEFLOCCULATING	DEFORMATIONAL	DEGENERATED	DEGREASINGS
DEFINITENESS	DEFLOCCULATION	DEFORMATIONS	DEGENERATELY	DEGREELESS
DEFINITENESSES	DEFLOCCULATIONS	DEFORMATIVE	DEGENERATENESS	DEGRESSION
DEFINITION	DEFLORATED	DEFORMEDLY	DEGENERATES	DEGRESSIONS
DEFINITIONAL	DEFLORATES	DEFORMEDNESS	DEGENERATING	DEGRESSIVE
DEFINITIONS	DEFLORATING	DEFORMEDNESSES	DEGENERATION	DEGRESSIVELY
DEFINITISE	DEFLORATION	DEFORMITIES	DEGENERATIONIST	DEGRINGOLADE
DEFINITISED	DEFLORATIONS	DEFRAGGERS	DEGENERATIONS	DEGRINGOLADED
DEFINITISES	DEFLOWERED	DEFRAGGING	DEGENERATIVE	DEGRINGOLADES
DEFINITISING	DEFLOWERER	DEFRAGGINGS	DEGENEROUS	DEGRINGOLADING
DEFINITIVE	DEFLOWERERS	DEFRAGMENT	DEGLACIATED	DEGRINGOLER
DEFINITIVELY	DEFLOWERING	DEFRAGMENTED	DEGLACIATION	DEGRINGOLERED
DEFINITIVENESS	DEFLUXIONS	DEFRAGMENTING	DEGLACIATIONS	DEGRINGOLERING
DEFINITIVES	DEFOCUSING	DEFRAGMENTS	DEGLAMORISATION	DEGRINGOLERS
DEFINITIZE	DEFOCUSSED	DEFRAUDATION	DEGLAMORISE	DEGUSTATED
DEFINITIZED	DEFOCUSSES	DEFRAUDATIONS	DEGLAMORISED	DEGUSTATES
DEFINITIZES	DEFOCUSSING	DEFRAUDERS	DEGLAMORISES	DEGUSTATING
DEFINITIZING	DEFOLIANTS	DEFRAUDING	DEGLAMORISING	DEGUSTATION
DEFINITUDE	DEFOLIATED	DEFRAUDMENT	DEGLAMORIZATION	DEGUSTATIONS
DEFINITUDES	DEFOLIATES	DEFRAUDMENTS	DEGLAMORIZE	DEGUSTATORY
DEFLAGRABILITY	DEFOLIATING	DEFRAYABLE	DEGLAMORIZED	DEHISCENCE
DEFLAGRABLE	DEFOLIATION	DEFRAYMENT	DEGLAMORIZES	DEHISCENCES
DEFLAGRATE	DEFOLIATIONS	DEFRAYMENTS	DEGLAMORIZING	DEHORTATION
DEFLAGRATED	DEFOLIATOR	DEFREEZING	DEGLUTINATE	DEHORTATIONS
DEFLAGRATES	DEFOLIATORS	DEFRIENDED	DEGLUTINATED	DEHORTATIVE
DEFLAGRATING	DEFORCEMENT	DEFRIENDING	DEGLUTINATES	DEHORTATORY
DEFLAGRATION	DEFORCEMENTS	DEFROCKING	DEGLUTINATING	DEHUMANISATION
DEFLAGRATIONS	DEFORCIANT	DEFROSTERS	DEGLUTINATION	DEHUMANISATIONS
DEFLAGRATOR	DEFORCIANTS	DEFROSTING	DEGLUTINATIONS	DEHUMANISE
DEFLAGRATORS	DEFORCIATION	DEFROSTINGS	DEGLUTITION	DEHUMANISED
DEFLATIONARY	DEFORCIATIONS	DEFTNESSES	DEGLUTITIONS	DEHUMANISES
DEFLATIONIST	DEFORESTATION	DEFUELLING	DEGLUTITIVE	DEHUMANISING
DEFLATIONISTS	DEFORESTATIONS	DEFUNCTION	DEGLUTITORY	DEHUMANIZATION

DEHUMANIZATIONS	DEIFICATIONS	DELECTABILITY	DELIBERATORS	DELIQUESCE
DEHUMANIZE	DEINDEXATION	DELECTABLE	DELICACIES	DELIQUESCED
DEHUMANIZED	DEINDEXATIONS	DELECTABLENESS	DELICATELY	DELIQUESCENCE
DEHUMANIZES	DEINDEXING	DELECTABLES	DELICATENESS	DELIQUESCENCES
DEHUMANIZING	DEINDIVIDUATION	DELECTABLY	DELICATENESSES	DELIQUESCENT
DEHUMIDIFIED	DEINDUSTRIALISE	DELECTATED	DELICATESSEN	DELIQUESCES
DEHUMIDIFIER	DEINDUSTRIALIZE	DELECTATES	DELICATESSENS	DELIQUESCING
DEHUMIDIFIERS	DEINONYCHUS	DELECTATING	DELICENSED	DELIQUIUMS
DEHUMIDIFIES	DEINONYCHUSES	DELECTATION	DELICENSES	DELIRATION
DEHUMIDIFY	DEINOSAURS	DELECTATIONS	DELICENSING	DELIRATIONS
DEHUMIDIFYING	DEINOTHERE	DELEGACIES	DELICIOUSLY	DELIRIFACIENT
DEHYDRATED	DEINOTHERES	DELEGATEES	DELICIOUSNESS	DELIRIFACIENTS
DEHYDRATER	DEINOTHERIA	DELEGATING	DELICIOUSNESSES	DELIRIOUSLY
DEHYDRATERS	DEINOTHERIUM	DELEGATION	DELIGATION	DELIRIOUSNESS
DEHYDRATES	DEINOTHERIUMS	DELEGATIONS	DELIGATIONS	DELIRIOUSNESSES
DEHYDRATING	DEIONISATION	DELEGATORS	DELIGHTEDLY	DELITESCENCE
DEHYDRATION	DEIONISATIONS	DELEGITIMATION	DELIGHTEDNESS	DELITESCENCES
DEHYDRATIONS	DEIONISERS	DELEGITIMATIONS	DELIGHTEDNESSES	DELITESCENT
DEHYDRATOR	DEIONISING	DELEGITIMISE	DELIGHTERS	DELIVERABILITY
DEHYDRATORS	DEIONIZATION	DELEGITIMISED	DELIGHTFUL	DELIVERABLE
DEHYDROGENASE	DEIONIZATIONS	DELEGITIMISES	DELIGHTFULLY	DELIVERABLES
DEHYDROGENASES	DEIONIZERS	DELEGITIMISING	DELIGHTFULNESS	DELIVERANCE
DEHYDROGENATE	DEIONIZING	DELEGITIMIZE	DELIGHTING	DELIVERANCES
DEHYDROGENATED	DEIPNOSOPHIST	DELEGITIMIZED	DELIGHTLESS	DELIVERERS
DEHYDROGENATES	DEIPNOSOPHISTS	DELEGITIMIZES	DELIGHTSOME	DELIVERIES
DEHYDROGENATING	DEISTICALLY	DELEGITIMIZING	DELIMITATE	DELIVERING
DEHYDROGENATION	DEJECTEDLY	DELETERIOUS	DELIMITATED	DELIVERYMAN
DEHYDROGENISE	DEJECTEDNESS	DELETERIOUSLY	DELIMITATES	DELIVERYMEN
DEHYDROGENISED	DEJECTEDNESSES	DELETERIOUSNESS	DELIMITATING	DELOCALISATION
DEHYDROGENISES	DEJECTIONS	DELEVERAGE	DELIMITATION	DELOCALISATIONS
DEHYDROGENISING	DEKALITERS	DELEVERAGED	DELIMITATIONS	DELOCALISE
DEHYDROGENIZE	DEKALITRES	DELEVERAGES	DELIMITATIVE	DELOCALISED
DEHYDROGENIZED	DEKALOGIES	DELEVERAGING	DELIMITERS	DELOCALISES
DEHYDROGENIZES	DEKAMETERS	DELEVERAGINGS	DELIMITING	DELOCALISING
DEHYDROGENIZING	DEKAMETRES	DELFTWARES	DELINEABLE	DELOCALIZATION
DEHYDRORETINOL	DEKAMETRIC	DELIBATING	DELINEATED	DELOCALIZATIONS
DEHYDRORETINOLS	DELAMINATE	DELIBATION	DELINEATES	DELOCALIZE
DEHYPNOTISATION	DELAMINATED	DELIBATIONS	DELINEATING	DELOCALIZED
DEHYPNOTISE	DELAMINATES	DELIBERATE	DELINEATION	DELOCALIZES
DEHYPNOTISED	DELAMINATING	DELIBERATED	DELINEATIONS	DELOCALIZING
DEHYPNOTISES	DELAMINATION	DELIBERATELY	DELINEATIVE	DELPHICALLY
DEHYPNOTISING	DELAMINATIONS	DELIBERATENESS	DELINEATOR	DELPHINIUM
DEHYPNOTIZATION	DELAPSIONS	DELIBERATES	DELINEATORS	DELPHINIUMS
DEHYPNOTIZE	DELASSEMENT	DELIBERATING	DELINEAVIT	DELPHINOID
DEHYPNOTIZED	DELASSEMENTS	DELIBERATION	DELINQUENCIES	DELPHINOIDS
DEHYPNOTIZES	DELAYERING	DELIBERATIONS	DELINQUENCY	DELTIOLOGIES
DEHYPNOTIZING	DELAYERINGS	DELIBERATIVE	DELINQUENT	DELTIOLOGIST
DEICTICALLY	DELAYINGLY	DELIBERATIVELY	DELINQUENTLY	DELTIOLOGISTS
DEIFICATION	DELECTABILITIES	DELIBERATOR	DELINQUENTS	DELTIOLOGY

DELTOIDEUS	DEMARCATED	DEMILITARIZING	DEMOBILIZES	DEMOLISHMENT
DELUDINGLY	DEMARCATES	DEMIMONDAINE	DEMOBILIZING	DEMOLISHMENTS
DELUNDUNGS	DEMARCATING	DEMIMONDAINES	DEMOCRACIES	DEMOLITION
DELUSIONAL	DEMARCATION	DEMIMONDES	DEMOCRATIC	DEMOLITIONIST
DELUSIONARY	DEMARCATIONS	DEMINERALISE	DEMOCRATICAL	DEMOLITIONISTS
DELUSIONIST	DEMARCATOR	DEMINERALISED	DEMOCRATICALLY	DEMOLITIONS
DELUSIONISTS	DEMARCATORS	DEMINERALISER	DEMOCRATIES	DEMOLOGIES
DELUSIVELY	DEMARKATION	DEMINERALISERS	DEMOCRATIFIABLE	DEMONESSES
DELUSIVENESS	DEMARKATIONS	DEMINERALISES	DEMOCRATISATION	DEMONETARISE
DELUSIVENESSES	DEMARKETED	DEMINERALISING	DEMOCRATISE	DEMONETARISED
DELUSTERED	DEMARKETING	DEMINERALIZE	DEMOCRATISED	DEMONETARISES
DELUSTERING	DEMATERIALISE	DEMINERALIZED	DEMOCRATISER	DEMONETARISING
DELUSTRANT	DEMATERIALISED	DEMINERALIZER	DEMOCRATISERS	DEMONETARIZE
DELUSTRANTS	DEMATERIALISES	DEMINERALIZERS	DEMOCRATISES	DEMONETARIZED
DELUSTRING	DEMATERIALISING	DEMINERALIZES	DEMOCRATISING	DEMONETARIZES
DEMAGNETISATION	DEMATERIALIZE	DEMINERALIZING	DEMOCRATIST	DEMONETARIZING
DEMAGNETISE	DEMATERIALIZED	DEMIPIQUES	DEMOCRATISTS	DEMONETISATION
DEMAGNETISED	DEMATERIALIZES	DEMIRELIEF	DEMOCRATIZATION	DEMONETISATIONS
DEMAGNETISER	DEMATERIALIZING	DEMIRELIEFS	DEMOCRATIZE	DEMONETISE
DEMAGNETISERS	DEMEANOURS	DEMIREPDOM	DEMOCRATIZED	DEMONETISED
DEMAGNETISES	DEMEASNURE	DEMIREPDOMS	DEMOCRATIZER	DEMONETISES
DEMAGNETISING	DEMEASNURES	DEMISEMIQUAVER	DEMOCRATIZERS	DEMONETISING
DEMAGNETIZATION	DEMENTATED	DEMISEMIQUAVERS	DEMOCRATIZES	DEMONETIZATION
DEMAGNETIZE	DEMENTATES	DEMISEXUAL	DEMOCRATIZING	DEMONETIZATIONS
DEMAGNETIZED	DEMENTATING	DEMISEXUALITIES	DEMODULATE	DEMONETIZE
DEMAGNETIZER	DEMENTEDLY	DEMISEXUALITY	DEMODULATED	DEMONETIZED
DEMAGNETIZERS	DEMENTEDNESS	DEMISEXUALS	DEMODULATES	DEMONETIZES
DEMAGNETIZES	DEMENTEDNESSES	DEMISSIONS	DEMODULATING	DEMONETIZING
DEMAGNETIZING	DEMERGERED	DEMISTINGS	DEMODULATION	DEMONIACAL
DEMAGOGICAL	DEMERGERING	DEMITASSES	DEMODULATIONS	DEMONIACALLY
DEMAGOGICALLY	DEMERITING	DEMIURGEOUS	DEMODULATOR	DEMONIACISM
DEMAGOGIES	DEMERITORIOUS	DEMIURGICAL	DEMODULATORS	DEMONIACISMS
DEMAGOGING	DEMERITORIOUSLY	DEMIURGICALLY	DEMOGRAPHER	DEMONIANISM
DEMAGOGISM	DEMERSIONS	DEMIURGUSES	DEMOGRAPHERS	DEMONIANISMS
DEMAGOGISMS	DEMIBASTION	DEMIVEGGES	DEMOGRAPHIC	DEMONICALLY
DEMAGOGUED	DEMIBASTIONS	DEMIVIERGE	DEMOGRAPHICAL	DEMONISATION
DEMAGOGUERIES	DEMICANTON	DEMIVIERGES	DEMOGRAPHICALLY	DEMONISATIONS
DEMAGOGUERY	DEMICANTONS	DEMIVOLTES	DEMOGRAPHICS	DEMONISING
DEMAGOGUES	DEMIGODDESS	DEMIWORLDS	DEMOGRAPHIES	DEMONIZATION
DEMAGOGUING	DEMIGODDESSES	DEMOBILISATION	DEMOGRAPHIST	DEMONIZATIONS
DEMAGOGUISM	DEMIGRATION	DEMOBILISATIONS	DEMOGRAPHISTS	DEMONIZING
DEMAGOGUISMS	DEMIGRATIONS	DEMOBILISE	DEMOGRAPHY	DEMONOCRACIES
DEMANDABLE	DEMILITARISE	DEMOBILISED	DEMOISELLE	DEMONOCRACY
DEMANDANTS	DEMILITARISED	DEMOBILISES	DEMOISELLES	DEMONOLATER
DEMANDINGLY	DEMILITARISES	DEMOBILISING	DEMOLISHED	DEMONOLATERS
DEMANDINGNESS	DEMILITARISING	DEMOBILIZATION	DEMOLISHER	DEMONOLATRIES
DEMANDINGNESSES	DEMILITARIZE	DEMOBILIZATIONS	DEMOLISHERS	DEMONOLATRY
DEMANNINGS	DEMILITARIZED	DEMOBILIZE	DEMOLISHES	DEMONOLOGIC
DEMANTOIDS	DEMILITARIZES	DEMOBILIZED	DEMOLISHING	DEMONOLOGICAL

DEMONOLOGIES	DEMOUNTABLE	DEMYTHOLOGIZES	DENDROLATRIES	DENIZATIONS
DEMONOLOGIST	DEMOUNTING	DEMYTHOLOGIZING	DENDROLATRY	DENIZENING
DEMONOLOGISTS	DEMULCENTS	DENATIONALISE	DENDROLOGIC	DENIZENSHIP
DEMONOLOGY	DEMULSIFICATION	DENATIONALISED	DENDROLOGICAL	DENIZENSHIPS
DEMONOMANIA	DEMULSIFIED	DENATIONALISES	DENDROLOGIES	DENOMINABLE
DEMONOMANIAS	DEMULSIFIER	DENATIONALISING	DENDROLOGIST	DENOMINATE
DEMONSTRABILITY	DEMULSIFIERS	DENATIONALIZE	DENDROLOGISTS	DENOMINATED
DEMONSTRABLE	DEMULSIFIES	DENATIONALIZED	DENDROLOGOUS	DENOMINATES
DEMONSTRABLY	DEMULSIFYING	DENATIONALIZES	DENDROLOGY	DENOMINATING
DEMONSTRATE	DEMULTIPLEXER	DENATIONALIZING	DENDROMETER	DENOMINATION
DEMONSTRATED	DEMULTIPLEXERS	DENATURALISE	DENDROMETERS	DENOMINATIONAL
DEMONSTRATES	DEMURENESS	DENATURALISED	DENDROPHIS	DENOMINATIONS
DEMONSTRATING	DEMURENESSES	DENATURALISES	DENDROPHISES	DENOMINATIVE
DEMONSTRATION	DEMURRABLE	DENATURALISING	DENEGATION	DENOMINATIVELY
DEMONSTRATIONAL	DEMURRAGES	DENATURALIZE	DENEGATIONS	DENOMINATIVES
DEMONSTRATIONS	DEMUTUALISATION	DENATURALIZED	DENERVATED	DENOMINATOR
DEMONSTRATIVE	DEMUTUALISE	DENATURALIZES	DENERVATES	DENOMINATORS
DEMONSTRATIVELY	DEMUTUALISED	DENATURALIZING	DENERVATING	DENOTATING
DEMONSTRATIVES	DEMUTUALISES	DENATURANT	DENERVATION	DENOTATION
DEMONSTRATOR	DEMUTUALISING	DENATURANTS	DENERVATIONS	DENOTATIONS
DEMONSTRATORS	DEMUTUALIZATION	DENATURATION	DENIABILITIES	DENOTATIVE
DEMONSTRATORY	DEMUTUALIZE	DENATURATIONS	DENIABILITY	DENOTATIVELY
DEMORALISATION	DEMUTUALIZED	DENATURING	DENIALISMS	DENOTEMENT
DEMORALISATIONS	DEMUTUALIZES	DENATURISE	DENIALISTS	DENOTEMENTS
DEMORALISE	DEMUTUALIZING	DENATURISED	DENIGRATED	DENOUEMENT
DEMORALISED	DEMYELINATE	DENATURISES	DENIGRATES	DENOUEMENTS
DEMORALISER	DEMYELINATED	DENATURISING	DENIGRATING	DENOUNCEMENT
DEMORALISERS	DEMYELINATES	DENATURIZE	DENIGRATION	DENOUNCEMENTS
DEMORALISES	DEMYELINATING	DENATURIZED	DENIGRATIONS	DENOUNCERS
DEMORALISING	DEMYELINATION	DENATURIZES	DENIGRATIVE	DENOUNCING
DEMORALISINGLY	DEMYELINATIONS	DENATURIZING	DENIGRATOR	DENSENESSES
DEMORALIZATION	DEMYSTIFICATION	DENAZIFICATION	DENIGRATORS	DENSIFICATION
DEMORALIZATIONS	DEMYSTIFIED	DENAZIFICATIONS	DENIGRATORY	DENSIFICATIONS
DEMORALIZE	DEMYSTIFIES	DENAZIFIED	DENISATION	DENSIFIERS
DEMORALIZED	DEMYSTIFYING	DENAZIFIES	DENISATIONS	DENSIFYING
DEMORALIZER	DEMYTHIFICATION	DENAZIFYING	DENITRATED	DENSIMETER
DEMORALIZERS	DEMYTHIFIED	DENDRACHATE	DENITRATES	DENSIMETERS
DEMORALIZES	DEMYTHIFIES	DENDRACHATES	DENITRATING	DENSIMETRIC
DEMORALIZING	DEMYTHIFYING	DENDRIFORM	DENITRATION	DENSIMETRIES
DEMORALIZINGLY	DEMYTHOLOGISE	DENDRIMERS	DENITRATIONS	DENSIMETRY
DEMOSCENES	DEMYTHOLOGISED	DENDRITICAL	DENITRIFICATION	DENSITOMETER
DEMOTICIST	DEMYTHOLOGISER	DENDRITICALLY	DENITRIFICATOR	DENSITOMETERS
DEMOTICISTS	DEMYTHOLOGISERS	DENDROBIUM	DENITRIFICATORS	DENSITOMETRIC
DEMOTIVATE	DEMYTHOLOGISES	DENDROBIUMS	DENITRIFIED	DENSITOMETRIES
DEMOTIVATED	DEMYTHOLOGISING	DENDROGLYPH	DENITRIFIER	DENSITOMETRY
DEMOTIVATES	DEMYTHOLOGIZE	DENDROGLYPHS	DENITRIFIERS	DENTALISED
DEMOTIVATING	DEMYTHOLOGIZED	DENDROGRAM	DENITRIFIES	DENTALISES
DEMOTIVATION	DEMYTHOLOGIZER	DENDROGRAMS	DENITRIFYING	DENTALISING
DEMOTIVATIONS	DEMYTHOLOGIZERS	DENDROIDAL	DENIZATION	DENTALITIES

D

DENTALIUMS
DENTALIZED
DENTALIZES
DENTALIZING
DENTATIONS
DENTICARES
DENTICULATE
DENTICULATED
DENTICULATELY
DENTICULATION
DENTICULATIONS
DENTIFRICE
DENTIFRICES
DENTIGEROUS
DENTILABIAL
DENTILINGUAL
DENTILINGUALS
DENTIROSTRAL
DENTISTRIES
DENTITIONS
DENTURISMS
DENTURISTS
DENUCLEARISE
DENUCLEARISED
DENUCLEARISES
DENUCLEARISING
DENUCLEARIZE
DENUCLEARIZED
DENUCLEARIZES
DENUCLEARIZING
DENUDATING
DENUDATION
DENUDATIONS
DENUDEMENT
DENUDEMENTS
DENUMERABILITY
DENUMERABLE
DENUMERABLY
DENUNCIATE
DENUNCIATED
DENUNCIATES
DENUNCIATING
DENUNCIATION
DENUNCIATIONS
DENUNCIATIVE
DENUNCIATOR
DENUNCIATORS
DENUNCIATORY
DEOBSTRUENT

DEOBSTRUENTS
DEODORANTS
DEODORISATION
DEODORISATIONS
DEODORISED
DEODORISER
DEODORISERS
DEODORISES
DEODORISING
DEODORIZATION
DEODORIZATIONS
DEODORIZED
DEODORIZER
DEODORIZERS
DEODORIZES
DEODORIZING
DEONTOLOGICAL
DEONTOLOGIES
DEONTOLOGIST
DEONTOLOGISTS
DEONTOLOGY
DEOPPILATE
DEOPPILATED
DEOPPILATES
DEOPPILATING
DEOPPILATION
DEOPPILATIONS
DEOPPILATIVE
DEOPPILATIVES
DEORBITING
DEOXIDATED
DEOXIDATES
DEOXIDATING
DEOXIDATION
DEOXIDATIONS
DEOXIDISATION
DEOXIDISATIONS
DEOXIDISED
DEOXIDISER
DEOXIDISERS
DEOXIDISES
DEOXIDISING
DEOXIDIZATION
DEOXIDIZATIONS
DEOXIDIZED
DEOXIDIZER
DEOXIDIZERS
DEOXIDIZES
DEOXIDIZING

DEOXYCORTONE
DEOXYCORTONES
DEOXYGENATE
DEOXYGENATED
DEOXYGENATES
DEOXYGENATING
DEOXYGENATION
DEOXYGENATIONS
DEOXYGENISE
DEOXYGENISED
DEOXYGENISES
DEOXYGENISING
DEOXYGENIZE
DEOXYGENIZED
DEOXYGENIZES
DEOXYGENIZING
DEOXYRIBOSE
DEOXYRIBOSES
DEPAINTING
DEPANNEURS
DEPARTEMENT
DEPARTEMENTS
DEPARTINGS
DEPARTMENT
DEPARTMENTAL
DEPARTMENTALISE
DEPARTMENTALISM
DEPARTMENTALIZE
DEPARTMENTALLY
DEPARTMENTS
DEPARTURES
DEPASTURED
DEPASTURES
DEPASTURING
DEPAUPERATE
DEPAUPERATED
DEPAUPERATES
DEPAUPERATING
DEPAUPERISE
DEPAUPERISED
DEPAUPERISES
DEPAUPERISING
DEPAUPERIZE
DEPAUPERIZED
DEPAUPERIZES
DEPAUPERIZING
DEPEINCTED
DEPEINCTING
DEPENDABILITIES

DEPENDABILITY
DEPENDABLE
DEPENDABLENESS
DEPENDABLY
DEPENDANCE
DEPENDANCES
DEPENDANCIES
DEPENDANCY
DEPENDANTS
DEPENDENCE
DEPENDENCES
DEPENDENCIES
DEPENDENCY
DEPENDENTLY
DEPENDENTS
DEPENDINGLY
DEPEOPLING
DEPERSONALISE
DEPERSONALISED
DEPERSONALISES
DEPERSONALISING
DEPERSONALIZE
DEPERSONALIZED
DEPERSONALIZES
DEPERSONALIZING
DEPHLEGMATE
DEPHLEGMATED
DEPHLEGMATES
DEPHLEGMATING
DEPHLEGMATION
DEPHLEGMATIONS
DEPHLEGMATOR
DEPHLEGMATORS
DEPHLOGISTICATE
DEPHOSPHORYLATE
DEPICTIONS
DEPICTURED
DEPICTURES
DEPICTURING
DEPIGMENTATION
DEPIGMENTATIONS
DEPIGMENTED
DEPIGMENTING
DEPIGMENTS
DEPILATING
DEPILATION
DEPILATIONS
DEPILATORIES
DEPILATORS

DEPILATORY
DEPLATFORM
DEPLATFORMED
DEPLATFORMING
DEPLATFORMS
DEPLENISHED
DEPLENISHES
DEPLENISHING
DEPLETABLE
DEPLETIONS
DEPLORABILITIES
DEPLORABILITY
DEPLORABLE
DEPLORABLENESS
DEPLORABLY
DEPLORATION
DEPLORATIONS
DEPLORINGLY
DEPLOYABLE
DEPLOYMENT
DEPLOYMENTS
DEPLUMATION
DEPLUMATIONS
DEPOLARISATION
DEPOLARISATIONS
DEPOLARISE
DEPOLARISED
DEPOLARISER
DEPOLARISERS
DEPOLARISES
DEPOLARISING
DEPOLARIZATION
DEPOLARIZATIONS
DEPOLARIZE
DEPOLARIZED
DEPOLARIZER
DEPOLARIZERS
DEPOLARIZES
DEPOLARIZING
DEPOLISHED
DEPOLISHES
DEPOLISHING
DEPOLITICISE
DEPOLITICISED
DEPOLITICISES
DEPOLITICISING
DEPOLITICIZE
DEPOLITICIZED
DEPOLITICIZES

DEPOLITICIZING	DEPRECATIONS	DEPRESSURIZED	DERAIGNMENT	DEREPRESSED
DEPOLYMERISE	DEPRECATIVE	DEPRESSURIZES	DERAIGNMENTS	DEREPRESSES
DEPOLYMERISED	DEPRECATIVELY	DEPRESSURIZING	DERAILLEUR	DEREPRESSING
DEPOLYMERISES	DEPRECATOR	DEPRIVABLE	DERAILLEURS	DEREPRESSION
DEPOLYMERISING	DEPRECATORILY	DEPRIVATION	DERAILMENT	DEREPRESSIONS
DEPOLYMERIZE	DEPRECATORS	DEPRIVATIONS	DERAILMENTS	DEREQUISITION
DEPOLYMERIZED	DEPRECATORY	DEPRIVATIVE	DERANGEMENT	DEREQUISITIONED
DEPOLYMERIZES	DEPRECIABLE	DEPRIVEMENT	DERANGEMENTS	DEREQUISITIONS
DEPOLYMERIZING	DEPRECIATE	DEPRIVEMENTS	DERATIONED	DERESTRICT
DEPOPULATE	DEPRECIATED	DEPROGRAMED	DERATIONING	DERESTRICTED
DEPOPULATED	DEPRECIATES	DEPROGRAMING	DEREALISATION	DERESTRICTING
DEPOPULATES	DEPRECIATING	DEPROGRAMME	DEREALISATIONS	DERESTRICTION
DEPOPULATING	DEPRECIATINGLY	DEPROGRAMMED	DEREALIZATION	DERESTRICTIONS
DEPOPULATION	DEPRECIATION	DEPROGRAMMER	DEREALIZATIONS	DERESTRICTS
DEPOPULATIONS	DEPRECIATIONS	DEPROGRAMMERS	DERECOGNISE	DERIDINGLY
DEPOPULATOR	DEPRECIATIVE	DEPROGRAMMES	DERECOGNISED	DERISIVELY
DEPOPULATORS	DEPRECIATOR	DEPROGRAMMING	DERECOGNISES	DERISIVENESS
DEPORTABLE	DEPRECIATORS	DEPROGRAMS	DERECOGNISING	DERISIVENESSES
DEPORTATION	DEPRECIATORY	DEPURATING	DERECOGNITION	DERIVATING
DEPORTATIONS	DEPREDATED	DEPURATION	DERECOGNITIONS	DERIVATION
DEPORTMENT	DEPREDATES	DEPURATIONS	DERECOGNIZE	DERIVATIONAL
DEPORTMENTS	DEPREDATING	DEPURATIVE	DERECOGNIZED	DERIVATIONIST
DEPOSITARIES	DEPREDATION	DEPURATIVES	DERECOGNIZES	DERIVATIONISTS
DEPOSITARY	DEPREDATIONS	DEPURATORS	DERECOGNIZING	DERIVATIONS
DEPOSITATION	DEPREDATOR	DEPURATORY	DEREGISTER	DERIVATISATION
DEPOSITATIONS	DEPREDATORS	DEPUTATION	DEREGISTERED	DERIVATISATIONS
DEPOSITING	DEPREDATORY	DEPUTATIONS	DEREGISTERING	DERIVATISE
DEPOSITION	DEPREHENDED	DEPUTISATION	DEREGISTERS	DERIVATISED
DEPOSITIONAL	DEPREHENDING	DEPUTISATIONS	DEREGISTRATION	DERIVATISES
DEPOSITIONS	DEPREHENDS	DEPUTISING	DEREGISTRATIONS	DERIVATISING
DEPOSITIVE	DEPRESSANT	DEPUTIZATION	DEREGULATE	DERIVATIVE
DEPOSITORIES	DEPRESSANTS	DEPUTIZATIONS	DEREGULATED	DERIVATIVELY
DEPOSITORS	DEPRESSIBLE	DEPUTIZING	DEREGULATES	DERIVATIVENESS
DEPOSITORY	DEPRESSING	DEQUEUEING	DEREGULATING	DERIVATIVES
DEPRAVATION	DEPRESSINGLY	DERACIALISE	DEREGULATION	DERIVATIZATION
DEPRAVATIONS	DEPRESSION	DERACIALISED	DEREGULATIONS	DERIVATIZATIONS
DEPRAVEDLY	DEPRESSIONS	DERACIALISES	DEREGULATOR	DERIVATIZE
DEPRAVEDNESS	DEPRESSIVE	DERACIALISING	DEREGULATORS	DERIVATIZED
DEPRAVEDNESSES	DEPRESSIVELY	DERACIALIZE	DEREGULATORY	DERIVATIZES
DEPRAVEMENT	DEPRESSIVENESS	DERACIALIZED	DERELICTION	DERIVATIZING
DEPRAVEMENTS	DEPRESSIVES	DERACIALIZES	DERELICTIONS	DERMABRASION
DEPRAVINGLY	DEPRESSOMOTOR	DERACIALIZING	DERELIGIONISE	DERMABRASIONS
DEPRAVITIES	DEPRESSOMOTORS	DERACINATE	DERELIGIONISED	DERMAPLANING
DEPRECABLE	DEPRESSORS	DERACINATED	DERELIGIONISES	DERMAPLANINGS
DEPRECATED	DEPRESSURISE	DERACINATES	DERELIGIONISING	DERMAPTERAN
DEPRECATES	DEPRESSURISED	DERACINATING	DERELIGIONIZE	DERMAPTERANS
DEPRECATING	DEPRESSURISES	DERACINATION	DERELIGIONIZED	DERMATITIDES
DEPRECATINGLY	DEPRESSURISING	DERACINATIONS	DERELIGIONIZES	DERMATITIS
DEPRECATION	DEPRESSURIZE	DERAIGNING	DERELIGIONIZING	DERMATITISES

DERMATOGEN	DESACRALIZE	DESCHOOLED	DESENSITISES	DESICCATORS
DERMATOGENS	DESACRALIZED	DESCHOOLER	DESENSITISING	DESIDERATA
DERMATOGLYPHIC	DESACRALIZES	DESCHOOLERS	DESENSITIZATION	DESIDERATE
DERMATOGLYPHICS	DESACRALIZING	DESCHOOLING	DESENSITIZE	DESIDERATED
DERMATOGRAPHIA	DESAGREMENT	DESCHOOLINGS	DESENSITIZED	DESIDERATES
DERMATOGRAPHIAS	DESAGREMENTS	DESCRAMBLE	DESENSITIZER	DESIDERATING
DERMATOGRAPHIC	DESALINATE	DESCRAMBLED	DESENSITIZERS	DESIDERATION
DERMATOGRAPHIES	DESALINATED	DESCRAMBLER	DESENSITIZES	DESIDERATIONS
DERMATOGRAPHY	DESALINATES	DESCRAMBLERS	DESENSITIZING	DESIDERATIVE
DERMATOLOGIC	DESALINATING	DESCRAMBLES	DESERPIDINE	DESIDERATIVES
DERMATOLOGICAL	DESALINATION	DESCRAMBLING	DESERPIDINES	DESIDERATUM
DERMATOLOGIES	DESALINATIONS	DESCRIBABLE	DESERTIFICATION	DESIDERIUM
DERMATOLOGIST	DESALINATOR	DESCRIBERS	DESERTIFIED	DESIDERIUMS
DERMATOLOGISTS	DESALINATORS	DESCRIBING	DESERTIFIES	DESIGNABLE
DERMATOLOGY	DESALINISATION	DESCRIPTION	DESERTIFYING	DESIGNATED
DERMATOMAL	DESALINISATIONS	DESCRIPTIONS	DESERTIONS	DESIGNATES
DERMATOMES	DESALINISE	DESCRIPTIVE	DESERTISATION	DESIGNATING
DERMATOMIC	DESALINISED	DESCRIPTIVELY	DESERTISATIONS	DESIGNATION
DERMATOMYOSITIS	DESALINISES	DESCRIPTIVENESS	DESERTIZATION	DESIGNATIONS
DERMATOPHYTE	DESALINISING	DESCRIPTIVISM	DESERTIZATIONS	DESIGNATIVE
DERMATOPHYTES	DESALINIZATION	DESCRIPTIVISMS	DESERTLESS	DESIGNATOR
DERMATOPHYTIC	DESALINIZATIONS	DESCRIPTIVIST	DESERVEDLY	DESIGNATORS
DERMATOPHYTOSES	DESALINIZE	DESCRIPTOR	DESERVEDNESS	DESIGNATORY
DERMATOPHYTOSIS	DESALINIZED	DESCRIPTORS	DESERVEDNESSES	DESIGNEDLY
DERMATOPLASTIC	DESALINIZES	DESCRIVING	DESERVINGLY	DESIGNINGLY
DERMATOPLASTIES	DESALINIZING	DESECRATED	DESERVINGNESS	DESIGNINGS
DERMATOPLASTY	DESALTINGS	DESECRATER	DESERVINGNESSES	DESIGNLESS
DERMATOSES	DESATURATE	DESECRATERS	DESERVINGS	DESIGNMENT
DERMATOSIS	DESATURATED	DESECRATES	DESEXUALISATION	DESIGNMENTS
DERMESTIDS	DESATURATES	DESECRATING	DESEXUALISE	DESILVERED
DERMOGRAPHIES	DESATURATING	DESECRATION	DESEXUALISED	DESILVERING
DERMOGRAPHY	DESATURATION	DESECRATIONS	DESEXUALISES	DESILVERISATION
DEROGATELY	DESATURATIONS	DESECRATOR	DESEXUALISING	DESILVERISE
DEROGATING	DESCANTERS	DESECRATORS	DESEXUALIZATION	DESILVERISED
DEROGATION	DESCANTING	DESEGREGATE	DESEXUALIZE	DESILVERISES
DEROGATIONS	DESCENDABLE	DESEGREGATED	DESEXUALIZED	DESILVERISING
DEROGATIVE	DESCENDANT	DESEGREGATES	DESEXUALIZES	DESILVERIZATION
DEROGATIVELY	DESCENDANTS	DESEGREGATING	DESEXUALIZING	DESILVERIZE
DEROGATORILY	DESCENDENT	DESEGREGATION	DESHABILLE	DESILVERIZED
DEROGATORINESS	DESCENDENTS	DESEGREGATIONS	DESHABILLES	DESILVERIZES
DEROGATORY	DESCENDERS	DESELECTED	DESICCANTS	DESILVERIZING
DERRICKING	DESCENDEUR	DESELECTING	DESICCATED	DESINENCES
DERRINGERS	DESCENDEURS	DESELECTION	DESICCATES	DESINENTIAL
DESACRALISATION	DESCENDIBLE	DESELECTIONS	DESICCATING	DESIPIENCE
DESACRALISE	DESCENDING	DESENSITISATION	DESICCATION	DESIPIENCES
DESACRALISED	DESCENDINGS	DESENSITISE	DESICCATIONS	DESIPRAMINE
DESACRALISES	DESCENSION	DESENSITISED	DESICCATIVE	DESIPRAMINES
DESACRALISING	DESCENSIONAL	DESENSITISER	DESICCATIVES	DESIRABILITIES
DESACRALIZATION	DESCENSIONS	DESENSITISERS	DESICCATOR	DESIRABILITY

DESIRABLENESS	DESPERATION	DESPUMATES	DESTITUTES	DESULFURISERS
DESIRABLENESSES	DESPERATIONS	DESPUMATING	DESTITUTING	DESULFURISES
DESIRABLES	DESPICABILITIES	DESPUMATION	DESTITUTION	DESULFURISING
DESIRELESS	DESPICABILITY	DESPUMATIONS	DESTITUTIONS	DESULFURIZATION
DESIROUSLY	DESPICABLE	DESQUAMATE	DESTOCKING	DESULFURIZE
DESIROUSNESS	DESPICABLENESS	DESQUAMATED	DESTREAMED	DESULFURIZED
DESIROUSNESSES	DESPICABLY	DESQUAMATES	DESTREAMING	DESULFURIZER
DESISTANCE	DESPIRITUALISE	DESQUAMATING	DESTRESSED	DESULFURIZERS
DESISTANCES	DESPIRITUALISED	DESQUAMATION	DESTRESSES	DESULFURIZES
DESISTENCE	DESPIRITUALISES	DESQUAMATIONS	DESTRESSING	DESULFURIZING
DESISTENCES	DESPIRITUALIZE	DESQUAMATIVE	DESTROYABLE	DESULPHURATE
DESKILLING	DESPIRITUALIZED	DESQUAMATORIES	DESTROYERS	DESULPHURATED
DESKILLINGS	DESPIRITUALIZES	DESQUAMATORY	DESTROYING	DESULPHURATES
DESMODIUMS	DESPISABLE	DESSERTSPOON	DESTRUCTED	DESULPHURATING
DESMODROMIC	DESPISEDNESS	DESSERTSPOONFUL	DESTRUCTIBILITY	DESULPHURATION
DESMOSOMAL	DESPISEDNESSES	DESSERTSPOONS	DESTRUCTIBLE	DESULPHURATIONS
DESMOSOMES	DESPISEMENT	DESSIATINE	DESTRUCTING	DESULPHURED
DESNOODING	DESPISEMENTS	DESSIATINES	DESTRUCTION	DESULPHURING
DESOBLIGEANTE	DESPISINGLY	DESSIGNMENT	DESTRUCTIONAL	DESULPHURISE
DESOBLIGEANTES	DESPITEFUL	DESSIGNMENTS	DESTRUCTIONIST	DESULPHURISED
DESOLATELY	DESPITEFULLY	DESSYATINE	DESTRUCTIONISTS	DESULPHURISER
DESOLATENESS	DESPITEFULNESS	DESSYATINES	DESTRUCTIONS	DESULPHURISERS
DESOLATENESSES	DESPITEOUS	DESSYATINS	DESTRUCTIVE	DESULPHURISES
DESOLATERS	DESPITEOUSLY	DESTABILISATION	DESTRUCTIVELY	DESULPHURISING
DESOLATING	DESPITEOUSNESS	DESTABILISE	DESTRUCTIVENESS	DESULPHURIZE
DESOLATINGLY	DESPOILERS	DESTABILISED	DESTRUCTIVES	DESULPHURIZED
DESOLATION	DESPOILING	DESTABILISER	DESTRUCTIVISM	DESULPHURIZER
DESOLATIONS	DESPOILINGS	DESTABILISERS	DESTRUCTIVISMS	DESULPHURIZERS
DESOLATORS	DESPOILMENT	DESTABILISES	DESTRUCTIVIST	DESULPHURIZES
DESOLATORY	DESPOILMENTS	DESTABILISING	DESTRUCTIVISTS	DESULPHURIZING
DESORIENTE	DESPOLIATION	DESTABILIZATION	DESTRUCTIVITIES	DESULPHURS
DESORPTION	DESPOLIATIONS	DESTABILIZE	DESTRUCTIVITY	DESULTORILY
DESORPTIONS	DESPONDENCE	DESTABILIZED	DESTRUCTOR	DESULTORINESS
DESOXYRIBOSE	DESPONDENCES	DESTABILIZER	DESTRUCTORS	DESULTORINESSES
DESOXYRIBOSES	DESPONDENCIES	DESTABILIZERS	DESTRUCTOS	DETACHABILITIES
DESPAIRERS	DESPONDENCY	DESTABILIZES	DESUETUDES	DETACHABILITY
DESPAIRFUL	DESPONDENT	DESTABILIZING	DESUGARING	DETACHABLE
DESPAIRING	DESPONDENTLY	DESTAINING	DESULFURATE	DETACHABLY
DESPAIRINGLY	DESPONDING	DESTEMPERED	DESULFURATED	DETACHEDLY
DESPATCHED	DESPONDINGLY	DESTEMPERING	DESULFURATES	DETACHEDNESS
DESPATCHER	DESPONDINGS	DESTEMPERS	DESULFURATING	DETACHEDNESSES
DESPATCHERS	DESPOTATES	DESTINATED	DESULFURATION	DETACHMENT
DESPATCHES	DESPOTICAL	DESTINATES	DESULFURATIONS	DETACHMENTS
DESPATCHING	DESPOTICALLY	DESTINATING	DESULFURED	DETAILEDLY
DESPERADOES	DESPOTICALNESS	DESTINATION	DESULFURING	DETAILEDNESS
DESPERADOS	DESPOTISMS	DESTINATIONS	DESULFURISATION	DETAILEDNESSES
DESPERATELY	DESPOTOCRACIES	DESTITUTED	DESULFURISE	DETAILINGS
DESPERATENESS	DESPOTOCRACY	DESTITUTENESS	DESULFURISED	DETAINABLE
DESPERATENESSES	DESPUMATED	DESTITUTENESSES	DESULFURISER	DETAINMENT

DETAINMENTS
DETANGLERS
DETANGLING
DETASSELED
DETASSELING
DETASSELLED
DETASSELLING
DETECTABILITIES
DETECTABILITY
DETECTABLE
DETECTIBLE
DETECTIONS
DETECTIVELIKE
DETECTIVES
DETECTIVIST
DETECTIVISTS
DETECTOPHONE
DETECTOPHONES
DETECTORIST
DETECTORISTS
DETENTIONS
DETENTISTS
DETERGENCE
DETERGENCES
DETERGENCIES
DETERGENCY
DETERGENTS
DETERIORATE
DETERIORATED
DETERIORATES
DETERIORATING
DETERIORATION
DETERIORATIONS
DETERIORATIVE
DETERIORISM
DETERIORISMS
DETERIORITIES
DETERIORITY
DETERMENTS
DETERMINABILITY
DETERMINABLE
DETERMINABLY
DETERMINACIES
DETERMINACY
DETERMINANT
DETERMINANTAL
DETERMINANTS
DETERMINATE
DETERMINATED

DETERMINATELY
DETERMINATENESS
DETERMINATES
DETERMINATING
DETERMINATION
DETERMINATIONS
DETERMINATIVE
DETERMINATIVELY
DETERMINATIVES
DETERMINATOR
DETERMINATORS
DETERMINED
DETERMINEDLY
DETERMINEDNESS
DETERMINER
DETERMINERS
DETERMINES
DETERMINING
DETERMINISM
DETERMINISMS
DETERMINIST
DETERMINISTIC
DETERMINISTS
DETERRABILITIES
DETERRABILITY
DETERRABLE
DETERRENCE
DETERRENCES
DETERRENTLY
DETERRENTS
DETERSIONS
DETERSIVES
DETESTABILITIES
DETESTABILITY
DETESTABLE
DETESTABLENESS
DETESTABLY
DETESTATION
DETESTATIONS
DETHATCHED
DETHATCHES
DETHATCHING
DETHRONEMENT
DETHRONEMENTS
DETHRONERS
DETHRONING
DETHRONINGS
DETHRONISE
DETHRONISED

DETHRONISES
DETHRONISING
DETHRONIZE
DETHRONIZED
DETHRONIZES
DETHRONIZING
DETONABILITIES
DETONABILITY
DETONATABLE
DETONATING
DETONATION
DETONATIONS
DETONATIVE
DETONATORS
DETORSIONS
DETORTIONS
DETOXICANT
DETOXICANTS
DETOXICATE
DETOXICATED
DETOXICATES
DETOXICATING
DETOXICATION
DETOXICATIONS
DETOXIFICATION
DETOXIFICATIONS
DETOXIFIED
DETOXIFIES
DETOXIFYING
DETRACTING
DETRACTINGLY
DETRACTINGS
DETRACTION
DETRACTIONS
DETRACTIVE
DETRACTIVELY
DETRACTORS
DETRACTORY
DETRACTRESS
DETRACTRESSES
DETRAINING
DETRAINMENT
DETRAINMENTS
DETRAQUEES
DETRIBALISATION
DETRIBALISE
DETRIBALISED
DETRIBALISES
DETRIBALISING

DETRIBALIZATION
DETRIBALIZE
DETRIBALIZED
DETRIBALIZES
DETRIBALIZING
DETRIMENTAL
DETRIMENTALLY
DETRIMENTALS
DETRIMENTS
DETRITIONS
DETRITOVORE
DETRITOVORES
DETRUNCATE
DETRUNCATED
DETRUNCATES
DETRUNCATING
DETRUNCATION
DETRUNCATIONS
DETRUSIONS
DETUMESCENCE
DETUMESCENCES
DETUMESCENT
DEUTERAGONIST
DEUTERAGONISTS
DEUTERANOMALIES
DEUTERANOMALOUS
DEUTERANOMALY
DEUTERANOPE
DEUTERANOPES
DEUTERANOPIA
DEUTERANOPIAS
DEUTERANOPIC
DEUTERATED
DEUTERATES
DEUTERATING
DEUTERATION
DEUTERATIONS
DEUTERIDES
DEUTERIUMS
DEUTEROGAMIES
DEUTEROGAMIST
DEUTEROGAMISTS
DEUTEROGAMY
DEUTEROPLASM
DEUTEROPLASMS
DEUTEROSCOPIC
DEUTEROSCOPIES
DEUTEROSCOPY
DEUTEROSTOME

DEUTEROSTOMES
DEUTEROTOKIES
DEUTEROTOKY
DEUTOPLASM
DEUTOPLASMIC
DEUTOPLASMS
DEUTOPLASTIC
DEVALORISATION
DEVALORISATIONS
DEVALORISE
DEVALORISED
DEVALORISES
DEVALORISING
DEVALORIZATION
DEVALORIZATIONS
DEVALORIZE
DEVALORIZED
DEVALORIZES
DEVALORIZING
DEVALUATED
DEVALUATES
DEVALUATING
DEVALUATION
DEVALUATIONS
DEVANAGARI
DEVANAGARIS
DEVASTATED
DEVASTATES
DEVASTATING
DEVASTATINGLY
DEVASTATION
DEVASTATIONS
DEVASTATIVE
DEVASTATOR
DEVASTATORS
DEVASTAVIT
DEVASTAVITS
DEVELOPABLE
DEVELOPERS
DEVELOPING
DEVELOPMENT
DEVELOPMENTAL
DEVELOPMENTALLY
DEVELOPMENTS
DEVELOPPES
DEVERBATIVE
DEVERBATIVES
DEVIANCIES
DEVIATIONISM

DEVIATIONISMS	DEVOTEDNESSES	DEXTROROTATORY	DIACRITICAL	DIAKINESES
DEVIATIONIST	DEVOTEMENT	DEXTRORSAL	DIACRITICALLY	DIAKINESIS
DEVIATIONISTS	DEVOTEMENTS	DEXTRORSELY	DIACRITICS	DIALECTALLY
DEVIATIONS	DEVOTIONAL	DEXTROUSLY	DIACTINISM	DIALECTICAL
DEVILESSES	DEVOTIONALIST	DEXTROUSNESS	DIACTINISMS	DIALECTICALLY
DEVILFISHES	DEVOTIONALISTS	DEXTROUSNESSES	DIADELPHOUS	DIALECTICIAN
DEVILISHLY	DEVOTIONALITIES	DEZINCKING	DIADOCHIES	DIALECTICIANS
DEVILISHNESS	DEVOTIONALITY	DHARMSALAS	DIADROMOUS	DIALECTICISM
DEVILISHNESSES	DEVOTIONALLY	DHARMSHALA	DIAGENESES	DIALECTICISMS
DEVILMENTS	DEVOTIONALNESS	DHARMSHALAS	DIAGENESIS	DIALECTICS
DEVILSHIPS	DEVOTIONALS	DIABETICAL	DIAGENETIC	DIALECTOLOGICAL
DEVILTRIES	DEVOTIONIST	DIABETOGENIC	DIAGENETICALLY	DIALECTOLOGIES
DEVILWOODS	DEVOTIONISTS	DIABETOLOGIST	DIAGEOTROPIC	DIALECTOLOGIST
DEVIOUSNESS	DEVOURINGLY	DIABETOLOGISTS	DIAGEOTROPISM	DIALECTOLOGISTS
DEVIOUSNESSES	DEVOURMENT	DIABLERIES	DIAGEOTROPISMS	DIALECTOLOGY
DEVITALISATION	DEVOURMENTS	DIABOLICAL	DIAGNOSABILITY	DIALLAGOID
DEVITALISATIONS	DEVOUTNESS	DIABOLICALLY	DIAGNOSABLE	DIALOGICAL
DEVITALISE	DEVOUTNESSES	DIABOLICALNESS	DIAGNOSEABLE	DIALOGICALLY
DEVITALISED	DEVVELLING	DIABOLISED	DIAGNOSING	DIALOGISED
DEVITALISES	DEWATERERS	DIABOLISES	DIAGNOSTIC	DIALOGISES
DEVITALISING	DEWATERING	DIABOLISING	DIAGNOSTICAL	DIALOGISING
DEVITALIZATION	DEWATERINGS	DIABOLISMS	DIAGNOSTICALLY	DIALOGISMS
DEVITALIZATIONS	DEWBERRIES	DIABOLISTS	DIAGNOSTICIAN	DIALOGISTIC
DEVITALIZE	DEWINESSES	DIABOLIZED	DIAGNOSTICIANS	DIALOGISTICAL
DEVITALIZED	DEXAMETHASONE	DIABOLIZES	DIAGNOSTICS	DIALOGISTS
DEVITALIZES	DEXAMETHASONES	DIABOLIZING	DIAGOMETER	DIALOGITES
DEVITALIZING	DEXAMPHETAMINE	DIABOLOGIES	DIAGOMETERS	DIALOGIZED
DEVITRIFICATION	DEXAMPHETAMINES	DIABOLOLOGIES	DIAGONALISABLE	DIALOGIZES
DEVITRIFIED	DEXIOTROPIC	DIABOLOLOGY	DIAGONALISATION	DIALOGIZING
DEVITRIFIES	DEXTERITIES	DIACATHOLICON	DIAGONALISE	DIALOGUERS
DEVITRIFYING	DEXTEROUSLY	DIACATHOLICONS	DIAGONALISED	DIALOGUING
DEVOCALISE	DEXTEROUSNESS	DIACAUSTIC	DIAGONALISES	DIALYPETALOUS
DEVOCALISED	DEXTEROUSNESSES	DIACAUSTICS	DIAGONALISING	DIALYSABILITIES
DEVOCALISES	DEXTERWISE	DIACHRONIC	DIAGONALIZABLE	DIALYSABILITY
DEVOCALISING	DEXTRALITIES	DIACHRONICALLY	DIAGONALIZATION	DIALYSABLE
DEVOCALIZE	DEXTRALITY	DIACHRONIES	DIAGONALIZE	DIALYSATES
DEVOCALIZED	DEXTRANASE	DIACHRONISM	DIAGONALIZED	DIALYSATION
DEVOCALIZES	DEXTRANASES	DIACHRONISMS	DIAGONALIZES	DIALYSATIONS
DEVOCALIZING	DEXTROCARDIA	DIACHRONISTIC	DIAGONALIZING	DIALYTICALLY
DEVOICINGS	DEXTROCARDIAC	DIACHRONOUS	DIAGONALLY	DIALYZABILITIES
DEVOLUTION	DEXTROCARDIACS	DIACHYLONS	DIAGRAMING	DIALYZABILITY
DEVOLUTIONARY	DEXTROCARDIAS	DIACHYLUMS	DIAGRAMMABLE	DIALYZABLE
DEVOLUTIONIST	DEXTROGLUCOSE	DIACODIONS	DIAGRAMMATIC	DIALYZATES
DEVOLUTIONISTS	DEXTROGLUCOSES	DIACODIUMS	DIAGRAMMATICAL	DIALYZATION
DEVOLUTIONS	DEXTROGYRATE	DIACONATES	DIAGRAMMED	DIALYZATIONS
DEVOLVEMENT	DEXTROGYRE	DIACONICON	DIAGRAMMING	DIAMAGNETIC
DEVOLVEMENTS	DEXTROROTARY	DIACONICONS	DIAGRAPHIC	DIAMAGNETICALLY
DEVONPORTS	DEXTROROTATION	DIACOUSTIC	DIAHELIOTROPIC	DIAMAGNETISM
DEVOTEDNESS	DEXTROROTATIONS	DIACOUSTICS	DIAHELIOTROPISM	DIAMAGNETISMS

D

DIAMAGNETS	DIAPOPHYSES	DIATOMITES	DICHLORVOSES	DICKCISSELS
DIAMANTIFEROUS	DIAPOPHYSIAL	DIATONICALLY	DICHOGAMIC	DICKEYBIRD
DIAMANTINE	DIAPOPHYSIS	DIATONICISM	DICHOGAMIES	DICKEYBIRDS
DIAMETRALLY	DIAPOSITIVE	DIATONICISMS	DICHOGAMOUS	DICKYBIRDS
DIAMETRICAL	DIAPOSITIVES	DIATRETUMS	DICHONDRAS	DICLINISMS
DIAMETRICALLY	DIAPYETICS	DIATRIBIST	DICHOTICALLY	DICOTYLEDON
DIAMONDBACK	DIARCHICAL	DIATRIBISTS	DICHOTOMIC	DICOTYLEDONOUS
DIAMONDBACKS	DIARRHETIC	DIATROPISM	DICHOTOMIES	DICOTYLEDONS
DIAMONDIFEROUS	DIARRHOEAL	DIATROPISMS	DICHOTOMISATION	DICOUMARIN
DIAMONDING	DIARRHOEAS	DIAZEUCTIC	DICHOTOMISE	DICOUMARINS
DIAMORPHINE	DIARRHOEIC	DIAZOMETHANE	DICHOTOMISED	DICOUMAROL
DIAMORPHINES	DIARTHRODIAL	DIAZOMETHANES	DICHOTOMISES	DICOUMAROLS
DIANTHUSES	DIARTHROSES	DIAZONIUMS	DICHOTOMISING	DICROTISMS
DIAPASONAL	DIARTHROSIS	DIAZOTISATION	DICHOTOMIST	DICTATIONAL
DIAPASONIC	DIASCORDIUM	DIAZOTISATIONS	DICHOTOMISTS	DICTATIONS
DIAPAUSING	DIASCORDIUMS	DIAZOTISED	DICHOTOMIZATION	DICTATORIAL
DIAPEDESES	DIASKEUAST	DIAZOTISES	DICHOTOMIZE	DICTATORIALLY
DIAPEDESIS	DIASKEUASTS	DIAZOTISING	DICHOTOMIZED	DICTATORIALNESS
DIAPEDETIC	DIASTALSES	DIAZOTIZATION	DICHOTOMIZES	DICTATORSHIP
DIAPERINGS	DIASTALSIS	DIAZOTIZATIONS	DICHOTOMIZING	DICTATORSHIPS
DIAPHANEITIES	DIASTALTIC	DIAZOTIZED	DICHOTOMOUS	DICTATRESS
DIAPHANEITY	DIASTEMATA	DIAZOTIZES	DICHOTOMOUSLY	DICTATRESSES
DIAPHANOMETER	DIASTEMATIC	DIAZOTIZING	DICHOTOMOUSNESS	DICTATRICES
DIAPHANOMETERS	DIASTEREOISOMER	DIBASICITIES	DICHROISCOPE	DICTATRIXES
DIAPHANOUS	DIASTEREOMER	DIBASICITY	DICHROISCOPES	DICTATURES
DIAPHANOUSLY	DIASTEREOMERIC	DIBENZOFURAN	DICHROISCOPIC	DICTIONALLY
DIAPHANOUSNESS	DIASTEREOMERS	DIBENZOFURANS	DICHROISMS	DICTIONARIES
DIAPHONIES	DIASTROPHIC	DIBRANCHIATE	DICHROITES	DICTIONARY
DIAPHORASE	DIASTROPHICALLY	DIBRANCHIATES	DICHROITIC	DICTYOGENS
DIAPHORASES	DIASTROPHISM	DIBROMIDES	DICHROMACIES	DICTYOPTERAN
DIAPHORESES	DIASTROPHISMS	DICACITIES	DICHROMACY	DICTYOPTERANS
DIAPHORESIS	DIATESSARON	DICACODYLS	DICHROMATE	DICTYOSOME
DIAPHORETIC	DIATESSARONS	DICARBOXYLIC	DICHROMATES	DICTYOSOMES
DIAPHORETICS	DIATHERMACIES	DICARPELLARY	DICHROMATIC	DICTYOSTELE
DIAPHOTOTROPIC	DIATHERMACY	DICASTERIES	DICHROMATICISM	DICTYOSTELES
DIAPHOTOTROPIES	DIATHERMAL	DICENTRICS	DICHROMATICISMS	DICUMAROLS
DIAPHOTOTROPISM	DIATHERMANCIES	DICEPHALISM	DICHROMATICS	DICYNODONT
DIAPHOTOTROPY	DIATHERMANCY	DICEPHALISMS	DICHROMATISM	DICYNODONTS
DIAPHRAGMAL	DIATHERMANEITY	DICEPHALOUS	DICHROMATISMS	DIDACTICAL
DIAPHRAGMATIC	DIATHERMANOUS	DICHASIALLY	DICHROMATS	DIDACTICALLY
DIAPHRAGMATITIS	DIATHERMIA	DICHLAMYDEOUS	DICHROMISM	DIDACTICISM
DIAPHRAGMED	DIATHERMIAS	DICHLORACETIC	DICHROMISMS	DIDACTICISMS
DIAPHRAGMING	DIATHERMIC	DICHLORIDE	DICHROOSCOPE	DIDACTYLISM
DIAPHRAGMITIS	DIATHERMIES	DICHLORIDES	DICHROOSCOPES	DIDACTYLISMS
DIAPHRAGMITISES	DIATHERMOUS	DICHLOROBENZENE	DICHROOSCOPIC	DIDACTYLOUS
DIAPHRAGMS	DIATOMACEOUS	DICHLOROETHANE	DICHROSCOPE	DIDASCALIC
DIAPHYSEAL	DIATOMICITIES	DICHLOROETHANES	DICHROSCOPES	DIDELPHIAN
DIAPHYSIAL	DIATOMICITY	DICHLOROMETHANE	DICHROSCOPIC	DIDELPHIDS
DIAPIRISMS	DIATOMISTS	DICHLORVOS	DICKCISSEL	DIDELPHINE

DIDELPHOUS	DIEZEUGMENONS	DIFFUSEDNESS	DIGITATION	DIGRESSIVENESS
DIDGERIDOO	DIFFARREATION	DIFFUSEDNESSES	DIGITATIONS	DIHYBRIDISM
DIDGERIDOOS	DIFFARREATIONS	DIFFUSENESS	DIGITIFORM	DIHYBRIDISMS
DIDJERIDOO	DIFFERENCE	DIFFUSENESSES	DIGITIGRADE	DIHYDROCODEINE
DIDJERIDOOS	DIFFERENCED	DIFFUSIBILITIES	DIGITIGRADES	DIHYDROCODEINES
DIDJERIDUS	DIFFERENCES	DIFFUSIBILITY	DIGITISATION	DIHYDROGEN
DIDRACHMAS	DIFFERENCIED	DIFFUSIBLE	DIGITISATIONS	DIJUDICATE
DIDYNAMIAN	DIFFERENCIES	DIFFUSIBLENESS	DIGITISERS	DIJUDICATED
DIDYNAMIES	DIFFERENCING	DIFFUSIONAL	DIGITISING	DIJUDICATES
DIDYNAMOUS	DIFFERENCY	DIFFUSIONISM	DIGITIZATION	DIJUDICATING
DIECIOUSLY	DIFFERENCYING	DIFFUSIONISMS	DIGITIZATIONS	DIJUDICATION
DIECIOUSNESS	DIFFERENTIA	DIFFUSIONIST	DIGITIZERS	DIJUDICATIONS
DIECIOUSNESSES	DIFFERENTIABLE	DIFFUSIONISTS	DIGITIZING	DILACERATE
DIEFFENBACHIA	DIFFERENTIAE	DIFFUSIONS	DIGITONINS	DILACERATED
DIEFFENBACHIAS	DIFFERENTIAL	DIFFUSIVELY	DIGITORIUM	DILACERATES
DIELECTRIC	DIFFERENTIALLY	DIFFUSIVENESS	DIGITORIUMS	DILACERATING
DIELECTRICALLY	DIFFERENTIALS	DIFFUSIVENESSES	DIGITOXIGENIN	DILACERATION
DIELECTRICS	DIFFERENTIATE	DIFFUSIVITIES	DIGITOXIGENINS	DILACERATIONS
DIENCEPHALA	DIFFERENTIATED	DIFFUSIVITY	DIGITOXINS	DILAPIDATE
DIENCEPHALIC	DIFFERENTIATES	DIFUNCTIONAL	DIGLADIATE	DILAPIDATED
DIENCEPHALON	DIFFERENTIATING	DIFUNCTIONALS	DIGLADIATED	DILAPIDATES
DIENCEPHALONS	DIFFERENTIATION	DIGASTRICS	DIGLADIATES	DILAPIDATING
DIESELINGS	DIFFERENTIATOR	DIGESTANTS	DIGLADIATING	DILAPIDATION
DIESELISATION	DIFFERENTIATORS	DIGESTEDLY	DIGLADIATION	DILAPIDATIONS
DIESELISATIONS	DIFFERENTLY	DIGESTIBILITIES	DIGLADIATIONS	DILAPIDATOR
DIESELISED	DIFFERENTNESS	DIGESTIBILITY	DIGLADIATOR	DILAPIDATORS
DIESELISES	DIFFERENTNESSES	DIGESTIBLE	DIGLADIATORS	DILATABILITIES
DIESELISING	DIFFICULTIES	DIGESTIBLENESS	DIGLOSSIAS	DILATABILITY
DIESELIZATION	DIFFICULTLY	DIGESTIBLY	DIGLYCERIDE	DILATABLENESS
DIESELIZATIONS	DIFFICULTY	DIGESTIONAL	DIGLYCERIDES	DILATABLENESSES
DIESELIZED	DIFFIDENCE	DIGESTIONS	DIGNIFICATION	DILATANCIES
DIESELIZES	DIFFIDENCES	DIGESTIVELY	DIGNIFICATIONS	DILATATION
DIESELIZING	DIFFIDENTLY	DIGESTIVES	DIGNIFIEDLY	DILATATIONAL
DIESELLING	DIFFORMITIES	DIGITALINS	DIGNIFIEDNESS	DILATATIONS
DIESELLINGS	DIFFORMITY	DIGITALISATION	DIGNIFIEDNESSES	DILATATORS
DIESINKERS	DIFFRACTED	DIGITALISATIONS	DIGNIFYING	DILATOMETER
DIESTRUSES	DIFFRACTING	DIGITALISE	DIGNITARIES	DILATOMETERS
DIETARIANS	DIFFRACTION	DIGITALISED	DIGONEUTIC	DILATOMETRIC
DIETETICAL	DIFFRACTIONS	DIGITALISES	DIGONEUTISM	DILATOMETRIES
DIETETICALLY	DIFFRACTIVE	DIGITALISING	DIGONEUTISMS	DILATOMETRY
DIETHYLAMIDE	DIFFRACTIVELY	DIGITALISM	DIGRAPHICALLY	DILATORILY
DIETHYLAMIDES	DIFFRACTIVENESS	DIGITALISMS	DIGRESSERS	DILATORINESS
DIETHYLAMINE	DIFFRACTOMETER	DIGITALIZATION	DIGRESSING	DILATORINESSES
DIETHYLAMINES	DIFFRACTOMETERS	DIGITALIZATIONS	DIGRESSION	DILEMMATIC
DIETHYLENE	DIFFRACTOMETRIC	DIGITALIZE	DIGRESSIONAL	DILETTANTE
DIETHYLENES	DIFFRACTOMETRY	DIGITALIZED	DIGRESSIONARY	DILETTANTEISH
DIETICIANS	DIFFRANGIBILITY	DIGITALIZES	DIGRESSIONS	DILETTANTEISM
DIETITIANS	DIFFRANGIBLE	DIGITALIZING	DIGRESSIVE	DILETTANTEISMS
DIEZEUGMENON	DIFFUSEDLY	DIGITATELY	DIGRESSIVELY	DILETTANTES

D

DILETTANTI	DIMIDIATING	DINOSAURIC	DIPHENYLKETONE	DIPLODOCUSES
DILETTANTISH	DIMIDIATION	DINOTHERES	DIPHENYLKETONES	DIPLOGENESES
DILETTANTISM	DIMIDIATIONS	DINOTHERIA	DIPHOSGENE	DIPLOGENESIS
DILETTANTISMS	DIMINISHABLE	DINOTHERIUM	DIPHOSGENES	DIPLOIDIES
DILIGENCES	DIMINISHED	DINOTHERIUMS	DIPHOSPHATE	DIPLOMACIES
DILIGENTLY	DIMINISHES	DINOTURBATION	DIPHOSPHATES	DIPLOMAING
DILLYDALLIED	DIMINISHING	DINOTURBATIONS	DIPHTHERIA	DIPLOMATED
DILLYDALLIES	DIMINISHINGLY	DINUCLEOTIDE	DIPHTHERIAL	DIPLOMATES
DILLYDALLY	DIMINISHINGS	DINUCLEOTIDES	DIPHTHERIAS	DIPLOMATESE
DILLYDALLYING	DIMINISHMENT	DIOECIOUSLY	DIPHTHERIC	DIPLOMATESES
DILTIAZEMS	DIMINISHMENTS	DIOECIOUSNESS	DIPHTHERITIC	DIPLOMATIC
DILUCIDATE	DIMINUENDO	DIOECIOUSNESSES	DIPHTHERITIS	DIPLOMATICAL
DILUCIDATED	DIMINUENDOES	DIOESTRUSES	DIPHTHERITISES	DIPLOMATICALLY
DILUCIDATES	DIMINUENDOS	DIOICOUSLY	DIPHTHEROID	DIPLOMATICS
DILUCIDATING	DIMINUTION	DIOICOUSNESS	DIPHTHEROIDS	DIPLOMATING
DILUCIDATION	DIMINUTIONS	DIOICOUSNESSES	DIPHTHONGAL	DIPLOMATISE
DILUCIDATIONS	DIMINUTIVAL	DIOPHYSITE	DIPHTHONGALLY	DIPLOMATISED
DILUTABLES	DIMINUTIVE	DIOPHYSITES	DIPHTHONGED	DIPLOMATISES
DILUTENESS	DIMINUTIVELY	DIOPTOMETER	DIPHTHONGIC	DIPLOMATISING
DILUTENESSES	DIMINUTIVENESS	DIOPTOMETERS	DIPHTHONGING	DIPLOMATIST
DILUTIONARY	DIMINUTIVES	DIOPTOMETRIES	DIPHTHONGISE	DIPLOMATISTS
DILUVIALISM	DIMORPHISM	DIOPTOMETRY	DIPHTHONGISED	DIPLOMATIZE
DILUVIALISMS	DIMORPHISMS	DIOPTRICAL	DIPHTHONGISES	DIPLOMATIZED
DILUVIALIST	DIMORPHOUS	DIOPTRICALLY	DIPHTHONGISING	DIPLOMATIZES
DILUVIALISTS	DIMPLEMENT	DIORISTICAL	DIPHTHONGIZE	DIPLOMATIZING
DIMENHYDRINATE	DIMPLEMENTS	DIORISTICALLY	DIPHTHONGIZED	DIPLOMATOLOGIES
DIMENHYDRINATES	DINANDERIE	DIORTHOSES	DIPHTHONGIZES	DIPLOMATOLOGY
DIMENSIONAL	DINANDERIES	DIORTHOSIS	DIPHTHONGIZING	DIPLONEMAS
DIMENSIONALITY	DINARCHIES	DIORTHOTIC	DIPHTHONGS	DIPLOPHASE
DIMENSIONALLY	DINGDONGED	DIOSCOREACEOUS	DIPHYCERCAL	DIPLOPHASES
DIMENSIONED	DINGDONGING	DIOSGENINS	DIPHYLETIC	DIPLOSPEAK
DIMENSIONING	DINGINESSES	DIOTHELETE	DIPHYLLOUS	DIPLOSPEAKS
DIMENSIONLESS	DINGLEBERRIES	DIOTHELETES	DIPHYODONT	DIPLOSTEMONOUS
DIMENSIONS	DINGLEBERRY	DIOTHELETIC	DIPHYODONTS	DIPLOTENES
DIMERCAPROL	DINITROBENZENE	DIOTHELETICAL	DIPHYSITES	DIPNETTING
DIMERCAPROLS	DINITROBENZENES	DIOTHELISM	DIPHYSITISM	DIPPERFULS
DIMERISATION	DINITROGEN	DIOTHELISMS	DIPHYSITISMS	DIPPINESSES
DIMERISATIONS	DINITROPHENOL	DIOTHELITE	DIPLEIDOSCOPE	DIPRIONIDIAN
DIMERISING	DINITROPHENOLS	DIOTHELITES	DIPLEIDOSCOPES	DIPROPELLANT
DIMERIZATION	DINNERLESS	DIOXONITRIC	DIPLOBIONT	DIPROPELLANTS
DIMERIZATIONS	DINNERTIME	DIPEPTIDASE	DIPLOBIONTIC	DIPROTODON
DIMERIZING	DINNERTIMES	DIPEPTIDASES	DIPLOBIONTS	DIPROTODONS
DIMETHOATE	DINNERWARE	DIPEPTIDES	DIPLOBLASTIC	DIPROTODONT
DIMETHOATES	DINNERWARES	DIPETALOUS	DIPLOCARDIAC	DIPROTODONTID
DIMETHYLAMINE	DINOCERASES	DIPHENHYDRAMINE	DIPLOCOCCAL	DIPROTODONTIDS
DIMETHYLAMINES	DINOFLAGELLATE	DIPHENYLAMINE	DIPLOCOCCI	DIPROTODONTS
DIMETHYLANILINE	DINOFLAGELLATES	DIPHENYLAMINES	DIPLOCOCCIC	DIPSOMANIA
DIMIDIATED	DINOMANIAS	DIPHENYLENE	DIPLOCOCCUS	DIPSOMANIAC
DIMIDIATES	DINOSAURIAN	DIPHENYLENIMINE	DIPLODOCUS	DIPSOMANIACAL

DIPSOMANIACS	DISABUSING	DISAFFILIATES	DISANCHORS	DISAPPROVE
DIPSOMANIAS	DISACCHARID	DISAFFILIATING	DISANIMATE	DISAPPROVED
DIPSWITCHES	DISACCHARIDASE	DISAFFILIATION	DISANIMATED	DISAPPROVER
DIPTERISTS	DISACCHARIDASES	DISAFFILIATIONS	DISANIMATES	DISAPPROVERS
DIPTEROCARP	DISACCHARIDE	DISAFFIRMANCE	DISANIMATING	DISAPPROVES
DIPTEROCARPOUS	DISACCHARIDES	DISAFFIRMANCES	DISANNEXED	DISAPPROVING
DIPTEROCARPS	DISACCHARIDS	DISAFFIRMATION	DISANNEXES	DISAPPROVINGLY
DIPTEROSES	DISACCOMMODATE	DISAFFIRMATIONS	DISANNEXING	DISARMAMENT
DIRECTEDNESS	DISACCOMMODATED	DISAFFIRMED	DISANNULLED	DISARMAMENTS
DIRECTEDNESSES	DISACCOMMODATES	DISAFFIRMING	DISANNULLER	DISARMINGLY
DIRECTIONAL	DISACCORDANT	DISAFFIRMS	DISANNULLERS	DISARRANGE
DIRECTIONALITY	DISACCORDED	DISAFFOREST	DISANNULLING	DISARRANGED
DIRECTIONLESS	DISACCORDING	DISAFFORESTED	DISANNULLINGS	DISARRANGEMENT
DIRECTIONS	DISACCORDS	DISAFFORESTING	DISANNULMENT	DISARRANGEMENTS
DIRECTIVES	DISACCREDIT	DISAFFORESTMENT	DISANNULMENTS	DISARRANGES
DIRECTIVITIES	DISACCREDITED	DISAFFORESTS	DISANOINTED	DISARRANGING
DIRECTIVITY	DISACCREDITING	DISAGGREGATE	DISANOINTING	DISARRAYED
DIRECTNESS	DISACCREDITS	DISAGGREGATED	DISANOINTS	DISARRAYING
DIRECTNESSES	DISACCUSTOM	DISAGGREGATES	DISAPPAREL	DISARTICULATE
DIRECTORATE	DISACCUSTOMED	DISAGGREGATING	DISAPPARELLED	DISARTICULATED
DIRECTORATES	DISACCUSTOMING	DISAGGREGATION	DISAPPARELLING	DISARTICULATES
DIRECTORIAL	DISACCUSTOMS	DISAGGREGATIONS	DISAPPARELS	DISARTICULATING
DIRECTORIALLY	DISACKNOWLEDGE	DISAGGREGATIVE	DISAPPEARANCE	DISARTICULATION
DIRECTORIES	DISACKNOWLEDGED	DISAGREEABILITY	DISAPPEARANCES	DISARTICULATOR
DIRECTORSHIP	DISACKNOWLEDGES	DISAGREEABLE	DISAPPEARED	DISARTICULATORS
DIRECTORSHIPS	DISADORNED	DISAGREEABLES	DISAPPEARING	DISASSEMBLE
DIRECTRESS	DISADORNING	DISAGREEABLY	DISAPPEARS	DISASSEMBLED
DIRECTRESSES	DISADVANCE	DISAGREEING	DISAPPLICATION	DISASSEMBLER
DIRECTRICE	DISADVANCED	DISAGREEMENT	DISAPPLICATIONS	DISASSEMBLERS
DIRECTRICES	DISADVANCES	DISAGREEMENTS	DISAPPLIED	DISASSEMBLES
DIRECTRIXES	DISADVANCING	DISALLOWABLE	DISAPPLIES	DISASSEMBLIES
DIREFULNESS	DISADVANTAGE	DISALLOWANCE	DISAPPLYING	DISASSEMBLING
DIREFULNESSES	DISADVANTAGED	DISALLOWANCES	DISAPPOINT	DISASSEMBLY
DIREMPTING	DISADVANTAGEOUS	DISALLOWED	DISAPPOINTED	DISASSIMILATE
DIREMPTION	DISADVANTAGES	DISALLOWING	DISAPPOINTEDLY	DISASSIMILATED
DIREMPTIONS	DISADVANTAGING	DISALLYING	DISAPPOINTING	DISASSIMILATES
DIRENESSES	DISADVENTURE	DISAMBIGUATE	DISAPPOINTINGLY	DISASSIMILATING
DIRIGIBILITIES	DISADVENTURES	DISAMBIGUATED	DISAPPOINTMENT	DISASSIMILATION
DIRIGIBILITY	DISADVENTUROUS	DISAMBIGUATES	DISAPPOINTMENTS	DISASSIMILATIVE
DIRIGIBLES	DISAFFECTED	DISAMBIGUATING	DISAPPOINTS	DISASSOCIATE
DIRIGISMES	DISAFFECTEDLY	DISAMBIGUATION	DISAPPROBATION	DISASSOCIATED
DIRTINESSES	DISAFFECTEDNESS	DISAMBIGUATIONS	DISAPPROBATIONS	DISASSOCIATES
DISABILITIES	DISAFFECTING	DISAMENITIES	DISAPPROBATIVE	DISASSOCIATING
DISABILITY	DISAFFECTION	DISAMENITY	DISAPPROBATORY	DISASSOCIATION
DISABLEMENT	DISAFFECTIONATE	DISANALOGIES	DISAPPROPRIATE	DISASSOCIATIONS
DISABLEMENTS	DISAFFECTIONS	DISANALOGOUS	DISAPPROPRIATED	DISASTROUS
DISABLISMS	DISAFFECTS	DISANALOGY	DISAPPROPRIATES	DISASTROUSLY
DISABLISTS	DISAFFILIATE	DISANCHORED	DISAPPROVAL	DISATTIRED
DISABUSALS	DISAFFILIATED	DISANCHORING	DISAPPROVALS	DISATTIRES

D

DISATTIRING	DISBOSOMED	DISCEPTATORIAL	DISCIPLINES	DISCOMEDUSANS
DISATTRIBUTION	DISBOSOMING	DISCEPTATORS	DISCIPLING	DISCOMFITED
DISATTRIBUTIONS	DISBOWELED	DISCEPTING	DISCIPLINING	DISCOMFITER
DISATTUNED	DISBOWELING	DISCERNABLE	DISCIPULAR	DISCOMFITERS
DISATTUNES	DISBOWELLED	DISCERNABLY	DISCISSION	DISCOMFITING
DISATTUNING	DISBOWELLING	DISCERNERS	DISCISSIONS	DISCOMFITS
DISAUTHORISE	DISBRANCHED	DISCERNIBLE	DISCLAIMED	DISCOMFITURE
DISAUTHORISED	DISBRANCHES	DISCERNIBLY	DISCLAIMER	DISCOMFITURES
DISAUTHORISES	DISBRANCHING	DISCERNING	DISCLAIMERS	DISCOMFORT
DISAUTHORISING	DISBUDDING	DISCERNINGLY	DISCLAIMING	DISCOMFORTABLE
DISAUTHORIZE	DISBURDENED	DISCERNMENT	DISCLAMATION	DISCOMFORTED
DISAUTHORIZED	DISBURDENING	DISCERNMENTS	DISCLAMATIONS	DISCOMFORTING
DISAUTHORIZES	DISBURDENMENT	DISCERPIBILITY	DISCLIMAXES	DISCOMFORTS
DISAUTHORIZING	DISBURDENMENTS	DISCERPIBLE	DISCLOSERS	DISCOMMEND
DISAVAUNCE	DISBURDENS	DISCERPING	DISCLOSING	DISCOMMENDABLE
DISAVAUNCED	DISBURSABLE	DISCERPTIBLE	DISCLOSURE	DISCOMMENDATION
DISAVAUNCES	DISBURSALS	DISCERPTION	DISCLOSURES	DISCOMMENDED
DISAVAUNCING	DISBURSEMENT	DISCERPTIONS	DISCOBOLOS	DISCOMMENDING
DISAVENTROUS	DISBURSEMENTS	DISCERPTIVE	DISCOBOLUS	DISCOMMENDS
DISAVENTURE	DISBURSERS	DISCHARGEABLE	DISCOBOLUSES	DISCOMMISSION
DISAVENTURES	DISBURSING	DISCHARGED	DISCOGRAPHER	DISCOMMISSIONED
DISAVOUCHED	DISBURTHEN	DISCHARGEE	DISCOGRAPHERS	DISCOMMISSIONS
DISAVOUCHES	DISBURTHENED	DISCHARGEES	DISCOGRAPHIC	DISCOMMODE
DISAVOUCHING	DISBURTHENING	DISCHARGER	DISCOGRAPHICAL	DISCOMMODED
DISAVOWABLE	DISBURTHENS	DISCHARGERS	DISCOGRAPHIES	DISCOMMODES
DISAVOWALS	DISCALCEATE	DISCHARGES	DISCOGRAPHY	DISCOMMODING
DISAVOWEDLY	DISCALCEATES	DISCHARGING	DISCOLOGIES	DISCOMMODIOUS
DISAVOWERS	DISCANDERING	DISCHUFFED	DISCOLOGIST	DISCOMMODIOUSLY
DISAVOWING	DISCANDERINGS	DISCHURCHED	DISCOLOGISTS	DISCOMMODITIES
DISBANDING	DISCANDIED	DISCHURCHES	DISCOLORATION	DISCOMMODITY
DISBANDMENT	DISCANDIES	DISCHURCHING	DISCOLORATIONS	DISCOMMONED
DISBANDMENTS	DISCANDYING	DISCIPLESHIP	DISCOLORED	DISCOMMONING
DISBARKING	DISCANDYINGS	DISCIPLESHIPS	DISCOLORING	DISCOMMONS
DISBARMENT	DISCANTERS	DISCIPLINABLE	DISCOLORMENT	DISCOMMUNITIES
DISBARMENTS	DISCANTING	DISCIPLINAL	DISCOLORMENTS	DISCOMMUNITY
DISBARRING	DISCAPACITATE	DISCIPLINANT	DISCOLOURATION	DISCOMPOSE
DISBELIEFS	DISCAPACITATED	DISCIPLINANTS	DISCOLOURATIONS	DISCOMPOSED
DISBELIEVE	DISCAPACITATES	DISCIPLINARIA	DISCOLOURED	DISCOMPOSEDLY
DISBELIEVED	DISCAPACITATING	DISCIPLINARIAN	DISCOLOURING	DISCOMPOSES
DISBELIEVER	DISCARDABLE	DISCIPLINARIANS	DISCOLOURMENT	DISCOMPOSING
DISBELIEVERS	DISCARDERS	DISCIPLINARILY	DISCOLOURMENTS	DISCOMPOSINGLY
DISBELIEVES	DISCARDING	DISCIPLINARITY	DISCOLOURS	DISCOMPOSURE
DISBELIEVING	DISCARDMENT	DISCIPLINARIUM	DISCOMBOBERATE	DISCOMPOSURES
DISBELIEVINGLY	DISCARDMENTS	DISCIPLINARIUMS	DISCOMBOBERATED	DISCOMYCETE
DISBENCHED	DISCARNATE	DISCIPLINARY	DISCOMBOBERATES	DISCOMYCETES
DISBENCHES	DISCEPTATION	DISCIPLINE	DISCOMBOBULATE	DISCOMYCETOUS
DISBENCHING	DISCEPTATIONS	DISCIPLINED	DISCOMBOBULATED	DISCONCERT
DISBENEFIT	DISCEPTATIOUS	DISCIPLINER	DISCOMBOBULATES	DISCONCERTED
DISBENEFITS	DISCEPTATOR	DISCIPLINERS	DISCOMEDUSAN	DISCONCERTEDLY

DISCONCERTING	DISCONTINUE	DISCOURAGING	DISCRETIVE	DISDAINFUL
DISCONCERTINGLY	DISCONTINUED	DISCOURAGINGLY	DISCRETIVELY	DISDAINFULLY
DISCONCERTION	DISCONTINUER	DISCOURING	DISCRETIVES	DISDAINFULNESS
DISCONCERTIONS	DISCONTINUERS	DISCOURSAL	DISCRIMINABLE	DISDAINING
DISCONCERTMENT	DISCONTINUES	DISCOURSED	DISCRIMINABLY	DISEASEDNESS
DISCONCERTMENTS	DISCONTINUING	DISCOURSER	DISCRIMINANT	DISEASEDNESSES
DISCONCERTS	DISCONTINUITIES	DISCOURSERS	DISCRIMINANTS	DISEASEFUL
DISCONFIRM	DISCONTINUITY	DISCOURSES	DISCRIMINATE	DISECONOMIES
DISCONFIRMATION	DISCONTINUOUS	DISCOURSING	DISCRIMINATED	DISECONOMY
DISCONFIRMED	DISCONTINUOUSLY	DISCOURSIVE	DISCRIMINATELY	DISEMBARKATION
DISCONFIRMING	DISCOPHILE	DISCOURTEISE	DISCRIMINATES	DISEMBARKATIONS
DISCONFIRMS	DISCOPHILES	DISCOURTEOUS	DISCRIMINATING	DISEMBARKED
DISCONFORMABLE	DISCOPHORAN	DISCOURTEOUSLY	DISCRIMINATION	DISEMBARKING
DISCONFORMITIES	DISCOPHORANS	DISCOURTESIES	DISCRIMINATIONS	DISEMBARKMENT
DISCONFORMITY	DISCOPHOROUS	DISCOURTESY	DISCRIMINATIVE	DISEMBARKMENTS
DISCONNECT	DISCORDANCE	DISCOVERABLE	DISCRIMINATOR	DISEMBARKS
DISCONNECTED	DISCORDANCES	DISCOVERED	DISCRIMINATORS	DISEMBARRASS
DISCONNECTEDLY	DISCORDANCIES	DISCOVERER	DISCRIMINATORY	DISEMBARRASSED
DISCONNECTER	DISCORDANCY	DISCOVERERS	DISCROWNED	DISEMBARRASSES
DISCONNECTERS	DISCORDANT	DISCOVERIES	DISCROWNING	DISEMBARRASSING
DISCONNECTING	DISCORDANTLY	DISCOVERING	DISCULPATE	DISEMBELLISH
DISCONNECTION	DISCORDFUL	DISCOVERTURE	DISCULPATED	DISEMBELLISHED
DISCONNECTIONS	DISCORDING	DISCOVERTURES	DISCULPATES	DISEMBELLISHES
DISCONNECTIVE	DISCORPORATE	DISCREDITABLE	DISCULPATING	DISEMBELLISHING
DISCONNECTS	DISCORPORATED	DISCREDITABLY	DISCUMBERED	DISEMBITTER
DISCONNEXION	DISCORPORATES	DISCREDITED	DISCUMBERING	DISEMBITTERED
DISCONNEXIONS	DISCORPORATING	DISCREDITING	DISCUMBERS	DISEMBITTERING
DISCONSENT	DISCOTHEQUE	DISCREDITS	DISCURSION	DISEMBITTERS
DISCONSENTED	DISCOTHEQUES	DISCREETER	DISCURSIONS	DISEMBODIED
DISCONSENTING	DISCOUNSEL	DISCREETEST	DISCURSIST	DISEMBODIES
DISCONSENTS	DISCOUNSELLED	DISCREETLY	DISCURSISTS	DISEMBODIMENT
DISCONSOLATE	DISCOUNSELLING	DISCREETNESS	DISCURSIVE	DISEMBODIMENTS
DISCONSOLATELY	DISCOUNSELS	DISCREETNESSES	DISCURSIVELY	DISEMBODYING
DISCONSOLATION	DISCOUNTABLE	DISCREPANCE	DISCURSIVENESS	DISEMBOGUE
DISCONSOLATIONS	DISCOUNTED	DISCREPANCES	DISCURSORY	DISEMBOGUED
DISCONTENT	DISCOUNTENANCE	DISCREPANCIES	DISCURSUSES	DISEMBOGUEMENT
DISCONTENTED	DISCOUNTENANCED	DISCREPANCY	DISCUSSABLE	DISEMBOGUEMENTS
DISCONTENTEDLY	DISCOUNTENANCES	DISCREPANT	DISCUSSANT	DISEMBOGUES
DISCONTENTFUL	DISCOUNTER	DISCREPANTLY	DISCUSSANTS	DISEMBOGUING
DISCONTENTING	DISCOUNTERS	DISCRETELY	DISCUSSERS	DISEMBOSOM
DISCONTENTMENT	DISCOUNTING	DISCRETENESS	DISCUSSIBLE	DISEMBOSOMED
DISCONTENTMENTS	DISCOURAGE	DISCRETENESSES	DISCUSSING	DISEMBOSOMING
DISCONTENTS	DISCOURAGEABLE	DISCRETEST	DISCUSSION	DISEMBOSOMS
DISCONTIGUITIES	DISCOURAGED	DISCRETION	DISCUSSIONAL	DISEMBOWEL
DISCONTIGUITY	DISCOURAGEMENT	DISCRETIONAL	DISCUSSIONS	DISEMBOWELED
DISCONTIGUOUS	DISCOURAGEMENTS	DISCRETIONALLY	DISCUSSIVE	DISEMBOWELING
DISCONTINUANCE	DISCOURAGER	DISCRETIONARILY	DISCUSSIVES	DISEMBOWELLED
DISCONTINUANCES	DISCOURAGERS	DISCRETIONARY	DISCUTIENT	DISEMBOWELLING
DISCONTINUATION	DISCOURAGES	DISCRETIONS	DISCUTIENTS	DISEMBOWELMENT

DISEMBOWELMENTS

DISEMBOWELMENTS DISENCLOSED DISENTANGLING DISENVIRONED DISFIGURING
DISEMBOWELS DISENCLOSES DISENTHRAL DISENVIRONING DISFLESHED
DISEMBRANGLE DISENCLOSING DISENTHRALL DISENVIRONS DISFLESHES
DISEMBRANGLED DISENCUMBER DISENTHRALLED DISEPALOUS DISFLESHING
DISEMBRANGLES DISENCUMBERED DISENTHRALLING DISEQUILIBRATE DISFLUENCIES
DISEMBRANGLING DISENCUMBERING DISENTHRALLMENT DISEQUILIBRATED DISFLUENCY
DISEMBROIL DISENCUMBERMENT DISENTHRALLS DISEQUILIBRATES DISFORESTATION
DISEMBROILED DISENCUMBERS DISENTHRALMENT DISEQUILIBRIA DISFORESTATIONS
DISEMBROILING DISENCUMBRANCE DISENTHRALMENTS DISEQUILIBRIUM DISFORESTED
DISEMBROILS DISENCUMBRANCES DISENTHRALS DISEQUILIBRIUMS DISFORESTING
DISEMBURDEN DISENDOWED DISENTHRONE DISESPOUSE DISFORESTS
DISEMBURDENED DISENDOWER DISENTHRONED DISESPOUSED DISFORMING
DISEMBURDENING DISENDOWERS DISENTHRONES DISESPOUSES DISFRANCHISE
DISEMBURDENS DISENDOWING DISENTHRONING DISESPOUSING DISFRANCHISED
DISEMPLOYED DISENDOWMENT DISENTITLE DISESTABLISH DISFRANCHISES
DISEMPLOYING DISENDOWMENTS DISENTITLED DISESTABLISHED DISFRANCHISING
DISEMPLOYMENT DISENFRANCHISE DISENTITLES DISESTABLISHES DISFROCKED
DISEMPLOYMENTS DISENFRANCHISED DISENTITLING DISESTABLISHING DISFROCKING
DISEMPLOYS DISENFRANCHISES DISENTOMBED DISESTEEMED DISFUNCTION
DISEMPOWER DISENGAGED DISENTOMBING DISESTEEMING DISFUNCTIONAL
DISEMPOWERED DISENGAGEDNESS DISENTOMBS DISESTEEMS DISFUNCTIONS
DISEMPOWERING DISENGAGEMENT DISENTRAIL DISESTIMATION DISFURNISH
DISEMPOWERMENT DISENGAGEMENTS DISENTRAILED DISESTIMATIONS DISFURNISHED
DISEMPOWERMENTS DISENGAGES DISENTRAILING DISFAVORED DISFURNISHES
DISEMPOWERS DISENGAGING DISENTRAILS DISFAVORER DISFURNISHING
DISEMVOWEL DISENNOBLE DISENTRAIN DISFAVORERS DISFURNISHMENT
DISEMVOWELLED DISENNOBLED DISENTRAINED DISFAVORING DISFURNISHMENTS
DISEMVOWELLING DISENNOBLES DISENTRAINING DISFAVOURED DISGARNISH
DISEMVOWELS DISENNOBLING DISENTRAINMENT DISFAVOURER DISGARNISHED
DISENABLED DISENROLLED DISENTRAINMENTS DISFAVOURERS DISGARNISHES
DISENABLEMENT DISENROLLING DISENTRAINS DISFAVOURING DISGARNISHING
DISENABLEMENTS DISENROLLINGS DISENTRANCE DISFAVOURS DISGARRISON
DISENABLES DISENSHROUD DISENTRANCED DISFEATURE DISGARRISONED
DISENABLING DISENSHROUDED DISENTRANCEMENT DISFEATURED DISGARRISONING
DISENCHAIN DISENSHROUDING DISENTRANCES DISFEATUREMENT DISGARRISONS
DISENCHAINED DISENSHROUDS DISENTRANCING DISFEATUREMENTS DISGAVELLED
DISENCHAINING DISENSLAVE DISENTRAYLE DISFEATURES DISGAVELLING
DISENCHAINS DISENSLAVED DISENTRAYLED DISFEATURING DISGAVELLINGS
DISENCHANT DISENSLAVES DISENTRAYLES DISFELLOWSHIP DISGESTING
DISENCHANTED DISENSLAVING DISENTRAYLING DISFELLOWSHIPED DISGESTION
DISENCHANTER DISENTAILED DISENTWINE DISFELLOWSHIPS DISGESTIONS
DISENCHANTERS DISENTAILING DISENTWINED DISFIGURATION DISGLORIFIED
DISENCHANTING DISENTAILMENT DISENTWINES DISFIGURATIONS DISGLORIFIES
DISENCHANTINGLY DISENTAILMENTS DISENTWINING DISFIGURED DISGLORIFY
DISENCHANTMENT DISENTAILS DISENVELOP DISFIGUREMENT DISGLORIFYING
DISENCHANTMENTS DISENTANGLE DISENVELOPED DISFIGUREMENTS DISGORGEMENT
DISENCHANTRESS DISENTANGLED DISENVELOPING DISFIGURER DISGORGEMENTS
DISENCHANTS DISENTANGLEMENT DISENVELOPS DISFIGURERS DISGORGERS
DISENCLOSE DISENTANGLES DISENVIRON DISFIGURES DISGORGING

DISGOSPELLING	DISHALLOWING	DISHONORERS	DISIMPRISONING	DISINGENUITIES
DISGOWNING	DISHALLOWS	DISHONORING	DISIMPRISONMENT	DISINGENUITY
DISGRACEFUL	DISHARMONIC	DISHONOURABLE	DISIMPRISONS	DISINGENUOUS
DISGRACEFULLY	DISHARMONIES	DISHONOURABLY	DISIMPROVE	DISINGENUOUSLY
DISGRACEFULNESS	DISHARMONIOUS	DISHONOURED	DISIMPROVED	DISINHERISON
DISGRACERS	DISHARMONIOUSLY	DISHONOURER	DISIMPROVES	DISINHERISONS
DISGRACING	DISHARMONISE	DISHONOURERS	DISIMPROVING	DISINHERIT
DISGRACIOUS	DISHARMONISED	DISHONOURING	DISINCARCERATE	DISINHERITANCE
DISGRADATION	DISHARMONISES	DISHONOURS	DISINCARCERATED	DISINHERITANCES
DISGRADATIONS	DISHARMONISING	DISHORNING	DISINCARCERATES	DISINHERITED
DISGRADING	DISHARMONIZE	DISHORSING	DISINCENTIVE	DISINHERITING
DISGREGATION	DISHARMONIZED	DISHOUSING	DISINCENTIVES	DISINHERITS
DISGREGATIONS	DISHARMONIZES	DISHTOWELS	DISINCLINATION	DISINHIBIT
DISGRUNTLE	DISHARMONIZING	DISHUMOURED	DISINCLINATIONS	DISINHIBITED
DISGRUNTLED	DISHARMONY	DISHUMOURING	DISINCLINE	DISINHIBITING
DISGRUNTLEMENT	DISHCLOTHS	DISHUMOURS	DISINCLINED	DISINHIBITION
DISGRUNTLEMENTS	DISHCLOUTS	DISHWASHER	DISINCLINES	DISINHIBITIONS
DISGRUNTLES	DISHDASHAS	DISHWASHERS	DISINCLINING	DISINHIBITORY
DISGRUNTLING	DISHDASHES	DISHWATERS	DISINCLOSE	DISINHIBITS
DISGUISABLE	DISHEARTEN	DISILLUDED	DISINCLOSED	DISINHUMED
DISGUISEDLY	DISHEARTENED	DISILLUDES	DISINCLOSES	DISINHUMES
DISGUISEDNESS	DISHEARTENING	DISILLUDING	DISINCLOSING	DISINHUMING
DISGUISEDNESSES	DISHEARTENINGLY	DISILLUMINATE	DISINCORPORATE	DISINTEGRABLE
DISGUISELESS	DISHEARTENMENT	DISILLUMINATED	DISINCORPORATED	DISINTEGRATE
DISGUISEMENT	DISHEARTENMENTS	DISILLUMINATES	DISINCORPORATES	DISINTEGRATED
DISGUISEMENTS	DISHEARTENS	DISILLUMINATING	DISINFECTANT	DISINTEGRATES
DISGUISERS	DISHELMING	DISILLUSION	DISINFECTANTS	DISINTEGRATING
DISGUISING	DISHERISON	DISILLUSIONARY	DISINFECTED	DISINTEGRATION
DISGUISINGS	DISHERISONS	DISILLUSIONED	DISINFECTING	DISINTEGRATIONS
DISGUSTEDLY	DISHERITED	DISILLUSIONING	DISINFECTION	DISINTEGRATIVE
DISGUSTEDNESS	DISHERITING	DISILLUSIONISE	DISINFECTIONS	DISINTEGRATOR
DISGUSTEDNESSES	DISHERITOR	DISILLUSIONISED	DISINFECTOR	DISINTEGRATORS
DISGUSTFUL	DISHERITORS	DISILLUSIONISES	DISINFECTORS	DISINTEREST
DISGUSTFULLY	DISHEVELED	DISILLUSIONIZE	DISINFECTS	DISINTERESTED
DISGUSTFULNESS	DISHEVELING	DISILLUSIONIZED	DISINFESTANT	DISINTERESTEDLY
DISGUSTING	DISHEVELLED	DISILLUSIONIZES	DISINFESTANTS	DISINTERESTING
DISGUSTINGLY	DISHEVELLING	DISILLUSIONMENT	DISINFESTATION	DISINTERESTS
DISGUSTINGNESS	DISHEVELMENT	DISILLUSIONS	DISINFESTATIONS	DISINTERMEDIATE
DISHABILITATE	DISHEVELMENTS	DISILLUSIVE	DISINFESTED	DISINTERMENT
DISHABILITATED	DISHOARDED	DISIMAGINE	DISINFESTING	DISINTERMENTS
DISHABILITATES	DISHOARDING	DISIMAGINED	DISINFESTS	DISINTERRED
DISHABILITATING	DISHONESTIES	DISIMAGINES	DISINFLATION	DISINTERRING
DISHABILITATION	DISHONESTLY	DISIMAGINING	DISINFLATIONARY	DISINTHRAL
DISHABILLE	DISHONESTY	DISIMMURED	DISINFLATIONS	DISINTHRALLED
DISHABILLES	DISHONORABLE	DISIMMURES	DISINFORMATION	DISINTHRALLING
DISHABITED	DISHONORABLY	DISIMMURING	DISINFORMATIONS	DISINTHRALLINGS
DISHABITING	DISHONORARY	DISIMPASSIONED	DISINFORMED	DISINTHRALS
DISHABLING	DISHONORED	DISIMPRISON	DISINFORMING	DISINTOXICATE
DISHALLOWED	DISHONORER	DISIMPRISONED	DISINFORMS	DISINTOXICATED

DISINTOXICATES DISLIKABLE DISMAYFULLY DISOBLIGINGLY DISPARATENESSES
DISINTOXICATING DISLIKEABLE DISMAYINGLY DISOBLIGINGNESS DISPARATES
DISINTOXICATION DISLIKEFUL DISMAYLING DISOPERATION DISPARITIES
DISINTRICATE DISLIKENED DISMEMBERED DISOPERATIONS DISPARKING
DISINTRICATED DISLIKENESS DISMEMBERER DISORDERED DISPARTING
DISINTRICATES DISLIKENESSES DISMEMBERERS DISORDEREDLY DISPASSION
DISINTRICATING DISLIKENING DISMEMBERING DISORDEREDNESS DISPASSIONATE
DISINURING DISLIMBING DISMEMBERMENT DISORDERING DISPASSIONATELY
DISINVENTED DISLIMNING DISMEMBERMENTS DISORDERLIES DISPASSIONS
DISINVENTING DISLINKING DISMEMBERS DISORDERLINESS DISPATCHED
DISINVENTS DISLOADING DISMISSALS DISORDERLY DISPATCHER
DISINVESTED DISLOCATED DISMISSIBLE DISORDINATE DISPATCHERS
DISINVESTING DISLOCATEDLY DISMISSING DISORDINATELY DISPATCHES
DISINVESTITURE DISLOCATES DISMISSION DISORGANIC DISPATCHFUL
DISINVESTITURES DISLOCATING DISMISSIONS DISORGANISATION DISPATCHING
DISINVESTMENT DISLOCATION DISMISSIVE DISORGANISE DISPATHIES
DISINVESTMENTS DISLOCATIONS DISMISSIVELY DISORGANISED DISPAUPERED
DISINVESTS DISLODGEMENT DISMISSORY DISORGANISER DISPAUPERING
DISINVIGORATE DISLODGEMENTS DISMOUNTABLE DISORGANISERS DISPAUPERISE
DISINVIGORATED DISLODGING DISMOUNTED DISORGANISES DISPAUPERISED
DISINVIGORATES DISLODGMENT DISMOUNTING DISORGANISING DISPAUPERISES
DISINVIGORATING DISLODGMENTS DISMUTATION DISORGANIZATION DISPAUPERISING
DISINVITED DISLOIGNED DISMUTATIONS DISORGANIZE DISPAUPERIZE
DISINVITES DISLOIGNING DISNATURALISE DISORGANIZED DISPAUPERIZED
DISINVITING DISLOYALLY DISNATURALISED DISORGANIZER DISPAUPERIZES
DISINVOLVE DISLOYALTIES DISNATURALISES DISORGANIZERS DISPAUPERIZING
DISINVOLVED DISLOYALTY DISNATURALISING DISORGANIZES DISPAUPERS
DISINVOLVES DISLUSTRED DISNATURALIZE DISORGANIZING DISPELLERS
DISINVOLVING DISLUSTRES DISNATURALIZED DISORIENTATE DISPELLING
DISJECTING DISLUSTRING DISNATURALIZES DISORIENTATED DISPENCING
DISJECTION DISMALITIES DISNATURALIZING DISORIENTATES DISPENDING
DISJECTIONS DISMALLEST DISNATURED DISORIENTATING DISPENSABILITY
DISJOINABLE DISMALNESS DISNATURES DISORIENTATION DISPENSABLE
DISJOINING DISMALNESSES DISNATURING DISORIENTATIONS DISPENSABLENESS
DISJOINTED DISMANNING DISNESTING DISORIENTED DISPENSABLY
DISJOINTEDLY DISMANTLED DISOBEDIENCE DISORIENTING DISPENSARIES
DISJOINTEDNESS DISMANTLEMENT DISOBEDIENCES DISORIENTS DISPENSARY
DISJOINTING DISMANTLEMENTS DISOBEDIENT DISOWNMENT DISPENSATION
DISJUNCTION DISMANTLER DISOBEDIENTLY DISOWNMENTS DISPENSATIONAL
DISJUNCTIONS DISMANTLERS DISOBEYERS DISPARAGED DISPENSATIONS
DISJUNCTIVE DISMANTLES DISOBEYING DISPARAGEMENT DISPENSATIVE
DISJUNCTIVELY DISMANTLING DISOBLIGATION DISPARAGEMENTS DISPENSATIVELY
DISJUNCTIVES DISMANTLINGS DISOBLIGATIONS DISPARAGER DISPENSATOR
DISJUNCTOR DISMASKING DISOBLIGATORY DISPARAGERS DISPENSATORIES
DISJUNCTORS DISMASTING DISOBLIGED DISPARAGES DISPENSATORILY
DISJUNCTURE DISMASTMENT DISOBLIGEMENT DISPARAGING DISPENSATORS
DISJUNCTURES DISMASTMENTS DISOBLIGEMENTS DISPARAGINGLY DISPENSATORY
DISLEAFING DISMAYEDNESS DISOBLIGES DISPARATELY DISPENSERS
DISLEAVING DISMAYEDNESSES DISOBLIGING DISPARATENESS DISPENSING

DISPEOPLED	DISPLEASEDLY	DISPOSSESSOR	DISPROVERS	DISQUIETNESS
DISPEOPLES	DISPLEASEDNESS	DISPOSSESSORS	DISPROVIDE	DISQUIETNESSES
DISPEOPLING	DISPLEASES	DISPOSSESSORY	DISPROVIDED	DISQUIETOUS
DISPERMOUS	DISPLEASING	DISPOSTING	DISPROVIDES	DISQUIETUDE
DISPERSALS	DISPLEASINGLY	DISPOSURES	DISPROVIDING	DISQUIETUDES
DISPERSANT	DISPLEASINGNESS	DISPRAISED	DISPROVING	DISQUISITION
DISPERSANTS	DISPLEASURE	DISPRAISER	DISPUNGING	DISQUISITIONAL
DISPERSEDLY	DISPLEASURED	DISPRAISERS	DISPURSING	DISQUISITIONARY
DISPERSEDNESS	DISPLEASURES	DISPRAISES	DISPURVEYANCE	DISQUISITIONS
DISPERSEDNESSES	DISPLEASURING	DISPRAISING	DISPURVEYANCES	DISQUISITIVE
DISPERSERS	DISPLENISH	DISPRAISINGLY	DISPURVEYED	DISQUISITORY
DISPERSIBLE	DISPLENISHED	DISPREADED	DISPURVEYING	DISRANKING
DISPERSING	DISPLENISHES	DISPREADING	DISPURVEYS	DISREGARDED
DISPERSION	DISPLENISHING	DISPREDDEN	DISPUTABILITIES	DISREGARDER
DISPERSIONS	DISPLENISHMENT	DISPREDDING	DISPUTABILITY	DISREGARDERS
DISPERSIVE	DISPLENISHMENTS	DISPRINCED	DISPUTABLE	DISREGARDFUL
DISPERSIVELY	DISPLODING	DISPRISONED	DISPUTABLENESS	DISREGARDFULLY
DISPERSIVENESS	DISPLOSION	DISPRISONING	DISPUTABLY	DISREGARDING
DISPERSOID	DISPLOSIONS	DISPRISONS	DISPUTANTS	DISREGARDS
DISPERSOIDS	DISPLUMING	DISPRIVACIED	DISPUTATION	DISRELATED
DISPIRITED	DISPONDAIC	DISPRIVILEGE	DISPUTATIONS	DISRELATION
DISPIRITEDLY	DISPONDEES	DISPRIVILEGED	DISPUTATIOUS	DISRELATIONS
DISPIRITEDNESS	DISPONGING	DISPRIVILEGES	DISPUTATIOUSLY	DISRELISHED
DISPIRITING	DISPORTING	DISPRIVILEGING	DISPUTATIVE	DISRELISHES
DISPIRITINGLY	DISPORTMENT	DISPRIZING	DISPUTATIVELY	DISRELISHING
DISPIRITMENT	DISPORTMENTS	DISPROFESS	DISPUTATIVENESS	DISREMEMBER
DISPIRITMENTS	DISPOSABILITIES	DISPROFESSED	DISQUALIFIABLE	DISREMEMBERED
DISPITEOUS	DISPOSABILITY	DISPROFESSES	DISQUALIFIED	DISREMEMBERING
DISPITEOUSLY	DISPOSABLE	DISPROFESSING	DISQUALIFIER	DISREMEMBERS
DISPITEOUSNESS	DISPOSABLENESS	DISPROFITED	DISQUALIFIERS	DISREPAIRS
DISPLACEABLE	DISPOSABLES	DISPROFITING	DISQUALIFIES	DISREPUTABILITY
DISPLACEMENT	DISPOSEDLY	DISPROFITS	DISQUALIFY	DISREPUTABLE
DISPLACEMENTS	DISPOSINGLY	DISPROOVED	DISQUALIFYING	DISREPUTABLY
DISPLACERS	DISPOSINGS	DISPROOVES	DISQUANTITIED	DISREPUTATION
DISPLACING	DISPOSITION	DISPROOVING	DISQUANTITIES	DISREPUTATIONS
DISPLANTATION	DISPOSITIONAL	DISPROPERTIED	DISQUANTITY	DISREPUTES
DISPLANTATIONS	DISPOSITIONED	DISPROPERTIES	DISQUANTITYING	DISRESPECT
DISPLANTED	DISPOSITIONS	DISPROPERTY	DISQUIETED	DISRESPECTABLE
DISPLANTING	DISPOSITIVE	DISPROPERTYING	DISQUIETEDLY	DISRESPECTED
DISPLAYABLE	DISPOSITIVELY	DISPROPORTION	DISQUIETEDNESS	DISRESPECTFUL
DISPLAYERS	DISPOSITIVES	DISPROPORTIONAL	DISQUIETEN	DISRESPECTFULLY
DISPLAYING	DISPOSITOR	DISPROPORTIONED	DISQUIETENED	DISRESPECTING
DISPLEASANCE	DISPOSITORS	DISPROPORTIONS	DISQUIETENING	DISRESPECTS
DISPLEASANCES	DISPOSSESS	DISPROPRIATE	DISQUIETENS	DISROBEMENT
DISPLEASANT	DISPOSSESSED	DISPROPRIATED	DISQUIETFUL	DISROBEMENTS
DISPLEASANTED	DISPOSSESSES	DISPROPRIATES	DISQUIETING	DISROOTING
DISPLEASANTING	DISPOSSESSING	DISPROPRIATING	DISQUIETINGLY	DISRUPTERS
DISPLEASANTS	DISPOSSESSION	DISPROVABLE	DISQUIETIVE	DISRUPTING
DISPLEASED	DISPOSSESSIONS	DISPROVALS	DISQUIETLY	DISRUPTION

DISRUPTIONS

DISRUPTIONS
DISRUPTIVE
DISRUPTIVELY
DISRUPTIVENESS
DISRUPTORS
DISSATISFACTION
DISSATISFACTORY
DISSATISFIED
DISSATISFIEDLY
DISSATISFIES
DISSATISFY
DISSATISFYING
DISSAVINGS
DISSEATING
DISSECTIBLE
DISSECTING
DISSECTINGS
DISSECTION
DISSECTIONS
DISSECTIVE
DISSECTORS
DISSEISEES
DISSEISING
DISSEISINS
DISSEISORS
DISSEIZEES
DISSEIZING
DISSEIZINS
DISSEIZORS
DISSELBOOM
DISSELBOOMS
DISSEMBLANCE
DISSEMBLANCES
DISSEMBLED
DISSEMBLER
DISSEMBLERS
DISSEMBLES
DISSEMBLIES
DISSEMBLING
DISSEMBLINGLY
DISSEMBLINGS
DISSEMINATE
DISSEMINATED
DISSEMINATES
DISSEMINATING
DISSEMINATION
DISSEMINATIONS
DISSEMINATIVE
DISSEMINATOR

DISSEMINATORS
DISSEMINULE
DISSEMINULES
DISSENSION
DISSENSIONS
DISSENSUSES
DISSENTERISH
DISSENTERISM
DISSENTERISMS
DISSENTERS
DISSENTIENCE
DISSENTIENCES
DISSENTIENCIES
DISSENTIENCY
DISSENTIENT
DISSENTIENTLY
DISSENTIENTS
DISSENTING
DISSENTINGLY
DISSENTION
DISSENTIONS
DISSENTIOUS
DISSEPIMENT
DISSEPIMENTAL
DISSEPIMENTS
DISSERTATE
DISSERTATED
DISSERTATES
DISSERTATING
DISSERTATION
DISSERTATIONAL
DISSERTATIONIST
DISSERTATIONS
DISSERTATIVE
DISSERTATOR
DISSERTATORS
DISSERTING
DISSERVICE
DISSERVICEABLE
DISSERVICES
DISSERVING
DISSEVERANCE
DISSEVERANCES
DISSEVERATION
DISSEVERATIONS
DISSEVERED
DISSEVERING
DISSEVERMENT
DISSEVERMENTS

DISSHEATHE
DISSHEATHED
DISSHEATHES
DISSHEATHING
DISSHIVERED
DISSHIVERING
DISSHIVERS
DISSIDENCE
DISSIDENCES
DISSIDENTLY
DISSIDENTS
DISSILIENCE
DISSILIENCES
DISSILIENT
DISSIMILAR
DISSIMILARITIES
DISSIMILARITY
DISSIMILARLY
DISSIMILARS
DISSIMILATE
DISSIMILATED
DISSIMILATES
DISSIMILATING
DISSIMILATION
DISSIMILATIONS
DISSIMILATIVE
DISSIMILATORY
DISSIMILES
DISSIMILITUDE
DISSIMILITUDES
DISSIMULATE
DISSIMULATED
DISSIMULATES
DISSIMULATING
DISSIMULATION
DISSIMULATIONS
DISSIMULATIVE
DISSIMULATOR
DISSIMULATORS
DISSIPABLE
DISSIPATED
DISSIPATEDLY
DISSIPATEDNESS
DISSIPATER
DISSIPATERS
DISSIPATES
DISSIPATING
DISSIPATION
DISSIPATIONS

DISSIPATIVE
DISSIPATOR
DISSIPATORS
DISSOCIABILITY
DISSOCIABLE
DISSOCIABLENESS
DISSOCIABLY
DISSOCIALISE
DISSOCIALISED
DISSOCIALISES
DISSOCIALISING
DISSOCIALITIES
DISSOCIALITY
DISSOCIALIZE
DISSOCIALIZED
DISSOCIALIZES
DISSOCIALIZING
DISSOCIATE
DISSOCIATED
DISSOCIATES
DISSOCIATING
DISSOCIATION
DISSOCIATIONS
DISSOCIATIVE
DISSOLUBILITIES
DISSOLUBILITY
DISSOLUBLE
DISSOLUBLENESS
DISSOLUTELY
DISSOLUTENESS
DISSOLUTENESSES
DISSOLUTES
DISSOLUTION
DISSOLUTIONISM
DISSOLUTIONISMS
DISSOLUTIONIST
DISSOLUTIONISTS
DISSOLUTIONS
DISSOLUTIVE
DISSOLVABILITY
DISSOLVABLE
DISSOLVABLENESS
DISSOLVENT
DISSOLVENTS
DISSOLVERS
DISSOLVING
DISSOLVINGS
DISSONANCE
DISSONANCES

DISSONANCIES
DISSONANCY
DISSONANTLY
DISSUADABLE
DISSUADERS
DISSUADING
DISSUASION
DISSUASIONS
DISSUASIVE
DISSUASIVELY
DISSUASIVENESS
DISSUASIVES
DISSUASORIES
DISSUASORY
DISSUNDERED
DISSUNDERING
DISSUNDERS
DISSYLLABIC
DISSYLLABIFIED
DISSYLLABIFIES
DISSYLLABIFY
DISSYLLABIFYING
DISSYLLABISM
DISSYLLABISMS
DISSYLLABLE
DISSYLLABLES
DISSYMMETRIC
DISSYMMETRICAL
DISSYMMETRIES
DISSYMMETRY
DISTAINING
DISTANCELESS
DISTANCING
DISTANTNESS
DISTANTNESSES
DISTASTEFUL
DISTASTEFULLY
DISTASTEFULNESS
DISTASTING
DISTELFINK
DISTELFINKS
DISTEMPERATE
DISTEMPERATURE
DISTEMPERATURES
DISTEMPERED
DISTEMPERING
DISTEMPERS
DISTENDERS
DISTENDING

DISTENSIBILITY	DISTINGUEE	DISTRESSED	DISTURBANCE	DITCHDIGGERS
DISTENSIBLE	DISTINGUISH	DISTRESSER	DISTURBANCES	DITCHWATER
DISTENSILE	DISTINGUISHABLE	DISTRESSERS	DISTURBANT	DITCHWATERS
DISTENSION	DISTINGUISHABLY	DISTRESSES	DISTURBANTS	DITHEISTIC
DISTENSIONS	DISTINGUISHED	DISTRESSFUL	DISTURBATIVE	DITHEISTICAL
DISTENSIVE	DISTINGUISHER	DISTRESSFULLY	DISTURBERS	DITHELETES
DISTENTION	DISTINGUISHERS	DISTRESSFULNESS	DISTURBING	DITHELETIC
DISTENTIONS	DISTINGUISHES	DISTRESSING	DISTURBINGLY	DITHELETICAL
DISTHRONED	DISTINGUISHING	DISTRESSINGLY	DISUBSTITUTED	DITHELETISM
DISTHRONES	DISTINGUISHMENT	DISTRESSINGS	DISULFATES	DITHELETISMS
DISTHRONING	DISTORTEDLY	DISTRIBUEND	DISULFIDES	DITHELISMS
DISTHRONISE	DISTORTEDNESS	DISTRIBUENDS	DISULFIRAM	DITHELITISM
DISTHRONISED	DISTORTEDNESSES	DISTRIBUTABLE	DISULFIRAMS	DITHELITISMS
DISTHRONISES	DISTORTERS	DISTRIBUTARIES	DISULFOTON	DITHERIEST
DISTHRONISING	DISTORTING	DISTRIBUTARY	DISULFOTONS	DITHERINGS
DISTHRONIZE	DISTORTION	DISTRIBUTE	DISULPHATE	DITHIOCARBAMATE
DISTHRONIZED	DISTORTIONAL	DISTRIBUTED	DISULPHATES	DITHIOCARBAMIC
DISTHRONIZES	DISTORTIONS	DISTRIBUTEE	DISULPHIDE	DITHIONATE
DISTHRONIZING	DISTORTIVE	DISTRIBUTEES	DISULPHIDES	DITHIONATES
DISTICHOUS	DISTRACTABLE	DISTRIBUTER	DISULPHURET	DITHIONITE
DISTICHOUSLY	DISTRACTED	DISTRIBUTERS	DISULPHURETS	DITHIONITES
DISTILLABLE	DISTRACTEDLY	DISTRIBUTES	DISULPHURIC	DITHIONOUS
DISTILLAND	DISTRACTEDNESS	DISTRIBUTING	DISUNIONIST	DITHYRAMBIC
DISTILLANDS	DISTRACTER	DISTRIBUTION	DISUNIONISTS	DITHYRAMBICALLY
DISTILLATE	DISTRACTERS	DISTRIBUTIONAL	DISUNITERS	DITHYRAMBIST
DISTILLATES	DISTRACTIBILITY	DISTRIBUTIONS	DISUNITIES	DITHYRAMBISTS
DISTILLATION	DISTRACTIBLE	DISTRIBUTIVE	DISUNITING	DITHYRAMBS
DISTILLATIONS	DISTRACTING	DISTRIBUTIVELY	DISUTILITIES	DITRANSITIVE
DISTILLATORY	DISTRACTINGLY	DISTRIBUTIVES	DISUTILITY	DITRANSITIVES
DISTILLERIES	DISTRACTION	DISTRIBUTIVITY	DISVALUING	DITRIGLYPH
DISTILLERS	DISTRACTIONS	DISTRIBUTOR	DISVOUCHED	DITRIGLYPHIC
DISTILLERY	DISTRACTIVE	DISTRIBUTORS	DISVOUCHES	DITRIGLYPHS
DISTILLING	DISTRACTIVELY	DISTRIBUTORSHIP	DISVOUCHING	DITROCHEAN
DISTILLINGS	DISTRACTOR	DISTRICTED	DISWORSHIP	DITROCHEES
DISTILMENT	DISTRACTORS	DISTRICTING	DISWORSHIPED	DITSINESSES
DISTILMENTS	DISTRAINABLE	DISTRINGAS	DISWORSHIPING	DITTANDERS
DISTINCTER	DISTRAINED	DISTRINGASES	DISWORSHIPPED	DITTOGRAPHIC
DISTINCTEST	DISTRAINEE	DISTROUBLE	DISWORSHIPPING	DITTOGRAPHIES
DISTINCTION	DISTRAINEES	DISTROUBLED	DISWORSHIPS	DITTOGRAPHY
DISTINCTIONS	DISTRAINER	DISTROUBLES	DISYLLABIC	DITTOLOGIES
DISTINCTIVE	DISTRAINERS	DISTROUBLING	DISYLLABIFIED	DITZINESSES
DISTINCTIVELY	DISTRAINING	DISTRUSTED	DISYLLABIFIES	DIURETICALLY
DISTINCTIVENESS	DISTRAINMENT	DISTRUSTER	DISYLLABIFY	DIURETICALNESS
DISTINCTIVES	DISTRAINMENTS	DISTRUSTERS	DISYLLABIFYING	DIURNALIST
DISTINCTLY	DISTRAINOR	DISTRUSTFUL	DISYLLABISM	DIURNALISTS
DISTINCTNESS	DISTRAINORS	DISTRUSTFULLY	DISYLLABISMS	DIUTURNITIES
DISTINCTNESSES	DISTRAINTS	DISTRUSTFULNESS	DISYLLABLE	DIUTURNITY
DISTINCTURE	DISTRAUGHT	DISTRUSTING	DISYLLABLES	DIVAGATING
DISTINCTURES	DISTRAUGHTLY	DISTRUSTLESS	DITCHDIGGER	DIVAGATION

DIVAGATIONS	DIVERTICULATED	DIVISIONISMS	DOCKWORKER	DOCUMENTATION
DIVALENCES	DIVERTICULITIS	DIVISIONIST	DOCKWORKERS	DOCUMENTATIONAL
DIVALENCIES	DIVERTICULOSES	DIVISIONISTS	DOCQUETING	DOCUMENTATIONS
DIVARICATE	DIVERTICULOSIS	DIVISIVELY	DOCTORANDS	DOCUMENTED
DIVARICATED	DIVERTICULUM	DIVISIVENESS	DOCTORATED	DOCUMENTER
DIVARICATELY	DIVERTIMENTI	DIVISIVENESSES	DOCTORATES	DOCUMENTERS
DIVARICATES	DIVERTIMENTO	DIVORCEABLE	DOCTORATING	DOCUMENTING
DIVARICATING	DIVERTIMENTOS	DIVORCEMENT	DOCTORESSES	DODDERIEST
DIVARICATINGLY	DIVERTINGLY	DIVORCEMENTS	DOCTORINGS	DODDIPOLLS
DIVARICATION	DIVERTISEMENT	DIVULGATED	DOCTORLESS	DODDYPOLLS
DIVARICATIONS	DIVERTISEMENTS	DIVULGATER	DOCTORSHIP	DODECAGONAL
DIVARICATOR	DIVERTISSEMENT	DIVULGATERS	DOCTORSHIPS	DODECAGONS
DIVARICATORS	DIVERTISSEMENTS	DIVULGATES	DOCTRESSES	DODECAGYNIAN
DIVEBOMBED	DIVESTIBLE	DIVULGATING	DOCTRINAIRE	DODECAGYNOUS
DIVEBOMBING	DIVESTITURE	DIVULGATION	DOCTRINAIRES	DODECAHEDRA
DIVELLICATE	DIVESTITURES	DIVULGATIONS	DOCTRINAIRISM	DODECAHEDRAL
DIVELLICATED	DIVESTMENT	DIVULGATOR	DOCTRINAIRISMS	DODECAHEDRON
DIVELLICATES	DIVESTMENTS	DIVULGATORS	DOCTRINALITIES	DODECAHEDRONS
DIVELLICATING	DIVESTURES	DIVULGEMENT	DOCTRINALITY	DODECANDROUS
DIVERGEMENT	DIVIDEDNESS	DIVULGEMENTS	DOCTRINALLY	DODECANOIC
DIVERGEMENTS	DIVIDEDNESSES	DIVULGENCE	DOCTRINARIAN	DODECAPHONIC
DIVERGENCE	DIVIDENDLESS	DIVULGENCES	DOCTRINARIANISM	DODECAPHONIES
DIVERGENCES	DIVINATION	DIVULSIONS	DOCTRINARIANS	DODECAPHONISM
DIVERGENCIES	DIVINATIONS	DIZENMENTS	DOCTRINARISM	DODECAPHONISMS
DIVERGENCY	DIVINATORIAL	DIZZINESSES	DOCTRINARISMS	DODECAPHONIST
DIVERGENTLY	DIVINATORS	DIZZYINGLY	DOCTRINISM	DODECAPHONISTS
DIVERGINGLY	DIVINATORY	DJELLABAHS	DOCTRINISMS	DODECAPHONY
DIVERSENESS	DIVINENESS	DOBSONFLIES	DOCTRINIST	DODECASTYLE
DIVERSENESSES	DIVINENESSES	DOCENTSHIP	DOCTRINISTS	DODECASTYLES
DIVERSIFIABLE	DIVINERESS	DOCENTSHIPS	DOCUDRAMAS	DODECASYLLABIC
DIVERSIFICATION	DIVINERESSES	DOCHMIACAL	DOCUMENTABLE	DODECASYLLABLE
DIVERSIFIED	DIVINIFIED	DOCHMIUSES	DOCUMENTAL	DODECASYLLABLES
DIVERSIFIER	DIVINIFIES	DOCIBILITIES	DOCUMENTALIST	DODGEBALLS
DIVERSIFIERS	DIVINIFYING	DOCIBILITY	DOCUMENTALISTS	DODGINESSES
DIVERSIFIES	DIVINISATION	DOCIBLENESS	DOCUMENTARIAN	DOGARESSAS
DIVERSIFORM	DIVINISATIONS	DOCIBLENESSES	DOCUMENTARIANS	DOGBERRIES
DIVERSIFYING	DIVINISING	DOCILITIES	DOCUMENTARIES	DOGBERRYISM
DIVERSIONAL	DIVINITIES	DOCIMASIES	DOCUMENTARILY	DOGBERRYISMS
DIVERSIONARY	DIVINIZATION	DOCIMASTIC	DOCUMENTARISE	DOGCATCHER
DIVERSIONIST	DIVINIZATIONS	DOCIMOLOGIES	DOCUMENTARISED	DOGCATCHERS
DIVERSIONISTS	DIVINIZING	DOCIMOLOGY	DOCUMENTARISES	DOGFIGHTING
DIVERSIONS	DIVISIBILITIES	DOCKISATION	DOCUMENTARISING	DOGFIGHTINGS
DIVERSITIES	DIVISIBILITY	DOCKISATIONS	DOCUMENTARIST	DOGFOODING
DIVERTIBILITIES	DIVISIBLENESS	DOCKIZATION	DOCUMENTARISTS	DOGFOODINGS
DIVERTIBILITY	DIVISIBLENESSES	DOCKIZATIONS	DOCUMENTARIZE	DOGGEDNESS
DIVERTIBLE	DIVISIONAL	DOCKMASTER	DOCUMENTARIZED	DOGGEDNESSES
DIVERTICULA	DIVISIONALLY	DOCKMASTERS	DOCUMENTARIZES	DOGGINESSES
DIVERTICULAR	DIVISIONARY	DOCKWALLOPER	DOCUMENTARIZING	DOGGISHNESS
DIVERTICULATE	DIVISIONISM	DOCKWALLOPERS	DOCUMENTARY	DOGGISHNESSES

DOGGONEDER	DOLESOMELY	DOLOROUSLY	DOMINATION	DOORKNOCKS
DOGGONEDEST	DOLICHOCEPHAL	DOLOROUSNESS	DOMINATIONS	DOORNBOOMS
DOGLEGGING	DOLICHOCEPHALIC	DOLOROUSNESSES	DOMINATIVE	DOORPLATES
DOGMATICAL	DOLICHOCEPHALS	DOLOSTONES	DOMINATORS	DOORSTEPPED
DOGMATICALLY	DOLICHOCEPHALY	DOLPHINARIA	DOMINATRICES	DOORSTEPPER
DOGMATICALNESS	DOLICHOSAURUS	DOLPHINARIUM	DOMINATRIX	DOORSTEPPERS
DOGMATISATION	DOLICHOSAURUSES	DOLPHINARIUMS	DOMINATRIXES	DOORSTEPPING
DOGMATISATIONS	DOLICHOSES	DOLPHINETS	DOMINEERED	DOORSTEPPINGS
DOGMATISED	DOLICHURUS	DOLPHINFISH	DOMINEERING	DOORSTONES
DOGMATISER	DOLICHURUSES	DOLPHINFISHES	DOMINEERINGLY	DOPAMINERGIC
DOGMATISERS	DOLLARBIRD	DOLTISHNESS	DOMINEERINGNESS	DOPESHEETS
DOGMATISES	DOLLARBIRDS	DOLTISHNESSES	DOMINICKER	DOPEYNESSES
DOGMATISING	DOLLARFISH	DOMESTICABLE	DOMINICKERS	DOPINESSES
DOGMATISMS	DOLLARFISHES	DOMESTICAL	DOMINIQUES	DOPPELGANGER
DOGMATISTS	DOLLARISATION	DOMESTICALLY	DONATARIES	DOPPELGANGERS
DOGMATIZATION	DOLLARISATIONS	DOMESTICATE	DONATISTIC	DOPPLERITE
DOGMATIZATIONS	DOLLARISED	DOMESTICATED	DONATISTICAL	DOPPLERITES
DOGMATIZED	DOLLARISES	DOMESTICATES	DONATORIES	DORBEETLES
DOGMATIZER	DOLLARISING	DOMESTICATING	DONENESSES	DORKINESSES
DOGMATIZERS	DOLLARIZATION	DOMESTICATION	DONEPEZILS	DORMANCIES
DOGMATIZES	DOLLARIZATIONS	DOMESTICATIONS	DONKEYWORK	DORMITIONS
DOGMATIZING	DOLLARIZED	DOMESTICATIVE	DONKEYWORKS	DORMITIVES
DOGMATOLOGIES	DOLLARIZES	DOMESTICATOR	DONNICKERS	DORMITORIES
DOGMATOLOGY	DOLLARIZING	DOMESTICATORS	DONNISHNESS	DORONICUMS
DOGNAPINGS	DOLLARLESS	DOMESTICISE	DONNISHNESSES	DORSIBRANCHIATE
DOGNAPPERS	DOLLAROCRACIES	DOMESTICISED	DONNYBROOK	DORSIFEROUS
DOGNAPPING	DOLLAROCRACY	DOMESTICISES	DONNYBROOKS	DORSIFIXED
DOGNAPPINGS	DOLLARSHIP	DOMESTICISING	DONORSHIPS	DORSIFLEXED
DOGROBBERS	DOLLARSHIPS	DOMESTICITIES	DOODLEBUGS	DORSIFLEXES
DOGSBODIED	DOLLHOUSES	DOMESTICITY	DOOHICKEYS	DORSIFLEXING
DOGSBODIES	DOLLINESSES	DOMESTICIZE	DOOHICKIES	DORSIFLEXION
DOGSBODYING	DOLLISHNESS	DOMESTICIZED	DOOMSAYERS	DORSIFLEXIONS
DOGSBODYINGS	DOLLISHNESSES	DOMESTICIZES	DOOMSAYING	DORSIGRADE
DOGSLEDDED	DOLLYBIRDS	DOMESTICIZING	DOOMSAYINGS	DORSIVENTRAL
DOGSLEDDER	DOLOMITISATION	DOMESTIQUE	DOOMSDAYER	DORSIVENTRALITY
DOGSLEDDERS	DOLOMITISATIONS	DOMESTIQUES	DOOMSDAYERS	DORSIVENTRALLY
DOGSLEDDING	DOLOMITISE	DOMICILIARY	DOOMWATCHED	DORSOLATERAL
DOGSLEDDINGS	DOLOMITISED	DOMICILIATE	DOOMWATCHER	DORSOLUMBAR
DOGTROTTED	DOLOMITISES	DOMICILIATED	DOOMWATCHERS	DORSOVENTRAL
DOGTROTTING	DOLOMITISING	DOMICILIATES	DOOMWATCHES	DORSOVENTRALITY
DOGWATCHES	DOLOMITIZATION	DOMICILIATING	DOOMWATCHING	DORSOVENTRALLY
DOLABRIFORM	DOLOMITIZATIONS	DOMICILIATION	DOOMWATCHINGS	DORTINESSES
DOLCELATTE	DOLOMITIZE	DOMICILIATIONS	DOORFRAMES	DOSEMETERS
DOLCELATTES	DOLOMITIZED	DOMICILING	DOORKEEPER	DOSIMETERS
DOLCEMENTE	DOLOMITIZES	DOMINANCES	DOORKEEPERS	DOSIMETRIC
DOLEFULLER	DOLOMITIZING	DOMINANCIES	DOORKNOCKED	DOSIMETRICIAN
DOLEFULLEST	DOLORIFEROUS	DOMINANTLY	DOORKNOCKER	DOSIMETRICIANS
DOLEFULNESS	DOLORIMETRIES	DOMINATING	DOORKNOCKERS	DOSIMETRIES
DOLEFULNESSES	DOLORIMETRY	DOMINATINGLY	DOORKNOCKING	DOSIMETRIST

DOSIMETRISTS	DOVEISHNESS	DOWNSCALING	DOXYCYCLINES	DRAGOONING
DOSIOLOGIES	DOVEISHNESSES	DOWNSHIFTED	DOZINESSES	DRAGSTRIPS
DOSOLOGIES	DOVETAILED	DOWNSHIFTER	DRABBINESS	DRAGSVILLE
DOSSHOUSES	DOVETAILING	DOWNSHIFTERS	DRABBINESSES	DRAGSVILLES
DOTARDLIER	DOVETAILINGS	DOWNSHIFTING	DRABBLINGS	DRAINBOARD
DOTARDLIEST	DOVISHNESS	DOWNSHIFTINGS	DRABNESSES	DRAINBOARDS
DOTCOMMERS	DOVISHNESSES	DOWNSHIFTS	DRACONIANISM	DRAINLAYER
DOTTINESSES	DOWDINESSES	DOWNSIZERS	DRACONIANISMS	DRAINLAYERS
DOUBLEHEADER	DOWELLINGS	DOWNSIZING	DRACONICALLY	DRAINPIPES
DOUBLEHEADERS	DOWFNESSES	DOWNSIZINGS	DRACONISMS	DRAKESTONE
DOUBLENESS	DOWITCHERS	DOWNSLIDES	DRACONITES	DRAKESTONES
DOUBLENESSES	DOWNBURSTS	DOWNSLOPES	DRACONTIASES	DRAMATICAL
DOUBLESPEAK	DOWNCOMERS	DOWNSPOUTS	DRACONTIASIS	DRAMATICALLY
DOUBLESPEAKER	DOWNCRYING	DOWNSTAGES	DRACUNCULI	DRAMATICISM
DOUBLESPEAKERS	DOWNDRAFTS	DOWNSTAIRS	DRACUNCULIASES	DRAMATICISMS
DOUBLESPEAKS	DOWNDRAUGHT	DOWNSTAIRSES	DRACUNCULIASIS	DRAMATISABLE
DOUBLETHINK	DOWNDRAUGHTS	DOWNSTATER	DRACUNCULUS	DRAMATISATION
DOUBLETHINKS	DOWNFALLEN	DOWNSTATERS	DRACUNCULUSES	DRAMATISATIONS
DOUBLETONS	DOWNFORCES	DOWNSTATES	DRAFTINESS	DRAMATISED
DOUBLETREE	DOWNGRADED	DOWNSTREAM	DRAFTINESSES	DRAMATISER
DOUBLETREES	DOWNGRADES	DOWNSTROKE	DRAFTSMANSHIP	DRAMATISERS
DOUBTFULLY	DOWNGRADING	DOWNSTROKES	DRAFTSMANSHIPS	DRAMATISES
DOUBTFULNESS	DOWNHEARTED	DOWNSWINGS	DRAFTSPERSON	DRAMATISING
DOUBTFULNESSES	DOWNHEARTEDLY	DOWNTHREAD	DRAFTSPERSONS	DRAMATISTS
DOUBTINGLY	DOWNHEARTEDNESS	DOWNTHROWS	DRAFTSWOMAN	DRAMATIZABLE
DOUBTLESSLY	DOWNHILLER	DOWNTOWNER	DRAFTSWOMEN	DRAMATIZATION
DOUBTLESSNESS	DOWNHILLERS	DOWNTOWNERS	DRAGGINGLY	DRAMATIZATIONS
DOUBTLESSNESSES	DOWNINESSES	DOWNTRENDED	DRAGGLETAILED	DRAMATIZED
DOUCENESSES	DOWNLIGHTER	DOWNTRENDING	DRAGHOUNDS	DRAMATIZER
DOUCEPERES	DOWNLIGHTERS	DOWNTRENDS	DRAGONESSES	DRAMATIZERS
DOUCHEBAGS	DOWNLIGHTS	DOWNTRODDEN	DRAGONFLIES	DRAMATIZES
DOUGHBALLS	DOWNLINKED	DOWNTURNED	DRAGONHEAD	DRAMATIZING
DOUGHFACED	DOWNLINKING	DOWNVOTING	DRAGONHEADS	DRAMATURGE
DOUGHFACES	DOWNLOADABLE	DOWNWARDLY	DRAGONISED	DRAMATURGES
DOUGHINESS	DOWNLOADED	DOWNWARDNESS	DRAGONISES	DRAMATURGIC
DOUGHINESSES	DOWNLOADING	DOWNWARDNESSES	DRAGONISING	DRAMATURGICAL
DOUGHNUTLIKE	DOWNLOADINGS	DOWNWASHES	DRAGONISMS	DRAMATURGICALLY
DOUGHNUTTED	DOWNLOOKED	DOWNZONING	DRAGONIZED	DRAMATURGIES
DOUGHNUTTING	DOWNPLAYED	DOXOGRAPHER	DRAGONIZES	DRAMATURGIST
DOUGHNUTTINGS	DOWNPLAYING	DOXOGRAPHERS	DRAGONIZING	DRAMATURGISTS
DOUGHTIEST	DOWNRATING	DOXOGRAPHIC	DRAGONLIKE	DRAMATURGS
DOUGHTINESS	DOWNREGULATION	DOXOGRAPHIES	DRAGONNADE	DRAMATURGY
DOUGHTINESSES	DOWNREGULATIONS	DOXOGRAPHY	DRAGONNADED	DRAPABILITIES
DOULOCRACIES	DOWNRIGHTLY	DOXOLOGICAL	DRAGONNADES	DRAPABILITY
DOULOCRACY	DOWNRIGHTNESS	DOXOLOGICALLY	DRAGONNADING	DRAPEABILITIES
DOUPPIONIS	DOWNRIGHTNESSES	DOXOLOGIES	DRAGONROOT	DRAPEABILITY
DOURNESSES	DOWNRUSHES	DOXORUBICIN	DRAGONROOTS	DRAPERYING
DOUROUCOULI	DOWNSCALED	DOXORUBICINS	DRAGOONAGE	DRASTICALLY
DOUROUCOULIS	DOWNSCALES	DOXYCYCLINE	DRAGOONAGES	DRATCHELLS

DRAUGHTBOARD	DREAMCATCHERS	DRILLABILITIES	DROPFORGED	DRUNKALOGUE
DRAUGHTBOARDS	DREAMERIES	DRILLABILITY	DROPFORGES	DRUNKALOGUES
DRAUGHTERS	DREAMFULLY	DRILLHOLES	DROPFORGING	DRUNKATHON
DRAUGHTIER	DREAMFULNESS	DRILLMASTER	DROPKICKER	DRUNKATHONS
DRAUGHTIEST	DREAMFULNESSES	DRILLMASTERS	DROPKICKERS	DRUNKENNESS
DRAUGHTILY	DREAMHOLES	DRILLSHIPS	DROPLIGHTS	DRUNKENNESSES
DRAUGHTINESS	DREAMINESS	DRILLSTOCK	DROPPERFUL	DRUNKOMETER
DRAUGHTINESSES	DREAMINESSES	DRILLSTOCKS	DROPPERFULS	DRUNKOMETERS
DRAUGHTING	DREAMINGLY	DRINKABILITIES	DROPPERSFUL	DRUPACEOUS
DRAUGHTMAN	DREAMLANDS	DRINKABILITY	DROPSICALLY	DRYASDUSTS
DRAUGHTMEN	DREAMLESSLY	DRINKABLENESS	DROPSONDES	DRYBEATING
DRAUGHTPROOF	DREAMLESSNESS	DRINKABLENESSES	DROPSTONES	DRYOPITHECINE
DRAUGHTPROOFED	DREAMLESSNESSES	DRINKABLES	DROSERACEOUS	DRYOPITHECINES
DRAUGHTPROOFING	DREAMTIMES	DRIPSTONES	DROSOMETER	DRYSALTERIES
DRAUGHTPROOFS	DREAMWHILE	DRIVABILITIES	DROSOMETERS	DRYSALTERS
DRAUGHTSMAN	DREAMWHILES	DRIVABILITY	DROSOPHILA	DRYSALTERY
DRAUGHTSMANSHIP	DREAMWORLD	DRIVEABILITIES	DROSOPHILAE	DRYWALLERS
DRAUGHTSMEN	DREAMWORLDS	DRIVEABILITY	DROSOPHILAS	DRYWALLING
DRAUGHTSPERSON	DREARIHEAD	DRIVELINES	DROSSINESS	DRYWALLINGS
DRAUGHTSPERSONS	DREARIHEADS	DRIVELLERS	DROSSINESSES	DUALISTICALLY
DRAUGHTSWOMAN	DREARIHOOD	DRIVELLING	DROUGHTIER	DUATHLETES
DRAUGHTSWOMEN	DREARIHOODS	DRIVENNESS	DROUGHTIEST	DUBIOSITIES
DRAWBRIDGE	DREARIMENT	DRIVENNESSES	DROUGHTINESS	DUBIOUSNESS
DRAWBRIDGES	DREARIMENTS	DRIVERLESS	DROUGHTINESSES	DUBIOUSNESSES
DRAWERFULS	DREARINESS	DRIVESHAFT	DROUTHIEST	DUBITANCIES
DRAWKNIVES	DREARINESSES	DRIVESHAFTS	DROUTHINESS	DUBITATING
DRAWLINGLY	DREARISOME	DRIVETHROUGH	DROUTHINESSES	DUBITATION
DRAWLINGNESS	DRECKSILLS	DRIVETHROUGHS	DROWSIHEAD	DUBITATIONS
DRAWLINGNESSES	DREGGINESS	DRIVETRAIN	DROWSIHEADS	DUBITATIVE
DRAWNWORKS	DREGGINESSES	DRIVETRAINS	DROWSIHEDS	DUBITATIVELY
DRAWPLATES	DREIKANTER	DRIZZLIEST	DROWSINESS	DUCHESSING
DRAWSHAVES	DREIKANTERS	DRIZZLINGLY	DROWSINESSES	DUCKBOARDS
DRAWSTRING	DRENCHINGS	DROICHIEST	DRUCKENNESS	DUCKSHOVED
DRAWSTRINGS	DREPANIUMS	DROLLERIES	DRUCKENNESSES	DUCKSHOVER
DRAYHORSES	DRERIHEADS	DROLLNESSES	DRUDGERIES	DUCKSHOVERS
DREADFULLY	DRESSGUARD	DROMEDARES	DRUDGINGLY	DUCKSHOVES
DREADFULNESS	DRESSGUARDS	DROMEDARIES	DRUGMAKERS	DUCKSHOVING
DREADFULNESSES	DRESSINESS	DROMOPHOBIA	DRUGSTORES	DUCKSHOVINGS
DREADLESSLY	DRESSINESSES	DROMOPHOBIAS	DRUIDESSES	DUCKWALKED
DREADLESSNESS	DRESSMAKER	DRONISHNESS	DRUMBEATER	DUCKWALKING
DREADLESSNESSES	DRESSMAKERS	DRONISHNESSES	DRUMBEATERS	DUCTILENESS
DREADLOCKED	DRESSMAKES	DRONKVERDRIET	DRUMBEATING	DUCTILENESSES
DREADLOCKS	DRESSMAKING	DROOLWORTHIER	DRUMBEATINGS	DUCTILITIES
DREADNAUGHT	DRESSMAKINGS	DROOLWORTHIEST	DRUMBLEDOR	DUDENESSES
DREADNAUGHTS	DRIBBLIEST	DROOLWORTHY	DRUMBLEDORS	DUENNASHIP
DREADNOUGHT	DRIBBLINGS	DROOPINESS	DRUMBLEDRANE	DUENNASHIPS
DREADNOUGHTS	DRICKSIEST	DROOPINESSES	DRUMBLEDRANES	DUFFERDOMS
DREAMBOATS	DRIFTINGLY	DROOPINGLY	DRUMFISHES	DUFFERISMS
DREAMCATCHER	DRIFTWOODS	DROPCLOTHS	DRUMSTICKS	DUIKERBOKS

DUKKERIPEN	DUNDERFUNK	DUPLICATURE	DYNAMICISTS	DYSCHROIAS
DUKKERIPENS	DUNDERFUNKS	DUPLICATURES	DYNAMISING	DYSCRASIAS
DULCAMARAS	DUNDERHEAD	DUPLICIDENT	DYNAMISTIC	DYSCRASITE
DULCETNESS	DUNDERHEADED	DUPLICITIES	DYNAMITARD	DYSCRASITES
DULCETNESSES	DUNDERHEADISM	DUPLICITOUS	DYNAMITARDS	DYSENTERIC
DULCIFICATION	DUNDERHEADISMS	DUPLICITOUSLY	DYNAMITERS	DYSENTERIES
DULCIFICATIONS	DUNDERHEADS	DURABILITIES	DYNAMITING	DYSFUNCTION
DULCIFLUOUS	DUNDERPATE	DURABILITY	DYNAMIZING	DYSFUNCTIONAL
DULCIFYING	DUNDERPATES	DURABLENESS	DYNAMOELECTRIC	DYSFUNCTIONS
DULCILOQUIES	DUNDREARIES	DURABLENESSES	DYNAMOGENESES	DYSGENESES
DULCILOQUY	DUNGEONERS	DURALUMINIUM	DYNAMOGENESIS	DYSGENESIS
DULCIMORES	DUNGEONING	DURALUMINIUMS	DYNAMOGENIES	DYSGRAPHIA
DULCITUDES	DUNIEWASSAL	DURALUMINS	DYNAMOGENY	DYSGRAPHIAS
DULLNESSES	DUNIEWASSALS	DURATIONAL	DYNAMOGRAPH	DYSGRAPHIC
DULLSVILLE	DUNIWASSAL	DURCHKOMPONIERT	DYNAMOGRAPHS	DYSGRAPHICS
DULLSVILLES	DUNIWASSALS	DURCHKOMPONIRT	DYNAMOMETER	DYSHARMONIC
DULOCRACIES	DUNNIEWASSAL	DURICRUSTS	DYNAMOMETERS	DYSKINESIA
DUMBFOUNDED	DUNNIEWASSALS	DUROMETERS	DYNAMOMETRIC	DYSKINESIAS
DUMBFOUNDER	DUODECENNIAL	DUSKINESSES	DYNAMOMETRICAL	DYSKINETIC
DUMBFOUNDERED	DUODECILLION	DUSKISHNESS	DYNAMOMETRIES	DYSLECTICS
DUMBFOUNDERING	DUODECILLIONS	DUSKISHNESSES	DYNAMOMETRY	DYSLOGISTIC
DUMBFOUNDERS	DUODECIMAL	DUSKNESSES	DYNAMOTORS	DYSLOGISTICALLY
DUMBFOUNDING	DUODECIMALLY	DUSTCLOTHS	DYNASTICAL	DYSMENORRHEA
DUMBFOUNDS	DUODECIMALS	DUSTCOVERS	DYNASTICALLY	DYSMENORRHEAL
DUMBLEDORE	DUODECIMOS	DUSTINESSES	DYNASTICISM	DYSMENORRHEAS
DUMBLEDORES	DUODENECTOMIES	DUSTSHEETS	DYNASTICISMS	DYSMENORRHEIC
DUMBNESSES	DUODENECTOMY	DUSTSTORMS	DYNORPHINS	DYSMENORRHOEA
DUMBPHONES	DUODENITIS	DUTEOUSNESS	DYOPHYSITE	DYSMENORRHOEAL
DUMBSIZING	DUODENITISES	DUTEOUSNESSES	DYOPHYSITES	DYSMENORRHOEAS
DUMBSTRICKEN	DUOPOLISTIC	DUTIABILITIES	DYOTHELETE	DYSMENORRHOEIC
DUMBSTRUCK	DUOPOLISTS	DUTIABILITY	DYOTHELETES	DYSMORPHIC
DUMBWAITER	DUOPSONIES	DUTIFULNESS	DYOTHELETIC	DYSMORPHOPHOBIA
DUMBWAITERS	DUPABILITIES	DUTIFULNESSES	DYOTHELETICAL	DYSMORPHOPHOBIC
DUMFOUNDED	DUPABILITY	DUUMVIRATE	DYOTHELETISM	DYSPAREUNIA
DUMFOUNDER	DUPLEXINGS	DUUMVIRATES	DYOTHELETISMS	DYSPAREUNIAS
DUMFOUNDERED	DUPLEXITIES	DWARFISHLY	DYOTHELISM	DYSPATHETIC
DUMFOUNDERING	DUPLICABILITIES	DWARFISHNESS	DYOTHELISMS	DYSPATHIES
DUMFOUNDERS	DUPLICABILITY	DWARFISHNESSES	DYOTHELITE	DYSPEPSIAS
DUMFOUNDING	DUPLICABLE	DWARFNESSES	DYOTHELITES	DYSPEPSIES
DUMMELHEAD	DUPLICANDS	DWINDLEMENT	DYOTHELITIC	DYSPEPTICAL
DUMMELHEADS	DUPLICATED	DWINDLEMENTS	DYOTHELITICAL	DYSPEPTICALLY
DUMMINESSES	DUPLICATELY	DYADICALLY	DYSAESTHESIA	DYSPEPTICS
DUMORTIERITE	DUPLICATES	DYARCHICAL	DYSAESTHESIAS	DYSPHAGIAS
DUMORTIERITES	DUPLICATING	DYEABILITIES	DYSAESTHETIC	DYSPHAGIES
DUMOSITIES	DUPLICATION	DYEABILITY	DYSARTHRIA	DYSPHASIAS
DUMPINESSES	DUPLICATIONS	DYINGNESSES	DYSARTHRIAS	DYSPHASICS
DUMPISHNESS	DUPLICATIVE	DYNAMETERS	DYSBINDINS	DYSPHEMISM
DUMPISHNESSES	DUPLICATOR	DYNAMICALLY	DYSCALCULIA	DYSPHEMISMS
DUMPTRUCKS	DUPLICATORS	DYNAMICIST	DYSCALCULIAS	DYSPHEMISTIC

DYSPHONIAS	DYSPROSIUMS	DYSSYNERGIC	DYSTELEOLOGY	DYSTROPHIA
DYSPHORIAS	DYSRHYTHMIA	DYSSYNERGIES	DYSTHESIAS	DYSTROPHIAS
DYSPLASIAS	DYSRHYTHMIAS	DYSSYNERGY	DYSTHYMIAC	DYSTROPHIC
DYSPLASTIC	DYSRHYTHMIC	DYSTELEOLOGICAL	DYSTHYMIACS	DYSTROPHIES
DYSPRACTIC	DYSRHYTHMICS	DYSTELEOLOGIES	DYSTHYMIAS	DYSTROPHIN
DYSPRAXIAS	DYSSYNERGIA	DYSTELEOLOGIST	DYSTHYMICS	DYSTROPHINS
DYSPROSIUM	DYSSYNERGIAS	DYSTELEOLOGISTS	DYSTOPIANS	DZIGGETAIS

D

E

EAGERNESSES	EARTHSHAKER	EBIONISING	ECCHYMOTIC	ECHOICALLY
EAGLEHAWKS	EARTHSHAKERS	EBIONITISM	ECCLESIARCH	ECHOLALIAS
EAGLESTONE	EARTHSHAKING	EBIONITISMS	ECCLESIARCHS	ECHOLOCATION
EAGLESTONES	EARTHSHAKINGLY	EBIONIZING	ECCLESIAST	ECHOLOCATIONS
EAGLEWOODS	EARTHSHATTERING	EBOULEMENT	ECCLESIASTIC	ECHOPRAXES
EARBASHERS	EARTHSHINE	EBOULEMENTS	ECCLESIASTICAL	ECHOPRAXIA
EARBASHING	EARTHSHINES	EBRACTEATE	ECCLESIASTICISM	ECHOPRAXIAS
EARBASHINGS	EARTHSTARS	EBRACTEOLATE	ECCLESIASTICS	ECHOPRAXIS
EARLIERISE	EARTHWARDS	EBRILLADES	ECCLESIASTS	ECHOVIRUSES
EARLIERISED	EARTHWAXES	EBRIOSITIES	ECCLESIOLATER	ECLAIRCISSEMENT
EARLIERISES	EARTHWOLVES	EBULLIENCE	ECCLESIOLATERS	ECLAMPSIAS
EARLIERISING	EARTHWOMAN	EBULLIENCES	ECCLESIOLATRIES	ECLAMPSIES
EARLIERIZE	EARTHWOMEN	EBULLIENCIES	ECCLESIOLATRY	ECLECTICALLY
EARLIERIZED	EARTHWORKS	EBULLIENCY	ECCLESIOLOGICAL	ECLECTICISM
EARLIERIZES	EARTHWORMS	EBULLIENTLY	ECCLESIOLOGIES	ECLECTICISMS
EARLIERIZING	EARWIGGIER	EBULLIOMETER	ECCLESIOLOGIST	ECLIPSISES
EARLINESSES	EARWIGGIEST	EBULLIOMETERS	ECCLESIOLOGISTS	ECLIPTICALLY
EARLYWOODS	EARWIGGING	EBULLIOMETRIES	ECCLESIOLOGY	ECOCATASTROPHE
EARMARKING	EARWIGGINGS	EBULLIOMETRY	ECCOPROTIC	ECOCATASTROPHES
EARNESTNESS	EARWITNESS	EBULLIOSCOPE	ECCOPROTICS	ECOCENTRIC
EARNESTNESSES	EARWITNESSES	EBULLIOSCOPES	ECCREMOCARPI	ECOCLIMATE
EARSPLITTING	EASEFULNESS	EBULLIOSCOPIC	ECCREMOCARPUS	ECOCLIMATES
EARTHBOUND	EASEFULNESSES	EBULLIOSCOPICAL	ECCREMOCARPUSES	ECOFEMINISM
EARTHENWARE	EASINESSES	EBULLIOSCOPIES	ECCRINOLOGIES	ECOFEMINISMS
EARTHENWARES	EASSELGATE	EBULLIOSCOPY	ECCRINOLOGY	ECOFEMINIST
EARTHFALLS	EASSELWARD	EBULLITION	ECDYSIASTS	ECOFEMINISTS
EARTHFLAXES	EASTERLIES	EBULLITIONS	ECHELONING	ECOFRIENDLIER
EARTHINESS	EASTERLING	EBURNATION	ECHEVERIAS	ECOFRIENDLIEST
EARTHINESSES	EASTERLINGS	EBURNATIONS	ECHIDNINES	ECOFRIENDLY
EARTHLIEST	EASTERMOST	EBURNIFICATION	ECHINACEAS	ECOLOGICAL
EARTHLIGHT	EASTERNERS	EBURNIFICATIONS	ECHINOCOCCI	ECOLOGICALLY
EARTHLIGHTS	EASTERNMOST	ECARDINATE	ECHINOCOCCOSES	ECOLOGISTS
EARTHLINESS	EASTWARDLY	ECBLASTESES	ECHINOCOCCOSIS	ECOMMERCES
EARTHLINESSES	EASYGOINGNESS	ECBLASTESIS	ECHINOCOCCUS	ECOMOVEMENT
EARTHLINGS	EASYGOINGNESSES	ECCALEOBION	ECHINODERM	ECOMOVEMENTS
EARTHMOVER	EAVESDRIPS	ECCALEOBIONS	ECHINODERMAL	ECOMUSEUMS
EARTHMOVERS	EAVESDROPPED	ECCENTRICAL	ECHINODERMATOUS	ECONOBOXES
EARTHMOVING	EAVESDROPPER	ECCENTRICALLY	ECHINODERMS	ECONOMETER
EARTHMOVINGS	EAVESDROPPERS	ECCENTRICITIES	ECHIUROIDS	ECONOMETERS
EARTHQUAKE	EAVESDROPPING	ECCENTRICITY	ECHOCARDIOGRAM	ECONOMETRIC
EARTHQUAKED	EAVESDROPPINGS	ECCENTRICS	ECHOCARDIOGRAMS	ECONOMETRICAL
EARTHQUAKES	EAVESDROPS	ECCHYMOSED	ECHOGRAPHIES	ECONOMETRICALLY
EARTHQUAKING	EAVESTROUGH	ECCHYMOSES	ECHOGRAPHS	ECONOMETRICIAN
EARTHRISES	EAVESTROUGHS	ECCHYMOSIS	ECHOGRAPHY	ECONOMETRICIANS

ECONOMETRICS
ECONOMETRIST
ECONOMETRISTS
ECONOMICAL
ECONOMICALLY
ECONOMISATION
ECONOMISATIONS
ECONOMISED
ECONOMISER
ECONOMISERS
ECONOMISES
ECONOMISING
ECONOMISMS
ECONOMISTIC
ECONOMISTS
ECONOMIZATION
ECONOMIZATIONS
ECONOMIZED
ECONOMIZER
ECONOMIZERS
ECONOMIZES
ECONOMIZING
ECOPHOBIAS
ECOPHYSIOLOGIES
ECOPHYSIOLOGY
ECOREGIONS
ECOSPECIES
ECOSPECIFIC
ECOSPHERES
ECOSSAISES
ECOSYSTEMS
ECOTARIANISM
ECOTARIANISMS
ECOTARIANS
ECOTECTURE
ECOTECTURES
ECOTERRORISM
ECOTERRORISMS
ECOTERRORIST
ECOTERRORISTS
ECOTOURING
ECOTOURISM
ECOTOURISMS
ECOTOURIST
ECOTOURISTS
ECOTOXICOLOGIES
ECOTOXICOLOGIST
ECOTOXICOLOGY
ECOTYPICALLY

ECPHONESES
ECPHONESIS
ECPHRACTIC
ECPHRACTICS
ECRITOIRES
ECSTASISED
ECSTASISES
ECSTASISING
ECSTASIZED
ECSTASIZES
ECSTASIZING
ECSTASYING
ECSTATICALLY
ECTHLIPSES
ECTHLIPSIS
ECTOBLASTIC
ECTOBLASTS
ECTOCRINES
ECTODERMAL
ECTODERMIC
ECTOENZYME
ECTOENZYMES
ECTOGENESES
ECTOGENESIS
ECTOGENETIC
ECTOGENICALLY
ECTOGENIES
ECTOGENOUS
ECTOMORPHIC
ECTOMORPHIES
ECTOMORPHS
ECTOMORPHY
ECTOMYCORRHIZA
ECTOMYCORRHIZAE
ECTOMYCORRHIZAS
ECTOPARASITE
ECTOPARASITES
ECTOPARASITIC
ECTOPHYTES
ECTOPHYTIC
ECTOPICALLY
ECTOPLASMIC
ECTOPLASMS
ECTOPLASTIC
ECTOPROCTS
ECTOSARCOUS
ECTOTHERMIC
ECTOTHERMS
ECTOTROPHIC

ECTROPIONS
ECTROPIUMS
ECTYPOGRAPHIES
ECTYPOGRAPHY
ECUMENICAL
ECUMENICALISM
ECUMENICALISMS
ECUMENICALLY
ECUMENICISM
ECUMENICISMS
ECUMENICIST
ECUMENICISTS
ECUMENICITIES
ECUMENICITY
ECUMENISMS
ECUMENISTS
ECZEMATOUS
EDACIOUSLY
EDACIOUSNESS
EDACIOUSNESSES
EDAPHICALLY
EDAPHOLOGIES
EDAPHOLOGY
EDELWEISSES
EDENTULATE
EDENTULOUS
EDGINESSES
EDIBILITIES
EDIBLENESS
EDIBLENESSES
EDIFICATION
EDIFICATIONS
EDIFICATORY
EDIFYINGLY
EDITIONING
EDITORIALISE
EDITORIALISED
EDITORIALISER
EDITORIALISERS
EDITORIALISES
EDITORIALISING
EDITORIALIST
EDITORIALISTS
EDITORIALIZE
EDITORIALIZED
EDITORIALIZER
EDITORIALIZERS
EDITORIALIZES
EDITORIALIZING

EDITORIALLY
EDITORIALS
EDITORSHIP
EDITORSHIPS
EDITRESSES
EDRIOPHTHALMIAN
EDRIOPHTHALMIC
EDRIOPHTHALMOUS
EDUCABILITIES
EDUCABILITY
EDUCATABILITIES
EDUCATABILITY
EDUCATABLE
EDUCATEDNESS
EDUCATEDNESSES
EDUCATIONAL
EDUCATIONALIST
EDUCATIONALISTS
EDUCATIONALLY
EDUCATIONESE
EDUCATIONESES
EDUCATIONIST
EDUCATIONISTS
EDUCATIONS
EDUCEMENTS
EDULCORANT
EDULCORATE
EDULCORATED
EDULCORATES
EDULCORATING
EDULCORATION
EDULCORATIONS
EDULCORATIVE
EDULCORATOR
EDULCORATORS
EDUTAINMENT
EDUTAINMENTS
EELGRASSES
EERINESSES
EFFACEABLE
EFFACEMENT
EFFACEMENTS
EFFECTIBLE
EFFECTIVELY
EFFECTIVENESS
EFFECTIVENESSES
EFFECTIVES
EFFECTIVITIES
EFFECTIVITY

EFFECTLESS
EFFECTUALITIES
EFFECTUALITY
EFFECTUALLY
EFFECTUALNESS
EFFECTUALNESSES
EFFECTUATE
EFFECTUATED
EFFECTUATES
EFFECTUATING
EFFECTUATION
EFFECTUATIONS
EFFEMINACIES
EFFEMINACY
EFFEMINATE
EFFEMINATED
EFFEMINATELY
EFFEMINATENESS
EFFEMINATES
EFFEMINATING
EFFEMINISE
EFFEMINISED
EFFEMINISES
EFFEMINISING
EFFEMINIZE
EFFEMINIZED
EFFEMINIZES
EFFEMINIZING
EFFERENCES
EFFERENTLY
EFFERVESCE
EFFERVESCED
EFFERVESCENCE
EFFERVESCENCES
EFFERVESCENCIES
EFFERVESCENCY
EFFERVESCENT
EFFERVESCENTLY
EFFERVESCES
EFFERVESCIBLE
EFFERVESCING
EFFERVESCINGLY
EFFETENESS
EFFETENESSES
EFFICACIES
EFFICACIOUS
EFFICACIOUSLY
EFFICACIOUSNESS
EFFICACITIES

E

EFFICACITY	EGLANDULAR	EIGHTFOILS	ELASMOBRANCHS	ELECTIVELY
EFFICIENCE	EGLANDULOSE	EIGHTIETHS	ELASMOSAUR	ELECTIVENESS
EFFICIENCES	EGLANTINES	EIGHTPENCE	ELASMOSAURS	ELECTIVENESSES
EFFICIENCIES	EGOCENTRIC	EIGHTPENCES	ELASTANCES	ELECTIVITIES
EFFICIENCY	EGOCENTRICAL	EIGHTPENNY	ELASTICALLY	ELECTIVITY
EFFICIENTLY	EGOCENTRICALLY	EIGHTSCORE	ELASTICATE	ELECTORALLY
EFFICIENTS	EGOCENTRICITIES	EIGHTSCORES	ELASTICATED	ELECTORATE
EFFIERCING	EGOCENTRICITY	EIGHTSOMES	ELASTICATES	ELECTORATES
EFFIGURATE	EGOCENTRICS	EINSTEINIUM	ELASTICATING	ELECTORESS
EFFIGURATION	EGOCENTRISM	EINSTEINIUMS	ELASTICATION	ELECTORESSES
EFFIGURATIONS	EGOCENTRISMS	EIRENICALLY	ELASTICATIONS	ELECTORIAL
EFFLEURAGE	EGOISTICAL	EIRENICONS	ELASTICISE	ELECTORIALLY
EFFLEURAGED	EGOISTICALLY	EISTEDDFOD	ELASTICISED	ELECTORSHIP
EFFLEURAGES	EGOMANIACAL	EISTEDDFODAU	ELASTICISES	ELECTORSHIPS
EFFLEURAGING	EGOMANIACALLY	EISTEDDFODIC	ELASTICISING	ELECTRESSES
EFFLORESCE	EGOMANIACS	EISTEDDFODS	ELASTICITIES	ELECTRICAL
EFFLORESCED	EGOSURFING	EJACULATED	ELASTICITY	ELECTRICALLY
EFFLORESCENCE	EGOTHEISMS	EJACULATES	ELASTICIZE	ELECTRICALS
EFFLORESCENCES	EGOTISTICAL	EJACULATING	ELASTICIZED	ELECTRICIAN
EFFLORESCENT	EGOTISTICALLY	EJACULATION	ELASTICIZES	ELECTRICIANS
EFFLORESCES	EGREGIOUSLY	EJACULATIONS	ELASTICIZING	ELECTRICITIES
EFFLORESCING	EGREGIOUSNESS	EJACULATIVE	ELASTICNESS	ELECTRICITY
EFFLUENCES	EGREGIOUSNESSES	EJACULATOR	ELASTICNESSES	ELECTRIFIABLE
EFFLUVIUMS	EGRESSIONS	EJACULATORS	ELASTOMERIC	ELECTRIFICATION
EFFLUXIONS	EGRESSIVES	EJACULATORY	ELASTOMERS	ELECTRIFIED
EFFORTFULLY	EGURGITATE	EJECTAMENTA	ELATEDNESS	ELECTRIFIER
EFFORTFULNESS	EGURGITATED	EJECTIVELY	ELATEDNESSES	ELECTRIFIERS
EFFORTFULNESSES	EGURGITATES	EJECTMENTS	ELATERITES	ELECTRIFIES
EFFORTLESS	EGURGITATING	EKISTICIAN	ELATERIUMS	ELECTRIFYING
EFFORTLESSLY	EICOSANOID	EKISTICIANS	ELBOWROOMS	ELECTRIFYINGLY
EFFORTLESSNESS	EICOSANOIDS	ELABORATED	ELDERBERRIES	ELECTRISATION
EFFRONTERIES	EIDERDOWNS	ELABORATELY	ELDERBERRY	ELECTRISATIONS
EFFRONTERY	EIDETICALLY	ELABORATENESS	ELDERCARES	ELECTRISED
EFFULGENCE	EIDOGRAPHS	ELABORATENESSES	ELDERFLOWER	ELECTRISES
EFFULGENCES	EIGENFREQUENCY	ELABORATES	ELDERFLOWERS	ELECTRISING
EFFULGENTLY	EIGENFUNCTION	ELABORATING	ELDERLINESS	ELECTRIZATION
EFFUSIOMETER	EIGENFUNCTIONS	ELABORATION	ELDERLINESSES	ELECTRIZATIONS
EFFUSIOMETERS	EIGENMODES	ELABORATIONS	ELDERSHIPS	ELECTRIZED
EFFUSIVELY	EIGENTONES	ELABORATIVE	ELECAMPANE	ELECTRIZES
EFFUSIVENESS	EIGENVALUE	ELABORATOR	ELECAMPANES	ELECTRIZING
EFFUSIVENESSES	EIGENVALUES	ELABORATORIES	ELECTABILITIES	ELECTROACOUSTIC
EGALITARIAN	EIGENVECTOR	ELABORATORS	ELECTABILITY	ELECTROACTIVE
EGALITARIANISM	EIGENVECTORS	ELABORATORY	ELECTIONEER	ELECTROACTIVITY
EGALITARIANISMS	EIGHTBALLS	ELAEAGNUSES	ELECTIONEERED	ELECTROANALYSES
EGALITARIANS	EIGHTEENMO	ELAEOLITES	ELECTIONEERER	ELECTROANALYSIS
EGAREMENTS	EIGHTEENMOS	ELAEOPTENE	ELECTIONEERERS	ELECTROANALYTIC
EGGBEATERS	EIGHTEENTH	ELAEOPTENES	ELECTIONEERING	ELECTROBIOLOGY
EGGHEADEDNESS	EIGHTEENTHLY	ELAIOSOMES	ELECTIONEERINGS	ELECTROCAUTERY
EGGHEADEDNESSES	EIGHTEENTHS	ELASMOBRANCH	ELECTIONEERS	ELECTROCEMENT

ELECTROCEMENTS	ELECTROGRAPHY	ELECTROMOTOR	ELECTROSONDE	ELEOPTENES
ELECTROCHEMIC	ELECTROING	ELECTROMOTORS	ELECTROSONDES	ELEPHANTIASES
ELECTROCHEMICAL	ELECTROJET	ELECTROMYOGRAM	ELECTROSTATIC	ELEPHANTIASIC
ELECTROCHEMIST	ELECTROJETS	ELECTROMYOGRAMS	ELECTROSTATICS	ELEPHANTIASIS
ELECTROCHEMISTS	ELECTROKINETIC	ELECTROMYOGRAPH	ELECTROSURGERY	ELEPHANTINE
ELECTROCHROMIC	ELECTROKINETICS	ELECTRONEGATIVE	ELECTROSURGICAL	ELEPHANTOID
ELECTROCLASH	ELECTROLESS	ELECTRONIC	ELECTROTECHNICS	ELEPIDOTES
ELECTROCLASHES	ELECTROLIER	ELECTRONICA	ELECTROTHERAPY	ELEUTHERARCH
ELECTROCULTURE	ELECTROLIERS	ELECTRONICALLY	ELECTROTHERMAL	ELEUTHERARCHS
ELECTROCULTURES	ELECTROLOGIES	ELECTRONICAS	ELECTROTHERMIC	ELEUTHERIAN
ELECTROCUTE	ELECTROLOGIST	ELECTRONICS	ELECTROTHERMICS	ELEUTHEROCOCCI
ELECTROCUTED	ELECTROLOGISTS	ELECTRONVOLT	ELECTROTHERMIES	ELEUTHEROCOCCUS
ELECTROCUTES	ELECTROLOGY	ELECTRONVOLTS	ELECTROTHERMY	ELEUTHERODACTYL
ELECTROCUTING	ELECTROLYSATION	ELECTROOSMOSES	ELECTROTINT	ELEUTHEROMANIA
ELECTROCUTION	ELECTROLYSE	ELECTROOSMOSIS	ELECTROTINTS	ELEUTHEROMANIAS
ELECTROCUTIONS	ELECTROLYSED	ELECTROOSMOTIC	ELECTROTONIC	ELEUTHEROPHOBIA
ELECTROCYTE	ELECTROLYSER	ELECTROPHILE	ELECTROTONUS	ELEUTHEROPHOBIC
ELECTROCYTES	ELECTROLYSERS	ELECTROPHILES	ELECTROTONUSES	ELEVATIONAL
ELECTRODEPOSIT	ELECTROLYSES	ELECTROPHILIC	ELECTROTYPE	ELEVATIONS
ELECTRODEPOSITS	ELECTROLYSING	ELECTROPHONE	ELECTROTYPED	ELEVENTHLY
ELECTRODERMAL	ELECTROLYSIS	ELECTROPHONES	ELECTROTYPER	ELFISHNESS
ELECTRODES	ELECTROLYTE	ELECTROPHONIC	ELECTROTYPERS	ELFISHNESSES
ELECTRODIALYSES	ELECTROLYTES	ELECTROPHORESE	ELECTROTYPES	ELICITABLE
ELECTRODIALYSIS	ELECTROLYTIC	ELECTROPHORESED	ELECTROTYPIC	ELICITATION
ELECTRODIALYTIC	ELECTROLYTICS	ELECTROPHORESES	ELECTROTYPIES	ELICITATIONS
ELECTRODYNAMIC	ELECTROLYZATION	ELECTROPHORESIS	ELECTROTYPING	ELIGIBILITIES
ELECTRODYNAMICS	ELECTROLYZE	ELECTROPHORETIC	ELECTROTYPIST	ELIGIBILITY
ELECTROFISHING	ELECTROLYZED	ELECTROPHORI	ELECTROTYPISTS	ELIMINABILITIES
ELECTROFISHINGS	ELECTROLYZER	ELECTROPHORUS	ELECTROTYPY	ELIMINABILITY
ELECTROFLUOR	ELECTROLYZERS	ELECTROPHORUSES	ELECTROVALENCE	ELIMINABLE
ELECTROFLUORS	ELECTROLYZES	ELECTROPLATE	ELECTROVALENCES	ELIMINANTS
ELECTROFORM	ELECTROLYZING	ELECTROPLATED	ELECTROVALENCY	ELIMINATED
ELECTROFORMED	ELECTROMAGNET	ELECTROPLATER	ELECTROVALENT	ELIMINATES
ELECTROFORMING	ELECTROMAGNETIC	ELECTROPLATERS	ELECTROVALENTLY	ELIMINATING
ELECTROFORMINGS	ELECTROMAGNETS	ELECTROPLATES	ELECTROWEAK	ELIMINATION
ELECTROFORMS	ELECTROMER	ELECTROPLATING	ELECTROWINNING	ELIMINATIONS
ELECTROGEN	ELECTROMERIC	ELECTROPLATINGS	ELECTROWINNINGS	ELIMINATIVE
ELECTROGENESES	ELECTROMERISM	ELECTROPOLAR	ELECTUARIES	ELIMINATIVISM
ELECTROGENESIS	ELECTROMERISMS	ELECTROPOP	ELEDOISINS	ELIMINATIVISMS
ELECTROGENIC	ELECTROMERS	ELECTROPOPS	ELEEMOSYNARY	ELIMINATOR
ELECTROGENS	ELECTROMETER	ELECTROPOSITIVE	ELEGANCIES	ELIMINATORS
ELECTROGILDING	ELECTROMETERS	ELECTROPUNCTURE	ELEGIACALLY	ELIMINATORY
ELECTROGILDINGS	ELECTROMETRIC	ELECTRORECEPTOR	ELEMENTALISM	ELLIPSOGRAPH
ELECTROGRAM	ELECTROMETRICAL	ELECTRORHEOLOGY	ELEMENTALISMS	ELLIPSOGRAPHS
ELECTROGRAMS	ELECTROMETRIES	ELECTROSCOPE	ELEMENTALLY	ELLIPSOIDAL
ELECTROGRAPH	ELECTROMETRY	ELECTROSCOPES	ELEMENTALS	ELLIPSOIDS
ELECTROGRAPHIC	ELECTROMOTANCE	ELECTROSCOPIC	ELEMENTARILY	ELLIPTICAL
ELECTROGRAPHIES	ELECTROMOTANCES	ELECTROSHOCK	ELEMENTARINESS	ELLIPTICALLY
ELECTROGRAPHS	ELECTROMOTIVE	ELECTROSHOCKS	ELEMENTARY	ELLIPTICALNESS

ELLIPTICALS	ELYTRIGEROUS	EMBARKATION	EMBLAZONER	EMBONPOINT
ELLIPTICITIES	EMACIATING	EMBARKATIONS	EMBLAZONERS	EMBONPOINTS
ELLIPTICITY	EMACIATION	EMBARKMENT	EMBLAZONING	EMBORDERED
ELOCUTIONARY	EMACIATIONS	EMBARKMENTS	EMBLAZONMENT	EMBORDERING
ELOCUTIONIST	EMALANGENI	EMBARQUEMENT	EMBLAZONMENTS	EMBOSCATAS
ELOCUTIONISTS	EMANATIONAL	EMBARQUEMENTS	EMBLAZONRIES	EMBOSOMING
ELOCUTIONS	EMANATIONS	EMBARRASSABLE	EMBLAZONRY	EMBOSSABLE
ELOIGNMENT	EMANATISTS	EMBARRASSED	EMBLEMATIC	EMBOSSINGS
ELOIGNMENTS	EMANCIPATE	EMBARRASSEDLY	EMBLEMATICAL	EMBOSSMENT
ELOINMENTS	EMANCIPATED	EMBARRASSES	EMBLEMATICALLY	EMBOSSMENTS
ELONGATING	EMANCIPATES	EMBARRASSING	EMBLEMATISE	EMBOTHRIUM
ELONGATION	EMANCIPATING	EMBARRASSINGLY	EMBLEMATISED	EMBOTHRIUMS
ELONGATIONS	EMANCIPATION	EMBARRASSMENT	EMBLEMATISES	EMBOUCHURE
ELOPEMENTS	EMANCIPATIONIST	EMBARRASSMENTS	EMBLEMATISING	EMBOUCHURES
ELOQUENCES	EMANCIPATIONS	EMBARRINGS	EMBLEMATIST	EMBOUNDING
ELOQUENTLY	EMANCIPATIVE	EMBASEMENT	EMBLEMATISTS	EMBOURGEOISE
ELSEWHITHER	EMANCIPATOR	EMBASEMENTS	EMBLEMATIZE	EMBOURGEOISED
ELUCIDATED	EMANCIPATORS	EMBASSADES	EMBLEMATIZED	EMBOURGEOISES
ELUCIDATES	EMANCIPATORY	EMBASSADOR	EMBLEMATIZES	EMBOURGEOISING
ELUCIDATING	EMANCIPIST	EMBASSADORS	EMBLEMATIZING	EMBOWELING
ELUCIDATION	EMANCIPISTS	EMBASSAGES	EMBLEMENTS	EMBOWELLED
ELUCIDATIONS	EMARGINATE	EMBATTLEMENT	EMBLEMISED	EMBOWELLING
ELUCIDATIVE	EMARGINATED	EMBATTLEMENTS	EMBLEMISES	EMBOWELMENT
ELUCIDATOR	EMARGINATELY	EMBATTLING	EMBLEMISING	EMBOWELMENTS
ELUCIDATORS	EMARGINATES	EMBAYMENTS	EMBLEMIZED	EMBOWERING
ELUCIDATORY	EMARGINATING	EMBEDDINGS	EMBLEMIZES	EMBOWERMENT
ELUCUBRATE	EMARGINATION	EMBEDMENTS	EMBLEMIZING	EMBOWERMENTS
ELUCUBRATED	EMARGINATIONS	EMBELLISHED	EMBLOOMING	EMBOWMENTS
ELUCUBRATES	EMASCULATE	EMBELLISHER	EMBLOSSOMED	EMBRACEABLE
ELUCUBRATING	EMASCULATED	EMBELLISHERS	EMBLOSSOMING	EMBRACEMENT
ELUCUBRATION	EMASCULATES	EMBELLISHES	EMBLOSSOMS	EMBRACEMENTS
ELUCUBRATIONS	EMASCULATING	EMBELLISHING	EMBODIMENT	EMBRACEORS
ELUSIVENESS	EMASCULATION	EMBELLISHINGLY	EMBODIMENTS	EMBRACERIES
ELUSIVENESSES	EMASCULATIONS	EMBELLISHMENT	EMBOITEMENT	EMBRACINGLY
ELUSORINESS	EMASCULATIVE	EMBELLISHMENTS	EMBOITEMENTS	EMBRACINGNESS
ELUSORINESSES	EMASCULATOR	EMBEZZLEMENT	EMBOLDENED	EMBRACINGNESSES
ELUTRIATED	EMASCULATORS	EMBEZZLEMENTS	EMBOLDENER	EMBRAIDING
ELUTRIATES	EMASCULATORY	EMBEZZLERS	EMBOLDENERS	EMBRANCHMENT
ELUTRIATING	EMBALLINGS	EMBEZZLING	EMBOLDENING	EMBRANCHMENTS
ELUTRIATION	EMBALMINGS	EMBIGGENED	EMBOLECTOMIES	EMBRANGLED
ELUTRIATIONS	EMBALMMENT	EMBIGGENING	EMBOLECTOMY	EMBRANGLEMENT
ELUTRIATOR	EMBALMMENTS	EMBITTERED	EMBOLISATION	EMBRANGLEMENTS
ELUTRIATORS	EMBANKMENT	EMBITTERER	EMBOLISATIONS	EMBRANGLES
ELUVIATING	EMBANKMENTS	EMBITTERERS	EMBOLISING	EMBRANGLING
ELUVIATION	EMBARCADERO	EMBITTERING	EMBOLISMAL	EMBRASURED
ELUVIATIONS	EMBARCADEROS	EMBITTERINGS	EMBOLISMIC	EMBRASURES
ELVISHNESS	EMBARCATION	EMBITTERMENT	EMBOLIZATION	EMBRAZURES
ELVISHNESSES	EMBARCATIONS	EMBITTERMENTS	EMBOLIZATIONS	EMBREADING
ELYTRIFORM	EMBARGOING	EMBLAZONED	EMBOLIZING	EMBREATHED

EMBREATHES	EMBRYOTOMY	EMOLUMENTARY	EMPATHISED	EMPIRICUTIC
EMBREATHING	EMBRYULCIA	EMOLUMENTS	EMPATHISES	EMPLACEMENT
EMBRITTLED	EMBRYULCIAS	EMOTIONABLE	EMPATHISING	EMPLACEMENTS
EMBRITTLEMENT	EMENDATING	EMOTIONALISE	EMPATHISTS	EMPLASTERED
EMBRITTLEMENTS	EMENDATION	EMOTIONALISED	EMPATHIZED	EMPLASTERING
EMBRITTLES	EMENDATIONS	EMOTIONALISES	EMPATHIZES	EMPLASTERS
EMBRITTLING	EMENDATORS	EMOTIONALISING	EMPATHIZING	EMPLASTICS
EMBROCATED	EMENDATORY	EMOTIONALISM	EMPATRONED	EMPLASTRON
EMBROCATES	EMERGENCES	EMOTIONALISMS	EMPATRONING	EMPLASTRONS
EMBROCATING	EMERGENCIES	EMOTIONALIST	EMPEACHING	EMPLASTRUM
EMBROCATION	EMERGENTLY	EMOTIONALISTIC	EMPENNAGES	EMPLASTRUMS
EMBROCATIONS	EMETICALLY	EMOTIONALISTS	EMPEOPLING	EMPLEACHED
EMBROGLIOS	EMETOPHOBIA	EMOTIONALITIES	EMPERISHED	EMPLEACHES
EMBROIDERED	EMETOPHOBIAS	EMOTIONALITY	EMPERISHES	EMPLEACHING
EMBROIDERER	EMICATIONS	EMOTIONALIZE	EMPERISHING	EMPLECTONS
EMBROIDERERS	EMIGRATING	EMOTIONALIZED	EMPERISING	EMPLECTUMS
EMBROIDERIES	EMIGRATION	EMOTIONALIZES	EMPERIZING	EMPLONGING
EMBROIDERING	EMIGRATIONAL	EMOTIONALIZING	EMPERORSHIP	EMPLOYABILITIES
EMBROIDERS	EMIGRATIONIST	EMOTIONALLY	EMPERORSHIPS	EMPLOYABILITY
EMBROIDERY	EMIGRATIONISTS	EMOTIONLESS	EMPHASISED	EMPLOYABLE
EMBROILERS	EMIGRATIONS	EMOTIONLESSLY	EMPHASISES	EMPLOYABLES
EMBROILING	EMIGRATORY	EMOTIONLESSNESS	EMPHASISING	EMPLOYMENT
EMBROILMENT	EMINENCIES	EMOTIVENESS	EMPHASIZED	EMPLOYMENTS
EMBROILMENTS	EMINENTIAL	EMOTIVENESSES	EMPHASIZES	EMPOISONED
EMBROWNING	EMISSARIES	EMOTIVISMS	EMPHASIZING	EMPOISONING
EMBRUEMENT	EMISSIVITIES	EMOTIVITIES	EMPHATICAL	EMPOISONMENT
EMBRUEMENTS	EMISSIVITY	EMPACKETED	EMPHATICALLY	EMPOISONMENTS
EMBRYECTOMIES	EMITTANCES	EMPACKETING	EMPHATICALNESS	EMPOLDERED
EMBRYECTOMY	EMMARBLING	EMPALEMENT	EMPHRACTIC	EMPOLDERING
EMBRYOGENESES	EMMENAGOGIC	EMPALEMENTS	EMPHRACTICS	EMPOVERISH
EMBRYOGENESIS	EMMENAGOGUE	EMPANELING	EMPHYSEMAS	EMPOVERISHED
EMBRYOGENETIC	EMMENAGOGUES	EMPANELLED	EMPHYSEMATOUS	EMPOVERISHER
EMBRYOGENIC	EMMENOLOGIES	EMPANELLING	EMPHYSEMIC	EMPOVERISHERS
EMBRYOGENIES	EMMENOLOGY	EMPANELMENT	EMPHYSEMICS	EMPOVERISHES
EMBRYOGENY	EMMETROPES	EMPANELMENTS	EMPHYTEUSES	EMPOVERISHING
EMBRYOLOGIC	EMMETROPIA	EMPANOPLIED	EMPHYTEUSIS	EMPOVERISHMENT
EMBRYOLOGICAL	EMMETROPIAS	EMPANOPLIES	EMPHYTEUTIC	EMPOVERISHMENTS
EMBRYOLOGICALLY	EMMETROPIC	EMPANOPLYING	EMPIECEMENT	EMPOWERING
EMBRYOLOGIES	EMOLLESCENCE	EMPARADISE	EMPIECEMENTS	EMPOWERMENT
EMBRYOLOGIST	EMOLLESCENCES	EMPARADISED	EMPIERCING	EMPOWERMENTS
EMBRYOLOGISTS	EMOLLIATED	EMPARADISES	EMPIGHTING	EMPRESSEMENT
EMBRYOLOGY	EMOLLIATES	EMPARADISING	EMPIRICALLY	EMPRESSEMENTS
EMBRYONATE	EMOLLIATING	EMPARLAUNCE	EMPIRICALNESS	EMPTINESSES
EMBRYONATED	EMOLLIENCE	EMPARLAUNCES	EMPIRICALNESSES	EMPURPLING
EMBRYONICALLY	EMOLLIENCES	EMPASSIONATE	EMPIRICALS	EMPYREUMATA
EMBRYOPHYTE	EMOLLIENTS	EMPASSIONED	EMPIRICISM	EMPYREUMATIC
EMBRYOPHYTES	EMOLLITION	EMPATHETIC	EMPIRICISMS	EMPYREUMATICAL
EMBRYOTICALLY	EMOLLITIONS	EMPATHETICALLY	EMPIRICIST	EMPYREUMATISE
EMBRYOTOMIES	EMOLUMENTAL	EMPATHICALLY	EMPIRICISTS	EMPYREUMATISED

EMPYREUMATISES	ENANTHEMAS	ENCARPUSES	ENCHARGING	ENCOMIASTIC
EMPYREUMATISING	ENANTIODROMIA	ENCASEMENT	ENCHARMING	ENCOMIASTICAL
EMPYREUMATIZE	ENANTIODROMIAS	ENCASEMENTS	ENCHEASONS	ENCOMIASTICALLY
EMPYREUMATIZED	ENANTIODROMIC	ENCASHABLE	ENCHEERING	ENCOMIASTS
EMPYREUMATIZES	ENANTIOMER	ENCASHMENT	ENCHEIRIDIA	ENCOMIENDA
EMPYREUMATIZING	ENANTIOMERIC	ENCASHMENTS	ENCHEIRIDION	ENCOMIENDAS
EMULATIONS	ENANTIOMERS	ENCAUSTICALLY	ENCHEIRIDIONS	ENCOMPASSED
EMULATIVELY	ENANTIOMORPH	ENCAUSTICS	ENCHILADAS	ENCOMPASSES
EMULATRESS	ENANTIOMORPHIC	ENCEPHALALGIA	ENCHIRIDIA	ENCOMPASSING
EMULATRESSES	ENANTIOMORPHIES	ENCEPHALALGIAS	ENCHIRIDION	ENCOMPASSMENT
EMULGENCES	ENANTIOMORPHISM	ENCEPHALIC	ENCHIRIDIONS	ENCOMPASSMENTS
EMULOUSNESS	ENANTIOMORPHOUS	ENCEPHALIN	ENCHONDROMA	ENCOPRESES
EMULOUSNESSES	ENANTIOMORPHS	ENCEPHALINE	ENCHONDROMAS	ENCOPRESIS
EMULSIFIABLE	ENANTIOMORPHY	ENCEPHALINES	ENCHONDROMATA	ENCOPRETIC
EMULSIFICATION	ENANTIOPATHIES	ENCEPHALINS	ENCHONDROMATOUS	ENCOUNTERED
EMULSIFICATIONS	ENANTIOPATHY	ENCEPHALITIC	ENCINCTURE	ENCOUNTERER
EMULSIFIED	ENANTIOSES	ENCEPHALITIDES	ENCINCTURED	ENCOUNTERERS
EMULSIFIER	ENANTIOSIS	ENCEPHALITIS	ENCINCTURES	ENCOUNTERING
EMULSIFIERS	ENANTIOSTYLIES	ENCEPHALITISES	ENCINCTURING	ENCOUNTERS
EMULSIFIES	ENANTIOSTYLOUS	ENCEPHALITOGEN	ENCIPHERED	ENCOURAGED
EMULSIFYING	ENANTIOSTYLY	ENCEPHALITOGENS	ENCIPHERER	ENCOURAGEMENT
EMULSIONISE	ENANTIOTROPIC	ENCEPHALOCELE	ENCIPHERERS	ENCOURAGEMENTS
EMULSIONISED	ENANTIOTROPIES	ENCEPHALOCELES	ENCIPHERING	ENCOURAGER
EMULSIONISES	ENANTIOTROPY	ENCEPHALOGRAM	ENCIPHERMENT	ENCOURAGERS
EMULSIONISING	ENARRATION	ENCEPHALOGRAMS	ENCIPHERMENTS	ENCOURAGES
EMULSIONIZE	ENARRATIONS	ENCEPHALOGRAPH	ENCIRCLEMENT	ENCOURAGING
EMULSIONIZED	ENARTHRODIAL	ENCEPHALOGRAPHS	ENCIRCLEMENTS	ENCOURAGINGLY
EMULSIONIZES	ENARTHROSES	ENCEPHALOGRAPHY	ENCIRCLING	ENCOURAGINGS
EMULSIONIZING	ENARTHROSIS	ENCEPHALOID	ENCLASPING	ENCRADLING
EMULSOIDAL	ENCAMPMENT	ENCEPHALOMA	ENCLITICALLY	ENCREASING
EMUNCTIONS	ENCAMPMENTS	ENCEPHALOMAS	ENCLOISTER	ENCRIMSONED
EMUNCTORIES	ENCANTHISES	ENCEPHALOMATA	ENCLOISTERED	ENCRIMSONING
ENABLEMENT	ENCAPSULATE	ENCEPHALON	ENCLOISTERING	ENCRIMSONS
ENABLEMENTS	ENCAPSULATED	ENCEPHALONS	ENCLOISTERS	ENCRINITAL
ENACTMENTS	ENCAPSULATES	ENCEPHALOPATHIC	ENCLOSABLE	ENCRINITES
ENALAPRILS	ENCAPSULATING	ENCEPHALOPATHY	ENCLOSURES	ENCRINITIC
ENAMELINGS	ENCAPSULATION	ENCEPHALOTOMIES	ENCLOTHING	ENCROACHED
ENAMELISTS	ENCAPSULATIONS	ENCEPHALOTOMY	ENCLOUDING	ENCROACHER
ENAMELLERS	ENCAPSULED	ENCEPHALOUS	ENCODEMENT	ENCROACHERS
ENAMELLING	ENCAPSULES	ENCHAINING	ENCODEMENTS	ENCROACHES
ENAMELLINGS	ENCAPSULING	ENCHAINMENT	ENCOIGNURE	ENCROACHING
ENAMELLIST	ENCARNALISE	ENCHAINMENTS	ENCOIGNURES	ENCROACHINGLY
ENAMELLISTS	ENCARNALISED	ENCHANTERS	ENCOLORING	ENCROACHMENT
ENAMELWARE	ENCARNALISES	ENCHANTING	ENCOLOURED	ENCROACHMENTS
ENAMELWARES	ENCARNALISING	ENCHANTINGLY	ENCOLOURING	ENCRUSTATION
ENAMELWORK	ENCARNALIZE	ENCHANTMENT	ENCOLPIONS	ENCRUSTATIONS
ENAMELWORKS	ENCARNALIZED	ENCHANTMENTS	ENCOLPIUMS	ENCRUSTING
ENAMORADOS	ENCARNALIZES	ENCHANTRESS	ENCOMENDERO	ENCRUSTMENT
ENAMOURING	ENCARNALIZING	ENCHANTRESSES	ENCOMENDEROS	ENCRUSTMENTS

E

ENCRYPTING	ENDAMOEBAS	ENDOCARDIAL	ENDOLYMPHS	ENDOPROCTS
ENCRYPTION	ENDAMOEBIC	ENDOCARDITIC	ENDOMETRIA	ENDORADIOSONDE
ENCRYPTIONS	ENDANGERED	ENDOCARDITIDES	ENDOMETRIAL	ENDORADIOSONDES
ENCULTURATE	ENDANGERER	ENDOCARDITIS	ENDOMETRIOSES	ENDORHIZAL
ENCULTURATED	ENDANGERERS	ENDOCARDITISES	ENDOMETRIOSIS	ENDORPHINS
ENCULTURATES	ENDANGERING	ENDOCARDIUM	ENDOMETRITIS	ENDORSABLE
ENCULTURATING	ENDANGERMENT	ENDOCARPAL	ENDOMETRITISES	ENDORSATION
ENCULTURATION	ENDANGERMENTS	ENDOCARPIC	ENDOMETRIUM	ENDORSATIONS
ENCULTURATIONS	ENDARCHIES	ENDOCENTRIC	ENDOMITOSES	ENDORSEMENT
ENCULTURATIVE	ENDARTERECTOMY	ENDOCHONDRAL	ENDOMITOSIS	ENDORSEMENTS
ENCUMBERED	ENDEARINGLY	ENDOCHYLOUS	ENDOMITOTIC	ENDOSCOPES
ENCUMBERING	ENDEARINGNESS	ENDOCRANIA	ENDOMIXISES	ENDOSCOPIC
ENCUMBERINGLY	ENDEARINGNESSES	ENDOCRANIAL	ENDOMORPHIC	ENDOSCOPICALLY
ENCUMBERMENT	ENDEARMENT	ENDOCRANIUM	ENDOMORPHIES	ENDOSCOPIES
ENCUMBERMENTS	ENDEARMENTS	ENDOCRINAL	ENDOMORPHISM	ENDOSCOPIST
ENCUMBRANCE	ENDEAVORED	ENDOCRINES	ENDOMORPHISMS	ENDOSCOPISTS
ENCUMBRANCER	ENDEAVORER	ENDOCRINIC	ENDOMORPHS	ENDOSKELETAL
ENCUMBRANCERS	ENDEAVORERS	ENDOCRINOLOGIC	ENDOMORPHY	ENDOSKELETON
ENCUMBRANCES	ENDEAVORING	ENDOCRINOLOGIES	ENDOMYCORRHIZA	ENDOSKELETONS
ENCURTAINED	ENDEAVORMENT	ENDOCRINOLOGIST	ENDONEURIA	ENDOSMOMETER
ENCURTAINING	ENDEAVORMENTS	ENDOCRINOLOGY	ENDONEURIUM	ENDOSMOMETERS
ENCURTAINS	ENDEAVOURED	ENDOCRINOPATHIC	ENDONUCLEASE	ENDOSMOMETRIC
ENCYCLICAL	ENDEAVOURER	ENDOCRINOPATHY	ENDONUCLEASES	ENDOSMOSES
ENCYCLICALS	ENDEAVOURERS	ENDOCRINOUS	ENDONUCLEOLYTIC	ENDOSMOSIS
ENCYCLOPAEDIA	ENDEAVOURING	ENDOCRITIC	ENDOPARASITE	ENDOSMOTIC
ENCYCLOPAEDIAS	ENDEAVOURMENT	ENDOCUTICLE	ENDOPARASITES	ENDOSMOTICALLY
ENCYCLOPAEDIC	ENDEAVOURMENTS	ENDOCUTICLES	ENDOPARASITIC	ENDOSPERMIC
ENCYCLOPAEDICAL	ENDEAVOURS	ENDOCYTOSES	ENDOPARASITISM	ENDOSPERMS
ENCYCLOPAEDISM	ENDECAGONS	ENDOCYTOSIS	ENDOPARASITISMS	ENDOSPORES
ENCYCLOPAEDISMS	ENDEIXISES	ENDOCYTOTIC	ENDOPEPTIDASE	ENDOSPOROUS
ENCYCLOPAEDIST	ENDEMICALLY	ENDODERMAL	ENDOPEPTIDASES	ENDOSTEALLY
ENCYCLOPAEDISTS	ENDEMICITIES	ENDODERMIC	ENDOPEROXIDE	ENDOSTOSES
ENCYCLOPEDIA	ENDEMICITY	ENDODERMIS	ENDOPEROXIDES	ENDOSTOSIS
ENCYCLOPEDIAN	ENDEMIOLOGIES	ENDODERMISES	ENDOPHAGIES	ENDOSTYLES
ENCYCLOPEDIAS	ENDEMIOLOGY	ENDODONTAL	ENDOPHAGOUS	ENDOSULFAN
ENCYCLOPEDIC	ENDENIZENED	ENDODONTIC	ENDOPHITIC	ENDOSULFANS
ENCYCLOPEDICAL	ENDENIZENING	ENDODONTICALLY	ENDOPHYLLOUS	ENDOSYMBIONT
ENCYCLOPEDISM	ENDENIZENS	ENDODONTICS	ENDOPHYTES	ENDOSYMBIONTS
ENCYCLOPEDISMS	ENDERGONIC	ENDODONTIST	ENDOPHYTIC	ENDOSYMBIOSES
ENCYCLOPEDIST	ENDERMATIC	ENDODONTISTS	ENDOPHYTICALLY	ENDOSYMBIOSIS
ENCYCLOPEDISTS	ENDERMATICAL	ENDOENZYME	ENDOPLASMIC	ENDOSYMBIOTIC
ENCYSTATION	ENDERMICAL	ENDOENZYMES	ENDOPLASMS	ENDOTHECIA
ENCYSTATIONS	ENDLESSNESS	ENDOGAMIES	ENDOPLASTIC	ENDOTHECIAL
ENCYSTMENT	ENDLESSNESSES	ENDOGAMOUS	ENDOPLEURA	ENDOTHECIUM
ENCYSTMENTS	ENDOBIOTIC	ENDOGENIES	ENDOPLEURAS	ENDOTHELIA
ENDAMAGEMENT	ENDOBLASTIC	ENDOGENOUS	ENDOPODITE	ENDOTHELIAL
ENDAMAGEMENTS	ENDOBLASTS	ENDOGENOUSLY	ENDOPODITES	ENDOTHELIOID
ENDAMAGING	ENDOCARDIA	ENDOLITHIC	ENDOPOLYPLOID	ENDOTHELIOMA
ENDAMOEBAE	ENDOCARDIAC	ENDOLYMPHATIC	ENDOPOLYPLOIDY	ENDOTHELIOMAS

ENDOTHELIOMATA	ENFELONING	ENGARRISONS	ENGROSSMENT	ENJOINDERS
ENDOTHELIUM	ENFEOFFING	ENGENDERED	ENGROSSMENTS	ENJOINMENT
ENDOTHERMAL	ENFEOFFMENT	ENGENDERER	ENGUARDING	ENJOINMENTS
ENDOTHERMIC	ENFEOFFMENTS	ENGENDERERS	ENGULFMENT	ENJOYABLENESS
ENDOTHERMICALLY	ENFESTERED	ENGENDERING	ENGULFMENTS	ENJOYABLENESSES
ENDOTHERMIES	ENFETTERED	ENGENDERMENT	ENGULPHING	ENJOYMENTS
ENDOTHERMISM	ENFETTERING	ENGENDERMENTS	ENGYSCOPES	ENKEPHALIN
ENDOTHERMISMS	ENFEVERING	ENGENDRURE	ENHANCEMENT	ENKEPHALINE
ENDOTHERMS	ENFIERCING	ENGENDRURES	ENHANCEMENTS	ENKEPHALINES
ENDOTHERMY	ENFILADING	ENGENDURES	ENHARMONIC	ENKEPHALINS
ENDOTOXINS	ENFLESHING	ENGINEERED	ENHARMONICAL	ENKERNELLED
ENDOTRACHEAL	ENFLEURAGE	ENGINEERING	ENHARMONICALLY	ENKERNELLING
ENDOTROPHIC	ENFLEURAGES	ENGINEERINGS	ENHEARSING	ENKINDLERS
ENDOWMENTS	ENFLOWERED	ENGINERIES	ENHEARTENED	ENKINDLING
ENDPLAYING	ENFLOWERING	ENGIRDLING	ENHEARTENING	ENLACEMENT
ENDUNGEONED	ENFOLDMENT	ENGLACIALLY	ENHEARTENS	ENLACEMENTS
ENDUNGEONING	ENFOLDMENTS	ENGLISHING	ENHUNGERED	ENLARGEABLE
ENDUNGEONS	ENFORCEABILITY	ENGLOOMING	ENHUNGERING	ENLARGEDLY
ENDURABILITIES	ENFORCEABLE	ENGLUTTING	ENHYDRITES	ENLARGEDNESS
ENDURABILITY	ENFORCEDLY	ENGORGEMENT	ENHYDRITIC	ENLARGEDNESSES
ENDURABLENESS	ENFORCEMENT	ENGORGEMENTS	ENHYDROSES	ENLARGEMENT
ENDURABLENESSES	ENFORCEMENTS	ENGOUEMENT	ENHYPOSTASIA	ENLARGEMENTS
ENDURANCES	ENFORESTED	ENGOUEMENTS	ENHYPOSTASIAS	ENLARGENED
ENDURINGLY	ENFORESTING	ENGOUMENTS	ENHYPOSTATIC	ENLARGENING
ENDURINGNESS	ENFOULDERED	ENGRAFFING	ENHYPOSTATISE	ENLEVEMENT
ENDURINGNESSES	ENFRAMEMENT	ENGRAFTATION	ENHYPOSTATISED	ENLEVEMENTS
ENERGETICAL	ENFRAMEMENTS	ENGRAFTATIONS	ENHYPOSTATISES	ENLIGHTENED
ENERGETICALLY	ENFRANCHISE	ENGRAFTING	ENHYPOSTATISING	ENLIGHTENER
ENERGETICS	ENFRANCHISED	ENGRAFTMENT	ENHYPOSTATIZE	ENLIGHTENERS
ENERGISATION	ENFRANCHISEMENT	ENGRAFTMENTS	ENHYPOSTATIZED	ENLIGHTENING
ENERGISATIONS	ENFRANCHISER	ENGRAILING	ENHYPOSTATIZES	ENLIGHTENMENT
ENERGISERS	ENFRANCHISERS	ENGRAILMENT	ENHYPOSTATIZING	ENLIGHTENMENTS
ENERGISING	ENFRANCHISES	ENGRAILMENTS	ENIGMATICAL	ENLIGHTENS
ENERGIZATION	ENFRANCHISING	ENGRAINEDLY	ENIGMATICALLY	ENLIGHTING
ENERGIZATIONS	ENFREEDOMED	ENGRAINEDNESS	ENIGMATISE	ENLISTMENT
ENERGIZERS	ENFREEDOMING	ENGRAINEDNESSES	ENIGMATISED	ENLISTMENTS
ENERGIZING	ENFREEDOMS	ENGRAINERS	ENIGMATISES	ENLIVENERS
ENERGUMENS	ENFREEZING	ENGRAINING	ENIGMATISING	ENLIVENING
ENERVATING	ENGAGEMENT	ENGRAMMATIC	ENIGMATIST	ENLIVENMENT
ENERVATION	ENGAGEMENTS	ENGRASPING	ENIGMATISTS	ENLIVENMENTS
ENERVATIONS	ENGAGINGLY	ENGRAVERIES	ENIGMATIZE	ENLUMINING
ENERVATIVE	ENGAGINGNESS	ENGRAVINGS	ENIGMATIZED	ENMESHMENT
ENERVATORS	ENGAGINGNESSES	ENGRENAGES	ENIGMATIZES	ENMESHMENTS
ENFACEMENT	ENGARLANDED	ENGRIEVING	ENIGMATIZING	ENNEAGONAL
ENFACEMENTS	ENGARLANDING	ENGROOVING	ENIGMATOGRAPHY	ENNEAGRAMS
ENFEEBLEMENT	ENGARLANDS	ENGROSSEDLY	ENJAMBEMENT	ENNEAHEDRA
ENFEEBLEMENTS	ENGARRISON	ENGROSSERS	ENJAMBEMENTS	ENNEAHEDRAL
ENFEEBLERS	ENGARRISONED	ENGROSSING	ENJAMBMENT	ENNEAHEDRON
ENFEEBLING	ENGARRISONING	ENGROSSINGLY	ENJAMBMENTS	ENNEAHEDRONS

ENNEANDRIAN	ENSAMPLING	ENSORCELLING	ENTEROCELES	ENTERTAINING
ENNEANDROUS	ENSANGUINATED	ENSORCELLMENT	ENTEROCENTESES	ENTERTAININGLY
ENNEASTYLE	ENSANGUINE	ENSORCELLMENTS	ENTEROCENTESIS	ENTERTAININGS
ENNEATHLON	ENSANGUINED	ENSORCELLS	ENTEROCOCCAL	ENTERTAINMENT
ENNEATHLONS	ENSANGUINES	ENSOULMENT	ENTEROCOCCI	ENTERTAINMENTS
ENNOBLEMENT	ENSANGUINING	ENSOULMENTS	ENTEROCOCCUS	ENTERTAINS
ENNOBLEMENTS	ENSCHEDULE	ENSPHERING	ENTEROCOEL	ENTERTAKEN
ENOKIDAKES	ENSCHEDULED	ENSTAMPING	ENTEROCOELE	ENTERTAKES
ENOKITAKES	ENSCHEDULES	ENSTATITES	ENTEROCOELES	ENTERTAKING
ENOLOGICAL	ENSCHEDULING	ENSTEEPING	ENTEROCOELIC	ENTERTISSUED
ENOLOGISTS	ENSCONCING	ENSTRUCTURED	ENTEROCOELOUS	ENTHALPIES
ENORMITIES	ENSCROLLED	ENSWATHEMENT	ENTEROCOELS	ENTHEOGENS
ENORMOUSLY	ENSCROLLING	ENSWATHEMENTS	ENTEROCOLITIDES	ENTHRALDOM
ENORMOUSNESS	ENSEPULCHRE	ENSWATHING	ENTEROCOLITIS	ENTHRALDOMS
ENORMOUSNESSES	ENSEPULCHRED	ENSWEEPING	ENTEROCOLITISES	ENTHRALLED
ENOUNCEMENT	ENSEPULCHRES	ENTABLATURE	ENTEROGASTRONE	ENTHRALLER
ENOUNCEMENTS	ENSEPULCHRING	ENTABLATURES	ENTEROGASTRONES	ENTHRALLERS
ENPHYTOTIC	ENSERFMENT	ENTABLEMENT	ENTEROHEPATITIS	ENTHRALLING
ENQUEUEING	ENSERFMENTS	ENTABLEMENTS	ENTEROKINASE	ENTHRALLMENT
ENQUIRATION	ENSHEATHED	ENTAILMENT	ENTEROKINASES	ENTHRALLMENTS
ENQUIRATIONS	ENSHEATHES	ENTAILMENTS	ENTEROLITH	ENTHRALMENT
ENRAGEMENT	ENSHEATHING	ENTAMOEBAE	ENTEROLITHS	ENTHRALMENTS
ENRAGEMENTS	ENSHELLING	ENTAMOEBAS	ENTEROPATHIES	ENTHRONEMENT
ENRANCKLED	ENSHELTERED	ENTANGLEMENT	ENTEROPATHY	ENTHRONEMENTS
ENRANCKLES	ENSHELTERING	ENTANGLEMENTS	ENTEROPNEUST	ENTHRONING
ENRANCKLING	ENSHELTERS	ENTANGLERS	ENTEROPNEUSTAL	ENTHRONISATION
ENRAPTURED	ENSHIELDED	ENTANGLING	ENTEROPNEUSTS	ENTHRONISATIONS
ENRAPTURES	ENSHIELDING	ENTELECHIES	ENTEROPTOSES	ENTHRONISE
ENRAPTURING	ENSHRINEES	ENTELLUSES	ENTEROPTOSIS	ENTHRONISED
ENRAUNGING	ENSHRINEMENT	ENTENDERED	ENTEROSTOMAL	ENTHRONISES
ENRAVISHED	ENSHRINEMENTS	ENTENDERING	ENTEROSTOMIES	ENTHRONISING
ENRAVISHES	ENSHRINING	ENTERCHAUNGE	ENTEROSTOMY	ENTHRONIZATION
ENRAVISHING	ENSHROUDED	ENTERCHAUNGED	ENTEROTOMIES	ENTHRONIZATIONS
ENREGIMENT	ENSHROUDING	ENTERCHAUNGES	ENTEROTOMY	ENTHRONIZE
ENREGIMENTED	ENSIGNCIES	ENTERCHAUNGING	ENTEROTOXIN	ENTHRONIZED
ENREGIMENTING	ENSIGNSHIP	ENTERDEALE	ENTEROTOXINS	ENTHRONIZES
ENREGIMENTS	ENSIGNSHIPS	ENTERDEALED	ENTEROVIRAL	ENTHRONIZING
ENREGISTER	ENSILABILITIES	ENTERDEALES	ENTEROVIRUS	ENTHUSIASM
ENREGISTERED	ENSILABILITY	ENTERDEALING	ENTEROVIRUSES	ENTHUSIASMS
ENREGISTERING	ENSILAGEING	ENTERECTOMIES	ENTERPRISE	ENTHUSIAST
ENREGISTERS	ENSILAGING	ENTERECTOMY	ENTERPRISED	ENTHUSIASTIC
ENRHEUMING	ENSLAVEMENT	ENTERITIDES	ENTERPRISER	ENTHUSIASTICAL
ENRICHMENT	ENSLAVEMENTS	ENTERITISES	ENTERPRISERS	ENTHUSIASTS
ENRICHMENTS	ENSNAREMENT	ENTEROBACTERIA	ENTERPRISES	ENTHYMEMATIC
ENROLLMENT	ENSNAREMENTS	ENTEROBACTERIAL	ENTERPRISING	ENTHYMEMATICAL
ENROLLMENTS	ENSNARLING	ENTEROBACTERIUM	ENTERPRISINGLY	ENTHYMEMES
ENROLMENTS	ENSORCELED	ENTEROBIASES	ENTERTAINED	ENTICEABLE
ENROUGHING	ENSORCELING	ENTEROBIASIS	ENTERTAINER	ENTICEMENT
ENROUNDING	ENSORCELLED	ENTEROCELE	ENTERTAINERS	ENTICEMENTS

ENTICINGLY	ENTOPLASTRAL	ENTREPRENEUR	ENVELOPERS	EOHIPPUSES
ENTICINGNESS	ENTOPLASTRON	ENTREPRENEURIAL	ENVELOPING	EOSINOPHIL
ENTICINGNESSES	ENTOPROCTS	ENTREPRENEURS	ENVELOPMENT	EOSINOPHILE
ENTIRENESS	ENTOURAGES	ENTREPRENEUSE	ENVELOPMENTS	EOSINOPHILES
ENTIRENESSES	ENTRAILING	ENTREPRENEUSES	ENVENOMING	EOSINOPHILIA
ENTIRETIES	ENTRAINEMENT	ENTROPICALLY	ENVENOMISATION	EOSINOPHILIAS
ENTITATIVE	ENTRAINEMENTS	ENTROPIONS	ENVENOMISATIONS	EOSINOPHILIC
ENTITLEMENT	ENTRAINERS	ENTROPIUMS	ENVENOMIZATION	EOSINOPHILOUS
ENTITLEMENTS	ENTRAINING	ENTRUSTING	ENVENOMIZATIONS	EOSINOPHILS
ENTOBLASTIC	ENTRAINMENT	ENTRUSTMENT	ENVERMEILED	EPAGOMENAL
ENTOBLASTS	ENTRAINMENTS	ENTRUSTMENTS	ENVERMEILING	EPANADIPLOSES
ENTODERMAL	ENTRAMMELED	ENTWINEMENT	ENVERMEILS	EPANADIPLOSIS
ENTODERMIC	ENTRAMMELING	ENTWINEMENTS	ENVIABLENESS	EPANALEPSES
ENTOILMENT	ENTRAMMELLED	ENTWISTING	ENVIABLENESSES	EPANALEPSIS
ENTOILMENTS	ENTRAMMELLING	ENUCLEATED	ENVIOUSNESS	EPANALEPTIC
ENTOMBMENT	ENTRAMMELS	ENUCLEATES	ENVIOUSNESSES	EPANAPHORA
ENTOMBMENTS	ENTRANCEMENT	ENUCLEATING	ENVIRONICS	EPANAPHORAL
ENTOMOFAUNA	ENTRANCEMENTS	ENUCLEATION	ENVIRONING	EPANAPHORAS
ENTOMOFAUNAE	ENTRANCEWAY	ENUCLEATIONS	ENVIRONMENT	EPANODOSES
ENTOMOFAUNAS	ENTRANCEWAYS	ENUMERABILITIES	ENVIRONMENTAL	EPANORTHOSES
ENTOMOLOGIC	ENTRANCING	ENUMERABILITY	ENVIRONMENTALLY	EPANORTHOSIS
ENTOMOLOGICAL	ENTRANCINGLY	ENUMERABLE	ENVIRONMENTS	EPANORTHOTIC
ENTOMOLOGICALLY	ENTRAPMENT	ENUMERATED	ENVISAGEMENT	EPARCHATES
ENTOMOLOGIES	ENTRAPMENTS	ENUMERATES	ENVISAGEMENTS	EPAULEMENT
ENTOMOLOGISE	ENTRAPPERS	ENUMERATING	ENVISAGING	EPAULEMENTS
ENTOMOLOGISED	ENTRAPPING	ENUMERATION	ENVISIONED	EPAULETTED
ENTOMOLOGISES	ENTREASURE	ENUMERATIONS	ENVISIONING	EPAULETTES
ENTOMOLOGISING	ENTREASURED	ENUMERATIVE	ENVOYSHIPS	EPEIROGENESES
ENTOMOLOGIST	ENTREASURES	ENUMERATOR	ENWALLOWED	EPEIROGENESIS
ENTOMOLOGISTS	ENTREASURING	ENUMERATORS	ENWALLOWING	EPEIROGENETIC
ENTOMOLOGIZE	ENTREATABLE	ENUNCIABLE	ENWHEELING	EPEIROGENIC
ENTOMOLOGIZED	ENTREATIES	ENUNCIATED	ENWRAPMENT	EPEIROGENICALLY
ENTOMOLOGIZES	ENTREATING	ENUNCIATES	ENWRAPMENTS	EPEIROGENIES
ENTOMOLOGIZING	ENTREATINGLY	ENUNCIATING	ENWRAPPING	EPEIROGENY
ENTOMOLOGY	ENTREATINGS	ENUNCIATION	ENWRAPPINGS	EPENCEPHALA
ENTOMOPHAGIES	ENTREATIVE	ENUNCIATIONS	ENWREATHED	EPENCEPHALIC
ENTOMOPHAGOUS	ENTREATMENT	ENUNCIATIVE	ENWREATHES	EPENCEPHALON
ENTOMOPHAGY	ENTREATMENTS	ENUNCIATIVELY	ENWREATHING	EPENCEPHALONS
ENTOMOPHILIES	ENTRECHATS	ENUNCIATOR	ENZOOTICALLY	EPENTHESES
ENTOMOPHILOUS	ENTRECOTES	ENUNCIATORS	ENZYMATICALLY	EPENTHESIS
ENTOMOPHILY	ENTREMESSE	ENUNCIATORY	ENZYMICALLY	EPENTHETIC
ENTOMOSTRACAN	ENTREMESSES	ENUREDNESS	ENZYMOLOGICAL	EPEOLATRIES
ENTOMOSTRACANS	ENTRENCHED	ENUREDNESSES	ENZYMOLOGIES	EPEXEGESES
ENTOMOSTRACOUS	ENTRENCHER	ENUREMENTS	ENZYMOLOGIST	EPEXEGESIS
ENTOPHYTAL	ENTRENCHERS	ENURESISES	ENZYMOLOGISTS	EPEXEGETIC
ENTOPHYTES	ENTRENCHES	ENVASSALLED	ENZYMOLOGY	EPEXEGETICAL
ENTOPHYTIC	ENTRENCHING	ENVASSALLING	ENZYMOLYSES	EPEXEGETICALLY
ENTOPHYTOUS	ENTRENCHMENT	ENVAULTING	ENZYMOLYSIS	EPHEBOPHILE
ENTOPLASTRA	ENTRENCHMENTS	ENVEIGLING	ENZYMOLYTIC	EPHEBOPHILES

E

EPHEBOPHILIA	EPICURISES	EPIGASTRIA	EPIGRAPHISTS	EPINEURIUMS
EPHEBOPHILIAS	EPICURISING	EPIGASTRIAL	EPILATIONS	EPINICIONS
EPHEDRINES	EPICURISMS	EPIGASTRIC	EPILEPSIES	EPINIKIANS
EPHEMERALITIES	EPICURIZED	EPIGASTRIUM	EPILEPTICAL	EPINIKIONS
EPHEMERALITY	EPICURIZES	EPIGENESES	EPILEPTICALLY	EPIPELAGIC
EPHEMERALLY	EPICURIZING	EPIGENESIS	EPILEPTICS	EPIPETALOUS
EPHEMERALNESS	EPICUTICLE	EPIGENESIST	EPILEPTIFORM	EPIPHANIES
EPHEMERALNESSES	EPICUTICLES	EPIGENESISTS	EPILEPTOGENIC	EPIPHANOUS
EPHEMERALS	EPICUTICULAR	EPIGENETIC	EPILEPTOID	EPIPHENOMENA
EPHEMERIDES	EPICYCLICAL	EPIGENETICALLY	EPILIMNION	EPIPHENOMENAL
EPHEMERIDIAN	EPICYCLOID	EPIGENETICIST	EPILIMNIONS	EPIPHENOMENALLY
EPHEMERIDS	EPICYCLOIDAL	EPIGENETICISTS	EPILOBIUMS	EPIPHENOMENON
EPHEMERIST	EPICYCLOIDS	EPIGENETICS	EPILOGISED	EPIPHONEMA
EPHEMERISTS	EPIDEICTIC	EPIGENISTS	EPILOGISES	EPIPHONEMAS
EPHEMERONS	EPIDEICTICAL	EPIGENOMES	EPILOGISING	EPIPHRAGMS
EPHEMEROPTERAN	EPIDEMICAL	EPIGLOTTAL	EPILOGISTIC	EPIPHYLLOUS
EPHEMEROPTERANS	EPIDEMICALLY	EPIGLOTTIC	EPILOGISTS	EPIPHYSEAL
EPHEMEROUS	EPIDEMICITIES	EPIGLOTTIDES	EPILOGIZED	EPIPHYSIAL
EPHORALTIES	EPIDEMICITY	EPIGLOTTIS	EPILOGIZES	EPIPHYTICAL
EPIBLASTIC	EPIDEMIOLOGIC	EPIGLOTTISES	EPILOGIZING	EPIPHYTICALLY
EPICALYCES	EPIDEMIOLOGICAL	EPIGNATHOUS	EPILOGUING	EPIPHYTISM
EPICALYXES	EPIDEMIOLOGIES	EPIGONISMS	EPILOGUISE	EPIPHYTISMS
EPICANTHIC	EPIDEMIOLOGIST	EPIGRAMMATIC	EPILOGUISED	EPIPHYTOLOGIES
EPICANTHUS	EPIDEMIOLOGISTS	EPIGRAMMATICAL	EPILOGUISES	EPIPHYTOLOGY
EPICARDIAC	EPIDEMIOLOGY	EPIGRAMMATISE	EPILOGUISING	EPIPHYTOTIC
EPICARDIAL	EPIDENDRONE	EPIGRAMMATISED	EPILOGUIZE	EPIPHYTOTICS
EPICARDIUM	EPIDENDRONES	EPIGRAMMATISER	EPILOGUIZED	EPIPLASTRA
EPICARDIUMS	EPIDENDRUM	EPIGRAMMATISERS	EPILOGUIZES	EPIPLASTRAL
EPICEDIANS	EPIDENDRUMS	EPIGRAMMATISES	EPILOGUIZING	EPIPLASTRON
EPICENISMS	EPIDERMISES	EPIGRAMMATISING	EPIMELETIC	EPIPOLISMS
EPICENTERS	EPIDERMOID	EPIGRAMMATISM	EPIMERASES	EPIROGENETIC
EPICENTRAL	EPIDERMOLYSES	EPIGRAMMATISMS	EPIMERISED	EPIROGENIC
EPICENTRES	EPIDERMOLYSIS	EPIGRAMMATIST	EPIMERISES	EPIROGENIES
EPICENTRUM	EPIDIASCOPE	EPIGRAMMATISTS	EPIMERISING	EPIRRHEMAS
EPICHEIREMA	EPIDIASCOPES	EPIGRAMMATIZE	EPIMERISMS	EPIRRHEMATA
EPICHEIREMAS	EPIDIDYMAL	EPIGRAMMATIZED	EPIMERIZED	EPIRRHEMATIC
EPICHEIREMATA	EPIDIDYMIDES	EPIGRAMMATIZER	EPIMERIZES	EPISCOPACIES
EPICHLOROHYDRIN	EPIDIDYMIS	EPIGRAMMATIZERS	EPIMERIZING	EPISCOPACY
EPICONDYLE	EPIDIDYMITIS	EPIGRAMMATIZES	EPIMORPHIC	EPISCOPALIAN
EPICONDYLES	EPIDIDYMITISES	EPIGRAMMATIZING	EPIMORPHOSES	EPISCOPALIANISM
EPICONDYLITIS	EPIDIORITE	EPIGRAPHED	EPIMORPHOSIS	EPISCOPALIANS
EPICONDYLITISES	EPIDIORITES	EPIGRAPHER	EPINASTICALLY	EPISCOPALISM
EPICONTINENTAL	EPIDOSITES	EPIGRAPHERS	EPINASTIES	EPISCOPALISMS
EPICRANIUM	EPIDOTISATION	EPIGRAPHIC	EPINEPHRIN	EPISCOPALLY
EPICRANIUMS	EPIDOTISATIONS	EPIGRAPHICAL	EPINEPHRINE	EPISCOPANT
EPICUREANISM	EPIDOTISED	EPIGRAPHICALLY	EPINEPHRINES	EPISCOPANTS
EPICUREANISMS	EPIDOTIZATION	EPIGRAPHIES	EPINEPHRINS	EPISCOPATE
EPICUREANS	EPIDOTIZATIONS	EPIGRAPHING	EPINEURIAL	EPISCOPATED
EPICURISED	EPIDOTIZED	EPIGRAPHIST	EPINEURIUM	EPISCOPATES

EPISCOPATING	EPISTOLIZES	EPITHETING	EQUALISATION	EQUILIBRATE
EPISCOPIES	EPISTOLIZING	EPITHETONS	EQUALISATIONS	EQUILIBRATED
EPISCOPISE	EPISTOLOGRAPHY	EPITHYMETIC	EQUALISERS	EQUILIBRATES
EPISCOPISED	EPISTROPHE	EPITOMICAL	EQUALISING	EQUILIBRATING
EPISCOPISES	EPISTROPHES	EPITOMISATION	EQUALITARIAN	EQUILIBRATION
EPISCOPISING	EPITAPHERS	EPITOMISATIONS	EQUALITARIANISM	EQUILIBRATIONS
EPISCOPIZE	EPITAPHIAL	EPITOMISED	EQUALITARIANS	EQUILIBRATOR
EPISCOPIZED	EPITAPHIAN	EPITOMISER	EQUALITIES	EQUILIBRATORS
EPISCOPIZES	EPITAPHING	EPITOMISERS	EQUALIZATION	EQUILIBRATORY
EPISCOPIZING	EPITAPHIST	EPITOMISES	EQUALIZATIONS	EQUILIBRIA
EPISEMATIC	EPITAPHISTS	EPITOMISING	EQUALIZERS	EQUILIBRIST
EPISEPALOUS	EPITAXIALLY	EPITOMISTS	EQUALIZING	EQUILIBRISTIC
EPISIOTOMIES	EPITHALAMIA	EPITOMIZATION	EQUALNESSES	EQUILIBRISTS
EPISIOTOMY	EPITHALAMIC	EPITOMIZATIONS	EQUANIMITIES	EQUILIBRITIES
EPISODICAL	EPITHALAMION	EPITOMIZED	EQUANIMITY	EQUILIBRITY
EPISODICALLY	EPITHALAMIUM	EPITOMIZER	EQUANIMOUS	EQUILIBRIUM
EPISOMALLY	EPITHALAMIUMS	EPITOMIZERS	EQUANIMOUSLY	EQUILIBRIUMS
EPISPASTIC	EPITHELIAL	EPITOMIZES	EQUATABILITIES	EQUIMOLECULAR
EPISPASTICS	EPITHELIALISE	EPITOMIZING	EQUATABILITY	EQUIMULTIPLE
EPISTASIES	EPITHELIALISED	EPITRACHELION	EQUATIONAL	EQUIMULTIPLES
EPISTAXISES	EPITHELIALISES	EPITRACHELIONS	EQUATIONALLY	EQUINITIES
EPISTEMICALLY	EPITHELIALISING	EPITROCHOID	EQUATORIAL	EQUINOCTIAL
EPISTEMICS	EPITHELIALIZE	EPITROCHOIDS	EQUATORIALLY	EQUINOCTIALLY
EPISTEMOLOGICAL	EPITHELIALIZED	EPIZEUXISES	EQUATORIALS	EQUINOCTIALS
EPISTEMOLOGIES	EPITHELIALIZES	EPIZOOTICALLY	EQUATORWARD	EQUINUMEROUS
EPISTEMOLOGIST	EPITHELIALIZING	EPIZOOTICS	EQUESTRIAN	EQUIPAGING
EPISTEMOLOGISTS	EPITHELIOID	EPIZOOTIES	EQUESTRIANISM	EQUIPARATE
EPISTEMOLOGY	EPITHELIOMA	EPIZOOTIOLOGIC	EQUESTRIANISMS	EQUIPARATED
EPISTERNAL	EPITHELIOMAS	EPIZOOTIOLOGIES	EQUESTRIANS	EQUIPARATES
EPISTERNUM	EPITHELIOMATA	EPIZOOTIOLOGY	EQUESTRIENNE	EQUIPARATING
EPISTERNUMS	EPITHELIOMATOUS	EPONYCHIUM	EQUESTRIENNES	EQUIPARATION
EPISTILBITE	EPITHELISATION	EPONYCHIUMS	EQUIANGULAR	EQUIPARATIONS
EPISTILBITES	EPITHELISATIONS	EPONYMOUSLY	EQUIANGULARITY	EQUIPARTITION
EPISTOLARIAN	EPITHELISE	EPOXIDATION	EQUIBALANCE	EQUIPARTITIONS
EPISTOLARIANS	EPITHELISED	EPOXIDATIONS	EQUIBALANCED	EQUIPMENTS
EPISTOLARIES	EPITHELISES	EPOXIDISED	EQUIBALANCES	EQUIPOISED
EPISTOLARY	EPITHELISING	EPOXIDISES	EQUIBALANCING	EQUIPOISES
EPISTOLATORY	EPITHELIUM	EPOXIDISING	EQUICALORIC	EQUIPOISING
EPISTOLERS	EPITHELIUMS	EPOXIDIZED	EQUIDIFFERENT	EQUIPOLLENCE
EPISTOLETS	EPITHELIZATION	EPOXIDIZES	EQUIDISTANCE	EQUIPOLLENCES
EPISTOLICAL	EPITHELIZATIONS	EPOXIDIZING	EQUIDISTANCES	EQUIPOLLENCIES
EPISTOLISE	EPITHELIZE	EPROUVETTE	EQUIDISTANT	EQUIPOLLENCY
EPISTOLISED	EPITHELIZED	EPROUVETTES	EQUIDISTANTLY	EQUIPOLLENT
EPISTOLISES	EPITHELIZES	EPULATIONS	EQUIFINALLY	EQUIPOLLENTLY
EPISTOLISING	EPITHELIZING	EPURATIONS	EQUILATERAL	EQUIPOLLENTS
EPISTOLIST	EPITHEMATA	EQUABILITIES	EQUILATERALLY	EQUIPONDERANCE
EPISTOLISTS	EPITHERMAL	EQUABILITY	EQUILATERALS	EQUIPONDERANCES
EPISTOLIZE	EPITHETICAL	EQUABLENESS	EQUILIBRANT	EQUIPONDERANCY
EPISTOLIZED	EPITHETICALLY	EQUABLENESSES	EQUILIBRANTS	EQUIPONDERANT

EQUIPONDERATE	ERADICATED	ERGONOVINES	EROTOLOGIES	ERYTHREMIA
EQUIPONDERATED	ERADICATES	ERGOPHOBIA	EROTOLOGIST	ERYTHREMIAS
EQUIPONDERATES	ERADICATING	ERGOPHOBIAS	EROTOLOGISTS	ERYTHRINAS
EQUIPONDERATING	ERADICATION	ERGOSTEROL	EROTOMANIA	ERYTHRISMAL
EQUIPOTENT	ERADICATIONS	ERGOSTEROLS	EROTOMANIAC	ERYTHRISMS
EQUIPOTENTIAL	ERADICATIVE	ERGOTAMINE	EROTOMANIACS	ERYTHRISTIC
EQUIPOTENTIALS	ERADICATOR	ERGOTAMINES	EROTOMANIAS	ERYTHRITES
EQUIPROBABILITY	ERADICATORS	ERGOTISING	EROTOPHOBIA	ERYTHRITIC
EQUIPROBABLE	ERASABILITIES	ERGOTIZING	EROTOPHOBIAS	ERYTHRITOL
EQUISETACEOUS	ERASABILITY	ERICACEOUS	ERRANTRIES	ERYTHRITOLS
EQUISETIFORM	ERASEMENTS	ERINACEOUS	ERRATICALLY	ERYTHROBLAST
EQUISETUMS	ERECTILITIES	ERIOMETERS	ERRATICISM	ERYTHROBLASTIC
EQUITABILITIES	ERECTILITY	ERIOPHOROUS	ERRATICISMS	ERYTHROBLASTS
EQUITABILITY	ERECTNESSES	ERIOPHORUM	ERRONEOUSLY	ERYTHROCYTE
EQUITABLENESS	EREMACAUSES	ERIOPHORUMS	ERRONEOUSNESS	ERYTHROCYTES
EQUITABLENESSES	EREMACAUSIS	ERIOPHYIDS	ERRONEOUSNESSES	ERYTHROCYTIC
EQUITATION	EREMITICAL	ERIOSTEMON	ERUBESCENCE	ERYTHROMELALGIA
EQUITATIONS	EREMITISMS	ERIOSTEMONS	ERUBESCENCES	ERYTHROMYCIN
EQUIVALENCE	EREMURUSES	ERISTICALLY	ERUBESCENCIES	ERYTHROMYCINS
EQUIVALENCES	ERETHISMIC	ERODABILITIES	ERUBESCENCY	ERYTHRONIUM
EQUIVALENCIES	ERETHISTIC	ERODABILITY	ERUBESCENT	ERYTHRONIUMS
EQUIVALENCY	ERGASTOPLASM	ERODIBILITIES	ERUBESCITE	ERYTHROPENIA
EQUIVALENT	ERGASTOPLASMIC	ERODIBILITY	ERUBESCITES	ERYTHROPENIAS
EQUIVALENTLY	ERGASTOPLASMS	EROGENEITIES	ERUCTATING	ERYTHROPHOBIA
EQUIVALENTS	ERGATANDROMORPH	EROGENEITY	ERUCTATION	ERYTHROPHOBIAS
EQUIVOCACIES	ERGATANERS	EROSIONALLY	ERUCTATIONS	ERYTHROPOIESES
EQUIVOCACY	ERGATIVITIES	EROSIVENESS	ERUCTATIVE	ERYTHROPOIESIS
EQUIVOCALITIES	ERGATIVITY	EROSIVENESSES	ERUDITENESS	ERYTHROPOIETIC
EQUIVOCALITY	ERGATOCRACIES	EROSIVITIES	ERUDITENESSES	ERYTHROPOIETIN
EQUIVOCALLY	ERGATOCRACY	EROTICALLY	ERUDITIONS	ERYTHROPOIETINS
EQUIVOCALNESS	ERGATOGYNE	EROTICISATION	ERUPTIONAL	ERYTHROPSIA
EQUIVOCALNESSES	ERGATOGYNES	EROTICISATIONS	ERUPTIVELY	ERYTHROPSIAS
EQUIVOCATE	ERGATOMORPH	EROTICISED	ERUPTIVENESS	ERYTHROSIN
EQUIVOCATED	ERGATOMORPHIC	EROTICISES	ERUPTIVENESSES	ERYTHROSINE
EQUIVOCATES	ERGATOMORPHS	EROTICISING	ERUPTIVITIES	ERYTHROSINES
EQUIVOCATING	ERGODICITIES	EROTICISMS	ERUPTIVITY	ERYTHROSINS
EQUIVOCATINGLY	ERGODICITY	EROTICISTS	ERVALENTAS	ERYTHROSINS
EQUIVOCATION	ERGOGRAPHS	EROTICIZATION	ERYSIPELAS	ESCABECHES
EQUIVOCATIONS	ERGOMANIAC	EROTICIZATIONS	ERYSIPELASES	ESCADRILLE
EQUIVOCATOR	ERGOMANIACS	EROTICIZED	ERYSIPELATOUS	ESCADRILLES
EQUIVOCATORS	ERGOMANIAS	EROTICIZES	ERYSIPELOID	ESCALADERS
EQUIVOCATORY	ERGOMETERS	EROTICIZING	ERYSIPELOIDS	ESCALADING
EQUIVOQUES	ERGOMETRIC	EROTISATION	ERYTHEMATIC	ESCALADOES
ERADIATING	ERGOMETRIES	EROTISATIONS	ERYTHEMATOUS	ESCALATING
ERADIATION	ERGONOMICALLY	EROTIZATION	ERYTHORBATE	ESCALATION
ERADIATIONS	ERGONOMICS	EROTIZATIONS	ERYTHORBATES	ESCALATIONS
ERADICABLE	ERGONOMIST	EROTOGENIC	ERYTHORBIC	ESCALATORS
ERADICABLY	ERGONOMISTS	EROTOGENOUS	ERYTHRAEMIA	ESCALATORY
ERADICANTS	ERGONOVINE	EROTOLOGICAL	ERYTHRAEMIAS	ESCALLONIA
				ESCALLONIAS

ESCALLOPED	ESOPHAGEAL	ESSENTIALNESS	ESTIMATIONS	ETERNALIZES
ESCALLOPING	ESOPHAGITIDES	ESSENTIALNESSES	ESTIMATIVE	ETERNALIZING
ESCALOPING	ESOPHAGITIS	ESSENTIALS	ESTIMATORS	ETERNALNESS
ESCAMOTAGE	ESOPHAGITISES	ESTABLISHABLE	ESTIPULATE	ETERNALNESSES
ESCAMOTAGES	ESOPHAGOSCOPE	ESTABLISHED	ESTIVATING	ETERNISATION
ESCAPADOES	ESOPHAGOSCOPES	ESTABLISHER	ESTIVATION	ETERNISATIONS
ESCAPELESS	ESOPHAGOSCOPIES	ESTABLISHERS	ESTIVATIONS	ETERNISING
ESCAPEMENT	ESOPHAGOSCOPY	ESTABLISHES	ESTIVATORS	ETERNITIES
ESCAPEMENTS	ESOPHAGUSES	ESTABLISHING	ESTOPPAGES	ETERNIZATION
ESCAPOLOGIES	ESOTERICALLY	ESTABLISHMENT	ESTRADIOLS	ETERNIZATIONS
ESCAPOLOGIST	ESOTERICAS	ESTABLISHMENTS	ESTRAMAZONE	ETERNIZING
ESCAPOLOGISTS	ESOTERICISM	ESTAFETTES	ESTRAMAZONES	ETHAMBUTOL
ESCAPOLOGY	ESOTERICISMS	ESTAMINETS	ESTRANGEDNESS	ETHAMBUTOLS
ESCARMOUCHE	ESOTERICIST	ESTANCIERO	ESTRANGEDNESSES	ETHANEDIOIC
ESCARMOUCHES	ESOTERICISTS	ESTANCIEROS	ESTRANGELO	ETHANEDIOL
ESCARPMENT	ESOTERISMS	ESTATESMAN	ESTRANGELOS	ETHANEDIOLS
ESCARPMENTS	ESOTROPIAS	ESTATESMEN	ESTRANGEMENT	ETHANOATES
ESCHAROTIC	ESPADRILLE	ESTERIFICATION	ESTRANGEMENTS	ETHANOLAMINE
ESCHAROTICS	ESPADRILLES	ESTERIFICATIONS	ESTRANGERS	ETHANOLAMINES
ESCHATOLOGIC	ESPAGNOLES	ESTERIFIED	ESTRANGHELO	ETHEOSTOMINE
ESCHATOLOGICAL	ESPAGNOLETTE	ESTERIFIES	ESTRANGHELOS	ETHEREALISATION
ESCHATOLOGIES	ESPAGNOLETTES	ESTERIFYING	ESTRANGING	ETHEREALISE
ESCHATOLOGIST	ESPALIERED	ESTERISATION	ESTRAPADES	ETHEREALISED
ESCHATOLOGISTS	ESPALIERING	ESTERISATIONS	ESTREATING	ETHEREALISES
ESCHATOLOGY	ESPECIALLY	ESTERIZATION	ESTREPEMENT	ETHEREALISING
ESCHEATABLE	ESPERANCES	ESTERIZATIONS	ESTREPEMENTS	ETHEREALITIES
ESCHEATAGE	ESPIEGLERIE	ESTHESIOGEN	ESTRIBUTOR	ETHEREALITY
ESCHEATAGES	ESPIEGLERIES	ESTHESIOGENS	ESTRIBUTORS	ETHEREALIZATION
ESCHEATING	ESPIONAGES	ESTHESISES	ESTRILDIDS	ETHEREALIZE
ESCHEATMENT	ESPLANADES	ESTHETICAL	ESTROGENIC	ETHEREALIZED
ESCHEATMENTS	ESPRESSIVO	ESTHETICALLY	ESTROGENICALLY	ETHEREALIZES
ESCHEATORS	ESQUIRESSES	ESTHETICIAN	ESURIENCES	ETHEREALIZING
ESCHSCHOLTZIA	ESSAYETTES	ESTHETICIANS	ESURIENCIES	ETHEREALLY
ESCHSCHOLTZIAS	ESSAYISTIC	ESTHETICISE	ESURIENTLY	ETHEREALNESS
ESCHSCHOLZIA	ESSENTIALISE	ESTHETICISED	ETEPIMELETIC	ETHEREALNESSES
ESCHSCHOLZIAS	ESSENTIALISED	ESTHETICISES	ETERNALISATION	ETHERIFICATION
ESCLANDRES	ESSENTIALISES	ESTHETICISING	ETERNALISATIONS	ETHERIFICATIONS
ESCOPETTES	ESSENTIALISING	ESTHETICISM	ETERNALISE	ETHERIFIED
ESCORTAGES	ESSENTIALISM	ESTHETICISMS	ETERNALISED	ETHERIFIES
ESCRIBANOS	ESSENTIALISMS	ESTHETICIST	ETERNALISES	ETHERIFYING
ESCRITOIRE	ESSENTIALIST	ESTHETICISTS	ETERNALISING	ETHERISATION
ESCRITOIRES	ESSENTIALISTS	ESTHETICIZE	ETERNALIST	ETHERISATIONS
ESCRITORIAL	ESSENTIALITIES	ESTHETICIZED	ETERNALISTS	ETHERISERS
ESCUTCHEON	ESSENTIALITY	ESTHETICIZES	ETERNALITIES	ETHERISING
ESCUTCHEONED	ESSENTIALIZE	ESTHETICIZING	ETERNALITY	ETHERIZATION
ESCUTCHEONS	ESSENTIALIZED	ESTIMABLENESS	ETERNALIZATION	ETHERIZATIONS
ESEMPLASIES	ESSENTIALIZES	ESTIMABLENESSES	ETERNALIZATIONS	ETHERIZERS
ESEMPLASTIC	ESSENTIALIZING	ESTIMATING	ETERNALIZE	ETHERIZING
ESEMPLASTICALLY	ESSENTIALLY	ESTIMATION	ETERNALIZED	ETHEROMANIA

E

ETHEROMANIAC	ETHNOLINGUISTS	ETYMOLOGISED	EUDEMONISTIC	EUNUCHISES
ETHEROMANIACS	ETHNOLOGIC	ETYMOLOGISES	EUDEMONISTICAL	EUNUCHISING
ETHEROMANIAS	ETHNOLOGICAL	ETYMOLOGISING	EUDEMONISTS	EUNUCHISMS
ETHICALITIES	ETHNOLOGICALLY	ETYMOLOGIST	EUDIALYTES	EUNUCHIZED
ETHICALITY	ETHNOLOGIES	ETYMOLOGISTS	EUDICOTYLEDON	EUNUCHIZES
ETHICALNESS	ETHNOLOGIST	ETYMOLOGIZE	EUDICOTYLEDONS	EUNUCHIZING
ETHICALNESSES	ETHNOLOGISTS	ETYMOLOGIZED	EUDIOMETER	EUNUCHOIDISM
ETHICISING	ETHNOMEDICINE	ETYMOLOGIZES	EUDIOMETERS	EUNUCHOIDISMS
ETHICIZING	ETHNOMEDICINES	ETYMOLOGIZING	EUDIOMETRIC	EUNUCHOIDS
ETHIONAMIDE	ETHNOMUSICOLOGY	EUBACTERIA	EUDIOMETRICAL	EUONYMUSES
ETHIONAMIDES	ETHNOSCIENCE	EUBACTERIUM	EUDIOMETRICALLY	EUPATORIUM
ETHIONINES	ETHNOSCIENCES	EUCALYPTOL	EUDIOMETRIES	EUPATORIUMS
ETHNARCHIES	ETHNOSTATE	EUCALYPTOLE	EUDIOMETRY	EUPATRIDAE
ETHNICALLY	ETHNOSTATES	EUCALYPTOLES	EUGENECIST	EUPEPTICITIES
ETHNICISMS	ETHOLOGICAL	EUCALYPTOLS	EUGENECISTS	EUPEPTICITY
ETHNICITIES	ETHOLOGICALLY	EUCALYPTUS	EUGENICALLY	EUPHAUSIACEAN
ETHNOBIOLOGIES	ETHOLOGIES	EUCALYPTUSES	EUGENICIST	EUPHAUSIACEANS
ETHNOBIOLOGY	ETHOLOGIST	EUCARYOTES	EUGENICISTS	EUPHAUSIDS
ETHNOBOTANICAL	ETHOLOGISTS	EUCARYOTIC	EUGEOSYNCLINAL	EUPHAUSIID
ETHNOBOTANIES	ETHOXYETHANE	EUCHARISES	EUGEOSYNCLINE	EUPHAUSIIDS
ETHNOBOTANIST	ETHOXYETHANES	EUCHARISTIC	EUGEOSYNCLINES	EUPHEMISED
ETHNOBOTANISTS	ETHYLAMINE	EUCHLORINE	EUGLENOIDS	EUPHEMISER
ETHNOBOTANY	ETHYLAMINES	EUCHLORINES	EUGLOBULIN	EUPHEMISERS
ETHNOCENTRIC	ETHYLATING	EUCHLORINS	EUGLOBULINS	EUPHEMISES
ETHNOCENTRICITY	ETHYLATION	EUCHOLOGIA	EUHARMONIC	EUPHEMISING
ETHNOCENTRISM	ETHYLATIONS	EUCHOLOGIES	EUHEMERISE	EUPHEMISMS
ETHNOCENTRISMS	ETHYLBENZENE	EUCHOLOGION	EUHEMERISED	EUPHEMISTIC
ETHNOCIDES	ETHYLBENZENES	EUCHROMATIC	EUHEMERISES	EUPHEMISTICALLY
ETHNOCRACIES	ETIOLATING	EUCHROMATIN	EUHEMERISING	EUPHEMISTS
ETHNOCRACY	ETIOLATION	EUCHROMATINS	EUHEMERISM	EUPHEMIZED
ETHNOGENIC	ETIOLATIONS	EUCRYPHIAS	EUHEMERISMS	EUPHEMIZER
ETHNOGENIES	ETIOLOGICAL	EUDAEMONIA	EUHEMERIST	EUPHEMIZERS
ETHNOGENIST	ETIOLOGICALLY	EUDAEMONIAS	EUHEMERISTIC	EUPHEMIZES
ETHNOGENISTS	ETIOLOGIES	EUDAEMONIC	EUHEMERISTS	EUPHEMIZING
ETHNOGRAPHER	ETIOLOGIST	EUDAEMONICS	EUHEMERIZE	EUPHONICAL
ETHNOGRAPHERS	ETIOLOGISTS	EUDAEMONIES	EUHEMERIZED	EUPHONICALLY
ETHNOGRAPHIC	ETIQUETTES	EUDAEMONISM	EUHEMERIZES	EUPHONIOUS
ETHNOGRAPHICA	ETONOGESTREL	EUDAEMONISMS	EUHEMERIZING	EUPHONIOUSLY
ETHNOGRAPHICAL	ETONOGESTRELS	EUDAEMONIST	EUKARYOTES	EUPHONIOUSNESS
ETHNOGRAPHIES	ETOURDERIE	EUDAEMONISTIC	EUKARYOTIC	EUPHONISED
ETHNOGRAPHY	ETOURDERIES	EUDAEMONISTICAL	EULOGISERS	EUPHONISES
ETHNOHISTORIAN	ETRANGERES	EUDAEMONISTS	EULOGISING	EUPHONISING
ETHNOHISTORIANS	ETYMOLOGICA	EUDAIMONISM	EULOGISTIC	EUPHONISMS
ETHNOHISTORIC	ETYMOLOGICAL	EUDAIMONISMS	EULOGISTICAL	EUPHONIUMS
ETHNOHISTORICAL	ETYMOLOGICALLY	EUDEMONIAS	EULOGISTICALLY	EUPHONIZED
ETHNOHISTORIES	ETYMOLOGICON	EUDEMONICS	EULOGIZERS	EUPHONIZES
ETHNOHISTORY	ETYMOLOGICUM	EUDEMONISM	EULOGIZING	EUPHONIZING
ETHNOLINGUIST	ETYMOLOGIES	EUDEMONISMS	EUMELANINS	EUPHORBIACEOUS
ETHNOLINGUISTIC	ETYMOLOGISE	EUDEMONIST	EUNUCHISED	EUPHORBIAS

EUPHORBIUM	EURYTHERMIC	EVACUATIONS	EVANGELIST	EVENTRATES
EUPHORBIUMS	EURYTHERMOUS	EVACUATIVE	EVANGELISTARIES	EVENTRATING
EUPHORIANT	EURYTHERMS	EVACUATIVES	EVANGELISTARION	EVENTRATION
EUPHORIANTS	EURYTHMICAL	EVACUATORS	EVANGELISTARY	EVENTRATIONS
EUPHORICALLY	EURYTHMICS	EVAGATIONS	EVANGELISTIC	EVENTUALISE
EUPHRASIAS	EURYTHMIES	EVAGINATED	EVANGELISTS	EVENTUALISED
EUPHRASIES	EURYTHMIST	EVAGINATES	EVANGELIZATION	EVENTUALISES
EUPHUISING	EURYTHMISTS	EVAGINATING	EVANGELIZATIONS	EVENTUALISING
EUPHUISTIC	EUSPORANGIATE	EVAGINATION	EVANGELIZE	EVENTUALITIES
EUPHUISTICAL	EUSTATICALLY	EVAGINATIONS	EVANGELIZED	EVENTUALITY
EUPHUISTICALLY	EUSTRESSES	EVALUATING	EVANGELIZER	EVENTUALIZE
EUPHUIZING	EUTECTOIDS	EVALUATION	EVANGELIZERS	EVENTUALIZED
EUPLASTICS	EUTHANASED	EVALUATIONS	EVANGELIZES	EVENTUALIZES
EUPLOIDIES	EUTHANASES	EVALUATIVE	EVANGELIZING	EVENTUALIZING
EURHYTHMIC	EUTHANASIA	EVALUATORS	EVANISHING	EVENTUALLY
EURHYTHMICAL	EUTHANASIAS	EVANESCENCE	EVANISHMENT	EVENTUATED
EURHYTHMICS	EUTHANASIAST	EVANESCENCES	EVANISHMENTS	EVENTUATES
EURHYTHMIES	EUTHANASIASTS	EVANESCENT	EVANITIONS	EVENTUATING
EURHYTHMIST	EUTHANASIC	EVANESCENTLY	EVAPORABILITIES	EVENTUATION
EURHYTHMISTS	EUTHANASIES	EVANESCING	EVAPORABILITY	EVENTUATIONS
EUROCHEQUE	EUTHANASING	EVANGELARIUM	EVAPORABLE	EVERBLOOMING
EUROCHEQUES	EUTHANATISE	EVANGELARIUMS	EVAPORATED	EVERDURING
EUROCREDIT	EUTHANATISED	EVANGELIAR	EVAPORATES	EVERGLADES
EUROCREDITS	EUTHANATISES	EVANGELIARIES	EVAPORATING	EVERGREENS
EUROCREEPS	EUTHANATISING	EVANGELIARION	EVAPORATION	EVERLASTING
EUROCURRENCIES	EUTHANATIZE	EVANGELIARIONS	EVAPORATIONS	EVERLASTINGLY
EUROCURRENCY	EUTHANATIZED	EVANGELIARIUM	EVAPORATIVE	EVERLASTINGNESS
EURODEPOSIT	EUTHANATIZES	EVANGELIARIUMS	EVAPORATOR	EVERLASTINGS
EURODEPOSITS	EUTHANATIZING	EVANGELIARS	EVAPORATORS	EVERYDAYNESS
EURODOLLAR	EUTHANAZED	EVANGELIARY	EVAPORIMETER	EVERYDAYNESSES
EURODOLLARS	EUTHANAZES	EVANGELICAL	EVAPORIMETERS	EVERYPLACE
EUROMARKET	EUTHANAZING	EVANGELICALISM	EVAPORITES	EVERYTHING
EUROMARKETS	EUTHANISED	EVANGELICALISMS	EVAPORITIC	EVERYWHENCE
EUROPHILES	EUTHANISES	EVANGELICALLY	EVAPOROGRAPH	EVERYWHERE
EUROPHILIA	EUTHANISING	EVANGELICALNESS	EVAPOROGRAPHS	EVERYWHITHER
EUROPHILIAS	EUTHANIZED	EVANGELICALS	EVAPOROMETER	EVERYWOMAN
EUROPHOBIA	EUTHANIZES	EVANGELICISM	EVAPOROMETERS	EVERYWOMEN
EUROPHOBIAS	EUTHANIZING	EVANGELICISMS	EVASIVENESS	EVIDENCING
EUROPHOBIC	EUTHENISTS	EVANGELIES	EVASIVENESSES	EVIDENTIAL
EUROTERMINAL	EUTHERIANS	EVANGELISATION	EVECTIONAL	EVIDENTIALLY
EUROTERMINALS	EUTHYROIDS	EVANGELISATIONS	EVENEMENTS	EVIDENTIARY
EURYBATHIC	EUTRAPELIA	EVANGELISE	EVENHANDED	EVILDOINGS
EURYHALINE	EUTRAPELIAS	EVANGELISED	EVENHANDEDLY	EVILNESSES
EURYOECIOUS	EUTRAPELIES	EVANGELISER	EVENHANDEDNESS	EVINCEMENT
EURYPTERID	EUTROPHICATION	EVANGELISERS	EVENNESSES	EVINCEMENTS
EURYPTERIDS	EUTROPHICATIONS	EVANGELISES	EVENTFULLY	EVISCERATE
EURYPTEROID	EUTROPHIES	EVANGELISING	EVENTFULNESS	EVISCERATED
EURYPTEROIDS	EVACUATING	EVANGELISM	EVENTFULNESSES	EVISCERATES
EURYTHERMAL	EVACUATION	EVANGELISMS	EVENTRATED	EVISCERATING

EVISCERATION	EXAGGERATIONS	EXCARNATING	EXCISIONAL	EXCOGITABLE
EVISCERATIONS	EXAGGERATIVE	EXCARNATION	EXCITABILITIES	EXCOGITATE
EVISCERATOR	EXAGGERATOR	EXCARNATIONS	EXCITABILITY	EXCOGITATED
EVISCERATORS	EXAGGERATORS	EXCAVATING	EXCITABLENESS	EXCOGITATES
EVITATIONS	EXAGGERATORY	EXCAVATION	EXCITABLENESSES	EXCOGITATING
EVITERNALLY	EXAHERTZES	EXCAVATIONAL	EXCITANCIES	EXCOGITATION
EVITERNITIES	EXALBUMINOUS	EXCAVATIONS	EXCITATION	EXCOGITATIONS
EVITERNITY	EXALTATION	EXCAVATORS	EXCITATIONS	EXCOGITATIVE
EVOCATIONS	EXALTATIONS	EXCEEDABLE	EXCITATIVE	EXCOGITATOR
EVOCATIVELY	EXALTEDNESS	EXCEEDINGLY	EXCITATORY	EXCOGITATORS
EVOCATIVENESS	EXALTEDNESSES	EXCELLENCE	EXCITEDNESS	EXCOMMUNICABLE
EVOCATIVENESSES	EXAMINABILITIES	EXCELLENCES	EXCITEDNESSES	EXCOMMUNICATE
EVOLUTIONAL	EXAMINABILITY	EXCELLENCIES	EXCITEMENT	EXCOMMUNICATED
EVOLUTIONARILY	EXAMINABLE	EXCELLENCY	EXCITEMENTS	EXCOMMUNICATES
EVOLUTIONARY	EXAMINANTS	EXCELLENTLY	EXCITINGLY	EXCOMMUNICATING
EVOLUTIONISM	EXAMINATES	EXCELSIORS	EXCLAIMERS	EXCOMMUNICATION
EVOLUTIONISMS	EXAMINATION	EXCENTRICS	EXCLAIMING	EXCOMMUNICATIVE
EVOLUTIONIST	EXAMINATIONAL	EXCEPTANTS	EXCLAMATION	EXCOMMUNICATOR
EVOLUTIONISTIC	EXAMINATIONS	EXCEPTIONABLE	EXCLAMATIONAL	EXCOMMUNICATORS
EVOLUTIONISTS	EXAMINATOR	EXCEPTIONABLY	EXCLAMATIONS	EXCOMMUNICATORY
EVOLUTIONS	EXAMINATORS	EXCEPTIONAL	EXCLAMATIVE	EXCOMMUNION
EVOLVEMENT	EXAMINERSHIP	EXCEPTIONALISM	EXCLAMATIVES	EXCOMMUNIONS
EVOLVEMENTS	EXAMINERSHIPS	EXCEPTIONALISMS	EXCLAMATORILY	EXCORIATED
EVONYMUSES	EXANIMATION	EXCEPTIONALITY	EXCLAMATORY	EXCORIATES
EVULGATING	EXANIMATIONS	EXCEPTIONALLY	EXCLAUSTRATION	EXCORIATING
EXACERBATE	EXANTHEMAS	EXCEPTIONALNESS	EXCLAUSTRATIONS	EXCORIATION
EXACERBATED	EXANTHEMATA	EXCEPTIONALS	EXCLOSURES	EXCORIATIONS
EXACERBATES	EXANTHEMATIC	EXCEPTIONS	EXCLUDABILITIES	EXCORTICATE
EXACERBATING	EXANTHEMATOUS	EXCEPTIOUS	EXCLUDABILITY	EXCORTICATED
EXACERBATION	EXARATIONS	EXCEPTLESS	EXCLUDABLE	EXCORTICATES
EXACERBATIONS	EXARCHATES	EXCERPTERS	EXCLUDIBILITIES	EXCORTICATING
EXACERBESCENCE	EXARCHISTS	EXCERPTIBLE	EXCLUDIBILITY	EXCORTICATION
EXACERBESCENCES	EXASPERATE	EXCERPTING	EXCLUDIBLE	EXCORTICATIONS
EXACTINGLY	EXASPERATED	EXCERPTINGS	EXCLUSIONARY	EXCREMENTA
EXACTINGNESS	EXASPERATEDLY	EXCERPTION	EXCLUSIONISM	EXCREMENTAL
EXACTINGNESSES	EXASPERATER	EXCERPTIONS	EXCLUSIONISMS	EXCREMENTITIAL
EXACTITUDE	EXASPERATERS	EXCERPTORS	EXCLUSIONIST	EXCREMENTITIOUS
EXACTITUDES	EXASPERATES	EXCESSIVELY	EXCLUSIONISTS	EXCREMENTS
EXACTMENTS	EXASPERATING	EXCESSIVENESS	EXCLUSIONS	EXCREMENTUM
EXACTNESSES	EXASPERATINGLY	EXCESSIVENESSES	EXCLUSIVELY	EXCRESCENCE
EXACTRESSES	EXASPERATION	EXCHANGEABILITY	EXCLUSIVENESS	EXCRESCENCES
EXAGGERATE	EXASPERATIONS	EXCHANGEABLE	EXCLUSIVENESSES	EXCRESCENCIES
EXAGGERATED	EXASPERATIVE	EXCHANGEABLY	EXCLUSIVES	EXCRESCENCY
EXAGGERATEDLY	EXASPERATOR	EXCHANGERS	EXCLUSIVISM	EXCRESCENT
EXAGGERATEDNESS	EXASPERATORS	EXCHANGING	EXCLUSIVISMS	EXCRESCENTIAL
EXAGGERATES	EXCAMBIONS	EXCHEQUERED	EXCLUSIVIST	EXCRESCENTLY
EXAGGERATING	EXCAMBIUMS	EXCHEQUERING	EXCLUSIVISTS	EXCRETIONS
EXAGGERATINGLY	EXCARNATED	EXCHEQUERS	EXCLUSIVITIES	EXCRETORIES
EXAGGERATION	EXCARNATES	EXCIPIENTS	EXCLUSIVITY	EXCRUCIATE

EXCRUCIATED	EXECUTIONERS	EXFILTRATING	EXHILARANT	EXODONTIAS
EXCRUCIATES	EXECUTIONS	EXFOLIANTS	EXHILARANTS	EXODONTICS
EXCRUCIATING	EXECUTIVELY	EXFOLIATED	EXHILARATE	EXODONTIST
EXCRUCIATINGLY	EXECUTIVES	EXFOLIATES	EXHILARATED	EXODONTISTS
EXCRUCIATION	EXECUTORIAL	EXFOLIATING	EXHILARATES	EXOENZYMES
EXCRUCIATIONS	EXECUTORSHIP	EXFOLIATION	EXHILARATING	EXOERYTHROCYTIC
EXCULPABLE	EXECUTORSHIPS	EXFOLIATIONS	EXHILARATINGLY	EXOGENETIC
EXCULPATED	EXECUTRESS	EXFOLIATIVE	EXHILARATION	EXOGENISMS
EXCULPATES	EXECUTRESSES	EXFOLIATOR	EXHILARATIONS	EXOGENOUSLY
EXCULPATING	EXECUTRICES	EXFOLIATORS	EXHILARATIVE	EXONERATED
EXCULPATION	EXECUTRIES	EXHALATION	EXHILARATOR	EXONERATES
EXCULPATIONS	EXECUTRIXES	EXHALATIONS	EXHILARATORS	EXONERATING
EXCULPATORY	EXEGETICAL	EXHAUSTEDLY	EXHILARATORY	EXONERATION
EXCURSIONED	EXEGETICALLY	EXHAUSTERS	EXHORTATION	EXONERATIONS
EXCURSIONING	EXEGETISTS	EXHAUSTIBILITY	EXHORTATIONS	EXONERATIVE
EXCURSIONISE	EXEMPLARILY	EXHAUSTIBLE	EXHORTATIVE	EXONERATOR
EXCURSIONISED	EXEMPLARINESS	EXHAUSTING	EXHORTATORY	EXONERATORS
EXCURSIONISES	EXEMPLARINESSES	EXHAUSTINGLY	EXHUMATING	EXONUCLEASE
EXCURSIONISING	EXEMPLARITIES	EXHAUSTION	EXHUMATION	EXONUCLEASES
EXCURSIONIST	EXEMPLARITY	EXHAUSTIONS	EXHUMATIONS	EXONUMISTS
EXCURSIONISTS	EXEMPLIFIABLE	EXHAUSTIVE	EXIGENCIES	EXOPARASITE
EXCURSIONIZE	EXEMPLIFICATION	EXHAUSTIVELY	EXIGUITIES	EXOPARASITES
EXCURSIONIZED	EXEMPLIFICATIVE	EXHAUSTIVENESS	EXIGUOUSLY	EXOPARASITIC
EXCURSIONIZES	EXEMPLIFIED	EXHAUSTIVITIES	EXIGUOUSNESS	EXOPEPTIDASE
EXCURSIONIZING	EXEMPLIFIER	EXHAUSTIVITY	EXIGUOUSNESSES	EXOPEPTIDASES
EXCURSIONS	EXEMPLIFIERS	EXHAUSTLESS	EXILEMENTS	EXOPHAGIES
EXCURSIVELY	EXEMPLIFIES	EXHAUSTLESSLY	EXIMIOUSLY	EXOPHAGOUS
EXCURSIVENESS	EXEMPLIFYING	EXHAUSTLESSNESS	EXISTENCES	EXOPHTHALMIA
EXCURSIVENESSES	EXEMPTIONS	EXHEREDATE	EXISTENTIAL	EXOPHTHALMIAS
EXCURSUSES	EXENTERATE	EXHEREDATED	EXISTENTIALISM	EXOPHTHALMIC
EXCUSABLENESS	EXENTERATED	EXHEREDATES	EXISTENTIALISMS	EXOPHTHALMOS
EXCUSABLENESSES	EXENTERATES	EXHEREDATING	EXISTENTIALIST	EXOPHTHALMOSES
EXCUSATORY	EXENTERATING	EXHEREDATION	EXISTENTIALISTS	EXOPHTHALMUS
EXECRABLENESS	EXENTERATION	EXHEREDATIONS	EXISTENTIALLY	EXOPHTHALMUSES
EXECRABLENESSES	EXENTERATIONS	EXHIBITERS	EXISTENTIALS	EXOPLANETS
EXECRATING	EXEQUATURS	EXHIBITING	EXOBIOLOGICAL	EXOPODITES
EXECRATION	EXERCISABLE	EXHIBITION	EXOBIOLOGIES	EXOPODITIC
EXECRATIONS	EXERCISERS	EXHIBITIONER	EXOBIOLOGIST	EXORABILITIES
EXECRATIVE	EXERCISING	EXHIBITIONERS	EXOBIOLOGISTS	EXORABILITY
EXECRATIVELY	EXERCITATION	EXHIBITIONISM	EXOBIOLOGY	EXORATIONS
EXECRATORS	EXERCITATIONS	EXHIBITIONISMS	EXOCENTRIC	EXORBITANCE
EXECRATORY	EXERCYCLES	EXHIBITIONIST	EXOCUTICLE	EXORBITANCES
EXECUTABLE	EXERGAMING	EXHIBITIONISTIC	EXOCUTICLES	EXORBITANCIES
EXECUTABLES	EXERGAMINGS	EXHIBITIONISTS	EXOCYTOSED	EXORBITANCY
EXECUTANCIES	EXERTAINMENT	EXHIBITIONS	EXOCYTOSES	EXORBITANT
EXECUTANCY	EXERTAINMENTS	EXHIBITIVE	EXOCYTOSING	EXORBITANTLY
EXECUTANTS	EXFILTRATE	EXHIBITIVELY	EXOCYTOSIS	EXORBITATE
EXECUTARIES	EXFILTRATED	EXHIBITORS	EXOCYTOTIC	EXORBITATED
EXECUTIONER	EXFILTRATES	EXHIBITORY	EXODERMISES	EXORBITATES

EXORBITATING	EXPANSIONISTIC	EXPECTORATION	EXPERIENCERS	EXPLANATORILY
EXORCISERS	EXPANSIONISTS	EXPECTORATIONS	EXPERIENCES	EXPLANATORY
EXORCISING	EXPANSIONS	EXPECTORATIVE	EXPERIENCING	EXPLANTATION
EXORCISTIC	EXPANSIVELY	EXPECTORATIVES	EXPERIENTIAL	EXPLANTATIONS
EXORCISTICAL	EXPANSIVENESS	EXPECTORATOR	EXPERIENTIALISM	EXPLANTING
EXORCIZERS	EXPANSIVENESSES	EXPECTORATORS	EXPERIENTIALIST	EXPLETIVELY
EXORCIZING	EXPANSIVITIES	EXPEDIENCE	EXPERIENTIALLY	EXPLETIVES
EXOSKELETAL	EXPANSIVITY	EXPEDIENCES	EXPERIMENT	EXPLICABLE
EXOSKELETON	EXPATIATED	EXPEDIENCIES	EXPERIMENTAL	EXPLICABLY
EXOSKELETONS	EXPATIATES	EXPEDIENCY	EXPERIMENTALISE	EXPLICATED
EXOSPHERES	EXPATIATING	EXPEDIENTIAL	EXPERIMENTALISM	EXPLICATES
EXOSPHERIC	EXPATIATION	EXPEDIENTIALLY	EXPERIMENTALIST	EXPLICATING
EXOSPHERICAL	EXPATIATIONS	EXPEDIENTLY	EXPERIMENTALIZE	EXPLICATION
EXOSPORIUM	EXPATIATIVE	EXPEDIENTS	EXPERIMENTALLY	EXPLICATIONS
EXOSPOROUS	EXPATIATOR	EXPEDITATE	EXPERIMENTATION	EXPLICATIVE
EXOTERICAL	EXPATIATORS	EXPEDITATED	EXPERIMENTATIVE	EXPLICATIVELY
EXOTERICALLY	EXPATIATORY	EXPEDITATES	EXPERIMENTED	EXPLICATOR
EXOTERICISM	EXPATRIATE	EXPEDITATING	EXPERIMENTER	EXPLICATORS
EXOTERICISMS	EXPATRIATED	EXPEDITATION	EXPERIMENTERS	EXPLICATORY
EXOTHERMAL	EXPATRIATES	EXPEDITATIONS	EXPERIMENTING	EXPLICITLY
EXOTHERMALLY	EXPATRIATING	EXPEDITELY	EXPERIMENTIST	EXPLICITNESS
EXOTHERMIC	EXPATRIATION	EXPEDITERS	EXPERIMENTISTS	EXPLICITNESSES
EXOTHERMICALLY	EXPATRIATIONS	EXPEDITING	EXPERIMENTS	EXPLOITABLE
EXOTHERMICITIES	EXPATRIATISM	EXPEDITION	EXPERTISED	EXPLOITAGE
EXOTHERMICITY	EXPATRIATISMS	EXPEDITIONARY	EXPERTISES	EXPLOITAGES
EXOTICALLY	EXPECTABLE	EXPEDITIONS	EXPERTISING	EXPLOITATION
EXOTICISED	EXPECTABLY	EXPEDITIOUS	EXPERTISMS	EXPLOITATIONS
EXOTICISES	EXPECTANCE	EXPEDITIOUSLY	EXPERTIZED	EXPLOITATIVE
EXOTICISING	EXPECTANCES	EXPEDITIOUSNESS	EXPERTIZES	EXPLOITATIVELY
EXOTICISMS	EXPECTANCIES	EXPEDITIVE	EXPERTIZING	EXPLOITERS
EXOTICISTS	EXPECTANCY	EXPEDITORS	EXPERTNESS	EXPLOITING
EXOTICIZED	EXPECTANTLY	EXPELLABLE	EXPERTNESSES	EXPLOITIVE
EXOTICIZES	EXPECTANTS	EXPELLANTS	EXPIATIONS	EXPLOITIVELY
EXOTICIZING	EXPECTATION	EXPELLENTS	EXPIRATION	EXPLORABLE
EXOTICNESS	EXPECTATIONAL	EXPENDABILITIES	EXPIRATIONS	EXPLORATION
EXOTICNESSES	EXPECTATIONS	EXPENDABILITY	EXPIRATORY	EXPLORATIONAL
EXOTROPIAS	EXPECTATIVE	EXPENDABLE	EXPISCATED	EXPLORATIONIST
EXPANDABILITIES	EXPECTATIVES	EXPENDABLES	EXPISCATES	EXPLORATIONISTS
EXPANDABILITY	EXPECTEDLY	EXPENDABLY	EXPISCATING	EXPLORATIONS
EXPANDABLE	EXPECTEDNESS	EXPENDITURE	EXPISCATION	EXPLORATIVE
EXPANSIBILITIES	EXPECTEDNESSES	EXPENDITURES	EXPISCATIONS	EXPLORATIVELY
EXPANSIBILITY	EXPECTINGLY	EXPENSIVELY	EXPISCATORY	EXPLORATORY
EXPANSIBLE	EXPECTINGS	EXPENSIVENESS	EXPLAINABLE	EXPLOSIBLE
EXPANSIBLY	EXPECTORANT	EXPENSIVENESSES	EXPLAINERS	EXPLOSIONS
EXPANSIONAL	EXPECTORANTS	EXPERIENCE	EXPLAINING	EXPLOSIVELY
EXPANSIONARY	EXPECTORATE	EXPERIENCEABLE	EXPLANATION	EXPLOSIVENESS
EXPANSIONISM	EXPECTORATED	EXPERIENCED	EXPLANATIONS	EXPLOSIVENESSES
EXPANSIONISMS	EXPECTORATES	EXPERIENCELESS	EXPLANATIVE	EXPLOSIVES
EXPANSIONIST	EXPECTORATING	EXPERIENCER	EXPLANATIVELY	EXPONENTIAL

EXPONENTIALLY	EXPRESSIONS	EXPURGATORS	EXTEMPORISATION	EXTENUATINGLY
EXPONENTIALS	EXPRESSIVE	EXPURGATORY	EXTEMPORISE	EXTENUATINGS
EXPONENTIATION	EXPRESSIVELY	EXQUISITELY	EXTEMPORISED	EXTENUATION
EXPONENTIATIONS	EXPRESSIVENESS	EXQUISITENESS	EXTEMPORISER	EXTENUATIONS
EXPORTABILITIES	EXPRESSIVITIES	EXQUISITENESSES	EXTEMPORISERS	EXTENUATIVE
EXPORTABILITY	EXPRESSIVITY	EXQUISITES	EXTEMPORISES	EXTENUATIVES
EXPORTABLE	EXPRESSMAN	EXSANGUINATE	EXTEMPORISING	EXTENUATOR
EXPORTATION	EXPRESSMEN	EXSANGUINATED	EXTEMPORIZATION	EXTENUATORS
EXPORTATIONS	EXPRESSNESS	EXSANGUINATES	EXTEMPORIZE	EXTENUATORY
EXPOSEDNESS	EXPRESSNESSES	EXSANGUINATING	EXTEMPORIZED	EXTERIORISATION
EXPOSEDNESSES	EXPRESSURE	EXSANGUINATION	EXTEMPORIZER	EXTERIORISE
EXPOSITING	EXPRESSURES	EXSANGUINATIONS	EXTEMPORIZERS	EXTERIORISED
EXPOSITION	EXPRESSWAY	EXSANGUINE	EXTEMPORIZES	EXTERIORISES
EXPOSITIONAL	EXPRESSWAYS	EXSANGUINED	EXTEMPORIZING	EXTERIORISING
EXPOSITIONS	EXPROBRATE	EXSANGUINEOUS	EXTENDABILITIES	EXTERIORITIES
EXPOSITIVE	EXPROBRATED	EXSANGUINITIES	EXTENDABILITY	EXTERIORITY
EXPOSITIVELY	EXPROBRATES	EXSANGUINITY	EXTENDABLE	EXTERIORIZATION
EXPOSITORILY	EXPROBRATING	EXSANGUINOUS	EXTENDEDLY	EXTERIORIZE
EXPOSITORS	EXPROBRATION	EXSCINDING	EXTENDEDNESS	EXTERIORIZED
EXPOSITORY	EXPROBRATIONS	EXSECTIONS	EXTENDEDNESSES	EXTERIORIZES
EXPOSITRESS	EXPROBRATIVE	EXSERTIONS	EXTENDIBILITIES	EXTERIORIZING
EXPOSITRESSES	EXPROBRATORY	EXSICCANTS	EXTENDIBILITY	EXTERIORLY
EXPOSTULATE	EXPROMISSION	EXSICCATED	EXTENDIBLE	EXTERMINABLE
EXPOSTULATED	EXPROMISSIONS	EXSICCATES	EXTENSIBILITIES	EXTERMINATE
EXPOSTULATES	EXPROMISSOR	EXSICCATING	EXTENSIBILITY	EXTERMINATED
EXPOSTULATING	EXPROMISSORS	EXSICCATION	EXTENSIBLE	EXTERMINATES
EXPOSTULATINGLY	EXPROPRIABLE	EXSICCATIONS	EXTENSIBLENESS	EXTERMINATING
EXPOSTULATION	EXPROPRIATE	EXSICCATIVE	EXTENSIFICATION	EXTERMINATION
EXPOSTULATIONS	EXPROPRIATED	EXSICCATOR	EXTENSIMETER	EXTERMINATIONS
EXPOSTULATIVE	EXPROPRIATES	EXSICCATORS	EXTENSIMETERS	EXTERMINATIVE
EXPOSTULATOR	EXPROPRIATING	EXSOLUTION	EXTENSIONAL	EXTERMINATOR
EXPOSTULATORS	EXPROPRIATION	EXSOLUTIONS	EXTENSIONALISM	EXTERMINATORS
EXPOSTULATORY	EXPROPRIATIONS	EXSTIPULATE	EXTENSIONALISMS	EXTERMINATORY
EXPOSTURES	EXPROPRIATOR	EXSTROPHIES	EXTENSIONALITY	EXTERMINED
EXPOUNDERS	EXPROPRIATORS	EXSUFFLATE	EXTENSIONALLY	EXTERMINES
EXPOUNDING	EXPUGNABLE	EXSUFFLATED	EXTENSIONIST	EXTERMINING
EXPRESSAGE	EXPUGNATION	EXSUFFLATES	EXTENSIONISTS	EXTERNALISATION
EXPRESSAGES	EXPUGNATIONS	EXSUFFLATING	EXTENSIONS	EXTERNALISE
EXPRESSERS	EXPULSIONS	EXSUFFLATION	EXTENSITIES	EXTERNALISED
EXPRESSIBLE	EXPUNCTING	EXSUFFLATIONS	EXTENSIVELY	EXTERNALISES
EXPRESSING	EXPUNCTION	EXSUFFLICATE	EXTENSIVENESS	EXTERNALISING
EXPRESSION	EXPUNCTIONS	EXTEMPORAL	EXTENSIVENESSES	EXTERNALISM
EXPRESSIONAL	EXPURGATED	EXTEMPORALLY	EXTENSIVISATION	EXTERNALISMS
EXPRESSIONISM	EXPURGATES	EXTEMPORANEITY	EXTENSIVIZATION	EXTERNALIST
EXPRESSIONISMS	EXPURGATING	EXTEMPORANEOUS	EXTENSOMETER	EXTERNALISTS
EXPRESSIONIST	EXPURGATION	EXTEMPORARILY	EXTENSOMETERS	EXTERNALITIES
EXPRESSIONISTIC	EXPURGATIONS	EXTEMPORARINESS	EXTENUATED	EXTERNALITY
EXPRESSIONISTS	EXPURGATOR	EXTEMPORARY	EXTENUATES	EXTERNALIZATION
EXPRESSIONLESS	EXPURGATORIAL	EXTEMPORES	EXTENUATING	EXTERNALIZE

EXTERNALIZED	EXTORTIONISTS	EXTRAMUNDANE	EXTRAVAGATION	EXTRUSIONS
EXTERNALIZES	EXTORTIONS	EXTRAMURAL	EXTRAVAGATIONS	EXTUBATING
EXTERNALIZING	EXTRABOLDS	EXTRAMURALLY	EXTRAVASATE	EXUBERANCE
EXTERNALLY	EXTRACANONICAL	EXTRAMUSICAL	EXTRAVASATED	EXUBERANCES
EXTERNSHIP	EXTRACELLULAR	EXTRANEITIES	EXTRAVASATES	EXUBERANCIES
EXTERNSHIPS	EXTRACELLULARLY	EXTRANEITY	EXTRAVASATING	EXUBERANCY
EXTEROCEPTIVE	EXTRACORPOREAL	EXTRANEOUS	EXTRAVASATION	EXUBERANTLY
EXTEROCEPTOR	EXTRACRANIAL	EXTRANEOUSLY	EXTRAVASATIONS	EXUBERATED
EXTEROCEPTORS	EXTRACTABILITY	EXTRANEOUSNESS	EXTRAVASCULAR	EXUBERATES
EXTERRITORIAL	EXTRACTABLE	EXTRANUCLEAR	EXTRAVEHICULAR	EXUBERATING
EXTERRITORIALLY	EXTRACTANT	EXTRAORDINAIRE	EXTRAVERSION	EXUDATIONS
EXTINCTING	EXTRACTANTS	EXTRAORDINARIES	EXTRAVERSIONS	EXULCERATE
EXTINCTION	EXTRACTIBLE	EXTRAORDINARILY	EXTRAVERSIVE	EXULCERATED
EXTINCTIONS	EXTRACTING	EXTRAORDINARY	EXTRAVERSIVELY	EXULCERATES
EXTINCTIVE	EXTRACTION	EXTRAPOLATE	EXTRAVERTED	EXULCERATING
EXTINCTURE	EXTRACTIONS	EXTRAPOLATED	EXTRAVERTING	EXULCERATION
EXTINCTURES	EXTRACTIVE	EXTRAPOLATES	EXTRAVERTLY	EXULCERATIONS
EXTINGUISH	EXTRACTIVELY	EXTRAPOLATING	EXTRAVERTS	EXULTANCES
EXTINGUISHABLE	EXTRACTIVES	EXTRAPOLATION	EXTREATING	EXULTANCIES
EXTINGUISHANT	EXTRACTORS	EXTRAPOLATIONS	EXTREMENESS	EXULTANTLY
EXTINGUISHANTS	EXTRACURRICULAR	EXTRAPOLATIVE	EXTREMENESSES	EXULTATION
EXTINGUISHED	EXTRADITABLE	EXTRAPOLATOR	EXTREMISMS	EXULTATIONS
EXTINGUISHER	EXTRADITED	EXTRAPOLATORS	EXTREMISTS	EXULTINGLY
EXTINGUISHERS	EXTRADITES	EXTRAPOLATORY	EXTREMITIES	EXURBANITE
EXTINGUISHES	EXTRADITING	EXTRAPOSED	EXTREMOPHILE	EXURBANITES
EXTINGUISHING	EXTRADITION	EXTRAPOSES	EXTREMOPHILES	EXUVIATING
EXTINGUISHMENT	EXTRADITIONS	EXTRAPOSING	EXTRICABLE	EXUVIATION
EXTINGUISHMENTS	EXTRADOSES	EXTRAPOSITION	EXTRICATED	EXUVIATIONS
EXTIRPABLE	EXTRADOTAL	EXTRAPOSITIONS	EXTRICATES	EYEBALLING
EXTIRPATED	EXTRADURAL	EXTRAPYRAMIDAL	EXTRICATING	EYEBRIGHTS
EXTIRPATES	EXTRADURALS	EXTRASENSORY	EXTRICATION	EYEBROWING
EXTIRPATING	EXTRAEMBRYONIC	EXTRASOLAR	EXTRICATIONS	EYEBROWLESS
EXTIRPATION	EXTRAFLORAL	EXTRASYSTOLE	EXTRINSICAL	EYEDNESSES
EXTIRPATIONS	EXTRAFORANEOUS	EXTRASYSTOLES	EXTRINSICALITY	EYEDROPPER
EXTIRPATIVE	EXTRAGALACTIC	EXTRATEXTUAL	EXTRINSICALLY	EYEDROPPERS
EXTIRPATOR	EXTRAHEPATIC	EXTRATROPICAL	EXTRINSICALS	EYEGLASSES
EXTIRPATORS	EXTRAJUDICIAL	EXTRAUTERINE	EXTROPIANS	EYELETEERS
EXTIRPATORY	EXTRAJUDICIALLY	EXTRAVAGANCE	EXTROVERSION	EYELETTING
EXTOLLINGLY	EXTRALEGAL	EXTRAVAGANCES	EXTROVERSIONS	EYEOPENERS
EXTOLLMENT	EXTRALEGALLY	EXTRAVAGANCIES	EXTROVERSIVE	EYEPATCHES
EXTOLLMENTS	EXTRALIMITAL	EXTRAVAGANCY	EXTROVERSIVELY	EYEPOPPERS
EXTOLMENTS	EXTRALIMITARY	EXTRAVAGANT	EXTROVERTED	EYESHADOWS
EXTORSIVELY	EXTRALINGUISTIC	EXTRAVAGANTLY	EXTROVERTING	EYESTRAINS
EXTORTIONARY	EXTRALITERARY	EXTRAVAGANZA	EXTROVERTLY	EYESTRINGS
EXTORTIONATE	EXTRALITIES	EXTRAVAGANZAS	EXTROVERTS	EYEWITNESS
EXTORTIONATELY	EXTRALOGICAL	EXTRAVAGATE	EXTRUDABILITIES	EYEWITNESSED
EXTORTIONER	EXTRAMARITAL	EXTRAVAGATED	EXTRUDABILITY	EYEWITNESSES
EXTORTIONERS	EXTRAMARITALLY	EXTRAVAGATES	EXTRUDABLE	EYEWITNESSING
EXTORTIONIST	EXTRAMETRICAL	EXTRAVAGATING	EXTRUSIBLE	

F

FABRICANTS	FACILENESSES	FACTITIOUSNESS	FAINEANCES	FALCONOIDS
FABRICATED	FACILITATE	FACTITIVELY	FAINEANCIES	FALCONRIES
FABRICATES	FACILITATED	FACTORABILITIES	FAINEANTISE	FALDERALED
FABRICATING	FACILITATES	FACTORABILITY	FAINEANTISES	FALDERALING
FABRICATION	FACILITATING	FACTORABLE	FAINNESSES	FALDISTORIES
FABRICATIONS	FACILITATION	FACTORAGES	FAINTHEARTED	FALDISTORY
FABRICATIVE	FACILITATIONS	FACTORIALLY	FAINTHEARTEDLY	FALDSTOOLS
FABRICATOR	FACILITATIVE	FACTORIALS	FAINTINGLY	FALLACIOUS
FABRICATORS	FACILITATOR	FACTORINGS	FAINTISHNESS	FALLACIOUSLY
FABRICKING	FACILITATORS	FACTORISATION	FAINTISHNESSES	FALLACIOUSNESS
FABRICKINGS	FACILITATORY	FACTORISATIONS	FAINTNESSES	FALLALERIES
FABULATING	FACILITIES	FACTORISED	FAIRGROUND	FALLALISHLY
FABULATORS	FACINERIOUS	FACTORISES	FAIRGROUNDS	FALLBOARDS
FABULISING	FACINOROUS	FACTORISING	FAIRLEADER	FALLFISHES
FABULISTIC	FACINOROUSNESS	FACTORIZATION	FAIRLEADERS	FALLIBILISM
FABULIZING	FACSIMILED	FACTORIZATIONS	FAIRNESSES	FALLIBILISMS
FABULOSITIES	FACSIMILEING	FACTORIZED	FAIRNITICKLE	FALLIBILIST
FABULOSITY	FACSIMILES	FACTORIZES	FAIRNITICKLES	FALLIBILISTS
FABULOUSLY	FACSIMILIST	FACTORIZING	FAIRNITICLE	FALLIBILITIES
FABULOUSNESS	FACSIMILISTS	FACTORSHIP	FAIRNITICLES	FALLIBILITY
FABULOUSNESSES	FACTICITIES	FACTORSHIPS	FAIRNYTICKLE	FALLIBLENESS
FACEBOOKED	FACTIONALISE	FACTORYLIKE	FAIRNYTICKLES	FALLIBLENESSES
FACEBOOKING	FACTIONALISED	FACTSHEETS	FAIRNYTICLE	FALLOWNESS
FACECLOTHS	FACTIONALISES	FACTUALISM	FAIRNYTICLES	FALLOWNESSES
FACELESSNESS	FACTIONALISING	FACTUALISMS	FAIRYFLOSS	FALSEFACES
FACELESSNESSES	FACTIONALISM	FACTUALIST	FAIRYFLOSSES	FALSEHOODS
FACELIFTED	FACTIONALISMS	FACTUALISTIC	FAIRYHOODS	FALSENESSES
FACELIFTING	FACTIONALIST	FACTUALISTS	FAIRYLANDS	FALSEWORKS
FACEPALMED	FACTIONALISTS	FACTUALITIES	FAITHCURES	FALSIDICAL
FACEPALMING	FACTIONALIZE	FACTUALITY	FAITHFULLY	FALSIFIABILITY
FACEPLANTED	FACTIONALIZED	FACTUALNESS	FAITHFULNESS	FALSIFIABLE
FACEPLANTING	FACTIONALIZES	FACTUALNESSES	FAITHFULNESSES	FALSIFICATION
FACEPLANTS	FACTIONALIZING	FACULTATIVE	FAITHLESSLY	FALSIFICATIONS
FACEPLATES	FACTIONALLY	FACULTATIVELY	FAITHLESSNESS	FALSIFIERS
FACEPRINTS	FACTIONARIES	FACUNDITIES	FAITHLESSNESSES	FALSIFYING
FACETIMING	FACTIONARY	FADDINESSES	FAITHWORTHIER	FALTERINGLY
FACETIOUSLY	FACTIONIST	FADDISHNESS	FAITHWORTHIEST	FALTERINGS
FACETIOUSNESS	FACTIONISTS	FADDISHNESSES	FAITHWORTHINESS	FAMILIARISATION
FACETIOUSNESSES	FACTIOUSLY	FADEDNESSES	FAITHWORTHY	FAMILIARISE
FACEWORKER	FACTIOUSNESS	FADELESSLY	FALANGISMS	FAMILIARISED
FACEWORKERS	FACTIOUSNESSES	FADOMETERS	FALANGISTS	FAMILIARISER
FACIALISTS	FACTITIOUS	FAGGOTINGS	FALCATIONS	FAMILIARISERS
FACILENESS	FACTITIOUSLY	FAGOTTISTS	FALCONIFORM	FAMILIARISES

FAMILIARISING	FANFARONADED	FARANDINES	FASCIATION	FASTIDIOUSNESS
FAMILIARITIES	FANFARONADES	FARANDOLES	FASCIATIONS	FASTIGIATE
FAMILIARITY	FANFARONADING	FARAWAYNESS	FASCICULAR	FASTIGIATED
FAMILIARIZATION	FANFARONAS	FARAWAYNESSES	FASCICULARLY	FASTIGIUMS
FAMILIARIZE	FANFOLDING	FARBOROUGH	FASCICULATE	FASTNESSES
FAMILIARIZED	FANGIRLING	FARBOROUGHS	FASCICULATED	FATALISTIC
FAMILIARIZER	FANTABULOUS	FARCEMEATS	FASCICULATELY	FATALISTICALLY
FAMILIARIZERS	FANTASISED	FARCICALITIES	FASCICULATION	FATALITIES
FAMILIARIZES	FANTASISER	FARCICALITY	FASCICULATIONS	FATALNESSES
FAMILIARIZING	FANTASISERS	FARCICALLY	FASCICULES	FATBRAINED
FAMILIARLY	FANTASISES	FARCICALNESS	FASCICULUS	FATEFULNESS
FAMILIARNESS	FANTASISING	FARCICALNESSES	FASCIITISES	FATEFULNESSES
FAMILIARNESSES	FANTASISTS	FARCIFYING	FASCINATED	FATHEADEDLY
FAMILICIDAL	FANTASIZED	FAREWELLED	FASCINATEDLY	FATHEADEDNESS
FAMILICIDE	FANTASIZER	FAREWELLING	FASCINATES	FATHEADEDNESSES
FAMILICIDES	FANTASIZERS	FARFETCHEDNESS	FASCINATING	FATHERHOOD
FAMILISTIC	FANTASIZES	FARINACEOUS	FASCINATINGLY	FATHERHOODS
FAMISHMENT	FANTASIZING	FARINOSELY	FASCINATION	FATHERINGS
FAMISHMENTS	FANTASMALLY	FARKLEBERRIES	FASCINATIONS	FATHERLAND
FAMOUSNESS	FANTASMICALLY	FARKLEBERRY	FASCINATIVE	FATHERLANDS
FAMOUSNESSES	FANTASQUES	FARMERESSES	FASCINATOR	FATHERLESS
FANATICALLY	FANTASTICAL	FARMERETTE	FASCINATORS	FATHERLESSNESS
FANATICALNESS	FANTASTICALITY	FARMERETTES	FASCIOLIASES	FATHERLIER
FANATICALNESSES	FANTASTICALLY	FARMHOUSES	FASCIOLIASIS	FATHERLIEST
FANATICISATION	FANTASTICALNESS	FARMSTEADS	FASCISTICALLY	FATHERLIKE
FANATICISATIONS	FANTASTICATE	FARMWORKER	FASCITISES	FATHERLINESS
FANATICISE	FANTASTICATED	FARMWORKERS	FASHIONABILITY	FATHERLINESSES
FANATICISED	FANTASTICATES	FARNARKELED	FASHIONABLE	FATHERSHIP
FANATICISES	FANTASTICATING	FARNARKELING	FASHIONABLENESS	FATHERSHIPS
FANATICISING	FANTASTICATION	FARNARKELINGS	FASHIONABLES	FATHOMABLE
FANATICISM	FANTASTICATIONS	FARNARKELS	FASHIONABLY	FATHOMETER
FANATICISMS	FANTASTICISM	FARRAGINOUS	FASHIONERS	FATHOMETERS
FANATICIZATION	FANTASTICISMS	FARRANDINE	FASHIONIER	FATHOMLESS
FANATICIZATIONS	FANTASTICO	FARRANDINES	FASHIONIEST	FATHOMLESSLY
FANATICIZE	FANTASTICOES	FARRIERIES	FASHIONING	FATHOMLESSNESS
FANATICIZED	FANTASTICS	FARROWINGS	FASHIONIST	FATIDICALLY
FANATICIZES	FANTASTRIES	FARSIGHTED	FASHIONISTA	FATIGABILITIES
FANATICIZING	FANTASYING	FARSIGHTEDLY	FASHIONISTAS	FATIGABILITY
FANCIFULLY	FANTASYLAND	FARSIGHTEDNESS	FASHIONISTS	FATIGABLENESS
FANCIFULNESS	FANTASYLANDS	FARTHERMORE	FASHIONMONGER	FATIGABLENESSES
FANCIFULNESSES	FANTOCCINI	FARTHERMOST	FASHIONMONGERS	FATIGATING
FANCIFYING	FARADISATION	FARTHINGALE	FASHIONMONGING	FATIGUABLE
FANCINESSES	FARADISATIONS	FARTHINGALES	FASHIOUSNESS	FATIGUABLENESS
FANCYWORKS	FARADISERS	FARTHINGLAND	FASHIOUSNESSES	FATIGUELESS
FANDABIDOZI	FARADISING	FARTHINGLANDS	FASTBALLER	FATIGUINGLY
FANDANGLES	FARADIZATION	FARTHINGLESS	FASTBALLERS	FATISCENCE
FANDANGOES	FARADIZATIONS	FARTHINGSWORTH	FASTENINGS	FATISCENCES
FANFARADES	FARADIZERS	FARTHINGSWORTHS	FASTIDIOUS	FATSHEDERA
FANFARONADE	FARADIZING	FASCIATELY	FASTIDIOUSLY	FATSHEDERAS

FATTENABLE	FEARFULNESS	FEATLINESS	FEDERARIES	FELLATIONS
FATTENINGS	FEARFULNESSES	FEATLINESSES	FEDERATING	FELLATRICES
FATTINESSES	FEARLESSLY	FEATURELESS	FEDERATION	FELLATRIXES
FATUOUSNESS	FEARLESSNESS	FEATURELESSNESS	FEDERATIONS	FELLFIELDS
FATUOUSNESSES	FEARLESSNESSES	FEATURETTE	FEDERATIVE	FELLMONGER
FAUCETRIES	FEARMONGER	FEATURETTES	FEDERATIVELY	FELLMONGERED
FAULCHIONS	FEARMONGERING	FEBRICITIES	FEDERATORS	FELLMONGERIES
FAULTFINDER	FEARMONGERINGS	FEBRICULAS	FEEBLEMINDED	FELLMONGERING
FAULTFINDERS	FEARMONGERS	FEBRICULES	FEEBLEMINDEDLY	FELLMONGERINGS
FAULTFINDING	FEARNAUGHT	FEBRIFACIENT	FEEBLENESS	FELLMONGERS
FAULTFINDINGS	FEARNAUGHTS	FEBRIFACIENTS	FEEBLENESSES	FELLMONGERY
FAULTINESS	FEARNOUGHT	FEBRIFEROUS	FEEDGRAINS	FELLNESSES
FAULTINESSES	FEARNOUGHTS	FEBRIFUGAL	FEEDINGSTUFF	FELLOWSHIP
FAULTLESSLY	FEARSOMELY	FEBRIFUGES	FEEDINGSTUFFS	FELLOWSHIPED
FAULTLESSNESS	FEARSOMENESS	FEBRILITIES	FEEDSTOCKS	FELLOWSHIPING
FAULTLESSNESSES	FEARSOMENESSES	FECKLESSLY	FEEDSTUFFS	FELLOWSHIPPED
FAULTLINES	FEASIBILITIES	FECKLESSNESS	FEEDTHROUGH	FELLOWSHIPPING
FAUNISTICALLY	FEASIBILITY	FECKLESSNESSES	FEEDTHROUGHS	FELLOWSHIPS
FAUXBOURDON	FEASIBLENESS	FECULENCES	FEEDWATERS	FELLWALKER
FAUXBOURDONS	FEASIBLENESSES	FECULENCIES	FEELINGLESS	FELLWALKERS
FAUXMANCES	FEATEOUSLY	FECUNDATED	FEELINGNESS	FELONIOUSLY
FAVIPIRAVIR	FEATHERBED	FECUNDATES	FEELINGNESSES	FELONIOUSNESS
FAVIPIRAVIRS	FEATHERBEDDED	FECUNDATING	FEIGNEDNESS	FELONIOUSNESSES
FAVORABLENESS	FEATHERBEDDING	FECUNDATION	FEIGNEDNESSES	FELQUISTES
FAVORABLENESSES	FEATHERBEDDINGS	FECUNDATIONS	FEIGNINGLY	FELSPATHIC
FAVOREDNESS	FEATHERBEDS	FECUNDATOR	FEISTINESS	FELSPATHOID
FAVOREDNESSES	FEATHERBRAIN	FECUNDATORS	FEISTINESSES	FELSPATHOIDS
FAVORINGLY	FEATHERBRAINED	FECUNDATORY	FELDSCHARS	FELSPATHOSE
FAVORITING	FEATHERBRAINS	FECUNDITIES	FELDSCHERS	FEMALENESS
FAVORITISM	FEATHEREDGE	FEDERACIES	FELDSPATHIC	FEMALENESSES
FAVORITISMS	FEATHEREDGED	FEDERALESE	FELDSPATHOID	FEMALITIES
FAVOURABLE	FEATHEREDGES	FEDERALESES	FELDSPATHOIDS	FEMETARIES
FAVOURABLENESS	FEATHEREDGING	FEDERALISATION	FELDSPATHOSE	FEMINACIES
FAVOURABLY	FEATHERHEAD	FEDERALISATIONS	FELDSPATHS	FEMINALITIES
FAVOUREDNESS	FEATHERHEADED	FEDERALISE	FELICITATE	FEMINALITY
FAVOUREDNESSES	FEATHERHEADS	FEDERALISED	FELICITATED	FEMINEITIES
FAVOURINGLY	FEATHERIER	FEDERALISES	FELICITATES	FEMINILITIES
FAVOURITED	FEATHERIEST	FEDERALISING	FELICITATING	FEMINILITY
FAVOURITES	FEATHERINESS	FEDERALISM	FELICITATION	FEMININELY
FAVOURITING	FEATHERINESSES	FEDERALISMS	FELICITATIONS	FEMININENESS
FAVOURITISM	FEATHERING	FEDERALIST	FELICITATOR	FEMININENESSES
FAVOURITISMS	FEATHERINGS	FEDERALISTIC	FELICITATORS	FEMININISM
FAVOURLESS	FEATHERLESS	FEDERALISTS	FELICITIES	FEMININISMS
FAWNINGNESS	FEATHERLIGHT	FEDERALIZATION	FELICITOUS	FEMININITIES
FAWNINGNESSES	FEATHERSTITCH	FEDERALIZATIONS	FELICITOUSLY	FEMININITY
FAZENDEIRO	FEATHERSTITCHED	FEDERALIZE	FELICITOUSNESS	FEMINISATION
FAZENDEIROS	FEATHERSTITCHES	FEDERALIZED	FELINENESS	FEMINISATIONS
FEARFULLER	FEATHERWEIGHT	FEDERALIZES	FELINENESSES	FEMINISING
FEARFULLEST	FEATHERWEIGHTS	FEDERALIZING	FELINITIES	FEMINISTIC

FEMINITIES	FERNTICKLED	FERROMAGNETIC	FERVENCIES	FETISHISTS
FEMINIZATION	FERNTICKLES	FERROMAGNETISM	FERVENTEST	FETISHIZATION
FEMINIZATIONS	FERNTICLED	FERROMAGNETISMS	FERVENTNESS	FETISHIZATIONS
FEMINIZING	FERNTICLES	FERROMAGNETS	FERVENTNESSES	FETISHIZED
FEMTOMETER	FERNYTICKLE	FERROMANGANESE	FERVESCENT	FETISHIZES
FEMTOMETERS	FERNYTICKLES	FERROMANGANESES	FERVIDITIES	FETISHIZING
FEMTOMETRE	FERNYTICLE	FERROMOLYBDENUM	FERVIDNESS	FETOLOGIES
FEMTOMETRES	FERNYTICLES	FERRONICKEL	FERVIDNESSES	FETOLOGIST
FEMTOSECOND	FEROCIOUSLY	FERRONICKELS	FESCENNINE	FETOLOGISTS
FEMTOSECONDS	FEROCIOUSNESS	FERRONIERE	FESTILOGIES	FETOPROTEIN
FENCELESSNESS	FEROCIOUSNESSES	FERRONIERES	FESTINATED	FETOPROTEINS
FENCELESSNESSES	FEROCITIES	FERRONNIERE	FESTINATELY	FETOSCOPES
FENCELINES	FERRANDINE	FERRONNIERES	FESTINATES	FETOSCOPIES
FENCEWIRES	FERRANDINES	FERROPRUSSIATE	FESTINATING	FETTERLESS
FENDERLESS	FERREDOXIN	FERROPRUSSIATES	FESTINATION	FETTERLOCK
FENESTELLA	FERREDOXINS	FERROSILICON	FESTINATIONS	FETTERLOCKS
FENESTELLAE	FERRELLING	FERROSILICONS	FESTIVALGOER	FETTUCCINE
FENESTELLAS	FERRETIEST	FERROSOFERRIC	FESTIVALGOERS	FETTUCCINES
FENESTRALS	FERRETINGS	FERROTYPED	FESTIVENESS	FETTUCCINI
FENESTRATE	FERRICYANIC	FERROTYPES	FESTIVENESSES	FETTUCCINIS
FENESTRATED	FERRICYANIDE	FERROTYPING	FESTIVITIES	FETTUCINES
FENESTRATES	FERRICYANIDES	FERRUGINEOUS	FESTOLOGIES	FETTUCINIS
FENESTRATING	FERRICYANOGEN	FERRUGINOUS	FESTOONERIES	FEUDALISATION
FENESTRATION	FERRICYANOGENS	FERRYBOATS	FESTOONERY	FEUDALISATIONS
FENESTRATIONS	FERRIFEROUS	FERTIGATED	FESTOONING	FEUDALISED
FENNELFLOWER	FERRIMAGNET	FERTIGATES	FESTSCHRIFT	FEUDALISES
FENNELFLOWERS	FERRIMAGNETIC	FERTIGATING	FESTSCHRIFTEN	FEUDALISING
FENUGREEKS	FERRIMAGNETISM	FERTIGATION	FESTSCHRIFTS	FEUDALISMS
FEOFFMENTS	FERRIMAGNETISMS	FERTIGATIONS	FETCHINGLY	FEUDALISTIC
FERACITIES	FERRIMAGNETS	FERTILENESS	FETICHISED	FEUDALISTS
FERETORIES	FERROCENES	FERTILENESSES	FETICHISES	FEUDALITIES
FERMENTABILITY	FERROCHROME	FERTILISABLE	FETICHISING	FEUDALIZATION
FERMENTABLE	FERROCHROMES	FERTILISATION	FETICHISMS	FEUDALIZATIONS
FERMENTATION	FERROCHROMIUM	FERTILISATIONS	FETICHISTIC	FEUDALIZED
FERMENTATIONS	FERROCHROMIUMS	FERTILISED	FETICHISTS	FEUDALIZES
FERMENTATIVE	FERROCONCRETE	FERTILISER	FETICHIZED	FEUDALIZING
FERMENTATIVELY	FERROCONCRETES	FERTILISERS	FETICHIZES	FEUDATORIES
FERMENTERS	FERROCYANIC	FERTILISES	FETICHIZING	FEUILLETES
FERMENTESCIBLE	FERROCYANIDE	FERTILISING	FETIDITIES	FEUILLETON
FERMENTING	FERROCYANIDES	FERTILITIES	FETIDNESSES	FEUILLETONISM
FERMENTITIOUS	FERROCYANOGEN	FERTILIZABLE	FETIPAROUS	FEUILLETONISMS
FERMENTIVE	FERROCYANOGENS	FERTILIZATION	FETISHISATION	FEUILLETONIST
FERMENTORS	FERROELECTRIC	FERTILIZATIONS	FETISHISATIONS	FEUILLETONISTIC
FERNALLIES	FERROELECTRICS	FERTILIZED	FETISHISED	FEUILLETONISTS
FERNITICKLE	FERROGRAMS	FERTILIZER	FETISHISES	FEUILLETONS
FERNITICKLES	FERROGRAPHIES	FERTILIZERS	FETISHISING	FEVERISHLY
FERNITICLE	FERROGRAPHY	FERTILIZES	FETISHISMS	FEVERISHNESS
FERNITICLES	FERROMAGNESIAN	FERTILIZING	FETISHISTIC	FEVERISHNESSES
FERNTICKLE	FERROMAGNET	FERULACEOUS	FETISHISTICALLY	FEVEROUSLY

ten to fifteen letter words | 839

FEVERROOTS	FIBRINOGENS	FICTIONEER	FIDUCIARIES	FILARIASIS
FEVERWEEDS	FIBRINOIDS	FICTIONEERING	FIDUCIARILY	FILATORIES
FEVERWORTS	FIBRINOLYSES	FICTIONEERINGS	FIELDBOOTS	FILCHINGLY
FIANCAILLES	FIBRINOLYSIN	FICTIONEERS	FIELDCRAFT	FILEFISHES
FIANCHETTI	FIBRINOLYSINS	FICTIONISATION	FIELDCRAFTS	FILIALNESS
FIANCHETTO	FIBRINOLYSIS	FICTIONISATIONS	FIELDFARES	FILIALNESSES
FIANCHETTOED	FIBRINOLYTIC	FICTIONISE	FIELDMOUSE	FILIATIONS
FIANCHETTOES	FIBRINOPEPTIDE	FICTIONISED	FIELDPIECE	FILIBUSTER
FIANCHETTOING	FIBRINOPEPTIDES	FICTIONISES	FIELDPIECES	FILIBUSTERED
FIANCHETTOS	FIBROADENOMA	FICTIONISING	FIELDSTONE	FILIBUSTERER
FIBERBOARD	FIBROADENOMAS	FICTIONIST	FIELDSTONES	FILIBUSTERERS
FIBERBOARDS	FIBROADENOMATA	FICTIONISTS	FIELDSTRIP	FILIBUSTERING
FIBERFILLS	FIBROBLAST	FICTIONIZATION	FIELDSTRIPPED	FILIBUSTERINGS
FIBERGLASS	FIBROBLASTIC	FICTIONIZATIONS	FIELDSTRIPPING	FILIBUSTERISM
FIBERGLASSED	FIBROBLASTS	FICTIONIZE	FIELDSTRIPS	FILIBUSTERISMS
FIBERGLASSES	FIBROCARTILAGE	FICTIONIZED	FIELDVOLES	FILIBUSTEROUS
FIBERGLASSING	FIBROCARTILAGES	FICTIONIZES	FIELDWARDS	FILIBUSTERS
FIBERISATION	FIBROCEMENT	FICTIONIZING	FIELDWORKER	FILICINEAN
FIBERISATIONS	FIBROCEMENTS	FICTITIOUS	FIELDWORKERS	FILIGRAINS
FIBERISING	FIBROCYSTIC	FICTITIOUSLY	FIELDWORKS	FILIGRANES
FIBERIZATION	FIBROCYTES	FICTITIOUSNESS	FIENDISHLY	FILIGREEING
FIBERIZATIONS	FIBROLINES	FICTIVENESS	FIENDISHNESS	FILIOPIETISTIC
FIBERIZING	FIBROLITES	FICTIVENESSES	FIENDISHNESSES	FILIPENDULOUS
FIBERSCOPE	FIBROMATOUS	FIDDIOUSED	FIERCENESS	FILLAGREED
FIBERSCOPES	FIBROMYALGIA	FIDDIOUSES	FIERCENESSES	FILLAGREEING
FIBREBOARD	FIBROMYALGIAS	FIDDIOUSING	FIERINESSES	FILLAGREES
FIBREBOARDS	FIBRONECTIN	FIDDLEBACK	FIFTEENERS	FILLESTERS
FIBREFILLS	FIBRONECTINS	FIDDLEBACKS	FIFTEENTHLY	FILLIPEENS
FIBREGLASS	FIBROSARCOMA	FIDDLEDEDEE	FIFTEENTHS	FILLISTERS
FIBREGLASSED	FIBROSARCOMAS	FIDDLEDEEDEE	FIGHTBACKS	FILMGOINGS
FIBREGLASSES	FIBROSARCOMATA	FIDDLEHEAD	FIGURABILITIES	FILMICALLY
FIBREGLASSING	FIBROSITIS	FIDDLEHEADS	FIGURABILITY	FILMINESSES
FIBREOPTIC	FIBROSITISES	FIDDLENECK	FIGURANTES	FILMMAKERS
FIBRESCOPE	FIBROUSNESS	FIDDLENECKS	FIGURATELY	FILMMAKING
FIBRESCOPES	FIBROUSNESSES	FIDDLESTICK	FIGURATION	FILMMAKINGS
FIBRILLARY	FIBROVASCULAR	FIDDLESTICKS	FIGURATIONS	FILMOGRAPHIES
FIBRILLATE	FICKLENESS	FIDDLEWOOD	FIGURATIVE	FILMOGRAPHY
FIBRILLATED	FICKLENESSES	FIDDLEWOODS	FIGURATIVELY	FILMSETTER
FIBRILLATES	FICTIONALISE	FIDEICOMMISSA	FIGURATIVENESS	FILMSETTERS
FIBRILLATING	FICTIONALISED	FIDEICOMMISSARY	FIGUREHEAD	FILMSETTING
FIBRILLATION	FICTIONALISES	FIDEICOMMISSUM	FIGUREHEADS	FILMSETTINGS
FIBRILLATIONS	FICTIONALISING	FIDELISMOS	FIGURELESS	FILMSTRIPS
FIBRILLIFORM	FICTIONALITIES	FIDELISTAS	FIGUREWORK	FILOPLUMES
FIBRILLINS	FICTIONALITY	FIDELITIES	FIGUREWORKS	FILOPODIUM
FIBRILLOSE	FICTIONALIZE	FIDGETIEST	FILAGGRINS	FILOSELLES
FIBRILLOUS	FICTIONALIZED	FIDGETINESS	FILAGREEING	FILOVIRUSES
FIBRINOGEN	FICTIONALIZES	FIDGETINESSES	FILAMENTARY	FILTERABILITIES
FIBRINOGENIC	FICTIONALIZING	FIDGETINGLY	FILAMENTOUS	FILTERABILITY
FIBRINOGENOUS	FICTIONALLY	FIDUCIALLY	FILARIASES	FILTERABLE

FILTERABLENESS	FINGERGLASS	FINNOCHIOS	FIRESCREEN	FISSIPARITIES
FILTHINESS	FINGERGLASSES	FINOCCHIOS	FIRESCREENS	FISSIPARITY
FILTHINESSES	FINGERGUARD	FIORATURAE	FIRESTONES	FISSIPAROUS
FILTRABILITIES	FINGERGUARDS	FIREBALLER	FIRESTORMS	FISSIPAROUSLY
FILTRABILITY	FINGERHOLD	FIREBALLERS	FIRETHORNS	FISSIPAROUSNESS
FILTRABLENESS	FINGERHOLDS	FIREBALLING	FIRETRUCKS	FISSIPEDAL
FILTRABLENESSES	FINGERHOLE	FIREBOARDS	FIREWALLED	FISSIPEDES
FILTRATABLE	FINGERHOLES	FIREBOMBED	FIREWALLING	FISSIROSTRAL
FILTRATING	FINGERINGS	FIREBOMBER	FIREWARDEN	FISTFIGHTS
FILTRATION	FINGERLESS	FIREBOMBERS	FIREWARDENS	FISTICUFFED
FILTRATIONS	FINGERLIKE	FIREBOMBING	FIREWATERS	FISTICUFFING
FIMBRIATED	FINGERLING	FIREBOMBINGS	FIRMAMENTAL	FISTICUFFS
FIMBRIATES	FINGERLINGS	FIREBRANDS	FIRMAMENTS	FITFULNESS
FIMBRIATING	FINGERMARK	FIREBREAKS	FIRMNESSES	FITFULNESSES
FIMBRIATION	FINGERMARKS	FIREBRICKS	FIRSTBORNS	FITTINGNESS
FIMBRIATIONS	FINGERNAIL	FIREBUSHES	FIRSTFRUITS	FITTINGNESSES
FIMBRILLATE	FINGERNAILS	FIRECRACKER	FIRSTLINGS	FIVEFINGER
FIMICOLOUS	FINGERPICK	FIRECRACKERS	FIRSTNESSES	FIVEFINGERS
FINABLENESS	FINGERPICKED	FIRECRESTS	FISCALISTS	FIVEPENCES
FINABLENESSES	FINGERPICKING	FIREDRAGON	FISHABILITIES	FIXEDNESSES
FINAGLINGS	FINGERPICKINGS	FIREDRAGONS	FISHABILITY	FIXTURELESS
FINALISATION	FINGERPICKS	FIREDRAKES	FISHBURGER	FIXTURINGS
FINALISATIONS	FINGERPLATE	FIREFANGED	FISHBURGERS	FIZGIGGING
FINALISERS	FINGERPLATES	FIREFANGING	FISHERFOLK	FIZZENLESS
FINALISING	FINGERPOST	FIREFIGHTER	FISHERWOMAN	FIZZINESSES
FINALISTIC	FINGERPOSTS	FIREFIGHTERS	FISHERWOMEN	FLABBERGAST
FINALITIES	FINGERPRINT	FIREFIGHTING	FISHFINGER	FLABBERGASTED
FINALIZATION	FINGERPRINTED	FIREFIGHTINGS	FISHFINGERS	FLABBERGASTING
FINALIZATIONS	FINGERPRINTING	FIREFIGHTS	FISHIFYING	FLABBERGASTS
FINALIZERS	FINGERPRINTINGS	FIREFLOATS	FISHINESSES	FLABBINESS
FINALIZING	FINGERPRINTS	FIREFLOODS	FISHMONGER	FLABBINESSES
FINANCIALIST	FINGERSTALL	FIREGUARDS	FISHMONGERS	FLABELLATE
FINANCIALISTS	FINGERSTALLS	FIREHOSING	FISHPLATES	FLABELLATION
FINANCIALLY	FINGERTIPS	FIREHOSINGS	FISHTAILED	FLABELLATIONS
FINANCIALS	FINICALITIES	FIREHOUSES	FISHTAILING	FLABELLIFORM
FINANCIERED	FINICALITY	FIRELIGHTER	FISHWIFELIER	FLACCIDEST
FINANCIERING	FINICALNESS	FIRELIGHTERS	FISHWIFELIEST	FLACCIDITIES
FINANCIERS	FINICALNESSES	FIRELIGHTS	FISHWIFELY	FLACCIDITY
FINANCINGS	FINICKETIER	FIREPLACED	FISHYBACKS	FLACCIDNESS
FINEABLENESS	FINICKETIEST	FIREPLACES	FISSICOSTATE	FLACCIDNESSES
FINEABLENESSES	FINICKIEST	FIREPOWERS	FISSILINGUAL	FLACKERIES
FINENESSES	FINICKINESS	FIREPROOFED	FISSILITIES	FLACKERING
FINESSINGS	FINICKINESSES	FIREPROOFING	FISSIONABILITY	FLACKETING
FINGERBOARD	FINICKINGS	FIREPROOFINGS	FISSIONABLE	FLAFFERING
FINGERBOARDS	FINISHINGS	FIREPROOFS	FISSIONABLES	FLAGELLANT
FINGERBOWL	FINITENESS	FIRESCAPED	FISSIONING	FLAGELLANTISM
FINGERBOWLS	FINITENESSES	FIRESCAPES	FISSIPALMATE	FLAGELLANTISMS
FINGERBREADTH	FINNICKIER	FIRESCAPING	FISSIPARISM	FLAGELLANTS
FINGERBREADTHS	FINNICKIEST	FIRESCAPINGS	FISSIPARISMS	FLAGELLATE

FLAGELLATED	FLAMEPROOFED	FLASHCUBES	FLAUGHTING	FLEECHMENTS
FLAGELLATES	FLAMEPROOFER	FLASHFORWARD	FLAUNCHING	FLEECINESS
FLAGELLATING	FLAMEPROOFERS	FLASHFORWARDS	FLAUNCHINGS	FLEECINESSES
FLAGELLATION	FLAMEPROOFING	FLASHINESS	FLAUNTIEST	FLEERINGLY
FLAGELLATIONS	FLAMEPROOFS	FLASHINESSES	FLAUNTINESS	FLEETINGLY
FLAGELLATOR	FLAMETHROWER	FLASHLAMPS	FLAUNTINESSES	FLEETINGNESS
FLAGELLATORS	FLAMETHROWERS	FLASHLIGHT	FLAUNTINGLY	FLEETINGNESSES
FLAGELLATORY	FLAMINGOES	FLASHLIGHTS	FLAVANONES	FLEETNESSES
FLAGELLIFEROUS	FLAMINICAL	FLASHMOBBING	FLAVESCENT	FLEHMENING
FLAGELLIFORM	FLAMMABILITIES	FLASHMOBBINGS	FLAVIVIRUS	FLEMISHING
FLAGELLINS	FLAMMABILITY	FLASHOVERS	FLAVIVIRUSES	FLEROVIUMS
FLAGELLOMANIA	FLAMMABLES	FLASHPACKER	FLAVONOIDS	FLESHHOODS
FLAGELLOMANIAC	FLAMMIFEROUS	FLASHPACKERS	FLAVOPROTEIN	FLESHINESS
FLAGELLOMANIACS	FLAMMULATED	FLASHPOINT	FLAVOPROTEINS	FLESHINESSES
FLAGELLOMANIAS	FLAMMULATION	FLASHPOINTS	FLAVOPURPURIN	FLESHLIEST
FLAGELLUMS	FLAMMULATIONS	FLASHTUBES	FLAVOPURPURINS	FLESHLINESS
FLAGEOLETS	FLANCHINGS	FLATBREADS	FLAVORFULLY	FLESHLINESSES
FLAGGINESS	FLANCONADE	FLATFISHES	FLAVORIEST	FLESHLINGS
FLAGGINESSES	FLANCONADES	FLATFOOTED	FLAVORINGS	FLESHMENTS
FLAGGINGLY	FLANGELESS	FLATFOOTING	FLAVORISTS	FLESHMONGER
FLAGITATED	FLANKERING	FLATLANDER	FLAVORLESS	FLESHMONGERS
FLAGITATES	FLANNELBOARD	FLATLANDERS	FLAVORSOME	FLESHWORMS
FLAGITATING	FLANNELBOARDS	FLATLINERS	FLAVOURDYNAMICS	FLETCHINGS
FLAGITATION	FLANNELETS	FLATLINING	FLAVOURERS	FLEURETTES
FLAGITATIONS	FLANNELETTE	FLATNESSES	FLAVOURFUL	FLEXECUTIVE
FLAGITIOUS	FLANNELETTES	FLATPICKED	FLAVOURFULLY	FLEXECUTIVES
FLAGITIOUSLY	FLANNELGRAPH	FLATPICKING	FLAVOURIER	FLEXIBILITIES
FLAGITIOUSNESS	FLANNELGRAPHS	FLATSCREEN	FLAVOURIEST	FLEXIBILITY
FLAGRANCES	FLANNELING	FLATSCREENS	FLAVOURING	FLEXIBLENESS
FLAGRANCIES	FLANNELLED	FLATSHARES	FLAVOURINGS	FLEXIBLENESSES
FLAGRANTLY	FLANNELLIER	FLATTENERS	FLAVOURIST	FLEXICURITIES
FLAGRANTNESS	FLANNELLIEST	FLATTENING	FLAVOURISTS	FLEXICURITY
FLAGRANTNESSES	FLANNELLING	FLATTERABLE	FLAVOURLESS	FLEXIHOURS
FLAGSTAFFS	FLANNELMOUTHED	FLATTERERS	FLAVOURSOME	FLEXIONLESS
FLAGSTAVES	FLAPDOODLE	FLATTERIES	FLAWLESSLY	FLEXITARIAN
FLAGSTICKS	FLAPDOODLES	FLATTERING	FLAWLESSNESS	FLEXITARIANISM
FLAGSTONES	FLAPPERHOOD	FLATTERINGLY	FLAWLESSNESSES	FLEXITARIANISMS
FLAKINESSES	FLAPPERHOODS	FLATTEROUS	FLEAHOPPER	FLEXITARIANS
FLAMBEEING	FLAPPERISH	FLATTEROUSLY	FLEAHOPPERS	FLEXITIMES
FLAMBOYANCE	FLAPTRACKS	FLATULENCE	FLECHETTES	FLEXOGRAPHIC
FLAMBOYANCES	FLAREBACKS	FLATULENCES	FLECKERING	FLEXOGRAPHIES
FLAMBOYANCIES	FLASHBACKED	FLATULENCIES	FLECTIONAL	FLEXOGRAPHY
FLAMBOYANCY	FLASHBACKING	FLATULENCY	FLECTIONLESS	FLEXTENSION
FLAMBOYANT	FLASHBACKS	FLATULENTLY	FLEDGELING	FLEXTENSIONS
FLAMBOYANTE	FLASHBANGS	FLATWASHES	FLEDGELINGS	FLEXTIMERS
FLAMBOYANTES	FLASHBOARD	FLATWATERS	FLEDGLINGS	FLEXUOUSLY
FLAMBOYANTLY	FLASHBOARDS	FLAUGHTERED	FLEECELESS	FLIBBERTIGIBBET
FLAMBOYANTS	FLASHBULBS	FLAUGHTERING	FLEECHINGS	FLICHTERED
FLAMEPROOF	FLASHCARDS	FLAUGHTERS	FLEECHMENT	FLICHTERING

FLICKERIER	FLOATATION	FLOPPINESSES	FLOWCHARTS	FLUKINESSES
FLICKERIEST	FLOATATIONS	FLOPTICALS	FLOWERAGES	FLUMMERIES
FLICKERING	FLOATBASES	FLORENTINE	FLOWERBEDS	FLUMMOXING
FLICKERINGLY	FLOATINGLY	FLORENTINES	FLOWERETTE	FLUNITRAZEPAM
FLICKERTAIL	FLOATPLANE	FLORESCENCE	FLOWERETTES	FLUNITRAZEPAMS
FLICKERTAILS	FLOATPLANES	FLORESCENCES	FLOWERHORN	FLUNKEYDOM
FLIGHTIEST	FLOCCILLATION	FLORESCENT	FLOWERIEST	FLUNKEYDOMS
FLIGHTINESS	FLOCCILLATIONS	FLORIATION	FLOWERINESS	FLUNKEYISH
FLIGHTINESSES	FLOCCULANT	FLORIATIONS	FLOWERINESSES	FLUNKEYISM
FLIGHTLESS	FLOCCULANTS	FLORIBUNDA	FLOWERINGS	FLUNKEYISMS
FLIMFLAMMED	FLOCCULATE	FLORIBUNDAS	FLOWERLESS	FLUNKYISMS
FLIMFLAMMER	FLOCCULATED	FLORICANES	FLOWERLIKE	FLUORAPATITE
FLIMFLAMMERIES	FLOCCULATES	FLORICULTURAL	FLOWERPOTS	FLUORAPATITES
FLIMFLAMMERS	FLOCCULATING	FLORICULTURE	FLOWINGNESS	FLUORESCED
FLIMFLAMMERY	FLOCCULATION	FLORICULTURES	FLOWINGNESSES	FLUORESCEIN
FLIMFLAMMING	FLOCCULATIONS	FLORICULTURIST	FLOWMETERS	FLUORESCEINE
FLIMSINESS	FLOCCULATOR	FLORICULTURISTS	FLOWSTONES	FLUORESCEINES
FLIMSINESSES	FLOCCULATORS	FLORIDEANS	FLUCTUATED	FLUORESCEINS
FLINCHINGLY	FLOCCULENCE	FLORIDEOUS	FLUCTUATES	FLUORESCENCE
FLINCHINGS	FLOCCULENCES	FLORIDITIES	FLUCTUATING	FLUORESCENCES
FLINDERING	FLOCCULENCIES	FLORIDNESS	FLUCTUATION	FLUORESCENT
FLINDERSIA	FLOCCULENCY	FLORIDNESSES	FLUCTUATIONAL	FLUORESCENTS
FLINDERSIAS	FLOCCULENT	FLORIFEROUS	FLUCTUATIONS	FLUORESCER
FLINTHEADS	FLOCCULENTLY	FLORIFEROUSNESS	FLUEGELHORN	FLUORESCERS
FLINTIFIED	FLOODGATES	FLORIGENIC	FLUEGELHORNS	FLUORESCES
FLINTIFIES	FLOODLIGHT	FLORILEGIA	FLUENTNESS	FLUORESCING
FLINTIFYING	FLOODLIGHTED	FLORILEGIUM	FLUENTNESSES	FLUORIDATE
FLINTINESS	FLOODLIGHTING	FLORISTICALLY	FLUFFBALLS	FLUORIDATED
FLINTINESSES	FLOODLIGHTINGS	FLORISTICS	FLUFFINESS	FLUORIDATES
FLINTLOCKS	FLOODLIGHTS	FLORISTRIES	FLUFFINESSES	FLUORIDATING
FLIPBOARDS	FLOODMARKS	FLOSCULOUS	FLUGELHORN	FLUORIDATION
FLIPCHARTS	FLOODPLAIN	FLOTATIONS	FLUGELHORNIST	FLUORIDATIONS
FLIPFLOPPED	FLOODPLAINS	FLOUNCIEST	FLUGELHORNISTS	FLUORIDISE
FLIPFLOPPING	FLOODTIDES	FLOUNCINGS	FLUGELHORNS	FLUORIDISED
FLIPPANCIES	FLOODWALLS	FLOUNDERED	FLUIDEXTRACT	FLUORIDISES
FLIPPANTLY	FLOODWATER	FLOUNDERING	FLUIDEXTRACTS	FLUORIDISING
FLIPPANTNESS	FLOODWATERS	FLOURISHED	FLUIDIFIED	FLUORIDIZE
FLIPPANTNESSES	FLOORBOARD	FLOURISHER	FLUIDIFIES	FLUORIDIZED
FLIRTATION	FLOORBOARDS	FLOURISHERS	FLUIDIFYING	FLUORIDIZES
FLIRTATIONS	FLOORCLOTH	FLOURISHES	FLUIDISATION	FLUORIDIZING
FLIRTATIOUS	FLOORCLOTHS	FLOURISHIER	FLUIDISATIONS	FLUORIMETER
FLIRTATIOUSLY	FLOORDROBE	FLOURISHIEST	FLUIDISERS	FLUORIMETERS
FLIRTATIOUSNESS	FLOORDROBES	FLOURISHING	FLUIDISING	FLUORIMETRIC
FLIRTINGLY	FLOORHEADS	FLOURISHINGLY	FLUIDITIES	FLUORIMETRIES
FLITTERING	FLOORSHOWS	FLOUTINGLY	FLUIDIZATION	FLUORIMETRY
FLITTERMICE	FLOORWALKER	FLOUTINGSTOCK	FLUIDIZATIONS	FLUORINATE
FLITTERMOUSE	FLOORWALKERS	FLOUTINGSTOCKS	FLUIDIZERS	FLUORINATED
FLOATABILITIES	FLOPHOUSES	FLOWCHARTING	FLUIDIZING	FLUORINATES
FLOATABILITY	FLOPPINESS	FLOWCHARTINGS	FLUIDNESSES	FLUORINATING

FLUORINATION	FLUSTRATIONS	FOCALIZATION	FOLLICULOUS	FOOTDRAGGER
FLUORINATIONS	FLUTEMOUTH	FOCALIZATIONS	FOLLOWABLE	FOOTDRAGGERS
FLUOROACETATE	FLUTEMOUTHS	FOCALIZING	FOLLOWERSHIP	FOOTDRAGGING
FLUOROACETATES	FLUTTERBOARD	FOCIMETERS	FOLLOWERSHIPS	FOOTDRAGGINGS
FLUOROCARBON	FLUTTERBOARDS	FOCOMETERS	FOLLOWINGS	FOOTFAULTED
FLUOROCARBONS	FLUTTERERS	FODDERINGS	FOLLOWSHIP	FOOTFAULTING
FLUOROCHROME	FLUTTERIER	FOEDERATUS	FOLLOWSHIPS	FOOTFAULTS
FLUOROCHROMES	FLUTTERIEST	FOETATIONS	FOMENTATION	FOOTGUARDS
FLUOROGRAPHIC	FLUTTERING	FOETICIDAL	FOMENTATIONS	FOOTLAMBERT
FLUOROGRAPHIES	FLUTTERINGLY	FOETICIDES	FONCTIONNAIRE	FOOTLAMBERTS
FLUOROGRAPHY	FLUTTERINGS	FOETIDNESS	FONCTIONNAIRES	FOOTLESSLY
FLUOROMETER	FLUVIALIST	FOETIDNESSES	FONDLINGLY	FOOTLESSNESS
FLUOROMETERS	FLUVIALISTS	FOETIPAROUS	FONDNESSES	FOOTLESSNESSES
FLUOROMETRIC	FLUVIATILE	FOETOSCOPIES	FONTANELLE	FOOTLIGHTS
FLUOROMETRIES	FLUVIOMARINE	FOETOSCOPY	FONTANELLES	FOOTLOCKER
FLUOROMETRY	FLUVOXAMINE	FOGGINESSES	FONTICULUS	FOOTLOCKERS
FLUOROPHORE	FLUVOXAMINES	FOGRAMITES	FONTINALIS	FOOTNOTING
FLUOROPHORES	FLUXIONALLY	FOGRAMITIES	FONTINALISES	FOOTPLATEMAN
FLUOROPHOSPHATE	FLUXIONARY	FOILSWOMAN	FOODLESSNESS	FOOTPLATEMEN
FLUOROSCOPE	FLUXIONIST	FOILSWOMEN	FOODLESSNESSES	FOOTPLATES
FLUOROSCOPED	FLUXIONISTS	FOISONLESS	FOODSTUFFS	FOOTPLATEWOMAN
FLUOROSCOPES	FLUXMETERS	FOLIACEOUS	FOOLBEGGED	FOOTPLATEWOMEN
FLUOROSCOPIC	FLYBLOWING	FOLIATIONS	FOOLFISHES	FOOTPRINTS
FLUOROSCOPIES	FLYBOARDING	FOLIATURES	FOOLHARDIER	FOOTSLOGGED
FLUOROSCOPING	FLYBOARDINGS	FOLKINESSES	FOOLHARDIEST	FOOTSLOGGER
FLUOROSCOPIST	FLYBRIDGES	FOLKISHNESS	FOOLHARDILY	FOOTSLOGGERS
FLUOROSCOPISTS	FLYCATCHER	FOLKISHNESSES	FOOLHARDINESS	FOOTSLOGGING
FLUOROSCOPY	FLYCATCHERS	FOLKLORISH	FOOLHARDINESSES	FOOTSLOGGINGS
FLUOROTYPE	FLYFISHERS	FOLKLORIST	FOOLHARDISE	FOOTSORENESS
FLUOROTYPES	FLYPITCHER	FOLKLORISTIC	FOOLHARDISES	FOOTSORENESSES
FLUOROURACIL	FLYPITCHERS	FOLKLORISTS	FOOLHARDIZE	FOOTSTALKS
FLUOROURACILS	FLYPITCHES	FOLKSINESS	FOOLHARDIZES	FOOTSTALLS
FLUORSPARS	FLYPOSTERS	FOLKSINESSES	FOOLISHEST	FOOTSTOCKS
FLUOXETINE	FLYPOSTING	FOLKSINGER	FOOLISHNESS	FOOTSTONES
FLUOXETINES	FLYPOSTINGS	FOLKSINGERS	FOOLISHNESSES	FOOTSTOOLED
FLUPHENAZINE	FLYRODDERS	FOLKSINGING	FOOTBALLENE	FOOTSTOOLS
FLUPHENAZINES	FLYSCREENS	FOLKSINGINGS	FOOTBALLENES	FOOTWEARIER
FLUSHNESSES	FLYSPECKED	FOLKSONOMIES	FOOTBALLER	FOOTWEARIEST
FLUSHWORKS	FLYSPECKING	FOLKSONOMY	FOOTBALLERS	FOPPISHNESS
FLUSTEREDLY	FLYSTRIKES	FOLKTRONICA	FOOTBALLING	FOPPISHNESSES
FLUSTERIER	FLYSWATTER	FOLKTRONICAS	FOOTBALLIST	FORAMINATED
FLUSTERIEST	FLYSWATTERS	FOLLICULAR	FOOTBALLISTS	FORAMINIFER
FLUSTERING	FLYWEIGHTS	FOLLICULATE	FOOTBOARDS	FORAMINIFERA
FLUSTERMENT	FOAMFLOWER	FOLLICULATED	FOOTBRAKES	FORAMINIFERAL
FLUSTERMENTS	FOAMFLOWERS	FOLLICULIN	FOOTBREADTH	FORAMINIFERAN
FLUSTRATED	FOAMINESSES	FOLLICULINS	FOOTBREADTHS	FORAMINIFERANS
FLUSTRATES	FOCALISATION	FOLLICULITIS	FOOTBRIDGE	FORAMINIFEROUS
FLUSTRATING	FOCALISATIONS	FOLLICULITISES	FOOTBRIDGES	FORAMINIFERS
FLUSTRATION	FOCALISING	FOLLICULOSE	FOOTCLOTHS	FORAMINOUS

FORBEARANCE	FORECASTERS	FOREHANDEDNESS	FOREPAYMENT	FORESIGNIFIES
FORBEARANCES	FORECASTING	FOREHANDING	FOREPAYMENTS	FORESIGNIFY
FORBEARANT	FORECASTINGS	FOREHENTING	FOREPLANNED	FORESIGNIFYING
FORBEARERS	FORECASTLE	FOREHOOVES	FOREPLANNING	FORESKIRTS
FORBEARING	FORECASTLES	FOREIGNERS	FOREPOINTED	FORESLACKED
FORBEARINGLY	FORECHECKED	FOREIGNISM	FOREPOINTING	FORESLACKING
FORBIDDALS	FORECHECKER	FOREIGNISMS	FOREPOINTS	FORESLACKS
FORBIDDANCE	FORECHECKERS	FOREIGNNESS	FOREQUARTER	FORESLOWED
FORBIDDANCES	FORECHECKING	FOREIGNNESSES	FOREQUARTERS	FORESLOWING
FORBIDDENLY	FORECHECKS	FOREJUDGED	FOREREACHED	FORESPEAKING
FORBIDDERS	FORECHOSEN	FOREJUDGEMENT	FOREREACHES	FORESPEAKS
FORBIDDING	FORECLOSABLE	FOREJUDGEMENTS	FOREREACHING	FORESPENDING
FORBIDDINGLY	FORECLOSED	FOREJUDGES	FOREREADING	FORESPENDS
FORBIDDINGNESS	FORECLOSES	FOREJUDGING	FOREREADINGS	FORESPOKEN
FORBIDDINGS	FORECLOSING	FOREJUDGMENT	FORERUNNER	FORESTAGES
FORCEDNESS	FORECLOSURE	FOREJUDGMENTS	FORERUNNERS	FORESTAIRS
FORCEDNESSES	FORECLOSURES	FOREKNOWABLE	FORERUNNING	FORESTALLED
FORCEFULLY	FORECLOTHS	FOREKNOWING	FORESAYING	FORESTALLER
FORCEFULNESS	FORECOURSE	FOREKNOWINGLY	FORESEEABILITY	FORESTALLERS
FORCEFULNESSES	FORECOURSES	FOREKNOWLEDGE	FORESEEABLE	FORESTALLING
FORCEMEATS	FORECOURTS	FOREKNOWLEDGES	FORESEEING	FORESTALLINGS
FORCEPSLIKE	FOREDAMNED	FORELADIES	FORESEEINGLY	FORESTALLMENT
FORCIBILITIES	FOREDATING	FORELAYING	FORESHADOW	FORESTALLMENTS
FORCIBILITY	FOREDOOMED	FORELENDING	FORESHADOWED	FORESTALLS
FORCIBLENESS	FOREDOOMING	FORELIFTED	FORESHADOWER	FORESTALMENT
FORCIBLENESSES	FOREFATHER	FORELIFTING	FORESHADOWERS	FORESTALMENTS
FORCIPATED	FOREFATHERLY	FORELOCKED	FORESHADOWING	FORESTATION
FORCIPATION	FOREFATHERS	FORELOCKING	FORESHADOWINGS	FORESTATIONS
FORCIPATIONS	FOREFEELING	FOREMANSHIP	FORESHADOWS	FORESTAYSAIL
FOREARMING	FOREFEELINGLY	FOREMANSHIPS	FORESHANKS	FORESTAYSAILS
FOREBITTER	FOREFENDED	FOREMASTMAN	FORESHEETS	FORESTLAND
FOREBITTERS	FOREFENDING	FOREMASTMEN	FORESHEWED	FORESTLANDS
FOREBODEMENT	FOREFINGER	FOREMEANING	FORESHEWING	FORESTLESS
FOREBODEMENTS	FOREFINGERS	FOREMENTIONED	FORESHOCKS	FORESTRIES
FOREBODERS	FOREFRONTS	FOREMOTHER	FORESHORES	FORESWEARING
FOREBODIES	FOREGATHER	FOREMOTHERS	FORESHORTEN	FORESWEARS
FOREBODING	FOREGATHERED	FORENIGHTS	FORESHORTENED	FORETASTED
FOREBODINGLY	FOREGATHERING	FORENSICALITIES	FORESHORTENING	FORETASTES
FOREBODINGNESS	FOREGATHERS	FORENSICALITY	FORESHORTENINGS	FORETASTING
FOREBODINGS	FOREGLEAMS	FORENSICALLY	FORESHORTENS	FORETAUGHT
FOREBRAINS	FOREGOINGS	FOREORDAIN	FORESHOWED	FORETEACHES
FORECABINS	FOREGONENESS	FOREORDAINED	FORESHOWING	FORETEACHING
FORECADDIE	FOREGONENESSES	FOREORDAINING	FORESIGHTED	FORETELLER
FORECADDIES	FOREGROUND	FOREORDAINMENT	FORESIGHTEDLY	FORETELLERS
FORECARRIAGE	FOREGROUNDED	FOREORDAINMENTS	FORESIGHTEDNESS	FORETELLING
FORECARRIAGES	FOREGROUNDING	FOREORDAINS	FORESIGHTFUL	FORETHINKER
FORECASTABLE	FOREGROUNDS	FOREORDINATION	FORESIGHTLESS	FORETHINKERS
FORECASTED	FOREHANDED	FOREORDINATIONS	FORESIGHTS	FORETHINKING
FORECASTER	FOREHANDEDLY	FOREPASSED	FORESIGNIFIED	FORETHINKS

FORETHOUGHT	FORGETFULNESSES	FORMALISMS	FORMULARISERS	FORSWEARERS
FORETHOUGHTFUL	FORGETTABLE	FORMALISTIC	FORMULARISES	FORSWEARING
FORETHOUGHTS	FORGETTERIES	FORMALISTICALLY	FORMULARISING	FORSWINKED
FORETOKENED	FORGETTERS	FORMALISTS	FORMULARISTIC	FORSWINKING
FORETOKENING	FORGETTERY	FORMALITER	FORMULARIZATION	FORSWORNNESS
FORETOKENINGS	FORGETTING	FORMALITIES	FORMULARIZE	FORSWORNNESSES
FORETOKENS	FORGETTINGLY	FORMALIZABLE	FORMULARIZED	FORSYTHIAS
FORETOPMAN	FORGETTINGS	FORMALIZATION	FORMULARIZER	FORTALICES
FORETOPMAST	FORGIVABLE	FORMALIZATIONS	FORMULARIZERS	FORTEPIANIST
FORETOPMASTS	FORGIVABLY	FORMALIZED	FORMULARIZES	FORTEPIANISTS
FORETOPMEN	FORGIVENESS	FORMALIZER	FORMULARIZING	FORTEPIANO
FORETRIANGLE	FORGIVENESSES	FORMALIZERS	FORMULATED	FORTEPIANOS
FORETRIANGLES	FORGIVINGLY	FORMALIZES	FORMULATES	FORTHCOMES
FOREVERMORE	FORGIVINGNESS	FORMALIZING	FORMULATING	FORTHCOMING
FOREVERNESS	FORGIVINGNESSES	FORMALNESS	FORMULATION	FORTHCOMINGNESS
FOREVERNESSES	FORGOTTENNESS	FORMALNESSES	FORMULATIONS	FORTHGOING
FOREVOUCHED	FORGOTTENNESSES	FORMAMIDES	FORMULATOR	FORTHGOINGS
FOREWARDED	FORHAILING	FORMATIONAL	FORMULATORS	FORTHINKING
FOREWARDING	FORHENTING	FORMATIONS	FORMULISED	FORTHOUGHT
FOREWARNED	FORHOOIEING	FORMATIVELY	FORMULISES	FORTHRIGHT
FOREWARNER	FORINSECAL	FORMATIVENESS	FORMULISING	FORTHRIGHTLY
FOREWARNERS	FORISFAMILIATE	FORMATIVENESSES	FORMULISMS	FORTHRIGHTNESS
FOREWARNING	FORISFAMILIATED	FORMATIVES	FORMULISTIC	FORTHRIGHTS
FOREWARNINGLY	FORISFAMILIATES	FORMATTERS	FORMULISTS	FORTIFIABLE
FOREWARNINGS	FORJUDGING	FORMATTING	FORMULIZED	FORTIFICATION
FOREWEIGHED	FORJUDGMENT	FORMATTINGS	FORMULIZES	FORTIFICATIONS
FOREWEIGHING	FORJUDGMENTS	FORMFITTING	FORMULIZING	FORTIFIERS
FOREWEIGHS	FORKEDNESS	FORMICARIA	FORNICATED	FORTIFYING
FORFAIRING	FORKEDNESSES	FORMICARIES	FORNICATES	FORTIFYINGLY
FORFAITERS	FORKINESSES	FORMICARIUM	FORNICATING	FORTILAGES
FORFAITING	FORKLIFTED	FORMICATED	FORNICATION	FORTISSIMI
FORFAITINGS	FORKLIFTING	FORMICATES	FORNICATIONS	FORTISSIMO
FORFEITABLE	FORLENDING	FORMICATING	FORNICATOR	FORTISSIMOS
FORFEITERS	FORLORNEST	FORMICATION	FORNICATORS	FORTISSISSIMO
FORFEITING	FORLORNNESS	FORMICATIONS	FORNICATRESS	FORTITUDES
FORFEITURE	FORLORNNESSES	FORMIDABILITIES	FORNICATRESSES	FORTITUDINOUS
FORFEITURES	FORMABILITIES	FORMIDABILITY	FORSAKENLY	FORTNIGHTLIES
FORFENDING	FORMABILITY	FORMIDABLE	FORSAKENNESS	FORTNIGHTLY
FORFEUCHEN	FORMALDEHYDE	FORMIDABLENESS	FORSAKENNESSES	FORTNIGHTS
FORFICULATE	FORMALDEHYDES	FORMIDABLY	FORSAKINGS	FORTRESSED
FORFOUGHEN	FORMALINES	FORMLESSLY	FORSLACKED	FORTRESSES
FORFOUGHTEN	FORMALISABLE	FORMLESSNESS	FORSLACKING	FORTRESSING
FORGATHERED	FORMALISATION	FORMLESSNESSES	FORSLOEING	FORTRESSLIKE
FORGATHERING	FORMALISATIONS	FORMULAICALLY	FORSLOWING	FORTUITIES
FORGATHERS	FORMALISED	FORMULARIES	FORSPEAKING	FORTUITISM
FORGEABILITIES	FORMALISER	FORMULARISATION	FORSPENDING	FORTUITISMS
FORGEABILITY	FORMALISERS	FORMULARISE	FORSTERITE	FORTUITIST
FORGETFULLY	FORMALISES	FORMULARISED	FORSTERITES	FORTUITISTS
FORGETFULNESS	FORMALISING	FORMULARISER	FORSWEARER	FORTUITOUS

FORTUITOUSLY	FOTHERGILLA	FOXHUNTINGS	FRACTOCUMULUS	FRANCHISEE
FORTUITOUSNESS	FOTHERGILLAS	FOXINESSES	FRACTOGRAPHIES	FRANCHISEES
FORTUNATELY	FOUDROYANT	FOXTROTTED	FRACTOGRAPHY	FRANCHISEMENT
FORTUNATENESS	FOUGHTIEST	FOXTROTTING	FRACTOSTRATI	FRANCHISEMENTS
FORTUNATENESSES	FOULBROODS	FOZINESSES	FRACTOSTRATUS	FRANCHISER
FORTUNATES	FOULDERING	FRABJOUSLY	FRACTURABLE	FRANCHISERS
FORTUNELESS	FOULMOUTHED	FRACTALITIES	FRACTURERS	FRANCHISES
FORTUNISED	FOULNESSES	FRACTALITY	FRACTURING	FRANCHISING
FORTUNISES	FOUNDATION	FRACTIONAL	FRAGILENESS	FRANCHISOR
FORTUNISING	FOUNDATIONAL	FRACTIONALISE	FRAGILENESSES	FRANCHISORS
FORTUNIZED	FOUNDATIONALLY	FRACTIONALISED	FRAGILITIES	FRANCISATION
FORTUNIZES	FOUNDATIONARY	FRACTIONALISES	FRAGMENTAL	FRANCISATIONS
FORTUNIZING	FOUNDATIONER	FRACTIONALISING	FRAGMENTALLY	FRANCISING
FORWANDERED	FOUNDATIONERS	FRACTIONALISM	FRAGMENTARILY	FRANCIZATION
FORWANDERING	FOUNDATIONLESS	FRACTIONALISMS	FRAGMENTARINESS	FRANCIZATIONS
FORWANDERS	FOUNDATIONS	FRACTIONALIST	FRAGMENTARY	FRANCIZING
FORWARDERS	FOUNDERING	FRACTIONALISTS	FRAGMENTATE	FRANCOLINS
FORWARDEST	FOUNDEROUS	FRACTIONALIZE	FRAGMENTATED	FRANCOMANIA
FORWARDING	FOUNDLINGS	FRACTIONALIZED	FRAGMENTATES	FRANCOMANIAS
FORWARDINGS	FOUNDRESSES	FRACTIONALIZES	FRAGMENTATING	FRANCOPHIL
FORWARDNESS	FOUNTAINED	FRACTIONALIZING	FRAGMENTATION	FRANCOPHILE
FORWARDNESSES	FOUNTAINHEAD	FRACTIONALLY	FRAGMENTATIONS	FRANCOPHILES
FORWARNING	FOUNTAINHEADS	FRACTIONARY	FRAGMENTED	FRANCOPHILS
FORWASTING	FOUNTAINING	FRACTIONATE	FRAGMENTING	FRANCOPHOBE
FORWEARIED	FOUNTAINLESS	FRACTIONATED	FRAGMENTISE	FRANCOPHOBES
FORWEARIES	FOURCHETTE	FRACTIONATES	FRAGMENTISED	FRANCOPHOBIA
FORWEARYING	FOURCHETTES	FRACTIONATING	FRAGMENTISES	FRANCOPHOBIAS
FOSCARNETS	FOURDRINIER	FRACTIONATION	FRAGMENTISING	FRANCOPHONE
FOSSICKERS	FOURDRINIERS	FRACTIONATIONS	FRAGMENTIZE	FRANCOPHONES
FOSSICKING	FOURFOLDNESS	FRACTIONATOR	FRAGMENTIZED	FRANGIBILITIES
FOSSICKINGS	FOURFOLDNESSES	FRACTIONATORS	FRAGMENTIZES	FRANGIBILITY
FOSSILIFEROUS	FOURPENCES	FRACTIONED	FRAGMENTIZING	FRANGIBLENESS
FOSSILISABLE	FOURPENNIES	FRACTIONING	FRAGRANCED	FRANGIBLENESSES
FOSSILISATION	FOURPLEXES	FRACTIONISATION	FRAGRANCES	FRANGIPANE
FOSSILISATIONS	FOURRAGERE	FRACTIONISE	FRAGRANCIES	FRANGIPANES
FOSSILISED	FOURRAGERES	FRACTIONISED	FRAGRANCING	FRANGIPANI
FOSSILISES	FOURSCORTH	FRACTIONISES	FRAGRANTLY	FRANGIPANIS
FOSSILISING	FOURSQUARE	FRACTIONISING	FRAGRANTNESS	FRANGIPANNI
FOSSILIZABLE	FOURSQUARELY	FRACTIONIZATION	FRAGRANTNESSES	FRANKALMOIGN
FOSSILIZATION	FOURSQUARENESS	FRACTIONIZE	FRAICHEURS	FRANKALMOIGNS
FOSSILIZATIONS	FOURTEENER	FRACTIONIZED	FRAILNESSES	FRANKFORTS
FOSSILIZED	FOURTEENERS	FRACTIONIZES	FRAMBESIAS	FRANKFURTER
FOSSILIZES	FOURTEENTH	FRACTIONIZING	FRAMBOESIA	FRANKFURTERS
FOSSILIZING	FOURTEENTHLY	FRACTIONLET	FRAMBOESIAS	FRANKFURTS
FOSTERAGES	FOURTEENTHS	FRACTIONLETS	FRAMBOISES	FRANKINCENSE
FOSTERINGS	FOVEOLATED	FRACTIOUSLY	FRAMESHIFT	FRANKINCENSES
FOSTERLING	FOXBERRIES	FRACTIOUSNESS	FRAMESHIFTS	FRANKLINITE
FOSTERLINGS	FOXHUNTERS	FRACTIOUSNESSES	FRAMEWORKS	FRANKLINITES
FOSTRESSES	FOXHUNTING	FRACTOCUMULI	FRANCHISED	FRANKNESSES

FRANKPLEDGE	FREAKINESS	FREEMASONIC	FRENETICNESSES	FRIENDINGS
FRANKPLEDGES	FREAKINESSES	FREEMASONRIES	FRENZIEDLY	FRIENDLESS
FRANSERIAS	FREAKISHLY	FREEMASONRY	FREQUENCES	FRIENDLESSNESS
FRANTICALLY	FREAKISHNESS	FREEMASONS	FREQUENCIES	FRIENDLIER
FRANTICNESS	FREAKISHNESSES	FREENESSES	FREQUENTABLE	FRIENDLIES
FRANTICNESSES	FRECKLIEST	FREEPHONES	FREQUENTATION	FRIENDLIEST
FRATCHETIER	FRECKLINGS	FREESHEETS	FREQUENTATIONS	FRIENDLILY
FRATCHETIEST	FREEBASERS	FREESTANDING	FREQUENTATIVE	FRIENDLINESS
FRATCHIEST	FREEBASING	FREESTONES	FREQUENTATIVES	FRIENDLINESSES
FRATERNALISM	FREEBOARDS	FREESTYLED	FREQUENTED	FRIENDSHIP
FRATERNALISMS	FREEBOOTED	FREESTYLER	FREQUENTER	FRIENDSHIPS
FRATERNALLY	FREEBOOTER	FREESTYLERS	FREQUENTERS	FRIEZELIKE
FRATERNISATION	FREEBOOTERIES	FREESTYLES	FREQUENTEST	FRIGATOONS
FRATERNISATIONS	FREEBOOTERS	FREESTYLING	FREQUENTING	FRIGHTENED
FRATERNISE	FREEBOOTERY	FREESTYLINGS	FREQUENTLY	FRIGHTENER
FRATERNISED	FREEBOOTIES	FREETHINKER	FREQUENTNESS	FRIGHTENERS
FRATERNISER	FREEBOOTING	FREETHINKERS	FREQUENTNESSES	FRIGHTENING
FRATERNISERS	FREEBOOTINGS	FREETHINKING	FRESCOINGS	FRIGHTENINGLY
FRATERNISES	FREECOOLING	FREETHINKINGS	FRESCOISTS	FRIGHTFULLY
FRATERNISING	FREECOOLINGS	FREEWHEELED	FRESHENERS	FRIGHTFULNESS
FRATERNITIES	FREECYCLED	FREEWHEELER	FRESHENING	FRIGHTFULNESSES
FRATERNITY	FREECYCLES	FREEWHEELERS	FRESHERDOM	FRIGHTSOME
FRATERNIZATION	FREECYCLING	FREEWHEELING	FRESHERDOMS	FRIGIDARIA
FRATERNIZATIONS	FREEDIVERS	FREEWHEELINGLY	FRESHMANSHIP	FRIGIDARIUM
FRATERNIZE	FREEDIVING	FREEWHEELINGS	FRESHMANSHIPS	FRIGIDITIES
FRATERNIZED	FREEDIVINGS	FREEWHEELS	FRESHNESSES	FRIGIDNESS
FRATERNIZER	FREEDWOMAN	FREEWRITES	FRESHWATER	FRIGIDNESSES
FRATERNIZERS	FREEDWOMEN	FREEWRITING	FRESHWATERS	FRIGORIFIC
FRATERNIZES	FREEGANISM	FREEWRITINGS	FRETBOARDS	FRIGORIFICO
FRATERNIZING	FREEGANISMS	FREEWRITTEN	FRETFULNESS	FRIGORIFICOS
FRATRICIDAL	FREEHANDED	FREEZINGLY	FRETFULNESSES	FRIKKADELS
FRATRICIDE	FREEHANDEDLY	FREIGHTAGE	FRIABILITIES	FRILLERIES
FRATRICIDES	FREEHANDEDNESS	FREIGHTAGES	FRIABILITY	FRILLINESS
FRAUDFULLY	FREEHEARTED	FREIGHTERS	FRIABLENESS	FRILLINESSES
FRAUDSTERS	FREEHEARTEDLY	FREIGHTING	FRIABLENESSES	FRINGELESS
FRAUDULENCE	FREEHOLDER	FREIGHTLESS	FRIARBIRDS	FRINGELIKE
FRAUDULENCES	FREEHOLDERS	FREMESCENCE	FRICANDEAU	FRINGILLACEOUS
FRAUDULENCIES	FREELANCED	FREMESCENCES	FRICANDEAUS	FRINGILLID
FRAUDULENCY	FREELANCER	FREMESCENT	FRICANDEAUX	FRINGILLIFORM
FRAUDULENT	FREELANCERS	FREMITUSES	FRICANDOES	FRINGILLINE
FRAUDULENTLY	FREELANCES	FRENCHIFICATION	FRICASSEED	FRIPONNERIE
FRAUDULENTNESS	FREELANCING	FRENCHIFIED	FRICASSEEING	FRIPONNERIES
FRAUGHTAGE	FREELOADED	FRENCHIFIES	FRICASSEES	FRIPPERERS
FRAUGHTAGES	FREELOADER	FRENCHIFYING	FRICATIVES	FRIPPERIES
FRAUGHTEST	FREELOADERS	FRENETICAL	FRICTIONAL	FRISKINESS
FRAUGHTING	FREELOADING	FRENETICALLY	FRICTIONALLY	FRISKINESSES
FRAXINELLA	FREELOADINGS	FRENETICISM	FRICTIONLESS	FRISKINGLY
FRAXINELLAS	FREEMARTIN	FRENETICISMS	FRICTIONLESSLY	FRITHBORHS
FREAKERIES	FREEMARTINS	FRENETICNESS	FRIEDCAKES	FRITHSOKEN

FRITHSOKENS	FRONTIERED	FROWSTIEST	FRUITINESS	FULFILLMENTS
FRITHSTOOL	FRONTIERING	FROWSTINESS	FRUITINESSES	FULFILMENT
FRITHSTOOLS	FRONTIERSMAN	FROWSTINESSES	FRUITLESSLY	FULFILMENTS
FRITILLARIA	FRONTIERSMEN	FROWZINESS	FRUITLESSNESS	FULGENCIES
FRITILLARIAS	FRONTIERSWOMAN	FROWZINESSES	FRUITLESSNESSES	FULGURATED
FRITILLARIES	FRONTIERSWOMEN	FROZENNESS	FRUITWOODS	FULGURATES
FRITILLARY	FRONTISPIECE	FROZENNESSES	FRUITWORMS	FULGURATING
FRITTERERS	FRONTISPIECED	FRUCTIFEROUS	FRUMENTACEOUS	FULGURATION
FRITTERING	FRONTISPIECES	FRUCTIFEROUSLY	FRUMENTARIOUS	FULGURATIONS
FRIVOLITIES	FRONTISPIECING	FRUCTIFICATION	FRUMENTATION	FULGURITES
FRIVOLLERS	FRONTLESSLY	FRUCTIFICATIONS	FRUMENTATIONS	FULIGINOSITIES
FRIVOLLING	FRONTLINER	FRUCTIFIED	FRUMENTIES	FULIGINOSITY
FRIVOLOUSLY	FRONTLINERS	FRUCTIFIER	FRUMPINESS	FULIGINOUS
FRIVOLOUSNESS	FRONTLINES	FRUCTIFIERS	FRUMPINESSES	FULIGINOUSLY
FRIVOLOUSNESSES	FRONTLISTS	FRUCTIFIES	FRUMPISHLY	FULIGINOUSNESS
FRIZZINESS	FRONTOGENESES	FRUCTIFYING	FRUMPISHNESS	FULLBLOODS
FRIZZINESSES	FRONTOGENESIS	FRUCTIVOROUS	FRUMPISHNESSES	FULLERENES
FRIZZLIEST	FRONTOGENETIC	FRUCTUARIES	FRUSEMIDES	FULLERIDES
FRIZZLINESS	FRONTOLYSES	FRUCTUATED	FRUSTRATED	FULLERITES
FRIZZLINESSES	FRONTOLYSIS	FRUCTUATES	FRUSTRATER	FULLMOUTHED
FROGFISHES	FRONTPAGED	FRUCTUATING	FRUSTRATERS	FULLNESSES
FROGGERIES	FRONTPAGES	FRUCTUATION	FRUSTRATES	FULMINANTS
FROGHOPPER	FRONTPAGING	FRUCTUATIONS	FRUSTRATING	FULMINATED
FROGHOPPERS	FRONTRUNNER	FRUCTUOUSLY	FRUSTRATINGLY	FULMINATES
FROGMARCHED	FRONTRUNNERS	FRUCTUOUSNESS	FRUSTRATION	FULMINATING
FROGMARCHES	FRONTRUNNING	FRUCTUOUSNESSES	FRUSTRATIONS	FULMINATION
FROGMARCHING	FRONTRUNNINGS	FRUGALISTA	FRUTESCENCE	FULMINATIONS
FROGMOUTHS	FRONTWARDS	FRUGALISTAS	FRUTESCENCES	FULMINATOR
FROGSPAWNS	FROSTBITES	FRUGALISTS	FRUTESCENT	FULMINATORS
FROLICKERS	FROSTBITING	FRUGALITIES	FRUTIFYING	FULMINATORY
FROLICKIER	FROSTBITINGS	FRUGALNESS	FUCIVOROUS	FULMINEOUS
FROLICKIEST	FROSTBITTEN	FRUGALNESSES	FUCOXANTHIN	FULSOMENESS
FROLICKING	FROSTBOUND	FRUGIFEROUS	FUCOXANTHINS	FULSOMENESSES
FROLICSOME	FROSTFISHES	FRUGIVORES	FUGACIOUSLY	FUMATORIES
FROLICSOMELY	FROSTINESS	FRUGIVOROUS	FUGACIOUSNESS	FUMATORIUM
FROLICSOMENESS	FROSTINESSES	FRUITARIAN	FUGACIOUSNESSES	FUMATORIUMS
FROMENTIES	FROSTLINES	FRUITARIANISM	FUGACITIES	FUMBLINGLY
FRONDESCENCE	FROSTWORKS	FRUITARIANISMS	FUGGINESSES	FUMBLINGNESS
FRONDESCENCES	FROTHERIES	FRUITARIANS	FUGITATION	FUMBLINGNESSES
FRONDESCENT	FROTHINESS	FRUITCAKES	FUGITATIONS	FUMIGATING
FRONDIFEROUS	FROTHINESSES	FRUITERERS	FUGITIVELY	FUMIGATION
FRONTAGERS	FROUGHIEST	FRUITERESS	FUGITIVENESS	FUMIGATIONS
FRONTALITIES	FROUZINESS	FRUITERESSES	FUGITIVENESSES	FUMIGATORS
FRONTALITY	FROUZINESSES	FRUITERIES	FUGITOMETER	FUMIGATORY
FRONTBENCHER	FROWARDNESS	FRUITFULLER	FUGITOMETERS	FUMITORIES
FRONTBENCHERS	FROWARDNESSES	FRUITFULLEST	FULFILLERS	FUMOSITIES
FRONTCOURT	FROWNINGLY	FRUITFULLY	FULFILLING	FUNAMBULATE
FRONTCOURTS	FROWSINESS	FRUITFULNESS	FULFILLINGS	FUNAMBULATED
FRONTENISES	FROWSINESSES	FRUITFULNESSES	FULFILLMENT	FUNAMBULATES

FUNAMBULATING	FUNDAMENTS	FURBELOWING	FURTHERSOME	FUSTIANIZES
FUNAMBULATION	FUNDHOLDER	FURBISHERS	FURTIVENESS	FUSTIANIZING
FUNAMBULATIONS	FUNDHOLDERS	FURBISHING	FURTIVENESSES	FUSTIGATED
FUNAMBULATOR	FUNDHOLDING	FURCATIONS	FURUNCULAR	FUSTIGATES
FUNAMBULATORS	FUNDHOLDINGS	FURCIFEROUS	FURUNCULOSES	FUSTIGATING
FUNAMBULATORY	FUNDRAISED	FURFURACEOUS	FURUNCULOSIS	FUSTIGATION
FUNAMBULISM	FUNDRAISER	FURFURACEOUSLY	FURUNCULOUS	FUSTIGATIONS
FUNAMBULISMS	FUNDRAISERS	FURFURALDEHYDE	FUSHIONLESS	FUSTIGATOR
FUNAMBULIST	FUNDRAISES	FURFURALDEHYDES	FUSIBILITIES	FUSTIGATORS
FUNAMBULISTS	FUNDRAISING	FURFUROLES	FUSIBILITY	FUSTIGATORY
FUNCTIONAL	FUNDRAISINGS	FURIOSITIES	FUSIBLENESS	FUSTILARIAN
FUNCTIONALISM	FUNEREALLY	FURIOUSNESS	FUSIBLENESSES	FUSTILARIANS
FUNCTIONALISMS	FUNGIBILITIES	FURIOUSNESSES	FUSILLADED	FUSTILIRIAN
FUNCTIONALIST	FUNGIBILITY	FURLOUGHED	FUSILLADES	FUSTILIRIANS
FUNCTIONALISTIC	FUNGICIDAL	FURLOUGHING	FUSILLADING	FUSTILLIRIAN
FUNCTIONALISTS	FUNGICIDALLY	FURMENTIES	FUSILLATION	FUSTILLIRIANS
FUNCTIONALITIES	FUNGICIDES	FURNIMENTS	FUSILLATIONS	FUSTINESSES
FUNCTIONALITY	FUNGISTATIC	FURNISHERS	FUSIONISMS	FUSULINIDS
FUNCTIONALLY	FUNGISTATICALLY	FURNISHING	FUSIONISTS	FUTILENESS
FUNCTIONALS	FUNGISTATS	FURNISHINGS	FUSIONLESS	FUTILENESSES
FUNCTIONARIES	FUNGOSITIES	FURNISHMENT	FUSSBUDGET	FUTILITARIAN
FUNCTIONARY	FUNICULARS	FURNISHMENTS	FUSSBUDGETIER	FUTILITARIANISM
FUNCTIONATE	FUNICULATE	FURNITURES	FUSSBUDGETIEST	FUTILITARIANS
FUNCTIONATED	FUNKINESSES	FUROSEMIDE	FUSSBUDGETS	FUTILITIES
FUNCTIONATES	FUNNELFORM	FUROSEMIDES	FUSSBUDGETY	FUTURELESS
FUNCTIONATING	FUNNELLING	FURRIERIES	FUSSINESSES	FUTURELESSNESS
FUNCTIONED	FUNNINESSES	FURRINESSES	FUSTANELLA	FUTURISTIC
FUNCTIONING	FURACIOUSNESS	FURROWIEST	FUSTANELLAS	FUTURISTICALLY
FUNCTIONLESS	FURACIOUSNESSES	FURROWLESS	FUSTANELLE	FUTURISTICS
FUNDAMENTAL	FURACITIES	FURSHLUGGINER	FUSTANELLES	FUTURITIES
FUNDAMENTALISM	FURALDEHYDE	FURTHCOMING	FUSTIANISE	FUTURITION
FUNDAMENTALISMS	FURALDEHYDES	FURTHCOMINGS	FUSTIANISED	FUTURITIONS
FUNDAMENTALIST	FURANOSIDE	FURTHERANCE	FUSTIANISES	FUTUROLOGICAL
FUNDAMENTALISTS	FURANOSIDES	FURTHERANCES	FUSTIANISING	FUTUROLOGIES
FUNDAMENTALITY	FURAZOLIDONE	FURTHERERS	FUSTIANIST	FUTUROLOGIST
FUNDAMENTALLY	FURAZOLIDONES	FURTHERING	FUSTIANISTS	FUTUROLOGISTS
FUNDAMENTALNESS	FURBEARERS	FURTHERMORE	FUSTIANIZE	FUTUROLOGY
FUNDAMENTALS	FURBELOWED	FURTHERMOST	FUSTIANIZED	FUZZINESSES

G

GABAPENTIN	GAINSAYING	GALANTAMINE	GALLIASSES	GALLSICKNESSES
GABAPENTINS	GAINSAYINGS	GALANTAMINES	GALLICISATION	GALLSTONES
GABARDINES	GAINSHARING	GALANTINES	GALLICISATIONS	GALLUMPHED
GABBINESSES	GAINSHARINGS	GALAVANTED	GALLICISED	GALLUMPHING
GABBLEMENT	GAINSTRIVE	GALAVANTING	GALLICISES	GALLYGASKINS
GABBLEMENTS	GAINSTRIVED	GALDRAGONS	GALLICISING	GALRAVAGED
GABBROITIC	GAINSTRIVEN	GALENGALES	GALLICISMS	GALRAVAGES
GABERDINES	GAINSTRIVES	GALENICALS	GALLICIZATION	GALRAVAGING
GABERLUNZIE	GAINSTRIVING	GALEOPITHECINE	GALLICIZATIONS	GALRAVITCH
GABERLUNZIES	GAINSTROVE	GALEOPITHECOID	GALLICIZED	GALRAVITCHED
GABIONADES	GAITERLESS	GALIMATIAS	GALLICIZES	GALRAVITCHES
GABIONAGES	GALABIYAHS	GALIMATIASES	GALLICIZING	GALRAVITCHING
GABIONNADE	GALACTAGOGUE	GALINGALES	GALLIGASKINS	GALUMPHERS
GABIONNADES	GALACTAGOGUES	GALIONGEES	GALLIMAUFRIES	GALUMPHING
GADGETEERS	GALACTICOS	GALIVANTED	GALLIMAUFRY	GALVANICAL
GADGETIEST	GALACTOMETER	GALIVANTING	GALLINACEAN	GALVANICALLY
GADGETRIES	GALACTOMETERS	GALLABEAHS	GALLINACEANS	GALVANISATION
GADOLINITE	GALACTOMETRIES	GALLABIAHS	GALLINACEOUS	GALVANISATIONS
GADOLINITES	GALACTOMETRY	GALLABIEHS	GALLINAZOS	GALVANISED
GADOLINIUM	GALACTOPHOROUS	GALLABIYAH	GALLINIPPER	GALVANISER
GADOLINIUMS	GALACTOPOIESES	GALLABIYAHS	GALLINIPPERS	GALVANISERS
GADROONING	GALACTOPOIESIS	GALLABIYAS	GALLINULES	GALVANISES
GADROONINGS	GALACTOPOIETIC	GALLABIYEH	GALLISISED	GALVANISING
GADZOOKERIES	GALACTOPOIETICS	GALLABIYEHS	GALLISISES	GALVANISMS
GADZOOKERY	GALACTORRHEA	GALLAMINES	GALLISISING	GALVANISTS
GAELICISED	GALACTORRHEAS	GALLANTEST	GALLISIZED	GALVANIZATION
GAELICISES	GALACTORRHOEA	GALLANTING	GALLISIZES	GALVANIZATIONS
GAELICISING	GALACTORRHOEAS	GALLANTNESS	GALLISIZING	GALVANIZED
GAELICISMS	GALACTOSAEMIA	GALLANTNESSES	GALLIVANTED	GALVANIZER
GAELICIZED	GALACTOSAEMIAS	GALLANTRIES	GALLIVANTING	GALVANIZERS
GAELICIZES	GALACTOSAEMIC	GALLBLADDER	GALLIVANTS	GALVANIZES
GAELICIZING	GALACTOSAMINE	GALLBLADDERS	GALLIWASPS	GALVANIZING
GAILLARDIA	GALACTOSAMINES	GALLEASSES	GALLOGLASS	GALVANOMETER
GAILLARDIAS	GALACTOSEMIA	GALLERISTS	GALLOGLASSES	GALVANOMETERS
GAINFULNESS	GALACTOSEMIAS	GALLERYGOER	GALLONAGES	GALVANOMETRIC
GAINFULNESSES	GALACTOSEMIC	GALLERYGOERS	GALLOPADED	GALVANOMETRICAL
GAINGIVING	GALACTOSES	GALLERYING	GALLOPADES	GALVANOMETRIES
GAINGIVINGS	GALACTOSIDASE	GALLERYITE	GALLOPADING	GALVANOMETRY
GAINLESSNESS	GALACTOSIDASES	GALLERYITES	GALLOWGLASS	GALVANOPLASTIC
GAINLESSNESSES	GALACTOSIDE	GALLIAMBIC	GALLOWGLASSES	GALVANOPLASTIES
GAINLINESS	GALACTOSIDES	GALLIAMBICS	GALLOWSNESS	GALVANOPLASTY
GAINLINESSES	GALACTOSYL	GALLIARDISE	GALLOWSNESSES	GALVANOSCOPE
GAINSAYERS	GALACTOSYLS	GALLIARDISES	GALLSICKNESS	GALVANOSCOPES

GALVANOSCOPIC	GAMINESQUE	GANNISTERS	GARNISHEED	GASPINESSES
GALVANOSCOPIES	GAMINESSES	GANTELOPES	GARNISHEEING	GASSINESSES
GALVANOSCOPY	GAMMERSTANG	GANTLETING	GARNISHEEMENT	GASTEROPOD
GALVANOTROPIC	GAMMERSTANGS	GAOLBREAKING	GARNISHEEMENTS	GASTEROPODOUS
GALVANOTROPISM	GAMMOCKING	GAOLBREAKS	GARNISHEES	GASTEROPODS
GALVANOTROPISMS	GAMMONINGS	GAOLBROKEN	GARNISHERS	GASTHAUSER
GAMAHUCHED	GAMOGENESES	GAOLERESSES	GARNISHING	GASTHAUSES
GAMAHUCHES	GAMOGENESIS	GARAGISTES	GARNISHINGS	GASTIGHTNESS
GAMAHUCHING	GAMOGENETIC	GARBAGEMAN	GARNISHMENT	GASTIGHTNESSES
GAMARUCHED	GAMOGENETICAL	GARBAGEMEN	GARNISHMENTS	GASTNESSES
GAMARUCHES	GAMOGENETICALLY	GARBAGIEST	GARNISHORS	GASTRAEUMS
GAMARUCHING	GAMOPETALOUS	GARBOLOGIES	GARNISHRIES	GASTRALGIA
GAMBADOING	GAMOPHYLLOUS	GARBOLOGIST	GARNITURES	GASTRALGIAS
GAMBOLLING	GAMOSEPALOUS	GARBOLOGISTS	GAROTTINGS	GASTRALGIC
GAMEBREAKER	GAMOTROPIC	GARBURATOR	GARRETEERS	GASTRECTOMIES
GAMEBREAKERS	GAMOTROPISM	GARBURATORS	GARRISONED	GASTRECTOMY
GAMEFISHES	GAMOTROPISMS	GARDENFULS	GARRISONING	GASTRITIDES
GAMEKEEPER	GAMYNESSES	GARDENINGS	GARROTTERS	GASTRITISES
GAMEKEEPERS	GANDERISMS	GARDENLESS	GARROTTING	GASTROCNEMII
GAMEKEEPING	GANGBANGED	GARDEROBES	GARROTTINGS	GASTROCNEMIUS
GAMEKEEPINGS	GANGBANGER	GARGANTUAN	GARRULITIES	GASTROCOLIC
GAMENESSES	GANGBANGERS	GARGANTUAS	GARRULOUSLY	GASTRODUODENAL
GAMESMANSHIP	GANGBANGING	GARGARISED	GARRULOUSNESS	GASTROENTERIC
GAMESMANSHIPS	GANGBOARDS	GARGARISES	GARRULOUSNESSES	GASTROENTERITIC
GAMESOMELY	GANGBUSTER	GARGARISING	GARRYOWENS	GASTROENTERITIS
GAMESOMENESS	GANGBUSTERS	GARGARISMS	GASBAGGING	GASTROLITH
GAMESOMENESSES	GANGBUSTING	GARGARIZED	GASCONADED	GASTROLITHS
GAMETANGIA	GANGBUSTINGS	GARGARIZES	GASCONADER	GASTROLOGER
GAMETANGIAL	GANGLIATED	GARGARIZING	GASCONADERS	GASTROLOGERS
GAMETANGIUM	GANGLIFORM	GARGOYLISM	GASCONADES	GASTROLOGICAL
GAMETICALLY	GANGLIONATED	GARGOYLISMS	GASCONADING	GASTROLOGIES
GAMETOCYTE	GANGLIONIC	GARIBALDIS	GASCONISMS	GASTROLOGIST
GAMETOCYTES	GANGLIOSIDE	GARISHNESS	GASEOUSNESS	GASTROLOGISTS
GAMETOGENESES	GANGLIOSIDES	GARISHNESSES	GASEOUSNESSES	GASTROLOGY
GAMETOGENESIS	GANGMASTER	GARLANDAGE	GASHLINESS	GASTROMANCIES
GAMETOGENIC	GANGMASTERS	GARLANDAGES	GASHLINESSES	GASTROMANCY
GAMETOGENIES	GANGPLANKS	GARLANDING	GASHOLDERS	GASTRONOME
GAMETOGENOUS	GANGRENING	GARLANDLESS	GASIFIABLE	GASTRONOMER
GAMETOGENY	GANGRENOUS	GARLANDRIES	GASIFICATION	GASTRONOMERS
GAMETOPHORE	GANGSHAGGED	GARLICKIER	GASIFICATIONS	GASTRONOMES
GAMETOPHORES	GANGSHAGGING	GARLICKIEST	GASLIGHTED	GASTRONOMIC
GAMETOPHORIC	GANGSTERDOM	GARLICKING	GASLIGHTING	GASTRONOMICAL
GAMETOPHYTE	GANGSTERDOMS	GARMENTING	GASLIGHTINGS	GASTRONOMICALLY
GAMETOPHYTES	GANGSTERISH	GARMENTLESS	GASOMETERS	GASTRONOMICS
GAMETOPHYTIC	GANGSTERISM	GARMENTURE	GASOMETRIC	GASTRONOMIES
GAMEYNESSES	GANGSTERISMS	GARMENTURES	GASOMETRICAL	GASTRONOMIST
GAMIFICATION	GANGSTERLAND	GARNETIFEROUS	GASOMETRIES	GASTRONOMISTS
GAMIFICATIONS	GANGSTERLANDS	GARNIERITE	GASPEREAUS	GASTRONOMY
GAMINERIES	GANNETRIES	GARNIERITES	GASPEREAUX	GASTROPODAN

G

G

GASTROPODANS	GAUFFERING	GELANDESPRUNGS	GEMMINESSES	GENERALISE
GASTROPODOUS	GAUFFERINGS	GELATINATE	GEMMIPAROUS	GENERALISED
GASTROPODS	GAULEITERS	GELATINATED	GEMMIPAROUSLY	GENERALISER
GASTROPORN	GAULTHERIA	GELATINATES	GEMMOLOGICAL	GENERALISERS
GASTROPORNS	GAULTHERIAS	GELATINATING	GEMMOLOGIES	GENERALISES
GASTROPUBS	GAUNTLETED	GELATINATION	GEMMOLOGIST	GENERALISING
GASTROSCOPE	GAUNTLETING	GELATINATIONS	GEMMOLOGISTS	GENERALISM
GASTROSCOPES	GAUNTNESSES	GELATINISATION	GEMMULATION	GENERALISMS
GASTROSCOPIC	GAUSSMETER	GELATINISATIONS	GEMMULATIONS	GENERALISSIMO
GASTROSCOPIES	GAUSSMETERS	GELATINISE	GEMOLOGICAL	GENERALISSIMOS
GASTROSCOPIST	GAUZINESSES	GELATINISED	GEMOLOGIES	GENERALIST
GASTROSCOPISTS	GAVELKINDS	GELATINISER	GEMOLOGIST	GENERALISTS
GASTROSCOPY	GAWKIHOODS	GELATINISERS	GEMOLOGISTS	GENERALITIES
GASTROSOPH	GAWKINESSES	GELATINISES	GEMUTLICHKEIT	GENERALITY
GASTROSOPHER	GAWKISHNESS	GELATINISING	GEMUTLICHKEITS	GENERALIZABLE
GASTROSOPHERS	GAWKISHNESSES	GELATINIZATION	GENDARMERIE	GENERALIZATION
GASTROSOPHIES	GAYCATIONS	GELATINIZATIONS	GENDARMERIES	GENERALIZATIONS
GASTROSOPHS	GAZEHOUNDS	GELATINIZE	GENDARMERY	GENERALIZE
GASTROSOPHY	GAZETTEERED	GELATINIZED	GENDERISED	GENERALIZED
GASTROSTOMIES	GAZETTEERING	GELATINIZER	GENDERISES	GENERALIZER
GASTROSTOMY	GAZETTEERISH	GELATINIZERS	GENDERISING	GENERALIZERS
GASTROTOMIES	GAZETTEERS	GELATINIZES	GENDERIZED	GENERALIZES
GASTROTOMY	GAZILLIONAIRE	GELATINIZING	GENDERIZES	GENERALIZING
GASTROTRICH	GAZILLIONAIRES	GELATINOID	GENDERIZING	GENERALLED
GASTROTRICHS	GAZILLIONS	GELATINOIDS	GENDERLESS	GENERALLING
GASTROVASCULAR	GAZUMPINGS	GELATINOUS	GENDERQUEER	GENERALNESS
GASTRULATE	GAZUNDERED	GELATINOUSLY	GENDERQUEERS	GENERALNESSES
GASTRULATED	GAZUNDERER	GELATINOUSNESS	GENEALOGIC	GENERALSHIP
GASTRULATES	GAZUNDERERS	GELIDITIES	GENEALOGICAL	GENERALSHIPS
GASTRULATING	GAZUNDERING	GELIDNESSES	GENEALOGICALLY	GENERATING
GASTRULATION	GEALOUSIES	GELIGNITES	GENEALOGIES	GENERATION
GASTRULATIONS	GEANTICLINAL	GELLIFLOWRE	GENEALOGISE	GENERATIONAL
GATECRASHED	GEANTICLINE	GELLIFLOWRES	GENEALOGISED	GENERATIONALLY
GATECRASHER	GEANTICLINES	GELSEMINES	GENEALOGISES	GENERATIONISM
GATECRASHERS	GEARCHANGE	GELSEMININE	GENEALOGISING	GENERATIONISMS
GATECRASHES	GEARCHANGES	GELSEMININES	GENEALOGIST	GENERATIONS
GATECRASHING	GEARSHIFTS	GELSEMIUMS	GENEALOGISTS	GENERATIVE
GATEHOUSES	GEARSTICKS	GEMEINSCHAFT	GENEALOGIZE	GENERATORS
GATEKEEPER	GEARWHEELS	GEMEINSCHAFTEN	GENEALOGIZED	GENERATRICES
GATEKEEPERS	GEEKINESSES	GEMEINSCHAFTS	GENEALOGIZES	GENERATRIX
GATEKEEPING	GEEKSPEAKS	GEMFIBROZIL	GENEALOGIZING	GENERICALLY
GATEKEEPINGS	GEFUFFLING	GEMFIBROZILS	GENECOLOGIES	GENERICNESS
GATHERABLE	GEGENSCHEIN	GEMINATELY	GENECOLOGY	GENERICNESSES
GATHERINGS	GEGENSCHEINS	GEMINATING	GENERALATE	GENEROSITIES
GAUCHENESS	GEHLENITES	GEMINATION	GENERALATES	GENEROSITY
GAUCHENESSES	GEITONOGAMIES	GEMINATIONS	GENERALCIES	GENEROUSLY
GAUCHERIES	GEITONOGAMOUS	GEMMACEOUS	GENERALISABLE	GENEROUSNESS
GAUDEAMUSES	GEITONOGAMY	GEMMATIONS	GENERALISATION	GENEROUSNESSES
GAUDINESSES	GELANDESPRUNG	GEMMIFEROUS	GENERALISATIONS	GENETHLIAC

GENETHLIACAL	GENOTYPING	GENTLEMANSHIP	GEOCHRONOLOGIC	GEOMAGNETICALLY
GENETHLIACALLY	GENOUILLERE	GENTLEMANSHIPS	GEOCHRONOLOGIES	GEOMAGNETISM
GENETHLIACON	GENOUILLERES	GENTLENESS	GEOCHRONOLOGIST	GEOMAGNETISMS
GENETHLIACONS	GENSDARMES	GENTLENESSE	GEOCHRONOLOGY	GEOMAGNETIST
GENETHLIACS	GENTAMICIN	GENTLENESSES	GEOCORONAE	GEOMAGNETISTS
GENETHLIALOGIC	GENTAMICINS	GENTLEPERSON	GEOCORONAS	GEOMANCERS
GENETHLIALOGIES	GENTEELEST	GENTLEPERSONS	GEODEMOGRAPHICS	GEOMANCIES
GENETHLIALOGY	GENTEELISE	GENTLEWOMAN	GEODESICAL	GEOMECHANICS
GENETICALLY	GENTEELISED	GENTLEWOMANLIER	GEODESISTS	GEOMEDICAL
GENETICIST	GENTEELISES	GENTLEWOMANLY	GEODETICAL	GEOMEDICINE
GENETICISTS	GENTEELISH	GENTLEWOMEN	GEODETICALLY	GEOMEDICINES
GENETOTROPHIC	GENTEELISING	GENTRIFICATION	GEODYNAMIC	GEOMETRICAL
GENETRICES	GENTEELISM	GENTRIFICATIONS	GEODYNAMICAL	GEOMETRICALLY
GENETRIXES	GENTEELISMS	GENTRIFIED	GEODYNAMICIST	GEOMETRICIAN
GENEVRETTE	GENTEELIZE	GENTRIFIER	GEODYNAMICISTS	GEOMETRICIANS
GENEVRETTES	GENTEELIZED	GENTRIFIERS	GEODYNAMICS	GEOMETRICS
GENIALISED	GENTEELIZES	GENTRIFIES	GEOENGINEERING	GEOMETRIDS
GENIALISES	GENTEELIZING	GENTRIFYING	GEOENGINEERINGS	GEOMETRIES
GENIALISING	GENTEELNESS	GENUFLECTED	GEOFENCING	GEOMETRISATION
GENIALITIES	GENTEELNESSES	GENUFLECTING	GEOGNOSIES	GEOMETRISATIONS
GENIALIZED	GENTIANACEOUS	GENUFLECTION	GEOGNOSTIC	GEOMETRISE
GENIALIZES	GENTIANELLA	GENUFLECTIONS	GEOGNOSTICAL	GEOMETRISED
GENIALIZING	GENTIANELLAS	GENUFLECTOR	GEOGNOSTICALLY	GEOMETRISES
GENIALNESS	GENTILESSE	GENUFLECTORS	GEOGRAPHER	GEOMETRISING
GENIALNESSES	GENTILESSES	GENUFLECTS	GEOGRAPHERS	GEOMETRIST
GENICULATE	GENTILHOMME	GENUFLEXION	GEOGRAPHIC	GEOMETRISTS
GENICULATED	GENTILISED	GENUFLEXIONS	GEOGRAPHICAL	GEOMETRIZATION
GENICULATELY	GENTILISES	GENUINENESS	GEOGRAPHICALLY	GEOMETRIZATIONS
GENICULATES	GENTILISING	GENUINENESSES	GEOGRAPHIES	GEOMETRIZE
GENICULATING	GENTILISMS	GEOBOTANIC	GEOHYDROLOGIC	GEOMETRIZED
GENICULATION	GENTILITIAL	GEOBOTANICAL	GEOHYDROLOGIES	GEOMETRIZES
GENICULATIONS	GENTILITIAN	GEOBOTANIES	GEOHYDROLOGIST	GEOMETRIZING
GENISTEINS	GENTILITIES	GEOBOTANIST	GEOHYDROLOGISTS	GEOMORPHIC
GENITALIAL	GENTILITIOUS	GEOBOTANISTS	GEOHYDROLOGY	GEOMORPHOGENIC
GENITIVALLY	GENTILIZED	GEOCACHERS	GEOLATRIES	GEOMORPHOGENIES
GENITIVELY	GENTILIZES	GEOCACHING	GEOLINGUISTICS	GEOMORPHOGENIST
GENITOURINARY	GENTILIZING	GEOCACHINGS	GEOLOCATION	GEOMORPHOGENY
GENITRICES	GENTILSHOMMES	GEOCARPIES	GEOLOCATIONS	GEOMORPHOLOGIC
GENITRIXES	GENTLEFOLK	GEOCENTRIC	GEOLOGIANS	GEOMORPHOLOGIES
GENLOCKING	GENTLEFOLKS	GEOCENTRICAL	GEOLOGICAL	GEOMORPHOLOGIST
GENLOCKINGS	GENTLEHOOD	GEOCENTRICALLY	GEOLOGICALLY	GEOMORPHOLOGY
GENOCIDAIRE	GENTLEHOODS	GEOCENTRICISM	GEOLOGISED	GEOPHAGIAS
GENOCIDAIRES	GENTLEMANHOOD	GEOCENTRICISMS	GEOLOGISES	GEOPHAGIES
GENOPHOBIA	GENTLEMANHOODS	GEOCHEMICAL	GEOLOGISING	GEOPHAGISM
GENOPHOBIAS	GENTLEMANLIER	GEOCHEMICALLY	GEOLOGISTS	GEOPHAGISMS
GENOTYPICAL	GENTLEMANLIEST	GEOCHEMIST	GEOLOGIZED	GEOPHAGIST
GENOTYPICALLY	GENTLEMANLIKE	GEOCHEMISTRIES	GEOLOGIZES	GEOPHAGISTS
GENOTYPICITIES	GENTLEMANLINESS	GEOCHEMISTRY	GEOLOGIZING	GEOPHAGOUS
GENOTYPICITY	GENTLEMANLY	GEOCHEMISTS	GEOMAGNETIC	GEOPHILOUS

GEOPHYSICAL	GEOTHERMIC	GERMINATOR	GESTATIONAL	GIANTHOODS
GEOPHYSICALLY	GEOTHERMOMETER	GERMINATORS	GESTATIONS	GIANTLIEST
GEOPHYSICIST	GEOTHERMOMETERS	GERMINESSES	GESTATORIAL	GIANTSHIPS
GEOPHYSICISTS	GEOTROPICALLY	GERMOPHOBE	GESTICULANT	GIARDIASES
GEOPHYSICS	GEOTROPISM	GERMOPHOBES	GESTICULATE	GIARDIASIS
GEOPOLITICAL	GEOTROPISMS	GERMOPHOBIA	GESTICULATED	GIBBERELLIC
GEOPOLITICALLY	GERANIACEOUS	GERMOPHOBIAS	GESTICULATES	GIBBERELLIN
GEOPOLITICIAN	GERATOLOGICAL	GERMPLASMS	GESTICULATING	GIBBERELLINS
GEOPOLITICIANS	GERATOLOGIES	GERONTOCRACIES	GESTICULATION	GIBBERINGS
GEOPOLITICS	GERATOLOGIST	GERONTOCRACY	GESTICULATIONS	GIBBERISHES
GEOPONICAL	GERATOLOGISTS	GERONTOCRAT	GESTICULATIVE	GIBBETTING
GEOPRESSURED	GERATOLOGY	GERONTOCRATIC	GESTICULATOR	GIBBOSITIES
GEORGETTES	GERFALCONS	GERONTOCRATS	GESTICULATORS	GIBBOUSNESS
GEOSCIENCE	GERIATRICIAN	GERONTOLOGIC	GESTICULATORY	GIBBOUSNESSES
GEOSCIENCES	GERIATRICIANS	GERONTOLOGICAL	GESTURALLY	GIDDINESSES
GEOSCIENTIFIC	GERIATRICS	GERONTOLOGIES	GESUNDHEIT	GIFTEDNESS
GEOSCIENTIST	GERIATRIST	GERONTOLOGIST	GETTERINGS	GIFTEDNESSES
GEOSCIENTISTS	GERIATRISTS	GERONTOLOGISTS	GEWURZTRAMINER	GIFTWRAPPED
GEOSPATIAL	GERMANDERS	GERONTOLOGY	GEWURZTRAMINERS	GIFTWRAPPING
GEOSPHERES	GERMANENESS	GERONTOMORPHIC	GEYSERITES	GIFTWRAPPINGS
GEOSTATICS	GERMANENESSES	GERONTOPHIL	GHASTFULLY	GIGACYCLES
GEOSTATIONARY	GERMANISATION	GERONTOPHILE	GHASTLIEST	GIGAHERTZES
GEOSTRATEGIC	GERMANISATIONS	GERONTOPHILES	GHASTLINESS	GIGANTESQUE
GEOSTRATEGICAL	GERMANISED	GERONTOPHILIA	GHASTLINESSES	GIGANTICALLY
GEOSTRATEGIES	GERMANISES	GERONTOPHILIAS	GHASTNESSES	GIGANTICIDE
GEOSTRATEGIST	GERMANISING	GERONTOPHILS	GHETTOISATION	GIGANTICIDES
GEOSTRATEGISTS	GERMANITES	GERONTOPHOBE	GHETTOISATIONS	GIGANTICNESS
GEOSTRATEGY	GERMANIUMS	GERONTOPHOBES	GHETTOISED	GIGANTICNESSES
GEOSTROPHIC	GERMANIZATION	GERONTOPHOBIA	GHETTOISES	GIGANTISMS
GEOSTROPHICALLY	GERMANIZATIONS	GERONTOPHOBIAS	GHETTOISING	GIGANTOLOGIES
GEOSYNCHRONOUS	GERMANIZED	GERRYMANDER	GHETTOIZATION	GIGANTOLOGY
GEOSYNCLINAL	GERMANIZES	GERRYMANDERED	GHETTOIZATIONS	GIGANTOMACHIA
GEOSYNCLINE	GERMANIZING	GERRYMANDERER	GHETTOIZED	GIGANTOMACHIAS
GEOSYNCLINES	GERMAPHOBE	GERRYMANDERERS	GHETTOIZES	GIGANTOMACHIES
GEOTACTICAL	GERMAPHOBES	GERRYMANDERING	GHETTOIZING	GIGANTOMACHY
GEOTACTICALLY	GERMAPHOBIA	GERRYMANDERINGS	GHOSTLIEST	GIGGLESOME
GEOTAGGING	GERMAPHOBIAS	GERRYMANDERS	GHOSTLINESS	GIGGLINGLY
GEOTECHNIC	GERMICIDAL	GERUNDIVAL	GHOSTLINESSES	GIGMANITIES
GEOTECHNICAL	GERMICIDES	GERUNDIVELY	GHOSTWRITE	GILDSWOMAN
GEOTECHNICS	GERMINABILITIES	GERUNDIVES	GHOSTWRITER	GILDSWOMEN
GEOTECHNOLOGIES	GERMINABILITY	GESELLSCHAFT	GHOSTWRITERS	GILLFLIRTS
GEOTECHNOLOGY	GERMINABLE	GESELLSCHAFTEN	GHOSTWRITES	GILLIFLOWER
GEOTECTONIC	GERMINALLY	GESELLSCHAFTS	GHOSTWRITING	GILLIFLOWERS
GEOTECTONICALLY	GERMINATED	GESNERIADS	GHOSTWRITTEN	GILLNETTED
GEOTECTONICS	GERMINATES	GESSAMINES	GHOSTWROTE	GILLNETTER
GEOTEXTILE	GERMINATING	GESTALTISM	GHOULISHLY	GILLNETTERS
GEOTEXTILES	GERMINATION	GESTALTISMS	GHOULISHNESS	GILLNETTING
GEOTHERMAL	GERMINATIONS	GESTALTIST	GHOULISHNESSES	GILLRAVAGE
GEOTHERMALLY	GERMINATIVE	GESTALTISTS	GIANTESSES	GILLRAVAGED

G

GILLRAVAGES	GIRANDOLAS	GLADWRAPPED	GLARINESSES	GLEAMINGLY
GILLRAVAGING	GIRANDOLES	GLADWRAPPING	GLARINGNESS	GLEEFULNESS
GILLRAVITCH	GIRDLECAKE	GLAIKETNESS	GLARINGNESSES	GLEEFULNESSES
GILLRAVITCHED	GIRDLECAKES	GLAIKETNESSES	GLASNOSTIAN	GLEEMAIDEN
GILLRAVITCHES	GIRDLESCONE	GLAIKITNESS	GLASNOSTIC	GLEEMAIDENS
GILLRAVITCHING	GIRDLESCONES	GLAIKITNESSES	GLASSBLOWER	GLEGNESSES
GILLYFLOWER	GIRDLESTEAD	GLAIRINESS	GLASSBLOWERS	GLEISATION
GILLYFLOWERS	GIRDLESTEADS	GLAIRINESSES	GLASSBLOWING	GLEISATIONS
GILRAVAGED	GIRLFRIEND	GLAMORISATION	GLASSBLOWINGS	GLEIZATION
GILRAVAGER	GIRLFRIENDS	GLAMORISATIONS	GLASSCLOTH	GLEIZATIONS
GILRAVAGERS	GIRLISHNESS	GLAMORISED	GLASSCLOTHS	GLENDOVEER
GILRAVAGES	GIRLISHNESSES	GLAMORISER	GLASSCUTTER	GLENDOVEERS
GILRAVAGING	GIRTHLINES	GLAMORISERS	GLASSCUTTERS	GLENGARRIES
GILRAVITCH	GISMOLOGIES	GLAMORISES	GLASSHOUSE	GLIBNESSES
GILRAVITCHED	GITTARONES	GLAMORISING	GLASSHOUSES	GLIDEPATHS
GILRAVITCHES	GITTERNING	GLAMORIZATION	GLASSIFIED	GLIMMERIER
GILRAVITCHING	GIVENNESSES	GLAMORIZATIONS	GLASSIFIES	GLIMMERIEST
GILSONITES	GIZMOLOGIES	GLAMORIZED	GLASSIFYING	GLIMMERING
GIMBALLING	GLABRESCENT	GLAMORIZER	GLASSINESS	GLIMMERINGLY
GIMCRACKERIES	GLABROUSNESS	GLAMORIZERS	GLASSINESSES	GLIMMERINGS
GIMCRACKERY	GLABROUSNESSES	GLAMORIZES	GLASSMAKER	GLIOBLASTOMA
GIMMICKIER	GLACIALIST	GLAMORIZING	GLASSMAKERS	GLIOBLASTOMAS
GIMMICKIEST	GLACIALISTS	GLAMOROUSLY	GLASSMAKING	GLIOBLASTOMATA
GIMMICKING	GLACIATING	GLAMOROUSNESS	GLASSMAKINGS	GLIOMATOSES
GIMMICKRIES	GLACIATION	GLAMOROUSNESSES	GLASSPAPER	GLIOMATOSIS
GINGELLIES	GLACIATIONS	GLAMOURING	GLASSPAPERED	GLIOMATOUS
GINGERADES	GLACIOLOGIC	GLAMOURISE	GLASSPAPERING	GLISSADERS
GINGERBREAD	GLACIOLOGICAL	GLAMOURISED	GLASSPAPERS	GLISSADING
GINGERBREADED	GLACIOLOGIES	GLAMOURISES	GLASSWARES	GLISSANDOS
GINGERBREADIER	GLACIOLOGIST	GLAMOURISING	GLASSWORKER	GLISTENING
GINGERBREADIEST	GLACIOLOGISTS	GLAMOURIZE	GLASSWORKERS	GLISTENINGLY
GINGERBREADS	GLACIOLOGY	GLAMOURIZED	GLASSWORKS	GLISTERING
GINGERBREADY	GLADDENERS	GLAMOURIZES	GLASSWORMS	GLISTERINGLY
GINGERIEST	GLADDENING	GLAMOURIZING	GLASSWORTS	GLITCHIEST
GINGERLIER	GLADFULNESS	GLAMOURLESS	GLASSYHEADED	GLITTERAND
GINGERLIEST	GLADFULNESSES	GLAMOUROUS	GLAUBERITE	GLITTERATI
GINGERLINESS	GLADIATORIAL	GLAMOUROUSLY	GLAUBERITES	GLITTERIER
GINGERLINESSES	GLADIATORIAN	GLAMOUROUSNESS	GLAUCESCENCE	GLITTERIEST
GINGERROOT	GLADIATORS	GLAMOURPUSS	GLAUCESCENCES	GLITTERING
GINGERROOTS	GLADIATORSHIP	GLAMOURPUSSES	GLAUCESCENT	GLITTERINGLY
GINGERSNAP	GLADIATORSHIPS	GLAMPSITES	GLAUCOMATOUS	GLITTERINGS
GINGERSNAPS	GLADIATORY	GLANCINGLY	GLAUCONITE	GLITZINESS
GINGIVECTOMIES	GLADIOLUSES	GLANDEROUS	GLAUCONITES	GLITZINESSES
GINGIVECTOMY	GLADNESSES	GLANDIFEROUS	GLAUCONITIC	GLOATINGLY
GINGIVITIS	GLADSOMELY	GLANDIFORM	GLAUCOUSLY	GLOBALISATION
GINGIVITISES	GLADSOMENESS	GLANDULARLY	GLAUCOUSNESS	GLOBALISATIONS
GINGLIMOID	GLADSOMENESSES	GLANDULIFEROUS	GLAUCOUSNESSES	GLOBALISED
GIPSYHOODS	GLADSOMEST	GLANDULOUS	GLAZIERIES	GLOBALISES
GIPSYWORTS	GLADSTONES	GLANDULOUSLY	GLAZINESSES	GLOBALISING

GLOBALISMS	GLORIFICATIONS	GLUCONEOGENESES	GLUTTONISING	GLYCOSYLATE
GLOBALISTS	GLORIFIERS	GLUCONEOGENESIS	GLUTTONIZE	GLYCOSYLATED
GLOBALIZATION	GLORIFYING	GLUCONEOGENIC	GLUTTONIZED	GLYCOSYLATES
GLOBALIZATIONS	GLORIOUSLY	GLUCOPHORE	GLUTTONIZES	GLYCOSYLATING
GLOBALIZED	GLORIOUSNESS	GLUCOPHORES	GLUTTONIZING	GLYCOSYLATION
GLOBALIZES	GLORIOUSNESSES	GLUCOPROTEIN	GLUTTONOUS	GLYCOSYLATIONS
GLOBALIZING	GLOSSARIAL	GLUCOPROTEINS	GLUTTONOUSLY	GLYOXALINE
GLOBEFISHES	GLOSSARIALLY	GLUCOSAMINE	GLUTTONOUSNESS	GLYOXALINES
GLOBEFLOWER	GLOSSARIES	GLUCOSAMINES	GLYCAEMIAS	GLYPHOGRAPH
GLOBEFLOWERS	GLOSSARIST	GLUCOSIDAL	GLYCATIONS	GLYPHOGRAPHER
GLOBESITIES	GLOSSARISTS	GLUCOSIDASE	GLYCERALDEHYDE	GLYPHOGRAPHERS
GLOBETROTS	GLOSSATORS	GLUCOSIDASES	GLYCERALDEHYDES	GLYPHOGRAPHIC
GLOBETROTTED	GLOSSECTOMIES	GLUCOSIDES	GLYCERIDES	GLYPHOGRAPHICAL
GLOBETROTTER	GLOSSECTOMY	GLUCOSIDIC	GLYCERIDIC	GLYPHOGRAPHIES
GLOBETROTTERS	GLOSSEMATICS	GLUCOSURIA	GLYCERINATE	GLYPHOGRAPHS
GLOBETROTTING	GLOSSINESS	GLUCOSURIAS	GLYCERINATED	GLYPHOGRAPHY
GLOBETROTTINGS	GLOSSINESSES	GLUCOSURIC	GLYCERINATES	GLYPHOSATE
GLOBIGERINA	GLOSSINGLY	GLUCURONIC	GLYCERINATING	GLYPHOSATES
GLOBIGERINAE	GLOSSITISES	GLUCURONIDASE	GLYCERINES	GLYPTODONT
GLOBIGERINAS	GLOSSODYNIA	GLUCURONIDASES	GLYCOCOLLS	GLYPTODONTS
GLOBOSENESS	GLOSSODYNIAS	GLUCURONIDE	GLYCOGENESES	GLYPTOGRAPHER
GLOBOSENESSES	GLOSSOGRAPHER	GLUCURONIDES	GLYCOGENESIS	GLYPTOGRAPHERS
GLOBOSITIES	GLOSSOGRAPHERS	GLUEYNESSES	GLYCOGENETIC	GLYPTOGRAPHIC
GLOBULARITIES	GLOSSOGRAPHICAL	GLUINESSES	GLYCOGENIC	GLYPTOGRAPHICAL
GLOBULARITY	GLOSSOGRAPHIES	GLUMACEOUS	GLYCOGENOLYSES	GLYPTOGRAPHIES
GLOBULARLY	GLOSSOGRAPHY	GLUMIFEROUS	GLYCOGENOLYSIS	GLYPTOGRAPHY
GLOBULARNESS	GLOSSOLALIA	GLUMNESSES	GLYCOGENOLYTIC	GLYPTOTHECA
GLOBULARNESSES	GLOSSOLALIAS	GLUTAMATES	GLYCOLIPID	GLYPTOTHECAE
GLOBULIFEROUS	GLOSSOLALIST	GLUTAMINASE	GLYCOLIPIDS	GMELINITES
GLOBULITES	GLOSSOLALISTS	GLUTAMINASES	GLYCOLYSES	GNAPHALIUM
GLOCHIDIATE	GLOSSOLARYNGEAL	GLUTAMINES	GLYCOLYSIS	GNAPHALIUMS
GLOCHIDIUM	GLOSSOLOGICAL	GLUTAMINIC	GLYCOLYTIC	GNASHINGLY
GLOCKENSPIEL	GLOSSOLOGIES	GLUTARALDEHYDE	GLYCONEOGENESES	GNATCATCHER
GLOCKENSPIELS	GLOSSOLOGIST	GLUTARALDEHYDES	GLYCONEOGENESIS	GNATCATCHERS
GLOMERATED	GLOSSOLOGISTS	GLUTATHIONE	GLYCOPEPTIDE	GNATHONICAL
GLOMERATES	GLOSSOLOGY	GLUTATHIONES	GLYCOPEPTIDES	GNATHONICALLY
GLOMERATING	GLOTTIDEAN	GLUTETHIMIDE	GLYCOPHYTE	GNATHOSTOMATOUS
GLOMERATION	GLOTTOGONIC	GLUTETHIMIDES	GLYCOPHYTES	GNATHOSTOME
GLOMERATIONS	GLOTTOLOGIES	GLUTINOSITIES	GLYCOPHYTIC	GNATHOSTOMES
GLOMERULAR	GLOTTOLOGY	GLUTINOSITY	GLYCOPROTEIN	GNEISSITIC
GLOMERULATE	GLOVEBOXES	GLUTINOUSLY	GLYCOPROTEINS	GNETOPHYTE
GLOMERULES	GLOWERINGLY	GLUTINOUSNESS	GLYCOSIDASE	GNETOPHYTES
GLOMERULUS	GLOWSTICKS	GLUTINOUSNESSES	GLYCOSIDASES	GNOMICALLY
GLOOMFULLY	GLUCINIUMS	GLUTTINGLY	GLYCOSIDES	GNOMONICAL
GLOOMINESS	GLUCOCORTICOID	GLUTTONIES	GLYCOSIDIC	GNOMONICALLY
GLOOMINESSES	GLUCOCORTICOIDS	GLUTTONISE	GLYCOSIDICALLY	GNOMONOLOGIES
GLOOMSTERS	GLUCOKINASE	GLUTTONISED	GLYCOSURIA	GNOMONOLOGY
GLORIFIABLE	GLUCOKINASES	GLUTTONISES	GLYCOSURIAS	GNOSEOLOGIES
GLORIFICATION	GLUCONATES	GLUTTONISH	GLYCOSURIC	GNOSEOLOGY

GNOSIOLOGIES	GODDAMNDEST	GOLDSINNIES	GONIOMETRIC	GOOSEFISHES
GNOSIOLOGY	GODDAMNEDEST	GOLDSMITHERIES	GONIOMETRICAL	GOOSEFLESH
GNOSTICALLY	GODDAMNING	GOLDSMITHERY	GONIOMETRICALLY	GOOSEFLESHES
GNOSTICISM	GODDAUGHTER	GOLDSMITHRIES	GONIOMETRIES	GOOSEFOOTS
GNOSTICISMS	GODDAUGHTERS	GOLDSMITHRY	GONIOMETRY	GOOSEGRASS
GNOTOBIOLOGICAL	GODDESSHOOD	GOLDSMITHS	GONIOSCOPE	GOOSEGRASSES
GNOTOBIOLOGIES	GODDESSHOODS	GOLDSPINKS	GONIOSCOPES	GOOSEHERDS
GNOTOBIOLOGY	GODFATHERED	GOLDSTICKS	GONOCOCCAL	GOOSENECKED
GNOTOBIOSES	GODFATHERING	GOLDSTONES	GONOCOCCIC	GOOSENECKS
GNOTOBIOSIS	GODFATHERS	GOLDTHREAD	GONOCOCCOID	GOOSINESSES
GNOTOBIOTE	GODFORSAKEN	GOLDTHREADS	GONOCOCCUS	GOPHERWOOD
GNOTOBIOTES	GODLESSNESS	GOLIARDERIES	GONOPHORES	GOPHERWOODS
GNOTOBIOTIC	GODLESSNESSES	GOLIARDERY	GONOPHORIC	GORBELLIES
GNOTOBIOTICALLY	GODLIKENESS	GOLIARDIES	GONOPHOROUS	GORBLIMEYS
GNOTOBIOTICS	GODLIKENESSES	GOLIATHISE	GONORRHEAL	GORBLIMIES
GOALKEEPER	GODLINESSES	GOLIATHISED	GONORRHEAS	GOREHOUNDS
GOALKEEPERS	GODMOTHERED	GOLIATHISES	GONORRHEIC	GORGEOUSLY
GOALKEEPING	GODMOTHERING	GOLIATHISING	GONORRHOEA	GORGEOUSNESS
GOALKEEPINGS	GODMOTHERS	GOLIATHIZE	GONORRHOEAL	GORGEOUSNESSES
GOALKICKER	GODPARENTS	GOLIATHIZED	GONORRHOEAS	GORGONEION
GOALKICKERS	GODROONING	GOLIATHIZES	GONORRHOEIC	GORGONIANS
GOALKICKING	GODROONINGS	GOLIATHIZING	GOODFELLAS	GORGONISED
GOALKICKINGS	GOFFERINGS	GOLOMYNKAS	GOODFELLOW	GORGONISES
GOALMOUTHS	GOGGLEBOXES	GOLOPTIOUS	GOODFELLOWS	GORGONISING
GOALSCORER	GOITROGENIC	GOLUPTIOUS	GOODFELLOWSHIP	GORGONIZED
GOALSCORERS	GOITROGENICITY	GOMBEENISM	GOODFELLOWSHIPS	GORGONIZES
GOALTENDER	GOITROGENS	GOMBEENISMS	GOODINESSES	GORGONIZING
GOALTENDERS	GOLDARNING	GONADECTOMIES	GOODLIHEAD	GORILLAGRAM
GOALTENDING	GOLDBEATER	GONADECTOMISED	GOODLIHEADS	GORILLAGRAMS
GOALTENDINGS	GOLDBEATERS	GONADECTOMIZED	GOODLINESS	GORINESSES
GOATFISHES	GOLDBRICKED	GONADECTOMY	GOODLINESSES	GORMANDISE
GOATISHNESS	GOLDBRICKING	GONADOTROPHIC	GOODLYHEAD	GORMANDISED
GOATISHNESSES	GOLDBRICKS	GONADOTROPHIN	GOODLYHEADS	GORMANDISER
GOATSBEARD	GOLDCRESTS	GONADOTROPHINS	GOODNESSES	GORMANDISERS
GOATSBEARDS	GOLDENBERRIES	GONADOTROPIC	GOODNIGHTS	GORMANDISES
GOATSUCKER	GOLDENBERRY	GONADOTROPIN	GOODWILLED	GORMANDISING
GOATSUCKERS	GOLDENEYES	GONADOTROPINS	GOOEYNESSES	GORMANDISINGS
GOBBELINES	GOLDENNESS	GONDOLIERS	GOOFINESSES	GORMANDISM
GOBBLEDEGOOK	GOLDENNESSES	GONENESSES	GOOGLEWHACK	GORMANDISMS
GOBBLEDEGOOKS	GOLDENRODS	GONFALONIER	GOOGLEWHACKS	GORMANDIZE
GOBBLEDYGOOK	GOLDENSEAL	GONFALONIERS	GOOGOLPLEX	GORMANDIZED
GOBBLEDYGOOKS	GOLDENSEALS	GONGORISTIC	GOOGOLPLEXES	GORMANDIZER
GOBSMACKED	GOLDFIELDS	GONIATITES	GOOINESSES	GORMANDIZERS
GOBSTOPPER	GOLDFINCHES	GONIATITOID	GOONEYBIRD	GORMANDIZES
GOBSTOPPERS	GOLDFINNIES	GONIATITOIDS	GOONEYBIRDS	GORMANDIZING
GOCHUJANGS	GOLDFISHES	GONIMOBLAST	GOOPINESSES	GORMANDIZINGS
GODAMNDEST	GOLDILOCKS	GONIMOBLASTS	GOOSANDERS	GOSLARITES
GODCHILDREN	GOLDILOCKSES	GONIOMETER	GOOSEBERRIES	GOSPELISED
GODDAMMING	GOLDMINERS	GONIOMETERS	GOOSEBERRY	GOSPELISES

GOSPELISING	GOUVERNANTES	GRADABILITY	GRAMINIVOROUS	GRANDEESHIP
GOSPELIZED	GOVERNABILITIES	GRADABLENESS	GRAMINOLOGIES	GRANDEESHIPS
GOSPELIZES	GOVERNABILITY	GRADABLENESSES	GRAMINOLOGY	GRANDFATHER
GOSPELIZING	GOVERNABLE	GRADATIONAL	GRAMMALOGUE	GRANDFATHERED
GOSPELLERS	GOVERNABLENESS	GRADATIONALLY	GRAMMALOGUES	GRANDFATHERING
GOSPELLIER	GOVERNALLS	GRADATIONED	GRAMMARIAN	GRANDFATHERLIER
GOSPELLIEST	GOVERNANCE	GRADATIONS	GRAMMARIANS	GRANDFATHERLY
GOSPELLING	GOVERNANCES	GRADATORIES	GRAMMARLESS	GRANDFATHERS
GOSPELLINGS	GOVERNANTE	GRADDANING	GRAMMATICAL	GRANDIFLORA
GOSPELLISE	GOVERNANTES	GRADELIEST	GRAMMATICALITY	GRANDIFLORAS
GOSPELLISED	GOVERNESSED	GRADIENTER	GRAMMATICALLY	GRANDILOQUENCE
GOSPELLISES	GOVERNESSES	GRADIENTERS	GRAMMATICALNESS	GRANDILOQUENCES
GOSPELLISING	GOVERNESSIER	GRADIOMETER	GRAMMATICASTER	GRANDILOQUENT
GOSPELLIZE	GOVERNESSIEST	GRADIOMETERS	GRAMMATICASTERS	GRANDILOQUENTLY
GOSPELLIZED	GOVERNESSING	GRADUALISM	GRAMMATICISE	GRANDILOQUOUS
GOSPELLIZES	GOVERNESSY	GRADUALISMS	GRAMMATICISED	GRANDIOSELY
GOSPELLIZING	GOVERNMENT	GRADUALIST	GRAMMATICISES	GRANDIOSENESS
GOSSAMERIER	GOVERNMENTAL	GRADUALISTIC	GRAMMATICISING	GRANDIOSENESSES
GOSSAMERIEST	GOVERNMENTALISE	GRADUALISTS	GRAMMATICISM	GRANDIOSITIES
GOSSIPIEST	GOVERNMENTALISM	GRADUALITIES	GRAMMATICISMS	GRANDIOSITY
GOSSIPINGLY	GOVERNMENTALIST	GRADUALITY	GRAMMATICIZE	GRANDMAMAS
GOSSIPINGS	GOVERNMENTALIZE	GRADUALNESS	GRAMMATICIZED	GRANDMAMMA
GOSSIPMONGER	GOVERNMENTALLY	GRADUALNESSES	GRAMMATICIZES	GRANDMAMMAS
GOSSIPMONGERS	GOVERNMENTESE	GRADUATESHIP	GRAMMATICIZING	GRANDMASTER
GOSSIPPERS	GOVERNMENTESES	GRADUATESHIPS	GRAMMATIST	GRANDMASTERS
GOSSIPPING	GOVERNMENTS	GRADUATING	GRAMMATISTS	GRANDMOTHER
GOSSIPRIES	GOVERNORATE	GRADUATION	GRAMMATOLOGIES	GRANDMOTHERLIER
GOTHICALLY	GOVERNORATES	GRADUATIONS	GRAMMATOLOGIST	GRANDMOTHERLY
GOTHICISED	GOVERNORSHIP	GRADUATORS	GRAMMATOLOGISTS	GRANDMOTHERS
GOTHICISES	GOVERNORSHIPS	GRAECISING	GRAMMATOLOGY	GRANDNEPHEW
GOTHICISING	GOWDSPINKS	GRAECIZING	GRAMOPHONE	GRANDNEPHEWS
GOTHICISMS	GOWPENFULS	GRAFFITIED	GRAMOPHONES	GRANDNESSES
GOTHICIZED	GRACEFULLER	GRAFFITIING	GRAMOPHONIC	GRANDNIECE
GOTHICIZES	GRACEFULLEST	GRAFFITING	GRAMOPHONICALLY	GRANDNIECES
GOTHICIZING	GRACEFULLY	GRAFFITIST	GRAMOPHONIES	GRANDPAPAS
GOURDINESS	GRACEFULNESS	GRAFFITISTS	GRAMOPHONIST	GRANDPARENT
GOURDINESSES	GRACEFULNESSES	GRAINFIELD	GRAMOPHONISTS	GRANDPARENTAL
GOURMANDISE	GRACELESSLY	GRAINFIELDS	GRAMOPHONY	GRANDPARENTHOOD
GOURMANDISED	GRACELESSNESS	GRAININESS	GRANADILLA	GRANDPARENTS
GOURMANDISES	GRACELESSNESSES	GRAININESSES	GRANADILLAS	GRANDSIRES
GOURMANDISING	GRACILENESS	GRALLATORIAL	GRANDADDIES	GRANDSTAND
GOURMANDISM	GRACILENESSES	GRALLOCHED	GRANDAUNTS	GRANDSTANDED
GOURMANDISMS	GRACILITIES	GRALLOCHING	GRANDBABIES	GRANDSTANDER
GOURMANDIZE	GRACIOSITIES	GRAMERCIES	GRANDCHILD	GRANDSTANDERS
GOURMANDIZED	GRACIOSITY	GRAMICIDIN	GRANDCHILDREN	GRANDSTANDING
GOURMANDIZES	GRACIOUSLY	GRAMICIDINS	GRANDDADDIES	GRANDSTANDINGS
GOURMANDIZING	GRACIOUSNESS	GRAMINACEOUS	GRANDDADDY	GRANDSTANDS
GOUTINESSES	GRACIOUSNESSES	GRAMINEOUS	GRANDDAUGHTER	GRANDSTOOD
GOUVERNANTE	GRADABILITIES	GRAMINICOLOUS	GRANDDAUGHTERS	GRANDUNCLE

GRANDUNCLES	GRANTSMANSHIPS	GRAPHITISE	GRASSWRACKS	GRAVIDNESS
GRANGERISATION	GRANULARITIES	GRAPHITISED	GRATEFULLER	GRAVIDNESSES
GRANGERISATIONS	GRANULARITY	GRAPHITISES	GRATEFULLEST	GRAVIMETER
GRANGERISE	GRANULARLY	GRAPHITISING	GRATEFULLY	GRAVIMETERS
GRANGERISED	GRANULATED	GRAPHITIZABLE	GRATEFULNESS	GRAVIMETRIC
GRANGERISER	GRANULATER	GRAPHITIZATION	GRATEFULNESSES	GRAVIMETRICAL
GRANGERISERS	GRANULATERS	GRAPHITIZATIONS	GRATICULATION	GRAVIMETRICALLY
GRANGERISES	GRANULATES	GRAPHITIZE	GRATICULATIONS	GRAVIMETRIES
GRANGERISING	GRANULATING	GRAPHITIZED	GRATICULES	GRAVIMETRY
GRANGERISM	GRANULATION	GRAPHITIZES	GRATIFICATION	GRAVIPERCEPTION
GRANGERISMS	GRANULATIONS	GRAPHITIZING	GRATIFICATIONS	GRAVITASES
GRANGERIZATION	GRANULATIVE	GRAPHITOID	GRATIFIERS	GRAVITATED
GRANGERIZATIONS	GRANULATOR	GRAPHOLECT	GRATIFYING	GRAVITATER
GRANGERIZE	GRANULATORS	GRAPHOLECTS	GRATIFYINGLY	GRAVITATERS
GRANGERIZED	GRANULIFEROUS	GRAPHOLOGIC	GRATILLITIES	GRAVITATES
GRANGERIZER	GRANULIFORM	GRAPHOLOGICAL	GRATILLITY	GRAVITATING
GRANGERIZERS	GRANULITES	GRAPHOLOGIES	GRATINATED	GRAVITATION
GRANGERIZES	GRANULITIC	GRAPHOLOGIST	GRATINATES	GRAVITATIONAL
GRANGERIZING	GRANULITISATION	GRAPHOLOGISTS	GRATINATING	GRAVITATIONALLY
GRANITELIKE	GRANULITIZATION	GRAPHOLOGY	GRATINEEING	GRAVITATIONS
GRANITEWARE	GRANULOCYTE	GRAPHOMANIA	GRATITUDES	GRAVITATIVE
GRANITEWARES	GRANULOCYTES	GRAPHOMANIAS	GRATUITIES	GRAVITINOS
GRANITIFICATION	GRANULOCYTIC	GRAPHOMOTOR	GRATUITOUS	GRAVITOMETER
GRANITIFORM	GRANULOMAS	GRAPHOPHOBIA	GRATUITOUSLY	GRAVITOMETERS
GRANITISATION	GRANULOMATA	GRAPHOPHOBIAS	GRATUITOUSNESS	GRAYBEARDED
GRANITISATIONS	GRANULOMATOUS	GRAPINESSES	GRATULATED	GRAYBEARDS
GRANITISED	GRANULOSES	GRAPLEMENT	GRATULATES	GRAYFISHES
GRANITISES	GRANULOSIS	GRAPLEMENTS	GRATULATING	GRAYHEADED
GRANITISING	GRAPEFRUIT	GRAPPLINGS	GRATULATION	GRAYHOUNDS
GRANITITES	GRAPEFRUITS	GRAPTOLITE	GRATULATIONS	GRAYLISTED
GRANITIZATION	GRAPELOUSE	GRAPTOLITES	GRATULATORY	GRAYLISTING
GRANITIZATIONS	GRAPESEEDS	GRAPTOLITIC	GRAUNCHERS	GRAYNESSES
GRANITIZED	GRAPESHOTS	GRASPINGLY	GRAUNCHING	GRAYSTONES
GRANITIZES	GRAPESTONE	GRASPINGNESS	GRAVADLAXES	GRAYWACKES
GRANITIZING	GRAPESTONES	GRASPINGNESSES	GRAVEDIGGER	GRAYWATERS
GRANITOIDS	GRAPETREES	GRASSBIRDS	GRAVEDIGGERS	GRAYWETHER
GRANIVORES	GRAPEVINES	GRASSFINCH	GRAVELLIER	GRAYWETHERS
GRANIVOROUS	GRAPHEMICALLY	GRASSFINCHES	GRAVELLIEST	GREASEBALL
GRANNIEING	GRAPHEMICS	GRASSFIRES	GRAVELLING	GREASEBALLS
GRANODIORITE	GRAPHICACIES	GRASSHOOKS	GRAVENESSES	GREASEBAND
GRANODIORITES	GRAPHICACY	GRASSHOPPER	GRAVEOLENT	GREASEBANDS
GRANODIORITIC	GRAPHICALLY	GRASSHOPPERS	GRAVEROBBER	GREASEBUSH
GRANOLITHIC	GRAPHICALNESS	GRASSINESS	GRAVEROBBERS	GREASEBUSHES
GRANOLITHICS	GRAPHICALNESSES	GRASSINESSES	GRAVESIDES	GREASELESS
GRANOLITHS	GRAPHICNESS	GRASSLANDS	GRAVESITES	GREASEPAINT
GRANOPHYRE	GRAPHICNESSES	GRASSPLOTS	GRAVESTONE	GREASEPAINTS
GRANOPHYRES	GRAPHITISABLE	GRASSQUITS	GRAVESTONES	GREASEPROOF
GRANOPHYRIC	GRAPHITISATION	GRASSROOTS	GRAVEYARDS	GREASEPROOFS
GRANTSMANSHIP	GRAPHITISATIONS	GRASSWRACK	GRAVIDITIES	GREASEWOOD

GREASEWOODS	GREENHOUSE	GREGARIOUSLY	GRIFFINISH	GROSGRAINS
GREASINESS	GREENHOUSES	GREGARIOUSNESS	GRIFFINISM	GROSSIERETE
GREASINESSES	GREENISHNESS	GREISENISATION	GRIFFINISMS	GROSSIERETES
GREATCOATED	GREENISHNESSES	GREISENISATIONS	GRILLERIES	GROSSNESSES
GREATCOATS	GREENKEEPER	GREISENISE	GRILLROOMS	GROSSULARITE
GREATENING	GREENKEEPERS	GREISENISED	GRILLSTEAK	GROSSULARITES
GREATHEARTED	GREENLIGHT	GREISENISES	GRILLSTEAKS	GROSSULARS
GREATHEARTEDLY	GREENLIGHTED	GREISENISING	GRILLWORKS	GROTESQUELY
GREATNESSES	GREENLIGHTING	GREISENIZATION	GRIMACINGLY	GROTESQUENESS
GRECIANISE	GREENLIGHTS	GREISENIZATIONS	GRIMALKINS	GROTESQUENESSES
GRECIANISED	GREENLINGS	GREISENIZE	GRIMINESSES	GROTESQUER
GRECIANISES	GREENMAILED	GREISENIZED	GRIMLOOKED	GROTESQUERIE
GRECIANISING	GREENMAILER	GREISENIZES	GRIMNESSES	GROTESQUERIES
GRECIANIZE	GREENMAILERS	GREISENIZING	GRINDELIAS	GROTESQUERY
GRECIANIZED	GREENMAILING	GREMOLATAS	GRINDERIES	GROTESQUES
GRECIANIZES	GREENMAILS	GRENADIERS	GRINDHOUSE	GROTESQUEST
GRECIANIZING	GREENNESSES	GRENADILLA	GRINDHOUSES	GROTTINESS
GREEDHEADS	GREENOCKITE	GRENADILLAS	GRINDINGLY	GROTTINESSES
GREEDINESS	GREENOCKITES	GRENADINES	GRINDSTONE	GROUCHIEST
GREEDINESSES	GREENROOMS	GRESSORIAL	GRINDSTONES	GROUCHINESS
GREENBACKER	GREENSANDS	GRESSORIOUS	GRINNINGLY	GROUCHINESSES
GREENBACKERS	GREENSHANK	GREVILLEAS	GRIPPINGLY	GROUNDAGES
GREENBACKISM	GREENSHANKS	GREWHOUNDS	GRISAILLES	GROUNDBAIT
GREENBACKISMS	GREENSICKNESS	GREWSOMEST	GRISEOFULVIN	GROUNDBAITED
GREENBACKS	GREENSICKNESSES	GREYBEARDED	GRISEOFULVINS	GROUNDBAITING
GREENBELTS	GREENSKEEPER	GREYBEARDS	GRISLINESS	GROUNDBAITS
GREENBONES	GREENSKEEPERS	GREYHEADED	GRISLINESSES	GROUNDBREAKER
GREENBOTTLE	GREENSOMES	GREYHOUNDS	GRISTLIEST	GROUNDBREAKERS
GREENBOTTLES	GREENSPEAK	GREYLISTED	GRISTLINESS	GROUNDBREAKING
GREENBRIER	GREENSPEAKS	GREYLISTING	GRISTLINESSES	GROUNDBREAKINGS
GREENBRIERS	GREENSTICK	GREYNESSES	GRISTMILLS	GROUNDBURST
GREENCLOTH	GREENSTONE	GREYSCALES	GRITSTONES	GROUNDBURSTS
GREENCLOTHS	GREENSTONES	GREYSTONES	GRITTINESS	GROUNDEDLY
GREENERIES	GREENSTUFF	GREYWACKES	GRITTINESSES	GROUNDFISH
GREENFIELD	GREENSTUFFS	GREYWETHER	GRIVATIONS	GROUNDFISHES
GREENFIELDS	GREENSWARD	GREYWETHERS	GRIZZLIEST	GROUNDHOGS
GREENFINCH	GREENSWARDS	GRIDDLEBREAD	GROANINGLY	GROUNDINGS
GREENFINCHES	GREENWASHED	GRIDDLEBREADS	GROATSWORTH	GROUNDLESS
GREENFLIES	GREENWASHES	GRIDDLECAKE	GROATSWORTHS	GROUNDLESSLY
GREENGAGES	GREENWASHING	GRIDDLECAKES	GROCETERIA	GROUNDLESSNESS
GREENGROCER	GREENWASHINGS	GRIDIRONED	GROCETERIAS	GROUNDLING
GREENGROCERIES	GREENWEEDS	GRIDIRONING	GROGGERIES	GROUNDLINGS
GREENGROCERS	GREENWINGS	GRIDLOCKED	GROGGINESS	GROUNDMASS
GREENGROCERY	GREENWOODS	GRIDLOCKING	GROGGINESSES	GROUNDMASSES
GREENHANDS	GREGARIANISM	GRIEVANCES	GROMMETING	GROUNDNUTS
GREENHEADS	GREGARIANISMS	GRIEVINGLY	GROOVELESS	GROUNDOUTS
GREENHEART	GREGARINES	GRIEVOUSLY	GROOVELIKE	GROUNDPLOT
GREENHEARTS	GREGARINIAN	GRIEVOUSNESS	GROOVINESS	GROUNDPLOTS
GREENHORNS	GREGARIOUS	GRIEVOUSNESSES	GROOVINESSES	GROUNDPROX

G

GROUNDPROXES	GRUBSTAKED	GUARDHOUSES	GUILDSWOMAN	GUNPOWDERS
GROUNDSELL	GRUBSTAKER	GUARDIANSHIP	GUILDSWOMEN	GUNPOWDERY
GROUNDSELLS	GRUBSTAKERS	GUARDIANSHIPS	GUILEFULLY	GUNRUNNERS
GROUNDSELS	GRUBSTAKES	GUARDRAILS	GUILEFULNESS	GUNRUNNING
GROUNDSHARE	GRUBSTAKING	GUARDROOMS	GUILEFULNESSES	GUNRUNNINGS
GROUNDSHARED	GRUBSTREET	GUARDSHIPS	GUILELESSLY	GUNSLINGER
GROUNDSHARES	GRUDGELESS	GUARISHING	GUILELESSNESS	GUNSLINGERS
GROUNDSHARING	GRUDGINGLY	GUAYABERAS	GUILELESSNESSES	GUNSLINGING
GROUNDSHEET	GRUELINGLY	GUBERNACULA	GUILLEMETS	GUNSLINGINGS
GROUNDSHEETS	GRUELLINGLY	GUBERNACULAR	GUILLEMOTS	GUNSMITHING
GROUNDSILL	GRUELLINGS	GUBERNACULUM	GUILLOCHED	GUNSMITHINGS
GROUNDSILLS	GRUESOMELY	GUBERNATION	GUILLOCHES	GURGITATION
GROUNDSKEEPER	GRUESOMENESS	GUBERNATIONS	GUILLOCHING	GURGITATIONS
GROUNDSKEEPERS	GRUESOMENESSES	GUBERNATOR	GUILLOTINE	GUSHINESSES
GROUNDSMAN	GRUESOMEST	GUBERNATORIAL	GUILLOTINED	GUSSETINGS
GROUNDSMEN	GRUFFNESSES	GUBERNATORS	GUILLOTINER	GUSTATIONS
GROUNDSPEED	GRUMBLIEST	GUBERNIYAS	GUILLOTINERS	GUSTATORILY
GROUNDSPEEDS	GRUMBLINGLY	GUDGEONING	GUILLOTINES	GUSTINESSES
GROUNDSWELL	GRUMBLINGS	GUERDONERS	GUILLOTINING	GUTBUCKETS
GROUNDSWELLS	GRUMMETING	GUERDONING	GUILTINESS	GUTLESSNESS
GROUNDWATER	GRUMNESSES	GUERILLAISM	GUILTINESSES	GUTLESSNESSES
GROUNDWATERS	GRUMPINESS	GUERILLAISMS	GUILTLESSLY	GUTSINESSES
GROUNDWOOD	GRUMPINESSES	GUERRILLAISM	GUILTLESSNESS	GUTTATIONS
GROUNDWOODS	GRUMPISHLY	GUERRILLAISMS	GUILTLESSNESSES	GUTTERBLOOD
GROUNDWORK	GRUMPISHNESS	GUERRILLAS	GUITARFISH	GUTTERBLOODS
GROUNDWORKS	GRUMPISHNESSES	GUERRILLERO	GUITARFISHES	GUTTERIEST
GROUPTHINK	GRUNTINGLY	GUERRILLEROS	GUITARISTS	GUTTERINGS
GROUPTHINKS	GUACAMOLES	GUESSINGLY	GULLIBILITIES	GUTTERSNIPE
GROUPUSCULE	GUACHAMOLE	GUESSTIMATE	GULLIBILITY	GUTTERSNIPES
GROUPUSCULES	GUACHAMOLES	GUESSTIMATED	GULOSITIES	GUTTERSNIPISH
GROUPWARES	GUACHAROES	GUESSTIMATES	GUMMIFEROUS	GUTTIFEROUS
GROUPWORKS	GUANABANAS	GUESSTIMATING	GUMMINESSES	GUTTURALISATION
GROUSELIKE	GUANAZOLOS	GUESSWORKS	GUMMOSITIES	GUTTURALISE
GROVELINGLY	GUANCIALES	GUESTBOOKS	GUMSHIELDS	GUTTURALISED
GROVELINGS	GUANETHIDINE	GUESTENING	GUMSHOEING	GUTTURALISES
GROVELLERS	GUANETHIDINES	GUESTHOUSE	GUMSUCKERS	GUTTURALISING
GROVELLING	GUANIDINES	GUESTHOUSES	GUNCOTTONS	GUTTURALISM
GROVELLINGLY	GUANIFEROUS	GUESTIMATE	GUNFIGHTER	GUTTURALISMS
GROVELLINGS	GUANOSINES	GUESTIMATED	GUNFIGHTERS	GUTTURALITIES
GROWLERIES	GUARANTEED	GUESTIMATES	GUNFIGHTING	GUTTURALITY
GROWLINESS	GUARANTEEING	GUESTIMATING	GUNFIGHTINGS	GUTTURALIZATION
GROWLINESSES	GUARANTEES	GUIDEBOOKS	GUNKHOLING	GUTTURALIZE
GROWLINGLY	GUARANTIED	GUIDELINES	GUNMANSHIP	GUTTURALIZED
GROWTHIEST	GUARANTIES	GUIDEPOSTS	GUNMANSHIPS	GUTTURALIZES
GROWTHINESS	GUARANTORS	GUIDESHIPS	GUNNERSHIP	GUTTURALIZING
GROWTHINESSES	GUARANTYING	GUIDEWORDS	GUNNERSHIPS	GUTTURALLY
GROWTHISTS	GUARDEDNESS	GUIDWILLIE	GUNNYSACKS	GUTTURALNESS
GRUBBINESS	GUARDEDNESSES	GUILDHALLS	GUNPOWDERIER	GUTTURALNESSES
GRUBBINESSES	GUARDHOUSE	GUILDSHIPS	GUNPOWDERIEST	GYMNASIARCH

GYMNASIARCHS	GYNAECOLOGIC	GYNECOCRACY	GYNOMONOECIOUS	GYROCOPTERS
GYMNASIAST	GYNAECOLOGICAL	GYNECOCRATIC	GYNOMONOECISM	GYROFREQUENCIES
GYMNASIASTS	GYNAECOLOGIES	GYNECOLOGIC	GYNOMONOECISMS	GYROFREQUENCY
GYMNASIUMS	GYNAECOLOGIST	GYNECOLOGICAL	GYNOPHOBES	GYROMAGNETIC
GYMNASTICAL	GYNAECOLOGISTS	GYNECOLOGIES	GYNOPHOBIA	GYROMAGNETISM
GYMNASTICALLY	GYNAECOLOGY	GYNECOLOGIST	GYNOPHOBIAS	GYROMAGNETISMS
GYMNASTICS	GYNAECOMAST	GYNECOLOGISTS	GYNOPHOBIC	GYROMANCIES
GYMNORHINAL	GYNAECOMASTIA	GYNECOLOGY	GYNOPHOBICS	GYROPILOTS
GYMNOSOPHIES	GYNAECOMASTIAS	GYNECOMASTIA	GYNOPHORES	GYROPLANES
GYMNOSOPHIST	GYNAECOMASTIES	GYNECOMASTIAS	GYNOPHORIC	GYROSCOPES
GYMNOSOPHISTS	GYNAECOMASTS	GYNIATRICS	GYNOSTEMIA	GYROSCOPIC
GYMNOSOPHS	GYNAECOMASTY	GYNIATRIES	GYNOSTEMIUM	GYROSCOPICALLY
GYMNOSOPHY	GYNANDRIES	GYNIOLATRIES	GYPSIFEROUS	GYROSCOPICS
GYMNOSPERM	GYNANDRISM	GYNIOLATRY	GYPSOPHILA	GYROSTABILISER
GYMNOSPERMIES	GYNANDRISMS	GYNOCRACIES	GYPSOPHILAS	GYROSTABILISERS
GYMNOSPERMOUS	GYNANDROMORPH	GYNOCRATIC	GYPSYHOODS	GYROSTABILIZER
GYMNOSPERMS	GYNANDROMORPHIC	GYNODIOECIOUS	GYPSYWORTS	GYROSTABILIZERS
GYMNOSPERMY	GYNANDROMORPHS	GYNODIOECISM	GYRATIONAL	GYROSTATIC
GYNAECEUMS	GYNANDROMORPHY	GYNODIOECISMS	GYRFALCONS	GYROSTATICALLY
GYNAECOCRACIES	GYNANDROUS	GYNOGENESES	GYROCOMPASS	GYROSTATICS
GYNAECOCRACY	GYNARCHIES	GYNOGENESIS	GYROCOMPASSES	GYROVAGUES
GYNAECOCRATIC	GYNECOCRACIES	GYNOGENETIC	GYROCOPTER	

G

H

HAANEPOOTS
HABERDASHER
HABERDASHERIES
HABERDASHERS
HABERDASHERY
HABERDINES
HABERGEONS
HABILATORY
HABILIMENT
HABILIMENTS
HABILITATE
HABILITATED
HABILITATES
HABILITATING
HABILITATION
HABILITATIONS
HABILITATOR
HABILITATORS
HABITABILITIES
HABITABILITY
HABITABLENESS
HABITABLENESSES
HABITATION
HABITATIONAL
HABITATIONS
HABITAUNCE
HABITAUNCES
HABITUALLY
HABITUALNESS
HABITUALNESSES
HABITUATED
HABITUATES
HABITUATING
HABITUATION
HABITUATIONS
HABITUDINAL
HACENDADOS
HACIENDADO
HACIENDADOS
HACKAMORES
HACKATHONS
HACKBERRIES
HACKBUTEER

HACKBUTEERS
HACKBUTTER
HACKBUTTERS
HACKERAZZI
HACKERAZZIS
HACKERAZZO
HACKMATACK
HACKMATACKS
HACKNEYING
HACKNEYISM
HACKNEYISMS
HACKNEYMAN
HACKNEYMEN
HACKSAWING
HACKTIVISM
HACKTIVISMS
HACKTIVIST
HACKTIVISTS
HACQUETONS
HADROSAURS
HADROSAURUS
HADROSAURUSES
HAECCEITIES
HAEMACHROME
HAEMACHROMES
HAEMACYTOMETER
HAEMACYTOMETERS
HAEMAGGLUTINATE
HAEMAGGLUTININ
HAEMAGGLUTININS
HAEMAGOGUE
HAEMAGOGUES
HAEMANGIOMA
HAEMANGIOMAS
HAEMANGIOMATA
HAEMATEINS
HAEMATEMESES
HAEMATEMESIS
HAEMATINIC
HAEMATINICS
HAEMATITES
HAEMATITIC
HAEMATOBLAST

HAEMATOBLASTIC
HAEMATOBLASTS
HAEMATOCELE
HAEMATOCELES
HAEMATOCRIT
HAEMATOCRITS
HAEMATOCRYAL
HAEMATOGENESES
HAEMATOGENESIS
HAEMATOGENETIC
HAEMATOGENIC
HAEMATOGENOUS
HAEMATOLOGIC
HAEMATOLOGICAL
HAEMATOLOGIES
HAEMATOLOGIST
HAEMATOLOGISTS
HAEMATOLOGY
HAEMATOLYSES
HAEMATOLYSIS
HAEMATOMAS
HAEMATOMATA
HAEMATOPHAGOUS
HAEMATOPOIESES
HAEMATOPOIESIS
HAEMATOPOIETIC
HAEMATOSES
HAEMATOSIS
HAEMATOTHERMAL
HAEMATOXYLIC
HAEMATOXYLIN
HAEMATOXYLINS
HAEMATOXYLON
HAEMATOXYLONS
HAEMATOZOA
HAEMATOZOON
HAEMATURIA
HAEMATURIAS
HAEMATURIC
HAEMOCHROME
HAEMOCHROMES
HAEMOCOELS
HAEMOCONIA

HAEMOCONIAS
HAEMOCYANIN
HAEMOCYANINS
HAEMOCYTES
HAEMOCYTOMETER
HAEMOCYTOMETERS
HAEMODIALYSER
HAEMODIALYSERS
HAEMODIALYSES
HAEMODIALYSIS
HAEMODIALYZER
HAEMODIALYZERS
HAEMODILUTION
HAEMODILUTIONS
HAEMODYNAMIC
HAEMODYNAMICS
HAEMOFLAGELLATE
HAEMOGLOBIN
HAEMOGLOBINS
HAEMOGLOBINURIA
HAEMOGLOBINURIC
HAEMOLYMPH
HAEMOLYMPHS
HAEMOLYSED
HAEMOLYSES
HAEMOLYSIN
HAEMOLYSING
HAEMOLYSINS
HAEMOLYSIS
HAEMOLYTIC
HAEMOLYZED
HAEMOLYZES
HAEMOLYZING
HAEMOPHILE
HAEMOPHILES
HAEMOPHILIA
HAEMOPHILIAC
HAEMOPHILIACS
HAEMOPHILIAS
HAEMOPHILIC
HAEMOPHILIOID
HAEMOPHOBIA
HAEMOPHOBIAS

HAEMOPOIESES
HAEMOPOIESIS
HAEMOPOIETIC
HAEMOPROTEIN
HAEMOPROTEINS
HAEMOPTYSES
HAEMOPTYSIS
HAEMORRHAGE
HAEMORRHAGED
HAEMORRHAGES
HAEMORRHAGIC
HAEMORRHAGING
HAEMORRHAGINGS
HAEMORRHOID
HAEMORRHOIDAL
HAEMORRHOIDS
HAEMOSIDERIN
HAEMOSIDERINS
HAEMOSTASES
HAEMOSTASIA
HAEMOSTASIAS
HAEMOSTASIS
HAEMOSTATIC
HAEMOSTATICS
HAEMOSTATS
HAEMOTOXIC
HAEMOTOXIN
HAEMOTOXINS
HAGBERRIES
HAGBUTEERS
HAGBUTTERS
HAGGADICAL
HAGGADISTIC
HAGGADISTS
HAGGARDNESS
HAGGARDNESSES
HAGGISHNESS
HAGGISHNESSES
HAGIARCHIES
HAGIOCRACIES
HAGIOCRACY
HAGIOGRAPHER
HAGIOGRAPHERS

HAGIOGRAPHIC	HAIRSPRINGS	HALLUCINANTS	HALTERBROKE	HANDBALLED
HAGIOGRAPHICAL	HAIRSTREAK	HALLUCINATE	HALTERBROKEN	HANDBALLER
HAGIOGRAPHIES	HAIRSTREAKS	HALLUCINATED	HALTERNECK	HANDBALLERS
HAGIOGRAPHIST	HAIRSTYLES	HALLUCINATES	HALTERNECKS	HANDBALLING
HAGIOGRAPHISTS	HAIRSTYLING	HALLUCINATING	HALTINGNESS	HANDBARROW
HAGIOGRAPHY	HAIRSTYLINGS	HALLUCINATION	HALTINGNESSES	HANDBARROWS
HAGIOLATER	HAIRSTYLIST	HALLUCINATIONAL	HAMADRYADES	HANDBASKET
HAGIOLATERS	HAIRSTYLISTS	HALLUCINATIONS	HAMADRYADS	HANDBASKETS
HAGIOLATRIES	HAIRWEAVING	HALLUCINATIVE	HAMADRYASES	HANDBRAKES
HAGIOLATROUS	HAIRWEAVINGS	HALLUCINATOR	HAMAMELIDACEOUS	HANDBREADTH
HAGIOLATRY	HAIRYBACKS	HALLUCINATORS	HAMAMELISES	HANDBREADTHS
HAGIOLOGIC	HALACHISTS	HALLUCINATORY	HAMANTASCH	HANDCLASPS
HAGIOLOGICAL	HALAKHISTS	HALLUCINOGEN	HAMANTASCHEN	HANDCRAFTED
HAGIOLOGIES	HALBERDIER	HALLUCINOGENIC	HAMARTHRITIS	HANDCRAFTING
HAGIOLOGIST	HALBERDIERS	HALLUCINOGENICS	HAMARTHRITISES	HANDCRAFTS
HAGIOLOGISTS	HALCYONIAN	HALLUCINOGENS	HAMARTIOLOGIES	HANDCRAFTSMAN
HAGIOSCOPE	HALENESSES	HALLUCINOSES	HAMARTIOLOGY	HANDCRAFTSMEN
HAGIOSCOPES	HALFENDEALE	HALLUCINOSIS	HAMBURGERS	HANDCUFFED
HAGIOSCOPIC	HALFENDEALES	HALOBIONTIC	HAMESUCKEN	HANDCUFFING
HAILSTONES	HALFHEARTED	HALOBIONTS	HAMESUCKENS	HANDEDNESS
HAILSTORMS	HALFHEARTEDLY	HALOBIOTIC	HAMFATTERED	HANDEDNESSES
HAIRBRAINED	HALFHEARTEDNESS	HALOCARBON	HAMFATTERING	HANDFASTED
HAIRBREADTH	HALFNESSES	HALOCARBONS	HAMFATTERS	HANDFASTING
HAIRBREADTHS	HALFPENNIES	HALOCLINES	HAMMERCLOTH	HANDFASTINGS
HAIRBRUSHES	HALFPENNYWORTH	HALOGENATE	HAMMERCLOTHS	HANDFEEDING
HAIRCLOTHS	HALFPENNYWORTHS	HALOGENATED	HAMMERHEAD	HANDGLASSES
HAIRCUTTER	HALFSERIOUSLY	HALOGENATES	HAMMERHEADED	HANDICAPPED
HAIRCUTTERS	HALFTRACKS	HALOGENATING	HAMMERHEADS	HANDICAPPER
HAIRCUTTING	HALFWITTED	HALOGENATION	HAMMERINGS	HANDICAPPERS
HAIRCUTTINGS	HALFWITTEDLY	HALOGENATIONS	HAMMERKOPS	HANDICAPPING
HAIRDRESSER	HALFWITTEDNESS	HALOGENOID	HAMMERLESS	HANDICRAFT
HAIRDRESSERS	HALIEUTICS	HALOGENOUS	HAMMERLOCK	HANDICRAFTER
HAIRDRESSING	HALIPLANKTON	HALOGETONS	HAMMERLOCKS	HANDICRAFTERS
HAIRDRESSINGS	HALIPLANKTONS	HALOMORPHIC	HAMMERSTONE	HANDICRAFTS
HAIRDRIERS	HALLALLING	HALOPERIDOL	HAMMERSTONES	HANDICRAFTSMAN
HAIRDRYERS	HALLEFLINTA	HALOPERIDOLS	HAMMERTOES	HANDICRAFTSMEN
HAIRINESSES	HALLEFLINTAS	HALOPHILES	HAMMINESSES	HANDICUFFS
HAIRLESSES	HALLELUIAH	HALOPHILIC	HAMPEREDNESS	HANDINESSES
HAIRLESSNESS	HALLELUIAHS	HALOPHILIES	HAMPEREDNESSES	HANDIWORKS
HAIRLESSNESSES	HALLELUJAH	HALOPHILOUS	HAMSHACKLE	HANDKERCHER
HAIRPIECES	HALLELUJAHS	HALOPHOBES	HAMSHACKLED	HANDKERCHERS
HAIRSBREADTH	HALLMARKED	HALOPHYTES	HAMSHACKLES	HANDKERCHIEF
HAIRSBREADTHS	HALLMARKING	HALOPHYTIC	HAMSHACKLING	HANDKERCHIEFS
HAIRSPLITTER	HALLOWEDNESS	HALOPHYTISM	HAMSTRINGED	HANDKERCHIEVES
HAIRSPLITTERS	HALLOWEDNESSES	HALOPHYTISMS	HAMSTRINGING	HANDLANGER
HAIRSPLITTING	HALLOYSITE	HALOTHANES	HAMSTRINGS	HANDLANGERS
HAIRSPLITTINGS	HALLOYSITES	HALTERBREAK	HANDBAGGED	HANDLEABLE
HAIRSPRAYS	HALLSTANDS	HALTERBREAKING	HANDBAGGING	HANDLEBARS
HAIRSPRING	HALLUCINANT	HALTERBREAKS	HANDBAGGINGS	HANDLELESS

HANDLINERS	HANDYWORKS	HAPTOTROPISM	HARDINGGRASS	HARMONIOUSNESS
HANDMAIDEN	HANGABILITIES	HAPTOTROPISMS	HARDINGGRASSES	HARMONIPHON
HANDMAIDENS	HANGABILITY	HARAMZADAS	HARDLINERS	HARMONIPHONE
HANDPASSED	HANGARAGES	HARAMZADIS	HARDMOUTHED	HARMONIPHONES
HANDPASSES	HANKERINGS	HARANGUERS	HARDNESSES	HARMONIPHONS
HANDPASSING	HANSARDISE	HARANGUING	HARDSCAPES	HARMONISABLE
HANDPHONES	HANSARDISED	HARASSEDLY	HARDSCRABBLE	HARMONISATION
HANDPICKED	HANSARDISES	HARASSINGLY	HARDSCRABBLES	HARMONISATIONS
HANDPICKING	HANSARDISING	HARASSINGS	HARDSTANDING	HARMONISED
HANDPRESSES	HANSARDIZE	HARASSMENT	HARDSTANDINGS	HARMONISER
HANDPRINTS	HANSARDIZED	HARASSMENTS	HARDSTANDS	HARMONISERS
HANDSBREADTH	HANSARDIZES	HARBINGERED	HARDWAREMAN	HARMONISES
HANDSBREADTHS	HANSARDIZING	HARBINGERING	HARDWAREMEN	HARMONISING
HANDSELING	HANSELLING	HARBINGERS	HARDWIRING	HARMONISTIC
HANDSELLED	HANTAVIRUS	HARBORAGES	HARDWORKING	HARMONISTICALLY
HANDSELLING	HANTAVIRUSES	HARBORFULS	HAREBRAINED	HARMONISTS
HANDSHAKES	HAPAXANTHIC	HARBORLESS	HARESTAILS	HARMONIUMIST
HANDSHAKING	HAPAXANTHOUS	HARBORMASTER	HARIOLATED	HARMONIUMISTS
HANDSHAKINGS	HAPHAZARDLY	HARBORMASTERS	HARIOLATES	HARMONIUMS
HANDSOMELY	HAPHAZARDNESS	HARBORSIDE	HARIOLATING	HARMONIZABLE
HANDSOMENESS	HAPHAZARDNESSES	HARBOURAGE	HARIOLATION	HARMONIZATION
HANDSOMENESSES	HAPHAZARDRIES	HARBOURAGES	HARIOLATIONS	HARMONIZATIONS
HANDSOMEST	HAPHAZARDRY	HARBOURERS	HARLEQUINADE	HARMONIZED
HANDSPIKES	HAPHAZARDS	HARBOURFUL	HARLEQUINADES	HARMONIZER
HANDSPRING	HAPHTARAHS	HARBOURFULS	HARLEQUINED	HARMONIZERS
HANDSPRINGS	HAPHTAROTH	HARBOURING	HARLEQUINING	HARMONIZES
HANDSTAFFS	HAPLESSNESS	HARBOURLESS	HARLEQUINS	HARMONIZING
HANDSTAMPED	HAPLESSNESSES	HARBOURSIDE	HARLOTRIES	HARMONOGRAM
HANDSTAMPING	HAPLOBIONT	HARBOURSIDES	HARMALINES	HARMONOGRAMS
HANDSTAMPS	HAPLOBIONTIC	HARDBACKED	HARMATTANS	HARMONOGRAPH
HANDSTANDS	HAPLOBIONTS	HARDBOARDS	HARMDOINGS	HARMONOGRAPHS
HANDSTAVES	HAPLOGRAPHIES	HARDBODIES	HARMFULNESS	HARMONOMETER
HANDSTROKE	HAPLOGRAPHY	HARDBOUNDS	HARMFULNESSES	HARMONOMETERS
HANDSTROKES	HAPLOGROUP	HARDCOVERS	HARMLESSLY	HARMOSTIES
HANDSTURNS	HAPLOGROUPS	HARDENINGS	HARMLESSNESS	HARMOTOMES
HANDTOWELS	HAPLOIDIES	HARDFISTED	HARMLESSNESSES	HARNESSERS
HANDWHEELS	HAPLOLOGIC	HARDGRASSES	HARMOLODIC	HARNESSING
HANDWORKED	HAPLOLOGIES	HARDHANDED	HARMOLODICS	HARNESSLESS
HANDWORKER	HAPLOSTEMONOUS	HARDHANDEDNESS	HARMONICAL	HARPOONEER
HANDWORKERS	HAPLOTYPES	HARDHEADED	HARMONICALLY	HARPOONEERS
HANDWRINGER	HAPPENCHANCE	HARDHEADEDLY	HARMONICAS	HARPOONERS
HANDWRINGERS	HAPPENCHANCES	HARDHEADEDNESS	HARMONICHORD	HARPOONING
HANDWRITES	HAPPENINGS	HARDHEARTED	HARMONICHORDS	HARPSICHORD
HANDWRITING	HAPPENSTANCE	HARDHEARTEDLY	HARMONICIST	HARPSICHORDIST
HANDWRITINGS	HAPPENSTANCES	HARDHEARTEDNESS	HARMONICISTS	HARPSICHORDISTS
HANDWRITTEN	HAPPINESSES	HARDIHEADS	HARMONICON	HARPSICHORDS
HANDWROUGHT	HAPTOGLOBIN	HARDIHOODS	HARMONICONS	HARQUEBUSE
HANDYPERSON	HAPTOGLOBINS	HARDIMENTS	HARMONIOUS	HARQUEBUSES
HANDYPERSONS	HAPTOTROPIC	HARDINESSES	HARMONIOUSLY	HARQUEBUSIER

HARQUEBUSIERS	HATCHELLERS	HAWTHORNIEST	HEADMASTERSHIPS	HEALTHINESSES
HARQUEBUSS	HATCHELLING	HAYCATIONS	HEADMISTRESS	HEALTHISMS
HARQUEBUSSES	HATCHERIES	HAYMAKINGS	HEADMISTRESSES	HEALTHLESS
HARROWINGLY	HATCHETIER	HAZARDABLE	HEADMISTRESSIER	HEALTHLESSNESS
HARROWINGS	HATCHETIEST	HAZARDIZES	HEADMISTRESSY	HEALTHSOME
HARROWMENT	HATCHETTITE	HAZARDOUSLY	HEADPEACES	HEAPSTEADS
HARROWMENTS	HATCHETTITES	HAZARDOUSNESS	HEADPHONES	HEARKENERS
HARRUMPHED	HATCHLINGS	HAZARDOUSNESSES	HEADPIECES	HEARKENING
HARRUMPHING	HATCHMENTS	HAZARDRIES	HEADQUARTER	HEARTACHES
HARSHENING	HATEFULNESS	HAZELWOODS	HEADQUARTERED	HEARTBEATS
HARSHNESSES	HATEFULNESSES	HAZINESSES	HEADQUARTERING	HEARTBREAK
HARTBEESES	HATELESSNESS	HEADACHIER	HEADQUARTERS	HEARTBREAKER
HARTBEESTS	HATELESSNESSES	HEADACHIEST	HEADREACHED	HEARTBREAKERS
HARTEBEEST	HATEWORTHIER	HEADBANGED	HEADREACHES	HEARTBREAKING
HARTEBEESTS	HATEWORTHIEST	HEADBANGING	HEADREACHING	HEARTBREAKINGLY
HARTSHORNS	HATEWORTHY	HEADBANGINGS	HEADSCARVES	HEARTBREAKS
HARUMPHING	HATINATORS	HEADBOARDS	HEADSHAKES	HEARTBROKE
HARUSPICAL	HATLESSNESS	HEADBOROUGH	HEADSHEETS	HEARTBROKEN
HARUSPICATE	HATLESSNESSES	HEADBOROUGHS	HEADSHRINKER	HEARTBROKENLY
HARUSPICATED	HAUBERGEON	HEADBUTTED	HEADSHRINKERS	HEARTBROKENNESS
HARUSPICATES	HAUBERGEONS	HEADBUTTING	HEADSPACES	HEARTBURNING
HARUSPICATING	HAUGHTIEST	HEADCHAIRS	HEADSPRING	HEARTBURNINGS
HARUSPICATION	HAUGHTINESS	HEADCHEESE	HEADSPRINGS	HEARTBURNS
HARUSPICATIONS	HAUGHTINESSES	HEADCHEESES	HEADSQUARE	HEARTENERS
HARUSPICES	HAUNTINGLY	HEADCLOTHS	HEADSQUARES	HEARTENING
HARUSPICIES	HAUSFRAUEN	HEADCOUNTS	HEADSTALLS	HEARTENINGLY
HARVESTABLE	HAUSSMANNISE	HEADDRESSES	HEADSTANDS	HEARTHRUGS
HARVESTERS	HAUSSMANNISED	HEADFISHES	HEADSTICKS	HEARTHSTONE
HARVESTING	HAUSSMANNISES	HEADFOREMOST	HEADSTOCKS	HEARTHSTONES
HARVESTINGS	HAUSSMANNISING	HEADFRAMES	HEADSTONES	HEARTIKINS
HARVESTLESS	HAUSSMANNIZE	HEADGUARDS	HEADSTREAM	HEARTINESS
HARVESTMAN	HAUSSMANNIZED	HEADHUNTED	HEADSTREAMS	HEARTINESSES
HARVESTMEN	HAUSSMANNIZES	HEADHUNTER	HEADSTRONG	HEARTLANDS
HARVESTTIME	HAUSSMANNIZING	HEADHUNTERS	HEADSTRONGLY	HEARTLESSLY
HARVESTTIMES	HAUSTELLATE	HEADHUNTING	HEADSTRONGNESS	HEARTLESSNESS
HASENPFEFFER	HAUSTELLUM	HEADHUNTINGS	HEADTEACHER	HEARTLESSNESSES
HASENPFEFFERS	HAUSTORIAL	HEADINESSES	HEADTEACHERS	HEARTLINGS
HASHEESHES	HAUSTORIUM	HEADLEASES	HEADWAITER	HEARTRENDING
HASSOCKIER	HAVERSACKS	HEADLESSNESS	HEADWAITERS	HEARTRENDINGLY
HASSOCKIEST	HAVERSINES	HEADLESSNESSES	HEADWATERS	HEARTSEASE
HASTEFULLY	HAWFINCHES	HEADLIGHTS	HEADWORKER	HEARTSEASES
HASTINESSES	HAWKISHNESS	HEADLINERS	HEADWORKERS	HEARTSEEDS
HATBRUSHES	HAWKISHNESSES	HEADLINING	HEALTHCARE	HEARTSICKNESS
HATCHABILITIES	HAWKSBEARD	HEADMASTER	HEALTHCARES	HEARTSICKNESSES
HATCHABILITY	HAWKSBEARDS	HEADMASTERLIER	HEALTHFULLY	HEARTSINKS
HATCHBACKS	HAWKSBILLS	HEADMASTERLIEST	HEALTHFULNESS	HEARTSOMELY
HATCHELING	HAWSEHOLES	HEADMASTERLY	HEALTHFULNESSES	HEARTSOMENESS
HATCHELLED	HAWSEPIPES	HEADMASTERS	HEALTHIEST	HEARTSOMENESSES
HATCHELLER	HAWTHORNIER	HEADMASTERSHIP	HEALTHINESS	HEARTSORES

HEARTSTRING	HEAVYHEARTEDLY	HECTOMETER	HELDENTENORS	HELIOLATRIES
HEARTSTRINGS	HEAVYWEIGHT	HECTOMETERS	HELIACALLY	HELIOLATROUS
HEARTTHROB	HEAVYWEIGHTS	HECTOMETRE	HELIANTHEMUM	HELIOLATRY
HEARTTHROBS	HEBDOMADAL	HECTOMETRES	HELIANTHEMUMS	HELIOLITHIC
HEARTWARMING	HEBDOMADALLY	HECTORINGLY	HELIANTHUS	HELIOLOGIES
HEARTWATER	HEBDOMADAR	HECTORINGS	HELIANTHUSES	HELIOMETER
HEARTWATERS	HEBDOMADARIES	HECTORISMS	HELIBUSSES	HELIOMETERS
HEARTWOODS	HEBDOMADARS	HECTORSHIP	HELICHRYSUM	HELIOMETRIC
HEARTWORMS	HEBDOMADARY	HECTORSHIPS	HELICHRYSUMS	HELIOMETRICAL
HEATEDNESS	HEBDOMADER	HECTOSTERE	HELICITIES	HELIOMETRICALLY
HEATEDNESSES	HEBDOMADERS	HECTOSTERES	HELICLINES	HELIOMETRIES
HEATHBERRIES	HEBEPHRENIA	HEDGEBILLS	HELICOGRAPH	HELIOMETRY
HEATHBERRY	HEBEPHRENIAC	HEDGEHOPPED	HELICOGRAPHS	HELIOPAUSE
HEATHBIRDS	HEBEPHRENIACS	HEDGEHOPPER	HELICOIDAL	HELIOPAUSES
HEATHCOCKS	HEBEPHRENIAS	HEDGEHOPPERS	HELICOIDALLY	HELIOPHILOUS
HEATHENDOM	HEBEPHRENIC	HEDGEHOPPING	HELICONIAS	HELIOPHOBIC
HEATHENDOMS	HEBEPHRENICS	HEDGEHOPPINGS	HELICOPTED	HELIOPHYTE
HEATHENESSE	HEBETATING	HEDONICALLY	HELICOPTER	HELIOPHYTES
HEATHENESSES	HEBETATION	HEDONISTIC	HELICOPTERED	HELIOSCIOPHYTE
HEATHENISE	HEBETATIONS	HEDONISTICALLY	HELICOPTERING	HELIOSCIOPHYTES
HEATHENISED	HEBETATIVE	HEDYPHANES	HELICOPTERS	HELIOSCOPE
HEATHENISES	HEBETUDINOSITY	HEDYSARUMS	HELICOPTING	HELIOSCOPES
HEATHENISH	HEBETUDINOUS	HEEDFULNESS	HELICTITES	HELIOSCOPIC
HEATHENISHLY	HEBRAISATION	HEEDFULNESSES	HELIDROMES	HELIOSPHERE
HEATHENISHNESS	HEBRAISATIONS	HEEDINESSES	HELILIFTED	HELIOSPHERES
HEATHENISING	HEBRAISING	HEEDLESSLY	HELILIFTING	HELIOSTATIC
HEATHENISM	HEBRAIZATION	HEEDLESSNESS	HELIOCENTRIC	HELIOSTATS
HEATHENISMS	HEBRAIZATIONS	HEEDLESSNESSES	HELIOCENTRICISM	HELIOTACTIC
HEATHENIZE	HEBRAIZING	HEELPIECES	HELIOCENTRICITY	HELIOTAXES
HEATHENIZED	HECKELPHONE	HEELPLATES	HELIOCHROME	HELIOTAXIS
HEATHENIZES	HECKELPHONES	HEFTINESSES	HELIOCHROMES	HELIOTHERAPIES
HEATHENIZING	HECOGENINS	HEGEMONIAL	HELIOCHROMIC	HELIOTHERAPY
HEATHENNESS	HECTICALLY	HEGEMONICAL	HELIOCHROMIES	HELIOTROPE
HEATHENNESSES	HECTOCOTYLI	HEGEMONIES	HELIOCHROMY	HELIOTROPES
HEATHENRIES	HECTOCOTYLUS	HEGEMONISM	HELIOGRAMS	HELIOTROPIC
HEATHERIER	HECTOGRAMME	HEGEMONISMS	HELIOGRAPH	HELIOTROPICAL
HEATHERIEST	HECTOGRAMMES	HEGEMONIST	HELIOGRAPHED	HELIOTROPICALLY
HEATHFOWLS	HECTOGRAMS	HEGEMONISTS	HELIOGRAPHER	HELIOTROPIES
HEATHLANDS	HECTOGRAPH	HEGUMENIES	HELIOGRAPHERS	HELIOTROPIN
HEATSTROKE	HECTOGRAPHED	HEGUMENOSES	HELIOGRAPHIC	HELIOTROPINS
HEATSTROKES	HECTOGRAPHIC	HEIGHTENED	HELIOGRAPHICAL	HELIOTROPISM
HEAVENLIER	HECTOGRAPHIES	HEIGHTENER	HELIOGRAPHIES	HELIOTROPISMS
HEAVENLIEST	HECTOGRAPHING	HEIGHTENERS	HELIOGRAPHING	HELIOTROPY
HEAVENLINESS	HECTOGRAPHS	HEIGHTENING	HELIOGRAPHS	HELIOTYPED
HEAVENLINESSES	HECTOGRAPHY	HEIGHTISMS	HELIOGRAPHY	HELIOTYPES
HEAVENWARD	HECTOLITER	HEINOUSNESS	HELIOGRAVURE	HELIOTYPIC
HEAVENWARDS	HECTOLITERS	HEINOUSNESSES	HELIOGRAVURES	HELIOTYPIES
HEAVINESSES	HECTOLITRE	HEKTOGRAMS	HELIOLATER	HELIOTYPING
HEAVYHEARTED	HECTOLITRES	HELDENTENOR	HELIOLATERS	HELIOZOANS

HELIPILOTS	HELPLESSLY	HEMATOXYLINS	HEMIMORPHITE	HEMODIALYZER
HELISKIING	HELPLESSNESS	HEMATOZOON	HEMIMORPHITES	HEMODIALYZERS
HELISKIINGS	HELPLESSNESSES	HEMATURIAS	HEMIMORPHY	HEMODILUTION
HELISPHERIC	HELVETIUMS	HEMELYTRAL	HEMIONUSES	HEMODILUTIONS
HELISPHERICAL	HEMACHROME	HEMELYTRON	HEMIOPSIAS	HEMODYNAMIC
HELLACIOUS	HEMACHROMES	HEMELYTRUM	HEMIPARASITE	HEMODYNAMICALLY
HELLACIOUSLY	HEMACYTOMETER	HEMERALOPIA	HEMIPARASITES	HEMODYNAMICS
HELLBENDER	HEMACYTOMETERS	HEMERALOPIAS	HEMIPARASITIC	HEMOFLAGELLATE
HELLBENDERS	HEMAGGLUTINATE	HEMERALOPIC	HEMIPLEGIA	HEMOFLAGELLATES
HELLBROTHS	HEMAGGLUTINATED	HEMEROCALLIS	HEMIPLEGIAS	HEMOGLOBIN
HELLDIVERS	HEMAGGLUTINATES	HEMEROCALLISES	HEMIPLEGIC	HEMOGLOBINS
HELLEBORES	HEMAGGLUTININ	HEMERYTHRIN	HEMIPLEGICS	HEMOGLOBINURIA
HELLEBORINE	HEMAGGLUTININS	HEMERYTHRINS	HEMIPTERAL	HEMOGLOBINURIAS
HELLEBORINES	HEMAGOGUES	HEMIACETAL	HEMIPTERAN	HEMOGLOBINURIC
HELLENISATION	HEMANGIOMA	HEMIACETALS	HEMIPTERANS	HEMOLYMPHS
HELLENISATIONS	HEMANGIOMAS	HEMIALGIAS	HEMIPTERON	HEMOLYSING
HELLENISED	HEMANGIOMATA	HEMIANOPIA	HEMIPTERONS	HEMOLYSINS
HELLENISES	HEMATEMESES	HEMIANOPIAS	HEMIPTEROUS	HEMOLYZING
HELLENISING	HEMATEMESIS	HEMIANOPIC	HEMISPACES	HEMOPHILES
HELLENIZATION	HEMATINICS	HEMIANOPSIA	HEMISPHERE	HEMOPHILIA
HELLENIZATIONS	HEMATOBLAST	HEMIANOPSIAS	HEMISPHERES	HEMOPHILIAC
HELLENIZED	HEMATOBLASTIC	HEMIANOPTIC	HEMISPHERIC	HEMOPHILIACS
HELLENIZES	HEMATOBLASTS	HEMICELLULOSE	HEMISPHERICAL	HEMOPHILIAS
HELLENIZING	HEMATOCELE	HEMICELLULOSES	HEMISPHEROID	HEMOPHILIC
HELLGRAMITE	HEMATOCELES	HEMICHORDATE	HEMISPHEROIDAL	HEMOPHILICS
HELLGRAMITES	HEMATOCRIT	HEMICHORDATES	HEMISPHEROIDS	HEMOPHILIOID
HELLGRAMMITE	HEMATOCRITS	HEMICRANIA	HEMISTICHAL	HEMOPOIESES
HELLGRAMMITES	HEMATOCRYAL	HEMICRANIAS	HEMISTICHS	HEMOPOIESIS
HELLHOUNDS	HEMATOGENESES	HEMICRYPTOPHYTE	HEMITERPENE	HEMOPOIETIC
HELLISHNESS	HEMATOGENESIS	HEMICRYSTALLINE	HEMITERPENES	HEMOPROTEIN
HELLISHNESSES	HEMATOGENETIC	HEMICYCLES	HEMITROPAL	HEMOPROTEINS
HELLSCAPES	HEMATOGENIC	HEMICYCLIC	HEMITROPES	HEMOPTYSES
HELMETINGS	HEMATOGENOUS	HEMIELYTRA	HEMITROPIC	HEMOPTYSIS
HELMETLIKE	HEMATOLOGIC	HEMIELYTRAL	HEMITROPIES	HEMORRHAGE
HELMINTHIASES	HEMATOLOGICAL	HEMIELYTRON	HEMITROPISM	HEMORRHAGED
HELMINTHIASIS	HEMATOLOGIES	HEMIHEDRAL	HEMITROPISMS	HEMORRHAGES
HELMINTHIC	HEMATOLOGIST	HEMIHEDRIES	HEMITROPOUS	HEMORRHAGIC
HELMINTHICS	HEMATOLOGISTS	HEMIHEDRISM	HEMIZYGOUS	HEMORRHAGING
HELMINTHOID	HEMATOLOGY	HEMIHEDRISMS	HEMOCHROMATOSES	HEMORRHAGINGS
HELMINTHOLOGIC	HEMATOLYSES	HEMIHEDRON	HEMOCHROMATOSIS	HEMORRHOID
HELMINTHOLOGIES	HEMATOLYSIS	HEMIHEDRONS	HEMOCHROME	HEMORRHOIDAL
HELMINTHOLOGIST	HEMATOMATA	HEMIHYDRATE	HEMOCHROMES	HEMORRHOIDALS
HELMINTHOLOGY	HEMATOPHAGOUS	HEMIHYDRATED	HEMOCONIAS	HEMORRHOIDS
HELMINTHOUS	HEMATOPOIESES	HEMIHYDRATES	HEMOCYANIN	HEMOSIDERIN
HELMSMANSHIP	HEMATOPOIESIS	HEMIMETABOLOUS	HEMOCYANINS	HEMOSIDERINS
HELMSMANSHIPS	HEMATOPOIETIC	HEMIMORPHIC	HEMOCYTOMETER	HEMOSTASES
HELOPHYTES	HEMATOPORPHYRIN	HEMIMORPHIES	HEMOCYTOMETERS	HEMOSTASIA
HELPFULNESS	HEMATOTHERMAL	HEMIMORPHISM	HEMODIALYSES	HEMOSTASIAS
HELPFULNESSES	HEMATOXYLIN	HEMIMORPHISMS	HEMODIALYSIS	HEMOSTASIS

H

HEMOSTATIC
HEMOSTATICS
HEMOTOXINS
HEMSTITCHED
HEMSTITCHER
HEMSTITCHERS
HEMSTITCHES
HEMSTITCHING
HENCEFORTH
HENCEFORWARD
HENCEFORWARDS
HENCHPERSON
HENCHPERSONS
HENCHWOMAN
HENCHWOMEN
HENDECAGON
HENDECAGONAL
HENDECAGONS
HENDECAHEDRA
HENDECAHEDRON
HENDECAHEDRONS
HENDECASYLLABIC
HENDECASYLLABLE
HENDIADYSES
HENOTHEISM
HENOTHEISMS
HENOTHEIST
HENOTHEISTIC
HENOTHEISTS
HENPECKERIES
HENPECKERY
HENPECKING
HEORTOLOGICAL
HEORTOLOGIES
HEORTOLOGIST
HEORTOLOGISTS
HEORTOLOGY
HEPARINISED
HEPARINIZED
HEPARINOID
HEPATECTOMIES
HEPATECTOMISED
HEPATECTOMIZED
HEPATECTOMY
HEPATICOLOGICAL
HEPATICOLOGIES
HEPATICOLOGIST
HEPATICOLOGISTS
HEPATICOLOGY

HEPATISATION
HEPATISATIONS
HEPATISING
HEPATITIDES
HEPATITISES
HEPATIZATION
HEPATIZATIONS
HEPATIZING
HEPATOCELLULAR
HEPATOCYTE
HEPATOCYTES
HEPATOGENOUS
HEPATOLOGIES
HEPATOLOGIST
HEPATOLOGISTS
HEPATOLOGY
HEPATOMATA
HEPATOMEGALIES
HEPATOMEGALY
HEPATOPANCREAS
HEPATOSCOPIES
HEPATOSCOPY
HEPATOTOXIC
HEPATOTOXICITY
HEPHTHEMIMER
HEPHTHEMIMERAL
HEPHTHEMIMERS
HEPTACHLOR
HEPTACHLORS
HEPTACHORD
HEPTACHORDS
HEPTADECANOIC
HEPTAGLOTS
HEPTAGONAL
HEPTAGYNOUS
HEPTAHEDRA
HEPTAHEDRAL
HEPTAHEDRON
HEPTAHEDRONS
HEPTAMEROUS
HEPTAMETER
HEPTAMETERS
HEPTAMETRICAL
HEPTANDROUS
HEPTANGULAR
HEPTAPODIC
HEPTAPODIES
HEPTARCHAL
HEPTARCHIC

HEPTARCHIES
HEPTARCHIST
HEPTARCHISTS
HEPTASTICH
HEPTASTICHS
HEPTASYLLABIC
HEPTATHLETE
HEPTATHLETES
HEPTATHLON
HEPTATHLONS
HEPTATONIC
HEPTAVALENT
HERALDICALLY
HERALDISTS
HERALDRIES
HERALDSHIP
HERALDSHIPS
HERBACEOUS
HERBACEOUSLY
HERBALISMS
HERBALISTS
HERBARIANS
HERBARIUMS
HERBICIDAL
HERBICIDALLY
HERBICIDES
HERBIVORES
HERBIVORIES
HERBIVOROUS
HERBIVOROUSLY
HERBIVOROUSNESS
HERBOLOGIES
HERBORISATION
HERBORISATIONS
HERBORISED
HERBORISES
HERBORISING
HERBORISTS
HERBORIZATION
HERBORIZATIONS
HERBORIZED
HERBORIZES
HERBORIZING
HERCOGAMIES
HERCOGAMOUS
HERCULESES
HERCYNITES
HEREABOUTS
HEREAFTERS

HEREDITABILITY
HEREDITABLE
HEREDITABLY
HEREDITAMENT
HEREDITAMENTS
HEREDITARIAN
HEREDITARIANISM
HEREDITARIANIST
HEREDITARIANS
HEREDITARILY
HEREDITARINESS
HEREDITARY
HEREDITIES
HEREDITIST
HEREDITISTS
HEREINABOVE
HEREINAFTER
HEREINBEFORE
HEREINBELOW
HERENESSES
HERESIARCH
HERESIARCHS
HERESIOGRAPHER
HERESIOGRAPHERS
HERESIOGRAPHIES
HERESIOGRAPHY
HERESIOLOGIES
HERESIOLOGIST
HERESIOLOGISTS
HERESIOLOGY
HERESTHETIC
HERESTHETICAL
HERESTHETICIAN
HERESTHETICIANS
HERESTHETICS
HERETICALLY
HERETICATE
HERETICATED
HERETICATES
HERETICATING
HERETOFORE
HERETOFORES
HERETRICES
HERETRIXES
HERIOTABLE
HERITABILITIES
HERITABILITY
HERITRESSES
HERITRICES

HERITRIXES
HERKOGAMIES
HERMANDADS
HERMAPHRODITE
HERMAPHRODITES
HERMAPHRODITIC
HERMAPHRODITISM
HERMATYPIC
HERMENEUTIC
HERMENEUTICAL
HERMENEUTICALLY
HERMENEUTICS
HERMENEUTIST
HERMENEUTISTS
HERMETICAL
HERMETICALLY
HERMETICISM
HERMETICISMS
HERMETICITIES
HERMETICITY
HERMETISMS
HERMETISTS
HERMITAGES
HERMITESSES
HERMITICAL
HERMITICALLY
HERMITISMS
HERMITRIES
HERNIATING
HERNIATION
HERNIATIONS
HERNIORRHAPHIES
HERNIORRHAPHY
HERNIOTOMIES
HERNIOTOMY
HEROICALLY
HEROICALNESS
HEROICALNESSES
HEROICISED
HEROICISES
HEROICISING
HEROICIZED
HEROICIZES
HEROICIZING
HEROICNESS
HEROICNESSES
HEROICOMIC
HEROICOMICAL
HEROINISMS

HERONSHAWS	HETERAUXESIS	HETEROECISM	HETEROLYSIS	HETEROSEXISTS
HERPESVIRUS	HETEROAROMATIC	HETEROECISMS	HETEROLYTIC	HETEROSEXUAL
HERPESVIRUSES	HETEROATOM	HETEROFLEXIBLE	HETEROMEROUS	HETEROSEXUALITY
HERPETOFAUNA	HETEROATOMS	HETEROFLEXIBLES	HETEROMORPHIC	HETEROSEXUALLY
HERPETOFAUNAE	HETEROAUXIN	HETEROGAMETE	HETEROMORPHIES	HETEROSEXUALS
HERPETOFAUNAS	HETEROAUXINS	HETEROGAMETES	HETEROMORPHISM	HETEROSOCIAL
HERPETOLOGIC	HETEROBLASTIC	HETEROGAMETIC	HETEROMORPHISMS	HETEROSOCIALITY
HERPETOLOGICAL	HETEROBLASTIES	HETEROGAMETIES	HETEROMORPHOUS	HETEROSOMATOUS
HERPETOLOGIES	HETEROBLASTY	HETEROGAMETY	HETEROMORPHY	HETEROSPECIFIC
HERPETOLOGIST	HETEROCARPOUS	HETEROGAMIES	HETERONOMIES	HETEROSPECIFICS
HERPETOLOGISTS	HETEROCERCAL	HETEROGAMOUS	HETERONOMOUS	HETEROSPORIES
HERPETOLOGY	HETEROCERCALITY	HETEROGAMY	HETERONOMOUSLY	HETEROSPOROUS
HERRENVOLK	HETEROCERCIES	HETEROGENEITIES	HETERONOMY	HETEROSPORY
HERRENVOLKS	HETEROCERCY	HETEROGENEITY	HETERONORMATIVE	HETEROSTROPHIC
HERRIMENTS	HETEROCHROMATIC	HETEROGENEOUS	HETERONYMOUS	HETEROSTROPHIES
HERRINGBONE	HETEROCHROMATIN	HETEROGENEOUSLY	HETERONYMOUSLY	HETEROSTROPHY
HERRINGBONED	HETEROCHROMOUS	HETEROGENESES	HETERONYMS	HETEROSTYLED
HERRINGBONES	HETEROCHRONIC	HETEROGENESIS	HETEROOUSIAN	HETEROSTYLIES
HERRINGBONING	HETEROCHRONIES	HETEROGENETIC	HETEROOUSIANS	HETEROSTYLISM
HERRINGERS	HETEROCHRONISM	HETEROGENIC	HETEROPHIL	HETEROSTYLISMS
HERRYMENTS	HETEROCHRONISMS	HETEROGENIES	HETEROPHILE	HETEROSTYLOUS
HERSTORIES	HETEROCHRONOUS	HETEROGENOUS	HETEROPHILES	HETEROSTYLY
HESITANCES	HETEROCHRONY	HETEROGENY	HETEROPHILS	HETEROTACTIC
HESITANCIES	HETEROCLITE	HETEROGONIC	HETEROPHONIES	HETEROTACTOUS
HESITANTLY	HETEROCLITES	HETEROGONIES	HETEROPHONY	HETEROTAXES
HESITATERS	HETEROCLITIC	HETEROGONOUS	HETEROPHYLLIES	HETEROTAXIA
HESITATING	HETEROCLITOUS	HETEROGONOUSLY	HETEROPHYLLOUS	HETEROTAXIAS
HESITATINGLY	HETEROCONT	HETEROGONY	HETEROPHYLLY	HETEROTAXIC
HESITATION	HETEROCONTS	HETEROGRAFT	HETEROPLASIA	HETEROTAXIES
HESITATIONS	HETEROCYCLE	HETEROGRAFTS	HETEROPLASIAS	HETEROTAXIS
HESITATIVE	HETEROCYCLES	HETEROGRAPHIC	HETEROPLASTIC	HETEROTAXY
HESITATORS	HETEROCYCLIC	HETEROGRAPHICAL	HETEROPLASTIES	HETEROTHALLIC
HESITATORY	HETEROCYCLICS	HETEROGRAPHIES	HETEROPLASTY	HETEROTHALLIES
HESPERIDIA	HETEROCYST	HETEROGRAPHY	HETEROPLOID	HETEROTHALLISM
HESPERIDIN	HETEROCYSTOUS	HETEROGYNOUS	HETEROPLOIDIES	HETEROTHALLISMS
HESPERIDINS	HETEROCYSTS	HETEROKARYON	HETEROPLOIDS	HETEROTHALLY
HESPERIDIUM	HETERODACTYL	HETEROKARYONS	HETEROPLOIDY	HETEROTHERMAL
HESSONITES	HETERODACTYLOUS	HETEROKARYOSES	HETEROPODS	HETEROTOPIA
HETAERISMIC	HETERODACTYLS	HETEROKARYOSIS	HETEROPOLAR	HETEROTOPIAS
HETAERISMS	HETERODONT	HETEROKARYOTIC	HETEROPOLARITY	HETEROTOPIC
HETAERISTIC	HETERODOXIES	HETEROKONT	HETEROPTERAN	HETEROTOPIES
HETAERISTS	HETERODOXY	HETEROKONTAN	HETEROPTERANS	HETEROTOPOUS
HETAIRISMIC	HETERODUPLEX	HETEROKONTS	HETEROPTEROUS	HETEROTOPY
HETAIRISMS	HETERODUPLEXES	HETEROLECITHAL	HETEROSCEDASTIC	HETEROTROPH
HETAIRISTIC	HETERODYNE	HETEROLOGIES	HETEROSCIAN	HETEROTROPHIC
HETAIRISTS	HETERODYNED	HETEROLOGOUS	HETEROSCIANS	HETEROTROPHIES
HETERARCHIES	HETERODYNES	HETEROLOGOUSLY	HETEROSEXISM	HETEROTROPHS
HETERARCHY	HETERODYNING	HETEROLOGY	HETEROSEXISMS	HETEROTROPHY
HETERAUXESES	HETEROECIOUS	HETEROLYSES	HETEROSEXIST	HETEROTYPIC

HETEROTYPICAL	HEXAHEMERON	HEXYLRESORCINOL	HIERACOSPHINGES	HIEROGRAPHIES
HETEROUSIAN	HEXAHEMERONS	HIBAKUSHAS	HIERACOSPHINX	HIEROGRAPHS
HETEROUSIANS	HEXAHYDRATE	HIBERNACLE	HIERACOSPHINXES	HIEROGRAPHY
HETEROZYGOSES	HEXAHYDRATED	HIBERNACLES	HIERARCHAL	HIEROLATRIES
HETEROZYGOSIS	HEXAHYDRATES	HIBERNACULA	HIERARCHIC	HIEROLATRY
HETEROZYGOSITY	HEXAMERISM	HIBERNACULUM	HIERARCHICAL	HIEROLOGIC
HETEROZYGOTE	HEXAMERISMS	HIBERNATED	HIERARCHICALLY	HIEROLOGICAL
HETEROZYGOTES	HEXAMEROUS	HIBERNATES	HIERARCHIES	HIEROLOGIES
HETEROZYGOUS	HEXAMETERS	HIBERNATING	HIERARCHISE	HIEROLOGIST
HETHERWARD	HEXAMETHONIUM	HIBERNATION	HIERARCHISED	HIEROLOGISTS
HETMANATES	HEXAMETHONIUMS	HIBERNATIONS	HIERARCHISES	HIEROMANCIES
HETMANSHIP	HEXAMETRAL	HIBERNATOR	HIERARCHISING	HIEROMANCY
HETMANSHIPS	HEXAMETRIC	HIBERNATORS	HIERARCHISM	HIEROPHANT
HEULANDITE	HEXAMETRICAL	HIBERNICISATION	HIERARCHISMS	HIEROPHANTIC
HEULANDITES	HEXAMETRISE	HIBERNICISE	HIERARCHIZE	HIEROPHANTS
HEURISTICALLY	HEXAMETRISED	HIBERNICISED	HIERARCHIZED	HIEROPHOBIA
HEURISTICS	HEXAMETRISES	HIBERNICISES	HIERARCHIZES	HIEROPHOBIAS
HEXACHLORETHANE	HEXAMETRISING	HIBERNICISING	HIERARCHIZING	HIEROPHOBIC
HEXACHLORIDE	HEXAMETRIST	HIBERNICIZATION	HIERATICAL	HIEROPHOBICS
HEXACHLORIDES	HEXAMETRISTS	HIBERNICIZE	HIERATICALLY	HIEROSCOPIES
HEXACHLOROPHANE	HEXAMETRIZE	HIBERNICIZED	HIERATICAS	HIEROSCOPY
HEXACHLOROPHENE	HEXAMETRIZED	HIBERNICIZES	HIEROCRACIES	HIERURGICAL
HEXACHORDS	HEXAMETRIZES	HIBERNICIZING	HIEROCRACY	HIERURGIES
HEXACOSANOIC	HEXAMETRIZING	HIBERNISATION	HIEROCRATIC	HIGHBALLED
HEXACTINAL	HEXANDRIAN	HIBERNISATIONS	HIEROCRATICAL	HIGHBALLING
HEXACTINELLID	HEXANDROUS	HIBERNISED	HIEROCRATS	HIGHBINDER
HEXACTINELLIDS	HEXANGULAR	HIBERNISES	HIERODULES	HIGHBINDERS
HEXADACTYLIC	HEXAPLARIAN	HIBERNISING	HIERODULIC	HIGHBLOODED
HEXADACTYLOUS	HEXAPLARIC	HIBERNIZATION	HIEROGLYPH	HIGHBROWED
HEXADECANE	HEXAPLOIDIES	HIBERNIZATIONS	HIEROGLYPHED	HIGHBROWISM
HEXADECANES	HEXAPLOIDS	HIBERNIZED	HIEROGLYPHIC	HIGHBROWISMS
HEXADECANOIC	HEXAPLOIDY	HIBERNIZES	HIEROGLYPHICAL	HIGHBUSHES
HEXADECIMAL	HEXAPODIES	HIBERNIZING	HIEROGLYPHICS	HIGHCHAIRS
HEXADECIMALS	HEXARCHIES	HIBISCUSES	HIEROGLYPHING	HIGHERMOST
HEXADECYLS	HEXASTICHAL	HICCOUGHED	HIEROGLYPHIST	HIGHFALUTIN
HEXAEMERIC	HEXASTICHIC	HICCOUGHING	HIEROGLYPHISTS	HIGHFALUTING
HEXAEMERON	HEXASTICHON	HICCUPIEST	HIEROGLYPHS	HIGHFALUTINGS
HEXAEMERONS	HEXASTICHONS	HICCUPPING	HIEROGRAMMAT	HIGHFALUTINS
HEXAFLUORIDE	HEXASTICHS	HIDALGOISH	HIEROGRAMMATE	HIGHFLIERS
HEXAFLUORIDES	HEXASTYLES	HIDALGOISM	HIEROGRAMMATES	HIGHFLYERS
HEXAGONALLY	HEXATEUCHAL	HIDALGOISMS	HIEROGRAMMATIC	HIGHJACKED
HEXAGRAMMOID	HEXATHLONS	HIDDENITES	HIEROGRAMMATIST	HIGHJACKER
HEXAGRAMMOIDS	HEXAVALENT	HIDDENMOST	HIEROGRAMMATS	HIGHJACKERS
HEXAGYNIAN	HEXOBARBITAL	HIDDENNESS	HIEROGRAMS	HIGHJACKING
HEXAGYNOUS	HEXOBARBITALS	HIDDENNESSES	HIEROGRAPH	HIGHJACKINGS
HEXAHEDRAL	HEXOKINASE	HIDEOSITIES	HIEROGRAPHER	HIGHLANDER
HEXAHEDRON	HEXOKINASES	HIDEOUSNESS	HIEROGRAPHERS	HIGHLANDERS
HEXAHEDRONS	HEXOSAMINIDASE	HIDEOUSNESSES	HIEROGRAPHIC	HIGHLIGHTED
HEXAHEMERIC	HEXOSAMINIDASES	HIERACIUMS	HIEROGRAPHICAL	HIGHLIGHTER

HIGHLIGHTERS	HIPPEASTRUM	HIPPURITIC	HISTIOLOGY	HISTORICIZES
HIGHLIGHTING	HIPPEASTRUMS	HIPSTERDOM	HISTIOPHOROID	HISTORICIZING
HIGHLIGHTS	HIPPIATRIC	HIPSTERDOMS	HISTOBLAST	HISTORIETTE
HIGHLINERS	HIPPIATRICS	HIPSTERISM	HISTOBLASTS	HISTORIETTES
HIGHLINING	HIPPIATRIES	HIPSTERISMS	HISTOCHEMICAL	HISTORIFIED
HIGHLININGS	HIPPIATRIST	HIRCOCERVUS	HISTOCHEMICALLY	HISTORIFIES
HIGHNESSES	HIPPIATRISTS	HIRCOCERVUSES	HISTOCHEMIST	HISTORIFYING
HIGHTAILED	HIPPIEDOMS	HIRCOSITIES	HISTOCHEMISTRY	HISTORIOGRAPHER
HIGHTAILING	HIPPIENESS	HIRSELLING	HISTOCHEMISTS	HISTORIOGRAPHIC
HIGHWAYMAN	HIPPIENESSES	HIRSELLINGS	HISTOCOMPATIBLE	HISTORIOGRAPHY
HIGHWAYMEN	HIPPINESSES	HIRSUTENESS	HISTOGENESES	HISTORIOLOGIES
HIGHWROUGHT	HIPPOCAMPAL	HIRSUTENESSES	HISTOGENESIS	HISTORIOLOGY
HIJACKINGS	HIPPOCAMPI	HIRSUTISMS	HISTOGENETIC	HISTORISMS
HILARIOUSLY	HIPPOCAMPUS	HIRUDINEAN	HISTOGENIC	HISTORYING
HILARIOUSNESS	HIPPOCENTAUR	HIRUDINEANS	HISTOGENICALLY	HISTRIONIC
HILARIOUSNESSES	HIPPOCENTAURS	HIRUDINOID	HISTOGENIES	HISTRIONICAL
HILARITIES	HIPPOCRASES	HIRUDINOUS	HISTOGRAMS	HISTRIONICALLY
HILLBILLIES	HIPPOCREPIAN	HISPANICISE	HISTOLOGIC	HISTRIONICISM
HILLCRESTS	HIPPOCREPIANS	HISPANICISED	HISTOLOGICAL	HISTRIONICISMS
HILLINESSES	HIPPODAMES	HISPANICISES	HISTOLOGICALLY	HISTRIONICS
HILLOCKIER	HIPPODAMIST	HISPANICISING	HISTOLOGIES	HISTRIONISM
HILLOCKIEST	HIPPODAMISTS	HISPANICISM	HISTOLOGIST	HISTRIONISMS
HILLSLOPES	HIPPODAMOUS	HISPANICISMS	HISTOLOGISTS	HITCHHIKED
HILLWALKER	HIPPODROME	HISPANICIZE	HISTOLYSES	HITCHHIKER
HILLWALKERS	HIPPODROMES	HISPANICIZED	HISTOLYSIS	HITCHHIKERS
HILLWALKING	HIPPODROMIC	HISPANICIZES	HISTOLYTIC	HITCHHIKES
HILLWALKINGS	HIPPOGRIFF	HISPANICIZING	HISTOLYTICALLY	HITCHHIKING
HINDBERRIES	HIPPOGRIFFS	HISPANIDAD	HISTOPATHOLOGIC	HITCHHIKINGS
HINDBRAINS	HIPPOGRYPH	HISPANIDADS	HISTOPATHOLOGY	HITHERMOST
HINDCASTED	HIPPOGRYPHS	HISPANIOLISE	HISTOPHYSIOLOGY	HITHERSIDE
HINDCASTING	HIPPOLOGIES	HISPANIOLISED	HISTOPLASMOSES	HITHERSIDES
HINDERANCE	HIPPOLOGIST	HISPANIOLISES	HISTOPLASMOSIS	HITHERWARD
HINDERANCES	HIPPOLOGISTS	HISPANIOLISING	HISTORIANS	HITHERWARDS
HINDERINGLY	HIPPOMANES	HISPANIOLIZE	HISTORIATED	HOACTZINES
HINDERINGS	HIPPOPHAGIES	HISPANIOLIZED	HISTORICAL	HOARFROSTS
HINDERLAND	HIPPOPHAGIST	HISPANIOLIZES	HISTORICALLY	HOARHOUNDS
HINDERLANDS	HIPPOPHAGISTS	HISPANIOLIZING	HISTORICALNESS	HOARINESSES
HINDERLANS	HIPPOPHAGOUS	HISPANISMS	HISTORICISE	HOARSENESS
HINDERLINGS	HIPPOPHAGY	HISPIDITIES	HISTORICISED	HOARSENESSES
HINDERLINS	HIPPOPHILE	HISTAMINASE	HISTORICISES	HOARSENING
HINDERMOST	HIPPOPHILES	HISTAMINASES	HISTORICISING	HOBBITRIES
HINDFOREMOST	HIPPOPHOBE	HISTAMINERGIC	HISTORICISM	HOBBLEBUSH
HINDQUARTER	HIPPOPHOBES	HISTAMINES	HISTORICISMS	HOBBLEBUSHES
HINDQUARTERS	HIPPOPOTAMI	HISTAMINIC	HISTORICIST	HOBBLEDEHOY
HINDRANCES	HIPPOPOTAMIAN	HISTIDINES	HISTORICISTS	HOBBLEDEHOYDOM
HINDSHANKS	HIPPOPOTAMIC	HISTIOCYTE	HISTORICITIES	HOBBLEDEHOYDOMS
HINDSIGHTS	HIPPOPOTAMUS	HISTIOCYTES	HISTORICITY	HOBBLEDEHOYHOOD
HINTERLAND	HIPPOPOTAMUSES	HISTIOCYTIC	HISTORICIZE	HOBBLEDEHOYISH
HINTERLANDS	HIPPURITES	HISTIOLOGIES	HISTORICIZED	HOBBLEDEHOYISM

H

HOBBLEDEHOYISMS	HOLIDAYMAKER	HOLOPHRASTIC	HOMEOPATHY	HOMEWORKING
HOBBLEDEHOYS	HOLIDAYMAKERS	HOLOPHYTES	HOMEOSTASES	HOMEWORKINGS
HOBBLINGLY	HOLINESSES	HOLOPHYTIC	HOMEOSTASIS	HOMEWRECKER
HOBBYHORSE	HOLISTICALLY	HOLOPHYTISM	HOMEOSTATIC	HOMEWRECKERS
HOBBYHORSED	HOLLANDAISE	HOLOPHYTISMS	HOMEOTELEUTON	HOMEYNESSES
HOBBYHORSES	HOLLANDAISES	HOLOPLANKTON	HOMEOTELEUTONS	HOMICIDALLY
HOBBYHORSING	HOLLOWARES	HOLOPLANKTONS	HOMEOTHERM	HOMILETICAL
HOBGOBLINISM	HOLLOWNESS	HOLOSTERIC	HOMEOTHERMAL	HOMILETICALLY
HOBGOBLINISMS	HOLLOWNESSES	HOLOTHURIAN	HOMEOTHERMIC	HOMILETICS
HOBGOBLINRIES	HOLLOWWARE	HOLOTHURIANS	HOMEOTHERMIES	HOMINESSES
HOBGOBLINRY	HOLLOWWARES	HOLSTERING	HOMEOTHERMISM	HOMINISATION
HOBGOBLINS	HOLLYHOCKS	HOLYSTONED	HOMEOTHERMISMS	HOMINISATIONS
HOBJOBBERS	HOLOBENTHIC	HOLYSTONES	HOMEOTHERMOUS	HOMINISING
HOBJOBBING	HOLOBLASTIC	HOLYSTONING	HOMEOTHERMS	HOMINIZATION
HOBJOBBINGS	HOLOBLASTICALLY	HOMALOGRAPHIC	HOMEOTHERMY	HOMINIZATIONS
HOBNAILING	HOLOCAINES	HOMALOIDAL	HOMEOTYPIC	HOMINIZING
HOBNOBBERS	HOLOCAUSTAL	HOMEBIRTHS	HOMEOTYPICAL	HOMOBLASTIC
HOBNOBBIER	HOLOCAUSTIC	HOMEBODIES	HOMEOWNERS	HOMOBLASTIES
HOBNOBBIEST	HOLOCAUSTS	HOMEBUYERS	HOMEOWNERSHIP	HOMOBLASTY
HOBNOBBING	HOLOCRYSTALLINE	HOMECOMERS	HOMEOWNERSHIPS	HOMOCENTRIC
HOCHMAGANDIES	HOLODISCUS	HOMECOMING	HOMEPLACES	HOMOCENTRICALLY
HOCHMAGANDY	HOLODISCUSES	HOMECOMINGS	HOMEPORTED	HOMOCERCAL
HODGEPODGE	HOLOENZYME	HOMECRAFTS	HOMEPORTING	HOMOCERCIES
HODGEPODGES	HOLOENZYMES	HOMEGOINGS	HOMESCHOOL	HOMOCHLAMYDEOUS
HODMANDODS	HOLOGAMIES	HOMELESSNESS	HOMESCHOOLED	HOMOCHROMATIC
HODOGRAPHIC	HOLOGRAPHED	HOMELESSNESSES	HOMESCHOOLER	HOMOCHROMATISM
HODOGRAPHS	HOLOGRAPHER	HOMELINESS	HOMESCHOOLERS	HOMOCHROMATISMS
HODOMETERS	HOLOGRAPHERS	HOMELINESSES	HOMESCHOOLING	HOMOCHROMIES
HODOMETRIES	HOLOGRAPHIC	HOMEMAKERS	HOMESCHOOLS	HOMOCHROMOUS
HODOSCOPES	HOLOGRAPHICALLY	HOMEMAKING	HOMESCREETCH	HOMOCHROMY
HOGGISHNESS	HOLOGRAPHIES	HOMEMAKINGS	HOMESCREETCHES	HOMOCYCLIC
HOGGISHNESSES	HOLOGRAPHING	HOMEOBOXES	HOMESHORING	HOMOCYSTEINE
HOIDENISHNESS	HOLOGRAPHS	HOMEOMERIC	HOMESHORINGS	HOMOCYSTEINES
HOIDENISHNESSES	HOLOGRAPHY	HOMEOMERIES	HOMESICKNESS	HOMOEOMERIC
HOJATOLESLAM	HOLOGYNIES	HOMEOMEROUS	HOMESICKNESSES	HOMOEOMERIES
HOJATOLESLAMS	HOLOHEDRAL	HOMEOMORPH	HOMESOURCING	HOMOEOMEROUS
HOJATOLISLAM	HOLOHEDRISM	HOMEOMORPHIC	HOMESOURCINGS	HOMOEOMERY
HOJATOLISLAMS	HOLOHEDRISMS	HOMEOMORPHIES	HOMESTALLS	HOMOEOMORPH
HOKEYNESSES	HOLOHEDRON	HOMEOMORPHISM	HOMESTANDS	HOMOEOMORPHIC
HOKEYPOKEY	HOLOHEDRONS	HOMEOMORPHISMS	HOMESTEADED	HOMOEOMORPHIES
HOKEYPOKEYS	HOLOMETABOLIC	HOMEOMORPHOUS	HOMESTEADER	HOMOEOMORPHISM
HOKINESSES	HOLOMETABOLISM	HOMEOMORPHS	HOMESTEADERS	HOMOEOMORPHISMS
HOKYPOKIES	HOLOMETABOLISMS	HOMEOMORPHY	HOMESTEADING	HOMOEOMORPHOUS
HOLARCHIES	HOLOMETABOLOUS	HOMEOPATHIC	HOMESTEADINGS	HOMOEOMORPHS
HOLDERBATS	HOLOMORPHIC	HOMEOPATHICALLY	HOMESTEADS	HOMOEOMORPHY
HOLDERSHIP	HOLOPHOTAL	HOMEOPATHIES	HOMESTRETCH	HOMOEOPATH
HOLDERSHIPS	HOLOPHOTES	HOMEOPATHIST	HOMESTRETCHES	HOMOEOPATHIC
HOLIDAYERS	HOLOPHRASE	HOMEOPATHISTS	HOMEWORKER	HOMOEOPATHIES
HOLIDAYING	HOLOPHRASES	HOMEOPATHS	HOMEWORKERS	HOMOEOPATHIST

HOMOEOPATHISTS	HOMOGENIZERS	HOMOMORPHIES	HOMOSEXUALISTS	HONEYCOMBS
HOMOEOPATHS	HOMOGENIZES	HOMOMORPHISM	HOMOSEXUALITIES	HONEYCREEPER
HOMOEOPATHY	HOMOGENIZING	HOMOMORPHISMS	HOMOSEXUALITY	HONEYCREEPERS
HOMOEOSTASES	HOMOGENOUS	HOMOMORPHOSES	HOMOSEXUALLY	HONEYDEWED
HOMOEOSTASIS	HOMOGONIES	HOMOMORPHOSIS	HOMOSEXUALS	HONEYEATER
HOMOEOSTATIC	HOMOGONOUS	HOMOMORPHOUS	HOMOSOCIAL	HONEYEATERS
HOMOEOTELEUTON	HOMOGONOUSLY	HOMOMORPHS	HOMOSOCIALITIES	HONEYGUIDE
HOMOEOTELEUTONS	HOMOGRAFTS	HOMOMORPHY	HOMOSOCIALITY	HONEYGUIDES
HOMOEOTHERM	HOMOGRAPHIC	HOMONUCLEAR	HOMOSPORIES	HONEYMONTH
HOMOEOTHERMAL	HOMOGRAPHIES	HOMONYMIES	HOMOSPOROUS	HONEYMONTHED
HOMOEOTHERMIC	HOMOGRAPHS	HOMONYMITIES	HOMOSTYLIES	HONEYMONTHING
HOMOEOTHERMOUS	HOMOGRAPHY	HOMONYMITY	HOMOTAXIAL	HONEYMONTHS
HOMOEOTHERMS	HOMOIOMEROUS	HOMONYMOUS	HOMOTAXIALLY	HONEYMOONED
HOMOEOTYPIC	HOMOIOTHERM	HOMONYMOUSLY	HOMOTHALLIC	HONEYMOONER
HOMOEOTYPICAL	HOMOIOTHERMAL	HOMOOUSIAN	HOMOTHALLIES	HONEYMOONERS
HOMOEROTIC	HOMOIOTHERMIC	HOMOOUSIANS	HOMOTHALLISM	HONEYMOONING
HOMOEROTICALLY	HOMOIOTHERMIES	HOMOPHILES	HOMOTHALLISMS	HONEYMOONS
HOMOEROTICISM	HOMOIOTHERMS	HOMOPHOBES	HOMOTHALLY	HONEYSUCKER
HOMOEROTICISMS	HOMOIOTHERMY	HOMOPHOBIA	HOMOTHERMAL	HONEYSUCKERS
HOMOEROTISM	HOMOIOUSIAN	HOMOPHOBIAS	HOMOTHERMIC	HONEYSUCKLE
HOMOEROTISMS	HOMOIOUSIANS	HOMOPHOBIC	HOMOTHERMIES	HONEYSUCKLED
HOMOGAMETIC	HOMOLOGATE	HOMOPHONES	HOMOTHERMOUS	HONEYSUCKLES
HOMOGAMIES	HOMOLOGATED	HOMOPHONIC	HOMOTHERMY	HONEYTRAPS
HOMOGAMOUS	HOMOLOGATES	HOMOPHONICALLY	HOMOTONIES	HONORABILITIES
HOMOGENATE	HOMOLOGATING	HOMOPHONIES	HOMOTONOUS	HONORABILITY
HOMOGENATES	HOMOLOGATION	HOMOPHONOUS	HOMOTRANSPLANT	HONORABLENESS
HOMOGENEITIES	HOMOLOGATIONS	HOMOPHYLIES	HOMOTRANSPLANTS	HONORABLENESSES
HOMOGENEITY	HOMOLOGICAL	HOMOPHYLLIC	HOMOTYPIES	HONORARIES
HOMOGENEOUS	HOMOLOGICALLY	HOMOPLASIES	HOMOUSIANS	HONORARILY
HOMOGENEOUSLY	HOMOLOGIES	HOMOPLASMIES	HOMOZYGOSES	HONORARIUM
HOMOGENEOUSNESS	HOMOLOGISE	HOMOPLASMY	HOMOZYGOSIS	HONORARIUMS
HOMOGENESES	HOMOLOGISED	HOMOPLASTIC	HOMOZYGOSITIES	HONORIFICAL
HOMOGENESIS	HOMOLOGISER	HOMOPLASTICALLY	HOMOZYGOSITY	HONORIFICALLY
HOMOGENETIC	HOMOLOGISERS	HOMOPLASTIES	HOMOZYGOTE	HONORIFICS
HOMOGENETICAL	HOMOLOGISES	HOMOPLASTY	HOMOZYGOTES	HONOURABILITIES
HOMOGENIES	HOMOLOGISING	HOMOPOLARITIES	HOMOZYGOTIC	HONOURABILITY
HOMOGENISATION	HOMOLOGIZE	HOMOPOLARITY	HOMOZYGOUS	HONOURABLE
HOMOGENISATIONS	HOMOLOGIZED	HOMOPOLYMER	HOMOZYGOUSLY	HONOURABLENESS
HOMOGENISE	HOMOLOGIZER	HOMOPOLYMERIC	HOMUNCULAR	HONOURABLY
HOMOGENISED	HOMOLOGIZERS	HOMOPOLYMERS	HOMUNCULES	HONOURLESS
HOMOGENISER	HOMOLOGIZES	HOMOPTERAN	HOMUNCULUS	HOODEDNESS
HOMOGENISERS	HOMOLOGIZING	HOMOPTERANS	HONESTNESS	HOODEDNESSES
HOMOGENISES	HOMOLOGOUMENA	HOMOPTEROUS	HONESTNESSES	HOODLUMISH
HOMOGENISING	HOMOLOGOUS	HOMORGANIC	HONEYBELLS	HOODLUMISM
HOMOGENIZATION	HOMOLOGRAPHIC	HOMOSCEDASTIC	HONEYBUNCH	HOODLUMISMS
HOMOGENIZATIONS	HOMOLOGUES	HOMOSEXUAL	HONEYBUNCHES	HOODOOISMS
HOMOGENIZE	HOMOLOGUMENA	HOMOSEXUALISM	HONEYCOMBED	HOODWINKED
HOMOGENIZED	HOMOLOSINE	HOMOSEXUALISMS	HONEYCOMBING	HOODWINKER
HOMOGENIZER	HOMOMORPHIC	HOMOSEXUALIST	HONEYCOMBINGS	HOODWINKERS

HOODWINKING	HORNBLENDIC	HORRIPILATED	HORSEWOMAN	HOTFOOTING
HOOFPRINTS	HORNEDNESS	HORRIPILATES	HORSEWOMEN	HOTHEADEDLY
HOOKCHECKS	HORNEDNESSES	HORRIPILATING	HORSINESSES	HOTHEADEDNESS
HOOKEDNESS	HORNFELSES	HORRIPILATION	HORTATIONS	HOTHEADEDNESSES
HOOKEDNESSES	HORNFISHES	HORRIPILATIONS	HORTATIVELY	HOTHOUSING
HOOLACHANS	HORNINESSES	HORRISONANT	HORTATORILY	HOTHOUSINGS
HOOLIGANISM	HORNLESSNESS	HORRISONOUS	HORTENSIAS	HOTPRESSED
HOOLIGANISMS	HORNLESSNESSES	HORSEBACKS	HORTICULTURAL	HOTPRESSES
HOOPHOUSES	HORNSTONES	HORSEBEANS	HORTICULTURALLY	HOTPRESSING
HOOPSKIRTS	HORNSWOGGLE	HORSEBOXES	HORTICULTURE	HOTTENTOTS
HOOTANANNIE	HORNSWOGGLED	HORSEFEATHERS	HORTICULTURES	HOUGHMAGANDIE
HOOTANANNIES	HORNSWOGGLES	HORSEFLESH	HORTICULTURIST	HOUGHMAGANDIES
HOOTANANNY	HORNSWOGGLING	HORSEFLESHES	HORTICULTURISTS	HOUNDFISHES
HOOTENANNIE	HORNWRACKS	HORSEFLIES	HOSANNAING	HOURGLASSES
HOOTENANNIES	HORNYHEADS	HORSEHAIRS	HOSPITABLE	HOURPLATES
HOOTENANNY	HORNYWINKS	HORSEHEADS	HOSPITABLENESS	HOUSEBOATER
HOOTNANNIE	HOROGRAPHER	HORSEHIDES	HOSPITABLY	HOUSEBOATERS
HOOTNANNIES	HOROGRAPHERS	HORSELAUGH	HOSPITAGES	HOUSEBOATS
HOOVERINGS	HOROGRAPHIES	HORSELAUGHS	HOSPITALER	HOUSEBOUND
HOPEFULNESS	HOROGRAPHY	HORSELEECH	HOSPITALERS	HOUSEBREAK
HOPEFULNESSES	HOROLOGERS	HORSELEECHES	HOSPITALES	HOUSEBREAKER
HOPELESSLY	HOROLOGICAL	HORSEMANSHIP	HOSPITALISATION	HOUSEBREAKERS
HOPELESSNESS	HOROLOGIES	HORSEMANSHIPS	HOSPITALISE	HOUSEBREAKING
HOPELESSNESSES	HOROLOGION	HORSEMEATS	HOSPITALISED	HOUSEBREAKINGS
HOPLOLOGIES	HOROLOGIONS	HORSEMINTS	HOSPITALISES	HOUSEBREAKS
HOPLOLOGIST	HOROLOGIST	HORSEPLAYER	HOSPITALISING	HOUSEBROKE
HOPLOLOGISTS	HOROLOGISTS	HORSEPLAYERS	HOSPITALIST	HOUSEBROKEN
HOPPERCARS	HOROLOGIUM	HORSEPLAYS	HOSPITALISTS	HOUSECARLS
HOPPINESSES	HOROMETRICAL	HORSEPONDS	HOSPITALITIES	HOUSECLEAN
HOPSACKING	HOROMETRIES	HORSEPOWER	HOSPITALITY	HOUSECLEANED
HOPSACKINGS	HOROSCOPES	HORSEPOWERS	HOSPITALIZATION	HOUSECLEANING
HOPSCOTCHED	HOROSCOPIC	HORSEPOXES	HOSPITALIZE	HOUSECLEANINGS
HOPSCOTCHES	HOROSCOPIES	HORSERACES	HOSPITALIZED	HOUSECLEANS
HOPSCOTCHING	HOROSCOPIST	HORSERADISH	HOSPITALIZES	HOUSECOATS
HOREHOUNDS	HOROSCOPISTS	HORSERADISHES	HOSPITALIZING	HOUSECRAFT
HORIATIKIS	HORRENDOUS	HORSESHITS	HOSPITALLER	HOUSECRAFTS
HORIZONLESS	HORRENDOUSLY	HORSESHOED	HOSPITALLERS	HOUSEDRESS
HORIZONTAL	HORRENDOUSNESS	HORSESHOEING	HOSTELINGS	HOUSEDRESSES
HORIZONTALITIES	HORRIBLENESS	HORSESHOEINGS	HOSTELLERS	HOUSEFATHER
HORIZONTALITY	HORRIBLENESSES	HORSESHOER	HOSTELLING	HOUSEFATHERS
HORIZONTALLY	HORRIDNESS	HORSESHOERS	HOSTELLINGS	HOUSEFLIES
HORIZONTALNESS	HORRIDNESSES	HORSESHOES	HOSTELRIES	HOUSEFRONT
HORIZONTALS	HORRIFICALLY	HORSETAILS	HOSTESSING	HOUSEFRONTS
HORMOGONIA	HORRIFICATION	HORSEWEEDS	HOSTILITIES	HOUSEGUEST
HORMOGONIUM	HORRIFICATIONS	HORSEWHIPPED	HOTCHPOTCH	HOUSEGUESTS
HORMONALLY	HORRIFYING	HORSEWHIPPER	HOTCHPOTCHES	HOUSEHOLDER
HORMONELIKE	HORRIFYINGLY	HORSEWHIPPERS	HOTDOGGERS	HOUSEHOLDERS
HORNBLENDE	HORRIPILANT	HORSEWHIPPING	HOTDOGGING	HOUSEHOLDERSHIP
HORNBLENDES	HORRIPILATE	HORSEWHIPS	HOTELLINGS	HOUSEHOLDS

HOUSEHUSBAND	HOUSEWIVES	HUGEOUSNESSES	HUMECTATES	HUMORLESSLY
HOUSEHUSBANDS	HOUSEWORKER	HULLABALLOO	HUMECTATING	HUMORLESSNESS
HOUSEKEEPER	HOUSEWORKERS	HULLABALLOOS	HUMECTATION	HUMORLESSNESSES
HOUSEKEEPERS	HOUSEWORKS	HULLABALOO	HUMECTATIONS	HUMOROUSLY
HOUSEKEEPING	HOUSEWRAPS	HULLABALOOS	HUMECTIVES	HUMOROUSNESS
HOUSEKEEPINGS	HOUSTONIAS	HUMANENESS	HUMGRUFFIAN	HUMOROUSNESSES
HOUSEKEEPS	HOVERBOARD	HUMANENESSES	HUMGRUFFIANS	HUMORSOMENESS
HOUSELEEKS	HOVERBOARDS	HUMANHOODS	HUMGRUFFIN	HUMORSOMENESSES
HOUSELESSNESS	HOVERCRAFT	HUMANISATION	HUMGRUFFINS	HUMOURLESS
HOUSELESSNESSES	HOVERCRAFTS	HUMANISATIONS	HUMICOLOUS	HUMOURLESSLY
HOUSELIGHTS	HOVERFLIES	HUMANISERS	HUMIDIFICATION	HUMOURLESSNESS
HOUSELINES	HOVERINGLY	HUMANISING	HUMIDIFICATIONS	HUMOURSOME
HOUSELINGS	HOVERPORTS	HUMANISTIC	HUMIDIFIED	HUMOURSOMENESS
HOUSELLING	HOVERTRAIN	HUMANISTICALLY	HUMIDIFIER	HUMPBACKED
HOUSELLINGS	HOVERTRAINS	HUMANITARIAN	HUMIDIFIERS	HUMPINESSES
HOUSEMAIDS	HOWLROUNDS	HUMANITARIANISM	HUMIDIFIES	HUNCHBACKED
HOUSEMASTER	HOWSOMDEVER	HUMANITARIANIST	HUMIDIFYING	HUNCHBACKS
HOUSEMASTERS	HOWSOMEVER	HUMANITARIANS	HUMIDISTAT	HUNDREDERS
HOUSEMATES	HOWTOWDIES	HUMANITIES	HUMIDISTATS	HUNDREDFOLD
HOUSEMISTRESS	HOYDENHOOD	HUMANIZATION	HUMIDITIES	HUNDREDFOLDS
HOUSEMISTRESSES	HOYDENHOODS	HUMANIZATIONS	HUMIDNESSES	HUNDREDORS
HOUSEMOTHER	HOYDENISHNESS	HUMANIZERS	HUMIFICATION	HUNDREDTHS
HOUSEMOTHERS	HOYDENISHNESSES	HUMANIZING	HUMIFICATIONS	HUNDREDWEIGHT
HOUSEPAINTER	HOYDENISMS	HUMANKINDS	HUMILIATED	HUNDREDWEIGHTS
HOUSEPAINTERS	HUBRISTICALLY	HUMANNESSES	HUMILIATES	HUNGERINGLY
HOUSEPARENT	HUCKABACKS	HUMBLEBEES	HUMILIATING	HUNGRINESS
HOUSEPARENTS	HUCKLEBERRIES	HUMBLEBRAG	HUMILIATINGLY	HUNGRINESSES
HOUSEPERSON	HUCKLEBERRY	HUMBLEBRAGGED	HUMILIATION	HUNTIEGOWK
HOUSEPERSONS	HUCKLEBERRYING	HUMBLEBRAGGING	HUMILIATIONS	HUNTIEGOWKED
HOUSEPLANT	HUCKLEBERRYINGS	HUMBLEBRAGS	HUMILIATIVE	HUNTIEGOWKING
HOUSEPLANTS	HUCKLEBONE	HUMBLENESS	HUMILIATOR	HUNTIEGOWKS
HOUSEROOMS	HUCKLEBONES	HUMBLENESSES	HUMILIATORS	HUNTRESSES
HOUSESITTING	HUCKSTERAGE	HUMBLESSES	HUMILIATORY	HUNTSMANSHIP
HOUSEWARES	HUCKSTERAGES	HUMBLINGLY	HUMILITIES	HUNTSMANSHIPS
HOUSEWARMING	HUCKSTERED	HUMBUCKERS	HUMMELLERS	HUPAITHRIC
HOUSEWARMINGS	HUCKSTERESS	HUMBUGGABLE	HUMMELLING	HURLBARROW
HOUSEWIFELIER	HUCKSTERESSES	HUMBUGGERIES	HUMMELLINGS	HURLBARROWS
HOUSEWIFELIEST	HUCKSTERIES	HUMBUGGERS	HUMMINGBIRD	HURRICANES
HOUSEWIFELINESS	HUCKSTERING	HUMBUGGERY	HUMMINGBIRDS	HURRICANOES
HOUSEWIFELY	HUCKSTERISM	HUMBUGGING	HUMMOCKIER	HURRIEDNESS
HOUSEWIFERIES	HUCKSTERISMS	HUMDINGERS	HUMMOCKIEST	HURRIEDNESSES
HOUSEWIFERY	HUCKSTRESS	HUMDRUMNESS	HUMMOCKING	HURRYINGLY
HOUSEWIFESHIP	HUCKSTRESSES	HUMDRUMNESSES	HUMORALISM	HURTFULNESS
HOUSEWIFESHIPS	HUDIBRASTIC	HUMDUDGEON	HUMORALISMS	HURTFULNESSES
HOUSEWIFESKEP	HUFFINESSES	HUMDUDGEONS	HUMORALIST	HURTLEBERRIES
HOUSEWIFESKEPS	HUFFISHNESS	HUMDURGEON	HUMORALISTS	HURTLEBERRY
HOUSEWIFEY	HUFFISHNESSES	HUMDURGEONS	HUMORESQUE	HURTLESSLY
HOUSEWIFIER	HUGENESSES	HUMECTANTS	HUMORESQUES	HURTLESSNESS
HOUSEWIFIEST	HUGEOUSNESS	HUMECTATED	HUMORISTIC	HURTLESSNESSES

HUSBANDAGE	HYBRIDISTS	HYDROBIOLOGICAL	HYDRODYNAMICS	HYDROLOGIC
HUSBANDAGES	HYBRIDITIES	HYDROBIOLOGIES	HYDROELASTIC	HYDROLOGICAL
HUSBANDERS	HYBRIDIZABLE	HYDROBIOLOGIST	HYDROELECTRIC	HYDROLOGICALLY
HUSBANDING	HYBRIDIZATION	HYDROBIOLOGISTS	HYDROEXTRACTOR	HYDROLOGIES
HUSBANDLAND	HYBRIDIZATIONS	HYDROBIOLOGY	HYDROEXTRACTORS	HYDROLOGIST
HUSBANDLANDS	HYBRIDIZED	HYDROBROMIC	HYDROFLUORIC	HYDROLOGISTS
HUSBANDLESS	HYBRIDIZER	HYDROCARBON	HYDROFOILS	HYDROLYSABLE
HUSBANDLIER	HYBRIDIZERS	HYDROCARBONS	HYDROFORMING	HYDROLYSATE
HUSBANDLIEST	HYBRIDIZES	HYDROCASTS	HYDROFORMINGS	HYDROLYSATES
HUSBANDLIKE	HYBRIDIZING	HYDROCELES	HYDROGENASE	HYDROLYSATION
HUSBANDMAN	HYBRIDOMAS	HYDROCELLULOSE	HYDROGENASES	HYDROLYSATIONS
HUSBANDMEN	HYBRIDOMATA	HYDROCELLULOSES	HYDROGENATE	HYDROLYSED
HUSBANDRIES	HYDANTOINS	HYDROCEPHALI	HYDROGENATED	HYDROLYSER
HUSHABYING	HYDATHODES	HYDROCEPHALIC	HYDROGENATES	HYDROLYSERS
HUSHPUPPIES	HYDATIDIFORM	HYDROCEPHALICS	HYDROGENATING	HYDROLYSES
HUSKINESSES	HYDNOCARPATE	HYDROCEPHALIES	HYDROGENATION	HYDROLYSING
HYACINTHINE	HYDNOCARPATES	HYDROCEPHALOID	HYDROGENATIONS	HYDROLYSIS
HYALINISATION	HYDNOCARPIC	HYDROCEPHALOUS	HYDROGENATOR	HYDROLYTES
HYALINISATIONS	HYDRAEMIAS	HYDROCEPHALUS	HYDROGENATORS	HYDROLYTIC
HYALINISED	HYDRAGOGUE	HYDROCEPHALUSES	HYDROGENISATION	HYDROLYTICALLY
HYALINISES	HYDRAGOGUES	HYDROCEPHALY	HYDROGENISE	HYDROLYZABLE
HYALINISING	HYDRALAZINE	HYDROCHLORIC	HYDROGENISED	HYDROLYZATE
HYALINIZATION	HYDRALAZINES	HYDROCHLORIDE	HYDROGENISES	HYDROLYZATES
HYALINIZATIONS	HYDRANGEAS	HYDROCHLORIDES	HYDROGENISING	HYDROLYZATION
HYALINIZED	HYDRARGYRAL	HYDROCHORE	HYDROGENIZATION	HYDROLYZATIONS
HYALINIZES	HYDRARGYRIA	HYDROCHORES	HYDROGENIZE	HYDROLYZED
HYALINIZING	HYDRARGYRIAS	HYDROCHORIC	HYDROGENIZED	HYDROLYZER
HYALOMELAN	HYDRARGYRIC	HYDROCODONE	HYDROGENIZES	HYDROLYZERS
HYALOMELANE	HYDRARGYRISM	HYDROCODONES	HYDROGENIZING	HYDROLYZES
HYALOMELANES	HYDRARGYRISMS	HYDROCOLLOID	HYDROGENOLYSES	HYDROLYZING
HYALOMELANS	HYDRARGYRUM	HYDROCOLLOIDAL	HYDROGENOLYSIS	HYDROMAGNETIC
HYALONEMAS	HYDRARGYRUMS	HYDROCOLLOIDS	HYDROGENOUS	HYDROMAGNETICS
HYALOPHANE	HYDRARTHROSES	HYDROCORAL	HYDROGEOLOGICAL	HYDROMANCER
HYALOPHANES	HYDRARTHROSIS	HYDROCORALLINE	HYDROGEOLOGIES	HYDROMANCERS
HYALOPLASM	HYDRASTINE	HYDROCORALLINES	HYDROGEOLOGIST	HYDROMANCIES
HYALOPLASMIC	HYDRASTINES	HYDROCORALS	HYDROGEOLOGISTS	HYDROMANCY
HYALOPLASMS	HYDRASTININE	HYDROCORTISONE	HYDROGEOLOGY	HYDROMANIA
HYALURONIC	HYDRASTININES	HYDROCORTISONES	HYDROGRAPH	HYDROMANIAS
HYALURONIDASE	HYDRASTISES	HYDROCRACK	HYDROGRAPHER	HYDROMANTIC
HYALURONIDASES	HYDRATIONS	HYDROCRACKED	HYDROGRAPHERS	HYDROMECHANICAL
HYBRIDISABLE	HYDRAULICALLY	HYDROCRACKER	HYDROGRAPHIC	HYDROMECHANICS
HYBRIDISATION	HYDRAULICKED	HYDROCRACKERS	HYDROGRAPHICAL	HYDROMEDUSA
HYBRIDISATIONS	HYDRAULICKING	HYDROCRACKING	HYDROGRAPHIES	HYDROMEDUSAE
HYBRIDISED	HYDRAULICKINGS	HYDROCRACKINGS	HYDROGRAPHS	HYDROMEDUSAN
HYBRIDISER	HYDRAULICS	HYDROCRACKS	HYDROGRAPHY	HYDROMEDUSANS
HYBRIDISERS	HYDRAZIDES	HYDROCYANIC	HYDROKINETIC	HYDROMEDUSAS
HYBRIDISES	HYDRAZINES	HYDRODYNAMIC	HYDROKINETICAL	HYDROMEDUSOID
HYBRIDISING	HYDRICALLY	HYDRODYNAMICAL	HYDROKINETICS	HYDROMEDUSOIDS
HYBRIDISMS	HYDROACOUSTICS	HYDRODYNAMICIST	HYDROLASES	HYDROMETALLURGY

HYDROMETEOR	HYDROPHYTON	HYDROSULPHITE	HYDROXYUREAS	HYGROSTATS
HYDROMETEORS	HYDROPHYTONS	HYDROSULPHITES	HYDROXYZINE	HYLOGENESES
HYDROMETER	HYDROPHYTOUS	HYDROSULPHURIC	HYDROXYZINES	HYLOGENESIS
HYDROMETERS	HYDROPLANE	HYDROSULPHUROUS	HYDROZINCITE	HYLOMORPHIC
HYDROMETRIC	HYDROPLANED	HYDROTACTIC	HYDROZINCITES	HYLOMORPHISM
HYDROMETRICAL	HYDROPLANES	HYDROTAXES	HYDROZOANS	HYLOMORPHISMS
HYDROMETRICALLY	HYDROPLANING	HYDROTAXIS	HYETOGRAPH	HYLOPATHISM
HYDROMETRIES	HYDROPNEUMATIC	HYDROTHECA	HYETOGRAPHIC	HYLOPATHISMS
HYDROMETRY	HYDROPOLYP	HYDROTHECAE	HYETOGRAPHICAL	HYLOPATHIST
HYDROMORPHIC	HYDROPOLYPS	HYDROTHERAPIC	HYETOGRAPHIES	HYLOPATHISTS
HYDRONAUTS	HYDROPONIC	HYDROTHERAPIES	HYETOGRAPHS	HYLOPHAGOUS
HYDRONEPHROSES	HYDROPONICALLY	HYDROTHERAPIST	HYETOGRAPHY	HYLOPHYTES
HYDRONEPHROSIS	HYDROPONICS	HYDROTHERAPISTS	HYETOLOGIES	HYLOTHEISM
HYDRONEPHROTIC	HYDROPOWER	HYDROTHERAPY	HYETOMETER	HYLOTHEISMS
HYDRONICALLY	HYDROPOWERS	HYDROTHERMAL	HYETOMETERS	HYLOTHEIST
HYDRONIUMS	HYDROPSIES	HYDROTHERMALLY	HYETOMETROGRAPH	HYLOTHEISTS
HYDROPATHIC	HYDROPULTS	HYDROTHORACES	HYGIENICALLY	HYLOTOMOUS
HYDROPATHICAL	HYDROQUINOL	HYDROTHORACIC	HYGIENISTS	HYLOZOICAL
HYDROPATHICALLY	HYDROQUINOLS	HYDROTHORAX	HYGRISTORS	HYLOZOISMS
HYDROPATHICS	HYDROQUINONE	HYDROTHORAXES	HYGROCHASIES	HYLOZOISTIC
HYDROPATHIES	HYDROQUINONES	HYDROTROPIC	HYGROCHASTIC	HYLOZOISTICALLY
HYDROPATHIST	HYDROSCOPE	HYDROTROPICALLY	HYGROCHASY	HYLOZOISTS
HYDROPATHISTS	HYDROSCOPES	HYDROTROPISM	HYGRODEIKS	HYMENAEANS
HYDROPATHS	HYDROSCOPIC	HYDROTROPISMS	HYGROGRAPH	HYMENEALLY
HYDROPATHY	HYDROSCOPICAL	HYDROVANES	HYGROGRAPHIC	HYMENOPHORE
HYDROPEROXIDE	HYDROSEEDED	HYDROXIDES	HYGROGRAPHICAL	HYMENOPHORES
HYDROPEROXIDES	HYDROSEEDING	HYDROXIUMS	HYGROGRAPHS	HYMENOPLASTIES
HYDROPHANE	HYDROSEEDINGS	HYDROXONIUM	HYGROLOGIES	HYMENOPLASTY
HYDROPHANES	HYDROSEEDS	HYDROXONIUMS	HYGROMETER	HYMENOPTERA
HYDROPHANOUS	HYDROSERES	HYDROXYACETIC	HYGROMETERS	HYMENOPTERAN
HYDROPHILE	HYDROSOLIC	HYDROXYAPATITE	HYGROMETRIC	HYMENOPTERANS
HYDROPHILES	HYDROSOMAL	HYDROXYAPATITES	HYGROMETRICAL	HYMENOPTERON
HYDROPHILIC	HYDROSOMATA	HYDROXYBUTYRATE	HYGROMETRICALLY	HYMENOPTERONS
HYDROPHILICITY	HYDROSOMATOUS	HYDROXYCITRIC	HYGROMETRIES	HYMENOPTEROUS
HYDROPHILIES	HYDROSOMES	HYDROXYLAMINE	HYGROMETRY	HYMNODICAL
HYDROPHILITE	HYDROSPACE	HYDROXYLAMINES	HYGROPHILE	HYMNODISTS
HYDROPHILITES	HYDROSPACES	HYDROXYLAPATITE	HYGROPHILES	HYMNOGRAPHER
HYDROPHILOUS	HYDROSPHERE	HYDROXYLASE	HYGROPHILOUS	HYMNOGRAPHERS
HYDROPHILY	HYDROSPHERES	HYDROXYLASES	HYGROPHOBE	HYMNOGRAPHIES
HYDROPHOBIA	HYDROSPHERIC	HYDROXYLATE	HYGROPHOBES	HYMNOGRAPHY
HYDROPHOBIAS	HYDROSTATIC	HYDROXYLATED	HYGROPHYTE	HYMNOLOGIC
HYDROPHOBIC	HYDROSTATICAL	HYDROXYLATES	HYGROPHYTES	HYMNOLOGICAL
HYDROPHOBICITY	HYDROSTATICALLY	HYDROXYLATING	HYGROPHYTIC	HYMNOLOGIES
HYDROPHOBOUS	HYDROSTATICS	HYDROXYLATION	HYGROSCOPE	HYMNOLOGIST
HYDROPHONE	HYDROSTATS	HYDROXYLATIONS	HYGROSCOPES	HYMNOLOGISTS
HYDROPHONES	HYDROSULPHATE	HYDROXYLIC	HYGROSCOPIC	HYOPLASTRA
HYDROPHYTE	HYDROSULPHATES	HYDROXYPROLINE	HYGROSCOPICAL	HYOPLASTRAL
HYDROPHYTES	HYDROSULPHIDE	HYDROXYPROLINES	HYGROSCOPICALLY	HYOPLASTRON
HYDROPHYTIC	HYDROSULPHIDES	HYDROXYUREA	HYGROSCOPICITY	HYOSCYAMINE

H

HYOSCYAMINES	HYPERBARIC	HYPERCHARGES	HYPEREXCITED	HYPERINVOLUTION
HYOSCYAMUS	HYPERBARICALLY	HYPERCHARGING	HYPEREXCITEMENT	HYPERIRRITABLE
HYOSCYAMUSES	HYPERBATIC	HYPERCIVILISED	HYPEREXCRETION	HYPERKALAEMIA
HYPABYSSAL	HYPERBATICALLY	HYPERCIVILIZED	HYPEREXCRETIONS	HYPERKALAEMIAS
HYPABYSSALLY	HYPERBATON	HYPERCOAGULABLE	HYPEREXTEND	HYPERKALAEMIC
HYPAESTHESIA	HYPERBATONS	HYPERCOLOR	HYPEREXTENDED	HYPERKALEMIA
HYPAESTHESIAS	HYPERBOLAE	HYPERCOLORS	HYPEREXTENDING	HYPERKALEMIAS
HYPAESTHESIC	HYPERBOLAEON	HYPERCOLOUR	HYPEREXTENDS	HYPERKALEMIC
HYPAETHRAL	HYPERBOLAEONS	HYPERCOLOURS	HYPEREXTENSION	HYPERKERATOSES
HYPAETHRON	HYPERBOLAS	HYPERCOMPLEX	HYPEREXTENSIONS	HYPERKERATOSIS
HYPAETHRONS	HYPERBOLES	HYPERCONSCIOUS	HYPERFASTIDIOUS	HYPERKERATOTIC
HYPALGESIA	HYPERBOLIC	HYPERCORRECT	HYPERFOCAL	HYPERKINESES
HYPALGESIAS	HYPERBOLICAL	HYPERCORRECTION	HYPERFUNCTION	HYPERKINESIA
HYPALGESIC	HYPERBOLICALLY	HYPERCORRECTLY	HYPERFUNCTIONAL	HYPERKINESIAS
HYPALLACTIC	HYPERBOLISE	HYPERCRITIC	HYPERFUNCTIONS	HYPERKINESIS
HYPALLAGES	HYPERBOLISED	HYPERCRITICAL	HYPERGAMIES	HYPERKINETIC
HYPANTHIAL	HYPERBOLISES	HYPERCRITICALLY	HYPERGAMOUS	HYPERLINKED
HYPANTHIUM	HYPERBOLISING	HYPERCRITICISE	HYPERGEOMETRIC	HYPERLINKING
HYPERACIDITIES	HYPERBOLISM	HYPERCRITICISED	HYPERGLYCAEMIA	HYPERLINKS
HYPERACIDITY	HYPERBOLISMS	HYPERCRITICISES	HYPERGLYCAEMIAS	HYPERLIPAEMIA
HYPERACTION	HYPERBOLIST	HYPERCRITICISM	HYPERGLYCAEMIC	HYPERLIPAEMIAS
HYPERACTIONS	HYPERBOLISTS	HYPERCRITICISMS	HYPERGLYCEMIA	HYPERLIPAEMIC
HYPERACTIVE	HYPERBOLIZE	HYPERCRITICIZE	HYPERGLYCEMIAS	HYPERLIPEMIA
HYPERACTIVES	HYPERBOLIZED	HYPERCRITICIZED	HYPERGLYCEMIC	HYPERLIPEMIAS
HYPERACTIVITIES	HYPERBOLIZES	HYPERCRITICIZES	HYPERGOLIC	HYPERLIPEMIC
HYPERACTIVITY	HYPERBOLIZING	HYPERCRITICS	HYPERGOLICALLY	HYPERLIPIDAEMIA
HYPERACUITIES	HYPERBOLOID	HYPERCUBES	HYPERHIDROSES	HYPERLIPIDAEMIC
HYPERACUITY	HYPERBOLOIDAL	HYPERDACTYL	HYPERHIDROSIS	HYPERLIPIDEMIA
HYPERACUSES	HYPERBOLOIDS	HYPERDACTYLIES	HYPERICINS	HYPERLIPIDEMIAS
HYPERACUSIS	HYPERBOREAN	HYPERDACTYLY	HYPERICUMS	HYPERLIPIDEMIC
HYPERACUTE	HYPERBOREANS	HYPERDORIAN	HYPERIDROSES	HYPERLOCAL
HYPERACUTENESS	HYPERCALCAEMIA	HYPERDULIA	HYPERIDROSIS	HYPERLYDIAN
HYPERADRENALISM	HYPERCALCAEMIAS	HYPERDULIAS	HYPERIMMUNE	HYPERMANIA
HYPERAEMIA	HYPERCALCAEMIC	HYPERDULIC	HYPERIMMUNISE	HYPERMANIAS
HYPERAEMIAS	HYPERCALCEMIA	HYPERDULICAL	HYPERIMMUNISED	HYPERMANIC
HYPERAEMIC	HYPERCALCEMIAS	HYPEREFFICIENT	HYPERIMMUNISES	HYPERMARKET
HYPERAESTHESIA	HYPERCALCEMIC	HYPEREMESES	HYPERIMMUNISING	HYPERMARKETS
HYPERAESTHESIAS	HYPERCAPNIA	HYPEREMESIS	HYPERIMMUNIZE	HYPERMARTS
HYPERAESTHESIC	HYPERCAPNIAS	HYPEREMETIC	HYPERIMMUNIZED	HYPERMASCULINE
HYPERAESTHETIC	HYPERCAPNIC	HYPEREMIAS	HYPERIMMUNIZES	HYPERMEDIA
HYPERAGGRESSIVE	HYPERCARBIA	HYPEREMOTIONAL	HYPERIMMUNIZING	HYPERMEDIAS
HYPERALERT	HYPERCARBIAS	HYPERENDEMIC	HYPERINFLATED	HYPERMETABOLIC
HYPERALGESIA	HYPERCATABOLISM	HYPERENERGETIC	HYPERINFLATION	HYPERMETABOLISM
HYPERALGESIAS	HYPERCATALECTIC	HYPERESTHESIA	HYPERINFLATIONS	HYPERMETER
HYPERALGESIC	HYPERCATALEXES	HYPERESTHESIAS	HYPERINOSES	HYPERMETERS
HYPERAROUSAL	HYPERCATALEXIS	HYPERESTHETIC	HYPERINOSIS	HYPERMETRIC
HYPERAROUSALS	HYPERCAUTIOUS	HYPEREUTECTIC	HYPERINOTIC	HYPERMETRICAL
HYPERAWARE	HYPERCHARGE	HYPEREUTECTOID	HYPERINSULINISM	HYPERMETROPIA
HYPERAWARENESS	HYPERCHARGED	HYPEREXCITABLE	HYPERINTENSE	HYPERMETROPIAS

HYPERMETROPIC	HYPERPLANES	HYPERSALINITY	HYPERTHERMAL	HYPHENATION
HYPERMETROPICAL	HYPERPLASIA	HYPERSALIVATION	HYPERTHERMIA	HYPHENATIONS
HYPERMETROPIES	HYPERPLASIAS	HYPERSARCOMA	HYPERTHERMIAS	HYPHENISATION
HYPERMETROPY	HYPERPLASTIC	HYPERSARCOMAS	HYPERTHERMIC	HYPHENISATIONS
HYPERMILING	HYPERPLOID	HYPERSARCOMATA	HYPERTHERMIES	HYPHENISED
HYPERMILINGS	HYPERPLOIDIES	HYPERSARCOSES	HYPERTHERMY	HYPHENISES
HYPERMNESIA	HYPERPLOIDS	HYPERSARCOSIS	HYPERTHYMIA	HYPHENISING
HYPERMNESIAS	HYPERPLOIDY	HYPERSECRETION	HYPERTHYMIAS	HYPHENISMS
HYPERMNESIC	HYPERPNEAS	HYPERSECRETIONS	HYPERTHYROID	HYPHENIZATION
HYPERMOBILITIES	HYPERPNEIC	HYPERSENSITISE	HYPERTHYROIDISM	HYPHENIZATIONS
HYPERMOBILITY	HYPERPNOEA	HYPERSENSITISED	HYPERTHYROIDS	HYPHENIZED
HYPERMODERN	HYPERPNOEAS	HYPERSENSITISES	HYPERTONIA	HYPHENIZES
HYPERMODERNISM	HYPERPOLARISE	HYPERSENSITIVE	HYPERTONIAS	HYPHENIZING
HYPERMODERNISMS	HYPERPOLARISED	HYPERSENSITIZE	HYPERTONIC	HYPHENLESS
HYPERMODERNIST	HYPERPOLARISES	HYPERSENSITIZED	HYPERTONICITIES	HYPNAGOGIC
HYPERMODERNISTS	HYPERPOLARISING	HYPERSENSITIZES	HYPERTONICITY	HYPNOANALYSES
HYPERMUTABILITY	HYPERPOLARIZE	HYPERSENSUAL	HYPERTROPHIC	HYPNOANALYSIS
HYPERMUTABLE	HYPERPOLARIZED	HYPERSEXUAL	HYPERTROPHICAL	HYPNOANALYTIC
HYPERNATRAEMIA	HYPERPOLARIZES	HYPERSEXUALITY	HYPERTROPHIED	HYPNOBIRTHING
HYPERNATRAEMIAS	HYPERPOLARIZING	HYPERSOMNIA	HYPERTROPHIES	HYPNOBIRTHINGS
HYPERNATREMIA	HYPERPOWER	HYPERSOMNIAS	HYPERTROPHOUS	HYPNOGENESES
HYPERNATREMIAS	HYPERPOWERS	HYPERSOMNOLENCE	HYPERTROPHY	HYPNOGENESIS
HYPERNOVAE	HYPERPRODUCER	HYPERSONIC	HYPERTROPHYING	HYPNOGENETIC
HYPERNOVAS	HYPERPRODUCERS	HYPERSONICALLY	HYPERTYPICAL	HYPNOGENIC
HYPERNYMIES	HYPERPRODUCTION	HYPERSONICS	HYPERURBANISM	HYPNOGENIES
HYPEROPIAS	HYPERPROSEXIA	HYPERSPACE	HYPERURBANISMS	HYPNOGENOUS
HYPEROREXIA	HYPERPROSEXIAS	HYPERSPACES	HYPERURICAEMIA	HYPNOGOGIC
HYPEROREXIAS	HYPERPYRETIC	HYPERSPATIAL	HYPERURICAEMIAS	HYPNOIDISE
HYPEROSMIA	HYPERPYREXIA	HYPERSTATIC	HYPERURICEMIA	HYPNOIDISED
HYPEROSMIAS	HYPERPYREXIAL	HYPERSTHENE	HYPERURICEMIAS	HYPNOIDISES
HYPEROSTOSES	HYPERPYREXIAS	HYPERSTHENES	HYPERVELOCITIES	HYPNOIDISING
HYPEROSTOSIS	HYPERRATIONAL	HYPERSTHENIA	HYPERVELOCITY	HYPNOIDIZE
HYPEROSTOSISES	HYPERREACTIVE	HYPERSTHENIAS	HYPERVENTILATE	HYPNOIDIZED
HYPEROSTOTIC	HYPERREACTIVITY	HYPERSTHENIC	HYPERVENTILATED	HYPNOIDIZES
HYPEROXIDE	HYPERREACTOR	HYPERSTHENITE	HYPERVENTILATES	HYPNOIDIZING
HYPEROXIDES	HYPERREACTORS	HYPERSTHENITES	HYPERVIGILANCE	HYPNOLOGIC
HYPERPARASITE	HYPERREALISM	HYPERSTIMULATE	HYPERVIGILANCES	HYPNOLOGICAL
HYPERPARASITES	HYPERREALISMS	HYPERSTIMULATED	HYPERVIGILANT	HYPNOLOGIES
HYPERPARASITIC	HYPERREALIST	HYPERSTIMULATES	HYPERVIRULENT	HYPNOLOGIST
HYPERPARASITISM	HYPERREALISTIC	HYPERSTRESS	HYPERVISCOSITY	HYPNOLOGISTS
HYPERPHAGIA	HYPERREALISTS	HYPERSTRESSES	HYPERVISOR	HYPNOPAEDIA
HYPERPHAGIAS	HYPERREALITIES	HYPERSURFACE	HYPERVISORS	HYPNOPAEDIAS
HYPERPHAGIC	HYPERREALITY	HYPERSURFACES	HYPESTHESIA	HYPNOPHOBIA
HYPERPHRYGIAN	HYPERREALS	HYPERTENSE	HYPESTHESIAS	HYPNOPHOBIAS
HYPERPHYSICAL	HYPERRESPONSIVE	HYPERTENSION	HYPESTHESIC	HYPNOPOMPIC
HYPERPHYSICALLY	HYPERROMANTIC	HYPERTENSIONS	HYPHAEMIAS	HYPNOTHERAPIES
HYPERPIGMENTED	HYPERROMANTICS	HYPERTENSIVE	HYPHENATED	HYPNOTHERAPIST
HYPERPITUITARY	HYPERSALINE	HYPERTENSIVES	HYPHENATES	HYPNOTHERAPISTS
HYPERPLANE	HYPERSALINITIES	HYPERTEXTS	HYPHENATING	HYPNOTHERAPY

HYPNOTICALLY	HYPOCHONDRIASIS	HYPOGLYCEMICS	HYPOPHYGES	HYPOSTATIZATION
HYPNOTISABILITY	HYPOCHONDRIASM	HYPOGNATHISM	HYPOPHYSEAL	HYPOSTATIZE
HYPNOTISABLE	HYPOCHONDRIASMS	HYPOGNATHISMS	HYPOPHYSECTOMY	HYPOSTATIZED
HYPNOTISATION	HYPOCHONDRIAST	HYPOGNATHOUS	HYPOPHYSES	HYPOSTATIZES
HYPNOTISATIONS	HYPOCHONDRIASTS	HYPOGYNIES	HYPOPHYSIAL	HYPOSTATIZING
HYPNOTISED	HYPOCHONDRIUM	HYPOGYNOUS	HYPOPHYSIS	HYPOSTHENIA
HYPNOTISER	HYPOCORISM	HYPOKALAEMIA	HYPOPITUITARISM	HYPOSTHENIAS
HYPNOTISERS	HYPOCORISMA	HYPOKALAEMIAS	HYPOPITUITARY	HYPOSTHENIC
HYPNOTISES	HYPOCORISMAS	HYPOKALAEMIC	HYPOPLASIA	HYPOSTOMES
HYPNOTISING	HYPOCORISMS	HYPOKALEMIA	HYPOPLASIAS	HYPOSTRESS
HYPNOTISMS	HYPOCORISTIC	HYPOKALEMIAS	HYPOPLASTIC	HYPOSTRESSES
HYPNOTISTIC	HYPOCORISTICAL	HYPOKALEMIC	HYPOPLASTIES	HYPOSTROPHE
HYPNOTISTS	HYPOCOTYLOUS	HYPOLIMNIA	HYPOPLASTRA	HYPOSTROPHES
HYPNOTIZABILITY	HYPOCOTYLS	HYPOLIMNION	HYPOPLASTRON	HYPOSTYLES
HYPNOTIZABLE	HYPOCRISIES	HYPOLIMNIONS	HYPOPLASTY	HYPOSULPHATE
HYPNOTIZATION	HYPOCRITES	HYPOLYDIAN	HYPOPLOIDIES	HYPOSULPHATES
HYPNOTIZATIONS	HYPOCRITIC	HYPOMAGNESAEMIA	HYPOPLOIDS	HYPOSULPHITE
HYPNOTIZED	HYPOCRITICAL	HYPOMAGNESEMIA	HYPOPLOIDY	HYPOSULPHITES
HYPNOTIZER	HYPOCRITICALLY	HYPOMAGNESEMIAS	HYPOPNOEAS	HYPOSULPHURIC
HYPNOTIZERS	HYPOCRYSTALLINE	HYPOMANIAS	HYPOSENSITISE	HYPOSULPHUROUS
HYPNOTIZES	HYPOCYCLOID	HYPOMANICS	HYPOSENSITISED	HYPOTACTIC
HYPNOTIZING	HYPOCYCLOIDAL	HYPOMENORRHEA	HYPOSENSITISES	HYPOTENSION
HYPOACIDITIES	HYPOCYCLOIDS	HYPOMENORRHEAS	HYPOSENSITISING	HYPOTENSIONS
HYPOACIDITY	HYPODERMAL	HYPOMENORRHOEA	HYPOSENSITIZE	HYPOTENSIVE
HYPOAEOLIAN	HYPODERMAS	HYPOMENORRHOEAS	HYPOSENSITIZED	HYPOTENSIVES
HYPOALLERGENIC	HYPODERMIC	HYPOMIXOLYDIAN	HYPOSENSITIZES	HYPOTENUSE
HYPOBLASTIC	HYPODERMICALLY	HYPOMORPHIC	HYPOSENSITIZING	HYPOTENUSES
HYPOBLASTS	HYPODERMICS	HYPOMORPHS	HYPOSPADIAS	HYPOTHALAMI
HYPOCALCAEMIA	HYPODERMIS	HYPONASTIC	HYPOSPADIASES	HYPOTHALAMIC
HYPOCALCAEMIAS	HYPODERMISES	HYPONASTICALLY	HYPOSTASES	HYPOTHALAMUS
HYPOCALCAEMIC	HYPODIPLOID	HYPONASTIES	HYPOSTASIS	HYPOTHECAE
HYPOCALCEMIA	HYPODIPLOIDIES	HYPONATRAEMIA	HYPOSTASISATION	HYPOTHECARY
HYPOCALCEMIAS	HYPODIPLOIDY	HYPONATRAEMIAS	HYPOSTASISE	HYPOTHECATE
HYPOCALCEMIC	HYPODORIAN	HYPONATREMIA	HYPOSTASISED	HYPOTHECATED
HYPOCAUSTS	HYPOEUTECTIC	HYPONATREMIAS	HYPOSTASISES	HYPOTHECATES
HYPOCENTER	HYPOEUTECTOID	HYPONITRITE	HYPOSTASISING	HYPOTHECATING
HYPOCENTERS	HYPOGAEOUS	HYPONITRITES	HYPOSTASIZATION	HYPOTHECATION
HYPOCENTRAL	HYPOGASTRIA	HYPONITROUS	HYPOSTASIZE	HYPOTHECATIONS
HYPOCENTRE	HYPOGASTRIC	HYPONYMIES	HYPOSTASIZED	HYPOTHECATOR
HYPOCENTRES	HYPOGASTRIUM	HYPOPHARYNGES	HYPOSTASIZES	HYPOTHECATORS
HYPOCHLORITE	HYPOGENOUS	HYPOPHARYNX	HYPOSTASIZING	HYPOTHENUSE
HYPOCHLORITES	HYPOGLOSSAL	HYPOPHARYNXES	HYPOSTATIC	HYPOTHENUSES
HYPOCHLOROUS	HYPOGLOSSALS	HYPOPHOSPHATE	HYPOSTATICAL	HYPOTHERMAL
HYPOCHONDRIA	HYPOGLYCAEMIA	HYPOPHOSPHATES	HYPOSTATICALLY	HYPOTHERMIA
HYPOCHONDRIAC	HYPOGLYCAEMIAS	HYPOPHOSPHITE	HYPOSTATISATION	HYPOTHERMIAS
HYPOCHONDRIACAL	HYPOGLYCAEMIC	HYPOPHOSPHITES	HYPOSTATISE	HYPOTHERMIC
HYPOCHONDRIACS	HYPOGLYCEMIA	HYPOPHOSPHORIC	HYPOSTATISED	HYPOTHESES
HYPOCHONDRIAS	HYPOGLYCEMIAS	HYPOPHOSPHOROUS	HYPOSTATISES	HYPOTHESIS
HYPOCHONDRIASES	HYPOGLYCEMIC	HYPOPHRYGIAN	HYPOSTATISING	HYPOTHESISE

HYPOTHESISED	HYPOTHETIZE	HYPOXAEMIC	HYPSOPHOBE	HYSTERESIS
HYPOTHESISER	HYPOTHETIZED	HYPOXANTHINE	HYPSOPHOBES	HYSTERETIC
HYPOTHESISERS	HYPOTHETIZES	HYPOXANTHINES	HYPSOPHOBIA	HYSTERETICALLY
HYPOTHESISES	HYPOTHETIZING	HYPOXEMIAS	HYPSOPHOBIAS	HYSTERICAL
HYPOTHESISING	HYPOTHYMIA	HYPSOCHROME	HYPSOPHYLL	HYSTERICALLY
HYPOTHESIST	HYPOTHYMIAS	HYPSOCHROMES	HYPSOPHYLLARY	HYSTERICKY
HYPOTHESISTS	HYPOTHYROID	HYPSOCHROMIC	HYPSOPHYLLS	HYSTERITIS
HYPOTHESIZE	HYPOTHYROIDISM	HYPSOGRAPHIC	HYRACOIDEAN	HYSTERITISES
HYPOTHESIZED	HYPOTHYROIDISMS	HYPSOGRAPHICAL	HYRACOIDEANS	HYSTEROGENIC
HYPOTHESIZER	HYPOTHYROIDS	HYPSOGRAPHIES	HYSTERANTHOUS	HYSTEROGENIES
HYPOTHESIZERS	HYPOTONIAS	HYPSOGRAPHY	HYSTERECTOMIES	HYSTEROGENY
HYPOTHESIZES	HYPOTONICITIES	HYPSOMETER	HYSTERECTOMISE	HYSTEROIDAL
HYPOTHESIZING	HYPOTONICITY	HYPSOMETERS	HYSTERECTOMISED	HYSTEROMANIA
HYPOTHETIC	HYPOTROCHOID	HYPSOMETRIC	HYSTERECTOMISES	HYSTEROMANIAS
HYPOTHETICAL	HYPOTROCHOIDS	HYPSOMETRICAL	HYSTERECTOMIZE	HYSTEROTOMIES
HYPOTHETICALLY	HYPOTYPOSES	HYPSOMETRICALLY	HYSTERECTOMIZED	HYSTEROTOMY
HYPOTHETISE	HYPOTYPOSIS	HYPSOMETRIES	HYSTERECTOMIZES	HYSTRICOMORPH
HYPOTHETISED	HYPOVENTILATION	HYPSOMETRIST	HYSTERECTOMY	HYSTRICOMORPHIC
HYPOTHETISES	HYPOXAEMIA	HYPSOMETRISTS	HYSTERESES	HYSTRICOMORPHS
HYPOTHETISING	HYPOXAEMIAS	HYPSOMETRY	HYSTERESIAL	

H

IAMBICALLY	ICHTHYOLITE	ICONOGRAPHIES	IDEALISTIC	IDEOLOGIES
IAMBOGRAPHER	ICHTHYOLITES	ICONOGRAPHY	IDEALISTICALLY	IDEOLOGISE
IAMBOGRAPHERS	ICHTHYOLITIC	ICONOLATER	IDEALITIES	IDEOLOGISED
IATROCHEMICAL	ICHTHYOLOGIC	ICONOLATERS	IDEALIZATION	IDEOLOGISES
IATROCHEMIST	ICHTHYOLOGICAL	ICONOLATRIES	IDEALIZATIONS	IDEOLOGISING
IATROCHEMISTRY	ICHTHYOLOGIES	ICONOLATROUS	IDEALIZERS	IDEOLOGIST
IATROCHEMISTS	ICHTHYOLOGIST	ICONOLATRY	IDEALIZING	IDEOLOGISTS
IATROGENIC	ICHTHYOLOGISTS	ICONOLOGICAL	IDEALNESSES	IDEOLOGIZE
IATROGENICALLY	ICHTHYOLOGY	ICONOLOGIES	IDEALOGIES	IDEOLOGIZED
IATROGENICITIES	ICHTHYOPHAGIES	ICONOLOGIST	IDEALOGUES	IDEOLOGIZES
IATROGENICITY	ICHTHYOPHAGIST	ICONOLOGISTS	IDEATIONAL	IDEOLOGIZING
IATROGENIES	ICHTHYOPHAGISTS	ICONOMACHIES	IDEATIONALLY	IDEOLOGUES
IBUPROFENS	ICHTHYOPHAGOUS	ICONOMACHIST	IDEMPOTENCIES	IDEOPHONES
ICEBOATERS	ICHTHYOPHAGY	ICONOMACHISTS	IDEMPOTENCY	IDEOPOLISES
ICEBOATING	ICHTHYOPSID	ICONOMACHY	IDEMPOTENT	IDEOPRAXIST
ICEBOATINGS	ICHTHYOPSIDAN	ICONOMATIC	IDEMPOTENTS	IDEOPRAXISTS
ICEBREAKER	ICHTHYOPSIDANS	ICONOMATICISM	IDENTICALLY	IDIOBLASTIC
ICEBREAKERS	ICHTHYOPSIDS	ICONOMATICISMS	IDENTICALNESS	IDIOBLASTS
ICEBREAKING	ICHTHYORNIS	ICONOMETER	IDENTICALNESSES	IDIOCRACIES
ICEFISHING	ICHTHYORNISES	ICONOMETERS	IDENTIFIABLE	IDIOCRATIC
ICHNEUMONS	ICHTHYOSAUR	ICONOMETRIES	IDENTIFIABLY	IDIOGLOSSIA
ICHNOFOSSIL	ICHTHYOSAURI	ICONOMETRY	IDENTIFICATION	IDIOGLOSSIAS
ICHNOFOSSILS	ICHTHYOSAURIAN	ICONOPHILISM	IDENTIFICATIONS	IDIOGRAPHIC
ICHNOGRAPHIC	ICHTHYOSAURIANS	ICONOPHILISMS	IDENTIFIED	IDIOGRAPHS
ICHNOGRAPHICAL	ICHTHYOSAURS	ICONOPHILIST	IDENTIFIER	IDIOLECTAL
ICHNOGRAPHIES	ICHTHYOSAURUS	ICONOPHILISTS	IDENTIFIERS	IDIOLECTIC
ICHNOGRAPHY	ICHTHYOSAURUSES	ICONOSCOPE	IDENTIFIES	IDIOMATICAL
ICHNOLITES	ICHTHYOSES	ICONOSCOPES	IDENTIFYING	IDIOMATICALLY
ICHNOLOGICAL	ICHTHYOSIS	ICONOSTASES	IDENTIKITS	IDIOMATICALNESS
ICHNOLOGIES	ICHTHYOTIC	ICONOSTASIS	IDENTITARIAN	IDIOMATICNESS
ICHTHYOCOLLA	ICKINESSES	ICOSAHEDRA	IDENTITARIANS	IDIOMATICNESSES
ICHTHYOCOLLAS	ICONICALLY	ICOSAHEDRAL	IDENTITIES	IDIOMORPHIC
ICHTHYODORULITE	ICONICITIES	ICOSAHEDRON	IDEOGRAMIC	IDIOMORPHICALLY
ICHTHYODORYLITE	ICONIFYING	ICOSAHEDRONS	IDEOGRAMMATIC	IDIOMORPHISM
ICHTHYOFAUNA	ICONOCLASM	ICOSANDRIAN	IDEOGRAMMIC	IDIOMORPHISMS
ICHTHYOFAUNAE	ICONOCLASMS	ICOSANDROUS	IDEOGRAPHIC	IDIOPATHIC
ICHTHYOFAUNAL	ICONOCLAST	ICOSITETRAHEDRA	IDEOGRAPHICAL	IDIOPATHICALLY
ICHTHYOFAUNAS	ICONOCLASTIC	ICTERICALS	IDEOGRAPHICALLY	IDIOPATHIES
ICHTHYOIDAL	ICONOCLASTS	ICTERITIOUS	IDEOGRAPHIES	IDIOPHONES
ICHTHYOIDS	ICONOGRAPHER	IDEALISATION	IDEOGRAPHS	IDIOPHONIC
ICHTHYOLATRIES	ICONOGRAPHERS	IDEALISATIONS	IDEOGRAPHY	IDIOPLASMATIC
ICHTHYOLATROUS	ICONOGRAPHIC	IDEALISERS	IDEOLOGICAL	IDIOPLASMIC
ICHTHYOLATRY	ICONOGRAPHICAL	IDEALISING	IDEOLOGICALLY	IDIOPLASMS

IDIORHYTHMIC	IGNOBILITIES	ILLEGITIMATED	ILLUMINANCES	ILLUSTRATORY
IDIORRHYTHMIC	IGNOBILITY	ILLEGITIMATELY	ILLUMINANT	ILLUSTRIOUS
IDIOSYNCRASIES	IGNOBLENESS	ILLEGITIMATES	ILLUMINANTS	ILLUSTRIOUSLY
IDIOSYNCRASY	IGNOBLENESSES	ILLEGITIMATING	ILLUMINATE	ILLUSTRIOUSNESS
IDIOSYNCRATIC	IGNOMINIES	ILLEGITIMATION	ILLUMINATED	ILLUSTRISSIMO
IDIOSYNCRATICAL	IGNOMINIOUS	ILLEGITIMATIONS	ILLUMINATES	ILLUVIATED
IDIOTHERMOUS	IGNOMINIOUSLY	ILLIBERALISE	ILLUMINATI	ILLUVIATES
IDIOTICALLY	IGNOMINIOUSNESS	ILLIBERALISED	ILLUMINATING	ILLUVIATING
IDIOTICALNESS	IGNORAMUSES	ILLIBERALISES	ILLUMINATINGLY	ILLUVIATION
IDIOTICALNESSES	IGNORANCES	ILLIBERALISING	ILLUMINATION	ILLUVIATIONS
IDIOTICONS	IGNORANTLY	ILLIBERALISM	ILLUMINATIONAL	IMAGEBOARD
IDLENESSES	IGNORANTNESS	ILLIBERALISMS	ILLUMINATIONS	IMAGEBOARDS
IDOLATRESS	IGNORANTNESSES	ILLIBERALITIES	ILLUMINATIVE	IMAGINABLE
IDOLATRESSES	IGNORATION	ILLIBERALITY	ILLUMINATO	IMAGINABLENESS
IDOLATRIES	IGNORATIONS	ILLIBERALIZE	ILLUMINATOR	IMAGINABLY
IDOLATRISE	IGUANODONS	ILLIBERALIZED	ILLUMINATORS	IMAGINARIES
IDOLATRISED	ILEOSTOMIES	ILLIBERALIZES	ILLUMINERS	IMAGINARILY
IDOLATRISER	ILLAQUEABLE	ILLIBERALIZING	ILLUMINING	IMAGINARINESS
IDOLATRISERS	ILLAQUEATE	ILLIBERALLY	ILLUMINISM	IMAGINARINESSES
IDOLATRISES	ILLAQUEATED	ILLIBERALNESS	ILLUMINISMS	IMAGINATION
IDOLATRISING	ILLAQUEATES	ILLIBERALNESSES	ILLUMINIST	IMAGINATIONAL
IDOLATRIZE	ILLAQUEATING	ILLICITNESS	ILLUMINISTS	IMAGINATIONS
IDOLATRIZED	ILLAQUEATION	ILLICITNESSES	ILLUSIONAL	IMAGINATIVE
IDOLATRIZER	ILLAQUEATIONS	ILLIMITABILITY	ILLUSIONARY	IMAGINATIVELY
IDOLATRIZERS	ILLATIVELY	ILLIMITABLE	ILLUSIONED	IMAGINATIVENESS
IDOLATRIZES	ILLAUDABLE	ILLIMITABLENESS	ILLUSIONISM	IMAGINEERED
IDOLATRIZING	ILLAUDABLY	ILLIMITABLY	ILLUSIONISMS	IMAGINEERING
IDOLATROUS	ILLAWARRAS	ILLIMITATION	ILLUSIONIST	IMAGINEERS
IDOLATROUSLY	ILLEGALISATION	ILLIMITATIONS	ILLUSIONISTIC	IMAGININGS
IDOLATROUSNESS	ILLEGALISATIONS	ILLIQUATION	ILLUSIONISTS	IMAGINISTS
IDOLISATION	ILLEGALISE	ILLIQUATIONS	ILLUSIVELY	IMAGISTICALLY
IDOLISATIONS	ILLEGALISED	ILLIQUIDITIES	ILLUSIVENESS	IMBALANCED
IDOLIZATION	ILLEGALISES	ILLIQUIDITY	ILLUSIVENESSES	IMBALANCES
IDOLIZATIONS	ILLEGALISING	ILLITERACIES	ILLUSORILY	IMBECILELY
IDOLOCLAST	ILLEGALITIES	ILLITERACY	ILLUSORINESS	IMBECILICALLY
IDOLOCLASTS	ILLEGALITY	ILLITERATE	ILLUSORINESSES	IMBECILITIES
IDONEITIES	ILLEGALIZATION	ILLITERATELY	ILLUSTRATABLE	IMBECILITY
IDOXURIDINE	ILLEGALIZATIONS	ILLITERATENESS	ILLUSTRATE	IMBIBITION
IDOXURIDINES	ILLEGALIZE	ILLITERATES	ILLUSTRATED	IMBIBITIONAL
IDYLLICALLY	ILLEGALIZED	ILLOCUTION	ILLUSTRATEDS	IMBIBITIONS
IFFINESSES	ILLEGALIZES	ILLOCUTIONARY	ILLUSTRATES	IMBITTERED
IGNESCENTS	ILLEGALIZING	ILLOCUTIONS	ILLUSTRATING	IMBITTERING
IGNIMBRITE	ILLEGIBILITIES	ILLOGICALITIES	ILLUSTRATION	IMBOLDENED
IGNIMBRITES	ILLEGIBILITY	ILLOGICALITY	ILLUSTRATIONAL	IMBOLDENING
IGNIPOTENT	ILLEGIBLENESS	ILLOGICALLY	ILLUSTRATIONS	IMBORDERED
IGNITABILITIES	ILLEGIBLENESSES	ILLOGICALNESS	ILLUSTRATIVE	IMBORDERING
IGNITABILITY	ILLEGITIMACIES	ILLOGICALNESSES	ILLUSTRATIVELY	IMBOSOMING
IGNITIBILITIES	ILLEGITIMACY	ILLUMINABLE	ILLUSTRATOR	IMBOWERING
IGNITIBILITY	ILLEGITIMATE	ILLUMINANCE	ILLUSTRATORS	IMBRANGLED

IMBRANGLES	IMMANENTISTS	IMMERGENCE	IMMISSIONS	IMMORTALISATION
IMBRANGLING	IMMANENTLY	IMMERGENCES	IMMITIGABILITY	IMMORTALISE
IMBRICATED	IMMANITIES	IMMERITOUS	IMMITIGABLE	IMMORTALISED
IMBRICATELY	IMMANTLING	IMMERSIBLE	IMMITIGABLY	IMMORTALISER
IMBRICATES	IMMARCESCIBLE	IMMERSIONISM	IMMITTANCE	IMMORTALISERS
IMBRICATING	IMMARGINATE	IMMERSIONISMS	IMMITTANCES	IMMORTALISES
IMBRICATION	IMMATERIAL	IMMERSIONIST	IMMIXTURES	IMMORTALISING
IMBRICATIONS	IMMATERIALISE	IMMERSIONISTS	IMMOBILISATION	IMMORTALITIES
IMBROCCATA	IMMATERIALISED	IMMERSIONS	IMMOBILISATIONS	IMMORTALITY
IMBROCCATAS	IMMATERIALISES	IMMETHODICAL	IMMOBILISE	IMMORTALIZATION
IMBROGLIOS	IMMATERIALISING	IMMETHODICALLY	IMMOBILISED	IMMORTALIZE
IMBROWNING	IMMATERIALISM	IMMIGRANCIES	IMMOBILISER	IMMORTALIZED
IMBRUEMENT	IMMATERIALISMS	IMMIGRANCY	IMMOBILISERS	IMMORTALIZER
IMBRUEMENTS	IMMATERIALIST	IMMIGRANTS	IMMOBILISES	IMMORTALIZERS
IMBUEMENTS	IMMATERIALISTS	IMMIGRATED	IMMOBILISING	IMMORTALIZES
IMIDACLOPRID	IMMATERIALITIES	IMMIGRATES	IMMOBILISM	IMMORTALIZING
IMIDACLOPRIDS	IMMATERIALITY	IMMIGRATING	IMMOBILISMS	IMMORTALLY
IMIDAZOLES	IMMATERIALIZE	IMMIGRATION	IMMOBILITIES	IMMORTELLE
IMINAZOLES	IMMATERIALIZED	IMMIGRATIONAL	IMMOBILITY	IMMORTELLES
IMINOUREAS	IMMATERIALIZES	IMMIGRATIONS	IMMOBILIZATION	IMMOTILITIES
IMIPRAMINE	IMMATERIALIZING	IMMIGRATOR	IMMOBILIZATIONS	IMMOTILITY
IMIPRAMINES	IMMATERIALLY	IMMIGRATORS	IMMOBILIZE	IMMOVABILITIES
IMITABILITIES	IMMATERIALNESS	IMMIGRATORY	IMMOBILIZED	IMMOVABILITY
IMITABILITY	IMMATURELY	IMMINENCES	IMMOBILIZER	IMMOVABLENESS
IMITABLENESS	IMMATURENESS	IMMINENCIES	IMMOBILIZERS	IMMOVABLENESSES
IMITABLENESSES	IMMATURENESSES	IMMINENTLY	IMMOBILIZES	IMMOVABLES
IMITANCIES	IMMATUREST	IMMINENTNESS	IMMOBILIZING	IMMOVEABILITIES
IMITATIONAL	IMMATURITIES	IMMINENTNESSES	IMMODERACIES	IMMOVEABILITY
IMITATIONS	IMMATURITY	IMMINGLING	IMMODERACY	IMMOVEABLE
IMITATIVELY	IMMEASURABILITY	IMMINUTION	IMMODERATE	IMMOVEABLENESS
IMITATIVENESS	IMMEASURABLE	IMMINUTIONS	IMMODERATELY	IMMOVEABLES
IMITATIVENESSES	IMMEASURABLY	IMMISCIBILITIES	IMMODERATENESS	IMMOVEABLY
IMMACULACIES	IMMEASURED	IMMISCIBILITY	IMMODERATION	IMMUNIFACIENT
IMMACULACY	IMMEDIACIES	IMMISCIBLE	IMMODERATIONS	IMMUNISATION
IMMACULATE	IMMEDIATELY	IMMISCIBLY	IMMODESTER	IMMUNISATIONS
IMMACULATELY	IMMEDIATENESS	IMMISERATION	IMMODESTEST	IMMUNISERS
IMMACULATENESS	IMMEDIATENESSES	IMMISERATIONS	IMMODESTIES	IMMUNISING
IMMANACLED	IMMEDIATISM	IMMISERISATION	IMMODESTLY	IMMUNITIES
IMMANACLES	IMMEDIATISMS	IMMISERISATIONS	IMMOLATING	IMMUNIZATION
IMMANACLING	IMMEDICABLE	IMMISERISE	IMMOLATION	IMMUNIZATIONS
IMMANATION	IMMEDICABLENESS	IMMISERISED	IMMOLATIONS	IMMUNIZERS
IMMANATIONS	IMMEDICABLY	IMMISERISES	IMMOLATORS	IMMUNIZING
IMMANENCES	IMMEMORIAL	IMMISERISING	IMMOMENTOUS	IMMUNOASSAY
IMMANENCIES	IMMEMORIALLY	IMMISERIZATION	IMMORALISM	IMMUNOASSAYABLE
IMMANENTAL	IMMENSENESS	IMMISERIZATIONS	IMMORALISMS	IMMUNOASSAYIST
IMMANENTISM	IMMENSENESSES	IMMISERIZE	IMMORALIST	IMMUNOASSAYISTS
IMMANENTISMS	IMMENSITIES	IMMISERIZED	IMMORALISTS	IMMUNOASSAYS
IMMANENTIST	IMMENSURABILITY	IMMISERIZES	IMMORALITIES	IMMUNOBLOT
IMMANENTISTIC	IMMENSURABLE	IMMISERIZING	IMMORALITY	IMMUNOBLOTS

IMMUNOBLOTTING	IMMUTABILITIES	IMPARTIBILITY	IMPEDANCES	IMPERCIPIENCE
IMMUNOBLOTTINGS	IMMUTABILITY	IMPARTIBLE	IMPEDIMENT	IMPERCIPIENCES
IMMUNOCHEMICAL	IMMUTABLENESS	IMPARTIBLY	IMPEDIMENTA	IMPERCIPIENT
IMMUNOCHEMIST	IMMUTABLENESSES	IMPARTMENT	IMPEDIMENTAL	IMPERCIPIENTLY
IMMUNOCHEMISTRY	IMPACTIONS	IMPARTMENTS	IMPEDIMENTARY	IMPERFECTER
IMMUNOCHEMISTS	IMPACTITES	IMPASSABILITIES	IMPEDIMENTS	IMPERFECTEST
IMMUNOCOMPETENT	IMPAINTING	IMPASSABILITY	IMPEDINGLY	IMPERFECTIBLE
IMMUNOCOMPLEX	IMPAIRABLE	IMPASSABLE	IMPEDITIVE	IMPERFECTION
IMMUNOCOMPLEXES	IMPAIRINGS	IMPASSABLENESS	IMPELLENTS	IMPERFECTIONS
IMMUNODEFICIENT	IMPAIRMENT	IMPASSABLY	IMPENDENCE	IMPERFECTIVE
IMMUNODIAGNOSES	IMPAIRMENTS	IMPASSIBILITIES	IMPENDENCES	IMPERFECTIVELY
IMMUNODIAGNOSIS	IMPALEMENT	IMPASSIBILITY	IMPENDENCIES	IMPERFECTIVES
IMMUNODIFFUSION	IMPALEMENTS	IMPASSIBLE	IMPENDENCY	IMPERFECTLY
IMMUNOGENESES	IMPALPABILITIES	IMPASSIBLENESS	IMPENETRABILITY	IMPERFECTNESS
IMMUNOGENESIS	IMPALPABILITY	IMPASSIBLY	IMPENETRABLE	IMPERFECTNESSES
IMMUNOGENETIC	IMPALPABLE	IMPASSIONATE	IMPENETRABLY	IMPERFECTS
IMMUNOGENETICAL	IMPALPABLY	IMPASSIONED	IMPENETRATE	IMPERFORABLE
IMMUNOGENETICS	IMPALUDISM	IMPASSIONEDLY	IMPENETRATED	IMPERFORATE
IMMUNOGENIC	IMPALUDISMS	IMPASSIONEDNESS	IMPENETRATES	IMPERFORATED
IMMUNOGENICALLY	IMPANATION	IMPASSIONING	IMPENETRATING	IMPERFORATION
IMMUNOGENICITY	IMPANATIONS	IMPASSIONS	IMPENETRATION	IMPERFORATIONS
IMMUNOGENS	IMPANELING	IMPASSIVELY	IMPENETRATIONS	IMPERIALISE
IMMUNOGLOBULIN	IMPANELLED	IMPASSIVENESS	IMPENITENCE	IMPERIALISED
IMMUNOGLOBULINS	IMPANELLING	IMPASSIVENESSES	IMPENITENCES	IMPERIALISES
IMMUNOLOGIC	IMPANELMENT	IMPASSIVITIES	IMPENITENCIES	IMPERIALISING
IMMUNOLOGICAL	IMPANELMENTS	IMPASSIVITY	IMPENITENCY	IMPERIALISM
IMMUNOLOGICALLY	IMPANNELLED	IMPASTATION	IMPENITENT	IMPERIALISMS
IMMUNOLOGIES	IMPANNELLING	IMPASTATIONS	IMPENITENTLY	IMPERIALIST
IMMUNOLOGIST	IMPARADISE	IMPATIENCE	IMPENITENTNESS	IMPERIALISTIC
IMMUNOLOGISTS	IMPARADISED	IMPATIENCES	IMPENITENTS	IMPERIALISTS
IMMUNOLOGY	IMPARADISES	IMPATIENTLY	IMPERATIVAL	IMPERIALITIES
IMMUNOMODULATOR	IMPARADISING	IMPEACHABILITY	IMPERATIVE	IMPERIALITY
IMMUNOPATHOLOGY	IMPARIDIGITATE	IMPEACHABLE	IMPERATIVELY	IMPERIALIZE
IMMUNOPHORESES	IMPARIPINNATE	IMPEACHERS	IMPERATIVENESS	IMPERIALIZED
IMMUNOPHORESIS	IMPARISYLLABIC	IMPEACHING	IMPERATIVES	IMPERIALIZES
IMMUNOREACTION	IMPARITIES	IMPEACHMENT	IMPERATORIAL	IMPERIALIZING
IMMUNOREACTIONS	IMPARKATION	IMPEACHMENTS	IMPERATORIALLY	IMPERIALLY
IMMUNOREACTIVE	IMPARKATIONS	IMPEARLING	IMPERATORS	IMPERIALNESS
IMMUNOSORBENT	IMPARLANCE	IMPECCABILITIES	IMPERATORSHIP	IMPERIALNESSES
IMMUNOSORBENTS	IMPARLANCES	IMPECCABILITY	IMPERATORSHIPS	IMPERILING
IMMUNOSTIMULANT	IMPARTABLE	IMPECCABLE	IMPERCEABLE	IMPERILLED
IMMUNOSUPPRESS	IMPARTATION	IMPECCABLY	IMPERCEIVABLE	IMPERILLING
IMMUNOTHERAPIES	IMPARTATIONS	IMPECCANCIES	IMPERCEPTIBLE	IMPERILMENT
IMMUNOTHERAPY	IMPARTIALITIES	IMPECCANCY	IMPERCEPTIBLY	IMPERILMENTS
IMMUNOTOXIC	IMPARTIALITY	IMPECUNIOSITIES	IMPERCEPTION	IMPERIOUSLY
IMMUNOTOXIN	IMPARTIALLY	IMPECUNIOSITY	IMPERCEPTIONS	IMPERIOUSNESS
IMMUNOTOXINS	IMPARTIALNESS	IMPECUNIOUS	IMPERCEPTIVE	IMPERIOUSNESSES
IMMUREMENT	IMPARTIALNESSES	IMPECUNIOUSLY	IMPERCEPTIVELY	IMPERISHABILITY
IMMUREMENTS	IMPARTIBILITIES	IMPECUNIOUSNESS	IMPERCEPTIVITY	IMPERISHABLE

IMPERISHABLES	IMPERVIABLENESS	IMPLAUSIBLE	IMPOCKETED	IMPOSITIONS
IMPERISHABLY	IMPERVIOUS	IMPLAUSIBLENESS	IMPOCKETING	IMPOSSIBILISM
IMPERMANENCE	IMPERVIOUSLY	IMPLAUSIBLY	IMPOLDERED	IMPOSSIBILISMS
IMPERMANENCES	IMPERVIOUSNESS	IMPLEACHED	IMPOLDERING	IMPOSSIBILIST
IMPERMANENCIES	IMPETICOSSED	IMPLEACHES	IMPOLICIES	IMPOSSIBILISTS
IMPERMANENCY	IMPETICOSSES	IMPLEACHING	IMPOLITELY	IMPOSSIBILITIES
IMPERMANENT	IMPETICOSSING	IMPLEADABLE	IMPOLITENESS	IMPOSSIBILITY
IMPERMANENTLY	IMPETIGINES	IMPLEADERS	IMPOLITENESSES	IMPOSSIBLE
IMPERMEABILITY	IMPETIGINOUS	IMPLEADING	IMPOLITEST	IMPOSSIBLENESS
IMPERMEABLE	IMPETRATED	IMPLEDGING	IMPOLITICAL	IMPOSSIBLES
IMPERMEABLENESS	IMPETRATES	IMPLEMENTAL	IMPOLITICALLY	IMPOSSIBLY
IMPERMEABLY	IMPETRATING	IMPLEMENTATION	IMPOLITICLY	IMPOSTHUMATE
IMPERMISSIBLE	IMPETRATION	IMPLEMENTATIONS	IMPOLITICNESS	IMPOSTHUMATED
IMPERMISSIBLY	IMPETRATIONS	IMPLEMENTED	IMPOLITICNESSES	IMPOSTHUMATES
IMPERSCRIPTIBLE	IMPETRATIVE	IMPLEMENTER	IMPONDERABILIA	IMPOSTHUMATING
IMPERSEVERANT	IMPETRATOR	IMPLEMENTERS	IMPONDERABILITY	IMPOSTHUMATION
IMPERSISTENT	IMPETRATORS	IMPLEMENTING	IMPONDERABLE	IMPOSTHUMATIONS
IMPERSONAL	IMPETRATORY	IMPLEMENTOR	IMPONDERABLES	IMPOSTHUME
IMPERSONALISE	IMPETUOSITIES	IMPLEMENTORS	IMPONDERABLY	IMPOSTHUMED
IMPERSONALISED	IMPETUOSITY	IMPLEMENTS	IMPONDEROUS	IMPOSTHUMES
IMPERSONALISES	IMPETUOUSLY	IMPLETIONS	IMPORTABILITIES	IMPOSTOROUS
IMPERSONALISING	IMPETUOUSNESS	IMPLEXIONS	IMPORTABILITY	IMPOSTROUS
IMPERSONALITIES	IMPETUOUSNESSES	IMPLEXUOUS	IMPORTABLE	IMPOSTUMATE
IMPERSONALITY	IMPICTURED	IMPLICATED	IMPORTANCE	IMPOSTUMATED
IMPERSONALIZE	IMPIERCEABLE	IMPLICATES	IMPORTANCES	IMPOSTUMATES
IMPERSONALIZED	IMPIGNORATE	IMPLICATING	IMPORTANCIES	IMPOSTUMATING
IMPERSONALIZES	IMPIGNORATED	IMPLICATION	IMPORTANCY	IMPOSTUMATION
IMPERSONALIZING	IMPIGNORATES	IMPLICATIONAL	IMPORTANTLY	IMPOSTUMATIONS
IMPERSONALLY	IMPIGNORATING	IMPLICATIONS	IMPORTATION	IMPOSTUMED
IMPERSONATE	IMPIGNORATION	IMPLICATIVE	IMPORTATIONS	IMPOSTUMES
IMPERSONATED	IMPIGNORATIONS	IMPLICATIVELY	IMPORTINGS	IMPOSTURES
IMPERSONATES	IMPINGEMENT	IMPLICATIVENESS	IMPORTUNACIES	IMPOSTUROUS
IMPERSONATING	IMPINGEMENTS	IMPLICATURE	IMPORTUNACY	IMPOTENCES
IMPERSONATION	IMPIOUSNESS	IMPLICATURES	IMPORTUNATE	IMPOTENCIES
IMPERSONATIONS	IMPIOUSNESSES	IMPLICITIES	IMPORTUNATELY	IMPOTENTLY
IMPERSONATOR	IMPISHNESS	IMPLICITLY	IMPORTUNATENESS	IMPOTENTNESS
IMPERSONATORS	IMPISHNESSES	IMPLICITNESS	IMPORTUNED	IMPOTENTNESSES
IMPERTINENCE	IMPLACABILITIES	IMPLICITNESSES	IMPORTUNELY	IMPOUNDABLE
IMPERTINENCES	IMPLACABILITY	IMPLODENTS	IMPORTUNER	IMPOUNDAGE
IMPERTINENCIES	IMPLACABLE	IMPLORATION	IMPORTUNERS	IMPOUNDAGES
IMPERTINENCY	IMPLACABLENESS	IMPLORATIONS	IMPORTUNES	IMPOUNDERS
IMPERTINENT	IMPLACABLY	IMPLORATOR	IMPORTUNING	IMPOUNDING
IMPERTINENTLY	IMPLACENTAL	IMPLORATORS	IMPORTUNINGS	IMPOUNDMENT
IMPERTURBABLE	IMPLANTABLE	IMPLORATORY	IMPORTUNITIES	IMPOUNDMENTS
IMPERTURBABLY	IMPLANTATION	IMPLORINGLY	IMPORTUNITY	IMPOVERISH
IMPERTURBATION	IMPLANTATIONS	IMPLOSIONS	IMPOSINGLY	IMPOVERISHED
IMPERTURBATIONS	IMPLANTERS	IMPLOSIVELY	IMPOSINGNESS	IMPOVERISHER
IMPERVIABILITY	IMPLANTING	IMPLOSIVES	IMPOSINGNESSES	IMPOVERISHERS
IMPERVIABLE	IMPLAUSIBILITY	IMPLUNGING	IMPOSITION	IMPOVERISHES

IMPOVERISHING	IMPRESSIONALLY	IMPROPRIETY	IMPUDENTNESSES	INACTIVENESS
IMPOVERISHMENT	IMPRESSIONISM	IMPROVABILITIES	IMPUDICITIES	INACTIVENESSES
IMPOVERISHMENTS	IMPRESSIONISMS	IMPROVABILITY	IMPUDICITY	INACTIVITIES
IMPOWERING	IMPRESSIONIST	IMPROVABLE	IMPUGNABLE	INACTIVITY
IMPRACTICABLE	IMPRESSIONISTIC	IMPROVABLENESS	IMPUGNATION	INADAPTABLE
IMPRACTICABLY	IMPRESSIONISTS	IMPROVABLY	IMPUGNATIONS	INADAPTATION
IMPRACTICAL	IMPRESSIONS	IMPROVEMENT	IMPUGNMENT	INADAPTATIONS
IMPRACTICALITY	IMPRESSIVE	IMPROVEMENTS	IMPUGNMENTS	INADAPTIVE
IMPRACTICALLY	IMPRESSIVELY	IMPROVIDENCE	IMPUISSANCE	INADEQUACIES
IMPRACTICALNESS	IMPRESSIVENESS	IMPROVIDENCES	IMPUISSANCES	INADEQUACY
IMPRECATED	IMPRESSMENT	IMPROVIDENT	IMPUISSANT	INADEQUATE
IMPRECATES	IMPRESSMENTS	IMPROVIDENTLY	IMPULSIONS	INADEQUATELY
IMPRECATING	IMPRESSURE	IMPROVINGLY	IMPULSIVELY	INADEQUATENESS
IMPRECATION	IMPRESSURES	IMPROVISATE	IMPULSIVENESS	INADEQUATES
IMPRECATIONS	IMPRIMATUR	IMPROVISATED	IMPULSIVENESSES	INADMISSIBILITY
IMPRECATORY	IMPRIMATURS	IMPROVISATES	IMPULSIVITIES	INADMISSIBLE
IMPRECISELY	IMPRINTERS	IMPROVISATING	IMPULSIVITY	INADMISSIBLY
IMPRECISENESS	IMPRINTING	IMPROVISATION	IMPUNDULUS	INADVERTENCE
IMPRECISENESSES	IMPRINTINGS	IMPROVISATIONAL	IMPUNITIES	INADVERTENCES
IMPRECISION	IMPRISONABLE	IMPROVISATIONS	IMPURENESS	INADVERTENCIES
IMPRECISIONS	IMPRISONED	IMPROVISATOR	IMPURENESSES	INADVERTENCY
IMPREDICATIVE	IMPRISONER	IMPROVISATORE	IMPURITIES	INADVERTENT
IMPREGNABILITY	IMPRISONERS	IMPROVISATORES	IMPURPLING	INADVERTENTLY
IMPREGNABLE	IMPRISONING	IMPROVISATORI	IMPUTABILITIES	INADVISABILITY
IMPREGNABLENESS	IMPRISONMENT	IMPROVISATORIAL	IMPUTABILITY	INADVISABLE
IMPREGNABLY	IMPRISONMENTS	IMPROVISATORS	IMPUTABLENESS	INADVISABLENESS
IMPREGNANT	IMPROBABILITIES	IMPROVISATORY	IMPUTABLENESSES	INADVISABLY
IMPREGNANTS	IMPROBABILITY	IMPROVISATRICE	IMPUTATION	INALIENABILITY
IMPREGNATABLE	IMPROBABLE	IMPROVISATRICES	IMPUTATIONS	INALIENABLE
IMPREGNATE	IMPROBABLENESS	IMPROVISATRIX	IMPUTATIVE	INALIENABLENESS
IMPREGNATED	IMPROBABLY	IMPROVISATRIXES	IMPUTATIVELY	INALIENABLY
IMPREGNATES	IMPROBATION	IMPROVISED	INABILITIES	INALTERABILITY
IMPREGNATING	IMPROBATIONS	IMPROVISER	INABSTINENCE	INALTERABLE
IMPREGNATION	IMPROBITIES	IMPROVISERS	INABSTINENCES	INALTERABLENESS
IMPREGNATIONS	IMPROMPTUS	IMPROVISES	INACCESSIBILITY	INALTERABLY
IMPREGNATOR	IMPROPERER	IMPROVISING	INACCESSIBLE	INAMORATAS
IMPREGNATORS	IMPROPEREST	IMPROVISOR	INACCESSIBLY	INAMORATOS
IMPREGNING	IMPROPERLY	IMPROVISORS	INACCURACIES	INANENESSES
IMPRESARIO	IMPROPERNESS	IMPROVVISATORE	INACCURACY	INANIMATELY
IMPRESARIOS	IMPROPERNESSES	IMPROVVISATORES	INACCURATE	INANIMATENESS
IMPRESCRIPTIBLE	IMPROPRIATE	IMPROVVISATRICE	INACCURATELY	INANIMATENESSES
IMPRESCRIPTIBLY	IMPROPRIATED	IMPRUDENCE	INACCURATENESS	INANIMATION
IMPRESSERS	IMPROPRIATES	IMPRUDENCES	INACTIVATE	INANIMATIONS
IMPRESSIBILITY	IMPROPRIATING	IMPRUDENTLY	INACTIVATED	INANITIONS
IMPRESSIBLE	IMPROPRIATION	IMPSONITES	INACTIVATES	INAPPARENT
IMPRESSING	IMPROPRIATIONS	IMPUDENCES	INACTIVATING	INAPPARENTLY
IMPRESSION	IMPROPRIATOR	IMPUDENCIES	INACTIVATION	INAPPEASABLE
IMPRESSIONABLE	IMPROPRIATORS	IMPUDENTLY	INACTIVATIONS	INAPPELLABLE
IMPRESSIONAL	IMPROPRIETIES	IMPUDENTNESS	INACTIVELY	INAPPETENCE

INAPPETENCES	INAUGURATE	INCAPABLENESS	INCATENATED	INCHOATELY
INAPPETENCIES	INAUGURATED	INCAPABLENESSES	INCATENATES	INCHOATENESS
INAPPETENCY	INAUGURATES	INCAPABLES	INCATENATING	INCHOATENESSES
INAPPETENT	INAUGURATING	INCAPACIOUS	INCATENATION	INCHOATING
INAPPLICABILITY	INAUGURATION	INCAPACIOUSNESS	INCATENATIONS	INCHOATION
INAPPLICABLE	INAUGURATIONS	INCAPACITANT	INCAUTIONS	INCHOATIONS
INAPPLICABLY	INAUGURATOR	INCAPACITANTS	INCAUTIOUS	INCHOATIVE
INAPPOSITE	INAUGURATORS	INCAPACITATE	INCAUTIOUSLY	INCHOATIVELY
INAPPOSITELY	INAUGURATORY	INCAPACITATED	INCAUTIOUSNESS	INCHOATIVES
INAPPOSITENESS	INAURATING	INCAPACITATES	INCEDINGLY	INCIDENCES
INAPPRECIABLE	INAUSPICIOUS	INCAPACITATING	INCENDIARIES	INCIDENTAL
INAPPRECIABLY	INAUSPICIOUSLY	INCAPACITATION	INCENDIARISM	INCIDENTALLY
INAPPRECIATION	INAUTHENTIC	INCAPACITATIONS	INCENDIARISMS	INCIDENTALNESS
INAPPRECIATIONS	INAUTHENTICITY	INCAPACITIES	INCENDIARY	INCIDENTALS
INAPPRECIATIVE	INBOUNDING	INCAPACITY	INCENDIVITIES	INCINERATE
INAPPREHENSIBLE	INBREATHED	INCAPSULATE	INCENDIVITY	INCINERATED
INAPPREHENSION	INBREATHES	INCAPSULATED	INCENSATION	INCINERATES
INAPPREHENSIONS	INBREATHING	INCAPSULATES	INCENSATIONS	INCINERATING
INAPPREHENSIVE	INBREEDERS	INCAPSULATING	INCENSEMENT	INCINERATION
INAPPROACHABLE	INBREEDING	INCAPSULATION	INCENSEMENTS	INCINERATIONS
INAPPROACHABLY	INBREEDINGS	INCAPSULATIONS	INCENSORIES	INCINERATOR
INAPPROPRIATE	INBRINGING	INCARCERATE	INCENTIVELY	INCINERATORS
INAPPROPRIATELY	INBRINGINGS	INCARCERATED	INCENTIVES	INCIPIENCE
INAPTITUDE	INBURSTING	INCARCERATES	INCENTIVISATION	INCIPIENCES
INAPTITUDES	INCALCULABILITY	INCARCERATING	INCENTIVISE	INCIPIENCIES
INAPTNESSES	INCALCULABLE	INCARCERATION	INCENTIVISED	INCIPIENCY
INARGUABLE	INCALCULABLY	INCARCERATIONS	INCENTIVISES	INCIPIENTLY
INARGUABLY	INCALESCENCE	INCARCERATOR	INCENTIVISING	INCISIFORM
INARTICULACIES	INCALESCENCES	INCARCERATORS	INCENTIVIZATION	INCISIVELY
INARTICULACY	INCALESCENT	INCARDINATE	INCENTIVIZE	INCISIVENESS
INARTICULATE	INCANDESCE	INCARDINATED	INCENTIVIZED	INCISIVENESSES
INARTICULATELY	INCANDESCED	INCARDINATES	INCENTIVIZES	INCISORIAL
INARTICULATES	INCANDESCENCE	INCARDINATING	INCENTIVIZING	INCITATION
INARTICULATION	INCANDESCENCES	INCARDINATION	INCEPTIONS	INCITATIONS
INARTICULATIONS	INCANDESCENCIES	INCARDINATIONS	INCEPTIVELY	INCITATIVE
INARTIFICIAL	INCANDESCENCY	INCARNADINE	INCEPTIVES	INCITATIVES
INARTIFICIALLY	INCANDESCENT	INCARNADINED	INCERTAINTIES	INCITEMENT
INARTISTIC	INCANDESCENTLY	INCARNADINES	INCERTAINTY	INCITEMENTS
INARTISTICALLY	INCANDESCENTS	INCARNADINING	INCERTITUDE	INCITINGLY
INATTENTION	INCANDESCES	INCARNATED	INCERTITUDES	INCIVILITIES
INATTENTIONS	INCANDESCING	INCARNATES	INCESSANCIES	INCIVILITY
INATTENTIVE	INCANTATION	INCARNATING	INCESSANCY	INCLASPING
INATTENTIVELY	INCANTATIONAL	INCARNATION	INCESSANTLY	INCLEMENCIES
INATTENTIVENESS	INCANTATIONS	INCARNATIONS	INCESSANTNESS	INCLEMENCY
INAUDIBILITIES	INCANTATOR	INCARVILLEA	INCESSANTNESSES	INCLEMENTLY
INAUDIBILITY	INCANTATORS	INCARVILLEAS	INCESTUOUS	INCLEMENTNESS
INAUDIBLENESS	INCANTATORY	INCASEMENT	INCESTUOUSLY	INCLEMENTNESSES
INAUDIBLENESSES	INCAPABILITIES	INCASEMENTS	INCESTUOUSNESS	INCLINABLE
INAUGURALS	INCAPABILITY	INCATENATE	INCHARITABLE	INCLINABLENESS

INCLINATION	INCOMBUSTIBLES	INCOMPREHENSION	INCONSISTENCES	INCOORDINATIONS
INCLINATIONAL	INCOMBUSTIBLY	INCOMPREHENSIVE	INCONSISTENCIES	INCORONATE
INCLINATIONS	INCOMMENSURABLE	INCOMPRESSIBLE	INCONSISTENCY	INCORONATED
INCLINATORIA	INCOMMENSURABLY	INCOMPRESSIBLY	INCONSISTENT	INCORONATION
INCLINATORIUM	INCOMMENSURATE	INCOMPUTABILITY	INCONSISTENTLY	INCORONATIONS
INCLINATORY	INCOMMISCIBLE	INCOMPUTABLE	INCONSOLABILITY	INCORPORABLE
INCLININGS	INCOMMODED	INCOMPUTABLY	INCONSOLABLE	INCORPORAL
INCLINOMETER	INCOMMODES	INCOMUNICADO	INCONSOLABLY	INCORPORALL
INCLINOMETERS	INCOMMODING	INCONCEIVABLE	INCONSONANCE	INCORPORATE
INCLIPPING	INCOMMODIOUS	INCONCEIVABLES	INCONSONANCES	INCORPORATED
INCLOSABLE	INCOMMODIOUSLY	INCONCEIVABLY	INCONSONANT	INCORPORATES
INCLOSURES	INCOMMODITIES	INCONCINNITIES	INCONSONANTLY	INCORPORATING
INCLUDABLE	INCOMMODITY	INCONCINNITY	INCONSPICUOUS	INCORPORATION
INCLUDEDNESS	INCOMMUNICABLE	INCONCINNOUS	INCONSPICUOUSLY	INCORPORATIONS
INCLUDEDNESSES	INCOMMUNICABLY	INCONCLUSION	INCONSTANCIES	INCORPORATIVE
INCLUDIBLE	INCOMMUNICADO	INCONCLUSIONS	INCONSTANCY	INCORPORATOR
INCLUSIONS	INCOMMUNICATIVE	INCONCLUSIVE	INCONSTANT	INCORPORATORS
INCLUSIVELY	INCOMMUTABILITY	INCONCLUSIVELY	INCONSTANTLY	INCORPOREAL
INCLUSIVENESS	INCOMMUTABLE	INCONDENSABLE	INCONSTRUABLE	INCORPOREALITY
INCLUSIVENESSES	INCOMMUTABLY	INCONDENSIBLE	INCONSUMABLE	INCORPOREALLY
INCLUSIVITIES	INCOMPARABILITY	INCONDITELY	INCONSUMABLY	INCORPOREITIES
INCLUSIVITY	INCOMPARABLE	INCONFORMITIES	INCONTESTABLE	INCORPOREITY
INCOAGULABLE	INCOMPARABLY	INCONFORMITY	INCONTESTABLY	INCORPSING
INCOERCIBLE	INCOMPARED	INCONGRUENCE	INCONTIGUOUS	INCORRECTLY
INCOGITABILITY	INCOMPATIBILITY	INCONGRUENCES	INCONTIGUOUSLY	INCORRECTNESS
INCOGITABLE	INCOMPATIBLE	INCONGRUENT	INCONTINENCE	INCORRECTNESSES
INCOGITANCIES	INCOMPATIBLES	INCONGRUENTLY	INCONTINENCES	INCORRIGIBILITY
INCOGITANCY	INCOMPATIBLY	INCONGRUITIES	INCONTINENCIES	INCORRIGIBLE
INCOGITANT	INCOMPETENCE	INCONGRUITY	INCONTINENCY	INCORRIGIBLES
INCOGITATIVE	INCOMPETENCES	INCONGRUOUS	INCONTINENT	INCORRIGIBLY
INCOGNISABLE	INCOMPETENCIES	INCONGRUOUSLY	INCONTINENTLY	INCORRODIBLE
INCOGNISANCE	INCOMPETENCY	INCONGRUOUSNESS	INCONTROLLABLE	INCORROSIBLE
INCOGNISANCES	INCOMPETENT	INCONSCIENT	INCONTROLLABLY	INCORRUPTED
INCOGNISANT	INCOMPETENTLY	INCONSCIENTLY	INCONVENIENCE	INCORRUPTIBLE
INCOGNITAS	INCOMPETENTS	INCONSCIONABLE	INCONVENIENCED	INCORRUPTIBLES
INCOGNITOS	INCOMPLETE	INCONSCIOUS	INCONVENIENCES	INCORRUPTIBLY
INCOGNIZABLE	INCOMPLETELY	INCONSECUTIVE	INCONVENIENCIES	INCORRUPTION
INCOGNIZANCE	INCOMPLETENESS	INCONSECUTIVELY	INCONVENIENCING	INCORRUPTIONS
INCOGNIZANCES	INCOMPLETION	INCONSEQUENCE	INCONVENIENCY	INCORRUPTIVE
INCOGNIZANT	INCOMPLETIONS	INCONSEQUENCES	INCONVENIENT	INCORRUPTLY
INCOHERENCE	INCOMPLIANCE	INCONSEQUENT	INCONVENIENTLY	INCORRUPTNESS
INCOHERENCES	INCOMPLIANCES	INCONSEQUENTIAL	INCONVERSABLE	INCORRUPTNESSES
INCOHERENCIES	INCOMPLIANCIES	INCONSEQUENTLY	INCONVERSANT	INCRASSATE
INCOHERENCY	INCOMPLIANCY	INCONSIDERABLE	INCONVERTIBLE	INCRASSATED
INCOHERENT	INCOMPLIANT	INCONSIDERABLY	INCONVERTIBLY	INCRASSATES
INCOHERENTLY	INCOMPLIANTLY	INCONSIDERATE	INCONVINCIBLE	INCRASSATING
INCOHERENTNESS	INCOMPOSED	INCONSIDERATELY	INCONVINCIBLY	INCRASSATION
INCOHESIVE	INCOMPOSITE	INCONSIDERATION	INCOORDINATE	INCRASSATIONS
INCOMBUSTIBLE	INCOMPOSSIBLE	INCONSISTENCE	INCOORDINATION	INCRASSATIVE

INCRASSATIVES	INCROSSBREEDING	INCUNABLES	INDECISIVELY	INDEMONSTRABLY
INCREASABLE	INCROSSBREEDS	INCUNABULA	INDECISIVENESS	INDENTATION
INCREASEDLY	INCROSSING	INCUNABULAR	INDECLINABLE	INDENTATIONS
INCREASEFUL	INCRUSTANT	INCUNABULIST	INDECLINABLY	INDENTIONS
INCREASERS	INCRUSTANTS	INCUNABULISTS	INDECOMPOSABLE	INDENTURED
INCREASING	INCRUSTATION	INCUNABULUM	INDECOROUS	INDENTURES
INCREASINGLY	INCRUSTATIONS	INCURABILITIES	INDECOROUSLY	INDENTURESHIP
INCREASINGS	INCRUSTING	INCURABILITY	INDECOROUSNESS	INDENTURESHIPS
INCREATELY	INCRUSTMENT	INCURABLENESS	INDECORUMS	INDENTURING
INCREDIBILITIES	INCRUSTMENTS	INCURABLENESSES	INDEFATIGABLE	INDEPENDENCE
INCREDIBILITY	INCUBATING	INCURABLES	INDEFATIGABLY	INDEPENDENCES
INCREDIBLE	INCUBATION	INCURIOSITIES	INDEFEASIBILITY	INDEPENDENCIES
INCREDIBLENESS	INCUBATIONAL	INCURIOSITY	INDEFEASIBLE	INDEPENDENCY
INCREDIBLY	INCUBATIONS	INCURIOUSLY	INDEFEASIBLY	INDEPENDENT
INCREDULITIES	INCUBATIVE	INCURIOUSNESS	INDEFECTIBILITY	INDEPENDENTLY
INCREDULITY	INCUBATORS	INCURIOUSNESSES	INDEFECTIBLE	INDEPENDENTS
INCREDULOUS	INCUBATORY	INCURRABLE	INDEFECTIBLY	INDESCRIBABLE
INCREDULOUSLY	INCULCATED	INCURRENCE	INDEFENSIBILITY	INDESCRIBABLES
INCREDULOUSNESS	INCULCATES	INCURRENCES	INDEFENSIBLE	INDESCRIBABLY
INCREMATED	INCULCATING	INCURSIONS	INDEFENSIBLY	INDESIGNATE
INCREMATES	INCULCATION	INCURVATED	INDEFINABILITY	INDESTRUCTIBLE
INCREMATING	INCULCATIONS	INCURVATES	INDEFINABLE	INDESTRUCTIBLY
INCREMATION	INCULCATIVE	INCURVATING	INDEFINABLENESS	INDETECTABLE
INCREMATIONS	INCULCATOR	INCURVATION	INDEFINABLES	INDETECTIBLE
INCREMENTAL	INCULCATORS	INCURVATIONS	INDEFINABLY	INDETERMINABLE
INCREMENTALISM	INCULCATORY	INCURVATURE	INDEFINITE	INDETERMINABLY
INCREMENTALISMS	INCULPABILITIES	INCURVATURES	INDEFINITELY	INDETERMINACIES
INCREMENTALIST	INCULPABILITY	INCURVITIES	INDEFINITENESS	INDETERMINACY
INCREMENTALISTS	INCULPABLE	INDAGATING	INDEFINITES	INDETERMINATE
INCREMENTALLY	INCULPABLENESS	INDAGATION	INDEHISCENCE	INDETERMINATELY
INCREMENTALS	INCULPABLY	INDAGATIONS	INDEHISCENCES	INDETERMINATION
INCREMENTED	INCULPATED	INDAGATIVE	INDEHISCENT	INDETERMINED
INCREMENTING	INCULPATES	INDAGATORS	INDELIBILITIES	INDETERMINISM
INCREMENTS	INCULPATING	INDAGATORY	INDELIBILITY	INDETERMINISMS
INCRESCENT	INCULPATION	INDAPAMIDE	INDELIBLENESS	INDETERMINIST
INCRETIONARY	INCULPATIONS	INDAPAMIDES	INDELIBLENESSES	INDETERMINISTIC
INCRETIONS	INCULPATIVE	INDEBTEDNESS	INDELICACIES	INDETERMINISTS
INCRIMINATE	INCULPATORY	INDEBTEDNESSES	INDELICACY	INDEXATION
INCRIMINATED	INCUMBENCIES	INDECENCIES	INDELICATE	INDEXATIONS
INCRIMINATES	INCUMBENCY	INDECENTER	INDELICATELY	INDEXICALS
INCRIMINATING	INCUMBENTLY	INDECENTEST	INDELICATENESS	INDEXTERITIES
INCRIMINATION	INCUMBENTS	INDECENTLY	INDEMNIFICATION	INDEXTERITY
INCRIMINATIONS	INCUMBERED	INDECIDUATE	INDEMNIFIED	INDEXTROUS
INCRIMINATOR	INCUMBERING	INDECIDUOUS	INDEMNIFIER	INDICATABLE
INCRIMINATORS	INCUMBERINGLY	INDECIPHERABLE	INDEMNIFIERS	INDICATING
INCRIMINATORY	INCUMBRANCE	INDECIPHERABLY	INDEMNIFIES	INDICATION
INCROSSBRED	INCUMBRANCER	INDECISION	INDEMNIFYING	INDICATIONAL
INCROSSBREDS	INCUMBRANCERS	INDECISIONS	INDEMNITIES	INDICATIONS
INCROSSBREED	INCUMBRANCES	INDECISIVE	INDEMONSTRABLE	INDICATIVE

INDICATIVELY	INDIGESTION	INDISPOSITION	INDIVIDUATED	INDUBITABLENESS
INDICATIVES	INDIGESTIONS	INDISPOSITIONS	INDIVIDUATES	INDUBITABLY
INDICATORS	INDIGESTIVE	INDISPUTABILITY	INDIVIDUATING	INDUCEMENT
INDICATORY	INDIGNANCE	INDISPUTABLE	INDIVIDUATION	INDUCEMENTS
INDICOLITE	INDIGNANCES	INDISPUTABLY	INDIVIDUATIONS	INDUCIBILITIES
INDICOLITES	INDIGNANTLY	INDISSOCIABLE	INDIVIDUATOR	INDUCIBILITY
INDICTABLE	INDIGNATION	INDISSOCIABLY	INDIVIDUATORS	INDUCTANCE
INDICTABLY	INDIGNATIONS	INDISSOLUBILITY	INDIVIDUUM	INDUCTANCES
INDICTIONAL	INDIGNIFIED	INDISSOLUBLE	INDIVISIBILITY	INDUCTILITIES
INDICTIONS	INDIGNIFIES	INDISSOLUBLY	INDIVISIBLE	INDUCTILITY
INDICTMENT	INDIGNIFYING	INDISSOLVABLE	INDIVISIBLENESS	INDUCTIONAL
INDICTMENTS	INDIGNITIES	INDISSUADABLE	INDIVISIBLES	INDUCTIONS
INDIFFERENCE	INDIGOLITE	INDISSUADABLY	INDIVISIBLY	INDUCTIVELY
INDIFFERENCES	INDIGOLITES	INDISTINCT	INDOCILITIES	INDUCTIVENESS
INDIFFERENCIES	INDIGOTINS	INDISTINCTION	INDOCILITY	INDUCTIVENESSES
INDIFFERENCY	INDINAVIRS	INDISTINCTIONS	INDOCTRINATE	INDUCTIVITIES
INDIFFERENT	INDIRECTION	INDISTINCTIVE	INDOCTRINATED	INDUCTIVITY
INDIFFERENTISM	INDIRECTIONS	INDISTINCTIVELY	INDOCTRINATES	INDULGENCE
INDIFFERENTISMS	INDIRECTLY	INDISTINCTLY	INDOCTRINATING	INDULGENCED
INDIFFERENTIST	INDIRECTNESS	INDISTINCTNESS	INDOCTRINATION	INDULGENCES
INDIFFERENTISTS	INDIRECTNESSES	INDISTRIBUTABLE	INDOCTRINATIONS	INDULGENCIES
INDIFFERENTLY	INDIRUBINS	INDITEMENT	INDOCTRINATOR	INDULGENCING
INDIFFERENTS	INDISCERNIBLE	INDITEMENTS	INDOCTRINATORS	INDULGENCY
INDIGENCES	INDISCERNIBLY	INDIVERTIBLE	INDOLEACETIC	INDULGENTLY
INDIGENCIES	INDISCERPTIBLE	INDIVERTIBLY	INDOLEBUTYRIC	INDULGINGLY
INDIGENISATION	INDISCIPLINABLE	INDIVIDABLE	INDOLENCES	INDUMENTUM
INDIGENISATIONS	INDISCIPLINE	INDIVIDUAL	INDOLENCIES	INDUMENTUMS
INDIGENISE	INDISCIPLINED	INDIVIDUALISE	INDOLENTLY	INDUPLICATE
INDIGENISED	INDISCIPLINES	INDIVIDUALISED	INDOMETACIN	INDUPLICATED
INDIGENISES	INDISCOVERABLE	INDIVIDUALISER	INDOMETACINS	INDUPLICATION
INDIGENISING	INDISCREET	INDIVIDUALISERS	INDOMETHACIN	INDUPLICATIONS
INDIGENITIES	INDISCREETER	INDIVIDUALISES	INDOMETHACINS	INDURATING
INDIGENITY	INDISCREETEST	INDIVIDUALISING	INDOMITABILITY	INDURATION
INDIGENIZATION	INDISCREETLY	INDIVIDUALISM	INDOMITABLE	INDURATIONS
INDIGENIZATIONS	INDISCREETNESS	INDIVIDUALISMS	INDOMITABLENESS	INDURATIVE
INDIGENIZE	INDISCRETE	INDIVIDUALIST	INDOMITABLY	INDUSTRIAL
INDIGENIZED	INDISCRETELY	INDIVIDUALISTIC	INDOPHENOL	INDUSTRIALISE
INDIGENIZES	INDISCRETENESS	INDIVIDUALISTS	INDOPHENOLS	INDUSTRIALISED
INDIGENIZING	INDISCRETION	INDIVIDUALITIES	INDORSABLE	INDUSTRIALISES
INDIGENOUS	INDISCRETIONARY	INDIVIDUALITY	INDORSATION	INDUSTRIALISING
INDIGENOUSLY	INDISCRETIONS	INDIVIDUALIZE	INDORSATIONS	INDUSTRIALISM
INDIGENOUSNESS	INDISCRIMINATE	INDIVIDUALIZED	INDORSEMENT	INDUSTRIALISMS
INDIGENTLY	INDISPENSABLE	INDIVIDUALIZER	INDORSEMENTS	INDUSTRIALIST
INDIGESTED	INDISPENSABLES	INDIVIDUALIZERS	INDRAUGHTS	INDUSTRIALISTS
INDIGESTIBILITY	INDISPENSABLY	INDIVIDUALIZES	INDRENCHED	INDUSTRIALIZE
INDIGESTIBLE	INDISPOSED	INDIVIDUALIZING	INDRENCHES	INDUSTRIALIZED
INDIGESTIBLES	INDISPOSEDNESS	INDIVIDUALLY	INDRENCHING	INDUSTRIALIZES
INDIGESTIBLY	INDISPOSES	INDIVIDUALS	INDUBITABILITY	INDUSTRIALIZING
INDIGESTING	INDISPOSING	INDIVIDUATE	INDUBITABLE	INDUSTRIALLY

INDUSTRIALS	INELABORATE	INERASABLY	INEXISTENCY	INEXTENSIBILITY
INDUSTRIES	INELABORATED	INERASIBLE	INEXISTENT	INEXTENSIBLE
INDUSTRIOUS	INELABORATELY	INERASIBLY	INEXORABILITIES	INEXTENSION
INDUSTRIOUSLY	INELABORATES	INERRABILITIES	INEXORABILITY	INEXTENSIONS
INDUSTRIOUSNESS	INELABORATING	INERRABILITY	INEXORABLE	INEXTIRPABLE
INDUSTRYWIDE	INELASTICALLY	INERRABLENESS	INEXORABLENESS	INEXTRICABILITY
INDWELLERS	INELASTICITIES	INERRABLENESSES	INEXORABLY	INEXTRICABLE
INDWELLING	INELASTICITY	INERRANCIES	INEXPANSIBLE	INEXTRICABLY
INDWELLINGS	INELEGANCE	INERTIALLY	INEXPECTANCIES	INFALLIBISM
INEARTHING	INELEGANCES	INERTNESSES	INEXPECTANCY	INFALLIBISMS
INEBRIANTS	INELEGANCIES	INESCAPABLE	INEXPECTANT	INFALLIBIST
INEBRIATED	INELEGANCY	INESCAPABLY	INEXPECTATION	INFALLIBISTS
INEBRIATES	INELEGANTLY	INESCULENT	INEXPECTATIONS	INFALLIBILITIES
INEBRIATING	INELIGIBILITIES	INESCUTCHEON	INEXPEDIENCE	INFALLIBILITY
INEBRIATION	INELIGIBILITY	INESCUTCHEONS	INEXPEDIENCES	INFALLIBLE
INEBRIATIONS	INELIGIBLE	INESSENTIAL	INEXPEDIENCIES	INFALLIBLENESS
INEBRIETIES	INELIGIBLENESS	INESSENTIALITY	INEXPEDIENCY	INFALLIBLES
INEDIBILITIES	INELIGIBLES	INESSENTIALS	INEXPEDIENT	INFALLIBLY
INEDIBILITY	INELIGIBLY	INESTIMABILITY	INEXPEDIENTLY	INFAMISING
INEDUCABILITIES	INELOQUENCE	INESTIMABLE	INEXPENSIVE	INFAMIZING
INEDUCABILITY	INELOQUENCES	INESTIMABLENESS	INEXPENSIVELY	INFAMONISE
INEDUCABLE	INELOQUENT	INESTIMABLY	INEXPENSIVENESS	INFAMONISED
INEFFABILITIES	INELOQUENTLY	INEVITABILITIES	INEXPERIENCE	INFAMONISES
INEFFABILITY	INELUCTABILITY	INEVITABILITY	INEXPERIENCED	INFAMONISING
INEFFABLENESS	INELUCTABLE	INEVITABLE	INEXPERIENCES	INFAMONIZE
INEFFABLENESSES	INELUCTABLY	INEVITABLENESS	INEXPERTLY	INFAMONIZED
INEFFACEABILITY	INELUDIBILITIES	INEVITABLES	INEXPERTNESS	INFAMONIZES
INEFFACEABLE	INELUDIBILITY	INEVITABLY	INEXPERTNESSES	INFAMONIZING
INEFFACEABLY	INELUDIBLE	INEXACTITUDE	INEXPIABLE	INFAMOUSLY
INEFFECTIVE	INELUDIBLY	INEXACTITUDES	INEXPIABLENESS	INFAMOUSNESS
INEFFECTIVELY	INENARRABLE	INEXACTNESS	INEXPIABLY	INFAMOUSNESSES
INEFFECTIVENESS	INEPTITUDE	INEXACTNESSES	INEXPLAINABLE	INFANGTHIEF
INEFFECTUAL	INEPTITUDES	INEXCITABLE	INEXPLAINABLY	INFANGTHIEFS
INEFFECTUALITY	INEPTNESSES	INEXCUSABILITY	INEXPLICABILITY	INFANTEERS
INEFFECTUALLY	INEQUALITIES	INEXCUSABLE	INEXPLICABLE	INFANTHOOD
INEFFECTUALNESS	INEQUALITY	INEXCUSABLENESS	INEXPLICABLY	INFANTHOODS
INEFFICACIES	INEQUATION	INEXCUSABLY	INEXPLICIT	INFANTICIDAL
INEFFICACIOUS	INEQUATIONS	INEXECRABLE	INEXPLICITLY	INFANTICIDE
INEFFICACIOUSLY	INEQUIPOTENT	INEXECUTABLE	INEXPLICITNESS	INFANTICIDES
INEFFICACITIES	INEQUITABLE	INEXECUTION	INEXPRESSIBLE	INFANTILISATION
INEFFICACITY	INEQUITABLENESS	INEXECUTIONS	INEXPRESSIBLES	INFANTILISE
INEFFICACY	INEQUITABLY	INEXHAUSTED	INEXPRESSIBLY	INFANTILISED
INEFFICIENCIES	INEQUITIES	INEXHAUSTIBLE	INEXPRESSIVE	INFANTILISES
INEFFICIENCY	INEQUIVALVE	INEXHAUSTIBLY	INEXPRESSIVELY	INFANTILISING
INEFFICIENT	INEQUIVALVED	INEXHAUSTIVE	INEXPUGNABILITY	INFANTILISM
INEFFICIENTLY	INERADICABILITY	INEXISTANT	INEXPUGNABLE	INFANTILISMS
INEFFICIENTS	INERADICABLE	INEXISTENCE	INEXPUGNABLY	INFANTILITIES
INEGALITARIAN	INERADICABLY	INEXISTENCES	INEXPUNGIBLE	INFANTILITY
INEGALITARIANS	INERASABLE	INEXISTENCIES	INEXTENDED	INFANTILIZATION

INFANTILIZE	INFERRABLE	INFINITIVE	INFLECTORS	INFORMATICIANS
INFANTILIZED	INFERRIBLE	INFINITIVELY	INFLEXIBILITIES	INFORMATICS
INFANTILIZES	INFERTILELY	INFINITIVES	INFLEXIBILITY	INFORMATION
INFANTILIZING	INFERTILITIES	INFINITUDE	INFLEXIBLE	INFORMATIONAL
INFANTRIES	INFERTILITY	INFINITUDES	INFLEXIBLENESS	INFORMATIONALLY
INFANTRYMAN	INFESTANTS	INFIRMARER	INFLEXIBLY	INFORMATIONS
INFANTRYMEN	INFESTATION	INFIRMARERS	INFLEXIONAL	INFORMATISATION
INFARCTION	INFESTATIONS	INFIRMARIAN	INFLEXIONALLY	INFORMATISE
INFARCTIONS	INFEUDATION	INFIRMARIANS	INFLEXIONLESS	INFORMATISED
INFATUATED	INFEUDATIONS	INFIRMARIES	INFLEXIONS	INFORMATISES
INFATUATEDLY	INFIBULATE	INFIRMITIES	INFLEXURES	INFORMATISING
INFATUATES	INFIBULATED	INFIRMNESS	INFLICTABLE	INFORMATIVE
INFATUATING	INFIBULATES	INFIRMNESSES	INFLICTERS	INFORMATIVELY
INFATUATION	INFIBULATING	INFIXATION	INFLICTING	INFORMATIVENESS
INFATUATIONS	INFIBULATION	INFIXATIONS	INFLICTION	INFORMATIZATION
INFEASIBILITIES	INFIBULATIONS	INFLAMABLE	INFLICTIONS	INFORMATIZE
INFEASIBILITY	INFIDELITIES	INFLAMINGLY	INFLICTIVE	INFORMATIZED
INFEASIBLE	INFIDELITY	INFLAMMABILITY	INFLICTORS	INFORMATIZES
INFEASIBLENESS	INFIELDERS	INFLAMMABLE	INFLORESCENCE	INFORMATIZING
INFECTANTS	INFIELDSMAN	INFLAMMABLENESS	INFLORESCENCES	INFORMATORILY
INFECTIONS	INFIELDSMEN	INFLAMMABLES	INFLORESCENT	INFORMATORY
INFECTIOUS	INFIGHTERS	INFLAMMABLY	INFLOWINGS	INFORMEDLY
INFECTIOUSLY	INFIGHTING	INFLAMMATION	INFLUENCEABLE	INFORMIDABLE
INFECTIOUSNESS	INFIGHTINGS	INFLAMMATIONS	INFLUENCED	INFORMINGLY
INFECTIVELY	INFILLINGS	INFLAMMATORILY	INFLUENCER	INFORTUNES
INFECTIVENESS	INFILTRATE	INFLAMMATORY	INFLUENCERS	INFOSPHERE
INFECTIVENESSES	INFILTRATED	INFLATABLE	INFLUENCES	INFOSPHERES
INFECTIVITIES	INFILTRATES	INFLATABLES	INFLUENCING	INFOTAINMENT
INFECTIVITY	INFILTRATING	INFLATEDLY	INFLUENTIAL	INFOTAINMENTS
INFECUNDITIES	INFILTRATION	INFLATEDNESS	INFLUENTIALLY	INFRACOSTAL
INFECUNDITY	INFILTRATIONS	INFLATEDNESSES	INFLUENTIALS	INFRACTING
INFEFTMENT	INFILTRATIVE	INFLATINGLY	INFLUENZAL	INFRACTION
INFEFTMENTS	INFILTRATOR	INFLATIONARY	INFLUENZAS	INFRACTIONS
INFELICITIES	INFILTRATORS	INFLATIONISM	INFLUXIONS	INFRACTORS
INFELICITOUS	INFINITANT	INFLATIONISMS	INFOGRAPHIC	INFRAGRANT
INFELICITOUSLY	INFINITARY	INFLATIONIST	INFOGRAPHICS	INFRAHUMAN
INFELICITY	INFINITATE	INFLATIONISTS	INFOLDINGS	INFRAHUMANS
INFEOFFING	INFINITATED	INFLATIONS	INFOLDMENT	INFRALAPSARIAN
INFERENCES	INFINITATES	INFLATUSES	INFOLDMENTS	INFRALAPSARIANS
INFERENCING	INFINITATING	INFLECTABLE	INFOMANIAS	INFRAMAXILLARY
INFERENCINGS	INFINITELY	INFLECTEDNESS	INFOMERCIAL	INFRANGIBILITY
INFERENTIAL	INFINITENESS	INFLECTEDNESSES	INFOMERCIALS	INFRANGIBLE
INFERENTIALLY	INFINITENESSES	INFLECTING	INFOPRENEURIAL	INFRANGIBLENESS
INFERIORITIES	INFINITESIMAL	INFLECTION	INFORMABLE	INFRANGIBLY
INFERIORITY	INFINITESIMALLY	INFLECTIONAL	INFORMALITIES	INFRAORBITAL
INFERIORLY	INFINITESIMALS	INFLECTIONALLY	INFORMALITY	INFRAPOSED
INFERNALITIES	INFINITIES	INFLECTIONLESS	INFORMALLY	INFRAPOSITION
INFERNALITY	INFINITIVAL	INFLECTIONS	INFORMANTS	INFRAPOSITIONS
INFERNALLY	INFINITIVALLY	INFLECTIVE	INFORMATICIAN	INFRASONIC

INFRASOUND	INGEMINATED	INGREDIENT	INHARMONIOUS	INIMICALNESS
INFRASOUNDS	INGEMINATES	INGREDIENTS	INHARMONIOUSLY	INIMICALNESSES
INFRASPECIFIC	INGEMINATING	INGRESSION	INHAUSTING	INIMICITIOUS
INFRASTRUCTURAL	INGEMINATION	INGRESSIONS	INHEARSING	INIMITABILITIES
INFRASTRUCTURE	INGEMINATIONS	INGRESSIVE	INHERENCES	INIMITABILITY
INFRASTRUCTURES	INGENERATE	INGRESSIVENESS	INHERENCIES	INIMITABLE
INFREQUENCE	INGENERATED	INGRESSIVES	INHERENTLY	INIMITABLENESS
INFREQUENCES	INGENERATES	INGROOVING	INHERITABILITY	INIMITABLY
INFREQUENCIES	INGENERATING	INGROSSING	INHERITABLE	INIQUITIES
INFREQUENCY	INGENERATION	INGROUNDED	INHERITABLENESS	INIQUITOUS
INFREQUENT	INGENERATIONS	INGROUNDING	INHERITABLY	INIQUITOUSLY
INFREQUENTLY	INGENIOUSLY	INGROWNNESS	INHERITANCE	INIQUITOUSNESS
INFRINGEMENT	INGENIOUSNESS	INGROWNNESSES	INHERITANCES	INITIALERS
INFRINGEMENTS	INGENIOUSNESSES	INGULFMENT	INHERITING	INITIALING
INFRINGERS	INGENUITIES	INGULFMENTS	INHERITORS	INITIALISATION
INFRINGING	INGENUOUSLY	INGULPHING	INHERITRESS	INITIALISATIONS
INFRUCTUOUS	INGENUOUSNESS	INGURGITATE	INHERITRESSES	INITIALISE
INFRUCTUOUSLY	INGENUOUSNESSES	INGURGITATED	INHERITRICES	INITIALISED
INFUNDIBULA	INGESTIBLE	INGURGITATES	INHERITRIX	INITIALISES
INFUNDIBULAR	INGESTIONS	INGURGITATING	INHERITRIXES	INITIALISING
INFUNDIBULATE	INGLENEUKS	INGURGITATION	INHIBITABLE	INITIALISM
INFUNDIBULIFORM	INGLENOOKS	INGURGITATIONS	INHIBITEDLY	INITIALISMS
INFUNDIBULUM	INGLORIOUS	INHABITABILITY	INHIBITERS	INITIALIZATION
INFURIATED	INGLORIOUSLY	INHABITABLE	INHIBITING	INITIALIZATIONS
INFURIATELY	INGLORIOUSNESS	INHABITANCE	INHIBITION	INITIALIZE
INFURIATES	INGRAFTATION	INHABITANCES	INHIBITIONS	INITIALIZED
INFURIATING	INGRAFTATIONS	INHABITANCIES	INHIBITIVE	INITIALIZES
INFURIATINGLY	INGRAFTING	INHABITANCY	INHIBITORS	INITIALIZING
INFURIATION	INGRAFTMENT	INHABITANT	INHIBITORY	INITIALLED
INFURIATIONS	INGRAFTMENTS	INHABITANTS	INHOLDINGS	INITIALLER
INFUSCATED	INGRAINEDLY	INHABITATION	INHOMOGENEITIES	INITIALLERS
INFUSIBILITIES	INGRAINEDNESS	INHABITATIONS	INHOMOGENEITY	INITIALLING
INFUSIBILITY	INGRAINEDNESSES	INHABITERS	INHOMOGENEOUS	INITIALNESS
INFUSIBLENESS	INGRAINERS	INHABITING	INHOSPITABLE	INITIALNESSES
INFUSIBLENESSES	INGRAINING	INHABITIVENESS	INHOSPITABLY	INITIATING
INFUSIONISM	INGRATEFUL	INHABITORS	INHOSPITALITIES	INITIATION
INFUSIONISMS	INGRATIATE	INHABITRESS	INHOSPITALITY	INITIATIONS
INFUSIONIST	INGRATIATED	INHABITRESSES	INHUMANELY	INITIATIVE
INFUSIONISTS	INGRATIATES	INHALATION	INHUMANEST	INITIATIVELY
INFUSORIAL	INGRATIATING	INHALATIONAL	INHUMANITIES	INITIATIVES
INFUSORIAN	INGRATIATINGLY	INHALATIONS	INHUMANITY	INITIATORIES
INFUSORIANS	INGRATIATION	INHALATORIUM	INHUMANNESS	INITIATORS
INFUSORIES	INGRATIATIONS	INHALATORIUMS	INHUMANNESSES	INITIATORY
INGATHERED	INGRATIATORY	INHALATORS	INHUMATING	INITIATRESS
INGATHERER	INGRATITUDE	INHARMONIC	INHUMATION	INITIATRESSES
INGATHERERS	INGRATITUDES	INHARMONICAL	INHUMATIONS	INITIATRICES
INGATHERING	INGRAVESCENCE	INHARMONICITIES	INIMICALITIES	INITIATRIX
INGATHERINGS	INGRAVESCENCES	INHARMONICITY	INIMICALITY	INITIATRIXES
INGEMINATE	INGRAVESCENT	INHARMONIES	INIMICALLY	INJECTABLE

INJECTABLES	INNOMINABLE	INOCULABILITIES	INORGANIZATIONS	INRUSHINGS
INJECTANTS	INNOMINABLES	INOCULABILITY	INORGANIZED	INSALIVATE
INJECTIONS	INNOMINATE	INOCULABLE	INOSCULATE	INSALIVATED
INJELLYING	INNOVATING	INOCULANTS	INOSCULATED	INSALIVATES
INJOINTING	INNOVATION	INOCULATED	INOSCULATES	INSALIVATING
INJUDICIAL	INNOVATIONAL	INOCULATES	INOSCULATING	INSALIVATION
INJUDICIALLY	INNOVATIONIST	INOCULATING	INOSCULATION	INSALIVATIONS
INJUDICIOUS	INNOVATIONISTS	INOCULATION	INOSCULATIONS	INSALUBRIOUS
INJUDICIOUSLY	INNOVATIONS	INOCULATIONS	INOSILICATE	INSALUBRIOUSLY
INJUDICIOUSNESS	INNOVATIVE	INOCULATIVE	INOSILICATES	INSALUBRITIES
INJUNCTING	INNOVATIVELY	INOCULATOR	INPATIENTS	INSALUBRITY
INJUNCTION	INNOVATIVENESS	INOCULATORS	INPAYMENTS	INSALUTARY
INJUNCTIONS	INNOVATORS	INOCULATORY	INPOURINGS	INSANENESS
INJUNCTIVE	INNOVATORY	INODOROUSLY	INQUIETING	INSANENESSES
INJUNCTIVELY	INNOXIOUSLY	INODOROUSNESS	INQUIETUDE	INSANITARINESS
INJURIOUSLY	INNOXIOUSNESS	INODOROUSNESSES	INQUIETUDES	INSANITARY
INJURIOUSNESS	INNOXIOUSNESSES	INOFFENSIVE	INQUILINES	INSANITATION
INJURIOUSNESSES	INNUENDOED	INOFFENSIVELY	INQUILINIC	INSANITATIONS
INJUSTICES	INNUENDOES	INOFFENSIVENESS	INQUILINICS	INSANITIES
INKBERRIES	INNUENDOING	INOFFICIOUS	INQUILINISM	INSATIABILITIES
INKHOLDERS	INNUMERABILITY	INOFFICIOUSLY	INQUILINISMS	INSATIABILITY
INKINESSES	INNUMERABLE	INOFFICIOUSNESS	INQUILINITIES	INSATIABLE
INMARRIAGE	INNUMERABLENESS	INOPERABILITIES	INQUILINITY	INSATIABLENESS
INMARRIAGES	INNUMERABLY	INOPERABILITY	INQUILINOUS	INSATIABLY
INMIGRANTS	INNUMERACIES	INOPERABLE	INQUINATED	INSATIATELY
INNATENESS	INNUMERACY	INOPERABLENESS	INQUINATES	INSATIATENESS
INNATENESSES	INNUMERATE	INOPERABLY	INQUINATING	INSATIATENESSES
INNAVIGABLE	INNUMERATES	INOPERATIVE	INQUINATION	INSATIETIES
INNAVIGABLY	INNUMEROUS	INOPERATIVENESS	INQUINATIONS	INSCIENCES
INNERMOSTS	INNUTRIENT	INOPERCULATE	INQUIRATION	INSCONCING
INNERNESSES	INNUTRITION	INOPERCULATES	INQUIRATIONS	INSCRIBABLE
INNERSOLES	INNUTRITIONS	INOPPORTUNE	INQUIRENDO	INSCRIBABLENESS
INNERSPRING	INNUTRITIOUS	INOPPORTUNELY	INQUIRENDOS	INSCRIBERS
INNERVATED	INOBEDIENCE	INOPPORTUNENESS	INQUIRINGLY	INSCRIBING
INNERVATES	INOBEDIENCES	INOPPORTUNITIES	INQUISITION	INSCRIPTION
INNERVATING	INOBEDIENT	INOPPORTUNITY	INQUISITIONAL	INSCRIPTIONAL
INNERVATION	INOBEDIENTLY	INORDINACIES	INQUISITIONIST	INSCRIPTIONS
INNERVATIONS	INOBSERVABLE	INORDINACY	INQUISITIONISTS	INSCRIPTIVE
INNERWEARS	INOBSERVANCE	INORDINATE	INQUISITIONS	INSCRIPTIVELY
INNKEEPERS	INOBSERVANCES	INORDINATELY	INQUISITIVE	INSCROLLED
INNOCENCES	INOBSERVANT	INORDINATENESS	INQUISITIVELY	INSCROLLING
INNOCENCIES	INOBSERVANTLY	INORDINATION	INQUISITIVENESS	INSCRUTABILITY
INNOCENTER	INOBSERVATION	INORDINATIONS	INQUISITOR	INSCRUTABLE
INNOCENTEST	INOBSERVATIONS	INORGANICALLY	INQUISITORIAL	INSCRUTABLENESS
INNOCENTLY	INOBTRUSIVE	INORGANICS	INQUISITORIALLY	INSCRUTABLY
INNOCUITIES	INOBTRUSIVELY	INORGANISATION	INQUISITORS	INSCULPING
INNOCUOUSLY	INOBTRUSIVENESS	INORGANISATIONS	INQUISITRESS	INSCULPTURE
INNOCUOUSNESS	INOCCUPATION	INORGANISED	INQUISITRESSES	INSCULPTURED
INNOCUOUSNESSES	INOCCUPATIONS	INORGANIZATION	INQUISITURIENT	INSCULPTURES

INSCULPTURING	INSENSUOUS	INSINUATINGLY	INSOLVABILITIES	INSPIRITED
INSECTARIA	INSENTIENCE	INSINUATION	INSOLVABILITY	INSPIRITER
INSECTARIES	INSENTIENCES	INSINUATIONS	INSOLVABLE	INSPIRITERS
INSECTARIUM	INSENTIENCIES	INSINUATIVE	INSOLVABLY	INSPIRITING
INSECTARIUMS	INSENTIENCY	INSINUATOR	INSOLVENCIES	INSPIRITINGLY
INSECTICIDAL	INSENTIENT	INSINUATORS	INSOLVENCY	INSPIRITMENT
INSECTICIDALLY	INSEPARABILITY	INSINUATORY	INSOLVENTS	INSPIRITMENTS
INSECTICIDE	INSEPARABLE	INSIPIDEST	INSOMNIACS	INSPISSATE
INSECTICIDES	INSEPARABLENESS	INSIPIDITIES	INSOMNIOUS	INSPISSATED
INSECTIFORM	INSEPARABLES	INSIPIDITY	INSOMNOLENCE	INSPISSATES
INSECTIFUGE	INSEPARABLY	INSIPIDNESS	INSOMNOLENCES	INSPISSATING
INSECTIFUGES	INSEPARATE	INSIPIDNESSES	INSOUCIANCE	INSPISSATION
INSECTIONS	INSERTABLE	INSIPIENCE	INSOUCIANCES	INSPISSATIONS
INSECTIVORE	INSERTIONAL	INSIPIENCES	INSOUCIANT	INSPISSATOR
INSECTIVORES	INSERTIONS	INSIPIENTLY	INSOUCIANTLY	INSPISSATORS
INSECTIVOROUS	INSESSORIAL	INSISTENCE	INSOULMENT	INSTABILITIES
INSECTOLOGIES	INSEVERABLE	INSISTENCES	INSOULMENTS	INSTABILITY
INSECTOLOGIST	INSHEATHED	INSISTENCIES	INSOURCING	INSTAGRAMMED
INSECTOLOGISTS	INSHEATHES	INSISTENCY	INSOURCINGS	INSTAGRAMMING
INSECTOLOGY	INSHEATHING	INSISTENTLY	INSPANNING	INSTAGRAMS
INSECURELY	INSHELLING	INSISTINGLY	INSPECTABLE	INSTALLANT
INSECURENESS	INSHELTERED	INSNAREMENT	INSPECTING	INSTALLANTS
INSECURENESSES	INSHELTERING	INSNAREMENTS	INSPECTINGLY	INSTALLATION
INSECUREST	INSHELTERS	INSOBRIETIES	INSPECTION	INSTALLATIONS
INSECURITIES	INSHIPPING	INSOBRIETY	INSPECTIONAL	INSTALLERS
INSECURITY	INSHRINEES	INSOCIABILITIES	INSPECTIONS	INSTALLING
INSELBERGE	INSHRINEMENT	INSOCIABILITY	INSPECTIVE	INSTALLMENT
INSELBERGS	INSHRINEMENTS	INSOCIABLE	INSPECTORAL	INSTALLMENTS
INSEMINATE	INSHRINING	INSOCIABLY	INSPECTORATE	INSTALMENT
INSEMINATED	INSIDIOUSLY	INSOLATING	INSPECTORATES	INSTALMENTS
INSEMINATES	INSIDIOUSNESS	INSOLATION	INSPECTORIAL	INSTANCIES
INSEMINATING	INSIDIOUSNESSES	INSOLATIONS	INSPECTORS	INSTANCING
INSEMINATION	INSIGHTFUL	INSOLENCES	INSPECTORSHIP	INSTANTANEITIES
INSEMINATIONS	INSIGHTFULLY	INSOLENTLY	INSPECTORSHIPS	INSTANTANEITY
INSEMINATOR	INSIGNIFICANCE	INSOLIDITIES	INSPHERING	INSTANTANEOUS
INSEMINATORS	INSIGNIFICANCES	INSOLIDITY	INSPIRABLE	INSTANTANEOUSLY
INSENSATELY	INSIGNIFICANCY	INSOLUBILISE	INSPIRATION	INSTANTIAL
INSENSATENESS	INSIGNIFICANT	INSOLUBILISED	INSPIRATIONAL	INSTANTIATE
INSENSATENESSES	INSIGNIFICANTLY	INSOLUBILISES	INSPIRATIONALLY	INSTANTIATED
INSENSIBILITIES	INSIGNIFICATIVE	INSOLUBILISING	INSPIRATIONISM	INSTANTIATES
INSENSIBILITY	INSINCERELY	INSOLUBILITIES	INSPIRATIONISMS	INSTANTIATING
INSENSIBLE	INSINCERER	INSOLUBILITY	INSPIRATIONIST	INSTANTIATION
INSENSIBLENESS	INSINCEREST	INSOLUBILIZE	INSPIRATIONISTS	INSTANTIATIONS
INSENSIBLY	INSINCERITIES	INSOLUBILIZED	INSPIRATIONS	INSTANTNESS
INSENSITIVE	INSINCERITY	INSOLUBILIZES	INSPIRATIVE	INSTANTNESSES
INSENSITIVELY	INSINEWING	INSOLUBILIZING	INSPIRATOR	INSTARRING
INSENSITIVENESS	INSINUATED	INSOLUBLENESS	INSPIRATORS	INSTATEMENT
INSENSITIVITIES	INSINUATES	INSOLUBLENESSES	INSPIRATORY	INSTATEMENTS
INSENSITIVITY	INSINUATING	INSOLUBLES	INSPIRINGLY	INSTAURATION

INSTAURATIONS	INSTRUCTIBLE	INSULARISM	INTACTNESSES	INTELLIGENCER
INSTAURATOR	INSTRUCTING	INSULARISMS	INTAGLIATED	INTELLIGENCERS
INSTAURATORS	INSTRUCTION	INSULARITIES	INTAGLIOED	INTELLIGENCES
INSTIGATED	INSTRUCTIONAL	INSULARITY	INTAGLIOES	INTELLIGENT
INSTIGATES	INSTRUCTIONS	INSULATING	INTAGLIOING	INTELLIGENTIAL
INSTIGATING	INSTRUCTIVE	INSULATION	INTANGIBILITIES	INTELLIGENTLY
INSTIGATINGLY	INSTRUCTIVELY	INSULATIONS	INTANGIBILITY	INTELLIGENTSIA
INSTIGATION	INSTRUCTIVENESS	INSULATORS	INTANGIBLE	INTELLIGENTSIAS
INSTIGATIONS	INSTRUCTOR	INSULINASE	INTANGIBLENESS	INTELLIGENTZIA
INSTIGATIVE	INSTRUCTORS	INSULINASES	INTANGIBLES	INTELLIGENTZIAS
INSTIGATOR	INSTRUCTORSHIP	INSULSITIES	INTANGIBLY	INTELLIGIBILITY
INSTIGATORS	INSTRUCTORSHIPS	INSULTABLE	INTEGRABILITIES	INTELLIGIBLE
INSTILLATION	INSTRUCTRESS	INSULTINGLY	INTEGRABILITY	INTELLIGIBLY
INSTILLATIONS	INSTRUCTRESSES	INSULTMENT	INTEGRABLE	INTEMERATE
INSTILLERS	INSTRUMENT	INSULTMENTS	INTEGRALITIES	INTEMERATELY
INSTILLING	INSTRUMENTAL	INSUPERABILITY	INTEGRALITY	INTEMERATENESS
INSTILLMENT	INSTRUMENTALISM	INSUPERABLE	INTEGRALLY	INTEMPERANCE
INSTILLMENTS	INSTRUMENTALIST	INSUPERABLENESS	INTEGRANDS	INTEMPERANCES
INSTILMENT	INSTRUMENTALITY	INSUPERABLY	INTEGRANTS	INTEMPERANT
INSTILMENTS	INSTRUMENTALLY	INSUPPORTABLE	INTEGRATED	INTEMPERANTS
INSTINCTIVE	INSTRUMENTALS	INSUPPORTABLY	INTEGRATES	INTEMPERATE
INSTINCTIVELY	INSTRUMENTATION	INSUPPRESSIBLE	INTEGRATING	INTEMPERATELY
INSTINCTIVITIES	INSTRUMENTED	INSUPPRESSIBLY	INTEGRATION	INTEMPERATENESS
INSTINCTIVITY	INSTRUMENTING	INSURABILITIES	INTEGRATIONIST	INTEMPESTIVE
INSTINCTUAL	INSTRUMENTS	INSURABILITY	INTEGRATIONISTS	INTEMPESTIVELY
INSTINCTUALLY	INSUBJECTION	INSURANCER	INTEGRATIONS	INTEMPESTIVITY
INSTITORIAL	INSUBJECTIONS	INSURANCERS	INTEGRATIVE	INTENDANCE
INSTITUTED	INSUBORDINATE	INSURANCES	INTEGRATOR	INTENDANCES
INSTITUTER	INSUBORDINATELY	INSURGENCE	INTEGRATORS	INTENDANCIES
INSTITUTERS	INSUBORDINATES	INSURGENCES	INTEGRITIES	INTENDANCY
INSTITUTES	INSUBORDINATION	INSURGENCIES	INTEGUMENT	INTENDANTS
INSTITUTING	INSUBSTANTIAL	INSURGENCY	INTEGUMENTAL	INTENDEDLY
INSTITUTION	INSUBSTANTIALLY	INSURGENTLY	INTEGUMENTARY	INTENDERED
INSTITUTIONAL	INSUFFERABLE	INSURGENTS	INTEGUMENTS	INTENDERING
INSTITUTIONALLY	INSUFFERABLY	INSURMOUNTABLE	INTELLECTED	INTENDMENT
INSTITUTIONARY	INSUFFICIENCE	INSURMOUNTABLY	INTELLECTION	INTENDMENTS
INSTITUTIONS	INSUFFICIENCES	INSURRECTION	INTELLECTIONS	INTENERATE
INSTITUTIST	INSUFFICIENCIES	INSURRECTIONAL	INTELLECTIVE	INTENERATED
INSTITUTISTS	INSUFFICIENCY	INSURRECTIONARY	INTELLECTIVELY	INTENERATES
INSTITUTIVE	INSUFFICIENT	INSURRECTIONISM	INTELLECTS	INTENERATING
INSTITUTIVELY	INSUFFICIENTLY	INSURRECTIONIST	INTELLECTUAL	INTENERATION
INSTITUTOR	INSUFFLATE	INSURRECTIONS	INTELLECTUALISE	INTENERATIONS
INSTITUTORS	INSUFFLATED	INSUSCEPTIBLE	INTELLECTUALISM	INTENSATED
INSTREAMING	INSUFFLATES	INSUSCEPTIBLY	INTELLECTUALIST	INTENSATES
INSTREAMINGS	INSUFFLATING	INSUSCEPTIVE	INTELLECTUALITY	INTENSATING
INSTRESSED	INSUFFLATION	INSUSCEPTIVELY	INTELLECTUALIZE	INTENSATIVE
INSTRESSES	INSUFFLATIONS	INSWATHING	INTELLECTUALLY	INTENSATIVES
INSTRESSING	INSUFFLATOR	INSWINGERS	INTELLECTUALS	INTENSENESS
INSTRUCTED	INSUFFLATORS	INTACTNESS	INTELLIGENCE	INTENSENESSES

INTENSIFICATION	INTERANNUAL	INTERCEPTERS	INTERCOLONIALLY	INTERCROPPED
INTENSIFIED	INTERARCHED	INTERCEPTING	INTERCOLUMNAR	INTERCROPPING
INTENSIFIER	INTERARCHES	INTERCEPTION	INTERCOMMUNAL	INTERCROPS
INTENSIFIERS	INTERARCHING	INTERCEPTIONS	INTERCOMMUNE	INTERCROSS
INTENSIFIES	INTERATOMIC	INTERCEPTIVE	INTERCOMMUNED	INTERCROSSED
INTENSIFYING	INTERBASIN	INTERCEPTOR	INTERCOMMUNES	INTERCROSSES
INTENSIONAL	INTERBEDDED	INTERCEPTORS	INTERCOMMUNING	INTERCROSSING
INTENSIONALITY	INTERBEDDING	INTERCEPTS	INTERCOMMUNION	INTERCRURAL
INTENSIONALLY	INTERBEDDINGS	INTERCESSION	INTERCOMMUNIONS	INTERCULTURAL
INTENSIONS	INTERBEHAVIOR	INTERCESSIONAL	INTERCOMMUNITY	INTERCULTURALLY
INTENSITIES	INTERBEHAVIORAL	INTERCESSIONS	INTERCOMPANY	INTERCULTURE
INTENSITIVE	INTERBEHAVIORS	INTERCESSOR	INTERCOMPARE	INTERCULTURES
INTENSITIVES	INTERBEHAVIOUR	INTERCESSORIAL	INTERCOMPARED	INTERCURRENCE
INTENSIVELY	INTERBEHAVIOURS	INTERCESSORS	INTERCOMPARES	INTERCURRENCES
INTENSIVENESS	INTERBLEND	INTERCESSORY	INTERCOMPARING	INTERCURRENT
INTENSIVENESSES	INTERBLENDED	INTERCHAIN	INTERCOMPARISON	INTERCURRENTLY
INTENSIVES	INTERBLENDING	INTERCHAINED	INTERCONNECT	INTERCURRENTS
INTENTIONAL	INTERBLENDS	INTERCHAINING	INTERCONNECTED	INTERCUTTING
INTENTIONALITY	INTERBOROUGH	INTERCHAINS	INTERCONNECTING	INTERDASHED
INTENTIONALLY	INTERBRAIN	INTERCHANGE	INTERCONNECTION	INTERDASHES
INTENTIONED	INTERBRAINS	INTERCHANGEABLE	INTERCONNECTOR	INTERDASHING
INTENTIONS	INTERBRANCH	INTERCHANGEABLY	INTERCONNECTORS	INTERDEALER
INTENTNESS	INTERBREED	INTERCHANGED	INTERCONNECTS	INTERDEALERS
INTENTNESSES	INTERBREEDING	INTERCHANGEMENT	INTERCONNEXION	INTERDEALING
INTERABANG	INTERBREEDINGS	INTERCHANGER	INTERCONNEXIONS	INTERDEALS
INTERABANGS	INTERBREEDS	INTERCHANGERS	INTERCONVERSION	INTERDEALT
INTERACTANT	INTERBROKER	INTERCHANGES	INTERCONVERT	INTERDENTAL
INTERACTANTS	INTERCALAR	INTERCHANGING	INTERCONVERTED	INTERDENTALLY
INTERACTED	INTERCALARILY	INTERCHANNEL	INTERCONVERTING	INTERDEPEND
INTERACTING	INTERCALARY	INTERCHAPTER	INTERCONVERTS	INTERDEPENDED
INTERACTION	INTERCALATE	INTERCHAPTERS	INTERCOOLED	INTERDEPENDENCE
INTERACTIONAL	INTERCALATED	INTERCHURCH	INTERCOOLER	INTERDEPENDENCY
INTERACTIONISM	INTERCALATES	INTERCIPIENT	INTERCOOLERS	INTERDEPENDENT
INTERACTIONISMS	INTERCALATING	INTERCIPIENTS	INTERCOOLING	INTERDEPENDING
INTERACTIONIST	INTERCALATION	INTERCLASS	INTERCOOLS	INTERDEPENDS
INTERACTIONISTS	INTERCALATIONS	INTERCLAVICLE	INTERCORPORATE	INTERDIALECTAL
INTERACTIONS	INTERCALATIVE	INTERCLAVICLES	INTERCORRELATE	INTERDICTED
INTERACTIVE	INTERCAMPUS	INTERCLAVICULAR	INTERCORRELATED	INTERDICTING
INTERACTIVELY	INTERCASTE	INTERCLUDE	INTERCORRELATES	INTERDICTION
INTERACTIVITIES	INTERCEDED	INTERCLUDED	INTERCORTICAL	INTERDICTIONS
INTERACTIVITY	INTERCEDENT	INTERCLUDES	INTERCOSTAL	INTERDICTIVE
INTERAGENCY	INTERCEDER	INTERCLUDING	INTERCOSTALLY	INTERDICTIVELY
INTERALLELIC	INTERCEDERS	INTERCLUSION	INTERCOSTALS	INTERDICTOR
INTERALLIED	INTERCEDES	INTERCLUSIONS	INTERCOUNTRY	INTERDICTORS
INTERAMBULACRA	INTERCEDING	INTERCLUSTER	INTERCOUNTY	INTERDICTORY
INTERAMBULACRAL	INTERCELLULAR	INTERCOASTAL	INTERCOUPLE	INTERDICTS
INTERAMBULACRUM	INTERCENSAL	INTERCOLLEGIATE	INTERCOURSE	INTERDIFFUSE
INTERANIMATION	INTERCEPTED	INTERCOLLINE	INTERCOURSES	INTERDIFFUSED
INTERANIMATIONS	INTERCEPTER	INTERCOLONIAL	INTERCRATER	INTERDIFFUSES

INTERDIFFUSING	INTERFERINGLY	INTERGRADED	INTERJECTING	INTERLENDING
INTERDIFFUSION	INTERFEROGRAM	INTERGRADES	INTERJECTION	INTERLENDS
INTERDIFFUSIONS	INTERFEROGRAMS	INTERGRADIENT	INTERJECTIONAL	INTERLEUKIN
INTERDIGITAL	INTERFEROMETER	INTERGRADING	INTERJECTIONARY	INTERLEUKINS
INTERDIGITATE	INTERFEROMETERS	INTERGRAFT	INTERJECTIONS	INTERLIBRARY
INTERDIGITATED	INTERFEROMETRIC	INTERGRAFTED	INTERJECTOR	INTERLINEAL
INTERDIGITATES	INTERFEROMETRY	INTERGRAFTING	INTERJECTORS	INTERLINEALLY
INTERDIGITATING	INTERFERON	INTERGRAFTS	INTERJECTORY	INTERLINEAR
INTERDIGITATION	INTERFERONS	INTERGRANULAR	INTERJECTS	INTERLINEARLY
INTERDINED	INTERFERTILE	INTERGROUP	INTERJECTURAL	INTERLINEARS
INTERDINES	INTERFERTILITY	INTERGROUPS	INTERJOINED	INTERLINEATE
INTERDINING	INTERFIBER	INTERGROWING	INTERJOINING	INTERLINEATED
INTERDISTRICT	INTERFIBRE	INTERGROWN	INTERJOINS	INTERLINEATES
INTERDIVISIONAL	INTERFILED	INTERGROWS	INTERKINESES	INTERLINEATING
INTERDOMINION	INTERFILES	INTERGROWTH	INTERKINESIS	INTERLINEATION
INTERELECTRODE	INTERFILING	INTERGROWTHS	INTERKNITS	INTERLINEATIONS
INTERELECTRON	INTERFLOWED	INTERINDIVIDUAL	INTERKNITTED	INTERLINED
INTERELECTRONIC	INTERFLOWING	INTERINDUSTRY	INTERKNITTING	INTERLINER
INTEREPIDEMIC	INTERFLOWS	INTERINFLUENCE	INTERKNOTS	INTERLINERS
INTERESSED	INTERFLUENCE	INTERINFLUENCED	INTERKNOTTED	INTERLINES
INTERESSES	INTERFLUENCES	INTERINFLUENCES	INTERKNOTTING	INTERLINGUA
INTERESSING	INTERFLUENT	INTERINVOLVE	INTERLACED	INTERLINGUAL
INTERESTED	INTERFLUOUS	INTERINVOLVED	INTERLACEDLY	INTERLINGUALLY
INTERESTEDLY	INTERFLUVE	INTERINVOLVES	INTERLACEMENT	INTERLINGUAS
INTERESTEDNESS	INTERFLUVES	INTERINVOLVING	INTERLACEMENTS	INTERLINING
INTERESTING	INTERFLUVIAL	INTERIONIC	INTERLACES	INTERLININGS
INTERESTINGLY	INTERFOLDED	INTERIORISATION	INTERLACING	INTERLINKED
INTERESTINGNESS	INTERFOLDING	INTERIORISE	INTERLACUSTRINE	INTERLINKING
INTERETHNIC	INTERFOLDS	INTERIORISED	INTERLAMINAR	INTERLINKS
INTERFACED	INTERFOLIATE	INTERIORISES	INTERLAMINATE	INTERLOANS
INTERFACES	INTERFOLIATED	INTERIORISING	INTERLAMINATED	INTERLOBULAR
INTERFACIAL	INTERFOLIATES	INTERIORITIES	INTERLAMINATES	INTERLOCAL
INTERFACIALLY	INTERFOLIATING	INTERIORITY	INTERLAMINATING	INTERLOCATION
INTERFACING	INTERFRATERNITY	INTERIORIZATION	INTERLAMINATION	INTERLOCATIONS
INTERFACINGS	INTERFRETTED	INTERIORIZE	INTERLAPPED	INTERLOCKED
INTERFACULTY	INTERFRONTAL	INTERIORIZED	INTERLAPPING	INTERLOCKER
INTERFAITH	INTERFUSED	INTERIORIZES	INTERLARDED	INTERLOCKERS
INTERFAMILIAL	INTERFUSES	INTERIORIZING	INTERLARDING	INTERLOCKING
INTERFAMILY	INTERFUSING	INTERIORLY	INTERLARDS	INTERLOCKS
INTERFASCICULAR	INTERFUSION	INTERISLAND	INTERLAYER	INTERLOCUTION
INTERFEMORAL	INTERFUSIONS	INTERJACENCIES	INTERLAYERED	INTERLOCUTIONS
INTERFERED	INTERGALACTIC	INTERJACENCY	INTERLAYERING	INTERLOCUTOR
INTERFERENCE	INTERGENERATION	INTERJACENT	INTERLAYERINGS	INTERLOCUTORILY
INTERFERENCES	INTERGENERIC	INTERJACULATE	INTERLAYERS	INTERLOCUTORS
INTERFERENTIAL	INTERGLACIAL	INTERJACULATED	INTERLAYING	INTERLOCUTORY
INTERFERER	INTERGLACIALS	INTERJACULATES	INTERLEAVE	INTERLOCUTRESS
INTERFERERS	INTERGRADATION	INTERJACULATING	INTERLEAVED	INTERLOCUTRICE
INTERFERES	INTERGRADATIONS	INTERJACULATORY	INTERLEAVES	INTERLOCUTRICES
INTERFERING	INTERGRADE	INTERJECTED	INTERLEAVING	INTERLOCUTRIX

INTERLOCUTRIXES	INTERMEDIATORS	INTERMODULATION	INTEROCEAN	INTERPERMEATES
INTERLOOPED	INTERMEDIATORY	INTERMOLECULAR	INTEROCEANIC	INTERPERMEATING
INTERLOOPING	INTERMEDIN	INTERMONTANE	INTEROCEPTION	INTERPERSONAL
INTERLOOPS	INTERMEDINS	INTERMOUNTAIN	INTEROCEPTIONS	INTERPERSONALLY
INTERLOPED	INTERMEDIUM	INTERMUNDANE	INTEROCEPTIVE	INTERPETIOLAR
INTERLOPER	INTERMEDIUMS	INTERMURED	INTEROCEPTOR	INTERPHALANGEAL
INTERLOPERS	INTERMEMBRANE	INTERMURES	INTEROCEPTORS	INTERPHASE
INTERLOPES	INTERMENSTRUAL	INTERMURING	INTEROCULAR	INTERPHASES
INTERLOPING	INTERMENTS	INTERMUSCULAR	INTEROFFICE	INTERPHONE
INTERLUDED	INTERMESHED	INTERNALISATION	INTEROPERABLE	INTERPHONES
INTERLUDES	INTERMESHES	INTERNALISE	INTEROPERATIVE	INTERPILASTER
INTERLUDIAL	INTERMESHING	INTERNALISED	INTERORBITAL	INTERPILASTERS
INTERLUDING	INTERMETALLIC	INTERNALISES	INTERORGAN	INTERPLANETARY
INTERLUNAR	INTERMETALLICS	INTERNALISING	INTEROSCULANT	INTERPLANT
INTERLUNARY	INTERMEZZI	INTERNALITIES	INTEROSCULATE	INTERPLANTED
INTERLUNATION	INTERMEZZO	INTERNALITY	INTEROSCULATED	INTERPLANTING
INTERLUNATIONS	INTERMEZZOS	INTERNALIZATION	INTEROSCULATES	INTERPLANTS
INTERMARGINAL	INTERMIGRATION	INTERNALIZE	INTEROSCULATING	INTERPLAYED
INTERMARRIAGE	INTERMIGRATIONS	INTERNALIZED	INTEROSCULATION	INTERPLAYING
INTERMARRIAGES	INTERMINABILITY	INTERNALIZES	INTEROSSEAL	INTERPLAYS
INTERMARRIED	INTERMINABLE	INTERNALIZING	INTEROSSEOUS	INTERPLEAD
INTERMARRIES	INTERMINABLY	INTERNALLY	INTERPAGED	INTERPLEADED
INTERMARRY	INTERMINGLE	INTERNALNESS	INTERPAGES	INTERPLEADER
INTERMARRYING	INTERMINGLED	INTERNALNESSES	INTERPAGING	INTERPLEADERS
INTERMATTED	INTERMINGLES	INTERNATIONAL	INTERPANDEMIC	INTERPLEADING
INTERMATTING	INTERMINGLING	INTERNATIONALLY	INTERPARIETAL	INTERPLEADS
INTERMAXILLA	INTERMISSION	INTERNATIONALS	INTERPARISH	INTERPLEURAL
INTERMAXILLAE	INTERMISSIONS	INTERNECINE	INTERPAROCHIAL	INTERPLUVIAL
INTERMAXILLARY	INTERMISSIVE	INTERNECIVE	INTERPAROXYSMAL	INTERPLUVIALS
INTERMEDDLE	INTERMITOTIC	INTERNEURAL	INTERPARTICLE	INTERPOINT
INTERMEDDLED	INTERMITTED	INTERNEURON	INTERPARTY	INTERPOINTS
INTERMEDDLER	INTERMITTENCE	INTERNEURONAL	INTERPELLANT	INTERPOLABLE
INTERMEDDLERS	INTERMITTENCES	INTERNEURONS	INTERPELLANTS	INTERPOLAR
INTERMEDDLES	INTERMITTENCIES	INTERNISTS	INTERPELLATE	INTERPOLATE
INTERMEDDLING	INTERMITTENCY	INTERNMENT	INTERPELLATED	INTERPOLATED
INTERMEDIA	INTERMITTENT	INTERNMENTS	INTERPELLATES	INTERPOLATER
INTERMEDIACIES	INTERMITTENTLY	INTERNODAL	INTERPELLATING	INTERPOLATERS
INTERMEDIACY	INTERMITTER	INTERNODES	INTERPELLATION	INTERPOLATES
INTERMEDIAL	INTERMITTERS	INTERNODIAL	INTERPELLATIONS	INTERPOLATING
INTERMEDIARIES	INTERMITTING	INTERNSHIP	INTERPELLATOR	INTERPOLATION
INTERMEDIARY	INTERMITTINGLY	INTERNSHIPS	INTERPELLATORS	INTERPOLATIONS
INTERMEDIATE	INTERMITTOR	INTERNUCLEAR	INTERPENETRABLE	INTERPOLATIVE
INTERMEDIATED	INTERMITTORS	INTERNUCLEON	INTERPENETRANT	INTERPOLATOR
INTERMEDIATELY	INTERMIXED	INTERNUCLEONIC	INTERPENETRATE	INTERPOLATORS
INTERMEDIATES	INTERMIXES	INTERNUCLEOTIDE	INTERPENETRATED	INTERPONED
INTERMEDIATING	INTERMIXING	INTERNUNCIAL	INTERPENETRATES	INTERPONES
INTERMEDIATION	INTERMIXTURE	INTERNUNCIO	INTERPERCEPTUAL	INTERPONING
INTERMEDIATIONS	INTERMIXTURES	INTERNUNCIOS	INTERPERMEATE	INTERPOPULATION
INTERMEDIATOR	INTERMODAL	INTEROBSERVER	INTERPERMEATED	INTERPOSABLE

INTERPOSAL	INTERRAILERS	INTERRUPTIBLE	INTERSPATIALLY	INTERTEXTUALLY
INTERPOSALS	INTERRAILING	INTERRUPTING	INTERSPECIES	INTERTEXTURE
INTERPOSED	INTERRAILS	INTERRUPTION	INTERSPECIFIC	INTERTEXTURES
INTERPOSER	INTERRAMAL	INTERRUPTIONS	INTERSPERSAL	INTERTIDAL
INTERPOSERS	INTERREGAL	INTERRUPTIVE	INTERSPERSALS	INTERTIDALLY
INTERPOSES	INTERREGES	INTERRUPTIVELY	INTERSPERSE	INTERTILLAGE
INTERPOSING	INTERREGIONAL	INTERRUPTOR	INTERSPERSED	INTERTILLAGES
INTERPOSITION	INTERREGNA	INTERRUPTORS	INTERSPERSEDLY	INTERTILLED
INTERPOSITIONS	INTERREGNAL	INTERRUPTS	INTERSPERSES	INTERTILLING
INTERPRETABLE	INTERREGNUM	INTERSCAPULAR	INTERSPERSING	INTERTILLS
INTERPRETABLY	INTERREGNUMS	INTERSCHOLASTIC	INTERSPERSION	INTERTISSUED
INTERPRETATE	INTERRELATE	INTERSCHOOL	INTERSPERSIONS	INTERTRAFFIC
INTERPRETATED	INTERRELATED	INTERSCRIBE	INTERSPINAL	INTERTRAFFICS
INTERPRETATES	INTERRELATEDLY	INTERSCRIBED	INTERSPINOUS	INTERTRIAL
INTERPRETATING	INTERRELATES	INTERSCRIBES	INTERSTADIAL	INTERTRIBAL
INTERPRETATION	INTERRELATING	INTERSCRIBING	INTERSTADIALS	INTERTRIGO
INTERPRETATIONS	INTERRELATION	INTERSECTED	INTERSTAGE	INTERTRIGOS
INTERPRETATIVE	INTERRELATIONS	INTERSECTING	INTERSTATE	INTERTROOP
INTERPRETED	INTERRELIGIOUS	INTERSECTION	INTERSTATES	INTERTROPICAL
INTERPRETER	INTERRENAL	INTERSECTIONAL	INTERSTATION	INTERTWINE
INTERPRETERS	INTERROBANG	INTERSECTIONS	INTERSTELLAR	INTERTWINED
INTERPRETERSHIP	INTERROBANGS	INTERSECTS	INTERSTELLARY	INTERTWINEMENT
INTERPRETESS	INTERROGABLE	INTERSEGMENT	INTERSTERILE	INTERTWINEMENTS
INTERPRETESSES	INTERROGANT	INTERSEGMENTAL	INTERSTERILITY	INTERTWINES
INTERPRETING	INTERROGANTS	INTERSEGMENTS	INTERSTICE	INTERTWINING
INTERPRETIVE	INTERROGATE	INTERSENSORY	INTERSTICES	INTERTWININGLY
INTERPRETIVELY	INTERROGATED	INTERSEPTAL	INTERSTIMULUS	INTERTWININGS
INTERPRETRESS	INTERROGATEE	INTERSERTAL	INTERSTITIAL	INTERTWIST
INTERPRETRESSES	INTERROGATEES	INTERSERTED	INTERSTITIALLY	INTERTWISTED
INTERPRETS	INTERROGATES	INTERSERTING	INTERSTITIALS	INTERTWISTING
INTERPROVINCIAL	INTERROGATING	INTERSERTS	INTERSTRAIN	INTERTWISTINGLY
INTERPROXIMAL	INTERROGATINGLY	INTERSERVICE	INTERSTRAND	INTERTWISTS
INTERPSYCHIC	INTERROGATION	INTERSESSION	INTERSTRATIFIED	INTERUNION
INTERPUNCTION	INTERROGATIONAL	INTERSESSIONS	INTERSTRATIFIES	INTERUNIONS
INTERPUNCTIONS	INTERROGATIONS	INTERSEXES	INTERSTRATIFY	INTERUNIVERSITY
INTERPUNCTUATE	INTERROGATIVE	INTERSEXUAL	INTERSUBJECTIVE	INTERURBAN
INTERPUNCTUATED	INTERROGATIVELY	INTERSEXUALISM	INTERSYSTEM	INTERVALES
INTERPUNCTUATES	INTERROGATIVES	INTERSEXUALISMS	INTERTANGLE	INTERVALLEY
INTERPUPILLARY	INTERROGATOR	INTERSEXUALITY	INTERTANGLED	INTERVALLIC
INTERQUARTILE	INTERROGATORIES	INTERSEXUALLY	INTERTANGLEMENT	INTERVALLUM
INTERRACIAL	INTERROGATORILY	INTERSEXUALS	INTERTANGLES	INTERVALLUMS
INTERRACIALLY	INTERROGATORS	INTERSIDEREAL	INTERTANGLING	INTERVALOMETER
INTERRADIAL	INTERROGATORY	INTERSOCIETAL	INTERTARSAL	INTERVALOMETERS
INTERRADIALLY	INTERROGEE	INTERSOCIETY	INTERTENTACULAR	INTERVARSITY
INTERRADII	INTERROGEES	INTERSPACE	INTERTERMINAL	INTERVEINED
INTERRADIUS	INTERRUPTED	INTERSPACED	INTERTERMS	INTERVEINING
INTERRADIUSES	INTERRUPTEDLY	INTERSPACES	INTERTEXTS	INTERVEINS
INTERRAILED	INTERRUPTER	INTERSPACING	INTERTEXTUAL	INTERVENED
INTERRAILER	INTERRUPTERS	INTERSPATIAL	INTERTEXTUALITY	INTERVENER

INTERVENERS	INTERWREATHES	INTOLERATIONS	INTRAGALACTIC	INTRASPECIES
INTERVENES	INTERWREATHING	INTONATING	INTRAGENIC	INTRASPECIFIC
INTERVENIENT	INTERWROUGHT	INTONATION	INTRAMEDULLARY	INTRASTATE
INTERVENING	INTERZONAL	INTONATIONAL	INTRAMERCURIAL	INTRATELLURIC
INTERVENOR	INTERZONES	INTONATIONS	INTRAMOLECULAR	INTRATHECAL
INTERVENORS	INTESTACIES	INTONATORS	INTRAMUNDANE	INTRATHECALLY
INTERVENTION	INTESTATES	INTONINGLY	INTRAMURAL	INTRATHORACIC
INTERVENTIONAL	INTESTINAL	INTORSIONS	INTRAMURALLY	INTRAUTERINE
INTERVENTIONISM	INTESTINALLY	INTORTIONS	INTRAMURALS	INTRAVASATION
INTERVENTIONIST	INTESTINES	INTOXICABLE	INTRAMUSCULAR	INTRAVASATIONS
INTERVENTIONS	INTHRALLED	INTOXICANT	INTRAMUSCULARLY	INTRAVASCULAR
INTERVENTOR	INTHRALLING	INTOXICANTS	INTRANASAL	INTRAVASCULARLY
INTERVENTORS	INTHRONING	INTOXICATE	INTRANASALLY	INTRAVENOUS
INTERVERTEBRAL	INTIFADAHS	INTOXICATED	INTRANATIONAL	INTRAVENOUSLY
INTERVIEWED	INTIFADEHS	INTOXICATEDLY	INTRANSIGEANCE	INTRAVERSABLE
INTERVIEWEE	INTIMACIES	INTOXICATES	INTRANSIGEANCES	INTRAVITAL
INTERVIEWEES	INTIMATELY	INTOXICATING	INTRANSIGEANT	INTRAVITALLY
INTERVIEWER	INTIMATENESS	INTOXICATINGLY	INTRANSIGEANTLY	INTRAVITAM
INTERVIEWERS	INTIMATENESSES	INTOXICATION	INTRANSIGEANTS	INTRAZONAL
INTERVIEWING	INTIMATERS	INTOXICATIONS	INTRANSIGENCE	INTREATABLE
INTERVIEWS	INTIMATING	INTOXICATIVE	INTRANSIGENCES	INTREATFULL
INTERVILLAGE	INTIMATION	INTOXICATOR	INTRANSIGENCIES	INTREATING
INTERVISIBILITY	INTIMATIONS	INTOXICATORS	INTRANSIGENCY	INTREATINGLY
INTERVISIBLE	INTIMIDATE	INTOXIMETER	INTRANSIGENT	INTREATINGS
INTERVISITATION	INTIMIDATED	INTOXIMETERS	INTRANSIGENTISM	INTREATIVE
INTERVITAL	INTIMIDATES	INTRACAPSULAR	INTRANSIGENTIST	INTREATMENT
INTERVOCALIC	INTIMIDATING	INTRACARDIAC	INTRANSIGENTLY	INTREATMENTS
INTERVOLVE	INTIMIDATINGLY	INTRACARDIAL	INTRANSIGENTS	INTRENCHANT
INTERVOLVED	INTIMIDATION	INTRACARDIALLY	INTRANSITIVE	INTRENCHED
INTERVOLVES	INTIMIDATIONS	INTRACAVITARY	INTRANSITIVELY	INTRENCHER
INTERVOLVING	INTIMIDATOR	INTRACELLULAR	INTRANSITIVES	INTRENCHERS
INTERWEAVE	INTIMIDATORS	INTRACELLULARLY	INTRANSITIVITY	INTRENCHES
INTERWEAVED	INTIMIDATORY	INTRACEREBRAL	INTRANSMISSIBLE	INTRENCHING
INTERWEAVEMENT	INTIMISTES	INTRACEREBRALLY	INTRANSMUTABLE	INTRENCHMENT
INTERWEAVEMENTS	INTIMITIES	INTRACOMPANY	INTRANUCLEAR	INTRENCHMENTS
INTERWEAVER	INTINCTION	INTRACRANIAL	INTRAOCULAR	INTREPIDITIES
INTERWEAVERS	INTINCTIONS	INTRACRANIALLY	INTRAOCULARLY	INTREPIDITY
INTERWEAVES	INTITULING	INTRACTABILITY	INTRAPARIETAL	INTREPIDLY
INTERWEAVING	INTOLERABILITY	INTRACTABLE	INTRAPARTUM	INTREPIDNESS
INTERWINDING	INTOLERABLE	INTRACTABLENESS	INTRAPERITONEAL	INTREPIDNESSES
INTERWINDS	INTOLERABLENESS	INTRACTABLY	INTRAPERSONAL	INTRICACIES
INTERWORKED	INTOLERABLY	INTRACUTANEOUS	INTRAPETIOLAR	INTRICATELY
INTERWORKING	INTOLERANCE	INTRADERMAL	INTRAPLATE	INTRICATENESS
INTERWORKINGS	INTOLERANCES	INTRADERMALLY	INTRAPOPULATION	INTRICATENESSES
INTERWORKS	INTOLERANT	INTRADERMIC	INTRAPRENEUR	INTRIGANTE
INTERWOUND	INTOLERANTLY	INTRADERMICALLY	INTRAPRENEURIAL	INTRIGANTES
INTERWOVEN	INTOLERANTNESS	INTRADOSES	INTRAPRENEURS	INTRIGANTS
INTERWREATHE	INTOLERANTS	INTRAFALLOPIAN	INTRAPSYCHIC	INTRIGUANT
INTERWREATHED	INTOLERATION	INTRAFASCICULAR	INTRASEXUAL	INTRIGUANTE

INTRIGUANTES	INTROSPECTIONS	INTUMESCENCIES	INVALIDATION	INVENTIONLESS
INTRIGUANTS	INTROSPECTIVE	INTUMESCENCY	INVALIDATIONS	INVENTIONS
INTRIGUERS	INTROSPECTIVELY	INTUMESCENT	INVALIDATOR	INVENTIVELY
INTRIGUING	INTROSPECTS	INTUMESCES	INVALIDATORS	INVENTIVENESS
INTRIGUINGLY	INTROSUSCEPTION	INTUMESCING	INVALIDEST	INVENTIVENESSES
INTRINSICAL	INTROVERSIBLE	INTURBIDATE	INVALIDHOOD	INVENTORIABLE
INTRINSICALITY	INTROVERSION	INTURBIDATED	INVALIDHOODS	INVENTORIAL
INTRINSICALLY	INTROVERSIONS	INTURBIDATES	INVALIDING	INVENTORIALLY
INTRINSICALNESS	INTROVERSIVE	INTURBIDATING	INVALIDINGS	INVENTORIED
INTRINSICATE	INTROVERSIVELY	INTUSSUSCEPT	INVALIDISM	INVENTORIES
INTRODUCED	INTROVERTED	INTUSSUSCEPTED	INVALIDISMS	INVENTORYING
INTRODUCER	INTROVERTING	INTUSSUSCEPTING	INVALIDITIES	INVENTRESS
INTRODUCERS	INTROVERTIVE	INTUSSUSCEPTION	INVALIDITY	INVENTRESSES
INTRODUCES	INTROVERTS	INTUSSUSCEPTIVE	INVALIDNESS	INVERACITIES
INTRODUCIBLE	INTRUDINGLY	INTUSSUSCEPTS	INVALIDNESSES	INVERACITY
INTRODUCING	INTRUSIONAL	INTWINEMENT	INVALUABLE	INVERITIES
INTRODUCTION	INTRUSIONIST	INTWINEMENTS	INVALUABLENESS	INVERNESSES
INTRODUCTIONS	INTRUSIONISTS	INTWISTING	INVALUABLY	INVERSIONS
INTRODUCTIVE	INTRUSIONS	INUMBRATED	INVARIABILITIES	INVERTASES
INTRODUCTORILY	INTRUSIVELY	INUMBRATES	INVARIABILITY	INVERTEBRAL
INTRODUCTORY	INTRUSIVENESS	INUMBRATING	INVARIABLE	INVERTEBRATE
INTROFYING	INTRUSIVENESSES	INUNCTIONS	INVARIABLENESS	INVERTEBRATES
INTROGRESSANT	INTRUSIVES	INUNDATING	INVARIABLES	INVERTEDLY
INTROGRESSANTS	INTRUSTING	INUNDATION	INVARIABLY	INVERTIBILITIES
INTROGRESSION	INTRUSTMENT	INUNDATIONS	INVARIANCE	INVERTIBILITY
INTROGRESSIONS	INTRUSTMENTS	INUNDATORS	INVARIANCES	INVERTIBLE
INTROGRESSIVE	INTUBATING	INUNDATORY	INVARIANCIES	INVESTABLE
INTROITUSES	INTUBATION	INURBANELY	INVARIANCY	INVESTIBLE
INTROJECTED	INTUBATIONS	INURBANITIES	INVARIANTS	INVESTIGABLE
INTROJECTING	INTUITABLE	INURBANITY	INVASIVELY	INVESTIGATE
INTROJECTION	INTUITIONAL	INUREDNESS	INVASIVENESS	INVESTIGATED
INTROJECTIONS	INTUITIONALISM	INUREDNESSES	INVASIVENESSES	INVESTIGATES
INTROJECTIVE	INTUITIONALISMS	INUREMENTS	INVEAGLING	INVESTIGATING
INTROJECTS	INTUITIONALIST	INURNMENTS	INVECTIVELY	INVESTIGATION
INTROMISSIBLE	INTUITIONALISTS	INUSITATION	INVECTIVENESS	INVESTIGATIONAL
INTROMISSION	INTUITIONALLY	INUSITATIONS	INVECTIVENESSES	INVESTIGATIONS
INTROMISSIONS	INTUITIONISM	INUTILITIES	INVECTIVES	INVESTIGATIVE
INTROMISSIVE	INTUITIONISMS	INUTTERABLE	INVEIGHERS	INVESTIGATOR
INTROMITTED	INTUITIONIST	INVAGINABLE	INVEIGHING	INVESTIGATORS
INTROMITTENT	INTUITIONISTS	INVAGINATE	INVEIGLEMENT	INVESTIGATORY
INTROMITTER	INTUITIONS	INVAGINATED	INVEIGLEMENTS	INVESTITIVE
INTROMITTERS	INTUITIVELY	INVAGINATES	INVEIGLERS	INVESTITURE
INTROMITTING	INTUITIVENESS	INVAGINATING	INVEIGLING	INVESTITURES
INTRORSELY	INTUITIVENESSES	INVAGINATION	INVENDIBILITIES	INVESTMENT
INTROSPECT	INTUITIVISM	INVAGINATIONS	INVENDIBILITY	INVESTMENTS
INTROSPECTED	INTUITIVISMS	INVALIDATE	INVENDIBLE	INVETERACIES
INTROSPECTING	INTUMESCED	INVALIDATED	INVENTABLE	INVETERACY
INTROSPECTION	INTUMESCENCE	INVALIDATES	INVENTIBLE	INVETERATE
INTROSPECTIONAL	INTUMESCENCES	INVALIDATING	INVENTIONAL	INVETERATELY

INVETERATENESS	INVITATION	INWRAPMENTS	IRASCIBILITIES	IRONWORKERS
INVIABILITIES	INVITATIONAL	INWRAPPING	IRASCIBILITY	IRRADIANCE
INVIABILITY	INVITATIONALS	INWRAPPINGS	IRASCIBLENESS	IRRADIANCES
INVIABLENESS	INVITATIONS	INWREATHED	IRASCIBLENESSES	IRRADIANCIES
INVIABLENESSES	INVITATORIES	INWREATHES	IRATENESSES	IRRADIANCY
INVIDIOUSLY	INVITATORY	INWREATHING	IREFULNESS	IRRADIATED
INVIDIOUSNESS	INVITEMENT	IODINATING	IREFULNESSES	IRRADIATES
INVIDIOUSNESSES	INVITEMENTS	IODINATION	IRENICALLY	IRRADIATING
INVIGILATE	INVITINGLY	IODINATIONS	IRENICISMS	IRRADIATION
INVIGILATED	INVITINGNESS	IODISATION	IRENOLOGIES	IRRADIATIONS
INVIGILATES	INVITINGNESSES	IODISATIONS	IRIDACEOUS	IRRADIATIVE
INVIGILATING	INVOCATING	IODIZATION	IRIDECTOMIES	IRRADIATOR
INVIGILATION	INVOCATION	IODIZATIONS	IRIDECTOMY	IRRADIATORS
INVIGILATIONS	INVOCATIONAL	IODOMETRIC	IRIDESCENCE	IRRADICABLE
INVIGILATOR	INVOCATIONS	IODOMETRICAL	IRIDESCENCES	IRRADICABLY
INVIGILATORS	INVOCATIVE	IODOMETRICALLY	IRIDESCENT	IRRADICATE
INVIGORANT	INVOCATORS	IODOMETRIES	IRIDESCENTLY	IRRADICATED
INVIGORANTS	INVOCATORY	IONICITIES	IRIDISATION	IRRADICATES
INVIGORATE	INVOICINGS	IONISATION	IRIDISATIONS	IRRADICATING
INVIGORATED	INVOLUCELLA	IONISATIONS	IRIDIZATION	IRRATIONAL
INVIGORATES	INVOLUCELLATE	IONIZATION	IRIDIZATIONS	IRRATIONALISE
INVIGORATING	INVOLUCELLATED	IONIZATIONS	IRIDOCYTES	IRRATIONALISED
INVIGORATINGLY	INVOLUCELLUM	IONOPAUSES	IRIDOLOGIES	IRRATIONALISES
INVIGORATION	INVOLUCELS	IONOPHORES	IRIDOLOGIST	IRRATIONALISING
INVIGORATIONS	INVOLUCRAL	IONOPHORESES	IRIDOLOGISTS	IRRATIONALISM
INVIGORATIVE	INVOLUCRATE	IONOPHORESIS	IRIDOSMINE	IRRATIONALISMS
INVIGORATIVELY	INVOLUCRES	IONOSONDES	IRIDOSMINES	IRRATIONALIST
INVIGORATOR	INVOLUCRUM	IONOSPHERE	IRIDOSMIUM	IRRATIONALISTIC
INVIGORATORS	INVOLUNTARILY	IONOSPHERES	IRIDOSMIUMS	IRRATIONALISTS
INVINCIBILITIES	INVOLUNTARINESS	IONOSPHERIC	IRIDOTOMIES	IRRATIONALITIES
INVINCIBILITY	INVOLUNTARY	IONOSPHERICALLY	IRISATIONS	IRRATIONALITY
INVINCIBLE	INVOLUTEDLY	IONOTROPIC	IRKSOMENESS	IRRATIONALIZE
INVINCIBLENESS	INVOLUTELY	IONOTROPIES	IRKSOMENESSES	IRRATIONALIZED
INVINCIBLY	INVOLUTING	IONTOPHORESES	IRONFISTED	IRRATIONALIZES
INVIOLABILITIES	INVOLUTION	IONTOPHORESIS	IRONHANDED	IRRATIONALIZING
INVIOLABILITY	INVOLUTIONAL	IONTOPHORETIC	IRONHEARTED	IRRATIONALLY
INVIOLABLE	INVOLUTIONS	IPECACUANHA	IRONICALLY	IRRATIONALNESS
INVIOLABLENESS	INVOLVEDLY	IPECACUANHAS	IRONICALNESS	IRRATIONALS
INVIOLABLY	INVOLVEMENT	IPRATROPIUM	IRONICALNESSES	IRREALISABLE
INVIOLACIES	INVOLVEMENTS	IPRATROPIUMS	IRONMASTER	IRREALITIES
INVIOLATED	INVULNERABILITY	IPRINDOLES	IRONMASTERS	IRREALIZABLE
INVIOLATELY	INVULNERABLE	IPRONIAZID	IRONMONGER	IRREBUTTABLE
INVIOLATENESS	INVULNERABLY	IPRONIAZIDS	IRONMONGERIES	IRRECEPTIVE
INVIOLATENESSES	INVULTUATION	IPSELATERAL	IRONMONGERS	IRRECIPROCAL
INVISIBILITIES	INVULTUATIONS	IPSILATERAL	IRONMONGERY	IRRECIPROCITIES
INVISIBILITY	INWARDNESS	IPSILATERALLY	IRONNESSES	IRRECIPROCITY
INVISIBLENESS	INWARDNESSES	IRACUNDITIES	IRONSMITHS	IRRECLAIMABLE
INVISIBLENESSES	INWORKINGS	IRACUNDITY	IRONSTONES	IRRECLAIMABLY
INVISIBLES	INWRAPMENT	IRACUNDULOUS	IRONWORKER	IRRECOGNISABLE

IRRECOGNITION	IRREGULARLY	IRREPREHENSIBLY	IRREVOCABILITY	ISOANTIBODY
IRRECOGNITIONS	IRREGULARS	IRREPRESSIBLE	IRREVOCABLE	ISOANTIGEN
IRRECOGNIZABLE	IRRELATION	IRREPRESSIBLY	IRREVOCABLENESS	ISOANTIGENIC
IRRECONCILABLE	IRRELATIONS	IRREPROACHABLE	IRREVOCABLY	ISOANTIGENS
IRRECONCILABLES	IRRELATIVE	IRREPROACHABLY	IRRIDENTAS	ISOBARISMS
IRRECONCILABLY	IRRELATIVELY	IRREPRODUCIBLE	IRRIGATING	ISOBAROMETRIC
IRRECONCILED	IRRELATIVENESS	IRREPROVABLE	IRRIGATION	ISOBILATERAL
IRRECONCILEMENT	IRRELEVANCE	IRREPROVABLY	IRRIGATIONAL	ISOBUTANES
IRRECOVERABLE	IRRELEVANCES	IRRESISTANCE	IRRIGATIONS	ISOBUTENES
IRRECOVERABLY	IRRELEVANCIES	IRRESISTANCES	IRRIGATIVE	ISOBUTYLENE
IRRECUSABLE	IRRELEVANCY	IRRESISTIBILITY	IRRIGATORS	ISOBUTYLENES
IRRECUSABLY	IRRELEVANT	IRRESISTIBLE	IRRITABILITIES	ISOCALORIC
IRREDEEMABILITY	IRRELEVANTLY	IRRESISTIBLY	IRRITABILITY	ISOCARBOXAZID
IRREDEEMABLE	IRRELIEVABLE	IRRESOLUBILITY	IRRITABLENESS	ISOCARBOXAZIDS
IRREDEEMABLES	IRRELIGION	IRRESOLUBLE	IRRITABLENESSES	ISOCHASMIC
IRREDEEMABLY	IRRELIGIONIST	IRRESOLUBLY	IRRITANCIES	ISOCHEIMAL
IRREDENTAS	IRRELIGIONISTS	IRRESOLUTE	IRRITATEDLY	ISOCHEIMALS
IRREDENTISM	IRRELIGIONS	IRRESOLUTELY	IRRITATING	ISOCHEIMENAL
IRREDENTISMS	IRRELIGIOUS	IRRESOLUTENESS	IRRITATINGLY	ISOCHEIMENALS
IRREDENTIST	IRRELIGIOUSLY	IRRESOLUTION	IRRITATION	ISOCHEIMIC
IRREDENTISTS	IRRELIGIOUSNESS	IRRESOLUTIONS	IRRITATIONS	ISOCHIMALS
IRREDUCIBILITY	IRREMEABLE	IRRESOLVABILITY	IRRITATIVE	ISOCHROMATIC
IRREDUCIBLE	IRREMEABLY	IRRESOLVABLE	IRRITATORS	ISOCHROMOSOME
IRREDUCIBLENESS	IRREMEDIABLE	IRRESOLVABLY	IRROTATIONAL	ISOCHROMOSOMES
IRREDUCIBLY	IRREMEDIABLY	IRRESPECTIVE	IRRUPTIONS	ISOCHRONAL
IRREDUCTIBILITY	IRREMISSIBILITY	IRRESPECTIVELY	IRRUPTIVELY	ISOCHRONALLY
IRREDUCTION	IRREMISSIBLE	IRRESPIRABLE	IRUKANDJIS	ISOCHRONES
IRREDUCTIONS	IRREMISSIBLY	IRRESPONSIBLE	ISABELLINE	ISOCHRONISE
IRREFLECTION	IRREMISSION	IRRESPONSIBLES	ISABELLINES	ISOCHRONISED
IRREFLECTIONS	IRREMISSIONS	IRRESPONSIBLY	ISALLOBARIC	ISOCHRONISES
IRREFLECTIVE	IRREMISSIVE	IRRESPONSIVE	ISALLOBARS	ISOCHRONISING
IRREFLEXION	IRREMOVABILITY	IRRESPONSIVELY	ISAPOSTOLIC	ISOCHRONISM
IRREFLEXIONS	IRREMOVABLE	IRRESTRAINABLE	ISCHAEMIAS	ISOCHRONISMS
IRREFLEXIVE	IRREMOVABLENESS	IRRESUSCITABLE	ISCHURETIC	ISOCHRONIZE
IRREFORMABILITY	IRREMOVABLY	IRRESUSCITABLY	ISCHURETICS	ISOCHRONIZED
IRREFORMABLE	IRRENOWNED	IRRETENTION	ISEIKONIAS	ISOCHRONIZES
IRREFORMABLY	IRREPAIRABLE	IRRETENTIONS	ISENTROPIC	ISOCHRONIZING
IRREFRAGABILITY	IRREPARABILITY	IRRETENTIVE	ISENTROPICALLY	ISOCHRONOUS
IRREFRAGABLE	IRREPARABLE	IRRETENTIVENESS	ISINGLASSES	ISOCHRONOUSLY
IRREFRAGABLY	IRREPARABLENESS	IRRETRIEVABLE	ISLOMANIAS	ISOCHROOUS
IRREFRANGIBLE	IRREPARABLY	IRRETRIEVABLY	ISMATICALNESS	ISOCLINALS
IRREFRANGIBLY	IRREPEALABILITY	IRREVERENCE	ISMATICALNESSES	ISOCLINICS
IRREFUTABILITY	IRREPEALABLE	IRREVERENCES	ISOAGGLUTININ	ISOCRACIES
IRREFUTABLE	IRREPEALABLY	IRREVERENT	ISOAGGLUTININS	ISOCRYMALS
IRREFUTABLENESS	IRREPLACEABLE	IRREVERENTIAL	ISOALLOXAZINE	ISOCYANATE
IRREFUTABLY	IRREPLACEABLY	IRREVERENTLY	ISOALLOXAZINES	ISOCYANATES
IRREGARDLESS	IRREPLEVIABLE	IRREVERSIBILITY	ISOAMINILE	ISOCYANIDE
IRREGULARITIES	IRREPLEVISABLE	IRREVERSIBLE	ISOAMINILES	ISOCYANIDES
IRREGULARITY	IRREPREHENSIBLE	IRREVERSIBLY	ISOANTIBODIES	ISODIAMETRIC

ISODIAMETRICAL	ISOLATABLE	ISOPACHYTE	ISOTENISCOPES	ITALICIZED
ISODIAPHERE	ISOLATIONISM	ISOPACHYTES	ISOTHERALS	ITALICIZES
ISODIAPHERES	ISOLATIONISMS	ISOPERIMETER	ISOTHERMAL	ITALICIZING
ISODIMORPHIC	ISOLATIONIST	ISOPERIMETERS	ISOTHERMALLY	ITCHINESSES
ISODIMORPHISM	ISOLATIONISTS	ISOPERIMETRICAL	ISOTHERMALS	ITEMISATION
ISODIMORPHISMS	ISOLATIONS	ISOPERIMETRIES	ISOTONICALLY	ITEMISATIONS
ISODIMORPHOUS	ISOLECITHAL	ISOPERIMETRY	ISOTONICITIES	ITEMIZATION
ISODONTALS	ISOLEUCINE	ISOPIESTIC	ISOTONICITY	ITEMIZATIONS
ISODYNAMIC	ISOLEUCINES	ISOPIESTICALLY	ISOTOPICALLY	ITERATIONS
ISODYNAMICS	ISOMAGNETIC	ISOPLETHIC	ISOTRETINOIN	ITERATIVELY
ISOELECTRIC	ISOMAGNETICS	ISOPLUVIAL	ISOTRETINOINS	ITERATIVENESS
ISOELECTRONIC	ISOMERASES	ISOPLUVIALS	ISOTROPICALLY	ITERATIVENESSES
ISOENZYMATIC	ISOMERISATION	ISOPOLITIES	ISOTROPIES	ITEROPARITIES
ISOENZYMES	ISOMERISATIONS	ISOPRENALINE	ISOTROPISM	ITEROPARITY
ISOENZYMIC	ISOMERISED	ISOPRENALINES	ISOTROPISMS	ITEROPAROUS
ISOFLAVONE	ISOMERISES	ISOPRENOID	ISOTROPOUS	ITHYPHALLI
ISOFLAVONES	ISOMERISING	ISOPRENOIDS	ISOXSUPRINE	ITHYPHALLIC
ISOGAMETES	ISOMERISMS	ISOPROPYLS	ISOXSUPRINES	ITHYPHALLICS
ISOGAMETIC	ISOMERIZATION	ISOPROTERENOL	ISPAGHULAS	ITHYPHALLUS
ISOGENETIC	ISOMERIZATIONS	ISOPROTERENOLS	ITACOLUMITE	ITHYPHALLUSES
ISOGEOTHERM	ISOMERIZED	ISOPTERANS	ITACOLUMITES	ITINERACIES
ISOGEOTHERMAL	ISOMERIZES	ISOPTEROUS	ITALIANATE	ITINERANCIES
ISOGEOTHERMALS	ISOMERIZING	ISOPYCNALS	ITALIANATED	ITINERANCY
ISOGEOTHERMIC	ISOMETRICAL	ISOPYCNICS	ITALIANATES	ITINERANTLY
ISOGEOTHERMICS	ISOMETRICALLY	ISORHYTHMIC	ITALIANATING	ITINERANTS
ISOGEOTHERMS	ISOMETRICS	ISOSEISMAL	ITALIANISE	ITINERARIES
ISOGLOSSAL	ISOMETRIES	ISOSEISMALS	ITALIANISED	ITINERATED
ISOGLOSSES	ISOMETROPIA	ISOSEISMIC	ITALIANISES	ITINERATES
ISOGLOSSIC	ISOMETROPIAS	ISOSEISMICS	ITALIANISING	ITINERATING
ISOGLOTTAL	ISOMORPHIC	ISOSMOTICALLY	ITALIANIZE	ITINERATION
ISOGLOTTIC	ISOMORPHICALLY	ISOSPONDYLOUS	ITALIANIZED	ITINERATIONS
ISOGRAFTED	ISOMORPHISM	ISOSPORIES	ITALIANIZES	IVERMECTIN
ISOGRAFTING	ISOMORPHISMS	ISOSPOROUS	ITALIANIZING	IVERMECTINS
ISOHYETALS	ISOMORPHOUS	ISOSTACIES	ITALICISATION	IVORYBILLS
ISOIMMUNISATION	ISONIAZIDE	ISOSTASIES	ITALICISATIONS	IVORYWOODS
ISOIMMUNIZATION	ISONIAZIDES	ISOSTATICALLY	ITALICISED	IZVESTIYAS
ISOKINETIC	ISONIAZIDS	ISOSTEMONOUS	ITALICISES	
ISOKONTANS	ISONITRILE	ISOSTHENURIA	ITALICISING	
ISOLABILITIES	ISONITRILES	ISOSTHENURIAS	ITALICIZATION	
ISOLABILITY	ISOOCTANES	ISOTENISCOPE	ITALICIZATIONS	

J

JABBERINGLY	JACKSCREWS	JAMBOKKING	JASPERIZED	JELLYBEANS
JABBERINGS	JACKSHAFTS	JAMBOLANAS	JASPERIZES	JELLYFISHES
JABBERWOCK	JACKSMELTS	JAMBUSTERS	JASPERIZING	JELLYGRAPH
JABBERWOCKIES	JACKSMITHS	JANISARIES	JASPERWARE	JELLYGRAPHED
JABBERWOCKS	JACKSNIPES	JANISSARIES	JASPERWARES	JELLYGRAPHING
JABBERWOCKY	JACKSTAFFS	JANITORIAL	JASPIDEOUS	JELLYGRAPHS
JABORANDIS	JACKSTAVES	JANITORSHIP	JASPILITES	JELLYROLLS
JABOTICABA	JACKSTONES	JANITORSHIPS	JAUNDICING	JEMMINESSES
JABOTICABAS	JACKSTRAWS	JANITRESSES	JAUNTINESS	JENNETINGS
JACARANDAS	JACQUERIES	JANITRIXES	JAUNTINESSES	JEOPARDERS
JACKALLING	JACTATIONS	JANIZARIAN	JAUNTINGLY	JEOPARDIED
JACKALOPES	JACTITATION	JANIZARIES	JAVELINING	JEOPARDIES
JACKANAPES	JACTITATIONS	JANNEYINGS	JAWBATIONS	JEOPARDING
JACKANAPESES	JACULATING	JAPANISING	JAWBONINGS	JEOPARDISE
JACKAROOED	JACULATION	JAPANIZING	JAWBREAKER	JEOPARDISED
JACKAROOING	JACULATIONS	JAPONAISERIE	JAWBREAKERS	JEOPARDISES
JACKASSERIES	JACULATORS	JAPONAISERIES	JAWBREAKING	JEOPARDISING
JACKASSERY	JACULATORY	JARDINIERE	JAWBREAKINGLY	JEOPARDIZE
JACKBOOTED	JADEDNESSES	JARDINIERES	JAWCRUSHER	JEOPARDIZED
JACKBOOTING	JADISHNESS	JARGONEERS	JAWCRUSHERS	JEOPARDIZES
JACKEROOED	JADISHNESSES	JARGONELLE	JAYHAWKERS	JEOPARDIZING
JACKEROOING	JAGDWURSTS	JARGONELLES	JAYWALKERS	JEOPARDOUS
JACKETLESS	JAGGEDNESS	JARGONIEST	JAYWALKING	JEOPARDOUSLY
JACKFISHES	JAGGEDNESSES	JARGONISATION	JAYWALKINGS	JEOPARDYING
JACKFRUITS	JAGGHERIES	JARGONISATIONS	JAZZINESSES	JEQUERITIES
JACKHAMMER	JAGHIRDARS	JARGONISED	JEALOUSEST	JEQUIRITIES
JACKHAMMERED	JAGUARONDI	JARGONISES	JEALOUSHOOD	JERFALCONS
JACKHAMMERING	JAGUARONDIS	JARGONISING	JEALOUSHOODS	JERKINESSES
JACKHAMMERS	JAGUARUNDI	JARGONISTIC	JEALOUSIES	JERKINHEAD
JACKKNIFED	JAGUARUNDIS	JARGONISTS	JEALOUSING	JERKINHEADS
JACKKNIFES	JAILBREAKER	JARGONIZATION	JEALOUSNESS	JERKWATERS
JACKKNIFING	JAILBREAKERS	JARGONIZATIONS	JEALOUSNESSES	JERRYMANDER
JACKKNIVES	JAILBREAKING	JARGONIZED	JEANSWEARS	JERRYMANDERED
JACKLIGHTED	JAILBREAKS	JARGONIZES	JEISTIECOR	JERRYMANDERING
JACKLIGHTING	JAILBROKEN	JARGONIZING	JEISTIECORS	JERRYMANDERS
JACKLIGHTS	JAILERESSES	JARLSBERGS	JEJUNENESS	JESSAMINES
JACKPLANES	JAILHOUSES	JAROVISING	JEJUNENESSES	JESSERANTS
JACKPOTTED	JAILORESSES	JAROVIZING	JEJUNITIES	JETSTREAMS
JACKPOTTING	JALOALLOFANE	JASMONATES	JEJUNOSTOMIES	JETTATURAS
JACKRABBIT	JALOALLOFANES	JASPERIEST	JEJUNOSTOMY	JETTINESSES
JACKRABBITS	JAMAHIRIYA	JASPERISED	JELLIFICATION	JETTISONABLE
JACKROLLED	JAMAHIRIYAS	JASPERISES	JELLIFICATIONS	JETTISONED
JACKROLLING	JAMBALAYAS	JASPERISING	JELLIFYING	JETTISONING

JEWELFISHES	JOCULARITIES	JOURNALISER	JUBILARIANS	JUNGLEGYMS
JEWELLERIES	JOCULARITY	JOURNALISERS	JUBILATING	JUNGLELIKE
JEWELWEEDS	JOCULATORS	JOURNALISES	JUBILATION	JUNIORATES
JICKAJOGGED	JOCUNDITIES	JOURNALISING	JUBILATIONS	JUNIORITIES
JICKAJOGGING	JOCUNDNESS	JOURNALISM	JUDDERIEST	JUNKERDOMS
JICKAJOGGINGS	JOCUNDNESSES	JOURNALISMS	JUDGEMENTAL	JUNKETEERED
JIGAJIGGED	JOGTROTTED	JOURNALIST	JUDGEMENTALLY	JUNKETEERING
JIGAJIGGING	JOGTROTTING	JOURNALISTIC	JUDGEMENTS	JUNKETEERS
JIGAJOGGED	JOHANNESES	JOURNALISTS	JUDGESHIPS	JUNKETINGS
JIGAJOGGING	JOHNNYCAKE	JOURNALIZATION	JUDGMATICAL	JUNKETTERS
JIGAMAREES	JOHNNYCAKES	JOURNALIZATIONS	JUDGMATICALLY	JUNKETTING
JIGGERMAST	JOHNSONGRASS	JOURNALIZE	JUDGMENTAL	JUNKINESSES
JIGGERMASTS	JOHNSONGRASSES	JOURNALIZED	JUDGMENTALLY	JURIDICALLY
JIGGUMBOBS	JOINTEDNESS	JOURNALIZER	JUDICATION	JURISCONSULT
JILLFLIRTS	JOINTEDNESSES	JOURNALIZERS	JUDICATIONS	JURISCONSULTS
JIMPNESSES	JOINTNESSES	JOURNALIZES	JUDICATIVE	JURISDICTION
JIMSONWEED	JOINTRESSES	JOURNALIZING	JUDICATORIAL	JURISDICTIONAL
JIMSONWEEDS	JOINTURESS	JOURNALLED	JUDICATORIES	JURISDICTIONS
JINGOISTIC	JOINTURESSES	JOURNALLING	JUDICATORS	JURISDICTIVE
JINGOISTICALLY	JOINTURING	JOURNALLINGS	JUDICATORY	JURISPRUDENCE
JINRICKSHA	JOINTWEEDS	JOURNEYERS	JUDICATURE	JURISPRUDENCES
JINRICKSHAS	JOINTWORMS	JOURNEYING	JUDICATURES	JURISPRUDENT
JINRICKSHAW	JOKESMITHS	JOURNEYMAN	JUDICIALLY	JURISPRUDENTIAL
JINRICKSHAWS	JOKINESSES	JOURNEYMEN	JUDICIARIES	JURISPRUDENTS
JINRIKISHA	JOLIOTIUMS	JOURNEYWORK	JUDICIARILY	JURISTICAL
JINRIKISHAS	JOLLEYINGS	JOURNEYWORKS	JUDICIOUSLY	JURISTICALLY
JINRIKSHAS	JOLLIFICATION	JOUYSAUNCE	JUDICIOUSNESS	JUSTICESHIP
JITTERBUGGED	JOLLIFICATIONS	JOUYSAUNCES	JUDICIOUSNESSES	JUSTICESHIPS
JITTERBUGGING	JOLLIFYING	JOVIALITIES	JUGGERNAUT	JUSTICIABILITY
JITTERBUGS	JOLLIMENTS	JOVIALNESS	JUGGERNAUTS	JUSTICIABLE
JITTERIEST	JOLLINESSES	JOVIALNESSES	JUGGLERIES	JUSTICIALISM
JITTERINESS	JOLLYBOATS	JOVIALTIES	JUGGLINGLY	JUSTICIALISMS
JITTERINESSES	JOLLYHEADS	JOVYSAUNCE	JUGLANDACEOUS	JUSTICIARIES
JOBCENTRES	JOLTERHEAD	JOVYSAUNCES	JUGULATING	JUSTICIARS
JOBERNOWLS	JOLTERHEADS	JOWLINESSES	JUGULATION	JUSTICIARSHIP
JOBHOLDERS	JONNYCAKES	JOYFULLEST	JUGULATIONS	JUSTICIARSHIPS
JOBLESSNESS	JOSEPHINITE	JOYFULNESS	JUICEHEADS	JUSTICIARY
JOBLESSNESSES	JOSEPHINITES	JOYFULNESSES	JUICINESSES	JUSTIFIABILITY
JOBSEEKERS	JOSTLEMENT	JOYLESSNESS	JULIENNING	JUSTIFIABLE
JOBSWORTHS	JOSTLEMENTS	JOYLESSNESSES	JUMBLINGLY	JUSTIFIABLENESS
JOCKEYISMS	JOUISANCES	JOYOUSNESS	JUMBOISING	JUSTIFIABLY
JOCKEYSHIP	JOURNALESE	JOYOUSNESSES	JUMBOIZING	JUSTIFICATION
JOCKEYSHIPS	JOURNALESES	JOYPOPPERS	JUMHOURIYA	JUSTIFICATIONS
JOCKSTRAPS	JOURNALING	JOYPOPPING	JUMHOURIYAS	JUSTIFICATIVE
JOCKTELEGS	JOURNALINGS	JOYRIDINGS	JUMPINESSES	JUSTIFICATOR
JOCOSENESS	JOURNALISATION	JUBILANCES	JUMPSCARES	JUSTIFICATORS
JOCOSENESSES	JOURNALISATIONS	JUBILANCIES	JUNCACEOUS	JUSTIFICATORY
JOCOSERIOUS	JOURNALISE	JUBILANTLY	JUNCTIONAL	JUSTIFIERS
JOCOSITIES	JOURNALISED	JUBILARIAN	JUNEATINGS	JUSTIFYING

JUSTNESSES	JUVENESCENT	JUVENILENESSES	JUXTAPOSED	JUXTAPOSITION
JUVENESCENCE	JUVENILELY	JUVENILITIES	JUXTAPOSES	JUXTAPOSITIONAL
JUVENESCENCES	JUVENILENESS	JUVENILITY	JUXTAPOSING	JUXTAPOSITIONS

J

K

KABALISTIC	KALSOMINES	KARYOLOGISTS	KEELYVINES	KERATOMATA
KABARAGOYA	KALSOMINING	KARYOLYMPH	KEENNESSES	KERATOMETER
KABARAGOYAS	KAMELAUKION	KARYOLYMPHS	KEEPERLESS	KERATOMETERS
KABBALISMS	KAMELAUKIONS	KARYOLYSES	KEEPERSHIP	KERATOPHYRE
KABBALISTIC	KAMERADING	KARYOLYSIS	KEEPERSHIPS	KERATOPHYRES
KABBALISTS	KANAMYCINS	KARYOLYTIC	KEEPSAKIER	KERATOPLASTIC
KABELJOUWS	KANGAROOED	KARYOMAPPING	KEEPSAKIEST	KERATOPLASTIES
KACHAHARIS	KANGAROOING	KARYOMAPPINGS	KEESHONDEN	KERATOPLASTY
KACHUMBERS	KANTIKOYED	KARYOPLASM	KEFUFFLING	KERATOTOMIES
KADAITCHAS	KANTIKOYING	KARYOPLASMIC	KEKERENGUS	KERATOTOMY
KAFFEEKLATSCH	KAOLINISED	KARYOPLASMS	KELPFISHES	KERAUNOGRAPH
KAFFEEKLATSCHES	KAOLINISES	KARYOSOMES	KELYPHITIC	KERAUNOGRAPHS
KAHIKATEAS	KAOLINISING	KARYOTYPED	KENNELLING	KERBLOOEYS
KAHIKATOAS	KAOLINITES	KARYOTYPES	KENNETTING	KERBSTONES
KAIKAWAKAS	KAOLINITIC	KARYOTYPIC	KENOGENESES	KERCHIEFED
KAIKOMAKOS	KAOLINIZED	KARYOTYPICAL	KENOGENESIS	KERCHIEFING
KAILYAIRDS	KAOLINIZES	KARYOTYPICALLY	KENOGENETIC	KERCHIEVES
KAINOGENESES	KAOLINIZING	KARYOTYPING	KENOGENETICALLY	KERFUFFLED
KAINOGENESIS	KAOLINOSES	KATABOLICALLY	KENOPHOBIA	KERFUFFLES
KAINOGENETIC	KAOLINOSIS	KATABOLISM	KENOPHOBIAS	KERFUFFLING
KAIROMONES	KAPELLMEISTER	KATABOLISMS	KENOTICIST	KERMESITES
KAISERDOMS	KAPELLMEISTERS	KATABOTHRON	KENOTICISTS	KERNELLIER
KAISERISMS	KARABINERS	KATABOTHRONS	KENSPECKLE	KERNELLIEST
KAISERSHIP	KARANGAING	KATADROMOUS	KENTLEDGES	KERNELLING
KAISERSHIPS	KARATEISTS	KATATHERMOMETER	KERATECTOMIES	KERNICTERUS
KAKISTOCRACIES	KARMICALLY	KATAVOTHRON	KERATECTOMY	KERNICTERUSES
KAKISTOCRACY	KARSTIFICATION	KATAVOTHRONS	KERATINISATION	KERNMANTEL
KALAMKARIS	KARSTIFICATIONS	KATHAKALIS	KERATINISATIONS	KERPLUNKED
KALANCHOES	KARSTIFIED	KATHAREVOUSA	KERATINISE	KERPLUNKING
KALASHNIKOV	KARSTIFIES	KATHAREVOUSAS	KERATINISED	KERSANTITE
KALASHNIKOVS	KARSTIFYING	KATHAROMETER	KERATINISES	KERSANTITES
KALEIDOPHONE	KARUHIRUHI	KATHAROMETERS	KERATINISING	KERSEYMERE
KALEIDOPHONES	KARUHIRUHIS	KATZENJAMMER	KERATINIZATION	KERSEYMERES
KALEIDOSCOPE	KARYOGAMIC	KATZENJAMMERS	KERATINIZATIONS	KERYGMATIC
KALEIDOSCOPES	KARYOGAMIES	KAWANATANGA	KERATINIZE	KETCHUPIER
KALEIDOSCOPIC	KARYOGRAMS	KAWANATANGAS	KERATINIZED	KETCHUPIEST
KALENDARED	KARYOKINESES	KAZATSKIES	KERATINIZES	KETOACIDOSES
KALENDARING	KARYOKINESIS	KAZILLIONS	KERATINIZING	KETOACIDOSIS
KALIPHATES	KARYOKINETIC	KEELHALING	KERATINOPHILIC	KETOGENESES
KALLIKREIN	KARYOLOGIC	KEELHAULED	KERATINOUS	KETOGENESIS
KALLIKREINS	KARYOLOGICAL	KEELHAULING	KERATITIDES	KETONAEMIA
KALLITYPES	KARYOLOGIES	KEELHAULINGS	KERATITISES	KETONAEMIAS
KALSOMINED	KARYOLOGIST	KEELIVINES	KERATOGENOUS	KETONEMIAS

KETONURIAS	KIBBITZERS	KILOCURIES	KINEMATOGRAPHIC	KINGFISHES
KETOSTEROID	KIBBITZING	KILOCYCLES	KINEMATOGRAPHS	KINGLIHOOD
KETOSTEROIDS	KIBBUTZNIK	KILOGAUSSES	KINEMATOGRAPHY	KINGLIHOODS
KETTLEBELL	KIBBUTZNIKS	KILOGRAMME	KINESCOPED	KINGLINESS
KETTLEBELLS	KICKABOUTS	KILOGRAMMES	KINESCOPES	KINGLINESSES
KETTLEDRUM	KICKAROUND	KILOHERTZES	KINESCOPING	KINGMAKERS
KETTLEDRUMMER	KICKAROUNDS	KILOJOULES	KINESIATRIC	KINGSNAKES
KETTLEDRUMMERS	KICKBOARDS	KILOLITERS	KINESIATRICS	KINKINESSES
KETTLEDRUMS	KICKBOXERS	KILOLITRES	KINESIOLOGIES	KINNIKINIC
KETTLEFULS	KICKBOXING	KILOMETERS	KINESIOLOGIST	KINNIKINICK
KETTLESTITCH	KICKBOXINGS	KILOMETRES	KINESIOLOGISTS	KINNIKINICKS
KETTLESTITCHES	KICKFLIPPED	KILOMETRIC	KINESIOLOGY	KINNIKINICS
KEYBOARDED	KICKFLIPPING	KILOMETRICAL	KINESIPATH	KINNIKINNICK
KEYBOARDER	KICKPLATES	KILOPARSEC	KINESIPATHIC	KINNIKINNICKS
KEYBOARDERS	KICKSHAWSES	KILOPARSECS	KINESIPATHIES	KINTLEDGES
KEYBOARDING	KICKSORTER	KILOPASCAL	KINESIPATHIST	KIRBIGRIPS
KEYBOARDINGS	KICKSORTERS	KILOPASCALS	KINESIPATHISTS	KIRKYAIRDS
KEYBOARDIST	KICKSTANDS	KILOTONNES	KINESIPATHS	KIRSCHWASSER
KEYBOARDISTS	KICKSTARTED	KIMBERLITE	KINESIPATHY	KIRSCHWASSERS
KEYBUTTONS	KICKSTARTING	KIMBERLITES	KINESITHERAPIES	KISSAGRAMS
KEYLOGGERS	KICKSTARTS	KINAESTHESES	KINESITHERAPY	KISSOGRAMS
KEYLOGGING	KIDDIEWINK	KINAESTHESIA	KINESTHESES	KISSPEPTIN
KEYLOGGINGS	KIDDIEWINKIE	KINAESTHESIAS	KINESTHESIA	KISSPEPTINS
KEYPRESSES	KIDDIEWINKIES	KINAESTHESIS	KINESTHESIAS	KITCHENALIA
KEYPUNCHED	KIDDIEWINKS	KINAESTHETIC	KINESTHESIS	KITCHENALIAS
KEYPUNCHER	KIDDISHNESS	KINDERGARTEN	KINESTHETIC	KITCHENDOM
KEYPUNCHERS	KIDDISHNESSES	KINDERGARTENER	KINESTHETICALLY	KITCHENDOMS
KEYPUNCHES	KIDDYWINKS	KINDERGARTENERS	KINETHEODOLITE	KITCHENERS
KEYPUNCHING	KIDNAPINGS	KINDERGARTENS	KINETHEODOLITES	KITCHENETS
KEYSTONING	KIDNAPPEES	KINDERGARTNER	KINETICALLY	KITCHENETTE
KEYSTROKED	KIDNAPPERS	KINDERGARTNERS	KINETICIST	KITCHENETTES
KEYSTROKES	KIDNAPPING	KINDERSPIEL	KINETICISTS	KITCHENING
KEYSTROKING	KIDNAPPINGS	KINDERSPIELS	KINETOCHORE	KITCHENMAID
KEYSTROKINGS	KIDNEYLIKE	KINDHEARTED	KINETOCHORES	KITCHENMAIDS
KEYWORKERS	KIDOLOGIES	KINDHEARTEDLY	KINETOGRAPH	KITCHENWARE
KHALIFATES	KIDOLOGIST	KINDHEARTEDNESS	KINETOGRAPHS	KITCHENWARES
KHANSAMAHS	KIDOLOGISTS	KINDLESSLY	KINETONUCLEI	KITEBOARDS
KHEDIVATES	KIESELGUHR	KINDLINESS	KINETONUCLEUS	KITESURFER
KHEDIVIATE	KIESELGUHRS	KINDLINESSES	KINETONUCLEUSES	KITESURFERS
KHEDIVIATES	KIESELGURS	KINDNESSES	KINETOPLAST	KITESURFING
KHIDMATGAR	KIESERITES	KINDREDNESS	KINETOPLASTS	KITESURFINGS
KHIDMATGARS	KILDERKINS	KINDREDNESSES	KINETOSCOPE	KITSCHIEST
KHIDMUTGAR	KILLIFISHES	KINDREDSHIP	KINETOSCOPES	KITSCHIFIED
KHIDMUTGARS	KILLIKINICK	KINDREDSHIPS	KINETOSOME	KITSCHIFIES
KHITMATGAR	KILLIKINICKS	KINEMATICAL	KINETOSOMES	KITSCHIFYING
KHITMATGARS	KILOAMPERE	KINEMATICALLY	KINGCRAFTS	KITSCHNESS
KHITMUTGAR	KILOAMPERES	KINEMATICS	KINGDOMLESS	KITSCHNESSES
KHITMUTGARS	KILOCALORIE	KINEMATOGRAPH	KINGFISHER	KITTENIEST
KHUSKHUSES	KILOCALORIES	KINEMATOGRAPHER	KINGFISHERS	KITTENISHLY

KITTENISHNESS	KNACKINESS	KNOBBLIEST	KOEKSISTERS	KRIEGSSPIEL
KITTENISHNESSES	KNACKINESSES	KNOBKERRIE	KOHLRABIES	KRIEGSSPIELS
KITTIWAKES	KNACKWURST	KNOBKERRIES	KOHUTUHUTU	KROMESKIES
KIWIFRUITS	KNACKWURSTS	KNOBSTICKS	KOHUTUHUTUS	KRUGERRAND
KIWISPORTS	KNAGGINESS	KNOCKABOUT	KOLINSKIES	KRUGERRANDS
KLANGFARBE	KNAGGINESSES	KNOCKABOUTS	KOLKHOZNIK	KRUMMHORNS
KLANGFARBES	KNAPSACKED	KNOCKBACKS	KOLKHOZNIKI	KRYOMETERS
KLEBSIELLA	KNAVESHIPS	KNOCKDOWNS	KOLKHOZNIKS	KRYPTONITE
KLEBSIELLAS	KNAVISHNESS	KNOCKWURST	KOMONDOROCK	KRYPTONITES
KLEINHUISIE	KNAVISHNESSES	KNOCKWURSTS	KOMONDOROK	KUMARAHOUS
KLEINHUISIES	KNEEBOARDED	KNOTGRASSES	KOMPROMATS	KUMMERBUND
KLENDUSITIES	KNEEBOARDING	KNOTTINESS	KONIMETERS	KUMMERBUNDS
KLENDUSITY	KNEEBOARDS	KNOTTINESSES	KONIOLOGIES	KUNDALINIS
KLEPHTISMS	KNEECAPPED	KNOWABLENESS	KONISCOPES	KURBASHING
KLEPTOCRACIES	KNEECAPPING	KNOWABLENESSES	KOOKABURRA	KURCHATOVIUM
KLEPTOCRACY	KNEECAPPINGS	KNOWINGEST	KOOKABURRAS	KURCHATOVIUMS
KLEPTOCRAT	KNEEPIECES	KNOWINGNESS	KOOKINESSES	KURDAITCHA
KLEPTOCRATIC	KNEVELLING	KNOWINGNESSES	KOTAHITANGA	KURDAITCHAS
KLEPTOCRATS	KNICKERBOCKER	KNOWLEDGABILITY	KOTAHITANGAS	KURFUFFLED
KLEPTOMANIA	KNICKERBOCKERS	KNOWLEDGABLE	KOTTABOSES	KURFUFFLES
KLEPTOMANIAC	KNICKKNACK	KNOWLEDGABLY	KOTUKUTUKU	KURFUFFLING
KLEPTOMANIACS	KNICKKNACKS	KNOWLEDGEABLE	KOTUKUTUKUS	KURRAJONGS
KLEPTOMANIAS	KNICKPOINT	KNOWLEDGEABLY	KOULIBIACA	KURTOSISES
KLETTERSCHUH	KNICKPOINTS	KNOWLEDGED	KOULIBIACAS	KVETCHIEST
KLETTERSCHUHE	KNIFEPOINT	KNOWLEDGES	KOURBASHED	KVETCHINESS
KLINOSTATS	KNIFEPOINTS	KNOWLEDGING	KOURBASHES	KVETCHINESSES
KLIPSPRINGER	KNIFERESTS	KNUBBLIEST	KOURBASHING	KVETCHINGS
KLIPSPRINGERS	KNIGHTAGES	KNUCKLEBALL	KOUSKOUSES	KWASHIORKOR
KLONDIKERS	KNIGHTHEAD	KNUCKLEBALLER	KOWHAIWHAI	KWASHIORKORS
KLONDIKING	KNIGHTHEADS	KNUCKLEBALLERS	KOWHAIWHAIS	KYANISATION
KLONDYKERS	KNIGHTHOOD	KNUCKLEBALLS	KRAKOWIAKS	KYANISATIONS
KLONDYKING	KNIGHTHOODS	KNUCKLEBONE	KRAUTROCKS	KYANIZATION
KLOOCHMANS	KNIGHTLESS	KNUCKLEBONES	KREASOTING	KYANIZATIONS
KLOOTCHMAN	KNIGHTLIER	KNUCKLEDUSTER	KREMLINOLOGIES	KYMOGRAPHIC
KLOOTCHMANS	KNIGHTLIEST	KNUCKLEDUSTERS	KREMLINOLOGIST	KYMOGRAPHIES
KLOOTCHMEN	KNIGHTLINESS	KNUCKLEHEAD	KREMLINOLOGISTS	KYMOGRAPHS
KLUTZINESS	KNIGHTLINESSES	KNUCKLEHEADED	KREMLINOLOGY	KYMOGRAPHY
KLUTZINESSES	KNIPHOFIAS	KNUCKLEHEADS	KREOSOTING	
KNACKERIES	KNOBBINESS	KNUCKLIEST	KRIEGSPIEL	
KNACKERING	KNOBBINESSES	KOEKSISTER	KRIEGSPIELS	

K

L

LABANOTATION	LABOURISMS	LACHRYMATOR	LACTATIONALLY	LAEOTROPIC
LABANOTATIONS	LABOURISTS	LACHRYMATORIES	LACTATIONS	LAEVIGATED
LABDACISMS	LABOURITES	LACHRYMATORS	LACTESCENCE	LAEVIGATES
LABEFACTATION	LABOURSAVING	LACHRYMATORY	LACTESCENCES	LAEVIGATING
LABEFACTATIONS	LABOURSOME	LACHRYMOSE	LACTESCENT	LAEVOGYRATE
LABEFACTION	LABRADOODLE	LACHRYMOSELY	LACTIFEROUS	LAEVOGYRES
LABEFACTIONS	LABRADOODLES	LACHRYMOSITIES	LACTIFEROUSNESS	LAEVOROTARY
LABELLABLE	LABRADORESCENT	LACHRYMOSITY	LACTIFLUOUS	LAEVOROTATION
LABELLINGS	LABRADORITE	LACINESSES	LACTIVISMS	LAEVOROTATIONS
LABELLISTS	LABRADORITES	LACINIATED	LACTIVISTS	LAEVOROTATORY
LABELMATES	LABYRINTHAL	LACINIATION	LACTOBACILLI	LAEVULOSES
LABIALISATION	LABYRINTHIAN	LACINIATIONS	LACTOBACILLUS	LAGENIFORM
LABIALISATIONS	LABYRINTHIC	LACKADAISICAL	LACTOFLAVIN	LAGERPHONE
LABIALISED	LABYRINTHICAL	LACKADAISICALLY	LACTOFLAVINS	LAGERPHONES
LABIALISES	LABYRINTHICALLY	LACKADAISY	LACTOGENIC	LAGGARDLIER
LABIALISING	LABYRINTHINE	LACKLUSTER	LACTOGLOBULIN	LAGGARDLIEST
LABIALISMS	LABYRINTHITIS	LACKLUSTERS	LACTOGLOBULINS	LAGGARDNESS
LABIALITIES	LABYRINTHITISES	LACKLUSTRE	LACTOMETER	LAGGARDNESSES
LABIALIZATION	LABYRINTHODONT	LACKLUSTRES	LACTOMETERS	LAGNIAPPES
LABIALIZATIONS	LABYRINTHODONTS	LACONICALLY	LACTOPROTEIN	LAGOMORPHIC
LABIALIZED	LABYRINTHS	LACONICISM	LACTOPROTEINS	LAGOMORPHOUS
LABIALIZES	LACCOLITES	LACONICISMS	LACTOSCOPE	LAGOMORPHS
LABIALIZING	LACCOLITHIC	LACQUERERS	LACTOSCOPES	LAICISATION
LABILITIES	LACCOLITHS	LACQUERING	LACTOSURIA	LAICISATIONS
LABIODENTAL	LACCOLITIC	LACQUERINGS	LACTOSURIAS	LAICIZATION
LABIODENTALS	LACEMAKERS	LACQUERWARE	LACTOVEGETARIAN	LAICIZATIONS
LABIONASAL	LACEMAKING	LACQUERWARES	LACTULOSES	LAIRDLIEST
LABIONASALS	LACEMAKINGS	LACQUERWORK	LACUNOSITIES	LAIRDSHIPS
LABIOVELAR	LACERABILITIES	LACQUERWORKS	LACUNOSITY	LAKEFRONTS
LABIOVELARS	LACERABILITY	LACQUEYING	LACUSTRINE	LAKESHORES
LABORATORIES	LACERATING	LACRIMARIES	LADDERIEST	LALAPALOOZA
LABORATORY	LACERATION	LACRIMATION	LADDERLIKE	LALAPALOOZAS
LABOREDNESS	LACERATIONS	LACRIMATIONS	LADDERPROOF	LALLAPALOOZA
LABOREDNESSES	LACERATIVE	LACRIMATOR	LADDISHNESS	LALLAPALOOZAS
LABORINGLY	LACERTIANS	LACRIMATORS	LADDISHNESSES	LALLATIONS
LABORIOUSLY	LACERTILIAN	LACRIMATORY	LADIESWEAR	LALLYGAGGED
LABORIOUSNESS	LACERTILIANS	LACRYMATOR	LADIESWEARS	LALLYGAGGING
LABORIOUSNESSES	LACERTINES	LACRYMATORS	LADYFINGER	LAMASERAIS
LABORSAVING	LACHRYMALS	LACRYMATORY	LADYFINGERS	LAMASERIES
LABOUREDLY	LACHRYMARIES	LACTALBUMIN	LADYFISHES	LAMBASTING
LABOUREDNESS	LACHRYMARY	LACTALBUMINS	LADYLIKENESS	LAMBDACISM
LABOUREDNESSES	LACHRYMATION	LACTARIANS	LADYLIKENESSES	LAMBDACISMS
LABOURINGLY	LACHRYMATIONS	LACTATIONAL	LADYNESSES	LAMBDOIDAL

LAMBENCIES	LAMINECTOMIES	LANDAULETS	LANDSCAPERS	LANKNESSES
LAMBITIVES	LAMINECTOMY	LANDAULETTE	LANDSCAPES	LANOSITIES
LAMBREQUIN	LAMINGTONS	LANDAULETTES	LANDSCAPING	LANSQUENET
LAMBREQUINS	LAMINITISES	LANDBOARDING	LANDSCAPINGS	LANSQUENETS
LAMBRUSCOS	LAMMERGEIER	LANDBOARDINGS	LANDSCAPIST	LANTERLOOS
LAMBSWOOLS	LAMMERGEIERS	LANDBOARDS	LANDSCAPISTS	LANTERNING
LAMEBRAINED	LAMMERGEYER	LANDDAMNED	LANDSHARKS	LANTERNIST
LAMEBRAINS	LAMMERGEYERS	LANDDAMNES	LANDSKIPPED	LANTERNISTS
LAMELLARLY	LAMPADARIES	LANDDAMNING	LANDSKIPPING	LANTHANIDE
LAMELLATED	LAMPADEDROMIES	LANDDROSES	LANDSKNECHT	LANTHANIDES
LAMELLATELY	LAMPADEDROMY	LANDDROSTS	LANDSKNECHTS	LANTHANONS
LAMELLATION	LAMPADEPHORIA	LANDFILLED	LANDSLIDDEN	LANTHANUMS
LAMELLATIONS	LAMPADEPHORIAS	LANDFILLING	LANDSLIDES	LANUGINOSE
LAMELLIBRANCH	LAMPADISTS	LANDFILLINGS	LANDSLIDING	LANUGINOUS
LAMELLIBRANCHS	LAMPADOMANCIES	LANDFORCES	LANDWAITER	LANUGINOUSNESS
LAMELLICORN	LAMPADOMANCY	LANDGRAVATE	LANDWAITERS	LANZKNECHT
LAMELLICORNS	LAMPBLACKED	LANDGRAVATES	LANDWASHES	LANZKNECHTS
LAMELLIFORM	LAMPBLACKING	LANDGRAVES	LANGBEINITE	LAODICEANS
LAMELLIROSTRAL	LAMPBLACKS	LANDGRAVIATE	LANGBEINITES	LAPAROSCOPE
LAMELLIROSTRATE	LAMPHOLDER	LANDGRAVIATES	LANGLAUFER	LAPAROSCOPES
LAMELLOSITIES	LAMPHOLDERS	LANDGRAVINE	LANGLAUFERS	LAPAROSCOPIC
LAMELLOSITY	LAMPLIGHTER	LANDGRAVINES	LANGOSTINO	LAPAROSCOPIES
LAMENESSES	LAMPLIGHTERS	LANDHOLDER	LANGOSTINOS	LAPAROSCOPIST
LAMENTABLE	LAMPLIGHTS	LANDHOLDERS	LANGOUSTES	LAPAROSCOPISTS
LAMENTABLENESS	LAMPOONERIES	LANDHOLDING	LANGOUSTINE	LAPAROSCOPY
LAMENTABLY	LAMPOONERS	LANDHOLDINGS	LANGOUSTINES	LAPAROTOMIES
LAMENTATION	LAMPOONERY	LANDLADIES	LANGRIDGES	LAPAROTOMY
LAMENTATIONS	LAMPOONING	LANDLESSNESS	LANGSPIELS	LAPIDARIAN
LAMENTEDLY	LAMPOONIST	LANDLESSNESSES	LANGUAGELESS	LAPIDARIES
LAMENTINGLY	LAMPOONISTS	LANDLOCKED	LANGUAGING	LAPIDARIST
LAMENTINGS	LAMPROPHYRE	LANDLOPERS	LANGUESCENT	LAPIDARISTS
LAMESTREAM	LAMPROPHYRES	LANDLORDISM	LANGUETTES	LAPIDATING
LAMESTREAMS	LAMPROPHYRIC	LANDLORDISMS	LANGUIDNESS	LAPIDATION
LAMINARIAN	LAMPSHADES	LANDLUBBER	LANGUIDNESSES	LAPIDATIONS
LAMINARIANS	LAMPSHELLS	LANDLUBBERLY	LANGUISHED	LAPIDESCENCE
LAMINARIAS	LAMPSTANDS	LANDLUBBERS	LANGUISHER	LAPIDESCENCES
LAMINARINS	LANCEJACKS	LANDLUBBING	LANGUISHERS	LAPIDESCENT
LAMINARISE	LANCEOLATE	LANDMARKED	LANGUISHES	LAPIDICOLOUS
LAMINARISED	LANCEOLATED	LANDMARKING	LANGUISHING	LAPIDIFICATION
LAMINARISES	LANCEOLATELY	LANDMASSES	LANGUISHINGLY	LAPIDIFICATIONS
LAMINARISING	LANCEWOODS	LANDMINING	LANGUISHINGS	LAPIDIFIED
LAMINARIZE	LANCINATED	LANDMININGS	LANGUISHMENT	LAPIDIFIES
LAMINARIZED	LANCINATES	LANDOWNERS	LANGUISHMENTS	LAPIDIFYING
LAMINARIZES	LANCINATING	LANDOWNERSHIP	LANGUOROUS	LAPILLIFORM
LAMINARIZING	LANCINATION	LANDOWNERSHIPS	LANGUOROUSLY	LAPSTRAKES
LAMINATING	LANCINATIONS	LANDOWNING	LANGUOROUSNESS	LAPSTREAKS
LAMINATION	LANDAMMANN	LANDOWNINGS	LANIFEROUS	LARCENISTS
LAMINATIONS	LANDAMMANNS	LANDSCAPED	LANIGEROUS	LARCENOUSLY
LAMINATORS	LANDAMMANS	LANDSCAPER	LANKINESSES	LARCHWOODS

LARDACEOUS	LARYNGOSPASM	LATHERIEST	LAUGHABLENESSES	LAVEROCKED
LARDALITES	LARYNGOSPASMS	LATHYRISMS	LAUGHINGLY	LAVEROCKING
LARGEHEARTED	LARYNGOTOMIES	LATHYRITIC	LAUGHINGSTOCK	LAVISHMENT
LARGEMOUTH	LARYNGOTOMY	LATHYRUSES	LAUGHINGSTOCKS	LAVISHMENTS
LARGEMOUTHS	LASCIVIOUS	LATICIFEROUS	LAUGHLINES	LAVISHNESS
LARGENESSES	LASCIVIOUSLY	LATICIFERS	LAUGHWORTHIER	LAVISHNESSES
LARGHETTOS	LASCIVIOUSNESS	LATICLAVES	LAUGHWORTHIEST	LAVOLTAING
LARGITIONS	LASERDISCS	LATIFUNDIA	LAUGHWORTHY	LAWBREAKER
LARKINESSES	LASERDISKS	LATIFUNDIO	LAUNCEGAYE	LAWBREAKERS
LARKISHNESS	LASERWORTS	LATIFUNDIOS	LAUNCEGAYES	LAWBREAKING
LARKISHNESSES	LASSITUDES	LATIFUNDIUM	LAUNCHINGS	LAWBREAKINGS
LARRIKINISM	LASTINGNESS	LATIMERIAS	LAUNCHPADS	LAWFULNESS
LARRIKINISMS	LASTINGNESSES	LATINISATION	LAUNDERERS	LAWFULNESSES
LARVACEOUS	LATCHSTRING	LATINISATIONS	LAUNDERETTE	LAWGIVINGS
LARVICIDAL	LATCHSTRINGS	LATINISING	LAUNDERETTES	LAWLESSNESS
LARVICIDED	LATECOMERS	LATINITIES	LAUNDERING	LAWLESSNESSES
LARVICIDES	LATEENRIGGED	LATINIZATION	LAUNDERINGS	LAWMAKINGS
LARVICIDING	LATENESSES	LATINIZATIONS	LAUNDRESSES	LAWMONGERS
LARVIKITES	LATENSIFICATION	LATINIZING	LAUNDRETTE	LAWNMOWERS
LARVIPAROUS	LATERALING	LATIROSTRAL	LAUNDRETTES	LAWRENCIUM
LARYNGEALLY	LATERALISATION	LATIROSTRATE	LAUNDRYMAN	LAWRENCIUMS
LARYNGEALS	LATERALISATIONS	LATISEPTATE	LAUNDRYMEN	LAWYERINGS
LARYNGECTOMEE	LATERALISE	LATITANCIES	LAUNDRYWOMAN	LAWYERLIER
LARYNGECTOMEES	LATERALISED	LATITATION	LAUNDRYWOMEN	LAWYERLIEST
LARYNGECTOMIES	LATERALISES	LATITATIONS	LAURACEOUS	LAWYERLIKE
LARYNGECTOMISED	LATERALISING	LATITUDINAL	LAURDALITE	LAXATIVENESS
LARYNGECTOMIZED	LATERALITIES	LATITUDINALLY	LAURDALITES	LAXATIVENESSES
LARYNGECTOMY	LATERALITY	LATITUDINARIAN	LAUREATESHIP	LAYBACKING
LARYNGISMUS	LATERALIZATION	LATITUDINARIANS	LAUREATESHIPS	LAYMANISED
LARYNGISMUSES	LATERALIZATIONS	LATITUDINOUS	LAUREATING	LAYMANISES
LARYNGITIC	LATERALIZE	LATRATIONS	LAUREATION	LAYMANISING
LARYNGITIDES	LATERALIZED	LATROCINIA	LAUREATIONS	LAYMANIZED
LARYNGITIS	LATERALIZES	LATROCINIES	LAURELLING	LAYMANIZES
LARYNGITISES	LATERALIZING	LATROCINIUM	LAURUSTINE	LAYMANIZING
LARYNGOLOGIC	LATERALLED	LATTERMATH	LAURUSTINES	LAYPERSONS
LARYNGOLOGICAL	LATERALLING	LATTERMATHS	LAURUSTINUS	LAZARETTES
LARYNGOLOGIES	LATERBORNS	LATTERMOST	LAURUSTINUSES	LAZARETTOS
LARYNGOLOGIST	LATERIGRADE	LATTICEWORK	LAURVIKITE	LAZINESSES
LARYNGOLOGISTS	LATERISATION	LATTICEWORKS	LAURVIKITES	LEACHABILITIES
LARYNGOLOGY	LATERISATIONS	LATTICINGS	LAVALIERES	LEACHABILITY
LARYNGOPHONIES	LATERISING	LATTICINIO	LAVALLIERE	LEADENNESS
LARYNGOPHONY	LATERITIOUS	LAUDABILITIES	LAVALLIERES	LEADENNESSES
LARYNGOSCOPE	LATERIZATION	LAUDABILITY	LAVATIONAL	LEADERBOARD
LARYNGOSCOPES	LATERIZATIONS	LAUDABLENESS	LAVATORIAL	LEADERBOARDS
LARYNGOSCOPIC	LATERIZING	LAUDABLENESSES	LAVATORIES	LEADERENES
LARYNGOSCOPIES	LATEROVERSION	LAUDATIONS	LAVENDERED	LEADERETTE
LARYNGOSCOPIST	LATEROVERSIONS	LAUDATIVES	LAVENDERING	LEADERETTES
LARYNGOSCOPISTS	LATESCENCE	LAUDATORIES	LAVERBREAD	LEADERLESS
LARYNGOSCOPY	LATESCENCES	LAUGHABLENESS	LAVERBREADS	LEADERSHIP

LEADERSHIPS	LEATHERLEAFS	LEGATESHIP	LEGITIMACY	LEISHMANIA
LEADPLANTS	LEATHERLEAVES	LEGATESHIPS	LEGITIMATE	LEISHMANIAE
LEADSCREWS	LEATHERLIKE	LEGATIONARY	LEGITIMATED	LEISHMANIAL
LEAFCUTTER	LEATHERNECK	LEGATISSIMO	LEGITIMATELY	LEISHMANIAS
LEAFCUTTERS	LEATHERNECKS	LEGATORIAL	LEGITIMATENESS	LEISHMANIASES
LEAFHOPPER	LEATHERWOOD	LEGENDARIES	LEGITIMATES	LEISHMANIASIS
LEAFHOPPERS	LEATHERWOODS	LEGENDARILY	LEGITIMATING	LEISHMANIOSES
LEAFINESSES	LEATHERWORK	LEGENDISED	LEGITIMATION	LEISHMANIOSIS
LEAFLESSNESS	LEATHERWORKS	LEGENDISES	LEGITIMATIONS	LEISTERING
LEAFLESSNESSES	LEAVENINGS	LEGENDISING	LEGITIMATISE	LEISURABLE
LEAFLETEER	LEBENSRAUM	LEGENDISTS	LEGITIMATISED	LEISURABLY
LEAFLETEERS	LEBENSRAUMS	LEGENDIZED	LEGITIMATISES	LEISURELIER
LEAFLETERS	LECHEROUSLY	LEGENDIZES	LEGITIMATISING	LEISURELIEST
LEAFLETING	LECHEROUSNESS	LEGENDIZING	LEGITIMATIZE	LEISURELINESS
LEAFLETTED	LECHEROUSNESSES	LEGENDRIES	LEGITIMATIZED	LEISURELINESSES
LEAFLETTING	LECITHINASE	LEGERDEMAIN	LEGITIMATIZES	LEISUREWEAR
LEAFSTALKS	LECITHINASES	LEGERDEMAINIST	LEGITIMATIZING	LEISUREWEARS
LEAGUERING	LECTIONARIES	LEGERDEMAINISTS	LEGITIMATOR	LEITMOTIFS
LEAKINESSES	LECTIONARY	LEGERDEMAINS	LEGITIMATORS	LEITMOTIVS
LEANNESSES	LECTISTERNIA	LEGERITIES	LEGITIMISATION	LEMMATISATION
LEAPFROGGED	LECTISTERNIUM	LEGGINESSES	LEGITIMISATIONS	LEMMATISATIONS
LEAPFROGGING	LECTISTERNIUMS	LEGIBILITIES	LEGITIMISE	LEMMATISED
LEARINESSES	LECTORATES	LEGIBILITY	LEGITIMISED	LEMMATISES
LEARNABILITIES	LECTORSHIP	LEGIBLENESS	LEGITIMISER	LEMMATISING
LEARNABILITY	LECTORSHIPS	LEGIBLENESSES	LEGITIMISERS	LEMMATIZATION
LEARNEDNESS	LECTOTYPES	LEGIONARIES	LEGITIMISES	LEMMATIZATIONS
LEARNEDNESSES	LECTRESSES	LEGIONELLA	LEGITIMISING	LEMMATIZED
LEASEBACKS	LECTURESHIP	LEGIONELLAE	LEGITIMISM	LEMMATIZES
LEASEHOLDER	LECTURESHIPS	LEGIONELLAS	LEGITIMISMS	LEMMATIZING
LEASEHOLDERS	LECYTHIDACEOUS	LEGIONNAIRE	LEGITIMIST	LEMMINGLIKE
LEASEHOLDS	LECYTHISES	LEGIONNAIRES	LEGITIMISTIC	LEMNISCATE
LEASTAWAYS	LEDERHOSEN	LEGISLATED	LEGITIMISTS	LEMNISCATES
LEATHERBACK	LEECHCRAFT	LEGISLATES	LEGITIMIZATION	LEMONFISHES
LEATHERBACKS	LEECHCRAFTS	LEGISLATING	LEGITIMIZATIONS	LEMONGRASS
LEATHERBOUND	LEERINESSES	LEGISLATION	LEGITIMIZE	LEMONGRASSES
LEATHERETTE	LEETSPEAKS	LEGISLATIONS	LEGITIMIZED	LEMONWOODS
LEATHERETTES	LEFTWARDLY	LEGISLATIVE	LEGITIMIZER	LENGTHENED
LEATHERGOODS	LEGALISATION	LEGISLATIVELY	LEGITIMIZERS	LENGTHENER
LEATHERHEAD	LEGALISATIONS	LEGISLATIVES	LEGITIMIZES	LENGTHENERS
LEATHERHEADS	LEGALISERS	LEGISLATOR	LEGITIMIZING	LENGTHENING
LEATHERIER	LEGALISING	LEGISLATORIAL	LEGLESSNESS	LENGTHIEST
LEATHERIEST	LEGALISTIC	LEGISLATORS	LEGLESSNESSES	LENGTHINESS
LEATHERINESS	LEGALISTICALLY	LEGISLATORSHIP	LEGUMINOUS	LENGTHINESSES
LEATHERINESSES	LEGALITIES	LEGISLATORSHIPS	LEGWARMERS	LENGTHSMAN
LEATHERING	LEGALIZATION	LEGISLATRESS	LEIOMYOMAS	LENGTHSMEN
LEATHERINGS	LEGALIZATIONS	LEGISLATRESSES	LEIOMYOMATA	LENGTHWAYS
LEATHERJACKET	LEGALIZERS	LEGISLATURE	LEIOTRICHIES	LENGTHWISE
LEATHERJACKETS	LEGALIZING	LEGISLATURES	LEIOTRICHOUS	LENIENCIES
LEATHERLEAF	LEGATARIES	LEGITIMACIES	LEIOTRICHY	LENITIVELY

LENOCINIUM	LEPROSERIES	LETTERBOXING	LEUCOPENIA	LEUKOPENIAS
LENOCINIUMS	LEPROSITIES	LETTERBOXINGS	LEUCOPENIAS	LEUKOPENIC
LENTAMENTE	LEPROUSNESS	LETTERFORM	LEUCOPENIC	LEUKOPLAKIA
LENTICELLATE	LEPROUSNESSES	LETTERFORMS	LEUCOPLAKIA	LEUKOPLAKIAS
LENTICULAR	LEPTOCEPHALI	LETTERHEAD	LEUCOPLAKIAS	LEUKOPLAKIC
LENTICULARLY	LEPTOCEPHALIC	LETTERHEADS	LEUCOPLAKIC	LEUKOPOIESES
LENTICULARS	LEPTOCEPHALOUS	LETTERINGS	LEUCOPLAST	LEUKOPOIESIS
LENTICULES	LEPTOCEPHALUS	LETTERLESS	LEUCOPLASTID	LEUKOPOIETIC
LENTIGINES	LEPTOCERCAL	LETTERPRESS	LEUCOPLASTIDS	LEUKORRHEA
LENTIGINOSE	LEPTODACTYL	LETTERPRESSES	LEUCOPLASTS	LEUKORRHEAL
LENTIGINOUS	LEPTODACTYLOUS	LETTERSETS	LEUCOPOIESES	LEUKORRHEAS
LENTISSIMO	LEPTODACTYLS	LETTERSPACING	LEUCOPOIESIS	LEUKOTOMES
LENTIVIRUS	LEPTOKURTIC	LETTERSPACINGS	LEUCOPOIETIC	LEUKOTOMIES
LENTIVIRUSES	LEPTOPHOSES	LEUCAEMIAS	LEUCORRHOEA	LEUKOTRIENE
LEONTIASES	LEPTOPHYLLOUS	LEUCAEMOGEN	LEUCORRHOEAL	LEUKOTRIENES
LEONTIASIS	LEPTORRHINE	LEUCAEMOGENESES	LEUCORRHOEAS	LEVANTINES
LEONTOPODIUM	LEPTOSOMATIC	LEUCAEMOGENESIS	LEUCOTOMES	LEVELHEADED
LEONTOPODIUMS	LEPTOSOMES	LEUCAEMOGENIC	LEUCOTOMIES	LEVELHEADEDNESS
LEOPARDESS	LEPTOSOMIC	LEUCAEMOGENS	LEUKAEMIAS	LEVELLINGS
LEOPARDESSES	LEPTOSPIRAL	LEUCHAEMIA	LEUKAEMOGEN	LEVELNESSES
LEOPARDSKIN	LEPTOSPIRE	LEUCHAEMIAS	LEUKAEMOGENESES	LEVERAGING
LEOPARDSKINS	LEPTOSPIRES	LEUCITOHEDRA	LEUKAEMOGENESIS	LEVIATHANS
LEPIDODENDROID	LEPTOSPIROSES	LEUCITOHEDRON	LEUKAEMOGENIC	LEVIGATING
LEPIDODENDROIDS	LEPTOSPIROSIS	LEUCITOHEDRONS	LEUKAEMOGENS	LEVIGATION
LEPIDOLITE	LEPTOTENES	LEUCOBLAST	LEUKEMOGEN	LEVIGATIONS
LEPIDOLITES	LESBIANISM	LEUCOBLASTS	LEUKEMOGENESES	LEVIGATORS
LEPIDOMELANE	LESBIANISMS	LEUCOCIDIN	LEUKEMOGENESIS	LEVIRATICAL
LEPIDOMELANES	LESPEDEZAS	LEUCOCIDINS	LEUKEMOGENIC	LEVIRATION
LEPIDOPTERA	LESSEESHIP	LEUCOCRATIC	LEUKEMOGENS	LEVIRATIONS
LEPIDOPTERAN	LESSEESHIPS	LEUCOCYTES	LEUKOBLAST	LEVITATING
LEPIDOPTERANS	LESSENINGS	LEUCOCYTHAEMIA	LEUKOBLASTS	LEVITATION
LEPIDOPTERIST	LESSONINGS	LEUCOCYTHAEMIAS	LEUKOCIDIN	LEVITATIONAL
LEPIDOPTERISTS	LETHALITIES	LEUCOCYTIC	LEUKOCIDINS	LEVITATIONS
LEPIDOPTEROLOGY	LETHARGICAL	LEUCOCYTOLYSES	LEUKOCYTES	LEVITATORS
LEPIDOPTERON	LETHARGICALLY	LEUCOCYTOLYSIS	LEUKOCYTIC	LEVITICALLY
LEPIDOPTERONS	LETHARGIED	LEUCOCYTOPENIA	LEUKOCYTOLYSES	LEVOROTARY
LEPIDOPTEROUS	LETHARGIES	LEUCOCYTOPENIAS	LEUKOCYTOLYSIS	LEVOROTATORY
LEPIDOSIREN	LETHARGISE	LEUCOCYTOSES	LEUKOCYTOPENIA	LEWDNESSES
LEPIDOSIRENS	LETHARGISED	LEUCOCYTOSIS	LEUKOCYTOPENIAS	LEXICALISATION
LEPRECHAUN	LETHARGISES	LEUCOCYTOTIC	LEUKOCYTOSES	LEXICALISATIONS
LEPRECHAUNISH	LETHARGISING	LEUCODEPLETED	LEUKOCYTOSIS	LEXICALISE
LEPRECHAUNS	LETHARGIZE	LEUCODERMA	LEUKOCYTOTIC	LEXICALISED
LEPRECHAWN	LETHARGIZED	LEUCODERMAL	LEUKODEPLETED	LEXICALISES
LEPRECHAWNS	LETHARGIZES	LEUCODERMAS	LEUKODERMA	LEXICALISING
LEPROMATOUS	LETHARGIZING	LEUCODERMIA	LEUKODERMAL	LEXICALITIES
LEPROSARIA	LETHIFEROUS	LEUCODERMIAS	LEUKODERMAS	LEXICALITY
LEPROSARIUM	LETROZOLES	LEUCODERMIC	LEUKODERMIC	LEXICALIZATION
LEPROSARIUMS	LETTERBOXED	LEUCOMAINE	LEUKODYSTROPHY	LEXICALIZATIONS
LEPROSERIE	LETTERBOXES	LEUCOMAINES	LEUKOPENIA	LEXICALIZE

L

LEXICALIZED	LIBERALIZATION	LICENTIATE	LIFELESSLY	LIGHTWEIGHT
LEXICALIZES	LIBERALIZATIONS	LICENTIATES	LIFELESSNESS	LIGHTWEIGHTS
LEXICALIZING	LIBERALIZE	LICENTIATESHIP	LIFELESSNESSES	LIGHTWOODS
LEXICOGRAPHER	LIBERALIZED	LICENTIATESHIPS	LIFELIKENESS	LIGNICOLOUS
LEXICOGRAPHERS	LIBERALIZER	LICENTIATION	LIFELIKENESSES	LIGNIFICATION
LEXICOGRAPHIC	LIBERALIZERS	LICENTIATIONS	LIFEMANSHIP	LIGNIFICATIONS
LEXICOGRAPHICAL	LIBERALIZES	LICENTIOUS	LIFEMANSHIPS	LIGNIFYING
LEXICOGRAPHIES	LIBERALIZING	LICENTIOUSLY	LIFESAVERS	LIGNIPERDOUS
LEXICOGRAPHIST	LIBERALNESS	LICENTIOUSNESS	LIFESAVING	LIGNIVOROUS
LEXICOGRAPHISTS	LIBERALNESSES	LICHANOSES	LIFESAVINGS	LIGNOCAINE
LEXICOGRAPHY	LIBERATING	LICHENISMS	LIFESTYLER	LIGNOCAINES
LEXICOLOGICAL	LIBERATION	LICHENISTS	LIFESTYLERS	LIGNOCELLULOSE
LEXICOLOGICALLY	LIBERATIONISM	LICHENOLOGICAL	LIFESTYLES	LIGNOCELLULOSES
LEXICOLOGIES	LIBERATIONISMS	LICHENOLOGIES	LIFEWORLDS	LIGNOCELLULOSIC
LEXICOLOGIST	LIBERATIONIST	LICHENOLOGIST	LIGAMENTAL	LIGNOSULFONATE
LEXICOLOGISTS	LIBERATIONISTS	LICHENOLOGISTS	LIGAMENTARY	LIGNOSULFONATES
LEXICOLOGY	LIBERATIONS	LICHENOLOGY	LIGAMENTOUS	LIGULIFLORAL
LEXIGRAPHIC	LIBERATORS	LICHTLYING	LIGATURING	LIGUSTRUMS
LEXIGRAPHICAL	LIBERATORY	LICITNESSES	LIGHTBULBS	LIKABILITIES
LEXIGRAPHIES	LIBERTARIAN	LICKERISHLY	LIGHTENERS	LIKABILITY
LEXIGRAPHY	LIBERTARIANISM	LICKERISHNESS	LIGHTENING	LIKABLENESS
LEYLANDIIS	LIBERTARIANISMS	LICKERISHNESSES	LIGHTENINGS	LIKABLENESSES
LHERZOLITE	LIBERTARIANS	LICKPENNIES	LIGHTERAGE	LIKEABILITIES
LHERZOLITES	LIBERTICIDAL	LICKSPITTLE	LIGHTERAGES	LIKEABILITY
LIABILITIES	LIBERTICIDE	LICKSPITTLES	LIGHTERING	LIKEABLENESS
LIABLENESS	LIBERTICIDES	LIDOCAINES	LIGHTERMAN	LIKEABLENESSES
LIABLENESSES	LIBERTINAGE	LIEBFRAUMILCH	LIGHTERMEN	LIKELIHOOD
LIBATIONAL	LIBERTINAGES	LIEBFRAUMILCHS	LIGHTFACED	LIKELIHOODS
LIBATIONARY	LIBERTINES	LIENHOLDER	LIGHTFACES	LIKELINESS
LIBECCHIOS	LIBERTINISM	LIENHOLDERS	LIGHTFASTNESS	LIKELINESSES
LIBELLANTS	LIBERTINISMS	LIENTERIES	LIGHTFASTNESSES	LIKENESSES
LIBELLINGS	LIBIDINALLY	LIEUTENANCIES	LIGHTHEARTED	LILANGENIS
LIBELLOUSLY	LIBIDINIST	LIEUTENANCY	LIGHTHEARTEDLY	LILIACEOUS
LIBELOUSLY	LIBIDINISTS	LIEUTENANT	LIGHTHOUSE	LILLIPUTIAN
LIBERALISATION	LIBIDINOSITIES	LIEUTENANTRIES	LIGHTHOUSEMAN	LILLIPUTIANS
LIBERALISATIONS	LIBIDINOSITY	LIEUTENANTRY	LIGHTHOUSEMEN	LILTINGNESS
LIBERALISE	LIBIDINOUS	LIEUTENANTS	LIGHTHOUSES	LILTINGNESSES
LIBERALISED	LIBIDINOUSLY	LIEUTENANTSHIP	LIGHTLYING	LIMACIFORM
LIBERALISER	LIBIDINOUSNESS	LIEUTENANTSHIPS	LIGHTNESSES	LIMACOLOGIES
LIBERALISERS	LIBRAIRIES	LIFEBLOODS	LIGHTNINGED	LIMACOLOGIST
LIBERALISES	LIBRARIANS	LIFEBOATMAN	LIGHTNINGS	LIMACOLOGISTS
LIBERALISING	LIBRARIANSHIP	LIFEBOATMEN	LIGHTPLANE	LIMACOLOGY
LIBERALISM	LIBRARIANSHIPS	LIFEGUARDED	LIGHTPLANES	LIMBERNESS
LIBERALISMS	LIBRATIONAL	LIFEGUARDING	LIGHTPROOF	LIMBERNESSES
LIBERALIST	LIBRATIONS	LIFEGUARDS	LIGHTSHIPS	LIMBURGITE
LIBERALISTIC	LIBRETTIST	LIFEHACKED	LIGHTSOMELY	LIMBURGITES
LIBERALISTS	LIBRETTISTS	LIFEHACKER	LIGHTSOMENESS	LIMELIGHTED
LIBERALITIES	LICENSABLE	LIFEHACKERS	LIGHTSOMENESSES	LIMELIGHTER
LIBERALITY	LICENSURES	LIFEHACKING	LIGHTTIGHT	LIMELIGHTERS

LIMELIGHTING	LINEARITIES	LIONHEARTEDNESS	LIQUEFACTION	LIQUORISHNESS
LIMELIGHTS	LINEARIZATION	LIONISATION	LIQUEFACTIONS	LIQUORISHNESSES
LIMERENCES	LINEARIZATIONS	LIONISATIONS	LIQUEFACTIVE	LIRIODENDRA
LIMESCALES	LINEARIZED	LIONIZATION	LIQUEFIABLE	LIRIODENDRON
LIMESTONES	LINEARIZES	LIONIZATIONS	LIQUEFIERS	LIRIODENDRONS
LIMEWASHES	LINEARIZING	LIPECTOMIES	LIQUEFYING	LISSENCEPHALOUS
LIMEWATERS	LINEATIONS	LIPGLOSSES	LIQUESCENCE	LISSOMENESS
LIMICOLINE	LINEBACKER	LIPIDOPLAST	LIQUESCENCES	LISSOMENESSES
LIMICOLOUS	LINEBACKERS	LIPIDOPLASTS	LIQUESCENCIES	LISSOMNESS
LIMINESSES	LINEBACKING	LIPOCHROME	LIQUESCENCY	LISSOMNESSES
LIMITABLENESS	LINEBACKINGS	LIPOCHROMES	LIQUESCENT	LISSOTRICHOUS
LIMITABLENESSES	LINEBREEDING	LIPODYSTROPHIES	LIQUESCING	LISTENABILITIES
LIMITARIAN	LINEBREEDINGS	LIPODYSTROPHY	LIQUEURING	LISTENABILITY
LIMITARIANS	LINECASTER	LIPOGENESES	LIQUIDAMBAR	LISTENABLE
LIMITATION	LINECASTERS	LIPOGENESIS	LIQUIDAMBARS	LISTENERSHIP
LIMITATIONAL	LINECASTING	LIPOGRAMMATIC	LIQUIDATED	LISTENERSHIPS
LIMITATIONS	LINECASTINGS	LIPOGRAMMATISM	LIQUIDATES	LISTENINGS
LIMITATIVE	LINENFOLDS	LIPOGRAMMATISMS	LIQUIDATING	LISTERIOSES
LIMITEDNESS	LINEOLATED	LIPOGRAMMATIST	LIQUIDATION	LISTERIOSIS
LIMITEDNESSES	LINERBOARD	LIPOGRAMMATISTS	LIQUIDATIONISM	LISTLESSLY
LIMITINGLY	LINERBOARDS	LIPOGRAPHIES	LIQUIDATIONISMS	LISTLESSNESS
LIMITLESSLY	LINESCORES	LIPOGRAPHY	LIQUIDATIONIST	LISTLESSNESSES
LIMITLESSNESS	LINGBERRIES	LIPOMATOSES	LIQUIDATIONISTS	LITENESSES
LIMITLESSNESSES	LINGERINGLY	LIPOMATOSIS	LIQUIDATIONS	LITERACIES
LIMITROPHE	LINGERINGS	LIPOMATOUS	LIQUIDATOR	LITERALISATION
LIMIVOROUS	LINGONBERRIES	LIPOPHILIC	LIQUIDATORS	LITERALISATIONS
LIMNOLOGIC	LINGONBERRY	LIPOPLASTS	LIQUIDIEST	LITERALISE
LIMNOLOGICAL	LINGUIFORM	LIPOPROTEIN	LIQUIDISED	LITERALISED
LIMNOLOGICALLY	LINGUISTER	LIPOPROTEINS	LIQUIDISER	LITERALISER
LIMNOLOGIES	LINGUISTERS	LIPOSCULPTURE	LIQUIDISERS	LITERALISERS
LIMNOLOGIST	LINGUISTIC	LIPOSCULPTURES	LIQUIDISES	LITERALISES
LIMNOLOGISTS	LINGUISTICAL	LIPOSUCKED	LIQUIDISING	LITERALISING
LIMNOPHILOUS	LINGUISTICALLY	LIPOSUCKING	LIQUIDITIES	LITERALISM
LIMOUSINES	LINGUISTICIAN	LIPOSUCTION	LIQUIDIZED	LITERALISMS
LIMPIDITIES	LINGUISTICIANS	LIPOSUCTIONS	LIQUIDIZER	LITERALIST
LIMPIDNESS	LINGUISTICS	LIPOTROPIC	LIQUIDIZERS	LITERALISTIC
LIMPIDNESSES	LINGUISTRIES	LIPOTROPIES	LIQUIDIZES	LITERALISTS
LIMPNESSES	LINGUISTRY	LIPOTROPIN	LIQUIDIZING	LITERALITIES
LINCOMYCIN	LINGULATED	LIPOTROPINS	LIQUIDNESS	LITERALITY
LINCOMYCINS	LINISHINGS	LIPPINESSES	LIQUIDNESSES	LITERALIZATION
LINCRUSTAS	LINKSLANDS	LIPPITUDES	LIQUIDUSES	LITERALIZATIONS
LINEALITIES	LINOLEATES	LIPREADERS	LIQUIFACTION	LITERALIZE
LINEAMENTAL	LINOTYPERS	LIPREADING	LIQUIFACTIONS	LITERALIZED
LINEAMENTS	LINOTYPING	LIPREADINGS	LIQUIFACTIVE	LITERALIZER
LINEARISATION	LINTSTOCKS	LIPSTICKED	LIQUIFIABLE	LITERALIZERS
LINEARISATIONS	LINTWHITES	LIPSTICKING	LIQUIFIERS	LITERALIZES
LINEARISED	LIONCELLES	LIQUATIONS	LIQUIFYING	LITERALIZING
LINEARISES	LIONFISHES	LIQUEFACIENT	LIQUORICES	LITERALNESS
LINEARISING	LIONHEARTED	LIQUEFACIENTS	LIQUORISHLY	LITERALNESSES

LITERARILY

LITERARILY	LITHOLATRY	LITHOTRIPSY	LITURGIOLOGIES	LIVRAISONS
LITERARINESS	LITHOLOGIC	LITHOTRIPTER	LITURGIOLOGIST	LIXIVIATED
LITERARINESSES	LITHOLOGICAL	LITHOTRIPTERS	LITURGIOLOGISTS	LIXIVIATES
LITERARYISM	LITHOLOGICALLY	LITHOTRIPTIC	LITURGIOLOGY	LIXIVIATING
LITERARYISMS	LITHOLOGIES	LITHOTRIPTICS	LITURGISMS	LIXIVIATION
LITERATELY	LITHOLOGIST	LITHOTRIPTIST	LITURGISTIC	LIXIVIATIONS
LITERATENESS	LITHOLOGISTS	LITHOTRIPTISTS	LITURGISTS	LOADMASTER
LITERATENESSES	LITHOMANCIES	LITHOTRIPTOR	LIVABILITIES	LOADMASTERS
LITERATION	LITHOMANCY	LITHOTRIPTORS	LIVABILITY	LOADSAMONEY
LITERATIONS	LITHOMARGE	LITHOTRITE	LIVABLENESS	LOADSAMONEYS
LITERATORS	LITHOMARGES	LITHOTRITES	LIVABLENESSES	LOADSAMONIES
LITERATURE	LITHOMETEOR	LITHOTRITIC	LIVEABILITIES	LOADSPACES
LITERATURED	LITHOMETEORS	LITHOTRITICS	LIVEABILITY	LOADSTONES
LITERATURES	LITHONTHRYPTIC	LITHOTRITIES	LIVEABLENESS	LOAMINESSES
LITEROSITIES	LITHONTHRYPTICS	LITHOTRITISE	LIVEABLENESSES	LOANSHIFTS
LITEROSITY	LITHONTRIPTIC	LITHOTRITISED	LIVEABOARD	LOATHEDNESS
LITHAEMIAS	LITHONTRIPTICS	LITHOTRITISES	LIVEABOARDS	LOATHEDNESSES
LITHENESSES	LITHONTRIPTIST	LITHOTRITISING	LIVEBLOGGED	LOATHFULNESS
LITHESOMENESS	LITHONTRIPTISTS	LITHOTRITIST	LIVEBLOGGER	LOATHFULNESSES
LITHESOMENESSES	LITHONTRIPTOR	LITHOTRITISTS	LIVEBLOGGERS	LOATHINGLY
LITHIFICATION	LITHONTRIPTORS	LITHOTRITIZE	LIVEBLOGGING	LOATHLIEST
LITHIFICATIONS	LITHOPHAGOUS	LITHOTRITIZED	LIVEBLOGGINGS	LOATHLINESS
LITHIFYING	LITHOPHANE	LITHOTRITIZES	LIVELIHEAD	LOATHLINESSES
LITHISTIDS	LITHOPHANES	LITHOTRITIZING	LIVELIHEADS	LOATHNESSES
LITHOCHROMATIC	LITHOPHILOUS	LITHOTRITOR	LIVELIHOOD	LOATHSOMELY
LITHOCHROMATICS	LITHOPHYSA	LITHOTRITORS	LIVELIHOODS	LOATHSOMENESS
LITHOCHROMIES	LITHOPHYSAE	LITHOTRITY	LIVELINESS	LOATHSOMENESSES
LITHOCHROMY	LITHOPHYSE	LITHOTYPES	LIVELINESSES	LOBECTOMIES
LITHOCLAST	LITHOPHYSES	LITIGATING	LIVENESSES	LOBLOLLIES
LITHOCLASTS	LITHOPHYTE	LITIGATION	LIVERISHLY	LOBOTOMIES
LITHOCYSTS	LITHOPHYTES	LITIGATIONS	LIVERISHNESS	LOBOTOMISE
LITHODOMOUS	LITHOPHYTIC	LITIGATORS	LIVERISHNESSES	LOBOTOMISED
LITHOGENOUS	LITHOPONES	LITIGIOUSLY	LIVERLEAVES	LOBOTOMISES
LITHOGLYPH	LITHOPRINT	LITIGIOUSNESS	LIVERMORIUM	LOBOTOMISING
LITHOGLYPHS	LITHOPRINTS	LITIGIOUSNESSES	LIVERMORIUMS	LOBOTOMIZE
LITHOGRAPH	LITHOSPERMUM	LITTERATEUR	LIVERWORTS	LOBOTOMIZED
LITHOGRAPHED	LITHOSPERMUMS	LITTERATEURS	LIVERWURST	LOBOTOMIZES
LITHOGRAPHER	LITHOSPHERE	LITTERBAGS	LIVERWURSTS	LOBOTOMIZING
LITHOGRAPHERS	LITHOSPHERES	LITTERBUGS	LIVESTOCKS	LOBSCOUSES
LITHOGRAPHIC	LITHOSPHERIC	LITTERIEST	LIVESTREAM	LOBSTERERS
LITHOGRAPHICAL	LITHOSTATIC	LITTERMATE	LIVESTREAMED	LOBSTERING
LITHOGRAPHIES	LITHOTOMES	LITTERMATES	LIVESTREAMING	LOBSTERINGS
LITHOGRAPHING	LITHOTOMIC	LITTLENECK	LIVESTREAMS	LOBSTERLIKE
LITHOGRAPHS	LITHOTOMICAL	LITTLENECKS	LIVETRAPPED	LOBSTERMAN
LITHOGRAPHY	LITHOTOMIES	LITTLENESS	LIVETRAPPING	LOBSTERMEN
LITHOLAPAXIES	LITHOTOMIST	LITTLENESSES	LIVIDITIES	LOBTAILING
LITHOLAPAXY	LITHOTOMISTS	LITTLEWORTH	LIVIDNESSES	LOBTAILINGS
LITHOLATRIES	LITHOTOMOUS	LITURGICAL	LIVINGNESS	LOBULATION
LITHOLATROUS	LITHOTRIPSIES	LITURGICALLY	LIVINGNESSES	LOBULATIONS

LOCALISABILITY	LOCULAMENT	LOGOGRAPHERS	LONGCLOTHS	LOPHOPHORATE
LOCALISABLE	LOCULAMENTS	LOGOGRAPHIC	LONGEVITIES	LOPHOPHORE
LOCALISATION	LOCULATION	LOGOGRAPHICAL	LONGHAIRED	LOPHOPHORES
LOCALISATIONS	LOCULATIONS	LOGOGRAPHICALLY	LONGHEADED	LOPINAVIRS
LOCALISERS	LOCULICIDAL	LOGOGRAPHIES	LONGHEADEDNESS	LOPSIDEDLY
LOCALISING	LOCUTIONARY	LOGOGRAPHS	LONGHOUSES	LOPSIDEDNESS
LOCALISTIC	LOCUTORIES	LOGOGRAPHY	LONGICAUDATE	LOPSIDEDNESSES
LOCALITIES	LODESTONES	LOGOGRIPHIC	LONGICORNS	LOQUACIOUS
LOCALIZABILITY	LODGEMENTS	LOGOGRIPHS	LONGINQUITIES	LOQUACIOUSLY
LOCALIZABLE	LODGEPOLES	LOGOMACHIES	LONGINQUITY	LOQUACIOUSNESS
LOCALIZATION	LOFTINESSES	LOGOMACHIST	LONGIPENNATE	LOQUACITIES
LOCALIZATIONS	LOGAGRAPHIA	LOGOMACHISTS	LONGIROSTRAL	LORAZEPAMS
LOCALIZERS	LOGAGRAPHIAS	LOGOPAEDIC	LONGITUDES	LORDLINESS
LOCALIZING	LOGANBERRIES	LOGOPAEDICS	LONGITUDINAL	LORDLINESSES
LOCALNESSES	LOGANBERRY	LOGOPEDICS	LONGITUDINALLY	LORDOLATRIES
LOCATEABLE	LOGANIACEOUS	LOGOPHILES	LONGJUMPED	LORDOLATRY
LOCATIONAL	LOGAOEDICS	LOGORRHEAS	LONGJUMPING	LORGNETTES
LOCATIONALLY	LOGARITHMIC	LOGORRHEIC	LONGLEAVES	LORICATING
LOCKHOUSES	LOGARITHMICAL	LOGORRHOEA	LONGLINERS	LORICATION
LOCKKEEPER	LOGARITHMICALLY	LOGORRHOEAS	LONGLISTED	LORICATIONS
LOCKKEEPERS	LOGARITHMS	LOGOTHETES	LONGLISTING	LORNNESSES
LOCKMAKERS	LOGGERHEAD	LOGOTYPIES	LONGNESSES	LOSABLENESS
LOCKSMITHERIES	LOGGERHEADED	LOGROLLERS	LONGPRIMER	LOSABLENESSES
LOCKSMITHERY	LOGGERHEADS	LOGROLLING	LONGPRIMERS	LOSSMAKERS
LOCKSMITHING	LOGICALITIES	LOGROLLINGS	LONGSHOREMAN	LOSSMAKING
LOCKSMITHINGS	LOGICALITY	LOINCLOTHS	LONGSHOREMEN	LOSTNESSES
LOCKSMITHS	LOGICALNESS	LOITERINGLY	LONGSHORING	LOTHNESSES
LOCKSTITCH	LOGICALNESSES	LOITERINGS	LONGSHORINGS	LOTUSLANDS
LOCKSTITCHED	LOGICISING	LOLLAPALOOSA	LONGSIGHTED	LOUDHAILER
LOCKSTITCHES	LOGICIZING	LOLLAPALOOSAS	LONGSIGHTEDNESS	LOUDHAILERS
LOCKSTITCHING	LOGINESSES	LOLLAPALOOZA	LONGSOMELY	LOUDMOUTHED
LOCOMOBILE	LOGISTICAL	LOLLAPALOOZAS	LONGSOMENESS	LOUDMOUTHS
LOCOMOBILES	LOGISTICALLY	LOLLOPIEST	LONGSOMENESSES	LOUDNESSES
LOCOMOBILITIES	LOGISTICIAN	LOLLYGAGGED	LONGWEARING	LOUDSPEAKER
LOCOMOBILITY	LOGISTICIANS	LOLLYGAGGING	LOOKALIKES	LOUDSPEAKERS
LOCOMOTING	LOGJAMMING	LOMENTACEOUS	LOONINESSES	LOUNDERING
LOCOMOTION	LOGJAMMINGS	LONELINESS	LOOPHOLING	LOUNDERINGS
LOCOMOTIONS	LOGNORMALITIES	LONELINESSES	LOOPINESSES	LOUNGEWEAR
LOCOMOTIVE	LOGNORMALITY	LONENESSES	LOOSEBOXES	LOUNGEWEARS
LOCOMOTIVELY	LOGNORMALLY	LONESOMELY	LOOSENESSES	LOUNGINGLY
LOCOMOTIVENESS	LOGOCENTRISM	LONESOMENESS	LOOSENINGS	LOUSEWORTS
LOCOMOTIVES	LOGOCENTRISMS	LONESOMENESSES	LOOSESTRIFE	LOUSINESSES
LOCOMOTIVITIES	LOGODAEDALIC	LONGAEVOUS	LOOSESTRIFES	LOUTISHNESS
LOCOMOTIVITY	LOGODAEDALIES	LONGANIMITIES	LOOYENWORK	LOUTISHNESSES
LOCOMOTORS	LOGODAEDALUS	LONGANIMITY	LOOYENWORKS	LOVABILITIES
LOCOMOTORY	LOGODAEDALUSES	LONGANIMOUS	LOPGRASSES	LOVABILITY
LOCOPLANTS	LOGODAEDALY	LONGBOARDS	LOPHOBRANCH	LOVABLENESS
LOCORESTIVE	LOGOGRAMMATIC	LONGBOWMAN	LOPHOBRANCHIATE	LOVABLENESSES
LOCTICIANS	LOGOGRAPHER	LONGBOWMEN	LOPHOBRANCHS	LOVASTATIN

LOVASTATINS	LOYALNESSES	LUCUBRATORS	LUMINESCED	LUSTFULNESSES
LOVEABILITIES	LOZENGIEST	LUCULENTLY	LUMINESCENCE	LUSTIHEADS
LOVEABILITY	LUBBERLIER	LUDICROUSLY	LUMINESCENCES	LUSTIHOODS
LOVEABLENESS	LUBBERLIEST	LUDICROUSNESS	LUMINESCENT	LUSTINESSES
LOVEABLENESSES	LUBBERLINESS	LUDICROUSNESSES	LUMINESCES	LUSTRATING
LOVELESSLY	LUBBERLINESSES	LUETICALLY	LUMINESCING	LUSTRATION
LOVELESSNESS	LUBRICANTS	LUFTMENSCH	LUMINIFEROUS	LUSTRATIONS
LOVELESSNESSES	LUBRICATED	LUFTMENSCHEN	LUMINOSITIES	LUSTRATIVE
LOVELIGHTS	LUBRICATES	LUGUBRIOUS	LUMINOSITY	LUSTRELESS
LOVELIHEAD	LUBRICATING	LUGUBRIOUSLY	LUMINOUSLY	LUSTREWARE
LOVELIHEADS	LUBRICATION	LUGUBRIOUSNESS	LUMINOUSNESS	LUSTREWARES
LOVELINESS	LUBRICATIONAL	LUKEWARMISH	LUMINOUSNESSES	LUSTROUSLY
LOVELINESSES	LUBRICATIONS	LUKEWARMLY	LUMISTEROL	LUSTROUSNESS
LOVELORNNESS	LUBRICATIVE	LUKEWARMNESS	LUMISTEROLS	LUSTROUSNESSES
LOVELORNNESSES	LUBRICATOR	LUKEWARMNESSES	LUMPECTOMIES	LUTEINISATION
LOVEMAKERS	LUBRICATORS	LUKEWARMTH	LUMPECTOMY	LUTEINISATIONS
LOVEMAKING	LUBRICIOUS	LUKEWARMTHS	LUMPFISHES	LUTEINISED
LOVEMAKINGS	LUBRICIOUSLY	LULLABYING	LUMPINESSES	LUTEINISES
LOVESICKNESS	LUBRICITIES	LUMBAGINOUS	LUMPISHNESS	LUTEINISING
LOVESICKNESSES	LUBRICOUSLY	LUMBERINGLY	LUMPISHNESSES	LUTEINIZATION
LOVESTRUCK	LUBRITORIA	LUMBERINGNESS	LUMPSUCKER	LUTEINIZATIONS
LOVEWORTHIER	LUBRITORIUM	LUMBERINGNESSES	LUMPSUCKERS	LUTEINIZED
LOVEWORTHIES	LUBRITORIUMS	LUMBERINGS	LUNARNAUTS	LUTEINIZES
LOVEWORTHIEST	LUCIDITIES	LUMBERJACK	LUNATICALLY	LUTEINIZING
LOVEWORTHY	LUCIDNESSES	LUMBERJACKET	LUNCHBOXES	LUTEOTROPHIC
LOVINGNESS	LUCIFERASE	LUMBERJACKETS	LUNCHBREAK	LUTEOTROPHIN
LOVINGNESSES	LUCIFERASES	LUMBERJACKS	LUNCHBREAKS	LUTEOTROPHINS
LOWBALLING	LUCIFERINS	LUMBERSOME	LUNCHEONED	LUTEOTROPIC
LOWBALLINGS	LUCIFEROUS	LUMBERSOMENESS	LUNCHEONETTE	LUTEOTROPIN
LOWBROWISM	LUCIFUGOUS	LUMBERYARD	LUNCHEONETTES	LUTEOTROPINS
LOWBROWISMS	LUCKENBOOTH	LUMBERYARDS	LUNCHEONING	LUTESTRING
LOWERCASED	LUCKENBOOTHS	LUMBOSACRAL	LUNCHMEATS	LUTESTRINGS
LOWERCASES	LUCKENGOWAN	LUMBRICALES	LUNCHPAILS	LUVVIEDOMS
LOWERCASING	LUCKENGOWANS	LUMBRICALIS	LUNCHROOMS	LUXULIANITE
LOWERCLASSMAN	LUCKINESSES	LUMBRICALISES	LUNCHTIMES	LUXULIANITES
LOWERCLASSMEN	LUCKLESSLY	LUMBRICALS	LUNGFISHES	LUXULLIANITE
LOWERINGLY	LUCKLESSNESS	LUMBRICIFORM	LUNINESSES	LUXULLIANITES
LOWLANDERS	LUCKLESSNESSES	LUMBRICOID	LUNKHEADED	LUXULYANITE
LOWLIGHTED	LUCKPENNIES	LUMBRICUSES	LURIDNESSES	LUXULYANITES
LOWLIGHTING	LUCRATIVELY	LUMINAIRES	LUSCIOUSLY	LUXURIANCE
LOWLIHEADS	LUCRATIVENESS	LUMINANCES	LUSCIOUSNESS	LUXURIANCES
LOWLINESSES	LUCRATIVENESSES	LUMINARIAS	LUSCIOUSNESSES	LUXURIANCIES
LOWSENINGS	LUCTATIONS	LUMINARIES	LUSHNESSES	LUXURIANCY
LOXODROMES	LUCUBRATED	LUMINARISM	LUSKISHNESS	LUXURIANTLY
LOXODROMIC	LUCUBRATES	LUMINARISMS	LUSKISHNESSES	LUXURIATED
LOXODROMICAL	LUCUBRATING	LUMINARIST	LUSTERLESS	LUXURIATES
LOXODROMICALLY	LUCUBRATION	LUMINARISTS	LUSTERWARE	LUXURIATING
LOXODROMICS	LUCUBRATIONS	LUMINATION	LUSTERWARES	LUXURIATION
LOXODROMIES	LUCUBRATOR	LUMINATIONS	LUSTFULNESS	LUXURIATIONS

LUXURIOUSLY	LYMPHANGIOMATA	LYMPHOGRANULOMA	LYOPHILISE	LYSIGENOUS
LUXURIOUSNESS	LYMPHANGITIC	LYMPHOGRAPHIC	LYOPHILISED	LYSIMETERS
LUXURIOUSNESSES	LYMPHANGITIDES	LYMPHOGRAPHIES	LYOPHILISER	LYSIMETRIC
LYCANTHROPE	LYMPHANGITIS	LYMPHOGRAPHY	LYOPHILISERS	LYSOGENICITIES
LYCANTHROPES	LYMPHANGITISES	LYMPHOKINE	LYOPHILISES	LYSOGENICITY
LYCANTHROPIC	LYMPHATICALLY	LYMPHOKINES	LYOPHILISING	LYSOGENIES
LYCANTHROPIES	LYMPHATICS	LYMPHOMATA	LYOPHILIZATION	LYSOGENISATION
LYCANTHROPIST	LYMPHOADENOMA	LYMPHOMATOID	LYOPHILIZATIONS	LYSOGENISATIONS
LYCANTHROPISTS	LYMPHOADENOMAS	LYMPHOMATOSES	LYOPHILIZE	LYSOGENISE
LYCANTHROPY	LYMPHOADENOMATA	LYMPHOMATOSIS	LYOPHILIZED	LYSOGENISED
LYCHNOSCOPE	LYMPHOBLAST	LYMPHOMATOUS	LYOPHILIZER	LYSOGENISES
LYCHNOSCOPES	LYMPHOBLASTIC	LYMPHOPENIA	LYOPHILIZERS	LYSOGENISING
LYCOPODIUM	LYMPHOBLASTS	LYMPHOPENIAS	LYOPHILIZES	LYSOGENIZATION
LYCOPODIUMS	LYMPHOCYTE	LYMPHOPOIESES	LYOPHILIZING	LYSOGENIZATIONS
LYMPHADENITIS	LYMPHOCYTES	LYMPHOPOIESIS	LYOSORPTION	LYSOGENIZE
LYMPHADENITISES	LYMPHOCYTIC	LYMPHOPOIETIC	LYOSORPTIONS	LYSOGENIZED
LYMPHADENOPATHY	LYMPHOCYTOPENIA	LYMPHOSARCOMA	LYRICALNESS	LYSOGENIZES
LYMPHANGIAL	LYMPHOCYTOSES	LYMPHOSARCOMAS	LYRICALNESSES	LYSOGENIZING
LYMPHANGIOGRAM	LYMPHOCYTOSIS	LYMPHOSARCOMATA	LYRICISING	LYSOLECITHIN
LYMPHANGIOGRAMS	LYMPHOCYTOTIC	LYMPHOTROPHIC	LYRICIZING	LYSOLECITHINS
LYMPHANGIOMA	LYMPHOGRAM	LYOPHILISATION	LYSERGIDES	LYTHRACEOUS
LYMPHANGIOMAS	LYMPHOGRAMS	LYOPHILISATIONS	LYSIGENETIC	

L

M

MACABERESQUE	MACHIAVELLIAN	MACRENCEPHALY	MACROECONOMIC	MACROPHYLUM
MACADAMIAS	MACHIAVELLIANS	MACROAGGREGATE	MACROECONOMICS	MACROPHYSICS
MACADAMISATION	MACHICOLATE	MACROAGGREGATED	MACROEVOLUTION	MACROPHYTE
MACADAMISATIONS	MACHICOLATED	MACROAGGREGATES	MACROEVOLUTIONS	MACROPHYTES
MACADAMISE	MACHICOLATES	MACROBIOTA	MACROFAUNA	MACROPHYTIC
MACADAMISED	MACHICOLATING	MACROBIOTAS	MACROFAUNAE	MACROPINACOID
MACADAMISER	MACHICOLATION	MACROBIOTE	MACROFAUNAS	MACROPINACOIDS
MACADAMISERS	MACHICOLATIONS	MACROBIOTES	MACROFLORA	MACROPINAKOID
MACADAMISES	MACHINABILITIES	MACROBIOTIC	MACROFLORAE	MACROPINAKOIDS
MACADAMISING	MACHINABILITY	MACROBIOTICS	MACROFLORAS	MACROPRISM
MACADAMIZATION	MACHINABLE	MACROCARPA	MACROFOSSIL	MACROPRISMS
MACADAMIZATIONS	MACHINATED	MACROCARPAS	MACROFOSSILS	MACROPRUDENTIAL
MACADAMIZE	MACHINATES	MACROCEPHALIA	MACROGAMETE	MACROPSIAS
MACADAMIZED	MACHINATING	MACROCEPHALIAS	MACROGAMETES	MACROPTEROUS
MACADAMIZER	MACHINATION	MACROCEPHALIC	MACROGLIAS	MACROSCALE
MACADAMIZERS	MACHINATIONS	MACROCEPHALIES	MACROGLOBULIN	MACROSCALES
MACADAMIZES	MACHINATOR	MACROCEPHALOUS	MACROGLOBULINS	MACROSCOPIC
MACADAMIZING	MACHINATORS	MACROCEPHALY	MACROGRAPH	MACROSCOPICALLY
MACARISING	MACHINEABILITY	MACROCLIMATE	MACROGRAPHIC	MACROSOCIOLOGY
MACARIZING	MACHINEABLE	MACROCLIMATES	MACROGRAPHS	MACROSPORANGIA
MACARONICALLY	MACHINEGUN	MACROCLIMATIC	MACROLIDES	MACROSPORANGIUM
MACARONICS	MACHINEGUNNED	MACROCODES	MACROLOGIES	MACROSPORE
MACARONIES	MACHINEGUNNING	MACROCOPIES	MACROMARKETING	MACROSPORES
MACCARONIES	MACHINEGUNS	MACROCOSMIC	MACROMARKETINGS	MACROSTRUCTURAL
MACCARONIS	MACHINELESS	MACROCOSMICALLY	MACROMERES	MACROSTRUCTURE
MACCHERONCINI	MACHINELIKE	MACROCOSMS	MACROMOLECULAR	MACROSTRUCTURES
MACCHERONCINIS	MACHINEMAN	MACROCYCLE	MACROMOLECULE	MACROZAMIA
MACCHIATOS	MACHINEMEN	MACROCYCLES	MACROMOLECULES	MACROZAMIAS
MACEBEARER	MACHINERIES	MACROCYCLIC	MACROMOLES	MACTATIONS
MACEBEARERS	MACHINIMAS	MACROCYSTS	MACROMUTATION	MACULATING
MACEDOINES	MACHININGS	MACROCYTES	MACROMUTATIONS	MACULATION
MACERANDUBA	MACHINISTS	MACROCYTIC	MACRONUCLEAR	MACULATIONS
MACERANDUBAS	MACHMETERS	MACROCYTOSES	MACRONUCLEI	MACULATURE
MACERATERS	MACHTPOLITIK	MACROCYTOSIS	MACRONUCLEUS	MACULATURES
MACERATING	MACHTPOLITIKS	MACRODACTYL	MACRONUCLEUSES	MADBRAINED
MACERATION	MACINTOSHES	MACRODACTYLIC	MACRONUTRIENT	MADDENINGLY
MACERATIONS	MACKINTOSH	MACRODACTYLIES	MACRONUTRIENTS	MADDENINGNESS
MACERATIVE	MACKINTOSHES	MACRODACTYLOUS	MACROPHAGE	MADDENINGNESSES
MACERATORS	MACONOCHIE	MACRODACTYLS	MACROPHAGES	MADEFACTION
MACHAIRODONT	MACONOCHIES	MACRODACTYLY	MACROPHAGIC	MADEFACTIONS
MACHAIRODONTS	MACRENCEPHALIA	MACRODIAGONAL	MACROPHAGOUS	MADELEINES
MACHIAVELIAN	MACRENCEPHALIAS	MACRODIAGONALS	MACROPHOTOGRAPH	MADEMOISELLE
MACHIAVELIANS	MACRENCEPHALIES	MACRODOMES	MACROPHYLA	MADEMOISELLES

MADERISATION	MAGISTRANDS	MAGNETOGRAPH	MAIDENHAIRS	MAINSTREAMINGS
MADERISATIONS	MAGISTRATE	MAGNETOGRAPHS	MAIDENHEAD	MAINSTREAMS
MADERISING	MAGISTRATES	MAGNETOMETER	MAIDENHEADS	MAINSTREETING
MADERIZATION	MAGISTRATESHIP	MAGNETOMETERS	MAIDENHOOD	MAINSTREETINGS
MADERIZATIONS	MAGISTRATESHIPS	MAGNETOMETRIC	MAIDENHOODS	MAINTAINABILITY
MADERIZING	MAGISTRATIC	MAGNETOMETRIES	MAIDENLIER	MAINTAINABLE
MADONNAISH	MAGISTRATICAL	MAGNETOMETRY	MAIDENLIEST	MAINTAINED
MADONNAWISE	MAGISTRATICALLY	MAGNETOMOTIVE	MAIDENLIKE	MAINTAINER
MADRASSAHS	MAGISTRATURE	MAGNETOPAUSE	MAIDENLINESS	MAINTAINERS
MADREPORAL	MAGISTRATURES	MAGNETOPAUSES	MAIDENLINESSES	MAINTAINING
MADREPORES	MAGMATISMS	MAGNETOSPHERE	MAIDENWEED	MAINTENANCE
MADREPORIAN	MAGNALIUMS	MAGNETOSPHERES	MAIDENWEEDS	MAINTENANCED
MADREPORIANS	MAGNANIMITIES	MAGNETOSPHERIC	MAIDISHNESS	MAINTENANCES
MADREPORIC	MAGNANIMITY	MAGNETOSTATIC	MAIDISHNESSES	MAINTENANCING
MADREPORITE	MAGNANIMOUS	MAGNETOSTATICS	MAIDSERVANT	MAINTOPMAST
MADREPORITES	MAGNANIMOUSLY	MAGNETRONS	MAIDSERVANTS	MAINTOPMASTS
MADREPORITIC	MAGNANIMOUSNESS	MAGNIFIABLE	MAIEUTICAL	MAINTOPSAIL
MADRIGALESQUE	MAGNATESHIP	MAGNIFICAL	MAILABILITIES	MAINTOPSAILS
MADRIGALIAN	MAGNATESHIPS	MAGNIFICALLY	MAILABILITY	MAISONETTE
MADRIGALIST	MAGNESITES	MAGNIFICAT	MAILCOACHES	MAISONETTES
MADRIGALISTS	MAGNESIUMS	MAGNIFICATION	MAILGRAMMED	MAISONNETTE
MADRILENES	MAGNESSTONE	MAGNIFICATIONS	MAILGRAMMING	MAISONNETTES
MAELSTROMS	MAGNESSTONES	MAGNIFICATS	MAILMERGED	MAISTERDOME
MAENADICALLY	MAGNETICAL	MAGNIFICENCE	MAILMERGES	MAISTERDOMES
MAENADISMS	MAGNETICALLY	MAGNIFICENCES	MAILMERGING	MAISTERING
MAFFICKERS	MAGNETICIAN	MAGNIFICENT	MAILPOUCHES	MAISTRINGS
MAFFICKING	MAGNETICIANS	MAGNIFICENTLY	MAILSHOTTED	MAJESTICAL
MAFFICKINGS	MAGNETISABLE	MAGNIFICENTNESS	MAILSHOTTING	MAJESTICALLY
MAGALOGUES	MAGNETISATION	MAGNIFICOES	MAIMEDNESS	MAJESTICALNESS
MAGAZINIST	MAGNETISATIONS	MAGNIFICOS	MAIMEDNESSES	MAJESTICNESS
MAGAZINISTS	MAGNETISED	MAGNIFIERS	MAINBRACES	MAJESTICNESSES
MAGDALENES	MAGNETISER	MAGNIFYING	MAINFRAMES	MAJOLICAWARE
MAGGOTIEST	MAGNETISERS	MAGNILOQUENCE	MAINLANDER	MAJOLICAWARES
MAGGOTORIA	MAGNETISES	MAGNILOQUENCES	MAINLANDERS	MAJORDOMOS
MAGGOTORIUM	MAGNETISING	MAGNILOQUENT	MAINLINERS	MAJORETTES
MAGIANISMS	MAGNETISMS	MAGNILOQUENTLY	MAINLINING	MAJORETTING
MAGISTERIAL	MAGNETISTS	MAGNITUDES	MAINLININGS	MAJORETTINGS
MAGISTERIALLY	MAGNETITES	MAGNITUDINOUS	MAINPERNOR	MAJORITAIRE
MAGISTERIALNESS	MAGNETITIC	MAGNOLIACEOUS	MAINPERNORS	MAJORITAIRES
MAGISTERIES	MAGNETIZABLE	MAGSTRIPES	MAINPRISED	MAJORITARIAN
MAGISTERIUM	MAGNETIZATION	MAHARAJAHS	MAINPRISES	MAJORITARIANISM
MAGISTERIUMS	MAGNETIZATIONS	MAHARANEES	MAINPRISING	MAJORITARIANS
MAGISTRACIES	MAGNETIZED	MAHARISHIS	MAINSHEETS	MAJORITIES
MAGISTRACY	MAGNETIZER	MAHATMAISM	MAINSPRING	MAJORSHIPS
MAGISTRALITIES	MAGNETIZERS	MAHATMAISMS	MAINSPRINGS	MAJUSCULAR
MAGISTRALITY	MAGNETIZES	MAHLSTICKS	MAINSTAGES	MAJUSCULES
MAGISTRALLY	MAGNETIZING	MAHOGANIES	MAINSTREAM	MAKEREADIES
MAGISTRALS	MAGNETOCHEMICAL	MAIASAURAS	MAINSTREAMED	MAKESHIFTS
MAGISTRAND	MAGNETOELECTRIC	MAIDENHAIR	MAINSTREAMING	MAKEWEIGHT

MAKEWEIGHTS	MALAPROPIAN	MALEVOLENCES	MALLOWPUFF	MAMMAPLASTIES
MAKUNOUCHI	MALAPROPISM	MALEVOLENT	MALLOWPUFFS	MAMMAPLASTY
MAKUNOUCHIS	MALAPROPISMS	MALEVOLENTLY	MALMSTONES	MAMMECTOMIES
MALABSORPTION	MALAPROPIST	MALFEASANCE	MALNOURISHED	MAMMECTOMY
MALABSORPTIONS	MALAPROPISTS	MALFEASANCES	MALNUTRITION	MAMMETRIES
MALACHITES	MALAPROPOS	MALFEASANT	MALNUTRITIONS	MAMMIFEROUS
MALACOLOGICAL	MALARIOLOGIES	MALFEASANTS	MALOCCLUDED	MAMMILLARIA
MALACOLOGIES	MALARIOLOGIST	MALFORMATION	MALOCCLUSION	MAMMILLARIAS
MALACOLOGIST	MALARIOLOGISTS	MALFORMATIONS	MALOCCLUSIONS	MAMMILLARY
MALACOLOGISTS	MALARIOLOGY	MALFUNCTION	MALODOROUS	MAMMILLATE
MALACOLOGY	MALASSIMILATION	MALFUNCTIONED	MALODOROUSLY	MAMMILLATED
MALACOPHILIES	MALATHIONS	MALFUNCTIONING	MALODOROUSNESS	MAMMILLATION
MALACOPHILOUS	MALAXATING	MALFUNCTIONINGS	MALOLACTIC	MAMMILLATIONS
MALACOPHILY	MALAXATION	MALFUNCTIONS	MALONYLUREA	MAMMILLIFORM
MALACOPHYLLOUS	MALAXATIONS	MALICIOUSLY	MALONYLUREAS	MAMMITIDES
MALACOPTERYGIAN	MALAXATORS	MALICIOUSNESS	MALPIGHIACEOUS	MAMMOCKING
MALACOSTRACAN	MALCONFORMATION	MALICIOUSNESSES	MALPIGHIAS	MAMMOGENIC
MALACOSTRACANS	MALCONTENT	MALIGNANCE	MALPOSITION	MAMMOGRAMS
MALACOSTRACOUS	MALCONTENTED	MALIGNANCES	MALPOSITIONS	MAMMOGRAPH
MALADAPTATION	MALCONTENTEDLY	MALIGNANCIES	MALPRACTICE	MAMMOGRAPHIC
MALADAPTATIONS	MALCONTENTS	MALIGNANCY	MALPRACTICES	MAMMOGRAPHIES
MALADAPTED	MALDEPLOYMENT	MALIGNANTLY	MALPRACTITIONER	MAMMOGRAPHS
MALADAPTIVE	MALDEPLOYMENTS	MALIGNANTS	MALPRESENTATION	MAMMOGRAPHY
MALADAPTIVELY	MALDISTRIBUTION	MALIGNITIES	MALTALENTS	MAMMONISMS
MALADDRESS	MALEDICENT	MALIGNMENT	MALTINESSES	MAMMONISTIC
MALADDRESSES	MALEDICTED	MALIGNMENTS	MALTODEXTRIN	MAMMONISTS
MALADJUSTED	MALEDICTING	MALIMPRINTED	MALTODEXTRINS	MAMMONITES
MALADJUSTIVE	MALEDICTION	MALIMPRINTING	MALTREATED	MAMMOPLASTIES
MALADJUSTMENT	MALEDICTIONS	MALIMPRINTINGS	MALTREATER	MAMMOPLASTY
MALADJUSTMENTS	MALEDICTIVE	MALINGERED	MALTREATERS	MANAGEABILITIES
MALADMINISTER	MALEDICTORY	MALINGERER	MALTREATING	MANAGEABILITY
MALADMINISTERED	MALEFACTION	MALINGERERS	MALTREATMENT	MANAGEABLE
MALADMINISTERS	MALEFACTIONS	MALINGERIES	MALTREATMENTS	MANAGEABLENESS
MALADROITLY	MALEFACTOR	MALINGERING	MALVACEOUS	MANAGEABLY
MALADROITNESS	MALEFACTORS	MALLANDERS	MALVERSATION	MANAGEMENT
MALADROITNESSES	MALEFACTORY	MALLEABILITIES	MALVERSATIONS	MANAGEMENTAL
MALADROITS	MALEFACTRESS	MALLEABILITY	MALVOISIES	MANAGEMENTS
MALAGUENAS	MALEFACTRESSES	MALLEABLENESS	MAMAGUYING	MANAGERESS
MALAGUETTA	MALEFFECTS	MALLEABLENESSES	MAMILLATED	MANAGERESSES
MALAGUETTAS	MALEFICALLY	MALLEATING	MAMILLATION	MANAGERIAL
MALAKATOONE	MALEFICENCE	MALLEATION	MAMILLATIONS	MANAGERIALISM
MALAKATOONES	MALEFICENCES	MALLEATIONS	MAMILLIFORM	MANAGERIALISMS
MALAPERTLY	MALEFICENT	MALLEIFORM	MAMMALIANS	MANAGERIALIST
MALAPERTNESS	MALEFICIAL	MALLEMAROKING	MAMMALIFEROUS	MANAGERIALISTS
MALAPERTNESSES	MALENESSES	MALLEMAROKINGS	MAMMALITIES	MANAGERIALLY
MALAPPORTIONED	MALENGINES	MALLEMUCKS	MAMMALOGICAL	MANAGERSHIP
MALAPPROPRIATE	MALENTENDU	MALLENDERS	MAMMALOGIES	MANAGERSHIPS
MALAPPROPRIATED	MALENTENDUS	MALLEOLUSES	MAMMALOGIST	MANCHESTER
MALAPPROPRIATES	MALEVOLENCE	MALLOPHAGOUS	MAMMALOGISTS	MANCHESTERS

MANCHINEEL	MANGABEIRA	MANIFESTOED	MANOEUVRER	MANUFACTORY
MANCHINEELS	MANGABEIRAS	MANIFESTOES	MANOEUVRERS	MANUFACTURABLE
MANCIPATED	MANGALSUTRA	MANIFESTOING	MANOEUVRES	MANUFACTURAL
MANCIPATES	MANGALSUTRAS	MANIFESTOS	MANOEUVRING	MANUFACTURE
MANCIPATING	MANGANATES	MANIFOLDED	MANOEUVRINGS	MANUFACTURED
MANCIPATION	MANGANESES	MANIFOLDER	MANOMETERS	MANUFACTURER
MANCIPATIONS	MANGANESIAN	MANIFOLDERS	MANOMETRIC	MANUFACTURERS
MANCIPATORY	MANGANIFEROUS	MANIFOLDING	MANOMETRICAL	MANUFACTURES
MANDAMUSED	MANGANITES	MANIFOLDLY	MANOMETRICALLY	MANUFACTURING
MANDAMUSES	MANGELWURZEL	MANIFOLDNESS	MANOMETRIES	MANUFACTURINGS
MANDAMUSING	MANGELWURZELS	MANIFOLDNESSES	MANORIALISM	MANUMISSION
MANDARINATE	MANGEMANGE	MANIPULABILITY	MANORIALISMS	MANUMISSIONS
MANDARINATES	MANGEMANGES	MANIPULABLE	MANOSCOPIES	MANUMITTED
MANDARINES	MANGETOUTS	MANIPULARS	MANRIKIGUSARI	MANUMITTER
MANDARINIC	MANGINESSES	MANIPULATABLE	MANRIKIGUSARIS	MANUMITTERS
MANDARINISM	MANGOLDWURZEL	MANIPULATE	MANSCAPING	MANUMITTING
MANDARINISMS	MANGOLDWURZELS	MANIPULATED	MANSCAPINGS	MANURANCES
MANDATARIES	MANGOSTANS	MANIPULATES	MANSERVANT	MANUSCRIPT
MANDATORIES	MANGOSTEEN	MANIPULATING	MANSIONARIES	MANUSCRIPTS
MANDATORILY	MANGOSTEENS	MANIPULATION	MANSIONARY	MANZANILLA
MANDIBULAR	MANGOUSTES	MANIPULATIONS	MANSLAUGHTER	MANZANILLAS
MANDIBULATE	MANGULATED	MANIPULATIVE	MANSLAUGHTERS	MANZANITAS
MANDIBULATED	MANGULATES	MANIPULATIVELY	MANSLAYERS	MAPMAKINGS
MANDIBULATES	MANGULATING	MANIPULATIVES	MANSONRIES	MAPPEMONDS
MANDILIONS	MANHANDLED	MANIPULATOR	MANSPLAINED	MAQUILADORA
MANDIOCCAS	MANHANDLES	MANIPULATORS	MANSPLAINING	MAQUILADORAS
MANDOLINES	MANHANDLING	MANIPULATORY	MANSPLAININGS	MAQUILLAGE
MANDOLINIST	MANHATTANS	MANLINESSES	MANSPLAINS	MAQUILLAGES
MANDOLINISTS	MANHUNTERS	MANNEQUINS	MANSPREADING	MAQUISARDS
MANDRAGORA	MANIACALLY	MANNERISMS	MANSPREADINGS	MARABUNTAS
MANDRAGORAS	MANICOTTIS	MANNERISTIC	MANSPREADS	MARANATHAS
MANDUCABLE	MANICURING	MANNERISTICAL	MANSUETUDE	MARASCHINO
MANDUCATED	MANICURIST	MANNERISTICALLY	MANSUETUDES	MARASCHINOS
MANDUCATES	MANICURISTS	MANNERISTS	MANTELLETTA	MARASMUSES
MANDUCATING	MANIFESTABLE	MANNERLESS	MANTELLETTAS	MARATHONER
MANDUCATION	MANIFESTANT	MANNERLESSNESS	MANTELPIECE	MARATHONERS
MANDUCATIONS	MANIFESTANTS	MANNERLIER	MANTELPIECES	MARATHONING
MANDUCATORY	MANIFESTATION	MANNERLIEST	MANTELSHELF	MARATHONINGS
MANDYLIONS	MANIFESTATIONAL	MANNERLINESS	MANTELSHELVES	MARAUDINGS
MANEUVERABILITY	MANIFESTATIONS	MANNERLINESSES	MANTELTREE	MARBELISED
MANEUVERABLE	MANIFESTATIVE	MANNIFEROUS	MANTELTREES	MARBELISES
MANEUVERED	MANIFESTED	MANNISHNESS	MANTICALLY	MARBELISING
MANEUVERER	MANIFESTER	MANNISHNESSES	MANTICORAS	MARBELIZED
MANEUVERERS	MANIFESTERS	MANOEUVERED	MANTICORES	MARBELIZES
MANEUVERING	MANIFESTIBLE	MANOEUVERING	MANTLETREE	MARBELIZING
MANEUVERINGS	MANIFESTING	MANOEUVERS	MANTLETREES	MARBLEISED
MANFULLEST	MANIFESTLY	MANOEUVRABILITY	MANTYHOSES	MARBLEISES
MANFULNESS	MANIFESTNESS	MANOEUVRABLE	MANUBRIUMS	MARBLEISING
MANFULNESSES	MANIFESTNESSES	MANOEUVRED	MANUFACTORIES	MARBLEIZED

MARBLEIZES	MARGINALIZATION	MARKETABILITY	MARMELIZES	MARSHLOCKSES
MARBLEIZING	MARGINALIZE	MARKETABLE	MARMELIZING	MARSHMALLOW
MARBLEWOOD	MARGINALIZED	MARKETABLENESS	MARMOREALLY	MARSHMALLOWIER
MARBLEWOODS	MARGINALIZES	MARKETABLY	MAROONINGS	MARSHMALLOWIEST
MARCANTANT	MARGINALIZING	MARKETEERS	MARPRELATE	MARSHMALLOWS
MARCANTANTS	MARGINALLY	MARKETINGS	MARPRELATED	MARSHMALLOWY
MARCASITES	MARGINATED	MARKETISATION	MARPRELATES	MARSHWORTS
MARCASITICAL	MARGINATES	MARKETISATIONS	MARPRELATING	MARSIPOBRANCH
MARCATISSIMO	MARGINATING	MARKETISED	MARQUESSATE	MARSIPOBRANCHS
MARCELLERS	MARGINATION	MARKETISES	MARQUESSATES	MARSQUAKES
MARCELLING	MARGINATIONS	MARKETISING	MARQUESSES	MARSUPIALIAN
MARCESCENCE	MARGRAVATE	MARKETIZATION	MARQUETERIE	MARSUPIALIANS
MARCESCENCES	MARGRAVATES	MARKETIZATIONS	MARQUETERIES	MARSUPIALS
MARCESCENT	MARGRAVIAL	MARKETIZED	MARQUETRIES	MARSUPIANS
MARCESCIBLE	MARGRAVIATE	MARKETIZES	MARQUISATE	MARTELLANDO
MARCHANTIA	MARGRAVIATES	MARKETIZING	MARQUISATES	MARTELLANDOS
MARCHANTIAS	MARGRAVINE	MARKETPLACE	MARQUISETTE	MARTELLATO
MARCHIONESS	MARGRAVINES	MARKETPLACES	MARQUISETTES	MARTELLATOS
MARCHIONESSES	MARGUERITA	MARKSMANSHIP	MARRIAGEABILITY	MARTELLING
MARCHLANDS	MARGUERITAS	MARKSMANSHIPS	MARRIAGEABLE	MARTENSITE
MARCHPANES	MARGUERITE	MARKSWOMAN	MARROWBONE	MARTENSITES
MARCONIGRAM	MARGUERITES	MARKSWOMEN	MARROWBONES	MARTENSITIC
MARCONIGRAMS	MARIALITES	MARLACIOUS	MARROWFATS	MARTENSITICALLY
MARCONIGRAPH	MARICULTURE	MARLINESPIKE	MARROWIEST	MARTIALISM
MARCONIGRAPHED	MARICULTURES	MARLINESPIKES	MARROWLESS	MARTIALISMS
MARCONIGRAPHING	MARICULTURIST	MARLINGSPIKE	MARROWSKIED	MARTIALIST
MARCONIGRAPHS	MARICULTURISTS	MARLINGSPIKES	MARROWSKIES	MARTIALISTS
MARCONIING	MARIGRAPHS	MARLINSPIKE	MARROWSKYING	MARTIALNESS
MARESCHALS	MARIHUANAS	MARLINSPIKES	MARSEILLES	MARTIALNESSES
MARGARINES	MARIJUANAS	MARLSTONES	MARSHALCIES	MARTINETISH
MARGARITAS	MARIMBAPHONE	MARMALADES	MARSHALERS	MARTINETISM
MARGARITES	MARIMBAPHONES	MARMALISED	MARSHALING	MARTINETISMS
MARGARITIC	MARIMBISTS	MARMALISES	MARSHALINGS	MARTINGALE
MARGARITIFEROUS	MARINADING	MARMALISING	MARSHALLED	MARTINGALES
MARGENTING	MARINATING	MARMALIZED	MARSHALLER	MARTINGALS
MARGHERITA	MARINATION	MARMALIZES	MARSHALLERS	MARTYRDOMS
MARGHERITAS	MARINATIONS	MARMALIZING	MARSHALLING	MARTYRISATION
MARGINALIA	MARIONBERRIES	MARMARISED	MARSHALLINGS	MARTYRISATIONS
MARGINALISATION	MARIONBERRY	MARMARISES	MARSHALSHIP	MARTYRISED
MARGINALISE	MARIONETTE	MARMARISING	MARSHALSHIPS	MARTYRISES
MARGINALISED	MARIONETTES	MARMARIZED	MARSHBUCKS	MARTYRISING
MARGINALISES	MARISCHALLED	MARMARIZES	MARSHELDER	MARTYRIZATION
MARGINALISING	MARISCHALLING	MARMARIZING	MARSHELDERS	MARTYRIZATIONS
MARGINALISM	MARISCHALS	MARMAROSES	MARSHINESS	MARTYRIZED
MARGINALISMS	MARIVAUDAGE	MARMAROSIS	MARSHINESSES	MARTYRIZES
MARGINALIST	MARIVAUDAGES	MARMELISED	MARSHLANDER	MARTYRIZING
MARGINALISTS	MARKEDNESS	MARMELISES	MARSHLANDERS	MARTYROLOGIC
MARGINALITIES	MARKEDNESSES	MARMELISING	MARSHLANDS	MARTYROLOGICAL
MARGINALITY	MARKETABILITIES	MARMELIZED	MARSHLOCKS	MARTYROLOGIES

MARTYROLOGIST	MASOCHISMS	MASTERLINESSES	MASTURBATE	MATERIALISTIC
MARTYROLOGISTS	MASOCHISTIC	MASTERMIND	MASTURBATED	MATERIALISTICAL
MARTYROLOGY	MASOCHISTICALLY	MASTERMINDED	MASTURBATES	MATERIALISTS
MARVELLERS	MASOCHISTS	MASTERMINDING	MASTURBATING	MATERIALITIES
MARVELLING	MASONICALLY	MASTERMINDS	MASTURBATION	MATERIALITY
MARVELLOUS	MASQUERADE	MASTERPIECE	MASTURBATIONS	MATERIALIZATION
MARVELLOUSLY	MASQUERADED	MASTERPIECES	MASTURBATOR	MATERIALIZE
MARVELLOUSNESS	MASQUERADER	MASTERSHIP	MASTURBATORS	MATERIALIZED
MARVELOUSLY	MASQUERADERS	MASTERSHIPS	MASTURBATORY	MATERIALIZER
MARVELOUSNESS	MASQUERADES	MASTERSINGER	MATACHINAS	MATERIALIZERS
MARVELOUSNESSES	MASQUERADING	MASTERSINGERS	MATAGOURIS	MATERIALIZES
MARZIPANNED	MASSACRERS	MASTERSTROKE	MATCHBOARD	MATERIALIZING
MARZIPANNING	MASSACRING	MASTERSTROKES	MATCHBOARDING	MATERIALLY
MASCARAING	MASSAGISTS	MASTERWORK	MATCHBOARDINGS	MATERIALNESS
MASCARPONE	MASSARANDUBA	MASTERWORKS	MATCHBOARDS	MATERIALNESSES
MASCARPONES	MASSARANDUBAS	MASTERWORT	MATCHBOOKS	MATERNALISM
MASCULINELY	MASSASAUGA	MASTERWORTS	MATCHBOXES	MATERNALISMS
MASCULINENESS	MASSASAUGAS	MASTHEADED	MATCHLESSLY	MATERNALISTIC
MASCULINENESSES	MASSERANDUBA	MASTHEADING	MATCHLESSNESS	MATERNALLY
MASCULINES	MASSERANDUBAS	MASTHOUSES	MATCHLESSNESSES	MATERNITIES
MASCULINISATION	MASSETERIC	MASTICABLE	MATCHLOCKS	MATEYNESSES
MASCULINISE	MASSIFICATION	MASTICATED	MATCHMAKER	MATFELLONS
MASCULINISED	MASSIFICATIONS	MASTICATES	MATCHMAKERS	MATGRASSES
MASCULINISES	MASSINESSES	MASTICATING	MATCHMAKES	MATHEMATIC
MASCULINISING	MASSIVENESS	MASTICATION	MATCHMAKING	MATHEMATICAL
MASCULINISM	MASSIVENESSES	MASTICATIONS	MATCHMAKINGS	MATHEMATICALLY
MASCULINISMS	MASSOTHERAPIES	MASTICATOR	MATCHMARKED	MATHEMATICIAN
MASCULINIST	MASSOTHERAPIST	MASTICATORIES	MATCHMARKING	MATHEMATICIANS
MASCULINISTS	MASSOTHERAPISTS	MASTICATORS	MATCHMARKS	MATHEMATICISE
MASCULINITIES	MASSOTHERAPY	MASTICATORY	MATCHPLAYS	MATHEMATICISED
MASCULINITY	MASSPRIEST	MASTIGOPHORAN	MATCHSTICK	MATHEMATICISES
MASCULINIZATION	MASSPRIESTS	MASTIGOPHORANS	MATCHSTICKS	MATHEMATICISING
MASCULINIZE	MASSYMORES	MASTIGOPHORE	MATCHWOODS	MATHEMATICISM
MASCULINIZED	MASTECTOMIES	MASTIGOPHORES	MATELASSES	MATHEMATICISMS
MASCULINIZES	MASTECTOMY	MASTIGOPHORIC	MATELLASSE	MATHEMATICIZE
MASCULINIZING	MASTERATES	MASTIGOPHOROUS	MATELLASSES	MATHEMATICIZED
MASCULISMS	MASTERCLASS	MASTITIDES	MATELOTTES	MATHEMATICIZES
MASCULISTS	MASTERCLASSES	MASTITISES	MATERFAMILIAS	MATHEMATICIZING
MASHGICHIM	MASTERDOMS	MASTODONIC	MATERFAMILIASES	MATHEMATICS
MASKALLONGE	MASTERFULLY	MASTODONTIC	MATERIALISATION	MATHEMATISATION
MASKALLONGES	MASTERFULNESS	MASTODONTS	MATERIALISE	MATHEMATISE
MASKALONGE	MASTERFULNESSES	MASTODYNIA	MATERIALISED	MATHEMATISED
MASKALONGES	MASTERHOOD	MASTODYNIAS	MATERIALISER	MATHEMATISES
MASKANONGE	MASTERHOODS	MASTOIDECTOMIES	MATERIALISERS	MATHEMATISING
MASKANONGES	MASTERINGS	MASTOIDECTOMY	MATERIALISES	MATHEMATIZATION
MASKINONGE	MASTERLESS	MASTOIDITIDES	MATERIALISING	MATHEMATIZE
MASKINONGES	MASTERLIER	MASTOIDITIS	MATERIALISM	MATHEMATIZED
MASKIROVKA	MASTERLIEST	MASTOIDITISES	MATERIALISMS	MATHEMATIZES
MASKIROVKAS	MASTERLINESS	MASTOPEXIES	MATERIALIST	MATHEMATIZING

M

MATINESSES	MATROCLINY	MAVERICKED	MEADOWSWEETS	MECHANICALLY
MATRESFAMILIAS	MATRONAGES	MAVERICKING	MEAGERNESS	MECHANICALNESS
MATRIARCHAL	MATRONHOOD	MAVOURNEEN	MEAGERNESSES	MECHANICALS
MATRIARCHALISM	MATRONHOODS	MAVOURNEENS	MEAGRENESS	MECHANICIAN
MATRIARCHALISMS	MATRONISED	MAVOURNINS	MEAGRENESSES	MECHANICIANS
MATRIARCHATE	MATRONISES	MAWKISHNESS	MEALINESSES	MECHANISABLE
MATRIARCHATES	MATRONISING	MAWKISHNESSES	MEALYMOUTHED	MECHANISATION
MATRIARCHIC	MATRONIZED	MAWMETRIES	MEANDERERS	MECHANISATIONS
MATRIARCHIES	MATRONIZES	MAXIDRESSES	MEANDERING	MECHANISED
MATRIARCHS	MATRONIZING	MAXILLARIES	MEANDERINGLY	MECHANISER
MATRIARCHY	MATRONLIER	MAXILLIPED	MEANDERINGS	MECHANISERS
MATRICIDAL	MATRONLIEST	MAXILLIPEDARY	MEANINGFUL	MECHANISES
MATRICIDES	MATRONLINESS	MAXILLIPEDE	MEANINGFULLY	MECHANISING
MATRICLINIC	MATRONLINESSES	MAXILLIPEDES	MEANINGFULNESS	MECHANISMS
MATRICLINOUS	MATRONSHIP	MAXILLIPEDS	MEANINGLESS	MECHANISTIC
MATRICULANT	MATRONSHIPS	MAXILLOFACIAL	MEANINGLESSLY	MECHANISTICALLY
MATRICULANTS	MATRONYMIC	MAXILLULAE	MEANINGLESSNESS	MECHANISTS
MATRICULAR	MATRONYMICS	MAXIMALIST	MEANNESSES	MECHANIZABLE
MATRICULAS	MATROYSHKA	MAXIMALISTS	MEANWHILES	MECHANIZATION
MATRICULATE	MATROYSHKAS	MAXIMAPHILIES	MEASLINESS	MECHANIZATIONS
MATRICULATED	MATRYOSHKA	MAXIMAPHILY	MEASLINESSES	MECHANIZED
MATRICULATES	MATRYOSHKAS	MAXIMATION	MEASURABILITIES	MECHANIZER
MATRICULATING	MATRYOSHKI	MAXIMATIONS	MEASURABILITY	MECHANIZERS
MATRICULATION	MATSUTAKES	MAXIMISATION	MEASURABLE	MECHANIZES
MATRICULATIONS	MATTAMORES	MAXIMISATIONS	MEASURABLENESS	MECHANIZING
MATRICULATOR	MATTERIEST	MAXIMISERS	MEASURABLY	MECHANOCHEMICAL
MATRICULATORS	MATTERLESS	MAXIMISING	MEASUREDLY	MECHANOMORPHISM
MATRICULATORY	MATTIFYING	MAXIMIZATION	MEASUREDNESS	MECHANORECEPTOR
MATRIFOCAL	MATTRASSES	MAXIMIZATIONS	MEASUREDNESSES	MECHANOTHERAPY
MATRIFOCALITIES	MATTRESSES	MAXIMIZERS	MEASURELESS	MECHATRONIC
MATRIFOCALITY	MATURATING	MAXIMIZING	MEASURELESSLY	MECHATRONICS
MATRILINEAL	MATURATION	MAYFLOWERS	MEASURELESSNESS	MECLIZINES
MATRILINEALLY	MATURATIONAL	MAYONNAISE	MEASUREMENT	MECONOPSES
MATRILINEAR	MATURATIONS	MAYONNAISES	MEASUREMENTS	MECONOPSIS
MATRILINIES	MATURATIVE	MAYORALTIES	MEASURINGS	MEDAILLONS
MATRILOCAL	MATURENESS	MAYORESSES	MEATINESSES	MEDALLIONED
MATRILOCALITIES	MATURENESSES	MAYORSHIPS	MEATLOAVES	MEDALLIONING
MATRILOCALITY	MATURITIES	MAYSTERDOME	MEATPACKER	MEDALLIONS
MATRILOCALLY	MATUTINALLY	MAYSTERDOMES	MEATPACKERS	MEDALLISTS
MATRIMONIAL	MAUDLINISM	MAZARINADE	MEATPACKING	MEDALPLAYS
MATRIMONIALLY	MAUDLINISMS	MAZARINADES	MEATPACKINGS	MEDDLESOME
MATRIMONIES	MAUDLINNESS	MAZEDNESSES	MEATSCREEN	MEDDLESOMELY
MATRIOSHKA	MAUDLINNESSES	MAZINESSES	MEATSCREENS	MEDDLESOMENESS
MATRIOSHKAS	MAULSTICKS	MEADOWIEST	MEATSPACES	MEDDLINGLY
MATRIOSHKI	MAUMETRIES	MEADOWLAND	MECAMYLAMINE	MEDEVACING
MATROCLINAL	MAUNDERERS	MEADOWLANDS	MECAMYLAMINES	MEDEVACKED
MATROCLINIC	MAUNDERING	MEADOWLARK	MECHANICAL	MEDEVACKING
MATROCLINIES	MAUNDERINGS	MEADOWLARKS	MECHANICALISM	MEDIAEVALISM
MATROCLINOUS	MAUSOLEUMS	MEADOWSWEET	MECHANICALISMS	MEDIAEVALISMS

MEDIAEVALIST	MEDICAMENTOUS	MEFLOQUINES	MEGALOMANIC	MEGATONNAGE
MEDIAEVALISTIC	MEDICAMENTS	MEGACEPHALIC	MEGALOPOLIS	MEGATONNAGES
MEDIAEVALISTS	MEDICASTER	MEGACEPHALIES	MEGALOPOLISES	MEGAVERTEBRATE
MEDIAEVALLY	MEDICASTERS	MEGACEPHALOUS	MEGALOPOLITAN	MEGAVERTEBRATES
MEDIAEVALS	MEDICATING	MEGACEPHALY	MEGALOPOLITANS	MEGAVITAMIN
MEDIAGENIC	MEDICATION	MEGACHURCH	MEGALOPSES	MEGAVITAMINS
MEDIASTINA	MEDICATIONS	MEGACHURCHES	MEGALOSAUR	MEIOFAUNAE
MEDIASTINAL	MEDICATIVE	MEGACITIES	MEGALOSAURI	MEIOFAUNAL
MEDIASTINUM	MEDICINABLE	MEGACORPORATION	MEGALOSAURIAN	MEIOFAUNAS
MEDIATENESS	MEDICINALLY	MEGACURIES	MEGALOSAURIANS	MEIOSPORES
MEDIATENESSES	MEDICINALS	MEGACYCLES	MEGALOSAURS	MEIOTICALLY
MEDIATIONAL	MEDICINERS	MEGADEATHS	MEGALOSAURUS	MEITNERIUM
MEDIATIONS	MEDICINING	MEGADROUGHT	MEGANEWTON	MEITNERIUMS
MEDIATISATION	MEDICOLEGAL	MEGADROUGHTS	MEGANEWTONS	MEKOMETERS
MEDIATISATIONS	MEDIEVALISM	MEGAFARADS	MEGAPARSEC	MELACONITE
MEDIATISED	MEDIEVALISMS	MEGAFAUNAE	MEGAPARSECS	MELACONITES
MEDIATISES	MEDIEVALIST	MEGAFAUNAL	MEGAPHONED	MELALEUCAS
MEDIATISING	MEDIEVALISTIC	MEGAFAUNAS	MEGAPHONES	MELAMPODES
MEDIATIZATION	MEDIEVALISTS	MEGAFLORAE	MEGAPHONIC	MELANAEMIA
MEDIATIZATIONS	MEDIEVALLY	MEGAFLORAS	MEGAPHONICALLY	MELANAEMIAS
MEDIATIZED	MEDIOCRACIES	MEGAGAMETE	MEGAPHONING	MELANCHOLIA
MEDIATIZES	MEDIOCRACY	MEGAGAMETES	MEGAPHYLLS	MELANCHOLIAC
MEDIATIZING	MEDIOCRITIES	MEGAGAMETOPHYTE	MEGAPIXELS	MELANCHOLIACS
MEDIATORIAL	MEDIOCRITY	MEGAGAUSSES	MEGAPLEXES	MELANCHOLIAE
MEDIATORIALLY	MEDITATING	MEGAHERBIVORE	MEGAPOLISES	MELANCHOLIAS
MEDIATORSHIP	MEDITATION	MEGAHERBIVORES	MEGAPOLITAN	MELANCHOLIC
MEDIATORSHIPS	MEDITATIONS	MEGAHERTZES	MEGAPOLITANS	MELANCHOLICALLY
MEDIATRESS	MEDITATIVE	MEGAJOULES	MEGAPROJECT	MELANCHOLICS
MEDIATRESSES	MEDITATIVELY	MEGAKARYOCYTE	MEGAPROJECTS	MELANCHOLIES
MEDIATRICES	MEDITATIVENESS	MEGAKARYOCYTES	MEGAQUAKES	MELANCHOLILY
MEDIATRIXES	MEDITATORS	MEGAKARYOCYTIC	MEGASCOPES	MELANCHOLINESS
MEDICALISATION	MEDITERRANEAN	MEGALITERS	MEGASCOPIC	MELANCHOLIOUS
MEDICALISATIONS	MEDIUMISTIC	MEGALITHIC	MEGASCOPICALLY	MELANCHOLY
MEDICALISE	MEDIUMSHIP	MEGALITRES	MEGASPORANGIA	MELANEMIAS
MEDICALISED	MEDIUMSHIPS	MEGALOBLAST	MEGASPORANGIUM	MELANISATION
MEDICALISES	MEDIVACING	MEGALOBLASTIC	MEGASPORES	MELANISATIONS
MEDICALISING	MEDIVACKED	MEGALOBLASTS	MEGASPORIC	MELANISING
MEDICALIZATION	MEDIVACKING	MEGALOCARDIA	MEGASPOROPHYLL	MELANISTIC
MEDICALIZATIONS	MEDRESSEHS	MEGALOCARDIAS	MEGASPOROPHYLLS	MELANIZATION
MEDICALIZE	MEDULLATED	MEGALOCEPHALIC	MEGASTORES	MELANIZATIONS
MEDICALIZED	MEDULLOBLASTOMA	MEGALOCEPHALIES	MEGASTORMS	MELANIZING
MEDICALIZES	MEDUSIFORM	MEGALOCEPHALOUS	MEGASTRUCTURE	MELANOBLAST
MEDICALIZING	MEEKNESSES	MEGALOCEPHALY	MEGASTRUCTURES	MELANOBLASTS
MEDICAMENT	MEERSCHAUM	MEGALODONS	MEGATECHNOLOGY	MELANOCHROI
MEDICAMENTAL	MEERSCHAUMS	MEGALOMANIA	MEGATHERES	MELANOCHROIC
MEDICAMENTALLY	MEETINGHOUSE	MEGALOMANIAC	MEGATHERIAN	MELANOCHROOUS
MEDICAMENTARY	MEETINGHOUSES	MEGALOMANIACAL	MEGATHREAD	MELANOCYTE
MEDICAMENTED	MEETNESSES	MEGALOMANIACS	MEGATHREADS	MELANOCYTES
MEDICAMENTING	MEFLOQUINE	MEGALOMANIAS	MEGATHRUST	MELANOGENESES

M

MELANOGENESIS	MELLOPHONES	MEMBRANOUS	MENDACIOUS	MENSTRUATIONS
MELANOMATA	MELLOTRONS	MEMBRANOUSLY	MENDACIOUSLY	MENSTRUOUS
MELANOPHORE	MELLOWIEST	MEMBRILLOS	MENDACIOUSNESS	MENSTRUUMS
MELANOPHORES	MELLOWNESS	MEMOIRISMS	MENDACITIES	MENSURABILITIES
MELANOSITIES	MELLOWNESSES	MEMOIRISTS	MENDELEVIUM	MENSURABILITY
MELANOSITY	MELLOWSPEAK	MEMORABILE	MENDELEVIUMS	MENSURABLE
MELANOSOME	MELLOWSPEAKS	MEMORABILIA	MENDICANCIES	MENSURATION
MELANOSOMES	MELOCOTONS	MEMORABILITIES	MENDICANCY	MENSURATIONAL
MELANOTROPIN	MELOCOTOON	MEMORABILITY	MENDICANTS	MENSURATIONS
MELANOTROPINS	MELOCOTOONS	MEMORABLENESS	MENDICITIES	MENSURATIVE
MELANTERITE	MELODICALLY	MEMORABLENESSES	MENINGIOMA	MENTALESES
MELANTERITES	MELODIOUSLY	MEMORANDUM	MENINGIOMAS	MENTALISMS
MELANURIAS	MELODIOUSNESS	MEMORANDUMS	MENINGIOMATA	MENTALISTIC
MELAPHYRES	MELODIOUSNESSES	MEMORATIVE	MENINGITIC	MENTALISTICALLY
MELASTOMACEOUS	MELODISERS	MEMORIALISATION	MENINGITIDES	MENTALISTS
MELASTOMES	MELODISING	MEMORIALISE	MENINGITIS	MENTALITIES
MELATONINS	MELODIZERS	MEMORIALISED	MENINGITISES	MENTATIONS
MELIACEOUS	MELODIZING	MEMORIALISER	MENINGOCELE	MENTHACEOUS
MELICOTTON	MELODRAMAS	MEMORIALISERS	MENINGOCELES	MENTHOLATED
MELICOTTONS	MELODRAMATIC	MEMORIALISES	MENINGOCOCCAL	MENTICIDES
MELIORABLE	MELODRAMATICS	MEMORIALISING	MENINGOCOCCI	MENTIONABLE
MELIORATED	MELODRAMATISE	MEMORIALIST	MENINGOCOCCIC	MENTIONERS
MELIORATES	MELODRAMATISED	MEMORIALISTS	MENINGOCOCCUS	MENTIONING
MELIORATING	MELODRAMATISES	MEMORIALIZATION	MENISCECTOMIES	MENTONNIERE
MELIORATION	MELODRAMATISING	MEMORIALIZE	MENISCECTOMY	MENTONNIERES
MELIORATIONS	MELODRAMATIST	MEMORIALIZED	MENISCUSES	MENTORINGS
MELIORATIVE	MELODRAMATISTS	MEMORIALIZER	MENISPERMACEOUS	MENTORSHIP
MELIORATIVES	MELODRAMATIZE	MEMORIALIZERS	MENISPERMUM	MENTORSHIPS
MELIORATOR	MELODRAMATIZED	MEMORIALIZES	MENISPERMUMS	MENUISIERS
MELIORATORS	MELODRAMATIZES	MEMORIALIZING	MENOLOGIES	MEPACRINES
MELIORISMS	MELODRAMATIZING	MEMORIALLY	MENOMINEES	MEPERIDINE
MELIORISTIC	MELODRAMES	MEMORISABLE	MENOPAUSAL	MEPERIDINES
MELIORISTS	MELOMANIAC	MEMORISATION	MENOPAUSES	MEPHITICAL
MELIORITIES	MELOMANIACS	MEMORISATIONS	MENOPAUSIC	MEPHITICALLY
MELIPHAGOUS	MELOMANIAS	MEMORISERS	MENOPOLISES	MEPHITISES
MELISMATIC	MELONGENES	MEMORISING	MENORRHAGIA	MEPHITISMS
MELLIFEROUS	MELOXICAMS	MEMORIZABLE	MENORRHAGIAS	MEPROBAMATE
MELLIFICATION	MELPHALANS	MEMORIZATION	MENORRHAGIC	MEPROBAMATES
MELLIFICATIONS	MELTABILITIES	MEMORIZATIONS	MENORRHEAS	MERBROMINS
MELLIFLUENCE	MELTABILITY	MEMORIZERS	MENORRHOEA	MERCANTILE
MELLIFLUENCES	MELTINGNESS	MEMORIZING	MENORRHOEAS	MERCANTILISM
MELLIFLUENT	MELTINGNESSES	MEMORIZINGS	MENSCHIEST	MERCANTILISMS
MELLIFLUENTLY	MELTWATERS	MENACINGLY	MENSERVANTS	MERCANTILIST
MELLIFLUOUS	MELUNGEONS	MENADIONES	MENSTRUALLY	MERCANTILISTIC
MELLIFLUOUSLY	MEMBERLESS	MENAGERIES	MENSTRUATE	MERCANTILISTS
MELLIFLUOUSNESS	MEMBERSHIP	MENAQUINONE	MENSTRUATED	MERCAPTANS
MELLIPHAGOUS	MEMBERSHIPS	MENAQUINONES	MENSTRUATES	MERCAPTIDE
MELLIVOROUS	MEMBRANACEOUS	MENARCHEAL	MENSTRUATING	MERCAPTIDES
MELLOPHONE	MEMBRANEOUS	MENARCHIAL	MENSTRUATION	MERCAPTOPURINE

MERCAPTOPURINES	MERCIFYING	MERITOCRAT	MESENCHYME	MESOCEPHALY
MERCENARIES	MERCILESSLY	MERITOCRATIC	MESENCHYMES	MESOCRANIES
MERCENARILY	MERCILESSNESS	MERITOCRATS	MESENTERIAL	MESOCRATIC
MERCENARINESS	MERCILESSNESSES	MERITORIOUS	MESENTERIC	MESOCYCLONE
MERCENARINESSES	MERCURATED	MERITORIOUSLY	MESENTERIES	MESOCYCLONES
MERCENARISM	MERCURATES	MERITORIOUSNESS	MESENTERITIS	MESODERMAL
MERCENARISMS	MERCURATING	MERMAIDENS	MESENTERITISES	MESODERMIC
MERCERISATION	MERCURATION	MEROBLASTIC	MESENTERON	MESOGASTRIA
MERCERISATIONS	MERCURATIONS	MEROBLASTICALLY	MESENTERONIC	MESOGASTRIC
MERCERISED	MERCURIALISE	MEROGENESES	MESHUGAASEN	MESOGASTRIUM
MERCERISER	MERCURIALISED	MEROGENESIS	MESHUGASEN	MESOGLOEAS
MERCERISERS	MERCURIALISES	MEROGENETIC	MESHUGGENAH	MESOGNATHIES
MERCERISES	MERCURIALISING	MEROGONIES	MESHUGGENAHS	MESOGNATHISM
MERCERISING	MERCURIALISM	MEROMORPHIC	MESHUGGENEH	MESOGNATHISMS
MERCERIZATION	MERCURIALISMS	MEROMYOSIN	MESHUGGENEHS	MESOGNATHOUS
MERCERIZATIONS	MERCURIALIST	MEROMYOSINS	MESHUGGENER	MESOGNATHY
MERCERIZED	MERCURIALISTS	MERONYMIES	MESHUGGENERS	MESOHIPPUS
MERCERIZER	MERCURIALITIES	MEROPIDANS	MESITYLENE	MESOHIPPUSES
MERCERIZERS	MERCURIALITY	MEROPLANKTON	MESITYLENES	MESOKURTIC
MERCERIZES	MERCURIALIZE	MEROPLANKTONS	MESMERICAL	MESOMERISM
MERCERIZING	MERCURIALIZED	MEROZOITES	MESMERICALLY	MESOMERISMS
MERCHANDISE	MERCURIALIZES	MERPEOPLES	MESMERISATION	MESOMORPHIC
MERCHANDISED	MERCURIALIZING	MERRIMENTS	MESMERISATIONS	MESOMORPHIES
MERCHANDISER	MERCURIALLY	MERRINESSES	MESMERISED	MESOMORPHISM
MERCHANDISERS	MERCURIALNESS	MERRYMAKER	MESMERISER	MESOMORPHISMS
MERCHANDISES	MERCURIALNESSES	MERRYMAKERS	MESMERISERS	MESOMORPHOUS
MERCHANDISING	MERCURIALS	MERRYMAKING	MESMERISES	MESOMORPHS
MERCHANDISINGS	MERCURISED	MERRYMAKINGS	MESMERISING	MESOMORPHY
MERCHANDIZE	MERCURISES	MERRYTHOUGHT	MESMERISMS	MESONEPHRIC
MERCHANDIZED	MERCURISING	MERRYTHOUGHTS	MESMERISTS	MESONEPHROI
MERCHANDIZER	MERCURIZED	MERVEILLEUSE	MESMERIZATION	MESONEPHROS
MERCHANDIZERS	MERCURIZES	MERVEILLEUSES	MESMERIZATIONS	MESONEPHROSES
MERCHANDIZES	MERCURIZING	MERVEILLEUX	MESMERIZED	MESOPAUSES
MERCHANDIZING	MERDIVOROUS	MERVEILLEUXES	MESMERIZER	MESOPELAGIC
MERCHANDIZINGS	MEREOLOGICAL	MESALLIANCE	MESMERIZERS	MESOPHILES
MERCHANTABILITY	MEREOLOGIES	MESALLIANCES	MESMERIZES	MESOPHILIC
MERCHANTABLE	MERESTONES	MESATICEPHALIC	MESMERIZING	MESOPHYLLIC
MERCHANTED	MERETRICIOUS	MESATICEPHALIES	MESNALTIES	MESOPHYLLOUS
MERCHANTING	MERETRICIOUSLY	MESATICEPHALOUS	MESOAMERICAN	MESOPHYLLS
MERCHANTINGS	MERGANSERS	MESATICEPHALY	MESOBENTHOS	MESOPHYTES
MERCHANTLIKE	MERIDIONAL	MESCALINES	MESOBENTHOSES	MESOPHYTIC
MERCHANTMAN	MERIDIONALITIES	MESCALISMS	MESOBLASTIC	MESOSCAPHE
MERCHANTMEN	MERIDIONALITY	MESDEMOISELLES	MESOBLASTS	MESOSCAPHES
MERCHANTRIES	MERIDIONALLY	MESENCEPHALA	MESOCEPHALIC	MESOSPHERE
MERCHANTRY	MERIDIONALS	MESENCEPHALIC	MESOCEPHALICS	MESOSPHERES
MERCHILDREN	MERISTEMATIC	MESENCEPHALON	MESOCEPHALIES	MESOSPHERIC
MERCIFULLY	MERISTICALLY	MESENCEPHALONS	MESOCEPHALISM	MESOTHELIA
MERCIFULNESS	MERITOCRACIES	MESENCHYMAL	MESOCEPHALISMS	MESOTHELIAL
MERCIFULNESSES	MERITOCRACY	MESENCHYMATOUS	MESOCEPHALOUS	MESOTHELIOMA

M

MESOTHELIOMAS	METABOTROPIC	METAGRABOLISES	METALLOCENES	METAMORPHOSIS
MESOTHELIOMATA	METACARPAL	METAGRABOLISING	METALLOGENETIC	METAMORPHOUS
MESOTHELIUM	METACARPALS	METAGRABOLIZE	METALLOGENIC	METANALYSES
MESOTHELIUMS	METACARPUS	METAGRABOLIZED	METALLOGENIES	METANALYSIS
MESOTHERAPIES	METACENTER	METAGRABOLIZES	METALLOGENY	METANARRATIVE
MESOTHERAPY	METACENTERS	METAGRABOLIZING	METALLOGRAPHER	METANARRATIVES
MESOTHORACES	METACENTRE	METAGROBOLISE	METALLOGRAPHERS	METANEPHRIC
MESOTHORACIC	METACENTRES	METAGROBOLISED	METALLOGRAPHIC	METANEPHROI
MESOTHORAX	METACENTRIC	METAGROBOLISES	METALLOGRAPHIES	METANEPHROS
MESOTHORAXES	METACENTRICS	METAGROBOLISING	METALLOGRAPHIST	METAPERIODIC
MESOTHORIUM	METACERCARIA	METAGROBOLIZE	METALLOGRAPHY	METAPHASES
MESOTHORIUMS	METACERCARIAE	METAGROBOLIZED	METALLOIDAL	METAPHONIES
MESOTROPHIC	METACERCARIAL	METAGROBOLIZES	METALLOIDS	METAPHORIC
MESQUINERIE	METACERCARIAS	METAGROBOLIZING	METALLOPHONE	METAPHORICAL
MESQUINERIES	METACHROMATIC	METALANGUAGE	METALLOPHONES	METAPHORICALLY
MESSAGINGS	METACHROMATISM	METALANGUAGES	METALLURGIC	METAPHORIST
MESSALINES	METACHROMATISMS	METALCORES	METALLURGICAL	METAPHORISTS
MESSEIGNEURS	METACHRONISM	METALDEHYDE	METALLURGICALLY	METAPHOSPHATE
MESSENGERED	METACHRONISMS	METALDEHYDES	METALLURGIES	METAPHOSPHATES
MESSENGERING	METACHROSES	METALEPSES	METALLURGIST	METAPHOSPHORIC
MESSENGERS	METACHROSIS	METALEPSIS	METALLURGISTS	METAPHRASE
MESSIAHSHIP	METACINNABARITE	METALEPTIC	METALLURGY	METAPHRASED
MESSIAHSHIPS	METACOGNITION	METALEPTICAL	METALMARKS	METAPHRASES
MESSIANICALLY	METACOGNITIONS	METALHEADS	METALSMITH	METAPHRASING
MESSIANISM	METACOMPUTER	METALINGUISTIC	METALSMITHS	METAPHRASIS
MESSIANISMS	METACOMPUTERS	METALINGUISTICS	METALWARES	METAPHRAST
MESSINESSES	METACOMPUTING	METALISATION	METALWORKER	METAPHRASTIC
MESTRANOLS	METACOMPUTINGS	METALISATIONS	METALWORKERS	METAPHRASTICAL
METABISULPHITE	METAETHICAL	METALISING	METALWORKING	METAPHRASTS
METABISULPHITES	METAETHICS	METALIZATION	METALWORKINGS	METAPHYSIC
METABOLICALLY	METAFEMALE	METALIZATIONS	METALWORKS	METAPHYSICAL
METABOLIES	METAFEMALES	METALIZING	METAMATERIAL	METAPHYSICALLY
METABOLISABLE	METAFICTION	METALLICALLY	METAMATERIALS	METAPHYSICIAN
METABOLISE	METAFICTIONAL	METALLIDING	METAMATHEMATICS	METAPHYSICIANS
METABOLISED	METAFICTIONIST	METALLIDINGS	METAMERICALLY	METAPHYSICISE
METABOLISES	METAFICTIONISTS	METALLIFEROUS	METAMERISM	METAPHYSICISED
METABOLISING	METAFICTIONS	METALLINGS	METAMERISMS	METAPHYSICISES
METABOLISM	METAGALACTIC	METALLISATION	METAMICTISATION	METAPHYSICISING
METABOLISMS	METAGALAXIES	METALLISATIONS	METAMICTIZATION	METAPHYSICIST
METABOLITE	METAGALAXY	METALLISED	METAMORPHIC	METAPHYSICISTS
METABOLITES	METAGENESES	METALLISES	METAMORPHICALLY	METAPHYSICIZE
METABOLIZABLE	METAGENESIS	METALLISING	METAMORPHISM	METAPHYSICIZED
METABOLIZE	METAGENETIC	METALLISTS	METAMORPHISMS	METAPHYSICIZES
METABOLIZED	METAGENETICALLY	METALLIZATION	METAMORPHIST	METAPHYSICIZING
METABOLIZES	METAGNATHISM	METALLIZATIONS	METAMORPHISTS	METAPHYSICS
METABOLIZING	METAGNATHISMS	METALLIZED	METAMORPHOSE	METAPLASES
METABOLOME	METAGNATHOUS	METALLIZES	METAMORPHOSED	METAPLASIA
METABOLOMES	METAGRABOLISE	METALLIZING	METAMORPHOSES	METAPLASIAS
METABOLOMICS	METAGRABOLISED	METALLOCENE	METAMORPHOSING	METAPLASIS

METAPLASMIC	METATHESIS	METEOROGRAPH	METHODICALNESS	METHYLMERCURY
METAPLASMS	METATHESISE	METEOROGRAPHIC	METHODISATION	METHYLPHENIDATE
METAPLASTIC	METATHESISED	METEOROGRAPHS	METHODISATIONS	METHYLPHENOL
METAPOLITICAL	METATHESISES	METEOROIDAL	METHODISED	METHYLPHENOLS
METAPOLITICS	METATHESISING	METEOROIDS	METHODISER	METHYLTHIONINE
METAPROTEIN	METATHESIZE	METEOROLITE	METHODISERS	METHYLTHIONINES
METAPROTEINS	METATHESIZED	METEOROLITES	METHODISES	METHYLXANTHINE
METAPSYCHIC	METATHESIZES	METEOROLOGIC	METHODISING	METHYLXANTHINES
METAPSYCHICAL	METATHESIZING	METEOROLOGICAL	METHODISMS	METHYSERGIDE
METAPSYCHICS	METATHETIC	METEOROLOGIES	METHODISTIC	METHYSERGIDES
METAPSYCHOLOGY	METATHETICAL	METEOROLOGIST	METHODISTS	METICULOSITIES
METARCHONS	METATHETICALLY	METEOROLOGISTS	METHODIZATION	METICULOSITY
METASEQUOIA	METATHORACES	METEOROLOGY	METHODIZATIONS	METICULOUS
METASEQUOIAS	METATHORACIC	METERSTICK	METHODIZED	METICULOUSLY
METASILICATE	METATHORAX	METERSTICKS	METHODIZER	METICULOUSNESS
METASILICATES	METATHORAXES	METESTICKS	METHODIZERS	METOCLOPRAMIDE
METASILICIC	METATUNGSTIC	METESTROUS	METHODIZES	METOCLOPRAMIDES
METASOMATA	METAVANADIC	METESTRUSES	METHODIZING	METOESTROUS
METASOMATIC	METAVERSES	METFORMINS	METHODOLOGICAL	METOESTRUS
METASOMATISM	METAXYLEMS	METHACRYLATE	METHODOLOGIES	METOESTRUSES
METASOMATISMS	METECDYSES	METHACRYLATES	METHODOLOGIST	METONYMICAL
METASOMATOSES	METECDYSIS	METHACRYLIC	METHODOLOGISTS	METONYMICALLY
METASOMATOSIS	METEMPIRIC	METHADONES	METHODOLOGY	METONYMIES
METASTABILITIES	METEMPIRICAL	METHAEMOGLOBIN	METHOMANIA	METOPOSCOPIC
METASTABILITY	METEMPIRICALLY	METHAEMOGLOBINS	METHOMANIAS	METOPOSCOPICAL
METASTABLE	METEMPIRICISM	METHAMPHETAMINE	METHOTREXATE	METOPOSCOPIES
METASTABLES	METEMPIRICISMS	METHANAMIDE	METHOTREXATES	METOPOSCOPIST
METASTABLY	METEMPIRICIST	METHANAMIDES	METHOXIDES	METOPOSCOPISTS
METASTASES	METEMPIRICISTS	METHANATION	METHOXYBENZENE	METOPOSCOPY
METASTASIS	METEMPIRICS	METHANATIONS	METHOXYBENZENES	METRALGIAS
METASTASISE	METEMPSYCHOSES	METHANOMETER	METHOXYCHLOR	METRESTICK
METASTASISED	METEMPSYCHOSIS	METHANOMETERS	METHOXYCHLORS	METRESTICKS
METASTASISES	METEMPSYCHOSIST	METHANOYLS	METHOXYFLURANE	METRICALLY
METASTASISING	METENCEPHALA	METHAQUALONE	METHOXYFLURANES	METRICATED
METASTASIZE	METENCEPHALIC	METHAQUALONES	METHYLAMINE	METRICATES
METASTASIZED	METENCEPHALON	METHEDRINE	METHYLAMINES	METRICATING
METASTASIZES	METENCEPHALONS	METHEDRINES	METHYLASES	METRICATION
METASTASIZING	METEORICALLY	METHEGLINS	METHYLATED	METRICATIONS
METASTATIC	METEORISMS	METHEMOGLOBIN	METHYLATES	METRICIANS
METASTATICALLY	METEORISTS	METHEMOGLOBINS	METHYLATING	METRICISED
METATARSAL	METEORITAL	METHENAMINE	METHYLATION	METRICISES
METATARSALS	METEORITES	METHENAMINES	METHYLATIONS	METRICISING
METATARSUS	METEORITIC	METHICILLIN	METHYLATOR	METRICISMS
METATHEORETICAL	METEORITICAL	METHICILLINS	METHYLATORS	METRICISTS
METATHEORIES	METEORITICIST	METHINKETH	METHYLCELLULOSE	METRICIZED
METATHEORY	METEORITICISTS	METHIONINE	METHYLDOPA	METRICIZES
METATHERIAN	METEORITICS	METHIONINES	METHYLDOPAS	METRICIZING
METATHERIANS	METEOROGRAM	METHODICAL	METHYLENES	METRIFICATION
METATHESES	METEOROGRAMS	METHODICALLY	METHYLMERCURIES	METRIFICATIONS

ten to fifteen letter words | 937

METRIFIERS	MIAROLITIC	MICROBREWERIES	MICROCOPYING	MICROFARAD
METRIFONATE	MIASMATICAL	MICROBREWERS	MICROCOPYINGS	MICROFARADS
METRIFONATES	MIASMATOUS	MICROBREWERY	MICROCOSMIC	MICROFAUNA
METRIFYING	MIASMICALLY	MICROBREWING	MICROCOSMICAL	MICROFAUNAE
METRITISES	MICRIFYING	MICROBREWINGS	MICROCOSMICALLY	MICROFAUNAL
METROLOGIC	MICROAEROPHILE	MICROBREWS	MICROCOSMOS	MICROFAUNAS
METROLOGICAL	MICROAEROPHILES	MICROBUBBLES	MICROCOSMOSES	MICROFELSITIC
METROLOGICALLY	MICROAEROPHILIC	MICROBURST	MICROCOSMS	MICROFIBER
METROLOGIES	MICROAGGRESSION	MICROBURSTS	MICROCRACK	MICROFIBERS
METROLOGIST	MICROAMPERE	MICROBUSES	MICROCRACKED	MICROFIBRE
METROLOGISTS	MICROAMPERES	MICROBUSSES	MICROCRACKING	MICROFIBRES
METROMANIA	MICROANALYSES	MICROCAPSULE	MICROCRACKINGS	MICROFIBRIL
METROMANIAS	MICROANALYSIS	MICROCAPSULES	MICROCRACKS	MICROFIBRILLAR
METRONIDAZOLE	MICROANALYST	MICROCARDS	MICROCREDIT	MICROFIBRILS
METRONIDAZOLES	MICROANALYSTS	MICROCASSETTE	MICROCREDITS	MICROFICHE
METRONOMES	MICROANALYTIC	MICROCASSETTES	MICROCRYSTAL	MICROFICHES
METRONOMIC	MICROANALYTICAL	MICROCELEBRITY	MICROCRYSTALS	MICROFILAMENT
METRONOMICAL	MICROANATOMICAL	MICROCEPHAL	MICROCULTURAL	MICROFILAMENTS
METRONOMICALLY	MICROANATOMIES	MICROCEPHALIC	MICROCULTURE	MICROFILARIA
METRONYMIC	MICROANATOMY	MICROCEPHALICS	MICROCULTURES	MICROFILARIAE
METRONYMICS	MICROARRAY	MICROCEPHALIES	MICROCURIE	MICROFILARIAL
METROPLEXES	MICROARRAYS	MICROCEPHALOUS	MICROCURIES	MICROFILING
METROPOLIS	MICROBALANCE	MICROCEPHALS	MICROCURRENT	MICROFILINGS
METROPOLISES	MICROBALANCES	MICROCEPHALY	MICROCURRENTS	MICROFILMABLE
METROPOLITAN	MICROBAROGRAPH	MICROCHEMICAL	MICROCYTES	MICROFILMED
METROPOLITANATE	MICROBAROGRAPHS	MICROCHEMISTRY	MICROCYTIC	MICROFILMER
METROPOLITANISE	MICROBEADS	MICROCHIPPED	MICRODETECTION	MICROFILMERS
METROPOLITANISM	MICROBEAMS	MICROCHIPPING	MICRODETECTIONS	MICROFILMING
METROPOLITANIZE	MICROBIOLOGIC	MICROCHIPS	MICRODETECTOR	MICROFILMS
METROPOLITANS	MICROBIOLOGICAL	MICROCIRCUIT	MICRODETECTORS	MICROFILTER
METROPOLITICAL	MICROBIOLOGIES	MICROCIRCUITRY	MICRODISSECTION	MICROFILTERS
METRORRHAGIA	MICROBIOLOGIST	MICROCIRCUITS	MICRODONTOUS	MICROFINANCE
METRORRHAGIAS	MICROBIOLOGISTS	MICROCLIMATE	MICRODOSED	MICROFINANCES
METROSEXUAL	MICROBIOLOGY	MICROCLIMATES	MICRODOSES	MICROFLOPPIES
METROSEXUALS	MICROBIOME	MICROCLIMATIC	MICRODOSING	MICROFLOPPY
METROSTYLE	MICROBIOMES	MICROCLINE	MICRODRIVE	MICROFLORA
METROSTYLES	MICROBIOTA	MICROCLINES	MICRODRIVES	MICROFLORAE
METTLESOME	MICROBIOTAS	MICROCOCCAL	MICRODRONE	MICROFLORAL
METTLESOMENESS	MICROBLADE	MICROCOCCI	MICRODRONES	MICROFLORAS
MEZCALINES	MICROBLADED	MICROCOCCUS	MICROEARTHQUAKE	MICROFORMS
MEZZALUNAS	MICROBLADES	MICROCODES	MICROECONOMIC	MICROFOSSIL
MEZZANINES	MICROBLADING	MICROCOMPONENT	MICROECONOMICS	MICROFOSSILS
MEZZOTINTED	MICROBLADINGS	MICROCOMPONENTS	MICROELECTRODE	MICROFUNGI
MEZZOTINTER	MICROBLOGGER	MICROCOMPUTER	MICROELECTRODES	MICROFUNGUS
MEZZOTINTERS	MICROBLOGGERS	MICROCOMPUTERS	MICROELECTRONIC	MICROFUNGUSES
MEZZOTINTING	MICROBLOGGING	MICROCOMPUTING	MICROELEMENT	MICROGAMETE
MEZZOTINTO	MICROBLOGGINGS	MICROCOMPUTINGS	MICROELEMENTS	MICROGAMETES
MEZZOTINTOS	MICROBLOGS	MICROCOPIED	MICROEVOLUTION	MICROGAMETOCYTE
MEZZOTINTS	MICROBREWER	MICROCOPIES	MICROEVOLUTIONS	MICROGENERATION

MICROGLIAS	MICROLOGICALLY	MICRONISATIONS	MICROPIPET	MICRORADIOGRAPH
MICROGRAMS	MICROLOGIES	MICRONISED	MICROPIPETS	MICROREADER
MICROGRANITE	MICROLOGIST	MICRONISES	MICROPIPETTE	MICROREADERS
MICROGRANITES	MICROLOGISTS	MICRONISING	MICROPIPETTES	MICROSATELLITE
MICROGRANITIC	MICROLUCES	MICRONIZATION	MICROPLANKTON	MICROSATELLITES
MICROGRAPH	MICROLUXES	MICRONIZATIONS	MICROPLANKTONS	MICROSCALE
MICROGRAPHED	MICROMANAGE	MICRONIZED	MICROPLASTIC	MICROSCALES
MICROGRAPHER	MICROMANAGED	MICRONIZES	MICROPLASTICS	MICROSCOPE
MICROGRAPHERS	MICROMANAGEMENT	MICRONIZING	MICROPOLIS	MICROSCOPES
MICROGRAPHIC	MICROMANAGER	MICRONUCLEI	MICROPOLISES	MICROSCOPIC
MICROGRAPHICS	MICROMANAGERS	MICRONUCLEUS	MICROPORES	MICROSCOPICAL
MICROGRAPHIES	MICROMANAGES	MICRONUCLEUSES	MICROPOROSITIES	MICROSCOPICALLY
MICROGRAPHING	MICROMANAGING	MICRONUTRIENT	MICROPOROSITY	MICROSCOPIES
MICROGRAPHS	MICROMARKETING	MICRONUTRIENTS	MICROPOROUS	MICROSCOPIST
MICROGRAPHY	MICROMARKETINGS	MICROORGANISM	MICROPOWER	MICROSCOPISTS
MICROGRAVITIES	MICROMERES	MICROORGANISMS	MICROPOWERS	MICROSCOPY
MICROGRAVITY	MICROMESHES	MICROPARASITE	MICROPRINT	MICROSECOND
MICROGREEN	MICROMETEORITE	MICROPARASITES	MICROPRINTED	MICROSECONDS
MICROGREENS	MICROMETEORITES	MICROPARASITIC	MICROPRINTING	MICROSEISM
MICROGRIDS	MICROMETEORITIC	MICROPARTICLE	MICROPRINTINGS	MICROSEISMIC
MICROGROOVE	MICROMETEOROID	MICROPARTICLES	MICROPRINTS	MICROSEISMICAL
MICROGROOVES	MICROMETEOROIDS	MICROPARTIES	MICROPRISM	MICROSEISMICITY
MICROHABITAT	MICROMETER	MICROPARTY	MICROPRISMS	MICROSEISMS
MICROHABITATS	MICROMETERS	MICROPAYMENT	MICROPROBE	MICROSITES
MICROHERBS	MICROMETHOD	MICROPAYMENTS	MICROPROBES	MICROSKIRT
MICROIMAGE	MICROMETHODS	MICROPEGMATITE	MICROPROCESSING	MICROSKIRTS
MICROIMAGES	MICROMETRE	MICROPEGMATITES	MICROPROCESSOR	MICROSLEEP
MICROINCHES	MICROMETRES	MICROPEGMATITIC	MICROPROCESSORS	MICROSLEEPS
MICROINJECT	MICROMETRIC	MICROPHAGE	MICROPROGRAM	MICROSMATIC
MICROINJECTED	MICROMETRICAL	MICROPHAGES	MICROPROGRAMS	MICROSOMAL
MICROINJECTING	MICROMETRIES	MICROPHAGOUS	MICROPROJECTION	MICROSOMES
MICROINJECTION	MICROMETRY	MICROPHONE	MICROPROJECTOR	MICROSPECIES
MICROINJECTIONS	MICROMICROCURIE	MICROPHONES	MICROPROJECTORS	MICROSPHERE
MICROINJECTS	MICROMICROFARAD	MICROPHONIC	MICROPSIAS	MICROSPHERES
MICROLIGHT	MICROMILLIMETER	MICROPHONICS	MICROPTEROUS	MICROSPHERICAL
MICROLIGHTING	MICROMILLIMETRE	MICROPHOTOGRAPH	MICROPUBLISHER	MICROSPORANGIA
MICROLIGHTINGS	MICROMINIATURE	MICROPHOTOMETER	MICROPUBLISHERS	MICROSPORANGIUM
MICROLIGHTS	MICROMINIS	MICROPHOTOMETRY	MICROPUBLISHING	MICROSPORE
MICROLITER	MICROMOBILITIES	MICROPHYLL	MICROPULSATION	MICROSPORES
MICROLITERS	MICROMOBILITY	MICROPHYLLOUS	MICROPULSATIONS	MICROSPORIC
MICROLITES	MICROMOLAR	MICROPHYLLS	MICROPUMPS	MICROSPORIDIAN
MICROLITHIC	MICROMOLES	MICROPHYSICAL	MICROPUNCTURE	MICROSPOROCYTE
MICROLITHS	MICROMORPHOLOGY	MICROPHYSICALLY	MICROPUNCTURES	MICROSPOROCYTES
MICROLITIC	MICROMORTS	MICROPHYSICIST	MICROPYLAR	MICROSPOROPHYLL
MICROLITRE	MICRONATION	MICROPHYSICISTS	MICROPYLES	MICROSPOROUS
MICROLITRES	MICRONATIONS	MICROPHYSICS	MICROPYROMETER	MICROSTATE
MICROLOANS	MICRONEEDLE	MICROPHYTE	MICROPYROMETERS	MICROSTATES
MICROLOGIC	MICRONEEDLES	MICROPHYTES	MICROQUAKE	MICROSTOMATOUS
MICROLOGICAL	MICRONISATION	MICROPHYTIC	MICROQUAKES	MICROSTOMOUS

M

MICROSTRUCTURAL	MICROWAVING	MIDSHIPMATES	MILITARIZE	MILLESIMALLY
MICROSTRUCTURE	MICROWIRES	MIDSHIPMEN	MILITARIZED	MILLESIMALS
MICROSTRUCTURES	MICROWORLD	MIDSTORIES	MILITARIZES	MILLHOUSES
MICROSURGEON	MICROWORLDS	MIDSTREAMS	MILITARIZING	MILLIAMPERE
MICROSURGEONS	MICROWRITER	MIDSUMMERS	MILITATING	MILLIAMPERES
MICROSURGERIES	MICROWRITERS	MIDWATCHES	MILITATION	MILLIARIES
MICROSURGERY	MICRURGIES	MIDWESTERN	MILITATIONS	MILLICURIE
MICROSURGICAL	MICTURATED	MIDWIFERIES	MILITIAMAN	MILLICURIES
MICROSWITCH	MICTURATES	MIDWINTERS	MILITIAMEN	MILLIDEGREE
MICROSWITCHES	MICTURATING	MIFEPRISTONE	MILKFISHES	MILLIDEGREES
MICROTARGET	MICTURITION	MIFEPRISTONES	MILKINESSES	MILLIGRAMME
MICROTARGETED	MICTURITIONS	MIFFINESSES	MILKSHAKES	MILLIGRAMMES
MICROTARGETING	MIDDELMANNETJIE	MIGHTINESS	MILKSOPISM	MILLIGRAMS
MICROTARGETINGS	MIDDELSKOT	MIGHTINESSES	MILKSOPISMS	MILLIHENRIES
MICROTARGETS	MIDDELSKOTS	MIGMATITES	MILKSOPPIER	MILLIHENRY
MICROTECHNIC	MIDDENSTEAD	MIGNONETTE	MILKSOPPIEST	MILLIHENRYS
MICROTECHNICS	MIDDENSTEADS	MIGNONETTES	MILKSOPPING	MILLILAMBERT
MICROTECHNIQUE	MIDDLEBREAKER	MIGRAINEUR	MILKTOASTS	MILLILAMBERTS
MICROTECHNIQUES	MIDDLEBREAKERS	MIGRAINEURS	MILLBOARDS	MILLILITER
MICROTECHNOLOGY	MIDDLEBROW	MIGRAINOUS	MILLEFEUILLE	MILLILITERS
MICROTOMES	MIDDLEBROWED	MIGRATIONAL	MILLEFEUILLES	MILLILITRE
MICROTOMIC	MIDDLEBROWISM	MIGRATIONIST	MILLEFIORI	MILLILITRES
MICROTOMICAL	MIDDLEBROWISMS	MIGRATIONISTS	MILLEFIORIS	MILLILUCES
MICROTOMIES	MIDDLEBROWS	MIGRATIONS	MILLEFLEUR	MILLILUXES
MICROTOMIST	MIDDLEBUSTER	MILDEWIEST	MILLEFLEURS	MILLIMETER
MICROTOMISTS	MIDDLEBUSTERS	MILDNESSES	MILLENARIAN	MILLIMETERS
MICROTONAL	MIDDLEMOST	MILEOMETER	MILLENARIANISM	MILLIMETRE
MICROTONALITIES	MIDDLEWARE	MILEOMETERS	MILLENARIANISMS	MILLIMETRES
MICROTONALITY	MIDDLEWARES	MILESTONES	MILLENARIANS	MILLIMICRON
MICROTONALLY	MIDDLEWEIGHT	MILITANCES	MILLENARIES	MILLIMICRONS
MICROTONES	MIDDLEWEIGHTS	MILITANCIES	MILLENARISM	MILLIMOLAR
MICROTUBES	MIDDLINGLY	MILITANTLY	MILLENARISMS	MILLIMOLES
MICROTUBULAR	MIDFIELDER	MILITANTNESS	MILLENNIAL	MILLINERIES
MICROTUBULE	MIDFIELDERS	MILITANTNESSES	MILLENNIALISM	MILLIONAIRE
MICROTUBULES	MIDIBUSSES	MILITARIES	MILLENNIALISMS	MILLIONAIRES
MICROTUNNELING	MIDINETTES	MILITARILY	MILLENNIALIST	MILLIONAIRESS
MICROTUNNELINGS	MIDISKIRTS	MILITARISATION	MILLENNIALISTS	MILLIONAIRESSES
MICROTUNNELLING	MIDLANDERS	MILITARISATIONS	MILLENNIALLY	MILLIONARY
MICROVASCULAR	MIDLATITUDE	MILITARISE	MILLENNIALS	MILLIONFOLD
MICROVILLAR	MIDLATITUDES	MILITARISED	MILLENNIANISM	MILLIONNAIRE
MICROVILLI	MIDLITTORAL	MILITARISES	MILLENNIANISMS	MILLIONNAIRES
MICROVILLOUS	MIDLITTORALS	MILITARISING	MILLENNIARISM	MILLIONNAIRESS
MICROVILLUS	MIDNIGHTLY	MILITARISM	MILLENNIARISMS	MILLIONTHS
MICROVOLTS	MIDRASHOTH	MILITARISMS	MILLENNIUM	MILLIOSMOL
MICROWATTS	MIDSAGITTAL	MILITARIST	MILLENNIUMS	MILLIOSMOLS
MICROWAVABLE	MIDSECTION	MILITARISTIC	MILLEPEDES	MILLIPEDES
MICROWAVEABLE	MIDSECTIONS	MILITARISTS	MILLEPORES	MILLIPROBE
MICROWAVED	MIDSHIPMAN	MILITARIZATION	MILLERITES	MILLIPROBES
MICROWAVES	MIDSHIPMATE	MILITARIZATIONS	MILLESIMAL	MILLIRADIAN

MILLIRADIANS	MINDFULNESSES	MINESTRONE	MINIFICATION	MINISYSTEMS
MILLIROENTGEN	MINDLESSLY	MINESTRONES	MINIFICATIONS	MINITOWERS
MILLIROENTGENS	MINDLESSNESS	MINESWEEPER	MINIFLOPPIES	MINITRACKS
MILLISECOND	MINDLESSNESSES	MINESWEEPERS	MINIFLOPPY	MINIVOLLEY
MILLISECONDS	MINDSCAPES	MINESWEEPING	MINIMALISM	MINIVOLLEYS
MILLISIEVERT	MINDSHARES	MINESWEEPINGS	MINIMALISMS	MINNESINGER
MILLISIEVERTS	MINEFIELDS	MINEWORKER	MINIMALIST	MINNESINGERS
MILLIVOLTS	MINEHUNTER	MINEWORKERS	MINIMALISTIC	MINNICKING
MILLIWATTS	MINEHUNTERS	MINGIMINGI	MINIMALISTS	MINNOCKING
MILLOCRACIES	MINELAYERS	MINGIMINGIS	MINIMARKET	MINORITAIRE
MILLOCRACY	MINELAYING	MINGINESSES	MINIMARKETS	MINORITAIRES
MILLOCRATS	MINELAYINGS	MINGLEMENT	MINIMAXING	MINORITIES
MILLSCALES	MINERALISABLE	MINGLEMENTS	MINIMISATION	MINORSHIPS
MILLSTONES	MINERALISATION	MINGLINGLY	MINIMISATIONS	MINOXIDILS
MILLSTREAM	MINERALISATIONS	MINIATIONS	MINIMISERS	MINSTRELSIES
MILLSTREAMS	MINERALISE	MINIATURED	MINIMISING	MINSTRELSY
MILLWHEELS	MINERALISED	MINIATURES	MINIMIZATION	MINUSCULAR
MILLWRIGHT	MINERALISER	MINIATURING	MINIMIZATIONS	MINUSCULES
MILLWRIGHTS	MINERALISERS	MINIATURISATION	MINIMIZERS	MINUTENESS
MILOMETERS	MINERALISES	MINIATURISE	MINIMIZING	MINUTENESSES
MILQUETOAST	MINERALISING	MINIATURISED	MINIRUGBIES	MIRABELLES
MILQUETOASTS	MINERALIST	MINIATURISES	MINISCHOOL	MIRABILISES
MIMEOGRAPH	MINERALISTS	MINIATURISING	MINISCHOOLS	MIRACIDIAL
MIMEOGRAPHED	MINERALIZABLE	MINIATURIST	MINISCULES	MIRACIDIUM
MIMEOGRAPHING	MINERALIZATION	MINIATURISTIC	MINISERIES	MIRACULOUS
MIMEOGRAPHS	MINERALIZATIONS	MINIATURISTS	MINISKIRTED	MIRACULOUSLY
MIMETICALLY	MINERALIZE	MINIATURIZATION	MINISKIRTS	MIRACULOUSNESS
MIMIVIRUSES	MINERALIZED	MINIATURIZE	MINISTATES	MIRANDISED
MIMMICKING	MINERALIZER	MINIATURIZED	MINISTERED	MIRANDISES
MIMOGRAPHER	MINERALIZERS	MINIATURIZES	MINISTERIA	MIRANDISING
MIMOGRAPHERS	MINERALIZES	MINIATURIZING	MINISTERIAL	MIRANDIZED
MIMOGRAPHIES	MINERALIZING	MINIBEASTS	MINISTERIALIST	MIRANDIZES
MIMOGRAPHY	MINERALOGIC	MINIBIKERS	MINISTERIALISTS	MIRANDIZING
MIMOSACEOUS	MINERALOGICAL	MINIBREAKS	MINISTERIALLY	MIRIFICALLY
MINACIOUSLY	MINERALOGICALLY	MINIBUDGET	MINISTERING	MIRINESSES
MINACITIES	MINERALOGIES	MINIBUDGETS	MINISTERIUM	MIRKINESSES
MINATORIAL	MINERALOGISE	MINIBUSSES	MINISTERSHIP	MIRRORINGS
MINATORIALLY	MINERALOGISED	MINICABBING	MINISTERSHIPS	MIRRORLIKE
MINATORILY	MINERALOGISES	MINICABBINGS	MINISTRANT	MIRRORWISE
MINAUDERIE	MINERALOGISING	MINICALCULATOR	MINISTRANTS	MIRTHFULLY
MINAUDERIES	MINERALOGIST	MINICALCULATORS	MINISTRATION	MIRTHFULNESS
MINAUDIERE	MINERALOGISTS	MINICASSETTE	MINISTRATIONS	MIRTHFULNESSES
MINAUDIERES	MINERALOGIZE	MINICASSETTES	MINISTRATIVE	MIRTHLESSLY
MINCEMEATS	MINERALOGIZED	MINICOMPUTER	MINISTRESS	MIRTHLESSNESS
MINDBLOWER	MINERALOGIZES	MINICOMPUTERS	MINISTRESSES	MIRTHLESSNESSES
MINDBLOWERS	MINERALOGIZING	MINICOURSE	MINISTRIES	MISACCEPTATION
MINDEDNESS	MINERALOGY	MINICOURSES	MINISTROKE	MISACCEPTATIONS
MINDEDNESSES	MINESHAFTS	MINIDISHES	MINISTROKES	MISADAPTED
MINDFULNESS	MINESTONES	MINIDRESSES	MINISYSTEM	MISADAPTING

M

MISADDRESS	MISANTHROPE	MISASSIGNING	MISBESTOWED	MISCEGENATION
MISADDRESSED	MISANTHROPES	MISASSIGNS	MISBESTOWING	MISCEGENATIONAL
MISADDRESSES	MISANTHROPIC	MISASSUMED	MISBESTOWS	MISCEGENATIONS
MISADDRESSING	MISANTHROPICAL	MISASSUMES	MISBIASING	MISCEGENATOR
MISADJUSTED	MISANTHROPIES	MISASSUMING	MISBIASSED	MISCEGENATORS
MISADJUSTING	MISANTHROPIST	MISASSUMPTION	MISBIASSES	MISCEGENES
MISADJUSTS	MISANTHROPISTS	MISASSUMPTIONS	MISBIASSING	MISCEGENETIC
MISADVENTURE	MISANTHROPOS	MISATONING	MISBILLING	MISCEGENIST
MISADVENTURED	MISANTHROPOSES	MISATTRIBUTE	MISBINDING	MISCEGENISTS
MISADVENTURER	MISANTHROPY	MISATTRIBUTED	MISBRANDED	MISCEGINES
MISADVENTURERS	MISAPPLICATION	MISATTRIBUTES	MISBRANDING	MISCELLANARIAN
MISADVENTURES	MISAPPLICATIONS	MISATTRIBUTING	MISBUILDING	MISCELLANARIANS
MISADVENTUROUS	MISAPPLIED	MISATTRIBUTION	MISBUTTONED	MISCELLANEA
MISADVERTENCE	MISAPPLIES	MISATTRIBUTIONS	MISBUTTONING	MISCELLANEOUS
MISADVERTENCES	MISAPPLYING	MISAUNTERS	MISBUTTONS	MISCELLANEOUSLY
MISADVICES	MISAPPRAISAL	MISAVERRED	MISCALCULATE	MISCELLANIES
MISADVISED	MISAPPRAISALS	MISAVERRING	MISCALCULATED	MISCELLANIST
MISADVISEDLY	MISAPPRECIATE	MISAWARDED	MISCALCULATES	MISCELLANISTS
MISADVISEDNESS	MISAPPRECIATED	MISAWARDING	MISCALCULATING	MISCELLANY
MISADVISES	MISAPPRECIATES	MISBALANCE	MISCALCULATION	MISCHALLENGE
MISADVISING	MISAPPRECIATING	MISBALANCED	MISCALCULATIONS	MISCHALLENGES
MISALIGNED	MISAPPRECIATION	MISBALANCES	MISCALCULATOR	MISCHANCED
MISALIGNING	MISAPPRECIATIVE	MISBALANCING	MISCALCULATORS	MISCHANCEFUL
MISALIGNMENT	MISAPPREHEND	MISBECOMES	MISCALLERS	MISCHANCES
MISALIGNMENTS	MISAPPREHENDED	MISBECOMING	MISCALLING	MISCHANCIER
MISALLEGED	MISAPPREHENDING	MISBECOMINGNESS	MISCANTHUS	MISCHANCIEST
MISALLEGES	MISAPPREHENDS	MISBEGINNING	MISCANTHUSES	MISCHANCING
MISALLEGING	MISAPPREHENSION	MISBEGOTTEN	MISCAPTION	MISCHANNEL
MISALLIANCE	MISAPPREHENSIVE	MISBEHAVED	MISCAPTIONED	MISCHANNELED
MISALLIANCES	MISAPPROPRIATE	MISBEHAVER	MISCAPTIONING	MISCHANNELING
MISALLOCATE	MISAPPROPRIATED	MISBEHAVERS	MISCAPTIONS	MISCHANNELLED
MISALLOCATED	MISAPPROPRIATES	MISBEHAVES	MISCARRIAGE	MISCHANNELLING
MISALLOCATES	MISARRANGE	MISBEHAVING	MISCARRIAGES	MISCHANNELS
MISALLOCATING	MISARRANGED	MISBEHAVIOR	MISCARRIED	MISCHANTER
MISALLOCATION	MISARRANGEMENT	MISBEHAVIORS	MISCARRIES	MISCHANTERS
MISALLOCATIONS	MISARRANGEMENTS	MISBEHAVIOUR	MISCARRYING	MISCHARACTERISE
MISALLOTMENT	MISARRANGES	MISBEHAVIOURS	MISCASTING	MISCHARACTERIZE
MISALLOTMENTS	MISARRANGING	MISBELIEFS	MISCATALOG	MISCHARGED
MISALLOTTED	MISARTICULATE	MISBELIEVE	MISCATALOGED	MISCHARGES
MISALLOTTING	MISARTICULATED	MISBELIEVED	MISCATALOGING	MISCHARGING
MISALLYING	MISARTICULATES	MISBELIEVER	MISCATALOGS	MISCHIEFED
MISALTERED	MISARTICULATING	MISBELIEVERS	MISCATALOGUE	MISCHIEFING
MISALTERING	MISASSAYED	MISBELIEVES	MISCATALOGUED	MISCHIEVOUS
MISANALYSES	MISASSAYING	MISBELIEVING	MISCATALOGUES	MISCHIEVOUSLY
MISANALYSIS	MISASSEMBLE	MISBESEEMED	MISCATALOGUING	MISCHIEVOUSNESS
MISANDRIES	MISASSEMBLED	MISBESEEMING	MISCEGENATE	MISCHMETAL
MISANDRIST	MISASSEMBLES	MISBESEEMS	MISCEGENATED	MISCHMETALS
MISANDRISTS	MISASSEMBLING	MISBESTOWAL	MISCEGENATES	MISCHOICES
MISANDROUS	MISASSIGNED	MISBESTOWALS	MISCEGENATING	MISCHOOSES

MISCHOOSING	MISCONNECT	MISCREATING	MISDIALLING	MISENTERING
MISCIBILITIES	MISCONNECTED	MISCREATION	MISDIETING	MISENTREAT
MISCIBILITY	MISCONNECTING	MISCREATIONS	MISDIGHTED	MISENTREATED
MISCITATION	MISCONNECTION	MISCREATIVE	MISDIGHTING	MISENTREATING
MISCITATIONS	MISCONNECTIONS	MISCREATOR	MISDIRECTED	MISENTREATS
MISCLAIMED	MISCONNECTS	MISCREATORS	MISDIRECTING	MISENTRIES
MISCLAIMING	MISCONSTER	MISCREAUNCE	MISDIRECTION	MISERABILISM
MISCLASSED	MISCONSTERED	MISCREAUNCES	MISDIRECTIONS	MISERABILISMS
MISCLASSES	MISCONSTERING	MISCREDITED	MISDIRECTS	MISERABILIST
MISCLASSIFIED	MISCONSTERS	MISCREDITING	MISDISTRIBUTION	MISERABILISTS
MISCLASSIFIES	MISCONSTRUCT	MISCREDITS	MISDIVIDED	MISERABLENESS
MISCLASSIFY	MISCONSTRUCTED	MISCUTTING	MISDIVIDES	MISERABLENESSES
MISCLASSIFYING	MISCONSTRUCTING	MISDEALERS	MISDIVIDING	MISERABLES
MISCLASSING	MISCONSTRUCTION	MISDEALING	MISDIVISION	MISERABLISM
MISCOINING	MISCONSTRUCTS	MISDEEMFUL	MISDIVISIONS	MISERABLISMS
MISCOLORED	MISCONSTRUE	MISDEEMING	MISDOUBTED	MISERABLIST
MISCOLORING	MISCONSTRUED	MISDEEMINGS	MISDOUBTFUL	MISERABLISTS
MISCOLOURED	MISCONSTRUES	MISDEFINED	MISDOUBTING	MISERICORD
MISCOLOURING	MISCONSTRUING	MISDEFINES	MISDRAWING	MISERICORDE
MISCOLOURS	MISCONTENT	MISDEFINING	MISDRAWINGS	MISERICORDES
MISCOMPREHEND	MISCONTENTED	MISDEMEANANT	MISDREADED	MISERICORDS
MISCOMPREHENDED	MISCONTENTING	MISDEMEANANTS	MISDREADING	MISERLIEST
MISCOMPREHENDS	MISCONTENTMENT	MISDEMEANED	MISDRIVING	MISERLINESS
MISCOMPUTATION	MISCONTENTMENTS	MISDEMEANING	MISEDITING	MISERLINESSES
MISCOMPUTATIONS	MISCONTENTS	MISDEMEANOR	MISEDUCATE	MISESTEEMED
MISCOMPUTE	MISCOOKING	MISDEMEANORS	MISEDUCATED	MISESTEEMING
MISCOMPUTED	MISCOPYING	MISDEMEANOUR	MISEDUCATES	MISESTEEMS
MISCOMPUTES	MISCORRECT	MISDEMEANOURS	MISEDUCATING	MISESTIMATE
MISCOMPUTING	MISCORRECTED	MISDEMEANS	MISEDUCATION	MISESTIMATED
MISCONCEIT	MISCORRECTING	MISDESCRIBE	MISEDUCATIONS	MISESTIMATES
MISCONCEITED	MISCORRECTION	MISDESCRIBED	MISEMPHASES	MISESTIMATING
MISCONCEITING	MISCORRECTIONS	MISDESCRIBES	MISEMPHASIS	MISESTIMATION
MISCONCEITS	MISCORRECTS	MISDESCRIBING	MISEMPHASISE	MISESTIMATIONS
MISCONCEIVE	MISCORRELATION	MISDESCRIPTION	MISEMPHASISED	MISEVALUATE
MISCONCEIVED	MISCORRELATIONS	MISDESCRIPTIONS	MISEMPHASISES	MISEVALUATED
MISCONCEIVER	MISCOUNSEL	MISDESERTS	MISEMPHASISING	MISEVALUATES
MISCONCEIVERS	MISCOUNSELLED	MISDEVELOP	MISEMPHASIZE	MISEVALUATING
MISCONCEIVES	MISCOUNSELLING	MISDEVELOPED	MISEMPHASIZED	MISEVALUATION
MISCONCEIVING	MISCOUNSELLINGS	MISDEVELOPING	MISEMPHASIZES	MISEVALUATIONS
MISCONCEPTION	MISCOUNSELS	MISDEVELOPS	MISEMPHASIZING	MISFALLING
MISCONCEPTIONS	MISCOUNTED	MISDEVOTION	MISEMPLOYED	MISFARINGS
MISCONDUCT	MISCOUNTING	MISDEVOTIONS	MISEMPLOYING	MISFEASANCE
MISCONDUCTED	MISCREANCE	MISDIAGNOSE	MISEMPLOYMENT	MISFEASANCES
MISCONDUCTING	MISCREANCES	MISDIAGNOSED	MISEMPLOYMENTS	MISFEASORS
MISCONDUCTS	MISCREANCIES	MISDIAGNOSES	MISEMPLOYS	MISFEATURE
MISCONJECTURE	MISCREANCY	MISDIAGNOSING	MISENROLLED	MISFEATURED
MISCONJECTURED	MISCREANTS	MISDIAGNOSIS	MISENROLLING	MISFEATURES
MISCONJECTURES	MISCREATED	MISDIALING	MISENROLLS	MISFEATURING
MISCONJECTURING	MISCREATES	MISDIALLED	MISENTERED	MISFEEDING

MISFEIGNED	MISGUGGLING	MISINFORMING	MISLEEKING	MISOBSERVANCE
MISFEIGNING	MISGUIDANCE	MISINFORMS	MISLIGHTED	MISOBSERVANCES
MISFIELDED	MISGUIDANCES	MISINSTRUCT	MISLIGHTING	MISOBSERVE
MISFIELDING	MISGUIDEDLY	MISINSTRUCTED	MISLIKINGS	MISOBSERVED
MISFITTING	MISGUIDEDNESS	MISINSTRUCTING	MISLIPPENED	MISOBSERVES
MISFOCUSED	MISGUIDEDNESSES	MISINSTRUCTION	MISLIPPENING	MISOBSERVING
MISFOCUSES	MISGUIDERS	MISINSTRUCTIONS	MISLIPPENS	MISOCAPNIC
MISFOCUSING	MISGUIDING	MISINSTRUCTS	MISLOCATED	MISOGAMIES
MISFOCUSSED	MISHALLOWED	MISINTELLIGENCE	MISLOCATES	MISOGAMIST
MISFOCUSSES	MISHANDLED	MISINTENDED	MISLOCATING	MISOGAMISTS
MISFOCUSSING	MISHANDLES	MISINTENDING	MISLOCATION	MISOGYNIES
MISFOLDING	MISHANDLING	MISINTENDS	MISLOCATIONS	MISOGYNIST
MISFORMATION	MISHANDLINGS	MISINTERPRET	MISLODGING	MISOGYNISTIC
MISFORMATIONS	MISHANTERS	MISINTERPRETED	MISLUCKING	MISOGYNISTICAL
MISFORMING	MISHAPPENED	MISINTERPRETER	MISMANAGED	MISOGYNISTS
MISFORTUNE	MISHAPPENING	MISINTERPRETERS	MISMANAGEMENT	MISOGYNOUS
MISFORTUNED	MISHAPPENS	MISINTERPRETING	MISMANAGEMENTS	MISOLOGIES
MISFORTUNES	MISHAPPING	MISINTERPRETS	MISMANAGER	MISOLOGIST
MISFRAMING	MISHEARING	MISINTERRED	MISMANAGERS	MISOLOGISTS
MISFUNCTION	MISHEGAASEN	MISINTERRING	MISMANAGES	MISONEISMS
MISFUNCTIONED	MISHGUGGLE	MISJOINDER	MISMANAGING	MISONEISTIC
MISFUNCTIONING	MISHGUGGLED	MISJOINDERS	MISMANNERS	MISONEISTS
MISFUNCTIONS	MISHGUGGLES	MISJOINING	MISMARKING	MISORDERED
MISGAUGING	MISHGUGGLING	MISJUDGEMENT	MISMARRIAGE	MISORDERING
MISGENDERED	MISHITTING	MISJUDGEMENTS	MISMARRIAGES	MISORIENTATION
MISGENDERING	MISHMASHES	MISJUDGERS	MISMARRIED	MISORIENTATIONS
MISGENDERS	MISHMOSHES	MISJUDGING	MISMARRIES	MISORIENTED
MISGIVINGS	MISHUGASES	MISJUDGMENT	MISMARRYING	MISORIENTING
MISGOVERNANCE	MISIDENTIFIED	MISJUDGMENTS	MISMATCHED	MISORIENTS
MISGOVERNANCES	MISIDENTIFIES	MISKEEPING	MISMATCHES	MISPACKAGE
MISGOVERNAUNCE	MISIDENTIFY	MISKENNING	MISMATCHING	MISPACKAGED
MISGOVERNAUNCES	MISIDENTIFYING	MISKICKING	MISMATCHMENT	MISPACKAGES
MISGOVERNED	MISIMPRESSION	MISKNOWING	MISMATCHMENTS	MISPACKAGING
MISGOVERNING	MISIMPRESSIONS	MISKNOWLEDGE	MISMATINGS	MISPAINTED
MISGOVERNMENT	MISIMPROVE	MISKNOWLEDGES	MISMEASURE	MISPAINTING
MISGOVERNMENTS	MISIMPROVED	MISLABELED	MISMEASURED	MISPARSING
MISGOVERNOR	MISIMPROVEMENT	MISLABELING	MISMEASUREMENT	MISPARTING
MISGOVERNORS	MISIMPROVEMENTS	MISLABELLED	MISMEASUREMENTS	MISPATCHED
MISGOVERNS	MISIMPROVES	MISLABELLING	MISMEASURES	MISPATCHES
MISGRADING	MISIMPROVING	MISLABORED	MISMEASURING	MISPATCHING
MISGRAFTED	MISINFERRED	MISLABORING	MISMEETING	MISPENNING
MISGRAFTING	MISINFERRING	MISLABOURED	MISMETERED	MISPERCEIVE
MISGROWING	MISINFORMANT	MISLABOURING	MISMETERING	MISPERCEIVED
MISGROWTHS	MISINFORMANTS	MISLABOURS	MISMETRING	MISPERCEIVES
MISGUESSED	MISINFORMATION	MISLEADERS	MISNOMERED	MISPERCEIVING
MISGUESSES	MISINFORMATIONS	MISLEADING	MISNOMERING	MISPERCEPTION
MISGUESSING	MISINFORMED	MISLEADINGLY	MISNUMBERED	MISPERCEPTIONS
MISGUGGLED	MISINFORMER	MISLEARNED	MISNUMBERING	MISPERSUADE
MISGUGGLES	MISINFORMERS	MISLEARNING	MISNUMBERS	MISPERSUADED

MISPERSUADES	MISPRONOUNCING	MISRENDERED	MISSIONING	MISSUMMATIONS
MISPERSUADING	MISPROPORTION	MISRENDERING	MISSIONISATION	MISTAKABLE
MISPERSUASION	MISPROPORTIONED	MISRENDERS	MISSIONISATIONS	MISTAKABLY
MISPERSUASIONS	MISPROPORTIONS	MISREPORTED	MISSIONISE	MISTAKEABLE
MISPHRASED	MISPUNCTUATE	MISREPORTER	MISSIONISED	MISTAKEABLY
MISPHRASES	MISPUNCTUATED	MISREPORTERS	MISSIONISER	MISTAKENLY
MISPHRASING	MISPUNCTUATES	MISREPORTING	MISSIONISERS	MISTAKENNESS
MISPICKELS	MISPUNCTUATING	MISREPORTS	MISSIONISES	MISTAKENNESSES
MISPLACEMENT	MISPUNCTUATION	MISREPRESENT	MISSIONISING	MISTAKINGS
MISPLACEMENTS	MISPUNCTUATIONS	MISREPRESENTED	MISSIONIZATION	MISTEACHES
MISPLACING	MISQUOTATION	MISREPRESENTER	MISSIONIZATIONS	MISTEACHING
MISPLANNED	MISQUOTATIONS	MISREPRESENTERS	MISSIONIZE	MISTELLING
MISPLANNING	MISQUOTERS	MISREPRESENTING	MISSIONIZED	MISTEMPERED
MISPLANTED	MISQUOTING	MISREPRESENTS	MISSIONIZER	MISTEMPERING
MISPLANTING	MISRAISING	MISROUTEING	MISSIONIZERS	MISTEMPERS
MISPLAYING	MISREADING	MISROUTING	MISSIONIZES	MISTENDING
MISPLEADED	MISREADINGS	MISSAYINGS	MISSIONIZING	MISTERMING
MISPLEADING	MISRECKONED	MISSEATING	MISSISHNESS	MISTHINKING
MISPLEADINGS	MISRECKONING	MISSEEMING	MISSISHNESSES	MISTHOUGHT
MISPLEASED	MISRECKONINGS	MISSEEMINGS	MISSORTING	MISTHOUGHTS
MISPLEASES	MISRECKONS	MISSELLING	MISSOUNDED	MISTHROWING
MISPLEASING	MISRECOLLECTION	MISSELLINGS	MISSOUNDING	MISTIGRISES
MISPOINTED	MISRECORDED	MISSENDING	MISSPACING	MISTIMINGS
MISPOINTING	MISRECORDING	MISSENSING	MISSPEAKING	MISTINESSES
MISPOISING	MISRECORDS	MISSETTING	MISSPELLED	MISTITLING
MISPOSITION	MISREFERENCE	MISSHAPENLY	MISSPELLING	MISTLETOES
MISPOSITIONED	MISREFERENCED	MISSHAPENNESS	MISSPELLINGS	MISTOUCHED
MISPOSITIONING	MISREFERENCES	MISSHAPENNESSES	MISSPENDER	MISTOUCHES
MISPOSITIONS	MISREFERENCING	MISSHAPERS	MISSPENDERS	MISTOUCHING
MISPRAISED	MISREFERRED	MISSHAPING	MISSPENDING	MISTRACING
MISPRAISES	MISREFERRING	MISSHEATHED	MISSTAMPED	MISTRAINED
MISPRAISING	MISREGARDED	MISSILEERS	MISSTAMPING	MISTRAINING
MISPRICING	MISREGARDING	MISSILEMAN	MISSTARTED	MISTRANSCRIBE
MISPRINTED	MISREGARDS	MISSILEMEN	MISSTARTING	MISTRANSCRIBED
MISPRINTING	MISREGISTER	MISSILERIES	MISSTATEMENT	MISTRANSCRIBES
MISPRISING	MISREGISTERED	MISSILRIES	MISSTATEMENTS	MISTRANSCRIBING
MISPRISION	MISREGISTERING	MISSIOLOGIES	MISSTATING	MISTRANSLATE
MISPRISIONS	MISREGISTERS	MISSIOLOGY	MISSTEERED	MISTRANSLATED
MISPRIZERS	MISREGISTRATION	MISSIONARIES	MISSTEERING	MISTRANSLATES
MISPRIZING	MISRELATED	MISSIONARISE	MISSTEPPED	MISTRANSLATING
MISPROGRAM	MISRELATES	MISSIONARISED	MISSTEPPING	MISTRANSLATION
MISPROGRAMED	MISRELATING	MISSIONARISES	MISSTOPPED	MISTRANSLATIONS
MISPROGRAMING	MISRELATION	MISSIONARISING	MISSTOPPING	MISTRAYNED
MISPROGRAMMED	MISRELATIONS	MISSIONARIZE	MISSTRICKEN	MISTREADING
MISPROGRAMMING	MISRELYING	MISSIONARIZED	MISSTRIKES	MISTREADINGS
MISPROGRAMS	MISREMEMBER	MISSIONARIZES	MISSTRIKING	MISTREATED
MISPRONOUNCE	MISREMEMBERED	MISSIONARIZING	MISSTYLING	MISTREATING
MISPRONOUNCED	MISREMEMBERING	MISSIONARY	MISSUITING	MISTREATMENT
MISPRONOUNCES	MISREMEMBERS	MISSIONERS	MISSUMMATION	MISTREATMENTS

MISTRESSED	MITHRIDATIC	MNEMONISTS	MODERNISED	MOISTURISE
MISTRESSES	MITHRIDATISE	MNEMOTECHNIC	MODERNISER	MOISTURISED
MISTRESSING	MITHRIDATISED	MNEMOTECHNICS	MODERNISERS	MOISTURISER
MISTRESSLESS	MITHRIDATISES	MNEMOTECHNIST	MODERNISES	MOISTURISERS
MISTRESSLIER	MITHRIDATISING	MNEMOTECHNISTS	MODERNISING	MOISTURISES
MISTRESSLIEST	MITHRIDATISM	MOBCASTING	MODERNISMS	MOISTURISING
MISTRESSLY	MITHRIDATISMS	MOBCASTINGS	MODERNISTIC	MOISTURIZE
MISTRUSTED	MITHRIDATIZE	MOBILISABLE	MODERNISTICALLY	MOISTURIZED
MISTRUSTER	MITHRIDATIZED	MOBILISATION	MODERNISTS	MOISTURIZER
MISTRUSTERS	MITHRIDATIZES	MOBILISATIONS	MODERNITIES	MOISTURIZERS
MISTRUSTFUL	MITHRIDATIZING	MOBILISERS	MODERNIZATION	MOISTURIZES
MISTRUSTFULLY	MITIGATING	MOBILISING	MODERNIZATIONS	MOISTURIZING
MISTRUSTFULNESS	MITIGATION	MOBILITIES	MODERNIZED	MOITHERING
MISTRUSTING	MITIGATIONS	MOBILIZABLE	MODERNIZER	MOLALITIES
MISTRUSTINGLY	MITIGATIVE	MOBILIZATION	MODERNIZERS	MOLARITIES
MISTRUSTLESS	MITIGATIVES	MOBILIZATIONS	MODERNIZES	MOLASSESES
MISTRYSTED	MITIGATORS	MOBILIZERS	MODERNIZING	MOLDABILITIES
MISTRYSTING	MITIGATORY	MOBILIZING	MODERNNESS	MOLDABILITY
MISTUTORED	MITOCHONDRIA	MOBLOGGERS	MODERNNESSES	MOLDAVITES
MISTUTORING	MITOCHONDRIAL	MOBOCRACIES	MODIFIABILITIES	MOLDBOARDS
MISUNDERSTAND	MITOCHONDRION	MOBOCRATIC	MODIFIABILITY	MOLDINESSES
MISUNDERSTANDS	MITOGENETIC	MOBOCRATICAL	MODIFIABLE	MOLECATCHER
MISUNDERSTOOD	MITOGENICITIES	MOCHINESSES	MODIFIABLENESS	MOLECATCHERS
MISUTILISATION	MITOGENICITY	MOCKERNUTS	MODIFICATION	MOLECULARITIES
MISUTILISATIONS	MITOMYCINS	MOCKINGBIRD	MODIFICATIONS	MOLECULARITY
MISUTILIZATION	MITOTICALLY	MOCKINGBIRDS	MODIFICATIVE	MOLECULARLY
MISUTILIZATIONS	MITRAILLES	MOCKUMENTARIES	MODIFICATORY	MOLENDINAR
MISVALUING	MITRAILLEUR	MOCKUMENTARY	MODILLIONS	MOLENDINARIES
MISVENTURE	MITRAILLEURS	MODAFINILS	MODISHNESS	MOLENDINARS
MISVENTURES	MITRAILLEUSE	MODALISTIC	MODISHNESSES	MOLENDINARY
MISVENTUROUS	MITRAILLEUSES	MODALITIES	MODULABILITIES	MOLESTATION
MISVOCALISATION	MITREWORTS	MODELLINGS	MODULABILITY	MOLESTATIONS
MISVOCALIZATION	MITTIMUSES	MODELLISTS	MODULARISED	MOLIMINOUS
MISWANDRED	MIXABILITIES	MODERATELY	MODULARITIES	MOLLIFIABLE
MISWEENING	MIXABILITY	MODERATENESS	MODULARITY	MOLLIFICATION
MISWENDING	MIXEDNESSES	MODERATENESSES	MODULARIZED	MOLLIFICATIONS
MISWORDING	MIXMASTERS	MODERATING	MODULATING	MOLLIFIERS
MISWORDINGS	MIXOBARBARIC	MODERATION	MODULATION	MOLLIFYING
MISWORSHIP	MIXOLOGIES	MODERATIONS	MODULATIONS	MOLLITIOUS
MISWORSHIPPED	MIXOLOGIST	MODERATISM	MODULATIVE	MOLLUSCANS
MISWORSHIPPING	MIXOLOGISTS	MODERATISMS	MODULATORS	MOLLUSCICIDAL
MISWORSHIPPINGS	MIXOLYDIAN	MODERATORS	MODULATORY	MOLLUSCICIDE
MISWORSHIPS	MIXOTROPHIC	MODERATORSHIP	MOISTENERS	MOLLUSCICIDES
MISWRITING	MIZENMASTS	MODERATORSHIPS	MOISTENING	MOLLUSCOID
MISWRITTEN	MIZZENMAST	MODERATRICES	MOISTIFIED	MOLLUSCOIDAL
MITERWORTS	MIZZENMASTS	MODERATRIX	MOISTIFIES	MOLLUSCOIDS
MITHRADATIC	MIZZONITES	MODERATRIXES	MOISTIFYING	MOLLUSCOUS
MITHRADATIC	MNEMONICAL	MODERNISATION	MOISTNESSES	MOLLUSKANS
MITHRIDATE	MNEMONICALLY	MODERNISATIONS	MOISTURELESS	MOLLYCODDLE
MITHRIDATES				

MOLLYCODDLED	MONARCHICAL	MONEYLENDING	MONKFISHES	MONOCLINAL
MOLLYCODDLER	MONARCHICALLY	MONEYLENDINGS	MONKISHNESS	MONOCLINALLY
MOLLYCODDLERS	MONARCHIES	MONEYMAKER	MONKISHNESSES	MONOCLINALS
MOLLYCODDLES	MONARCHISE	MONEYMAKERS	MONKSHOODS	MONOCLINES
MOLLYCODDLING	MONARCHISED	MONEYMAKING	MONOACIDIC	MONOCLINIC
MOLLYCODDLINGS	MONARCHISES	MONEYMAKINGS	MONOAMINERGIC	MONOCLINISM
MOLLYHAWKS	MONARCHISING	MONEYSPINNING	MONOAMINES	MONOCLINISMS
MOLLYMAWKS	MONARCHISM	MONEYWORTS	MONOATOMIC	MONOCLINOUS
MOLOCHISED	MONARCHISMS	MONGERINGS	MONOBLEPSES	MONOCLONAL
MOLOCHISES	MONARCHIST	MONGRELISATION	MONOBLEPSIS	MONOCLONALS
MOLOCHISING	MONARCHISTIC	MONGRELISATIONS	MONOCARBOXYLIC	MONOCOQUES
MOLOCHIZED	MONARCHISTS	MONGRELISE	MONOCARDIAN	MONOCOTYLEDON
MOLOCHIZES	MONARCHIZE	MONGRELISED	MONOCARDIANS	MONOCOTYLEDONS
MOLOCHIZING	MONARCHIZED	MONGRELISER	MONOCARPELLARY	MONOCOTYLS
MOLYBDATES	MONARCHIZES	MONGRELISERS	MONOCARPIC	MONOCRACIES
MOLYBDENITE	MONARCHIZING	MONGRELISES	MONOCARPOUS	MONOCRATIC
MOLYBDENITES	MONASTERIAL	MONGRELISING	MONOCEROSES	MONOCROPPED
MOLYBDENOSES	MONASTERIES	MONGRELISM	MONOCEROUS	MONOCROPPING
MOLYBDENOSIS	MONASTICAL	MONGRELISMS	MONOCHASIA	MONOCRYSTAL
MOLYBDENOUS	MONASTICALLY	MONGRELIZATION	MONOCHASIAL	MONOCRYSTALLINE
MOLYBDENUM	MONASTICISM	MONGRELIZATIONS	MONOCHASIUM	MONOCRYSTALS
MOLYBDENUMS	MONASTICISMS	MONGRELIZE	MONOCHLAMYDEOUS	MONOCULARLY
MOLYBDOSES	MONAURALLY	MONGRELIZED	MONOCHLORIDE	MONOCULARS
MOLYBDOSIS	MONCHIQUITE	MONGRELIZER	MONOCHLORIDES	MONOCULOUS
MOMENTANEOUS	MONCHIQUITES	MONGRELIZERS	MONOCHORDS	MONOCULTURAL
MOMENTARILY	MONDEGREEN	MONGRELIZES	MONOCHROIC	MONOCULTURE
MOMENTARINESS	MONDEGREENS	MONGRELIZING	MONOCHROICS	MONOCULTURES
MOMENTARINESSES	MONECIOUSLY	MONGRELLIER	MONOCHROMACIES	MONOCYCLES
MOMENTOUSLY	MONERGISMS	MONGRELLIEST	MONOCHROMACY	MONOCYCLIC
MOMENTOUSNESS	MONESTROUS	MONILIASES	MONOCHROMASIES	MONOCYTOID
MOMENTOUSNESSES	MONETARILY	MONILIASIS	MONOCHROMASY	MONODACTYLOUS
MOMPRENEUR	MONETARISM	MONILIFORM	MONOCHROMAT	MONODELPHIAN
MOMPRENEURS	MONETARISMS	MONISTICAL	MONOCHROMATE	MONODELPHIANS
MONACHISMS	MONETARIST	MONISTICALLY	MONOCHROMATES	MONODELPHIC
MONACHISTS	MONETARISTS	MONITORIAL	MONOCHROMATIC	MONODELPHOUS
MONACTINAL	MONETISATION	MONITORIALLY	MONOCHROMATICS	MONODICALLY
MONACTINES	MONETISATIONS	MONITORIES	MONOCHROMATISM	MONODISPERSE
MONADELPHOUS	MONETISING	MONITORING	MONOCHROMATISMS	MONODRAMAS
MONADICALLY	MONETIZATION	MONITORINGS	MONOCHROMATOR	MONODRAMATIC
MONADIFORM	MONETIZATIONS	MONITORSHIP	MONOCHROMATORS	MONOECIOUS
MONADISTIC	MONETIZING	MONITORSHIPS	MONOCHROMATS	MONOECIOUSLY
MONADNOCKS	MONEYBELTS	MONITRESSES	MONOCHROME	MONOECISMS
MONADOLOGIES	MONEYBOXES	MONKEYGLAND	MONOCHROMES	MONOESTERS
MONADOLOGY	MONEYCHANGER	MONKEYISMS	MONOCHROMIC	MONOFILAMENT
MONANDRIES	MONEYCHANGERS	MONKEYPODS	MONOCHROMICAL	MONOFILAMENTS
MONANDROUS	MONEYGRUBBING	MONKEYPOTS	MONOCHROMIES	MONOGAMIES
MONANTHOUS	MONEYGRUBBINGS	MONKEYPOXES	MONOCHROMIST	MONOGAMIST
MONARCHALLY	MONEYLENDER	MONKEYSHINE	MONOCHROMISTS	MONOGAMISTIC
MONARCHIAL	MONEYLENDERS	MONKEYSHINES	MONOCHROMY	MONOGAMISTS

MONOGAMOUS	MONOHYDRIC	MONOMANIACAL	MONOPHTHONGIZE	MONOPRIONIDIAN
MONOGAMOUSLY	MONOHYDROGEN	MONOMANIACALLY	MONOPHTHONGIZED	MONOPROPELLANT
MONOGAMOUSNESS	MONOHYDROXY	MONOMANIACS	MONOPHTHONGIZES	MONOPROPELLANTS
MONOGASTRIC	MONOICOUSLY	MONOMANIAS	MONOPHTHONGS	MONOPSONIES
MONOGENEAN	MONOLATERS	MONOMEROUS	MONOPHYLETIC	MONOPSONIST
MONOGENEANS	MONOLATRIES	MONOMETALLIC	MONOPHYLIES	MONOPSONISTIC
MONOGENESES	MONOLATRIST	MONOMETALLISM	MONOPHYLLOUS	MONOPSONISTS
MONOGENESIS	MONOLATRISTS	MONOMETALLISMS	MONOPHYODONT	MONOPTERAL
MONOGENETIC	MONOLATROUS	MONOMETALLIST	MONOPHYODONTS	MONOPTEROI
MONOGENICALLY	MONOLAYERS	MONOMETALLISTS	MONOPHYSITE	MONOPTERON
MONOGENIES	MONOLINGUAL	MONOMETERS	MONOPHYSITES	MONOPTEROS
MONOGENISM	MONOLINGUALISM	MONOMETRIC	MONOPHYSITIC	MONOPTEROSES
MONOGENISMS	MONOLINGUALISMS	MONOMETRICAL	MONOPHYSITISM	MONOPTOTES
MONOGENIST	MONOLINGUALS	MONOMOLECULAR	MONOPHYSITISMS	MONOPULSES
MONOGENISTIC	MONOLINGUIST	MONOMOLECULARLY	MONOPITCHES	MONORCHIDISM
MONOGENISTS	MONOLINGUISTS	MONOMORPHEMIC	MONOPLANES	MONORCHIDISMS
MONOGENOUS	MONOLITHIC	MONOMORPHIC	MONOPLEGIA	MONORCHIDS
MONOGLYCERIDE	MONOLITHICALLY	MONOMORPHISM	MONOPLEGIAS	MONORCHISM
MONOGLYCERIDES	MONOLOGGED	MONOMORPHISMS	MONOPLEGIC	MONORCHISMS
MONOGONIES	MONOLOGGING	MONOMORPHOUS	MONOPLEGICS	MONORHINAL
MONOGRAMED	MONOLOGICAL	MONOMYARIAN	MONOPLOIDS	MONORHINES
MONOGRAMING	MONOLOGIES	MONOMYARIANS	MONOPODIAL	MONORHYMED
MONOGRAMMATIC	MONOLOGISE	MONONUCLEAR	MONOPODIALLY	MONORHYMES
MONOGRAMMED	MONOLOGISED	MONONUCLEARS	MONOPODIAS	MONOSACCHARIDE
MONOGRAMMER	MONOLOGISES	MONONUCLEATE	MONOPODIES	MONOSACCHARIDES
MONOGRAMMERS	MONOLOGISING	MONONUCLEATED	MONOPODIUM	MONOSATURATED
MONOGRAMMING	MONOLOGIST	MONONUCLEOSES	MONOPOLIES	MONOSEMIES
MONOGRAPHED	MONOLOGISTS	MONONUCLEOSIS	MONOPOLISATION	MONOSEPALOUS
MONOGRAPHER	MONOLOGIZE	MONONUCLEOTIDE	MONOPOLISATIONS	MONOSKIERS
MONOGRAPHERS	MONOLOGIZED	MONONUCLEOTIDES	MONOPOLISE	MONOSKIING
MONOGRAPHIC	MONOLOGIZES	MONOPETALOUS	MONOPOLISED	MONOSKIINGS
MONOGRAPHICAL	MONOLOGIZING	MONOPHAGIES	MONOPOLISER	MONOSODIUM
MONOGRAPHICALLY	MONOLOGUED	MONOPHAGOUS	MONOPOLISERS	MONOSOMICS
MONOGRAPHIES	MONOLOGUES	MONOPHASES	MONOPOLISES	MONOSOMIES
MONOGRAPHING	MONOLOGUING	MONOPHASIC	MONOPOLISING	MONOSPACED
MONOGRAPHIST	MONOLOGUISE	MONOPHOBIA	MONOPOLISM	MONOSPECIFIC
MONOGRAPHISTS	MONOLOGUISED	MONOPHOBIAS	MONOPOLISMS	MONOSPECIFICITY
MONOGRAPHS	MONOLOGUISES	MONOPHOBIC	MONOPOLIST	MONOSPERMAL
MONOGRAPHY	MONOLOGUISING	MONOPHOBICS	MONOPOLISTIC	MONOSPERMOUS
MONOGYNIAN	MONOLOGUIST	MONOPHONIC	MONOPOLISTS	MONOSTABLE
MONOGYNIES	MONOLOGUISTS	MONOPHONICALLY	MONOPOLIZATION	MONOSTELES
MONOGYNIST	MONOLOGUIZE	MONOPHONIES	MONOPOLIZATIONS	MONOSTELIC
MONOGYNISTS	MONOLOGUIZED	MONOPHOSPHATE	MONOPOLIZE	MONOSTELIES
MONOGYNOUS	MONOLOGUIZES	MONOPHOSPHATES	MONOPOLIZED	MONOSTICHIC
MONOHYBRID	MONOLOGUIZING	MONOPHTHONG	MONOPOLIZER	MONOSTICHOUS
MONOHYBRIDS	MONOMACHIA	MONOPHTHONGAL	MONOPOLIZERS	MONOSTICHS
MONOHYDRATE	MONOMACHIAS	MONOPHTHONGISE	MONOPOLIZES	MONOSTOMOUS
MONOHYDRATED	MONOMACHIES	MONOPHTHONGISED	MONOPOLIZING	MONOSTROPHE
MONOHYDRATES	MONOMANIAC	MONOPHTHONGISES	MONOPRINTS	MONOSTROPHES

MONOSTROPHIC	MONOTONICITY	MONTAGNARD	MOONPHASES	MORATORIUMS
MONOSTROPHICS	MONOTONIES	MONTAGNARDS	MOONQUAKES	MORBIDEZZA
MONOSTYLAR	MONOTONING	MONTBRETIA	MOONRAKERS	MORBIDEZZAS
MONOSTYLOUS	MONOTONISE	MONTBRETIAS	MOONRAKING	MORBIDITIES
MONOSYLLABIC	MONOTONISED	MONTELIMAR	MOONRAKINGS	MORBIDNESS
MONOSYLLABICITY	MONOTONISES	MONTELIMARS	MOONSCAPES	MORBIDNESSES
MONOSYLLABISM	MONOTONISING	MONTGOLFIER	MOONSHINED	MORBIFEROUS
MONOSYLLABISMS	MONOTONIZE	MONTGOLFIERS	MOONSHINER	MORBIFICALLY
MONOSYLLABLE	MONOTONIZED	MONTHLINGS	MOONSHINERS	MORBILLIFORM
MONOSYLLABLES	MONOTONIZES	MONTHSLONG	MOONSHINES	MORBILLIVIRUS
MONOSYMMETRIC	MONOTONIZING	MONTICELLITE	MOONSHINIER	MORBILLIVIRUSES
MONOSYMMETRICAL	MONOTONOUS	MONTICELLITES	MOONSHINIEST	MORBILLOUS
MONOSYMMETRIES	MONOTONOUSLY	MONTICOLOUS	MOONSHINING	MORDACIOUS
MONOSYMMETRY	MONOTONOUSNESS	MONTICULATE	MOONSHININGS	MORDACIOUSLY
MONOSYNAPTIC	MONOTREMATOUS	MONTICULES	MOONSTONES	MORDACIOUSNESS
MONOTASKED	MONOTREMES	MONTICULOUS	MOONSTRICKEN	MORDACITIES
MONOTASKING	MONOTRICHIC	MONTICULUS	MOONSTRIKE	MORDANCIES
MONOTASKINGS	MONOTRICHOUS	MONTICULUSES	MOONSTRIKES	MORDANTING
MONOTELEPHONE	MONOTROCHS	MONTMORILLONITE	MOONSTRUCK	MORENESSES
MONOTELEPHONES	MONOUNSATURATE	MONUMENTAL	MOONWALKED	MORGANATIC
MONOTERPENE	MONOUNSATURATED	MONUMENTALISE	MOONWALKER	MORGANATICALLY
MONOTERPENES	MONOUNSATURATES	MONUMENTALISED	MOONWALKERS	MORGANITES
MONOTHALAMIC	MONOVALENCE	MONUMENTALISES	MOONWALKING	MORGELLONS
MONOTHALAMOUS	MONOVALENCES	MONUMENTALISING	MOORBUZZARD	MORGENSTERN
MONOTHECAL	MONOVALENCIES	MONUMENTALITIES	MOORBUZZARDS	MORGENSTERNS
MONOTHECOUS	MONOVALENCY	MONUMENTALITY	MOOSEBIRDS	MORIBUNDITIES
MONOTHEISM	MONOVALENT	MONUMENTALIZE	MOOSEHAIRS	MORIBUNDITY
MONOTHEISMS	MONOXYLONS	MONUMENTALIZED	MOOSEHIDES	MORIBUNDLY
MONOTHEIST	MONOXYLOUS	MONUMENTALIZES	MOOSEWOODS	MORIGERATE
MONOTHEISTIC	MONOZYGOTIC	MONUMENTALIZING	MOOSEYARDS	MORIGERATED
MONOTHEISTICAL	MONOZYGOUS	MONUMENTALLY	MOOTNESSES	MORIGERATES
MONOTHEISTS	MONSEIGNEUR	MONUMENTED	MOPINESSES	MORIGERATING
MONOTHELETE	MONSEIGNEURS	MONUMENTING	MOPISHNESS	MORIGERATION
MONOTHELETES	MONSIGNORI	MONZONITES	MOPISHNESSES	MORIGERATIONS
MONOTHELETIC	MONSIGNORIAL	MONZONITIC	MORALISATION	MORIGEROUS
MONOTHELETICAL	MONSIGNORS	MOODINESSES	MORALISATIONS	MORONICALLY
MONOTHELETISM	MONSTERING	MOONCALVES	MORALISERS	MORONITIES
MONOTHELETISMS	MONSTERINGS	MOONCHILDREN	MORALISING	MOROSENESS
MONOTHELISM	MONSTRANCE	MOONCRAFTS	MORALISINGS	MOROSENESSES
MONOTHELISMS	MONSTRANCES	MOONFISHES	MORALISTIC	MOROSITIES
MONOTHELITE	MONSTROSITIES	MOONFLOWER	MORALISTICALLY	MORPHACTIN
MONOTHELITES	MONSTROSITY	MOONFLOWERS	MORALITIES	MORPHACTINS
MONOTHELITISM	MONSTROUSLY	MOONINESSES	MORALIZATION	MORPHALLAXES
MONOTHELITISMS	MONSTROUSNESS	MOONLIGHTED	MORALIZATIONS	MORPHALLAXIS
MONOTHERAPIES	MONSTROUSNESSES	MOONLIGHTER	MORALIZERS	MORPHEMICALLY
MONOTHERAPY	MONSTRUOSITIES	MOONLIGHTERS	MORALIZING	MORPHEMICS
MONOTOCOUS	MONSTRUOSITY	MOONLIGHTING	MORALIZINGS	MORPHINISM
MONOTONICALLY	MONSTRUOUS	MOONLIGHTINGS	MORASSIEST	MORPHINISMS
MONOTONICITIES	MONTADALES	MOONLIGHTS	MORATORIUM	MORPHINOMANIA

MORPHINOMANIAC	MORTALIZES	MOSSPLANTS	MOTIVELESSNESS	MOUDIEWORT
MORPHINOMANIACS	MORTALIZING	MOSSTROOPER	MOTIVITIES	MOUDIEWORTS
MORPHINOMANIAS	MORTARBOARD	MOSSTROOPERS	MOTOCROSSES	MOUDIWARTS
MORPHOGENESES	MORTARBOARDS	MOTETTISTS	MOTONEURON	MOUDIWORTS
MORPHOGENESIS	MORTARIEST	MOTHBALLED	MOTONEURONAL	MOULDABILITIES
MORPHOGENETIC	MORTARLESS	MOTHBALLING	MOTONEURONS	MOULDABILITY
MORPHOGENIC	MORTCLOTHS	MOTHERBOARD	MOTORBICYCLE	MOULDBOARD
MORPHOGENIES	MORTGAGEABLE	MOTHERBOARDS	MOTORBICYCLES	MOULDBOARDS
MORPHOGENS	MORTGAGEES	MOTHERCRAFT	MOTORBIKED	MOULDERING
MORPHOGENY	MORTGAGERS	MOTHERCRAFTS	MOTORBIKES	MOULDINESS
MORPHOGRAPHER	MORTGAGING	MOTHERESES	MOTORBIKING	MOULDINESSES
MORPHOGRAPHERS	MORTGAGORS	MOTHERFUCKER	MOTORBOATED	MOULDWARPS
MORPHOGRAPHIES	MORTICIANS	MOTHERFUCKERS	MOTORBOATER	MOULDYWARP
MORPHOGRAPHY	MORTIFEROUS	MOTHERFUCKING	MOTORBOATERS	MOULDYWARPS
MORPHOLINE	MORTIFEROUSNESS	MOTHERHOOD	MOTORBOATING	MOUNDBIRDS
MORPHOLINES	MORTIFICATION	MOTHERHOODS	MOTORBOATINGS	MOUNTAINBOARD
MORPHOLINO	MORTIFICATIONS	MOTHERHOUSE	MOTORBOATS	MOUNTAINBOARDER
MORPHOLINOS	MORTIFIERS	MOTHERHOUSES	MOTORBUSES	MOUNTAINBOARDS
MORPHOLOGIC	MORTIFYING	MOTHERIEST	MOTORBUSSES	MOUNTAINED
MORPHOLOGICAL	MORTIFYINGLY	MOTHERINGS	MOTORCADED	MOUNTAINEER
MORPHOLOGICALLY	MORTIFYINGS	MOTHERLAND	MOTORCADES	MOUNTAINEERED
MORPHOLOGIES	MORTUARIES	MOTHERLANDS	MOTORCADING	MOUNTAINEERING
MORPHOLOGIST	MORULATION	MOTHERLESS	MOTORCOACH	MOUNTAINEERINGS
MORPHOLOGISTS	MORULATIONS	MOTHERLESSNESS	MOTORCOACHES	MOUNTAINEERS
MORPHOLOGY	MOSAICALLY	MOTHERLIER	MOTORCYCLE	MOUNTAINIER
MORPHOMETRIC	MOSAICISMS	MOTHERLIEST	MOTORCYCLED	MOUNTAINIEST
MORPHOMETRICS	MOSAICISTS	MOTHERLINESS	MOTORCYCLES	MOUNTAINOUS
MORPHOMETRIES	MOSAICKING	MOTHERLINESSES	MOTORCYCLING	MOUNTAINOUSLY
MORPHOMETRY	MOSAICKINGS	MOTHERWORT	MOTORCYCLINGS	MOUNTAINOUSNESS
MORPHOPHONEME	MOSAICLIKE	MOTHERWORTS	MOTORCYCLIST	MOUNTAINSIDE
MORPHOPHONEMES	MOSASAURUS	MOTHPROOFED	MOTORCYCLISTS	MOUNTAINSIDES
MORPHOPHONEMIC	MOSBOLLETJIE	MOTHPROOFER	MOTORHOMES	MOUNTAINTOP
MORPHOPHONEMICS	MOSBOLLETJIES	MOTHPROOFERS	MOTORICALLY	MOUNTAINTOPS
MORPHOPHONOLOGY	MOSCHATELS	MOTHPROOFING	MOTORISATION	MOUNTEBANK
MORPHOSYNTAX	MOSCHIFEROUS	MOTHPROOFS	MOTORISATIONS	MOUNTEBANKED
MORPHOSYNTAXES	MOSCOVIUMS	MOTILITIES	MOTORISING	MOUNTEBANKERIES
MORPHOTROPIC	MOSKONFYTS	MOTIONISTS	MOTORIZATION	MOUNTEBANKERY
MORPHOTROPIES	MOSQUITOES	MOTIONLESS	MOTORIZATIONS	MOUNTEBANKING
MORPHOTROPY	MOSQUITOEY	MOTIONLESSLY	MOTORIZING	MOUNTEBANKINGS
MORSELLING	MOSQUITOFISH	MOTIONLESSNESS	MOTORMOUTH	MOUNTEBANKISM
MORSELLINGS	MOSQUITOFISHES	MOTIVATING	MOTORMOUTHS	MOUNTEBANKISMS
MORTADELLA	MOSQUITOIER	MOTIVATION	MOTORSHIPS	MOUNTEBANKS
MORTADELLAS	MOSQUITOIEST	MOTIVATIONAL	MOTORTRUCK	MOUNTENANCE
MORTADELLE	MOSSBACKED	MOTIVATIONALLY	MOTORTRUCKS	MOUNTENANCES
MORTALISED	MOSSBLUITER	MOTIVATIONS	MOTOSCAFOS	MOUNTENAUNCE
MORTALISES	MOSSBLUITERS	MOTIVATIVE	MOUCHARABIES	MOUNTENAUNCES
MORTALISING	MOSSBUNKER	MOTIVATORS	MOUCHARABY	MOURNFULLER
MORTALITIES	MOSSBUNKERS	MOTIVELESS	MOUDIEWART	MOURNFULLEST
MORTALIZED	MOSSINESSES	MOTIVELESSLY	MOUDIEWARTS	MOURNFULLY

MOURNFULNESS	MOVELESSNESS	MUCOPEPTIDE	MUKHABARATS	MULTICHANNEL
MOURNFULNESSES	MOVELESSNESSES	MUCOPEPTIDES	MULBERRIES	MULTICHARACTER
MOURNINGLY	MOVIEGOERS	MUCOPROTEIN	MULIEBRITIES	MULTICIDES
MOURNIVALS	MOVIEGOING	MUCOPROTEINS	MULIEBRITY	MULTICIPITAL
MOURVEDRES	MOVIEGOINGS	MUCOPURULENT	MULISHNESS	MULTICLIENT
MOUSEBIRDS	MOVIELANDS	MUCOSANGUINEOUS	MULISHNESSES	MULTICOATED
MOUSEOVERS	MOVIEMAKER	MUCOSITIES	MULLAHISMS	MULTICOLOR
MOUSEPIECE	MOVIEMAKERS	MUCOVISCIDOSES	MULLARKIES	MULTICOLORED
MOUSEPIECES	MOVIEMAKING	MUCOVISCIDOSIS	MULLIGATAWNIES	MULTICOLORS
MOUSETAILS	MOVIEMAKINGS	MUCRONATED	MULLIGATAWNY	MULTICOLOUR
MOUSETRAPPED	MOWBURNING	MUCRONATION	MULLIGRUBS	MULTICOLOURED
MOUSETRAPPING	MOWBURNINGS	MUCRONATIONS	MULLIONING	MULTICOLOURS
MOUSETRAPPINGS	MOWDIEWART	MUDCAPPING	MULLOCKIER	MULTICOLUMN
MOUSETRAPS	MOWDIEWARTS	MUDCAPPINGS	MULLOCKIEST	MULTICOMPONENT
MOUSINESSES	MOWDIEWORT	MUDDINESSES	MULTANGULAR	MULTICONDUCTOR
MOUSQUETAIRE	MOWDIEWORTS	MUDDLEDNESS	MULTANIMOUS	MULTICOPIES
MOUSQUETAIRES	MOXIBUSTION	MUDDLEDNESSES	MULTARTICULATE	MULTICOSTATE
MOUSSELIKE	MOXIBUSTIONS	MUDDLEHEAD	MULTEITIES	MULTICOUNTY
MOUSSELINE	MOYGASHELS	MUDDLEHEADED	MULTIACCESS	MULTICOURSE
MOUSSELINES	MOZZARELLA	MUDDLEHEADEDLY	MULTIACCESSES	MULTICULTI
MOUSTACHED	MOZZARELLAS	MUDDLEHEADS	MULTIAGENCY	MULTICULTIS
MOUSTACHES	MRIDAMGAMS	MUDDLEMENT	MULTIANGULAR	MULTICULTURAL
MOUSTACHIAL	MRIDANGAMS	MUDDLEMENTS	MULTIARMED	MULTICULTURALLY
MOUSTACHIO	MUCEDINOUS	MUDDLINGLY	MULTIARTICULATE	MULTICURIE
MOUSTACHIOED	MUCHNESSES	MUDHOPPERS	MULTIAUTHOR	MULTICURRENCIES
MOUSTACHIOS	MUCIDITIES	MUDLARKING	MULTIAXIAL	MULTICURRENCY
MOUTHBREATHER	MUCIDNESSES	MUDLOGGERS	MULTIBARREL	MULTICUSPID
MOUTHBREATHERS	MUCIFEROUS	MUDLOGGING	MULTIBARRELED	MULTICUSPIDATE
MOUTHBREEDER	MUCILAGINOUS	MUDLOGGINGS	MULTIBARRELLED	MULTICUSPIDS
MOUTHBREEDERS	MUCILAGINOUSLY	MUDPUPPIES	MULTIBARRELS	MULTICYCLE
MOUTHBROODER	MUCINOGENS	MUDSKIPPER	MULTIBILLION	MULTICYCLES
MOUTHBROODERS	MUCKAMUCKED	MUDSKIPPERS	MULTIBLADED	MULTICYLINDER
MOUTHFEELS	MUCKAMUCKING	MUDSLINGER	MULTIBRANCHED	MULTIDENTATE
MOUTHPARTS	MUCKAMUCKS	MUDSLINGERS	MULTIBUILDING	MULTIDIALECTAL
MOUTHPIECE	MUCKENDERS	MUDSLINGING	MULTICAMERATE	MULTIDIGITATE
MOUTHPIECES	MUCKINESSES	MUDSLINGINGS	MULTICAMPUS	MULTIDISCIPLINE
MOUTHWASHES	MUCKRAKERS	MUFFETTEES	MULTICAPITATE	MULTIDIVISIONAL
MOUTHWATERING	MUCKRAKING	MUFFINEERS	MULTICARBON	MULTIDOMAIN
MOUTHWATERINGLY	MUCKRAKINGS	MUGEARITES	MULTICASTS	MULTIELECTRODE
MOUVEMENTE	MUCKSPREAD	MUGGINESSES	MULTICAULINE	MULTIELEMENT
MOVABILITIES	MUCKSPREADER	MUGWUMPERIES	MULTICAUSAL	MULTIEMPLOYER
MOVABILITY	MUCKSPREADERS	MUGWUMPERY	MULTICELLED	MULTIEMPLOYERS
MOVABLENESS	MUCKSPREADING	MUGWUMPISH	MULTICELLULAR	MULTIENGINE
MOVABLENESSES	MUCKSPREADS	MUGWUMPISM	MULTICENTER	MULTIENGINED
MOVEABILITIES	MUCKSWEATS	MUGWUMPISMS	MULTICENTRAL	MULTIENZYME
MOVEABILITY	MUCKYMUCKS	MUJAHEDDIN	MULTICENTRE	MULTIETHNIC
MOVEABLENESS	MUCOCUTANEOUS	MUJAHEDEEN	MULTICENTRIC	MULTIETHNICS
MOVEABLENESSES	MUCOLYTICS	MUJAHIDEEN	MULTICHAIN	MULTIFACED
MOVELESSLY	MUCOMEMBRANOUS	MUKHABARAT	MULTICHAMBERED	MULTIFACETED

MULTIFACTOR	MULTILEVELLED	MULTIORGASMIC	MULTIPLIER	MULTISPECIES
MULTIFACTORIAL	MULTILINEAL	MULTIPACKS	MULTIPLIERS	MULTISPECTRAL
MULTIFAMILIES	MULTILINEAR	MULTIPANED	MULTIPLIES	MULTISPEED
MULTIFAMILY	MULTILINES	MULTIPARAE	MULTIPLYING	MULTISPIRAL
MULTIFARIOUS	MULTILINGUAL	MULTIPARAMETER	MULTIPOINT	MULTISPORT
MULTIFARIOUSLY	MULTILINGUALISM	MULTIPARAS	MULTIPOLAR	MULTISTAGE
MULTIFIDLY	MULTILINGUALLY	MULTIPARITIES	MULTIPOLARITIES	MULTISTANDARD
MULTIFIDOUS	MULTILINGUIST	MULTIPARITY	MULTIPOLARITY	MULTISTATE
MULTIFILAMENT	MULTILINGUISTS	MULTIPAROUS	MULTIPOLES	MULTISTEMMED
MULTIFILAMENTS	MULTILOBATE	MULTIPARTICLE	MULTIPOTENT	MULTISTOREY
MULTIFLASH	MULTILOBED	MULTIPARTITE	MULTIPOTENTIAL	MULTISTOREYS
MULTIFLORA	MULTILOBES	MULTIPARTY	MULTIPOWER	MULTISTORIED
MULTIFLORAS	MULTILOBULAR	MULTIPARTYISM	MULTIPRESENCE	MULTISTORIES
MULTIFLOROUS	MULTILOBULATE	MULTIPARTYISMS	MULTIPRESENCES	MULTISTORY
MULTIFOCAL	MULTILOCATIONAL	MULTIPEDES	MULTIPRESENT	MULTISTRANDED
MULTIFOCALS	MULTILOCULAR	MULTIPHASE	MULTIPROBLEM	MULTISTRIKE
MULTIFOILS	MULTILOCULATE	MULTIPHASIC	MULTIPROCESSING	MULTISTRIKES
MULTIFOLIATE	MULTILOQUENCE	MULTIPHOTON	MULTIPROCESSOR	MULTISULCATE
MULTIFOLIOLATE	MULTILOQUENCES	MULTIPICTURE	MULTIPROCESSORS	MULTISYLLABIC
MULTIFORMITIES	MULTILOQUENT	MULTIPIECE	MULTIPRODUCT	MULTISYSTEM
MULTIFORMITY	MULTILOQUIES	MULTIPISTON	MULTIPRONGED	MULTITALENTED
MULTIFORMS	MULTILOQUOUS	MULTIPLANE	MULTIPURPOSE	MULTITASKED
MULTIFREQUENCY	MULTILOQUY	MULTIPLANES	MULTIRACIAL	MULTITASKING
MULTIFUNCTION	MULTIMANNED	MULTIPLANT	MULTIRACIALISM	MULTITASKINGS
MULTIFUNCTIONAL	MULTIMEDIA	MULTIPLAYER	MULTIRACIALISMS	MULTITASKS
MULTIGENES	MULTIMEDIAS	MULTIPLAYERS	MULTIRACIALLY	MULTITERMINAL
MULTIGENIC	MULTIMEGATON	MULTIPLETS	MULTIRAMIFIED	MULTITHREADING
MULTIGRADE	MULTIMEGAWATT	MULTIPLEXED	MULTIRANGE	MULTITHREADINGS
MULTIGRADES	MULTIMEGAWATTS	MULTIPLEXER	MULTIREGIONAL	MULTITIERED
MULTIGRAIN	MULTIMEMBER	MULTIPLEXERS	MULTIRELIGIOUS	MULTITONED
MULTIGRAVIDA	MULTIMETALLIC	MULTIPLEXES	MULTIROOMED	MULTITONES
MULTIGRAVIDAE	MULTIMETER	MULTIPLEXING	MULTISCIENCE	MULTITOOLS
MULTIGRAVIDAS	MULTIMETERS	MULTIPLEXINGS	MULTISCIENCES	MULTITOUCH
MULTIGROUP	MULTIMILLENNIAL	MULTIPLEXOR	MULTISCREEN	MULTITOWERED
MULTIHEADED	MULTIMILLION	MULTIPLEXORS	MULTISCREENS	MULTITRACK
MULTIHOSPITAL	MULTIMODAL	MULTIPLIABLE	MULTISENSE	MULTITRACKED
MULTIHULLS	MULTIMODES	MULTIPLICABLE	MULTISENSORY	MULTITRACKING
MULTIJUGATE	MULTIMOLECULAR	MULTIPLICAND	MULTISEPTATE	MULTITRACKS
MULTIJUGOUS	MULTINATION	MULTIPLICANDS	MULTISERIAL	MULTITRILLION
MULTILANES	MULTINATIONAL	MULTIPLICATE	MULTISERIATE	MULTITRILLIONS
MULTILATERAL	MULTINATIONALS	MULTIPLICATES	MULTISERVICE	MULTITUDES
MULTILATERALISM	MULTINOMIAL	MULTIPLICATION	MULTISIDED	MULTITUDINARY
MULTILATERALIST	MULTINOMIALS	MULTIPLICATIONS	MULTISKILL	MULTITUDINOUS
MULTILATERALLY	MULTINOMINAL	MULTIPLICATIVE	MULTISKILLED	MULTITUDINOUSLY
MULTILAYER	MULTINUCLEAR	MULTIPLICATOR	MULTISKILLING	MULTIUNION
MULTILAYERED	MULTINUCLEATE	MULTIPLICATORS	MULTISKILLINGS	MULTIUTILITIES
MULTILAYERS	MULTINUCLEATED	MULTIPLICITIES	MULTISKILLS	MULTIUTILITY
MULTILEVEL	MULTINUCLEOLAR	MULTIPLICITY	MULTISONANT	MULTIVALENCE
MULTILEVELED	MULTINUCLEOLATE	MULTIPLIED	MULTISOURCE	MULTIVALENCES

MULTIVALENCIES	MUNDANENESSES	MURMURATIONS	MUSICALIZATIONS	MUTABLENESSES
MULTIVALENCY	MUNDANITIES	MURMURINGLY	MUSICALIZE	MUTAGENESES
MULTIVALENT	MUNDIFICATION	MURMURINGS	MUSICALIZED	MUTAGENESIS
MULTIVALENTS	MUNDIFICATIONS	MURMUROUSLY	MUSICALIZES	MUTAGENICALLY
MULTIVARIABLE	MUNDIFICATIVE	MURTHERERS	MUSICALIZING	MUTAGENICITIES
MULTIVARIATE	MUNDIFICATIVES	MURTHERING	MUSICALNESS	MUTAGENICITY
MULTIVARIOUS	MUNDIFYING	MUSCADELLE	MUSICALNESSES	MUTAGENISE
MULTIVERSE	MUNDUNGUSES	MUSCADELLES	MUSICIANER	MUTAGENISED
MULTIVERSES	MUNICIPALISE	MUSCADINES	MUSICIANERS	MUTAGENISES
MULTIVERSITIES	MUNICIPALISED	MUSCARDINE	MUSICIANLIER	MUTAGENISING
MULTIVERSITY	MUNICIPALISES	MUSCARDINES	MUSICIANLIEST	MUTAGENIZE
MULTIVIBRATOR	MUNICIPALISING	MUSCARINES	MUSICIANLY	MUTAGENIZED
MULTIVIBRATORS	MUNICIPALISM	MUSCARINIC	MUSICIANSHIP	MUTAGENIZES
MULTIVIOUS	MUNICIPALISMS	MUSCATORIA	MUSICIANSHIPS	MUTAGENIZING
MULTIVITAMIN	MUNICIPALIST	MUSCATORIUM	MUSICOLOGICAL	MUTATIONAL
MULTIVITAMINS	MUNICIPALISTS	MUSCAVADOS	MUSICOLOGICALLY	MUTATIONALLY
MULTIVOCAL	MUNICIPALITIES	MUSCOLOGIES	MUSICOLOGIES	MUTATIONIST
MULTIVOCALS	MUNICIPALITY	MUSCOVADOS	MUSICOLOGIST	MUTATIONISTS
MULTIVOLTINE	MUNICIPALIZE	MUSCOVITES	MUSICOLOGISTS	MUTENESSES
MULTIVOLUME	MUNICIPALIZED	MUSCULARITIES	MUSICOLOGY	MUTESSARIF
MULTIWARHEAD	MUNICIPALIZES	MUSCULARITY	MUSICOTHERAPIES	MUTESSARIFAT
MULTIWAVELENGTH	MUNICIPALIZING	MUSCULARLY	MUSICOTHERAPY	MUTESSARIFATS
MULTIWINDOW	MUNICIPALLY	MUSCULATION	MUSKELLUNGE	MUTESSARIFS
MULTIWINDOWS	MUNICIPALS	MUSCULATIONS	MUSKELLUNGES	MUTILATING
MULTOCULAR	MUNIFICENCE	MUSCULATURE	MUSKETEERS	MUTILATION
MULTUNGULATE	MUNIFICENCES	MUSCULATURES	MUSKETOONS	MUTILATIONS
MULTUNGULATES	MUNIFICENT	MUSCULOSKELETAL	MUSKETRIES	MUTILATIVE
MUMBLECORE	MUNIFICENTLY	MUSEOLOGICAL	MUSKINESSES	MUTILATORS
MUMBLECORES	MUNIFICENTNESS	MUSEOLOGIES	MUSKMELONS	MUTINEERED
MUMBLEMENT	MUNIFIENCE	MUSEOLOGIST	MUSQUASHES	MUTINEERING
MUMBLEMENTS	MUNIFIENCES	MUSEOLOGISTS	MUSQUETOON	MUTINOUSLY
MUMBLETYPEG	MUNITIONED	MUSHINESSES	MUSQUETOONS	MUTINOUSNESS
MUMBLETYPEGS	MUNITIONEER	MUSHMOUTHS	MUSSELCRACKER	MUTINOUSNESSES
MUMBLINGLY	MUNITIONEERS	MUSHROOMED	MUSSELCRACKERS	MUTOSCOPES
MUMCHANCES	MUNITIONER	MUSHROOMER	MUSSINESSES	MUTTERATION
MUMMERINGS	MUNITIONERS	MUSHROOMERS	MUSSITATED	MUTTERATIONS
MUMMICHOGS	MUNITIONETTE	MUSHROOMIER	MUSSITATES	MUTTERINGLY
MUMMIFICATION	MUNITIONETTES	MUSHROOMIEST	MUSSITATING	MUTTERINGS
MUMMIFICATIONS	MUNITIONING	MUSHROOMING	MUSSITATION	MUTTONBIRD
MUMMIFORMS	MURDERABILIA	MUSHROOMINGS	MUSSITATIONS	MUTTONBIRDER
MUMMIFYING	MURDERBALL	MUSICALISATION	MUSTACHIOED	MUTTONBIRDERS
MUMPISHNESS	MURDERBALLS	MUSICALISATIONS	MUSTACHIOS	MUTTONBIRDS
MUMPISHNESSES	MURDERESSES	MUSICALISE	MUSTARDIER	MUTTONCHOPS
MUMPRENEUR	MURDEROUSLY	MUSICALISED	MUSTARDIEST	MUTTONFISH
MUMPRENEURS	MURDEROUSNESS	MUSICALISES	MUSTELINES	MUTTONFISHES
MUMPSIMUSES	MURDEROUSNESSES	MUSICALISING	MUSTINESSES	MUTTONHEAD
MUMSINESSES	MURGEONING	MUSICALITIES	MUTABILITIES	MUTTONHEADED
MUNCHABLES	MURKINESSES	MUSICALITY	MUTABILITY	MUTTONHEADS
MUNDANENESS	MURMURATION	MUSICALIZATION	MUTABLENESS	MUTTONIEST

M

MUTUALISATION	MYCOPLASMATA	MYLONITISED	MYRINGITIS	MYSTIFICATION
MUTUALISATIONS	MYCOPLASMOSES	MYLONITISES	MYRINGITISES	MYSTIFICATIONS
MUTUALISED	MYCOPLASMOSIS	MYLONITISING	MYRINGOSCOPE	MYSTIFIERS
MUTUALISES	MYCORHIZAE	MYLONITIZATION	MYRINGOSCOPES	MYSTIFYING
MUTUALISING	MYCORHIZAL	MYLONITIZATIONS	MYRINGOTOMIES	MYSTIFYINGLY
MUTUALISMS	MYCORHIZAS	MYLONITIZE	MYRINGOTOMY	MYTHICALLY
MUTUALISTIC	MYCORRHIZA	MYLONITIZED	MYRIORAMAS	MYTHICISATION
MUTUALISTS	MYCORRHIZAE	MYLONITIZES	MYRIOSCOPE	MYTHICISATIONS
MUTUALITIES	MYCORRHIZAL	MYLONITIZING	MYRIOSCOPES	MYTHICISED
MUTUALIZATION	MYCORRHIZAS	MYOBLASTIC	MYRISTICIVOROUS	MYTHICISER
MUTUALIZATIONS	MYCOTOXICOLOGY	MYOCARDIAL	MYRMECOCHORIES	MYTHICISERS
MUTUALIZED	MYCOTOXICOSES	MYOCARDIOGRAPH	MYRMECOCHORY	MYTHICISES
MUTUALIZES	MYCOTOXICOSIS	MYOCARDIOGRAPHS	MYRMECOLOGIC	MYTHICISING
MUTUALIZING	MYCOTOXINS	MYOCARDIOPATHY	MYRMECOLOGICAL	MYTHICISMS
MUTUALNESS	MYCOTOXOLOGIES	MYOCARDITIS	MYRMECOLOGIES	MYTHICISTS
MUTUALNESSES	MYCOTOXOLOGY	MYOCARDITISES	MYRMECOLOGIST	MYTHICIZATION
MUZZINESSES	MYCOTROPHIC	MYOCARDIUM	MYRMECOLOGISTS	MYTHICIZATIONS
MYASTHENIA	MYCOVIRUSES	MYOCLONUSES	MYRMECOLOGY	MYTHICIZED
MYASTHENIAS	MYDRIATICS	MYOELECTRIC	MYRMECOPHAGOUS	MYTHICIZER
MYASTHENIC	MYELENCEPHALA	MYOELECTRICAL	MYRMECOPHILE	MYTHICIZERS
MYASTHENICS	MYELENCEPHALIC	MYOFIBRILLAR	MYRMECOPHILES	MYTHICIZES
MYCETOLOGIES	MYELENCEPHALON	MYOFIBRILS	MYRMECOPHILIES	MYTHICIZING
MYCETOLOGY	MYELENCEPHALONS	MYOFILAMENT	MYRMECOPHILOUS	MYTHMAKERS
MYCETOMATA	MYELINATED	MYOFILAMENTS	MYRMECOPHILY	MYTHMAKING
MYCETOMATOUS	MYELITIDES	MYOGLOBINS	MYRMIDONES	MYTHMAKINGS
MYCETOPHAGOUS	MYELITISES	MYOGRAPHIC	MYRMIDONIAN	MYTHOGENESES
MYCETOZOAN	MYELOBLAST	MYOGRAPHICAL	MYROBALANS	MYTHOGENESIS
MYCETOZOANS	MYELOBLASTIC	MYOGRAPHICALLY	MYRTACEOUS	MYTHOGRAPHER
MYCOBACTERIA	MYELOBLASTS	MYOGRAPHIES	MYSOPHOBES	MYTHOGRAPHERS
MYCOBACTERIAL	MYELOCYTES	MYOGRAPHIST	MYSOPHOBIA	MYTHOGRAPHIES
MYCOBACTERIUM	MYELOCYTIC	MYOGRAPHISTS	MYSOPHOBIAS	MYTHOGRAPHY
MYCOBIONTS	MYELOFIBROSES	MYOINOSITOL	MYSOPHOBIC	MYTHOLOGER
MYCODOMATIA	MYELOFIBROSIS	MYOINOSITOLS	MYSOPHOBICS	MYTHOLOGERS
MYCODOMATIUM	MYELOFIBROTIC	MYOLOGICAL	MYSTAGOGIC	MYTHOLOGIAN
MYCOFLORAE	MYELOGENOUS	MYOLOGISTS	MYSTAGOGICAL	MYTHOLOGIANS
MYCOFLORAS	MYELOGRAMS	MYOMANCIES	MYSTAGOGICALLY	MYTHOLOGIC
MYCOLOGICAL	MYELOGRAPHIES	MYOMECTOMIES	MYSTAGOGIES	MYTHOLOGICAL
MYCOLOGICALLY	MYELOGRAPHY	MYOMECTOMY	MYSTAGOGUE	MYTHOLOGICALLY
MYCOLOGIES	MYELOMATOID	MYOPATHIES	MYSTAGOGUES	MYTHOLOGIES
MYCOLOGIST	MYELOMATOUS	MYOPHILIES	MYSTAGOGUS	MYTHOLOGISATION
MYCOLOGISTS	MYELOPATHIC	MYOPHILOUS	MYSTAGOGUSES	MYTHOLOGISE
MYCOPHAGIES	MYELOPATHIES	MYOPICALLY	MYSTERIOUS	MYTHOLOGISED
MYCOPHAGIST	MYELOPATHY	MYOSITISES	MYSTERIOUSLY	MYTHOLOGISER
MYCOPHAGISTS	MYIOPHILIES	MYOSOTISES	MYSTERIOUSNESS	MYTHOLOGISERS
MYCOPHAGOUS	MYIOPHILOUS	MYOSTATINS	MYSTICALLY	MYTHOLOGISES
MYCOPHILES	MYLOHYOIDS	MYRIADFOLD	MYSTICALNESS	MYTHOLOGISING
MYCOPLASMA	MYLONITISATION	MYRIADFOLDS	MYSTICALNESSES	MYTHOLOGIST
MYCOPLASMAL	MYLONITISATIONS	MYRIAPODAN	MYSTICETES	MYTHOLOGISTS
MYCOPLASMAS	MYLONITISE	MYRIAPODOUS	MYSTICISMS	MYTHOLOGIZATION

MYTHOLOGIZE
MYTHOLOGIZED
MYTHOLOGIZER
MYTHOLOGIZERS
MYTHOLOGIZES
MYTHOLOGIZING
MYTHOMANES
MYTHOMANIA

MYTHOMANIAC
MYTHOMANIACS
MYTHOMANIAS
MYTHOPOEIA
MYTHOPOEIAS
MYTHOPOEIC
MYTHOPOEISM
MYTHOPOEISMS

MYTHOPOEIST
MYTHOPOEISTS
MYTHOPOESES
MYTHOPOESIS
MYTHOPOETIC
MYTHOPOETICAL
MYTHOPOETS
MYTILIFORM

MYXAMOEBAE
MYXAMOEBAS
MYXEDEMATOUS
MYXOEDEMAS
MYXOEDEMATOUS
MYXOEDEMIC
MYXOMATOSES
MYXOMATOSIS

MYXOMATOUS
MYXOMYCETE
MYXOMYCETES
MYXOMYCETOUS
MYXOVIRUSES

M

N

NABOBERIES
NABOBESSES
NACHTMAALS
NAFFNESSES
NAIFNESSES
NAILBITERS
NAILBRUSHES
NAISSANCES
NAIVENESSES
NAKEDNESSES
NALBUPHINE
NALBUPHINES
NALORPHINE
NALORPHINES
NALTREXONE
NALTREXONES
NAMASKARAM
NAMASKARAMS
NAMAYCUSHES
NAMECHECKED
NAMECHECKING
NAMECHECKS
NAMELESSLY
NAMELESSNESS
NAMELESSNESSES
NAMEPLATES
NAMEWORTHIER
NAMEWORTHIEST
NAMEWORTHY
NANDROLONE
NANDROLONES
NANISATION
NANISATIONS
NANIZATION
NANIZATIONS
NANNOPLANKTON
NANNOPLANKTONS
NANOGRAMME
NANOGRAMMES
NANOGRASSES
NANOMATERIAL
NANOMATERIALS
NANOMEDICINE

NANOMEDICINES
NANOMETERS
NANOMETRES
NANOPARTICLE
NANOPARTICLES
NANOPHYSICS
NANOPLANKTON
NANOPLANKTONS
NANOPUBLISHING
NANOPUBLISHINGS
NANOSECOND
NANOSECONDS
NANOTECHNOLOGY
NANOTESLAS
NANOWORLDS
NAPHTHALENE
NAPHTHALENES
NAPHTHALIC
NAPHTHALIN
NAPHTHALINE
NAPHTHALINES
NAPHTHALINS
NAPHTHALISE
NAPHTHALISED
NAPHTHALISES
NAPHTHALISING
NAPHTHALIZE
NAPHTHALIZED
NAPHTHALIZES
NAPHTHALIZING
NAPHTHENES
NAPHTHENIC
NAPHTHYLAMINE
NAPHTHYLAMINES
NAPOLEONITE
NAPOLEONITES
NAPPINESSES
NAPRAPATHIES
NAPRAPATHY
NARCISSISM
NARCISSISMS
NARCISSIST
NARCISSISTIC

NARCISSISTS
NARCISSUSES
NARCOANALYSES
NARCOANALYSIS
NARCOCATHARSES
NARCOCATHARSIS
NARCOHYPNOSES
NARCOHYPNOSIS
NARCOLEPSIES
NARCOLEPSY
NARCOLEPTIC
NARCOLEPTICS
NARCOSYNTHESES
NARCOSYNTHESIS
NARCOTERRORISM
NARCOTERRORISMS
NARCOTERRORIST
NARCOTERRORISTS
NARCOTICALLY
NARCOTINES
NARCOTISATION
NARCOTISATIONS
NARCOTISED
NARCOTISES
NARCOTISING
NARCOTISMS
NARCOTISTS
NARCOTIZATION
NARCOTIZATIONS
NARCOTIZED
NARCOTIZES
NARCOTIZING
NARGHILIES
NARGHILLIES
NARGUILEHS
NARRATABLE
NARRATIONAL
NARRATIONS
NARRATIVELY
NARRATIVES
NARRATOLOGICAL
NARRATOLOGIES
NARRATOLOGIST

NARRATOLOGISTS
NARRATOLOGY
NARROWBAND
NARROWBANDS
NARROWCAST
NARROWCASTED
NARROWCASTING
NARROWCASTINGS
NARROWCASTS
NARROWINGS
NARROWNESS
NARROWNESSES
NASALISATION
NASALISATIONS
NASALISING
NASALITIES
NASALIZATION
NASALIZATIONS
NASALIZING
NASCENCIES
NASEBERRIES
NASOFRONTAL
NASOGASTRIC
NASOLACRYMAL
NASOPHARYNGEAL
NASOPHARYNGES
NASOPHARYNX
NASOPHARYNXES
NASTINESSES
NASTURTIUM
NASTURTIUMS
NATALITIAL
NATALITIES
NATATIONAL
NATATORIAL
NATATORIUM
NATATORIUMS
NATHELESSE
NATIONALISATION
NATIONALISE
NATIONALISED
NATIONALISER
NATIONALISERS

NATIONALISES
NATIONALISING
NATIONALISM
NATIONALISMS
NATIONALIST
NATIONALISTIC
NATIONALISTS
NATIONALITIES
NATIONALITY
NATIONALIZATION
NATIONALIZE
NATIONALIZED
NATIONALIZER
NATIONALIZERS
NATIONALIZES
NATIONALIZING
NATIONALLY
NATIONHOOD
NATIONHOODS
NATIONLESS
NATIONWIDE
NATIVENESS
NATIVENESSES
NATIVISTIC
NATIVITIES
NATRIURESES
NATRIURESIS
NATRIURESISES
NATRIURETIC
NATRIURETICS
NATROLITES
NATTERIEST
NATTERJACK
NATTERJACKS
NATTINESSES
NATURALISATION
NATURALISATIONS
NATURALISE
NATURALISED
NATURALISES
NATURALISING
NATURALISM
NATURALISMS

NATURALIST	NAVIGATIONS	NECESSARIANISMS	NECROMANIAS	NECTARIVOROUS
NATURALISTIC	NAVIGATORS	NECESSARIANS	NECROMANTIC	NECTOCALYCES
NATURALISTS	NAYSAYINGS	NECESSARIES	NECROMANTICAL	NECTOCALYX
NATURALIZATION	NAZIFICATION	NECESSARILY	NECROMANTICALLY	NEEDCESSITIES
NATURALIZATIONS	NAZIFICATIONS	NECESSARINESS	NECROPHAGOUS	NEEDCESSITY
NATURALIZE	NEANDERTAL	NECESSARINESSES	NECROPHILE	NEEDFULNESS
NATURALIZED	NEANDERTALER	NECESSITARIAN	NECROPHILES	NEEDFULNESSES
NATURALIZES	NEANDERTALERS	NECESSITARIANS	NECROPHILIA	NEEDINESSES
NATURALIZING	NEANDERTALS	NECESSITATE	NECROPHILIAC	NEEDLECORD
NATURALNESS	NEANDERTHAL	NECESSITATED	NECROPHILIACS	NEEDLECORDS
NATURALNESSES	NEANDERTHALER	NECESSITATES	NECROPHILIAS	NEEDLECRAFT
NATURISTIC	NEANDERTHALERS	NECESSITATING	NECROPHILIC	NEEDLECRAFTS
NATUROPATH	NEANDERTHALOID	NECESSITATION	NECROPHILIES	NEEDLEFISH
NATUROPATHIC	NEANDERTHALS	NECESSITATIONS	NECROPHILISM	NEEDLEFISHES
NATUROPATHIES	NEAPOLITAN	NECESSITATIVE	NECROPHILISMS	NEEDLEFULS
NATUROPATHS	NEAPOLITANS	NECESSITIED	NECROPHILOUS	NEEDLELESS
NATUROPATHY	NEARNESSES	NECESSITIES	NECROPHILS	NEEDLELIKE
NAUGAHYDES	NEARSHORED	NECESSITOUS	NECROPHILY	NEEDLEPOINT
NAUGHTIEST	NEARSHORES	NECESSITOUSLY	NECROPHOBE	NEEDLEPOINTED
NAUGHTINESS	NEARSHORING	NECESSITOUSNESS	NECROPHOBES	NEEDLEPOINTING
NAUGHTINESSES	NEARSIGHTED	NECKCLOTHS	NECROPHOBIA	NEEDLEPOINTS
NAUMACHIAE	NEARSIGHTEDLY	NECKERCHIEF	NECROPHOBIAS	NEEDLESSLY
NAUMACHIAS	NEARSIGHTEDNESS	NECKERCHIEFS	NECROPHOBIC	NEEDLESSNESS
NAUMACHIES	NEARTHROSES	NECKERCHIEVES	NECROPHOROUS	NEEDLESSNESSES
NAUPLIIFORM	NEARTHROSIS	NECKLACING	NECROPOLEIS	NEEDLESTICK
NAUSEATING	NEATNESSES	NECKLACINGS	NECROPOLES	NEEDLESTICKS
NAUSEATINGLY	NEBBISHERS	NECKPIECES	NECROPOLIS	NEEDLEWOMAN
NAUSEATION	NEBBISHIER	NECKVERSES	NECROPOLISES	NEEDLEWOMEN
NAUSEATIONS	NEBBISHIEST	NECROBIOSES	NECROPSIED	NEEDLEWORK
NAUSEATIVE	NEBENKERNS	NECROBIOSIS	NECROPSIES	NEEDLEWORKER
NAUSEOUSLY	NEBUCHADNEZZAR	NECROBIOTIC	NECROPSYING	NEEDLEWORKERS
NAUSEOUSNESS	NEBUCHADNEZZARS	NECROGRAPHER	NECROSCOPIC	NEEDLEWORKS
NAUSEOUSNESSES	NEBULISATION	NECROGRAPHERS	NECROSCOPICAL	NEESBERRIES
NAUTICALLY	NEBULISATIONS	NECROLATER	NECROSCOPIES	NEFARIOUSLY
NAUTILOIDS	NEBULISERS	NECROLATERS	NECROSCOPY	NEFARIOUSNESS
NAUTILUSES	NEBULISING	NECROLATRIES	NECROTISED	NEFARIOUSNESSES
NAVARCHIES	NEBULIZATION	NECROLATRY	NECROTISES	NEGATIONAL
NAVELWORTS	NEBULIZATIONS	NECROLOGIC	NECROTISING	NEGATIONIST
NAVICULARE	NEBULIZERS	NECROLOGICAL	NECROTIZED	NEGATIONISTS
NAVICULARES	NEBULIZING	NECROLOGIES	NECROTIZES	NEGATIVELY
NAVICULARS	NEBULOSITIES	NECROLOGIST	NECROTIZING	NEGATIVENESS
NAVIGABILITIES	NEBULOSITY	NECROLOGISTS	NECROTOMIES	NEGATIVENESSES
NAVIGABILITY	NEBULOUSLY	NECROMANCER	NECROTROPH	NEGATIVING
NAVIGABLENESS	NEBULOUSNESS	NECROMANCERS	NECROTROPHIC	NEGATIVISM
NAVIGABLENESSES	NEBULOUSNESSES	NECROMANCIES	NECROTROPHS	NEGATIVISMS
NAVIGATING	NECESSAIRE	NECROMANCY	NECTAREOUS	NEGATIVIST
NAVIGATION	NECESSAIRES	NECROMANIA	NECTAREOUSNESS	NEGATIVISTIC
NAVIGATIONAL	NECESSARIAN	NECROMANIAC	NECTARIFEROUS	NEGATIVISTS
NAVIGATIONALLY	NECESSARIANISM	NECROMANIACS	NECTARINES	NEGATIVITIES

N

NEGATIVITY	NEIGHBORLINESS	NEOCLASSICAL	NEONICOTINOIDS	NEOTERIZING
NEGLECTABLE	NEIGHBORLY	NEOCLASSICISM	NEONOMIANISM	NEOTROPICS
NEGLECTEDNESS	NEIGHBOURED	NEOCLASSICISMS	NEONOMIANISMS	NEOVITALISM
NEGLECTEDNESSES	NEIGHBOURHOOD	NEOCLASSICIST	NEONOMIANS	NEOVITALISMS
NEGLECTERS	NEIGHBOURHOODS	NEOCLASSICISTS	NEOORTHODOX	NEOVITALIST
NEGLECTFUL	NEIGHBOURING	NEOCOLONIAL	NEOORTHODOXIES	NEOVITALISTS
NEGLECTFULLY	NEIGHBOURLESS	NEOCOLONIALISM	NEOORTHODOXY	NEPENTHEAN
NEGLECTFULNESS	NEIGHBOURLIER	NEOCOLONIALISMS	NEOPAGANISE	NEPHALISMS
NEGLECTING	NEIGHBOURLIEST	NEOCOLONIALIST	NEOPAGANISED	NEPHALISTS
NEGLECTINGLY	NEIGHBOURLINESS	NEOCOLONIALISTS	NEOPAGANISES	NEPHELINES
NEGLECTION	NEIGHBOURLY	NEOCONSERVATISM	NEOPAGANISING	NEPHELINIC
NEGLECTIONS	NEIGHBOURS	NEOCONSERVATIVE	NEOPAGANISM	NEPHELINITE
NEGLECTIVE	NELUMBIUMS	NEOCORTEXES	NEOPAGANISMS	NEPHELINITES
NEGLECTORS	NEMATHELMINTH	NEOCORTICAL	NEOPAGANIZE	NEPHELINITIC
NEGLIGEABLE	NEMATHELMINTHIC	NEOCORTICES	NEOPAGANIZED	NEPHELITES
NEGLIGENCE	NEMATHELMINTHS	NEODYMIUMS	NEOPAGANIZES	NEPHELOMETER
NEGLIGENCES	NEMATICIDAL	NEOGENESES	NEOPAGANIZING	NEPHELOMETERS
NEGLIGENTLY	NEMATICIDE	NEOGENESIS	NEOPHILIAC	NEPHELOMETRIC
NEGLIGIBILITIES	NEMATICIDES	NEOGENETIC	NEOPHILIACS	NEPHELOMETRIES
NEGLIGIBILITY	NEMATOBLAST	NEOGOTHICS	NEOPHILIAS	NEPHELOMETRY
NEGLIGIBLE	NEMATOBLASTS	NEOGRAMMARIAN	NEOPHOBIAS	NEPHOGRAMS
NEGLIGIBLENESS	NEMATOCIDAL	NEOGRAMMARIANS	NEOPILINAS	NEPHOGRAPH
NEGLIGIBLY	NEMATOCIDE	NEOLIBERAL	NEOPLASIAS	NEPHOGRAPHS
NEGOCIANTS	NEMATOCIDES	NEOLIBERALISM	NEOPLASTIC	NEPHOLOGIC
NEGOTIABILITIES	NEMATOCYST	NEOLIBERALISMS	NEOPLASTICISM	NEPHOLOGICAL
NEGOTIABILITY	NEMATOCYSTIC	NEOLIBERALS	NEOPLASTICISMS	NEPHOLOGIES
NEGOTIABLE	NEMATOCYSTS	NEOLITHICS	NEOPLASTICIST	NEPHOLOGIST
NEGOTIANTS	NEMATODIRIASES	NEOLOGIANS	NEOPLASTICISTS	NEPHOLOGISTS
NEGOTIATED	NEMATODIRIASIS	NEOLOGICAL	NEOPLASTIES	NEPHOSCOPE
NEGOTIATES	NEMATODIRUS	NEOLOGICALLY	NEOPRONOUN	NEPHOSCOPES
NEGOTIATING	NEMATODIRUSES	NEOLOGISED	NEOPRONOUNS	NEPHRALGIA
NEGOTIATION	NEMATOLOGICAL	NEOLOGISES	NEOREALISM	NEPHRALGIAS
NEGOTIATIONS	NEMATOLOGIES	NEOLOGISING	NEOREALISMS	NEPHRALGIC
NEGOTIATOR	NEMATOLOGIST	NEOLOGISMS	NEOREALIST	NEPHRALGIES
NEGOTIATORS	NEMATOLOGISTS	NEOLOGISTIC	NEOREALISTIC	NEPHRECTOMIES
NEGOTIATORY	NEMATOLOGY	NEOLOGISTICAL	NEOREALISTS	NEPHRECTOMISE
NEGOTIATRESS	NEMATOPHORE	NEOLOGISTICALLY	NEOSTIGMINE	NEPHRECTOMISED
NEGOTIATRESSES	NEMATOPHORES	NEOLOGISTS	NEOSTIGMINES	NEPHRECTOMISES
NEGOTIATRICES	NEMERTEANS	NEOLOGIZED	NEOTEINIAS	NEPHRECTOMISING
NEGOTIATRIX	NEMERTIANS	NEOLOGIZES	NEOTERICAL	NEPHRECTOMIZE
NEGOTIATRIXES	NEMERTINES	NEOLOGIZING	NEOTERICALLY	NEPHRECTOMIZED
NEGRITUDES	NEMOPHILAS	NEONATALLY	NEOTERICALS	NEPHRECTOMIZES
NEIGHBORED	NEOANTHROPIC	NEONATICIDE	NEOTERISED	NEPHRECTOMIZING
NEIGHBORHOOD	NEOARSPHENAMINE	NEONATICIDES	NEOTERISES	NEPHRECTOMY
NEIGHBORHOODS	NEOCAPITALISM	NEONATOLOGIES	NEOTERISING	NEPHRIDIAL
NEIGHBORING	NEOCAPITALISMS	NEONATOLOGIST	NEOTERISMS	NEPHRIDIUM
NEIGHBORLESS	NEOCAPITALIST	NEONATOLOGISTS	NEOTERISTS	NEPHRITICAL
NEIGHBORLIER	NEOCAPITALISTS	NEONATOLOGY	NEOTERIZED	NEPHRITICS
NEIGHBORLIEST	NEOCLASSIC	NEONICOTINOID	NEOTERIZES	NEPHRITIDES

NEPHRITISES	NETHERMORES	NEUROBIOLOGY	NEUROHUMORS	NEUROPTERAN
NEPHROBLASTOMA	NETHERMOST	NEUROBLAST	NEUROHUMOUR	NEUROPTERANS
NEPHROBLASTOMAS	NETHERSTOCK	NEUROBLASTOMA	NEUROHUMOURS	NEUROPTERIST
NEPHROLEPIS	NETHERSTOCKS	NEUROBLASTOMAS	NEUROHYPNOLOGY	NEUROPTERISTS
NEPHROLEPISES	NETHERWARD	NEUROBLASTOMATA	NEUROHYPOPHYSES	NEUROPTERON
NEPHROLOGICAL	NETHERWARDS	NEUROBLASTS	NEUROHYPOPHYSIS	NEUROPTERONS
NEPHROLOGIES	NETHERWORLD	NEUROCHEMICAL	NEUROLEMMA	NEUROPTEROUS
NEPHROLOGIST	NETHERWORLDS	NEUROCHEMICALS	NEUROLEMMAS	NEURORADIOLOGY
NEPHROLOGISTS	NETIQUETTE	NEUROCHEMIST	NEUROLEPTIC	NEUROSCIENCE
NEPHROLOGY	NETIQUETTES	NEUROCHEMISTRY	NEUROLEPTICS	NEUROSCIENCES
NEPHROPATHIC	NETMINDERS	NEUROCHEMISTS	NEUROLINGUIST	NEUROSCIENTIFIC
NEPHROPATHIES	NETSURFERS	NEUROCHIPS	NEUROLINGUISTIC	NEUROSCIENTIST
NEPHROPATHY	NETSURFING	NEUROCOELE	NEUROLINGUISTS	NEUROSCIENTISTS
NEPHROPEXIES	NETSURFINGS	NEUROCOELES	NEUROLOGIC	NEUROSECRETION
NEPHROPEXY	NETTLELIKE	NEUROCOELS	NEUROLOGICAL	NEUROSECRETIONS
NEPHROPTOSES	NETTLESOME	NEUROCOGNITIVE	NEUROLOGICALLY	NEUROSECRETORY
NEPHROPTOSIS	NETWORKERS	NEUROCOMPUTER	NEUROLOGIES	NEUROSENSORY
NEPHROSCOPE	NETWORKING	NEUROCOMPUTERS	NEUROLOGIST	NEUROSPORA
NEPHROSCOPES	NETWORKINGS	NEUROCOMPUTING	NEUROLOGISTS	NEUROSPORAS
NEPHROSCOPIES	NEURALGIAS	NEUROCOMPUTINGS	NEUROLYSES	NEUROSURGEON
NEPHROSCOPY	NEURAMINIC	NEURODIVERGENT	NEUROLYSIS	NEUROSURGEONS
NEPHROSTOME	NEURAMINIDASE	NEURODIVERSE	NEUROMARKETING	NEUROSURGERIES
NEPHROSTOMES	NEURAMINIDASES	NEURODIVERSITY	NEUROMARKETINGS	NEUROSURGERY
NEPHROTICS	NEURASTHENIA	NEUROECTODERMAL	NEUROMASTS	NEUROSURGICAL
NEPHROTOMIES	NEURASTHENIAC	NEUROENDOCRINE	NEUROMATOUS	NEUROSURGICALLY
NEPHROTOMY	NEURASTHENIACS	NEUROETHOLOGIES	NEUROMINORITIES	NEUROSYPHILIS
NEPHROTOXIC	NEURASTHENIAS	NEUROETHOLOGY	NEUROMINORITY	NEUROSYPHILISES
NEPHROTOXICITY	NEURASTHENIC	NEUROFEEDBACK	NEUROMOTOR	NEUROTICALLY
NEPOTISTIC	NEURASTHENICS	NEUROFEEDBACKS	NEUROMUSCULAR	NEUROTICISM
NEPTUNIUMS	NEURATIONS	NEUROFIBRIL	NEUROPATHIC	NEUROTICISMS
NERDINESSES	NEURECTOMIES	NEUROFIBRILAR	NEUROPATHICAL	NEUROTOMIES
NERVATIONS	NEURECTOMY	NEUROFIBRILLAR	NEUROPATHICALLY	NEUROTOMIST
NERVATURES	NEURILEMMA	NEUROFIBRILLARY	NEUROPATHIES	NEUROTOMISTS
NERVELESSLY	NEURILEMMAL	NEUROFIBRILS	NEUROPATHIST	NEUROTOXIC
NERVELESSNESS	NEURILEMMAS	NEUROFIBROMA	NEUROPATHISTS	NEUROTOXICITIES
NERVELESSNESSES	NEURILITIES	NEUROFIBROMAS	NEUROPATHOLOGIC	NEUROTOXICITY
NERVINESSES	NEURITIDES	NEUROFIBROMATA	NEUROPATHOLOGY	NEUROTOXIN
NERVOSITIES	NEURITISES	NEUROGENESES	NEUROPATHS	NEUROTOXINS
NERVOUSNESS	NEUROACTIVE	NEUROGENESIS	NEUROPATHY	NEUROTROPHIC
NERVOUSNESSES	NEUROANATOMIC	NEUROGENIC	NEUROPEPTIDE	NEUROTROPHIES
NERVURATION	NEUROANATOMICAL	NEUROGENICALLY	NEUROPEPTIDES	NEUROTROPHY
NERVURATIONS	NEUROANATOMIES	NEUROGLIAL	NEUROPHYSIOLOGY	NEUROTROPIC
NESCIENCES	NEUROANATOMIST	NEUROGLIAS	NEUROPLASM	NEUROTYPICAL
NESHNESSES	NEUROANATOMISTS	NEUROGRAMS	NEUROPLASMS	NEUROVASCULAR
NESSELRODE	NEUROANATOMY	NEUROHORMONAL	NEUROPLASTIC	NEURULATION
NESSELRODES	NEUROBIOLOGICAL	NEUROHORMONE	NEUROPLASTICITY	NEURULATIONS
NETBALLERS	NEUROBIOLOGIES	NEUROHORMONES	NEUROPSYCHIATRY	NEURYPNOLOGIES
NETHERLINGS	NEUROBIOLOGIST	NEUROHUMOR	NEUROPSYCHOLOGY	NEURYPNOLOGY
NETHERMORE	NEUROBIOLOGISTS	NEUROHUMORAL	NEUROPTERA	NEUTERINGS

ten to fifteen letter words | 959

NEUTRALISATION	NEWSBREAKS	NIAISERIES	NIDIFICATIONS	NIGHTMARISHNESS
NEUTRALISATIONS	NEWSCASTER	NIALAMIDES	NIDIFUGOUS	NIGHTPIECE
NEUTRALISE	NEWSCASTERS	NIBBLINGLY	NIDULATION	NIGHTPIECES
NEUTRALISED	NEWSCASTING	NICCOLITES	NIDULATIONS	NIGHTRIDER
NEUTRALISER	NEWSCASTINGS	NICENESSES	NIFEDIPINE	NIGHTRIDERS
NEUTRALISERS	NEWSDEALER	NICKELIFEROUS	NIFEDIPINES	NIGHTRIDING
NEUTRALISES	NEWSDEALERS	NICKELINES	NIFFNAFFED	NIGHTRIDINGS
NEUTRALISING	NEWSFLASHES	NICKELISED	NIFFNAFFING	NIGHTSCOPE
NEUTRALISM	NEWSGROUPS	NICKELISES	NIFTINESSES	NIGHTSCOPES
NEUTRALISMS	NEWSHOUNDS	NICKELISING	NIGGARDING	NIGHTSHADE
NEUTRALIST	NEWSINESSES	NICKELIZED	NIGGARDISE	NIGHTSHADES
NEUTRALISTIC	NEWSLETTER	NICKELIZES	NIGGARDISES	NIGHTSHIRT
NEUTRALISTS	NEWSLETTERS	NICKELIZING	NIGGARDIZE	NIGHTSHIRTS
NEUTRALITIES	NEWSMAGAZINE	NICKELLING	NIGGARDIZES	NIGHTSIDES
NEUTRALITY	NEWSMAGAZINES	NICKELODEON	NIGGARDLIER	NIGHTSPOTS
NEUTRALIZATION	NEWSMAKERS	NICKELODEONS	NIGGARDLIEST	NIGHTSTAND
NEUTRALIZATIONS	NEWSMONGER	NICKERNUTS	NIGGARDLINESS	NIGHTSTANDS
NEUTRALIZE	NEWSMONGERS	NICKNAMERS	NIGGARDLINESSES	NIGHTSTICK
NEUTRALIZED	NEWSPAPERDOM	NICKNAMING	NIGGLINGLY	NIGHTSTICKS
NEUTRALIZER	NEWSPAPERDOMS	NICKPOINTS	NIGHNESSES	NIGHTTIDES
NEUTRALIZERS	NEWSPAPERED	NICKSTICKS	NIGHTBIRDS	NIGHTTIMES
NEUTRALIZES	NEWSPAPERING	NICKUMPOOP	NIGHTBLIND	NIGHTWALKER
NEUTRALIZING	NEWSPAPERISM	NICKUMPOOPS	NIGHTCLASS	NIGHTWALKERS
NEUTRALNESS	NEWSPAPERISMS	NICOMPOOPS	NIGHTCLASSES	NIGHTWATCHMAN
NEUTRALNESSES	NEWSPAPERMAN	NICOTIANAS	NIGHTCLOTHES	NIGHTWATCHMEN
NEUTRETTOS	NEWSPAPERMEN	NICOTINAMIDE	NIGHTCLUBBED	NIGHTWEARS
NEUTRINOLESS	NEWSPAPERS	NICOTINAMIDES	NIGHTCLUBBER	NIGRESCENCE
NEUTROPENIA	NEWSPAPERWOMAN	NICOTINISM	NIGHTCLUBBERS	NIGRESCENCES
NEUTROPENIAS	NEWSPAPERWOMEN	NICOTINISMS	NIGHTCLUBBING	NIGRESCENT
NEUTROPHIL	NEWSPEOPLE	NICROSILAL	NIGHTCLUBBINGS	NIGRIFYING
NEUTROPHILE	NEWSPERSON	NICROSILALS	NIGHTCLUBS	NIGRITUDES
NEUTROPHILES	NEWSPERSONS	NICTATIONS	NIGHTDRESS	NIGROMANCIES
NEUTROPHILIC	NEWSPRINTS	NICTITATED	NIGHTDRESSES	NIGROMANCY
NEUTROPHILS	NEWSREADER	NICTITATES	NIGHTFALLS	NIGROSINES
NEVERMINDS	NEWSREADERS	NICTITATING	NIGHTFARING	NIHILISTIC
NEVERTHELESS	NEWSSHEETS	NICTITATION	NIGHTFIRES	NIHILITIES
NEVERTHEMORE	NEWSSTANDS	NICTITATIONS	NIGHTGEARS	NIKETHAMIDE
NEWFANGLED	NEWSTRADES	NIDAMENTAL	NIGHTGLOWS	NIKETHAMIDES
NEWFANGLEDLY	NEWSWEEKLIES	NIDAMENTUM	NIGHTGOWNS	NILPOTENTS
NEWFANGLEDNESS	NEWSWEEKLY	NIDDERINGS	NIGHTHAWKS	NIMBLENESS
NEWFANGLENESS	NEWSWORTHIER	NIDDERLING	NIGHTINGALE	NIMBLENESSES
NEWFANGLENESSES	NEWSWORTHIEST	NIDDERLINGS	NIGHTINGALES	NIMBLESSES
NEWFANGLES	NEWSWORTHINESS	NIDERLINGS	NIGHTLIFES	NIMBLEWITS
NEWISHNESS	NEWSWORTHY	NIDICOLOUS	NIGHTLIVES	NIMBLEWITTED
NEWISHNESSES	NEWSWRITING	NIDIFICATE	NIGHTMARES	NIMBOSTRATI
NEWMARKETS	NEWSWRITINGS	NIDIFICATED	NIGHTMARIER	NIMBOSTRATUS
NEWSAGENCIES	NEXTNESSES	NIDIFICATES	NIGHTMARIEST	NIMBYNESSES
NEWSAGENCY	NIACINAMIDE	NIDIFICATING	NIGHTMARISH	NINCOMPOOP
NEWSAGENTS	NIACINAMIDES	NIDIFICATION	NIGHTMARISHLY	NINCOMPOOPERIES

NINCOMPOOPERY	NITROGELATINE	NOBLEWOMEN	NOISOMENESSES	NOMOGRAPHIC
NINCOMPOOPS	NITROGELATINES	NOCHELLING	NOMADICALLY	NOMOGRAPHICAL
NINEPENCES	NITROGELATINS	NOCICEPTIVE	NOMADISATION	NOMOGRAPHICALLY
NINEPENNIES	NITROGENASE	NOCICEPTOR	NOMADISATIONS	NOMOGRAPHIES
NINESCORES	NITROGENASES	NOCICEPTORS	NOMADISING	NOMOGRAPHS
NINETEENTH	NITROGENISATION	NOCIRECEPTOR	NOMADIZATION	NOMOGRAPHY
NINETEENTHLIES	NITROGENISE	NOCIRECEPTORS	NOMADIZATIONS	NOMOLOGICAL
NINETEENTHLY	NITROGENISED	NOCTAMBULATION	NOMADIZING	NOMOLOGICALLY
NINETEENTHS	NITROGENISES	NOCTAMBULATIONS	NOMARCHIES	NOMOLOGIES
NINETIETHS	NITROGENISING	NOCTAMBULISM	NOMENCLATIVE	NOMOLOGIST
NINHYDRINS	NITROGENIZATION	NOCTAMBULISMS	NOMENCLATOR	NOMOLOGISTS
NINNYHAMMER	NITROGENIZE	NOCTAMBULIST	NOMENCLATORIAL	NOMOTHETES
NINNYHAMMERS	NITROGENIZED	NOCTAMBULISTS	NOMENCLATORS	NOMOTHETIC
NIPCHEESES	NITROGENIZES	NOCTILUCAE	NOMENCLATURAL	NOMOTHETICAL
NIPPERKINS	NITROGENIZING	NOCTILUCAS	NOMENCLATURE	NONABRASIVE
NIPPINESSES	NITROGENOUS	NOCTILUCENCE	NOMENCLATURES	NONABSORBABLE
NIPPLEWORT	NITROGLYCERIN	NOCTILUCENCES	NOMENKLATURA	NONABSORBENT
NIPPLEWORTS	NITROGLYCERINE	NOCTILUCENT	NOMENKLATURAS	NONABSORPTIVE
NISBERRIES	NITROGLYCERINES	NOCTILUCOUS	NOMINALISATION	NONABSTRACT
NITPICKERS	NITROGLYCERINS	NOCTIVAGANT	NOMINALISATIONS	NONACADEMIC
NITPICKIER	NITROMETER	NOCTIVAGANTS	NOMINALISE	NONACADEMICS
NITPICKIEST	NITROMETERS	NOCTIVAGATION	NOMINALISED	NONACCEPTANCE
NITPICKING	NITROMETHANE	NOCTIVAGATIONS	NOMINALISES	NONACCEPTANCES
NITPICKINGS	NITROMETHANES	NOCTIVAGOUS	NOMINALISING	NONACCIDENTAL
NITRAMINES	NITROMETRIC	NOCTUARIES	NOMINALISM	NONACCOUNTABLE
NITRANILINE	NITROPARAFFIN	NOCTURNALITIES	NOMINALISMS	NONACCREDITED
NITRANILINES	NITROPARAFFINS	NOCTURNALITY	NOMINALIST	NONACCRUAL
NITRATINES	NITROPHILOUS	NOCTURNALLY	NOMINALISTIC	NONACHIEVEMENT
NITRATIONS	NITROSAMINE	NOCTURNALS	NOMINALISTS	NONACHIEVEMENTS
NITRAZEPAM	NITROSAMINES	NOCUOUSNESS	NOMINALIZATION	NONACQUISITIVE
NITRAZEPAMS	NITROSATION	NOCUOUSNESSES	NOMINALIZATIONS	NONACTINGS
NITRIDINGS	NITROSATIONS	NODALISING	NOMINALIZE	NONACTIONS
NITRIFIABLE	NITROTOLUENE	NODALITIES	NOMINALIZED	NONACTIVATED
NITRIFICATION	NITROTOLUENES	NODALIZING	NOMINALIZES	NONADAPTIVE
NITRIFICATIONS	NITWITTEDNESS	NODOSITIES	NOMINALIZING	NONADDICTIVE
NITRIFIERS	NITWITTEDNESSES	NODULATION	NOMINATELY	NONADDICTS
NITRIFYING	NITWITTERIES	NODULATIONS	NOMINATING	NONADDITIVE
NITROBACTERIA	NITWITTERY	NOEMATICAL	NOMINATION	NONADDITIVITIES
NITROBACTERIUM	NOBBINESSES	NOEMATICALLY	NOMINATIONS	NONADDITIVITY
NITROBENZENE	NOBILESSES	NOGOODNIKS	NOMINATIVAL	NONADHESIVE
NITROBENZENES	NOBILITATE	NOISELESSLY	NOMINATIVALLY	NONADIABATIC
NITROCELLULOSE	NOBILITATED	NOISELESSNESS	NOMINATIVE	NONADJACENT
NITROCELLULOSES	NOBILITATES	NOISELESSNESSES	NOMINATIVELY	NONADMIRER
NITROCHLOROFORM	NOBILITATING	NOISEMAKER	NOMINATIVES	NONADMIRERS
NITROCOTTON	NOBILITATION	NOISEMAKERS	NOMINATORS	NONADMISSION
NITROCOTTONS	NOBILITATIONS	NOISEMAKING	NOMOCRACIES	NONADMISSIONS
NITROFURAN	NOBILITIES	NOISEMAKINGS	NOMOGENIES	NONAESTHETIC
NITROFURANS	NOBLENESSES	NOISINESSES	NOMOGRAPHER	NONAFFILIATED
NITROGELATIN	NOBLEWOMAN	NOISOMENESS	NOMOGRAPHERS	NONAFFLUENT

NONAGENARIAN	NONASSERTIVE	NONBROADCAST	NONCHURCHGOER	NONCOMMUNITY
NONAGENARIANS	NONASSOCIATED	NONBUILDING	NONCHURCHGOERS	NONCOMMUTATIVE
NONAGESIMAL	NONASTRONOMICAL	NONBURNABLE	NONCHURCHING	NONCOMPARABLE
NONAGESIMALS	NONATHLETE	NONBUSINESS	NONCIRCULAR	NONCOMPATIBLE
NONAGGRESSION	NONATHLETES	NONCABINET	NONCIRCULATING	NONCOMPETITION
NONAGGRESSIONS	NONATHLETIC	NONCALLABLE	NONCITIZEN	NONCOMPETITIONS
NONAGGRESSIVE	NONATTACHED	NONCALORIC	NONCITIZENS	NONCOMPETITIVE
NONAGRICULTURAL	NONATTACHMENT	NONCANCELABLE	NONCLANDESTINE	NONCOMPETITOR
NONALCOHOLIC	NONATTACHMENTS	NONCANCELLABLE	NONCLASSES	NONCOMPETITORS
NONALGEBRAIC	NONATTENDANCE	NONCANCEROUS	NONCLASSICAL	NONCOMPLETION
NONALIGNED	NONATTENDANCES	NONCANDIDACIES	NONCLASSIFIED	NONCOMPLETIONS
NONALIGNMENT	NONATTENDER	NONCANDIDACY	NONCLASSROOM	NONCOMPLEX
NONALIGNMENTS	NONATTENDERS	NONCANDIDATE	NONCLERICAL	NONCOMPLIANCE
NONALLELIC	NONATTRIBUTABLE	NONCANDIDATES	NONCLINICAL	NONCOMPLIANCES
NONALLERGENIC	NONAUDITORY	NONCAPITAL	NONCLOGGING	NONCOMPLICATED
NONALLERGIC	NONAUTHORS	NONCAPITALIST	NONCOERCIVE	NONCOMPLYING
NONALPHABETIC	NONAUTOMATED	NONCAPITALISTS	NONCOGNITIVE	NONCOMPLYINGS
NONALUMINIUM	NONAUTOMATIC	NONCARBOHYDRATE	NONCOGNITIVISM	NONCOMPOSER
NONALUMINUM	NONAUTOMOTIVE	NONCARCINOGEN	NONCOGNITIVISMS	NONCOMPOSERS
NONAMBIGUOUS	NONAUTONOMOUS	NONCARCINOGENIC	NONCOHERENT	NONCOMPOUND
NONANALYTIC	NONAVAILABILITY	NONCARCINOGENS	NONCOINCIDENCE	NONCOMPRESSIBLE
NONANATOMIC	NONBACTERIAL	NONCARDIAC	NONCOINCIDENCES	NONCOMPUTER
NONANSWERED	NONBANKING	NONCARRIER	NONCOLLECTOR	NONCOMPUTERISED
NONANSWERING	NONBARBITURATE	NONCARRIERS	NONCOLLECTORS	NONCOMPUTERIZED
NONANSWERS	NONBARBITURATES	NONCELEBRATION	NONCOLLEGE	NONCONCEPTUAL
NONANTAGONISTIC	NONBEARING	NONCELEBRATIONS	NONCOLLEGIATE	NONCONCERN
NONANTIBIOTIC	NONBEHAVIORAL	NONCELEBRITIES	NONCOLLINEAR	NONCONCERNS
NONANTIBIOTICS	NONBEHAVIOURAL	NONCELEBRITY	NONCOLORED	NONCONCLUSION
NONANTIGENIC	NONBELIEFS	NONCELLULAR	NONCOLORFAST	NONCONCLUSIONS
NONAPPEARANCE	NONBELIEVER	NONCELLULOSIC	NONCOLOURED	NONCONCURRED
NONAPPEARANCES	NONBELIEVERS	NONCELLULOSICS	NONCOLOURFAST	NONCONCURRENCE
NONAQUATIC	NONBELLIGERENCY	NONCENTRAL	NONCOLOURS	NONCONCURRENCES
NONAQUEOUS	NONBELLIGERENT	NONCERTIFICATED	NONCOMBATANT	NONCONCURRENT
NONARBITRARY	NONBELLIGERENTS	NONCERTIFIED	NONCOMBATANTS	NONCONCURRING
NONARCHITECT	NONBETTING	NONCHALANCE	NONCOMBATIVE	NONCONCURS
NONARCHITECTS	NONBINDING	NONCHALANCES	NONCOMBUSTIBLE	NONCONDENSABLE
NONARCHITECTURE	NONBIOGRAPHICAL	NONCHALANT	NONCOMBUSTIBLES	NONCONDITIONED
NONARGUMENT	NONBIOLOGICAL	NONCHALANTLY	NONCOMMERCIAL	NONCONDUCTING
NONARGUMENTS	NONBIOLOGICALLY	NONCHARACTER	NONCOMMISSIONED	NONCONDUCTION
NONARISTOCRATIC	NONBIOLOGIST	NONCHARACTERS	NONCOMMITMENT	NONCONDUCTIONS
NONAROMATIC	NONBIOLOGISTS	NONCHARISMATIC	NONCOMMITMENTS	NONCONDUCTIVE
NONAROMATICS	NONBONDING	NONCHARISMATICS	NONCOMMITTAL	NONCONDUCTOR
NONARRIVAL	NONBOTANIST	NONCHAUVINIST	NONCOMMITTALLY	NONCONDUCTORS
NONARRIVALS	NONBOTANISTS	NONCHAUVINISTS	NONCOMMITTALS	NONCONFERENCE
NONARTISTIC	NONBREAKABLE	NONCHEMICAL	NONCOMMITTED	NONCONFIDENCE
NONARTISTS	NONBREATHING	NONCHEMICALS	NONCOMMUNICANT	NONCONFIDENCES
NONASCETIC	NONBREEDER	NONCHROMOSOMAL	NONCOMMUNICANTS	NONCONFIDENTIAL
NONASCETICS	NONBREEDERS	NONCHURCHED	NONCOMMUNIST	NONCONFLICTING
NONASPIRIN	NONBREEDING	NONCHURCHES	NONCOMMUNISTS	NONCONFORM

NONCONFORMANCE	NONCOOPERATION	NONDEFORMING	NONDISJUNCTION	NONEMPHATIC
NONCONFORMANCES	NONCOOPERATIONS	NONDEGENERATE	NONDISJUNCTIONS	NONEMPIRICAL
NONCONFORMED	NONCOOPERATIVE	NONDEGRADABLE	NONDISPERSIVE	NONEMPLOYEE
NONCONFORMER	NONCOOPERATOR	NONDELEGATE	NONDISRUPTIVE	NONEMPLOYEES
NONCONFORMERS	NONCOOPERATORS	NONDELEGATES	NONDISTINCTIVE	NONEMPLOYMENT
NONCONFORMING	NONCOPLANAR	NONDELIBERATE	NONDIVERGENT	NONEMPLOYMENTS
NONCONFORMINGS	NONCORPORATE	NONDELINQUENT	NONDIVERSIFIED	NONENCAPSULATED
NONCONFORMISM	NONCORRELATION	NONDELINQUENTS	NONDIVIDING	NONENFORCEMENT
NONCONFORMISMS	NONCORRELATIONS	NONDELIVERIES	NONDOCTORS	NONENFORCEMENTS
NONCONFORMIST	NONCORRODIBLE	NONDELIVERY	NONDOCTRINAIRE	NONENGAGEMENT
NONCONFORMISTS	NONCORRODING	NONDEMANDING	NONDOCUMENTARY	NONENGAGEMENTS
NONCONFORMITIES	NONCORROSIVE	NONDEMANDS	NONDOGMATIC	NONENGINEERING
NONCONFORMITY	NONCOUNTRIES	NONDEMOCRATIC	NONDOMESTIC	NONENTITIES
NONCONFORMS	NONCOUNTRY	NONDEPARTMENTAL	NONDOMICILED	NONENTRIES
NONCONGRUENT	NONCOVERAGE	NONDEPENDENT	NONDOMINANT	NONENZYMATIC
NONCONJUGATED	NONCOVERAGES	NONDEPENDENTS	NONDORMANT	NONENZYMIC
NONCONNECTION	NONCREATIVE	NONDEPLETABLE	NONDRAMATIC	NONEQUILIBRIA
NONCONNECTIONS	NONCREATIVITIES	NONDEPLETING	NONDRINKER	NONEQUILIBRIUM
NONCONSCIOUS	NONCREATIVITY	NONDEPOSITION	NONDRINKERS	NONEQUILIBRIUMS
NONCONSECUTIVE	NONCREDENTIALED	NONDEPOSITIONS	NONDRINKING	NONEQUIVALENCE
NONCONSENSUAL	NONCRIMINAL	NONDEPRESSED	NONDRIVERS	NONEQUIVALENCES
NONCONSERVATION	NONCRIMINALS	NONDERIVATIVE	NONDURABLE	NONEQUIVALENT
NONCONSERVATIVE	NONCRITICAL	NONDESCRIPT	NONDURABLES	NONESSENTIAL
NONCONSOLIDATED	NONCROSSOVER	NONDESCRIPTIVE	NONEARNING	NONESSENTIALS
NONCONSTANT	NONCROSSOVERS	NONDESCRIPTLY	NONECONOMIC	NONESTABLISHED
NONCONSTRUCTION	NONCRUSHABLE	NONDESCRIPTNESS	NONECONOMIST	NONESTERIFIED
NONCONSTRUCTIVE	NONCRYSTALLINE	NONDESCRIPTS	NONECONOMISTS	NONESUCHES
NONCONSUMER	NONCULINARY	NONDESTRUCTIVE	NONEDIBLES	NONETHELESS
NONCONSUMERS	NONCULTIVATED	NONDETACHABLE	NONEDITORIAL	NONETHICAL
NONCONSUMING	NONCULTIVATION	NONDEVELOPMENT	NONEDUCATION	NONETHNICS
NONCONSUMPTION	NONCULTIVATIONS	NONDEVELOPMENTS	NONEDUCATIONAL	NONEVALUATIVE
NONCONSUMPTIONS	NONCULTURAL	NONDEVIANT	NONEFFECTIVE	NONEVIDENCE
NONCONSUMPTIVE	NONCUMULATIVE	NONDIABETIC	NONEFFECTIVES	NONEVIDENCES
NONCONTACT	NONCURRENT	NONDIABETICS	NONELASTIC	NONEXCLUSIVE
NONCONTACTS	NONCUSTODIAL	NONDIALYSABLE	NONELECTED	NONEXECUTIVE
NONCONTAGIOUS	NONCUSTOMER	NONDIALYZABLE	NONELECTION	NONEXECUTIVES
NONCONTEMPORARY	NONCUSTOMERS	NONDIAPAUSING	NONELECTIONS	NONEXEMPTS
NONCONTIGUOUS	NONCYCLICAL	NONDIDACTIC	NONELECTIVE	NONEXISTENCE
NONCONTINGENT	NONDANCERS	NONDIFFUSIBLE	NONELECTRIC	NONEXISTENCES
NONCONTINUOUS	NONDEALERS	NONDIMENSIONAL	NONELECTRICAL	NONEXISTENT
NONCONTRACT	NONDECEPTIVE	NONDIPLOMATIC	NONELECTRICALS	NONEXISTENTIAL
NONCONTRACTUAL	NONDECISION	NONDIRECTED	NONELECTRICS	NONEXISTENTS
NONCONTRIBUTING	NONDECISIONS	NONDIRECTIONAL	NONELECTROLYTE	NONEXPENDABLE
NONCONTRIBUTORY	NONDECREASING	NONDIRECTIVE	NONELECTROLYTES	NONEXPERIMENTAL
NONCONTROLLABLE	NONDEDUCTIBLE	NONDISABLED	NONELECTRONIC	NONEXPERTS
NONCONTROLLED	NONDEDUCTIVE	NONDISCLOSURE	NONELEMENTARY	NONEXPLANATORY
NONCONTROLLING	NONDEFENCE	NONDISCLOSURES	NONEMERGENCIES	NONEXPLOITATION
NONCONVENTIONAL	NONDEFENSE	NONDISCOUNT	NONEMERGENCY	NONEXPLOITATIVE
NONCONVERTIBLE	NONDEFERRABLE	NONDISCURSIVE	NONEMOTIONAL	NONEXPLOITIVE

NONEXPLOSIVE	NONGOLFERS	NONIMPLICATIONS	NONINTERFERENCE	NONLOGICAL
NONEXPOSED	NONGONOCOCCAL	NONIMPORTATION	NONINTERSECTING	NONLOGICALLY
NONFACTORS	NONGOVERNMENT	NONIMPORTATIONS	NONINTERVENTION	NONLUMINOUS
NONFACTUAL	NONGOVERNMENTAL	NONINCLUSION	NONINTIMIDATING	NONMAGNETIC
NONFACULTIES	NONGRADUATE	NONINCLUSIONS	NONINTOXICANT	NONMAINSTREAM
NONFACULTY	NONGRADUATES	NONINCREASING	NONINTOXICANTS	NONMALICIOUS
NONFAMILIAL	NONGRAMMATICAL	NONINCUMBENT	NONINTOXICATING	NONMALIGNANT
NONFAMILIES	NONGRANULAR	NONINCUMBENTS	NONINTRUSIVE	NONMALLEABLE
NONFARMERS	NONGREGARIOUS	NONINDEPENDENCE	NONINTUITIVE	NONMANAGEMENT
NONFATTENING	NONGROWING	NONINDICTABLE	NONINVASIVE	NONMANAGERIAL
NONFEASANCE	NONGROWTHS	NONINDIGENOUS	NONINVOLVED	NONMANDATORY
NONFEASANCES	NONHAEMOLYTIC	NONINDIVIDUAL	NONINVOLVEMENT	NONMARITAL
NONFEDERAL	NONHALOGENATED	NONINDIVIDUALS	NONINVOLVEMENTS	NONMARKETS
NONFEDERATED	NONHAPPENING	NONINDUCTIVE	NONIONISING	NONMATERIAL
NONFEEDING	NONHAPPENINGS	NONINDUSTRIAL	NONIONIZING	NONMATHEMATICAL
NONFEMINIST	NONHARMONIC	NONINDUSTRY	NONIRRADIATED	NONMATRICULATED
NONFEMINISTS	NONHAZARDOUS	NONINFECTED	NONIRRIGATED	NONMEANINGFUL
NONFERROUS	NONHEMOLYTIC	NONINFECTIOUS	NONIRRITANT	NONMEASURABLE
NONFICTION	NONHEREDITARY	NONINFECTIVE	NONIRRITANTS	NONMECHANICAL
NONFICTIONAL	NONHIERARCHICAL	NONINFESTED	NONIRRITATING	NONMECHANISTIC
NONFICTIONALLY	NONHISTONE	NONINFLAMMABLE	NONJOINDER	NONMEDICAL
NONFICTIONS	NONHISTORICAL	NONINFLAMMATORY	NONJOINDERS	NONMEETING
NONFIGURATIVE	NONHOMOGENEITY	NONINFLATIONARY	NONJOINERS	NONMEETINGS
NONFILAMENTOUS	NONHOMOGENEOUS	NONINFLECTIONAL	NONJUDGEMENTAL	NONMEMBERS
NONFILTERABLE	NONHOMOLOGOUS	NONINFLUENCE	NONJUDGMENTAL	NONMEMBERSHIP
NONFINANCIAL	NONHOMOSEXUAL	NONINFLUENCES	NONJUDICIAL	NONMEMBERSHIPS
NONFISSIONABLE	NONHOMOSEXUALS	NONINFORMATION	NONJUSTICIABLE	NONMERCURIAL
NONFLAMMABILITY	NONHORMONAL	NONINFORMATIONS	NONKOSHERS	NONMETALLIC
NONFLAMMABLE	NONHOSPITAL	NONINFRINGEMENT	NONLADDERING	NONMETAMERIC
NONFLOWERING	NONHOSPITALISED	NONINITIAL	NONLANDOWNER	NONMETAPHORICAL
NONFLUENCIES	NONHOSPITALIZED	NONINITIATE	NONLANDOWNERS	NONMETRICAL
NONFLUENCY	NONHOSTILE	NONINITIATES	NONLANGUAGE	NONMETROPOLITAN
NONFLUORESCENT	NONHOUSING	NONINSECTICIDAL	NONLANGUAGES	NONMICROBIAL
NONFORFEITABLE	NONHUNTERS	NONINSECTS	NONLAWYERS	NONMIGRANT
NONFORFEITURE	NONHUNTING	NONINSTALLMENT	NONLEGUMES	NONMIGRANTS
NONFORFEITURES	NONHYGROSCOPIC	NONINSTALLMENTS	NONLEGUMINOUS	NONMIGRATORY
NONFREEZING	NONHYSTERICAL	NONINSTALMENT	NONLEXICAL	NONMILITANT
NONFRIVOLOUS	NONIDENTICAL	NONINSTRUMENTAL	NONLIBRARIAN	NONMILITANTS
NONFULFILLMENT	NONIDENTITIES	NONINSURANCE	NONLIBRARIANS	NONMILITARY
NONFULFILLMENTS	NONIDENTITY	NONINSURANCES	NONLIBRARY	NONMIMETIC
NONFULFILMENT	NONIDEOLOGICAL	NONINSURED	NONLINEARITIES	NONMINORITIES
NONFULFILMENTS	NONILLIONS	NONINTEGRAL	NONLINEARITY	NONMINORITY
NONFUNCTIONAL	NONILLIONTH	NONINTEGRATED	NONLINGUISTIC	NONMODERNS
NONFUNCTIONING	NONILLIONTHS	NONINTELLECTUAL	NONLIQUIDS	NONMOLECULAR
NONGASEOUS	NONIMITATIVE	NONINTERACTING	NONLITERAL	NONMONETARIST
NONGENETIC	NONIMMIGRANT	NONINTERACTIVE	NONLITERARY	NONMONETARISTS
NONGENITAL	NONIMMIGRANTS	NONINTERCOURSE	NONLITERATE	NONMONETARY
NONGEOMETRICAL	NONIMPACTS	NONINTERCOURSES	NONLITERATES	NONMONOGAMOUS
NONGLAMOROUS	NONIMPLICATION	NONINTEREST	NONLIVINGS	NONMORTALS

NONMOTILITIES	NONOPERATING	NONPHYSICIAN	NONPUNITIVE	NONRENEWALS
NONMOTILITY	NONOPERATIONAL	NONPHYSICIANS	NONPURPOSIVE	NONREPAYABLE
NONMOTORISED	NONOPERATIVE	NONPLASTIC	NONQUANTIFIABLE	NONREPRODUCTIVE
NONMOTORIZED	NONOPTIMAL	NONPLASTICS	NONQUANTITATIVE	NONRESIDENCE
NONMUNICIPAL	NONORGANIC	NONPLAYERS	NONRACIALLY	NONRESIDENCES
NONMUSICAL	NONORGASMIC	NONPLAYING	NONRACISMS	NONRESIDENCIES
NONMUSICALS	NONORTHODOX	NONPLUSING	NONRADIOACTIVE	NONRESIDENCY
NONMUSICIAN	NONOVERLAPPING	NONPLUSSED	NONRAILROAD	NONRESIDENT
NONMUSICIANS	NONOXIDISING	NONPLUSSES	NONRANDOMNESS	NONRESIDENTIAL
NONMUTANTS	NONOXIDIZING	NONPLUSSING	NONRANDOMNESSES	NONRESIDENTS
NONMYELINATED	NONPARALLEL	NONPOISONOUS	NONRATIONAL	NONRESISTANCE
NONMYSTICAL	NONPARAMETRIC	NONPOLARISABLE	NONREACTIVE	NONRESISTANCES
NONNARRATIVE	NONPARASITIC	NONPOLARIZABLE	NONREACTOR	NONRESISTANT
NONNATIONAL	NONPAREILS	NONPOLITICAL	NONREACTORS	NONRESISTANTS
NONNATIONALS	NONPARENTS	NONPOLITICALLY	NONREADERS	NONRESONANT
NONNATIVES	NONPARITIES	NONPOLITICIAN	NONREADING	NONRESPONDENT
NONNATURAL	NONPARTICIPANT	NONPOLITICIANS	NONREADINGS	NONRESPONDENTS
NONNECESSITIES	NONPARTICIPANTS	NONPOLLUTING	NONREALISTIC	NONRESPONDER
NONNECESSITY	NONPARTIES	NONPOPULAR	NONRECEIPT	NONRESPONDERS
NONNEGATIVE	NONPARTISAN	NONPORTABLE	NONRECEIPTS	NONRESPONSE
NONNEGLIGENT	NONPARTISANSHIP	NONPOSSESSION	NONRECIPROCAL	NONRESPONSES
NONNEGOTIABLE	NONPARTIZAN	NONPOSSESSIONS	NONRECOGNITION	NONRESPONSIVE
NONNEGOTIABLES	NONPARTIZANSHIP	NONPRACTICAL	NONRECOGNITIONS	NONRESTRICTED
NONNETWORK	NONPASSERINE	NONPRACTICING	NONRECOMBINANT	NONRESTRICTIVE
NONNITROGENOUS	NONPASSIVE	NONPRACTISING	NONRECOMBINANTS	NONRETRACTILE
NONNORMATIVE	NONPATHOGENIC	NONPREGNANT	NONRECOURSE	NONRETROACTIVE
NONNUCLEAR	NONPAYMENT	NONPREHENSILE	NONRECOVERABLE	NONRETURNABLE
NONNUCLEATED	NONPAYMENTS	NONPRESCRIPTION	NONRECURRENT	NONRETURNABLES
NONNUMERICAL	NONPECUNIARY	NONPRINTING	NONRECURRING	NONREUSABLE
NONNUTRITIOUS	NONPERFORMANCE	NONPROBLEM	NONRECYCLABLE	NONREVERSIBLE
NONNUTRITIVE	NONPERFORMANCES	NONPROBLEMS	NONRECYCLABLES	NONRHOTICITIES
NONOBJECTIVE	NONPERFORMER	NONPRODUCING	NONREDUCING	NONRHOTICITY
NONOBJECTIVISM	NONPERFORMERS	NONPRODUCTIVE	NONREDUNDANT	NONRIOTERS
NONOBJECTIVISMS	NONPERFORMING	NONPRODUCTIVITY	NONREFILLABLE	NONRIOTING
NONOBJECTIVIST	NONPERISHABLE	NONPROFESSIONAL	NONREFLECTING	NONROTATING
NONOBJECTIVISTS	NONPERISHABLES	NONPROFESSORIAL	NONREFLECTIVE	NONROUTINE
NONOBJECTIVITY	NONPERMANENT	NONPROFITS	NONREFLEXIVE	NONRUMINANT
NONOBSCENE	NONPERMISSIVE	NONPROGRAM	NONREFUNDABLE	NONRUMINANTS
NONOBSERVANCE	NONPERSISTENT	NONPROGRAMMER	NONREGIMENTAL	NONRUNNERS
NONOBSERVANCES	NONPERSONAL	NONPROGRAMMERS	NONREGULATED	NONSALABLE
NONOBSERVANT	NONPERSONS	NONPROGRESSIVE	NONREGULATION	NONSALEABLE
NONOBVIOUS	NONPETROLEUM	NONPROPRIETARY	NONREIGNING	NONSAPONIFIABLE
NONOBVIOUSES	NONPHILOSOPHER	NONPROSSED	NONRELATIVE	NONSCHEDULED
NONOCCUPATIONAL	NONPHILOSOPHERS	NONPROSSES	NONRELATIVES	NONSCIENCE
NONOCCURRENCE	NONPHONEMIC	NONPROSSING	NONRELATIVISTIC	NONSCIENCES
NONOCCURRENCES	NONPHONETIC	NONPROTEIN	NONRELEVANT	NONSCIENTIFIC
NONOFFICIAL	NONPHOSPHATE	NONPSYCHIATRIC	NONRELIGIOUS	NONSCIENTIST
NONOFFICIALS	NONPHOTOGRAPHIC	NONPSYCHIATRIST	NONRENEWABLE	NONSCIENTISTS
NONOPERATIC	NONPHYSICAL	NONPSYCHOTIC	NONRENEWAL	NONSEASONAL

N

NONSECRETOR	NONSPECIFICITY	NONSYNCHRONOUS	NONUNIQUENESSES	NOREPINEPHRINE
NONSECRETORS	NONSPECTACULAR	NONSYSTEMATIC	NONUNIVERSAL	NOREPINEPHRINES
NONSECRETORY	NONSPECTRAL	NONSYSTEMIC	NONUNIVERSITY	NORETHINDRONE
NONSECRETS	NONSPECULAR	NONSYSTEMS	NONUTILITARIAN	NORETHINDRONES
NONSECTARIAN	NONSPECULATIVE	NONTACTICAL	NONUTILITIES	NORETHISTERONE
NONSEDIMENTABLE	NONSPEECHES	NONTALKERS	NONUTILITY	NORETHISTERONES
NONSEGREGATED	NONSPHERICAL	NONTAXABLE	NONUTOPIAN	NORMALCIES
NONSEGREGATION	NONSPORTING	NONTEACHING	NONVALIDITIES	NORMALISABLE
NONSEGREGATIONS	NONSTAINING	NONTECHNICAL	NONVALIDITY	NORMALISATION
NONSELECTED	NONSTANDARD	NONTEMPORAL	NONVANISHING	NORMALISATIONS
NONSELECTIVE	NONSTAPLES	NONTENURED	NONVASCULAR	NORMALISED
NONSENSATIONAL	NONSTARTER	NONTERMINAL	NONVECTORS	NORMALISER
NONSENSICAL	NONSTARTERS	NONTERMINALS	NONVEGETARIAN	NORMALISERS
NONSENSICALITY	NONSTATIONARY	NONTERMINATING	NONVEGETARIANS	NORMALISES
NONSENSICALLY	NONSTATISTICAL	NONTEXTUAL	NONVENEREAL	NORMALISING
NONSENSICALNESS	NONSTATIVE	NONTHEATRICAL	NONVENOMOUS	NORMALITIES
NONSENSITIVE	NONSTATIVES	NONTHEISMS	NONVERBALLY	NORMALIZABLE
NONSENSUOUS	NONSTATUTORY	NONTHEISTIC	NONVETERAN	NORMALIZATION
NONSENTENCE	NONSTELLAR	NONTHEISTS	NONVETERANS	NORMALIZATIONS
NONSENTENCES	NONSTEROID	NONTHEOLOGICAL	NONVIEWERS	NORMALIZED
NONSEPTATE	NONSTEROIDAL	NONTHEORETICAL	NONVINTAGE	NORMALIZER
NONSEQUENTIAL	NONSTEROIDS	NONTHERAPEUTIC	NONVINTAGES	NORMALIZERS
NONSERIALS	NONSTORIES	NONTHERMAL	NONVIOLENCE	NORMALIZES
NONSERIOUS	NONSTRATEGIC	NONTHINKING	NONVIOLENCES	NORMALIZING
NONSHRINKABLE	NONSTRIATED	NONTHINKINGS	NONVIOLENT	NORMATIVELY
NONSIGNERS	NONSTRIKING	NONTHREATENING	NONVIOLENTLY	NORMATIVENESS
NONSIGNIFICANT	NONSTRUCTURAL	NONTOBACCO	NONVIRGINS	NORMATIVENESSES
NONSIGNIFICANTS	NONSTRUCTURED	NONTOTALITARIAN	NONVISCOUS	NORMOGLYCAEMIA
NONSIMULTANEOUS	NONSTUDENT	NONTRADING	NONVOCATIONAL	NORMOGLYCAEMIAS
NONSINKABLE	NONSTUDENTS	NONTRADITIONAL	NONVOLATILE	NORMOGLYCAEMIC
NONSINUSOIDAL	NONSUBJECT	NONTRANSFERABLE	NONVOLCANIC	NORMOGLYCEMIA
NONSKATERS	NONSUBJECTIVE	NONTRANSITIVE	NONVOLUNTARY	NORMOGLYCEMIAS
NONSKELETAL	NONSUBJECTS	NONTREATMENT	NONWINNING	NORMOGLYCEMIC
NONSKILLED	NONSUBSIDISED	NONTREATMENTS	NONWORKERS	NORMOTENSION
NONSMOKERS	NONSUBSIDIZED	NONTRIVIAL	NONWORKING	NORMOTENSIONS
NONSMOKING	NONSUCCESS	NONTROPICAL	NONWRITERS	NORMOTENSIVE
NONSOCIALIST	NONSUCCESSES	NONTURBULENT	NONYELLOWING	NORMOTENSIVES
NONSOCIALISTS	NONSUITING	NONTYPICAL	NOODLEDOMS	NORMOTHERMIA
NONSOLUTION	NONSUPERVISORY	NONUNANIMOUS	NOOGENESES	NORMOTHERMIAS
NONSOLUTIONS	NONSUPPORT	NONUNIFORM	NOOGENESIS	NORMOTHERMIC
NONSOLVENT	NONSUPPORTS	NONUNIFORMITIES	NOOMETRIES	NOROVIRUSES
NONSPATIAL	NONSURGICAL	NONUNIFORMITY	NOOSPHERES	NORSELLERS
NONSPEAKER	NONSWIMMER	NONUNIONISED	NOOTROPICS	NORSELLING
NONSPEAKERS	NONSWIMMERS	NONUNIONISM	NORADRENALIN	NORTHBOUND
NONSPEAKING	NONSYLLABIC	NONUNIONISMS	NORADRENALINE	NORTHCOUNTRYMAN
NONSPECIALIST	NONSYLLABICS	NONUNIONIST	NORADRENALINES	NORTHCOUNTRYMEN
NONSPECIALISTS	NONSYMBOLIC	NONUNIONISTS	NORADRENALINS	NORTHEASTER
NONSPECIFIC	NONSYMMETRIC	NONUNIONIZED	NORADRENERGIC	NORTHEASTERLIES
NONSPECIFICALLY	NONSYMMETRICAL	NONUNIQUENESS	NORDICITIES	NORTHEASTERLY

NORTHEASTERN	NOSOGRAPHERS	NOTEDNESSES	NOTWORKINGS	NOVODAMUSES
NORTHEASTERS	NOSOGRAPHIC	NOTEPAPERS	NOUGATINES	NOWCASTING
NORTHEASTS	NOSOGRAPHIES	NOTEWORTHIER	NOUMENALISM	NOWCASTINGS
NORTHEASTWARD	NOSOGRAPHY	NOTEWORTHIEST	NOUMENALISMS	NOXIOUSNESS
NORTHEASTWARDLY	NOSOLOGICAL	NOTEWORTHILY	NOUMENALIST	NOXIOUSNESSES
NORTHEASTWARDS	NOSOLOGICALLY	NOTEWORTHINESS	NOUMENALISTS	NUBBINESSES
NORTHERING	NOSOLOGIES	NOTEWORTHY	NOUMENALITIES	NUBIFEROUS
NORTHERLIES	NOSOLOGIST	NOTHINGARIAN	NOUMENALITY	NUBIGENOUS
NORTHERLINESS	NOSOLOGISTS	NOTHINGARIANISM	NOUMENALLY	NUBILITIES
NORTHERLINESSES	NOSOPHOBIA	NOTHINGARIANS	NOURISHABLE	NUCIFEROUS
NORTHERMOST	NOSOPHOBIAS	NOTHINGBURGER	NOURISHERS	NUCIVOROUS
NORTHERNER	NOSTALGIAS	NOTHINGBURGERS	NOURISHING	NUCLEARISATION
NORTHERNERS	NOSTALGICALLY	NOTHINGISM	NOURISHINGLY	NUCLEARISATIONS
NORTHERNISE	NOSTALGICS	NOTHINGISMS	NOURISHMENT	NUCLEARISE
NORTHERNISED	NOSTALGIST	NOTHINGNESS	NOURISHMENTS	NUCLEARISED
NORTHERNISES	NOSTALGISTS	NOTHINGNESSES	NOURITURES	NUCLEARISES
NORTHERNISING	NOSTOLOGIC	NOTICEABILITIES	NOURRITURE	NUCLEARISING
NORTHERNISM	NOSTOLOGICAL	NOTICEABILITY	NOURRITURES	NUCLEARIZATION
NORTHERNISMS	NOSTOLOGIES	NOTICEABLE	NOUSELLING	NUCLEARIZATIONS
NORTHERNIZE	NOSTOMANIA	NOTICEABLY	NOVACULITE	NUCLEARIZE
NORTHERNIZED	NOSTOMANIAS	NOTICEBOARD	NOVACULITES	NUCLEARIZED
NORTHERNIZES	NOSTOPATHIES	NOTICEBOARDS	NOVELETTES	NUCLEARIZES
NORTHERNIZING	NOSTOPATHY	NOTIFIABLE	NOVELETTISH	NUCLEARIZING
NORTHERNMOST	NOSTRADAMIC	NOTIFICATION	NOVELETTIST	NUCLEATING
NORTHLANDS	NOTABILITIES	NOTIFICATIONS	NOVELETTISTS	NUCLEATION
NORTHWARDLY	NOTABILITY	NOTIONALIST	NOVELISATION	NUCLEATIONS
NORTHWARDS	NOTABLENESS	NOTIONALISTS	NOVELISATIONS	NUCLEATORS
NORTHWESTER	NOTABLENESSES	NOTIONALITIES	NOVELISERS	NUCLEOCAPSID
NORTHWESTERLIES	NOTAPHILIC	NOTIONALITY	NOVELISING	NUCLEOCAPSIDS
NORTHWESTERLY	NOTAPHILIES	NOTIONALLY	NOVELISTIC	NUCLEOLATE
NORTHWESTERN	NOTAPHILISM	NOTIONISTS	NOVELISTICALLY	NUCLEOLATED
NORTHWESTERS	NOTAPHILISMS	NOTOCHORDAL	NOVELIZATION	NUCLEONICALLY
NORTHWESTS	NOTAPHILIST	NOTOCHORDS	NOVELIZATIONS	NUCLEONICS
NORTHWESTWARD	NOTAPHILISTS	NOTODONTID	NOVELIZERS	NUCLEOPHILE
NORTHWESTWARDLY	NOTARIALLY	NOTODONTIDS	NOVELIZING	NUCLEOPHILES
NORTHWESTWARDS	NOTARISATION	NOTONECTAL	NOVEMDECILLION	NUCLEOPHILIC
NORTRIPTYLINE	NOTARISATIONS	NOTORIETIES	NOVEMDECILLIONS	NUCLEOPHILICITY
NORTRIPTYLINES	NOTARISING	NOTORIOUSLY	NOVENARIES	NUCLEOPLASM
NOSEBANDED	NOTARIZATION	NOTORIOUSNESS	NOVICEHOOD	NUCLEOPLASMATIC
NOSEBLEEDING	NOTARIZATIONS	NOTORIOUSNESSES	NOVICEHOODS	NUCLEOPLASMIC
NOSEBLEEDINGS	NOTARIZING	NOTORNISES	NOVICESHIP	NUCLEOPLASMS
NOSEBLEEDS	NOTARYSHIP	NOTOTHERIUM	NOVICESHIPS	NUCLEOPROTEIN
NOSEDIVING	NOTARYSHIPS	NOTOTHERIUMS	NOVICIATES	NUCLEOPROTEINS
NOSEGUARDS	NOTATIONAL	NOTOUNGULATE	NOVITIATES	NUCLEOSIDE
NOSEPIECES	NOTCHBACKS	NOTOUNGULATES	NOVOBIOCIN	NUCLEOSIDES
NOSEWHEELS	NOTCHELING	NOTUNGULATE	NOVOBIOCINS	NUCLEOSOMAL
NOSINESSES	NOTCHELLED	NOTUNGULATES	NOVOCAINES	NUCLEOSOME
NOSOCOMIAL	NOTCHELLING	NOTWITHSTANDING	NOVOCENTENARIES	NUCLEOSOMES
NOSOGRAPHER	NOTEBANDIS	NOTWORKING	NOVOCENTENARY	NUCLEOSYNTHESES

N

NUCLEOSYNTHESIS	NUMBERLESSNESS	NUMISMATISTS	NURTURABLE	NYCTAGINACEOUS
NUCLEOSYNTHETIC	NUMBERPLATE	NUMISMATOLOGIES	NURTURANCE	NYCTALOPES
NUCLEOTIDASE	NUMBERPLATES	NUMISMATOLOGIST	NURTURANCES	NYCTALOPIA
NUCLEOTIDASES	NUMBFISHES	NUMISMATOLOGY	NUTATIONAL	NYCTALOPIAS
NUCLEOTIDE	NUMBNESSES	NUMMULATED	NUTBUTTERS	NYCTALOPIC
NUCLEOTIDES	NUMBNUTSES	NUMMULATION	NUTCRACKER	NYCTANTHOUS
NUDENESSES	NUMBSKULLED	NUMMULATIONS	NUTCRACKERS	NYCTINASTIC
NUDIBRANCH	NUMBSKULLS	NUMMULINES	NUTGRASSES	NYCTINASTIES
NUDIBRANCHIATE	NUMERABILITIES	NUMMULITES	NUTHATCHES	NYCTINASTY
NUDIBRANCHIATES	NUMERABILITY	NUMMULITIC	NUTJOBBERS	NYCTITROPIC
NUDIBRANCHS	NUMERACIES	NUMSKULLED	NUTMEGGIER	NYCTITROPISM
NUDICAUDATE	NUMERAIRES	NUNCIATURE	NUTMEGGIEST	NYCTITROPISMS
NUDICAULOUS	NUMERATING	NUNCIATURES	NUTMEGGING	NYCTOPHOBIA
NUGATORINESS	NUMERATION	NUNCUPATED	NUTPECKERS	NYCTOPHOBIAS
NUGATORINESSES	NUMERATIONS	NUNCUPATES	NUTRACEUTICAL	NYCTOPHOBIC
NUGGETIEST	NUMERATIVE	NUNCUPATING	NUTRACEUTICALS	NYMPHAEACEOUS
NUGGETTING	NUMERATORS	NUNCUPATION	NUTRIGENETICS	NYMPHAEUMS
NUISANCERS	NUMERICALLY	NUNCUPATIONS	NUTRIGENOMICS	NYMPHALIDS
NULLIFICATION	NUMEROLOGICAL	NUNCUPATIVE	NUTRIMENTAL	NYMPHETTES
NULLIFICATIONS	NUMEROLOGIES	NUNCUPATORY	NUTRIMENTS	NYMPHLIEST
NULLIFIDIAN	NUMEROLOGIST	NUNNATIONS	NUTRITIONAL	NYMPHOLEPSIES
NULLIFIDIANS	NUMEROLOGISTS	NUNNISHNESS	NUTRITIONALLY	NYMPHOLEPSY
NULLIFIERS	NUMEROLOGY	NUNNISHNESSES	NUTRITIONARY	NYMPHOLEPT
NULLIFYING	NUMEROSITIES	NUPTIALITIES	NUTRITIONIST	NYMPHOLEPTIC
NULLIPARAE	NUMEROSITY	NUPTIALITY	NUTRITIONISTS	NYMPHOLEPTS
NULLIPARAS	NUMEROUSLY	NURSEHOUND	NUTRITIONS	NYMPHOMANIA
NULLIPARITIES	NUMEROUSNESS	NURSEHOUNDS	NUTRITIOUS	NYMPHOMANIAC
NULLIPARITY	NUMEROUSNESSES	NURSELINGS	NUTRITIOUSLY	NYMPHOMANIACAL
NULLIPAROUS	NUMINOUSES	NURSEMAIDED	NUTRITIOUSNESS	NYMPHOMANIACS
NULLIPORES	NUMINOUSNESS	NURSEMAIDING	NUTRITIVELY	NYMPHOMANIAS
NULLNESSES	NUMINOUSNESSES	NURSEMAIDS	NUTRITIVES	NYSTAGMOID
NUMBERABLE	NUMISMATIC	NURSERYMAID	NUTTINESSES	NYSTAGMUSES
NUMBERINGS	NUMISMATICALLY	NURSERYMAIDS	NYCHTHEMERAL	
NUMBERLESS	NUMISMATICS	NURSERYMAN	NYCHTHEMERON	
NUMBERLESSLY	NUMISMATIST	NURSERYMEN	NYCHTHEMERONS	

N

OAFISHNESS	OBJECTIVAL	OBLIGATELY	OBNUBILATES	OBSERVATIONAL
OAFISHNESSES	OBJECTIVATE	OBLIGATING	OBNUBILATING	OBSERVATIONALLY
OAKENSHAWS	OBJECTIVATED	OBLIGATION	OBNUBILATION	OBSERVATIONS
OAKINESSES	OBJECTIVATES	OBLIGATIONAL	OBNUBILATIONS	OBSERVATIVE
OARSMANSHIP	OBJECTIVATING	OBLIGATIONS	OBREPTIONS	OBSERVATOR
OARSMANSHIPS	OBJECTIVATION	OBLIGATIVE	OBREPTITIOUS	OBSERVATORIES
OASTHOUSES	OBJECTIVATIONS	OBLIGATORILY	OBSCENENESS	OBSERVATORS
OBBLIGATOS	OBJECTIVELY	OBLIGATORINESS	OBSCENENESSES	OBSERVATORY
OBCOMPRESSED	OBJECTIVENESS	OBLIGATORS	OBSCENITIES	OBSERVINGLY
OBDURACIES	OBJECTIVENESSES	OBLIGATORY	OBSCURANTIC	OBSESSIONAL
OBDURATELY	OBJECTIVES	OBLIGEMENT	OBSCURANTISM	OBSESSIONALLY
OBDURATENESS	OBJECTIVISE	OBLIGEMENTS	OBSCURANTISMS	OBSESSIONIST
OBDURATENESSES	OBJECTIVISED	OBLIGINGLY	OBSCURANTIST	OBSESSIONISTS
OBDURATING	OBJECTIVISES	OBLIGINGNESS	OBSCURANTISTS	OBSESSIONS
OBDURATION	OBJECTIVISING	OBLIGINGNESSES	OBSCURANTS	OBSESSIVELY
OBDURATIONS	OBJECTIVISM	OBLIQUATION	OBSCURATION	OBSESSIVENESS
OBEDIENCES	OBJECTIVISMS	OBLIQUATIONS	OBSCURATIONS	OBSESSIVENESSES
OBEDIENTIAL	OBJECTIVIST	OBLIQUENESS	OBSCUREMENT	OBSESSIVES
OBEDIENTIARIES	OBJECTIVISTIC	OBLIQUENESSES	OBSCUREMENTS	OBSIDIONAL
OBEDIENTIARY	OBJECTIVISTS	OBLIQUITIES	OBSCURENESS	OBSIDIONARY
OBEDIENTLY	OBJECTIVITIES	OBLIQUITOUS	OBSCURENESSES	OBSIGNATED
OBEISANCES	OBJECTIVITY	OBLITERATE	OBSCURITIES	OBSIGNATES
OBEISANTLY	OBJECTIVIZE	OBLITERATED	OBSECRATED	OBSIGNATING
OBELISCOID	OBJECTIVIZED	OBLITERATES	OBSECRATES	OBSIGNATION
OBELISKOID	OBJECTIVIZES	OBLITERATING	OBSECRATING	OBSIGNATIONS
OBESENESSES	OBJECTIVIZING	OBLITERATION	OBSECRATION	OBSIGNATORY
OBESOGENIC	OBJECTLESS	OBLITERATIONS	OBSECRATIONS	OBSOLESCED
OBFUSCATED	OBJECTLESSNESS	OBLITERATIVE	OBSEQUIOUS	OBSOLESCENCE
OBFUSCATES	OBJURATION	OBLITERATOR	OBSEQUIOUSLY	OBSOLESCENCES
OBFUSCATING	OBJURATIONS	OBLITERATORS	OBSEQUIOUSNESS	OBSOLESCENT
OBFUSCATION	OBJURGATED	OBLIVIOUSLY	OBSERVABILITIES	OBSOLESCENTLY
OBFUSCATIONS	OBJURGATES	OBLIVIOUSNESS	OBSERVABILITY	OBSOLESCES
OBFUSCATORY	OBJURGATING	OBLIVIOUSNESSES	OBSERVABLE	OBSOLESCING
OBITUARIES	OBJURGATION	OBLIVISCENCE	OBSERVABLENESS	OBSOLETELY
OBITUARIST	OBJURGATIONS	OBLIVISCENCES	OBSERVABLES	OBSOLETENESS
OBITUARISTS	OBJURGATIVE	OBMUTESCENCE	OBSERVABLY	OBSOLETENESSES
OBJECTIFICATION	OBJURGATOR	OBMUTESCENCES	OBSERVANCE	OBSOLETING
OBJECTIFIED	OBJURGATORS	OBMUTESCENT	OBSERVANCES	OBSOLETION
OBJECTIFIES	OBJURGATORY	OBNOXIOUSLY	OBSERVANCIES	OBSOLETIONS
OBJECTIFYING	OBLANCEOLATE	OBNOXIOUSNESS	OBSERVANCY	OBSOLETISM
OBJECTIONABLE	OBLATENESS	OBNOXIOUSNESSES	OBSERVANTLY	OBSOLETISMS
OBJECTIONABLY	OBLATENESSES	OBNUBILATE	OBSERVANTS	OBSTETRICAL
OBJECTIONS	OBLATIONAL	OBNUBILATED	OBSERVATION	OBSTETRICALLY

OBSTETRICIAN

OBSTETRICIAN	OBTEMPERING	OCCIDENTALISED	OCEANOLOGIES	OCTENNIALLY
OBSTETRICIANS	OBTENTIONS	OCCIDENTALISES	OCEANOLOGIST	OCTILLIONS
OBSTETRICS	OBTESTATION	OCCIDENTALISING	OCEANOLOGISTS	OCTILLIONTH
OBSTINACIES	OBTESTATIONS	OCCIDENTALISM	OCEANOLOGY	OCTILLIONTHS
OBSTINATELY	OBTRUDINGS	OCCIDENTALISMS	OCELLATION	OCTINGENARIES
OBSTINATENESS	OBTRUNCATE	OCCIDENTALIST	OCELLATIONS	OCTINGENARY
OBSTINATENESSES	OBTRUNCATED	OCCIDENTALISTS	OCHLOCRACIES	OCTINGENTENARY
OBSTIPATION	OBTRUNCATES	OCCIDENTALIZE	OCHLOCRACY	OCTOCENTENARIES
OBSTIPATIONS	OBTRUNCATING	OCCIDENTALIZED	OCHLOCRATIC	OCTOCENTENARY
OBSTREPERATE	OBTRUSIONS	OCCIDENTALIZES	OCHLOCRATICAL	OCTODECILLION
OBSTREPERATED	OBTRUSIVELY	OCCIDENTALIZING	OCHLOCRATICALLY	OCTODECILLIONS
OBSTREPERATES	OBTRUSIVENESS	OCCIDENTALLY	OCHLOCRATS	OCTODECIMO
OBSTREPERATING	OBTRUSIVENESSES	OCCIDENTALS	OCHLOPHOBIA	OCTODECIMOS
OBSTREPEROUS	OBTUNDENTS	OCCIPITALLY	OCHLOPHOBIAC	OCTOGENARIAN
OBSTREPEROUSLY	OBTUNDITIES	OCCIPITALS	OCHLOPHOBIACS	OCTOGENARIANS
OBSTRICTION	OBTURATING	OCCLUDENTS	OCHLOPHOBIAS	OCTOGENARIES
OBSTRICTIONS	OBTURATION	OCCLUSIONS	OCHLOPHOBIC	OCTOGENARY
OBSTROPALOUS	OBTURATIONS	OCCLUSIVENESS	OCHLOPHOBICS	OCTOGYNOUS
OBSTROPULOUS	OBTURATORS	OCCLUSIVENESSES	OCHRACEOUS	OCTOHEDRON
OBSTRUCTED	OBTUSENESS	OCCLUSIVES	OCHROLEUCOUS	OCTOHEDRONS
OBSTRUCTER	OBTUSENESSES	OCCULTATION	OCTACHORDAL	OCTONARIAN
OBSTRUCTERS	OBTUSITIES	OCCULTATIONS	OCTACHORDS	OCTONARIANS
OBSTRUCTING	OBUMBRATED	OCCULTISMS	OCTAGONALLY	OCTONARIES
OBSTRUCTINGLY	OBUMBRATES	OCCULTISTS	OCTAHEDRAL	OCTONARIUS
OBSTRUCTION	OBUMBRATING	OCCULTNESS	OCTAHEDRALLY	OCTONOCULAR
OBSTRUCTIONAL	OBUMBRATION	OCCULTNESSES	OCTAHEDRITE	OCTOPETALOUS
OBSTRUCTIONALLY	OBUMBRATIONS	OCCUPANCES	OCTAHEDRITES	OCTOPLOIDS
OBSTRUCTIONISM	OBVENTIONS	OCCUPANCIES	OCTAHEDRON	OCTOPODANS
OBSTRUCTIONISMS	OBVERSIONS	OCCUPATING	OCTAHEDRONS	OCTOPODOUS
OBSTRUCTIONIST	OBVIATIONS	OCCUPATION	OCTAMEROUS	OCTOPUSHER
OBSTRUCTIONISTS	OBVIOUSNESS	OCCUPATIONAL	OCTAMETERS	OCTOPUSHERS
OBSTRUCTIONS	OBVIOUSNESSES	OCCUPATIONALLY	OCTANDRIAN	OCTOPUSHES
OBSTRUCTIVE	OBVOLUTION	OCCUPATIONS	OCTANDROUS	OCTOSEPALOUS
OBSTRUCTIVELY	OBVOLUTIONS	OCCUPATIVE	OCTANEDIOIC	OCTOSTICHOUS
OBSTRUCTIVENESS	OBVOLUTIVE	OCCURRENCE	OCTANGULAR	OCTOSTYLES
OBSTRUCTIVES	OCCASIONAL	OCCURRENCES	OCTAPEPTIDE	OCTOSYLLABIC
OBSTRUCTOR	OCCASIONALISM	OCCURRENTS	OCTAPEPTIDES	OCTOSYLLABICS
OBSTRUCTORS	OCCASIONALISMS	OCEANARIUM	OCTAPLOIDIES	OCTOSYLLABLE
OBSTRUENTS	OCCASIONALIST	OCEANARIUMS	OCTAPLOIDS	OCTOSYLLABLES
OBTAINABILITIES	OCCASIONALISTS	OCEANFRONT	OCTAPLOIDY	OCTOTHORPS
OBTAINABILITY	OCCASIONALITIES	OCEANFRONTS	OCTAPODIES	OCTUPLICATE
OBTAINABLE	OCCASIONALITY	OCEANGOING	OCTARCHIES	OCTUPLICATES
OBTAINMENT	OCCASIONALLY	OCEANOGRAPHER	OCTASTICHON	OCULARISTS
OBTAINMENTS	OCCASIONED	OCEANOGRAPHERS	OCTASTICHONS	OCULOMOTOR
OBTEMPERATE	OCCASIONER	OCEANOGRAPHIC	OCTASTICHOUS	ODALISQUES
OBTEMPERATED	OCCASIONERS	OCEANOGRAPHICAL	OCTASTICHS	ODDSMAKERS
OBTEMPERATES	OCCASIONING	OCEANOGRAPHIES	OCTASTROPHIC	ODIOUSNESS
OBTEMPERATING	OCCIDENTAL	OCEANOGRAPHY	OCTASTYLES	ODIOUSNESSES
OBTEMPERED	OCCIDENTALISE	OCEANOLOGICAL	OCTAVALENT	ODOMETRIES

ODONATISTS	ODORIPHORE	OFFERTORIES	OFTENNESSES	OLIGOCYTHAEMIA
ODONATOLOGIES	ODORIPHORES	OFFHANDEDLY	OFTENTIMES	OLIGOCYTHAEMIAS
ODONATOLOGIST	ODOROUSNESS	OFFHANDEDNESS	OGANESSONS	OLIGOCYTHEMIA
ODONATOLOGISTS	ODOROUSNESSES	OFFHANDEDNESSES	OILINESSES	OLIGOCYTHEMIAS
ODONATOLOGY	OECOLOGICAL	OFFICEHOLDER	OINOLOGIES	OLIGODENDROCYTE
ODONTALGIA	OECOLOGICALLY	OFFICEHOLDERS	OLDFANGLED	OLIGODENDROGLIA
ODONTALGIAS	OECOLOGIES	OFFICERING	OLEAGINOUS	OLIGOGENES
ODONTALGIC	OECOLOGIST	OFFICIALDOM	OLEAGINOUSLY	OLIGOMERIC
ODONTALGIES	OECOLOGISTS	OFFICIALDOMS	OLEAGINOUSNESS	OLIGOMERISATION
ODONTOBLAST	OECUMENICAL	OFFICIALESE	OLEANDOMYCIN	OLIGOMERIZATION
ODONTOBLASTIC	OECUMENICALLY	OFFICIALESES	OLEANDOMYCINS	OLIGOMEROUS
ODONTOBLASTS	OEDEMATOSE	OFFICIALISM	OLECRANONS	OLIGONUCLEOTIDE
ODONTOCETE	OEDEMATOUS	OFFICIALISMS	OLEIFEROUS	OLIGOPEPTIDE
ODONTOCETES	OEDOMETERS	OFFICIALITIES	OLEOGRAPHIC	OLIGOPEPTIDES
ODONTOGENIC	OENOLOGICAL	OFFICIALITY	OLEOGRAPHIES	OLIGOPHAGIES
ODONTOGENIES	OENOLOGIES	OFFICIALLY	OLEOGRAPHS	OLIGOPHAGOUS
ODONTOGENY	OENOLOGIST	OFFICIALTIES	OLEOGRAPHY	OLIGOPHAGY
ODONTOGLOSSUM	OENOLOGISTS	OFFICIALTY	OLEOMARGARIN	OLIGOPOLIES
ODONTOGLOSSUMS	OENOMANCIES	OFFICIANTS	OLEOMARGARINE	OLIGOPOLISTIC
ODONTOGRAPH	OENOMANIAS	OFFICIARIES	OLEOMARGARINES	OLIGOPSONIES
ODONTOGRAPHIES	OENOMETERS	OFFICIATED	OLEOMARGARINS	OLIGOPSONISTIC
ODONTOGRAPHS	OENOPHILES	OFFICIATES	OLEOPHILIC	OLIGOPSONY
ODONTOGRAPHY	OENOPHILIES	OFFICIATING	OLEORESINOUS	OLIGOSACCHARIDE
ODONTOLITE	OENOPHILIST	OFFICIATION	OLEORESINS	OLIGOSPERMIA
ODONTOLITES	OENOPHILISTS	OFFICIATIONS	OLERACEOUS	OLIGOSPERMIAS
ODONTOLOGIC	OENOTHERAS	OFFICIATOR	OLFACTIBLE	OLIGOTROPHIC
ODONTOLOGICAL	OESOPHAGEAL	OFFICIATORS	OLFACTIONS	OLIGOTROPHIES
ODONTOLOGIES	OESOPHAGITIS	OFFICINALLY	OLFACTOLOGIES	OLIGOTROPHY
ODONTOLOGIST	OESOPHAGITISES	OFFICINALS	OLFACTOLOGIST	OLIGURESES
ODONTOLOGISTS	OESOPHAGOSCOPE	OFFICIOUSLY	OLFACTOLOGISTS	OLIGURESIS
ODONTOLOGY	OESOPHAGOSCOPES	OFFICIOUSNESS	OLFACTOLOGY	OLIGURETIC
ODONTOMATA	OESOPHAGOSCOPY	OFFICIOUSNESSES	OLFACTOMETER	OLINGUITOS
ODONTOMATOUS	OESOPHAGUS	OFFISHNESS	OLFACTOMETERS	OLIVACEOUS
ODONTOPHOBIA	OESOPHAGUSES	OFFISHNESSES	OLFACTOMETRIES	OLIVENITES
ODONTOPHOBIAS	OESTRADIOL	OFFLOADING	OLFACTOMETRY	OLIVEWOODS
ODONTOPHORAL	OESTRADIOLS	OFFPRINTED	OLFACTORIES	OLIVINITIC
ODONTOPHORAN	OESTROGENIC	OFFPRINTING	OLFACTRONICS	OLOGOANING
ODONTOPHORANS	OESTROGENICALLY	OFFSADDLED	OLIGAEMIAS	OLOLIUQUIS
ODONTOPHORE	OESTROGENS	OFFSADDLES	OLIGARCHAL	OMBROGENOUS
ODONTOPHORES	OFFENCEFUL	OFFSADDLING	OLIGARCHIC	OMBROMETER
ODONTOPHOROUS	OFFENCELESS	OFFSCOURING	OLIGARCHICAL	OMBROMETERS
ODONTORHYNCHOUS	OFFENDEDLY	OFFSCOURINGS	OLIGARCHICALLY	OMBROPHILE
ODONTORNITHES	OFFENDRESS	OFFSEASONS	OLIGARCHIES	OMBROPHILES
ODONTOSTOMATOUS	OFFENDRESSES	OFFSETABLE	OLIGOCHAETE	OMBROPHILOUS
ODORIFEROUS	OFFENSELESS	OFFSETTING	OLIGOCHAETES	OMBROPHILS
ODORIFEROUSLY	OFFENSIVELY	OFFSETTINGS	OLIGOCHROME	OMBROPHOBE
ODORIFEROUSNESS	OFFENSIVENESS	OFFSHORING	OLIGOCHROMES	OMBROPHOBES
ODORIMETRIES	OFFENSIVENESSES	OFFSHORINGS	OLIGOCLASE	OMBROPHOBOUS
ODORIMETRY	OFFENSIVES	OFFSPRINGS	OLIGOCLASES	OMBUDSMANSHIP

OMBUDSMANSHIPS	OMNISEXUALITY	ONEIROLOGY	ONTOLOGISTS	OPENMOUTHEDNESS
OMINOUSNESS	OMNISEXUALS	ONEIROMANCER	ONYCHITISES	OPENNESSES
OMINOUSNESSES	OMNISHAMBLES	ONEIROMANCERS	ONYCHOCRYPTOSES	OPERABILITIES
OMISSIVENESS	OMNIVORIES	ONEIROMANCIES	ONYCHOCRYPTOSIS	OPERABILITY
OMISSIVENESSES	OMNIVOROUS	ONEIROMANCY	ONYCHOMANCIES	OPERAGOERS
OMITTANCES	OMNIVOROUSLY	ONEIROSCOPIES	ONYCHOMANCY	OPERAGOING
OMMATIDIAL	OMNIVOROUSNESS	ONEIROSCOPIST	ONYCHOPHAGIES	OPERAGOINGS
OMMATIDIUM	OMOPHAGIAS	ONEIROSCOPISTS	ONYCHOPHAGIST	OPERATICALLY
OMMATOPHORE	OMOPHAGIES	ONEIROSCOPY	ONYCHOPHAGISTS	OPERATIONAL
OMMATOPHORES	OMOPHAGOUS	ONEROUSNESS	ONYCHOPHAGY	OPERATIONALISM
OMMATOPHOROUS	OMOPHORION	ONEROUSNESSES	ONYCHOPHORAN	OPERATIONALISMS
OMNIBENEVOLENCE	OMOPLATOSCOPIES	ONGOINGNESS	ONYCHOPHORANS	OPERATIONALIST
OMNIBENEVOLENT	OMOPLATOSCOPY	ONGOINGNESSES	OOGAMOUSLY	OPERATIONALISTS
OMNIBUSSES	OMPHACITES	ONIONSKINS	OOJAMAFLIP	OPERATIONALLY
OMNICOMPETENCE	OMPHALOMANCIES	ONOCENTAUR	OOJAMAFLIPS	OPERATIONISM
OMNICOMPETENCES	OMPHALOMANCY	ONOCENTAURS	OOMPAHPAHS	OPERATIONISMS
OMNICOMPETENT	OMPHALOSKEPSES	ONOMASIOLOGIES	OOPHORECTOMIES	OPERATIONIST
OMNIDIRECTIONAL	OMPHALOSKEPSIS	ONOMASIOLOGY	OOPHORECTOMISE	OPERATIONISTS
OMNIFARIOUS	ONAGRACEOUS	ONOMASTICALLY	OOPHORECTOMISED	OPERATIONS
OMNIFARIOUSLY	ONBOARDING	ONOMASTICIAN	OOPHORECTOMISES	OPERATISED
OMNIFARIOUSNESS	ONBOARDINGS	ONOMASTICIANS	OOPHORECTOMIZE	OPERATISES
OMNIFEROUS	ONCHOCERCIASES	ONOMASTICON	OOPHORECTOMIZED	OPERATISING
OMNIFICENCE	ONCHOCERCIASIS	ONOMASTICONS	OOPHORECTOMIZES	OPERATIVELY
OMNIFICENCES	ONCOGENESES	ONOMASTICS	OOPHORECTOMY	OPERATIVENESS
OMNIFICENT	ONCOGENESIS	ONOMATOLOGIES	OOPHORITIC	OPERATIVENESSES
OMNIFORMITIES	ONCOGENETICIST	ONOMATOLOGIST	OOPHORITIS	OPERATIVES
OMNIFORMITY	ONCOGENETICISTS	ONOMATOLOGISTS	OOPHORITISES	OPERATIVITIES
OMNIGENOUS	ONCOGENICITIES	ONOMATOLOGY	OOZINESSES	OPERATIVITY
OMNIPARITIES	ONCOGENICITY	ONOMATOPOEIA	OPACIFIERS	OPERATIZED
OMNIPARITY	ONCOGENOUS	ONOMATOPOEIAS	OPACIFYING	OPERATIZES
OMNIPAROUS	ONCOLOGICAL	ONOMATOPOEIC	OPALESCENCE	OPERATIZING
OMNIPATIENT	ONCOLOGIES	ONOMATOPOESES	OPALESCENCES	OPERATORLESS
OMNIPOTENCE	ONCOLOGIST	ONOMATOPOESIS	OPALESCENT	OPERCULARS
OMNIPOTENCES	ONCOLOGISTS	ONOMATOPOETIC	OPALESCENTLY	OPERCULATE
OMNIPOTENCIES	ONCOLYTICS	ONOMATOPOIESES	OPALESCING	OPERCULATED
OMNIPOTENCY	ONCOMETERS	ONOMATOPOIESIS	OPAQUENESS	OPERCULUMS
OMNIPOTENT	ONCORNAVIRUS	ONSETTINGS	OPAQUENESSES	OPERETTIST
OMNIPOTENTLY	ONCORNAVIRUSES	ONSHORINGS	OPEIDOSCOPE	OPERETTISTS
OMNIPOTENTS	ONCOTOMIES	ONSLAUGHTS	OPEIDOSCOPES	OPEROSENESS
OMNIPRESENCE	ONCOVIRUSES	ONTOGENESES	OPENABILITIES	OPEROSENESSES
OMNIPRESENCES	ONDOGRAPHS	ONTOGENESIS	OPENABILITY	OPEROSITIES
OMNIPRESENT	ONEIRICALLY	ONTOGENETIC	OPENHANDED	OPHICALCITE
OMNIRANGES	ONEIROCRITIC	ONTOGENETICALLY	OPENHANDEDLY	OPHICALCITES
OMNISCIENCE	ONEIROCRITICAL	ONTOGENICALLY	OPENHANDEDNESS	OPHICLEIDE
OMNISCIENCES	ONEIROCRITICISM	ONTOGENIES	OPENHEARTED	OPHICLEIDES
OMNISCIENT	ONEIROCRITICS	ONTOLOGICAL	OPENHEARTEDLY	OPHIDIARIA
OMNISCIENTLY	ONEIRODYNIA	ONTOLOGICALLY	OPENHEARTEDNESS	OPHIDIARIUM
OMNISEXUAL	ONEIRODYNIAS	ONTOLOGIES	OPENMOUTHED	OPHIDIARIUMS
OMNISEXUALITIES	ONEIROLOGIES	ONTOLOGIST	OPENMOUTHEDLY	OPHIOLATER

OPHIOLATERS	OPINIONATOR	OPPORTUNENESSES	OPSONIFIED	OPTOMETRIST
OPHIOLATRIES	OPINIONATORS	OPPORTUNISM	OPSONIFIES	OPTOMETRISTS
OPHIOLATROUS	OPINIONIST	OPPORTUNISMS	OPSONIFYING	OPTOPHONES
OPHIOLATRY	OPINIONISTS	OPPORTUNIST	OPSONISATION	OPULENCIES
OPHIOLITES	OPISOMETER	OPPORTUNISTIC	OPSONISATIONS	ORACULARITIES
OPHIOLITIC	OPISOMETERS	OPPORTUNISTS	OPSONISING	ORACULARITY
OPHIOLOGIC	OPISTHOBRANCH	OPPORTUNITIES	OPSONIZATION	ORACULARLY
OPHIOLOGICAL	OPISTHOBRANCHS	OPPORTUNITY	OPSONIZATIONS	ORACULARNESS
OPHIOLOGIES	OPISTHOCOELIAN	OPPOSABILITIES	OPSONIZING	ORACULARNESSES
OPHIOLOGIST	OPISTHOCOELOUS	OPPOSABILITY	OPTATIVELY	ORACULOUSLY
OPHIOLOGISTS	OPISTHODOMOI	OPPOSELESS	OPTIMALISATION	ORACULOUSNESS
OPHIOMORPH	OPISTHODOMOS	OPPOSINGLY	OPTIMALISATIONS	ORACULOUSNESSES
OPHIOMORPHIC	OPISTHOGLOSSAL	OPPOSITELY	OPTIMALISE	ORANGEADES
OPHIOMORPHOUS	OPISTHOGNATHISM	OPPOSITENESS	OPTIMALISED	ORANGERIES
OPHIOMORPHS	OPISTHOGNATHOUS	OPPOSITENESSES	OPTIMALISES	ORANGEWOOD
OPHIOPHAGOUS	OPISTHOGRAPH	OPPOSITION	OPTIMALISING	ORANGEWOODS
OPHIOPHILIST	OPISTHOGRAPHIC	OPPOSITIONAL	OPTIMALITIES	ORANGUTANS
OPHIOPHILISTS	OPISTHOGRAPHIES	OPPOSITIONISM	OPTIMALITY	ORATORIANS
OPHIUROIDS	OPISTHOGRAPHS	OPPOSITIONISMS	OPTIMALIZATION	ORATORICAL
OPHTHALMIA	OPISTHOGRAPHY	OPPOSITIONIST	OPTIMALIZATIONS	ORATORICALLY
OPHTHALMIAS	OPISTHOSOMA	OPPOSITIONISTS	OPTIMALIZE	ORATRESSES
OPHTHALMIC	OPISTHOSOMATA	OPPOSITIONLESS	OPTIMALIZED	ORBICULARES
OPHTHALMIST	OPISTHOTONIC	OPPOSITIONS	OPTIMALIZES	ORBICULARIS
OPHTHALMISTS	OPISTHOTONOS	OPPOSITIVE	OPTIMALIZING	ORBICULARITIES
OPHTHALMITIS	OPISTHOTONOSES	OPPRESSING	OPTIMISATION	ORBICULARITY
OPHTHALMITISES	OPOBALSAMS	OPPRESSINGLY	OPTIMISATIONS	ORBICULARLY
OPHTHALMOLOGIC	OPODELDOCS	OPPRESSION	OPTIMISERS	ORBICULATE
OPHTHALMOLOGIES	OPOPANAXES	OPPRESSIONS	OPTIMISING	ORBICULATED
OPHTHALMOLOGIST	OPOTHERAPIES	OPPRESSIVE	OPTIMISTIC	ORCHARDING
OPHTHALMOLOGY	OPOTHERAPY	OPPRESSIVELY	OPTIMISTICAL	ORCHARDINGS
OPHTHALMOMETER	OPPIGNERATE	OPPRESSIVENESS	OPTIMISTICALLY	ORCHARDIST
OPHTHALMOMETERS	OPPIGNERATED	OPPRESSORS	OPTIMIZATION	ORCHARDISTS
OPHTHALMOMETRY	OPPIGNERATES	OPPROBRIOUS	OPTIMIZATIONS	ORCHARDMAN
OPHTHALMOPHOBIA	OPPIGNERATING	OPPROBRIOUSLY	OPTIMIZERS	ORCHARDMEN
OPHTHALMOPLEGIA	OPPIGNERATION	OPPROBRIOUSNESS	OPTIMIZING	ORCHESOGRAPHIES
OPHTHALMOSCOPE	OPPIGNERATIONS	OPPROBRIUM	OPTIONALITIES	ORCHESOGRAPHY
OPHTHALMOSCOPES	OPPIGNORATE	OPPROBRIUMS	OPTIONALITY	ORCHESTICS
OPHTHALMOSCOPIC	OPPIGNORATED	OPPUGNANCIES	OPTIONALLY	ORCHESTRAL
OPHTHALMOSCOPY	OPPIGNORATES	OPPUGNANCY	OPTOACOUSTIC	ORCHESTRALIST
OPINICUSES	OPPIGNORATING	OPPUGNANTLY	OPTOELECTRONIC	ORCHESTRALISTS
OPINIONATE	OPPIGNORATION	OPPUGNANTS	OPTOELECTRONICS	ORCHESTRALLY
OPINIONATED	OPPIGNORATIONS	OPSIMATHIES	OPTOKINETIC	ORCHESTRAS
OPINIONATEDLY	OPPILATING	OPSIOMETER	OPTOLOGIES	ORCHESTRATE
OPINIONATEDNESS	OPPILATION	OPSIOMETERS	OPTOLOGIST	ORCHESTRATED
OPINIONATELY	OPPILATIONS	OPSOMANIAC	OPTOLOGISTS	ORCHESTRATER
OPINIONATES	OPPILATIVE	OPSOMANIACS	OPTOMETERS	ORCHESTRATERS
OPINIONATING	OPPONENCIES	OPSOMANIAS	OPTOMETRIC	ORCHESTRATES
OPINIONATIVE	OPPORTUNELY	OPSONIFICATION	OPTOMETRICAL	ORCHESTRATING
OPINIONATIVELY	OPPORTUNENESS	OPSONIFICATIONS	OPTOMETRIES	ORCHESTRATION

ORCHESTRATIONAL	OREOGRAPHICAL	ORGANOGENY	ORIENTATIONS	ORNITHOLOGIC
ORCHESTRATIONS	OREOGRAPHICALLY	ORGANOGRAM	ORIENTATOR	ORNITHOLOGICAL
ORCHESTRATOR	OREOGRAPHIES	ORGANOGRAMS	ORIENTATORS	ORNITHOLOGIES
ORCHESTRATORS	OREOGRAPHY	ORGANOGRAPHIC	ORIENTEERED	ORNITHOLOGIST
ORCHESTRIC	OREOLOGICAL	ORGANOGRAPHICAL	ORIENTEERING	ORNITHOLOGISTS
ORCHESTRINA	OREOLOGIES	ORGANOGRAPHIES	ORIENTEERINGS	ORNITHOLOGY
ORCHESTRINAS	OREOLOGIST	ORGANOGRAPHIST	ORIENTEERS	ORNITHOMANCIES
ORCHESTRION	OREOLOGISTS	ORGANOGRAPHISTS	ORIFLAMMES	ORNITHOMANCY
ORCHESTRIONS	OREPEARCHED	ORGANOGRAPHY	ORIGINALITIES	ORNITHOMANTIC
ORCHIDACEOUS	OREPEARCHES	ORGANOLEPTIC	ORIGINALITY	ORNITHOMORPH
ORCHIDECTOMIES	OREPEARCHING	ORGANOLOGICAL	ORIGINALLY	ORNITHOMORPHIC
ORCHIDECTOMY	ORGANELLES	ORGANOLOGIES	ORIGINATED	ORNITHOMORPHS
ORCHIDEOUS	ORGANICALLY	ORGANOLOGIST	ORIGINATES	ORNITHOPHILIES
ORCHIDISTS	ORGANICISM	ORGANOLOGISTS	ORIGINATING	ORNITHOPHILOUS
ORCHIDLIKE	ORGANICISMS	ORGANOLOGY	ORIGINATION	ORNITHOPHILY
ORCHIDOLOGIES	ORGANICIST	ORGANOMERCURIAL	ORIGINATIONS	ORNITHOPHOBIA
ORCHIDOLOGIST	ORGANICISTIC	ORGANOMETALLIC	ORIGINATIVE	ORNITHOPHOBIAS
ORCHIDOLOGISTS	ORGANICISTS	ORGANOMETALLICS	ORIGINATIVELY	ORNITHOPOD
ORCHIDOLOGY	ORGANICITIES	ORGANOPHOSPHATE	ORIGINATOR	ORNITHOPODS
ORCHIDOMANIA	ORGANICITY	ORGANOSOLS	ORIGINATORS	ORNITHOPTER
ORCHIDOMANIAC	ORGANISABILITY	ORGANOTHERAPIES	ORINASALLY	ORNITHOPTERS
ORCHIDOMANIACS	ORGANISABLE	ORGANOTHERAPY	ORISMOLOGICAL	ORNITHORHYNCHUS
ORCHIDOMANIAS	ORGANISATION	ORGANZINES	ORISMOLOGIES	ORNITHOSAUR
ORCHIECTOMIES	ORGANISATIONAL	ORGASMICALLY	ORISMOLOGY	ORNITHOSAURS
ORCHIECTOMY	ORGANISATIONS	ORGASTICALLY	ORNAMENTAL	ORNITHOSCOPIES
ORCHITISES	ORGANISERS	ORGIASTICALLY	ORNAMENTALLY	ORNITHOSCOPY
ORDAINABLE	ORGANISING	ORICALCHES	ORNAMENTALS	ORNITHOSES
ORDAINMENT	ORGANISINGS	ORICHALCEOUS	ORNAMENTATION	ORNITHOSIS
ORDAINMENTS	ORGANISMAL	ORIENTALISE	ORNAMENTATIONS	OROBANCHACEOUS
ORDERLINESS	ORGANISMALLY	ORIENTALISED	ORNAMENTED	OROGENESES
ORDERLINESSES	ORGANISMIC	ORIENTALISES	ORNAMENTER	OROGENESIS
ORDINAIRES	ORGANISMICALLY	ORIENTALISING	ORNAMENTERS	OROGENETIC
ORDINANCES	ORGANISTRUM	ORIENTALISM	ORNAMENTING	OROGENETICALLY
ORDINARIER	ORGANISTRUMS	ORIENTALISMS	ORNAMENTIST	OROGENICALLY
ORDINARIES	ORGANITIES	ORIENTALIST	ORNAMENTISTS	OROGRAPHER
ORDINARIEST	ORGANIZABILITY	ORIENTALISTS	ORNATENESS	OROGRAPHERS
ORDINARILY	ORGANIZABLE	ORIENTALITIES	ORNATENESSES	OROGRAPHIC
ORDINARINESS	ORGANIZATION	ORIENTALITY	ORNERINESS	OROGRAPHICAL
ORDINARINESSES	ORGANIZATIONAL	ORIENTALIZE	ORNERINESSES	OROGRAPHICALLY
ORDINATELY	ORGANIZATIONS	ORIENTALIZED	ORNITHICHNITE	OROGRAPHIES
ORDINATING	ORGANIZERS	ORIENTALIZES	ORNITHICHNITES	OROLOGICAL
ORDINATION	ORGANIZING	ORIENTALIZING	ORNITHINES	OROLOGICALLY
ORDINATIONS	ORGANIZINGS	ORIENTALLY	ORNITHISCHIAN	OROLOGISTS
ORDONNANCE	ORGANOCHLORINE	ORIENTATED	ORNITHISCHIANS	OROMAXILLARY
ORDONNANCES	ORGANOCHLORINES	ORIENTATES	ORNITHODELPHIAN	OROPHARYNGEAL
ORECCHIETTE	ORGANOGENESES	ORIENTATING	ORNITHODELPHIC	OROPHARYNGES
ORECCHIETTES	ORGANOGENESIS	ORIENTATION	ORNITHODELPHOUS	OROPHARYNX
ORECCHIETTI	ORGANOGENETIC	ORIENTATIONAL	ORNITHOGALUM	OROPHARYNXES
OREOGRAPHIC	ORGANOGENIES	ORIENTATIONALLY	ORNITHOGALUMS	OROROTUNDITIES

OROROTUNDITY	ORTHOEPICALLY	ORTHOPAEDIST	ORTHOSCOPES	OSCITATION
OROTUNDITIES	ORTHOEPIES	ORTHOPAEDISTS	ORTHOSCOPIC	OSCITATIONS
OROTUNDITY	ORTHOEPIST	ORTHOPAEDY	ORTHOSILICATE	OSCULATING
ORPHANAGES	ORTHOEPISTS	ORTHOPEDIA	ORTHOSILICATES	OSCULATION
ORPHANHOOD	ORTHOGENESES	ORTHOPEDIAS	ORTHOSILICIC	OSCULATIONS
ORPHANHOODS	ORTHOGENESIS	ORTHOPEDIC	ORTHOSTATIC	OSCULATORIES
ORPHANISMS	ORTHOGENETIC	ORTHOPEDICAL	ORTHOSTICHIES	OSCULATORY
ORPHARIONS	ORTHOGENIC	ORTHOPEDICALLY	ORTHOSTICHOUS	OSMETERIUM
ORPHEOREON	ORTHOGENICALLY	ORTHOPEDICS	ORTHOSTICHY	OSMIDROSES
ORPHEOREONS	ORTHOGENICS	ORTHOPEDIES	ORTHOTISTS	OSMIDROSIS
ORPHICALLY	ORTHOGNATHIC	ORTHOPEDIST	ORTHOTONES	OSMIRIDIUM
ORRISROOTS	ORTHOGNATHIES	ORTHOPEDISTS	ORTHOTONESES	OSMIRIDIUMS
ORTANIQUES	ORTHOGNATHISM	ORTHOPHOSPHATE	ORTHOTONESIS	OSMOLALITIES
ORTHOBORATE	ORTHOGNATHISMS	ORTHOPHOSPHATES	ORTHOTONIC	OSMOLALITY
ORTHOBORATES	ORTHOGNATHOUS	ORTHOPHOSPHORIC	ORTHOTOPIC	OSMOLARITIES
ORTHOBORIC	ORTHOGNATHY	ORTHOPHYRE	ORTHOTROPIC	OSMOLARITY
ORTHOCAINE	ORTHOGONAL	ORTHOPHYRES	ORTHOTROPIES	OSMOMETERS
ORTHOCAINES	ORTHOGONALISE	ORTHOPHYRIC	ORTHOTROPISM	OSMOMETRIC
ORTHOCENTER	ORTHOGONALISED	ORTHOPINAKOID	ORTHOTROPISMS	OSMOMETRICALLY
ORTHOCENTERS	ORTHOGONALISES	ORTHOPINAKOIDS	ORTHOTROPOUS	OSMOMETRIES
ORTHOCENTRE	ORTHOGONALISING	ORTHOPNOEA	ORTHOTROPY	OSMOREGULATION
ORTHOCENTRES	ORTHOGONALITIES	ORTHOPNOEAS	ORTHOTUNGSTIC	OSMOREGULATIONS
ORTHOCEPHALIC	ORTHOGONALITY	ORTHOPRAXES	ORTHOVANADIC	OSMOREGULATORY
ORTHOCEPHALIES	ORTHOGONALIZE	ORTHOPRAXIES	ORYCTOLOGIES	OSMOTICALLY
ORTHOCEPHALOUS	ORTHOGONALIZED	ORTHOPRAXIS	ORYCTOLOGY	OSMUNDINES
ORTHOCEPHALY	ORTHOGONALIZES	ORTHOPRAXY	OSCILLATED	OSSIFEROUS
ORTHOCHROMATIC	ORTHOGONALIZING	ORTHOPRISM	OSCILLATES	OSSIFICATION
ORTHOCHROMATISM	ORTHOGONALLY	ORTHOPRISMS	OSCILLATING	OSSIFICATIONS
ORTHOCLASE	ORTHOGRADE	ORTHOPSYCHIATRY	OSCILLATION	OSSIFRAGAS
ORTHOCLASES	ORTHOGRAPH	ORTHOPTERA	OSCILLATIONAL	OSSIFRAGES
ORTHOCLASTIC	ORTHOGRAPHER	ORTHOPTERAN	OSCILLATIONS	OSSIVOROUS
ORTHOCOUSINS	ORTHOGRAPHERS	ORTHOPTERANS	OSCILLATIVE	OSTEICHTHYAN
ORTHODIAGONAL	ORTHOGRAPHIC	ORTHOPTERIST	OSCILLATOR	OSTEICHTHYANS
ORTHODIAGONALS	ORTHOGRAPHICAL	ORTHOPTERISTS	OSCILLATORS	OSTEITIDES
ORTHODONTIA	ORTHOGRAPHIES	ORTHOPTEROID	OSCILLATORY	OSTEITISES
ORTHODONTIAS	ORTHOGRAPHIST	ORTHOPTEROIDS	OSCILLOGRAM	OSTENSIBILITIES
ORTHODONTIC	ORTHOGRAPHISTS	ORTHOPTEROLOGY	OSCILLOGRAMS	OSTENSIBILITY
ORTHODONTICALLY	ORTHOGRAPHS	ORTHOPTERON	OSCILLOGRAPH	OSTENSIBLE
ORTHODONTICS	ORTHOGRAPHY	ORTHOPTEROUS	OSCILLOGRAPHIC	OSTENSIBLY
ORTHODONTIST	ORTHOHYDROGEN	ORTHOPTERS	OSCILLOGRAPHIES	OSTENSIVELY
ORTHODONTISTS	ORTHOHYDROGENS	ORTHOPTICS	OSCILLOGRAPHS	OSTENSORIA
ORTHODOXES	ORTHOMOLECULAR	ORTHOPTIST	OSCILLOGRAPHY	OSTENSORIES
ORTHODOXIES	ORTHOMORPHIC	ORTHOPTISTS	OSCILLOSCOPE	OSTENSORIUM
ORTHODOXLY	ORTHONORMAL	ORTHOPYROXENE	OSCILLOSCOPES	OSTENTATION
ORTHODROMIC	ORTHOPAEDIC	ORTHOPYROXENES	OSCILLOSCOPIC	OSTENTATIONS
ORTHODROMICS	ORTHOPAEDICAL	ORTHOREXIA	OSCITANCES	OSTENTATIOUS
ORTHODROMIES	ORTHOPAEDICALLY	ORTHOREXIAS	OSCITANCIES	OSTENTATIOUSLY
ORTHODROMY	ORTHOPAEDICS	ORTHORHOMBIC	OSCITANTLY	OSTEOARTHRITIC
ORTHOEPICAL	ORTHOPAEDIES	ORTHOSCOPE	OSCITATING	OSTEOARTHRITICS

OSTEOARTHRITIS	OSTEOPETROSES	OSTRICHLIKE	OUTBARGAINING	OUTBULGING
OSTEOARTHROSES	OSTEOPETROSIS	OTHERGATES	OUTBARGAINS	OUTBULKING
OSTEOARTHROSIS	OSTEOPHYTE	OTHERGUESS	OUTBARKING	OUTBULLIED
OSTEOBLAST	OSTEOPHYTES	OTHERNESSES	OUTBARRING	OUTBULLIES
OSTEOBLASTIC	OSTEOPHYTIC	OTHERWHERE	OUTBAWLING	OUTBULLYING
OSTEOBLASTS	OSTEOPLASTIC	OTHERWHILE	OUTBEAMING	OUTBURNING
OSTEOCLASES	OSTEOPLASTIES	OTHERWHILES	OUTBEGGING	OUTBURSTING
OSTEOCLASIS	OSTEOPLASTY	OTHERWORLD	OUTBIDDERS	OUTCALLING
OSTEOCLAST	OSTEOPOROSES	OTHERWORLDISH	OUTBIDDING	OUTCAPERED
OSTEOCLASTIC	OSTEOPOROSIS	OTHERWORLDLIER	OUTBITCHED	OUTCAPERING
OSTEOCLASTS	OSTEOPOROTIC	OTHERWORLDLIEST	OUTBITCHES	OUTCASTEING
OSTEOCOLLA	OSTEOSARCOMA	OTHERWORLDLY	OUTBITCHING	OUTCASTING
OSTEOCOLLAS	OSTEOSARCOMAS	OTHERWORLDS	OUTBLAZING	OUTCATCHES
OSTEOCYTES	OSTEOSARCOMATA	OTIOSENESS	OUTBLEATED	OUTCATCHING
OSTEODERMAL	OSTEOSISES	OTIOSENESSES	OUTBLEATING	OUTCAVILED
OSTEODERMATOUS	OSTEOTOMES	OTIOSITIES	OUTBLESSED	OUTCAVILING
OSTEODERMIC	OSTEOTOMIES	OTOLARYNGOLOGY	OUTBLESSES	OUTCAVILLED
OSTEODERMOUS	OSTLERESSES	OTOLOGICAL	OUTBLESSING	OUTCAVILLING
OSTEODERMS	OSTRACEANS	OTOLOGISTS	OUTBLOOMED	OUTCHARGED
OSTEOFIBROSES	OSTRACEOUS	OTOPLASTIES	OUTBLOOMING	OUTCHARGES
OSTEOFIBROSIS	OSTRACISABLE	OTORRHOEAS	OUTBLUFFED	OUTCHARGING
OSTEOGENESES	OSTRACISED	OTOSCLEROSES	OUTBLUFFING	OUTCHARMED
OSTEOGENESIS	OSTRACISER	OTOSCLEROSIS	OUTBLUSHED	OUTCHARMING
OSTEOGENETIC	OSTRACISERS	OTOSCOPIES	OUTBLUSHES	OUTCHEATED
OSTEOGENIC	OSTRACISES	OTOTOXICITIES	OUTBLUSHING	OUTCHEATING
OSTEOGENIES	OSTRACISING	OTOTOXICITY	OUTBLUSTER	OUTCHIDDEN
OSTEOGENOUS	OSTRACISMS	OTTERHOUND	OUTBLUSTERED	OUTCHIDING
OSTEOGRAPHIES	OSTRACIZABLE	OTTERHOUNDS	OUTBLUSTERING	OUTCLASSED
OSTEOGRAPHY	OSTRACIZED	OTTRELITES	OUTBLUSTERS	OUTCLASSES
OSTEOLOGICAL	OSTRACIZER	OUANANICHE	OUTBOASTED	OUTCLASSING
OSTEOLOGICALLY	OSTRACIZERS	OUANANICHES	OUTBOASTING	OUTCLIMBED
OSTEOLOGIES	OSTRACIZES	OUBLIETTES	OUTBRAGGED	OUTCLIMBING
OSTEOLOGIST	OSTRACIZING	OUGHTLINGS	OUTBRAGGING	OUTCOACHED
OSTEOLOGISTS	OSTRACODAN	OUGHTNESSES	OUTBRAVING	OUTCOACHES
OSTEOMALACIA	OSTRACODERM	OUROBOROSES	OUTBRAWLED	OUTCOACHING
OSTEOMALACIAL	OSTRACODERMS	OUROLOGIES	OUTBRAWLING	OUTCOMPETE
OSTEOMALACIAS	OSTRACODES	OUROSCOPIES	OUTBRAZENED	OUTCOMPETED
OSTEOMALACIC	OSTRACODOUS	OUTACHIEVE	OUTBRAZENING	OUTCOMPETES
OSTEOMYELITIS	OSTREACEOUS	OUTACHIEVED	OUTBRAZENS	OUTCOMPETING
OSTEOMYELITISES	OSTREICULTURE	OUTACHIEVES	OUTBREAKING	OUTCOOKING
OSTEOPATHIC	OSTREICULTURES	OUTACHIEVING	OUTBREATHE	OUTCOUNTED
OSTEOPATHICALLY	OSTREICULTURIST	OUTARGUING	OUTBREATHED	OUTCOUNTING
OSTEOPATHIES	OSTREOPHAGE	OUTBACKERS	OUTBREATHES	OUTCRAFTIED
OSTEOPATHIST	OSTREOPHAGES	OUTBALANCE	OUTBREATHING	OUTCRAFTIES
OSTEOPATHISTS	OSTREOPHAGIES	OUTBALANCED	OUTBREEDING	OUTCRAFTYING
OSTEOPATHS	OSTREOPHAGOUS	OUTBALANCES	OUTBREEDINGS	OUTCRAWLED
OSTEOPATHY	OSTREOPHAGY	OUTBALANCING	OUTBRIBING	OUTCRAWLING
OSTEOPENIA	OSTRICHISM	OUTBARGAIN	OUTBUILDING	OUTCROPPED
OSTEOPENIAS	OSTRICHISMS	OUTBARGAINED	OUTBUILDINGS	OUTCROPPING

OUTCROPPINGS	OUTDROPPED	OUTFROWNED	OUTHAULERS	OUTLAUNCING
OUTCROSSED	OUTDROPPING	OUTFROWNING	OUTHEARING	OUTLAWRIES
OUTCROSSES	OUTDUELING	OUTFUMBLED	OUTHITTING	OUTLEADING
OUTCROSSING	OUTDUELLED	OUTFUMBLES	OUTHOMERED	OUTLEAPING
OUTCROSSINGS	OUTDUELLING	OUTFUMBLING	OUTHOMERING	OUTLEARNED
OUTCROWDED	OUTDWELLED	OUTGAINING	OUTHOWLING	OUTLEARNING
OUTCROWDING	OUTDWELLING	OUTGALLOPED	OUTHUMORED	OUTLODGING
OUTCROWING	OUTEARNING	OUTGALLOPING	OUTHUMORING	OUTLODGINGS
OUTCURSING	OUTECHOING	OUTGALLOPS	OUTHUMOURED	OUTLOOKING
OUTDACIOUS	OUTERCOATS	OUTGAMBLED	OUTHUMOURING	OUTLUSTERED
OUTDANCING	OUTERCOURSE	OUTGAMBLES	OUTHUMOURS	OUTLUSTERING
OUTDATEDLY	OUTERCOURSES	OUTGAMBLING	OUTHUNTING	OUTLUSTERS
OUTDATEDNESS	OUTERWEARS	OUTGASSING	OUTHUSTLED	OUTLUSTRED
OUTDATEDNESSES	OUTFABLING	OUTGASSINGS	OUTHUSTLES	OUTLUSTRES
OUTDAZZLED	OUTFANGTHIEF	OUTGENERAL	OUTHUSTLING	OUTLUSTRING
OUTDAZZLES	OUTFANGTHIEVES	OUTGENERALED	OUTINTRIGUE	OUTMANEUVER
OUTDAZZLING	OUTFASTING	OUTGENERALING	OUTINTRIGUED	OUTMANEUVERED
OUTDEBATED	OUTFAWNING	OUTGENERALLED	OUTINTRIGUES	OUTMANEUVERING
OUTDEBATES	OUTFEASTED	OUTGENERALLING	OUTINTRIGUING	OUTMANEUVERS
OUTDEBATING	OUTFEASTING	OUTGENERALS	OUTJESTING	OUTMANIPULATE
OUTDELIVER	OUTFEELING	OUTGIVINGS	OUTJETTING	OUTMANIPULATED
OUTDELIVERED	OUTFENCING	OUTGLARING	OUTJETTINGS	OUTMANIPULATES
OUTDELIVERING	OUTFIELDER	OUTGLEAMED	OUTJINXING	OUTMANIPULATING
OUTDELIVERS	OUTFIELDERS	OUTGLEAMING	OUTJOCKEYED	OUTMANNING
OUTDESIGNED	OUTFIGHTING	OUTGLITTER	OUTJOCKEYING	OUTMANOEUVRE
OUTDESIGNING	OUTFIGHTINGS	OUTGLITTERED	OUTJOCKEYS	OUTMANOEUVRED
OUTDESIGNS	OUTFIGURED	OUTGLITTERING	OUTJUGGLED	OUTMANOEUVRES
OUTDISTANCE	OUTFIGURES	OUTGLITTERS	OUTJUGGLES	OUTMANOEUVRING
OUTDISTANCED	OUTFIGURING	OUTGLOWING	OUTJUGGLING	OUTMANTLED
OUTDISTANCES	OUTFINDING	OUTGNAWING	OUTJUMPING	OUTMANTLES
OUTDISTANCING	OUTFISHING	OUTGOINGNESS	OUTJUTTING	OUTMANTLING
OUTDODGING	OUTFITTERS	OUTGOINGNESSES	OUTJUTTINGS	OUTMARCHED
OUTDOORSIER	OUTFITTING	OUTGRINNED	OUTKEEPING	OUTMARCHES
OUTDOORSIEST	OUTFITTINGS	OUTGRINNING	OUTKICKING	OUTMARCHING
OUTDOORSMAN	OUTFLANKED	OUTGROSSED	OUTKILLING	OUTMARRIAGE
OUTDOORSMANSHIP	OUTFLANKING	OUTGROSSES	OUTKISSING	OUTMARRIAGES
OUTDOORSMEN	OUTFLASHED	OUTGROSSING	OUTLANDERS	OUTMASTERED
OUTDOORSWOMAN	OUTFLASHES	OUTGROWING	OUTLANDISH	OUTMASTERING
OUTDOORSWOMEN	OUTFLASHING	OUTGROWTHS	OUTLANDISHLY	OUTMASTERS
OUTDRAGGED	OUTFLINGING	OUTGUESSED	OUTLANDISHNESS	OUTMATCHED
OUTDRAGGING	OUTFLOATED	OUTGUESSES	OUTLASHING	OUTMATCHES
OUTDRAWING	OUTFLOATING	OUTGUESSING	OUTLASTING	OUTMATCHING
OUTDREAMED	OUTFLOWING	OUTGUIDING	OUTLAUGHED	OUTMEASURE
OUTDREAMING	OUTFLOWINGS	OUTGUNNING	OUTLAUGHING	OUTMEASURED
OUTDRESSED	OUTFLUSHED	OUTGUSHING	OUTLAUNCED	OUTMEASURES
OUTDRESSES	OUTFLUSHES	OUTHANDLED	OUTLAUNCES	OUTMEASURING
OUTDRESSING	OUTFLUSHING	OUTHANDLES	OUTLAUNCHED	OUTMODEDLY
OUTDRINKING	OUTFOOLING	OUTHANDLING	OUTLAUNCHES	OUTMODEDNESS
OUTDRIVING	OUTFOOTING	OUTHARBORS	OUTLAUNCHING	OUTMODEDNESSES

OUTMUSCLED	OUTPLOTTING	OUTQUOTING	OUTROOTING	OUTSNORING
OUTMUSCLES	OUTPOINTED	OUTRAGEOUS	OUTRUNNERS	OUTSOARING
OUTMUSCLING	OUTPOINTING	OUTRAGEOUSLY	OUTRUNNING	OUTSOURCED
OUTNIGHTED	OUTPOLITICK	OUTRAGEOUSNESS	OUTRUSHING	OUTSOURCER
OUTNIGHTING	OUTPOLITICKED	OUTRAISING	OUTSAILING	OUTSOURCERS
OUTNUMBERED	OUTPOLITICKING	OUTRANGING	OUTSAVORED	OUTSOURCES
OUTNUMBERING	OUTPOLITICKS	OUTRANKING	OUTSAVORING	OUTSOURCING
OUTNUMBERS	OUTPOLLING	OUTREACHED	OUTSAVOURED	OUTSOURCINGS
OUTOFFICES	OUTPOPULATE	OUTREACHES	OUTSAVOURING	OUTSPANNED
OUTORGANISE	OUTPOPULATED	OUTREACHING	OUTSAVOURS	OUTSPANNING
OUTORGANISED	OUTPOPULATES	OUTREADING	OUTSCHEMED	OUTSPARKLE
OUTORGANISES	OUTPOPULATING	OUTREASONED	OUTSCHEMES	OUTSPARKLED
OUTORGANISING	OUTPORTERS	OUTREASONING	OUTSCHEMING	OUTSPARKLES
OUTORGANIZE	OUTPOURERS	OUTREASONS	OUTSCOLDED	OUTSPARKLING
OUTORGANIZED	OUTPOURING	OUTREBOUND	OUTSCOLDING	OUTSPEAKING
OUTORGANIZES	OUTPOURINGS	OUTREBOUNDED	OUTSCOOPED	OUTSPECKLE
OUTORGANIZING	OUTPOWERED	OUTREBOUNDING	OUTSCOOPING	OUTSPECKLES
OUTPAINTED	OUTPOWERING	OUTREBOUNDS	OUTSCORING	OUTSPEEDED
OUTPAINTING	OUTPRAYING	OUTRECKONED	OUTSCORNED	OUTSPEEDING
OUTPASSING	OUTPREACHED	OUTRECKONING	OUTSCORNING	OUTSPELLED
OUTPASSION	OUTPREACHES	OUTRECKONS	OUTSCREAMED	OUTSPELLING
OUTPASSIONED	OUTPREACHING	OUTRECUIDANCE	OUTSCREAMING	OUTSPENDING
OUTPASSIONING	OUTPREENED	OUTRECUIDANCES	OUTSCREAMS	OUTSPOKENLY
OUTPASSIONS	OUTPREENING	OUTREDDENED	OUTSELLING	OUTSPOKENNESS
OUTPATIENT	OUTPRESSED	OUTREDDENING	OUTSERVING	OUTSPOKENNESSES
OUTPATIENTS	OUTPRESSES	OUTREDDENS	OUTSETTING	OUTSPORTED
OUTPEEPING	OUTPRESSING	OUTREDDING	OUTSETTINGS	OUTSPORTING
OUTPEERING	OUTPRICING	OUTREDDINGS	OUTSETTLEMENT	OUTSPREADING
OUTPEOPLED	OUTPRIZING	OUTREIGNED	OUTSETTLEMENTS	OUTSPREADS
OUTPEOPLES	OUTPRODUCE	OUTREIGNING	OUTSHAMING	OUTSPRINGING
OUTPEOPLING	OUTPRODUCED	OUTRELIEFS	OUTSHINING	OUTSPRINGS
OUTPERFORM	OUTPRODUCES	OUTREPRODUCE	OUTSHOOTING	OUTSPRINTED
OUTPERFORMED	OUTPRODUCING	OUTREPRODUCED	OUTSHOUTED	OUTSPRINTING
OUTPERFORMING	OUTPROMISE	OUTREPRODUCES	OUTSHOUTING	OUTSPRINTS
OUTPERFORMS	OUTPROMISED	OUTREPRODUCING	OUTSIDERNESS	OUTSTANDING
OUTPITCHED	OUTPROMISES	OUTRIDINGS	OUTSIDERNESSES	OUTSTANDINGLY
OUTPITCHES	OUTPROMISING	OUTRIGGERS	OUTSINGING	OUTSTARING
OUTPITCHING	OUTPSYCHED	OUTRIGGING	OUTSINNING	OUTSTARTED
OUTPITYING	OUTPSYCHING	OUTRIGGINGS	OUTSITTING	OUTSTARTING
OUTPLACEMENT	OUTPULLING	OUTRIGHTLY	OUTSKATING	OUTSTATING
OUTPLACEMENTS	OUTPUNCHED	OUTRINGING	OUTSLEEPING	OUTSTATION
OUTPLACERS	OUTPUNCHES	OUTRIVALED	OUTSLICKED	OUTSTATIONS
OUTPLACING	OUTPUNCHING	OUTRIVALING	OUTSLICKING	OUTSTAYING
OUTPLANNED	OUTPURSUED	OUTRIVALLED	OUTSMARTED	OUTSTEERED
OUTPLANNING	OUTPURSUES	OUTRIVALLING	OUTSMARTING	OUTSTEERING
OUTPLAYING	OUTPURSUING	OUTROARING	OUTSMELLED	OUTSTEPPED
OUTPLODDED	OUTPUSHING	OUTROCKING	OUTSMELLING	OUTSTEPPING
OUTPLODDING	OUTPUTTING	OUTROLLING	OUTSMILING	OUTSTRAINED
OUTPLOTTED	OUTQUARTERS	OUTROOPERS	OUTSMOKING	OUTSTRAINING

OUTSTRAINS	OUTTHROWING	OUTWELLING	OVERACCENTUATE	OVERARRANGE
OUTSTRETCH	OUTTHRUSTED	OUTWHIRLED	OVERACCENTUATED	OVERARRANGED
OUTSTRETCHED	OUTTHRUSTING	OUTWHIRLING	OVERACCENTUATES	OVERARRANGES
OUTSTRETCHES	OUTTHRUSTS	OUTWICKING	OVERACHIEVE	OVERARRANGING
OUTSTRETCHING	OUTTONGUED	OUTWILLING	OVERACHIEVED	OVERARTICULATE
OUTSTRIDDEN	OUTTONGUES	OUTWINDING	OVERACHIEVEMENT	OVERARTICULATED
OUTSTRIDED	OUTTONGUING	OUTWINGING	OVERACHIEVER	OVERARTICULATES
OUTSTRIDES	OUTTOPPING	OUTWINNING	OVERACHIEVERS	OVERASSERT
OUTSTRIDING	OUTTOWERED	OUTWISHING	OVERACHIEVES	OVERASSERTED
OUTSTRIKES	OUTTOWERING	OUTWITTING	OVERACHIEVING	OVERASSERTING
OUTSTRIKING	OUTTRADING	OUTWORKERS	OVERACTING	OVERASSERTION
OUTSTRIPPED	OUTTRAVELED	OUTWORKING	OVERACTION	OVERASSERTIONS
OUTSTRIPPING	OUTTRAVELING	OUTWORTHED	OVERACTIONS	OVERASSERTIVE
OUTSTRIVEN	OUTTRAVELLED	OUTWORTHING	OVERACTIVE	OVERASSERTS
OUTSTRIVES	OUTTRAVELLING	OUTWRESTED	OVERACTIVITIES	OVERASSESSMENT
OUTSTRIVING	OUTTRAVELS	OUTWRESTING	OVERACTIVITY	OVERASSESSMENTS
OUTSTROKES	OUTTRICKED	OUTWRESTLE	OVERADJUSTMENT	OVERATTENTION
OUTSTUDIED	OUTTRICKING	OUTWRESTLED	OVERADJUSTMENTS	OVERATTENTIONS
OUTSTUDIES	OUTTROTTED	OUTWRESTLES	OVERADVERTISE	OVERATTENTIVE
OUTSTUDYING	OUTTROTTING	OUTWRESTLING	OVERADVERTISED	OVERBAKING
OUTSTUNTED	OUTTRUMPED	OUTWRITING	OVERADVERTISES	OVERBALANCE
OUTSTUNTING	OUTTRUMPING	OUTWRITTEN	OVERADVERTISING	OVERBALANCED
OUTSULKING	OUTVALUING	OUTWROUGHT	OVERADVERTIZE	OVERBALANCES
OUTSUMMING	OUTVAUNTED	OUTYELLING	OVERADVERTIZED	OVERBALANCING
OUTSWEARING	OUTVAUNTING	OUTYELPING	OVERADVERTIZES	OVERBEARING
OUTSWEEPING	OUTVENOMED	OUTYIELDED	OVERADVERTIZING	OVERBEARINGLY
OUTSWEETEN	OUTVENOMING	OUTYIELDING	OVERAGGRESSIVE	OVERBEARINGNESS
OUTSWEETENED	OUTVILLAIN	OUVIRANDRA	OVERAMBITIOUS	OVERBEATEN
OUTSWEETENING	OUTVILLAINED	OUVIRANDRAS	OVERAMPLIFIED	OVERBEATING
OUTSWEETENS	OUTVILLAINING	OVALBUMINS	OVERANALYSE	OVERBEJEWELED
OUTSWELLED	OUTVILLAINS	OVALNESSES	OVERANALYSED	OVERBEJEWELLED
OUTSWELLING	OUTVOICING	OVARIECTOMIES	OVERANALYSES	OVERBETTED
OUTSWIMMING	OUTWAITING	OVARIECTOMISED	OVERANALYSING	OVERBETTING
OUTSWINGER	OUTWALKING	OVARIECTOMIZED	OVERANALYSIS	OVERBETTINGS
OUTSWINGERS	OUTWARDNESS	OVARIECTOMY	OVERANALYTICAL	OVERBIDDEN
OUTSWINGING	OUTWARDNESSES	OVARIOTOMIES	OVERANALYZE	OVERBIDDER
OUTSWOLLEN	OUTWARRING	OVARIOTOMIST	OVERANALYZED	OVERBIDDERS
OUTTALKING	OUTWASTING	OVARIOTOMISTS	OVERANALYZES	OVERBIDDING
OUTTASKING	OUTWATCHED	OVARIOTOMY	OVERANALYZING	OVERBIDDINGS
OUTTELLING	OUTWATCHES	OVARITIDES	OVERANXIETIES	OVERBILLED
OUTTHANKED	OUTWATCHING	OVARITISES	OVERANXIETY	OVERBILLING
OUTTHANKING	OUTWEARIED	OVERABOUND	OVERANXIOUS	OVERBLANKET
OUTTHIEVED	OUTWEARIES	OVERABOUNDED	OVERAPPLICATION	OVERBLANKETS
OUTTHIEVES	OUTWEARING	OVERABOUNDING	OVERARCHED	OVERBLEACH
OUTTHIEVING	OUTWEARYING	OVERABOUNDS	OVERARCHES	OVERBLEACHED
OUTTHINKING	OUTWEEDING	OVERABSTRACT	OVERARCHING	OVERBLEACHES
OUTTHOUGHT	OUTWEEPING	OVERABUNDANCE	OVERARMING	OVERBLEACHING
OUTTHROBBED	OUTWEIGHED	OVERABUNDANCES	OVERAROUSAL	OVERBLOUSE
OUTTHROBBING	OUTWEIGHING	OVERABUNDANT	OVERAROUSALS	OVERBLOUSES

OVERBLOWING
OVERBOILED
OVERBOILING
OVERBOLDLY
OVERBOOKED
OVERBOOKING
OVERBOOKINGS
OVERBORROW
OVERBORROWED
OVERBORROWING
OVERBORROWS
OVERBOUGHT
OVERBOUNDED
OVERBOUNDING
OVERBOUNDS
OVERBRAKED
OVERBRAKES
OVERBRAKING
OVERBREATHING
OVERBREATHINGS
OVERBREEDING
OVERBREEDS
OVERBRIDGE
OVERBRIDGED
OVERBRIDGES
OVERBRIDGING
OVERBRIEFED
OVERBRIEFING
OVERBRIEFS
OVERBRIGHT
OVERBRIMMED
OVERBRIMMING
OVERBROWED
OVERBROWING
OVERBROWSE
OVERBROWSED
OVERBROWSES
OVERBROWSING
OVERBRUTAL
OVERBUILDING
OVERBUILDS
OVERBULKED
OVERBULKING
OVERBURDEN
OVERBURDENED
OVERBURDENING
OVERBURDENS
OVERBURDENSOME
OVERBURNED

OVERBURNING
OVERBURTHEN
OVERBURTHENED
OVERBURTHENING
OVERBURTHENS
OVERBUSIED
OVERBUSIES
OVERBUSYING
OVERBUYING
OVERCALLED
OVERCALLING
OVERCANOPIED
OVERCANOPIES
OVERCANOPY
OVERCANOPYING
OVERCAPACITIES
OVERCAPACITY
OVERCAPITALISE
OVERCAPITALISED
OVERCAPITALISES
OVERCAPITALIZE
OVERCAPITALIZED
OVERCAPITALIZES
OVERCAREFUL
OVERCARRIED
OVERCARRIES
OVERCARRYING
OVERCASTED
OVERCASTING
OVERCASTINGS
OVERCATCHES
OVERCATCHING
OVERCAUGHT
OVERCAUTION
OVERCAUTIONS
OVERCAUTIOUS
OVERCAUTIOUSLY
OVERCENTRALISE
OVERCENTRALISED
OVERCENTRALISES
OVERCENTRALIZE
OVERCENTRALIZED
OVERCENTRALIZES
OVERCHARGE
OVERCHARGED
OVERCHARGES
OVERCHARGING
OVERCHARGINGS
OVERCHECKS

OVERCHILLED
OVERCHILLING
OVERCHILLS
OVERCIVILISED
OVERCIVILIZED
OVERCLAIMED
OVERCLAIMING
OVERCLAIMS
OVERCLASSES
OVERCLASSIFIED
OVERCLASSIFIES
OVERCLASSIFY
OVERCLASSIFYING
OVERCLEANED
OVERCLEANING
OVERCLEANS
OVERCLEARED
OVERCLEARING
OVERCLEARS
OVERCLEVER
OVERCLOCKED
OVERCLOCKER
OVERCLOCKERS
OVERCLOCKING
OVERCLOCKINGS
OVERCLOCKS
OVERCLOUDED
OVERCLOUDING
OVERCLOUDS
OVERCLOYED
OVERCLOYING
OVERCLUBBED
OVERCLUBBING
OVERCOACHED
OVERCOACHES
OVERCOACHING
OVERCOATING
OVERCOATINGS
OVERCOLORED
OVERCOLORING
OVERCOLORS
OVERCOLOUR
OVERCOLOURED
OVERCOLOURING
OVERCOLOURS
OVERCOMERS
OVERCOMING
OVERCOMMIT
OVERCOMMITMENT

OVERCOMMITMENTS
OVERCOMMITS
OVERCOMMITTED
OVERCOMMITTING
OVERCOMMUNICATE
OVERCOMPENSATE
OVERCOMPENSATED
OVERCOMPENSATES
OVERCOMPLEX
OVERCOMPLIANCE
OVERCOMPLIANCES
OVERCOMPLICATE
OVERCOMPLICATED
OVERCOMPLICATES
OVERCOMPRESS
OVERCOMPRESSED
OVERCOMPRESSES
OVERCOMPRESSING
OVERCONCERN
OVERCONCERNED
OVERCONCERNING
OVERCONCERNS
OVERCONFIDENCE
OVERCONFIDENCES
OVERCONFIDENT
OVERCONFIDENTLY
OVERCONSCIOUS
OVERCONSTRUCT
OVERCONSTRUCTED
OVERCONSTRUCTS
OVERCONSUME
OVERCONSUMED
OVERCONSUMES
OVERCONSUMING
OVERCONSUMPTION
OVERCONTROL
OVERCONTROLLED
OVERCONTROLLING
OVERCONTROLS
OVERCOOKED
OVERCOOKING
OVERCOOLED
OVERCOOLING
OVERCORRECT
OVERCORRECTED
OVERCORRECTING
OVERCORRECTION
OVERCORRECTIONS
OVERCORRECTS

OVERCOUNTED
OVERCOUNTING
OVERCOUNTS
OVERCOVERED
OVERCOVERING
OVERCOVERS
OVERCRAMMED
OVERCRAMMING
OVERCRAMMINGS
OVERCRAWED
OVERCRAWING
OVERCREDULITIES
OVERCREDULITY
OVERCREDULOUS
OVERCRITICAL
OVERCROPPED
OVERCROPPING
OVERCROWDED
OVERCROWDING
OVERCROWDINGS
OVERCROWDS
OVERCROWED
OVERCROWING
OVERCULTIVATION
OVERCURING
OVERCUTTING
OVERCUTTINGS
OVERDARING
OVERDECKED
OVERDECKING
OVERDECORATE
OVERDECORATED
OVERDECORATES
OVERDECORATING
OVERDECORATION
OVERDECORATIONS
OVERDEEPENING
OVERDELICATE
OVERDEMANDING
OVERDEPENDENCE
OVERDEPENDENCES
OVERDEPENDENT
OVERDESIGN
OVERDESIGNED
OVERDESIGNING
OVERDESIGNS
OVERDETERMINED
OVERDEVELOP
OVERDEVELOPED

OVERDEVELOPING	OVERDRIVES	OVEREMPLOYMENT	OVEREXPANDING	OVERFEARING
OVERDEVELOPMENT	OVERDRIVING	OVEREMPLOYMENTS	OVEREXPANDS	OVERFEEDING
OVERDEVELOPS	OVERDRYING	OVERENAMORED	OVEREXPANSION	OVERFEEDINGS
OVERDEVIATE	OVERDUBBED	OVERENAMOURED	OVEREXPANSIONS	OVERFERTILISE
OVERDEVIATED	OVERDUBBING	OVERENCOURAGE	OVEREXPECTATION	OVERFERTILISED
OVERDEVIATES	OVERDUSTED	OVERENCOURAGED	OVEREXPLAIN	OVERFERTILISES
OVERDEVIATING	OVERDUSTING	OVERENCOURAGES	OVEREXPLAINED	OVERFERTILISING
OVERDIAGNOSES	OVERDYEING	OVERENCOURAGING	OVEREXPLAINING	OVERFERTILIZE
OVERDIAGNOSIS	OVEREAGERNESS	OVERENERGETIC	OVEREXPLAINS	OVERFERTILIZED
OVERDILUTED	OVEREAGERNESSES	OVERENGINEER	OVEREXPLICIT	OVERFERTILIZES
OVERDIRECT	OVEREARNEST	OVERENGINEERED	OVEREXPLOIT	OVERFERTILIZING
OVERDIRECTED	OVEREASIER	OVERENGINEERING	OVEREXPLOITED	OVERFILLED
OVERDIRECTING	OVEREASIEST	OVERENGINEERS	OVEREXPLOITING	OVERFILLING
OVERDIRECTS	OVEREATERS	OVERENROLLED	OVEREXPLOITS	OVERFINENESS
OVERDISCOUNT	OVEREATING	OVERENTERTAINED	OVEREXPOSE	OVERFINENESSES
OVERDISCOUNTED	OVEREATINGS	OVERENTHUSIASM	OVEREXPOSED	OVERFINISHED
OVERDISCOUNTING	OVEREDITED	OVERENTHUSIASMS	OVEREXPOSES	OVERFISHED
OVERDISCOUNTS	OVEREDITING	OVEREQUIPPED	OVEREXPOSING	OVERFISHES
OVERDIVERSITIES	OVEREDUCATE	OVEREQUIPPING	OVEREXPOSURE	OVERFISHING
OVERDIVERSITY	OVEREDUCATED	OVEREQUIPS	OVEREXPOSURES	OVERFISHINGS
OVERDOCUMENT	OVEREDUCATES	OVERESTIMATE	OVEREXTEND	OVERFLIGHT
OVERDOCUMENTED	OVEREDUCATING	OVERESTIMATED	OVEREXTENDED	OVERFLIGHTS
OVERDOCUMENTING	OVEREDUCATION	OVERESTIMATES	OVEREXTENDING	OVERFLOODED
OVERDOCUMENTS	OVEREDUCATIONS	OVERESTIMATING	OVEREXTENDS	OVERFLOODING
OVERDOMINANCE	OVEREFFUSIVE	OVERESTIMATION	OVEREXTENSION	OVERFLOODS
OVERDOMINANCES	OVEREGGING	OVERESTIMATIONS	OVEREXTENSIONS	OVERFLOURISH
OVERDOMINANT	OVERELABORATE	OVEREVALUATION	OVEREXTRACTION	OVERFLOURISHED
OVERDOSAGE	OVERELABORATED	OVEREVALUATIONS	OVEREXTRACTIONS	OVERFLOURISHES
OVERDOSAGES	OVERELABORATES	OVEREXAGGERATE	OVEREXTRAVAGANT	OVERFLOURISHING
OVERDOSING	OVERELABORATING	OVEREXAGGERATED	OVEREXUBERANT	OVERFLOWED
OVERDRAFTS	OVERELABORATION	OVEREXAGGERATES	OVEREYEING	OVERFLOWING
OVERDRAMATIC	OVEREMBELLISH	OVEREXCITABLE	OVERFACILE	OVERFLOWINGLY
OVERDRAMATISE	OVEREMBELLISHED	OVEREXCITE	OVERFALLEN	OVERFLOWINGS
OVERDRAMATISED	OVEREMBELLISHES	OVEREXCITED	OVERFALLING	OVERFLUSHES
OVERDRAMATISES	OVEREMOTED	OVEREXCITEMENT	OVERFAMILIAR	OVERFLYING
OVERDRAMATISING	OVEREMOTES	OVEREXCITEMENTS	OVERFAMILIARITY	OVERFOCUSED
OVERDRAMATIZE	OVEREMOTING	OVEREXCITES	OVERFASTIDIOUS	OVERFOCUSES
OVERDRAMATIZED	OVEREMOTIONAL	OVEREXCITING	OVERFATIGUE	OVERFOCUSING
OVERDRAMATIZES	OVEREMPHASES	OVEREXERCISE	OVERFATIGUED	OVERFOCUSSED
OVERDRAMATIZING	OVEREMPHASIS	OVEREXERCISED	OVERFATIGUES	OVERFOCUSSES
OVERDRAUGHT	OVEREMPHASISE	OVEREXERCISES	OVERFATIGUING	OVERFOCUSSING
OVERDRAUGHTS	OVEREMPHASISED	OVEREXERCISING	OVERFAVORED	OVERFOLDED
OVERDRAWING	OVEREMPHASISES	OVEREXERTED	OVERFAVORING	OVERFOLDING
OVERDRESSED	OVEREMPHASISING	OVEREXERTING	OVERFAVORS	OVERFONDLY
OVERDRESSES	OVEREMPHASIZE	OVEREXERTION	OVERFAVOUR	OVERFONDNESS
OVERDRESSING	OVEREMPHASIZED	OVEREXERTIONS	OVERFAVOURED	OVERFONDNESSES
OVERDRINKING	OVEREMPHASIZES	OVEREXERTS	OVERFAVOURING	OVERFORWARD
OVERDRINKS	OVEREMPHASIZING	OVEREXPAND	OVERFAVOURS	OVERFORWARDNESS
OVERDRIVEN	OVEREMPHATIC	OVEREXPANDED	OVERFEARED	OVERFRAUGHT

OVERFREEDOM	OVERGLAMORIZES	OVERHAILING	OVERHUNTINGS	OVERINTENSITY
OVERFREEDOMS	OVERGLAMORIZING	OVERHALING	OVERHYPING	OVERINVESTMENT
OVERFREELY	OVERGLANCE	OVERHANDED	OVERIDEALISE	OVERINVESTMENTS
OVERFREIGHT	OVERGLANCED	OVERHANDING	OVERIDEALISED	OVERISSUANCE
OVERFREIGHTING	OVERGLANCES	OVERHANDLE	OVERIDEALISES	OVERISSUANCES
OVERFREIGHTS	OVERGLANCING	OVERHANDLED	OVERIDEALISING	OVERISSUED
OVERFULFIL	OVERGLAZED	OVERHANDLES	OVERIDEALIZE	OVERISSUES
OVERFULFILL	OVERGLAZES	OVERHANDLING	OVERIDEALIZED	OVERISSUING
OVERFULFILLED	OVERGLAZING	OVERHANGING	OVERIDEALIZES	OVERJOYING
OVERFULFILLING	OVERGLOOMED	OVERHAPPIER	OVERIDEALIZING	OVERJUMPED
OVERFULFILLS	OVERGLOOMING	OVERHAPPIEST	OVERIDENTIFIED	OVERJUMPING
OVERFULFILS	OVERGLOOMS	OVERHARVEST	OVERIDENTIFIES	OVERKEEPING
OVERFULLNESS	OVERGOADED	OVERHARVESTED	OVERIDENTIFY	OVERKILLED
OVERFULLNESSES	OVERGOADING	OVERHARVESTING	OVERIDENTIFYING	OVERKILLING
OVERFULNESS	OVERGOINGS	OVERHARVESTS	OVERIMAGINATIVE	OVERKINDNESS
OVERFULNESSES	OVERGORGED	OVERHASTES	OVERIMPRESS	OVERKINDNESSES
OVERFUNDED	OVERGORGES	OVERHASTILY	OVERIMPRESSED	OVERLABORED
OVERFUNDING	OVERGORGING	OVERHASTINESS	OVERIMPRESSES	OVERLABORING
OVERFUNDINGS	OVERGOVERN	OVERHASTINESSES	OVERIMPRESSING	OVERLABORS
OVERFUSSIER	OVERGOVERNED	OVERHATING	OVERINCLINED	OVERLABOUR
OVERFUSSIEST	OVERGOVERNING	OVERHAULED	OVERINDULGE	OVERLABOURED
OVERGALLED	OVERGOVERNS	OVERHAULING	OVERINDULGED	OVERLABOURING
OVERGALLING	OVERGRADED	OVERHEAPED	OVERINDULGENCE	OVERLABOURS
OVERGANGING	OVERGRADES	OVERHEAPING	OVERINDULGENCES	OVERLADING
OVERGARMENT	OVERGRADING	OVERHEARING	OVERINDULGENT	OVERLANDED
OVERGARMENTS	OVERGRAINED	OVERHEATED	OVERINDULGES	OVERLANDER
OVERGEARED	OVERGRAINER	OVERHEATING	OVERINDULGING	OVERLANDERS
OVERGEARING	OVERGRAINERS	OVERHEATINGS	OVERINFLATE	OVERLANDING
OVERGENERALISE	OVERGRAINING	OVERHENTING	OVERINFLATED	OVERLAPPED
OVERGENERALISED	OVERGRAINS	OVERHITTING	OVERINFLATES	OVERLAPPING
OVERGENERALISES	OVERGRASSED	OVERHOLDING	OVERINFLATING	OVERLARDED
OVERGENERALIZE	OVERGRASSES	OVERHOLIER	OVERINFLATION	OVERLARDING
OVERGENERALIZED	OVERGRASSING	OVERHOLIEST	OVERINFLATIONS	OVERLAUNCH
OVERGENERALIZES	OVERGRAZED	OVERHOMOGENISE	OVERINFORM	OVERLAUNCHED
OVERGENEROSITY	OVERGRAZES	OVERHOMOGENISED	OVERINFORMED	OVERLAUNCHES
OVERGENEROUS	OVERGRAZING	OVERHOMOGENISES	OVERINFORMING	OVERLAUNCHING
OVERGENEROUSLY	OVERGRAZINGS	OVERHOMOGENIZE	OVERINFORMS	OVERLAVISH
OVERGETTING	OVERGREEDIER	OVERHOMOGENIZED	OVERINGENIOUS	OVERLAYING
OVERGILDED	OVERGREEDIEST	OVERHOMOGENIZES	OVERINGENUITIES	OVERLAYINGS
OVERGILDING	OVERGREEDY	OVERHONORED	OVERINGENUITY	OVERLEAPED
OVERGIRDED	OVERGREENED	OVERHONORING	OVERINSISTENT	OVERLEAPING
OVERGIRDING	OVERGREENING	OVERHONORS	OVERINSURANCE	OVERLEARNED
OVERGIVING	OVERGREENS	OVERHONOUR	OVERINSURANCES	OVERLEARNING
OVERGLAMORISE	OVERGROUND	OVERHONOURED	OVERINSURE	OVERLEARNS
OVERGLAMORISED	OVERGROWING	OVERHONOURING	OVERINSURED	OVERLEARNT
OVERGLAMORISES	OVERGROWTH	OVERHONOURS	OVERINSURES	OVERLEATHER
OVERGLAMORISING	OVERGROWTHS	OVERHOPING	OVERINSURING	OVERLEATHERS
OVERGLAMORIZE	OVERHAILED	OVERHUNTED	OVERINTENSE	OVERLEAVEN
OVERGLAMORIZED	OVERHAILES	OVERHUNTING	OVERINTENSITIES	OVERLEAVENED

OVERLEAVENING	OVERMASTING	OVERNICELY	OVERPAINTING	OVERPLAYED
OVERLEAVENS	OVERMATCHED	OVERNICENESS	OVERPAINTS	OVERPLAYING
OVERLENDING	OVERMATCHES	OVERNICENESSES	OVERPARTED	OVERPLOTTED
OVERLENGTH	OVERMATCHING	OVERNIGHTED	OVERPARTICULAR	OVERPLOTTING
OVERLENGTHEN	OVERMATTER	OVERNIGHTER	OVERPARTING	OVERPLOTTINGS
OVERLENGTHENED	OVERMATTERS	OVERNIGHTERS	OVERPASSED	OVERPLUSES
OVERLENGTHENING	OVERMATURE	OVERNIGHTING	OVERPASSES	OVERPLUSSES
OVERLENGTHENS	OVERMATURITIES	OVERNIGHTS	OVERPASSING	OVERPLYING
OVERLENGTHS	OVERMATURITY	OVERNOURISH	OVERPAYING	OVERPOISED
OVERLETTING	OVERMEASURE	OVERNOURISHED	OVERPAYMENT	OVERPOISES
OVERLEVERAGED	OVERMEASURED	OVERNOURISHES	OVERPAYMENTS	OVERPOISING
OVERLIGHTED	OVERMEASURES	OVERNOURISHING	OVERPEDALED	OVERPOLICE
OVERLIGHTING	OVERMEASURING	OVERNUTRITION	OVERPEDALING	OVERPOLICED
OVERLIGHTS	OVERMEDICATE	OVERNUTRITIONS	OVERPEDALLED	OVERPOLICES
OVERLITERAL	OVERMEDICATED	OVEROBVIOUS	OVERPEDALLING	OVERPOLICING
OVERLITERARY	OVERMEDICATES	OVEROFFICE	OVERPEDALLINGS	OVERPOPULATE
OVERLIVING	OVERMEDICATING	OVEROFFICED	OVERPEDALS	OVERPOPULATED
OVERLOADED	OVERMEDICATION	OVEROFFICES	OVERPEERED	OVERPOPULATES
OVERLOADING	OVERMEDICATIONS	OVEROFFICING	OVERPEERING	OVERPOPULATING
OVERLOCKED	OVERMELTED	OVEROPERATE	OVERPEOPLE	OVERPOPULATION
OVERLOCKER	OVERMELTING	OVEROPERATED	OVERPEOPLED	OVERPOPULATIONS
OVERLOCKERS	OVERMERRIER	OVEROPERATES	OVERPEOPLES	OVERPOSTED
OVERLOCKING	OVERMERRIEST	OVEROPERATING	OVERPEOPLING	OVERPOSTING
OVERLOCKINGS	OVERMIGHTIER	OVEROPINIONATED	OVERPERCHED	OVERPOTENT
OVERLOOKED	OVERMIGHTIEST	OVEROPTIMISM	OVERPERCHES	OVERPOWERED
OVERLOOKER	OVERMIGHTY	OVEROPTIMISMS	OVERPERCHING	OVERPOWERING
OVERLOOKERS	OVERMILKED	OVEROPTIMIST	OVERPERSUADE	OVERPOWERINGLY
OVERLOOKING	OVERMILKING	OVEROPTIMISTIC	OVERPERSUADED	OVERPOWERS
OVERLORDED	OVERMINING	OVEROPTIMISTS	OVERPERSUADES	OVERPRAISE
OVERLORDING	OVERMIXING	OVERORCHESTRATE	OVERPERSUADING	OVERPRAISED
OVERLORDSHIP	OVERMODEST	OVERORGANISE	OVERPERSUASION	OVERPRAISES
OVERLORDSHIPS	OVERMODESTLY	OVERORGANISED	OVERPERSUASIONS	OVERPRAISING
OVERLOVING	OVERMOUNTED	OVERORGANISES	OVERPESSIMISTIC	OVERPRECISE
OVERMANAGE	OVERMOUNTING	OVERORGANISING	OVERPICTURE	OVERPREPARATION
OVERMANAGED	OVERMOUNTS	OVERORGANIZE	OVERPICTURED	OVERPREPARE
OVERMANAGES	OVERMUCHES	OVERORGANIZED	OVERPICTURES	OVERPREPARED
OVERMANAGING	OVERMULTIPLIED	OVERORGANIZES	OVERPICTURING	OVERPREPARES
OVERMANIES	OVERMULTIPLIES	OVERORGANIZING	OVERPITCHED	OVERPREPARING
OVERMANNED	OVERMULTIPLY	OVERORNAMENT	OVERPITCHES	OVERPRESCRIBE
OVERMANNERED	OVERMULTIPLYING	OVERORNAMENTED	OVERPITCHING	OVERPRESCRIBED
OVERMANNING	OVERMULTITUDE	OVERORNAMENTING	OVERPLACED	OVERPRESCRIBES
OVERMANNINGS	OVERMULTITUDED	OVERORNAMENTS	OVERPLAIDED	OVERPRESCRIBING
OVERMANTEL	OVERMULTITUDES	OVERPACKAGE	OVERPLAIDS	OVERPRESSED
OVERMANTELS	OVERMULTITUDING	OVERPACKAGED	OVERPLANNED	OVERPRESSES
OVERMASTED	OVERMUSCLED	OVERPACKAGES	OVERPLANNING	OVERPRESSING
OVERMASTER	OVERNAMING	OVERPACKAGING	OVERPLANNINGS	OVERPRESSURE
OVERMASTERED	OVERNETTED	OVERPACKED	OVERPLANTED	OVERPRESSURES
OVERMASTERING	OVERNETTING	OVERPACKING	OVERPLANTING	OVERPRICED
OVERMASTERS	OVERNETTINGS	OVERPAINTED	OVERPLANTS	OVERPRICES

OVERPRICING
OVERPRINTED
OVERPRINTING
OVERPRINTS
OVERPRIVILEGED
OVERPRIZED
OVERPRIZES
OVERPRIZING
OVERPROCESS
OVERPROCESSED
OVERPROCESSES
OVERPROCESSING
OVERPRODUCE
OVERPRODUCED
OVERPRODUCES
OVERPRODUCING
OVERPRODUCTION
OVERPRODUCTIONS
OVERPROGRAM
OVERPROGRAMED
OVERPROGRAMING
OVERPROGRAMMED
OVERPROGRAMMING
OVERPROGRAMS
OVERPROMISE
OVERPROMISED
OVERPROMISES
OVERPROMISING
OVERPROMOTE
OVERPROMOTED
OVERPROMOTES
OVERPROMOTING
OVERPROOFS
OVERPROPORTION
OVERPROPORTIONS
OVERPROTECT
OVERPROTECTED
OVERPROTECTING
OVERPROTECTION
OVERPROTECTIONS
OVERPROTECTIVE
OVERPROTECTS
OVERPUMPED
OVERPUMPING
OVERQUALIFIED
OVERRACKED
OVERRACKING
OVERRAKING
OVERRANKED

OVERRANKING
OVERRASHLY
OVERRASHNESS
OVERRASHNESSES
OVERRATING
OVERRAUGHT
OVERREACHED
OVERREACHER
OVERREACHERS
OVERREACHES
OVERREACHING
OVERREACTED
OVERREACTING
OVERREACTION
OVERREACTIONS
OVERREACTS
OVERREADING
OVERRECKON
OVERRECKONED
OVERRECKONING
OVERRECKONS
OVERREDDED
OVERREDDING
OVERREFINE
OVERREFINED
OVERREFINEMENT
OVERREFINEMENTS
OVERREFINES
OVERREFINING
OVERREGULATE
OVERREGULATED
OVERREGULATES
OVERREGULATING
OVERREGULATION
OVERREGULATIONS
OVERRELIANCE
OVERRELIANCES
OVERRENNING
OVERREPORT
OVERREPORTED
OVERREPORTING
OVERREPORTS
OVERREPRESENTED
OVERRESPOND
OVERRESPONDED
OVERRESPONDING
OVERRESPONDS
OVERRIDDEN
OVERRIDERS

OVERRIDING
OVERRIPENED
OVERRIPENESS
OVERRIPENESSES
OVERRIPENING
OVERRIPENS
OVERROASTED
OVERROASTING
OVERROASTS
OVERRUFFED
OVERRUFFING
OVERRULERS
OVERRULING
OVERRULINGS
OVERRUNNER
OVERRUNNERS
OVERRUNNING
OVERSAILED
OVERSAILING
OVERSALTED
OVERSALTING
OVERSANGUINE
OVERSATURATE
OVERSATURATED
OVERSATURATES
OVERSATURATING
OVERSATURATION
OVERSATURATIONS
OVERSAUCED
OVERSAUCES
OVERSAUCING
OVERSAVING
OVERSCALED
OVERSCHUTCHT
OVERSCORED
OVERSCORES
OVERSCORING
OVERSCRUPULOUS
OVERSCUTCHED
OVERSECRETION
OVERSECRETIONS
OVERSEEDED
OVERSEEDING
OVERSEEING
OVERSELLING
OVERSENSITIVE
OVERSENSITIVITY
OVERSERIOUS
OVERSERIOUSLY

OVERSERVED
OVERSERVES
OVERSERVICE
OVERSERVICED
OVERSERVICES
OVERSERVICING
OVERSERVING
OVERSETTING
OVERSEWING
OVERSHADED
OVERSHADES
OVERSHADING
OVERSHADOW
OVERSHADOWED
OVERSHADOWING
OVERSHADOWS
OVERSHARED
OVERSHARES
OVERSHARING
OVERSHINES
OVERSHINING
OVERSHIRTS
OVERSHOOTING
OVERSHOOTS
OVERSHOWER
OVERSHOWERED
OVERSHOWERING
OVERSHOWERS
OVERSIGHTS
OVERSIMPLE
OVERSIMPLIFIED
OVERSIMPLIFIES
OVERSIMPLIFY
OVERSIMPLIFYING
OVERSIMPLISTIC
OVERSIMPLY
OVERSIZING
OVERSKATED
OVERSKATES
OVERSKATING
OVERSKIPPED
OVERSKIPPING
OVERSKIRTS
OVERSLAUGH
OVERSLAUGHED
OVERSLAUGHING
OVERSLAUGHS
OVERSLEEPING
OVERSLEEPS

OVERSLEEVE
OVERSLEEVES
OVERSLIPPED
OVERSLIPPING
OVERSMOKED
OVERSMOKES
OVERSMOKING
OVERSOAKED
OVERSOAKING
OVERSOLICITOUS
OVERSOWING
OVERSPECIALISE
OVERSPECIALISED
OVERSPECIALISES
OVERSPECIALIZE
OVERSPECIALIZED
OVERSPECIALIZES
OVERSPECULATE
OVERSPECULATED
OVERSPECULATES
OVERSPECULATING
OVERSPECULATION
OVERSPENDER
OVERSPENDERS
OVERSPENDING
OVERSPENDINGS
OVERSPENDS
OVERSPICED
OVERSPICES
OVERSPICING
OVERSPILLED
OVERSPILLING
OVERSPILLS
OVERSPREAD
OVERSPREADING
OVERSPREADS
OVERSTABILITIES
OVERSTABILITY
OVERSTAFFED
OVERSTAFFING
OVERSTAFFINGS
OVERSTAFFS
OVERSTAINED
OVERSTAINING
OVERSTAINS
OVERSTANDING
OVERSTANDS
OVERSTARED
OVERSTARES

OVERSTARING	OVERSTRIDING	OVERSWOLLEN	OVERTOWERED	OVERVEILING
OVERSTATED	OVERSTRIKE	OVERTAKING	OVERTOWERING	OVERVIOLENT
OVERSTATEMENT	OVERSTRIKES	OVERTAKINGS	OVERTOWERS	OVERVOLTAGE
OVERSTATEMENTS	OVERSTRIKING	OVERTALKATIVE	OVERTRADED	OVERVOLTAGES
OVERSTATES	OVERSTRODE	OVERTALKED	OVERTRADES	OVERVOTING
OVERSTATING	OVERSTRONG	OVERTALKING	OVERTRADING	OVERWARIER
OVERSTAYED	OVERSTROOKE	OVERTASKED	OVERTRADINGS	OVERWARIEST
OVERSTAYER	OVERSTRUCK	OVERTASKING	OVERTRAINED	OVERWARMED
OVERSTAYERS	OVERSTRUCTURED	OVERTAUGHT	OVERTRAINING	OVERWARMING
OVERSTAYING	OVERSTRUNG	OVERTAXATION	OVERTRAINS	OVERWASHES
OVERSTEERED	OVERSTUDIED	OVERTAXATIONS	OVERTREATED	OVERWATCHED
OVERSTEERING	OVERSTUDIES	OVERTAXING	OVERTREATING	OVERWATCHES
OVERSTEERS	OVERSTUDYING	OVERTEACHES	OVERTREATMENT	OVERWATCHING
OVERSTEPPED	OVERSTUFFED	OVERTEACHING	OVERTREATMENTS	OVERWATERED
OVERSTEPPING	OVERSTUFFING	OVERTEDIOUS	OVERTREATS	OVERWATERING
OVERSTIMULATE	OVERSTUFFS	OVERTEEMED	OVERTRICKS	OVERWATERS
OVERSTIMULATED	OVERSUBSCRIBE	OVERTEEMING	OVERTRIMMED	OVERWEARIED
OVERSTIMULATES	OVERSUBSCRIBED	OVERTHINKING	OVERTRIMMING	OVERWEARIES
OVERSTIMULATING	OVERSUBSCRIBES	OVERTHINKS	OVERTRIPPED	OVERWEARING
OVERSTIMULATION	OVERSUBSCRIBING	OVERTHINNED	OVERTRIPPING	OVERWEARYING
OVERSTINKING	OVERSUBTLE	OVERTHINNING	OVERTRUMPED	OVERWEATHER
OVERSTINKS	OVERSUBTLETIES	OVERTHOUGHT	OVERTRUMPING	OVERWEATHERED
OVERSTIRRED	OVERSUBTLETY	OVERTHROWER	OVERTRUMPS	OVERWEATHERING
OVERSTIRRING	OVERSUDSED	OVERTHROWERS	OVERTRUSTED	OVERWEATHERS
OVERSTOCKED	OVERSUDSES	OVERTHROWING	OVERTRUSTING	OVERWEENED
OVERSTOCKING	OVERSUDSING	OVERTHROWN	OVERTRUSTS	OVERWEENING
OVERSTOCKS	OVERSUPPED	OVERTHROWS	OVERTURING	OVERWEENINGLY
OVERSTOREY	OVERSUPPING	OVERTHRUST	OVERTURNED	OVERWEENINGNESS
OVERSTOREYS	OVERSUPPLIED	OVERTHRUSTS	OVERTURNER	OVERWEENINGS
OVERSTORIES	OVERSUPPLIES	OVERTHWART	OVERTURNERS	OVERWEIGHED
OVERSTRAIN	OVERSUPPLY	OVERTHWARTED	OVERTURNING	OVERWEIGHING
OVERSTRAINED	OVERSUPPLYING	OVERTHWARTING	OVERTYPING	OVERWEIGHS
OVERSTRAINING	OVERSUSPICIOUS	OVERTHWARTS	OVERURGING	OVERWEIGHT
OVERSTRAINS	OVERSWAYED	OVERTIGHTEN	OVERUTILISATION	OVERWEIGHTED
OVERSTRESS	OVERSWAYING	OVERTIGHTENED	OVERUTILISE	OVERWEIGHTING
OVERSTRESSED	OVERSWEARING	OVERTIGHTENING	OVERUTILISED	OVERWEIGHTS
OVERSTRESSES	OVERSWEARS	OVERTIGHTENS	OVERUTILISES	OVERWETTED
OVERSTRESSING	OVERSWEETEN	OVERTIMELY	OVERUTILISING	OVERWETTING
OVERSTRETCH	OVERSWEETENED	OVERTIMERS	OVERUTILIZATION	OVERWHELMED
OVERSTRETCHED	OVERSWEETENING	OVERTIMING	OVERUTILIZE	OVERWHELMING
OVERSTRETCHES	OVERSWEETENS	OVERTIPPED	OVERUTILIZED	OVERWHELMINGLY
OVERSTRETCHING	OVERSWEETNESS	OVERTIPPING	OVERUTILIZES	OVERWHELMINGS
OVERSTREWED	OVERSWEETNESSES	OVERTIRING	OVERUTILIZING	OVERWHELMS
OVERSTREWING	OVERSWELLED	OVERTNESSES	OVERVALUATION	OVERWILIER
OVERSTREWN	OVERSWELLING	OVERTOILED	OVERVALUATIONS	OVERWILIEST
OVERSTREWS	OVERSWELLS	OVERTOILING	OVERVALUED	OVERWINDED
OVERSTRIDDEN	OVERSWIMMING	OVERTOPPED	OVERVALUES	OVERWINDING
OVERSTRIDE	OVERSWINGING	OVERTOPPING	OVERVALUING	OVERWINGED
OVERSTRIDES	OVERSWINGS	OVERTOPPINGS	OVERVEILED	OVERWINGING

OVERWINTER OVERZEALOUS OXACILLINS OXYCEPHALY OXYHYDROGENS
OVERWINTERED OVERZEALOUSLY OXALACETATE OXYCODONES OXYMORONIC
OVERWINTERING OVERZEALOUSNESS OXALACETATES OXYGENASES OXYMORONICALLY
OVERWINTERS OVIPARITIES OXALOACETATE OXYGENATED OXYPHENBUTAZONE
OVERWISELY OVIPAROUSLY OXALOACETATES OXYGENATES OXYRHYNCHUS
OVERWITHHELD OVIPOSITED OXALOACETIC OXYGENATING OXYRHYNCHUSES
OVERWITHHOLD OVIPOSITING OXIDATIONAL OXYGENATION OXYSULPHIDE
OVERWITHHOLDING OVIPOSITION OXIDATIONS OXYGENATIONS OXYSULPHIDES
OVERWITHHOLDS OVIPOSITIONAL OXIDATIVELY OXYGENATOR OXYTETRACYCLINE
OVERWORKED OVIPOSITIONS OXIDIMETRIC OXYGENATORS OXYURIASES
OVERWORKING OVIPOSITOR OXIDIMETRIES OXYGENISED OXYURIASIS
OVERWRAPPED OVIPOSITORS OXIDIMETRY OXYGENISER OYSTERCATCHER
OVERWRAPPING OVIRAPTORS OXIDISABLE OXYGENISERS OYSTERCATCHERS
OVERWRESTED OVOVIVIPARITIES OXIDISATION OXYGENISES OYSTERINGS
OVERWRESTING OVOVIVIPARITY OXIDISATIONS OXYGENISING OZOCERITES
OVERWRESTLE OVOVIVIPAROUS OXIDIZABLE OXYGENIZED OZOKERITES
OVERWRESTLED OVOVIVIPAROUSLY OXIDIZATION OXYGENIZER OZONATIONS
OVERWRESTLES OVULATIONS OXIDIZATIONS OXYGENIZERS OZONIFEROUS
OVERWRESTLING OVULIFEROUS OXIDOREDUCTASE OXYGENIZES OZONISATION
OVERWRESTS OWERLOUPEN OXIDOREDUCTASES OXYGENIZING OZONISATIONS
OVERWRITES OWERLOUPING OXIMETRIES OXYGENLESS OZONIZATION
OVERWRITING OWERLOUPIT OXYACETYLENE OXYHAEMOGLOBIN OZONIZATIONS
OVERWRITTEN OWLISHNESS OXYACETYLENES OXYHAEMOGLOBINS OZONOLYSES
OVERWROUGHT OWLISHNESSES OXYCEPHALIC OXYHEMOGLOBIN OZONOLYSIS
OVERYEARED OWNERSHIPS OXYCEPHALIES OXYHEMOGLOBINS OZONOSPHERE
OVERYEARING OWRECOMING OXYCEPHALOUS OXYHYDROGEN OZONOSPHERES

P

PACEMAKERS	PACKBOARDS	PAEDAGOGIC	PAEDOTRIBES	PAINTERLINESSES
PACEMAKING	PACKCLOTHS	PAEDAGOGUE	PAEDOTROPHIES	PAINTINESS
PACEMAKINGS	PACKETISED	PAEDAGOGUES	PAEDOTROPHY	PAINTINESSES
PACESETTER	PACKETISES	PAEDERASTIC	PAGANISATION	PAINTRESSES
PACESETTERS	PACKETISING	PAEDERASTIES	PAGANISATIONS	PAINTWORKS
PACESETTING	PACKETIZED	PAEDERASTS	PAGANISERS	PAKIRIKIRI
PACESETTINGS	PACKETIZES	PAEDERASTY	PAGANISING	PAKIRIKIRIS
PACHYCARPOUS	PACKETIZING	PAEDEUTICS	PAGANISTIC	PALACINKES
PACHYDACTYL	PACKFRAMES	PAEDIATRIC	PAGANISTICALLY	PALAEANTHROPIC
PACHYDACTYLOUS	PACKHORSES	PAEDIATRICIAN	PAGANIZATION	PALAEBIOLOGIES
PACHYDERMAL	PACKINGHOUSE	PAEDIATRICIANS	PAGANIZATIONS	PALAEBIOLOGIST
PACHYDERMATOUS	PACKINGHOUSES	PAEDIATRICS	PAGANIZERS	PALAEBIOLOGISTS
PACHYDERMIA	PACKNESSES	PAEDIATRIES	PAGANIZING	PALAEBIOLOGY
PACHYDERMIAS	PACKSADDLE	PAEDIATRIST	PAGEANTRIES	PALAEETHNOLOGY
PACHYDERMIC	PACKSADDLES	PAEDIATRISTS	PAGINATING	PALAEOANTHROPIC
PACHYDERMOUS	PACKSHEETS	PAEDOBAPTISM	PAGINATION	PALAEOARTIST
PACHYDERMS	PACKSTAFFS	PAEDOBAPTISMS	PAGINATIONS	PALAEOARTISTS
PACHYMENINGITIS	PACKTHREAD	PAEDOBAPTIST	PAIDEUTICS	PALAEOARTS
PACHYMETER	PACKTHREADS	PAEDOBAPTISTS	PAILLASSES	PALAEOBIOLOGIC
PACHYMETERS	PACLITAXEL	PAEDODONTIC	PAILLETTES	PALAEOBIOLOGIES
PACHYSANDRA	PACLITAXELS	PAEDODONTICS	PAINFULLER	PALAEOBIOLOGIST
PACHYSANDRAS	PACTIONING	PAEDOGENESES	PAINFULLEST	PALAEOBIOLOGY
PACHYTENES	PADDLEBALL	PAEDOGENESIS	PAINFULNESS	PALAEOBOTANIC
PACIFIABLE	PADDLEBALLS	PAEDOGENETIC	PAINFULNESSES	PALAEOBOTANICAL
PACIFICALLY	PADDLEBOARD	PAEDOGENIC	PAINKILLER	PALAEOBOTANIES
PACIFICATE	PADDLEBOARDS	PAEDOLOGICAL	PAINKILLERS	PALAEOBOTANIST
PACIFICATED	PADDLEBOAT	PAEDOLOGIES	PAINKILLING	PALAEOBOTANISTS
PACIFICATES	PADDLEBOATS	PAEDOLOGIST	PAINLESSLY	PALAEOBOTANY
PACIFICATING	PADDLEFISH	PAEDOLOGISTS	PAINLESSNESS	PALAEOCENE
PACIFICATION	PADDLEFISHES	PAEDOMORPHIC	PAINLESSNESSES	PALAEOCLIMATE
PACIFICATIONS	PADDOCKING	PAEDOMORPHISM	PAINSTAKER	PALAEOCLIMATES
PACIFICATOR	PADDYMELON	PAEDOMORPHISMS	PAINSTAKERS	PALAEOCLIMATIC
PACIFICATORS	PADDYMELONS	PAEDOMORPHOSES	PAINSTAKING	PALAEOCRYSTIC
PACIFICATORY	PADDYWACKED	PAEDOMORPHOSIS	PAINSTAKINGLY	PALAEOCURRENT
PACIFICISM	PADDYWACKING	PAEDOPHILE	PAINSTAKINGNESS	PALAEOCURRENTS
PACIFICISMS	PADDYWACKS	PAEDOPHILES	PAINSTAKINGS	PALAEOECOLOGIC
PACIFICIST	PADDYWHACK	PAEDOPHILIA	PAINTBALLING	PALAEOECOLOGIES
PACIFICISTS	PADDYWHACKS	PAEDOPHILIAC	PAINTBALLINGS	PALAEOECOLOGIST
PACIFISTIC	PADEMELONS	PAEDOPHILIACS	PAINTBALLS	PALAEOECOLOGY
PACIFISTICALLY	PADEREROES	PAEDOPHILIAS	PAINTBOXES	PALAEOETHNOLOGY
PACKABILITIES	PADLOCKING	PAEDOPHILIC	PAINTBRUSH	PALAEOGAEA
PACKABILITY	PADRONISMS	PAEDOPHILICS	PAINTBRUSHES	PALAEOGAEAS
PACKAGINGS	PADYMELONS	PAEDOTRIBE	PAINTERLINESS	PALAEOGEOGRAPHY

PALAEOGRAPHER	PALATALISED	PALEOLOGIES	PALISADOES	PALMETTOES
PALAEOGRAPHERS	PALATALISES	PALEOMAGNETIC	PALISADOING	PALMHOUSES
PALAEOGRAPHIC	PALATALISING	PALEOMAGNETISM	PALISANDER	PALMIFICATION
PALAEOGRAPHICAL	PALATALIZATION	PALEOMAGNETISMS	PALISANDERS	PALMIFICATIONS
PALAEOGRAPHIES	PALATALIZATIONS	PALEOMAGNETIST	PALLADIOUS	PALMIPEDES
PALAEOGRAPHIST	PALATALIZE	PALEOMAGNETISTS	PALLADIUMS	PALMISTERS
PALAEOGRAPHISTS	PALATALIZED	PALEONTOLOGIC	PALLASITES	PALMISTRIES
PALAEOGRAPHY	PALATALIZES	PALEONTOLOGICAL	PALLBEARER	PALMITATES
PALAEOLIMNOLOGY	PALATALIZING	PALEONTOLOGIES	PALLBEARERS	PALMPRINTS
PALAEOLITH	PALATIALLY	PALEONTOLOGIST	PALLESCENCE	PALOVERDES
PALAEOLITHIC	PALATIALNESS	PALEONTOLOGISTS	PALLESCENCES	PALPABILITIES
PALAEOLITHS	PALATIALNESSES	PALEONTOLOGY	PALLESCENT	PALPABILITY
PALAEOLOGIES	PALATINATE	PALEOPATHOLOGY	PALLETISATION	PALPABLENESS
PALAEOLOGY	PALATINATES	PALEOZOOLOGICAL	PALLETISATIONS	PALPABLENESSES
PALAEOMAGNETIC	PALAVERERS	PALEOZOOLOGIES	PALLETISED	PALPATIONS
PALAEOMAGNETISM	PALAVERING	PALEOZOOLOGIST	PALLETISER	PALPEBRATE
PALAEOMAGNETIST	PALEACEOUS	PALEOZOOLOGISTS	PALLETISERS	PALPEBRATED
PALAEONTOGRAPHY	PALEMPORES	PALEOZOOLOGY	PALLETISES	PALPEBRATES
PALAEONTOLOGIES	PALENESSES	PALFRENIER	PALLETISING	PALPEBRATING
PALAEONTOLOGIST	PALEOARTIST	PALFRENIERS	PALLETIZATION	PALPITATED
PALAEONTOLOGY	PALEOARTISTS	PALIFICATION	PALLETIZATIONS	PALPITATES
PALAEOPATHOLOGY	PALEOBIOLOGIC	PALIFICATIONS	PALLETIZED	PALPITATING
PALAEOPEDOLOGY	PALEOBIOLOGICAL	PALILALIAS	PALLETIZER	PALPITATION
PALAEOPHYTOLOGY	PALEOBIOLOGIES	PALILLOGIES	PALLETIZERS	PALPITATIONS
PALAEOSOLS	PALEOBIOLOGIST	PALIMONIES	PALLETIZES	PALSGRAVES
PALAEOTYPE	PALEOBIOLOGISTS	PALIMPSEST	PALLETIZING	PALSGRAVINE
PALAEOTYPES	PALEOBIOLOGY	PALIMPSESTS	PALLIAMENT	PALSGRAVINES
PALAEOTYPIC	PALEOBOTANIC	PALINDROME	PALLIAMENTS	PALTRINESS
PALAEOZOOLOGIES	PALEOBOTANICAL	PALINDROMES	PALLIASSES	PALTRINESSES
PALAEOZOOLOGIST	PALEOBOTANIES	PALINDROMIC	PALLIATING	PALUDAMENT
PALAEOZOOLOGY	PALEOBOTANIST	PALINDROMICAL	PALLIATION	PALUDAMENTA
PALAESTRAE	PALEOBOTANISTS	PALINDROMIST	PALLIATIONS	PALUDAMENTS
PALAESTRAL	PALEOBOTANY	PALINDROMISTS	PALLIATIVE	PALUDAMENTUM
PALAESTRAS	PALEOECOLOGIC	PALINGENESES	PALLIATIVELY	PALUDAMENTUMS
PALAESTRIC	PALEOECOLOGICAL	PALINGENESIA	PALLIATIVES	PALUDICOLOUS
PALAESTRICAL	PALEOECOLOGIES	PALINGENESIAS	PALLIATORS	PALUDINOUS
PALAFITTES	PALEOECOLOGIST	PALINGENESIES	PALLIATORY	PALUSTRIAN
PALAGONITE	PALEOECOLOGISTS	PALINGENESIS	PALLIDITIES	PALUSTRINE
PALAGONITES	PALEOECOLOGY	PALINGENESIST	PALLIDNESS	PALYNOLOGIC
PALAMPORES	PALEOGEOGRAPHIC	PALINGENESISTS	PALLIDNESSES	PALYNOLOGICAL
PALANKEENS	PALEOGEOGRAPHY	PALINGENESY	PALMACEOUS	PALYNOLOGICALLY
PALANQUINS	PALEOGRAPHER	PALINGENETIC	PALMATIFID	PALYNOLOGIES
PALATABILITIES	PALEOGRAPHERS	PALINGENETICAL	PALMATIONS	PALYNOLOGIST
PALATABILITY	PALEOGRAPHIC	PALINODIES	PALMATIPARTITE	PALYNOLOGISTS
PALATABLENESS	PALEOGRAPHICAL	PALINOPIAS	PALMATISECT	PALYNOLOGY
PALATABLENESSES	PALEOGRAPHIES	PALINOPSIA	PALMCORDER	PAMPELMOOSE
PALATALISATION	PALEOGRAPHY	PALINOPSIAS	PALMCORDERS	PAMPELMOOSES
PALATALISATIONS	PALEOLITHIC	PALISADING	PALMERWORM	PAMPELMOUSE
PALATALISE	PALEOLITHS	PALISADOED	PALMERWORMS	PAMPELMOUSES

PAMPEREDNESS	PANDAEMONIUMS	PANESTHESIAS	PANOPHTHALMIA	PANTALETTES
PAMPEREDNESSES	PANDANACEOUS	PANETELLAS	PANOPHTHALMIAS	PANTALONES
PAMPERINGS	PANDANUSES	PANETTONES	PANOPHTHALMITIS	PANTALOONED
PAMPHLETED	PANDATIONS	PANFISHING	PANOPTICAL	PANTALOONERIES
PAMPHLETEER	PANDECTIST	PANFISHINGS	PANOPTICALLY	PANTALOONERY
PAMPHLETEERED	PANDECTISTS	PANGENESES	PANOPTICON	PANTALOONS
PAMPHLETEERING	PANDEMONIAC	PANGENESIS	PANOPTICONS	PANTDRESSES
PAMPHLETEERINGS	PANDEMONIACAL	PANGENETIC	PANORAMICALLY	PANTECHNICON
PAMPHLETEERS	PANDEMONIAN	PANGENETICALLY	PANPHARMACON	PANTECHNICONS
PAMPHLETING	PANDEMONIANS	PANGRAMMATIST	PANPHARMACONS	PANTHEISMS
PAMPOOTIES	PANDEMONIC	PANGRAMMATISTS	PANPSYCHISM	PANTHEISTIC
PANACHAEAS	PANDEMONIUM	PANHANDLED	PANPSYCHISMS	PANTHEISTICAL
PANAESTHESIA	PANDEMONIUMS	PANHANDLER	PANPSYCHIST	PANTHEISTICALLY
PANAESTHESIAS	PANDERESSES	PANHANDLERS	PANPSYCHISTIC	PANTHEISTS
PANAESTHETISM	PANDERINGS	PANHANDLES	PANPSYCHISTS	PANTHENOLS
PANAESTHETISMS	PANDERISMS	PANHANDLING	PANRADIOMETER	PANTHEOLOGIES
PANARITIUM	PANDERMITE	PANHARMONICON	PANRADIOMETERS	PANTHEOLOGIST
PANARITIUMS	PANDERMITES	PANHARMONICONS	PANSEXUALISM	PANTHEOLOGISTS
PANARTHRITIS	PANDICULATION	PANHELLENIC	PANSEXUALISMS	PANTHEOLOGY
PANARTHRITISES	PANDICULATIONS	PANHELLENION	PANSEXUALIST	PANTHERESS
PANATELLAS	PANDOWDIES	PANHELLENIONS	PANSEXUALISTS	PANTHERESSES
PANBROILED	PANDURATED	PANHELLENIUM	PANSEXUALITIES	PANTHERINE
PANBROILING	PANDURIFORM	PANHELLENIUMS	PANSEXUALITY	PANTHERISH
PANCHAYATS	PANEGOISMS	PANICKIEST	PANSEXUALS	PANTIHOSES
PANCHROMATIC	PANEGYRICA	PANICMONGER	PANSOPHICAL	PANTILINGS
PANCHROMATISM	PANEGYRICAL	PANICMONGERS	PANSOPHICALLY	PANTISOCRACIES
PANCHROMATISMS	PANEGYRICALLY	PANICULATE	PANSOPHIES	PANTISOCRACY
PANCOSMISM	PANEGYRICON	PANICULATED	PANSOPHISM	PANTISOCRAT
PANCOSMISMS	PANEGYRICS	PANICULATELY	PANSOPHISMS	PANTISOCRATIC
PANCRATIAN	PANEGYRIES	PANIDIOMORPHIC	PANSOPHIST	PANTISOCRATICAL
PANCRATIAST	PANEGYRISE	PANIFICATION	PANSOPHISTS	PANTISOCRATIST
PANCRATIASTS	PANEGYRISED	PANIFICATIONS	PANSPERMATIC	PANTISOCRATISTS
PANCRATIST	PANEGYRISES	PANISLAMIST	PANSPERMATISM	PANTISOCRATS
PANCRATISTS	PANEGYRISING	PANJANDARUM	PANSPERMATISMS	PANTOFFLES
PANCRATIUM	PANEGYRIST	PANJANDARUMS	PANSPERMATIST	PANTOGRAPH
PANCRATIUMS	PANEGYRISTS	PANJANDRUM	PANSPERMATISTS	PANTOGRAPHER
PANCREASES	PANEGYRIZE	PANJANDRUMS	PANSPERMIA	PANTOGRAPHERS
PANCREATECTOMY	PANEGYRIZED	PANLEUCOPENIA	PANSPERMIAS	PANTOGRAPHIC
PANCREATIC	PANEGYRIZES	PANLEUCOPENIAS	PANSPERMIC	PANTOGRAPHICAL
PANCREATIN	PANEGYRIZING	PANLEUKOPENIA	PANSPERMIES	PANTOGRAPHIES
PANCREATINS	PANELLINGS	PANLEUKOPENIAS	PANSPERMISM	PANTOGRAPHS
PANCREATITIDES	PANELLISED	PANLOGISMS	PANSPERMISMS	PANTOGRAPHY
PANCREATITIS	PANELLISTS	PANMIXISES	PANSPERMIST	PANTOMIMED
PANCREATITISES	PANELLIZED	PANNICULUS	PANSPERMISTS	PANTOMIMES
PANCREOZYMIN	PANENTHEISM	PANNICULUSES	PANTAGAMIES	PANTOMIMIC
PANCREOZYMINS	PANENTHEISMS	PANNIKELLS	PANTAGRAPH	PANTOMIMICAL
PANCYTOPENIA	PANENTHEIST	PANOMPHAEAN	PANTAGRAPHS	PANTOMIMICALLY
PANCYTOPENIAS	PANENTHEISTS	PANOPHOBIA	PANTALEONS	PANTOMIMING
PANDAEMONIUM	PANESTHESIA	PANOPHOBIAS	PANTALETTED	PANTOMIMIST

PANTOMIMISTS	PAPERHANGERS	PARABEMATIC	PARACLETES	PARAFFINIC
PANTOPHAGIES	PAPERHANGING	PARABIOSES	PARACROSTIC	PARAFFINIER
PANTOPHAGIST	PAPERHANGINGS	PARABIOSIS	PARACROSTICS	PARAFFINIEST
PANTOPHAGISTS	PAPERINESS	PARABIOTIC	PARACYANOGEN	PARAFFINING
PANTOPHAGOUS	PAPERINESSES	PARABIOTICALLY	PARACYANOGENS	PARAFFINOID
PANTOPHAGY	PAPERKNIFE	PARABLASTIC	PARADIDDLE	PARAGENESES
PANTOPHOBIA	PAPERKNIVES	PARABLASTS	PARADIDDLED	PARAGENESIA
PANTOPHOBIAS	PAPERMAKER	PARABLEPSES	PARADIDDLES	PARAGENESIAS
PANTOPRAGMATIC	PAPERMAKERS	PARABLEPSIES	PARADIDDLING	PARAGENESIS
PANTOPRAGMATICS	PAPERMAKING	PARABLEPSIS	PARADIGMATIC	PARAGENETIC
PANTOSCOPE	PAPERMAKINGS	PARABLEPSY	PARADIGMATICAL	PARAGENETICALLY
PANTOSCOPES	PAPERWARES	PARABLEPTIC	PARADISAIC	PARAGLIDED
PANTOSCOPIC	PAPERWEIGHT	PARABOLANUS	PARADISAICAL	PARAGLIDER
PANTOTHENATE	PAPERWEIGHTS	PARABOLANUSES	PARADISAICALLY	PARAGLIDERS
PANTOTHENATES	PAPERWORKS	PARABOLICAL	PARADISEAN	PARAGLIDES
PANTOTHENIC	PAPETERIES	PARABOLICALLY	PARADISIAC	PARAGLIDING
PANTOUFLES	PAPILIONACEOUS	PARABOLISATION	PARADISIACAL	PARAGLIDINGS
PANTROPICAL	PAPILLATED	PARABOLISATIONS	PARADISIACALLY	PARAGLOSSA
PANTRYMAID	PAPILLIFEROUS	PARABOLISE	PARADISIAL	PARAGLOSSAE
PANTRYMAIDS	PAPILLIFORM	PARABOLISED	PARADISIAN	PARAGLOSSAL
PANTSUITED	PAPILLITIS	PARABOLISES	PARADISICAL	PARAGLOSSATE
PANTYHOSES	PAPILLITISES	PARABOLISING	PARADOCTOR	PARAGNATHISM
PANTYWAIST	PAPILLOMAS	PARABOLIST	PARADOCTORS	PARAGNATHISMS
PANTYWAISTS	PAPILLOMATA	PARABOLISTS	PARADOXERS	PARAGNATHOUS
PANZEROTTI	PAPILLOMATOSES	PARABOLIZATION	PARADOXICAL	PARAGNOSES
PANZEROTTO	PAPILLOMATOSIS	PARABOLIZATIONS	PARADOXICALITY	PARAGNOSIS
PANZEROTTOS	PAPILLOMATOUS	PARABOLIZE	PARADOXICALLY	PARAGOGICAL
PANZOOTICS	PAPILLOMAVIRUS	PARABOLIZED	PARADOXICALNESS	PARAGOGICALLY
PAPALISING	PAPILLOTES	PARABOLIZES	PARADOXIDIAN	PARAGOGUES
PAPALIZING	PAPILLULATE	PARABOLIZING	PARADOXIES	PARAGONING
PAPAPRELATIST	PAPILLULES	PARABOLOID	PARADOXIST	PARAGONITE
PAPAPRELATISTS	PAPOVAVIRUS	PARABOLOIDAL	PARADOXISTS	PARAGONITES
PAPAVERACEOUS	PAPOVAVIRUSES	PARABOLOIDS	PARADOXOLOGIES	PARAGRAMMATIST
PAPAVERINE	PAPPARDELLE	PARABRAKES	PARADOXOLOGY	PARAGRAMMATISTS
PAPAVERINES	PAPPARDELLES	PARACASEIN	PARADOXURE	PARAGRAPHED
PAPAVEROUS	PAPRIKASES	PARACASEINS	PARADOXURES	PARAGRAPHER
PAPERBACKED	PAPRIKASHES	PARACENTESES	PARADOXURINE	PARAGRAPHERS
PAPERBACKER	PAPULATION	PARACENTESIS	PARADOXURINES	PARAGRAPHIA
PAPERBACKERS	PAPULATIONS	PARACETAMOL	PARADROPPED	PARAGRAPHIAS
PAPERBACKING	PAPULIFEROUS	PARACETAMOLS	PARADROPPING	PARAGRAPHIC
PAPERBACKS	PAPYRACEOUS	PARACHRONISM	PARAENESES	PARAGRAPHICAL
PAPERBARKS	PAPYROLOGICAL	PARACHRONISMS	PARAENESIS	PARAGRAPHICALLY
PAPERBOARD	PAPYROLOGIES	PARACHUTED	PARAENETIC	PARAGRAPHING
PAPERBOARDS	PAPYROLOGIST	PARACHUTES	PARAENETICAL	PARAGRAPHIST
PAPERBOUND	PAPYROLOGISTS	PARACHUTIC	PARAESTHESIA	PARAGRAPHISTS
PAPERBOUNDS	PAPYROLOGY	PARACHUTING	PARAESTHESIAS	PARAGRAPHS
PAPERCLIPS	PARABAPTISM	PARACHUTINGS	PARAESTHETIC	PARAHELIOTROPIC
PAPERGIRLS	PARABAPTISMS	PARACHUTIST	PARAFFINED	PARAHYDROGEN
PAPERHANGER	PARABEMATA	PARACHUTISTS	PARAFFINES	PARAHYDROGENS

PARAINFLUENZA	PARALLELIZES	PARAMASTOIDS	PARAMOUNCY	PARAPHRASERS
PARAINFLUENZAS	PARALLELIZING	PARAMATTAS	PARAMOUNTCIES	PARAPHRASES
PARAJOURNALISM	PARALLELLED	PARAMECIUM	PARAMOUNTCY	PARAPHRASING
PARAJOURNALISMS	PARALLELLING	PARAMECIUMS	PARAMOUNTLY	PARAPHRAST
PARAKEELYA	PARALLELLY	PARAMEDICAL	PARAMOUNTS	PARAPHRASTIC
PARAKEELYAS	PARALLELOGRAM	PARAMEDICALS	PARAMYLUMS	PARAPHRASTICAL
PARAKELIAS	PARALLELOGRAMS	PARAMEDICO	PARAMYXOVIRUS	PARAPHRASTS
PARAKITING	PARALLELOPIPED	PARAMEDICOS	PARAMYXOVIRUSES	PARAPHRAXES
PARAKITINGS	PARALLELOPIPEDA	PARAMEDICS	PARANEPHRIC	PARAPHRAXIA
PARALALIAS	PARALLELOPIPEDS	PARAMENSTRUA	PARANEPHROS	PARAPHRAXIAS
PARALANGUAGE	PARALLELWISE	PARAMENSTRUUM	PARANEPHROSES	PARAPHRAXIS
PARALANGUAGES	PARALOGIAS	PARAMENSTRUUMS	PARANOEICS	PARAPHRENIA
PARALDEHYDE	PARALOGIES	PARAMETERISE	PARANOIACS	PARAPHRENIAS
PARALDEHYDES	PARALOGISE	PARAMETERISED	PARANOICALLY	PARAPHYSATE
PARALEGALS	PARALOGISED	PARAMETERISES	PARANOIDAL	PARAPHYSES
PARALEIPOMENA	PARALOGISES	PARAMETERISING	PARANORMAL	PARAPHYSIS
PARALEIPOMENON	PARALOGISING	PARAMETERIZE	PARANORMALITIES	PARAPINEAL
PARALEIPSES	PARALOGISM	PARAMETERIZED	PARANORMALITY	PARAPLANNER
PARALEIPSIS	PARALOGISMS	PARAMETERIZES	PARANORMALLY	PARAPLANNERS
PARALEXIAS	PARALOGIST	PARAMETERIZING	PARANORMALS	PARAPLEGIA
PARALIMNION	PARALOGISTIC	PARAMETERS	PARANTHELIA	PARAPLEGIAS
PARALIMNIONS	PARALOGISTS	PARAMETRAL	PARANTHELION	PARAPLEGIC
PARALINGUISTIC	PARALOGIZE	PARAMETRIC	PARANTHROPUS	PARAPLEGICS
PARALINGUISTICS	PARALOGIZED	PARAMETRICAL	PARANTHROPUSES	PARAPODIAL
PARALIPOMENA	PARALOGIZES	PARAMETRICALLY	PARANYMPHS	PARAPODIUM
PARALIPOMENON	PARALOGIZING	PARAMETRISATION	PARAPARESES	PARAPOPHYSES
PARALIPSES	PARALOGUES	PARAMETRISE	PARAPARESIS	PARAPOPHYSIAL
PARALIPSIS	PARALYMPIC	PARAMETRISED	PARAPARETIC	PARAPOPHYSIS
PARALLACTIC	PARALYMPICS	PARAMETRISES	PARAPENTES	PARAPRAXES
PARALLACTICAL	PARALYSATION	PARAMETRISING	PARAPENTING	PARAPRAXIS
PARALLACTICALLY	PARALYSATIONS	PARAMETRIZATION	PARAPENTINGS	PARAPRAXISES
PARALLAXES	PARALYSERS	PARAMETRIZE	PARAPERIODIC	PARAPSYCHIC
PARALLELED	PARALYSING	PARAMETRIZED	PARAPHASIA	PARAPSYCHICAL
PARALLELEPIPED	PARALYSINGLY	PARAMETRIZES	PARAPHASIAS	PARAPSYCHISM
PARALLELEPIPEDA	PARALYTICALLY	PARAMETRIZING	PARAPHASIC	PARAPSYCHISMS
PARALLELEPIPEDS	PARALYTICS	PARAMILITARIES	PARAPHERNALIA	PARAPSYCHOLOGY
PARALLELING	PARALYZATION	PARAMILITARY	PARAPHILIA	PARAPSYCHOSES
PARALLELINGS	PARALYZATIONS	PARAMNESIA	PARAPHILIAC	PARAPSYCHOSIS
PARALLELISE	PARALYZERS	PARAMNESIAS	PARAPHILIACS	PARAQUADRATE
PARALLELISED	PARALYZING	PARAMOECIA	PARAPHILIAS	PARAQUADRATES
PARALLELISES	PARALYZINGLY	PARAMOECIUM	PARAPHIMOSES	PARAQUITOS
PARALLELISING	PARAMAECIA	PARAMORPHIC	PARAPHIMOSIS	PARARHYMES
PARALLELISM	PARAMAECIUM	PARAMORPHINE	PARAPHONIA	PARAROSANILINE
PARALLELISMS	PARAMAGNET	PARAMORPHINES	PARAPHONIAS	PARAROSANILINES
PARALLELIST	PARAMAGNETIC	PARAMORPHISM	PARAPHONIC	PARARTHRIA
PARALLELISTIC	PARAMAGNETISM	PARAMORPHISMS	PARAPHRASABLE	PARARTHRIAS
PARALLELISTS	PARAMAGNETISMS	PARAMORPHOUS	PARAPHRASE	PARASAILED
PARALLELIZE	PARAMAGNETS	PARAMORPHS	PARAPHRASED	PARASAILING
PARALLELIZED	PARAMASTOID	PARAMOUNCIES	PARAPHRASER	PARASAILINGS

PARASCENDER	PARASITOSIS	PARBREAKED	PARENTHESISES	PARLEMENTS
PARASCENDERS	PARASKIING	PARBREAKING	PARENTHESISING	PARLEYVOOED
PARASCENDING	PARASKIINGS	PARBUCKLED	PARENTHESIZE	PARLEYVOOING
PARASCENDINGS	PARASOMNIA	PARBUCKLES	PARENTHESIZED	PARLEYVOOS
PARASCENIA	PARASOMNIAS	PARBUCKLING	PARENTHESIZES	PARLIAMENT
PARASCENIUM	PARASPHENOID	PARCELLING	PARENTHESIZING	PARLIAMENTARIAN
PARASCEVES	PARASPHENOIDS	PARCELWISE	PARENTHETIC	PARLIAMENTARILY
PARASCIENCE	PARASTATAL	PARCENARIES	PARENTHETICAL	PARLIAMENTARISM
PARASCIENCES	PARASTATALS	PARCHEDNESS	PARENTHETICALLY	PARLIAMENTARY
PARASELENAE	PARASTICHIES	PARCHEDNESSES	PARENTHOOD	PARLIAMENTING
PARASELENE	PARASTICHOUS	PARCHEESIS	PARENTHOODS	PARLIAMENTINGS
PARASELENIC	PARASTICHY	PARCHMENTIER	PARENTINGS	PARLIAMENTS
PARASEXUAL	PARASUICIDE	PARCHMENTIEST	PARENTLESS	PARLOURMAID
PARASEXUALITIES	PARASUICIDES	PARCHMENTISE	PARESTHESIA	PARLOURMAIDS
PARASEXUALITY	PARASYMBIONT	PARCHMENTISED	PARESTHESIAS	PARLOUSNESS
PARASHIOTH	PARASYMBIONTS	PARCHMENTISES	PARESTHETIC	PARLOUSNESSES
PARASITAEMIA	PARASYMBIOSES	PARCHMENTISING	PARFLECHES	PARMACITIE
PARASITAEMIAS	PARASYMBIOSIS	PARCHMENTIZE	PARFLESHES	PARMACITIES
PARASITEMIA	PARASYMBIOTIC	PARCHMENTIZED	PARFOCALISE	PARMIGIANA
PARASITEMIAS	PARASYMPATHETIC	PARCHMENTIZES	PARFOCALISED	PARMIGIANO
PARASITICAL	PARASYNAPSES	PARCHMENTIZING	PARFOCALISES	PARMIGIANOS
PARASITICALLY	PARASYNAPSIS	PARCHMENTS	PARFOCALISING	PAROCCIPITAL
PARASITICALNESS	PARASYNAPTIC	PARCHMENTY	PARFOCALITIES	PAROCCIPITALS
PARASITICIDAL	PARASYNTHESES	PARCIMONIES	PARFOCALITY	PAROCHIALISE
PARASITICIDE	PARASYNTHESIS	PARDALISES	PARFOCALIZE	PAROCHIALISED
PARASITICIDES	PARASYNTHETA	PARDALOTES	PARFOCALIZED	PAROCHIALISES
PARASITISATION	PARASYNTHETIC	PARDONABLE	PARFOCALIZES	PAROCHIALISING
PARASITISATIONS	PARASYNTHETON	PARDONABLENESS	PARFOCALIZING	PAROCHIALISM
PARASITISE	PARATACTIC	PARDONABLY	PARGASITES	PAROCHIALISMS
PARASITISED	PARATACTICAL	PARDONINGS	PARGETINGS	PAROCHIALITIES
PARASITISES	PARATACTICALLY	PARDONLESS	PARGETTERS	PAROCHIALITY
PARASITISING	PARATANIWHA	PAREGORICS	PARGETTING	PAROCHIALIZE
PARASITISM	PARATANIWHAS	PAREIDOLIA	PARGETTINGS	PAROCHIALIZED
PARASITISMS	PARATHESES	PAREIDOLIAS	PARGYLINES	PAROCHIALIZES
PARASITIZATION	PARATHESIS	PARENCEPHALA	PARHELIACAL	PAROCHIALIZING
PARASITIZATIONS	PARATHIONS	PARENCEPHALON	PARHELIONS	PAROCHIALLY
PARASITIZE	PARATHORMONE	PARENCHYMA	PARHYPATES	PAROCHINES
PARASITIZED	PARATHORMONES	PARENCHYMAL	PARIPINNATE	PARODISTIC
PARASITIZES	PARATHYROID	PARENCHYMAS	PARISCHANE	PAROECIOUS
PARASITIZING	PARATHYROIDS	PARENCHYMATA	PARISCHANES	PAROECISMS
PARASITOID	PARATROOPER	PARENCHYMATOUS	PARISCHANS	PAROEMIACS
PARASITOIDS	PARATROOPERS	PARENTAGES	PARISHIONER	PAROEMIOGRAPHER
PARASITOLOGIC	PARATROOPS	PARENTALLY	PARISHIONERS	PAROEMIOGRAPHY
PARASITOLOGICAL	PARATUNGSTIC	PARENTERAL	PARISYLLABIC	PAROEMIOLOGIES
PARASITOLOGIES	PARATYPHOID	PARENTERALLY	PARKINSONIAN	PAROEMIOLOGY
PARASITOLOGIST	PARATYPHOIDS	PARENTHESES	PARKINSONIANS	PARONOMASIA
PARASITOLOGISTS	PARAWALKER	PARENTHESIS	PARKINSONISM	PARONOMASIAS
PARASITOLOGY	PARAWALKERS	PARENTHESISE	PARKINSONISMS	PARONOMASIES
PARASITOSES	PARBOILING	PARENTHESISED	PARKLEAVES	PARONOMASTIC

PARONOMASTICAL	PARTHENOGENESIS	PARTICULARISE	PARTURIENCIES	PASSEMEASURES
PARONOMASY	PARTHENOGENETIC	PARTICULARISED	PARTURIENCY	PASSEMENTED
PARONYCHIA	PARTHENOSPORE	PARTICULARISER	PARTURIENT	PASSEMENTERIE
PARONYCHIAL	PARTHENOSPORES	PARTICULARISERS	PARTURIENTS	PASSEMENTERIES
PARONYCHIAS	PARTIALISE	PARTICULARISES	PARTURIFACIENT	PASSEMENTING
PARONYMIES	PARTIALISED	PARTICULARISING	PARTURIFACIENTS	PASSEMENTS
PARONYMOUS	PARTIALISES	PARTICULARISM	PARTURITION	PASSENGERS
PARONYMOUSLY	PARTIALISING	PARTICULARISMS	PARTURITIONS	PASSEPIEDS
PAROTIDITIC	PARTIALISM	PARTICULARIST	PARTYGOERS	PASSERIFORM
PAROTIDITIS	PARTIALISMS	PARTICULARISTIC	PARURETICS	PASSERINES
PAROTIDITISES	PARTIALIST	PARTICULARISTS	PARVANIMITIES	PASSIBILITIES
PAROTITIDES	PARTIALISTS	PARTICULARITIES	PARVANIMITY	PASSIBILITY
PAROTITISES	PARTIALITIES	PARTICULARITY	PARVIFOLIATE	PASSIBLENESS
PAROXETINE	PARTIALITY	PARTICULARIZE	PARVOLINES	PASSIBLENESSES
PAROXETINES	PARTIALIZE	PARTICULARIZED	PARVOVIRUS	PASSIFLORA
PAROXYSMAL	PARTIALIZED	PARTICULARIZER	PARVOVIRUSES	PASSIFLORACEOUS
PAROXYSMALLY	PARTIALIZES	PARTICULARIZERS	PASIGRAPHIC	PASSIFLORAS
PAROXYSMIC	PARTIALIZING	PARTICULARIZES	PASIGRAPHICAL	PASSIMETER
PAROXYTONE	PARTIALLED	PARTICULARIZING	PASIGRAPHIES	PASSIMETERS
PAROXYTONES	PARTIALLING	PARTICULARLY	PASIGRAPHY	PASSIONALS
PAROXYTONIC	PARTIALNESS	PARTICULARNESS	PASODOBLES	PASSIONARIES
PARQUETING	PARTIALNESSES	PARTICULARS	PASQUEFLOWER	PASSIONARY
PARQUETRIES	PARTIBILITIES	PARTICULATE	PASQUEFLOWERS	PASSIONATE
PARQUETTED	PARTIBILITY	PARTICULATES	PASQUILANT	PASSIONATED
PARQUETTING	PARTICIPABLE	PARTISANLY	PASQUILANTS	PASSIONATELY
PARRAKEETS	PARTICIPANT	PARTISANSHIP	PASQUILERS	PASSIONATENESS
PARRAMATTA	PARTICIPANTLY	PARTISANSHIPS	PASQUILLED	PASSIONATES
PARRAMATTAS	PARTICIPANTS	PARTITIONED	PASQUILLING	PASSIONATING
PARRHESIAS	PARTICIPATE	PARTITIONER	PASQUINADE	PASSIONFLOWER
PARRICIDAL	PARTICIPATED	PARTITIONERS	PASQUINADED	PASSIONFLOWERS
PARRICIDES	PARTICIPATES	PARTITIONING	PASQUINADER	PASSIONING
PARRITCHES	PARTICIPATING	PARTITIONIST	PASQUINADERS	PASSIONLESS
PARROCKING	PARTICIPATION	PARTITIONISTS	PASQUINADES	PASSIONLESSLY
PARROQUETS	PARTICIPATIONAL	PARTITIONMENT	PASQUINADING	PASSIONLESSNESS
PARROTFISH	PARTICIPATIONS	PARTITIONMENTS	PASSABLENESS	PASSIVATED
PARROTFISHES	PARTICIPATIVE	PARTITIONS	PASSABLENESSES	PASSIVATES
PARROTIEST	PARTICIPATOR	PARTITIVELY	PASSACAGLIA	PASSIVATING
PARROTRIES	PARTICIPATORS	PARTITIVES	PASSACAGLIAS	PASSIVATION
PARSIMONIES	PARTICIPATORY	PARTITURAS	PASSAGEWAY	PASSIVATIONS
PARSIMONIOUS	PARTICIPIAL	PARTIZANLY	PASSAGEWAYS	PASSIVENESS
PARSIMONIOUSLY	PARTICIPIALLY	PARTIZANSHIP	PASSAGEWORK	PASSIVENESSES
PARSONAGES	PARTICIPIALS	PARTIZANSHIPS	PASSAGEWORKS	PASSIVISMS
PARSONICAL	PARTICIPLE	PARTNERING	PASSALONGS	PASSIVISTS
PARTAKINGS	PARTICIPLES	PARTNERINGS	PASSAMENTED	PASSIVITIES
PARTHENOCARPIC	PARTICLEBOARD	PARTNERLESS	PASSAMENTING	PASSMENTED
PARTHENOCARPIES	PARTICLEBOARDS	PARTNERSHIP	PASSAMENTS	PASSMENTING
PARTHENOCARPOUS	PARTICOLORED	PARTNERSHIPS	PASSAMEZZO	PASSPHRASE
PARTHENOCARPY	PARTICOLOURED	PARTRIDGEBERRY	PASSAMEZZOS	PASSPHRASES
PARTHENOGENESES	PARTICULAR	PARTRIDGES	PASSEMEASURE	PASSPORTED

PASSPORTING	PASTOURELLES	PATHLESSNESS	PATRIALISE	PATRIMONIALLY
PASTEBOARD	PASTRYCOOK	PATHLESSNESSES	PATRIALISED	PATRIMONIES
PASTEBOARDS	PASTRYCOOKS	PATHOBIOLOGIES	PATRIALISES	PATRIOTICALLY
PASTEDOWNS	PASTURABLE	PATHOBIOLOGY	PATRIALISING	PATRIOTISM
PASTELISTS	PASTURAGES	PATHOGENES	PATRIALISM	PATRIOTISMS
PASTELLIST	PASTURELAND	PATHOGENESES	PATRIALISMS	PATRISTICAL
PASTELLISTS	PASTURELANDS	PATHOGENESIS	PATRIALITIES	PATRISTICALLY
PASTEURELLA	PASTURELESS	PATHOGENETIC	PATRIALITY	PATRISTICISM
PASTEURELLAE	PATAPHYSICS	PATHOGENIC	PATRIALIZATION	PATRISTICISMS
PASTEURELLAS	PATCHBOARD	PATHOGENICITIES	PATRIALIZATIONS	PATRISTICS
PASTEURISATION	PATCHBOARDS	PATHOGENICITY	PATRIALIZE	PATROCLINAL
PASTEURISATIONS	PATCHCOCKE	PATHOGENIES	PATRIALIZED	PATROCLINIC
PASTEURISE	PATCHCOCKES	PATHOGENOUS	PATRIALIZES	PATROCLINIES
PASTEURISED	PATCHERIES	PATHOGNOMIES	PATRIALIZING	PATROCLINOUS
PASTEURISER	PATCHINESS	PATHOGNOMONIC	PATRIARCHAL	PATROCLINY
PASTEURISERS	PATCHINESSES	PATHOGNOMY	PATRIARCHALISM	PATROLLERS
PASTEURISES	PATCHOCKES	PATHOGRAPHIES	PATRIARCHALISMS	PATROLLING
PASTEURISING	PATCHOULIES	PATHOGRAPHY	PATRIARCHALLY	PATROLOGICAL
PASTEURISM	PATCHOULIS	PATHOLOGIC	PATRIARCHATE	PATROLOGIES
PASTEURISMS	PATCHWORKED	PATHOLOGICAL	PATRIARCHATES	PATROLOGIST
PASTEURIZATION	PATCHWORKING	PATHOLOGICALLY	PATRIARCHIES	PATROLOGISTS
PASTEURIZATIONS	PATCHWORKS	PATHOLOGIES	PATRIARCHISM	PATROLWOMAN
PASTEURIZE	PATELLECTOMIES	PATHOLOGISE	PATRIARCHISMS	PATROLWOMEN
PASTEURIZED	PATELLECTOMY	PATHOLOGISED	PATRIARCHS	PATRONAGED
PASTEURIZER	PATELLIFORM	PATHOLOGISES	PATRIARCHY	PATRONAGES
PASTEURIZERS	PATELLOFEMORAL	PATHOLOGISING	PATRIATING	PATRONAGING
PASTEURIZES	PATENTABILITIES	PATHOLOGIST	PATRIATION	PATRONESSES
PASTEURIZING	PATENTABILITY	PATHOLOGISTS	PATRIATIONS	PATRONISATION
PASTICCIOS	PATENTABLE	PATHOLOGIZE	PATRICIANLY	PATRONISATIONS
PASTICHEUR	PATERCOVES	PATHOLOGIZED	PATRICIANS	PATRONISED
PASTICHEURS	PATEREROES	PATHOLOGIZES	PATRICIATE	PATRONISER
PASTINESSES	PATERFAMILIAS	PATHOLOGIZING	PATRICIATES	PATRONISERS
PASTITSIOS	PATERFAMILIASES	PATHOPHOBIA	PATRICIDAL	PATRONISES
PASTNESSES	PATERNALISM	PATHOPHOBIAS	PATRICIDES	PATRONISING
PASTORALES	PATERNALISMS	PATHOPHYSIOLOGY	PATRICLINIC	PATRONISINGLY
PASTORALISM	PATERNALIST	PATIBULARY	PATRICLINOUS	PATRONIZATION
PASTORALISMS	PATERNALISTIC	PATIENTEST	PATRIFOCAL	PATRONIZATIONS
PASTORALIST	PATERNALISTS	PATIENTING	PATRIFOCALITIES	PATRONIZED
PASTORALISTS	PATERNALLY	PATINATING	PATRIFOCALITY	PATRONIZER
PASTORALLY	PATERNITIES	PATINATION	PATRILINEAGE	PATRONIZERS
PASTORALNESS	PATERNOSTER	PATINATIONS	PATRILINEAGES	PATRONIZES
PASTORALNESSES	PATERNOSTERS	PATINISING	PATRILINEAL	PATRONIZING
PASTORATES	PATHBREAKING	PATINIZING	PATRILINEALLY	PATRONIZINGLY
PASTORIUMS	PATHETICAL	PATISSERIE	PATRILINEAR	PATRONLESS
PASTORLIER	PATHETICALLY	PATISSERIES	PATRILINEARLY	PATRONLIER
PASTORLIEST	PATHFINDER	PATISSIERS	PATRILINIES	PATRONLIEST
PASTORSHIP	PATHFINDERS	PATRESFAMILIAS	PATRILOCAL	PATRONYMIC
PASTORSHIPS	PATHFINDING	PATRIALISATION	PATRILOCALLY	PATRONYMICS
PASTOURELLE	PATHFINDINGS	PATRIALISATIONS	PATRIMONIAL	PATROONSHIP

PATROONSHIPS PEACEABLENESSES PEASOUPERS PEDAGOGICAL PEDESTALLING
PATTERNING PEACEFULLER PEBBLEDASH PEDAGOGICALLY PEDESTRIAN
PATTERNINGS PEACEFULLEST PEBBLEDASHED PEDAGOGICS PEDESTRIANISE
PATTERNLESS PEACEFULLY PEBBLEDASHES PEDAGOGIES PEDESTRIANISED
PATTRESSES PEACEFULNESS PEBBLEDASHING PEDAGOGISM PEDESTRIANISES
PATULOUSLY PEACEFULNESSES PEBBLEWEAVE PEDAGOGISMS PEDESTRIANISING
PATULOUSNESS PEACEKEEPER PEBBLEWEAVES PEDAGOGUED PEDESTRIANISM
PATULOUSNESSES PEACEKEEPERS PECCABILITIES PEDAGOGUERIES PEDESTRIANISMS
PAUCILOQUENT PEACEKEEPING PECCABILITY PEDAGOGUERY PEDESTRIANIZE
PAUGHTIEST PEACEKEEPINGS PECCADILLO PEDAGOGUES PEDESTRIANIZED
PAULOWNIAS PEACELESSNESS PECCADILLOES PEDAGOGUING PEDESTRIANIZES
PAUNCHIEST PEACELESSNESSES PECCADILLOS PEDAGOGUISH PEDESTRIANIZING
PAUNCHINESS PEACEMAKER PECCANCIES PEDAGOGUISHNESS PEDESTRIANS
PAUNCHINESSES PEACEMAKERS PECKISHNESS PEDAGOGUISM PEDETENTOUS
PAUPERDOMS PEACEMAKING PECKISHNESSES PEDAGOGUISMS PEDIATRICIAN
PAUPERESSES PEACEMAKINGS PECTINACEOUS PEDALBOATS PEDIATRICIANS
PAUPERISATION PEACETIMES PECTINATED PEDALLINGS PEDIATRICS
PAUPERISATIONS PEACHBLOWS PECTINATELY PEDANTICAL PEDIATRIST
PAUPERISED PEACHERINO PECTINATION PEDANTICALLY PEDIATRISTS
PAUPERISES PEACHERINOS PECTINATIONS PEDANTICISE PEDICELLARIA
PAUPERISING PEACHINESS PECTINESTERASE PEDANTICISED PEDICELLARIAE
PAUPERISMS PEACHINESSES PECTINESTERASES PEDANTICISES PEDICELLATE
PAUPERIZATION PEACOCKERIES PECTINEUSES PEDANTICISING PEDICULATE
PAUPERIZATIONS PEACOCKERY PECTISABLE PEDANTICISM PEDICULATED
PAUPERIZED PEACOCKIER PECTISATION PEDANTICISMS PEDICULATES
PAUPERIZES PEACOCKIEST PECTISATIONS PEDANTICIZE PEDICULATION
PAUPERIZING PEACOCKING PECTIZABLE PEDANTICIZED PEDICULATIONS
PAUPIETTES PEACOCKISH PECTIZATION PEDANTICIZES PEDICULOSES
PAUSEFULLY PEAKEDNESS PECTIZATIONS PEDANTICIZING PEDICULOSIS
PAUSELESSLY PEAKEDNESSES PECTOLITES PEDANTISED PEDICULOUS
PAVEMENTED PEAKINESSES PECTORALLY PEDANTISES PEDICURING
PAVEMENTING PEANUTTIER PECTORILOQUIES PEDANTISING PEDICURIST
PAVILIONED PEANUTTIEST PECTORILOQUY PEDANTISMS PEDICURISTS
PAVILIONING PEARLASHES PECULATING PEDANTIZED PEDIMENTAL
PAVONAZZOS PEARLESCENCE PECULATION PEDANTIZES PEDIMENTED
PAWKINESSES PEARLESCENCES PECULATIONS PEDANTIZING PEDIPALPUS
PAWNBROKER PEARLESCENT PECULATORS PEDANTOCRACIES PEDOGENESES
PAWNBROKERS PEARLINESS PECULIARISE PEDANTOCRACY PEDOGENESIS
PAWNBROKING PEARLINESSES PECULIARISED PEDANTOCRAT PEDOGENETIC
PAWNBROKINGS PEARLWARES PECULIARISES PEDANTOCRATIC PEDOLOGICAL
PAWNTICKET PEARLWORTS PECULIARISING PEDANTOCRATS PEDOLOGIES
PAWNTICKETS PEARMONGER PECULIARITIES PEDANTRIES PEDOLOGIST
PAYCHEQUES PEARMONGERS PECULIARITY PEDDLERIES PEDOLOGISTS
PAYMASTERS PEARTNESSES PECULIARIZE PEDERASTIC PEDOMETERS
PAYNIMRIES PEASANTIER PECULIARIZED PEDERASTIES PEDOPHILES
PAYSAGISTS PEASANTIEST PECULIARIZES PEDEREROES PEDOPHILIA
PAYWALLING PEASANTRIES PECULIARIZING PEDESTALED PEDOPHILIAC
PEABERRIES PEASHOOTER PECULIARLY PEDESTALING PEDOPHILIACS
PEACEABLENESS PEASHOOTERS PECUNIARILY PEDESTALLED PEDOPHILIAS

P

PEDOPHILIC	PELLUCIDITY	PENELOPISED	PENICILLIN	PENNYWINKLES
PEDOPHILICS	PELLUCIDLY	PENELOPISES	PENICILLINASE	PENNYWORTH
PEDUNCULAR	PELLUCIDNESS	PENELOPISING	PENICILLINASES	PENNYWORTHS
PEDUNCULATE	PELLUCIDNESSES	PENELOPIZE	PENICILLINS	PENNYWORTS
PEDUNCULATED	PELMANISMS	PENELOPIZED	PENICILLIUM	PENOLOGICAL
PEDUNCULATION	PELOLOGIES	PENELOPIZES	PENICILLIUMS	PENOLOGICALLY
PEDUNCULATIONS	PELOTHERAPIES	PENELOPIZING	PENICILLUS	PENOLOGIES
PEELGARLIC	PELOTHERAPY	PENEPLAINS	PENINSULAR	PENOLOGIST
PEELGARLICS	PELTATIONS	PENEPLANATION	PENINSULARITIES	PENOLOGISTS
PEERLESSLY	PELTMONGER	PENEPLANATIONS	PENINSULARITY	PENONCELLE
PEERLESSNESS	PELTMONGERS	PENEPLANES	PENINSULAS	PENONCELLES
PEERLESSNESSES	PELVIMETER	PENETRABILITIES	PENINSULATE	PENPUSHERS
PEEVISHNESS	PELVIMETERS	PENETRABILITY	PENINSULATED	PENPUSHING
PEEVISHNESSES	PELVIMETRIES	PENETRABLE	PENINSULATES	PENPUSHINGS
PEGMATITES	PELVIMETRY	PENETRABLENESS	PENINSULATING	PENSEROSOS
PEGMATITIC	PELYCOSAUR	PENETRABLY	PENISTONES	PENSIEROSO
PEIRASTICALLY	PELYCOSAURS	PENETRALIA	PENITENCES	PENSILENESS
PEJORATING	PEMPHIGOID	PENETRALIAN	PENITENCIES	PENSILENESSES
PEJORATION	PEMPHIGOIDS	PENETRANCE	PENITENTIAL	PENSILITIES
PEJORATIONS	PEMPHIGOUS	PENETRANCES	PENITENTIALLY	PENSILITY
PEJORATIVE	PEMPHIGUSES	PENETRANCIES	PENITENTIALS	PENSIONABLE
PEJORATIVELY	PENALISATION	PENETRANCY	PENITENTIARIES	PENSIONARIES
PEJORATIVES	PENALISATIONS	PENETRANTS	PENITENTIARY	PENSIONARY
PELARGONIC	PENALISING	PENETRATED	PENITENTLY	PENSIONEER
PELARGONIUM	PENALITIES	PENETRATES	PENMANSHIP	PENSIONERS
PELARGONIUMS	PENALIZATION	PENETRATING	PENMANSHIPS	PENSIONING
PELECYPODS	PENALIZATIONS	PENETRATINGLY	PENNACEOUS	PENSIONLESS
PELLAGRINS	PENALIZING	PENETRATION	PENNALISMS	PENSIONNAT
PELLAGROUS	PENANNULAR	PENETRATIONS	PENNATULACEOUS	PENSIONNATS
PELLETIFIED	PENCILINGS	PENETRATIVE	PENNATULAE	PENSIVENESS
PELLETIFIES	PENCILLERS	PENETRATIVELY	PENNATULAS	PENSIVENESSES
PELLETIFYING	PENCILLING	PENETRATIVENESS	PENNILESSLY	PENSTEMONS
PELLETISATION	PENCILLINGS	PENETRATOR	PENNILESSNESS	PENTABARBITAL
PELLETISATIONS	PENDENCIES	PENETRATORS	PENNILESSNESSES	PENTABARBITALS
PELLETISED	PENDENTIVE	PENETROMETER	PENNILLION	PENTACHORD
PELLETISER	PENDENTIVES	PENETROMETERS	PENNINITES	PENTACHORDS
PELLETISERS	PENDICLERS	PENFRIENDS	PENNONCELLE	PENTACRINOID
PELLETISES	PENDRAGONS	PENGUINERIES	PENNONCELLES	PENTACRINOIDS
PELLETISING	PENDRAGONSHIP	PENGUINERY	PENNONCELS	PENTACTINAL
PELLETIZATION	PENDRAGONSHIPS	PENGUINRIES	PENNYCRESS	PENTACYCLIC
PELLETIZATIONS	PENDULATED	PENHOLDERS	PENNYCRESSES	PENTADACTYL
PELLETIZED	PENDULATES	PENICILLAMINE	PENNYLANDS	PENTADACTYLE
PELLETIZER	PENDULATING	PENICILLAMINES	PENNYROYAL	PENTADACTYLES
PELLETIZERS	PENDULOSITIES	PENICILLATE	PENNYROYALS	PENTADACTYLIC
PELLETIZES	PENDULOSITY	PENICILLATELY	PENNYWEIGHT	PENTADACTYLIES
PELLETIZING	PENDULOUSLY	PENICILLATION	PENNYWEIGHTS	PENTADACTYLISM
PELLICULAR	PENDULOUSNESS	PENICILLATIONS	PENNYWHISTLE	PENTADACTYLISMS
PELLITORIES	PENDULOUSNESSES	PENICILLIA	PENNYWHISTLES	PENTADACTYLOUS
PELLUCIDITIES	PENELOPISE	PENICILLIFORM	PENNYWINKLE	PENTADACTYLS
				PENTADACTYLY

PENTADELPHOUS	PENTASTYLE	PENURIOUSNESSES	PEPTONISATIONS	PERCEPTIVITY
PENTAGONAL	PENTASTYLES	PEOPLEHOOD	PEPTONISED	PERCEPTUAL
PENTAGONALLY	PENTASYLLABIC	PEOPLEHOODS	PEPTONISER	PERCEPTUALLY
PENTAGONALS	PENTATEUCHAL	PEOPLELESS	PEPTONISERS	PERCHERIES
PENTAGRAMS	PENTATHLETE	PEPEROMIAS	PEPTONISES	PERCHERONS
PENTAGRAPH	PENTATHLETES	PEPPERBOXES	PEPTONISING	PERCHLORATE
PENTAGRAPHS	PENTATHLON	PEPPERCORN	PEPTONIZATION	PERCHLORATES
PENTAGYNIAN	PENTATHLONS	PEPPERCORNIER	PEPTONIZATIONS	PERCHLORIC
PENTAGYNOUS	PENTATHLUM	PEPPERCORNIEST	PEPTONIZED	PERCHLORIDE
PENTAHEDRA	PENTATHLUMS	PEPPERCORNS	PEPTONIZER	PERCHLORIDES
PENTAHEDRAL	PENTATOMIC	PEPPERCORNY	PEPTONIZERS	PERCHLOROETHENE
PENTAHEDRON	PENTATONIC	PEPPERGRASS	PEPTONIZES	PERCIFORMS
PENTAHEDRONS	PENTAVALENCE	PEPPERGRASSES	PEPTONIZING	PERCIPIENCE
PENTAHYDRATE	PENTAVALENCES	PEPPERIDGE	PERACIDITIES	PERCIPIENCES
PENTAHYDRATES	PENTAVALENCIES	PEPPERIDGES	PERACIDITY	PERCIPIENCIES
PENTALOGIES	PENTAVALENCY	PEPPERIEST	PERADVENTURE	PERCIPIENCY
PENTALPHAS	PENTAVALENT	PEPPERINESS	PERADVENTURES	PERCIPIENT
PENTAMERIES	PENTAZOCINE	PEPPERINESSES	PERAEOPODS	PERCIPIENTLY
PENTAMERISM	PENTAZOCINES	PEPPERINGS	PERAMBULATE	PERCIPIENTS
PENTAMERISMS	PENTECONTER	PEPPERMILL	PERAMBULATED	PERCOCTING
PENTAMEROUS	PENTECONTERS	PEPPERMILLS	PERAMBULATES	PERCOIDEAN
PENTAMETER	PENTETERIC	PEPPERMINT	PERAMBULATING	PERCOIDEANS
PENTAMETERS	PENTHEMIMER	PEPPERMINTIER	PERAMBULATION	PERCOLABLE
PENTAMIDINE	PENTHEMIMERAL	PEPPERMINTIEST	PERAMBULATIONS	PERCOLATED
PENTAMIDINES	PENTHEMIMERS	PEPPERMINTS	PERAMBULATOR	PERCOLATES
PENTANDRIAN	PENTHOUSED	PEPPERMINTY	PERAMBULATORS	PERCOLATING
PENTANDROUS	PENTHOUSES	PEPPERONIS	PERAMBULATORY	PERCOLATION
PENTANGLES	PENTHOUSING	PEPPERTREE	PERBORATES	PERCOLATIONS
PENTANGULAR	PENTIMENTI	PEPPERTREES	PERCALINES	PERCOLATIVE
PENTAPEPTIDE	PENTIMENTO	PEPPERWORT	PERCEIVABILITY	PERCOLATOR
PENTAPEPTIDES	PENTLANDITE	PEPPERWORTS	PERCEIVABLE	PERCOLATORS
PENTAPLOID	PENTLANDITES	PEPPINESSES	PERCEIVABLY	PERCURRENT
PENTAPLOIDIES	PENTOBARBITAL	PEPSINATED	PERCEIVERS	PERCURSORY
PENTAPLOIDS	PENTOBARBITALS	PEPSINATES	PERCEIVING	PERCUSSANT
PENTAPLOIDY	PENTOBARBITONE	PEPSINATING	PERCEIVINGS	PERCUSSING
PENTAPODIC	PENTOBARBITONES	PEPSINOGEN	PERCENTAGE	PERCUSSION
PENTAPODIES	PENTOSANES	PEPSINOGENS	PERCENTAGES	PERCUSSIONAL
PENTAPOLIS	PENTOSIDES	PEPTALKING	PERCENTILE	PERCUSSIONIST
PENTAPOLISES	PENTOXIDES	PEPTICITIES	PERCENTILES	PERCUSSIONISTS
PENTAPOLITAN	PENTSTEMON	PEPTIDASES	PERCEPTIBILITY	PERCUSSIONS
PENTAPRISM	PENTSTEMONS	PEPTIDOGLYCAN	PERCEPTIBLE	PERCUSSIVE
PENTAPRISMS	PENTYLENES	PEPTIDOGLYCANS	PERCEPTIBLY	PERCUSSIVELY
PENTAQUARK	PENULTIMAS	PEPTISABLE	PERCEPTION	PERCUSSIVENESS
PENTAQUARKS	PENULTIMATE	PEPTISATION	PERCEPTIONAL	PERCUSSORS
PENTARCHICAL	PENULTIMATELY	PEPTISATIONS	PERCEPTIONS	PERCUTANEOUS
PENTARCHIES	PENULTIMATES	PEPTIZABLE	PERCEPTIVE	PERCUTANEOUSLY
PENTASTICH	PENUMBROUS	PEPTIZATION	PERCEPTIVELY	PERCUTIENT
PENTASTICHOUS	PENURIOUSLY	PEPTIZATIONS	PERCEPTIVENESS	PERCUTIENTS
PENTASTICHS	PENURIOUSNESS	PEPTONISATION	PERCEPTIVITIES	PERDENDOSI

PERDITIONABLE	PERFECTIBILISMS	PERFORATIONS	PERICENTRAL	PERIGENESES
PERDITIONS	PERFECTIBILIST	PERFORATIVE	PERICENTRE	PERIGENESIS
PERDUELLION	PERFECTIBILISTS	PERFORATOR	PERICENTRES	PERIGLACIAL
PERDUELLIONS	PERFECTIBILITY	PERFORATORS	PERICENTRIC	PERIGONIAL
PERDURABILITIES	PERFECTIBLE	PERFORATORY	PERICHAETIA	PERIGONIUM
PERDURABILITY	PERFECTING	PERFORATUS	PERICHAETIAL	PERIGYNIES
PERDURABLE	PERFECTION	PERFORATUSES	PERICHAETIUM	PERIGYNOUS
PERDURABLY	PERFECTIONATE	PERFORMABILITY	PERICHONDRAL	PERIHELIAL
PERDURANCE	PERFECTIONATED	PERFORMABLE	PERICHONDRIA	PERIHELION
PERDURANCES	PERFECTIONATES	PERFORMANCE	PERICHONDRIAL	PERIHEPATIC
PERDURATION	PERFECTIONATING	PERFORMANCES	PERICHONDRIUM	PERIHEPATITIS
PERDURATIONS	PERFECTIONISM	PERFORMATIVE	PERICHORESES	PERIHEPATITISES
PEREGRINATE	PERFECTIONISMS	PERFORMATIVELY	PERICHORESIS	PERIKARYAL
PEREGRINATED	PERFECTIONIST	PERFORMATIVES	PERICHYLOUS	PERIKARYON
PEREGRINATES	PERFECTIONISTIC	PERFORMATORY	PERICLASES	PERILOUSLY
PEREGRINATING	PERFECTIONISTS	PERFORMERS	PERICLASTIC	PERILOUSNESS
PEREGRINATION	PERFECTIONS	PERFORMING	PERICLINAL	PERILOUSNESSES
PEREGRINATIONS	PERFECTIVE	PERFORMINGS	PERICLINES	PERILYMPHS
PEREGRINATOR	PERFECTIVELY	PERFUMELESS	PERICLITATE	PERIMENOPAUSAL
PEREGRINATORS	PERFECTIVENESS	PERFUMERIES	PERICLITATED	PERIMENOPAUSE
PEREGRINATORY	PERFECTIVES	PERFUMIERS	PERICLITATES	PERIMENOPAUSES
PEREGRINES	PERFECTIVITIES	PERFUMIEST	PERICLITATING	PERIMETERS
PEREGRINITIES	PERFECTIVITY	PERFUNCTORILY	PERICRANIA	PERIMETRAL
PEREGRINITY	PERFECTNESS	PERFUNCTORINESS	PERICRANIAL	PERIMETRIC
PEREIOPODS	PERFECTNESSES	PERFUNCTORY	PERICRANIUM	PERIMETRICAL
PEREMPTORILY	PERFECTORS	PERFUSATES	PERICRANIUMS	PERIMETRICALLY
PEREMPTORINESS	PERFERVIDITIES	PERFUSIONIST	PERICULOUS	PERIMETRIES
PEREMPTORY	PERFERVIDITY	PERFUSIONISTS	PERICYCLES	PERIMORPHIC
PERENNATED	PERFERVIDLY	PERFUSIONS	PERICYCLIC	PERIMORPHISM
PERENNATES	PERFERVIDNESS	PERGAMENEOUS	PERICYNTHIA	PERIMORPHISMS
PERENNATING	PERFERVIDNESSES	PERGAMENTACEOUS	PERICYNTHION	PERIMORPHOUS
PERENNATION	PERFERVORS	PERGUNNAHS	PERICYNTHIONS	PERIMORPHS
PERENNATIONS	PERFERVOUR	PERIASTRON	PERIDERMAL	PERIMYSIUM
PERENNIALITIES	PERFERVOURS	PERIASTRONS	PERIDERMIC	PERINAEUMS
PERENNIALITY	PERFICIENT	PERIBLASTS	PERIDESMIA	PERINATALLY
PERENNIALLY	PERFICIENTS	PERICARDIA	PERIDESMIUM	PERINEPHRIA
PERENNIALS	PERFIDIOUS	PERICARDIAC	PERIDINIAN	PERINEPHRIC
PERENNIBRANCH	PERFIDIOUSLY	PERICARDIAL	PERIDINIANS	PERINEPHRITIS
PERENNIBRANCHS	PERFIDIOUSNESS	PERICARDIAN	PERIDINIUM	PERINEPHRITISES
PERENNITIES	PERFLUOROCARBON	PERICARDITIC	PERIDINIUMS	PERINEPHRIUM
PERESTROIKA	PERFOLIATE	PERICARDITIDES	PERIDOTITE	PERINEURAL
PERESTROIKAS	PERFOLIATION	PERICARDITIS	PERIDOTITES	PERINEURIA
PERFECTATION	PERFOLIATIONS	PERICARDITISES	PERIDOTITIC	PERINEURIAL
PERFECTATIONS	PERFORABLE	PERICARDIUM	PERIDROMES	PERINEURITIC
PERFECTERS	PERFORANSES	PERICARDIUMS	PERIEGESES	PERINEURITIS
PERFECTEST	PERFORATED	PERICARPIAL	PERIEGESIS	PERINEURITISES
PERFECTIBILIAN	PERFORATES	PERICARPIC	PERIGASTRIC	PERINEURIUM
PERFECTIBILIANS	PERFORATING	PERICENTER	PERIGASTRITIS	PERIODATES
PERFECTIBILISM	PERFORATION	PERICENTERS	PERIGASTRITISES	PERIODICAL

PERIODICALIST	PERIPETIAN	PERISSODACTYL	PERIWIGGED	PERMEATION
PERIODICALISTS	PERIPETIAS	PERISSODACTYLE	PERIWIGGING	PERMEATIONS
PERIODICALLY	PERIPETIES	PERISSODACTYLES	PERIWINKLE	PERMEATIVE
PERIODICALS	PERIPHERAL	PERISSODACTYLIC	PERIWINKLES	PERMEATORS
PERIODICITIES	PERIPHERALITIES	PERISSODACTYLS	PERJINKETY	PERMETHRIN
PERIODICITY	PERIPHERALITY	PERISSOLOGIES	PERJINKITIES	PERMETHRINS
PERIODIDES	PERIPHERALLY	PERISSOLOGY	PERJINKITY	PERMILLAGE
PERIODISATION	PERIPHERALS	PERISSOSYLLABIC	PERJURIOUS	PERMILLAGES
PERIODISATIONS	PERIPHERIC	PERISTALITH	PERJURIOUSLY	PERMISSIBILITY
PERIODISED	PERIPHERICAL	PERISTALITHS	PERKINESSES	PERMISSIBLE
PERIODISES	PERIPHERIES	PERISTALSES	PERLEMOENS	PERMISSIBLENESS
PERIODISING	PERIPHONIC	PERISTALSIS	PERLOCUTION	PERMISSIBLY
PERIODIZATION	PERIPHRASE	PERISTALTIC	PERLOCUTIONARY	PERMISSION
PERIODIZATIONS	PERIPHRASED	PERISTALTICALLY	PERLOCUTIONS	PERMISSIONS
PERIODIZED	PERIPHRASES	PERISTERITE	PERLUSTRATE	PERMISSIVE
PERIODIZES	PERIPHRASING	PERISTERITES	PERLUSTRATED	PERMISSIVELY
PERIODIZING	PERIPHRASIS	PERISTERONIC	PERLUSTRATES	PERMISSIVENESS
PERIODONTAL	PERIPHRASTIC	PERISTOMAL	PERLUSTRATING	PERMITTANCE
PERIODONTALLY	PERIPHRASTICAL	PERISTOMATIC	PERLUSTRATION	PERMITTANCES
PERIODONTIA	PERIPHYTIC	PERISTOMES	PERLUSTRATIONS	PERMITTEES
PERIODONTIAS	PERIPHYTON	PERISTOMIAL	PERMABEARS	PERMITTERS
PERIODONTIC	PERIPHYTONS	PERISTREPHIC	PERMABULLS	PERMITTING
PERIODONTICALLY	PERIPLASMS	PERISTYLAR	PERMACULTURE	PERMITTIVITIES
PERIODONTICS	PERIPLASTS	PERISTYLES	PERMACULTURES	PERMITTIVITY
PERIODONTIST	PERIPLUSES	PERITECTIC	PERMADEATH	PERMUTABILITIES
PERIODONTISTS	PERIPROCTS	PERITECTICS	PERMADEATHS	PERMUTABILITY
PERIODONTITIS	PERIPTERAL	PERITHECIA	PERMAFROST	PERMUTABLE
PERIODONTITISES	PERIPTERIES	PERITHECIAL	PERMAFROSTS	PERMUTABLENESS
PERIODONTOLOGY	PERISARCAL	PERITHECIUM	PERMALINKS	PERMUTABLY
PERIONYCHIA	PERISARCOUS	PERITONAEA	PERMALLOYS	PERMUTATED
PERIONYCHIUM	PERISCIANS	PERITONAEAL	PERMANENCE	PERMUTATES
PERIOSTEAL	PERISCOPES	PERITONAEUM	PERMANENCES	PERMUTATING
PERIOSTEUM	PERISCOPIC	PERITONAEUMS	PERMANENCIES	PERMUTATION
PERIOSTITIC	PERISCOPICALLY	PERITONEAL	PERMANENCY	PERMUTATIONAL
PERIOSTITIDES	PERISELENIA	PERITONEALLY	PERMANENTLY	PERMUTATIONS
PERIOSTITIS	PERISELENIUM	PERITONEOSCOPY	PERMANENTNESS	PERNANCIES
PERIOSTITISES	PERISHABILITIES	PERITONEUM	PERMANENTNESSES	PERNICIOUS
PERIOSTRACUM	PERISHABILITY	PERITONEUMS	PERMANENTS	PERNICIOUSLY
PERIOSTRACUMS	PERISHABLE	PERITONITIC	PERMANGANATE	PERNICIOUSNESS
PERIPATETIC	PERISHABLENESS	PERITONITIS	PERMANGANATES	PERNICKETIER
PERIPATETICAL	PERISHABLES	PERITONITISES	PERMANGANIC	PERNICKETIEST
PERIPATETICALLY	PERISHABLY	PERITRACKS	PERMEABILITIES	PERNICKETINESS
PERIPATETICISM	PERISHINGLY	PERITRICHA	PERMEABILITY	PERNICKETY
PERIPATETICISMS	PERISPERMAL	PERITRICHOUS	PERMEABLENESS	PERNOCTATE
PERIPATETICS	PERISPERMIC	PERITRICHOUSLY	PERMEABLENESSES	PERNOCTATED
PERIPATUSES	PERISPERMS	PERITRICHS	PERMEAMETER	PERNOCTATES
PERIPETEIA	PERISPOMENA	PERITYPHLITIS	PERMEAMETERS	PERNOCTATING
PERIPETEIAN	PERISPOMENON	PERITYPHLITISES	PERMEANCES	PERNOCTATION
PERIPETEIAS	PERISPOMENONS	PERIVITELLINE	PERMEATING	PERNOCTATIONS

PERONEUSES	PERPETUANCES	PERSEVERATES	PERSONALITIES	PERSPICUITIES
PERORATING	PERPETUATE	PERSEVERATING	PERSONALITY	PERSPICUITY
PERORATION	PERPETUATED	PERSEVERATION	PERSONALIZATION	PERSPICUOUS
PERORATIONAL	PERPETUATES	PERSEVERATIONS	PERSONALIZE	PERSPICUOUSLY
PERORATIONS	PERPETUATING	PERSEVERATIVE	PERSONALIZED	PERSPICUOUSNESS
PERORATORS	PERPETUATION	PERSEVERATOR	PERSONALIZES	PERSPIRABLE
PEROVSKIAS	PERPETUATIONS	PERSEVERATORS	PERSONALIZING	PERSPIRATE
PEROVSKITE	PERPETUATOR	PERSEVERED	PERSONALLY	PERSPIRATED
PEROVSKITES	PERPETUATORS	PERSEVERES	PERSONALTIES	PERSPIRATES
PEROXIDASE	PERPETUITIES	PERSEVERING	PERSONALTY	PERSPIRATING
PEROXIDASES	PERPETUITY	PERSEVERINGLY	PERSONATED	PERSPIRATION
PEROXIDATION	PERPHENAZINE	PERSICARIA	PERSONATES	PERSPIRATIONS
PEROXIDATIONS	PERPHENAZINES	PERSICARIAS	PERSONATING	PERSPIRATORY
PEROXIDING	PERPLEXEDLY	PERSIENNES	PERSONATINGS	PERSPIRIER
PEROXIDISE	PERPLEXEDNESS	PERSIFLAGE	PERSONATION	PERSPIRIEST
PEROXIDISED	PERPLEXEDNESSES	PERSIFLAGES	PERSONATIONS	PERSPIRING
PEROXIDISES	PERPLEXERS	PERSIFLEUR	PERSONATIVE	PERSPIRINGLY
PEROXIDISING	PERPLEXING	PERSIFLEURS	PERSONATOR	PERSTRINGE
PEROXIDIZE	PERPLEXINGLY	PERSIMMONS	PERSONATORS	PERSTRINGED
PEROXIDIZED	PERPLEXITIES	PERSISTENCE	PERSONHOOD	PERSTRINGES
PEROXIDIZES	PERPLEXITY	PERSISTENCES	PERSONHOODS	PERSTRINGING
PEROXIDIZING	PERQUISITE	PERSISTENCIES	PERSONIFIABLE	PERSUADABILITY
PEROXISOMAL	PERQUISITES	PERSISTENCY	PERSONIFICATION	PERSUADABLE
PEROXISOME	PERQUISITION	PERSISTENT	PERSONIFIED	PERSUADERS
PEROXISOMES	PERQUISITIONS	PERSISTENTLY	PERSONIFIER	PERSUADING
PEROXYSULPHURIC	PERQUISITOR	PERSISTENTS	PERSONIFIERS	PERSUASIBILITY
PERPENDICULAR	PERQUISITORS	PERSISTERS	PERSONIFIES	PERSUASIBLE
PERPENDICULARLY	PERRUQUIER	PERSISTING	PERSONIFYING	PERSUASION
PERPENDICULARS	PERRUQUIERS	PERSISTINGLY	PERSONISED	PERSUASIONS
PERPENDING	PERSCRUTATION	PERSISTIVE	PERSONISES	PERSUASIVE
PERPETRABLE	PERSCRUTATIONS	PERSNICKETIER	PERSONISING	PERSUASIVELY
PERPETRATE	PERSECUTED	PERSNICKETIEST	PERSONIZED	PERSUASIVENESS
PERPETRATED	PERSECUTEE	PERSNICKETINESS	PERSONIZES	PERSUASIVES
PERPETRATES	PERSECUTEES	PERSNICKETY	PERSONIZING	PERSUASORY
PERPETRATING	PERSECUTES	PERSONABLE	PERSONNELS	PERSULFATE
PERPETRATION	PERSECUTING	PERSONABLENESS	PERSONPOWER	PERSULFATES
PERPETRATIONS	PERSECUTION	PERSONABLY	PERSONPOWERS	PERSULFURIC
PERPETRATOR	PERSECUTIONS	PERSONAGES	PERSPECTIVAL	PERSULPHATE
PERPETRATORS	PERSECUTIVE	PERSONALIA	PERSPECTIVE	PERSULPHATES
PERPETUABLE	PERSECUTOR	PERSONALISATION	PERSPECTIVELY	PERSULPHURIC
PERPETUALISM	PERSECUTORS	PERSONALISE	PERSPECTIVES	PERSWADING
PERPETUALISMS	PERSECUTORY	PERSONALISED	PERSPECTIVISM	PERTAINING
PERPETUALIST	PERSEITIES	PERSONALISES	PERSPECTIVISMS	PERTINACIOUS
PERPETUALISTS	PERSELINES	PERSONALISING	PERSPECTIVIST	PERTINACIOUSLY
PERPETUALITIES	PERSEVERANCE	PERSONALISM	PERSPECTIVISTS	PERTINACITIES
PERPETUALITY	PERSEVERANCES	PERSONALISMS	PERSPICACIOUS	PERTINACITY
PERPETUALLY	PERSEVERANT	PERSONALIST	PERSPICACIOUSLY	PERTINENCE
PERPETUALS	PERSEVERATE	PERSONALISTIC	PERSPICACITIES	PERTINENCES
PERPETUANCE	PERSEVERATED	PERSONALISTS	PERSPICACITY	PERTINENCIES

PERTINENCY	PERVICACIOUS	PETITENESS	PETROGRAPHICAL	PETULANCES
PERTINENTLY	PERVICACITIES	PETITENESSES	PETROGRAPHIES	PETULANCIES
PERTINENTS	PERVICACITY	PETITIONARY	PETROGRAPHY	PETULANTLY
PERTNESSES	PERVIOUSLY	PETITIONED	PETROLAGES	PEWHOLDERS
PERTURBABLE	PERVIOUSNESS	PETITIONER	PETROLATUM	PEWTERIEST
PERTURBABLY	PERVIOUSNESSES	PETITIONERS	PETROLATUMS	PHACOLITES
PERTURBANCE	PESCATARIAN	PETITIONING	PETROLEOUS	PHACOLITHS
PERTURBANCES	PESCATARIANS	PETITIONINGS	PETROLEUMS	PHAELONION
PERTURBANT	PESCETARIAN	PETITIONIST	PETROLEURS	PHAELONIONS
PERTURBANTS	PESCETARIANS	PETITIONISTS	PETROLEUSE	PHAENOGAMIC
PERTURBATE	PESHMERGAS	PETNAPINGS	PETROLEUSES	PHAENOGAMOUS
PERTURBATED	PESKINESSES	PETNAPPERS	PETROLHEAD	PHAENOGAMS
PERTURBATES	PESSIMISMS	PETNAPPING	PETROLHEADS	PHAENOLOGIES
PERTURBATING	PESSIMISTIC	PETNAPPINGS	PETROLIFEROUS	PHAENOLOGY
PERTURBATION	PESSIMISTICAL	PETRICHORS	PETROLLING	PHAENOMENA
PERTURBATIONAL	PESSIMISTICALLY	PETRIFACTION	PETROLOGIC	PHAENOMENON
PERTURBATIONS	PESSIMISTS	PETRIFACTIONS	PETROLOGICAL	PHAENOTYPE
PERTURBATIVE	PESTERINGLY	PETRIFACTIVE	PETROLOGICALLY	PHAENOTYPED
PERTURBATOR	PESTERMENT	PETRIFICATION	PETROLOGIES	PHAENOTYPES
PERTURBATORIES	PESTERMENTS	PETRIFICATIONS	PETROLOGIST	PHAENOTYPING
PERTURBATORS	PESTHOUSES	PETRIFIERS	PETROLOGISTS	PHAEOMELANIN
PERTURBATORY	PESTICIDAL	PETRIFYING	PETROMONEY	PHAEOMELANINS
PERTURBEDLY	PESTICIDES	PETRISSAGE	PETROMONEYS	PHAGEDAENA
PERTURBERS	PESTIFEROUS	PETRISSAGES	PETROMONIES	PHAGEDAENAS
PERTURBING	PESTIFEROUSLY	PETROCHEMICAL	PETRONELLA	PHAGEDAENIC
PERTURBINGLY	PESTIFEROUSNESS	PETROCHEMICALLY	PETRONELLAS	PHAGEDENAS
PERTUSIONS	PESTILENCE	PETROCHEMICALS	PETROPHYSICAL	PHAGEDENIC
PERTUSSISES	PESTILENCES	PETROCHEMIST	PETROPHYSICIST	PHAGOCYTES
PERVASIONS	PESTILENTIAL	PETROCHEMISTRY	PETROPHYSICISTS	PHAGOCYTIC
PERVASIVELY	PESTILENTIALLY	PETROCHEMISTS	PETROPHYSICS	PHAGOCYTICAL
PERVASIVENESS	PESTILENTLY	PETROCURRENCIES	PETROPOUNDS	PHAGOCYTISE
PERVASIVENESSES	PESTOLOGICAL	PETROCURRENCY	PETROSTATE	PHAGOCYTISED
PERVERSELY	PESTOLOGIES	PETRODOLLAR	PETROSTATES	PHAGOCYTISES
PERVERSENESS	PESTOLOGIST	PETRODOLLARS	PETTEDNESS	PHAGOCYTISING
PERVERSENESSES	PESTOLOGISTS	PETRODROME	PETTEDNESSES	PHAGOCYTISM
PERVERSEST	PETAHERTZES	PETRODROMES	PETTICHAPS	PHAGOCYTISMS
PERVERSION	PETALIFEROUS	PETROGENESES	PETTICHAPSES	PHAGOCYTIZE
PERVERSIONS	PETALODIES	PETROGENESIS	PETTICOATED	PHAGOCYTIZED
PERVERSITIES	PETALOMANIA	PETROGENETIC	PETTICOATS	PHAGOCYTIZES
PERVERSITY	PETALOMANIAS	PETROGENIES	PETTIFOGGED	PHAGOCYTIZING
PERVERSIVE	PETAMETERS	PETROGLYPH	PETTIFOGGER	PHAGOCYTOSE
PERVERTEDLY	PETAMETRES	PETROGLYPHIC	PETTIFOGGERIES	PHAGOCYTOSED
PERVERTEDNESS	PETAURINES	PETROGLYPHIES	PETTIFOGGERS	PHAGOCYTOSES
PERVERTEDNESSES	PETAURISTS	PETROGLYPHS	PETTIFOGGERY	PHAGOCYTOSING
PERVERTERS	PETCHARIES	PETROGLYPHY	PETTIFOGGING	PHAGOCYTOSIS
PERVERTIBLE	PETERSHAMS	PETROGRAMS	PETTIFOGGINGS	PHAGOCYTOTIC
PERVERTING	PETHIDINES	PETROGRAPHER	PETTINESSES	PHAGOMANIA
PERVIATING	PETIOLATED	PETROGRAPHERS	PETTISHNESS	PHAGOMANIAC
PERVICACIES	PETIOLULES	PETROGRAPHIC	PETTISHNESSES	PHAGOMANIACS

PHAGOMANIAS	PHANTASMAGORIES	PHARMACOPEIA	PHENACAINE	PHENOMENALISM
PHAGOPHOBIA	PHANTASMAGORY	PHARMACOPEIAL	PHENACAINES	PHENOMENALISMS
PHAGOPHOBIAS	PHANTASMAL	PHARMACOPEIAS	PHENACETIN	PHENOMENALIST
PHAGOSOMES	PHANTASMALIAN	PHARMACOPOEIA	PHENACETINS	PHENOMENALISTIC
PHALANGEAL	PHANTASMALITIES	PHARMACOPOEIAL	PHENACITES	PHENOMENALISTS
PHALANGERS	PHANTASMALITY	PHARMACOPOEIAN	PHENAKISMS	PHENOMENALITIES
PHALANGIDS	PHANTASMALLY	PHARMACOPOEIANS	PHENAKISTOSCOPE	PHENOMENALITY
PHALANGIST	PHANTASMATA	PHARMACOPOEIAS	PHENAKITES	PHENOMENALIZE
PHALANGISTS	PHANTASMIC	PHARMACOPOEIC	PHENANTHRENE	PHENOMENALIZED
PHALANSTERIAN	PHANTASMICAL	PHARMACOPOEIST	PHENANTHRENES	PHENOMENALIZES
PHALANSTERIANS	PHANTASMICALLY	PHARMACOPOEISTS	PHENARSAZINE	PHENOMENALIZING
PHALANSTERIES	PHANTASTIC	PHARMACOPOLIST	PHENARSAZINES	PHENOMENALLY
PHALANSTERISM	PHANTASTICS	PHARMACOPOLISTS	PHENAZINES	PHENOMENAS
PHALANSTERISMS	PHANTASTRIES	PHARMACOTHERAPY	PHENCYCLIDINE	PHENOMENISE
PHALANSTERIST	PHANTASTRY	PHARYNGALS	PHENCYCLIDINES	PHENOMENISED
PHALANSTERISTS	PHANTASYING	PHARYNGEAL	PHENETICIST	PHENOMENISES
PHALANSTERY	PHANTOMATIC	PHARYNGEALS	PHENETICISTS	PHENOMENISING
PHALAROPES	PHANTOMISH	PHARYNGITIC	PHENETIDINE	PHENOMENISM
PHALLICALLY	PHANTOMLIKE	PHARYNGITIDES	PHENETIDINES	PHENOMENISMS
PHALLICISM	PHANTOSMES	PHARYNGITIS	PHENETOLES	PHENOMENIST
PHALLICISMS	PHARISAICAL	PHARYNGITISES	PHENFORMIN	PHENOMENISTS
PHALLICIST	PHARISAICALLY	PHARYNGOLOGICAL	PHENFORMINS	PHENOMENIZE
PHALLICISTS	PHARISAICALNESS	PHARYNGOLOGIES	PHENGOPHOBIA	PHENOMENIZED
PHALLOCENTRIC	PHARISAISM	PHARYNGOLOGIST	PHENGOPHOBIAS	PHENOMENIZES
PHALLOCENTRISM	PHARISAISMS	PHARYNGOLOGISTS	PHENMETRAZINE	PHENOMENIZING
PHALLOCENTRISMS	PHARISEEISM	PHARYNGOLOGY	PHENMETRAZINES	PHENOMENOLOGIES
PHALLOCRAT	PHARISEEISMS	PHARYNGOSCOPE	PHENOBARBITAL	PHENOMENOLOGIST
PHALLOCRATIC	PHARMACEUTIC	PHARYNGOSCOPES	PHENOBARBITALS	PHENOMENOLOGY
PHALLOCRATS	PHARMACEUTICAL	PHARYNGOSCOPIC	PHENOBARBITONE	PHENOMENON
PHALLOIDIN	PHARMACEUTICALS	PHARYNGOSCOPIES	PHENOBARBITONES	PHENOMENONS
PHALLOIDINS	PHARMACEUTICS	PHARYNGOSCOPY	PHENOBARBS	PHENOTHIAZINE
PHANEROGAM	PHARMACEUTIST	PHARYNGOTOMIES	PHENOCOPIES	PHENOTHIAZINES
PHANEROGAMIC	PHARMACEUTISTS	PHARYNGOTOMY	PHENOCRYST	PHENOTYPED
PHANEROGAMOUS	PHARMACIES	PHASCOGALE	PHENOCRYSTIC	PHENOTYPES
PHANEROGAMS	PHARMACIST	PHASCOGALES	PHENOCRYSTS	PHENOTYPIC
PHANEROPHYTE	PHARMACISTS	PHASEDOWNS	PHENOLATED	PHENOTYPICAL
PHANEROPHYTES	PHARMACODYNAMIC	PHASEOLINS	PHENOLATES	PHENOTYPICALLY
PHANSIGARS	PHARMACOGENOMIC	PHATICALLY	PHENOLATING	PHENOTYPING
PHANTASIAST	PHARMACOGNOSIES	PHEASANTRIES	PHENOLOGICAL	PHENOXIDES
PHANTASIASTS	PHARMACOGNOSIST	PHEASANTRY	PHENOLOGICALLY	PHENTOLAMINE
PHANTASIED	PHARMACOGNOSTIC	PHELLODERM	PHENOLOGIES	PHENTOLAMINES
PHANTASIES	PHARMACOGNOSY	PHELLODERMAL	PHENOLOGIST	PHENYLALANIN
PHANTASIME	PHARMACOKINETIC	PHELLODERMS	PHENOLOGISTS	PHENYLALANINE
PHANTASIMES	PHARMACOLOGIC	PHELLOGENETIC	PHENOLPHTHALEIN	PHENYLALANINES
PHANTASIMS	PHARMACOLOGICAL	PHELLOGENIC	PHENOMENAL	PHENYLALANINS
PHANTASMAGORIA	PHARMACOLOGIES	PHELLOGENS	PHENOMENALISE	PHENYLAMINE
PHANTASMAGORIAL	PHARMACOLOGIST	PHELLOPLASTIC	PHENOMENALISED	PHENYLAMINES
PHANTASMAGORIAS	PHARMACOLOGISTS	PHELLOPLASTICS	PHENOMENALISES	PHENYLBUTAZONE
PHANTASMAGORIC	PHARMACOLOGY	PHELONIONS	PHENOMENALISING	PHENYLBUTAZONES

PHENYLENES	PHILIPPINAS	PHILOSOPHERS	PHLEBOTOMIES	PHONASTHENIAS
PHENYLEPHRINE	PHILIPPINE	PHILOSOPHES	PHLEBOTOMISE	PHONATHONS
PHENYLEPHRINES	PHILIPPINES	PHILOSOPHESS	PHLEBOTOMISED	PHONATIONS
PHENYLKETONURIA	PHILISTIAS	PHILOSOPHESSES	PHLEBOTOMISES	PHONAUTOGRAPH
PHENYLKETONURIC	PHILISTINE	PHILOSOPHIC	PHLEBOTOMISING	PHONAUTOGRAPHIC
PHENYLMETHYL	PHILISTINES	PHILOSOPHICAL	PHLEBOTOMIST	PHONAUTOGRAPHS
PHENYLMETHYLS	PHILISTINISM	PHILOSOPHICALLY	PHLEBOTOMISTS	PHONECARDS
PHENYLTHIOUREA	PHILISTINISMS	PHILOSOPHIES	PHLEBOTOMIZE	PHONEMATIC
PHENYLTHIOUREAS	PHILLABEGS	PHILOSOPHISE	PHLEBOTOMIZED	PHONEMATICALLY
PHENYTOINS	PHILLIBEGS	PHILOSOPHISED	PHLEBOTOMIZES	PHONEMICALLY
PHEROMONAL	PHILLIPSITE	PHILOSOPHISER	PHLEBOTOMIZING	PHONEMICISATION
PHEROMONES	PHILLIPSITES	PHILOSOPHISERS	PHLEBOTOMY	PHONEMICISE
PHIALIFORM	PHILLUMENIES	PHILOSOPHISES	PHLEGMAGOGIC	PHONEMICISED
PHILADELPHUS	PHILLUMENIST	PHILOSOPHISING	PHLEGMAGOGICS	PHONEMICISES
PHILADELPHUSES	PHILLUMENISTS	PHILOSOPHISINGS	PHLEGMAGOGUE	PHONEMICISING
PHILANDERED	PHILLUMENY	PHILOSOPHISM	PHLEGMAGOGUES	PHONEMICIST
PHILANDERER	PHILODENDRA	PHILOSOPHISMS	PHLEGMASIA	PHONEMICISTS
PHILANDERERS	PHILODENDRON	PHILOSOPHIST	PHLEGMASIAS	PHONEMICIZATION
PHILANDERING	PHILODENDRONS	PHILOSOPHISTIC	PHLEGMATIC	PHONEMICIZE
PHILANDERINGS	PHILOGYNIES	PHILOSOPHISTS	PHLEGMATICAL	PHONEMICIZED
PHILANDERS	PHILOGYNIST	PHILOSOPHIZE	PHLEGMATICALLY	PHONEMICIZES
PHILANTHROPE	PHILOGYNISTS	PHILOSOPHIZED	PHLEGMATICNESS	PHONEMICIZING
PHILANTHROPES	PHILOGYNOUS	PHILOSOPHIZER	PHLEGMIEST	PHONENDOSCOPE
PHILANTHROPIC	PHILOLOGER	PHILOSOPHIZERS	PHLEGMONIC	PHONENDOSCOPES
PHILANTHROPICAL	PHILOLOGERS	PHILOSOPHIZES	PHLEGMONOID	PHONETICAL
PHILANTHROPIES	PHILOLOGIAN	PHILOSOPHIZING	PHLEGMONOUS	PHONETICALLY
PHILANTHROPIST	PHILOLOGIANS	PHILOSOPHIZINGS	PHLOGISTIC	PHONETICIAN
PHILANTHROPISTS	PHILOLOGIC	PHILOSOPHY	PHLOGISTICATE	PHONETICIANS
PHILANTHROPOID	PHILOLOGICAL	PHILOXENIA	PHLOGISTICATED	PHONETICISATION
PHILANTHROPOIDS	PHILOLOGICALLY	PHILOXENIAS	PHLOGISTICATES	PHONETICISE
PHILANTHROPY	PHILOLOGIES	PHILTERING	PHLOGISTICATING	PHONETICISED
PHILATELIC	PHILOLOGIST	PHISNOMIES	PHLOGISTON	PHONETICISES
PHILATELICALLY	PHILOLOGISTS	PHLEBECTOMIES	PHLOGISTONS	PHONETICISING
PHILATELIES	PHILOLOGUE	PHLEBECTOMY	PHLOGOPITE	PHONETICISM
PHILATELIST	PHILOLOGUES	PHLEBITIDES	PHLOGOPITES	PHONETICISMS
PHILATELISTS	PHILOMATHIC	PHLEBITISES	PHLORIZINS	PHONETICIST
PHILAVERIES	PHILOMATHICAL	PHLEBOGRAM	PHLYCTAENA	PHONETICISTS
PHILHARMONIC	PHILOMATHIES	PHLEBOGRAMS	PHLYCTAENAE	PHONETICIZATION
PHILHARMONICS	PHILOMATHS	PHLEBOGRAPHIC	PHLYCTENAE	PHONETICIZE
PHILHELLENE	PHILOMATHY	PHLEBOGRAPHIES	PHOCOMELIA	PHONETICIZED
PHILHELLENES	PHILOMELAS	PHLEBOGRAPHY	PHOCOMELIAS	PHONETICIZES
PHILHELLENIC	PHILOPENAS	PHLEBOLITE	PHOCOMELIC	PHONETICIZING
PHILHELLENISM	PHILOPOENA	PHLEBOLITES	PHOCOMELIES	PHONETISATION
PHILHELLENISMS	PHILOPOENAS	PHLEBOLOGIES	PHOENIXISM	PHONETISATIONS
PHILHELLENIST	PHILOSOPHASTER	PHLEBOLOGY	PHOENIXISMS	PHONETISED
PHILHELLENISTS	PHILOSOPHASTERS	PHLEBOSCLEROSES	PHOENIXLIKE	PHONETISES
PHILHORSES	PHILOSOPHE	PHLEBOSCLEROSIS	PHOLIDOSES	PHONETISING
PHILIPPICS	PHILOSOPHER	PHLEBOTOMIC	PHOLIDOSIS	PHONETISMS
PHILIPPINA	PHILOSOPHERESS	PHLEBOTOMICAL	PHONASTHENIA	PHONETISTS

P

PHONETIZATION	PHONOTACTICS	PHOSPHOLIPID	PHOSPHORYLATING	PHOTOCOMPOSING
PHONETIZATIONS	PHONOTYPED	PHOSPHOLIPIDS	PHOSPHORYLATION	PHOTOCONDUCTING
PHONETIZED	PHONOTYPER	PHOSPHONIC	PHOSPHORYLATIVE	PHOTOCONDUCTION
PHONETIZES	PHONOTYPERS	PHOSPHONIUM	PHOSPHORYLS	PHOTOCONDUCTIVE
PHONETIZING	PHONOTYPES	PHOSPHONIUMS	PHOSPHURET	PHOTOCONDUCTOR
PHONEYNESS	PHONOTYPIC	PHOSPHOPROTEIN	PHOSPHURETS	PHOTOCONDUCTORS
PHONEYNESSES	PHONOTYPICAL	PHOSPHOPROTEINS	PHOSPHURETTED	PHOTOCOPIABLE
PHONICALLY	PHONOTYPIES	PHOSPHORATE	PHOTICALLY	PHOTOCOPIED
PHONINESSES	PHONOTYPING	PHOSPHORATED	PHOTOACTINIC	PHOTOCOPIER
PHONMETERS	PHONOTYPIST	PHOSPHORATES	PHOTOACTIVE	PHOTOCOPIERS
PHONOCAMPTIC	PHONOTYPISTS	PHOSPHORATING	PHOTOAUTOTROPH	PHOTOCOPIES
PHONOCAMPTICS	PHORMINGES	PHOSPHORES	PHOTOAUTOTROPHS	PHOTOCOPYING
PHONOCARDIOGRAM	PHOSGENITE	PHOSPHORESCE	PHOTOBATHIC	PHOTOCOPYINGS
PHONOCHEMISTRY	PHOSGENITES	PHOSPHORESCED	PHOTOBIOLOGIC	PHOTOCURRENT
PHONOFIDDLE	PHOSPHATASE	PHOSPHORESCENCE	PHOTOBIOLOGICAL	PHOTOCURRENTS
PHONOFIDDLES	PHOSPHATASES	PHOSPHORESCENT	PHOTOBIOLOGIES	PHOTODEGRADABLE
PHONOGRAMIC	PHOSPHATED	PHOSPHORESCES	PHOTOBIOLOGIST	PHOTODETECTOR
PHONOGRAMICALLY	PHOSPHATES	PHOSPHORESCING	PHOTOBIOLOGISTS	PHOTODETECTORS
PHONOGRAMMIC	PHOSPHATIC	PHOSPHORET	PHOTOBIOLOGY	PHOTODIODE
PHONOGRAMS	PHOSPHATIDE	PHOSPHORETS	PHOTOBLOGGED	PHOTODIODES
PHONOGRAPH	PHOSPHATIDES	PHOSPHORETTED	PHOTOBLOGGING	PHOTODISKS
PHONOGRAPHER	PHOSPHATIDIC	PHOSPHORIC	PHOTOBLOGS	PHOTODISSOCIATE
PHONOGRAPHERS	PHOSPHATIDYL	PHOSPHORISE	PHOTOBOMBED	PHOTODUPLICATE
PHONOGRAPHIC	PHOSPHATIDYLS	PHOSPHORISED	PHOTOBOMBING	PHOTODUPLICATED
PHONOGRAPHIES	PHOSPHATING	PHOSPHORISES	PHOTOBOMBS	PHOTODUPLICATES
PHONOGRAPHIST	PHOSPHATISATION	PHOSPHORISING	PHOTOCALLS	PHOTODYNAMIC
PHONOGRAPHISTS	PHOSPHATISE	PHOSPHORISM	PHOTOCARDS	PHOTODYNAMICS
PHONOGRAPHS	PHOSPHATISED	PHOSPHORISMS	PHOTOCATALYSES	PHOTOELASTIC
PHONOGRAPHY	PHOSPHATISES	PHOSPHORITE	PHOTOCATALYSIS	PHOTOELASTICITY
PHONOLITES	PHOSPHATISING	PHOSPHORITES	PHOTOCATALYTIC	PHOTOELECTRIC
PHONOLITIC	PHOSPHATIZATION	PHOSPHORITIC	PHOTOCATHODE	PHOTOELECTRICAL
PHONOLOGIC	PHOSPHATIZE	PHOSPHORIZE	PHOTOCATHODES	PHOTOELECTRODE
PHONOLOGICAL	PHOSPHATIZED	PHOSPHORIZED	PHOTOCELLS	PHOTOELECTRODES
PHONOLOGICALLY	PHOSPHATIZES	PHOSPHORIZES	PHOTOCHEMICAL	PHOTOELECTRON
PHONOLOGIES	PHOSPHATIZING	PHOSPHORIZING	PHOTOCHEMICALLY	PHOTOELECTRONIC
PHONOLOGIST	PHOSPHATURIA	PHOSPHOROLYSES	PHOTOCHEMIST	PHOTOELECTRONS
PHONOLOGISTS	PHOSPHATURIAS	PHOSPHOROLYSIS	PHOTOCHEMISTRY	PHOTOEMISSION
PHONOMETER	PHOSPHATURIC	PHOSPHOROLYTIC	PHOTOCHEMISTS	PHOTOEMISSIONS
PHONOMETERS	PHOSPHENES	PHOSPHOROSCOPE	PHOTOCHROMIC	PHOTOEMISSIVE
PHONOMETRIC	PHOSPHIDES	PHOSPHOROSCOPES	PHOTOCHROMICS	PHOTOENGRAVE
PHONOMETRICAL	PHOSPHINES	PHOSPHOROUS	PHOTOCHROMIES	PHOTOENGRAVED
PHONOPHOBIA	PHOSPHITES	PHOSPHORUS	PHOTOCHROMISM	PHOTOENGRAVER
PHONOPHOBIAS	PHOSPHOCREATIN	PHOSPHORUSES	PHOTOCHROMISMS	PHOTOENGRAVERS
PHONOPHORE	PHOSPHOCREATINE	PHOSPHORYL	PHOTOCHROMY	PHOTOENGRAVES
PHONOPHORES	PHOSPHOCREATINS	PHOSPHORYLASE	PHOTOCOMPOSE	PHOTOENGRAVING
PHONOPORES	PHOSPHOKINASE	PHOSPHORYLASES	PHOTOCOMPOSED	PHOTOENGRAVINGS
PHONOSCOPE	PHOSPHOKINASES	PHOSPHORYLATE	PHOTOCOMPOSER	PHOTOEXCITATION
PHONOSCOPES	PHOSPHOLIPASE	PHOSPHORYLATED	PHOTOCOMPOSERS	PHOTOEXCITED
PHONOTACTIC	PHOSPHOLIPASES	PHOSPHORYLATES	PHOTOCOMPOSES	PHOTOFINISHER

P

PHOTOFINISHERS	PHOTOIONISE	PHOTOMOSAIC	PHOTOPHORESES	PHOTOSETTING
PHOTOFINISHING	PHOTOIONISED	PHOTOMOSAICS	PHOTOPHORESIS	PHOTOSETTINGS
PHOTOFINISHINGS	PHOTOIONISES	PHOTOMULTIPLIER	PHOTOPLAYS	PHOTOSHOOT
PHOTOFISSION	PHOTOIONISING	PHOTOMURAL	PHOTOPOLYMER	PHOTOSHOOTS
PHOTOFISSIONS	PHOTOIONIZATION	PHOTOMURALS	PHOTOPOLYMERS	PHOTOSHOPPED
PHOTOFLASH	PHOTOIONIZE	PHOTONASTIC	PHOTOPOSITIVE	PHOTOSHOPPING
PHOTOFLASHES	PHOTOIONIZED	PHOTONASTIES	PHOTOPRODUCT	PHOTOSHOPS
PHOTOFLOOD	PHOTOIONIZES	PHOTONASTY	PHOTOPRODUCTION	PHOTOSPHERE
PHOTOFLOODS	PHOTOIONIZING	PHOTONEGATIVE	PHOTOPRODUCTS	PHOTOSPHERES
PHOTOFLUOROGRAM	PHOTOJOURNALISM	PHOTONEUTRON	PHOTOPSIAS	PHOTOSPHERIC
PHOTOGELATIN	PHOTOJOURNALIST	PHOTONEUTRONS	PHOTOPSIES	PHOTOSTATED
PHOTOGELATINE	PHOTOKINESES	PHOTONOVEL	PHOTOREACTION	PHOTOSTATIC
PHOTOGENES	PHOTOKINESIS	PHOTONOVELS	PHOTOREACTIONS	PHOTOSTATING
PHOTOGENIC	PHOTOKINETIC	PHOTONUCLEAR	PHOTOREACTIVE	PHOTOSTATS
PHOTOGENICALLY	PHOTOLITHO	PHOTOOXIDATION	PHOTOREALISM	PHOTOSTATTED
PHOTOGENIES	PHOTOLITHOGRAPH	PHOTOOXIDATIONS	PHOTOREALISMS	PHOTOSTATTING
PHOTOGEOLOGIC	PHOTOLITHOS	PHOTOOXIDATIVE	PHOTOREALIST	PHOTOSYNTHATE
PHOTOGEOLOGICAL	PHOTOLUMINESCE	PHOTOOXIDISE	PHOTOREALISTIC	PHOTOSYNTHATES
PHOTOGEOLOGIES	PHOTOLUMINESCED	PHOTOOXIDISED	PHOTOREALISTS	PHOTOSYNTHESES
PHOTOGEOLOGIST	PHOTOLUMINESCES	PHOTOOXIDISES	PHOTORECEPTION	PHOTOSYNTHESIS
PHOTOGEOLOGISTS	PHOTOLYSABLE	PHOTOOXIDISING	PHOTORECEPTIONS	PHOTOSYNTHESISE
PHOTOGEOLOGY	PHOTOLYSED	PHOTOOXIDIZE	PHOTORECEPTIVE	PHOTOSYNTHESIZE
PHOTOGLYPH	PHOTOLYSES	PHOTOOXIDIZED	PHOTORECEPTOR	PHOTOSYNTHETIC
PHOTOGLYPHIC	PHOTOLYSING	PHOTOOXIDIZES	PHOTORECEPTORS	PHOTOSYSTEM
PHOTOGLYPHIES	PHOTOLYSIS	PHOTOOXIDIZING	PHOTOREDUCE	PHOTOSYSTEMS
PHOTOGLYPHS	PHOTOLYTIC	PHOTOPERIOD	PHOTOREDUCED	PHOTOTACTIC
PHOTOGLYPHY	PHOTOLYTICALLY	PHOTOPERIODIC	PHOTOREDUCES	PHOTOTACTICALLY
PHOTOGRAMMETRIC	PHOTOLYZABLE	PHOTOPERIODISM	PHOTOREDUCING	PHOTOTAXES
PHOTOGRAMMETRY	PHOTOLYZED	PHOTOPERIODISMS	PHOTOREDUCTION	PHOTOTAXIES
PHOTOGRAMS	PHOTOLYZES	PHOTOPERIODS	PHOTOREDUCTIONS	PHOTOTAXIS
PHOTOGRAPH	PHOTOLYZING	PHOTOPHASE	PHOTOREFRACTIVE	PHOTOTELEGRAM
PHOTOGRAPHED	PHOTOMACHINE	PHOTOPHASES	PHOTORESIST	PHOTOTELEGRAMS
PHOTOGRAPHER	PHOTOMACHINES	PHOTOPHILIC	PHOTORESISTS	PHOTOTELEGRAPH
PHOTOGRAPHERS	PHOTOMACROGRAPH	PHOTOPHILIES	PHOTOSCANNED	PHOTOTELEGRAPHS
PHOTOGRAPHIC	PHOTOMAPPED	PHOTOPHILOUS	PHOTOSCANNING	PHOTOTELEGRAPHY
PHOTOGRAPHICAL	PHOTOMAPPING	PHOTOPHILS	PHOTOSCANS	PHOTOTHERAPIES
PHOTOGRAPHIES	PHOTOMASKS	PHOTOPHILY	PHOTOSENSITISE	PHOTOTHERAPY
PHOTOGRAPHING	PHOTOMECHANICAL	PHOTOPHOBE	PHOTOSENSITISED	PHOTOTHERMAL
PHOTOGRAPHIST	PHOTOMETER	PHOTOPHOBES	PHOTOSENSITISER	PHOTOTHERMALLY
PHOTOGRAPHISTS	PHOTOMETERS	PHOTOPHOBIA	PHOTOSENSITISES	PHOTOTHERMIC
PHOTOGRAPHS	PHOTOMETRIC	PHOTOPHOBIAS	PHOTOSENSITIVE	PHOTOTONIC
PHOTOGRAPHY	PHOTOMETRICALLY	PHOTOPHOBIC	PHOTOSENSITIZE	PHOTOTONUS
PHOTOGRAVURE	PHOTOMETRIES	PHOTOPHONE	PHOTOSENSITIZED	PHOTOTONUSES
PHOTOGRAVURES	PHOTOMETRIST	PHOTOPHONES	PHOTOSENSITIZER	PHOTOTOPOGRAPHY
PHOTOINDUCED	PHOTOMETRISTS	PHOTOPHONIC	PHOTOSENSITIZES	PHOTOTOXIC
PHOTOINDUCTION	PHOTOMETRY	PHOTOPHONIES	PHOTOSENSOR	PHOTOTOXICITIES
PHOTOINDUCTIONS	PHOTOMICROGRAPH	PHOTOPHONY	PHOTOSENSORS	PHOTOTOXICITY
PHOTOINDUCTIVE	PHOTOMONTAGE	PHOTOPHORE	PHOTOSETTER	PHOTOTRANSISTOR
PHOTOIONISATION	PHOTOMONTAGES	PHOTOPHORES	PHOTOSETTERS	PHOTOTROPE

PHOTOTROPES	PHREATOPHYTE	PHYCOLOGICAL	PHYLOGENESIS	PHYSIOGRAPHIES
PHOTOTROPH	PHREATOPHYTES	PHYCOLOGIES	PHYLOGENETIC	PHYSIOGRAPHY
PHOTOTROPHIC	PHREATOPHYTIC	PHYCOLOGIST	PHYLOGENIC	PHYSIOLATER
PHOTOTROPHS	PHRENESIAC	PHYCOLOGISTS	PHYLOGENIES	PHYSIOLATERS
PHOTOTROPIC	PHRENETICAL	PHYCOMYCETE	PHYSALISES	PHYSIOLATRIES
PHOTOTROPICALLY	PHRENETICALLY	PHYCOMYCETES	PHYSHARMONICA	PHYSIOLATRY
PHOTOTROPIES	PHRENETICNESS	PHYCOMYCETOUS	PHYSHARMONICAS	PHYSIOLOGIC
PHOTOTROPISM	PHRENETICNESSES	PHYCOPHAEIN	PHYSIATRIC	PHYSIOLOGICAL
PHOTOTROPISMS	PHRENETICS	PHYCOPHAEINS	PHYSIATRICAL	PHYSIOLOGICALLY
PHOTOTROPY	PHRENITIDES	PHYCOXANTHIN	PHYSIATRICS	PHYSIOLOGIES
PHOTOTUBES	PHRENITISES	PHYCOXANTHINS	PHYSIATRIES	PHYSIOLOGIST
PHOTOTYPED	PHRENOLOGIC	PHYLACTERIC	PHYSIATRIST	PHYSIOLOGISTS
PHOTOTYPES	PHRENOLOGICAL	PHYLACTERICAL	PHYSIATRISTS	PHYSIOLOGUS
PHOTOTYPESET	PHRENOLOGICALLY	PHYLACTERIES	PHYSICALISM	PHYSIOLOGUSES
PHOTOTYPESETS	PHRENOLOGIES	PHYLACTERY	PHYSICALISMS	PHYSIOLOGY
PHOTOTYPESETTER	PHRENOLOGISE	PHYLARCHIES	PHYSICALIST	PHYSIOPATHOLOGY
PHOTOTYPIC	PHRENOLOGISED	PHYLAXISES	PHYSICALISTIC	PHYSIOTHERAPIES
PHOTOTYPICALLY	PHRENOLOGISES	PHYLESISES	PHYSICALISTS	PHYSIOTHERAPIST
PHOTOTYPIES	PHRENOLOGISING	PHYLETICALLY	PHYSICALITIES	PHYSIOTHERAPY
PHOTOTYPING	PHRENOLOGIST	PHYLLARIES	PHYSICALITY	PHYSITHEISM
PHOTOTYPOGRAPHY	PHRENOLOGISTS	PHYLLOCLAD	PHYSICALLY	PHYSITHEISMS
PHOTOVOLTAIC	PHRENOLOGIZE	PHYLLOCLADE	PHYSICALNESS	PHYSITHEISTIC
PHOTOVOLTAICS	PHRENOLOGIZED	PHYLLOCLADES	PHYSICALNESSES	PHYSOCLISTOUS
PHOTOXYLOGRAPHY	PHRENOLOGIZES	PHYLLOCLADS	PHYSICIANCIES	PHYSOSTIGMIN
PHOTOZINCOGRAPH	PHRENOLOGIZING	PHYLLODIAL	PHYSICIANCY	PHYSOSTIGMINE
PHRAGMOPLAST	PHRENOLOGY	PHYLLODIES	PHYSICIANER	PHYSOSTIGMINES
PHRAGMOPLASTS	PHRENSICAL	PHYLLODIUM	PHYSICIANERS	PHYSOSTIGMINS
PHRASELESS	PHRENSYING	PHYLLOMANIA	PHYSICIANS	PHYSOSTOMOUS
PHRASEMAKER	PHRONTISTERIES	PHYLLOMANIAS	PHYSICIANSHIP	PHYTOALEXIN
PHRASEMAKERS	PHRONTISTERY	PHYLLOPHAGOUS	PHYSICIANSHIPS	PHYTOALEXINS
PHRASEMAKING	PHTHALATES	PHYLLOPLANE	PHYSICISMS	PHYTOBENTHOS
PHRASEMAKINGS	PHTHALEINS	PHYLLOPLANES	PHYSICISTS	PHYTOBENTHOSES
PHRASEMONGER	PHTHALOCYANIN	PHYLLOPODS	PHYSICKING	PHYTOCHEMICAL
PHRASEMONGERING	PHTHALOCYANINE	PHYLLOQUINONE	PHYSICOCHEMICAL	PHYTOCHEMICALLY
PHRASEMONGERS	PHTHALOCYANINES	PHYLLOQUINONES	PHYSIOCRACIES	PHYTOCHEMICALS
PHRASEOGRAM	PHTHALOCYANINS	PHYLLOSILICATE	PHYSIOCRACY	PHYTOCHEMIST
PHRASEOGRAMS	PHTHIRIASES	PHYLLOSILICATES	PHYSIOCRAT	PHYTOCHEMISTRY
PHRASEOGRAPH	PHTHIRIASIS	PHYLLOSPHERE	PHYSIOCRATIC	PHYTOCHEMISTS
PHRASEOGRAPHIC	PHTHISICAL	PHYLLOSPHERES	PHYSIOCRATS	PHYTOCHROME
PHRASEOGRAPHIES	PHTHISICKY	PHYLLOTACTIC	PHYSIOGNOMIC	PHYTOCHROMES
PHRASEOGRAPHS	PHYCOBILIN	PHYLLOTACTICAL	PHYSIOGNOMICAL	PHYTOESTROGEN
PHRASEOGRAPHY	PHYCOBILINS	PHYLLOTAXES	PHYSIOGNOMIES	PHYTOESTROGENS
PHRASEOLOGIC	PHYCOBIONT	PHYLLOTAXIES	PHYSIOGNOMIST	PHYTOFLAGELLATE
PHRASEOLOGICAL	PHYCOBIONTS	PHYLLOTAXIS	PHYSIOGNOMISTS	PHYTOGENESES
PHRASEOLOGIES	PHYCOCYANIN	PHYLLOTAXY	PHYSIOGNOMY	PHYTOGENESIS
PHRASEOLOGIST	PHYCOCYANINS	PHYLLOXERA	PHYSIOGRAPHER	PHYTOGENETIC
PHRASEOLOGISTS	PHYCOCYANS	PHYLLOXERAE	PHYSIOGRAPHERS	PHYTOGENETICAL
PHRASEOLOGY	PHYCOERYTHRIN	PHYLLOXERAS	PHYSIOGRAPHIC	PHYTOGENIC
PHREAKINGS	PHYCOERYTHRINS	PHYLOGENESES	PHYSIOGRAPHICAL	PHYTOGENIES

PHYTOGEOGRAPHER	PIANISSIMO	PICKELHAUBE	PICTORIALISTS	PIEMONTITES
PHYTOGEOGRAPHIC	PIANISSIMOS	PICKELHAUBES	PICTORIALIZE	PIEPOWDERS
PHYTOGEOGRAPHY	PIANISSISSIMO	PICKERELWEED	PICTORIALIZED	PIERCEABLE
PHYTOGRAPHER	PIANISTICALLY	PICKERELWEEDS	PICTORIALIZES	PIERCINGLY
PHYTOGRAPHERS	PIANOFORTE	PICKETBOAT	PICTORIALIZING	PIERCINGNESS
PHYTOGRAPHIC	PIANOFORTES	PICKETBOATS	PICTORIALLY	PIERCINGNESSES
PHYTOGRAPHIES	PIANOLISTS	PICKETINGS	PICTORIALNESS	PIERRETTES
PHYTOGRAPHY	PICADILLOS	PICKINESSES	PICTORIALNESSES	PIETISTICAL
PHYTOHORMONE	PICARESQUE	PICKLEBALL	PICTORIALS	PIETISTICALLY
PHYTOHORMONES	PICARESQUES	PICKLEBALLER	PICTORICAL	PIEZOCHEMISTRY
PHYTOLITHS	PICAROONED	PICKLEBALLERS	PICTORICALLY	PIEZOELECTRIC
PHYTOLOGICAL	PICAROONING	PICKLEBALLS	PICTUREGOER	PIEZOMAGNETIC
PHYTOLOGICALLY	PICAYUNISH	PICKPOCKET	PICTUREGOERS	PIEZOMAGNETISM
PHYTOLOGIES	PICAYUNISHLY	PICKPOCKETED	PICTUREPHONE	PIEZOMAGNETISMS
PHYTOLOGIST	PICAYUNISHNESS	PICKPOCKETING	PICTUREPHONES	PIEZOMETER
PHYTOLOGISTS	PICCADILLIES	PICKPOCKETS	PICTURESQUE	PIEZOMETERS
PHYTONADIONE	PICCADILLO	PICKTHANKS	PICTURESQUELY	PIEZOMETRIC
PHYTONADIONES	PICCADILLOES	PICNICKERS	PICTURESQUENESS	PIEZOMETRICALLY
PHYTOPATHOGEN	PICCADILLOS	PICNICKIER	PICTURISATION	PIEZOMETRIES
PHYTOPATHOGENIC	PICCADILLS	PICNICKIEST	PICTURISATIONS	PIEZOMETRY
PHYTOPATHOGENS	PICCADILLY	PICNICKING	PICTURISED	PIFFERAROS
PHYTOPATHOLOGY	PICCALILLI	PICOCURIES	PICTURISES	PIGEONHOLE
PHYTOPHAGIC	PICCALILLIS	PICOFARADS	PICTURISING	PIGEONHOLED
PHYTOPHAGIES	PICCOLOIST	PICOMETERS	PICTURIZATION	PIGEONHOLER
PHYTOPHAGOUS	PICCOLOISTS	PICOMETRES	PICTURIZATIONS	PIGEONHOLERS
PHYTOPHAGY	PICHICIAGO	PICORNAVIRUS	PICTURIZED	PIGEONHOLES
PHYTOPLANKTER	PICHICIAGOS	PICORNAVIRUSES	PICTURIZES	PIGEONHOLING
PHYTOPLANKTERS	PICHICIEGO	PICOSECOND	PICTURIZING	PIGEONITES
PHYTOPLANKTON	PICHICIEGOS	PICOSECONDS	PIDDLINGLY	PIGEONRIES
PHYTOPLANKTONIC	PICHOLINES	PICOWAVING	PIDGINISATION	PIGEONWING
PHYTOPLANKTONS	PICKABACKED	PICQUETING	PIDGINISATIONS	PIGEONWINGS
PHYTOSANITARY	PICKABACKING	PICROCARMINE	PIDGINISED	PIGGINESSES
PHYTOSOCIOLOGY	PICKABACKS	PICROCARMINES	PIDGINISES	PIGGISHNESS
PHYTOSTEROL	PICKADILLIES	PICROTOXIN	PIDGINISING	PIGGISHNESSES
PHYTOSTEROLS	PICKADILLO	PICROTOXINS	PIDGINIZATION	PIGGYBACKED
PHYTOTHERAPIES	PICKADILLOES	PICTARNIES	PIDGINIZATIONS	PIGGYBACKING
PHYTOTHERAPY	PICKADILLOS	PICTOGRAMS	PIDGINIZED	PIGGYBACKS
PHYTOTOMIES	PICKADILLS	PICTOGRAPH	PIDGINIZES	PIGHEADEDLY
PHYTOTOMIST	PICKADILLY	PICTOGRAPHIC	PIDGINIZING	PIGHEADEDNESS
PHYTOTOMISTS	PICKAPACKED	PICTOGRAPHIES	PIECEMEALED	PIGHEADEDNESSES
PHYTOTOXIC	PICKAPACKING	PICTOGRAPHS	PIECEMEALING	PIGMENTARY
PHYTOTOXICITIES	PICKAPACKS	PICTOGRAPHY	PIECEMEALS	PIGMENTATION
PHYTOTOXICITY	PICKAROONS	PICTORIALISE	PIECEWORKER	PIGMENTATIONS
PHYTOTOXIN	PICKBACKED	PICTORIALISED	PIECEWORKERS	PIGMENTING
PHYTOTOXINS	PICKBACKING	PICTORIALISES	PIECEWORKS	PIGMENTOSA
PHYTOTRONS	PICKEDNESS	PICTORIALISING	PIEDMONTITE	PIGMENTOSAS
PIACULARITIES	PICKEDNESSES	PICTORIALISM	PIEDMONTITES	PIGNERATED
PIACULARITY	PICKEERERS	PICTORIALISMS	PIEDNESSES	PIGNERATES
PIANISSIMI	PICKEERING	PICTORIALIST	PIEMONTITE	PIGNERATING

PIGNERATION	PILLARLESS	PINCHPOINTS	PINNYWINKLES	PIQUANCIES
PIGNERATIONS	PILLICOCKS	PINCUSHION	PINOCYTOSES	PIQUANTNESS
PIGNORATED	PILLIONING	PINCUSHIONS	PINOCYTOSIS	PIQUANTNESSES
PIGNORATES	PILLIONIST	PINEALECTOMIES	PINOCYTOTIC	PIRACETAMS
PIGNORATING	PILLIONISTS	PINEALECTOMISE	PINOCYTOTICALLY	PIRATICALLY
PIGNORATION	PILLIWINKS	PINEALECTOMISED	PINPOINTED	PIRLICUING
PIGNORATIONS	PILLORISED	PINEALECTOMISES	PINPOINTING	PIROPLASMA
PIGSCONCES	PILLORISES	PINEALECTOMIZE	PINPRICKED	PIROPLASMATA
PIGSTICKED	PILLORISING	PINEALECTOMIZED	PINPRICKING	PIROPLASMS
PIGSTICKER	PILLORIZED	PINEALECTOMIZES	PINSETTERS	PIROUETTED
PIGSTICKERS	PILLORIZES	PINEALECTOMY	PINSPOTTED	PIROUETTER
PIGSTICKING	PILLORIZING	PINEAPPLES	PINSPOTTER	PIROUETTERS
PIGSTICKINGS	PILLORYING	PINFEATHER	PINSPOTTERS	PIROUETTES
PIKEMINNOW	PILLOWCASE	PINFEATHERS	PINSPOTTING	PIROUETTING
PIKEMINNOWS	PILLOWCASES	PINFOLDING	PINSTRIPED	PISCATORIAL
PIKEPERCHES	PILLOWIEST	PINGRASSES	PINSTRIPES	PISCATORIALLY
PIKESTAFFS	PILLOWSLIP	PINGUEFIED	PINTADERAS	PISCATRICES
PIKESTAVES	PILLOWSLIPS	PINGUEFIES	PINTUCKING	PISCATRIXES
PILASTERED	PILNIEWINKS	PINGUEFYING	PINTUCKINGS	PISCICOLOUS
PILEORHIZA	PILOCARPIN	PINGUIDITIES	PINWHEELED	PISCICULTURAL
PILEORHIZAS	PILOCARPINE	PINGUIDITY	PINWHEELING	PISCICULTURALLY
PILFERABLE	PILOCARPINES	PINGUITUDE	PINWRENCHES	PISCICULTURE
PILFERAGES	PILOCARPINS	PINGUITUDES	PIONEERING	PISCICULTURES
PILFERINGLY	PILOSITIES	PINHEADEDNESS	PIOUSNESSES	PISCICULTURIST
PILFERINGS	PILOTFISHES	PINHEADEDNESSES	PIPECLAYED	PISCICULTURISTS
PILFERPROOF	PILOTHOUSE	PINHOOKERS	PIPECLAYING	PISCIFAUNA
PILGARLICK	PILOTHOUSES	PINKERTONS	PIPEFISHES	PISCIFAUNAE
PILGARLICKS	PIMPERNELS	PINKINESSES	PIPEFITTER	PISCIFAUNAS
PILGARLICKY	PIMPLINESS	PINKISHNESS	PIPEFITTERS	PISCIVORES
PILGARLICS	PIMPLINESSES	PINKISHNESSES	PIPEFITTING	PISCIVOROUS
PILGRIMAGE	PIMPMOBILE	PINKNESSES	PIPEFITTINGS	PISSASPHALT
PILGRIMAGED	PIMPMOBILES	PINKWASHED	PIPELINING	PISSASPHALTS
PILGRIMAGER	PINACOIDAL	PINKWASHES	PIPELININGS	PISTACHIOS
PILGRIMAGERS	PINACOTHECA	PINKWASHING	PIPERACEOUS	PISTAREENS
PILGRIMAGES	PINACOTHECAE	PINKWASHINGS	PIPERAZINE	PISTILLARY
PILGRIMAGING	PINAKOIDAL	PINNACLING	PIPERAZINES	PISTILLATE
PILGRIMERS	PINAKOTHEK	PINNATIFID	PIPERIDINE	PISTILLODE
PILGRIMING	PINAKOTHEKS	PINNATIFIDLY	PIPERIDINES	PISTILLODES
PILGRIMISE	PINBALLING	PINNATIONS	PIPERONALS	PISTOLEERS
PILGRIMISED	PINCERLIKE	PINNATIPARTITE	PIPESTONES	PISTOLEROS
PILGRIMISES	PINCHBECKS	PINNATIPED	PIPINESSES	PISTOLIERS
PILGRIMISING	PINCHCOCKS	PINNATISECT	PIPISTRELLE	PISTOLLING
PILGRIMIZE	PINCHCOMMONS	PINNIEWINKLE	PIPISTRELLES	PITAPATTED
PILGRIMIZED	PINCHCOMMONSES	PINNIEWINKLES	PIPISTRELS	PITAPATTING
PILGRIMIZES	PINCHFISTS	PINNIPEDES	PIPIWHARAUROA	PITCHBENDS
PILGRIMIZING	PINCHINGLY	PINNIPEDIAN	PIPIWHARAUROAS	PITCHBLENDE
PILIFEROUS	PINCHPENNIES	PINNIPEDIANS	PIPSISSEWA	PITCHBLENDES
PILLAGINGS	PINCHPENNY	PINNULATED	PIPSISSEWAS	PITCHERFUL
PILLARISTS	PINCHPOINT	PINNYWINKLE	PIPSQUEAKS	PITCHERFULS

PITCHERSFUL	PIXELLATED	PLAGIARISED	PLAINTLESS	PLANLESSNESS
PITCHFORKED	PIXELLATES	PLAGIARISER	PLAINWORKS	PLANLESSNESSES
PITCHFORKING	PIXELLATING	PLAGIARISERS	PLAISTERED	PLANOBLAST
PITCHFORKS	PIXELLATION	PLAGIARISES	PLAISTERING	PLANOBLASTS
PITCHINESS	PIXELLATIONS	PLAGIARISING	PLANARIANS	PLANOCONVEX
PITCHINESSES	PIXILATING	PLAGIARISM	PLANARITIES	PLANOGAMETE
PITCHOMETER	PIXILATION	PLAGIARISMS	PLANATIONS	PLANOGAMETES
PITCHOMETERS	PIXILATIONS	PLAGIARIST	PLANCHETTE	PLANOGRAMS
PITCHPERSON	PIXILLATED	PLAGIARISTIC	PLANCHETTES	PLANOGRAPHIC
PITCHPERSONS	PIXILLATES	PLAGIARISTS	PLANELOADS	PLANOGRAPHIES
PITCHPINES	PIXILLATING	PLAGIARIZE	PLANENESSES	PLANOGRAPHY
PITCHPIPES	PIXILLATION	PLAGIARIZED	PLANESIDES	PLANOMETER
PITCHPOLED	PIXILLATIONS	PLAGIARIZER	PLANETARIA	PLANOMETERS
PITCHPOLES	PIXINESSES	PLAGIARIZERS	PLANETARIES	PLANOMETRIC
PITCHPOLING	PIZAZZIEST	PLAGIARIZES	PLANETARIUM	PLANOMETRICALLY
PITCHSTONE	PIZZAIOLAS	PLAGIARIZING	PLANETARIUMS	PLANOMETRIES
PITCHSTONES	PIZZAIOLOS	PLAGIOCEPHALIES	PLANETESIMAL	PLANOMETRY
PITCHWOMAN	PIZZAZZIER	PLAGIOCEPHALY	PLANETESIMALS	PLANTAGINACEOUS
PITCHWOMEN	PIZZAZZIEST	PLAGIOCLASE	PLANETICAL	PLANTATION
PITEOUSNESS	PIZZICATOS	PLAGIOCLASES	PLANETLIKE	PLANTATIONS
PITEOUSNESSES	PLACABILITIES	PLAGIOCLASTIC	PLANETOIDAL	PLANTIGRADE
PITHECANTHROPI	PLACABILITY	PLAGIOCLIMAX	PLANETOIDS	PLANTIGRADES
PITHECANTHROPUS	PLACABLENESS	PLAGIOCLIMAXES	PLANETOLOGICAL	PLANTLINGS
PITHECOIDS	PLACABLENESSES	PLAGIOSTOMATOUS	PLANETOLOGIES	PLANTOCRACIES
PITHINESSES	PLACARDING	PLAGIOSTOME	PLANETOLOGIST	PLANTOCRACY
PITHIVIERS	PLACATINGLY	PLAGIOSTOMES	PLANETOLOGISTS	PLANTSWOMAN
PITIABLENESS	PLACATIONS	PLAGIOSTOMOUS	PLANETOLOGY	PLANTSWOMEN
PITIABLENESSES	PLACEHOLDER	PLAGIOTROPIC	PLANETWIDE	PLANULIFORM
PITIFULLER	PLACEHOLDERS	PLAGIOTROPISM	PLANGENCIES	PLAQUETTES
PITIFULLEST	PLACEKICKED	PLAGIOTROPISMS	PLANGENTLY	PLASMAGELS
PITIFULNESS	PLACEKICKER	PLAGIOTROPOUS	PLANIGRAMS	PLASMAGENE
PITIFULNESSES	PLACEKICKERS	PLAGUELIKE	PLANIGRAPH	PLASMAGENES
PITILESSLY	PLACEKICKING	PLAGUESOME	PLANIGRAPHIES	PLASMAGENIC
PITILESSNESS	PLACEKICKS	PLAINCHANT	PLANIGRAPHS	PLASMALEMMA
PITILESSNESSES	PLACELESSLY	PLAINCHANTS	PLANIGRAPHY	PLASMALEMMAS
PITMASTERS	PLACEMENTS	PLAINCLOTHES	PLANIMETER	PLASMAPHERESES
PITTOSPORUM	PLACENTALS	PLAINCLOTHESMAN	PLANIMETERS	PLASMAPHERESIS
PITTOSPORUMS	PLACENTATE	PLAINCLOTHESMEN	PLANIMETRIC	PLASMASOLS
PITUITARIES	PLACENTATION	PLAINNESSES	PLANIMETRICAL	PLASMATICAL
PITUITRINS	PLACENTATIONS	PLAINSONGS	PLANIMETRICALLY	PLASMINOGEN
PITYRIASES	PLACENTIFORM	PLAINSPOKEN	PLANIMETRIES	PLASMINOGENS
PITYRIASIS	PLACENTOLOGIES	PLAINSPOKENNESS	PLANIMETRY	PLASMODESM
PITYROSPORUM	PLACENTOLOGY	PLAINSTANES	PLANISHERS	PLASMODESMA
PITYROSPORUMS	PLACIDITIES	PLAINSTONES	PLANISHING	PLASMODESMAS
PIWAKAWAKA	PLACIDNESS	PLAINTEXTS	PLANISPHERE	PLASMODESMATA
PIWAKAWAKAS	PLACIDNESSES	PLAINTIFFS	PLANISPHERES	PLASMODESMS
PIXELATING	PLACODERMS	PLAINTIVELY	PLANISPHERIC	PLASMODIAL
PIXELATION	PLAGIARIES	PLAINTIVENESS	PLANKTONIC	PLASMODIUM
PIXELATIONS	PLAGIARISE	PLAINTIVENESSES	PLANLESSLY	PLASMOGAMIES

PLASMOGAMY	PLASTICIZER	PLATINIRIDIUMS	PLATYPUSES	PLEASANCES
PLASMOLYSE	PLASTICIZERS	PLATINISATION	PLATYRRHINE	PLEASANTER
PLASMOLYSED	PLASTICIZES	PLATINISATIONS	PLATYRRHINES	PLEASANTEST
PLASMOLYSES	PLASTICIZING	PLATINISED	PLATYRRHINIAN	PLEASANTLY
PLASMOLYSING	PLASTICKIER	PLATINISES	PLATYRRHINIANS	PLEASANTNESS
PLASMOLYSIS	PLASTICKIEST	PLATINISING	PLAUDITORY	PLEASANTNESSES
PLASMOLYTIC	PLASTIDIAL	PLATINIZATION	PLAUSIBILITIES	PLEASANTRIES
PLASMOLYTICALLY	PLASTIDULE	PLATINIZATIONS	PLAUSIBILITY	PLEASANTRY
PLASMOLYZE	PLASTIDULES	PLATINIZED	PLAUSIBLENESS	PLEASINGLY
PLASMOLYZED	PLASTILINA	PLATINIZES	PLAUSIBLENESSES	PLEASINGNESS
PLASMOLYZES	PLASTILINAS	PLATINIZING	PLAYABILITIES	PLEASINGNESSES
PLASMOLYZING	PLASTINATION	PLATINOCYANIC	PLAYABILITY	PLEASURABILITY
PLASMOSOMA	PLASTINATIONS	PLATINOCYANIDE	PLAYACTING	PLEASURABLE
PLASMOSOMATA	PLASTIQUES	PLATINOCYANIDES	PLAYACTINGS	PLEASURABLENESS
PLASMOSOME	PLASTISOLS	PLATINOIDS	PLAYACTORS	PLEASURABLY
PLASMOSOMES	PLASTOCYANIN	PLATINOTYPE	PLAYBUSSES	PLEASUREFUL
PLASTERBOARD	PLASTOCYANINS	PLATINOTYPES	PLAYDOUGHS	PLEASURELESS
PLASTERBOARDS	PLASTOGAMIES	PLATITUDES	PLAYFELLOW	PLEASURERS
PLASTERERS	PLASTOGAMY	PLATITUDINAL	PLAYFELLOWS	PLEASURING
PLASTERIER	PLASTOMETER	PLATITUDINARIAN	PLAYFIELDS	PLEBEIANISE
PLASTERIEST	PLASTOMETERS	PLATITUDINISE	PLAYFULNESS	PLEBEIANISED
PLASTERINESS	PLASTOMETRIC	PLATITUDINISED	PLAYFULNESSES	PLEBEIANISES
PLASTERINESSES	PLASTOMETRIES	PLATITUDINISER	PLAYGOINGS	PLEBEIANISING
PLASTERING	PLASTOMETRY	PLATITUDINISERS	PLAYGROUND	PLEBEIANISM
PLASTERINGS	PLASTOQUINONE	PLATITUDINISES	PLAYGROUNDS	PLEBEIANISMS
PLASTERSTONE	PLASTOQUINONES	PLATITUDINISING	PLAYGROUPS	PLEBEIANIZE
PLASTERSTONES	PLATANACEOUS	PLATITUDINIZE	PLAYHOUSES	PLEBEIANIZED
PLASTERWORK	PLATEAUING	PLATITUDINIZED	PLAYLEADER	PLEBEIANIZES
PLASTERWORKS	PLATEGLASS	PLATITUDINIZER	PLAYLEADERS	PLEBEIANIZING
PLASTICALLY	PLATEGLASSES	PLATITUDINIZERS	PLAYLISTED	PLEBEIANLY
PLASTICATED	PLATELAYER	PLATITUDINIZES	PLAYLISTING	PLEBIFICATION
PLASTICENE	PLATELAYERS	PLATITUDINIZING	PLAYMAKERS	PLEBIFICATIONS
PLASTICENES	PLATELAYING	PLATITUDINOUS	PLAYMAKING	PLEBIFYING
PLASTICINE	PLATELAYINGS	PLATITUDINOUSLY	PLAYMAKINGS	PLEBISCITARY
PLASTICINES	PLATEMAKER	PLATONICALLY	PLAYREADER	PLEBISCITE
PLASTICISATION	PLATEMAKERS	PLATONISMS	PLAYREADERS	PLEBISCITES
PLASTICISATIONS	PLATEMAKING	PLATOONING	PLAYSCAPES	PLECOPTERAN
PLASTICISE	PLATEMAKINGS	PLATTELAND	PLAYSCHOOL	PLECOPTERANS
PLASTICISED	PLATEMARKED	PLATTELANDS	PLAYSCHOOLS	PLECOPTEROUS
PLASTICISER	PLATEMARKING	PLATTERFUL	PLAYTHINGS	PLECTOGNATH
PLASTICISERS	PLATEMARKS	PLATTERFULS	PLAYTHROUGH	PLECTOGNATHIC
PLASTICISES	PLATERESQUE	PLATTERSFUL	PLAYTHROUGHS	PLECTOGNATHOUS
PLASTICISING	PLATFORMED	PLATYCEPHALIC	PLAYWRIGHT	PLECTOGNATHS
PLASTICITIES	PLATFORMER	PLATYCEPHALOUS	PLAYWRIGHTING	PLECTOPTEROUS
PLASTICITY	PLATFORMERS	PLATYFISHES	PLAYWRIGHTINGS	PLEDGEABLE
PLASTICIZATION	PLATFORMING	PLATYHELMINTH	PLAYWRIGHTS	PLEINAIRISM
PLASTICIZATIONS	PLATFORMINGS	PLATYHELMINTHIC	PLAYWRITING	PLEINAIRISMS
PLASTICIZE	PLATINIFEROUS	PLATYHELMINTHS	PLAYWRITINGS	PLEINAIRIST
PLASTICIZED	PLATINIRIDIUM	PLATYKURTIC	PLEADINGLY	PLEINAIRISTS

PLEIOCHASIA	PLEONECTIC	PLEXIMETRY	PLUCKINESS	PLURALIZES
PLEIOCHASIUM	PLEONEXIAS	PLIABILITIES	PLUCKINESSES	PLURALIZING
PLEIOMERIES	PLEROCERCOID	PLIABILITY	PLUGBOARDS	PLURILITERAL
PLEIOMEROUS	PLEROCERCOIDS	PLIABLENESS	PLUGUGLIES	PLURILOCULAR
PLEIOTAXIES	PLEROMATIC	PLIABLENESSES	PLUMASSIER	PLURIPARAE
PLEIOTROPIC	PLEROPHORIA	PLIANTNESS	PLUMASSIERS	PLURIPARAS
PLEIOTROPIES	PLEROPHORIAS	PLIANTNESSES	PLUMBAGINACEOUS	PLURIPOTENT
PLEIOTROPISM	PLEROPHORIES	PLICATENESS	PLUMBAGINOUS	PLURIPRESENCE
PLEIOTROPISMS	PLEROPHORY	PLICATENESSES	PLUMBERIES	PLURIPRESENCES
PLEIOTROPY	PLESIOSAUR	PLICATIONS	PLUMBIFEROUS	PLURISERIAL
PLEISTOCENE	PLESIOSAURIAN	PLICATURES	PLUMBISOLVENCY	PLURISERIATE
PLENARTIES	PLESIOSAURIANS	PLODDINGLY	PLUMBISOLVENT	PLUSHINESS
PLENILUNAR	PLESIOSAURS	PLODDINGNESS	PLUMBNESSES	PLUSHINESSES
PLENILUNES	PLESSIMETER	PLODDINGNESSES	PLUMBOSOLVENCY	PLUSHNESSES
PLENIPOTENCE	PLESSIMETERS	PLOTLESSNESS	PLUMBOSOLVENT	PLUTOCRACIES
PLENIPOTENCES	PLESSIMETRIC	PLOTLESSNESSES	PLUMDAMASES	PLUTOCRACY
PLENIPOTENCIES	PLESSIMETRIES	PLOTTERING	PLUMIGEROUS	PLUTOCRATIC
PLENIPOTENCY	PLESSIMETRY	PLOTTINGLY	PLUMMETING	PLUTOCRATICAL
PLENIPOTENT	PLETHORICAL	PLOUGHABLE	PLUMOSITIES	PLUTOCRATICALLY
PLENIPOTENTIAL	PLETHORICALLY	PLOUGHBACK	PLUMPENING	PLUTOCRATS
PLENIPOTENTIARY	PLETHYSMOGRAM	PLOUGHBACKS	PLUMPNESSES	PLUTOLATRIES
PLENISHERS	PLETHYSMOGRAMS	PLOUGHBOYS	PLUMULACEOUS	PLUTOLATRY
PLENISHING	PLETHYSMOGRAPH	PLOUGHGATE	PLUMULARIAN	PLUTOLOGIES
PLENISHINGS	PLETHYSMOGRAPHS	PLOUGHGATES	PLUMULARIANS	PLUTOLOGIST
PLENISHMENT	PLETHYSMOGRAPHY	PLOUGHHEAD	PLUNDERABLE	PLUTOLOGISTS
PLENISHMENTS	PLEURAPOPHYSES	PLOUGHHEADS	PLUNDERAGE	PLUTONISMS
PLENITUDES	PLEURAPOPHYSIS	PLOUGHINGS	PLUNDERAGES	PLUTONIUMS
PLENITUDINOUS	PLEURISIES	PLOUGHLAND	PLUNDERERS	PLUTONOMIES
PLENTEOUSLY	PLEURITICAL	PLOUGHLANDS	PLUNDERING	PLUTONOMIST
PLENTEOUSNESS	PLEURITICS	PLOUGHMANSHIP	PLUNDEROUS	PLUTONOMISTS
PLENTEOUSNESSES	PLEURITISES	PLOUGHMANSHIPS	PLUPERFECT	PLUVIOMETER
PLENTIFULLY	PLEUROCARPOUS	PLOUGHSHARE	PLUPERFECTS	PLUVIOMETERS
PLENTIFULNESS	PLEUROCENTESES	PLOUGHSHARES	PLURALISATION	PLUVIOMETRIC
PLENTIFULNESSES	PLEUROCENTESIS	PLOUGHSTAFF	PLURALISATIONS	PLUVIOMETRICAL
PLENTITUDE	PLEURODONT	PLOUGHSTAFFS	PLURALISED	PLUVIOMETRIES
PLENTITUDES	PLEURODONTS	PLOUGHTAIL	PLURALISER	PLUVIOMETRY
PLEOCHROIC	PLEURODYNIA	PLOUGHTAILS	PLURALISERS	PLYOMETRIC
PLEOCHROISM	PLEURODYNIAS	PLOUGHWISE	PLURALISES	PLYOMETRICS
PLEOCHROISMS	PLEURONIAS	PLOUGHWRIGHT	PLURALISING	PNEUMATHODE
PLEOMORPHIC	PLEUROPNEUMONIA	PLOUGHWRIGHTS	PLURALISMS	PNEUMATHODES
PLEOMORPHIES	PLEUROTOMIES	PLOUTERING	PLURALISTIC	PNEUMATICAL
PLEOMORPHISM	PLEUROTOMY	PLOVERIEST	PLURALISTICALLY	PNEUMATICALLY
PLEOMORPHISMS	PLEUSTONIC	PLOWMANSHIP	PLURALISTS	PNEUMATICITIES
PLEOMORPHOUS	PLEXIGLASS	PLOWMANSHIPS	PLURALITIES	PNEUMATICITY
PLEOMORPHY	PLEXIGLASSES	PLOWSHARES	PLURALIZATION	PNEUMATICS
PLEONASTES	PLEXIMETER	PLOWSTAFFS	PLURALIZATIONS	PNEUMATOLOGICAL
PLEONASTIC	PLEXIMETERS	PLOWTERING	PLURALIZED	PNEUMATOLOGIES
PLEONASTICAL	PLEXIMETRIC	PLOWWRIGHT	PLURALIZER	PNEUMATOLOGIST
PLEONASTICALLY	PLEXIMETRIES	PLOWWRIGHTS	PLURALIZERS	PNEUMATOLOGISTS

PNEUMATOLOGY	POCKETABLE	PODOSPHERE	POIGNANCES	POLARIMETRIES
PNEUMATOLYSES	POCKETBIKE	PODOSPHERES	POIGNANCIES	POLARIMETRY
PNEUMATOLYSIS	POCKETBIKES	PODSOLISATION	POIGNANTLY	POLARISABILITY
PNEUMATOLYTIC	POCKETBOOK	PODSOLISATIONS	POIKILITIC	POLARISABLE
PNEUMATOMETER	POCKETBOOKS	PODSOLISED	POIKILOCYTE	POLARISATION
PNEUMATOMETERS	POCKETFULS	PODSOLISES	POIKILOCYTES	POLARISATIONS
PNEUMATOMETRIES	POCKETKNIFE	PODSOLISING	POIKILOTHERM	POLARISCOPE
PNEUMATOMETRY	POCKETKNIVES	PODSOLIZATION	POIKILOTHERMAL	POLARISCOPES
PNEUMATOPHORE	POCKETLESS	PODSOLIZATIONS	POIKILOTHERMIC	POLARISCOPIC
PNEUMATOPHORES	POCKETPHONE	PODSOLIZED	POIKILOTHERMIES	POLARISERS
PNEUMECTOMIES	POCKETPHONES	PODSOLIZES	POIKILOTHERMISM	POLARISING
PNEUMECTOMY	POCKETSFUL	PODSOLIZING	POIKILOTHERMS	POLARITIES
PNEUMOBACILLI	POCKMANKIES	PODZOLISATION	POIKILOTHERMY	POLARIZABILITY
PNEUMOBACILLUS	POCKMANTIE	PODZOLISATIONS	POINCIANAS	POLARIZABLE
PNEUMOCOCCAL	POCKMANTIES	PODZOLISED	POINDEXTER	POLARIZATION
PNEUMOCOCCI	POCKMARKED	PODZOLISES	POINDEXTERS	POLARIZATIONS
PNEUMOCOCCUS	POCKMARKING	PODZOLISING	POINSETTIA	POLARIZERS
PNEUMOCONIOSES	POCKPITTED	PODZOLIZATION	POINSETTIAS	POLARIZING
PNEUMOCONIOSIS	POCOCURANTE	PODZOLIZATIONS	POINTEDNESS	POLAROGRAM
PNEUMOCONIOTIC	POCOCURANTEISM	PODZOLIZED	POINTEDNESSES	POLAROGRAMS
PNEUMOCONIOTICS	POCOCURANTEISMS	PODZOLIZES	POINTELLES	POLAROGRAPH
PNEUMOCYSTIS	POCOCURANTES	PODZOLIZING	POINTILLES	POLAROGRAPHIC
PNEUMOCYSTISES	POCOCURANTISM	POENOLOGIES	POINTILLISM	POLAROGRAPHIES
PNEUMODYNAMICS	POCOCURANTISMS	POETASTERIES	POINTILLISME	POLAROGRAPHS
PNEUMOGASTRIC	POCOCURANTIST	POETASTERING	POINTILLISMES	POLAROGRAPHY
PNEUMOGASTRICS	POCOCURANTISTS	POETASTERINGS	POINTILLISMS	POLEMARCHS
PNEUMOGRAM	POCULIFORM	POETASTERS	POINTILLIST	POLEMICALLY
PNEUMOGRAMS	PODAGRICAL	POETASTERY	POINTILLISTE	POLEMICISE
PNEUMOGRAPH	PODARGUSES	POETASTRIES	POINTILLISTES	POLEMICISED
PNEUMOGRAPHS	PODCASTERS	POETICALLY	POINTILLISTIC	POLEMICISES
PNEUMOKONIOSES	PODCASTING	POETICALNESS	POINTILLISTS	POLEMICISING
PNEUMOKONIOSIS	PODCASTINGS	POETICALNESSES	POINTLESSLY	POLEMICIST
PNEUMONECTOMIES	PODGINESSES	POETICISED	POINTLESSNESS	POLEMICISTS
PNEUMONECTOMY	PODIATRIES	POETICISES	POINTLESSNESSES	POLEMICIZE
PNEUMONIAS	PODIATRIST	POETICISING	POISONABLE	POLEMICIZED
PNEUMONICS	PODIATRISTS	POETICISMS	POISONINGS	POLEMICIZES
PNEUMONITIDES	PODOCONIOSES	POETICIZED	POISONOUSLY	POLEMICIZING
PNEUMONITIS	PODOCONIOSIS	POETICIZES	POISONOUSNESS	POLEMISING
PNEUMONITISES	PODOLOGIES	POETICIZING	POISONOUSNESSES	POLEMIZING
PNEUMONOLOGIES	PODOLOGIST	POETICULES	POISONWOOD	POLEMONIACEOUS
PNEUMONOLOGIST	PODOLOGISTS	POETRESSES	POISONWOODS	POLEMONIUM
PNEUMONOLOGISTS	PODOPHTHALMOUS	POGONOPHORAN	POKEBERRIES	POLEMONIUMS
PNEUMONOLOGY	PODOPHYLIN	POGONOPHORANS	POKELOGANS	POLIANITES
PNEUMOTHORACES	PODOPHYLINS	POGONOTOMIES	POKERISHLY	POLICEWOMAN
PNEUMOTHORAX	PODOPHYLLI	POGONOTOMY	POKERWORKS	POLICEWOMEN
PNEUMOTHORAXES	PODOPHYLLIN	POGROMISTS	POKINESSES	POLICYHOLDER
PNICTOGENS	PODOPHYLLINS	POHUTUKAWA	POLARIMETER	POLICYHOLDERS
POACHINESS	PODOPHYLLUM	POHUTUKAWAS	POLARIMETERS	POLICYMAKER
POACHINESSES	PODOPHYLLUMS	POIGNADOES	POLARIMETRIC	POLICYMAKERS

POLIOMYELITIDES	POLLENATES	POLTROONERIES	POLYCHASIUM	POLYCYTHEMIC
POLIOMYELITIS	POLLENATING	POLTROONERY	POLYCHETES	POLYDACTYL
POLIOMYELITISES	POLLENIFEROUS	POLVERINES	POLYCHETOUS	POLYDACTYLIES
POLIORCETIC	POLLENISER	POLYACRYLAMIDE	POLYCHLORINATED	POLYDACTYLISM
POLIORCETICS	POLLENISERS	POLYACRYLAMIDES	POLYCHLOROPRENE	POLYDACTYLISMS
POLIOVIRUS	POLLENIZER	POLYACTINAL	POLYCHOTOMIES	POLYDACTYLOUS
POLIOVIRUSES	POLLENIZERS	POLYACTINE	POLYCHOTOMOUS	POLYDACTYLS
POLISHABLE	POLLENOSES	POLYACTINES	POLYCHOTOMY	POLYDACTYLY
POLISHINGS	POLLENOSIS	POLYADELPHOUS	POLYCHREST	POLYDAEMONISM
POLISHMENT	POLLICITATION	POLYALCOHOL	POLYCHRESTS	POLYDAEMONISMS
POLISHMENTS	POLLICITATIONS	POLYALCOHOLS	POLYCHROIC	POLYDEMONISM
POLITBUROS	POLLINATED	POLYAMIDES	POLYCHROISM	POLYDEMONISMS
POLITENESS	POLLINATES	POLYAMINES	POLYCHROISMS	POLYDIPSIA
POLITENESSES	POLLINATING	POLYAMORIES	POLYCHROMATIC	POLYDIPSIAS
POLITESSES	POLLINATION	POLYAMOROUS	POLYCHROMATISM	POLYDIPSIC
POLITICALISE	POLLINATIONS	POLYANDRIES	POLYCHROMATISMS	POLYDISPERSE
POLITICALISED	POLLINATOR	POLYANDROUS	POLYCHROME	POLYDISPERSITY
POLITICALISES	POLLINATORS	POLYANTHAS	POLYCHROMED	POLYELECTROLYTE
POLITICALISING	POLLINIFEROUS	POLYANTHUS	POLYCHROMES	POLYEMBRYONATE
POLITICALIZE	POLLINISED	POLYANTHUSES	POLYCHROMIC	POLYEMBRYONIC
POLITICALIZED	POLLINISER	POLYARCHIES	POLYCHROMIES	POLYEMBRYONIES
POLITICALIZES	POLLINISERS	POLYARTHRITIDES	POLYCHROMING	POLYEMBRYONY
POLITICALIZING	POLLINISES	POLYARTHRITIS	POLYCHROMOUS	POLYESTERS
POLITICALLY	POLLINISING	POLYARTHRITISES	POLYCHROMY	POLYESTROUS
POLITICASTER	POLLINIZED	POLYATOMIC	POLYCISTRONIC	POLYETHENE
POLITICASTERS	POLLINIZER	POLYAXIALS	POLYCLINIC	POLYETHENES
POLITICIAN	POLLINIZERS	POLYAXONIC	POLYCLINICS	POLYETHYLENE
POLITICIANS	POLLINIZES	POLYBAGGED	POLYCLONAL	POLYETHYLENES
POLITICISATION	POLLINIZING	POLYBAGGING	POLYCLONALS	POLYGALACEOUS
POLITICISATIONS	POLLINOSES	POLYBASITE	POLYCOTTON	POLYGAMIES
POLITICISE	POLLINOSIS	POLYBASITES	POLYCOTTONS	POLYGAMISE
POLITICISED	POLLTAKERS	POLYBUTADIENE	POLYCOTYLEDON	POLYGAMISED
POLITICISES	POLLUCITES	POLYBUTADIENES	POLYCOTYLEDONS	POLYGAMISES
POLITICISING	POLLUSIONS	POLYCARBONATE	POLYCROTIC	POLYGAMISING
POLITICIZATION	POLLUTANTS	POLYCARBONATES	POLYCROTISM	POLYGAMIST
POLITICIZATIONS	POLLUTEDLY	POLYCARBOXYLATE	POLYCROTISMS	POLYGAMISTS
POLITICIZE	POLLUTEDNESS	POLYCARBOXYLIC	POLYCRYSTAL	POLYGAMIZE
POLITICIZED	POLLUTEDNESSES	POLYCARPELLARY	POLYCRYSTALLINE	POLYGAMIZED
POLITICIZES	POLLUTIONS	POLYCARPIC	POLYCRYSTALS	POLYGAMIZES
POLITICIZING	POLLYANNAISH	POLYCARPIES	POLYCULTURE	POLYGAMIZING
POLITICKED	POLLYANNAISM	POLYCARPOUS	POLYCULTURES	POLYGAMOUS
POLITICKER	POLLYANNAISMS	POLYCENTRIC	POLYCYCLIC	POLYGAMOUSLY
POLITICKERS	POLLYANNAS	POLYCENTRICS	POLYCYCLICS	POLYGENESES
POLITICKING	POLLYANNISH	POLYCENTRISM	POLYCYSTIC	POLYGENESIS
POLITICKINGS	POLONAISES	POLYCENTRISMS	POLYCYTHAEMIA	POLYGENETIC
POLITICOES	POLONISING	POLYCHAETE	POLYCYTHAEMIAS	POLYGENETICALLY
POLITIQUES	POLONIZING	POLYCHAETES	POLYCYTHAEMIC	POLYGENIES
POLLARDING	POLTERGEIST	POLYCHAETOUS	POLYCYTHEMIA	POLYGENISM
POLLENATED	POLTERGEISTS	POLYCHASIA	POLYCYTHEMIAS	POLYGENISMS

POLYGENIST POLYHYBRIDS POLYNEURITIDES POLYPLOIDAL POLYSYLLABLE
POLYGENISTS POLYHYDRIC POLYNEURITIS POLYPLOIDIC POLYSYLLABLES
POLYGENOUS POLYHYDROXY POLYNEURITISES POLYPLOIDIES POLYSYLLOGISM
POLYGLOTISM POLYIMIDES POLYNOMIAL POLYPLOIDS POLYSYLLOGISMS
POLYGLOTISMS POLYISOPRENE POLYNOMIALISM POLYPLOIDY POLYSYNAPTIC
POLYGLOTTAL POLYISOPRENES POLYNOMIALISMS POLYPODIES POLYSYNDETON
POLYGLOTTIC POLYLEMMAS POLYNOMIALS POLYPODOUS POLYSYNDETONS
POLYGLOTTISM POLYLINGUAL POLYNUCLEAR POLYPROPENE POLYSYNTHESES
POLYGLOTTISMS POLYLYSINE POLYNUCLEATE POLYPROPENES POLYSYNTHESIS
POLYGLOTTOUS POLYLYSINES POLYNUCLEOTIDE POLYPROPYLENE POLYSYNTHESISM
POLYGLOTTS POLYMASTIA POLYNUCLEOTIDES POLYPROPYLENES POLYSYNTHESISMS
POLYGONACEOUS POLYMASTIAS POLYOLEFIN POLYPROTODONT POLYSYNTHETIC
POLYGONALLY POLYMASTIC POLYOLEFINS POLYPROTODONTS POLYSYNTHETICAL
POLYGONATUM POLYMASTICS POLYOMINOES POLYPTYCHS POLYSYNTHETISM
POLYGONATUMS POLYMASTIES POLYOMINOS POLYRHYTHM POLYSYNTHETISMS
POLYGONIES POLYMASTISM POLYONYMIC POLYRHYTHMIC POLYTECHNIC
POLYGONUMS POLYMASTISMS POLYONYMIES POLYRHYTHMS POLYTECHNICAL
POLYGRAPHED POLYMATHIC POLYONYMOUS POLYRIBOSOMAL POLYTECHNICS
POLYGRAPHER POLYMATHIES POLYPARIES POLYRIBOSOME POLYTENIES
POLYGRAPHERS POLYMERASE POLYPARIUM POLYRIBOSOMES POLYTHALAMOUS
POLYGRAPHIC POLYMERASES POLYPEPTIDE POLYSACCHARIDE POLYTHEISM
POLYGRAPHICALLY POLYMERIDE POLYPEPTIDES POLYSACCHARIDES POLYTHEISMS
POLYGRAPHIES POLYMERIDES POLYPEPTIDIC POLYSACCHAROSE POLYTHEIST
POLYGRAPHING POLYMERIES POLYPETALOUS POLYSACCHAROSES POLYTHEISTIC
POLYGRAPHIST POLYMERISATION POLYPHAGIA POLYSEMANT POLYTHEISTICAL
POLYGRAPHISTS POLYMERISATIONS POLYPHAGIAS POLYSEMANTS POLYTHEISTS
POLYGRAPHS POLYMERISE POLYPHAGIES POLYSEMIES POLYTHENES
POLYGRAPHY POLYMERISED POLYPHAGOUS POLYSEMOUS POLYTOCOUS
POLYGYNIAN POLYMERISES POLYPHARMACIES POLYSEPALOUS POLYTONALISM
POLYGYNIES POLYMERISING POLYPHARMACY POLYSILOXANE POLYTONALISMS
POLYGYNIST POLYMERISM POLYPHASIC POLYSILOXANES POLYTONALIST
POLYGYNISTS POLYMERISMS POLYPHENOL POLYSOMICS POLYTONALISTS
POLYGYNOUS POLYMERIZATION POLYPHENOLIC POLYSOMIES POLYTONALITIES
POLYHALITE POLYMERIZATIONS POLYPHENOLS POLYSORBATE POLYTONALITY
POLYHALITES POLYMERIZE POLYPHLOESBOEAN POLYSORBATES POLYTONALLY
POLYHEDRAL POLYMERIZED POLYPHLOISBIC POLYSTICHOUS POLYTROPHIC
POLYHEDRIC POLYMERIZES POLYPHONES POLYSTYLAR POLYTUNNEL
POLYHEDRON POLYMERIZING POLYPHONIC POLYSTYLES POLYTUNNELS
POLYHEDRONS POLYMEROUS POLYPHONICALLY POLYSTYRENE POLYTYPICAL
POLYHEDROSES POLYMORPHIC POLYPHONIES POLYSTYRENES POLYTYPING
POLYHEDROSIS POLYMORPHICALLY POLYPHONIST POLYSULFIDE POLYUNSATURATE
POLYHISTOR POLYMORPHISM POLYPHONISTS POLYSULFIDES POLYUNSATURATED
POLYHISTORIAN POLYMORPHISMS POLYPHONOUS POLYSULPHIDE POLYUNSATURATES
POLYHISTORIANS POLYMORPHOUS POLYPHONOUSLY POLYSULPHIDES POLYURETHAN
POLYHISTORIC POLYMORPHOUSLY POLYPHOSPHORIC POLYSYLLABIC POLYURETHANE
POLYHISTORIES POLYMORPHS POLYPHYLETIC POLYSYLLABICAL POLYURETHANES
POLYHISTORS POLYMYOSITIS POLYPHYLLOUS POLYSYLLABICISM POLYURETHANS
POLYHISTORY POLYMYOSITISES POLYPHYODONT POLYSYLLABISM POLYVALENCE
POLYHYBRID POLYMYXINS POLYPIDOMS POLYSYLLABISMS POLYVALENCES

POLYVALENCIES	PONDERATING	POPLINETTES	PORCELLANISED	PORPHYRITE
POLYVALENCY	PONDERATION	POPMOBILITIES	PORCELLANISES	PORPHYRITES
POLYVALENT	PONDERATIONS	POPMOBILITY	PORCELLANISING	PORPHYRITIC
POLYVINYLIDENE	PONDERINGLY	POPPERINGS	PORCELLANITE	PORPHYROGENITE
POLYVINYLIDENES	PONDERMENT	POPPYCOCKS	PORCELLANITES	PORPHYROGENITES
POLYVINYLS	PONDERMENTS	POPPYHEADS	PORCELLANIZE	PORPHYROID
POLYWATERS	PONDEROSAS	POPULARISATION	PORCELLANIZED	PORPHYROIDS
POLYZOARIA	PONDEROSITIES	POPULARISATIONS	PORCELLANIZES	PORPHYROPSIN
POLYZOARIAL	PONDEROSITY	POPULARISE	PORCELLANIZING	PORPHYROPSINS
POLYZOARIES	PONDEROUSLY	POPULARISED	PORCELLANOUS	PORPHYROUS
POLYZOARIUM	PONDEROUSNESS	POPULARISER	PORCHETTAS	PORPOISING
POMATUMING	PONDEROUSNESSES	POPULARISERS	PORCUPINES	PORRACEOUS
POMEGRANATE	PONDOKKIES	POPULARISES	PORCUPINIER	PORRECTING
POMEGRANATES	PONEROLOGIES	POPULARISING	PORCUPINIEST	PORRECTION
POMICULTURE	PONEROLOGY	POPULARIST	PORCUPINISH	PORRECTIONS
POMICULTURES	PONIARDING	POPULARITIES	PORIFERANS	PORRENGERS
POMIFEROUS	PONTIANACS	POPULARITY	PORIFEROUS	PORRIDGIER
POMMELLING	PONTIANAKS	POPULARIZATION	PORINESSES	PORRIDGIEST
POMOERIUMS	PONTICELLO	POPULARIZATIONS	PORISMATIC	PORRIGINOUS
POMOLOGICAL	PONTICELLOS	POPULARIZE	PORISMATICAL	PORRINGERS
POMOLOGICALLY	PONTIFICAL	POPULARIZED	PORISTICAL	PORTABELLA
POMOLOGIES	PONTIFICALITIES	POPULARIZER	PORKINESSES	PORTABELLAS
POMOLOGIST	PONTIFICALITY	POPULARIZERS	PORLOCKING	PORTABELLO
POMOLOGISTS	PONTIFICALLY	POPULARIZES	PORNIFICATION	PORTABELLOS
POMOSEXUAL	PONTIFICALS	POPULARIZING	PORNIFICATIONS	PORTABILITIES
POMOSEXUALS	PONTIFICATE	POPULATING	PORNOCRACIES	PORTABILITY
POMPADOURED	PONTIFICATED	POPULATION	PORNOCRACY	PORTAMENTI
POMPADOURS	PONTIFICATES	POPULATIONAL	PORNOGRAPHER	PORTAMENTO
POMPELMOOSE	PONTIFICATING	POPULATIONS	PORNOGRAPHERS	PORTAPACKS
POMPELMOOSES	PONTIFICATION	POPULISTIC	PORNOGRAPHIC	PORTATIVES
POMPELMOUS	PONTIFICATIONS	POPULOUSLY	PORNOGRAPHIES	PORTCULLIS
POMPELMOUSE	PONTIFICATOR	POPULOUSNESS	PORNOGRAPHY	PORTCULLISED
POMPELMOUSES	PONTIFICATORS	POPULOUSNESSES	PORNOTOPIA	PORTCULLISES
POMPHOLYGOUS	PONTIFICES	PORBEAGLES	PORNOTOPIAN	PORTCULLISING
POMPHOLYXES	PONTIFYING	PORCELAINEOUS	PORNOTOPIAS	PORTENDING
POMPOSITIES	PONTLEVISES	PORCELAINISE	POROGAMIES	PORTENTOUS
POMPOUSNESS	PONTONEERS	PORCELAINISED	POROMERICS	PORTENTOUSLY
POMPOUSNESSES	PONTONIERS	PORCELAINISES	POROSCOPES	PORTENTOUSNESS
PONDERABILITIES	PONTONNIER	PORCELAINISING	POROSCOPIC	PORTEOUSES
PONDERABILITY	PONTONNIERS	PORCELAINIZE	POROSCOPIES	PORTERAGES
PONDERABLE	PONTOONERS	PORCELAINIZED	POROSITIES	PORTERESSES
PONDERABLES	PONTOONING	PORCELAINIZES	POROUSNESS	PORTERHOUSE
PONDERABLY	PONYTAILED	PORCELAINIZING	POROUSNESSES	PORTERHOUSES
PONDERANCE	POORHOUSES	PORCELAINLIKE	PORPENTINE	PORTFOLIOS
PONDERANCES	POORMOUTHED	PORCELAINOUS	PORPENTINES	PORTHORSES
PONDERANCIES	POORMOUTHING	PORCELAINS	PORPHYRIAS	PORTHOUSES
PONDERANCY	POORMOUTHS	PORCELANEOUS	PORPHYRIES	PORTIONERS
PONDERATED	POORNESSES	PORCELLANEOUS	PORPHYRINS	PORTIONING
PONDERATES	POPLINETTE	PORCELLANISE	PORPHYRIOS	PORTIONIST

PORTIONISTS	POSITRONIUMS	POSTCARDLIKE	POSTERISATIONS	POSTILIONS
PORTIONLESS	POSOLOGICAL	POSTCLASSIC	POSTERISED	POSTILLATE
PORTLINESS	POSOLOGIES	POSTCLASSICAL	POSTERISES	POSTILLATED
PORTLINESSES	POSSESSABLE	POSTCODING	POSTERISING	POSTILLATES
PORTMANTEAU	POSSESSEDLY	POSTCOITAL	POSTERITIES	POSTILLATING
PORTMANTEAUS	POSSESSEDNESS	POSTCOLLEGE	POSTERIZATION	POSTILLATION
PORTMANTEAUX	POSSESSEDNESSES	POSTCOLLEGIATE	POSTERIZATIONS	POSTILLATIONS
PORTMANTLE	POSSESSING	POSTCOLONIAL	POSTERIZED	POSTILLATOR
PORTMANTLES	POSSESSION	POSTCONCEPTION	POSTERIZES	POSTILLATORS
PORTMANTUA	POSSESSIONAL	POSTCONCERT	POSTERIZING	POSTILLERS
PORTMANTUAS	POSSESSIONARY	POSTCONQUEST	POSTEROLATERAL	POSTILLING
PORTOBELLO	POSSESSIONATE	POSTCONSONANTAL	POSTERUPTIVE	POSTILLION
PORTOBELLOS	POSSESSIONATES	POSTCONVENTION	POSTEXERCISE	POSTILLIONS
PORTOLANOS	POSSESSIONED	POSTCOPULATORY	POSTEXILIAN	POSTIMPACT
PORTRAITED	POSSESSIONLESS	POSTCORONARY	POSTEXILIC	POSTIMPERIAL
PORTRAITING	POSSESSIONS	POSTCRANIAL	POSTEXPERIENCE	POSTINAUGURAL
PORTRAITIST	POSSESSIVE	POSTCRANIALLY	POSTEXPOSURE	POSTINDUSTRIAL
PORTRAITISTS	POSSESSIVELY	POSTCRISIS	POSTFEMINISM	POSTINFECTION
PORTRAITURE	POSSESSIVENESS	POSTDATING	POSTFEMINISMS	POSTINJECTION
PORTRAITURES	POSSESSIVES	POSTDEADLINE	POSTFEMINIST	POSTINOCULATION
PORTRAYABLE	POSSESSORS	POSTDEBATE	POSTFEMINISTS	POSTIRRADIATION
PORTRAYALS	POSSESSORSHIP	POSTDEBUTANTE	POSTFIXING	POSTISCHEMIC
PORTRAYERS	POSSESSORSHIPS	POSTDELIVERY	POSTFLIGHT	POSTISOLATION
PORTRAYING	POSSESSORY	POSTDEPRESSION	POSTFORMED	POSTLANDING
PORTREEVES	POSSIBILISM	POSTDEVALUATION	POSTFORMING	POSTLAPSARIAN
PORTRESSES	POSSIBILISMS	POSTDILUVIAL	POSTFRACTURE	POSTLAUNCH
PORTULACACEOUS	POSSIBILIST	POSTDILUVIAN	POSTFREEZE	POSTLIBERATION
PORTULACAS	POSSIBILISTS	POSTDILUVIANS	POSTGANGLIONIC	POSTLIMINARY
PORWIGGLES	POSSIBILITIES	POSTDIVESTITURE	POSTGLACIAL	POSTLIMINIA
POSHNESSES	POSSIBILITY	POSTDIVORCE	POSTGRADUATE	POSTLIMINIARY
POSITIONAL	POSSIBLEST	POSTDOCTORAL	POSTGRADUATES	POSTLIMINIES
POSITIONALITIES	POSTABORTION	POSTDOCTORALS	POSTGRADUATION	POSTLIMINIOUS
POSITIONALITY	POSTACCIDENT	POSTDOCTORATE	POSTGRADUATIONS	POSTLIMINIUM
POSITIONALLY	POSTADOLESCENT	POSTDOCTORATES	POSTHARVEST	POSTLIMINOUS
POSITIONED	POSTADOLESCENTS	POSTEDITING	POSTHASTES	POSTLIMINY
POSITIONING	POSTAMPUTATION	POSTEDITINGS	POSTHEATED	POSTLITERATE
POSITIONINGS	POSTAPOCALYPSE	POSTELECTION	POSTHEATING	POSTMARITAL
POSITIVELY	POSTAPOCALYPSES	POSTEMBRYONAL	POSTHEMORRHAGIC	POSTMARKED
POSITIVENESS	POSTAPOCALYPTIC	POSTEMBRYONIC	POSTHOLDER	POSTMARKING
POSITIVENESSES	POSTARREST	POSTEMERGENCE	POSTHOLDERS	POSTMASTECTOMY
POSITIVEST	POSTATOMIC	POSTEMERGENCY	POSTHOLIDAY	POSTMASTER
POSITIVISM	POSTATTACK	POSTEPILEPTIC	POSTHOLOCAUST	POSTMASTERS
POSITIVISMS	POSTBELLUM	POSTERBOARD	POSTHORSES	POSTMASTERSHIP
POSITIVIST	POSTBIBLICAL	POSTERBOARDS	POSTHOSPITAL	POSTMASTERSHIPS
POSITIVISTIC	POSTBOURGEOIS	POSTERIORITIES	POSTHOUSES	POSTMATING
POSITIVISTS	POSTBUSSES	POSTERIORITY	POSTHUMOUS	POSTMEDIEVAL
POSITIVITIES	POSTCAPITALIST	POSTERIORLY	POSTHUMOUSLY	POSTMENOPAUSAL
POSITIVITY	POSTCARDED	POSTERIORS	POSTHUMOUSNESS	POSTMENSTRUAL
POSITRONIUM	POSTCARDING	POSTERISATION	POSTHYPNOTIC	POSTMERIDIAN

POSTMIDNIGHT	POSTPUBERTIES	POSTULATUM	POTENTILLA	POURPARLER
POSTMILLENARIAN	POSTPUBERTY	POSTURINGS	POTENTILLAS	POURPARLERS
POSTMILLENNIAL	POSTPUBESCENT	POSTURISED	POTENTIOMETER	POURPOINTS
POSTMISTRESS	POSTPUBESCENTS	POSTURISES	POTENTIOMETERS	POURSEWING
POSTMISTRESSES	POSTRECESSION	POSTURISING	POTENTIOMETRIC	POURTRAHED
POSTMODERN	POSTRETIREMENT	POSTURISTS	POTENTIOMETRIES	POURTRAICT
POSTMODERNISM	POSTRIDERS	POSTURIZED	POTENTIOMETRY	POURTRAICTS
POSTMODERNISMS	POSTROMANTIC	POSTURIZES	POTENTISED	POURTRAYED
POSTMODERNIST	POSTROMANTICS	POSTURIZING	POTENTISES	POURTRAYING
POSTMODERNISTS	POSTSCENIUM	POSTVACCINAL	POTENTISING	POUSOWDIES
POSTMODERNS	POSTSCENIUMS	POSTVACCINATION	POTENTIZED	POUSSETTED
POSTMODIFIED	POSTSCRIPT	POSTVAGOTOMY	POTENTIZES	POUSSETTES
POSTMODIFIES	POSTSCRIPTS	POSTVASECTOMY	POTENTIZING	POUSSETTING
POSTMODIFY	POSTSEASON	POSTVOCALIC	POTENTNESS	POUTASSOUS
POSTMODIFYING	POSTSEASONS	POSTWEANING	POTENTNESSES	POUTHERING
POSTMORTEM	POSTSECONDARY	POSTWORKSHOP	POTHECARIES	POWDERIEST
POSTMORTEMS	POSTSTIMULATION	POTABILITIES	POTHERIEST	POWDERINGS
POSTNATALLY	POSTSTIMULATORY	POTABILITY	POTHOLDERS	POWDERLESS
POSTNEONATAL	POSTSTIMULUS	POTABLENESS	POTHOLINGS	POWDERLIKE
POSTNUPTIAL	POSTSTRIKE	POTABLENESSES	POTHUNTERS	POWELLISED
POSTOCULAR	POSTSURGICAL	POTAMOGETON	POTHUNTING	POWELLISES
POSTOCULARS	POSTSYNAPTIC	POTAMOGETONS	POTHUNTINGS	POWELLISING
POSTOPERATIVE	POSTSYNCED	POTAMOLOGICAL	POTICARIES	POWELLITES
POSTOPERATIVELY	POSTSYNCHRONISE	POTAMOLOGIES	POTICHOMANIA	POWELLIZED
POSTORBITAL	POSTSYNCHRONIZE	POTAMOLOGIST	POTICHOMANIAS	POWELLIZES
POSTORGASMIC	POSTSYNCING	POTAMOLOGISTS	POTLATCHED	POWELLIZING
POSTPARTUM	POSTTENSION	POTAMOLOGY	POTLATCHES	POWERBANDS
POSTPERSON	POSTTENSIONED	POTASSIUMS	POTLATCHING	POWERBOATING
POSTPERSONS	POSTTENSIONING	POTATOBUGS	POTOMETERS	POWERBOATINGS
POSTPOLLINATION	POSTTENSIONS	POTBELLIED	POTPOURRIS	POWERBOATS
POSTPONABLE	POSTTRANSFUSION	POTBELLIES	POTSHOTTING	POWERFULLY
POSTPONEMENT	POSTTRAUMATIC	POTBOILERS	POTSHOTTINGS	POWERFULNESS
POSTPONEMENTS	POSTTREATMENT	POTBOILING	POTTERINGLY	POWERFULNESSES
POSTPONENCE	POSTTREATMENTS	POTBOILINGS	POTTERINGS	POWERHOUSE
POSTPONENCES	POSTULANCIES	POTENTATES	POTTINESSES	POWERHOUSES
POSTPONERS	POSTULANCY	POTENTIALITIES	POTTINGARS	POWERLESSLY
POSTPONING	POSTULANTS	POTENTIALITY	POTTINGERS	POWERLESSNESS
POSTPOSING	POSTULANTSHIP	POTENTIALLY	POTTYMOUTH	POWERLESSNESSES
POSTPOSITION	POSTULANTSHIPS	POTENTIALS	POTTYMOUTHS	POWERLIFTER
POSTPOSITIONAL	POSTULATED	POTENTIARIES	POTWALLERS	POWERLIFTERS
POSTPOSITIONS	POSTULATES	POTENTIARY	POULTERERS	POWERLIFTING
POSTPOSITIVE	POSTULATING	POTENTIATE	POULTICING	POWERLIFTINGS
POSTPOSITIVELY	POSTULATION	POTENTIATED	POULTROONE	POWERPLAYS
POSTPOSITIVES	POSTULATIONAL	POTENTIATES	POULTROONES	POWERSLIDE
POSTPRANDIAL	POSTULATIONALLY	POTENTIATING	POULTRYMAN	POWERSLIDES
POSTPRIMARY	POSTULATIONS	POTENTIATION	POULTRYMEN	POWERSLIDING
POSTPRISON	POSTULATOR	POTENTIATIONS	POUNDCAKES	POWERTRAIN
POSTPRODUCTION	POSTULATORS	POTENTIATOR	POUNDSHOPS	POWERTRAINS
POSTPRODUCTIONS	POSTULATORY	POTENTIATORS	POURBOIRES	POWERWASHED

P

POWERWASHES	PRAENOMENS	PRAISEWORTHILY	PREACHINESS	PREAMBULATORY
POWERWASHING	PRAENOMINA	PRAISEWORTHY	PREACHINESSES	PREAMPLIFIER
POWSOWDIES	PRAENOMINAL	PRAISINGLY	PREACHINGLY	PREAMPLIFIERS
POXVIRUSES	PRAENOMINALLY	PRALLTRILLER	PREACHINGS	PREANAESTHETIC
POZZOLANAS	PRAEPOSTOR	PRALLTRILLERS	PREACHMENT	PREANAESTHETICS
POZZOLANIC	PRAEPOSTORS	PRANAYAMAS	PREACHMENTS	PREANESTHETIC
POZZUOLANA	PRAESIDIUM	PRANCINGLY	PREACQUAINT	PREANNOUNCE
POZZUOLANAS	PRAESIDIUMS	PRANDIALLY	PREACQUAINTANCE	PREANNOUNCED
PRACHARAKS	PRAETORIAL	PRANKINGLY	PREACQUAINTED	PREANNOUNCES
PRACTICABILITY	PRAETORIAN	PRANKISHLY	PREACQUAINTING	PREANNOUNCING
PRACTICABLE	PRAETORIANS	PRANKISHNESS	PREACQUAINTS	PREAPPLIED
PRACTICABLENESS	PRAETORIUM	PRANKISHNESSES	PREACQUISITION	PREAPPLIES
PRACTICABLY	PRAETORIUMS	PRANKSTERS	PREADAMITE	PREAPPLYING
PRACTICALISM	PRAETORSHIP	PRASEODYMIUM	PREADAMITES	PREAPPOINT
PRACTICALISMS	PRAETORSHIPS	PRASEODYMIUMS	PREADAPTATION	PREAPPOINTED
PRACTICALIST	PRAGMATICAL	PRATFALLEN	PREADAPTATIONS	PREAPPOINTING
PRACTICALISTS	PRAGMATICALITY	PRATFALLING	PREADAPTED	PREAPPOINTS
PRACTICALITIES	PRAGMATICALLY	PRATINCOLE	PREADAPTING	PREAPPROVE
PRACTICALITY	PRAGMATICALNESS	PRATINCOLES	PREADAPTIVE	PREAPPROVED
PRACTICALLY	PRAGMATICISM	PRATTLEBOX	PREADJUSTED	PREAPPROVES
PRACTICALNESS	PRAGMATICISMS	PRATTLEBOXES	PREADJUSTING	PREAPPROVING
PRACTICALNESSES	PRAGMATICIST	PRATTLEMENT	PREADJUSTS	PREARRANGE
PRACTICALS	PRAGMATICISTS	PRATTLEMENTS	PREADMISSION	PREARRANGED
PRACTICERS	PRAGMATICS	PRATTLINGLY	PREADMISSIONS	PREARRANGEMENT
PRACTICIAN	PRAGMATISATION	PRAXEOLOGICAL	PREADMITTED	PREARRANGEMENTS
PRACTICIANS	PRAGMATISATIONS	PRAXEOLOGIES	PREADMITTING	PREARRANGES
PRACTICING	PRAGMATISE	PRAXEOLOGY	PREADMONISH	PREARRANGING
PRACTICKED	PRAGMATISED	PRAXINOSCOPE	PREADMONISHED	PREASSEMBLED
PRACTICKING	PRAGMATISER	PRAXINOSCOPES	PREADMONISHES	PREASSIGNED
PRACTICUMS	PRAGMATISERS	PRAYERFULLY	PREADMONISHING	PREASSIGNING
PRACTIQUES	PRAGMATISES	PRAYERFULNESS	PREADMONITION	PREASSIGNS
PRACTISANT	PRAGMATISING	PRAYERFULNESSES	PREADMONITIONS	PREASSURANCE
PRACTISANTS	PRAGMATISM	PRAYERLESS	PREADOLESCENCE	PREASSURANCES
PRACTISERS	PRAGMATISMS	PRAYERLESSLY	PREADOLESCENCES	PREASSURED
PRACTISING	PRAGMATIST	PRAYERLESSNESS	PREADOLESCENT	PREASSURES
PRACTITIONER	PRAGMATISTIC	PREABSORBED	PREADOLESCENTS	PREASSURING
PRACTITIONERS	PRAGMATISTS	PREABSORBING	PREADOPTED	PREATTUNED
PRACTOLOLS	PRAGMATIZATION	PREABSORBS	PREADOPTING	PREATTUNES
PRAEAMBLES	PRAGMATIZATIONS	PREACCUSED	PREAGRICULTURAL	PREATTUNING
PRAECOCIAL	PRAGMATIZE	PREACCUSES	PREALLOTTED	PREAUDIENCE
PRAECORDIAL	PRAGMATIZED	PREACCUSING	PREALLOTTING	PREAUDIENCES
PRAEDIALITIES	PRAGMATIZER	PREACHABLE	PREALTERED	PREAVERRED
PRAEDIALITY	PRAGMATIZERS	PREACHERSHIP	PREALTERING	PREAVERRING
PRAEFECTORIAL	PRAGMATIZES	PREACHERSHIPS	PREAMBLING	PREAXIALLY
PRAELECTED	PRAGMATIZING	PREACHIEST	PREAMBULARY	PREBENDARIES
PRAELECTING	PRAISEACHS	PREACHIFIED	PREAMBULATE	PREBENDARY
PRAELUDIUM	PRAISELESS	PREACHIFIES	PREAMBULATED	PREBIBLICAL
PRAEMUNIRE	PRAISEWORTHIER	PREACHIFYING	PREAMBULATES	PREBIDDING
PRAEMUNIRES	PRAISEWORTHIEST	PREACHIFYINGS	PREAMBULATING	PREBIDDINGS

PREBILLING	PRECEDENTIALLY	PRECIOUSES	PRECLEARANCE	PRECOMPUTES
PREBINDING	PRECEDENTLY	PRECIOUSLY	PRECLEARANCES	PRECOMPUTING
PREBIOLOGIC	PRECEDENTS	PRECIOUSNESS	PRECLEARED	PRECONCEIT
PREBIOLOGICAL	PRECENSORED	PRECIOUSNESSES	PRECLEARING	PRECONCEITED
PREBIOTICS	PRECENSORING	PRECIPICED	PRECLINICAL	PRECONCEITING
PREBLESSED	PRECENSORS	PRECIPICES	PRECLINICALLY	PRECONCEITS
PREBLESSES	PRECENTING	PRECIPITABILITY	PRECLUDABLE	PRECONCEIVE
PREBLESSING	PRECENTORIAL	PRECIPITABLE	PRECLUDING	PRECONCEIVED
PREBOARDED	PRECENTORS	PRECIPITANCE	PRECLUSION	PRECONCEIVES
PREBOARDING	PRECENTORSHIP	PRECIPITANCES	PRECLUSIONS	PRECONCEIVING
PREBOILING	PRECENTORSHIPS	PRECIPITANCIES	PRECLUSIVE	PRECONCEPTION
PREBOOKING	PRECENTRESS	PRECIPITANCY	PRECLUSIVELY	PRECONCEPTIONS
PREBREAKFAST	PRECENTRESSES	PRECIPITANT	PRECOCIALS	PRECONCERT
PREBUDGETS	PRECENTRICES	PRECIPITANTLY	PRECOCIOUS	PRECONCERTED
PREBUILDING	PRECENTRIX	PRECIPITANTNESS	PRECOCIOUSLY	PRECONCERTEDLY
PREBUTTALS	PRECENTRIXES	PRECIPITANTS	PRECOCIOUSNESS	PRECONCERTING
PRECALCULI	PRECEPTIAL	PRECIPITATE	PRECOCITIES	PRECONCERTS
PRECALCULUS	PRECEPTIVE	PRECIPITATED	PRECOGNISANT	PRECONCILIAR
PRECALCULUSES	PRECEPTIVELY	PRECIPITATELY	PRECOGNISE	PRECONDEMN
PRECANCELATION	PRECEPTORAL	PRECIPITATENESS	PRECOGNISED	PRECONDEMNED
PRECANCELATIONS	PRECEPTORATE	PRECIPITATES	PRECOGNISES	PRECONDEMNING
PRECANCELED	PRECEPTORATES	PRECIPITATING	PRECOGNISING	PRECONDEMNS
PRECANCELING	PRECEPTORIAL	PRECIPITATION	PRECOGNITION	PRECONDITION
PRECANCELLATION	PRECEPTORIALS	PRECIPITATIONS	PRECOGNITIONS	PRECONDITIONED
PRECANCELLED	PRECEPTORIES	PRECIPITATIVE	PRECOGNITIVE	PRECONDITIONING
PRECANCELLING	PRECEPTORS	PRECIPITATOR	PRECOGNIZANT	PRECONDITIONS
PRECANCELS	PRECEPTORSHIP	PRECIPITATORS	PRECOGNIZE	PRECONISATION
PRECANCEROUS	PRECEPTORSHIPS	PRECIPITIN	PRECOGNIZED	PRECONISATIONS
PRECANCERS	PRECEPTORY	PRECIPITINOGEN	PRECOGNIZES	PRECONISED
PRECAPITALIST	PRECEPTRESS	PRECIPITINOGENS	PRECOGNIZING	PRECONISES
PRECARIATS	PRECEPTRESSES	PRECIPITINS	PRECOGNOSCE	PRECONISING
PRECARIOUS	PRECESSING	PRECIPITOUS	PRECOGNOSCED	PRECONIZATION
PRECARIOUSLY	PRECESSION	PRECIPITOUSLY	PRECOGNOSCES	PRECONIZATIONS
PRECARIOUSNESS	PRECESSIONAL	PRECIPITOUSNESS	PRECOGNOSCING	PRECONIZED
PRECARITIES	PRECESSIONALLY	PRECISENESS	PRECOLLEGE	PRECONIZES
PRECASTING	PRECESSIONS	PRECISENESSES	PRECOLLEGIATE	PRECONIZING
PRECAUTION	PRECHARGED	PRECISIANISM	PRECOLONIAL	PRECONQUEST
PRECAUTIONAL	PRECHARGES	PRECISIANISMS	PRECOMBUSTION	PRECONSCIOUS
PRECAUTIONARY	PRECHARGING	PRECISIANIST	PRECOMBUSTIONS	PRECONSCIOUSES
PRECAUTIONED	PRECHECKED	PRECISIANISTS	PRECOMMITMENT	PRECONSCIOUSLY
PRECAUTIONING	PRECHECKING	PRECISIANS	PRECOMMITMENTS	PRECONSONANTAL
PRECAUTIONS	PRECHILLED	PRECISIONISM	PRECOMPETITIVE	PRECONSTRUCT
PRECAUTIOUS	PRECHILLING	PRECISIONISMS	PRECOMPOSE	PRECONSTRUCTED
PRECEDENCE	PRECHOOSES	PRECISIONIST	PRECOMPOSED	PRECONSTRUCTING
PRECEDENCES	PRECHOOSING	PRECISIONISTS	PRECOMPOSES	PRECONSTRUCTION
PRECEDENCIES	PRECHRISTIAN	PRECISIONS	PRECOMPOSING	PRECONSTRUCTS
PRECEDENCY	PRECIEUSES	PRECLASSICAL	PRECOMPUTE	PRECONSUME
PRECEDENTED	PRECIOSITIES	PRECLEANED	PRECOMPUTED	PRECONSUMED
PRECEDENTIAL	PRECIOSITY	PRECLEANING	PRECOMPUTER	PRECONSUMES

PRECONSUMING	PREDEFINITIONS	PREDEVELOP	PREDIGESTS	PREELECTRIC
PRECONTACT	PREDELIVERIES	PREDEVELOPED	PREDIKANTS	PREEMBARGO
PRECONTACTS	PREDELIVERY	PREDEVELOPING	PREDILECTED	PREEMERGENCE
PRECONTRACT	PREDENTARY	PREDEVELOPMENT	PREDILECTION	PREEMERGENT
PRECONTRACTED	PREDENTATE	PREDEVELOPMENTS	PREDILECTIONS	PREEMINENCE
PRECONTRACTING	PREDEPARTURE	PREDEVELOPS	PREDINNERS	PREEMINENCES
PRECONTRACTS	PREDEPOSIT	PREDEVOTED	PREDISCHARGE	PREEMINENT
PRECONVENTION	PREDEPOSITED	PREDEVOTES	PREDISCOVERIES	PREEMINENTLY
PRECONVICTION	PREDEPOSITING	PREDEVOTING	PREDISCOVERY	PREEMPLOYMENT
PRECONVICTIONS	PREDEPOSITS	PREDIABETES	PREDISPOSAL	PREEMPTING
PRECOOKERS	PREDESIGNATE	PREDIABETESES	PREDISPOSALS	PREEMPTION
PRECOOKING	PREDESIGNATED	PREDIABETIC	PREDISPOSE	PREEMPTIONS
PRECOOLING	PREDESIGNATES	PREDIABETICS	PREDISPOSED	PREEMPTIVE
PRECOPULATORY	PREDESIGNATING	PREDIALITIES	PREDISPOSES	PREEMPTIVELY
PRECORDIAL	PREDESIGNATION	PREDIALITY	PREDISPOSING	PREEMPTORS
PRECREASED	PREDESIGNATIONS	PREDICABILITIES	PREDISPOSITION	PREENACTED
PRECREASES	PREDESIGNATORY	PREDICABILITY	PREDISPOSITIONS	PREENACTING
PRECREASING	PREDESIGNED	PREDICABLE	PREDISTRIBUTION	PREENROLLMENT
PRECRITICAL	PREDESIGNING	PREDICABLENESS	PREDNISOLONE	PREERECTED
PRECURRERS	PREDESIGNS	PREDICABLES	PREDNISOLONES	PREERECTING
PRECURSING	PREDESTINABLE	PREDICAMENT	PREDNISONE	PREESTABLISH
PRECURSIVE	PREDESTINARIAN	PREDICAMENTAL	PREDNISONES	PREESTABLISHED
PRECURSORS	PREDESTINARIANS	PREDICAMENTS	PREDOCTORAL	PREESTABLISHES
PRECURSORY	PREDESTINATE	PREDICANTS	PREDOMINANCE	PREESTABLISHING
PRECUTTING	PREDESTINATED	PREDICATED	PREDOMINANCES	PREETHICAL
PRECYCLING	PREDESTINATES	PREDICATES	PREDOMINANCIES	PREEXCITED
PREDACEOUS	PREDESTINATING	PREDICATING	PREDOMINANCY	PREEXCITES
PREDACEOUSNESS	PREDESTINATION	PREDICATION	PREDOMINANT	PREEXCITING
PREDACIOUS	PREDESTINATIONS	PREDICATIONS	PREDOMINANTLY	PREEXEMPTED
PREDACIOUSNESS	PREDESTINATIVE	PREDICATIVE	PREDOMINATE	PREEXEMPTING
PREDACITIES	PREDESTINATOR	PREDICATIVELY	PREDOMINATED	PREEXEMPTS
PREDATIONS	PREDESTINATORS	PREDICATOR	PREDOMINATELY	PREEXISTED
PREDATISMS	PREDESTINE	PREDICATORS	PREDOMINATES	PREEXISTENCE
PREDATORILY	PREDESTINED	PREDICATORY	PREDOMINATING	PREEXISTENCES
PREDATORINESS	PREDESTINES	PREDICTABILITY	PREDOMINATION	PREEXISTENT
PREDATORINESSES	PREDESTINIES	PREDICTABLE	PREDOMINATIONS	PREEXISTING
PREDECEASE	PREDESTINING	PREDICTABLENESS	PREDOMINATOR	PREEXPERIMENT
PREDECEASED	PREDESTINY	PREDICTABLY	PREDOMINATORS	PREEXPOSED
PREDECEASES	PREDETERMINABLE	PREDICTERS	PREDOOMING	PREEXPOSES
PREDECEASING	PREDETERMINATE	PREDICTING	PREDRILLED	PREEXPOSING
PREDECESSOR	PREDETERMINE	PREDICTION	PREDRILLING	PREFABBING
PREDECESSORS	PREDETERMINED	PREDICTIONS	PREDYNASTIC	PREFABRICATE
PREDEDUCTED	PREDETERMINER	PREDICTIVE	PREECLAMPSIA	PREFABRICATED
PREDEDUCTING	PREDETERMINERS	PREDICTIVELY	PREECLAMPSIAS	PREFABRICATES
PREDEDUCTS	PREDETERMINES	PREDICTORS	PREECLAMPTIC	PREFABRICATING
PREDEFINED	PREDETERMINING	PREDIGESTED	PREEDITING	PREFABRICATION
PREDEFINES	PREDETERMINISM	PREDIGESTING	PREELECTED	PREFABRICATIONS
PREDEFINING	PREDETERMINISMS	PREDIGESTION	PREELECTING	PREFABRICATOR
PREDEFINITION	PREDEVALUATION	PREDIGESTIONS	PREELECTION	PREFABRICATORS

PREFASCIST	PREFLIGHTED	PREGUSTATION	PREINSERTED	PRELAUNCHED
PREFATORIAL	PREFLIGHTING	PREGUSTATIONS	PREINSERTING	PRELAUNCHES
PREFATORIALLY	PREFLIGHTS	PREHALLUCES	PREINSERTS	PRELAUNCHING
PREFATORILY	PREFLORATION	PREHANDLED	PREINTERVIEW	PRELECTING
PREFECTORIAL	PREFLORATIONS	PREHANDLES	PREINTERVIEWED	PRELECTION
PREFECTSHIP	PREFOCUSED	PREHANDLING	PREINTERVIEWING	PRELECTIONS
PREFECTSHIPS	PREFOCUSES	PREHARDENED	PREINTERVIEWS	PRELECTORS
PREFECTURAL	PREFOCUSING	PREHARDENING	PREINVASION	PRELEXICAL
PREFECTURE	PREFOCUSSED	PREHARDENS	PREINVITED	PRELIBATION
PREFECTURES	PREFOCUSSES	PREHARVEST	PREINVITES	PRELIBATIONS
PREFERABILITIES	PREFOCUSSING	PREHARVESTS	PREINVITING	PRELIMINARIES
PREFERABILITY	PREFOLIATION	PREHEADACHE	PREJUDGEMENT	PRELIMINARILY
PREFERABLE	PREFOLIATIONS	PREHEATERS	PREJUDGEMENTS	PRELIMINARY
PREFERABLENESS	PREFORMATION	PREHEATING	PREJUDGERS	PRELIMITED
PREFERABLY	PREFORMATIONISM	PREHEMINENCE	PREJUDGING	PRELIMITING
PREFERENCE	PREFORMATIONIST	PREHEMINENCES	PREJUDGMENT	PRELINGUAL
PREFERENCES	PREFORMATIONS	PREHENDING	PREJUDGMENTS	PRELINGUALLY
PREFERENTIAL	PREFORMATIVE	PREHENSIBLE	PREJUDICANT	PRELITERACIES
PREFERENTIALISM	PREFORMATIVES	PREHENSILE	PREJUDICATE	PRELITERACY
PREFERENTIALIST	PREFORMATS	PREHENSILITIES	PREJUDICATED	PRELITERARY
PREFERENTIALITY	PREFORMATTED	PREHENSILITY	PREJUDICATES	PRELITERATE
PREFERENTIALLY	PREFORMATTING	PREHENSION	PREJUDICATING	PRELITERATES
PREFERMENT	PREFORMING	PREHENSIONS	PREJUDICATION	PRELOADING
PREFERMENTS	PREFORMULATE	PREHENSIVE	PREJUDICATIONS	PRELOCATED
PREFERRABLE	PREFORMULATED	PREHENSORIAL	PREJUDICATIVE	PRELOCATES
PREFERRERS	PREFORMULATES	PREHENSORS	PREJUDICED	PRELOCATING
PREFERRING	PREFORMULATING	PREHENSORY	PREJUDICES	PRELOGICAL
PREFIGURATE	PREFRANKED	PREHISTORIAN	PREJUDICIAL	PRELUDIOUS
PREFIGURATED	PREFRANKING	PREHISTORIANS	PREJUDICIALLY	PRELUNCHEON
PREFIGURATES	PREFREEZES	PREHISTORIC	PREJUDICIALNESS	PRELUNCHEONS
PREFIGURATING	PREFREEZING	PREHISTORICAL	PREJUDICING	PRELUSIONS
PREFIGURATION	PREFRESHMAN	PREHISTORICALLY	PREJUDIZES	PRELUSIVELY
PREFIGURATIONS	PREFRESHMEN	PREHISTORIES	PREKINDERGARTEN	PRELUSORILY
PREFIGURATIVE	PREFRONTAL	PREHISTORY	PRELAPSARIAN	PREMALIGNANT
PREFIGURATIVELY	PREFRONTALS	PREHOLIDAY	PRELATESHIP	PREMANDIBULAR
PREFIGURED	PREFULGENT	PREHOMINID	PRELATESHIPS	PREMANDIBULARS
PREFIGUREMENT	PREFUNDING	PREHOMINIDS	PRELATESSES	PREMANUFACTURE
PREFIGUREMENTS	PREGANGLIONIC	PREIGNITION	PRELATICAL	PREMANUFACTURED
PREFIGURES	PREGENITAL	PREIGNITIONS	PRELATICALLY	PREMANUFACTURES
PREFIGURING	PREGLACIAL	PREIMPLANTATION	PRELATIONS	PREMARITAL
PREFINANCE	PREGNABILITIES	PREIMPOSED	PRELATISED	PREMARITALLY
PREFINANCED	PREGNABILITY	PREIMPOSES	PRELATISES	PREMARKETED
PREFINANCES	PREGNANCES	PREIMPOSING	PRELATISING	PREMARKETING
PREFINANCING	PREGNANCIES	PREINAUGURAL	PRELATISMS	PREMARKETS
PREFINANCINGS	PREGNANTLY	PREINDUCTION	PRELATISTS	PREMARRIAGE
PREFIXALLY	PREGNENOLONE	PREINDUSTRIAL	PRELATIZED	PREMATURELY
PREFIXIONS	PREGNENOLONES	PREINFORMED	PRELATIZES	PREMATURENESS
PREFIXTURE	PREGROWTHS	PREINFORMING	PRELATIZING	PREMATURENESSES
PREFIXTURES	PREGUIDING	PREINFORMS	PRELATURES	PREMATURES

P

PREMATURITIES PREMOISTENED PRENUMBERS PREPARATORS PREPOSITORS
PREMATURITY PREMOISTENING PRENUPTIAL PREPARATORY PREPOSSESS
PREMAXILLA PREMOISTENS PRENUPTIALS PREPAREDLY PREPOSSESSED
PREMAXILLAE PREMOLDING PREOBTAINED PREPAREDNESS PREPOSSESSES
PREMAXILLARIES PREMONISHED PREOBTAINING PREPAREDNESSES PREPOSSESSING
PREMAXILLARY PREMONISHES PREOBTAINS PREPASTING PREPOSSESSINGLY
PREMAXILLAS PREMONISHING PREOCCUPANCIES PREPATELLAR PREPOSSESSION
PREMEASURE PREMONISHMENT PREOCCUPANCY PREPAYABLE PREPOSSESSIONS
PREMEASURED PREMONISHMENTS PREOCCUPANT PREPAYMENT PREPOSTEROUS
PREMEASURES PREMONITION PREOCCUPANTS PREPAYMENTS PREPOSTEROUSLY
PREMEASURING PREMONITIONS PREOCCUPATE PREPENSELY PREPOSTORS
PREMEDICAL PREMONITIVE PREOCCUPATED PREPENSING PREPOTENCE
PREMEDICALLY PREMONITOR PREOCCUPATES PREPENSIVE PREPOTENCES
PREMEDICATE PREMONITORILY PREOCCUPATING PREPERFORMANCE PREPOTENCIES
PREMEDICATED PREMONITORS PREOCCUPATION PREPLACING PREPOTENCY
PREMEDICATES PREMONITORY PREOCCUPATIONS PREPLANNED PREPOTENTLY
PREMEDICATING PREMOTIONS PREOCCUPIED PREPLANNING PREPPINESS
PREMEDICATION PREMOULDED PREOCCUPIES PREPLANTING PREPPINESSES
PREMEDICATIONS PREMOULDING PREOCCUPYING PREPOLLENCE PREPRANDIAL
PREMEDIEVAL PREMOVEMENT PREOCULARS PREPOLLENCES PREPREPARED
PREMEDITATE PREMOVEMENTS PREOPENING PREPOLLENCIES PREPRESIDENTIAL
PREMEDITATED PREMUNITION PREOPERATIONAL PREPOLLENCY PREPRESSES
PREMEDITATEDLY PREMUNITIONS PREOPERATIVE PREPOLLENT PREPRICING
PREMEDITATES PREMYCOTIC PREOPERATIVELY PREPOLLICES PREPRIMARIES
PREMEDITATING PRENATALLY PREOPTIONS PREPONDERANCE PREPRIMARY
PREMEDITATION PRENEGOTIATE PREORDAINED PREPONDERANCES PREPRINTED
PREMEDITATIONS PRENEGOTIATED PREORDAINING PREPONDERANCIES PREPRINTING
PREMEDITATIVE PRENEGOTIATES PREORDAINMENT PREPONDERANCY PREPROCESS
PREMEDITATOR PRENEGOTIATING PREORDAINMENTS PREPONDERANT PREPROCESSED
PREMEDITATORS PRENEGOTIATION PREORDAINS PREPONDERANTLY PREPROCESSES
PREMEIOTIC PRENEGOTIATIONS PREORDERED PREPONDERATE PREPROCESSING
PREMENOPAUSAL PRENOMINAL PREORDERING PREPONDERATED PREPROCESSOR
PREMENSTRUAL PRENOMINALLY PREORDINANCE PREPONDERATELY PREPROCESSORS
PREMENSTRUALLY PRENOMINATE PREORDINANCES PREPONDERATES PREPRODUCTION
PREMIERING PRENOMINATED PREORDINATION PREPONDERATING PREPRODUCTIONS
PREMIERSHIP PRENOMINATES PREORDINATIONS PREPONDERATION PREPROFESSIONAL
PREMIERSHIPS PRENOMINATING PREOVULATORY PREPONDERATIONS PREPROGRAM
PREMIGRATION PRENOMINATION PREPACKAGE PREPORTION PREPROGRAMED
PREMILLENARIAN PRENOMINATIONS PREPACKAGED PREPORTIONED PREPROGRAMING
PREMILLENARIANS PRENOTIFICATION PREPACKAGES PREPORTIONING PREPROGRAMMED
PREMILLENNIAL PRENOTIFIED PREPACKAGING PREPORTIONS PREPROGRAMMING
PREMILLENNIALLY PRENOTIFIES PREPACKING PREPOSITION PREPROGRAMMINGS
PREMILLENNIALS PRENOTIFYING PREPARATION PREPOSITIONAL PREPROGRAMS
PREMISSING PRENOTIONS PREPARATIONS PREPOSITIONALLY PREPSYCHEDELIC
PREMODIFICATION PRENTICESHIP PREPARATIVE PREPOSITIONS PREPUBERAL
PREMODIFIED PRENTICESHIPS PREPARATIVELY PREPOSITIVE PREPUBERTAL
PREMODIFIES PRENTICING PREPARATIVES PREPOSITIVELY PREPUBERTIES
PREMODIFYING PRENUMBERED PREPARATOR PREPOSITIVES PREPUBERTY
PREMOISTEN PRENUMBERING PREPARATORILY PREPOSITOR PREPUBESCENCE

PREPUBESCENCES	PREROGATIVES	PRESCHOOLERS	PRESENTATIONIST	PRESHAPING
PREPUBESCENT	PREROLLING	PRESCHOOLS	PRESENTATIONS	PRESHIPPED
PREPUBESCENTS	PREROMANTIC	PRESCIENCE	PRESENTATIVE	PRESHIPPING
PREPUBLICATION	PREROMANTICS	PRESCIENCES	PRESENTEEISM	PRESHOWING
PREPUBLICATIONS	PRESAGEFUL	PRESCIENTIFIC	PRESENTEEISMS	PRESHRINKING
PREPUNCHED	PRESAGEFULLY	PRESCIENTLY	PRESENTEES	PRESHRINKS
PREPUNCHES	PRESAGEMENT	PRESCINDED	PRESENTENCE	PRESHRUNKEN
PREPUNCHING	PRESAGEMENTS	PRESCINDENT	PRESENTENCED	PRESIDENCIES
PREPUNCTUAL	PRESANCTIFIED	PRESCINDING	PRESENTENCES	PRESIDENCY
PREPURCHASE	PRESANCTIFIES	PRESCISSION	PRESENTENCING	PRESIDENTESS
PREPURCHASED	PRESANCTIFY	PRESCISSIONS	PRESENTERS	PRESIDENTESSES
PREPURCHASES	PRESANCTIFYING	PRESCORING	PRESENTIAL	PRESIDENTIAL
PREPURCHASING	PRESBYACOUSES	PRESCREENED	PRESENTIALITIES	PRESIDENTIALLY
PREQUALIFIED	PRESBYACOUSIS	PRESCREENING	PRESENTIALITY	PRESIDENTS
PREQUALIFIES	PRESBYACUSES	PRESCREENS	PRESENTIALLY	PRESIDENTSHIP
PREQUALIFY	PRESBYACUSIS	PRESCRIBED	PRESENTIENT	PRESIDENTSHIPS
PREQUALIFYING	PRESBYCOUSES	PRESCRIBER	PRESENTIMENT	PRESIDIARY
PREREADING	PRESBYCOUSIS	PRESCRIBERS	PRESENTIMENTAL	PRESIDIUMS
PRERECESSION	PRESBYCUSES	PRESCRIBES	PRESENTIMENTS	PRESIFTING
PRERECORDED	PRESBYCUSIS	PRESCRIBING	PRESENTING	PRESIGNALED
PRERECORDING	PRESBYOPES	PRESCRIBINGS	PRESENTISM	PRESIGNALING
PRERECORDS	PRESBYOPIA	PRESCRIPTIBLE	PRESENTISMS	PRESIGNALLED
PREREGISTER	PRESBYOPIAS	PRESCRIPTION	PRESENTIST	PRESIGNALLING
PREREGISTERED	PRESBYOPIC	PRESCRIPTIONS	PRESENTISTS	PRESIGNALS
PREREGISTERING	PRESBYOPICS	PRESCRIPTIVE	PRESENTIVE	PRESIGNIFIED
PREREGISTERS	PRESBYOPIES	PRESCRIPTIVELY	PRESENTIVENESS	PRESIGNIFIES
PREREGISTRATION	PRESBYTERAL	PRESCRIPTIVISM	PRESENTIVES	PRESIGNIFY
PREREHEARSAL	PRESBYTERATE	PRESCRIPTIVISMS	PRESENTMENT	PRESIGNIFYING
PREREHEARSALS	PRESBYTERATES	PRESCRIPTIVIST	PRESENTMENTS	PRESLAUGHTER
PRERELEASE	PRESBYTERIAL	PRESCRIPTIVISTS	PRESENTNESS	PRESLICING
PRERELEASED	PRESBYTERIALLY	PRESCRIPTS	PRESENTNESSES	PRESOAKING
PRERELEASES	PRESBYTERIALS	PRESEASONS	PRESERVABILITY	PRESOLVING
PRERELEASING	PRESBYTERIAN	PRESELECTED	PRESERVABLE	PRESORTING
PREREQUIRE	PRESBYTERIANISE	PRESELECTING	PRESERVABLY	PRESPECIFIED
PREREQUIRED	PRESBYTERIANISM	PRESELECTION	PRESERVATION	PRESPECIFIES
PREREQUIRES	PRESBYTERIANIZE	PRESELECTIONS	PRESERVATIONIST	PRESPECIFY
PREREQUIRING	PRESBYTERIANS	PRESELECTOR	PRESERVATIONS	PRESPECIFYING
PREREQUISITE	PRESBYTERIES	PRESELECTORS	PRESERVATIVE	PRESSBOARD
PREREQUISITES	PRESBYTERS	PRESELECTS	PRESERVATIVES	PRESSBOARDS
PRERETIREMENT	PRESBYTERSHIP	PRESELLING	PRESERVATORIES	PRESSGANGS
PREREVIEWED	PRESBYTERSHIPS	PRESENSION	PRESERVATORY	PRESSINGLY
PREREVIEWING	PRESBYTERY	PRESENSIONS	PRESERVERS	PRESSINGNESS
PREREVIEWS	PRESBYTISM	PRESENTABILITY	PRESERVICE	PRESSINGNESSES
PREREVISIONIST	PRESBYTISMS	PRESENTABLE	PRESERVING	PRESSMARKS
PREREVOLUTION	PRESCHEDULE	PRESENTABLENESS	PRESETTING	PRESSROOMS
PRERINSING	PRESCHEDULED	PRESENTABLY	PRESETTLED	PRESSURELESS
PREROGATIVE	PRESCHEDULES	PRESENTATION	PRESETTLEMENT	PRESSURING
PREROGATIVED	PRESCHEDULING	PRESENTATIONAL	PRESETTLES	PRESSURISATION
PREROGATIVELY	PRESCHOOLER	PRESENTATIONISM	PRESETTLING	PRESSURISATIONS

PRESSURISE	PRESTRUCTURES	PRETENSIONED	PRETTIFIED	PREVENTIBLY
PRESSURISED	PRESTRUCTURING	PRETENSIONING	PRETTIFIER	PREVENTING
PRESSURISER	PRESUMABLE	PRETENSIONLESS	PRETTIFIERS	PREVENTION
PRESSURISERS	PRESUMABLY	PRETENSIONS	PRETTIFIES	PREVENTIONS
PRESSURISES	PRESUMEDLY	PRETENSIVE	PRETTIFYING	PREVENTIVE
PRESSURISING	PRESUMINGLY	PRETENTIOUS	PRETTINESS	PREVENTIVELY
PRESSURIZATION	PRESUMMITS	PRETENTIOUSLY	PRETTINESSES	PREVENTIVENESS
PRESSURIZATIONS	PRESUMPTION	PRETENTIOUSNESS	PRETTYISMS	PREVENTIVES
PRESSURIZE	PRESUMPTIONS	PRETERHUMAN	PRETZELLED	PREVIEWERS
PRESSURIZED	PRESUMPTIVE	PRETERISTS	PRETZELLING	PREVIEWING
PRESSURIZER	PRESUMPTIVELY	PRETERITENESS	PREUNIFICATION	PREVIOUSLY
PRESSURIZERS	PRESUMPTIVENESS	PRETERITENESSES	PREUNITING	PREVIOUSNESS
PRESSURIZES	PRESUMPTUOUS	PRETERITES	PREUNIVERSITY	PREVIOUSNESSES
PRESSURIZING	PRESUMPTUOUSLY	PRETERITION	PREVAILERS	PREVISIONAL
PRESSWOMAN	PRESUPPOSE	PRETERITIONS	PREVAILING	PREVISIONARY
PRESSWOMEN	PRESUPPOSED	PRETERITIVE	PREVAILINGLY	PREVISIONED
PRESSWORKS	PRESUPPOSES	PRETERMINAL	PREVAILMENT	PREVISIONING
PRESTAMPED	PRESUPPOSING	PRETERMINATION	PREVAILMENTS	PREVISIONS
PRESTAMPING	PRESUPPOSITION	PRETERMINATIONS	PREVALENCE	PREVISITED
PRESTATION	PRESUPPOSITIONS	PRETERMISSION	PREVALENCES	PREVISITING
PRESTATIONS	PRESURGERY	PRETERMISSIONS	PREVALENCIES	PREVOCALIC
PRESTERILISE	PRESURMISE	PRETERMITS	PREVALENCY	PREVOCALICALLY
PRESTERILISED	PRESURMISES	PRETERMITTED	PREVALENTLY	PREVOCATIONAL
PRESTERILISES	PRESURVEYED	PRETERMITTER	PREVALENTNESS	PREWARMING
PRESTERILISING	PRESURVEYING	PRETERMITTERS	PREVALENTNESSES	PREWARNING
PRESTERILIZE	PRESURVEYS	PRETERMITTING	PREVALENTS	PREWASHING
PRESTERILIZED	PRESWEETEN	PRETERNATURAL	PREVALUING	PREWEANING
PRESTERILIZES	PRESWEETENED	PRETERNATURALLY	PREVARICATE	PREWEIGHED
PRESTERILIZING	PRESWEETENING	PRETERPERFECT	PREVARICATED	PREWEIGHING
PRESTERNUM	PRESWEETENS	PRETERPERFECTS	PREVARICATES	PREWORKING
PRESTERNUMS	PRESYMPTOMATIC	PRETESTING	PREVARICATING	PREWRAPPED
PRESTIDIGITATOR	PRESYNAPTIC	PRETEXTING	PREVARICATION	PREWRAPPING
PRESTIGEFUL	PRESYNAPTICALLY	PRETEXTINGS	PREVARICATIONS	PREWRITING
PRESTIGIATOR	PRETASTING	PRETHEATER	PREVARICATOR	PREWRITINGS
PRESTIGIATORS	PRETELEVISION	PRETHEATRE	PREVARICATORS	PREWRITTEN
PRESTIGIOUS	PRETELLING	PRETORIANS	PREVENANCIES	PRICELESSLY
PRESTIGIOUSLY	PRETENCELESS	PRETORSHIP	PREVENANCY	PRICELESSNESS
PRESTIGIOUSNESS	PRETENDANT	PRETORSHIPS	PREVENIENCE	PRICELESSNESSES
PRESTISSIMO	PRETENDANTS	PRETOURNAMENT	PREVENIENCES	PRICINESSES
PRESTISSIMOS	PRETENDEDLY	PRETRAINED	PREVENIENT	PRICKLIEST
PRESTORAGE	PRETENDENT	PRETRAINING	PREVENIENTLY	PRICKLINESS
PRESTORING	PRETENDENTS	PRETREATED	PREVENTABILITY	PRICKLINESSES
PRESTRESSED	PRETENDERS	PRETREATING	PREVENTABLE	PRICKLINGS
PRESTRESSES	PRETENDERSHIP	PRETREATMENT	PREVENTABLY	PRICKWOODS
PRESTRESSING	PRETENDERSHIPS	PRETREATMENTS	PREVENTATIVE	PRIDEFULLY
PRESTRICTION	PRETENDING	PRETRIMMED	PREVENTATIVES	PRIDEFULNESS
PRESTRICTIONS	PRETENDINGLY	PRETRIMMING	PREVENTERS	PRIDEFULNESSES
PRESTRUCTURE	PRETENSELESS	PRETTIFICATION	PREVENTIBILITY	PRIESTCRAFT
PRESTRUCTURED	PRETENSION	PRETTIFICATIONS	PREVENTIBLE	PRIESTCRAFTS

PRIESTESSES	PRIMITIVISMS	PRINCESSLIER	PRISMATOID	PRIZEWINNER
PRIESTHOOD	PRIMITIVIST	PRINCESSLIEST	PRISMATOIDAL	PRIZEWINNERS
PRIESTHOODS	PRIMITIVISTIC	PRINCESSLY	PRISMATOIDS	PRIZEWINNING
PRIESTLIER	PRIMITIVISTS	PRINCIFIED	PRISMOIDAL	PRIZEWOMAN
PRIESTLIEST	PRIMITIVITIES	PRINCIPALITIES	PRISONMENT	PRIZEWOMEN
PRIESTLIKE	PRIMITIVITY	PRINCIPALITY	PRISONMENTS	PROABORTION
PRIESTLINESS	PRIMNESSES	PRINCIPALLY	PRISSINESS	PROACTIONS
PRIESTLINESSES	PRIMOGENIAL	PRINCIPALNESS	PRISSINESSES	PROAIRESES
PRIESTLING	PRIMOGENIT	PRINCIPALNESSES	PRISTINELY	PROAIRESIS
PRIESTLINGS	PRIMOGENITAL	PRINCIPALS	PRIVATDOCENT	PROBABILIORISM
PRIESTSHIP	PRIMOGENITARY	PRINCIPALSHIP	PRIVATDOCENTS	PROBABILIORISMS
PRIESTSHIPS	PRIMOGENITIVE	PRINCIPALSHIPS	PRIVATDOZENT	PROBABILIORIST
PRIGGERIES	PRIMOGENITIVES	PRINCIPATE	PRIVATDOZENTS	PROBABILIORISTS
PRIGGISHLY	PRIMOGENITOR	PRINCIPATES	PRIVATEERED	PROBABILISM
PRIGGISHNESS	PRIMOGENITORS	PRINCIPIAL	PRIVATEERING	PROBABILISMS
PRIGGISHNESSES	PRIMOGENITRICES	PRINCIPIUM	PRIVATEERINGS	PROBABILIST
PRIMAEVALLY	PRIMOGENITRIX	PRINCIPLED	PRIVATEERS	PROBABILISTIC
PRIMALITIES	PRIMOGENITRIXES	PRINCIPLES	PRIVATEERSMAN	PROBABILISTS
PRIMAQUINE	PRIMOGENITS	PRINCIPLING	PRIVATEERSMEN	PROBABILITIES
PRIMAQUINES	PRIMOGENITURE	PRINTABILITIES	PRIVATENESS	PROBABILITY
PRIMARINESS	PRIMOGENITURES	PRINTABILITY	PRIVATENESSES	PROBATIONAL
PRIMARINESSES	PRIMORDIAL	PRINTABLENESS	PRIVATIONS	PROBATIONALLY
PRIMARYING	PRIMORDIALISM	PRINTABLENESSES	PRIVATISATION	PROBATIONARIES
PRIMATESHIP	PRIMORDIALISMS	PRINTERIES	PRIVATISATIONS	PROBATIONARY
PRIMATESHIPS	PRIMORDIALITIES	PRINTHEADS	PRIVATISED	PROBATIONER
PRIMATIALS	PRIMORDIALITY	PRINTMAKER	PRIVATISER	PROBATIONERS
PRIMATICAL	PRIMORDIALLY	PRINTMAKERS	PRIVATISERS	PROBATIONERSHIP
PRIMATOLOGICAL	PRIMORDIALS	PRINTMAKING	PRIVATISES	PROBATIONS
PRIMATOLOGIES	PRIMORDIUM	PRINTMAKINGS	PRIVATISING	PROBATIVELY
PRIMATOLOGIST	PRIMROSIER	PRINTWHEEL	PRIVATISMS	PROBENECID
PRIMATOLOGISTS	PRIMROSIEST	PRINTWHEELS	PRIVATISTS	PROBENECIDS
PRIMATOLOGY	PRIMROSING	PRINTWORKS	PRIVATIVELY	PROBIOTICS
PRIMAVERAS	PRIMULACEOUS	PRIORESSES	PRIVATIVES	PROBLEMATIC
PRIMENESSES	PRIMULINES	PRIORITIES	PRIVATIZATION	PROBLEMATICAL
PRIMEVALLY	PRINCEDOMS	PRIORITISATION	PRIVATIZATIONS	PROBLEMATICALLY
PRIMIGENIAL	PRINCEHOOD	PRIORITISATIONS	PRIVATIZED	PROBLEMATICS
PRIMIGRAVIDA	PRINCEHOODS	PRIORITISE	PRIVATIZER	PROBLEMIST
PRIMIGRAVIDAE	PRINCEKINS	PRIORITISED	PRIVATIZERS	PROBLEMISTS
PRIMIGRAVIDAS	PRINCELETS	PRIORITISES	PRIVATIZES	PROBOSCIDEAN
PRIMIPARAE	PRINCELIER	PRIORITISING	PRIVATIZING	PROBOSCIDEANS
PRIMIPARAS	PRINCELIEST	PRIORITIZATION	PRIVILEGED	PROBOSCIDES
PRIMIPARITIES	PRINCELIKE	PRIORITIZATIONS	PRIVILEGES	PROBOSCIDIAN
PRIMIPARITY	PRINCELINESS	PRIORITIZE	PRIVILEGING	PROBOSCIDIANS
PRIMIPAROUS	PRINCELINESSES	PRIORITIZED	PRIZEFIGHT	PROBOSCISES
PRIMITIVELY	PRINCELING	PRIORITIZES	PRIZEFIGHTER	PROBOULEUTIC
PRIMITIVENESS	PRINCELINGS	PRIORITIZING	PRIZEFIGHTERS	PROBUSINESS
PRIMITIVENESSES	PRINCESHIP	PRIORSHIPS	PRIZEFIGHTING	PROCACIOUS
PRIMITIVES	PRINCESHIPS	PRISMATICAL	PRIZEFIGHTINGS	PROCACITIES
PRIMITIVISM	PRINCESSES	PRISMATICALLY	PRIZEFIGHTS	PROCAMBIAL

PROCAMBIUM	PROCESSIONS	PROCRYPTIC	PROCURATORS	PROFANATORY
PROCAMBIUMS	PROCESSORS	PROCRYPTICALLY	PROCURATORSHIP	PROFANENESS
PROCAPITALIST	PROCESSUAL	PROCTALGIA	PROCURATORSHIPS	PROFANENESSES
PROCARBAZINE	PROCHRONISM	PROCTALGIAS	PROCURATORY	PROFANITIES
PROCARBAZINES	PROCHRONISMS	PROCTITIDES	PROCUREMENT	PROFASCIST
PROCARYONS	PROCIDENCE	PROCTITISES	PROCUREMENTS	PROFECTITIOUS
PROCARYOTE	PROCIDENCES	PROCTODAEA	PROCURESSES	PROFEMINIST
PROCARYOTES	PROCLAIMANT	PROCTODAEAL	PROCUREURS	PROFESSEDLY
PROCARYOTIC	PROCLAIMANTS	PROCTODAEUM	PROCURINGS	PROFESSING
PROCATHEDRAL	PROCLAIMED	PROCTODAEUMS	PROCYONIDS	PROFESSION
PROCATHEDRALS	PROCLAIMER	PROCTODEAL	PRODIGALISE	PROFESSIONAL
PROCEDURAL	PROCLAIMERS	PROCTODEUM	PRODIGALISED	PROFESSIONALISE
PROCEDURALLY	PROCLAIMING	PROCTODEUMS	PRODIGALISES	PROFESSIONALISM
PROCEDURALS	PROCLAMATION	PROCTOLOGIC	PRODIGALISING	PROFESSIONALIST
PROCEDURES	PROCLAMATIONS	PROCTOLOGICAL	PRODIGALITIES	PROFESSIONALIZE
PROCEEDERS	PROCLAMATORY	PROCTOLOGIES	PRODIGALITY	PROFESSIONALLY
PROCEEDING	PROCLITICS	PROCTOLOGIST	PRODIGALIZE	PROFESSIONALS
PROCEEDINGS	PROCLIVITIES	PROCTOLOGISTS	PRODIGALIZED	PROFESSIONS
PROCELEUSMATIC	PROCLIVITY	PROCTOLOGY	PRODIGALIZES	PROFESSORATE
PROCELEUSMATICS	PROCOELOUS	PROCTORAGE	PRODIGALIZING	PROFESSORATES
PROCELLARIAN	PROCONSULAR	PROCTORAGES	PRODIGALLY	PROFESSORESS
PROCELLARIANS	PROCONSULATE	PROCTORIAL	PRODIGIOSITIES	PROFESSORESSES
PROCEPHALIC	PROCONSULATES	PROCTORIALLY	PRODIGIOSITY	PROFESSORIAL
PROCERCOID	PROCONSULS	PROCTORING	PRODIGIOUS	PROFESSORIALLY
PROCERCOIDS	PROCONSULSHIP	PROCTORISE	PRODIGIOUSLY	PROFESSORIAT
PROCEREBRA	PROCONSULSHIPS	PROCTORISED	PRODIGIOUSNESS	PROFESSORIATE
PROCEREBRAL	PROCRASTINATE	PROCTORISES	PRODITORIOUS	PROFESSORIATES
PROCEREBRUM	PROCRASTINATED	PROCTORISING	PRODNOSING	PROFESSORIATS
PROCEREBRUMS	PROCRASTINATES	PROCTORIZE	PRODROMATA	PROFESSORS
PROCERITIES	PROCRASTINATING	PROCTORIZED	PRODUCEMENT	PROFESSORSHIP
PROCESSABILITY	PROCRASTINATION	PROCTORIZES	PRODUCEMENTS	PROFESSORSHIPS
PROCESSABLE	PROCRASTINATIVE	PROCTORIZING	PRODUCIBILITIES	PROFFERERS
PROCESSERS	PROCRASTINATOR	PROCTORSHIP	PRODUCIBILITY	PROFFERING
PROCESSIBILITY	PROCRASTINATORS	PROCTORSHIPS	PRODUCIBLE	PROFICIENCE
PROCESSIBLE	PROCRASTINATORY	PROCTOSCOPE	PRODUCTIBILITY	PROFICIENCES
PROCESSING	PROCREANTS	PROCTOSCOPES	PRODUCTILE	PROFICIENCIES
PROCESSINGS	PROCREATED	PROCTOSCOPIC	PRODUCTION	PROFICIENCY
PROCESSION	PROCREATES	PROCTOSCOPIES	PRODUCTIONAL	PROFICIENT
PROCESSIONAL	PROCREATING	PROCTOSCOPY	PRODUCTIONS	PROFICIENTLY
PROCESSIONALIST	PROCREATION	PROCUMBENT	PRODUCTIVE	PROFICIENTS
PROCESSIONALLY	PROCREATIONAL	PROCURABLE	PRODUCTIVELY	PROFILINGS
PROCESSIONALS	PROCREATIONS	PROCURACIES	PRODUCTIVENESS	PROFILISTS
PROCESSIONARIES	PROCREATIVE	PROCURANCE	PRODUCTIVITIES	PROFITABILITIES
PROCESSIONARY	PROCREATIVENESS	PROCURANCES	PRODUCTIVITY	PROFITABILITY
PROCESSIONED	PROCREATOR	PROCURATION	PROEMBRYOS	PROFITABLE
PROCESSIONER	PROCREATORS	PROCURATIONS	PROENZYMES	PROFITABLENESS
PROCESSIONERS	PROCRUSTEAN	PROCURATOR	PROESTRUSES	PROFITABLY
PROCESSIONING	PROCRYPSES	PROCURATORIAL	PROFANATION	PROFITEERED
PROCESSIONINGS	PROCRYPSIS	PROCURATORIES	PROFANATIONS	PROFITEERING

PROFITEERINGS	PROGLOTTID	PROGRESSISM	PROJECTIVE	PROLIFERATED
PROFITEERS	PROGLOTTIDEAN	PROGRESSISMS	PROJECTIVELY	PROLIFERATES
PROFITEROLE	PROGLOTTIDES	PROGRESSIST	PROJECTIVITIES	PROLIFERATING
PROFITEROLES	PROGLOTTIDS	PROGRESSISTS	PROJECTIVITY	PROLIFERATION
PROFITINGS	PROGLOTTIS	PROGRESSIVE	PROJECTIZATION	PROLIFERATIONS
PROFITLESS	PROGNATHIC	PROGRESSIVELY	PROJECTIZATIONS	PROLIFERATIVE
PROFITLESSLY	PROGNATHISM	PROGRESSIVENESS	PROJECTMENT	PROLIFEROUS
PROFITWISE	PROGNATHISMS	PROGRESSIVES	PROJECTMENTS	PROLIFEROUSLY
PROFLIGACIES	PROGNATHOUS	PROGRESSIVISM	PROJECTORS	PROLIFICACIES
PROFLIGACY	PROGNOSING	PROGRESSIVISMS	PROJECTURE	PROLIFICACY
PROFLIGATE	PROGNOSTIC	PROGRESSIVIST	PROJECTURES	PROLIFICAL
PROFLIGATELY	PROGNOSTICATE	PROGRESSIVISTIC	PROKARYONS	PROLIFICALLY
PROFLIGATES	PROGNOSTICATED	PROGRESSIVISTS	PROKARYOTE	PROLIFICATION
PROFLUENCE	PROGNOSTICATES	PROGRESSIVITIES	PROKARYOTES	PROLIFICATIONS
PROFLUENCES	PROGNOSTICATING	PROGRESSIVITY	PROKARYOTIC	PROLIFICITIES
PROFOUNDER	PROGNOSTICATION	PROGYMNASIA	PROKARYOTS	PROLIFICITY
PROFOUNDEST	PROGNOSTICATIVE	PROGYMNASIUM	PROLACTINS	PROLIFICNESS
PROFOUNDLY	PROGNOSTICATOR	PROGYMNASIUMS	PROLAMINES	PROLIFICNESSES
PROFOUNDNESS	PROGNOSTICATORS	PROHIBITED	PROLAPSING	PROLIXIOUS
PROFOUNDNESSES	PROGNOSTICS	PROHIBITER	PROLAPSUSES	PROLIXITIES
PROFULGENT	PROGRADATION	PROHIBITERS	PROLATENESS	PROLIXNESS
PROFUNDITIES	PROGRADATIONS	PROHIBITING	PROLATENESSES	PROLIXNESSES
PROFUNDITY	PROGRADING	PROHIBITION	PROLATIONS	PROLOCUTION
PROFUSENESS	PROGRAMABLE	PROHIBITIONARY	PROLEGOMENA	PROLOCUTIONS
PROFUSENESSES	PROGRAMERS	PROHIBITIONISM	PROLEGOMENAL	PROLOCUTOR
PROFUSIONS	PROGRAMING	PROHIBITIONISMS	PROLEGOMENARY	PROLOCUTORS
PROGENITIVE	PROGRAMINGS	PROHIBITIONIST	PROLEGOMENON	PROLOCUTORSHIP
PROGENITIVENESS	PROGRAMMABILITY	PROHIBITIONISTS	PROLEGOMENOUS	PROLOCUTORSHIPS
PROGENITOR	PROGRAMMABLE	PROHIBITIONS	PROLEPTICAL	PROLOCUTRICES
PROGENITORIAL	PROGRAMMABLES	PROHIBITIVE	PROLEPTICALLY	PROLOCUTRIX
PROGENITORS	PROGRAMMATIC	PROHIBITIVELY	PROLETARIAN	PROLOCUTRIXES
PROGENITORSHIP	PROGRAMMED	PROHIBITIVENESS	PROLETARIANISE	PROLOGISED
PROGENITORSHIPS	PROGRAMMER	PROHIBITOR	PROLETARIANISED	PROLOGISES
PROGENITRESS	PROGRAMMERS	PROHIBITORS	PROLETARIANISES	PROLOGISING
PROGENITRESSES	PROGRAMMES	PROHIBITORY	PROLETARIANISM	PROLOGISTS
PROGENITRICES	PROGRAMMING	PROINSULIN	PROLETARIANISMS	PROLOGIZED
PROGENITRIX	PROGRAMMINGS	PROINSULINS	PROLETARIANIZE	PROLOGIZES
PROGENITRIXES	PROGRESSED	PROJECTABLE	PROLETARIANIZED	PROLOGIZING
PROGENITURE	PROGRESSES	PROJECTILE	PROLETARIANIZES	PROLOGUING
PROGENITURES	PROGRESSING	PROJECTILES	PROLETARIANNESS	PROLOGUISE
PROGESTATIONAL	PROGRESSION	PROJECTING	PROLETARIANS	PROLOGUISED
PROGESTERONE	PROGRESSIONAL	PROJECTINGS	PROLETARIAT	PROLOGUISES
PROGESTERONES	PROGRESSIONALLY	PROJECTION	PROLETARIATE	PROLOGUISING
PROGESTINS	PROGRESSIONARY	PROJECTIONAL	PROLETARIATES	PROLOGUIZE
PROGESTOGEN	PROGRESSIONISM	PROJECTIONIST	PROLETARIATS	PROLOGUIZED
PROGESTOGENIC	PROGRESSIONISMS	PROJECTIONISTS	PROLETARIES	PROLOGUIZES
PROGESTOGENS	PROGRESSIONIST	PROJECTIONS	PROLICIDAL	PROLOGUIZING
PROGGINSES	PROGRESSIONISTS	PROJECTISATION	PROLICIDES	PROLONGABLE
PROGLOTTIC	PROGRESSIONS	PROJECTISATIONS	PROLIFERATE	PROLONGATE

PROLONGATED	PROMOTIONAL	PRONOUNCEDLY	PROPAGANDIZER	PROPHESIABLE
PROLONGATES	PROMOTIONS	PRONOUNCEMENT	PROPAGANDIZERS	PROPHESIED
PROLONGATING	PROMOTIVENESS	PRONOUNCEMENTS	PROPAGANDIZES	PROPHESIER
PROLONGATION	PROMOTIVENESSES	PRONOUNCER	PROPAGANDIZING	PROPHESIERS
PROLONGATIONS	PROMPTBOOK	PRONOUNCERS	PROPAGATED	PROPHESIES
PROLONGERS	PROMPTBOOKS	PRONOUNCES	PROPAGATES	PROPHESYING
PROLONGING	PROMPTINGS	PRONOUNCING	PROPAGATING	PROPHESYINGS
PROLONGMENT	PROMPTITUDE	PRONOUNCINGS	PROPAGATION	PROPHETESS
PROLONGMENTS	PROMPTITUDES	PRONUCLEAR	PROPAGATIONAL	PROPHETESSES
PROLUSIONS	PROMPTNESS	PRONUCLEARIST	PROPAGATIONS	PROPHETHOOD
PROMACHOSES	PROMPTNESSES	PRONUCLEARISTS	PROPAGATIVE	PROPHETHOODS
PROMENADED	PROMPTUARIES	PRONUCLEUS	PROPAGATOR	PROPHETICAL
PROMENADER	PROMPTUARY	PRONUCLEUSES	PROPAGATORS	PROPHETICALLY
PROMENADERS	PROMPTURES	PRONUNCIAMENTO	PROPAGULES	PROPHETICISM
PROMENADES	PROMULGATE	PRONUNCIAMENTOS	PROPAGULUM	PROPHETICISMS
PROMENADING	PROMULGATED	PRONUNCIATION	PROPANEDIOIC	PROPHETISM
PROMETHAZINE	PROMULGATES	PRONUNCIATIONAL	PROPANONES	PROPHETISMS
PROMETHAZINES	PROMULGATING	PRONUNCIATIONS	PROPAROXYTONE	PROPHETSHIP
PROMETHEUM	PROMULGATION	PRONUNCIOS	PROPAROXYTONES	PROPHETSHIPS
PROMETHEUMS	PROMULGATIONS	PROOEMIONS	PROPELLANT	PROPHYLACTIC
PROMETHIUM	PROMULGATOR	PROOEMIUMS	PROPELLANTS	PROPHYLACTICS
PROMETHIUMS	PROMULGATORS	PROOFREADER	PROPELLENT	PROPHYLAXES
PROMILITARY	PROMULGING	PROOFREADERS	PROPELLENTS	PROPHYLAXIS
PROMINENCE	PROMUSCIDATE	PROOFREADING	PROPELLERS	PROPINQUITIES
PROMINENCES	PROMUSCIDES	PROOFREADINGS	PROPELLING	PROPINQUITY
PROMINENCIES	PROMYCELIA	PROOFREADS	PROPELLINGS	PROPIONATE
PROMINENCY	PROMYCELIAL	PROOFROOMS	PROPELLORS	PROPIONATES
PROMINENTLY	PROMYCELIUM	PROPAEDEUTIC	PROPELMENT	PROPITIABLE
PROMINENTNESS	PRONATIONS	PROPAEDEUTICAL	PROPELMENTS	PROPITIATE
PROMINENTNESSES	PRONATORES	PROPAEDEUTICS	PROPENDENT	PROPITIATED
PROMINENTS	PRONENESSES	PROPAGABILITIES	PROPENDING	PROPITIATES
PROMISCUITIES	PRONEPHRIC	PROPAGABILITY	PROPENSELY	PROPITIATING
PROMISCUITY	PRONEPHROI	PROPAGABLE	PROPENSENESS	PROPITIATION
PROMISCUOUS	PRONEPHROS	PROPAGABLENESS	PROPENSENESSES	PROPITIATIONS
PROMISCUOUSLY	PRONEPHROSES	PROPAGANDA	PROPENSION	PROPITIATIOUS
PROMISCUOUSNESS	PRONGBUCKS	PROPAGANDAS	PROPENSIONS	PROPITIATIVE
PROMISEFUL	PRONGHORNS	PROPAGANDISE	PROPENSITIES	PROPITIATOR
PROMISELESS	PRONOMINAL	PROPAGANDISED	PROPENSITY	PROPITIATORIES
PROMISINGLY	PRONOMINALISE	PROPAGANDISER	PROPENSIVE	PROPITIATORILY
PROMISSIVE	PRONOMINALISED	PROPAGANDISERS	PROPERDINS	PROPITIATORS
PROMISSORILY	PRONOMINALISES	PROPAGANDISES	PROPERISPOMENA	PROPITIATORY
PROMISSORS	PRONOMINALISING	PROPAGANDISING	PROPERISPOMENON	PROPITIOUS
PROMISSORY	PRONOMINALIZE	PROPAGANDISM	PROPERNESS	PROPITIOUSLY
PROMONARCHIST	PRONOMINALIZED	PROPAGANDISMS	PROPERNESSES	PROPITIOUSNESS
PROMONTORIES	PRONOMINALIZES	PROPAGANDIST	PROPERTIED	PROPLASTID
PROMONTORY	PRONOMINALIZING	PROPAGANDISTIC	PROPERTIES	PROPLASTIDS
PROMOTABILITIES	PRONOMINALLY	PROPAGANDISTS	PROPERTYING	PROPODEONS
PROMOTABILITY	PRONOUNCEABLE	PROPAGANDIZE	PROPERTYLESS	PROPODEUMS
PROMOTABLE	PRONOUNCED	PROPAGANDIZED	PROPHECIES	PROPOLISES

PROPONENTS	PROPRIETORS	PROSAICISM	PROSELYTISING	PROSPECTION
PROPORTION	PROPRIETORSHIP	PROSAICISMS	PROSELYTISM	PROSPECTIONS
PROPORTIONABLE	PROPRIETORSHIPS	PROSAICNESS	PROSELYTISMS	PROSPECTIVE
PROPORTIONABLY	PROPRIETRESS	PROSAICNESSES	PROSELYTIZATION	PROSPECTIVELY
PROPORTIONAL	PROPRIETRESSES	PROSATEURS	PROSELYTIZE	PROSPECTIVENESS
PROPORTIONALITY	PROPRIETRICES	PROSAUROPOD	PROSELYTIZED	PROSPECTIVES
PROPORTIONALLY	PROPRIETRIX	PROSAUROPODS	PROSELYTIZER	PROSPECTLESS
PROPORTIONALS	PROPRIETRIXES	PROSCENIUM	PROSELYTIZERS	PROSPECTOR
PROPORTIONATE	PROPRIOCEPTION	PROSCENIUMS	PROSELYTIZES	PROSPECTORS
PROPORTIONATED	PROPRIOCEPTIONS	PROSCIUTTI	PROSELYTIZING	PROSPECTUS
PROPORTIONATELY	PROPRIOCEPTIVE	PROSCIUTTO	PROSEMINAR	PROSPECTUSES
PROPORTIONATES	PROPRIOCEPTOR	PROSCIUTTOS	PROSEMINARS	PROSPERING
PROPORTIONATING	PROPRIOCEPTORS	PROSCRIBED	PROSENCEPHALA	PROSPERITIES
PROPORTIONED	PROPROCTOR	PROSCRIBER	PROSENCEPHALIC	PROSPERITY
PROPORTIONING	PROPROCTORS	PROSCRIBERS	PROSENCEPHALON	PROSPEROUS
PROPORTIONINGS	PROPUGNATION	PROSCRIBES	PROSENCHYMA	PROSPEROUSLY
PROPORTIONLESS	PROPUGNATIONS	PROSCRIBING	PROSENCHYMAS	PROSPEROUSNESS
PROPORTIONMENT	PROPULSION	PROSCRIPTION	PROSENCHYMATA	PROSTACYCLIN
PROPORTIONMENTS	PROPULSIONS	PROSCRIPTIONS	PROSENCHYMATOUS	PROSTACYCLINS
PROPORTIONS	PROPULSIVE	PROSCRIPTIVE	PROSEUCHAE	PROSTAGLANDIN
PROPOSABLE	PROPULSORS	PROSCRIPTIVELY	PROSIFYING	PROSTAGLANDINS
PROPOSITAE	PROPULSORY	PROSCRIPTS	PROSILIENCIES	PROSTANTHERA
PROPOSITION	PROPYLAEUM	PROSECTING	PROSILIENCY	PROSTANTHERAS
PROPOSITIONAL	PROPYLAMINE	PROSECTORIAL	PROSILIENT	PROSTATECTOMIES
PROPOSITIONALLY	PROPYLAMINES	PROSECTORS	PROSIMIANS	PROSTATECTOMY
PROPOSITIONED	PROPYLENES	PROSECTORSHIP	PROSINESSES	PROSTATISM
PROPOSITIONING	PROPYLITES	PROSECTORSHIPS	PROSLAMBANOMENE	PROSTATISMS
PROPOSITIONS	PROPYLITISATION	PROSECUTABLE	PROSLAVERY	PROSTATITIS
PROPOSITUS	PROPYLITISE	PROSECUTED	PROSOBRANCH	PROSTATITISES
PROPOUNDED	PROPYLITISED	PROSECUTES	PROSOBRANCHS	PROSTERNUM
PROPOUNDER	PROPYLITISES	PROSECUTING	PROSODIANS	PROSTERNUMS
PROPOUNDERS	PROPYLITISING	PROSECUTION	PROSODICAL	PROSTHESES
PROPOUNDING	PROPYLITIZATION	PROSECUTIONS	PROSODICALLY	PROSTHESIS
PROPOXYPHENE	PROPYLITIZE	PROSECUTOR	PROSODISTS	PROSTHETIC
PROPOXYPHENES	PROPYLITIZED	PROSECUTORIAL	PROSOPAGNOSIA	PROSTHETICALLY
PROPRAETOR	PROPYLITIZES	PROSECUTORS	PROSOPAGNOSIAS	PROSTHETICS
PROPRAETORIAL	PROPYLITIZING	PROSECUTRICES	PROSOPOGRAPHER	PROSTHETIST
PROPRAETORIAN	PRORATABLE	PROSECUTRIX	PROSOPOGRAPHERS	PROSTHETISTS
PROPRAETORS	PRORATIONS	PROSECUTRIXES	PROSOPOGRAPHIES	PROSTHODONTIA
PROPRANOLOL	PRORECTORS	PROSELYTED	PROSOPOGRAPHY	PROSTHODONTIAS
PROPRANOLOLS	PROROGATED	PROSELYTES	PROSOPOPEIA	PROSTHODONTICS
PROPRETORS	PROROGATES	PROSELYTIC	PROSOPOPEIAL	PROSTHODONTIST
PROPRIETARIES	PROROGATING	PROSELYTING	PROSOPOPEIAS	PROSTHODONTISTS
PROPRIETARILY	PROROGATION	PROSELYTISATION	PROSOPOPOEIA	PROSTITUTE
PROPRIETARY	PROROGATIONS	PROSELYTISE	PROSOPOPOEIAL	PROSTITUTED
PROPRIETIES	PROROGUING	PROSELYTISED	PROSOPOPOEIAS	PROSTITUTES
PROPRIETOR	PROSAICALLY	PROSELYTISER	PROSPECTED	PROSTITUTING
PROPRIETORIAL	PROSAICALNESS	PROSELYTISERS	PROSPECTING	PROSTITUTION
PROPRIETORIALLY	PROSAICALNESSES	PROSELYTISES	PROSPECTINGS	PROSTITUTIONS

PROSTITUTOR	PROTECTORS	PROTESTORS	PROTOCTISTS	PROTOPLASMIC
PROSTITUTORS	PROTECTORSHIP	PROTHALAMIA	PROTODERMS	PROTOPLASMS
PROSTOMIAL	PROTECTORSHIPS	PROTHALAMION	PROTOGALAXIES	PROTOPLAST
PROSTOMIUM	PROTECTORY	PROTHALAMIUM	PROTOGALAXY	PROTOPLASTIC
PROSTRATED	PROTECTRESS	PROTHALLIA	PROTOGENIC	PROTOPLASTS
PROSTRATES	PROTECTRESSES	PROTHALLIAL	PROTOGINES	PROTOPORPHYRIN
PROSTRATING	PROTECTRICES	PROTHALLIC	PROTOGYNIES	PROTOPORPHYRINS
PROSTRATION	PROTECTRIX	PROTHALLIUM	PROTOGYNOUS	PROTOSPATAIRE
PROSTRATIONS	PROTECTRIXES	PROTHALLOID	PROTOHISTORIAN	PROTOSPATAIRES
PROSYLLOGISM	PROTEIFORM	PROTHALLUS	PROTOHISTORIANS	PROTOSPATHAIRE
PROSYLLOGISMS	PROTEINACEOUS	PROTHALLUSES	PROTOHISTORIC	PROTOSPATHAIRES
PROTACTINIUM	PROTEINASE	PROTHETICALLY	PROTOHISTORIES	PROTOSPATHARIUS
PROTACTINIUMS	PROTEINASES	PROTHONOTARIAL	PROTOHISTORY	PROTOSTARS
PROTAGONISM	PROTEINOUS	PROTHONOTARIAT	PROTOHUMAN	PROTOSTELE
PROTAGONISMS	PROTEINURIA	PROTHONOTARIATS	PROTOHUMANS	PROTOSTELES
PROTAGONIST	PROTEINURIAS	PROTHONOTARIES	PROTOLANGUAGE	PROTOSTELIC
PROTAGONISTS	PROTENDING	PROTHONOTARY	PROTOLANGUAGES	PROTOSTOME
PROTAMINES	PROTENSION	PROTHORACES	PROTOLITHIC	PROTOSTOMES
PROTANDRIES	PROTENSIONS	PROTHORACIC	PROTOMARTYR	PROTOTHERIAN
PROTANDROUS	PROTENSITIES	PROTHORAXES	PROTOMARTYRS	PROTOTHERIANS
PROTANOMALIES	PROTENSITY	PROTHROMBIN	PROTOMORPHIC	PROTOTROPH
PROTANOMALOUS	PROTENSIVE	PROTHROMBINS	PROTONATED	PROTOTROPHIC
PROTANOMALY	PROTENSIVELY	PROTISTANS	PROTONATES	PROTOTROPHIES
PROTANOPES	PROTEOCLASTIC	PROTISTOLOGIES	PROTONATING	PROTOTROPHS
PROTANOPIA	PROTEOGLYCAN	PROTISTOLOGIST	PROTONATION	PROTOTROPHY
PROTANOPIAS	PROTEOGLYCANS	PROTISTOLOGISTS	PROTONATIONS	PROTOTYPAL
PROTANOPIC	PROTEOLYSE	PROTISTOLOGY	PROTONEMAL	PROTOTYPED
PROTEACEOUS	PROTEOLYSED	PROTOACTINIUM	PROTONEMATA	PROTOTYPES
PROTECTANT	PROTEOLYSES	PROTOACTINIUMS	PROTONEMATAL	PROTOTYPIC
PROTECTANTS	PROTEOLYSING	PROTOAVISES	PROTONOTARIAL	PROTOTYPICAL
PROTECTERS	PROTEOLYSIS	PROTOCHORDATE	PROTONOTARIAT	PROTOTYPICALLY
PROTECTING	PROTEOLYTIC	PROTOCHORDATES	PROTONOTARIATS	PROTOTYPING
PROTECTINGLY	PROTEOLYTICALLY	PROTOCOCCAL	PROTONOTARIES	PROTOXIDES
PROTECTION	PROTEOMICS	PROTOCOLED	PROTONOTARY	PROTOXYLEM
PROTECTIONISM	PROTERANDRIES	PROTOCOLIC	PROTOPATHIC	PROTOXYLEMS
PROTECTIONISMS	PROTERANDROUS	PROTOCOLING	PROTOPATHIES	PROTOZOANS
PROTECTIONIST	PROTERANDRY	PROTOCOLISE	PROTOPATHY	PROTOZOOLOGICAL
PROTECTIONISTS	PROTEROGYNIES	PROTOCOLISED	PROTOPHILIC	PROTOZOOLOGIES
PROTECTIONS	PROTEROGYNOUS	PROTOCOLISES	PROTOPHLOEM	PROTOZOOLOGIST
PROTECTIVE	PROTEROGYNY	PROTOCOLISING	PROTOPHLOEMS	PROTOZOOLOGISTS
PROTECTIVELY	PROTERVITIES	PROTOCOLIST	PROTOPHYTE	PROTOZOOLOGY
PROTECTIVENESS	PROTERVITY	PROTOCOLISTS	PROTOPHYTES	PROTOZOONS
PROTECTIVES	PROTESTANT	PROTOCOLIZE	PROTOPHYTIC	PROTRACTED
PROTECTORAL	PROTESTANTS	PROTOCOLIZED	PROTOPLANET	PROTRACTEDLY
PROTECTORATE	PROTESTATION	PROTOCOLIZES	PROTOPLANETARY	PROTRACTEDNESS
PROTECTORATES	PROTESTATIONS	PROTOCOLIZING	PROTOPLANETS	PROTRACTIBLE
PROTECTORIAL	PROTESTERS	PROTOCOLLED	PROTOPLASM	PROTRACTILE
PROTECTORIES	PROTESTING	PROTOCOLLING	PROTOPLASMAL	PROTRACTING
PROTECTORLESS	PROTESTINGLY	PROTOCTIST	PROTOPLASMATIC	PROTRACTION

PROTRACTIONS	PROVENANCE	PROVIRUSES	PRUDENTIALITIES	PSAMMOPHYTIC
PROTRACTIVE	PROVENANCES	PROVISIONAL	PRUDENTIALITY	PSELLISMUS
PROTRACTOR	PROVENDERED	PROVISIONALLY	PRUDENTIALLY	PSELLISMUSES
PROTRACTORS	PROVENDERING	PROVISIONALS	PRUDENTIALS	PSEPHOANALYSES
PROTREPTIC	PROVENDERS	PROVISIONARIES	PRUDISHNESS	PSEPHOANALYSIS
PROTREPTICAL	PROVENIENCE	PROVISIONARY	PRUDISHNESSES	PSEPHOLOGICAL
PROTREPTICS	PROVENIENCES	PROVISIONED	PRURIENCES	PSEPHOLOGICALLY
PROTRUDABLE	PROVENTRICULAR	PROVISIONER	PRURIENCIES	PSEPHOLOGIES
PROTRUDENT	PROVENTRICULI	PROVISIONERS	PRURIENTLY	PSEPHOLOGIST
PROTRUDING	PROVENTRICULUS	PROVISIONING	PRURIGINOUS	PSEPHOLOGISTS
PROTRUSIBLE	PROVERBIAL	PROVISIONS	PRURITUSES	PSEPHOLOGY
PROTRUSILE	PROVERBIALISE	PROVISORILY	PRUSSIANISATION	PSEUDAESTHESIA
PROTRUSION	PROVERBIALISED	PROVITAMIN	PRUSSIANISE	PSEUDAESTHESIAS
PROTRUSIONS	PROVERBIALISES	PROVITAMINS	PRUSSIANISED	PSEUDARTHROSES
PROTRUSIVE	PROVERBIALISING	PROVOCABLE	PRUSSIANISES	PSEUDARTHROSIS
PROTRUSIVELY	PROVERBIALISM	PROVOCANTS	PRUSSIANISING	PSEUDEPIGRAPH
PROTRUSIVENESS	PROVERBIALISMS	PROVOCATEUR	PRUSSIANIZATION	PSEUDEPIGRAPHA
PROTUBERANCE	PROVERBIALIST	PROVOCATEURS	PRUSSIANIZE	PSEUDEPIGRAPHIC
PROTUBERANCES	PROVERBIALISTS	PROVOCATION	PRUSSIANIZED	PSEUDEPIGRAPHON
PROTUBERANCIES	PROVERBIALIZE	PROVOCATIONS	PRUSSIANIZES	PSEUDEPIGRAPHS
PROTUBERANCY	PROVERBIALIZED	PROVOCATIVE	PRUSSIANIZING	PSEUDEPIGRAPHY
PROTUBERANT	PROVERBIALIZES	PROVOCATIVELY	PRUSSIATES	PSEUDERIES
PROTUBERANTLY	PROVERBIALIZING	PROVOCATIVENESS	PSALIGRAPHIES	PSEUDIMAGINES
PROTUBERATE	PROVERBIALLY	PROVOCATIVES	PSALIGRAPHY	PSEUDIMAGO
PROTUBERATED	PROVERBING	PROVOCATOR	PSALMBOOKS	PSEUDIMAGOES
PROTUBERATES	PROVIDABLE	PROVOCATORS	PSALMODICAL	PSEUDIMAGOS
PROTUBERATING	PROVIDENCE	PROVOCATORY	PSALMODIES	PSEUDOACID
PROTUBERATION	PROVIDENCES	PROVOKABLE	PSALMODISE	PSEUDOACIDS
PROTUBERATIONS	PROVIDENTIAL	PROVOKEMENT	PSALMODISED	PSEUDOALLELE
PROUDHEARTED	PROVIDENTIALLY	PROVOKEMENTS	PSALMODISES	PSEUDOALLELES
PROUDNESSES	PROVIDENTLY	PROVOKINGLY	PSALMODISING	PSEUDOARTHROSES
PROUSTITES	PROVINCEWIDE	PROVOLONES	PSALMODIST	PSEUDOARTHROSIS
PROVABILITIES	PROVINCIAL	PROVOSTRIES	PSALMODISTS	PSEUDOBULB
PROVABILITY	PROVINCIALISE	PROVOSTSHIP	PSALMODIZE	PSEUDOBULBS
PROVABLENESS	PROVINCIALISED	PROVOSTSHIPS	PSALMODIZED	PSEUDOCARP
PROVABLENESSES	PROVINCIALISES	PROWLINGLY	PSALMODIZES	PSEUDOCARPOUS
PROVANTING	PROVINCIALISING	PROXIMALLY	PSALMODIZING	PSEUDOCARPS
PROVASCULAR	PROVINCIALISM	PROXIMATELY	PSALTERERS	PSEUDOCIDE
PROVEABILITIES	PROVINCIALISMS	PROXIMATENESS	PSALTERIAN	PSEUDOCIDES
PROVEABILITY	PROVINCIALIST	PROXIMATENESSES	PSALTERIES	PSEUDOCLASSIC
PROVEABLENESS	PROVINCIALISTS	PROXIMATION	PSALTERIUM	PSEUDOCLASSICS
PROVEABLENESSES	PROVINCIALITIES	PROXIMATIONS	PSALTRESSES	PSEUDOCODE
PROVECTION	PROVINCIALITY	PROXIMITIES	PSAMMOPHIL	PSEUDOCODES
PROVECTIONS	PROVINCIALIZE	PROZYMITES	PSAMMOPHILE	PSEUDOCOEL
PROVEDITOR	PROVINCIALIZED	PRUDENTIAL	PSAMMOPHILES	PSEUDOCOELOM
PROVEDITORE	PROVINCIALIZES	PRUDENTIALISM	PSAMMOPHILOUS	PSEUDOCOELOMATE
PROVEDITORES	PROVINCIALIZING	PRUDENTIALISMS	PSAMMOPHILS	PSEUDOCOELOMS
PROVEDITORS	PROVINCIALLY	PRUDENTIALIST	PSAMMOPHYTE	PSEUDOCOELS
PROVEDORES	PROVINCIALS	PRUDENTIALISTS	PSAMMOPHYTES	PSEUDOCYESES

P

PSEUDOCYESIS	PSEUDOSOLUTION	PSYCHICISTS	PSYCHOGENETIC	PSYCHOMACHY
PSEUDOEPHEDRINE	PSEUDOSOLUTIONS	PSYCHOACOUSTIC	PSYCHOGENETICAL	PSYCHOMETER
PSEUDOGRAPH	PSEUDOSYMMETRY	PSYCHOACOUSTICS	PSYCHOGENETICS	PSYCHOMETERS
PSEUDOGRAPHIES	PSEUDOVECTOR	PSYCHOACTIVE	PSYCHOGENIC	PSYCHOMETRIC
PSEUDOGRAPHS	PSEUDOVECTORS	PSYCHOANALYSE	PSYCHOGENICALLY	PSYCHOMETRICAL
PSEUDOGRAPHY	PSILANTHROPIC	PSYCHOANALYSED	PSYCHOGERIATRIC	PSYCHOMETRICIAN
PSEUDOLOGIA	PSILANTHROPIES	PSYCHOANALYSER	PSYCHOGNOSES	PSYCHOMETRICS
PSEUDOLOGIAS	PSILANTHROPISM	PSYCHOANALYSERS	PSYCHOGNOSIS	PSYCHOMETRIES
PSEUDOLOGIES	PSILANTHROPISMS	PSYCHOANALYSES	PSYCHOGNOSTIC	PSYCHOMETRIST
PSEUDOLOGUE	PSILANTHROPIST	PSYCHOANALYSING	PSYCHOGONIES	PSYCHOMETRISTS
PSEUDOLOGUES	PSILANTHROPISTS	PSYCHOANALYSIS	PSYCHOGONY	PSYCHOMETRY
PSEUDOLOGY	PSILANTHROPY	PSYCHOANALYST	PSYCHOGRAM	PSYCHOMOTOR
PSEUDOMARTYR	PSILOCYBIN	PSYCHOANALYSTS	PSYCHOGRAMS	PSYCHONEUROSES
PSEUDOMARTYRS	PSILOCYBINS	PSYCHOANALYTIC	PSYCHOGRAPH	PSYCHONEUROSIS
PSEUDOMEMBRANE	PSILOMELANE	PSYCHOANALYZE	PSYCHOGRAPHIC	PSYCHONEUROTIC
PSEUDOMEMBRANES	PSILOMELANES	PSYCHOANALYZED	PSYCHOGRAPHICAL	PSYCHONEUROTICS
PSEUDOMONAD	PSILOPHYTE	PSYCHOANALYZER	PSYCHOGRAPHICS	PSYCHONOMIC
PSEUDOMONADES	PSILOPHYTES	PSYCHOANALYZERS	PSYCHOGRAPHIES	PSYCHONOMICS
PSEUDOMONADS	PSILOPHYTIC	PSYCHOANALYZES	PSYCHOGRAPHS	PSYCHOPATH
PSEUDOMONAS	PSITTACINE	PSYCHOANALYZING	PSYCHOGRAPHY	PSYCHOPATHIC
PSEUDOMORPH	PSITTACINES	PSYCHOBABBLE	PSYCHOHISTORIAN	PSYCHOPATHICS
PSEUDOMORPHIC	PSITTACOSES	PSYCHOBABBLED	PSYCHOHISTORIES	PSYCHOPATHIES
PSEUDOMORPHISM	PSITTACOSIS	PSYCHOBABBLER	PSYCHOHISTORY	PSYCHOPATHIST
PSEUDOMORPHISMS	PSITTACOTIC	PSYCHOBABBLERS	PSYCHOKINESES	PSYCHOPATHISTS
PSEUDOMORPHOUS	PSORIATICS	PSYCHOBABBLES	PSYCHOKINESIS	PSYCHOPATHOLOGY
PSEUDOMORPHS	PSYCHAGOGUE	PSYCHOBABBLING	PSYCHOKINETIC	PSYCHOPATHS
PSEUDOMUTUALITY	PSYCHAGOGUES	PSYCHOBILLIES	PSYCHOLINGUIST	PSYCHOPATHY
PSEUDONYMITIES	PSYCHASTHENIA	PSYCHOBILLY	PSYCHOLINGUISTS	PSYCHOPHILIES
PSEUDONYMITY	PSYCHASTHENIAS	PSYCHOBIOGRAPHY	PSYCHOLOGIC	PSYCHOPHILY
PSEUDONYMOUS	PSYCHASTHENIC	PSYCHOBIOLOGIC	PSYCHOLOGICAL	PSYCHOPHYSICAL
PSEUDONYMOUSLY	PSYCHASTHENICS	PSYCHOBIOLOGIES	PSYCHOLOGICALLY	PSYCHOPHYSICIST
PSEUDONYMS	PSYCHEDELIA	PSYCHOBIOLOGIST	PSYCHOLOGIES	PSYCHOPHYSICS
PSEUDOPODAL	PSYCHEDELIAS	PSYCHOBIOLOGY	PSYCHOLOGISE	PSYCHOPOMP
PSEUDOPODIA	PSYCHEDELIC	PSYCHOCHEMICAL	PSYCHOLOGISED	PSYCHOPOMPS
PSEUDOPODIAL	PSYCHEDELICALLY	PSYCHOCHEMICALS	PSYCHOLOGISES	PSYCHOSEXUAL
PSEUDOPODIUM	PSYCHEDELICS	PSYCHOCHEMISTRY	PSYCHOLOGISING	PSYCHOSEXUALITY
PSEUDOPODS	PSYCHIATER	PSYCHODELIA	PSYCHOLOGISM	PSYCHOSEXUALLY
PSEUDOPREGNANCY	PSYCHIATERS	PSYCHODELIAS	PSYCHOLOGISMS	PSYCHOSOCIAL
PSEUDOPREGNANT	PSYCHIATRIC	PSYCHODELIC	PSYCHOLOGIST	PSYCHOSOCIALLY
PSEUDORANDOM	PSYCHIATRICAL	PSYCHODELICALLY	PSYCHOLOGISTIC	PSYCHOSOCIOLOGY
PSEUDOSCALAR	PSYCHIATRICALLY	PSYCHODRAMA	PSYCHOLOGISTS	PSYCHOSOMATIC
PSEUDOSCALARS	PSYCHIATRIES	PSYCHODRAMAS	PSYCHOLOGIZE	PSYCHOSOMATICS
PSEUDOSCIENCE	PSYCHIATRIST	PSYCHODRAMATIC	PSYCHOLOGIZED	PSYCHOSOMIMETIC
PSEUDOSCIENCES	PSYCHIATRISTS	PSYCHODYNAMIC	PSYCHOLOGIZES	PSYCHOSURGEON
PSEUDOSCIENTIST	PSYCHIATRY	PSYCHODYNAMICS	PSYCHOLOGIZING	PSYCHOSURGEONS
PSEUDOSCOPE	PSYCHICALLY	PSYCHOGALVANIC	PSYCHOLOGY	PSYCHOSURGERIES
PSEUDOSCOPES	PSYCHICISM	PSYCHOGASES	PSYCHOMACHIA	PSYCHOSURGERY
PSEUDOSCORPION	PSYCHICISMS	PSYCHOGENESES	PSYCHOMACHIAS	PSYCHOSURGICAL
PSEUDOSCORPIONS	PSYCHICIST	PSYCHOGENESIS	PSYCHOMACHIES	PSYCHOSYNTHESES

P

PSYCHOSYNTHESIS	PTERYLOGRAPHIC	PUERILISMS	PULSATILITIES	PUMMELLINGS
PSYCHOTECHNICS	PTERYLOGRAPHIES	PUERILITIES	PULSATILITY	PUMPERNICKEL
PSYCHOTHERAPIES	PTERYLOGRAPHY	PUERPERALLY	PULSATILLA	PUMPERNICKELS
PSYCHOTHERAPIST	PTERYLOSES	PUERPERIUM	PULSATILLAS	PUMPHOUSES
PSYCHOTHERAPY	PTERYLOSIS	PUFFERFISH	PULSATIONS	PUMPKINSEED
PSYCHOTICALLY	PTOCHOCRACIES	PUFFERFISHES	PULSATIVELY	PUMPKINSEEDS
PSYCHOTICISM	PTOCHOCRACY	PUFFINESSES	PULSEBEATS	PUNCHBALLS
PSYCHOTICISMS	PTYALAGOGIC	PUFFTALOONAS	PULSELESSNESS	PUNCHBOARD
PSYCHOTICS	PTYALAGOGUE	PUFTALOONAS	PULSELESSNESSES	PUNCHBOARDS
PSYCHOTOMIMETIC	PTYALAGOGUES	PUFTALOONIES	PULSIMETER	PUNCHBOWLS
PSYCHOTOXIC	PTYALISING	PUFTALOONS	PULSIMETERS	PUNCHINELLO
PSYCHOTROPIC	PTYALIZING	PUGGINESSES	PULSOMETER	PUNCHINELLOES
PSYCHOTROPICS	PUBCRAWLER	PUGILISTIC	PULSOMETERS	PUNCHINELLOS
PSYCHROMETER	PUBCRAWLERS	PUGILISTICAL	PULTACEOUS	PUNCHINESS
PSYCHROMETERS	PUBERULENT	PUGILISTICALLY	PULTRUDING	PUNCHINESSES
PSYCHROMETRIC	PUBERULOUS	PUGNACIOUS	PULTRUSION	PUNCHLINES
PSYCHROMETRICAL	PUBESCENCE	PUGNACIOUSLY	PULTRUSIONS	PUNCTATION
PSYCHROMETRIES	PUBESCENCES	PUGNACIOUSNESS	PULVERABLE	PUNCTATIONS
PSYCHROMETRY	PUBLICALLY	PUGNACITIES	PULVERATION	PUNCTATORS
PSYCHROPHILIC	PUBLICATION	PUISSANCES	PULVERATIONS	PUNCTILIOS
PTARMIGANS	PUBLICATIONS	PUISSANTLY	PULVERINES	PUNCTILIOUS
PTERANODON	PUBLICISED	PUISSAUNCE	PULVERISABLE	PUNCTILIOUSLY
PTERANODONS	PUBLICISES	PUISSAUNCES	PULVERISATION	PUNCTILIOUSNESS
PTERIDINES	PUBLICISING	PULCHRITUDE	PULVERISATIONS	PUNCTUALIST
PTERIDOLOGICAL	PUBLICISTS	PULCHRITUDES	PULVERISED	PUNCTUALISTS
PTERIDOLOGIES	PUBLICITIES	PULCHRITUDINOUS	PULVERISER	PUNCTUALITIES
PTERIDOLOGIST	PUBLICIZED	PULLULATED	PULVERISERS	PUNCTUALITY
PTERIDOLOGISTS	PUBLICIZES	PULLULATES	PULVERISES	PUNCTUALLY
PTERIDOLOGY	PUBLICIZING	PULLULATING	PULVERISING	PUNCTUATED
PTERIDOMANIA	PUBLICNESS	PULLULATION	PULVERIZABLE	PUNCTUATES
PTERIDOMANIAS	PUBLICNESSES	PULLULATIONS	PULVERIZATION	PUNCTUATING
PTERIDOPHILIST	PUBLISHABLE	PULMOBRANCH	PULVERIZATIONS	PUNCTUATION
PTERIDOPHILISTS	PUBLISHERS	PULMOBRANCHIATE	PULVERIZED	PUNCTUATIONIST
PTERIDOPHYTE	PUBLISHING	PULMOBRANCHS	PULVERIZER	PUNCTUATIONISTS
PTERIDOPHYTES	PUBLISHINGS	PULMONATES	PULVERIZERS	PUNCTUATIONS
PTERIDOPHYTIC	PUBLISHMENT	PULMONOLOGIES	PULVERIZES	PUNCTUATIVE
PTERIDOPHYTOUS	PUBLISHMENTS	PULMONOLOGIST	PULVERIZING	PUNCTUATOR
PTERIDOSPERM	PUCCINIACEOUS	PULMONOLOGISTS	PULVERULENCE	PUNCTUATORS
PTERIDOSPERMS	PUCKERIEST	PULMONOLOGY	PULVERULENCES	PUNCTULATE
PTERODACTYL	PUCKEROOED	PULPBOARDS	PULVERULENT	PUNCTULATED
PTERODACTYLE	PUCKISHNESS	PULPIFYING	PULVILISED	PUNCTULATES
PTERODACTYLES	PUCKISHNESSES	PULPINESSES	PULVILIZED	PUNCTULATING
PTERODACTYLS	PUDDENINGS	PULPITEERED	PULVILLIFORM	PUNCTULATION
PTEROSAURIAN	PUDDINGIER	PULPITEERING	PULVILLING	PUNCTULATIONS
PTEROSAURIANS	PUDDINGIEST	PULPITEERS	PULVILLIOS	PUNCTURABLE
PTEROSAURS	PUDGINESSES	PULPITRIES	PULVINATED	PUNCTURATION
PTERYGIALS	PUDIBUNDITIES	PULPSTONES	PULVINULES	PUNCTURATIONS
PTERYGIUMS	PUDIBUNDITY	PULSATANCE	PUMICATING	PUNCTURERS
PTERYGOIDS	PUDICITIES	PULSATANCES	PUMMELLING	PUNCTURING

PUNDIGRION	PURGATIVES	PURSERSHIP	PUTREFYING	PYKNODYSOSTOSES
PUNDIGRIONS	PURGATORIAL	PURSERSHIPS	PUTRESCENCE	PYKNODYSOSTOSIS
PUNDITRIES	PURGATORIALLY	PURSINESSES	PUTRESCENCES	PYKNOMETER
PUNDONORES	PURGATORIAN	PURSUANCES	PUTRESCENT	PYKNOMETERS
PUNGENCIES	PURGATORIANS	PURSUANTLY	PUTRESCIBILITY	PYKNOSOMES
PUNICACEOUS	PURGATORIES	PURSUINGLY	PUTRESCIBLE	PYLORECTOMIES
PUNINESSES	PURIFICATION	PURSUIVANT	PUTRESCIBLES	PYLORECTOMY
PUNISHABILITIES	PURIFICATIONS	PURSUIVANTS	PUTRESCINE	PYOGENESES
PUNISHABILITY	PURIFICATIVE	PURTENANCE	PUTRESCINES	PYOGENESIS
PUNISHABLE	PURIFICATOR	PURTENANCES	PUTRIDITIES	PYORRHOEAL
PUNISHINGLY	PURIFICATORS	PURULENCES	PUTRIDNESS	PYORRHOEAS
PUNISHMENT	PURIFICATORY	PURULENCIES	PUTRIDNESSES	PYORRHOEIC
PUNISHMENTS	PURISTICAL	PURULENTLY	PUTRIFICATION	PYRACANTHA
PUNITIVELY	PURISTICALLY	PURVEYANCE	PUTRIFICATIONS	PYRACANTHAS
PUNITIVENESS	PURITANICAL	PURVEYANCES	PUTSCHISTS	PYRACANTHS
PUNITIVENESSES	PURITANICALLY	PUSCHKINIA	PUTTYROOTS	PYRALIDIDS
PUNKINESSES	PURITANICALNESS	PUSCHKINIAS	PUZZLEDOMS	PYRAMIDALLY
PUPIGEROUS	PURITANISE	PUSHCHAIRS	PUZZLEHEADED	PYRAMIDICAL
PUPILABILITIES	PURITANISED	PUSHFULNESS	PUZZLEMENT	PYRAMIDICALLY
PUPILABILITY	PURITANISES	PUSHFULNESSES	PUZZLEMENTS	PYRAMIDING
PUPILARITIES	PURITANISING	PUSHINESSES	PUZZLINGLY	PYRAMIDION
PUPILARITY	PURITANISM	PUSHINGNESS	PUZZOLANAS	PYRAMIDIONS
PUPILLAGES	PURITANISMS	PUSHINGNESSES	PYCNIDIOSPORE	PYRAMIDIST
PUPILLARITIES	PURITANIZE	PUSILLANIMITIES	PYCNIDIOSPORES	PYRAMIDISTS
PUPILLARITY	PURITANIZED	PUSILLANIMITY	PYCNOCONIDIA	PYRAMIDOLOGIES
PUPILLATED	PURITANIZES	PUSILLANIMOUS	PYCNOCONIDIUM	PYRAMIDOLOGIST
PUPILLATES	PURITANIZING	PUSILLANIMOUSLY	PYCNODYSOSTOSES	PYRAMIDOLOGISTS
PUPILLATING	PURLICUING	PUSSYFOOTED	PYCNODYSOSTOSIS	PYRAMIDOLOGY
PUPILSHIPS	PURLOINERS	PUSSYFOOTER	PYCNOGONID	PYRAMIDONS
PUPIPAROUS	PURLOINING	PUSSYFOOTERS	PYCNOGONIDS	PYRANOMETER
PUPPETEERED	PUROMYCINS	PUSSYFOOTING	PYCNOGONOID	PYRANOMETERS
PUPPETEERING	PURPLEHEART	PUSSYFOOTINGS	PYCNOGONOIDS	PYRANOSIDE
PUPPETEERS	PURPLEHEARTS	PUSSYFOOTS	PYCNOMETER	PYRANOSIDES
PUPPETLIKE	PURPLENESS	PUSTULANTS	PYCNOMETERS	PYRARGYRITE
PUPPETRIES	PURPLENESSES	PUSTULATED	PYCNOMETRIC	PYRARGYRITES
PUPPYHOODS	PURPORTEDLY	PUSTULATES	PYCNOSOMES	PYRENEITES
PURBLINDLY	PURPORTING	PUSTULATING	PYCNOSPORE	PYRENOCARP
PURBLINDNESS	PURPORTLESS	PUSTULATION	PYCNOSPORES	PYRENOCARPS
PURBLINDNESSES	PURPOSEFUL	PUSTULATIONS	PYCNOSTYLE	PYRENOMYCETOUS
PURCHASABILITY	PURPOSEFULLY	PUTANGITANGI	PYCNOSTYLES	PYRETHRINS
PURCHASABLE	PURPOSEFULNESS	PUTANGITANGIS	PYELITISES	PYRETHROID
PURCHASERS	PURPOSELESS	PUTATIVELY	PYELOGRAMS	PYRETHROIDS
PURCHASING	PURPOSELESSLY	PUTONGHUAS	PYELOGRAPHIC	PYRETHRUMS
PURCHASINGS	PURPOSELESSNESS	PUTREFACIENT	PYELOGRAPHIES	PYRETOLOGIES
PURDONIUMS	PURPOSIVELY	PUTREFACTION	PYELOGRAPHY	PYRETOLOGY
PUREBLOODS	PURPOSIVENESS	PUTREFACTIONS	PYELONEPHRITIC	PYRETOTHERAPIES
PURENESSES	PURPOSIVENESSES	PUTREFACTIVE	PYELONEPHRITIS	PYRETOTHERAPY
PURGATIONS	PURPRESTURE	PUTREFIABLE	PYGARGUSES	PYRGEOMETER
PURGATIVELY	PURPRESTURES	PUTREFIERS	PYGOSTYLES	PYRGEOMETERS

PYRHELIOMETER	PYROCLASTIC	PYROLUSITE	PYROPHOBIA	PYROTECHNICIAN
PYRHELIOMETERS	PYROCLASTICS	PYROLUSITES	PYROPHOBIAS	PYROTECHNICIANS
PYRHELIOMETRIC	PYROCLASTS	PYROLYSABLE	PYROPHOBIC	PYROTECHNICS
PYRIDOSTIGMINE	PYROELECTRIC	PYROLYSATE	PYROPHOBICS	PYROTECHNIES
PYRIDOSTIGMINES	PYROELECTRICITY	PYROLYSATES	PYROPHONES	PYROTECHNIST
PYRIDOXALS	PYROELECTRICS	PYROLYSERS	PYROPHORIC	PYROTECHNISTS
PYRIDOXAMINE	PYROGALLATE	PYROLYSING	PYROPHOROUS	PYROTECHNY
PYRIDOXAMINES	PYROGALLATES	PYROLYTICALLY	PYROPHORUS	PYROVANADIC
PYRIDOXINE	PYROGALLIC	PYROLYZABLE	PYROPHORUSES	PYROXENITE
PYRIDOXINES	PYROGALLOL	PYROLYZATE	PYROPHOSPHATE	PYROXENITES
PYRIDOXINS	PYROGALLOLS	PYROLYZATES	PYROPHOSPHATES	PYROXENITIC
PYRIMETHAMINE	PYROGENETIC	PYROLYZERS	PYROPHOSPHORIC	PYROXENOID
PYRIMETHAMINES	PYROGENICITIES	PYROLYZING	PYROPHOTOGRAPH	PYROXENOIDS
PYRIMIDINE	PYROGENICITY	PYROMAGNETIC	PYROPHOTOGRAPHS	PYROXYLINE
PYRIMIDINES	PYROGENOUS	PYROMANCER	PYROPHOTOGRAPHY	PYROXYLINES
PYRITHIAMINE	PYROGNOSTIC	PYROMANCERS	PYROPHOTOMETER	PYROXYLINS
PYRITHIAMINES	PYROGNOSTICS	PYROMANCIES	PYROPHOTOMETERS	PYRRHICIST
PYRITIFEROUS	PYROGRAPHER	PYROMANIAC	PYROPHOTOMETRY	PYRRHICISTS
PYRITISING	PYROGRAPHERS	PYROMANIACAL	PYROPHYLLITE	PYRRHOTINE
PYRITIZING	PYROGRAPHIC	PYROMANIACS	PYROPHYLLITES	PYRRHOTINES
PYRITOHEDRA	PYROGRAPHIES	PYROMANIAS	PYROSCOPES	PYRRHOTITE
PYRITOHEDRAL	PYROGRAPHY	PYROMANTIC	PYROSTATIC	PYRRHOTITES
PYRITOHEDRON	PYROGRAVURE	PYROMERIDE	PYROSULFITE	PYRRHULOXIA
PYRITOHEDRONS	PYROGRAVURES	PYROMERIDES	PYROSULFITES	PYRRHULOXIAS
PYROBALLOGIES	PYROKINESES	PYROMETALLURGY	PYROSULPHATE	PYRROLIDINE
PYROBALLOGY	PYROKINESIS	PYROMETERS	PYROSULPHATES	PYRROLIDINES
PYROCATECHIN	PYROLATERS	PYROMETRIC	PYROSULPHURIC	PYTHOGENIC
PYROCATECHINS	PYROLATRIES	PYROMETRICAL	PYROTARTARIC	PYTHONESSES
PYROCATECHOL	PYROLIGNEOUS	PYROMETRICALLY	PYROTARTRATE	PYTHONOMORPH
PYROCATECHOLS	PYROLIGNIC	PYROMETRIES	PYROTARTRATES	PYTHONOMORPHS
PYROCERAMS	PYROLISING	PYROMORPHITE	PYROTECHNIC	
PYROCHEMICAL	PYROLIZING	PYROMORPHITES	PYROTECHNICAL	
PYROCHEMICALLY	PYROLOGIES	PYRONINOPHILIC	PYROTECHNICALLY	

P

QABALISTIC	QUADRENNIALS	QUADRIPLEGIC	QUADRUPLETS	QUALIFYINGS
QINGHAOSUS	QUADRENNIUM	QUADRIPLEGICS	QUADRUPLEX	QUALITATIVE
QUACKERIES	QUADRENNIUMS	QUADRIPOLE	QUADRUPLEXED	QUALITATIVELY
QUACKSALVER	QUADRICEPS	QUADRIPOLES	QUADRUPLEXES	QUALMISHLY
QUACKSALVERS	QUADRICEPSES	QUADRIREME	QUADRUPLEXING	QUALMISHNESS
QUACKSALVING	QUADRICIPITAL	QUADRIREMES	QUADRUPLICATE	QUALMISHNESSES
QUADCOPTER	QUADRICONE	QUADRISECT	QUADRUPLICATED	QUANDARIES
QUADCOPTERS	QUADRICONES	QUADRISECTED	QUADRUPLICATES	QUANGOCRACIES
QUADPLEXES	QUADRIENNIA	QUADRISECTING	QUADRUPLICATING	QUANGOCRACY
QUADRAGENARIAN	QUADRIENNIAL	QUADRISECTION	QUADRUPLICATION	QUANTIFIABLE
QUADRAGENARIANS	QUADRIENNIUM	QUADRISECTIONS	QUADRUPLICITIES	QUANTIFICATION
QUADRAGESIMAL	QUADRIENNIUMS	QUADRISECTS	QUADRUPLICITY	QUANTIFICATIONS
QUADRANGLE	QUADRIFARIOUS	QUADRISYLLABIC	QUADRUPLIES	QUANTIFIED
QUADRANGLES	QUADRIFOLIATE	QUADRISYLLABICS	QUADRUPLING	QUANTIFIER
QUADRANGULAR	QUADRIFORM	QUADRISYLLABLE	QUADRUPOLE	QUANTIFIERS
QUADRANGULARLY	QUADRIGEMINAL	QUADRISYLLABLES	QUADRUPOLES	QUANTIFIES
QUADRANTAL	QUADRIGEMINATE	QUADRIVALENCE	QUAESITUMS	QUANTIFYING
QUADRANTES	QUADRIGEMINOUS	QUADRIVALENCES	QUAESTIONARIES	QUANTISATION
QUADRAPHONIC	QUADRILATERAL	QUADRIVALENCIES	QUAESTIONARY	QUANTISATIONS
QUADRAPHONICS	QUADRILATERALS	QUADRIVALENCY	QUAESTORIAL	QUANTISERS
QUADRAPHONIES	QUADRILINGUAL	QUADRIVALENT	QUAESTORSHIP	QUANTISING
QUADRAPHONY	QUADRILITERAL	QUADRIVALENTS	QUAESTORSHIPS	QUANTITATE
QUADRAPLEGIA	QUADRILITERALS	QUADRIVIAL	QUAESTUARIES	QUANTITATED
QUADRAPLEGIAS	QUADRILLED	QUADRIVIUM	QUAESTUARY	QUANTITATES
QUADRAPLEGIC	QUADRILLER	QUADRIVIUMS	QUAGGINESS	QUANTITATING
QUADRAPLEGICS	QUADRILLERS	QUADROPHONIC	QUAGGINESSES	QUANTITATION
QUADRASONIC	QUADRILLES	QUADROPHONICS	QUAGMIRIER	QUANTITATIONS
QUADRASONICS	QUADRILLING	QUADROPHONIES	QUAGMIRIEST	QUANTITATIVE
QUADRATICAL	QUADRILLION	QUADROPHONY	QUAGMIRING	QUANTITATIVELY
QUADRATICALLY	QUADRILLIONS	QUADROTORS	QUAINTNESS	QUANTITIES
QUADRATICS	QUADRILLIONTH	QUADRUMANE	QUAINTNESSES	QUANTITIVE
QUADRATING	QUADRILLIONTHS	QUADRUMANES	QUAKINESSES	QUANTITIVELY
QUADRATRICES	QUADRILOCULAR	QUADRUMANOUS	QUALIFIABLE	QUANTIVALENCE
QUADRATRIX	QUADRINGENARIES	QUADRUMANS	QUALIFICATION	QUANTIVALENCES
QUADRATRIXES	QUADRINGENARY	QUADRUMVIR	QUALIFICATIONS	QUANTIVALENT
QUADRATURA	QUADRINOMIAL	QUADRUMVIRATE	QUALIFICATIVE	QUANTIZATION
QUADRATURE	QUADRINOMIALS	QUADRUMVIRATES	QUALIFICATIVES	QUANTIZATIONS
QUADRATURES	QUADRIPARTITE	QUADRUMVIRS	QUALIFICATOR	QUANTIZERS
QUADRATUSES	QUADRIPARTITION	QUADRUPEDAL	QUALIFICATORS	QUANTIZING
QUADRELLAS	QUADRIPHONIC	QUADRUPEDS	QUALIFICATORY	QUANTOMETER
QUADRENNIA	QUADRIPHONICS	QUADRUPLED	QUALIFIEDLY	QUANTOMETERS
QUADRENNIAL	QUADRIPLEGIA	QUADRUPLES	QUALIFIERS	QUAQUAVERSAL
QUADRENNIALLY	QUADRIPLEGIAS	QUADRUPLET	QUALIFYING	QUAQUAVERSALLY

QUARANTINE	QUARTERMASTER	QUEASINESS	QUESTIONEES	QUIESCENCIES
QUARANTINED	QUARTERMASTERS	QUEASINESSES	QUESTIONER	QUIESCENCY
QUARANTINES	QUARTERMISTRESS	QUEBRACHOS	QUESTIONERS	QUIESCENTLY
QUARANTINING	QUARTERSAW	QUEECHIEST	QUESTIONING	QUIETENERS
QUARENDENS	QUARTERSAWED	QUEENCAKES	QUESTIONINGLY	QUIETENING
QUARENDERS	QUARTERSAWING	QUEENCRAFT	QUESTIONINGS	QUIETENINGS
QUARRELERS	QUARTERSAWN	QUEENCRAFTS	QUESTIONIST	QUIETISTIC
QUARRELING	QUARTERSAWS	QUEENFISHES	QUESTIONISTS	QUIETNESSES
QUARRELINGS	QUARTERSTAFF	QUEENHOODS	QUESTIONLESS	QUILLBACKS
QUARRELLED	QUARTERSTAFFS	QUEENLIEST	QUESTIONLESSLY	QUILLWORKS
QUARRELLER	QUARTERSTAVES	QUEENLINESS	QUESTIONNAIRE	QUILLWORTS
QUARRELLERS	QUARTETTES	QUEENLINESSES	QUESTIONNAIRES	QUINACRINE
QUARRELLING	QUARTODECIMAN	QUEENSHIPS	QUESTORIAL	QUINACRINES
QUARRELLINGS	QUARTODECIMANS	QUEENSIDES	QUESTORSHIP	QUINALBARBITONE
QUARRELLOUS	QUARTZIEST	QUEERCORES	QUESTORSHIPS	QUINAQUINA
QUARRELSOME	QUARTZIFEROUS	QUEERITIES	QUESTRISTS	QUINAQUINAS
QUARRELSOMELY	QUARTZITES	QUEERNESSES	QUETIAPINE	QUINCENTENARIES
QUARRELSOMENESS	QUARTZITIC	QUELQUECHOSE	QUETIAPINES	QUINCENTENARY
QUARRENDER	QUASICRYSTAL	QUELQUECHOSES	QUIBBLINGLY	QUINCENTENNIAL
QUARRENDERS	QUASICRYSTALS	QUENCHABLE	QUIBBLINGS	QUINCENTENNIALS
QUARRIABLE	QUASIPARTICLE	QUENCHINGS	QUICKBEAMS	QUINCUNCIAL
QUARRINGTON	QUASIPARTICLES	QUENCHLESS	QUICKENERS	QUINCUNCIALLY
QUARRINGTONS	QUASIPERIODIC	QUENCHLESSLY	QUICKENING	QUINCUNXES
QUARRYINGS	QUATERCENTENARY	QUERCETINS	QUICKENINGS	QUINCUNXIAL
QUARRYMASTER	QUATERNARIES	QUERCETUMS	QUICKLIMES	QUINDECAGON
QUARRYMASTERS	QUATERNARY	QUERCITINS	QUICKNESSES	QUINDECAGONS
QUARTATION	QUATERNATE	QUERCITRON	QUICKSANDS	QUINDECAPLET
QUARTATIONS	QUATERNION	QUERCITRONS	QUICKSILVER	QUINDECAPLETS
QUARTERAGE	QUATERNIONIST	QUERIMONIES	QUICKSILVERED	QUINDECENNIAL
QUARTERAGES	QUATERNIONISTS	QUERIMONIOUS	QUICKSILVERIER	QUINDECENNIALS
QUARTERBACK	QUATERNIONS	QUERIMONIOUSLY	QUICKSILVERIEST	QUINDECILLION
QUARTERBACKED	QUATERNITIES	QUERNSTONE	QUICKSILVERING	QUINDECILLIONS
QUARTERBACKING	QUATERNITY	QUERNSTONES	QUICKSILVERINGS	QUINGENTENARIES
QUARTERBACKINGS	QUATORZAIN	QUERSPRUNG	QUICKSILVERISH	QUINGENTENARY
QUARTERBACKS	QUATORZAINS	QUERSPRUNGS	QUICKSILVERS	QUINIDINES
QUARTERDECK	QUATREFEUILLE	QUERULOUSLY	QUICKSILVERY	QUINOLINES
QUARTERDECKER	QUATREFEUILLES	QUERULOUSNESS	QUICKSTEPPED	QUINOLONES
QUARTERDECKERS	QUATREFOIL	QUERULOUSNESSES	QUICKSTEPPING	QUINQUAGENARIAN
QUARTERDECKS	QUATREFOILS	QUERYINGLY	QUICKSTEPS	QUINQUAGESIMAL
QUARTERERS	QUATTROCENTISM	QUESADILLA	QUICKTHORN	QUINQUECOSTATE
QUARTERFINAL	QUATTROCENTISMS	QUESADILLAS	QUICKTHORNS	QUINQUEFARIOUS
QUARTERFINALIST	QUATTROCENTIST	QUESTINGLY	QUIDDANIED	QUINQUEFOLIATE
QUARTERFINALS	QUATTROCENTISTS	QUESTIONABILITY	QUIDDANIES	QUINQUENNIA
QUARTERING	QUATTROCENTO	QUESTIONABLE	QUIDDANYING	QUINQUENNIAD
QUARTERINGS	QUATTROCENTOS	QUESTIONABLY	QUIDDITATIVE	QUINQUENNIADS
QUARTERLIES	QUAVERIEST	QUESTIONARIES	QUIDDITCHES	QUINQUENNIAL
QUARTERLIFE	QUAVERINGLY	QUESTIONARY	QUIDDITIES	QUINQUENNIALLY
QUARTERLIGHT	QUAVERINGS	QUESTIONED	QUIESCENCE	QUINQUENNIALS
QUARTERLIGHTS	QUEACHIEST	QUESTIONEE	QUIESCENCES	QUINQUENNIUM

QUINQUENNIUMS

QUINQUENNIUMS QUINTETTES QUIRKINESS QUIXOTISMS QUODLIBETIC
QUINQUEPARTITE QUINTILLION QUIRKINESSES QUIXOTRIES QUODLIBETICAL
QUINQUEREME QUINTILLIONS QUISLINGISM QUIZMASTER QUODLIBETICALLY
QUINQUEREMES QUINTILLIONTH QUISLINGISMS QUIZMASTERS QUODLIBETS
QUINQUEVALENCE QUINTILLIONTHS QUITCLAIMED QUIZZERIES QUOTABILITIES
QUINQUEVALENCES QUINTUPLED QUITCLAIMING QUIZZICALITIES QUOTABILITY
QUINQUEVALENCY QUINTUPLES QUITCLAIMS QUIZZICALITY QUOTABLENESS
QUINQUEVALENT QUINTUPLET QUITTANCED QUIZZICALLY QUOTABLENESSES
QUINQUINAS QUINTUPLETS QUITTANCES QUIZZIFICATION QUOTATIONS
QUINQUIVALENCE QUINTUPLICATE QUITTANCING QUIZZIFICATIONS QUOTATIOUS
QUINQUIVALENCES QUINTUPLICATED QUIVERFULS QUIZZIFIED QUOTATIVES
QUINQUIVALENCY QUINTUPLICATES QUIVERIEST QUIZZIFIES QUOTEWORTHIER
QUINQUIVALENT QUINTUPLICATING QUIVERINGLY QUIZZIFYING QUOTEWORTHIEST
QUINTESSENCE QUINTUPLICATION QUIVERINGS QUIZZINESS QUOTEWORTHY
QUINTESSENCES QUINTUPLIES QUIVERSFUL QUIZZINESSES QUOTIDIANS
QUINTESSENTIAL QUINTUPLING QUIXOTICAL QUODLIBETARIAN QUOTITIONS
QUINTESSENTIALS QUIRISTERS QUIXOTICALLY QUODLIBETARIANS

R

RABATMENTS	RACEWALKING	RADIALITIES	RADIOACTIVATE	RADIOIODINE
RABATTEMENT	RACEWALKINGS	RADIALIZATION	RADIOACTIVATED	RADIOIODINES
RABATTEMENTS	RACHIOTOMIES	RADIALIZATIONS	RADIOACTIVATES	RADIOISOTOPE
RABATTINGS	RACHIOTOMY	RADIALIZED	RADIOACTIVATING	RADIOISOTOPES
RABBINATES	RACHISCHISES	RADIALIZES	RADIOACTIVATION	RADIOISOTOPIC
RABBINICAL	RACHISCHISIS	RADIALIZING	RADIOACTIVE	RADIOLABEL
RABBINICALLY	RACHITIDES	RADIANCIES	RADIOACTIVELY	RADIOLABELED
RABBINISMS	RACHITISES	RADIATIONAL	RADIOACTIVITIES	RADIOLABELING
RABBINISTIC	RACIALISED	RADIATIONLESS	RADIOACTIVITY	RADIOLABELLED
RABBINISTS	RACIALISES	RADIATIONS	RADIOAUTOGRAPH	RADIOLABELLING
RABBINITES	RACIALISING	RADICALISATION	RADIOAUTOGRAPHS	RADIOLABELS
RABBITBRUSH	RACIALISMS	RADICALISATIONS	RADIOAUTOGRAPHY	RADIOLARIAN
RABBITBRUSHES	RACIALISTIC	RADICALISE	RADIOBIOLOGIC	RADIOLARIANS
RABBITFISH	RACIALISTS	RADICALISED	RADIOBIOLOGICAL	RADIOLOCATION
RABBITFISHES	RACIALIZED	RADICALISES	RADIOBIOLOGIES	RADIOLOCATIONAL
RABBITIEST	RACIALIZES	RADICALISING	RADIOBIOLOGIST	RADIOLOCATIONS
RABBITINGS	RACIALIZING	RADICALISM	RADIOBIOLOGISTS	RADIOLOGIC
RABBITRIES	RACIATIONS	RADICALISMS	RADIOBIOLOGY	RADIOLOGICAL
RABBLEMENT	RACINESSES	RADICALISTIC	RADIOCARBON	RADIOLOGICALLY
RABBLEMENTS	RACKABONES	RADICALITIES	RADIOCARBONS	RADIOLOGIES
RABIDITIES	RACKETEERED	RADICALITY	RADIOCHEMICAL	RADIOLOGIST
RABIDNESSES	RACKETEERING	RADICALIZATION	RADIOCHEMICALLY	RADIOLOGISTS
RACCAHOUTS	RACKETEERINGS	RADICALIZATIONS	RADIOCHEMIST	RADIOLUCENCIES
RACECOURSE	RACKETEERS	RADICALIZE	RADIOCHEMISTRY	RADIOLUCENCY
RACECOURSES	RACKETIEST	RADICALIZED	RADIOCHEMISTS	RADIOLUCENT
RACEGOINGS	RACKETRIES	RADICALIZES	RADIOECOLOGIES	RADIOLYSES
RACEHORSES	RACONTEURING	RADICALIZING	RADIOECOLOGY	RADIOLYSIS
RACEMATION	RACONTEURINGS	RADICALNESS	RADIOELEMENT	RADIOLYTIC
RACEMATIONS	RACONTEURS	RADICALNESSES	RADIOELEMENTS	RADIOMETER
RACEMISATION	RACONTEUSE	RADICATING	RADIOGENIC	RADIOMETERS
RACEMISATIONS	RACONTEUSES	RADICATION	RADIOGOLDS	RADIOMETRIC
RACEMISING	RACQUETBALL	RADICATIONS	RADIOGONIOMETER	RADIOMETRICALLY
RACEMIZATION	RACQUETBALLS	RADICCHIOS	RADIOGONIOMETRY	RADIOMETRIES
RACEMIZATIONS	RACQUETING	RADICELLOSE	RADIOGRAMS	RADIOMETRY
RACEMIZING	RACTOPAMINE	RADICICOLOUS	RADIOGRAPH	RADIOMICROMETER
RACEMOSELY	RACTOPAMINES	RADICIFORM	RADIOGRAPHED	RADIOMIMETIC
RACEMOUSLY	RADARSCOPE	RADICIVOROUS	RADIOGRAPHER	RADIONUCLIDE
RACETRACKER	RADARSCOPES	RADICULOSE	RADIOGRAPHERS	RADIONUCLIDES
RACETRACKERS	RADIALISATION	RADIESTHESIA	RADIOGRAPHIC	RADIOPACITIES
RACETRACKS	RADIALISATIONS	RADIESTHESIAS	RADIOGRAPHIES	RADIOPACITY
RACEWALKED	RADIALISED	RADIESTHESIST	RADIOGRAPHING	RADIOPAGER
RACEWALKER	RADIALISES	RADIESTHESISTS	RADIOGRAPHS	RADIOPAGERS
RACEWALKERS	RADIALISING	RADIESTHETIC	RADIOGRAPHY	RADIOPAGING

R

RADIOPAGINGS	RADIOTELETYPES	RAINMAKINGS	RAMPAGEOUSNESS	RANIVOROUS
RADIOPAQUE	RADIOTHERAPIES	RAINPROOFED	RAMPAGINGS	RANKNESSES
RADIOPHONE	RADIOTHERAPIST	RAINPROOFING	RAMPALLIAN	RANKSHIFTED
RADIOPHONES	RADIOTHERAPISTS	RAINPROOFS	RAMPALLIANS	RANKSHIFTING
RADIOPHONIC	RADIOTHERAPY	RAINSPOUTS	RAMPANCIES	RANKSHIFTS
RADIOPHONICALLY	RADIOTHERMIES	RAINSQUALL	RAMPARTING	RANSACKERS
RADIOPHONICS	RADIOTHERMY	RAINSQUALLS	RAMPAUGING	RANSACKING
RADIOPHONIES	RADIOTHONS	RAINSTICKS	RAMRODDING	RANSACKINGS
RADIOPHONIST	RADIOTHORIUM	RAINSTORMS	RAMSHACKLE	RANSHACKLE
RADIOPHONISTS	RADIOTHORIUMS	RAINWASHED	RANCELLING	RANSHACKLED
RADIOPHONY	RADIOTOXIC	RAINWASHES	RANCHERIAS	RANSHACKLES
RADIOPHOSPHORUS	RADIOTRACER	RAINWASHING	RANCHERIES	RANSHACKLING
RADIOPHOTO	RADIOTRACERS	RAINWATERS	RANCHETTES	RANSHAKLED
RADIOPHOTOS	RADULIFORM	RAISINIEST	RANCHLANDS	RANSHAKLES
RADIOPROTECTION	RAFFINATES	RAISONNEUR	RANCIDITIES	RANSHAKLING
RADIOPROTECTIVE	RAFFINOSES	RAISONNEURS	RANCIDNESS	RANSOMABLE
RADIORESISTANT	RAFFISHNESS	RAIYATWARI	RANCIDNESSES	RANSOMLESS
RADIOSCOPE	RAFFISHNESSES	RAIYATWARIS	RANCOROUSLY	RANSOMWARE
RADIOSCOPES	RAFFLESIAS	RAJAHSHIPS	RANCOROUSNESS	RANSOMWARES
RADIOSCOPIC	RAFTERINGS	RAJPRAMUKH	RANCOROUSNESSES	RANTERISMS
RADIOSCOPICALLY	RAGAMUFFIN	RAJPRAMUKHS	RANDINESSES	RANTIPOLED
RADIOSCOPIES	RAGAMUFFINS	RAKEHELLIER	RANDOMISATION	RANTIPOLES
RADIOSCOPY	RAGGAMUFFIN	RAKEHELLIEST	RANDOMISATIONS	RANTIPOLING
RADIOSENSITISE	RAGGAMUFFINS	RAKESHAMES	RANDOMISED	RANUNCULACEOUS
RADIOSENSITISED	RAGGEDIEST	RAKISHNESS	RANDOMISER	RANUNCULUS
RADIOSENSITISES	RAGGEDNESS	RAKISHNESSES	RANDOMISERS	RANUNCULUSES
RADIOSENSITIVE	RAGGEDNESSES	RALLENTANDI	RANDOMISES	RAPACIOUSLY
RADIOSENSITIZE	RAGMATICAL	RALLENTANDO	RANDOMISING	RAPACIOUSNESS
RADIOSENSITIZED	RAGPICKERS	RALLENTANDOS	RANDOMIZATION	RAPACIOUSNESSES
RADIOSENSITIZES	RAILBUSSES	RALLYCROSS	RANDOMIZATIONS	RAPACITIES
RADIOSONDE	RAILLERIES	RALLYCROSSES	RANDOMIZED	RAPIDITIES
RADIOSONDES	RAILROADED	RALLYINGLY	RANDOMIZER	RAPIDNESSES
RADIOSTRONTIUM	RAILROADER	RAMAPITHECINE	RANDOMIZERS	RAPIERLIKE
RADIOSTRONTIUMS	RAILROADERS	RAMAPITHECINES	RANDOMIZES	RAPPELLING
RADIOTELEGRAM	RAILROADING	RAMBLINGLY	RANDOMIZING	RAPPELLINGS
RADIOTELEGRAMS	RAILROADINGS	RAMBOUILLET	RANDOMNESS	RAPPORTAGE
RADIOTELEGRAPH	RAILWAYMAN	RAMBOUILLETS	RANDOMNESSES	RAPPORTAGES
RADIOTELEGRAPHS	RAILWAYMEN	RAMBUNCTIOUS	RANDOMWISE	RAPPORTEUR
RADIOTELEGRAPHY	RAILWORKER	RAMBUNCTIOUSLY	RANGATIRAS	RAPPORTEURS
RADIOTELEMETER	RAILWORKERS	RAMENTACEOUS	RANGATIRATANGA	RAPPROCHEMENT
RADIOTELEMETERS	RAINBOWIER	RAMGUNSHOCH	RANGATIRATANGAS	RAPPROCHEMENTS
RADIOTELEMETRIC	RAINBOWIEST	RAMIFICATION	RANGEFINDER	RAPSCALLION
RADIOTELEMETRY	RAINBOWLIKE	RAMIFICATIONS	RANGEFINDERS	RAPSCALLIONS
RADIOTELEPHONE	RAINCHECKS	RAMMISHNESS	RANGEFINDING	RAPTATORIAL
RADIOTELEPHONED	RAINFOREST	RAMMISHNESSES	RANGEFINDINGS	RAPTNESSES
RADIOTELEPHONES	RAINFORESTS	RAMOSITIES	RANGELANDS	RAPTURELESS
RADIOTELEPHONIC	RAININESSES	RAMPACIOUS	RANGERSHIP	RAPTURISED
RADIOTELEPHONY	RAINMAKERS	RAMPAGEOUS	RANGERSHIPS	RAPTURISES
RADIOTELETYPE	RAINMAKING	RAMPAGEOUSLY	RANGINESSES	RAPTURISING

R

RAPTURISTS	RATEABILITY	RATTENINGS	REABSORBED	REACTIONARIES
RAPTURIZED	RATEABLENESS	RATTINESSES	REABSORBING	REACTIONARISM
RAPTURIZES	RATEABLENESSES	RATTLEBAGS	REABSORPTION	REACTIONARISMS
RAPTURIZING	RATEMETERS	RATTLEBOXES	REABSORPTIONS	REACTIONARIST
RAPTUROUSLY	RATEPAYERS	RATTLEBRAIN	REACCEDING	REACTIONARISTS
RAPTUROUSNESS	RATHERIPES	RATTLEBRAINED	REACCELERATE	REACTIONARY
RAPTUROUSNESSES	RATHSKELLER	RATTLEBRAINS	REACCELERATED	REACTIONARYISM
RAREFACTION	RATHSKELLERS	RATTLEPODS	REACCELERATES	REACTIONARYISMS
RAREFACTIONAL	RATIFIABLE	RATTLESNAKE	REACCELERATING	REACTIONISM
RAREFACTIONS	RATIFICATION	RATTLESNAKES	REACCENTED	REACTIONISMS
RAREFACTIVE	RATIFICATIONS	RATTLETRAP	REACCENTING	REACTIONIST
RAREFIABLE	RATIOCINATE	RATTLETRAPS	REACCEPTED	REACTIONISTS
RAREFICATION	RATIOCINATED	RATTLINGLY	REACCEPTING	REACTIVATE
RAREFICATIONAL	RATIOCINATES	RATTOONING	REACCESSION	REACTIVATED
RAREFICATIONS	RATIOCINATING	RAUCOUSNESS	REACCESSIONS	REACTIVATES
RARENESSES	RATIOCINATION	RAUCOUSNESSES	REACCLAIMED	REACTIVATING
RASCAILLES	RATIOCINATIONS	RAUNCHIEST	REACCLAIMING	REACTIVATION
RASCALDOMS	RATIOCINATIVE	RAUNCHINESS	REACCLAIMS	REACTIVATIONS
RASCALISMS	RATIOCINATOR	RAUNCHINESSES	REACCLIMATISE	REACTIVELY
RASCALITIES	RATIOCINATORS	RAUWOLFIAS	REACCLIMATISED	REACTIVENESS
RASCALLIER	RATIOCINATORY	RAVAGEMENT	REACCLIMATISES	REACTIVENESSES
RASCALLIEST	RATIONALES	RAVAGEMENTS	REACCLIMATISING	REACTIVITIES
RASCALLION	RATIONALISABLE	RAVELLIEST	REACCLIMATIZE	REACTIVITY
RASCALLIONS	RATIONALISATION	RAVELLINGS	REACCLIMATIZED	REACTUATED
RASHNESSES	RATIONALISE	RAVELMENTS	REACCLIMATIZES	REACTUATES
RASPATORIES	RATIONALISED	RAVENINGLY	REACCLIMATIZING	REACTUATING
RASPBERRIES	RATIONALISER	RAVENOUSLY	REACCREDIT	READABILITIES
RASPINESSES	RATIONALISERS	RAVENOUSNESS	REACCREDITATION	READABILITY
RASTAFARIAN	RATIONALISES	RAVENOUSNESSES	REACCREDITED	READABLENESS
RASTAFARIANS	RATIONALISING	RAVIGOTTES	REACCREDITING	READABLENESSES
RASTAFARIS	RATIONALISM	RAVISHINGLY	REACCREDITS	READAPTATION
RASTERISED	RATIONALISMS	RAVISHMENT	REACCUSING	READAPTATIONS
RASTERISES	RATIONALIST	RAVISHMENTS	REACCUSTOM	READAPTING
RASTERISING	RATIONALISTIC	RAWINSONDE	REACCUSTOMED	READDICTED
RASTERIZED	RATIONALISTS	RAWINSONDES	REACCUSTOMING	READDICTING
RASTERIZES	RATIONALITIES	RAWMAISHES	REACCUSTOMS	READDRESSED
RASTERIZING	RATIONALITY	RAYGRASSES	REACQUAINT	READDRESSES
RATABILITIES	RATIONALIZABLE	RAYLESSNESS	REACQUAINTANCE	READDRESSING
RATABILITY	RATIONALIZATION	RAYLESSNESSES	REACQUAINTANCES	READERLIER
RATABLENESS	RATIONALIZE	RAZMATAZES	REACQUAINTED	READERLIEST
RATABLENESSES	RATIONALIZED	RAZORBACKS	REACQUAINTING	READERSHIP
RATAPLANNED	RATIONALIZER	RAZORBILLS	REACQUAINTS	READERSHIPS
RATAPLANNING	RATIONALIZERS	RAZORCLAMS	REACQUIRED	READINESSES
RATATOUILLE	RATIONALIZES	RAZORFISHES	REACQUIRES	READJUSTABLE
RATATOUILLES	RATIONALIZING	RAZZAMATAZZ	REACQUIRING	READJUSTED
RATBAGGERIES	RATIONALLY	RAZZAMATAZZES	REACQUISITION	READJUSTER
RATBAGGERY	RATIONALNESS	RAZZBERRIES	REACQUISITIONS	READJUSTERS
RATCHETING	RATIONALNESSES	RAZZMATAZZ	REACTANCES	READJUSTING
RATEABILITIES	RATIONINGS	RAZZMATAZZES	REACTIONAL	READJUSTMENT

R

READJUSTMENTS	REALIGNMENT	REANOINTED	REAROUSALS	REASSIGNMENT
READMISSION	REALIGNMENTS	REANOINTING	REAROUSING	REASSIGNMENTS
READMISSIONS	REALISABILITIES	REANSWERED	REARRANGED	REASSORTED
READMITTANCE	REALISABILITY	REANSWERING	REARRANGEMENT	REASSORTING
READMITTANCES	REALISABLE	REAPPARELED	REARRANGEMENTS	REASSORTMENT
READMITTED	REALISABLY	REAPPARELING	REARRANGER	REASSORTMENTS
READMITTING	REALISATION	REAPPARELLED	REARRANGERS	REASSUMING
READOPTING	REALISATIONS	REAPPARELLING	REARRANGES	REASSUMPTION
READOPTION	REALISTICALLY	REAPPARELS	REARRANGING	REASSUMPTIONS
READOPTIONS	REALIZABILITIES	REAPPEARANCE	REARRESTED	REASSURANCE
READORNING	REALIZABILITY	REAPPEARANCES	REARRESTING	REASSURANCES
READVANCED	REALIZABLE	REAPPEARED	REARTICULATE	REASSURERS
READVANCES	REALIZABLY	REAPPEARING	REARTICULATED	REASSURING
READVANCING	REALIZATION	REAPPLICATION	REARTICULATES	REASSURINGLY
READVERTISE	REALIZATIONS	REAPPLICATIONS	REARTICULATING	REASTINESS
READVERTISED	REALLOCATE	REAPPLYING	REASCENDED	REASTINESSES
READVERTISEMENT	REALLOCATED	REAPPOINTED	REASCENDING	REATTACHED
READVERTISES	REALLOCATES	REAPPOINTING	REASCENSION	REATTACHES
READVERTISING	REALLOCATING	REAPPOINTMENT	REASCENSIONS	REATTACHING
READVERTIZE	REALLOCATION	REAPPOINTMENTS	REASONABILITIES	REATTACHMENT
READVERTIZED	REALLOCATIONS	REAPPOINTS	REASONABILITY	REATTACHMENTS
READVERTIZEMENT	REALLOTMENT	REAPPORTION	REASONABLE	REATTACKED
READVERTIZES	REALLOTMENTS	REAPPORTIONED	REASONABLENESS	REATTACKING
READVERTIZING	REALLOTTED	REAPPORTIONING	REASONABLY	REATTAINED
READVISING	REALLOTTING	REAPPORTIONMENT	REASONEDLY	REATTAINING
READYMADES	REALNESSES	REAPPORTIONS	REASONINGS	REATTEMPTED
REAEDIFIED	REALPOLITIK	REAPPRAISAL	REASONLESS	REATTEMPTING
REAEDIFIES	REALPOLITIKER	REAPPRAISALS	REASONLESSLY	REATTEMPTS
REAEDIFYED	REALPOLITIKERS	REAPPRAISE	REASSAILED	REATTRIBUTE
REAEDIFYES	REALPOLITIKS	REAPPRAISED	REASSAILING	REATTRIBUTED
REAEDIFYING	REALTERING	REAPPRAISEMENT	REASSEMBLAGE	REATTRIBUTES
REAFFIRMATION	REAMENDING	REAPPRAISEMENTS	REASSEMBLAGES	REATTRIBUTING
REAFFIRMATIONS	REAMENDMENT	REAPPRAISER	REASSEMBLE	REATTRIBUTION
REAFFIRMED	REAMENDMENTS	REAPPRAISERS	REASSEMBLED	REATTRIBUTIONS
REAFFIRMING	REANALYSED	REAPPRAISES	REASSEMBLES	REAUTHORISATION
REAFFIXING	REANALYSES	REAPPRAISING	REASSEMBLIES	REAUTHORISE
REAFFOREST	REANALYSING	REAPPROPRIATE	REASSEMBLING	REAUTHORISED
REAFFORESTATION	REANALYSIS	REAPPROPRIATED	REASSEMBLY	REAUTHORISES
REAFFORESTED	REANALYZED	REAPPROPRIATES	REASSERTED	REAUTHORISING
REAFFORESTING	REANALYZES	REAPPROPRIATING	REASSERTING	REAUTHORIZATION
REAFFORESTS	REANALYZING	REAPPROVED	REASSERTION	REAUTHORIZE
REAGENCIES	REANIMATED	REAPPROVES	REASSERTIONS	REAUTHORIZED
REAGGREGATE	REANIMATES	REAPPROVING	REASSESSED	REAUTHORIZES
REAGGREGATED	REANIMATING	REARGUARDS	REASSESSES	REAUTHORIZING
REAGGREGATES	REANIMATION	REARGUMENT	REASSESSING	REAVAILING
REAGGREGATING	REANIMATIONS	REARGUMENTS	REASSESSMENT	REAWAKENED
REAGGREGATION	REANNEXATION	REARHORSES	REASSESSMENTS	REAWAKENING
REAGGREGATIONS	REANNEXATIONS	REARMAMENT	REASSIGNED	REAWAKENINGS
REALIGNING	REANNEXING	REARMAMENTS	REASSIGNING	REBALANCED

REBALANCES	REBROADCASTS	RECANALISES	RECEIVABILITIES	RECESSIVES
REBALANCING	REBUILDING	RECANALISING	RECEIVABILITY	RECHALLENGE
REBAPTISED	REBUILDINGS	RECANALIZATION	RECEIVABLE	RECHALLENGED
REBAPTISES	REBUKEFULLY	RECANALIZATIONS	RECEIVABLENESS	RECHALLENGES
REBAPTISING	REBUKINGLY	RECANALIZE	RECEIVABLES	RECHALLENGING
REBAPTISMS	REBUTMENTS	RECANALIZED	RECEIVERSHIP	RECHANGING
REBAPTIZED	REBUTTABLE	RECANALIZES	RECEIVERSHIPS	RECHANNELED
REBAPTIZES	REBUTTONED	RECANALIZING	RECEIVINGS	RECHANNELING
REBAPTIZING	REBUTTONING	RECANTATION	RECEMENTED	RECHANNELLED
REBARBATIVE	RECALCITRANCE	RECANTATIONS	RECEMENTING	RECHANNELLING
REBARBATIVELY	RECALCITRANCES	RECAPITALISE	RECENSIONS	RECHANNELS
REBATEABLE	RECALCITRANCIES	RECAPITALISED	RECENSORED	RECHARGEABLE
REBATEMENT	RECALCITRANCY	RECAPITALISES	RECENSORING	RECHARGERS
REBATEMENTS	RECALCITRANT	RECAPITALISING	RECENTNESS	RECHARGING
REBBETZINS	RECALCITRANTS	RECAPITALIZE	RECENTNESSES	RECHARTERED
REBEGINNING	RECALCITRATE	RECAPITALIZED	RECENTRIFUGE	RECHARTERING
REBELLIONS	RECALCITRATED	RECAPITALIZES	RECENTRIFUGED	RECHARTERS
REBELLIOUS	RECALCITRATES	RECAPITALIZING	RECENTRIFUGES	RECHARTING
REBELLIOUSLY	RECALCITRATING	RECAPITULATE	RECENTRIFUGING	RECHAUFFES
REBELLIOUSNESS	RECALCITRATION	RECAPITULATED	RECENTRING	RECHEATING
REBELLOWED	RECALCITRATIONS	RECAPITULATES	RECEPTACLE	RECHECKING
REBELLOWING	RECALCULATE	RECAPITULATING	RECEPTACLES	RECHIPPING
REBIRTHERS	RECALCULATED	RECAPITULATION	RECEPTACULA	RECHIPPINGS
REBIRTHING	RECALCULATES	RECAPITULATIONS	RECEPTACULAR	RECHOOSING
REBIRTHINGS	RECALCULATING	RECAPITULATIVE	RECEPTACULUM	RECHOREOGRAPH
REBLENDING	RECALCULATION	RECAPITULATORY	RECEPTIBILITIES	RECHOREOGRAPHED
REBLOCHONS	RECALCULATIONS	RECAPPABLE	RECEPTIBILITY	RECHOREOGRAPHS
REBLOOMERS	RECALESCED	RECAPTIONS	RECEPTIBLE	RECHRISTEN
REBLOOMING	RECALESCENCE	RECAPTURED	RECEPTIONIST	RECHRISTENED
REBLOSSOMED	RECALESCENCES	RECAPTURER	RECEPTIONISTS	RECHRISTENING
REBLOSSOMING	RECALESCENT	RECAPTURERS	RECEPTIONS	RECHRISTENS
REBLOSSOMS	RECALESCES	RECAPTURES	RECEPTIVELY	RECHROMATOGRAPH
REBOARDING	RECALESCING	RECAPTURING	RECEPTIVENESS	RECIDIVISM
REBOATIONS	RECALIBRATE	RECARPETED	RECEPTIVENESSES	RECIDIVISMS
REBORROWED	RECALIBRATED	RECARPETING	RECEPTIVITIES	RECIDIVIST
REBORROWING	RECALIBRATES	RECARRYING	RECEPTIVITY	RECIDIVISTIC
REBOTTLING	RECALIBRATING	RECATALOGED	RECERTIFICATION	RECIDIVISTS
REBOUNDERS	RECALIBRATION	RECATALOGING	RECERTIFIED	RECIDIVOUS
REBOUNDING	RECALIBRATIONS	RECATALOGS	RECERTIFIES	RECIPIENCE
REBOUNDINGS	RECALLABILITIES	RECATALOGUE	RECERTIFYING	RECIPIENCES
REBRANCHED	RECALLABILITY	RECATALOGUED	RECESSIONAL	RECIPIENCIES
REBRANCHES	RECALLABLE	RECATALOGUES	RECESSIONALS	RECIPIENCY
REBRANCHING	RECALLMENT	RECATALOGUING	RECESSIONARY	RECIPIENTS
REBRANDING	RECALLMENTS	RECATCHING	RECESSIONISTA	RECIPROCAL
REBRANDINGS	RECALMENTS	RECAUTIONED	RECESSIONISTAS	RECIPROCALITIES
REBREEDING	RECANALISATION	RECAUTIONING	RECESSIONS	RECIPROCALITY
REBROADCAST	RECANALISATIONS	RECAUTIONS	RECESSIVELY	RECIPROCALLY
REBROADCASTED	RECANALISE	RECEIPTING	RECESSIVENESS	RECIPROCALS
REBROADCASTING	RECANALISED	RECEIPTORS	RECESSIVENESSES	RECIPROCANT

RECIPROCANTS	RECLEANING	RECOGNIZES	RECOMMENCING	RECOMPUTATION
RECIPROCATE	RECLIMBING	RECOGNIZING	RECOMMENDABLE	RECOMPUTATIONS
RECIPROCATED	RECLINABLE	RECOGNIZOR	RECOMMENDABLY	RECOMPUTED
RECIPROCATES	RECLINATION	RECOGNIZORS	RECOMMENDATION	RECOMPUTES
RECIPROCATING	RECLINATIONS	RECOILLESS	RECOMMENDATIONS	RECOMPUTING
RECIPROCATION	RECLOSABLE	RECOINAGES	RECOMMENDATORY	RECONCEIVE
RECIPROCATIONS	RECLOTHING	RECOLLECTED	RECOMMENDED	RECONCEIVED
RECIPROCATIVE	RECLUSENESS	RECOLLECTEDLY	RECOMMENDER	RECONCEIVES
RECIPROCATOR	RECLUSENESSES	RECOLLECTEDNESS	RECOMMENDERS	RECONCEIVING
RECIPROCATORS	RECLUSIONS	RECOLLECTING	RECOMMENDING	RECONCENTRATE
RECIPROCATORY	RECLUSIVELY	RECOLLECTION	RECOMMENDS	RECONCENTRATED
RECIPROCITIES	RECLUSIVENESS	RECOLLECTIONS	RECOMMISSION	RECONCENTRATES
RECIPROCITY	RECLUSIVENESSES	RECOLLECTIVE	RECOMMISSIONED	RECONCENTRATING
RECIRCLING	RECLUSORIES	RECOLLECTIVELY	RECOMMISSIONING	RECONCENTRATION
RECIRCULATE	RECODIFICATION	RECOLLECTS	RECOMMISSIONS	RECONCEPTION
RECIRCULATED	RECODIFICATIONS	RECOLONISATION	RECOMMITMENT	RECONCEPTIONS
RECIRCULATES	RECODIFIED	RECOLONISATIONS	RECOMMITMENTS	RECONCEPTUALISE
RECIRCULATING	RECODIFIES	RECOLONISE	RECOMMITTAL	RECONCEPTUALIZE
RECIRCULATION	RECODIFYING	RECOLONISED	RECOMMITTALS	RECONCILABILITY
RECIRCULATIONS	RECOGNISABILITY	RECOLONISES	RECOMMITTED	RECONCILABLE
RECITALIST	RECOGNISABLE	RECOLONISING	RECOMMITTING	RECONCILABLY
RECITALISTS	RECOGNISABLY	RECOLONIZATION	RECOMPACTED	RECONCILED
RECITATION	RECOGNISANCE	RECOLONIZATIONS	RECOMPACTING	RECONCILEMENT
RECITATIONIST	RECOGNISANCES	RECOLONIZE	RECOMPACTS	RECONCILEMENTS
RECITATIONISTS	RECOGNISANT	RECOLONIZED	RECOMPENCE	RECONCILER
RECITATIONS	RECOGNISED	RECOLONIZES	RECOMPENCES	RECONCILERS
RECITATIVE	RECOGNISEE	RECOLONIZING	RECOMPENSABLE	RECONCILES
RECITATIVES	RECOGNISEES	RECOLORING	RECOMPENSE	RECONCILIATION
RECITATIVI	RECOGNISER	RECOLOURED	RECOMPENSED	RECONCILIATIONS
RECITATIVO	RECOGNISERS	RECOLOURING	RECOMPENSER	RECONCILIATORY
RECITATIVOS	RECOGNISES	RECOMBINANT	RECOMPENSERS	RECONCILING
RECKLESSLY	RECOGNISING	RECOMBINANTS	RECOMPENSES	RECONDENSATION
RECKLESSNESS	RECOGNISOR	RECOMBINATION	RECOMPENSING	RECONDENSATIONS
RECKLESSNESSES	RECOGNISORS	RECOMBINATIONAL	RECOMPILATION	RECONDENSE
RECKONINGS	RECOGNITION	RECOMBINATIONS	RECOMPILATIONS	RECONDENSED
RECLADDING	RECOGNITIONS	RECOMBINED	RECOMPILED	RECONDENSES
RECLAIMABLE	RECOGNITIVE	RECOMBINES	RECOMPILES	RECONDENSING
RECLAIMABLY	RECOGNITORY	RECOMBINING	RECOMPILING	RECONDITELY
RECLAIMANT	RECOGNIZABILITY	RECOMFORTED	RECOMPOSED	RECONDITENESS
RECLAIMANTS	RECOGNIZABLE	RECOMFORTING	RECOMPOSES	RECONDITENESSES
RECLAIMERS	RECOGNIZABLY	RECOMFORTLESS	RECOMPOSING	RECONDITION
RECLAIMING	RECOGNIZANCE	RECOMFORTS	RECOMPOSITION	RECONDITIONED
RECLAMATION	RECOGNIZANCES	RECOMFORTURE	RECOMPOSITIONS	RECONDITIONING
RECLAMATIONS	RECOGNIZANT	RECOMFORTURES	RECOMPRESS	RECONDITIONS
RECLASPING	RECOGNIZED	RECOMMENCE	RECOMPRESSED	RECONDUCTED
RECLASSIFIED	RECOGNIZEE	RECOMMENCED	RECOMPRESSES	RECONDUCTING
RECLASSIFIES	RECOGNIZEES	RECOMMENCEMENT	RECOMPRESSING	RECONDUCTS
RECLASSIFY	RECOGNIZER	RECOMMENCEMENTS	RECOMPRESSION	RECONFERRED
RECLASSIFYING	RECOGNIZERS	RECOMMENCES	RECOMPRESSIONS	RECONFERRING

RECONFIGURATION RECONSIDERING RECONTOURED RECOVERABLENESS RECRUITINGS
RECONFIGURE RECONSIDERS RECONTOURING RECOVEREES RECRUITMENT
RECONFIGURED RECONSIGNED RECONTOURS RECOVERERS RECRUITMENTS
RECONFIGURES RECONSIGNING RECONVALESCE RECOVERIES RECRYSTALLISE
RECONFIGURING RECONSIGNS RECONVALESCED RECOVERING RECRYSTALLISED
RECONFINED RECONSOLED RECONVALESCENCE RECOVERORS RECRYSTALLISES
RECONFINES RECONSOLES RECONVALESCENT RECOWERING RECRYSTALLISING
RECONFINING RECONSOLIDATE RECONVALESCES RECREANCES RECRYSTALLIZE
RECONFIRMATION RECONSOLIDATED RECONVALESCING RECREANCIES RECRYSTALLIZED
RECONFIRMATIONS RECONSOLIDATES RECONVENED RECREANTLY RECRYSTALLIZES
RECONFIRMED RECONSOLIDATING RECONVENES RECREATING RECRYSTALLIZING
RECONFIRMING RECONSOLIDATION RECONVENING RECREATION RECTANGLED
RECONFIRMS RECONSOLING RECONVERSION RECREATIONAL RECTANGLES
RECONNAISSANCE RECONSTITUENT RECONVERSIONS RECREATIONALLY RECTANGULAR
RECONNAISSANCES RECONSTITUENTS RECONVERTED RECREATIONIST RECTANGULARITY
RECONNECTED RECONSTITUTABLE RECONVERTING RECREATIONISTS RECTANGULARLY
RECONNECTING RECONSTITUTE RECONVERTS RECREATIONS RECTIFIABILITY
RECONNECTION RECONSTITUTED RECONVEYANCE RECREATIVE RECTIFIABLE
RECONNECTIONS RECONSTITUTES RECONVEYANCES RECREATIVELY RECTIFICATION
RECONNECTS RECONSTITUTING RECONVEYED RECREATORS RECTIFICATIONS
RECONNOISSANCE RECONSTITUTION RECONVEYING RECREMENTAL RECTIFIERS
RECONNOISSANCES RECONSTITUTIONS RECONVICTED RECREMENTITIAL RECTIFYING
RECONNOITER RECONSTRUCT RECONVICTING RECREMENTITIOUS RECTILINEAL
RECONNOITERED RECONSTRUCTED RECONVICTION RECREMENTS RECTILINEALLY
RECONNOITERER RECONSTRUCTIBLE RECONVICTIONS RECRIMINATE RECTILINEAR
RECONNOITERERS RECONSTRUCTING RECONVICTS RECRIMINATED RECTILINEARITY
RECONNOITERING RECONSTRUCTION RECONVINCE RECRIMINATES RECTILINEARLY
RECONNOITERS RECONSTRUCTIONS RECONVINCED RECRIMINATING RECTIPETALIES
RECONNOITRE RECONSTRUCTIVE RECONVINCES RECRIMINATION RECTIPETALITIES
RECONNOITRED RECONSTRUCTOR RECONVINCING RECRIMINATIONS RECTIPETALITY
RECONNOITRER RECONSTRUCTORS RECORDABLE RECRIMINATIVE RECTIPETALY
RECONNOITRERS RECONSTRUCTS RECORDATION RECRIMINATOR RECTIROSTRAL
RECONNOITRES RECONSULTED RECORDATIONS RECRIMINATORS RECTISERIAL
RECONNOITRING RECONSULTING RECORDERSHIP RECRIMINATORY RECTITISES
RECONNOITRINGS RECONSULTS RECORDERSHIPS RECROSSING RECTITUDES
RECONQUERED RECONTACTED RECORDINGS RECROWNING RECTITUDINOUS
RECONQUERING RECONTACTING RECORDISTS RECRUDESCE RECTOCELES
RECONQUERS RECONTACTS RECOUNTALS RECRUDESCED RECTORATES
RECONQUEST RECONTAMINATE RECOUNTERS RECRUDESCENCE RECTORESSES
RECONQUESTS RECONTAMINATED RECOUNTING RECRUDESCENCES RECTORIALS
RECONSECRATE RECONTAMINATES RECOUNTMENT RECRUDESCENCIES RECTORSHIP
RECONSECRATED RECONTAMINATING RECOUNTMENTS RECRUDESCENCY RECTORSHIPS
RECONSECRATES RECONTAMINATION RECOUPABLE RECRUDESCENT RECTRESSES
RECONSECRATING RECONTEXTUALISE RECOUPLING RECRUDESCES RECTRICIAL
RECONSECRATION RECONTEXTUALIZE RECOUPMENT RECRUDESCING RECULTIVATE
RECONSECRATIONS RECONTINUE RECOUPMENTS RECRUITABLE RECULTIVATED
RECONSIDER RECONTINUED RECOURSING RECRUITALS RECULTIVATES
RECONSIDERATION RECONTINUES RECOVERABILITY RECRUITERS RECULTIVATING
RECONSIDERED RECONTINUING RECOVERABLE RECRUITING RECUMBENCE

RECUMBENCES	REDDISHNESS	REDEMPTIVELY	REDINTEGRATIONS	REDISTRIBUTION
RECUMBENCIES	REDDISHNESSES	REDEMPTORY	REDINTEGRATIVE	REDISTRIBUTIONS
RECUMBENCY	REDECIDING	REDEPLOYED	REDIRECTED	REDISTRIBUTIVE
RECUMBENTLY	REDECORATE	REDEPLOYING	REDIRECTING	REDISTRICT
RECUPERABLE	REDECORATED	REDEPLOYMENT	REDIRECTION	REDISTRICTED
RECUPERATE	REDECORATES	REDEPLOYMENTS	REDIRECTIONS	REDISTRICTING
RECUPERATED	REDECORATING	REDEPOSITED	REDISBURSE	REDISTRICTINGS
RECUPERATES	REDECORATION	REDEPOSITING	REDISBURSED	REDISTRICTS
RECUPERATING	REDECORATIONS	REDEPOSITS	REDISBURSES	REDIVIDING
RECUPERATION	REDECORATOR	REDESCENDED	REDISBURSING	REDIVISION
RECUPERATIONS	REDECORATORS	REDESCENDING	REDISCOUNT	REDIVISIONS
RECUPERATIVE	REDECRAFTS	REDESCENDS	REDISCOUNTABLE	REDIVORCED
RECUPERATOR	REDEDICATE	REDESCRIBE	REDISCOUNTED	REDIVORCES
RECUPERATORS	REDEDICATED	REDESCRIBED	REDISCOUNTING	REDIVORCING
RECUPERATORY	REDEDICATES	REDESCRIBES	REDISCOUNTS	REDLININGS
RECURELESS	REDEDICATING	REDESCRIBING	REDISCOVER	REDOLENCES
RECURRENCE	REDEDICATION	REDESCRIPTION	REDISCOVERED	REDOLENCIES
RECURRENCES	REDEDICATIONS	REDESCRIPTIONS	REDISCOVERER	REDOLENTLY
RECURRENCIES	REDEEMABILITIES	REDESIGNED	REDISCOVERERS	REDOUBLEMENT
RECURRENCY	REDEEMABILITY	REDESIGNING	REDISCOVERIES	REDOUBLEMENTS
RECURRENTLY	REDEEMABLE	REDETERMINATION	REDISCOVERING	REDOUBLERS
RECURRINGLY	REDEEMABLENESS	REDETERMINE	REDISCOVERS	REDOUBLING
RECURSIONS	REDEEMABLY	REDETERMINED	REDISCOVERY	REDOUBTABLE
RECURSIVELY	REDEEMLESS	REDETERMINES	REDISCUSSED	REDOUBTABLENESS
RECURSIVENESS	REDEFEATED	REDETERMINING	REDISCUSSES	REDOUBTABLY
RECURSIVENESSES	REDEFEATING	REDEVELOPED	REDISCUSSING	REDOUBTING
RECURVIROSTRAL	REDEFECTED	REDEVELOPER	REDISPLAYED	REDOUNDING
RECUSANCES	REDEFECTING	REDEVELOPERS	REDISPLAYING	REDOUNDINGS
RECUSANCIES	REDEFINING	REDEVELOPING	REDISPLAYS	REDRAFTING
RECUSATION	REDEFINITION	REDEVELOPMENT	REDISPOSED	REDREAMING
RECUSATIONS	REDEFINITIONS	REDEVELOPMENTS	REDISPOSES	REDRESSABLE
RECYCLABLE	REDELIVERANCE	REDEVELOPS	REDISPOSING	REDRESSALS
RECYCLABLES	REDELIVERANCES	REDIALLING	REDISPOSITION	REDRESSERS
RECYCLATES	REDELIVERED	REDICTATED	REDISPOSITIONS	REDRESSIBLE
RECYCLEABLE	REDELIVERER	REDICTATES	REDISSOLUTION	REDRESSING
RECYCLEABLES	REDELIVERERS	REDICTATING	REDISSOLUTIONS	REDRESSIVE
RECYCLINGS	REDELIVERIES	REDIGESTED	REDISSOLVE	REDRESSORS
RECYCLISTS	REDELIVERING	REDIGESTING	REDISSOLVED	REDRILLING
REDACTIONAL	REDELIVERS	REDIGESTION	REDISSOLVES	REDRUTHITE
REDACTIONS	REDELIVERY	REDIGESTIONS	REDISSOLVING	REDRUTHITES
REDACTORIAL	REDEMANDED	REDIGRESSED	REDISTILLATION	REDSHIFTED
REDAMAGING	REDEMANDING	REDIGRESSES	REDISTILLATIONS	REDSHIRTED
REDARGUING	REDEMPTIBLE	REDIGRESSING	REDISTILLED	REDSHIRTING
REDBAITERS	REDEMPTION	REDINGOTES	REDISTILLING	REDSTREAKS
REDBAITING	REDEMPTIONAL	REDINTEGRATE	REDISTILLS	REDUCETARIAN
REDBELLIES	REDEMPTIONER	REDINTEGRATED	REDISTRIBUTE	REDUCETARIANISM
REDBREASTS	REDEMPTIONERS	REDINTEGRATES	REDISTRIBUTED	REDUCETARIANS
REDCURRANT	REDEMPTIONS	REDINTEGRATING	REDISTRIBUTES	REDUCIBILITIES
REDCURRANTS	REDEMPTIVE	REDINTEGRATION	REDISTRIBUTING	REDUCIBILITY

R

REDUCIBLENESS	REEMBARKING	REENFORCES	REESTIMATE	REFASTENED
REDUCIBLENESSES	REEMBODIED	REENFORCING	REESTIMATED	REFASTENING
REDUCTANTS	REEMBODIES	REENGAGEMENT	REESTIMATES	REFECTIONER
REDUCTASES	REEMBODYING	REENGAGEMENTS	REESTIMATING	REFECTIONERS
REDUCTIONAL	REEMBRACED	REENGAGING	REEVALUATE	REFECTIONS
REDUCTIONISM	REEMBRACES	REENGINEER	REEVALUATED	REFECTORIAN
REDUCTIONISMS	REEMBRACING	REENGINEERED	REEVALUATES	REFECTORIANS
REDUCTIONIST	REEMBROIDER	REENGINEERING	REEVALUATING	REFECTORIES
REDUCTIONISTIC	REEMBROIDERED	REENGINEERS	REEVALUATION	REFEEDINGS
REDUCTIONISTS	REEMBROIDERING	REENGRAVED	REEVALUATIONS	REFEREEING
REDUCTIONS	REEMBROIDERS	REENGRAVES	REEVESHIPS	REFEREEINGS
REDUCTIVELY	REEMERGENCE	REENGRAVING	REEXAMINATION	REFERENCED
REDUCTIVENESS	REEMERGENCES	REENJOYING	REEXAMINATIONS	REFERENCER
REDUCTIVENESSES	REEMERGING	REENLARGED	REEXAMINED	REFERENCERS
REDUCTIVES	REEMISSION	REENLARGES	REEXAMINES	REFERENCES
REDUNDANCE	REEMISSIONS	REENLARGING	REEXAMINING	REFERENCING
REDUNDANCES	REEMITTING	REENLISTED	REEXECUTED	REFERENCINGS
REDUNDANCIES	REEMPHASES	REENLISTING	REEXECUTES	REFERENDARIES
REDUNDANCY	REEMPHASIS	REENLISTMENT	REEXECUTING	REFERENDARY
REDUNDANTLY	REEMPHASISE	REENLISTMENTS	REEXHIBITED	REFERENDUM
REDUPLICATE	REEMPHASISED	REENROLLED	REEXHIBITING	REFERENDUMS
REDUPLICATED	REEMPHASISES	REENROLLING	REEXHIBITS	REFERENTIAL
REDUPLICATES	REEMPHASISING	REENSLAVED	REEXPELLED	REFERENTIALITY
REDUPLICATING	REEMPHASIZE	REENSLAVES	REEXPELLING	REFERENTIALLY
REDUPLICATION	REEMPHASIZED	REENSLAVING	REEXPERIENCE	REFERRABLE
REDUPLICATIONS	REEMPHASIZES	REENTERING	REEXPERIENCED	REFERRIBLE
REDUPLICATIVE	REEMPHASIZING	REENTHRONE	REEXPERIENCES	REFIGHTING
REDUPLICATIVELY	REEMPLOYED	REENTHRONED	REEXPERIENCING	REFIGURING
REEDIFYING	REEMPLOYING	REENTHRONES	REEXPLAINED	REFILLABLE
REEDINESSES	REEMPLOYMENT	REENTHRONING	REEXPLAINING	REFILTERED
REEDITIONS	REEMPLOYMENTS	REENTRANCE	REEXPLAINS	REFILTERING
REEDUCATED	REENACTING	REENTRANCES	REEXPLORED	REFINANCED
REEDUCATES	REENACTMENT	REENTRANTS	REEXPLORES	REFINANCES
REEDUCATING	REENACTMENTS	REEQUIPMENT	REEXPLORING	REFINANCING
REEDUCATION	REENACTORS	REEQUIPMENTS	REEXPORTATION	REFINANCINGS
REEDUCATIONS	REENCOUNTER	REEQUIPPED	REEXPORTATIONS	REFINEDNESS
REEDUCATIVE	REENCOUNTERED	REEQUIPPING	REEXPORTED	REFINEDNESSES
REEFPOINTS	REENCOUNTERING	REERECTING	REEXPORTING	REFINEMENT
REEJECTING	REENCOUNTERS	REESCALATE	REEXPOSING	REFINEMENTS
REELECTING	REENDOWING	REESCALATED	REEXPOSURE	REFINERIES
REELECTION	REENERGISE	REESCALATES	REEXPOSURES	REFINISHED
REELECTIONS	REENERGISED	REESCALATING	REEXPRESSED	REFINISHER
REELEVATED	REENERGISES	REESCALATION	REEXPRESSES	REFINISHERS
REELEVATES	REENERGISING	REESCALATIONS	REEXPRESSING	REFINISHES
REELEVATING	REENERGIZE	REESTABLISH	REFASHIONED	REFINISHING
REELIGIBILITIES	REENERGIZED	REESTABLISHED	REFASHIONING	REFITMENTS
REELIGIBILITY	REENERGIZES	REESTABLISHES	REFASHIONMENT	REFITTINGS
REELIGIBLE	REENERGIZING	REESTABLISHING	REFASHIONMENTS	REFLAGGING
REEMBARKED	REENFORCED	REESTABLISHMENT	REFASHIONS	REFLATIONARY

REFLATIONS	REFLOATING	REFORTIFIES	REFRESHFULLY	REFURBISHMENT
REFLECTANCE	REFLOODING	REFORTIFYING	REFRESHING	REFURBISHMENTS
REFLECTANCES	REFLOWERED	REFOULEMENT	REFRESHINGLY	REFURNISHED
REFLECTERS	REFLOWERING	REFOULEMENTS	REFRESHMENT	REFURNISHES
REFLECTING	REFLOWERINGS	REFOUNDATION	REFRESHMENTS	REFURNISHING
REFLECTINGLY	REFLOWINGS	REFOUNDATIONS	REFRIGERANT	REFUSENIKS
REFLECTION	REFLUENCES	REFOUNDERS	REFRIGERANTS	REFUTABILITIES
REFLECTIONAL	REFOCILLATE	REFOUNDING	REFRIGERATE	REFUTABILITY
REFLECTIONLESS	REFOCILLATED	REFRACTABLE	REFRIGERATED	REFUTATION
REFLECTIONS	REFOCILLATES	REFRACTARIES	REFRIGERATES	REFUTATIONS
REFLECTIVE	REFOCILLATING	REFRACTARY	REFRIGERATING	REGAINABLE
REFLECTIVELY	REFOCILLATION	REFRACTILE	REFRIGERATION	REGAINMENT
REFLECTIVENESS	REFOCILLATIONS	REFRACTING	REFRIGERATIONS	REGAINMENTS
REFLECTIVITIES	REFOCUSING	REFRACTION	REFRIGERATIVE	REGALEMENT
REFLECTIVITY	REFOCUSSED	REFRACTIONS	REFRIGERATOR	REGALEMENTS
REFLECTOGRAM	REFOCUSSES	REFRACTIVE	REFRIGERATORIES	REGALITIES
REFLECTOGRAMS	REFOCUSSING	REFRACTIVELY	REFRIGERATORS	REGALNESSES
REFLECTOGRAPH	REFORESTATION	REFRACTIVENESS	REFRIGERATORY	REGARDABLE
REFLECTOGRAPHS	REFORESTATIONS	REFRACTIVITIES	REFRINGENCE	REGARDFULLY
REFLECTOGRAPHY	REFORESTED	REFRACTIVITY	REFRINGENCES	REGARDFULNESS
REFLECTOMETER	REFORESTING	REFRACTOMETER	REFRINGENCIES	REGARDFULNESSES
REFLECTOMETERS	REFORMABILITIES	REFRACTOMETERS	REFRINGENCY	REGARDLESS
REFLECTOMETRIES	REFORMABILITY	REFRACTOMETRIC	REFRINGENT	REGARDLESSLY
REFLECTOMETRY	REFORMABLE	REFRACTOMETRIES	REFRINGING	REGARDLESSNESS
REFLECTORISE	REFORMADES	REFRACTOMETRY	REFRONTING	REGATHERED
REFLECTORISED	REFORMADOES	REFRACTORIES	REFUELABLE	REGATHERING
REFLECTORISES	REFORMADOS	REFRACTORILY	REFUELINGS	REGELATING
REFLECTORISING	REFORMATES	REFRACTORINESS	REFUELLABLE	REGELATION
REFLECTORIZE	REFORMATION	REFRACTORS	REFUELLING	REGELATIONS
REFLECTORIZED	REFORMATIONAL	REFRACTORY	REFUELLINGS	REGENERABLE
REFLECTORIZES	REFORMATIONIST	REFRACTURE	REFUGEEISM	REGENERACIES
REFLECTORIZING	REFORMATIONISTS	REFRACTURED	REFUGEEISMS	REGENERACY
REFLECTORS	REFORMATIONS	REFRACTURES	REFULGENCE	REGENERATE
REFLEXIBILITIES	REFORMATIVE	REFRACTURING	REFULGENCES	REGENERATED
REFLEXIBILITY	REFORMATORIES	REFRAINERS	REFULGENCIES	REGENERATELY
REFLEXIBLE	REFORMATORY	REFRAINING	REFULGENCY	REGENERATENESS
REFLEXIONAL	REFORMATTED	REFRAINMENT	REFULGENTLY	REGENERATES
REFLEXIONS	REFORMATTING	REFRAINMENTS	REFUNDABILITIES	REGENERATING
REFLEXIVELY	REFORMINGS	REFRANGIBILITY	REFUNDABILITY	REGENERATION
REFLEXIVENESS	REFORMISMS	REFRANGIBLE	REFUNDABLE	REGENERATIONS
REFLEXIVENESSES	REFORMISTS	REFRANGIBLENESS	REFUNDINGS	REGENERATIVE
REFLEXIVES	REFORMULATE	REFREEZING	REFUNDMENT	REGENERATIVELY
REFLEXIVITIES	REFORMULATED	REFRESHENED	REFUNDMENTS	REGENERATOR
REFLEXIVITY	REFORMULATES	REFRESHENER	REFURBISHED	REGENERATORS
REFLEXOLOGICAL	REFORMULATING	REFRESHENERS	REFURBISHER	REGENERATORY
REFLEXOLOGIES	REFORMULATION	REFRESHENING	REFURBISHERS	REGENTSHIP
REFLEXOLOGIST	REFORMULATIONS	REFRESHENS	REFURBISHES	REGENTSHIPS
REFLEXOLOGISTS	REFORTIFICATION	REFRESHERS	REFURBISHING	REGGAETONS
REFLEXOLOGY	REFORTIFIED	REFRESHFUL	REFURBISHINGS	REGIMENTAL

R

REGIMENTALLY	REGREDIENCES	REGULIZING	REHYDRATABLE	REIMPLANTS
REGIMENTALS	REGREENING	REGURGITANT	REHYDRATED	REIMPORTATION
REGIMENTATION	REGREETING	REGURGITANTS	REHYDRATES	REIMPORTATIONS
REGIMENTATIONS	REGRESSING	REGURGITATE	REHYDRATING	REIMPORTED
REGIMENTED	REGRESSION	REGURGITATED	REHYDRATION	REIMPORTER
REGIMENTING	REGRESSIONS	REGURGITATES	REHYDRATIONS	REIMPORTERS
REGIONALISATION	REGRESSIVE	REGURGITATING	REHYPNOTISE	REIMPORTING
REGIONALISE	REGRESSIVELY	REGURGITATION	REHYPNOTISED	REIMPOSING
REGIONALISED	REGRESSIVENESS	REGURGITATIONS	REHYPNOTISES	REIMPOSITION
REGIONALISES	REGRESSIVITIES	REHABILITANT	REHYPNOTISING	REIMPOSITIONS
REGIONALISING	REGRESSIVITY	REHABILITANTS	REHYPNOTIZE	REIMPRESSION
REGIONALISM	REGRESSORS	REHABILITATE	REHYPNOTIZED	REIMPRESSIONS
REGIONALISMS	REGRETFULLY	REHABILITATED	REHYPNOTIZES	REINCARNATE
REGIONALIST	REGRETFULNESS	REHABILITATES	REHYPNOTIZING	REINCARNATED
REGIONALISTIC	REGRETFULNESSES	REHABILITATING	REICHSMARK	REINCARNATES
REGIONALISTS	REGRETTABLE	REHABILITATION	REICHSMARKS	REINCARNATING
REGIONALIZATION	REGRETTABLY	REHABILITATIONS	REIDENTIFIED	REINCARNATION
REGIONALIZE	REGRETTERS	REHABILITATIVE	REIDENTIFIES	REINCARNATIONS
REGIONALIZED	REGRETTING	REHABILITATOR	REIDENTIFY	REINCITING
REGIONALIZES	REGRINDING	REHABILITATORS	REIDENTIFYING	REINCORPORATE
REGIONALIZING	REGROOMING	REHAMMERED	REIFICATION	REINCORPORATED
REGIONALLY	REGROOVING	REHAMMERING	REIFICATIONS	REINCORPORATES
REGISSEURS	REGROUPING	REHANDLING	REIFICATORY	REINCORPORATING
REGISTERABLE	REGROUPINGS	REHANDLINGS	REIGNITING	REINCORPORATION
REGISTERED	REGUERDONED	REHARDENED	REIGNITION	REINCREASE
REGISTERER	REGUERDONING	REHARDENING	REIGNITIONS	REINCREASED
REGISTERERS	REGUERDONS	REHEARINGS	REILLUMINE	REINCREASES
REGISTERING	REGULARISATION	REHEARSALS	REILLUMINED	REINCREASING
REGISTRABLE	REGULARISATIONS	REHEARSERS	REILLUMINES	REINCURRED
REGISTRANT	REGULARISE	REHEARSING	REILLUMING	REINCURRING
REGISTRANTS	REGULARISED	REHEARSINGS	REILLUMINING	REINDEXING
REGISTRARIES	REGULARISES	REHEATINGS	REIMAGINED	REINDICTED
REGISTRARS	REGULARISING	REHOSPITALISE	REIMAGINES	REINDICTING
REGISTRARSHIP	REGULARITIES	REHOSPITALISED	REIMAGINING	REINDICTMENT
REGISTRARSHIPS	REGULARITY	REHOSPITALISES	REIMBURSABLE	REINDICTMENTS
REGISTRARY	REGULARIZATION	REHOSPITALISING	REIMBURSED	REINDUCING
REGISTRATION	REGULARIZATIONS	REHOSPITALIZE	REIMBURSEMENT	REINDUCTED
REGISTRATIONAL	REGULARIZE	REHOSPITALIZED	REIMBURSEMENTS	REINDUCTING
REGISTRATIONS	REGULARIZED	REHOSPITALIZES	REIMBURSER	REINDUSTRIALISE
REGISTRIES	REGULARIZES	REHOSPITALIZING	REIMBURSERS	REINDUSTRIALIZE
REGLORIFIED	REGULARIZING	REHOUSINGS	REIMBURSES	REINFECTED
REGLORIFIES	REGULATING	REHUMANISE	REIMBURSING	REINFECTING
REGLORIFYING	REGULATION	REHUMANISED	REIMMERSED	REINFECTION
REGLOSSING	REGULATIONS	REHUMANISES	REIMMERSES	REINFECTIONS
REGNANCIES	REGULATIVE	REHUMANISING	REIMMERSING	REINFESTATION
REGRAFTING	REGULATIVELY	REHUMANIZE	REIMPLANTATION	REINFESTATIONS
REGRANTING	REGULATORS	REHUMANIZED	REIMPLANTATIONS	REINFLAMED
REGRATINGS	REGULATORY	REHUMANIZES	REIMPLANTED	REINFLAMES
REGREDIENCE	REGULISING	REHUMANIZING	REIMPLANTING	REINFLAMING

REINFLATED	REINSPECTION	REINTERRED	REISTAFELS	REJUVENESCED
REINFLATES	REINSPECTIONS	REINTERRING	REITERANCE	REJUVENESCENCE
REINFLATING	REINSPECTS	REINTERROGATE	REITERANCES	REJUVENESCENCES
REINFLATION	REINSPIRED	REINTERROGATED	REITERATED	REJUVENESCENT
REINFLATIONS	REINSPIRES	REINTERROGATES	REITERATEDLY	REJUVENESCES
REINFORCEABLE	REINSPIRING	REINTERROGATING	REITERATES	REJUVENESCING
REINFORCED	REINSPIRIT	REINTERROGATION	REITERATING	REJUVENISE
REINFORCEMENT	REINSPIRITED	REINTERVIEW	REITERATION	REJUVENISED
REINFORCEMENTS	REINSPIRITING	REINTERVIEWED	REITERATIONS	REJUVENISES
REINFORCER	REINSPIRITS	REINTERVIEWING	REITERATIVE	REJUVENISING
REINFORCERS	REINSTALLATION	REINTERVIEWS	REITERATIVELY	REJUVENIZE
REINFORCES	REINSTALLATIONS	REINTRODUCE	REITERATIVES	REJUVENIZED
REINFORCING	REINSTALLED	REINTRODUCED	REJACKETED	REJUVENIZES
REINFORMED	REINSTALLING	REINTRODUCES	REJACKETING	REJUVENIZING
REINFORMING	REINSTALLS	REINTRODUCING	REJECTABLE	REKEYBOARD
REINFUNDED	REINSTALMENT	REINTRODUCTION	REJECTAMENTA	REKEYBOARDED
REINFUNDING	REINSTALMENTS	REINTRODUCTIONS	REJECTIBLE	REKEYBOARDING
REINFUSING	REINSTATED	REINVADING	REJECTINGLY	REKEYBOARDS
REINHABITED	REINSTATEMENT	REINVASION	REJECTIONIST	REKINDLING
REINHABITING	REINSTATEMENTS	REINVASIONS	REJECTIONISTS	REKINDLINGS
REINHABITS	REINSTATES	REINVENTED	REJECTIONS	REKNITTING
REINITIATE	REINSTATING	REINVENTING	REJIGGERED	REKNITTINGS
REINITIATED	REINSTATION	REINVENTION	REJIGGERING	REKNOTTING
REINITIATES	REINSTATIONS	REINVENTIONS	REJOICEFUL	REKNOTTINGS
REINITIATING	REINSTATOR	REINVESTED	REJOICEMENT	RELABELING
REINJECTED	REINSTATORS	REINVESTIGATE	REJOICEMENTS	RELABELLED
REINJECTING	REINSTITUTE	REINVESTIGATED	REJOICINGLY	RELABELLING
REINJECTION	REINSTITUTED	REINVESTIGATES	REJOICINGS	RELACQUERED
REINJECTIONS	REINSTITUTES	REINVESTIGATING	REJOINDERS	RELACQUERING
REINJURIES	REINSTITUTING	REINVESTIGATION	REJOINDURE	RELACQUERS
REINJURING	REINSTITUTION	REINVESTING	REJOINDURES	RELANDSCAPE
REINNERVATE	REINSTITUTIONS	REINVESTMENT	REJONEADOR	RELANDSCAPED
REINNERVATED	REINSURANCE	REINVESTMENTS	REJONEADORA	RELANDSCAPES
REINNERVATES	REINSURANCES	REINVIGORATE	REJONEADORAS	RELANDSCAPING
REINNERVATING	REINSURERS	REINVIGORATED	REJONEADORES	RELATABILITIES
REINNERVATION	REINSURING	REINVIGORATES	REJOURNING	RELATABILITY
REINNERVATIONS	REINTEGRATE	REINVIGORATING	REJUGGLING	RELATEDNESS
REINOCULATE	REINTEGRATED	REINVIGORATION	REJUSTIFIED	RELATEDNESSES
REINOCULATED	REINTEGRATES	REINVIGORATIONS	REJUSTIFIES	RELATIONAL
REINOCULATES	REINTEGRATING	REINVIGORATOR	REJUSTIFYING	RELATIONALLY
REINOCULATING	REINTEGRATION	REINVIGORATORS	REJUVENATE	RELATIONISM
REINOCULATION	REINTEGRATIONS	REINVITING	REJUVENATED	RELATIONISMS
REINOCULATIONS	REINTEGRATIVE	REINVOKING	REJUVENATES	RELATIONIST
REINSERTED	REINTERMENT	REINVOLVED	REJUVENATING	RELATIONISTS
REINSERTING	REINTERMENTS	REINVOLVES	REJUVENATION	RELATIONLESS
REINSERTION	REINTERPRET	REINVOLVING	REJUVENATIONS	RELATIONSHIP
REINSERTIONS	REINTERPRETED	REIOYNDURE	REJUVENATOR	RELATIONSHIPS
REINSPECTED	REINTERPRETING	REIOYNDURES	REJUVENATORS	RELATIVELY
REINSPECTING	REINTERPRETS	REISSUABLE	REJUVENESCE	RELATIVENESS

RELATIVENESSES	RELETTERING	RELINQUISHES	REMANDMENT	REMEDILESS
RELATIVISATION	RELEVANCES	RELINQUISHING	REMANDMENTS	REMEDILESSLY
RELATIVISATIONS	RELEVANCIES	RELINQUISHMENT	REMANENCES	REMEDILESSNESS
RELATIVISE	RELEVANTLY	RELINQUISHMENTS	REMANENCIES	REMEMBERABILITY
RELATIVISED	RELIABILITIES	RELIQUAIRE	REMANUFACTURE	REMEMBERABLE
RELATIVISES	RELIABILITY	RELIQUAIRES	REMANUFACTURED	REMEMBERABLY
RELATIVISING	RELIABLENESS	RELIQUARIES	REMANUFACTURER	REMEMBERED
RELATIVISM	RELIABLENESSES	RELIQUEFIED	REMANUFACTURERS	REMEMBERER
RELATIVISMS	RELICENSED	RELIQUEFIES	REMANUFACTURES	REMEMBERERS
RELATIVIST	RELICENSES	RELIQUEFYING	REMANUFACTURING	REMEMBERING
RELATIVISTIC	RELICENSING	RELIQUIFIED	REMARKABILITIES	REMEMBRANCE
RELATIVISTS	RELICENSURE	RELIQUIFIES	REMARKABILITY	REMEMBRANCER
RELATIVITIES	RELICENSURES	RELIQUIFYING	REMARKABLE	REMEMBRANCERS
RELATIVITIST	RELICTIONS	RELISHABLE	REMARKABLENESS	REMEMBRANCES
RELATIVITISTS	RELIEFLESS	RELISTENED	REMARKABLES	REMERCYING
RELATIVITY	RELIEVABLE	RELISTENING	REMARKABLY	REMIGATING
RELATIVIZATION	RELIEVEDLY	RELIVERING	REMARKETED	REMIGATION
RELATIVIZATIONS	RELIGHTING	RELLISHING	REMARKETING	REMIGATIONS
RELATIVIZE	RELIGIEUSE	RELOCATABLE	REMARRIAGE	REMIGRATED
RELATIVIZED	RELIGIEUSES	RELOCATEES	REMARRIAGES	REMIGRATES
RELATIVIZES	RELIGIONARIES	RELOCATING	REMARRYING	REMIGRATING
RELATIVIZING	RELIGIONARY	RELOCATION	REMASTERED	REMIGRATION
RELAUNCHED	RELIGIONER	RELOCATIONS	REMASTERING	REMIGRATIONS
RELAUNCHES	RELIGIONERS	RELOCATORS	REMATCHING	REMILITARISE
RELAUNCHING	RELIGIONISE	RELUBRICATE	REMATERIALISE	REMILITARISED
RELAUNDERED	RELIGIONISED	RELUBRICATED	REMATERIALISED	REMILITARISES
RELAUNDERING	RELIGIONISES	RELUBRICATES	REMATERIALISES	REMILITARISING
RELAUNDERS	RELIGIONISING	RELUBRICATING	REMATERIALISING	REMILITARIZE
RELAXATION	RELIGIONISM	RELUBRICATION	REMATERIALIZE	REMILITARIZED
RELAXATIONS	RELIGIONISMS	RELUBRICATIONS	REMATERIALIZED	REMILITARIZES
RELAXATIVE	RELIGIONIST	RELUCTANCE	REMATERIALIZES	REMILITARIZING
RELAXATIVES	RELIGIONISTS	RELUCTANCES	REMATERIALIZING	REMINERALISE
RELAXEDNESS	RELIGIONIZE	RELUCTANCIES	REMDESIVIR	REMINERALISED
RELAXEDNESSES	RELIGIONIZED	RELUCTANCY	REMDESIVIRS	REMINERALISES
RELEARNING	RELIGIONIZES	RELUCTANTLY	REMEASURED	REMINERALISING
RELEASABLE	RELIGIONIZING	RELUCTATED	REMEASUREMENT	REMINERALIZE
RELEASEMENT	RELIGIONLESS	RELUCTATES	REMEASUREMENTS	REMINERALIZED
RELEASEMENTS	RELIGIOSELY	RELUCTATING	REMEASURES	REMINERALIZES
RELEGATABLE	RELIGIOSITIES	RELUCTATION	REMEASURING	REMINERALIZING
RELEGATING	RELIGIOSITY	RELUCTATIONS	REMEDIABILITIES	REMINISCED
RELEGATION	RELIGIOSOS	RELUCTIVITIES	REMEDIABILITY	REMINISCENCE
RELEGATIONS	RELIGIOUSES	RELUCTIVITY	REMEDIABLE	REMINISCENCES
RELENTINGS	RELIGIOUSLY	RELUMINING	REMEDIABLY	REMINISCENT
RELENTLESS	RELIGIOUSNESS	REMAILINGS	REMEDIALLY	REMINISCENTIAL
RELENTLESSLY	RELIGIOUSNESSES	REMAINDERED	REMEDIATED	REMINISCENTLY
RELENTLESSNESS	RELINQUISH	REMAINDERING	REMEDIATES	REMINISCENTS
RELENTMENT	RELINQUISHED	REMAINDERMAN	REMEDIATING	REMINISCER
RELENTMENTS	RELINQUISHER	REMAINDERMEN	REMEDIATION	REMINISCERS
RELETTERED	RELINQUISHERS	REMAINDERS	REMEDIATIONS	REMINISCES

R

REMINISCING	REMONETISED	REMORTGAGED	RENASCENCE	RENOGRAPHIC
REMISSIBILITIES	REMONETISES	REMORTGAGES	RENASCENCES	RENOGRAPHIES
REMISSIBILITY	REMONETISING	REMORTGAGING	RENATIONALISE	RENOGRAPHY
REMISSIBLE	REMONETIZATION	REMOTENESS	RENATIONALISED	RENOMINATE
REMISSIBLENESS	REMONETIZATIONS	REMOTENESSES	RENATIONALISES	RENOMINATED
REMISSIBLY	REMONETIZE	REMOTIVATE	RENATIONALISING	RENOMINATES
REMISSIONS	REMONETIZED	REMOTIVATED	RENATIONALIZE	RENOMINATING
REMISSIVELY	REMONETIZES	REMOTIVATES	RENATIONALIZED	RENOMINATION
REMISSNESS	REMONETIZING	REMOTIVATING	RENATIONALIZES	RENOMINATIONS
REMISSNESSES	REMONSTRANCE	REMOTIVATION	RENATIONALIZING	RENORMALISATION
REMITMENTS	REMONSTRANCES	REMOTIVATIONS	RENATURATION	RENORMALISE
REMITTABLE	REMONSTRANT	REMOULADES	RENATURATIONS	RENORMALISED
REMITTANCE	REMONSTRANTLY	REMOULDING	RENATURING	RENORMALISES
REMITTANCES	REMONSTRANTS	REMOUNTING	RENCONTRED	RENORMALISING
REMITTENCE	REMONSTRATE	REMOUNTINGS	RENCONTRES	RENORMALIZATION
REMITTENCES	REMONSTRATED	REMOVABILITIES	RENCONTRING	RENORMALIZE
REMITTENCIES	REMONSTRATES	REMOVABILITY	RENCOUNTER	RENORMALIZED
REMITTENCY	REMONSTRATING	REMOVABLENESS	RENCOUNTERED	RENORMALIZES
REMITTENTLY	REMONSTRATINGLY	REMOVABLENESSES	RENCOUNTERING	RENORMALIZING
REMIXTURES	REMONSTRATION	REMOVALIST	RENCOUNTERS	RENOSTERVELD
REMOBILISATION	REMONSTRATIONS	REMOVALISTS	RENDERABLE	RENOSTERVELDS
REMOBILISATIONS	REMONSTRATIVE	REMOVEABLE	RENDERINGS	RENOTIFIED
REMOBILISE	REMONSTRATIVELY	REMOVEDNESS	RENDEZVOUS	RENOTIFIES
REMOBILISED	REMONSTRATOR	REMOVEDNESSES	RENDEZVOUSED	RENOTIFYING
REMOBILISES	REMONSTRATORS	REMUNERABILITY	RENDEZVOUSES	RENOUNCEABLE
REMOBILISING	REMONSTRATORY	REMUNERABLE	RENDEZVOUSING	RENOUNCEMENT
REMOBILIZATION	REMONTANTS	REMUNERATE	RENDITIONED	RENOUNCEMENTS
REMOBILIZATIONS	REMONTOIRE	REMUNERATED	RENDITIONING	RENOUNCERS
REMOBILIZE	REMONTOIRES	REMUNERATES	RENDITIONS	RENOUNCING
REMOBILIZED	REMONTOIRS	REMUNERATING	RENEAGUING	RENOVASCULAR
REMOBILIZES	REMORALISATION	REMUNERATION	RENEGADING	RENOVATING
REMOBILIZING	REMORALISATIONS	REMUNERATIONS	RENEGADOES	RENOVATION
REMODELERS	REMORALISE	REMUNERATIVE	RENEGATION	RENOVATIONS
REMODELING	REMORALISED	REMUNERATIVELY	RENEGATIONS	RENOVATIVE
REMODELINGS	REMORALISES	REMUNERATOR	RENEGOTIABLE	RENOVATORS
REMODELLED	REMORALISING	REMUNERATORS	RENEGOTIATE	RENSSELAERITE
REMODELLER	REMORALIZATION	REMUNERATORY	RENEGOTIATED	RENSSELAERITES
REMODELLERS	REMORALIZATIONS	REMURMURED	RENEGOTIATES	RENTABILITIES
REMODELLING	REMORALIZE	REMURMURING	RENEGOTIATING	RENTABILITY
REMODELLINGS	REMORALIZED	REMYTHOLOGISE	RENEGOTIATION	RENTALLERS
REMODIFIED	REMORALIZES	REMYTHOLOGISED	RENEGOTIATIONS	RENUMBERED
REMODIFIES	REMORALIZING	REMYTHOLOGISES	RENEWABILITIES	RENUMBERING
REMODIFYING	REMORSEFUL	REMYTHOLOGISING	RENEWABILITY	RENUNCIATE
REMOISTENED	REMORSEFULLY	REMYTHOLOGIZE	RENEWABLES	RENUNCIATES
REMOISTENING	REMORSEFULNESS	REMYTHOLOGIZED	RENEWEDNESS	RENUNCIATION
REMOISTENS	REMORSELESS	REMYTHOLOGIZES	RENEWEDNESSES	RENUNCIATIONS
REMONETISATION	REMORSELESSLY	REMYTHOLOGIZING	RENFORCING	RENUNCIATIVE
REMONETISATIONS	REMORSELESSNESS	RENAISSANCE	RENITENCES	RENUNCIATORY
REMONETISE	REMORTGAGE	RENAISSANCES	RENITENCIES	RENVERSEMENT

RENVERSEMENTS	REORGANIZATIONS	REPANELING	REPELLINGLY	REPLANNING
RENVERSING	REORGANIZE	REPANELLED	REPENTANCE	REPLANTATION
REOBJECTED	REORGANIZED	REPANELLING	REPENTANCES	REPLANTATIONS
REOBJECTING	REORGANIZER	REPAPERING	REPENTANTLY	REPLANTING
REOBSERVED	REORGANIZERS	REPARABILITIES	REPENTANTS	REPLASTERED
REOBSERVES	REORGANIZES	REPARABILITY	REPENTINGLY	REPLASTERING
REOBSERVING	REORGANIZING	REPARATION	REPEOPLING	REPLASTERS
REOBTAINED	REORIENTATE	REPARATIONS	REPERCUSSED	REPLEADERS
REOBTAINING	REORIENTATED	REPARATIVE	REPERCUSSES	REPLEADING
REOCCUPATION	REORIENTATES	REPARATORY	REPERCUSSING	REPLEDGING
REOCCUPATIONS	REORIENTATING	REPARTEEING	REPERCUSSION	REPLENISHABLE
REOCCUPIED	REORIENTATION	REPARTITION	REPERCUSSIONS	REPLENISHED
REOCCUPIES	REORIENTATIONS	REPARTITIONED	REPERCUSSIVE	REPLENISHER
REOCCUPYING	REORIENTED	REPARTITIONING	REPERTOIRE	REPLENISHERS
REOCCURRED	REORIENTING	REPARTITIONS	REPERTOIRES	REPLENISHES
REOCCURRENCE	REOUTFITTED	REPASSAGES	REPERTORIAL	REPLENISHING
REOCCURRENCES	REOUTFITTING	REPASTURES	REPERTORIES	REPLENISHMENT
REOCCURRING	REOVIRUSES	REPATCHING	REPERUSALS	REPLENISHMENTS
REOFFENDED	REOXIDATION	REPATRIATE	REPERUSING	REPLETENESS
REOFFENDER	REOXIDATIONS	REPATRIATED	REPETITEUR	REPLETENESSES
REOFFENDERS	REOXIDISED	REPATRIATES	REPETITEURS	REPLETIONS
REOFFENDING	REOXIDISES	REPATRIATING	REPETITEUSE	REPLEVIABLE
REOFFERING	REOXIDISING	REPATRIATION	REPETITEUSES	REPLEVINED
REOPENINGS	REOXIDIZED	REPATRIATIONS	REPETITION	REPLEVINING
REOPERATED	REOXIDIZES	REPATRIATOR	REPETITIONAL	REPLEVISABLE
REOPERATES	REOXIDIZING	REPATRIATORS	REPETITIONARY	REPLEVYING
REOPERATING	REOXYGENATE	REPATTERNED	REPETITIONS	REPLICABILITIES
REOPERATION	REOXYGENATED	REPATTERNING	REPETITIOUS	REPLICABILITY
REOPERATIONS	REOXYGENATES	REPATTERNS	REPETITIOUSLY	REPLICABLE
REOPPOSING	REOXYGENATING	REPAYMENTS	REPETITIOUSNESS	REPLICANTS
REORCHESTRATE	REPACIFIED	REPEALABLE	REPETITIVE	REPLICASES
REORCHESTRATED	REPACIFIES	REPEATABILITIES	REPETITIVELY	REPLICATED
REORCHESTRATES	REPACIFYING	REPEATABILITY	REPETITIVENESS	REPLICATES
REORCHESTRATING	REPACKAGED	REPEATABLE	REPHOTOGRAPH	REPLICATING
REORCHESTRATION	REPACKAGER	REPEATEDLY	REPHOTOGRAPHED	REPLICATION
REORDAINED	REPACKAGERS	REPEATINGS	REPHOTOGRAPHING	REPLICATIONS
REORDAINING	REPACKAGES	REPECHAGES	REPHOTOGRAPHS	REPLICATIVE
REORDERING	REPACKAGING	REPELLANCE	REPHRASING	REPLICATOR
REORDINATION	REPAGINATE	REPELLANCES	REPHRASINGS	REPLICATORS
REORDINATIONS	REPAGINATED	REPELLANCIES	REPIGMENTED	REPLOTTING
REORGANISATION	REPAGINATES	REPELLANCY	REPIGMENTING	REPLOUGHED
REORGANISATIONS	REPAGINATING	REPELLANTLY	REPIGMENTS	REPLOUGHING
REORGANISE	REPAGINATION	REPELLANTS	REPINEMENT	REPLUMBING
REORGANISED	REPAGINATIONS	REPELLENCE	REPINEMENTS	REPLUNGING
REORGANISER	REPAINTING	REPELLENCES	REPININGLY	REPOINTING
REORGANISERS	REPAINTINGS	REPELLENCIES	REPLACEABILITY	REPOINTINGS
REORGANISES	REPAIRABILITIES	REPELLENCY	REPLACEABLE	REPOLARISATION
REORGANISING	REPAIRABILITY	REPELLENTLY	REPLACEMENT	REPOLARISATIONS
REORGANIZATION	REPAIRABLE	REPELLENTS	REPLACEMENTS	REPOLARISE

R

REPOLARISED	REPOSSESSION	REPRESSION	REPROACHFULNESS	REPROGRAPHIC
REPOLARISES	REPOSSESSIONS	REPRESSIONIST	REPROACHING	REPROGRAPHICS
REPOLARISING	REPOSSESSOR	REPRESSIONISTS	REPROACHINGLY	REPROGRAPHIES
REPOLARIZATION	REPOSSESSORS	REPRESSIONS	REPROACHLESS	REPROGRAPHY
REPOLARIZATIONS	REPOTTINGS	REPRESSIVE	REPROBACIES	REPROOFING
REPOLARIZE	REPOUSSAGE	REPRESSIVELY	REPROBANCE	REPROVABLE
REPOLARIZED	REPOUSSAGES	REPRESSIVENESS	REPROBANCES	REPROVINGLY
REPOLARIZES	REPOUSSOIR	REPRESSORS	REPROBATED	REPROVISION
REPOLARIZING	REPOUSSOIRS	REPRESSURISE	REPROBATER	REPROVISIONED
REPOLISHED	REPOWERING	REPRESSURISED	REPROBATERS	REPROVISIONING
REPOLISHES	REPREEVING	REPRESSURISES	REPROBATES	REPROVISIONS
REPOLISHING	REPREHENDABLE	REPRESSURISING	REPROBATING	REPTATIONS
REPOPULARISE	REPREHENDED	REPRESSURIZE	REPROBATION	REPTILIANLY
REPOPULARISED	REPREHENDER	REPRESSURIZED	REPROBATIONARY	REPTILIANS
REPOPULARISES	REPREHENDERS	REPRESSURIZES	REPROBATIONS	REPTILIFEROUS
REPOPULARISING	REPREHENDING	REPRESSURIZING	REPROBATIVE	REPTILIFORM
REPOPULARIZE	REPREHENDS	REPRIEVABLE	REPROBATIVELY	REPTILIOUS
REPOPULARIZED	REPREHENSIBLE	REPRIEVALS	REPROBATOR	REPTILOIDS
REPOPULARIZES	REPREHENSIBLY	REPRIEVERS	REPROBATORS	REPUBLICAN
REPOPULARIZING	REPREHENSION	REPRIEVING	REPROBATORY	REPUBLICANISE
REPOPULATE	REPREHENSIONS	REPRIMANDED	REPROCESSED	REPUBLICANISED
REPOPULATED	REPREHENSIVE	REPRIMANDING	REPROCESSES	REPUBLICANISES
REPOPULATES	REPREHENSIVELY	REPRIMANDS	REPROCESSING	REPUBLICANISING
REPOPULATING	REPREHENSORY	REPRINTERS	REPROCESSINGS	REPUBLICANISM
REPOPULATION	REPRESENTABLE	REPRINTING	REPRODUCED	REPUBLICANISMS
REPOPULATIONS	REPRESENTAMEN	REPRISTINATE	REPRODUCER	REPUBLICANIZE
REPORTABLE	REPRESENTAMENS	REPRISTINATED	REPRODUCERS	REPUBLICANIZED
REPORTAGES	REPRESENTANT	REPRISTINATES	REPRODUCES	REPUBLICANIZES
REPORTEDLY	REPRESENTANTS	REPRISTINATING	REPRODUCIBILITY	REPUBLICANIZING
REPORTINGLY	REPRESENTATION	REPRISTINATION	REPRODUCIBLE	REPUBLICANS
REPORTINGS	REPRESENTATIONS	REPRISTINATIONS	REPRODUCIBLES	REPUBLICATION
REPORTORIAL	REPRESENTATIVE	REPRIVATISATION	REPRODUCIBLY	REPUBLICATIONS
REPORTORIALLY	REPRESENTATIVES	REPRIVATISE	REPRODUCING	REPUBLISHED
REPOSEDNESS	REPRESENTED	REPRIVATISED	REPRODUCTION	REPUBLISHER
REPOSEDNESSES	REPRESENTEE	REPRIVATISES	REPRODUCTIONS	REPUBLISHERS
REPOSEFULLY	REPRESENTEES	REPRIVATISING	REPRODUCTIVE	REPUBLISHES
REPOSEFULNESS	REPRESENTER	REPRIVATIZATION	REPRODUCTIVELY	REPUBLISHING
REPOSEFULNESSES	REPRESENTERS	REPRIVATIZE	REPRODUCTIVES	REPUDIABLE
REPOSITING	REPRESENTING	REPRIVATIZED	REPRODUCTIVITY	REPUDIATED
REPOSITION	REPRESENTMENT	REPRIVATIZES	REPROGRAMED	REPUDIATES
REPOSITIONED	REPRESENTMENTS	REPRIVATIZING	REPROGRAMING	REPUDIATING
REPOSITIONING	REPRESENTOR	REPROACHABLE	REPROGRAMMABLE	REPUDIATION
REPOSITIONS	REPRESENTORS	REPROACHABLY	REPROGRAMME	REPUDIATIONIST
REPOSITORIES	REPRESENTS	REPROACHED	REPROGRAMMED	REPUDIATIONISTS
REPOSITORS	REPRESSERS	REPROACHER	REPROGRAMMES	REPUDIATIONS
REPOSITORY	REPRESSIBILITY	REPROACHERS	REPROGRAMMING	REPUDIATIVE
REPOSSESSED	REPRESSIBLE	REPROACHES	REPROGRAMS	REPUDIATOR
REPOSSESSES	REPRESSIBLY	REPROACHFUL	REPROGRAPHER	REPUDIATORS
REPOSSESSING	REPRESSING	REPROACHFULLY	REPROGRAPHERS	REPUGNANCE

REPUGNANCES	REQUISITENESSES	REREMINDING	RESECTABLE	RESERVICED
REPUGNANCIES	REQUISITES	REREPEATED	RESECTIONAL	RESERVICES
REPUGNANCY	REQUISITION	REREPEATING	RESECTIONS	RESERVICING
REPUGNANTLY	REQUISITIONARY	REREVIEWED	RESECURING	RESERVISTS
REPULSIONS	REQUISITIONED	REREVIEWING	RESEGREGATE	RESERVOIRED
REPULSIVELY	REQUISITIONING	REREVISING	RESEGREGATED	RESERVOIRING
REPULSIVENESS	REQUISITIONIST	REROUTEING	RESEGREGATES	RESERVOIRS
REPULSIVENESSES	REQUISITIONISTS	RESADDLING	RESEGREGATING	RESETTABLE
REPUNCTUATION	REQUISITIONS	RESALEABLE	RESEGREGATION	RESETTLEMENT
REPUNCTUATIONS	REQUISITOR	RESALUTING	RESEGREGATIONS	RESETTLEMENTS
REPURCHASE	REQUISITORIES	RESAMPLING	RESEIZURES	RESETTLING
REPURCHASED	REQUISITORS	RESCHEDULE	RESELECTED	RESHAPINGS
REPURCHASES	REQUISITORY	RESCHEDULED	RESELECTING	RESHARPENED
REPURCHASING	REQUITABLE	RESCHEDULES	RESELECTION	RESHARPENING
REPURIFIED	REQUITEFUL	RESCHEDULING	RESELECTIONS	RESHARPENS
REPURIFIES	REQUITELESS	RESCHEDULINGS	RESEMBLANCE	RESHINGLED
REPURIFYING	REQUITEMENT	RESCHOOLED	RESEMBLANCES	RESHINGLES
REPURPOSED	REQUITEMENTS	RESCHOOLING	RESEMBLANT	RESHINGLING
REPURPOSES	REQUITTING	RESCINDABLE	RESEMBLERS	RESHIPMENT
REPURPOSING	REQUOYLING	RESCINDERS	RESEMBLING	RESHIPMENTS
REPURSUING	RERADIATED	RESCINDING	RESENSITISE	RESHIPPERS
REPUTABILITIES	RERADIATES	RESCINDMENT	RESENSITISED	RESHIPPING
REPUTABILITY	RERADIATING	RESCINDMENTS	RESENSITISES	RESHOOTING
REPUTATION	RERADIATION	RESCISSIBLE	RESENSITISING	RESHORINGS
REPUTATIONAL	RERADIATIONS	RESCISSION	RESENSITIZE	RESHOWERED
REPUTATIONLESS	RERAILINGS	RESCISSIONS	RESENSITIZED	RESHOWERING
REPUTATIONS	REREADINGS	RESCISSORY	RESENSITIZES	RESHOWINGS
REPUTATIVE	REREBRACES	RESCREENED	RESENSITIZING	RESHUFFLED
REPUTATIVELY	RERECORDED	RESCREENING	RESENTENCE	RESHUFFLES
REPUTELESS	RERECORDING	RESCRIPTED	RESENTENCED	RESHUFFLING
REQUALIFIED	REREDORTER	RESCRIPTING	RESENTENCES	RESIDENCES
REQUALIFIES	REREDORTERS	RESCRIPTION	RESENTENCING	RESIDENCIES
REQUALIFYING	REREDOSSES	RESCRIPTIONS	RESENTFULLY	RESIDENTER
REQUESTERS	REREGISTER	RESCULPTED	RESENTFULNESS	RESIDENTERS
REQUESTING	REREGISTERED	RESCULPTING	RESENTFULNESSES	RESIDENTIAL
REQUESTORS	REREGISTERING	RESEALABLE	RESENTINGLY	RESIDENTIALLY
REQUICKENED	REREGISTERS	RESEARCHABLE	RESENTMENT	RESIDENTIARIES
REQUICKENING	REREGISTRATION	RESEARCHED	RESENTMENTS	RESIDENTIARY
REQUICKENS	REREGISTRATIONS	RESEARCHER	RESERPINES	RESIDENTSHIP
REQUIESCAT	REREGULATE	RESEARCHERS	RESERVABLE	RESIDENTSHIPS
REQUIESCATS	REREGULATED	RESEARCHES	RESERVATION	RESIDUALLY
REQUIGHTED	REREGULATES	RESEARCHFUL	RESERVATIONIST	RESIGHTING
REQUIGHTING	REREGULATING	RESEARCHING	RESERVATIONISTS	RESIGNATION
REQUIRABLE	REREGULATION	RESEARCHIST	RESERVATIONS	RESIGNATIONS
REQUIREMENT	REREGULATIONS	RESEARCHISTS	RESERVATORIES	RESIGNEDLY
REQUIREMENTS	RERELEASED	RESEASONED	RESERVATORY	RESIGNEDNESS
REQUIRINGS	RERELEASES	RESEASONING	RESERVEDLY	RESIGNEDNESSES
REQUISITELY	RERELEASING	RESECTABILITIES	RESERVEDNESS	RESIGNMENT
REQUISITENESS	REREMINDED	RESECTABILITY	RESERVEDNESSES	RESIGNMENTS

R

RESILEMENT	RESKETCHING	RESONANCES	RESPELLINGS	RESPONSIBLE
RESILEMENTS	RESKILLING	RESONANTLY	RESPIRABILITIES	RESPONSIBLENESS
RESILIENCE	RESKILLINGS	RESONATING	RESPIRABILITY	RESPONSIBLY
RESILIENCES	RESKINNING	RESONATION	RESPIRABLE	RESPONSIONS
RESILIENCIES	RESMELTING	RESONATIONS	RESPIRATION	RESPONSIVE
RESILIENCY	RESMOOTHED	RESONATORS	RESPIRATIONAL	RESPONSIVELY
RESILIENTLY	RESMOOTHING	RESORBENCE	RESPIRATIONS	RESPONSIVENESS
RESILVERED	RESNATRONS	RESORBENCES	RESPIRATOR	RESPONSORIAL
RESILVERING	RESOCIALISATION	RESORCINAL	RESPIRATORS	RESPONSORIALS
RESINATING	RESOCIALISE	RESORCINOL	RESPIRATORY	RESPONSORIES
RESINIFEROUS	RESOCIALISED	RESORCINOLS	RESPIRITUALISE	RESPONSORS
RESINIFICATION	RESOCIALISES	RESORPTION	RESPIRITUALISED	RESPONSORY
RESINIFICATIONS	RESOCIALISING	RESORPTIONS	RESPIRITUALISES	RESPONSUMS
RESINIFIED	RESOCIALIZATION	RESORPTIVE	RESPIRITUALIZE	RESPOOLING
RESINIFIES	RESOCIALIZE	RESOUNDING	RESPIRITUALIZED	RESPOTTING
RESINIFYING	RESOCIALIZED	RESOUNDINGLY	RESPIRITUALIZES	RESPRAYING
RESINISING	RESOCIALIZES	RESOURCEFUL	RESPIROLOGIES	RESPREADING
RESINIZING	RESOCIALIZING	RESOURCEFULLY	RESPIROLOGIST	RESPRINGING
RESINOUSLY	RESOFTENED	RESOURCEFULNESS	RESPIROLOGISTS	RESPROUTED
RESINOUSNESS	RESOFTENING	RESOURCELESS	RESPIROLOGY	RESPROUTING
RESINOUSNESSES	RESOLDERED	RESOURCING	RESPIROMETER	RESSALDARS
RESIPISCENCE	RESOLDERING	RESOURCINGS	RESPIROMETERS	RESSENTIMENT
RESIPISCENCES	RESOLIDIFIED	RESPAWNING	RESPIROMETRIC	RESSENTIMENTS
RESIPISCENCIES	RESOLIDIFIES	RESPEAKING	RESPIROMETRIES	RESTABILISE
RESIPISCENCY	RESOLIDIFY	RESPECIFIED	RESPIROMETRY	RESTABILISED
RESIPISCENT	RESOLIDIFYING	RESPECIFIES	RESPITELESS	RESTABILISES
RESISTANCE	RESOLUBILITIES	RESPECIFYING	RESPLENDED	RESTABILISING
RESISTANCES	RESOLUBILITY	RESPECTABILISE	RESPLENDENCE	RESTABILIZE
RESISTANTS	RESOLUBLENESS	RESPECTABILISED	RESPLENDENCES	RESTABILIZED
RESISTENTS	RESOLUBLENESSES	RESPECTABILISES	RESPLENDENCIES	RESTABILIZES
RESISTIBILITIES	RESOLUTELY	RESPECTABILITY	RESPLENDENCY	RESTABILIZING
RESISTIBILITY	RESOLUTENESS	RESPECTABILIZE	RESPLENDENT	RESTABLING
RESISTIBLE	RESOLUTENESSES	RESPECTABILIZED	RESPLENDENTLY	RESTACKING
RESISTIBLY	RESOLUTEST	RESPECTABILIZES	RESPLENDING	RESTAFFING
RESISTINGLY	RESOLUTION	RESPECTABLE	RESPLICING	RESTAMPING
RESISTIVELY	RESOLUTIONER	RESPECTABLENESS	RESPLITTING	RESTARTABLE
RESISTIVENESS	RESOLUTIONERS	RESPECTABLES	RESPONDENCE	RESTARTERS
RESISTIVENESSES	RESOLUTIONIST	RESPECTABLY	RESPONDENCES	RESTARTING
RESISTIVITIES	RESOLUTIONISTS	RESPECTANT	RESPONDENCIES	RESTATEMENT
RESISTIVITY	RESOLUTIONS	RESPECTERS	RESPONDENCY	RESTATEMENTS
RESISTLESS	RESOLUTIVE	RESPECTFUL	RESPONDENT	RESTATIONED
RESISTLESSLY	RESOLVABILITIES	RESPECTFULLY	RESPONDENTIA	RESTATIONING
RESISTLESSNESS	RESOLVABILITY	RESPECTFULNESS	RESPONDENTIAS	RESTATIONS
RESITTINGS	RESOLVABLE	RESPECTING	RESPONDENTS	RESTAURANT
RESITUATED	RESOLVABLENESS	RESPECTIVE	RESPONDERS	RESTAURANTEUR
RESITUATES	RESOLVEDLY	RESPECTIVELY	RESPONDING	RESTAURANTEURS
RESITUATING	RESOLVEDNESS	RESPECTIVENESS	RESPONSELESS	RESTAURANTS
RESKETCHED	RESOLVEDNESSES	RESPECTLESS	RESPONSERS	RESTAURATEUR
RESKETCHES	RESOLVENTS	RESPELLING	RESPONSIBILITY	RESTAURATEURS

RESTAURATION	RESTRAINED	RESUBJECTED	RESUSCITANT	RETAILORED
RESTAURATIONS	RESTRAINEDLY	RESUBJECTING	RESUSCITANTS	RETAILORING
RESTEMMING	RESTRAINEDNESS	RESUBJECTS	RESUSCITATE	RETAINABLE
RESTFULLER	RESTRAINER	RESUBMISSION	RESUSCITATED	RETAINERSHIP
RESTFULLEST	RESTRAINERS	RESUBMISSIONS	RESUSCITATES	RETAINERSHIPS
RESTFULNESS	RESTRAINING	RESUBMITTED	RESUSCITATING	RETAINMENT
RESTFULNESSES	RESTRAININGS	RESUBMITTING	RESUSCITATION	RETAINMENTS
RESTHARROW	RESTRAINTS	RESULTANTLY	RESUSCITATIONS	RETALIATED
RESTHARROWS	RESTRENGTHEN	RESULTANTS	RESUSCITATIVE	RETALIATES
RESTIMULATE	RESTRENGTHENED	RESULTATIVE	RESUSCITATOR	RETALIATING
RESTIMULATED	RESTRENGTHENING	RESULTATIVES	RESUSCITATORS	RETALIATION
RESTIMULATES	RESTRENGTHENS	RESULTLESS	RESUSPENDED	RETALIATIONIST
RESTIMULATING	RESTRESSED	RESULTLESSNESS	RESUSPENDING	RETALIATIONISTS
RESTIMULATION	RESTRESSES	RESUMMONED	RESUSPENDS	RETALIATIONS
RESTIMULATIONS	RESTRESSING	RESUMMONING	RESVERATROL	RETALIATIVE
RESTITCHED	RESTRETCHED	RESUMPTION	RESVERATROLS	RETALIATOR
RESTITCHES	RESTRETCHES	RESUMPTIONS	RESWALLOWED	RETALIATORS
RESTITCHING	RESTRETCHING	RESUMPTIVE	RESWALLOWING	RETALIATORY
RESTITUTED	RESTRICKEN	RESUMPTIVELY	RESWALLOWS	RETALLYING
RESTITUTES	RESTRICTED	RESUPINATE	RESYNCHRONISE	RETARDANTS
RESTITUTING	RESTRICTEDLY	RESUPINATION	RESYNCHRONISED	RETARDATION
RESTITUTION	RESTRICTEDNESS	RESUPINATIONS	RESYNCHRONISES	RETARDATIONS
RESTITUTIONISM	RESTRICTING	RESUPPLIED	RESYNCHRONISING	RETARDATIVE
RESTITUTIONISMS	RESTRICTION	RESUPPLIES	RESYNCHRONIZE	RETARDATORY
RESTITUTIONIST	RESTRICTIONISM	RESUPPLYING	RESYNCHRONIZED	RETARDMENT
RESTITUTIONISTS	RESTRICTIONISMS	RESURFACED	RESYNCHRONIZES	RETARDMENTS
RESTITUTIONS	RESTRICTIONIST	RESURFACER	RESYNCHRONIZING	RETARGETED
RESTITUTIVE	RESTRICTIONISTS	RESURFACERS	RESYNTHESES	RETARGETING
RESTITUTOR	RESTRICTIONS	RESURFACES	RESYNTHESIS	RETCONNING
RESTITUTORS	RESTRICTIVE	RESURFACING	RESYNTHESISE	RETEACHING
RESTITUTORY	RESTRICTIVELY	RESURGENCE	RESYNTHESISED	RETELLINGS
RESTIVENESS	RESTRICTIVENESS	RESURGENCES	RESYNTHESISES	RETEMPERED
RESTIVENESSES	RESTRICTIVES	RESURRECTED	RESYNTHESISING	RETEMPERING
RESTLESSLY	RESTRIKING	RESURRECTING	RESYNTHESIZE	RETENTIONIST
RESTLESSNESS	RESTRINGED	RESURRECTION	RESYNTHESIZED	RETENTIONISTS
RESTLESSNESSES	RESTRINGEING	RESURRECTIONAL	RESYNTHESIZES	RETENTIONS
RESTOCKING	RESTRINGENT	RESURRECTIONARY	RESYNTHESIZING	RETENTIVELY
RESTORABLE	RESTRINGENTS	RESURRECTIONISE	RESYSTEMATISE	RETENTIVENESS
RESTORABLENESS	RESTRINGES	RESURRECTIONISM	RESYSTEMATISED	RETENTIVENESSES
RESTORATION	RESTRINGING	RESURRECTIONIST	RESYSTEMATISES	RETENTIVES
RESTORATIONISM	RESTRIVING	RESURRECTIONIZE	RESYSTEMATISING	RETENTIVITIES
RESTORATIONISMS	RESTRUCTURE	RESURRECTIONS	RESYSTEMATIZE	RETENTIVITY
RESTORATIONIST	RESTRUCTURED	RESURRECTIVE	RESYSTEMATIZED	RETESTIFIED
RESTORATIONISTS	RESTRUCTURES	RESURRECTOR	RESYSTEMATIZES	RETESTIFIES
RESTORATIONS	RESTRUCTURING	RESURRECTORS	RESYSTEMATIZING	RETESTIFYING
RESTORATIVE	RESTRUCTURINGS	RESURRECTS	RETACKLING	RETEXTURED
RESTORATIVELY	RESTUDYING	RESURVEYED	RETAILINGS	RETEXTURES
RESTORATIVES	RESTUFFING	RESURVEYING	RETAILMENT	RETEXTURING
RESTRAINABLE	RESTUMPING	RESUSCITABLE	RETAILMENTS	RETHINKERS

RETHINKING	RETIREMENT	RETRANSLATE	RETROACTIVELY	RETROGRESSES
RETHINKINGS	RETIREMENTS	RETRANSLATED	RETROACTIVENESS	RETROGRESSING
RETHREADED	RETIRINGLY	RETRANSLATES	RETROACTIVITIES	RETROGRESSION
RETHREADING	RETIRINGNESS	RETRANSLATING	RETROACTIVITY	RETROGRESSIONAL
RETICELLAS	RETIRINGNESSES	RETRANSLATION	RETROBULBAR	RETROGRESSIONS
RETICENCES	RETORSIONS	RETRANSLATIONS	RETROCEDED	RETROGRESSIVE
RETICENCIES	RETORTIONS	RETRANSMISSION	RETROCEDENCE	RETROGRESSIVELY
RETICENTLY	RETOTALING	RETRANSMISSIONS	RETROCEDENCES	RETROJECTED
RETICULARLY	RETOTALLED	RETRANSMIT	RETROCEDENT	RETROJECTING
RETICULARY	RETOTALLING	RETRANSMITS	RETROCEDES	RETROJECTION
RETICULATE	RETOUCHABLE	RETRANSMITTED	RETROCEDING	RETROJECTIONS
RETICULATED	RETOUCHERS	RETRANSMITTING	RETROCESSION	RETROJECTS
RETICULATELY	RETOUCHING	RETREADING	RETROCESSIONS	RETROLENTAL
RETICULATES	RETOUCHINGS	RETREATANT	RETROCESSIVE	RETROMINGENCIES
RETICULATING	RETRACEABLE	RETREATANTS	RETROCHOIR	RETROMINGENCY
RETICULATION	RETRACEMENT	RETREATERS	RETROCHOIRS	RETROMINGENT
RETICULATIONS	RETRACEMENTS	RETREATING	RETROCOGNITION	RETROMINGENTS
RETICULOCYTE	RETRACKING	RETRENCHABLE	RETROCOGNITIONS	RETROPACKS
RETICULOCYTES	RETRACTABILITY	RETRENCHED	RETRODICTED	RETROPERITONEAL
RETICULUMS	RETRACTABLE	RETRENCHES	RETRODICTING	RETROPHILIA
RETIGHTENED	RETRACTATION	RETRENCHING	RETRODICTION	RETROPHILIAC
RETIGHTENING	RETRACTATIONS	RETRENCHMENT	RETRODICTIONS	RETROPHILIACS
RETIGHTENS	RETRACTIBILITY	RETRENCHMENTS	RETRODICTIVE	RETROPHILIAS
RETINACULA	RETRACTIBLE	RETRIBUTED	RETRODICTS	RETROPULSION
RETINACULAR	RETRACTILE	RETRIBUTES	RETROENGINE	RETROPULSIONS
RETINACULUM	RETRACTILITIES	RETRIBUTING	RETROENGINES	RETROPULSIVE
RETINALITE	RETRACTILITY	RETRIBUTION	RETROFIRED	RETROREFLECTION
RETINALITES	RETRACTING	RETRIBUTIONS	RETROFIRES	RETROREFLECTIVE
RETINISPORA	RETRACTION	RETRIBUTIVE	RETROFIRING	RETROREFLECTOR
RETINISPORAS	RETRACTIONS	RETRIBUTIVELY	RETROFITTED	RETROREFLECTORS
RETINITIDES	RETRACTIVE	RETRIBUTOR	RETROFITTING	RETROROCKET
RETINITISES	RETRACTIVELY	RETRIBUTORS	RETROFITTINGS	RETROROCKETS
RETINOBLASTOMA	RETRACTORS	RETRIBUTORY	RETROFLECTED	RETRORSELY
RETINOBLASTOMAS	RETRAINABLE	RETRIEVABILITY	RETROFLECTION	RETROSEXUAL
RETINOPATHIES	RETRAINEES	RETRIEVABLE	RETROFLECTIONS	RETROSEXUALS
RETINOPATHY	RETRAINING	RETRIEVABLENESS	RETROFLEXED	RETROSPECT
RETINOSCOPE	RETRAININGS	RETRIEVABLY	RETROFLEXES	RETROSPECTED
RETINOSCOPES	RETRANSFER	RETRIEVALS	RETROFLEXING	RETROSPECTING
RETINOSCOPIC	RETRANSFERRED	RETRIEVEMENT	RETROFLEXION	RETROSPECTION
RETINOSCOPIES	RETRANSFERRING	RETRIEVEMENTS	RETROFLEXIONS	RETROSPECTIONS
RETINOSCOPIST	RETRANSFERS	RETRIEVERS	RETROGRADATION	RETROSPECTIVE
RETINOSCOPISTS	RETRANSFORM	RETRIEVING	RETROGRADATIONS	RETROSPECTIVELY
RETINOSCOPY	RETRANSFORMED	RETRIEVINGS	RETROGRADE	RETROSPECTIVES
RETINOSPORA	RETRANSFORMING	RETRIMMING	RETROGRADED	RETROSPECTS
RETINOSPORAS	RETRANSFORMS	RETROACTED	RETROGRADELY	RETROUSSAGE
RETINOTECTAL	RETRANSFUSE	RETROACTING	RETROGRADES	RETROUSSAGES
RETIRACIES	RETRANSFUSED	RETROACTION	RETROGRADING	RETROVERSE
RETIREDNESS	RETRANSFUSES	RETROACTIONS	RETROGRESS	RETROVERSION
RETIREDNESSES	RETRANSFUSING	RETROACTIVE	RETROGRESSED	RETROVERSIONS

R

RETROVERTED	REVACCINATIONS	REVELATIONAL	REVERIFIES	REVISIONIST
RETROVERTING	REVALENTAS	REVELATIONIST	REVERIFYING	REVISIONISTS
RETROVERTS	REVALIDATE	REVELATIONISTS	REVERSEDLY	REVISITANT
RETROVIRAL	REVALIDATED	REVELATIONS	REVERSELESS	REVISITANTS
RETROVIRUS	REVALIDATES	REVELATIVE	REVERSIBILITIES	REVISITATION
RETROVIRUSES	REVALIDATING	REVELATORS	REVERSIBILITY	REVISITATIONS
RETURNABILITIES	REVALIDATION	REVELATORY	REVERSIBLE	REVISITING
RETURNABILITY	REVALIDATIONS	REVELLINGS	REVERSIBLES	REVISUALISATION
RETURNABLE	REVALORISATION	REVELMENTS	REVERSIBLY	REVISUALIZATION
RETURNABLES	REVALORISATIONS	REVENDICATE	REVERSINGS	REVITALISATION
RETURNERSHIP	REVALORISE	REVENDICATED	REVERSIONAL	REVITALISATIONS
RETURNERSHIPS	REVALORISED	REVENDICATES	REVERSIONALLY	REVITALISE
RETURNLESS	REVALORISES	REVENDICATING	REVERSIONARIES	REVITALISED
RETURNSHIP	REVALORISING	REVENDICATION	REVERSIONARY	REVITALISES
RETURNSHIPS	REVALORIZATION	REVENDICATIONS	REVERSIONER	REVITALISING
RETWEETING	REVALORIZATIONS	REVENGEFUL	REVERSIONERS	REVITALIZATION
RETWISTING	REVALORIZE	REVENGEFULLY	REVERSIONS	REVITALIZATIONS
REUNIFICATION	REVALORIZED	REVENGEFULNESS	REVERSISES	REVITALIZE
REUNIFICATIONS	REVALORIZES	REVENGELESS	REVERTANTS	REVITALIZED
REUNIFYING	REVALORIZING	REVENGEMENT	REVERTIBLE	REVITALIZES
REUNIONISM	REVALUATED	REVENGEMENTS	REVESTIARIES	REVITALIZING
REUNIONISMS	REVALUATES	REVENGINGLY	REVESTIARY	REVIVABILITIES
REUNIONIST	REVALUATING	REVENGINGS	REVESTRIES	REVIVABILITY
REUNIONISTIC	REVALUATION	REVERBATORIES	REVETMENTS	REVIVALISM
REUNIONISTS	REVALUATIONS	REVERBATORY	REVIBRATED	REVIVALISMS
REUNITABLE	REVAMPINGS	REVERBERANT	REVIBRATES	REVIVALIST
REUPHOLSTER	REVANCHISM	REVERBERANTLY	REVIBRATING	REVIVALISTIC
REUPHOLSTERED	REVANCHISMS	REVERBERATE	REVICTUALED	REVIVALISTS
REUPHOLSTERING	REVANCHIST	REVERBERATED	REVICTUALING	REVIVEMENT
REUPHOLSTERS	REVANCHISTS	REVERBERATES	REVICTUALLED	REVIVEMENTS
REUPTAKING	REVARNISHED	REVERBERATING	REVICTUALLING	REVIVESCENCE
REUSABILITIES	REVARNISHES	REVERBERATION	REVICTUALS	REVIVESCENCES
REUSABILITY	REVARNISHING	REVERBERATIONS	REVIEWABLE	REVIVESCENCIES
REUTILISATION	REVEALABILITIES	REVERBERATIVE	REVILEMENT	REVIVESCENCY
REUTILISATIONS	REVEALABILITY	REVERBERATOR	REVILEMENTS	REVIVESCENT
REUTILISED	REVEALABLE	REVERBERATORIES	REVILINGLY	REVIVIFICATION
REUTILISES	REVEALINGLY	REVERBERATORS	REVINDICATE	REVIVIFICATIONS
REUTILISING	REVEALINGNESS	REVERBERATORY	REVINDICATED	REVIVIFIED
REUTILIZATION	REVEALINGNESSES	REVERENCED	REVINDICATES	REVIVIFIES
REUTILIZATIONS	REVEALINGS	REVERENCER	REVINDICATING	REVIVIFYING
REUTILIZED	REVEALMENT	REVERENCERS	REVINDICATION	REVIVINGLY
REUTILIZES	REVEALMENTS	REVERENCES	REVINDICATIONS	REVIVISCENCE
REUTILIZING	REVEGETATE	REVERENCING	REVIOLATED	REVIVISCENCES
REUTTERING	REVEGETATED	REVERENTIAL	REVIOLATES	REVIVISCENCIES
REVACCINATE	REVEGETATES	REVERENTIALLY	REVIOLATING	REVIVISCENCY
REVACCINATED	REVEGETATING	REVERENTLY	REVISIONAL	REVIVISCENT
REVACCINATES	REVEGETATION	REVERENTNESS	REVISIONARY	REVOCABILITIES
REVACCINATING	REVEGETATIONS	REVERENTNESSES	REVISIONISM	REVOCABILITY
REVACCINATION	REVELATION	REVERIFIED	REVISIONISMS	REVOCABLENESS

REVOCABLENESSES	REWATERING	RHAPSODIZED	RHEUMATOID	RHINOSCOPIC
REVOCATION	REWEIGHING	RHAPSODIZES	RHEUMATOIDALLY	RHINOSCOPIES
REVOCATIONS	REWIDENING	RHAPSODIZING	RHEUMATOLOGICAL	RHINOSCOPY
REVOCATORY	REWILDINGS	RHEOCHORDS	RHEUMATOLOGIES	RHINOTHECA
REVOKABILITIES	REWINDINGS	RHEOLOGICAL	RHEUMATOLOGIST	RHINOTHECAE
REVOKABILITY	REWORDINGS	RHEOLOGICALLY	RHEUMATOLOGISTS	RHINOVIRUS
REVOKEMENT	REWORKINGS	RHEOLOGIES	RHEUMATOLOGY	RHINOVIRUSES
REVOKEMENTS	REWRAPPING	RHEOLOGIST	RHIGOLENES	RHIPIDIONS
REVOLTINGLY	REWRITABLE	RHEOLOGISTS	RHINENCEPHALA	RHIPIDIUMS
REVOLUTION	REWRITEABLE	RHEOMETERS	RHINENCEPHALIC	RHIZANTHOUS
REVOLUTIONAL	RHABDOCOELE	RHEOMETRIC	RHINENCEPHALON	RHIZOCARPIC
REVOLUTIONARIES	RHABDOCOELES	RHEOMETRICAL	RHINENCEPHALONS	RHIZOCARPOUS
REVOLUTIONARILY	RHABDOLITH	RHEOMETRIES	RHINESTONE	RHIZOCARPS
REVOLUTIONARY	RHABDOLITHS	RHEOMORPHIC	RHINESTONED	RHIZOCAULS
REVOLUTIONER	RHABDOMANCER	RHEOMORPHISM	RHINESTONES	RHIZOCEPHALAN
REVOLUTIONERS	RHABDOMANCERS	RHEOMORPHISMS	RHINITIDES	RHIZOCEPHALANS
REVOLUTIONISE	RHABDOMANCIES	RHEOPHILES	RHINITISES	RHIZOCEPHALOUS
REVOLUTIONISED	RHABDOMANCY	RHEORECEPTOR	RHINOCERICAL	RHIZOCTONIA
REVOLUTIONISER	RHABDOMANTIST	RHEORECEPTORS	RHINOCEROI	RHIZOCTONIAS
REVOLUTIONISERS	RHABDOMANTISTS	RHEOSCOPES	RHINOCEROS	RHIZOGENETIC
REVOLUTIONISES	RHABDOMERE	RHEOSTATIC	RHINOCEROSES	RHIZOGENIC
REVOLUTIONISING	RHABDOMERES	RHEOTACTIC	RHINOCEROT	RHIZOGENOUS
REVOLUTIONISM	RHABDOMYOMA	RHEOTROPES	RHINOCEROTE	RHIZOMATOUS
REVOLUTIONISMS	RHABDOMYOMAS	RHEOTROPIC	RHINOCEROTES	RHIZOMORPH
REVOLUTIONIST	RHABDOMYOMATA	RHEOTROPISM	RHINOCEROTIC	RHIZOMORPHOUS
REVOLUTIONISTS	RHABDOSPHERE	RHEOTROPISMS	RHINOLALIA	RHIZOMORPHS
REVOLUTIONIZE	RHABDOSPHERES	RHETORICAL	RHINOLALIAS	RHIZOPHAGOUS
REVOLUTIONIZED	RHABDOVIRUS	RHETORICALLY	RHINOLITHS	RHIZOPHILOUS
REVOLUTIONIZER	RHABDOVIRUSES	RHETORICIAN	RHINOLOGICAL	RHIZOPHORE
REVOLUTIONIZERS	RHACHIDIAL	RHETORICIANS	RHINOLOGIES	RHIZOPHORES
REVOLUTIONIZES	RHACHILLAS	RHETORISED	RHINOLOGIST	RHIZOPLANE
REVOLUTIONIZING	RHACHITISES	RHETORISES	RHINOLOGISTS	RHIZOPLANES
REVOLUTIONS	RHADAMANTHINE	RHETORISING	RHINOPHONIA	RHIZOPODAN
REVOLVABLE	RHAGADIFORM	RHETORIZED	RHINOPHONIAS	RHIZOPODANS
REVOLVABLY	RHAMNACEOUS	RHETORIZES	RHINOPHYMA	RHIZOPODOUS
REVOLVENCIES	RHAMPHOTHECA	RHETORIZING	RHINOPHYMAS	RHIZOPUSES
REVOLVENCY	RHAMPHOTHECAE	RHEUMATEESE	RHINOPLASTIC	RHIZOSPHERE
REVOLVINGLY	RHAPONTICS	RHEUMATEESES	RHINOPLASTIES	RHIZOSPHERES
REVOLVINGS	RHAPSODICAL	RHEUMATICAL	RHINOPLASTY	RHIZOTOMIES
REVULSIONARY	RHAPSODICALLY	RHEUMATICALLY	RHINORRHAGIA	RHODAMINES
REVULSIONS	RHAPSODIES	RHEUMATICKY	RHINORRHAGIAS	RHODANATES
REVULSIVELY	RHAPSODISE	RHEUMATICS	RHINORRHOEA	RHODANISED
REVULSIVES	RHAPSODISED	RHEUMATISE	RHINORRHOEAL	RHODANISES
REWAKENING	RHAPSODISES	RHEUMATISES	RHINORRHOEAS	RHODANISING
REWARDABLE	RHAPSODISING	RHEUMATISM	RHINOSCLEROMA	RHODANIZED
REWARDABLENESS	RHAPSODIST	RHEUMATISMAL	RHINOSCLEROMAS	RHODANIZES
REWARDINGLY	RHAPSODISTIC	RHEUMATISMS	RHINOSCLEROMATA	RHODANIZING
REWARDLESS	RHAPSODISTS	RHEUMATIZE	RHINOSCOPE	RHODOCHROSITE
REWATCHING	RHAPSODIZE	RHEUMATIZES	RHINOSCOPES	RHODOCHROSITES

R

RHODODAPHNE	RHUMBATRON	RIBGRASSES	RIDICULING	RIJKSDAALER
RHODODAPHNES	RHUMBATRONS	RIBOFLAVIN	RIDICULOUS	RIJKSDAALERS
RHODODENDRA	RHYMESTERS	RIBOFLAVINE	RIDICULOUSLY	RIJSTAFELS
RHODODENDRON	RHYNCHOCOEL	RIBOFLAVINES	RIDICULOUSNESS	RIJSTTAFEL
RHODODENDRONS	RHYNCHOCOELS	RIBOFLAVINS	RIEBECKITE	RIJSTTAFELS
RHODOLITES	RHYNCHODONT	RIBONUCLEASE	RIEBECKITES	RIMINESSES
RHODOMONTADE	RHYNCHOPHORE	RIBONUCLEASES	RIFACIMENTI	RIMOSITIES
RHODOMONTADED	RHYNCHOPHORES	RIBONUCLEIC	RIFACIMENTO	RINDERPEST
RHODOMONTADES	RHYNCHOPHOROUS	RIBONUCLEOSIDE	RIFACIMENTOS	RINDERPESTS
RHODOMONTADING	RHYPAROGRAPHER	RIBONUCLEOSIDES	RIFAMPICIN	RINFORZANDO
RHODONITES	RHYPAROGRAPHERS	RIBONUCLEOTIDE	RIFAMPICINS	RINGBARKED
RHODOPHANE	RHYPAROGRAPHIC	RIBONUCLEOTIDES	RIFAMYCINS	RINGBARKING
RHODOPHANES	RHYPAROGRAPHIES	RICEFIELDS	RIFENESSES	RINGHALSES
RHODOPSINS	RHYPAROGRAPHY	RICEGRASSES	RIFLEBIRDS	RINGLEADER
RHOEADINES	RHYTHMICAL	RICERCARES	RIGAMAROLE	RINGLEADERS
RHOICISSUS	RHYTHMICALLY	RICERCATAS	RIGAMAROLES	RINGLETIER
RHOICISSUSES	RHYTHMICITIES	RICHNESSES	RIGHTABLENESS	RINGLETIEST
RHOMBENCEPHALA	RHYTHMICITY	RICINOLEIC	RIGHTABLENESSES	RINGMASTER
RHOMBENCEPHALON	RHYTHMISATION	RICKBURNER	RIGHTENING	RINGMASTERS
RHOMBENPORPHYR	RHYTHMISATIONS	RICKBURNERS	RIGHTEOUSLY	RINGSIDERS
RHOMBENPORPHYRS	RHYTHMISED	RICKETIEST	RIGHTEOUSNESS	RINGSTANDS
RHOMBENPORPHYRY	RHYTHMISES	RICKETINESS	RIGHTEOUSNESSES	RINGSTRAKED
RHOMBOHEDRA	RHYTHMISING	RICKETINESSES	RIGHTFULLY	RINGTOSSES
RHOMBOHEDRAL	RHYTHMISTS	RICKETTIER	RIGHTFULNESS	RINKHALSES
RHOMBOHEDRON	RHYTHMIZATION	RICKETTIEST	RIGHTFULNESSES	RINSABILITIES
RHOMBOHEDRONS	RHYTHMIZATIONS	RICKETTSIA	RIGHTNESSES	RINSABILITY
RHOMBOIDAL	RHYTHMIZED	RICKETTSIAE	RIGHTSIZED	RINSIBILITIES
RHOMBOIDEI	RHYTHMIZES	RICKETTSIAL	RIGHTSIZES	RINSIBILITY
RHOMBOIDES	RHYTHMIZING	RICKETTSIAS	RIGHTSIZING	RINTHEREOUT
RHOMBOIDEUS	RHYTHMLESS	RICKSTANDS	RIGHTSIZINGS	RINTHEREOUTS
RHOMBPORPHYRIES	RHYTHMOMETER	RICKSTICKS	RIGHTWARDLY	RIOTOUSNESS
RHOMBPORPHYRY	RHYTHMOMETERS	RICOCHETED	RIGHTWARDS	RIOTOUSNESSES
RHOPALISMS	RHYTHMOPOEIA	RICOCHETING	RIGIDIFICATION	RIPENESSES
RHOPALOCERAL	RHYTHMOPOEIAS	RICOCHETTED	RIGIDIFICATIONS	RIPIDOLITE
RHOPALOCEROUS	RHYTHMUSES	RICOCHETTING	RIGIDIFIED	RIPIDOLITES
RHOTACISED	RHYTIDECTOMIES	RIDABILITIES	RIGIDIFIES	RIPIENISTS
RHOTACISES	RHYTIDECTOMY	RIDABILITY	RIGIDIFYING	RIPPLINGLY
RHOTACISING	RHYTIDOMES	RIDDLINGLY	RIGIDISING	RIPRAPPING
RHOTACISMS	RIBALDRIES	RIDERSHIPS	RIGIDITIES	RIPSNORTER
RHOTACISTIC	RIBATTUTAS	RIDESHARED	RIGIDIZING	RIPSNORTERS
RHOTACISTS	RIBAUDRIES	RIDESHARES	RIGIDNESSES	RIPSNORTING
RHOTACIZED	RIBAVIRINS	RIDESHARING	RIGMAROLES	RIPSNORTINGLY
RHOTACIZES	RIBBONFISH	RIDESHARINGS	RIGORISTIC	RISIBILITIES
RHOTACIZING	RIBBONFISHES	RIDGEBACKS	RIGOROUSLY	RISIBILITY
RHOTICITIES	RIBBONIEST	RIDGELINES	RIGOROUSNESS	RISKINESSES
RHUBARBIER	RIBBONLIKE	RIDGELINGS	RIGOROUSNESSES	RISORGIMENTO
RHUBARBIEST	RIBBONRIES	RIDGEPOLES	RIGSDALERS	RISORGIMENTOS
RHUBARBING	RIBBONWOOD	RIDGETREES	RIGWIDDIES	RISTRETTOS
RHUBARBINGS	RIBBONWOODS	RIDICULERS	RIGWOODIES	RITARDANDI

R

RITARDANDO	RIVETINGLY	ROCKBURSTS	ROENTGENOLOGIST	ROMANTICALITIES
RITARDANDOS	ROADABILITIES	ROCKCRESSES	ROENTGENOLOGY	ROMANTICALITY
RITONAVIRS	ROADABILITY	ROCKETEERS	ROENTGENOPAQUE	ROMANTICALLY
RITORNELLE	ROADBLOCKED	ROCKETRIES	ROENTGENOSCOPE	ROMANTICISATION
RITORNELLES	ROADBLOCKING	ROCKETSONDE	ROENTGENOSCOPES	ROMANTICISE
RITORNELLI	ROADBLOCKS	ROCKETSONDES	ROENTGENOSCOPIC	ROMANTICISED
RITORNELLO	ROADCRAFTS	ROCKFISHES	ROENTGENOSCOPY	ROMANTICISES
RITORNELLOS	ROADHEADER	ROCKHOPPER	ROGUESHIPS	ROMANTICISING
RITORNELLS	ROADHEADERS	ROCKHOPPERS	ROGUISHNESS	ROMANTICISM
RITOURNELLE	ROADHOLDING	ROCKHOUNDING	ROGUISHNESSES	ROMANTICISMS
RITOURNELLES	ROADHOLDINGS	ROCKHOUNDINGS	ROISTERERS	ROMANTICIST
RITUALISATION	ROADHOUSES	ROCKHOUNDS	ROISTERING	ROMANTICISTS
RITUALISATIONS	ROADMAKING	ROCKINESSES	ROISTERINGS	ROMANTICIZATION
RITUALISED	ROADMAKINGS	ROCKSHAFTS	ROISTEROUS	ROMANTICIZE
RITUALISES	ROADMENDER	ROCKSLIDES	ROISTEROUSLY	ROMANTICIZED
RITUALISING	ROADMENDERS	ROCKSTEADIES	ROLLCOLLAR	ROMANTICIZES
RITUALISMS	ROADROLLER	ROCKSTEADY	ROLLCOLLARS	ROMANTICIZING
RITUALISTIC	ROADROLLERS	ROCKWATERS	ROLLERBALL	ROMELDALES
RITUALISTICALLY	ROADRUNNER	RODENTICIDE	ROLLERBALLS	ROMPISHNESS
RITUALISTS	ROADRUNNERS	RODENTICIDES	ROLLERBLADE	ROMPISHNESSES
RITUALIZATION	ROADSTEADS	RODFISHERS	ROLLERBLADED	RONDOLETTO
RITUALIZATIONS	ROADWORTHIER	RODFISHING	ROLLERBLADER	RONDOLETTOS
RITUALIZED	ROADWORTHIES	RODFISHINGS	ROLLERBLADERS	RONTGENISATION
RITUALIZES	ROADWORTHIEST	RODGERSIAS	ROLLERBLADES	RONTGENISATIONS
RITUALIZING	ROADWORTHINESS	RODOMONTADE	ROLLERBLADING	RONTGENISE
RITUXIMABS	ROADWORTHY	RODOMONTADED	ROLLERBLADINGS	RONTGENISED
RITZINESSES	ROASTERIES	RODOMONTADER	ROLLERCOASTER	RONTGENISES
RIVALESSES	ROBERDSMAN	RODOMONTADERS	ROLLERCOASTERED	RONTGENISING
RIVALISING	ROBERDSMEN	RODOMONTADES	ROLLERCOASTERS	RONTGENIZATION
RIVALITIES	ROBERTSMAN	RODOMONTADING	ROLLERDROME	RONTGENIZATIONS
RIVALIZING	ROBERTSMEN	ROENTGENISATION	ROLLERDROMES	RONTGENIZE
RIVALSHIPS	ROBOCALLED	ROENTGENISE	ROLLICKIER	RONTGENIZED
RIVERBANKS	ROBOCALLING	ROENTGENISED	ROLLICKIEST	RONTGENIZES
RIVERBOATS	ROBORATING	ROENTGENISES	ROLLICKING	RONTGENIZING
RIVERCRAFT	ROBOTICALLY	ROENTGENISING	ROLLICKINGS	RONTGENOGRAM
RIVERCRAFTS	ROBOTISATION	ROENTGENIUM	ROLLOCKING	RONTGENOGRAMS
RIVERFRONT	ROBOTISATIONS	ROENTGENIUMS	ROLLOCKINGS	RONTGENOGRAPH
RIVERFRONTS	ROBOTISING	ROENTGENIZATION	ROMANCICAL	RONTGENOGRAPHS
RIVERHEADS	ROBOTIZATION	ROENTGENIZE	ROMANCINGS	RONTGENOGRAPHY
RIVERSCAPE	ROBOTIZATIONS	ROENTGENIZED	ROMANESCOS	RONTGENOLOGICAL
RIVERSCAPES	ROBOTIZING	ROENTGENIZES	ROMANICITE	RONTGENOLOGIES
RIVERSIDES	ROBUSTIOUS	ROENTGENIZING	ROMANICITES	RONTGENOLOGIST
RIVERWALKS	ROBUSTIOUSLY	ROENTGENOGRAM	ROMANISATION	RONTGENOLOGISTS
RIVERWARDS	ROBUSTIOUSNESS	ROENTGENOGRAMS	ROMANISATIONS	RONTGENOLOGY
RIVERWEEDS	ROBUSTNESS	ROENTGENOGRAPH	ROMANISING	RONTGENOPAQUE
RIVERWORTHIER	ROBUSTNESSES	ROENTGENOGRAPHS	ROMANIZATION	RONTGENOSCOPE
RIVERWORTHIEST	ROCAMBOLES	ROENTGENOGRAPHY	ROMANIZATIONS	RONTGENOSCOPES
RIVERWORTHINESS	ROCKABILLIES	ROENTGENOLOGIC	ROMANIZING	RONTGENOSCOPIC
RIVERWORTHY	ROCKABILLY	ROENTGENOLOGIES	ROMANTICAL	RONTGENOSCOPIES

RONTGENOSCOPY	ROTATIONAL	ROUGHHEWED	ROUSTABOUT	RUBBISHING
RONTGENOTHERAPY	ROTATIVELY	ROUGHHEWING	ROUSTABOUTS	RUBBISHLIER
ROOFLESSNESS	ROTAVATING	ROUGHHOUSE	ROUTEMARCH	RUBBISHLIEST
ROOFLESSNESSES	ROTAVATORS	ROUGHHOUSED	ROUTEMARCHED	RUBBLEWORK
ROOFSCAPES	ROTAVIRUSES	ROUGHHOUSES	ROUTEMARCHES	RUBBLEWORKS
ROOMINESSES	ROTGRASSES	ROUGHHOUSING	ROUTEMARCHING	RUBEFACIENT
ROOTEDNESS	ROTIFERANS	ROUGHHOUSINGS	ROUTINEERS	RUBEFACIENTS
ROOTEDNESSES	ROTIFEROUS	ROUGHNECKED	ROUTINISATION	RUBEFACTION
ROOTINESSES	ROTISSERIE	ROUGHNECKING	ROUTINISATIONS	RUBEFACTIONS
ROOTLESSNESS	ROTISSERIED	ROUGHNECKS	ROUTINISED	RUBELLITES
ROOTLESSNESSES	ROTISSERIEING	ROUGHNESSES	ROUTINISES	RUBESCENCE
ROOTSERVER	ROTISSERIES	ROUGHRIDER	ROUTINISING	RUBESCENCES
ROOTSERVERS	ROTOGRAPHED	ROUGHRIDERS	ROUTINISMS	RUBIACEOUS
ROOTSINESS	ROTOGRAPHING	ROULETTING	ROUTINISTS	RUBICELLES
ROOTSINESSES	ROTOGRAPHS	ROUNCEVALS	ROUTINIZATION	RUBICONING
ROOTSTALKS	ROTOGRAVURE	ROUNDABOUT	ROUTINIZATIONS	RUBICUNDITIES
ROOTSTOCKS	ROTOGRAVURES	ROUNDABOUTATION	ROUTINIZED	RUBICUNDITY
ROPEDANCER	ROTORCRAFT	ROUNDABOUTED	ROUTINIZES	RUBIGINOSE
ROPEDANCERS	ROTORCRAFTS	ROUNDABOUTEDLY	ROUTINIZING	RUBIGINOUS
ROPEDANCING	ROTOSCOPED	ROUNDABOUTILITY	ROWANBERRIES	RUBRICALLY
ROPEDANCINGS	ROTOSCOPES	ROUNDABOUTING	ROWANBERRY	RUBRICATED
ROPEWALKER	ROTOSCOPING	ROUNDABOUTLY	ROWDINESSES	RUBRICATES
ROPEWALKERS	ROTOTILLED	ROUNDABOUTNESS	ROWDYDOWED	RUBRICATING
ROPINESSES	ROTOTILLER	ROUNDABOUTS	ROWDYDOWING	RUBRICATION
ROQUEFORTS	ROTOTILLERS	ROUNDARCHED	ROYALISING	RUBRICATIONS
ROQUELAURE	ROTOTILLING	ROUNDBALLS	ROYALISTIC	RUBRICATOR
ROQUELAURES	ROTOVATING	ROUNDEDNESS	ROYALIZING	RUBRICATORS
ROSANILINE	ROTOVATORS	ROUNDEDNESSES	ROYALMASTS	RUBRICIANS
ROSANILINES	ROTTENNESS	ROUNDELAYS	ROYSTERERS	RUBYTHROAT
ROSANILINS	ROTTENNESSES	ROUNDHANDS	ROYSTERING	RUBYTHROATS
ROSEBUSHES	ROTTENSTONE	ROUNDHEADED	ROYSTEROUS	RUCTATIONS
ROSEFINCHES	ROTTENSTONED	ROUNDHEADEDNESS	RUBBERIEST	RUDBECKIAS
ROSEFISHES	ROTTENSTONES	ROUNDHEELS	RUBBERISED	RUDDERHEAD
ROSEMALING	ROTTENSTONING	ROUNDHOUSE	RUBBERISES	RUDDERHEADS
ROSEMALINGS	ROTTWEILER	ROUNDHOUSES	RUBBERISING	RUDDERLESS
ROSEMARIES	ROTTWEILERS	ROUNDNESSES	RUBBERIZED	RUDDERPOST
ROSETTINGS	ROTUNDITIES	ROUNDTABLE	RUBBERIZES	RUDDERPOSTS
ROSEWATERS	ROTUNDNESS	ROUNDTABLES	RUBBERIZING	RUDDERSTOCK
ROSINESSES	ROTUNDNESSES	ROUNDTRIPPING	RUBBERLIKE	RUDDERSTOCKS
ROSINWEEDS	ROUGHBACKS	ROUNDTRIPPINGS	RUBBERNECK	RUDDINESSES
ROSMARINES	ROUGHCASTED	ROUNDTRIPS	RUBBERNECKED	RUDENESSES
ROSTELLATE	ROUGHCASTER	ROUNDWOODS	RUBBERNECKER	RUDIMENTAL
ROSTELLUMS	ROUGHCASTERS	ROUNDWORMS	RUBBERNECKERS	RUDIMENTALLY
ROSTERINGS	ROUGHCASTING	ROUSEABOUT	RUBBERNECKING	RUDIMENTARILY
ROSTROCARINATE	ROUGHCASTS	ROUSEABOUTS	RUBBERNECKS	RUDIMENTARINESS
ROSTROCARINATES	ROUGHDRIED	ROUSEDNESS	RUBBERWEAR	RUDIMENTARY
ROTACHUTES	ROUGHDRIES	ROUSEDNESSES	RUBBERWEARS	RUEFULNESS
ROTAMETERS	ROUGHDRYING	ROUSEMENTS	RUBBISHIER	RUEFULNESSES
ROTAPLANES	ROUGHENING	ROUSSETTES	RUBBISHIEST	RUFESCENCE

R

RUFESCENCES	RUMBLINGLY	RUMMISHING	RUSHINESSES	RUSTICWORKS
RUFFIANING	RUMBULLION	RUMMLEGUMPTION	RUSHLIGHTS	RUSTINESSES
RUFFIANISH	RUMBULLIONS	RUMMLEGUMPTIONS	RUSSETIEST	RUSTLINGLY
RUFFIANISM	RUMBUNCTIOUS	RUMORMONGER	RUSSETINGS	RUSTPROOFED
RUFFIANISMS	RUMBUSTICAL	RUMORMONGERING	RUSSETTING	RUSTPROOFING
RUGGEDISATION	RUMBUSTIOUS	RUMORMONGERINGS	RUSSETTINGS	RUSTPROOFINGS
RUGGEDISATIONS	RUMBUSTIOUSLY	RUMORMONGERS	RUSSIFYING	RUSTPROOFS
RUGGEDISED	RUMBUSTIOUSNESS	RUMRUNNERS	RUSTBUCKET	RUTHENIOUS
RUGGEDISES	RUMELGUMPTION	RUNAROUNDS	RUSTBUCKETS	RUTHENIUMS
RUGGEDISING	RUMELGUMPTIONS	RUNECRAFTS	RUSTICALLY	RUTHERFORD
RUGGEDIZATION	RUMFUSTIAN	RUNNINESSES	RUSTICATED	RUTHERFORDIUM
RUGGEDIZATIONS	RUMFUSTIANS	RUNTINESSES	RUSTICATES	RUTHERFORDIUMS
RUGGEDIZED	RUMGUMPTION	RUPESTRIAN	RUSTICATING	RUTHERFORDS
RUGGEDIZES	RUMGUMPTIONS	RUPICOLINE	RUSTICATINGS	RUTHFULNESS
RUGGEDIZING	RUMINANTLY	RUPICOLOUS	RUSTICATION	RUTHFULNESSES
RUGGEDNESS	RUMINATING	RUPTURABLE	RUSTICATIONS	RUTHLESSLY
RUGGEDNESSES	RUMINATINGLY	RUPTUREWORT	RUSTICATOR	RUTHLESSNESS
RUGGELACHS	RUMINATION	RUPTUREWORTS	RUSTICATORS	RUTHLESSNESSES
RUGOSITIES	RUMINATIONS	RURALISATION	RUSTICISED	RUTTINESSES
RUINATIONS	RUMINATIVE	RURALISATIONS	RUSTICISES	RUTTISHNESS
RUINOUSNESS	RUMINATIVELY	RURALISING	RUSTICISING	RUTTISHNESSES
RUINOUSNESSES	RUMINATORS	RURALITIES	RUSTICISMS	RYBAUDRYES
RULERSHIPS	RUMLEGUMPTION	RURALIZATION	RUSTICITIES	RYEGRASSES
RUMBLEDETHUMP	RUMLEGUMPTIONS	RURALIZATIONS	RUSTICIZED	
RUMBLEDETHUMPS	RUMMELGUMPTION	RURALIZING	RUSTICIZES	
RUMBLEGUMPTION	RUMMELGUMPTIONS	RURALNESSES	RUSTICIZING	
RUMBLEGUMPTIONS	RUMMINESSES	RURIDECANAL	RUSTICWORK	

R

S

SABADILLAS	SACCHARIMETRY	SACERDOTALISTS	SACRIFICER	SADOMASOCHISM
SABBATARIAN	SACCHARINE	SACERDOTALIZE	SACRIFICERS	SADOMASOCHISMS
SABBATICAL	SACCHARINELY	SACERDOTALIZED	SACRIFICES	SADOMASOCHIST
SABBATICALS	SACCHARINES	SACERDOTALIZES	SACRIFICIAL	SADOMASOCHISTIC
SABBATISED	SACCHARINITIES	SACERDOTALIZING	SACRIFICIALLY	SADOMASOCHISTS
SABBATISES	SACCHARINITY	SACERDOTALLY	SACRIFICING	SAFECRACKER
SABBATISING	SACCHARINS	SACHEMDOMS	SACRIFYING	SAFECRACKERS
SABBATISMS	SACCHARISATION	SACHEMSHIP	SACRILEGES	SAFECRACKING
SABBATIZED	SACCHARISATIONS	SACHEMSHIPS	SACRILEGIOUS	SAFECRACKINGS
SABBATIZES	SACCHARISE	SACKCLOTHS	SACRILEGIOUSLY	SAFEGUARDED
SABBATIZING	SACCHARISED	SACRALGIAS	SACRILEGIST	SAFEGUARDING
SABERMETRICIAN	SACCHARISES	SACRALISATION	SACRILEGISTS	SAFEGUARDS
SABERMETRICIANS	SACCHARISING	SACRALISATIONS	SACRISTANS	SAFEKEEPING
SABERMETRICS	SACCHARIZATION	SACRALISED	SACRISTIES	SAFEKEEPINGS
SABLEFISHES	SACCHARIZATIONS	SACRALISES	SACROCOCCYGEAL	SAFELIGHTS
SABOTAGING	SACCHARIZE	SACRALISING	SACROCOSTAL	SAFENESSES
SABRETACHE	SACCHARIZED	SACRALITIES	SACROCOSTALS	SAFFLOWERS
SABRETACHES	SACCHARIZES	SACRALIZATION	SACROILIAC	SAFFRONIER
SABREWINGS	SACCHARIZING	SACRALIZATIONS	SACROILIACS	SAFFRONIEST
SABULOSITIES	SACCHAROID	SACRALIZED	SACROILIITIS	SAFRANINES
SABULOSITY	SACCHAROIDAL	SACRALIZES	SACROILIITISES	SAGACIOUSLY
SABURRATION	SACCHAROIDS	SACRALIZING	SACROSANCT	SAGACIOUSNESS
SABURRATIONS	SACCHAROMETER	SACRAMENTAL	SACROSANCTITIES	SAGACIOUSNESSES
SACAHUISTA	SACCHAROMETERS	SACRAMENTALISM	SACROSANCTITY	SAGACITIES
SACAHUISTAS	SACCHAROMETRIES	SACRAMENTALISMS	SACROSANCTNESS	SAGANASHES
SACAHUISTE	SACCHAROMETRY	SACRAMENTALIST	SADDLEBACK	SAGAPENUMS
SACAHUISTES	SACCHAROMYCES	SACRAMENTALISTS	SADDLEBACKED	SAGEBRUSHES
SACCADICALLY	SACCHAROMYCETES	SACRAMENTALITY	SADDLEBACKS	SAGENESSES
SACCHARASE	SACCHAROSE	SACRAMENTALLY	SADDLEBAGS	SAGINATING
SACCHARASES	SACCHAROSES	SACRAMENTALNESS	SADDLEBILL	SAGINATION
SACCHARATE	SACCHARUMS	SACRAMENTALS	SADDLEBILLS	SAGINATIONS
SACCHARATED	SACCULATED	SACRAMENTARIAN	SADDLEBOWS	SAGITTALLY
SACCHARATES	SACCULATION	SACRAMENTARIANS	SADDLEBRED	SAGITTARIES
SACCHARIDE	SACCULATIONS	SACRAMENTARIES	SADDLEBREDS	SAGITTIFORM
SACCHARIDES	SACCULIFORM	SACRAMENTARY	SADDLECLOTH	SAILBOARDED
SACCHARIFEROUS	SACERDOTAL	SACRAMENTED	SADDLECLOTHS	SAILBOARDER
SACCHARIFIED	SACERDOTALISE	SACRAMENTING	SADDLELESS	SAILBOARDERS
SACCHARIFIES	SACERDOTALISED	SACRAMENTS	SADDLERIES	SAILBOARDING
SACCHARIFY	SACERDOTALISES	SACRARIUMS	SADDLEROOM	SAILBOARDINGS
SACCHARIFYING	SACERDOTALISING	SACREDNESS	SADDLEROOMS	SAILBOARDS
SACCHARIMETER	SACERDOTALISM	SACREDNESSES	SADDLETREE	SAILBOATER
SACCHARIMETERS	SACERDOTALISMS	SACRIFICEABLE	SADDLETREES	SAILBOATERS
SACCHARIMETRIES	SACERDOTALIST	SACRIFICED	SADISTICALLY	SAILBOATING

SAILBOATINGS	SALERATUSES	SALINOMETERS	SALTATIONISTS	SALVABLENESSES
SAILCLOTHS	SALESCLERK	SALINOMETRIC	SALTATIONS	SALVAGEABILITY
SAILFISHES	SALESCLERKS	SALINOMETRIES	SALTATORIAL	SALVAGEABLE
SAILMAKERS	SALESGIRLS	SALINOMETRY	SALTATORIOUS	SALVARSANS
SAILMAKING	SALESLADIES	SALIVATING	SALTBUSHES	SALVATIONAL
SAILMAKINGS	SALESMANSHIP	SALIVATION	SALTCELLAR	SALVATIONISM
SAILORINGS	SALESMANSHIPS	SALIVATIONS	SALTCELLARS	SALVATIONISMS
SAILORLESS	SALESPEOPLE	SALIVATORS	SALTCHUCKER	SALVATIONIST
SAILORLIER	SALESPERSON	SALLENDERS	SALTCHUCKERS	SALVATIONISTS
SAILORLIEST	SALESPERSONS	SALLOWIEST	SALTCHUCKS	SALVATIONS
SAILORLIKE	SALESROOMS	SALLOWNESS	SALTFISHES	SALVATORIES
SAILPLANED	SALESWOMAN	SALLOWNESSES	SALTIGRADE	SALVERFORM
SAILPLANER	SALESWOMEN	SALLYPORTS	SALTIGRADES	SALVIFICAL
SAILPLANERS	SALIAUNCES	SALMAGUNDI	SALTIMBANCO	SALVIFICALLY
SAILPLANES	SALICACEOUS	SALMAGUNDIES	SALTIMBANCOS	SALVINIACEOUS
SAILPLANING	SALICETUMS	SALMAGUNDIS	SALTIMBOCCA	SAMARIFORM
SAILPLANINGS	SALICIONAL	SALMAGUNDY	SALTIMBOCCAS	SAMARITANS
SAINTESSES	SALICIONALS	SALMANASER	SALTINESSES	SAMARSKITE
SAINTFOINS	SALICORNIA	SALMANASERS	SALTIREWISE	SAMARSKITES
SAINTHOODS	SALICORNIAS	SALMANAZAR	SALTISHNESS	SAMENESSES
SAINTLIEST	SALICYLAMIDE	SALMANAZARS	SALTISHNESSES	SAMEYNESSES
SAINTLINESS	SALICYLAMIDES	SALMONBERRIES	SALTNESSES	SAMNITISES
SAINTLINESSES	SALICYLATE	SALMONBERRY	SALTPETERS	SAMPLERIES
SAINTLINGS	SALICYLATED	SALMONELLA	SALTPETREMAN	SANATORIUM
SAINTPAULIA	SALICYLATES	SALMONELLAE	SALTPETREMEN	SANATORIUMS
SAINTPAULIAS	SALICYLATING	SALMONELLAS	SALTPETRES	SANBENITOS
SAINTSHIPS	SALICYLISM	SALMONELLOSES	SALTSHAKER	SANCTIFIABLE
SALABILITIES	SALICYLISMS	SALMONELLOSIS	SALTSHAKERS	SANCTIFICATION
SALABILITY	SALIENCIES	SALMONIEST	SALTWATERS	SANCTIFICATIONS
SALABLENESS	SALIENTIAN	SALMONOIDS	SALUBRIOUS	SANCTIFIED
SALABLENESSES	SALIENTIANS	SALOMETERS	SALUBRIOUSLY	SANCTIFIEDLY
SALACIOUSLY	SALIFEROUS	SALOPETTES	SALUBRIOUSNESS	SANCTIFIER
SALACIOUSNESS	SALIFIABLE	SALPIGLOSSES	SALUBRITIES	SANCTIFIERS
SALACIOUSNESSES	SALIFICATION	SALPIGLOSSIS	SALURETICS	SANCTIFIES
SALACITIES	SALIFICATIONS	SALPIGLOSSISES	SALUTARILY	SANCTIFYING
SALAMANDER	SALIMETERS	SALPINGECTOMIES	SALUTARINESS	SANCTIFYINGLY
SALAMANDERS	SALIMETRIC	SALPINGECTOMY	SALUTARINESSES	SANCTIFYINGS
SALAMANDRIAN	SALIMETRIES	SALPINGIAN	SALUTATION	SANCTIMONIES
SALAMANDRIANS	SALINATING	SALPINGITIC	SALUTATIONAL	SANCTIMONIOUS
SALAMANDRINE	SALINATION	SALPINGITIS	SALUTATIONS	SANCTIMONIOUSLY
SALAMANDROID	SALINATIONS	SALPINGITISES	SALUTATORIAN	SANCTIMONY
SALAMANDROIDS	SALINISATION	SALSOLACEOUS	SALUTATORIANS	SANCTIONABLE
SALANGANES	SALINISATIONS	SALSUGINOUS	SALUTATORIES	SANCTIONED
SALBUTAMOL	SALINISING	SALTARELLI	SALUTATORILY	SANCTIONEER
SALBUTAMOLS	SALINITIES	SALTARELLO	SALUTATORY	SANCTIONEERS
SALEABILITIES	SALINIZATION	SALTARELLOS	SALUTIFEROUS	SANCTIONER
SALEABILITY	SALINIZATIONS	SALTATIONISM	SALVABILITIES	SANCTIONERS
SALEABLENESS	SALINIZING	SALTATIONISMS	SALVABILITY	SANCTIONING
SALEABLENESSES	SALINOMETER	SALTATIONIST	SALVABLENESS	SANCTIONLESS

SANCTITIES	SANDPAPERS	SANITATING	SAPONIFIED	SARCOCYSTISES
SANCTITUDE	SANDPAPERY	SANITATION	SAPONIFIER	SARCODINES
SANCTITUDES	SANDPIPERS	SANITATIONIST	SAPONIFIERS	SARCOIDOSES
SANCTUARIES	SANDSPOUTS	SANITATIONISTS	SAPONIFIES	SARCOIDOSIS
SANCTUARISE	SANDSTONES	SANITATIONS	SAPONIFYING	SARCOLEMMA
SANCTUARISED	SANDSTORMS	SANITISATION	SAPOTACEOUS	SARCOLEMMAL
SANCTUARISES	SANDSUCKER	SANITISATIONS	SAPPANWOOD	SARCOLEMMAS
SANCTUARISING	SANDSUCKERS	SANITISERS	SAPPANWOODS	SARCOLEMMATA
SANCTUARIZE	SANDWICHED	SANITISING	SAPPERMENT	SARCOLOGIES
SANCTUARIZED	SANDWICHES	SANITIZATION	SAPPHIRINE	SARCOMATOID
SANCTUARIZES	SANDWICHING	SANITIZATIONS	SAPPHIRINES	SARCOMATOSES
SANCTUARIZING	SANENESSES	SANITIZERS	SAPPINESSES	SARCOMATOSIS
SANDALLING	SANGFROIDS	SANITIZING	SAPRAEMIAS	SARCOMATOUS
SANDALWOOD	SANGUIFEROUS	SANITORIUM	SAPROBIONT	SARCOMERES
SANDALWOODS	SANGUIFICATION	SANITORIUMS	SAPROBIONTS	SARCOPENIA
SANDARACHS	SANGUIFICATIONS	SANNYASINS	SAPROBIOTIC	SARCOPENIAS
SANDBAGGED	SANGUIFIED	SANSCULOTTE	SAPROBITIES	SARCOPHAGAL
SANDBAGGER	SANGUIFIES	SANSCULOTTERIE	SAPROGENIC	SARCOPHAGI
SANDBAGGERS	SANGUIFYING	SANSCULOTTERIES	SAPROGENICITIES	SARCOPHAGOUS
SANDBAGGING	SANGUINARIA	SANSCULOTTES	SAPROGENICITY	SARCOPHAGUS
SANDBLASTED	SANGUINARIAS	SANSCULOTTIC	SAPROGENOUS	SARCOPHAGUSES
SANDBLASTER	SANGUINARILY	SANSCULOTTIDES	SAPROLEGNIA	SARCOPLASM
SANDBLASTERS	SANGUINARINESS	SANSCULOTTISH	SAPROLEGNIAS	SARCOPLASMIC
SANDBLASTING	SANGUINARY	SANSCULOTTISM	SAPROLITES	SARCOPLASMS
SANDBLASTINGS	SANGUINELY	SANSCULOTTISMS	SAPROLITIC	SARCOSOMAL
SANDBLASTS	SANGUINENESS	SANSCULOTTIST	SAPROPELIC	SARCOSOMES
SANDCASTLE	SANGUINENESSES	SANSCULOTTISTS	SAPROPELITE	SARDONIANS
SANDCASTLES	SANGUINEOUS	SANSEVIERIA	SAPROPELITES	SARDONICAL
SANDCRACKS	SANGUINEOUSNESS	SANSEVIERIAS	SAPROPHAGOUS	SARDONICALLY
SANDERLING	SANGUINING	SANTALACEOUS	SAPROPHYTE	SARDONICISM
SANDERLINGS	SANGUINITIES	SANTOLINAS	SAPROPHYTES	SARDONICISMS
SANDERSWOOD	SANGUINITY	SANTONICAS	SAPROPHYTIC	SARDONYXES
SANDERSWOODS	SANGUINIVOROUS	SAPANWOODS	SAPROPHYTICALLY	SARGASSOES
SANDFISHES	SANGUINOLENCIES	SAPIDITIES	SAPROPHYTISM	SARGASSUMS
SANDGLASSES	SANGUINOLENCY	SAPIDNESSES	SAPROPHYTISMS	SARKINESSES
SANDGROPER	SANGUINOLENT	SAPIENCIES	SAPROTROPH	SARMENTACEOUS
SANDGROPERS	SANGUIVOROUS	SAPIENTIAL	SAPROTROPHIC	SARMENTOSE
SANDGROUSE	SANITARIAN	SAPIENTIALLY	SAPROTROPHS	SARMENTOUS
SANDGROUSES	SANITARIANISM	SAPINDACEOUS	SAPSUCKERS	SARPANCHES
SANDINESSES	SANITARIANISMS	SAPLESSNESS	SARABANDES	SARRACENIA
SANDLOTTER	SANITARIANS	SAPLESSNESSES	SARBACANES	SARRACENIACEOUS
SANDLOTTERS	SANITARIES	SAPODILLAS	SARCASTICALLY	SARRACENIAS
SANDPAINTING	SANITARILY	SAPOGENINS	SARCENCHYMATOUS	SARRUSOPHONE
SANDPAINTINGS	SANITARINESS	SAPONACEOUS	SARCENCHYME	SARRUSOPHONES
SANDPAPERED	SANITARINESSES	SAPONACEOUSNESS	SARCENCHYMES	SARSAPARILLA
SANDPAPERIER	SANITARIST	SAPONARIAS	SARCOCARPS	SARSAPARILLAS
SANDPAPERIEST	SANITARISTS	SAPONIFIABLE	SARCOCOLLA	SARTORIALLY
SANDPAPERING	SANITARIUM	SAPONIFICATION	SARCOCOLLAS	SARTORIUSES
SANDPAPERINGS	SANITARIUMS	SAPONIFICATIONS	SARCOCYSTIS	SASKATOONS

S

SASQUATCHES	SATIRISERS	SAUCERLESS	SAXICAVOUS	SCALENOHEDRA
SASSAFRASES	SATIRISING	SAUCERLIKE	SAXICOLINE	SCALENOHEDRON
SASSARARAS	SATIRIZABLE	SAUCINESSES	SAXICOLOUS	SCALENOHEDRONS
SASSINESSES	SATIRIZATION	SAUCISSONS	SAXIFRAGACEOUS	SCALETAILS
SASSOLITES	SATIRIZATIONS	SAUERBRATEN	SAXIFRAGES	SCALEWORKS
SASSYWOODS	SATIRIZERS	SAUERBRATENS	SAXITOXINS	SCALINESSES
SATANICALLY	SATIRIZING	SAUERKRAUT	SAXOPHONES	SCALLAWAGS
SATANICALNESS	SATISFACTION	SAUERKRAUTS	SAXOPHONIC	SCALLOPERS
SATANICALNESSES	SATISFACTIONS	SAUNTERERS	SAXOPHONIST	SCALLOPING
SATANITIES	SATISFACTORILY	SAUNTERING	SAXOPHONISTS	SCALLOPINGS
SATANOLOGIES	SATISFACTORY	SAUNTERINGLY	SCABBARDED	SCALLOPINI
SATANOLOGY	SATISFIABLE	SAUNTERINGS	SCABBARDING	SCALLOPINIS
SATANOPHANIES	SATISFICED	SAURISCHIAN	SCABBARDLESS	SCALLYWAGS
SATANOPHANY	SATISFICER	SAURISCHIANS	SCABBEDNESS	SCALOGRAMS
SATANOPHOBIA	SATISFICERS	SAUROGNATHOUS	SCABBEDNESSES	SCALOPPINE
SATANOPHOBIAS	SATISFICES	SAUROPODOUS	SCABBINESS	SCALOPPINES
SATCHELFUL	SATISFICING	SAUROPSIDAN	SCABBINESSES	SCALOPPINI
SATCHELFULS	SATISFICINGS	SAUROPSIDANS	SCABERULOUS	SCALPELLIC
SATCHELLED	SATISFIERS	SAUROPTERYGIAN	SCABIOUSES	SCALPELLIFORM
SATCHELSFUL	SATISFYING	SAUROPTERYGIANS	SCABRIDITIES	SCALPRIFORM
SATEDNESSES	SATISFYINGLY	SAUSSURITE	SCABRIDITY	SCAMBAITING
SATELLITED	SATURABILITIES	SAUSSURITES	SCABROUSLY	SCAMBAITINGS
SATELLITES	SATURABILITY	SAUSSURITIC	SCABROUSNESS	SCAMBLINGLY
SATELLITIC	SATURATERS	SAVABLENESS	SCABROUSNESSES	SCAMBLINGS
SATELLITING	SATURATING	SAVABLENESSES	SCAFFOLAGE	SCAMMONIATE
SATELLITISE	SATURATION	SAVAGEDOMS	SCAFFOLAGES	SCAMMONIES
SATELLITISED	SATURATIONS	SAVAGENESS	SCAFFOLDAGE	SCAMPERERS
SATELLITISES	SATURATORS	SAVAGENESSES	SCAFFOLDAGES	SCAMPERING
SATELLITISING	SATURNALIA	SAVAGERIES	SCAFFOLDED	SCAMPERINGS
SATELLITIUM	SATURNALIAN	SAVEABLENESS	SCAFFOLDER	SCAMPISHLY
SATELLITIUMS	SATURNALIANLY	SAVEABLENESSES	SCAFFOLDERS	SCAMPISHNESS
SATELLITIZE	SATURNALIAS	SAVEGARDED	SCAFFOLDING	SCAMPISHNESSES
SATELLITIZED	SATURNIIDS	SAVEGARDING	SCAFFOLDINGS	SCANDALING
SATELLITIZES	SATURNINELY	SAVINGNESS	SCAGLIOLAS	SCANDALISATION
SATELLITIZING	SATURNINITIES	SAVINGNESSES	SCAITHLESS	SCANDALISATIONS
SATIABILITIES	SATURNINITY	SAVORINESS	SCALABILITIES	SCANDALISE
SATIABILITY	SATURNISMS	SAVORINESSES	SCALABILITY	SCANDALISED
SATIATIONS	SATURNISTS	SAVOURIEST	SCALABLENESS	SCANDALISER
SATINETTAS	SATYAGRAHA	SAVOURINESS	SCALABLENESSES	SCANDALISERS
SATINETTES	SATYAGRAHAS	SAVOURINESSES	SCALARIFORM	SCANDALISES
SATINFLOWER	SATYAGRAHI	SAVOURLESS	SCALARIFORMLY	SCANDALISING
SATINFLOWERS	SATYAGRAHIS	SAVVINESSES	SCALATIONS	SCANDALIZATION
SATINWOODS	SATYRESQUE	SAWBONESES	SCALDBERRIES	SCANDALIZATIONS
SATIRICALLY	SATYRESSES	SAWDUSTIER	SCALDBERRY	SCANDALIZE
SATIRICALNESS	SATYRIASES	SAWDUSTIEST	SCALDFISHES	SCANDALIZED
SATIRICALNESSES	SATYRIASIS	SAWDUSTING	SCALDHEADS	SCANDALIZER
SATIRISABLE	SAUCEBOATS	SAWGRASSES	SCALDSHIPS	SCANDALIZERS
SATIRISATION	SAUCEBOXES	SAWMILLERS	SCALEBOARD	SCANDALIZES
SATIRISATIONS	SAUCERFULS	SAWTIMBERS	SCALEBOARDS	SCANDALIZING

SCANDALLED	SCARABAEIST	SCATOPHAGOUS	SCENARIZED	SCHEMATISED
SCANDALLING	SCARABAEISTS	SCATOPHAGY	SCENARIZES	SCHEMATISES
SCANDALMONGER	SCARABAEOID	SCATTERABLE	SCENARIZING	SCHEMATISING
SCANDALMONGERS	SCARABAEOIDS	SCATTERATION	SCENESHIFTER	SCHEMATISM
SCANDALOUS	SCARABAEUS	SCATTERATIONS	SCENESHIFTERS	SCHEMATISMS
SCANDALOUSLY	SCARABAEUSES	SCATTERBRAIN	SCENESTERS	SCHEMATIST
SCANDALOUSNESS	SCARABOIDS	SCATTERBRAINED	SCENICALLY	SCHEMATISTS
SCANSORIAL	SCARAMOUCH	SCATTERBRAINS	SCENOGRAPHER	SCHEMATIZATION
SCANTINESS	SCARAMOUCHE	SCATTEREDLY	SCENOGRAPHERS	SCHEMATIZATIONS
SCANTINESSES	SCARAMOUCHED	SCATTERERS	SCENOGRAPHIC	SCHEMATIZE
SCANTITIES	SCARAMOUCHES	SCATTERGOOD	SCENOGRAPHICAL	SCHEMATIZED
SCANTLINGS	SCARAMOUCHING	SCATTERGOODS	SCENOGRAPHIES	SCHEMATIZES
SCANTNESSES	SCARCEMENT	SCATTERGRAM	SCENOGRAPHY	SCHEMATIZING
SCAPEGALLOWS	SCARCEMENTS	SCATTERGRAMS	SCENTLESSNESS	SCHEMINGLY
SCAPEGALLOWSES	SCARCENESS	SCATTERGUN	SCENTLESSNESSES	SCHEMOZZLE
SCAPEGOATED	SCARCENESSES	SCATTERGUNS	SCEPTERING	SCHEMOZZLED
SCAPEGOATING	SCARCITIES	SCATTERIER	SCEPTERLESS	SCHEMOZZLES
SCAPEGOATINGS	SCARECROWS	SCATTERIEST	SCEPTICALLY	SCHEMOZZLING
SCAPEGOATISM	SCAREHEADS	SCATTERING	SCEPTICISM	SCHERZANDI
SCAPEGOATISMS	SCAREMONGER	SCATTERINGLY	SCEPTICISMS	SCHERZANDO
SCAPEGOATS	SCAREMONGERING	SCATTERINGS	SCEPTRELESS	SCHERZANDOS
SCAPEGRACE	SCAREMONGERINGS	SCATTERLING	SCEUOPHYLACIA	SCHIAVONES
SCAPEGRACES	SCAREMONGERS	SCATTERLINGS	SCEUOPHYLACIUM	SCHILLERISATION
SCAPEMENTS	SCAREWARES	SCATTERMOUCH	SCEUOPHYLACIUMS	SCHILLERISE
SCAPEWHEEL	SCARFISHES	SCATTERMOUCHES	SCEUOPHYLAX	SCHILLERISED
SCAPEWHEELS	SCARFSKINS	SCATTEROMETER	SCEUOPHYLAXES	SCHILLERISES
SCAPHOCEPHALI	SCARIFICATION	SCATTEROMETERS	SCHADENFREUDE	SCHILLERISING
SCAPHOCEPHALIC	SCARIFICATIONS	SCATTERSHOT	SCHADENFREUDES	SCHILLERIZATION
SCAPHOCEPHALICS	SCARIFICATOR	SCATTINESS	SCHALSTEIN	SCHILLERIZE
SCAPHOCEPHALIES	SCARIFICATORS	SCATTINESSES	SCHALSTEINS	SCHILLERIZED
SCAPHOCEPHALISM	SCARIFIERS	SCATURIENT	SCHAPPEING	SCHILLERIZES
SCAPHOCEPHALOUS	SCARIFYING	SCAVENGERED	SCHATCHENS	SCHILLERIZING
SCAPHOCEPHALUS	SCARIFYINGLY	SCAVENGERIES	SCHECHITAH	SCHILLINGS
SCAPHOCEPHALY	SCARINESSES	SCAVENGERING	SCHECHITAHS	SCHINDYLESES
SCAPHOPODS	SCARLATINA	SCAVENGERINGS	SCHECHITAS	SCHINDYLESIS
SCAPIGEROUS	SCARLATINAL	SCAVENGERS	SCHECKLATON	SCHINDYLETIC
SCAPOLITES	SCARLATINAS	SCAVENGERY	SCHECKLATONS	SCHIPPERKE
SCAPULARIES	SCARLETING	SCAVENGING	SCHEDULERS	SCHIPPERKES
SCAPULATED	SCARPERING	SCAVENGINGS	SCHEDULING	SCHISMATIC
SCAPULIMANCIES	SCATHEFULNESS	SCAZONTICS	SCHEDULINGS	SCHISMATICAL
SCAPULIMANCY	SCATHEFULNESSES	SCELERATES	SCHEELITES	SCHISMATICALLY
SCAPULIMANTIC	SCATHELESS	SCENARISATION	SCHEFFLERA	SCHISMATICALS
SCAPULOMANCIES	SCATHINGLY	SCENARISATIONS	SCHEFFLERAS	SCHISMATICS
SCAPULOMANCY	SCATOLOGIC	SCENARISED	SCHEMATICAL	SCHISMATISE
SCAPULOMANTIC	SCATOLOGICAL	SCENARISES	SCHEMATICALLY	SCHISMATISED
SCARABAEAN	SCATOLOGIES	SCENARISING	SCHEMATICS	SCHISMATISES
SCARABAEANS	SCATOLOGIST	SCENARISTS	SCHEMATISATION	SCHISMATISING
SCARABAEID	SCATOLOGISTS	SCENARIZATION	SCHEMATISATIONS	SCHISMATIZE
SCARABAEIDS	SCATOPHAGIES	SCENARIZATIONS	SCHEMATISE	SCHISMATIZED

S

SCHISMATIZES	SCHLEPPERS	SCHOLARLIER	SCHOOLMATE	SCIENTIZED
SCHISMATIZING	SCHLEPPIER	SCHOLARLIEST	SCHOOLMATES	SCIENTIZES
SCHISTOSITIES	SCHLEPPIEST	SCHOLARLINESS	SCHOOLMISTRESS	SCIENTIZING
SCHISTOSITY	SCHLEPPING	SCHOLARLINESSES	SCHOOLMISTRESSY	SCINCOIDIAN
SCHISTOSOMAL	SCHLIERENS	SCHOLARSHIP	SCHOOLROOM	SCINCOIDIANS
SCHISTOSOME	SCHLIMAZEL	SCHOLARSHIPS	SCHOOLROOMS	SCINDAPSUS
SCHISTOSOMES	SCHLIMAZELS	SCHOLASTIC	SCHOOLTEACHER	SCINDAPSUSES
SCHISTOSOMIASES	SCHLOCKERS	SCHOLASTICAL	SCHOOLTEACHERS	SCINTIGRAM
SCHISTOSOMIASIS	SCHLOCKEYS	SCHOLASTICALLY	SCHOOLTEACHING	SCINTIGRAMS
SCHIZAEACEOUS	SCHLOCKIER	SCHOLASTICATE	SCHOOLTEACHINGS	SCINTIGRAPHIC
SCHIZANTHUS	SCHLOCKIEST	SCHOLASTICATES	SCHOOLTIDE	SCINTIGRAPHIES
SCHIZANTHUSES	SCHLUMBERGERA	SCHOLASTICISM	SCHOOLTIDES	SCINTIGRAPHY
SCHIZOCARP	SCHLUMBERGERAS	SCHOLASTICISMS	SCHOOLTIME	SCINTILLAE
SCHIZOCARPIC	SCHLUMPIER	SCHOLASTICS	SCHOOLTIMES	SCINTILLANT
SCHIZOCARPOUS	SCHLUMPIEST	SCHOLIASTIC	SCHOOLWARD	SCINTILLANTLY
SCHIZOCARPS	SCHLUMPING	SCHOLIASTS	SCHOOLWARDS	SCINTILLAS
SCHIZOGENESES	SCHMALTZES	SCHOOLBAGS	SCHOOLWORK	SCINTILLASCOPE
SCHIZOGENESIS	SCHMALTZIER	SCHOOLBOOK	SCHOOLWORKS	SCINTILLASCOPES
SCHIZOGENETIC	SCHMALTZIEST	SCHOOLBOOKS	SCHOOLYARD	SCINTILLATE
SCHIZOGENIC	SCHMALZIER	SCHOOLBOYISH	SCHOOLYARDS	SCINTILLATED
SCHIZOGNATHOUS	SCHMALZIEST	SCHOOLBOYS	SCHORLACEOUS	SCINTILLATES
SCHIZOGONIC	SCHMEARING	SCHOOLCHILD	SCHORLOMITE	SCINTILLATING
SCHIZOGONIES	SCHMECKERS	SCHOOLCHILDREN	SCHORLOMITES	SCINTILLATINGLY
SCHIZOGONOUS	SCHMECKING	SCHOOLCRAFT	SCHOTTISCHE	SCINTILLATION
SCHIZOGONY	SCHMEERING	SCHOOLCRAFTS	SCHOTTISCHES	SCINTILLATIONS
SCHIZOIDAL	SCHMICKEST	SCHOOLDAYS	SCHRECKLICH	SCINTILLATOR
SCHIZOMYCETE	SCHMOOSING	SCHOOLERIES	SCHTUMMEST	SCINTILLATORS
SCHIZOMYCETES	SCHMOOZERS	SCHOOLFELLOW	SCHTUPPING	SCINTILLISCAN
SCHIZOMYCETIC	SCHMOOZIER	SCHOOLFELLOWS	SCHUSSBOOMER	SCINTILLISCANS
SCHIZOMYCETOUS	SCHMOOZIEST	SCHOOLGIRL	SCHUSSBOOMERS	SCINTILLOMETER
SCHIZOPHRENE	SCHMOOZING	SCHOOLGIRLISH	SCHVITZING	SCINTILLOMETERS
SCHIZOPHRENES	SCHMUCKIER	SCHOOLGIRLS	SCHWARMEREI	SCINTILLON
SCHIZOPHRENETIC	SCHMUCKIEST	SCHOOLGOING	SCHWARMEREIS	SCINTILLONS
SCHIZOPHRENIA	SCHMUCKING	SCHOOLGOINGS	SCHWARMERISCH	SCINTILLOSCOPE
SCHIZOPHRENIAS	SCHMUTTERS	SCHOOLHOUSE	SCHWARZLOT	SCINTILLOSCOPES
SCHIZOPHRENIC	SCHNAPPERS	SCHOOLHOUSES	SCHWARZLOTS	SCINTISCAN
SCHIZOPHRENICS	SCHNAPPSES	SCHOOLINGS	SCIAENOIDS	SCINTISCANNER
SCHIZOPHYCEOUS	SCHNAUZERS	SCHOOLKIDS	SCIAMACHIES	SCINTISCANNERS
SCHIZOPHYTE	SCHNITZELS	SCHOOLMAID	SCIENTIFIC	SCINTISCANS
SCHIZOPHYTES	SCHNOODLES	SCHOOLMAIDS	SCIENTIFICAL	SCIOLISTIC
SCHIZOPHYTIC	SCHNORKELED	SCHOOLMARM	SCIENTIFICALLY	SCIOMACHIES
SCHIZOPODAL	SCHNORKELING	SCHOOLMARMISH	SCIENTIFICITIES	SCIOMANCER
SCHIZOPODOUS	SCHNORKELLED	SCHOOLMARMS	SCIENTIFICITY	SCIOMANCERS
SCHIZOPODS	SCHNORKELLING	SCHOOLMASTER	SCIENTISED	SCIOMANCIES
SCHIZOTHYMIA	SCHNORKELS	SCHOOLMASTERED	SCIENTISES	SCIOMANTIC
SCHIZOTHYMIAS	SCHNORRERS	SCHOOLMASTERING	SCIENTISING	SCIOPHYTES
SCHIZOTHYMIC	SCHNORRING	SCHOOLMASTERISH	SCIENTISMS	SCIOPHYTIC
SCHLEMIELS	SCHNOZZLES	SCHOOLMASTERLY	SCIENTISTIC	SCIOSOPHIES
SCHLEMIHLS	SCHOLARCHS	SCHOOLMASTERS	SCIENTISTS	SCIRRHOSITIES

S

SCIRRHOSITY	SCLEROTICS	SCOPOPHILIAC	SCOUNDRELLY	SCRAPPIEST
SCIRRHUSES	SCLEROTINS	SCOPOPHILIACS	SCOUNDRELS	SCRAPPINESS
SCISSIPARITIES	SCLEROTIOID	SCOPOPHILIAS	SCOURGINGS	SCRAPPINESSES
SCISSIPARITY	SCLEROTISATION	SCOPOPHILIC	SCOUTCRAFT	SCRAPPINGS
SCISSORERS	SCLEROTISATIONS	SCOPOPHOBIA	SCOUTCRAFTS	SCRAPYARDS
SCISSORING	SCLEROTISE	SCOPOPHOBIAS	SCOUTHERED	SCRATCHBACK
SCISSORTAIL	SCLEROTISED	SCOPTOPHILIA	SCOUTHERING	SCRATCHBACKS
SCISSORTAILS	SCLEROTISES	SCOPTOPHILIAS	SCOUTHERINGS	SCRATCHBOARD
SCISSORWISE	SCLEROTISING	SCOPTOPHOBIA	SCOUTMASTER	SCRATCHBOARDS
SCITAMINEOUS	SCLEROTITIS	SCOPTOPHOBIAS	SCOUTMASTERS	SCRATCHBUILD
SCLAUNDERS	SCLEROTITISES	SCORBUTICALLY	SCOWDERING	SCRATCHBUILDER
SCLEREIDES	SCLEROTIUM	SCORCHINGLY	SCOWDERINGS	SCRATCHBUILDERS
SCLERENCHYMA	SCLEROTIZATION	SCORCHINGNESS	SCOWLINGLY	SCRATCHBUILDING
SCLERENCHYMAS	SCLEROTIZATIONS	SCORCHINGNESSES	SCOWTHERED	SCRATCHBUILDS
SCLERENCHYMATA	SCLEROTIZE	SCORCHINGS	SCOWTHERING	SCRATCHBUILT
SCLERIASES	SCLEROTIZED	SCORDATURA	SCRABBLERS	SCRATCHCARD
SCLERIASIS	SCLEROTIZES	SCORDATURAS	SCRABBLIER	SCRATCHCARDS
SCLERITISES	SCLEROTIZING	SCOREBOARD	SCRABBLIEST	SCRATCHERS
SCLEROCAULIES	SCLEROTOMIES	SCOREBOARDS	SCRABBLING	SCRATCHIER
SCLEROCAULOUS	SCLEROTOMY	SCORECARDS	SCRABBLINGS	SCRATCHIES
SCLEROCAULY	SCOFFINGLY	SCOREKEEPER	SCRAGGEDNESS	SCRATCHIEST
SCLERODERM	SCOLDINGLY	SCOREKEEPERS	SCRAGGEDNESSES	SCRATCHILY
SCLERODERMA	SCOLECIFORM	SCORELINES	SCRAGGIEST	SCRATCHINESS
SCLERODERMAS	SCOLECITES	SCORESHEET	SCRAGGINESS	SCRATCHINESSES
SCLERODERMATA	SCOLLOPING	SCORESHEETS	SCRAGGINESSES	SCRATCHING
SCLERODERMATOUS	SCOLOPACEOUS	SCORIACEOUS	SCRAGGLIER	SCRATCHINGLY
SCLERODERMIA	SCOLOPENDRA	SCORIFICATION	SCRAGGLIEST	SCRATCHINGS
SCLERODERMIAS	SCOLOPENDRAS	SCORIFICATIONS	SCRAGGLING	SCRATCHLESS
SCLERODERMIC	SCOLOPENDRID	SCORIFIERS	SCRAICHING	SCRATCHPLATE
SCLERODERMITE	SCOLOPENDRIDS	SCORIFYING	SCRAIGHING	SCRATCHPLATES
SCLERODERMITES	SCOLOPENDRIFORM	SCORNFULLY	SCRAMBLERS	SCRATTLING
SCLERODERMOUS	SCOLOPENDRINE	SCORNFULNESS	SCRAMBLING	SCRAUCHING
SCLERODERMS	SCOLOPENDRIUM	SCORNFULNESSES	SCRAMBLINGLY	SCRAUGHING
SCLEROMALACIA	SCOLOPENDRIUMS	SCORODITES	SCRAMBLINGS	SCRAVELING
SCLEROMALACIAS	SCOLYTOIDS	SCORPAENID	SCRANCHING	SCRAVELLED
SCLEROMATA	SCOMBROIDS	SCORPAENIDS	SCRANNIEST	SCRAVELLING
SCLEROMETER	SCOMFISHED	SCORPAENOID	SCRAPBOOKED	SCRAWLIEST
SCLEROMETERS	SCOMFISHES	SCORPAENOIDS	SCRAPBOOKING	SCRAWLINGLY
SCLEROMETRIC	SCOMFISHING	SCORPIOIDS	SCRAPBOOKINGS	SCRAWLINGS
SCLEROPHYLL	SCONCHEONS	SCORPIONIC	SCRAPBOOKS	SCRAWNIEST
SCLEROPHYLLIES	SCOOTCHING	SCORZONERA	SCRAPEGOOD	SCRAWNINESS
SCLEROPHYLLOUS	SCOOTERING	SCORZONERAS	SCRAPEGOODS	SCRAWNINESSES
SCLEROPHYLLS	SCOOTERIST	SCOTODINIA	SCRAPEGUTS	SCREAKIEST
SCLEROPHYLLY	SCOOTERISTS	SCOTODINIAS	SCRAPEPENNIES	SCREAKINGS
SCLEROPROTEIN	SCOPELOIDS	SCOTOMATOUS	SCRAPEPENNY	SCREAMINGLY
SCLEROPROTEINS	SCOPOLAMINE	SCOTOMETER	SCRAPERBOARD	SCREAMINGS
SCLEROSING	SCOPOLAMINES	SCOTOMETERS	SCRAPERBOARDS	SCREECHERS
SCLEROTALS	SCOPOLINES	SCOUNDRELLIER	SCRAPHEAPS	SCREECHIER
SCLEROTIAL	SCOPOPHILIA	SCOUNDRELLIEST	SCRAPPAGES	SCREECHIEST

SCREECHING	SCRIEVEBOARDS	SCRIPTURALISMS	SCRUBBABLE	SCRUTINISERS
SCREEDINGS	SCRIGGLIER	SCRIPTURALIST	SCRUBBIEST	SCRUTINISES
SCREENABLE	SCRIGGLIEST	SCRIPTURALISTS	SCRUBBINESS	SCRUTINISING
SCREENAGER	SCRIGGLING	SCRIPTURALLY	SCRUBBINESSES	SCRUTINISINGLY
SCREENAGERS	SCRIMMAGED	SCRIPTURES	SCRUBBINGS	SCRUTINIZE
SCREENCAST	SCRIMMAGER	SCRIPTURISM	SCRUBLANDS	SCRUTINIZED
SCREENCASTS	SCRIMMAGERS	SCRIPTURISMS	SCRUBWOMAN	SCRUTINIZER
SCREENCRAFT	SCRIMMAGES	SCRIPTURIST	SCRUBWOMEN	SCRUTINIZERS
SCREENCRAFTS	SCRIMMAGING	SCRIPTURISTS	SCRUFFIEST	SCRUTINIZES
SCREENFULS	SCRIMPIEST	SCRIPTWRITER	SCRUFFINESS	SCRUTINIZING
SCREENINGS	SCRIMPINESS	SCRIPTWRITERS	SCRUFFINESSES	SCRUTINIZINGLY
SCREENLAND	SCRIMPINESSES	SCRIPTWRITING	SCRUMDOWNS	SCRUTINOUS
SCREENLANDS	SCRIMPINGS	SCRIPTWRITINGS	SCRUMMAGED	SCRUTINOUSLY
SCREENLIKE	SCRIMPNESS	SCRITCHING	SCRUMMAGER	SCRUTOIRES
SCREENPLAY	SCRIMPNESSES	SCRITCHINGS	SCRUMMAGERS	SCUDDALERS
SCREENPLAYS	SCRIMSHANDER	SCRIVEBOARD	SCRUMMAGES	SCUFFLINGS
SCREENSAVER	SCRIMSHANDERED	SCRIVEBOARDS	SCRUMMAGING	SCULDUDDERIES
SCREENSAVERS	SCRIMSHANDERING	SCRIVENERS	SCRUMMIEST	SCULDUDDERY
SCREENSHOT	SCRIMSHANDERS	SCRIVENERSHIP	SCRUMPLING	SCULDUDDRIES
SCREENSHOTS	SCRIMSHANDIED	SCRIVENERSHIPS	SCRUMPOXES	SCULDUDDRY
SCREENSHOTTED	SCRIMSHANDIES	SCRIVENING	SCRUMPTIOUS	SCULDUGGERIES
SCREENSHOTTING	SCRIMSHANDY	SCRIVENINGS	SCRUMPTIOUSLY	SCULDUGGERY
SCREENWRITER	SCRIMSHANDYING	SCROBBLING	SCRUMPTIOUSNESS	SCULLERIES
SCREENWRITERS	SCRIMSHANK	SCROBICULAR	SCRUNCHEON	SCULPTINGS
SCREENWRITING	SCRIMSHANKED	SCROBICULATE	SCRUNCHEONS	SCULPTRESS
SCREENWRITINGS	SCRIMSHANKER	SCROBICULATED	SCRUNCHIER	SCULPTRESSES
SCREEVINGS	SCRIMSHANKERS	SCROBICULE	SCRUNCHIES	SCULPTURAL
SCREICHING	SCRIMSHANKING	SCROBICULES	SCRUNCHIEST	SCULPTURALLY
SCREIGHING	SCRIMSHANKS	SCROFULOUS	SCRUNCHING	SCULPTURED
SCREWBALLS	SCRIMSHAWED	SCROFULOUSLY	SCRUNCHINGS	SCULPTURES
SCREWBEANS	SCRIMSHAWING	SCROFULOUSNESS	SCRUNCHINS	SCULPTURESQUE
SCREWDRIVER	SCRIMSHAWS	SCROGGIEST	SCRUNCHION	SCULPTURESQUELY
SCREWDRIVERS	SCRIMSHONER	SCROLLABLE	SCRUNCHIONS	SCULPTURING
SCREWHEADS	SCRIMSHONERS	SCROLLINGS	SCRUNTIEST	SCULPTURINGS
SCREWINESS	SCRIPHOLDER	SCROLLWISE	SCRUPLELESS	SCUMBERING
SCREWINESSES	SCRIPHOLDERS	SCROLLWORK	SCRUPULOSITIES	SCUMBLINGS
SCREWWORMS	SCRIPOPHILE	SCROLLWORKS	SCRUPULOSITY	SCUMFISHED
SCRIBACIOUS	SCRIPOPHILES	SCROOCHING	SCRUPULOUS	SCUMFISHES
SCRIBACIOUSNESS	SCRIPOPHILIES	SCROOTCHED	SCRUPULOUSLY	SCUMFISHING
SCRIBBLEMENT	SCRIPOPHILIST	SCROOTCHES	SCRUPULOUSNESS	SCUNCHEONS
SCRIBBLEMENTS	SCRIPOPHILISTS	SCROOTCHING	SCRUTABILITIES	SCUNGILLIS
SCRIBBLERS	SCRIPOPHILY	SCROPHULARIA	SCRUTABILITY	SCUNNERING
SCRIBBLIER	SCRIPPAGES	SCROPHULARIAS	SCRUTATORS	SCUPPERING
SCRIBBLIEST	SCRIPTORIA	SCROUNGERS	SCRUTINEER	SCUPPERNONG
SCRIBBLING	SCRIPTORIAL	SCROUNGIER	SCRUTINEERS	SCUPPERNONGS
SCRIBBLINGLY	SCRIPTORIUM	SCROUNGIEST	SCRUTINIES	SCURFINESS
SCRIBBLINGS	SCRIPTORIUMS	SCROUNGING	SCRUTINISE	SCURFINESSES
SCRIECHING	SCRIPTURAL	SCROUNGINGS	SCRUTINISED	SCURRILITIES
SCRIEVEBOARD	SCRIPTURALISM	SCROWDGING	SCRUTINISER	SCURRILITY

S

SCURRILOUS	SEAMINESSES	SEBORRHOEA	SECRETIVELY	SECTORISES
SCURRILOUSLY	SEAMLESSLY	SEBORRHOEAL	SECRETIVENESS	SECTORISING
SCURRILOUSNESS	SEAMLESSNESS	SEBORRHOEAS	SECRETIVENESSES	SECTORIZATION
SCURRIOURS	SEAMLESSNESSES	SEBORRHOEIC	SECRETNESS	SECTORIZATIONS
SCURVINESS	SEAMSTRESS	SECERNENTS	SECRETNESSES	SECTORIZED
SCURVINESSES	SEAMSTRESSES	SECERNMENT	SECRETORIES	SECTORIZES
SCUTATIONS	SEAMSTRESSIES	SECERNMENTS	SECTARIANISE	SECTORIZING
SCUTCHEONLESS	SEAMSTRESSY	SECESSIONAL	SECTARIANISED	SECULARISATION
SCUTCHEONS	SEANNACHIE	SECESSIONISM	SECTARIANISES	SECULARISATIONS
SCUTCHINGS	SEANNACHIES	SECESSIONISMS	SECTARIANISING	SECULARISE
SCUTELLATE	SEAQUARIUM	SECESSIONIST	SECTARIANISM	SECULARISED
SCUTELLATED	SEAQUARIUMS	SECESSIONISTS	SECTARIANISMS	SECULARISER
SCUTELLATION	SEARCHABLE	SECESSIONS	SECTARIANIZE	SECULARISERS
SCUTELLATIONS	SEARCHINGLY	SECLUDEDLY	SECTARIANIZED	SECULARISES
SCUTTERING	SEARCHINGNESS	SECLUDEDNESS	SECTARIANIZES	SECULARISING
SCUTTLEBUTT	SEARCHINGNESSES	SECLUDEDNESSES	SECTARIANIZING	SECULARISM
SCUTTLEBUTTS	SEARCHINGS	SECLUSIONIST	SECTARIANS	SECULARISMS
SCUTTLEFUL	SEARCHLESS	SECLUSIONISTS	SECTILITIES	SECULARIST
SCUTTLEFULS	SEARCHLIGHT	SECLUSIONS	SECTIONALISE	SECULARISTIC
SCUTTLINGS	SEARCHLIGHTS	SECLUSIVELY	SECTIONALISED	SECULARISTS
SCUZZBALLS	SEAREDNESS	SECLUSIVENESS	SECTIONALISES	SECULARITIES
SCYPHIFORM	SEAREDNESSES	SECLUSIVENESSES	SECTIONALISING	SECULARITY
SCYPHISTOMA	SEARNESSES	SECOBARBITAL	SECTIONALISM	SECULARIZATION
SCYPHISTOMAE	SEASICKEST	SECOBARBITALS	SECTIONALISMS	SECULARIZATIONS
SCYPHISTOMAS	SEASICKNESS	SECONDARIES	SECTIONALIST	SECULARIZE
SCYPHOZOAN	SEASICKNESSES	SECONDARILY	SECTIONALISTS	SECULARIZED
SCYPHOZOANS	SEASONABILITIES	SECONDARINESS	SECTIONALIZE	SECULARIZER
SCYTHELIKE	SEASONABILITY	SECONDARINESSES	SECTIONALIZED	SECULARIZERS
SDEIGNFULL	SEASONABLE	SECONDHAND	SECTIONALIZES	SECULARIZES
SDEIGNFULLY	SEASONABLENESS	SECONDINGS	SECTIONALIZING	SECULARIZING
SDRUCCIOLA	SEASONABLY	SECONDMENT	SECTIONALLY	SECUNDINES
SEABEACHES	SEASONALITIES	SECONDMENTS	SECTIONALS	SECUNDOGENITURE
SEABORGIUM	SEASONALITY	SECRETAGES	SECTIONING	SECURANCES
SEABORGIUMS	SEASONALLY	SECRETAGOGIC	SECTIONISATION	SECUREMENT
SEABOTTLES	SEASONALNESS	SECRETAGOGUE	SECTIONISATIONS	SECUREMENTS
SEACHANGER	SEASONALNESSES	SECRETAGOGUES	SECTIONISE	SECURENESS
SEACHANGERS	SEASONINGS	SECRETAIRE	SECTIONISED	SECURENESSES
SEACUNNIES	SEASONLESS	SECRETAIRES	SECTIONISES	SECURIFORM
SEAFARINGS	SEASTRANDS	SECRETARIAL	SECTIONISING	SECURITANS
SEAGRASSES	SEAWEEDIER	SECRETARIAT	SECTIONIZATION	SECURITIES
SEALIFTING	SEAWEEDIEST	SECRETARIATE	SECTIONIZATIONS	SECURITISATION
SEALIONING	SEAWORTHIER	SECRETARIATES	SECTIONIZE	SECURITISATIONS
SEALIONINGS	SEAWORTHIEST	SECRETARIATS	SECTIONIZED	SECURITISE
SEALPOINTS	SEAWORTHINESS	SECRETARIES	SECTIONIZES	SECURITISED
SEAMANLIER	SEAWORTHINESSES	SECRETARYSHIP	SECTIONIZING	SECURITISES
SEAMANLIEST	SEBIFEROUS	SECRETARYSHIPS	SECTORIALS	SECURITISING
SEAMANLIKE	SEBORRHEAL	SECRETIONAL	SECTORISATION	SECURITIZATION
SEAMANSHIP	SEBORRHEAS	SECRETIONARY	SECTORISATIONS	SECURITIZATIONS
SEAMANSHIPS	SEBORRHEIC	SECRETIONS	SECTORISED	SECURITIZE

SECURITIZED	SEEMELESSE	SEISMICALLY	SELECTORATES	SEMAPHORICALLY
SECURITIZES	SEEMINGNESS	SEISMICITIES	SELECTORIAL	SEMAPHORING
SECURITIZING	SEEMINGNESSES	SEISMICITY	SELEGILINE	SEMASIOLOGICAL
SECUROCRAT	SEEMLIHEAD	SEISMOGRAM	SELEGILINES	SEMASIOLOGIES
SECUROCRATS	SEEMLIHEADS	SEISMOGRAMS	SELENIFEROUS	SEMASIOLOGIST
SEDATENESS	SEEMLIHEDS	SEISMOGRAPH	SELENOCENTRIC	SEMASIOLOGISTS
SEDATENESSES	SEEMLINESS	SEISMOGRAPHER	SELENODONT	SEMASIOLOGY
SEDENTARILY	SEEMLINESSES	SEISMOGRAPHERS	SELENODONTS	SEMATOLOGIES
SEDENTARINESS	SEEMLYHEDS	SEISMOGRAPHIC	SELENOGRAPH	SEMATOLOGY
SEDENTARINESSES	SEERSUCKER	SEISMOGRAPHICAL	SELENOGRAPHER	SEMBLABLES
SEDGELANDS	SEERSUCKERS	SEISMOGRAPHIES	SELENOGRAPHERS	SEMBLANCES
SEDIGITATED	SEETHINGLY	SEISMOGRAPHS	SELENOGRAPHIC	SEMBLATIVE
SEDIMENTABLE	SEGHOLATES	SEISMOGRAPHY	SELENOGRAPHICAL	SEMEIOLOGIC
SEDIMENTARILY	SEGMENTALLY	SEISMOLOGIC	SELENOGRAPHIES	SEMEIOLOGICAL
SEDIMENTARY	SEGMENTARY	SEISMOLOGICAL	SELENOGRAPHIST	SEMEIOLOGIES
SEDIMENTATION	SEGMENTATE	SEISMOLOGICALLY	SELENOGRAPHISTS	SEMEIOLOGIST
SEDIMENTATIONS	SEGMENTATION	SEISMOLOGIES	SELENOGRAPHS	SEMEIOLOGISTS
SEDIMENTED	SEGMENTATIONS	SEISMOLOGIST	SELENOGRAPHY	SEMEIOLOGY
SEDIMENTING	SEGMENTING	SEISMOLOGISTS	SELENOLOGICAL	SEMEIOTICALLY
SEDIMENTOLOGIC	SEGREGABLE	SEISMOLOGY	SELENOLOGIES	SEMEIOTICIAN
SEDIMENTOLOGIES	SEGREGANTS	SEISMOMETER	SELENOLOGIST	SEMEIOTICIANS
SEDIMENTOLOGIST	SEGREGATED	SEISMOMETERS	SELENOLOGISTS	SEMEIOTICS
SEDIMENTOLOGY	SEGREGATES	SEISMOMETRIC	SELENOLOGY	SEMELPARITIES
SEDIMENTOUS	SEGREGATING	SEISMOMETRICAL	SELFISHNESS	SEMELPARITY
SEDITIONARIES	SEGREGATION	SEISMOMETRIES	SELFISHNESSES	SEMELPAROUS
SEDITIONARY	SEGREGATIONAL	SEISMOMETRY	SELFLESSLY	SEMESTERED
SEDITIOUSLY	SEGREGATIONIST	SEISMONASTIC	SELFLESSNESS	SEMESTERING
SEDITIOUSNESS	SEGREGATIONISTS	SEISMONASTIES	SELFLESSNESSES	SEMESTERINGS
SEDITIOUSNESSES	SEGREGATIONS	SEISMONASTY	SELFNESSES	SEMESTRIAL
SEDUCEABLE	SEGREGATIVE	SEISMOSCOPE	SELFSAMENESS	SEMIABSTRACT
SEDUCEMENT	SEGREGATOR	SEISMOSCOPES	SELFSAMENESSES	SEMIABSTRACTION
SEDUCEMENTS	SEGREGATORS	SEISMOSCOPIC	SELLOTAPED	SEMIANGLES
SEDUCINGLY	SEGUIDILLA	SELACHIANS	SELLOTAPES	SEMIANNUAL
SEDUCTIONS	SEGUIDILLAS	SELAGINELLA	SELLOTAPING	SEMIANNUALLY
SEDUCTIVELY	SEIGNEURIAL	SELAGINELLAS	SELTZOGENE	SEMIAQUATIC
SEDUCTIVENESS	SEIGNEURIE	SELDOMNESS	SELTZOGENES	SEMIARBOREAL
SEDUCTIVENESSES	SEIGNEURIES	SELDOMNESSES	SELVEDGING	SEMIARIDITIES
SEDUCTRESS	SEIGNIORAGE	SELECTABLE	SEMAINIERS	SEMIARIDITY
SEDUCTRESSES	SEIGNIORAGES	SELECTIONIST	SEMANTEMES	SEMIAUTOMATED
SEDULITIES	SEIGNIORALTIES	SELECTIONISTS	SEMANTICAL	SEMIAUTOMATIC
SEDULOUSLY	SEIGNIORALTY	SELECTIONS	SEMANTICALLY	SEMIAUTOMATICS
SEDULOUSNESS	SEIGNIORIAL	SELECTIVELY	SEMANTICIST	SEMIAUTONOMOUS
SEDULOUSNESSES	SEIGNIORIES	SELECTIVENESS	SEMANTICISTS	SEMIBASEMENT
SEECATCHES	SEIGNIORSHIP	SELECTIVENESSES	SEMANTIDES	SEMIBASEMENTS
SEECATCHIE	SEIGNIORSHIPS	SELECTIVITIES	SEMANTRONS	SEMIBREVES
SEEDEATERS	SEIGNORAGE	SELECTIVITY	SEMAPHORED	SEMICARBAZIDE
SEEDINESSES	SEIGNORAGES	SELECTNESS	SEMAPHORES	SEMICARBAZIDES
SEEDNESSES	SEIGNORIAL	SELECTNESSES	SEMAPHORIC	SEMICARBAZONE
SEEDSTOCKS	SEIGNORIES	SELECTORATE	SEMAPHORICAL	SEMICARBAZONES

S

SEMICENTENNIAL	SEMIDIAMETERS	SEMIMONTHLY	SEMIPERMANENT	SEMPERVIVUMS
SEMICENTENNIALS	SEMIDIURNAL	SEMIMYSTICAL	SEMIPERMEABLE	SEMPITERNAL
SEMICHORUS	SEMIDIVINE	SEMINALITIES	SEMIPLUMES	SEMPITERNALLY
SEMICHORUSES	SEMIDOCUMENTARY	SEMINALITY	SEMIPOLITICAL	SEMPITERNITIES
SEMICIRCLE	SEMIDOMINANT	SEMINARIAL	SEMIPOPULAR	SEMPITERNITY
SEMICIRCLED	SEMIDRIEST	SEMINARIAN	SEMIPORCELAIN	SEMPITERNUM
SEMICIRCLES	SEMIDRYING	SEMINARIANS	SEMIPORCELAINS	SEMPITERNUMS
SEMICIRCULAR	SEMIDWARFS	SEMINARIES	SEMIPORNOGRAPHY	SEMPSTERING
SEMICIRCULARLY	SEMIDWARVES	SEMINARIST	SEMIPOSTAL	SEMPSTERINGS
SEMICIRQUE	SEMIELLIPTICAL	SEMINARISTS	SEMIPOSTALS	SEMPSTRESS
SEMICIRQUES	SEMIEMPIRICAL	SEMINATING	SEMIPRECIOUS	SEMPSTRESSES
SEMICIVILISED	SEMIEVERGREEN	SEMINATION	SEMIPRIVATE	SEMPSTRESSING
SEMICIVILIZED	SEMIFEUDAL	SEMINATIONS	SEMIPUBLIC	SEMPSTRESSINGS
SEMICLASSIC	SEMIFINALIST	SEMINATURAL	SEMIQUAVER	SENARMONTITE
SEMICLASSICAL	SEMIFINALISTS	SEMINIFEROUS	SEMIQUAVERS	SENARMONTITES
SEMICLASSICS	SEMIFINALS	SEMINOMADIC	SEMIREFINED	SENATORIAL
SEMICOLONIAL	SEMIFINISHED	SEMINOMADS	SEMIRELIGIOUS	SENATORIALLY
SEMICOLONIALISM	SEMIFITTED	SEMINOMATA	SEMIRETIRED	SENATORIAN
SEMICOLONIES	SEMIFLEXIBLE	SEMINUDITIES	SEMIRETIREMENT	SENATORSHIP
SEMICOLONS	SEMIFLUIDIC	SEMINUDITY	SEMIRETIREMENTS	SENATORSHIPS
SEMICOLONY	SEMIFLUIDITIES	SEMIOCHEMICAL	SEMIROUNDS	SENECTITUDE
SEMICOMATOSE	SEMIFLUIDITY	SEMIOCHEMICALS	SEMISACRED	SENECTITUDES
SEMICOMMERCIAL	SEMIFLUIDS	SEMIOFFICIAL	SEMISECRET	SENESCENCE
SEMICONDUCTING	SEMIFORMAL	SEMIOFFICIALLY	SEMISEDENTARY	SENESCENCES
SEMICONDUCTION	SEMIFREDDI	SEMIOLOGIC	SEMISHRUBBY	SENESCHALS
SEMICONDUCTIONS	SEMIFREDDO	SEMIOLOGICAL	SEMISKILLED	SENESCHALSHIP
SEMICONDUCTOR	SEMIFREDDOS	SEMIOLOGICALLY	SEMISOLIDS	SENESCHALSHIPS
SEMICONDUCTORS	SEMIGLOBES	SEMIOLOGIES	SEMISOLUSES	SENHORITAS
SEMICONSCIOUS	SEMIGLOBULAR	SEMIOLOGIST	SEMISUBMERSIBLE	SENILITIES
SEMICONSCIOUSLY	SEMIGLOSSES	SEMIOLOGISTS	SEMISYNTHETIC	SENIORITIES
SEMICONSONANT	SEMIGROUPS	SEMIOPAQUE	SEMITERETE	SENNACHIES
SEMICONSONANTS	SEMIHOBOES	SEMIOTICALLY	SEMITERRESTRIAL	SENSATIONAL
SEMICRYSTALLIC	SEMILEGENDARY	SEMIOTICIAN	SEMITONALLY	SENSATIONALISE
SEMICRYSTALLINE	SEMILETHAL	SEMIOTICIANS	SEMITONICALLY	SENSATIONALISED
SEMICYLINDER	SEMILETHALS	SEMIOTICIST	SEMITRAILER	SENSATIONALISES
SEMICYLINDERS	SEMILIQUID	SEMIOTICISTS	SEMITRAILERS	SENSATIONALISM
SEMICYLINDRICAL	SEMILIQUIDS	SEMIOVIPAROUS	SEMITRANSLUCENT	SENSATIONALISMS
SEMIDARKNESS	SEMILITERATE	SEMIPALMATE	SEMITRANSPARENT	SENSATIONALIST
SEMIDARKNESSES	SEMILITERATES	SEMIPALMATED	SEMITROPIC	SENSATIONALISTS
SEMIDEIFIED	SEMILOGARITHMIC	SEMIPALMATION	SEMITROPICAL	SENSATIONALIZE
SEMIDEIFIES	SEMILUCENT	SEMIPALMATIONS	SEMITROPICS	SENSATIONALIZED
SEMIDEIFYING	SEMILUNATE	SEMIPARASITE	SEMITRUCKS	SENSATIONALIZES
SEMIDEPONENT	SEMILUSTROUS	SEMIPARASITES	SEMIVITREOUS	SENSATIONALLY
SEMIDEPONENTS	SEMIMANUFACTURE	SEMIPARASITIC	SEMIVOCALIC	SENSATIONISM
SEMIDESERT	SEMIMENSTRUAL	SEMIPARASITISM	SEMIVOWELS	SENSATIONISMS
SEMIDESERTS	SEMIMETALLIC	SEMIPARASITISMS	SEMIWEEKLIES	SENSATIONIST
SEMIDETACHED	SEMIMETALS	SEMIPELLUCID	SEMIWEEKLY	SENSATIONISTS
SEMIDETACHEDS	SEMIMONASTIC	SEMIPERIMETER	SEMIYEARLY	SENSATIONLESS
SEMIDIAMETER	SEMIMONTHLIES	SEMIPERIMETERS	SEMPERVIVUM	SENSATIONS

S

SENSELESSLY	SENSUALISTS	SEPARABLENESS	SEPTENTRIONES	SEQUELIZED
SENSELESSNESS	SENSUALITIES	SEPARABLENESSES	SEPTENTRIONS	SEQUELIZES
SENSELESSNESSES	SENSUALITY	SEPARATELY	SEPTICAEMIA	SEQUELIZING
SENSIBILIA	SENSUALIZATION	SEPARATENESS	SEPTICAEMIAS	SEQUENCERS
SENSIBILITIES	SENSUALIZATIONS	SEPARATENESSES	SEPTICAEMIC	SEQUENCIES
SENSIBILITY	SENSUALIZE	SEPARATING	SEPTICALLY	SEQUENCING
SENSIBLENESS	SENSUALIZED	SEPARATION	SEPTICEMIA	SEQUENCINGS
SENSIBLENESSES	SENSUALIZES	SEPARATIONISM	SEPTICEMIAS	SEQUENTIAL
SENSIBLEST	SENSUALIZING	SEPARATIONISMS	SEPTICEMIC	SEQUENTIALITIES
SENSITISATION	SENSUALNESS	SEPARATIONIST	SEPTICIDAL	SEQUENTIALITY
SENSITISATIONS	SENSUALNESSES	SEPARATIONISTS	SEPTICIDALLY	SEQUENTIALLY
SENSITISED	SENSUOSITIES	SEPARATIONS	SEPTICITIES	SEQUESTERED
SENSITISER	SENSUOSITY	SEPARATISM	SEPTIFEROUS	SEQUESTERING
SENSITISERS	SENSUOUSLY	SEPARATISMS	SEPTIFRAGAL	SEQUESTERS
SENSITISES	SENSUOUSNESS	SEPARATIST	SEPTILATERAL	SEQUESTRABLE
SENSITISING	SENSUOUSNESSES	SEPARATISTIC	SEPTILLION	SEQUESTRAL
SENSITIVELY	SENTENCERS	SEPARATISTS	SEPTILLIONS	SEQUESTRANT
SENSITIVENESS	SENTENCING	SEPARATIVE	SEPTILLIONTH	SEQUESTRANTS
SENSITIVENESSES	SENTENCINGS	SEPARATIVELY	SEPTILLIONTHS	SEQUESTRATE
SENSITIVES	SENTENTIAE	SEPARATIVENESS	SEPTIMOLES	SEQUESTRATED
SENSITIVITIES	SENTENTIAL	SEPARATORIES	SEPTIVALENT	SEQUESTRATES
SENSITIVITY	SENTENTIALLY	SEPARATORS	SEPTUAGENARIAN	SEQUESTRATING
SENSITIZATION	SENTENTIOUS	SEPARATORY	SEPTUAGENARIANS	SEQUESTRATION
SENSITIZATIONS	SENTENTIOUSLY	SEPARATRICES	SEPTUAGENARIES	SEQUESTRATIONS
SENSITIZED	SENTENTIOUSNESS	SEPARATRIX	SEPTUAGENARY	SEQUESTRATOR
SENSITIZER	SENTIENCES	SEPARATUMS	SEPTUPLETS	SEQUESTRATORS
SENSITIZERS	SENTIENCIES	SEPIOLITES	SEPTUPLICATE	SEQUESTRUM
SENSITIZES	SENTIENTLY	SEPIOSTAIRE	SEPTUPLICATES	SEQUESTRUMS
SENSITIZING	SENTIMENTAL	SEPIOSTAIRES	SEPTUPLING	SERAPHICAL
SENSITOMETER	SENTIMENTALISE	SEPTATIONS	SEPULCHERED	SERAPHICALLY
SENSITOMETERS	SENTIMENTALISED	SEPTAVALENT	SEPULCHERING	SERAPHINES
SENSITOMETRIC	SENTIMENTALISES	SEPTEMVIRATE	SEPULCHERS	SERASKIERATE
SENSITOMETRIES	SENTIMENTALISM	SEPTEMVIRATES	SEPULCHRAL	SERASKIERATES
SENSITOMETRY	SENTIMENTALISMS	SEPTEMVIRI	SEPULCHRALLY	SERASKIERS
SENSOMOTOR	SENTIMENTALIST	SEPTEMVIRS	SEPULCHRED	SERENADERS
SENSORIALLY	SENTIMENTALISTS	SEPTENARIES	SEPULCHRES	SERENADING
SENSORIMOTOR	SENTIMENTALITY	SEPTENARII	SEPULCHRING	SERENATING
SENSORINEURAL	SENTIMENTALIZE	SEPTENARIUS	SEPULCHROUS	SERENDIPITIES
SENSORIUMS	SENTIMENTALIZED	SEPTENDECILLION	SEPULTURAL	SERENDIPITIST
SENSUALISATION	SENTIMENTALIZES	SEPTENNATE	SEPULTURED	SERENDIPITISTS
SENSUALISATIONS	SENTIMENTALLY	SEPTENNATES	SEPULTURES	SERENDIPITOUS
SENSUALISE	SENTIMENTS	SEPTENNIAL	SEPULTURING	SERENDIPITOUSLY
SENSUALISED	SENTINELED	SEPTENNIALLY	SEQUACIOUS	SERENDIPITY
SENSUALISES	SENTINELING	SEPTENNIUM	SEQUACIOUSLY	SERENENESS
SENSUALISING	SENTINELLED	SEPTENNIUMS	SEQUACIOUSNESS	SERENENESSES
SENSUALISM	SENTINELLING	SEPTENTRIAL	SEQUACITIES	SERENITIES
SENSUALISMS	SEPALODIES	SEPTENTRION	SEQUELISED	SERGEANCIES
SENSUALIST	SEPARABILITIES	SEPTENTRIONAL	SEQUELISES	SERGEANTIES
SENSUALISTIC	SEPARABILITY	SEPTENTRIONALLY	SEQUELISING	SERGEANTSHIP

SERGEANTSHIPS	SERMONETTES	SERPENTIFORM	SERRIEDNESSES	SESQUICENTENARY
SERIALISATION	SERMONICAL	SERPENTINE	SERRULATED	SESQUIOXIDE
SERIALISATIONS	SERMONINGS	SERPENTINED	SERRULATION	SESQUIOXIDES
SERIALISED	SERMONISED	SERPENTINELY	SERRULATIONS	SESQUIPEDAL
SERIALISES	SERMONISER	SERPENTINES	SERTULARIAN	SESQUIPEDALIAN
SERIALISING	SERMONISERS	SERPENTINIC	SERTULARIANS	SESQUIPEDALIANS
SERIALISMS	SERMONISES	SERPENTINING	SERVANTHOOD	SESQUIPEDALITY
SERIALISTS	SERMONISING	SERPENTININGLY	SERVANTHOODS	SESQUIPEDALS
SERIALITIES	SERMONISINGS	SERPENTININGS	SERVANTING	SESQUIPLICATE
SERIALIZATION	SERMONIZED	SERPENTINISE	SERVANTLESS	SESQUISULPHIDE
SERIALIZATIONS	SERMONIZER	SERPENTINISED	SERVANTRIES	SESQUISULPHIDES
SERIALIZED	SERMONIZERS	SERPENTINISES	SERVANTSHIP	SESQUITERPENE
SERIALIZES	SERMONIZES	SERPENTINISING	SERVANTSHIPS	SESQUITERPENES
SERIALIZING	SERMONIZING	SERPENTINITE	SERVEWARES	SESQUITERTIA
SERIATIONS	SERMONIZINGS	SERPENTINITES	SERVICEABILITY	SESQUITERTIAS
SERICICULTURE	SEROCONVERSION	SERPENTINIZE	SERVICEABLE	SESSILITIES
SERICICULTURES	SEROCONVERSIONS	SERPENTINIZED	SERVICEABLENESS	SESSIONALLY
SERICICULTURIST	SEROCONVERT	SERPENTINIZES	SERVICEABLY	SESTERTIUM
SERICITISATION	SEROCONVERTED	SERPENTINIZING	SERVICEBERRIES	SESTERTIUS
SERICITISATIONS	SEROCONVERTING	SERPENTINOUS	SERVICEBERRY	SETACEOUSLY
SERICITIZATION	SEROCONVERTS	SERPENTISE	SERVICELESS	SETIFEROUS
SERICITIZATIONS	SERODIAGNOSES	SERPENTISED	SERVICEMAN	SETIGEROUS
SERICTERIA	SERODIAGNOSIS	SERPENTISES	SERVICEMEN	SETTERWORT
SERICTERIUM	SERODIAGNOSTIC	SERPENTISING	SERVICEWOMAN	SETTERWORTS
SERICULTURAL	SEROGROUPS	SERPENTIZE	SERVICEWOMEN	SETTLEABLE
SERICULTURE	SEROLOGICAL	SERPENTIZED	SERVICINGS	SETTLEDNESS
SERICULTURES	SEROLOGICALLY	SERPENTIZES	SERVIETTES	SETTLEDNESSES
SERICULTURIST	SEROLOGIES	SERPENTIZING	SERVILENESS	SETTLEMENT
SERICULTURISTS	SEROLOGIST	SERPENTLIKE	SERVILENESSES	SETTLEMENTS
SERIGRAPHER	SEROLOGISTS	SERPENTRIES	SERVILISMS	SEVENPENCE
SERIGRAPHERS	SERONEGATIVE	SERPIGINES	SERVILITIES	SEVENPENCES
SERIGRAPHIC	SERONEGATIVITY	SERPIGINOUS	SERVITORIAL	SEVENPENNIES
SERIGRAPHIES	SEROPOSITIVE	SERPIGINOUSLY	SERVITORSHIP	SEVENPENNY
SERIGRAPHS	SEROPOSITIVITY	SERPULITES	SERVITORSHIPS	SEVENTEENS
SERIGRAPHY	SEROPURULENT	SERRADELLA	SERVITRESS	SEVENTEENTH
SERINETTES	SEROSITIES	SERRADELLAS	SERVITRESSES	SEVENTEENTHLY
SERIOCOMIC	SEROTAXONOMIES	SERRADILLA	SERVITUDES	SEVENTEENTHS
SERIOCOMICAL	SEROTAXONOMY	SERRADILLAS	SERVOCONTROL	SEVENTIETH
SERIOCOMICALLY	SEROTHERAPIES	SERRANOIDS	SERVOCONTROLS	SEVENTIETHS
SERIOUSNESS	SEROTHERAPY	SERRASALMO	SERVOMECHANICAL	SEVERABILITIES
SERIOUSNESSES	SEROTINIES	SERRASALMOS	SERVOMECHANISM	SEVERABILITY
SERJEANCIES	SEROTINOUS	SERRATIONS	SERVOMECHANISMS	SEVERALFOLD
SERJEANTIES	SEROTONERGIC	SERRATIROSTRAL	SERVOMOTOR	SEVERALTIES
SERJEANTRIES	SEROTONINERGIC	SERRATULATE	SERVOMOTORS	SEVERANCES
SERJEANTRY	SEROTONINS	SERRATURES	SESQUIALTER	SEVERENESS
SERJEANTSHIP	SEROTYPING	SERRATUSES	SESQUIALTERA	SEVERENESSES
SERJEANTSHIPS	SEROTYPINGS	SERREFILES	SESQUIALTERAS	SEVERITIES
SERMONEERS	SEROUSNESS	SERRICORNS	SESQUIALTERS	SEWABILITIES
SERMONETTE	SEROUSNESSES	SERRIEDNESS	SESQUICARBONATE	SEWABILITY

S

SEXAGENARIAN	SEXTUPLIES	SHADOWLIKE	SHAMPOOING	SHARKSKINS
SEXAGENARIANS	SEXTUPLING	SHAGGEDNESS	SHANACHIES	SHARKSUCKER
SEXAGENARIES	SEXTUPLYING	SHAGGEDNESSES	SHANDRYDAN	SHARKSUCKERS
SEXAGENARY	SEXUALISATION	SHAGGINESS	SHANDRYDANS	SHARPBENDER
SEXAGESIMAL	SEXUALISATIONS	SHAGGINESSES	SHANDYGAFF	SHARPBENDERS
SEXAGESIMALLY	SEXUALISED	SHAGGYMANE	SHANDYGAFFS	SHARPENERS
SEXAGESIMALS	SEXUALISES	SHAGGYMANES	SHANGHAIED	SHARPENING
SEXAHOLICS	SEXUALISING	SHAGREENED	SHANGHAIER	SHARPENINGS
SEXANGULAR	SEXUALISMS	SHAGTASTIC	SHANGHAIERS	SHARPNESSES
SEXANGULARLY	SEXUALISTS	SHAHTOOSHES	SHANGHAIING	SHARPSHOOTER
SEXAVALENT	SEXUALITIES	SHAKEDOWNS	SHANKBONES	SHARPSHOOTERS
SEXCAPADES	SEXUALIZATION	SHAKINESSES	SHANKPIECE	SHARPSHOOTING
SEXCENTENARIES	SEXUALIZATIONS	SHAKSHUKAS	SHANKPIECES	SHARPSHOOTINGS
SEXCENTENARY	SEXUALIZED	SHAKUHACHI	SHANTYTOWN	SHARPTAILS
SEXDECILLION	SEXUALIZES	SHAKUHACHIS	SHANTYTOWNS	SHASHLICKS
SEXDECILLIONS	SEXUALIZING	SHALLOWEST	SHAPELESSLY	SHATOOSHES
SEXENNIALLY	SFORZANDOS	SHALLOWING	SHAPELESSNESS	SHATTERERS
SEXENNIALS	SHABBINESS	SHALLOWINGS	SHAPELESSNESSES	SHATTERIER
SEXERCISES	SHABBINESSES	SHALLOWNESS	SHAPELIEST	SHATTERIEST
SEXINESSES	SHABRACQUE	SHALLOWNESSES	SHAPELINESS	SHATTERING
SEXIVALENT	SHABRACQUES	SHAMANISMS	SHAPELINESSES	SHATTERINGLY
SEXLESSNESS	SHACKLEBONE	SHAMANISTIC	SHAPESHIFTER	SHATTERPROOF
SEXLESSNESSES	SHACKLEBONES	SHAMANISTS	SHAPESHIFTERS	SHAUCHLIER
SEXLOCULAR	SHACKTOWNS	SHAMATEURISM	SHAPESHIFTING	SHAUCHLIEST
SEXOLOGICAL	SHADBERRIES	SHAMATEURISMS	SHAPESHIFTINGS	SHAUCHLING
SEXOLOGIES	SHADBUSHES	SHAMATEURS	SHAPEWEARS	SHAVASANAS
SEXOLOGIST	SHADCHANIM	SHAMBLIEST	SHARAWADGI	SHAVELINGS
SEXOLOGISTS	SHADINESSES	SHAMBLINGS	SHARAWADGIS	SHAVETAILS
SEXPARTITE	SHADKHANIM	SHAMBOLICALLY	SHARAWAGGI	SHEARLINGS
SEXPLOITATION	SHADOWBANNED	SHAMEFACED	SHARAWAGGIS	SHEARWATER
SEXPLOITATIONS	SHADOWBANNING	SHAMEFACEDLY	SHAREABILITIES	SHEARWATERS
SEXTARIUSES	SHADOWBANS	SHAMEFACEDNESS	SHAREABILITY	SHEATFISHES
SEXTILLION	SHADOWBOXED	SHAMEFASTNESS	SHARECROPPED	SHEATHBILL
SEXTILLIONS	SHADOWBOXES	SHAMEFASTNESSES	SHARECROPPER	SHEATHBILLS
SEXTILLIONTH	SHADOWBOXING	SHAMEFULLY	SHARECROPPERS	SHEATHFISH
SEXTILLIONTHS	SHADOWCAST	SHAMEFULNESS	SHARECROPPING	SHEATHFISHES
SEXTODECIMO	SHADOWCASTED	SHAMEFULNESSES	SHARECROPPINGS	SHEATHIEST
SEXTODECIMOS	SHADOWCASTING	SHAMELESSLY	SHARECROPS	SHEATHINGS
SEXTONESSES	SHADOWCASTINGS	SHAMELESSNESS	SHAREFARMER	SHEATHLESS
SEXTONSHIP	SHADOWCASTS	SHAMELESSNESSES	SHAREFARMERS	SHEATHLIKE
SEXTONSHIPS	SHADOWGRAPH	SHAMEWORTHIER	SHAREHOLDER	SHEBAGGING
SEXTORTION	SHADOWGRAPHIES	SHAMEWORTHIEST	SHAREHOLDERS	SHEBAGGINGS
SEXTORTIONS	SHADOWGRAPHS	SHAMEWORTHY	SHAREHOLDING	SHEBEENERS
SEXTUPLETS	SHADOWGRAPHY	SHAMIANAHS	SHAREHOLDINGS	SHEBEENING
SEXTUPLICATE	SHADOWIEST	SHAMIYANAH	SHAREMILKER	SHEBEENINGS
SEXTUPLICATED	SHADOWINESS	SHAMIYANAHS	SHAREMILKERS	SHECHITAHS
SEXTUPLICATES	SHADOWINESSES	SHAMMASHIM	SHARENTING	SHECKLATON
SEXTUPLICATING	SHADOWINGS	SHAMOISING	SHARENTINGS	SHECKLATONS
SEXTUPLIED	SHADOWLESS	SHAMPOOERS	SHAREWARES	SHEEPBERRIES

S

SHEEPBERRY	SHELLFISHES	SHERIFFDOMS	SHIMOZZLES	SHIRTSLEEVES
SHEEPCOTES	SHELLINESS	SHERIFFSHIP	SHINGLIEST	SHIRTTAILED
SHEEPFOLDS	SHELLINESSES	SHERIFFSHIPS	SHINGLINGS	SHIRTTAILING
SHEEPHEADS	SHELLPROOF	SHERLOCKED	SHINGUARDS	SHIRTTAILS
SHEEPHERDER	SHELLSHOCK	SHERLOCKING	SHININESSES	SHIRTWAIST
SHEEPHERDERS	SHELLSHOCKED	SHEWBREADS	SHININGNESS	SHIRTWAISTED
SHEEPHERDING	SHELLSHOCKS	SHIBBOLETH	SHININGNESSES	SHIRTWAISTER
SHEEPHERDINGS	SHELLWORKS	SHIBBOLETHS	SHINLEAVES	SHIRTWAISTERS
SHEEPISHLY	SHELLYCOAT	SHIBUICHIS	SHINNERIES	SHIRTWAISTS
SHEEPISHNESS	SHELLYCOATS	SHIDDUCHIM	SHINNEYING	SHITCANNED
SHEEPISHNESSES	SHELTERBELT	SHIELDINGS	SHINPLASTER	SHITCANNING
SHEEPSHANK	SHELTERBELTS	SHIELDLESS	SHINPLASTERS	SHITHOUSES
SHEEPSHANKS	SHELTERERS	SHIELDLIKE	SHINSPLINTS	SHITPOSTED
SHEEPSHEAD	SHELTERIER	SHIELDLING	SHIPBOARDS	SHITPOSTER
SHEEPSHEADS	SHELTERIEST	SHIELDLINGS	SHIPBROKER	SHITPOSTERS
SHEEPSHEARER	SHELTERING	SHIELDRAKE	SHIPBROKERS	SHITPOSTING
SHEEPSHEARERS	SHELTERINGS	SHIELDRAKES	SHIPBUILDER	SHITSTORMS
SHEEPSHEARING	SHELTERLESS	SHIELDWALL	SHIPBUILDERS	SHITTIMWOOD
SHEEPSHEARINGS	SHEMOZZLED	SHIELDWALLS	SHIPBUILDING	SHITTIMWOODS
SHEEPSKINS	SHEMOZZLES	SHIFTINESS	SHIPBUILDINGS	SHITTINESS
SHEEPTRACK	SHEMOZZLING	SHIFTINESSES	SHIPFITTER	SHITTINESSES
SHEEPTRACKS	SHENANIGAN	SHIFTLESSLY	SHIPFITTERS	SHIVAREEING
SHEEPWALKS	SHENANIGANS	SHIFTLESSNESS	SHIPLAPPED	SHIVERIEST
SHEERNESSES	SHEPHERDED	SHIFTLESSNESSES	SHIPLAPPING	SHIVERINGLY
SHEETROCKED	SHEPHERDESS	SHIFTSTICK	SHIPLAPPINGS	SHIVERINGS
SHEETROCKING	SHEPHERDESSES	SHIFTSTICKS	SHIPMASTER	SHLEMIEHLS
SHEETROCKS	SHEPHERDING	SHIFTWORKS	SHIPMASTERS	SHLEMOZZLE
SHEIKHDOMS	SHEPHERDINGS	SHIGELLOSES	SHIPOWNERS	SHLEMOZZLED
SHELDDUCKS	SHEPHERDLESS	SHIGELLOSIS	SHIPPOUNDS	SHLEMOZZLES
SHELDRAKES	SHEPHERDLING	SHIKARRING	SHIPWRECKED	SHLEMOZZLING
SHELFROOMS	SHEPHERDLINGS	SHILLABERS	SHIPWRECKING	SHLEPPIEST
SHELFTALKER	SHERARDISATION	SHILLALAHS	SHIPWRECKS	SHLIMAZELS
SHELFTALKERS	SHERARDISATIONS	SHILLELAGH	SHIPWRIGHT	SHLOCKIEST
SHELLACKED	SHERARDISE	SHILLELAGHS	SHIPWRIGHTS	SHLUMPIEST
SHELLACKER	SHERARDISED	SHILLELAHS	SHIRETOWNS	SHMALTZIER
SHELLACKERS	SHERARDISES	SHILLINGLESS	SHIRRALEES	SHMALTZIEST
SHELLACKING	SHERARDISING	SHILLINGSWORTH	SHIRTBANDS	SHMOOZIEST
SHELLACKINGS	SHERARDIZATION	SHILLINGSWORTHS	SHIRTDRESS	SHMUCKIEST
SHELLBACKS	SHERARDIZATIONS	SHILLYSHALLIED	SHIRTDRESSES	SHOALINESS
SHELLBARKS	SHERARDIZE	SHILLYSHALLIER	SHIRTFRONT	SHOALINESSES
SHELLBOUND	SHERARDIZED	SHILLYSHALLIERS	SHIRTFRONTED	SHOALNESSES
SHELLCRACKER	SHERARDIZES	SHILLYSHALLIES	SHIRTFRONTING	SHOCKABILITIES
SHELLCRACKERS	SHERARDIZING	SHILLYSHALLY	SHIRTFRONTS	SHOCKABILITY
SHELLDRAKE	SHEREEFIAN	SHILLYSHALLYING	SHIRTINESS	SHOCKHEADED
SHELLDRAKES	SHERGOTTITE	SHIMMERIER	SHIRTINESSES	SHOCKINGLY
SHELLDUCKS	SHERGOTTITES	SHIMMERIEST	SHIRTMAKER	SHOCKINGNESS
SHELLFIRES	SHERIFFALTIES	SHIMMERING	SHIRTMAKERS	SHOCKINGNESSES
SHELLFISHERIES	SHERIFFALTY	SHIMMERINGLY	SHIRTSLEEVE	SHOCKPROOF
SHELLFISHERY	SHERIFFDOM	SHIMMERINGS	SHIRTSLEEVED	SHOCKSTALL

S

SHOCKSTALLS	SHOPWALKER	SHORTSWORD	SHOWERPROOFING	SHRIMPINGS
SHOCKUMENTARIES	SHOPWALKERS	SHORTSWORDS	SHOWERPROOFINGS	SHRIMPLIKE
SHOCKUMENTARY	SHOPWINDOW	SHORTWAVED	SHOWERPROOFS	SHRINELIKE
SHODDINESS	SHOPWINDOWS	SHORTWAVES	SHOWGROUND	SHRINKABLE
SHODDINESSES	SHOREBIRDS	SHORTWAVING	SHOWGROUNDS	SHRINKAGES
SHOEBLACKS	SHOREFRONT	SHOTCRETES	SHOWINESSES	SHRINKFLATION
SHOEBRUSHES	SHOREFRONTS	SHOTFIRERS	SHOWJUMPED	SHRINKFLATIONS
SHOEGAZING	SHORELINES	SHOTGUNNED	SHOWJUMPER	SHRINKINGLY
SHOEGAZINGS	SHORESIDES	SHOTGUNNER	SHOWJUMPERS	SHRINKPACK
SHOEHORNED	SHOREWARDS	SHOTGUNNERS	SHOWJUMPING	SHRINKPACKS
SHOEHORNING	SHOREWEEDS	SHOTGUNNING	SHOWJUMPINGS	SHRITCHING
SHOEMAKERS	SHORTARSES	SHOTMAKERS	SHOWMANCES	SHRIVELING
SHOEMAKING	SHORTBOARD	SHOTMAKING	SHOWMANLIER	SHRIVELLED
SHOEMAKINGS	SHORTBOARDS	SHOTMAKINGS	SHOWMANLIEST	SHRIVELLING
SHOESHINES	SHORTBREAD	SHOULDERED	SHOWMANSHIP	SHROFFAGES
SHOESTRING	SHORTBREADS	SHOULDERING	SHOWMANSHIPS	SHROUDIEST
SHOESTRINGS	SHORTCAKES	SHOULDERINGS	SHOWPEOPLE	SHROUDINGS
SHOGGLIEST	SHORTCHANGE	SHOUTHERED	SHOWPERSON	SHROUDLESS
SHOGUNATES	SHORTCHANGED	SHOUTHERING	SHOWPERSONS	SHRUBBERIED
SHONGOLOLO	SHORTCHANGER	SHOUTINGLY	SHOWPIECES	SHRUBBERIES
SHONGOLOLOS	SHORTCHANGERS	SHOUTLINES	SHOWPLACES	SHRUBBIEST
SHOOGIEING	SHORTCHANGES	SHOVELBOARD	SHOWROOMING	SHRUBBINESS
SHOOGLIEST	SHORTCHANGING	SHOVELBOARDS	SHOWROOMINGS	SHRUBBINESSES
SHOOTAROUND	SHORTCOMING	SHOVELFULS	SHOWRUNNER	SHRUBLANDS
SHOOTAROUNDS	SHORTCOMINGS	SHOVELHEAD	SHOWRUNNERS	SHTETELACH
SHOOTDOWNS	SHORTCRUST	SHOVELHEADS	SHOWSTOPPER	SHTICKIEST
SHOPAHOLIC	SHORTCUTTING	SHOVELLERS	SHOWSTOPPERS	SHTREIMELS
SHOPAHOLICS	SHORTENERS	SHOVELLING	SHOWSTOPPING	SHUBUNKINS
SHOPAHOLISM	SHORTENING	SHOVELNOSE	SHOWWOMANSHIP	SHUDDERIER
SHOPAHOLISMS	SHORTENINGS	SHOVELNOSES	SHOWWOMANSHIPS	SHUDDERIEST
SHOPBOARDS	SHORTFALLS	SHOVELSFUL	SHREDDIEST	SHUDDERING
SHOPBREAKER	SHORTGOWNS	SHOWBIZZES	SHREDDINGS	SHUDDERINGLY
SHOPBREAKERS	SHORTHAIRED	SHOWBIZZIER	SHREWDNESS	SHUDDERINGS
SHOPBREAKING	SHORTHAIRS	SHOWBIZZIEST	SHREWDNESSES	SHUDDERSOME
SHOPBREAKINGS	SHORTHANDED	SHOWBOATED	SHREWISHLY	SHUFFLEBOARD
SHOPFITTER	SHORTHANDS	SHOWBOATER	SHREWISHNESS	SHUFFLEBOARDS
SHOPFITTERS	SHORTHEADS	SHOWBOATERS	SHREWISHNESSES	SHUFFLINGLY
SHOPFRONTS	SHORTHORNS	SHOWBOATING	SHREWMOUSE	SHUFFLINGS
SHOPHOUSES	SHORTLISTED	SHOWBREADS	SHRIECHING	SHUNAMITISM
SHOPKEEPER	SHORTLISTING	SHOWCASING	SHRIEKIEST	SHUNAMITISMS
SHOPKEEPERS	SHORTLISTS	SHOWERHEAD	SHRIEKINGLY	SHUNPIKERS
SHOPKEEPING	SHORTNESSES	SHOWERHEADS	SHRIEKINGS	SHUNPIKING
SHOPKEEPINGS	SHORTSHEET	SHOWERIEST	SHRIEVALTIES	SHUNPIKINGS
SHOPLIFTED	SHORTSHEETED	SHOWERINESS	SHRIEVALTY	SHUTTERBUG
SHOPLIFTER	SHORTSHEETING	SHOWERINESSES	SHRILLIEST	SHUTTERBUGS
SHOPLIFTERS	SHORTSHEETS	SHOWERINGS	SHRILLINGS	SHUTTERING
SHOPLIFTING	SHORTSIGHTED	SHOWERLESS	SHRILLNESS	SHUTTERINGS
SHOPLIFTINGS	SHORTSIGHTEDLY	SHOWERPROOF	SHRILLNESSES	SHUTTERLESS
SHOPSOILED	SHORTSTOPS	SHOWERPROOFED	SHRIMPIEST	SHUTTLECOCK

SHUTTLECOCKED	SICKNURSINGS	SIDESWIPERS	SIGNALISATION	SILENTIARY
SHUTTLECOCKING	SIDDHUISMS	SIDESWIPES	SIGNALISATIONS	SILENTNESS
SHUTTLECOCKS	SIDEARMERS	SIDESWIPING	SIGNALISED	SILENTNESSES
SHUTTLELESS	SIDEARMING	SIDETABLES	SIGNALISES	SILHOUETTE
SHUTTLEWISE	SIDEBOARDS	SIDETRACKED	SIGNALISING	SILHOUETTED
SHYLOCKING	SIDEBURNED	SIDETRACKING	SIGNALIZATION	SILHOUETTES
SIALAGOGIC	SIDECHAIRS	SIDETRACKS	SIGNALIZATIONS	SILHOUETTING
SIALAGOGUE	SIDECHECKS	SIDEWHEELER	SIGNALIZED	SILHOUETTIST
SIALAGOGUES	SIDEDNESSES	SIDEWHEELERS	SIGNALIZES	SILHOUETTISTS
SIALOGOGIC	SIDEDRESSES	SIDEWHEELS	SIGNALIZING	SILICATING
SIALOGOGUE	SIDELEVERS	SIDEWINDER	SIGNALLERS	SILICICOLOUS
SIALOGOGUES	SIDELIGHTS	SIDEWINDERS	SIGNALLING	SILICIFEROUS
SIALOGRAMS	SIDELINERS	SIEGECRAFT	SIGNALLINGS	SILICIFICATION
SIALOGRAPHIES	SIDELINING	SIEGECRAFTS	SIGNALMENT	SILICIFICATIONS
SIALOGRAPHY	SIDEPIECES	SIEGEWORKS	SIGNALMENTS	SILICIFIED
SIALOLITHS	SIDERATING	SIFFLEUSES	SIGNATORIES	SILICIFIES
SIALORRHOEA	SIDERATION	SIGHTLESSLY	SIGNATURES	SILICIFYING
SIALORRHOEAS	SIDERATIONS	SIGHTLESSNESS	SIGNBOARDS	SILICONISED
SIBILANCES	SIDEREALLY	SIGHTLESSNESSES	SIGNEURIES	SILICONIZED
SIBILANCIES	SIDEROLITE	SIGHTLIEST	SIGNIFIABLE	SILICOTICS
SIBILANTLY	SIDEROLITES	SIGHTLINES	SIGNIFICANCE	SILICULOSE
SIBILATING	SIDEROPENIA	SIGHTLINESS	SIGNIFICANCES	SILIQUACEOUS
SIBILATION	SIDEROPENIAS	SIGHTLINESSES	SIGNIFICANCIES	SILKALENES
SIBILATIONS	SIDEROPHILE	SIGHTSCREEN	SIGNIFICANCY	SILKALINES
SIBILATORS	SIDEROPHILES	SIGHTSCREENS	SIGNIFICANT	SILKGROWER
SIBILATORY	SIDEROPHILIC	SIGHTSEEING	SIGNIFICANTLY	SILKGROWERS
SICCATIVES	SIDEROPHILIN	SIGHTSEEINGS	SIGNIFICANTS	SILKINESSES
SICILIANAS	SIDEROPHILINS	SIGHTSEERS	SIGNIFICATE	SILKOLINES
SICILIANOS	SIDEROSTAT	SIGHTWORTHIER	SIGNIFICATES	SILKSCREEN
SICILIENNE	SIDEROSTATIC	SIGHTWORTHIEST	SIGNIFICATION	SILKSCREENED
SICILIENNES	SIDEROSTATS	SIGHTWORTHY	SIGNIFICATIONS	SILKSCREENING
SICKENINGLY	SIDESADDLE	SIGILLARIAN	SIGNIFICATIVE	SILKSCREENS
SICKENINGS	SIDESADDLES	SIGILLARIANS	SIGNIFICATIVELY	SILLIMANITE
SICKERNESS	SIDESHOOTS	SIGILLARID	SIGNIFICATOR	SILLIMANITES
SICKERNESSES	SIDESLIPPED	SIGILLARIDS	SIGNIFICATORS	SILLINESSES
SICKISHNESS	SIDESLIPPING	SIGILLATION	SIGNIFICATORY	SILTATIONS
SICKISHNESSES	SIDESPLITS	SIGILLATIONS	SIGNIFIEDS	SILTSTONES
SICKLAEMIA	SIDESPLITTING	SIGMATIONS	SIGNIFIERS	SILVERBACK
SICKLAEMIAS	SIDESPLITTINGLY	SIGMATISMS	SIGNIFYING	SILVERBACKS
SICKLAEMIC	SIDESTEPPED	SIGMATRONS	SIGNIFYINGS	SILVERBERRIES
SICKLEBILL	SIDESTEPPER	SIGMOIDALLY	SIGNIORIES	SILVERBERRY
SICKLEBILLS	SIDESTEPPERS	SIGMOIDECTOMIES	SIGNORINAS	SILVERBILL
SICKLEMIAS	SIDESTEPPING	SIGMOIDECTOMY	SIGNPOSTED	SILVERBILLS
SICKLINESS	SIDESTEPPINGS	SIGMOIDOSCOPE	SIGNPOSTING	SILVEREYES
SICKLINESSES	SIDESTREAM	SIGMOIDOSCOPES	SIGNPOSTINGS	SILVERFISH
SICKNESSES	SIDESTROKE	SIGMOIDOSCOPIC	SIKORSKIES	SILVERFISHES
SICKNURSED	SIDESTROKES	SIGMOIDOSCOPIES	SILDENAFIL	SILVERHORN
SICKNURSES	SIDESWIPED	SIGMOIDOSCOPY	SILDENAFILS	SILVERHORNS
SICKNURSING	SIDESWIPER	SIGNALINGS	SILENTIARIES	SILVERIEST

S

SILVERINESS	SIMONIACALLY	SIMVASTATIN	SINGSONGIEST	SINOLOGISTS
SILVERINESSES	SIMONISING	SIMVASTATINS	SINGSONGING	SINOLOGUES
SILVERINGS	SIMONIZING	SINANTHROPUS	SINGSPIELS	SINSEMILLA
SILVERISED	SIMPERINGLY	SINANTHROPUSES	SINGULARISATION	SINSEMILLAS
SILVERISES	SIMPERINGS	SINARCHISM	SINGULARISE	SINTERABILITIES
SILVERISING	SIMPLEMINDED	SINARCHISMS	SINGULARISED	SINTERABILITY
SILVERIZED	SIMPLEMINDEDLY	SINARCHIST	SINGULARISES	SINTERIEST
SILVERIZES	SIMPLENESS	SINARCHISTS	SINGULARISING	SINUATIONS
SILVERIZING	SIMPLENESSES	SINARQUISM	SINGULARISM	SINUITISES
SILVERLING	SIMPLESSES	SINARQUISMS	SINGULARISMS	SINUOSITIES
SILVERLINGS	SIMPLETONS	SINARQUIST	SINGULARIST	SINUOUSNESS
SILVERPOINT	SIMPLICIAL	SINARQUISTS	SINGULARISTS	SINUOUSNESSES
SILVERPOINTS	SIMPLICIALLY	SINCERENESS	SINGULARITIES	SINUPALLIAL
SILVERSIDE	SIMPLICIDENTATE	SINCERENESSES	SINGULARITY	SINUPALLIATE
SILVERSIDES	SIMPLICITER	SINCERITIES	SINGULARIZATION	SINUSITISES
SILVERSKIN	SIMPLICITIES	SINCIPITAL	SINGULARIZE	SINUSOIDAL
SILVERSKINS	SIMPLICITY	SINDONOLOGIES	SINGULARIZED	SINUSOIDALLY
SILVERSMITH	SIMPLIFIABLE	SINDONOLOGIST	SINGULARIZES	SIPHONAGES
SILVERSMITHING	SIMPLIFICATION	SINDONOLOGISTS	SINGULARIZING	SIPHONOGAM
SILVERSMITHINGS	SIMPLIFICATIONS	SINDONOLOGY	SINGULARLY	SIPHONOGAMIES
SILVERSMITHS	SIMPLIFICATIVE	SINDONOPHANIES	SINGULARNESS	SIPHONOGAMS
SILVERTAIL	SIMPLIFICATOR	SINDONOPHANY	SINGULARNESSES	SIPHONOGAMY
SILVERTAILS	SIMPLIFICATORS	SINECURISM	SINGULTUSES	SIPHONOPHORE
SILVERTIPS	SIMPLIFIED	SINECURISMS	SINICISING	SIPHONOPHORES
SILVERWARE	SIMPLIFIER	SINECURIST	SINICIZING	SIPHONOPHOROUS
SILVERWARES	SIMPLIFIERS	SINECURISTS	SINISTERITIES	SIPHONOSTELE
SILVERWEED	SIMPLIFIES	SINEWINESS	SINISTERITY	SIPHONOSTELES
SILVERWEEDS	SIMPLIFYING	SINEWINESSES	SINISTERLY	SIPHONOSTELIC
SILVESTRIAN	SIMPLISTES	SINFONIETTA	SINISTERNESS	SIPHUNCLES
SILVICULTURAL	SIMPLISTIC	SINFONIETTAS	SINISTERNESSES	SIPUNCULID
SILVICULTURALLY	SIMPLISTICALLY	SINFULNESS	SINISTERWISE	SIPUNCULIDS
SILVICULTURE	SIMULACRES	SINFULNESSES	SINISTRALITIES	SIPUNCULOID
SILVICULTURES	SIMULACRUM	SINGABLENESS	SINISTRALITY	SIPUNCULOIDS
SILVICULTURIST	SIMULACRUMS	SINGABLENESSES	SINISTRALLY	SIRENISING
SILVICULTURISTS	SIMULATING	SINGALONGS	SINISTRALS	SIRENIZING
SILYMARINS	SIMULATION	SINGLEDOMS	SINISTRODEXTRAL	SIRONISING
SIMAROUBACEOUS	SIMULATIONS	SINGLEHOOD	SINISTRORSAL	SIRONIZING
SIMAROUBAS	SIMULATIVE	SINGLEHOODS	SINISTRORSALLY	SISERARIES
SIMARUBACEOUS	SIMULATIVELY	SINGLENESS	SINISTRORSE	SISSINESSES
SIMILARITIES	SIMULATORS	SINGLENESSES	SINISTRORSELY	SISSYNESSES
SIMILARITY	SIMULATORY	SINGLESTICK	SINISTROUS	SISTERHOOD
SIMILATIVE	SIMULCASTED	SINGLESTICKS	SINISTROUSLY	SISTERHOODS
SIMILISING	SIMULCASTING	SINGLETONS	SINLESSNESS	SISTERLESS
SIMILITUDE	SIMULCASTS	SINGLETRACK	SINLESSNESSES	SISTERLIER
SIMILITUDES	SIMULTANEITIES	SINGLETRACKS	SINNINGIAS	SISTERLIEST
SIMILIZING	SIMULTANEITY	SINGLETREE	SINOATRIAL	SISTERLIKE
SIMILLIMUM	SIMULTANEOUS	SINGLETREES	SINOLOGICAL	SISTERLINESS
SIMILLIMUMS	SIMULTANEOUSES	SINGSONGED	SINOLOGIES	SISTERLINESSES
SIMONIACAL	SIMULTANEOUSLY	SINGSONGIER	SINOLOGIST	SITATUNGAS

S

SITIOLOGIES	SKELETALLY	SKIJUMPERS	SKIRMISHINGS	SKYSURFING
SITIOPHOBIA	SKELETOGENOUS	SKIKJORERS	SKITTERIER	SKYSURFINGS
SITIOPHOBIAS	SKELETONIC	SKIKJORING	SKITTERIEST	SKYWATCHED
SITOLOGIES	SKELETONISE	SKIKJORINGS	SKITTERING	SKYWATCHES
SITOPHOBIA	SKELETONISED	SKILFULNESS	SKITTISHLY	SKYWATCHING
SITOPHOBIAS	SKELETONISER	SKILFULNESSES	SKITTISHNESS	SKYWRITERS
SITOSTEROL	SKELETONISERS	SKILLCENTRE	SKITTISHNESSES	SKYWRITING
SITOSTEROLS	SKELETONISES	SKILLCENTRES	SKORDALIAS	SKYWRITINGS
SITUATIONAL	SKELETONISING	SKILLESSNESS	SKREEGHING	SKYWRITTEN
SITUATIONALLY	SKELETONIZE	SKILLESSNESSES	SKREIGHING	SLABBERERS
SITUATIONISM	SKELETONIZED	SKILLFULLY	SKRIECHING	SLABBERIER
SITUATIONISMS	SKELETONIZER	SKILLFULNESS	SKRIEGHING	SLABBERIEST
SITUATIONS	SKELETONIZERS	SKILLFULNESSES	SKRIMMAGED	SLABBERING
SITUTUNGAS	SKELETONIZES	SKILLIGALEE	SKRIMMAGES	SLABBINESS
SITZKRIEGS	SKELETONIZING	SKILLIGALEES	SKRIMMAGING	SLABBINESSES
SIXPENNIES	SKELLOCHED	SKILLIGOLEE	SKRIMSHANK	SLABSTONES
SIXTEENERS	SKELLOCHING	SKILLIGOLEES	SKRIMSHANKED	SLACKENERS
SIXTEENMOS	SKELTERING	SKIMBOARDED	SKRIMSHANKER	SLACKENING
SIXTEENTHLY	SKEPTICALLY	SKIMBOARDER	SKRIMSHANKERS	SLACKENINGS
SIXTEENTHS	SKEPTICALNESS	SKIMBOARDERS	SKRIMSHANKING	SLACKLINING
SIZABLENESS	SKEPTICALNESSES	SKIMBOARDING	SKRIMSHANKS	SLACKLININGS
SIZABLENESSES	SKEPTICISM	SKIMBOARDS	SKULDUDDERIES	SLACKNESSES
SIZARSHIPS	SKEPTICISMS	SKIMMINGLY	SKULDUDDERY	SLACKTIVISM
SIZEABLENESS	SKETCHABILITIES	SKIMMINGTON	SKULDUGGERIES	SLACKTIVISMS
SIZEABLENESSES	SKETCHABILITY	SKIMMINGTONS	SKULDUGGERY	SLACKTIVIST
SIZINESSES	SKETCHABLE	SKIMOBILED	SKULKINGLY	SLACKTIVISTS
SIZZLINGLY	SKETCHBOOK	SKIMOBILES	SKULLDUGGERIES	SLACTIVISM
SJAMBOKING	SKETCHBOOKS	SKIMOBILING	SKULLDUGGERY	SLACTIVISMS
SJAMBOKKED	SKETCHIEST	SKIMPINESS	SKUMMERING	SLACTIVIST
SJAMBOKKING	SKETCHINESS	SKIMPINESSES	SKUNKBIRDS	SLACTIVISTS
SKAITHLESS	SKETCHINESSES	SKIMPINGLY	SKUNKBUSHES	SLAISTERED
SKALDSHIPS	SKETCHPADS	SKINFLICKS	SKUNKWEEDS	SLAISTERIES
SKANKINESS	SKEUOMORPH	SKINFLINTIER	SKUTTERUDITE	SLAISTERING
SKANKINESSES	SKEUOMORPHIC	SKINFLINTIEST	SKUTTERUDITES	SLALOMISTS
SKATEBOARD	SKEUOMORPHISM	SKINFLINTS	SKYBRIDGES	SLAMDANCED
SKATEBOARDED	SKEUOMORPHISMS	SKINFLINTY	SKYDIVINGS	SLAMDANCES
SKATEBOARDER	SKEUOMORPHS	SKINNINESS	SKYJACKERS	SLAMDANCING
SKATEBOARDERS	SKEWBACKED	SKINNINESSES	SKYJACKING	SLAMMAKINS
SKATEBOARDING	SKEWNESSES	SKINTIGHTER	SKYJACKINGS	SLAMMERKIN
SKATEBOARDINGS	SKIAGRAPHS	SKINTIGHTEST	SKYLARKERS	SLAMMERKINS
SKATEBOARDS	SKIAMACHIES	SKINTIGHTS	SKYLARKING	SLANDERERS
SKATEPARKS	SKIASCOPES	SKIPPERING	SKYLARKINGS	SLANDERING
SKATEPUNKS	SKIASCOPIES	SKIPPERINGS	SKYLIGHTED	SLANDEROUS
SKEDADDLED	SKIBOBBERS	SKIPPINGLY	SKYROCKETED	SLANDEROUSLY
SKEDADDLER	SKIBOBBING	SKIRMISHED	SKYROCKETING	SLANDEROUSNESS
SKEDADDLERS	SKIBOBBINGS	SKIRMISHER	SKYROCKETS	SLANGINESS
SKEDADDLES	SKIDDOOING	SKIRMISHERS	SKYSCRAPER	SLANGINESSES
SKEDADDLING	SKIDOOINGS	SKIRMISHES	SKYSCRAPERS	SLANGINGLY
SKELDERING	SKIJORINGS	SKIRMISHING	SKYSURFERS	SLANGUAGES

SLANTENDICULAR	SLEAZEBALLS	SLEUTHHOUNDS	SLIPSHEETED	SLOPESIDES
SLANTINDICULAR	SLEAZINESS	SLEUTHINGS	SLIPSHEETING	SLOPINGNESS
SLANTINGLY	SLEAZINESSES	SLICKENERS	SLIPSHEETS	SLOPINGNESSES
SLANTINGWAYS	SLEDGEHAMMER	SLICKENING	SLIPSHODDINESS	SLOPPINESS
SLAPDASHED	SLEDGEHAMMERED	SLICKENSIDE	SLIPSHODNESS	SLOPPINESSES
SLAPDASHES	SLEDGEHAMMERING	SLICKENSIDED	SLIPSHODNESSES	SLOPWORKER
SLAPDASHING	SLEDGEHAMMERS	SLICKENSIDES	SLIPSLOPPIER	SLOPWORKERS
SLAPHAPPIER	SLEECHIEST	SLICKNESSES	SLIPSLOPPIEST	SLOTHFULLY
SLAPHAPPIEST	SLEEKENING	SLICKROCKS	SLIPSLOPPY	SLOTHFULNESS
SLAPSTICKS	SLEEKNESSES	SLICKSTERS	SLIPSTREAM	SLOTHFULNESSES
SLASHFESTS	SLEEKSTONE	SLICKSTONE	SLIPSTREAMED	SLOUCHIEST
SLASHINGLY	SLEEKSTONES	SLICKSTONES	SLIPSTREAMING	SLOUCHINESS
SLATHERING	SLEEPINESS	SLIDDERIER	SLIPSTREAMS	SLOUCHINESSES
SLATINESSES	SLEEPINESSES	SLIDDERIEST	SLITHERIER	SLOUCHINGLY
SLATTERING	SLEEPLESSLY	SLIDDERING	SLITHERIEST	SLOUGHIEST
SLATTERNLIER	SLEEPLESSNESS	SLIDESHOWS	SLITHERING	SLOVENLIER
SLATTERNLIEST	SLEEPLESSNESSES	SLIGHTINGLY	SLIVOVICAS	SLOVENLIEST
SLATTERNLINESS	SLEEPOVERS	SLIGHTNESS	SLIVOVICES	SLOVENLIKE
SLATTERNLY	SLEEPSUITS	SLIGHTNESSES	SLIVOVITZES	SLOVENLINESS
SLAUGHTERABLE	SLEEPWALKED	SLIMEBALLS	SLIVOWITZES	SLOVENLINESSES
SLAUGHTERED	SLEEPWALKER	SLIMINESSES	SLOBBERERS	SLOVENRIES
SLAUGHTERER	SLEEPWALKERS	SLIMNASTICS	SLOBBERIER	SLOWCOACHES
SLAUGHTERERS	SLEEPWALKING	SLIMNESSES	SLOBBERIEST	SLOWNESSES
SLAUGHTERHOUSE	SLEEPWALKINGS	SLIMPSIEST	SLOBBERING	SLUBBERING
SLAUGHTERHOUSES	SLEEPWALKS	SLINGBACKS	SLOBBISHNESS	SLUBBERINGLY
SLAUGHTERIES	SLEEPWEARS	SLINGSHOTS	SLOBBISHNESSES	SLUBBERINGS
SLAUGHTERING	SLEEPYHEAD	SLINGSTONE	SLOCKDOLAGER	SLUGGABEDS
SLAUGHTERMAN	SLEEPYHEADED	SLINGSTONES	SLOCKDOLAGERS	SLUGGARDISE
SLAUGHTERMEN	SLEEPYHEADS	SLINKINESS	SLOCKDOLIGER	SLUGGARDISED
SLAUGHTEROUS	SLEETINESS	SLINKINESSES	SLOCKDOLIGERS	SLUGGARDISES
SLAUGHTEROUSLY	SLEETINESSES	SLINKSKINS	SLOCKDOLOGER	SLUGGARDISING
SLAUGHTERS	SLEEVEHAND	SLINKWEEDS	SLOCKDOLOGERS	SLUGGARDIZE
SLAUGHTERY	SLEEVEHANDS	SLIPCOVERED	SLOCKENING	SLUGGARDIZED
SLAVEHOLDER	SLEEVELESS	SLIPCOVERING	SLOEBUSHES	SLUGGARDIZES
SLAVEHOLDERS	SLEEVELETS	SLIPCOVERS	SLOETHORNS	SLUGGARDIZING
SLAVEHOLDING	SLEEVELIKE	SLIPDRESSES	SLOGANEERED	SLUGGARDLIER
SLAVEHOLDINGS	SLEIGHINGS	SLIPFORMED	SLOGANEERING	SLUGGARDLIEST
SLAVERINGLY	SLENDEREST	SLIPFORMING	SLOGANEERINGS	SLUGGARDLINESS
SLAVERINGS	SLENDERISE	SLIPNOOSES	SLOGANEERS	SLUGGARDLY
SLAVISHNESS	SLENDERISED	SLIPPERIER	SLOGANISED	SLUGGARDNESS
SLAVISHNESSES	SLENDERISES	SLIPPERIEST	SLOGANISES	SLUGGARDNESSES
SLAVOCRACIES	SLENDERISING	SLIPPERILY	SLOGANISING	SLUGGISHLY
SLAVOCRACY	SLENDERIZE	SLIPPERINESS	SLOGANISINGS	SLUGGISHNESS
SLAVOCRATS	SLENDERIZED	SLIPPERINESSES	SLOGANIZED	SLUGGISHNESSES
SLAVOPHILE	SLENDERIZES	SLIPPERING	SLOGANIZES	SLUGHORNES
SLAVOPHILES	SLENDERIZING	SLIPPERWORT	SLOGANIZING	SLUICEGATE
SLAVOPHILS	SLENDERNESS	SLIPPERWORTS	SLOGANIZINGS	SLUICEGATES
SLEAZEBAGS	SLENDERNESSES	SLIPPINESS	SLOMMOCKED	SLUICELIKE
SLEAZEBALL	SLEUTHHOUND	SLIPPINESSES	SLOMMOCKING	SLUICEWAYS

SLUMBERERS	SMALMINESSES	SMITHEREENS	SMOULDERINGLY	SNAPSHOOTER
SLUMBERFUL	SMARAGDINE	SMITHERIES	SMOULDERINGS	SNAPSHOOTERS
SLUMBERIER	SMARAGDITE	SMITHSONITE	SMOULDRIER	SNAPSHOOTING
SLUMBERIEST	SMARAGDITES	SMITHSONITES	SMOULDRIEST	SNAPSHOOTINGS
SLUMBERING	SMARMINESS	SMOKEBOARD	SMUDGELESS	SNAPSHOTTED
SLUMBERINGLY	SMARMINESSES	SMOKEBOARDS	SMUDGINESS	SNAPSHOTTING
SLUMBERINGS	SMARTARSED	SMOKEBOXES	SMUDGINESSES	SNARLINGLY
SLUMBERLAND	SMARTARSES	SMOKEBUSHES	SMUGGERIES	SNATCHIEST
SLUMBERLANDS	SMARTASSES	SMOKEHOODS	SMUGGLINGS	SNATCHINGLY
SLUMBERLESS	SMARTENING	SMOKEHOUSE	SMUGNESSES	SNATCHINGS
SLUMBEROUS	SMARTINGLY	SMOKEHOUSES	SMUTCHIEST	SNAZZINESS
SLUMBEROUSLY	SMARTMOUTH	SMOKEJACKS	SMUTTINESS	SNAZZINESSES
SLUMBEROUSNESS	SMARTMOUTHS	SMOKELESSLY	SMUTTINESSES	SNEAKBOXES
SLUMBERSOME	SMARTNESSES	SMOKELESSNESS	SNACKETTES	SNEAKINESS
SLUMBROUSLY	SMARTPHONE	SMOKELESSNESSES	SNAGGLETEETH	SNEAKINESSES
SLUMBROUSNESS	SMARTPHONES	SMOKEPROOF	SNAGGLETOOTH	SNEAKINGLY
SLUMBROUSNESSES	SMARTWATCH	SMOKESCREEN	SNAGGLETOOTHED	SNEAKINGNESS
SLUMGULLION	SMARTWATCHES	SMOKESCREENS	SNAILERIES	SNEAKINGNESSES
SLUMGULLIONS	SMARTWEEDS	SMOKESTACK	SNAILFISHES	SNEAKISHLY
SLUMMOCKED	SMARTYPANTS	SMOKESTACKS	SNAKEBIRDS	SNEAKISHNESS
SLUMMOCKING	SMASHEROOS	SMOKETIGHT	SNAKEBITES	SNEAKISHNESSES
SLUMPFLATION	SMASHINGLY	SMOKINESSES	SNAKEBITTEN	SNEAKSBIES
SLUMPFLATIONARY	SMASHMOUTH	SMOLDERING	SNAKEFISHES	SNEERINGLY
SLUMPFLATIONS	SMATTERERS	SMOOCHIEST	SNAKEHEADS	SNEESHINGS
SLUNGSHOTS	SMATTERING	SMOOTHABLE	SNAKEMOUTH	SNEEZELESS
SLUSHINESS	SMATTERINGLY	SMOOTHBORE	SNAKEMOUTHS	SNEEZEWEED
SLUSHINESSES	SMATTERINGS	SMOOTHBORED	SNAKEROOTS	SNEEZEWEEDS
SLUTCHIEST	SMEARCASES	SMOOTHBORES	SNAKESKINS	SNEEZEWOOD
SLUTTERIES	SMEARINESS	SMOOTHENED	SNAKESTONE	SNEEZEWOODS
SLUTTINESS	SMEARINESSES	SMOOTHENING	SNAKESTONES	SNEEZEWORT
SLUTTINESSES	SMELLINESS	SMOOTHINGS	SNAKEWEEDS	SNEEZEWORTS
SLUTTISHLY	SMELLINESSES	SMOOTHNESS	SNAKEWOODS	SNICKERERS
SLUTTISHNESS	SMELTERIES	SMOOTHNESSES	SNAKINESSES	SNICKERIER
SLUTTISHNESSES	SMICKERING	SMOOTHPATE	SNAKISHNESS	SNICKERIEST
SMACKDOWNS	SMICKERINGS	SMOOTHPATES	SNAKISHNESSES	SNICKERING
SMACKEROOS	SMIERCASES	SMORGASBORD	SNAPDRAGON	SNICKERSNEE
SMACKHEADS	SMIFLIGATE	SMORGASBORDS	SNAPDRAGONS	SNICKERSNEED
SMALLCLOTHES	SMIFLIGATED	SMORREBROD	SNAPHANCES	SNICKERSNEEING
SMALLHOLDER	SMIFLIGATES	SMORREBRODS	SNAPHAUNCE	SNICKERSNEES
SMALLHOLDERS	SMIFLIGATING	SMOTHERERS	SNAPHAUNCES	SNIDENESSES
SMALLHOLDING	SMILACACEOUS	SMOTHERIER	SNAPHAUNCH	SNIFFINESS
SMALLHOLDINGS	SMILINGNESS	SMOTHERIEST	SNAPHAUNCHES	SNIFFINESSES
SMALLMOUTH	SMILINGNESSES	SMOTHERINESS	SNAPPERING	SNIFFINGLY
SMALLMOUTHS	SMIRKINGLY	SMOTHERINESSES	SNAPPINESS	SNIFFISHLY
SMALLNESSES	SMITHCRAFT	SMOTHERING	SNAPPINESSES	SNIFFISHNESS
SMALLPOXES	SMITHCRAFTS	SMOTHERINGLY	SNAPPINGLY	SNIFFISHNESSES
SMALLSWORD	SMITHEREEN	SMOTHERINGS	SNAPPISHLY	SNIFFLIEST
SMALLSWORDS	SMITHEREENED	SMOULDERED	SNAPPISHNESS	SNIFTERING
SMALMINESS	SMITHEREENING	SMOULDERING	SNAPPISHNESSES	SNIGGERERS

SNIGGERING	SNORKELLING	SNOWPLOUGHED	SOCDOLAGER	SOCIOLINGUIST
SNIGGERINGLY	SNORKELLINGS	SNOWPLOUGHING	SOCDOLAGERS	SOCIOLINGUISTIC
SNIGGERINGS	SNORTINGLY	SNOWPLOUGHS	SOCDOLIGER	SOCIOLINGUISTS
SNIGGLINGS	SNOTTERIES	SNOWPLOWED	SOCDOLIGERS	SOCIOLOGESE
SNIPEFISHES	SNOTTERING	SNOWPLOWING	SOCDOLOGER	SOCIOLOGESES
SNIPERSCOPE	SNOTTINESS	SNOWSCAPES	SOCDOLOGERS	SOCIOLOGIC
SNIPERSCOPES	SNOTTINESSES	SNOWSHOEING	SOCIABILITIES	SOCIOLOGICAL
SNIPPERSNAPPER	SNOWBALLED	SNOWSHOEINGS	SOCIABILITY	SOCIOLOGICALLY
SNIPPERSNAPPERS	SNOWBALLING	SNOWSHOERS	SOCIABLENESS	SOCIOLOGIES
SNIPPETIER	SNOWBERRIES	SNOWSLIDES	SOCIABLENESSES	SOCIOLOGISM
SNIPPETIEST	SNOWBLADER	SNOWSNAKES	SOCIALISABLE	SOCIOLOGISMS
SNIPPETINESS	SNOWBLADERS	SNOWSTORMS	SOCIALISATION	SOCIOLOGIST
SNIPPETINESSES	SNOWBLADES	SNOWSURFING	SOCIALISATIONS	SOCIOLOGISTIC
SNIPPINESS	SNOWBLADING	SNOWSURFINGS	SOCIALISED	SOCIOLOGISTS
SNIPPINESSES	SNOWBLADINGS	SNOWTUBING	SOCIALISER	SOCIOMETRIC
SNITCHIEST	SNOWBLINKS	SNOWTUBINGS	SOCIALISERS	SOCIOMETRIES
SNIVELIEST	SNOWBLOWER	SNUBBINESS	SOCIALISES	SOCIOMETRIST
SNIVELINGS	SNOWBLOWERS	SNUBBINESSES	SOCIALISING	SOCIOMETRISTS
SNIVELLERS	SNOWBOARDED	SNUBBINGLY	SOCIALISINGS	SOCIOMETRY
SNIVELLIER	SNOWBOARDER	SNUBNESSES	SOCIALISMS	SOCIOPATHIC
SNIVELLIEST	SNOWBOARDERS	SNUFFBOXES	SOCIALISTIC	SOCIOPATHIES
SNIVELLING	SNOWBOARDING	SNUFFINESS	SOCIALISTICALLY	SOCIOPATHS
SNIVELLINGS	SNOWBOARDINGS	SNUFFINESSES	SOCIALISTS	SOCIOPATHY
SNOBBERIES	SNOWBOARDS	SNUFFLIEST	SOCIALITES	SOCIOPOLITICAL
SNOBBISHLY	SNOWBRUSHES	SNUFFLINGS	SOCIALITIES	SOCIORELIGIOUS
SNOBBISHNESS	SNOWBUSHES	SNUGGERIES	SOCIALIZABLE	SOCIOSEXUAL
SNOBBISHNESSES	SNOWCAPPED	SNUGGLIEST	SOCIALIZATION	SOCKDOLAGER
SNOBBOCRACIES	SNOWCLONES	SNUGNESSES	SOCIALIZATIONS	SOCKDOLAGERS
SNOBBOCRACY	SNOWCOACHES	SOAPBERRIES	SOCIALIZED	SOCKDOLIGER
SNOBOCRACIES	SNOWDRIFTS	SOAPBOXING	SOCIALIZER	SOCKDOLIGERS
SNOBOCRACY	SNOWFIELDS	SOAPDISHES	SOCIALIZERS	SOCKDOLOGER
SNOBOGRAPHER	SNOWFLAKES	SOAPFISHES	SOCIALIZES	SOCKDOLOGERS
SNOBOGRAPHERS	SNOWFLECKS	SOAPFLAKES	SOCIALIZING	SODALITIES
SNOBOGRAPHIES	SNOWFLICKS	SOAPINESSES	SOCIALIZINGS	SODBUSTERS
SNOBOGRAPHY	SNOWGLOBES	SOAPOLALLIE	SOCIALNESS	SODDENNESS
SNOCOACHES	SNOWINESSES	SOAPOLALLIES	SOCIALNESSES	SODDENNESSES
SNOLLYGOSTER	SNOWMAKERS	SOAPSTONES	SOCIATIONS	SODICITIES
SNOLLYGOSTERS	SNOWMAKING	SOAPSUDSIER	SOCIETALLY	SODOMISING
SNOOKERING	SNOWMOBILE	SOAPSUDSIEST	SOCIOBIOLOGICAL	SODOMITICAL
SNOOPERSCOPE	SNOWMOBILED	SOBERINGLY	SOCIOBIOLOGIES	SODOMITICALLY
SNOOPERSCOPES	SNOWMOBILER	SOBERISING	SOCIOBIOLOGIST	SODOMIZING
SNOOTINESS	SNOWMOBILERS	SOBERIZING	SOCIOBIOLOGISTS	SOFTBALLER
SNOOTINESSES	SNOWMOBILES	SOBERNESSES	SOCIOBIOLOGY	SOFTBALLERS
SNORKELERS	SNOWMOBILING	SOBERSIDED	SOCIOCULTURAL	SOFTBOUNDS
SNORKELING	SNOWMOBILINGS	SOBERSIDEDNESS	SOCIOCULTURALLY	SOFTCOVERS
SNORKELINGS	SNOWMOBILIST	SOBERSIDES	SOCIOECONOMIC	SOFTENINGS
SNORKELLED	SNOWMOBILISTS	SOBOLIFEROUS	SOCIOGRAMS	SOFTHEADED
SNORKELLER	SNOWMOULDS	SOBRIETIES	SOCIOHISTORICAL	SOFTHEADEDLY
SNORKELLERS	SNOWPLOUGH	SOBRIQUETS	SOCIOLECTS	SOFTHEADEDNESS

SOFTHEARTED	SOLECISTICALLY	SOLICITUDES	SOLIPSISTS	SOLVABILITIES
SOFTHEARTEDLY	SOLECIZING	SOLIDARISM	SOLITAIRES	SOLVABILITY
SOFTHEARTEDNESS	SOLEMNESSES	SOLIDARISMS	SOLITARIAN	SOLVABLENESS
SOFTNESSES	SOLEMNIFICATION	SOLIDARIST	SOLITARIANS	SOLVABLENESSES
SOFTSCAPES	SOLEMNIFIED	SOLIDARISTIC	SOLITARIES	SOLVATIONS
SOFTSHELLS	SOLEMNIFIES	SOLIDARISTS	SOLITARILY	SOLVENCIES
SOGDOLAGER	SOLEMNIFYING	SOLIDARITIES	SOLITARINESS	SOLVENTLESS
SOGDOLAGERS	SOLEMNISATION	SOLIDARITY	SOLITARINESSES	SOLVOLYSES
SOGDOLIGER	SOLEMNISATIONS	SOLIDATING	SOLITUDINARIAN	SOLVOLYSIS
SOGDOLIGERS	SOLEMNISED	SOLIDIFIABLE	SOLITUDINARIANS	SOLVOLYTIC
SOGDOLOGER	SOLEMNISER	SOLIDIFICATION	SOLITUDINOUS	SOMAESTHESIA
SOGDOLOGERS	SOLEMNISERS	SOLIDIFICATIONS	SOLIVAGANT	SOMAESTHESIAS
SOGGINESSES	SOLEMNISES	SOLIDIFIED	SOLIVAGANTS	SOMAESTHESIS
SOILINESSES	SOLEMNISING	SOLIDIFIER	SOLLICKERS	SOMAESTHESISES
SOJOURNERS	SOLEMNITIES	SOLIDIFIERS	SOLMISATION	SOMAESTHETIC
SOJOURNING	SOLEMNIZATION	SOLIDIFIES	SOLMISATIONS	SOMASCOPES
SOJOURNINGS	SOLEMNIZATIONS	SOLIDIFYING	SOLMIZATION	SOMATICALLY
SOJOURNMENT	SOLEMNIZED	SOLIDITIES	SOLMIZATIONS	SOMATOFORM
SOJOURNMENTS	SOLEMNIZER	SOLIDNESSES	SOLONCHAKS	SOMATOGENIC
SOKEMANRIES	SOLEMNIZERS	SOLIDUNGULATE	SOLONETSES	SOMATOLOGIC
SOLACEMENT	SOLEMNIZES	SOLIDUNGULATES	SOLONETZES	SOMATOLOGICAL
SOLACEMENTS	SOLEMNIZING	SOLIDUNGULOUS	SOLONETZIC	SOMATOLOGICALLY
SOLANACEOUS	SOLEMNNESS	SOLIFIDIAN	SOLONISATION	SOMATOLOGIES
SOLARIMETER	SOLEMNNESSES	SOLIFIDIANISM	SOLONISATIONS	SOMATOLOGIST
SOLARIMETERS	SOLENESSES	SOLIFIDIANISMS	SOLONIZATION	SOMATOLOGISTS
SOLARISATION	SOLENETTES	SOLIFIDIANS	SOLONIZATIONS	SOMATOLOGY
SOLARISATIONS	SOLENODONS	SOLIFLUCTION	SOLSTITIAL	SOMATOMEDIN
SOLARISING	SOLENOIDAL	SOLIFLUCTIONS	SOLSTITIALLY	SOMATOMEDINS
SOLARIZATION	SOLENOIDALLY	SOLIFLUXION	SOLUBILISATION	SOMATOPLASM
SOLARIZATIONS	SOLEPLATES	SOLIFLUXIONS	SOLUBILISATIONS	SOMATOPLASMS
SOLARIZING	SOLEPRINTS	SOLILOQUIES	SOLUBILISE	SOMATOPLASTIC
SOLDATESQUE	SOLFATARAS	SOLILOQUISE	SOLUBILISED	SOMATOPLEURAL
SOLDERABILITIES	SOLFATARIC	SOLILOQUISED	SOLUBILISES	SOMATOPLEURE
SOLDERABILITY	SOLFEGGIOS	SOLILOQUISER	SOLUBILISING	SOMATOPLEURES
SOLDERABLE	SOLFERINOS	SOLILOQUISERS	SOLUBILITIES	SOMATOPLEURIC
SOLDERINGS	SOLICITANT	SOLILOQUISES	SOLUBILITY	SOMATOSENSORY
SOLDIERIES	SOLICITANTS	SOLILOQUISING	SOLUBILIZATION	SOMATOSTATIN
SOLDIERING	SOLICITATION	SOLILOQUIST	SOLUBILIZATIONS	SOMATOSTATINS
SOLDIERINGS	SOLICITATIONS	SOLILOQUISTS	SOLUBILIZE	SOMATOTENSIC
SOLDIERLIER	SOLICITIES	SOLILOQUIZE	SOLUBILIZED	SOMATOTONIA
SOLDIERLIEST	SOLICITING	SOLILOQUIZED	SOLUBILIZES	SOMATOTONIAS
SOLDIERLIKE	SOLICITINGS	SOLILOQUIZER	SOLUBILIZING	SOMATOTONIC
SOLDIERLINESS	SOLICITORS	SOLILOQUIZERS	SOLUBLENESS	SOMATOTONICS
SOLDIERLINESSES	SOLICITORSHIP	SOLILOQUIZES	SOLUBLENESSES	SOMATOTROPHIC
SOLDIERSHIP	SOLICITORSHIPS	SOLILOQUIZING	SOLUTIONAL	SOMATOTROPHIN
SOLDIERSHIPS	SOLICITOUS	SOLIPEDOUS	SOLUTIONED	SOMATOTROPHINS
SOLECISING	SOLICITOUSLY	SOLIPSISMS	SOLUTIONING	SOMATOTROPIC
SOLECISTIC	SOLICITOUSNESS	SOLIPSISTIC	SOLUTIONIST	SOMATOTROPIN
SOLECISTICAL	SOLICITUDE	SOLIPSISTICALLY	SOLUTIONISTS	SOMATOTROPINE

S

SOMATOTROPINES	SOMNAMBULIC	SONICATING	SOPHISTICATES	SORROWFULNESS
SOMATOTROPINS	SOMNAMBULISM	SONICATION	SOPHISTICATING	SORROWFULNESSES
SOMATOTYPE	SOMNAMBULISMS	SONICATIONS	SOPHISTICATION	SORROWINGS
SOMATOTYPED	SOMNAMBULIST	SONICATORS	SOPHISTICATIONS	SORROWLESS
SOMATOTYPES	SOMNAMBULISTIC	SONIFEROUS	SOPHISTICATOR	SORTATIONS
SOMATOTYPING	SOMNAMBULISTS	SONNETEERING	SOPHISTICATORS	SORTILEGER
SOMBERNESS	SOMNIATING	SONNETEERINGS	SOPHISTRIES	SORTILEGERS
SOMBERNESSES	SOMNIATIVE	SONNETEERS	SOPHOMORES	SORTILEGES
SOMBRENESS	SOMNIATORY	SONNETISED	SOPHOMORIC	SORTILEGIES
SOMBRENESSES	SOMNIFACIENT	SONNETISES	SOPHOMORICAL	SORTITIONS
SOMBRERITE	SOMNIFACIENTS	SONNETISING	SOPORIFEROUS	SOSTENUTOS
SOMBRERITES	SOMNIFEROUS	SONNETIZED	SOPORIFEROUSLY	SOTERIOLOGIC
SOMEBODIES	SOMNIFEROUSLY	SONNETIZES	SOPORIFICALLY	SOTERIOLOGICAL
SOMEPLACES	SOMNILOQUENCE	SONNETIZING	SOPORIFICS	SOTERIOLOGIES
SOMERSAULT	SOMNILOQUENCES	SONNETTING	SOPPINESSES	SOTERIOLOGY
SOMERSAULTED	SOMNILOQUIES	SONOFABITCH	SOPRANINOS	SOTTISHNESS
SOMERSAULTING	SOMNILOQUISE	SONOGRAPHER	SOPRANISTS	SOTTISHNESSES
SOMERSAULTS	SOMNILOQUISED	SONOGRAPHERS	SORBABILITIES	SOTTISIERS
SOMERSETED	SOMNILOQUISES	SONOGRAPHIES	SORBABILITY	SOUBRETTES
SOMERSETING	SOMNILOQUISING	SONOGRAPHS	SORBEFACIENT	SOUBRETTISH
SOMERSETTED	SOMNILOQUISM	SONOGRAPHY	SORBEFACIENTS	SOUBRIQUET
SOMERSETTING	SOMNILOQUISMS	SONOMETERS	SORBITISATION	SOUBRIQUETS
SOMESTHESIA	SOMNILOQUIST	SONORITIES	SORBITISATIONS	SOULDIERED
SOMESTHESIAS	SOMNILOQUISTS	SONOROUSLY	SORBITISED	SOULDIERING
SOMESTHESIS	SOMNILOQUIZE	SONOROUSNESS	SORBITISES	SOULFULNESS
SOMESTHESISES	SOMNILOQUIZED	SONOROUSNESSES	SORBITISING	SOULFULNESSES
SOMESTHETIC	SOMNILOQUIZES	SOOTERKINS	SORBITIZATION	SOULLESSLY
SOMETHINGS	SOMNILOQUIZING	SOOTFLAKES	SORBITIZATIONS	SOULLESSNESS
SOMEWHENCE	SOMNILOQUOUS	SOOTHERING	SORBITIZED	SOULLESSNESSES
SOMEWHERES	SOMNILOQUY	SOOTHFASTLY	SORBITIZES	SOUNDALIKE
SOMEWHILES	SOMNOLENCE	SOOTHFASTNESS	SORBITIZING	SOUNDALIKES
SOMEWHITHER	SOMNOLENCES	SOOTHFASTNESSES	SORCERESSES	SOUNDBITES
SOMMELIERS	SOMNOLENCIES	SOOTHINGLY	SORDAMENTE	SOUNDBOARD
SOMNAMBULANCE	SOMNOLENCY	SOOTHINGNESS	SORDIDNESS	SOUNDBOARDS
SOMNAMBULANCES	SOMNOLENTLY	SOOTHINGNESSES	SORDIDNESSES	SOUNDBOXES
SOMNAMBULANT	SOMNOLESCENT	SOOTHSAYER	SOREHEADED	SOUNDCARDS
SOMNAMBULANTS	SONGCRAFTS	SOOTHSAYERS	SOREHEADEDLY	SOUNDINGLY
SOMNAMBULAR	SONGFULNESS	SOOTHSAYING	SOREHEADEDNESS	SOUNDLESSLY
SOMNAMBULARY	SONGFULNESSES	SOOTHSAYINGS	SORENESSES	SOUNDLESSNESS
SOMNAMBULATE	SONGLESSLY	SOOTINESSES	SORICIDENT	SOUNDLESSNESSES
SOMNAMBULATED	SONGOLOLOS	SOPAIPILLA	SORORIALLY	SOUNDNESSES
SOMNAMBULATES	SONGSHEETS	SOPAIPILLAS	SORORICIDAL	SOUNDPOSTS
SOMNAMBULATING	SONGSMITHS	SOPAPILLAS	SORORICIDE	SOUNDPROOF
SOMNAMBULATION	SONGSTRESS	SOPHISTERS	SORORICIDES	SOUNDPROOFED
SOMNAMBULATIONS	SONGSTRESSES	SOPHISTICAL	SORORISING	SOUNDPROOFING
SOMNAMBULATOR	SONGWRITER	SOPHISTICALLY	SORORITIES	SOUNDPROOFINGS
SOMNAMBULATORS	SONGWRITERS	SOPHISTICATE	SORORIZING	SOUNDPROOFS
SOMNAMBULE	SONGWRITING	SOPHISTICATED	SORRINESSES	SOUNDSCAPE
SOMNAMBULES	SONGWRITINGS	SOPHISTICATEDLY	SORROWFULLY	SOUNDSCAPES

SOUNDSTAGE	SOUTHERNLY	SOYBURGERS	SPANAKOPITAS	SPARROWHAWKS
SOUNDSTAGES	SOUTHERNMOST	SPACEBANDS	SPANCELING	SPARROWLIKE
SOUNDTRACK	SOUTHERNNESS	SPACEBORNE	SPANCELLED	SPARSENESS
SOUNDTRACKED	SOUTHERNNESSES	SPACECRAFT	SPANCELLING	SPARSENESSES
SOUNDTRACKING	SOUTHERNWOOD	SPACECRAFTS	SPANGHEWED	SPARSITIES
SOUNDTRACKS	SOUTHERNWOODS	SPACEFARING	SPANGHEWING	SPARTEINES
SOUPINESSES	SOUTHLANDER	SPACEFARINGS	SPANGLIEST	SPARTERIES
SOUPSPOONS	SOUTHLANDERS	SPACEFLIGHT	SPANGLINGS	SPARTICLES
SOURCEBOOK	SOUTHLANDS	SPACEFLIGHTS	SPANIELLED	SPASMATICAL
SOURCEBOOKS	SOUTHSAYING	SPACEPLANE	SPANIELLING	SPASMODICAL
SOURCELESS	SOUTHWARDLY	SPACEPLANES	SPANIOLATE	SPASMODICALLY
SOURDELINE	SOUTHWARDS	SPACEPORTS	SPANIOLATED	SPASMODIST
SOURDELINES	SOUTHWESTER	SPACESHIPS	SPANIOLATES	SPASMODISTS
SOURDOUGHS	SOUTHWESTERLIES	SPACESUITS	SPANIOLATING	SPASMOLYTIC
SOURNESSES	SOUTHWESTERLY	SPACETIMES	SPANIOLISE	SPASMOLYTICS
SOURPUSSES	SOUTHWESTERN	SPACEWALKED	SPANIOLISED	SPASTICALLY
SOUSAPHONE	SOUTHWESTERS	SPACEWALKER	SPANIOLISES	SPASTICITIES
SOUSAPHONES	SOUTHWESTS	SPACEWALKERS	SPANIOLISING	SPASTICITY
SOUSAPHONIST	SOUTHWESTWARD	SPACEWALKING	SPANIOLIZE	SPATANGOID
SOUSAPHONISTS	SOUTHWESTWARDLY	SPACEWALKS	SPANIOLIZED	SPATANGOIDS
SOUTENEURS	SOUTHWESTWARDS	SPACEWOMAN	SPANIOLIZES	SPATCHCOCK
SOUTERRAIN	SOUVENIRED	SPACEWOMEN	SPANIOLIZING	SPATCHCOCKED
SOUTERRAINS	SOUVENIRING	SPACINESSES	SPANKINGLY	SPATCHCOCKING
SOUTHBOUND	SOUVLAKIAS	SPACIOUSLY	SPANOKOPITA	SPATCHCOCKS
SOUTHEASTER	SOVENANCES	SPACIOUSNESS	SPANOKOPITAS	SPATHACEOUS
SOUTHEASTERLIES	SOVEREIGNLY	SPACIOUSNESSES	SPARAGMATIC	SPATHIPHYLLUM
SOUTHEASTERLY	SOVEREIGNS	SPADASSINS	SPARAGRASS	SPATHIPHYLLUMS
SOUTHEASTERN	SOVEREIGNTIES	SPADEFISHES	SPARAGRASSES	SPATHULATE
SOUTHEASTERS	SOVEREIGNTIST	SPADEFOOTS	SPARAXISES	SPATIALISATION
SOUTHEASTS	SOVEREIGNTISTS	SPADEWORKS	SPARENESSES	SPATIALISATIONS
SOUTHEASTWARD	SOVEREIGNTY	SPADICEOUS	SPARGANIUM	SPATIALITIES
SOUTHEASTWARDS	SOVIETISATION	SPADICIFLORAL	SPARGANIUMS	SPATIALITY
SOUTHERING	SOVIETISATIONS	SPADILLIOS	SPARINGNESS	SPATIALIZATION
SOUTHERLIES	SOVIETISED	SPAGHETTIFIED	SPARINGNESSES	SPATIALIZATIONS
SOUTHERLINESS	SOVIETISES	SPAGHETTIFIES	SPARKISHLY	SPATIOTEMPORAL
SOUTHERLINESSES	SOVIETISING	SPAGHETTIFY	SPARKLEBERRIES	SPATTERDASH
SOUTHERMOST	SOVIETISMS	SPAGHETTIFYING	SPARKLEBERRY	SPATTERDASHES
SOUTHERNER	SOVIETISTIC	SPAGHETTILIKE	SPARKLESSLY	SPATTERDOCK
SOUTHERNERS	SOVIETISTS	SPAGHETTINI	SPARKLIEST	SPATTERDOCKS
SOUTHERNISE	SOVIETIZATION	SPAGHETTINIS	SPARKLINGLY	SPATTERING
SOUTHERNISED	SOVIETIZATIONS	SPAGHETTIS	SPARKLINGS	SPATTERWORK
SOUTHERNISES	SOVIETIZED	SPAGIRISTS	SPARKPLUGGED	SPATTERWORKS
SOUTHERNISING	SOVIETIZES	SPAGYRICAL	SPARKPLUGGING	SPEAKEASIES
SOUTHERNISM	SOVIETIZING	SPAGYRICALLY	SPARKPLUGS	SPEAKERINE
SOUTHERNISMS	SOVIETOLOGICAL	SPAGYRISTS	SPARROWFART	SPEAKERINES
SOUTHERNIZE	SOVIETOLOGIST	SPALLATION	SPARROWFARTS	SPEAKERPHONE
SOUTHERNIZED	SOVIETOLOGISTS	SPALLATIONS	SPARROWGRASS	SPEAKERPHONES
SOUTHERNIZES	SOVRANTIES	SPANAEMIAS	SPARROWGRASSES	SPEAKERSHIP
SOUTHERNIZING	SOWBELLIES	SPANAKOPITA	SPARROWHAWK	SPEAKERSHIPS

S

SPEAKINGLY	SPECIESIST	SPECTRALITY	SPEECHFULNESS	SPELEOLOGICAL
SPEARCARRIER	SPECIESISTS	SPECTRALLY	SPEECHFULNESSES	SPELEOLOGIES
SPEARCARRIERS	SPECIFIABLE	SPECTRALNESS	SPEECHIFICATION	SPELEOLOGIST
SPEARFISHED	SPECIFICAL	SPECTRALNESSES	SPEECHIFIED	SPELEOLOGISTS
SPEARFISHES	SPECIFICALLY	SPECTROGRAM	SPEECHIFIER	SPELEOLOGY
SPEARFISHING	SPECIFICATE	SPECTROGRAMS	SPEECHIFIERS	SPELEOTHEM
SPEARHEADED	SPECIFICATED	SPECTROGRAPH	SPEECHIFIES	SPELEOTHEMS
SPEARHEADING	SPECIFICATES	SPECTROGRAPHIC	SPEECHIFYING	SPELEOTHERAPIES
SPEARHEADS	SPECIFICATING	SPECTROGRAPHIES	SPEECHIFYINGS	SPELEOTHERAPY
SPEARMINTS	SPECIFICATION	SPECTROGRAPHS	SPEECHLESS	SPELLBINDER
SPEARWORTS	SPECIFICATIONS	SPECTROGRAPHY	SPEECHLESSLY	SPELLBINDERS
SPECIALEST	SPECIFICATIVE	SPECTROLOGICAL	SPEECHLESSNESS	SPELLBINDING
SPECIALISATION	SPECIFICATORY	SPECTROLOGIES	SPEECHMAKER	SPELLBINDINGLY
SPECIALISATIONS	SPECIFICITIES	SPECTROLOGY	SPEECHMAKERS	SPELLBINDS
SPECIALISE	SPECIFICITY	SPECTROMETER	SPEECHMAKING	SPELLBOUND
SPECIALISED	SPECIFIERS	SPECTROMETERS	SPEECHMAKINGS	SPELLCHECK
SPECIALISER	SPECIFYING	SPECTROMETRIC	SPEECHWRITER	SPELLCHECKED
SPECIALISERS	SPECIOCIDE	SPECTROMETRIES	SPEECHWRITERS	SPELLCHECKER
SPECIALISES	SPECIOCIDES	SPECTROMETRY	SPEEDBALLED	SPELLCHECKERS
SPECIALISING	SPECIOSITIES	SPECTROSCOPE	SPEEDBALLING	SPELLCHECKING
SPECIALISM	SPECIOSITY	SPECTROSCOPES	SPEEDBALLINGS	SPELLCHECKS
SPECIALISMS	SPECIOUSLY	SPECTROSCOPIC	SPEEDBALLS	SPELLDOWNS
SPECIALIST	SPECIOUSNESS	SPECTROSCOPICAL	SPEEDBOATING	SPELLICANS
SPECIALISTIC	SPECIOUSNESSES	SPECTROSCOPIES	SPEEDBOATINGS	SPELLINGLY
SPECIALISTS	SPECKLEDNESS	SPECTROSCOPIST	SPEEDBOATS	SPELLSTOPT
SPECIALITIES	SPECKLEDNESSES	SPECTROSCOPISTS	SPEEDFREAK	SPELUNKERS
SPECIALITY	SPECKSIONEER	SPECTROSCOPY	SPEEDFREAKS	SPELUNKING
SPECIALIZATION	SPECKSIONEERS	SPECULARITIES	SPEEDFULLY	SPELUNKINGS
SPECIALIZATIONS	SPECKTIONEER	SPECULARITY	SPEEDINESS	SPENDTHRIFT
SPECIALIZE	SPECKTIONEERS	SPECULARLY	SPEEDINESSES	SPENDTHRIFTS
SPECIALIZED	SPECTACLED	SPECULATED	SPEEDOMETER	SPERMACETI
SPECIALIZER	SPECTACLES	SPECULATES	SPEEDOMETERS	SPERMACETIS
SPECIALIZERS	SPECTACULAR	SPECULATING	SPEEDREADING	SPERMADUCT
SPECIALIZES	SPECTACULARITY	SPECULATION	SPEEDREADS	SPERMADUCTS
SPECIALIZING	SPECTACULARLY	SPECULATIONS	SPEEDRUNNING	SPERMAGONIA
SPECIALLED	SPECTACULARS	SPECULATIST	SPEEDSKATING	SPERMAGONIUM
SPECIALLING	SPECTATING	SPECULATISTS	SPEEDSKATINGS	SPERMAPHYTE
SPECIALNESS	SPECTATORIAL	SPECULATIVE	SPEEDSTERS	SPERMAPHYTES
SPECIALNESSES	SPECTATORS	SPECULATIVELY	SPEEDWALKS	SPERMAPHYTIC
SPECIALOGS	SPECTATORSHIP	SPECULATIVENESS	SPEEDWELLS	SPERMARIES
SPECIALOGUE	SPECTATORSHIPS	SPECULATOR	SPELAEOLOGICAL	SPERMARIUM
SPECIALOGUES	SPECTATRESS	SPECULATORS	SPELAEOLOGIES	SPERMATHECA
SPECIALTIES	SPECTATRESSES	SPECULATORY	SPELAEOLOGIST	SPERMATHECAE
SPECIATING	SPECTATRICES	SPECULATRICE	SPELAEOLOGISTS	SPERMATHECAL
SPECIATION	SPECTATRIX	SPECULATRICES	SPELAEOLOGY	SPERMATHECAS
SPECIATIONAL	SPECTATRIXES	SPECULATRIX	SPELAEOTHEM	SPERMATIAL
SPECIATIONS	SPECTINOMYCIN	SPECULATRIXES	SPELAEOTHEMS	SPERMATICAL
SPECIESISM	SPECTINOMYCINS	SPEECHCRAFT	SPELDERING	SPERMATICALLY
SPECIESISMS	SPECTRALITIES	SPEECHCRAFTS	SPELDRINGS	SPERMATICS

SPERMATIDS	SPERMIOGENESIS	SPHENOPSID	SPHRAGISTICS	SPIFLICATIONS
SPERMATIUM	SPERMIOGENETIC	SPHENOPSIDS	SPHYGMOGRAM	SPIKEFISHES
SPERMATOBLAST	SPERMOGONE	SPHERELESS	SPHYGMOGRAMS	SPIKENARDS
SPERMATOBLASTIC	SPERMOGONES	SPHERELIKE	SPHYGMOGRAPH	SPIKINESSES
SPERMATOBLASTS	SPERMOGONIA	SPHERICALITIES	SPHYGMOGRAPHIC	SPILLIKINS
SPERMATOCELE	SPERMOGONIUM	SPHERICALITY	SPHYGMOGRAPHIES	SPILLOVERS
SPERMATOCELES	SPERMOPHILE	SPHERICALLY	SPHYGMOGRAPHS	SPILOSITES
SPERMATOCIDAL	SPERMOPHILES	SPHERICALNESS	SPHYGMOGRAPHY	SPINACENES
SPERMATOCIDE	SPERMOPHYTE	SPHERICALNESSES	SPHYGMOLOGIES	SPINACEOUS
SPERMATOCIDES	SPERMOPHYTES	SPHERICITIES	SPHYGMOLOGY	SPINACHIER
SPERMATOCYTE	SPERMOPHYTIC	SPHERICITY	SPHYGMOMETER	SPINACHIEST
SPERMATOCYTES	SPERRYLITE	SPHERISTERION	SPHYGMOMETERS	SPINACHLIKE
SPERMATOGENESES	SPERRYLITES	SPHERISTERIONS	SPHYGMOPHONE	SPINARAMAS
SPERMATOGENESIS	SPESSARTINE	SPHEROCYTE	SPHYGMOPHONES	SPINDLELEGS
SPERMATOGENETIC	SPESSARTINES	SPHEROCYTES	SPHYGMOSCOPE	SPINDLESHANKS
SPERMATOGENIC	SPESSARTITE	SPHEROCYTOSES	SPHYGMOSCOPES	SPINDLIEST
SPERMATOGENIES	SPESSARTITES	SPHEROCYTOSIS	SPHYGMUSES	SPINDLINGS
SPERMATOGENOUS	SPETSNAZES	SPHEROIDAL	SPICEBERRIES	SPINDRIFTS
SPERMATOGENY	SPETZNAZES	SPHEROIDALLY	SPICEBERRY	SPINELESSLY
SPERMATOGONIA	SPEWINESSES	SPHEROIDICALLY	SPICEBUSHES	SPINELESSNESS
SPERMATOGONIAL	SPHACELATE	SPHEROIDICITIES	SPICILEGES	SPINELESSNESSES
SPERMATOGONIUM	SPHACELATED	SPHEROIDICITY	SPICINESSES	SPINESCENCE
SPERMATOPHORAL	SPHACELATES	SPHEROIDISATION	SPICULATED	SPINESCENCES
SPERMATOPHORE	SPHACELATING	SPHEROIDISE	SPICULATION	SPINESCENT
SPERMATOPHORES	SPHACELATION	SPHEROIDISED	SPICULATIONS	SPINIFEROUS
SPERMATOPHYTE	SPHACELATIONS	SPHEROIDISES	SPIDERIEST	SPINIFEXES
SPERMATOPHYTES	SPHACELUSES	SPHEROIDISING	SPIDERLIKE	SPINIGEROUS
SPERMATOPHYTIC	SPHAERIDIA	SPHEROIDIZATION	SPIDERWEBS	SPINIGRADE
SPERMATORRHEA	SPHAERIDIUM	SPHEROIDIZE	SPIDERWOOD	SPINIGRADES
SPERMATORRHEAS	SPHAERITES	SPHEROIDIZED	SPIDERWOODS	SPININESSES
SPERMATORRHOEA	SPHAEROCRYSTAL	SPHEROIDIZES	SPIDERWORK	SPINMEISTER
SPERMATORRHOEAS	SPHAEROCRYSTALS	SPHEROIDIZING	SPIDERWORKS	SPINMEISTERS
SPERMATOTHECA	SPHAEROSIDERITE	SPHEROMETER	SPIDERWORT	SPINNAKERS
SPERMATOTHECAE	SPHAGNICOLOUS	SPHEROMETERS	SPIDERWORTS	SPINNERETS
SPERMATOTHECAS	SPHAGNOLOGIES	SPHEROPLAST	SPIEGELEISEN	SPINNERETTE
SPERMATOZOA	SPHAGNOLOGIST	SPHEROPLASTS	SPIEGELEISENS	SPINNERETTES
SPERMATOZOAL	SPHAGNOLOGISTS	SPHERULITE	SPIFFINESS	SPINNERIES
SPERMATOZOAN	SPHAGNOLOGY	SPHERULITES	SPIFFINESSES	SPINNERULE
SPERMATOZOANS	SPHAIRISTIKE	SPHERULITIC	SPIFFLICATE	SPINNERULES
SPERMATOZOIC	SPHAIRISTIKES	SPHINCTERAL	SPIFFLICATED	SPINOSITIES
SPERMATOZOID	SPHALERITE	SPHINCTERIAL	SPIFFLICATES	SPINSTERDOM
SPERMATOZOIDS	SPHALERITES	SPHINCTERIC	SPIFFLICATING	SPINSTERDOMS
SPERMATOZOON	SPHENDONES	SPHINCTERS	SPIFFLICATION	SPINSTERHOOD
SPERMICIDAL	SPHENODONS	SPHINGOMYELIN	SPIFFLICATIONS	SPINSTERHOODS
SPERMICIDE	SPHENODONT	SPHINGOMYELINS	SPIFLICATE	SPINSTERIAL
SPERMICIDES	SPHENODONTS	SPHINGOSINE	SPIFLICATED	SPINSTERIAN
SPERMIDUCT	SPHENOGRAM	SPHINGOSINES	SPIFLICATES	SPINSTERISH
SPERMIDUCTS	SPHENOGRAMS	SPHINXLIKE	SPIFLICATING	SPINSTERLIER
SPERMIOGENESES	SPHENOIDAL	SPHRAGISTIC	SPIFLICATION	SPINSTERLIEST

S

SPINSTERLY	SPIRITUALITIES	SPIROPHORE	SPLEENFULLY	SPLINTWOODS
SPINSTERSHIP	SPIRITUALITY	SPIROPHORES	SPLEENIEST	SPLITTINGS
SPINSTERSHIPS	SPIRITUALIZE	SPIRULINAE	SPLEENLESS	SPLITTISMS
SPINSTRESS	SPIRITUALIZED	SPIRULINAS	SPLEENLIKE	SPLITTISTS
SPINSTRESSES	SPIRITUALIZER	SPISSITUDE	SPLEENSTONE	SPLODGIEST
SPINTHARISCOPE	SPIRITUALIZERS	SPISSITUDES	SPLEENSTONES	SPLODGINESS
SPINTHARISCOPES	SPIRITUALIZES	SPITBALLED	SPLEENWORT	SPLODGINESSES
SPINULESCENT	SPIRITUALIZING	SPITBALLING	SPLEENWORTS	SPLOOSHING
SPINULIFEROUS	SPIRITUALLY	SPITCHCOCK	SPLENATIVE	SPLOTCHIER
SPIRACULAR	SPIRITUALNESS	SPITCHCOCKED	SPLENDIDER	SPLOTCHIEST
SPIRACULATE	SPIRITUALNESSES	SPITCHCOCKING	SPLENDIDEST	SPLOTCHILY
SPIRACULUM	SPIRITUALS	SPITCHCOCKS	SPLENDIDIOUS	SPLOTCHINESS
SPIRALIFORM	SPIRITUALTIES	SPITCHERED	SPLENDIDLY	SPLOTCHINESSES
SPIRALISER	SPIRITUALTY	SPITCHERING	SPLENDIDNESS	SPLOTCHING
SPIRALISERS	SPIRITUELLE	SPITEFULLER	SPLENDIDNESSES	SPLURGIEST
SPIRALISMS	SPIRITUOSITIES	SPITEFULLEST	SPLENDIDOUS	SPLUTTERED
SPIRALISTS	SPIRITUOSITY	SPITEFULLY	SPLENDIFEROUS	SPLUTTERER
SPIRALITIES	SPIRITUOUS	SPITEFULNESS	SPLENDIFEROUSLY	SPLUTTERERS
SPIRALIZER	SPIRITUOUSNESS	SPITEFULNESSES	SPLENDOROUS	SPLUTTERIER
SPIRALIZERS	SPIRITUSES	SPITSTICKER	SPLENDOURS	SPLUTTERIEST
SPIRALLING	SPIRKETTING	SPITSTICKERS	SPLENDROUS	SPLUTTERING
SPIRASTERS	SPIRKETTINGS	SPITTLEBUG	SPLENECTOMIES	SPLUTTERINGLY
SPIRATIONS	SPIROCHAETAEMIA	SPITTLEBUGS	SPLENECTOMISE	SPLUTTERINGS
SPIRIFEROUS	SPIROCHAETAL	SPITTLIEST	SPLENECTOMISED	SPODOGRAMS
SPIRILLOSES	SPIROCHAETE	SPIVVERIES	SPLENECTOMISES	SPODOMANCIES
SPIRILLOSIS	SPIROCHAETES	SPLANCHNIC	SPLENECTOMISING	SPODOMANCY
SPIRITEDLY	SPIROCHAETOSES	SPLANCHNOCELE	SPLENECTOMIZE	SPODOMANTIC
SPIRITEDNESS	SPIROCHAETOSIS	SPLANCHNOCELES	SPLENECTOMIZED	SPODUMENES
SPIRITEDNESSES	SPIROCHETAL	SPLANCHNOLOGIES	SPLENECTOMIZES	SPOILFIVES
SPIRITINGS	SPIROCHETE	SPLANCHNOLOGY	SPLENECTOMIZING	SPOILSPORT
SPIRITISMS	SPIROCHETEMIA	SPLASHBACK	SPLENECTOMY	SPOILSPORTS
SPIRITISTIC	SPIROCHETEMIAS	SPLASHBACKS	SPLENETICAL	SPOKESHAVE
SPIRITISTS	SPIROCHETES	SPLASHBOARD	SPLENETICALLY	SPOKESHAVES
SPIRITLESS	SPIROCHETOSES	SPLASHBOARDS	SPLENETICS	SPOKESMANSHIP
SPIRITLESSLY	SPIROCHETOSIS	SPLASHDOWN	SPLENISATION	SPOKESMANSHIPS
SPIRITLESSNESS	SPIROGRAMS	SPLASHDOWNS	SPLENISATIONS	SPOKESPEOPLE
SPIRITOUSNESS	SPIROGRAPH	SPLASHIEST	SPLENITISES	SPOKESPERSON
SPIRITOUSNESSES	SPIROGRAPHIC	SPLASHINESS	SPLENIUSES	SPOKESPERSONS
SPIRITUALISE	SPIROGRAPHIES	SPLASHINESSES	SPLENIZATION	SPOKESWOMAN
SPIRITUALISED	SPIROGRAPHS	SPLASHINGS	SPLENIZATIONS	SPOKESWOMEN
SPIRITUALISER	SPIROGRAPHY	SPLASHPROOF	SPLENOMEGALIES	SPOLIATING
SPIRITUALISERS	SPIROGYRAS	SPLATCHING	SPLENOMEGALY	SPOLIATION
SPIRITUALISES	SPIROMETER	SPLATTERED	SPLEUCHANS	SPOLIATIONS
SPIRITUALISING	SPIROMETERS	SPLATTERING	SPLINTERED	SPOLIATIVE
SPIRITUALISM	SPIROMETRIC	SPLATTERPUNK	SPLINTERIER	SPOLIATORS
SPIRITUALISMS	SPIROMETRIES	SPLATTERPUNKS	SPLINTERIEST	SPOLIATORY
SPIRITUALIST	SPIROMETRY	SPLATTINGS	SPLINTERING	SPONDAICAL
SPIRITUALISTIC	SPIRONOLACTONE	SPLAYFOOTED	SPLINTLIKE	SPONDOOLICKS
SPIRITUALISTS	SPIRONOLACTONES	SPLAYFOOTEDLY	SPLINTWOOD	SPONDULICKS

SPONDYLITIC	SPOONHOOKS	SPORTABILITIES	SPORULATION	SPRIGHTING
SPONDYLITICS	SPOONWORMS	SPORTABILITY	SPORULATIONS	SPRIGHTLESS
SPONDYLITIDES	SPORADICAL	SPORTANCES	SPORULATIVE	SPRIGHTLIER
SPONDYLITIS	SPORADICALLY	SPORTBIKES	SPOTLESSLY	SPRIGHTLIEST
SPONDYLITISES	SPORADICALNESS	SPORTCASTER	SPOTLESSNESS	SPRIGHTLINESS
SPONDYLOLYSES	SPORANGIAL	SPORTCASTERS	SPOTLESSNESSES	SPRIGHTLINESSES
SPONDYLOLYSIS	SPORANGIOLA	SPORTCOATS	SPOTLIGHTED	SPRIGTAILS
SPONDYLOSES	SPORANGIOLE	SPORTFISHERMAN	SPOTLIGHTING	SPRINGALDS
SPONDYLOSIS	SPORANGIOLES	SPORTFISHERMEN	SPOTLIGHTS	SPRINGBOARD
SPONDYLOSISES	SPORANGIOLUM	SPORTFISHING	SPOTTEDNESS	SPRINGBOARDS
SPONDYLOUS	SPORANGIOPHORE	SPORTFISHINGS	SPOTTEDNESSES	SPRINGBOKS
SPONGEABLE	SPORANGIOPHORES	SPORTFULLY	SPOTTINESS	SPRINGBUCK
SPONGEBAGS	SPORANGIOSPORE	SPORTFULNESS	SPOTTINESSES	SPRINGBUCKS
SPONGELIKE	SPORANGIOSPORES	SPORTFULNESSES	SPOUSELESS	SPRINGEING
SPONGEWARE	SPORANGIUM	SPORTINESS	SPOYLEFULL	SPRINGHAAS
SPONGEWARES	SPORICIDAL	SPORTINESSES	SPRACHGEFUHL	SPRINGHALT
SPONGEWOOD	SPORICIDES	SPORTINGLY	SPRACHGEFUHLS	SPRINGHALTS
SPONGEWOODS	SPORIDESMS	SPORTIVELY	SPRACKLING	SPRINGHASE
SPONGICOLOUS	SPOROCARPS	SPORTIVENESS	SPRADDLING	SPRINGHEAD
SPONGIFORM	SPOROCYSTIC	SPORTIVENESSES	SPRANGLING	SPRINGHEADS
SPONGINESS	SPOROCYSTS	SPORTSCAST	SPRATTLING	SPRINGHOUSE
SPONGINESSES	SPOROCYTES	SPORTSCASTER	SPRAUCHLED	SPRINGHOUSES
SPONGIOBLAST	SPOROGENESES	SPORTSCASTERS	SPRAUCHLES	SPRINGIEST
SPONGIOBLASTIC	SPOROGENESIS	SPORTSCASTS	SPRAUCHLING	SPRINGINESS
SPONGIOBLASTS	SPOROGENIC	SPORTSMANLIER	SPRAUNCIER	SPRINGINESSES
SPONGOLOGIES	SPOROGENIES	SPORTSMANLIEST	SPRAUNCIEST	SPRINGINGS
SPONGOLOGIST	SPOROGENOUS	SPORTSMANLIKE	SPRAWLIEST	SPRINGKEEPER
SPONGOLOGISTS	SPOROGONIA	SPORTSMANLY	SPREADABILITIES	SPRINGKEEPERS
SPONGOLOGY	SPOROGONIAL	SPORTSMANSHIP	SPREADABILITY	SPRINGLESS
SPONSIONAL	SPOROGONIC	SPORTSMANSHIPS	SPREADABLE	SPRINGLETS
SPONSORIAL	SPOROGONIES	SPORTSPEOPLE	SPREADEAGLED	SPRINGLIKE
SPONSORING	SPOROGONIUM	SPORTSPERSON	SPREADINGLY	SPRINGTAIL
SPONSORSHIP	SPOROPHORE	SPORTSPERSONS	SPREADINGS	SPRINGTAILS
SPONSORSHIPS	SPOROPHORES	SPORTSWASH	SPREADSHEET	SPRINGTIDE
SPONTANEITIES	SPOROPHORIC	SPORTSWASHED	SPREADSHEETS	SPRINGTIDES
SPONTANEITY	SPOROPHOROUS	SPORTSWASHES	SPREAGHERIES	SPRINGTIME
SPONTANEOUS	SPOROPHYLL	SPORTSWASHING	SPREAGHERY	SPRINGTIMES
SPONTANEOUSLY	SPOROPHYLLS	SPORTSWASHINGS	SPREATHING	SPRINGWATER
SPONTANEOUSNESS	SPOROPHYLS	SPORTSWEAR	SPRECHERIES	SPRINGWATERS
SPOOFERIES	SPOROPHYTE	SPORTSWEARS	SPRECHGESANG	SPRINGWOOD
SPOOKERIES	SPOROPHYTES	SPORTSWOMAN	SPRECHGESANGS	SPRINGWOODS
SPOOKINESS	SPOROPHYTIC	SPORTSWOMEN	SPRECHSTIMME	SPRINGWORT
SPOOKINESSES	SPOROPOLLENIN	SPORTSWRITER	SPRECHSTIMMES	SPRINGWORTS
SPOONBAITS	SPOROPOLLENINS	SPORTSWRITERS	SPREETHING	SPRINKLERED
SPOONBILLS	SPOROTRICHOSES	SPORTSWRITING	SPREKELIAS	SPRINKLERING
SPOONDRIFT	SPOROTRICHOSIS	SPORTSWRITINGS	SPRIGGIEST	SPRINKLERS
SPOONDRIFTS	SPOROZOANS	SPORULATED	SPRIGHTFUL	SPRINKLING
SPOONERISM	SPOROZOITE	SPORULATES	SPRIGHTFULLY	SPRINKLINGS
SPOONERISMS	SPOROZOITES	SPORULATING	SPRIGHTFULNESS	SPRINTINGS

SPRITEFULLY	SQUADRONAL	SQUATTERED	SQUINNIEST	STABBINGLY
SPRITEFULNESS	SQUADRONED	SQUATTERING	SQUINNYING	STABILATES
SPRITEFULNESSES	SQUADRONES	SQUATTIEST	SQUINTIEST	STABILISATION
SPRITELIER	SQUADRONING	SQUATTINESS	SQUINTINGLY	STABILISATIONS
SPRITELIEST	SQUAILINGS	SQUATTINESSES	SQUINTINGS	STABILISATOR
SPRITSAILS	SQUALIDEST	SQUATTINGS	SQUIRALITIES	STABILISATORS
SPRITZIEST	SQUALIDITIES	SQUATTLING	SQUIRALITY	STABILISED
SPROUTINGS	SQUALIDITY	SQUATTOCRACIES	SQUIRALTIES	STABILISER
SPRUCENESS	SQUALIDNESS	SQUATTOCRACY	SQUIRARCHAL	STABILISERS
SPRUCENESSES	SQUALIDNESSES	SQUAWBUSHES	SQUIRARCHICAL	STABILISES
SPRYNESSES	SQUALLIEST	SQUAWFISHES	SQUIRARCHIES	STABILISING
SPUILZIEING	SQUALLINGS	SQUAWKIEST	SQUIRARCHS	STABILITIES
SPULEBLADE	SQUAMATION	SQUAWKINGS	SQUIRARCHY	STABILIZATION
SPULEBLADES	SQUAMATIONS	SQUAWROOTS	SQUIREAGES	STABILIZATIONS
SPULYIEING	SQUAMELLAS	SQUEAKERIES	SQUIREARCH	STABILIZATOR
SPULZIEING	SQUAMIFORM	SQUEAKIEST	SQUIREARCHAL	STABILIZATORS
SPUMESCENCE	SQUAMOSALS	SQUEAKINESS	SQUIREARCHICAL	STABILIZED
SPUMESCENCES	SQUAMOSELY	SQUEAKINESSES	SQUIREARCHIES	STABILIZER
SPUMESCENT	SQUAMOSENESS	SQUEAKINGLY	SQUIREARCHS	STABILIZERS
SPUNBONDED	SQUAMOSENESSES	SQUEAKINGS	SQUIREARCHY	STABILIZES
SPUNKINESS	SQUAMOSITIES	SQUEALINGS	SQUIREDOMS	STABILIZING
SPUNKINESSES	SQUAMOSITY	SQUEAMISHLY	SQUIREHOOD	STABLEBOYS
SPURGALLED	SQUAMOUSLY	SQUEAMISHNESS	SQUIREHOODS	STABLEMATE
SPURGALLING	SQUAMOUSNESS	SQUEAMISHNESSES	SQUIRELIKE	STABLEMATES
SPURIOSITIES	SQUAMOUSNESSES	SQUEEGEEING	SQUIRELING	STABLENESS
SPURIOSITY	SQUAMULOSE	SQUEEZABILITIES	SQUIRELINGS	STABLENESSES
SPURIOUSLY	SQUANDERED	SQUEEZABILITY	SQUIRESHIP	STABLISHED
SPURIOUSNESS	SQUANDERER	SQUEEZABLE	SQUIRESHIPS	STABLISHES
SPURIOUSNESSES	SQUANDERERS	SQUEEZIEST	SQUIRESSES	STABLISHING
SPUTTERERS	SQUANDERING	SQUEEZINGS	SQUIRMIEST	STABLISHMENT
SPUTTERIER	SQUANDERINGLY	SQUEGGINGS	SQUIRMINGLY	STABLISHMENTS
SPUTTERIEST	SQUANDERINGS	SQUELCHERS	SQUIRRELED	STACATIONED
SPUTTERING	SQUANDERMANIA	SQUELCHIER	SQUIRRELFISH	STACATIONER
SPUTTERINGLY	SQUANDERMANIAS	SQUELCHIEST	SQUIRRELFISHES	STACATIONERS
SPUTTERINGS	SQUAREHEAD	SQUELCHING	SQUIRRELIER	STACATIONING
SPYCATCHER	SQUAREHEADS	SQUELCHINGS	SQUIRRELIEST	STACATIONS
SPYCATCHERS	SQUARENESS	SQUETEAGUE	SQUIRRELING	STACCATISSIMO
SPYGLASSES	SQUARENESSES	SQUETEAGUES	SQUIRRELLED	STACKROOMS
SPYMASTERS	SQUAREWISE	SQUIBBINGS	SQUIRRELLIER	STACKYARDS
SQUABASHED	SQUARISHLY	SQUIDGIEST	SQUIRRELLIEST	STACTOMETER
SQUABASHER	SQUARISHNESS	SQUIFFIEST	SQUIRRELLING	STACTOMETERS
SQUABASHERS	SQUARISHNESSES	SQUIGGLERS	SQUIRRELLY	STADDLESTONE
SQUABASHES	SQUARSONAGE	SQUIGGLIER	SQUIRTINGS	STADDLESTONES
SQUABASHING	SQUARSONAGES	SQUIGGLIEST	SQUISHIEST	STADHOLDER
SQUABBIEST	SQUASHABLE	SQUIGGLING	SQUISHINESS	STADHOLDERATE
SQUABBLERS	SQUASHIEST	SQUILGEEING	SQUISHINESSES	STADHOLDERATES
SQUABBLING	SQUASHINESS	SQUILLIONS	SQUOOSHIER	STADHOLDERS
SQUABBLINGS	SQUASHINESSES	SQUINANCIES	SQUOOSHIEST	STADHOLDERSHIP
SQUADOOSHES	SQUATNESSES	SQUINCHING	SQUOOSHING	STADHOLDERSHIPS

STADIOMETER	STAIRCASES	STALLINGER	STANDARDIZING	STARCHEDLY
STADIOMETERS	STAIRCASING	STALLINGERS	STANDARDLESS	STARCHEDNESS
STADTHOLDER	STAIRCASINGS	STALLMASTER	STANDARDLY	STARCHEDNESSES
STADTHOLDERATE	STAIRFOOTS	STALLMASTERS	STANDDOWNS	STARCHIEST
STADTHOLDERATES	STAIRHEADS	STALWARTLY	STANDFASTS	STARCHINESS
STADTHOLDERS	STAIRLIFTS	STALWARTNESS	STANDFIRST	STARCHINESSES
STADTHOLDERSHIP	STAIRSTEPPED	STALWARTNESSES	STANDFIRSTS	STARCHLIKE
STAFFRIDER	STAIRSTEPPING	STALWORTHS	STANDGALES	STARDRIFTS
STAFFRIDERS	STAIRSTEPS	STAMINEOUS	STANDISHES	STARFISHED
STAFFROOMS	STAIRWELLS	STAMINIFEROUS	STANDOFFISH	STARFISHES
STAGECOACH	STAIRWORKS	STAMINODES	STANDOFFISHLY	STARFLOWER
STAGECOACHES	STAKEHOLDER	STAMINODIA	STANDOFFISHNESS	STARFLOWERS
STAGECOACHING	STAKEHOLDERS	STAMINODIES	STANDOVERS	STARFRUITS
STAGECOACHINGS	STAKHANOVISM	STAMINODIUM	STANDPATTER	STARFUCKER
STAGECOACHMAN	STAKHANOVISMS	STAMMERERS	STANDPATTERS	STARFUCKERS
STAGECOACHMEN	STAKHANOVITE	STAMMERING	STANDPATTISM	STARFUCKING
STAGECRAFT	STAKHANOVITES	STAMMERINGLY	STANDPATTISMS	STARFUCKINGS
STAGECRAFTS	STAKTOMETER	STAMMERINGS	STANDPIPES	STARGAZERS
STAGEHANDS	STAKTOMETERS	STAMPEDERS	STANDPOINT	STARGAZING
STAGEHEADS	STALACTICAL	STAMPEDING	STANDPOINTS	STARGAZINGS
STAGESTRUCK	STALACTIFORM	STAMPEDOED	STANDSTILL	STARKENING
STAGFLATION	STALACTITAL	STAMPEDOING	STANDSTILLS	STARKNESSES
STAGFLATIONARY	STALACTITE	STANCHABLE	STANNARIES	STARLIGHTED
STAGFLATIONS	STALACTITED	STANCHELLED	STANNATORS	STARLIGHTS
STAGGERBUSH	STALACTITES	STANCHELLING	STANNIFEROUS	STARMONGER
STAGGERBUSHES	STALACTITIC	STANCHERED	STANNOTYPE	STARMONGERS
STAGGERERS	STALACTITICAL	STANCHERING	STANNOTYPES	STAROSTIES
STAGGERIER	STALACTITICALLY	STANCHINGS	STAPEDECTOMIES	STARRINESS
STAGGERIEST	STALACTITIFORM	STANCHIONED	STAPEDECTOMY	STARRINESSES
STAGGERING	STALACTITIOUS	STANCHIONING	STAPEDIUSES	STARSHINES
STAGGERINGLY	STALAGMITE	STANCHIONS	STAPHYLINE	STARSTONES
STAGGERINGS	STALAGMITES	STANCHLESS	STAPHYLINID	STARSTRUCK
STAGHOUNDS	STALAGMITIC	STANCHNESS	STAPHYLINIDS	STARTINGLY
STAGINESSES	STALAGMITICAL	STANCHNESSES	STAPHYLITIS	STARTLEMENT
STAGNANCES	STALAGMITICALLY	STANDARDBRED	STAPHYLITISES	STARTLEMENTS
STAGNANCIES	STALAGMOMETER	STANDARDBREDS	STAPHYLOCOCCAL	STARTLIEST
STAGNANTLY	STALAGMOMETERS	STANDARDISATION	STAPHYLOCOCCI	STARTLINGLY
STAGNATING	STALAGMOMETRIES	STANDARDISE	STAPHYLOCOCCIC	STARTLINGS
STAGNATION	STALAGMOMETRY	STANDARDISED	STAPHYLOCOCCUS	STARVATION
STAGNATIONS	STALEMATED	STANDARDISER	STAPHYLOMA	STARVATIONS
STAIDNESSES	STALEMATES	STANDARDISERS	STAPHYLOMAS	STARVELING
STAINABILITIES	STALEMATING	STANDARDISES	STAPHYLOMATA	STARVELINGS
STAINABILITY	STALENESSES	STANDARDISING	STAPHYLOPLASTIC	STASIDIONS
STAINLESSES	STALKINESS	STANDARDIZATION	STAPHYLOPLASTY	STASIMORPHIES
STAINLESSLY	STALKINESSES	STANDARDIZE	STAPHYLORRHAPHY	STASIMORPHY
STAINLESSNESS	STALLENGER	STANDARDIZED	STARBOARDED	STATECRAFT
STAINLESSNESSES	STALLENGERS	STANDARDIZER	STARBOARDING	STATECRAFTS
STAINPROOF	STALLHOLDER	STANDARDIZERS	STARBOARDS	STATEHOODS
STAIRCASED	STALLHOLDERS	STANDARDIZES	STARBURSTS	STATEHOUSE

STATEHOUSES	STATUESQUE	STEAMBOATS	STEELWORKERS	STEGOMYIAS
STATELESSNESS	STATUESQUELY	STEAMERING	STEELWORKING	STEGOPHILIST
STATELESSNESSES	STATUESQUENESS	STEAMFITTER	STEELWORKINGS	STEGOPHILISTS
STATELIEST	STATUETTES	STEAMFITTERS	STEELWORKS	STEGOSAURIAN
STATELINESS	STATUSIEST	STEAMINESS	STEELYARDS	STEGOSAURIANS
STATELINESSES	STATUTABLE	STEAMINESSES	STEENBRASES	STEGOSAURS
STATEMENTED	STATUTABLY	STEAMPUNKS	STEENBUCKS	STEGOSAURUS
STATEMENTING	STATUTORILY	STEAMROLLED	STEENKIRKS	STEGOSAURUSES
STATEMENTINGS	STAUNCHABLE	STEAMROLLER	STEEPDOWNE	STEINBOCKS
STATEMENTS	STAUNCHERS	STEAMROLLERED	STEEPEDOWNE	STEINKIRKS
STATEROOMS	STAUNCHEST	STEAMROLLERING	STEEPENING	STELLARATOR
STATESMANLIER	STAUNCHING	STEAMROLLERS	STEEPINESS	STELLARATORS
STATESMANLIEST	STAUNCHINGS	STEAMROLLING	STEEPINESSES	STELLATELY
STATESMANLIKE	STAUNCHLESS	STEAMROLLS	STEEPLEBUSH	STELLERIDAN
STATESMANLY	STAUNCHNESS	STEAMSHIPS	STEEPLEBUSHES	STELLERIDANS
STATESMANSHIP	STAUNCHNESSES	STEAMTIGHT	STEEPLECHASE	STELLERIDS
STATESMANSHIPS	STAUROLITE	STEAMTIGHTNESS	STEEPLECHASED	STELLIFEROUS
STATESPERSON	STAUROLITES	STEAROPTENE	STEEPLECHASER	STELLIFIED
STATESPERSONS	STAUROLITIC	STEAROPTENES	STEEPLECHASERS	STELLIFIES
STATESWOMAN	STAUROSCOPE	STEARSMATE	STEEPLECHASES	STELLIFORM
STATESWOMEN	STAUROSCOPES	STEARSMATES	STEEPLECHASING	STELLIFYING
STATICALLY	STAUROSCOPIC	STEATOCELE	STEEPLECHASINGS	STELLIFYINGS
STATICKIER	STAVESACRE	STEATOCELES	STEEPLEJACK	STELLIONATE
STATICKIEST	STAVESACRES	STEATOHEPATITIS	STEEPLEJACKS	STELLIONATES
STATIONARIES	STAVUDINES	STEATOLYSES	STEEPNESSES	STELLULARLY
STATIONARILY	STAYCATION	STEATOLYSIS	STEERAGEWAY	STELLULATE
STATIONARINESS	STAYCATIONED	STEATOMATOUS	STEERAGEWAYS	STEMMATOUS
STATIONARY	STAYCATIONER	STEATOPYGA	STEERLINGS	STEMMERIES
STATIONERIES	STAYCATIONERS	STEATOPYGAS	STEERSMATE	STEMWINDER
STATIONERS	STAYCATIONING	STEATOPYGIA	STEERSMATES	STEMWINDERS
STATIONERY	STAYCATIONS	STEATOPYGIAS	STEGANOGRAM	STENCHIEST
STATIONING	STAYMAKERS	STEATOPYGIC	STEGANOGRAMS	STENCILERS
STATIONMASTER	STEADFASTLY	STEATOPYGOUS	STEGANOGRAPH	STENCILING
STATIONMASTERS	STEADFASTNESS	STEATORRHEA	STEGANOGRAPHER	STENCILINGS
STATISTICAL	STEADFASTNESSES	STEATORRHEAS	STEGANOGRAPHERS	STENCILLED
STATISTICALLY	STEADINESS	STEATORRHOEA	STEGANOGRAPHIC	STENCILLER
STATISTICIAN	STEADINESSES	STEATORRHOEAS	STEGANOGRAPHIES	STENCILLERS
STATISTICIANS	STEAKETTES	STEDFASTLY	STEGANOGRAPHIST	STENCILLING
STATISTICS	STEAKHOUSE	STEDFASTNESS	STEGANOGRAPHS	STENCILLINGS
STATOBLAST	STEAKHOUSES	STEDFASTNESSES	STEGANOGRAPHY	STENOBATHIC
STATOBLASTS	STEALINGLY	STEELHEADS	STEGANOPOD	STENOBATHS
STATOCYSTS	STEALTHFUL	STEELINESS	STEGANOPODOUS	STENOCARDIA
STATOLATRIES	STEALTHIER	STEELINESSES	STEGANOPODS	STENOCARDIAS
STATOLATRY	STEALTHIEST	STEELMAKER	STEGNOTICS	STENOCHROME
STATOLITHIC	STEALTHILY	STEELMAKERS	STEGOCARPOUS	STENOCHROMES
STATOLITHS	STEALTHINESS	STEELMAKING	STEGOCEPHALIAN	STENOCHROMIES
STATOSCOPE	STEALTHINESSES	STEELMAKINGS	STEGOCEPHALIANS	STENOCHROMY
STATOSCOPES	STEALTHING	STEELWARES	STEGOCEPHALOUS	STENOGRAPH
STATUARIES	STEALTHINGS	STEELWORKER	STEGODONTS	STENOGRAPHED

STENOGRAPHER	STEPHANOTISES	STEREOGRAM	STEREOTAXIC	STERNALGIC
STENOGRAPHERS	STEPLADDER	STEREOGRAMS	STEREOTAXICALLY	STERNBOARD
STENOGRAPHIC	STEPLADDERS	STEREOGRAPH	STEREOTAXIS	STERNBOARDS
STENOGRAPHICAL	STEPMOTHER	STEREOGRAPHED	STEREOTOMIES	STERNEBRAE
STENOGRAPHIES	STEPMOTHERLIER	STEREOGRAPHIC	STEREOTOMY	STERNFASTS
STENOGRAPHING	STEPMOTHERLIEST	STEREOGRAPHICAL	STEREOTROPIC	STERNFOREMOST
STENOGRAPHIST	STEPMOTHERLY	STEREOGRAPHIES	STEREOTROPISM	STERNNNESSES
STENOGRAPHISTS	STEPMOTHERS	STEREOGRAPHING	STEREOTROPISMS	STERNOCOSTAL
STENOGRAPHS	STEPPARENT	STEREOGRAPHS	STEREOTYPE	STERNOTRIBE
STENOGRAPHY	STEPPARENTING	STEREOGRAPHY	STEREOTYPED	STERNPORTS
STENOHALINE	STEPPARENTINGS	STEREOISOMER	STEREOTYPER	STERNPOSTS
STENOPAEIC	STEPPARENTS	STEREOISOMERIC	STEREOTYPERS	STERNSHEET
STENOPETALOUS	STEPSISTER	STEREOISOMERISM	STEREOTYPES	STERNSHEETS
STENOPHAGOUS	STEPSISTERS	STEREOISOMERS	STEREOTYPIC	STERNUTATION
STENOPHYLLOUS	STEPSTOOLS	STEREOISOMETRIC	STEREOTYPICAL	STERNUTATIONS
STENOTHERM	STERADIANS	STEREOLOGICAL	STEREOTYPICALLY	STERNUTATIVE
STENOTHERMAL	STERCORACEOUS	STEREOLOGICALLY	STEREOTYPIES	STERNUTATIVES
STENOTHERMS	STERCORANISM	STEREOLOGIES	STEREOTYPING	STERNUTATOR
STENOTOPIC	STERCORANISMS	STEREOLOGY	STEREOTYPINGS	STERNUTATORIES
STENOTROPIC	STERCORANIST	STEREOMETER	STEREOTYPIST	STERNUTATORS
STENOTYPED	STERCORANISTS	STEREOMETERS	STEREOTYPISTS	STERNUTATORY
STENOTYPER	STERCORARIES	STEREOMETRIC	STEREOTYPY	STERNWARDS
STENOTYPERS	STERCORARIOUS	STEREOMETRICAL	STEREOVISION	STERNWORKS
STENOTYPES	STERCORARY	STEREOMETRIES	STEREOVISIONS	STEROIDOGENESES
STENOTYPIC	STERCORATE	STEREOMETRY	STERICALLY	STEROIDOGENESIS
STENOTYPIES	STERCORATED	STEREOPHONIC	STERIGMATA	STEROIDOGENIC
STENOTYPING	STERCORATES	STEREOPHONIES	STERILANTS	STERTOROUS
STENOTYPIST	STERCORATING	STEREOPHONY	STERILISABLE	STERTOROUSLY
STENOTYPISTS	STERCORICOLOUS	STEREOPSES	STERILISATION	STERTOROUSNESS
STENTMASTER	STERCULIACEOUS	STEREOPSIS	STERILISATIONS	STETHOSCOPE
STENTMASTERS	STERCULIAS	STEREOPTICON	STERILISED	STETHOSCOPES
STENTORIAN	STEREOACUITIES	STEREOPTICONS	STERILISER	STETHOSCOPIC
STEPBAIRNS	STEREOACUITY	STEREOPTICS	STERILISERS	STETHOSCOPIES
STEPBROTHER	STEREOBATE	STEREOREGULAR	STERILISES	STETHOSCOPIST
STEPBROTHERS	STEREOBATES	STEREOSCOPE	STERILISING	STETHOSCOPISTS
STEPCHILDREN	STEREOBATIC	STEREOSCOPES	STERILITIES	STETHOSCOPY
STEPDANCER	STEREOBLIND	STEREOSCOPIC	STERILIZABLE	STEVEDORED
STEPDANCERS	STEREOCARD	STEREOSCOPICAL	STERILIZATION	STEVEDORES
STEPDANCING	STEREOCARDS	STEREOSCOPIES	STERILIZATIONS	STEVEDORING
STEPDANCINGS	STEREOCHEMICAL	STEREOSCOPIST	STERILIZED	STEVEDORINGS
STEPDAUGHTER	STEREOCHEMISTRY	STEREOSCOPISTS	STERILIZER	STEVENGRAPH
STEPDAUGHTERS	STEREOCHROME	STEREOSCOPY	STERILIZERS	STEVENGRAPHS
STEPFAMILIES	STEREOCHROMED	STEREOSONIC	STERILIZES	STEWARDESS
STEPFAMILY	STEREOCHROMES	STEREOSPECIFIC	STERILIZING	STEWARDESSES
STEPFATHER	STEREOCHROMIES	STEREOTACTIC	STERLINGLY	STEWARDING
STEPFATHERS	STEREOCHROMING	STEREOTACTICAL	STERLINGNESS	STEWARDRIES
STEPHANITE	STEREOCHROMY	STEREOTAXES	STERLINGNESSES	STEWARDSHIP
STEPHANITES	STEREOGNOSES	STEREOTAXIA	STERNALGIA	STEWARDSHIPS
STEPHANOTIS	STEREOGNOSIS	STEREOTAXIAS	STERNALGIAS	STEWARTRIES

S

STIACCIATO	STIFFENERS	STILLBORNS	STINKWEEDS	STOCKBROKINGS
STIACCIATOS	STIFFENING	STILLHOUSE	STINKWOODS	STOCKFISHES
STIBIALISM	STIFFENINGS	STILLHOUSES	STINTEDNESS	STOCKHOLDER
STIBIALISMS	STIFFNESSES	STILLICIDE	STINTEDNESSES	STOCKHOLDERS
STICCADOES	STIFFWARES	STILLICIDES	STINTINGLY	STOCKHOLDING
STICCATOES	STIFLINGLY	STILLIFORM	STIPELLATE	STOCKHOLDINGS
STICHARION	STIGMARIAN	STILLNESSES	STIPENDIARIES	STOCKHORNS
STICHARIONS	STIGMARIANS	STILLROOMS	STIPENDIARY	STOCKHORSE
STICHICALLY	STIGMASTEROL	STILPNOSIDERITE	STIPENDIATE	STOCKHORSES
STICHIDIUM	STIGMASTEROLS	STILTBIRDS	STIPENDIATED	STOCKINESS
STICHOLOGIES	STIGMATICAL	STILTEDNESS	STIPENDIATES	STOCKINESSES
STICHOLOGY	STIGMATICALLY	STILTEDNESSES	STIPENDIATING	STOCKINETS
STICHOMETRIC	STIGMATICS	STILTINESS	STIPITIFORM	STOCKINETTE
STICHOMETRICAL	STIGMATIFEROUS	STILTINESSES	STIPPLINGS	STOCKINETTES
STICHOMETRIES	STIGMATISATION	STIMPMETER	STIPULABLE	STOCKINGED
STICHOMETRY	STIGMATISATIONS	STIMPMETERS	STIPULACEOUS	STOCKINGER
STICHOMYTHIA	STIGMATISE	STIMULABLE	STIPULATED	STOCKINGERS
STICHOMYTHIAS	STIGMATISED	STIMULANCIES	STIPULATES	STOCKINGLESS
STICHOMYTHIC	STIGMATISER	STIMULANCY	STIPULATING	STOCKISHLY
STICHOMYTHIES	STIGMATISERS	STIMULANTS	STIPULATION	STOCKISHNESS
STICHOMYTHY	STIGMATISES	STIMULATED	STIPULATIONS	STOCKISHNESSES
STICKABILITIES	STIGMATISING	STIMULATER	STIPULATOR	STOCKJOBBER
STICKABILITY	STIGMATISM	STIMULATERS	STIPULATORS	STOCKJOBBERIES
STICKBALLS	STIGMATISMS	STIMULATES	STIPULATORY	STOCKJOBBERS
STICKERING	STIGMATIST	STIMULATING	STIRABOUTS	STOCKJOBBERY
STICKHANDLE	STIGMATISTS	STIMULATINGLY	STIRPICULTURE	STOCKJOBBING
STICKHANDLED	STIGMATIZATION	STIMULATION	STIRPICULTURES	STOCKJOBBINGS
STICKHANDLER	STIGMATIZATIONS	STIMULATIONS	STIRRINGLY	STOCKKEEPER
STICKHANDLERS	STIGMATIZE	STIMULATIVE	STITCHCRAFT	STOCKKEEPERS
STICKHANDLES	STIGMATIZED	STIMULATIVES	STITCHCRAFTS	STOCKLISTS
STICKHANDLING	STIGMATIZER	STIMULATOR	STITCHERIES	STOCKLOCKS
STICKHANDLINGS	STIGMATIZERS	STIMULATORS	STITCHINGS	STOCKPICKER
STICKINESS	STIGMATIZES	STIMULATORY	STITCHWORK	STOCKPICKERS
STICKINESSES	STIGMATIZING	STINGAREES	STITCHWORKS	STOCKPILED
STICKLEADER	STIGMATOPHILIA	STINGBULLS	STITCHWORT	STOCKPILER
STICKLEADERS	STIGMATOPHILIAS	STINGFISHES	STITCHWORTS	STOCKPILERS
STICKLEBACK	STIGMATOPHILIST	STINGINESS	STOCCADOES	STOCKPILES
STICKLEBACKS	STIGMATOSE	STINGINESSES	STOCHASTIC	STOCKPILING
STICKLINGS	STILBESTROL	STINGINGLY	STOCHASTICALLY	STOCKPILINGS
STICKSEEDS	STILBESTROLS	STINGINGNESS	STOCKADING	STOCKPUNISHT
STICKTIGHT	STILBOESTROL	STINGINGNESSES	STOCKBREEDER	STOCKROOMS
STICKTIGHTS	STILBOESTROLS	STINKBIRDS	STOCKBREEDERS	STOCKROUTE
STICKWEEDS	STILETTOED	STINKEROOS	STOCKBREEDING	STOCKROUTES
STICKWORKS	STILETTOES	STINKHORNS	STOCKBREEDINGS	STOCKTAKEN
STICKYBEAK	STILETTOING	STINKINGLY	STOCKBROKER	STOCKTAKES
STICKYBEAKED	STILLATORIES	STINKINGNESS	STOCKBROKERAGE	STOCKTAKING
STICKYBEAKING	STILLATORY	STINKINGNESSES	STOCKBROKERAGES	STOCKTAKINGS
STICKYBEAKS	STILLBIRTH	STINKSTONE	STOCKBROKERS	STOCKWORKS
STIDDIEING	STILLBIRTHS	STINKSTONES	STOCKBROKING	STOCKYARDS

S

STODGINESS	STOMATOLOGICAL	STONEWASHED	STORYBOOKS	STRAIGHTEDGED
STODGINESSES	STOMATOLOGIES	STONEWASHES	STORYETTES	STRAIGHTEDGES
STOECHIOLOGICAL	STOMATOLOGIST	STONEWASHING	STORYLINES	STRAIGHTEN
STOECHIOLOGIES	STOMATOLOGISTS	STONEWORKER	STORYTELLER	STRAIGHTENED
STOECHIOLOGY	STOMATOLOGY	STONEWORKERS	STORYTELLERS	STRAIGHTENER
STOECHIOMETRIC	STOMATOPLASTIES	STONEWORKS	STORYTELLING	STRAIGHTENERS
STOECHIOMETRIES	STOMATOPLASTY	STONEWORTS	STORYTELLINGS	STRAIGHTENING
STOECHIOMETRY	STOMATOPOD	STONINESSES	STORYTIMES	STRAIGHTENS
STOICALNESS	STOMATOPODS	STONISHING	STOTTERING	STRAIGHTER
STOICALNESSES	STOMODAEAL	STONKERING	STOUTENING	STRAIGHTEST
STOICHEIOLOGIES	STOMODAEUM	STONYHEARTED	STOUTHEARTED	STRAIGHTFORTH
STOICHEIOLOGY	STOMODAEUMS	STOOLBALLS	STOUTHEARTEDLY	STRAIGHTFORWARD
STOICHEIOMETRIC	STOMODEUMS	STOOPBALLS	STOUTHERIE	STRAIGHTING
STOICHEIOMETRY	STONEBOATS	STOOPINGLY	STOUTHERIES	STRAIGHTISH
STOICHIOLOGICAL	STONEBORER	STOPLIGHTS	STOUTHRIEF	STRAIGHTJACKET
STOICHIOLOGIES	STONEBORERS	STOPPERING	STOUTHRIEFS	STRAIGHTJACKETS
STOICHIOLOGY	STONEBRASH	STOPWATCHES	STOUTNESSES	STRAIGHTLACED
STOICHIOMETRIC	STONEBRASHES	STORECARDS	STOVEPIPES	STRAIGHTLY
STOICHIOMETRIES	STONEBREAK	STOREFRONT	STOVEWOODS	STRAIGHTNESS
STOICHIOMETRY	STONEBREAKER	STOREFRONTS	STRABISMAL	STRAIGHTNESSES
STOITERING	STONEBREAKERS	STOREHOUSE	STRABISMIC	STRAIGHTWAY
STOKEHOLDS	STONEBREAKS	STOREHOUSES	STRABISMICAL	STRAIGHTWAYS
STOKEHOLES	STONECASTS	STOREKEEPER	STRABISMOMETER	STRAINEDLY
STOLENWISE	STONECHATS	STOREKEEPERS	STRABISMOMETERS	STRAININGS
STOLIDITIES	STONECROPS	STOREKEEPING	STRABISMUS	STRAITENED
STOLIDNESS	STONECUTTER	STOREKEEPINGS	STRABISMUSES	STRAITENING
STOLIDNESSES	STONECUTTERS	STOREROOMS	STRABOMETER	STRAITJACKET
STOLONIFEROUS	STONECUTTING	STORESHIPS	STRABOMETERS	STRAITJACKETED
STOMACHACHE	STONECUTTINGS	STORIETTES	STRABOTOMIES	STRAITJACKETING
STOMACHACHES	STONEFISHES	STORIOLOGIES	STRABOTOMY	STRAITJACKETS
STOMACHALS	STONEFLIES	STORIOLOGIST	STRACCHINI	STRAITLACED
STOMACHERS	STONEGROUND	STORIOLOGISTS	STRACCHINO	STRAITLACEDLY
STOMACHFUL	STONEHANDS	STORIOLOGY	STRADDLEBACK	STRAITLACEDNESS
STOMACHFULNESS	STONEHORSE	STORKSBILL	STRADDLERS	STRAITNESS
STOMACHFULS	STONEHORSES	STORKSBILLS	STRADDLING	STRAITNESSES
STOMACHICAL	STONELESSNESS	STORMBIRDS	STRAGGLERS	STRAITWAISTCOAT
STOMACHICS	STONELESSNESSES	STORMBOUND	STRAGGLIER	STRAMACONS
STOMACHIER	STONEMASON	STORMCOCKS	STRAGGLIEST	STRAMASHED
STOMACHIEST	STONEMASONRIES	STORMFULLY	STRAGGLING	STRAMASHES
STOMACHING	STONEMASONRY	STORMFULNESS	STRAGGLINGLY	STRAMASHING
STOMACHLESS	STONEMASONS	STORMFULNESSES	STRAGGLINGS	STRAMAZONS
STOMACHOUS	STONESHOTS	STORMINESS	STRAICHTER	STRAMINEOUS
STOMATITIC	STONEWALLED	STORMINESSES	STRAICHTEST	STRAMONIES
STOMATITIDES	STONEWALLER	STORMPROOF	STRAIGHTAWAY	STRAMONIUM
STOMATITIS	STONEWALLERS	STORMSTAYED	STRAIGHTAWAYS	STRAMONIUMS
STOMATITISES	STONEWALLING	STORYBOARD	STRAIGHTBRED	STRANDEDNESS
STOMATODAEA	STONEWALLINGS	STORYBOARDED	STRAIGHTBREDS	STRANDEDNESSES
STOMATODAEUM	STONEWALLS	STORYBOARDING	STRAIGHTED	STRANDFLAT
STOMATOGASTRIC	STONEWARES	STORYBOARDS	STRAIGHTEDGE	STRANDFLATS

S

STRANDLINE	STRATEGIST	STRAUGHTEST	STREETKEEPERS	STREPTOCARPUS
STRANDLINES	STRATEGISTS	STRAUGHTING	STREETLAMP	STREPTOCARPUSES
STRANDWOLF	STRATEGIZE	STRAVAGING	STREETLAMPS	STREPTOCOCCAL
STRANDWOLVES	STRATEGIZED	STRAVAIGED	STREETLIGHT	STREPTOCOCCI
STRANGENESS	STRATEGIZES	STRAVAIGER	STREETLIGHTS	STREPTOCOCCIC
STRANGENESSES	STRATEGIZING	STRAVAIGERS	STREETROOM	STREPTOCOCCUS
STRANGERED	STRATHSPEY	STRAVAIGING	STREETROOMS	STREPTOKINASE
STRANGERING	STRATHSPEYS	STRAWBERRIES	STREETSCAPE	STREPTOKINASES
STRANGLEHOLD	STRATICULATE	STRAWBERRY	STREETSCAPES	STREPTOLYSIN
STRANGLEHOLDS	STRATICULATION	STRAWBOARD	STREETSMART	STREPTOLYSINS
STRANGLEMENT	STRATICULATIONS	STRAWBOARDS	STREETWALKER	STREPTOMYCES
STRANGLEMENTS	STRATIFICATION	STRAWFLOWER	STREETWALKERS	STREPTOMYCETE
STRANGLERS	STRATIFICATIONS	STRAWFLOWERS	STREETWALKING	STREPTOMYCETES
STRANGLING	STRATIFIED	STRAWWEIGHT	STREETWALKINGS	STREPTOMYCIN
STRANGULATE	STRATIFIES	STRAWWEIGHTS	STREETWARD	STREPTOMYCINS
STRANGULATED	STRATIFORM	STRAWWORMS	STREETWARDS	STREPTOSOLEN
STRANGULATES	STRATIFYING	STRAYLINGS	STREETWEAR	STREPTOSOLENS
STRANGULATING	STRATIGRAPHER	STREAKIEST	STREETWEARS	STREPTOTHRICIN
STRANGULATION	STRATIGRAPHERS	STREAKINESS	STREETWISE	STREPTOTHRICINS
STRANGULATIONS	STRATIGRAPHIC	STREAKINESSES	STREIGNING	STRESSBUSTER
STRANGURIES	STRATIGRAPHICAL	STREAKINGS	STRELITZES	STRESSBUSTERS
STRAPHANGED	STRATIGRAPHIES	STREAKLIKE	STRELITZIA	STRESSBUSTING
STRAPHANGER	STRATIGRAPHIST	STREAMBEDS	STRELITZIAS	STRESSFULLY
STRAPHANGERS	STRATIGRAPHISTS	STREAMERED	STRENGTHEN	STRESSFULNESS
STRAPHANGING	STRATIGRAPHY	STREAMIEST	STRENGTHENED	STRESSFULNESSES
STRAPHANGINGS	STRATOCRACIES	STREAMINESS	STRENGTHENER	STRESSIEST
STRAPHANGS	STRATOCRACY	STREAMINESSES	STRENGTHENERS	STRESSLESS
STRAPLESSES	STRATOCRAT	STREAMINGLY	STRENGTHENING	STRESSLESSNESS
STRAPLINES	STRATOCRATIC	STREAMINGS	STRENGTHENINGS	STRETCHABILITY
STRAPONTIN	STRATOCRATS	STREAMLESS	STRENGTHENS	STRETCHABLE
STRAPONTINS	STRATOCUMULI	STREAMLETS	STRENGTHFUL	STRETCHERED
STRAPPADOED	STRATOCUMULUS	STREAMLIKE	STRENGTHLESS	STRETCHERING
STRAPPADOES	STRATOPAUSE	STREAMLINE	STRENUITIES	STRETCHERS
STRAPPADOING	STRATOPAUSES	STREAMLINED	STRENUOSITIES	STRETCHIER
STRAPPADOS	STRATOSPHERE	STREAMLINER	STRENUOSITY	STRETCHIEST
STRAPPIEST	STRATOSPHERES	STREAMLINERS	STRENUOUSLY	STRETCHINESS
STRAPPINGS	STRATOSPHERIC	STREAMLINES	STRENUOUSNESS	STRETCHINESSES
STRAPWORTS	STRATOSPHERICAL	STREAMLING	STRENUOUSNESSES	STRETCHING
STRATAGEMS	STRATOTANKER	STREAMLINGS	STREPEROUS	STRETCHINGS
STRATEGETIC	STRATOTANKERS	STREAMLINING	STREPHOSYMBOLIA	STRETCHLESS
STRATEGETICAL	STRATOVOLCANO	STREAMLININGS	STREPITANT	STRETCHMARKS
STRATEGICAL	STRATOVOLCANOES	STREAMSIDE	STREPITATION	STREWMENTS
STRATEGICALLY	STRATOVOLCANOS	STREAMSIDES	STREPITATIONS	STRIATIONS
STRATEGICS	STRAUCHTED	STREETAGES	STREPITOSO	STRIATURES
STRATEGIES	STRAUCHTER	STREETBOYS	STREPITOUS	STRICKENLY
STRATEGISE	STRAUCHTEST	STREETCARS	STREPSIPTEROUS	STRICKLING
STRATEGISED	STRAUCHTING	STREETFULS	STREPTOBACILLI	STRICTIONS
STRATEGISES	STRAUGHTED	STREETIEST	STREPTOBACILLUS	STRICTNESS
STRATEGISING	STRAUGHTER	STREETKEEPER	STREPTOCARPI	STRICTNESSES

STRICTURED	STRINGHALT	STROBOSCOPE	STROPHIOLE	STRYCHNISMS
STRICTURES	STRINGHALTED	STROBOSCOPES	STROPHIOLES	STUBBINESS
STRIDDLING	STRINGHALTS	STROBOSCOPIC	STROPHOIDS	STUBBINESSES
STRIDELEGGED	STRINGIEST	STROBOSCOPICAL	STROPHULUS	STUBBLIEST
STRIDELEGS	STRINGINESS	STROBOTRON	STROPPIEST	STUBBORNED
STRIDENCES	STRINGINESSES	STROBOTRONS	STROPPINESS	STUBBORNER
STRIDENCIES	STRINGINGS	STRODDLING	STROPPINESSES	STUBBORNEST
STRIDENTLY	STRINGLESS	STROGANOFF	STROUDINGS	STUBBORNING
STRIDEWAYS	STRINGLIKE	STROGANOFFS	STROUPACHS	STUBBORNLY
STRIDULANCE	STRINGPIECE	STROKEPLAY	STRUCTURAL	STUBBORNNESS
STRIDULANCES	STRINGPIECES	STROLLINGS	STRUCTURALISE	STUBBORNNESSES
STRIDULANT	STRINGYBARK	STROMATOLITE	STRUCTURALISED	STUCCOWORK
STRIDULANTLY	STRINGYBARKS	STROMATOLITES	STRUCTURALISES	STUCCOWORKS
STRIDULATE	STRINKLING	STROMATOLITIC	STRUCTURALISING	STUDDINGSAIL
STRIDULATED	STRINKLINGS	STROMATOUS	STRUCTURALISM	STUDDINGSAILS
STRIDULATES	STRIPAGRAM	STROMBOLIS	STRUCTURALISMS	STUDENTIER
STRIDULATING	STRIPAGRAMS	STROMBULIFEROUS	STRUCTURALIST	STUDENTIEST
STRIDULATION	STRIPELESS	STROMBULIFORM	STRUCTURALISTS	STUDENTRIES
STRIDULATIONS	STRIPINESS	STROMBUSES	STRUCTURALIZE	STUDENTSHIP
STRIDULATOR	STRIPINESSES	STRONGARMED	STRUCTURALIZED	STUDENTSHIPS
STRIDULATORS	STRIPLINGS	STRONGARMING	STRUCTURALIZES	STUDFISHES
STRIDULATORY	STRIPOGRAM	STRONGARMS	STRUCTURALIZING	STUDHORSES
STRIDULOUS	STRIPOGRAMS	STRONGBOXES	STRUCTURALLY	STUDIEDNESS
STRIDULOUSLY	STRIPPABLE	STRONGHOLD	STRUCTURATION	STUDIEDNESSES
STRIDULOUSNESS	STRIPPAGRAM	STRONGHOLDS	STRUCTURATIONS	STUDIOUSLY
STRIFELESS	STRIPPAGRAMS	STRONGNESS	STRUCTURED	STUDIOUSNESS
STRIGIFORM	STRIPPERGRAM	STRONGNESSES	STRUCTURELESS	STUDIOUSNESSES
STRIKEBOUND	STRIPPERGRAMS	STRONGPOINT	STRUCTURES	STUFFINESS
STRIKEBREAKER	STRIPPINGS	STRONGPOINTS	STRUCTURING	STUFFINESSES
STRIKEBREAKERS	STRIPTEASE	STRONGROOM	STRUGGLERS	STULTIFICATION
STRIKEBREAKING	STRIPTEASER	STRONGROOMS	STRUGGLING	STULTIFICATIONS
STRIKEBREAKINGS	STRIPTEASERS	STRONGYLES	STRUGGLINGLY	STULTIFIED
STRIKELESS	STRIPTEASES	STRONGYLOID	STRUGGLINGS	STULTIFIER
STRIKEOUTS	STRIVINGLY	STRONGYLOIDOSES	STRUMITISES	STULTIFIERS
STRIKEOVER	STROBILACEOUS	STRONGYLOIDOSIS	STRUMPETED	STULTIFIES
STRIKEOVERS	STROBILATE	STRONGYLOIDS	STRUMPETING	STULTIFYING
STRIKINGLY	STROBILATED	STRONGYLOSES	STRUTHIOID	STUMBLEBUM
STRIKINGNESS	STROBILATES	STRONGYLOSIS	STRUTHIOIDS	STUMBLEBUMS
STRIKINGNESSES	STROBILATING	STRONTIANITE	STRUTHIOUS	STUMBLIEST
STRINGBOARD	STROBILATION	STRONTIANITES	STRUTTINGLY	STUMBLINGLY
STRINGBOARDS	STROBILATIONS	STRONTIANS	STRUTTINGS	STUMPINESS
STRINGCOURSE	STROBILIFORM	STRONTIUMS	STRYCHNIAS	STUMPINESSES
STRINGCOURSES	STROBILINE	STROPHANTHIN	STRYCHNINE	STUMPWORKS
STRINGENCIES	STROBILISATION	STROPHANTHINS	STRYCHNINED	STUNNINGLY
STRINGENCY	STROBILISATIONS	STROPHANTHUS	STRYCHNINES	STUNTEDNESS
STRINGENDO	STROBILIZATION	STROPHANTHUSES	STRYCHNINING	STUNTEDNESSES
STRINGENTLY	STROBILIZATIONS	STROPHICAL	STRYCHNINISM	STUNTWOMAN
STRINGENTNESS	STROBILOID	STROPHIOLATE	STRYCHNINISMS	STUNTWOMEN
STRINGENTNESSES	STROBILUSES	STROPHIOLATED	STRYCHNISM	STUPEFACIENT

STUPEFACIENTS	STYLOPISED	SUBALTERNITIES	SUBCALIBER	SUBCLASSED
STUPEFACTION	STYLOPISES	SUBALTERNITY	SUBCALIBRE	SUBCLASSES
STUPEFACTIONS	STYLOPISING	SUBALTERNS	SUBCANTORS	SUBCLASSIFIED
STUPEFACTIVE	STYLOPIZED	SUBANGULAR	SUBCAPSULAR	SUBCLASSIFIES
STUPEFIERS	STYLOPIZES	SUBANTARCTIC	SUBCARDINAL	SUBCLASSIFY
STUPEFYING	STYLOPIZING	SUBAPOSTOLIC	SUBCARDINALS	SUBCLASSIFYING
STUPEFYINGLY	STYLOPODIA	SUBAPPEARANCE	SUBCARRIER	SUBCLASSING
STUPENDIOUS	STYLOPODIUM	SUBAPPEARANCES	SUBCARRIERS	SUBCLAUSES
STUPENDOUS	STYLOSTIXES	SUBAQUATIC	SUBCATEGORIES	SUBCLAVIAN
STUPENDOUSLY	STYLOSTIXIS	SUBAQUEOUS	SUBCATEGORISE	SUBCLAVIANS
STUPENDOUSNESS	STYPTICITIES	SUBARACHNOID	SUBCATEGORISED	SUBCLAVICULAR
STUPIDITIES	STYPTICITY	SUBARACHNOIDAL	SUBCATEGORISES	SUBCLIMACTIC
STUPIDNESS	STYRACACEOUS	SUBARACHNOIDS	SUBCATEGORISING	SUBCLIMAXES
STUPIDNESSES	STYROFOAMS	SUBARBOREAL	SUBCATEGORIZE	SUBCLINICAL
STUPRATING	SUABILITIES	SUBARBORESCENT	SUBCATEGORIZED	SUBCLINICALLY
STUPRATION	SUASIVENESS	SUBARCTICS	SUBCATEGORIZES	SUBCLUSTER
STUPRATIONS	SUASIVENESSES	SUBARCUATE	SUBCATEGORIZING	SUBCLUSTERED
STURDINESS	SUAVENESSES	SUBARCUATION	SUBCATEGORY	SUBCLUSTERING
STURDINESSES	SUAVEOLENT	SUBARCUATIONS	SUBCAVITIES	SUBCLUSTERS
STUTTERERS	SUBABDOMINAL	SUBARRATION	SUBCEILING	SUBCOLLECTION
STUTTERING	SUBACETATE	SUBARRATIONS	SUBCEILINGS	SUBCOLLECTIONS
STUTTERINGLY	SUBACETATES	SUBARRHATION	SUBCELESTIAL	SUBCOLLEGE
STUTTERINGS	SUBACIDITIES	SUBARRHATIONS	SUBCELESTIALS	SUBCOLLEGES
STYLEBOOKS	SUBACIDITY	SUBARTICLE	SUBCELLARS	SUBCOLLEGIATE
STYLELESSNESS	SUBACIDNESS	SUBARTICLES	SUBCELLULAR	SUBCOLONIES
STYLELESSNESSES	SUBACIDNESSES	SUBASSEMBLE	SUBCENTERS	SUBCOMMISSION
STYLIFEROUS	SUBACTIONS	SUBASSEMBLED	SUBCENTRAL	SUBCOMMISSIONED
STYLISATION	SUBACUTELY	SUBASSEMBLES	SUBCENTRALLY	SUBCOMMISSIONER
STYLISATIONS	SUBADOLESCENT	SUBASSEMBLIES	SUBCENTRES	SUBCOMMISSIONS
STYLISHNESS	SUBADOLESCENTS	SUBASSEMBLING	SUBCEPTION	SUBCOMMITTEE
STYLISHNESSES	SUBAERIALLY	SUBASSEMBLY	SUBCEPTIONS	SUBCOMMITTEES
STYLISTICALLY	SUBAFFLUENT	SUBASSOCIATION	SUBCHANTER	SUBCOMMUNITIES
STYLISTICS	SUBAGENCIES	SUBASSOCIATIONS	SUBCHANTERS	SUBCOMMUNITY
STYLITISMS	SUBAGGREGATE	SUBATMOSPHERIC	SUBCHAPTER	SUBCOMPACT
STYLIZATION	SUBAGGREGATES	SUBATOMICS	SUBCHAPTERS	SUBCOMPACTS
STYLIZATIONS	SUBAGGREGATION	SUBAUDIBLE	SUBCHARTER	SUBCOMPONENT
STYLOBATES	SUBAGGREGATIONS	SUBAUDITION	SUBCHARTERED	SUBCOMPONENTS
STYLOGRAPH	SUBAHDARIES	SUBAUDITIONS	SUBCHARTERING	SUBCONSCIOUS
STYLOGRAPHIC	SUBAHSHIPS	SUBAURICULAR	SUBCHARTERS	SUBCONSCIOUSES
STYLOGRAPHICAL	SUBALLIANCE	SUBAVERAGE	SUBCHASERS	SUBCONSCIOUSLY
STYLOGRAPHIES	SUBALLIANCES	SUBAXILLARY	SUBCHELATE	SUBCONSULS
STYLOGRAPHS	SUBALLOCATION	SUBBASEMENT	SUBCHLORIDE	SUBCONTIGUOUS
STYLOGRAPHY	SUBALLOCATIONS	SUBBASEMENTS	SUBCHLORIDES	SUBCONTINENT
STYLOLITES	SUBALTERNANT	SUBBITUMINOUS	SUBCIRCUIT	SUBCONTINENTAL
STYLOLITIC	SUBALTERNANTS	SUBBRANCHES	SUBCIRCUITS	SUBCONTINENTS
STYLOMETRIES	SUBALTERNATE	SUBBUREAUS	SUBCIVILISATION	SUBCONTINUOUS
STYLOMETRY	SUBALTERNATES	SUBBUREAUX	SUBCIVILISED	SUBCONTRACT
STYLOPHONE	SUBALTERNATION	SUBCABINET	SUBCIVILIZATION	SUBCONTRACTED
STYLOPHONES	SUBALTERNATIONS	SUBCABINETS	SUBCIVILIZED	SUBCONTRACTING

SUBCONTRACTINGS	SUBDEPARTMENTS	SUBEPIDERMAL	SUBINDICATE	SUBJECTABILITY
SUBCONTRACTOR	SUBDEPUTIES	SUBEQUATORIAL	SUBINDICATED	SUBJECTABLE
SUBCONTRACTORS	SUBDERMALLY	SUBERISATION	SUBINDICATES	SUBJECTIFIED
SUBCONTRACTS	SUBDEVELOPMENT	SUBERISATIONS	SUBINDICATING	SUBJECTIFIES
SUBCONTRAOCTAVE	SUBDEVELOPMENTS	SUBERISING	SUBINDICATION	SUBJECTIFY
SUBCONTRARIES	SUBDIACONAL	SUBERIZATION	SUBINDICATIONS	SUBJECTIFYING
SUBCONTRARIETY	SUBDIACONATE	SUBERIZATIONS	SUBINDICATIVE	SUBJECTING
SUBCONTRARY	SUBDIACONATES	SUBERIZING	SUBINDICES	SUBJECTION
SUBCOOLING	SUBDIALECT	SUBFACTORIAL	SUBINDUSTRIES	SUBJECTIONS
SUBCORDATE	SUBDIALECTS	SUBFACTORIALS	SUBINDUSTRY	SUBJECTIVE
SUBCORIACEOUS	SUBDIRECTOR	SUBFAMILIES	SUBINFEUDATE	SUBJECTIVELY
SUBCORTEXES	SUBDIRECTORS	SUBFERTILE	SUBINFEUDATED	SUBJECTIVENESS
SUBCORTICAL	SUBDISCIPLINE	SUBFERTILITIES	SUBINFEUDATES	SUBJECTIVES
SUBCORTICES	SUBDISCIPLINES	SUBFERTILITY	SUBINFEUDATING	SUBJECTIVISE
SUBCOSTALS	SUBDISTRICT	SUBFEUDATION	SUBINFEUDATION	SUBJECTIVISED
SUBCOUNTIES	SUBDISTRICTS	SUBFEUDATIONS	SUBINFEUDATIONS	SUBJECTIVISES
SUBCRANIAL	SUBDIVIDABLE	SUBFEUDATORY	SUBINFEUDATORY	SUBJECTIVISING
SUBCRITICAL	SUBDIVIDED	SUBFOLDERS	SUBINFEUDED	SUBJECTIVISM
SUBCRUSTAL	SUBDIVIDER	SUBFOSSILS	SUBINFEUDING	SUBJECTIVISMS
SUBCULTURAL	SUBDIVIDERS	SUBFREEZING	SUBINFEUDS	SUBJECTIVIST
SUBCULTURALLY	SUBDIVIDES	SUBFUSCOUS	SUBINHIBITORY	SUBJECTIVISTIC
SUBCULTURE	SUBDIVIDING	SUBGENERATION	SUBINSINUATION	SUBJECTIVISTS
SUBCULTURED	SUBDIVISIBLE	SUBGENERATIONS	SUBINSINUATIONS	SUBJECTIVITIES
SUBCULTURES	SUBDIVISION	SUBGENERIC	SUBINSPECTOR	SUBJECTIVITY
SUBCULTURING	SUBDIVISIONAL	SUBGENERICALLY	SUBINSPECTORS	SUBJECTIVIZE
SUBCURATIVE	SUBDIVISIONS	SUBGENUSES	SUBINTELLECTION	SUBJECTIVIZED
SUBCUTANEOUS	SUBDIVISIVE	SUBGLACIAL	SUBINTELLIGENCE	SUBJECTIVIZES
SUBCUTANEOUSLY	SUBDOMINANT	SUBGLACIALLY	SUBINTELLIGITUR	SUBJECTIVIZING
SUBCUTISES	SUBDOMINANTS	SUBGLOBOSE	SUBINTERVAL	SUBJECTLESS
SUBDEACONATE	SUBDUCTING	SUBGLOBULAR	SUBINTERVALS	SUBJECTSHIP
SUBDEACONATES	SUBDUCTION	SUBGOVERNMENT	SUBINTRANT	SUBJECTSHIPS
SUBDEACONRIES	SUBDUCTIONS	SUBGOVERNMENTS	SUBINTRODUCE	SUBJOINDER
SUBDEACONRY	SUBDUEDNESS	SUBGROUPED	SUBINTRODUCED	SUBJOINDERS
SUBDEACONS	SUBDUEDNESSES	SUBGROUPING	SUBINTRODUCES	SUBJOINING
SUBDEACONSHIP	SUBDUEMENT	SUBHARMONIC	SUBINTRODUCING	SUBJUGABLE
SUBDEACONSHIPS	SUBDUEMENTS	SUBHARMONICS	SUBINVOLUTION	SUBJUGATED
SUBDEALERS	SUBDUPLICATE	SUBHASTATION	SUBINVOLUTIONS	SUBJUGATES
SUBDEANERIES	SUBECONOMIC	SUBHASTATIONS	SUBIRRIGATE	SUBJUGATING
SUBDEANERY	SUBECONOMIES	SUBHEADING	SUBIRRIGATED	SUBJUGATION
SUBDEBUTANTE	SUBECONOMY	SUBHEADINGS	SUBIRRIGATES	SUBJUGATIONS
SUBDEBUTANTES	SUBEDITING	SUBIMAGINAL	SUBIRRIGATING	SUBJUGATOR
SUBDECANAL	SUBEDITORIAL	SUBIMAGINES	SUBIRRIGATION	SUBJUGATORS
SUBDECISION	SUBEDITORS	SUBIMAGOES	SUBIRRIGATIONS	SUBJUNCTION
SUBDECISIONS	SUBEDITORSHIP	SUBINCISED	SUBITANEOUS	SUBJUNCTIONS
SUBDELIRIA	SUBEDITORSHIPS	SUBINCISES	SUBITISING	SUBJUNCTIVE
SUBDELIRIOUS	SUBEMPLOYED	SUBINCISING	SUBITIZING	SUBJUNCTIVELY
SUBDELIRIUM	SUBEMPLOYMENT	SUBINCISION	SUBJACENCIES	SUBJUNCTIVES
SUBDELIRIUMS	SUBEMPLOYMENTS	SUBINCISIONS	SUBJACENCY	SUBKINGDOM
SUBDEPARTMENT	SUBENTRIES	SUBINDEXES	SUBJACENTLY	SUBKINGDOMS

S

SUBLANCEOLATE	SUBLITERATES	SUBMICRONS	SUBNETWORKS	SUBORDINATORS
SUBLANGUAGE	SUBLITERATURE	SUBMICROSCOPIC	SUBNORMALITIES	SUBORGANISATION
SUBLANGUAGES	SUBLITERATURES	SUBMILLIMETER	SUBNORMALITY	SUBORGANIZATION
SUBLAPSARIAN	SUBLITTORAL	SUBMILLIMETERS	SUBNORMALLY	SUBORNATION
SUBLAPSARIANISM	SUBLITTORALS	SUBMILLIMETRE	SUBNORMALS	SUBORNATIONS
SUBLAPSARIANS	SUBLUXATED	SUBMILLIMETRES	SUBNUCLEAR	SUBORNATIVE
SUBLATIONS	SUBLUXATES	SUBMINIATURE	SUBNUCLEUS	SUBOSCINES
SUBLEASING	SUBLUXATING	SUBMINIATURES	SUBNUCLEUSES	SUBPANATION
SUBLESSEES	SUBLUXATION	SUBMINIATURISE	SUBOCCIPITAL	SUBPANATIONS
SUBLESSORS	SUBLUXATIONS	SUBMINIATURISED	SUBOCEANIC	SUBPARAGRAPH
SUBLETHALLY	SUBMANAGER	SUBMINIATURISES	SUBOCTAVES	SUBPARAGRAPHS
SUBLETTERS	SUBMANAGERS	SUBMINIATURIZE	SUBOCTUPLE	SUBPARALLEL
SUBLETTING	SUBMANDIBULAR	SUBMINIATURIZED	SUBOFFICER	SUBPENAING
SUBLETTINGS	SUBMANDIBULARS	SUBMINIATURIZES	SUBOFFICERS	SUBPERIODS
SUBLIBRARIAN	SUBMANIFOLD	SUBMINIMAL	SUBOFFICES	SUBPHRENIC
SUBLIBRARIANS	SUBMANIFOLDS	SUBMINISTER	SUBOPERCULA	SUBPHYLUMS
SUBLICENSE	SUBMARGINAL	SUBMINISTERED	SUBOPERCULAR	SUBPOENAED
SUBLICENSED	SUBMARGINALLY	SUBMINISTERING	SUBOPERCULUM	SUBPOENAING
SUBLICENSES	SUBMARINED	SUBMINISTERS	SUBOPERCULUMS	SUBPOPULATION
SUBLICENSING	SUBMARINER	SUBMISSIBLE	SUBOPTIMAL	SUBPOPULATIONS
SUBLIEUTENANCY	SUBMARINERS	SUBMISSION	SUBOPTIMISATION	SUBPOTENCIES
SUBLIEUTENANT	SUBMARINES	SUBMISSIONS	SUBOPTIMISE	SUBPOTENCY
SUBLIEUTENANTS	SUBMARINING	SUBMISSIVE	SUBOPTIMISED	SUBPREFECT
SUBLIMABLE	SUBMARKETS	SUBMISSIVELY	SUBOPTIMISES	SUBPREFECTS
SUBLIMATED	SUBMATRICES	SUBMISSIVENESS	SUBOPTIMISING	SUBPREFECTURE
SUBLIMATES	SUBMATRIXES	SUBMISSNESS	SUBOPTIMIZATION	SUBPREFECTURES
SUBLIMATING	SUBMAXILLARIES	SUBMISSNESSES	SUBOPTIMIZE	SUBPRIMATE
SUBLIMATION	SUBMAXILLARY	SUBMITTABLE	SUBOPTIMIZED	SUBPRIMATES
SUBLIMATIONS	SUBMAXIMAL	SUBMITTALS	SUBOPTIMIZES	SUBPRINCIPAL
SUBLIMENESS	SUBMEDIANT	SUBMITTERS	SUBOPTIMIZING	SUBPRINCIPALS
SUBLIMENESSES	SUBMEDIANTS	SUBMITTING	SUBOPTIMUM	SUBPRIORESS
SUBLIMINAL	SUBMENTUMS	SUBMITTINGS	SUBOPTIMUMS	SUBPRIORESSES
SUBLIMINALLY	SUBMERGEMENT	SUBMOLECULE	SUBORBICULAR	SUBPROBLEM
SUBLIMINALS	SUBMERGEMENTS	SUBMOLECULES	SUBORBITAL	SUBPROBLEMS
SUBLIMINGS	SUBMERGENCE	SUBMONTANE	SUBORDINAL	SUBPROCESS
SUBLIMISED	SUBMERGENCES	SUBMONTANELY	SUBORDINANCIES	SUBPROCESSES
SUBLIMISES	SUBMERGIBILITY	SUBMUCOSAE	SUBORDINANCY	SUBPRODUCT
SUBLIMISING	SUBMERGIBLE	SUBMUCOSAL	SUBORDINARIES	SUBPRODUCTS
SUBLIMITIES	SUBMERGIBLES	SUBMUCOSAS	SUBORDINARY	SUBPROFESSIONAL
SUBLIMIZED	SUBMERGING	SUBMULTIPLE	SUBORDINATE	SUBPROGRAM
SUBLIMIZES	SUBMERSIBILITY	SUBMULTIPLES	SUBORDINATED	SUBPROGRAMS
SUBLIMIZING	SUBMERSIBLE	SUBMUNITION	SUBORDINATELY	SUBPROJECT
SUBLINEATION	SUBMERSIBLES	SUBMUNITIONS	SUBORDINATENESS	SUBPROJECTS
SUBLINEATIONS	SUBMERSING	SUBNASCENT	SUBORDINATES	SUBPROLETARIAT
SUBLINGUAL	SUBMERSION	SUBNATIONAL	SUBORDINATING	SUBPROLETARIATS
SUBLITERACIES	SUBMERSIONS	SUBNATURAL	SUBORDINATION	SUBRATIONAL
SUBLITERACY	SUBMETACENTRIC	SUBNETWORK	SUBORDINATIONS	SUBREFERENCE
SUBLITERARY	SUBMETACENTRICS	SUBNETWORKED	SUBORDINATIVE	SUBREFERENCES
SUBLITERATE	SUBMICROGRAM	SUBNETWORKING	SUBORDINATOR	SUBREGIONAL

S

SUBREGIONS	SUBSENSIBLE	SUBSISTENCES	SUBSTANTIATE	SUBSTRACTS
SUBRENTING	SUBSENTENCE	SUBSISTENT	SUBSTANTIATED	SUBSTRATAL
SUBREPTION	SUBSENTENCES	SUBSISTENTIAL	SUBSTANTIATES	SUBSTRATES
SUBREPTIONS	SUBSEQUENCE	SUBSISTERS	SUBSTANTIATING	SUBSTRATIVE
SUBREPTITIOUS	SUBSEQUENCES	SUBSISTING	SUBSTANTIATION	SUBSTRATOSPHERE
SUBREPTITIOUSLY	SUBSEQUENT	SUBSOCIALLY	SUBSTANTIATIONS	SUBSTRATUM
SUBREPTIVE	SUBSEQUENTIAL	SUBSOCIETIES	SUBSTANTIATIVE	SUBSTRATUMS
SUBREPTIVELY	SUBSEQUENTLY	SUBSOCIETY	SUBSTANTIATOR	SUBSTRUCTED
SUBROGATED	SUBSEQUENTNESS	SUBSOILERS	SUBSTANTIATORS	SUBSTRUCTING
SUBROGATES	SUBSEQUENTS	SUBSOILING	SUBSTANTIVAL	SUBSTRUCTION
SUBROGATING	SUBSERVIENCE	SUBSOILINGS	SUBSTANTIVALLY	SUBSTRUCTIONS
SUBROGATION	SUBSERVIENCES	SUBSONICALLY	SUBSTANTIVE	SUBSTRUCTS
SUBROGATIONS	SUBSERVIENCIES	SUBSPECIALISE	SUBSTANTIVELY	SUBSTRUCTURAL
SUBROUTINE	SUBSERVIENCY	SUBSPECIALISED	SUBSTANTIVENESS	SUBSTRUCTURE
SUBROUTINES	SUBSERVIENT	SUBSPECIALISES	SUBSTANTIVES	SUBSTRUCTURES
SUBSAMPLED	SUBSERVIENTLY	SUBSPECIALISING	SUBSTANTIVISE	SUBSULTIVE
SUBSAMPLES	SUBSERVIENTS	SUBSPECIALIST	SUBSTANTIVISED	SUBSULTORILY
SUBSAMPLING	SUBSERVING	SUBSPECIALISTS	SUBSTANTIVISES	SUBSULTORY
SUBSATELLITE	SUBSESSILE	SUBSPECIALITIES	SUBSTANTIVISING	SUBSULTUSES
SUBSATELLITES	SUBSHRUBBY	SUBSPECIALITY	SUBSTANTIVITIES	SUBSUMABLE
SUBSATURATED	SUBSIDENCE	SUBSPECIALIZE	SUBSTANTIVITY	SUBSUMPTION
SUBSATURATION	SUBSIDENCES	SUBSPECIALIZED	SUBSTANTIVIZE	SUBSUMPTIONS
SUBSATURATIONS	SUBSIDENCIES	SUBSPECIALIZES	SUBSTANTIVIZED	SUBSUMPTIVE
SUBSCAPULAR	SUBSIDENCY	SUBSPECIALIZING	SUBSTANTIVIZES	SUBSURFACE
SUBSCAPULARS	SUBSIDIARIAT	SUBSPECIALTIES	SUBSTANTIVIZING	SUBSURFACES
SUBSCHEMATA	SUBSIDIARIATS	SUBSPECIALTY	SUBSTATION	SUBSYSTEMS
SUBSCIENCE	SUBSIDIARIES	SUBSPECIES	SUBSTATIONS	SUBTACKSMAN
SUBSCIENCES	SUBSIDIARILY	SUBSPECIFIC	SUBSTELLAR	SUBTACKSMEN
SUBSCRIBABLE	SUBSIDIARINESS	SUBSPECIFICALLY	SUBSTERNAL	SUBTANGENT
SUBSCRIBED	SUBSIDIARITIES	SUBSPINOUS	SUBSTITUENT	SUBTANGENTS
SUBSCRIBER	SUBSIDIARITY	SUBSPONTANEOUS	SUBSTITUENTS	SUBTEMPERATE
SUBSCRIBERS	SUBSIDIARY	SUBSTANCELESS	SUBSTITUTABLE	SUBTENANCIES
SUBSCRIBES	SUBSIDISABLE	SUBSTANCES	SUBSTITUTE	SUBTENANCY
SUBSCRIBING	SUBSIDISATION	SUBSTANDARD	SUBSTITUTED	SUBTENANTS
SUBSCRIBINGS	SUBSIDISATIONS	SUBSTANTIAL	SUBSTITUTES	SUBTENDING
SUBSCRIPTION	SUBSIDISED	SUBSTANTIALISE	SUBSTITUTING	SUBTENURES
SUBSCRIPTIONS	SUBSIDISER	SUBSTANTIALISED	SUBSTITUTION	SUBTERFUGE
SUBSCRIPTIVE	SUBSIDISERS	SUBSTANTIALISES	SUBSTITUTIONAL	SUBTERFUGES
SUBSCRIPTS	SUBSIDISES	SUBSTANTIALISM	SUBSTITUTIONARY	SUBTERMINAL
SUBSECRETARIES	SUBSIDISING	SUBSTANTIALISMS	SUBSTITUTIONS	SUBTERNATURAL
SUBSECRETARY	SUBSIDIZABLE	SUBSTANTIALIST	SUBSTITUTIVE	SUBTERRAIN
SUBSECTION	SUBSIDIZATION	SUBSTANTIALISTS	SUBSTITUTIVELY	SUBTERRAINS
SUBSECTIONS	SUBSIDIZATIONS	SUBSTANTIALITY	SUBSTITUTIVITY	SUBTERRANE
SUBSECTORS	SUBSIDIZED	SUBSTANTIALIZE	SUBSTRACTED	SUBTERRANEAN
SUBSEGMENT	SUBSIDIZER	SUBSTANTIALIZED	SUBSTRACTING	SUBTERRANEANLY
SUBSEGMENTS	SUBSIDIZERS	SUBSTANTIALIZES	SUBSTRACTION	SUBTERRANEANS
SUBSEIZURE	SUBSIDIZES	SUBSTANTIALLY	SUBSTRACTIONS	SUBTERRANEOUS
SUBSEIZURES	SUBSIDIZING	SUBSTANTIALNESS	SUBSTRACTOR	SUBTERRANEOUSLY
SUBSELLIUM	SUBSISTENCE	SUBSTANTIALS	SUBSTRACTORS	SUBTERRANES

S

SUBTERRENE	SUBTREASURER	SUBVERSIVE	SUCCESSIVELY	SUCKERFISHES
SUBTERRENES	SUBTREASURERS	SUBVERSIVELY	SUCCESSIVENESS	SUCKFISHES
SUBTERRESTRIAL	SUBTREASURIES	SUBVERSIVENESS	SUCCESSLESS	SUCKHOLING
SUBTERRESTRIALS	SUBTREASURY	SUBVERSIVES	SUCCESSLESSLY	SUCKINESSES
SUBTEXTUAL	SUBTRIANGULAR	SUBVERTEBRAL	SUCCESSLESSNESS	SUCRALFATE
SUBTHERAPEUTIC	SUBTRIPLICATE	SUBVERTERS	SUCCESSORAL	SUCRALFATES
SUBTHRESHOLD	SUBTROPICAL	SUBVERTICAL	SUCCESSORS	SUCRALOSES
SUBTILENESS	SUBTROPICALLY	SUBVERTING	SUCCESSORSHIP	SUCTIONING
SUBTILENESSES	SUBTROPICS	SUBVIRUSES	SUCCESSORSHIPS	SUCTORIANS
SUBTILISATION	SUBTRUDING	SUBVISIBLE	SUCCINATES	SUDATORIES
SUBTILISATIONS	SUBTWEETED	SUBVITREOUS	SUCCINCTER	SUDATORIUM
SUBTILISED	SUBTWEETING	SUBVOCALISATION	SUCCINCTEST	SUDATORIUMS
SUBTILISER	SUBTYPICAL	SUBVOCALISE	SUCCINCTLY	SUDDENNESS
SUBTILISERS	SUBUMBRELLA	SUBVOCALISED	SUCCINCTNESS	SUDDENNESSES
SUBTILISES	SUBUMBRELLAR	SUBVOCALISES	SUCCINCTNESSES	SUDDENTIES
SUBTILISIN	SUBUMBRELLAS	SUBVOCALISING	SUCCINCTORIA	SUDORIFEROUS
SUBTILISING	SUBUNGULATE	SUBVOCALIZATION	SUCCINCTORIES	SUDORIFICS
SUBTILISINS	SUBUNGULATES	SUBVOCALIZE	SUCCINCTORIUM	SUDORIPAROUS
SUBTILITIES	SUBURBANISATION	SUBVOCALIZED	SUCCINCTORIUMS	SUEABILITIES
SUBTILIZATION	SUBURBANISE	SUBVOCALIZES	SUCCINCTORY	SUEABILITY
SUBTILIZATIONS	SUBURBANISED	SUBVOCALIZING	SUCCINITES	SUFFERABLE
SUBTILIZED	SUBURBANISES	SUBVOCALLY	SUCCINYLCHOLINE	SUFFERABLENESS
SUBTILIZER	SUBURBANISING	SUBWARDENS	SUCCORABLE	SUFFERABLY
SUBTILIZERS	SUBURBANISM	SUBWOOFERS	SUCCORLESS	SUFFERANCE
SUBTILIZES	SUBURBANISMS	SUBWRITERS	SUCCOTASHES	SUFFERANCES
SUBTILIZING	SUBURBANITE	SUCCEDANEA	SUCCOURABLE	SUFFERINGLY
SUBTILTIES	SUBURBANITES	SUCCEDANEOUS	SUCCOURERS	SUFFERINGS
SUBTITLING	SUBURBANITIES	SUCCEDANEUM	SUCCOURING	SUFFICIENCE
SUBTITLINGS	SUBURBANITY	SUCCEDANEUMS	SUCCOURLESS	SUFFICIENCES
SUBTITULAR	SUBURBANIZATION	SUCCEDENTS	SUCCUBUSES	SUFFICIENCIES
SUBTLENESS	SUBURBANIZE	SUCCEEDABLE	SUCCULENCE	SUFFICIENCY
SUBTLENESSES	SUBURBANIZED	SUCCEEDERS	SUCCULENCES	SUFFICIENT
SUBTLETIES	SUBURBANIZES	SUCCEEDING	SUCCULENCIES	SUFFICIENTLY
SUBTOTALED	SUBURBANIZING	SUCCEEDINGLY	SUCCULENCY	SUFFICIENTS
SUBTOTALING	SUBURBICARIAN	SUCCENTORS	SUCCULENTLY	SUFFICINGNESS
SUBTOTALLED	SUBVARIANT	SUCCENTORSHIP	SUCCULENTS	SUFFICINGNESSES
SUBTOTALLING	SUBVARIANTS	SUCCENTORSHIPS	SUCCUMBERS	SUFFIGANCE
SUBTOTALLY	SUBVARIETIES	SUCCESSANTLY	SUCCUMBING	SUFFIGANCES
SUBTRACTED	SUBVARIETY	SUCCESSFUL	SUCCURSALE	SUFFISANCE
SUBTRACTER	SUBVASSALS	SUCCESSFULLY	SUCCURSALES	SUFFISANCES
SUBTRACTERS	SUBVENTION	SUCCESSFULNESS	SUCCURSALS	SUFFIXATION
SUBTRACTING	SUBVENTIONARY	SUCCESSION	SUCCUSSATION	SUFFIXATIONS
SUBTRACTION	SUBVENTIONS	SUCCESSIONAL	SUCCUSSATIONS	SUFFIXIONS
SUBTRACTIONS	SUBVERSALS	SUCCESSIONALLY	SUCCUSSING	SUFFLATING
SUBTRACTIVE	SUBVERSING	SUCCESSIONIST	SUCCUSSION	SUFFLATION
SUBTRACTOR	SUBVERSION	SUCCESSIONISTS	SUCCUSSIONS	SUFFLATIONS
SUBTRACTORS	SUBVERSIONARIES	SUCCESSIONLESS	SUCCUSSIVE	SUFFOCATED
SUBTRAHEND	SUBVERSIONARY	SUCCESSIONS	SUCHNESSES	SUFFOCATES
SUBTRAHENDS	SUBVERSIONS	SUCCESSIVE	SUCKERFISH	SUFFOCATING

SUFFOCATINGLY	SUGGESTIONISES	SULFHYDRYLS	SULPHAMATE	SULPHURIEST
SUFFOCATINGS	SUGGESTIONISING	SULFINPYRAZONE	SULPHAMATES	SULPHURING
SUFFOCATION	SUGGESTIONISM	SULFINPYRAZONES	SULPHANILAMIDE	SULPHURISATION
SUFFOCATIONS	SUGGESTIONISMS	SULFONAMIDE	SULPHANILAMIDES	SULPHURISATIONS
SUFFOCATIVE	SUGGESTIONIST	SULFONAMIDES	SULPHATASE	SULPHURISE
SUFFRAGANS	SUGGESTIONISTS	SULFONATED	SULPHATASES	SULPHURISED
SUFFRAGANSHIP	SUGGESTIONIZE	SULFONATES	SULPHATHIAZOLE	SULPHURISES
SUFFRAGANSHIPS	SUGGESTIONIZED	SULFONATING	SULPHATHIAZOLES	SULPHURISING
SUFFRAGETTE	SUGGESTIONIZES	SULFONATION	SULPHATING	SULPHURIZATION
SUFFRAGETTES	SUGGESTIONIZING	SULFONATIONS	SULPHATION	SULPHURIZATIONS
SUFFRAGETTISM	SUGGESTIONS	SULFONIUMS	SULPHATIONS	SULPHURIZE
SUFFRAGETTISMS	SUGGESTIVE	SULFONMETHANE	SULPHHYDRYL	SULPHURIZED
SUFFRAGISM	SUGGESTIVELY	SULFONMETHANES	SULPHHYDRYLS	SULPHURIZES
SUFFRAGISMS	SUGGESTIVENESS	SULFONYLUREA	SULPHINPYRAZONE	SULPHURIZING
SUFFRAGIST	SUICIDALLY	SULFONYLUREAS	SULPHINYLS	SULPHUROUS
SUFFRAGISTS	SUICIDOLOGIES	SULFOXIDES	SULPHONAMIDE	SULPHUROUSLY
SUFFRUTESCENT	SUICIDOLOGIST	SULFURATED	SULPHONAMIDES	SULPHUROUSNESS
SUFFRUTICOSE	SUICIDOLOGISTS	SULFURATES	SULPHONATE	SULPHURWORT
SUFFUMIGATE	SUICIDOLOGY	SULFURATING	SULPHONATED	SULPHURWORTS
SUFFUMIGATED	SUITABILITIES	SULFURATION	SULPHONATES	SULPHURYLS
SUFFUMIGATES	SUITABILITY	SULFURATIONS	SULPHONATING	SULTANATES
SUFFUMIGATING	SUITABLENESS	SULFUREOUS	SULPHONATION	SULTANESSES
SUFFUMIGATION	SUITABLENESSES	SULFURETED	SULPHONATIONS	SULTANSHIP
SUFFUMIGATIONS	SUITRESSES	SULFURETING	SULPHONIUM	SULTANSHIPS
SUFFUSIONS	SULCALISED	SULFURETTED	SULPHONIUMS	SULTRINESS
SUGARALLIE	SULCALISES	SULFURETTING	SULPHONMETHANE	SULTRINESSES
SUGARALLIES	SULCALISING	SULFURIEST	SULPHONMETHANES	SUMBITCHES
SUGARBERRIES	SULCALIZED	SULFURISATION	SULPHONYLS	SUMMABILITIES
SUGARBERRY	SULCALIZES	SULFURISATIONS	SULPHONYLUREA	SUMMABILITY
SUGARBUSHES	SULCALIZING	SULFURISED	SULPHONYLUREAS	SUMMARINESS
SUGARCANES	SULCATIONS	SULFURISES	SULPHOXIDE	SUMMARINESSES
SUGARCOATED	SULFACETAMIDE	SULFURISING	SULPHOXIDES	SUMMARISABLE
SUGARCOATING	SULFACETAMIDES	SULFURIZATION	SULPHURATE	SUMMARISATION
SUGARCOATS	SULFADIAZINE	SULFURIZATIONS	SULPHURATED	SUMMARISATIONS
SUGARHOUSE	SULFADIAZINES	SULFURIZED	SULPHURATES	SUMMARISED
SUGARHOUSES	SULFADIMIDINE	SULFURIZES	SULPHURATING	SUMMARISER
SUGARINESS	SULFADIMIDINES	SULFURIZING	SULPHURATION	SUMMARISERS
SUGARINESSES	SULFADOXINE	SULFUROUSLY	SULPHURATIONS	SUMMARISES
SUGARLOAVES	SULFADOXINES	SULFUROUSNESS	SULPHURATOR	SUMMARISING
SUGARPLUMS	SULFAMATES	SULFUROUSNESSES	SULPHURATORS	SUMMARISTS
SUGGESTERS	SULFAMETHAZINE	SULKINESSES	SULPHUREOUS	SUMMARIZABLE
SUGGESTIBILITY	SULFAMETHAZINES	SULLENNESS	SULPHUREOUSLY	SUMMARIZATION
SUGGESTIBLE	SULFANILAMIDE	SULLENNESSES	SULPHUREOUSNESS	SUMMARIZATIONS
SUGGESTIBLENESS	SULFANILAMIDES	SULPHACETAMIDE	SULPHURETED	SUMMARIZED
SUGGESTIBLY	SULFATASES	SULPHACETAMIDES	SULPHURETING	SUMMARIZER
SUGGESTING	SULFATHIAZOLE	SULPHADIAZINE	SULPHURETS	SUMMARIZERS
SUGGESTION	SULFATHIAZOLES	SULPHADIAZINES	SULPHURETTED	SUMMARIZES
SUGGESTIONISE	SULFATIONS	SULPHADOXINE	SULPHURETTING	SUMMARIZING
SUGGESTIONISED	SULFHYDRYL	SULPHADOXINES	SULPHURIER	SUMMATIONAL

SUMMATIONS	SUNDERANCE	SUPERACHIEVER	SUPERBOARDS	SUPERCLASSES
SUMMERHOUSE	SUNDERANCES	SUPERACHIEVERS	SUPERBOMBER	SUPERCLEAN
SUMMERHOUSES	SUNDERINGS	SUPERACTIVE	SUPERBOMBERS	SUPERCLUBS
SUMMERIEST	SUNDERMENT	SUPERACTIVITIES	SUPERBOMBS	SUPERCLUSTER
SUMMERINESS	SUNDERMENTS	SUPERACTIVITY	SUPERBRAIN	SUPERCLUSTERS
SUMMERINESSES	SUNDOWNERS	SUPERACUTE	SUPERBRAINS	SUPERCOILED
SUMMERINGS	SUNDOWNING	SUPERADDED	SUPERBRATS	SUPERCOILING
SUMMERLESS	SUNDRENCHED	SUPERADDING	SUPERBRIGHT	SUPERCOILS
SUMMERLIER	SUNDRESSES	SUPERADDITION	SUPERBUREAUCRAT	SUPERCOLLIDER
SUMMERLIEST	SUNFLOWERS	SUPERADDITIONAL	SUPERCABINET	SUPERCOLLIDERS
SUMMERLIKE	SUNGAZINGS	SUPERADDITIONS	SUPERCABINETS	SUPERCOLOSSAL
SUMMERLONG	SUNGLASSES	SUPERAGENCIES	SUPERCALENDER	SUPERCOLUMNAR
SUMMERSAULT	SUNLESSNESS	SUPERAGENCY	SUPERCALENDERED	SUPERCOMPUTER
SUMMERSAULTED	SUNLESSNESSES	SUPERAGENT	SUPERCALENDERS	SUPERCOMPUTERS
SUMMERSAULTING	SUNLOUNGER	SUPERAGENTS	SUPERCAPACITOR	SUPERCOMPUTING
SUMMERSAULTS	SUNLOUNGERS	SUPERALLOY	SUPERCAPACITORS	SUPERCOMPUTINGS
SUMMERSETS	SUNNINESSES	SUPERALLOYS	SUPERCARGO	SUPERCONDUCT
SUMMERSETTED	SUNPORCHES	SUPERALTAR	SUPERCARGOES	SUPERCONDUCTED
SUMMERSETTING	SUNRISINGS	SUPERALTARS	SUPERCARGOS	SUPERCONDUCTING
SUMMERTIDE	SUNSCREENING	SUPERALTERN	SUPERCARGOSHIP	SUPERCONDUCTION
SUMMERTIDES	SUNSCREENINGS	SUPERALTERNS	SUPERCARGOSHIPS	SUPERCONDUCTIVE
SUMMERTIME	SUNSCREENS	SUPERAMBITIOUS	SUPERCARRIER	SUPERCONDUCTOR
SUMMERTIMES	SUNSEEKERS	SUPERANNUABLE	SUPERCARRIERS	SUPERCONDUCTORS
SUMMERWEIGHT	SUNSETTING	SUPERANNUATE	SUPERCAUTIOUS	SUPERCONDUCTS
SUMMERWOOD	SUNSETTINGS	SUPERANNUATED	SUPERCEDED	SUPERCONFIDENCE
SUMMERWOODS	SUNSHINIER	SUPERANNUATES	SUPERCEDES	SUPERCONFIDENT
SUMMITEERS	SUNSHINIEST	SUPERANNUATING	SUPERCEDING	SUPERCONTINENT
SUMMITLESS	SUNSPOTTED	SUPERANNUATION	SUPERCELESTIAL	SUPERCONTINENTS
SUMMITRIES	SUNSTROKES	SUPERANNUATIONS	SUPERCELLS	SUPERCONVENIENT
SUMMONABLE	SUNTANNING	SUPERATHLETE	SUPERCENTER	SUPERCOOLED
SUMMONSING	SUNTANNINGS	SUPERATHLETES	SUPERCENTERS	SUPERCOOLING
SUMPHISHNESS	SUNWORSHIPPER	SUPERATING	SUPERCHARGE	SUPERCOOLS
SUMPHISHNESSES	SUNWORSHIPPERS	SUPERATION	SUPERCHARGED	SUPERCOVER
SUMPSIMUSES	SUOVETAURILIA	SUPERATIONS	SUPERCHARGER	SUPERCOVERS
SUMPTUOSITIES	SUOVETAURILIAS	SUPERATOMS	SUPERCHARGERS	SUPERCRIMINAL
SUMPTUOSITY	SUPERABILITIES	SUPERBANKS	SUPERCHARGES	SUPERCRIMINALS
SUMPTUOUSLY	SUPERABILITY	SUPERBAZAAR	SUPERCHARGING	SUPERCRITICAL
SUMPTUOUSNESS	SUPERABLENESS	SUPERBAZAARS	SUPERCHERIE	SUPERCURRENT
SUMPTUOUSNESSES	SUPERABLENESSES	SUPERBAZAR	SUPERCHERIES	SUPERCURRENTS
SUNBATHERS	SUPERABOUND	SUPERBAZARS	SUPERCHURCH	SUPERDAINTIER
SUNBATHING	SUPERABOUNDED	SUPERBIKES	SUPERCHURCHES	SUPERDAINTIEST
SUNBATHINGS	SUPERABOUNDING	SUPERBITCH	SUPERCILIARIES	SUPERDAINTY
SUNBEAMIER	SUPERABOUNDS	SUPERBITCHES	SUPERCILIARY	SUPERDELEGATE
SUNBEAMIEST	SUPERABSORBENT	SUPERBITIES	SUPERCILIOUS	SUPERDELEGATES
SUNBERRIES	SUPERABSORBENTS	SUPERBLOCK	SUPERCILIOUSLY	SUPERDELUXE
SUNBONNETED	SUPERABUNDANCE	SUPERBLOCKS	SUPERCITIES	SUPERDENSE
SUNBONNETS	SUPERABUNDANCES	SUPERBNESS	SUPERCIVILISED	SUPERDIPLOMAT
SUNBURNING	SUPERABUNDANT	SUPERBNESSES	SUPERCIVILIZED	SUPERDIPLOMATS
SUNDERABLE	SUPERABUNDANTLY	SUPERBOARD	SUPERCLASS	SUPERDOMINANT

SUPERDOMINANTS	SUPERFEMALE	SUPERGIANTS	SUPERHUMANLY	SUPERJACENT
SUPEREFFECTIVE	SUPERFEMALES	SUPERGLACIAL	SUPERHUMANNESS	SUPERJOCKS
SUPEREFFICIENCY	SUPERFETATE	SUPERGLUED	SUPERHUMANS	SUPERJUMBO
SUPEREFFICIENT	SUPERFETATED	SUPERGLUEING	SUPERHUMERAL	SUPERJUMBOS
SUPEREGOIST	SUPERFETATES	SUPERGLUES	SUPERHUMERALS	SUPERKINGDOM
SUPEREGOISTS	SUPERFETATING	SUPERGLUING	SUPERHYPED	SUPERKINGDOMS
SUPERELASTIC	SUPERFETATION	SUPERGOVERNMENT	SUPERHYPES	SUPERLARGE
SUPERELEVATE	SUPERFETATIONS	SUPERGRAPHICS	SUPERHYPING	SUPERLATIVE
SUPERELEVATED	SUPERFICIAL	SUPERGRASS	SUPERIMPORTANT	SUPERLATIVELY
SUPERELEVATES	SUPERFICIALISE	SUPERGRASSES	SUPERIMPOSABLE	SUPERLATIVENESS
SUPERELEVATING	SUPERFICIALISED	SUPERGRAVITIES	SUPERIMPOSE	SUPERLATIVES
SUPERELEVATION	SUPERFICIALISES	SUPERGRAVITY	SUPERIMPOSED	SUPERLAWYER
SUPERELEVATIONS	SUPERFICIALITY	SUPERGROUP	SUPERIMPOSES	SUPERLAWYERS
SUPERELITE	SUPERFICIALIZE	SUPERGROUPS	SUPERIMPOSING	SUPERLIGHT
SUPERELITES	SUPERFICIALIZED	SUPERGROWTH	SUPERIMPOSITION	SUPERLINER
SUPEREMINENCE	SUPERFICIALIZES	SUPERGROWTHS	SUPERINCUMBENCE	SUPERLINERS
SUPEREMINENCES	SUPERFICIALLY	SUPERHARDEN	SUPERINCUMBENCY	SUPERLOADS
SUPEREMINENT	SUPERFICIALNESS	SUPERHARDENED	SUPERINCUMBENT	SUPERLOBBYIST
SUPEREMINENTLY	SUPERFICIALS	SUPERHARDENING	SUPERINDIVIDUAL	SUPERLOBBYISTS
SUPEREROGANT	SUPERFICIES	SUPERHARDENS	SUPERINDUCE	SUPERLOYALIST
SUPEREROGATE	SUPERFINENESS	SUPERHEATED	SUPERINDUCED	SUPERLOYALISTS
SUPEREROGATED	SUPERFINENESSES	SUPERHEATER	SUPERINDUCEMENT	SUPERLUMINAL
SUPEREROGATES	SUPERFIRMS	SUPERHEATERS	SUPERINDUCES	SUPERLUNAR
SUPEREROGATING	SUPERFIXES	SUPERHEATING	SUPERINDUCING	SUPERLUNARY
SUPEREROGATION	SUPERFLACK	SUPERHEATS	SUPERINDUCTION	SUPERLUXURIES
SUPEREROGATIONS	SUPERFLACKS	SUPERHEAVIES	SUPERINDUCTIONS	SUPERLUXURIOUS
SUPEREROGATIVE	SUPERFLUID	SUPERHEAVY	SUPERINFECT	SUPERLUXURY
SUPEREROGATOR	SUPERFLUIDITIES	SUPERHELICAL	SUPERINFECTED	SUPERLYING
SUPEREROGATORS	SUPERFLUIDITY	SUPERHELICES	SUPERINFECTING	SUPERMACHO
SUPEREROGATORY	SUPERFLUIDS	SUPERHELIX	SUPERINFECTION	SUPERMAJORITIES
SUPERESSENTIAL	SUPERFLUITIES	SUPERHELIXES	SUPERINFECTIONS	SUPERMAJORITY
SUPERETTES	SUPERFLUITY	SUPERHEROES	SUPERINFECTS	SUPERMALES
SUPEREVIDENT	SUPERFLUOUS	SUPERHEROINE	SUPERINSULATED	SUPERMARKET
SUPEREXALT	SUPERFLUOUSLY	SUPERHEROINES	SUPERINTEND	SUPERMARKETS
SUPEREXALTATION	SUPERFLUOUSNESS	SUPERHETERODYNE	SUPERINTENDED	SUPERMARTS
SUPEREXALTED	SUPERFLUXES	SUPERHIGHWAY	SUPERINTENDENCE	SUPERMASCULINE
SUPEREXALTING	SUPERFOETATION	SUPERHIGHWAYS	SUPERINTENDENCY	SUPERMASSIVE
SUPEREXALTS	SUPERFOETATIONS	SUPERHIVES	SUPERINTENDENT	SUPERMAXES
SUPEREXCELLENCE	SUPERFOODS	SUPERHUMAN	SUPERINTENDENTS	SUPERMEMBRANE
SUPEREXCELLENT	SUPERFRONTAL	SUPERHUMANISE	SUPERINTENDING	SUPERMEMBRANES
SUPEREXPENSIVE	SUPERFRONTALS	SUPERHUMANISED	SUPERINTENDS	SUPERMICRO
SUPEREXPRESS	SUPERFUNDS	SUPERHUMANISES	SUPERINTENSITY	SUPERMICROS
SUPEREXPRESSES	SUPERFUSED	SUPERHUMANISING	SUPERIORESS	SUPERMILITANT
SUPERFAMILIES	SUPERFUSES	SUPERHUMANITIES	SUPERIORESSES	SUPERMILITANTS
SUPERFAMILY	SUPERFUSING	SUPERHUMANITY	SUPERIORITIES	SUPERMINDS
SUPERFARMS	SUPERFUSION	SUPERHUMANIZE	SUPERIORITY	SUPERMINIS
SUPERFATTED	SUPERFUSIONS	SUPERHUMANIZED	SUPERIORLY	SUPERMINISTER
SUPERFECTA	SUPERGENES	SUPERHUMANIZES	SUPERIORSHIP	SUPERMINISTERS
SUPERFECTAS	SUPERGIANT	SUPERHUMANIZING	SUPERIORSHIPS	SUPERMODEL

SUPERMODELS	SUPERORDINARY	SUPERPLUSES	SUPERSAURS	SUPERSEXUALITY
SUPERMODERN	SUPERORDINATE	SUPERPOLITE	SUPERSAVER	SUPERSHARP
SUPERMOONS	SUPERORDINATED	SUPERPOLYMER	SUPERSAVERS	SUPERSHOWS
SUPERMOTOS	SUPERORDINATES	SUPERPOLYMERS	SUPERSCALAR	SUPERSINGER
SUPERMUNDANE	SUPERORDINATING	SUPERPORTS	SUPERSCALE	SUPERSINGERS
SUPERNACULA	SUPERORDINATION	SUPERPOSABLE	SUPERSCHOOL	SUPERSIZED
SUPERNACULAR	SUPERORGANIC	SUPERPOSED	SUPERSCHOOLS	SUPERSIZES
SUPERNACULUM	SUPERORGANICISM	SUPERPOSES	SUPERSCOUT	SUPERSIZING
SUPERNALLY	SUPERORGANICIST	SUPERPOSING	SUPERSCOUTS	SUPERSLEUTH
SUPERNANNIES	SUPERORGANISM	SUPERPOSITION	SUPERSCREEN	SUPERSLEUTHS
SUPERNANNY	SUPERORGANISMS	SUPERPOSITIONS	SUPERSCREENS	SUPERSLICK
SUPERNATANT	SUPERORGASM	SUPERPOWER	SUPERSCRIBE	SUPERSMART
SUPERNATANTS	SUPERORGASMS	SUPERPOWERED	SUPERSCRIBED	SUPERSMOOTH
SUPERNATATION	SUPEROVULATE	SUPERPOWERFUL	SUPERSCRIBES	SUPERSONIC
SUPERNATATIONS	SUPEROVULATED	SUPERPOWERS	SUPERSCRIBING	SUPERSONICALLY
SUPERNATED	SUPEROVULATES	SUPERPRAISE	SUPERSCRIPT	SUPERSONICS
SUPERNATES	SUPEROVULATING	SUPERPRAISED	SUPERSCRIPTION	SUPERSOUND
SUPERNATING	SUPEROVULATION	SUPERPRAISES	SUPERSCRIPTIONS	SUPERSOUNDS
SUPERNATION	SUPEROVULATIONS	SUPERPRAISING	SUPERSCRIPTS	SUPERSPECIAL
SUPERNATIONAL	SUPEROXIDE	SUPERPREMIUM	SUPERSECRECIES	SUPERSPECIALIST
SUPERNATIONALLY	SUPEROXIDES	SUPERPREMIUMS	SUPERSECRECY	SUPERSPECIALS
SUPERNATIONS	SUPERPARASITISM	SUPERPROFIT	SUPERSECRET	SUPERSPECIES
SUPERNATURAL	SUPERPARTICLE	SUPERPROFITS	SUPERSECRETS	SUPERSPECTACLE
SUPERNATURALISE	SUPERPARTICLES	SUPERQUALITIES	SUPERSEDABLE	SUPERSPECTACLES
SUPERNATURALISM	SUPERPATRIOT	SUPERQUALITY	SUPERSEDEAS	SUPERSPEED
SUPERNATURALIST	SUPERPATRIOTIC	SUPERRACES	SUPERSEDEASES	SUPERSPEEDS
SUPERNATURALIZE	SUPERPATRIOTISM	SUPERREALISM	SUPERSEDED	SUPERSPIES
SUPERNATURALLY	SUPERPATRIOTS	SUPERREALISMS	SUPERSEDENCE	SUPERSPREADER
SUPERNATURALS	SUPERPEOPLE	SUPERREALIST	SUPERSEDENCES	SUPERSPREADERS
SUPERNATURE	SUPERPERSON	SUPERREALISTS	SUPERSEDER	SUPERSTARDOM
SUPERNATURES	SUPERPERSONAL	SUPERREFINE	SUPERSEDERE	SUPERSTARDOMS
SUPERNORMAL	SUPERPERSONS	SUPERREFINED	SUPERSEDERES	SUPERSTARS
SUPERNORMALITY	SUPERPHENOMENA	SUPERREFINES	SUPERSEDERS	SUPERSTATE
SUPERNORMALLY	SUPERPHENOMENON	SUPERREFINING	SUPERSEDES	SUPERSTATES
SUPERNOVAE	SUPERPHONE	SUPERREGIONAL	SUPERSEDING	SUPERSTATION
SUPERNOVAS	SUPERPHONES	SUPERREGIONALS	SUPERSEDURE	SUPERSTATIONS
SUPERNUMERARIES	SUPERPHOSPHATE	SUPERROADS	SUPERSEDURES	SUPERSTIMULATE
SUPERNUMERARY	SUPERPHOSPHATES	SUPERROMANTIC	SUPERSELLER	SUPERSTIMULATED
SUPERNURSE	SUPERPHYLA	SUPERSAFETIES	SUPERSELLERS	SUPERSTIMULATES
SUPERNURSES	SUPERPHYLUM	SUPERSAFETY	SUPERSELLING	SUPERSTITION
SUPERNUTRIENT	SUPERPHYSICAL	SUPERSALES	SUPERSELLS	SUPERSTITIONS
SUPERNUTRIENTS	SUPERPIMPS	SUPERSALESMAN	SUPERSENSIBLE	SUPERSTITIOUS
SUPERNUTRITION	SUPERPLANE	SUPERSALESMEN	SUPERSENSIBLY	SUPERSTITIOUSLY
SUPERNUTRITIONS	SUPERPLANES	SUPERSALTS	SUPERSENSITIVE	SUPERSTOCK
SUPEROCTAVE	SUPERPLASTIC	SUPERSATURATE	SUPERSENSORY	SUPERSTOCKS
SUPEROCTAVES	SUPERPLASTICITY	SUPERSATURATED	SUPERSENSUAL	SUPERSTORE
SUPERORDER	SUPERPLASTICS	SUPERSATURATES	SUPERSESSION	SUPERSTORES
SUPERORDERS	SUPERPLAYER	SUPERSATURATING	SUPERSESSIONS	SUPERSTORM
SUPERORDINAL	SUPERPLAYERS	SUPERSATURATION	SUPERSEXES	SUPERSTORMS

SUPERSTRATA	SUPERTRAMS	SUPINENESS	SUPPLICATION	SUPPRESSER
SUPERSTRATUM	SUPERTRUCK	SUPINENESSES	SUPPLICATIONS	SUPPRESSERS
SUPERSTRATUMS	SUPERTRUCKS	SUPPEAGOES	SUPPLICATORY	SUPPRESSES
SUPERSTRENGTH	SUPERTWIST	SUPPEDANEA	SUPPLICATS	SUPPRESSIBILITY
SUPERSTRENGTHS	SUPERTWISTS	SUPPEDANEUM	SUPPLICAVIT	SUPPRESSIBLE
SUPERSTRIKE	SUPERUSERS	SUPPERLESS	SUPPLICAVITS	SUPPRESSING
SUPERSTRIKES	SUPERVENED	SUPPERTIME	SUPPLYMENT	SUPPRESSION
SUPERSTRING	SUPERVENES	SUPPERTIMES	SUPPLYMENTS	SUPPRESSIONS
SUPERSTRINGS	SUPERVENIENCE	SUPPLANTATION	SUPPORTABILITY	SUPPRESSIVE
SUPERSTRONG	SUPERVENIENCES	SUPPLANTATIONS	SUPPORTABLE	SUPPRESSIVENESS
SUPERSTRUCT	SUPERVENIENT	SUPPLANTED	SUPPORTABLENESS	SUPPRESSOR
SUPERSTRUCTED	SUPERVENING	SUPPLANTER	SUPPORTABLY	SUPPRESSORS
SUPERSTRUCTING	SUPERVENTION	SUPPLANTERS	SUPPORTANCE	SUPPURATED
SUPERSTRUCTION	SUPERVENTIONS	SUPPLANTING	SUPPORTANCES	SUPPURATES
SUPERSTRUCTIONS	SUPERVIRILE	SUPPLEJACK	SUPPORTERS	SUPPURATING
SUPERSTRUCTIVE	SUPERVIRTUOSI	SUPPLEJACKS	SUPPORTING	SUPPURATION
SUPERSTRUCTS	SUPERVIRTUOSO	SUPPLEMENT	SUPPORTINGS	SUPPURATIONS
SUPERSTRUCTURAL	SUPERVIRTUOSOS	SUPPLEMENTAL	SUPPORTIVE	SUPPURATIVE
SUPERSTRUCTURE	SUPERVIRULENT	SUPPLEMENTALLY	SUPPORTIVELY	SUPPURATIVES
SUPERSTRUCTURES	SUPERVISAL	SUPPLEMENTALS	SUPPORTIVENESS	SUPRACHIASMIC
SUPERSTUDS	SUPERVISALS	SUPPLEMENTARIES	SUPPORTLESS	SUPRACHOROIDAL
SUPERSUBTILE	SUPERVISED	SUPPLEMENTARILY	SUPPORTMENT	SUPRACILIARY
SUPERSUBTLE	SUPERVISEE	SUPPLEMENTARY	SUPPORTMENTS	SUPRACOSTAL
SUPERSUBTLETIES	SUPERVISEES	SUPPLEMENTATION	SUPPORTRESS	SUPRACRUSTAL
SUPERSUBTLETY	SUPERVISES	SUPPLEMENTED	SUPPORTRESSES	SUPRAGLOTTAL
SUPERSURGEON	SUPERVISING	SUPPLEMENTER	SUPPORTURE	SUPRALAPSARIAN
SUPERSURGEONS	SUPERVISION	SUPPLEMENTERS	SUPPORTURES	SUPRALAPSARIANS
SUPERSWEET	SUPERVISIONS	SUPPLEMENTING	SUPPOSABLE	SUPRALIMINAL
SUPERSYMMETRIC	SUPERVISOR	SUPPLEMENTS	SUPPOSABLY	SUPRALIMINALLY
SUPERSYMMETRIES	SUPERVISORS	SUPPLENESS	SUPPOSEDLY	SUPRALUNAR
SUPERSYMMETRY	SUPERVISORSHIP	SUPPLENESSES	SUPPOSINGS	SUPRAMAXILLARY
SUPERSYSTEM	SUPERVISORSHIPS	SUPPLETION	SUPPOSITION	SUPRAMOLECULAR
SUPERSYSTEMS	SUPERVISORY	SUPPLETIONS	SUPPOSITIONAL	SUPRAMOLECULE
SUPERTANKER	SUPERVOLUTE	SUPPLETIVE	SUPPOSITIONALLY	SUPRAMOLECULES
SUPERTANKERS	SUPERWAIFS	SUPPLETIVES	SUPPOSITIONARY	SUPRAMUNDANE
SUPERTASKS	SUPERWAVES	SUPPLETORILY	SUPPOSITIONLESS	SUPRANATIONAL
SUPERTAXES	SUPERWEAPON	SUPPLETORY	SUPPOSITIONS	SUPRANATIONALLY
SUPERTEACHER	SUPERWEAPONS	SUPPLIABLE	SUPPOSITIOUS	SUPRAOPTIC
SUPERTEACHERS	SUPERWEEDS	SUPPLIANCE	SUPPOSITIOUSLY	SUPRAORBITAL
SUPERTERRANEAN	SUPERWIDES	SUPPLIANCES	SUPPOSITITIOUS	SUPRAPUBIC
SUPERTERRIFIC	SUPERWIVES	SUPPLIANTLY	SUPPOSITIVE	SUPRARATIONAL
SUPERTHICK	SUPERWOMAN	SUPPLIANTS	SUPPOSITIVELY	SUPRARENAL
SUPERTHRILLER	SUPERWOMEN	SUPPLICANT	SUPPOSITIVES	SUPRARENALS
SUPERTHRILLERS	SUPERYACHT	SUPPLICANTS	SUPPOSITORIES	SUPRASEGMENTAL
SUPERTIGHT	SUPERYACHTS	SUPPLICATE	SUPPOSITORY	SUPRASENSIBLE
SUPERTITLE	SUPINATING	SUPPLICATED	SUPPRESSANT	SUPRATEMPORAL
SUPERTITLES	SUPINATION	SUPPLICATES	SUPPRESSANTS	SUPRAVITAL
SUPERTONIC	SUPINATIONS	SUPPLICATING	SUPPRESSED	SUPRAVITALLY
SUPERTONICS	SUPINATORS	SUPPLICATINGLY	SUPPRESSEDLY	SUPREMACIES

SUPREMACISM	SURFCASTINGS	SURPRISING	SURTARBRANDS	SUSPECTEDNESS
SUPREMACISMS	SURFEITERS	SURPRISINGLY	SURTURBRAND	SUSPECTEDNESSES
SUPREMACIST	SURFEITING	SURPRISINGNESS	SURTURBRANDS	SUSPECTERS
SUPREMACISTS	SURFEITINGS	SURPRISINGS	SURVEILING	SUSPECTFUL
SUPREMATISM	SURFFISHES	SURPRIZING	SURVEILLANCE	SUSPECTING
SUPREMATISMS	SURFPERCHES	SURQUEDIES	SURVEILLANCES	SUSPECTLESS
SUPREMATIST	SURFRIDDEN	SURQUEDRIES	SURVEILLANT	SUSPENDERED
SUPREMATISTS	SURFRIDERS	SURREALISM	SURVEILLANTS	SUSPENDERS
SUPREMENESS	SURFRIDING	SURREALISMS	SURVEILLED	SUSPENDIBILITY
SUPREMENESSES	SURFRIDINGS	SURREALIST	SURVEILLES	SUSPENDIBLE
SUPREMITIES	SURGEONCIES	SURREALISTIC	SURVEILLING	SUSPENDING
SURADDITION	SURGEONFISH	SURREALISTS	SURVEYABLE	SUSPENSEFUL
SURADDITIONS	SURGEONFISHES	SURREBUTTAL	SURVEYANCE	SUSPENSEFULLY
SURBASEMENT	SURGEONSHIP	SURREBUTTALS	SURVEYANCES	SUSPENSEFULNESS
SURBASEMENTS	SURGEONSHIPS	SURREBUTTED	SURVEYINGS	SUSPENSELESS
SURBEDDING	SURGICALLY	SURREBUTTER	SURVEYORSHIP	SUSPENSERS
SURCEASING	SURJECTION	SURREBUTTERS	SURVEYORSHIPS	SUSPENSIBILITY
SURCHARGED	SURJECTIONS	SURREBUTTING	SURVIEWING	SUSPENSIBLE
SURCHARGEMENT	SURJECTIVE	SURREJOINDER	SURVIVABILITIES	SUSPENSION
SURCHARGEMENTS	SURLINESSES	SURREJOINDERS	SURVIVABILITY	SUSPENSIONS
SURCHARGER	SURMASTERS	SURREJOINED	SURVIVABLE	SUSPENSIVE
SURCHARGERS	SURMISABLE	SURREJOINING	SURVIVALISM	SUSPENSIVELY
SURCHARGES	SURMISINGS	SURREJOINS	SURVIVALISMS	SUSPENSIVENESS
SURCHARGING	SURMISTRESS	SURRENDERED	SURVIVALIST	SUSPENSOID
SURCINGLED	SURMISTRESSES	SURRENDEREE	SURVIVALISTS	SUSPENSOIDS
SURCINGLES	SURMOUNTABLE	SURRENDEREES	SURVIVANCE	SUSPENSORIA
SURCINGLING	SURMOUNTED	SURRENDERER	SURVIVANCES	SUSPENSORIAL
SURCULUSES	SURMOUNTER	SURRENDERERS	SURVIVORSHIP	SUSPENSORIES
SUREFOOTED	SURMOUNTERS	SURRENDERING	SURVIVORSHIPS	SUSPENSORIUM
SUREFOOTEDLY	SURMOUNTING	SURRENDEROR	SUSCEPTANCE	SUSPENSORS
SUREFOOTEDNESS	SURMOUNTINGS	SURRENDERORS	SUSCEPTANCES	SUSPENSORY
SURENESSES	SURMULLETS	SURRENDERS	SUSCEPTIBILITY	SUSPERCOLLATE
SURETYSHIP	SURNOMINAL	SURRENDRIES	SUSCEPTIBLE	SUSPERCOLLATED
SURETYSHIPS	SURPASSABLE	SURREPTITIOUS	SUSCEPTIBLENESS	SUSPERCOLLATES
SURFACELESS	SURPASSERS	SURREPTITIOUSLY	SUSCEPTIBLY	SUSPERCOLLATING
SURFACEMAN	SURPASSING	SURROGACIES	SUSCEPTIVE	SUSPICIONAL
SURFACEMEN	SURPASSINGLY	SURROGATED	SUSCEPTIVENESS	SUSPICIONED
SURFACINGS	SURPASSINGNESS	SURROGATES	SUSCEPTIVITIES	SUSPICIONING
SURFACTANT	SURPLUSAGE	SURROGATESHIP	SUSCEPTIVITY	SUSPICIONLESS
SURFACTANTS	SURPLUSAGES	SURROGATESHIPS	SUSCEPTORS	SUSPICIONS
SURFBOARDED	SURPLUSING	SURROGATING	SUSCIPIENT	SUSPICIOUS
SURFBOARDER	SURPLUSSED	SURROGATION	SUSCIPIENTS	SUSPICIOUSLY
SURFBOARDERS	SURPLUSSES	SURROGATIONS	SUSCITATED	SUSPICIOUSNESS
SURFBOARDING	SURPLUSSING	SURROGATUM	SUSCITATES	SUSPIRATION
SURFBOARDINGS	SURPRINTED	SURROGATUMS	SUSCITATING	SUSPIRATIONS
SURFBOARDS	SURPRINTING	SURROUNDED	SUSCITATION	SUSPIRIOUS
SURFCASTER	SURPRISALS	SURROUNDING	SUSCITATIONS	SUSTAINABILITY
SURFCASTERS	SURPRISEDLY	SURROUNDINGS	SUSPECTABLE	SUSTAINABLE
SURFCASTING	SURPRISERS	SURTARBRAND	SUSPECTEDLY	SUSTAINABLY

SUSTAINEDLY	SWALLOWERS	SWEEPSTAKE	SWINDLINGS	SWIVELLING
SUSTAINERS	SWALLOWING	SWEEPSTAKES	SWINEHERDS	SWOLLENNESS
SUSTAINING	SWALLOWTAIL	SWEETBREAD	SWINEHOODS	SWOLLENNESSES
SUSTAININGLY	SWALLOWTAILS	SWEETBREADS	SWINEPOXES	SWOONINGLY
SUSTAININGS	SWALLOWWORT	SWEETBRIAR	SWINESTONE	SWOOPSTAKE
SUSTAINMENT	SWALLOWWORTS	SWEETBRIARS	SWINESTONES	SWORDBEARER
SUSTAINMENTS	SWAMPINESS	SWEETBRIER	SWINGBEATS	SWORDBEARERS
SUSTENANCE	SWAMPINESSES	SWEETBRIERS	SWINGBOATS	SWORDBILLS
SUSTENANCES	SWAMPLANDS	SWEETCORNS	SWINGEINGLY	SWORDCRAFT
SUSTENTACULA	SWANKINESS	SWEETENERS	SWINGINGER	SWORDCRAFTS
SUSTENTACULAR	SWANKINESSES	SWEETENING	SWINGINGEST	SWORDFERNS
SUSTENTACULUM	SWANNERIES	SWEETENINGS	SWINGINGLY	SWORDFISHES
SUSTENTATE	SWANSDOWNS	SWEETFISHES	SWINGLETREE	SWORDPLAYER
SUSTENTATED	SWARAJISMS	SWEETHEART	SWINGLETREES	SWORDPLAYERS
SUSTENTATES	SWARAJISTS	SWEETHEARTED	SWINGLINGS	SWORDPLAYS
SUSTENTATING	SWARTHIEST	SWEETHEARTING	SWINGOMETER	SWORDPROOF
SUSTENTATION	SWARTHINESS	SWEETHEARTINGS	SWINGOMETERS	SWORDSMANSHIP
SUSTENTATIONS	SWARTHINESSES	SWEETHEARTS	SWINGTREES	SWORDSMANSHIPS
SUSTENTATIVE	SWARTHNESS	SWEETIEWIFE	SWINISHNESS	SWORDSTICK
SUSTENTATOR	SWARTHNESSES	SWEETIEWIVES	SWINISHNESSES	SWORDSTICKS
SUSTENTATORS	SWARTNESSES	SWEETISHLY	SWIRLINGLY	SWORDSWOMAN
SUSTENTION	SWASHBUCKLE	SWEETISHNESS	SWISHINGLY	SWORDSWOMEN
SUSTENTIONS	SWASHBUCKLED	SWEETISHNESSES	SWITCHABLE	SWORDTAILS
SUSTENTIVE	SWASHBUCKLER	SWEETMEATS	SWITCHBACK	SYBARITICAL
SUSURRATED	SWASHBUCKLERS	SWEETNESSES	SWITCHBACKED	SYBARITICALLY
SUSURRATES	SWASHBUCKLES	SWEETSHOPS	SWITCHBACKING	SYBARITISH
SUSURRATING	SWASHBUCKLING	SWEETVELDS	SWITCHBACKS	SYBARITISM
SUSURRATION	SWASHWORKS	SWEETWATER	SWITCHBLADE	SYBARITISMS
SUSURRATIONS	SWATCHBOOK	SWEETWATERS	SWITCHBLADES	SYCOPHANCIES
SUSURRUSES	SWATCHBOOKS	SWEETWOODS	SWITCHBOARD	SYCOPHANCY
SUTLERSHIP	SWATHEABLE	SWEIRNESSES	SWITCHBOARDS	SYCOPHANTIC
SUTLERSHIPS	SWATTERING	SWELLFISHES	SWITCHEROO	SYCOPHANTICAL
SUTTEEISMS	SWAYBACKED	SWELLHEADED	SWITCHEROOS	SYCOPHANTICALLY
SUTTLETIES	SWEARWORDS	SWELLHEADEDNESS	SWITCHGEAR	SYCOPHANTISE
SUTURATION	SWEATBANDS	SWELLHEADS	SWITCHGEARS	SYCOPHANTISED
SUTURATIONS	SWEATBOXES	SWELLINGLY	SWITCHGIRL	SYCOPHANTISES
SUZERAINTIES	SWEATERDRESS	SWELTERING	SWITCHGIRLS	SYCOPHANTISH
SUZERAINTY	SWEATERDRESSES	SWELTERINGLY	SWITCHGRASS	SYCOPHANTISHLY
SVARABHAKTI	SWEATINESS	SWELTERINGS	SWITCHGRASSES	SYCOPHANTISING
SVARABHAKTIS	SWEATINESSES	SWELTRIEST	SWITCHIEST	SYCOPHANTISM
SVELTENESS	SWEATPANTS	SWEPTWINGS	SWITCHINGS	SYCOPHANTISMS
SVELTENESSES	SWEATSHIRT	SWERVELESS	SWITCHLIKE	SYCOPHANTIZE
SWAGGERERS	SWEATSHIRTS	SWIFTNESSES	SWITCHOVER	SYCOPHANTIZED
SWAGGERING	SWEATSHOPS	SWIMFEEDER	SWITCHOVERS	SYCOPHANTIZES
SWAGGERINGLY	SWEATSUITS	SWIMFEEDERS	SWITCHYARD	SYCOPHANTIZING
SWAGGERINGS	SWEEPBACKS	SWIMMERETS	SWITCHYARDS	SYCOPHANTLIER
SWAINISHNESS	SWEEPINGLY	SWIMMINGLY	SWITHERING	SYCOPHANTLIEST
SWAINISHNESSES	SWEEPINGNESS	SWIMMINGNESS	SWIVELBLOCK	SYCOPHANTLY
SWALLOWABLE	SWEEPINGNESSES	SWIMMINGNESSES	SWIVELBLOCKS	SYCOPHANTRIES

SYCOPHANTRY
SYCOPHANTS
SYLLABARIA
SYLLABARIES
SYLLABARIUM
SYLLABICAL
SYLLABICALLY
SYLLABICATE
SYLLABICATED
SYLLABICATES
SYLLABICATING
SYLLABICATION
SYLLABICATIONS
SYLLABICITIES
SYLLABICITY
SYLLABIFICATION
SYLLABIFIED
SYLLABIFIES
SYLLABIFYING
SYLLABISED
SYLLABISES
SYLLABISING
SYLLABISMS
SYLLABIZED
SYLLABIZES
SYLLABIZING
SYLLABLING
SYLLABOGRAM
SYLLABOGRAMS
SYLLABOGRAPHIES
SYLLABOGRAPHY
SYLLABUSES
SYLLEPTICAL
SYLLEPTICALLY
SYLLOGISATION
SYLLOGISATIONS
SYLLOGISED
SYLLOGISER
SYLLOGISERS
SYLLOGISES
SYLLOGISING
SYLLOGISMS
SYLLOGISTIC
SYLLOGISTICAL
SYLLOGISTICALLY
SYLLOGISTICS
SYLLOGISTS
SYLLOGIZATION
SYLLOGIZATIONS

SYLLOGIZED
SYLLOGIZER
SYLLOGIZERS
SYLLOGIZES
SYLLOGIZING
SYLPHIDINE
SYLVANITES
SYLVESTRAL
SYLVESTRIAN
SYLVICULTURAL
SYLVICULTURE
SYLVICULTURES
SYLVINITES
SYMBIONTIC
SYMBIONTICALLY
SYMBIOTICAL
SYMBIOTICALLY
SYMBOLICAL
SYMBOLICALLY
SYMBOLICALNESS
SYMBOLISATION
SYMBOLISATIONS
SYMBOLISED
SYMBOLISER
SYMBOLISERS
SYMBOLISES
SYMBOLISING
SYMBOLISMS
SYMBOLISTIC
SYMBOLISTICAL
SYMBOLISTICALLY
SYMBOLISTS
SYMBOLIZATION
SYMBOLIZATIONS
SYMBOLIZED
SYMBOLIZER
SYMBOLIZERS
SYMBOLIZES
SYMBOLIZING
SYMBOLLING
SYMBOLOGICAL
SYMBOLOGIES
SYMBOLOGIST
SYMBOLOGISTS
SYMBOLOGRAPHIES
SYMBOLOGRAPHY
SYMBOLOLATRIES
SYMBOLOLATRY
SYMBOLOLOGIES

SYMBOLOLOGY
SYMMETALISM
SYMMETALISMS
SYMMETALLIC
SYMMETALLISM
SYMMETALLISMS
SYMMETRIAN
SYMMETRIANS
SYMMETRICAL
SYMMETRICALLY
SYMMETRICALNESS
SYMMETRIES
SYMMETRISATION
SYMMETRISATIONS
SYMMETRISE
SYMMETRISED
SYMMETRISES
SYMMETRISING
SYMMETRIZATION
SYMMETRIZATIONS
SYMMETRIZE
SYMMETRIZED
SYMMETRIZES
SYMMETRIZING
SYMMETROPHOBIA
SYMMETROPHOBIAS
SYMPATHECTOMIES
SYMPATHECTOMY
SYMPATHETIC
SYMPATHETICAL
SYMPATHETICALLY
SYMPATHETICS
SYMPATHIES
SYMPATHINS
SYMPATHIQUE
SYMPATHISE
SYMPATHISED
SYMPATHISER
SYMPATHISERS
SYMPATHISES
SYMPATHISING
SYMPATHIZE
SYMPATHIZED
SYMPATHIZER
SYMPATHIZERS
SYMPATHIZES
SYMPATHIZING
SYMPATHOLYTIC
SYMPATHOLYTICS

SYMPATHOMIMETIC
SYMPATRICALLY
SYMPATRIES
SYMPETALIES
SYMPETALOUS
SYMPHILIES
SYMPHILISM
SYMPHILISMS
SYMPHILOUS
SYMPHONICALLY
SYMPHONIES
SYMPHONION
SYMPHONIONS
SYMPHONIOUS
SYMPHONIOUSLY
SYMPHONIST
SYMPHONISTS
SYMPHYLOUS
SYMPHYSEAL
SYMPHYSEOTOMIES
SYMPHYSEOTOMY
SYMPHYSIAL
SYMPHYSIOTOMIES
SYMPHYSIOTOMY
SYMPHYSTIC
SYMPIESOMETER
SYMPIESOMETERS
SYMPLASTIC
SYMPODIALLY
SYMPOSIACS
SYMPOSIARCH
SYMPOSIARCHS
SYMPOSIAST
SYMPOSIASTS
SYMPOSIUMS
SYMPTOMATIC
SYMPTOMATICAL
SYMPTOMATICALLY
SYMPTOMATISE
SYMPTOMATISED
SYMPTOMATISES
SYMPTOMATISING
SYMPTOMATIZE
SYMPTOMATIZED
SYMPTOMATIZES
SYMPTOMATIZING
SYMPTOMATOLOGIC
SYMPTOMATOLOGY
SYMPTOMLESS

SYMPTOMOLOGICAL
SYMPTOMOLOGIES
SYMPTOMOLOGY
SYNADELPHITE
SYNADELPHITES
SYNAERESES
SYNAERESIS
SYNAESTHESES
SYNAESTHESIA
SYNAESTHESIAS
SYNAESTHESIS
SYNAESTHETIC
SYNAGOGICAL
SYNAGOGUES
SYNALEPHAS
SYNALLAGMATIC
SYNALOEPHA
SYNALOEPHAS
SYNANDRIUM
SYNANDROUS
SYNANTHEROUS
SYNANTHESES
SYNANTHESIS
SYNANTHETIC
SYNANTHIES
SYNANTHOUS
SYNAPHEIAS
SYNAPOSEMATIC
SYNAPOSEMATISM
SYNAPOSEMATISMS
SYNAPTASES
SYNAPTICAL
SYNAPTICALLY
SYNAPTOSOMAL
SYNAPTOSOME
SYNAPTOSOMES
SYNARCHIES
SYNARTHRODIAL
SYNARTHRODIALLY
SYNARTHROSES
SYNARTHROSIS
SYNASTRIES
SYNAXARION
SYNBIOTICS
SYNCARPIES
SYNCARPOUS
SYNCHONDROSES
SYNCHONDROSIS
SYNCHORESES

S

SYNCHORESIS	SYNCOPATING	SYNDICSHIP	SYNOECIOSIS	SYNTACTICS
SYNCHROFLASH	SYNCOPATION	SYNDICSHIPS	SYNOECIOUS	SYNTAGMATA
SYNCHROFLASHES	SYNCOPATIONS	SYNDIOTACTIC	SYNOECISED	SYNTAGMATIC
SYNCHROMESH	SYNCOPATIVE	SYNDYASMIAN	SYNOECISES	SYNTAGMATITE
SYNCHROMESHES	SYNCOPATOR	SYNECDOCHE	SYNOECISING	SYNTAGMATITES
SYNCHRONAL	SYNCOPATORS	SYNECDOCHES	SYNOECISMS	SYNTECTICAL
SYNCHRONEITIES	SYNCRETISATION	SYNECDOCHIC	SYNOECIZED	SYNTENOSES
SYNCHRONEITY	SYNCRETISATIONS	SYNECDOCHICAL	SYNOECIZES	SYNTENOSIS
SYNCHRONIC	SYNCRETISE	SYNECDOCHICALLY	SYNOECIZING	SYNTERESES
SYNCHRONICAL	SYNCRETISED	SYNECDOCHISM	SYNOECOLOGIES	SYNTERESIS
SYNCHRONICALLY	SYNCRETISES	SYNECDOCHISMS	SYNOECOLOGY	SYNTEXISES
SYNCHRONICITIES	SYNCRETISING	SYNECOLOGIC	SYNOEKETES	SYNTHESISATION
SYNCHRONICITY	SYNCRETISM	SYNECOLOGICAL	SYNONYMATIC	SYNTHESISATIONS
SYNCHRONIES	SYNCRETISMS	SYNECOLOGICALLY	SYNONYMICAL	SYNTHESISE
SYNCHRONISATION	SYNCRETIST	SYNECOLOGIES	SYNONYMICON	SYNTHESISED
SYNCHRONISE	SYNCRETISTIC	SYNECOLOGIST	SYNONYMICONS	SYNTHESISER
SYNCHRONISED	SYNCRETISTS	SYNECOLOGISTS	SYNONYMIES	SYNTHESISERS
SYNCHRONISER	SYNCRETIZATION	SYNECOLOGY	SYNONYMISE	SYNTHESISES
SYNCHRONISERS	SYNCRETIZATIONS	SYNECPHONESES	SYNONYMISED	SYNTHESISING
SYNCHRONISES	SYNCRETIZE	SYNECPHONESIS	SYNONYMISES	SYNTHESIST
SYNCHRONISING	SYNCRETIZED	SYNECTICALLY	SYNONYMISING	SYNTHESISTS
SYNCHRONISM	SYNCRETIZES	SYNEIDESES	SYNONYMIST	SYNTHESIZATION
SYNCHRONISMS	SYNCRETIZING	SYNEIDESIS	SYNONYMISTS	SYNTHESIZATIONS
SYNCHRONISTIC	SYNDACTYLIES	SYNERGETIC	SYNONYMITIES	SYNTHESIZE
SYNCHRONISTICAL	SYNDACTYLISM	SYNERGETICALLY	SYNONYMITY	SYNTHESIZED
SYNCHRONIZATION	SYNDACTYLISMS	SYNERGICALLY	SYNONYMIZE	SYNTHESIZER
SYNCHRONIZE	SYNDACTYLOUS	SYNERGISED	SYNONYMIZED	SYNTHESIZERS
SYNCHRONIZED	SYNDACTYLS	SYNERGISES	SYNONYMIZES	SYNTHESIZES
SYNCHRONIZER	SYNDACTYLY	SYNERGISING	SYNONYMIZING	SYNTHESIZING
SYNCHRONIZERS	SYNDERESES	SYNERGISMS	SYNONYMOUS	SYNTHESPIAN
SYNCHRONIZES	SYNDERESIS	SYNERGISTIC	SYNONYMOUSLY	SYNTHESPIANS
SYNCHRONIZING	SYNDESISES	SYNERGISTICALLY	SYNONYMOUSNESS	SYNTHETASE
SYNCHRONOLOGIES	SYNDESMOSES	SYNERGISTS	SYNOPSISED	SYNTHETASES
SYNCHRONOLOGY	SYNDESMOSIS	SYNERGIZED	SYNOPSISES	SYNTHETICAL
SYNCHRONOSCOPE	SYNDESMOTIC	SYNERGIZES	SYNOPSISING	SYNTHETICALLY
SYNCHRONOSCOPES	SYNDETICAL	SYNERGIZING	SYNOPSIZED	SYNTHETICISM
SYNCHRONOUS	SYNDETICALLY	SYNESTHESIA	SYNOPSIZES	SYNTHETICISMS
SYNCHRONOUSLY	SYNDICALISM	SYNESTHESIAS	SYNOPSIZING	SYNTHETICS
SYNCHRONOUSNESS	SYNDICALISMS	SYNESTHETIC	SYNOPTICAL	SYNTHETISATION
SYNCHROSCOPE	SYNDICALIST	SYNGENESES	SYNOPTICALLY	SYNTHETISATIONS
SYNCHROSCOPES	SYNDICALISTIC	SYNGENESIOUS	SYNOPTISTIC	SYNTHETISE
SYNCHROTRON	SYNDICALISTS	SYNGENESIS	SYNOPTISTS	SYNTHETISED
SYNCHROTRONS	SYNDICATED	SYNGENETIC	SYNOSTOSES	SYNTHETISER
SYNCLASTIC	SYNDICATES	SYNGNATHOUS	SYNOSTOSIS	SYNTHETISERS
SYNCLINALS	SYNDICATING	SYNKARYONIC	SYNOVIALLY	SYNTHETISES
SYNCLINORIA	SYNDICATION	SYNKARYONS	SYNOVITISES	SYNTHETISING
SYNCLINORIUM	SYNDICATIONS	SYNODICALLY	SYNSEPALOUS	SYNTHETISM
SYNCOPATED	SYNDICATOR	SYNOECETES	SYNTACTICAL	SYNTHETISMS
SYNCOPATES	SYNDICATORS	SYNOECIOSES	SYNTACTICALLY	SYNTHETIST

S

SYNTHETISTS	SYPHILISATIONS	SYPHILOPHOBIAS	SYSTEMATISATION	SYSTEMATOLOGY
SYNTHETIZATION	SYPHILISED	SYPHONAGES	SYSTEMATISE	SYSTEMICALLY
SYNTHETIZATIONS	SYPHILISES	SYRINGITIS	SYSTEMATISED	SYSTEMISATION
SYNTHETIZE	SYPHILISING	SYRINGITISES	SYSTEMATISER	SYSTEMISATIONS
SYNTHETIZED	SYPHILITIC	SYRINGOMYELIA	SYSTEMATISERS	SYSTEMISED
SYNTHETIZER	SYPHILITICALLY	SYRINGOMYELIAS	SYSTEMATISES	SYSTEMISER
SYNTHETIZERS	SYPHILITICS	SYRINGOMYELIC	SYSTEMATISING	SYSTEMISERS
SYNTHETIZES	SYPHILIZATION	SYRINGOTOMIES	SYSTEMATISM	SYSTEMISES
SYNTHETIZING	SYPHILIZATIONS	SYRINGOTOMY	SYSTEMATISMS	SYSTEMISING
SYNTHRONUS	SYPHILIZED	SYSSARCOSES	SYSTEMATIST	SYSTEMIZATION
SYNTONICALLY	SYPHILIZES	SYSSARCOSIS	SYSTEMATISTS	SYSTEMIZATIONS
SYNTONISED	SYPHILIZING	SYSSARCOTIC	SYSTEMATIZATION	SYSTEMIZED
SYNTONISES	SYPHILOLOGIES	SYSTEMATIC	SYSTEMATIZE	SYSTEMIZER
SYNTONISING	SYPHILOLOGIST	SYSTEMATICAL	SYSTEMATIZED	SYSTEMIZERS
SYNTONIZED	SYPHILOLOGISTS	SYSTEMATICALLY	SYSTEMATIZER	SYSTEMIZES
SYNTONIZES	SYPHILOLOGY	SYSTEMATICIAN	SYSTEMATIZERS	SYSTEMIZING
SYNTONIZING	SYPHILOMAS	SYSTEMATICIANS	SYSTEMATIZES	SYSTEMLESS
SYPHERINGS	SYPHILOMATA	SYSTEMATICNESS	SYSTEMATIZING	SYZYGETICALLY
SYPHILISATION	SYPHILOPHOBIA	SYSTEMATICS	SYSTEMATOLOGIES	

T

TABASHEERS	TABULARIZED	TACHYLITIC	TAENIACIDE	TAINTLESSLY
TABBOULEHS	TABULARIZES	TACHYLYTES	TAENIACIDES	TAKINGNESS
TABBYHOODS	TABULARIZING	TACHYLYTIC	TAENIAFUGE	TAKINGNESSES
TABEFACTION	TABULATING	TACHYMETER	TAENIAFUGES	TALBOTYPES
TABEFACTIONS	TABULATION	TACHYMETERS	TAFFETASES	TALEBEARER
TABELLIONS	TABULATIONS	TACHYMETRIC	TAFFETIEST	TALEBEARERS
TABERNACLE	TABULATORS	TACHYMETRICAL	TAFFETISED	TALEBEARING
TABERNACLED	TABULATORY	TACHYMETRICALLY	TAFFETIZED	TALEBEARINGS
TABERNACLES	TACAMAHACS	TACHYMETRIES	TAGLIARINI	TALEGALLAS
TABERNACLING	TACHEOMETER	TACHYMETRY	TAGLIARINIS	TALENTLESS
TABERNACULAR	TACHEOMETERS	TACHYPHASIA	TAGLIATELLE	TALETELLER
TABESCENCE	TACHEOMETRIC	TACHYPHASIAS	TAGLIATELLES	TALETELLERS
TABESCENCES	TACHEOMETRICAL	TACHYPHRASIA	TAHSILDARS	TALETELLING
TABLANETTE	TACHEOMETRIES	TACHYPHRASIAS	TAIKONAUTS	TALETELLINGS
TABLANETTES	TACHEOMETRY	TACHYPHYLAXES	TAILBOARDS	TALISMANIC
TABLATURES	TACHISTOSCOPE	TACHYPHYLAXIS	TAILCOATED	TALISMANICAL
TABLECLOTH	TACHISTOSCOPES	TACHYPNEAS	TAILENDERS	TALISMANICALLY
TABLECLOTHS	TACHISTOSCOPIC	TACHYPNOEA	TAILGATERS	TALKABILITIES
TABLELANDS	TACHOGRAMS	TACHYPNOEAS	TAILGATING	TALKABILITY
TABLEMATES	TACHOGRAPH	TACITNESSES	TAILGATINGS	TALKATHONS
TABLESPOON	TACHOGRAPHS	TACITURNITIES	TAILHOPPING	TALKATIVELY
TABLESPOONFUL	TACHOMETER	TACITURNITY	TAILHOPPINGS	TALKATIVENESS
TABLESPOONFULS	TACHOMETERS	TACITURNLY	TAILLESSLY	TALKATIVENESSES
TABLESPOONS	TACHOMETRIC	TACKBOARDS	TAILLESSNESS	TALKINESSES
TABLESPOONSFUL	TACHOMETRICAL	TACKETIEST	TAILLESSNESSES	TALLGRASSES
TABLETOPPED	TACHOMETRICALLY	TACKIFIERS	TAILLIGHTS	TALLIATING
TABLETTING	TACHOMETRIES	TACKIFYING	TAILORBIRD	TALLNESSES
TABLEWARES	TACHOMETRY	TACKINESSES	TAILORBIRDS	TALLOWIEST
TABLOIDIER	TACHYARRHYTHMIA	TACMAHACKS	TAILORESSES	TALLYHOING
TABLOIDIEST	TACHYCARDIA	TACTFULNESS	TAILORINGS	TALLYSHOPS
TABOGGANED	TACHYCARDIAC	TACTFULNESSES	TAILORMADE	TALLYWOMAN
TABOGGANING	TACHYCARDIAS	TACTICALLY	TAILORMAKE	TALLYWOMEN
TABOPARESES	TACHYGRAPH	TACTICIANS	TAILORMAKES	TALMUDISMS
TABOPARESIS	TACHYGRAPHER	TACTICITIES	TAILORMAKING	TAMABILITIES
TABULARISATION	TACHYGRAPHERS	TACTILISTS	TAILPIECES	TAMABILITY
TABULARISATIONS	TACHYGRAPHIC	TACTILITIES	TAILPIPING	TAMABLENESS
TABULARISE	TACHYGRAPHICAL	TACTLESSLY	TAILPLANES	TAMABLENESSES
TABULARISED	TACHYGRAPHIES	TACTLESSNESS	TAILSLIDES	TAMARILLOS
TABULARISES	TACHYGRAPHIST	TACTLESSNESSES	TAILSPINNED	TAMBOURERS
TABULARISING	TACHYGRAPHISTS	TACTUALITIES	TAILSPINNING	TAMBOURINE
TABULARIZATION	TACHYGRAPHS	TACTUALITY	TAILSTOCKS	TAMBOURINES
TABULARIZATIONS	TACHYGRAPHY	TADALAFILS	TAILWATERS	TAMBOURING
TABULARIZE	TACHYLITES	TAEKWONDOS	TAILWHEELS	TAMBOURINIST

TAMBOURINISTS	TANTALISING	TARAMASALATA	TARRINESSES	TATTERDEMALION
TAMBOURINS	TANTALISINGLY	TARAMASALATAS	TARSALGIAS	TATTERDEMALIONS
TAMEABILITIES	TANTALISINGS	TARANTARAED	TARSOMETATARSAL	TATTERDEMALLION
TAMEABILITY	TANTALISMS	TARANTARAING	TARSOMETATARSI	TATTERIEST
TAMEABLENESS	TANTALITES	TARANTARAS	TARSOMETATARSUS	TATTERSALL
TAMEABLENESSES	TANTALIZATION	TARANTASES	TARTANALIA	TATTERSALLS
TAMELESSNESS	TANTALIZATIONS	TARANTASSES	TARTANALIAS	TATTINESSES
TAMELESSNESSES	TANTALIZED	TARANTELLA	TARTANRIES	TATTLETALE
TAMENESSES	TANTALIZER	TARANTELLAS	TARTAREOUS	TATTLETALED
TAMOXIFENS	TANTALIZERS	TARANTISMS	TARTARISATION	TATTLETALES
TAMPERINGS	TANTALIZES	TARANTISTS	TARTARISATIONS	TATTLETALING
TAMPERPROOF	TANTALIZING	TARANTULAE	TARTARISED	TATTLINGLY
TAMPONADES	TANTALIZINGLY	TARANTULAS	TARTARISES	TATTOOISTS
TAMPONAGES	TANTALIZINGS	TARATANTARA	TARTARISING	TAUNTINGLY
TANDEMWISE	TANTALUSES	TARATANTARAED	TARTARIZATION	TAUROBOLIA
TANGENCIES	TANTAMOUNT	TARATANTARAING	TARTARIZATIONS	TAUROBOLIUM
TANGENTALLY	TANTARARAS	TARATANTARAS	TARTARIZED	TAUROMACHIAN
TANGENTIAL	TANZANITES	TARAXACUMS	TARTARIZES	TAUROMACHIES
TANGENTIALITIES	TAPERINGLY	TARBOGGINED	TARTARIZING	TAUROMACHY
TANGENTIALITY	TAPERNESSES	TARBOGGINING	TARTINESSES	TAUROMORPHOUS
TANGENTIALLY	TAPERSTICK	TARBOGGINS	TARTNESSES	TAUTNESSES
TANGERINES	TAPERSTICKS	TARBOOSHES	TARTRAZINE	TAUTOCHRONE
TANGHININS	TAPESCRIPT	TARBOUCHES	TARTRAZINES	TAUTOCHRONES
TANGIBILITIES	TAPESCRIPTS	TARBOUSHES	TASEOMETER	TAUTOCHRONISM
TANGIBILITY	TAPESTRIED	TARDIGRADE	TASEOMETERS	TAUTOCHRONISMS
TANGIBLENESS	TAPESTRIES	TARDIGRADES	TASIMETERS	TAUTOCHRONOUS
TANGIBLENESSES	TAPESTRYING	TARDINESSES	TASIMETRIC	TAUTOLOGIC
TANGINESSES	TAPHEPHOBIA	TARGETABLE	TASIMETRIES	TAUTOLOGICAL
TANGLEFOOT	TAPHEPHOBIAS	TARGETEERS	TASKMASTER	TAUTOLOGICALLY
TANGLEFOOTS	TAPHEPHOBIC	TARGETINGS	TASKMASTERS	TAUTOLOGIES
TANGLEMENT	TAPHONOMIC	TARGETITIS	TASKMISTRESS	TAUTOLOGISE
TANGLEMENTS	TAPHONOMICAL	TARGETITISES	TASKMISTRESSES	TAUTOLOGISED
TANGLESOME	TAPHONOMIES	TARGETLESS	TASSELIEST	TAUTOLOGISES
TANGLEWEED	TAPHONOMIST	TARIFFICATION	TASSELLIER	TAUTOLOGISING
TANGLEWEEDS	TAPHONOMISTS	TARIFFICATIONS	TASSELLIEST	TAUTOLOGISM
TANGLINGLY	TAPHOPHOBIA	TARIFFLESS	TASSELLING	TAUTOLOGISMS
TANISTRIES	TAPHOPHOBIAS	TARMACADAM	TASSELLINGS	TAUTOLOGIST
TANKBUSTER	TAPHROGENESES	TARMACADAMS	TASTEFULLY	TAUTOLOGISTS
TANKBUSTERS	TAPHROGENESIS	TARMACKING	TASTEFULNESS	TAUTOLOGIZE
TANKBUSTING	TAPOTEMENT	TARNATIONS	TASTEFULNESSES	TAUTOLOGIZED
TANKBUSTINGS	TAPOTEMENTS	TARNISHABLE	TASTELESSLY	TAUTOLOGIZES
TANOREXICS	TAPSALTEERIE	TARNISHERS	TASTELESSNESS	TAUTOLOGIZING
TANTALATES	TAPSALTEERIES	TARNISHING	TASTELESSNESSES	TAUTOLOGOUS
TANTALISATION	TAPSIETEERIE	TARPAULING	TASTEMAKER	TAUTOLOGOUSLY
TANTALISATIONS	TAPSIETEERIES	TARPAULINGS	TASTEMAKERS	TAUTOMERIC
TANTALISED	TAPSTRESSES	TARPAULINS	TASTINESSES	TAUTOMERISM
TANTALISER	TARABISHES	TARRADIDDLE	TATAHASHES	TAUTOMERISMS
TANTALISERS	TARADIDDLE	TARRADIDDLES	TATPURUSHA	TAUTOMETRIC
TANTALISES	TARADIDDLES	TARRIANCES	TATPURUSHAS	TAUTOMETRICAL

TAUTONYMIC	TEACHABLENESSES	TECHNICIAN	TECHNOLOGIZES	TEETHRIDGES
TAUTONYMIES	TEACHERLESS	TECHNICIANS	TECHNOLOGIZING	TEETOTALED
TAUTONYMOUS	TEACHERLIER	TECHNICISE	TECHNOLOGY	TEETOTALER
TAUTOPHONIC	TEACHERLIEST	TECHNICISED	TECHNOMANIA	TEETOTALERS
TAUTOPHONICAL	TEACHERSHIP	TECHNICISES	TECHNOMANIAC	TEETOTALING
TAUTOPHONIES	TEACHERSHIPS	TECHNICISING	TECHNOMANIACS	TEETOTALISM
TAUTOPHONY	TEACUPFULS	TECHNICISM	TECHNOMANIAS	TEETOTALISMS
TAWDRINESS	TEACUPSFUL	TECHNICISMS	TECHNOMUSIC	TEETOTALIST
TAWDRINESSES	TEAKETTLES	TECHNICIST	TECHNOMUSICS	TEETOTALISTS
TAWHEOWHEO	TEARFULNESS	TECHNICISTS	TECHNOPHILE	TEETOTALLED
TAWHEOWHEOS	TEARFULNESSES	TECHNICIZE	TECHNOPHILES	TEETOTALLER
TAWNINESSES	TEARGASSED	TECHNICIZED	TECHNOPHILIA	TEETOTALLERS
TAXABILITIES	TEARGASSES	TECHNICIZES	TECHNOPHILIAS	TEETOTALLING
TAXABILITY	TEARGASSING	TECHNICIZING	TECHNOPHOBE	TEETOTALLY
TAXABLENESS	TEARINESSES	TECHNICOLOR	TECHNOPHOBES	TEGUMENTAL
TAXABLENESSES	TEARJERKER	TECHNICOLORED	TECHNOPHOBIA	TEGUMENTARY
TAXAMETERS	TEARJERKERS	TECHNICOLORS	TECHNOPHOBIAS	TEHSILDARS
TAXATIONAL	TEARLESSLY	TECHNICOLOUR	TECHNOPHOBIC	TEICHOPSIA
TAXIDERMAL	TEARSHEETS	TECHNICOLOURED	TECHNOPHOBICS	TEICHOPSIAS
TAXIDERMIC	TEARSTAINED	TECHNICOLOURS	TECHNOPOLE	TEINOSCOPE
TAXIDERMIES	TEARSTAINS	TECHNIKONS	TECHNOPOLES	TEINOSCOPES
TAXIDERMISE	TEARSTRIPS	TECHNIQUES	TECHNOPOLIS	TEKNONYMIES
TAXIDERMISED	TEASELINGS	TECHNOBABBLE	TECHNOPOLISES	TEKNONYMOUS
TAXIDERMISES	TEASELLERS	TECHNOBABBLES	TECHNOPOLITAN	TELAESTHESIA
TAXIDERMISING	TEASELLING	TECHNOCRACIES	TECHNOPOLITANS	TELAESTHESIAS
TAXIDERMIST	TEASELLINGS	TECHNOCRACY	TECHNOPOPS	TELAESTHETIC
TAXIDERMISTS	TEASPOONFUL	TECHNOCRAT	TECHNOSPEAK	TELANGIECTASES
TAXIDERMIZE	TEASPOONFULS	TECHNOCRATIC	TECHNOSPEAKS	TELANGIECTASIA
TAXIDERMIZED	TEASPOONSFUL	TECHNOCRATS	TECHNOSTRESS	TELANGIECTASIAS
TAXIDERMIZES	TEATASTERS	TECHNOFEAR	TECHNOSTRESSES	TELANGIECTASIS
TAXIDERMIZING	TEAZELLING	TECHNOFEARS	TECHNOSTRUCTURE	TELANGIECTATIC
TAXIMETERS	TECHINESSES	TECHNOFERENCE	TECTIBRANCH	TELAUTOGRAPHIC
TAXIPLANES	TECHNETIUM	TECHNOFERENCES	TECTIBRANCHIATE	TELAUTOGRAPHIES
TAXONOMERS	TECHNETIUMS	TECHNOGRAPHIES	TECTIBRANCHS	TELAUTOGRAPHY
TAXONOMICAL	TECHNETRONIC	TECHNOGRAPHY	TECTONICALLY	TELEARCHICS
TAXONOMICALLY	TECHNICALISE	TECHNOJUNKIE	TECTONISMS	TELEBANKING
TAXONOMIES	TECHNICALISED	TECHNOJUNKIES	TECTRICIAL	TELEBANKINGS
TAXONOMIST	TECHNICALISES	TECHNOLOGIC	TEDIOSITIES	TELEBRIDGE
TAXONOMISTS	TECHNICALISING	TECHNOLOGICAL	TEDIOUSNESS	TELEBRIDGES
TAXPAYINGS	TECHNICALITIES	TECHNOLOGICALLY	TEDIOUSNESSES	TELECAMERA
TAYASSUIDS	TECHNICALITY	TECHNOLOGIES	TEDIOUSOME	TELECAMERAS
TAYBERRIES	TECHNICALIZE	TECHNOLOGISE	TEEMINGNESS	TELECASTED
TCHOTCHKES	TECHNICALIZED	TECHNOLOGISED	TEEMINGNESSES	TELECASTER
TCHOUKBALL	TECHNICALIZES	TECHNOLOGISES	TEENTSIEST	TELECASTERS
TCHOUKBALLS	TECHNICALIZING	TECHNOLOGISING	TEENYBOPPER	TELECASTING
TEABERRIES	TECHNICALLY	TECHNOLOGIST	TEENYBOPPERS	TELECHIRIC
TEACHABILITIES	TECHNICALNESS	TECHNOLOGISTS	TEETERBOARD	TELECOMMAND
TEACHABILITY	TECHNICALNESSES	TECHNOLOGIZE	TEETERBOARDS	TELECOMMANDS
TEACHABLENESS	TECHNICALS	TECHNOLOGIZED	TEETHRIDGE	TELECOMMUTE

TELECOMMUTED	TELEGRAPHY	TELEOSTEANS	TELEPRINTS	TELEVANGELICAL
TELECOMMUTER	TELEHEALTH	TELEOSTOME	TELEPROCESSING	TELEVANGELISM
TELECOMMUTERS	TELEHEALTHS	TELEOSTOMES	TELEPROCESSINGS	TELEVANGELISMS
TELECOMMUTES	TELEJOURNALISM	TELEOSTOMOUS	TELERECORD	TELEVANGELIST
TELECOMMUTING	TELEJOURNALISMS	TELEPATHED	TELERECORDED	TELEVANGELISTS
TELECOMMUTINGS	TELEJOURNALIST	TELEPATHIC	TELERECORDING	TELEVERITE
TELECONFERENCE	TELEJOURNALISTS	TELEPATHICALLY	TELERECORDINGS	TELEVERITES
TELECONFERENCES	TELEKINESES	TELEPATHIES	TELERECORDS	TELEVIEWED
TELECONNECTION	TELEKINESIS	TELEPATHING	TELERGICALLY	TELEVIEWER
TELECONNECTIONS	TELEKINETIC	TELEPATHISE	TELEROBOTS	TELEVIEWERS
TELECONTROL	TELEKINETICALLY	TELEPATHISED	TELESCIENCE	TELEVIEWING
TELECONTROLS	TELEMARKED	TELEPATHISES	TELESCIENCES	TELEVIEWINGS
TELECONVERTER	TELEMARKETER	TELEPATHISING	TELESCOPED	TELEVISERS
TELECONVERTERS	TELEMARKETERS	TELEPATHIST	TELESCOPES	TELEVISING
TELECOPIES	TELEMARKETING	TELEPATHISTS	TELESCOPIC	TELEVISION
TELECOTTAGE	TELEMARKETINGS	TELEPATHIZE	TELESCOPICAL	TELEVISIONAL
TELECOTTAGES	TELEMARKING	TELEPATHIZED	TELESCOPICALLY	TELEVISIONALLY
TELECOTTAGING	TELEMATICS	TELEPATHIZES	TELESCOPIES	TELEVISIONARY
TELECOTTAGINGS	TELEMEDICINE	TELEPATHIZING	TELESCOPIFORM	TELEVISIONS
TELECOURSE	TELEMEDICINES	TELEPHEMES	TELESCOPING	TELEVISORS
TELECOURSES	TELEMEETING	TELEPHERIQUE	TELESCOPIST	TELEVISUAL
TELEDILDONICS	TELEMEETINGS	TELEPHERIQUES	TELESCOPISTS	TELEVISUALLY
TELEFACSIMILE	TELEMESSAGE	TELEPHONED	TELESCREEN	TELEWORKED
TELEFACSIMILES	TELEMESSAGES	TELEPHONER	TELESCREENS	TELEWORKER
TELEFAXING	TELEMETERED	TELEPHONERS	TELESELLING	TELEWORKERS
TELEFERIQUE	TELEMETERING	TELEPHONES	TELESELLINGS	TELEWORKING
TELEFERIQUES	TELEMETERS	TELEPHONIC	TELESERVICES	TELEWORKINGS
TELEGENICALLY	TELEMETRIC	TELEPHONICALLY	TELESHOPPED	TELEWRITER
TELEGNOSES	TELEMETRICAL	TELEPHONIES	TELESHOPPING	TELEWRITERS
TELEGNOSIS	TELEMETRICALLY	TELEPHONING	TELESHOPPINGS	TELFERAGES
TELEGNOSTIC	TELEMETRIES	TELEPHONIST	TELESMATIC	TELICITIES
TELEGONIES	TELENCEPHALA	TELEPHONISTS	TELESMATICAL	TELIOSPORE
TELEGONOUS	TELENCEPHALIC	TELEPHONITIS	TELESMATICALLY	TELIOSPORES
TELEGRAMMATIC	TELENCEPHALON	TELEPHONITISES	TELESOFTWARE	TELLERSHIP
TELEGRAMMED	TELENCEPHALONS	TELEPHOTOGRAPH	TELESOFTWARES	TELLERSHIPS
TELEGRAMMIC	TELEOLOGIC	TELEPHOTOGRAPHS	TELESTEREOSCOPE	TELLURATES
TELEGRAMMING	TELEOLOGICAL	TELEPHOTOGRAPHY	TELESTHESIA	TELLURETTED
TELEGRAPHED	TELEOLOGICALLY	TELEPHOTOS	TELESTHESIAS	TELLURIANS
TELEGRAPHER	TELEOLOGIES	TELEPOINTS	TELESTHETIC	TELLURIDES
TELEGRAPHERS	TELEOLOGISM	TELEPORTATION	TELESTICHS	TELLURIONS
TELEGRAPHESE	TELEOLOGISMS	TELEPORTATIONS	TELESURGERIES	TELLURISED
TELEGRAPHESES	TELEOLOGIST	TELEPORTED	TELESURGERY	TELLURISES
TELEGRAPHIC	TELEOLOGISTS	TELEPORTING	TELETYPESETTING	TELLURISING
TELEGRAPHICALLY	TELEONOMIC	TELEPRESENCE	TELETYPEWRITER	TELLURITES
TELEGRAPHIES	TELEONOMIES	TELEPRESENCES	TELETYPEWRITERS	TELLURIUMS
TELEGRAPHING	TELEOSAURIAN	TELEPRINTED	TELETYPING	TELLURIZED
TELEGRAPHIST	TELEOSAURIANS	TELEPRINTER	TELEUTOSPORE	TELLURIZES
TELEGRAPHISTS	TELEOSAURS	TELEPRINTERS	TELEUTOSPORES	TELLURIZING
TELEGRAPHS	TELEOSTEAN	TELEPRINTING	TELEUTOSPORIC	TELLUROMETER

T

TELLUROMETERS	TEMPESTING	TEMPTATIONS	TENDERIZATION	TENNESSINE
TELNETTING	TEMPESTIVE	TEMPTATIOUS	TENDERIZATIONS	TENNESSINES
TELOCENTRIC	TEMPESTUOUS	TEMPTINGLY	TENDERIZED	TENORRHAPHIES
TELOCENTRICS	TEMPESTUOUSLY	TEMPTINGNESS	TENDERIZER	TENORRHAPHY
TELOMERASE	TEMPESTUOUSNESS	TEMPTINGNESSES	TENDERIZERS	TENOSYNOVITIS
TELOMERASES	TEMPOLABILE	TEMPTRESSES	TENDERIZES	TENOSYNOVITISES
TELOMERISATION	TEMPORALISE	TEMULENCES	TENDERIZING	TENOTOMIES
TELOMERISATIONS	TEMPORALISED	TEMULENCIES	TENDERLING	TENOTOMIST
TELOMERIZATION	TEMPORALISES	TEMULENTLY	TENDERLINGS	TENOTOMISTS
TELOMERIZATIONS	TEMPORALISING	TENABILITIES	TENDERLOIN	TENOVAGINITIS
TELOPHASES	TEMPORALITIES	TENABILITY	TENDERLOINS	TENOVAGINITISES
TELOPHASIC	TEMPORALITY	TENABLENESS	TENDERNESS	TENPINNERS
TELPHERAGE	TEMPORALIZE	TENABLENESSES	TENDERNESSES	TENPOUNDER
TELPHERAGES	TEMPORALIZED	TENACIOUSLY	TENDEROMETER	TENPOUNDERS
TELPHERING	TEMPORALIZES	TENACIOUSNESS	TENDEROMETERS	TENSENESSES
TELPHERLINE	TEMPORALIZING	TENACIOUSNESSES	TENDINITIDES	TENSIBILITIES
TELPHERLINES	TEMPORALLY	TENACITIES	TENDINITIS	TENSIBILITY
TELPHERMAN	TEMPORALNESS	TENACULUMS	TENDINITISES	TENSIBLENESS
TELPHERMEN	TEMPORALNESSES	TENAILLONS	TENDONITIDES	TENSIBLENESSES
TELPHERWAY	TEMPORALTIES	TENANTABLE	TENDONITIS	TENSILENESS
TELPHERWAYS	TEMPORALTY	TENANTLESS	TENDONITISES	TENSILENESSES
TEMAZEPAMS	TEMPORANEOUS	TENANTRIES	TENDOVAGINITIS	TENSILITIES
TEMERARIOUS	TEMPORARIES	TENANTSHIP	TENDRESSES	TENSIMETER
TEMERARIOUSLY	TEMPORARILY	TENANTSHIPS	TENDRILLAR	TENSIMETERS
TEMERARIOUSNESS	TEMPORARINESS	TENDENCIAL	TENDRILLED	TENSIOMETER
TEMERITIES	TEMPORARINESSES	TENDENCIALLY	TENDRILLIER	TENSIOMETERS
TEMEROUSLY	TEMPORISATION	TENDENCIES	TENDRILLIEST	TENSIOMETRIC
TEMPERABILITIES	TEMPORISATIONS	TENDENCIOUS	TENDRILLOUS	TENSIOMETRIES
TEMPERABILITY	TEMPORISED	TENDENCIOUSLY	TENDRILOUS	TENSIOMETRY
TEMPERABLE	TEMPORISER	TENDENCIOUSNESS	TENEBRIFIC	TENSIONALLY
TEMPERALITIE	TEMPORISERS	TENDENTIAL	TENEBRIONID	TENSIONERS
TEMPERALITIES	TEMPORISES	TENDENTIALLY	TENEBRIONIDS	TENSIONING
TEMPERAMENT	TEMPORISING	TENDENTIOUS	TENEBRIOUS	TENSIONLESS
TEMPERAMENTAL	TEMPORISINGLY	TENDENTIOUSLY	TENEBRIOUSNESS	TENTACULAR
TEMPERAMENTALLY	TEMPORISINGS	TENDENTIOUSNESS	TENEBRISMS	TENTACULATE
TEMPERAMENTFUL	TEMPORIZATION	TENDERABLE	TENEBRISTS	TENTACULIFEROUS
TEMPERAMENTS	TEMPORIZATIONS	TENDERFEET	TENEBRITIES	TENTACULITE
TEMPERANCE	TEMPORIZED	TENDERFOOT	TENEBROSITIES	TENTACULITES
TEMPERANCES	TEMPORIZER	TENDERFOOTS	TENEBROSITY	TENTACULOID
TEMPERATED	TEMPORIZERS	TENDERHEARTED	TENEBROUSNESS	TENTACULUM
TEMPERATELY	TEMPORIZES	TENDERHEARTEDLY	TENEBROUSNESSES	TENTATIONS
TEMPERATENESS	TEMPORIZING	TENDERINGS	TENEMENTAL	TENTATIVELY
TEMPERATENESSES	TEMPORIZINGLY	TENDERISATION	TENEMENTARY	TENTATIVENESS
TEMPERATES	TEMPORIZINGS	TENDERISATIONS	TENEMENTED	TENTATIVENESSES
TEMPERATING	TEMPTABILITIES	TENDERISED	TENESMUSES	TENTATIVES
TEMPERATIVE	TEMPTABILITY	TENDERISER	TENIACIDES	TENTERHOOK
TEMPERATURE	TEMPTABLENESS	TENDERISERS	TENIAFUGES	TENTERHOOKS
TEMPERATURES	TEMPTABLENESSES	TENDERISES	TENNANTITE	TENTIGINOUS
TEMPERINGS	TEMPTATION	TENDERISING	TENNANTITES	TENTMAKERS

TENUIROSTRAL	TEREBRATULAS	TERNEPLATES	TERRITORIALITY	TESTACEOUS
TENUOUSNESS	TEREPHTHALATE	TEROTECHNOLOGY	TERRITORIALIZE	TESTAMENTAL
TENUOUSNESSES	TEREPHTHALATES	TERPENELESS	TERRITORIALIZED	TESTAMENTAR
TENURIALLY	TEREPHTHALIC	TERPENOIDS	TERRITORIALIZES	TESTAMENTARILY
TEPEFACTION	TERGIVERSANT	TERPINEOLS	TERRITORIALLY	TESTAMENTARY
TEPEFACTIONS	TERGIVERSANTS	TERPOLYMER	TERRITORIALS	TESTAMENTS
TEPHIGRAMS	TERGIVERSATE	TERPOLYMERS	TERRITORIED	TESTATIONS
TEPHROITES	TERGIVERSATED	TERPSICHOREAL	TERRITORIES	TESTATRICES
TEPHROMANCIES	TERGIVERSATES	TERPSICHOREAN	TERRORISATION	TESTATRIXES
TEPHROMANCY	TERGIVERSATING	TERRACELESS	TERRORISATIONS	TESTCROSSED
TEPIDARIUM	TERGIVERSATION	TERRACETTE	TERRORISED	TESTCROSSES
TEPIDITIES	TERGIVERSATIONS	TERRACETTES	TERRORISER	TESTCROSSING
TEPIDNESSES	TERGIVERSATOR	TERRACINGS	TERRORISERS	TESTERNING
TERAHERTZES	TERGIVERSATORS	TERRACOTTA	TERRORISES	TESTICULAR
TERAMETERS	TERGIVERSATORY	TERRACOTTAS	TERRORISING	TESTICULATE
TERATOCARCINOMA	TERMAGANCIES	TERRAFORMED	TERRORISMS	TESTICULATED
TERATOGENESES	TERMAGANCY	TERRAFORMING	TERRORISTIC	TESTIFICATE
TERATOGENESIS	TERMAGANTLY	TERRAFORMINGS	TERRORISTS	TESTIFICATES
TERATOGENIC	TERMAGANTS	TERRAFORMS	TERRORIZATION	TESTIFICATION
TERATOGENICIST	TERMINABILITIES	TERRAMARAS	TERRORIZATIONS	TESTIFICATIONS
TERATOGENICISTS	TERMINABILITY	TERRAMARES	TERRORIZED	TESTIFICATOR
TERATOGENICITY	TERMINABLE	TERRAQUEOUS	TERRORIZER	TESTIFICATORS
TERATOGENIES	TERMINABLENESS	TERRARIUMS	TERRORIZERS	TESTIFICATORY
TERATOGENS	TERMINABLY	TERREMOTIVE	TERRORIZES	TESTIFIERS
TERATOGENY	TERMINALLY	TERREPLEIN	TERRORIZING	TESTIFYING
TERATOLOGIC	TERMINATED	TERREPLEINS	TERRORLESS	TESTIMONIAL
TERATOLOGICAL	TERMINATES	TERRESTRIAL	TERSANCTUS	TESTIMONIALISE
TERATOLOGIES	TERMINATING	TERRESTRIALLY	TERSANCTUSES	TESTIMONIALISED
TERATOLOGIST	TERMINATION	TERRESTRIALNESS	TERSENESSES	TESTIMONIALISES
TERATOLOGISTS	TERMINATIONAL	TERRESTRIALS	TERTIARIES	TESTIMONIALIZE
TERATOLOGY	TERMINATIONS	TERRIBILITIES	TERVALENCIES	TESTIMONIALIZED
TERATOMATA	TERMINATIVE	TERRIBILITY	TERVALENCY	TESTIMONIALIZES
TERATOMATOUS	TERMINATIVELY	TERRIBLENESS	TESCHENITE	TESTIMONIALS
TERATOPHOBIA	TERMINATOR	TERRIBLENESSES	TESCHENITES	TESTIMONIED
TERATOPHOBIAS	TERMINATORS	TERRICOLES	TESSARAGLOT	TESTIMONIES
TERCENTENARIES	TERMINATORY	TERRICOLOUS	TESSELATED	TESTIMONYING
TERCENTENARY	TERMINISMS	TERRIFICALLY	TESSELATES	TESTINESSES
TERCENTENNIAL	TERMINISTS	TERRIFIERS	TESSELATING	TESTOSTERONE
TERCENTENNIALS	TERMINOLOGICAL	TERRIFYING	TESSELLATE	TESTOSTERONES
TEREBINTHINE	TERMINOLOGIES	TERRIFYINGLY	TESSELLATED	TESTUDINAL
TEREBINTHS	TERMINOLOGIST	TERRIGENOUS	TESSELLATES	TESTUDINARY
TEREBRANTS	TERMINOLOGISTS	TERRITORIAL	TESSELLATING	TESTUDINEOUS
TEREBRATED	TERMINOLOGY	TERRITORIALISE	TESSELLATION	TESTUDINES
TEREBRATES	TERMINUSES	TERRITORIALISED	TESSELLATIONS	TETANICALLY
TEREBRATING	TERMITARIA	TERRITORIALISES	TESSERACTS	TETANISATION
TEREBRATION	TERMITARIES	TERRITORIALISM	TESSITURAS	TETANISATIONS
TEREBRATIONS	TERMITARIUM	TERRITORIALISMS	TESTABILITIES	TETANISING
TEREBRATULA	TERMITARIUMS	TERRITORIALIST	TESTABILITY	TETANIZATION
TEREBRATULAE	TERNEPLATE	TERRITORIALISTS	TESTACEANS	TETANIZATIONS

TETANIZING	TETRAETHYL	TETRAPOLISES	TETROXIDES	THALIDOMIDE
TETARTOHEDRAL	TETRAETHYLLEAD	TETRAPOLITAN	TEUTONISED	THALIDOMIDES
TETARTOHEDRALLY	TETRAETHYLLEADS	TETRAPTERAN	TEUTONISES	THALLIFORM
TETARTOHEDRISM	TETRAETHYLS	TETRAPTEROUS	TEUTONISING	THALLOPHYTE
TETARTOHEDRISMS	TETRAFLUORIDE	TETRAPTOTE	TEUTONIZED	THALLOPHYTES
TETCHINESS	TETRAFLUORIDES	TETRAPTOTES	TEUTONIZES	THALLOPHYTIC
TETCHINESSES	TETRAGONAL	TETRAPYRROLE	TEUTONIZING	THANATISMS
TETHERBALL	TETRAGONALLY	TETRAPYRROLES	TEXTBOOKISH	THANATISTS
TETHERBALLS	TETRAGONALNESS	TETRARCHATE	TEXTPHONES	THANATOGNOMONIC
TETRABASIC	TETRAGONOUS	TETRARCHATES	TEXTSPEAKS	THANATOGRAPHIES
TETRABASICITIES	TETRAGRAMMATON	TETRARCHIC	TEXTUALISM	THANATOGRAPHY
TETRABASICITY	TETRAGRAMMATONS	TETRARCHICAL	TEXTUALISMS	THANATOLOGICAL
TETRABORATE	TETRAGRAMS	TETRARCHIES	TEXTUALIST	THANATOLOGIES
TETRABORATES	TETRAGYNIAN	TETRASEMIC	TEXTUALISTS	THANATOLOGIST
TETRABRACH	TETRAGYNOUS	TETRASPORANGIA	TEXTUARIES	THANATOLOGISTS
TETRABRACHS	TETRAHEDRA	TETRASPORANGIUM	TEXTURALLY	THANATOLOGY
TETRABRANCHIATE	TETRAHEDRAL	TETRASPORE	TEXTURELESS	THANATOPHOBIA
TETRACAINE	TETRAHEDRALLY	TETRASPORES	TEXTURINGS	THANATOPHOBIAS
TETRACAINES	TETRAHEDRITE	TETRASPORIC	TEXTURISED	THANATOPSES
TETRACHLORIDE	TETRAHEDRITES	TETRASPOROUS	TEXTURISES	THANATOPSIS
TETRACHLORIDES	TETRAHEDRON	TETRASTICH	TEXTURISING	THANATOSES
TETRACHORD	TETRAHEDRONS	TETRASTICHAL	TEXTURIZED	THANATOSIS
TETRACHORDAL	TETRAHYDROFURAN	TETRASTICHIC	TEXTURIZES	THANEHOODS
TETRACHORDS	TETRAHYMENA	TETRASTICHOUS	TEXTURIZING	THANESHIPS
TETRACHOTOMIES	TETRAHYMENAS	TETRASTICHS	THALAMENCEPHALA	THANKFULLER
TETRACHOTOMOUS	TETRALOGIES	TETRASTYLE	THALAMICALLY	THANKFULLEST
TETRACHOTOMY	TETRAMERAL	TETRASTYLES	THALAMIFLORAL	THANKFULLY
TETRACHROMACIES	TETRAMERIC	TETRASYLLABIC	THALASSAEMIA	THANKFULNESS
TETRACHROMACY	TETRAMERISM	TETRASYLLABICAL	THALASSAEMIAS	THANKFULNESSES
TETRACHROMAT	TETRAMERISMS	TETRASYLLABLE	THALASSAEMIC	THANKLESSLY
TETRACHROMATS	TETRAMEROUS	TETRASYLLABLES	THALASSAEMICS	THANKLESSNESS
TETRACTINAL	TETRAMETER	TETRATHEISM	THALASSEMIA	THANKLESSNESSES
TETRACTINALS	TETRAMETERS	TETRATHEISMS	THALASSEMIAS	THANKSGIVER
TETRACTINE	TETRAMETHYL	TETRATHLON	THALASSEMIC	THANKSGIVERS
TETRACTINES	TETRAMETHYLLEAD	TETRATHLONS	THALASSEMICS	THANKSGIVING
TETRACYCLIC	TETRAMORPHIC	TETRATOMIC	THALASSIAN	THANKSGIVINGS
TETRACYCLINE	TETRANDRIAN	TETRAVALENCE	THALASSIANS	THANKWORTHIER
TETRACYCLINES	TETRANDROUS	TETRAVALENCES	THALASSOCRACIES	THANKWORTHIEST
TETRADACTYL	TETRAPLEGIA	TETRAVALENCIES	THALASSOCRACY	THANKWORTHILY
TETRADACTYLIES	TETRAPLEGIAS	TETRAVALENCY	THALASSOCRAT	THANKWORTHINESS
TETRADACTYLOUS	TETRAPLEGIC	TETRAVALENT	THALASSOCRATS	THANKWORTHY
TETRADACTYLS	TETRAPLOID	TETRAVALENTS	THALASSOGRAPHER	THARBOROUGH
TETRADACTYLY	TETRAPLOIDIES	TETRAZOLIUM	THALASSOGRAPHIC	THARBOROUGHS
TETRADITES	TETRAPLOIDS	TETRAZOLIUMS	THALASSOGRAPHY	THATCHIEST
TETRADRACHM	TETRAPLOIDY	TETRAZZINI	THALASSOTHERAPY	THATCHINGS
TETRADRACHMS	TETRAPODIC	TETRODOTOXIN	THALATTOCRACIES	THATCHLESS
TETRADYMITE	TETRAPODIES	TETRODOTOXINS	THALATTOCRACY	THATNESSES
TETRADYMITES	TETRAPODOUS	TETROTOXIN	THALICTRUM	THAUMASITE
TETRADYNAMOUS	TETRAPOLIS	TETROTOXINS	THALICTRUMS	THAUMASITES

THAUMATINS	THEATRICALISM	THENARDITES	THEOLOGIZE	THEORETICAL
THAUMATOGENIES	THEATRICALISMS	THENCEFORTH	THEOLOGIZED	THEORETICALLY
THAUMATOGENY	THEATRICALITIES	THENCEFORWARD	THEOLOGIZER	THEORETICIAN
THAUMATOGRAPHY	THEATRICALITY	THENCEFORWARDS	THEOLOGIZERS	THEORETICIANS
THAUMATOLATRIES	THEATRICALIZE	THEOBROMINE	THEOLOGIZES	THEORETICS
THAUMATOLATRY	THEATRICALIZED	THEOBROMINES	THEOLOGIZING	THEORIQUES
THAUMATOLOGIES	THEATRICALIZES	THEOCENTRIC	THEOLOGOUMENA	THEORISATION
THAUMATOLOGY	THEATRICALIZING	THEOCENTRICISM	THEOLOGOUMENON	THEORISATIONS
THAUMATROPE	THEATRICALLY	THEOCENTRICISMS	THEOLOGUES	THEORISERS
THAUMATROPES	THEATRICALNESS	THEOCENTRICITY	THEOMACHIES	THEORISING
THAUMATROPICAL	THEATRICALS	THEOCENTRISM	THEOMACHIST	THEORIZATION
THAUMATURGE	THEATRICISE	THEOCENTRISMS	THEOMACHISTS	THEORIZATIONS
THAUMATURGES	THEATRICISED	THEOCRACIES	THEOMANCIES	THEORIZERS
THAUMATURGIC	THEATRICISES	THEOCRASIES	THEOMANIAC	THEORIZING
THAUMATURGICAL	THEATRICISING	THEOCRATIC	THEOMANIACS	THEOSOPHER
THAUMATURGICS	THEATRICISM	THEOCRATICAL	THEOMANIAS	THEOSOPHERS
THAUMATURGIES	THEATRICISMS	THEOCRATICALLY	THEOMANTIC	THEOSOPHIC
THAUMATURGISM	THEATRICIZE	THEODICEAN	THEOMORPHIC	THEOSOPHICAL
THAUMATURGISMS	THEATRICIZED	THEODICEANS	THEOMORPHISM	THEOSOPHICALLY
THAUMATURGIST	THEATRICIZES	THEODICIES	THEOMORPHISMS	THEOSOPHIES
THAUMATURGISTS	THEATRICIZING	THEODOLITE	THEONOMIES	THEOSOPHISE
THAUMATURGUS	THEATROMANIA	THEODOLITES	THEONOMOUS	THEOSOPHISED
THAUMATURGUSES	THEATROMANIAS	THEODOLITIC	THEOPATHETIC	THEOSOPHISES
THAUMATURGY	THEATROPHONE	THEOGONICAL	THEOPATHIC	THEOSOPHISING
THEANTHROPIC	THEATROPHONES	THEOGONIES	THEOPATHIES	THEOSOPHISM
THEANTHROPIES	THECODONTS	THEOGONIST	THEOPHAGIES	THEOSOPHISMS
THEANTHROPISM	THEFTUOUSLY	THEOGONISTS	THEOPHAGOUS	THEOSOPHIST
THEANTHROPISMS	THEGNLIEST	THEOLOGASTER	THEOPHANIC	THEOSOPHISTICAL
THEANTHROPIST	THEIRSELVES	THEOLOGASTERS	THEOPHANIES	THEOSOPHISTS
THEANTHROPISTS	THEISTICAL	THEOLOGATE	THEOPHANOUS	THEOSOPHIZE
THEANTHROPY	THEISTICALLY	THEOLOGATES	THEOPHOBIA	THEOSOPHIZED
THEARCHIES	THELEMENTS	THEOLOGERS	THEOPHOBIAC	THEOSOPHIZES
THEATERGOER	THELITISES	THEOLOGIAN	THEOPHOBIACS	THEOSOPHIZING
THEATERGOERS	THELYTOKIES	THEOLOGIANS	THEOPHOBIAS	THEOTECHNIC
THEATERGOING	THELYTOKOUS	THEOLOGICAL	THEOPHOBIST	THEOTECHNIES
THEATERGOINGS	THEMATICALLY	THEOLOGICALLY	THEOPHOBISTS	THEOTECHNY
THEATERLAND	THEMATISATION	THEOLOGIES	THEOPHORIC	THERALITES
THEATERLANDS	THEMATISATIONS	THEOLOGISATION	THEOPHYLLINE	THERAPEUSES
THEATREGOER	THEMATISED	THEOLOGISATIONS	THEOPHYLLINES	THERAPEUSIS
THEATREGOERS	THEMATISES	THEOLOGISE	THEOPNEUST	THERAPEUTIC
THEATREGOING	THEMATISING	THEOLOGISED	THEOPNEUSTIC	THERAPEUTICAL
THEATREGOINGS	THEMATIZATION	THEOLOGISER	THEOPNEUSTIES	THERAPEUTICALLY
THEATRELAND	THEMATIZATIONS	THEOLOGISERS	THEOPNEUSTY	THERAPEUTICS
THEATRELANDS	THEMATIZED	THEOLOGISES	THEORBISTS	THERAPEUTIST
THEATRICAL	THEMATIZES	THEOLOGISING	THEOREMATIC	THERAPEUTISTS
THEATRICALISE	THEMATIZING	THEOLOGIST	THEOREMATICAL	THERAPISED
THEATRICALISED	THEMSELVES	THEOLOGISTS	THEOREMATICALLY	THERAPISES
THEATRICALISES	THENABOUTS	THEOLOGIZATION	THEOREMATIST	THERAPISING
THEATRICALISING	THENARDITE	THEOLOGIZATIONS	THEOREMATISTS	THERAPISTS

THERAPIZED	THERMIDORS	THERMOGRAPHS	THERMOSETS	THICKENING
THERAPIZES	THERMIONIC	THERMOGRAPHY	THERMOSETTING	THICKENINGS
THERAPIZING	THERMIONICS	THERMOHALINE	THERMOSIPHON	THICKETIER
THERAPSIDS	THERMISTOR	THERMOJUNCTION	THERMOSIPHONS	THICKETIEST
THEREABOUT	THERMISTORS	THERMOJUNCTIONS	THERMOSPHERE	THICKHEADED
THEREABOUTS	THERMOBALANCE	THERMOLABILE	THERMOSPHERES	THICKHEADEDNESS
THEREAFTER	THERMOBALANCES	THERMOLABILITY	THERMOSPHERIC	THICKHEADS
THEREAGAINST	THERMOBARIC	THERMOLOGIES	THERMOSTABILITY	THICKLEAVES
THEREAMONG	THERMOBAROGRAPH	THERMOLOGY	THERMOSTABLE	THICKNESSES
THEREANENT	THERMOBAROMETER	THERMOLYSES	THERMOSTAT	THICKSKINS
THEREBESIDE	THERMOCHEMICAL	THERMOLYSIS	THERMOSTATED	THIEVERIES
THEREINAFTER	THERMOCHEMIST	THERMOLYTIC	THERMOSTATIC	THIEVISHLY
THEREINBEFORE	THERMOCHEMISTRY	THERMOMAGNETIC	THERMOSTATICS	THIEVISHNESS
THERENESSES	THERMOCHEMISTS	THERMOMETER	THERMOSTATING	THIEVISHNESSES
THERETHROUGH	THERMOCHROMIC	THERMOMETERS	THERMOSTATS	THIGHBONES
THERETOFORE	THERMOCHROMIES	THERMOMETRIC	THERMOSTATTED	THIGMOTACTIC
THEREUNDER	THERMOCHROMISM	THERMOMETRICAL	THERMOSTATTING	THIGMOTAXES
THEREWITHAL	THERMOCHROMISMS	THERMOMETRIES	THERMOTACTIC	THIGMOTAXIS
THEREWITHIN	THERMOCHROMY	THERMOMETRY	THERMOTAXES	THIGMOTROPIC
THERIANTHROPIC	THERMOCLINE	THERMOMOTOR	THERMOTAXIC	THIGMOTROPISM
THERIANTHROPISM	THERMOCLINES	THERMOMOTORS	THERMOTAXIS	THIGMOTROPISMS
THERIOLATRIES	THERMOCOUPLE	THERMONASTIES	THERMOTENSILE	THIMBLEBERRIES
THERIOLATRY	THERMOCOUPLES	THERMONASTY	THERMOTHERAPIES	THIMBLEBERRY
THERIOMORPH	THERMODURIC	THERMONUCLEAR	THERMOTHERAPY	THIMBLEFUL
THERIOMORPHIC	THERMODYNAMIC	THERMOPERIODIC	THERMOTICAL	THIMBLEFULS
THERIOMORPHISM	THERMODYNAMICAL	THERMOPERIODISM	THERMOTICS	THIMBLERIG
THERIOMORPHISMS	THERMODYNAMICS	THERMOPHIL	THERMOTOLERANT	THIMBLERIGGED
THERIOMORPHOSES	THERMOELECTRIC	THERMOPHILE	THERMOTROPIC	THIMBLERIGGER
THERIOMORPHOSIS	THERMOELECTRON	THERMOPHILES	THERMOTROPICS	THIMBLERIGGERS
THERIOMORPHOUS	THERMOELECTRONS	THERMOPHILIC	THERMOTROPISM	THIMBLERIGGING
THERIOMORPHS	THERMOELEMENT	THERMOPHILOUS	THERMOTROPISMS	THIMBLERIGGINGS
THERMAESTHESIA	THERMOELEMENTS	THERMOPHILS	THEROLOGIES	THIMBLERIGS
THERMAESTHESIAS	THERMOFORM	THERMOPHYLLOUS	THEROPHYTE	THIMBLESFUL
THERMALISATION	THERMOFORMABLE	THERMOPILE	THEROPHYTES	THIMBLEWEED
THERMALISATIONS	THERMOFORMED	THERMOPILES	THEROPODAN	THIMBLEWEEDS
THERMALISE	THERMOFORMING	THERMOPLASTIC	THEROPODANS	THIMBLEWIT
THERMALISED	THERMOFORMS	THERMOPLASTICS	THERSITICAL	THIMBLEWITS
THERMALISES	THERMOGENESES	THERMORECEPTOR	THESAURUSES	THIMBLEWITTED
THERMALISING	THERMOGENESIS	THERMORECEPTORS	THESMOTHETE	THIMEROSAL
THERMALIZATION	THERMOGENETIC	THERMOREGULATE	THESMOTHETES	THIMEROSALS
THERMALIZATIONS	THERMOGENIC	THERMOREGULATED	THETICALLY	THINGAMABOB
THERMALIZE	THERMOGENOUS	THERMOREGULATES	THEURGICAL	THINGAMABOBS
THERMALIZED	THERMOGRAM	THERMOREGULATOR	THEURGICALLY	THINGAMAJIG
THERMALIZES	THERMOGRAMS	THERMOREMANENCE	THEURGISTS	THINGAMAJIGS
THERMALIZING	THERMOGRAPH	THERMOREMANENT	THIABENDAZOLE	THINGAMIES
THERMESTHESIA	THERMOGRAPHER	THERMOSCOPE	THIABENDAZOLES	THINGAMYBOB
THERMESTHESIAS	THERMOGRAPHERS	THERMOSCOPES	THIAMINASE	THINGAMYBOBS
THERMETTES	THERMOGRAPHIC	THERMOSCOPIC	THIAMINASES	THINGAMYJIG
THERMICALLY	THERMOGRAPHIES	THERMOSCOPICAL	THICKENERS	THINGAMYJIGS

T

THINGHOODS	THIOSULFURIC	THORNBACKS	THRAIPINGS	THRENODISTS
THINGINESS	THIOSULPHATE	THORNBILLS	THRALLDOMS	THREONINES
THINGINESSES	THIOSULPHATES	THORNBIRDS	THRAPPLING	THRESHINGS
THINGLINESS	THIOSULPHURIC	THORNBUSHES	THRASHIEST	THRESHOLDS
THINGLINESSES	THIOURACIL	THORNHEDGE	THRASHINGS	THRIFTIEST
THINGNESSES	THIOURACILS	THORNHEDGES	THRASONICAL	THRIFTINESS
THINGUMABOB	THIRDBOROUGH	THORNINESS	THRASONICALLY	THRIFTINESSES
THINGUMABOBS	THIRDBOROUGHS	THORNINESSES	THREADBARE	THRIFTLESS
THINGUMAJIG	THIRDSTREAM	THORNPROOF	THREADBARENESS	THRIFTLESSLY
THINGUMAJIGS	THIRDSTREAMS	THORNPROOFS	THREADBARER	THRIFTLESSNESS
THINGUMBOB	THIRSTIEST	THORNTAILS	THREADBAREST	THRILLIEST
THINGUMBOBS	THIRSTINESS	THORNTREES	THREADFINS	THRILLINGLY
THINGUMMIES	THIRSTINESSES	THOROUGHBASS	THREADIEST	THRILLINGNESS
THINGUMMYBOB	THIRSTLESS	THOROUGHBASSES	THREADINESS	THRILLINGNESSES
THINGUMMYBOBS	THIRTEENTH	THOROUGHBRACE	THREADINESSES	THRIVELESS
THINGUMMYJIG	THIRTEENTHLY	THOROUGHBRACED	THREADLESS	THRIVINGLY
THINGUMMYJIGS	THIRTEENTHS	THOROUGHBRACES	THREADLIKE	THRIVINGNESS
THINKABLENESS	THIRTIETHS	THOROUGHBRED	THREADMAKER	THRIVINGNESSES
THINKABLENESSES	THIRTYFOLD	THOROUGHBREDS	THREADMAKERS	THROATIEST
THINKINGLY	THIRTYSOMETHING	THOROUGHER	THREADWORM	THROATINESS
THINKINGNESS	THISNESSES	THOROUGHEST	THREADWORMS	THROATINESSES
THINKINGNESSES	THISTLEDOWN	THOROUGHFARE	THREATENED	THROATLASH
THINKPIECE	THISTLEDOWNS	THOROUGHFARES	THREATENER	THROATLASHES
THINKPIECES	THISTLIEST	THOROUGHGOING	THREATENERS	THROATLATCH
THINNESSES	THITHERWARD	THOROUGHGOINGLY	THREATENING	THROATLATCHES
THIOALCOHOL	THITHERWARDS	THOROUGHLY	THREATENINGLY	THROATWORT
THIOALCOHOLS	THIXOTROPE	THOROUGHNESS	THREATENINGS	THROATWORTS
THIOBACILLI	THIXOTROPES	THOROUGHNESSES	THREEFOLDNESS	THROBBINGLY
THIOBACILLUS	THIXOTROPIC	THOROUGHPACED	THREEFOLDNESSES	THROBBINGS
THIOBARBITURATE	THIXOTROPIES	THOROUGHPIN	THREENESSES	THROMBECTOMIES
THIOCARBAMIDE	THIXOTROPY	THOROUGHPINS	THREEPEATED	THROMBECTOMY
THIOCARBAMIDES	THOLEIITES	THOROUGHWAX	THREEPEATING	THROMBOCYTE
THIOCYANATE	THOLEIITIC	THOROUGHWAXES	THREEPEATS	THROMBOCYTES
THIOCYANATES	THOLOBATES	THOROUGHWORT	THREEPENCE	THROMBOCYTIC
THIOCYANIC	THORACENTESES	THOROUGHWORTS	THREEPENCES	THROMBOEMBOLIC
THIODIGLYCOL	THORACENTESIS	THOUGHTCAST	THREEPENCEWORTH	THROMBOEMBOLISM
THIODIGLYCOLS	THORACICALLY	THOUGHTCASTS	THREEPENNIES	THROMBOGEN
THIOFURANS	THORACOCENTESES	THOUGHTFUL	THREEPENNY	THROMBOGENS
THIOPENTAL	THORACOCENTESIS	THOUGHTFULLY	THREEPENNYWORTH	THROMBOKINASE
THIOPENTALS	THORACOPLASTIES	THOUGHTFULNESS	THREEQUELS	THROMBOKINASES
THIOPENTONE	THORACOPLASTY	THOUGHTLESS	THREESCORE	THROMBOLYSES
THIOPENTONES	THORACOSCOPE	THOUGHTLESSLY	THREESCORES	THROMBOLYSIS
THIOPHENES	THORACOSCOPES	THOUGHTLESSNESS	THREESOMES	THROMBOLYTIC
THIORIDAZINE	THORACOSTOMIES	THOUGHTWAY	THREMMATOLOGIES	THROMBOLYTICS
THIORIDAZINES	THORACOSTOMY	THOUGHTWAYS	THREMMATOLOGY	THROMBOPHILIA
THIOSINAMINE	THORACOTOMIES	THOUSANDFOLD	THRENETICAL	THROMBOPHILIAS
THIOSINAMINES	THORACOTOMY	THOUSANDFOLDS	THRENODIAL	THROMBOPLASTIC
THIOSULFATE	THORIANITE	THOUSANDTH	THRENODIES	THROMBOPLASTIN
THIOSULFATES	THORIANITES	THOUSANDTHS	THRENODIST	THROMBOPLASTINS

THROMBOSED	THUMBPIECE	THUNDERSTORMS	THYROTROPHIC	TIEBREAKER
THROMBOSES	THUMBPIECES	THUNDERSTRICKEN	THYROTROPHIN	TIEBREAKERS
THROMBOSING	THUMBPRINT	THUNDERSTRIKE	THYROTROPHINS	TIEMANNITE
THROMBOSIS	THUMBPRINTS	THUNDERSTRIKES	THYROTROPIC	TIEMANNITES
THROMBOTIC	THUMBSCREW	THUNDERSTRIKING	THYROTROPIN	TIERCELETS
THROMBOXANE	THUMBSCREWS	THUNDERSTROKE	THYROTROPINS	TIERCERONS
THROMBOXANES	THUMBSTALL	THUNDERSTROKES	THYROXINES	TIGERISHLY
THRONELESS	THUMBSTALLS	THUNDERSTRUCK	THYRSOIDAL	TIGERISHNESS
THRONGINGS	THUMBSTICK	THURIFEROUS	THYSANOPTEROUS	TIGERISHNESSES
THROPPLING	THUMBSTICKS	THURIFICATION	THYSANURAN	TIGERLIEST
THROTTLEABLE	THUMBTACKED	THURIFICATIONS	THYSANURANS	TIGERWOODS
THROTTLEHOLD	THUMBTACKING	THURIFYING	THYSANUROUS	TIGGYWINKLE
THROTTLEHOLDS	THUMBTACKS	THUSNESSES	TIBIOFIBULA	TIGGYWINKLES
THROTTLERS	THUMBWHEEL	THWACKINGS	TIBIOFIBULAE	TIGHTASSED
THROTTLING	THUMBWHEELS	THWARTEDLY	TIBIOFIBULAS	TIGHTASSES
THROTTLINGS	THUMPINGLY	THWARTINGLY	TIBIOTARSI	TIGHTENERS
THROUGHFARE	THUNBERGIA	THWARTINGS	TIBIOTARSUS	TIGHTENING
THROUGHFARES	THUNBERGIAS	THWARTSHIP	TIBOUCHINA	TIGHTENINGS
THROUGHGAUN	THUNDERBIRD	THWARTSHIPS	TIBOUCHINAS	TIGHTFISTED
THROUGHGAUNS	THUNDERBIRDS	THWARTWAYS	TICHORRHINE	TIGHTFISTEDNESS
THROUGHITHER	THUNDERBOLT	THWARTWISE	TICHORRHINES	TIGHTISHLY
THROUGHOTHER	THUNDERBOLTS	THYLACINES	TICKETINGS	TIGHTNESSES
THROUGHOUT	THUNDERBOX	THYLAKOIDS	TICKETLESS	TIGHTROPES
THROUGHPUT	THUNDERBOXES	THYMECTOMIES	TICKETTYBOO	TIGHTWIRES
THROUGHPUTS	THUNDERCLAP	THYMECTOMISE	TICKLEASSES	TIGRISHNESS
THROUGHWAY	THUNDERCLAPS	THYMECTOMISED	TICKLISHLY	TIGRISHNESSES
THROUGHWAYS	THUNDERCLOUD	THYMECTOMISES	TICKLISHNESS	TIKINAGANS
THROWAWAYS	THUNDERCLOUDS	THYMECTOMISING	TICKLISHNESSES	TIKOLOSHES
THROWBACKS	THUNDERERS	THYMECTOMIZE	TICKTACKED	TIKTAALIKS
THROWDOWNS	THUNDERFLASH	THYMECTOMIZED	TICKTACKING	TILEFISHES
THROWOVERS	THUNDERFLASHES	THYMECTOMIZES	TICKTACKTOE	TILIACEOUS
THROWSTERS	THUNDERHEAD	THYMECTOMIZING	TICKTACKTOES	TILLANDSIA
THRUMMIEST	THUNDERHEADS	THYMECTOMY	TICKTOCKED	TILLANDSIAS
THRUMMINGLY	THUNDERIER	THYMELAEACEOUS	TICKTOCKING	TILLERINGS
THRUMMINGS	THUNDERIEST	THYMIDINES	TICTACKING	TILLERLESS
THRUPENNIES	THUNDERING	THYMIDYLIC	TICTOCKING	TILTMETERS
THRUPPENCE	THUNDERINGLY	THYMOCYTES	TIDDLEDYWINK	TILTROTORS
THRUPPENCES	THUNDERINGS	THYRATRONS	TIDDLEDYWINKS	TIMBERDOODLE
THRUPPENNIES	THUNDERLESS	THYRISTORS	TIDDLEYWINK	TIMBERDOODLES
THRUPPENNY	THUNDEROUS	THYROCALCITONIN	TIDDLEYWINKS	TIMBERHEAD
THRUSHLIKE	THUNDEROUSLY	THYROGLOBULIN	TIDDLYWINK	TIMBERHEADS
THRUSTINGS	THUNDEROUSNESS	THYROGLOBULINS	TIDDLYWINKS	TIMBERIEST
THRUTCHING	THUNDERSHOWER	THYROIDECTOMIES	TIDEWAITER	TIMBERINGS
THUDDINGLY	THUNDERSHOWERS	THYROIDECTOMY	TIDEWAITERS	TIMBERLAND
THUGGERIES	THUNDERSNOW	THYROIDITIDES	TIDEWATERS	TIMBERLANDS
THUMBHOLES	THUNDERSNOWS	THYROIDITIS	TIDINESSES	TIMBERLINE
THUMBIKINS	THUNDERSTONE	THYROIDITISES	TIDIVATING	TIMBERLINES
THUMBLINGS	THUNDERSTONES	THYROTOXICOSES	TIDIVATION	TIMBERWORK
THUMBNAILS	THUNDERSTORM	THYROTOXICOSIS	TIDIVATIONS	TIMBERWORKS

T

TIMBERYARD	TIMETABLINGS	TIPTRONICS	TITTIVATING	TOCOPHOBIA
TIMBERYARDS	TIMEWORKER	TIRAILLEUR	TITTIVATION	TOCOPHOBIAS
TIMBRELLED	TIMEWORKERS	TIRAILLEURS	TITTIVATIONS	TODDLERHOOD
TIMBROLOGIES	TIMIDITIES	TIREDNESSES	TITTIVATOR	TODDLERHOODS
TIMBROLOGIST	TIMIDNESSES	TIRELESSLY	TITTIVATORS	TOENAILING
TIMBROLOGISTS	TIMOCRACIES	TIRELESSNESS	TITTLEBATS	TOERAGGERS
TIMBROLOGY	TIMOCRATIC	TIRELESSNESSES	TITTUPIEST	TOFFISHNESS
TIMBROMANIA	TIMOCRATICAL	TIREMAKERS	TITTUPPIER	TOFFISHNESSES
TIMBROMANIAC	TIMOROUSLY	TIRESOMELY	TITTUPPIEST	TOGAVIRUSES
TIMBROMANIACS	TIMOROUSNESS	TIRESOMENESS	TITTUPPING	TOGETHERNESS
TIMBROMANIAS	TIMOROUSNESSES	TIRESOMENESSES	TITUBANCIES	TOGETHERNESSES
TIMBROPHILIES	TIMPANISTS	TIROCINIUM	TITUBATING	TOILETINGS
TIMBROPHILIST	TINCTORIAL	TIROCINIUMS	TITUBATION	TOILETRIES
TIMBROPHILISTS	TINCTORIALLY	TITANESSES	TITUBATIONS	TOILFULNESS
TIMBROPHILY	TINCTURING	TITANICALLY	TITULARIES	TOILFULNESSES
TIMEFRAMES	TINDERBOXES	TITANIFEROUS	TITULARITIES	TOILINETTE
TIMEKEEPER	TINDERIEST	TITANOSAUR	TITULARITY	TOILINETTES
TIMEKEEPERS	TINGLINGLY	TITANOSAURS	TOADEATERS	TOILSOMELY
TIMEKEEPING	TINGUAITES	TITANOTHERE	TOADFISHES	TOILSOMENESS
TIMEKEEPINGS	TININESSES	TITANOTHERES	TOADFLAXES	TOILSOMENESSES
TIMELESSLY	TINKERINGS	TITARAKURA	TOADGRASSES	TOKENISTIC
TIMELESSNESS	TINKERTOYS	TITARAKURAS	TOADRUSHES	TOKOLOGIES
TIMELESSNESSES	TINKLINGLY	TITHINGMAN	TOADSTONES	TOKOLOSHES
TIMELINESS	TINNINESSES	TITHINGMEN	TOADSTOOLS	TOKOLOSHIS
TIMELINESSES	TINNITUSES	TITILLATED	TOASTMASTER	TOKOPHOBIA
TIMENOGUYS	TINPLATING	TITILLATES	TOASTMASTERS	TOKOPHOBIAS
TIMEPASSED	TINSELIEST	TITILLATING	TOASTMISTRESS	TOKTOKKIES
TIMEPASSES	TINSELLIER	TITILLATINGLY	TOASTMISTRESSES	TOLBUTAMIDE
TIMEPASSING	TINSELLIEST	TITILLATION	TOBACCANALIAN	TOLBUTAMIDES
TIMEPIECES	TINSELLING	TITILLATIONS	TOBACCANALIANS	TOLERABILITIES
TIMEPLEASER	TINSELRIES	TITILLATIVE	TOBACCOLESS	TOLERABILITY
TIMEPLEASERS	TINSMITHING	TITILLATOR	TOBACCONIST	TOLERABLENESS
TIMESAVERS	TINSMITHINGS	TITILLATORS	TOBACCONISTS	TOLERABLENESSES
TIMESAVING	TINTINESSES	TITIPOUNAMU	TOBOGGANED	TOLERANCES
TIMESCALES	TINTINNABULA	TITIPOUNAMUS	TOBOGGANER	TOLERANTLY
TIMESERVER	TINTINNABULANT	TITIVATING	TOBOGGANERS	TOLERATING
TIMESERVERS	TINTINNABULAR	TITIVATION	TOBOGGANING	TOLERATION
TIMESERVING	TINTINNABULARY	TITIVATIONS	TOBOGGANINGS	TOLERATIONISM
TIMESERVINGS	TINTINNABULATE	TITIVATORS	TOBOGGANIST	TOLERATIONISMS
TIMESHARES	TINTINNABULATED	TITLEHOLDER	TOBOGGANISTS	TOLERATIONIST
TIMESHIFTED	TINTINNABULATES	TITLEHOLDERS	TOBOGGINED	TOLERATIONISTS
TIMESHIFTING	TINTINNABULOUS	TITLEHOLDING	TOBOGGINING	TOLERATIONS
TIMESHIFTS	TINTINNABULUM	TITRATABLE	TOCCATELLA	TOLERATIVE
TIMESTAMPED	TINTOMETER	TITRATIONS	TOCCATELLAS	TOLERATORS
TIMESTAMPING	TINTOMETERS	TITRIMETRIC	TOCCATINAS	TOLLBOOTHS
TIMESTAMPS	TINTOOKIES	TITTERINGLY	TOCHERLESS	TOLLBRIDGE
TIMETABLED	TIPPYTOEING	TITTERINGS	TOCOLOGIES	TOLLBRIDGES
TIMETABLES	TIPSIFYING	TITTIVATED	TOCOPHEROL	TOLLDISHES
TIMETABLING	TIPSINESSES	TITTIVATES	TOCOPHEROLS	TOLLGATING

TOLLHOUSES	TONOMETRIC	TOPAZOLITES	TOPONYMISTS	TORRENTIALLY
TOLLKEEPER	TONOMETRIES	TOPCROSSES	TOPOPHILIA	TORRENTING
TOLLKEEPERS	TONOPLASTS	TOPDRESSED	TOPOPHILIAS	TORRENTUOUS
TOLUIDIDES	TONSILITIS	TOPDRESSES	TOPSCORING	TORRIDITIES
TOLUIDINES	TONSILITISES	TOPDRESSING	TOPSOILING	TORRIDNESS
TOMAHAWKED	TONSILLARY	TOPDRESSINGS	TOPSOILINGS	TORRIDNESSES
TOMAHAWKING	TONSILLECTOMIES	TOPECTOMIES	TOPSTITCHED	TORRIFYING
TOMATILLOES	TONSILLECTOMY	TOPGALLANT	TOPSTITCHES	TORSIBILITIES
TOMATILLOS	TONSILLITIC	TOPGALLANTS	TOPSTITCHING	TORSIBILITY
TOMATOIEST	TONSILLITIDES	TOPHACEOUS	TOPWORKING	TORSIOGRAPH
TOMBOYISHLY	TONSILLITIS	TOPIARISTS	TORBANITES	TORSIOGRAPHS
TOMBOYISHNESS	TONSILLITISES	TOPICALITIES	TORBERNITE	TORSIONALLY
TOMBOYISHNESSES	TONSILLOTOMIES	TOPICALITY	TORBERNITES	TORTELLINI
TOMBSTONES	TONSILLOTOMY	TOPKNOTTED	TORCHBEARER	TORTELLINIS
TOMBSTONING	TOOLCHESTS	TOPLESSNESS	TORCHBEARERS	TORTFEASOR
TOMBSTONINGS	TOOLHOLDER	TOPLESSNESSES	TORCHIERES	TORTFEASORS
TOMCATTING	TOOLHOLDERS	TOPLOFTICAL	TORCHLIGHT	TORTICOLLAR
TOMCATTINGS	TOOLHOUSES	TOPLOFTIER	TORCHLIGHTS	TORTICOLLIS
TOMFOOLERIES	TOOLMAKERS	TOPLOFTIEST	TORCHWOODS	TORTICOLLISES
TOMFOOLERY	TOOLMAKING	TOPLOFTILY	TORMENTEDLY	TORTILITIES
TOMFOOLING	TOOLMAKINGS	TOPLOFTINESS	TORMENTERS	TORTILLONS
TOMFOOLISH	TOOLPUSHER	TOPLOFTINESSES	TORMENTILS	TORTIOUSLY
TOMFOOLISHNESS	TOOLPUSHERS	TOPMAKINGS	TORMENTING	TORTOISESHELL
TOMOGRAPHIC	TOOLPUSHES	TOPMINNOWS	TORMENTINGLY	TORTOISESHELLS
TOMOGRAPHIES	TOOTHACHES	TOPNOTCHER	TORMENTINGS	TORTRICIDS
TOMOGRAPHS	TOOTHBRUSH	TOPNOTCHERS	TORMENTORS	TORTUOSITIES
TOMOGRAPHY	TOOTHBRUSHES	TOPOCENTRIC	TORMENTUMS	TORTUOSITY
TOMOPHOBES	TOOTHBRUSHING	TOPOCHEMISTRIES	TOROIDALLY	TORTUOUSLY
TOMOPHOBIA	TOOTHBRUSHINGS	TOPOCHEMISTRY	TOROSITIES	TORTUOUSNESS
TOMOPHOBIAS	TOOTHCOMBS	TOPOGRAPHER	TORPEDINOUS	TORTUOUSNESSES
TOMOPHOBIC	TOOTHFISHES	TOPOGRAPHERS	TORPEDOERS	TORTUREDLY
TOMOPHOBICS	TOOTHINESS	TOPOGRAPHIC	TORPEDOING	TORTURESOME
TONALITIES	TOOTHINESSES	TOPOGRAPHICAL	TORPEDOIST	TORTURINGLY
TONALITIVE	TOOTHPASTE	TOPOGRAPHICALLY	TORPEDOISTS	TORTURINGS
TONELESSLY	TOOTHPASTES	TOPOGRAPHIES	TORPEFYING	TORTUROUSLY
TONELESSNESS	TOOTHPICKS	TOPOGRAPHS	TORPESCENCE	TOSSICATED
TONELESSNESSES	TOOTHSHELL	TOPOGRAPHY	TORPESCENCES	TOSTICATED
TONETICALLY	TOOTHSHELLS	TOPOISOMERASE	TORPESCENT	TOSTICATION
TONGUELESS	TOOTHSOMELY	TOPOISOMERASES	TORPIDITIES	TOSTICATIONS
TONGUELETS	TOOTHSOMENESS	TOPOLOGICAL	TORPIDNESS	TOTALISATION
TONGUELIKE	TOOTHSOMENESSES	TOPOLOGICALLY	TORPIDNESSES	TOTALISATIONS
TONGUESTER	TOOTHWASHES	TOPOLOGIES	TORPITUDES	TOTALISATOR
TONGUESTERS	TOOTHWORTS	TOPOLOGIST	TORPORIFIC	TOTALISATORS
TONICITIES	TOPAGNOSES	TOPOLOGISTS	TORREFACTION	TOTALISERS
TONISHNESS	TOPAGNOSIA	TOPOMETRIES	TORREFACTIONS	TOTALISING
TONISHNESSES	TOPAGNOSIAS	TOPONYMICAL	TORREFYING	TOTALISTIC
TONNISHNESS	TOPAGNOSIS	TOPONYMICS	TORRENTIAL	TOTALITARIAN
TONNISHNESSES	TOPARCHIES	TOPONYMIES	TORRENTIALITIES	TOTALITARIANISE
TONOMETERS	TOPAZOLITE	TOPONYMIST	TORRENTIALITY	TOTALITARIANISM

TOTALITARIANIZE	TOURBILLON	TOXICOMANIA	TRACHELATE	TRADECRAFT
TOTALITARIANS	TOURBILLONS	TOXICOMANIAS	TRACHEOLAR	TRADECRAFTS
TOTALITIES	TOURISTICALLY	TOXICOPHAGOUS	TRACHEOLES	TRADEMARKED
TOTALIZATION	TOURISTIER	TOXICOPHOBIA	TRACHEOPHYTE	TRADEMARKING
TOTALIZATIONS	TOURISTIEST	TOXICOPHOBIAS	TRACHEOPHYTES	TRADEMARKS
TOTALIZATOR	TOURMALINE	TOXIGENICITIES	TRACHEOSCOPIES	TRADENAMES
TOTALIZATORS	TOURMALINES	TOXIGENICITY	TRACHEOSCOPY	TRADERSHIP
TOTALIZERS	TOURMALINIC	TOXIPHAGOUS	TRACHEOSTOMIES	TRADERSHIPS
TOTALIZING	TOURNAMENT	TOXIPHOBIA	TRACHEOSTOMY	TRADESCANTIA
TOTAQUINES	TOURNAMENTS	TOXIPHOBIAC	TRACHEOTOMIES	TRADESCANTIAS
TOTEMICALLY	TOURNEYERS	TOXIPHOBIACS	TRACHEOTOMY	TRADESFOLK
TOTEMISTIC	TOURNEYING	TOXIPHOBIAS	TRACHINUSES	TRADESFOLKS
TOTIPALMATE	TOURNIQUET	TOXOCARIASES	TRACHITISES	TRADESMANLIKE
TOTIPALMATION	TOURNIQUETS	TOXOCARIASIS	TRACHOMATOUS	TRADESPEOPLE
TOTIPALMATIONS	TOURTIERES	TOXOPHILIES	TRACHYPTERUS	TRADESPEOPLES
TOTIPOTENCIES	TOVARICHES	TOXOPHILITE	TRACHYPTERUSES	TRADESPERSON
TOTIPOTENCY	TOVARISCHES	TOXOPHILITES	TRACHYTOID	TRADESPERSONS
TOTIPOTENT	TOVARISHES	TOXOPHILITIC	TRACKBALLS	TRADESWOMAN
TOTTERIEST	TOWARDLINESS	TOXOPLASMA	TRACKERBALL	TRADESWOMEN
TOTTERINGLY	TOWARDLINESSES	TOXOPLASMAS	TRACKERBALLS	TRADITIONAL
TOTTERINGS	TOWARDNESS	TOXOPLASMIC	TRACKLAYER	TRADITIONALISE
TOUCHABLENESS	TOWARDNESSES	TOXOPLASMOSES	TRACKLAYERS	TRADITIONALISED
TOUCHABLENESSES	TOWELETTES	TOXOPLASMOSIS	TRACKLAYING	TRADITIONALISES
TOUCHBACKS	TOWELLINGS	TOYISHNESS	TRACKLAYINGS	TRADITIONALISM
TOUCHDOWNS	TOWERINGLY	TOYISHNESSES	TRACKLEMENT	TRADITIONALISMS
TOUCHHOLES	TOWNHOUSES	TRABEATION	TRACKLEMENTS	TRADITIONALIST
TOUCHINESS	TOWNSCAPED	TRABEATIONS	TRACKLESSLY	TRADITIONALISTS
TOUCHINESSES	TOWNSCAPES	TRABECULAE	TRACKLESSNESS	TRADITIONALITY
TOUCHINGLY	TOWNSCAPING	TRABECULAR	TRACKLESSNESSES	TRADITIONALIZE
TOUCHINGNESS	TOWNSCAPINGS	TRABECULAS	TRACKROADS	TRADITIONALIZED
TOUCHINGNESSES	TOWNSFOLKS	TRABECULATE	TRACKSIDES	TRADITIONALIZES
TOUCHLINES	TOWNSPEOPLE	TRABECULATED	TRACKSUITS	TRADITIONALLY
TOUCHMARKS	TOWNSPEOPLES	TRACASSERIE	TRACKWALKER	TRADITIONARILY
TOUCHPAPER	TOWNSWOMAN	TRACASSERIES	TRACKWALKERS	TRADITIONARY
TOUCHPAPERS	TOWNSWOMEN	TRACEABILITIES	TRACTABILITIES	TRADITIONER
TOUCHPOINT	TOXALBUMIN	TRACEABILITY	TRACTABILITY	TRADITIONERS
TOUCHPOINTS	TOXALBUMINS	TRACEABLENESS	TRACTABLENESS	TRADITIONIST
TOUCHSCREEN	TOXAPHENES	TRACEABLENESSES	TRACTABLENESSES	TRADITIONISTS
TOUCHSCREENS	TOXICATION	TRACELESSLY	TRACTARIAN	TRADITIONLESS
TOUCHSTONE	TOXICATIONS	TRACHEARIAN	TRACTARIANS	TRADITIONS
TOUCHSTONES	TOXICITIES	TRACHEARIANS	TRACTATORS	TRADITORES
TOUCHTONES	TOXICOGENIC	TRACHEARIES	TRACTILITIES	TRADUCEMENT
TOUCHWOODS	TOXICOLOGIC	TRACHEATED	TRACTILITY	TRADUCEMENTS
TOUGHENERS	TOXICOLOGICAL	TRACHEATES	TRACTIONAL	TRADUCIANISM
TOUGHENING	TOXICOLOGICALLY	TRACHEIDAL	TRACTORATION	TRADUCIANISMS
TOUGHENINGS	TOXICOLOGIES	TRACHEIDES	TRACTORATIONS	TRADUCIANIST
TOUGHNESSES	TOXICOLOGIST	TRACHEITIDES	TRACTORFEED	TRADUCIANISTIC
TOURBILLION	TOXICOLOGISTS	TRACHEITIS	TRACTORFEEDS	TRADUCIANISTS
TOURBILLIONS	TOXICOLOGY	TRACHEITISES	TRACTRICES	TRADUCIANS

TRADUCIBLE	TRAILINGLY	TRAMPOLINED	TRANSACTED	TRANSCRIBERS
TRADUCINGLY	TRAINABILITIES	TRAMPOLINER	TRANSACTING	TRANSCRIBES
TRADUCINGS	TRAINABILITY	TRAMPOLINERS	TRANSACTINIDE	TRANSCRIBING
TRADUCTION	TRAINBANDS	TRAMPOLINES	TRANSACTINIDES	TRANSCRIPT
TRADUCTIONS	TRAINBEARER	TRAMPOLINING	TRANSACTION	TRANSCRIPTASE
TRADUCTIVE	TRAINBEARERS	TRAMPOLININGS	TRANSACTIONAL	TRANSCRIPTASES
TRAFFICABILITY	TRAINEESHIP	TRAMPOLINIST	TRANSACTIONALLY	TRANSCRIPTION
TRAFFICABLE	TRAINEESHIPS	TRAMPOLINISTS	TRANSACTIONS	TRANSCRIPTIONAL
TRAFFICATOR	TRAINLOADS	TRAMPOLINS	TRANSACTOR	TRANSCRIPTIONS
TRAFFICATORS	TRAINSPOTTER	TRANCELIKE	TRANSACTORS	TRANSCRIPTIVE
TRAFFICKED	TRAINSPOTTERISH	TRANQUILER	TRANSALPINE	TRANSCRIPTIVELY
TRAFFICKER	TRAINSPOTTERS	TRANQUILEST	TRANSALPINES	TRANSCRIPTOME
TRAFFICKERS	TRAINWRECK	TRANQUILISATION	TRANSAMINASE	TRANSCRIPTOMES
TRAFFICKIER	TRAINWRECKS	TRANQUILISE	TRANSAMINASES	TRANSCRIPTS
TRAFFICKIEST	TRAIPSINGS	TRANQUILISED	TRANSAMINATION	TRANSCULTURAL
TRAFFICKING	TRAITORESS	TRANQUILISER	TRANSAMINATIONS	TRANSCURRENT
TRAFFICKINGS	TRAITORESSES	TRANQUILISERS	TRANSANDEAN	TRANSCUTANEOUS
TRAFFICLESS	TRAITORHOOD	TRANQUILISES	TRANSANDINE	TRANSDERMAL
TRAGACANTH	TRAITORHOODS	TRANQUILISING	TRANSATLANTIC	TRANSDUCED
TRAGACANTHS	TRAITORISM	TRANQUILISINGLY	TRANSAXLES	TRANSDUCER
TRAGEDIANS	TRAITORISMS	TRANQUILITIES	TRANSCALENCIES	TRANSDUCERS
TRAGEDIENNE	TRAITOROUS	TRANQUILITY	TRANSCALENCY	TRANSDUCES
TRAGEDIENNES	TRAITOROUSLY	TRANQUILIZATION	TRANSCALENT	TRANSDUCING
TRAGELAPHINE	TRAITOROUSNESS	TRANQUILIZE	TRANSCAUCASIAN	TRANSDUCTANT
TRAGELAPHS	TRAITORSHIP	TRANQUILIZED	TRANSCEIVER	TRANSDUCTANTS
TRAGICALLY	TRAITORSHIPS	TRANQUILIZER	TRANSCEIVERS	TRANSDUCTION
TRAGICALNESS	TRAITRESSES	TRANQUILIZERS	TRANSCENDED	TRANSDUCTIONAL
TRAGICALNESSES	TRAJECTILE	TRANQUILIZES	TRANSCENDENCE	TRANSDUCTIONS
TRAGICOMEDIES	TRAJECTING	TRANQUILIZING	TRANSCENDENCES	TRANSDUCTOR
TRAGICOMEDY	TRAJECTION	TRANQUILIZINGLY	TRANSCENDENCIES	TRANSDUCTORS
TRAGICOMIC	TRAJECTIONS	TRANQUILLER	TRANSCENDENCY	TRANSECTED
TRAGICOMICAL	TRAJECTORIES	TRANQUILLEST	TRANSCENDENT	TRANSECTING
TRAGICOMICALLY	TRAJECTORY	TRANQUILLISE	TRANSCENDENTAL	TRANSECTION
TRAILBASTON	TRALATICIOUS	TRANQUILLISED	TRANSCENDENTALS	TRANSECTIONS
TRAILBASTONS	TRALATITIOUS	TRANQUILLISER	TRANSCENDENTLY	TRANSENNAS
TRAILBLAZER	TRAMELLING	TRANQUILLISERS	TRANSCENDENTS	TRANSEPTAL
TRAILBLAZERS	TRAMMELERS	TRANQUILLISES	TRANSCENDING	TRANSEPTATE
TRAILBLAZING	TRAMMELING	TRANQUILLISING	TRANSCENDINGLY	TRANSEPTED
TRAILBLAZINGS	TRAMMELLED	TRANQUILLITIES	TRANSCENDS	TRANSEXUAL
TRAILBREAKER	TRAMMELLER	TRANQUILLITY	TRANSCODED	TRANSEXUALISM
TRAILBREAKERS	TRAMMELLERS	TRANQUILLIZE	TRANSCODER	TRANSEXUALISMS
TRAILERABLE	TRAMMELLING	TRANQUILLIZED	TRANSCODERS	TRANSEXUALITIES
TRAILERING	TRAMONTANA	TRANQUILLIZER	TRANSCODES	TRANSEXUALITY
TRAILERINGS	TRAMONTANAS	TRANQUILLIZERS	TRANSCODING	TRANSEXUALS
TRAILERIST	TRAMONTANE	TRANQUILLIZES	TRANSCRANIAL	TRANSFECTED
TRAILERISTS	TRAMONTANES	TRANQUILLIZING	TRANSCRIBABLE	TRANSFECTING
TRAILERITE	TRAMPETTES	TRANQUILLY	TRANSCRIBE	TRANSFECTION
TRAILERITES	TRAMPLINGS	TRANQUILNESS	TRANSCRIBED	TRANSFECTIONS
TRAILHEADS	TRAMPOLINE	TRANQUILNESSES	TRANSCRIBER	TRANSFECTS

TRANSFEMININE	TRANSFORMISTS	TRANSHUMANT	TRANSLATABILITY	TRANSMIGRANTS
TRANSFERABILITY	TRANSFORMS	TRANSHUMANTS	TRANSLATABLE	TRANSMIGRATE
TRANSFERABLE	TRANSFUSABLE	TRANSHUMED	TRANSLATED	TRANSMIGRATED
TRANSFERAL	TRANSFUSED	TRANSHUMES	TRANSLATES	TRANSMIGRATES
TRANSFERALS	TRANSFUSER	TRANSHUMING	TRANSLATING	TRANSMIGRATING
TRANSFERASE	TRANSFUSERS	TRANSIENCE	TRANSLATION	TRANSMIGRATION
TRANSFERASES	TRANSFUSES	TRANSIENCES	TRANSLATIONAL	TRANSMIGRATIONS
TRANSFEREE	TRANSFUSIBLE	TRANSIENCIES	TRANSLATIONALLY	TRANSMIGRATIVE
TRANSFEREES	TRANSFUSING	TRANSIENCY	TRANSLATIONS	TRANSMIGRATOR
TRANSFERENCE	TRANSFUSION	TRANSIENTLY	TRANSLATIVE	TRANSMIGRATORS
TRANSFERENCES	TRANSFUSIONAL	TRANSIENTNESS	TRANSLATIVES	TRANSMIGRATORY
TRANSFERENTIAL	TRANSFUSIONIST	TRANSIENTNESSES	TRANSLATOR	TRANSMISSIBLE
TRANSFEROR	TRANSFUSIONISTS	TRANSIENTS	TRANSLATORIAL	TRANSMISSION
TRANSFERORS	TRANSFUSIONS	TRANSILIENCE	TRANSLATORS	TRANSMISSIONAL
TRANSFERRABLE	TRANSFUSIVE	TRANSILIENCES	TRANSLATORY	TRANSMISSIONS
TRANSFERRAL	TRANSFUSIVELY	TRANSILIENCIES	TRANSLEITHAN	TRANSMISSIVE
TRANSFERRALS	TRANSGENDER	TRANSILIENCY	TRANSLITERATE	TRANSMISSIVELY
TRANSFERRED	TRANSGENDERED	TRANSILIENT	TRANSLITERATED	TRANSMISSIVITY
TRANSFERRER	TRANSGENDERS	TRANSILLUMINATE	TRANSLITERATES	TRANSMISSOMETER
TRANSFERRERS	TRANSGENES	TRANSISTHMIAN	TRANSLITERATING	TRANSMITTABLE
TRANSFERRIBLE	TRANSGENESES	TRANSISTOR	TRANSLITERATION	TRANSMITTAL
TRANSFERRIN	TRANSGENESIS	TRANSISTORISE	TRANSLITERATOR	TRANSMITTALS
TRANSFERRING	TRANSGENIC	TRANSISTORISED	TRANSLITERATORS	TRANSMITTANCE
TRANSFERRINS	TRANSGENICS	TRANSISTORISES	TRANSLOCATE	TRANSMITTANCES
TRANSFIGURATION	TRANSGRESS	TRANSISTORISING	TRANSLOCATED	TRANSMITTANCIES
TRANSFIGURE	TRANSGRESSED	TRANSISTORIZE	TRANSLOCATES	TRANSMITTANCY
TRANSFIGURED	TRANSGRESSES	TRANSISTORIZED	TRANSLOCATING	TRANSMITTED
TRANSFIGUREMENT	TRANSGRESSING	TRANSISTORIZES	TRANSLOCATION	TRANSMITTER
TRANSFIGURES	TRANSGRESSION	TRANSISTORIZING	TRANSLOCATIONS	TRANSMITTERS
TRANSFIGURING	TRANSGRESSIONAL	TRANSISTORS	TRANSLUCENCE	TRANSMITTIBLE
TRANSFINITE	TRANSGRESSIONS	TRANSITABLE	TRANSLUCENCES	TRANSMITTING
TRANSFIXED	TRANSGRESSIVE	TRANSITING	TRANSLUCENCIES	TRANSMITTIVITY
TRANSFIXES	TRANSGRESSIVELY	TRANSITION	TRANSLUCENCY	TRANSMOGRIFIED
TRANSFIXING	TRANSGRESSOR	TRANSITIONAL	TRANSLUCENT	TRANSMOGRIFIES
TRANSFIXION	TRANSGRESSORS	TRANSITIONALLY	TRANSLUCENTLY	TRANSMOGRIFY
TRANSFIXIONS	TRANSHIPMENT	TRANSITIONALS	TRANSLUCID	TRANSMOGRIFYING
TRANSFORMABLE	TRANSHIPMENTS	TRANSITIONARY	TRANSLUCIDITIES	TRANSMONTANE
TRANSFORMATION	TRANSHIPPED	TRANSITIONED	TRANSLUCIDITY	TRANSMONTANES
TRANSFORMATIONS	TRANSHIPPER	TRANSITIONING	TRANSLUMENAL	TRANSMOUNTAIN
TRANSFORMATIVE	TRANSHIPPERS	TRANSITIONS	TRANSLUMINAL	TRANSMOVED
TRANSFORMED	TRANSHIPPING	TRANSITIVE	TRANSLUNAR	TRANSMOVES
TRANSFORMER	TRANSHIPPINGS	TRANSITIVELY	TRANSLUNARY	TRANSMOVING
TRANSFORMERS	TRANSHISTORICAL	TRANSITIVENESS	TRANSMANCHE	TRANSMUNDANE
TRANSFORMING	TRANSHUMANCE	TRANSITIVES	TRANSMARINE	TRANSMUTABILITY
TRANSFORMINGS	TRANSHUMANCES	TRANSITIVITIES	TRANSMASCULINE	TRANSMUTABLE
TRANSFORMISM	TRANSHUMANISM	TRANSITIVITY	TRANSMEMBRANE	TRANSMUTABLY
TRANSFORMISMS	TRANSHUMANISMS	TRANSITORILY	TRANSMEWED	TRANSMUTATION
TRANSFORMIST	TRANSHUMANIST	TRANSITORINESS	TRANSMEWING	TRANSMUTATIONAL
TRANSFORMISTIC	TRANSHUMANISTS	TRANSITORY	TRANSMIGRANT	TRANSMUTATIONS

TRANSMUTATIVE	TRANSPLANT	TRANSPUTERS	TRANSVALUING	TRASHINESS
TRANSMUTED	TRANSPLANTABLE	TRANSSEXUAL	TRANSVERSAL	TRASHINESSES
TRANSMUTER	TRANSPLANTATION	TRANSSEXUALISM	TRANSVERSALITY	TRASHTRIES
TRANSMUTERS	TRANSPLANTED	TRANSSEXUALISMS	TRANSVERSALLY	TRATTORIAS
TRANSMUTES	TRANSPLANTER	TRANSSEXUALITY	TRANSVERSALS	TRAUCHLING
TRANSMUTING	TRANSPLANTERS	TRANSSEXUALS	TRANSVERSE	TRAUMATICALLY
TRANSNATIONAL	TRANSPLANTING	TRANSSHAPE	TRANSVERSED	TRAUMATISATION
TRANSNATURAL	TRANSPLANTINGS	TRANSSHAPED	TRANSVERSELY	TRAUMATISATIONS
TRANSNESSES	TRANSPLANTS	TRANSSHAPES	TRANSVERSENESS	TRAUMATISE
TRANSOCEANIC	TRANSPOLAR	TRANSSHAPING	TRANSVERSES	TRAUMATISED
TRANSONICS	TRANSPONDER	TRANSSHIPMENT	TRANSVERSING	TRAUMATISES
TRANSPACIFIC	TRANSPONDERS	TRANSSHIPMENTS	TRANSVERSION	TRAUMATISING
TRANSPADANE	TRANSPONDOR	TRANSSHIPPED	TRANSVERSIONS	TRAUMATISM
TRANSPARENCE	TRANSPONDORS	TRANSSHIPPER	TRANSVERTER	TRAUMATISMS
TRANSPARENCES	TRANSPONTINE	TRANSSHIPPERS	TRANSVERTERS	TRAUMATIZATION
TRANSPARENCIES	TRANSPORTABLE	TRANSSHIPPING	TRANSVESTED	TRAUMATIZATIONS
TRANSPARENCY	TRANSPORTAL	TRANSSHIPPINGS	TRANSVESTIC	TRAUMATIZE
TRANSPARENT	TRANSPORTALS	TRANSSHIPS	TRANSVESTING	TRAUMATIZED
TRANSPARENTISE	TRANSPORTANCE	TRANSSONIC	TRANSVESTISM	TRAUMATIZES
TRANSPARENTISED	TRANSPORTANCES	TRANSTHORACIC	TRANSVESTISMS	TRAUMATIZING
TRANSPARENTISES	TRANSPORTATION	TRANSUBSTANTIAL	TRANSVESTIST	TRAUMATOLOGICAL
TRANSPARENTIZE	TRANSPORTATIONS	TRANSUDATE	TRANSVESTISTS	TRAUMATOLOGIES
TRANSPARENTIZED	TRANSPORTED	TRANSUDATES	TRANSVESTITE	TRAUMATOLOGY
TRANSPARENTIZES	TRANSPORTEDLY	TRANSUDATION	TRANSVESTITES	TRAUMATONASTIES
TRANSPARENTLY	TRANSPORTEDNESS	TRANSUDATIONS	TRANSVESTITISM	TRAUMATONASTY
TRANSPARENTNESS	TRANSPORTER	TRANSUDATORY	TRANSVESTITISMS	TRAVAILING
TRANSPERSON	TRANSPORTERS	TRANSUDING	TRANSVESTS	TRAVELATOR
TRANSPERSONAL	TRANSPORTING	TRANSUMING	TRAPANNERS	TRAVELATORS
TRANSPERSONS	TRANSPORTINGLY	TRANSUMPTION	TRAPANNING	TRAVELINGS
TRANSPHOBE	TRANSPORTINGS	TRANSUMPTIONS	TRAPESINGS	TRAVELLERS
TRANSPHOBES	TRANSPORTIVE	TRANSUMPTIVE	TRAPEZIFORM	TRAVELLING
TRANSPHOBIA	TRANSPORTS	TRANSUMPTS	TRAPEZISTS	TRAVELLINGS
TRANSPHOBIAS	TRANSPOSABILITY	TRANSURANIAN	TRAPEZIUMS	TRAVELOGUE
TRANSPHOBIC	TRANSPOSABLE	TRANSURANIC	TRAPEZIUSES	TRAVELOGUES
TRANSPICUOUS	TRANSPOSAL	TRANSURANICS	TRAPEZOHEDRA	TRAVERSABLE
TRANSPICUOUSLY	TRANSPOSALS	TRANSURANIUM	TRAPEZOHEDRAL	TRAVERSALS
TRANSPIERCE	TRANSPOSED	TRANSURETHRAL	TRAPEZOHEDRON	TRAVERSERS
TRANSPIERCED	TRANSPOSER	TRANSVAGINAL	TRAPEZOHEDRONS	TRAVERSING
TRANSPIERCES	TRANSPOSERS	TRANSVALUATE	TRAPEZOIDAL	TRAVERSINGS
TRANSPIERCING	TRANSPOSES	TRANSVALUATED	TRAPEZOIDS	TRAVERTINE
TRANSPIRABLE	TRANSPOSING	TRANSVALUATES	TRAPNESTED	TRAVERTINES
TRANSPIRATION	TRANSPOSINGS	TRANSVALUATING	TRAPNESTING	TRAVERTINS
TRANSPIRATIONAL	TRANSPOSITION	TRANSVALUATION	TRAPPINESS	TRAVESTIED
TRANSPIRATIONS	TRANSPOSITIONAL	TRANSVALUATIONS	TRAPPINESSES	TRAVESTIES
TRANSPIRATORY	TRANSPOSITIONS	TRANSVALUE	TRAPSHOOTER	TRAVESTYING
TRANSPIRED	TRANSPOSITIVE	TRANSVALUED	TRAPSHOOTERS	TRAVOLATOR
TRANSPIRES	TRANSPOSON	TRANSVALUER	TRAPSHOOTING	TRAVOLATORS
TRANSPIRING	TRANSPOSONS	TRANSVALUERS	TRAPSHOOTINGS	TRAWLERMAN
TRANSPLACENTAL	TRANSPUTER	TRANSVALUES	TRASHERIES	TRAWLERMEN

TRAYCLOTHS
TRAYMOBILE
TRAYMOBILES
TRAZODONES
TREACHERER
TREACHERERS
TREACHERIES
TREACHEROUS
TREACHEROUSLY
TREACHEROUSNESS
TREACHETOUR
TREACHETOURS
TREACHOURS
TREACLIEST
TREACLINESS
TREACLINESSES
TREADLINGS
TREADMILLS
TREADWHEEL
TREADWHEELS
TREASONABLE
TREASONABLENESS
TREASONABLY
TREASONOUS
TREASURABLE
TREASURELESS
TREASURERS
TREASURERSHIP
TREASURERSHIPS
TREASURIES
TREASURING
TREATABILITIES
TREATABILITY
TREATMENTS
TREATYLESS
TREBBIANOS
TREBLENESS
TREBLENESSES
TREBUCHETS
TREBUCKETS
TRECENTIST
TRECENTISTS
TREDECILLION
TREDECILLIONS
TREDRILLES
TREEHOPPER
TREEHOPPERS
TREEHOUSES
TREELESSNESS

TREELESSNESSES
TREENWARES
TREGETOURS
TREHALOSES
TREILLAGED
TREILLAGES
TREKSCHUIT
TREKSCHUITS
TRELLISING
TRELLISWORK
TRELLISWORKS
TREMATODES
TREMATOIDS
TREMBLEMENT
TREMBLEMENTS
TREMBLIEST
TREMBLINGLY
TREMBLINGS
TREMENDOUS
TREMENDOUSLY
TREMENDOUSNESS
TREMOLANDI
TREMOLANDO
TREMOLANDOS
TREMOLANTS
TREMOLITES
TREMOLITIC
TREMORLESS
TREMULANTS
TREMULATED
TREMULATES
TREMULATING
TREMULOUSLY
TREMULOUSNESS
TREMULOUSNESSES
TRENCHANCIES
TRENCHANCY
TRENCHANTLY
TRENCHARDS
TRENCHERMAN
TRENCHERMEN
TRENDIFIED
TRENDIFIES
TRENDIFYING
TRENDINESS
TRENDINESSES
TRENDSETTER
TRENDSETTERS
TRENDSETTING

TRENDSETTINGS
TRENDYISMS
TREPANATION
TREPANATIONS
TREPANNERS
TREPANNING
TREPANNINGS
TREPHINATION
TREPHINATIONS
TREPHINERS
TREPHINING
TREPHININGS
TREPIDATION
TREPIDATIONS
TREPIDATORY
TREPONEMAL
TREPONEMAS
TREPONEMATA
TREPONEMATOSES
TREPONEMATOSIS
TREPONEMATOUS
TREPONEMES
TRESPASSED
TRESPASSER
TRESPASSERS
TRESPASSES
TRESPASSING
TRESTLETREE
TRESTLETREES
TRESTLEWORK
TRESTLEWORKS
TRETINOINS
TREVALLIES
TRIABLENESS
TRIABLENESSES
TRIACETATE
TRIACETATES
TRIACONTER
TRIACONTERS
TRIACTINAL
TRIADELPHOUS
TRIADICALLY
TRIALITIES
TRIALLINGS
TRIALLISTS
TRIALOGUES
TRIALWARES
TRIAMCINOLONE
TRIAMCINOLONES

TRIANDRIAN
TRIANDROUS
TRIANGULAR
TRIANGULARITIES
TRIANGULARITY
TRIANGULARLY
TRIANGULATE
TRIANGULATED
TRIANGULATELY
TRIANGULATES
TRIANGULATING
TRIANGULATION
TRIANGULATIONS
TRIAPSIDAL
TRIARCHIES
TRIATHLETE
TRIATHLETES
TRIATHLONS
TRIATOMICALLY
TRIAXIALITIES
TRIAXIALITY
TRIBADISMS
TRIBALISMS
TRIBALISTIC
TRIBALISTS
TRIBESPEOPLE
TRIBESWOMAN
TRIBESWOMEN
TRIBOELECTRIC
TRIBOLOGICAL
TRIBOLOGIES
TRIBOLOGIST
TRIBOLOGISTS
TRIBOMETER
TRIBOMETERS
TRIBRACHIAL
TRIBRACHIC
TRIBROMOETHANOL
TRIBROMOMETHANE
TRIBULATED
TRIBULATES
TRIBULATING
TRIBULATION
TRIBULATIONS
TRIBUNATES
TRIBUNESHIP
TRIBUNESHIPS
TRIBUNICIAL
TRIBUNICIAN

TRIBUNITIAL
TRIBUNITIAN
TRIBUTARIES
TRIBUTARILY
TRIBUTARINESS
TRIBUTARINESSES
TRICAMERAL
TRICARBOXYLIC
TRICARPELLARY
TRICENTENARIES
TRICENTENARY
TRICENTENNIAL
TRICENTENNIALS
TRICEPHALOUS
TRICERATOPS
TRICERATOPSES
TRICERIONS
TRICHIASES
TRICHIASIS
TRICHINELLA
TRICHINELLAE
TRICHINELLAS
TRICHINIASES
TRICHINIASIS
TRICHINISATION
TRICHINISATIONS
TRICHINISE
TRICHINISED
TRICHINISES
TRICHINISING
TRICHINIZATION
TRICHINIZATIONS
TRICHINIZE
TRICHINIZED
TRICHINIZES
TRICHINIZING
TRICHINOSE
TRICHINOSED
TRICHINOSES
TRICHINOSING
TRICHINOSIS
TRICHINOTIC
TRICHINOUS
TRICHLORACETIC
TRICHLORFON
TRICHLORFONS
TRICHLORIDE
TRICHLORIDES
TRICHLOROACETIC

TRICHLOROETHANE	TRICHROISM	TRICROTOUS	TRIGAMISTS	TRILINGUALLY
TRICHLORPHON	TRICHROISMS	TRICUSPIDAL	TRIGEMINAL	TRILITERAL
TRICHLORPHONS	TRICHROMACIES	TRICUSPIDATE	TRIGEMINALS	TRILITERALISM
TRICHOBACTERIA	TRICHROMACY	TRICUSPIDS	TRIGEMINUS	TRILITERALISMS
TRICHOCYST	TRICHROMAT	TRICYCLERS	TRIGGERFISH	TRILITERALS
TRICHOCYSTIC	TRICHROMATIC	TRICYCLICS	TRIGGERFISHES	TRILITHONS
TRICHOCYSTS	TRICHROMATISM	TRICYCLING	TRIGGERING	TRILLIONAIRE
TRICHOGYNE	TRICHROMATISMS	TRICYCLINGS	TRIGGERLESS	TRILLIONAIRES
TRICHOGYNES	TRICHROMATS	TRICYCLIST	TRIGGERMAN	TRILLIONTH
TRICHOGYNIAL	TRICHROMIC	TRICYCLISTS	TRIGGERMEN	TRILLIONTHS
TRICHOGYNIC	TRICHROMICS	TRIDACTYLOUS	TRIGLYCERIDE	TRILOBATED
TRICHOLOGICAL	TRICHRONOUS	TRIDENTATE	TRIGLYCERIDES	TRILOBITES
TRICHOLOGIES	TRICHURIASES	TRIDIMENSIONAL	TRIGLYPHIC	TRILOBITIC
TRICHOLOGIST	TRICHURIASIS	TRIDOMINIA	TRIGLYPHICAL	TRILOCULAR
TRICHOLOGISTS	TRICKERIES	TRIDOMINIUM	TRIGNESSES	TRIMERISMS
TRICHOLOGY	TRICKINESS	TRIDOMINIUMS	TRIGONALLY	TRIMESTERS
TRICHOMONACIDAL	TRICKINESSES	TRIDYMITES	TRIGONOMETER	TRIMESTRAL
TRICHOMONACIDE	TRICKISHLY	TRIENNIALLY	TRIGONOMETERS	TRIMESTRIAL
TRICHOMONACIDES	TRICKISHNESS	TRIENNIALS	TRIGONOMETRIC	TRIMETHADIONE
TRICHOMONAD	TRICKISHNESSES	TRIENNIUMS	TRIGONOMETRICAL	TRIMETHADIONES
TRICHOMONADAL	TRICKLIEST	TRIERARCHAL	TRIGONOMETRIES	TRIMETHOPRIM
TRICHOMONADS	TRICKLINGLY	TRIERARCHIES	TRIGONOMETRY	TRIMETHOPRIMS
TRICHOMONAL	TRICKLINGS	TRIERARCHS	TRIGRAMMATIC	TRIMETHYLAMINE
TRICHOMONIASES	TRICKSIEST	TRIERARCHY	TRIGRAMMIC	TRIMETHYLAMINES
TRICHOMONIASIS	TRICKSINESS	TRIETHIODIDE	TRIGRAPHIC	TRIMETHYLENE
TRICHOPHYTON	TRICKSINESSES	TRIETHIODIDES	TRIHALOMETHANE	TRIMETHYLENES
TRICHOPHYTONS	TRICKSTERING	TRIETHYLAMINE	TRIHALOMETHANES	TRIMETRICAL
TRICHOPHYTOSES	TRICKSTERINGS	TRIETHYLAMINES	TRIHEDRALS	TRIMETROGON
TRICHOPHYTOSIS	TRICKSTERS	TRIFACIALS	TRIHEDRONS	TRIMETROGONS
TRICHOPTERAN	TRICKTRACK	TRIFARIOUS	TRIHYBRIDS	TRIMMINGLY
TRICHOPTERANS	TRICKTRACKS	TRIFFIDIAN	TRIHYDRATE	TRIMNESSES
TRICHOPTERIST	TRICLINIUM	TRIFFIDIER	TRIHYDRATED	TRIMOLECULAR
TRICHOPTERISTS	TRICLOSANS	TRIFFIDIEST	TRIHYDRATES	TRIMONTHLY
TRICHOPTEROUS	TRICOLETTE	TRIFLINGLY	TRIHYDROXY	TRIMORPHIC
TRICHOTHECENE	TRICOLETTES	TRIFLINGNESS	TRIIODOMETHANE	TRIMORPHISM
TRICHOTHECENES	TRICOLORED	TRIFLINGNESSES	TRIIODOMETHANES	TRIMORPHISMS
TRICHOTOMIC	TRICOLOURED	TRIFLUOPERAZINE	TRILATERAL	TRIMORPHOUS
TRICHOTOMIES	TRICOLOURS	TRIFLURALIN	TRILATERALISM	TRIMPHONES
TRICHOTOMISE	TRICONSONANTAL	TRIFLURALINS	TRILATERALISMS	TRINACRIAN
TRICHOTOMISED	TRICONSONANTIC	TRIFOLIATE	TRILATERALIST	TRINACRIFORM
TRICHOTOMISES	TRICORNERED	TRIFOLIATED	TRILATERALISTS	TRINISCOPE
TRICHOTOMISING	TRICORPORATE	TRIFOLIOLATE	TRILATERALLY	TRINISCOPES
TRICHOTOMIZE	TRICORPORATED	TRIFOLIUMS	TRILATERALS	TRINITARIAN
TRICHOTOMIZED	TRICOSTATE	TRIFURCATE	TRILATERATION	TRINITARIANS
TRICHOTOMIZES	TRICOTEUSE	TRIFURCATED	TRILATERATIONS	TRINITRATE
TRICHOTOMIZING	TRICOTEUSES	TRIFURCATES	TRILINEATE	TRINITRATES
TRICHOTOMOUS	TRICOTINES	TRIFURCATING	TRILINGUAL	TRINITRINS
TRICHOTOMOUSLY	TRICROTISM	TRIFURCATION	TRILINGUALISM	TRINITROBENZENE
TRICHOTOMY	TRICROTISMS	TRIFURCATIONS	TRILINGUALISMS	TRINITROCRESOL

TRINITROCRESOLS	TRIPHYLITE	TRISECTORS	TRITICALNESS	TRIVIALISTS
TRINITROPHENOL	TRIPHYLITES	TRISECTRICES	TRITICALNESSES	TRIVIALITIES
TRINITROPHENOLS	TRIPHYLLOUS	TRISECTRIX	TRITICEOUS	TRIVIALITY
TRINITROTOLUENE	TRIPINNATE	TRISKELION	TRITICISMS	TRIVIALIZATION
TRINITROTOLUOL	TRIPINNATELY	TRISKELIONS	TRITUBERCULAR	TRIVIALIZATIONS
TRINITROTOLUOLS	TRIPITAKAS	TRISOCTAHEDRA	TRITUBERCULATE	TRIVIALIZE
TRINKETERS	TRIPLENESS	TRISOCTAHEDRAL	TRITUBERCULIES	TRIVIALIZED
TRINKETING	TRIPLENESSES	TRISOCTAHEDRON	TRITUBERCULISM	TRIVIALIZES
TRINKETINGS	TRIPLETAIL	TRISOCTAHEDRONS	TRITUBERCULISMS	TRIVIALIZING
TRINKETRIES	TRIPLETAILS	TRISTEARIN	TRITUBERCULY	TRIVIALNESS
TRINOCULAR	TRIPLEXING	TRISTEARINS	TRITURABLE	TRIVIALNESSES
TRINOMIALISM	TRIPLICATE	TRISTESSES	TRITURATED	TRIWEEKLIES
TRINOMIALISMS	TRIPLICATED	TRISTFULLY	TRITURATES	TROCHAICALLY
TRINOMIALIST	TRIPLICATES	TRISTFULNESS	TRITURATING	TROCHANTER
TRINOMIALISTS	TRIPLICATING	TRISTFULNESSES	TRITURATION	TROCHANTERAL
TRINOMIALLY	TRIPLICATION	TRISTICHIC	TRITURATIONS	TROCHANTERIC
TRINOMIALS	TRIPLICATIONS	TRISTICHOUS	TRITURATOR	TROCHANTERS
TRINUCLEOTIDE	TRIPLICITIES	TRISTIMULUS	TRITURATORS	TROCHEAMETER
TRINUCLEOTIDES	TRIPLICITY	TRISUBSTITUTED	TRIUMPHALISM	TROCHEAMETERS
TRIOECIOUS	TRIPLOBLASTIC	TRISULCATE	TRIUMPHALISMS	TROCHELMINTH
TRIOXOBORIC	TRIPLOIDIES	TRISULFIDE	TRIUMPHALIST	TROCHELMINTHS
TRIOXYGENS	TRIPMETERS	TRISULFIDES	TRIUMPHALISTS	TROCHILUSES
TRIPALMITIN	TRIPPERIER	TRISULPHIDE	TRIUMPHALS	TROCHISCUS
TRIPALMITINS	TRIPPERIEST	TRISULPHIDES	TRIUMPHANT	TROCHISCUSES
TRIPARTISM	TRIPPERISH	TRISYLLABIC	TRIUMPHANTLY	TROCHLEARS
TRIPARTISMS	TRIPPINGLY	TRISYLLABICAL	TRIUMPHERIES	TROCHOIDAL
TRIPARTITE	TRIPTEROUS	TRISYLLABICALLY	TRIUMPHERS	TROCHOIDALLY
TRIPARTITELY	TRIPTYQUES	TRISYLLABLE	TRIUMPHERY	TROCHOMETER
TRIPARTITION	TRIPUDIARY	TRISYLLABLES	TRIUMPHING	TROCHOMETERS
TRIPARTITIONS	TRIPUDIATE	TRITAGONIST	TRIUMPHINGS	TROCHOPHORE
TRIPEHOUND	TRIPUDIATED	TRITAGONISTS	TRIUMVIRAL	TROCHOPHORES
TRIPEHOUNDS	TRIPUDIATES	TRITANOPES	TRIUMVIRATE	TROCHOSPHERE
TRIPERSONAL	TRIPUDIATING	TRITANOPIA	TRIUMVIRATES	TROCHOSPHERES
TRIPERSONALISM	TRIPUDIATION	TRITANOPIAS	TRIUMVIRIES	TROCHOTRON
TRIPERSONALISMS	TRIPUDIATIONS	TRITANOPIC	TRIUMVIRIES	TROCHOTRONS
TRIPERSONALIST	TRIQUETRAE	TRITENESSES	TRIUNITIES	TROCTOLITE
TRIPERSONALISTS	TRIQUETRAL	TRITERNATE	TRIVALENCE	TROCTOLITES
TRIPERSONALITY	TRIQUETRAS	TRITHEISMS	TRIVALENCES	TROGLODYTE
TRIPETALOUS	TRIQUETROUS	TRITHEISTIC	TRIVALENCIES	TROGLODYTES
TRIPHAMMER	TRIQUETROUSLY	TRITHEISTICAL	TRIVALENCY	TROGLODYTIC
TRIPHAMMERS	TRIQUETRUM	TRITHEISTS	TRIVALVULAR	TROGLODYTICAL
TRIPHENYLAMINE	TRIRADIATE	TRITHIONATE	TRIVIALISATION	TROGLODYTISM
TRIPHENYLAMINES	TRIRADIATELY	TRITHIONATES	TRIVIALISATIONS	TROGLODYTISMS
TRIPHIBIOUS	TRISACCHARIDE	TRITHIONIC	TRIVIALISE	TROLLEYBUS
TRIPHOSPHATE	TRISACCHARIDES	TRITIATING	TRIVIALISED	TROLLEYBUSES
TRIPHOSPHATES	TRISAGIONS	TRITIATION	TRIVIALISES	TROLLEYBUSSES
TRIPHTHONG	TRISECTING	TRITIATIONS	TRIVIALISING	TROLLEYING
TRIPHTHONGAL	TRISECTION	TRITICALES	TRIVIALISM	TROLLIUSES
TRIPHTHONGS	TRISECTIONS	TRITICALLY	TRIVIALISMS	TROLLOPEES

TROLLOPIER	TROPICALISED	TROUBLESHOOTERS	TRUMPETINGS	TRUTHINESS
TROLLOPIEST	TROPICALISES	TROUBLESHOOTING	TRUMPETLIKE	TRUTHINESSES
TROLLOPING	TROPICALISING	TROUBLESHOOTS	TRUMPETWEED	TRUTHLESSNESS
TROLLOPISH	TROPICALITIES	TROUBLESHOT	TRUMPETWEEDS	TRUTHLESSNESSES
TROMBICULID	TROPICALITY	TROUBLESOME	TRUNCATELY	TRYINGNESS
TROMBICULIDS	TROPICALIZATION	TROUBLESOMELY	TRUNCATING	TRYINGNESSES
TROMBIDIASES	TROPICALIZE	TROUBLESOMENESS	TRUNCATINGS	TRYPAFLAVINE
TROMBIDIASIS	TROPICALIZED	TROUBLINGS	TRUNCATION	TRYPAFLAVINES
TROMBONIST	TROPICALIZES	TROUBLOUSLY	TRUNCATIONS	TRYPANOCIDAL
TROMBONISTS	TROPICALIZING	TROUBLOUSNESS	TRUNCHEONED	TRYPANOCIDE
TROMOMETER	TROPICALLY	TROUBLOUSNESSES	TRUNCHEONER	TRYPANOCIDES
TROMOMETERS	TROPICBIRD	TROUGHINGS	TRUNCHEONERS	TRYPANOSOMAL
TROMOMETRIC	TROPICBIRDS	TROUGHLIKE	TRUNCHEONING	TRYPANOSOME
TROOPSHIPS	TROPISMATIC	TROUNCINGS	TRUNCHEONS	TRYPANOSOMES
TROOSTITES	TROPOCOLLAGEN	TROUSERING	TRUNKFISHES	TRYPANOSOMIASES
TROPAEOLIN	TROPOCOLLAGENS	TROUSERINGS	TRUNKSLEEVE	TRYPANOSOMIASIS
TROPAEOLINS	TROPOLOGIC	TROUSERLESS	TRUNKSLEEVES	TRYPANOSOMIC
TROPAEOLUM	TROPOLOGICAL	TROUSSEAUS	TRUNKWORKS	TRYPARSAMIDE
TROPAEOLUMS	TROPOLOGICALLY	TROUSSEAUX	TRUNNIONED	TRYPARSAMIDES
TROPARIONS	TROPOLOGIES	TROUTLINGS	TRUSTABILITIES	TRYPSINOGEN
TROPEOLINS	TROPOMYOSIN	TROUTSTONE	TRUSTABILITY	TRYPSINOGENS
TROPHALLACTIC	TROPOMYOSINS	TROUTSTONES	TRUSTAFARIAN	TRYPTAMINE
TROPHALLAXES	TROPOPAUSE	TROUVAILLE	TRUSTAFARIANS	TRYPTAMINES
TROPHALLAXIS	TROPOPAUSES	TROUVAILLES	TRUSTBUSTER	TRYPTOPHAN
TROPHESIAL	TROPOPHILOUS	TROWELLERS	TRUSTBUSTERS	TRYPTOPHANE
TROPHESIES	TROPOPHYTE	TROWELLING	TRUSTBUSTING	TRYPTOPHANES
TROPHICALLY	TROPOPHYTES	TRUANTINGS	TRUSTBUSTINGS	TRYPTOPHANS
TROPHOBIOSES	TROPOPHYTIC	TRUANTRIES	TRUSTEEING	TSAREVICHES
TROPHOBIOSIS	TROPOSCATTER	TRUANTSHIP	TRUSTEESHIP	TSAREVITCH
TROPHOBIOTIC	TROPOSCATTERS	TRUANTSHIPS	TRUSTEESHIPS	TSAREVITCHES
TROPHOBLAST	TROPOSPHERE	TRUCKLINES	TRUSTFULLY	TSCHERNOSEM
TROPHOBLASTIC	TROPOSPHERES	TRUCKLINGS	TRUSTFULNESS	TSCHERNOSEMS
TROPHOBLASTS	TROPOSPHERIC	TRUCKLOADS	TRUSTFULNESSES	TSESAREVICH
TROPHOLOGIES	TROPOTAXES	TRUCKMASTER	TRUSTINESS	TSESAREVICHES
TROPHOLOGY	TROPOTAXIS	TRUCKMASTERS	TRUSTINESSES	TSESAREVITCH
TROPHONEUROSES	TROTHPLIGHT	TRUCKSTOPS	TRUSTINGLY	TSESAREVITCHES
TROPHONEUROSIS	TROTHPLIGHTED	TRUCULENCE	TRUSTINGNESS	TSESAREVNA
TROPHOPLASM	TROTHPLIGHTING	TRUCULENCES	TRUSTINGNESSES	TSESAREVNAS
TROPHOPLASMS	TROTHPLIGHTS	TRUCULENCIES	TRUSTLESSLY	TSESAREWICH
TROPHOTACTIC	TROUBADOUR	TRUCULENCY	TRUSTLESSNESS	TSESAREWICHES
TROPHOTAXES	TROUBADOURS	TRUCULENTLY	TRUSTLESSNESSES	TSESAREWITCH
TROPHOTAXIS	TROUBLEDLY	TRUEHEARTED	TRUSTWORTHIER	TSESAREWITCHES
TROPHOTROPIC	TROUBLEFREE	TRUEHEARTEDNESS	TRUSTWORTHIEST	TSORRISSES
TROPHOTROPISM	TROUBLEMAKER	TRUENESSES	TRUSTWORTHILY	TSOTSITAAL
TROPHOTROPISMS	TROUBLEMAKERS	TRUEPENNIES	TRUSTWORTHINESS	TSOTSITAALS
TROPHOZOITE	TROUBLEMAKING	TRUFFLINGS	TRUSTWORTHY	TSUNAMIGENIC
TROPHOZOITES	TROUBLEMAKINGS	TRUMPERIES	TRUTHFULLY	TSUTSUGAMUSHI
TROPICALISATION	TROUBLESHOOT	TRUMPETERS	TRUTHFULNESS	TSUTSUGAMUSHIS
TROPICALISE	TROUBLESHOOTER	TRUMPETING	TRUTHFULNESSES	TUBBINESSES

T

TUBECTOMIES	TUBULATING	TUMESCENTLY	TURBIDIMETER	TURGIDITIES
TUBERACEOUS	TUBULATION	TUMIDITIES	TURBIDIMETERS	TURGIDNESS
TUBERCULAR	TUBULATIONS	TUMIDNESSES	TURBIDIMETRIC	TURGIDNESSES
TUBERCULARLY	TUBULATORS	TUMORGENIC	TURBIDIMETRIES	TURMOILING
TUBERCULARS	TUBULATURE	TUMORGENICITIES	TURBIDIMETRY	TURNABOUTS
TUBERCULATE	TUBULATURES	TUMORGENICITY	TURBIDITES	TURNAGAINS
TUBERCULATED	TUBULIFLORAL	TUMORIGENESES	TURBIDITIES	TURNAROUND
TUBERCULATELY	TUBULIFLOROUS	TUMORIGENESIS	TURBIDNESS	TURNAROUNDS
TUBERCULATION	TUBULOUSLY	TUMORIGENIC	TURBIDNESSES	TURNBROACH
TUBERCULATIONS	TUCKAMORES	TUMORIGENICITY	TURBINACIOUS	TURNBROACHES
TUBERCULES	TUCKERBAGS	TUMULOSITIES	TURBINATED	TURNBUCKLE
TUBERCULIN	TUCKERBOXES	TUMULOSITY	TURBINATES	TURNBUCKLES
TUBERCULINS	TUFFACEOUS	TUMULTUARY	TURBINATION	TURNIPIEST
TUBERCULISATION	TUFFTAFFETA	TUMULTUATE	TURBINATIONS	TURNROUNDS
TUBERCULISE	TUFFTAFFETAS	TUMULTUATED	TURBOCHARGE	TURNSTILES
TUBERCULISED	TUFFTAFFETIES	TUMULTUATES	TURBOCHARGED	TURNSTONES
TUBERCULISES	TUFFTAFFETY	TUMULTUATING	TURBOCHARGER	TURNTABLES
TUBERCULISING	TUFTAFFETA	TUMULTUATION	TURBOCHARGERS	TURNTABLIST
TUBERCULIZATION	TUFTAFFETAS	TUMULTUATIONS	TURBOCHARGES	TURNTABLISTS
TUBERCULIZE	TUFTAFFETIES	TUMULTUOUS	TURBOCHARGING	TURNVEREIN
TUBERCULIZED	TUFTAFFETY	TUMULTUOUSLY	TURBOCHARGINGS	TURNVEREINS
TUBERCULIZES	TUILLETTES	TUMULTUOUSNESS	TURBOELECTRIC	TUROPHILES
TUBERCULIZING	TUILYIEING	TUNABILITIES	TURBOGENERATOR	TURPENTINE
TUBERCULOID	TUILZIEING	TUNABILITY	TURBOGENERATORS	TURPENTINED
TUBERCULOMA	TUITIONARY	TUNABLENESS	TURBOMACHINERY	TURPENTINES
TUBERCULOMAS	TULARAEMIA	TUNABLENESSES	TURBOPROPS	TURPENTINIER
TUBERCULOMATA	TULARAEMIAS	TUNBELLIED	TURBOSHAFT	TURPENTINIEST
TUBERCULOSE	TULARAEMIC	TUNBELLIES	TURBOSHAFTS	TURPENTINING
TUBERCULOSED	TULAREMIAS	TUNEFULNESS	TURBULATOR	TURPENTINY
TUBERCULOSES	TULIPOMANIA	TUNEFULNESSES	TURBULATORS	TURPITUDES
TUBERCULOSIS	TULIPOMANIAS	TUNELESSLY	TURBULENCE	TURQUOISES
TUBERCULOUS	TULIPWOODS	TUNELESSNESS	TURBULENCES	TURRIBANTS
TUBERCULOUSLY	TUMATAKURU	TUNELESSNESSES	TURBULENCIES	TURRICULATE
TUBERCULUM	TUMATAKURUS	TUNESMITHS	TURBULENCY	TURRICULATED
TUBERIFEROUS	TUMBLEBUGS	TUNGSTATES	TURBULENTLY	TURTLEBACK
TUBERIFORM	TUMBLEDOWN	TUNGSTITES	TURCOPOLES	TURTLEBACKS
TUBEROSITIES	TUMBLEHOME	TUNNELINGS	TURCOPOLIER	TURTLEDOVE
TUBEROSITY	TUMBLEHOMES	TUNNELLERS	TURCOPOLIERS	TURTLEDOVES
TUBICOLOUS	TUMBLERFUL	TUNNELLIKE	TURDUCKENS	TURTLEHEAD
TUBIFICIDS	TUMBLERFULS	TUNNELLING	TURFGRASSES	TURTLEHEADS
TUBIFLOROUS	TUMBLERSFUL	TUNNELLINGS	TURFINESSES	TURTLENECK
TUBOCURARINE	TUMBLESETS	TUPPENNIES	TURFSKIING	TURTLENECKED
TUBOCURARINES	TUMBLEWEED	TUPTOWINGS	TURFSKIINGS	TURTLENECKS
TUBOPLASTIES	TUMBLEWEEDS	TURACOVERDIN	TURGENCIES	TUSSOCKIER
TUBOPLASTY	TUMEFACIENT	TURACOVERDINS	TURGESCENCE	TUSSOCKIEST
TUBULARIAN	TUMEFACTION	TURANGAWAEWAE	TURGESCENCES	TUTELARIES
TUBULARIANS	TUMEFACTIONS	TURANGAWAEWAES	TURGESCENCIES	TUTIORISMS
TUBULARITIES	TUMESCENCE	TURBELLARIAN	TURGESCENCY	TUTIORISTS
TUBULARITY	TUMESCENCES	TURBELLARIANS	TURGESCENT	TUTORESSES

T

TUTORIALLY	TWILIGHTED	TYMPANITIS	TYPHOGENIC	TYRANNICIDE
TUTORISING	TWILIGHTING	TYMPANITISES	TYPHOIDINS	TYRANNICIDES
TUTORIZING	TWINBERRIES	TYNDALLIMETRIES	TYPICALITIES	TYRANNISED
TUTORSHIPS	TWINFLOWER	TYNDALLIMETRY	TYPICALITY	TYRANNISER
TUTOYERING	TWINFLOWERS	TYPECASTER	TYPICALNESS	TYRANNISERS
TUTWORKERS	TWINKLIEST	TYPECASTERS	TYPICALNESSES	TYRANNISES
TUTWORKMAN	TWINKLINGS	TYPECASTING	TYPIFICATION	TYRANNISING
TUTWORKMEN	TWISTABILITIES	TYPECASTINGS	TYPIFICATIONS	TYRANNIZED
TWADDLIEST	TWISTABILITY	TYPEFOUNDER	TYPOGRAPHED	TYRANNIZER
TWADDLINGS	TWITCHIEST	TYPEFOUNDERS	TYPOGRAPHER	TYRANNIZERS
TWALPENNIES	TWITCHINGS	TYPEFOUNDING	TYPOGRAPHERS	TYRANNIZES
TWANGINGLY	TWITTERATI	TYPEFOUNDINGS	TYPOGRAPHIA	TYRANNIZING
TWANGLINGLY	TWITTERERS	TYPEFOUNDRIES	TYPOGRAPHIC	TYRANNOSAUR
TWANGLINGS	TWITTERIER	TYPEFOUNDRY	TYPOGRAPHICAL	TYRANNOSAURS
TWATTLINGS	TWITTERIEST	TYPESCRIPT	TYPOGRAPHICALLY	TYRANNOSAURUS
TWAYBLADES	TWITTERING	TYPESCRIPTS	TYPOGRAPHIES	TYRANNOSAURUSES
TWEEDINESS	TWITTERINGLY	TYPESETTER	TYPOGRAPHING	TYRANNOUSLY
TWEEDINESSES	TWITTERINGS	TYPESETTERS	TYPOGRAPHIST	TYRANNOUSNESS
TWEEDLEDEE	TWITTINGLY	TYPESETTING	TYPOGRAPHISTS	TYRANNOUSNESSES
TWEEDLEDEED	TWOFOLDNESS	TYPESETTINGS	TYPOGRAPHS	TYREMAKERS
TWEEDLEDEEING	TWOFOLDNESSES	TYPESTYLES	TYPOGRAPHY	TYROCIDINE
TWEEDLEDEES	TWOPENCEWORTH	TYPEWRITER	TYPOLOGICAL	TYROCIDINES
TWEENAGERS	TWOPENCEWORTHS	TYPEWRITERS	TYPOLOGICALLY	TYROCIDINS
TWEENESSES	TWOPENNIES	TYPEWRITES	TYPOLOGIES	TYROGLYPHID
TWELVEFOLD	TWOSEATERS	TYPEWRITING	TYPOLOGIST	TYROGLYPHIDS
TWELVEMONTH	TYCOONATES	TYPEWRITINGS	TYPOLOGISTS	TYROPITTAS
TWELVEMONTHS	TYCOONERIES	TYPEWRITTEN	TYPOMANIAS	TYROSINASE
TWENTIETHS	TYLECTOMIES	TYPHACEOUS	TYPOTHETAE	TYROSINASES
TWENTYFOLD	TYMPANIFORM	TYPHLITISES	TYRANNESSES	TYROTHRICIN
TWENTYFOLDS	TYMPANISTS	TYPHLOLOGIES	TYRANNICAL	TYROTHRICINS
TWICHILDREN	TYMPANITES	TYPHLOLOGY	TYRANNICALLY	
TWIDDLIEST	TYMPANITESES	TYPHLOSOLE	TYRANNICALNESS	
TWIDDLINGS	TYMPANITIC	TYPHLOSOLES	TYRANNICIDAL	

T

U

UBERSEXUAL	ULTIMATENESS	ULTRAFILTRATE	ULTRAMODERNISMS	ULTRASENSUAL
UBERSEXUALS	ULTIMATENESSES	ULTRAFILTRATES	ULTRAMODERNIST	ULTRASERIOUS
UBIQUARIAN	ULTIMATING	ULTRAFILTRATION	ULTRAMODERNISTS	ULTRASHARP
UBIQUINONE	ULTIMATUMS	ULTRAGLAMOROUS	ULTRAMONTANE	ULTRASHORT
UBIQUINONES	ULTIMOGENITURE	ULTRAHAZARDOUS	ULTRAMONTANES	ULTRASIMPLE
UBIQUITARIAN	ULTIMOGENITURES	ULTRAHEATED	ULTRAMONTANISM	ULTRASLICK
UBIQUITARIANISM	ULTRABASIC	ULTRAHEATING	ULTRAMONTANISMS	ULTRASMALL
UBIQUITARIANS	ULTRABASICS	ULTRAHEATS	ULTRAMONTANIST	ULTRASMART
UBIQUITARY	ULTRACAREFUL	ULTRAHEAVIER	ULTRAMONTANISTS	ULTRASMOOTH
UBIQUITIES	ULTRACASUAL	ULTRAHEAVIEST	ULTRAMUNDANE	ULTRASONIC
UBIQUITINATION	ULTRACAUTIOUS	ULTRAHEAVY	ULTRANATIONAL	ULTRASONICALLY
UBIQUITINATIONS	ULTRACENTRIFUGE	ULTRAHUMAN	ULTRAORTHODOX	ULTRASONICS
UBIQUITINS	ULTRACIVILISED	ULTRAISTIC	ULTRAPATRIOTIC	ULTRASONOGRAPHY
UBIQUITOUS	ULTRACIVILIZED	ULTRALARGE	ULTRAPHYSICAL	ULTRASOUND
UBIQUITOUSLY	ULTRACLEAN	ULTRALEFTISM	ULTRAPOWERFUL	ULTRASOUNDS
UBIQUITOUSNESS	ULTRACOMMERCIAL	ULTRALEFTISMS	ULTRAPRACTICAL	ULTRASTRUCTURAL
UDOMETRIES	ULTRACOMPACT	ULTRALEFTIST	ULTRAPRECISE	ULTRASTRUCTURE
UFOLOGICAL	ULTRACOMPETENT	ULTRALEFTISTS	ULTRAPRECISION	ULTRASTRUCTURES
UFOLOGISTS	ULTRACONVENIENT	ULTRALEFTS	ULTRAPRECISIONS	ULTRATINIER
UGLIFICATION	ULTRACREPIDATE	ULTRALIBERAL	ULTRAQUIET	ULTRATINIEST
UGLIFICATIONS	ULTRACREPIDATED	ULTRALIBERALISM	ULTRARADICAL	ULTRAVACUA
UGLINESSES	ULTRACREPIDATES	ULTRALIBERALS	ULTRARADICALS	ULTRAVACUUM
UGSOMENESS	ULTRACRITICAL	ULTRALIGHT	ULTRARAPID	ULTRAVACUUMS
UGSOMENESSES	ULTRADEMOCRATIC	ULTRALIGHTS	ULTRAREFIED	ULTRAVIOLENCE
UINTAHITES	ULTRADENSE	ULTRAMAFIC	ULTRARATIONAL	ULTRAVIOLENCES
UINTATHERE	ULTRADISTANCE	ULTRAMARATHON	ULTRAREALISM	ULTRAVIOLENT
UINTATHERES	ULTRADISTANT	ULTRAMARATHONER	ULTRAREALISMS	ULTRAVIOLET
UITLANDERS	ULTRADRIER	ULTRAMARATHONS	ULTRAREALIST	ULTRAVIOLETS
ULCERATING	ULTRADRIEST	ULTRAMARINE	ULTRAREALISTIC	ULTRAVIRILE
ULCERATION	ULTRADRYER	ULTRAMARINES	ULTRAREALISTS	ULTRAVIRILITIES
ULCERATIONS	ULTRADRYEST	ULTRAMASCULINE	ULTRAREFINED	ULTRAVIRILITY
ULCERATIVE	ULTRAEFFICIENT	ULTRAMICRO	ULTRARELIABLE	ULTRAVIRUS
ULCEROGENIC	ULTRAENERGETIC	ULTRAMICROMETER	ULTRARIGHT	ULTRAVIRUSES
ULCEROUSLY	ULTRAEXCLUSIVE	ULTRAMICROSCOPE	ULTRARIGHTISM	ULTRAWIDEBAND
ULCEROUSNESS	ULTRAFAMILIAR	ULTRAMICROSCOPY	ULTRARIGHTISMS	ULTRAWIDEBANDS
ULCEROUSNESSES	ULTRAFASTIDIOUS	ULTRAMICROTOME	ULTRARIGHTIST	ULTRONEOUS
ULOTRICHIES	ULTRAFEMININE	ULTRAMICROTOMES	ULTRARIGHTISTS	ULTRONEOUSLY
ULOTRICHOUS	ULTRAFICHE	ULTRAMICROTOMY	ULTRARIGHTS	ULTRONEOUSNESS
ULSTERETTE	ULTRAFICHES	ULTRAMILITANT	ULTRAROMANTIC	ULULATIONS
ULSTERETTES	ULTRAFILTER	ULTRAMILITANTS	ULTRAROYALIST	UMBELLATED
ULTERIORLY	ULTRAFILTERED	ULTRAMINIATURE	ULTRAROYALISTS	UMBELLATELY
ULTIMACIES	ULTRAFILTERING	ULTRAMODERN	ULTRASECRET	UMBELLIFER
ULTIMATELY	ULTRAFILTERS	ULTRAMODERNISM	ULTRASENSITIVE	UMBELLIFEROUS

UMBELLIFERS	UNACCLIMATISED	UNAESTHETIC	UNANCHORED	UNAPPREHENSIVE
UMBELLULATE	UNACCLIMATIZED	UNAFFECTED	UNANCHORING	UNAPPRISED
UMBELLULES	UNACCOMMODATED	UNAFFECTEDLY	UNANESTHETISED	UNAPPROACHABLE
UMBILICALLY	UNACCOMMODATING	UNAFFECTEDNESS	UNANESTHETIZED	UNAPPROACHABLY
UMBILICALS	UNACCOMPANIED	UNAFFECTING	UNANIMATED	UNAPPROACHED
UMBILICATE	UNACCOMPLISHED	UNAFFECTIONATE	UNANIMITIES	UNAPPROPRIATE
UMBILICATED	UNACCOUNTABLE	UNAFFILIATED	UNANIMOUSLY	UNAPPROPRIATED
UMBILICATION	UNACCOUNTABLY	UNAFFLUENT	UNANIMOUSNESS	UNAPPROPRIATES
UMBILICATIONS	UNACCOUNTED	UNAFFORDABLE	UNANIMOUSNESSES	UNAPPROPRIATING
UMBILICUSES	UNACCREDITED	UNAGGRESSIVE	UNANNEALED	UNAPPROVED
UMBILIFORM	UNACCULTURATED	UNAGREEABLE	UNANNOTATED	UNAPPROVING
UMBONATION	UNACCUSABLE	UNALIENABLE	UNANNOUNCED	UNAPPROVINGLY
UMBONATIONS	UNACCUSABLY	UNALIENABLY	UNANSWERABILITY	UNAPTNESSES
UMBRACULATE	UNACCUSTOMED	UNALIENATED	UNANSWERABLE	UNARGUABLE
UMBRACULIFORM	UNACCUSTOMEDLY	UNALLEVIATED	UNANSWERABLY	UNARGUABLY
UMBRACULUM	UNACHIEVABLE	UNALLOCATED	UNANSWERED	UNARMOURED
UMBRAGEOUS	UNACHIEVED	UNALLOTTED	UNANTICIPATED	UNARRANGED
UMBRAGEOUSLY	UNACKNOWLEDGED	UNALLOWABLE	UNANTICIPATEDLY	UNARROGANT
UMBRAGEOUSNESS	UNACQUAINT	UNALLURING	UNAPOLOGETIC	UNARTFULLY
UMBRATICAL	UNACQUAINTANCE	UNALTERABILITY	UNAPOLOGISING	UNARTICULATE
UMBRATILES	UNACQUAINTANCES	UNALTERABLE	UNAPOLOGIZING	UNARTICULATED
UMBRATILOUS	UNACQUAINTED	UNALTERABLENESS	UNAPOSTOLIC	UNARTIFICIAL
UMBRELLAED	UNACQUAINTING	UNALTERABLY	UNAPOSTOLICAL	UNARTIFICIALLY
UMBRELLAING	UNACQUAINTS	UNALTERING	UNAPOSTOLICALLY	UNARTISTIC
UMBRELLOES	UNACTIVING	UNAMBIGUOUS	UNAPPALLED	UNARTISTLIKE
UMBRIFEROUS	UNACTORISH	UNAMBIGUOUSLY	UNAPPARELLED	UNASCENDABLE
UMPIRESHIP	UNACTUATED	UNAMBITIOUS	UNAPPARELLING	UNASCENDED
UMPIRESHIPS	UNADAPTABLE	UNAMBITIOUSLY	UNAPPARELS	UNASCENDIBLE
UMPTEENTHS	UNADDRESSED	UNAMBIVALENT	UNAPPARENT	UNASCERTAINABLE
UNABASHEDLY	UNADJUDICATED	UNAMBIVALENTLY	UNAPPEALABLE	UNASCERTAINED
UNABATEDLY	UNADJUSTED	UNAMENABLE	UNAPPEALABLY	UNASHAMEDLY
UNABBREVIATED	UNADMIRING	UNAMENDABLE	UNAPPEALING	UNASHAMEDNESS
UNABOLISHED	UNADMITTED	UNAMIABILITIES	UNAPPEALINGLY	UNASHAMEDNESSES
UNABRIDGED	UNADMONISHED	UNAMIABILITY	UNAPPEASABLE	UNASPIRATED
UNABROGATED	UNADOPTABLE	UNAMIABLENESS	UNAPPEASABLY	UNASPIRING
UNABSOLVED	UNADULTERATE	UNAMIABLENESSES	UNAPPEASED	UNASPIRINGLY
UNABSORBED	UNADULTERATED	UNAMORTISED	UNAPPETISING	UNASPIRINGNESS
UNABSORBENT	UNADULTERATEDLY	UNAMORTIZED	UNAPPETISINGLY	UNASSAILABILITY
UNACADEMIC	UNADVENTROUS	UNAMPLIFIED	UNAPPETIZING	UNASSAILABLE
UNACADEMICALLY	UNADVENTUROUS	UNAMUSABLE	UNAPPETIZINGLY	UNASSAILABLY
UNACCENTED	UNADVENTUROUSLY	UNAMUSINGLY	UNAPPLAUSIVE	UNASSAILED
UNACCENTUATED	UNADVERTISED	UNANAESTHETISED	UNAPPLICABLE	UNASSEMBLED
UNACCEPTABILITY	UNADVERTIZED	UNANAESTHETIZED	UNAPPOINTED	UNASSERTIVE
UNACCEPTABLE	UNADVISABLE	UNANALYSABLE	UNAPPRECIATED	UNASSERTIVELY
UNACCEPTABLY	UNADVISABLENESS	UNANALYSED	UNAPPRECIATION	UNASSIGNABLE
UNACCEPTANCE	UNADVISABLY	UNANALYTIC	UNAPPRECIATIONS	UNASSIGNED
UNACCEPTANCES	UNADVISEDLY	UNANALYTICAL	UNAPPRECIATIVE	UNASSIMILABLE
UNACCEPTED	UNADVISEDNESS	UNANALYZABLE	UNAPPREHENDED	UNASSIMILATED
UNACCLIMATED	UNADVISEDNESSES	UNANALYZED	UNAPPREHENSIBLE	UNASSISTED

UNASSISTEDLY	UNAWARENESS	UNBELIEVABLY	UNBLAMABLY	UNBREECHED
UNASSISTING	UNAWARENESSES	UNBELIEVED	UNBLAMEABLE	UNBREECHES
UNASSOCIATED	UNBAILABLE	UNBELIEVER	UNBLAMEABLY	UNBREECHING
UNASSUAGEABLE	UNBALANCED	UNBELIEVERS	UNBLEACHED	UNBRIBABLE
UNASSUAGED	UNBALANCES	UNBELIEVES	UNBLEMISHED	UNBRIDGEABLE
UNASSUMING	UNBALANCING	UNBELIEVING	UNBLENCHED	UNBRIDLEDLY
UNASSUMINGLY	UNBALLASTED	UNBELIEVINGLY	UNBLENCHING	UNBRIDLEDNESS
UNASSUMINGNESS	UNBANDAGED	UNBELIEVINGNESS	UNBLESSEDNESS	UNBRIDLEDNESSES
UNATHLETIC	UNBANDAGES	UNBELLIGERENT	UNBLESSEDNESSES	UNBRIDLING
UNATONABLE	UNBANDAGING	UNBENDABLE	UNBLESSING	UNBRILLIANT
UNATTACHED	UNBANNINGS	UNBENDINGLY	UNBLINDFOLD	UNBROKENLY
UNATTAINABLE	UNBAPTISED	UNBENDINGNESS	UNBLINDFOLDED	UNBROKENNESS
UNATTAINABLY	UNBAPTISES	UNBENDINGNESSES	UNBLINDFOLDING	UNBROKENNESSES
UNATTAINTED	UNBAPTISING	UNBENDINGS	UNBLINDFOLDS	UNBROTHERLIKE
UNATTEMPTED	UNBAPTIZED	UNBENEFICED	UNBLINDING	UNBROTHERLY
UNATTENDED	UNBAPTIZES	UNBENEFICIAL	UNBLINKING	UNBUCKLING
UNATTENDING	UNBAPTIZING	UNBENEFITED	UNBLINKINGLY	UNBUDGEABLE
UNATTENTIVE	UNBARBERED	UNBENEFITTED	UNBLISSFUL	UNBUDGEABLY
UNATTENUATED	UNBARRICADE	UNBENIGHTED	UNBLOCKING	UNBUDGETED
UNATTESTED	UNBARRICADED	UNBENIGNANT	UNBLOODIED	UNBUDGINGLY
UNATTRACTIVE	UNBARRICADES	UNBENIGNLY	UNBLOODIER	UNBUFFERED
UNATTRACTIVELY	UNBARRICADING	UNBESEEMED	UNBLOODIEST	UNBUILDABLE
UNATTRIBUTABLE	UNBATTERED	UNBESEEMING	UNBLUSHING	UNBUILDING
UNATTRIBUTED	UNBEARABLE	UNBESEEMINGLY	UNBLUSHINGLY	UNBULKIEST
UNAUGMENTED	UNBEARABLENESS	UNBESOUGHT	UNBLUSHINGNESS	UNBUNDLERS
UNAUSPICIOUS	UNBEARABLY	UNBESPEAKING	UNBOASTFUL	UNBUNDLING
UNAUTHENTIC	UNBEATABLE	UNBESPEAKS	UNBONNETED	UNBUNDLINGS
UNAUTHENTICATED	UNBEATABLY	UNBESPOKEN	UNBONNETING	UNBURDENED
UNAUTHENTICITY	UNBEAUTIFUL	UNBESTOWED	UNBORROWED	UNBURDENING
UNAUTHORISED	UNBEAUTIFULLY	UNBETRAYED	UNBOSOMERS	UNBUREAUCRATIC
UNAUTHORITATIVE	UNBEAVERED	UNBETTERABLE	UNBOSOMING	UNBURNABLE
UNAUTHORIZED	UNBECOMING	UNBETTERED	UNBOTTLING	UNBURNISHED
UNAUTOMATED	UNBECOMINGLY	UNBEWAILED	UNBOTTOMED	UNBURROWED
UNAVAILABILITY	UNBECOMINGNESS	UNBIASEDLY	UNBOUNCIER	UNBURROWING
UNAVAILABLE	UNBECOMINGS	UNBIASEDNESS	UNBOUNCIEST	UNBURTHENED
UNAVAILABLENESS	UNBEDIMMED	UNBIASEDNESSES	UNBOUNDEDLY	UNBURTHENING
UNAVAILABLY	UNBEDINNED	UNBIASINGS	UNBOUNDEDNESS	UNBURTHENS
UNAVAILING	UNBEFITTING	UNBIASSEDLY	UNBOUNDEDNESSES	UNBUSINESSLIKE
UNAVAILINGLY	UNBEFRIENDED	UNBIASSEDNESS	UNBOWDLERISED	UNBUTTERED
UNAVAILINGNESS	UNBEGETTING	UNBIASSEDNESSES	UNBOWDLERIZED	UNBUTTONED
UNAVERTABLE	UNBEGINNING	UNBIASSING	UNBRACKETED	UNBUTTONING
UNAVERTIBLE	UNBEGOTTEN	UNBIASSINGS	UNBRAIDING	UNCALCIFIED
UNAVOIDABILITY	UNBEGUILED	UNBIBLICAL	UNBRANCHED	UNCALCINED
UNAVOIDABLE	UNBEGUILES	UNBINDINGS	UNBREACHABLE	UNCALCULATED
UNAVOIDABLENESS	UNBEGUILING	UNBIRTHDAY	UNBREACHED	UNCALCULATING
UNAVOIDABLY	UNBEHOLDEN	UNBIRTHDAYS	UNBREAKABLE	UNCALIBRATED
UNAVOWEDLY	UNBEKNOWNST	UNBISHOPED	UNBREATHABLE	UNCALLOUSED
UNAWAKENED	UNBELIEVABILITY	UNBISHOPING	UNBREATHED	UNCANCELED
UNAWAKENING	UNBELIEVABLE	UNBLAMABLE	UNBREATHING	UNCANCELING

UNCANCELLED	UNCERTIFICATED	UNCHILDLIKE	UNCLAMPING	UNCLUTTERED
UNCANCELLING	UNCERTIFIED	UNCHIVALROUS	UNCLARIFIED	UNCLUTTERING
UNCANDIDLY	UNCHAINING	UNCHIVALROUSLY	UNCLARITIES	UNCLUTTERS
UNCANDIDNESS	UNCHAIRING	UNCHLORINATED	UNCLASPING	UNCOALESCE
UNCANDIDNESSES	UNCHALLENGEABLE	UNCHOREOGRAPHED	UNCLASSICAL	UNCOALESCED
UNCANDOURS	UNCHALLENGEABLY	UNCHRISTEN	UNCLASSIER	UNCOALESCES
UNCANNIEST	UNCHALLENGED	UNCHRISTENED	UNCLASSIEST	UNCOALESCING
UNCANNINESS	UNCHALLENGING	UNCHRISTENING	UNCLASSIFIABLE	UNCOATINGS
UNCANNINESSES	UNCHANCIER	UNCHRISTENS	UNCLASSIFIED	UNCODIFIED
UNCANONICAL	UNCHANCIEST	UNCHRISTIAN	UNCLEANEST	UNCOERCIVE
UNCANONICALNESS	UNCHANGEABILITY	UNCHRISTIANED	UNCLEANLIER	UNCOERCIVELY
UNCANONISE	UNCHANGEABLE	UNCHRISTIANING	UNCLEANLIEST	UNCOFFINED
UNCANONISED	UNCHANGEABLY	UNCHRISTIANISE	UNCLEANLINESS	UNCOFFINING
UNCANONISES	UNCHANGING	UNCHRISTIANISED	UNCLEANLINESSES	UNCOLLECTABLE
UNCANONISING	UNCHANGINGLY	UNCHRISTIANISES	UNCLEANNESS	UNCOLLECTABLES
UNCANONIZE	UNCHANGINGNESS	UNCHRISTIANIZE	UNCLEANNESSES	UNCOLLECTED
UNCANONIZED	UNCHANNELED	UNCHRISTIANIZED	UNCLEANSED	UNCOLLECTIBLE
UNCANONIZES	UNCHANNELLED	UNCHRISTIANIZES	UNCLEAREST	UNCOLLECTIBLES
UNCANONIZING	UNCHAPERONED	UNCHRISTIANLIKE	UNCLEARNESS	UNCOLOURED
UNCAPITALISED	UNCHARGING	UNCHRISTIANLY	UNCLEARNESSES	UNCOMATABLE
UNCAPITALIZED	UNCHARIEST	UNCHRISTIANS	UNCLENCHED	UNCOMBATIVE
UNCAPSIZABLE	UNCHARISMATIC	UNCHRONICLED	UNCLENCHES	UNCOMBINED
UNCAPTIONED	UNCHARITABLE	UNCHRONOLOGICAL	UNCLENCHING	UNCOMBINES
UNCAPTIVATED	UNCHARITABLY	UNCHURCHED	UNCLERICAL	UNCOMBINING
UNCAPTURABLE	UNCHARITIES	UNCHURCHES	UNCLESHIPS	UNCOMEATABLE
UNCARPETED	UNCHARMING	UNCHURCHING	UNCLIMBABLE	UNCOMELIER
UNCASTRATED	UNCHARNELLED	UNCHURCHLY	UNCLIMBABLENESS	UNCOMELIEST
UNCATALOGED	UNCHARNELLING	UNCILIATED	UNCLINCHED	UNCOMELINESS
UNCATALOGUED	UNCHARNELS	UNCINARIAS	UNCLINCHES	UNCOMELINESSES
UNCATCHABLE	UNCHARTERED	UNCINARIASES	UNCLINCHING	UNCOMFIEST
UNCATCHIER	UNCHASTELY	UNCINARIASIS	UNCLIPPING	UNCOMFORTABLE
UNCATCHIEST	UNCHASTENED	UNCINEMATIC	UNCLOAKING	UNCOMFORTABLY
UNCATEGORISABLE	UNCHASTENESS	UNCIPHERED	UNCLOGGING	UNCOMFORTED
UNCATEGORIZABLE	UNCHASTENESSES	UNCIPHERING	UNCLOISTER	UNCOMMENDABLE
UNCEASINGLY	UNCHASTEST	UNCIRCULATED	UNCLOISTERED	UNCOMMENDABLY
UNCEASINGNESS	UNCHASTISABLE	UNCIRCUMCISED	UNCLOISTERING	UNCOMMENDED
UNCEASINGNESSES	UNCHASTISED	UNCIRCUMCISION	UNCLOISTERS	UNCOMMERCIAL
UNCELEBRATED	UNCHASTITIES	UNCIRCUMCISIONS	UNCLOTHING	UNCOMMITTED
UNCENSORED	UNCHASTITY	UNCIRCUMSCRIBED	UNCLOUDEDLY	UNCOMMONER
UNCENSORIOUS	UNCHASTIZABLE	UNCIVILISED	UNCLOUDEDNESS	UNCOMMONEST
UNCENSURED	UNCHASTIZED	UNCIVILISEDLY	UNCLOUDEDNESSES	UNCOMMONLY
UNCEREBRAL	UNCHAUVINISTIC	UNCIVILISEDNESS	UNCLOUDIER	UNCOMMONNESS
UNCEREMONIOUS	UNCHECKABLE	UNCIVILITIES	UNCLOUDIEST	UNCOMMONNESSES
UNCEREMONIOUSLY	UNCHECKING	UNCIVILITY	UNCLOUDING	UNCOMMUNICABLE
UNCERTAINLY	UNCHEERFUL	UNCIVILIZED	UNCLUBABLE	UNCOMMUNICATED
UNCERTAINNESS	UNCHEERFULLY	UNCIVILIZEDLY	UNCLUBBABLE	UNCOMMUNICATIVE
UNCERTAINNESSES	UNCHEERFULNESS	UNCIVILIZEDNESS	UNCLUTCHED	UNCOMMUTED
UNCERTAINTIES	UNCHEWABLE	UNCIVILNESS	UNCLUTCHES	UNCOMPACTED
UNCERTAINTY	UNCHILDING	UNCIVILNESSES	UNCLUTCHING	UNCOMPANIED

UNCOMPANIONABLE	UNCONFINABLE	UNCONSTANT	UNCOSTLIER	UNCUMBERED
UNCOMPANIONED	UNCONFINED	UNCONSTRAINABLE	UNCOSTLIEST	UNCURBABLE
UNCOMPASSIONATE	UNCONFINEDLY	UNCONSTRAINED	UNCOUNSELLED	UNCURTAILED
UNCOMPELLED	UNCONFINES	UNCONSTRAINEDLY	UNCOUNTABLE	UNCURTAINED
UNCOMPELLING	UNCONFINING	UNCONSTRAINT	UNCOUPLERS	UNCURTAINING
UNCOMPENSATED	UNCONFIRMED	UNCONSTRAINTS	UNCOUPLING	UNCURTAINS
UNCOMPETITIVE	UNCONFORMABLE	UNCONSTRICTED	UNCOURAGEOUS	UNCUSTOMARILY
UNCOMPLACENT	UNCONFORMABLY	UNCONSTRUCTED	UNCOURTEOUS	UNCUSTOMARY
UNCOMPLAINING	UNCONFORMING	UNCONSTRUCTIVE	UNCOURTLIER	UNCUSTOMED
UNCOMPLAININGLY	UNCONFORMITIES	UNCONSUMED	UNCOURTLIEST	UNCYNICALLY
UNCOMPLAISANT	UNCONFORMITY	UNCONSUMMATED	UNCOURTLINESS	UNDANCEABLE
UNCOMPLAISANTLY	UNCONFOUNDED	UNCONTAINABLE	UNCOURTLINESSES	UNDAUNTABLE
UNCOMPLETED	UNCONFUSED	UNCONTAMINATED	UNCOUTHEST	UNDAUNTEDLY
UNCOMPLIANT	UNCONFUSEDLY	UNCONTEMNED	UNCOUTHNESS	UNDAUNTEDNESS
UNCOMPLICATED	UNCONFUSES	UNCONTEMPLATED	UNCOUTHNESSES	UNDAUNTEDNESSES
UNCOMPLIMENTARY	UNCONFUSING	UNCONTEMPORARY	UNCOVENANTED	UNDAUNTING
UNCOMPLYING	UNCONGEALED	UNCONTENTIOUS	UNCOVERING	UNDAZZLING
UNCOMPOSABLE	UNCONGEALING	UNCONTESTABLE	UNCRAZIEST	UNDEBARRED
UNCOMPOUNDED	UNCONGEALS	UNCONTESTED	UNCREATEDNESS	UNDEBATABLE
UNCOMPREHENDED	UNCONGENIAL	UNCONTRACTED	UNCREATEDNESSES	UNDEBATABLY
UNCOMPREHENDING	UNCONGENIALITY	UNCONTRADICTED	UNCREATING	UNDEBAUCHED
UNCOMPREHENSIVE	UNCONJECTURED	UNCONTRIVED	UNCREATIVE	UNDECADENT
UNCOMPROMISABLE	UNCONJUGAL	UNCONTROLLABLE	UNCREDENTIALED	UNDECAGONS
UNCOMPROMISING	UNCONJUGATED	UNCONTROLLABLY	UNCREDIBLE	UNDECEIVABLE
UNCOMPUTERISED	UNCONJUNCTIVE	UNCONTROLLED	UNCREDITABLE	UNDECEIVED
UNCOMPUTERIZED	UNCONNECTED	UNCONTROLLEDLY	UNCREDITED	UNDECEIVER
UNCONCEALABLE	UNCONNECTEDLY	UNCONTROVERSIAL	UNCRIPPLED	UNDECEIVERS
UNCONCEALED	UNCONNECTEDNESS	UNCONTROVERTED	UNCRITICAL	UNDECEIVES
UNCONCEALING	UNCONNIVING	UNCONVENTIONAL	UNCRITICALLY	UNDECEIVING
UNCONCEIVABLE	UNCONQUERABLE	UNCONVERSABLE	UNCROSSABLE	UNDECIDABILITY
UNCONCEIVABLY	UNCONQUERABLY	UNCONVERSANT	UNCROSSING	UNDECIDABLE
UNCONCEIVED	UNCONQUERED	UNCONVERTED	UNCROWNING	UNDECIDEDLY
UNCONCERNED	UNCONSCIENTIOUS	UNCONVERTIBLE	UNCRUMPLED	UNDECIDEDNESS
UNCONCERNEDLY	UNCONSCIONABLE	UNCONVICTED	UNCRUMPLES	UNDECIDEDNESSES
UNCONCERNEDNESS	UNCONSCIONABLY	UNCONVINCED	UNCRUMPLING	UNDECIDEDS
UNCONCERNING	UNCONSCIOUS	UNCONVINCING	UNCRUSHABLE	UNDECILLION
UNCONCERNMENT	UNCONSCIOUSES	UNCONVINCINGLY	UNCRYSTALLISED	UNDECILLIONS
UNCONCERNMENTS	UNCONSCIOUSLY	UNCONVOYED	UNCRYSTALLIZED	UNDECIMOLE
UNCONCERNS	UNCONSCIOUSNESS	UNCOOPERATIVE	UNCTIONLESS	UNDECIMOLES
UNCONCERTED	UNCONSECRATE	UNCOOPERATIVELY	UNCTUOSITIES	UNDECIPHERABLE
UNCONCILIATORY	UNCONSECRATED	UNCOORDINATED	UNCTUOSITY	UNDECIPHERED
UNCONCLUSIVE	UNCONSECRATES	UNCOPYRIGHTABLE	UNCTUOUSLY	UNDECISIVE
UNCONCOCTED	UNCONSECRATING	UNCOQUETTISH	UNCTUOUSNESS	UNDECLARED
UNCONDITIONAL	UNCONSENTANEOUS	UNCORRECTABLE	UNCTUOUSNESSES	UNDECLINING
UNCONDITIONALLY	UNCONSENTING	UNCORRECTED	UNCUCKOLDED	UNDECOMPOSABLE
UNCONDITIONED	UNCONSIDERED	UNCORRELATED	UNCULTIVABLE	UNDECOMPOSED
UNCONDUCIVE	UNCONSIDERING	UNCORROBORATED	UNCULTIVATABLE	UNDECORATED
UNCONFEDERATED	UNCONSOLED	UNCORRUPTED	UNCULTIVATED	UNDEDICATED
UNCONFESSED	UNCONSOLIDATED	UNCORSETED	UNCULTURED	UNDEFEATABLE

UNDEFEATED	UNDERBAKED	UNDERBUSHED	UNDERCRESTED	UNDEREMPHASISED
UNDEFENDED	UNDERBAKES	UNDERBUSHES	UNDERCRESTING	UNDEREMPHASISES
UNDEFINABLE	UNDERBAKING	UNDERBUSHING	UNDERCRESTS	UNDEREMPHASIZE
UNDEFOLIATED	UNDERBEARER	UNDERBUYING	UNDERCROFT	UNDEREMPHASIZED
UNDEFORMED	UNDERBEARERS	UNDERCAPITALISE	UNDERCROFTS	UNDEREMPHASIZES
UNDEIFYING	UNDERBEARING	UNDERCAPITALIZE	UNDERCURRENT	UNDEREMPLOYED
UNDELAYING	UNDERBEARINGS	UNDERCARDS	UNDERCURRENTS	UNDEREMPLOYMENT
UNDELECTABLE	UNDERBEARS	UNDERCARRIAGE	UNDERCUTTING	UNDERESTIMATE
UNDELEGATED	UNDERBELLIES	UNDERCARRIAGES	UNDERDAMPER	UNDERESTIMATED
UNDELETING	UNDERBELLY	UNDERCARTS	UNDERDAMPERS	UNDERESTIMATES
UNDELIBERATE	UNDERBIDDER	UNDERCASTS	UNDERDECKS	UNDERESTIMATING
UNDELIGHTED	UNDERBIDDERS	UNDERCHARGE	UNDERDELIVER	UNDERESTIMATION
UNDELIGHTFUL	UNDERBIDDING	UNDERCHARGED	UNDERDELIVERED	UNDEREXPLOIT
UNDELIGHTS	UNDERBITES	UNDERCHARGES	UNDERDELIVERING	UNDEREXPLOITED
UNDELIVERABLE	UNDERBITING	UNDERCHARGING	UNDERDELIVERS	UNDEREXPLOITING
UNDELIVERED	UNDERBITTEN	UNDERCLASS	UNDERDEVELOP	UNDEREXPLOITS
UNDEMANDING	UNDERBLANKET	UNDERCLASSES	UNDERDEVELOPED	UNDEREXPOSE
UNDEMARCATED	UNDERBLANKETS	UNDERCLASSMAN	UNDERDEVELOPING	UNDEREXPOSED
UNDEMOCRATIC	UNDERBODIES	UNDERCLASSMEN	UNDERDEVELOPS	UNDEREXPOSES
UNDEMONSTRABLE	UNDERBOOBS	UNDERCLAYS	UNDERDOERS	UNDEREXPOSING
UNDEMONSTRATED	UNDERBORNE	UNDERCLIFF	UNDERDOING	UNDEREXPOSURE
UNDEMONSTRATIVE	UNDERBOSSES	UNDERCLIFFS	UNDERDOSED	UNDEREXPOSURES
UNDENIABLE	UNDERBOUGH	UNDERCLOTHE	UNDERDOSES	UNDERFEEDING
UNDENIABLENESS	UNDERBOUGHS	UNDERCLOTHED	UNDERDOSING	UNDERFEEDINGS
UNDENIABLY	UNDERBOUGHT	UNDERCLOTHES	UNDERDRAIN	UNDERFEEDS
UNDEPENDABLE	UNDERBREATH	UNDERCLOTHING	UNDERDRAINAGE	UNDERFELTS
UNDEPENDING	UNDERBREATHS	UNDERCLOTHINGS	UNDERDRAINAGES	UNDERFINANCED
UNDEPLORED	UNDERBREEDING	UNDERCLUBBED	UNDERDRAINED	UNDERFINISHED
UNDEPRAVED	UNDERBREEDINGS	UNDERCLUBBING	UNDERDRAINING	UNDERFIRED
UNDEPRECIATED	UNDERBRIDGE	UNDERCLUBS	UNDERDRAINS	UNDERFIRES
UNDEPRESSED	UNDERBRIDGES	UNDERCOATED	UNDERDRAWERS	UNDERFIRING
UNDEPRIVED	UNDERBRIMS	UNDERCOATING	UNDERDRAWING	UNDERFISHED
UNDERACHIEVE	UNDERBRUSH	UNDERCOATINGS	UNDERDRAWINGS	UNDERFISHES
UNDERACHIEVED	UNDERBRUSHED	UNDERCOATS	UNDERDRAWN	UNDERFISHING
UNDERACHIEVER	UNDERBRUSHES	UNDERCOOKED	UNDERDRAWS	UNDERFLOOR
UNDERACHIEVERS	UNDERBRUSHING	UNDERCOOKING	UNDERDRESS	UNDERFLOWS
UNDERACHIEVES	UNDERBUDDED	UNDERCOOKS	UNDERDRESSED	UNDERFONGED
UNDERACHIEVING	UNDERBUDDING	UNDERCOOLED	UNDERDRESSES	UNDERFONGING
UNDERACTED	UNDERBUDGET	UNDERCOOLING	UNDERDRESSING	UNDERFONGS
UNDERACTING	UNDERBUDGETED	UNDERCOOLS	UNDERDRIVE	UNDERFOOTED
UNDERACTION	UNDERBUDGETING	UNDERCOUNT	UNDERDRIVES	UNDERFOOTING
UNDERACTIONS	UNDERBUDGETS	UNDERCOUNTED	UNDEREARTH	UNDERFOOTS
UNDERACTIVE	UNDERBUILD	UNDERCOUNTING	UNDEREARTHS	UNDERFULFIL
UNDERACTIVITIES	UNDERBUILDER	UNDERCOUNTS	UNDEREATEN	UNDERFULFILL
UNDERACTIVITY	UNDERBUILDERS	UNDERCOVER	UNDEREATING	UNDERFULFILLED
UNDERACTOR	UNDERBUILDING	UNDERCOVERT	UNDEREDUCATED	UNDERFULFILLING
UNDERACTORS	UNDERBUILDS	UNDERCOVERTS	UNDEREMPHASES	UNDERFULFILLS
UNDERAGENT	UNDERBUILT	UNDERCRACKERS	UNDEREMPHASIS	UNDERFULFILS
UNDERAGENTS	UNDERBURNT	UNDERCREST	UNDEREMPHASISE	UNDERFUNDED

UNDERFUNDING	UNDERINVESTS	UNDERMINDE	UNDERPLANT	UNDERRATING
UNDERFUNDINGS	UNDERJAWED	UNDERMINDED	UNDERPLANTED	UNDERREACT
UNDERFUNDS	UNDERKEEPER	UNDERMINDES	UNDERPLANTING	UNDERREACTED
UNDERGARMENT	UNDERKEEPERS	UNDERMINDING	UNDERPLANTS	UNDERREACTING
UNDERGARMENTS	UNDERKEEPING	UNDERMINED	UNDERPLAYED	UNDERREACTION
UNDERGIRDED	UNDERKEEPS	UNDERMINER	UNDERPLAYING	UNDERREACTIONS
UNDERGIRDING	UNDERKILLS	UNDERMINERS	UNDERPLAYS	UNDERREACTS
UNDERGIRDS	UNDERKINGDOM	UNDERMINES	UNDERPLOTS	UNDERREPORT
UNDERGLAZE	UNDERKINGDOMS	UNDERMINING	UNDERPOPULATED	UNDERREPORTED
UNDERGLAZES	UNDERKINGS	UNDERMININGS	UNDERPOWERED	UNDERREPORTING
UNDERGOERS	UNDERLAPPED	UNDERNAMED	UNDERPRAISE	UNDERREPORTS
UNDERGOING	UNDERLAPPING	UNDERNEATH	UNDERPRAISED	UNDERRUNNING
UNDERGOWNS	UNDERLAYER	UNDERNEATHS	UNDERPRAISES	UNDERRUNNINGS
UNDERGRADS	UNDERLAYERS	UNDERNICENESS	UNDERPRAISING	UNDERSATURATED
UNDERGRADUATE	UNDERLAYING	UNDERNICENESSES	UNDERPREPARED	UNDERSAYING
UNDERGRADUATES	UNDERLAYMENT	UNDERNOTED	UNDERPRICE	UNDERSCORE
UNDERGRADUETTE	UNDERLAYMENTS	UNDERNOTES	UNDERPRICED	UNDERSCORED
UNDERGRADUETTES	UNDERLEASE	UNDERNOTING	UNDERPRICES	UNDERSCORES
UNDERGROUND	UNDERLEASED	UNDERNOURISH	UNDERPRICING	UNDERSCORING
UNDERGROUNDER	UNDERLEASES	UNDERNOURISHED	UNDERPRICINGS	UNDERSCORINGS
UNDERGROUNDERS	UNDERLEASING	UNDERNOURISHES	UNDERPRISE	UNDERSCRUB
UNDERGROUNDS	UNDERLEAVES	UNDERNOURISHING	UNDERPRISED	UNDERSCRUBS
UNDERGROVE	UNDERLETTER	UNDERNTIME	UNDERPRISES	UNDERSEALED
UNDERGROVES	UNDERLETTERS	UNDERNTIMES	UNDERPRISING	UNDERSEALING
UNDERGROWN	UNDERLETTING	UNDERNUTRITION	UNDERPRIVILEGED	UNDERSEALINGS
UNDERGROWTH	UNDERLETTINGS	UNDERNUTRITIONS	UNDERPRIZE	UNDERSEALS
UNDERGROWTHS	UNDERLEVERAGED	UNDEROCCUPIED	UNDERPRIZED	UNDERSECRETARY
UNDERHAIRS	UNDERLIERS	UNDERPAINTING	UNDERPRIZES	UNDERSELLER
UNDERHANDED	UNDERLINED	UNDERPAINTINGS	UNDERPRIZING	UNDERSELLERS
UNDERHANDEDLY	UNDERLINEN	UNDERPANTS	UNDERPRODUCE	UNDERSELLING
UNDERHANDEDNESS	UNDERLINENS	UNDERPARTS	UNDERPRODUCED	UNDERSELLS
UNDERHANDING	UNDERLINES	UNDERPASSES	UNDERPRODUCES	UNDERSELVES
UNDERHANDS	UNDERLINGS	UNDERPASSION	UNDERPRODUCING	UNDERSENSE
UNDERHEATED	UNDERLINING	UNDERPASSIONS	UNDERPRODUCTION	UNDERSENSES
UNDERHEATING	UNDERLININGS	UNDERPAYING	UNDERPROOF	UNDERSERVED
UNDERHEATS	UNDERLOADED	UNDERPAYMENT	UNDERPROPPED	UNDERSETTING
UNDERHITTING	UNDERLOADING	UNDERPAYMENTS	UNDERPROPPER	UNDERSEXED
UNDERHONEST	UNDERLOADS	UNDERPEEPED	UNDERPROPPERS	UNDERSHAPEN
UNDERINFLATED	UNDERLOOKER	UNDERPEEPING	UNDERPROPPING	UNDERSHERIFF
UNDERINFLATION	UNDERLOOKERS	UNDERPEEPS	UNDERPROPS	UNDERSHERIFFS
UNDERINFLATIONS	UNDERLYING	UNDERPEOPLED	UNDERPUBLICISED	UNDERSHIRT
UNDERINSURE	UNDERLYINGLY	UNDERPERFORM	UNDERPUBLICIZED	UNDERSHIRTED
UNDERINSURED	UNDERMANNED	UNDERPERFORMED	UNDERQUALIFIED	UNDERSHIRTS
UNDERINSURES	UNDERMANNING	UNDERPERFORMING	UNDERQUOTE	UNDERSHOOT
UNDERINSURING	UNDERMANNINGS	UNDERPERFORMS	UNDERQUOTED	UNDERSHOOTING
UNDERINVEST	UNDERMASTED	UNDERPINNED	UNDERQUOTES	UNDERSHOOTS
UNDERINVESTED	UNDERMEANING	UNDERPINNING	UNDERQUOTING	UNDERSHORTS
UNDERINVESTING	UNDERMEANINGS	UNDERPINNINGS	UNDERRATED	UNDERSHRUB
UNDERINVESTMENT	UNDERMENTIONED	UNDERPITCH	UNDERRATES	UNDERSHRUBS

UNDERSIDES	UNDERSTOCKING	UNDERTONES	UNDERWORKING	UNDETERMINED
UNDERSIGNED	UNDERSTOCKS	UNDERTRICK	UNDERWORKS	UNDETERRED
UNDERSIGNING	UNDERSTOOD	UNDERTRICKS	UNDERWORLD	UNDEVELOPED
UNDERSIGNS	UNDERSTOREY	UNDERTRUMP	UNDERWORLDS	UNDEVIATING
UNDERSIZED	UNDERSTOREYS	UNDERTRUMPED	UNDERWRITE	UNDEVIATINGLY
UNDERSKIES	UNDERSTORIES	UNDERTRUMPING	UNDERWRITER	UNDIAGNOSABLE
UNDERSKINKER	UNDERSTORY	UNDERTRUMPS	UNDERWRITERS	UNDIAGNOSED
UNDERSKINKERS	UNDERSTRAPPER	UNDERUSING	UNDERWRITES	UNDIALECTICAL
UNDERSKIRT	UNDERSTRAPPERS	UNDERUTILISE	UNDERWRITING	UNDIDACTIC
UNDERSKIRTS	UNDERSTRAPPING	UNDERUTILISED	UNDERWRITINGS	UNDIFFERENCED
UNDERSLEEVE	UNDERSTRATA	UNDERUTILISES	UNDERWRITTEN	UNDIGESTED
UNDERSLEEVES	UNDERSTRATUM	UNDERUTILISING	UNDERWROTE	UNDIGESTIBLE
UNDERSLUNG	UNDERSTRATUMS	UNDERUTILIZE	UNDERWROUGHT	UNDIGHTING
UNDERSOILS	UNDERSTRENGTH	UNDERUTILIZED	UNDESCENDABLE	UNDIGNIFIED
UNDERSONGS	UNDERSTUDIED	UNDERUTILIZES	UNDESCENDED	UNDIGNIFIES
UNDERSOWED	UNDERSTUDIES	UNDERUTILIZING	UNDESCENDIBLE	UNDIGNIFYING
UNDERSOWING	UNDERSTUDY	UNDERVALUATION	UNDESCRIBABLE	UNDIMINISHABLE
UNDERSPEND	UNDERSTUDYING	UNDERVALUATIONS	UNDESCRIBED	UNDIMINISHED
UNDERSPENDING	UNDERSUBSCRIBED	UNDERVALUE	UNDESCRIED	UNDIPLOMATIC
UNDERSPENDINGS	UNDERSUPPLIED	UNDERVALUED	UNDESERVED	UNDIRECTED
UNDERSPENDS	UNDERSUPPLIES	UNDERVALUER	UNDESERVEDLY	UNDISAPPOINTING
UNDERSPENT	UNDERSUPPLY	UNDERVALUERS	UNDESERVEDNESS	UNDISCERNED
UNDERSPINS	UNDERSUPPLYING	UNDERVALUES	UNDESERVER	UNDISCERNEDLY
UNDERSTAFFED	UNDERSURFACE	UNDERVALUING	UNDESERVERS	UNDISCERNIBLE
UNDERSTAFFING	UNDERSURFACES	UNDERVESTS	UNDESERVES	UNDISCERNIBLY
UNDERSTAFFINGS	UNDERTAKABLE	UNDERVIEWER	UNDESERVING	UNDISCERNING
UNDERSTAND	UNDERTAKEN	UNDERVIEWERS	UNDESERVINGLY	UNDISCERNINGS
UNDERSTANDABLE	UNDERTAKER	UNDERVOICE	UNDESIGNATED	UNDISCHARGED
UNDERSTANDABLY	UNDERTAKERS	UNDERVOICES	UNDESIGNED	UNDISCIPLINABLE
UNDERSTANDED	UNDERTAKES	UNDERVOTES	UNDESIGNEDLY	UNDISCIPLINE
UNDERSTANDER	UNDERTAKING	UNDERWATER	UNDESIGNEDNESS	UNDISCIPLINED
UNDERSTANDERS	UNDERTAKINGS	UNDERWATERS	UNDESIGNING	UNDISCIPLINES
UNDERSTANDING	UNDERTAXED	UNDERWEARS	UNDESIRABILITY	UNDISCLOSED
UNDERSTANDINGLY	UNDERTAXES	UNDERWEIGHT	UNDESIRABLE	UNDISCOMFITED
UNDERSTANDINGS	UNDERTAXING	UNDERWEIGHTS	UNDESIRABLENESS	UNDISCORDANT
UNDERSTANDS	UNDERTENANCIES	UNDERWHELM	UNDESIRABLES	UNDISCORDING
UNDERSTATE	UNDERTENANCY	UNDERWHELMED	UNDESIRABLY	UNDISCOURAGED
UNDERSTATED	UNDERTENANT	UNDERWHELMING	UNDESIRING	UNDISCOVERABLE
UNDERSTATEDLY	UNDERTENANTS	UNDERWHELMS	UNDESIROUS	UNDISCOVERABLY
UNDERSTATEMENT	UNDERTHINGS	UNDERWINGS	UNDESPAIRING	UNDISCOVERED
UNDERSTATEMENTS	UNDERTHIRST	UNDERWIRED	UNDESPAIRINGLY	UNDISCUSSABLE
UNDERSTATES	UNDERTHIRSTS	UNDERWIRES	UNDESPATCHED	UNDISCUSSED
UNDERSTATING	UNDERTHRUST	UNDERWIRING	UNDESPOILED	UNDISCUSSIBLE
UNDERSTEER	UNDERTHRUSTING	UNDERWIRINGS	UNDESTROYED	UNDISGUISABLE
UNDERSTEERED	UNDERTHRUSTS	UNDERWOODS	UNDETECTABLE	UNDISGUISED
UNDERSTEERING	UNDERTIMED	UNDERWOOLS	UNDETECTED	UNDISGUISEDLY
UNDERSTEERS	UNDERTIMES	UNDERWORKED	UNDETERMINABLE	UNDISHONOURED
UNDERSTOCK	UNDERTINTS	UNDERWORKER	UNDETERMINATE	UNDISMANTLED
UNDERSTOCKED	UNDERTONED	UNDERWORKERS	UNDETERMINATION	UNDISMAYED

UNDISORDERED	UNDOUBTING	UNEDUCABLE	UNENTERPRISING	UNEXCITABLE
UNDISPATCHED	UNDOUBTINGLY	UNEDUCATED	UNENTERTAINED	UNEXCITING
UNDISPENSED	UNDRAINABLE	UNEFFECTED	UNENTERTAINING	UNEXCLUDED
UNDISPOSED	UNDRAMATIC	UNELABORATE	UNENTHRALLED	UNEXCLUSIVE
UNDISPUTABLE	UNDRAMATICALLY	UNELABORATED	UNENTHUSIASTIC	UNEXCLUSIVELY
UNDISPUTED	UNDRAMATISED	UNELECTABLE	UNENTITLED	UNEXECUTED
UNDISPUTEDLY	UNDRAMATIZED	UNELECTRIFIED	UNENVIABLE	UNEXEMPLIFIED
UNDISSEMBLED	UNDREADING	UNEMBARRASSED	UNENVIABLY	UNEXERCISED
UNDISSOCIATED	UNDREAMING	UNEMBELLISHED	UNEQUALLED	UNEXHAUSTED
UNDISSOLVED	UNDRESSING	UNEMBITTERED	UNEQUIPPED	UNEXPANDED
UNDISSOLVING	UNDRESSINGS	UNEMBODIED	UNEQUITABLE	UNEXPECTANT
UNDISTEMPERED	UNDRINKABLE	UNEMOTIONAL	UNEQUIVOCABLE	UNEXPECTED
UNDISTILLED	UNDRIVEABLE	UNEMOTIONALLY	UNEQUIVOCABLY	UNEXPECTEDLY
UNDISTINCTIVE	UNDROOPING	UNEMOTIONED	UNEQUIVOCAL	UNEXPECTEDNESS
UNDISTINGUISHED	UNDROSSIER	UNEMPHASISED	UNEQUIVOCALLY	UNEXPENDED
UNDISTORTED	UNDROSSIEST	UNEMPHASIZED	UNEQUIVOCALNESS	UNEXPENSIVE
UNDISTRACTED	UNDULANCES	UNEMPHATIC	UNERASABLE	UNEXPENSIVELY
UNDISTRACTEDLY	UNDULANCIES	UNEMPHATICALLY	UNERRINGLY	UNEXPERIENCED
UNDISTRACTING	UNDULATELY	UNEMPIRICAL	UNERRINGNESS	UNEXPERIENT
UNDISTRIBUTED	UNDULATING	UNEMPLOYABILITY	UNERRINGNESSES	UNEXPIATED
UNDISTURBED	UNDULATINGLY	UNEMPLOYABLE	UNESCAPABLE	UNEXPLAINABLE
UNDISTURBEDLY	UNDULATION	UNEMPLOYABLES	UNESCORTED	UNEXPLAINED
UNDISTURBING	UNDULATIONIST	UNEMPLOYED	UNESSENCED	UNEXPLODED
UNDIVERSIFIED	UNDULATIONISTS	UNEMPLOYEDS	UNESSENCES	UNEXPLOITED
UNDIVERTED	UNDULATIONS	UNEMPLOYMENT	UNESSENCING	UNEXPLORED
UNDIVERTING	UNDULATORS	UNEMPLOYMENTS	UNESSENTIAL	UNEXPRESSED
UNDIVESTED	UNDULATORY	UNENCHANTED	UNESSENTIALLY	UNEXPRESSIBLE
UNDIVESTEDLY	UNDUPLICATED	UNENCLOSED	UNESSENTIALS	UNEXPRESSIVE
UNDIVIDABLE	UNDUTIFULLY	UNENCOURAGING	UNESTABLISHED	UNEXPUGNABLE
UNDIVIDEDLY	UNDUTIFULNESS	UNENCUMBERED	UNESTHETIC	UNEXPURGATED
UNDIVIDEDNESS	UNDUTIFULNESSES	UNENDANGERED	UNETHICALLY	UNEXTENDED
UNDIVIDEDNESSES	UNDYINGNESS	UNENDEARED	UNEVALUATED	UNEXTENUATED
UNDIVORCED	UNDYINGNESSES	UNENDEARING	UNEVANGELICAL	UNEXTINGUISHED
UNDIVULGED	UNEARMARKED	UNENDINGLY	UNEVENNESS	UNEXTRAORDINARY
UNDOCTORED	UNEARTHING	UNENDINGNESS	UNEVENNESSES	UNFADINGLY
UNDOCTRINAIRE	UNEARTHLIER	UNENDINGNESSES	UNEVENTFUL	UNFADINGNESS
UNDOCTRINAIRES	UNEARTHLIEST	UNENDURABLE	UNEVENTFULLY	UNFADINGNESSES
UNDOCUMENTED	UNEARTHLINESS	UNENDURABLENESS	UNEVENTFULNESS	UNFAILINGLY
UNDOGMATIC	UNEARTHLINESSES	UNENDURABLY	UNEVIDENCED	UNFAILINGNESS
UNDOGMATICALLY	UNEASINESS	UNENFORCEABLE	UNEXACTING	UNFAILINGNESSES
UNDOMESTIC	UNEASINESSES	UNENFORCED	UNEXAGGERATED	UNFAIRNESS
UNDOMESTICATE	UNEATABLENESS	UNENJOYABLE	UNEXAMINED	UNFAIRNESSES
UNDOMESTICATED	UNEATABLENESSES	UNENLARGED	UNEXAMPLED	UNFAITHFUL
UNDOMESTICATES	UNECCENTRIC	UNENLIGHTENED	UNEXCAVATED	UNFAITHFULLY
UNDOMESTICATING	UNECLIPSED	UNENLIGHTENING	UNEXCELLED	UNFAITHFULNESS
UNDOUBLING	UNECOLOGICAL	UNENQUIRING	UNEXCEPTIONABLE	UNFALLIBLE
UNDOUBTABLE	UNECONOMIC	UNENRICHED	UNEXCEPTIONABLY	UNFALSIFIABLE
UNDOUBTEDLY	UNECONOMICAL	UNENSLAVED	UNEXCEPTIONAL	UNFALTERING
UNDOUBTFUL	UNEDIFYING	UNENTAILED	UNEXCEPTIONALLY	UNFALTERINGLY

UNFAMILIAR	UNFEUDALISING	UNFORCEDLY	UNFRAUGHTS	UNGENEROSITY
UNFAMILIARITIES	UNFEUDALIZE	UNFORCIBLE	UNFREEDOMS	UNGENEROUS
UNFAMILIARITY	UNFEUDALIZED	UNFORDABLE	UNFREEZING	UNGENEROUSLY
UNFAMILIARLY	UNFEUDALIZES	UNFOREBODING	UNFREEZINGS	UNGENITURED
UNFANCIEST	UNFEUDALIZING	UNFOREKNOWABLE	UNFREQUENT	UNGENTEELLY
UNFASHIONABLE	UNFILIALLY	UNFOREKNOWN	UNFREQUENTED	UNGENTILITIES
UNFASHIONABLY	UNFILLABLE	UNFORESEEABLE	UNFREQUENTING	UNGENTILITY
UNFASHIONED	UNFILLETED	UNFORESEEING	UNFREQUENTLY	UNGENTLEMANLIER
UNFASTENED	UNFILTERABLE	UNFORESEEN	UNFREQUENTS	UNGENTLEMANLIKE
UNFASTENING	UNFILTERED	UNFORESKINNED	UNFRIENDED	UNGENTLEMANLY
UNFASTIDIOUS	UNFILTRABLE	UNFORESTED	UNFRIENDEDNESS	UNGENTLENESS
UNFATHERED	UNFINDABLE	UNFORETOLD	UNFRIENDING	UNGENTLENESSES
UNFATHERLIER	UNFINISHED	UNFOREWARNED	UNFRIENDLIER	UNGENTLEST
UNFATHERLIEST	UNFINISHING	UNFORFEITED	UNFRIENDLIEST	UNGENTRIFIED
UNFATHERLY	UNFINISHINGS	UNFORGETTABLE	UNFRIENDLILY	UNGENUINENESS
UNFATHOMABLE	UNFITNESSES	UNFORGETTABLY	UNFRIENDLINESS	UNGENUINENESSES
UNFATHOMABLY	UNFITTEDNESS	UNFORGIVABLE	UNFRIENDLY	UNGERMINATED
UNFATHOMED	UNFITTEDNESSES	UNFORGIVABLY	UNFRIENDSHIP	UNGETATABLE
UNFAULTIER	UNFITTINGLY	UNFORGIVEN	UNFRIENDSHIPS	UNGHOSTLIER
UNFAULTIEST	UNFIXEDNESS	UNFORGIVENESS	UNFRIGHTED	UNGHOSTLIEST
UNFAVORABLE	UNFIXEDNESSES	UNFORGIVENESSES	UNFRIGHTENED	UNGIMMICKY
UNFAVORABLENESS	UNFIXITIES	UNFORGIVING	UNFRIVOLOUS	UNGIRTHING
UNFAVORABLY	UNFLAGGING	UNFORGIVINGNESS	UNFROCKING	UNGLACIATED
UNFAVORITE	UNFLAGGINGLY	UNFORGOTTEN	UNFRUCTUOUS	UNGLAMORISED
UNFAVOURABLE	UNFLAMBOYANT	UNFORMALISED	UNFRUITFUL	UNGLAMORIZED
UNFAVOURABLY	UNFLAPPABILITY	UNFORMALIZED	UNFRUITFULLY	UNGLAMOROUS
UNFAVOURED	UNFLAPPABLE	UNFORMATTED	UNFRUITFULNESS	UNGLITZIER
UNFAVOURITE	UNFLAPPABLENESS	UNFORMIDABLE	UNFULFILLABLE	UNGLITZIEST
UNFEARFULLY	UNFLAPPABLY	UNFORMULATED	UNFULFILLED	UNGODLIEST
UNFEASIBLE	UNFLASHIER	UNFORSAKEN	UNFULFILLING	UNGODLINESS
UNFEATHERED	UNFLASHIEST	UNFORTHCOMING	UNFUNNIEST	UNGODLINESSES
UNFEATURED	UNFLATTERING	UNFORTIFIED	UNFURNISHED	UNGOVERNABLE
UNFEELINGLY	UNFLATTERINGLY	UNFORTUNATE	UNFURNISHES	UNGOVERNABLY
UNFEELINGNESS	UNFLAVORED	UNFORTUNATELY	UNFURNISHING	UNGOVERNED
UNFEELINGNESSES	UNFLAVOURED	UNFORTUNATENESS	UNFURROWED	UNGRACEFUL
UNFEIGNEDLY	UNFLESHING	UNFORTUNATES	UNFUSSIEST	UNGRACEFULLY
UNFEIGNEDNESS	UNFLESHLIER	UNFORTUNED	UNGAINLIER	UNGRACEFULNESS
UNFEIGNEDNESSES	UNFLESHLIEST	UNFORTUNES	UNGAINLIEST	UNGRACIOUS
UNFEIGNING	UNFLINCHING	UNFOSSILIFEROUS	UNGAINLINESS	UNGRACIOUSLY
UNFELLOWED	UNFLINCHINGLY	UNFOSSILISED	UNGAINLINESSES	UNGRACIOUSNESS
UNFEMININE	UNFLUSHING	UNFOSSILIZED	UNGAINSAID	UNGRAMMATIC
UNFERMENTED	UNFLUSTERED	UNFOSTERED	UNGAINSAYABLE	UNGRAMMATICAL
UNFERTILISED	UNFOCUSSED	UNFOUGHTEN	UNGALLANTLY	UNGRAMMATICALLY
UNFERTILIZED	UNFOLDINGS	UNFOUNDEDLY	UNGARMENTED	UNGRASPABLE
UNFETTERED	UNFOLDMENT	UNFOUNDEDNESS	UNGARNERED	UNGRATEFUL
UNFETTERING	UNFOLDMENTS	UNFOUNDEDNESSES	UNGARNISHED	UNGRATEFULLY
UNFEUDALISE	UNFOLLOWED	UNFRANCHISED	UNGARTERED	UNGRATEFULNESS
UNFEUDALISED	UNFOLLOWING	UNFRAUGHTED	UNGATHERED	UNGRATIFIED
UNFEUDALISES	UNFORBIDDEN	UNFRAUGHTING	UNGENEROSITIES	UNGREEDIER

U

UNGREEDIEST	UNHARMFULLY	UNHOMELIEST	UNIDEALISMS	UNIMAGINABLY
UNGREENEST	UNHARMONIOUS	UNHOMELIKE	UNIDEALISTIC	UNIMAGINATIVE
UNGROUNDED	UNHARNESSED	UNHOMOGENISED	UNIDENTIFIABLE	UNIMAGINATIVELY
UNGROUNDEDLY	UNHARNESSES	UNHOMOGENIZED	UNIDENTIFIED	UNIMAGINED
UNGROUNDEDNESS	UNHARNESSING	UNHONOURED	UNIDEOLOGICAL	UNIMMORTAL
UNGROUPING	UNHARVESTED	UNHOPEFULLY	UNIDIMENSIONAL	UNIMMUNISED
UNGRUDGING	UNHASTIEST	UNHOSPITABLE	UNIDIOMATIC	UNIMMUNIZED
UNGRUDGINGLY	UNHATTINGS	UNHOUSELED	UNIDIOMATICALLY	UNIMOLECULAR
UNGUARDEDLY	UNHAZARDED	UNHOUZZLED	UNIDIRECTIONAL	UNIMPAIRED
UNGUARDEDNESS	UNHAZARDOUS	UNHUMANISE	UNIFICATION	UNIMPARTED
UNGUARDEDNESSES	UNHEALABLE	UNHUMANISED	UNIFICATIONS	UNIMPASSIONED
UNGUARDING	UNHEALTHFUL	UNHUMANISES	UNIFLOROUS	UNIMPEACHABLE
UNGUENTARIA	UNHEALTHFULLY	UNHUMANISING	UNIFOLIATE	UNIMPEACHABLY
UNGUENTARIES	UNHEALTHFULNESS	UNHUMANIZE	UNIFOLIOLATE	UNIMPEACHED
UNGUENTARIUM	UNHEALTHIER	UNHUMANIZED	UNIFORMEST	UNIMPEDEDLY
UNGUENTARY	UNHEALTHIEST	UNHUMANIZES	UNIFORMING	UNIMPLORED
UNGUERDONED	UNHEALTHILY	UNHUMANIZING	UNIFORMITARIAN	UNIMPORTANCE
UNGUESSABLE	UNHEALTHINESS	UNHUMOROUS	UNIFORMITARIANS	UNIMPORTANCES
UNGUICULATE	UNHEALTHINESSES	UNHURRIEDLY	UNIFORMITIES	UNIMPORTANT
UNGUICULATED	UNHEARSING	UNHURRYING	UNIFORMITY	UNIMPORTUNED
UNGUICULATES	UNHEARTING	UNHURTFULLY	UNIFORMNESS	UNIMPOSING
UNGUILTIER	UNHEEDEDLY	UNHURTFULNESS	UNIFORMNESSES	UNIMPREGNATED
UNGUILTIEST	UNHEEDFULLY	UNHURTFULNESSES	UNIGENITURE	UNIMPRESSED
UNGULIGRADE	UNHEEDIEST	UNHUSBANDED	UNIGENITURES	UNIMPRESSIBLE
UNHABITABLE	UNHEEDINGLY	UNHYDROLYSED	UNIGNORABLE	UNIMPRESSIVE
UNHABITUATED	UNHELMETED	UNHYDROLYZED	UNILABIATE	UNIMPRISONED
UNHACKNEYED	UNHELPABLE	UNHYGIENIC	UNILATERAL	UNIMPROVED
UNHALLOWED	UNHELPFULLY	UNHYPHENATED	UNILATERALISM	UNIMPUGNABLE
UNHALLOWING	UNHELPFULNESS	UNHYSTERICAL	UNILATERALISMS	UNINAUGURATED
UNHAMPERED	UNHELPFULNESSES	UNHYSTERICALLY	UNILATERALIST	UNINCHANTED
UNHANDIEST	UNHERALDED	UNIAXIALLY	UNILATERALISTS	UNINCLOSED
UNHANDINESS	UNHEROICAL	UNICAMERAL	UNILATERALITIES	UNINCORPORATED
UNHANDINESSES	UNHEROICALLY	UNICAMERALISM	UNILATERALITY	UNINCUMBERED
UNHANDSELLED	UNHESITATING	UNICAMERALISMS	UNILATERALLY	UNINDEARED
UNHANDSOME	UNHESITATINGLY	UNICAMERALIST	UNILINGUAL	UNINDENTED
UNHANDSOMELY	UNHIDEBOUND	UNICAMERALISTS	UNILINGUALISM	UNINDICTED
UNHANDSOMENESS	UNHINDERED	UNICAMERALLY	UNILINGUALISMS	UNINFECTED
UNHAPPENED	UNHINGEMENT	UNICELLULAR	UNILINGUALIST	UNINFLAMED
UNHAPPENING	UNHINGEMENTS	UNICELLULARITY	UNILINGUALISTS	UNINFLAMMABLE
UNHAPPENINGS	UNHISTORIC	UNICENTRAL	UNILINGUALS	UNINFLATED
UNHAPPIEST	UNHISTORICAL	UNICOLORATE	UNILITERAL	UNINFLECTED
UNHAPPINESS	UNHITCHING	UNICOLORED	UNILLUMINATED	UNINFLUENCED
UNHAPPINESSES	UNHOARDING	UNICOLOROUS	UNILLUMINATING	UNINFLUENTIAL
UNHAPPYING	UNHOLINESS	UNICOLOURED	UNILLUMINED	UNINFORCEABLE
UNHARBOURED	UNHOLINESSES	UNICOSTATE	UNILLUSIONED	UNINFORCED
UNHARBOURING	UNHOLSTERED	UNICYCLING	UNILLUSTRATED	UNINFORMATIVE
UNHARBOURS	UNHOLSTERING	UNICYCLIST	UNILOBULAR	UNINFORMATIVELY
UNHARDENED	UNHOLSTERS	UNICYCLISTS	UNILOCULAR	UNINFORMED
UNHARDIEST	UNHOMELIER	UNIDEALISM	UNIMAGINABLE	UNINFORMING

UNINGRATIATING	UNINTOXICATING	UNITISATIONS	UNKENNELLING	UNLEAVENED
UNINHABITABLE	UNINTRODUCED	UNITIZATION	UNKINDLIER	UNLEISURED
UNINHABITED	UNINUCLEAR	UNITIZATIONS	UNKINDLIEST	UNLEISURELY
UNINHIBITED	UNINUCLEATE	UNIVALENCE	UNKINDLINESS	UNLESSONED
UNINHIBITEDLY	UNINVENTIVE	UNIVALENCES	UNKINDLINESSES	UNLETTABLE
UNINHIBITEDNESS	UNINVESTED	UNIVALENCIES	UNKINDNESS	UNLETTERED
UNINITIATE	UNINVIDIOUS	UNIVALENCY	UNKINDNESSES	UNLEVELING
UNINITIATED	UNINVITING	UNIVALENTS	UNKINGLIER	UNLEVELLED
UNINITIATES	UNINVOLVED	UNIVALVULAR	UNKINGLIEST	UNLEVELLING
UNINOCULATED	UNIONISATION	UNIVARIANT	UNKINGLIKE	UNLIBERATED
UNINQUIRING	UNIONISATIONS	UNIVARIATE	UNKNIGHTED	UNLIBIDINOUS
UNINQUISITIVE	UNIONISERS	UNIVERSALISABLE	UNKNIGHTING	UNLICENSED
UNINSCRIBED	UNIONISING	UNIVERSALISE	UNKNIGHTLIER	UNLIFELIKE
UNINSPECTED	UNIONISTIC	UNIVERSALISED	UNKNIGHTLIEST	UNLIGHTENED
UNINSPIRED	UNIONIZATION	UNIVERSALISES	UNKNIGHTLINESS	UNLIGHTSOME
UNINSPIRING	UNIONIZATIONS	UNIVERSALISING	UNKNIGHTLY	UNLIKEABLE
UNINSTALLED	UNIONIZERS	UNIVERSALISM	UNKNITTING	UNLIKELIER
UNINSTALLING	UNIONIZING	UNIVERSALISMS	UNKNOTTING	UNLIKELIEST
UNINSTALLS	UNIPARENTAL	UNIVERSALIST	UNKNOWABILITIES	UNLIKELIHOOD
UNINSTRUCTED	UNIPARENTALLY	UNIVERSALISTIC	UNKNOWABILITY	UNLIKELIHOODS
UNINSTRUCTIVE	UNIPARTITE	UNIVERSALISTS	UNKNOWABLE	UNLIKELINESS
UNINSULATED	UNIPERSONAL	UNIVERSALITIES	UNKNOWABLENESS	UNLIKELINESSES
UNINSURABLE	UNIPERSONALITY	UNIVERSALITY	UNKNOWABLES	UNLIKENESS
UNINSUREDS	UNIPOLARITIES	UNIVERSALIZABLE	UNKNOWABLY	UNLIKENESSES
UNINTEGRATED	UNIPOLARITY	UNIVERSALIZE	UNKNOWINGLY	UNLIMBERED
UNINTELLECTUAL	UNIQUENESS	UNIVERSALIZED	UNKNOWINGNESS	UNLIMBERING
UNINTELLIGENCE	UNIQUENESSES	UNIVERSALIZES	UNKNOWINGNESSES	UNLIMITEDLY
UNINTELLIGENCES	UNIRONICALLY	UNIVERSALIZING	UNKNOWINGS	UNLIMITEDNESS
UNINTELLIGENT	UNIRRADIATED	UNIVERSALLY	UNKNOWLEDGEABLE	UNLIMITEDNESSES
UNINTELLIGENTLY	UNIRRIGATED	UNIVERSALNESS	UNKNOWNNESS	UNLIQUEFIED
UNINTELLIGIBLE	UNISEPTATE	UNIVERSALNESSES	UNKNOWNNESSES	UNLIQUIDATED
UNINTELLIGIBLY	UNISERIALLY	UNIVERSALS	UNLABELLED	UNLIQUORED
UNINTENDED	UNISERIATE	UNIVERSITARIAN	UNLABORING	UNLISTENABLE
UNINTENTIONAL	UNISERIATELY	UNIVERSITIES	UNLABORIOUS	UNLISTENED
UNINTENTIONALLY	UNISEXUALITIES	UNIVERSITY	UNLABOURED	UNLISTENING
UNINTEREST	UNISEXUALITY	UNIVOCALLY	UNLABOURING	UNLITERARY
UNINTERESTED	UNISEXUALLY	UNIVOLTINE	UNLADYLIKE	UNLIVEABLE
UNINTERESTEDLY	UNISONALLY	UNJAUNDICED	UNLAMENTED	UNLIVELIER
UNINTERESTING	UNISONANCE	UNJOINTING	UNLATCHING	UNLIVELIEST
UNINTERESTINGLY	UNISONANCES	UNJUSTIFIABLE	UNLAUNDERED	UNLIVELINESS
UNINTERESTS	UNITARIANISM	UNJUSTIFIABLY	UNLAWFULLY	UNLIVELINESSES
UNINTERMITTED	UNITARIANISMS	UNJUSTIFIED	UNLAWFULNESS	UNLOADINGS
UNINTERMITTEDLY	UNITARIANS	UNJUSTNESS	UNLAWFULNESSES	UNLOCALISED
UNINTERMITTING	UNITARITIES	UNJUSTNESSES	UNLEARNABLE	UNLOCALIZED
UNINTERPRETABLE	UNITEDNESS	UNKEMPTNESS	UNLEARNEDLY	UNLOCKABLE
UNINTERPRETED	UNITEDNESSES	UNKEMPTNESSES	UNLEARNEDNESS	UNLOOSENED
UNINTERRUPTED	UNITHOLDER	UNKENNELED	UNLEARNEDNESSES	UNLOOSENING
UNINTERRUPTEDLY	UNITHOLDERS	UNKENNELING	UNLEARNING	UNLORDLIER
UNINTIMIDATED	UNITISATION	UNKENNELLED	UNLEASHING	UNLORDLIEST

UNLOVEABLE	UNMASKINGS	UNMERITING	UNMORTISING	UNNILHEXIUM
UNLOVELIER	UNMASTERED	UNMERRIEST	UNMOTHERLIER	UNNILHEXIUMS
UNLOVELIEST	UNMATCHABLE	UNMETABOLISED	UNMOTHERLIEST	UNNILPENTIUM
UNLOVELINESS	UNMATCHING	UNMETABOLIZED	UNMOTHERLY	UNNILPENTIUMS
UNLOVELINESSES	UNMATERIAL	UNMETALLED	UNMOTIVATED	UNNILQUADIUM
UNLOVERLIKE	UNMATERIALISED	UNMETAPHORICAL	UNMOULDING	UNNILQUADIUMS
UNLOVINGLY	UNMATERIALIZED	UNMETAPHYSICAL	UNMOUNTING	UNNILSEPTIUM
UNLOVINGNESS	UNMATERNAL	UNMETHODICAL	UNMOVEABLE	UNNILSEPTIUMS
UNLOVINGNESSES	UNMATHEMATICAL	UNMETHODISED	UNMOVEABLY	UNNOISIEST
UNLUCKIEST	UNMATRICULATED	UNMETHODIZED	UNMUFFLING	UNNOTICEABLE
UNLUCKINESS	UNMEANINGLY	UNMETRICAL	UNMUNITIONED	UNNOTICEABLY
UNLUCKINESSES	UNMEANINGNESS	UNMILITARY	UNMURMURING	UNNOTICING
UNLUXURIANT	UNMEANINGNESSES	UNMINDFULLY	UNMURMURINGLY	UNNOURISHED
UNLUXURIOUS	UNMEASURABLE	UNMINDFULNESS	UNMUSICALLY	UNNOURISHING
UNMACADAMISED	UNMEASURABLY	UNMINDFULNESSES	UNMUSICALNESS	UNNUMBERED
UNMACADAMIZED	UNMEASURED	UNMINGLING	UNMUSICALNESSES	UNNURTURED
UNMAGNIFIED	UNMEASUREDLY	UNMINISTERIAL	UNMUTILATED	UNOBEDIENT
UNMAIDENLY	UNMECHANIC	UNMIRACULOUS	UNMUZZLING	UNOBJECTIONABLE
UNMAILABLE	UNMECHANICAL	UNMISSABLE	UNMUZZLINGS	UNOBJECTIONABLY
UNMAINTAINABLE	UNMECHANISE	UNMISTAKABLE	UNMYELINATED	UNOBLIGING
UNMAINTAINED	UNMECHANISED	UNMISTAKABLY	UNNAMEABLE	UNOBNOXIOUS
UNMALICIOUS	UNMECHANISES	UNMISTAKEABLE	UNNATIVING	UNOBSCURED
UNMALICIOUSLY	UNMECHANISING	UNMISTAKEABLY	UNNATURALISE	UNOBSERVABLE
UNMALLEABILITY	UNMECHANIZE	UNMISTRUSTFUL	UNNATURALISED	UNOBSERVABLES
UNMALLEABLE	UNMECHANIZED	UNMITERING	UNNATURALISES	UNOBSERVANCE
UNMANACLED	UNMECHANIZES	UNMITIGABLE	UNNATURALISING	UNOBSERVANCES
UNMANACLES	UNMECHANIZING	UNMITIGABLY	UNNATURALIZE	UNOBSERVANT
UNMANACLING	UNMEDIATED	UNMITIGATED	UNNATURALIZED	UNOBSERVED
UNMANAGEABLE	UNMEDICATED	UNMITIGATEDLY	UNNATURALIZES	UNOBSERVEDLY
UNMANAGEABLY	UNMEDICINABLE	UNMITIGATEDNESS	UNNATURALIZING	UNOBSERVING
UNMANFULLY	UNMEDITATED	UNMODERATED	UNNATURALLY	UNOBSTRUCTED
UNMANIPULATED	UNMEETNESS	UNMODERNISED	UNNATURALNESS	UNOBSTRUCTIVE
UNMANLIEST	UNMEETNESSES	UNMODERNIZED	UNNATURALNESSES	UNOBTAINABLE
UNMANLINESS	UNMELLOWED	UNMODIFIABLE	UNNAVIGABLE	UNOBTAINED
UNMANLINESSES	UNMELODIOUS	UNMODIFIED	UNNAVIGATED	UNOBTRUSIVE
UNMANNERED	UNMELODIOUSNESS	UNMODULATED	UNNECESSARILY	UNOBTRUSIVELY
UNMANNEREDLY	UNMEMORABLE	UNMOISTENED	UNNECESSARINESS	UNOBTRUSIVENESS
UNMANNERLIER	UNMEMORABLY	UNMOLESTED	UNNECESSARY	UNOCCUPIED
UNMANNERLIEST	UNMENTIONABLE	UNMONITORED	UNNEEDFULLY	UNOFFENDED
UNMANNERLINESS	UNMENTIONABLES	UNMORALISED	UNNEGOTIABLE	UNOFFENDING
UNMANNERLY	UNMENTIONABLY	UNMORALISING	UNNEIGHBORED	UNOFFENSIVE
UNMANTLING	UNMENTIONED	UNMORALITIES	UNNEIGHBORLY	UNOFFICERED
UNMANUFACTURED	UNMERCENARY	UNMORALITY	UNNEIGHBOURED	UNOFFICIAL
UNMARKETABLE	UNMERCHANTABLE	UNMORALIZED	UNNEIGHBOURLY	UNOFFICIALLY
UNMARRIABLE	UNMERCIFUL	UNMORALIZING	UNNERVINGLY	UNOFFICIOUS
UNMARRIAGEABLE	UNMERCIFULLY	UNMORTGAGED	UNNEUROTIC	UNOPENABLE
UNMARRIEDS	UNMERCIFULNESS	UNMORTIFIED	UNNEWSWORTHIER	UNOPERATIVE
UNMARRYING	UNMERITABLE	UNMORTISED	UNNEWSWORTHIEST	UNOPPOSING
UNMASCULINE	UNMERITEDLY	UNMORTISES	UNNEWSWORTHY	UNOPPRESSIVE

UNORDAINED	UNPARDONING	UNPERILOUS	UNPLUGGING	UNPREDICTABLES
UNORDERING	UNPARENTAL	UNPERISHABLE	UNPLUMBING	UNPREDICTABLY
UNORDINARY	UNPARENTED	UNPERISHED	UNPOETICAL	UNPREDICTED
UNORGANISED	UNPARLIAMENTARY	UNPERISHING	UNPOETICALLY	UNPREDICTING
UNORGANIZED	UNPASSABLE	UNPERJURED	UNPOETICALNESS	UNPREDICTS
UNORIGINAL	UNPASSABLENESS	UNPERPETRATED	UNPOISONED	UNPREFERRED
UNORIGINALITIES	UNPASSIONATE	UNPERPLEXED	UNPOISONING	UNPREGNANT
UNORIGINALITY	UNPASSIONED	UNPERPLEXES	UNPOLARISABLE	UNPREJUDICED
UNORIGINALS	UNPASTEURISED	UNPERPLEXING	UNPOLARISED	UNPREJUDICEDLY
UNORIGINATE	UNPASTEURIZED	UNPERSECUTED	UNPOLARIZABLE	UNPRELATICAL
UNORIGINATED	UNPASTORAL	UNPERSONED	UNPOLARIZED	UNPREMEDITABLE
UNORNAMENTAL	UNPASTURED	UNPERSONING	UNPOLICIED	UNPREMEDITATED
UNORNAMENTED	UNPATENTABLE	UNPERSUADABLE	UNPOLISHABLE	UNPREMEDITATION
UNORTHODOX	UNPATENTED	UNPERSUADED	UNPOLISHED	UNPREOCCUPIED
UNORTHODOXIES	UNPATHETIC	UNPERSUASIVE	UNPOLISHES	UNPREPARED
UNORTHODOXLY	UNPATHWAYED	UNPERTURBED	UNPOLISHING	UNPREPAREDLY
UNORTHODOXY	UNPATRIOTIC	UNPERVERTED	UNPOLITELY	UNPREPAREDNESS
UNOSSIFIED	UNPATRIOTICALLY	UNPERVERTING	UNPOLITENESS	UNPREPARES
UNOSTENTATIOUS	UNPATRONISED	UNPERVERTS	UNPOLITENESSES	UNPREPARING
UNOVERCOME	UNPATRONIZED	UNPHILOSOPHIC	UNPOLITICAL	UNPREPOSSESSED
UNOVERTHROWN	UNPATTERNED	UNPHILOSOPHICAL	UNPOLLUTED	UNPREPOSSESSING
UNOXIDISED	UNPAVILIONED	UNPHONETIC	UNPOPULARITIES	UNPRESCRIBED
UNOXIDIZED	UNPEACEABLE	UNPICKABLE	UNPOPULARITY	UNPRESENTABLE
UNOXYGENATED	UNPEACEABLENESS	UNPICTURESQUE	UNPOPULARLY	UNPRESSURED
UNPACIFIED	UNPEACEFUL	UNPIGMENTED	UNPOPULATED	UNPRESSURISED
UNPACKINGS	UNPEACEFULLY	UNPILLARED	UNPOPULOUS	UNPRESSURIZED
UNPAINTABLE	UNPEDANTIC	UNPILLOWED	UNPORTIONED	UNPRESUMING
UNPAINTING	UNPEDIGREED	UNPITIFULLY	UNPOSSESSED	UNPRESUMPTUOUS
UNPALATABILITY	UNPEERABLE	UNPITIFULNESS	UNPOSSESSING	UNPRETENDING
UNPALATABLE	UNPENSIONED	UNPITIFULNESSES	UNPOSSIBLE	UNPRETENDINGLY
UNPALATABLY	UNPEOPLING	UNPITYINGLY	UNPOWDERED	UNPRETENTIOUS
UNPAMPERED	UNPEPPERED	UNPLAITING	UNPRACTICABLE	UNPRETENTIOUSLY
UNPANELLED	UNPERCEIVABLE	UNPLASTERED	UNPRACTICAL	UNPRETTIER
UNPANELLING	UNPERCEIVABLY	UNPLASTICISED	UNPRACTICALITY	UNPRETTIEST
UNPANNELLED	UNPERCEIVED	UNPLASTICIZED	UNPRACTICALLY	UNPRETTINESS
UNPANNELLING	UNPERCEIVEDLY	UNPLAUSIBLE	UNPRACTICALNESS	UNPRETTINESSES
UNPAPERING	UNPERCEPTIVE	UNPLAUSIBLY	UNPRACTICED	UNPREVAILING
UNPARADISE	UNPERCHING	UNPLAUSIVE	UNPRACTICEDNESS	UNPREVENTABLE
UNPARADISED	UNPERFECTED	UNPLAYABLE	UNPRACTISED	UNPREVENTED
UNPARADISES	UNPERFECTION	UNPLEASANT	UNPRACTISEDNESS	UNPRIESTED
UNPARADISING	UNPERFECTIONS	UNPLEASANTLY	UNPRAISEWORTHY	UNPRIESTING
UNPARAGONED	UNPERFECTLY	UNPLEASANTNESS	UNPRAISING	UNPRIESTLIER
UNPARALLEL	UNPERFECTNESS	UNPLEASANTRIES	UNPREACHED	UNPRIESTLIEST
UNPARALLELED	UNPERFECTNESSES	UNPLEASANTRY	UNPREACHES	UNPRIESTLY
UNPARASITISED	UNPERFORATED	UNPLEASING	UNPREACHING	UNPRINCELIER
UNPARASITIZED	UNPERFORMABLE	UNPLEASINGLY	UNPRECEDENTED	UNPRINCELIEST
UNPARDONABLE	UNPERFORMED	UNPLEASURABLE	UNPRECEDENTEDLY	UNPRINCELY
UNPARDONABLY	UNPERFORMING	UNPLEASURABLY	UNPREDESTINED	UNPRINCIPLED
UNPARDONED	UNPERFUMED	UNPLOUGHED	UNPREDICTABLE	UNPRINTABLE

U

UNPRINTABLENESS	UNPROSPEROUS	UNQUALITIED	UNREALISMS	UNRECURING
UNPRINTABLY	UNPROSPEROUSLY	UNQUANTIFIABLE	UNREALISTIC	UNRECYCLABLE
UNPRISABLE	UNPROTECTED	UNQUANTIFIED	UNREALISTICALLY	UNRECYCLABLES
UNPRISONED	UNPROTECTEDNESS	UNQUANTISED	UNREALITIES	UNREDEEMABLE
UNPRISONING	UNPROTESTANTISE	UNQUANTIZED	UNREALIZABLE	UNREDEEMED
UNPRIVILEGED	UNPROTESTANTIZE	UNQUARRIED	UNREALIZED	UNREDRESSED
UNPRIZABLE	UNPROTESTED	UNQUEENING	UNREALIZES	UNREDUCIBLE
UNPROBLEMATIC	UNPROTESTING	UNQUEENLIER	UNREALIZING	UNREFLECTED
UNPROCEDURAL	UNPROVABLE	UNQUEENLIEST	UNREASONABLE	UNREFLECTING
UNPROCESSED	UNPROVIDED	UNQUEENLIKE	UNREASONABLY	UNREFLECTINGLY
UNPROCLAIMED	UNPROVIDEDLY	UNQUENCHABLE	UNREASONED	UNREFLECTIVE
UNPROCURABLE	UNPROVIDENT	UNQUENCHABLY	UNREASONING	UNREFLECTIVELY
UNPRODUCED	UNPROVIDES	UNQUENCHED	UNREASONINGLY	UNREFORMABLE
UNPRODUCTIVE	UNPROVIDING	UNQUESTIONABLE	UNRECALLABLE	UNREFORMED
UNPRODUCTIVELY	UNPROVISIONED	UNQUESTIONABLY	UNRECALLED	UNREFRACTED
UNPRODUCTIVITY	UNPROVOCATIVE	UNQUESTIONED	UNRECALLING	UNREFRESHED
UNPROFANED	UNPROVOKED	UNQUESTIONING	UNRECAPTURABLE	UNREFRESHING
UNPROFESSED	UNPROVOKEDLY	UNQUESTIONINGLY	UNRECEIPTED	UNREFRIGERATED
UNPROFESSIONAL	UNPROVOKES	UNQUICKENED	UNRECEIVED	UNREGARDED
UNPROFESSIONALS	UNPROVOKING	UNQUIETEST	UNRECEPTIVE	UNREGARDING
UNPROFITABILITY	UNPUBLICISED	UNQUIETING	UNRECIPROCATED	UNREGENERACIES
UNPROFITABLE	UNPUBLICIZED	UNQUIETNESS	UNRECKONABLE	UNREGENERACY
UNPROFITABLY	UNPUBLISHABLE	UNQUIETNESSES	UNRECKONED	UNREGENERATE
UNPROFITED	UNPUBLISHED	UNQUOTABLE	UNRECLAIMABLE	UNREGENERATED
UNPROFITING	UNPUCKERED	UNRANSOMED	UNRECLAIMABLY	UNREGENERATELY
UNPROFITINGS	UNPUCKERING	UNRATIFIED	UNRECLAIMED	UNREGENERATES
UNPROGRAMMABLE	UNPUNCTUAL	UNRAVELING	UNRECOGNISABLE	UNREGIMENTED
UNPROGRAMMED	UNPUNCTUALITIES	UNRAVELLED	UNRECOGNISABLY	UNREGISTERED
UNPROGRESSIVE	UNPUNCTUALITY	UNRAVELLER	UNRECOGNISED	UNREGRETTED
UNPROGRESSIVELY	UNPUNCTUATED	UNRAVELLERS	UNRECOGNISING	UNREGULATED
UNPROHIBITED	UNPUNISHABLE	UNRAVELLING	UNRECOGNIZABLE	UNREHEARSED
UNPROJECTED	UNPUNISHABLY	UNRAVELLINGS	UNRECOGNIZABLY	UNREINFORCED
UNPROLIFIC	UNPUNISHED	UNRAVELMENT	UNRECOGNIZED	UNREJOICED
UNPROMISED	UNPURCHASABLE	UNRAVELMENTS	UNRECOGNIZING	UNREJOICING
UNPROMISING	UNPURCHASEABLE	UNRAVISHED	UNRECOLLECTED	UNRELATIVE
UNPROMISINGLY	UNPURCHASED	UNREACHABLE	UNRECOMMENDABLE	UNRELEASED
UNPROMPTED	UNPURIFIED	UNREACTIVE	UNRECOMMENDED	UNRELENTING
UNPRONOUNCEABLE	UNPURPOSED	UNREADABILITIES	UNRECOMPENSED	UNRELENTINGLY
UNPRONOUNCED	UNPURVAIDE	UNREADABILITY	UNRECONCILABLE	UNRELENTINGNESS
UNPROPERLY	UNPURVEYED	UNREADABLE	UNRECONCILABLY	UNRELENTOR
UNPROPERTIED	UNPUTDOWNABLE	UNREADABLENESS	UNRECONCILED	UNRELENTORS
UNPROPHETIC	UNPUZZLING	UNREADABLY	UNRECONCILIABLE	UNRELIABILITIES
UNPROPHETICAL	UNQUALIFIABLE	UNREADIEST	UNRECONSTRUCTED	UNRELIABILITY
UNPROPITIOUS	UNQUALIFIED	UNREADINESS	UNRECORDED	UNRELIABLE
UNPROPITIOUSLY	UNQUALIFIEDLY	UNREADINESSES	UNRECOUNTED	UNRELIABLENESS
UNPROPORTIONATE	UNQUALIFIEDNESS	UNREALISABLE	UNRECOVERABLE	UNRELIABLY
UNPROPORTIONED	UNQUALIFIES	UNREALISED	UNRECOVERABLY	UNRELIEVABLE
UNPROPOSED	UNQUALIFYING	UNREALISES	UNRECOVERED	UNRELIEVED
UNPROPPING	UNQUALITED	UNREALISING	UNRECTIFIED	UNRELIEVEDLY

UNRELIGIOUS	UNREPRESSED	UNRESTRAINEDLY	UNRIVETTING	UNSATISFACTION
UNRELIGIOUSLY	UNREPRIEVABLE	UNRESTRAINT	UNROADWORTHY	UNSATISFACTIONS
UNRELISHED	UNREPRIEVED	UNRESTRAINTS	UNROMANISED	UNSATISFACTORY
UNRELUCTANT	UNREPRIMANDED	UNRESTRICTED	UNROMANIZED	UNSATISFIABLE
UNREMAINING	UNREPROACHED	UNRESTRICTEDLY	UNROMANTIC	UNSATISFIED
UNREMARKABLE	UNREPROACHFUL	UNRETARDED	UNROMANTICAL	UNSATISFIEDNESS
UNREMARKABLY	UNREPROACHING	UNRETENTIVE	UNROMANTICALLY	UNSATISFYING
UNREMARKED	UNREPRODUCIBLE	UNRETIRING	UNROMANTICISED	UNSATURATE
UNREMEDIED	UNREPROVABLE	UNRETOUCHED	UNROMANTICIZED	UNSATURATED
UNREMEMBERED	UNREPROVED	UNRETURNABLE	UNROOSTING	UNSATURATES
UNREMEMBERING	UNREPROVING	UNRETURNED	UNROUNDING	UNSATURATION
UNREMINISCENT	UNREPUGNANT	UNRETURNING	UNRUFFABLE	UNSATURATIONS
UNREMITTED	UNREPULSABLE	UNRETURNINGLY	UNRUFFLEDNESS	UNSAVORIER
UNREMITTEDLY	UNREQUESTED	UNREVEALABLE	UNRUFFLEDNESSES	UNSAVORIEST
UNREMITTENT	UNREQUIRED	UNREVEALED	UNRUFFLING	UNSAVORILY
UNREMITTENTLY	UNREQUISITE	UNREVEALING	UNRULIMENT	UNSAVORINESS
UNREMITTING	UNREQUITED	UNREVENGED	UNRULIMENTS	UNSAVORINESSES
UNREMITTINGLY	UNREQUITEDLY	UNREVENGEFUL	UNRULINESS	UNSAVOURIER
UNREMITTINGNESS	UNRESCINDED	UNREVEREND	UNRULINESSES	UNSAVOURIEST
UNREMORSEFUL	UNRESENTED	UNREVERENT	UNRUPTURED	UNSAVOURILY
UNREMORSEFULLY	UNRESENTFUL	UNREVERSED	UNSADDLING	UNSAVOURINESS
UNREMORSELESS	UNRESENTING	UNREVERTED	UNSAFENESS	UNSAVOURINESSES
UNREMOVABLE	UNRESERVED	UNREVIEWABLE	UNSAFENESSES	UNSAYABLES
UNREMUNERATIVE	UNRESERVEDLY	UNREVIEWED	UNSAFETIES	UNSCABBARD
UNRENDERED	UNRESERVEDNESS	UNREVOLUTIONARY	UNSAILORLIKE	UNSCABBARDED
UNRENOWNED	UNRESERVES	UNREWARDED	UNSAINTING	UNSCABBARDING
UNREPAIRABLE	UNRESISTANT	UNREWARDEDLY	UNSAINTLIER	UNSCABBARDS
UNREPAIRED	UNRESISTED	UNREWARDING	UNSAINTLIEST	UNSCALABLE
UNREPEALABLE	UNRESISTIBLE	UNRHETORICAL	UNSAINTLINESS	UNSCARIEST
UNREPEALED	UNRESISTING	UNRHYTHMIC	UNSAINTLINESSES	UNSCAVENGERED
UNREPEATABLE	UNRESISTINGLY	UNRHYTHMICAL	UNSALABILITIES	UNSCEPTRED
UNREPEATED	UNRESOLVABLE	UNRHYTHMICALLY	UNSALABILITY	UNSCHEDULED
UNREPELLED	UNRESOLVED	UNRIDDLEABLE	UNSALARIED	UNSCHOLARLIKE
UNREPENTANCE	UNRESOLVEDNESS	UNRIDDLERS	UNSALEABILITIES	UNSCHOLARLY
UNREPENTANCES	UNRESPECTABLE	UNRIDDLING	UNSALEABILITY	UNSCHOOLED
UNREPENTANT	UNRESPECTABLES	UNRIDEABLE	UNSALEABLE	UNSCIENTIFIC
UNREPENTANTLY	UNRESPECTED	UNRIGHTEOUS	UNSALEABLY	UNSCISSORED
UNREPENTED	UNRESPECTIVE	UNRIGHTEOUSLY	UNSALVAGEABLE	UNSCORCHED
UNREPENTING	UNRESPITED	UNRIGHTEOUSNESS	UNSANCTIFIED	UNSCOTTIFIED
UNREPENTINGLY	UNRESPONSIVE	UNRIGHTFUL	UNSANCTIFIES	UNSCRAMBLE
UNREPINING	UNRESPONSIVELY	UNRIGHTFULLY	UNSANCTIFY	UNSCRAMBLED
UNREPININGLY	UNRESTFULNESS	UNRIGHTFULNESS	UNSANCTIFYING	UNSCRAMBLER
UNREPLACEABLE	UNRESTFULNESSES	UNRIGHTING	UNSANCTIONED	UNSCRAMBLERS
UNREPLENISHED	UNRESTINGLY	UNRIPENESS	UNSANDALLED	UNSCRAMBLES
UNREPORTABLE	UNRESTINGNESS	UNRIPENESSES	UNSANITARY	UNSCRAMBLING
UNREPORTED	UNRESTINGNESSES	UNRIPPINGS	UNSATIABLE	UNSCRATCHED
UNREPOSEFUL	UNRESTORED	UNRIVALLED	UNSATIATED	UNSCREENED
UNREPOSING	UNRESTRAINABLE	UNRIVETING	UNSATIATING	UNSCREWING
UNREPRESENTED	UNRESTRAINED	UNRIVETTED	UNSATIRICAL	UNSCRIPTED

UNSCRIPTURAL	UNSENSITISED	UNSHIFTING	UNSMOKABLE	UNSPECIALISED
UNSCRIPTURALLY	UNSENSITIVE	UNSHINGLED	UNSMOOTHED	UNSPECIALIZED
UNSCRUPLED	UNSENSITIZED	UNSHIPPING	UNSMOOTHING	UNSPECIFIABLE
UNSCRUPULOSITY	UNSENSUALISE	UNSHOCKABLE	UNSMOTHERABLE	UNSPECIFIC
UNSCRUPULOUS	UNSENSUALISED	UNSHOOTING	UNSNAGGING	UNSPECIFICALLY
UNSCRUPULOUSLY	UNSENSUALISES	UNSHOTTING	UNSNAPPING	UNSPECIFIED
UNSCRUTINISED	UNSENSUALISING	UNSHOUTING	UNSNARLING	UNSPECTACLED
UNSCRUTINIZED	UNSENSUALIZE	UNSHOWERED	UNSNECKING	UNSPECTACULAR
UNSCULPTURED	UNSENSUALIZED	UNSHOWIEST	UNSOBERING	UNSPECULATIVE
UNSEALABLE	UNSENSUALIZES	UNSHRINKABLE	UNSOCIABILITIES	UNSPELLING
UNSEARCHABLE	UNSENSUALIZING	UNSHRINKING	UNSOCIABILITY	UNSPHERING
UNSEARCHABLES	UNSENTENCED	UNSHRINKINGLY	UNSOCIABLE	UNSPIRITED
UNSEARCHABLY	UNSENTIMENTAL	UNSHROUDED	UNSOCIABLENESS	UNSPIRITUAL
UNSEARCHED	UNSEPARABLE	UNSHROUDING	UNSOCIABLY	UNSPIRITUALISE
UNSEASONABLE	UNSEPARATED	UNSHRUBBED	UNSOCIALISED	UNSPIRITUALISED
UNSEASONABLY	UNSEPULCHRED	UNSHUNNABLE	UNSOCIALISM	UNSPIRITUALISES
UNSEASONED	UNSERIOUSNESS	UNSHUTTERED	UNSOCIALISMS	UNSPIRITUALIZE
UNSEASONEDNESS	UNSERIOUSNESSES	UNSHUTTERING	UNSOCIALITIES	UNSPIRITUALIZED
UNSEASONING	UNSERVICEABLE	UNSHUTTERS	UNSOCIALITY	UNSPIRITUALIZES
UNSEAWORTHINESS	UNSETTLEDLY	UNSHUTTING	UNSOCIALIZED	UNSPIRITUALLY
UNSEAWORTHY	UNSETTLEDNESS	UNSIGHTEDLY	UNSOCIALLY	UNSPLINTERABLE
UNSECONDED	UNSETTLEDNESSES	UNSIGHTING	UNSOCKETED	UNSPOOLING
UNSECRETED	UNSETTLEMENT	UNSIGHTLIER	UNSOCKETING	UNSPORTING
UNSECRETING	UNSETTLEMENTS	UNSIGHTLIEST	UNSOFTENED	UNSPORTSMANLIKE
UNSECTARIAN	UNSETTLING	UNSIGHTLINESS	UNSOFTENING	UNSPOTTEDNESS
UNSECTARIANISM	UNSETTLINGLY	UNSIGHTLINESSES	UNSOLDERED	UNSPOTTEDNESSES
UNSECTARIANISMS	UNSETTLINGS	UNSINEWING	UNSOLDERING	UNSPRINKLED
UNSECTARIANS	UNSHACKLED	UNSINKABLE	UNSOLDIERLIKE	UNSTABLENESS
UNSEEMINGS	UNSHACKLES	UNSINNOWED	UNSOLDIERLY	UNSTABLENESSES
UNSEEMLIER	UNSHACKLING	UNSISTERED	UNSOLICITED	UNSTABLEST
UNSEEMLIEST	UNSHADOWABLE	UNSISTERLINESS	UNSOLICITOUS	UNSTACKING
UNSEEMLINESS	UNSHADOWED	UNSISTERLY	UNSOLIDITIES	UNSTAIDNESS
UNSEEMLINESSES	UNSHADOWING	UNSIZEABLE	UNSOLIDITY	UNSTAIDNESSES
UNSEGMENTED	UNSHAKABLE	UNSKILFULLY	UNSOLVABLE	UNSTAINABLE
UNSEGREGATED	UNSHAKABLENESS	UNSKILFULNESS	UNSONSIEST	UNSTANCHABLE
UNSEISABLE	UNSHAKABLY	UNSKILFULNESSES	UNSOPHISTICATE	UNSTANCHED
UNSEIZABLE	UNSHAKEABLE	UNSKILLFUL	UNSOPHISTICATED	UNSTANDARDISED
UNSELECTED	UNSHAKEABLENESS	UNSKILLFULLY	UNSOUNDABLE	UNSTANDARDIZED
UNSELECTIVE	UNSHAKEABLY	UNSKILLFULNESS	UNSOUNDEST	UNSTARCHED
UNSELECTIVELY	UNSHAKENLY	UNSLAKABLE	UNSOUNDNESS	UNSTARCHES
UNSELFCONSCIOUS	UNSHAPELIER	UNSLEEPING	UNSOUNDNESSES	UNSTARCHING
UNSELFISHLY	UNSHAPELIEST	UNSLEEPINGS	UNSPARINGLY	UNSTARRIER
UNSELFISHNESS	UNSHARPENED	UNSLINGING	UNSPARINGNESS	UNSTARRIEST
UNSELFISHNESSES	UNSHEATHED	UNSLIPPING	UNSPARINGNESSES	UNSTARTLING
UNSELLABLE	UNSHEATHES	UNSLUICING	UNSPARRING	UNSTATESMANLIKE
UNSEMINARIED	UNSHEATHING	UNSLUMBERING	UNSPEAKABLE	UNSTATUTABLE
UNSENSATIONAL	UNSHELLING	UNSLUMBROUS	UNSPEAKABLENESS	UNSTATUTABLY
UNSENSIBLE	UNSHELTERED	UNSMILINGLY	UNSPEAKABLY	UNSTAUNCHABLE
UNSENSIBLY	UNSHIELDED	UNSMIRCHED	UNSPEAKING	UNSTAUNCHED

UNSTEADFAST	UNSTRINGING	UNSUPPORTED	UNSYMPATHISING	UNTERRIFYING
UNSTEADFASTLY	UNSTRIPPED	UNSUPPORTEDLY	UNSYMPATHIZING	UNTESTABLE
UNSTEADFASTNESS	UNSTRIPPING	UNSUPPOSABLE	UNSYMPATHY	UNTETHERED
UNSTEADIED	UNSTRUCTURED	UNSUPPRESSED	UNSYNCHRONISED	UNTETHERING
UNSTEADIER	UNSTUFFIER	UNSURFACED	UNSYNCHRONIZED	UNTHANKFUL
UNSTEADIES	UNSTUFFIEST	UNSURMISED	UNSYSTEMATIC	UNTHANKFULLY
UNSTEADIEST	UNSUBDUABLE	UNSURMOUNTABLE	UNSYSTEMATICAL	UNTHANKFULNESS
UNSTEADILY	UNSUBJECTED	UNSURPASSABLE	UNSYSTEMATISED	UNTHATCHED
UNSTEADINESS	UNSUBJECTING	UNSURPASSABLY	UNSYSTEMATIZED	UNTHATCHES
UNSTEADINESSES	UNSUBJECTS	UNSURPASSED	UNSYSTEMIC	UNTHATCHING
UNSTEADYING	UNSUBLIMATED	UNSURPRISED	UNTACKLING	UNTHEOLOGICAL
UNSTEELING	UNSUBLIMED	UNSURPRISING	UNTAILORED	UNTHEORETICAL
UNSTEPPING	UNSUBMERGED	UNSURPRISINGLY	UNTAINTEDLY	UNTHICKENED
UNSTERCORATED	UNSUBMISSIVE	UNSURVEYED	UNTAINTEDNESS	UNTHINKABILITY
UNSTEREOTYPED	UNSUBMITTING	UNSUSCEPTIBLE	UNTAINTEDNESSES	UNTHINKABLE
UNSTERILISED	UNSUBSCRIBE	UNSUSPECTED	UNTAINTING	UNTHINKABLENESS
UNSTERILIZED	UNSUBSCRIBED	UNSUSPECTEDLY	UNTALENTED	UNTHINKABLY
UNSTICKING	UNSUBSCRIBER	UNSUSPECTEDNESS	UNTAMABLENESS	UNTHINKING
UNSTIFFENED	UNSUBSCRIBERS	UNSUSPECTING	UNTAMABLENESSES	UNTHINKINGLY
UNSTIFFENING	UNSUBSCRIBES	UNSUSPECTINGLY	UNTAMEABLE	UNTHINKINGNESS
UNSTIFFENS	UNSUBSCRIBING	UNSUSPENDED	UNTAMEABLENESS	UNTHOROUGH
UNSTIGMATISED	UNSUBSIDISED	UNSUSPICION	UNTAMEABLY	UNTHOUGHTFUL
UNSTIGMATIZED	UNSUBSIDIZED	UNSUSPICIONS	UNTAMEDNESS	UNTHOUGHTFULLY
UNSTIMULATED	UNSUBSTANTIAL	UNSUSPICIOUS	UNTAMEDNESSES	UNTHREADED
UNSTINTING	UNSUBSTANTIALLY	UNSUSPICIOUSLY	UNTANGIBLE	UNTHREADING
UNSTINTINGLY	UNSUBSTANTIATED	UNSUSTAINABLE	UNTANGLING	UNTHREATENED
UNSTITCHED	UNSUBTLEST	UNSUSTAINABLY	UNTARNISHED	UNTHREATENING
UNSTITCHES	UNSUCCEEDED	UNSUSTAINED	UNTASTEFUL	UNTHRESHED
UNSTITCHING	UNSUCCESSES	UNSUSTAINING	UNTEACHABLE	UNTHRIFTIER
UNSTOCKING	UNSUCCESSFUL	UNSWADDLED	UNTEACHABLENESS	UNTHRIFTIEST
UNSTOCKINGED	UNSUCCESSFULLY	UNSWADDLES	UNTEACHING	UNTHRIFTIHEAD
UNSTOOPING	UNSUCCESSIVE	UNSWADDLING	UNTEARABLE	UNTHRIFTIHEADS
UNSTOPPABLE	UNSUCCOURED	UNSWALLOWED	UNTECHNICAL	UNTHRIFTILY
UNSTOPPABLY	UNSUFFERABLE	UNSWATHING	UNTELLABLE	UNTHRIFTINESS
UNSTOPPERED	UNSUFFICIENT	UNSWAYABLE	UNTEMPERED	UNTHRIFTINESSES
UNSTOPPERING	UNSUITABILITIES	UNSWEARING	UNTEMPERING	UNTHRIFTYHEAD
UNSTOPPERS	UNSUITABILITY	UNSWEARINGS	UNTENABILITIES	UNTHRIFTYHEADS
UNSTOPPING	UNSUITABLE	UNSWEETENED	UNTENABILITY	UNTHRIFTYHED
UNSTRAINED	UNSUITABLENESS	UNSWERVING	UNTENABLENESS	UNTHRIFTYHEDS
UNSTRAPPED	UNSUITABLY	UNSWERVINGLY	UNTENABLENESSES	UNTHRONING
UNSTRAPPING	UNSUMMERED	UNSYLLABLED	UNTENANTABLE	UNTIDINESS
UNSTRATIFIED	UNSUMMONED	UNSYMMETRICAL	UNTENANTED	UNTIDINESSES
UNSTREAMED	UNSUNNIEST	UNSYMMETRICALLY	UNTENANTING	UNTILLABLE
UNSTRENGTHENED	UNSUPERFLUOUS	UNSYMMETRIES	UNTENDERED	UNTIMBERED
UNSTRESSED	UNSUPERVISED	UNSYMMETRISED	UNTENDERLY	UNTIMELIER
UNSTRESSES	UNSUPPLENESS	UNSYMMETRIZED	UNTENTIEST	UNTIMELIEST
UNSTRESSING	UNSUPPLENESSES	UNSYMMETRY	UNTERMINATED	UNTIMELINESS
UNSTRIATED	UNSUPPLIED	UNSYMPATHETIC	UNTERRESTRIAL	UNTIMELINESSES
UNSTRINGED	UNSUPPORTABLE	UNSYMPATHIES	UNTERRIFIED	UNTIMEOUSLY

UNTINCTURED · UNTRENCHED · UNUTTERABLES · UNWARINESSES · UNWIELDIEST
UNTIRINGLY · UNTRENDIER · UNUTTERABLY · UNWARRANTABLE · UNWIELDILY
UNTOCHERED · UNTRENDIEST · UNVACCINATED · UNWARRANTABLY · UNWIELDINESS
UNTOGETHER · UNTRESPASSING · UNVALUABLE · UNWARRANTED · UNWIELDINESSES
UNTORMENTED · UNTRIMMING · UNVANQUISHABLE · UNWARRANTEDLY · UNWIELDLILY
UNTORTURED · UNTROUBLED · UNVANQUISHED · UNWASHEDNESS · UNWIELDLINESS
UNTOUCHABILITY · UNTROUBLEDLY · UNVARIABLE · UNWASHEDNESSES · UNWIELDLINESSES
UNTOUCHABLE · UNTRUENESS · UNVARIEGATED · UNWATCHABLE · UNWIFELIER
UNTOUCHABLES · UNTRUENESSES · UNVARNISHED · UNWATCHFUL · UNWIFELIEST
UNTOWARDLINESS · UNTRUSSERS · UNVARYINGLY · UNWATCHFULLY · UNWIFELIKE
UNTOWARDLY · UNTRUSSING · UNVEILINGS · UNWATCHFULNESS · UNWILLINGLY
UNTOWARDNESS · UNTRUSSINGS · UNVENDIBLE · UNWATERING · UNWILLINGNESS
UNTOWARDNESSES · UNTRUSTFUL · UNVENERABLE · UNWAVERING · UNWILLINGNESSES
UNTRACEABLE · UNTRUSTIER · UNVENTILATED · UNWAVERINGLY · UNWINDABLE
UNTRACKING · UNTRUSTIEST · UNVERACIOUS · UNWEAKENED · UNWINDINGS
UNTRACTABLE · UNTRUSTINESS · UNVERACITIES · UNWEAPONED · UNWINKINGLY
UNTRACTABLENESS · UNTRUSTINESSES · UNVERACITY · UNWEAPONING · UNWINNABLE
UNTRADITIONAL · UNTRUSTING · UNVERBALISED · UNWEARABLE · UNWINNOWED
UNTRADITIONALLY · UNTRUSTWORTHILY · UNVERBALIZED · UNWEARABLES · UNWISENESS
UNTRAMMELED · UNTRUSTWORTHY · UNVERIFIABILITY · UNWEARIABLE · UNWISENESSES
UNTRAMMELLED · UNTRUTHFUL · UNVERIFIABLE · UNWEARIABLY · UNWITCHING
UNTRAMPLED · UNTRUTHFULLY · UNVERIFIED · UNWEARIEDLY · UNWITHDRAWING
UNTRANQUIL · UNTRUTHFULNESS · UNVIOLATED · UNWEARIEDNESS · UNWITHERED
UNTRANSFERABLE · UNTUCKERED · UNVIRTUOUS · UNWEARIEDNESSES · UNWITHERING
UNTRANSFERRABLE · UNTUMULTUOUS · UNVIRTUOUSLY · UNWEARIEST · UNWITHHELD
UNTRANSFORMED · UNTUNABLENESS · UNVISITABLE · UNWEARYING · UNWITHHOLDEN
UNTRANSLATABLE · UNTUNABLENESSES · UNVISORING · UNWEARYINGLY · UNWITHHOLDING
UNTRANSLATABLY · UNTUNEABLE · UNVITIATED · UNWEATHERED · UNWITHSTOOD
UNTRANSLATED · UNTUNEABLENESS · UNVITRIFIABLE · UNWEDGABLE · UNWITNESSED
UNTRANSMIGRATED · UNTUNEABLY · UNVITRIFIED · UNWEDGEABLE · UNWITTIEST
UNTRANSMISSIBLE · UNTUNEFULLY · UNVIZARDED · UNWEETINGLY · UNWITTINGLY
UNTRANSMITTED · UNTUNEFULNESS · UNVIZARDING · UNWEIGHING · UNWITTINGNESS
UNTRANSMUTABLE · UNTUNEFULNESSES · UNVOCALISED · UNWEIGHTED · UNWITTINGNESSES
UNTRANSMUTED · UNTURNABLE · UNVOCALIZED · UNWEIGHTING · UNWOMANING
UNTRANSPARENT · UNTWISTING · UNVOICINGS · UNWEIGHTINGS · UNWOMANLIER
UNTRAVELED · UNTWISTINGS · UNVOYAGEABLE · UNWELCOMED · UNWOMANLIEST
UNTRAVELLED · UNTYPICALLY · UNVULGARISE · UNWELCOMELY · UNWOMANLINESS
UNTRAVERSABLE · UNTYREABLE · UNVULGARISED · UNWELCOMENESS · UNWOMANLINESSES
UNTRAVERSED · UNUNUNIUMS · UNVULGARISES · UNWELCOMENESSES · UNWONTEDLY
UNTREADING · UNUPLIFTED · UNVULGARISING · UNWELCOMING · UNWONTEDNESS
UNTREASURE · UNUSEFULLY · UNVULGARIZE · UNWELLNESS · UNWONTEDNESSES
UNTREASURED · UNUSEFULNESS · UNVULGARIZED · UNWELLNESSES · UNWORKABILITIES
UNTREASURES · UNUSEFULNESSES · UNVULGARIZES · UNWESTERNISED · UNWORKABILITY
UNTREASURING · UNUSUALNESS · UNVULGARIZING · UNWESTERNIZED · UNWORKABLE
UNTREATABLE · UNUSUALNESSES · UNVULNERABLE · UNWHISTLEABLE · UNWORKMANLIKE
UNTREMBLING · UNUTILISED · UNWANDERING · UNWHOLESOME · UNWORLDLIER
UNTREMBLINGLY · UNUTILIZED · UNWARENESS · UNWHOLESOMELY · UNWORLDLIEST
UNTREMENDOUS · UNUTTERABLE · UNWARENESSES · UNWHOLESOMENESS · UNWORLDLINESS
UNTREMULOUS · UNUTTERABLENESS · UNWARINESS · UNWIELDIER · UNWORLDLINESSES

UNWORSHIPFUL	UPGRADABILITIES	UPRIGHTEOUSLY	UPTITLINGS	URBANOLOGY
UNWORSHIPPED	UPGRADABILITY	UPRIGHTING	UPTRAINING	URCEOLUSES
UNWORTHIER	UPGRADABLE	UPRIGHTNESS	UPTURNINGS	UREDINIOSPORE
UNWORTHIES	UPGRADATION	UPRIGHTNESSES	UPVALUATION	UREDINIOSPORES
UNWORTHIEST	UPGRADATIONS	UPROARIOUS	UPVALUATIONS	UREDINIUMS
UNWORTHILY	UPGRADEABILITY	UPROARIOUSLY	UPWARDNESS	UREDIOSPORE
UNWORTHINESS	UPGRADEABLE	UPROARIOUSNESS	UPWARDNESSES	UREDIOSPORES
UNWORTHINESSES	UPGROWINGS	UPROOTEDNESS	UPWELLINGS	UREDOSORUS
UNWOUNDABLE	UPHEAPINGS	UPROOTEDNESSES	UPWHIRLING	UREDOSPORE
UNWRAPPING	UPHILLWARD	UPROOTINGS	URALITISATION	UREDOSPORES
UNWREATHED	UPHOARDING	UPSELLINGS	URALITISATIONS	UREOTELISM
UNWREATHES	UPHOISTING	UPSETTABLE	URALITISED	UREOTELISMS
UNWREATHING	UPHOLDINGS	UPSETTINGLY	URALITISES	URETERITIS
UNWRINKLED	UPHOLSTERED	UPSETTINGS	URALITISING	URETERITISES
UNWRINKLES	UPHOLSTERER	UPSHIFTING	URALITIZATION	URETHANING
UNWRINKLING	UPHOLSTERERS	UPSHOOTING	URALITIZATIONS	URETHRITIC
UNYIELDING	UPHOLSTERIES	UPSIDEOWNE	URALITIZED	URETHRITIDES
UNYIELDINGLY	UPHOLSTERING	UPSITTINGS	URALITIZES	URETHRITIS
UNYIELDINGNESS	UPHOLSTERS	UPSKILLING	URALITIZING	URETHRITISES
UPBRAIDERS	UPHOLSTERY	UPSKIRTING	URANALYSES	URETHROSCOPE
UPBRAIDING	UPHOLSTRESS	UPSKIRTINGS	URANALYSIS	URETHROSCOPES
UPBRAIDINGLY	UPHOLSTRESSES	UPSPEAKING	URANINITES	URETHROSCOPIC
UPBRAIDINGS	UPHOORDING	UPSPEARING	URANOGRAPHER	URETHROSCOPIES
UPBREAKING	UPKNITTING	UPSPRINGING	URANOGRAPHERS	URETHROSCOPY
UPBRINGING	UPLIFTINGLY	UPSTANDING	URANOGRAPHIC	URICOSURIC
UPBRINGINGS	UPLIFTINGS	UPSTANDINGNESS	URANOGRAPHICAL	URICOTELIC
UPBUILDERS	UPLIGHTERS	UPSTARTING	URANOGRAPHIES	URICOTELISM
UPBUILDING	UPLIGHTING	UPSTEPPING	URANOGRAPHIST	URICOTELISMS
UPBUILDINGS	UPLIGHTINGS	UPSTEPPINGS	URANOGRAPHISTS	URINAEMIAS
UPBUOYANCE	UPLINKINGS	UPSTIRRING	URANOGRAPHY	URINALYSES
UPBUOYANCES	UPMANSHIPS	UPSTREAMED	URANOLOGIES	URINALYSIS
UPBURSTING	UPMARKETED	UPSTREAMING	URANOMETRIES	URINATIONS
UPCATCHING	UPMARKETING	UPSTRETCHED	URANOMETRY	URINIFEROUS
UPCHEERING	UPPERCASED	UPSURGENCE	URANOPLASTIES	URINIPAROUS
UPCHUCKING	UPPERCASES	UPSURGENCES	URANOPLASTY	URINOGENITAL
UPCLIMBING	UPPERCASING	UPSWARMING	URBANENESS	URINOLOGIES
UPCOUNTRIES	UPPERCLASSMAN	UPSWEEPING	URBANENESSES	URINOMETER
UPCURRENTS	UPPERCLASSMEN	UPSWELLING	URBANISATION	URINOMETERS
UPDATEABLE	UPPERCUTTING	UPSWINGING	URBANISATIONS	URINOSCOPIES
UPDRAGGING	UPPERPARTS	UPTALKINGS	URBANISING	URINOSCOPY
UPDRAGGINGS	UPPERWORKS	UPTHROWING	URBANISTIC	UROBILINOGEN
UPDRAUGHTS	UPPISHNESS	UPTHRUSTED	URBANISTICALLY	UROBILINOGENS
UPFILLINGS	UPPISHNESSES	UPTHRUSTING	URBANITIES	UROBOROSES
UPFLASHING	UPPITINESS	UPTHUNDERED	URBANIZATION	UROCHORDAL
UPFLINGING	UPPITINESSES	UPTHUNDERING	URBANIZATIONS	UROCHORDATE
UPFOLLOWED	UPPITYNESS	UPTHUNDERS	URBANIZING	UROCHORDATES
UPFOLLOWING	UPPITYNESSES	UPTIGHTEST	URBANOLOGIES	UROCHROMES
UPGATHERED	UPPROPPING	UPTIGHTNESS	URBANOLOGIST	URODYNAMICS
UPGATHERING	UPREACHING	UPTIGHTNESSES	URBANOLOGISTS	UROGENITAL

U

UROGENITALS	URTICATIONS	USUCAPIONS	UTILISABLE	UTOPIANIZED
UROGRAPHIC	USABILITIES	USUCAPTIBLE	UTILISATION	UTOPIANIZER
UROGRAPHIES	USABLENESS	USUCAPTING	UTILISATIONS	UTOPIANIZERS
UROKINASES	USABLENESSES	USUCAPTION	UTILITARIAN	UTOPIANIZES
UROLAGNIAS	USEABILITIES	USUCAPTIONS	UTILITARIANISE	UTOPIANIZING
UROLITHIASES	USEABILITY	USUFRUCTED	UTILITARIANISED	UTRICULARIA
UROLITHIASIS	USEABLENESS	USUFRUCTING	UTILITARIANISES	UTRICULARIAS
UROLOGICAL	USEABLENESSES	USUFRUCTUARIES	UTILITARIANISM	UTRICULATE
UROLOGISTS	USEFULNESS	USUFRUCTUARY	UTILITARIANISMS	UTRICULITIS
UROPOIESES	USEFULNESSES	USURIOUSLY	UTILITARIANIZE	UTRICULITISES
UROPOIESIS	USELESSNESS	USURIOUSNESS	UTILITARIANIZED	UTTERABLENESS
UROPYGIUMS	USELESSNESSES	USURIOUSNESSES	UTILITARIANIZES	UTTERABLENESSES
UROSCOPIES	USHERESSES	USURPATION	UTILITARIANS	UTTERANCES
UROSCOPIST	USHERETTES	USURPATIONS	UTILIZABLE	UTTERMOSTS
UROSCOPISTS	USHERSHIPS	USURPATIVE	UTILIZATION	UTTERNESSES
UROSTEGITE	USQUEBAUGH	USURPATORY	UTILIZATIONS	UVAROVITES
UROSTEGITES	USQUEBAUGHS	USURPATURE	UTOPIANISE	UVULITISES
UROSTHENIC	USTILAGINEOUS	USURPATURES	UTOPIANISED	UXORICIDAL
UROSTOMIES	USTILAGINOUS	USURPINGLY	UTOPIANISER	UXORICIDES
URTICACEOUS	USTULATING	UTERECTOMIES	UTOPIANISERS	UXORILOCAL
URTICARIAL	USTULATION	UTERECTOMY	UTOPIANISES	UXORIOUSLY
URTICARIAS	USTULATIONS	UTERITISES	UTOPIANISING	UXORIOUSNESS
URTICARIOUS	USUALNESSES	UTEROGESTATION	UTOPIANISM	UXORIOUSNESSES
URTICATING	USUCAPIENT	UTEROGESTATIONS	UTOPIANISMS	
URTICATION	USUCAPIENTS	UTEROTOMIES	UTOPIANIZE	

U

V

VACANTNESS	VAGABONDAGE	VALEDICTIONS	VALVASSORS	VANQUISHES
VACANTNESSES	VAGABONDAGES	VALEDICTORIAN	VALVULITIS	VANQUISHING
VACATIONED	VAGABONDED	VALEDICTORIANS	VALVULITISES	VANQUISHMENT
VACATIONER	VAGABONDING	VALEDICTORIES	VAMPIRISED	VANQUISHMENTS
VACATIONERS	VAGABONDISE	VALEDICTORY	VAMPIRISES	VANTAGELESS
VACATIONING	VAGABONDISED	VALENTINES	VAMPIRISING	VANTBRACES
VACATIONIST	VAGABONDISES	VALERIANACEOUS	VAMPIRISMS	VANTBRASSES
VACATIONISTS	VAGABONDISH	VALETUDINARIAN	VAMPIRIZED	VAPIDITIES
VACATIONLAND	VAGABONDISING	VALETUDINARIANS	VAMPIRIZES	VAPIDNESSES
VACATIONLANDS	VAGABONDISM	VALETUDINARIES	VAMPIRIZING	VAPORABILITIES
VACATIONLESS	VAGABONDISMS	VALETUDINARY	VANADIATES	VAPORABILITY
VACCINATED	VAGABONDIZE	VALIANCIES	VANADINITE	VAPORESCENCE
VACCINATES	VAGABONDIZED	VALIANTNESS	VANADINITES	VAPORESCENCES
VACCINATING	VAGABONDIZES	VALIANTNESSES	VANASPATIS	VAPORESCENT
VACCINATION	VAGABONDIZING	VALIDATING	VANCOMYCIN	VAPORETTOS
VACCINATIONS	VAGARIOUSLY	VALIDATION	VANCOMYCINS	VAPORIFORM
VACCINATOR	VAGILITIES	VALIDATIONS	VANDALISATION	VAPORIMETER
VACCINATORS	VAGINECTOMIES	VALIDATORS	VANDALISATIONS	VAPORIMETERS
VACCINATORY	VAGINECTOMY	VALIDATORY	VANDALISED	VAPORISABLE
VACCINIUMS	VAGINICOLINE	VALIDITIES	VANDALISES	VAPORISATION
VACCINOLOGIES	VAGINICOLOUS	VALIDNESSES	VANDALISING	VAPORISATIONS
VACCINOLOGIST	VAGINISMUS	VALLATIONS	VANDALISMS	VAPORISERS
VACCINOLOGISTS	VAGINISMUSES	VALLECULAE	VANDALISTIC	VAPORISHNESS
VACCINOLOGY	VAGINITIDES	VALLECULAR	VANDALIZATION	VAPORISHNESSES
VACILLATED	VAGINITISES	VALLECULAS	VANDALIZATIONS	VAPORISING
VACILLATES	VAGOTOMIES	VALLECULATE	VANDALIZED	VAPORIZABLE
VACILLATING	VAGOTONIAS	VALORISATION	VANDALIZES	VAPORIZATION
VACILLATINGLY	VAGOTROPIC	VALORISATIONS	VANDALIZING	VAPORIZATIONS
VACILLATION	VAGRANCIES	VALORISING	VANGUARDISM	VAPORIZERS
VACILLATIONS	VAGRANTNESS	VALORIZATION	VANGUARDISMS	VAPORIZING
VACILLATOR	VAGRANTNESSES	VALORIZATIONS	VANGUARDIST	VAPOROSITIES
VACILLATORS	VAGUENESSES	VALORIZING	VANGUARDISTS	VAPOROSITY
VACILLATORY	VAINGLORIED	VALOROUSLY	VANISHINGLY	VAPOROUSLY
VACUATIONS	VAINGLORIES	VALPOLICELLA	VANISHINGS	VAPOROUSNESS
VACUOLATED	VAINGLORIOUS	VALPOLICELLAS	VANISHMENT	VAPOROUSNESSES
VACUOLATION	VAINGLORIOUSLY	VALPROATES	VANISHMENTS	VAPORWARES
VACUOLATIONS	VAINGLORYING	VALUABLENESS	VANITORIES	VAPORWAVES
VACUOLISATION	VAINNESSES	VALUABLENESSES	VANPOOLING	VAPOURABILITIES
VACUOLISATIONS	VAIVODESHIP	VALUATIONAL	VANPOOLINGS	VAPOURABILITY
VACUOLIZATION	VAIVODESHIPS	VALUATIONALLY	VANQUISHABLE	VAPOURABLE
VACUOLIZATIONS	VAJAZZLING	VALUATIONS	VANQUISHED	VAPOURIEST
VACUOUSNESS	VAJAZZLINGS	VALUELESSNESS	VANQUISHER	VAPOURINGLY
VACUOUSNESSES	VALEDICTION	VALUELESSNESSES	VANQUISHERS	VAPOURINGS

VAPOURISHNESS	VARIOLATOR	VASECTOMISING	VATICINATORS	VEGETATIVELY
VAPOURISHNESSES	VARIOLATORS	VASECTOMIZE	VATICINATORY	VEGETATIVENESS
VAPOURLESS	VARIOLISATION	VASECTOMIZED	VAUDEVILLE	VEGGIEBURGER
VAPOURWARE	VARIOLISATIONS	VASECTOMIZES	VAUDEVILLEAN	VEGGIEBURGERS
VAPOURWARES	VARIOLITES	VASECTOMIZING	VAUDEVILLEANS	VEHEMENCES
VAPOURWAVE	VARIOLITIC	VASELINING	VAUDEVILLES	VEHEMENCIES
VAPOURWAVES	VARIOLIZATION	VASOACTIVE	VAUDEVILLIAN	VEHEMENTLY
VAPULATING	VARIOLIZATIONS	VASOACTIVITIES	VAUDEVILLIANS	VEILLEUSES
VAPULATION	VARIOLOIDS	VASOACTIVITY	VAUDEVILLIST	VEINSTONES
VAPULATIONS	VARIOMETER	VASOCONSTRICTOR	VAUDEVILLISTS	VEINSTUFFS
VARIABILITIES	VARIOMETERS	VASODILATATION	VAULTINGLY	VELARISATION
VARIABILITY	VARIOUSNESS	VASODILATATIONS	VAUNTERIES	VELARISATIONS
VARIABLENESS	VARIOUSNESSES	VASODILATATORY	VAUNTINGLY	VELARISING
VARIABLENESSES	VARISCITES	VASODILATION	VAVASORIES	VELARIZATION
VARIATIONAL	VARITYPING	VASODILATIONS	VECTOGRAPH	VELARIZATIONS
VARIATIONALLY	VARITYPIST	VASODILATOR	VECTOGRAPHS	VELARIZING
VARIATIONIST	VARITYPISTS	VASODILATORS	VECTORIALLY	VELDSCHOEN
VARIATIONISTS	VARLETESSES	VASODILATORY	VECTORINGS	VELDSCHOENS
VARIATIONS	VARLETRIES	VASOINHIBITOR	VECTORISATION	VELDSKOENS
VARICELLAR	VARNISHERS	VASOINHIBITORS	VECTORISATIONS	VELITATION
VARICELLAS	VARNISHIER	VASOINHIBITORY	VECTORISED	VELITATIONS
VARICELLATE	VARNISHIEST	VASOPRESSIN	VECTORISES	VELLEITIES
VARICELLOID	VARNISHING	VASOPRESSINS	VECTORISING	VELLENAGES
VARICELLOUS	VARNISHINGS	VASOPRESSOR	VECTORIZATION	VELLICATED
VARICOCELE	VARSOVIENNE	VASOPRESSORS	VECTORIZATIONS	VELLICATES
VARICOCELES	VARSOVIENNES	VASOSPASMS	VECTORIZED	VELLICATING
VARICOLORED	VASCULARISATION	VASOSPASTIC	VECTORIZES	VELLICATION
VARICOLOURED	VASCULARISE	VASOTOCINS	VECTORIZING	VELLICATIONS
VARICOSITIES	VASCULARISED	VASOTOMIES	VECTORSCOPE	VELLICATIVE
VARICOSITY	VASCULARISES	VASSALAGES	VECTORSCOPES	VELOCIMETER
VARICOTOMIES	VASCULARISING	VASSALESSES	VEDUTISTAS	VELOCIMETERS
VARICOTOMY	VASCULARITIES	VASSALISED	VEGANISING	VELOCIMETRIES
VARIEDNESS	VASCULARITY	VASSALISES	VEGANIZING	VELOCIMETRY
VARIEDNESSES	VASCULARIZATION	VASSALISING	VEGEBURGER	VELOCIPEDE
VARIEGATED	VASCULARIZE	VASSALIZED	VEGEBURGERS	VELOCIPEDEAN
VARIEGATES	VASCULARIZED	VASSALIZES	VEGETABLES	VELOCIPEDEANS
VARIEGATING	VASCULARIZES	VASSALIZING	VEGETABLIER	VELOCIPEDED
VARIEGATION	VASCULARIZING	VASSALLING	VEGETABLIEST	VELOCIPEDER
VARIEGATIONS	VASCULARLY	VASSALRIES	VEGETARIAN	VELOCIPEDERS
VARIEGATOR	VASCULATURE	VASTIDITIES	VEGETARIANISM	VELOCIPEDES
VARIEGATORS	VASCULATURES	VASTITUDES	VEGETARIANISMS	VELOCIPEDIAN
VARIETALLY	VASCULIFORM	VASTNESSES	VEGETARIANS	VELOCIPEDIANS
VARIFOCALS	VASCULITIDES	VATICINATE	VEGETATING	VELOCIPEDING
VARIFORMLY	VASCULITIS	VATICINATED	VEGETATINGS	VELOCIPEDIST
VARIOLATED	VASCULITISES	VATICINATES	VEGETATION	VELOCIPEDISTS
VARIOLATES	VASECTOMIES	VATICINATING	VEGETATIONAL	VELOCIRAPTOR
VARIOLATING	VASECTOMISE	VATICINATION	VEGETATIONS	VELOCIRAPTORS
VARIOLATION	VASECTOMISED	VATICINATIONS	VEGETATIOUS	VELOCITIES
VARIOLATIONS	VASECTOMISES	VATICINATOR	VEGETATIVE	VELODROMES

VELOUTINES	VENESECTION	VENTRICULUS	VERBALISTS	VERIFIABLY
VELUTINOUS	VENESECTIONS	VENTRILOQUAL	VERBALITIES	VERIFICATION
VELVETEENED	VENGEANCES	VENTRILOQUIAL	VERBALIZATION	VERIFICATIONS
VELVETEENS	VENGEFULLY	VENTRILOQUIALLY	VERBALIZATIONS	VERIFICATIVE
VELVETIEST	VENGEFULNESS	VENTRILOQUIES	VERBALIZED	VERIFICATORY
VELVETINESS	VENGEFULNESSES	VENTRILOQUISE	VERBALIZER	VERISIMILAR
VELVETINESSES	VENGEMENTS	VENTRILOQUISED	VERBALIZERS	VERISIMILARLY
VELVETINGS	VENIALITIES	VENTRILOQUISES	VERBALIZES	VERISIMILITIES
VELVETLIKE	VENIALNESS	VENTRILOQUISING	VERBALIZING	VERISIMILITUDE
VENALITIES	VENIALNESSES	VENTRILOQUISM	VERBALLING	VERISIMILITUDES
VENATICALLY	VENIPUNCTURE	VENTRILOQUISMS	VERBARIANS	VERISIMILITY
VENATIONAL	VENIPUNCTURES	VENTRILOQUIST	VERBASCUMS	VERISIMILOUS
VENATORIAL	VENISECTION	VENTRILOQUISTIC	VERBENACEOUS	VERITABLENESS
VENDETTIST	VENISECTIONS	VENTRILOQUISTS	VERBERATED	VERITABLENESSES
VENDETTISTS	VENOGRAPHIC	VENTRILOQUIZE	VERBERATES	VERJUICING
VENDIBILITIES	VENOGRAPHICAL	VENTRILOQUIZED	VERBERATING	VERKRAMPTE
VENDIBILITY	VENOGRAPHIES	VENTRILOQUIZES	VERBERATION	VERKRAMPTES
VENDIBLENESS	VENOGRAPHY	VENTRILOQUIZING	VERBERATIONS	VERMEILING
VENDIBLENESSES	VENOLOGIES	VENTRILOQUOUS	VERBICIDES	VERMEILLED
VENDITATION	VENOMOUSLY	VENTRILOQUY	VERBIFICATION	VERMEILLES
VENDITATIONS	VENOMOUSNESS	VENTRIPOTENT	VERBIFICATIONS	VERMEILLING
VENDITIONS	VENOMOUSNESSES	VENTROLATERAL	VERBIFYING	VERMICELLI
VENEERINGS	VENOSCLEROSES	VENTROMEDIAL	VERBIGERATE	VERMICELLIS
VENEFICALLY	VENOSCLEROSIS	VENTURESOME	VERBIGERATED	VERMICIDAL
VENEFICIOUS	VENOSITIES	VENTURESOMELY	VERBIGERATES	VERMICIDES
VENEFICIOUSLY	VENOUSNESS	VENTURESOMENESS	VERBIGERATING	VERMICULAR
VENEFICOUS	VENOUSNESSES	VENTURINGLY	VERBIGERATION	VERMICULARLY
VENEFICOUSLY	VENTIDUCTS	VENTURINGS	VERBIGERATIONS	VERMICULATE
VENENATING	VENTIFACTS	VENTUROUSLY	VERBOSENESS	VERMICULATED
VENEPUNCTURE	VENTILABLE	VENTUROUSNESS	VERBOSENESSES	VERMICULATES
VENEPUNCTURES	VENTILATED	VENTUROUSNESSES	VERBOSITIES	VERMICULATING
VENERABILITIES	VENTILATES	VERACIOUSLY	VERDANCIES	VERMICULATION
VENERABILITY	VENTILATING	VERACIOUSNESS	VERDIGRISED	VERMICULATIONS
VENERABLENESS	VENTILATION	VERACIOUSNESSES	VERDIGRISES	VERMICULES
VENERABLENESSES	VENTILATIONS	VERACITIES	VERDIGRISING	VERMICULITE
VENERABLES	VENTILATIVE	VERANDAHED	VERDURELESS	VERMICULITES
VENERATING	VENTILATOR	VERAPAMILS	VERGEBOARD	VERMICULOUS
VENERATION	VENTILATORS	VERATRIDINE	VERGEBOARDS	VERMICULTURE
VENERATIONAL	VENTILATORY	VERATRIDINES	VERGENCIES	VERMICULTURES
VENERATIONS	VENTOSITIES	VERATRINES	VERGERSHIP	VERMIFUGAL
VENERATIVE	VENTRICLES	VERBALISATION	VERGERSHIPS	VERMIFUGES
VENERATIVENESS	VENTRICOSE	VERBALISATIONS	VERIDICALITIES	VERMILIONED
VENERATORS	VENTRICOSITIES	VERBALISED	VERIDICALITY	VERMILIONING
VENEREALLY	VENTRICOSITY	VERBALISER	VERIDICALLY	VERMILIONS
VENEREOLOGICAL	VENTRICOUS	VERBALISERS	VERIDICOUS	VERMILLING
VENEREOLOGIES	VENTRICULAR	VERBALISES	VERIFIABILITIES	VERMILLION
VENEREOLOGIST	VENTRICULE	VERBALISING	VERIFIABILITY	VERMILLIONS
VENEREOLOGISTS	VENTRICULES	VERBALISMS	VERIFIABLE	VERMINATED
VENEREOLOGY	VENTRICULI	VERBALISTIC	VERIFIABLENESS	VERMINATES

V

VERMINATING	VERSICOLOR	VESICATING	VEXILLARIES	VICARSHIPS
VERMINATION	VERSICOLORED	VESICATION	VEXILLATION	VICEGERENCIES
VERMINATIONS	VERSICOLOUR	VESICATIONS	VEXILLATIONS	VICEGERENCY
VERMINIEST	VERSICOLOURED	VESICATORIES	VEXILLOLOGIC	VICEGERENT
VERMINOUSLY	VERSICULAR	VESICATORY	VEXILLOLOGICAL	VICEGERENTS
VERMINOUSNESS	VERSIFICATION	VESICULARITIES	VEXILLOLOGIES	VICEREGALLY
VERMINOUSNESSES	VERSIFICATIONS	VESICULARITY	VEXILLOLOGIST	VICEREGENT
VERMIVOROUS	VERSIFICATOR	VESICULARLY	VEXILLOLOGISTS	VICEREGENTS
VERNACULAR	VERSIFICATORS	VESICULATE	VEXILLOLOGY	VICEREINES
VERNACULARISE	VERSIFIERS	VESICULATED	VEXINGNESS	VICEROYALTIES
VERNACULARISED	VERSIFYING	VESICULATES	VEXINGNESSES	VICEROYALTY
VERNACULARISES	VERSIONERS	VESICULATING	VIABILITIES	VICEROYSHIP
VERNACULARISING	VERSIONING	VESICULATION	VIBRACULAR	VICEROYSHIPS
VERNACULARISM	VERSIONINGS	VESICULATIONS	VIBRACULARIA	VICHYSSOIS
VERNACULARISMS	VERSIONIST	VESICULOSE	VIBRACULARIUM	VICHYSSOISE
VERNACULARIST	VERSIONISTS	VESPERTILIAN	VIBRACULOID	VICHYSSOISES
VERNACULARISTS	VERSLIBRIST	VESPERTILIONID	VIBRACULUM	VICINITIES
VERNACULARITIES	VERSLIBRISTE	VESPERTILIONIDS	VIBRAHARPIST	VICIOSITIES
VERNACULARITY	VERSLIBRISTES	VESPERTILIONINE	VIBRAHARPISTS	VICIOUSNESS
VERNACULARIZE	VERSLIBRISTS	VESPERTINAL	VIBRAHARPS	VICIOUSNESSES
VERNACULARIZED	VERTEBRALLY	VESPERTINE	VIBRANCIES	VICISSITUDE
VERNACULARIZES	VERTEBRATE	VESPIARIES	VIBRAPHONE	VICISSITUDES
VERNACULARIZING	VERTEBRATED	VESTIARIES	VIBRAPHONES	VICISSITUDINARY
VERNACULARLY	VERTEBRATES	VESTIBULAR	VIBRAPHONIST	VICISSITUDINOUS
VERNACULARS	VERTEBRATION	VESTIBULED	VIBRAPHONISTS	VICOMTESSE
VERNALISATION	VERTEBRATIONS	VESTIBULES	VIBRATILITIES	VICOMTESSES
VERNALISATIONS	VERTICALITIES	VESTIBULING	VIBRATILITY	VICTIMHOOD
VERNALISED	VERTICALITY	VESTIBULITIS	VIBRATINGLY	VICTIMHOODS
VERNALISES	VERTICALLY	VESTIBULITISES	VIBRATIONAL	VICTIMISATION
VERNALISING	VERTICALNESS	VESTIBULUM	VIBRATIONLESS	VICTIMISATIONS
VERNALITIES	VERTICALNESSES	VESTIGIALLY	VIBRATIONS	VICTIMISED
VERNALIZATION	VERTICILLASTER	VESTIMENTAL	VIBRATIUNCLE	VICTIMISER
VERNALIZATIONS	VERTICILLASTERS	VESTIMENTARY	VIBRATIUNCLES	VICTIMISERS
VERNALIZED	VERTICILLATE	VESTIMENTS	VIBRATOLESS	VICTIMISES
VERNALIZES	VERTICILLATED	VESTITURES	VIBROFLOTATION	VICTIMISING
VERNALIZING	VERTICILLATELY	VESTMENTAL	VIBROFLOTATIONS	VICTIMIZATION
VERNATIONS	VERTICILLATION	VESTMENTED	VIBROGRAPH	VICTIMIZATIONS
VERNISSAGE	VERTICILLATIONS	VESUVIANITE	VIBROGRAPHS	VICTIMIZED
VERNISSAGES	VERTICILLIUM	VESUVIANITES	VIBROMETER	VICTIMIZER
VERRUCIFORM	VERTICILLIUMS	VETCHLINGS	VIBROMETERS	VICTIMIZERS
VERRUCOSITIES	VERTICITIES	VETERINARIAN	VICARESSES	VICTIMIZES
VERRUCOSITY	VERTIGINES	VETERINARIANS	VICARIANCE	VICTIMIZING
VERSABILITIES	VERTIGINOUS	VETERINARIES	VICARIANCES	VICTIMLESS
VERSABILITY	VERTIGINOUSLY	VETERINARY	VICARIANTS	VICTIMOLOGIES
VERSATILELY	VERTIGINOUSNESS	VETTURINOS	VICARIATES	VICTIMOLOGIST
VERSATILENESS	VERTIPORTS	VEXATIOUSLY	VICARIOUSLY	VICTIMOLOGISTS
VERSATILENESSES	VERUMONTANA	VEXATIOUSNESS	VICARIOUSNESS	VICTIMOLOGY
VERSATILITIES	VERUMONTANUM	VEXATIOUSNESSES	VICARIOUSNESSES	VICTORESSES
VERSATILITY	VERUMONTANUMS	VEXEDNESSES	VICARLIEST	VICTORIANA

V

VICTORIANAS	VIEWLESSLY	VILLANELLE	VINEGARETTES	VIPERISHLY
VICTORINES	VIEWPHONES	VILLANELLES	VINEGARIER	VIPEROUSLY
VICTORIOUS	VIEWPOINTS	VILLANOUSLY	VINEGARIEST	VIRAGINIAN
VICTORIOUSLY	VIGILANCES	VILLEGGIATURA	VINEGARING	VIRAGINOUS
VICTORIOUSNESS	VIGILANTES	VILLEGGIATURAS	VINEGARISH	VIRALITIES
VICTORYLESS	VIGILANTISM	VILLEINAGE	VINEGARRETTE	VIREONINES
VICTRESSES	VIGILANTISMS	VILLEINAGES	VINEGARRETTES	VIRESCENCE
VICTUALAGE	VIGILANTLY	VILLENAGES	VINEGARROON	VIRESCENCES
VICTUALAGES	VIGILANTNESS	VILLIACOES	VINEGARROONS	VIRGINALIST
VICTUALERS	VIGILANTNESSES	VILLIAGOES	VINEYARDIST	VIRGINALISTS
VICTUALING	VIGINTILLION	VILLICATION	VINEYARDISTS	VIRGINALLED
VICTUALLAGE	VIGINTILLIONS	VILLICATIONS	VINICULTURAL	VIRGINALLING
VICTUALLAGES	VIGNETTERS	VILLOSITIES	VINICULTURE	VIRGINALLY
VICTUALLED	VIGNETTING	VINAIGRETTE	VINICULTURES	VIRGINHOOD
VICTUALLER	VIGNETTINGS	VINAIGRETTES	VINICULTURIST	VIRGINHOODS
VICTUALLERS	VIGNETTIST	VINBLASTINE	VINICULTURISTS	VIRGINITIES
VICTUALLESS	VIGNETTISTS	VINBLASTINES	VINIFEROUS	VIRGINIUMS
VICTUALLING	VIGORISHES	VINCIBILITIES	VINIFICATION	VIRIDESCENCE
VIDEOCASSETTE	VIGOROUSLY	VINCIBILITY	VINIFICATIONS	VIRIDESCENCES
VIDEOCASSETTES	VIGOROUSNESS	VINCIBLENESS	VINIFICATOR	VIRIDESCENT
VIDEOCONFERENCE	VIGOROUSNESSES	VINCIBLENESSES	VINIFICATORS	VIRIDITIES
VIDEODISCS	VIKINGISMS	VINCRISTINE	VINOLOGIES	VIRILESCENCE
VIDEODISKS	VILDNESSES	VINCRISTINES	VINOLOGIST	VIRILESCENCES
VIDEOGRAMS	VILENESSES	VINDEMIATE	VINOLOGISTS	VIRILESCENT
VIDEOGRAPHER	VILIFICATION	VINDEMIATED	VINOSITIES	VIRILISATION
VIDEOGRAPHERS	VILIFICATIONS	VINDEMIATES	VINTAGINGS	VIRILISATIONS
VIDEOGRAPHIES	VILIPENDED	VINDEMIATING	VINYLCYANIDE	VIRILISING
VIDEOGRAPHY	VILIPENDER	VINDICABILITIES	VINYLCYANIDES	VIRILITIES
VIDEOLANDS	VILIPENDERS	VINDICABILITY	VINYLIDENE	VIRILIZATION
VIDEOPHILE	VILIPENDING	VINDICABLE	VINYLIDENES	VIRILIZATIONS
VIDEOPHILES	VILLAGERIES	VINDICATED	VIOLABILITIES	VIRILIZING
VIDEOPHONE	VILLAGIEST	VINDICATES	VIOLABILITY	VIROLOGICAL
VIDEOPHONES	VILLAGIOES	VINDICATING	VIOLABLENESS	VIROLOGICALLY
VIDEOPHONIC	VILLAGISATION	VINDICATION	VIOLABLENESSES	VIROLOGIES
VIDEOTAPED	VILLAGISATIONS	VINDICATIONS	VIOLACEOUS	VIROLOGIST
VIDEOTAPES	VILLAGIZATION	VINDICATIVE	VIOLATIONS	VIROLOGISTS
VIDEOTAPING	VILLAGIZATIONS	VINDICATIVENESS	VIOLENTING	VIRTUALISATION
VIDEOTELEPHONE	VILLAGREES	VINDICATOR	VIOLINISTIC	VIRTUALISATIONS
VIDEOTELEPHONES	VILLAINAGE	VINDICATORILY	VIOLINISTICALLY	VIRTUALISE
VIDEOTEXES	VILLAINAGES	VINDICATORS	VIOLINISTS	VIRTUALISED
VIDEOTEXTS	VILLAINESS	VINDICATORY	VIOLONCELLI	VIRTUALISES
VIDEOTHEQUE	VILLAINESSES	VINDICATRESS	VIOLONCELLIST	VIRTUALISING
VIDEOTHEQUES	VILLAINIES	VINDICATRESSES	VIOLONCELLISTS	VIRTUALISM
VIDSCREENS	VILLAINOUS	VINDICTIVE	VIOLONCELLO	VIRTUALISMS
VIEWERSHIP	VILLAINOUSLY	VINDICTIVELY	VIOLONCELLOS	VIRTUALIST
VIEWERSHIPS	VILLAINOUSNESS	VINDICTIVENESS	VIOSTEROLS	VIRTUALISTS
VIEWFINDER	VILLANAGES	VINEDRESSER	VIPASSANAS	VIRTUALITIES
VIEWFINDERS	VILLANELLA	VINEDRESSERS	VIPERFISHES	VIRTUALITY
VIEWINESSES	VILLANELLAS	VINEGARETTE	VIPERIFORM	VIRTUALIZATION

V

VIRTUALIZATIONS	VISCOUNTCY	VITALISING	VITRAILLIST	VITUPERATES
VIRTUALIZE	VISCOUNTESS	VITALISTIC	VITRAILLISTS	VITUPERATING
VIRTUALIZED	VISCOUNTESSES	VITALISTICALLY	VITRECTOMIES	VITUPERATION
VIRTUALIZES	VISCOUNTIES	VITALITIES	VITRECTOMY	VITUPERATIONS
VIRTUALIZING	VISCOUNTSHIP	VITALIZATION	VITREORETINAL	VITUPERATIVE
VIRTUELESS	VISCOUNTSHIPS	VITALIZATIONS	VITREOSITIES	VITUPERATIVELY
VIRTUOSITIES	VISCOUSNESS	VITALIZERS	VITREOSITY	VITUPERATOR
VIRTUOSITY	VISCOUSNESSES	VITALIZING	VITREOUSES	VITUPERATORS
VIRTUOSOSHIP	VISIBILITIES	VITALNESSES	VITREOUSLY	VITUPERATORY
VIRTUOSOSHIPS	VISIBILITY	VITAMINISE	VITREOUSNESS	VIVACIOUSLY
VIRTUOUSLY	VISIBLENESS	VITAMINISED	VITREOUSNESSES	VIVACIOUSNESS
VIRTUOUSNESS	VISIBLENESSES	VITAMINISES	VITRESCENCE	VIVACIOUSNESSES
VIRTUOUSNESSES	VISIOGENIC	VITAMINISING	VITRESCENCES	VIVACISSIMO
VIRULENCES	VISIONALLY	VITAMINIZE	VITRESCENT	VIVACITIES
VIRULENCIES	VISIONARIES	VITAMINIZED	VITRESCIBILITY	VIVANDIERE
VIRULENTLY	VISIONARINESS	VITAMINIZES	VITRESCIBLE	VIVANDIERES
VIRULIFEROUS	VISIONARINESSES	VITAMINIZING	VITRIFACTION	VIVANDIERS
VISAGISTES	VISIONINGS	VITASCOPES	VITRIFACTIONS	VIVERRINES
VISCACHERA	VISIONISTS	VITATIVENESS	VITRIFACTURE	VIVIANITES
VISCACHERAS	VISIONLESS	VITATIVENESSES	VITRIFACTURES	VIVIDITIES
VISCERALLY	VISIOPHONE	VITELLARIES	VITRIFIABILITY	VIVIDNESSES
VISCERATED	VISIOPHONES	VITELLICLE	VITRIFIABLE	VIVIFICATION
VISCERATES	VISITATION	VITELLICLES	VITRIFICATION	VIVIFICATIONS
VISCERATING	VISITATIONAL	VITELLIGENOUS	VITRIFICATIONS	VIVIPARIES
VISCEROMOTOR	VISITATIONS	VITELLINES	VITRIFYING	VIVIPARISM
VISCEROPTOSES	VISITATIVE	VITELLOGENESES	VITRIOLATE	VIVIPARISMS
VISCEROPTOSIS	VISITATORIAL	VITELLOGENESIS	VITRIOLATED	VIVIPARITIES
VISCEROTONIA	VISITATORS	VITELLOGENIC	VITRIOLATES	VIVIPARITY
VISCEROTONIAS	VISITORIAL	VITELLUSES	VITRIOLATING	VIVIPAROUS
VISCEROTONIC	VISITRESSES	VITIATIONS	VITRIOLATION	VIVIPAROUSLY
VISCIDITIES	VISUALISATION	VITICETUMS	VITRIOLATIONS	VIVIPAROUSNESS
VISCIDNESS	VISUALISATIONS	VITICOLOUS	VITRIOLING	VIVISECTED
VISCIDNESSES	VISUALISED	VITICULTURAL	VITRIOLISATION	VIVISECTING
VISCOELASTIC	VISUALISER	VITICULTURALLY	VITRIOLISATIONS	VIVISECTION
VISCOELASTICITY	VISUALISERS	VITICULTURE	VITRIOLISE	VIVISECTIONAL
VISCOMETER	VISUALISES	VITICULTURER	VITRIOLISED	VIVISECTIONALLY
VISCOMETERS	VISUALISING	VITICULTURERS	VITRIOLISES	VIVISECTIONIST
VISCOMETRIC	VISUALISTS	VITICULTURES	VITRIOLISING	VIVISECTIONISTS
VISCOMETRICAL	VISUALITIES	VITICULTURIST	VITRIOLIZATION	VIVISECTIONS
VISCOMETRIES	VISUALIZATION	VITICULTURISTS	VITRIOLIZATIONS	VIVISECTIVE
VISCOMETRY	VISUALIZATIONS	VITIFEROUS	VITRIOLIZE	VIVISECTOR
VISCOSIMETER	VISUALIZED	VITILITIGATE	VITRIOLIZED	VIVISECTORIA
VISCOSIMETERS	VISUALIZER	VITILITIGATED	VITRIOLIZES	VIVISECTORIUM
VISCOSIMETRIC	VISUALIZERS	VITILITIGATES	VITRIOLIZING	VIVISECTORIUMS
VISCOSIMETRICAL	VISUALIZES	VITILITIGATING	VITRIOLLED	VIVISECTORS
VISCOSIMETRIES	VISUALIZING	VITILITIGATION	VITRIOLLING	VIVISEPULTURE
VISCOSIMETRY	VITALISATION	VITILITIGATIONS	VITUPERABLE	VIVISEPULTURES
VISCOSITIES	VITALISATIONS	VITIOSITIES	VITUPERATE	VIXENISHLY
VISCOUNTCIES	VITALISERS	VITRAILLED	VITUPERATED	VIXENISHNESS

VIXENISHNESSES	VODCASTING	VOLCANISING	VOLUMINOUS	VOORKAMERS
VIZIERATES	VODCASTINGS	VOLCANISMS	VOLUMINOUSLY	VOORTREKKER
VIZIERSHIP	VOETGANGER	VOLCANISTS	VOLUMINOUSNESS	VOORTREKKERS
VIZIERSHIPS	VOETGANGERS	VOLCANIZATION	VOLUMISERS	VORACIOUSLY
VIZIRSHIPS	VOETSTOETS	VOLCANIZATIONS	VOLUMISING	VORACIOUSNESS
VOCABULARIAN	VOETSTOOTS	VOLCANIZED	VOLUMIZERS	VORACIOUSNESSES
VOCABULARIANS	VOGUISHNESS	VOLCANIZES	VOLUMIZING	VORACITIES
VOCABULARIED	VOGUISHNESSES	VOLCANIZING	VOLUMOMETER	VORAGINOUS
VOCABULARIES	VOICEFULNESS	VOLCANOLOGIC	VOLUMOMETERS	VORTICALLY
VOCABULARY	VOICEFULNESSES	VOLCANOLOGICAL	VOLUNTARIES	VORTICELLA
VOCABULIST	VOICELESSLY	VOLCANOLOGIES	VOLUNTARILY	VORTICELLAE
VOCABULISTS	VOICELESSNESS	VOLCANOLOGIST	VOLUNTARINESS	VORTICELLAS
VOCALICALLY	VOICELESSNESSES	VOLCANOLOGISTS	VOLUNTARINESSES	VORTICISMS
VOCALISATION	VOICEMAILS	VOLCANOLOGY	VOLUNTARISM	VORTICISTS
VOCALISATIONS	VOICEOVERS	VOLITATING	VOLUNTARISMS	VORTICITIES
VOCALISERS	VOICEPRINT	VOLITATION	VOLUNTARIST	VORTICULAR
VOCALISING	VOICEPRINTS	VOLITATIONAL	VOLUNTARISTIC	VORTIGINOUS
VOCALITIES	VOIDABLENESS	VOLITATIONS	VOLUNTARISTS	VOTARESSES
VOCALIZATION	VOIDABLENESSES	VOLITIONAL	VOLUNTARYISM	VOTIVENESS
VOCALIZATIONS	VOIDNESSES	VOLITIONALLY	VOLUNTARYISMS	VOTIVENESSES
VOCALIZERS	VOISINAGES	VOLITIONARY	VOLUNTARYIST	VOUCHERING
VOCALIZING	VOITURIERS	VOLITIONLESS	VOLUNTARYISTS	VOUCHSAFED
VOCALNESSES	VOIVODESHIP	VOLITORIAL	VOLUNTATIVE	VOUCHSAFEMENT
VOCATIONAL	VOIVODESHIPS	VOLKSLIEDER	VOLUNTATIVES	VOUCHSAFEMENTS
VOCATIONALISM	VOLATILENESS	VOLKSRAADS	VOLUNTEERED	VOUCHSAFES
VOCATIONALISMS	VOLATILENESSES	VOLLEYBALL	VOLUNTEERING	VOUCHSAFING
VOCATIONALIST	VOLATILISABLE	VOLLEYBALLS	VOLUNTEERISM	VOUCHSAFINGS
VOCATIONALISTS	VOLATILISATION	VOLPLANING	VOLUNTEERISMS	VOUSSOIRED
VOCATIONALLY	VOLATILISATIONS	VOLTAMETER	VOLUNTEERS	VOUSSOIRING
VOCATIVELY	VOLATILISE	VOLTAMETERS	VOLUNTOURISM	VOUTSAFING
VOCICULTURAL	VOLATILISED	VOLTAMETRIC	VOLUNTOURISMS	VOWELISATION
VOCIFERANCE	VOLATILISES	VOLTAMMETER	VOLUPTUARIES	VOWELISATIONS
VOCIFERANCES	VOLATILISING	VOLTAMMETERS	VOLUPTUARY	VOWELISING
VOCIFERANT	VOLATILITIES	VOLTIGEURS	VOLUPTUOSITIES	VOWELIZATION
VOCIFERANTS	VOLATILITY	VOLTINISMS	VOLUPTUOSITY	VOWELIZATIONS
VOCIFERATE	VOLATILIZABLE	VOLTMETERS	VOLUPTUOUS	VOWELIZING
VOCIFERATED	VOLATILIZATION	VOLUBILITIES	VOLUPTUOUSLY	VOWELLIEST
VOCIFERATES	VOLATILIZATIONS	VOLUBILITY	VOLUPTUOUSNESS	VOYAGEABLE
VOCIFERATING	VOLATILIZE	VOLUBLENESS	VOLUTATION	VOYEURISMS
VOCIFERATION	VOLATILIZED	VOLUBLENESSES	VOLUTATIONS	VOYEURISTIC
VOCIFERATIONS	VOLATILIZES	VOLUMENOMETER	VOLVULUSES	VOYEURISTICALLY
VOCIFERATOR	VOLATILIZING	VOLUMENOMETERS	VOMERONASAL	VRAICKINGS
VOCIFERATORS	VOLCANICALLY	VOLUMETERS	VOMITORIES	VRAISEMBLANCE
VOCIFEROSITIES	VOLCANICITIES	VOLUMETRIC	VOMITORIUM	VRAISEMBLANCES
VOCIFEROSITY	VOLCANICITY	VOLUMETRICAL	VOMITURITION	VRYSTATERS
VOCIFEROUS	VOLCANISATION	VOLUMETRICALLY	VOMITURITIONS	VULCANICITIES
VOCIFEROUSLY	VOLCANISATIONS	VOLUMETRIES	VOODOOISMS	VULCANICITY
VOCIFEROUSNESS	VOLCANISED	VOLUMINOSITIES	VOODOOISTIC	VULCANISABLE
VODCASTERS	VOLCANISES	VOLUMINOSITY	VOODOOISTS	VULCANISATE

V

VULCANISATES
VULCANISATION
VULCANISATIONS
VULCANISED
VULCANISER
VULCANISERS
VULCANISES
VULCANISING
VULCANISMS
VULCANISTS
VULCANITES
VULCANIZABLE
VULCANIZATE

VULCANIZATES
VULCANIZATION
VULCANIZATIONS
VULCANIZED
VULCANIZER
VULCANIZERS
VULCANIZES
VULCANIZING
VULCANOLOGIC
VULCANOLOGICAL
VULCANOLOGIES
VULCANOLOGIST
VULCANOLOGISTS

VULCANOLOGY
VULGARIANS
VULGARISATION
VULGARISATIONS
VULGARISED
VULGARISER
VULGARISERS
VULGARISES
VULGARISING
VULGARISMS
VULGARITIES
VULGARIZATION
VULGARIZATIONS

VULGARIZED
VULGARIZER
VULGARIZERS
VULGARIZES
VULGARIZING
VULNERABILITIES
VULNERABILITY
VULNERABLE
VULNERABLENESS
VULNERABLY
VULNERARIES
VULNERATED
VULNERATES

VULNERATING
VULNERATION
VULNERATIONS
VULPECULAR
VULPICIDES
VULPINISMS
VULPINITES
VULTURISMS
VULVITISES
VULVOVAGINAL
VULVOVAGINITIS

W

WACKINESSES	WAITERHOOD	WALLPAPERED	WAPINSHAWS	WARMNESSES
WADSETTERS	WAITERHOODS	WALLPAPERING	WAPPENSCHAW	WARMONGERING
WADSETTING	WAITERINGS	WALLPAPERS	WAPPENSCHAWING	WARMONGERINGS
WAFFLESTOMPER	WAITLISTED	WALLPEPPER	WAPPENSCHAWINGS	WARMONGERS
WAFFLESTOMPERS	WAITLISTING	WALLPEPPERS	WAPPENSCHAWS	WARRANDICE
WAGELESSNESS	WAITPEOPLE	WALLPOSTER	WAPPENSHAW	WARRANDICES
WAGELESSNESSES	WAITPERSON	WALLPOSTERS	WAPPENSHAWING	WARRANDING
WAGENBOOMS	WAITPERSONS	WALLYBALLS	WAPPENSHAWINGS	WARRANTABILITY
WAGEWORKER	WAITRESSED	WALLYDRAGS	WAPPENSHAWS	WARRANTABLE
WAGEWORKERS	WAITRESSES	WALLYDRAIGLE	WARBLINGLY	WARRANTABLENESS
WAGGISHNESS	WAITRESSING	WALLYDRAIGLES	WARBONNETS	WARRANTABLY
WAGGISHNESSES	WAITRESSINGS	WALNUTWOOD	WARCHALKER	WARRANTEES
WAGGLINGLY	WAITSTAFFS	WALNUTWOODS	WARCHALKERS	WARRANTERS
WAGGONETTE	WAKEBOARDED	WAMBENGERS	WARCHALKING	WARRANTIED
WAGGONETTES	WAKEBOARDER	WAMBLINESS	WARCHALKINGS	WARRANTIES
WAGGONLESS	WAKEBOARDERS	WAMBLINESSES	WARDENRIES	WARRANTING
WAGGONLOAD	WAKEBOARDING	WAMBLINGLY	WARDENSHIP	WARRANTINGS
WAGGONLOADS	WAKEBOARDINGS	WAMPISHING	WARDENSHIPS	WARRANTISE
WAGHALTERS	WAKEBOARDS	WAMPUMPEAG	WARDERSHIP	WARRANTISED
WAGONETTES	WAKEFULNESS	WAMPUMPEAGS	WARDERSHIPS	WARRANTISES
WAGONLOADS	WAKEFULNESSES	WANCHANCIE	WARDRESSES	WARRANTISING
WAGONWRIGHT	WALDFLUTES	WANDERINGLY	WARDROBERS	WARRANTIZE
WAGONWRIGHTS	WALDGRAVES	WANDERINGS	WARDROBING	WARRANTIZED
WAINSCOTED	WALDGRAVINE	WANDERLUST	WAREHOUSED	WARRANTIZES
WAINSCOTING	WALDGRAVINES	WANDERLUSTS	WAREHOUSEMAN	WARRANTIZING
WAINSCOTINGS	WALDSTERBEN	WANRESTFUL	WAREHOUSEMEN	WARRANTLESS
WAINSCOTTED	WALDSTERBENS	WANTHRIVEN	WAREHOUSER	WARRANTORS
WAINSCOTTING	WALKABOUTS	WANTONISED	WAREHOUSERS	WARRANTYING
WAINSCOTTINGS	WALKATHONS	WANTONISES	WAREHOUSES	WARRIORESS
WAINWRIGHT	WALKINGSTICK	WANTONISING	WAREHOUSING	WARRIORESSES
WAINWRIGHTS	WALKINGSTICKS	WANTONIZED	WAREHOUSINGS	WASHABILITIES
WAISTBANDS	WALKSHORTS	WANTONIZES	WARFARINGS	WASHABILITY
WAISTBELTS	WALLBOARDS	WANTONIZING	WARGAMINGS	WASHATERIA
WAISTCLOTH	WALLCHARTS	WANTONNESS	WARIBASHIS	WASHATERIAS
WAISTCLOTHS	WALLCLIMBER	WANTONNESSES	WARINESSES	WASHBASINS
WAISTCOATED	WALLCLIMBERS	WANWORDIER	WARLIKENESS	WASHBOARDS
WAISTCOATEER	WALLCOVERING	WANWORDIEST	WARLIKENESSES	WASHCLOTHS
WAISTCOATEERS	WALLCOVERINGS	WAPENSCHAW	WARLOCKRIES	WASHERWOMAN
WAISTCOATING	WALLFISHES	WAPENSCHAWS	WARLORDISM	WASHERWOMEN
WAISTCOATINGS	WALLFLOWER	WAPENSHAWS	WARLORDISMS	WASHETERIA
WAISTCOATS	WALLFLOWERS	WAPENTAKES	WARMBLOODS	WASHETERIAS
WAISTLINES	WALLOPINGS	WAPINSCHAW	WARMHEARTED	WASHHOUSES
WAITERAGES	WALLOWINGS	WAPINSCHAWS	WARMHEARTEDNESS	WASHINESSES

WASHINGTONIA	WATCHSTRAPS	WATERHEADS	WATERTHRUSH	WEALTHINESS
WASHINGTONIAS	WATCHTOWER	WATERHOLES	WATERTHRUSHES	WEALTHINESSES
WASHSTANDS	WATCHTOWERS	WATERINESS	WATERTIGHT	WEALTHLESS
WASPINESSES	WATCHWORDS	WATERINESSES	WATERTIGHTNESS	WEAPONEERED
WASPISHNESS	WATERBIRDS	WATERISHNESS	WATERWEEDS	WEAPONEERING
WASPISHNESSES	WATERBOARDING	WATERISHNESSES	WATERWHEEL	WEAPONEERINGS
WASSAILERS	WATERBOARDINGS	WATERLEAFS	WATERWHEELS	WEAPONEERS
WASSAILING	WATERBORNE	WATERLEAVES	WATERWORKS	WEAPONISED
WASSAILINGS	WATERBRAIN	WATERLESSNESS	WATERZOOIS	WEAPONISES
WASSAILRIES	WATERBRAINS	WATERLESSNESSES	WATTLEBARK	WEAPONISING
WASTEBASKET	WATERBUCKS	WATERLILIES	WATTLEBARKS	WEAPONIZED
WASTEBASKETS	WATERBUSES	WATERLINES	WATTLEBIRD	WEAPONIZES
WASTEFULLY	WATERBUSSES	WATERLOGGED	WATTLEBIRDS	WEAPONIZING
WASTEFULNESS	WATERCOLOR	WATERLOGGING	WATTLEWORK	WEAPONLESS
WASTEFULNESSES	WATERCOLORIST	WATERLOGGINGS	WATTLEWORKS	WEAPONRIES
WASTELANDS	WATERCOLORISTS	WATERMANSHIP	WATTMETERS	WEARABILITIES
WASTENESSES	WATERCOLORS	WATERMANSHIPS	WAULKMILLS	WEARABILITY
WASTEPAPER	WATERCOLOUR	WATERMARKED	WAVEFRONTS	WEARIFULLY
WASTEPAPERS	WATERCOLOURIST	WATERMARKING	WAVEGUIDES	WEARIFULNESS
WASTERFULLY	WATERCOLOURISTS	WATERMARKS	WAVELENGTH	WEARIFULNESSES
WASTERFULNESS	WATERCOLOURS	WATERMELON	WAVELENGTHS	WEARILESSLY
WASTERFULNESSES	WATERCOOLER	WATERMELONS	WAVELESSLY	WEARINESSES
WASTEWATER	WATERCOOLERS	WATERMILLS	WAVELLITES	WEARISOMELY
WASTEWATERS	WATERCOURSE	WATERPARKS	WAVEMETERS	WEARISOMENESS
WASTEWEIRS	WATERCOURSES	WATERPOWER	WAVERINGLY	WEARISOMENESSES
WASTNESSES	WATERCRAFT	WATERPOWERS	WAVERINGNESS	WEARYINGLY
WATCHABLES	WATERCRAFTS	WATERPOXES	WAVERINGNESSES	WEASELIEST
WATCHBANDS	WATERCRESS	WATERPROOF	WAVESHAPES	WEASELLERS
WATCHBOXES	WATERCRESSES	WATERPROOFED	WAVETABLES	WEASELLIER
WATCHCASES	WATERDRIVE	WATERPROOFER	WAVINESSES	WEASELLIEST
WATCHCRIES	WATERDRIVES	WATERPROOFERS	WAXBERRIES	WEASELLING
WATCHDOGGED	WATERFALLS	WATERPROOFING	WAXFLOWERS	WEATHERABILITY
WATCHDOGGING	WATERFINDER	WATERPROOFINGS	WAXINESSES	WEATHERABLE
WATCHDOGGINGS	WATERFINDERS	WATERPROOFNESS	WAXWORKERS	WEATHERBOARD
WATCHFULLY	WATERFLOOD	WATERPROOFS	WAYFARINGS	WEATHERBOARDED
WATCHFULNESS	WATERFLOODED	WATERQUAKE	WAYMARKING	WEATHERBOARDING
WATCHFULNESSES	WATERFLOODING	WATERQUAKES	WAYMENTING	WEATHERBOARDS
WATCHGLASS	WATERFLOODINGS	WATERSCAPE	WAYWARDNESS	WEATHERCAST
WATCHGLASSES	WATERFLOODS	WATERSCAPES	WAYWARDNESSES	WEATHERCASTER
WATCHGUARD	WATERFOWLER	WATERSHEDS	WAYZGOOSES	WEATHERCASTERS
WATCHGUARDS	WATERFOWLERS	WATERSIDER	WEAKENINGS	WEATHERCASTS
WATCHLISTS	WATERFOWLING	WATERSIDERS	WEAKFISHES	WEATHERCLOTH
WATCHMAKER	WATERFOWLINGS	WATERSIDES	WEAKHEARTED	WEATHERCLOTHS
WATCHMAKERS	WATERFOWLS	WATERSKIING	WEAKISHNESS	WEATHERCOCK
WATCHMAKING	WATERFRONT	WATERSKIINGS	WEAKISHNESSES	WEATHERCOCKED
WATCHMAKINGS	WATERFRONTS	WATERSMEET	WEAKLINESS	WEATHERCOCKING
WATCHSPRING	WATERGATES	WATERSMEETS	WEAKLINESSES	WEATHERCOCKS
WATCHSPRINGS	WATERGLASS	WATERSPOUT	WEAKNESSES	WEATHERERS
WATCHSTRAP	WATERGLASSES	WATERSPOUTS	WEALTHIEST	WEATHERGIRL

W

WEATHERGIRLS	WEEDINESSES	WELLNESSES	WHALEBACKS	WHEELSPINS
WEATHERGLASS	WEEDKILLER	WELLSPRING	WHALEBOATS	WHEELWORKS
WEATHERGLASSES	WEEDKILLERS	WELLSPRINGS	WHALEBONES	WHEELWRIGHT
WEATHERING	WEEKENDERS	WELTANSCHAUUNG	WHAREPUNIS	WHEELWRIGHTS
WEATHERINGS	WEEKENDING	WELTANSCHAUUNGS	WHARFINGER	WHEESHTING
WEATHERISATION	WEEKENDINGS	WELTERWEIGHT	WHARFINGERS	WHEEZINESS
WEATHERISATIONS	WEEKNIGHTS	WELTERWEIGHTS	WHARFMASTER	WHEEZINESSES
WEATHERISE	WEELDLESSE	WELTSCHMERZ	WHARFMASTERS	WHEEZINGLY
WEATHERISED	WEEPINESSES	WELTSCHMERZES	WHATABOUTERIES	WHENCEFORTH
WEATHERISES	WEEVILIEST	WELWITSCHIA	WHATABOUTERY	WHENCESOEVER
WEATHERISING	WEEVILLIER	WELWITSCHIAS	WHATABOUTISM	WHENSOEVER
WEATHERIZATION	WEEVILLIEST	WENSLEYDALE	WHATABOUTISMS	WHEREABOUT
WEATHERIZATIONS	WEIGHBOARD	WENSLEYDALES	WHATABOUTS	WHEREABOUTS
WEATHERIZE	WEIGHBOARDS	WENTLETRAP	WHATCHAMACALLIT	WHEREAFTER
WEATHERIZED	WEIGHBRIDGE	WENTLETRAPS	WHATNESSES	WHEREAGAINST
WEATHERIZES	WEIGHBRIDGES	WEREWOLFERIES	WHATSERNAME	WHEREFORES
WEATHERIZING	WEIGHTAGES	WEREWOLFERY	WHATSERNAMES	WHEREINSOEVER
WEATHERLIER	WEIGHTIEST	WEREWOLFISH	WHATSHERNAME	WHERENESSES
WEATHERLIEST	WEIGHTINESS	WEREWOLFISM	WHATSHERNAMES	WHERESOEVER
WEATHERLINESS	WEIGHTINESSES	WEREWOLFISMS	WHATSHISNAME	WHERETHROUGH
WEATHERLINESSES	WEIGHTINGS	WEREWOLVES	WHATSHISNAMES	WHEREUNDER
WEATHERMAN	WEIGHTLESS	WERNERITES	WHATSISNAME	WHEREUNTIL
WEATHERMEN	WEIGHTLESSLY	WERWOLFISH	WHATSISNAMES	WHEREWITHAL
WEATHERMOST	WEIGHTLESSNESS	WESTERINGS	WHATSITSNAME	WHEREWITHALS
WEATHEROMETER	WEIGHTLIFTER	WESTERLIES	WHATSITSNAMES	WHEREWITHS
WEATHEROMETERS	WEIGHTLIFTERS	WESTERLINESS	WHATSOEVER	WHERRETING
WEATHERPERSON	WEIGHTLIFTING	WESTERLINESSES	WHATSOMEVER	WHERRITING
WEATHERPERSONS	WEIGHTLIFTINGS	WESTERNERS	WHEATFIELD	WHETSTONES
WEATHERPROOF	WEIMARANER	WESTERNISATION	WHEATFIELDS	WHEWELLITE
WEATHERPROOFED	WEIMARANERS	WESTERNISATIONS	WHEATGERMS	WHEWELLITES
WEATHERPROOFING	WEIRDNESSES	WESTERNISE	WHEATGRASS	WHEYISHNESS
WEATHERPROOFS	WEISENHEIMER	WESTERNISED	WHEATGRASSES	WHEYISHNESSES
WEATHERWOMAN	WEISENHEIMERS	WESTERNISES	WHEATLANDS	WHICHSOEVER
WEATHERWOMEN	WELCOMENESS	WESTERNISING	WHEATMEALS	WHICKERING
WEATHERWORN	WELCOMENESSES	WESTERNISM	WHEATWORMS	WHIDDERING
WEAVERBIRD	WELCOMINGLY	WESTERNISMS	WHEEDLESOME	WHIFFLERIES
WEAVERBIRDS	WELDABILITIES	WESTERNIZATION	WHEEDLINGLY	WHIFFLETREE
WEBCASTERS	WELDABILITY	WESTERNIZATIONS	WHEEDLINGS	WHIFFLETREES
WEBCASTING	WELDMESHES	WESTERNIZE	WHEELBARROW	WHIFFLINGS
WEBCASTINGS	WELFARISMS	WESTERNIZED	WHEELBARROWED	WHIGGAMORE
WEBCHATTED	WELFARISTIC	WESTERNIZES	WHEELBARROWING	WHIGGAMORES
WEBCHATTING	WELFARISTS	WESTERNIZING	WHEELBARROWS	WHIGMALEERIE
WEBLIOGRAPHIES	WELFARITES	WESTERNMOST	WHEELBASES	WHIGMALEERIES
WEBLIOGRAPHY	WELLBEINGS	WESTWARDLY	WHEELCHAIR	WHIGMALEERY
WEBLOGGERS	WELLHOUSES	WETTABILITIES	WHEELCHAIRS	WHILLYWHAED
WEBLOGGING	WELLINGTON	WETTABILITY	WHEELHORSE	WHILLYWHAING
WEBLOGGINGS	WELLINGTONIA	WHAIKORERO	WHEELHORSES	WHILLYWHAS
WEBMASTERS	WELLINGTONIAS	WHAIKOREROS	WHEELHOUSE	WHILLYWHAW
WEEDICIDES	WELLINGTONS	WHAKAPAPAS	WHEELHOUSES	WHILLYWHAWED

W

WHILLYWHAWING	WHIRLABOUTS	WHITENINGS	WHOLESALER	WIDESPREAD
WHILLYWHAWS	WHIRLBLAST	WHITESMITH	WHOLESALERS	WIDOWBIRDS
WHIMBERRIES	WHIRLBLASTS	WHITESMITHS	WHOLESALES	WIDOWERHOOD
WHIMPERERS	WHIRLIGIGS	WHITETAILS	WHOLESALING	WIDOWERHOODS
WHIMPERING	WHIRLINGLY	WHITETHORN	WHOLESALINGS	WIDOWHOODS
WHIMPERINGLY	WHIRLPOOLS	WHITETHORNS	WHOLESOMELY	WIELDINESS
WHIMPERINGS	WHIRLWINDS	WHITETHROAT	WHOLESOMENESS	WIELDINESSES
WHIMSICALITIES	WHIRLYBIRD	WHITETHROATS	WHOLESOMENESSES	WIENERWURST
WHIMSICALITY	WHIRLYBIRDS	WHITEWALLS	WHOLESOMER	WIENERWURSTS
WHIMSICALLY	WHIRRETING	WHITEWARES	WHOLESOMEST	WIFELINESS
WHIMSICALNESS	WHISKERANDO	WHITEWASHED	WHOLESTITCH	WIFELINESSES
WHIMSICALNESSES	WHISKERANDOED	WHITEWASHER	WHOLESTITCHES	WIGWAGGERS
WHIMSINESS	WHISKERANDOS	WHITEWASHERS	WHOLEWHEAT	WIGWAGGING
WHIMSINESSES	WHISKERIER	WHITEWASHES	WHOMSOEVER	WIKIALITIES
WHINBERRIES	WHISKERIEST	WHITEWASHING	WHOREHOUSE	WIKITORIAL
WHINGDINGS	WHISKEYFIED	WHITEWASHINGS	WHOREHOUSES	WIKITORIALS
WHINGEINGLY	WHISKIFIED	WHITEWATER	WHOREMASTER	WILDCATTED
WHINGEINGS	WHISPERERS	WHITEWINGS	WHOREMASTERIES	WILDCATTER
WHININESSES	WHISPERIER	WHITEWOODS	WHOREMASTERLY	WILDCATTERS
WHINSTONES	WHISPERIEST	WHITEYWOOD	WHOREMASTERS	WILDCATTING
WHIPCORDIER	WHISPERING	WHITEYWOODS	WHOREMASTERY	WILDCATTINGS
WHIPCORDIEST	WHISPERINGLY	WHITHERING	WHOREMISTRESS	WILDEBEEST
WHIPCRACKS	WHISPERINGS	WHITHERSOEVER	WHOREMISTRESSES	WILDEBEESTS
WHIPLASHED	WHISPEROUSLY	WHITHERWARD	WHOREMONGER	WILDERMENT
WHIPLASHES	WHISTLEABLE	WHITHERWARDS	WHOREMONGERIES	WILDERMENTS
WHIPLASHING	WHISTLEBLOWING	WHITISHNESS	WHOREMONGERS	WILDERNESS
WHIPPERSNAPPER	WHISTLEBLOWINGS	WHITISHNESSES	WHOREMONGERY	WILDERNESSES
WHIPPERSNAPPERS	WHISTLINGLY	WHITLEATHER	WHORISHNESS	WILDFLOWER
WHIPPETING	WHISTLINGS	WHITLEATHERS	WHORISHNESSES	WILDFLOWERS
WHIPPETINGS	WHITEBAITS	WHITTAWERS	WHORTLEBERRIES	WILDFOWLER
WHIPPINESS	WHITEBASSES	WHITTERICK	WHORTLEBERRY	WILDFOWLERS
WHIPPINESSES	WHITEBEAMS	WHITTERICKS	WHOSESOEVER	WILDFOWLING
WHIPPLETREE	WHITEBEARD	WHITTERING	WHUNSTANES	WILDFOWLINGS
WHIPPLETREES	WHITEBEARDS	WHITTLINGS	WHYDUNNITS	WILDGRAVES
WHIPPOORWILL	WHITEBOARD	WHIZZBANGS	WICKEDNESS	WILDNESSES
WHIPPOORWILLS	WHITEBOARDS	WHIZZINGLY	WICKEDNESSES	WILFULNESS
WHIPSAWING	WHITEBOYISM	WHODUNITRIES	WICKERWORK	WILFULNESSES
WHIPSNAKES	WHITEBOYISMS	WHODUNITRY	WICKERWORKS	WILINESSES
WHIPSTAFFS	WHITECOATS	WHODUNNITRIES	WICKETKEEPER	WILLEMITES
WHIPSTALLED	WHITECOMBS	WHODUNNITRY	WICKETKEEPERS	WILLFULNESS
WHIPSTALLING	WHITEDAMPS	WHODUNNITS	WICKTHINGS	WILLFULNESSES
WHIPSTALLS	WHITEFACES	WHOLEFOODS	WIDDERSHINS	WILLIEWAUGHT
WHIPSTITCH	WHITEFISHES	WHOLEGRAIN	WIDEAWAKES	WILLIEWAUGHTS
WHIPSTITCHED	WHITEFLIES	WHOLEGRAINS	WIDEBODIES	WILLINGEST
WHIPSTITCHES	WHITEHEADS	WHOLEHEARTED	WIDECHAPPED	WILLINGNESS
WHIPSTITCHING	WHITELISTED	WHOLEHEARTEDLY	WIDEMOUTHED	WILLINGNESSES
WHIPSTOCKS	WHITELISTING	WHOLEMEALS	WIDENESSES	WILLOWHERB
WHIPTAILED	WHITELISTS	WHOLENESSES	WIDERSHINS	WILLOWHERBS
WHIRLABOUT	WHITENESSES	WHOLESALED	WIDESCREEN	WILLOWIEST

WILLOWLIKE	WINDOWPANES	WINSOMENESS	WIREHAIRED	WITCHWEEDS
WILLOWWARE	WINDOWSILL	WINSOMENESSES	WIRELESSED	WITENAGEMOT
WILLOWWARES	WINDOWSILLS	WINTERBERRIES	WIRELESSES	WITENAGEMOTE
WILLPOWERS	WINDPROOFED	WINTERBERRY	WIRELESSING	WITENAGEMOTES
WIMPINESSES	WINDPROOFING	WINTERBOURNE	WIRELESSLY	WITENAGEMOTS
WIMPISHNESS	WINDPROOFS	WINTERBOURNES	WIREPHOTOS	WITGATBOOM
WIMPISHNESSES	WINDROWERS	WINTERCRESS	WIREPULLER	WITGATBOOMS
WINCEYETTE	WINDROWING	WINTERCRESSES	WIREPULLERS	WITHDRAWABLE
WINCEYETTES	WINDSCREEN	WINTERFEED	WIREPULLING	WITHDRAWAL
WINCHESTER	WINDSCREENS	WINTERFEEDING	WIREPULLINGS	WITHDRAWALS
WINCHESTERS	WINDSHAKES	WINTERFEEDS	WIRETAPPED	WITHDRAWER
WINCOPIPES	WINDSHIELD	WINTERGREEN	WIRETAPPER	WITHDRAWERS
WINDBAGGERIES	WINDSHIELDS	WINTERGREENS	WIRETAPPERS	WITHDRAWING
WINDBAGGERY	WINDSTORMS	WINTERIEST	WIRETAPPING	WITHDRAWMENT
WINDBLASTS	WINDSUCKER	WINTERINESS	WIRETAPPINGS	WITHDRAWMENTS
WINDBREAKER	WINDSUCKERS	WINTERINESSES	WIREWALKER	WITHDRAWNNESS
WINDBREAKERS	WINDSURFED	WINTERISATION	WIREWALKERS	WITHDRAWNNESSES
WINDBREAKS	WINDSURFER	WINTERISATIONS	WIREWORKER	WITHEREDNESS
WINDBURNED	WINDSURFERS	WINTERISED	WIREWORKERS	WITHEREDNESSES
WINDBURNING	WINDSURFING	WINTERISES	WIREWORKING	WITHERINGLY
WINDCHEATER	WINDSURFINGS	WINTERISING	WIREWORKINGS	WITHERINGS
WINDCHEATERS	WINDTHROWS	WINTERIZATION	WIRINESSES	WITHERITES
WINDCHILLS	WINEBERRIES	WINTERIZATIONS	WISECRACKED	WITHERSHINS
WINDFALLEN	WINEBIBBER	WINTERIZED	WISECRACKER	WITHHOLDEN
WINDFLOWER	WINEBIBBERS	WINTERIZES	WISECRACKERS	WITHHOLDER
WINDFLOWERS	WINEBIBBING	WINTERIZING	WISECRACKING	WITHHOLDERS
WINDGALLED	WINEBIBBINGS	WINTERKILL	WISECRACKS	WITHHOLDING
WINDHOVERS	WINEGLASSES	WINTERKILLED	WISENESSES	WITHHOLDMENT
WINDINESSES	WINEGLASSFUL	WINTERKILLING	WISENHEIMER	WITHHOLDMENTS
WINDJAMMER	WINEGLASSFULS	WINTERKILLINGS	WISENHEIMERS	WITHINDOORS
WINDJAMMERS	WINEGROWER	WINTERKILLS	WISHFULNESS	WITHOUTDOORS
WINDJAMMING	WINEGROWERS	WINTERLESS	WISHFULNESSES	WITHSTANDER
WINDJAMMINGS	WINEGROWING	WINTERLIER	WISHTONWISH	WITHSTANDERS
WINDLASSED	WINEGROWINGS	WINTERLIEST	WISHTONWISHES	WITHSTANDING
WINDLASSES	WINEMAKERS	WINTERLINESS	WISPINESSES	WITHSTANDS
WINDLASSING	WINEMAKING	WINTERLINESSES	WISTFULNESS	WITHYWINDS
WINDLESSLY	WINEMAKINGS	WINTERTIDE	WISTFULNESSES	WITLESSNESS
WINDLESSNESS	WINEPRESSES	WINTERTIDES	WITBLITSES	WITLESSNESSES
WINDLESSNESSES	WINGCHAIRS	WINTERTIME	WITCHBROOM	WITNESSABLE
WINDLESTRAE	WINGLESSNESS	WINTERTIMES	WITCHBROOMS	WITNESSERS
WINDLESTRAES	WINGLESSNESSES	WINTERWEIGHT	WITCHCRAFT	WITNESSING
WINDLESTRAW	WINGSPREAD	WINTRINESS	WITCHCRAFTS	WITTICISMS
WINDLESTRAWS	WINGSPREADS	WINTRINESSES	WITCHERIES	WITTINESSES
WINDMILLED	WINNABILITIES	WIREDRAWER	WITCHETTIES	WITWANTONED
WINDMILLING	WINNABILITY	WIREDRAWERS	WITCHGRASS	WITWANTONING
WINDOWIEST	WINNINGEST	WIREDRAWING	WITCHGRASSES	WITWANTONS
WINDOWINGS	WINNINGNESS	WIREDRAWINGS	WITCHHOODS	WIZARDLIER
WINDOWLESS	WINNINGNESSES	WIREFRAMES	WITCHINGLY	WIZARDLIEST
WINDOWPANE	WINNOWINGS	WIREGRASSES	WITCHKNOTS	WIZARDRIES

W

WOADWAXENS WONDERINGS WOODHOUSES WOOLSORTER WORKMANLIEST
WOBBEGONGS WONDERKIDS WOODINESSES WOOLSORTERS WORKMANLIKE
WOBBLINESS WONDERLAND WOODLANDER WOOMERANGS WORKMANSHIP
WOBBLINESSES WONDERLANDS WOODLANDERS WOOZINESSES WORKMANSHIPS
WOEBEGONENESS WONDERLESS WOODLESSNESS WORCESTERBERRY WORKMASTER
WOEBEGONENESSES WONDERMENT WOODLESSNESSES WORCESTERS WORKMASTERS
WOEFULLEST WONDERMENTS WOODNESSES WORDBREAKS WORKMISTRESS
WOEFULNESS WONDERMONGER WOODPECKER WORDCOUNTS WORKMISTRESSES
WOEFULNESSES WONDERMONGERING WOODPECKERS WORDINESSES WORKPEOPLE
WOFULNESSES WONDERMONGERS WOODPRINTS WORDISHNESS WORKPIECES
WOKENESSES WONDERSTRUCK WOODREEVES WORDISHNESSES WORKPLACES
WOLFBERRIES WONDERWORK WOODRUSHES WORDLESSLY WORKPRINTS
WOLFFISHES WONDERWORKS WOODSCREWS WORDLESSNESS WORKSHEETS
WOLFHOUNDS WONDROUSLY WOODSHEDDED WORDLESSNESSES WORKSHOPPED
WOLFISHNESS WONDROUSNESS WOODSHEDDING WORDMONGER WORKSHOPPING
WOLFISHNESSES WONDROUSNESSES WOODSHEDDINGS WORDMONGERS WORKSPACES
WOLFRAMITE WONKINESSES WOODSHOCKS WORDSEARCH WORKSTATION
WOLFRAMITES WONTEDNESS WOODSHRIKE WORDSEARCHES WORKSTATIONS
WOLFSBANES WONTEDNESSES WOODSHRIKES WORDSMITHERIES WORKSTREAM
WOLLASTONITE WOODBLOCKS WOODSMOKES WORDSMITHERY WORKSTREAMS
WOLLASTONITES WOODBORERS WOODSPITES WORDSMITHS WORKTABLES
WOLVERENES WOODBURYTYPE WOODSTONES WORKABILITIES WORKWATCHER
WOLVERINES WOODBURYTYPES WOODSTOVES WORKABILITY WORKWATCHERS
WOMANFULLY WOODCARVER WOODSWALLOW WORKABLENESS WORLDBEATS
WOMANHOODS WOODCARVERS WOODSWALLOWS WORKABLENESSES WORLDBUILDING
WOMANISERS WOODCARVING WOODTHRUSH WORKAHOLIC WORLDBUILDINGS
WOMANISHLY WOODCARVINGS WOODTHRUSHES WORKAHOLICS WORLDLIEST
WOMANISHNESS WOODCHOPPER WOODWAXENS WORKAHOLISM WORLDLINESS
WOMANISHNESSES WOODCHOPPERS WOODWORKER WORKAHOLISMS WORLDLINESSES
WOMANISING WOODCHUCKS WOODWORKERS WORKAROUND WORLDLINGS
WOMANISINGS WOODCRAFTS WOODWORKING WORKAROUNDS WORLDSCALE
WOMANIZERS WOODCRAFTSMAN WOODWORKINGS WORKBASKET WORLDSCALES
WOMANIZING WOODCRAFTSMEN WOOLGATHERER WORKBASKETS WORLDVIEWS
WOMANIZINGS WOODCUTTER WOOLGATHERERS WORKBENCHES WORMINESSES
WOMANKINDS WOODCUTTERS WOOLGATHERING WORKERISTS WORMWHEELS
WOMANLIEST WOODCUTTING WOOLGATHERINGS WORKERLESS WORNNESSES
WOMANLINESS WOODCUTTINGS WOOLGROWER WORKFELLOW WORRIMENTS
WOMANLINESSES WOODENHEAD WOOLGROWERS WORKFELLOWS WORRISOMELY
WOMANNESSES WOODENHEADED WOOLGROWING WORKFORCES WORRISOMENESS
WOMANPOWER WOODENHEADS WOOLGROWINGS WORKGROUPS WORRISOMENESSES
WOMANPOWERS WOODENNESS WOOLINESSES WORKHORSES WORRYINGLY
WOMENFOLKS WOODENNESSES WOOLLINESS WORKHOUSES WORRYWARTS
WOMENKINDS WOODENTOPS WOOLLINESSES WORKINGMAN WORSENESSES
WOMENSWEAR WOODENWARE WOOLLYBACK WORKINGMEN WORSENINGS
WOMENSWEARS WOODENWARES WOOLLYBACKS WORKINGWOMAN WORSHIPABLE
WONDERFULLY WOODGRAINS WOOLLYBUTT WORKINGWOMEN WORSHIPERS
WONDERFULNESS WOODGROUSE WOOLLYBUTTS WORKLESSNESS WORSHIPFUL
WONDERFULNESSES WOODGROUSES WOOLLYFOOT WORKLESSNESSES WORSHIPFULLY
WONDERINGLY WOODHORSES WOOLLYFOOTS WORKMANLIER WORSHIPFULNESS

WORSHIPING	WRAITHLIKE	WREATHLESS	WRINKLELESS	WRONGDOINGS
WORSHIPLESS	WRANGLERSHIP	WREATHLIKE	WRINKLIEST	WRONGFULLY
WORSHIPPED	WRANGLERSHIPS	WRECKFISHES	WRISTBANDS	WRONGFULNESS
WORSHIPPER	WRANGLESOME	WRECKMASTER	WRISTLOCKS	WRONGFULNESSES
WORSHIPPERS	WRANGLINGS	WRECKMASTERS	WRISTWATCH	WRONGHEADED
WORSHIPPING	WRAPAROUND	WRENCHINGLY	WRISTWATCHES	WRONGHEADEDLY
WORTHINESS	WRAPAROUNDS	WRENCHINGS	WRITEDOWNS	WRONGHEADEDNESS
WORTHINESSES	WRAPPERING	WRESTLINGS	WRITERESSES	WRONGNESSES
WORTHLESSLY	WRAPROUNDS	WRETCHEDER	WRITERLIER	WRONGOUSLY
WORTHLESSNESS	WRATHFULLY	WRETCHEDEST	WRITERLIEST	WULFENITES
WORTHLESSNESSES	WRATHFULNESS	WRETCHEDLY	WRITERSHIP	WUNDERKIND
WORTHWHILE	WRATHFULNESSES	WRETCHEDNESS	WRITERSHIPS	WUNDERKINDER
WORTHWHILENESS	WRATHINESS	WRETCHEDNESSES	WRITHINGLY	WUNDERKINDS
WOUNDINGLY	WRATHINESSES	WRIGGLIEST	WRONGDOERS	WYANDOTTES
WOUNDWORTS	WREATHIEST	WRIGGLINGS	WRONGDOING	WYLIECOATS

XANTHATION	XENODIAGNOSES	XENOTRANSPLANTS	XEROPHYTIC	XYLOGENOUS
XANTHATIONS	XENODIAGNOSIS	XENOTROPIC	XEROPHYTICALLY	XYLOGRAPHED
XANTHOCHROIA	XENODIAGNOSTIC	XERANTHEMUM	XEROPHYTISM	XYLOGRAPHER
XANTHOCHROIAS	XENODOCHIUM	XERANTHEMUMS	XEROPHYTISMS	XYLOGRAPHERS
XANTHOCHROIC	XENODOCHIUMS	XERISCAPED	XERORADIOGRAPHY	XYLOGRAPHIC
XANTHOCHROID	XENOGAMIES	XERISCAPES	XEROSTOMAS	XYLOGRAPHICAL
XANTHOCHROIDS	XENOGAMOUS	XERISCAPING	XEROSTOMATA	XYLOGRAPHIES
XANTHOCHROISM	XENOGENEIC	XEROCHASIES	XEROSTOMIA	XYLOGRAPHING
XANTHOCHROISMS	XENOGENESES	XERODERMAE	XEROSTOMIAS	XYLOGRAPHS
XANTHOCHROMIA	XENOGENESIS	XERODERMAS	XEROTHERMIC	XYLOGRAPHY
XANTHOCHROMIAS	XENOGENETIC	XERODERMATIC	XEROTRIPSES	XYLOIDINES
XANTHOCHROOUS	XENOGENIES	XERODERMATOUS	XEROTRIPSIS	XYLOLOGIES
XANTHOMATA	XENOGENOUS	XERODERMIA	XIPHIHUMERALIS	XYLOMETERS
XANTHOMATOUS	XENOGLOSSIA	XERODERMIAS	XIPHIPLASTRA	XYLOPHAGAN
XANTHOMELANOUS	XENOGLOSSIAS	XERODERMIC	XIPHIPLASTRAL	XYLOPHAGANS
XANTHOPHYL	XENOGLOSSIES	XEROGRAPHER	XIPHIPLASTRALS	XYLOPHAGES
XANTHOPHYLL	XENOGLOSSY	XEROGRAPHERS	XIPHIPLASTRON	XYLOPHAGOUS
XANTHOPHYLLOUS	XENOGRAFTS	XEROGRAPHIC	XIPHISTERNA	XYLOPHILOUS
XANTHOPHYLLS	XENOLITHIC	XEROGRAPHICALLY	XIPHISTERNUM	XYLOPHONES
XANTHOPHYLS	XENOMANIAS	XEROGRAPHIES	XIPHISTERNUMS	XYLOPHONIC
XANTHOPSIA	XENOMENIAS	XEROGRAPHY	XIPHOPAGIC	XYLOPHONIST
XANTHOPSIAS	XENOMORPHIC	XEROMORPHIC	XIPHOPAGOUS	XYLOPHONISTS
XANTHOPTERIN	XENOMORPHICALLY	XEROMORPHOUS	XIPHOPAGUS	XYLOPYROGRAPHY
XANTHOPTERINE	XENOPHILES	XEROMORPHS	XIPHOPAGUSES	XYLORIMBAS
XANTHOPTERINES	XENOPHOBES	XEROPHAGIES	XIPHOPHYLLOUS	XYLOTOMIES
XANTHOPTERINS	XENOPHOBIA	XEROPHILES	XIPHOSURAN	XYLOTOMIST
XANTHOXYLS	XENOPHOBIAS	XEROPHILIES	XIPHOSURANS	XYLOTOMISTS
XENARTHRAL	XENOPHOBIC	XEROPHILOUS	XYLOBALSAMUM	XYLOTOMOUS
XENOBIOTIC	XENOPHOBICALLY	XEROPHTHALMIA	XYLOBALSAMUMS	XYLOTYPOGRAPHIC
XENOBIOTICS	XENOPHOBIES	XEROPHTHALMIAS	XYLOCARPOUS	XYLOTYPOGRAPHY
XENOBLASTS	XENOPLASTIC	XEROPHTHALMIC	XYLOCHROME	XYRIDACEOUS
XENOCRYSTS	XENOTRANSPLANT	XEROPHYTES	XYLOCHROMES	

Y

YACHTSMANSHIP	YELLOWBARK	YELLOWWARE	YESTERNIGHT	YOURSELVES
YACHTSMANSHIPS	YELLOWBARKS	YELLOWWARES	YESTERNIGHTS	YOUTHENING
YACHTSWOMAN	YELLOWBIRD	YELLOWWEED	YESTERYEAR	YOUTHFULLY
YACHTSWOMEN	YELLOWBIRDS	YELLOWWEEDS	YESTERYEARS	YOUTHFULNESS
YAFFINGALE	YELLOWCAKE	YELLOWWOOD	YIELDABLENESS	YOUTHFULNESSES
YAFFINGALES	YELLOWCAKES	YELLOWWOODS	YIELDABLENESSES	YOUTHHEADS
YAMMERINGS	YELLOWFINS	YELLOWWORT	YIELDINGLY	YOUTHHOODS
YARBOROUGH	YELLOWHAMMER	YELLOWWORTS	YIELDINGNESS	YOUTHQUAKE
YARBOROUGHS	YELLOWHAMMERS	YEOMANRIES	YIELDINGNESSES	YOUTHQUAKES
YARDLIGHTS	YELLOWHEAD	YERSINIOSES	YOCTOSECOND	YPSILIFORM
YARDMASTER	YELLOWHEADS	YERSINIOSIS	YOCTOSECONDS	YTHUNDERED
YARDMASTERS	YELLOWIEST	YESTERDAYS	YODELLINGS	YTTERBITES
YARDSTICKS	YELLOWISHNESS	YESTEREVEN	YOHIMBINES	YTTERBIUMS
YATTERINGLY	YELLOWISHNESSES	YESTEREVENING	YOKEFELLOW	YTTRIFEROUS
YATTERINGS	YELLOWLEGS	YESTEREVENINGS	YOKEFELLOWS	YUCKINESSES
YEARNINGLY	YELLOWNESS	YESTEREVENS	YOTTABYTES	YUMBERRIES
YEASTINESS	YELLOWNESSES	YESTEREVES	YOUNGBERRIES	YUMMINESSES
YEASTINESSES	YELLOWTAIL	YESTERMORN	YOUNGBERRY	YUPPIEDOMS
YELLOCHING	YELLOWTAILS	YESTERMORNING	YOUNGLINGS	YUPPIFICATION
YELLOWBACK	YELLOWTHROAT	YESTERMORNINGS	YOUNGNESSES	YUPPIFICATIONS
YELLOWBACKS	YELLOWTHROATS	YESTERMORNS	YOUNGSTERS	YUPPIFYING

Z

ZABAGLIONE	ZESTFULNESS	ZINGIBERACEOUS	ZOOGEOGRAPHY	ZOOPHILISTS
ZABAGLIONES	ZESTFULNESSES	ZINJANTHROPI	ZOOGLOEOID	ZOOPHILOUS
ZALAMBDODONT	ZESTINESSES	ZINJANTHROPUS	ZOOGONIDIA	ZOOPHOBIAS
ZALAMBDODONTS	ZETTABYTES	ZINJANTHROPUSES	ZOOGONIDIUM	ZOOPHOBOUS
ZAMBOORAKS	ZEUGLODONT	ZINKENITES	ZOOGRAFTING	ZOOPHYSIOLOGIES
ZAMINDARIES	ZEUGLODONTS	ZINKIFEROUS	ZOOGRAFTINGS	ZOOPHYSIOLOGIST
ZAMINDARIS	ZEUGMATICALLY	ZINKIFICATION	ZOOGRAPHER	ZOOPHYSIOLOGY
ZANAMIVIRS	ZIBELLINES	ZINKIFICATIONS	ZOOGRAPHERS	ZOOPHYTICAL
ZANINESSES	ZIDOVUDINE	ZINKIFYING	ZOOGRAPHIC	ZOOPHYTOID
ZANTEDESCHIA	ZIDOVUDINES	ZINZIBERACEOUS	ZOOGRAPHICAL	ZOOPHYTOLOGICAL
ZANTEDESCHIAS	ZIGZAGGEDNESS	ZIPLININGS	ZOOGRAPHIES	ZOOPHYTOLOGIES
ZANTEWOODS	ZIGZAGGEDNESSES	ZIPLOCKING	ZOOGRAPHIST	ZOOPHYTOLOGIST
ZANTHOXYLS	ZIGZAGGERIES	ZIPPINESSES	ZOOGRAPHISTS	ZOOPHYTOLOGISTS
ZANTHOXYLUM	ZIGZAGGERS	ZIRCALLOYS	ZOOKEEPERS	ZOOPHYTOLOGY
ZANTHOXYLUMS	ZIGZAGGERY	ZIRCONIUMS	ZOOLATRIAS	ZOOPLANKTER
ZAPATEADOS	ZIGZAGGIER	ZITHERISTS	ZOOLATRIES	ZOOPLANKTERS
ZAPOTILLAS	ZIGZAGGIEST	ZIZYPHUSES	ZOOLATROUS	ZOOPLANKTON
ZEALOTISMS	ZIGZAGGING	ZOANTHARIAN	ZOOLOGICAL	ZOOPLANKTONIC
ZEALOTRIES	ZILLIONAIRE	ZOANTHARIANS	ZOOLOGICALLY	ZOOPLANKTONS
ZEALOUSNESS	ZILLIONAIRES	ZOANTHROPIC	ZOOLOGISTS	ZOOPLASTIC
ZEALOUSNESSES	ZILLIONTHS	ZOANTHROPIES	ZOOMAGNETIC	ZOOPLASTIES
ZEAXANTHIN	ZINCIFEROUS	ZOANTHROPY	ZOOMAGNETISM	ZOOPSYCHOLOGIES
ZEAXANTHINS	ZINCIFICATION	ZOECHROMES	ZOOMAGNETISMS	ZOOPSYCHOLOGY
ZEBRAFISHES	ZINCIFICATIONS	ZOMBIELIKE	ZOOMANCIES	ZOOSCOPIES
ZEBRAWOODS	ZINCIFYING	ZOMBIFICATION	ZOOMETRICAL	ZOOSPERMATIC
ZEBRINNIES	ZINCKENITE	ZOMBIFICATIONS	ZOOMETRIES	ZOOSPERMIA
ZEITGEBERS	ZINCKENITES	ZOMBIFYING	ZOOMORPHIC	ZOOSPERMIUM
ZEITGEISTIER	ZINCKIFICATION	ZOOCEPHALIC	ZOOMORPHIES	ZOOSPORANGIA
ZEITGEISTIEST	ZINCKIFICATIONS	ZOOCHEMICAL	ZOOMORPHISM	ZOOSPORANGIAL
ZEITGEISTS	ZINCKIFIED	ZOOCHEMISTRIES	ZOOMORPHISMS	ZOOSPORANGIUM
ZEITGEISTY	ZINCKIFIES	ZOOCHEMISTRY	ZOONOMISTS	ZOOSPOROUS
ZELATRICES	ZINCKIFYING	ZOOCHORIES	ZOOPATHIES	ZOOSTEROLS
ZELATRIXES	ZINCOGRAPH	ZOOCHOROUS	ZOOPATHOLOGIES	ZOOTECHNICAL
ZELOPHOBIA	ZINCOGRAPHER	ZOOCULTURE	ZOOPATHOLOGY	ZOOTECHNICS
ZELOPHOBIAS	ZINCOGRAPHERS	ZOOCULTURES	ZOOPERISTS	ZOOTECHNIES
ZELOPHOBIC	ZINCOGRAPHIC	ZOODENDRIA	ZOOPHAGANS	ZOOTHAPSES
ZELOPHOBICS	ZINCOGRAPHICAL	ZOODENDRIUM	ZOOPHAGIES	ZOOTHAPSIS
ZELOTYPIAS	ZINCOGRAPHIES	ZOOGAMETES	ZOOPHAGOUS	ZOOTHECIAL
ZEMINDARIES	ZINCOGRAPHS	ZOOGEOGRAPHER	ZOOPHILIAS	ZOOTHECIUM
ZEMINDARIS	ZINCOGRAPHY	ZOOGEOGRAPHERS	ZOOPHILIES	ZOOTHEISMS
ZEOLITIFORM	ZINCOLYSES	ZOOGEOGRAPHIC	ZOOPHILISM	ZOOTHEISTIC
ZEPTOSECOND	ZINCOLYSIS	ZOOGEOGRAPHICAL	ZOOPHILISMS	ZOOTHERAPIES
ZEPTOSECONDS	ZINFANDELS	ZOOGEOGRAPHIES	ZOOPHILIST	ZOOTHERAPY

ZOOTOMICAL	ZWISCHENZUG	ZYGOCACTUSES	ZYGOMYCETE	ZYMOLOGICAL
ZOOTOMICALLY	ZWISCHENZUGS	ZYGOCARDIAC	ZYGOMYCETES	ZYMOLOGIES
ZOOTOMISTS	ZWITTERION	ZYGODACTYL	ZYGOMYCETOUS	ZYMOLOGIST
ZOOTROPHIC	ZWITTERIONIC	ZYGODACTYLIC	ZYGOPHYLLACEOUS	ZYMOLOGISTS
ZOOTROPHIES	ZWITTERIONS	ZYGODACTYLISM	ZYGOPHYTES	ZYMOMETERS
ZOOTSUITER	ZYGANTRUMS	ZYGODACTYLISMS	ZYGOPLEURAL	ZYMOSIMETER
ZOOTSUITERS	ZYGAPOPHYSEAL	ZYGODACTYLOUS	ZYGOSITIES	ZYMOSIMETERS
ZOOXANTHELLA	ZYGAPOPHYSES	ZYGODACTYLS	ZYGOSPERMS	ZYMOTECHNIC
ZOOXANTHELLAE	ZYGAPOPHYSIAL	ZYGOMATICS	ZYGOSPHENE	ZYMOTECHNICAL
ZORBONAUTS	ZYGAPOPHYSIS	ZYGOMORPHIC	ZYGOSPHENES	ZYMOTECHNICS
ZUCCHETTOS	ZYGOBRANCH	ZYGOMORPHIES	ZYGOSPORES	ZYMOTICALLY
ZUGZWANGED	ZYGOBRANCHIATE	ZYGOMORPHISM	ZYGOSPORIC	
ZUGZWANGING	ZYGOBRANCHIATES	ZYGOMORPHISMS	ZYGOTICALLY	
ZUMBOORUKS	ZYGOBRANCHS	ZYGOMORPHOUS	ZYMOGENESES	
ZWANZIGERS	ZYGOCACTUS	ZYGOMORPHY	ZYMOGENESIS	

Z